REAL
REAL ORIGINAL

전국연합학력평가
3개년 기출 모의고사

고1 영어 [16회]

Contents

● 모바일 학습 영단어 QR 코드 제공

[모바일 영어 듣기 **MP3** 이용 방법]
① 스마트폰으로 **QR** 코드 스캔하기
② 입시플라이 or www.ipsifly.com 입력
   모바일 홈페이지 [듣기 **자료실**] 이용

교재의 구성과 특징

실전은 연습처럼! 연습은 실전처럼! 「리얼 오리지널」

수능 시험장에 가면 낯선 환경과 긴장감 때문에 실력을 제대로 발휘 못하는 경우가 많습니다. 실전 연습은 여러분의 실력이 됩니다.

01

실제 시험지와 똑같은 문제지

고1 영어 전국연합 모의고사는 총 16회분의 문제가 수록되어 있으며, 실전과 동일하게 학습할 수 있습니다.

❶ 리얼 오리지널 모의고사는 실제 시험지의 크기와 느낌을 그대로 살려 실전과 동일한 조건 속에서 문제를 풀어 볼 수 있습니다.

❷ 문제를 풀기 전에 먼저 학습 체크표에 학습 날짜와 시간을 기록 하고, [70분] 타이머를 작동해 실전처럼 풀어 보십시오.

02

특별 부록 [실전 모의고사] 4회

3·6·9·11월 전국연합 학력평가와 고1 학교 시험을 대비해 실전 모의고사 4회분을 제공합니다.

❶ 3·6·9·11월 시행되는 고1 학력평가와 1·2학기 학교 시험을 완벽 대비할 수 있습니다.

❷ 실전 모의고사는 고1 학력평가 문항 중 우수 문항만을 재구성한 문제로 학력평가와 내신을 대비해 꼭 풀어 봐야 합니다.

03

고1 학력평가 + 학교시험 대비

연 4회 [3월·6월·9월·11월] 시행되는 전국연합 학력평가와 고1 학교 내신까지 대비해 학습할 수 있습니다.

❶ 월별로 시행되는 학력평가를 대비해 12회분 문제를 풀어 보면 실제 시험에서 실력을 마음껏 발휘할 수 있습니다.

❷ 학교 시험에 학력평가 문제를 변형하거나 지문을 활용해 문제를 출제하는 학교가 많아 내신까지 대비할 수 있습니다.

★ 해설편 앞 부분에 「SPEED 정답 체크 표」가 있습니다.
오려서 정답을 확인하거나 책갈피로 사용하시면 됩니다.

04
VOCA LIST & 어휘 리뷰 TEST

회차별로 쉬운 단어부터 어려운 단어까지 모든 단어를 정리한
VOCA LIST와 [어휘 리뷰 TEST]를 제공합니다.

❶ 모의고사 회차별 문항 순서대로 어휘를 수록했으며 문제편 뒤에
회차별로 정리한 VOCA LIST를 제공합니다.

❷ 매회 기출문제로 학습한 후 [어휘 리뷰 TEST]로 단어를 복습하면
어휘력과 독해력이 쑥쑥 올라갑니다.

※ 모바일로 영단어를 학습할 수 있도록 VOCA 상단에 QR 코드를 제공합니다.

05
[딕테이션 TEST]로 듣기 만점

영어 영역 절대평가 1등급을 위해 놓칠 수 없는 딕테이션
테스트를 매회 [총 16회분]을 수록했습니다.

❶ 딕테이션에 한글 발문을 추가 수록했으며, 듣기 어려운 발음에
★로 표기하여 연음과 핵심 표현을 익힐 수 있습니다.

❷ 전회분 [QR 코드]를 수록해 바로 듣기가 가능하며 일반배속,
1.25배속, 1.5배속, 1.75배속, 2배속으로 청취 가능합니다.

※ QR 코드를 스캔 후 화면 우측에 있는 [⋮]을 클릭 후 재생 속도를 선택하세요.

06
입체적 해설 & 문제 해결 꿀 팁

혼자서도 학습이 충분하도록 자세한 [입체적 해설]과 함께
고난도 문제는 문제 해결 꿀~팁까지 수록을 했습니다.

❶ 자세한 입체적 해설로 직독직해, 구문 풀이가 수록되어 있으며
혼자서도 학습이 충분하도록 명쾌한 해설을 수록했습니다.

❷ 영어에서 등급을 가르는 고난도 문제는 많이 틀린 이유와 함께
문제 해결 꿀 팁까지 명쾌한 해설을 수록했습니다.

STUDY 플래너 & 등급 컷

① 문제를 풀기 전 먼저 〈학습 체크표〉에 학습 날짜와 시간을 기록하세요.
② 회분별 기출 문제는 영역별로 정해진 시간 안에 푸는 습관을 기르세요.
③ 정답 확인 후 점수와 등급을 적고 성적 변화를 체크하면서 학습 계획을 세우세요.
④ **리얼 오리지널**은 실제 수능 시험과 똑같이 학습하는 교재이므로 실전을 연습하는 것처럼 문제를 풀어 보세요.

● 영어영역 | 시험 개요

문항 수	문항당 배점	문항별 점수 표기	원점수 만점	시험 시간	문항 형태
45문항	2점, 3점	• 3점 문항에 점수 표시 • 점수 표시 없는 문항 모두 2점	100점	70분	5지 선다형

● 영어영역 | 등급 컷 원점수

회분	학습 날짜	학습 시간	틀린 문제	채점 결과		등급 컷 원점수							
				점수	등급	1등급	2등급	3등급	4등급	5등급	6등급	7등급	8등급
01회 2024학년도 3월	월 일	시 분 ~ 시 분				90	80	70	60	50	40	30	20
02회 2023학년도 3월	월 일	시 분 ~ 시 분				90	80	70	60	50	40	30	20
03회 2022학년도 3월	월 일	시 분 ~ 시 분				90	80	70	60	50	40	30	20
04회 2024학년도 6월	월 일	시 분 ~ 시 분				90	80	70	60	50	40	30	20
05회 2023학년도 6월	월 일	시 분 ~ 시 분				90	80	70	60	50	40	30	20
06회 2022학년도 6월	월 일	시 분 ~ 시 분				90	80	70	60	50	40	30	20
07회 2024학년도 9월	월 일	시 분 ~ 시 분				90	80	70	60	50	40	30	20
08회 2023학년도 9월	월 일	시 분 ~ 시 분				90	80	70	60	50	40	30	20
09회 2022학년도 9월	월 일	시 분 ~ 시 분				90	80	70	60	50	40	30	20
10회 2023학년도 11월	월 일	시 분 ~ 시 분				90	80	70	60	50	40	30	20
11회 2022학년도 11월	월 일	시 분 ~ 시 분				90	80	70	60	50	40	30	20
12회 2021학년도 11월	월 일	시 분 ~ 시 분				90	80	70	60	50	40	30	20

※ 〈영어영역〉은 절대 평가에 의한 등급 구분 점수입니다.

● [특별 부록] 실전 모의고사

회분	학습 날짜	학습 시간	채점 결과	틀린 문제	시간 부족 문제
01회 3월 대비 실전 모의고사	월 일	시 분 ~ 시 분			
02회 6월 대비 실전 모의고사	월 일	시 분 ~ 시 분			
03회 9월 대비 실전 모의고사	월 일	시 분 ~ 시 분			
04회 11월 대비 실전 모의고사	월 일	시 분 ~ 시 분			

2024학년도 3월 고1 전국연합학력평가 문제지

1

01회

제 3 교시

영어 영역

01회

● 문항수 45개 | 배점 100점 | 제한 시간 70분

● 점수 표시가 없는 문항은 모두 2점

1번부터 17번까지는 듣고 답하는 문제입니다. 1번부터 15번까지는 한 번만 들려주고, 16번부터 17번까지는 두 번 들려줍니다. 방송을 잘 듣고 답을 하시기 바랍니다.

1. 다음을 듣고, 남자가 하는 말의 목적으로 가장 적절한 것을 고르시오.

① 학교 체육관 공사 일정을 알리려고
② 학교 수업 시간표 조정을 안내하려고
③ 학교 통학 시 대중교통 이용을 권장하려고
④ 학교 방과 후 수업 신청 방식을 설명하려고
⑤ 학교 셔틀버스 운행 시간 변경을 공지하려고

2. 대화를 듣고, 여자의 의견으로 가장 적절한 것을 고르시오.

① 전기 자전거 이용 전에 배터리 상태를 점검하여야 한다.
② 전기 자전거 운행에 관한 규정이 더 엄격해야 한다.
③ 전기 자전거의 속도 규정에 대한 논의가 필요하다.
④ 전기 자전거 구입 시 가격을 고려해야 한다.
⑤ 전기 자전거 이용 시 헬멧을 착용해야 한다.

3. 다음을 듣고, 여자가 하는 말의 요지로 가장 적절한 것을 고르시오.

① 학업 목표를 분명히 설정하는 것이 필요하다.
② 친구와의 협력은 학교생활의 중요한 덕목이다.
③ 과제 제출 마감 기한을 확인하고 준수해야 한다.
④ 적절한 휴식이 성공적인 과업 수행의 핵심 요소이다.
⑤ 할 일의 목록을 활용하는 것이 시간 관리에 유용하다.

4. 대화를 듣고, 그림에서 대화의 내용과 일치하지 않는 것을 고르시오.

5. 대화를 듣고, 남자가 할 일로 가장 적절한 것을 고르시오.

① 따뜻한 옷 챙기기   ② 체스 세트 가져가기
③ 읽을 책 고르기   ④ 간편식 구매하기
⑤ 침낭 준비하기

6. 대화를 듣고, 여자가 지불할 금액을 고르시오. [3점]

① $15   ② $20   ③ $27   ④ $30   ⑤ $33

7. 대화를 듣고, 남자가 체육 대회 연습을 할 수 없는 이유를 고르시오.

① 시험공부를 해야 해서
② 동아리 면접이 있어서
③ 축구화를 가져오지 않아서
④ 다리가 완전히 회복되지 않아서
⑤ 가족 식사 모임에 참석해야 해서

8. 대화를 듣고, Science Open Lab Program에 관해 언급되지 않은 것을 고르시오.

① 지원 가능 학년   ② 실험 재료 구입 필요성
③ 지원서 제출 기한   ④ 참가 인원수
⑤ 시상 여부

9. Triwood High School Volunteer Program에 관한 다음 내용을 듣고, 일치하지 않는 것을 고르시오.

① 노인을 도와주는 봉사 활동이다.
② 봉사자는 대면으로 활동한다.
③ 스마트폰 사용 방법 교육을 한다.
④ 봉사자는 매주 토요일에 세 시간씩 참여한다.
⑤ 지원자는 이메일로 참가 신청서를 보내야 한다.

10. 다음 표를 보면서 대화를 듣고, 여자가 주문할 휴대용 선풍기를 고르시오.

Portable Fan

	Model	Number of Speed Options	Color	LED Display	Price
①	A	1	blue	X	$15
②	B	3	white	O	$26
③	C	3	yellow	X	$31
④	D	4	pink	X	$37
⑤	E	5	green	O	$42

11. 대화를 듣고, 남자의 마지막 말에 대한 여자의 응답으로 가장 적절한 것을 고르시오.

① I can help you find it.
② I already bought a new one.
③ I had it before biology class.
④ You should report it to the police.
⑤ It was a birthday gift from my dad.

12. 대화를 듣고, 여자의 마지막 말에 대한 남자의 응답으로 가장 적절한 것을 고르시오.

① Thank you. Everything looks delicious.
② Yes. I have an appointment this Saturday.
③ You're welcome. I made it with my dad's recipe.
④ Sounds good. What time did you make a reservation?
⑤ That's too bad. Why don't we try another restaurant?

13. 대화를 듣고, 남자의 마지막 말에 대한 여자의 응답으로 가장 적절한 것을 고르시오. [3점]

Woman: _____

① No problem. You can find other projects at the organization.
② Sure. Let's choose one from your old children's books.
③ Congratulations. You finally made your first audiobook.
④ I hope so. You're going to be a wonderful writer.
⑤ Exactly. Kids grow faster than you think.

14. 대화를 듣고, 여자의 마지막 말에 대한 남자의 응답으로 가장 적절한 것을 고르시오.

Man: _____

① Well, let's do the presentation together.
② Cheer up! I know you did your best.
③ Yes, I got a good grade on science.
④ Wow! it was a really nice presentation.
⑤ Right. I have already finished the project.

15. 다음 상황 설명을 듣고, Robert가 Michelle에게 할 말로 가장 적절한 것을 고르시오. [3점]

Robert: _____

① When can I use the library?
② Where can I find the library?
③ How can I join the reading club?
④ Why do you want to go to the library?
⑤ What time does the lost and found open?

[16 ~ 17] 다음을 듣고, 물음에 답하시오.

16. 남자가 하는 말의 주제로 가장 적절한 것은?

① useful foods to relieve coughs
② importance of proper food recipes
③ various causes of cough symptoms
④ traditional home remedies for fever
⑤ connection between weather and cough

17. 언급된 음식 재료가 <u>아닌</u> 것은?

① ginger
② lemon
③ pineapple
④ honey
⑤ banana

┌─────────────────────────────────────┐
│ 이제 듣기 문제가 끝났습니다. 18번부터는 문제지의 지시 │
│ 에 따라 답을 하시기 바랍니다.   │
└─────────────────────────────────────┘

18. 다음 글의 목적으로 가장 적절한 것은?

> Dear Ms. Jane Watson,
>
>   I am John Austin, a science teacher at Crestville High School. Recently I was impressed by the latest book you wrote about the environment. Also my students read your book and had a class discussion about it. They are big fans of your book, so I'd like to ask you to visit our school and give a special lecture. We can set the date and time to suit your schedule. Having you at our school would be a fantastic experience for the students. We would be very grateful if you could come.
>
> Best regards,
> John Austin

① 환경 보호의 중요성을 강조하려고
② 글쓰기에서 주의할 점을 알려 주려고
③ 특강 강사로 작가의 방문을 요청하려고
④ 작가의 팬 사인회 일정 변경을 공지하려고
⑤ 작가가 쓴 책의 내용에 관하여 문의하려고

19. 다음 글에 드러난 Sarah의 심경 변화로 가장 적절한 것은?

  Marilyn and her three-year-old daughter, Sarah, took a trip to the beach, where Sarah built her first sandcastle. Moments later, an enormous wave destroyed Sarah's castle. In response to the loss of her sandcastle, tears streamed down Sarah's cheeks and her heart was broken. She ran to Marilyn, saying she would never build a sandcastle again. Marilyn said, "Part of the joy of building a sandcastle is that, in the end, we give it as a gift to the ocean." Sarah loved this idea and responded with enthusiasm to the idea of building another castle—this time, even closer to the water so the ocean would get its gift sooner!

① sad → excited   ② envious → anxious
③ bored → joyful   ④ relaxed → regretful
⑤ nervous → surprised

20. 다음 글에서 필자가 주장하는 바로 가장 적절한 것은?

  Magic is what we all wish for to happen in our life. Do you love the movie *Cinderella* like me? Well, in real life, you can also create magic. Here's the trick. Write down all the real-time challenges that you face and deal with. Just change the challenge statement into positive statements. Let me give you an example here. If you struggle with getting up early in the morning, then write a positive statement such as "I get up early in the morning at 5:00 am every day." Once you write these statements, get ready to witness magic and confidence. You will be surprised that just by writing these statements, there is a shift in the way you think and act. Suddenly you feel more powerful and positive.

① 목표한 바를 꼭 이루려면 생각을 곧바로 행동으로 옮겨라.
② 자신감을 얻으려면 어려움을 긍정적인 진술로 바꿔 써라.
③ 어려운 일을 해결하려면 주변 사람에게 도움을 청하라.
④ 일상에서 자신감을 향상하려면 틈틈이 마술을 배워라.
⑤ 실생활에서 마주하는 도전을 피하지 말고 견뎌 내라.

21. 밑줄 친 push animal senses into Aristotelian buckets가 다음 글에서 의미하는 바로 가장 적절한 것은? [3점]

Consider the seemingly simple question *How many senses are there?* Around 2,370 years ago, Aristotle wrote that there are five, in both humans and animals — sight, hearing, smell, taste, and touch. However, according to the philosopher Fiona Macpherson, there are reasons to doubt it. For a start, Aristotle missed a few in humans: the perception of your own body which is different from touch and the sense of balance which has links to both touch and vision. Other animals have senses that are even harder to categorize. Many vertebrates have a different sense system for detecting odors. Some snakes can detect the body heat of their prey. These examples tell us that "senses cannot be clearly divided into a limited number of specific kinds," Macpherson wrote in *The Senses*. Instead of trying to push animal senses into Aristotelian buckets, we should study them for what they are.

* vertebrate: 척추동물 ** odor: 냄새

① sort various animal senses into fixed categories
② keep a balanced view to understand real senses
③ doubt the traditional way of dividing all senses
④ ignore the lessons on senses from Aristotle
⑤ analyze more animals to find real senses

22. 다음 글의 요지로 가장 적절한 것은?

When we think of leaders, we may think of people such as Abraham Lincoln or Martin Luther King, Jr. If you consider the historical importance and far-reaching influence of these individuals, leadership might seem like a noble and high goal. But like all of us, these people started out as students, workers, and citizens who possessed ideas about how some aspect of daily life could be improved on a larger scale. Through diligence and experience, they improved upon their ideas by sharing them with others, seeking their opinions and feedback and constantly looking for the best way to accomplish goals for a group. Thus we all have the potential to be leaders at school, in our communities, and at work, regardless of age or experience.

* diligence: 근면

① 훌륭한 리더는 고귀한 목표를 위해 희생적인 삶을 산다.
② 위대한 인물은 위기의 순간에 뛰어난 결단력을 발휘한다.
③ 공동체를 위한 아이디어를 발전시키는 누구나 리더가 될 수 있다.
④ 다른 사람의 의견을 경청하는 자세는 목표 달성에 가장 중요하다.
⑤ 근면하고 경험이 풍부한 사람들은 경제적으로 성공할 수 있다.

23. 다음 글의 주제로 가장 적절한 것은?

Crop rotation is the process in which farmers change the crops they grow in their fields in a special order. For example, if a farmer has three fields, he or she may grow carrots in the first field, green beans in the second, and tomatoes in the third. The next year, green beans will be in the first field, tomatoes in the second field, and carrots will be in the third. In year three, the crops will rotate again. By the fourth year, the crops will go back to their original order. Each crop enriches the soil for the next crop. This type of farming is sustainable because the soil stays healthy.

* sustainable: 지속 가능한

① advantage of crop rotation in maintaining soil health
② influence of purchasing organic food on farmers
③ ways to choose three important crops for rich soil
④ danger of growing diverse crops in small spaces
⑤ negative impact of crop rotation on the environment

24. 다음 글의 제목으로 가장 적절한 것은?

Working around the whole painting, rather than concentrating on one area at a time, will mean you can stop at any point and the painting can be considered "finished." Artists often find it difficult to know when to stop painting, and it can be tempting to keep on adding more to your work. It is important to take a few steps back from the painting from time to time to assess your progress. Putting too much into a painting can spoil its impact and leave it looking overworked. If you find yourself struggling to decide whether you have finished, take a break and come back to it later with fresh eyes. Then you can decide whether any areas of your painting would benefit from further refinement.

* tempting: 유혹하는 ** refinement: 정교하게 꾸밈

① Drawing Inspiration from Diverse Artists
② Don't Spoil Your Painting by Leaving It Incomplete
③ Art Interpretation: Discover Meanings in a Painting
④ Do Not Put Down Your Brush: The More, the Better
⑤ Avoid Overwork and Find the Right Moment to Finish

25. 다음 도표의 내용과 일치하지 <u>않는</u> 것은?

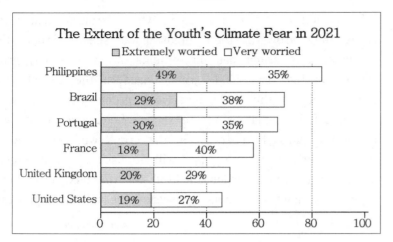

The Extent of the Youth's Climate Fear in 2021

□ Extremely worried □ Very worried

Country	Extremely worried	Very worried
Philippines	49%	35%
Brazil	29%	38%
Portugal	30%	35%
France	18%	40%
United Kingdom	20%	29%
United States	19%	27%

The above graph shows the extent to which young people aged 16−25 in six countries had fear about climate change in 2021. ① The Philippines had the highest percentage of young people who said they were extremely or very worried, at 84 percent, followed by 67 percent in Brazil. ② More than 60 percent of young people in Portugal said they were extremely worried or very worried. ③ In France, the percentage of young people who were extremely worried was higher than that of young people who were very worried. ④ In the United Kingdom, the percentage of young generation who said that they were very worried was 29 percent. ⑤ In the United States, the total percentage of extremely worried and very worried youth was the smallest among the six countries.

26. Jaroslav Heyrovsky에 관한 다음 글의 내용과 일치하지 <u>않는</u> 것은?

Jaroslav Heyrovsky was born in Prague on December 20, 1890, as the fifth child of Leopold Heyrovsky. In 1901 Jaroslav went to a secondary school called the Akademicke Gymnasium. Rather than Latin and Greek, he showed a strong interest in the natural sciences. At Czech University in Prague he studied chemistry, physics, and mathematics. From 1910 to 1914 he continued his studies at University College, London. Throughout the First World War, Jaroslav served in a military hospital. In 1926, Jaroslav became the first Professor of Physical Chemistry at Charles University in Prague. He won the Nobel Prize in chemistry in 1959.

① 라틴어와 그리스어보다 자연 과학에 강한 흥미를 보였다.
② Czech University에서 화학, 물리학 및 수학을 공부했다.
③ 1910년부터 1914년까지 런던에서 학업을 이어 나갔다.
④ 제1차 세계 대전이 끝난 후 군 병원에 복무했다.
⑤ 1959년에 노벨 화학상을 수상했다.

27. Spring Tea Class for Young People에 관한 다음 안내문의 내용과 일치하지 <u>않는</u> 것은?

Spring Tea Class for Young People

Join us for a delightful Spring Tea Class for young people, where you'll experience the taste of tea from various cultures around the world.

Class Schedule
• Friday, April 5 (4:30 p.m. − 6:00 p.m.)
• Saturday, April 6 (9:30 a.m. − 11:00 a.m.)

Details
• We will give you tea and snacks.
• We offer special tips for hosting a tea party.

Participation Fee
• Age 13 − 15: $25 per person
• Age 16 − 18: $30 per person

Note
If you have any food allergy, you should email us in advance at youth@seasonteaclass.com.

① 수강생은 전 세계 다양한 문화권의 차를 경험할 수 있다.
② 금요일 수업은 오후에 1시간 30분 동안 진행된다.
③ 수강생에게 차와 간식을 제공할 것이다.
④ 15세 이하의 수강생은 30달러의 참가비를 내야 한다.
⑤ 음식 알레르기가 있는 수강생은 이메일을 미리 보내야 한다.

28. Clothes Upcycling Contest 2024에 관한 다음 안내문의 내용과 일치하는 것은?

Clothes Upcycling Contest 2024

Are you passionate about fashion and the environment? Then we have a contest for you!

• **Participants**
 − Anyone living in Lakewood, aged 11 to 18

• **How to participate**
 − Take before and after photos of your upcycled clothes.
 − Email the photos at lovelw@lwplus.com.
 − Send in the photos from April 14 to May 12.

• **Winning Prize**
 − A $100 gift card to use at local shops
 − The winner will be announced on our website on May 30.

For more details, visit our website www.lovelwplus.com.

① Lakewood에 사는 사람이면 누구든지 참가할 수 있다.
② 참가자는 출품 사진을 직접 방문하여 제출해야 한다.
③ 참가자는 5월 14일까지 출품 사진을 제출할 수 있다.
④ 우승 상품은 지역 상점에서 쓸 수 있는 기프트 카드이다.
⑤ 지역 신문을 통해 우승자를 발표한다.

29. 다음 글의 밑줄 친 부분 중, 어법상 틀린 것은? [3점]

It would be hard to overstate how important meaningful work is to human beings — work ① that provides a sense of fulfillment and empowerment. Those who have found deeper meaning in their careers find their days much more energizing and satisfying, and ② to count their employment as one of their greatest sources of joy and pride. Sonya Lyubomirsky, professor of psychology at the University of California, has conducted numerous workplace studies ③ showing that when people are more fulfilled on the job, they not only produce higher quality work and a greater output, but also generally earn higher incomes. Those most satisfied with their work ④ are also much more likely to be happier with their lives overall. For her book *Happiness at Work*, researcher Jessica Pryce-Jones conducted a study of 3,000 workers in seventy-nine countries, ⑤ finding that those who took greater satisfaction from their work were 150 percent more likely to have a happier life overall.

* numerous: 수많은

30. 다음 글의 밑줄 친 부분 중, 문맥상 낱말의 쓰임이 적절하지 않은 것은? [3점]

The rate of speed at which one is traveling will greatly determine the ability to process detail in the environment. In evolutionary terms, human senses are adapted to the ① speed at which humans move through space under their own power while walking. Our ability to distinguish detail in the environment is therefore ideally ② suited to movement at speeds of perhaps five miles per hour and under. The fastest users of the street, motorists, therefore have a much more limited ability to process details along the street — a motorist simply has ③ enough time or ability to appreciate design details. On the other hand, pedestrian travel, being much slower, allows for the ④ appreciation of environmental detail. Joggers and bicyclists fall somewhere in between these polar opposites; while they travel faster than pedestrians, their rate of speed is ordinarily much ⑤ slower than that of the typical motorist.

* distinguish: 구별하다 ** pedestrian: 보행자

[31 ~ 34] 다음 빈칸에 들어갈 말로 가장 적절한 것을 고르시오.

31. Every species has certain climatic requirements — what degree of heat or cold it can endure, for example. When the climate changes, the places that satisfy those requirements change, too. Species are forced to follow. All creatures are capable of some degree of _____. Even creatures that appear immobile, like trees and barnacles, are capable of dispersal at some stage of their life — as a seed, in the case of the tree, or as a larva, in the case of the barnacle. A creature must get from the place it is born — often occupied by its parent — to a place where it can survive, grow, and reproduce. From fossils, scientists know that even creatures like trees moved with surprising speed during past periods of climate change.

* barnacle: 따개비 ** dispersal: 분산
*** fossil: 화석

① endurance
② movement
③ development
④ transformation
⑤ communication

32. No respectable boss would say, "I make it a point to discourage my staff from speaking up, and I maintain a culture that prevents disagreeing viewpoints from ever getting aired." If anything, most bosses even say that they are pro-dissent. This idea can be found throughout the series of conversations with corporate, university, and nonprofit leaders, published weekly in the business sections of newspapers. In the interviews, the featured leaders are asked about their management techniques, and regularly claim to continually encourage _____ from more junior staffers. As Bot Pittman remarked in one of these conversations: "I want us to listen to these dissenters because they may intend to tell you why we can't do something, but if you listen hard, what they're really telling you is what you must do to get something done." [3점]

* dissent: 반대

① unconditional loyalty
② positive attitude
③ internal protest
④ competitive atmosphere
⑤ outstanding performance

33. One of the most striking characteristics of a sleeping animal or person is that they do not respond normally to environmental stimuli. If you open the eyelids of a sleeping mammal the eyes will not see normally—they _____.
Some visual information apparently gets in, but it is not normally processed as it is shortened or weakened; same with the other sensing systems. Stimuli are registered but not processed normally and they fail to wake the individual. Perceptual disengagement probably serves the function of protecting sleep, so some authors do not count it as part of the definition of sleep itself. But as sleep would be impossible without it, it seems essential to its definition. Nevertheless, many animals (including humans) use the intermediate state of drowsiness to derive some benefits of sleep without total perceptual disengagement. [3점]

* stimuli: 자극 ** disengagement: 이탈
*** drowsiness: 졸음

① get recovered easily
② will see much better
③ are functionally blind
④ are completely activated
⑤ process visual information

34. A number of research studies have shown how experts in a field often experience difficulties when introducing newcomers to that field. For example, in a genuine training situation, Dr Pamela Hinds found that people expert in using mobile phones were remarkably less accurate than novice phone users in judging how long it takes people to learn to use the phones. Experts can become insensitive to how hard a task is for the beginner, an effect referred to as the 'curse of knowledge'. Dr Hinds was able to show that as people acquired the skill, they then began to underestimate the level of difficulty of that skill. Her participants even underestimated how long it had taken themselves to acquire that skill in an earlier session. Knowing that experts forget how hard it was for them to learn, we can understand the need to _____, rather than making assumptions about how students 'should be' learning. [3점]

* novice: 초보

① focus on the new functions of digital devices
② apply new learning theories recently released
③ develop varieties of methods to test students
④ forget the difficulties that we have had as students
⑤ look at the learning process through students' eyes

35. 다음 글에서 전체 흐름과 관계 <u>없는</u> 문장은?

A group of psychologists studied individuals with severe mental illness who experienced weekly group music therapy, including singing familiar songs and composing original songs. ① The results showed that the group music therapy improved the quality of participants' life, with those participating in a greater number of sessions experiencing the greatest benefits. ② Focusing on singing, another group of psychologists reviewed articles on the efficacy of group singing as a mental health treatment for individuals living with a mental health condition in a community setting. ③ The findings showed that, when people with mental health conditions participated in a choir, their mental health and wellbeing significantly improved. ④ The negative effects of music were greater than the psychologists expected. ⑤ Group singing provided enjoyment, improved emotional states, developed a sense of belonging and enhanced self-confidence.

* therapy: 치료 ** efficacy: 효능

[36~37] 주어진 글 다음에 이어질 글의 순서로 가장 적절한 것을 고르시오.

36.

In many sports, people realized the difficulties and even impossibilities of young children participating fully in many adult sport environments.

(A) As examples, baseball has T ball, football has flag football and junior soccer uses a smaller and lighter ball and (sometimes) a smaller field. All have junior competitive structures where children play for shorter time periods and often in smaller teams.

(B) In a similar way, tennis has adapted the court areas, balls and rackets to make them more appropriate for children under 10. The adaptations are progressive and relate to the age of the child.

(C) They found the road to success for young children is unlikely if they play on adult fields, courts or arenas with equipment that is too large, too heavy or too fast for them to handle while trying to compete in adult-style competition. Common sense has prevailed: different sports have made adaptations for children.

* prevail: 널리 퍼지다

① (A) - (C) - (B)   ② (B) - (A) - (C)
③ (B) - (C) - (A)   ④ (C) - (A) - (B)
⑤ (C) - (B) - (A)

37.

With no horses available, the Inca empire excelled at delivering messages on foot.

(A) When a messenger neared the next hut, he began to call out and repeated the message three or four times to the one who was running out to meet him. The Inca empire could relay messages 1,000 miles (1,610 km) in three or four days under good conditions.

(B) The messengers were stationed on the royal roads to deliver the Inca king's orders and reports coming from his lands. Called Chasquis, they lived in groups of four to six in huts, placed from one to two miles apart along the roads.

(C) They were all young men and especially good runners who watched the road in both directions. If they caught sight of another messenger coming, they hurried out to meet them. The Inca built the huts on high ground, in sight of one another. [3점]

* excel: 탁월하다 ** messenger: 전령

① (A) − (C) − (B) ② (B) − (A) − (C)
③ (B) − (C) − (A) ④ (C) − (A) − (B)
⑤ (C) − (B) − (A)

[38~39] 글의 흐름으로 보아, 주어진 문장이 들어가기에 가장 적절한 곳을 고르시오.

38.

Research in the 1980s and 1990s, however, demonstrated that the "tongue map" explanation of how we taste was, in fact, totally wrong.

The tongue was mapped into separate areas where certain tastes were registered: sweetness at the tip, sourness on the sides, and bitterness at the back of the mouth. (①) As it turns out, the map was a misinterpretation and mistranslation of research conducted in Germany at the turn of the twentieth century. (②) Today, leading taste researchers believe that taste buds are not grouped according to specialty. (③) Sweetness, saltiness, bitterness, and sourness can be tasted everywhere in the mouth, although they may be perceived at a little different intensities at different sites. (④) Moreover, the mechanism at work is not place, but time. (⑤) It's not that you taste sweetness at the tip of your tongue, but rather that you register that perception *first*.

* taste bud: 미뢰

39.

Environmental factors can also determine how the animal will respond during the treatment.

No two animals are alike. (①) Animals from the same litter will display some of the same features, but will not be exactly the same as each other; therefore, they may not respond in entirely the same way during a healing session. (②) For instance, a cat in a rescue center will respond very differently than a cat within a domestic home environment. (③) In addition, animals that experience healing for physical illness will react differently than those accepting healing for emotional confusion. (④) With this in mind, every healing session needs to be explored differently, and each healing treatment should be adjusted to suit the specific needs of the animal. (⑤) You will learn as you go; healing is a constant learning process.

* litter: (한 배에서 태어난) 새끼들

40. 다음 글의 내용을 한 문장으로 요약하고자 한다. 빈칸 (A), (B)에 들어갈 말로 가장 적절한 것은?

The mind has parts that are known as the conscious mind and the subconscious mind. The subconscious mind is very fast to act and doesn't deal with emotions. It deals with memories of your responses to life, your memories and recognition. However, the conscious mind is the one that you have more control over. You think. You can choose whether to carry on a thought or to add emotion to it and this is the part of your mind that lets you down frequently because — fueled by emotions — you make the wrong decisions time and time again. When your judgment is clouded by emotions, this puts in biases and all kinds of other negativities that hold you back. Scared of spiders? Scared of the dark? There are reasons for all of these fears, but they originate in the conscious mind. They only become real fears when the subconscious mind records your reactions.

↓

While the controllable conscious mind deals with thoughts and ___(A)___, the fast-acting subconscious mind stores your responses, ___(B)___ real fears.

	(A)		(B)
①	emotions	·······	forming
②	actions	·······	overcoming
③	emotions	·······	overcoming
④	actions	·······	avoiding
⑤	moralities	·······	forming

[41 ~ 42] 다음 글을 읽고, 물음에 답하시오.

Norms are everywhere, defining what is "normal" and guiding our interpretations of social life at every turn. As a simple example, there is a norm in Anglo society to say *Thank you* to strangers who have just done something to (a) help, such as open a door for you, point out that you've just dropped something, or give you directions. There is no law that forces you to say *Thank you*. But if people don't say *Thank you* in these cases it is marked. People expect that you will say it. You become responsible. (b) Failing to say it will be both surprising and worthy of criticism. Not knowing the norms of another community is the (c) central problem of cross-cultural communication. To continue the *Thank you* example, even though another culture may have an expression that appears translatable (many don't), there may be (d) similar norms for its usage, for example, such that you should say *Thank you* only when the cost someone has caused is considerable. In such a case it would sound ridiculous (i.e., unexpected, surprising, and worthy of criticism) if you were to thank someone for something so (e) minor as holding a door open for you.

41. 윗글의 제목으로 가장 적절한 것은?

① Norms: For Social Life and Cultural Communication
② Don't Forget to Say "Thank you" at Any Time
③ How to Be Responsible for Your Behaviors
④ Accept Criticism Without Hurting Yourself
⑤ How Did Diverse Languages Develop?

42. 밑줄 친 (a)~(e) 중에서 문맥상 낱말의 쓰임이 적절하지 <u>않은</u> 것은?

① (a)   ② (b)   ③ (c)   ④ (d)   ⑤ (e)

[43 ~ 45] 다음 글을 읽고, 물음에 답하시오.

(A)

Long ago, when the world was young, an old Native American spiritual leader Odawa had a dream on a high mountain. In his dream, Iktomi, the great spirit and searcher of wisdom, appeared to (a) him in the form of a spider. Iktomi spoke to him in a holy language.

(B)

Odawa shared Iktomi's lesson with (b) his people. Today, many Native Americans have dream catchers hanging above their beds. Dream catchers are believed to filter out bad dreams. The good dreams are captured in the web of life and carried with the people. The bad dreams pass through the hole in the web and are no longer a part of their lives.

(C)

When Iktomi finished speaking, he spun a web and gave it to Odawa. He said to Odawa, "The web is a perfect circle with a hole in the center. Use the web to help your people reach their goals. Make good use of their ideas, dreams, and visions. If (c) you believe in the great spirit, the web will catch your good ideas and the bad ones will go through the hole." Right after Odawa woke up, he went back to his village.

(D)

Iktomi told Odawa about the cycles of life. (d) He said, "We all begin our lives as babies, move on to childhood, and then to adulthood. Finally, we come to old age, where we must be taken care of as babies again." Iktomi also told (e) him that there are good and bad forces in each stage of life. "If we listen to the good forces, they will guide us in the right direction. But if we listen to the bad forces, they will lead us the wrong way and may harm us," Iktomi said.

43. 주어진 글 (A)에 이어질 내용을 순서에 맞게 배열한 것으로 가장 적절한 것은?

① (B) − (D) − (C)   ② (C) − (B) − (D)
③ (C) − (D) − (B)   ④ (D) − (B) − (C)
⑤ (D) − (C) − (B)

44. 밑줄 친 (a)~(e) 중에서 가리키는 대상이 나머지 넷과 <u>다른</u> 것은?

① (a)   ② (b)   ③ (c)   ④ (d)   ⑤ (e)

45. 윗글에 관한 내용으로 적절하지 <u>않은</u> 것은?

① Odawa는 높은 산에서 꿈을 꾸었다.
② 많은 미국 원주민은 드림캐처를 현관 위에 건다.
③ Iktomi는 Odawa에게 거미집을 짜서 주었다.
④ Odawa는 잠에서 깨자마자 자신의 마을로 돌아갔다.
⑤ Iktomi는 Odawa에게 삶의 순환에 대해 알려 주었다.

★ 확인 사항
○ 답안지의 해당란에 필요한 내용을 정확히 기입(표기) 했는지 확인하시오.

※ QR 코드를 스캔하시면 듣기 방송이 나옵니다. 듣기 방송을 들으며 다음 빈칸을 채우시오. ● 제한 시간 : 25분

01

다음을 듣고, 남자가 하는 말의 목적으로 가장 적절한 것을 고르시오.

M : Good afternoon, students! This is your vice principal, Jack Eliot. Due to the ✿ _____ _____ _____ _____, there's some damage on the road and the road condition is not good. So we decided to make some rearrangements to the _____ _____ _____ _____. From tomorrow, keep in mind that the bus schedule will be delayed by 15 minutes. We want to make sure all of you are safe. This bus schedule change will ✿ _____ _____ _____ _____. We appreciate your understanding and cooperation. Thank you for your attention!

02

대화를 듣고, 여자의 의견으로 가장 적절한 것을 고르시오.

W : Brian, I heard that you are thinking of _____ ____ _____ _____.

M : Yes, that's right.

W : That's good. But be careful when you ride it.

M : Yeah, I know what you mean. On my way here I saw a man riding an electric bicycle without ✿ _____ _____.

W : Some riders don't even _____ _____ ✿ _____ _____.

M : What do you mean by that?

W : These days many people ride electric bicycles on sidewalks.

M : Yes, it's so dangerous.

W : Right. There should be stricter rules about riding electric bicycles.

M : I totally agree with you.

03

다음을 듣고, 여자가 하는 말의 요지로 가장 적절한 것을 고르시오.

W : Hello, this is your student counselor, Susan Smith. You might be worried about your new school life as a freshman. You have a lot of things to do in the beginning of the year. Today, I'm going to give you a ____ _____ _____ ✿ _____. Make __ _____! Write down the tasks you have to do on a list and check off what you finish, one by one. By doing this, you won't miss the things you need to do. Using a todo list will help you _____ _____ _____ _____. Good luck to you and don't forget to start today.

04

대화를 듣고, 그림에서 대화의 내용과 일치하지 <u>않는</u> 것을 고르시오.

M : Hi, Amy. I heard that you've joined the English Newspaper Club.

W : Yes, Tom. I went to the club room yesterday and _____ __ _____ of it. Look.

M : Wow, the place looks nice. I like the lockers on the left.

W : Yes, they're good. We also have a ✿ _____ _____ _____ _____ _____.

M : It looks cool. What's that on the bookshelf?

W : Oh, that's the ✿ _____ _____ _____ _____ for 'Club of the Year'.

M : You must be very proud of it. There's also a computer on the right side of the room.

W : Yeah, we use the computer when we need it.

M : Great. I can see a newspaper on the table.

W : Yes, it was published last December.

05

대화를 듣고, 남자가 할 일로 가장 적절한 것을 고르시오.

W : Mike, I think we've got most of the _____ ✿ _____ _____ _____.

M : Yeah, the tent, sleeping bags, and cooking tools are all set.

W : Perfect. I bought some easy-to-cook meals and snacks for us.

M : Great. What about some warm clothes? It might get cold at night.

W : I've ✿ _____ _____ _____ _____ for us, too. Anything else we need to consider?

M : We need something fun for the camping night. I already packed some books to read.

W : How about _____ _____ _____?

M : Nice. I have a chess set at home.

W : Cool, can you bring it?

M : Of course! I'll take it with me.

06

대화를 듣고, 여자가 지불할 금액을 고르시오. [3점]

M : Hello, what can I help you with today?

W : Hi! I want to buy some ✿ _____ _____ _____. What's fresh today?

M : We just got some apples in.

W : How much are they?

M : They are ten dollars for one bag.

W : Fantastic! I'll take two bags of apples.

M : Okay, what else do you need?

W : I'd like to buy some carrots, too.

M : The carrots are five dollars ✪ _____ _____ _____. How many do you need?

W : I need two bags of carrots.

M : Okay, you need two bags of apples and two bags of carrots.

W : Right. And I have a coupon. I can get a discount with this, right?

M : Yes. You can get a _____ _____ _____ off the total price.

W : Good. Here's the coupon and my credit card.

07

대화를 듣고, 남자가 체육 대회 연습을 할 수 없는 이유를 고르시오.

W : Hey, Jake! How was your math test yesterday?

M : Better than I expected.

W : That's great. Let's go and _____ _____ _____ _____.

M : I'm so sorry but I can't make it.

W : Come on, Jake! Sports Day is just around the corner.

M : I know. That's why I brought my soccer shoes.

W : Then, why can't you practice today? Do you have a club interview?

M : No, I already had the interview last week.

W : Then, does your leg still hurt?

M : Not really, it's okay, now. Actually, I have to attend a _____ _____ ✪ _____ _____ for my mother's birthday.

W : Oh, that's important! Family always comes first. Are you available tomorrow, then?

M : Sure. Let's ✪ _____ _____ _____ the missed practice.

08

대화를 듣고, Science Open Lab Program에 관해 언급되지 않은 것을 고르시오.

W : Hey, Chris. Have you heard about the Science Open Lab Program?

M : Yes, I heard about it. But I don't know what it is exactly.

W : In that program, we can design any science experiment we want.

M : That sounds pretty cool. Do you want to join the program?

W : Sure, it's ✪ _____ _____ like us. Let's join it together.

M : Great! Do we need to buy some materials for experiments?

W : No, they'll prepare everything for us. We just need to send the application form online.

M : When is the _____ _____ ✪ _____?

W : It's tomorrow. We need to hurry.

M : Oh, I see. Is there any special prize?

W : Yes. I heard they're giving out prizes for the _____ _____ _____.

M : Perfect! I'm so excited.

09

Triwood High School Volunteer Program에 관한 다음 내용을 듣고, 일치하지 않는 것을 고르시오.

W : Hello, students! ✪ _____ _____ _____ _____ a chance to help others? Then, I recommend you to join Triwood High School Volunteer Program to help senior citizens. You're supposed to help the _____ _____ ✪ _____. You teach them how to use their smartphones for things such as sending text messages or taking pictures. You will also teach seniors how to use various apps. The program _____ _____ _____ to participate for two hours every Saturday. If you are interested in joining our program, please send us an application form through email.

10

다음 표를 보면서 대화를 듣고, 여자가 주문할 휴대용 선풍기를 고르시오.

M : Sophie, what are you looking for?

W : I'm trying to choose one of _____ ✪ _____ _____ as a gift for my friend Cathy.

M : Oh, let me help you. How many speed options do you think she would want?

W : She would like it if the fan has more than two options.

M : Okay, then, what color do you ✪ _____ _____?

W : Cathy's old one was white. I want to choose a different color.

M : Good idea. Do you want an LED display to show the remaining battery power?

W : Hmm, I don't think she will need it.

M : You're left with two options. Which one do you prefer?

W : Well, I'll _____ _____ _____ _____.

11

대화를 듣고, 남자의 마지막 말에 대한 여자의 응답으로 가장 적절한 것을 고르시오.

M : What's wrong, Jane? You _____ _____ _____.

W : I lost my purse! I ✪ _____ it for an hour, but I can't find it.

M : _____ _____ _____ last have it?

12

대화를 듣고, 여자의 마지막 말에 대한 남자의 응답으로 가장 적절한 것을 고르시오.

W : Honey, what do you _____ ___ _____ for lunch this Saturday?
M : I was thinking _____ _____ _____ the new Italian restaurant.
W : Hmm... I heard that it's hard to _____ ✿ _____ there these days.

13

대화를 듣고, 남자의 마지막 말에 대한 여자의 응답으로 가장 적절한 것을 고르시오. [3점]

M : Mom! I've started ___ _____ _____ for kids.
W : That's great! How did you get involved in that?
M : My teacher told me that a local organization is looking for students to record audiobooks.
W : Fantastic! Are you having fun with it?
M : Well, actually, _____ ✿ _____ _____ my voiceacting
W : Oh? Is that so?
M : Yes, it's ✿ __ _____ _____ to get the right tone for kids.
W : I'm sure you'll get better with practice soon.
M : Thanks. I'm trying my best.
W : That's wonderful. Anything I can help you with?
M : Can you recommend a good book for my audiobook recording?

14

대화를 듣고, 여자의 마지막 말에 대한 남자의 응답으로 가장 적절한 것을 고르시오.

W : Hi, Fred. What should we do for our history project?
M : Actually, I was thinking about it. ✿ _____ _____ _____ _____ the roles for the project?
W : Okay. Good idea. We have the research part, the visual material part, and the presentation part.
M : Hmm, is there any part you want to take on?
W : Well, I would like to do the research. I've been collecting news articles about history.
M : Excellent. You _____ _____ ___ gathering necessary information
W : Thanks. Can you handle the visual material?
M : Okay. I'll ✿ _____ _____ _____ ___. I have done it before.
W : All right. Then, the only part left is the presentation.

15

다음 상황 설명을 듣고, Robert가 Michelle에게 할 말로 가장 적절한 것을 고르시오. [3점]

W : Robert and Michelle _____ ✿ _____ _____ _____ _____ orientation. After short greetings, the teacher begins to explain student clubs, school activities, and school facilities. Robert is focusing very carefully on the explanation. However, while _____ _____ _____ _____ about the school library, Robert drops his pen. Trying to find his pen, Robert misses important information about ✿ _____ _____ _____ of the library, so now, Robert wants to ask Michelle when the library is open. In this situation, what would Robert most likely say to Michelle?

16~17

다음을 듣고, 물음에 답하시오.

M : Hello, listeners. Thank you for tuning in to our Happy Radio Show. Are you taking good care of your health in the early spring? Today, I want to recommend some foods that can _____ _____ ✿ _____ of a cough. Ginger is a popular home remedy for coughs. A cup of hot ginger tea can be helpful for reducing your cough. Lemon is a rich source of vitamin C. Lemon tea can help you ✿ _____ _____ _____. Surprisingly, pineapple is _____ _____ _____ ___ help relieve a cough. When you are suffering from a cough, eating bananas also helps to get rid of the symptoms more easily. These foods are rich in vitamins and they are recommended for people suffering from a cough. I hope you have a healthy week.

▶ 정답 : 해설편 014쪽

18
001 ☐ science ⓝ 과학
002 ☐ recently ⓐ 최근에
003 ☐ impressed ⓐ 감명을 받은
004 ☐ latest ⓐ 최신의, 최근의
005 ☐ discussion ⓝ 토론
006 ☐ special ⓐ 특별한
007 ☐ lecture ⓝ 강의
008 ☐ suit ⓥ 맞추다
009 ☐ schedule ⓝ 일정
010 ☐ fantastic ⓐ 굉장한, 멋진
011 ☐ experience ⓝ 경험
012 ☐ grateful ⓐ 감사한

19
013 ☐ daughter ⓝ 딸, 여식
014 ☐ sandcastle ⓝ 모래성
015 ☐ enormous ⓐ 거대한
016 ☐ wave ⓝ 파도, 물결
017 ☐ destroy ⓥ 부수다
018 ☐ response ⓝ 반응, 대응, 부응
019 ☐ stream ⓥ 흐르다
020 ☐ break ⓥ 깨어지다, 부서지다
021 ☐ ocean ⓝ 바다
022 ☐ respond ⓥ 반응하다
023 ☐ enthusiasm ⓝ 열정

20
024 ☐ magic ⓝ 마법, 마술
025 ☐ in real life 실제로
026 ☐ create ⓥ 창조하다
027 ☐ trick ⓝ 비결, 요령, 묘책
028 ☐ challenge ⓝ 어려움, 도전
029 ☐ deal ⓥ 다루다, 처리하다, 취급하다
030 ☐ statement ⓝ 진술
031 ☐ positive ⓐ 긍정적인
032 ☐ struggle ⓥ 어려움을 겪다
033 ☐ witness ⓥ 목격하다
034 ☐ confidence ⓝ 자신감
035 ☐ surprise ⓥ 놀라게 하다
036 ☐ shift ⓝ 변화
037 ☐ act ⓥ 행동하다
038 ☐ powerful ⓐ 강력한

21
039 ☐ consider ⓥ 고려하다
040 ☐ seemingly ⓐ 외견상으로, 겉보기에는
041 ☐ sense ⓝ 감각
042 ☐ sight ⓝ 시각
043 ☐ hearing ⓝ 청각
044 ☐ smell ⓝ 후각
045 ☐ taste ⓝ 미각
046 ☐ touch ⓝ 촉각
047 ☐ according to ~에 따르면
048 ☐ philosopher ⓝ 철학자
049 ☐ doubt ⓥ 의심하다
050 ☐ miss ⓥ 빠뜨리다, 빼놓다
051 ☐ perception ⓝ 인식
052 ☐ balance ⓝ 균형
053 ☐ link ⓝ 연결
054 ☐ categorize ⓥ 분류하다
055 ☐ vertebrates ⓝ 척추동물

056 ☐ detect ⓥ 감지하다
057 ☐ odor ⓝ 냄새
058 ☐ snake ⓝ 뱀
059 ☐ prey ⓝ 먹잇감
060 ☐ divide ⓥ 나누다
061 ☐ instead ⓐ 대신에
062 ☐ bucket ⓝ 양동이
063 ☐ category ⓝ 범주
064 ☐ traditional ⓐ 전통의, 전통적인

22
065 ☐ historical ⓐ 역사적인
066 ☐ importance ⓝ 중요성
067 ☐ far-reaching ⓐ 광범위한
068 ☐ influence ⓝ 영향력
069 ☐ noble ⓐ 고귀한
070 ☐ goal ⓝ 목표
071 ☐ worker ⓝ 노동자
072 ☐ citizen ⓝ 시민
073 ☐ possess ⓥ 가지다, 소유하다
074 ☐ aspect ⓝ 측면
075 ☐ improve ⓥ 개선하다
076 ☐ scale ⓝ 규모
077 ☐ diligence ⓝ 근면
078 ☐ share ⓥ 함께 쓰다, 공유하다
079 ☐ opinion ⓝ 의견
080 ☐ feedback ⓝ 피드백
081 ☐ constantly ⓐ 끊임없이
082 ☐ accomplish ⓥ 성취하다
083 ☐ potential ⓝ 잠재력
084 ☐ community ⓝ 공동체
085 ☐ regardless of ~와 관계없이

23
086 ☐ crop rotation ⓝ 윤작
087 ☐ farmer ⓝ 농부, 농장주, 농장 경영자
088 ☐ crop ⓝ 농작물, 수확물
089 ☐ field ⓝ 밭
090 ☐ order ⓝ 순서
091 ☐ carrot ⓝ 당근
092 ☐ bean ⓝ 콩
093 ☐ rotate ⓥ 순환하다
094 ☐ go back (앞에 있었던 일로) 돌아가다
095 ☐ original ⓐ 원래의
096 ☐ enrich ⓥ 비옥하게 하다
097 ☐ soil ⓝ 토양
098 ☐ sustainable ⓐ 지속 가능한
099 ☐ organic ⓐ 유기농의

24
100 ☐ painting ⓝ 그림
101 ☐ rather ⓐ 오히려, 차라리
102 ☐ concentrate ⓥ 집중하다
103 ☐ area ⓝ 범위, 영역
104 ☐ often ⓐ 흔히, 종종, 자주
105 ☐ important ⓐ 중요한
106 ☐ step ⓝ 걸음
107 ☐ back ⓥ 뒤로 물러서다
108 ☐ assess ⓥ 평가하다
109 ☐ spoil ⓥ 망쳐 놓다
110 ☐ impact ⓝ 영향(력)
111 ☐ overwork ⓥ 과하게 작업하다

112 ☐ decide ⓥ 결정하다
113 ☐ fresh ⓐ 새로운
114 ☐ benefit ⓥ 득을 보다

25
115 ☐ above ⓐ 위에
116 ☐ extent ⓝ 정도
117 ☐ fear ⓝ 공포, 두려움, 무서움
118 ☐ climate ⓝ 기후
119 ☐ extremely ⓐ 극도로
120 ☐ worry ⓥ 걱정하다
121 ☐ follow ⓥ 뒤를 잇다, 뒤따르다
122 ☐ generation ⓝ 세대

26
123 ☐ secondary school ⓝ 중등학교
124 ☐ natural science 자연 과학
125 ☐ chemistry ⓝ 화학
126 ☐ physics ⓝ 물리학
127 ☐ mathematics ⓝ 수학
128 ☐ continue ⓥ 계속하다, 지속하다
129 ☐ throughout ⓟⓡⓔⓟ 내내
130 ☐ served ⓥ 일하다, 복무하다
131 ☐ military ⓐ 군대의

27
132 ☐ delightful ⓐ 즐거운
133 ☐ experience ⓥ 경험하다
134 ☐ various ⓐ 다양한
135 ☐ culture ⓝ 문화
136 ☐ host ⓥ (파티 등을) 주최하다
137 ☐ in advance 미리

28
138 ☐ passionate ⓐ 열정적인
139 ☐ fashion ⓝ 패션, 의류
140 ☐ environment ⓝ 환경
141 ☐ contest ⓝ 대회
142 ☐ upcycled ⓐ 업사이클된
143 ☐ local ⓐ 지역의
144 ☐ announce ⓥ 발표하다

29
145 ☐ overstate ⓥ 과장해서 말하다
146 ☐ meaningful ⓐ 의미 있는, 중요한
147 ☐ provide ⓥ 제공하다
148 ☐ fulfillment ⓝ 성취감
149 ☐ empowerment ⓝ 권한
150 ☐ career ⓝ 직업, 경력
151 ☐ energizing ⓐ 활기찬
152 ☐ satisfying ⓐ 만족감을 주는
153 ☐ employment ⓝ 직업, 고용
154 ☐ source ⓝ 원천
155 ☐ pride ⓝ 자부심, 긍지
156 ☐ psychology ⓝ 심리
157 ☐ numerous ⓐ 수많은
158 ☐ workplace ⓝ 업무 현장, 직장
159 ☐ fulfilled ⓐ 성취감을 느끼는
160 ☐ quality ⓝ 질
161 ☐ output ⓝ 성과
162 ☐ generally ⓐ 일반적으로
163 ☐ earn ⓥ (돈을) 벌다

164 ☐ income ⓝ 수입
165 ☐ overall ⓐ 전반적으로
166 ☐ satisfaction ⓝ 만족(감)

30
167 ☐ rate ⓝ 빠르기
168 ☐ traveling ⓐ 이동하는, 움직이는
169 ☐ determine ⓥ 결정하다
170 ☐ ability ⓝ 능력
171 ☐ evolutionary ⓐ 진화의, 진화론적인
172 ☐ adapted ⓐ 맞추어진, 적응된
173 ☐ distinguish ⓥ 구별하다
174 ☐ ideally ⓐ 이상적으로
175 ☐ suited ⓐ 적합한
176 ☐ perhaps ⓐ 아마도
177 ☐ motorist ⓝ 운전자
178 ☐ limited ⓐ 제한된
179 ☐ appreciate ⓥ 감상하다, 제대로 인식하다
180 ☐ on the other hand 반면에
181 ☐ pedestrian ⓝ 보행자
182 ☐ allow for 가능하게 하다, 허락하다
183 ☐ appreciation ⓝ 감상
184 ☐ polar ⓐ 극과 극의
185 ☐ opposite ⓝ 반대의 것
186 ☐ ordinarily ⓐ 보통
187 ☐ typical ⓐ 전형적인

31
188 ☐ certain ⓐ 확실한, 틀림없는, 특정한
189 ☐ climatic ⓐ 기후의
190 ☐ requirement ⓝ 요건
191 ☐ degree ⓝ 정도
192 ☐ endure ⓥ 견디다
193 ☐ satisfy ⓥ 충족시키다
194 ☐ creature ⓝ 생명체
195 ☐ capable ⓐ ~을 할 수 있는
196 ☐ dispersal ⓝ 해산, 분산
197 ☐ appear ⓥ ~인 것 같다
198 ☐ immobile ⓐ 움직이지 않는
199 ☐ barnacle ⓝ 따개비
200 ☐ seed ⓝ 씨앗
201 ☐ larva ⓝ 유충
202 ☐ occupy ⓥ 점유하다
203 ☐ survive ⓥ 생존하다
204 ☐ reproduce ⓥ 번식하다
205 ☐ fossil ⓝ 화석

32
206 ☐ respectable ⓐ 존경할 만한
207 ☐ make it a point 반드시 ~하도록 하다
208 ☐ discourage ⓥ 못하게 하다
209 ☐ speak up 자유롭게 의견을 내다
210 ☐ maintain ⓥ 유지하다
211 ☐ prevent ⓥ 막다
212 ☐ disagree ⓥ 동의하지 않다
213 ☐ viewpoint ⓝ 관점
214 ☐ get aired 공공연히 알려지다
215 ☐ if anything 오히려
216 ☐ boss ⓝ (직장의) 상관, 상사
217 ☐ conversation ⓝ 대담, 대화
218 ☐ corporate ⓝ 기업
219 ☐ nonprofit ⓐ 비영리인

220 ☐ publish ⓥ 발행하다, 출판하다
221 ☐ section ⓝ (신문의) 난
222 ☐ feature ⓥ (기사로) 다루다
223 ☐ management ⓝ 경영
224 ☐ technique ⓝ 기법
225 ☐ regularly ⓐ𝖽 어김없이, 규칙적으로
226 ☐ claim ⓥ 주장하다
227 ☐ continually ⓐ𝖽 계속해서, 끊임없이
228 ☐ encourage ⓥ 격려하다, 장려하다
229 ☐ remark ⓥ 말하다
230 ☐ dissenter ⓝ 반대자
231 ☐ unconditional ⓐ 무조건의, 무제한의, 절대적인
232 ☐ loyalty ⓝ 충성
233 ☐ attitude ⓝ 태도, 사고방식
234 ☐ protest ⓝ 항의
235 ☐ atmosphere ⓝ 분위기, 기운

33
236 ☐ striking ⓐ 두드러진
237 ☐ characteristic ⓝ 특징
238 ☐ normally ⓐ𝖽 정상적으로
239 ☐ environmental ⓐ 환경의
240 ☐ stimulus ⓝ 자극 (pl. stimuli)
241 ☐ eyelid ⓝ 눈꺼풀
242 ☐ mammal ⓝ 포유류
243 ☐ functionally ⓐ𝖽 기능상
244 ☐ apparently ⓐ𝖽 분명히
245 ☐ process ⓥ 처리하다
246 ☐ shorten ⓥ 짧아지다
247 ☐ weaken ⓥ 약해지다
248 ☐ fail ⓥ 실패하다
249 ☐ perceptual ⓐ𝖽 지각의
250 ☐ disengagement ⓝ 이탈
251 ☐ probably ⓐ𝖽 아마
252 ☐ function ⓝ 기능
253 ☐ protect ⓥ 보호하다, 지키다
254 ☐ definition ⓝ (어떤 개념의) 정의
255 ☐ impossible ⓐ 불가능한
256 ☐ essential ⓐ 필수적인
257 ☐ intermediate ⓐ 중간의
258 ☐ derive ⓥ 얻다

34
259 ☐ research ⓝ 연구
260 ☐ expert ⓝ 전문가
261 ☐ difficulty ⓝ 어려움
262 ☐ introduce ⓥ 처음으로 경험하게 하다, 입문시키다
263 ☐ newcomer ⓝ 초보
264 ☐ genuine ⓐ 실제
265 ☐ situation ⓝ 상황, 처지, 환경
266 ☐ remarkably ⓐ𝖽 놀랍게
267 ☐ accurate ⓐ 정확한
268 ☐ novice ⓝ 초보자
269 ☐ judge ⓥ 판단하다
270 ☐ insensitive ⓐ 무감각한
271 ☐ effect ⓝ 결과, 효과
272 ☐ acquire ⓥ 습득하다
273 ☐ underestimate ⓥ 과소평가하다
274 ☐ participant ⓝ 참가자
275 ☐ session ⓝ 기간, 시간

276 ☐ assumption ⓝ 추정, 가정

35
277 ☐ psychologist ⓝ 심리학자
278 ☐ severe ⓐ 심각한
279 ☐ therapy ⓝ 치료, 요법
280 ☐ familiar ⓐ 익숙한, 친숙한
281 ☐ compose ⓥ 작곡하다
282 ☐ result ⓝ 결과
283 ☐ review ⓥ 검토하다
284 ☐ article ⓝ 기사, 논문
285 ☐ efficacy ⓝ 효능, 효험
286 ☐ mental health 정신 건강
287 ☐ treatment ⓝ 치료
288 ☐ finding ⓝ 결과
289 ☐ choir ⓝ 합창단
290 ☐ wellbeing ⓝ 행복
291 ☐ significantly ⓐ𝖽 상당히
292 ☐ enhance ⓥ 강화하다

36
293 ☐ realize ⓥ 깨닫다
294 ☐ impossibility ⓝ 불가능
295 ☐ competitive ⓐ 경쟁적인
296 ☐ structure ⓝ 구조
297 ☐ period ⓝ 기간
298 ☐ similar ⓐ 비슷한, 유사한
299 ☐ racket ⓝ 라켓
300 ☐ appropriate ⓐ 적절한
301 ☐ progressive ⓐ 점진적인
302 ☐ relate to ~와 관련되다
303 ☐ unlikely ⓐ ~할 것 같지 않은
304 ☐ arena ⓝ 경기장
305 ☐ equipment ⓝ 장비
306 ☐ handle ⓥ 다루다
307 ☐ compete ⓥ 경쟁하다
308 ☐ common sense ⓝ (일반인들의) 공통된 견해, 상식
309 ☐ adaptation ⓝ 조정

37
310 ☐ available ⓐ 구할 수 있는
311 ☐ empire ⓝ 제국
312 ☐ excel ⓥ 뛰어나다, 탁월하다
313 ☐ deliver ⓥ 전달하다
314 ☐ on foot 걸어서, 도보로
315 ☐ near ⓥ 다가가다
316 ☐ hut ⓝ 오두막, 막사
317 ☐ repeat ⓥ 반복하다
318 ☐ relay ⓥ 이어가다
319 ☐ condition ⓝ 사정, 상황
320 ☐ messenger ⓝ 전달자, 전령
321 ☐ station ⓥ 배치하다
322 ☐ royal ⓐ 왕의, 왕실의
323 ☐ report ⓥ 보고
324 ☐ apart ⓐ𝖽 떨어진
325 ☐ especially ⓐ𝖽 특히, 특별히
326 ☐ direction ⓝ 방향
327 ☐ hurry out 서둘러 나오다

38
328 ☐ demonstrate ⓥ 보여 주다

329 ☐ tongue ⓝ 혀
330 ☐ explanation ⓝ 설명
331 ☐ in fact 사실은
332 ☐ totally ⓐ𝖽 완전히, 전적으로
333 ☐ separate ⓐ 분리된, 독립된, 개별적인
334 ☐ register ⓥ 등록하다
335 ☐ sweetness ⓝ 단맛
336 ☐ tip ⓝ 끝
337 ☐ sourness ⓝ 신맛
338 ☐ bitterness ⓝ 쓴맛
339 ☐ turn out ~인 것으로 밝혀지다
340 ☐ map ⓥ (지도에) 구획하다
341 ☐ misinterpretation ⓝ 오해
342 ☐ mistranslation ⓝ 오역
343 ☐ conduct ⓥ 수행하다
344 ☐ taste bud (혀의) 미뢰
345 ☐ specialty ⓝ 특화된 분야
346 ☐ perceive ⓥ 지각하다
347 ☐ intensity ⓝ 강도
348 ☐ site ⓝ 위치
349 ☐ moreover ⓐ𝖽 게다가, 더욱이
350 ☐ mechanism ⓝ 기제

39
351 ☐ factor ⓝ 요인, 인자
352 ☐ alike ⓐ 서로 같은, 비슷한
353 ☐ litter ⓝ (개·돼지 등의) 한 배에서 난 새끼들
354 ☐ display ⓥ 보이다
355 ☐ feature ⓝ 특징, 특색
356 ☐ exactly ⓐ𝖽 정확히, 꼭, 틀림없이
357 ☐ each other 서로
358 ☐ therefore ⓐ𝖽 그런 까닭에
359 ☐ entirely ⓐ𝖽 완전히, 전부
360 ☐ healing ⓝ 치료
361 ☐ rescue ⓥ 구조하다
362 ☐ differently ⓐ𝖽 다르게, 같지 않게
363 ☐ domestic ⓐ 가정의
364 ☐ in addition (~에) 덧붙여, 게다가
365 ☐ illness ⓝ 질병
366 ☐ react ⓥ 반응하다
367 ☐ confusion ⓝ 동요, 혼란
368 ☐ explore ⓥ 탐구하다
369 ☐ specific ⓐ 특정한, 구체적인
370 ☐ constant ⓐ 끊임없는
371 ☐ process ⓝ 과정

40
372 ☐ conscious ⓐ 의식적인
373 ☐ subconscious ⓐ 잠재의식(적)
374 ☐ emotion ⓝ 감정, 정서
375 ☐ recognition ⓝ 인식
376 ☐ control ⓝ 통제력
377 ☐ carry on 계속 가다
378 ☐ frequently ⓐ𝖽 자주, 빈번히
379 ☐ fuel ⓥ (감정 등을) 부채질하다
380 ☐ judgment ⓝ 판단(력)
381 ☐ cloud ⓥ (기억력, 판단력 등을) 흐리게 하다
382 ☐ bias ⓝ 편견
383 ☐ negativity ⓝ 부정성
384 ☐ hold ⓥ 억누르다, 억제하다
385 ☐ scare ⓥ 무서워하다
386 ☐ originate ⓥ 비롯되다

41~42
387 ☐ norm ⓝ 규범
388 ☐ define ⓥ 규정하다
389 ☐ interpretation ⓝ 해석
390 ☐ society ⓝ 사회
391 ☐ stranger ⓝ 낯선 사람
392 ☐ drop ⓥ 떨어뜨리다
393 ☐ force ⓥ 강요하다
394 ☐ marked ⓐ 눈에 띄는
395 ☐ expect ⓥ 기대하다
396 ☐ responsible ⓐ 책임이 있는
397 ☐ worthy ⓐ 받을 만한
398 ☐ criticism ⓝ 비난
399 ☐ expression ⓝ 표현, 표출
400 ☐ central ⓐ 중심적인
401 ☐ translatable ⓐ 번역할 수 있는
402 ☐ cost ⓝ 대가, 비용
403 ☐ considerable ⓐ 상당한
404 ☐ ridiculous ⓐ 우스꽝스러운
405 ☐ unexpected ⓐ 예상치 못한
406 ☐ minor ⓐ 사소한

43~45
407 ☐ Native American ⓝ 미국 원주민
408 ☐ spiritual ⓐ 영적인
409 ☐ spirit ⓝ 정신, 영혼
410 ☐ wisdom ⓝ 지혜, 슬기, 현명함
411 ☐ holy ⓐ 성스러운
412 ☐ filter ⓥ 여과하다, 거르다
413 ☐ spin ⓥ 짜다 (과거형 spun)
414 ☐ cycle ⓝ 순환

● 채점 : 맞은 개수 _____ / 80

TEST A-B 각 단어의 뜻을 [A] 영어는 우리말로, [B] 우리말은 영어로 쓰시오.

A	English	Korean	B	Korean	English
01	suit		01	구조하다	
02	possess		02	특정한	
03	requirement		03	강의	
04	interpretation		04	규정하다	
05	detect		05	극도로	
06	definition		06	구조(물)	
07	intensity		07	습득하다	
08	enthusiasm		08	수입	
09	overwork		09	배치하다	
10	newcomer		10	무감각한	
11	endure		11	나누다	
12	bias		12	평가하다	
13	perceive		13	먹잇감	
14	register		14	규범	
15	noble		15	경기장	
16	equipment		16	성과	
17	compose		17	치료	
18	military		18	순환하다	
19	frequently		19	부수다	
20	statement		20	질병	

▶ A-D 정답 : 해설편 014쪽

TEST C-D 각 단어의 뜻을 골라 기호를 쓰시오.

C	English		Korean	D	Korean		English
01	witness	( )	ⓐ 이상적으로	01	변화	( )	ⓐ feature
02	remark	( )	ⓑ 말하다	02	오해	( )	ⓑ enrich
03	separate	( )	ⓒ 못하게 하다	03	가정의	( )	ⓒ progressive
04	on foot	( )	ⓓ 권한	04	(파티 등을) 주최하다	( )	ⓓ domestic
05	excel	( )	ⓔ 목격하다	05	행복	( )	ⓔ allow for
06	empowerment	( )	ⓕ 검토하다	06	가능하게 하다, 허락하다	( )	ⓕ marked
07	diligence	( )	ⓖ 개별적인	07	움직이지 않는	( )	ⓖ stream
08	on the other hand	( )	ⓗ 비롯되다	08	약해지다	( )	ⓗ concentrate
09	rate	( )	ⓘ 반면에	09	눈에 띄는	( )	ⓘ immobile
10	overall	( )	ⓙ 이어가다	10	(기사로) 다루다	( )	ⓙ misinterpretation
11	fulfillment	( )	ⓚ 즐거운	11	집중하다	( )	ⓚ wellbeing
12	delightful	( )	ⓛ 근면	12	번식하다	( )	ⓛ shift
13	relay	( )	ⓜ 전반적으로	13	극과 극의	( )	ⓜ get aired
14	review	( )	ⓝ 과소평가하다	14	떨어진	( )	ⓝ apart
15	overstate	( )	ⓞ 빠르기	15	점진적인	( )	ⓞ if anything
16	holy	( )	ⓟ 과장해서 말하다	16	받을 만한	( )	ⓟ polar
17	underestimate	( )	ⓠ 걸어서, 도보로	17	흐르다	( )	ⓠ host
18	discourage	( )	ⓡ 성스러운	18	비옥하게 하다	( )	ⓡ reproduce
19	originate	( )	ⓢ 성취감	19	오히려	( )	ⓢ worthy
20	ideally	( )	ⓣ 빼어나다, 탁월하다	20	공공연히 알려지다	( )	ⓣ weaken

2023학년도 3월 고1 전국연합학력평가 문제지

영어 영역

1

제 3 교시

02회

● 문항수 45개 | 배점 100점 | 제한 시간 70분

● 점수 표시가 없는 문항은 모두 2점

1번부터 17번까지는 듣고 답하는 문제입니다. 1번부터 15번까지는 한 번만 들려주고, 16번부터 17번까지는 두 번 들려줍니다. 방송을 잘 듣고 답을 하시기 바랍니다.

MP3

1. 다음을 듣고, 남자가 하는 말의 목적으로 가장 적절한 것을 고르시오.

① 아이스하키부의 우승을 알리려고
② 아이스하키부 훈련 일정을 공지하려고
③ 아이스하키부 신임 감독을 소개하려고
④ 아이스하키부 선수 모집을 안내하려고
⑤ 아이스하키부 경기의 관람을 독려하려고

2. 대화를 듣고, 여자의 의견으로 가장 적절한 것을 고르시오.

① 과다한 항생제 복용을 자제해야 한다.
② 오래된 약을 함부로 폐기해서는 안 된다.
③ 약을 복용할 때는 정해진 시간을 지켜야 한다.
④ 진료 전에 자신의 증상을 정확히 확인해야 한다.
⑤ 다른 사람에게 처방된 약을 복용해서는 안 된다.

3. 대화를 듣고, 두 사람의 관계를 가장 잘 나타낸 것을 고르시오.

① 관람객 – 박물관 관장
② 세입자 – 건물 관리인
③ 화가 – 미술관 직원
④ 고객 – 전기 기사
⑤ 의뢰인 – 건축사

4. 대화를 듣고, 그림에서 대화의 내용과 일치하지 않는 것을 고르시오.

5. 대화를 듣고, 남자가 할 일로 가장 적절한 것을 고르시오.

① 티켓 디자인하기   ② 포스터 게시하기
③ 블로그 개설하기   ④ 밴드부원 모집하기
⑤ 콘서트 장소 대여하기

6. 대화를 듣고, 여자가 지불할 금액을 고르시오. [3점]

① $70   ② $90   ③ $100   ④ $110   ⑤ $120

7. 대화를 듣고, 남자가 지갑을 구매하지 못한 이유를 고르시오.

① 해당 상품이 다 팔려서
② 브랜드명을 잊어버려서
③ 계산대의 줄이 길어서
④ 공항에 늦게 도착해서
⑤ 면세점이 문을 닫아서

8. 대화를 듣고, Youth Choir Audition에 관해 언급되지 않은 것을 고르시오.

① 지원 가능 연령   ② 날짜   ③ 심사 기준
④ 참가비   ⑤ 지원 방법

9. 2023 Career Week에 관한 다음 내용을 듣고, 일치하지 않는 것을 고르시오.

① 5일 동안 열릴 것이다.
② 미래 직업 탐색을 돕는 프로그램이 있을 것이다.
③ 프로그램 참가 인원에 제한이 있다.
④ 특별 강연이 마지막 날에 있을 것이다.
⑤ 등록은 5월 10일에 시작된다.

10. 다음 표를 보면서 대화를 듣고, 여자가 구입할 프라이팬을 고르시오.

Frying Pans

	Model	Price	Size (inches)	Material	Lid
①	A	$30	8	Aluminum	○
②	B	$32	9.5	Aluminum	○
③	C	$35	10	Stainless Steel	×
④	D	$40	11	Aluminum	×
⑤	E	$70	12.5	Stainless Steel	○

11. 대화를 듣고, 남자의 마지막 말에 대한 여자의 응답으로 가장 적절한 것을 고르시오.

① I don't think I can finish editing it by then.
② I learned it by myself through books.
③ This short movie is very interesting.
④ You should make another video clip.
⑤ I got an A⁺ on the team project.

12. 대화를 듣고, 여자의 마지막 말에 대한 남자의 응답으로 가장 적절한 것을 고르시오.

① All right. I'll come pick you up now.
② I'm sorry. The library is closed today.
③ No problem. You can borrow my book.
④ Thank you so much. I'll drop you off now.
⑤ Right. I've changed the interior of my office.

13. 대화를 듣고, 남자의 마지막 말에 대한 여자의 응답으로 가장 적절한 것을 고르시오.

Woman: _____

① Try these tomatoes and cucumbers.
② I didn't know peppers are good for skin.
③ Just wear comfortable clothes and shoes.
④ You can pick tomatoes when they are red.
⑤ I'll help you grow vegetables on your farm.

14. 대화를 듣고, 여자의 마지막 말에 대한 남자의 응답으로 가장 적절한 것을 고르시오. [3점]

Man: _____

① You're right. I'll meet her and apologize.
② I agree with you. That's why I did it.
③ Thank you. I appreciate your apology.
④ Don't worry. I don't think it's your fault.
⑤ Too bad. I hope the two of you get along.

15. 다음 상황 설명을 듣고, John이 Ted에게 할 말로 가장 적절한 것을 고르시오. [3점]

John: _____

① How can we find the best sunrise spot?
② Why do you go mountain climbing so often?
③ What time should we get up tomorrow morning?
④ When should we come down from the mountain top?
⑤ Where do we have to stay in the mountain at night?

[16 ~ 17] 다음을 듣고, 물음에 답하시오.

16. 여자가 하는 말의 주제로 가장 적절한 것은?

① indoor sports good for the elderly
② importance of learning rules in sports
③ best sports for families to enjoy together
④ useful tips for winning a sports game
⑤ history of traditional family sports

17. 언급된 스포츠가 <u>아닌</u> 것은?

① badminton
② basketball
③ table tennis
④ soccer
⑤ bowling

> 이제 듣기 문제가 끝났습니다. 18번부터는 문제지의 지시에 따라 답을 하시기 바랍니다.

18. 다음 글의 목적으로 가장 적절한 것은?

> To whom it may concern,
>
>   I am a resident of the Blue Sky Apartment. Recently I observed that the kid zone is in need of repairs. I want you to pay attention to the poor condition of the playground equipment in the zone. The swings are damaged, the paint is falling off, and some of the bolts on the slide are missing. The facilities have been in this terrible condition since we moved here. They are dangerous to the children playing there. Would you please have them repaired? I would appreciate your immediate attention to solve this matter.
>
> Yours sincerely,
> Nina Davis

① 아파트의 첨단 보안 설비를 홍보하려고
② 아파트 놀이터의 임시 폐쇄를 공지하려고
③ 아파트 놀이터 시설의 수리를 요청하려고
④ 아파트 놀이터 사고의 피해 보상을 촉구하려고
⑤ 아파트 공용 시설 사용 시 유의 사항을 안내하려고

19. 다음 글에 드러난 'I'의 심경 변화로 가장 적절한 것은?

  On a two-week trip in the Rocky Mountains, I saw a grizzly bear in its native habitat. At first, I felt joy as I watched the bear walk across the land. He stopped every once in a while to turn his head about, sniffing deeply. He was following the scent of something, and slowly I began to realize that this giant animal was smelling me! I froze. This was no longer a wonderful experience; it was now an issue of survival. The bear's motivation was to find meat to eat, and I was clearly on his menu.

* scent: 냄새

① sad → angry
② delighted → scared
③ satisfied → jealous
④ worried → relieved
⑤ frustrated → excited

20. 다음 글에서 필자가 주장하는 바로 가장 적절한 것은?

  It is difficult for any of us to maintain a constant level of attention throughout our working day. We all have body rhythms characterised by peaks and valleys of energy and alertness. You will achieve more, and feel confident as a benefit, if you schedule your most demanding tasks at times when you are best able to cope with them. If you haven't thought about energy peaks before, take a few days to observe yourself. Try to note the times when you are at your best. We are all different. For some, the peak will come first thing in the morning, but for others it may take a while to warm up.

* alertness: 기민함

① 부정적인 감정에 에너지를 낭비하지 말라.
② 자신의 신체 능력에 맞게 운동량을 조절하라.
③ 자기 성찰을 위한 아침 명상 시간을 확보하라.
④ 생산적인 하루를 보내려면 일을 균등하게 배분하라.
⑤ 자신의 에너지가 가장 높은 시간을 파악하여 활용하라.

21. 밑줄 친 The divorce of the hands from the head가 다음 글에서 의미하는 바로 가장 적절한 것은? [3점]

If we adopt technology, we need to pay its costs. Thousands of traditional livelihoods have been pushed aside by progress, and the lifestyles around those jobs removed. Hundreds of millions of humans today work at jobs they hate, producing things they have no love for. Sometimes these jobs cause physical pain, disability, or chronic disease. Technology creates many new jobs that are certainly dangerous. At the same time, mass education and media train humans to avoid low-tech physical work, to seek jobs working in the digital world. The divorce of the hands from the head puts a stress on the human mind. Indeed, the sedentary nature of the best-paying jobs is a health risk — for body and mind.

* chronic: 만성의   ** sedentary: 주로 앉아서 하는

① ignorance of modern technology
② endless competition in the labor market
③ not getting along well with our coworkers
④ working without any realistic goals for our career
⑤ our increasing use of high technology in the workplace

22. 다음 글의 요지로 가장 적절한 것은?

When students are starting their college life, they may approach every course, test, or learning task the same way, using what we like to call "the rubber-stamp approach." Think about it this way: Would you wear a tuxedo to a baseball game? A colorful dress to a funeral? A bathing suit to religious services? Probably not. You know there's appropriate dress for different occasions and settings. Skillful learners know that "putting on the same clothes" won't work for every class. They are flexible learners. They have different strategies and know when to use them. They know that you study for multiple-choice tests differently than you study for essay tests. And they not only know what to do, but they also know how to do it.

① 숙련된 학습자는 상황에 맞는 학습 전략을 사용할 줄 안다.
② 선다형 시험과 논술 시험은 평가의 형태와 목적이 다르다.
③ 문화마다 특정 행사와 상황에 맞는 복장 규정이 있다.
④ 학습의 양보다는 학습의 질이 학업 성과를 좌우한다.
⑤ 학습 목표가 명확할수록 성취 수준이 높아진다.

23. 다음 글의 주제로 가장 적절한 것은?

As the social and economic situation of countries got better, wage levels and working conditions improved. Gradually people were given more time off. At the same time, forms of transport improved and it became faster and cheaper to get to places. England's industrial revolution led to many of these changes. Railways, in the nineteenth century, opened up now famous seaside resorts such as Blackpool and Brighton. With the railways came many large hotels. In Canada, for example, the new coast-to-coast railway system made possible the building of such famous hotels as Banff Springs and Chateau Lake Louise in the Rockies. Later, the arrival of air transport opened up more of the world and led to tourism growth.

① factors that caused tourism expansion
② discomfort at a popular tourist destination
③ importance of tourism in society and economy
④ negative impacts of tourism on the environment
⑤ various types of tourism and their characteristics

24. 다음 글의 제목으로 가장 적절한 것은?

Success can lead you off your intended path and into a comfortable rut. If you are good at something and are well rewarded for doing it, you may want to keep doing it even if you stop enjoying it. The danger is that one day you look around and realize you're so deep in this comfortable rut that you can no longer see the sun or breathe fresh air; the sides of the rut have become so slippery that it would take a superhuman effort to climb out; and, effectively, you're stuck. And it's a situation that many working people worry they're in now. The poor employment market has left them feeling locked in what may be a secure, or even well-paying — but ultimately unsatisfying — job.

* rut: 틀에 박힌 생활

① Don't Compete with Yourself
② A Trap of a Successful Career
③ Create More Jobs for Young People
④ What Difficult Jobs Have in Common
⑤ A Road Map for an Influential Employer

25. 다음 도표의 내용과 일치하지 <u>않는</u> 것은?

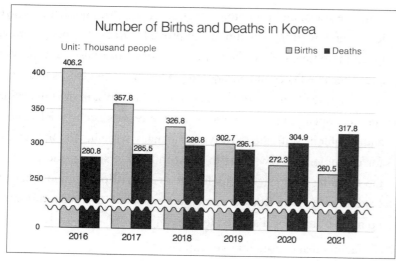

The above graph shows the number of births and deaths in Korea from 2016 to 2021. ① The number of births continued to decrease throughout the whole period. ② The gap between the number of births and deaths was the largest in 2016. ③ In 2019, the gap between the number of births and deaths was the smallest, with the number of births slightly larger than that of deaths. ④ The number of deaths increased steadily during the whole period, except the period from 2018 to 2019. ⑤ In 2021, the number of deaths was larger than that of births for the first time.

26. Lilian Bland에 관한 다음 글의 내용과 일치하지 <u>않는</u> 것은?

Lilian Bland was born in Kent, England in 1878. Unlike most other girls at the time she wore trousers and spent her time enjoying adventurous activities like horse riding and hunting. Lilian began her career as a sports and wildlife photographer for British newspapers. In 1910 she became the first woman to design, build, and fly her own airplane. In order to persuade her to try a slightly safer activity, Lilian's dad bought her a car. Soon Lilian was a master driver and ended up working as a car dealer. She never went back to flying but lived a long and exciting life nonetheless. She married, moved to Canada, and had a kid. Eventually, she moved back to England, and lived there for the rest of her life.

① 승마와 사냥 같은 모험적인 활동을 즐겼다.
② 스포츠와 야생 동물 사진작가로 경력을 시작했다.
③ 자신의 비행기를 설계하고 제작했다.
④ 자동차 판매원으로 일하기도 했다.
⑤ 캐나다에서 생의 마지막 기간을 보냈다.

27. Call for Articles에 관한 다음 안내문의 내용과 일치하지 <u>않는</u> 것은?

Call for Articles

Do you want to get your stories published? *New Dream Magazine* is looking for future writers! This event is open to anyone aged 13 to 18.

Articles
• Length of writing: 300−325 words
• Articles should also include high-quality color photos.

Rewards
• Five cents per word
• Five dollars per photo

Notes
• You should send us your phone number together with your writing.
• Please email your writing to us at article@ndmag.com.

① 13세에서 18세까지의 누구나 참여할 수 있다.
② 기사는 고화질 컬러 사진을 포함해야 한다.
③ 사진 한 장에 5센트씩 지급한다.
④ 전화번호를 원고와 함께 보내야 한다.
⑤ 원고를 이메일로 제출해야 한다.

28. Greenhill Roller Skating에 관한 다음 안내문의 내용과 일치하는 것은?

Greenhill Roller Skating

Join us for your chance to enjoy roller skating!

• Place: Greenhill Park, 351 Cypress Avenue
• Dates: Friday, April 7 − Sunday, April 9
• Time: 9 a.m. − 6 p.m.
• Fee: $8 per person for a 50-minute session

Details
− Admission will be on a first-come, first-served basis with no reservations.
− Children under the age of 10 must be accompanied by an adult.
− We will lend you our roller skates for free.

Contact the Community Center for more information at 013-234-6114.

① 오전 9시부터 오후 9시까지 운영한다.
② 이용료는 시간 제한 없이 1인당 8달러이다.
③ 입장하려면 예약이 필요하다.
④ 10세 미만 어린이는 어른과 동행해야 한다.
⑤ 추가 요금을 내면 롤러스케이트를 빌려준다.

29. 다음 글의 밑줄 친 부분 중, 어법상 틀린 것은? [3점]

The most noticeable human characteristic projected onto animals is ① <u>that</u> they can talk in human language. Physically, animal cartoon characters and toys ② <u>made</u> after animals are also most often deformed in such a way as to resemble humans. This is achieved by ③ <u>showing</u> them with humanlike facial features and deformed front legs to resemble human hands. In more recent animated movies the trend has been to show the animals in a more "natural" way. However, they still use their front legs ④ <u>like</u> human hands (for example, lions can pick up and lift small objects with one paw), and they still talk with an appropriate facial expression. A general strategy that is used to make the animal characters more emotionally appealing, both to children and adults, ⑤ <u>are</u> to give them enlarged and deformed childlike features.

* deform: 변형하다 ** paw: (동물의) 발

30. 다음 글의 밑줄 친 부분 중, 문맥상 낱말의 쓰임이 적절하지 <u>않은</u> 것은? [3점]

The major philosophical shift in the idea of selling came when industrial societies became more affluent, more competitive, and more geographically spread out during the 1940s and 1950s. This forced business to develop ① <u>closer</u> relations with buyers and clients, which in turn made business realize that it was not enough to produce a quality product at a reasonable price. In fact, it was equally ② <u>essential</u> to deliver products that customers actually wanted. Henry Ford produced his best-selling T-model Ford in one color only (black) in 1908, but in modern societies this was no longer ③ <u>possible</u>. The modernization of society led to a marketing revolution that ④ <u>strengthened</u> the view that production would create its own demand. Customers, and the desire to ⑤ <u>meet</u> their diverse and often complex needs, became the focus of business.

* affluent: 부유한

[31 ~ 34] 다음 빈칸에 들어갈 말로 가장 적절한 것을 고르시오.

31. People differ in how quickly they can reset their biological clocks to overcome jet lag, and the speed of recovery depends on the ＿＿＿＿＿＿ of travel. Generally, it's easier to fly westward and lengthen your day than it is to fly eastward and shorten it. This east-west difference in jet lag is sizable enough to have an impact on the performance of sports teams. Studies have found that teams flying westward perform significantly better than teams flying eastward in professional baseball and college football. A more recent study of more than 46,000 Major League Baseball games found additional evidence that eastward travel is tougher than westward travel.

* jet lag: 시차로 인한 피로감

① direction
② purpose
③ season
④ length
⑤ cost

32. If you want the confidence that comes from achieving what you set out to do each day, then it's important to understand ＿＿＿＿＿＿＿＿＿＿＿＿＿＿＿＿＿＿＿. Over-optimism about what can be achieved within a certain time frame is a problem. So work on it. Make a practice of estimating the amount of time needed alongside items on your 'things to do' list, and learn by experience when tasks take a greater or lesser time than expected. Give attention also to fitting the task to the available time. There are some tasks that you can only set about if you have a significant amount of time available. There is no point in trying to gear up for such a task when you only have a short period available. So schedule the time you need for the longer tasks and put the short tasks into the spare moments in between.

* gear up: 준비를 갖추다, 대비하다

① what benefits you can get
② how practical your tasks are
③ how long things are going to take
④ why failures are meaningful in life
⑤ why your leisure time should come first

33. In Lewis Carroll's *Through the Looking-Glass*, the Red Queen takes Alice on a race through the countryside. They run and they run, but then Alice discovers that they're still under the same tree that they started from. The Red Queen explains to Alice: "*here*, you see, it takes all the running you can do, to keep in the same place." Biologists sometimes use this Red Queen Effect to explain an evolutionary principle. If foxes evolve to run faster so they can catch more rabbits, then only the fastest rabbits will live long enough to make a new generation of bunnies that run even faster — in which case, of course, only the fastest foxes will catch enough rabbits to thrive and pass on their genes. Even though they might run, the two species _____. [3점]

* thrive: 번성하다

① just stay in place
② end up walking slowly
③ never run into each other
④ won't be able to adapt to changes
⑤ cannot run faster than their parents

34. Everything in the world around us was finished in the mind of its creator before it was started. The houses we live in, the cars we drive, and our clothing — all of these began with an idea. Each idea was then studied, refined and perfected before the first nail was driven or the first piece of cloth was cut. Long before the idea was turned into a physical reality, the mind had clearly pictured the finished product. The human being designs his or her own future through much the same process. We begin with an idea about how the future will be. Over a period of time we refine and perfect the vision. Before long, our every thought, decision and activity are all working in harmony to bring into existence what we _____. [3점]

* refine: 다듬다

① didn't even have the potential to accomplish
② have mentally concluded about the future
③ haven't been able to picture in our mind
④ considered careless and irresponsible
⑤ have observed in some professionals

35. 다음 글에서 전체 흐름과 관계 <u>없는</u> 문장은?

Whose story it is affects *what* the story is. Change the main character, and the focus of the story must also change. If we look at the events through another character's eyes, we will interpret them differently. ① We'll place our sympathies with someone new. ② When the conflict arises that is the heart of the story, we will be praying for a different outcome. ③ Consider, for example, how the tale of Cinderella would shift if told from the viewpoint of an evil stepsister. ④ We know Cinderella's kingdom does not exist, but we willingly go there anyway. ⑤ *Gone with the Wind* is Scarlett O'Hara's story, but what if we were shown the same events from the viewpoint of Rhett Butler or Melanie Wilkes?

* sympathy: 공감

[36 ~ 37] 주어진 글 다음에 이어질 글의 순서로 가장 적절한 것을 고르시오.

36.

> In the Old Stone Age, small bands of 20 to 60 people wandered from place to place in search of food. Once people began farming, they could settle down near their farms.

(A) While some workers grew crops, others built new houses and made tools. Village dwellers also learned to work together to do a task faster.

(B) For example, toolmakers could share the work of making stone axes and knives. By working together, they could make more tools in the same amount of time.

(C) As a result, towns and villages grew larger. Living in communities allowed people to organize themselves more efficiently. They could divide up the work of producing food and other things they needed.

* dweller: 거주자

① (A) − (C) − (B)   ② (B) − (A) − (C)
③ (B) − (C) − (A)   ④ (C) − (A) − (B)
⑤ (C) − (B) − (A)

37.

Natural processes form minerals in many ways. For example, hot melted rock material, called magma, cools when it reaches the Earth's surface, or even if it's trapped below the surface. As magma cools, its atoms lose heat energy, move closer together, and begin to combine into compounds.

(A) Also, the size of the crystals that form depends partly on how rapidly the magma cools. When magma cools slowly, the crystals that form are generally large enough to see with the unaided eye.

(B) During this process, atoms of the different compounds arrange themselves into orderly, repeating patterns. The type and amount of elements present in a magma partly determine which minerals will form.

(C) This is because the atoms have enough time to move together and form into larger crystals. When magma cools rapidly, the crystals that form will be small. In such cases, you can't easily see individual mineral crystals. [3점]

* compound: 화합물

① (A) − (C) − (B) ② (B) − (A) − (C)
③ (B) − (C) − (A) ④ (C) − (A) − (B)
⑤ (C) − (B) − (A)

[38 ~ 39] 글의 흐름으로 보아, 주어진 문장이 들어가기에 가장 적절한 곳을 고르시오.

38.

Bad carbohydrates, on the other hand, are simple sugars.

All carbohydrates are basically sugars. (①) Complex carbohydrates are the good carbohydrates for your body. (②) These complex sugar compounds are very difficult to break down and can trap other nutrients like vitamins and minerals in their chains. (③) As they slowly break down, the other nutrients are also released into your body, and can provide you with fuel for a number of hours. (④) Because their structure is not complex, they are easy to break down and hold few nutrients for your body other than the sugars from which they are made. (⑤) Your body breaks down these carbohydrates rather quickly and what it cannot use is converted to fat and stored in the body.

* carbohydrate: 탄수화물 ** convert: 바꾸다

39.

It was also found that those students who expected the lecturer to be warm tended to interact with him more.

People commonly make the mistaken assumption that because a person has one type of characteristic, then they automatically have other characteristics which go with it. (①) In one study, university students were given descriptions of a guest lecturer before he spoke to the group. (②) Half the students received a description containing the word 'warm', the other half were told the speaker was 'cold'. (③) The guest lecturer then led a discussion, after which the students were asked to give their impressions of him. (④) As expected, there were large differences between the impressions formed by the students, depending upon their original information of the lecturer. (⑤) This shows that different expectations not only affect the impressions we form but also our behaviour and the relationship which is formed. [3점]

40. 다음 글의 내용을 한 문장으로 요약하고자 한다. 빈칸 (A), (B)에 들어갈 말로 가장 적절한 것은?

To help decide what's risky and what's safe, who's trustworthy and who's not, we look for *social evidence*. From an evolutionary view, following the group is almost always positive for our prospects of survival. "If everyone's doing it, it must be a sensible thing to do," explains famous psychologist and best selling writer of *Influence*, Robert Cialdini. While we can frequently see this today in product reviews, even subtler cues within the environment can signal trustworthiness. Consider this: when you visit a local restaurant, are they busy? Is there a line outside or is it easy to find a seat? It is a hassle to wait, but a line can be a powerful cue that the food's tasty, and these seats are in demand. More often than not, it's good to adopt the practices of those around you.

* subtle: 미묘한 ** hassle: 성가신 일

↓

We tend to feel safe and secure in ___(A)___ when we decide how to act, particularly when faced with ___(B)___ conditions.

	(A)		(B)
①	numbers	......	uncertain
②	numbers	......	unrealistic
③	experiences	......	unrealistic
④	rules	......	uncertain
⑤	rules	......	unpleasant

[41 ~ 42] 다음 글을 읽고, 물음에 답하시오.

Chess masters shown a chess board in the middle of a game for 5 seconds with 20 to 30 pieces still in play can immediately reproduce the position of the pieces from memory. Beginners, of course, are able to place only a few. Now take the same pieces and place them on the board randomly and the (a) difference is much reduced. The expert's advantage is only for familiar patterns — those previously stored in memory. Faced with unfamiliar patterns, even when it involves the same familiar domain, the expert's advantage (b) disappears.

The beneficial effects of familiar structure on memory have been observed for many types of expertise, including music. People with musical training can reproduce short sequences of musical notation more accurately than those with no musical training when notes follow (c) unusual sequences, but the advantage is much reduced when the notes are ordered randomly. Expertise also improves memory for sequences of (d) movements. Experienced ballet dancers are able to repeat longer sequences of steps than less experienced dancers, and they can repeat a sequence of steps making up a routine better than steps ordered randomly. In each case, memory range is (e) increased by the ability to recognize familiar sequences and patterns.

* expertise: 전문 지식 ** sequence: 연속, 순서
*** musical notation: 악보

41. 윗글의 제목으로 가장 적절한 것은?

① How Can We Build Good Routines?
② Familiar Structures Help Us Remember
③ Intelligence Does Not Guarantee Expertise
④ Does Playing Chess Improve Your Memory?
⑤ Creative Art Performance Starts from Practice

42. 밑줄 친 (a) ~ (e) 중에서 문맥상 낱말의 쓰임이 적절하지 않은 것은?

① (a)   ② (b)   ③ (c)   ④ (d)   ⑤ (e)

[43 ~ 45] 다음 글을 읽고, 물음에 답하시오.

(A)

Once upon a time, there was a king who lived in a beautiful palace. While the king was away, a monster approached the gates of the palace. The monster was so ugly and smelly that the guards froze in shock. He passed the guards and sat on the king's throne. The guards soon came to their senses, went in, and shouted at the monster, demanding that (a) he get off the throne.

* throne: 왕좌

(B)

Eventually the king returned. He was wise and kind and saw what was happening. He knew what to do. He smiled and said to the monster, "Welcome to my palace!" He asked the monster if (b) he wanted a cup of coffee. The monster began to grow smaller as he drank the coffee.

(C)

The king offered (c) him some take-out pizza and fries. The guards immediately called for pizza. The monster continued to get smaller with the king's kind gestures. (d) He then offered the monster a full body massage. As the guards helped with the relaxing massage, the monster became tiny. With another act of kindness to the monster, he just disappeared.

(D)

With each bad word the guards used, the monster grew more ugly and smelly. The guards got even angrier — they began to brandish their swords to scare the monster away from the palace. But (e) he just grew bigger and bigger, eventually taking up the whole room. He grew more ugly and smelly than ever.

* brandish: 휘두르다

43. 주어진 글 (A)에 이어질 내용을 순서에 맞게 배열한 것으로 가장 적절한 것은?

① (B) - (D) - (C)   ② (C) - (B) - (D)
③ (C) - (D) - (B)   ④ (D) - (B) - (C)
⑤ (D) - (C) - (B)

44. 밑줄 친 (a) ~ (e) 중에서 가리키는 대상이 나머지 넷과 다른 것은?

① (a)   ② (b)   ③ (c)   ④ (d)   ⑤ (e)

45. 윗글에 관한 내용으로 적절하지 않은 것은?

① 왕이 없는 동안 괴물이 궁전 문으로 접근했다.
② 왕은 미소를 지으며 괴물에게 환영한다고 말했다.
③ 왕의 친절한 행동에 괴물의 몸이 계속 더 작아졌다.
④ 경비병들은 괴물을 마사지해 주기를 거부했다.
⑤ 경비병들은 겁을 주어 괴물을 쫓아내려 했다.

* 확인 사항
○ 답안지의 해당란에 필요한 내용을 정확히 기입(표기)했는지 확인하시오.

※ QR 코드를 스캔하시면 듣기 방송이 나옵니다. 듣기 방송을 들으며 다음 빈칸을 채우시오.   ● 제한 시간 : 25분

01

다음을 듣고, 남자가 하는 말의 목적으로 가장 적절한 것을 고르시오.

M : Hello, Villeford High School students. This is principal Aaron Clark. As a big fan of the Villeford ice hockey team, I'm very excited about the upcoming National High School Ice Hockey League. As you all know, the first game will be held in the Central Rink at 6 p.m. this Saturday. I want as many of you as possible to _____ _____ _____ _____ _____ to victory. I've seen them put in ____ _____ _____ ____ _____ to win the league. It will help them play better just to see you there cheering for them. I really hope to _____ _____ __ ____ _____. Thank you.

02

대화를 듣고, 여자의 의견으로 가장 적절한 것을 고르시오.

W : Honey, are you okay?

M : I'm afraid I've caught a cold. I've ✿ _____ __ _____ _____.

W : Why don't you go see a doctor?

M : Well, I don't think it's necessary. I've found some medicine in the cabinet. I'll take it.

W : You shouldn't take that medicine. That's what I got prescribed last week.

M : My symptoms are _____ ____ _____.

W : Honey, you _____ _____ _____ _____ _____ _____.

M : It's just a cold. I'll get better if I take your medicine.

W : It could be dangerous to take someone else's prescription.

M : Okay. Then I'll go see a doctor this afternoon.

03

대화를 듣고, 두 사람의 관계를 가장 잘 나타낸 것을 고르시오.

W : Hi, Mr. Thomson. How are your preparations going?

M : You arrived at the right time. I have something to tell you.

W : Okay. What is it?

M : Well, I'm afraid that we have to ✿ _____ _____ _____ _____ for your paintings.

W : May I ask why?

M : Sure. We have _____ _____ _____ there.

W : I see. Then where are you going to exhibit my works?

M : Our gallery is going to exhibit your paintings in the main hall.

W : Okay. _____ __ _____ __ _____ now?

M : Sure. Come with me.

04

대화를 듣고, 그림에서 대화의 내용과 일치하지 않는 것을 고르시오.

M : Hi, Grace. What are you looking at on your phone?

W : Hi, James. It's a photo I took when I did some volunteer work. We _____ _____ ____ __ _____ _____.

M : Let me see. Wow, I like the whale with the flower pattern.

W : I like it, too. _____ _____ _____ under the whale?

M : It's beautiful. What are these two chairs for?

W : You can take a picture sitting there. The painting becomes the background.

M : Oh, I see. Look at this tree! It has heart-shaped leaves.

W : That's right. We named it the Love Tree.

M : ✿ _____ _____ ____ ____ _____ _____ is lovely, too.

W : I hope a lot of people enjoy the painting.

05

대화를 듣고, 남자가 할 일로 가장 적절한 것을 고르시오.

M : Hi, Stella. How are you doing these days?

W : Hi, Ryan. I've been busy helping my granddad with his concert. He made a rock band with his friends.

M : There must be a lot of things to do.

W : Yeah. I _____ __ _____ for the concert yesterday.

M : What about posters and tickets?

W : Well, I've just finished designing a poster.

M : Then I think I can help you.

W : Really? How?

M : Actually, I have a music blog. I think I can _____ ____ _____ there.

W : That's great!

M : Just _____ _____ _____ ____ _____, and I'll post it online.

W : Thanks a lot.

06

대화를 듣고, 여자가 지불할 금액을 고르시오. [3점]

M : Good morning. How may I help you?

W : Hi. I want to _____ __ _____ ____.

M : Okay. You can choose from these coffee pots.

W : I like this one. How much is it?

M : It was originally $60, but it's now on sale for $50.

W : Okay, I'll buy it. I'd also like to buy this red tumbler.

M : Actually, ___ _____ ___ _____ _____. This smaller one is $20 and a bigger one is $30.

W : The smaller one would be ✿ _____ ___ _____ _____. I'll buy two smaller ones.

M : All right. Is there anything else you need?

W : No, that's all. Thank you.

M : Okay. How would you like to pay?

W : I'll pay by credit card. Here you are.

07

대화를 듣고, 남자가 지갑을 구매하지 못한 이유를 고르시오.

[Cell phone rings.]

W : Hi, Brian.

M : Hi, Mom. I'm in line to get on the plane.

W : Okay. By the way, did you ✿ _____ ____ ____ _____ _____ _____ in the airport?

M : Yes, but I couldn't buy the wallet you asked me to buy.

W : Did you forget the brand name?

M : No. I remembered that. I took a memo.

W : Then did you arrive late at the airport?

M : No, I had _____ _____ ____ _____.

W : Then why couldn't you buy the wallet?

M : Actually, because they were ____ _____ _____.

W : Oh, really?

M : Yeah. The wallet must be very popular.

W : Okay. Thanks for checking anyway.

08

대화를 듣고, Youth Choir Audition에 관해 언급되지 않은 것을 고르시오.

M : Lucy, look at this.

W : Wow. It's about the Youth Choir Audition.

M : Yes. It's open to anyone aged 13 to 18.

W : I'm interested in ✿ _____ _____ _____. When is it?

M : April 2nd, from 9 a.m. to 5 p.m.

W : The place for the audition is the Youth Training Center. It's _____ _____ _____ _____.

M : I think you should leave early in the morning.

W : That's no problem. ___ _____ ____ _____ _____?

M : No, it's free.

W : Good. I'll apply for the audition.

M : Then you should fill out an application form on this website.

W : All right. Thanks.

09

2023 Career Week에 관한 다음 내용을 듣고, 일치하지 않는 것을 고르시오.

W : Hello, Rosehill High School students! I'm your school counselor, Ms. Lee. I'm so happy to announce a special event, the 2023 Career Week. It'll be held from May 22nd ____ _____ _____. There will be many programs to help you ✿ _____ _____ _____ _____. Please kindly note that the number of participants for each program is limited to 20. A special lecture on future career choices will be presented ____ _____ _____ _____. Registration begins on May 10th. For more information, please visit our school website. I hope you can come and enjoy the 2023 Career Week!

10

다음 표를 보면서 대화를 듣고, 여자가 구입할 프라이팬을 고르시오.

M : Jessica, what are you doing?

W : I'm trying to buy one of these five frying pans.

M : Let me see. This frying pan seems pretty expensive.

W : Yeah. I don't want to spend more than $50.

M : Okay. And I think 9 to 12-inch frying pans will _____ _____ _____ ___ __ _____ _____.

W : I think so, too. An 8-inch frying pan seems too small for me.

M : What about the material? Stainless steel pans are good for fast cooking.

W : I know, but _____ _____ _____. I'll buy an aluminum pan.

M : Then you have two options left. Do you need a lid?

W : Of course. A lid ✿ _____ ____ _____ _____. I'll buy this one.

M : Good choice.

11

대화를 듣고, 남자의 마지막 말에 대한 여자의 응답으로 가장 적절한 것을 고르시오.

M : Have you finished your team's short-movie project?

W : Not yet. I'm still ✿ _____ ____ _____ _____.

M : Oh, you edit? _____ _____ _____ ___ _____ _____?

12

대화를 듣고, 여자의 마지막 말에 대한 남자의 응답으로 가장 적절한 것을 고르시오.

W : Daddy, are you still working now?

M : No, Emma. I'm about to _____ __ _____ _____ _____
_____ _____.

W : Great. ✿ _____? I'm at the
City Library near your office.

13

대화를 듣고, 남자의 마지막 말에 대한 여자의 응답으로 가장 적절한 것을 고르시오.

M : Claire, how's your farm doing?

W : Great! I ✿ _____ _____ _____
_____ and cucumbers last weekend. Do you want
some?

M : Of course. I'd like some very much.

W : Okay. I'll bring you some tomorrow.

M : Thanks. Are you going to the farm this weekend too?

W : Yes. The peppers are almost ✿ _____ ___ _____
_____.

M : Can I go with you? I'd like to look around your farm and help
you pick the peppers.

W : Sure. It would be fun to work on the farm together.

M : Sounds nice. Is there _____ _ _____ ___
_____?

14

대화를 듣고, 여자의 마지막 말에 대한 남자의 응답으로 가장 적절한 것을 고르시오.
[3점]

W : Daniel, what's wrong?

M : Hi, Leila. I ✿ _____ ___ _____ with Olivia.

W : Was it serious?

M : I'm not sure, but I think I made a mistake.

W : So that's why _____ _____ __ _____ _____.

M : Yeah. I want to get along with her, but she's still angry at me.

W : Did you say you're sorry to her?

M : Well, I texted her saying that I'm sorry.

W : I don't think it's a good idea to express your apology through a
text message.

M : Do you think so? Now I know why I haven't received any
response from her yet.

W : I think it'd be best to go and _____ ___ _____
_____.

15

다음 상황 설명을 듣고, John이 Ted에게 할 말로 가장 적절한 것을 고르시오. [3점]

M : Ted and John are college freshmen. They are climbing Green
Diamond Mountain together. Now they have reached the campsite
near the mountain top. After climbing the mountain all day, they
_____ __ _____ _____ at the campsite. While
drinking coffee, Ted suggests to John that they ✿ _____
_____ _____ at the mountain top the next morning. John
thinks it's a good idea. So, now John wants to ask Ted _____
_____ _____ _____ _____ ____ to see the
sunrise. In this situation, what would John most likely say to Ted?

16~17

다음을 듣고, 물음에 답하시오.

W : Good morning, everyone. Do you spend a lot of time with your
family? One of the best ways to spend time with your family is to
_____ _____ _____. Today, I will share
some of the best sports that families can play together. The first
one is badminton. The whole family can enjoy the sport
✿ _____ _____ _____. The second
one is basketball. You can easily find a basketball court near your
house. The third one is table tennis. ___ _____ _____ _____
_____ _____. The last one is bowling. Many
families have a great time playing it together. When you go home
today, how about playing one of these sports with your family?

18

001 to whom it may concern 담당자 귀하, 관계자 귀하
002 resident ⓝ 주민
003 observe ⓥ (보고) 알다, 관찰하다
004 in need of ~이 필요한
005 repair ⓝ 보수, 수리
006 pay attention to ~에 주의를 기울이다
007 condition ⓝ 상태
008 playground ⓝ 놀이터
009 equipment ⓝ 장비
010 swing ⓝ 그네
011 damaged ⓐ 손상된
012 fall off 벗겨지다, 떨어져 나가다
013 slide ⓝ 미끄럼틀
014 missing ⓐ 없어진, 실종된
015 facility ⓝ 시설
016 terrible ⓐ 끔찍한
017 immediate ⓐ 즉각적인
018 matter ⓝ 문제

19

019 grizzly bear (북미·러시아 일부 지역에 사는) 회색곰
020 native ⓐ 토착의, 토종의
021 habitat ⓝ 서식지
022 at first 처음에
023 joy ⓝ 기쁨, 즐거움
024 walk across ~을 횡단하다
025 every once in a while 이따금
026 turn about 뒤돌아보다, 방향을 바꾸다
027 sniff ⓥ 킁킁거리다
028 deeply ⓐⓓ 깊게
029 scent ⓝ 냄새
030 slowly ⓐⓓ 천천히
031 giant ⓐ 거대한
032 smell ⓥ 냄새 맡다
033 freeze 얼어붙다
034 no longer 더 이상 ~않다
035 issue ⓝ 문제, 이슈
036 survival ⓝ 생존
037 motivation ⓝ (행동의) 이유, 동기 (부여)
038 clearly ⓐⓓ 분명히
039 jealous ⓐ 질투하는
040 frustrated ⓐ 좌절한

20

041 maintain ⓥ 유지하다
042 constant ⓐ 지속적인
043 attention ⓝ 주의, 집중
044 throughout prep ~ 내내
045 working day 근무 시간대
046 characterise ⓥ ~을 특징으로 하다
047 peaks and valleys 정점과 저점, 부침, 성쇠
048 alertness ⓝ 기민함
049 achieve ⓥ 성취하다
050 confident ⓐ 자신감 있는
051 benefit ⓝ 이득
052 demanding ⓐ 까다로운, 힘든
053 cope with ~을 처리하다
054 warm up 준비가 되다, 몸을 풀다

21

055 adopt ⓥ 수용하다, 받아들이다
056 cost ⓝ 비용 ⓥ (~의 비용을) 치르게 하다
057 livelihood ⓝ 생계
058 push aside 밀어치우다
059 progress ⓝ 진보
060 remove ⓥ 제거하다
061 million ⓝ 100만
062 produce ⓥ 만들어내다
063 physical ⓐ 신체적인
064 disability ⓝ 장애
065 chronic ⓐ 만성의
066 certainly ⓐⓓ 분명히, 확실히
067 mass ⓝ (일반) 대중 ⓐ 대중의, 대량의
068 seek ⓥ 찾다, 추구하다
069 divorce A from B A와 B의 분리, A를 B로부터 분리시키다
070 put a stress on ~에 스트레스[부담]를 주다
071 sedentary ⓐ 주로 앉아서 하는
072 nature ⓝ 본성, 특성
073 health risk 건강상 위험
074 ignorance ⓝ 무지
075 endless ⓐ 끝없는
076 competition ⓝ 경쟁
077 labor market 노동 시장
078 get along (well) with ~와 잘 지내다
079 realistic ⓐ 현실적인

22

080 course ⓝ 수업, 강좌
081 rubber-stamp ⓝ 고무도장, 잘 살펴보지도 않고 무조건 허가하는 사람
082 colorful ⓐ 화려한, 색색의
083 funeral ⓝ 장례식
084 bathing suit 수영복
085 religious service 종교 의식
086 appropriate ⓐ 적절한
087 occasion ⓝ 상황, 경우
088 setting ⓝ 환경, 배경
089 skillful ⓐ 숙련된
090 flexible ⓐ 융통성 있는
091 strategy ⓝ 전략
092 multiple-choice test 객관식 시험, 선다형 시험

23

093 social ⓐ 사회적인
094 get better 나아지다, 개선되다
095 wage ⓝ 임금
096 working condition 근무 조건
097 improve ⓥ 향상되다
098 gradually ⓐⓓ 점차, 점점
099 time off 휴가
100 at the same time 동시에, 한편
101 transport ⓝ 운송, 이동
102 industrial revolution 산업 혁명
103 lead to ~을 초래하다
104 railway ⓝ 철도
105 seaside ⓝ 해변
106 arrival ⓝ 도래, 도착
107 tourism ⓝ 관광(업)

24

108 growth ⓝ 성장
109 factor ⓝ 요인
110 expansion ⓝ 확장
111 discomfort ⓝ 불편
112 tourist destination 관광지
113 impact ⓝ 영향, 여파
114 characteristic ⓝ 특징

24

115 intended ⓐ 의도된
116 path ⓝ 길
117 rut ⓝ 틀에 박힌 생활
118 be good at ~을 잘하다
119 be rewarded for ~에 대해 보상받다
120 look around 둘러보다
121 deep ⓐ 깊은
122 breathe ⓥ 호흡하다
123 slippery ⓐ 미끄러운
124 take effort to ~하는 데 (…한) 노력이 들다
125 superhuman ⓐ 초인적인
126 effectively ⓐⓓ 실질적으로, 사실상
127 be stuck 꼼짝 못하다
128 employment ⓝ 고용
129 well-paying ⓐ 보수가 좋은
130 ultimately ⓐⓓ 궁극적으로
131 unsatisfying ⓐ 불만족스러운
132 compete with ~와 경쟁하다
133 have ~ in common ~을 공통적으로 지니다
134 influential ⓐ 영향력 있는

25

135 the number of ~의 수
136 decrease ⓥ 감소하다
137 period ⓝ 기간
138 gap between A and B A와 B 사이의 격차
139 slightly ⓐⓓ 약간
140 steadily ⓐⓓ 꾸준히
141 except prep ~을 제외하고
142 for the first time 처음으로

26

143 unlike prep ~와 달리
144 at the time (과거) 당시에
145 trousers ⓝ 바지
146 spend time ~ing ~하면서 시간을 보내다
147 adventurous ⓐ 모험적인
148 horse riding 승마
149 hunting ⓝ 사냥
150 wildlife ⓝ 야생 동물
151 photographer ⓝ 사진 작가
152 design ⓥ 설계하다
153 persuade ⓥ 설득하다
154 safe ⓐ 안전한
155 end up ~ing 결국 ~하다
156 work as ~로서 일하다
157 car dealer 자동차 판매상
158 go back to ~로 되돌아가다
159 nonetheless ⓐⓓ 그럼에도 불구하고
160 have a kid 자식을 낳다
161 the rest of ~의 나머지

27

162 publish ⓥ 출간하다
163 be open to ~을 대상으로 하다
164 article ⓝ 기사
165 length ⓝ 길이
166 high-quality ⓐ 고품질의

28

167 session ⓝ (특정한 활동을 위한) 시간
168 admission ⓝ 입장
169 first-come, first-served 선착순
170 accompany ⓥ 동반하다
171 for free 공짜로

29

172 noticeable ⓐ 눈에 띄는, 두드러지는
173 characteristic ⓝ 특징
174 project onto ~에게 투영시키다
175 cartoon character 만화 캐릭터
176 deform ⓥ 변형하다
177 in such a way as to ~한 방식으로
178 resemble ⓥ ~와 닮다
179 humanlike ⓐ 인간 같은
180 animated movie 만화 영화
181 natural ⓐ 자연스러운
182 lift ⓥ 들어올리다
183 paw ⓝ (동물의) 발
184 facial expression 얼굴 표정
185 emotionally ⓐⓓ 정서적으로
186 appealing ⓐ 매력적인
187 enlarge ⓥ 확대하다
188 feature ⓝ 특징, 이목구비

30

189 major ⓐ 주요한, 큰
190 philosophical ⓐ 철학적인
191 shift ⓝ 변화, 전환 ⓥ 바뀌다
192 industrial ⓐ 산업의
193 affluent ⓐ 부유한
194 competitive ⓐ 경쟁적인
195 geographically ⓐⓓ 지리적으로
196 spread ⓥ 퍼지다
197 force ⓥ (~이) 어쩔 수 없이 …하게 하다
198 in turn 결과적으로
199 reasonable ⓐ 합리적인, 적당한
200 essential ⓐ 매우 중요한
201 best-selling ⓐ 가장 많이 팔리는, 베스트셀러인
202 modernization ⓝ 현대화
203 revolution ⓝ 혁명
204 strengthen ⓥ 강화하다
205 demand ⓝ 수요
206 complex ⓐ 복잡한

31

207 differ in ~에 관해 다르다
208 reset ⓥ 재설정하다
209 biological clock 체내 시계
210 overcome ⓥ 극복하다
211 jet lag 시차로 인한 피로감
212 recovery ⓝ 회복
213 depend on ~에 좌우되다

214 ☐ **westward** @ 서쪽으로
215 ☐ **lengthen** ⓥ 연장하다
216 ☐ **eastward** @ 동쪽으로
217 ☐ **shorten** ⓥ 단축하다
218 ☐ **sizable** @ 꽤 큰, 상당한
219 ☐ **have an impact on** ~에 영향을 주다
220 ☐ **performance** ⓝ (선수의) 경기력, 수행, 성과
221 ☐ **significantly** @ 상당히, 현저히
222 ☐ **additional** @ 추가적인
223 ☐ **tough** @ 어려운, 힘든

32
224 ☐ **confidence** ⓝ 자신감
225 ☐ **set out** 착수하다
226 ☐ **each day** 매일
227 ☐ **over-optimism** ⓝ 지나친 낙관주의
228 ☐ **time frame** (어떤 일에 쓸 수 있는) 시간(대)
229 ☐ **work on** ~에 공을 들이다
230 ☐ **make a practice of** ~을 습관으로 하다
231 ☐ **estimate** ⓥ 추산하다
232 ☐ **alongside** prep ~와 함께
233 ☐ **learn by experience** 경험을 통해 배우다
234 ☐ **than expected** 예상보다
235 ☐ **fit** ⓥ ~에 맞추다
236 ☐ **available** @ 이용 가능한
237 ☐ **set about** ~을 시작하다
238 ☐ **there is no point in** ~하는 것은 의미가 없다
239 ☐ **gear up** 준비를 갖추다, 대비하다
240 ☐ **spare** @ 여분의
241 ☐ **in between** 사이에
242 ☐ **practical** @ 현실성 있는, 타당한
243 ☐ **come first** 가장 중요하다, 최우선 고려 사항이다

33
244 ☐ **countryside** ⓝ 시골 지역
245 ☐ **discover** ⓥ 발견하다
246 ☐ **explain** ⓥ 설명하다
247 ☐ **biologist** ⓝ 생물학자
248 ☐ **evolutionary** @ 진화적인
249 ☐ **principle** ⓝ 원리
250 ☐ **evolve** ⓥ 진화하다, 발전하다
251 ☐ **generation** ⓝ 세대
252 ☐ **thrive** ⓥ 번성하다
253 ☐ **pass on** 물려주다
254 ☐ **gene** ⓝ 유전자
255 ☐ **species** ⓝ (생물) 종
256 ☐ **run into** ~을 우연히 만나다
257 ☐ **adapt to** ~에 적응하다

34
258 ☐ **creator** ⓝ 창조자
259 ☐ **clothing** ⓝ 옷, 의복
260 ☐ **begin with** ~로 시작되다
261 ☐ **refine** ⓥ 다듬다
262 ☐ **perfect** ⓥ 완성하다, 완벽하게 하다
263 ☐ **nail** ⓝ 못
264 ☐ **turn A into B** A를 B로 바꾸다
265 ☐ **picture** ⓥ 상상하다, 그리다
266 ☐ **finished product** 완제품

267 ☐ **process** ⓝ 과정
268 ☐ **over a period of time** 일정 기간에 걸쳐서
269 ☐ **before long** 머지않아
270 ☐ **in harmony** 조화롭게
271 ☐ **bring into existence** ~을 생겨나게 하다
272 ☐ **mentally** @ 머릿속에, 마음속으로
273 ☐ **careless** @ 조심성 없는
274 ☐ **irresponsible** @ 무책임한
275 ☐ **professional** ⓝ 전문가 @ 전문적인

35
276 ☐ **affect** ⓥ 영향을 미치다
277 ☐ **main character** 주인공
278 ☐ **look through** ~을 통해서 보다
279 ☐ **interpret** ⓥ 해석하다, 이해하다
280 ☐ **differently** @ 다르게
281 ☐ **sympathy** ⓝ 공감
282 ☐ **conflict** ⓝ 갈등
283 ☐ **arise** ⓥ 발생하다
284 ☐ **pray for** ~을 위해 기도하다
285 ☐ **outcome** ⓝ 결과
286 ☐ **tale** ⓝ 이야기
287 ☐ **shift** ⓥ 바꾸다
288 ☐ **viewpoint** ⓝ 관점
289 ☐ **evil** @ 사악한 ⓝ 악
290 ☐ **stepsister** ⓝ 의붓자매
291 ☐ **kingdom** ⓝ 왕국
292 ☐ **exist** ⓥ 존재하다
293 ☐ **willingly** @ 기꺼이
294 ☐ **what if** ~라면 어떨까

36
295 ☐ **Old Stone Age** 구석기 시대
296 ☐ **band** ⓝ (소규모) 무리
297 ☐ **wander** ⓥ 돌아다니다, 배회하다
298 ☐ **from place to place** 여기저기
299 ☐ **in search of** ~을 찾아서
300 ☐ **settle down** 정착하다
301 ☐ **crop** ⓝ 작물
302 ☐ **dweller** ⓝ 거주자
303 ☐ **work together** 함께 일하다, 협력하다
304 ☐ **share** ⓥ 나누다, 공유하다
305 ☐ **axe** ⓝ 도끼
306 ☐ **as a result** 그 결과
307 ☐ **community** ⓝ 공동체, 지역사회
308 ☐ **organize** ⓥ 조직하다, 정리하다
309 ☐ **efficiently** @ 효율적으로
310 ☐ **divide up** ~을 나누다

37
311 ☐ **form** ⓥ 형성하다
312 ☐ **mineral** ⓝ 광물
313 ☐ **in many ways** 많은 방법으로
314 ☐ **melt** ⓥ 녹이다, 녹다
315 ☐ **surface** ⓝ 표면
316 ☐ **trap** ⓥ 가두다
317 ☐ **below** prep ~의 아래에
318 ☐ **atom** ⓝ 원자
319 ☐ **combine into** ~로 결합되다
320 ☐ **compound** ⓝ 화합물
321 ☐ **crystal** ⓝ 결정체, 수정

322 ☐ **partly** @ 부분적으로
323 ☐ **rapidly** @ 빠르게
324 ☐ **with the unaided eye** 육안으로
325 ☐ **arrange** ⓥ 배열하다
326 ☐ **orderly** @ 질서 있는
327 ☐ **element** ⓝ 원소, 구성요소
328 ☐ **in such cases** 이런 경우에

38
329 ☐ **carbohydrate** ⓝ 탄수화물
330 ☐ **simple sugar** 단당류
331 ☐ **basically** @ 기본적으로
332 ☐ **break down** 분해하다
333 ☐ **nutrient** ⓝ 영양소
334 ☐ **chain** ⓝ 사슬
335 ☐ **release** ⓥ 방출하다
336 ☐ **provide A with B** A에게 B를 공급하다
337 ☐ **a number of** 많은
338 ☐ **structure** ⓝ 구조
339 ☐ **other than** ~ 외에
340 ☐ **be made from** ~로 구성되다
341 ☐ **rather** @ 다소, 상당히, 꽤
342 ☐ **convert** ⓥ 바꾸다
343 ☐ **store** ⓥ 저장하다, 보유하다

39
344 ☐ **lecturer** ⓝ 강사, 강연자
345 ☐ **interact with** ~와 상호작용하다
346 ☐ **commonly** @ 흔히
347 ☐ **mistaken** @ 잘못된, 틀린
348 ☐ **assumption** ⓝ 가정, 추정
349 ☐ **characteristic** ⓝ 특성
350 ☐ **automatically** @ 자동으로, 저절로
351 ☐ **go with** ~와 어울리다
352 ☐ **description** ⓝ 설명
353 ☐ **speak to** ~에게 말하다, 이야기를 걸다
354 ☐ **receive** ⓥ 받다
355 ☐ **contain** ⓥ 포함하다, (~이) 들어 있다
356 ☐ **be told** ~을 듣다
357 ☐ **discussion** ⓝ 토론, 논의
358 ☐ **impression** ⓝ 인상
359 ☐ **as expected** 예상된 대로
360 ☐ **original** @ 최초의, 원래의
361 ☐ **expectation** ⓝ 기대, 예상
362 ☐ **relationship** ⓝ 관계

40
363 ☐ **risky** @ 위험한
364 ☐ **trustworthy** @ 신뢰할 만한
365 ☐ **evidence** ⓝ 근거, 증거
366 ☐ **almost** @ 거의
367 ☐ **prospect** ⓝ 예상, 가망성
368 ☐ **sensible** @ 분별 있는, 현명한
369 ☐ **frequently** @ 자주, 빈번히
370 ☐ **product review** 상품평
371 ☐ **subtle** @ 미묘한
372 ☐ **cue** ⓝ 단서, 신호
373 ☐ **signal** ⓥ 알리다 ⓝ 신호
374 ☐ **local** @ 지역의, 현지의
375 ☐ **hassle** ⓝ 성가신 일
376 ☐ **tasty** @ 맛있는
377 ☐ **in demand** 수요가 많은

378 ☐ **more often than not** 대개
379 ☐ **practice** ⓝ 관례, 실행
380 ☐ **particularly** @ 특히
381 ☐ **faced with** ~와 직면한
382 ☐ **uncertain** @ 불확실한
383 ☐ **unrealistic** @ 비현실적인
384 ☐ **rule** ⓝ 규칙 ⓥ 지배하다
385 ☐ **unpleasant** @ 불쾌한

41~42
386 ☐ **master** ⓝ 달인, 고수
387 ☐ **chess board** 체스판
388 ☐ **in the middle of** ~의 한가운데에
389 ☐ **in play** 시합 중인
390 ☐ **reproduce** ⓥ 재현하다
391 ☐ **position** ⓝ 위치
392 ☐ **from memory** 외워서, 기억하여
393 ☐ **beginner** ⓝ 초심자
394 ☐ **only a few** 몇 안 되는 (것)
395 ☐ **place** ⓥ 놓다, 배치하다
396 ☐ **randomly** @ 무작위로
397 ☐ **reduce** ⓥ 줄이다, 감소시키다
398 ☐ **advantage** ⓝ 유리함, 이점
399 ☐ **familiar** @ 익숙한, 친숙한
400 ☐ **previously** @ 이전에, 사전에
401 ☐ **unfamiliar** @ 익숙지 않은, 낯선
402 ☐ **domain** ⓝ 영역, 분야
403 ☐ **disappear** ⓥ 사라지다
404 ☐ **beneficial** @ 유익한, 이로운
405 ☐ **expertise** ⓝ 전문 지식
406 ☐ **sequence** ⓝ 연속, 순서
407 ☐ **musical notation** 악보
408 ☐ **accurately** @ 정확하게
409 ☐ **unusual** @ 특이한
410 ☐ **movement** ⓝ 동작, 움직임
411 ☐ **experienced** @ 숙련된, 경험 많은
412 ☐ **routine** ⓝ 습관, (정해진) 춤 동작, 루틴
413 ☐ **guarantee** ⓥ 보장하다

43~45
414 ☐ **once upon a time** 옛날 옛적에
415 ☐ **palace** ⓝ 궁전
416 ☐ **approach** ⓥ 다가오다, 접근하다
417 ☐ **gate** ⓝ 문
418 ☐ **ugly** @ 추한
419 ☐ **smelly** @ 냄새 나는, 악취가 나는
420 ☐ **in shock** 충격을 받아
421 ☐ **throne** ⓝ 왕좌
422 ☐ **come to one's senses** 정신을 차리다
423 ☐ **shout at** ~을 향해 소리치다
424 ☐ **get off** ~을 떠나다
425 ☐ **wise** @ 현명한
426 ☐ **if** conj ~인지 아닌지
427 ☐ **take-out** @ 사서 가지고 가는
428 ☐ **call for** ~을 시키다, ~을 요구하다
429 ☐ **gesture** ⓝ 몸짓, (감정의) 표시, 표현
430 ☐ **massage** ⓝ 마사지
431 ☐ **tiny** @ 아주 작은
432 ☐ **brandish** ⓥ 휘두르다
433 ☐ **scare away** ~을 겁주어 쫓아버리다
434 ☐ **take up** ~을 차지하다
435 ☐ **than ever** 그 어느 때보다

TEST A-B 각 단어의 뜻을 [A] 영어는 우리말로, [B] 우리말은 영어로 쓰시오.

A	English	Korean		B	Korean	English
01	conflict			01	정착하다	
02	mineral			02	효율적으로	
03	carbohydrate			03	포함하다	
04	discussion			04	~을 겁주어 쫓아버리다	
05	unpleasant			05	발견하다	
06	approach			06	유전자	
07	guarantee			07	무작위로	
08	take up			08	지속적인	
09	willingly			09	(생물) 종	
10	release			10	조직하다, 정리하다	
11	scent			11	질투하는	
12	frustrated			12	이유, 동기부여	
13	confident			13	추산하다	
14	arise			14	돌아다니다, 배회하다	
15	combine into			15	원리	
16	cope with			16	인상	
17	adopt			17	공감	
18	adapt to			18	서식지	
19	maintain			19	기대, 예상	
20	call for			20	구조	

▶ A-D 정답 : 해설편 028쪽

TEST C-D 각 단어의 뜻을 골라 기호를 쓰시오.

C	English			Korean		D	Korean			English
01	picture	( )	ⓐ 화합물			01	질서 있는	( )	ⓐ stepsister
02	warm up	( )	ⓑ 규칙, 지배하다			02	영역, 분야	( )	ⓑ no longer
03	rule	( )	ⓒ 상상하다, 그리다			03	원소, 구성요소	( )	ⓒ careless
04	expertise	( )	ⓓ 영양소			04	무책임한	( )	ⓓ prospect
05	refine	( )	ⓔ 유익한, 이로운			05	근거, 증거	( )	ⓔ element
06	compound	( )	ⓕ 왕좌			06	위험한	( )	ⓕ interpret
07	faced with	( )	ⓖ ~내내			07	현실성 있는, 타당한	( )	ⓖ practice
08	alertness	( )	ⓗ 준비가 되다, 몸을 풀다			08	해석하다, 이해하다	( )	ⓗ orderly
09	run into	( )	ⓘ 다듬다			09	수요가 많은	( )	ⓘ familiar
10	thrive	( )	ⓙ 우연히 만나다			10	더 이상~ 않다	( )	ⓙ band
11	bring into existence	( )	ⓚ 결과			11	의붓자매	( )	ⓚ in demand
12	nutrient	( )	ⓛ 미묘한			12	조심성 없는	( )	ⓛ from memory
13	outcome	( )	ⓜ 전문지식			13	예상, 가망성	( )	ⓜ irresponsible
14	dweller	( )	ⓝ 이야기			14	익숙한, 친숙한	( )	ⓝ accurately
15	beneficial	( )	ⓞ 번성하다			15	관례, 실행	( )	ⓞ practical
16	throne	( )	ⓟ 거주자			16	(소규모) 무리	( )	ⓟ sequence
17	tale	( )	ⓠ ~을 생겨나게 하다			17	외워서, 기억하여	( )	ⓠ gesture
18	assumption	( )	ⓡ 기민함			18	연속, 순서	( )	ⓡ evidence
19	throughout	( )	ⓢ 가정			19	몸짓	( )	ⓢ domain
20	subtle	( )	ⓣ ~와 직면한			20	정확하게	( )	ⓣ risky

영어 영역

● 문항수 45개 | 배점 100점 | 제한 시간 70분　　● 점수 표시가 없는 문항은 모두 2점

1번부터 17번까지는 듣고 답하는 문제입니다. 1번부터 15번까지는 한 번만 들려주고, 16번부터 17번까지는 두 번 들려줍니다. 방송을 잘 듣고 답을 하시기 바랍니다.

MP3

1. 다음을 듣고, 남자가 하는 말의 목적으로 가장 적절한 것을 고르시오.

① 농구 리그 참가 등록 방법의 변경을 알리려고
② 확정된 농구 리그 시합 일정을 발표하려고
③ 농구 리그의 심판을 추가 모집하려고
④ 농구 리그 경기 관람을 권장하려고
⑤ 농구 리그 우승 상품을 안내하려고

2. 대화를 듣고, 여자의 의견으로 가장 적절한 것을 고르시오.

① 평소에 피부 상태를 잘 관찰할 필요가 있다.
② 여드름을 치료하려면 피부과 병원에 가야 한다.
③ 얼굴을 손으로 만지는 것은 얼굴 피부에 해롭다.
④ 지성 피부를 가진 사람은 자주 세수를 해야 한다.
⑤ 손을 자주 씻는 것은 감염병 예방에 도움이 된다.

3. 대화를 듣고, 두 사람의 관계를 가장 잘 나타낸 것을 고르시오.

① 방송 작가 – 연출자
② 만화가 – 환경 운동가
③ 촬영 감독 – 동화 작가
④ 토크쇼 진행자 – 기후학자
⑤ 제품 디자이너 – 영업 사원

4. 대화를 듣고, 그림에서 대화의 내용과 일치하지 않는 것을 고르시오.

5. 대화를 듣고, 여자가 남자에게 부탁한 일로 가장 적절한 것을 고르시오.

① 장난감 사 오기　　② 풍선 달기
③ 케이크 가져오기　　④ 탁자 옮기기
⑤ 아이들 데려오기

6. 대화를 듣고, 남자가 지불할 금액을 고르시오. [3점]

① $14　　② $16　　③ $18　　④ $20　　⑤ $22

7. 대화를 듣고, 두 사람이 오늘 실험을 할 수 없는 이유를 고르시오.

① 실험용 키트가 배달되지 않아서
② 실험 주제를 변경해야 해서
③ 과학실을 예약하지 못해서
④ 보고서를 작성해야 해서
⑤ 남자가 감기에 걸려서

8. 대화를 듣고, Stanville Free-cycle에 관해 언급되지 않은 것을 고르시오.

① 참가 대상　　② 행사 장소　　③ 주차 가능 여부
④ 행사 시작일　　⑤ 금지 품목

9. River Valley Music Camp에 관한 다음 내용을 듣고, 일치하지 않는 것을 고르시오.

① 4월 11일부터 5일 동안 진행된다.
② 학교 오케스트라 단원이 아니어도 참가할 수 있다.
③ 자신의 악기를 가져오거나 학교에서 빌릴 수 있다.
④ 마지막 날에 공연을 촬영한다.
⑤ 참가 인원에는 제한이 없다.

10. 다음 표를 보면서 대화를 듣고, 여자가 주문할 소형 진공청소기를 고르시오.

Handheld Vacuum Cleaners

	Model	Price	Working Time	Weight	Washable Filter
①	A	$50	8 minutes	2.5 kg	×
②	B	$80	12 minutes	2.0 kg	○
③	C	$100	15 minutes	1.8 kg	○
④	D	$120	20 minutes	1.8 kg	×
⑤	E	$150	25 minutes	1.6 kg	○

11. 대화를 듣고, 남자의 마지막 말에 대한 여자의 응답으로 가장 적절한 것을 고르시오.

① Why don't you rinse your eyes with clean water?
② Can you explain more about the air pollution?
③ I need to get myself a new pair of glasses.
④ I agree that fine dust is a serious problem.
⑤ We should go outside and take a walk.

12. 대화를 듣고, 여자의 마지막 말에 대한 남자의 응답으로 가장 적절한 것을 고르시오.

① That's not fair. I booked this seat first.
② Thank you. My friend will be glad to know it.
③ You're welcome. Feel free to ask me anything.
④ Not at all. I don't mind changing seats with you.
⑤ That's okay. I think the seat next to it is available.

영어 영역

13. 대화를 듣고, 남자의 마지막 말에 대한 여자의 응답으로 가장 적절한 것을 고르시오.

Woman: _____

① Smells good. Can I try the pizza?
② Great. I'll bring chips and popcorn.
③ No problem. I'll cancel the tickets.
④ Sorry. I don't like watching baseball.
⑤ Sure. Here's the hammer I borrowed.

14. 대화를 듣고, 여자의 마지막 말에 대한 남자의 응답으로 가장 적절한 것을 고르시오. [3점]

Man: _____

① Exactly. This is a best-selling novel.
② Sounds cool. I'll join a book club, too.
③ Not really. Books make good presents.
④ New year's resolutions are hard to keep.
⑤ Let's buy some books for your book club.

15. 다음 상황 설명을 듣고, Brian이 Sally에게 할 말로 가장 적절한 것을 고르시오. [3점]

Brian: _____

① You shouldn't touch a guide dog without permission.
② The dog would be happy if we give it some food.
③ I'm sure it's smart enough to be a guide dog.
④ I suggest that you walk your dog every day.
⑤ I'm afraid that dogs are not allowed in here.

[16 ~ 17] 다음을 듣고, 물음에 답하시오.

16. 여자가 하는 말의 주제로 가장 적절한 것은?

① activities that help build muscles
② ways to control stress in daily life
③ types of joint problems in elderly people
④ low-impact exercises for people with bad joints
⑤ importance of daily exercise for controlling weight

17. 언급된 운동이 <u>아닌</u> 것은?

① swimming
② cycling
③ horseback riding
④ bowling
⑤ walking

이제 듣기 문제가 끝났습니다. 18번부터는 문제지의 지시에 따라 답을 하시기 바랍니다.

---

18. 다음 글의 목적으로 가장 적절한 것은?

Dear Ms. Robinson,
 The Warblers Choir is happy to announce that we are invited to compete in the International Young Choir Competition. The competition takes place in London on May 20. Though we wish to participate in the event, we do not have the necessary funds to travel to London. So we are kindly asking you to support us by coming to our fundraising concert. It will be held on March 26. In this concert, we shall be able to show you how big our passion for music is. Thank you in advance for your kind support and help.
Sincerely,
Arnold Reynolds

① 합창 대회 결과를 공지하려고
② 모금 음악회 참석을 요청하려고
③ 음악회 개최 장소를 예약하려고
④ 합창곡 선정에 조언을 구하려고
⑤ 기부금 사용 내역을 보고하려고

19. 다음 글에 드러난 Zoe의 심경 변화로 가장 적절한 것은?

 The principal stepped on stage. "Now, I present this year's top academic award to the student who has achieved the highest placing." He smiled at the row of seats where twelve finalists had gathered. Zoe wiped a sweaty hand on her handkerchief and glanced at the other finalists. They all looked as pale and uneasy as herself. Zoe and one of the other finalists had won first placing in four subjects so it came down to how teachers ranked their hard work and confidence. "The Trophy for General Excellence is awarded to Miss Zoe Perry," the principal declared. "Could Zoe step this way, please?" Zoe felt as if she were in heaven. She walked into the thunder of applause with a big smile.

① hopeful → disappointed
② guilty → confident
③ nervous → delighted
④ angry → calm
⑤ relaxed → proud

20. 다음 글에서 필자가 주장하는 바로 가장 적절한 것은?

 When I was in the army, my instructors would show up in my barracks room, and the first thing they would inspect was our bed. It was a simple task, but every morning we were required to make our bed to perfection. It seemed a little ridiculous at the time, but the wisdom of this simple act has been proven to me many times over. If you make your bed every morning, you will have accomplished the first task of the day. It will give you a small sense of pride and it will encourage you to do another task and another. By the end of the day, that one task completed will have turned into many tasks completed. If you can't do little things right, you will never do the big things right.

* barracks room: (병영의) 생활관 ** accomplish: 성취하다

① 숙면을 위해서는 침대를 깔끔하게 관리해야 한다.
② 일의 효율성을 높이려면 협동심을 발휘해야 한다.
③ 올바른 습관을 기르려면 정해진 규칙을 따라야 한다.
④ 건강을 유지하기 위해서는 기상 시간이 일정해야 한다.
⑤ 큰일을 잘 이루려면 작은 일부터 제대로 수행해야 한다.

21. 밑줄 친 Leave those activities to the rest of the sheep이 다음 글에서 의미하는 바로 가장 적절한 것은? [3점]

A job search is not a passive task. When you are searching, you are not browsing, nor are you "just looking". Browsing is not an effective way to reach a goal you claim to want to reach. If you are acting with purpose, if you are serious about anything you chose to do, then you need to be direct, focused and whenever possible, clever. Everyone else searching for a job has the same goal, competing for the same jobs. You must do more than the rest of the herd. Regardless of how long it may take you to find and get the job you want, being proactive will logically get you results faster than if you rely only on browsing online job boards and emailing an occasional resume. Leave those activities to the rest of the sheep.

① Try to understand other job-seekers' feelings.
② Keep calm and stick to your present position.
③ Don't be scared of the job-seeking competition.
④ Send occasional emails to your future employers.
⑤ Be more active to stand out from other job-seekers.

22. 다음 글의 요지로 가장 적절한 것은?

Many people view sleep as merely a "down time" when their brain shuts off and their body rests. In a rush to meet work, school, family, or household responsibilities, people cut back on their sleep, thinking it won't be a problem, because all of these other activities seem much more important. But research reveals that a number of vital tasks carried out during sleep help to maintain good health and enable people to function at their best. While you sleep, your brain is hard at work forming the pathways necessary for learning and creating memories and new insights. Without enough sleep, you can't focus and pay attention or respond quickly. A lack of sleep may even cause mood problems. In addition, growing evidence shows that a continuous lack of sleep increases the risk for developing serious diseases.

* vital: 매우 중요한

① 수면은 건강 유지와 최상의 기능 발휘에 도움이 된다.
② 업무량이 증가하면 필요한 수면 시간도 증가한다.
③ 균형 잡힌 식단을 유지하면 뇌 기능이 향상된다.
④ 불면증은 주위 사람들에게 부정적인 영향을 미친다.
⑤ 꿈의 내용은 깨어 있는 시간 동안의 경험을 반영한다.

23. 다음 글의 주제로 가장 적절한 것은? [3점]

The whole of human society operates on knowing the future weather. For example, farmers in India know when the monsoon rains will come next year and so they know when to plant the crops. Farmers in Indonesia know there are two monsoon rains each year, so next year they can have two harvests. This is based on their knowledge of the past, as the monsoons have always come at about the same time each year in living memory. But the need to predict goes deeper than this; it influences every part of our lives. Our houses, roads, railways, airports, offices, and so on are all designed for the local climate. For example, in England all the houses have central heating, as the outside temperature is usually below 20°C, but no air-conditioning, as temperatures rarely go beyond 26°C, while in Australia the opposite is true: most houses have air-conditioning but rarely central heating.

① new technologies dealing with climate change
② difficulties in predicting the weather correctly
③ weather patterns influenced by rising temperatures
④ knowledge of the climate widely affecting our lives
⑤ traditional wisdom helping our survival in harsh climates

24. 다음 글의 제목으로 가장 적절한 것은?

Our ability to accurately recognize and label emotions is often referred to as *emotional granularity*. In the words of Harvard psychologist Susan David, "Learning to label emotions with a more nuanced vocabulary can be absolutely transformative." David explains that if we don't have a rich emotional vocabulary, it is difficult to communicate our needs and to get the support that we need from others. But those who are able to distinguish between a range of various emotions "do much, much better at managing the ups and downs of ordinary existence than those who see everything in black and white." In fact, research shows that the process of labeling emotional experience is related to greater emotion regulation and psychosocial well-being.

* nuanced: 미묘한 차이가 있는

① True Friendship Endures Emotional Arguments
② Detailed Labeling of Emotions Is Beneficial
③ Labeling Emotions: Easier Said Than Done
④ Categorize and Label Tasks for Efficiency
⑤ Be Brave and Communicate Your Needs

25. 다음 도표의 내용과 일치하지 <u>않는</u> 것은?

Percentage of UK People
Who Used Online Course and Online Learning Material
(in 2020, by age group)

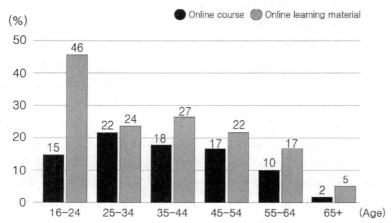

The above graph shows the percentage of people in the UK who used online courses and online learning materials, by age group in 2020. ① In each age group, the percentage of people who used online learning materials was higher than that of people who used online courses. ② The 25-34 age group had the highest percentage of people who used online courses in all the age groups. ③ Those aged 65 and older were the least likely to use online courses among the six age groups. ④ Among the six age groups, the gap between the percentage of people who used online courses and that of people who used online learning materials was the greatest in the 16-24 age group. ⑤ In each of the 35-44, 45-54, and 55-64 age groups, more than one in five people used online learning materials.

26. Antonie van Leeuwenhoek에 관한 다음 글의 내용과 일치하지 <u>않는</u> 것은?

Antonie van Leeuwenhoek was a scientist well known for his cell research. He was born in Delft, the Netherlands, on October 24, 1632. At the age of 16, he began to learn job skills in Amsterdam. At the age of 22, Leeuwenhoek returned to Delft. It wasn't easy for Leeuwenhoek to become a scientist. He knew only one language — Dutch — which was quite unusual for scientists of his time. But his curiosity was endless, and he worked hard. He had an important skill. He knew how to make things out of glass. This skill came in handy when he made lenses for his simple microscope. He saw tiny veins with blood flowing through them. He also saw living bacteria in pond water. He paid close attention to the things he saw and wrote down his observations. Since he couldn't draw well, he hired an artist to draw pictures of what he described.

* cell: 세포 ** vein: 혈관

① 세포 연구로 잘 알려진 과학자였다.
② 22살에 Delft로 돌아왔다.
③ 여러 개의 언어를 알았다.
④ 유리로 물건을 만드는 방법을 알고 있었다.
⑤ 화가를 고용하여 설명하는 것을 그리게 했다.

27. Rachel's Flower Class에 관한 다음 안내문의 내용과 일치하지 <u>않는</u> 것은?

Rachel's Flower Class
Make Your Life More Beautiful!

Class Schedule (Every Monday to Friday)

Flower Arrangement	11 a.m. — 12 p.m.
Flower Box Making	1 p.m. — 2 p.m.

Price
- \$50 for each class
  (flowers and other materials included)
- Bring your own scissors and a bag.

Other Info.
- You can sign up for classes either online or by phone.
- No refund for cancellations on the day of your class

To contact, visit www.rfclass.com or call 03-221-2131.

---

① 플라워 박스 만들기 수업은 오후 1시에 시작된다.
② 수강료에 꽃값과 다른 재료비가 포함된다.
③ 수강생은 가위와 가방을 가져와야 한다.
④ 수업 등록은 전화로만 할 수 있다.
⑤ 수업 당일 취소 시 환불을 받을 수 없다.

28. Nighttime Palace Tour에 관한 다음 안내문의 내용과 일치하는 것은?

Nighttime Palace Tour

Date: Friday, April 29 — Sunday, May 15

Time

Friday	7 p.m. — 8:30 p.m.
Saturday & Sunday	6 p.m. — 7:30 p.m.
	8 p.m. — 9:30 p.m.

Tickets & Booking
- \$15 per person (free for kids under 8)
- Bookings will be accepted up to 2 hours before the tour starts.

Program Activities
- Group tour with a tour guide (1 hour)
- Trying traditional foods and drinks (30 minutes)

※ You can try on traditional clothes with no extra charge.
※ For more information, please visit our website, www.palacenighttour.com.

---

① 금요일에는 하루에 두 번 투어가 운영된다.
② 8세 미만 어린이의 티켓은 5달러이다.
③ 예약은 투어 하루 전까지만 가능하다.
④ 투어 가이드의 안내 없이 궁궐을 둘러본다.
⑤ 추가 비용 없이 전통 의상을 입어 볼 수 있다.

29. 다음 글의 밑줄 친 부분 중, 어법상 <u>틀린</u> 것은?

We usually get along best with people who we think are like us. In fact, we seek them out. It's why places like Little Italy, Chinatown, and Koreatown ① <u>exist</u>. But I'm not just talking about race, skin color, or religion. I'm talking about people who share our values and look at the world the same way we ② <u>do</u>. As the saying goes, birds of a feather flock together. This is a very common human tendency ③ <u>what</u> is rooted in how our species developed. Imagine you are walking out in a forest. You would be conditioned to avoid something unfamiliar or foreign because there is a high likelihood that ④ <u>it</u> would be interested in killing you. Similarities make us ⑤ <u>relate</u> better to other people because we think they'll understand us on a deeper level than other people.

* species: 종(생물 분류의 기초 단위)

30. 다음 글의 밑줄 친 부분 중, 문맥상 낱말의 쓰임이 적절하지 <u>않은</u> 것은? [3점]

Rejection is an everyday part of our lives, yet most people can't handle it well. For many, it's so painful that they'd rather not ask for something at all than ask and ① <u>risk</u> rejection. Yet, as the old saying goes, if you don't ask, the answer is always no. Avoiding rejection ② <u>negatively</u> affects many aspects of your life. All of that happens only because you're not ③ <u>tough</u> enough to handle it. For this reason, consider rejection therapy. Come up with a ④ <u>request</u> or an activity that usually results in a rejection. Working in sales is one such example. Asking for discounts at the stores will also work. By deliberately getting yourself ⑤ <u>welcomed</u> you'll grow a thicker skin that will allow you to take on much more in life, thus making you more successful at dealing with unfavorable circumstances.

* deliberately: 의도적으로

[31~34] 다음 빈칸에 들어갈 말로 가장 적절한 것을 고르시오.

31. Generalization without specific examples that humanize writing is boring to the listener and to the reader. Who wants to read platitudes all day? Who wants to hear the words great, greater, best, smartest, finest, humanitarian, on and on and on without specific examples? Instead of using these 'nothing words,' leave them out completely and just describe the _____. There is nothing worse than reading a scene in a novel in which a main character is described up front as heroic or brave or tragic or funny, while thereafter, the writer quickly moves on to something else. That's no good, no good at all. You have to use less one word descriptions and more detailed, engaging descriptions if you want to make something real.

* platitude: 상투적인 말

① similarities
② particulars
③ fantasies
④ boredom
⑤ wisdom

32. Face-to-face interaction is a uniquely powerful — and sometimes the only — way to share many kinds of knowledge, from the simplest to the most complex. It is one of the best ways to stimulate new thinking and ideas, too. Most of us would have had difficulty learning how to tie a shoelace only from pictures, or how to do arithmetic from a book. Psychologist Mihàly Csikszentmihàlyi found, while studying high achievers, that a large number of Nobel Prize winners were the students of previous winners: they had access to the same literature as everyone else, but _____ made a crucial difference to their creativity. Within organisations this makes conversation both a crucial factor for high-level professional skills and the most important way of sharing everyday information.

* arithmetic: 계산 ** literature: (연구) 문헌

① natural talent
② regular practice
③ personal contact
④ complex knowledge
⑤ powerful motivation

33. Most times a foreign language is spoken in film, subtitles are used to translate the dialogue for the viewer. However, there are occasions when foreign dialogue is left unsubtitled (and thus incomprehensible to most of the target audience). This is often done if the movie is seen mainly from the viewpoint of a particular character who does not speak the language. Such absence of subtitles allows the audience to feel a similar sense of incomprehension and alienation that the character feels. An example of this is seen in *Not Without My Daughter*. The Persian language dialogue spoken by the Iranian characters is not subtitled because the main character Betty Mahmoody does not speak Persian and the audience is _____. [3점]

     * subtitle: 자막(을 넣다)   ** incomprehensible: 이해할 수 없는
                            *** alienation: 소외

① seeing the film from her viewpoint
② impressed by her language skills
③ attracted to her beautiful voice
④ participating in a heated debate
⑤ learning the language used in the film

34. One dynamic that can change dramatically in sport is the concept of the home-field advantage, in which perceived demands and resources seem to play a role. Under normal circumstances, the home ground would appear to provide greater perceived resources (fans, home field, and so on). However, researchers Roy Baumeister and Andrew Steinhilber were among the first to point out that these competitive factors can change; for example, the success percentage for home teams in the final games of a playoff or World Series seems to drop. Fans can become part of the perceived demands rather than resources under those circumstances. This change in perception can also explain why a team that's struggling at the start of the year will _____ to reduce perceived demands and pressures. [3점]

               * perceive: 인식하다   ** playoff: 우승 결정전

① often welcome a road trip
② avoid international matches
③ focus on increasing ticket sales
④ want to have an eco-friendly stadium
⑤ try to advertise their upcoming games

35. 다음 글에서 전체 흐름과 관계 <u>없는</u> 문장은?

Who hasn't used a cup of coffee to help themselves stay awake while studying? Mild stimulants commonly found in tea, coffee, or sodas possibly make you more attentive and, thus, better able to remember. ① However, you should know that stimulants are as likely to have negative effects on memory as they are to be beneficial. ② Even if they could improve performance at some level, the ideal doses are currently unknown. ③ If you are wide awake and well-rested, mild stimulation from caffeine can do little to further improve your memory performance. ④ In contrast, many studies have shown that drinking tea is healthier than drinking coffee. ⑤ Indeed, if you have too much of a stimulant, you will become nervous, find it difficult to sleep, and your memory performance will suffer.

               * stimulant: 자극제   ** dose: 복용량

[36 ~ 37] 주어진 글 다음에 이어질 글의 순서로 가장 적절한 것을 고르시오.

36.

> Toward the end of the 19th century, a new architectural attitude emerged. Industrial architecture, the argument went, was ugly and inhuman; past styles had more to do with pretension than what people needed in their homes.

(A) But they supplied people's needs perfectly and, at their best, had a beauty that came from the craftsman's skill and the rootedness of the house in its locality.

(B) Instead of these approaches, why not look at the way ordinary country builders worked in the past? They developed their craft skills over generations, demonstrating mastery of both tools and materials.

(C) Those materials were local, and used with simplicity — houses built this way had plain wooden floors and whitewashed walls inside.

                          * pretension: 허세, 가식

① (A) − (C) − (B)   ② (B) − (A) − (C)
③ (B) − (C) − (A)   ④ (C) − (A) − (B)
⑤ (C) − (B) − (A)

37.

> Robert Schumann once said, "The laws of morals are those of art." What the great man is saying here is that there is good music and bad music.

(A) It's the same with performances: a bad performance isn't necessarily the result of incompetence. Some of the worst performances occur when the performers, no matter how accomplished, are thinking more of themselves than of the music they're playing.

(B) The greatest music, even if it's tragic in nature, takes us to a world higher than ours; somehow the beauty uplifts us. Bad music, on the other hand, degrades us.

(C) These doubtful characters aren't really listening to what the composer is saying—they're just showing off, hoping that they'll have a great 'success' with the public. The performer's basic task is to try to understand the meaning of the music, and then to communicate it honestly to others. [3점]

* incompetence: 무능 ** degrade: 격하시키다

① (A) − (C) − (B) ② (B) − (A) − (C)
③ (B) − (C) − (A) ④ (C) − (A) − (B)
⑤ (C) − (B) − (A)

[38 ~ 39] 글의 흐름으로 보아, 주어진 문장이 들어가기에 가장 적절한 곳을 고르시오.

38.

> But, when there is biodiversity, the effects of a sudden change are not so dramatic.

When an ecosystem is biodiverse, wildlife have more opportunities to obtain food and shelter. Different species react and respond to changes in their environment differently. (①) For example, imagine a forest with only one type of plant in it, which is the only source of food and habitat for the entire forest food web. (②) Now, there is a sudden dry season and this plant dies. (③) Plant-eating animals completely lose their food source and die out, and so do the animals that prey upon them. (④) Different species of plants respond to the drought differently, and many can survive a dry season. (⑤) Many animals have a variety of food sources and don't just rely on one plant; now our forest ecosystem is no longer at the death! [3점]

* biodiversity: (생물학적) 종 다양성 ** habitat: 서식지

39.

> Since the dawn of civilization, our ancestors created myths and told legendary stories about the night sky.

We are connected to the night sky in many ways. (①) It has always inspired people to wonder and to imagine. (②) Elements of those narratives became embedded in the social and cultural identities of many generations. (③) On a practical level, the night sky helped past generations to keep track of time and create calendars —essential to developing societies as aids to farming and seasonal gathering. (④) For many centuries, it also provided a useful navigation tool, vital for commerce and for exploring new worlds. (⑤) Even in modern times, many people in remote areas of the planet observe the night sky for such practical purposes.

* embed: 깊이 새겨 두다 ** commerce: 무역

40. 다음 글의 내용을 한 문장으로 요약하고자 한다. 빈칸 (A), (B)에 들어갈 말로 가장 적절한 것은?

> The common blackberry (*Rubus allegheniensis*) has an amazing ability to move manganese from one layer of soil to another using its roots. This may seem like a funny talent for a plant to have, but it all becomes clear when you realize the effect it has on nearby plants. Manganese can be very harmful to plants, especially at high concentrations. Common blackberry is unaffected by damaging effects of this metal and has evolved two different ways of using manganese to its advantage. First, it redistributes manganese from deeper soil layers to shallow soil layers using its roots as a small pipe. Second, it absorbs manganese as it grows, concentrating the metal in its leaves. When the leaves drop and decay, their concentrated manganese deposits further poison the soil around the plant. For plants that are not immune to the toxic effects of manganese, this is very bad news. Essentially, the common blackberry eliminates competition by poisoning its neighbors with heavy metals.

* manganese: 망가니즈(금속 원소) ** deposit: 축적물

↓

> The common blackberry has an ability to __(A)__ the amount of manganese in the surrounding upper soil, which makes the nearby soil quite __(B)__ for other plants.

	(A)		(B)
①	increase	······	deadly
②	increase	······	advantageous
③	indicate	······	nutritious
④	reduce	······	dry
⑤	reduce	······	warm

[41 ~ 42] 다음 글을 읽고, 물음에 답하시오.

The longest journey we will make is the eighteen inches between our head and heart. If we take this journey, it can shorten our (a) misery in the world. Impatience, judgment, frustration, and anger reside in our heads. When we live in that place too long, it makes us (b) unhappy. But when we take the journey from our heads to our hearts, something shifts (c) inside. What if we were able to love everything that gets in our way? What if we tried loving the shopper who unknowingly steps in front of us in line, the driver who cuts us off in traffic, the swimmer who splashes us with water during a belly dive, or the reader who pens a bad online review of our writing?

Every person who makes us miserable is (d) like us — a human being, most likely doing the best they can, deeply loved by their parents, a child, or a friend. And how many times have we unknowingly stepped in front of someone in line? Cut someone off in traffic? Splashed someone in a pool? Or made a negative statement about something we've read? It helps to (e) deny that a piece of us resides in every person we meet.

* reside: (어떤 장소에) 있다

41. 윗글의 제목으로 가장 적절한 것은?

① Why It Is So Difficult to Forgive Others
② Even Acts of Kindness Can Hurt Somebody
③ Time Is the Best Healer for a Broken Heart
④ Celebrate the Happy Moments in Your Everyday Life
⑤ Understand Others to Save Yourself from Unhappiness

42. 밑줄 친 (a)~(e) 중에서 문맥상 낱말의 쓰임이 적절하지 않은 것은?

① (a)　② (b)　③ (c)　④ (d)　⑤ (e)

[43 ~ 45] 다음 글을 읽고, 물음에 답하시오.

(A)

One day a young man was walking along a road on his journey from one village to another. As he walked he noticed a monk working in the fields. The young man turned to the monk and said, "Excuse me. Do you mind if I ask (a) you a question?" "Not at all," replied the monk.

* monk: 수도승

(B)

A while later a middle-aged man journeyed down the same road and came upon the monk. "I am going to the village in the valley," said the man. "Do you know what it is like?" "I do," replied the monk, "but first tell (b) me about the village where you came from." "I've come from the village in the mountains," said the man. "It was a wonderful experience. I felt as though I was a member of the family in the village."

(C)

"I am traveling from the village in the mountains to the village in the valley and I was wondering if (c) you knew what it is like in the village in the valley." "Tell me," said the monk, "what was your experience of the village in the mountains?" "Terrible," replied the young man. "I am glad to be away from there. I found the people most unwelcoming. So tell (d) me, what can I expect in the village in the valley?" "I am sorry to tell you," said the monk, "but I think your experience will be much the same there." The young man lowered his head helplessly and walked on.

(D)

"Why did you feel like that?" asked the monk. "The elders gave me much advice, and people were kind and generous. I am sad to have left there. And what is the village in the valley like?" he asked again. "(e) I think you will find it much the same," replied the monk. "I'm glad to hear that," the middle-aged man said smiling and journeyed on.

43. 주어진 글 (A)에 이어질 내용을 순서에 맞게 배열한 것으로 가장 적절한 것은?

① (B) − (D) − (C)　② (C) − (B) − (D)
③ (C) − (D) − (B)　④ (D) − (B) − (C)
⑤ (D) − (C) − (B)

44. 밑줄 친 (a) ~ (e) 중에서 가리키는 대상이 나머지 넷과 다른 것은?

① (a)　② (b)　③ (c)　④ (d)　⑤ (e)

45. 윗글에 관한 내용으로 적절하지 않은 것은?

① 한 수도승이 들판에서 일하고 있었다.
② 중년 남자는 골짜기에 있는 마을로 가는 중이었다.
③ 수도승은 골짜기에 있는 마을에 대해 질문받았다.
④ 수도승의 말을 듣고 젊은이는 고개를 숙였다.
⑤ 중년 남자는 산속에 있는 마을을 떠나서 기쁘다고 말했다.

* 확인 사항
○ 답안지의 해당란에 필요한 내용을 정확히 기입(표기)했는지 확인하시오.

※ QR 코드를 스캔하시면 듣기 방송이 나옵니다. 듣기 방송을 들으며 다음 빈칸을 채우시오.
● 제한 시간 : 25분

01

다음을 듣고, 남자가 하는 말의 목적으로 가장 적절한 것을 고르시오.

M : Good afternoon, everybody. This is Student President Sam Wilson. As you know, the lunch basketball league will begin soon. Many students are interested in joining the league and waiting for the sign-up sheet _____ _____ _____ _____ at the gym. For easier access, we've decided to _____ _____ _____ _____. Instead of going to the gym to register, ✿ _____ _____ _____ _____ _____ _____ and fill out the registration form online. Thank you for listening and let's have a good league.

02

대화를 듣고, 여자의 의견으로 가장 적절한 것을 고르시오.

W : Daniel, what are you doing in front of the mirror?

M : I have skin problems these days. I'm trying to _____ _____ _____ on my face.

W : Pimples are really annoying, but I wouldn't do that.

M : Why not?

W : When you pop them with your hands, you're touching your face.

M : Are you saying that I _____ _____ _____ _____?

W : Exactly. You know our hands are covered with bacteria, right?

M : So?

W : You'll be spreading bacteria all over your face with your hands. It could ✿ _____ _____ _____ _____.

M : Oh, I didn't know that.

W : Touching your face with your hands is bad for your skin.

M : Okay, I got it.

03

대화를 듣고, 두 사람의 관계를 가장 잘 나타낸 것을 고르시오.

M : Excuse me. You're Chloe Jones, aren't you?

W : Yes, I am. Have we met before?

M : No, but I'm a big fan of yours. I've watched _____ _____ _____ _____ _____, and they're very inspiring.

W : Thank you. I'm so glad to hear that.

M : And, I also think your campaign about plastic pollution has been very successful.

W : ✿ _____ _____ _____ _____, that means a lot to me.

M : May I make a suggestion? I thought it'd be nice if more children could hear your ideas.

W : That's what I was thinking. Do you have any good ideas?

M : Actually, _____ _____ _____. Perhaps I can make comic books based on your work.

W : That is a wonderful idea. Can I contact you later to discuss it more?

M : Sure. By the way, my name is Jack Perse. Here's my business card.

04

대화를 듣고, 그림에서 대화의 내용과 일치하지 <u>않는</u> 것을 고르시오.

W : Yesterday, I decorated my fish tank like a beach.

M : I'd like to see it. Do you have a picture?

W : Sure. Here. [Pause] Do you recognize the boat in the bottom left corner?

M : Yes. It's the one I gave you, isn't it?

W : Right. It looks good in the fish tank, doesn't it?

M : It does. I love the beach chair in the center.

W : Yeah. I like it, too.

M : I see _____ _____ _____ _____ _____ _____.

W : Isn't it cute? And do you see these two surf boards on the right side of the picture?

M : Yeah. I like ✿ _____ _____ _____ _____ _____ _____ side by side.

W : I thought that'd look cool.

M : _____ _____ _____ _____ _____ _____ looks happy with its new home.

W : I hope so.

05

대화를 듣고, 여자가 남자에게 부탁한 일로 가장 적절한 것을 고르시오.

[Cell phone rings.]

M : Hello, honey. I'm on the way home. How's setting up Mike's birthday party going?

W : Good, but I still have stuff to do. Mike and his friends will get here soon.

M : Should I pick up the birthday cake?

W : No, that's okay. I already did that.

M : Then, do you want me to ✿ _____ _____ _____ _____ _____ _____ when I get there?

W : I'll take care of it. Can you _____ _____ _____ _____ to the front yard?

M : Sure. Are we having the party outside?

W : Yes. The weather is beautiful so I _____ _____ _____ _____.

M : Great. The kids can play with water guns in the front yard.

W : Good idea. I'll go to the garage and grab the water guns.

06

대화를 듣고, 남자가 지불할 금액을 고르시오. [3점]

W : Welcome to Green Eco Shop. How can I help you?

M : Hi, do you ✪ _____ _____ _____?

W : Yes, we have a few types over here. Which do you like?

M : Hmm.... How much are these?

W : They're $2 each. They are _____ _____ _____.

M : All right. I'll take four of them.

W : Excellent choice. Anything else?

M : I also _____ _____ _____.

W : They're right behind you. They're plastic-free and only $3 each.

M : Okay. I'll also take four of them. That'll be all.

W : If you have a store membership, you can get a 10% discount off the total price.

M : Great. I'm a member. Here are my credit and membership cards.

07

대화를 듣고, 두 사람이 오늘 실험을 할 수 없는 이유를 고르시오.

[Cell phone rings.]

M : Hey, Suji. Where are you?

W : I'm in the library _____ _____ _____. I'll be heading out to the science lab for our experiment in a couple of minutes.

M : I guess you haven't checked my message yet. We can't do the experiment today.

W : Really? Isn't the lab available today?

M : Yes, it is, but I canceled our reservation.

W : Why? Are you still _____ _____ _____ _____?

M : No, I'm fine now.

W : That's good. Then why aren't we doing the experiment today? We need to hand in the science report by next Monday.

M : Unfortunately, the experiment kit ✪ _____ _____ _____ _____. It'll arrive tomorrow.

W : Oh, well. The experiment _____ _____ _____ _____ _____, then.

08

대화를 듣고, Stanville Free-cycle에 관해 언급되지 않은 것을 고르시오.

W : Honey, did you see the poster about the Stanville Free-cycle?

M : Free-cycle? What is that?

W : It's another way of recycling. You give away items you don't need and anybody can take them for free.

M : Oh, it's like one man's garbage is _____ _____ _____. Who can participate?

W : It's open to everyone living in Stanville.

M : Great. _____ _____ _____ _____ _____?

W : At Rose Park on Second Street.

M : When does the event start?

W : It starts on April 12 and runs for a week.

M : Let's see what we can free-cycle, starting from the cupboard.

W : Okay. But ✪ _____ _____ _____ _____ _____ _____ _____ won't be accepted.

M : I see. I'll keep that in mind.

09

River Valley Music Camp에 관한 다음 내용을 듣고, 일치하지 <u>않는</u> 것을 고르시오.

M : Hello, River Valley High School students. This is your music teacher, Mr. Stailor. Starting on April 11, we are going to have the River Valley Music Camp for five days. You don't need to be a member of the school orchestra to join the camp. You may _____ _____ _____ _____ or you can borrow one from the school. On the last day of camp, we are going to film our performance and _____ _____ _____ _____ at the school summer festival. Please keep in mind the camp is ✪ _____ _____ _____ _____. Sign-ups start this Friday, on a first-come-first-served basis. Come and make music together!

10

다음 표를 보면서 대화를 듣고, 여자가 주문할 소형 진공청소기를 고르시오.

W : Ben, do you have a minute?

M : Sure. What is it?

W : I'm trying to buy a handheld vacuum cleaner among these five models. Could you help me choose one?

M : Okay. How much are you willing to spend?

W : No more than $130.

M : Then we can _____ _____ _____ _____. What about the working time?

W : I think it should be longer than 10 minutes.

M : Then that narrows it down to these three.

W : Should I go with one of the lighter ones?

M : Yes. Lighter ones are _____ _____ _____ while cleaning.

W : All right. What about the filter?

M : The one ✪ _____ _____ _____ would be a better choice.

W : I got it. Then I'll order this one.

11

대화를 듣고, 남자의 마지막 말에 대한 여자의 응답으로 가장 적절한 것을 고르시오.

M : _____ _____ _____ _____ today.

W : Too bad. Maybe some dust ✪ _____ _____ _____ _____.

M : You're probably right. What should I do?

12

대화를 듣고, 여자의 마지막 말에 대한 남자의 응답으로 가장 적절한 것을 고르시오.

W : Excuse me. Would you mind if I sit here?

M : I'm sorry, but it's my friend's seat. He'll be back in a minute.

W : Oh, I didn't know that. ✪ _____ _____ _____ _____.

13

대화를 듣고, 남자의 마지막 말에 대한 여자의 응답으로 가장 적절한 것을 고르시오.

M : Hey, Jasmine.

W : Hi, Kurt. Are you going to be at home tomorrow afternoon?

M : Yeah, I'm going to watch the baseball game with my friends at home.

W : Good. Can I ✪ _____ _____ _____ _____ and give you back the hammer I borrowed?

M : Sure. Come over any time. By the way, _____ _____ _____ _____ _____ and watch the game?

W : I'd love to. Which teams are playing?

M : Green Thunders and Black Dragons.

W : That'll be exciting. What time should I come?

M : Come at five. We'll have pizza before the game.

W : Perfect. Do you want me to bring anything?

M : Maybe _____ _____ _____ _____ while watching the game.

14

대화를 듣고, 여자의 마지막 말에 대한 남자의 응답으로 가장 적절한 것을 고르시오. [3점]

W : Hi, Tom.

M : Hi, Jane. What are you reading?

W : It's a novel by Charles Dickens. I'm going to talk about it with my book club members this weekend.

M : Oh, you're in a book club?

W : Yes. I joined it a few months ago. And now I read much more than before.

M : Really? Actually one of _____ _____ _____ _____ is to read more books.

W : Then, joining a book club will surely help.

M : Hmm.... What other benefits can I get if I join one?

W : You can also _____ _____ _____ with others.

M : That'd be nice.

W : Yeah, ✪ _____ _____ _____ _____ _____. I really recommend you to join a book club.

15

다음 상황 설명을 듣고, Brian이 Sally에게 할 말로 가장 적절한 것을 고르시오. [3점]

M : Brian and Sally are walking down the street together. A blind man and his guide dog are walking towards them. Sally likes dogs very much, so she ✪ _____ _____ _____ _____ _____ _____ _____. Brian doesn't think that Sally should do that. The guide dog needs to concentrate on guiding the blind person. If someone touches the dog, the dog can _____ _____ _____. So Brian wants to tell Sally _____ _____ _____ _____ _____ _____ without the permission of the dog owner. In this situation, what would Brian most likely say to Sally?

16~17

다음을 듣고, 물음에 답하시오.

W : Hello, everybody. Welcome to the health workshop. I'm Alanna Reyes, the head trainer from Eastwood Fitness Center. As you know, joints are body parts that _____ _____ _____. And doing certain physical activities puts stress on the joints. But the good news is that people with bad joints can still do certain exercises. They have ✪ _____ _____ _____ _____ _____. Here are some examples. The first is swimming. While swimming, the water supports your body weight. The second is cycling. You _____ _____ _____ _____ on the knee joints when you pedal smoothly. Horseback riding is another exercise that puts very little stress on your knees. Lastly, walking is great because it's low-impact, unlike running. If you have bad joints, _____ _____ _____ _____. Instead, stay active and stay healthy!

▶ 정답 : 해설편 **041**쪽

VOCA LIST 03

 회차별 영단어 QR 코드 ※ QR 코드를 스캔 후 모바일로 단어장처럼 학습할 수 있습니다.   ● 고1 2022학년도 3월

18
- 001 choir ⓝ 합창단
- 002 announce ⓥ 발표하다, 알리다
- 003 compete in ~에서 경쟁하다
- 004 takes place 열리다
- 005 participate in ~에 참가하다
- 006 support ⓥ 후원하다
- 007 fundraising ⓝ 모금
- 008 passion ⓝ 열정
- 009 in advance 미리, 앞서

19
- 010 present ⓥ 수여하다
- 011 academic ⓐ 학업의
- 012 row ⓝ 열, 횡렬
- 013 finalist ⓝ 최종 후보자, 결승 진출자
- 014 gather ⓥ 모이다
- 015 wipe ⓥ 닦다
- 016 sweaty ⓐ 땀에 젖은
- 017 handkerchief ⓝ 손수건
- 018 glance at ~을 흘긋 보다
- 019 pale ⓐ 창백한
- 020 uneasy ⓐ 불안한
- 021 subject ⓝ 과목
- 022 rank ⓥ 평가하다, 순위를 매기다
- 023 confidence ⓝ 자신감
- 024 declare ⓥ 선언[포고]하다, 공표하다
- 025 this way 이리로
- 026 applause ⓝ 박수갈채
- 027 guilty ⓐ 죄책감이 드는, 가책을 느끼는

20
- 028 instructor ⓝ 교사, 교관, 강사
- 029 barrack ⓝ 막사, 병영
- 030 inspect ⓥ 조사하다
- 031 task ⓝ 일, 과업, 과제
- 032 require ⓥ 필요[요구]하다
- 033 make the bed 잠자리를 정돈하다
- 034 perfection ⓝ 완벽, 완전
- 035 ridiculous ⓐ 우스꽝스러운
- 036 wisdom ⓝ 지혜
- 037 prove ⓥ 입증[증명]하다
- 038 accomplish ⓥ 완수하다, 성취하다
- 039 encourage ⓥ 용기를 북돋우다
- 040 complete ⓥ 완수하다
- 041 turn into ~로 바뀌다

21
- 042 job search 구직 활동
- 043 passive ⓐ 수동적인
- 044 browse ⓥ 훑어보다
- 045 reach ⓥ ~에 이르다, ~에 도착[도달]하다
- 046 goal ⓥ 목표
- 047 claim ⓥ 주장하다
- 048 purpose ⓝ 목적
- 049 serious ⓐ 진지한
- 050 clever ⓐ 영리한
- 051 else ⓐ 다른
- 052 rest ⓝ (어떤 것의) 나머지
- 053 herd ⓝ 무리
- 054 regardless of ~와 상관없이
- 055 proactive ⓐ 상황을 앞서서 주도하는

22
- 056 logically ⓐ 논리적으로
- 057 result ⓝ 결과
- 058 occasional ⓐ 가끔씩의
- 059 resume ⓝ 이력서
- 060 stand out from ~에서 두드러지다
- 061 sheep ⓝ 양, 어리석은 사람
- 062 view A as B A를 B로 보다
- 063 merely ⓐ 그저, 단순히
- 064 down time 정지 시간, 휴식 시간
- 065 shut off 멈추다
- 066 in a rush 서둘러
- 067 household ⓝ (한 집에 사는 사람들을 일컫는) 가정
- 068 responsibility ⓝ 책임
- 069 cut back on ~을 줄이다
- 070 activity ⓝ 활동
- 071 reveal ⓥ 밝히다
- 072 a number of 많은
- 073 vital ⓐ 매우 중요한
- 074 carry out ~을 수행하다
- 075 during prep 동안
- 076 maintain ⓥ 유지하다
- 077 enable ⓥ ~을 할 수 있게 하다
- 078 function ⓥ 기능하다
- 079 at one's best 최상의 수준으로
- 080 form ⓥ 형성하다
- 081 pathway ⓝ 경로
- 082 memory ⓝ 기억
- 083 insight ⓝ 통찰력
- 084 focus ⓥ 정신을 집중하다
- 085 pay attention 주의를 기울이다
- 086 respond ⓥ 반응하다
- 087 lack ⓝ 부족
- 088 cause ⓥ 일으키다
- 089 mood ⓝ 기분, 감정
- 090 in addition 게다가
- 091 grow ⓥ 커지다, 증대하다
- 092 evidence ⓝ 증거
- 093 risk ⓝ 위험
- 094 develop a disease 병을 키우다

23
- 095 whole ⓐ 전체
- 096 human society 인간 사회
- 097 operate ⓥ 운영되다, 돌아가다
- 098 monsoon ⓝ (동남아 여름철의) 몬순, 우기, 장마
- 099 plant ⓥ 심다
- 100 crop ⓝ 작물
- 101 harvest ⓝ 수확
- 102 knowledge ⓝ 지식
- 103 past ⓝ 과거
- 104 predict ⓥ 예측하다
- 105 influence ⓝ 영향을 미치다
- 106 railway ⓝ 철도
- 107 climate ⓝ 기후
- 108 central heating 중앙난방
- 109 temperature ⓝ 기온
- 110 below prep ~보다 아래에
- 111 air-conditioning ⓝ 냉방(기)

24
- 112 rarely ⓐ 거의 없게
- 113 beyond prep 위로
- 114 opposite ⓝ 정반대
- 115 technology ⓝ 과학기술
- 116 deal ⓥ 처리하다, 다루다
- 117 correctly ⓐ 정확하게
- 118 affect ⓥ 영향을 미치다
- 119 harsh ⓐ 혹독한
- 120 accurately ⓐ 정확하게
- 121 recognize ⓥ 인식하다
- 122 label ⓥ 이름을 붙이다
- 123 refer to A as B A를 B라고 부르다
- 124 granularity ⓝ 낟알 모양, 입상(粒狀)
- 125 psychologist ⓝ 심리학자
- 126 vocabulary ⓝ 어휘
- 127 absolutely ⓐ 절대적으로
- 128 transformative ⓐ 변화시키는
- 129 explain ⓥ 설명하다
- 130 communicate ⓥ 전달하다
- 131 support ⓥ 지지
- 132 distinguish ⓥ 구별하다
- 133 a range of 광범위한
- 134 various ⓐ 다양한
- 135 ups and downs 좋은 일과 궂은 일, 오르락내리락
- 136 ordinary ⓐ 평범한
- 137 existence ⓝ 존재
- 138 process ⓝ 과정
- 139 related to ~에 관련된
- 140 regulation ⓝ 통제
- 141 psychosocial ⓐ 심리사회적인
- 142 well-being ⓝ 행복
- 143 friendship ⓝ 우정, 교우관계
- 144 endure ⓥ 견디다, 참다, 인내하다
- 145 argument ⓝ 논쟁, 논의
- 146 beneficial ⓐ 유익한, 이로운
- 147 categorize ⓥ 분류하다
- 148 efficiency ⓝ 효율, 능률

25
- 149 course ⓝ 강의
- 150 learning material 학습 자료
- 151 age group 연령 집단
- 152 be the least likely to ~할 가능성이 가장 낮다

26
- 153 known for ~으로 알려진
- 154 job skill 직무 기술
- 155 Dutch ⓝ 네덜란드어
- 156 unusual ⓐ 드문
- 157 curiosity ⓝ 호기심
- 158 endless ⓐ 끝없는
- 159 make A out of B B로 A를 만들다
- 160 come in handy 도움이 되다
- 161 microscope ⓝ 현미경
- 162 vein ⓝ 정맥
- 163 flow ⓥ 흐르다
- 164 pond ⓝ 연못
- 165 pay attention to ~에 주의를 기울이다

27
- 166 observation ⓝ 관찰
- 167 hire ⓥ 고용하다
- 168 describe ⓥ 설명하다, 서술하다, 묘사하다
- 169 flower arrangement 꽃꽂이
- 170 material ⓝ 재료
- 171 scissor ⓝ 가위
- 172 sign up for ~에 등록하다
- 173 refund ⓝ 환불
- 174 cancellation ⓝ 취소
- 175 contact ⓥ 연락하다

28
- 176 palace ⓝ 궁전
- 177 book ⓥ 예약하다
- 178 traditional ⓐ 전통적인
- 179 extra charge 추가 비용, 할증요금
- 180 visit ⓝ 접촉 ⓥ 방문하다

29
- 181 get along with ~와 잘 지내다, 어울리다
- 182 seek out (오랫동안 공들여) 찾아다니다
- 183 exist ⓥ 존재하다
- 184 race ⓝ 인종
- 185 religion ⓝ 종교
- 186 value ⓝ 가치관
- 187 way ⓝ 방식
- 188 as the saying goes 속담에서 말하듯이, 옛말처럼
- 189 feather ⓝ 깃털
- 190 flock ⓥ 모이다, 무리 짓다
- 191 common ⓐ 흔한
- 192 tendency ⓝ 경향, 경향성
- 193 be rooted in ~에 뿌리박고 있다, ~에 원인이 있다
- 194 species ⓝ 종(생물 분류의 기초 단위)
- 195 be conditioned to ~에 조건화되어 있다
- 196 avoid ⓥ 피하다
- 197 unfamiliar ⓐ 친숙하지 않은
- 198 likelihood ⓝ 가능성
- 199 similarity ⓝ 유사점
- 200 relate to ~을 이해하다, ~에 공감하다

30
- 201 rejection ⓝ 거절
- 202 handle ⓥ 감당하다
- 203 painful ⓐ 고통스러운
- 204 rather ⓐ 오히려, 차라리
- 205 negative ⓐ 부정적인
- 206 tough ⓐ 강한
- 207 reason ⓝ 이유
- 208 consider ⓥ 고려하다
- 209 therapy ⓝ 요법
- 210 come up with ~을 생각해내다, 떠올리다
- 211 request ⓝ 요청
- 212 deliberately ⓐ 고의로, 의도적으로
- 213 grow a thick skin 무덤덤해지다, 둔감해지다
- 214 thus ⓐ 따라서, 그러므로
- 215 unfavorable ⓐ 호의적이지 않은
- 216 circumstance ⓝ 상황, 환경

31

217 □ generalization ⓝ 일반화
218 □ specific ⓐ 구체적인, 명확한
219 □ humanize ⓥ 인간적으로 만들다
220 □ platitude ⓝ 진부한 말, 상투적인 문구
221 □ finest ⓐ 가장 훌륭한
222 □ humanitarian ⓐ 인도주의적인
223 □ leave out ~을 빼다
224 □ completely ⓐⓓ 완전히, 전적으로
225 □ novel ⓝ 소설
226 □ main character 주인공
227 □ up front 대놓고
228 □ heroic ⓐ 대담한, 영웅적인
229 □ brave ⓐ 용감한
230 □ tragic ⓐ 비극적인
231 □ thereafter ⓐⓓ 그 후에
232 □ description ⓝ 묘사
233 □ at all 전혀
234 □ detailed ⓐ 세밀한
235 □ engaging ⓐ 마음을 끄는, 몰입시키는
236 □ boredom ⓝ 지루함

32

237 □ interaction ⓝ 상호 작용
238 □ uniquely ⓐⓓ 유례없이
239 □ powerful ⓐ 영향력 있는, 강력한
240 □ simplest ⓐ 가장 간단한
241 □ complex ⓐ 복잡한
242 □ stimulate ⓥ 자극하다
243 □ difficulty ⓝ 어려움
244 □ tie ⓥ 묶다
245 □ shoelace ⓝ 신발 끈
246 □ arithmetic ⓝ 산수
247 □ achiever ⓝ 성취도를 보이는 사람
248 □ previous ⓐ 이전의
249 □ crucial ⓐ 아주 중요한, 중대한, 경쟁적인
250 □ organization ⓝ 조직, 단체
251 □ conversation ⓝ 대화
252 □ factor ⓝ 요소

33

253 □ foreign ⓐ 외국의, 낯선
254 □ subtitle ⓝ (영화·텔레비전 화면의) 자막
255 □ translate ⓥ 번역하다, 통역하다
256 □ dialogue ⓝ 대화
257 □ viewer ⓝ 관객
258 □ occasion ⓝ 경우, 때
259 □ incomprehensible ⓐ 이해할 수 없는
260 □ target audience 주요 대상 관객
261 □ mainly ⓐⓓ 주로
262 □ viewpoint ⓝ 관점, 시점
263 □ particular ⓐ 특정한
264 □ absence ⓝ 부재
265 □ alienation ⓝ 소외
266 □ impressed ⓐ 감명[감동]을 받은
267 □ attract ⓥ 끌어당기다
268 □ participate ⓥ 참여하다

34

269 □ dynamic ⓝ 역학
270 □ dramatically ⓐⓓ 극적으로
271 □ concept ⓝ 개념

272 □ home-field advantage 홈 이점
273 □ perceive ⓥ 인지하다
274 □ demand ⓝ 부담, 요구
275 □ play a role in ~에 역할을 하다, 일조하다
276 □ provide ⓥ 제공하다
277 □ researcher ⓝ 연구원
278 □ point out 지적하다
279 □ competitive ⓐ 경쟁력 있는
280 □ appear ⓥ ~인 것같이 보이다
281 □ perception ⓝ 인식
282 □ struggling ⓐ 고전하는
283 □ reduce ⓥ 줄이다
284 □ road trip 장거리 자동차 여행
285 □ increase ⓥ 증가하다
286 □ advertise ⓥ (상품이나 서비스를) 광고하다
287 □ upcoming ⓐ 다가오는, 곧 있을

35

288 □ mild ⓐ 가벼운
289 □ stimulant ⓝ 자극제, 흥분제
290 □ commonly ⓐⓓ 흔히, 보통
291 □ attentive ⓐ 주의 깊은
292 □ likely ⓐ ~ 할 것 같은
293 □ have an effect on ~에 영향을 미치다
294 □ ideal ⓐ 이상적인
295 □ currently ⓐⓓ 현재
296 □ unknown ⓐ 알려지지 않은
297 □ wide awake 아주 잠이 깨어
298 □ well-rested 잘 쉰
299 □ further ⓐⓓ 더욱
300 □ in contrast 반면에
301 □ indeed ⓐⓓ 실제로
302 □ nervous ⓐ 신경이 과민한
303 □ suffer ⓥ 악화되다

36

304 □ architectural ⓐ 건축의
305 □ attitude ⓝ 사고방식
306 □ emerge ⓥ 나타나다, 출현하다
307 □ industrial ⓐ 산업의
308 □ inhuman ⓐ 비인간적인
309 □ pretension ⓝ 허세, 가식
310 □ supply ⓥ 공급하다
311 □ perfectly ⓐⓓ 완벽하게
312 □ craftsman ⓝ 장인
313 □ rootedness ⓝ 뿌리내림, 고착, 정착
314 □ locality ⓝ (~이 존재하는) 지역, 곳
315 □ instead ⓐⓓ 대신에
316 □ approach ⓝ 접근
317 □ craft ⓝ 공예
318 □ generation ⓝ 세대
319 □ demonstrate ⓥ 입증하다
320 □ mastery ⓝ 숙달한 기술
321 □ simplicity ⓝ 단순함
322 □ plain ⓐ 평범한, 단순한

37

323 □ moral ⓐ 도덕의
324 □ necessarily ⓐⓓ 반드시
325 □ incompetence ⓝ 무능
326 □ occur ⓥ 일어나다, 발생하다
327 □ accomplished ⓐ 숙달된, 기량이 뛰어난

328 □ in nature 사실상
329 □ somehow ⓐⓓ 어떻게든지
330 □ uplift ⓥ 고양시키다, 들어올리다
331 □ on the other hand 반면에
332 □ degrade ⓥ 격하시키다
333 □ doubtful ⓐ 미심쩍은
334 □ character ⓝ 사람, 등장인물
335 □ composer ⓝ 작곡가
336 □ show off 과시하다, 뽐내다
337 □ honestly ⓐⓓ 정직하게

38

338 □ biodiversity ⓝ 생물의 다양성
339 □ sudden ⓐ 갑작스러운
340 □ ecosystem ⓝ 생태계
341 □ wildlife ⓝ 야생 생물
342 □ opportunity ⓝ 기회
343 □ obtain ⓥ 얻다
344 □ shelter ⓝ 서식지
345 □ react ⓥ 작용하다
346 □ entire ⓐ 전체의
347 □ food web 먹이 그물, 먹이 사슬 체계
348 □ dry season 건기(乾期)
349 □ die out 멸종되다, 자취를 감추다
350 □ prey upon ~을 잡아먹다, 괴롭히다
351 □ drought ⓝ 가뭄
352 □ survive ⓥ 살아남다
353 □ rely ⓥ 의지하다
354 □ at the death 종말에 처한

39

355 □ dawn ⓝ 시작, 새벽
356 □ civilization ⓝ 문명
357 □ ancestor ⓝ 선조
358 □ myth ⓝ 신화
359 □ legendary ⓐ 전설의
360 □ connect ⓥ 연결되다
361 □ inspire ⓥ 영감을 주다
362 □ wonder ⓥ 궁금하다
363 □ element ⓝ 요소
364 □ narrative ⓝ 이야기
365 □ embed ⓥ ~ 을 깊이 새겨 두다, 끼워 넣다
366 □ identity ⓝ 정체성
367 □ practical ⓐ 실용적인
368 □ keep track of ~을 기록하다
369 □ calendar ⓝ 달력
370 □ aid ⓝ 보조 도구
371 □ farming ⓝ 농업
372 □ seasonal ⓐ 계절에 따른
373 □ gathering ⓝ 수집, 수확
374 □ navigation ⓝ 항해
375 □ commerce ⓝ 무역, 상업
376 □ explore ⓥ 탐험하다
377 □ remote ⓐ 멀리 떨어진
378 □ planet ⓝ 지구
379 □ observe ⓥ 관찰하다

40

380 □ layer ⓝ 층
381 □ soil ⓝ 토양
382 □ root ⓝ 뿌리
383 □ funny ⓐ 기이한

384 □ talent ⓝ 재능
385 □ nearby ⓝ 근처
386 □ manganese ⓝ 망가니즈(금속 원소)
387 □ harmful ⓐ 해로운, 유해한
388 □ concentration ⓝ 농도, 농축
389 □ unaffected ⓐ 영향을 받지 않은
390 □ damaging ⓐ 해로운
391 □ evolve ⓥ 발달시키다
392 □ redistribute ⓥ 재분배하다
393 □ shallow ⓐ 얕은
394 □ absorb ⓥ 흡수하다
395 □ concentrate ⓥ 모으다, 농축시키다
396 □ decay ⓥ 썩다
397 □ deposit ⓝ 축적물, 퇴적물
398 □ poison ⓥ (독성 물질로) 오염시키다, 중독시키다
399 □ be immune to ~에 면역이 있다
400 □ toxic ⓐ 유독한
401 □ essentially ⓐⓓ 본질적으로
402 □ eliminate ⓥ 제거하다
403 □ competition ⓝ 경쟁자
404 □ poisoning ⓝ 중독
405 □ neighbor ⓝ 이웃
406 □ surrounding ⓐ 주변의

41~42

407 □ shorten ⓥ 줄이다
408 □ misery ⓝ 불행, 비참함
409 □ impatience ⓝ 조급함
410 □ judgment ⓝ 비난
411 □ frustration ⓝ 좌절
412 □ anger ⓝ 분노
413 □ reside ⓥ 존재하다
414 □ shift ⓥ 바뀌다
415 □ get in one's way ~을 방해하다
416 □ unknowingly ⓐⓓ 무심코
417 □ cut off ~을 가로막다
418 □ in traffic 차량 흐름에서
419 □ splash ⓥ (물을) 튀기다, 끼얹다
420 □ pen ⓥ (글을) 쓰다
421 □ review ⓝ 후기
422 □ miserable ⓐ 비참한
423 □ human being 인간
424 □ child ⓝ 자녀
425 □ statement ⓝ 진술
426 □ deny ⓥ 부인하다
427 □ forgive ⓥ 용서하다

43~45

428 □ journey ⓝ 여정, 여행 ⓥ 여행하다
429 □ village ⓝ 마을
430 □ monk ⓝ 수도승
431 □ field ⓝ 들판
432 □ reply ⓥ 대답하다
433 □ middle-aged ⓐ 중년의
434 □ come upon ~을 우연히 만나다
435 □ valley ⓝ 골짜기
436 □ unwelcoming ⓐ 불친절한, 환영하지 않는
437 □ expect ⓥ 예상하다
438 □ helplessly ⓐⓓ 힘없이, 무기력하게
439 □ elder ⓝ 원로들, 어른들
440 □ generous ⓐ 관대한

● 채점 : 맞은 개수 _____ / 80

TEST A-B 각 단어의 뜻을 [A] 영어는 우리말로, [B] 우리말은 영어로 쓰시오.

A	English	Korean
01	announce	
02	responsibility	
03	passion	
04	gather	
05	task	
06	complete	
07	serious	
08	insight	
09	temperature	
10	recognize	
11	curiosity	
12	handle	
13	specific	
14	previous	
15	viewpoint	
16	reduce	
17	emerge	
18	ecosystem	
19	survive	
20	eliminate	

B	Korean	English
01	유지하다	
02	전달하다	
03	통제	
04	흐르다	
05	낯선	
06	마음을 끄는, 몰입시키는	
07	경쟁력 있는	
08	반드시	
09	재료	
10	영향을 미치다	
11	전통적인	
12	대답하다	
13	실제로	
14	관찰하다	
15	문명	
16	현재	
17	주장하다	
18	요소	
19	평범한, 단순한	
20	주로	

▶ A-D 정답 : 해설편 041쪽

TEST C-D 각 단어의 뜻을 골라 기호를 쓰시오.

C	English			Korean
01	harsh	(	)	ⓐ 인종
02	misery	(	)	ⓑ 환불
03	ridiculous	(	)	ⓒ 정반대
04	support	(	)	ⓓ 좌절
05	craftsman	(	)	ⓔ 기후
06	confidence	(	)	ⓕ 혹독한
07	distinguish	(	)	ⓖ 고려하다
08	climate	(	)	ⓗ 조급함
09	race	(	)	ⓘ 얻다
10	existence	(	)	ⓙ 얕은
11	shallow	(	)	ⓚ 우스꽝스러운
12	obtain	(	)	ⓛ 장인
13	opposite	(	)	ⓜ 자신감
14	frustration	(	)	ⓝ 존재
15	wisdom	(	)	ⓞ 구별하다
16	consider	(	)	ⓟ 불행, 비참함
17	wipe	(	)	ⓠ 농도, 농축
18	refund	(	)	ⓡ 후원하다
19	impatience	(	)	ⓢ 닦다
20	concentration	(	)	ⓣ 지혜

D	Korean			English
01	거절	(	)	ⓐ suffer
02	입증하다	(	)	ⓑ perception
03	구성	(	)	ⓒ accomplished
04	이력서	(	)	ⓓ element
05	번역하다, 통역하다	(	)	ⓔ occasional
06	수확	(	)	ⓕ fundraising
07	사고방식	(	)	ⓖ stimulate
08	가끔씩의	(	)	ⓗ resume
09	고양시키다, 들어 올리다	(	)	ⓘ construction
10	조사하다	(	)	ⓙ demonstrate
11	용감한	(	)	ⓚ instructor
12	모금	(	)	ⓛ harvest
13	악화되다	(	)	ⓜ generalization
14	숙달된, 기량이 뛰어난	(	)	ⓝ uplift
15	교사, 교관, 강사	(	)	ⓞ operate
16	요소	(	)	ⓟ rejection
17	자극하다	(	)	ⓠ inspect
18	인식	(	)	ⓡ translate
19	운영되다, 돌아가다	(	)	ⓢ brave
20	일반화	(	)	ⓣ attitude

2024학년도 6월 고1 전국연합학력평가 문제지 1

제 3 교시

영어 영역

04회

● 문항수 45개 | 배점 100점 | 제한 시간 70분

● 점수 표시가 없는 문항은 모두 2점

04회

1번부터 17번까지는 듣고 답하는 문제입니다. 1번부터 15번까지는 한 번만 들려주고, 16번부터 17번까지는 두 번 들려줍니다. 방송을 잘 듣고 답을 하시기 바랍니다.

1. 다음을 듣고, 여자가 하는 말의 목적으로 가장 적절한 것을 고르시오.

   ① 친환경 제품 사용을 홍보하려고
   ② 음식 대접에 대한 감사를 표하려고
   ③ 간식이 마련되어 있음을 안내하려고
   ④ 휴식 시간이 변경되었음을 공지하려고
   ⑤ 구내식당 메뉴에 관한 의견을 구하려고

2. 대화를 듣고, 남자의 의견으로 가장 적절한 것을 고르시오.

   ① 인공 지능에서 얻은 정보를 맹목적으로 믿어서는 안 된다.
   ② 출처를 밝히지 않고 타인의 표현을 인용해서는 안 된다.
   ③ 인공 지능의 도움을 통해 과제물의 질을 높일 수 있다.
   ④ 과제를 할 때 본인의 생각이 들어가는 것이 중요하다.
   ⑤ 기술의 변화에 맞추어 작업 방식을 바꿀 필요가 있다.

3. 다음을 듣고, 여자가 하는 말의 요지로 가장 적절한 것을 고르시오.

   ① 소셜 미디어는 원만한 대인관계 유지에 도움이 된다.
   ② 온라인에서는 자아가 다양한 모습으로 표출될 수 있다.
   ③ 소셜 미디어는 자존감에 부정적인 영향을 줄 수 있다.
   ④ 친밀한 관계일수록 상대의 언행에 쉽게 영향을 받는다.
   ⑤ 유명인 사생활 보호의 중요성은 종종 간과된다.

4. 대화를 듣고, 그림에서 대화의 내용과 일치하지 않는 것을 고르시오.

5. 대화를 듣고, 남자가 할 일로 가장 적절한 것을 고르시오.

   ① 과학 캠프 지원하기   ② 참가 실험 결정하기
   ③ 체크리스트 작성하기   ④ 실험 계획서 보여주기
   ⑤ 자기 소개 영상 촬영하기

6. 대화를 듣고, 여자가 지불할 금액을 고르시오. [3점]

   ① $50   ② $55   ③ $60   ④ $65   ⑤ $70

7. 대화를 듣고, 남자가 마술쇼에 갈 수 없는 이유를 고르시오.

   ① 록 콘서트에 가야 해서
   ② 다른 학교 축제에 가야 해서
   ③ 가족 중 아픈 사람이 있어서
   ④ 동아리 축제를 준비해야 해서
   ⑤ 삼촌 생일 파티에 참석해야 해서

8. 대화를 듣고, Victory Marathon에 관해 언급되지 않은 것을 고르시오.

   ① 행사 날짜   ② 신청 방법   ③ 출발 지점
   ④ 참가비   ⑤ 예상 참가 인원

9. Violet Hill Mentorship에 관한 다음 내용을 듣고, 일치하지 않는 것을 고르시오.

   ① 다음 주 금요일에 개최될 예정이다.
   ② 대학 생활에 관한 조언이 제공된다.
   ③ 신청 시 질문을 미리 제출해야 한다.
   ④ 신청 마감일은 다음 주 화요일이다.
   ⑤ 전공별 참가 가능한 인원은 20명이다.

10. 다음 표를 보면서 대화를 듣고, 두 사람이 구입할 무선 진공청소기를 고르시오.

Cordless Vacuum Cleaner

	Model	Battery Life	Price	Wet Cleaning	Color
①	A	1 hour	$300	×	Red
②	B	2 hours	$330	×	White
③	C	2 hours	$370	○	Red
④	D	3 hours	$390	○	White
⑤	E	3 hours	$410	○	Black

11. 대화를 듣고, 남자의 마지막 말에 대한 여자의 응답으로 가장 적절한 것을 고르시오.

   ① Fine. Let's talk about it over dinner.
   ② Okay. Be more responsible next time.
   ③ Great. I already ordered some pet food.
   ④ Too bad. I hope your cat gets well soon.
   ⑤ Sorry. I can't take care of your cat tonight.

12. 대화를 듣고, 여자의 마지막 말에 대한 남자의 응답으로 가장 적절한 것을 고르시오.

   ① I can't accept late assignments.
   ② You did an excellent job this time.
   ③ Upload your work to our school website.
   ④ Try to do your homework by yourself.
   ⑤ We can finish it before the next class.

13. 대화를 듣고, 남자의 마지막 말에 대한 여자의 응답으로 가장 적절한 것을 고르시오. [3점]

Woman: _____

① Yes. I can give you the phone number of the clinic I visited.
② I agree. Last evening's badminton match was awesome.
③ No problem. I'll teach you how to serve this time.
④ Too bad. I hope you recover from your knee injury soon.
⑤ You're right. Maybe I should start taking badminton lessons.

14. 대화를 듣고, 여자의 마지막 말에 대한 남자의 응답으로 가장 적절한 것을 고르시오. [3점]

Man: _____

① Sure. It seems like a perfect place for bears.
② Great. Let's think about the club name first.
③ My pleasure. I can always give you a ride.
④ I agree. It's hard to give up using plastics.
⑤ No worries. I'll get my bike repaired.

15. 다음 상황 설명을 듣고, Laura가 Tony에게 할 말로 가장 적절한 것을 고르시오.

Laura: _____

① I don't like visiting a hospital for medical checkups.
② I appreciate you taking me to the doctor today.
③ You'd better take a break for a few days.
④ You should finish your work before the deadline.
⑤ I'm afraid I can't reduce your workload right now.

[16~17] 다음을 듣고, 물음에 답하시오.

16. 남자가 하는 말의 주제로 가장 적절한 것은?

① relationships between media and voters
② common ways of promoting school policy
③ guidelines for student election campaigns
④ requirements for becoming a candidate
⑤ useful tips for winning school debates

17. 언급된 매체가 <u>아닌</u> 것은?

① social media   ② poster   ③ pamphlet
④ school newspaper   ⑤ school website

이제 듣기 문제가 끝났습니다. 18번부터는 문제지의 지시에 따라 답을 하시기 바랍니다.

---

18. 다음 글의 목적으로 가장 적절한 것은?

Dear Reader,

We always appreciate your support. As you know, our service is now available through an app. There has never been a better time to switch to an online membership of *TourTide Magazine*. At a 50% discount off your current print subscription, you can access a full year of online reading. Get new issues and daily web pieces at TourTide.com, read or listen to *TourTide Magazine* via the app, and get our members-only newsletter. You'll also gain access to our editors' selections of the best articles. Join today!

Yours,
TourTide Team

① 여행 일정 지연에 대해 사과하려고
② 잡지 온라인 구독을 권유하려고
③ 무료 잡지 신청을 홍보하려고
④ 여행 후기 모집을 안내하려고
⑤ 기사에 대한 독자 의견에 답변하려고

19. 다음 글에 드러난 'I'의 심경 변화로 가장 적절한 것은?

As I walked from the mailbox, my heart was beating rapidly. In my hands, I held the letter from the university I had applied to. I thought my grades were good enough to cross the line and my application letter was well-written, but was it enough? I hadn't slept a wink for days. As I carefully tore into the paper of the envelope, the letter slowly emerged with the opening phrase, "It is our great pleasure..." I shouted with joy, "I am in!" As I held the letter, I began to make a fantasy about my college life in a faraway city.

① relaxed   → upset   ② anxious   → delighted
③ guilty   → confident   ④ angry   → grateful
⑤ hopeful   → disappointed

20. 다음 글에서 필자가 주장하는 바로 가장 적절한 것은?

Having a messy room can add up to negative feelings and destructive thinking. Psychologists say that having a disorderly room can indicate a disorganized mental state. One of the professional tidying experts says that the moment you start cleaning your room, you also start changing your life and gaining new perspective. When you clean your surroundings, positive and good atmosphere follows. You can do more things efficiently and neatly. So, clean up your closets, organize your drawers, and arrange your things first, then peace of mind will follow.

① 자신의 공간을 정돈하여 긍정적 변화를 도모하라.
② 오랜 시간 고민하기보다는 일단 행동으로 옮겨라.
③ 무질서한 환경에서 창의적인 생각을 시도하라.
④ 장기 목표를 위해 단기 목표를 먼저 설정하라.
⑤ 반복되는 일상을 새로운 관점으로 관찰하라.

21. 밑줄 친 luxury real estate가 다음 글에서 의미하는 바로 가장 적절한 것은? [3점]

The soil of a farm field is forced to be the perfect environment for monoculture growth. This is achieved by adding nutrients in the form of fertilizer and water by way of irrigation. During the last fifty years, engineers and crop scientists have helped farmers become much more efficient at supplying exactly the right amount of both. World usage of fertilizer has tripled since 1969, and the global capacity for irrigation has almost doubled; we are feeding and watering our fields more than ever, and our crops are loving it. Unfortunately, these luxurious conditions have also excited the attention of certain agricultural undesirables. Because farm fields are loaded with nutrients and water relative to the natural land that surrounds them, they are desired as luxury real estate by every random weed in the area.

* monoculture: 단일 작물 재배 ** irrigation: (논,밭에) 물을 댐; 관개

① a farm where a scientist's aid is highly required
② a field abundant with necessities for plants
③ a district accessible only for the rich
④ a place that is conserved for ecology
⑤ a region with higher economic value

22. 다음 글의 요지로 가장 적절한 것은?

When it comes to helping out, you don't have to do much. All you have to do is come around and show that you care. If you notice someone who is lonely, you could go and sit with them. If you work with someone who eats lunch all by themselves, and you go and sit down with them, they will begin to be more social after a while, and they will owe it all to you. A person's happiness comes from attention. There are too many people out in the world who feel like everyone has forgotten them or ignored them. Even if you say hi to someone passing by, they will begin to feel better about themselves, like someone cares.

① 사소한 관심이 타인에게 도움이 될 수 있다.
② 사람마다 행복의 기준이 제각기 다르다.
③ 선행을 통해 자신을 되돌아볼 수 있다.
④ 원만한 대인 관계는 경청에서 비롯된다.
⑤ 현재에 대한 만족이 행복의 필수조건이다.

23. 다음 글의 주제로 가장 적절한 것은?

We often try to make cuts in our challenges and take the easy route. When taking the quick exit, we fail to acquire the strength to compete. We often take the easy route to improve our skills. Many of us never really work to achieve mastery in the key areas of life. These skills are key tools that can be useful to our career, health, and prosperity. Highly successful athletes don't win because of better equipment; they win by facing hardship to gain strength and skill. They win through preparation. It's the mental preparation, winning mindset, strategy, and skill that set them apart. Strength comes from struggle, not from taking the path of least resistance. Hardship is not just a lesson for the next time in front of us. Hardship will be the greatest teacher we will ever have in life.

① characteristics of well-equipped athletes
② difficulties in overcoming life's sudden challenges
③ relationship between personal habit and competence
④ risks of enduring hardship without any preparation
⑤ importance of confronting hardship in one's life

24. 다음 글의 제목으로 가장 적절한 것은?

Your behaviors are usually a reflection of your identity. What you do is an indication of the type of person you believe that you are — either consciously or nonconsciously. Research has shown that once a person believes in a particular aspect of their identity, they are more likely to act according to that belief. For example, people who identified as "being a voter" were more likely to vote than those who simply claimed "voting" was an action they wanted to perform. Similarly, the person who accepts exercise as the part of their identity doesn't have to convince themselves to train. Doing the right thing is easy. After all, when your behavior and your identity perfectly match, you are no longer pursuing behavior change. You are simply acting like the type of person you already believe yourself to be.

① Action Comes from Who You Think You Are
② The Best Practices for Gaining More Voters
③ Stop Pursuing Undesirable Behavior Change!
④ What to Do When Your Exercise Bores You
⑤ Your Actions Speak Louder than Your Words

25. 다음 도표의 내용과 일치하지 <u>않는</u> 것은?

Electronic Waste Collection and Recycling Rate by Region in 2016 and 2019

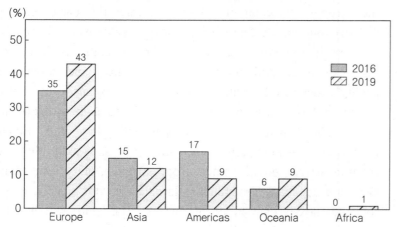

The above graph shows the electronic waste collection and recycling rate by region in 2016 and 2019. ① In both years, Europe showed the highest electronic waste collection and recycling rates. ② The electronic waste collection and recycling rate of Asia in 2019 was lower than in 2016. ③ The Americas ranked third both in 2016 and in 2019, with 17 percent and 9 percent respectively. ④ In both years, the electronic waste collection and recycling rates in Oceania remained under 10 percent. ⑤ Africa had the lowest electronic waste collection and recycling rates in both 2016 and 2019, showing the smallest gap between 2016 and 2019.

26. Fritz Zwicky에 관한 다음 글의 내용과 일치하지 <u>않는</u> 것은?

Fritz Zwicky, a memorable astrophysicist who coined the term 'supernova', was born in Varna, Bulgaria to a Swiss father and a Czech mother. At the age of six, he was sent to his grandparents who looked after him for most of his childhood in Switzerland. There, he received an advanced education in mathematics and physics. In 1925, he emigrated to the United States and continued his physics research at California Institute of Technology (Caltech). He developed numerous theories that have had a profound influence on the understanding of our universe in the early 21st century. After being appointed as a professor of astronomy at Caltech in 1942, he developed some of the earliest jet engines and holds more than 50 patents, many in jet propulsion.

* patent: 특허(권) ** propulsion: 추진(력)

① 불가리아의 Varna에서 태어났다.
② 스위스에서 수학과 물리학 교육을 받았다.
③ 미국으로 이주하여 연구를 이어갔다.
④ 우주 이해에 영향을 미친 수많은 이론을 발전시켰다.
⑤ 초창기 제트 엔진을 개발한 후 교수로 임용되었다.

27. Gourmet Baking Competition에 관한 다음 안내문의 내용과 일치하지 <u>않는</u> 것은?

Gourmet Baking Competition

Get out your cookbooks and dust off your greatest baking recipes.

When & Where
• 5 p.m. – 7 p.m. Saturday, August 3rd
• Gourmet Baking Studio

Registration
• Register online at www.bakeoff.org by July 25th.
• Anyone can participate in the competition.

Categories
• Pies, Cakes, and Cookies
• Each person can only enter one category.

Prizes & Gifts
• Prizes will be given to the top three in each category.
• Souvenirs will be given to every participant.

① 8월 3일 토요일에 개최된다.
② 온라인으로 참가 신청이 가능하다.
③ 누구나 참가할 수 있다.
④ 참가자 한 명이 여러 부문에 참여할 수 있다.
⑤ 모든 참가자에게 기념품이 제공될 것이다.

28. Winter Sports Program에 관한 다음 안내문의 내용과 일치하는 것은?

Winter Sports Program
Winter is coming! Let's have some fun together!

Time & Location
• Every Sunday in December from 1 p.m. to 3 p.m.
• Grand Blue Ice Rink

Lesson Details
• Ice Hockey, Speed Skating, and Figure Skating
• Participants must be 8 years of age or older.

Fee
• Ice Hockey: $200
• Speed Skating / Figure Skating: $150

Notice
• Skates and helmets will be provided for free.
• You should bring your own gloves.

※ For more information, visit www.wintersports.com.

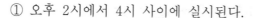

① 오후 2시에서 4시 사이에 실시된다.
② 네 종목의 강좌가 개설된다.
③ 참가 연령에 제한은 없다.
④ 모든 종목 강좌의 수강료는 같다.
⑤ 장갑은 각자 가져와야 한다.

29. 다음 글의 밑줄 친 부분 중, 어법상 틀린 것은? [3점]

The hunter-gatherer lifestyle, which can ① be described as "natural" to human beings, appears to have had much to recommend it. Examination of human remains from early hunter-gatherer societies ② has suggested that our ancestors enjoyed abundant food, obtainable without excessive effort, and suffered very few diseases. If this is true, it is not clear why so many humans settled in permanent villages and developed agriculture, growing crops and domesticating animals: cultivating fields was hard work, and it was in farming villages ③ what epidemic diseases first took root. Whatever its immediate effect on the lives of humans, the development of settlements and agriculture ④ undoubtedly led to a high increase in population density. This period, known as the New Stone Age, was a major turning point in human development, ⑤ opening the way to the growth of the first towns and cities, and eventually leading to settled "civilizations."

* remains: 유적, 유해 ** epidemic: 전염병의

30. 다음 글의 밑줄 친 부분 중, 문맥상 낱말의 쓰임이 적절하지 않은 것은? [3점]

Many human and non-human animals save commodities or money for future consumption. This behavior seems to reveal a preference of a ① delayed reward over an immediate one: the agent gives up some immediate pleasure in exchange for a future one. Thus the discounted value of the future reward should be ② greater than the un-discounted value of the present one. However, in some cases the agent does not wait for the envisioned occasion but uses their savings ③ prematurely. For example, early in the year an employee might set aside money to buy Christmas presents but then spend it on a summer vacation instead. Such cases could be examples of ④ weakness of will. That is, the agents may judge or resolve to spend their savings in a certain way for the greatest benefit but then act differently when temptation for immediate pleasure ⑤ disappears.

* envision: 계획하다

[31~34] 다음 빈칸에 들어갈 말로 가장 적절한 것을 고르시오.

31. The costs of _____ are well-documented. Martin Luther King Jr. lamented them when he described "that lovely poem that didn't get written because someone knocked on the door." Perhaps the most famous literary example happened in 1797 when Samuel Taylor Coleridge started writing his poem *Kubla Khan* from a dream he had but then was visited by an unexpected guest. For Coleridge, by coincidence, the untimely visitor came at a particularly bad time. He forgot his inspiration and left the work unfinished. While there are many documented cases of sudden disruptions that have had significant consequences for professionals in critical roles such as doctors, nurses, control room operators, stock traders, and pilots, they also impact most of us in our everyday lives, slowing down work productivity and generally increasing stress levels.

* lament: 슬퍼하다

① misunderstandings   ② interruptions
③ inequalities   ④ regulations
⑤ arguments

32. There's a lot of scientific evidence demonstrating that focused attention leads to _____. In animals rewarded for noticing sound (to hunt or to avoid being hunted for example), we find much larger auditory centers in the brain. In animals rewarded for sharp eyesight, the visual areas are larger. Brain scans of violinists provide more evidence, showing dramatic growth and expansion in regions of the cortex that represent the left hand, which has to finger the strings precisely, often at very high speed. Other studies have shown that the hippocampus, which is vital for spatial memory, is enlarged in taxi drivers. The point is that the physical architecture of the brain changes according to where we direct our attention and what we practice doing.

* cortex: (대뇌) 피질(皮質) ** hippocampus: (대뇌 측두엽의) 해마

① improved decision making
② the reshaping of the brain
③ long-term mental tiredness
④ the development of hand skills
⑤ increased levels of self-control

33. How did the human mind evolve? One possibility is that _____ caused our brains to evolve the way they did. A human tribe that could out-think its enemies, even slightly, possessed a vital advantage. The ability of your tribe to imagine and predict where and when a hostile enemy tribe might strike, and plan accordingly, gives your tribe a significant military advantage. The human mind became a weapon in the struggle for survival, a weapon far more decisive than any before it. And this mental advantage was applied, over and over, within each succeeding generation. The tribe that could out-think its opponents was more likely to succeed in battle and would then pass on the genes responsible for this mental advantage to its offspring. You and I are the descendants of the winners. [3점]

① physical power to easily hunt prey
② individual responsibility in one's inner circle
③ instinctive tendency to avoid natural disasters
④ superiority in the number of one's descendants
⑤ competition and conflicts with other human tribes

34. To find the hidden potential in teams, instead of brainstorming, we're better off shifting to a process called brainwriting. The initial steps are solo. You start by asking everyone to generate ideas separately. Next, you pool them and share them anonymously among the group. To preserve independent judgment, each member evaluates them on their own. Only then does the team come together to select and refine the most promising options. By _____ before choosing and elaborating them, teams can surface and advance possibilities that might not get attention otherwise. This brainwriting process makes sure that all ideas are brought to the table and all voices are brought into the conversation. It is especially effective in groups that struggle to achieve collective intelligence. [3점]

* anonymously: 익명으로 ** surface: 드러내다

① developing and assessing ideas individually
② presenting and discussing ideas out loud
③ assigning different roles to each member
④ coming to an agreement on these options
⑤ skipping the step of judging these options

35. 다음 글에서 전체 흐름과 관계 <u>없는</u> 문장은?

Simply giving employees a sense of agency—a feeling that they are in control, that they have genuine decision-making authority—can radically increase how much energy and focus they bring to their jobs. ① One 2010 study at a manufacturing plant in Ohio, for instance, carefully examined assembly-line workers who were empowered to make small decisions about their schedules and work environment. ② They designed their own uniforms and had authority over shifts while all the manufacturing processes and pay scales stayed the same. ③ It led to decreased efficiency because their decisions were not uniform or focused on meeting organizational goals. ④ Within two months, productivity at the plant increased by 20 percent, with workers taking shorter breaks and making fewer mistakes. ⑤ Giving employees a sense of control improved how much self-discipline they brought to their jobs.

* radically: 급격하게 ** shift: (근무) 교대

[36~37] 주어진 글 다음에 이어질 글의 순서로 가장 적절한 것을 고르시오.

36.

As businesses shift some core business activities to digital, such as sales, marketing, or archiving, it is assumed that the impact on the environment will be less negative.

(A) When we store bigger data on clouds, increased carbon emissions make our green clouds gray. The carbon footprint of an email is smaller than mail sent via a post office, but still, it causes four grams of CO_2, and it can be as much as 50 grams if the attachment is big.

(B) However, digital business activities can still threaten the environment. In some cases, the harm of digital businesses can be even more hazardous. A few decades ago, offices used to have much more paper waste since all documents were paper based.

(C) When workplaces shifted from paper to digital documents, invoices, and emails, it was a promising step to save trees. However, the cost of the Internet and electricity for the environment is neglected. A recent *Wired* report declared that most data centers' energy source is fossil fuels. [3점]

① (A) − (C) − (B) ② (B) − (A) − (C)
③ (B) − (C) − (A) ④ (C) − (A) − (B)
⑤ (C) − (B) − (A)

[해설편 p.050]

37.

> Problems often arise if an exotic species is suddenly introduced to an ecosystem.

(A) The grey had the edge because it can adapt its diet; it is able, for instance, to eat green acorns, while the red can only digest mature acorns. Within the same area of forest, grey squirrels can destroy the food supply before red squirrels even have a bite.

(B) Britain's red and grey squirrels provide a clear example. When the grey arrived from America in the 1870s, both squirrel species competed for the same food and habitat, which put the native red squirrel populations under pressure.

(C) Greys can also live more densely and in varied habitats, so have survived more easily when woodland has been destroyed. As a result, the red squirrel has come close to extinction in England.

* edge: 우위 ** acorn: 도토리

① (A) − (C) − (B)   ② (B) − (A) − (C)
③ (B) − (C) − (A)   ④ (C) − (A) − (B)
⑤ (C) − (B) − (A)

[38~39] 글의 흐름으로 보아, 주어진 문장이 들어가기에 가장 적절한 곳을 고르시오.

38.

> Farmers, on the other hand, could live in the same place year after year and did not have to worry about transporting young children long distances.

Growing crops forced people to stay in one place. Hunter−gatherers typically moved around frequently, and they had to be able to carry all their possessions with them every time they moved. (①) In particular, mothers had to carry their young children. (②) As a result, hunter−gatherer mothers could have only one baby every four years or so, spacing their births so that they never had to carry more than one child at a time. (③) Societies that settled down in one place were able to shorten their birth intervals from four years to about two. (④) This meant that each woman could have more children than her hunter−gatherer counterpart, which in turn resulted in rapid population growth among farming communities. (⑤) An increased population was actually an advantage to agricultural societies, because farming required large amounts of human labor.

* counterpart: (대응 관계에 있는) 상대

39.

> By comparison, birds with the longest childhoods, and those that migrate with their parents, tend to have the most efficient migration routes.

Spending time as children allows animals to learn about their environment. Without childhood, animals must rely more fully on hardware, and therefore be less flexible. (①) Among migratory bird species, those that are born knowing how, when, and where to migrate — those that are migrating entirely with instructions they were born with — sometimes have very inefficient migration routes. (②) These birds, born knowing how to migrate, don't adapt easily. (③) So when lakes dry up, forest becomes farmland, or climate change pushes breeding grounds farther north, those birds that are born knowing how to migrate keep flying by the old rules and maps. (④) Childhood facilitates the passing on of cultural information, and culture can evolve faster than genes. (⑤) Childhood gives flexibility in a changing world. [3점]

40. 다음 글의 내용을 한 문장으로 요약하고자 한다. 빈칸 (A), (B)에 들어갈 말로 가장 적절한 것은?

> Over the last several decades, scholars have developed standards for how best to create, organize, present, and preserve digital information for future generations. What has remained neglected for the most part, however, are the needs of people with disabilities. As a result, many of the otherwise most valuable digital resources are useless for people who are deaf or hard of hearing, as well as for people who are blind, have low vision, or have difficulty distinguishing particular colors. While professionals working in educational technology and commercial web design have made significant progress in meeting the needs of such users, some scholars creating digital projects all too often fail to take these needs into account. This situation would be much improved if more projects embraced the idea that we should always keep the largest possible audience in mind as we make design decisions, ensuring that our final product serves the needs of those with disabilities as well as those without.

↓

> The needs of people with disabilities have often been _____(A)_____ in digital projects, which could be changed by adopting a(n) _____(B)_____ design.

	(A)		(B)
①	overlooked	......	inclusive
②	accepted	......	practical
③	considered	......	inclusive
④	accepted	......	abstract
⑤	overlooked	......	abstract

[41~42] 다음 글을 읽고, 물음에 답하시오.

All humans, to an extent, seek activities that cause a degree of pain in order to experience pleasure, whether this is found in spicy food, strong massages, or stepping into a too-cold or too-hot bath. The key is that it is a 'safe threat'. The brain perceives the stimulus to be painful but ultimately (a) non-threatening. Interestingly, this could be similar to the way humor works: a 'safe threat' that causes pleasure by playfully violating norms. We feel uncomfortable, but safe. In this context, where (b) survival is clearly not in danger, the desire for pain is actually the desire for a reward, not suffering or punishment. This reward-like effect comes from the feeling of mastery over the pain. The closer you look at your chilli-eating habit, the more remarkable it seems. When the active ingredient of chillies — capsaicin — touches the tongue, it stimulates exactly the same receptor that is activated when any of these tissues are burned. Knowing that our body is firing off danger signals, but that we are actually completely safe, (c) produces pleasure. All children start off hating chilli, but many learn to derive pleasure from it through repeated exposure and knowing that they will never experience any real (d) joy. Interestingly, seeking pain for the pain itself appears to be (e) uniquely human. The only way scientists have trained animals to have a preference for chilli or to self-harm is to have the pain always directly associated with a pleasurable reward.

41. 윗글의 제목으로 가장 적절한 것은?

① The Secret Behind Painful Pleasures
② How 'Safe Threat' Changes into Real Pain
③ What Makes You Stronger, Pleasure or Pain?
④ How Does Your Body Detect Danger Signals?
⑤ Recipes to Change Picky Children's Eating Habits

42. 밑줄 친 (a)~(e) 중에서 문맥상 낱말의 쓰임이 적절하지 <u>않은</u> 것은?

① (a)　② (b)　③ (c)　④ (d)　⑤ (e)

[43~45] 다음 글을 읽고, 물음에 답하시오.

(A)

An airplane flew high above the deep blue seas far from any land. Flying the small plane was a student pilot who was sitting alongside an experienced flight instructor. As the student looked out the window, (a) she was filled with wonder and appreciation for the beauty of the world. Her instructor, meanwhile, waited patiently for the right time to start a surprise flight emergency training exercise.

(B)

Then, the student carefully flew low enough to see if she could find any ships making their way across the surface of the ocean. Now the instructor and the student could see some ships. Although the ships were far apart, they were all sailing in a line. With the line of ships in view, the student could see the way to home and safety. The student looked at (b) her in relief, who smiled proudly back at her student.

(C)

When the student began to panic, the instructor said, "Stay calm and steady. (c) You can do it." Calm as ever, the instructor told her student, "Difficult times always happen during flight. The most important thing is to focus on your flight in those situations." Those words encouraged the student to focus on flying the aircraft first. "Thank you, I think (d) I can make it," she said, "As I've been trained, I should search for visual markers."

(D)

When the plane hit a bit of turbulence, the instructor pushed a hidden button. Suddenly, all the monitors inside the plane flashed several times then went out completely! Now the student was in control of an airplane that was flying well, but (e) she had no indication of where she was or where she should go. She did have a map, but no other instruments. She was at a loss and then the plane shook again.

* turbulence: 난(亂)기류

43. 주어진 글 (A)에 이어질 내용을 순서에 맞게 배열한 것으로 가장 적절한 것은?

① (B) - (D) - (C)　　② (C) - (B) - (D)
③ (C) - (D) - (B)　　④ (D) - (B) - (C)
⑤ (D) - (C) - (B)

44. 밑줄 친 (a)~(e) 중에서 가리키는 대상이 나머지 넷과 <u>다른</u> 것은?

① (a)　② (b)　③ (c)　④ (d)　⑤ (e)

45. 윗글에 관한 내용으로 적절하지 <u>않은</u> 것은?

① 교관과 교육생이 소형 비행기에 타고 있었다.
② 배들은 서로 떨어져 있었지만 한 줄을 이루고 있었다.
③ 교관은 어려운 상황에서는 집중이 가장 중요하다고 말했다.
④ 비행기 내부의 모니터가 깜박이다가 다시 정상 작동했다.
⑤ 교육생은 지도 이외의 다른 도구는 가지고 있지 않았다.

* 확인 사항

o 답안지의 해당란에 필요한 내용을 정확히 기입(표기)했는지 확인하시오.

※ QR 코드를 스캔하시면 듣기 방송이 나옵니다. 듣기 방송을 들으며 다음 빈칸을 채우시오. ● 제한 시간 : 25분

01

다음을 듣고, 여자가 하는 말의 목적으로 가장 적절한 것을 고르시오.

[Chime bell rings.]

W : Attention, everyone! Our CEO, Mr. Wayne, has prepared a snack bar ✪ ____ _____ _____ _____ on last month's project. Please come down to the lobby and enjoy some delicious snacks. They'll ✪ ____ _____ _____ 4 p.m. You'll be impressed by the amazing variety, from crispy fries and hot dogs to fresh lemonade and coffee. It'd be great if you could bring _____ _____ _____ _____ for the drinks. See you there.

02

대화를 듣고, 남자의 의견으로 가장 적절한 것을 고르시오.

M : Hi, Pamela. Did you finish your history assignment?

W : Yes, Dad. I finished it quite easily with the help of AI.

M : Really? Do you mean you used ✪ ____ _____ _____ _____ _____ _____?

W : Yeah. I typed in the questions and AI gave me the answers right away.

M : Well, is it a good idea to do your homework that way?

W : Why not? It saves a lot of time and gives me just the information I need.

M : I _____ ___ _____ ____, too. But after trying it a couple of times, I found out AI sometimes uses false information as well.

W : Really? I didn't know that.

M : Yeah, you shouldn't blindly trust the answers from AI.

W : Okay. I'll ✪ _____ _____ ___ _____ next time.

03

다음을 듣고, 여자가 하는 말의 요지로 가장 적절한 것을 고르시오.

W : Hello, listeners. This is Kelly Watson's *Love Yourself*. Have you ever thought about your social media use? _____ _____ _____ _____ stay connected with others easily. However, it can make you compare yourself with others, too. For example, a celebrity's post about going on a ✪ _____ _____ _____ _____ you jealous. Continuously making such comparisons stops you from looking at yourself the way you truly are. You might think, "Why can't I have a better life?" and ✪ _____ _____ _____ _____ _____. As you can see, social media can have a negative effect on your self-esteem. I'll be right back with some tips for healthy social media use.

04

대화를 듣고, 그림에서 대화의 내용과 일치하지 <u>않는</u> 것을 고르시오.

W : Honey, I love this park!

M : Me, too. This park is so cool. But, oh, look! What's that in the tree?

W : It's just a ✪ _____ _____ ___ _____ tree's branches.

M : I guess some kids went home without their kite.

W : By the same tree, a woman is walking her dog. They look so lovely.

M : What about the little girl beside her?

W : You mean the girl _____ _____ _____ hand?

M : Right. She's adorable. And look there! Did you notice a basket full of flowers on the picnic mat?

W : Yes, right. It adds a touch of ✪ _____ ___ _____.

M : I think so, too. Oh, there's a fountain. Next to it, a man is playing the violin.

W : The melody is beautiful. I'm glad we came here.

05

대화를 듣고, 남자가 할 일로 가장 적절한 것을 고르시오.

M : Hey, Alice. I ✪ _____ _____ _____ _____ camp next week. What about you?

W : Me, too. But I didn't know that there were so many things to do before the camp.

M : Right. Would you like to ____ _____ _____ _____ together?

W : Hmm, let's see. Did you upload your introduction video to the website?

M : Yes, I tried to show my interest in science. Oh, hey, have you picked which experiment to work on?

W : Yes. I decided to participate in a biology experiment.

M : Me, too. Wasn't it difficult to make a plan for your experiment?

W : Actually, I haven't even started yet because I've never written a plan for a ✪ _____ _____ _____.

M : I'll show you mine after class. Maybe you can get some ideas.

W : Really? That'd be great. See you soon.

06

대화를 듣고, 여자가 지불할 금액을 고르시오. [3점]

W : Hi, I'm ✪ _____ _____ ___ _____ for my niece. She's going on a camping trip this summer.

M : Great. We have this blue backpack that has multiple pockets.

W : It looks stylish and functional. How much is it?

M : It's $50, but we have a ✪ _____ _____ _____ _____ backpacks today. Every backpack is 10% off.

W : That's a great deal! I'll take it.

M : I'm sure _____ _____ _____ _____ it. Do you need anything else?

W : Yes. I like this camping hat. How much is it?

M : It's $10, not on sale, though.

W : That's okay. I'll take it as well.

M : Gift wrapping for them would be a total of $5. Would you like gift wrapping?

W : Yes, please. Here's my credit card.

07

대화를 듣고, 남자가 마술쇼에 갈 수 <u>없는</u> 이유를 고르시오.

W : Hi, Chris. How was your weekend?

M : Hello, Martha. I went to a rock concert and had fun. How about you?

W : I've been ✪ _____ _____ _____ _____ festival.

M : Oh, what kind of activity are you preparing for the festival?

W : Our club members are _____ __ _____ _____. Come and watch us at 4 p.m. tomorrow if you are available.

M : I'd love to, but I can't make it.

W : Why? It'd be nice to have you there.

M : I'm sorry, but I ✪ _____ ___ _____ _____ uncle's birthday party.

W : Oh, I understand. I hope you have a wonderful time with your family.

M : Thank you, I will.

08

대화를 듣고, Victory Marathon에 관해 언급되지 <u>않은</u> 것을 고르시오.

W : Hey, Alex. Have you seen the announcement for the Victory Marathon?

M : Not yet, but I'm curious about it. When's the event?

W : It's on Saturday, July 13th.

M : Nice. Where will the race start?

W : It will start at William Stadium.

M : Oh, great. How much does it cost to participate?

W : It costs $30.

M : That's reasonable. How many _____ _____ _____ ?

W : Last year, there were around 5,000. They say they ✪ _____ _____ _____ _____ this year.

M : I didn't know that many people love marathons. I'm in!

W : Great. I ✪ _____ _____ ___ running with you.

09

Violet Hill Mentorship에 관한 다음 내용을 듣고, 일치하지 <u>않는</u> 것을 고르시오.

M : Good morning, students of Violet Hill High School. This is your principal speaking. I'm ✪ _____ __ _____ _____ the annual Violet Hill Mentorship will be held next Friday. Our school graduates ✪ _____ _____ _____ _____ in English literature, bioengineering, and theater and film will be giving some tips on university life. To register for this event, visit our school website and submit two questions you would like to ask them in advance. _____ _____ _____ ____ _____ is next Tuesday, so don't wait too long. And remember, the maximum number of participants for each major is 30 people. For more information, visit our school website.

10

다음 표를 보면서 대화를 듣고, 두 사람이 구입할 무선 진공 청소기를 고르시오.

M : Honey, look. This website's Summer Sale has just begun.

W : Oh, great. Why don't we buy a ✪ _____ _____ _____ ?

M : Sure. There are five bestsellers shown here.

W : Let's check the battery life first.

M : I think it should be at least two hours so that we don't have to charge it as often.

W : I agree. But let's not spend more than $400 on a vacuum cleaner.

M : Fine. Oh, some of these also have ✪ __ _____ _____ _____ .

W : I'd love that. With that function, we can definitely save a lot of time.

M : Okay. What about the color? The white one _____ _____ ___ _____.

W : Right. It'll match the color tone of our living room.

M : Perfect. So, let's buy this one.

W : Great.

11

대화를 듣고, 남자의 마지막 말에 대한 여자의 응답으로 가장 적절한 것을 고르시오.

M : Mom, I want to have a cat. Have you ever thought about ____ _____ __ ____?

W : Sweetie, having a pet requires ✪ _ _____ ___ _____ .

M : I'm _____ _____ _____ __. Mom, we could at least consider it.

12

대화를 듣고, 여자의 마지막 말에 대한 남자의 응답으로 가장 절한 것을 고르시오.

W : Jake, I completely forgot ✪ _____ _____ _____ . When's the deadline?

M : ✪ _____ _____ ___ _____ it by next Tuesday.

W : Phew, I _____ _____ _____ . Where should I submit it?

13

대화를 듣고, 남자의 마지막 말에 대한 여자의 응답으로 가장 적절한 것을 고르시오.　[3점]

M : Hey, Cindy. _____ _____ _____ _____ a lot of badminton these days?

W : No, I've been experiencing some pain in my knee since a badminton match last weekend.

M : I'm sorry to hear that. Did you go see a doctor?

W : Yes, I ✪ _____ __ _____ _____ yesterday.

M : I hope you feel better soon. By the way, have you ever taken a badminton lesson?

W : No, I haven't. Why are you asking?

M : In my experience, that kind of injury can ✪ _____ _____ _____ _____. A lesson might reduce the risk of any further injury.

W : Well, I thought I didn't need those lessons.

M : Cindy, if you want to keep playing badminton without any injuries, it's important to learn from an instructor to develop the right posture.

14

대화를 듣고, 여자의 마지막 말에 대한 남자의 응답으로 가장 적절한 것을 고르시오.　[3점]

W : Mike, don't you think _____ _____ ___ _____ of scary?

M : Right. The temperature seems higher than ever.

W : I heard it's putting a number of animals in danger these days.

M : Right. Maybe one day we ✪ _____ ___ _____ ____ see polar bears anymore.

W : That's not good. What can we do?

M : Use less plastic, plant more trees. Small things matter.

W : And maybe we can ride bikes instead of always asking for rides.

M : Yeah. Making a Tree-Planting Day at school ✪ _____ _____ ____ _____.

W : Absolutely. Then, why don't we make our own school club to put it into action?

15

다음 상황 설명을 듣고, Laura가 Tony에게 할 말로 가장 적절한 것을 고르시오.

W : Laura and Tony are close coworkers. Laura notices that Tony has been _____ _____ _____ and pale recently. One day, she asks Tony if he's not been feeling well lately, but Tony says he's just a bit tired from work. Laura knows that Tony sometimes works even on weekends ✪ _____ _____ __ _____ or getting any rest. However, this time, she is ✪ _____ _____ _____ _____ and wants him to take at least a couple of days off. In this situation, what would Laura most likely say to Tony

16~17

다음을 듣고, 물음에 답하시오.

M : Hello, Lincoln High School. This is David Newman, ✪ _____ _____ _____ _____ _____, and I'm speaking to you today to let you know about the upcoming election for next year's student representative. Candidates can now begin their campaigns, _____ _____ _____. First, they can share short promotional video clips on their social media, but the video clips must not be longer than 3 minutes. Second, candidates can display posters only in allowed areas, and it's important to keep the size to A3 or smaller, as larger posters will be removed without warning. Third, the use of ✪ _____ ___ _____, but they must only be distributed within the school campus. Lastly, there will be an online debate broadcast on our school website among the candidates three days before the election. It's important to be respectful toward the other candidates during the debate. Let's make this election a success.

▶ 정답 : 해설편 055쪽

회차별 영단어 QR 코드 ※ QR 코드를 스캔 후 모바일로 단어장처럼 학습할 수 있습니다. ● 고1 2024학년도 6월

18
001 □ appreciate ⓥ 감사하다
002 □ support ⓝ 지원
003 □ available ⓐ 가능한
004 □ switch ⓥ 전환하다
005 □ discount ⓝ 할인
006 □ current ⓐ 현재의
007 □ subscription ⓝ 구독료
008 □ access ⓥ 접근하다
009 □ a full year 만 1년
010 □ piece ⓝ (신문·잡지에 실린 한 편의) 기사
011 □ editor ⓝ 편집자
012 □ article ⓝ 기사

19
013 □ mailbox ⓝ 우편함
014 □ beat ⓥ 뛰다
015 □ rapidly 젧 빠르게
016 □ hold ⓥ 잡다, 쥐다
017 □ university ⓝ 대학교
018 □ apply ⓥ 지원하다
019 □ grade ⓝ 성적, 학점
020 □ good enough 만족스러운
021 □ application ⓝ 지원서
022 □ carefully 젧 조심스럽게, 신중히
023 □ envelope ⓝ 봉투
024 □ emerge ⓥ 나오다, 나타나다
025 □ faraway ⓐ 멀리 떨어진, 먼

20
026 □ messy ⓐ 지저분한
027 □ negative ⓐ 부정적인
028 □ feeling ⓝ 감정
029 □ destructive ⓐ 파괴적인
030 □ psychologist ⓝ 심리학자
031 □ disorderly ⓐ 무질서한, 난잡한, 어질러진
032 □ indicate ⓥ 가리키다
033 □ disorganized ⓐ 체계적이지 못한
034 □ expert ⓝ 전문가
035 □ moment ⓝ 순간
036 □ perspective ⓝ 관점, 시각
037 □ surrounding ⓝ 주변
038 □ positive ⓐ 긍정적인
039 □ atmosphere ⓝ 분위기
040 □ follow ⓥ 따라오다
041 □ efficiently 젧 효과적으로
042 □ neatly 젧 깔끔하게
043 □ closet ⓝ 벽장
044 □ drawer ⓝ 서랍
045 □ arrange ⓥ 정리하다, 배열하다

21
046 □ soil ⓝ 토양, 흙
047 □ farm ⓝ 농장
048 □ perfect ⓐ 완벽한
049 □ monoculture ⓝ 단일 작물 재배
050 □ achieve ⓥ 달성하다
051 □ nutrient ⓝ 영양소, 영양분
052 □ fertilizer ⓝ 비료
053 □ irrigation ⓝ 관개, 물 대기
054 □ crop ⓝ 작물
055 □ efficient ⓐ 효과적인

056 □ supply ⓥ 제공하다
057 □ amount ⓝ 양
058 □ capacity ⓝ 능력
059 □ luxurious ⓐ 사치스러운, 호화로운
060 □ agricultural ⓐ 농업의
061 □ undesirable ⓐ 바람직스럽지 못한, 달갑지 않은
062 □ relative ⓐ 비교상의
063 □ surround ⓥ 둘러싸다, 에워싸다
064 □ real estate 부동산

22
065 □ care ⓥ 관심을 가지다
066 □ notice ⓥ 알아차리다
067 □ lonely ⓐ 외로운
068 □ social ⓐ 사회적인
069 □ owe ⓥ 빚지다
070 □ attention ⓝ 관심
071 □ ignore ⓥ 무시하다
072 □ pass by 지나가다

23
073 □ often 젧 흔히, 종종, 자주
074 □ cut ⓝ 지름길
075 □ challenge ⓝ 도전
076 □ route ⓝ 길
077 □ fail ⓥ 실패하다
078 □ acquire ⓥ 얻다, 획득하다
079 □ strength ⓝ 힘, 기운
080 □ compete ⓥ 경쟁하다
081 □ mastery ⓝ 숙달
082 □ area ⓝ 영역
083 □ tool ⓝ 도구
084 □ useful ⓐ 유용한
085 □ prosperity ⓝ 번영
086 □ successful ⓐ 성공한, 성공적인
087 □ hardship ⓝ 고난
088 □ preparation ⓝ 준비
089 □ strategy ⓝ 계획, 전략
090 □ lesson ⓝ 교훈
091

24
092 □ usually 젧 보통, 대개
093 □ reflection ⓝ 반영
094 □ identity ⓝ 정체성
095 □ indication ⓝ 지시, 암시
096 □ type ⓝ 유형, 종류
097 □ consciously 젧 의식적으로
098 □ research ⓝ 연구
099 □ particular ⓐ 특정한
100 □ aspect ⓝ 측면
101 □ according to (지시·합의 등에) 따라
102 □ belief ⓝ 믿음, 확신, 신념
103 □ voter ⓝ 투표자, 유권자
104 □ similarly 젧 비슷하게
105 □ accept ⓥ 받아들이다
106 □ convince ⓥ 설득하다
107 □ train ⓥ 훈련하다
108 □ pursue ⓥ 추구하다

25
109 □ electronic ⓐ 전자의

110 □ collection ⓝ 수집, 수거
111 □ recycling ⓝ 재활용
112 □ rate ⓝ 비율, ~율
113 □ region ⓝ 지역
114 □ rank ⓥ (등급·등위·순위를) 차지하다
115 □ respectively 젧 각각
116 □ remain ⓥ 남다

26
117 □ memorable ⓐ 기억할만한
118 □ astrophysicist ⓝ 천체물리학자
119 □ coin ⓥ (단어를) 발명하다
120 □ term ⓝ 말, 전문어, 용어
121 □ supernova ⓝ 초신성
122 □ emigrate ⓥ 이주하다, 이민을 가다
123 □ develop ⓥ 발달시키다
124 □ numerous ⓐ 수많은
125 □ theory ⓝ 이론
126 □ astronomy ⓝ 천문학
127 □ patent ⓝ 특허권
128 □ propulsion ⓝ 추진력

27
129 □ gourmet ⓝ 미식가
130 □ competition ⓝ 경쟁
131 □ cookbook ⓝ 요리책
132 □ dust ⓝ 먼지
133 □ participate ⓥ 참여하다
134 □ category ⓝ 분류
135 □ enter ⓥ 응시하다, 출전하다
136 □ souvenir ⓝ 기념품

28
137 □ provide ⓥ 제공하다
138 □ bring ⓥ 가져오다
139 □ glove ⓝ 장갑
140 □ information ⓝ 정보

29
141 □ hunter-gatherer 수렵·채집인
142 □ lifestyle ⓝ 생활 방식
143 □ natural ⓐ 자연적인
144 □ appear ⓥ ~인 것같이 보이다
145 □ recommend ⓥ 추천하다
146 □ examination ⓝ 조사
147 □ remains ⓝ 유적, 유해
148 □ ancestor ⓝ 조상, 선조
149 □ abundant ⓐ 풍부한
150 □ obtainable ⓐ 얻을 수 있는
151 □ excessive ⓐ 지나친, 과도한
152 □ effort ⓝ 노력
153 □ suffer ⓥ 겪다
154 □ disease ⓝ 질병, 질환
155 □ settle ⓥ 정착하다
156 □ permanent ⓐ 영구적인
157 □ village ⓝ 마을
158 □ agriculture ⓝ 농업
159 □ domesticate ⓥ 길들이다
160 □ cultivate ⓥ 경작하다, 일구다
161 □ epidemic ⓐ 전염병의
162 □ settlement ⓝ 정착지
163 □ increase ⓝ 증가

164 □ population density 인구 밀도
165 □ period ⓝ 시기
166 □ New Stone Age 신석기 시대
167 □ turning point 전환점
168 □ eventually 젧 결국, 드디어
169 □ civilization ⓝ 문명

30
170 □ commodity ⓝ 상품
171 □ consumption ⓝ 소비
172 □ behavior ⓝ 행동
173 □ reveal ⓥ 드러내다
174 □ preference ⓝ 선호
175 □ reward ⓝ 보상
176 □ immediate ⓐ 즉각적인
177 □ agent ⓝ 행위자
178 □ exchange ⓥ 교환하다
179 □ discounted ⓐ 할인된
180 □ value ⓝ 가치
181 □ case ⓝ 경우, 사례
182 □ wait ⓥ 기다리다
183 □ envision ⓥ 계획하다
184 □ occasion ⓝ 기회
185 □ instead 젧 대신에
186 □ judge ⓥ 판단하다
187 □ resolve ⓥ 결심하다
188 □ benefit ⓝ 이익
189 □ temptation ⓝ 유혹

31
190 □ cost ⓝ 비용
191 □ interruption ⓝ 방해
192 □ lament ⓥ 애통하다, 슬퍼하다
193 □ describe ⓥ 묘사하다
194 □ poem ⓝ 시(詩)
195 □ famous ⓐ 유명한
196 □ literary ⓐ 문학적인
197 □ unexpected ⓐ 예기치 않은, 뜻밖의
198 □ guest ⓝ 손님
199 □ untimely 젧 때에 맞지 않게
200 □ visitor ⓝ 방문객
201 □ particularly 젧 특히, 특별히
202 □ inspiration ⓝ 영감

32
203 □ scientific ⓐ 과학적인
204 □ evidence ⓝ 증거
205 □ demonstrate ⓥ 입증하다
206 □ attention ⓝ 집중
207 □ auditory ⓐ 청각의
208 □ sharp ⓐ 예리한, 날카로운
209 □ eyesight ⓝ 시력
210 □ visual ⓐ 시각의
211 □ dramatic ⓐ 극적인
212 □ growth ⓝ 성장
213 □ expansion ⓝ 확장
214 □ cortex ⓝ 대뇌피질
215 □ represent ⓥ 나타내다
216 □ string ⓝ (악기의) 현(絃), 끈, 줄
217 □ precisely 젧 정확하게
218 □ hippocampus ⓝ 해마
219 □ vital ⓐ 필수적인

04회

220 spatial ⓐ 공간의, 공간적인
221 enlarge ⓥ 확대되다
222 physical ⓐ 물리적인
223 architecture ⓝ 구조, 구성
224 practice ⓥ 연습하다

33
225 evolve ⓥ 진화하다
226 possibility ⓝ 가능성
227 conflict ⓝ 갈등
228 tribe ⓝ 부족
229 enemy ⓝ 적
230 slightly ⓐⓓ 약간, 조금
231 possess ⓥ 점유하다, 소유하다, 가지다
232 advantage ⓝ 장점
233 imagine ⓥ 상상하다
234 predict ⓥ 예측하다
235 hostile ⓐ 적대적인
236 strike ⓥ 공격하다
237 accordingly ⓐⓓ (상황에) 부응해서, 그에 맞춰
238 significant ⓐ 중요한
239 military ⓐ 군사의
240 weapon ⓝ 무기
241 decisive ⓐ 결정적인
242 mental ⓐ 정신적인
243 over and over 반복해서
244 generation ⓝ 세대
245 opponent ⓝ 상대
246 battle ⓝ 전투
247 gene ⓝ 유전자
248 responsible ⓐ 책임지고 있는, 책임이 있는
249 offspring ⓝ 자식, 자손
250 descendant ⓝ 후손

34
251 hidden ⓐ 숨겨진
252 potential ⓝ 가능성
253 shift ⓥ 바꾸다
254 generate ⓥ 만들어 내다
255 separately ⓐⓓ 개별적으로
256 pool ⓥ 모으다
257 anonymously ⓐⓓ 익명으로
258 independent ⓐ 독립적인, 독립된
259 judgment ⓝ 판단
260 evaluate ⓥ 평가하다
261 select ⓥ 고르다, 선택하다
262 refine ⓥ 다듬다, 정제하다
263 promising ⓐ 유망한
264 elaborate ⓥ 잘 다듬다
265 surface ⓥ 드러내다
266 conversation ⓝ 대화
267 struggle ⓥ 다투다
268 collective ⓐ 집단의
269 intelligence ⓝ 지성

35
270 employee ⓝ 직원
271 agency ⓝ 주인
272 control ⓥ 통제하다
273 genuine ⓐ 진짜의
274 decision-making 의사 결정

275 authority ⓝ 권한
276 radically ⓐⓓ 급진적으로
277 plant ⓝ 공장
278 examine ⓥ 검사하다
279 assembly-line ⓐ 조립 라인의
280 empower ⓥ 권한을 주다
281 decision ⓝ 결정
282 schedule ⓝ 일정, 스케줄
283 work environment 작업환경
284 manufacturing processes 제조 공정
285 pay scale 급여 체계
286 stay ⓥ 머무르다, 그대로 있다
287 decrease ⓥ 줄다, 감소하다
288 efficiency ⓝ 효율성, 능률
289 organizational ⓐ 조직의
290 goal ⓝ 목표
291 productivity ⓝ 생산성
292 break ⓝ 휴식
293 mistake ⓝ 실수, 잘못

36
294 core ⓐ 핵심적인, 가장 중요한
295 activity ⓝ 활동
296 archiving ⓝ 파일 보관
297 environment ⓝ 환경
298 emission ⓝ 배출
299 carbon footprint 탄소 발자국
300 attachment ⓝ (이메일의) 첨부 파일
301 threaten ⓥ 위협하다
302 hazardous ⓐ 위험한
303 decade ⓝ 10년
304 waste ⓝ 쓰레기
305 document ⓝ 자료
306 workplace ⓝ 직장
307 invoice ⓝ 청구서
308 electricity ⓝ 전기
309 neglect ⓥ 방치하다, 간과하다
310 declare ⓥ 발표하다, 밝히다

37
311 exotic species 외래종
312 suddenly ⓐⓓ 갑자기
313 introduce ⓥ 소개하다
314 edge ⓝ 우위
315 for instance 예를 들어
316 ecosystem ⓝ 생태계
317 acorn ⓝ 도토리
318 digest ⓥ 소화하다, 소화시키다
319 mature ⓐ 익은, 성숙한
320 forest ⓝ 숲, 삼림
321 destroy ⓥ 파괴하다, 말살하다
322 supply ⓝ 공급
323 bite ⓥ 베어 물다
324 survive ⓥ 살아남다
325 woodland ⓝ 삼림 지대
326 as a result 결과적으로
327 extinction ⓝ 멸종

38
328 on the other hand 반면에, 다른 한편으로는
329 year after year 해마다, 매년

330 transport ⓥ 이송하다
331 distance ⓝ 거리
332 typically ⓐⓓ 일반적으로
333 frequently ⓐⓓ 자주
334 carry ⓥ 휴대하다, 가지고 다니다
335 possession ⓝ 소유물, 소지품
336 spacing ⓝ 간격
337 birth ⓝ 출산
338 at a time 한 번에
339 settled ⓐ 정착한
340 interval ⓝ 간격
341 counterpart ⓝ 상대
342 rapid ⓐ 빠른
343 population ⓝ 인구
344 agricultural society 농경 사회, 농업사회
345 labor ⓝ 노동

39
346 comparison ⓝ 비교
347 childhood ⓝ 유년기
348 migrate ⓥ 이주하다
349 migration ⓝ 이주
350 flexible ⓐ 유연한
351 migratory bird 철새
352 entirely ⓐⓓ 전적으로
353 instruction ⓝ 지시, 명령
354 inefficient ⓐ 비효율적인
355 adapt ⓥ 적응하다
356 dry up (강·호수 등이) 바싹 마르다
357 climate change 기후 변화
358 breeding ground (야생 동물의) 번식지
359 facilitate ⓥ 촉진하다
360 flexibility ⓝ 유연성

40
361 scholar ⓝ 학자
362 organize ⓥ 정리하다
363 present ⓥ 제공하다
364 preserve ⓥ 보존하다
365 disability ⓝ 장애
366 valuable ⓐ 가치가 큰, 소중한
367 resource ⓝ 원천
368 useless ⓐ 소용없는, 쓸모없는
369 distinguish ⓥ 구별하다
370 situation ⓝ 상황
371 improve ⓥ 개선되다, 나아지다
372 embrace ⓥ 받아들이다, 포옹하다
373 audience ⓝ 청중

41~42
374 extent ⓝ 정도
375 seek ⓥ 찾다
376 degree ⓝ 정도
377 pain ⓝ 고통
378 pleasure ⓝ 즐거움
379 spicy ⓐ 매운
380 step ⓥ 움직이다
381 threat ⓝ 협박, 위협
382 perceive ⓥ 인지하다
383 stimulus ⓝ 자극
384 painful ⓐ 고통스러운, 아픈
385 ultimately ⓐⓓ 궁극적으로, 결국

386 interestingly ⓐⓓ 흥미롭게, 재미있게
387 similar ⓐ 비슷한, 유사한
388 playfully ⓐⓓ 장난삼아, 재미있게
389 violate ⓥ 위반하다, 침해하다
390 norm ⓝ 규범
391 uncomfortable ⓐ 불편한, 불쾌한
392 context ⓝ (어떤 일의) 정황, 배경, 환경
393 desire ⓝ 욕구, 갈망
394 suffering ⓝ 고통
395 punishment ⓝ 처벌, 형벌
396 remarkable ⓐ 놀랄 만한, 놀라운
397 ingredient ⓝ 성분
398 receptor ⓝ 수용체
399 tissue ⓝ 조직
400 burn ⓥ 태우다
401 completely ⓐⓓ 완전히

43~45
402 alongside prep ~옆에, 나란히
403 experienced ⓐ 경험이 있는, 능숙한
404 instructor ⓝ 교관
405 wonder ⓝ 궁금증
406 appreciation ⓝ 감사
407 meanwhile ⓐⓓ 그 동안에
408 patiently ⓐⓓ 침착하게
409 emergency ⓝ 긴급 상황
410 relief ⓝ 안도
411 panic ⓥ 당황하다, 공포에 질리다
412 aircraft ⓝ 비행기
413 turbulence ⓝ 난기류

어휘 Review test 04

TEST A-B 각 단어의 뜻을 [A] 영어는 우리말로, [B] 우리말은 영어로 쓰시오.

A	English	Korean
01	envision	
02	article	
03	indication	
04	emission	
05	patent	
06	declare	
07	atmosphere	
08	beat	
09	distinguish	
10	auditory	
11	inspiration	
12	describe	
13	reveal	
14	route	
15	emergency	
16	rapidly	
17	preference	
18	appreciate	
19	surrounding	
20	examine	

B	Korean	English
01	부족	
02	전환하다	
03	증거	
04	안도	
05	간격	
06	지원하다	
07	비교	
08	능력	
09	이주하다	
10	다투다	
11	빠른	
12	노동	
13	생태계	
14	파괴적인	
15	처벌, 형벌	
16	자료	
17	보존하다	
18	기념품	
19	제공하다	
20	고난	

▶ A-D 정답 : 해설편 055쪽

TEST C-D 각 단어의 뜻을 골라 기호를 쓰시오.

C	English			Korean
01	pass by	(	)	ⓐ 지저분한
02	scholar	(	)	ⓑ 확장
03	descendant	(	)	ⓒ 번영
04	gourmet	(	)	ⓓ 미식가
05	interruption	(	)	ⓔ 비슷하게
06	hostile	(	)	ⓕ 입증하다
07	mastery	(	)	ⓖ 방해
08	similarly	(	)	ⓗ 소화하다, 소화시키다
09	digest	(	)	ⓘ 영구적인
10	demonstrate	(	)	ⓙ 결심하다
11	permanent	(	)	ⓚ 후손
12	opponent	(	)	ⓛ 숙달
13	lament	(	)	ⓜ 지나가다
14	prosperity	(	)	ⓝ 주인
15	expansion	(	)	ⓞ 슬퍼하다
16	bite	(	)	ⓟ 적대적인
17	resolve	(	)	ⓠ 핵심적인, 가장 중요한
18	messy	(	)	ⓡ 베어 물다
19	core	(	)	ⓢ 상대
20	agency	(	)	ⓣ 학자

D	Korean			English
01	정착한	(	)	ⓐ coin
02	위험한	(	)	ⓑ threat
03	궁금증	(	)	ⓒ dry up
04	침착하게	(	)	ⓓ facilitate
05	가져오다	(	)	ⓔ wonder
06	권한	(	)	ⓕ epidemic
07	(단어를) 발명하다	(	)	ⓖ seek
08	비행기	(	)	ⓗ patiently
09	찾다	(	)	ⓘ owe
10	즉각적인	(	)	ⓙ settled
11	촉진하다	(	)	ⓚ enlarge
12	추진력	(	)	ⓛ bring
13	조직	(	)	ⓜ disability
14	빚지다	(	)	ⓝ tissue
15	확대되다	(	)	ⓞ hazardous
16	각각	(	)	ⓟ immediate
17	협박, 위협	(	)	ⓠ authority
18	장애	(	)	ⓡ propulsion
19	전염병의	(	)	ⓢ aircraft
20	바싹 마르다	(	)	ⓣ respectively

2023학년도 6월 고1 전국연합학력평가 문제지

제 3 교시

영어 영역

05회

● 문항수 45개 | 배점 100점 | 제한 시간 70분

● 점수 표시가 없는 문항은 모두 2점

05회

1번부터 17번까지는 듣고 답하는 문제입니다. 1번부터 15번까지는 한 번만 들려주고, 16번부터 17번까지는 두 번 들려줍니다. 방송을 잘 듣고 답을 하시기 바랍니다.

MP3

1. 다음을 듣고, 여자가 하는 말의 목적으로 가장 적절한 것을 고르시오.

① 체육대회 종목을 소개하려고
② 대회 자원봉사자를 모집하려고
③ 학생 회장 선거 일정을 공지하려고
④ 경기 관람 규칙 준수를 당부하려고
⑤ 학교 홈페이지 주소 변경을 안내하려고

2. 대화를 듣고, 남자의 의견으로 가장 적절한 것을 고르시오.

① 산책은 창의적인 생각을 할 수 있게 돕는다.
② 식사 후 과격한 운동은 소화를 방해한다.
③ 지나친 스트레스는 집중력을 감소시킨다.
④ 독서를 통해 창의력을 증진할 수 있다.
⑤ 꾸준한 운동은 기초체력을 향상시킨다.

3. 대화를 듣고, 두 사람의 관계를 가장 잘 나타낸 것을 고르시오.

① 고객 – 우체국 직원
② 투숙객 – 호텔 지배인
③ 여행객 – 여행 가이드
④ 아파트 주민 – 경비원
⑤ 손님 – 옷가게 주인

4. 대화를 듣고, 그림에서 대화의 내용과 일치하지 <u>않는</u> 것을 고르시오.

5. 대화를 듣고, 남자가 할 일로 가장 적절한 것을 고르시오.

① 초대장 보내기
② 피자 주문하기
③ 거실 청소하기
④ 꽃다발 준비하기
⑤ 스마트폰 사러 가기

6. 대화를 듣고, 여자가 지불할 금액을 고르시오. [3점]

① $54   ② $60   ③ $72   ④ $76   ⑤ $80

7. 대화를 듣고, 남자가 록 콘서트에 갈 수 <u>없는</u> 이유를 고르시오.

① 일을 하러 가야 해서
② 피아노 연습을 해야 해서
③ 할머니를 뵈러 가야 해서
④ 친구의 개를 돌봐야 해서
⑤ 과제를 아직 끝내지 못해서

8. 대화를 듣고, Eco Day에 관해 언급되지 <u>않은</u> 것을 고르시오.

① 행사 시간   ② 행사 장소   ③ 참가비
④ 준비물   ⑤ 등록 방법

9. Eastville Dance Contest에 관한 다음 내용을 듣고, 일치하지 <u>않는</u> 것을 고르시오.

① 처음으로 개최되는 경연이다.
② 모든 종류의 춤이 허용된다.
③ 춤 영상을 8월 15일까지 업로드 해야 한다.
④ 학생들은 가장 좋아하는 영상에 투표할 수 있다.
⑤ 우승팀은 상으로 상품권을 받게 될 것이다.

10. 다음 표를 보면서 대화를 듣고, 두 사람이 구입할 정수기를 고르시오.

Water Purifiers

	Model	Price	Water Tank Capacity(liters)	Power-saving Mode	Warranty
①	A	$570	4	×	1 year
②	B	$650	5	○	1 year
③	C	$680	5	×	3 years
④	D	$740	5	○	3 years
⑤	E	$830	6	○	3 years

11. 대화를 듣고, 남자의 마지막 말에 대한 여자의 응답으로 가장 적절한 것을 고르시오.

① Great. We don't have to wait in line.
② All right. We can come back later.
③ Good job. Let's buy the tickets.
④ No worries. I will stand in line.
⑤ Too bad. I can't buy that car.

12. 대화를 듣고, 여자의 마지막 말에 대한 남자의 응답으로 가장 적절한 것을 고르시오.

① Yes. You can register online.
② Sorry. I can't see you next week.
③ Right. I should go to his office now.
④ Fantastic! I'll take the test tomorrow.
⑤ Of course. I can help him if he needs my help.

13. 대화를 듣고, 여자의 마지막 말에 대한 남자의 응답으로 가장 적절한 것을 고르시오. [3점]

Man: _____

① I agree. You can save a lot by buying secondhand.
② Great idea! Our message would make others smile.
③ Sorry. I forgot to write a message in the book.
④ Exactly. Taking notes during class is important.
⑤ Okay. We can arrive on time if we leave now.

14. 대화를 듣고, 남자의 마지막 말에 대한 여자의 응답으로 가장 적절한 것을 고르시오. [3점]

Woman: _____

① Why not? I can bring some food when we go camping.
② I'm sorry. That fishing equipment is not for sale.
③ I don't think so. The price is most important.
④ Really? I'd love to meet your family.
⑤ No problem. You can use my equipment.

15. 다음 상황 설명을 듣고, Violet이 Peter에게 할 말로 가장 적절한 것을 고르시오.

Violet: _____

① Will you join the science club together?
② Is it okay to use a card to pay for the drinks?
③ Why don't we donate our books to the library?
④ How about going to the cafeteria to have lunch?
⑤ Can you borrow the books for me with your card?

[16~17] 다음을 듣고, 물음에 답하시오.

16. 남자가 하는 말의 주제로 가장 적절한 것은?

① different causes of sleep disorders
② various ways to keep foods fresh
③ foods to improve quality of sleep
④ reasons for organic foods' popularity
⑤ origins of popular foods around the world

17. 언급된 음식이 아닌 것은?

① kiwi fruits   ② milk   ③ nuts
④ tomatoes   ⑤ honey

이제 듣기 문제가 끝났습니다. 18번부터는 문제지의 지시에 따라 답을 하시기 바랍니다.

18. 다음 글의 목적으로 가장 적절한 것은?

ACC Travel Agency Customers:

Have you ever wanted to enjoy a holiday in nature? This summer is the best time to turn your dream into reality. We have a perfect travel package for you. This travel package includes special trips to Lake Madison as well as massage and meditation to help you relax. Also, we provide yoga lessons taught by experienced instructors. If you book this package, you will enjoy all this at a reasonable price. We are sure that it will be an unforgettable experience for you. If you call us, we will be happy to give you more details.

① 여행 일정 변경을 안내하려고
② 패키지 여행 상품을 홍보하려고
③ 여행 상품 불만족에 대해 사과하려고
④ 여행 만족도 조사 참여를 부탁하려고
⑤ 패키지 여행 업무 담당자를 모집하려고

19. 다음 글에 드러난 'I'의 심경 변화로 가장 적절한 것은?

When I woke up in our hotel room, it was almost midnight. I didn't see my husband nor daughter. I called them, but I heard their phones ringing in the room. Feeling worried, I went outside and walked down the street, but they were nowhere to be found. When I decided I should ask someone for help, a crowd nearby caught my attention. I approached, hoping to find my husband and daughter, and suddenly I saw two familiar faces. I smiled, feeling calm. Just then, my daughter saw me and called, "Mom!" They were watching the magic show. Finally, I felt all my worries disappear.

① anxious   → relieved   ② delighted → unhappy
③ indifferent   → excited   ④ relaxed   → upset
⑤ embarrassed → proud

20. 다음 글에서 필자가 주장하는 바로 가장 적절한 것은?

Research shows that people who work have two calendars: one for work and one for their personal lives. Although it may seem sensible, having two separate calendars for work and personal life can lead to distractions. To check if something is missing, you will find yourself checking your to-do lists multiple times. Instead, organize all of your tasks in one place. It doesn't matter if you use digital or paper media. It's okay to keep your professional and personal tasks in one place. This will give you a good idea of how time is divided between work and home. This will allow you to make informed decisions about which tasks are most important.

① 결정한 것은 반드시 실행하도록 노력하라.
② 자신이 담당한 업무에 관한 전문성을 확보하라.
③ 업무 집중도를 높이기 위해 책상 위를 정돈하라.
④ 좋은 아이디어를 메모하는 습관을 길러라.
⑤ 업무와 개인 용무를 한 곳에 정리하라.

21. 밑줄 친 become unpaid ambassadors가 다음 글에서 의미하는 바로 가장 적절한 것은?

Why do you care how a customer reacts to a purchase? Good question. By understanding post-purchase behavior, you can understand the influence and the likelihood of whether a buyer will repurchase the product (and whether she will keep it or return it). You'll also determine whether the buyer will encourage others to purchase the product from you. Satisfied customers can become unpaid ambassadors for your business, so customer satisfaction should be on the top of your to-do list. People tend to believe the opinions of people they know. People trust friends over advertisements any day. They know that advertisements are paid to tell the "good side" and that they're used to persuade them to purchase products and services. By continually monitoring your customer's satisfaction after the sale, you have the ability to avoid negative word-of-mouth advertising.

① recommend products to others for no gain
② offer manufacturers feedback on products
③ become people who don't trust others' words
④ get rewards for advertising products overseas
⑤ buy products without worrying about the price

22. 다음 글의 요지로 가장 적절한 것은?

The promise of a computerized society, we were told, was that it would pass to machines all of the repetitive drudgery of work, allowing us humans to pursue higher purposes and to have more leisure time. It didn't work out this way. Instead of more time, most of us have less. Companies large and small have off-loaded work onto the backs of consumers. Things that used to be done for us, as part of the value-added service of working with a company, we are now expected to do ourselves. With air travel, we're now expected to complete our own reservations and check-in, jobs that used to be done by airline employees or travel agents. At the grocery store, we're expected to bag our own groceries and, in some supermarkets, to scan our own purchases.

* drudgery: 고된 일

① 컴퓨터 기반 사회에서는 여가 시간이 더 늘어난다.
② 회사 업무의 전산화는 업무 능률을 향상시킨다.
③ 컴퓨터화된 사회에서 소비자는 더 많은 일을 하게 된다.
④ 온라인 거래가 모든 소비자들을 만족시키기에는 한계가 있다.
⑤ 산업의 발전으로 인해 기계가 인간의 일자리를 대신하고 있다.

23. 다음 글의 주제로 가장 적절한 것은?

We tend to believe that we possess a host of socially desirable characteristics, and that we are free of most of those that are socially undesirable. For example, a large majority of the general public thinks that they are more intelligent, more fair-minded, less prejudiced, and more skilled behind the wheel of an automobile than the average person. This phenomenon is so reliable and ubiquitous that it has come to be known as the "Lake Wobegon effect," after Garrison Keillor's fictional community where "the women are strong, the men are good-looking, and all the children are above average." A survey of one million high school seniors found that 70% thought they were above average in leadership ability, and only 2% thought they were below average. In terms of ability to get along with others, *all* students thought they were above average, 60% thought they were in the top 10%, and 25% thought they were in the top 1%!

* ubiquitous: 도처에 있는

① importance of having a positive self-image as a leader
② our common belief that we are better than average
③ our tendency to think others are superior to us
④ reasons why we always try to be above average
⑤ danger of prejudice in building healthy social networks

24. 다음 글의 제목으로 가장 적절한 것은?

Few people will be surprised to hear that poverty tends to create stress: a 2006 study published in the American journal *Psychosomatic Medicine*, for example, noted that a lower socioeconomic status was associated with higher levels of stress hormones in the body. However, richer economies have their own distinct stresses. The key issue is time pressure. A 1999 study of 31 countries by American psychologist Robert Levine and Canadian psychologist Ara Norenzayan found that wealthier, more industrialized nations had a faster pace of life — which led to a higher standard of living, but at the same time left the population feeling a constant sense of urgency, as well as being more prone to heart disease. In effect, fast-paced productivity creates wealth, but it also leads people to feel time-poor when they lack the time to relax and enjoy themselves.

* prone: 걸리기 쉬운

① Why Are Even Wealthy Countries Not Free from Stress?
② In Search of the Path to Escaping the Poverty Trap
③ Time Management: Everything You Need to Know
④ How Does Stress Affect Human Bodies?
⑤ Sound Mind Wins the Game of Life!

25. 다음 도표의 내용과 일치하지 <u>않는</u> 것은?

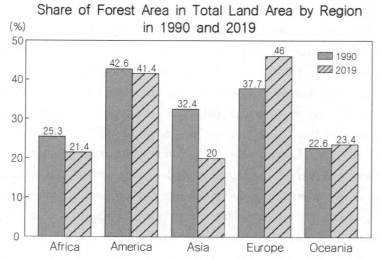

Share of Forest Area in Total Land Area by Region in 1990 and 2019

The above graph shows the share of forest area in total land area by region in 1990 and 2019. ① Africa's share of forest area in total land area was over 20% in both 1990 and 2019. ② The share of forest area in America was 42.6% in 1990, which was larger than that in 2019. ③ The share of forest area in Asia declined from 1990 to 2019 by more than 10 percentage points. ④ In 2019, the share of forest area in Europe was the largest among the five regions, more than three times that in Asia in the same year. ⑤ Oceania showed the smallest gap between 1990 and 2019 in terms of the share of forest area in total land area.

26. Gary Becker에 관한 다음 글의 내용과 일치하지 <u>않는</u> 것은?

Gary Becker was born in Pottsville, Pennsylvania in 1930 and grew up in Brooklyn, New York City. His father, who was not well educated, had a deep interest in financial and political issues. After graduating from high school, Becker went to Princeton University, where he majored in economics. He was dissatisfied with his economic education at Princeton University because "it didn't seem to be handling real problems." He earned a doctor's degree in economics from the University of Chicago in 1955. His doctoral paper on the economics of discrimination was mentioned by the Nobel Prize Committee as an important contribution to economics. Since 1985, Becker had written a regular economics column in *Business Week*, explaining economic analysis and ideas to the general public. In 1992, he was awarded the Nobel Prize in economic science.

* discrimination: 차별

① New York City의 Brooklyn에서 자랐다.
② 아버지는 금융과 정치 문제에 깊은 관심이 있었다.
③ Princeton University에서의 경제학 교육에 만족했다.
④ 1955년에 경제학 박사 학위를 취득했다.
⑤ *Business Week*에 경제학 칼럼을 기고했다.

27. 2023 Drone Racing Championship에 관한 다음 안내문의 내용과 일치하지 <u>않는</u> 것은?

2023 Drone Racing Championship

Are you the best drone racer? Then take the opportunity to prove you are the one!

When & Where
• 6 p.m. — 8 p.m., Sunday, July 9
• Lakeside Community Center

Requirements
• Participants: High school students only
• Bring your own drone for the race.

Prize
• $500 and a medal will be awarded to the winner.

Note
• The first 10 participants will get souvenirs.

For more details, please visit www.droneracing.com or call 313 - 6745 - 1189.

① 7월 9일 일요일에 개최된다.
② 고등학생만 참가할 수 있다.
③ 자신의 드론을 가져와야 한다.
④ 상금과 메달이 우승자에게 수여될 것이다.
⑤ 20명의 참가자가 기념품을 받을 것이다.

28. Summer Scuba Diving One-day Class에 관한 다음 안내문의 내용과 일치하는 것은?

Summer Scuba Diving One-day Class

Join our summer scuba diving lesson for beginners, and become an underwater explorer!

Schedule
• 10:00 - 12:00 Learning the basics
• 13:00 - 16:00 Practicing diving skills in a pool

Price
• Private lesson: $150
• Group lesson (up to 3 people): $100 per person
• Participants can rent our diving equipment for free.

Notice
• Participants must be 10 years old or over.
• Participants must register at least 5 days before the class begins.

For more information, please go to www.ssdiver.com.

① 오후 시간에 바다에서 다이빙 기술을 연습한다.
② 그룹 수업의 최대 정원은 4명이다.
③ 다이빙 장비를 유료로 대여할 수 있다.
④ 연령에 관계없이 참가할 수 있다.
⑤ 적어도 수업 시작 5일 전까지 등록해야 한다.

29. 다음 글의 밑줄 친 부분 중, 어법상 틀린 것은? [3점]

Although praise is one of the most powerful tools available for improving young children's behavior, it is equally powerful for improving your child's self-esteem. Preschoolers believe what their parents tell ① them in a very profound way. They do not yet have the cognitive sophistication to reason ② analytically and reject false information. If a preschool boy consistently hears from his mother ③ that he is smart and a good helper, he is likely to incorporate that information into his self-image. Thinking of himself as a boy who is smart and knows how to do things ④ being likely to make him endure longer in problem-solving efforts and increase his confidence in trying new and difficult tasks. Similarly, thinking of himself as the kind of boy who is a good helper will make him more likely to volunteer ⑤ to help with tasks at home and at preschool.

* profound: 뜻 깊은 ** sophistication: 정교화(함)

30. 다음 글의 밑줄 친 부분 중, 문맥상 낱말의 쓰임이 적절하지 않은 것은?

Advertisers often displayed considerable facility in ① adapting their claims to the market status of the goods they promoted. Fleischmann's yeast, for instance, was used as an ingredient for cooking homemade bread. Yet more and more people in the early 20th century were buying their bread from stores or bakeries, so consumer demand for yeast ② increased. The producer of Fleischmann's yeast hired the J. Walter Thompson advertising agency to come up with a different marketing strategy to ③ boost sales. No longer the "Soul of Bread," the Thompson agency first turned yeast into an important source of vitamins with significant health ④ benefits. Shortly thereafter, the advertising agency transformed yeast into a natural laxative. ⑤ Repositioning yeast helped increase sales.

* laxative: 완하제(배변을 쉽게 하는 약·음식·음료)

[31~34] 다음 빈칸에 들어갈 말로 가장 적절한 것을 고르시오.

31. Individuals who perform at a high level in their profession often have instant credibility with others. People admire them, they want to be like them, and they feel connected to them. When they speak, others listen — even if the area of their skill has nothing to do with the advice they give. Think about a world-famous basketball player. He has made more money from endorsements than he ever did playing basketball. Is it because of his knowledge of the products he endorses? No. It's because of what he can do with a basketball. The same can be said of an Olympic medalist swimmer. People listen to him because of what he can do in the pool. And when an actor tells us we should drive a certain car, we don't listen because of his expertise on engines. We listen because we admire his talent. _____ connects. If you possess a high level of ability in an area, others may desire to connect with you because of it.

* endorsement: (유명인의 텔레비전 등에서의 상품) 보증 선전

① Patience
② Sacrifice
③ Honesty
④ Excellence
⑤ Creativity

32. Think of the brain as a city. If you were to look out over a city and ask "where is the economy located?" you'd see there's no good answer to the question. Instead, the economy emerges from the interaction of all the elements — from the stores and the banks to the merchants and the customers. And so it is with the brain's operation: it doesn't happen in one spot. Just as in a city, no neighborhood of the brain _____. In brains and in cities, everything emerges from the interaction between residents, at all scales, locally and distantly. Just as trains bring materials and textiles into a city, which become processed into the economy, so the raw electrochemical signals from sensory organs are transported along superhighways of neurons. There the signals undergo processing and transformation into our conscious reality. [3점]

* electrochemical: 전기화학의

① operates in isolation
② suffers from rapid changes
③ resembles economic elements
④ works in a systematic way
⑤ interacts with another

33. Someone else's body language affects our own body, which then creates an emotional echo that makes us feel accordingly. As Louis Armstrong sang, "When you're smiling, the whole world smiles with you." If copying another's smile makes us feel happy, the emotion of the smiler has been transmitted via our body. Strange as it may sound, this theory states that _____.
For example, our mood can be improved by simply lifting up the corners of our mouth. If people are asked to bite down on a pencil lengthwise, taking care not to let the pencil touch their lips (thus forcing the mouth into a smile-like shape), they judge cartoons funnier than if they have been asked to frown. The primacy of the body is sometimes summarized in the phrase "I must be afraid, because I'm running." [3점]

* lengthwise: 길게 ** frown: 얼굴을 찡그리다

① language guides our actions
② emotions arise from our bodies
③ body language hides our feelings
④ what others say affects our mood
⑤ negative emotions easily disappear

34. _____ boosts sales. Brian Wansink, Professor of Marketing at Cornell University, investigated the effectiveness of this tactic in 1998. He persuaded three supermarkets in Sioux City, Iowa, to offer Campbell's soup at a small discount: 79 cents rather than 89 cents. The discounted soup was sold in one of three conditions: a control, where there was no limit on the volume of purchases, or two tests, where customers were limited to either four or twelve cans. In the unlimited condition shoppers bought 3.3 cans on average, whereas in the scarce condition, when there was a limit, they bought 5.3 on average. This suggests scarcity encourages sales. The findings are particularly strong because the test took place in a supermarket with genuine shoppers. It didn't rely on claimed data, nor was it held in a laboratory where consumers might behave differently. [3점]

* tactic: 전략

① Promoting products through social media
② Reducing the risk of producing poor quality items
③ Restricting the number of items customers can buy
④ Offering several options that customers find attractive
⑤ Emphasizing the safety of products with research data

35. 다음 글에서 전체 흐름과 관계 없는 문장은?

Although technology has the potential to increase productivity, it can also have a negative impact on productivity. For example, in many office environments workers sit at desks with computers and have access to the internet. ① They are able to check their personal e-mails and use social media whenever they want to. ② This can stop them from doing their work and make them less productive. ③ Introducing new technology can also have a negative impact on production when it causes a change to the production process or requires workers to learn a new system. ④ Using technology can enable businesses to produce more goods and to get more out of the other factors of production. ⑤ Learning to use new technology can be time consuming and stressful for workers and this can cause a decline in productivity.

[36~37] 주어진 글 다음에 이어질 글의 순서로 가장 적절한 것을 고르시오.

36.

Up until about 6,000 years ago, most people were farmers. Many lived in different places throughout the year, hunting for food or moving their livestock to areas with enough food.

(A) For example, priests wanted to know when to carry out religious ceremonies. This was when people first invented clocks — devices that show, measure, and keep track of passing time.

(B) There was no need to tell the time because life depended on natural cycles, such as the changing seasons or sunrise and sunset. Gradually more people started to live in larger settlements, and some needed to tell the time.

(C) Clocks have been important ever since. Today, clocks are used for important things such as setting busy airport timetables — if the time is incorrect, aeroplanes might crash into each other when taking off or landing! [3점]

① (A) − (C) − (B)
② (B) − (A) − (C)
③ (B) − (C) − (A)
④ (C) − (A) − (B)
⑤ (C) − (B) − (A)

37.

Managers are always looking for ways to increase productivity, which is the ratio of costs to output in production. Adam Smith, writing when the manufacturing industry was new, described a way that production could be made more efficient, known as the "division of labor."

(A) Because each worker specializes in one job, he or she can work much faster without changing from one task to another. Now 10 workers can produce thousands of pins in a day — a huge increase in productivity from the 200 they would have produced before.

(B) One worker could do all these tasks, and make 20 pins in a day. But this work can be divided into its separate processes, with a number of workers each performing one task.

(C) Making most manufactured goods involves several different processes using different skills. Smith's example was the manufacture of pins: the wire is straightened, sharpened, a head is put on, and then it is polished.

* ratio: 비율

① (A) − (C) − (B)　　② (B) − (A) − (C)
③ (B) − (C) − (A)　　④ (C) − (A) − (B)
⑤ (C) − (B) − (A)

[38~39] 글의 흐름으로 보아, 주어진 문장이 들어가기에 가장 적절한 곳을 고르시오.

38.

Yet we know that the face that stares back at us from the glass is not the same, cannot be the same, as it was 10 minutes ago.

Sometimes the pace of change is far slower. (①) The face you saw reflected in your mirror this morning probably appeared no different from the face you saw the day before — or a week or a month ago. (②) The proof is in your photo album: Look at a photograph taken of yourself 5 or 10 years ago and you see clear differences between the face in the snapshot and the face in your mirror. (③) If you lived in a world without mirrors for a year and then saw your reflection, you might be surprised by the change. (④) After an interval of 10 years without seeing yourself, you might not at first recognize the person peering from the mirror. (⑤) Even something as basic as our own face changes from moment to moment.

* peer: 응시하다

39.

As children absorb more evidence from the world around them, certain possibilities become much more likely and more useful and harden into knowledge or beliefs.

According to educational psychologist Susan Engel, curiosity begins to decrease as young as four years old. By the time we are adults, we have fewer questions and more default settings. As Henry James put it, "Disinterested curiosity is past, the mental grooves and channels set." (①) The decline in curiosity can be traced in the development of the brain through childhood. (②) Though smaller than the adult brain, the infant brain contains millions more neural connections. (③) The wiring, however, is a mess; the lines of communication between infant neurons are far less efficient than between those in the adult brain. (④) The baby's perception of the world is consequently both intensely rich and wildly disordered. (⑤) The neural pathways that enable those beliefs become faster and more automatic, while the ones that the child doesn't use regularly are pruned away. [3점]

* default setting: 기본값 ** groove: 고랑 *** prune: 가지치기하다

40. 다음 글의 내용을 한 문장으로 요약하고자 한다. 빈칸 (A), (B)에 들어갈 말로 가장 적절한 것은?

Nearly eight of ten U.S. adults believe there are "good foods" and "bad foods." Unless we're talking about spoiled stew, poison mushrooms, or something similar, however, no foods can be labeled as either good or bad. There are, however, combinations of foods that add up to a healthful or unhealthful diet. Consider the case of an adult who eats only foods thought of as "good" — for example, raw broccoli, apples, orange juice, boiled tofu, and carrots. Although all these foods are nutrient-dense, they do not add up to a healthy diet because they don't supply a wide enough variety of the nutrients we need. Or take the case of the teenager who occasionally eats fried chicken, but otherwise stays away from fried foods. The occasional fried chicken isn't going to knock his or her diet off track. But the person who eats fried foods every day, with few vegetables or fruits, and loads up on supersized soft drinks, candy, and chips for snacks has a bad diet.

↓

Unlike the common belief, defining foods as good or bad is not ___(A)___ ; in fact, a healthy diet is determined largely by what the diet is ___(B)___ .

	(A)		(B)
①	incorrect	.....	limited to
②	appropriate	.....	composed of
③	wrong	.....	aimed at
④	appropriate	.....	tested on
⑤	incorrect	.....	adjusted to

[41~42] 다음 글을 읽고, 물음에 답하시오.

Early hunter-gatherer societies had (a) <u>minimal</u> structure. A chief or group of elders usually led the camp or village. Most of these leaders had to hunt and gather along with the other members because the surpluses of food and other vital resources were seldom (b) <u>sufficient</u> to support a full-time chief or village council. The development of agriculture changed work patterns. Early farmers could reap 3-10 kg of grain from each 1 kg of seed planted. Part of this food/energy surplus was returned to the community and (c) <u>limited</u> support for nonfarmers such as chieftains, village councils, men who practice medicine, priests, and warriors. In return, the nonfarmers provided leadership and security for the farming population, enabling it to continue to increase food/energy yields and provide ever larger surpluses.

With improved technology and favorable conditions, agriculture produced consistent surpluses of the basic necessities, and population groups grew in size. These groups concentrated in towns and cities, and human tasks (d) <u>specialized</u> further. Specialists such as carpenters, blacksmiths, merchants, traders, and sailors developed their skills and became more efficient in their use of time and energy. The goods and services they provided brought about an (e) <u>improved</u> quality of life, a higher standard of living, and, for most societies, increased stability.

* reap: (농작물을) 베어들이다 ** chieftain: 수령, 두목

41. 윗글의 제목으로 가장 적절한 것은?

① How Agriculture Transformed Human Society
② The Dark Shadow of Agriculture: Repetition
③ How Can We Share Extra Food with the Poor?
④ Why Were Early Societies Destroyed by Agriculture?
⑤ The Advantages of Large Groups Over Small Groups in Farming

42. 밑줄 친 (a)~(e) 중에서 문맥상 낱말의 쓰임이 적절하지 <u>않은</u> 것은? [3점]

① (a)　② (b)　③ (c)　④ (d)　⑤ (e)

[43~45] 다음 글을 읽고, 물음에 답하시오.

(A)

A nurse took a tired, anxious soldier to the bedside. "Jack, your son is here," the nurse said to an old man lying on the bed. She had to repeat the words several times before the old man's eyes opened. Suffering from the severe pain because of heart disease, he barely saw the young uniformed soldier standing next to him. (a) <u>He</u> reached out his hand to the soldier.

(B)

Whenever the nurse came into the room, she heard the soldier say a few gentle words. The old man said nothing, only held tightly to (b) <u>him</u> all through the night. Just before dawn, the old man died. The soldier released the old man's hand and left the room to find the nurse. After she was told what happened, she went back to the room with him. The soldier hesitated for a while and asked, "Who was this man?"

(C)

She was surprised and asked, "Wasn't he your father?" "No, he wasn't. I've never met him before," the soldier replied. She asked, "Then why didn't you say something when I took you to (c) <u>him</u>?" He said, "I knew there had been a mistake, but when I realized that he was too sick to tell whether or not I was his son, I could see how much (d) <u>he</u> needed me. So, I stayed."

(D)

The soldier gently wrapped his fingers around the weak hand of the old man. The nurse brought a chair so that the soldier could sit beside the bed. All through the night the young soldier sat there, holding the old man's hand and offering (e) <u>him</u> words of support and comfort. Occasionally, she suggested that the soldier take a rest for a while. He politely said no.

43. 주어진 글 (A)에 이어질 내용을 순서에 맞게 배열한 것으로 가장 적절한 것은?

① (B) − (D) − (C)　　② (C) − (B) − (D)
③ (C) − (D) − (B)　　④ (D) − (B) − (C)
⑤ (D) − (C) − (B)

44. 밑줄 친 (a)~(e) 중에서 가리키는 대상이 나머지 넷과 <u>다른</u> 것은?

① (a)　② (b)　③ (c)　④ (d)　⑤ (e)

45. 윗글에 관한 내용으로 적절하지 <u>않은</u> 것은?

① 노인은 심장병으로 극심한 고통을 겪고 있었다.
② 군인은 간호사를 찾기 위해 병실을 나갔다.
③ 군인은 노인과 이전에 만난 적이 있다고 말했다.
④ 간호사는 군인이 앉을 수 있도록 의자를 가져왔다.
⑤ 군인은 잠시 쉬라는 간호사의 제안을 정중히 거절하였다.

★ 확인 사항
○ 답안지의 해당란에 필요한 내용을 정확히 기입(표기)했는지 확인하시오.

※ QR 코드를 스캔하시면 듣기 방송이 나옵니다. 듣기 방송을 들으며 다음 빈칸을 채우시오.   ● 제한 시간 : 25분

01

다음을 듣고, 여자가 하는 말의 목적으로 가장 적절한 것을 고르시오.

W : Good afternoon, everybody. This is your student council president, Monica Brown. Our school's annual e-sports competition will be held on the last day of the semester. For the competition, we need some volunteers to _____ _____ ____ _____.
If you're interested in helping us make the competition successful, please _____ _____ _____ _____ _____ _____ and email it to me. For more information, please visit our school website. I hope many of you _____ _____ ____. Thank you for listening.

02

대화를 듣고, 남자의 의견으로 가장 적절한 것을 고르시오.

M : Hannah, how's your design project going?
W : Hey, Aiden. I'm still working on it, but I'm 🔄 _____ _____ _____ _____.
M : Can you tell me what the problem is?
W : Hmm... [Pause] It's hard to think of creative ideas. I feel like I'm wasting my time.
M : I understand. Why don't you _____ __ _____?
W : How can that help me to _____ _____ _____?
M : It will actually make your brain more active. Then you'll see things differently.
W : But I don't have time for that.
M : You don't need a lot of time. Even a short walk will help you to come up with creative ideas.
W : Then I'll try it. Thanks for the tip.

03

대화를 듣고, 두 사람의 관계를 가장 잘 나타낸 것을 고르시오.

W : Excuse me. Could you please tell me where I can put this box?
M : Right here on this counter. How can I help you today?
W : I'd like to send this to Jeju Island.
M : Sure. Are there 🔄 _____ _____ _____ in the box?
W : No, there are only clothes in it.
M : Then, there should be no problem.
W : I see. What's the fastest way to send it?

M : You can send the package by express mail, but _____ ____ _____ _____.
W : That's okay. I want it to be delivered as soon as possible. When will it arrive in Jeju if it goes out today?
M : If you send it today, it will be there by this Friday.
W : Oh, Friday will be great. I'll ____ _____ ____ _____ _____.

04

대화를 듣고, 그림에서 대화의 내용과 일치하지 않는 것을 고르시오.

M : Kayla, I heard you _____ _____ ____ _____ _____ last weekend.
W : It was amazing! I've got a picture here. Look!
M : Oh, you're wearing the hat I gave you.
W : Yeah, I really like it.
M : Looks great. This boy playing the guitar next to you must be your brother Kevin.
W : You're right. He played while I sang.
M : Cool. Why did you 🔄 _____ _____ _____ _____?
W : That's for the audience. If they like our performance, they give us some money.
M: Oh, and you ____ ____ _____ _____!
W : I did. I recently bought them.
M : I see. And did you design that poster on the wall?
W : Yeah. My brother and I worked on it together.
M : It sounds like you really had a lot of fun!

05

대화를 듣고, 남자가 할 일로 가장 적절한 것을 고르시오.

W : Honey, are we ready for Jake's birthday party tomorrow?
M : I sent the invitation cards last week. What about other things?
W : I'm not sure. Let's check.
M : We are expecting a lot of guests. How about the dinner menu?
W : I haven't decided yet.
M : We won't have much time to cook, so let's just order pizza.
W : Okay. I'll do it tomorrow. _____ _____ ____ _____?
M : Oh, you mean the smartphone? I forgot to get it!
W : That's alright. Can you 🔄 ____ ___ ____ _____ _____ and buy it now?
M : No problem. I'll do it right away.
W : Good. Then, I'll _____ _____ ____ _____ _____ while you're out.

06

대화를 듣고, 여자가 지불할 금액을 고르시오. [3점]

M : Good morning! How can I help you?

W : Hi. I'm looking for a blanket and some cushions for my sofa.

M : Okay. We've got _____ ____ _____. Would you like to have a look?

W : Yes. How much is this green blanket?

M : That's $40.

W : Oh, I love the color green. Can you also show me some cushions that 🔍 ____ _____ _____ _____ _____?

M : Sure! How about these?

W : They look good. I need _____ ___ _____. How much are they?

M : The cushions are $20 each.

W : Okay. I'll take one green blanket and two cushions. Can I use this coupon?

M : Sure. It will give you 10% off the total.

W : Thanks! Here's my credit card.

07

대화를 듣고, 남자가 록 콘서트에 갈 수 없는 이유를 고르시오.

W : Hello, Justin. What are you doing?

M : Hi, Ellie. I'm doing my project for art class.

W : Can you 🔍 _____ ___ __ _____ _____ with me this Saturday? My sister gave me two tickets!

M : I'd love to! *[Pause]* But I'm afraid I can't.

W : Do you have to work that day?

M : No, I don't work on Saturdays.

W : Then, why not? I thought you really like rock music.

M : Of course I do. But I have to _____ _____ ___ _____ _____ _____ this Saturday.

W : Oh, really? Is your friend going somewhere?

M : He's _____ _____ _____ that day.

W : Okay, no problem. I'm sure I can find someone else to go with me.

08

대화를 듣고, Eco Day에 관해 언급되지 않은 것을 고르시오.

W : Scott, did you see this Eco Day poster?

M : No, not yet. Let me see. *[Pause]* It's an event for _____ ____ _____ while walking around a park.

W : Why don't we do it together? It's next Sunday from 10 a.m. to 5 p.m. M: Sounds good. I've been thinking a lot about the environment lately.

W : Me, too. Also, the event will be held in Eastside Park. You know, we often 🔍 _____ ___ _____ _____.

M : That's great. Oh, look at this. We have to bring our own gloves and small bags for the trash.

W : No problem. __ _____ _____. I can bring some for you as well.

M : Okay, thanks. Do we have to sign up for the event?

W : Yes. The poster says we can do it online.

M : Let's do it right now. I'm looking forward to it.

09

Eastville Dance Contest에 관한 다음 내용을 듣고, 일치하지 않는 것을 고르시오.

M : Hello, Eastville High School students. This is your P.E. teacher, Mr. Wilson. I'm pleased to let you know that we're hosting the first Eastville Dance Contest. Any Eastville students who love dancing can participate in the contest ____ __ _____. All kinds of dance are allowed. If you'd like to participate, please upload your team's dance video to our school website by August 15th. Students can 🔍 _____ _____ _____ _____ _____ from August 16th to 20th. The winning team will receive a trophy as a prize. Don't miss this great opportunity to _____ ____ _____ _____!

10

다음 표를 보면서 대화를 듣고, 두 사람이 구입할 정수기를 고르시오.

M : Honey, we need 🔍 __ _____ _____ for our new house.

W : You're right. Let's order one online.

M : Good idea. *[Clicking Sound]* Look! These are the five bestsellers.

W : I see. What's our budget?

M : Well, I don't want to spend more than 800 dollars.

W : Okay, how about the 🔍 _____ _____ _____?

M : I think the five-liter tank would be perfect for us.

W : I think so, too. And I like the ones with a power-saving mode.

M : Okay, then we can save electricity. Now, there are just two options left.

W : Let's 🔍 _____ ___ _____ _____. The longer, the better.

M : I agree. We should order this model.

11

대화를 듣고, 남자의 마지막 말에 대한 여자의 응답으로 가장 적절한 것을 고르시오.

M : Let's get inside. I'm so excited to see 🔍 _____ _____ _____.

W : Look over there. So many people are already standing in line to buy tickets.

M : Fortunately, I _____ _____ _____ _____.

12

대화를 듣고, 여자의 마지막 말에 대한 남자의 응답으로 가장 적절한 것을 고르시오.

W : Hi, Chris. Did you check your grade for the history test we took last week?

M : Yes. But I think there's ✪ _____ _____ _____ _____ _____.

W : Don't you think _____ _____ ____ _____ Mr. Morgan about it?

13

대화를 듣고, 여자의 마지막 말에 대한 남자의 응답으로 가장 적절한 것을 고르시오. [3점]

M : Mom, did you write this note?

W : What's that?

M : I found this in the book you gave me.

W : Oh, the one I bought for you ✪ ___ _____ _____ _____ last week?

M : Yes. At first I thought __ _____ _ _____, but it wasn't. It's a note with a message!

W : What does it say?

M : It says, "I hope you enjoy this book."

W : How sweet! That really _____ __ _____ to my face.

M : Yeah, mom. I love this message so much.

W : Well, then, why don't we leave a note if we resell this book later?

14

대화를 듣고, 남자의 마지막 말에 대한 여자의 응답으로 가장 적절한 것을 고르시오. [3점]

M : Do you have any plans for this weekend, Sandy?

W : Hey, Evan. I'm planning to go camping with my family.

M : I've never gone before. Do you go camping often?

W : Yes. Two or three times a month at least.

M : That's cool. Why do you like it so much?

W : I like _____ _____ ____ _____ with my family. It makes me feel closer to them.

M : I understand. It's like a family hobby, right?

W : Yes, you're right. Camping helps me ✪ _____ ____ _____ _____, too.

M : Sounds interesting. I'd love to try it.

W : If you go camping with your family, you'll see what I mean.

M : I wish I could, but I ✪ _____ _____ _____ _____ for it.

15

다음 상황 설명을 듣고, Violet이 Peter에게 할 말로 가장 적절한 것을 고르시오.

W : Violet and Peter are classmates. They're doing their ✪ _____ _____ _____ together. On Saturday morning, they meet at the public library. They decide to find the books they need in different sections of the library. Violet finds two useful books and tries to check them out. Unfortunately, she suddenly realizes that she didn't _____ _____ _____ _____. At that moment, Peter walks up to Violet. So, Violet wants to ask Peter to _____ _____ _____ _____ _____ _____ because she knows he has his library card. In this situation, what would Violet most likely say to Peter?

16~17

다음을 듣고, 물음에 답하시오.

M : Hello, everyone. I'm Shawn Collins, a doctor at Collins Sleep Clinic. Sleep is one of ✪ _____ _____ _____ _____ of our daily lives. So today, I'm going to introduce the best foods for helping you sleep better. First, kiwi fruits contain a high level of hormones that help you fall asleep more quickly, sleep longer, and wake up less during the night. Second, milk is ✪ _____ ___ _____ ___ and it calms the mind and nerves. If you drink a cup of milk before you go to bed, it will definitely help you get a good night's sleep. Third, nuts can help to produce the hormone that ✪ _____ _____ _____ _____ _____ and sends signals for the body to sleep at the right time. The last one is honey. Honey helps you sleep well because it reduces the hormone that keeps the brain awake! Now, I'll show you some delicious diet plans using these foods.

▶ 정답 : 해설편 **069**쪽

18

- 001 □ travel agency 여행사
- 002 □ turn A into B A를 B로 바꾸다
- 003 □ reality ⓝ 현실
- 004 □ A as well as B B뿐 아니라 A도
- 005 □ meditation ⓝ 명상
- 006 □ experienced ⓐ 경험 많은, 숙련된
- 007 □ instructor ⓝ 강사
- 008 □ reasonable ⓐ 적당한
- 009 □ unforgettable ⓐ 잊지 못할

19

- 010 □ midnight ⓝ 자정
- 011 □ ring ⓥ 울리다
- 012 □ worried ⓐ 걱정한
- 013 □ decide ⓥ 결심하다, 정하다
- 014 □ ask for help 도움을 요청하다
- 015 □ catch one's attention 관심을 끌다
- 016 □ approach ⓥ 다가가다
- 017 □ suddenly ⓐd 문득, 갑자기
- 018 □ familiar ⓐ 익숙한
- 019 □ disappear ⓥ 사라지다
- 020 □ anxious ⓐ 불안한
- 021 □ delighted ⓐ 기쁜
- 022 □ embarrassed ⓐ 당황한

20

- 023 □ personal life 사생활
- 024 □ sensible ⓐ 분별 있는, 현명한
- 025 □ separate ⓐ 별개의
- 026 □ lead to ~로 이어지다
- 027 □ distraction ⓝ 주의 분산, 정신을 흩뜨리는 것
- 028 □ missing ⓐ 빠진, 실종된
- 029 □ to-do list 할 일 목록
- 030 □ multiple ⓐ 여럿의, 다수의
- 031 □ organize ⓥ 정리하다
- 032 □ task ⓝ 일, 과업
- 033 □ professional ⓐ 직업의, 전문적인
- 034 □ divide ⓥ 나누다, 분배하다
- 035 □ make an informed decision 잘 알고 결정하다

21

- 036 □ react to ~에 반응하다
- 037 □ purchase ⓝ 구매 ⓥ 사다
- 038 □ likelihood ⓝ 가능성, 확률
- 039 □ whether ⓒonj ~인지 아닌지
- 040 □ buyer ⓝ 구매자
- 041 □ return ⓥ 반품하다
- 042 □ encourage ⓥ 격려하다
- 043 □ satisfied ⓐ 만족한
- 044 □ unpaid ⓐ 무급의
- 045 □ ambassador ⓝ (외교 시 나라를 대표하는) 대사, 사절
- 046 □ on the top of ~의 맨 위에
- 047 □ opinion ⓝ 의견, 생각
- 048 □ advertisement ⓝ 광고
- 049 □ be paid to 돈을 받고 ~하다
- 050 □ continually ⓐd 지속적으로
- 051 □ word-of-mouth ⓐ 구전의
- 052 □ for no gain 대가 없이
- 053 □ overseas ⓐd 해외에

22

- 054 □ computerize ⓥ 컴퓨터화하다
- 055 □ repetitive ⓐ 반복되는
- 056 □ drudgery ⓝ 고된 일
- 057 □ pursue ⓥ 추구하다
- 058 □ off-load 짐을 내리다, 떠넘기다
- 059 □ as part of ~의 일환으로
- 060 □ be expected to ~하도록 기대되다
- 061 □ complete ⓥ 완수하다 ⓐ 완전한
- 062 □ reservation ⓝ 예약
- 063 □ grocery store 슈퍼, 식료품 가게
- 064 □ scan ⓥ 스캔하다, 찍다, 훑다

23

- 065 □ possess ⓥ 지니다, 소유하다
- 066 □ a host of 여러, 다수의
- 067 □ socially ⓐd 사회적으로
- 068 □ desirable ⓐ 바람직한
- 069 □ characteristic ⓝ 특성
- 070 □ be free of ~가 없는
- 071 □ general public 일반 대중
- 072 □ intelligent ⓐ 지적인
- 073 □ fair-minded ⓐ 공정한
- 074 □ prejudiced ⓐ 고정 관념이 있는
- 075 □ skilled ⓐ 능숙한
- 076 □ behind the wheel 운전할 때, 핸들을 잡은
- 077 □ automobile ⓝ 자동차
- 078 □ phenomenon ⓝ 현상
- 079 □ reliable ⓐ 믿을 만한
- 080 □ ubiquitous ⓐ 도처에 있는
- 081 □ fictional ⓐ 허구의
- 082 □ good-looking ⓐ 잘생긴
- 083 □ million ⓝ 100만
- 084 □ high school senior 고교 졸업반
- 085 □ in terms of ~의 면에서
- 086 □ get along with ~와 어울리다
- 087 □ self-image 자아상(사람이 자기 자신에 대해 가진 이미지)
- 088 □ superior to ~보다 우월한
- 089 □ social network 사회적 네트워크

24

- 090 □ poverty ⓝ 가난
- 091 □ publish ⓥ 출판하다
- 092 □ socioeconomic ⓐ 사회경제적인
- 093 □ status ⓝ 지위
- 094 □ be associated with ~와 연관되다
- 095 □ distinct ⓐ 특유의, 독특한, 뚜렷한
- 096 □ time pressure 시간 압박
- 097 □ psychologist ⓝ 심리학자
- 098 □ wealthy ⓐ 부유한
- 099 □ industrialize ⓥ 산업화하다
- 100 □ nation ⓝ 나라
- 101 □ pace ⓝ 속도
- 102 □ standard of life 생활 수준
- 103 □ constant ⓐ 지속적인
- 104 □ urgency ⓝ 다급함
- 105 □ prone to ~에 걸리기 쉬운
- 106 □ productivity ⓝ 생산성
- 107 □ in search of ~을 찾아서
- 108 □ escape ⓥ 탈출하다, 빠져나가다
- 109 □ sound ⓐ 건전한

25

- 110 □ share ⓝ 점유율, 몫
- 111 □ region ⓝ 지역
- 112 □ decline ⓥ 감소하다, 줄어들다
- 113 □ percentage point 퍼센트포인트(백분율 간 격차)
- 114 □ more than ~ 이상
- 115 □ gap ⓝ 격차, 차이

26

- 116 □ well educated 교육을 많이 받은
- 117 □ financial ⓐ 재정적인
- 118 □ political ⓐ 정치적인
- 119 □ graduate from ~을 졸업하다
- 120 □ major in ~을 전공하다
- 121 □ handle ⓥ 다루다, 대처하다
- 122 □ earn ⓥ 얻다, 취득하다
- 123 □ doctor's degree 박사 학위
- 124 □ doctoral paper 박사 논문
- 125 □ discrimination ⓝ 차별
- 126 □ mention ⓥ 언급하다
- 127 □ contribution ⓝ 기여, 이바지
- 128 □ analysis ⓝ 분석
- 129 □ award ⓥ 상을 주다, 수여하다

27

- 130 □ drone ⓝ 드론, 무인 항공기
- 131 □ championship ⓝ 선수권
- 132 □ take an opportunity 기회를 잡다
- 133 □ prove ⓥ 증명하다
- 134 □ community center 주민센터
- 135 □ requirement ⓝ 필수 요건
- 136 □ bring ⓥ 가져오다, 지참하다
- 137 □ souvenir ⓝ 기념품

28

- 138 □ one-day class 일일 수업
- 139 □ underwater ⓐ 물속의, 수중의
- 140 □ explorer ⓝ 탐험가
- 141 □ basics ⓝ 기본, 필수적인 것들
- 142 □ private lesson 개인 레슨
- 143 □ equipment ⓝ 장비

29

- 144 □ praise ⓝ 칭찬
- 145 □ available ⓐ 이용할 수 있는
- 146 □ improve ⓥ 개선하다, 향상시키다
- 147 □ self-esteem ⓝ 자존감
- 148 □ preschooler ⓝ 미취학 아동
- 149 □ profound ⓐ 뜻 깊은
- 150 □ cognitive ⓐ 인지적인
- 151 □ sophistication ⓝ 정교화(함)
- 152 □ reason ⓥ 추론하다
- 153 □ analytically ⓐd 분석적으로
- 154 □ reject ⓥ 거부하다
- 155 □ consistently ⓐd 지속적으로
- 156 □ be likely to ~할 가능성이 크다
- 157 □ incorporate A into B A를 B로 통합 시키다
- 158 □ endure ⓥ 지속하다, 참다
- 159 □ problem-solving ⓝ 문제 해결
- 160 □ confidence ⓝ 자신감

30

- 161 □ display ⓥ 보이다, 전시하다
- 162 □ considerable ⓐ 상당한
- 163 □ facility ⓝ 능력, 재능
- 164 □ claim ⓥ 주장
- 165 □ goods ⓝ 상품, 재화
- 166 □ yeast ⓝ (반죽 발효에 쓰는) 효모, 이스트
- 167 □ ingredient ⓝ 재료
- 168 □ century ⓝ 100년, 세기
- 169 □ demand ⓝ 수요 ⓥ 요구하다
- 170 □ hire ⓥ 고용하다
- 171 □ come up with 떠올리다, 고안하다
- 172 □ strategy ⓝ 전략
- 173 □ boost ⓥ 촉진하다, 증진하다
- 174 □ sale ⓝ 매출, 판매
- 175 □ significant ⓐ 상당한, 중요한
- 176 □ shortly thereafter 그 후 얼마 안 되어
- 177 □ transform ⓥ 변모시키다
- 178 □ laxative ⓝ 완하제(배변을 쉽게 하는 약·음식·음료)
- 179 □ reposition ⓥ (제품의) 이미지를 바꾸다

31

- 180 □ perform ⓥ 수행하다
- 181 □ profession ⓝ 직업
- 182 □ instant ⓐ 즉각적인
- 183 □ credibility ⓝ 신뢰
- 184 □ admire ⓥ 존경하다
- 185 □ connected to ~에 연결된
- 186 □ even if 설령 ~일지라도
- 187 □ have nothing to do with ~와 관련이 없다
- 188 □ advice ⓝ 조언
- 189 □ world-famous ⓐ 세계적으로 유명한
- 190 □ make money 돈을 벌다
- 191 □ endorsement ⓝ (유명인의 텔레비전 등에서의 상품) 보증 선전
- 192 □ knowledge ⓝ 지식
- 193 □ endorse ⓥ (유명인이 광고에 나와 특정 상품을) 보증하다, 홍보하다
- 194 □ medalist ⓝ 메달리스트
- 195 □ certain ⓐ 특정한
- 196 □ expertise ⓝ 전문 지식
- 197 □ desire ⓥ 바라다, 열망하다
- 198 □ patience ⓝ 인내심
- 199 □ sacrifice ⓝ 희생
- 200 □ honesty ⓝ 정직

32

- 201 □ think of A as B A를 B로 여기다
- 202 □ look out ~을 내다보다
- 203 □ instead ⓐd 대신에
- 204 □ emerge ⓥ 나타나다, 생겨나다
- 205 □ element ⓝ 요소
- 206 □ merchant ⓝ 상인
- 207 □ operation ⓝ 작동, 작용
- 208 □ spot ⓝ 지점
- 209 □ neighborhood ⓝ 근방, 이웃, 지역
- 210 □ resident ⓝ 주민
- 211 □ scale ⓝ 규모
- 212 □ locally ⓐd 국지적으로
- 213 □ distantly ⓐd 멀리, 원거리로

214 ☐ textile ⓝ 직물
215 ☐ process ⓥ 가공하다, 처리하다
216 ☐ raw ⓐ 원재료의, 날것의
217 ☐ electrochemical ⓐ 전기화학의
218 ☐ sensory organ 감각 기관
219 ☐ transport ⓥ 수송하다, 실어 나르다
220 ☐ undergo ⓥ 거치다, 겪다
221 ☐ transformation ⓝ 변화, 변모
222 ☐ conscious ⓐ 의식적인
223 ☐ in isolation 고립되어
224 ☐ resemble ⓥ ~와 닮다
225 ☐ systematic ⓐ 체계적인

33
226 ☐ body language 신체 언어, 몸짓 언어
227 ☐ affect ⓥ 영향을 미치다
228 ☐ emotional ⓐ 정서적인
229 ☐ echo ⓝ 메아리
230 ☐ accordingly ⓐd 그에 따라
231 ☐ copy ⓥ 복사하다
232 ☐ transmit ⓥ 전달하다
233 ☐ via prep ~을 통해서
234 ☐ strange ⓐ 이상한
235 ☐ theory ⓝ 이론
236 ☐ state ⓥ 진술하다
237 ☐ mood ⓝ 기분, 분위기
238 ☐ lift up ~을 들어올리다
239 ☐ be asked to ~하도록 요청받다
240 ☐ bite down on ~을 깨물다
241 ☐ lengthwise ⓐd 길게
242 ☐ take care (not) to ~(하지 않)도록 주의하다
243 ☐ touch ⓥ 닿다, 만지다
244 ☐ judge ⓥ 판단하다
245 ☐ frown ⓥ 얼굴을 찡그리다
246 ☐ primacy ⓝ 우선함
247 ☐ summarize ⓥ 요약하다
248 ☐ arise from ~에서 생겨나다
249 ☐ hide ⓥ 숨기다

34
250 ☐ investigate ⓥ 조사하다
251 ☐ effectiveness ⓝ 유효성, 효과 있음
252 ☐ tactic ⓝ 전략
253 ☐ persuade ⓥ 설득하다
254 ☐ discount ⓝ 할인
255 ☐ rather than ~ 대신에
256 ☐ condition ⓝ 조건
257 ☐ control ⓝ 통제 집단(실험에서 처치를 가하지 않고 둔 집단)
258 ☐ limit ⓝ 제한 ⓥ 제한하다
259 ☐ volume ⓝ 양
260 ☐ unlimited ⓐ 제한되지 않은, 무제한의
261 ☐ on average 평균적으로
262 ☐ scarcity ⓝ 희소성
263 ☐ genuine ⓐ 진짜의
264 ☐ rely on ~에 의존하다
265 ☐ laboratory ⓝ 실험실
266 ☐ behave ⓥ 행동하다
267 ☐ differently ⓐd 다르게
268 ☐ attractive ⓐ 매력적인
269 ☐ emphasize ⓥ 강조하다

35
270 ☐ potential ⓝ 잠재력
271 ☐ negative ⓐ 부정적인
272 ☐ impact ⓝ 영향, 충격
273 ☐ have access to ~에 접근하다, ~을 이용하다
274 ☐ whenever conj ~할 때마다
275 ☐ stop A from B A가 B하지 못하게 막다
276 ☐ production ⓝ 생산, 제조
277 ☐ cause ⓥ 야기하다
278 ☐ require ⓥ 요구하다
279 ☐ enable ⓥ ~할 수 있게 하다
280 ☐ get A out of B B에게서 A를 얻어내다
281 ☐ factor ⓝ 요인, 요소
282 ☐ time-consuming ⓐ 시간이 많이 걸리는

36
283 ☐ up until ~에 이르기까지
284 ☐ throughout prep ~ 내내
285 ☐ hunt for ~을 사냥하다
286 ☐ livestock ⓝ 가축
287 ☐ carry out 수행하다
288 ☐ religious ⓐ 종교적인
289 ☐ invent ⓥ 발명하다
290 ☐ device ⓝ 장치
291 ☐ measure ⓥ 측정하다
292 ☐ keep track of ~을 추적하다, 기록하다
293 ☐ natural cycle 자연적 주기
294 ☐ sunrise ⓝ 일출, 해돋이
295 ☐ sunset ⓝ 일몰, 해넘이
296 ☐ gradually ⓐd 점차
297 ☐ settlement ⓝ 정착(지)
298 ☐ tell the time 시간을 알다
299 ☐ ever since 그 이후로
300 ☐ timetable ⓝ 시간표
301 ☐ crash into ~에 충돌하다
302 ☐ take off 이륙하다
303 ☐ land ⓥ 착륙하다

37
304 ☐ ratio ⓝ 비율
305 ☐ cost ⓝ 비용
306 ☐ output ⓝ 산출
307 ☐ manufacturing industry 제조업
308 ☐ describe ⓥ 설명하다
309 ☐ efficient ⓐ 효율적인
310 ☐ known as ~라고 알려진
311 ☐ division of labor 분업
312 ☐ specialize in ~에 특화되다
313 ☐ thousands of 수천의
314 ☐ a number of 많은
315 ☐ involve ⓥ 포함하다, 수반하다
316 ☐ straighten ⓥ 곧게 펴다
317 ☐ sharpen ⓥ 뾰족하게 하다
318 ☐ put on 끼우다, 달다, 입다, 착용하다
319 ☐ polish ⓥ 다듬다

38
320 ☐ stare back at ~을 마주 보다
321 ☐ far ⓐd (비교급 앞에서) 훨씬
322 ☐ reflect ⓥ 반사하다
323 ☐ probably ⓐd 아마도

324 ☐ appear ~인 것처럼 보이다
325 ☐ proof ⓝ 증거
326 ☐ clear ⓐ 명확한
327 ☐ snapshot ⓝ 스냅사진, 짧은 묘사
328 ☐ reflection ⓝ (물이나 거울에 비친) 그림자
329 ☐ surprised ⓐ 놀란
330 ☐ interval ⓝ 간격
331 ☐ at first 처음에
332 ☐ peer ⓥ 응시하다
333 ☐ basic ⓐ 기본적인
334 ☐ from moment to moment 시시각각

39
335 ☐ absorb ⓥ (정보를) 받아들이다
336 ☐ possibility ⓝ 가능성
337 ☐ harden ⓥ 굳어지다
338 ☐ belief ⓝ 믿음, 신념
339 ☐ educational ⓐ 교육의
340 ☐ curiosity ⓝ 호기심
341 ☐ decrease ⓥ 감소하다
342 ☐ default setting 기본값
343 ☐ disinterested ⓐ 무관심한
344 ☐ groove ⓝ 고랑
345 ☐ channel ⓝ 경로
346 ☐ development ⓝ 발달
347 ☐ childhood ⓝ 어린 시절
348 ☐ infant ⓝ 유아
349 ☐ neural ⓐ 신경의
350 ☐ mess ⓝ 엉망
351 ☐ perception ⓝ 지각, 인식
352 ☐ consequently ⓐd 그 결과
353 ☐ intensely ⓐd 대단히, 강렬하게
354 ☐ disordered ⓐ 무질서한
355 ☐ pathway ⓝ 경로
356 ☐ automatic ⓐ 자동적인
357 ☐ prune ⓥ 가지치기하다

40
358 ☐ nearly ⓐd 거의
359 ☐ unless conj ~하지 않는 한
360 ☐ spoiled ⓐ 상한
361 ☐ poison mushroom 독버섯
362 ☐ label A as B A를 B라고 분류하다
363 ☐ either A or B A 또는 B
364 ☐ combination ⓝ 조합
365 ☐ add up to 결국 ~이 되다
366 ☐ healthful ⓐ 건강에 좋은
367 ☐ broccoli ⓝ 브로콜리
368 ☐ tofu ⓝ 두부
369 ☐ nutrient-dense ⓐ 영양이 풍부한
370 ☐ supply ⓥ 공급하다
371 ☐ a wide variety of 매우 다양한
372 ☐ nutrient ⓝ 영양분
373 ☐ occasionally ⓐd 가끔
374 ☐ otherwise ⓐd 그렇지 않으면, 다른 경우에는
375 ☐ stay away from ~을 멀리하다
376 ☐ off track 제 길에서 벗어난
377 ☐ load up on ~로 배를 가득 채우다
378 ☐ unlike prep ~와 달리
379 ☐ largely ⓐd 대체로, 주로
380 ☐ composed of ~로 구성된

41~42
381 ☐ hunter-gatherer ⓝ 수렵 채집인
382 ☐ minimal ⓐ 최소한의
383 ☐ structure ⓝ 구조
384 ☐ chief ⓝ 추장, 족장, 우두머리
385 ☐ along with ~와 함께
386 ☐ surplus ⓝ 잉여, 흑자
387 ☐ vital ⓐ 필수적인, 매우 중요한
388 ☐ resource ⓝ 자원
389 ☐ seldom ⓐd ~할 때가 드물다, 좀처럼 ~하지 않다
390 ☐ sufficient ⓐ 충분한
391 ☐ support ⓥ 지원하다, 부양하다
392 ☐ full-time ⓐ 전임의, 정규직의
393 ☐ agriculture ⓝ 농업
394 ☐ reap ⓥ (농작물을) 베어들이다
395 ☐ grain ⓝ 곡물
396 ☐ plant ⓥ (식물을) 심다
397 ☐ community ⓝ 지역 사회
398 ☐ chieftain ⓝ 수령, 두목
399 ☐ practice medicine 의사로 개업하다, 의술을 행하다
400 ☐ priest ⓝ 성직자
401 ☐ warrior ⓝ 전사
402 ☐ security ⓝ 안보
403 ☐ yield ⓝ 수확량
404 ☐ favorable ⓐ 우호적인
405 ☐ basic necessity 기본 필수품
406 ☐ grow in size 규모가 커지다
407 ☐ concentrate ⓥ 집중되다
408 ☐ further ⓐd 더욱
409 ☐ carpenter ⓝ 목수
410 ☐ blacksmith ⓝ 대장장이
411 ☐ sailor ⓝ 선원
412 ☐ bring about ~을 야기하다, 초래하다, 가져오다
413 ☐ quality of life 삶의 질
414 ☐ stability ⓝ 안정성
415 ☐ shadow ⓝ 그림자

43~45
416 ☐ anxious ⓐ 불안한, 걱정하는
417 ☐ bedside ⓝ 침대 옆, 머리맡
418 ☐ lie on ~에 눕다
419 ☐ repeat ⓥ 반복하다
420 ☐ several ⓐ 몇몇의, 여럿의
421 ☐ severe ⓐ 극심한
422 ☐ heart disease 심장병
423 ☐ barely ⓐd 간신히 ~하다, 거의 못 ~하다
424 ☐ uniformed ⓐ 유니폼을 입은
425 ☐ reach out one's hand 손을 뻗다
426 ☐ gentle ⓐ 부드러운, 다정한
427 ☐ tightly ⓐd 꽉
428 ☐ through the night 밤새
429 ☐ dawn ⓝ 새벽
430 ☐ release ⓥ 놓다, 해방시키다
431 ☐ hesitate ⓥ 주저하다
432 ☐ for a while 잠시
433 ☐ take A to B A를 B에게 데려가다
434 ☐ wrap ⓥ 감싸다
435 ☐ take a rest 쉬다
436 ☐ politely ⓐd 정중하게

● 채점 : 맞은 개수 _____ / 80

TEST A-B 각 단어의 뜻을 [A] 영어는 우리말로, [B] 우리말은 영어로 쓰시오.

A	English	Korean
01	meditation	
02	anxious	
03	likelihood	
04	superior to	
05	fictional	
06	status	
07	consistently	
08	ask for help	
09	facility	
10	emerge	
11	peer	
12	surplus	
13	hesitate	
14	endure	
15	region	
16	distinct	
17	phenomenon	
18	desirable	
19	pursue	
20	distraction	

B	Korean	English
01	익숙한	
02	지니다, 소유하다	
03	생산성	
04	경험 많은, 숙련된	
05	무급의	
06	감소하다, 줄어들다	
07	상을 주다, 수여하다	
08	고용하다	
09	진술하다	
10	강조하다	
11	호기심	
12	간신히 ~하다, 거의 ~ 못하다	
13	필수적인, 매우 중요한	
14	안정성	
15	기여	
16	당황한	
17	상당한	
18	~로 구성된	
19	~하지 않는 한	
20	반사하다	

▶ A-D 정답 : 해설편 069쪽

TEST C-D 각 단어의 뜻을 골라 기호를 쓰시오.

C	English		Korean
01	instructor	( )	ⓐ 관심을 끌다
02	word-of-mouth	( )	ⓑ 분별 있는, 현명한
03	drudgery	( )	ⓒ 잘 알고 결정하다
04	prejudiced	( )	ⓓ 직업
05	industrialize	( )	ⓔ 거치다, 겪다
06	financial	( )	ⓕ 초래하다, 야기하다
07	strategy	( )	ⓖ (정보를) 받아들이다
08	profession	( )	ⓗ 강사
09	undergo	( )	ⓘ 얼굴을 찡그리다
10	frown	( )	ⓙ 무질서한
11	have access to	( )	ⓚ 전략
12	bring about	( )	ⓛ 극심한
13	severe	( )	ⓜ 미취학 아동
14	preschooler	( )	ⓝ 재정적인
15	catch one's attention	( )	ⓞ 구전의
16	sensible	( )	ⓟ ~에 접근하다, ~을 이용하다
17	make an informed decision	( )	ⓠ 산업화하다
18	absorb	( )	ⓡ 상한
19	spoiled	( )	ⓢ 고정 관념이 있는
20	disordered	( )	ⓣ 고된 일

D	Korean		English
01	기쁜	( )	ⓐ prone to
02	많은	( )	ⓑ analysis
03	자동차	( )	ⓒ self-esteem
04	기념품	( )	ⓓ ingredient
05	뜻깊은	( )	ⓔ livestock
06	비율	( )	ⓕ automobile
07	~에 걸리기 쉬운	( )	ⓖ delighted
08	분석	( )	ⓗ sophistication
09	인지적인	( )	ⓘ sacrifice
10	요약하다	( )	ⓙ genuine
11	차별	( )	ⓚ ratio
12	자존감	( )	ⓛ neural
13	재료	( )	ⓜ summarize
14	변모시키다	( )	ⓝ carry out
15	희생	( )	ⓞ transform
16	진짜의	( )	ⓟ cognitive
17	가축	( )	ⓠ profound
18	신경의	( )	ⓡ souvenir
19	수행하다	( )	ⓢ discrimination
20	정교화	( )	ⓣ a host of

2022학년도 6월 고1 전국연합학력평가 문제지   1

제 3 교시

영어 영역

06회

● 문항수 45개 | 배점 100점 | 제한 시간 70분

● 점수 표시가 없는 문항은 모두 2점

06회

1번부터 17번까지는 듣고 답하는 문제입니다. 1번부터 15번까지는 한 번만 들려주고, 16번부터 17번까지는 두 번 들려줍니다. 방송을 잘 듣고 답을 하시기 바랍니다.

1. 다음을 듣고, 남자가 하는 말의 목적으로 가장 적절한 것을 고르시오.
   ① 사생활 보호의 중요성을 강조하려고
   ② 건물 벽 페인트 작업을 공지하려고
   ③ 회사 근무시간 변경을 안내하려고
   ④ 새로운 직원 채용을 공고하려고
   ⑤ 친환경 제품 출시를 홍보하려고

2. 대화를 듣고, 여자의 의견으로 가장 적절한 것을 고르시오.
   ① 운전자는 제한 속도를 지켜야 한다.
   ② 교통경찰을 더 많이 배치해야 한다.
   ③ 보행자의 부주의가 교통사고를 유발한다.
   ④ 교통사고를 목격하면 즉시 신고해야 한다.
   ⑤ 대중교통을 이용하면 이동시간을 줄일 수 있다.

3. 대화를 듣고, 두 사람의 관계를 가장 잘 나타낸 것을 고르시오.
   ① 작가 – 출판사 직원   ② 관람객 – 박물관 해설사
   ③ 손님 – 주방장   ④ 탑승객 – 항공 승무원
   ⑤ 학생 – 사서

4. 대화를 듣고, 그림에서 대화의 내용과 일치하지 않는 것을 고르시오

5. 대화를 듣고, 남자가 할 일로 가장 적절한 것을 고르시오.
   ① 보고서 제출하기   ② 티켓 예매하기
   ③ 자전거 수리하기   ④ 축구 연습하기
   ⑤ 팝콘 구입하기

6. 대화를 듣고, 여자가 지불할 금액을 고르시오. [3점]
   ① $40   ② $60   ③ $80   ④ $100   ⑤ $120

7. 대화를 듣고, 남자가 음식 부스에 갈 수 없는 이유로 가장 적절한 것을 고르시오.
   ① 밴드 오디션 연습을 해야 해서
   ② 보드게임 부스를 설치해야 해서
   ③ 영어 프로젝트를 끝내야 해서
   ④ 샌드위치를 준비해야 해서
   ⑤ 친구를 만나러 가야 해서

8. 대화를 듣고, Spanish culture class에 관해 언급되지 않은 것을 고르시오.
   ① 강사   ② 활동 종류   ③ 수업 요일
   ④ 준비물   ⑤ 수강료

9. Summer Flea Market에 관한 다음 내용을 듣고, 일치하지 않는 것을 고르시오. [3점]
   ① 일주일 동안 진행된다.
   ② 학교 주차장에서 열린다.
   ③ 장난감, 양초와 같은 물품을 살 수 있다.
   ④ 상태가 좋은 중고 물품을 판매할 수 있다.
   ⑤ 첫날 방문하면 할인 쿠폰을 선물로 받는다.

10. 다음 표를 보면서 대화를 듣고, 여자가 구입할 운동화를 고르시오.

Sneakers

	Model	Price	Style	Waterproof	Color
①	A	$50	casual	×	black
②	B	$60	active	×	white
③	C	$65	casual	○	black
④	D	$70	casual	○	white
⑤	E	$85	active	○	white

11. 대화를 듣고, 여자의 마지막 말에 대한 남자의 응답으로 가장 적절한 것을 고르시오.
   ① All children's books are 20% off.
   ② It takes time to write a good article.
   ③ I like to read action adventure books.
   ④ There are too many advertisements on TV.
   ⑤ The store has been closed since last month.

12. 대화를 듣고, 남자의 마지막 말에 대한 여자의 응답으로 가장 적절한 것을 고르시오.
   ① You're welcome. I'm happy to help you.
   ② That's not true. I made it with your help.
   ③ Okay. Good food always makes me feel better.
   ④ Really? You should definitely visit the theater later.
   ⑤ Never mind. You'll do better on the next presentation.

13. 대화를 듣고, 여자의 마지막 말에 대한 남자의 응답으로 가장 적절한 것을 고르시오.

Man: _____

① I'm excited to buy a new guitar.
② Summer vacation starts on Friday.
③ You can find it on the school website.
④ Let's go to the school festival together.
⑤ You can get some rest during the vacation.

14. 대화를 듣고, 남자의 마지막 말에 대한 여자의 응답으로 가장 적절한 것을 고르시오.

Woman: _____

① I agree. There are many benefits of exercising at the gym.
② You're right. Not all exercise is helpful for your brain.
③ Don't worry. It's not too difficult for me to exercise.
④ That sounds great. Can I join the course, too?
⑤ That's too bad. I hope you get well soon.

15. 다음 상황 설명을 듣고, Ted가 Monica에게 할 말로 가장 적절한 것을 고르시오. [3점]

Ted: _____

① Can I draw your club members on the poster?
② Are you interested in joining my drawing club?
③ Could you tell me how to vote in the election?
④ Can you help me make posters for the election?
⑤ Would you run in the next school president election?

[16~17] 다음을 듣고, 물음에 답하시오.

16. 여자가 하는 말의 주제로 가장 적절한 것은?

① downsides of fatty food
② healthy foods for breakfast
③ ways to avoid eating snacks
④ easy foods to cook in 5 minutes
⑤ the importance of a balanced diet

17. 언급된 음식이 <u>아닌</u> 것은?

① eggs   ② cheese   ③ potatoes
④ yogurt   ⑤ berries

이제 듣기 문제가 끝났습니다. 18번부터는 문제지의 지시에 따라 답을 하시기 바랍니다.

18. 다음 글의 목적으로 가장 적절한 것은?

Dear Boat Tour Manager,

On March 15, my family was on one of your Glass Bottom Boat Tours. When we returned to our hotel, I discovered that I left behind my cell phone case. The case must have fallen off my lap and onto the floor when I took it off my phone to clean it. I would like to ask you to check if it is on your boat. Its color is black and it has my name on the inside. If you find the case, I would appreciate it if you would let me know.

Sincerely,
Sam Roberts

① 제품의 고장 원인을 문의하려고
② 분실물 발견 시 연락을 부탁하려고
③ 시설물의 철저한 관리를 당부하려고
④ 여행자 보험 가입 절차를 확인하려고
⑤ 분실물 센터 확장의 필요성을 건의하려고

19. 다음 글에 드러난 Matthew의 심경 변화로 가장 적절한 것은?

One Saturday morning, Matthew's mother told Matthew that she was going to take him to the park. A big smile came across his face. As he loved to play outside, he ate his breakfast and got dressed quickly so they could go. When they got to the park, Matthew ran all the way over to the swing set. That was his favorite thing to do at the park. But the swings were all being used. His mother explained that he could use the slide until a swing became available, but it was broken. Suddenly, his mother got a phone call and she told Matthew they had to leave. His heart sank.

① embarrassed → indifferent   ② excited → disappointed
③ cheerful   → ashamed   ④ nervous → touched
⑤ scared   → relaxed

20. 다음 글에서 필자가 주장하는 바로 가장 적절한 것은?

Meetings encourage creative thinking and can give you ideas that you may never have thought of on your own. However, on average, meeting participants consider about one third of meeting time to be unproductive. But you can make your meetings more productive and more useful by preparing well in advance. You should create a list of items to be discussed and share your list with other participants before a meeting. It allows them to know what to expect in your meeting and prepare to participate.

① 회의 결과는 빠짐없이 작성해서 공개해야 한다.
② 중요한 정보는 공식 회의를 통해 전달해야 한다.
③ 생산성 향상을 위해 정기적인 평가회가 필요하다.
④ 모든 참석자의 동의를 받아서 회의를 열어야 한다.
⑤ 회의에서 다룰 사항은 미리 작성해서 공유해야 한다.

21. 밑줄 친 put the glass down이 다음 글에서 의미하는 바로 가장 적절한 것은? [3점]

A psychology professor raised a glass of water while teaching stress management principles to her students, and asked them, "How heavy is this glass of water I'm holding?" Students shouted out various answers. The professor replied, "The absolute weight of this glass doesn't matter. It depends on how long I hold it. If I hold it for a minute, it's quite light. But, if I hold it for a day straight, it will cause severe pain in my arm, forcing me to drop the glass to the floor. In each case, the weight of the glass is the same, but the longer I hold it, the heavier it feels to me." As the class nodded their heads in agreement, she continued, "Your stresses in life are like this glass of water. If you still feel the weight of yesterday's stress, it's a strong sign that it's time to put the glass down."

① pour more water into the glass
② set a plan not to make mistakes
③ let go of the stress in your mind
④ think about the cause of your stress
⑤ learn to accept the opinions of others

22. 다음 글의 요지로 가장 적절한 것은?

Your emotions deserve attention and give you important pieces of information. However, they can also sometimes be an unreliable, inaccurate source of information. You may feel a certain way, but that does not mean those feelings are reflections of the truth. You may feel sad and conclude that your friend is angry with you when her behavior simply reflects that she's having a bad day. You may feel depressed and decide that you did poorly in an interview when you did just fine. Your feelings can mislead you into thinking things that are not supported by facts.

① 자신의 감정으로 인해 상황을 오해할 수 있다.
② 자신의 생각을 타인에게 강요해서는 안 된다.
③ 인간관계가 우리의 감정에 영향을 미친다.
④ 타인의 감정에 공감하는 자세가 필요하다.
⑤ 공동체를 위한 선택에는 보상이 따른다.

23. 다음 글의 주제로 가장 적절한 것은?

Every day, children explore and construct relationships among objects. Frequently, these relationships focus on how much or how many of something exists. Thus, children count — "One cookie, two shoes, three candles on the birthday cake, four children in the sandbox." Children compare — "Which has more? Which has fewer? Will there be enough?" Children calculate — "How many will fit? Now, I have five. I need one more." In all of these instances, children are developing a notion of quantity. Children reveal and investigate mathematical concepts through their own activities or experiences, such as figuring out how many crackers to take at snack time or sorting shells into piles.

① difficulties of children in learning how to count
② how children build mathematical understanding
③ why fingers are used in counting objects
④ importance of early childhood education
⑤ advantages of singing number songs

24. 다음 글의 제목으로 가장 적절한 것은?

Only a generation or two ago, mentioning the word *algorithms* would have drawn a blank from most people. Today, algorithms appear in every part of civilization. They are connected to everyday life. They're not just in your cell phone or your laptop but in your car, your house, your appliances, and your toys. Your bank is a huge web of algorithms, with humans turning the switches here and there. Algorithms schedule flights and then fly the airplanes. Algorithms run factories, trade goods, and keep records. If every algorithm suddenly stopped working, it would be the end of the world as we know it.

① We Live in an Age of Algorithms
② Mysteries of Ancient Civilizations
③ Dangers of Online Banking Algorithms
④ How Algorithms Decrease Human Creativity
⑤ Transportation: A Driving Force of Industry

25. 다음 도표의 내용과 일치하지 <u>않는</u> 것은?

Percent of U.S. Households with Pets

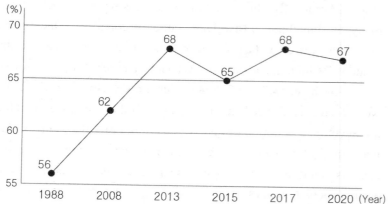

The graph above shows the percent of households with pets in the United States (U.S.) from 1988 to 2020. ① In 1988, more than half of U.S. households owned pets, and more than 6 out of 10 U.S. households owned pets from 2008 to 2020. ② In the period between 1988 and 2008, pet ownership increased among U.S. households by 6 percentage points. ③ From 2008 to 2013, pet ownership rose an additional 6 percentage points. ④ The percent of U.S. households with pets in 2013 was the same as that in 2017, which was 68 percent. ⑤ In 2015, the rate of U.S. households with pets was 3 percentage points lower than in 2020.

26. Claude Bolling에 관한 다음 글의 내용과 일치하지 <u>않는</u> 것은?

Pianist, composer, and big band leader, Claude Bolling, was born on April 10, 1930, in Cannes, France, but spent most of his life in Paris. He began studying classical music as a youth. He was introduced to the world of jazz by a schoolmate. Later, Bolling became interested in the music of Fats Waller, one of the most excellent jazz musicians. Bolling became famous as a teenager by winning the Best Piano Player prize at an amateur contest in France. He was also a successful film music composer, writing the music for more than one hundred films. In 1975, he collaborated with flutist Rampal and published *Suite for Flute and Jazz Piano Trio*, which he became most well-known for. He died in 2020, leaving two sons, David and Alexandre.

① 1930년에 프랑스에서 태어났다.
② 학교 친구를 통해 재즈를 소개받았다.
③ 20대에 Best Piano Player 상을 받았다.
④ 성공적인 영화 음악 작곡가였다.
⑤ 1975년에 플루트 연주자와 협업했다.

27. Kids Taekwondo Program에 관한 다음 안내문의 내용과 일치하지 <u>않는</u> 것은?

Kids Taekwondo Program
Enjoy our taekwondo program this summer vacation.

☐ **Schedule**
- Dates: August 8th − August 10th
- Time: 9:00 a.m. − 11:00 a.m.

☐ **Participants**
- Any child aged 5 and up

☐ **Activities**
- Self-defense training
- Team building games to develop social skills

☐ **Participation Fee**
- $50 per child (includes snacks)

☐ **Notice**
- What to bring: water bottle, towel
- What not to bring: chewing gum, expensive items

① 8월 8일부터 3일간 운영한다.
② 5세 이상의 어린이가 참가할 수 있다.
③ 자기 방어 훈련 활동을 한다.
④ 참가비에 간식비는 포함되지 않는다.
⑤ 물병과 수건을 가져와야 한다.

28. Moonlight Chocolate Factory Tour에 관한 다음 안내문의 내용과 일치하는 것은?

Moonlight Chocolate Factory Tour
Take this special tour and have a chance to enjoy our most popular chocolate bars.

☐ **Operating Hours**
- Monday − Friday, 2:00p.m. − 5:00 p.m.

☐ **Activities**
- Watching our chocolate-making process
- Tasting 3 types of chocolate (dark, milk, and mint chocolate)

☐ **Notice**
- Ticket price: $30
- Wearing a face mask is required.
- Taking pictures is not allowed inside the factory.

① 주말 오후 시간에 운영한다.
② 초콜릿 제조 과정을 볼 수 있다.
③ 네 가지 종류의 초콜릿을 시식한다.
④ 마스크 착용은 참여자의 선택 사항이다.
⑤ 공장 내부에서 사진 촬영이 가능하다.

29. 다음 글의 밑줄 친 부분 중, 어법상 틀린 것은?

Despite all the high-tech devices that seem to deny the need for paper, paper use in the United States ① has nearly doubled recently. We now consume more paper than ever: 400 million tons globally and growing. Paper is not the only resource ② that we are using more of. Technological advances often come with the promise of ③ using fewer materials. However, the reality is that they have historically caused more materials use, making us ④ dependently on more natural resources. The world now consumes far more "stuff" than it ever has. We use twenty-seven times more industrial minerals, such as gold, copper, and rare metals, than we ⑤ did just over a century ago. We also each individually use more resources. Much of that is due to our high-tech lifestyle.

* copper: 구리

30. 다음 글의 밑줄 친 부분 중, 문맥상 낱말의 쓰임이 적절하지 않은 것은? [3점]

Do you sometimes feel like you don't love your life? Like, deep inside, something is missing? That's because we are living someone else's life. We allow other people to ① influence our choices. We are trying to meet their expectations. Social pressure is deceiving — we are all impacted without noticing it. Before we realize we are losing ownership of our lives, we end up ② ignoring how other people live. Then, we can only see the greener grass — ours is never good enough. To regain that passion for the life you want, you must ③ recover control of your choices. No one but yourself can choose how you live. But, how? The first step to getting rid of expectations is to treat yourself ④ kindly. You can't truly love other people if you don't love yourself first. When we accept who we are, there's no room for other's ⑤ expectations.

[31~34] 다음 빈칸에 들어갈 말로 가장 적절한 것을 고르시오.

31. One of the big questions faced this past year was how to keep innovation rolling when people were working entirely virtually. But experts say that digital work didn't have a negative effect on innovation and creativity. Working within limits pushes us to solve problems. Overall, virtual meeting platforms put more constraints on communication and collaboration than face-to-face settings. For instance, with the press of a button, virtual meeting hosts can control the size of breakout groups and enforce time constraints; only one person can speak at a time; nonverbal signals, particularly those below the shoulders, are diminished; "seating arrangements" are assigned by the platform, not by individuals; and visual access to others may be limited by the size of each participant's screen. Such _____ are likely to stretch participants beyond their usual ways of thinking, boosting creativity.

① restrictions
② responsibilities
③ memories
④ coincidences
⑤ traditions

32. The law of demand is that the demand for goods and services increases as prices fall, and the demand falls as prices increase. *Giffen goods* are special types of products for which the traditional law of demand does not apply. Instead of switching to cheaper replacements, consumers demand more of giffen goods when the price increases and less of them when the price decreases. Taking an example, rice in China is a giffen good because people tend to purchase less of it when the price falls. The reason for this is, when the price of rice falls, people have more money to spend on other types of products such as meat and dairy and, therefore, change their spending pattern. On the other hand, as rice prices increase, people _____. [3점]

① order more meat
② consume more rice
③ try to get new jobs
④ increase their savings
⑤ start to invest overseas

33. In a study at Princeton University in 1992, research scientists looked at two different groups of mice. One group was made intellectually superior by modifying the gene for the glutamate receptor. Glutamate is a brain chemical that is necessary in learning. The other group was genetically manipulated to be intellectually inferior, also done by modifying the gene for the glutamate receptor. The smart mice were then raised in standard cages, while the inferior mice were raised in large cages with toys and exercise wheels and with lots of social interaction. At the end of the study, although the intellectually inferior mice were genetically handicapped, they were able to perform just as well as their genetic superiors. This was a real triumph for nurture over nature. Genes are turned on or off _____. [3점]

* glutamate: 글루타민산염   ** manipulate: 조작하다

① by themselves for survival
② free from social interaction
③ based on what is around you
④ depending on genetic superiority
⑤ so as to keep ourselves entertained

34. Researchers are working on a project that asks coastal towns how they are preparing for rising sea levels. Some towns have risk assessments; some towns even have a plan. But it's a rare town that is actually carrying out a plan. One reason we've failed to act on climate change is the common belief that _____. For decades, climate change was a prediction about the future, so scientists talked about it in the future tense. This became a habit — so that even today many scientists still use the future tense, even though we know that a climate crisis is ongoing. Scientists also often focus on regions most affected by the crisis, such as Bangladesh or the West Antarctic Ice Sheet, which for most Americans are physically remote. [3점]

① it is not related to science
② it is far away in time and space
③ energy efficiency matters the most
④ careful planning can fix the problem
⑤ it is too late to prevent it from happening

35. 다음 글에서 전체 흐름과 관계 <u>없는</u> 문장은?

According to Marguerite La Caze, fashion contributes to our lives and provides a medium for us to develop and exhibit important social virtues. ① Fashion may be beautiful, innovative, and useful; we can display creativity and good taste in our fashion choices. ② And in dressing with taste and care, we represent both self-respect and a concern for the pleasure of others. ③ There is no doubt that fashion can be a source of interest and pleasure which links us to each other. ④ Although the fashion industry developed first in Europe and America, today it is an international and highly globalized industry. ⑤ That is, fashion provides a sociable aspect along with opportunities to imagine oneself differently — to try on different identities.

* virtue: 가치

[36~37] 주어진 글 다음에 이어질 글의 순서로 가장 적절한 것을 고르시오.

36.

Mrs. Klein told her first graders to draw a picture of something to be thankful for. She thought that most of the class would draw turkeys or Thanksgiving tables. But Douglas drew something different.

(A) The class was so responsive that Mrs. Klein had almost forgotten about Douglas. After she had the others at work on another project, she asked Douglas whose hand it was. He answered softly, "It's yours. Thank you, Mrs. Klein."

(B) Douglas was a boy who usually spent time alone and stayed around her while his classmates went outside together during break time. What the boy drew was a hand. But whose hand? His image immediately attracted the other students' interest.

(C) So, everyone rushed to talk about whose hand it was. "It must be the hand of God that brings us food," said one student. "A farmer's," said a second student, "because they raise the turkeys." "It looks more like a police officer's," added another, "they protect us."

① (A) − (C) − (B)   ② (B) − (A) − (C)
③ (B) − (C) − (A)   ④ (C) − (A) − (B)
⑤ (C) − (B) − (A)

37.

> According to legend, once a vampire bites a person, that person turns into a vampire who seeks the blood of others. A researcher came up with some simple math, which proves that these highly popular creatures can't exist.

(A) In just two-and-a-half years, the original human population would all have become vampires with no humans left. But look around you. Have vampires taken over the world? No, because there's no such thing.

(B) If the first vampire came into existence that day and bit one person a month, there would have been two vampires by February 1st, 1600. A month later there would have been four, the next month eight, then sixteen, and so on.

(C) University of Central Florida physics professor Costas Efthimiou's work breaks down the myth. Suppose that on January 1st, 1600, the human population was just over five hundred million. [3점]

① (A) − (C) − (B) 　　② (B) − (A) − (C)
③ (B) − (C) − (A) 　　④ (C) − (A) − (B)
⑤ (C) − (B) − (A)

[38~39] 글의 흐름으로 보아, 주어진 문장이 들어가기에 가장 적절한 곳을 고르시오.

38.

> For example, if you rub your hands together quickly, they will get warmer.

Friction is a force between two surfaces that are sliding, or trying to slide, across each other. For example, when you try to push a book along the floor, friction makes this difficult. Friction always works in the direction opposite to the direction in which the object is moving, or trying to move. So, friction always slows a moving object down. (①) The amount of friction depends on the surface materials. (②) The rougher the surface is, the more friction is produced. (③) Friction also produces heat. (④) Friction can be a useful force because it prevents our shoes slipping on the floor when we walk and stops car tires skidding on the road. (⑤) When you walk, friction is caused between the tread on your shoes and the ground, acting to grip the ground and prevent sliding.

* skid: 미끄러지다 ** tread: 접지면, 바닥

39.

> But, a blind person will associate the same friend with a unique combination of experiences from their non-visual senses that act to represent that friend.

Humans born without sight are not able to collect visual experiences, so they understand the world entirely through their other senses. (①) As a result, people with blindness at birth develop an amazing ability to understand the world through the collection of experiences and memories that come from these non-visual senses. (②) The dreams of a person who has been without sight since birth can be just as vivid and imaginative as those of someone with normal vision. (③) They are unique, however, because their dreams are constructed from the non-visual experiences and memories they have collected. (④) A person with normal vision will dream about a familiar friend using visual memories of shape, lighting, and colour. (⑤) In other words, people blind at birth have similar overall dreaming experiences even though they do not dream in pictures.

40. 다음 글의 내용을 한 문장으로 요약하고자 한다. 빈칸 (A), (B)에 들어갈 말로 가장 적절한 것은? [3점]

> According to a study of Swedish adolescents, an important factor of adolescents' academic success is how they respond to challenges. The study reports that when facing difficulties, adolescents exposed to an authoritative parenting style are less likely to be passive, helpless, and afraid to fail. Another study of nine high schools in Wisconsin and northern California indicates that children of authoritative parents do well in school, because these parents put a lot of effort into getting involved in their children's school activities. That is, authoritative parents are significantly more likely to help their children with homework, to attend school programs, to watch their children in sports, and to help students select courses. Moreover, these parents are more aware of what their children do and how they perform in school. Finally, authoritative parents praise academic excellence and the importance of working hard more than other parents do.

⬇

> The studies above show that the children of authoritative parents often succeed academically, since they are more ___(A)___ to deal with their difficulties and are affected by their parents' ___(B)___ involvement.

	(A)		(B)
①	likely	……	random
②	willing	……	minimal
③	willing	……	active
④	hesitant	……	unwanted
⑤	hesitant	……	constant

[41~42] 다음 글을 읽고, 물음에 답하시오.

U.K. researchers say a bedtime of between 10 p.m. and 11 p.m. is best. They say people who go to sleep between these times have a (a) lower risk of heart disease. Six years ago, the researchers collected data on the sleep patterns of 80,000 volunteers. The volunteers had to wear a special watch for seven days so the researchers could collect data on their sleeping and waking times. The scientists then monitored the health of the volunteers. Around 3,000 volunteers later showed heart problems. They went to bed earlier or later than the (b) ideal 10 p.m. to 11 p.m. timeframe.

One of the authors of the study, Dr. David Plans, commented on his research and the (c) effects of bedtimes on the health of our heart. He said the study could not give a certain cause for their results, but it suggests that early or late bedtimes may be more likely to disrupt the body clock, with (d) positive consequences for cardiovascular health. He said that it was important for our body to wake up to the morning light, and that the worst time to go to bed was after midnight because it may (e) reduce the likelihood of seeing morning light which resets the body clock. He added that we risk cardiovascular disease if our body clock is not reset properly.

*disrupt: 혼란케 하다 **cardiovascular: 심장 혈관의

41. 윗글의 제목으로 가장 적절한 것은?

① The Best Bedtime for Your Heart
② Late Bedtimes Are a Matter of Age
③ For Sound Sleep: Turn Off the Light
④ Sleeping Patterns Reflect Personalities
⑤ Regular Exercise: A Miracle for Good Sleep

42. 밑줄 친 (a)~(e) 중에서 문맥상 낱말의 쓰임이 적절하지 않은 것은?

① (a) ② (b) ③ (c) ④ (d) ⑤ (e)

[43~45] 다음 글을 읽고, 물음에 답하시오.

(A)

Once, a farmer lost his precious watch while working in his barn. It may have appeared to be an ordinary watch to others, but it brought a lot of happy childhood memories to him. It was one of the most important things to (a) him. After searching for it for a long time, the old farmer became exhausted.

*barn: 헛간(곡물·건초 따위를 두는 곳)

(B)

The number of children looking for the watch slowly decreased and only a few tired children were left. The farmer gave up all hope of finding it and called off the search. Just when the farmer was closing the barn door, a little boy came up to him and asked the farmer to give him another chance. The farmer did not want to lose out on any chance of finding the watch so let (b) him in the barn.

(C)

After a little while the boy came out with the farmer's watch in his hand. (c) He was happily surprised and asked how he had succeeded to find the watch while everyone else had failed. He replied "I just sat there and tried listening for the sound of the watch. In silence, it was much easier to hear it and follow the direction of the sound." (d) He was delighted to get his watch back and rewarded the little boy as promised.

(D)

However, the tired farmer did not want to give up on the search for his watch and asked a group of children playing outside to help him. (e) He promised an attractive reward for the person who could find it. After hearing about the reward, the children hurried inside the barn and went through and round the entire pile of hay looking for the watch. After a long time searching for it, some of the children got tired and gave up.

43. 주어진 글 (A)에 이어질 내용을 순서에 맞게 배열한 것으로 가장 적절한 것은?

① (B) − (D) − (C)   ② (C) − (B) − (D)
③ (C) − (D) − (B)   ④ (D) − (B) − (C)
⑤ (D) − (C) − (B)

44. 밑줄 친 (a) ~ (e) 중에서 가리키는 대상이 나머지 넷과 다른 것은?

① (a) ② (b) ③ (c) ④ (d) ⑤ (e)

45. 윗글에 관한 내용으로 적절하지 않은 것은?

① 농부의 시계는 어린 시절의 행복한 기억을 불러일으켰다.
② 한 어린 소년이 농부에게 또 한 번의 기회를 달라고 요청했다.
③ 소년이 한 손에 농부의 시계를 들고 나왔다.
④ 아이들은 시계를 찾기 위해 헛간을 뛰쳐나왔다.
⑤ 아이들 중 일부는 지쳐서 시계 찾기를 포기했다.

* 확인 사항
◦ 답안지의 해당란에 필요한 내용을 정확히 기입(표기)했는지 확인하시오.

※ QR 코드를 스캔하시면 듣기 방송이 나옵니다. 듣기 방송을 들으며 다음 빈칸을 채우시오. ● 제한 시간 : 25분

01

다음을 듣고, 남자가 하는 말의 목적으로 가장 적절한 것을 고르시오.

M : Good afternoon, this is the building manager, Richard Carson. We are planning to _____ _____ _____ _____ on our building next week. The working hours will be from 9 a.m. to 6 p.m. Don't be ✿ _____ _____ _____ _____ outside your windows. Please keep your windows closed while they are painting. There might be some smell from the paint. But don't worry. It is totally _____ _____ _____. Sorry for any inconvenience and thank you for your cooperation.

02

대화를 듣고, 여자의 의견으로 가장 적절한 것을 고르시오.

M : Hello, Veronica.

W : Hi, Jason. I heard that you are trying to _____ _____ _____ _____ these days. How is it going?

M : You know what? I already got it. Look!

W : Oh, good for you! How was the driving test?

M : Well, while taking the driving test, I was very nervous because some people were driving so fast.

W : But there are speed limit signs everywhere.

M : Right, there are. But so ✿ _____ _____ _____ _____ _____ these days.

W : That's terrible. Those drivers could cause serious car accidents.

M : That's true. Driving too fast can be dangerous for everybody.

W : Exactly. In my opinion, all drivers should _____ _____ _____ _____.

M : I totally agree with you.

03

대화를 듣고, 두 사람의 관계를 가장 잘 나타낸 것을 고르시오.

W : Excuse me. Can you help me find some books for my homework?

M : Sure. What is your homework about?

W : It's for my history class. The topic is ✿ _____ _____ _____ _____ _____ _____.

M : What about this world history book?

W : It looks good. Do you have any other books?

M : I can also recommend this European history book.

W : Great. How many books can I borrow at a time?

M : You can _____ _____ _____ _____ for three weeks each.

W : Okay. I'll take these two books, then.

M : All right. *[Beep sound]* Don't forget to _____ _____ _____ _____.

04

대화를 듣고, 그림에서 대화의 내용과 일치하지 않는 것을 고르시오.

M : Honey, come to Lucy's room. Look at what I did for her.

W : It looks great. Is that _____ _____ _____?

M : Yes. That's right. She can sleep with the toy bear.

W : It's cute. Oh, and I like _____ _____ _____ on the wall.

M : The round clock goes well with the room, doesn't it? _____ _____ _____ the family picture next to the window?

W : That's so sweet. I also love the striped curtains on the window.

M : I'm happy you like them. What do you think of ✿ _____ _____ _____ _____ _____?

W : It is lovely. Lucy will feel safe and warm on the rug.

M : Looks like everything's prepared.

W : Thanks, honey. You've done a great job.

05

대화를 듣고, 남자가 할 일로 가장 적절한 것을 고르시오.

W : David, did you fix your bicycle yesterday?

M : Yes. Luckily, I was able to fix it by myself. How was your soccer practice, Christine?

W : A new coach came to our soccer club and we practiced very hard.

M : You must be so tired. Do you still want to see a movie this afternoon?

W : Of course, I booked the tickets two weeks ago.

M : All right. Let's get going.

W : Wait, did you _____ _____ _____ _____ to Mr. Smith? It's due today.

M : *[Pause]* Oh, no! I finished it but forgot to send it. What should I do?

W : Why don't you ✿ _____ _____ _____ _____ at the movie theater?

M : Good idea. I'll go home quickly and send the report, but can you _____ _____ _____ for me before I get there?

W : No problem. See you there.

06
대화를 듣고, 여자가 지불할 금액을 고르시오. [3점]

M : Good morning. Welcome to Happy Land.
W : Hello. I'd like to buy some tickets. How much are they?
M : $20 for the amusement park and $10 for the water park. How many tickets do you need?
W : We're five people in total, and we only _____ _____ _____ _____ _____ _____ _____.
M : Okay. Do you have any discount coupons?
W : I ✪ _____ _____ _____ _____ _____ from your website. It's my birthday today.
M : It's your birthday? Just let me check your ID, please.
W : Here you are.
M : Oh, happy birthday! With your birthday coupon, _____ _____ _____ _____.
W : That's great. Please give me five tickets including my ticket.
M : Let me see. That'll be four people at the original price, and one person with a birthday coupon.
W : Right. Here is my credit card.

07
대화를 듣고, 남자가 음식 부스에 갈 수 없는 이유로 가장 적절한 것을 고르시오.

W : Hi, Alex. How is it going?
M : I'm good. Thanks. I've just finished my English project. How about you, Tracy?
W : I'm _____ _____ _____ _____ for my food booth.
M : A food booth? What for?
W : My school festival is next Tuesday. I'm ✪ _____ _____ _____ _____ that day.
M : That is so cool. What is on the menu?
W : We're making sandwiches. You should come.
M : I'd love to, but I can't.
W : You can't? I was really looking forward to seeing you at my school.
M : I'm terribly sorry. I have to _____ _____ _____ _____ _____.
W : Oh, I see. Well, good luck with your audition.
M : Thank you.

08
대화를 듣고, Spanish culture class에 관해 언급되지 않은 것을 고르시오.

[Telephone rings.]
W : Hello, this is the World Culture Center. How can I help you?
M : Hi, I'm calling about a Spanish culture class for my teenage son.
W : Okay. We have an interesting class for teenagers.
M : Great. _____ _____ _____ _____?
W : A Korean teacher and a native speaker teach it together.

M : What kind of activities are there in the class?
W : Students can cook traditional foods, learn new words, and _____ _____ _____ _____ _____.
M : On what day is the class?
W : It's on Wednesday and Friday afternoons.
M : I see. Is there anything my son should prepare before the class?
W : He just needs to ✪ _____ _____ _____ _____ _____ _____. The center provides all the other class materials.
M : Perfect. Thanks for the information.

09
Summer Flea Market에 관한 다음 내용을 듣고, 일치하지 않는 것을 고르시오.
[3점]

W : Good afternoon, residents. This is the head of the Pineville Community Center. We're holding the Summer Flea Market for one week. It'll be held in the parking lot of Pineville Middle School. You can get _____ _____ _____ _____ _____ such as toys and candles at reasonable prices. You can also sell any of your own used items _____ _____ _____ _____ _____ _____. On the first day, every resident visiting the market will get ✪ _____ _____ _____ _____ _____ _____. For more information, please check out the community center's website.

10
다음 표를 보면서 대화를 듣고, 여자가 구입할 운동화를 고르시오.

W : Kyle, I'm looking for some sneakers. Can you help me find some good ones?
M : Of course. Let me see... *[Pause]* Look. These are the five best-selling ones.
W : Wow, they all look so cool. It's hard to choose among them.
M : Well, what's your budget?
W : I don't want to spend more than 80 dollars.
M : All right. Which style do you want, _____ _____ _____?
W : I prefer casual ones. I think they match my clothes better.
M : Good. And I'd like to ✪ _____ _____ _____ for rainy days.
W : Okay, I will take your advice.
M : So you have two options left. Which color do you prefer?
W : Most of my shoes are black, so I'll _____ _____ _____ this time.
M : You made a good choice.

11

대화를 듣고, 여자의 마지막 말에 대한 남자의 응답으로 가장 적절한 것을 고르시오.

W : Justin, what are you reading?

M : An advertisement. There's a special event at Will's Bookstore downtown.

W : ✪ _____ _____ _____ _____ _____ _____?

12

대화를 듣고, 남자의 마지막 말에 대한 여자의 응답으로 가장 적절한 것을 고르시오.

M : You look so worried. What's wrong, Liz?

W : I didn't do well on my presentation yesterday.

M : Sorry about that. To ✪ _____ _____ _____ _____ _____ _____ _____, how about having a nice meal?

13

대화를 듣고, 여자의 마지막 말에 대한 남자의 응답으로 가장 적절한 것을 고르시오.

M : Jenny, what class do you want to take this summer vacation?

W : Well, *[Pause]* I'm thinking of the guitar class.

M : Cool! I'm _____ _____ _____ _____ _____, too.

W : Really? It would be exciting if we took the class together.

M : I know, but I am thinking of taking a math class instead. I didn't do well on the final exam.

W : Oh, there is a math class? I didn't know that.

M : Yes. Mrs. Kim said she is offering _____ _____ _____ _____ _____ _____ _____.

W : That might be a good chance to improve my skills, too. ✪ _____ _____ _____ _____ _____ _____ for the math class?

14

대화를 듣고, 남자의 마지막 말에 대한 여자의 응답으로 가장 적절한 것을 고르시오.

M : Hi, Claire! How are you doing?

W : I'm good. You're looking great!

M : Thanks. ✪ _____ _____ _____ _____ these days.

W : I need to start working out, too. What kind of exercise do you do?

M : I do _____ _____ _____ _____ at home.

W : At home? Do you exercise alone?

M : Yes and no. I exercise online with other people.

W : Exercising online with others? What do you mean by that?

M : I'm taking an _____ _____ _____. We work out together on the Internet every evening at 7.

15

다음 상황 설명을 듣고, Ted가 Monica에게 할 말로 가장 적절한 것을 고르시오. [3점]

M : Ted is a high school student. He is planning to _____ _____ _____ _____ this year. He really wants to win the election. He thinks using posters is an effective way to ✪ _____ _____ _____ _____ on his schoolmates. But he is not good at drawing. His friend, Monica, is a member of a drawing club and she is good at drawing. So, he wants to ask her to _____ _____ _____ _____. In this situation, what would Ted most likely say to Monica?

16~17

다음을 듣고, 물음에 답하시오.

W : Good morning, listeners. This is your host Rachel at the Morning Radio Show. What do you eat for breakfast? Today I will _____ _____ _____ _____ _____ _____. Eggs are an excellent choice because they are high in protein. High-protein foods such as eggs provide energy for the brain. Cheese is another good option. It reduces hunger so it ✪ _____ _____ _____. Yogurt is also great to eat in the morning. It contains probiotics that _____ _____ _____. Eating berries such as blueberries or strawberries is another perfect way to start the morning. They are lower in sugar than most other fruits, but _____ _____ _____. Add them to yogurt for a tasty breakfast. Start every day with a healthy meal. Thank you.

▶ 정답 : 해설편 082쪽

18
001 □ return ⓥ 돌아오다
002 □ leave behind ~을 남겨놓고 오다
003 □ lap ⓝ 무릎
004 □ clean ⓥ 닦다
005 □ inside ⓐⓓ 안에
006 □ appreciate ⓥ 감사하다

19
007 □ take ⓥ 데리고 가다
008 □ dress ⓥ 옷을 입다
009 □ swing ⓝ 그네
010 □ favorite ⓐ 매우 좋아하는
011 □ available ⓐ 이용할 수 있는
012 □ sink ⓥ 가라앉다
013 □ embarrassed ⓐ 당황한
014 □ indifferent ⓐ 무관심한
015 □ disappointed ⓐ 실망한
016 □ ashamed ⓐ 수치스러운
017 □ nervous ⓐ 긴장한
018 □ touched ⓐ 감동한
019 □ scared ⓐ 겁에 질린
020 □ relaxed ⓐ 느긋한

20
021 □ encourage ⓥ 촉진하다, 격려하다
022 □ creative ⓐ 창의적인
023 □ on average 평균적으로
024 □ participant ⓝ 참가자
025 □ consider ⓥ 여기다
026 □ meeting time 회의 시간
027 □ unproductive ⓐ 비생산적인
028 □ productive ⓐ 생산적인
029 □ discuss ⓥ 논의하다
030 □ expect ⓥ 기대하다

21
031 □ psychology ⓝ 심리학
032 □ raise ⓥ (무엇을 위로) 들어 올리다
033 □ management ⓝ 관리
034 □ principle ⓝ 원칙, 원리
035 □ heavy ⓐ 무거운
036 □ shout ⓥ 외치다
037 □ various ⓐ 다양한
038 □ reply ⓥ 대답하다
039 □ absolute ⓐ (상대적이 아닌) 절대적인
040 □ matter ⓥ 중요하다
041 □ depend ⓥ ~에 달려 있다, 좌우되다
042 □ quite ⓐⓓ 꽤
043 □ straight ⓐⓓ 계속해서
044 □ severe ⓐ 심각한
045 □ pain ⓝ 아픔, 통증, 고통
046 □ case ⓝ 사례
047 □ nod ⓥ 끄덕이다
048 □ in agreement 동의하며
049 □ continue ⓥ 계속하다, 이어서 말하다
050 □ sign ⓝ 신호
051 □ put down ~을 내려놓다
052 □ pour ⓥ 쏟다, 붓다
053 □ mistake ⓝ 실수
054 □ let go of ~을 내려놓다, 버리다, 포기하다
055 □ opinion ⓝ 의견

22
056 □ deserve ⓥ ~을 받을 만하다
057 □ attention ⓝ 주목
058 □ unreliable ⓐ 믿을 만하지 않은
059 □ inaccurate ⓐ 부정확한
060 □ source of information 정보 출처
061 □ reflection ⓝ 반영
062 □ conclude ⓥ 결론을 내리다
063 □ behavior ⓝ 행동, 태도
064 □ depressed ⓐ 우울한
065 □ decide ⓥ 결정하다
066 □ poorly ⓐⓓ 좋지 못하게
067 □ interview ⓝ 면접
068 □ mislead A into B A를 속여 B하게 하다
069 □ support ⓥ 뒷받침하다, 지지하다

23
070 □ explore ⓥ 탐구하다
071 □ construct ⓥ 구성하다
072 □ relationship ⓝ 관계
073 □ object ⓝ 사물
074 □ frequently ⓐⓓ 자주, 종종, 빈번히
075 □ exist ⓥ 존재하다
076 □ thus ⓐⓓ 따라서
077 □ sandbox ⓝ (어린이가 안에서 노는) 모래놀이 통
078 □ compare ⓥ 비교하다
079 □ calculate ⓥ 계산하다
080 □ instance ⓝ 예시, 사례
081 □ notion ⓝ 개념
082 □ quantity ⓝ (측정 가능한) 양, 수량
083 □ reveal ⓥ 밝히다, 드러내다
084 □ investigate ⓥ 연구하다, 조사하다
085 □ concept ⓝ 개념
086 □ such as 예를 들어
087 □ sort A into B A를 B로 분류하다
088 □ shell ⓝ (조개 등의) 껍데기
089 □ advantage ⓝ 이점

24
090 □ generation ⓝ 세대
091 □ mention ⓥ 말하다, 언급하다
092 □ algorithm ⓝ 알고리즘, 연산
093 □ draw a blank 아무 반응을 얻지 못하다
094 □ civilization ⓝ 문명
095 □ connect ⓥ 이어지다, 연결되다
096 □ everyday life 일상생활
097 □ appliance ⓝ 가전 (제품)
098 □ here and there 여기저기에
099 □ fly an airplane 비행기를 운항하다
100 □ run ⓥ (사업체 등을) 운영하다
101 □ factory ⓝ 공장
102 □ trade ⓥ 거래하다, 교역하다
103 □ ancient ⓐ 고대의
104 □ decrease ⓥ 줄다, 감소하다
105 □ driving force 원동력

25
106 □ household ⓝ 가정, 가구
107 □ own ⓥ 보유하다, 소유하다
108 □ period ⓝ 기간, 시기
109 □ ownership ⓝ 보유, 소유(권)

26
110 □ rise ⓥ 오르다
111 □ additional ⓐ 추가의

26
112 □ composer ⓝ 작곡가
113 □ big band ⓝ (재즈의) 빅 밴드
114 □ classical music 고전 음악
115 □ youth ⓝ 젊은 시절, 청춘
116 □ introduce ⓥ 소개하다
117 □ musician ⓝ 음악가
118 □ film music 영화 음악
119 □ collaborate with ~와 협업하다
120 □ flutist ⓝ 플루티스트
121 □ publish ⓥ 발매하다, 출간하다
122 □ well-known ⓐ 잘 알려진, 유명한

27
123 □ self-defense ⓝ 자기 방어
124 □ training ⓝ 교육, 훈련, 연수
125 □ social skill 사교성
126 □ water bottle 물병
127 □ expensive ⓐ 비싼

28
128 □ have a chance to ~할 기회를 갖다
129 □ operating hour 운영 시간
130 □ process ⓝ 과정
131 □ require ⓥ 필요로 하다

29
132 □ despite ⓟⓡⓔⓟ ~에도 불구하고
133 □ high-tech ⓐ 첨단 기술의
134 □ device ⓝ 장치, 기기
135 □ deny ⓥ 부인[부정]하다
136 □ nearly ⓐⓓ 거의
137 □ recently ⓐⓓ 최근에
138 □ consume ⓥ 소비하다
139 □ globally ⓐⓓ 전 세계적으로
140 □ grow ⓥ 커지다, 늘다, 많아지다
141 □ resource ⓝ 자원
142 □ advance ⓝ 발전
143 □ promise ⓝ 가능성
144 □ material ⓝ 물질, 자재, 재료
145 □ historically ⓐⓓ 역사적으로
146 □ dependently ⓐⓓ 의존적으로, 남에게 의지하여
147 □ natural resources 천연자원
148 □ stuff ⓝ 재료
149 □ industrial ⓐ 산업의
150 □ mineral ⓝ 광물
151 □ copper ⓝ 구리
152 □ rare ⓐ 희귀한, 드문
153 □ ago ⓐⓓ (얼마의 시간) 전에
154 □ individually ⓐⓓ 개별적으로, 각각 따로
155 □ lifestyle ⓝ 생활 방식

30
156 □ sometimes ⓐⓓ 때때로, 가끔
157 □ missing ⓐ 빠진, 실종된
158 □ else ⓐⓓ 다른
159 □ meet the expectation 기대를 충족하다
160 □ pressure ⓝ 압박, 압력

31
161 □ deceiving ⓐ 현혹시키는, 속이는
162 □ impact ⓥ 영향을 미치다
163 □ realize ⓥ 깨닫다, 알아차리다
164 □ lose ⓥ 잃어버리다
165 □ ignore ⓥ 무시하다
166 □ regain ⓥ 되찾다
167 □ recover ⓥ 회복하다
168 □ get rid of ~을 없애다
169 □ expectation ⓝ 예상, 기대
170 □ treat ⓥ 대하다
171 □ accept ⓥ 받아들이다

31
172 □ face ⓥ 직면하다
173 □ innovation ⓝ 혁신
174 □ entirely ⓐⓓ 완전히
175 □ virtually ⓐⓓ (컴퓨터를 이용해) 가상으로
176 □ expert ⓝ 전문가
177 □ have a negative effect on ~에 부정적 영향을 미치다
178 □ solve ⓥ 해결하다
179 □ overall ⓐⓓ 전반적으로, 대체로
180 □ constraint ⓝ 제한, 한계, 통제
181 □ collaboration ⓝ 공동 작업, 협업
182 □ face-to-face ⓐ 대면하는
183 □ setting ⓝ 설정
184 □ for instance 예를 들어
185 □ press ⓥ 누르다
186 □ control ⓥ 제어하다
187 □ breakout group (전체에서 나누어진) 소집단
188 □ enforce ⓥ 시행하다
189 □ at a time 한 번에
190 □ nonverbal ⓐ 비언어적인
191 □ particularly ⓐⓓ 특히
192 □ shoulder ⓝ 어깨
193 □ diminish ⓥ 줄이다
194 □ seating arrangement 좌석 배치
195 □ assign ⓥ 배정하다, 할당하다
196 □ access ⓝ 접근
197 □ stretch ⓥ 늘이다, 확장하다
198 □ restriction ⓝ 제한점
199 □ responsibility ⓝ 책임
200 □ coincidence ⓝ 우연의 일치, 동시 발생
201 □ tradition ⓝ 전통
202 □ boost ⓥ 증진시키다

32
203 □ law ⓝ 법칙
204 □ demand ⓝ 수요 ⓥ 필요로 하다, 요구하다
205 □ increase ⓥ 증가하다
206 □ fall ⓥ (값이) 떨어지다
207 □ type ⓝ 유형
208 □ apply for ~에 적용되다
209 □ instead ⓐⓓ 대신에
210 □ switch to ~로 바꾸다
211 □ cheaper ⓐ 값이 더 싼
212 □ replacement ⓝ 대체(품)
213 □ consumer ⓝ 소비자
214 □ decrease ⓥ 내리다
215 □ tend ⓥ 경향이 있다
216 □ purchase ⓥ 구입하다

217 ☐ reason ⓝ 이유
218 ☐ dairy ⓝ 유제품
219 ☐ pattern ⓝ (정형화된) 양식, 패턴
220 ☐ on the other hand 다른 한편으로는, 반면에
221 ☐ invest ⓥ 투자하다
222 ☐ overseas ad 해외에

33
223 ☐ study ⓝ 연구
224 ☐ look ⓥ ~을 조사하다, 관찰하다
225 ☐ different ⓐ 다른
226 ☐ intellectually ad 지적으로
227 ☐ superior ⓐ 우수한
228 ☐ modify ⓥ 수정하다, 바꾸다
229 ☐ gene ⓝ 유전자
230 ☐ glutamate ⓝ 글루타민산염
231 ☐ receptor ⓝ 수용체
232 ☐ chemical ⓝ 화학 물질
233 ☐ necessary ⓐ 필요한
234 ☐ genetically ad 유전적으로
235 ☐ manipulate ⓥ 다루다, 조작하다
236 ☐ inferior ⓐ 열등한
237 ☐ cage ⓝ 우리
238 ☐ wheel ⓝ 바퀴
239 ☐ handicapped ⓐ 장애가 있는, 불리한 입장인
240 ☐ perform ⓥ 수행하다
241 ☐ as well as ~ 과 마찬가지로 잘
242 ☐ triumph ⓝ 승리
243 ☐ nurture ⓥ 양육
244 ☐ survival ⓝ 생존
245 ☐ free from ~ 없이, ~을 면하여
246 ☐ entertain ⓥ 즐겁게 해 주다

34
247 ☐ researcher ⓝ 연구원
248 ☐ coastal ⓐ 해안의
249 ☐ prepare ⓥ 준비하다
250 ☐ sea level 해수면
251 ☐ assessment ⓝ 평가
252 ☐ actually ad 실제로
253 ☐ carry out ~을 수행[이행]하다
254 ☐ climate change 기후 변화
255 ☐ belief ⓝ 믿음, 신념
256 ☐ decade ⓝ 10년간
257 ☐ prediction ⓝ 예측
258 ☐ tense ⓝ (문법) 시제
259 ☐ future tense 미래 시제
260 ☐ ongoing ⓐ 진행 중인
261 ☐ region ⓝ 지방, 지역
262 ☐ affect ⓥ 영향을 미치다
263 ☐ crisis ⓝ 위기
264 ☐ Antarctic ⓐ 남극의
265 ☐ ice sheet 빙상
266 ☐ physically ad 물리적으로, 신체적으로
267 ☐ remote ⓐ 멀리 떨어진
268 ☐ relate ⓥ 관련시키다
269 ☐ far away 멀리
270 ☐ energy efficiency 에너지 효율
271 ☐ careful ⓐ 신중한
272 ☐ prevent ⓥ 막다

35
273 ☐ contribute to ~에 기여하다, ~의 원인이 되다
274 ☐ provide ⓥ 제공하다
275 ☐ medium ⓝ 수단
276 ☐ exhibit ⓥ 보여주다, 드러내다
277 ☐ virtue ⓝ 가치
278 ☐ innovative ⓐ 혁신적인
279 ☐ useful ⓐ 유용한
280 ☐ display ⓥ 드러내다
281 ☐ taste ⓝ 취향
282 ☐ care ⓝ 관심
283 ☐ represent ⓥ 나타내다, 표현하다
284 ☐ self-respect ⓝ 자기 존중, 자존심
285 ☐ concern ⓝ 관심, 우려
286 ☐ pleasure ⓝ 기쁨, 즐거움
287 ☐ link A to B A와 B를 연결하다
288 ☐ highly ad 매우
289 ☐ sociable ⓐ 사교적인, 사람들과 어울리기 좋아하는
290 ☐ along with ~와 더불어
291 ☐ opportunity ⓝ 기회
292 ☐ identity ⓝ 정체성

36
293 ☐ thankful ⓐ 고맙게 생각하는, 감사하는
294 ☐ turkey ⓝ 칠면조
295 ☐ thanksgiving ⓝ 추수감사절
296 ☐ responsive ⓐ 즉각 반응하는, 관심을 보이는
297 ☐ forget ⓥ 잊다
298 ☐ softly ad 부드럽게
299 ☐ stay ⓥ 머무르다
300 ☐ classmate ⓝ 반 친구
301 ☐ break time 휴식 시간
302 ☐ immediately ad 즉시
303 ☐ attract one's interest ~의 관심을 끌다
304 ☐ raise ⓥ 기르다, 키우다
305 ☐ police officer 경찰관
306 ☐ protect ⓥ 보호하다, 지키다

37
307 ☐ according ad ~에 의하면
308 ☐ legend ⓝ 전설
309 ☐ vampire ⓝ 흡혈귀
310 ☐ turn ⓥ (…한 상태로) 변하다
311 ☐ seek ⓥ 구하다
312 ☐ prove ⓥ 입증[증명]하다
313 ☐ popular ⓐ 인기 있는, 대중적인
314 ☐ creature ⓝ 생명이 있는 존재, 생물
315 ☐ human ⓝ 인류
316 ☐ look around 둘러보다
317 ☐ take over ~을 지배하다, 장악하다
318 ☐ no such thing 그런 일은 없다
319 ☐ come into existence 생기다, 나타나다
320 ☐ break down 무너뜨리다
321 ☐ myth ⓝ 미신, (잘못된) 통념

38
322 ☐ rub ⓥ 문지르다
323 ☐ friction ⓝ 마찰
324 ☐ force ⓝ 힘

325 ☐ surface ⓝ 표면
326 ☐ slide ⓥ 미끄러지다
327 ☐ each other 서로
328 ☐ direction ⓝ 방향
329 ☐ opposite ⓐ 반대의
330 ☐ slow down ~을 느리게 하다
331 ☐ amount ⓝ 양
332 ☐ rough ⓐ 거친
333 ☐ slip ⓥ (넘어지거나 넘어질 뻔하게) 미끄러지다
334 ☐ slip ⓥ 미끄러지다
335 ☐ skid ⓥ 미끄러지다
336 ☐ tread ⓝ 접지면
337 ☐ act ⓥ 역할을 하다
338 ☐ grip ⓥ 붙잡다

39
339 ☐ blind person 맹인, 시각 장애인
340 ☐ associate A with B A와 B를 연결 짓다, 연상하다
341 ☐ unique ⓐ 독특한
342 ☐ combination ⓝ 조합
343 ☐ experience ⓝ 경험
344 ☐ non-visual 비시각적
345 ☐ sense ⓝ 감각
346 ☐ sight ⓝ 시력
347 ☐ collect ⓥ 모으다, 수집하다
348 ☐ understand ⓥ 이해하다
349 ☐ entirely ad 전적으로
350 ☐ result ⓝ 결과
351 ☐ amazing ⓐ 놀라운
352 ☐ ability ⓝ 능력
353 ☐ collection ⓝ 수집
354 ☐ dream ⓝ 꿈
355 ☐ vivid ⓐ 생생한
356 ☐ imaginative ⓐ 상상력이 풍부한
357 ☐ normal ⓐ 정상적인
358 ☐ vision ⓝ 시력
359 ☐ familiar ⓐ 익숙한, 친숙한
360 ☐ shape ⓝ 모양, 형태
361 ☐ in other words 다시 말해서
362 ☐ similar ⓐ 비슷한, 유사한

40
363 ☐ adolescent ⓝ 청소년
364 ☐ important ⓐ 중요한
365 ☐ factor ⓝ 요인
366 ☐ success ⓝ 성공
367 ☐ respond ⓥ 반응을 보이다
368 ☐ authoritative ⓐ 권위적인
369 ☐ parenting ⓝ 육아
370 ☐ passive ⓐ 수동적인, 소극적인
371 ☐ afraid ⓐ 두려워하는, 겁내는
372 ☐ indicate ⓥ 나타내다
373 ☐ involve ⓥ 관련시키다, 참여시키다
374 ☐ helpless ⓐ 무기력한
375 ☐ put effort into ~에 노력을 쏟다
376 ☐ significantly ad 상당히
377 ☐ homework ⓝ 숙제, 과제
378 ☐ attend ⓥ 참석하다, 참여하다
379 ☐ watch ⓥ 지켜보다
380 ☐ select ⓥ 선택하다

381 ☐ course ⓝ 강의, 과목
382 ☐ moreover ad 게다가, 더욱이
383 ☐ aware ⓐ 알고 있는
384 ☐ praise ⓥ 칭찬하다
385 ☐ random ⓐ 무작위적인
386 ☐ hesitant ⓐ 망설이는
387 ☐ constant ⓐ 지속적인

41~42
388 ☐ bedtime ⓝ 취침 시간
389 ☐ heart disease 심장병
390 ☐ volunteer ⓝ 지원자
391 ☐ monitor ⓥ 추적 관찰하다
392 ☐ health ⓝ 건강
393 ☐ go to bed 자다, 취침하다
394 ☐ ideal ⓐ 이상적인
395 ☐ timeframe ⓝ 기간, 시간
396 ☐ author ⓝ 저자
397 ☐ comment ⓥ 언급하다, 의견을 말하다
398 ☐ effect ⓝ 영향
399 ☐ certain ⓐ 확실한
400 ☐ cause ⓝ 원인
401 ☐ suggest ⓥ 암시하다, 시사하다
402 ☐ late ⓐ 늦은
403 ☐ disrupt ⓥ 혼란케 하다
404 ☐ body clock 생체 시계
405 ☐ consequence ⓝ 결과, 영향
406 ☐ cardiovascular ⓐ 심장 혈관의
407 ☐ midnight ⓝ 자정
408 ☐ likelihood ⓝ 가능성, 공산
409 ☐ reset ⓥ 다시 맞추다, 재설정하다
410 ☐ disease ⓝ 질환
411 ☐ properly ad 적절하게
412 ☐ sound ⓐ 좋은, 건전한
413 ☐ personality ⓝ 성격

43~45
414 ☐ farmer ⓝ 농부
415 ☐ watch ⓝ 시계
416 ☐ while conj ~하는 동안
417 ☐ barn ⓝ 헛간(곡물·건초 따위를 두는 곳)
418 ☐ ordinary ⓐ 평범한
419 ☐ others ⓝ 다른 사람들
420 ☐ bring ⓥ 가져다주다
421 ☐ childhood ⓝ 어린 시절
422 ☐ search ⓥ 찾아보다
423 ☐ for a long time 오랫동안
424 ☐ exhaust ⓥ 기진맥진하게 만들다
425 ☐ slowly ad 천천히, 서서히
426 ☐ tired ⓐ 지친
427 ☐ give up 포기하다
428 ☐ hope ⓝ 희망
429 ☐ precious ⓐ 소중한, 귀중한
430 ☐ call off ~을 중단하다, 멈추다
431 ☐ chance ⓝ 기회
432 ☐ lose out on ~을 놓치다, ~에게 지다
433 ☐ delight ⓥ 매우 기뻐하다
434 ☐ reward ⓥ 보상하다
435 ☐ promise ⓥ 약속하다
436 ☐ attractive ⓐ 매력적인
437 ☐ pile ⓝ 더미
438 ☐ hay ⓝ 건초

06회

● 채점 : 맞은 개수 _____ / 80

TEST A-B 각 단어의 뜻을 [A] 영어는 우리말로, [B] 우리말은 영어로 쓰시오.

A	English	Korean
01	deceiving	
02	attractive	
03	principle	
04	self-defense	
05	discuss	
06	explore	
07	physically	
08	grip	
09	reflection	
10	unreliable	
11	coincidence	
12	prediction	
13	genetically	
14	unique	
15	ownership	
16	quantity	
17	consequence	
18	nurture	
19	touched	
20	publish	

B	Korean	English
01	과정	
02	해외에	
03	소비하다	
04	참가자	
05	표면	
06	수정하다, 바꾸다	
07	기르다, 키우다	
08	우수한	
09	가정, 가구	
10	구성하다	
11	회복하다	
12	부정확한	
13	평가	
14	가라앉다	
15	역사적으로	
16	소개하다	
17	소중한, 귀중한	
18	제한, 한계	
19	언급하다, 의견을 말하다	
20	관심, 우려	

▶ A-D 정답 : 해설편 082쪽

TEST C-D 각 단어의 뜻을 골라 기호를 쓰시오.

C	English		Korean
01	missing	( )	ⓐ 즉각 반응하는, 관심을 보이는
02	embarrassed	( )	ⓑ 개념
03	deserve	( )	ⓒ 계산하다
04	responsive	( )	ⓓ 청소년
05	pour	( )	ⓔ 생생한
06	material	( )	ⓕ 심각한
07	combination	( )	ⓖ 거래하다, 교역하다
08	trade	( )	ⓗ 문지르다
09	vivid	( )	ⓘ 늘이다, 확장하다
10	investigate	( )	ⓙ 빠진, 실종된
11	replacement	( )	ⓚ 가전제품
12	notion	( )	ⓛ ~을 받을 만하다
13	authoritative	( )	ⓜ 쏟다, 붓다
14	adolescent	( )	ⓝ 당황한
15	rub	( )	ⓞ 열등한
16	appliance	( )	ⓟ 물질, 자재, 재료
17	severe	( )	ⓠ 연구하다, 조사하다
18	inferior	( )	ⓡ 조합
19	calculate	( )	ⓢ 권위적인
20	stretch	( )	ⓣ 대체품

D	Korean		English
01	상상력이 풍부한	( )	ⓐ reveal
02	사교적인	( )	ⓑ immediately
03	줄이다	( )	ⓒ support
04	미신, (잘못된) 통념	( )	ⓓ imaginative
05	준비하다	( )	ⓔ taste
06	산업의	( )	ⓕ enforce
07	세대	( )	ⓖ industrial
08	비생산적인	( )	ⓗ dairy
09	가능성, 공산	( )	ⓘ sociable
10	즉시	( )	ⓙ slide
11	안에	( )	ⓚ represent
12	유제품	( )	ⓛ unproductive
13	미끄러지다	( )	ⓜ author
14	나타내다, 표현하다	( )	ⓝ prepare
15	취향	( )	ⓞ diminish
16	밝히다, 드러내다	( )	ⓟ creature
17	시행하다	( )	ⓠ inside
18	저자	( )	ⓡ likelihood
19	생명이 있는 존재, 생물	( )	ⓢ generation
20	뒷받침하다, 지지하다	( )	ⓣ myth

제 3 교시

영어 영역

07회

● 문항수 45개 | 배점 100점 | 제한 시간 70분

● 점수 표시가 없는 문항은 모두 2점

1번부터 17번까지는 듣고 답하는 문제입니다. 1번부터 15번까지는 한 번만 들려주고, 16번부터 17번까지는 두 번 들려줍니다. 방송을 잘 듣고 답을 하시기 바랍니다.

1. 다음을 듣고, 여자가 하는 말의 목적으로 가장 적절한 것을 고르시오.

① 축제 기간 연장을 요청하려고
② 신설된 지하철 노선을 홍보하려고
③ 축제 당일의 지하철 연장 운행을 안내하려고
④ 축제 방문객에게 안전 수칙 준수를 당부하려고
⑤ 축제 기간 중 도심 교통 통제 구간을 공지하려고

2. 대화를 듣고, 남자의 의견으로 가장 적절한 것을 고르시오.

① 불규칙한 수면 습관은 청소년의 뇌 발달을 방해한다.
② 스마트폰의 화면 밝기를 조절하여 눈을 보호해야 한다.
③ 취침 전 스마트폰 사용을 줄여야 수면의 질이 높아진다.
④ 집중력 향상을 위해 디지털 기기 사용을 최소화해야 한다.
⑤ 일정한 시간에 취침하는 것이 생체 리듬 유지에 도움을 준다.

3. 다음을 듣고, 남자가 하는 말의 요지로 가장 적절한 것을 고르시오.

① 과도한 컴퓨터 사용은 스트레스 지수를 증가시킨다.
② 컴퓨터 관련 취미 활동은 IT 활용 능력을 향상시킨다.
③ 직업을 선택할 때 자신의 흥미와 적성을 고려해야 한다.
④ 다양한 악기 연주를 배우는 것은 인생을 풍요롭게 만든다.
⑤ 직업과 관련 없는 취미 활동이 스트레스 감소에 도움이 된다.

4. 대화를 듣고, 그림에서 대화의 내용과 일치하지 않는 것을 고르시오.

5. 대화를 듣고, 여자가 할 일로 가장 적절한 것을 고르시오.

① 선물 준비하기
② 온라인 초대장 보내기
③ 음식 주문하기
④ 초대 손님 명단 확인하기
⑤ 전시 부스 설치하기

6. 대화를 듣고, 남자가 지불할 금액을 고르시오. [3점]

① $63 ② $70 ③ $81 ④ $86 ⑤ $90

7. 대화를 듣고, 여자가 이번 주말에 등산을 갈 수 없는 이유를 고르시오.

① 아르바이트를 해야 해서
② 학교 시험공부를 해야 해서
③ 폭우로 인해 등산로가 폐쇄되어서
④ 경연을 위한 춤 연습을 해야 해서
⑤ 주문한 등산 장비가 도착하지 않아서

8. 대화를 듣고, Lakestate Apartment Yoga Program에 관해 언급되지 않은 것을 고르시오.

① 대상 연령   ② 운영 요일   ③ 모집 인원
④ 등록 방법   ⑤ 등록 준비물

9. Global Food Market에 관한 다음 내용을 듣고, 일치하지 않는 것을 고르시오.

① 학교 주차장에서 열린다.
② 이틀간 진행된다.
③ 8개 국가의 음식을 즐길 수 있다.
④ 음식마다 가격이 다르다.
⑤ 채식주의자를 위한 메뉴가 있다.

10. 다음 표를 보면서 대화를 듣고, 남자가 주문할 디지털 텀블러를 고르시오.

Digital Tumblers

	Model	Price	Size	Water Intake Display	Color
①	A	$35	350ml	×	White
②	B	$40	470ml	×	Gold
③	C	$45	470ml	○	Black
④	D	$55	550ml	○	White
⑤	E	$65	550ml	○	Gold

11. 대화를 듣고, 여자의 마지막 말에 대한 남자의 응답으로 가장 적절한 것을 고르시오.

① If it's too dry inside, you can easily get a cold.
② When you cough, you should cover your mouth.
③ You need to wash your hands not to get a cold.
④ It's really important to keep yourself warm.
⑤ Drinking water can make your skin soft.

12. 대화를 듣고, 남자의 마지막 말에 대한 여자의 응답으로 가장 적절한 것을 고르시오.

① Awesome. The new bookshelf looks good in your room.
② Right. Then, shall we sell them at a used bookstore?
③ I see. Can you borrow them from the library?
④ Okay. I'll buy you books in a good condition.
⑤ I'm sorry. I haven't finished the book yet.

13. 대화를 듣고, 여자의 마지막 말에 대한 남자의 응답으로 가장 적절한 것을 고르시오. [3점]

Man: _____

① I'll clarify each group member's specific role.
② I'll collect more data for our group research.
③ I should challenge myself for the competition.
④ I need to change the topic of our group project.
⑤ I'll let you know how to analyze data effectively.

14. 대화를 듣고, 남자의 마지막 말에 대한 여자의 응답으로 가장 적절한 것을 고르시오. [3점]

Woman: _____

① Trust me. When we eat makes a big difference.
② Okay. I'll check my meals to get in better shape.
③ Thank you for your tip. But I don't think I can do it.
④ Of course. I'll make sure to follow your workout routine.
⑤ Sure. That's why I didn't succeed at keeping a balanced diet.

15. 다음 상황 설명을 듣고, Julia가 Sophie에게 할 말로 가장 적절한 것을 고르시오.

Julia: _____

① Could you help me assemble my desk?
② Can you share where you bought your desk?
③ How about choosing a new computer together?
④ Why don't you repair the furniture by yourself?
⑤ Do you have any ideas for decorating my room?

[16~17] 다음을 듣고, 물음에 답하시오.

16. 여자가 하는 말의 주제로 가장 적절한 것은?

① material trends in the fashion industry
② benefits of making clothes from nature
③ tips to purchase natural material clothes
④ development of clothes washing methods
⑤ proper ways to wash natural material clothes

17. 언급된 소재가 <u>아닌</u> 것은?

① cotton   ② silk   ③ leather
④ linen   ⑤ wool

이제 듣기 문제가 끝났습니다. 18번부터는 문제지의 지시에 따라 답을 하시기 바랍니다.

18. 다음 글의 목적으로 가장 적절한 것은?

To whom it may concern,

I am writing to express my deep concern about the recent change made by Pittsburgh Train Station. The station had traditional ticket offices with staff before, but these have been replaced with ticket vending machines. However, individuals who are unfamiliar with these machines are now experiencing difficulty accessing the railway services. Since these individuals heavily relied on the staff assistance to be able to travel, they are in great need of ticket offices with staff in the station. Therefore, I am urging you to consider reopening the ticket offices. With the staff back in their positions, many people would regain access to the railway services. I look forward to your prompt attention to this matter and a positive resolution.

Sincerely,
Sarah Roberts

① 승차권 발매기 수리를 의뢰하려고
② 기차표 단체 예매 방법을 문의하려고
③ 기차 출발 시간 지연에 대해 항의하려고
④ 기차역 직원의 친절한 도움에 감사하려고
⑤ 기차역 유인 매표소 재운영을 요구하려고

19. 다음 글에 드러난 Jeevan의 심경 변화로 가장 적절한 것은?

All the actors on the stage were focused on their acting. Then, suddenly, Arthur fell into the corner of the stage. Jeevan immediately approached Arthur and found his heart wasn't beating. Jeevan began CPR. Jeevan worked silently, glancing sometimes at Arthur's face. He thought, "Please, start breathing again, please." Arthur's eyes were closed. Moments later, an older man in a grey suit appeared, swiftly kneeling beside Arthur's chest. "I'm Walter Jacobi. I'm a doctor." He announced with a calm voice. Jeevan wiped the sweat off his forehead. With combined efforts, Jeevan and Dr. Jacobi successfully revived Arthur. Arthur's eyes slowly opened. Finally, Jeevan was able to hear Arthur's breath again, thinking to himself, "Thank goodness. You're back."

① thrilled → bored
② ashamed → confident
③ hopeful → helpless
④ surprised → indifferent
⑤ desperate → relieved

20. 다음 글에서 필자가 주장하는 바로 가장 적절한 것은?

As the parent of a gifted child, you need to be aware of a certain common parent trap. Of course you are a proud parent, and you should be. While it is very easy to talk nonstop about your little genius and his or her remarkable behavior, this can be very stressful on your child. It is extremely important to limit your bragging behavior to your very close friends, or your parents. Gifted children feel pressured when their parents show them off too much. This behavior creates expectations that they may not be able to live up to, and also creates a false sense of self for your child. You want your child to be who they are, not who they seem to be as defined by their incredible achievements. If not, you could end up with a driven perfectionist child or perhaps a drop-out, or worse.

① 부모는 자녀를 다른 아이와 비교하지 말아야 한다.
② 부모는 자녀의 영재성을 지나치게 자랑하지 말아야 한다.
③ 영재교육 프로그램에 대한 맹목적인 믿음을 삼가야 한다.
④ 과도한 영재교육보다 자녀와의 좋은 관계 유지에 힘써야 한다.
⑤ 자녀의 독립성을 기르기 위해 자기 일은 스스로 하게 해야 한다.

21. 밑줄 친 "hanging out with the winners"가 다음 글에서 의미하는 바로 가장 적절한 것은?

One valuable technique for getting out of helplessness, depression, and situations which are predominantly being run by the thought, "I can't," is to choose to be with other persons who have resolved the problem with which we struggle. This is one of the great powers of self-help groups. When we are in a negative state, we have given a lot of energy to negative thought forms, and the positive thought forms are weak. Those who are in a higher vibration are free of the energy from their negative thoughts and have energized positive thought forms. Merely to be in their presence is beneficial. In some self-help groups, this is called "hanging out with the winners." The benefit here is on the psychic level of consciousness, and there is a transfer of positive energy and relighting of one's own latent positive thought forms.

* latent: 잠재적인

① staying with those who sacrifice themselves for others
② learning from people who have succeeded in competition
③ keeping relationships with people in a higher social position
④ spending time with those who need social skill development
⑤ being with positive people who have overcome negative states

22. 다음 글의 요지로 가장 적절한 것은?

Our emotions are thought to exist because they have contributed to our survival as a species. Fear has helped us avoid dangers, expressing anger helps us scare off threats, and expressing positive emotions helps us bond with others. From an evolutionary perspective, an emotion is a kind of "program" that, when triggered, directs many of our activities (including attention, perception, memory, movement, expressions, etc.). For example, fear makes us very attentive, narrows our perceptual focus to threatening stimuli, will cause us either to face a situation (fight) or avoid it (flight), and may cause us to remember an experience more acutely (so that we avoid the threat in the future). Regardless of the specific ways in which they activate our systems, the specific emotions we possess are thought to exist because they have helped us (as a species) survive challenges within our environment long ago. If they had not helped us adapt and survive, they would not have evolved with us.

① 과거의 경험이 현재의 감정에 영향을 미친다.
② 문명의 발달에 따라 인간의 감정은 다양화되어 왔다.
③ 감정은 인간이 생존하도록 도와왔기 때문에 존재한다.
④ 부정적인 감정은 긍정적인 감정보다 더 오래 기억된다.
⑤ 두려움의 원인을 파악함으로써 두려움을 없앨 수 있다.

23. 다음 글의 주제로 가장 적절한 것은?

By improving accessibility of the workplace for workers that are typically at a disadvantage in the labour market, AI can improve inclusiveness in the workplace. AI-powered assistive devices to aid workers with visual, speech or hearing difficulties are becoming more widespread, improving the access to, and the quality of work for people with disabilities. For example, speech recognition solutions for people with dysarthric voices, or live captioning systems for deaf and hard of hearing people can facilitate communication with colleagues and access to jobs where inter-personal communication is necessary. AI can also enhance the capabilities of low-skilled workers, with potentially positive effects on their wages and career prospects. For example, AI's capacity to translate written and spoken word in real-time can improve the performance of non-native speakers in the workplace. Moreover, recent developments in AI-powered text generators can instantly improve the performance of lower-skilled individuals in domains such as writing, coding or customer service.

* dysarthric: (신경 장애로 인한) 구음(構音) 장애의

① jobs replaced by AI in the labour market
② ethical issues caused by using AI in the workplace
③ necessity of using AI technology for language learning
④ impacts of AI on supporting workers with disadvantages
⑤ new designs of AI technology to cure people with disabilities

24. 다음 글의 제목으로 가장 적절한 것은?

Whales are highly efficient at carbon storage. When they die, each whale sequesters an average of 30 tons of carbon dioxide, taking that carbon out of the atmosphere for centuries. For comparison, the average tree absorbs only 48 pounds of CO_2 a year. From a climate perspective, each whale is the marine equivalent of thousands of trees. Whales also help sequester carbon by fertilizing the ocean as they release nutrient-rich waste, in turn increasing phytoplankton populations, which also sequester carbon — leading some scientists to call them the "engineers of marine ecosystems." In 2019, economists from the International Monetary Fund (IMF) estimated the value of the ecosystem services provided by each whale at over $2 million USD. They called for a new global program of economic incentives to return whale populations to preindustrial whaling levels as one example of a "nature-based solution" to climate change. Calls are now being made for a global whale restoration program, to slow down climate change.

* sequester: 격리하다 ** phytoplankton: 식물성 플랑크톤

① Saving Whales Saves the Earth and Us
② What Makes Whales Go Extinct in the Ocean
③ Why Is Overpopulation of Whales Dangerous?
④ Black Money: Lies about the Whaling Industry
⑤ Climate Change and Its Effect on Whale Habitats

25. 다음 도표의 내용과 일치하지 <u>않는</u> 것은?

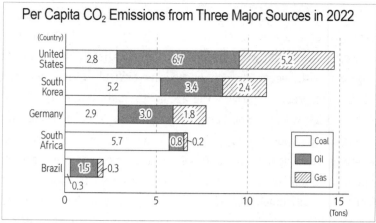

The above graph shows per capita CO_2 emissions from coal, oil, and gas by countries in 2022. ① The United States had the highest total per capita CO_2 emissions, even though its emissions from coal were the second lowest among the five countries shown. ② South Korea's total per capita CO_2 emissions were over 10 tons, ranking it the second highest among the countries shown. ③ Germany had lower CO_2 emissions per capita than South Korea in all three major sources respectively. ④ The per capita CO_2 emissions from coal in South Africa were over three times higher than those in Germany. ⑤ In Brazil, oil was the largest source of CO_2 emissions per capita among its three major sources, just as it was in the United States and Germany.

* per capita: 1인당

26. Émilie du Châtelet에 관한 다음 글의 내용과 일치하지 <u>않는</u> 것은?

Émilie du Châtelet, a French mathematician and physicist, was born in Paris in 1706. During her childhood, with her father's support, she was able to get mathematical and scientific education that most women of her time did not receive. In 1737, she submitted her paper on the nature of fire to a contest sponsored by the French Academy of Sciences, and it was published a year later. In her book, *Institutions de Physique*, Émilie du Châtelet explained the ideas of space and time in a way that is closer to what we understand in modern relativity than what was common during her time. Her most significant achievement was translating Isaac Newton's *Principia* into French near the end of her life. Émilie du Châtelet's work was not recognized in her time, but she is now remembered as a symbol of the Enlightenment and the struggle for women's participation in science.

① 어린 시절에 수학과 과학 교육을 받았다.
② 불의 속성에 관한 그녀의 논문이 1737년에 출간되었다.
③ *Institutions de Physique*에서 공간과 시간의 개념을 설명했다.
④ 아이작 뉴턴의 *Principia*를 프랑스어로 번역했다.
⑤ 이룩한 업적은 당대에 인정받지 못했다.

27. 2024 Young Inventors Robot Competition에 관한 다음 안내문의 내용과 일치하지 <u>않는</u> 것은?

2024 Young Inventors Robot Competition

Join us for an exciting day of the Young Inventors Robot Competition!

☐ **Categories**
 - Participants can compete in one of the following categories:
 · Robot Design · Robot Coding · Robot Remote Control

☐ **Date and Time**
 - September 28, 2024, 10 a.m. to 3 p.m.

☐ **Location**
 - Computer Lab, Oakwood University

☐ **Registration**
 - From August 1 to August 10, 2024
 - Open to high school students
 - Online registration only (www.younginventors.edu)

☐ **Awards**
 - In each competition category, three participants will be honored.
 · 1st place: $300 · 2nd place: $200 · 3rd place: $100

※ For more information, visit our website.

① 세 가지 분야 중 하나에 참가할 수 있다.
② 9월 28일에 5시간 동안 열린다.
③ 고등학생이 등록할 수 있다.
④ 등록은 온라인으로만 가능하다.
⑤ 수상자는 각 분야당 한 명이다.

28. Saintville Art Week Stamp Tour에 관한 다음 안내문의 내용과 일치하는 것은?

Saintville Art Week Stamp Tour

The 8th annual Saintville Art Week Stamp Tour is back this year! Anyone can participate in our event. Join us and enjoy exhibitions and new collections.

☐ **When:** The first week of October, 2024

☐ **Where:** Saintville Arts District

☐ **How:**
 Step 1. Take a stamp tour map from the Saintville Arts Center.
 Step 2. Get stamps from at least 3 out of 5 spots and receive your gift.
 - You can choose either an umbrella or a mug with printed artwork on it for your gift.

※ For more information, please visit our website at www.SaintvilleArtsCenter.com.

① 참가 대상에 제한이 있다.
② 10월 둘째 주에 진행된다.
③ Saintville Arts Center에서 스탬프 투어 지도를 받는다.
④ 적어도 다섯 곳에서 도장을 받아야 선물을 받는다.
⑤ 선물로 가방과 머그잔 중 하나를 고를 수 있다.

29. 다음 글의 밑줄 친 부분 중, 어법상 틀린 것은?

From an organizational viewpoint, one of the most fascinating examples of how any organization may contain many different types of culture ① is to recognize the functional operations of different departments within the organization. The varying departments and divisions within an organization will inevitably view any given situation from their own biased and prejudiced perspective. A department and its members will acquire "tunnel vision" which disallows them to see things as others see ② them. The very structure of organizations can create conflict. The choice of ③ whether the structure is "mechanistic" or "organic" can have a profound influence on conflict management. A mechanistic structure has a vertical hierarchy with many rules, many procedures, and many levels of management ④ involved in decision making. Organic structures are more horizontal in nature, ⑤ which decision making is less centralized and spread across the plane of the organization.

* hierarchy: 위계

30. 다음 글의 밑줄 친 부분 중, 문맥상 낱말의 쓰임이 적절하지 않은 것은? [3점]

An excellent alternative to calming traffic is removing it. Some cities ① reserve an extensive network of lanes and streets for bikes, pedestrians, and the occasional service vehicle. This motivates people to travel by bike rather than by car, making streets safer for everyone. As bicycles become more ② popular in a city, planners can convert more automobile lanes and entire streets to accommodate more of them. Nevertheless, even the most bikeable cities still ③ require motor vehicle lanes for taxis, emergency vehicles, and delivery trucks. Delivery vehicles are frequently a target of animus, but they are actually an essential component to making cities greener. A tightly packed delivery truck is a far more ④ inefficient transporter of goods than several hybrids carrying a few shopping bags each. Distributing food and other goods to neighborhood vendors ⑤ allows them to operate smaller stores close to homes so that residents can walk, rather than drive, to get their groceries.

* animus: 반감, 미움

[31~34] 다음 빈칸에 들어갈 말로 가장 적절한 것을 고르시오.

31. You hear again and again that some of the greatest composers were misunderstood in their own day. Not everyone could understand the compositions of Beethoven, Brahms, or Stravinsky in their day. The reason for this initial lack of acceptance is unfamiliarity. The musical forms, or ideas expressed within them, were completely new. And yet, this is exactly one of the things that makes them so great. Effective composers have their own ideas. Have you ever seen the classic movie *Amadeus*? The composer Antonio Salieri is the "host" of this movie; he's depicted as one of the most famous non-great composers — he lived at the time of Mozart and was completely overshadowed by him. Now, Salieri wasn't a bad composer; in fact, he was a very good one. But he wasn't one of the world's great composers because his work wasn't _____. What he wrote sounded just like what everyone else was composing at the time.

① simple
② original
③ familiar
④ conventional
⑤ understandable

32. Every time a new medium comes along — whether it's the invention of the printed book, or TV, or SNS — and you start to use it, it's like you are putting on a new kind of goggles, with their own special colors and lenses. Each set of goggles you put on makes you see things differently. So when you start to watch television, before you absorb the message of any particular TV show — whether it's *Wheel of Fortune* or *The Wire* — you start to see the world as being shaped like television itself. That's why Marshall McLuhan said that every time a new medium comes along — a new way for humans to communicate — it has buried in it a message. It is gently guiding us to _____.
The way information gets to you, McLuhan argued, is more important than the information itself. TV teaches you that the world is fast; that it's about surfaces and appearances. [3점]

① see the world according to a new set of codes
② ignore unfamiliar messages from new media
③ maintain steady focus and clear understanding
④ interpret information through a traditional lens
⑤ enjoy various media contents with one platform

33. Concepts are vital to human survival, but we must also be careful with them because concepts open the door to essentialism. They _____.
Stuart Firestein opens his book, *Ignorance*, with an old proverb, "It is very difficult to find a black cat in a dark room, especially when there is no cat." This statement beautifully sums up the search for essences. History has many examples of scientists who searched fruitlessly for an essence because they used the wrong concept to guide their hypotheses. Firestein gives the example of luminiferous ether, a mysterious substance that was thought to fill the universe so that light would have a medium to move through. The ether was a black cat, writes Firestein, and physicists had been theorizing in a dark room, and then experimenting in it, looking for evidence of a cat that did not exist. [3점]

① encourage us to see things that aren't present
② force scientists to simplify scientific theories
③ let us think science is essential and practical
④ drive physicists to explore philosophy
⑤ lead us to ignore the unknown

34. While social media attention is potentially an instrument to achieve ends like elite celebrity, some content creators desire ordinary fame as a social end in itself. Not unlike reality television stars, social media celebrities are often criticized for not having skills and talents associated with traditional, elite celebrity, such as acting or singing ability. This criticism highlights the fact that digital content creators face real barriers to crossing over to the sphere of elite celebrity. However, the criticism also misses the point that the phenomenon of ordinary celebrity _____. The elite celebrity is symbolized by the metaphor of the star, characterized by mystery and hierarchical distance and associated with naturalized qualities of talent and class. The ordinary celebrity attracts attention through regular and frequent interactions with other ordinary people. Achieving ordinary fame as a social media celebrity is like doing well at a game, because in this sphere, fame is nothing more nor less than relatively high scores on attention scales, the metrics of subscribers, followers, Likes, or clicks built into social media applications. [3점]

* sphere: 영역 ** metric: 측정 기준

① shifts to that of elite celebrity
② disappears gradually over time
③ focuses solely on talent and class
④ reconstructs the meaning of fame
⑤ restricts interactions with the public

35. 다음 글에서 전체 흐름과 관계 <u>없는</u> 문장은?

Why do we have the illusion that cramming for an exam is the best learning strategy? Because we are unable to differentiate between the various sections of our memory. Immediately after reading our textbook or our class notes, information is fully present in our mind. ① It sits in our conscious working memory, in an active form. ② We feel as if we know it, because it is present in our short-term storage space … but this short-term section has nothing to do with the long-term memory that we will need in order to recall the same information a few days later. ③ After a few seconds or minutes, working memory already starts disappearing, and after a few days, the effect becomes enormous: unless you retest your knowledge, memory vanishes. ④ Focusing on exploring new topics rather than reviewing the same material over and over again can improve your academic performance. ⑤ To get information into long-term memory, it is essential to study the material, then test yourself, rather than spend all your time studying.

* cram: 벼락 공부를 하다

[36~37] 주어진 글 다음에 이어질 글의 순서로 가장 적절한 것을 고르시오.

36.

> The discovery of mirror neurons has profoundly changed the way we think of a fundamental human capacity, learning by observation.

(A) You may not see the tongue stick out each time you stick yours out at your newborn, but if you do it many times, the tongue will come out more often than if you do something different. Babies babble and later start to imitate the sounds their parents produce.

(B) As children we learn a lot by observing what our parents and friends do. Newborns, in the first week of life, have an inborn tendency to stick out their tongue if their parents stick out theirs. Such imitation is not perfect.

(C) Later still, they play with vacuum cleaners and hammers in imitation of their parents. Our modern cultures, in which we write, speak, read, build spaceships and go to school, can work only because we are not restricted to the behavior we are born with or learn by trial and error. We can learn a lot by simply watching others.

* babble: 옹알이하다

① (A) − (C) − (B)   ② (B) − (A) − (C)
③ (B) − (C) − (A)   ④ (C) − (A) − (B)
⑤ (C) − (B) − (A)

[해설편 p.092]

37.

> Have you ever been surprised to hear a recording of your own voice? You might have thought, "Is that really what my voice sounds like?"

(A) There are two pathways through which we perceive our own voice when we speak. One is the route through which we perceive most external sounds, like waves that travel from the air through the outer, middle and inner ear.

(B) But because our vocal cords vibrate when we speak, there is a second internal path. Vibrations are conducted through our bones and stimulate our inner ears directly. Lower frequencies are emphasized along this pathway. That makes your voice sound deeper and richer to yourself than it may sound to other people.

(C) Maybe your accent is more pronounced in the recording than you realized, or your voice is higher than it seems to your own ears. This is of course quite a common experience. The explanation is actually fairly simple. [3점]

*vocal cords: 성대 **frequency: 주파수

① (A) – (C) – (B)   ② (B) – (A) – (C)
③ (B) – (C) – (A)   ④ (C) – (A) – (B)
⑤ (C) – (B) – (A)

[38~39] 글의 흐름으로 보아, 주어진 문장이 들어가기에 가장 적절한 곳을 고르시오.

38.

> "Homologous" traits, in contrast, may or may not have a common function, but they descended from a common ancestor and hence have some common structure that indicates their being "the same" organ.

Biologists distinguish two kinds of similarity. (①) "Analogous" traits are ones that have a common function but arose on different branches of the evolutionary tree and are in an important sense not "the same" organ. (②) The wings of birds and the wings of bees are both used for flight and are similar in some ways because anything used for flight has to be built in those ways, but they arose independently in evolution and have nothing in common beyond their use in flight. (③) The wing of a bat and the front leg of a horse have very different functions, but they are all modifications of the forelimb of the ancestor of all mammals. (④) As a result, they share nonfunctional traits like the number of bones and the ways they are connected. (⑤) To distinguish analogy from homology, biologists usually look at the overall architecture of the organs and focus on their most useless properties.

39.

> Thus, as global warming raises the temperature of marine waters, it is self-evident that the amount of dissolved oxygen will decrease.

Seawater contains an abundance of dissolved oxygen that all marine animals breathe to stay alive. (①) It has long been established in physics that cold water holds more dissolved oxygen than warm water does — this is one reason that cold polar seas are full of life while tropical oceans are blue, clear, and relatively poorly populated with living creatures. (②) This is a worrisome and potentially disastrous consequence if allowed to continue to an ecosystem-threatening level. (③) Now scientists have analyzed data indicating that the amount of dissolved oxygen in the oceans has been declining for more than a half century. (④) The data show that the ocean oxygen level has been falling more rapidly than the corresponding rise in water temperature. (⑤) Falling oxygen levels in water have the potential to impact the habitat of marine organisms worldwide and in recent years this has led to more frequent anoxic events that killed or displaced populations of fish, crabs, and many other organisms. [3점]

*dissolved: 용해된 **anoxic: 산소 결핍의

40. 다음 글의 내용을 한 문장으로 요약하고자 한다. 빈칸 (A), (B)에 들어갈 말로 가장 적절한 것은?

> Capuchins — New World Monkeys that live in large social groups — will, in captivity, trade with people all day long, especially if food is involved. *I give you this rock and you give me a treat to eat.* If you put two monkeys in cages next to each other, and offer them both slices of cucumber for the rocks they already have, they will happily eat the cucumbers. If, however, you give one monkey grapes instead — grapes being universally preferred to cucumbers — the monkey that is still receiving cucumbers will begin to throw them back at the experimenter. Even though she is still getting "paid" the same amount for her effort of sourcing rocks, and so her particular situation has not changed, the comparison to another makes the situation unfair. Furthermore, she is now willing to abandon all gains — the cucumbers themselves — to communicate her displeasure to the experimenter.

↓

> According to the passage, if the Capuchin monkey realizes the ___(A)___ in rewards compared to another monkey, she will ___(B)___ her rewards to express her feelings about the treatment, despite getting exactly the same rewards as before.

	(A)		(B)
①	benefit	......	protect
②	inequality	......	share
③	abundance	......	yield
④	inequality	......	reject
⑤	benefit	......	display

[41~42] 다음 글을 읽고, 물음에 답하시오.

Higher education has grown from an elite to a mass system across the world. In Europe and the USA, (a) increased rates of participation occurred in the decades after the Second World War. Between 2000 and 2014, rates of participation in higher education almost doubled from 19% to 34% across the world among the members of the population in the school-leaving age category (typically 18−23). The dramatic expansion of higher education has been marked by a wider range of institutions of higher learning and a more diverse demographic of students.

Changes from an elite system to a mass higher education system are associated with political needs to build a (b) specialised workforce for the economy. In theory, the expansion of higher education to develop a highly skilled workforce should diminish the role of examinations in the selection and control of students, initiating approaches to assessment which (c) block lifelong learning: assessment *for* learning and a focus on feedback for development. In reality, socio-political changes to expand higher education have set up a 'field of contradictions' for assessment in higher education. Mass higher education requires efficient approaches to assessment, such as examinations and multiple-choice quizzes, with minimalist, (d) impersonal, or standardised feedback, often causing students to focus more on grades than feedback. In contrast, the relatively small numbers of students in elite systems in the past (e) allowed for closer relationships between students and their teachers, with formative feedback shaping the minds, academic skills, and even the characters of students.

* demographic: 인구집단

41. 윗글의 제목으로 가장 적절한 것은?

① Is It Possible to Teach Without Assessment?
② Elite vs. Public: A History of Modern Class Society
③ Mass Higher Education and Its Reality in Assessment
④ Impacts of Mass Higher Education on Teachers' Status
⑤ Mass Higher Education Leads to Economic Development

42. 밑줄 친 (a)~(e) 중에서 문맥상 낱말의 쓰임이 적절하지 <u>않은</u> 것은? [3점]

① (a)   ② (b)   ③ (c)   ④ (d)   ⑤ (e)

[43~45] 다음 글을 읽고, 물음에 답하시오.

(A)

Once upon a time in the Iranian city of Shiraz, there lived the famous poet Sheikh Saadi. Like most other poets and philosophers, he led a very simple life. A rich merchant of Shiraz was preparing for his daughter's wedding and invited (a) him along with a lot of big businessmen of the town. The poet accepted the invitation and decided to attend.

(B)

The host personally led the poet to his seat and served out chicken soup to him. After a moment, the poet suddenly dipped the corner of his coat in the soup as if he fed it. All the guests were now staring at (b) him in surprise. The host said, "Sir, what are you doing?" The poet very calmly replied, "Now that I have put on expensive clothes, I see a world of difference here. All that I can say now is that this feast is meant for my clothes, not for me."

(C)

Seeing all this, the poet quietly left the party and went to a shop where he could rent clothes. There he chose a richly decorated coat, which made him look like a new person. With this coat, he entered the party and this time was welcomed with open arms. The host embraced him as (c) he would do to an old friend and complimented him on the clothes he was wearing. The poet did not say a word and allowed the host to lead (d) him to the dining room.

(D)

On the day of the wedding, the rich merchant, the host of the wedding, was receiving the guests at the gate. Many rich people of the town attended the wedding. They had come out in their best clothes. The poet wore simple clothes which were neither grand nor expensive. He waited for someone to approach him but no one gave (e) him as much as even a second glance. Even the host did not greet him and looked away.

43. 주어진 글 (A)에 이어질 내용을 순서에 맞게 배열한 것으로 가장 적절한 것은?

① (B) − (D) − (C)   ② (C) − (B) − (D)
③ (C) − (D) − (B)   ④ (D) − (B) − (C)
⑤ (D) − (C) − (B)

44. 밑줄 친 (a)~(e) 중에서 가리키는 대상이 나머지 넷과 <u>다른</u> 것은?

① (a)   ② (b)   ③ (c)   ④ (d)   ⑤ (e)

45. 윗글에 관한 내용으로 적절하지 <u>않은</u> 것은?

① 시인은 상인의 초대를 받아들였다.
② 상인은 시인의 외투 자락을 수프에 담갔다.
③ 시인은 옷을 빌릴 수 있는 가게로 갔다.
④ 결혼식 날 상인은 입구에서 손님을 맞이했다.
⑤ 마을의 많은 부유한 사람들이 결혼식에 참석했다.

---

* 확인 사항

○ 답안지의 해당란에 필요한 내용을 정확히 기입(표기)했는지 확인하시오.

※ QR 코드를 스캔하시면 듣기 방송이 나옵니다. 듣기 방송을 들으며 다음 빈칸을 채우시오. ● 제한 시간 : 25분

01

다음을 듣고, 여자가 하는 말의 목적으로 가장 적절한 것을 고르시오.

W : Hello! I'm Olivia Parker from Pineview City Subway. I have an announcement for this Saturday's fireworks festival. Many people ✿ _____ _____ ___ _____ and enjoy the festival late into the night. For smooth transportation and visitor safety, we're extending the operational hours of the subway on the day of the festival. The subway will run for an extra two hours after _____ _____ _____ _____ from the festival area stations. For a comfortable and safe journey from the event, we encourage you to take advantage of our extended subway services. We hope you enjoy this ✿ _____ _____ _____ _____. Thank you!

02

대화를 듣고, 남자의 의견으로 가장 적절한 것을 고르시오.

M : Hi, Emma. What's up? You look tired.

W : Hey, David. I always feel tired. Even though I sleep many hours, I guess I don't get any good sleep.

M : That's too bad. Is there anything you do _____ _____ ____ ___ _____?

W : I usually read webtoons on my smartphone for a few hours.

M : Ah, that's the problem. Having too much screen time right before bed is not good.

W : Really? But I'm so ✿ _____ ___ _____ time on my phone at night!

M : Long exposure to the screen light can make your brain stay awake.

W : I never knew using smartphones had a negative impact on sleep.

M : Reducing your smartphone use before going to bed ✿ _____ _____ _____ _____ of your sleep.

W : Okay, I can give it a try.

03

다음을 듣고, 남자가 하는 말의 요지로 가장 적절한 것을 고르시오.

M : Hello, listeners! Welcome to your *Daily Tips*. Today, I'll tell you a helpful way to relieve your stress. Recent research shows that having ✿ _____ _____ _____ ____ your job can significantly reduce stress. For example, if you work in IT, consider exploring activities that are far from the digital field. Playing the guitar might be a good option rather than playing computer games. Let's enjoy hobbies that are ✿ _____ _____ _____! That'll be the best way to get a refreshing break. Remember, a well-chosen hobby can ____ __ _____ _____ for stress relief. Tune in tomorrow for more helpful daily tips!

04

대화를 듣고, 그림에서 대화의 내용과 일치하지 <u>않는</u> 것을 고르시오.

M : Hey, Amy. Here is the new recording studio for our band. How do you like it?

W : Wow, these two speakers are impressive!

M : Yes, they are. The ✿ _____ _____ ___ _____.

W : Also, the long desk between the speakers looks great.

M : Yeah. And on the desk, there is a microphone. We can use it to give recording directions.

W : Nice. Oh, this chair looks comfortable. It could be _____ _____ _____ _____.

M : Agreed. And the rug under the chair gives the room a cozy feeling, doesn't it?

W : Yes, and I like the flower patterns on the rug.

M : I like it, too. How about the poster on the wall?

W : It's cool. This studio feels ✿ _____ _____ _____ _____ comes alive!

M : I'm glad you like this place.

W : Absolutely. I can't wait to start recording here.

05

대화를 듣고, 여자가 할 일로 가장 적절한 것을 고르시오.

W : Tony, I'm so excited for our Go-Green event!

M : Me too. The event is almost here. Why don't we ✿ ____ _____ _____ _____ together?

W : Okay. I think the exhibition booths are very important for our event. How are they going?

M : Almost ready. I'm working on the booth setup this afternoon. What about the welcome gifts?

W : I've already prepared ✿ _____ _____ _____.

M : Perfect! What's next?

W : We need to confirm the list of guests for the ceremony.

M : I double-checked the list. But I haven't sent the online invitation cards, yet.

W : No problem. I'll deal with it right away. How about the food and drinks?

M : I've scheduled food and drink services and I'll _____ _____ _____ with reusable dishes.

W : Nice! I'm confident our event will be a great success.

Dictation 07

06

대화를 듣고, 남자가 지불할 금액을 고르시오. [3점]

W : Welcome to the Riverside Camping store. How can I help you?
M : I'm looking for __ _____ _____ for my family. Can you recommend one?
W : Sure. How about this one? It's light and easy to fold, so it's ✿ _____ _____ _____.
M : It looks good. How much is it?
W : It comes in two sizes. The small one is 30 dollars and the large one is 50 dollars.
M : I'll buy the large one. Are there folding chairs, too?
W : Yep. These folding chairs might go well with the table. They're 10 dollars each.
M : Sounds good. I'll buy four of those chairs.
W : Okay. That's one large camping table and four chairs.
M : That's right. Can I use ✿ _____ _____ _____ _____?
W : Of course. You can get a 10% discount on the total price.
M : Perfect. Here's my credit card.

07

대화를 듣고, 여자가 이번 주말에 등산을 갈 수 없는 이유를 고르시오.

W : Lately, the weather has been lovely. This is a perfect time for climbing.
M : Indeed. Oh, would you like to ____ _____ _____ together?
W : Sounds awesome. I have all the climbing equipment.
M : Great. How about this upcoming weekend? I'll find a nice mountain for us.
W : Hold on, this weekend? I don't think I can make it then.
M : Really? All school tests are finally done, so I thought this weekend would be good for us.
W : Sorry, but I have ✿ _____ _____ ____ _____ this weekend.
M : Do you have a part-time job?
W : No. Actually, I need to practice dancing for the entire weekend.
M : Ah, for the dance ✿ _____ _____ _____ before?
W : Yes. Surprisingly, I made it through the first round, and it's the finals next Monday.
M : That's fantastic! I wish you the best of luck.

08

대화를 듣고, Lakestate Apartment Yoga Program에 관해 언급되지 않은 것을 고르시오.

W : Grandpa, take a look at this. It's a Lakestate Apartment Yoga Program poster.
M : Wow, a new ✿ _____ _____ _____ _____. I've always wanted to join a yoga program.
W : I know, and this one is only for those aged 60 and above.
M : That's perfect for me. [Pause] Oh, it says it's held at 8 a.m. every Tuesday and Friday.
W : It'll be a good time for you. You're an early bird.
M : Yes, I am. How do I register?
W : You just need to ✿ _____ _____ _____ _____ form at the apartment fitness center.
M : Okay, I think I'll go right now.
W : Good. But don't forget to _____ _____ ____ _____ with you.
M : Oh, do I need that for the registration?
W : Yes. It says that on the poster. Would you like me to go with you?
M : That would be lovely.

09

Global Food Market에 관한 다음 내용을 듣고, 일치하지 않는 것을 고르시오.

W : Good morning! This is Allison from the student council. I'm ✿ _____ ___ _____ the Global Food Market right here at Westhill High School. Get ready for a delicious journey around the world in the school parking lot. Our Global Food Market will take place for two days, on September 25th and 26th. You can enjoy food from eight different countries, including Mexico and France. And there's no need ___ _____ _____ _____. Every single dish is only five dollars. Wait! You don't eat meat? No problem! We also ✿ _____ _____ _____ _____. So, join us at the Global Food Market. It's not just about food, but a celebration of culture and diversity. Don't miss this chance to taste the world!

10

다음 표를 보면서 대화를 듣고, 남자가 주문할 디지털 텀블러를 고르시오.

W : Honey, what are you looking at?
M : I'm looking at digital tumblers. They show the temperature on an LED screen. Would you like to help me choose one?
W : Sure, let me see. [Pause] The price differs by model.
M : Hmm, I don't want to ✿ _____ _____ _____ 60 dollars.
W : That sounds reasonable. Look, there are various sizes to choose from.
M : Less than 400ml would be too small for me.
W : Alright. Oh, there's a new function. Do you need ✿ _____ _____ _____ _____? It'll show you how much water you drink in a day.
M : That sounds smart. I'd love to have it. Then, I have just two options left.
W : What color do you like? You have too many black items and they're boring.
M : Okay. I'll ____ _____ _____ that's not black. Then, I'll order this one.
W : Great idea!

11
대화를 듣고, 여자의 마지막 말에 대한 남자의 응답으로 가장 적절한 것을 고르시오.

W : I _____ __ _____ these days.

M : That's too bad. It's a good idea to ✪ _____ _____ _____ in your room.

W : Oh, how does that relate to a cold?

12
대화를 듣고, 남자의 마지막 말에 대한 여자의 응답으로 가장 적절한 것을 고르시오.

M : Mom, the bookshelf in my room is full of books. There's ____ _____ _____ new ones.

W : Well, how about ✪ _____ _____ ____ _____ you don't read anymore?

M : But _____ ___ _____ _____ in too good condition to throw away.

13
대화를 듣고, 여자의 마지막 말에 대한 남자의 응답으로 가장 적절한 것을 고르시오.　　　　　[3점]

W : Hey, Peter. How's your group project going?

M : Hello, Ms. Adams. It's my first time as a leader, so it's quite challenging.

W : I thought your group _____ _____ _____ _____.

M : Yes. We're all motivated and working hard, but progress is slow.

W : Well, what are you all working on at this moment?

M : Everyone is focusing on gathering data as much as possible.

W : Hmm, did you ✪ _____ _____ _____ to each member?

M : Oh, we haven't discussed it yet. We're not exactly sure who does what.

W : That's crucial. Otherwise, it can ✪ _____ ___ _____ _____ in a group project.

M : That makes sense. That's why our progress is not that fast.

W : Then, as the leader, what do you think you should do now?

14
대화를 듣고, 남자의 마지막 말에 대한 여자의 응답으로 가장 적절한 것을 고르시오.　　　　　[3점]

M : Hey, Emily! You're looking great these days.

W : Thanks, Isaac. I've been trying hard to get in better shape.

M : Good for you! I'm trying to get fit, too. But it's tough.

W : Haven't you been ✪ _____ _____ __ ____ lately?

M : Yeah, but I don't see a big difference. What's your secret?

W : Well, I started being careful _____ _____ __ _____.

M : You mean like not eating right before bed?

W : Kind of. I noticed I was eating a lot at night. So now I don't eat after 7 p.m.

M : Hmm... I don't know if that's ✪ _____ ___ _____ _____ in better shape.

15
다음 상황 설명을 듣고, Julia가 Sophie에게 할 말로 가장 적절한 것을 고르시오.

M : Julia is a college student, ✪ _____ _____. Recently, she ordered a new computer desk. Upon receiving the desk, she realized that the desk was a DIY product. It means she needs to put the pieces together to build the desk. However, it was ✪ _____ ___ _____ by herself. Julia knows that Sophie, her best friend, ___ _____ ___ _____ DIY furniture and enjoys it. So, Julia wants to ask Sophie to help her with the desk. In this situation, what would Julia most likely say to Sophie?

16~17
다음을 듣고, 물음에 답하시오.

W : Hello, *Family-Life* subscribers! These days, many people are looking for clothes made ✪ _____ _____ _____ for their family. Today, I'd like to introduce some tips for _____ ___ _____ _____ natural material clothes. First, for cotton, like 100% cotton t-shirts, you should hand-wash in cool water to avoid shrinking or wrinkling. Second, silk should be ✪ _____ _____ _____ _____ _____ to keep its shape and color. Also, when you dry silk clothes such as blouses, avoid direct sunlight and dry them in the shade. Third, linen is a sensitive material to wash. For example, to wash linen jackets, use vinegar instead of fabric softener. Lastly, for wool, the best way is to wash as little as possible. If you have to wash wool sweaters, use special wool washing soap. Apply these tips so you can keep and enjoy natural clothes for a longer time!

18

001 □ express ⓥ 표현하다
002 □ concern ⓥ 걱정
003 □ recent ⓐ 최근의
004 □ station ⓝ 역
005 □ traditional ⓐ 전통의, 전통적인
006 □ ticket office 매표소
007 □ staff ⓝ 직원
008 □ replace ⓥ 대신하다
009 □ vending machine 자동판매기
010 □ unfamiliar ⓐ 익숙하지 않은
011 □ experience ⓥ 경험하다
012 □ railway ⓝ 철도
013 □ rely ⓥ 의지하다
014 □ assistance ⓝ 도움
015 □ reopen ⓥ 다시 열다
016 □ position ⓝ 자리, 제자리
017 □ regain ⓥ 되찾다, 회복하다
018 □ prompt ⓐ 즉각적인, 지체 없는
019 □ resolution ⓝ 해결책

19

020 □ actor ⓝ 배우
021 □ stage ⓝ 무대
022 □ focus ⓥ 집중하다
023 □ acting ⓝ (연극·영화에서의) 연기
024 □ corner ⓝ 구석, 모서리, 모퉁이
025 □ immediately ⓐⓓ 즉시
026 □ approach ⓥ 접근하다
027 □ silently ⓐⓓ 아무 말 없이, 잠자코, 조용히
028 □ glance ⓥ 흘긋 보다
029 □ breathe ⓥ 호흡하다, 숨을 쉬다
030 □ appear ⓥ 나타나다
031 □ swiftly ⓐⓓ 신속히, 빨리
032 □ kneel ⓥ 무릎을 꿇다
033 □ chest ⓝ 가슴, 흉부
034 □ announce ⓥ 알리다
035 □ calm ⓐ 침착한, 차분한
036 □ wipe ⓥ 닦다
037 □ successfully ⓐⓓ 성공적으로
038 □ revive ⓥ 소생하다

20

039 □ gifted ⓐ 재능이 있는
040 □ be aware of 알고 있다
041 □ trap ⓝ 함정
042 □ proud ⓐ 자랑스러워하는, 자랑스러운
043 □ nonstop ⓐⓓ 중지 없이, 중단 없이
044 □ remarkable ⓐ 눈에 띄는
045 □ behavior ⓝ 행동, 행위, 처신
046 □ stressful ⓐ 스트레스가 많은
047 □ extremely ⓐⓓ 매우, 몹시
048 □ limit ⓥ 한정하다
049 □ brag ⓥ 자랑하다
050 □ expectation ⓝ 기대
051 □ false ⓐ 잘못된, 거짓된
052 □ incredible ⓐ 놀라운
053 □ achievement ⓝ 달성
054 □ perfectionist ⓝ 완벽주의자

21

055 □ valuable ⓐ 가치 있는

056 □ technique ⓝ 기술
057 □ helplessness ⓝ 무력감
058 □ depression ⓝ 우울증
059 □ predominantly ⓐⓓ 지배적인
060 □ resolve ⓥ 해결하다
061 □ struggle ⓥ 발버둥 치다, 몸부림치다, 싸우다
062 □ negative ⓐ 부정적인
063 □ state ⓝ 상태
064 □ positive ⓐ 긍정적인
065 □ weak ⓐ 약한, 힘이 없는
066 □ vibration ⓝ 진동
067 □ beneficial ⓐ 혜택의
068 □ consciousness ⓝ 의식
069 □ latent ⓐ 잠재적인

22

070 □ emotion ⓝ 감정
071 □ contribute ⓥ 기여하다
072 □ survival ⓝ 생존
073 □ species ⓝ 종(種)
074 □ avoid ⓥ 피하다
075 □ danger ⓝ 위험
076 □ scare off 겁을 줘 쫓아내다
077 □ threat ⓝ 협박, 위협
078 □ bond ⓥ 유대감을 형성하다
079 □ evolutionary ⓐ 진화의, 진화적인
080 □ perspective ⓝ 관점, 시각
081 □ trigger ⓥ 야기하다
082 □ direct ⓥ 지시하다
083 □ fear ⓝ 공포, 두려움, 무서움
084 □ attentive ⓐ 주의 깊은
085 □ perceptual ⓐ 지각의
086 □ threatening ⓐ 위협적인
087 □ stimulus ⓝ 자극(pl. stimuli)
088 □ regardless ⓐⓓ 상관하지 않고
089 □ specific ⓐ 특정한
090 □ activate ⓥ 활성화시키다
091 □ environment ⓝ 환경
092 □ adapt ⓥ 적응하다
093 □ evolve ⓥ 진화하다

23

094 □ improve ⓥ 향상시키다
095 □ accessibility ⓝ 접근, 접근하기 쉬움
096 □ workplace ⓝ 직장, 업무 현장
097 □ worker ⓝ 노동자
098 □ typically ⓐⓓ 보통, 일반적으로
099 □ disadvantage ⓝ 불리한 점
100 □ inclusiveness ⓝ 포괄성
101 □ assistive ⓐ 도와주는
102 □ device ⓝ 기기
103 □ aid ⓥ 돕다
104 □ widespread ⓐ 광범위한, 널리 퍼진
105 □ recognition ⓝ 알아봄, 인식
106 □ dysarthric ⓐ 구음 장애의
107 □ deaf ⓐ 청각 장애가 있는
108 □ facilitate ⓥ 용이하게 하다, 촉진하다
109 □ colleague ⓝ 동료
110 □ necessary ⓐ 필요한
111 □ enhance ⓥ 향상시키다
112 □ capability ⓝ 능력, 역량
113 □ wage ⓝ 임금

114 □ prospect ⓝ 전망
115 □ translate ⓥ 번역하다
116 □ development ⓝ 발달
117 □ instantly ⓐⓓ 즉각, 즉시
118 □ individual ⓝ 개인
119 □ domain ⓝ 영역, 분야

24

120 □ whale ⓝ 고래
121 □ efficient ⓐ 효율적인
122 □ carbon ⓝ 탄소
123 □ storage ⓝ 저장
124 □ sequester ⓥ 격리하다
125 □ average ⓐ 평균의
126 □ carbon dioxide 이산화탄소
127 □ atmosphere ⓝ 대기
128 □ comparison ⓝ 대조
129 □ climate ⓝ 기후
130 □ equivalent ⓐ 상응하는, 상당하는
131 □ fertilize ⓥ 비옥하게 하다
132 □ release ⓥ 풀어 주다, 놓아 주다, 방출하다
133 □ increase ⓥ 증가하다
134 □ phytoplankton ⓝ 식물성 플랑크톤
135 □ population ⓝ 개체군, 개체 수
136 □ ecosystem ⓝ 생태계
137 □ economist ⓝ 경제학자
138 □ estimate ⓥ 추산하다
139 □ preindustrial ⓐ 산업화 이전의, 산업 혁명 전의
140 □ solution ⓝ 해결책
141 □ restoration ⓝ 복원, 회복

25

142 □ per capita 1인당
143 □ emission ⓝ 배출량
144 □ coal ⓝ 석탄
145 □ rank ⓥ 순위에 들다
146 □ major ⓐ 주요한
147 □ source ⓝ 원천

26

148 □ mathematician ⓝ 수학자
149 □ physicist ⓝ 물리학자
150 □ childhood ⓝ 어린 시절
151 □ support ⓝ 지원
152 □ scientific ⓐ 과학의, 과학적인
153 □ receive ⓥ 받다
154 □ submit ⓥ 제출하다
155 □ paper ⓝ 논문
156 □ nature ⓝ 본질
157 □ publish ⓥ 출간하다
158 □ explain ⓥ 설명하다
159 □ relativity ⓝ 상대성 이론
160 □ significant ⓐ 중요한, 특별한 의미가 있는
161 □ recognize ⓥ 인정하다
162 □ enlightenment ⓝ (18세기의) 계몽주의 시대

27

163 □ inventor ⓝ 발명가
164 □ competition ⓝ 대회
165 □ category ⓝ 분류

166 □ remote ⓐ 원격의
167 □ registration ⓝ 등록
168 □ participant ⓝ 참여자

28

169 □ stamp ⓝ 도장
170 □ annual ⓐ 연간의
171 □ participate ⓥ 참여하다
172 □ event ⓝ 행사
173 □ join ⓥ 참여하다
174 □ exhibition ⓝ 전시회
175 □ collection ⓝ 수집품
176 □ district ⓝ 구역
177 □ spot ⓝ (특정한) 곳
178 □ umbrella ⓝ 우산, 양산

29

179 □ organizational ⓐ 구조적인
180 □ viewpoint ⓝ 시각
181 □ fascinate ⓥ 멋지다
182 □ organization ⓝ 조직, 단체, 기구
183 □ contain ⓥ 포함하다
184 □ type ⓝ 유형, 종류
185 □ functional ⓐ 기능상의, 기능적인
186 □ operation ⓝ 경영, 운용
187 □ department ⓝ 부서
188 □ division ⓝ (조직의) 분과
189 □ inevitably ⓐⓓ 필연적으로, 부득이
190 □ biased ⓐ 편향된, 선입견이 있는
191 □ prejudiced ⓐ 편견이 있는
192 □ acquire ⓥ 얻다
193 □ conflict ⓝ 갈등
194 □ choice ⓝ 선택
195 □ mechanistic ⓐ 기계적인
196 □ organic ⓐ 유기적인
197 □ profound ⓐ 깊은
198 □ influence ⓝ 영향
199 □ vertical ⓐ 수직의
200 □ hierarchy ⓝ 계급, 계층
201 □ procedure ⓝ 절차
202 □ horizontal ⓐ 수평의, 가로의
203 □ centralize ⓥ 중앙화하다, 중앙 집권화하다

30

204 □ excellent ⓐ 훌륭한
205 □ alternative ⓝ 대체
206 □ traffic ⓝ 교통
207 □ remove ⓥ 제거하다
208 □ extensive ⓐ 넓은, 광대한
209 □ lane ⓝ 차선
210 □ pedestrian ⓝ 보행자
211 □ occasional ⓐ 가끔의
212 □ rather ⓐⓓ 꽤, 약간, 상당히
213 □ popular ⓐ 인기 있는
214 □ convert ⓥ 바꾸다
215 □ automobile ⓝ 자동차
216 □ entire ⓐ 전체의, 온
217 □ accommodate ⓥ 공간을 제공하다, 수용하다
218 □ require ⓥ 필요하다, 필요로 하다
219 □ emergency ⓝ 비상사태, 긴급, 응급
220 □ delivery ⓝ 배송

221 ☐ frequently [ad] 자주, 흔히
222 ☐ target ⓝ 목표, 대상
223 ☐ animus ⓝ 반감, 적대감
224 ☐ actually [ad] 실제로, 정말로, 실지로
225 ☐ essential ⓐ 극히 중요한, 가장 중요한
226 ☐ component ⓝ 요소, 부품
227 ☐ tightly [ad] 단단히, 꽉

31
228 ☐ composer ⓝ 작곡가
229 ☐ misunderstand ⓥ 오해하다
230 ☐ composition ⓝ 구성
231 ☐ reason ⓝ 이유, 까닭, 사유
232 ☐ initial ⓐ 초기의
233 ☐ lack ⓝ 부족, 결핍
234 ☐ acceptance ⓝ 수락
235 ☐ unfamiliarity ⓝ 잘 모름, 익숙지 않음
236 ☐ completely [ad] 완전히
237 ☐ exactly [ad] 정확히, 꼭, 틀림없이
238 ☐ effective ⓐ 유능한
239 ☐ depict ⓥ 묘사하다
240 ☐ overshadow ⓥ 그늘지게 하다, 가리다

32
241 ☐ medium ⓝ 매체
242 ☐ come along 따라오다
243 ☐ invention ⓝ 발명
244 ☐ goggle ⓝ 고글
245 ☐ differently [ad] 다르게, 같지 않게
246 ☐ absorb ⓥ 흡수하다
247 ☐ particular ⓐ 특정한
248 ☐ communicate ⓥ 의사소통하다
249 ☐ bury ⓥ 묻다
250 ☐ gently [ad] 다정하게, 부드럽게
251 ☐ guide ⓥ 이끌다
252 ☐ argue ⓥ 주장하다
253 ☐ surface ⓝ 표면
254 ☐ appearance ⓝ 외모

33
255 ☐ concept ⓝ 개념
256 ☐ vital ⓐ 필수적인
257 ☐ careful ⓐ 조심스러운
258 ☐ essentialism ⓝ 본질주의
259 ☐ encourage ⓥ 부추기다
260 ☐ present ⓐ 있는, 존재하는
261 ☐ proverb ⓝ 속담
262 ☐ statement ⓝ 표현, 진술
263 ☐ sum up 요약하다
264 ☐ essence ⓝ 본질, 정수, 진수
265 ☐ fruitlessly [ad] 득 없이
266 ☐ hypothesis ⓝ 가설(*pl.* hypotheses)
267 ☐ luminiferous ⓐ 빛을 내는, 발광성의
268 ☐ mysterious ⓐ 신비한, 불가사의한
269 ☐ substance ⓝ 물질
270 ☐ medium ⓝ 도구
271 ☐ experiment ⓥ 실험하다
272 ☐ evidence ⓝ 증거
273 ☐ exist ⓥ 존재하다

34
274 ☐ attention ⓝ 관심

275 ☐ instrument ⓝ 도구
276 ☐ achieve ⓥ 달성하다
277 ☐ celebrity ⓝ 유명인
278 ☐ content ⓝ 콘텐츠
279 ☐ creator ⓝ 창작자
280 ☐ desire ⓥ 바라다, 원하다
281 ☐ ordinary ⓐ 평범한, 보통의, 일상적인
282 ☐ criticize ⓥ 비판하다
283 ☐ ability ⓝ 재능, 능력
284 ☐ highlight ⓥ 강조하다
285 ☐ barrier ⓝ 장벽
286 ☐ phenomenon ⓝ 현상
287 ☐ symbolize ⓥ 상징화하다
288 ☐ metaphor ⓝ 은유, 비유
289 ☐ characterize ⓥ 특징이 되다, 특징짓다
290 ☐ hierarchical ⓐ 계층제의, 계층에 따른
291 ☐ distance ⓝ 거리
292 ☐ attract attention 이목을 끌다
293 ☐ frequent ⓐ 잦은, 빈번한
294 ☐ interaction ⓝ 상호 작용
295 ☐ fame ⓝ 명성
296 ☐ sphere ⓝ 영역
297 ☐ relatively [ad] 상대적으로
298 ☐ subscriber ⓝ 구독자

35
299 ☐ illusion ⓝ 환각
300 ☐ cram ⓥ 벼락공부를 하다
301 ☐ strategy ⓝ 전략
302 ☐ differentiate ⓥ 차별화하다
303 ☐ section ⓝ 부분
304 ☐ memory ⓝ 기억
305 ☐ information ⓝ 정보
306 ☐ mind ⓝ 생각
307 ☐ conscious ⓐ 의식적인
308 ☐ disappear ⓥ 사라지다
309 ☐ effect ⓝ 효과
310 ☐ enormous ⓐ 막대한, 거대한
311 ☐ knowledge ⓝ 정보
312 ☐ vanish ⓥ 사라지다
313 ☐ performance ⓝ 실적, 성과

36
314 ☐ discovery ⓝ 발견
315 ☐ neuron ⓝ 뉴런
316 ☐ profoundly [ad] 풍부하게
317 ☐ fundamental ⓐ 기본적인
318 ☐ capacity ⓝ 능력
319 ☐ observation ⓝ 관찰
320 ☐ tongue ⓝ 혀
321 ☐ stick out ~을 내밀다
322 ☐ each time 언제나, 매번
323 ☐ newborn ⓝ 신생아
324 ☐ babble ⓥ 옹알이하다
325 ☐ observe ⓥ 관찰하다
326 ☐ imitation ⓝ 모방
327 ☐ vacuum cleaner 진공청소기
328 ☐ restrict ⓥ 제한하다
329 ☐ trial and error 시행착오

37
330 ☐ record ⓥ 녹음하다

331 ☐ pathway ⓝ 길
332 ☐ perceive ⓥ 인식하다
333 ☐ route ⓝ 경로, 길
334 ☐ external ⓐ 외부의
335 ☐ vocal cord ⓝ 성대
336 ☐ vibrate ⓥ 진동하다
337 ☐ internal ⓐ 내부의
338 ☐ path ⓝ 길, 경로
339 ☐ conduct ⓥ (열·전기·소리 등을) 전도하다
340 ☐ stimulate ⓥ 자극하다
341 ☐ directly [ad] 직접으로
342 ☐ frequency ⓝ 주파수
343 ☐ fairly [ad] 상당히, 꽤

38
344 ☐ biologist ⓝ 생물학자
345 ☐ similarity ⓝ 유사성
346 ☐ analogous ⓐ 유사한
347 ☐ arise ⓥ 생기다
348 ☐ branch ⓝ 나뭇가지
349 ☐ organ ⓝ 장기
350 ☐ independently [ad] 독립적으로
351 ☐ evolution ⓝ 진화
352 ☐ homologous ⓐ 상동의
353 ☐ trait ⓝ 특성
354 ☐ in contrast 그에 반해서, 그와 대조적으로
355 ☐ descend ⓥ 내려오다
356 ☐ common ⓐ 공통의
357 ☐ ancestor ⓝ 조상
358 ☐ hence [ad] 그러므로, 따라서
359 ☐ structure ⓝ 구조
360 ☐ indicate ⓥ 가리키다
361 ☐ modification ⓝ 변형
362 ☐ forelimb ⓝ (척추동물의) 앞다리
363 ☐ mammals ⓝ 포유류

39
364 ☐ abundance ⓝ 넘칠 만큼 많음, 다량
365 ☐ dissolved ⓐ 용해된
366 ☐ oxygen ⓝ 산소
367 ☐ establish ⓥ 확립하다, 수립하다
368 ☐ polar ⓐ 극지의
369 ☐ tropical ⓐ 열대 지방의, 열대의
370 ☐ poorly [ad] 부족하게
371 ☐ populate ⓥ 살다, 거주하다
372 ☐ creature ⓝ 생물
373 ☐ temperature ⓝ 온도
374 ☐ marine ⓐ 해양의
375 ☐ self-evident ⓐ 분명한
376 ☐ decrease ⓥ 감소하다
377 ☐ potentially [ad] 잠재적으로
378 ☐ disastrous ⓐ 재앙적인
379 ☐ consequence ⓝ 결과
380 ☐ analyze ⓥ 분석하다
381 ☐ rapidly [ad] 빨리, 급속히
382 ☐ correspond ⓥ 일치하다
383 ☐ anoxic ⓐ 산소 결핍의

40
384 ☐ large ⓐ 큰
385 ☐ social ⓐ 사회의
386 ☐ captivity ⓝ 감금, 억류, 포로

387 ☐ trade ⓥ 거래하다
388 ☐ involve ⓥ 포함하다
389 ☐ cage ⓝ 우리
390 ☐ cucumber ⓝ 오이
391 ☐ universally [ad] 공통적으로
392 ☐ prefer ⓥ 선호하다
393 ☐ experimenter ⓝ 실험자
394 ☐ effort ⓝ 노력
395 ☐ situation ⓝ 상황
396 ☐ unfair ⓐ 부당한
397 ☐ abandon ⓥ 버리다
398 ☐ displeasure ⓝ 불쾌감

41~42
399 ☐ elite ⓝ 엘리트
400 ☐ mass ⓝ 대량
401 ☐ participation ⓝ 참가
402 ☐ occur ⓥ 발생하다
403 ☐ education ⓝ 교육
404 ☐ population ⓝ 인구
405 ☐ diverse ⓐ 다양한
406 ☐ demographic ⓐ 인구학의
407 ☐ allow ⓥ 허락하다
408 ☐ relationship ⓝ 관계
409 ☐ formative ⓐ 형태적인
410 ☐ feedback ⓝ 평가

43~45
411 ☐ famous ⓐ 유명한
412 ☐ poet ⓝ 시인
413 ☐ philosopher ⓝ 철학가
414 ☐ prepare ⓥ 준비하다
415 ☐ invite ⓥ 초대하다
416 ☐ businessmen ⓝ 사업가
417 ☐ accept ⓥ 받아들이다
418 ☐ invitation ⓝ 초대장
419 ☐ attend ⓥ 참석하다

07회

● 채점 : 맞은 개수 _____ / 80

TEST A-B 각 단어의 뜻을 [A] 영어는 우리말로, [B] 우리말은 영어로 쓰시오.

A	English	Korean		B	Korean	English
01	express			01	기후	
02	concern			02	배출량	
03	regain			03	주요한	
04	approach			04	원천	
05	wipe			05	물리학자	
06	revive			06	지원	
07	remarkable			07	제출하다	
08	incredible			08	발명가	
09	achievement			09	분류	
10	predominantly			10	참여자	
11	state			11	연간의	
12	consciousness			12	참여하다	
13	contribute			13	전시회	
14	perspective			14	시각	
15	fear			15	기능상의, 기능적인	
16	assistive			16	얻다	
17	device			17	대체	
18	enhance			18	꽤, 약간, 상당히	
19	efficient			19	요소, 부품	
20	estimate			20	초기의	

▶ A-D 정답 : 해설편 097쪽

TEST C-D 각 단어의 뜻을 골라 기호를 쓰시오.

C	English			Korean	D	Korean			English
01	reason	( )	ⓐ 상호작용		01	공통의	( )	ⓐ involve
02	depict	( )	ⓑ 모방		02	내려오다	( )	ⓑ descend
03	particular	( )	ⓒ 전략		03	생기다	( )	ⓒ universally
04	communicate	( )	ⓓ 상징화되다		04	일치하다	( )	ⓓ establish
05	argue	( )	ⓔ 부분		05	확립하다, 수립하다	( )	ⓔ formative
06	vital	( )	ⓕ 능력		06	온도	( )	ⓕ trade
07	encourage	( )	ⓖ 자극하다		07	다양한	( )	ⓖ mass
08	exist	( )	ⓗ 묘사하다		08	발생하다	( )	ⓗ arise
09	symbolize	( )	ⓘ 이유, 까닭, 사유		09	대량	( )	ⓘ temperature
10	phenomenon	( )	ⓙ 현상		10	받아들이다	( )	ⓙ situation
11	interaction	( )	ⓚ 부추기다		11	초대하다	( )	ⓚ effort
12	conscious	( )	ⓛ 관찰		12	형태적인	( )	ⓛ occur
13	strategy	( )	ⓜ 필수적인		13	거래하다	( )	ⓜ diverse
14	section	( )	ⓝ 주장하다		14	상황	( )	ⓝ displeasure
15	observation	( )	ⓞ 존재하다		15	버리다	( )	ⓞ unfair
16	capacity	( )	ⓟ 내부의		16	불쾌감	( )	ⓟ invite
17	imitation	( )	ⓠ 의사소통하다		17	노력	( )	ⓠ accept
18	pathway	( )	ⓡ 의식적인		18	부당한	( )	ⓡ abandon
19	internal	( )	ⓢ 길		19	포함하다	( )	ⓢ common
20	stimulate	( )	ⓣ 특정한		20	공통적으로	( )	ⓣ correspond

영어 영역

● 문항수 45개 | 배점 100점 | 제한 시간 70분　　　　　● 점수 표시가 없는 문항은 모두 2점

1번부터 17번까지는 듣고 답하는 문제입니다. 1번부터 15번까지는 한 번만 들려주고, 16번부터 17번까지는 두 번 들려줍니다. 방송을 잘 듣고 답을 하시기 바랍니다.

1. 다음을 듣고, 남자가 하는 말의 목적으로 가장 적절한 것을 고르시오.
① 강당의 천장 수리 기간을 공지하려고
② 콘서트 관람 규칙 준수를 요청하려고
③ 학교 축제에서 공연할 동아리를 모집하려고
④ 폭우에 대비한 교실 시설 관리를 당부하려고
⑤ 학교 록 밴드 공연의 장소 변경을 안내하려고

2. 대화를 듣고, 여자의 의견으로 가장 적절한 것을 고르시오.
① 달리기를 할 때 적합한 신발을 신어야 한다.
② 운동을 한 후에 충분한 물을 섭취해야 한다.
③ 야외 활동 전에 일기예보를 확인하는 것이 좋다.
④ 달리기 전 스트레칭은 통증과 부상을 예방해 준다.
⑤ 초보자의 경우 달리는 거리를 점진적으로 늘려야 한다.

3. 대화를 듣고, 두 사람의 관계를 가장 잘 나타낸 것을 고르시오.
① 관객 – 영화감독　　　　② 연극 배우 – 시나리오 작가
③ 잡지 기자 – 의상 디자이너　④ 토크쇼 진행자 – 영화 평론가
⑤ 배우 지망생 – 연기 학원 강사

4. 대화를 듣고, 그림에서 대화의 내용과 일치하지 않는 것을 고르시오.

5. 대화를 듣고, 여자가 할 일로 가장 적절한 것을 고르시오.
① 관객용 의자 배치하기　　② 마이크 음향 점검하기
③ 공연 포스터 붙이기　　　④ 무대 조명 설치하기
⑤ 배터리 구매하기

6. 대화를 듣고, 남자가 지불할 금액을 고르시오. [3점]
① $37　　② $45　　③ $55　　④ $60　　⑤ $80

7. 대화를 듣고, 여자가 스키 여행을 갈 수 없는 이유를 고르시오.
① 카페에서 일해야 해서
② 숙소를 예약하지 못해서
③ 역사 시험 공부를 해야 해서
④ 수술받은 고양이를 돌봐야 해서
⑤ 캐나다에 사는 친척을 방문해야 해서

8. 대화를 듣고, Street Photography Contest에 관해 언급되지 않은 것을 고르시오.
① 참가 대상　　② 주제　　③ 심사 기준
④ 제출 마감일　　⑤ 우승 상품

9. Twin Stars Chocolate Day에 관한 다음 내용을 듣고, 일치하지 않는 것을 고르시오.
① 11월 12일 오후에 열린다.
② 초콜릿의 역사에 관한 강의가 진행된다.
③ 초콜릿 5개를 만든다.
④ 사전 등록 없이 참가할 수 있다.
⑤ 등록비에 재료비가 포함된다.

10. 다음 표를 보면서 대화를 듣고, 두 사람이 주문할 실내 사이클링 자전거를 고르시오.

Indoor Cycling Bikes

	Model	Price	Color	Foldable	Customer Rating
①	A	$100	White	×	★★★★
②	B	$150	Black	×	★★★
③	C	$190	Black	○	★★★★
④	D	$250	Black	○	★★★★★
⑤	E	$320	White	×	★★★★★

11. 대화를 듣고, 여자의 마지막 말에 대한 남자의 응답으로 가장 적절한 것을 고르시오.
① Sure. I'll send you a link to the website.
② It would look better in a different color.
③ Sorry. I forgot to bring your sweater.
④ You need your receipt to return it.
⑤ My brother bought it on sale, too.

12. 대화를 듣고, 남자의 마지막 말에 대한 여자의 응답으로 가장 적절한 것을 고르시오.
① Let's take the leftovers home.
② I prefer fried chicken over pizza.
③ I don't want to go out for lunch today.
④ I'll call the restaurant and check our order.
⑤ The letter was delivered to the wrong address.

13. 대화를 듣고, 여자의 마지막 말에 대한 남자의 응답으로 가장 적절한 것을 고르시오.

Man: _____

① You're right. I won't skip meals anymore.
② Thank you for the lunch you prepared for me.
③ You need to check when the cafeteria is open.
④ Trust me. I can teach you good table manners.
⑤ No problem. We'll finish the science project on time.

14. 대화를 듣고, 남자의 마지막 말에 대한 여자의 응답으로 가장 적절한 것을 고르시오. [3점]

Woman: _____

① No. It isn't difficult for me to learn Spanish.
② I'm glad you finally passed the vocabulary test.
③ Exactly. Learning a language starts with repetition.
④ It's very helpful to use a dictionary while writing.
⑤ You should turn in your homework by this afternoon.

15. 다음 상황 설명을 듣고, Brian이 Melissa에게 할 말로 가장 적절한 것을 고르시오. [3점]

Brian: _____

① Let's clean the classroom after art class.
② Did you remove the stickers from the board?
③ Please turn off the heater when you leave the room.
④ When is the final date to sign up for the design class?
⑤ Will you design stickers that encourage energy saving?

[16~17] 다음을 듣고, 물음에 답하시오.

16. 남자가 하는 말의 주제로 가장 적절한 것은?

① advantages of renting houses in cities
② reasons tourists prefer visiting old cities
③ ways cities deal with overtourism problems
④ correlation between cities' sizes and overtourism
⑤ how cities face their aging transportation systems

17. 언급된 도시가 <u>아닌</u> 것은?

① Barcelona　　② Amsterdam　　③ London
④ Venice　　⑤ Paris

이제 듣기 문제가 끝났습니다. 18번부터는 문제지의 지시에 따라 답을 하시기 바랍니다.

18. 다음 글의 목적으로 가장 적절한 것은?

Dear Professor Sanchez,

　My name is Ellis Wight, and I'm the director of the Alexandria Science Museum. We are holding a Chemistry Fair for local middle school students on Saturday, October 28. The goal of the fair is to encourage them to be interested in science through guided experiments. We are looking for college students who can help with the experiments during the event. I am contacting you to ask you to recommend some students from the chemistry department at your college who you think are qualified for this job. With their help, I'm sure the participants will have a great experience. I look forward to hearing from you soon.

Sincerely,
Ellis Wight

① 과학 박물관 내 시설 이용 제한을 안내하려고
② 화학 박람회 일정이 변경된 이유를 설명하려고
③ 중학생을 위한 화학 실험 특별 강연을 부탁하려고
④ 중학교 과학 수업용 실험 교재 집필을 의뢰하려고
⑤ 화학 박람회에서 실험을 도울 대학생 추천을 요청하려고

19. 다음 글에 나타난 'I'의 심경 변화로 가장 적절한 것은?

　Gregg and I had been rock climbing since sunrise and had had no problems. So we took a risk. "Look, the first bolt is right there. I can definitely climb out to it. Piece of cake," I persuaded Gregg, minutes before I found myself pinned. It wasn't a piece of cake. The rock was deceptively barren of handholds. I clumsily moved back and forth across the cliff face and ended up with nowhere to go...but down. The bolt that would save my life, if I could get to it, was about two feet above my reach. My arms trembled from exhaustion. I looked at Gregg. My body froze with fright from my neck down to my toes. Our rope was tied between us. If I fell, he would fall with me.

* barren of: ~이 없는

① joyful　→ bored　　　② confident → fearful
③ nervous → relieved　　④ regretful → pleased
⑤ grateful → annoyed

20. 다음 글에서 필자가 주장하는 바로 가장 적절한 것은?

　We are always teaching our children something by our words and our actions. They learn from seeing. They learn from hearing and from *overhearing*. Children share the values of their parents about the most important things in life. Our priorities and principles and our examples of good behavior can teach our children to take the high road when other roads look tempting. Remember that children do not learn the values that make up strong character simply by being *told* about them. They learn by seeing the people around them *act* on and *uphold* those values in their daily lives. Therefore show your child good examples of life by your action. In our daily lives, we can show our children that we respect others. We can show them our compassion and concern when others are suffering, and our own self-discipline, courage and honesty as we make difficult decisions.

① 자녀를 타인과 비교하는 말을 삼가야 한다.
② 자녀에게 행동으로 삶의 모범을 보여야 한다.
③ 칭찬을 통해 자녀의 바람직한 행동을 강화해야 한다.
④ 훈육을 하기 전에 자녀 스스로 생각할 시간을 주어야 한다.
⑤ 자녀가 새로운 것에 도전할 때 인내심을 가지고 지켜봐야 한다.

21. 밑줄 친 fall silently in the woods가 다음 글에서 의미하는 바로 가장 적절한 것은? [3점]

Most people have no doubt heard this question: If a tree falls in the forest and there is no one there to hear it fall, does it make a sound? The correct answer is no. Sound is more than pressure waves, and indeed there can be no sound without a hearer. And similarly, scientific communication is a two-way process. Just as a signal of any kind is useless unless it is perceived, a published scientific paper (signal) is useless unless it is both received *and* understood by its intended audience. Thus we can restate the axiom of science as follows: A scientific experiment is not complete until the results have been published *and understood*. Publication is no more than pressure waves unless the published paper is understood. Too many scientific papers fall silently in the woods.

* axiom: 자명한 이치

① fail to include the previous study
② end up being considered completely false
③ become useless because they are not published
④ focus on communication to meet public demands
⑤ are published yet readers don't understand them

22. 다음 글의 요지로 가장 적절한 것은?

We all negotiate every day, whether we realise it or not. Yet few people ever learn *how* to negotiate. Those who do usually learn the traditional, win-lose negotiating style rather than an approach that is likely to result in a win-win agreement. This old-school, adversarial approach may be useful in a one-off negotiation where you will probably not deal with that person again. However, such transactions are becoming increasingly rare, because most of us deal with the same people repeatedly — our spouses and children, our friends and colleagues, our customers and clients. In view of this, it's essential to achieve successful results for ourselves and maintain a healthy relationship with our negotiating partners at the same time. In today's interdependent world of business partnerships and long-term relationships, a win-win outcome is fast becoming the *only* acceptable result.

* adversarial: 적대적인

① 협상 상대의 단점뿐 아니라 장점을 철저히 분석해야 한다.
② 의사소통 과정에서 서로의 의도를 확인하는 것이 바람직하다.
③ 성공적인 협상을 위해 다양한 대안을 준비하는 것이 중요하다.
④ 양측에 유리한 협상을 통해 상대와 좋은 관계를 유지해야 한다.
⑤ 원만한 인간관계를 위해 상호독립성을 인정하는 것이 필요하다.

23. 다음 글의 주제로 가장 적절한 것은?

The interaction of workers from different cultural backgrounds with the host population might increase productivity due to positive externalities like knowledge spillovers. This is only an advantage up to a certain degree. When the variety of backgrounds is too large, fractionalization may cause excessive transaction costs for communication, which may lower productivity. Diversity not only impacts the labour market, but may also affect the quality of life in a location. A tolerant native population may value a multicultural city or region because of an increase in the range of available goods and services. On the other hand, diversity could be perceived as an unattractive feature if natives perceive it as a distortion of what they consider to be their national identity. They might even discriminate against other ethnic groups and they might fear that social conflicts between different foreign nationalities are imported into their own neighbourhood.

* externality: 외부 효과 ** fractionalization: 분열

① roles of culture in ethnic groups
② contrastive aspects of cultural diversity
③ negative perspectives of national identity
④ factors of productivity differences across countries
⑤ policies to protect minorities and prevent discrimination

24. 다음 글의 제목으로 가장 적절한 것은?

We think we are shaping our buildings. But really, our buildings and development are also shaping us. One of the best examples of this is the oldest-known construction: the ornately carved rings of standing stones at Göbekli Tepe in Turkey. Before these ancestors got the idea to erect standing stones some 12,000 years ago, they were hunter-gatherers. It appears that the erection of the multiple rings of megalithic stones took so long, and so many successive generations, that these innovators were forced to settle down to complete the construction works. In the process, they became the first farming society on Earth. This is an early example of a society constructing something that ends up radically remaking the society itself. Things are not so different in our own time.

* ornately: 화려하게 ** megalithic: 거석의

① Buildings Transform How We Live!
② Why Do We Build More Than We Need?
③ Copying Ancient Buildings for Creativity
④ Was Life Better in Hunter-gatherer Times?
⑤ Innovate Your Farm with New Constructions

25. 다음 도표의 내용과 일치하지 <u>않는</u> 것은?

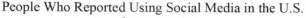

People Who Reported Using Social Media in the U.S.
(by age group)

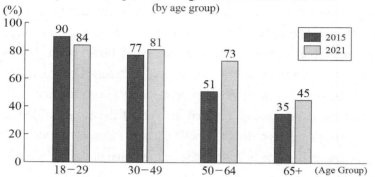

The graph above shows the percentages of people in different age groups who reported using social media in the United States in 2015 and 2021. ① In each of the given years, the 18-29 group had the highest percentage of people who said they used social media. ② In 2015, the percentage of people who reported using social media in the 30-49 group was more than twice that in the 65 and older group. ③ The percentage of people who said they used social media in the 50-64 group in 2021 was 22 percentage points higher than that in 2015. ④ In 2021, except for the 65 and older group, more than four-fifths of people in each age group reported using social media. ⑤ Among all the age groups, only the 18-29 group showed a decrease in the percentage of people who reported using social media from 2015 to 2021.

26. Bill Evans에 관한 다음 글의 내용과 일치하지 <u>않는</u> 것은?

American jazz pianist Bill Evans was born in New Jersey in 1929. His early training was in classical music. At the age of six, he began receiving piano lessons, later adding flute and violin. He earned bachelor's degrees in piano and music education from Southeastern Louisiana College in 1950. He went on to serve in the army from 1951 to 1954 and played flute in the Fifth Army Band. After serving in the military, he studied composition at the Mannes School of Music in New York. Composer George Russell admired his playing and hired Evans to record and perform his compositions. Evans became famous for recordings made from the late-1950s through the 1960s. He won his first Grammy Award in 1964 for his album *Conversations with Myself.* Evans' expressive piano works and his unique harmonic approach inspired a whole generation of musicians.

① 6세에 피아노 수업을 받기 시작했다.
② Southeastern Louisiana 대학에서 학위를 취득했다.
③ 군 복무 이후 뉴욕에서 작곡을 공부했다.
④ 작곡가 George Russell을 고용했다.
⑤ 1964년에 자신의 첫 번째 그래미상을 수상했다.

27. Silversmithing Class에 관한 다음 안내문의 내용과 일치하지 <u>않는</u> 것은?

Silversmithing Class

Kingston Club is offering a fine jewelry making class. Don't miss this great chance to make your own jewelry!

When & Where
· Saturday, October 21, 2023 (2 p.m. to 4 p.m.)
· Kingston Club studio

Registration
· Available only online
· Dates: October 1-14, 2023
· Fee: $40 (This includes all tools and materials.)
· Registration is limited to 6 people.

Note
· Participants must be at least 16 years old.
· No refund for cancellation on the day of the class

---

① 두 시간 동안 진행된다.
② 10월 1일부터 등록할 수 있다.
③ 등록 인원은 6명으로 제한된다.
④ 참가 연령에 제한이 없다.
⑤ 수업 당일 취소 시 환불이 불가하다.

28. 2023 Ocean Awareness Film Contest에 관한 다음 안내문의 내용과 일치하는 것은?

2023 Ocean Awareness Film Contest

Join our 7th annual film contest and show your knowledge of marine conservation.

☐ **Theme**
- Ocean Wildlife / Ocean Pollution
  (Choose one of the above.)

☐ **Guidelines**
- Participants: High school students
- Submission deadline: September 22, 2023
- The video must be between 10 and 15 minutes.
- All entries must be uploaded to our website.
- Only one entry per person

☐ **Prizes**
· 1st place: $100 · 2nd place: $70 · 3rd place: $50
  (Winners will be announced on our website.)

For more information, please visit www.oceanawareFC.com.

---

① 세 가지 주제 중 하나를 선택해야 한다.
② 중학생이 참가할 수 있다.
③ 영상은 10분을 넘길 수 없다.
④ 1인당 두 개까지 출품할 수 있다.
⑤ 수상자는 웹사이트에 공지될 것이다.

29. 다음 글의 밑줄 친 부분 중, 어법상 틀린 것은?

There is a reason the title "Monday Morning Quarterback" exists. Just read the comments on social media from fans discussing the weekend's games, and you quickly see how many people believe they could play, coach, and manage sport teams more ① successfully than those on the field. This goes for the boardroom as well. Students and professionals with years of training and specialized degrees in sport business may also find themselves ② being given advice on how to do their jobs from friends, family, or even total strangers without any expertise. Executives in sport management ③ have decades of knowledge and experience in their respective fields. However, many of them face criticism from fans and community members telling ④ themselves how to run their business. Very few people tell their doctor how to perform surgery or their accountant how to prepare their taxes, but many people provide feedback on ⑤ how sport organizations should be managed.

* boardroom: 이사회실

30. 다음 글의 밑줄 친 부분 중, 문맥상 낱말의 쓰임이 적절하지 않은 것은? [3점]

While moving is difficult for everyone, it is particularly stressful for children. They lose their sense of security and may feel disoriented when their routine is disrupted and all that is ① familiar is taken away. Young children, ages 3–6, are particularly affected by a move. Their understanding at this stage is quite literal, and it is ② easy for them to imagine beforehand a new home and their new room. Young children may have worries such as "Will I still be me in the new place?" and "Will my toys and bed come with us?" It is important to establish a balance between validating children's past experiences and focusing on helping them ③ adjust to the new place. Children need to have opportunities to share their backgrounds in a way that ④ respects their past as an important part of who they are. This contributes to building a sense of community, which is essential for all children, especially those in ⑤ transition.

[31~34] 다음 빈칸에 들어갈 말로 가장 적절한 것을 고르시오.

31. Many people are terrified to fly in airplanes. Often, this fear stems from a lack of control. The pilot is in control, not the passengers, and this lack of control instills fear. Many potential passengers are so afraid they choose to drive great distances to get to a destination instead of flying. But their decision to drive is based solely on emotion, not logic. Logic says that statistically, the odds of dying in a car crash are around 1 in 5,000, while the odds of dying in a plane crash are closer to 1 in 11 million. If you're going to take a risk, especially one that could possibly involve your well-being, wouldn't you want the odds in your favor? However, most people choose the option that will cause them the least amount of _____. Pay attention to the thoughts you have about taking the risk and make sure you're basing your decision on facts, not just feelings.

* instill: 스며들게 하다

① anxiety
② boredom
③ confidence
④ satisfaction
⑤ responsibility

32. The famous primatologist Frans de Waal, of Emory University, says humans downplay similarities between us and other animals as a way of maintaining our spot at the top of our imaginary ladder. Scientists, de Waal points out, can be some of the worst offenders — employing technical language to _____. They call "kissing" in chimps "mouth-to-mouth contact"; they call "friends" between primates "favorite affiliation partners"; they interpret evidence showing that crows and chimps can make tools as being somehow qualitatively different from the kind of toolmaking said to define humanity. If an animal can beat us at a cognitive task — like how certain bird species can remember the precise locations of thousands of seeds — they write it off as instinct, not intelligence. This and so many more tricks of language are what de Waal has termed "linguistic castration." The way we use our tongues to disempower animals, the way we invent words to maintain our spot at the top. [3점]

* primatologist: 영장류학자 ** affiliation: 제휴

① define human instincts
② overestimate chimps' intelligence
③ distance the other animals from us
④ identify animals' negative emotions
⑤ correct our misconceptions about nature

33. A key to engagement and achievement is providing students with _____. My scholarly work and my teaching have been deeply influenced by the work of Rosalie Fink. She interviewed twelve adults who were highly successful in their work, including a physicist, a biochemist, and a company CEO. All of them had dyslexia and had had significant problems with reading throughout their school years. While she expected to find that they had avoided reading and discovered ways to bypass it or compensate with other strategies for learning, she found the opposite. "To my surprise, I found that these dyslexics were enthusiastic readers...they rarely avoided reading. On the contrary, they sought out books." The pattern Fink discovered was that all of her subjects had been passionate in some personal interest. The areas of interest included religion, math, business, science, history, and biography. What mattered was that they read voraciously to find out more.

* dyslexia: 난독증   ** voraciously: 탐욕스럽게

① examples from official textbooks
② relevant texts they will be interested in
③ enough chances to exchange information
④ different genres for different age groups
⑤ early reading experience to develop logic skills

34. For many people, *ability* refers to intellectual competence, so they want everything they do to reflect how smart they are — writing a brilliant legal brief, getting the highest grade on a test, writing elegant computer code, saying something exceptionally wise or witty in a conversation. You could also define ability in terms of a particular skill or talent, such as how well one plays the piano, learns a language, or serves a tennis ball. Some people focus on their ability to be attractive, entertaining, up on the latest trends, or to have the newest gadgets. However ability may be defined, a problem occurs when _____.
The performance becomes the *only* measure of the person; nothing else is taken into account. An outstanding performance means an outstanding person; an average performance means an average person. Period. [3점]

① it is the sole determinant of one's self-worth
② you are distracted by others' achievements
③ there is too much competition in one field
④ you ignore feedback about a performance
⑤ it is not accompanied by effort

35. 다음 글에서 전체 흐름과 관계 <u>없는</u> 문장은? [3점]

Sensory nerves have specialized endings in the tissues that pick up a particular sensation. If, for example, you step on a sharp object such as a pin, nerve endings in the skin will transmit the pain sensation up your leg, up and along the spinal cord to the brain. ① While the pain itself is unpleasant, it is in fact acting as a protective mechanism for the foot. ② That is, you get used to the pain so the capacity with which you can avoid pain decreases. ③ Within the brain, nerves will connect to the area that controls speech, so that you may well shout 'ouch' or something rather less polite. ④ They will also connect to motor nerves that travel back down the spinal cord, and to the muscles in your leg that now contract quickly to lift your foot away from the painful object. ⑤ Sensory and motor nerves control almost all functions in the body — from the beating of the heart to the movement of the gut, sweating and just about everything else.

* spinal cord: 척수   ** gut: 장

[36~37] 주어진 글 다음에 이어질 글의 순서로 가장 적절한 것을 고르시오.

36.

> Maybe you've heard this joke: "How do you eat an elephant?" The answer is "one bite at a time."

(A) Common crystal habits include squares, triangles, and six-sided hexagons. Usually crystals form when liquids cool, such as when you create ice cubes. Many times, crystals form in ways that do not allow for perfect shapes. If conditions are too cold, too hot, or there isn't enough source material, they can form strange, twisted shapes.

(B) So, how do you "build" the Earth? That's simple, too: one atom at a time. Atoms are the basic building blocks of crystals, and since all rocks are made up of crystals, the more you know about atoms, the better. Crystals come in a variety of shapes that scientists call *habits*.

(C) But when conditions are right, we see beautiful displays. Usually, this involves a slow, steady environment where the individual atoms have plenty of time to join and fit perfectly into what's known as the *crystal lattice*. This is the basic structure of atoms that is seen time after time.

[3점]

① (A) – (C) – (B)   ② (B) – (A) – (C)
③ (B) – (C) – (A)   ④ (C) – (A) – (B)
⑤ (C) – (B) – (A)

37.

> When you pluck a guitar string it moves back and forth hundreds of times every second.

(A) The vibration of the wood creates more powerful waves in the air pressure, which travel away from the guitar. When the waves reach your eardrums they flex in and out the same number of times a second as the original string.

(B) Naturally, this movement is so fast that you cannot see it — you just see the blurred outline of the moving string. Strings vibrating in this way on their own make hardly any noise because strings are very thin and don't push much air about.

(C) But if you attach a string to a big hollow box (like a guitar body), then the vibration is amplified and the note is heard loud and clear. The vibration of the string is passed on to the wooden panels of the guitar body, which vibrate back and forth at the same rate as the string.

* pluck: (현악기를) 뜯다 ** amplify: 증폭시키다

① (A) – (C) – (B)   ② (B) – (A) – (C)
③ (B) – (C) – (A)   ④ (C) – (A) – (B)
⑤ (C) – (B) – (A)

[38~39] 글의 흐름으로 보아, 주어진 문장이 들어가기에 가장 적절한 곳을 고르시오.

38.

> Other individuals prefer integrating work and family roles all day long.

Boundaries between work and home are blurring as portable digital technology makes it increasingly possible to work anywhere, anytime. Individuals differ in how they like to manage their time to meet work and outside responsibilities. (①) Some people prefer to separate or segment roles so that boundary crossings are minimized. (②) For example, these people might keep separate email accounts for work and family and try to conduct work at the workplace and take care of family matters only during breaks and non-work time. (③) We've even noticed more of these "segmenters" carrying two phones — one for work and one for personal use. (④) Flexible schedules work well for these individuals because they enable greater distinction between time at work and time in other roles. (⑤) This might entail constantly trading text messages with children from the office, or monitoring emails at home and on vacation, rather than returning to work to find hundreds of messages in their inbox. [3점]

* entail: 수반하다

39.

> However, do not assume that a product is perfectly complementary, as customers may not be completely locked in to the product.

A "complementary good" is a product that is often consumed alongside another product. (①) For example, popcorn is a complementary good to a movie, while a travel pillow is a complementary good for a long plane journey. (②) When the popularity of one product increases, the sales of its complementary good also increase. (③) By producing goods that complement other products that are already (or about to be) popular, you can ensure a steady stream of demand for your product. (④) Some products enjoy perfect complementary status — they *have* to be consumed together, such as a lamp and a lightbulb. (⑤) For example, although motorists may seem required to purchase gasoline to run their cars, they can switch to electric cars.

40. 다음 글의 내용을 한 문장으로 요약하고자 한다. 빈칸 (A), (B)에 들어갈 말로 가장 적절한 것은?

> It's not news to anyone that we judge others based on their clothes. In general, studies that investigate these judgments find that people prefer clothing that matches expectations — surgeons in scrubs, little boys in blue — with one notable exception. A series of studies published in an article in June 2014 in the *Journal of Consumer Research* explored observers' reactions to people who broke established norms only slightly. In one scenario, a man at a black-tie affair was viewed as having higher status and competence when wearing a red bow tie. The researchers also found that valuing uniqueness increased audience members' ratings of the status and competence of a professor who wore red sneakers while giving a lecture. The results suggest that people judge these slight deviations from the norm as positive because they suggest that the individual is powerful enough to risk the social costs of such behaviors.

↓

> A series of studies show that people view an individual __(A)__ when the individual only slightly __(B)__ the norm for what people should wear.

	(A)		(B)
①	positively	……	challenges
②	negatively	……	challenges
③	indifferently	……	neglects
④	negatively	……	meets
⑤	positively	……	meets

[41~42] 다음 글을 읽고, 물음에 답하시오.

Claims that local food production cut greenhouse gas emissions by reducing the burning of transportation fuel are usually not well founded. Transport is the source of only 11 percent of greenhouse gas emissions within the food sector, so reducing the distance that food travels after it leaves the farm is far (a)less important than reducing wasteful energy use on the farm. Food coming from a distance can actually be better for the (b)climate, depending on how it was grown. For example, field-grown tomatoes shipped from Mexico in the winter months will have a smaller carbon footprint than (c)local winter tomatoes grown in a greenhouse. In the United Kingdom, lamb meat that travels 11,000 miles from New Zealand generates only one-quarter the carbon emissions per pound compared to British lamb because farmers in the United Kingdom raise their animals on feed (which must be produced using fossil fuels) rather than on clover pastureland.

When food does travel, what matters most is not the (d)distance traveled but the travel mode (surface versus air), and most of all the load size. Bulk loads of food can travel halfway around the world by ocean freight with a smaller carbon footprint, per pound delivered, than foods traveling just a short distance but in much (e)larger loads. For example, 18-wheelers carry much larger loads than pickup trucks so they can move food 100 times as far while burning only one-third as much gas per pound of food delivered.

* freight: 화물 운송

41. 윗글의 제목으로 가장 적절한 것은?

① Shorten the Route, Cut the Cost
② Is Local Food Always Better for the Earth?
③ Why Mass Production Ruins the Environment
④ New Technologies: What Matters in Agriculture
⑤ Reduce Food Waste for a Smaller Carbon Footprint

42. 밑줄 친 (a)~(e) 중에서 문맥상 낱말의 쓰임이 적절하지 <u>않은</u> 것은?

① (a)　　② (b)　　③ (c)　　④ (d)　　⑤ (e)

[43~45] 다음 글을 읽고, 물음에 답하시오.

(A)

Long ago, an old man built a grand temple at the center of his village. People traveled to worship at the temple. So the old man made arrangements for food and accommodation inside the temple itself. He needed someone who could look after the temple, so (a)he put up a notice: Manager needed.

(B)

When that young man left the temple, the old man called him and asked, "Will you take care of this temple?" The young man was surprised by the offer and replied, "I have no experience caring for a temple. I'm not even educated." The old man smiled and said, "I don't want any educated man. I want a qualified person." Confused, the young man asked, "But why do (b)you consider me a qualified person?"

(C)

The old man replied, "I buried a brick on the path to the temple. I watched for many days as people tripped over that brick. No one thought to remove it. But you dug up that brick." The young man said, "I haven't done anything great. It's the duty of every human being to think about others. (c)I only did my duty." The old man smiled and said, "Only people who know their duty and perform it are qualified people."

(D)

Seeing the notice, many people went to the old man. But he returned all the applicants after interviews, telling them, "I need a qualified person for this work." The old man would sit on the roof of (d)his house every morning, watching people go through the temple doors. One day, (e)he saw a young man come to the temple.

43. 주어진 글 (A)에 이어질 내용을 순서에 맞게 배열한 것으로 가장 적절한 것은?

① (B) − (D) − (C)　　② (C) − (B) − (D)
③ (C) − (D) − (B)　　④ (D) − (B) − (C)
⑤ (D) − (C) − (B)

44. 밑줄 친 (a)~(e) 중에서 가리키는 대상이 나머지 넷과 <u>다른</u> 것은?

① (a)　　② (b)　　③ (c)　　④ (d)　　⑤ (e)

45. 윗글에 관한 내용으로 적절하지 <u>않은</u> 것은?

① 노인은 마을 중심부에 사원을 지었다.
② 젊은이가 사원을 나설 때 노인이 그를 불렀다.
③ 젊은이는 노인의 제안에 놀랐다.
④ 노인은 사원으로 통하는 길에 묻혀있던 벽돌을 파냈다.
⑤ 공고를 보고 많은 사람들이 노인을 찾아갔다.

* 확인 사항

◦ 답안지의 해당란에 필요한 내용을 정확히 기입(표기)했는지 확인하시오.

※ QR 코드를 스캔하시면 듣기 방송이 나옵니다. 듣기 방송을 들으며 다음 빈칸을 채우시오. ● 제한 시간 : 25분

01

다음을 듣고, 남자가 하는 말의 목적으로 가장 적절한 것을 고르시오.

M : Attention, Fargo High School students. This is your music teacher, Mr. Nelson. Our school rock band was supposed to hold its concert in the auditorium today. I'm sure you've been looking forward to the concert. Unfortunately, the rain yesterday ✪ _____ __ _____ in the ceiling of the auditorium. The ceiling needs to be fixed, so we decided to _____ _____ _____ of the concert. The rock band will now perform in _____ _____ _____. The time for the concert hasn't changed. I hope you'll enjoy the performance.

02

대화를 듣고, 여자의 의견으로 가장 적절한 것을 고르시오.

W : Simon, are you doing anything after school?
M : Nothing special. What about you?
W : I'm planning to ____ _____ __ _____ in the park. It's a five-kilometer route.
M : The weather is perfect for running. Can I go with you?
W : Why not? [Pause] Wait! You're wearing slippers. Those aren't good for running.
M : It's okay. I can ✪ _____ ___ _____.
W : No way. Slippers aren't designed for running. You can get hurt if you run in them.
M : You mean I need to put on running shoes?
W : You got it. You need to _____ _____ _____ _____ for running.
M : All right. I'll go home and change.

03

대화를 듣고, 두 사람의 관계를 가장 잘 나타낸 것을 고르시오.

M : Good morning, Ms. Clapton. It's nice to meet you.
W : Nice to meet you, too. I'm __ _____ ___ _____ _____.
M : You ✪ _____ _____ _____ at the film festival this year. Congratulations!
W : Thank you. I was lucky to work with a great director and talented actors.
M : The clothes and accessories in the movie are impressive. How do you start ✪ _____ _____ _____?
W : I read the script to fully understand the characters. Then I research the characters' backgrounds.

M : That sounds like a lot of work. Which of the costumes from this film is your favorite?
W : It's hard to pick just one because I love all of my designs.
M : I totally understand. Thank you for sharing your story with the readers of our magazine.
W : It was my pleasure.

04

대화를 듣고, 그림에서 대화의 내용과 일치하지 않는 것을 고르시오.

W : Come look at the new reading room in the library.
M : Wow! It's much better than I thought.
W : Same here. I like ✪ _____ _____ ___ _____ _____ of the room.
M : The striped pattern of the rug makes the room feel warm.
W : I agree. I think putting the sofa between two plants was a good idea.
M : Right. We can sit there and read for hours.
W : There's a round clock on the wall.
M : I have the same clock at home. Oh, _____ _____ _____ _____ _____ is full of books.
W : We can read the books at the long table.
M : Yeah, it looks like a good place to read. _____ _____ on the table will make it easy to focus.
W : Good lighting is important for reading.
M : I can't wait to start using the reading room.

05

대화를 듣고, 여자가 할 일로 가장 적절한 것을 고르시오.

M : Kelly, the school musical is tomorrow. Shall we go over the final checklist together?
W : Let's do it. What's first? [Pause] Oh, the posters. We put them up around school last week.
M : Right. Do we _____ _____ _____ for the wireless microphones?
W : Yeah. I bought them yesterday. We should check that the microphones work well with the sound system.
M : I did that this morning. ✪ _____ _____ _____.
W : How about the stage lights?
M : They work perfectly. I think everyone will love the lighting design you made.
W : Really? Thanks. It looks like we've finished everything.
M : No, wait. The chairs for the audience haven't been arranged yet.
W : You're right! I'll ____ _____ _____ ___ _____ now.
M : The musical is going to be fantastic.

06

대화를 듣고, 남자가 지불할 금액을 고르시오. [3점]

W : Welcome to Libby's Flowers. How can I help you?
M : I'd like to order __ _____ _____ for my parents' wedding anniversary.
W : All right. Our rose baskets come in two sizes.
M : What are the options?
W : The regular size is 30 dollars, and the large size is 50 dollars.
M : Hmm.... I think the bigger one is better.
W : Good choice. So, you'll get one rose basket ___ ____ _____ _____. By the way, we're giving a 10-percent discount on all purchases this week.
M : Excellent! When will my order be ready?
W : It'll be ready around 11 a.m. If you can't pick it up, we ✪ _____ __ _____ _____. It's 10 dollars.
M : Oh, great. I'd like it to be delivered. Here's my credit card.

07

대화를 듣고, 여자가 스키 여행을 갈 수 없는 이유를 고르시오.

M : You seem busy this morning, Olivia.
W : I am. I had to see Professor Martin about my history test.
M : Oh, I see. Do you remember that our club's ski trip is this weekend?
W : Yeah. I heard that a nice ski resort has been booked for the trip.
M : I didn't know that. I'm so excited to go skiing at a nice resort.
W : I bet it'll be great, but I don't think I can go this time.
M : Why? You don't work at the cafe on the weekends, do you?
W : No, I don't. But I need to take care of my cat. She's ✪ _____.
M : Isn't there anyone else who can look after your cat?
W : _____ _____ _____ ____. My parents are ✪ _____ _____ ___ _____. They won't be back for two weeks.
M : I'm sorry that you can't join us.
W : Me, too. Have fun this weekend.

08

대화를 듣고, Street Photography Contest에 관해 언급되지 않은 것을 고르시오.

W : What are you doing, Tim?
M : I'm looking at the Street Photography Contest website.
W : I've heard about that. It's a contest for college students, right?
M : Actually, it's open to high school students, too. Why don't you try it?
W : Really? Maybe I will. Does the contest have a theme?
M : Sure. This year's theme is Daily Life.
W : That sounds interesting. When is the deadline?
M : You have to submit your photographs by September 15.
W : That's _____ _____ __ _____.
M : You should hurry and choose your photos. The winner will _____ __ _____ as a prize.
W : Okay! ✪ _____ _____ _____.

09

Twin Stars Chocolate Day에 관한 다음 내용을 듣고, 일치하지 않는 것을 고르시오.

M : Hello, listeners. I'm Charlie Anderson from the Twin Stars Chocolate Museum. I'm happy to introduce the Twin Stars Chocolate Day, a special opportunity to _____ _____ _____ _____ _____. It'll be held on November 12 from 1 p.m. to 4 p.m. First, you'll listen to a lecture about the history of chocolate. Then you'll have a chance to ✪ _____ _____ _____ _____ _____. At the end of the event, you'll make five chocolates yourself. If you want to take part in the event, you must register in advance. You can sign up on our website until November 1. The registration fee is 20 dollars, which includes ✪ _____ _____ ___ _____. Don't miss this sweet opportunity!

10

다음 표를 보면서 대화를 듣고, 두 사람이 주문할 실내 사이클링 자전거를 고르시오.

M : Honey, what are you looking at?
W : I'm looking at indoor cycling bikes. Would you like to choose one together?
M : Sure, let me see. [Pause] The price _____ ____ _____.
W : I don't want to pay more than 300 dollars. That's too expensive.
M : I agree. Which color do you like?
W : I prefer a dark color because it goes well with our living room.
M : Okay. Then we shouldn't get a white one. What do you think about the foldable one?
W : We definitely need that. It'll take up ✪ _____ _____ _____.
M : We have just two options left. Which one should we get?
W : I think we should go with the one with __ _____ _____ _____. The reviews are based on actual customers' experiences.
M : Sounds good. Let's order this one.

11

대화를 듣고, 여자의 마지막 말에 대한 남자의 응답으로 가장 적절한 것을 고르시오.

W : Jason, is that a new sweater? It looks good on you.
M : Thanks. I bought it online. It was on sale.
W : I'd love to _____ ____ _____ for my brother. Can you tell me ✪ _____ ___ _____ __?

12

대화를 듣고, 남자의 마지막 말에 대한 여자의 응답으로 가장 적절한 것을 고르시오.

M : Becky, did you order our food for dinner?

W : Yes. I ordered pizza _____ ____ _____ .

M : An hour ago? Delivery usually takes ✪ _____ _____ _____ _____ .

13

대화를 듣고, 여자의 마지막 말에 대한 남자의 응답으로 가장 적절한 것을 고르시오.

W : I haven't seen you in the cafeteria this week. _____ _____ _____ _____ ?

M : I've been in the library working on my science project.

W : Does that mean you've been skipping lunch?

M : Yeah. This project is really important for my grade.

W : You shouldn't do that. It's not good for your health.

M : Don't worry. I always _____ __ _____ _____ when I get home.

W : That's the problem. Skipping meals ✪ _____ _____ _____ later.

M : I hadn't thought of that. Then what should I do?

W : It's simple. You should eat regularly to stay healthy.

14

대화를 듣고, 남자의 마지막 말에 대한 여자의 응답으로 가장 적절한 것을 고르시오. [3점]

M : Excuse me, Ms. Lopez. Can I ask you something?

W : Sure, Tony. What can I do for you?

M : I want to do better in Spanish, but I don't know how to improve.

W : You seem to do well during class. Do you study when you're at home?

M : I do all my homework and try to _____ ____ _____ _____ every day.

W : That's a good start. Do you also _____ _____ _____ _____ repeatedly?

M : Do I need to do that? That sounds like it'll take a lot of time.

W : It does. But since you're still a beginner, you have to put in more effort to ✪ _____ _____ ___ new words.

M : I see. So are you suggesting that I practice them over and over?

15

다음 상황 설명을 듣고, Brian이 Melissa에게 할 말로 가장 적절한 것을 고르시오. [3점]

W : Brian is a class leader. He is passionate about environmental issues and saving energy. Recently, he's noticed that his classmates don't turn the lights off when they leave the classroom. Brian thinks ✪ _____ ___ _____ _____ . He wants to make stickers that remind his classmates to save energy by _____ _____ _____ _____ . He tells this idea to his classmate Melissa, and she agrees it's a good idea. Brian knows Melissa is a great artist, so he wants to _____ _____ ___ _____ stickers that encourage their classmates to save energy. In this situation, what would Brian most likely say to Melissa?

16~17

다음을 듣고, 물음에 답하시오.

M : Good afternoon, everyone. Last time, we learned that overtourism happens when there are too many visitors to a particular destination. Today, we'll learn how cities deal with ✪ _____ _____ _____ ____ _____ . First, some cities limit the number of hotels so there are _____ _____ _____ _____ ___ _____ . In Barcelona, building new hotels is not allowed in the city center. Second, other cities promote areas away from popular sites. For instance, Amsterdam encourages tourists to visit less-crowded areas. Third, many cities have tried to limit access. For example, Venice has tried to reduce tourism overall by stopping large cruise ships from docking on the island. Similarly, Paris has focused on reducing tourism to certain parts of the city by ✪ _____ _____ _____ . Now, let's watch some video clips.

▶ 정답 : 해설편 111쪽

18
001 hold ⓥ 개최하다
002 chemistry ⓝ 화학
003 fair ⓝ 박람회
004 local ⓐ 지역의, 지역의
005 experiment ⓝ 실험
006 college student 대학생
007 contact ⓥ 연락하다
008 recommend ⓥ 추천하다
009 department ⓝ 학과, 부서
010 qualified for ~에 적합한, 자격을 갖춘

19
011 rock climbing 암벽 등반
012 sunrise ⓝ 일출
013 take a risk 위험을 감수하다
014 bolt ⓝ 볼트, 나사못
015 definitely ⓐ 확실히, 분명히
016 piece of cake 식은 죽 먹기, 몹시 쉬운 일
017 pinned ⓐ 고정된
018 deceptively ⓐ 현혹될 정도로
019 handhold ⓝ (등반 도중) 손으로 잡을 수 있는 곳
020 clumsily ⓐ 서툴게
021 back and forth 이리저리
022 cliff ⓝ 절벽
023 end up with 결국 ~에 처하다
024 get to ~에 도착하다
025 exhaustion ⓝ 피로
026 freeze ⓥ 얼어붙다
027 fright ⓝ 공포
028 toe ⓝ 발가락
029 rope ⓝ 밧줄
030 tie ⓥ 묶다
031 confident ⓐ 자신 있는
032 fearful ⓐ 겁에 질린
033 regretful ⓐ 유감스러운, 후회하는

20
034 learn from ~로부터 배우다
035 overhear ⓥ 엿듣다, 우연히 듣다
036 value ⓝ 가치 ⓥ 중시하다
037 priority ⓝ 우선순위
038 principle ⓝ 원칙
039 take the high road 확실한 길로 가다
040 tempting ⓐ 유혹적인, 솔깃한
041 make up ~을 구성하다
042 act on ~에 따라 행동하다
043 uphold ⓥ 유지하다, 떠받치다
044 compassion ⓝ 연민
045 concern ⓝ 걱정, 우려
046 suffer ⓥ 고통받다, 괴로워하다
047 self-discipline ⓝ 자제
048 honesty ⓝ 정직

21
049 no doubt 분명히, 틀림없이
050 fall ⓥ 쓰러지다, 넘어지다
051 pressure wave 압력파(압력 크기의 변화로 생성되는 파동)
052 hearer ⓝ 청자
053 similarly ⓐ 비슷하게, 마찬가지로

054 scientific ⓐ 과학적인
055 signal ⓝ 신호 ⓥ 알리다
056 useless ⓐ 쓸모없는
057 publish ⓥ 출판하다, 게재하다
058 paper ⓝ 논문, 서류
059 intend ⓥ 목표로 하다, 의도하다
060 restate ⓥ (더 분명하게) 고쳐 말하다
061 as follows 다음과 같이
062 complete ⓐ 완성된
063 publication ⓝ 출판, 게재
064 no more than 단지 ~일 뿐인
065 previous ⓐ 이전의
066 false ⓐ 틀린
067 meet the demand 요구에 맞추다

22
068 negotiate ⓥ 협상하다
069 whether ~ or not ~이든 아니든
070 usually ⓐ 보통
071 traditional ⓐ 전통적인
072 approach ⓝ 접근법 ⓥ 접근하다
073 result in 결과적으로 ~을 낳다
074 agreement ⓝ 합의, 동의
075 old-school ⓐ 구식의
076 adversarial ⓐ 적대적인
077 one-off ⓐ 단 한 번의
078 transaction ⓝ 거래
079 increasingly ⓐ 점점 더
080 rare ⓐ 드문
081 repeatedly ⓐ 반복해서
082 spouse ⓝ 배우자
083 in view of ~을 고려하면
084 essential ⓐ 필수적인, 아주 중요한
085 maintain ⓥ 유지하다
086 interdependent ⓐ 상호 의존적인
087 long-term ⓐ 장기의
088 outcome ⓝ 결과, 성과
089 acceptable ⓐ 수용 가능한

23
090 interaction ⓝ 상호 작용
091 cultural ⓐ 문화적인
092 background ⓝ 배경
093 population ⓝ 인구
094 productivity ⓝ 생산성
095 due to ~ 때문에
096 externality ⓝ 외부 효과(의도하지 않았지만 부수적으로 따르는 결과)
097 knowledge spillover 지식의 확산
098 variety ⓝ 다양성
099 fractionalization ⓝ 분열
100 excessive ⓐ 과도한
101 cost ⓝ 비용, 대가
102 lower ⓥ 떨어뜨리다
103 impact ⓥ 영향을 주다, 충격을 주다
104 labo(u)r market 노동 시장
105 quality of life 삶의 질
106 tolerant ⓐ 관용적인
107 multicultural ⓐ 다문화의
108 range ⓝ 범위
109 on the other hand 반면에
110 perceive A as B A를 B로 인식하다

111 distortion ⓝ 왜곡
112 identity ⓝ 정체성
113 discriminate against ~을 차별하다
114 ethnic ⓐ 민족의
115 conflict ⓝ 갈등
116 import ⓥ 유입하다, 수입하다
117 contrastive ⓐ 대비되는, 대립적인
118 factor ⓝ 요인
119 policy ⓝ 정책

24
120 shape ⓥ 형성하다
121 construction ⓝ 건설, 구성
122 ornately ⓐ 화려하게
123 carve ⓥ 새기다
124 ancestor ⓝ 조상
125 erect ⓥ 세우다
126 hunter-gatherer ⓝ 수렵 채집인
127 multiple ⓐ 여럿의
128 megalithic ⓐ 거석의
129 successive ⓐ 연속된, 잇따른
130 innovator ⓝ 혁신가
131 be forced to 어쩔 수 없이 ~하다
132 settle down 정착하다
133 radically ⓐ 근본적으로, 급진적으로
134 transform ⓥ 바꾸다, 변모시키다

25
135 age group 연령 집단
136 social media 소셜 미디어
137 each ⓐ 각각 ⓐ 각각의
138 given ⓐ 주어진 prep ~을 고려하면
139 more than ~ 이상
140 except for ~을 제외하고
141 among prep ~ 중에서
142 decrease ⓝ 감소

26
143 add ⓥ 추가하다
144 flute ⓝ 플루트
145 earn ⓥ 얻다, 취득하다, 벌다
146 bachelor's degree 학사 학위
147 serve in the army 군 복무하다
148 military ⓝ 군대 ⓐ 군사적인
149 composition ⓝ 작곡
150 admire ⓥ 감탄하다, 존경하다
151 perform ⓥ 연주하다
152 recording ⓝ 음반, 녹음
153 expressive ⓐ 표현이 풍부한
154 unique ⓐ 독특한
155 harmonic ⓐ (음악) 화성의

27
156 silversmith ⓝ 은세공하는 사람
157 fine ⓐ 정교한, 미세한
158 jewelry ⓝ 보석
159 miss a chance 기회를 놓치다
160 registration ⓝ 등록
161 material ⓝ 재료
162 refund ⓝ 환불
163 cancellation ⓝ 취소
164 on the day of ~의 당일에

28
165 awareness ⓝ 인식, 앎
166 annual ⓐ 매년의
167 marine ⓐ 해양의
168 conservation ⓝ 보존
169 wildlife ⓝ 야생 생물
170 pollution ⓝ 오염
171 guideline ⓝ 지침
172 submission ⓝ 제출
173 entry ⓝ 출품작, 참가, 입장

29
174 comment ⓝ 논평, 지적
175 discuss ⓥ 토론하다
176 field ⓝ 경기장, 분야
177 boardroom ⓝ 이사회실
178 professional ⓝ 전문가
179 specialized ⓐ 전문화된
180 total stranger 생판 남
181 expertise ⓝ 전문 지식
182 executive ⓝ 임원, 중역
183 respective ⓐ 각자의
184 face ⓥ 마주하다, 직면하다
185 criticism ⓝ 비평
186 run ⓥ (가게나 사업을) 운영하다
187 accountant ⓝ 회계사
188 tax ⓝ 세금
189 organization ⓝ 조직, 단체

30
190 particularly ⓐ 특히
191 stressful ⓐ 스트레스가 되는
192 sense ⓝ 감각, 의식
193 security ⓝ 안정
194 disoriented ⓐ 혼란스러워 하는
195 routine ⓝ 일상, 루틴
196 disrupt ⓥ 무너뜨리다, 지장을 주다, 방해하다
197 familiar ⓐ 익숙한
198 take away 없애다, 빼앗다
199 understanding ⓝ 이해(력)
200 literal ⓐ 융통성 없는, 문자 그대로의
201 beforehand ⓐ 미리
202 establish ⓥ 설정하다, 쌓다
203 balance ⓝ 균형 ⓥ 균형을 맞추다
204 validate ⓥ 인정하다, 승인하다, 입증하다
205 adjust to ~에 적응하다
206 share ⓥ 나누다, 공유하다
207 contribute to ~에 기여하다, ~의 원인이 되다
208 transition ⓝ 변화

31
209 terrified ⓐ 겁에 질린
210 stem from ~에서 기원하다
211 lack ⓝ 부족, 결여
212 instill ⓥ 스며들게 하다, 주입하다
213 potential ⓐ 잠재적인
214 destination ⓝ 목적지
215 solely ⓐ 오로지
216 logic ⓝ 논리
217 statistically ⓐ 통계적으로
218 odds ⓝ 공산, 가능성

219 ☐ in one's favor ~에 유리한
220 ☐ crash ⑩ (차나 비행기의) 사고, 충돌
221 ☐ close to ~에 근접한
222 ☐ involve ⓥ ~와 관련 있다
223 ☐ well-being ⑩ 안녕, 행복
224 ☐ make sure 반드시 ~하다
225 ☐ base ⓥ ~에 근거를 두다, 기반으로 하다
226 ☐ anxiety ⑩ 불안
227 ☐ boredom ⑩ 지루함

32
228 ☐ primatologist ⑩ 영장류학자
229 ☐ downplay ⓥ 경시하다
230 ☐ similarity ⑩ 유사성
231 ☐ spot ⑩ 위치 ⓥ 파악하다
232 ☐ imaginary ⓐ 상상의
233 ☐ ladder ⑩ 사다리
234 ☐ offender ⑩ 범죄자, 나쁜 짓을 하는 사람
235 ☐ employ ⓥ 이용하다, 고용하다
236 ☐ technical ⓐ 전문적인
237 ☐ language ⑩ 언어
238 ☐ chimp ⑩ 침팬지
239 ☐ primate ⑩ 영장류
240 ☐ affiliation ⑩ 제휴
241 ☐ interpret A as B A를 B로 해석하다
242 ☐ crow ⑩ 까마귀
243 ☐ somehow ⓐⓓ 왠지, 어떻게든
244 ☐ qualitatively ⓐⓓ 질적으로
245 ☐ toolmaking ⑩ 도구 제작
246 ☐ define ⓥ 정의하다
247 ☐ humanity ⑩ 인류
248 ☐ beat ⓥ 이기다
249 ☐ cognitive ⓐ 인지적인
250 ☐ certain ⓐ 특정한
251 ☐ precise ⓐ 정확한
252 ☐ write off as ~라고 치부하다
253 ☐ instinct ⑩ 본능
254 ☐ intelligence ⑩ 지능
255 ☐ trick ⑩ 수법, 트릭
256 ☐ term ⓥ (특정 용어로) 칭하다 ⑩ 용어
257 ☐ disempower ⓥ ~로부터 힘을 빼앗다
258 ☐ overestimate ⓥ 과대평가하다
259 ☐ distance A from B A와 B 사이에 거리를 두다
260 ☐ identify ⓥ 식별하다, 알아보다, 확인하다
261 ☐ misconception ⑩ 오해

33
262 ☐ engagement ⑩ 참여, 몰입
263 ☐ achievement ⑩ 성취
264 ☐ provide A with B A에게 B를 제공하다
265 ☐ highly ⓐⓓ 매우
266 ☐ physicist ⑩ 물리학자
267 ☐ biochemist ⑩ 생화학자
268 ☐ dyslexia ⑩ 난독증
269 ☐ significant ⓐ 상당한, 심각한
270 ☐ throughout ⓟⓡⓔⓟ ~ 내내
271 ☐ discover ⓥ 찾아내다, 발견하다
272 ☐ bypass ⓥ 우회하다
273 ☐ compensate for ~을 보완하다, 보상하다
274 ☐ opposite ⓐ 정반대
275 ☐ enthusiastic ⓐ 열정적인, 열성적인

276 ☐ seek out ~을 찾아내다
277 ☐ subject ⑩ 실험 대상자
278 ☐ personal ⓐ 개인적인
279 ☐ religion ⑩ 종교
280 ☐ biography ⑩ (인물의) 전기
281 ☐ voraciously ⓐⓓ 탐욕스럽게
282 ☐ official ⓐ 공식적인
283 ☐ relevant ⓐ 적절한

34
284 ☐ refer to ~을 일컫다
285 ☐ competence ⑩ 능력, 역량
286 ☐ reflect ⓥ 반영하다
287 ☐ brilliant ⓐ 뛰어난
288 ☐ brief ⑩ (법률) 취지서, 의견서, 보고서
289 ☐ elegant ⓐ 명쾌한, 멋들어진
290 ☐ exceptionally ⓐⓓ 탁월하게
291 ☐ witty ⓐ 재치 있는
292 ☐ in terms of ~의 면에서
293 ☐ serve a ball 서브를 넣다
294 ☐ attractive ⓐ 매력적인
295 ☐ entertaining ⓐ 재미있는, 즐거움을 주는
296 ☐ gadget ⑩ 장비, 기기
297 ☐ measure ⑩ 척도
298 ☐ take into account ~을 고려하다, 참작하다
299 ☐ outstanding ⓐ 뛰어난
300 ☐ sole ⓐ 유일한
301 ☐ determinant ⑩ 결정 요소
302 ☐ self-worth ⑩ 자존감, 자부심
303 ☐ distracted ⓐ 정신이 팔린

35
304 ☐ sensory ⓐ 감각의
305 ☐ nerve ⑩ 신경
306 ☐ tissue ⑩ (생체) 조직
307 ☐ sensation ⑩ 감각
308 ☐ step on ~을 밟다
309 ☐ sharp ⓐ 날카로운, 예리한
310 ☐ transmit ⓥ 전달하다
311 ☐ spinal cord 척수
312 ☐ unpleasant ⓐ 불쾌한
313 ☐ protective mechanism 보호 기제
314 ☐ capacity ⑩ 능력
315 ☐ speech ⑩ 발화
316 ☐ lift ⓥ 들어올리다
317 ☐ painful ⓐ 고통스러운
318 ☐ motor ⓐ 운동 신경의
319 ☐ gut ⑩ 내장, 소화관
320 ☐ sweating ⑩ 발한, 땀이 남

36
321 ☐ bite ⑩ 한 입 (베어문 조각) ⓥ 베어 물다
322 ☐ crystal ⑩ 결정
323 ☐ hexagon ⑩ 육각형
324 ☐ liquid ⑩ 액체
325 ☐ ice cube 얼음 조각
326 ☐ allow for ~을 허용하다
327 ☐ twisted ⓐ 뒤틀린
328 ☐ atom ⑩ 원자
329 ☐ be made up of ~로 구성되다
330 ☐ steady ⓐ 안정된, 꾸준한
331 ☐ plenty of 많은

332 ☐ fit into ~에 들어 맞다
333 ☐ lattice ⑩ 격자 (모양)
334 ☐ time after time 자주, 매번, 되풀이해서

37
335 ☐ pluck ⓥ (현악기를) 뜯다
336 ☐ string ⑩ 줄, 현악기
337 ☐ vibration ⑩ 진동
338 ☐ eardrum ⑩ 고막
339 ☐ flex ⓥ (근육을) 수축시키다, (관절을) 구부리다
340 ☐ naturally ⓐⓓ 당연히
341 ☐ blur ⓥ 흐리게 하다
342 ☐ outline ⑩ 윤곽, 개요
343 ☐ hardly any 거의 전혀 ~않다
344 ☐ thin ⓐ 얇은
345 ☐ attach A to B A를 B에 부착하다
346 ☐ hollow ⓐ (속이) 빈
347 ☐ amplify ⓥ 증폭시키다
348 ☐ panel ⑩ 판
349 ☐ rate ⑩ 속도, 비율

38
350 ☐ integrate ⓥ 통합하다
351 ☐ all day long 하루 종일
352 ☐ boundary ⑩ 경계
353 ☐ portable ⓐ 휴대용의
354 ☐ outside ⑩ 외부의
355 ☐ responsibility ⑩ 책무, 책임
356 ☐ separate ⓥ 분리하다 ⓐ 분리된, 개별의
357 ☐ segment ⓥ 분할하다, 나누다
358 ☐ minimize ⓥ 최소화하다
359 ☐ account ⑩ 계정
360 ☐ conduct ⓥ 수행하다
361 ☐ workplace ⑩ 직장
362 ☐ break ⑩ 쉬는 시간
363 ☐ carry ⓥ 들고 다니다
364 ☐ flexible schedule 유연근무제
365 ☐ distinction ⑩ 구별
366 ☐ role ⑩ 역할
367 ☐ entail ⓥ 수반하다
368 ☐ constantly ⓐⓓ 계속
369 ☐ trade ⓥ 교환하다
370 ☐ monitor ⓥ 확인하다, 감독하다, 점검하다
371 ☐ on vacation 휴가 중인
372 ☐ inbox ⑩ 수신함

39
373 ☐ assume ⓥ 가정하다
374 ☐ complementary ⓐ 보완하는
375 ☐ locked in 갇힌, 고정된
376 ☐ alongside ⓟⓡⓔⓟ ~와 함께
377 ☐ pillow ⑩ 베개
378 ☐ journey ⑩ 여정
379 ☐ complement ⓥ 보완하다, 보충하다
380 ☐ ensure ⓥ 확실히 하다, 보장하다
381 ☐ stream ⑩ 흐름
382 ☐ status ⑩ 지위, 입지
383 ☐ lightbulb ⑩ 전구
384 ☐ motorist ⑩ 운전자
385 ☐ gasoline ⑩ 휘발유
386 ☐ switch to ~로 바꾸다
387 ☐ electric ⓐ 전기의

40
388 ☐ in general 일반적으로
389 ☐ investigate ⓥ 연구하다, 조사하다
390 ☐ match ⓥ 일치하다, 맞다, 부합하다
391 ☐ surgeon ⑩ 외과 의사
392 ☐ scrubs ⑩ 수술복
393 ☐ notable ⓐ 눈에 띄는
394 ☐ exception ⑩ 예외
395 ☐ explore ⓥ 탐구하다
396 ☐ reaction ⑩ 반응
397 ☐ established ⓐ 확립된, 정해진
398 ☐ black-tie affair 격식을 차리는 모임
399 ☐ bow tie 나비 넥타이
400 ☐ uniqueness ⑩ 독특함, 고유함
401 ☐ deviation ⑩ 일탈
402 ☐ powerful ⓐ 영향력 있는, 강력한
403 ☐ risk ⓥ 위태롭게 하다
404 ☐ challenge ⓥ 반박하다, 도전하다
405 ☐ negatively ⓐⓓ 부정적으로
406 ☐ neglect ⓥ 등한시하다, 소홀히 하다

41~42
407 ☐ production ⑩ 생산
408 ☐ greenhouse gas 온실가스
409 ☐ emission ⑩ 배출(량)
410 ☐ well founded 근거가 충분한
411 ☐ sector ⑩ 부문
412 ☐ wasteful ⓐ 낭비하는
413 ☐ climate ⑩ 기후
414 ☐ depending on ~에 따라
415 ☐ ship ⓥ 운송하다, 수송하다
416 ☐ carbon footprint 탄소 발자국
417 ☐ lamb ⑩ 어린 양
418 ☐ generate ⓥ 발생시키다, 생성하다
419 ☐ raise ⓥ 기르다, 키우다
420 ☐ feed ⑩ 사료, 먹이
421 ☐ fossil fuel 화석 연료
422 ☐ pastureland ⑩ 목초지
423 ☐ travel mode 이동 수단
424 ☐ surface ⑩ 지면
425 ☐ load ⑩ 적재(량) ⓥ (짐을) 싣다
426 ☐ bulk ⑩ 대량 ⓐ 대량의
427 ☐ freight ⑩ 화물 운송
428 ☐ pickup truck 픽업트럭, 소형 오픈 트럭
429 ☐ shorten ⓥ 짧게 줄이다
430 ☐ ruin ⓥ 파괴하다, 망치다
431 ☐ agriculture ⑩ 농업

43~45
432 ☐ grand ⓐ 큰, 위대한
433 ☐ temple ⑩ 사원, 절
434 ☐ worship ⓥ 예배하다
435 ☐ make arrangements for ~을 준비하다
436 ☐ accommodation ⑩ 숙소
437 ☐ care for ~을 관리하다, 돌보다
438 ☐ bury ⓥ 묻다
439 ☐ brick ⑩ 벽돌
440 ☐ path ⑩ 길
441 ☐ trip over ~에 걸려 넘어지다
442 ☐ dig up 파내다
443 ☐ duty ⑩ 의무
444 ☐ applicant ⑩ 지원자

● 채점 : 맞은 개수 _____ / 80

TEST A-B 각 단어의 뜻을 [A] 영어는 우리말로, [B] 우리말은 영어로 쓰시오.

A	English	Korean
01	fair	
02	take a risk	
03	no doubt	
04	knowledge spillover	
05	negotiate	
06	spouse	
07	discriminate against	
08	be forced to	
09	given	
10	awareness	
11	expertise	
12	adjust to	
13	enthusiastic	
14	take into account	
15	be made up with	
16	integrate	
17	complementary	
18	well founded	
19	worship	
20	uphold	

B	Korean	English
01	개최하다	
02	완성된	
03	자신 있는	
04	~이든 아니든	
05	필수적인, 아주 중요한	
06	결과, 성과	
07	인구	
08	건설, 구성	
09	보존	
10	목적지	
11	정확한	
12	~을 보완하다, 보상하다	
13	능력, 역량	
14	(생체) 조직	
15	진동	
16	분리하다	
17	지위, 입지	
18	운송하다, 수송하다	
19	의무	
20	확실히 하다, 보장하다	

▶ A-D 정답 : 해설편 111쪽

TEST C-D 각 단어의 뜻을 골라 기호를 쓰시오.

C	English			Korean
01	chemistry	(	)	ⓐ 고정된
02	pinned	(	)	ⓑ 요구에 맞추다
03	compassion	(	)	ⓒ 상호 의존적인
04	meet the demand	(	)	ⓓ 연속된, 잇따른
05	transaction	(	)	ⓔ 군 복무하다
06	interdependent	(	)	ⓕ 제출
07	lower	(	)	ⓖ 분할하다, 나누다
08	successive	(	)	ⓗ 연민
09	submission	(	)	ⓘ 화학
10	serve in the army	(	)	ⓙ ~에서 기원하다
11	executive	(	)	ⓚ 거래
12	stem from	(	)	ⓛ 발한, 땀이 남
13	overestimate	(	)	ⓜ 운전자
14	outstanding	(	)	ⓝ 화물 운송
15	sweating	(	)	ⓞ 외과 의사
16	segment	(	)	ⓟ 숙소
17	motorist	(	)	ⓠ 뛰어난
18	surgeon	(	)	ⓡ 과대평가하다
19	freight	(	)	ⓢ 임원, 중역
20	accommodation	(	)	ⓣ 떨어뜨리다

D	Korean			English
01	유혹적인, 솔깃한	(	)	ⓐ regretful
02	~에 적합한, 자격을 갖춘	(	)	ⓑ distortion
03	~를 목표로 하다, 의도하다	(	)	ⓒ factor
04	적대적인	(	)	ⓓ composition
05	배우자	(	)	ⓔ switch to
06	왜곡	(	)	ⓕ adversarial
07	요인	(	)	ⓖ intend
08	정착하다	(	)	ⓗ entail
09	오염	(	)	ⓘ tempting
10	작곡	(	)	ⓙ respective
11	유감스러운, 후회하는	(	)	ⓚ spouse
12	각자의	(	)	ⓛ pollution
13	공산, 가능성	(	)	ⓜ applicant
14	경시하다	(	)	ⓝ notable
15	난독증	(	)	ⓞ assume
16	수반하다	(	)	ⓟ odds
17	~로 바꾸다	(	)	ⓠ settle down
18	눈에 띄는	(	)	ⓡ qualified for
19	지원자	(	)	ⓢ dyslexia
20	가정하다	(	)	ⓣ downplay

● 문항수 45개 | 배점 100점 | 제한 시간 70분

● 점수 표시가 없는 문항은 모두 2점

1번부터 17번까지는 듣고 답하는 문제입니다. 1번부터 15번까지는 한 번만 들려주고, 16번부터 17번까지는 두 번 들려줍니다. 방송을 잘 듣고 답을 하시기 바랍니다.

1. 다음을 듣고, 여자가 하는 말의 목적으로 가장 적절한 것을 고르시오.
① 도서관 확장 이전을 공지하려고
② 도서관 이용 안내 영상을 소개하려고
③ 독서 습관 형성 프로그램을 홍보하려고
④ 독해력 향상 방안에 대한 의견을 구하려고
⑤ 독서 프로그램 만족도 조사 참여를 요청하려고

2. 대화를 듣고, 남자의 의견으로 가장 적절한 것을 고르시오.
① 중고품은 직접 만나서 거래해야 한다.
② 물품 구매 시 여러 제품을 비교해야 한다.
③ 계획적으로 예산을 세워 물품을 구매해야 한다.
④ 온라인 거래 시 개인 정보 유출에 유의해야 한다.
⑤ 중고품 구매 시 세부 사항을 꼼꼼히 확인해야 한다.

3. 대화를 듣고, 두 사람의 관계를 가장 잘 나타낸 것을 고르시오.
① 의사 – 간호사　　　② 안경사 – 고객
③ 보건 교사 – 학부모　　④ 사진사 – 모델
⑤ 앱 개발자 – 의뢰인

4. 대화를 듣고, 그림에서 대화의 내용과 일치하지 <u>않는</u> 것을 고르시오.

5. 대화를 듣고, 여자가 할 일로 가장 적절한 것을 고르시오.
① 식료품 주문하기　　② 자동차 수리 맡기기
③ 보고서 제출하기　　④ 고객 센터에 전화하기
⑤ 냉장고에 식료품 넣기

6. 대화를 듣고, 남자가 지불할 금액을 고르시오. [3점]
① $27　② $30　③ $36　④ $40　⑤ $45

7. 대화를 듣고, 여자가 가방을 구입한 이유를 고르시오.
① 유명 연예인들이 착용해서
② 재활용 소재를 사용해서
③ 많은 친구들이 추천해서
④ 디자인이 독특해서
⑤ 가격이 저렴해서

8. 대화를 듣고, Youth Street Dance Contest에 관해 언급되지 <u>않은</u> 것을 고르시오.
① 신청 마감일　　② 심사 기준　　③ 우승 상금액
④ 참가 부문　　　⑤ 신청 방법

9. Lakewoods Plogging에 관한 다음 내용을 듣고, 일치하지 <u>않는</u> 것을 고르시오.
① 참가자는 운동복과 운동화를 착용해야 한다.
② 쓰레기를 담을 봉투가 배부된다.
③ 10월 1일 오전 7시부터 진행될 것이다.
④ 학교 웹사이트에서 신청할 수 있다.
⑤ 참가자 모두 스포츠 양말을 받을 것이다.

10. 다음 표를 보면서 대화를 듣고, 두 사람이 주문할 휴대용 캠핑 히터를 고르시오.

Portable Camping Heater

	Model	Weight (kg)	Price	Energy Source	Customer Rating
①	A	4.2	$85	Oil	★★★
②	B	3.6	$90	Oil	★★★★
③	C	3.4	$92	Electricity	★★★★★
④	D	3.2	$95	Electricity	★★★★
⑤	E	2.8	$115	Electricity	★★★★★

11. 대화를 듣고, 여자의 마지막 말에 대한 남자의 응답으로 가장 적절한 것을 고르시오.
① You can join the tour, too.
② The bike wasn't that expensive.
③ I haven't decided the place, yet.
④ I'm going to rent a bike in the park.
⑤ Autumn is the best season for the tour.

12. 대화를 듣고, 남자의 마지막 말에 대한 여자의 응답으로 가장 적절한 것을 고르시오.
① Great. I'll be there at that time.
② Okay. I'll change my toothbrush.
③ Too bad. I hope you get well soon.
④ No worries. Your painkillers work well.
⑤ Sure. Let me know when he's available.

13. 대화를 듣고, 여자의 마지막 말에 대한 남자의 응답으로 가장 적절한 것을 고르시오.

Man: _____

① Fantastic! We'll be a really good team.
② Sorry. I don't understand why you like it.
③ Good idea! I'll find another partner for you.
④ No problem. I can use my racket to practice.
⑤ I know. Everyone loves watching sports competitions.

14. 대화를 듣고, 남자의 마지막 말에 대한 여자의 응답으로 가장 적절한 것을 고르시오. [3점]

Woman: _____

① Nice! I'm curious about what you'll ask.
② Sure. You should study hard for the quiz.
③ Okay. I'll make some questions right away.
④ All right. I'll see if I can add more pictures.
⑤ Don't worry. It won't take too long to answer.

15. 다음 상황 설명을 듣고, Ms. Olson이 Steven에게 할 말로 가장 적절한 것을 고르시오. [3점]

Ms. Olson: _____

① You can come see me any time you want.
② I'm happy to hear that you've met the CEO.
③ Why do you want to run a gaming company?
④ How about going to your role model's book-signing?
⑤ You should buy more books written by your role model.

[16 ~ 17] 다음을 듣고, 물음에 답하시오.

16. 남자가 하는 말의 주제로 가장 적절한 것은?

① tips for caring for musical instruments
② ways to choose a good musical instrument
③ effects of the weather on musical instruments
④ benefits of learning musical instruments as a child
⑤ difficulties of making your own musical instruments

17. 언급된 악기가 <u>아닌</u> 것은?

① flutes   ② trumpets   ③ pianos
④ drums   ⑤ guitars

이제 듣기 문제가 끝났습니다. 18번부터는 문제지의 지시에 따라 답을 하시기 바랍니다.

18. 다음 글의 목적으로 가장 적절한 것은?

Dear Parents/Guardians,

　Class parties will be held on the afternoon of Friday, December 16th, 2022. Children may bring in sweets, crisps, biscuits, cakes, and drinks. We are requesting that children do not bring in home-cooked or prepared food. All food should arrive in a sealed packet with the ingredients clearly listed. Fruit and vegetables are welcomed if they are pre-packed in a sealed packet from the shop. Please DO NOT send any food into school containing nuts as we have many children with severe nut allergies. Please check the ingredients of all food your children bring carefully. Thank you for your continued support and cooperation.

Yours sincerely,
Lisa Brown, Headteacher

① 학급 파티 일정 변경을 공지하려고
② 학교 식당의 새로운 메뉴를 소개하려고
③ 학생의 특정 음식 알레르기 여부를 조사하려고
④ 학부모의 적극적인 학급 파티 참여를 독려하려고
⑤ 학급 파티에 가져올 음식에 대한 유의 사항을 안내하려고

19. 다음 글에 나타난 'I'의 심경 변화로 가장 적절한 것은?

　It was two hours before the submission deadline and I still hadn't finished my news article. I sat at the desk, but suddenly, the typewriter didn't work. No matter how hard I tapped the keys, the levers wouldn't move to strike the paper. I started to realize that I would not be able to finish the article on time. Desperately, I rested the typewriter on my lap and started hitting each key with as much force as I could manage. Nothing happened. Thinking something might have happened inside of it, I opened the cover, lifted up the keys, and found the problem — a paper clip. The keys had no room to move. After picking it out, I pressed and pulled some parts. The keys moved smoothly again. I breathed deeply and smiled. Now I knew that I could finish my article on time.

① confident   →   nervous
② frustrated   →   relieved
③ bored   →   amazed
④ indifferent →   curious
⑤ excited   →   disappointed

20. 다음 글에서 필자가 주장하는 바로 가장 적절한 것은?

　Experts on writing say, "Get rid of as many words as possible." Each word must do something important. If it doesn't, get rid of it. Well, this doesn't work for speaking. It takes more words to introduce, express, and adequately elaborate an idea in speech than it takes in writing. Why is this so? While the reader can reread, the listener cannot rehear. Speakers do not come equipped with a replay button. Because listeners are easily distracted, they will miss many pieces of what a speaker says. If they miss the crucial sentence, they may never catch up. This makes it necessary for speakers to talk *longer* about their points, using more words on them than would be used to express the same idea in writing.

① 연설 시 중요한 정보는 천천히 말해야 한다.
② 좋은 글을 쓰려면 간결한 문장을 사용해야 한다.
③ 말하기 전에 신중히 생각하는 습관을 길러야 한다.
④ 글을 쓸 때보다 말할 때 더 많은 단어를 사용해야 한다.
⑤ 청중의 이해를 돕기 위해 미리 연설문을 제공해야 한다.

21. 밑줄 친 fire a customer가 다음 글에서 의미하는 바로 가장 적절한 것은?

Is the customer *always* right? When customers return a broken product to a famous company, which makes kitchen and bathroom fixtures, the company nearly always offers a replacement to maintain good customer relations. Still, "there are times you've got to say 'no,'" explains the warranty expert of the company, such as when a product is undamaged or has been abused. Entrepreneur Lauren Thorp, who owns an e-commerce company, says, "While the customer is 'always' right, sometimes you just have to fire a customer." When Thorp has tried everything to resolve a complaint and realizes that the customer will be dissatisfied no matter what, she returns her attention to the rest of her customers, who she says are "the reason for my success."

① deal with a customer's emergency
② delete a customer's purchasing record
③ reject a customer's unreasonable demand
④ uncover the hidden intention of a customer
⑤ rely on the power of an influential customer

22. 다음 글의 요지로 가장 적절한 것은?

A recent study from Carnegie Mellon University in Pittsburgh, called "When Too Much of a Good Thing May Be Bad," indicates that classrooms with too much decoration are a source of distraction for young children and directly affect their cognitive performance. Being visually overstimulated, the children have a great deal of difficulty concentrating and end up with worse academic results. On the other hand, if there is not much decoration on the classroom walls, the children are less distracted, spend more time on their activities, and learn more. So it's our job, in order to support their attention, to find the right balance between excessive decoration and the complete absence of it.

① 아이들의 집중을 돕기 위해 과도한 교실 장식을 지양할 필요가 있다.
② 아이들의 인성과 인지 능력을 균형 있게 발달시키는 것이 중요하다.
③ 아이들이 직접 교실을 장식하는 것은 창의력 발달에 도움이 된다.
④ 다양한 교실 활동은 아이들의 수업 참여도를 증진시킨다.
⑤ 풍부한 시각 자료는 아이들의 학습 동기를 높인다.

23. 다음 글의 주제로 가장 적절한 것은?

For creatures like us, evolution smiled upon those with a strong need to belong. Survival and reproduction are the criteria of success by natural selection, and forming relationships with other people can be useful for both survival and reproduction. Groups can share resources, care for sick members, scare off predators, fight together against enemies, divide tasks so as to improve efficiency, and contribute to survival in many other ways. In particular, if an individual and a group want the same resource, the group will generally prevail, so competition for resources would especially favor a need to belong. Belongingness will likewise promote reproduction, such as by bringing potential mates into contact with each other, and in particular by keeping parents together to care for their children, who are much more likely to survive if they have more than one caregiver.

① skills for the weak to survive modern life
② usefulness of belonging for human evolution
③ ways to avoid competition among social groups
④ roles of social relationships in children's education
⑤ differences between two major evolutionary theories

24. 다음 글의 제목으로 가장 적절한 것은?

Many people make a mistake of only operating along the safe zones, and in the process they miss the opportunity to achieve greater things. They do so because of a fear of the unknown and a fear of treading the unknown paths of life. Those that are brave enough to take those roads less travelled are able to get great returns and derive major satisfaction out of their courageous moves. Being overcautious will mean that you will miss attaining the greatest levels of your potential. You must learn to take those chances that many people around you will not take, because your success will flow from those bold decisions that you will take along the way.

* tread: 밟다

① More Courage Brings More Opportunities
② Travel: The Best Way to Make Friends
③ How to Turn Mistakes into Success
④ Satisfying Life? Share with Others
⑤ Why Is Overcoming Fear So Hard?

25. 다음 도표의 내용과 일치하지 <u>않는</u> 것은?

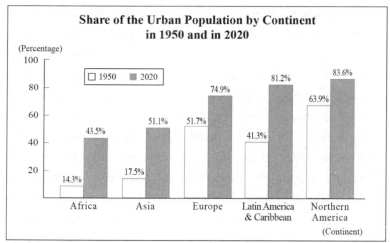

Share of the Urban Population by Continent in 1950 and in 2020

The graph above shows the share of the urban population by continent in 1950 and in 2020. ① For each continent, the share of the urban population in 2020 was larger than that in 1950. ② From 1950 to 2020, the share of the urban population in Africa increased from 14.3% to 43.5%. ③ The share of the urban population in Asia was the second lowest in 1950 but not in 2020. ④ In 1950, the share of the urban population in Europe was larger than that in Latin America and the Caribbean, whereas the reverse was true in 2020. ⑤ Among the five continents, Northern America was ranked in the first position for the share of the urban population in both 1950 and 2020.

26. Wilbur Smith에 관한 다음 글의 내용과 일치하지 <u>않는</u> 것은?

Wilbur Smith was a South African novelist specialising in historical fiction. Smith wanted to become a journalist, writing about social conditions in South Africa, but his father was never supportive of his writing and forced him to get a real job. Smith studied further and became a tax accountant, but he finally turned back to his love of writing. He wrote his first novel, *The Gods First Make Mad*, and had received 20 rejections by 1962. In 1964, Smith published another novel, *When the Lion Feeds*, and it went on to be successful, selling around the world. A famous actor and film producer bought the film rights for *When the Lion Feeds*, although no movie resulted. By the time of his death in 2021 he had published 49 novels, selling more than 140 million copies worldwide.

① 역사 소설을 전문으로 하는 소설가였다.
② 아버지는 그가 글 쓰는 것을 지지하지 않았다.
③ 첫 번째 소설은 1962년까지 20번 거절당했다.
④ 소설 *When the Lion Feeds*는 영화화되었다.
⑤ 죽기 전까지 49편의 소설을 출간했다.

27. 2022 Springfield Park Yoga Class에 관한 다음 안내문의 내용과 일치하지 <u>않는</u> 것은?

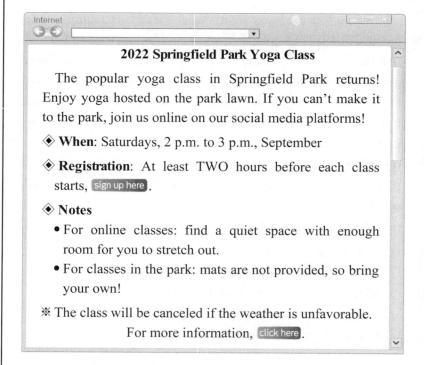

2022 Springfield Park Yoga Class

The popular yoga class in Springfield Park returns! Enjoy yoga hosted on the park lawn. If you can't make it to the park, join us online on our social media platforms!

◈ **When**: Saturdays, 2 p.m. to 3 p.m., September

◈ **Registration**: At least TWO hours before each class starts, sign up here.

◈ **Notes**
 • For online classes: find a quiet space with enough room for you to stretch out.
 • For classes in the park: mats are not provided, so bring your own!

※ The class will be canceled if the weather is unfavorable.
 For more information, click here.

① 온라인으로도 참여할 수 있다.
② 9월 중 토요일마다 진행된다.
③ 수업 시작 2시간 전까지 등록해야 한다.
④ 매트가 제공된다.
⑤ 날씨가 좋지 않으면 취소될 것이다.

28. Kenner High School's Water Challenge에 관한 다음 안내문의 내용과 일치하는 것은?

Kenner High School's Water Challenge

Kenner High School's Water Challenge is a new contest to propose measures against water pollution. Please share your ideas for dealing with water pollution!

Submission
- **How**: Submit your proposal by email to admin@khswater.edu.
- **When**: September 5, 2022 to September 23, 2022

Details
- Participants must enter in teams of four and can only join one team.
- Submission is limited to one proposal per team.
- Participants must use the proposal form provided on the website.

Prizes
- 1st: $50 gift certificate
- 2nd: $30 gift certificate
- 3rd: $10 gift certificate
Please visit www.khswater.edu to learn more about the challenge.

① 제안서는 직접 방문하여 제출해야 한다.
② 9월 23일부터 제안서를 제출할 수 있다.
③ 제안서는 한 팀당 4개까지 제출할 수 있다.
④ 제공된 제안서 양식을 사용해야 한다.
⑤ 2등은 10달러의 상품권을 받는다.

29. 다음 글의 밑줄 친 부분 중, 어법상 <u>틀린</u> 것은? [3점]

The human brain, it turns out, has shrunk in mass by about 10 percent since it ① <u>peaked</u> in size 15,000−30,000 years ago. One possible reason is that many thousands of years ago humans lived in a world of dangerous predators ② <u>where</u> they had to have their wits about them at all times to avoid being killed. Today, we have effectively domesticated ourselves and many of the tasks of survival — from avoiding immediate death to building shelters to obtaining food — ③ <u>has</u> been outsourced to the wider society. We are smaller than our ancestors too, and it is a characteristic of domestic animals ④ <u>that</u> they are generally smaller than their wild cousins. None of this may mean we are dumber — brain size is not necessarily an indicator of human intelligence — but it may mean that our brains today are wired up differently, and perhaps more efficiently, than ⑤ <u>those</u> of our ancestors.

30. 다음 글의 밑줄 친 부분 중, 문맥상 낱말의 쓰임이 적절하지 <u>않은</u> 것은? [3점]

It is widely believed that certain herbs somehow magically improve the work of certain organs, and "cure" specific diseases as a result. Such statements are unscientific and groundless. Sometimes herbs appear to work, since they tend to ① <u>increase</u> your blood circulation in an aggressive attempt by your body to eliminate them from your system. That can create a ② <u>temporary</u> feeling of a high, which makes it seem as if your health condition has improved. Also, herbs can have a placebo effect, just like any other method, thus helping you feel better. Whatever the case, it is your body that has the intelligence to ③ <u>regain</u> health, and not the herbs. How can herbs have the intelligence needed to direct your body into getting healthier? That is impossible. Try to imagine how herbs might come into your body and intelligently ④ <u>fix</u> your problems. If you try to do that, you will see how impossible it seems. Otherwise, it would mean that herbs are ⑤ <u>less</u> intelligent than the human body, which is truly hard to believe.

* placebo effect: 위약 효과

[31~34] 다음 빈칸에 들어갈 말로 가장 적절한 것을 고르시오.

31. We worry that the robots are taking our jobs, but just as common a problem is that the robots are taking our _____ . In the large warehouses so common behind the scenes of today's economy, human 'pickers' hurry around grabbing products off shelves and moving them to where they can be packed and dispatched. In their ears are headpieces: the voice of 'Jennifer', a piece of software, tells them where to go and what to do, controlling the smallest details of their movements. Jennifer breaks down instructions into tiny chunks, to minimise error and maximise productivity — for example, rather than picking eighteen copies of a book off a shelf, the human worker would be politely instructed to pick five. Then another five. Then yet another five. Then another three. Working in such conditions reduces people to machines made of flesh. Rather than asking us to think or adapt, the Jennifer unit takes over the thought process and treats workers as an inexpensive source of some visual processing and a pair of opposable thumbs. [3점]

* dispatch: 발송하다 ** chunk: 덩어리

① reliability
② judgment
③ endurance
④ sociability
⑤ cooperation

32. The prevailing view among developmental scientists is that people are active contributors to their own development. People are influenced by the physical and social contexts in which they live, but they also play a role in influencing their development by interacting with, and changing, those contexts. Even infants influence the world around them and construct their own development through their interactions. Consider an infant who smiles at each adult he sees; he influences his world because adults are likely to smile, use "baby talk," and play with him in response. The infant brings adults into close contact, making one-on-one interactions and creating opportunities for learning. By engaging the world around them, thinking, being curious, and interacting with people, objects, and the world around them, individuals of all ages are "_____."

① mirrors of their generation
② shields against social conflicts
③ explorers in their own career path
④ followers of their childhood dreams
⑤ manufacturers of their own development

33. The demand for freshness can _____.

While freshness is now being used as a term in food marketing as part of a return to nature, the demand for year-round supplies of fresh produce such as soft fruit and exotic vegetables has led to the widespread use of hot houses in cold climates and increasing reliance on total quality control — management by temperature control, use of pesticides and computer/satellite-based logistics. The demand for freshness has also contributed to concerns about food wastage. Use of 'best before', 'sell by' and 'eat by' labels has legally allowed institutional waste. Campaigners have exposed the scandal of over-production and waste. Tristram Stuart, one of the global band of anti-waste campaigners, argues that, with freshly made sandwiches, over-ordering is standard practice across the retail sector to avoid the appearance of empty shelf space, leading to high volumes of waste when supply regularly exceeds demand.

[3점]

* pesticide: 살충제 ** logistics: 물류, 유통

① have hidden environmental costs
② worsen the global hunger problem
③ bring about technological advances
④ improve nutrition and quality of food
⑤ diversify the diet of a local community

34. In the studies of Colin Cherry at the Massachusetts Institute for Technology back in the 1950s, his participants listened to voices in one ear at a time and then through both ears in an effort to determine whether we can listen to two people talk at the same time. One ear always contained a message that the listener had to repeat back (called "shadowing") while the other ear included people speaking. The trick was to see if you could totally focus on the main message and also hear someone talking in your other ear. Cleverly, Cherry found it was impossible for his participants to know whether the message in the other ear was spoken by a man or woman, in English or another language, or was even comprised of real words at all! In other words, people could not _____.

[3점]

① decide what they should do in the moment
② remember a message with too many words
③ analyze which information was more accurate
④ speak their own ideas while listening to others
⑤ process two pieces of information at the same time

35. 다음 글에서 전체 흐름과 관계 없는 문장은?

The fast-paced evolution of Information and Communication Technologies (ICTs) has radically transformed the dynamics and business models of the tourism and hospitality industry. ① This leads to new levels/forms of competitiveness among service providers and transforms the customer experience through new services. ② Creating unique experiences and providing convenient services to customers leads to satisfaction and, eventually, customer loyalty to the service provider or brand (i.e., hotels). ③ In particular, the most recent *technological* boost received by the tourism sector is represented by mobile applications. ④ Increasing competitiveness among service providers does not necessarily mean promoting quality of customer services. ⑤ Indeed, empowering tourists with mobile access to services such as hotel reservations, airline ticketing, and recommendations for local attractions generates strong interest and considerable profits.

* hospitality industry: 서비스업(호텔·식당업 등)

[36 ~ 37] 주어진 글 다음에 이어질 글의 순서로 가장 적절한 것을 고르시오.

36.

> With nearly a billion hungry people in the world, there is obviously no single cause.

(A) The reason people are hungry in those countries is that the products produced there can be sold on the world market for more than the local citizens can afford to pay for them. In the modern age you do not starve because you have no food, you starve because you have no money.

(B) However, far and away the biggest cause is poverty. Seventy-nine percent of the world's hungry live in nations that are net exporters of food. How can this be?

(C) So the problem really is that food is, in the grand scheme of things, too expensive and many people are too poor to buy it. The answer will be in continuing the trend of lowering the cost of food.

* net exporter: 순 수출국 ** scheme: 체계, 조직

① (A) − (C) − (B)   ② (B) − (A) − (C)
③ (B) − (C) − (A)   ④ (C) − (A) − (B)
⑤ (C) − (B) − (A)

37.

> Most people have a perfect time of day when they feel they are at their best, whether in the morning, evening, or afternoon.

(A) When your mind and body are less alert than at your "peak" hours, the muse of creativity awakens and is allowed to roam more freely. In other words, when your mental machinery is loose rather than standing at attention, the creativity flows.

(B) However, if the task you face demands creativity and novel ideas, it's best to tackle it at your "worst" time of day! So if you are an early bird, make sure to attack your creative task in the evening, and vice versa for night owls.

(C) Some of us are night owls, some early birds, and others in between may feel most active during the afternoon hours. If you are able to organize your day and divide your work, make it a point to deal with tasks that demand attention at your best time of the day. [3점]

* roam: (어슬렁어슬렁) 거닐다

① (A) − (C) − (B)   ② (B) − (A) − (C)
③ (B) − (C) − (A)   ④ (C) − (A) − (B)
⑤ (C) − (B) − (A)

[38~39] 글의 흐름으로 보아, 주어진 문장이 들어가기에 가장 적절한 곳을 고르시오.

38.

> Unfortunately, it is also likely to "crowd out" other activities that produce more sustainable social contributions to our social well-being.

Television is the number one leisure activity in the United States and Europe, consuming more than half of our free time. (①) We generally think of television as a way to relax, tune out, and escape from our troubles for a bit each day. (②) While this is true, there is increasing evidence that we are more motivated to tune in to our favorite shows and characters when we are feeling lonely or have a greater need for social connection. (③) Television watching does satisfy these social needs to some extent, at least in the short run. (④) The more television we watch, the less likely we are to volunteer our time or to spend time with people in our social networks. (⑤) In other words, the more time we make for *Friends*, the less time we have for friends in real life.

* *Friends*: 프렌즈(미국의 한 방송국에서 방영된 시트콤)

39.

> What we need is a reliable and reproducible method for measuring the relative hotness or coldness of objects rather than the rate of energy transfer.

We often associate the concept of temperature with how hot or cold an object feels when we touch it. In this way, our senses provide us with a qualitative indication of temperature. (①) Our senses, however, are unreliable and often mislead us. (②) For example, if you stand in bare feet with one foot on carpet and the other on a tile floor, the tile feels colder than the carpet *even though both are at the same temperature*. (③) The two objects feel different because tile transfers energy by heat at a higher rate than carpet does. (④) Your skin "measures" the rate of energy transfer by heat rather than the actual temperature. (⑤) Scientists have developed a variety of thermometers for making such quantitative measurements. [3점]

* thermometer: 온도계

40. 다음 글의 내용을 한 문장으로 요약하고자 한다. 빈칸 (A), (B)에 들어갈 말로 가장 적절한 것은?

> My colleagues and I ran an experiment testing two different messages meant to convince thousands of resistant alumni to make a donation. One message emphasized the opportunity to do good: donating would benefit students, faculty, and staff. The other emphasized the opportunity to feel good: donors would enjoy the warm glow of giving. The two messages were equally effective: in both cases, 6.5 percent of the unwilling alumni ended up donating. Then we combined them, because two reasons are better than one. Except they weren't. When we put the two reasons together, the giving rate dropped below 3 percent. Each reason alone was more than twice as effective as the two combined. The audience was already skeptical. When we gave them different kinds of reasons to donate, we triggered their awareness that someone was trying to persuade them — and they shielded themselves against it.

* alumni: 졸업생 ** skeptical: 회의적인

↓

> In the experiment mentioned above, when the two different reasons to donate were given _____(A)_____, the audience was less likely to be _____(B)_____ because they could recognize the intention to persuade them.

     (A)   (B)
① simultaneously ······ convinced
② separately ······ confused
③ frequently ······ annoyed
④ separately ······ satisfied
⑤ simultaneously ······ offended

[41 ~ 42] 다음 글을 읽고, 물음에 답하시오.

In a society that rejects the consumption of insects there are some individuals who overcome this rejection, but most will continue with this attitude. It may be very (a) difficult to convince an entire society that insects are totally suitable for consumption. However, there are examples in which this (b) reversal of attitudes about certain foods has happened to an entire society. Several examples in the past 120 years from European-American society are: considering lobster a luxury food instead of a food for servants and prisoners; considering sushi a safe and delicious food; and considering pizza not just a food for the rural poor of Sicily. In Latin American countries, where insects are already consumed, a portion of the population hates their consumption and (c) associates it with poverty. There are also examples of people who have had the habit of consuming them and (d) encouraged that habit due to shame, and because they do not want to be categorized as poor or uncivilized. According to Esther Katz, an anthropologist, if the consumption of insects as a food luxury is to be promoted, there would be more chances that some individuals who do not present this habit overcome ideas under which they were educated. And this could also help to (e) revalue the consumption of insects by those people who already eat them.

41. 윗글의 제목으로 가장 적절한 것은?

① The More Variety on the Table, The Healthier You Become
② Edible or Not? Change Your Perspectives on Insects
③ Insects: A Key to Solve the World Food Shortage
④ Don't Let Uniqueness in Food Culture Disappear
⑤ Experiencing Various Cultures by Food

42. 밑줄 친 (a)~(e) 중에서 문맥상 낱말의 쓰임이 적절하지 않은 것은?

① (a)　　② (b)　　③ (c)　　④ (d)　　⑤ (e)

[43 ~ 45] 다음 글을 읽고, 물음에 답하시오.

(A)

A boy had a place at the best school in town. In the morning, his granddad took him to the school. When (a) he went onto the playground with his grandson, the children surrounded them. "What a funny old man," one boy smirked. A girl with brown hair pointed at the pair and jumped up and down. Suddenly, the bell rang and the children ran off to their first lesson.

* smirk: 히죽히죽 웃다

(B)

In some schools the children completely ignored the old man and in others, they made fun of (b) him. When this happened, he would turn sadly and go home. Finally, he went onto the tiny playground of a very small school, and leant against the fence, exhausted. The bell rang, and the crowd of children ran out onto the playground. "Sir, are you all right? Shall I bring you a glass of water?" a voice said. "We've got a bench in the playground—come and sit down," another voice said. Soon a young teacher came out onto the playground.

(C)

The old man greeted (c) him and said: "Finally, I've found my grandson the best school in town." "You're mistaken, sir. Our school is not the best—it's small and cramped." The old man didn't argue with the teacher. Instead, he made arrangements for his grandson to join the school, and then the old man left. That evening, the boy's mom said to (d) him: "Dad, you can't even read. How do you know you've found the best teacher of all?" "Judge a teacher by his pupils," the old man replied.

* cramped: 비좁은

(D)

The old man took his grandson firmly by the hand, and led him out of the school gate. "Brilliant, I don't have to go to school!" the boy exclaimed. "You do, but not this one," his granddad replied. "I'll find you a school myself." Granddad took his grandson back to his own house, asked grandma to look after him, and went off to look for a teacher (e) himself. Every time he spotted a school, the old man went onto the playground, and waited for the children to come out at break time.

43. 주어진 글 (A)에 이어질 내용을 순서에 맞게 배열한 것으로 가장 적절한 것은?

① (B) − (D) − (C)　　② (C) − (B) − (D)
③ (C) − (D) − (B)　　④ (D) − (B) − (C)
⑤ (D) − (C) − (B)

44. 밑줄 친 (a)~(e) 중에서 가리키는 대상이 나머지 넷과 다른 것은?

① (a)　　② (b)　　③ (c)　　④ (d)　　⑤ (e)

45. 윗글에 관한 내용으로 적절하지 않은 것은?

① 갈색 머리 소녀가 노인과 소년을 향해 손가락질했다.
② 노인은 지쳐서 울타리에 기댔다.
③ 노인은 선생님과 논쟁을 벌였다.
④ 노인은 글을 읽을 줄 몰랐다.
⑤ 소년은 학교에 가지 않아도 된다고 소리쳤다.

＊ 확인 사항
○ 답안지의 해당란에 필요한 내용을 정확히 기입(표기)했는지 확인하시오.

※ QR 코드를 스캔하시면 듣기 방송이 나옵니다. 듣기 방송을 들으며 다음 빈칸을 채우시오.　　● 제한 시간 : 25분

01

다음을 듣고, 여자가 하는 말의 목적으로 가장 적절한 것을 고르시오.

W : Good evening, Vermont citizens. I'm Elizabeth Bowen, the Director of the Vermont City Library. I'd like to tell you about our online 15-Minute Book Reading program. This program is designed to help your children _____ _____ _____ _____ at home. Every day, individual tutoring is provided for 15 minutes. It's ✿ _____ _____ _____ your child's reading level! Don't hesitate to sign up your children _____ _____ _____ _____ to build their reading habits! For more information, please visit the Vermont City Library. Thank you.

02

대화를 듣고, 남자의 의견으로 가장 적절한 것을 고르시오.

M : Clara, why the long face?

W : Aw, Dad, I bought this hair dryer, but the cool air mode doesn't work.

M : Where did you get it?

W : I bought it second-hand online.

M : Did you check the condition before you ordered it?

W : I did, but I _____ _____ _____ _____ that said the cool air mode doesn't work.

M : Oh dear. It's important to check all the details when you buy second-hand items.

W : You're right. I was just so excited because it was _____ _____ _____ _____ _____ _____.

M : Some second-hand items are almost like new, but others are not. So, you should ✿ _____ _____ _____ _____ _____ _____ carefully.

W : Thanks, Dad. I'll keep that in mind.

03

대화를 듣고, 두 사람의 관계를 가장 잘 나타낸 것을 고르시오.

M : Hello, Ms. Adams! It's been a while since you were here.

W : Last time I came, you told me I should _____ _____ _____ every year.

M : That's right. When did you last visit us?

W : I guess I came here last October.

M : Okay. Then, let me _____ _____ _____. Please sit here. *[Pause]* Hmm... your eyesight got a little worse.

W : Yeah, maybe it's because I've been working on a computer for too long.

M : Actually, the blue light from computers and smartphones makes your eyes tired.

W : Really? Is there a lens that blocks the light?

M : Sure. You can wear these blue light blocking lenses.

W : That sounds perfect. But I'd like to _____ _____ _____ again.

M : No problem, you can just change the lenses. You can come ✿ _____ _____ _____ _____ _____ _____ _____.

W : Okay, thank you so much. See you then.

04

대화를 듣고, 그림에서 대화의 내용과 일치하지 않는 것을 고르시오.

W : Carl, what are you looking at?

M : Oh, hi, Amy. Come take a look. It's a picture of my grandparents' house. I was there last weekend.

W : What a beautiful house! There's even a pond under the tree!

M : Yes, my grandfather _____ _____ _____. And how about that flower-patterned tablecloth?

W : I love it. It makes the table look cozy.

M : Did you see the painting of a bear on the door?

W : Oh! Did you paint that?

M : Yeah, I did it when I was 8 years old.

W : It's cute. And there are two windows on the roof.

M : Right, we get a lot of sunlight through the windows.

W : I like that! And can you still ✿ _____ _____ _____ next to the house?

M : Of course. That's the best spot to _____ _____ _____.

W : Wow, your grandparents' house looks like a nice place!

05

대화를 듣고, 여자가 할 일로 가장 적절한 것을 고르시오.

M : Honey, there's a box in the doorway. What is it?

W : I ordered some groceries online. Would you bring it in?

M : Sure. Is this for the house-warming party today?

W : Yeah. Since I had to ✿ _____ _____ _____, I couldn't go shopping yesterday.

M : Sorry, I should've taken you to the market.

W : That's okay. You worked late to meet the deadline for your report. Would you open the box for me?

M : Sure. *[Pause]* Oh no, _____ _____ _____! Have a look.

W : Ah... that's never happened before.

M : Why don't we _____ _____ _____ _____ about it?

W : Okay. I'll do it right now.

M : While you do that, I'll put the other food in the fridge.

W : Thanks.

06

대화를 듣고, 남자가 지불할 금액을 고르시오. [3점]

W : Hello, welcome to Kelly's Bake Shop. How can I help you?

M : Hi, I'd like to _____.

W : Okay, we have two sizes. A small one is $25 and a large one is $35. Which one would you like?

M : Well, we're four people, so a large one would be good.

W : Great. _____?

M : No thanks, but can you ✿ _____ _____?

W : We can. It costs $5. What would you like the message to say?

M : Please write "Thank You Mom" on it.

W : Sure. It takes about half an hour. Is that okay?

M : No problem. Can I use this 10% off coupon?

W : Certainly. You get 10% off the total.

M : Thanks. Here's my credit card.

07

대화를 듣고, 여자가 가방을 구입한 이유를 고르시오.

M : Anna, I haven't seen you use this bag before. Did you buy a new one?

W : Hi, Jason. Yeah, I bought it online last week.

M : I saw ✿ _____ _____ on their social media.

W : Really? I didn't know that, but this bag seems to be popular.

M : It does, but its design isn't that unique. It's too plain.

W : Yeah, and it's a little expensive compared to other bags.

M : Well, then why did you buy it?

W : I bought it because it's _____ _____.

M : Oh, you're _____.

W : Exactly. So, I'm recommending it to all my friends.

M : Good idea. I'll check the website for more information.

08

대화를 듣고, Youth Street Dance Contest에 관해 언급되지 않은 것을 고르시오.

W : Jimmy, what are you doing with your smartphone?

M : I'm looking at a poster about the Youth Street Dance Contest.

W : Oh, isn't it a street dance contest for high school students?

M : Yeah. Why don't you enter? I know you're good at dancing.

W : Hmm... when is it?

M : The competition is October 22nd, but the _____ is September 30th.

W : Okay, good. I have a few months to practice.

M : And look! The winner gets $2,000!

W : That's amazing! What types of dancing are there?

M : It says participants should choose one of these three types: hip-hop, locking, and breakdancing.

W : I'm _____, so I'll enter with that. How do I apply?

M : You just ✿ _____ _____ and submit it by email.

W : Okay! It'll be a great experience for me to try out.

09

Lakewoods Plogging에 관한 다음 내용을 듣고, 일치하지 않는 것을 고르시오.

M : Hello, Lakewoods High School students! I'm Lawrence Cho, president of the student council. I'm happy to announce a special new event to _____ _____: Lakewoods Plogging! Since plogging is the activity of _____, all participants should ✿ _____ _____ _____. We provide eco-friendly bags for the trash, so you don't need to bring any. The event will be held on October 1st from 7 a.m. to 9 a.m. You can sign up for the event on the school website starting tomorrow. The first 30 participants will get a pair of sports socks. For more information, please visit our school website. Don't miss this fun opportunity!

10

다음 표를 보면서 대화를 듣고, 두 사람이 주문할 휴대용 캠핑 히터를 고르시오.

M : Honey, what are you doing?

W : I'm looking at a website to order a portable heater for winter camping. Would you like to choose one together?

M : Sure, let me see.

W : We should be able to carry it easily, so _____ _____ _____. I think we should get one of these under 4kg.

M : Good point. Oh, this one is pretty expensive.

W : I know. Let's choose one of these for less than $100.

M : Okay. And I think _____. What do you think?

W : I agree. It's safer to use.

M : Now we have these two models left.

W : I'd like the one ✿ _____ _____.

M : All right. Let's order this one.

11

대화를 듣고, 여자의 마지막 말에 대한 남자의 응답으로 가장 적절한 것을 고르시오.

W : Kevin, is this bike yours?

M : Yes, I ✿ _____ for my bike tour.

W : Really? _____ _____?

12

대화를 듣고, 남자의 마지막 말에 대한 여자의 응답으로 가장 적절한 것을 고르시오.

[Telephone rings.]

M : Hello, this is Ashley's Dental Clinic. How may I help you?

W : Hello, this is Emily Gibson. _____ _____ _____
_____ _____ _____ ? I ✪ _____ _____
_____ _____ .

M : Just a second. Let me check. *[Pause]* He's available at 4:30 this afternoon.

13

대화를 듣고, 여자의 마지막 말에 대한 남자의 응답으로 가장 적절한 것을 고르시오.

W : Hey, Justin. Do you know where those students are going?

M : They're probably going to the gym to practice badminton.

W : Why are so many students practicing badminton?

M : Haven't you heard about the School Badminton Tournament? Many of the students have already signed up for it.

W : Really? Why is it so popular?

M : The winners will _____ _____ _____ _____
and there are lots of other prizes as well.

W : That's nice! Why don't you sign up for it, too?

M : I'd like to, but ✪ _____ _____ _____ _____ .
And I haven't found a partner, yet.

W : Actually, I used to be a badminton player in my elementary school.

M : Wow! I have a top expert right here! _____ _____
_____ _____ _____ ?

W : Sure. Not an expert, but I can try.

14

대화를 듣고, 남자의 마지막 말에 대한 여자의 응답으로 가장 적절한 것을 고르시오. [3점]

M : Hey, Natalie. What are you doing on your computer?

W : Hi, Dave. I'm working on my presentation for social studies class. It's about _____ _____ _____ _____ .

M : Sounds interesting. Can I see it?

W : Sure. I'll introduce some games with these pictures.

M : That's a great idea, but I think you have too many words on the slides.

W : You're right. I'm worried it might be boring.

M : Then, how about ✪ _____ _____ _____ and using some questions? It would make your presentation more interesting.

W : Great idea! What do you think about True-or-False questions?

M : That's good. Your audience will be able to focus on your presentation while thinking about the answers.

W : But... what if they don't know the answers?

M : It doesn't matter. They'll _____ _____ _____
_____ _____ .

15

다음 상황 설명을 듣고, Ms. Olson이 Steven에게 할 말로 가장 적절한 것을 고르시오. [3점]

W : Steven is a high school student and Ms. Olson is a career counselor at his school. Steven has much interest in the video game industry. A few days ago, Ms. Olson recommended a book written by a CEO who _____ _____ _____
_____ _____ . After reading the book, Steven told her that the CEO is his role model. This morning, Ms. Olson hears the news that the CEO is going to ✪ _____ _____
_____ _____ _____ _____ .
She thinks Steven would love to _____ _____
_____ _____ _____ _____ . So, Ms. Olson wants to tell Steven that he should go see the CEO at the event. In this situation, what would Ms. Olson most likely say to Steven?

16~17

다음을 듣고, 물음에 답하시오.

M : Hello, students. Last class, we took a brief look at how to tune your musical instruments. Today, we're going to talk a bit about how to take care of and _____ _____ _____ .
First, let's take flutes. They may have moisture from the air blown through them, so you should clean and wipe the mouth piece before and after playing. Next are trumpets. They _____
_____ _____ _____ , so you should air dry the parts in a cool dry place, away from direct sunlight. And as for pianos, they don't need everyday care, but it's essential to protect the keys by covering them with a protective pad _____
_____ _____ _____ . The last ones are string instruments like guitars. Their strings need replacement. When you replace the strings, it's good to do it gradually, one at a time. Proper care can ✪ _____ _____ _____ of your musical instruments. I hope this lesson helps you to keep your musical instruments safe from damage.

▶ 정답 : 해설편 **125**쪽

18
001 □ guardian ⓝ 보호자
002 □ hold ⓥ (행사를) 열다, 개최하다
003 □ bring in 가져오다
004 □ home-cooked ⓐ 집에서 요리한
005 □ sealed ⓐ 밀봉한
006 □ packet ⓝ 꾸러미
007 □ ingredient ⓝ 성분, 재료
008 □ clearly ⓐⓓ 명확하게
009 □ welcome ⓥ 환영하다
010 □ pre-packed ⓐ 사전 포장된
011 □ contain ⓥ 포함하다, 함유하다
012 □ severe ⓐ 심각한
013 □ carefully ⓐⓓ 주의 깊게
014 □ continued ⓐ 지속적인
015 □ cooperation ⓝ 협조, 협력
016 □ headteacher ⓝ (공립학교) 교장

19
017 □ submission ⓝ 제출
018 □ deadline ⓝ 마감
019 □ article ⓝ 기사
020 □ work ⓥ 작동하다
021 □ strike ⓥ 치다, 때리다, 두드리다
022 □ be able to ~할 수 있다
023 □ on time 제시간에
024 □ desperately ⓐⓓ 필사적으로
025 □ rest ⓥ 놓다
026 □ lap ⓝ 무릎
027 □ lift up 들어올리다
028 □ pick out 빼다, 뽑다
029 □ smoothly ⓐⓓ 부드럽게
030 □ deeply ⓐⓓ 깊이
031 □ frustrated ⓐ 좌절한

20
032 □ get rid of ~을 제거하다
033 □ as ~ as possible 최대한 ~한
034 □ work for ~에 효과가 있다
035 □ express ⓥ 표현하다
036 □ adequately ⓐⓓ 적절하게
037 □ elaborate ⓥ 부연 설명하다, 자세히 말하다
038 □ speech ⓝ 연설, 말하기
039 □ reread ⓥ 다시 읽다
040 □ distract ⓥ 주의를 분산시키다
041 □ crucial ⓐ 아주 중요한
042 □ catch up 따라잡다
043 □ necessary ⓐ 필수적인, 필연적인
044 □ point ⓝ 요점

21
045 □ broken ⓐ 고장 난
046 □ fixture ⓝ 설비, 살림, 세간
047 □ replacement ⓝ 대체(품)
048 □ maintain ⓥ 유지하다
049 □ relation ⓝ 관계
050 □ warranty ⓝ (상품 품질) 보증
051 □ undamaged ⓐ 멀쩡한, 손상되지 않은
052 □ abuse ⓝ 남용하다
053 □ entrepreneur ⓝ 기업가, 사업가
054 □ own ⓥ 소유하다
055 □ e-commerce ⓝ 전자 상거래

056 □ fire ⓥ 해고하다
057 □ resolve ⓥ 해결하다
058 □ complaint ⓝ 불만
059 □ dissatisfied ⓐ 불만족한
060 □ the rest of ~의 나머지
061 □ reason ⓝ 이유
062 □ emergency ⓝ 응급 상황, 비상 사태
063 □ delete ⓥ 지우다, 삭제하다
064 □ purchasing record 구매 기록
065 □ reject ⓥ 거절하다
066 □ unreasonable ⓐ 불합리한
067 □ uncover ⓥ 드러내다, 밝히다
068 □ intention ⓝ 의도, 목적
069 □ rely on ~에 의존하다
070 □ influential ⓐ 영향력 있는

22
071 □ indicate ⓥ 보여주다, 나타내다
072 □ distraction ⓝ 주의 산만, 집중을 방해하는 것
073 □ cognitive ⓐ 인지적인
074 □ visually ⓐⓓ 시각적으로
075 □ overstimulate ⓥ 과도하게 자극하다
076 □ a great deal of 상당한, 큰, 많은
077 □ concentrate ⓥ 집중하다
078 □ end up with 결국 ~하다
079 □ academic ⓐ 학업의
080 □ support ⓥ 지지 ⓥ 지지하다, 돕다
081 □ attention ⓝ 집중, 주의
082 □ balance ⓝ 균형
083 □ excessive ⓐ 과도한
084 □ complete ⓐ 완전한
085 □ absence ⓝ 부재

23
086 □ creature ⓝ 생명체, 피조물
087 □ evolution ⓝ 진화
088 □ reproduction ⓝ 번식, 재생
089 □ criterion ⓝ 기준
090 □ natural selection 자연 선택
091 □ form ⓝ 양식, 서류 ⓥ 형성하다
092 □ care for ~을 돌보다
093 □ scare off ~을 겁주어 쫓아버리다
094 □ predator ⓝ 포식자
095 □ fight against ~에 맞서 싸우다
096 □ divide ⓥ 나누다
097 □ prevail ⓥ 우세하다
098 □ favor ⓥ 선호하다
099 □ belongingness ⓝ 소속, 귀속, 친밀감
100 □ likewise ⓐⓓ 마찬가지로
101 □ caregiver ⓝ 양육자

24
102 □ make a mistake of ~의 실수를 범하다
103 □ operate ⓥ 작동하다, 기능하다
104 □ safe zone 안전 구역
105 □ opportunity ⓝ 기회
106 □ achieve ⓥ 성취하다
107 □ fear ⓝ 공포
108 □ unknown ⓐ 미지의, 알지 못하는
109 □ path ⓝ 길
110 □ brave ⓐ 용감한
111 □ return ⓝ 보상

112 □ derive ⓥ 끌어내다, 도출하다
113 □ courageous ⓐ 용감한
114 □ overcautious ⓐ 지나치게 조심하는
115 □ attain ⓥ 달성하다, 얻다
116 □ potential ⓝ 잠재력
117 □ make friends 친구를 사귀다
118 □ satisfying ⓐ 만족스러운

25
119 □ share ⓝ 점유율
120 □ urban ⓐ 도시의
121 □ population ⓝ 인구(수)
122 □ continent ⓝ 대륙
123 □ whereas ⓒⓞⓝⓙ ~한 반면에
124 □ reverse ⓝ 반대, 역전, 전환
125 □ among ⓟⓡⓔⓟ ~ 중에서
126 □ rank ⓥ ~의 순위를 매기다, (입지를) 차지하다

26
127 □ novelist ⓝ 소설가
128 □ specialize in ~을 전문으로 하다
129 □ historical ⓐ 역사적인
130 □ fiction ⓝ 소설, 허구
131 □ journalist ⓝ 언론인, 저널리스트
132 □ condition ⓝ 상황, 환경
133 □ be supportive of ~을 지지하다
134 □ force ⓝ 강요하다 어쩔 수 없이 ~하게 만들다
135 □ tax accountant 세무사
136 □ turn back to ~로 돌아오다
137 □ publish ⓥ 출판하다
138 □ feed ⓥ 먹다, 먹이다
139 □ go on to 계속해서 ~하다
140 □ around the world 세계 곳곳에서
141 □ film rights 영화 판권, 상영권
142 □ by the time of ~할 무렵
143 □ worldwide ⓐⓓ 전 세계에

27
144 □ host ⓥ 열다, 개최하다
145 □ lawn ⓝ 잔디밭
146 □ make it 참석하다, 성공하다, 해내다
147 □ social media 소셜 미디어
148 □ registration ⓝ 등록
149 □ at least 적어도, 최소한
150 □ stretch out 몸을 뻗고 눕다
151 □ provide ⓥ 제공하다
152 □ bring ⓥ 가져오다, 지참하다
153 □ one's own 자기 자신의 (것)
154 □ unfavorable ⓐ (형편이) 나쁜, 우호적이지 않은

28
155 □ measure ⓝ 대책, 조치
156 □ against ⓟⓡⓔⓟ ~에 대항하여
157 □ water pollution 수질 오염
158 □ deal with ~을 다루다, ~에 대처하다
159 □ proposal ⓝ 제안서
160 □ be limited to ~로 제한되다
161 □ prize ⓝ 상(품)
162 □ gift certificate 상품권

29
163 □ turn out ~로 판명되다
164 □ shrink ⓥ 줄어들다
165 □ mass ⓝ 부피, 질량
166 □ about ⓐⓓ 대략, 약
167 □ peak ⓝ 정점 ⓥ 정점을 찍다
168 □ have one's wits about one ~의 기지를 발휘하다
169 □ at all times 항상, 늘
170 □ domesticate ⓥ 길들이다
171 □ immediate ⓐ 즉각적인, 임박한
172 □ shelter ⓝ 쉴 곳, 은신처
173 □ outsource ⓥ 외부에 위탁하다, 아웃소싱 하다
174 □ ancestor ⓝ 조상
175 □ domestic ⓐ 가정의
176 □ dumb ⓐ 어리석은
177 □ not necessarily 반드시 ~하지는 않은
178 □ indicator ⓝ 지표
179 □ intelligence ⓝ 지능
180 □ wire ⓥ 연결하다, 장착하다
181 □ differently than ~와는 다르게

30
182 □ certain ⓐ 특정한, 어떤
183 □ somehow ⓐⓓ 왜인지는 몰라도, 어떻게든
184 □ magically ⓐⓓ 마법처럼
185 □ cure ⓥ (병을) 치유하다, 낫게 하다
186 □ statement ⓝ 진술
187 □ unscientific ⓐ 비과학적인
188 □ groundless ⓐ 근거가 없는
189 □ appear to ~처럼 보이다
190 □ blood circulation 혈액 순환
191 □ aggressive ⓐ 적극적인, 공격적인
192 □ attempt ⓝ 시도, 노력
193 □ eliminate ⓥ 제거하다, 없애다
194 □ temporary ⓐ 일시적인
195 □ high ⓝ 도취감
196 □ health condition 건강 상태
197 □ method ⓝ 방법
198 □ whatever the case 어떤 경우이든지
199 □ regain ⓥ 되찾다, 회복하다
200 □ impossible ⓐ 불가능한
201 □ intelligently ⓐⓓ 똑똑하게, 현명하게, 지적으로

31
202 □ warehouse ⓝ 창고
203 □ picker ⓝ 수확자, 집는 사람
204 □ headpiece ⓝ 헤드폰, 머리에 쓰는 것, 지성, 판단력
205 □ break down 쪼개다
206 □ instruction ⓝ 지시
207 □ tiny ⓐ 아주 작은
208 □ productivity ⓝ 생산성
209 □ shelf ⓝ 선반
210 □ politely ⓐⓓ 정중하게, 예의 바르게
211 □ reduce ⓥ 전락시키다, 격하시키다
212 □ flesh ⓝ (사람, 동물의) 살
213 □ adapt ⓥ 적응하다
214 □ take over 지배하다, 장악하다
215 □ inexpensive ⓐ 값싼

216 ☐ **opposable** ⓐ 마주볼 수 있는	271 ☐ **contain** ⓥ 수용하다, 담다	326 ☐ **night owl** 저녁형 인간	380 ☐ **frequently** [ad] 자주
217 ☐ **reliability** ⓝ 신뢰성	272 ☐ **shadowing** ⓝ 섀도잉	327 ☐ **make it a point to** ~하기로 정하다, 으레 ~하다	381 ☐ **satisfied** ⓐ 만족한
218 ☐ **endurance** ⓝ 인내	273 ☐ **trick** ⓝ 속임수, 요령		382 ☐ **offend** ⓥ 공격하다, 기분 상하게 하다
219 ☐ **sociability** ⓝ 사교성	274 ☐ **totally** [ad] 완전히	**38**	
	275 ☐ **comprise** ⓥ ~을 구성하다	328 ☐ **unfortunately** [ad] 불행히도, 안타깝게도	**41~42**
32	276 ☐ **at all** (부정문 끝에서) 전혀, 아예	329 ☐ **crowd out** 몰아내다	383 ☐ **consumption** ⓝ 섭취, 소비
220 ☐ **prevailing** ⓐ 지배적인, 만연한	277 ☐ **analyze** ⓥ 분석하다	330 ☐ **produce** ⓥ 만들어내다	384 ☐ **individual** ⓝ 개인
221 ☐ **developmental** ⓐ 발달의	278 ☐ **accurate** ⓐ 정확한	331 ☐ **sustainable** ⓐ 지속 가능한	385 ☐ **overcome** ⓥ 극복하다
222 ☐ **active** ⓐ 적극적인, 능동적인	279 ☐ **process** ⓥ 처리하다	332 ☐ **contribution** ⓝ 기여, 이바지	386 ☐ **continue with** ~을 계속하다
223 ☐ **contributor** ⓝ 기여자		333 ☐ **consume** ⓥ 소비하다, 쓰다	387 ☐ **attitude** ⓝ 태도
224 ☐ **influence** ⓥ 영향을 주다	**35**	334 ☐ **free time** 자유 시간, 여가 시간	388 ☐ **convince** ⓥ 납득시키다, 설득하다
225 ☐ **physical** ⓐ 물리적인	280 ☐ **fast-paced** ⓐ 빠른	335 ☐ **think of A as B** A를 B로 여기다, 간주하다, 취급하다	389 ☐ **entire** ⓐ 온, 전체의
226 ☐ **context** ⓝ 상황, 맥락	281 ☐ **radically** [ad] 급진적으로	336 ☐ **tune out** 주의를 돌리다, 관심을 끄다	390 ☐ **suitable for** ~에 적합한
227 ☐ **play a role in** ~에서 역할을 하다	282 ☐ **transform** ⓥ 변모시키다	337 ☐ **escape from** ~로부터 도망치다	391 ☐ **reversal** ⓝ 역전
228 ☐ **interact with** ~와 상호작용하다	283 ☐ **dynamics** ⓝ 역학, 역동성	338 ☐ **a bit** 조금, 약간	392 ☐ **luxury** ⓝ 호사, 사치
229 ☐ **be likely to** ~할 가능성이 높다	284 ☐ **competitiveness** ⓝ 경쟁력, 경쟁적인 것	339 ☐ **tune in to** ~에 채널을 맞추다	393 ☐ **instead of** ~ 대신에
230 ☐ **baby talk** 아기 말(말을 배우는 유아나 어린 이에게 어른이 쓰는 말투)	285 ☐ **convenient** ⓐ 편리한	340 ☐ **satisfy** ⓥ 만족시키다, 충족하다	394 ☐ **servant** ⓝ 하인
231 ☐ **in response** (~에) 반응하여, 호응하여	286 ☐ **satisfaction** ⓝ 만족	341 ☐ **to some extent** 어느 정도	395 ☐ **prisoner** ⓝ 죄수
232 ☐ **close** ⓐ 친밀한	287 ☐ **loyalty** ⓝ 충성도	342 ☐ **in the short run** 단기적으로	396 ☐ **delicious** ⓐ 맛있는
233 ☐ **contact** ⓝ 접촉	288 ☐ **in particular** 특히		397 ☐ **the poor** 가난한 사람들
234 ☐ **one-on-one** ⓐ 일대일의	289 ☐ **technological** ⓐ 기술적인	**39**	398 ☐ **rural** ⓐ 시골의
235 ☐ **generation** ⓝ 세대	290 ☐ **boost** ⓝ 부상, 상승	343 ☐ **reliable** ⓐ 신뢰할 수 있는	399 ☐ **portion** ⓝ 일부, 부분
236 ☐ **shield** ⓝ 방패	291 ☐ **represent** ⓥ 대표하다, 나타내다	344 ☐ **reproducible** ⓐ 재현 가능한	400 ☐ **encourage** ⓥ 장려하다, 권장하다
237 ☐ **conflict** ⓝ 갈등	292 ☐ **application** ⓝ (휴대폰, 컴퓨터 등의) 응용 프로그램, 애플리케이션	345 ☐ **measure** ⓥ 측정하다	401 ☐ **due to** ~ 때문에
238 ☐ **career path** 진로	293 ☐ **empower** ⓥ 권한을 부여하다	346 ☐ **relative** ⓐ 상대적인	402 ☐ **shame** ⓝ 수치심
239 ☐ **manufacturer** ⓝ 생산자	294 ☐ **access** ⓝ 접근 (권한)	347 ☐ **object** ⓝ 물체	403 ☐ **categorize A as B** A를 B라고 분류하다
	295 ☐ **recommendation** ⓝ 추천, 권장	348 ☐ **rate** ⓝ 비율, 속도	404 ☐ **anthropologist** ⓝ 인류학자
33	296 ☐ **attraction** ⓝ (사람을 끄는) 명소, 명물, 매력	349 ☐ **energy transfer** 에너지 전도	405 ☐ **promote** ⓥ 장려하다, 촉진하다, 홍보하다, 증진하다
240 ☐ **demand** ⓝ 요구, 수요	297 ☐ **generate** ⓥ 만들어내다	350 ☐ **associate A with B** A를 B와 연관 짓다	406 ☐ **present** ⓥ 내보이다, 제시하다
241 ☐ **freshness** ⓝ 신선함	298 ☐ **profit** ⓝ 수익	351 ☐ **provide A with B** A에게 B를 제공하다	407 ☐ **revalue** ⓥ 재평가하다
242 ☐ **term** ⓝ 용어		352 ☐ **qualitative** ⓐ 정성적인, 질적인	408 ☐ **variety** ⓝ 종류, 다양성
243 ☐ **as part of** ~의 일환으로	**36**	353 ☐ **indication** ⓝ 지표, 암시, 조짐	409 ☐ **edible** ⓐ 먹을 수 있는
244 ☐ **nature** ⓝ 자연, 천성	299 ☐ **billion** ⓝ 10억	354 ☐ **mislead** ⓥ 잘못 이끌다	410 ☐ **shortage** ⓝ 부족
245 ☐ **year-round** ⓐ 연중 계속되는	300 ☐ **obviously** [ad] 분명히	355 ☐ **bare** ⓐ 맨, 벌거벗은	411 ☐ **uniqueness** ⓝ 고유성
246 ☐ **produce** ⓝ 농산물	301 ☐ **cause** ⓝ 원인	356 ☐ **actual** ⓐ 실제의	412 ☐ **disappear** ⓥ 사라지다
247 ☐ **exotic** ⓐ 외국의, 이국적인	302 ☐ **citizen** ⓝ 시민	357 ☐ **a variety of** 다양한	
248 ☐ **lead to** ~을 낳다, ~로 이어지다	303 ☐ **afford to** ~할 여유가 되다	358 ☐ **quantitative** ⓐ 정량적인	**43~45**
249 ☐ **widespread** ⓐ 광범위한	304 ☐ **pay for** ~을 지불하다, 대금을 치르다		413 ☐ **take A to B** A를 B로 데려다주다
250 ☐ **hot house** 온실	305 ☐ **modern** ⓐ 현대의	**40**	414 ☐ **playground** ⓝ 운동장, 놀이터
251 ☐ **reliance** ⓝ 의존	306 ☐ **starve** ⓥ 굶주리다	359 ☐ **colleague** ⓝ 동료	415 ☐ **grandson** ⓝ 손자
252 ☐ **quality control** 품질 관리	307 ☐ **far and away** 단연코, 훨씬	360 ☐ **mean to** ~하기를 의도하다	416 ☐ **surround** ⓥ 둘러싸다, 에워싸다
253 ☐ **temperature** ⓝ 온도	308 ☐ **poverty** ⓝ 가난, 빈곤	361 ☐ **resistant** ⓐ 저항하는	417 ☐ **point at** ~을 가리키다, 손가락질하다
254 ☐ **satellite** ⓝ 위성	309 ☐ **grand** ⓐ 거대한, 큰	362 ☐ **make a donation** 기부하다	418 ☐ **run off to** ~로 뛰어가다, 달아나다
255 ☐ **contribute to** ~의 원인이 되다	310 ☐ **continue** ⓥ 지속하다	363 ☐ **emphasize** ⓥ 강조하다	419 ☐ **ignore** ⓥ 무시하다
256 ☐ **concern** ⓝ 우려, 걱정	311 ☐ **trend** ⓝ 추세	364 ☐ **do good** 선행을 하다	420 ☐ **make fun of** ~을 조롱하다
257 ☐ **wastage** ⓝ 낭비(되는 양)	312 ☐ **lower** ⓥ 낮추다, 줄이다	365 ☐ **benefit** ⓥ ~에게 이득이 되다	421 ☐ **sadly** [ad] 슬프게
258 ☐ **institutional** ⓐ 제도적인, 기관의		366 ☐ **faculty** ⓝ 교직원	422 ☐ **lean against** ~에 기대다
259 ☐ **expose** ⓥ 폭로하다, 드러내다, 노출시키다	**37**	367 ☐ **donor** ⓝ 기부자	423 ☐ **fence** ⓝ 울타리
260 ☐ **over-production** ⓝ 과잉 생산	313 ☐ **whether A or B** A이든 B이든	368 ☐ **glow** ⓝ 빛, (기쁨이나 만족감을 동반한) 감정	424 ☐ **exhausted** ⓐ 지친, 소진된
261 ☐ **retail** ⓝ 소매	314 ☐ **alert** ⓐ 초롱초롱한, 기민한	369 ☐ **end up ~ing** 결국 ~하다	425 ☐ **crowd** ⓝ 무리, 군중
262 ☐ **sector** ⓝ 분야	315 ☐ **muse** ⓝ 뮤즈, 영감	370 ☐ **combine** ⓥ 합치다, 결합하다	426 ☐ **greet** ⓥ 인사하다
263 ☐ **appearance** ⓝ 모습, 외관	316 ☐ **freely** [ad] 자유롭게	371 ☐ **put together** 합치다	427 ☐ **You are mistaken.** 잘못 생각하고 계세요. 오해예요.
264 ☐ **worsen** ⓥ 악화시키다	317 ☐ **machinery** ⓝ 조직, 기계	372 ☐ **more than** ~ 이상	428 ☐ **argue with** ~와 논쟁하다
265 ☐ **bring about** ~을 가져오다, 야기하다	318 ☐ **loose** ⓐ 느슨한	373 ☐ **audience** ⓝ 관객, 청중	429 ☐ **make arrangements for** ~을 준비하다
266 ☐ **nutrition** ⓝ 영양	319 ☐ **stand at attention** 차렷 자세를 취하다	374 ☐ **trigger** ⓥ 유발하다	430 ☐ **pupil** ⓝ 학생, 제자
267 ☐ **diversify** ⓥ 다양화하다	320 ☐ **demand** ⓥ 요구하다	375 ☐ **awareness** ⓝ 인식, 의식	431 ☐ **firmly** [ad] 단단히, 꽉
	321 ☐ **novel** ⓐ 새로운, 신기한	376 ☐ **persuade** ⓥ 설득하다	432 ☐ **gate** ⓝ 문
34	322 ☐ **tackle** ⓥ 해결하다, 처리하다, 다루다	377 ☐ **shield** ⓥ 보호하다	433 ☐ **exclaim** ⓥ 소리치다, 외치다
268 ☐ **at a time** 한 번에	323 ☐ **early bird** 아침형 인간	378 ☐ **simultaneously** [ad] 동시에	434 ☐ **look after** ~을 돌보다
269 ☐ **in an effort to** ~하기 위해서	324 ☐ **make sure to** 반드시 ~하다	379 ☐ **separately** [ad] 따로, 별개로	435 ☐ **spot** ⓥ 찾다, 발견하다
270 ☐ **determine** ⓥ 판단하다	325 ☐ **vice versa** 그 반대도 같다		

09회

● 채점 : 맞은 개수 _____ / 80

TEST A-B 각 단어의 뜻을 [A] 영어는 우리말로, [B] 우리말은 영어로 쓰시오.

A	English	Korean		B	Korean	English
01	guardian			01	역학, 역동성	
02	tune out			02	일시적인	
03	fast-paced			03	부족	
04	sealed			04	친밀한	
05	domesticate			05	부드럽게	
06	elaborate			06	기업가, 사업가	
07	wire			07	찾다, 발견하다	
08	reproduction			08	불만족한	
09	derive			09	~을 구성하다	
10	criterion			10	인내	
11	unfavorable			11	줄어들다	
12	indicator			12	미지의, 알지 못하는	
13	reliance			13	수용하다, 담다	
14	starve			14	성분, 재료	
15	loose			15	근거가 없는	
16	institutional			16	둘러싸다, 에워싸다	
17	obviously			17	섭취, 소비	
18	sustainable			18	~에게 이득이 되다	
19	trigger			19	대책, 조치	
20	edible			20	우세하다	

▶ A-D 정답 : 해설편 125쪽

TEST C-D 각 단어의 뜻을 골라 기호를 쓰시오.

C	English		Korean		D	Korean		English
01	pre-packed	( )	ⓐ 다양화하다		01	치다, 때리다, 두드리다	( )	ⓐ firmly
02	distract	( )	ⓑ 멀쩡한, 손상되지 않은		02	위성	( )	ⓑ night owl
03	faculty	( )	ⓒ 재현 가능한		03	남용하다	( )	ⓒ qualitative
04	undamaged	( )	ⓓ 세무사		04	지배적인, 만연한	( )	ⓓ frustrated
05	bare	( )	ⓔ 경쟁력, 경쟁적인 것		05	저녁형 인간	( )	ⓔ exhausted
06	early bird	( )	ⓕ 사전 포장된		06	죄수	( )	ⓕ tiny
07	shame	( )	ⓖ 주의를 분산시키다		07	장려하다, 촉진하다, 홍보하다	( )	ⓖ courageous
08	diversify	( )	ⓗ 설비, 살림, 세간		08	창고	( )	ⓗ strike
09	reproducible	( )	ⓘ 외국의, 이국적인		09	충성도	( )	ⓘ prevailing
10	mass	( )	ⓙ 잘못 이끌다		10	좌절한	( )	ⓙ prisoner
11	tackle	( )	ⓚ 교직원		11	단단히, 꽉	( )	ⓚ abuse
12	population	( )	ⓛ 새로운, 신기한		12	시골의	( )	ⓛ ignore
13	overcome	( )	ⓜ 맨, 벌거벗은		13	마주볼 수 있는	( )	ⓜ satellite
14	natural selection	( )	ⓝ 수치심		14	정성적인, 질적인	( )	ⓝ rural
15	mislead	( )	ⓞ 부피, 질량		15	아주 작은	( )	ⓞ opposable
16	fixture	( )	ⓟ 해결하다, 처리하다, 다루다		16	속임수, 요령	( )	ⓟ trick
17	competitiveness	( )	ⓠ 자연 선택		17	발달의	( )	ⓠ warehouse
18	novel	( )	ⓡ 인구(수)		18	용감한	( )	ⓡ loyalty
19	exotic	( )	ⓢ 극복하다		19	지친, 소진된	( )	ⓢ promote
20	tax accountant	( )	ⓣ 아침형 인간		20	무시하다	( )	ⓣ developmental

2023학년도 11월 고1 전국연합학력평가 문제지

1

제 3 교시

영어 영역

10회

● 문항수 45개 | 배점 100점 | 제한 시간 70분

● 점수 표시가 없는 문항은 모두 2점

10회

1번부터 17번까지는 듣고 답하는 문제입니다. 1번부터 15번까지는 한 번만 들려주고, 16번부터 17번까지는 두 번 들려줍니다. 방송을 잘 듣고 답을 하시기 바랍니다.

1. 다음을 듣고, 남자가 하는 말의 목적으로 가장 적절한 것을 고르시오.

① 로봇 프로그램 만족도 조사 참여를 독려하려고
② 관람객을 위한 안내 로봇 서비스를 소개하려고
③ 전시 작품 해설 서비스 중단을 안내하려고
④ 오디오 가이드 대여 장소를 공지하려고
⑤ 전시관 온라인 예약 방법을 설명하려고

2. 대화를 듣고, 여자의 의견으로 가장 적절한 것을 고르시오.

① 번역 프로그램으로 번역한 글은 검토가 필요하다.
② 읽기 학습을 통해 쓰기 능력을 향상시킬 수 있다.
③ 글을 인용할 때는 출처를 명확히 밝혀야 한다.
④ 예상 독자를 고려하여 글을 작성해야 한다.
⑤ 번역기 사용은 외국어 학습에 효과적이다.

3. 대화를 듣고, 두 사람의 관계를 가장 잘 나타낸 것을 고르시오.

① 광고 제작자 - 사진작가
② 이사업체 직원 - 의뢰인
③ 고객 - 에어컨 설치 기사
④ 트럭 운전사 - 물류 창고 직원
⑤ 구매자 - 중고 물품 개인 판매자

4. 대화를 듣고, 그림에서 대화의 내용과 일치하지 <u>않는</u> 것을 고르시오.

5. 대화를 듣고, 남자가 할 일로 가장 적절한 것을 고르시오.

① 스티커 준비하기
② 안내문 게시하기
③ 급식 메뉴 선정하기
④ 설문 조사 실시하기
⑤ 우수 학급 시상하기

6. 대화를 듣고, 남자가 매달 지불할 금액을 고르시오.

① $20   ② $27   ③ $30   ④ $36   ⑤ $40

7. 대화를 듣고, 여자가 토크 쇼를 방청하러 갈 수 <u>없는</u> 이유를 고르시오.

① 가족 모임에 가야 해서
② 아르바이트를 해야 해서
③ 책 사인회를 준비해야 해서
④ 화학 프로젝트를 해야 해서
⑤ 친구 결혼식에 참석해야 해서

8. 대화를 듣고, Polar Bear Swim에 관해 언급되지 <u>않은</u> 것을 고르시오.

① 행사 날짜   ② 제출 서류   ③ 최대 참가 인원
④ 기념품   ⑤ 참가비

9. Walk in the Snow에 관한 다음 내용을 듣고, 일치하지 <u>않는</u> 것을 고르시오.

① 1일 투어 프로그램이다.
② 하이킹에 관심이 있는 누구든 참여할 수 있다.
③ 장비를 무료로 대여할 수 있다.
④ 학생에게 등록비 할인을 해 준다.
⑤ 참여하려면 사전에 등록해야 한다.

10. 다음 표를 보면서 대화를 듣고, 두 사람이 선택할 달력을 고르시오.

Calendar

	Product	Price	Format	Recyclable Paper	Theme
①	A	$8	standing desk	×	modern art
②	B	$10	standing desk	○	classic art
③	C	$12	standing desk	○	movie
④	D	$16	wall	○	nature
⑤	E	$22	wall	×	animal

11. 대화를 듣고, 여자의 마지막 말에 대한 남자의 응답으로 가장 적절한 것을 고르시오.

① I covered the worrying state of marine life.
② I sent an article to the biology department.
③ Whatever you did, let's not speak about it.
④ I spent lots of time preparing the speech.
⑤ The article was mainly read by students.

12. 대화를 듣고, 남자의 마지막 말에 대한 여자의 응답으로 가장 적절한 것을 고르시오.

① Take care. The weather is freezing cold.
② Good news. Thanks for letting me know.
③ Hurry up. The bus is leaving very soon.
④ Seriously? I'd better try walking, then.
⑤ Really? I was on the shuttle bus, too.

13. 대화를 듣고, 여자의 마지막 말에 대한 남자의 응답으로 가장 적절한 것을 고르시오. [3점]

Man: _____

① Definitely. That's why I got a refund for the app.
② Sorry. I should have repaired my tablet PC earlier.
③ Exactly. Documents were filed in alphabetical order.
④ I see. I'll give it some thought before buying this app.
⑤ Don't worry. I still have a few more days for the free trial.

14. 대화를 듣고, 남자의 마지막 말에 대한 여자의 응답으로 가장 적절한 것을 고르시오. [3점]

Woman: _____

① Good idea. Let's learn how to read sign language.
② You're right. That's because I wanted to help him.
③ Okay. Wish me luck in getting this volunteer work.
④ Trust me. I bet you'll be selected as a note-taker.
⑤ Wonderful. Thank you for taking notes for me in class.

15. 다음 상황 설명을 듣고, Tony가 Kate에게 할 말로 가장 적절한 것을 고르시오. [3점]

Tony: _____

① Why don't we post a review of this bakery?
② Let's give her the baker of the month award.
③ We'd better check if we're on the waiting list.
④ We should come later when the repairs are done.
⑤ How about finding a different bakery for the list?

[16 ~ 17] 다음을 듣고, 물음에 답하시오.

16. 여자가 하는 말의 주제로 가장 적절한 것은?

① fruits that can pose a risk to dogs' health
② ways to help dogs develop a taste for fruits
③ tips for protecting garden fruits from animals
④ reasons fruits should be included in dogs' diets
⑤ stories that use fruits and vegetables as characters

17. 언급된 과일이 <u>아닌</u> 것은?

① grapes   ② cherries   ③ avocados
④ grapefruits   ⑤ cranberries

┌───┐
│ 이제 듣기 문제가 끝났습니다. 18번부터는 문제지의 지시에 │
│ 따라 답을 하시기 바랍니다.   │
└───┘

18. 다음 글의 목적으로 가장 적절한 것은?

Dear Ms. MacAlpine,

 I was so excited to hear that your brand is opening a new shop on Bruns Street next month. I have always appreciated the way your brand helps women to feel more stylish and confident. I am writing in response to your ad in the Bruns Journal. I graduated from the Meline School of Fashion and have worked as a sales assistant at LoganMart for the last five years. During that time, I've developed strong customer service and sales skills, and now I would like to apply for the sales position in your clothing store. I am available for an interview at your earliest convenience. I look forward to hearing from you. Thank you for reading my letter.

Yours sincerely,
Grace Braddock

① 영업 시작일을 문의하려고
② 인터뷰 일정을 변경하려고
③ 디자인 공모전에 참가하려고
④ 제품 관련 문의에 답변하려고
⑤ 의류 매장 판매직에 지원하려고

19. 다음 글에 드러난 'I'의 심경 변화로 가장 적절한 것은?

 I had never seen a beach with such white sand or water that was such a beautiful shade of blue. Jane and I set up a blanket on the sand while looking forward to our ten days of honeymooning on an exotic island. "Look!" Jane waved her hand to point at the beautiful scene before us — and her gold wedding ring went flying off her hand. I tried to see where it went, but the sun hit my eyes and I lost track of it. I didn't want to lose her wedding ring, so I started looking in the area where I thought it had landed. However, the sand was so fine and I realized that anything heavy, like gold, would quickly sink and might never be found again.

① excited → frustrated   ② pleased → jealous
③ nervous → confident   ④ annoyed → grateful
⑤ relaxed → indifferent

20. 다음 글에서 필자가 주장하는 바로 가장 적절한 것은?

 Unfortunately, many people don't take personal responsibility for their own growth. Instead, they simply run the race laid out for them. They do well enough in school to keep advancing. Maybe they manage to get a good job at a well-run company. But so many think and act as if their learning journey ends with college. They have checked all the boxes in the life that was laid out for them and now lack a road map describing the right ways to move forward and continue to grow. In truth, that's when the journey really begins. When school is finished, your growth becomes voluntary. Like healthy eating habits or a regular exercise program, you need to commit to it and devote thought, time, and energy to it. Otherwise, it simply won't happen — and your life and career are likely to stop progressing as a result.

① 성공 경험을 위해 달성 가능한 목표를 수립해야 한다.
② 체계적인 경력 관리를 위해 전문가의 도움을 받아야 한다.
③ 건강을 위해 꾸준한 운동과 식습관 관리를 병행해야 한다.
④ 졸업 이후 성장을 위해 자발적으로 배움을 실천해야 한다.
⑤ 적성에 맞는 직업을 찾기 위해 학교 교육에 충실해야 한다.

21. 밑줄 친 our brain and the universe meet가 다음 글에서 의미하는 바로 가장 적절한 것은? [3점]

Many people take the commonsense view that color is an objective property of things, or of the light that bounces off them. They say a tree's leaves are green because they reflect green light — a greenness that is just as real as the leaves. Others argue that color doesn't inhabit the physical world at all but exists only in the eye or mind of the viewer. They maintain that if a tree fell in a forest and no one was there to see it, its leaves would be colorless — and so would everything else. They say there is no such *thing* as color; there are only the people who see it. Both positions are, in a way, correct. Color is objective *and* subjective — "the place," as Paul Cézanne put it, "where our brain and the universe meet." Color is created when light from the world is registered by the eyes and interpreted by the brain.

① we see things beyond the range of perception
② objects appear different by the change of light
③ your perspectives and others' reach an agreement
④ our mind and physical reality interact with each other
⑤ structures of the human brain and the universe are similar

22. 다음 글의 요지로 가장 적절한 것은?

When writing a novel, research for information needs to be done. The thing is that some kinds of fiction demand a higher level of detail: crime fiction, for example, or scientific thrillers. The information is never hard to find; one website for authors even organizes trips to police stations, so that crime writers can get it right. Often, a polite letter will earn you permission to visit a particular location and record all the details that you need. But remember that you will drive your readers to boredom if you think that you need to pack everything you discover into your work. The details that matter are those that reveal the human experience. The crucial thing is telling a story, finding the characters, the tension, and the conflict — not the train timetable or the building blueprint.

① 작품의 완성도는 작가의 경험의 양에 비례한다.
② 작가의 상상력은 가장 훌륭한 이야기 재료이다.
③ 소설에서 사건 전개에 대한 묘사는 구체적일수록 좋다.
④ 소설을 쓸 때 독자의 관심사를 먼저 고려하는 것이 중요하다.
⑤ 소설에 포함될 세부 사항은 인간의 경험을 드러내는 것이어야 한다.

23. 다음 글의 주제로 가장 적절한 것은?

Nearly everything has to go through your mouth to get to the rest of you, from food and air to bacteria and viruses. A healthy mouth can help your body get what it needs and prevent it from harm — with adequate space for air to travel to your lungs, and healthy teeth and gums that prevent harmful microorganisms from entering your bloodstream. From the moment you are created, oral health affects every aspect of your life. What happens in the mouth is usually just the tip of the iceberg and a reflection of what is happening in other parts of the body. Poor oral health can be a cause of a disease that affects the entire body. The microorganisms in an unhealthy mouth can enter the bloodstream and travel anywhere in the body, posing serious health risks.

* microorganism: 미생물

① the way the immune system fights viruses
② the effect of unhealthy eating habits on the body
③ the difficulty in raising awareness about oral health
④ the importance of oral health and its impact on the body
⑤ the relationship between oral health and emotional well-being

24. 다음 글의 제목으로 가장 적절한 것은?

Kids tire of their toys, college students get sick of cafeteria food, and sooner or later most of us lose interest in our favorite TV shows. The bottom line is that we humans are easily bored. But why should this be true? The answer lies buried deep in our nerve cells, which are designed to reduce their initial excited response to stimuli each time they occur. At the same time, these neurons enhance their responses to things that change — especially things that change quickly. We probably evolved this way because our ancestors got more survival value, for example, from attending to what was moving in a tree (such as a puma) than to the tree itself. Boredom in reaction to an unchanging environment turns down the level of neural excitation so that new stimuli (like our ancestor's hypothetical puma threat) stand out more. It's the neural equivalent of turning off a front door light to see the fireflies.

* neural: 신경의 ** hypothetical: 가정(假定)의, 가설상의
*** equivalent: (~와) 같은 것, 대응물

① The Brain's Brilliant Trick to Overcome Fear
② Boredom: Neural Mechanism for Detecting Change
③ Humans' Endless Desire to Pursue Familiar Experiences
④ The Destruction of Nature in Exchange for Human Survival
⑤ How Humans Changed the Environment to Their Advantage

25. 다음 도표의 내용과 일치하지 <u>않는</u> 것은?

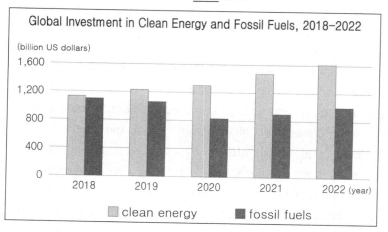

Global Investment in Clean Energy and Fossil Fuels, 2018-2022

(billion US dollars)

clean energy / fossil fuels

The above graph shows global energy investment in clean energy and in fossil fuels between 2018 and 2022. ① Since 2018 global energy investment in clean energy continued to rise, reaching its highest level in 2022. ② The investment gap between clean energy and fossil fuels in 2020 was larger than that in 2019. ③ Investment in fossil fuels was highest in 2018 and lowest in 2020. ④ In 2021, investment in clean energy exceeded 1,200 billion dollars, while investment in fossil fuels did not. ⑤ In 2022, the global investment in clean energy was more than double that of fossil fuels.

26. Frederick Douglass에 관한 다음 글의 내용과 일치하지 <u>않는</u> 것은?

Frederick Douglass was born into slavery at a farm in Maryland. His full name at birth was Frederick Augustus Washington Bailey. He changed his name to Frederick Douglass after he successfully escaped from slavery in 1838. He became a leader of the Underground Railroad — a network of people, places, and routes that helped enslaved people escape to the north. He assisted other runaway slaves until they could safely get to other areas in the north. As a slave, he had taught himself to read and write and he spread that knowledge to other slaves as well. Once free, he became a well-known abolitionist and strong believer in equality for all people including Blacks, Native Americans, women, and recent immigrants. He wrote several autobiographies describing his experiences as a slave. In addition to all this, he became the first African-American candidate for vice president of the United States.

* abolitionist: 노예제 폐지론자

① Maryland에서 노예로 태어났다.
② 노예들이 탈출하는 것을 돕는 조직의 리더가 되었다.
③ 다른 노예들로부터 읽고 쓰는 법을 배웠다.
④ 노예로서의 자신의 경험을 묘사한 자서전을 썼다.
⑤ 미국의 첫 아프리카계 미국인 부통령 후보가 되었다.

27. 2023 Australian Gateball Championships에 관한 다음 안내문의 내용과 일치하지 <u>않는</u> 것은?

2023 Australian Gateball Championships

The Diamond Coast is getting set to welcome the Australian Gateball Championships. Join this great outdoor competition and be the winner this year!

When & Where
‣ December 19 – 22, 2023
‣ Diamond Coast Performance Centre

Schedule of Matches
‣ Doubles matches (9 a.m. – 11 a.m.)
‣ Team matches (1 p.m. – 3 p.m.)

Prizes
‣ Every participant will receive a certificate for entry.
‣ Champions are awarded a medal.

Note
‣ Participation is free.
‣ Visit www.australiangateball.com for registration. (Registration on site is not available.)

① 4일 동안 진행된다.
② 복식 경기는 오전에 열린다.
③ 모든 참가자는 참가 증서를 받는다.
④ 참가비는 무료이다.
⑤ 현장에서 등록하는 것이 가능하다.

28. The Amazing Urban Adventure Quest에 관한 다음 안내문의 내용과 일치하는 것은?

The Amazing Urban Adventure Quest

Explore Central Park while solving clues and completing challenges! Guided by your smartphone, make your way among the well-known places in the park.

When & How
• Available 365 days a year (from sunrise to sunset)
• Start when you want.
• Get a stamp at each checkpoint.

Adventure Courses
• East Side: Starts at Twilight Gardens (no age limit)
• West Side: Starts at Strawberry Castle (over 15 years old)

Registration & Cost
• Sign up online at www.urbanquest.com.
• $40 for a team of 2-5 people
• Save 20% with discount code: CENTRALQUEST

① 참여하는 동안 스마트폰 사용은 금지된다.
② 일 년 내내 일몰 후 참여할 수 있다.
③ 서편 코스는 나이 제한이 없다.
④ 1인당 40달러의 요금이 든다.
⑤ 할인받을 수 있는 코드가 있다.

[해설편 p.132]

29. 다음 글의 밑줄 친 부분 중, 어법상 <u>틀린</u> 것은? [3점]

Some countries have proposed tougher guidelines for determining brain death when transplantation—transferring organs to others—is under consideration. In several European countries, there are legal requirements which specify ① that a whole team of doctors must agree over the diagnosis of death in the case of a potential donor. The reason for these strict regulations for diagnosing brain death in potential organ donors ② is, no doubt, to ease public fears of a premature diagnosis of brain death for the purpose of obtaining organs. But it is questionable whether these requirements reduce public suspicions as much as they create ③ them. They certainly maintain mistaken beliefs that diagnosing brain death is an unreliable process ④ lack precision. As a matter of consistency, at least, criteria for diagnosing the deaths of organ donors should be exactly the same as for those for ⑤ whom immediate burial or cremation is intended.

* diagnosis: 진단 ** donor: 기증자 *** cremation: 화장(火葬)

30. 다음 글의 밑줄 친 부분 중, 문맥상 낱말의 쓰임이 적절하지 <u>않은</u> 것은?

The term minimalism gives a negative impression to some people who think that it is all about sacrificing valuable possessions. This insecurity naturally stems from their ① attachment to their possessions. It is difficult to distance oneself from something that has been around for quite some time. Being an emotional animal, human beings give meaning to the things around them. So, the question arising here is that if minimalism will ② hurt one's emotions, why become a minimalist? The answer is very simple; the assumption of the question is fundamentally ③ wrong. Minimalism does not hurt emotions. You might feel a bit sad while getting rid of a useless item but sooner than later, this feeling will be ④ maintained by the joy of clarity. Minimalists never argue that you should leave every convenience of the modern era. They are of the view that you only need to ⑤ eliminate stuff that is unused or not going to be used in the near future.

[31~34] 다음 빈칸에 들어갈 말로 가장 적절한 것을 고르시오.

31. A remarkable characteristic of the visual system is that it has the ability of _____. Psychologist George M. Stratton made this clear in an impressive self-experiment. Stratton wore reversing glasses for several days, which literally turned the world upside down for him. In the beginning, this caused him great difficulties: just putting food in his mouth with a fork was a challenge for him. With time, however, his visual system adjusted to the new stimuli from reality, and he was able to act normally in his environment again, even seeing it upright when he concentrated. As he took off his reversing glasses, he was again confronted with problems: he used the wrong hand when he wanted to reach for something, for example. Fortunately, Stratton could reverse the perception, and he did not have to wear reversing glasses for the rest of his life. For him, everything returned to normal after one day.

* reverse: 뒤집다, 반전시키다

① adapting itself
② visualizing ideas
③ assessing distances
④ functioning irregularly
⑤ operating independently

32. Participants in a study were asked to answer questions like "Why does the moon have phases?" Half the participants were told to search for the answers on the internet, while the other half weren't allowed to do so. Then, in the second part of the study, all of the participants were presented with a new set of questions, such as "Why does Swiss cheese have holes?" These questions were unrelated to the ones asked during the first part of the study, so participants who used the internet had absolutely no advantage over those who hadn't. You would think that both sets of participants would be equally sure or unsure about how well they could answer the new questions. But those who used the internet in the first part of the study rated themselves as more knowledgeable than those who hadn't, even about questions they hadn't searched online for. The study suggests that having access to unrelated information was enough to _____.

* phase: (달의) 상(相)

① improve their judgment skills
② pump up their intellectual confidence
③ make them endure challenging situations
④ lead to a collaboration among the participants
⑤ motivate them to pursue in-depth knowledge

33. Anthropologist Gregory Bateson suggests that we tend to understand the world by _____.
Take platypuses. We might zoom in so closely to their fur that each hair appears different. We might also zoom out to the extent where it appears as a single, uniform object. We might take the platypus as an individual, or we might treat it as part of a larger unit such as a species or an ecosystem. It's possible to move between many of these perspectives, although we may need some additional tools and skills to zoom in on individual pieces of hair or zoom out to entire ecosystems. Crucially, however, we can only take up one perspective at a time. We can pay attention to the varied behavior of individual animals, look at what unites them into a single species, or look at them as part of bigger ecological patterns. Every possible perspective involves emphasizing certain aspects and ignoring others. [3점]

* anthropologist: 인류학자 ** platypus: 오리너구리

① using our experiences as a guide
② breaking the framework of old ideas
③ adding new information to what we know
④ focusing in on particular features within it
⑤ considering both bright and dark sides of it

34. Plato's realism includes all aspects of experience but is most easily explained by considering the nature of mathematical and geometrical objects such as circles. He asked the question, what is a circle? You might indicate a particular example carved into stone or drawn in the sand. However, Plato would point out that, if you looked closely enough, you would see that neither it, nor indeed any physical circle, was perfect. They all possessed flaws, and all were subject to change and decayed with time. So how can we talk about perfect circles if we cannot actually see or touch them? Plato's extraordinary answer was that the world we see is a poor reflection of a deeper unseen reality of *Forms*, or *universals*, where perfect cats chase perfect mice in perfect circles around perfect rocks. Plato believed that the *Forms* or *universals* are the true reality that exists in _____.
[3점]

① observable phenomena of the physical world
② our experiences shaped by external influences
③ an overlapping area between emotion and reason
④ an invisible but perfect world beyond our senses
⑤ our perception affected by stereotype or generalization

35. 다음 글에서 전체 흐름과 관계 없는 문장은?

In statistics, the law of large numbers describes a situation where having more data is better for making predictions. According to it, the more often an experiment is conducted, the closer the average of the results can be expected to match the true state of the world. ① For instance, on your first encounter with the game of roulette, you may have beginner's luck after betting on 7. ② But the more often you repeat this bet, the closer the relative frequency of wins and losses is expected to approach the true chance of winning, meaning that your luck will at some point fade away. ③ Each number's symbolic meanings can be interpreted in various ways and are promising in situations that may change unexpectedly. ④ Similarly, car insurers collect large amounts of data to figure out the chances that drivers will cause accidents, depending on their age, region, or car brand. ⑤ Both casinos and insurance industries rely on the law of large numbers to balance individual losses.

[36~37] 주어진 글 다음에 이어질 글의 순서로 가장 적절한 것을 고르시오.

36.

The adolescent brain is not fully developed until its early twenties. This means the way the adolescents' decision-making circuits integrate and process information may put them at a disadvantage.

(A) On the other hand, the limbic system matures earlier, playing a central role in processing emotional responses. Because of its earlier development, it is more likely to influence decision-making. Decision-making in the adolescent brain is led by emotional factors more than the perception of consequences.

(B) Due to these differences, there is an imbalance between feeling-based decision-making ruled by the more mature limbic system and logical-based decision-making by the not-yet-mature prefrontal cortex. This may explain why some teens are more likely to make bad decisions.

(C) One of their brain regions that matures later is the prefrontal cortex, which is the control center, tasked with thinking ahead and evaluating consequences. It is the area of the brain responsible for preventing you from sending off an initial angry text and modifying it with kinder words. [3점]

* integrate: 통합하다 ** limbic system: 대뇌변연계
*** prefrontal cortex: 전전두엽 피질

① (A) − (C) − (B) ② (B) − (A) − (C)
③ (B) − (C) − (A) ④ (C) − (A) − (B)
⑤ (C) − (B) − (A)

37.

> Despite the remarkable progress in deep-learning based facial recognition approaches in recent years, in terms of identification performance, they still have limitations. These limitations relate to the database used in the learning stage.

(A) To counteract this problem, researchers have developed models for face aging or digital de-aging. It is used to compensate for the differences in facial characteristics, which appear over a given time period.

(B) If the selected database does not contain enough instances, the result may be systematically affected. For example, the performance of a facial biometric system may decrease if the person to be identified was enrolled over 10 years ago.

(C) The factor to consider is that this person may experience changes in the texture of the face, particularly with the appearance of wrinkles and sagging skin. These changes may be highlighted by weight gain or loss.

* biometric: 생체 측정의 ** sagging: 처진

① (A) − (C) − (B)　　　② (B) − (A) − (C)
③ (B) − (C) − (A)　　　④ (C) − (A) − (B)
⑤ (C) − (B) − (A)

[38 ~ 39] 글의 흐름으로 보아, 주어진 문장이 들어가기에 가장 적절한 곳을 고르시오.

38.

> Leaving the contribution of that strategy to one side, the danger of creating more uniform crops is that they are more at risk when it comes to disasters.

The decline in the diversity of our food is an entirely human-made process. The biggest loss of crop diversity came in the decades that followed the Second World War. (①) In an attempt to save millions from extreme hunger, crop scientists found ways to produce grains such as rice and wheat on an enormous scale. (②) And thousands of traditional varieties were replaced by a small number of new super-productive ones. (③) The strategy worked spectacularly well, at least to begin with. (④) Because of it, grain production tripled, and between 1970 and 2020 the human population more than doubled. (⑤) Specifically, a global food system that depends on just a narrow selection of plants has a greater chance of not being able to survive diseases, pests and climate extremes.

* pest: 해충

39.

> A few years ago, Cuba altered that uniform style, modernizing it and perhaps conforming to other countries' style; interestingly, the national team has declined since that time.

Between 1940 and 2000, Cuba ruled the world baseball scene. They won 25 of the first 28 World Cups and 3 of 5 Olympic Games. (①) The Cubans were known for wearing uniforms covered in red from head to toe, a strong contrast to the more conservative North American style featuring grey or white pants. (②) Not only were their athletic talents superior, the Cubans appeared even stronger from just the colour of their uniforms. (③) A game would not even start and the opposing team would already be scared. (④) The country that ruled international baseball for decades has not been on top since that uniform change. (⑤) Traditions are important for a team; while a team brand or image can adjust to keep up with present times, if it abandons or neglects its roots, negative effects can surface.

* conservative: 보수적인

40. 다음 글의 내용을 한 문장으로 요약하고자 한다. 빈칸 (A), (B)에 들어갈 말로 가장 적절한 것은? [3점]

> Many of the first models of cultural evolution drew noticeable connections between culture and genes by using concepts from theoretical population genetics and applying them to culture. Cultural patterns of transmission, innovation, and selection are conceptually likened to genetic processes of transmission, mutation, and selection. However, these approaches had to be modified to account for the differences between genetic and cultural transmission. For example, we do not expect the cultural transmission to follow the rules of genetic transmission strictly. If two biological parents have different forms of a cultural trait, their child is not necessarily equally likely to acquire the mother's or father's form of that trait. Further, a child can acquire cultural traits not only from its parents but also from nonparental adults and peers; thus, the frequency of a cultural trait in the population is relevant beyond just the probability that an individual's parents had that trait.

* mutation: 돌연변이 ** relevant: 유의미한

↓

> Early cultural evolution models used the ___(A)___ between culture and genes but had to be revised since cultural transmission allows for more ___(B)___ factors than genetic transmission.

	(A)		(B)
①	similarity	⋯	diverse
②	similarity	⋯	limited
③	difference	⋯	flexible
④	difference	⋯	complicated
⑤	interaction	⋯	credible

[41 ~ 42] 다음 글을 읽고, 물음에 답하시오.

A ball thrown into the air is acted upon by the initial force given it, persisting as inertia of movement and tending to carry it in the same straight line, and by the constant pull of gravity downward, as well as by the resistance of the air. It moves, accordingly, in a (a) curved path. Now the path does not represent the working of any particular force; there is simply the (b) combination of the three elementary forces mentioned; but in a real sense, there is something in the total action besides the isolated action of three forces, namely, their joint action. In the same way, when two or more human individuals are together, their mutual relationships and their arrangement into a group are things which would not be (c) concealed if we confined our attention to each individual separately. The significance of group behavior is greatly (d) increased in the case of human beings by the fact that some of the tendencies to action of the individual are related definitely to other persons, and could not be aroused except by other persons acting as stimuli. An individual in complete (e) isolation would not reveal their competitive tendencies, their tendencies towards the opposite sex, their protective tendencies towards children. This shows that the traits of human nature do not fully appear until the individual is brought into relationships with other individuals.

* inertia: 관성 ** arouse: 유발하다

41. 윗글의 제목으로 가장 적절한 것은?

① Common Misunderstandings in Physics
② Collaboration: A Key to Success in Relationships
③ Interpersonal Traits and Their Impact on Science
④ Unbalanced Forces Causing Objects to Accelerate
⑤ Human Traits Uncovered by Interpersonal Relationships

42. 밑줄 친 (a)~(e) 중에서 문맥상 낱말의 쓰임이 적절하지 <u>않은</u> 것은? [3점]

① (a)   ② (b)   ③ (c)   ④ (d)   ⑤ (e)

[43 ~ 45] 다음 글을 읽고, 물음에 답하시오.

(A)

There once lived a man in a village who was not happy with his life. He was always troubled by one problem or another. One day, a saint with his guards stopped by his village. Many people heard the news and started going to him with their problems. The man also decided to visit the saint. Even after reaching the saint's place in the morning, (a) he didn't get the opportunity to meet him till evening.

(B)

But the saint also asked if the man could do a small job for him. He told the man to take care of a hundred camels in his group that night, saying "When all hundred camels sit down, you can go to sleep." The man agreed. The next morning when the saint met that man, (b) he asked if the man had slept well. Tired and sad, the man replied that he couldn't sleep even for a moment.

(C)

In fact, the man tried very hard but couldn't make all the camels sit at the same time because every time (c) he made one camel sit, another would stand up. The saint told him, "You realized that no matter how hard you try, you can't make all the camels sit down. If one problem is solved, for some reason, another will arise like the camels did. So, humans should enjoy life despite these problems."

(D)

When the man got to meet the saint, (d) he confessed that he was very unhappy with life because problems always surrounded him, like workplace tension or worries about his health. (e) He said, "Please give me a solution so that all the problems in my life will end and I can live peacefully." The saint smiled and said that he would answer the request the next day.

43. 주어진 글 (A)에 이어질 내용을 순서에 맞게 배열한 것으로 가장 적절한 것은?

① (B) - (D) - (C)   ② (C) - (B) - (D)
③ (C) - (D) - (B)   ④ (D) - (B) - (C)
⑤ (D) - (C) - (B)

44. 밑줄 친 (a)~(e) 중에서 가리키는 대상이 나머지 넷과 <u>다른</u> 것은?

① (a)   ② (b)   ③ (c)   ④ (d)   ⑤ (e)

45. 윗글에 관한 내용으로 적절하지 <u>않은</u> 것은?

① 많은 사람들이 자신들의 문제를 가지고 성자에게 갔다.
② 성자는 자신을 위해 작은 일을 해 줄 수 있는지 남자에게 물었다.
③ 성자는 남자가 낙타를 모두 재우면 잠을 자러 가도 좋다고 했다.
④ 성자는 문제가 있어도 인생을 즐겨야 한다고 말했다.
⑤ 성자는 남자의 요청에 대한 답을 다음 날 말해 주기로 했다.

※ 확인 사항

○ 답안지의 해당란에 필요한 내용을 정확히 기입(표기)했는지 확인하시오.

※ QR 코드를 스캔하시면 듣기 방송이 나옵니다. 듣기 방송을 들으며 다음 빈칸을 채우시오.
● 제한 시간 : 25분

01

다음을 듣고, 남자가 하는 말의 목적으로 가장 적절한 것을 고르시오.

[Cell phone rings.]

M : Hello, visitors. This is Scott Wolfman from the Edison Convention Center management office. We're doing our best to make sure that visitors have a wonderful experience in our convention center. As part of our effort, our center provides a robot guide service. ✿ _____ _____ _____ _____ of our exhibitions. Foreign languages, such as Chinese and Spanish, are available. And if you lose your way, the robot will accompany you to _____ _____ _____ ___ ____. So, please feel free to ask our friendly robot guide, ✿ _____ _____ _____ _____ _____. I hope this service makes your experience even better. Thank you.

02

대화를 듣고, 여자의 의견으로 가장 적절한 것을 고르시오.

W : Kevin, what are you doing?

M : Mom, I'm writing a letter to my sponsored child in Congo.

W : That's _____. Your French has gotten better and better.

M : Actually, I got help from a translation program.

W : I see. [Pause] Did you check the ✿ _____ _____ _____ _____ ___?

M : No, I didn't. Do you think I have to?

W : Yes. ✿ _____ _____ _____ _____ _____.

M : Well, I think the translation program does a better job than I can.

W : Not exactly. The translation could have meanings different from what you intended.

M : Hmm, you may be right. The translated text often loses the meaning of my original writing.

W : See? When translating a text with a translation program, you need to check the results.

M : Okay. Thanks for your advice.

03

대화를 듣고, 두 사람의 관계를 가장 잘 나타낸 것을 고르시오.

[Cell phone rings.]

M : Hello. This is Johnny. We've been messaging each other on the online marketplace.

W : Oh, hi. You have more questions about the air conditioner, right?

M : Yes. Could you tell me _____ _____ _____ _____ _____?

W : I bought it a year ago. It works well and is like new as you can see from the photo.

M : Then why do you want to sell it?

W : Because I don't need it anymore. I'm moving to a place with a built-in air conditioner.

M : I see. I'd like to buy it, then. It's $400, correct?

W : That's right. When ✿ _____ _____ _____ __ ____?

M : Maybe tomorrow. I need to find a truck ✿ _____ _____ _____.

W : Okay. Let me know when you're ready.

M : Thanks. I'll call you again.

04

대화를 듣고, 그림에서 대화의 내용과 일치하지 않는 것을 고르시오.

W : Hi, Benjamin. Did you finish your work for the student lounge design contest?

M : Yes. I'm confident that I'm going to win. Here's my design for it.

W : Awesome. Is that a hanging plant in front of the window?

M : Yes. The plant will ✿ _____ __ _____ _____ ___ _____ _____. What do you think about _____ _____ ____ _____ _____?

W : I love it. The slogan "TO THE WORLD" goes well with the world map.

M : I hope this place helps students dream big.

W : That's cool. And the two cushions on the sofa ✿ _____ _____ _____ _____ _____.

M : You're right. Check out the square-shaped table as well.

W : Good. It can be useful. Most of all, students will love the vending machine under the clock.

M : You bet!

05

대화를 듣고, 남자가 할 일로 가장 적절한 것을 고르시오.

M : Ms. Kim, Empty Your Plate Day is coming. How's the preparation going?

W : I've finally decided on the lunch menu for that day.

M : You did! How did you do that?

W : I did a survey of students' favorite foods.

M : Good idea! Can I help you with anything?

W : Actually, Mr. Han, I'm not sure ✿ _____ __ _____ ___ ___ _____.

M : How about ✿ _____ _____ ___ _____ with the fewest leftovers?

W : Sounds great. But how will we find that class?

M : You could give a sticker to the _____ _____ _____ _____ _____ _____ _____. And then, you can find the class with the most stickers.

W : Excellent. Could you prepare some stickers for me?

M : Sure. I'll do that for you.

W : Thanks. Then I'll put a notice on the bulletin board.

06

대화를 듣고, 남자가 매달 지불할 금액을 고르시오.

W : Welcome to Boom Telecom. How can I help you?

M : Hi. I'm thinking of changing my internet provider. _____ _____ _____ _____ _____ _____?

W : Okay. We have the Economic plan that's $20 per month. And the Supreme plan, which is faster, is $30 per month.

M : ✿ _____ _____ _____ _____.

W : Alright. We also have an OTT service for an extra $10 per month. What do you think?

M : Awesome. I'd like that as well.

W : Excellent choice. Then you'll have the Supreme plan with the OTT service, right?

M : Correct. Can I get a discount?

W : I'm afraid that the 10% discount promotion is over.

M : That's a shame. But I'll take it anyway.

W : Thank you. ✿ _____ _____ ____ ___ _____ _____ with your payment information.

M : Okay. [Writing sound] Here you are.

07

대화를 듣고, 여자가 토크 쇼를 방청하러 갈 수 없는 이유를 고르시오.

[Cell phone rings.]

M : Hi, Isabella.

W : Hi, Lorenzo. Did you finish your part-time job?

M : Yes. _____ ____ _____ _____ ___ a meeting for a chemistry project. What's up?

W : Your favorite talk show is *The Alice Mitchell Show*, right?

M : Yeah, I'm a big fan of hers. I even went to her book signing event.

W : I knew it! I got two tickets for her talk show. It's next Saturday evening.

M : Whoa! Can you please take me with you?

W : Actually, I'm not available that day. The tickets are all yours.

M : Wait, why can't you go? Is it because of the ✿ _____ _____ _____ ____ _____ ____ _____ _____?

W : No, that's in two weeks. Next Saturday I have to attend my friend's wedding.

M : Oh, I see. Then I'll ✿ _____ ____ _____ _____ _____. Thank you so much.

08

대화를 듣고, Polar Bear Swim에 관해 언급되지 않은 것을 고르시오.

W : Michael, look at this poster. The Polar Bear Swim will be held soon.

M : I know! I've been ✿ _____ _____ _____ _____ ___ ___. [Pause] It's on December 23rd.

W : Yeah. We can enjoy winter sea-swimming.

M : How nice! To join this event, we must hand in a medical check-up paper.

W : I think it's a good policy for everyone's health since the water is icy cold.

M : I agree. By the way, it says that there's a limit of 100 people.

W : Oh, we must hurry. Look! Registration starts this Saturday.

M : I'll _____ ___ _____ _____ ____ _____ _____ _____.

W : Great idea. And the entry fee is just $15.

M : Yes. And all entry fees ✿ _____ ____ _____ _____.

W : Cool. Let's have some icy fun while doing a good deed.

09

Walk in the Snow에 관한 다음 내용을 듣고, 일치하지 <u>않는</u> 것을 고르시오.

W : Hello, listeners! Are you a winter person? Then, Walk in the Snow might just be the adventure for you. It's a one-day tour program at Great White Mountain. Regardless of hiking experience, _____ _____ _____ _____ ___ hiking can participate in the tour. Participants ✿ _____ _____ _____ _____ _____ _____. But equipment is also available to rent for a small fee. The registration fee is $10, and we offer discounts to students. Don't forget that ✿ _____ _____ _____ _____ _____ ___ _____. For more information, please visit our website, www.walkinthesnow.com. Thank you.

10

다음 표를 보면서 대화를 듣고, 두 사람이 선택할 달력을 고르시오.

M : Honey, what are you looking at?

W : It's a brochure for a new calendar. Why don't we choose one together?

M : Great. How much do you want to spend?

W : I think more than $20 is not reasonable.

M : Agreed. How about trying a new format ✿ _____ ____ ___ _____ _____? We've only used wall calendars so far.

W : Good idea. Let's pick the standing desk format, then.

M : Okay. And I prefer _____ _____ _____ _____ _____.

W : Me, too. It's more eco-friendly than those that cannot be recycled.

M : Then, let's cross this out. Now, we have two options left. Which one do you prefer?

W : I think the classic art ✿ _____ _____ _____ _____ our interior design.

M : Good point. Then, let's choose this one.

11

대화를 듣고, 여자의 마지막 말에 대한 남자의 응답으로 가장 적절한 것을 고르시오.

W : Congratulations, Lucas! I heard ✿ _____ _____ _____ ____ _____ at the National Assembly.

M : Thanks. It's a real honor. I think the article I wrote in the newspaper made a strong impression.

W : _____ ____ _____ ____ _____. What did you mostly write about?

12

대화를 듣고, 남자의 마지막 말에 대한 여자의 응답으로 가장 적절한 것을 고르시오.

M : Claire, why are you sweating? It's pretty cold outside.

W : Hey, Jamie. _ _____ ___ ____ ___ _____ for class. ✪ _____
_____ _____ ___ _____ from the subway station to our
college, don't you think?

M : Yes, but the shuttle bus began running last week. You can take it
instead.

13

대화를 듣고, 여자의 마지막 말에 대한 남자의 응답으로 가장 적절한 것을 고르시오.
[3점]

W : Good morning, Pablo.

M : Hi, Eva. Look at my new tablet PC.

W : Wow. How do you like it?

M : It's ✪ _____ __ _____ _____ _____ ___
_____. But I have a small problem.

W : What is it? Maybe I can be of help.

M : This file works well on my laptop, but it won't open on my tablet.

W : ✪ _____ _____ _____ __ _____ _____ _____ _____ _____?
You need one to open the file on a tablet.

M : I already did that a week ago.

W : Then, I'll check a few things. *[Tapping sound]* I got it. The free
trial period of this app is over.

M : Oh, _____ _____ __ _____ _____. Do you
think I should pay for this app?

W : Well, it depends on you. You can consider it if you need this app.

14

대화를 듣고, 남자의 마지막 말에 대한 여자의 응답으로 가장 적절한 것을 고르시오.
[3점]

M : Hi, Naomi. What are you up to?

W : Hi. I'm looking for volunteer work. ✪ _____ _____
_____ _____?

M : Yes. I'm working as a note-taker.

W : You mean helping students with hearing difficulties?

M : Right. It ✪ _____ _____ _____
_____ _____ _____ _____.

W : Interesting. Could you tell me more?

M : I type everything during class, even jokes. The more detailed, the
more understandable.

W : It sounds like a unique and valuable experience.

M : Yeah. Are you thinking about joining?

W : Absolutely. But can I join in the middle of the semester?

M : It could be possible. I heard one member quit a few days ago.

W : Lucky me. ___ _____ ____ _____ _____ _____ _____?

M : Hmm, I'm not sure, but if you ask the student volunteer center,
you'll get an answer immediately.

15

다음 상황 설명을 듣고, Tony가 Kate에게 할 말로 가장 적절한 것을 고르시오. [3점]

M : Tony and Kate are members of the bread lovers club. They
✪ _____ ___ ____ __ __ _____ tour every month.
To make ✪ __ _____ _____ ____ __ _____, they're
sharing their ideas about must-visit bakeries. Kate proposes a
bakery whose bread she thinks is super delicious. However, Tony
finds out that the baker there quit and since then _____
_____ _____ _____ ____ _____ complaining
about the bread quality, getting worse. So, he wants to suggest
that they choose a better bakery for their where-to-go list. In this
situation, what would Tony most likely say to Kate?

16~17

다음을 듣고, 물음에 답하시오.

W : Hello, students. Last time, _____ _____ _____ _____
_____ _____ ____ to eat fruits and veggies. But what's good
for us isn't always good for animals. Today, let's find out what fruits
to avoid when feeding dogs. First, grapes are known to be highly
toxic to dogs. You should be careful because even a single grape
✪ _____ _____ _____ _____ _____.
Now, let's take a look at cherries. If a dog swallows their seeds, the
dog is likely to have difficulties breathing. Next, if your dog doesn't
eat avocados, it would be for the best. That's because eating large
amounts of avocados can make your dog sick. Finally, don't let
your dog snack on grapefruits. ✪ _____ _____
_____ ____ _____ _____ that some dogs can
develop stomach problems. Now, you may understand why some
fruits are said to be harmful to dogs. I hope this information will
help you and your dog in living a happy life.

▶ 정답 : 해설편 140쪽

18

001 appreciate ⓥ 진가를 알아보다
002 stylish ⓐ 멋진, 우아한
003 confident ⓐ 자신 있는
004 response ⓝ 대답, 응답
005 ad ⓝ 광고(advertisement)
006 graduate ⓥ 졸업하다
007 sales assistant 판매 보조원
008 customer ⓝ 손님, 고객
009 convenience ⓝ 편의
010 forward to ~ing ~하기를 고대하다

19

011 shade ⓝ 색조, 그늘
012 blanket ⓝ 담요
013 honeymoon ⓝ 신혼여행
014 exotic ⓐ 이국적인
015 wave ⓥ 흔들다
016 wedding ring 결혼반지
017 track ⓝ 방향, 길
018 land ⓥ 떨어지다
019 realize ⓥ 깨닫다
020 sink ⓥ 가라앉다

20

021 unfortunately ⓐ 안타깝게도
022 personal ⓐ 개인적인
023 responsibility ⓝ 책임감
024 growth ⓝ 성장
025 instead ⓐ 대신에
026 race ⓝ 경주, 달리기
027 lay out 놓이다
028 manage ⓥ 관리하다
029 well-run ⓐ 운영이 잘 되는
030 journey ⓝ 여행, 여정
031 lay ⓥ 놓다, 눕히다 (과거형, 과거분사 laid)
032 lack ⓥ 부족하다 ⓝ 부족
033 road map 지침, 로드 맵
034 voluntary ⓐ 자발적인
035 healthy ⓐ 건강한
036 regular ⓐ 규칙적인
037 commit ⓥ 헌신하다, 전념하다
038 devote ⓥ 쏟다, 몰두하다
039 otherwise ⓐ 그렇지 않으면
040 progress ⓝ 전진, 진행, 진척
041 as a result 결과적으로

21

042 commonsense ⓐ 상식적인
043 objective ⓐ 객관적인
044 property ⓝ 속성, 재산
045 bounce off 반사하다
046 reflect ⓥ 반사하다
047 greenness 녹색, 푸르름
048 argue ⓥ 주장하다, 논증하다
049 inhabit ⓥ ~에 존재하다
050 physical ⓐ 물리적인
051 mind ⓝ 마음, 정신
052 maintain ⓥ 주장하다
053 forest ⓝ 숲, 삼림
054 colorless ⓐ 무색의
055 position ⓝ 입장, 위치

056 in a way 어느 정도는, 어떤 면에서는
057 correct ⓐ 적절한, 옳은
058 subjective ⓐ 주관적인
059 register ⓥ 등록하다
060 interpret ⓥ 해석하다, 설명하다
061 range ⓝ 범위
062 perception ⓝ 인식
063 appear ⓥ 보이게 되다
064 perspective ⓝ 관점
065 interact ⓥ 상호 작용하다, 서로 영향을 끼치다
066 structure ⓝ 구조, 조직, 구성
067 similar ⓐ 비슷한, 유사한, 닮은

22

068 research ⓝ 연구, 조사
069 fiction ⓝ 소설
070 demand ⓥ 요구하다
071 detail ⓝ 세부 사항
072 scientific ⓐ 과학의
073 author ⓝ 작가
074 organize ⓥ 조직하다, 편성하다
075 police station 경찰서
076 crime ⓝ 범죄
077 often ⓐ 흔히, 종종, 자주
078 polite ⓐ 예의 바른, 공손한, 정중한
079 earn ⓥ 얻다
080 permission ⓝ 허락
081 record ⓥ 기록하다
082 drive ⓥ 만들다, 몰아가다
083 reader ⓝ 구독자
084 boredom ⓝ 지루함
085 crucial ⓐ 중대한, 결정인
086 conflict ⓝ 갈등
087 blueprint ⓝ 계획, 청사진

23

088 nearly ⓐ 거의
089 rest ⓝ 나머지
090 prevent ⓥ 막다
091 harm ⓝ 해, 피해, 손해
092 adequate ⓐ 충분한
093 lung ⓝ 폐
094 tooth ⓝ 이, 치아, 이빨 (pl. teeth)
095 gum ⓝ 잇몸
096 microorganisms ⓝ 미생물
097 bloodstream ⓝ 피의 흐름, 혈류
098 oral ⓐ 입의, 구강의
099 affect ⓥ 영향을 미치다
100 iceberg ⓝ 빙산
101 reflection ⓝ 반영
102 poor ⓐ 좋지 못한
103 entire ⓐ 전체의
104 serious ⓐ 심각한
105 risk ⓝ 위험, 위험 요소
106 immune system 면역 체계
107 awareness ⓝ 인식
108 impact ⓥ 영향을 주다
109 relationship ⓝ 관계, 관련

24

110 sick of ~에 실증나다

111 sooner or later 조만간, 머지않아
112 interest ⓝ 흥미
113 favorite ⓐ 마음에 드는, 매우 좋아하는
114 bottom line 요점
115 bury ⓥ 숨어있다
116 nerve cell 신경 세포
117 reduce ⓥ 줄이다, 감소시키다
118 initial ⓐ 처음의, 초기의
119 stimulus ⓝ 자극 (pl. stimuli)
120 occur ⓥ 일어나다, 발생하다
121 neuron ⓝ 뉴런(신경세포단위)
122 enhance ⓥ 강화하다
123 especially ⓐ 특히
124 probably ⓐ 아마도
125 evolve ⓥ 진화하다
126 ancestor ⓝ 조상
127 value ⓝ 가치
128 reaction ⓝ 반응, 반작용
129 environment ⓝ 환경
130 excitation ⓝ 자극
131 stimuli ⓝ 자극(stimulus)의 복수형
132 hypothetical ⓐ 가정의, 가상의
133 neural ⓐ 신경의
134 equivalent ⓝ 대응물
135 firefly ⓝ 반딧불이

25

136 investment ⓝ 투자, 투자액
137 fossil ⓝ 화석
138 fuel ⓝ 연료
139 reach ⓥ 도달하다
140 exceed ⓥ 초과하다
141 billion 10억

26

142 slavery ⓝ 노예
143 successfully ⓐ 성공적으로
144 escape ⓥ 달아나다, 탈출하다
145 route ⓝ 길
146 enslave ⓥ 노예로 만들다
147 assist ⓥ 돕다
148 runaway ⓐ 도망친, 탈주한
149 safely ⓐ 무사히, 안전하게
150 spread ⓥ 퍼뜨리다, 확산시키다
151 well-known 잘 알려진
152 abolitionist 노예제 폐지론자
153 believer ⓝ 믿는 사람, 신자, 신봉자
154 equality ⓝ 평등
155 Native American 아메리칸 원주민, 아메리칸 인디언
156 recent ⓐ 최근의
157 immigrant ⓝ 이민자, 이주민
158 several ⓐ 몇 개의
159 autobiography ⓝ 자서전
160 candidate ⓝ 후보자

27

161 get set 준비를 갖추다
162 outdoor ⓐ 집 밖의, 옥외의, 야외의
163 competition ⓝ 경기, 시합
164 participant ⓝ 참가자
165 receive ⓥ 받다

166 certificate ⓝ 증서, 증명서
167 entry ⓝ 참가
168 participation ⓝ 참가, 참여
169 registration ⓝ 등록

28

170 urban ⓐ 도시의, 도회지의
171 quest ⓝ 탐색, 탐구
172 explore ⓥ 탐험하다
173 solve ⓥ 해결하다
174 clue ⓝ 단서
175 complete ⓥ 완료하다
176 available ⓐ 이용할 수 있는
177 sunrise ⓝ 일출
178 sunset ⓝ 일몰
179 discount ⓝ 할인

29

180 propose ⓥ 제안하다
181 tough ⓐ 엄격한, 힘든
182 guideline ⓝ 지침
183 determine ⓥ 결정하다
184 brain death 뇌사
185 transplantation ⓝ 이식
186 transferring ⓝ 이동, 이송
187 organ ⓝ 장기
188 consideration ⓝ 고려, 숙고
189 legal ⓐ 법률의
190 requirement ⓝ 필요조건, 요건
191 specify ⓥ 구체화하다
192 diagnosis ⓝ 진단
193 potential ⓐ 잠재적인
194 donor ⓝ 기증자
195 strict ⓐ 엄격한
196 regulation ⓝ 규제
197 doubt ⓝ 의심, 의혹, 의문
198 ease ⓥ 완화시키다, 편하게 하다, 안심시키다
199 premature ⓐ 정상보다 이른
200 obtain ⓥ 얻다, 획득하다
201 questionable ⓐ 의심스러운, 미심쩍은
202 suspicion ⓝ 의심
203 certainly ⓐ 틀림없이, 분명히
204 belief ⓝ 생각, 신념
205 unreliable ⓐ 믿을 수 없는
206 consistency ⓝ 일관성
207 criteria ⓝ 기준
208 exactly ⓐ 정확히
209 immediate ⓐ 즉시
210 burial ⓝ 매장
211 cremation ⓝ 화장

30

212 term ⓝ 용어
213 impression ⓝ 인상
214 sacrifice ⓥ 희생하다
215 valuable ⓐ 가치 있는
216 possession ⓝ 소유
217 insecurity ⓝ 불안
218 stem ⓥ 비롯되다
219 attachment ⓝ 애착
220 distance ⓥ 거리를 두다
221 emotional ⓐ 정서의, 감정의

222 □ assumption ⓝ 가정
223 □ fundamentally ⓐ𝒹 근본적으로
224 □ get rid of 버리다
225 □ sooner than later 머지않아
226 □ maintain ⓥ 유지하다
227 □ clarity ⓥ 명료하다
228 □ era ⓝ 시대
229 □ eliminate ⓥ 제거하다
230 □ unused ⓐ 사용하지 않는

31
231 □ remarkable ⓐ 두드러진, 놀라운, 주목할만한
232 □ characteristic ⓝ 특징, 특질
233 □ visual ⓐ 시각의
234 □ ability ⓝ 능력, 수완, 역량
235 □ psychologist ⓝ 심리학자
236 □ impressive ⓐ 인상적인
237 □ self-experiment 자가 실험
238 □ reverse 뒤집다
239 □ literally ⓐ𝒹 문자 그대로, 정말로
240 □ upside down 거꾸로, 전도되어, 뒤집혀
241 □ adjust to ~에 적응하다
242 □ upright ⓐ 똑바른
243 □ concentrate ⓥ 집중하다
244 □ confront ⓥ 직면하다

32
245 □ phase ⓝ 상
246 □ allow ⓥ 허락하다
247 □ present ⓥ 제시하다
248 □ unrelated ⓐ 관계없는
249 □ absolutely ⓐ𝒹 전혀
250 □ advantage ⓝ 이점
251 □ equally ⓐ𝒹 동등하게
252 □ rate ⓥ 평가하다
253 □ knowledgeable ⓐ 아는 것이 많은, 많이 아는
254 □ access ⓥ 접근하다
255 □ pump up 부풀리다
256 □ intellectual ⓐ 지적인
257 □ confidence ⓝ 자신감, 확신
258 □ endure ⓥ 견디다
259 □ pursue ⓥ 추구하다
260 □ in-depth ⓐ 깊은

33
261 □ anthropologist ⓝ 인류학자
262 □ feature ⓝ 특색, 특징, 특성
263 □ platypus ⓝ 오리너구리
264 □ zoom in 확대하다
265 □ fur ⓝ 털
266 □ zoom out 축소하다
267 □ extent ⓝ 정도, 한도
268 □ object ⓝ 사물
269 □ treat ⓥ 다루다, 취급하다
270 □ ecosystem ⓝ 생태계
271 □ additional ⓐ 추가의
272 □ crucially ⓐ𝒹 결정적으로
273 □ take up 취하다
274 □ at a time 한 번에
275 □ attention ⓝ 주의, 주목

276 □ varied ⓐ 다양한
277 □ unite ⓥ 합하다
278 □ ecological ⓐ 생태계의
279 □ emphasize ⓥ 강조하다

34
280 □ aspect ⓝ 측면
281 □ explain ⓥ 설명하다
282 □ nature ⓝ 특성, 본성
283 □ geometrical ⓐ 기하학의
284 □ indicate ⓥ 가리키다
285 □ particular ⓐ 특정한
286 □ carved ⓐ 곡선의
287 □ point out 가리키다, 지적하다
288 □ indeed ⓐ𝒹 진정
289 □ possess ⓥ 소유하다
290 □ flaw ⓝ 결함
291 □ decay ⓥ 쇠하다, 부패하다
292 □ extraordinary ⓐ 비범한
293 □ form ⓝ 형상
294 □ universals ⓝ 보편자
295 □ chase ⓥ 쫓다
296 □ phenomena ⓝ 현상
297 □ overlapping ⓐ 중복된
298 □ stereotype ⓝ 고정관념
299 □ generalization ⓝ 일반화

35
300 □ statistics ⓝ 통계학
301 □ describe ⓥ 묘사하다, 말로 설명하다
302 □ situation ⓝ 상황, 처지, 환경
303 □ prediction ⓝ 예측
304 □ according to (진술·기록 등에) 따르면
305 □ experiment ⓝ 실험
306 □ conduct ⓥ 수행하다
307 □ average ⓝ 평균
308 □ encounter ⓥ 접하다, 만나다
309 □ beginner ⓝ 초보자
310 □ relative ⓐ 비교상의, 상대적인
311 □ frequency ⓝ 빈도
312 □ symbolic ⓐ 상징적인
313 □ promise ⓥ 유망하다
314 □ unexpectedly ⓐ𝒹 예상치 못하게
315 □ figure ⓝ 수치, 숫자
316 □ accident ⓝ 사고
317 □ insurance ⓝ 보험
318 □ rely on ~에 의존하다

36
319 □ adolescent ⓝ 청소년
320 □ decision-making ⓝ 의사 결정
321 □ circuit ⓝ 회로
322 □ integrate ⓥ 통합하다
323 □ disadvantage ⓝ 불리한 점, 약점
324 □ on the other hand 다른 한편으로는, 반면에
325 □ limbic system 대뇌변연계
326 □ mature ⓐ 성인의
327 □ be led by ~에 의해 이끌어지다
328 □ factor ⓝ 요인
329 □ consequence ⓝ 결과
330 □ imbalance ⓝ 불균형

331 □ prefrontal cortex 전전두엽 피질
332 □ region ⓝ 범위, 영역

37
333 □ facial ⓐ 얼굴의, 안면의
334 □ remarkable ⓐ 눈에 띄는
335 □ recognition ⓝ 식별
336 □ approach ⓥ 접근하다
337 □ in terms of ~에 관하여
338 □ identification ⓝ 인식
339 □ limitation ⓝ 한계
340 □ relate ⓥ 관련시키다
341 □ stage ⓝ 단계
342 □ counteract ⓥ 대응하다
343 □ de-aging ⓝ 노화 완화
344 □ compensate ⓥ 보완하다
345 □ biometric ⓐ 생물 측정의
346 □ decrease ⓥ 감소하다
347 □ identified ⓐ 확인된, 인정된, 식별된
348 □ enroll ⓥ 등록하다
349 □ texture ⓝ 감촉, 질감
350 □ appearance ⓝ 나타남, 출현
351 □ wrinkle ⓝ 주름
352 □ sagging ⓐ 처진

38
353 □ diversity ⓝ 다양성
354 □ decade ⓝ 수십 년의
355 □ attempt ⓥ 시도
356 □ wheat ⓝ 밀
357 □ scale ⓝ 규모
358 □ replace ⓥ 대체하다
359 □ super-productive ⓐ 초 생산적인
360 □ spectacularly ⓐ𝒹 굉장히
361 □ triple ⓥ 세배가 되다
362 □ contribution ⓝ 기여
363 □ strategy ⓝ 전략
364 □ uniform ⓝ 유니폼
365 □ depend on ~에 의존하다
366 □ disease ⓝ 질병
367 □ pest ⓝ 해충
368 □ extreme ⓝ 위기

39
369 □ be known for ~로 잘 알려진
370 □ covered in ~로 뒤덮인
371 □ toe ⓝ 발끝
372 □ contrast ⓝ 대조
373 □ conservative ⓐ 보수적인
374 □ alter ⓥ 바꾸다
375 □ modernize ⓥ 현대화하다
376 □ decline ⓥ 쇠퇴하다
377 □ abandon ⓥ 버리다
378 □ neglect ⓥ 방치하다, 등한하다

40
379 □ evolution ⓝ 진화
380 □ noticeable ⓐ 주목할 만한
381 □ concept ⓝ 개념
382 □ theoretical ⓐ 이론적인
383 □ genetics ⓝ 유전학
384 □ transmission ⓝ 전이

385 □ innovation ⓝ 혁신
386 □ link to ~에 접근하다
387 □ mutation ⓝ 돌연변이
388 □ modify ⓥ 수정하다
389 □ trait ⓝ 특징
390 □ acquire ⓥ 얻다
391 □ peer ⓝ 동료
392 □ probability ⓝ 개연성
393 □ revise ⓥ 수정하다
394 □ similarity ⓝ 유사성
395 □ diverse ⓐ 다양한
396 □ limited ⓐ 제한적인
397 □ difference ⓝ 다름
398 □ flexible ⓐ 유연한
399 □ complicated ⓐ 복잡한
400 □ interaction ⓝ 상호작용
401 □ credible ⓐ 믿을 수 있는

41~42
402 □ persist ⓥ 저항하다
403 □ inertia ⓝ 관성
404 □ carry ⓥ 나아가다
405 □ constant ⓐ 끊임없는
406 □ gravity ⓝ 중력
407 □ downward ⓐ 아래의
408 □ resistance ⓝ 저항
409 □ combination ⓝ 결합
410 □ elementary ⓐ 기본의
411 □ isolated ⓐ 고립된
412 □ joint ⓐ 공동의
413 □ mutual ⓐ 상호의
414 □ arrangement ⓝ 배치
415 □ conceal ⓥ 감추다
416 □ confined ⓐ 좁은
417 □ significance ⓝ 중요성
418 □ behavior ⓝ 행동
419 □ increase ⓥ 증가하다
420 □ tendency ⓝ 경향
421 □ arouse ⓥ 유발하다
422 □ reveal ⓥ 드러내다
423 □ competitive ⓐ 경쟁적인
424 □ opposite ⓐ 정반대의
425 □ toward ⓟⓡⓔⓟ ~향하여
426 □ bring into 끌어들이다

43~45
427 □ saint ⓝ 성자
428 □ guard ⓝ 경호원
429 □ stop by ~에 들르다
430 □ decide ⓥ 결심하다
431 □ opportunity ⓝ 기회
432 □ confess ⓥ 고백하다
433 □ surrounded ⓐ 둘러싸인
434 □ tension ⓝ 긴장
435 □ take care of ~을 돌보다
436 □ camel ⓝ 낙타
437 □ arise ⓥ 발생하다
438 □ despite ~에도 불구하고

● 채점 : 맞은 개수 _____ / 80

TEST A-B 각 단어의 뜻을 [A] 영어는 우리말로, [B] 우리말은 영어로 쓰시오.

A	English	Korean
01	confident	
02	convenience	
03	shade	
04	wave	
05	track	
06	growth	
07	devote	
08	responsibility	
09	commonsense	
10	objective	
11	reflect	
12	range	
13	demand	
14	drive	
15	prevent	
16	adequate	
17	awareness	
18	investment	
19	reach	
20	exceed	

B	Korean	English
01	평등	
02	증서, 증명서	
03	단서	
04	진단	
05	규제	
06	즉시	
07	구체화하다	
08	용어	
09	소유	
10	유지하다	
11	명료하다	
12	버리다	
13	시각의	
14	~에 적응하다	
15	똑바른	
16	뒤집다	
17	이점	
18	추구하다	
19	견디다	
20	관계없는	

▶ A-D 정답 : 해설편 140쪽

TEST C-D 각 단어의 뜻을 골라 기호를 쓰시오.

C	English	( )	Korean
01	decrease	( )	ⓐ 동등하게
02	spectacularly	( )	ⓑ 결정적으로
03	equally	( )	ⓒ 합하다
04	indeed	( )	ⓓ 가리키다
05	alter	( )	ⓔ 쇠하다, 부패하다
06	modify	( )	ⓕ 진정
07	neglect	( )	ⓖ 중복된
08	compensate	( )	ⓗ 고정관념
09	overlapping	( )	ⓘ 빈도
10	encounter	( )	ⓙ 접하다, 만나다
11	decay	( )	ⓚ 수정하다
12	frequency	( )	ⓛ 식별
13	disease	( )	ⓜ 감소하다
14	counteract	( )	ⓝ 보완하다
15	integrate	( )	ⓞ 대응하다
16	unite	( )	ⓟ 굉장히
17	recognition	( )	ⓠ 질병
18	indicate	( )	ⓡ 바꾸다
19	stereotype	( )	ⓢ 무시하다
20	crucially	( )	ⓣ 통합하다

D	Korean	( )	English
01	기본의	( )	ⓐ probability
02	조상	( )	ⓑ diverse
03	개연성	( )	ⓒ elementary
04	~향하여	( )	ⓓ reveal
05	이동, 이송	( )	ⓔ towards
06	고백하다	( )	ⓕ decide
07	다양한	( )	ⓖ confess
08	가정의, 가상의	( )	ⓗ surrounded
09	완료하다	( )	ⓘ opportunity
10	기회	( )	ⓙ fuel
11	둘러싸인	( )	ⓚ probably
12	자극	( )	ⓛ hypothetical
13	연료	( )	ⓜ excitation
14	아마도	( )	ⓝ ancestor
15	강화하다	( )	ⓞ enhance
16	시대	( )	ⓟ complete
17	두드러진, 놀라운, 주목할 만한	( )	ⓠ transferring
18	드러내다	( )	ⓡ era
19	결심하다	( )	ⓢ insecurity
20	불안	( )	ⓣ remarkable

제 3 교시

● 문항수 45개 | 배점 100점 | 제한 시간 70분

● 점수 표시가 없는 문항은 모두 2점

1번부터 17번까지는 듣고 답하는 문제입니다. 1번부터 15번까지는 한 번만 들려주고, 16번부터 17번까지는 두 번 들려줍니다. 방송을 잘 듣고 답을 하시기 바랍니다.

1. 다음을 듣고, 남자가 하는 말의 목적으로 가장 적절한 것을 고르시오.

① 얼음으로 덮인 일부 등산로 폐쇄를 공지하려고
② 등산객에게 야간 산행의 위험성을 경고하려고
③ 겨울 산행을 위한 안전 장비를 안내하려고
④ 긴급 제설에 필요한 작업자를 모집하려고
⑤ 일출 명소인 전망대를 소개하려고

2. 대화를 듣고, 남자의 의견으로 가장 적절한 것을 고르시오.

① 조리법을 있는 그대로 따를 필요는 없다.
② 요리 도구를 정기적으로 소독해야 한다.
③ 설탕 섭취는 단기 기억력을 향상시킨다.
④ 열량이 높은 음식은 건강에 좋지 않다.
⑤ 신선한 재료는 요리의 풍미를 높인다.

3. 대화를 듣고, 두 사람의 관계를 가장 잘 나타낸 것을 고르시오.

① 음악 평론가 – 방송 연출가   ② 작곡가 – 게임 제작자
③ 독자 – 웹툰 작가   ④ 삽화가 – 소설가
⑤ 영화감독 – 배우

4. 대화를 듣고, 그림에서 대화의 내용과 일치하지 않는 것을 고르시오

5. 대화를 듣고, 남자가 할 일로 가장 적절한 것을 고르시오.

① 음료 구매하기   ② 연필 준비하기
③ 의자 설치하기   ④ 마이크 점검하기
⑤ 스케치북 가져오기

6. 대화를 듣고, 여자가 지불할 금액을 고르시오. [3점]

① $17   ② $22   ③ $35   ④ $37   ⑤ $39

7. 대화를 듣고, 남자가 얼음낚시를 갈 수 없는 이유를 고르시오.

① 손목을 다쳐서
② 병원에 입원해야 해서
③ 직장에 출근해야 해서
④ 기상 여건이 나빠져서
⑤ 친구와 농구를 해야 해서

8. 대화를 듣고, Kids' Pottery Class에 관해 언급되지 않은 것을 고르시오.

① 날짜   ② 장소   ③ 수강 인원
④ 수강료   ⑤ 등록 방법

9. 2022 Online Whistling Championship에 관한 다음 내용을 듣고, 일치하지 않는 것을 고르시오.

① 좋아하는 어떤 노래든 선택할 수 있다.
② 12월 4일까지 동영상을 업로드해야 한다.
③ 녹음 시 마이크의 에코 효과를 반드시 꺼야 한다.
④ 운영진의 심사에 의해 수상자들이 결정될 것이다.
⑤ 결과는 웹사이트에 발표될 것이다.

10. 다음 표를 보면서 대화를 듣고, 두 사람이 선택할 커튼을 고르시오.

Curtains

	Product	Price	Care Instruction	Blackout	Color
①	A	$70	machine washable	×	navy
②	B	$80	machine washable	○	brown
③	C	$90	dry cleaning only	○	ivory
④	D	$95	machine washable	○	gray
⑤	E	$110	dry cleaning only	×	white

11. 대화를 듣고, 남자의 마지막 말에 대한 여자의 응답으로 가장 적절한 것을 고르시오.

① I've been waiting for 30 minutes.
② I've enjoyed this ride very much.
③ You're standing in the correct line.
④ I have enough time to wait for you.
⑤ You may end the construction in a year.

12. 대화를 듣고, 여자의 마지막 말에 대한 남자의 응답으로 가장 적절한 것을 고르시오.

① No way. I don't know who's lost.
② Okay. Let's see if he needs our help.
③ Exactly. Just stop crying like a child.
④ Sure. He loves walking around the park.
⑤ Thanks. We were worried about our son.

13. 대화를 듣고, 남자의 마지막 말에 대한 여자의 응답으로 가장 적절한 것을 고르시오. [3점]

Woman: _____

① Great. I believe my previous offer will benefit your company.
② I'm sorry. Your interview has been delayed to next Wednesday.
③ Good. Your effort will give a good impression on the interviewer.
④ Excellent. The second candidate's work experience caught my eye.
⑤ No worries. You can purchase nice clothes for the upcoming party.

14. 대화를 듣고, 여자의 마지막 말에 대한 남자의 응답으로 가장 적절한 것을 고르시오.

Man: _____

① Please wait. I'll be back with the shoes in a minute.
② Hurry up. You don't have enough time to do this.
③ Of course. You can get a refund for these shoes.
④ Don't worry. The color doesn't matter to me.
⑤ Sorry. The red ones are already sold out.

15. 다음 상황 설명을 듣고, Amelia가 Jacob 교수에게 할 말로 가장 적절한 것을 고르시오. [3점]

Amelia: _____

① Could you extend the deadline for the assignment?
② Would it be possible to change our appointment?
③ Why don't you join my final psychology project?
④ Do you want to meet at the information center?
⑤ How about visiting the doctor for a checkup?

[16~17] 다음을 듣고, 물음에 답하시오.

16. 여자가 하는 말의 주제로 가장 적절한 것은?

① ways to stop the spread of false information
② methods of delivering messages in the past
③ modes of communication in modern times
④ types of speeches according to purposes
⑤ means to survive in prehistoric times

17. 언급된 수단이 <u>아닌</u> 것은?

① drum   ② smoke   ③ pigeon
④ flag   ⑤ horse

> **이제 듣기 문제가 끝났습니다. 18번부터는 문제지의 지시에 따라 답을 하시기 바랍니다.**

18. 다음 글의 목적으로 가장 적절한 것은?

> Dear Mr. Krull,
>
> I have greatly enjoyed working at Trincom Enterprises as a sales manager. Since I joined in 2015, I have been a loyal and essential member of this company, and have developed innovative ways to contribute to the company. Moreover, in the last year alone, I have brought in two new major clients to the company, increasing the company's total sales by 5%. Also, I have voluntarily trained 5 new members of staff, totaling 35 hours. I would therefore request your consideration in raising my salary, which I believe reflects my performance as well as the industry average. I look forward to speaking with you soon.
>
> Kimberly Morss

① 부서 이동을 신청하려고
② 급여 인상을 요청하려고
③ 근무 시간 조정을 요구하려고
④ 기업 혁신 방안을 제안하려고
⑤ 신입 사원 연수에 대해 문의하려고

19. 다음 글에 드러난 'I'의 심경 변화로 가장 적절한 것은?

On one beautiful spring day, I was fully enjoying my day off. I arrived at the nail salon, and muted my cellphone so that I would be disconnected for the hour and feel calm and peaceful. I was so comfortable while I got a manicure. As I left the place, I checked my cellphone and saw four missed calls from a strange number. I knew immediately that something bad was coming, and I called back. A young woman answered and said that my father had fallen over a stone and was injured, now seated on a bench. I was really concerned since he had just recovered from his knee surgery. I rushed getting into my car to go see him.

① nervous → confident   ② relaxed → worried
③ excited → indifferent   ④ pleased → jealous
⑤ annoyed → grateful

20. 다음 글에서 필자가 주장하는 바로 가장 적절한 것은?

You already have a business and you're about to launch your blog so that you can sell your product. Unfortunately, here is where a 'business mind' can be a bad thing. Most people believe that to have a successful business blog promoting a product, they have to stay strictly 'on the topic.' If all you're doing is shamelessly promoting your product, then who is going to want to read the latest thing you're writing about? Instead, you need to give some useful or entertaining information away for free so that people have a reason to keep coming back. Only by doing this can you create an interested audience that you will then be able to sell to. So, the best way to be successful with a business blog is to write about things that your audience will be interested in.

① 인터넷 게시물에 대한 윤리적 기준을 세워야 한다.
② 블로그를 전문적으로 관리할 인력을 마련해야 한다.
③ 신제품 개발을 위해 상업용 블로그를 적극 활용해야 한다.
④ 상품에 대한 고객들의 반응을 정기적으로 분석할 필요가 있다.
⑤ 상업용 블로그는 사람들이 흥미 있어 할 정보를 제공해야 한다.

21. 밑줄 친 challenge this sacred cow가 다음 글에서 의미하는 바로 가장 적절한 것은? [3점]

Our language helps to reveal our deeper assumptions. Think of these revealing phrases: When we accomplish something important, we say it took "blood, sweat, and tears." We say important achievements are "hard-earned." We recommend a "hard day's work" when "day's work" would be enough. When we talk of "easy money," we are implying it was obtained through illegal or questionable means. We use the phrase "That's easy for you to say" as a criticism, usually when we are seeking to invalidate someone's opinion. It's like we all automatically accept that the "right" way is, inevitably, the harder one. In my experience this is hardly ever questioned. What would happen if you do challenge this sacred cow? We don't even pause to consider that something important and valuable could be made easy. What if the biggest thing keeping us from doing what matters is the false assumption that it has to take huge effort?

* invalidate: 틀렸음을 입증하다

① resist the tendency to avoid any hardship
② escape from the pressure of using formal language
③ doubt the solid belief that only hard work is worthy
④ abandon the old notion that money always comes first
⑤ break the superstition that holy animals bring good luck

22. 다음 글의 요지로 가장 적절한 것은?

The old saying is that "knowledge is power," but when it comes to scary, threatening news, research suggests the exact opposite. Frightening news can actually rob people of their inner sense of control, making them less likely to take care of themselves and other people. Public health research shows that when the news presents health-related information in a pessimistic way, people are actually less likely to take steps to protect themselves from illness as a result. A news article that's intended to warn people about increasing cancer rates, for example, can result in fewer people choosing to get screened for the disease because they're so terrified of what they might find. This is also true for issues such as climate change. When a news story is all doom and gloom, people feel depressed and become less interested in taking small, personal steps to fight ecological collapse.

① 두려움을 주는 뉴스는 사람들이 문제에 덜 대처하게 할 수 있다.
② 정보를 전달하는 시기에 따라 뉴스의 영향력이 달라질 수 있다.
③ 지속적인 환경 문제 보도가 사람들의 인식 변화를 가져온다.
④ 정보 제공의 지연은 정확한 문제 인식에 방해가 될 수 있다.
⑤ 출처가 불분명한 건강 정보는 사람들에게 유익하지 않다.

23. 다음 글의 주제로 가장 적절한 것은?

The most remarkable and unbelievable consequence of melting ice and rising seas is that together they are a kind of time machine, so real that they are altering the duration of our day. It works like this: As the glaciers melt and the seas rise, gravity forces more water toward the equator. This changes the shape of the Earth ever so slightly, making it fatter around the middle, which in turns slows the rotation of the planet similarly to the way a ballet dancer slows her spin by spreading out her arms. The slowdown isn't much, just a few thousandths of a second each year, but like the barely noticeable jump of rising seas every year, it adds up. When dinosaurs lived on the Earth, a day lasted only about twenty-three hours.

① cause of rising temperatures on the Earth
② principles of planets maintaining their shapes
③ implications of melting ice on marine biodiversity
④ way to keep track of time without using any device
⑤ impact of melting ice and rising seas on the length of a day

24. 다음 글의 제목으로 가장 적절한 것은?

Have you ever brought up an idea or suggestion to someone and heard them immediately say "No, that won't work."? You may have thought, "He/she didn't even give it a chance. How do they know it won't work?" When you are right about something, you close off the possibility of another viewpoint or opportunity. Being right about something means that "it is the way it is, period." You may be correct. Your particular way of seeing it may be true with the facts. However, considering the other option or the other person's point of view can be beneficial. If you see their side, you will see something new or, at worse, learn something about how the other person looks at life. Why would you think everyone sees and experiences life the way you do? Besides how boring that would be, it would eliminate all new opportunities, ideas, invention, and creativity.

① The Value of Being Honest
② Filter Out Negative Points of View
③ Keeping Your Word: A Road to Success
④ Being Right Can Block New Possibilities
⑤ Look Back When Everyone Looks Forward

25. 다음 도표의 내용과 일치하지 <u>않는</u> 것은?

Reasons for People Interested in Eating Less Meat and Non-meat Eaters in the UK (2018)

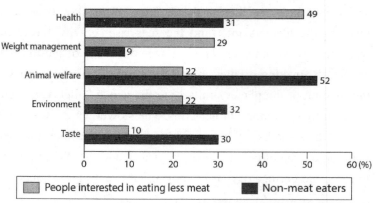

Health — 49 / 31
Weight management — 29 / 9
Animal welfare — 22 / 52
Environment — 22 / 32
Taste — 10 / 30

☐ People interested in eating less meat ■ Non-meat eaters

※ allowed to choose multiple reasons

The graph above shows the survey results on reasons for people interested in eating less meat and those eating no meat in the UK in 2018. ① For the group of people who are interested in eating less meat, health is the strongest motivator for doing so. ② For the group of non-meat eaters, animal welfare accounts for the largest percentage among all reasons, followed by environment, health, and taste. ③ The largest percentage point difference between the two groups is in animal welfare, whereas the smallest difference is in environment. ④ The percentage of non-meat eaters citing taste is four times higher than that of people interested in reducing their meat consumption citing taste. ⑤ Weight management ranks the lowest for people who don't eat meat, with less than 10 percent.

26. Margaret Knight에 관한 다음 글의 내용과 일치하지 <u>않는</u> 것은?

Margaret Knight was an exceptionally prolific inventor in the late 19th century; journalists occasionally compared her to Thomas Edison by nicknaming her "a woman Edison." From a young age, she built toys for her older brothers. After her father died, Knight's family moved to Manchester. Knight left school in 1850, at age 12, to earn money for her family at a nearby textile factory, where she witnessed a fellow worker injured by faulty equipment. That led her to create her first invention, a safety device for textile equipment, but she never earned money from the invention. She also invented a machine that cut, folded and glued flat-bottomed paper bags and was awarded her first patent in 1871 for it. It eliminated the need for workers to assemble them slowly by hand. Knight received 27 patents in her lifetime and entered the National Inventors Hall of Fame in 2006.

*prolific: 다작(多作)의 ** patent: 특허

① 기자들이 '여자 Edison'이라는 별명을 지어 주었다.
② 가족을 위해 돈을 벌려고 학교를 그만두었다.
③ 직물 장비에 쓰이는 안전장치를 발명하여 많은 돈을 벌었다.
④ 밑이 평평한 종이 가방을 자르고 접고 붙이는 기계를 발명했다.
⑤ 2006년에 국립 발명가 명예의 전당에 입성했다.

27. E-Waste Recycling Day에 관한 다음 안내문의 내용과 일치하지 <u>않는</u> 것은?

> **E-Waste Recycling Day**
> E-Waste Recycling Day is an annual event in our city. Bring your used electronics such as cell phones, tablets, and laptops to recycle. Go green!
>
> **When**
> Saturday, December 17, 2022
> 8:00 a.m. − 11:00 a.m.
>
> **Where**
> Lincoln Sports Center
>
> **Notes**
> • Items NOT accepted: light bulbs, batteries, and microwaves
> • All personal data on the devices must be wiped out in advance.
> • This event is free but open only to local residents.
>
> Please contact us at 986−571−0204 for more information.

① 3시간 동안 진행된다.
② Lincoln 스포츠 센터에서 열린다.
③ 전자레인지는 허용되지 않는 품목이다.
④ 기기 속 모든 개인 정보는 미리 삭제되어야 한다.
⑤ 거주 지역에 상관없이 참가할 수 있다.

28. Undersea Walking Activity에 관한 다음 안내문의 내용과 일치하는 것은?

> **Undersea Walking Activity**
> Enjoy a fascinating underwater walk on the ocean floor. Witness wonderful marine life on foot!
>
> **Age Requirement**
> 10 years or older
>
> **Operating Hours**
> from Tuesday to Sunday
> 9:00 a.m. − 4:00 p.m.
>
> **Price**
> $30 (insurance fee included)
>
> **What to Bring**
> swim suit and towel
>
> **Notes**
> • Experienced lifeguards accompany you throughout the activity.
> • With a special underwater helmet, you can wear glasses during the activity.
> • Reservations can be made on-site or online at www.seawalkwonder.com.

① 연중무휴로 운영된다.
② 가격에 보험료는 포함되어 있지 않다.
③ 숙련된 안전 요원이 활동 내내 동행한다.
④ 특수 수중 헬멧 착용 시 안경을 쓸 수 없다.
⑤ 현장 예약은 불가능하다.

29. 다음 글의 밑줄 친 부분 중, 어법상 <u>틀린</u> 것은? [3점]

You may have seen headlines in the news about some of the things machines powered by artificial intelligence can do. However, if you were to consider all the tasks ① <u>that</u> AI-powered machines could actually perform, it would be quite mind-blowing! One of the key features of artificial intelligence ② <u>is</u> that it enables machines to learn new things, rather than requiring programming specific to new tasks. Therefore, the core difference between computers of the future and ③ <u>those</u> of the past is that future computers will be able to learn and self-improve. In the near future, smart virtual assistants will know more about you than your closest friends and family members ④ <u>are</u>. Can you imagine how that might change our lives? These kinds of changes are exactly why it is so important ⑤ <u>to recognize</u> the implications that new technologies will have for our world.

30. 다음 글의 밑줄 친 부분 중, 문맥상 낱말의 쓰임이 적절하지 <u>않은</u> 것은? [3점]

Plant growth is controlled by a group of hormones called auxins found at the tips of stems and roots of plants. Auxins produced at the tips of stems tend to accumulate on the side of the stem that is in the shade. Accordingly, the auxins ① <u>stimulate</u> growth on the shaded side of the plant. Therefore, the shaded side grows faster than the side facing the sunlight. This phenomenon causes the stem to bend and appear to be growing ② <u>towards</u> the light. Auxins have the ③ <u>opposite</u> effect on the roots of plants. Auxins in the tips of roots tend to limit growth. If a root is horizontal in the soil, the auxins will accumulate on the lower side and interfere with its development. Therefore, the lower side of the root will grow ④ <u>faster</u> than the upper side. This will, in turn, cause the root to bend ⑤ <u>downwards</u>, with the tip of the root growing in that direction.

[31~34] 다음 빈칸에 들어갈 말로 가장 적절한 것을 고르시오.

31. To demonstrate how best to defeat the habit of delaying, Dan Ariely, a professor of psychology and behavioral economics, performed an experiment on students in three of his classes at MIT. He assigned all classes three reports over the course of the semester. The first class had to choose three due dates for themselves, up to and including the last day of class. The second had no deadlines — all three papers just had to be submitted by the last day of class. In his third class, he gave students three set deadlines over the course of the semester. At the end of the semester, he found that students with set deadlines received the best grades, the students with no deadlines had the worst, and those who could choose their own deadlines fell somewhere in the middle. Ariely concludes that _____ — whether by the professor or by students who recognize their own tendencies to delay things — improves self-control and performance.

① offering rewards
② removing obstacles
③ restricting freedom
④ increasing assignments
⑤ encouraging competition

32. The best way in which innovation changes our lives is by _____. The main theme of human history is that we become steadily more specialized in what we produce, and steadily more diversified in what we consume: we move away from unstable self-sufficiency to safer mutual interdependence. By concentrating on serving other people's needs for forty hours a week — which we call a job — you can spend the other seventy-two hours (not counting fifty-six hours in bed) relying on the services provided to you by other people. Innovation has made it possible to work for a fraction of a second in order to be able to afford to turn on an electric lamp for an hour, providing the quantity of light that would have required a whole day's work if you had to make it yourself by collecting and refining sesame oil or lamb fat to burn in a simple lamp, as much of humanity did in the not so distant past. [3점]

* a fraction of a second: 아주 짧은 시간 ** refine: 정제하다

① respecting the values of the old days
② enabling people to work for each other
③ providing opportunities to think creatively
④ satisfying customers with personalized services
⑤ introducing and commercializing unusual products

33. If you've ever made a poor choice, you might be interested in learning how to break that habit. One great way to trick your brain into doing so is to sign a "Ulysses Contract." The name of this life tip comes from the Greek myth about Ulysses, a captain whose ship sailed past the island of the Sirens, a tribe of dangerous women who lured victims to their death with their irresistible songs. Knowing that he would otherwise be unable to resist, Ulysses instructed his crew to stuff their ears with cotton and tie him to the ship's mast to prevent him from turning their ship towards the Sirens. It worked for him and you can do the same thing by _____. For example, if you want to stay off your cellphone and concentrate on your work, delete the apps that distract you or ask a friend to change your password!

* lure: 유혹하다 ** mast: 돛대

① letting go of all-or-nothing mindset
② finding reasons why you want to change
③ locking yourself out of your temptations
④ building a plan and tracking your progress
⑤ focusing on breaking one bad habit at a time

34. Our homes aren't just ecosystems, they're unique ones, hosting species that are adapted to indoor environments and pushing evolution in new directions. Indoor microbes, insects, and rats have all evolved the ability to survive our chemical attacks, developing resistance to antibacterials, insecticides, and poisons. German cockroaches are known to have developed a distaste for glucose, which is commonly used as bait in roach traps. Some indoor insects, which have fewer opportunities to feed than their outdoor counterparts, seem to have developed the ability to survive when food is limited. Dunn and other ecologists have suggested that as the planet becomes more developed and more urban, more species will _____. Over a long enough time period, indoor living could drive our evolution, too. Perhaps my indoorsy self represents the future of humanity.

[3점]

* glucose: 포도당 ** bait: 미끼

① produce chemicals to protect themselves
② become extinct with the destroyed habitats
③ evolve the traits they need to thrive indoors
④ compete with outside organisms to find their prey
⑤ break the boundaries between wildlife and humans

35. 다음 글에서 전체 흐름과 관계 없는 문장은?

Developing a personal engagement with poetry brings a number of benefits to you as an individual, in both a personal and a professional capacity. ① Writing poetry has been shown to have physical and mental benefits, with expressive writing found to improve immune system and lung function, diminish psychological distress, and enhance relationships. ② Poetry has long been used to aid different mental health needs, develop empathy, and reconsider our relationship with both natural and built environments. ③ Poetry is also an incredibly effective way of actively targeting the cognitive development period, improving your productivity and scientific creativity in the process. ④ Poetry is considered to be an easy and useful means of expressing emotions, but you fall into frustration when you realize its complexity. ⑤ In short, poetry has a lot to offer, if you give it the opportunity to do so.

* cognitive: 인지적인

[36~37] 주어진 글 다음에 이어질 글의 순서로 가장 적절한 것을 고르시오.

36.

Things are changing. It has been reported that 42 percent of jobs in Canada are at risk, and 62 percent of jobs in America will be in danger due to advances in automation.

(A) However, what's difficult to automate is the ability to creatively solve problems. Whereas workers in "doing" roles can be replaced by robots, the role of creatively solving problems is more dependent on an irreplaceable individual.

(B) You might say that the numbers seem a bit unrealistic, but the threat is real. One fast food franchise has a robot that can flip a burger in ten seconds. It is just a simple task but the robot could replace an entire crew.

(C) Highly skilled jobs are also at risk. A supercomputer, for instance, can suggest available treatments for specific illnesses in an automated way, drawing on the body of medical research and data on diseases.

① (A) － (C) － (B)   ② (B) － (A) － (C)
③ (B) － (C) － (A)   ④ (C) － (A) － (B)
⑤ (C) － (B) － (A)

37.

Each beech tree grows in a particular location and soil conditions can vary greatly in just a few yards. The soil can have a great deal of water or almost no water. It can be full of nutrients or not.

(A) This is taking place underground through the roots. Whoever has an abundance of sugar hands some over; whoever is running short gets help. Their network acts as a system to make sure that no trees fall too far behind.

(B) However, the rate is the same. Whether they are thick or thin, all the trees of the same species are using light to produce the same amount of sugar per leaf. Some trees have plenty of sugar and some have less, but the trees equalize this difference between them by transferring sugar.

(C) Accordingly, each tree grows more quickly or more slowly and produces more or less sugar, and thus you would expect every tree to be photosynthesizing at a different rate. [3점]

* photosynthesize: 광합성하다

① (A) − (C) − (B)
② (B) − (A) − (C)
③ (B) − (C) − (A)
④ (C) − (A) − (B)
⑤ (C) − (B) − (A)

[38~39] 글의 흐름으로 보아, 주어진 문장이 들어가기에 가장 적절한 곳을 고르시오.

38.

Nevertheless, language is enormously important in human life and contributes largely to our ability to cooperate with each other in dealing with the world.

Should we use language to understand mind or mind to understand language? (①) Analytic philosophy historically assumes that language is basic and that mind would make sense if proper use of language was appreciated. (②) Modern cognitive science, however, rightly judges that language is just one aspect of mind of great importance in human beings but not fundamental to all kinds of thinking. (③) Countless species of animals manage to navigate the world, solve problems, and learn without using language, through brain mechanisms that are largely preserved in the minds of humans. (④) There is no reason to assume that language is fundamental to mental operations. (⑤) Our species *homo sapiens* has been astonishingly successful, which depended in part on language, first as an effective contributor to collaborative problem solving and much later, as collective memory through written records. [3점]

* appreciate: (제대로) 인식하다

39.

If we could magically remove the glasses, we would find the two water bodies would not mix well.

Take two glasses of water. Put a little bit of orange juice into one and a little bit of lemon juice into the other. (①)What you have are essentially two glasses of water but with a completely different chemical makeup. (②) If we take the glass containing orange juice and heat it, we will still have two different glasses of water with different chemical makeups, but now they will also have different temperatures. (③) Perhaps they would mix a little where they met; however, they would remain separate because of their different chemical makeups and temperatures. (④) The warmer water would float on the surface of the cold water because of its lighter weight. (⑤) In the ocean we have bodies of water that differ in temperature and salt content; for this reason, they do not mix.

40. 다음 글의 내용을 한 문장으로 요약하고자 한다. 빈칸 (A), (B)에 들어갈 말로 가장 적절한 것은?

One of the most powerful tools to find meaning in our lives is reflective journaling — thinking back on and writing about what has happened to us. In the 1990s, Stanford University researchers asked undergraduate students on spring break to journal about their most important personal values and their daily activities; others were asked to write about only the good things that happened to them in the day. Three weeks later, the students who had written about their values were happier, healthier, and more confident about their ability to handle stress than the ones who had only focused on the good stuff. By reflecting on how their daily activities supported their values, students had gained a new perspective on those activities and choices. Little stresses and hassles were now demonstrations of their values in action. Suddenly, their lives were full of meaningful activities. And all they had to do was reflect and write about it — positively reframing their experiences with their personal values.

* hassle: 귀찮은 일

↓

Journaling about daily activities based on what we believe to be __(A)__ can make us feel that our life is meaningful by __(B)__ our experiences in a new way.

	(A)	(B)		(A)	(B)
①	factual	rethinking	②	worthwhile	rethinking
③	outdated	generalizing	④	objective	generalizing
⑤	demanding	describing			

[41~42] 다음 글을 읽고, 물음에 답하시오.

Mike May lost his sight at the age of three. Because he had spent the majority of his life adapting to being blind — and even cultivating a skiing career in this state — his other senses compensated by growing (a) stronger. However, when his sight was restored through a surgery in his forties, his entire perception of reality was (b) disrupted. Instead of being thrilled that he could see now, as he'd expected, his brain was so overloaded with new visual stimuli that the world became a frightening and overwhelming place. After he'd learned to know his family through touch and smell, he found that he couldn't recognize his children with his eyes, and this left him puzzled. Skiing also became a lot harder as he struggled to adapt to the visual stimulation.

This (c) confusion occurred because his brain hadn't yet learned to see. Though we often tend to assume our eyes function as video cameras which relay information to our brain, advances in neuroscientific research have proven that this is actually not the case. Instead, sight is a collaborative effort between our eyes and our brains, and the way we process (d) visual reality depends on the way these two communicate. If communication between our eyes and our brains is disturbed, our perception of reality is altered accordingly. And because other areas of May's brain had adapted to process information primarily through his other senses, the process of learning how to see was (e) easier than he'd anticipated.

41. 윗글의 제목으로 가장 적절한 것은?

① Eyes and Brain Working Together for Sight
② Visualization: A Useful Tool for Learning
③ Collaboration Between Vision and Sound
④ How to Ignore New Visual Stimuli
⑤ You See What You Believe

42. 밑줄 친 (a)~(e) 중에서 문맥상 낱말의 쓰임이 적절하지 않은 것은?

① (a) ② (b) ③ (c) ④ (d) ⑤ (e)

[43~45] 다음 글을 읽고, 물음에 답하시오.

(A)

On my daughter Marie's 8th birthday, she received a bunch of presents from her friends at school. That evening, with her favorite present, a teddy bear, in her arms, we went to a restaurant to celebrate her birthday. Our server, a friendly woman, noticed my daughter holding the teddy bear and said, "My daughter loves teddy bears, too." Then, we started chatting about (a) her family.

(B)

When Marie came back out, I asked her what she had been doing. She said that she gave her teddy bear to our server so that she could give it to (b) her daughter. I was surprised at her sudden action because I could see how much she loved that bear already. (c) She must have seen the look on my face, because she said, "I can't imagine being stuck in a hospital bed. I just want her to get better soon."

(C)

I felt moved by Marie's words as we walked toward the car. Then, our server ran out to our car and thanked Marie for her generosity. The server said that (d) she had never had anyone doing anything like that for her family before. Later, Marie said it was her best birthday ever. I was so proud of her empathy and warmth, and this was an unforgettable experience for our family.

(D)

The server mentioned during the conversation that her daughter was in the hospital with a broken leg. (e) She also said that Marie looked about the same age as her daughter. She was so kind and attentive all evening, and even gave Marie cookies for free. After we finished our meal, we paid the bill and began to walk to our car when unexpectedly Marie asked me to wait and ran back into the restaurant.

43. 주어진 글 (A)에 이어질 내용을 순서에 맞게 배열한 것으로 가장 적절한 것은?

① (B) − (D) − (C) ② (C) − (B) − (D)
③ (C) − (D) − (B) ④ (D) − (B) − (C)
⑤ (D) − (C) − (B)

44. 밑줄 친 (a)~(e) 중에서 가리키는 대상이 나머지 넷과 다른 것은?

① (a) ② (b) ③ (c) ④ (d) ⑤ (e)

45. 윗글에 관한 내용으로 적절하지 않은 것은?

① Marie는 테디 베어를 팔에 안고 식당에 갔다.
② 'I'는 Marie의 갑작스러운 행동에 놀랐다.
③ 종업원은 Marie의 관대함에 고마워했다.
④ 종업원은 자신의 딸이 팔이 부러져서 병원에 있다고 말했다.
⑤ 종업원은 Marie에게 쿠키를 무료로 주었다.

* 확인 사항
○ 답안지의 해당란에 필요한 내용을 정확히 기입(표기)했는지 확인하시오.

Dictation 11

✿ 표기에는 듣기 어려운 발음이 포함되어 있습니다. 귀 기울여 듣고 받아쓰세요.

● 고1 2022학년도 11월

※ QR 코드를 스캔하시면 듣기 방송이 나옵니다. 듣기 방송을 들으며 다음 빈칸을 채우시오.　　● 제한 시간 : 25분

01

다음을 듣고, 남자가 하는 말의 목적으로 가장 적절한 것을 고르시오.

[Chime bell rings.]

M : Good morning. This is Ethan Cooper from the Reindeer Mountain maintenance office. Last night, we had 20cm of heavy snow. Most of the snow ✿ _____ _____ _____ _____ _____ in the morning, but some of it froze in the shade. For hikers' safety, we've _____ _____ ___ _____ _____ covered with ice. At this moment, Sunrise Trail and Lakeview Trail are ✿ _____ _____ _____ . I'll make an announcement later when the trails are ready to be reopened. Until then, keep in mind that Sunrise Trail and Lakeview Trail are closed. Thank you.

02

대화를 듣고, 남자의 의견으로 가장 적절한 것을 고르시오.

M : Honey, what are you doing?

W : I'm looking for the measuring spoons. Do you know where they are?

M : They're in the first drawer. Why do you need them?

W : The recipe says four teaspoons of sugar.

M : Dear, you don't have to ✿ _____ _____ _____ _____ __ ___ .

W : What do you mean?

M : A recipe is _____ ____ _____ . You don't need to add the same amount of ingredients ___ _____ _____ _____ .

W : Hmm. Right. Sometimes the food is too sweet when I cook based on the recipe instructions.

M : See? You don't need to stick to the recipe.

W : Okay. I'll remember that.

03

대화를 듣고, 두 사람의 관계를 가장 잘 나타낸 것을 고르시오.

[Door knocks.]

W : Can I come in?

M : Yes. Oh, Ms. Smith. Did you read the email I sent?

W : I did. I liked _____ _____ _____ . The characters exploring space were very mysterious. How did you create the characters?

M : Actually, old science fiction movies inspired me to design those characters.

W : Interesting. Now, could you describe the main character more specifically? It'll be helpful when I compose the theme song for the character.

M : Well, he's ✿ __ _____ _____ . So, a strong, bold, and rhythmic sound would suit him.

W : Okay. Do you need anything else?

M : I also want you to _____ _____ _____ .

W : Of course. When do you need them?

M : By December 21st. I'd like to start putting the music into the game by then.

W : All right. Then I'll talk to you later.

04

대화를 듣고, 그림에서 대화의 내용과 일치하지 않는 것을 고르시오.

M : Hi, Chelsea. Did you finish your art assignment?

W : Oh, _____ _____ _____ _____ ? Yes. Here's the picture.

M : Wow, it's so creative. There is ✿ __ _____ _____ ___ _____ _____ .

W : Yes. I've always dreamed of a room with two floors. Look at the three light bulbs above the staircase.

M : They look very stylish. And I like the flower picture above the sofa. It'll ✿ _____ _____ ____ _____ _____ .

W : Thanks. Check out the square-shaped rug on the floor.

M : It goes well with this place. Oh, there is a bookshelf by the sofa.

W : You're right. I want to keep my favorite books nearby.

M : That's a good idea.

05

대화를 듣고, 남자가 할 일로 가장 적절한 것을 고르시오.

W : Jamie, is the cartoon artist on her way?

M : Yes. She'll arrive at our studio in an hour.

W : Perfect. Let's check if we have everything ready for our talk show.

M : Okay. I set up a chair for our guest yesterday.

W : Great. And I bought a drink and put it on the table.

M : Good. Did you prepare a pencil? The artist said she'll ✿ _____ ___ _____ during the live show.

W : Oh, she told me that she'll _____ _____ .

M : She did? Then we don't need it.

W : Yeah. By the way, where's the sketchbook?

M : Oops. I left it in my car. I'll ____ _____ __ ____ _____ .

W : Fine. Then I'll check the microphones.

M : Thanks.

Dictation 11

06

대화를 듣고, 여자가 지불할 금액을 고르시오. [3점]

M : Welcome to Crispy Fried Chicken. What would you like to order?

W : What kind of chicken do you have?

M : We only have two kinds. Fried chicken is $15 and barbecue chicken is $20.

W : I'll have one fried and one barbecue chicken.

M : Okay. Would you like _____ _____ _____ with your order? They're our most popular side dish.

W : How much are they?

M : One basket of potato chips is $2.

W : Then I'll _____ _____ _____.

M : ✪ _____ _____ ____ ____?

W : Yes. And can I use this coupon for a free soda?

M : Of course. You can grab any soda from the fridge.

W : Great. Here's my credit card.

07

대화를 듣고, 남자가 얼음낚시를 갈 수 없는 이유를 고르시오.

[Cell phone rings.]

W : Leo, I'm sorry I missed your call. What's up?

M : Well, I just called to tell you that I can't go ice fishing with you this weekend.

W : Oh, no. I heard the weather will be perfect this weekend.

M : I'm sorry. I really wish I could go.

W : Didn't you say you're off from work this weekend?

M : I am. It's not because of work. Actually, ✪ __ _____ _____ _____.

W : That's terrible. Are you okay?

M : Don't worry. I'll be fine.

W : _____ _____ _____ _____ _____?

M : I was playing basketball with a friend and ✪ _____ _____ _____.

W : Did you go to the hospital?

M : I did. The doctor told me that it'll be better in a month.

W : That's good. I hope you feel better soon.

08

대화를 듣고, Kids' Pottery Class에 관해 언급되지 않은 것을 고르시오.

M : Honey, look at this flyer about Kids' Pottery Class.

W : Okay. Let's take a look.

M : I think our little Austin would love to ✪ _____ _____ _____.

W : I think so, too. It says that the class is held on October 8th. We can take him there on that day.

M : Great. And it's held in Pottery Village. It's __ _____ _____ from our home.

W : That's so close. And check out the price. The class costs only $15.

M : That's reasonable. We should sign up. How can we register for the class?

W : It says you can _____ _____ _____ _____ to register online.

M : Okay. Let's do it right away.

09

2022 Online Whistling Championship에 관한 다음 내용을 듣고, 일치하지 않는 것을 고르시오.

W : Hello, listeners. The most interesting music competition is back! You can now sign up for the 2022 Online Whistling Championship. You can select any song that you like, but note that the length of your whistling video is _____ ____ _____ _____. To enter the competition, you must upload your video on our website by December 4th. When recording your whistling, be sure to turn off the echo effect on the microphone. Winners will be decided by _____ _____ _____. The result will be announced on our website. We look forward to ✪ _____ _____ _____.

10

다음 표를 보면서 대화를 듣고, 두 사람이 선택할 커튼을 고르시오.

M : Honey, I'm looking at a shopping site to choose _____ _____ _____ _____. But there are too many options to consider.

W : Okay. Let's pick one together.

M : I don't think we should spend more than $100.

W : I agree. Let's drop this one. And some of them are ✪ _____ _____ _____ ____ _____.

M : Fantastic. We won't have to pay for dry cleaning all the time.

W : Good for us. Let's cross out this one then. What about a blackout option?

M : We definitely need it. It'll _____ _____ _____, so we won't be disturbed. And which color do you like?

W : I don't mind any color except for gray.

M : Okay. Then we narrowed it down to one.

W : Well then, let's choose this one.

11

대화를 듣고, 남자의 마지막 말에 대한 여자의 응답으로 가장 적절한 것을 고르시오.

M : Excuse me. Is this really ✪ _____ _____ ____ _____ _____?

W : Yes. This is the line for the ride.

M : Oh, no. I can't believe it. There are so many people _____ ____ _____. How long have you been waiting here?

12

대화를 듣고, 여자의 마지막 말에 대한 남자의 응답으로 가장 적절한 것을 고르시오.

W : Chris, what are you looking at?
M : A little boy is crying and wandering around the park. He's ✪ _____ _____ _____.
W : Oh, I see him, too. We _____ _____ _____ if he's lost.

13

대화를 듣고, 남자의 마지막 말에 대한 여자의 응답으로 가장 적절한 것을 고르시오. [3점]

M : Hi, Ava.
W : Hi, Samuel. Are you all set for the job interview?
M : I'm still working on it. I've come up with a list of questions the interviewer might ask.
W : Good job. Preparing answers to those questions will help you for the interview.
M : But I think I'm not ready.
W : Hmm. Have you thought about how you'll make a good first impression?
M : ✪ _____ _____ ____ _____ _____?
W : You know a smile makes you look confident. Also, people _____ _____ ____ to give a favorable impression.
M : That's a good point.
W : I believe you'll get a good interview result with __ _____ _____ _____ ____ _____.
M : Okay. Then I'm going to practice smiling and look for my best suit.

14

대화를 듣고, 여자의 마지막 말에 대한 남자의 응답으로 가장 적절한 것을 고르시오.

W : Excuse me.
M : Yes, ma'am. How can I help you?
W : How much are those shoes?
M : They're $60. But today only, we're offering a 30% discount.
W : That's a good price. Do you have a size six?
M : Sure. Here they are. Take a seat here and try them on.
W : Thank you. *[Pause]* Well, these shoes are __ _____ _____ for me. Can I get a size six and a half?
M : I'm sorry. That size in this color is sold out.
W : Do you have these shoes ____ __ _____ _____?
M : Let me check. *[Typing sounds]* We have ✪ _____ _____ _____ ____ _____.
W : A green pair sounds good. I want to try them on.

15

다음 상황 설명을 듣고, Amelia가 Jacob 교수에게 할 말로 가장 적절한 것을 고르시오. [3점]

M : Amelia is a high school student. She is working on a psychology project. She thinks that an interview with an expert in the field will make her project even better. She emails Professor Jacob, who is ✪ __ _____ _____ _____. Even though he's busy, she manages to set up an interview with him. Unfortunately, on that morning, she _____ __ _____ _____ _____ _____. She knows this interview is important, and difficult to set up again. But she can't go meet him because of a severe stomachache. So she wants to ask him if he can _____ _____ _____. In this situation, what would Amelia most likely say to Professor Jacob?

16~17

다음을 듣고, 물음에 답하시오.

W : Good morning, students. These days we can easily send messages to each other using phones or computers. However, communication has not always been as simple as it is today. Here are a few ways people in the past used to carry their messages. First, some tribes used a special drum. They were able to send warnings or important information by ✪ _____ ____ _____ ____ _____. Next, other people used smoke to send messages _____ _____ _____. For example, our ancestors used smoke to signal attacks from enemies. Third, a pigeon was a reliable means of communication. It always found its way home with messages ✪ _____ ___ ____ _____. Finally, a horse was one of the most efficient ways to communicate. The horse with a messenger on its back delivered mail more quickly than runners. Now you may understand the ways of sending messages back in the old days. Then let's take a look in detail at each communication method.

▶ 정답 : 해설편 154쪽

회차별 영단어 QR 코드 ※ QR 코드를 스캔 후 모바일로 단어장처럼 학습할 수 있습니다. ● 고1 2022학년도 11월

18

001 ☐ enterprise ⓝ 기업
002 ☐ sales manager 영업 매니저
003 ☐ loyal ⓐ 충성스러운
004 ☐ essential ⓐ 핵심적인, 필수적인
005 ☐ innovative ⓐ 혁신적인
006 ☐ bring in ~을 데려오다
007 ☐ major ⓐ 주요한
008 ☐ increase ⓥ 증가시키다
009 ☐ voluntarily ⓐⓓ 자원해서
010 ☐ request ⓥ 요청하다
011 ☐ raise ⓥ 올리다, 높이다
012 ☐ reflect ⓥ 반영하다

19

013 ☐ day off 휴가
014 ☐ naill salon 네일 숍
015 ☐ mute ⓥ 음소거하다
016 ☐ disconnected ⓐ 단절된
017 ☐ calm ⓐ 차분한
018 ☐ comfortable ⓐ 편안한
019 ☐ missed call 부재중 전화
020 ☐ immediately ⓐⓓ 즉시
021 ☐ call back 전화를 회신하다
022 ☐ fall over ~에 걸려 넘어지다
023 ☐ concerned ⓐ 걱정되는
024 ☐ recover from ~로부터 회복하다
025 ☐ surgery ⓝ 수술
026 ☐ rush ⓥ 서두르다
027 ☐ nervous ⓐ 긴장한
028 ☐ relaxed ⓐ 느긋한, 여유로운
029 ☐ indifferent ⓐ 무관심한
030 ☐ jealous ⓐ 질투하는
031 ☐ annoyed ⓐ 짜증 난
032 ☐ grateful ⓐ 고마워하는

20

033 ☐ be about to 막 ~하려는 참이다
034 ☐ launch ⓥ 시작하다, 출시하다
035 ☐ unfortunately ⓐⓓ 안타깝게도
036 ☐ promote ⓥ 홍보하다
037 ☐ strictly ⓐⓓ 엄격하게
038 ☐ shamelessly ⓐⓓ 뻔뻔하게
039 ☐ latest ⓐ 최신의
040 ☐ give away 공짜로 주다, 거저 주다
041 ☐ useful ⓐ 유용한
042 ☐ entertaining ⓐ 재미있는
043 ☐ interested ⓐ 흥미를 느끼는
044 ☐ audience ⓝ 청중, 독자
045 ☐ successful ⓐ 성공적인

21

046 ☐ reveal ⓥ 드러내다
047 ☐ assumption ⓝ 가정, 추정
048 ☐ phrase ⓝ 구절
049 ☐ sweat ⓝ 땀
050 ☐ achievement ⓝ 성취, 성과
051 ☐ hard-earned ⓐ 힘들게 얻은
052 ☐ recommend ⓥ 권하다, 추천하다
053 ☐ obtain ⓥ 얻다, 획득하다
054 ☐ imply ⓥ 암시하다
055 ☐ illegal ⓐ 불법적인

056 ☐ questionable ⓐ 의심스러운
057 ☐ means ⓝ 수단
058 ☐ criticism ⓝ 비판
059 ☐ seek to ~하려고 추구하다
060 ☐ invalidate ⓥ 틀렸음을 입증하다
061 ☐ automatically ⓐⓓ 저절로
062 ☐ inevitably ⓐⓓ 불가피하게, 필연적으로
063 ☐ hardly ⓐⓓ 거의 ~않다
064 ☐ challenge ⓥ 도전하다, 이의를 제기하다
065 ☐ sacred ⓐ 성스러운
066 ☐ pause ⓥ 잠시 멈추다
067 ☐ valuable ⓐ 가치로운
068 ☐ huge ⓐ 거대한
069 ☐ hardship ⓝ 고난, 난관, 어려움
070 ☐ formal ⓐ 공식적인
071 ☐ doubt ⓥ 의심하다
072 ☐ solid ⓐ 확고한
073 ☐ abandon ⓥ 버리다
074 ☐ notion ⓝ 관념
075 ☐ superstition ⓝ 미신

22

076 ☐ when it comes to ~에 관해서
077 ☐ threatening ⓐ 겁을 주는
078 ☐ exact opposite 정반대
079 ☐ rob A of B A에게서 B를 빼앗다
080 ☐ sense of control 통제력
081 ☐ public health 공공 보건
082 ☐ present ⓥ 제시하다
083 ☐ pessimistic ⓐ 염세적인, 비관적인
084 ☐ take steps to ~하기 위해 조치를 취하다
085 ☐ illness ⓝ 질병
086 ☐ as a result 결과적으로
087 ☐ article ⓝ 기사
088 ☐ be intended to ~할 의도이다
089 ☐ warn ⓥ 경고하다
090 ☐ cancer ⓝ 암
091 ☐ rate ⓝ 비율
092 ☐ screen ⓥ (어떤 질병이 있는지) 검진하다
093 ☐ terrified ⓐ 겁에 질린
094 ☐ doom ⓝ 불운, 파멸
095 ☐ gloom ⓝ 우울, 어둠
096 ☐ collapse ⓝ 붕괴 ⓥ 쓰러지다

23

097 ☐ remarkable ⓐ 현저한, 두드러지는
098 ☐ consequence ⓝ 결과, 영향
099 ☐ melt ⓥ 녹다
100 ☐ alter ⓥ 바꾸다
101 ☐ duration ⓝ 지속 시간
102 ☐ glacier ⓝ 빙하
103 ☐ gravity ⓝ 중력
104 ☐ force ⓥ 강제하다
105 ☐ equator ⓝ 적도
106 ☐ slightly ⓐⓓ 약간
107 ☐ rotation ⓝ 회전
108 ☐ spin ⓝ 회전
109 ☐ spread out 벌리다, 펴지다
110 ☐ slowdown ⓝ 둔화, 지연
111 ☐ barely ⓐⓓ 거의 ~않다, 가까스로
112 ☐ noticeable ⓐ 분명한, 뚜렷한
113 ☐ add up 쌓이다, 축적되다

114 ☐ last ⓥ 지속되다
115 ☐ principle ⓝ 원리
116 ☐ implication ⓝ 영향
117 ☐ biodiversity ⓝ 생물 다양성
118 ☐ keep track of ~을 추적하다

24

119 ☐ bring up (화제를) 꺼내다, (아이디어를) 내놓다
120 ☐ suggestion ⓝ 제안
121 ☐ give a chance 기회를 주다
122 ☐ close off 차단하다
123 ☐ possibility ⓝ 가능성
124 ☐ viewpoint ⓝ 관점, 견해
125 ☐ period ⓝ (문장 끝에서) 끝, 이상이다, 더 말하지 마라
126 ☐ particular ⓐ 특정한
127 ☐ beneficial ⓐ 이로운
128 ☐ at worse 최소한, 적어도
129 ☐ besides ⓟⓡⓔⓟ ~을 제외하더라도, ~외에도 ⓐⓓ 게다가
130 ☐ eliminate ⓥ 제거하다
131 ☐ invention ⓝ 발명
132 ☐ filter out ~을 걸러내다, 여과하다
133 ☐ keep one's word 약속을 지키다
134 ☐ block ⓥ 차단하다
135 ☐ look back 뒤돌아보다

25

136 ☐ survey ⓝ 설문 조사
137 ☐ reason ⓝ 이유
138 ☐ meat ⓝ 고기
139 ☐ motivator ⓝ 동기 요인
140 ☐ welfare ⓝ 복지
141 ☐ account for ~을 차지하다
142 ☐ among ⓟⓡⓔⓟ ~ 중에서
143 ☐ followed by ~이 뒤를 잇다
144 ☐ environment ⓝ 환경
145 ☐ whereas ⓒⓞⓝⓙ ~한 반면에
146 ☐ cite ⓥ 언급하다, 인용하다
147 ☐ reduce ⓥ 줄이다
148 ☐ consumption ⓝ 소비
149 ☐ weight ⓝ 체중, 무게
150 ☐ rank ⓥ 순위가 ~이다

26

151 ☐ exceptionally ⓐⓓ 이례적으로, 특출나게
152 ☐ prolific ⓐ 다작한
153 ☐ inventor ⓝ 발명가
154 ☐ journalist ⓝ 기자
155 ☐ occasionally ⓐⓓ 가끔, 때때로
156 ☐ compare A to B A를 B와 비교하다, 견주다
157 ☐ nickname ⓥ 별명 짓다
158 ☐ leave school 학교를 그만두다
159 ☐ earn ⓥ 벌다
160 ☐ nearby ⓐ 근처의
161 ☐ witness ⓥ 목격하다
162 ☐ fellow ⓝ 동료
163 ☐ faulty ⓐ 결함이 있는
164 ☐ fold ⓥ 접다
165 ☐ glue ⓥ 접착하다

166 ☐ flat-bottomed ⓐ 밑이 평평한
167 ☐ award ⓥ 수여하다, 주다
168 ☐ patent ⓝ 특허
169 ☐ assemble ⓥ 조립하다
170 ☐ hall of fame 명예의 전당

27

171 ☐ e-waste ⓝ 전자 쓰레기
172 ☐ recycling ⓝ 재활용
173 ☐ laptop ⓝ 노트북 컴퓨터
174 ☐ green ⓐ 친환경적인
175 ☐ accept ⓥ 수용하다, 접수하다, 받다
176 ☐ microwave ⓝ 전자레인지
177 ☐ wipe out 지우다, 쓸어내다
178 ☐ in advance 미리
179 ☐ open to ~에게 개방되는
180 ☐ local resident 지역 주민

28

181 ☐ undersea ⓐ 해저의
182 ☐ fascinating ⓐ 매혹적인
183 ☐ ocean floor 해저
184 ☐ marine ⓐ 해양의
185 ☐ on foot 도보로
186 ☐ requirement ⓝ 필수 요건
187 ☐ operating hour 운영 시간
188 ☐ insurance fee 보험료
189 ☐ experienced ⓐ 숙련된
190 ☐ lifeguard ⓝ 안전 요원
191 ☐ accompany ⓥ 동행하다
192 ☐ throughout ⓟⓡⓔⓟ ~ 내내
193 ☐ on-site ⓐⓓ 현장에서 ⓐ 현장의

29

194 ☐ artificial intelligence 인공 지능
195 ☐ task ⓝ 과업, 일
196 ☐ perform ⓥ 수행하다
197 ☐ mind-blowing ⓐ 너무도 감동적인
198 ☐ feature ⓝ 특징
199 ☐ enable ⓥ ~이 …할 수 있게 하다
200 ☐ core ⓐ 핵심적인
201 ☐ self-improve ⓥ 자가 발전하다
202 ☐ virtual ⓐ 가상의
203 ☐ assistant ⓝ 조수, 비서
204 ☐ close ⓐ 친밀한, 가까운
205 ☐ exactly ⓐⓓ 바로, 정확히
206 ☐ recognize ⓥ 인식하다, 깨닫다

30

207 ☐ tip ⓝ 끝부분
208 ☐ stem ⓝ 줄기
209 ☐ accumulate ⓥ 축적되다, 쌓이다
210 ☐ accordingly ⓐⓓ 따라서
211 ☐ stimulate ⓥ 자극하다, 촉진하다
212 ☐ face ⓥ ~을 면하다, 마주보다
213 ☐ phenomenon ⓝ 현상
214 ☐ bend ⓥ 구부리다
215 ☐ limit ⓥ 제한하다
216 ☐ horizontal ⓐ 수평적인
217 ☐ interfere with ~을 방해하다
218 ☐ in turn 한편, 결국, 차례로
219 ☐ downward(s) ⓐⓓ 아래로

31

220 □ demonstrate ⓥ 입증하다
221 □ defeat ⓥ 무너뜨리다, 패배시키다
222 □ behavioral ⓐ 행동의
223 □ experiment ⓝ 실험 ⓥ 실험하다
224 □ assign ⓥ 할당하다
225 □ due date 마감일
226 □ for oneself 스스로
227 □ up to and including ~까지 포함해서
228 □ submit ⓥ 제출하다
229 □ set ⓐ 정해진
230 □ at the end of ~의 끝에
231 □ receive ⓥ 받다
232 □ in the middle 중간에
233 □ tendency ⓝ 경향, 성향
234 □ self-control ⓝ 자기 통제
235 □ obstacle ⓝ 장애물
236 □ restrict ⓥ 제한하다

32

237 □ innovation ⓝ 혁신
238 □ steadily ⓐⓓ 꾸준히
239 □ specialize ⓥ 전문화하다
240 □ diversify ⓥ 다양화하다
241 □ consume ⓥ 소비하다, 먹다, 마시다
242 □ unstable ⓐ 불안정한
243 □ self-sufficiency ⓝ 자급자족
244 □ mutual ⓐ 상호의
245 □ interdependence ⓝ 상호 의존성
246 □ concentrate on ~에 집중하다
247 □ serve one's needs ~의 필요를 충족하다, ~에게 도움이 되다
248 □ rely on ~에 의존하다
249 □ a fraction of a second 아주 짧은 시간
250 □ afford ⓥ ~할 여유가 있다
251 □ turn on ~을 켜다
252 □ quantity ⓝ 양
253 □ refine ⓥ 정제하다
254 □ sesame oil 참기름
255 □ lamb ⓝ (어린) 양
256 □ burn up 태우다
257 □ humanity ⓝ 인류
258 □ distant ⓐ 먼
259 □ satisfy ⓥ 만족시키다, 충족하다
260 □ personalize ⓥ 개인의 필요에 맞추다
261 □ commercialize ⓥ 상업화하다

33

262 □ make a choice 선택하다
263 □ break a habit 습관을 깨다
264 □ trick A into B A를 속여 B하게 하다
265 □ sign a contract 계약서에 서명하다
266 □ come from ~에서 기원하다
267 □ myth ⓝ 신화
268 □ sail ⓥ 항해하다
269 □ lure ⓥ 유혹하다
270 □ irresistible ⓐ 저항할 수 없는
271 □ resist ⓥ 저항하다
272 □ instruct ⓥ 지시하다, 가르치다
273 □ stuff ⓥ (속을) 채우다, 막다
274 □ tie ⓥ 묶다
275 □ mast ⓝ 돛대

276 □ prevent ⓥ 예방하다, 막다
277 □ distract ⓥ 주의를 분산시키다, 산만하게 하다
278 □ let go of ~을 놔주다, 내려놓다
279 □ all-or-nothing ⓐ 양자택일의, 이것 아니면 저것인
280 □ temptation ⓝ 유혹

34

281 □ ecosystem ⓝ 생태계
282 □ host ⓥ (손님을) 접대하다, 수용하다, (행사를) 주최하다
283 □ adapt ⓥ 적응시키다
284 □ indoor ⓐ 실내의
285 □ microbe ⓝ 미생물
286 □ resistance ⓝ 내성, 저항력
287 □ antibacterial ⓐ 항균성의 ⓝ 항균제
288 □ insecticide ⓝ 살충제
289 □ cockroach ⓝ 바퀴벌레
290 □ distaste ⓝ 혐오
291 □ glucose ⓝ 포도당
292 □ bait ⓝ 미끼
293 □ counterpart ⓝ 상대방, 대응물
294 □ ecologist ⓝ 생태학자
295 □ urban ⓐ 도시의, 도시적인
296 □ represent ⓥ 표현하다, 나타내다
297 □ extinct ⓐ 멸종한
298 □ habitat ⓝ 서식지
299 □ prey ⓝ 먹잇감

35

300 □ engagement ⓝ 관계, 참여
301 □ poetry ⓝ 시
302 □ individual ⓝ 개인 ⓐ 개인의
303 □ capacity ⓝ 능력, 역량
304 □ expressive ⓐ 표현적인
305 □ immune system 면역 체계
306 □ lung ⓝ 폐
307 □ diminish ⓥ 줄이다, 감소시키다
308 □ distress ⓝ 고통
309 □ enhance ⓥ 향상시키다
310 □ aid ⓥ 돕다, 원조하다
311 □ empathy ⓝ 공감, 감정 이입
312 □ incredibly ⓐⓓ 믿을 수 없을 정도로, 놀랍도록
313 □ cognitive ⓐ 인지적인
314 □ productivity ⓝ 생산성
315 □ frustration ⓝ 좌절
316 □ complexity ⓝ 복잡성

36

317 □ at risk 위험에 처한
318 □ due to ~로 인해
319 □ automation ⓝ 자동화
320 □ automate ⓥ 자동화하다
321 □ replace ⓥ 대체하다
322 □ dependent on ~에 의존하는
323 □ irreplaceable ⓐ 대체할 수 없는
324 □ unrealistic ⓐ 비현실적인
325 □ threat ⓝ 위협
326 □ flip ⓥ 뒤집다
327 □ entire ⓐ 전체의
328 □ crew ⓝ (전체) 직원, 승무원

37

329 □ highly ⓐⓓ 고도로, 매우
330 □ skilled ⓐ 숙련된
331 □ available ⓐ 이용 가능한
332 □ specific ⓐ 특정한, 구체적인
333 □ draw on ~을 이용하다

37

334 □ beech tree 너도밤나무
335 □ vary ⓥ 다르다
336 □ a great deal of 많은
337 □ nutrient ⓝ 영양소
338 □ underground ⓐⓓ 지하에서
339 □ abundance ⓝ 풍부함
340 □ hand over 건네주다
341 □ run short 부족해지다
342 □ act as ~의 역할을 하다
343 □ fall behind 뒤처지다
344 □ leaf ⓝ 이파리
345 □ plenty of 많은
346 □ equalize ⓥ 동등하게 하다
347 □ transfer ⓥ 전달하다
348 □ photosynthesize ⓥ 광합성하다

38

349 □ enormously ⓐⓓ 대단히, 거대하게
350 □ contribute to ~에 기여하다
351 □ cooperate with ~와 협력하다
352 □ deal with ~을 다루다, ~에 대처하다
353 □ analytic ⓐ 분석적인
354 □ philosophy ⓝ 철학
355 □ historically ⓐⓓ 역사적으로
356 □ make sense 이치에 맞다
357 □ appreciate ⓥ 제대로 인식하다
358 □ rightly ⓐⓓ 마땅히
359 □ aspect ⓝ 측면
360 □ fundamental ⓐ 근본적인
361 □ countless ⓐ 무수히 많은
362 □ navigate ⓥ 항해하다
363 □ preserve ⓥ 보존하다
364 □ operation ⓝ 작용
365 □ astonishingly ⓐⓓ 놀랍도록
366 □ in part 부분적으로
367 □ collaborative ⓐ 협력적인
368 □ collective ⓐ 집단적인

39

369 □ magically ⓐⓓ 희한하게, 마법처럼
370 □ remove ⓥ 제거하다
371 □ essentially ⓐⓓ 본질적으로
372 □ completely ⓐⓓ 완전히
373 □ makeup ⓝ 구성
374 □ contain ⓥ 포함하다
375 □ temperature ⓝ 온도
376 □ separate ⓐ 분리된
377 □ because of ~로 인해
378 □ float ⓥ 뜨다
379 □ surface ⓝ 표면
380 □ content ⓝ 함량

40

381 □ reflective ⓐ 성찰적인
382 □ journaling ⓝ 일기 쓰기

383 □ think back on ~에 대해 되돌아보다
384 □ undergraduate ⓐ 학부의
385 □ spring break 봄방학
386 □ daily activity 하루 활동, 일과
387 □ handle ⓥ 대처하다, 다루다
388 □ focus on ~에 집중하다
389 □ support ⓥ 뒷받침하다
390 □ perspective ⓝ 관점, 시각
391 □ hassle ⓝ 귀찮은 일
392 □ demonstration ⓝ 입증, 시연
393 □ in action 활동 중인, 작용 중인
394 □ be full of ~로 가득하다
395 □ meaningful ⓐ 유의미한
396 □ reframe ⓥ 재구성하다
397 □ based on ~에 근거해
398 □ factual ⓐ 사실적인
399 □ worthwhile ⓐ 가치 있는
400 □ outdated ⓐ 구식의
401 □ demanding ⓐ 까다로운, 힘든

41~42

402 □ lose one's sight 시력을 잃다
403 □ majority ⓝ 대다수, 대부분
404 □ cultivate ⓥ 갈고 닦다, 배양하다
405 □ state ⓝ 상태
406 □ compensate ⓥ 보충하다, 보상하다
407 □ restore ⓥ 회복하다, 복구하다
408 □ perception ⓝ 인식, 지각
409 □ disrupt ⓥ 지장을 주다, 방해하다
410 □ thrilled ⓐ 황홀한, 전율을 느끼는
411 □ overloaded ⓐ 과부하된
412 □ stimulus (pl. stimuli) ⓝ 자극
413 □ frightening ⓐ 겁을 주는, 두렵게 하는
414 □ overwhelming ⓐ 버거운, 압도적인
415 □ puzzled ⓐ 혼란스러운
416 □ struggle to ~하느라 고생하다
417 □ confusion ⓝ 혼란
418 □ relay ⓥ 전달하다
419 □ be not the case 사실이 아니다
420 □ primarily ⓐⓓ 주로
421 □ anticipate ⓥ 예상하다
422 □ visualization ⓝ 시각화
423 □ ignore ⓥ 무시하다

43~45

424 □ a bunch of 많은
425 □ present ⓝ 선물
426 □ server ⓝ 종업원
427 □ notice ⓥ 알아차리다
428 □ chat about ~에 관해 이야기하다
429 □ so that ~하도록, ~하기 위해
430 □ surprised ⓐ 놀란
431 □ sudden ⓐ 갑작스러운
432 □ get well (병 등이) 낫다
433 □ moved ⓐ 감동한
434 □ walk toward ~ 쪽으로 걷다
435 □ generosity ⓝ 관대함
436 □ unforgettable ⓐ 잊을 수 없는
437 □ conversation ⓝ 대화
438 □ attentive ⓐ 주의 깊은, 세심한
439 □ pay the bill 값을 치르다
440 □ unexpectedly ⓐⓓ 예기치 못하게

11회

● 채점 : 맞은 개수 _____ / 80

TEST A-B 각 단어의 뜻을 [A] 영어는 우리말로, [B] 우리말은 영어로 쓰시오.

A	English	Korean	B	Korean	English
01	grateful		01	핵심적인, 필수적인	
02	launch		02	~로부터 회복하다	
03	witness		03	빙하	
04	accompany		04	~외에도, 게다가	
05	bend		05	소비	
06	unstable		06	~할 여유가 있다	
07	beneficial		07	생산성	
08	irresistible		08	능력, 역량	
09	prey		09	자극하다, 촉진하다	
10	empathy		10	이치에 맞다	
11	replace		11	불법의	
12	contribute to		12	홍보하다	
13	reflective		13	질투하는	
14	get well		14	조립하다	
15	barely		15	공짜로 주다, 거저 주다	
16	criticism		16	매혹적인	
17	pessimistic		17	할당하다	
18	in advance		18	신화	
19	demonstrate		19	대다수, 대부분	
20	equalize		20	서식지	

▶ A-D 정답 : 해설편 154쪽

TEST C-D 각 단어의 뜻을 골라 기호를 쓰시오.

C	English			Korean	D	Korean			English
01	voluntarily	(	)	ⓐ 수술	01	기업	(	)	ⓐ take steps to
02	inevitably	(	)	ⓑ 최소한, 적어도	02	엄격하게	(	)	ⓑ keep one's word
03	rob A of B	(	)	ⓒ 인공지능	03	~하기 위해 조치를 취하다	(	)	ⓒ virtual
04	duration	(	)	ⓓ 수평적인	04	생물 다양성	(	)	ⓓ interfere with
05	at worse	(	)	ⓔ 장애물	05	언급하다, 인용하다	(	)	ⓔ tendency
06	account for	(	)	ⓕ 상호의	06	~을 방해하다	(	)	ⓕ personalize
07	prolific	(	)	ⓖ 주의를 분산시키다, 산만하게 하다	07	경향, 성향	(	)	ⓖ resistance
08	artificial intelligence	(	)	ⓗ 멸종한	08	주의 깊은, 세심한	(	)	ⓗ cultivate
09	obstacle	(	)	ⓘ 면역 체계	09	약속을 지키다	(	)	ⓘ enterprise
10	surgery	(	)	ⓙ 보충하다, 보상하다	10	개인의 필요에 맞추다	(	)	ⓙ let go of
11	horizontal	(	)	ⓚ ~을 차지하다	11	~을 놔주다, 내려놓다	(	)	ⓚ enhance
12	distract	(	)	ⓛ 지속 시간	12	내성, 저항력	(	)	ⓛ run short
13	extinct	(	)	ⓜ 다작한	13	가상의	(	)	ⓜ content
14	immune system	(	)	ⓝ 자원해서	14	향상시키다	(	)	ⓝ outdated
15	abundance	(	)	ⓞ 광합성하다	15	부족해지다	(	)	ⓞ attentive
16	photosynthesize	(	)	ⓟ 불가피하게, 필연적으로	16	함량	(	)	ⓟ perspective
17	makeup	(	)	ⓠ A에게서 B를 빼앗다	17	구식의	(	)	ⓠ biodiversity
18	compensate	(	)	ⓡ ~를 다루다, ~에 대처하다	18	갈고 닦다, 배양하다	(	)	ⓡ strictly
19	deal with	(	)	ⓢ 풍부함	19	관점, 시각	(	)	ⓢ worthwhile
20	mutual	(	)	ⓣ 구성	20	가치 있는	(	)	ⓣ cite

영어 영역

● 문항수 45개 | 배점 100점 | 제한 시간 70분　　　　　　　　● 점수 표시가 없는 문항은 모두 2점

1번부터 17번까지는 듣고 답하는 문제입니다. 1번부터 15번까지는 한 번만 들려주고, 16번부터 17번까지는 두 번 들려줍니다. 방송을 잘 듣고 답을 하시기 바랍니다.

1. 다음을 듣고, 남자가 하는 말의 목적으로 가장 적절한 것을 고르시오.
① 지하철 앱 출시를 홍보하려고
② 지하철 연장 운행을 안내하려고
③ 지하철 운행 지연에 대해 사과하려고
④ 지하철 시설 보수 공사 일정을 공지하려고
⑤ 지하철 내 영화 촬영에 대한 양해를 구하려고

2. 대화를 듣고, 여자의 의견으로 가장 적절한 것을 고르시오.
① 날씨가 더울수록 수분 보충이 중요하다.
② 적당한 준비 운동이 부상 위험을 줄인다.
③ 흐린 날에도 자외선 차단제를 발라야 한다.
④ 햇빛이 강한 날에는 야외 활동을 자제해야 한다.
⑤ 화상을 입었을 때 신속하게 응급 처치를 해야 한다.

3. 대화를 듣고, 두 사람의 관계를 가장 잘 나타낸 것을 고르시오.
① 세차장 직원 – 고객　　　② 청소 업체 직원 – 집주인
③ 중고차 판매원 – 구매자　④ 분실물 센터 직원 – 방문자
⑤ 액세서리 디자이너 – 의뢰인

4. 대화를 듣고, 그림에서 대화의 내용과 일치하지 않는 것을 고르시오.

5. 대화를 듣고, 남자가 할 일로 가장 적절한 것을 고르시오.
① 가방 준비하기　　　② 배지 가져오기
③ 스크린 점검하기　　④ 동영상 편집하기
⑤ 포스터 업로드하기

6. 대화를 듣고, 여자가 지불할 금액을 고르시오. [3점]
① $45　② $50　③ $54　④ $55　⑤ $60

7. 대화를 듣고, 남자가 London Walking Tour에 참여하지 못한 이유를 고르시오.
① 발목에 통증이 있어서
② 뮤지컬을 관람해야 해서
③ 투어 예약을 하지 못해서
④ 기념품을 사러 가야 해서
⑤ 날씨로 인해 투어가 취소되어서

8. 대화를 듣고, Winter Lake Festival에 관해 언급되지 않은 것을 고르시오.
① 기간　　　　② 장소　　　　③ 입장료
④ 기념품　　　⑤ 활동 종류

9. Mascot Design Contest에 관한 다음 내용을 듣고, 일치하지 않는 것을 고르시오.
① 팀을 사랑하는 누구든 참여할 수 있다.
② 디자인은 팀 슬로건과 관련되어야 한다.
③ 수상작은 팬 투표로 선정될 것이다.
④ 수상자는 상으로 시즌 티켓을 받게 될 것이다.
⑤ 참가 희망자는 디자인을 이메일로 보내야 한다.

10. 다음 표를 보면서 대화를 듣고, 두 사람이 예약할 캠핑장을 고르시오.

2021 Best Campsites

	Campsite	Location	Price (per night)	Type	Kids' Playground
①	A	Seaside	$65	tent	×
②	B	Jungle Hut	$70	tent	○
③	C	Rose Valley	$85	camping car	○
④	D	Blue Forest	$90	camping car	×
⑤	E	Pine Island	$110	camping car	○

11. 대화를 듣고, 남자의 마지막 말에 대한 여자의 응답으로 가장 적절한 것을 고르시오.
① It takes an hour by bus.
② It's bigger than your office.
③ You should've left home earlier.
④ The company moved last month.
⑤ I had a hard time getting the job.

12. 대화를 듣고, 여자의 마지막 말에 대한 남자의 응답으로 가장 적절한 것을 고르시오.
① Okay. I'll order a shrimp pizza.
② Thanks. You're good at cooking.
③ No. The pizza isn't delivered yet.
④ Sure. You can come over anytime.
⑤ Yes. Skipping meals is bad for your health.

13. 대화를 듣고, 남자의 마지막 말에 대한 여자의 응답으로 가장 적절한 것을 고르시오.

Woman: _____

① Too late. The meeting is already over.
② Sure. There are lots of French cookbooks.
③ I agree. You spend too much time reading.
④ No. We're not allowed to eat in the library.
⑤ You're right. I'll change the reservation now.

14. 대화를 듣고, 여자의 마지막 말에 대한 남자의 응답으로 가장 적절한 것을 고르시오. [3점]

Man: _____

① Sorry. I forgot to bring my laptop.
② Then, I'd like to replace the battery.
③ Well, the screen still doesn't work well.
④ Good. A new repair shop opened yesterday.
⑤ Actually, I don't have a receipt for a refund.

15. 다음 상황 설명을 듣고, Amy가 Terry에게 할 말로 가장 적절한 것을 고르시오. [3점]

Amy: _____

① How about using a colorful font on the poster?
② You'd better inform your friends of the concert.
③ Can you make the letter size bigger on the poster?
④ Why don't we hold a concert in the school festival?
⑤ You should put important information on the poster.

[16~17] 다음을 듣고, 물음에 답하시오.

16. 여자가 하는 말의 주제로 가장 적절한 것은?

① ways to prevent plant diseases
② factors that affect plant growth
③ benefits of growing plants at home
④ plants that can grow in shaded areas
⑤ materials that help plants grow in shade

17. 언급된 식물이 <u>아닌</u> 것은?

① lemon balm
② ivy
③ mint
④ camellia
⑤ lavender

이제 듣기 문제가 끝났습니다. 18번부터는 문제지의 지시에 따라 답을 하시기 바랍니다.

18. 다음 글의 목적으로 가장 적절한 것은?

> To the school librarian,
>
> I am Kyle Thomas, the president of the school's English writing club. I have planned activities that will increase the writing skills of our club members. One of the aims of these activities is to make us aware of various types of news media and the language used in printed newspaper articles. However, some old newspapers are not easy to access online. It is, therefore, my humble request to you to allow us to use old newspapers that have been stored in the school library. I would really appreciate it if you grant us permission.
>
> Yours truly,
> Kyle Thomas

① 도서관 이용 시간 연장을 건의하려고
② 신청한 도서의 대출 가능 여부를 문의하려고
③ 도서관에 보관 중인 자료 현황을 조사하려고
④ 글쓰기 동아리 신문의 도서관 비치를 부탁하려고
⑤ 도서관에 있는 오래된 신문의 사용 허락을 요청하려고

19. 다음 글에 드러난 "I"의 심경 변화로 가장 적절한 것은?

When my mom came home from the mall with a special present for me I was pretty sure I knew what it was. I was absolutely thrilled because I would soon communicate with a new cell phone! I was daydreaming about all of the cool apps and games I was going to download. But my mom smiled really big and handed me a book. I flipped through the pages, figuring that maybe she had hidden my new phone inside. But I slowly realized that my mom had not got me a phone and my present was just a little book, which was so different from what I had wanted.

① worried → furious
② surprised → relieved
③ ashamed → confident
④ anticipating → satisfied
⑤ excited → disappointed

20. 다음 글에서 필자가 주장하는 바로 가장 적절한 것은?

Some experts estimate that as much as half of what we communicate is done through the way we move our bodies. Paying attention to the nonverbal messages you send can make a significant difference in your relationship with students. In general, most students are often closely tuned in to their teacher's body language. For example, when your students first enter the classroom, their initial action is to look for their teacher. Think about how encouraging and empowering it is for a student when that teacher has a friendly greeting and a welcoming smile. Smiling at students — to let them know that you are glad to see them — does not require a great deal of time or effort, but it can make a significant difference in the classroom climate right from the start of class.

① 교사는 학생 간의 상호 작용을 주의 깊게 관찰해야 한다.
② 수업 시 교사는 학생의 수준에 맞는 언어를 사용해야 한다.
③ 학생과의 관계에서 교사는 비언어적 표현에 유의해야 한다.
④ 학교는 학생에게 다양한 역할 경험의 기회를 제공해야 한다.
⑤ 교사는 학생 안전을 위해 교실의 물리적 환경을 개선해야 한다.

[해설편 p.157]

21. 밑줄 친 <u>a slap in our own face</u>가 다음 글에서 의미하는 바로 가장 적절한 것은? [3점]

When it comes to climate change, many blame the fossil fuel industry for pumping greenhouse gases, the agricultural sector for burning rainforests, or the fashion industry for producing excessive clothes. But wait, what drives these industrial activities? Our consumption. Climate change is a summed product of each person's behavior. For example, the fossil fuel industry is a popular scapegoat in the climate crisis. But why do they drill and burn fossil fuels? We provide them strong financial incentives: some people regularly travel on airplanes and cars that burn fossil fuels. Some people waste electricity generated by burning fuel in power plants. Some people use and throw away plastic products derived from crude oil every day. Blaming the fossil fuel industry while engaging in these behaviors is <u>a slap in our own face</u>.

* scapegoat: 희생양

① giving the future generation room for change
② warning ourselves about the lack of natural resources
③ refusing to admit the benefits of fossil fuel production
④ failing to recognize our responsibility for climate change
⑤ starting to deal with environmental problems individually

22. 다음 글의 요지로 가장 적절한 것은?

Information is worthless if you never actually use it. Far too often, companies collect valuable customer information that ends up buried and never used. They must ensure their data is accessible for use at the appropriate times. For a hotel, one appropriate time for data usage is check-in at the front desk. I often check in at a hotel I've visited frequently, only for the people at the front desk to give no indication that they recognize me as a customer. The hotel must have stored a record of my visits, but they don't make that information accessible to the front desk clerks. They are missing a prime opportunity to utilize data to create a better experience focused on customer loyalty. Whether they have ten customers, ten thousand, or even ten million, the goal is the same: create a delightful customer experience that encourages loyalty.

① 기업 정보의 투명한 공개는 고객 만족도를 향상시킨다.
② 목표 고객층에 대한 분석은 기업의 이익 창출로 이어진다.
③ 고객 충성도를 높이기 위해 고객 정보가 활용될 필요가 있다.
④ 일관성 있는 호텔 서비스 제공을 통해 단골 고객을 확보할 수 있다.
⑤ 사생활 침해에 대한 우려로 고객 정보를 보관하는 데 어려움이 있다.

23. 다음 글의 주제로 가장 적절한 것은?

We used to think that the brain never changed, but according to the neuroscientist Richard Davidson, we now know that this is not true — specific brain circuits grow stronger through regular practice. He explains, "Well-being is fundamentally no different than learning to play the cello. If one practices the skills of well-being, one will get better at it." What this means is that you can actually train your brain to become more grateful, relaxed, or confident, by repeating experiences that evoke gratitude, relaxation, or confidence. Your brain is shaped by the thoughts you repeat. The more neurons fire as they are activated by repeated thoughts and activities, the faster they develop into neural pathways, which cause lasting changes in the brain. Or in the words of Donald Hebb, "Neurons that fire together wire together." This is such an encouraging premise: bottom line — we can intentionally create the habits for the brain to be happier.

* evoke: (감정을) 불러일으키다 ** premise: 전제

① possibility of forming brain habits for well-being
② role of brain circuits in improving body movements
③ importance of practice in playing musical instruments
④ effect of taking a break on enhancing memory capacity
⑤ difficulty of discovering how neurons in the brain work

24. 다음 글의 제목으로 가장 적절한 것은?

In modern times, society became more dynamic. Social mobility increased, and people began to exercise a higher degree of choice regarding, for instance, their profession, their marriage, or their religion. This posed a challenge to traditional roles in society. It was less evident that one needed to commit to the roles one was born into when alternatives could be realized. Increasing control over one's life choices became not only possible but desired. Identity then became a problem. It was no longer almost ready-made at birth but something to be discovered. Traditional role identities prescribed by society began to appear as masks imposed on people whose real self was to be found somewhere underneath.

* impose: 부여하다

① What Makes Our Modern Society So Competitive?
② How Modern Society Drives Us to Discover Our Identities
③ Social Masks: A Means to Build Trustworthy Relationships
④ The More Social Roles We Have, the Less Choice We Have
⑤ Increasing Social Mobility Leads Us to a More Equal Society

25. 다음 도표의 내용과 일치하지 <u>않는</u> 것은?

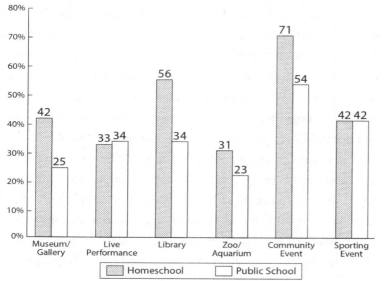

Percentage of U.S. Students Participating in Cultural Activities (2016)

The graph above shows the percentage of U.S. homeschooled and public school students participating in cultural activities in 2016. ① With the exception of live performances and sporting events, the percentage of homeschooled students participating in cultural activities was higher than that of public school students. ② For each group of students, community events accounted for the largest percentage among all cultural activities. ③ The percentage point difference between homeschooled students and their public school peers was largest in visiting libraries. ④ The percentage of homeschooled students visiting museums or galleries was more than twice that of public school students. ⑤ Going to zoos or aquariums ranked the lowest for both groups of students, with 31 and 23 percent respectively.

26. Bessie Coleman에 관한 다음 글의 내용과 일치하지 <u>않는</u> 것은?

Bessie Coleman was born in Texas in 1892. When she was eleven, she was told that the Wright brothers had flown their first plane. Since that moment, she dreamed about the day she would soar through the sky. At the age of 23, Coleman moved to Chicago, where she worked at a restaurant to save money for flying lessons. However, she had to travel to Paris to take flying lessons because American flight schools at the time admitted neither women nor Black people. In 1921, she finally became the first Black woman to earn an international pilot's license. She also studied flying acrobatics in Europe and made her first appearance in an airshow in New York in 1922. As a female pioneer of flight, she inspired the next generation to pursue their dreams of flying.

*flying acrobatics: 곡예 비행

① 11살 때 Wright 형제의 첫 비행 소식을 들었다.
② 비행 수업을 듣기 위해 파리로 가야 했다.
③ 국제 조종사 면허를 딴 최초의 흑인 여성이 되었다.
④ 유럽에서 에어쇼에 첫 출현을 했다.
⑤ 다음 세대가 비행의 꿈을 추구하도록 영감을 주었다.

27. 2021 Camptonville Nature Photo Contest에 관한 다음 안내문의 내용과 일치하지 <u>않는</u> 것은?

2021 Camptonville Nature Photo Contest

This is the fourth year of the annual Camptonville Nature Photo Contest. You can show the beauty of nature in Camptonville by sharing your most amazing photos!

Submission
- Upload a maximum of 20 photos onto our website www.camptonvillephotocontest.org.
- Deadline is December 1.

Prizes
• 1st Place: $500   • 2nd Place: $200   • 3rd Place: $100
(Winners will be posted on our website on December 31.)

Details
- All winning photos will be exhibited at City Hall.
- Please contact us at 122−861−3971 for further information.

---

① 매년 열리는 대회이며 올해가 네 번째이다.
② 최대 20장의 사진을 이메일로 제출해야 한다.
③ 제출 마감 기한은 12월 1일이다.
④ 수상자는 웹 사이트에 게시될 것이다.
⑤ 모든 수상작은 시청에 전시될 것이다.

28. Willow Valley Hot Air Balloon Ride에 관한 다음 안내문의 내용과 일치하는 것은?

Willow Valley Hot Air Balloon Ride

Enjoy the best views of Willow Valley from the sky with our hot air balloon ride!

• **Capacity**: up to 8 people including a pilot
• **Time Schedule**

Spring & Summer (from April to September)	5:00 a.m. − 7:00 a.m.
Autumn & Winter (from October to March)	6:00 a.m. − 8:00 a.m.

※ Duration of Flight: about 1 hour

• **Fee**: $150 per person (insurance not included)
• **Note**
- Reservations are required and must be made online.
- You can get a full refund up to 24 hours in advance.
- Visit www.willowvalleyballoon.com for more information.

---

① 조종사를 제외하고 8인까지 탈 수 있다.
② 여름에는 오전 6시에 시작한다.
③ 요금에 보험이 포함되어 있다.
④ 예약은 온라인으로 해야 한다.
⑤ 환불은 예외 없이 불가능하다.

29. 다음 글의 밑줄 친 부분 중, 어법상 틀린 것은? [3점]

The reduction of minerals in our food is the result of using pesticides and fertilizers ① that kill off beneficial bacteria, earthworms, and bugs in the soil that create many of the essential nutrients in the first place and prevent the uptake of nutrients into the plant. Fertilizing crops with nitrogen and potassium ② has led to declines in magnesium, zinc, iron and iodine. For example, there has been on average about a 30% decline in the magnesium content of wheat. This is partly due to potassium ③ being a blocker against magnesium absorption by plants. Lower magnesium levels in soil also ④ occurring with acidic soils and around 70% of the farmland on earth is now acidic. Thus, the overall characteristics of soil determine the accumulation of minerals in plants. Indeed, nowadays our soil is less healthy and so are the plants ⑤ grown on it.

* pesticide: 살충제

30. 다음 글의 밑줄 친 부분 중, 문맥상 낱말의 쓰임이 적절하지 않은 것은?

For species approaching extinction, zoos can act as a last chance for survival. ① Recovery programs are established to coordinate the efforts of field conservationists and wildlife authorities. As populations of those species ② diminish it is not unusual for zoos to start captive breeding programs. Captive breeding acts to protect against extinction. In some cases captive-bred individuals may be released back into the wild, supplementing wild populations. This is most successful in situations where individuals are at greatest threat during a ③ particular life stage. For example, turtle eggs may be removed from high-risk locations until after they hatch. This may ④ increase the number of turtles that survive to adulthood. Crocodile programs have also been successful in protecting eggs and hatchlings, ⑤ capturing hatchlings once they are better equipped to protect themselves.

* captive breeding: 포획 사육 ** hatch: 부화하다

[31~34] 다음 빈칸에 들어갈 말로 가장 적절한 것을 고르시오.

31. We don't send telegraphs to communicate anymore, but it's a great metaphor for giving advance notice. Sometimes, you must inform those close to you of upcoming change by conveying important information well in advance. There's a huge difference between saying, "From now on, we will do things differently," which doesn't give people enough time to understand and accept the change, and saying something like, "Starting next month, we're going to approach things differently." Telegraphing empowers people to _____. Telegraphing involves the art of seeing an upcoming event or circumstance and giving others enough time to process and accept the change. Telegraph anything that will take people out of what is familiar and comfortable to them. This will allow processing time for them to accept the circumstances and make the most of what's happening.

① unite   ② adapt   ③ object
④ compete   ⑤ recover

32. Not only does memory underlie our ability to think at all, it defines the content of our experiences and how we preserve them for years to come. Memory _____. If I were to suffer from heart failure and depend upon an artificial heart, I would be no less myself. If I lost an arm in an accident and had it replaced with an artificial arm, I would still be essentially *me*. As long as my mind and memories remain intact, I will continue to be the same person, no matter which part of my body (other than the brain) is replaced. On the other hand, when someone suffers from advanced Alzheimer's disease and his memories fade, people often say that he "is not himself anymore," or that it is as if the person "is no longer there," though his body remains unchanged.

* intact: 손상되지 않은

① makes us who we are
② has to do with our body
③ reflects what we expect
④ lets us understand others
⑤ helps us learn from the past

33. Over time, babies construct expectations about what sounds they will hear when. They hold in memory the sound patterns that occur on a regular basis. They make hypotheses like, "If I hear *this* sound first, it probably will be followed by *that* sound." Scientists conclude that much of babies' skill in learning language is due to their _____. For babies, this means that they appear to pay close attention to the patterns that repeat in language. They remember, in a systematic way, how often sounds occur, in what order, with what intervals, and with what changes of pitch. This memory store allows them to track, within the neural circuits of their brains, the frequency of sound patterns and to use this knowledge to make predictions about the meaning in patterns of sounds. [3점]

① lack of social pressures
② ability to calculate statistics
③ desire to interact with others
④ preference for simpler sounds
⑤ tendency to imitate caregivers

34. Some deep-sea organisms are known to use bioluminescence as a lure, to attract prey with a little glow imitating the movements of their favorite fish, or like fireflies, as a sexual attractant to find mates. While there are many possible evolutionary theories for the survival value of bioluminescence, one of the most fascinating is to _____. The color of almost all bioluminescent molecules is blue-green, the same color as the ocean above. By self-glowing blue-green, the creatures no longer cast a shadow or create a silhouette, especially when viewed from below against the brighter waters above. Rather, by glowing themselves, they can blend into the sparkles, reflections, and scattered blue-green glow of sunlight or moonlight. Thus, they are most likely making their own light not to see, but to be un-seen. [3점]

* bioluminescence: 생물 발광 ** lure: 가짜 미끼

① send a signal for help
② threaten enemies nearby
③ lift the veil of hidden prey
④ create a cloak of invisibility
⑤ serve as a navigation system

35. 다음 글에서 전체 흐름과 관계 <u>없는</u> 문장은?

Internet activist Eli Pariser noticed how online search algorithms encourage our human tendency to grab hold of everything that confirms the beliefs we already hold, while quietly ignoring information that doesn't match those beliefs. ① We set up a so-called "filter-bubble" around ourselves, where we are constantly exposed only to that material that we agree with. ② We are never challenged, never giving ourselves the opportunity to acknowledge the existence of diversity and difference. ③ Creating a difference that others don't have is a way to succeed in your field, leading to the creation of innovations. ④ In the best case, we become naive and sheltered, and in the worst, we become radicalized with extreme views, unable to imagine life outside our particular bubble. ⑤ The results are disastrous: intellectual isolation and the real distortion that comes with believing that the little world we create for ourselves is *the* world.

* naive: 세상을 모르는 ** radicalize: 과격하게 만들다

*** distortion: 왜곡

[36~37] 주어진 글 다음에 이어질 글의 순서로 가장 적절한 것을 고르시오.

36.

Roughly twenty years ago, brick-and-mortar stores began to give way to electronic commerce. For good or bad, the shift fundamentally changed consumers' perception of the shopping experience.

(A) Before long, the e-commerce book market naturally expanded to include additional categories, like CDs and DVDs. E-commerce soon snowballed into the enormous industry it is today, where you can buy everything from toilet paper to cars online.

(B) Nowhere was the shift more obvious than with book sales, which is how online bookstores got their start. Physical bookstores simply could not stock as many titles as a virtual bookstore could. There is only so much space available on a shelf.

(C) In addition to greater variety, online bookstores were also able to offer aggressive discounts thanks to their lower operating costs. The combination of lower prices and greater selection led to the slow, steady rise of online bookstores.

* brick-and-mortar: 오프라인 거래의

① (A) − (C) − (B)
② (B) − (A) − (C)
③ (B) − (C) − (A)
④ (C) − (A) − (B)
⑤ (C) − (B) − (A)

37.

Literary works, by their nature, suggest rather than explain; they imply rather than state their claims boldly and directly.

(A) What a text implies is often of great interest to us. And our work of figuring out a text's implications tests our analytical powers. In considering what a text suggests, we gain practice in making sense of texts.

(B) But whatever the proportion of a work's showing to telling, there is always something for readers to interpret. Thus we ask the question "What does the text suggest?" as a way to approach literary interpretation, as a way to begin thinking about a text's implications.

(C) This broad generalization, however, does not mean that works of literature do not include direct statements. Depending on when they were written and by whom, literary works may contain large amounts of direct telling and lesser amounts of suggestion and implication. [3점]

① (A) − (C) − (B)
② (B) − (A) − (C)
③ (B) − (C) − (A)
④ (C) − (A) − (B)
⑤ (C) − (B) − (A)

[38~39] 글의 흐름으로 보아, 주어진 문장이 들어가기에 가장 적절한 곳을 고르시오.

38.

Worse, some are contaminated with other substances and contain ingredients not listed on the label.

According to top nutrition experts, most nutrients are better absorbed and used by the body when consumed from a whole food instead of a supplement. (①) However, many people feel the need to take pills, powders, and supplements in an attempt to obtain nutrients and fill the gaps in their diets. (②) We hope these will give us more energy, prevent us from catching a cold in the winter, or improve our skin and hair. (③) But in reality, the large majority of supplements are artificial and may not even be completely absorbed by your body. (④) For example, a recent investigative report found heavy metals in 40 percent of 134 brands of protein powders on the market. (⑤) With little control and regulation, taking supplements is a gamble and often costly.

* contaminate: 오염시키다 ** supplement: 보충제

39.

But after this brief moment of rest, the pendulum swings back again and therefore part of the total energy is then given in the form of kinetic energy.

In general, kinetic energy is the energy associated with motion, while potential energy represents the energy which is "stored" in a physical system. Moreover, the total energy is always conserved. (①) But while the total energy remains unchanged, the kinetic and potential parts of the total energy can change all the time. (②) Imagine, for example, a pendulum which swings back and forth. (③) When it swings, it sweeps out an arc and then slows down as it comes closer to its highest point, where the pendulum does not move at all. (④) So at this point, the energy is completely given in terms of potential energy. (⑤) So as the pendulum swings, kinetic and potential energy constantly change into each other. [3점]

* pendulum: 추(錘) ** arc: 호(弧)

40. 다음 글의 내용을 한 문장으로 요약하고자 한다. 빈칸 (A), (B)에 들어갈 말로 가장 적절한 것은?

There is often a lot of uncertainty in the realm of science, which the general public finds uncomfortable. They don't want "informed guesses," they want certainties that make their lives easier, and science is often unequipped to meet these demands. In particular, the human body is fantastically complex, and some scientific answers can never be provided in black-or-white terms. All this is why the media tends to oversimplify scientific research when presenting it to the public. In their eyes, they're just "giving people what they want" as opposed to offering more accurate but complex information that very few people will read or understand. A perfect example of this is how people want definitive answers as to which foods are "good" and "bad." Scientifically speaking, there are no "good" and "bad" foods; rather, food quality exists on a continuum, meaning that some foods are *better* than others when it comes to general health and well-being.

* continuum: 연속(체)

↓

With regard to general health, science, by its nature, does not ___(A)___ the public's demands for certainty, which leads to the media giving less ___(B)___ answers to the public.

	(A)	(B)		(A)	(B)
①	satisfy	simple	②	satisfy	complicated
③	ignore	difficult	④	ignore	simple
⑤	reject	complicated			

[41~42] 다음 글을 읽고, 물음에 답하시오.

Since the turn of the twentieth century we've believed in genetic causes of diagnoses — a theory called genetic determinism. Under this model, our genes (and subsequent health) are determined at birth. We are "destined" to inherit certain diseases based on the misfortune of our DNA. Genetic determinism doesn't (a) consider the role of family backgrounds, traumas, habits, or anything else within the environment. In this dynamic we are not (b) active participants in our own health and wellness. Why would we be? If something is predetermined, it's not (c) necessary to look at anything beyond our DNA. But the more science has learned about the body and its interaction with the environment around it (in its various forms, from our nutrition to our relationships to our racially oppressive systems), the more (d) simplistic the story becomes. We are not merely expressions of coding but products of a remarkable variety of interactions that are both within and outside of our control. Once we see beyond the narrative that genetics are (e) destiny, we can take ownership of our health. This allows us to see how "choiceless" we once were and empowers us with the ability to create real and lasting change.

* oppressive: 억압적인

41. 윗글의 제목으로 가장 적절한 것은?

① Health Is in Our Hands, Not Only in Our Genes
② Genetics: A Solution to Enhance Human Wellness
③ How Did DNA Dominate Over Environment in Biology?
④ Never Be Confident in Your Health, but Keep Checking!
⑤ Why Scientific Innovation Affects Our Social Interactions

42. 밑줄 친 (a)~(e) 중에서 문맥상 낱말의 쓰임이 적절하지 <u>않은</u> 것은? [3점]

① (a)　　② (b)　　③ (c)　　④ (d)　　⑤ (e)

[43~45] 다음 글을 읽고, 물음에 답하시오.

(A)

One day a poor man brought a bunch of grapes to a prince as a gift. He was very excited to be able to bring a gift for (a) him because he was too poor to afford more. He placed the grapes beside the prince and said, "Oh, Prince, please accept this small gift from me." His face beamed with happiness as he offered his small gift.

(B)

If the prince had offered the grapes to them, they might have made funny faces and shown their distaste for the grapes. That would have hurt the feelings of that poor man. He thought to himself that it would be better to eat all of them cheerfully and please (b) him. He did not want to hurt the feelings of that poor man. Everyone around him was moved by his thoughtfulness.

(C)

The prince thanked him politely. As the man looked at him expectantly, the prince ate one grape. Then (c) he ate another one. Slowly the prince finished the whole bunch of grapes by himself. He did not offer grapes to anyone near him. The man who brought those grapes to (d) him was very pleased and left. The close friends of the prince who were around him were very surprised.

(D)

Usually the prince shared whatever he had with others. He would offer them whatever he was given and they would eat it together. This time was different. Without offering it to anyone, (e) he finished the bunch of grapes by himself. One of the friends asked, "Prince! How come you ate all the grapes by yourself and did not offer them to any one of us?" He smiled and said that he ate all the grapes by himself because the grapes were too sour.

43. 주어진 글 (A)에 이어질 내용을 순서에 맞게 배열한 것으로 가장 적절한 것은?

① (B) − (D) − (C)　　② (C) − (B) − (D)
③ (C) − (D) − (B)　　④ (D) − (B) − (C)
⑤ (D) − (C) − (B)

44. 밑줄 친 (a)~(e) 중에서 가리키는 대상이 나머지 넷과 <u>다른</u> 것은?

① (a)　　② (b)　　③ (c)　　④ (d)　　⑤ (e)

45. 윗글의 왕자에 관한 내용으로 적절하지 <u>않은</u> 것은?

① 가난한 남자에게 포도 한 송이를 선물로 받았다.
② 가난한 남자의 감정을 상하게 하고 싶지 않았다.
③ 곁에 있던 어떤 이에게도 포도를 권하지 않았다.
④ 가지고 있는 어떤 것이든 평소에 다른 사람들과 나눴다.
⑤ 포도가 너무 시어서 혼자 다 먹지 못했다.

* 확인 사항
○ 답안지의 해당란에 필요한 내용을 정확히 기입(표기)했는지 확인하시오.

※ QR 코드를 스캔하시면 듣기 방송이 나옵니다. 듣기 방송을 들으며 다음 빈칸을 채우시오. ● 제한 시간 : 25분

01

다음을 듣고, 남자가 하는 말의 목적으로 가장 적절한 것을 고르시오.

[Chime bell rings.]

M : Hello, passengers. I'm James Walker from the Greenville Subway System. As you know, the international film festival will be held in our city next month. Throughout the festival, some movies will _____ _____ _____ _____ _____ . So, for our citizens' convenience, the Greenville City Council has decided to _____ _____ _____ _____ _____ during the festival. All Greenville subway lines will run extra hours while the festival is going on. You can easily check ✪ _____ _____ _____ _____ _____ using the Greenville Subway App. I hope you can make the most of the festival experience with our services. Thank you.

02

대화를 듣고, 여자의 의견으로 가장 적절한 것을 고르시오.

W : Good morning, Jason. It's sports day today. Do you have everything you need?

M : Yes, Mom. I put a water bottle, some snacks, and a towel in my bag. Is there anything I forgot?

W : What about sunblock? Did you put it on?

M : Sunblock? It's not sunny outside.

W : Jason, you should wear sunblock _____ _____ _____ _____ _____ .

M : But I don't feel the sun in weather like this.

W : Even if you don't feel the sun on your skin, the harmful light from the sun can damage your skin because _____ _____ _____ _____ _____ .

M : Really? You mean I can still get a sunburn even on a cloudy day?

W : Yes. That's why you shouldn't ✪ _____ _____ _____ _____ even if it's not sunny outside.

M : I didn't know that. I'll put it on now.

03

대화를 듣고, 두 사람의 관계를 가장 잘 나타낸 것을 고르시오.

M : Hello, Ms. Green. You came just on time.

W : Really? I thought I was early.

M : No. Your car is over there. Follow me, please.

W : Wow. All the dirt is gone. It looks like a new car.

M : Yeah. But some stains were _____ _____ _____ . It's better to have your car washed right after it gets dirty.

W : I went on a business trip for a month, so I didn't have time. I'll keep that in mind.

M : Anyway, while cleaning the inside, we ✪ _____ _____ _____ under the driver's seat.

W : Really? I thought I had lost that. Thank you.

M : You're welcome. Would you like to pay _____ _____ _____ _____ _____ _____ ?

W : I'll pay in cash. Here you are.

M : Okay. *[Pause]* Here is your receipt. And this is a discount coupon for our car wash center. You can use it on your next visit.

W : That's nice. Thank you.

04

대화를 듣고, 그림에서 대화의 내용과 일치하지 않는 것을 고르시오.

W : Hi, Harry. Congratulations on your wedding. Did you finish decorating the new house?

M : I just finished the living room. Look at this picture, Linda.

W : Wow. I love ✪ _____ _____ _____ _____ _____ .

M : Thanks. Do you see those _____ _____ _____ _____ _____ ? My sister made them as wedding gifts.

W : That's lovely. Oh, you put a round table on the rug.

M : Yeah. We spend time reading books around the table. What do you think of the clock on the bookshelf?

W : It looks good in that room. By the way, is that a plant under the calendar?

M : Yes. I placed it there because the plant helps to _____ _____ _____ .

W : You decorated your house really well.

M : Thanks. I'll invite you over when we have the housewarming party.

05

대화를 듣고, 남자가 할 일로 가장 적절한 것을 고르시오.

M : Jane, the Stop Using Plastic campaign starts tomorrow. Let's do a final check.

W : Okay, Robin. I just finished _____ _____ _____ _____ about plastic waste.

M : Then, I'm going to check the screen that we'll use for the video.

W : No worries. I've already done it, and it works well.

M : That's nice. I _____ _____ _____ _____ on our organization's website.

W : Yeah. Some of my friends saw it and texted me they're coming.

M : My friends, too. They ✪ _____ _____ _____ interest in the _____ _____ _____ _____ . The bags are ready in that box.

W : Good. By the way, where are the badges you ordered for visitors?

M : Oh, I left the badges in my car. I'll bring them right away.

W : Great. It seems that everything is prepared.

06

대화를 듣고, 여자가 지불할 금액을 고르시오. [3점]

M : Welcome to Kids Clothing Club. How may I help you?

W : I'm looking for a muffler for my son. He's 5 years old.

M : Okay. Follow me. *[Pause]* This red muffler is one of the best sellers in our shop.

W : I love the color. How much is it?

M : It's $50. This one is popular ✿ _____ _____ _____ _____ _____ here.

W : Oh, that's my son's favorite character. I'll buy one red muffler, then.

M : Great. Anything else?

W : How much are _____ _____ _____ ?

M : A pair of socks is $5.

W : All right. I'll buy two pairs.

M : So, one red muffler and two pairs of winter socks, right?

W : Yes. Can I use _____ _____ _____ ?

M : Of course. With that coupon, you can get 10% off the total price.

W : Good. Here's my credit card.

07

대화를 듣고, 남자가 London Walking Tour에 참여하지 못한 이유를 고르시오.

W : Hi, Jeremy. How was your trip to London?

M : It was fantastic, Julia. I watched the musical you recommended.

W : Good. What about the London Walking Tour? Did you enjoy it?

M : Unfortunately, I _____ _____ _____ _____ .

W : Why? Didn't you say you booked it?

M : Yes. I made a reservation for the tour in advance.

W : Oh, was the tour canceled because of the weather?

M : No. The weather was no problem at all.

W : Then, why couldn't you join the tour?

M : Actually, _____ _____ _____ the day before the tour, so I had _____ _____ _____ _____ _____ . That's why I couldn't make it.

W : I'm sorry to hear that. Is it okay, now?

M : Yes. It's completely fine now. Oh, I forgot to ✿ _____ _____ _____ I bought for you. I'll bring it tomorrow.

W : That's so sweet. Thanks.

08

대화를 듣고, Winter Lake Festival에 관해 언급되지 않은 것을 고르시오.

M : What are you doing, Laura?

W : Hi, Tim. I'm looking for winter festivals to visit during vacation.

M : Is there anything good?

W : Yes, look at this. There is _____ _____ _____ _____ called the Winter Lake Festival.

M : Awesome. When does it start?

W : December 18th and it'll be held for two weeks.

M : Cool. Oh, it'll take place in Stevenson Park.

W : Great. It's near our school. If you don't have any plans during vacation, let's go together.

M : Of course. Is there an entrance fee?

W : Yes. Here, it says $3. It's not expensive.

M : Good. Look! There are ✿ _____ _____ _____ _____ to enjoy.

W : Yeah, there is ice skating, ice fishing, and _____ _____ .

M : They all sound exciting. Let's have fun there.

09

Mascot Design Contest에 관한 다음 내용을 듣고, 일치하지 <u>않는</u> 것을 고르시오.

W : Hello, supporters! I'm Christine Miller, manager of Western Football Club. This year, we're holding a Mascot Design Contest to celebrate our team's 1st championship. Anyone who loves our team can participate in this contest. The mascot design should be ✿ _____ _____ _____ _____ _____ "One team, one spirit." The winning design will be chosen through a fan vote. And the winner will receive _____ _____ _____ _____ _____ _____ . People who want to participate should send their design by email by December 5th. Show your creativity and love for our team _____ _____ _____ . For more information, please visit our website. Thank you.

10

다음 표를 보면서 대화를 듣고, 두 사람이 예약할 캠핑장을 고르시오.

W : Honey, what are you looking at?

M : This is a list of the best campsites in 2021. How about going to one of them next month?

W : Sounds great. Let me see. *[Pause]* There are five different campsites.

M : Yeah. Since we went to Seaside campsite last time, let's choose among the other four.

W : Good. Hmm, I don't want to spend more than $100 per night. It's too expensive.

M : I agree with that. What do you think of _____ _____ _____ _____ ?

W : Oh, I want to try it. It'll be a special experience.

M : Then, we can _____ _____ _____ _____ .

W : What about going to this campsite? Since this has ✿ _____ _____ _____ , our children can have more fun.

M : Cool! I'll make a reservation for this campsite.

11

대화를 듣고, 남자의 마지막 말에 대한 여자의 응답으로 가장 적절한 것을 고르시오.

M : Kate, I heard your company moved to a new office. How is it?

W : It's all good except one thing. It's _____ _____ _____ _____ .

M : Oh, really? ✿ _____ _____ _____ _____ _____ to get there?

12
대화를 듣고, 여자의 마지막 말에 대한 남자의 응답으로 가장 적절한 것을 고르시오.

W : Honey, you know my nephew is coming over this evening. How about _____ _____ _____ _____?

M : Sure. Which topping does he prefer, ✿ _____ _____ _____ _____?

W : Oh, he doesn't like beef. He loves seafood.

13
대화를 듣고, 남자의 마지막 말에 대한 여자의 응답으로 가장 적절한 것을 고르시오.

M : Honey, did you read this leaflet on the table?

W : Not yet. What's it about?

M : It says the local children's library is going to hold some events to _____ _____ _____.

W : Is there anything good?

M : Let me see. [Pause] There will be a Meet-the-Author event. Rebecca Moore is coming.

W : Oh, she's one of our son's favorite writers.

M : Yes. He'll be excited if he can _____ _____ _____ _____.

W : Let's take him to that event. When is it?

M : It's next Saturday, 1 p.m.

W : But we have a lunch reservation at the French restaurant at that time.

M : Oh, I forgot. Then ✿ _____ _____ _____ _____? It's a rare chance to meet the author.

14
대화를 듣고, 여자의 마지막 말에 대한 남자의 응답으로 가장 적절한 것을 고르시오.
[3점]

[Cell phone rings.]

W : This is Fairview Laptop Repair. How may I help you?

M : Hello, this is David Brown. _____ _____ _____ _____ this morning.

W : Oh, Mr. Brown. You requested the screen repair yesterday, right?

M : Yes. Is there any problem?

W : The screen is all repaired. But we found another problem with your laptop. You need to _____ _____ _____.

M : Oh, I didn't know that. How bad is it?

W : Even when the battery is fully charged, it ✿ _____ _____ _____ _____.

M : Really? How much does it cost to change the battery?

W : It's $70. It's on sale now.

M : That sounds great. But, I'm worried it'll delay the laptop pick-up time, 5 p.m. today.

W : Don't worry. You can still pick it up at that time.

15
다음 상황 설명을 듣고, Amy가 Terry에게 할 말로 가장 적절한 것을 고르시오. [3점]

M : Amy is the leader of a high school band and Terry is one of the band members. The band is going to hold a mini concert in the school festival, and Terry is in charge of making a concert poster. When he completes the poster, he shows it to the band members. Even though the poster has ✿ _____ _____ _____ _____, it's hard to read it because the size of the letters is too small. Amy thinks if Terry changes the font size to a larger one, it could be _____ _____ _____. So, Amy wants to suggest that Terry _____ _____ _____ _____ _____ _____ on the poster. In this situation, what would Amy most likely say to Terry?

16~17
다음을 듣고, 물음에 답하시오.

W : Hello, students. Previously, we discussed why gardening is a great hobby. But not everyone has a sunny front yard. So, today we'll learn about plants that grow even in shade. First, lemon balm _____ _____ _____ _____. So if your place is sunless, it's the plant you should choose. Next, ivy is _____ _____ _____ _____. Its ability to grow in shade makes it survive under trees where most plants can't. Also, there's mint. It lives well under low-light conditions, so you can grow it in a small pot indoors. Lastly, camellia grows better ✿ _____ _____ _____. Especially when it's a young plant, it needs protection from the sun. Many plants like these can live even in the shade. _____ _____ _____? Now, let's watch a video clip about how to grow these plants.

▶ 정답 : 해설편 **168**쪽

18
001 □ librarian ⓝ (도서관의) 사서
002 □ increase ⓥ ~를 강화하다, 증진시키다
003 □ aim ⓝ 목표, 목적
004 □ various ⓐ 다양한
005 □ news media 뉴스미디어, 뉴스 매체
006 □ newspaper ⓝ 신문
007 □ article ⓝ (신문·잡지의) 글, 기사
008 □ access ⓥ 접속하다, 접근하다
009 □ humble ⓐ 겸손한
010 □ allow ⓥ 허락하다, 허용하다
011 □ store ⓥ 보관하다
012 □ grant ⓥ (공식적으로) 주다

19
013 □ pretty ⓐⓓ 꽤, 매우
014 □ absolutely ⓐⓓ 완전히, 절대적으로
015 □ thrilled ⓐ 아주 신이 난, 황홀한
016 □ soon ⓐⓓ 곧, 머지않아
017 □ communicate ⓥ 의사소통을 하다
018 □ daydream ⓥ 공상하다
019 □ hand ⓥ 건네주다, 넘겨주다
020 □ flip through (책장을) 휙휙 넘기다, 훑어보다
021 □ figure ⓥ 생각하다
022 □ hide ⓥ 감추다, 숨기다
023 □ realize ⓥ 깨닫다
024 □ furious ⓐ 몹시 화가 난
025 □ confident ⓐ 자신감 있는
026 □ anticipate ⓥ 기대하다

20
027 □ expert ⓝ 전문가
028 □ estimate ⓥ 추정하다
029 □ as much as ~ 정도
030 □ way ⓝ 방법, 방식
031 □ attention ⓝ 주의, 주목
032 □ nonverbal ⓐ 비언어적인
033 □ significant ⓐ 상당한, 유의미한, 중요한
034 □ difference ⓝ 차이
035 □ in general 보통, 대개, 일반적으로
036 □ often ⓐⓓ 자주, 종종
037 □ closely ⓐⓓ 면밀하게, 밀접하게
038 □ tune in to ~에 맞추다
039 □ body language 몸짓 언어, 보디랭귀지
040 □ enter ⓥ 들어가다
041 □ initial ⓐ 초기의
042 □ action ⓝ 행동
043 □ look for 찾다
044 □ encourage ⓥ 격려하다
045 □ empower ⓥ 능력을 주다, 힘을 주다
046 □ friendly ⓐ 친근한, 다정한
047 □ greeting ⓝ 인사
048 □ require ⓥ 요구하다
049 □ a great deal of (양이) 많은
050 □ effort ⓝ 노력
051 □ climate ⓝ 분위기

21
052 □ climate change 기후 변화
053 □ blame A for B B에 대해 A를 탓하다
054 □ fossil fuel 화석 연료

055 □ industry ⓝ 산업
056 □ greenhouse gas 온실 가스
057 □ agricultural ⓐ 농업의
058 □ sector ⓝ 부분, 분야
059 □ burn ⓥ 태우다
060 □ rainforest ⓝ 열대 우림
061 □ excessive ⓐ 과다한
062 □ behavior ⓝ 행동, 행위
063 □ popular ⓐ 일반적인
064 □ scapegoat ⓝ 희생양
065 □ crisis ⓝ 위기
066 □ drill ⓥ (자원, 연료 등을) 시추하다, 구멍을 뚫다
067 □ provide ⓥ 제공하다
068 □ financial ⓐ 재정상의, 금융의
069 □ incentive ⓝ 동기
070 □ waste ⓥ 낭비하다
071 □ electricity ⓝ 전기 ⓥ 발생시키다, 만들어 내다
072 □ power plant 발전소
073 □ derive ⓥ 유래하다, 파생하다
074 □ crude oil 원유
075 □ slap ⓝ 철썩 때리기
076 □ generation ⓝ 세대
077 □ room ⓝ 여지, 기회
078 □ natural resources 천연 자원
079 □ recognize ⓥ 인식하다, 알아보다
080 □ responsibility ⓝ 책임, 책무
081 □ environmental problems 환경 문제
082 □ individually ⓐⓓ 개별적으로

22
083 □ worthless ⓐ 무가치한
084 □ company ⓝ 기업
085 □ valuable ⓐ 소중한, 귀중한
086 □ customer ⓝ 고객, 손님
087 □ end up 결국 ~이 되다
088 □ bury ⓥ 묻다
089 □ ensure ⓥ 보장하다
090 □ accessible ⓐ 접근 가능한, 이용 가능한
091 □ appropriate ⓐ 적절한
092 □ usage ⓝ 사용
093 □ frequently ⓐⓓ 자주
094 □ store ⓥ 저장하다, 보관하다
095 □ record ⓝ 기록
096 □ clerk ⓝ 직원
097 □ prime ⓐ 가장 적합한, 최적의
098 □ opportunity ⓝ 기회
099 □ indication ⓝ 표시, 징후
100 □ utilize ⓥ 이용하다
101 □ loyalty ⓝ 충성도
102 □ delightful ⓐ 즐거운, 기쁜

23
103 □ neuroscientist ⓝ 신경과학자
104 □ specific ⓐ 특정한
105 □ circuit ⓝ 회로
106 □ explain ⓥ 설명하다
107 □ fundamentally ⓐⓓ 기본적으로
108 □ train ⓥ 훈련하다
109 □ grateful ⓐ 감사하는
110 □ relaxed ⓐ 편안한

111 □ repeat ⓥ 반복하다
112 □ shape ⓥ 형성하다
113 □ fire ⓥ 발화[점화]되다
114 □ activate ⓥ 활성화하다
115 □ neural ⓐ 신경의
116 □ wire ⓥ 연결하다
117 □ premise ⓝ (주장의) 전제
118 □ bottom line 핵심, 요점, 결론
119 □ intentionally ⓐⓓ 의도적으로
120 □ possibility ⓝ 가능성
121 □ musical instrument 악기
122 □ enhance ⓥ 향상시키다
123 □ capacity ⓝ 용량

24
124 □ modern times 현대
125 □ society ⓝ 사회
126 □ dynamic ⓐ 역동적인
127 □ mobility ⓝ 유동성
128 □ degree ⓝ 정도
129 □ regarding ⓟⓡⓔⓟ ~에 관하여
130 □ for instance 예를 들어
131 □ profession ⓝ 직업
132 □ marriage ⓝ 결혼
133 □ religion ⓝ 종교
134 □ pose a challenge 도전하다, 이의를 제기하다
135 □ traditional ⓐ 전통의, 전통적인
136 □ evident ⓐ 명백한
137 □ commit to ~에 전념하다
138 □ alternative ⓝ 대안
139 □ control ⓝ 통제력
140 □ ready-made ⓐ 이미 주어진, 기성품의
141 □ prescribe ⓥ 규정하다, 처방하다
142 □ appear ⓥ 보이기 시작하다
143 □ underneath ⓐⓓ 아래
144 □ competitive ⓐ 경쟁적인
145 □ trustworthy ⓐ 신뢰할 수 있는

25
146 □ public school 공립학교
147 □ participate ⓥ 참여하다
148 □ with the exception of ~을 제외하고
149 □ account for ~을 차지하다
150 □ peer ⓝ 또래
151 □ gallery ⓝ 미술관
152 □ respectively ⓐⓓ 각각

26
153 □ moment ⓝ 때, 순간
154 □ dream ⓥ 꿈을 꾸다
155 □ soar ⓥ 솟아오르다
156 □ save money 돈을 모으다
157 □ admit ⓥ 입장[입학]을 허락하다
158 □ earn ⓥ 얻다, 획득하다
159 □ license ⓝ 면허증
160 □ also ⓐⓓ 또한
161 □ acrobatics ⓝ 곡예
162 □ appearance ⓝ 출현, 모습
163 □ pioneer ⓝ 선구자
164 □ inspire ⓥ 영감을 주다
165 □ pursue ⓥ 추구하다

27
166 □ annual ⓐ 매년 열리는
167 □ nature ⓝ 자연
168 □ submission ⓝ 제출
169 □ maximum ⓝ 최대
170 □ post ⓥ 게시하다
171 □ exhibit ⓥ 전시하다

28
172 □ pilot ⓝ 조종사
173 □ duration ⓝ (지속되는) 시간, 기간
174 □ flight ⓝ 비행
175 □ get a refund 환불을 받다
176 □ in advance 미리, 사전에

29
177 □ reduction ⓝ 감소
178 □ result ⓝ 결과
179 □ pesticide ⓝ 살충제, 농약
180 □ fertilizer ⓝ 비료
181 □ beneficial ⓐ 유익한, 이로운
182 □ earthworm ⓝ 지렁이
183 □ soil ⓝ 토양
184 □ essential ⓐ 필수적인, 본질적인
185 □ nutrient ⓝ 영양소, 영양분
186 □ in the first place 애초에, 우선
187 □ uptake ⓝ 흡수, 활용
188 □ fertilize ⓥ 비옥하게 하다, 비료를 주다
189 □ nitrogen ⓝ 질소
190 □ potassium ⓝ 칼륨
191 □ decline ⓝ 감소 ⓥ 감소하다
192 □ zinc ⓝ 아연
193 □ average ⓝ 평균
194 □ wheat ⓝ 밀
195 □ partly ⓐⓓ 부분적으로
196 □ blocker ⓝ 방해물, 차단제
197 □ absorption ⓝ 흡수
198 □ acidic ⓐ 산성의
199 □ farmland ⓝ 농지
200 □ characteristic ⓝ 특징, 특성
201 □ determine ⓥ 결정하다
202 □ accumulation ⓝ 축적

30
203 □ species ⓝ 종(種)
204 □ approach ⓥ ~에 이르다, ~에 가까워지다
205 □ extinction ⓝ 멸종
206 □ survival ⓝ 생존
207 □ recovery ⓝ 회복
208 □ establish ⓥ 수립하다
209 □ coordinate ⓥ 조직화하다, 통합하다
210 □ field ⓝ 현장
211 □ conservationist ⓝ 환경 보호 활동가
212 □ wildlife ⓝ 야생동물
213 □ authority ⓝ 당국
214 □ population ⓝ 개체수
215 □ diminish ⓥ 감소하다, 줄어들다
216 □ unusual ⓐ 드문
217 □ breeding ⓝ 사육, 번식
218 □ protect ⓥ 보호하다
219 □ release ⓥ 풀어 주다, 방생하다
220 □ supplement ⓥ 보충하다

221 ☐ threat ⓝ 위협
222 ☐ particular ⓐ 특정한
223 ☐ high-risk ⓐ 위험성이 높은
224 ☐ location ⓝ 위치, 장소
225 ☐ adulthood ⓝ 성체, 성인
226 ☐ hatchling ⓝ (갓 부화한) 유생
227 ☐ be equipped to ～할 준비를 갖추다

31
228 ☐ telegraph ⓝ 전보
229 ☐ anymore ⓐⓓ 더 이상
230 ☐ metaphor ⓝ 은유
231 ☐ advance ⓐ 사전의
232 ☐ notice ⓝ 통지, 통보
233 ☐ upcoming ⓐ 다가오는
234 ☐ convey ⓥ 전달하다
235 ☐ from now on 이제부터, 지금부터
236 ☐ accept ⓥ 받아들이다
237 ☐ involve ⓥ 포함하다
238 ☐ circumstance ⓝ 상황
239 ☐ familiar ⓐ 익숙한
240 ☐ comfortable ⓐ 편안한
241 ☐ make the most of ～을 최대한 활용하다
242 ☐ happen ⓥ (일, 사건 등이) 일어나다

32
243 ☐ underlie ⓥ (～의) 기반을 이루다
244 ☐ ability ⓝ 능력
245 ☐ define ⓥ 규정하다
246 ☐ preserve ⓥ 보존하다
247 ☐ for years 수년간, 몇 해 동안
248 ☐ suffer ⓥ 앓다, 병들다
249 ☐ heart failure 심부전, 심장 부전
250 ☐ artificial heart 인공 심장
251 ☐ accident ⓝ 사고
252 ☐ replace ⓥ 교체하다
253 ☐ essentially ⓐⓓ 본질적으로
254 ☐ intact ⓐ 손상되지 않은
255 ☐ continue ⓥ 계속되다
256 ☐ fade ⓥ 흐려지다, (빛이) 바래다
257 ☐ past ⓝ 과거

33
258 ☐ construct ⓥ 형성하다, 구성하다
259 ☐ expectation ⓝ 기대
260 ☐ occur ⓥ 일어나다, 발생하다
261 ☐ on a regular basis 규칙적으로
262 ☐ hypothesis ⓝ 가설
263 ☐ probably ⓐⓓ 아마도
264 ☐ follow ⓥ 따라가다[오다]
265 ☐ conclude ⓥ 결론을 내리다
266 ☐ close attention 세심한 주의
267 ☐ systematic ⓐ 체계적인
268 ☐ order ⓝ 순서
269 ☐ interval ⓝ 간격
270 ☐ track ⓥ 추적하다
271 ☐ frequency ⓝ 빈도
272 ☐ make a prediction 예측하다
273 ☐ calculate ⓥ 계산하다
274 ☐ statistics ⓝ 통계
275 ☐ interact ⓥ 소통하다
276 ☐ tendency ⓝ 성향, 경향

277 ☐ imitate ⓥ 모방하다, 흉내내다
278 ☐ caregiver ⓝ 간병인

34
279 ☐ deep-sea ⓐ 심해의
280 ☐ organism ⓝ 유기체, 생물
281 ☐ bioluminescence ⓝ 생물[생체] 발광
282 ☐ lure ⓝ 미끼
283 ☐ attractant ⓝ 유인 물질
284 ☐ prey ⓝ 먹이
285 ☐ firefly ⓝ 반딧불이
286 ☐ mate ⓝ 짝
287 ☐ evolutionary ⓐ 진화의
288 ☐ theory ⓝ 이론
289 ☐ survival value 생존가(생체의 특질이 생존·번식에 기여하는 유용성)
290 ☐ fascinating ⓐ 매력적인, 흥미로운
291 ☐ almost all 거의 모든, 거의 전부의
292 ☐ molecule ⓝ 분자
293 ☐ cast ⓥ 드리우다, 던지다
294 ☐ shadow ⓝ 그림자
295 ☐ silhouette ⓝ 실루엣, 윤곽
296 ☐ blend into ～에 섞이다
297 ☐ sparkle ⓝ 반짝거림, 광채
298 ☐ scatter ⓥ 흩뜨리다, 분산하다
299 ☐ threaten ⓥ 위협하다
300 ☐ cloak ⓝ 망토
301 ☐ invisibility ⓝ 보이지 않음

35
302 ☐ activist ⓝ 활동가
303 ☐ algorithm ⓝ 알고리즘, 연산
304 ☐ grab hold of ～을 (갑자기) 움켜잡다
305 ☐ confirm ⓥ 확인하다
306 ☐ belief ⓝ 신념, 확신
307 ☐ quietly ⓐⓓ 조용히
308 ☐ ignore ⓥ 무시하다
309 ☐ filter-bubble ⓝ 필터 버블(사용자가 인터넷 알고리즘에 의해 관심사에 맞는 정보만 제공받으며 왜곡된 인지 속에 갇히게 되는 것)
310 ☐ constantly ⓐⓓ 끊임없이, 지속적으로
311 ☐ expose ⓥ 노출시키다
312 ☐ agree ⓥ 동의하다
313 ☐ acknowledge ⓥ 인정하다
314 ☐ existence ⓝ 존재
315 ☐ diversity ⓝ 다양성
316 ☐ field ⓝ 분야
317 ☐ innovation ⓝ 혁신
318 ☐ shelter ⓥ 보호하다
319 ☐ radicalize ⓥ 과격하게 하다
320 ☐ extreme ⓐ 극단적인
321 ☐ view ⓝ 시각
322 ☐ disastrous ⓐ 참담한
323 ☐ intellectual ⓐ 지적인
324 ☐ isolation ⓝ 고립
325 ☐ distortion ⓝ 왜곡

36
326 ☐ roughly ⓐⓓ 약, 대략
327 ☐ brick-and-mortar ⓐ 소매(小賣)의, 오프라인 거래의
328 ☐ shift ⓥ 바꾸다

329 ☐ give way to ～로 바뀌다
330 ☐ electronic commerce 전자 상거래
331 ☐ perception ⓝ 인식
332 ☐ experience ⓝ 경험
333 ☐ before long 머지않아, 오래지 않아
334 ☐ e-commerce ⓝ 전자 상거래
335 ☐ naturally ⓐⓓ 자연스럽게
336 ☐ expand ⓥ 확장되다
337 ☐ additional ⓐ 추가의
338 ☐ snowball ⓥ 눈덩이처럼 커지다
339 ☐ enormous ⓐ 거대한
340 ☐ toilet paper (화장실용) 화장지
341 ☐ obvious ⓐ 분명한
342 ☐ title ⓝ 서적, 출판물
343 ☐ shelf ⓝ 책꽂이
344 ☐ offer ⓥ 제공하다
345 ☐ aggressive ⓐ 공격적인, (대단히) 적극적인
346 ☐ operating cost 운영비
347 ☐ combination ⓝ 결합
348 ☐ steady ⓐ 꾸준한

37
349 ☐ literary ⓐ 문학의
350 ☐ literary works 문학 작품
351 ☐ nature ⓝ 본질, 본성
352 ☐ suggest ⓥ 암시하다
353 ☐ imply ⓥ 함축하다
354 ☐ boldly ⓐⓓ 뚜렷하게, 대담하게
355 ☐ implication ⓝ 함축, 암시
356 ☐ analytical ⓐ 분석적인
357 ☐ consider ⓥ 고려하다
358 ☐ gain ⓥ 얻다
359 ☐ proportion ⓝ 비율
360 ☐ interpret ⓥ 해석하다
361 ☐ generalization ⓝ 일반화
362 ☐ direct ⓐ 직접적인
363 ☐ statement ⓝ 진술

38
364 ☐ contaminate ⓥ 오염시키다
365 ☐ substance ⓝ 물질
366 ☐ contain ⓥ ～이 들어있다
367 ☐ ingredient ⓝ 성분
368 ☐ nutrition ⓝ 영양
369 ☐ absorb ⓥ 흡수하다
370 ☐ whole food 자연식품
371 ☐ instead ⓐⓓ 대신에
372 ☐ supplement ⓝ 보충제
373 ☐ pill ⓝ 알약
374 ☐ powder ⓝ 분말, 가루
375 ☐ obtain ⓥ 얻다
376 ☐ fill the gap 부족한 부분을 채우다, 간격을 메우다
377 ☐ prevent ⓥ 막다, 예방하다
378 ☐ improve ⓥ 개선하다
379 ☐ artificial ⓐ 인위적인
380 ☐ completely ⓐⓓ 완전히
381 ☐ recent ⓐ 최근의
382 ☐ investigative ⓐ 조사의
383 ☐ heavy metal 중금속
384 ☐ protein ⓝ 단백질

385 ☐ regulation ⓝ 규제
386 ☐ gamble ⓝ 도박
387 ☐ costly ⓐ 대가가 큰, 많은 돈이 드는

39
388 ☐ brief ⓐ 짧은
389 ☐ pendulum ⓝ (시계의) 추
390 ☐ kinetic energy 운동 에너지
391 ☐ potential energy 위치 에너지
392 ☐ conserve ⓥ 보존하다
393 ☐ swing back and forth 앞뒤로 흔들리다
394 ☐ sweep out 쓸어내리다
395 ☐ arc ⓝ 호(弧)

40
396 ☐ uncertainty ⓝ 불확실성
397 ☐ realm ⓝ 영역
398 ☐ uncomfortable ⓐ 불편한
399 ☐ informed ⓐ 정보에 입각한
400 ☐ certainty ⓝ 확실성
401 ☐ demand ⓝ 요구
402 ☐ fantastically ⓐⓓ 환상적으로, 엄청나게
403 ☐ complex ⓐ 복잡한
404 ☐ black-or-white ⓐ 흑백논리의, 양자택일의
405 ☐ term ⓝ 말, 용어
406 ☐ tend ⓥ 경향이 있다
407 ☐ oversimplify ⓥ 지나치게 단순화하다
408 ☐ as opposed to ～와는 반대로, ～이 아니라
409 ☐ accurate ⓐ 정확한
410 ☐ definitive ⓐ 확정적인
411 ☐ continuum ⓝ 연속체
412 ☐ with regard to ～에 관하여

41~42
413 ☐ genetic ⓐ 유전적인
414 ☐ genetic determinism 유전자 결정론
415 ☐ gene ⓝ 유전자
416 ☐ diagnosis ⓝ 진단, 진찰
417 ☐ subsequent ⓐ 차후의, 그다음의
418 ☐ inherit ⓥ 물려받다
419 ☐ environment ⓝ 환경
420 ☐ predetermined ⓐ 미리 결정된
421 ☐ interaction ⓝ 상호 작용
422 ☐ racially ⓐⓓ 인종적으로
423 ☐ oppressive ⓐ 억압적인
424 ☐ simplistic ⓐ 단순한
425 ☐ merely ⓐⓓ 단지
426 ☐ expression ⓝ 표현
427 ☐ remarkable ⓐ 놀랄 만한
428 ☐ narrative ⓝ 이야기
429 ☐ take ownership of ～을 갖다, 소유하다

43~45
430 ☐ bunch ⓝ (포도 등의) 송이
431 ☐ place ⓥ 놓다, 두다
432 ☐ beside ⓟⓡⓔⓟ 옆에
433 ☐ beam with ～으로 환히 웃다
434 ☐ politely ⓐⓓ 정중하게
435 ☐ distaste ⓝ 불쾌감
436 ☐ thoughtfulness ⓝ 사려 깊음
437 ☐ expectantly ⓐⓓ 기대하여

● 채점 : 맞은 개수 _____ / 80

TEST A-B 각 단어의 뜻을 [A] 영어는 우리말로, [B] 우리말은 영어로 쓰시오.

A	English	Korean	B	Korean	English
01	drill		01	초기의	
02	anticipate		02	추정하다	
03	profession		03	상황	
04	ready-made		04	선구자	
05	extinction		05	표시, 징후	
06	daydream		06	면밀하게, 밀접하게	
07	enormous		07	전달하다	
08	uncertainty		08	기본적으로, 근본적으로	
09	fascinating		09	혁신	
10	bottom line		10	향상시키다	
11	empower		11	공격적인, (대단히) 적극적인	
12	annual		12	감소	
13	analytical		13	영감을 주다	
14	interval		14	본질, 본성	
15	accessible		15	각각	
16	excessive		16	부분, 분야	
17	essentially		17	보충하다	
18	regulation		18	물질	
19	sweep out		19	놀랄 만한	
20	systematic		20	필수적인, 본질적인	

▶ A-D 정답 : 해설편 168쪽

TEST C-D 각 단어의 뜻을 골라 기호를 쓰시오.

C	English		Korean	D	Korean		English
01	disastrous	( )	ⓐ 이용하다	01	(공식적으로) 주다	( )	ⓐ constantly
02	intentionally	( )	ⓑ 참담한	02	목표, 목적	( )	ⓑ worthless
03	thrilled	( )	ⓒ 해석하다	03	기대하여	( )	ⓒ characteristic
04	diagnosis	( )	ⓓ 불쾌감	04	운영비	( )	ⓓ crude oil
05	hypothesis	( )	ⓔ 흑백논리의, 양자택일의	05	흡수, 활용	( )	ⓔ fade
06	humble	( )	ⓕ 완전히, 절대적으로	06	드리우다, 던지다	( )	ⓕ uptake
07	underlie	( )	ⓖ 명백한	07	통계	( )	ⓖ expectantly
08	appropriate	( )	ⓗ 일반화	08	뚜렷하게, 대담하게	( )	ⓗ acknowledge
09	absolutely	( )	ⓘ 겸손한	09	보장하다	( )	ⓘ grant
10	prescribe	( )	ⓙ 의도적으로	10	지속적으로, 끊임없이	( )	ⓙ invisibility
11	distaste	( )	ⓚ 은유	11	특징, 특성	( )	ⓚ aim
12	utilize	( )	ⓛ 축적	12	농업의	( )	ⓛ ensure
13	evident	( )	ⓜ ~의 기반을 이루다	13	유전적인	( )	ⓜ operating cost
14	diminish	( )	ⓝ 아주 신이 난, 황홀한	14	인정하다	( )	ⓝ statistics
15	interpret	( )	ⓞ 적절한	15	보이지 않음	( )	ⓞ crisis
16	black-or-white	( )	ⓟ 단순한	16	원유	( )	ⓟ telegraph
17	metaphor	( )	ⓠ 진단, 진찰	17	무가치한	( )	ⓠ agricultural
18	simplistic	( )	ⓡ 가설	18	위기	( )	ⓡ boldly
19	generalization	( )	ⓢ 감소하다, 줄어들다	19	흐려지다, (빛이) 바래다	( )	ⓢ genetic
20	accumulation	( )	ⓣ 규정하다, 처방하다	20	전보	( )	ⓣ cast

1번부터 17번까지는 듣고 답하는 문제입니다. 1번부터 15번까지는 한 번만 들려주고, 16번부터 17번까지는 두 번 들려줍니다. 방송을 잘 듣고 답을 하시기 바랍니다.

MP3

1. 다음을 듣고, 남자가 하는 말의 목적으로 가장 적절한 것을 고르시오.

① 파손된 사물함 신고 절차를 안내하려고
② 사물함에 이름표를 부착할 것을 독려하려고
③ 사물함을 반드시 잠그고 다녀야 함을 강조하려고
④ 사물함 교체를 위해 사물함을 비울 것을 당부하려고
⑤ 사물함 사용에 대한 학생 설문 조사 참여를 요청하려고

2. 대화를 듣고, 여자의 의견으로 가장 적절한 것을 고르시오.

① 음식물을 들고 서점에 들어가면 안 된다.
② 서점에 의자를 비치하면 매출에 도움이 된다.
③ 서점은 책 외에 다양한 품목을 판매해야 한다.
④ 서점은 고객들에게 추천 도서 목록을 제공해야 한다.
⑤ 온라인 서점에서 책을 구매하는 것이 더 경제적이다.

3. 대화를 듣고, 두 사람의 관계를 가장 잘 나타낸 것을 고르시오.

① 미용사 – 고객   ② 화방 점원 – 화가
③ 미술관장 – 방문객   ④ 패션 디자이너 – 모델
⑤ 모자 가게 주인 – 손님

4. 대화를 듣고, 그림에서 대화의 내용과 일치하지 <u>않는</u> 것을 고르시오

5. 대화를 듣고, 남자가 여자를 위해 할 일로 가장 적절한 것을 고르시오

① 동아리 안내 책자 가져다주기
② 동아리 모임 장소 예약하기
③ 동아리 방에 함께 가기
④ 동아리 모임 일정 짜기
⑤ 동아리 가입 신청서 대신 제출하기

6. 대화를 듣고, 두 사람이 지불할 금액을 고르시오. [3점]

① $75   ② $80   ③ $85   ④ $105   ⑤ $110

7. 대화를 듣고, 여자가 뉴욕 여행을 취소한 이유를 고르시오.

① 부모님이 편찮으셔서
② 시골로 이사를 가게 되어서
③ 부모님 댁에서 휴가를 보내고 싶어서
④ 새로운 프로젝트를 맡게 되어서
⑤ 휴가 기간이 짧아져서

8. 대화를 듣고, Fun Town Amusement Park에 관해 언급되지 <u>않은</u> 것을 고르시오.

① 위치   ② 도착 소요 시간
③ 개장 시간   ④ 입장료
⑤ 특별 프로그램

9. 2019 Riverside High School Musical에 관한 다음 내용을 듣고, 일치하지 <u>않는</u> 것을 고르시오.

① 공연작은 *Shrek*이다.
② 공연을 위한 오디션은 작년 12월에 있었다.
③ 공연은 사흘간 진행된다.
④ 입장권은 1인당 8달러이다.
⑤ 입장권은 연극 동아리실에서 구입할 수 있다.

10. 다음 표를 보면서 대화를 듣고, 남자가 구매할 토스터를 고르시오.

Bestselling Toasters in K-Store

	Model	Number of Slices	Price	Color
①	A	1	$25	white
②	B	1	$30	silver
③	C	2	$40	white
④	D	4	$45	silver
⑤	E	4	$55	silver

11. 대화를 듣고, 여자의 마지막 말에 대한 남자의 응답으로 가장 적절한 것을 고르시오.

① Sorry, but I'd rather go to Spain by myself.
② No, I'm taking a class in the community center.
③ Yes, you need to eat healthy food for your brain.
④ Yeah, you don't have to worry about your brain.
⑤ Well, I'm not interested in learning Spanish.

12. 대화를 듣고, 남자의 마지막 말에 대한 여자의 응답으로 가장 적절한 것을 고르시오.

① But I haven't finished writing it.
② Yes, I can help you study history.
③ Okay, let's go to the teacher's office.
④ Well, take your time to write the essay.
⑤ Sorry, but I didn't bring my essay today.

13. 대화를 듣고, 남자의 마지막 말에 대한 여자의 응답으로 가장 적절한 것을 고르시오.

Woman: _____

① You're right. That's why I chose this book.
② That makes sense. I'll switch to an easier book.
③ Okay. I'll choose one from the bestseller list next time.
④ Don't worry. It's not too difficult for me to read.
⑤ Yeah. I'll join the book club to read more books.

14. 대화를 듣고, 여자의 마지막 말에 대한 남자의 응답으로 가장 적절한 것을 고르시오. [3점]

Man: _____

① Well, I'm not sure if your son likes it.
② No, it's dangerous to leave kids home alone.
③ Of course, they are not safe even for adults.
④ That's why it's difficult to find drones for kids.
⑤ Yes, as long as you get a right drone for his age.

15. 다음 상황 설명을 듣고, Lily가 John에게 할 말로 가장 적절한 것을 고르시오. [3점]

Lily: _____

① Why don't you run for class president?
② Please give me a hand putting up the poster.
③ How about changing your slogan in the poster?
④ Will you help me make a slogan for the election?
⑤ Tell me how to keep good relationships with classmates.

[16 ~ 17] 다음을 듣고, 물음에 답하시오.

16. 여자가 하는 말의 주제로 가장 적절한 것은?

① proverbs that have animals in them
② different proverbs in various cultures
③ why proverbs are difficult to understand
④ importance of studying animals' behavior
⑤ advantages of teaching values through proverbs

17. 언급된 동물이 <u>아닌</u> 것은?

① birds　② mice　③ cows　④ chickens　⑤ dogs

이제 듣기 문제가 끝났습니다. 18번부터는 문제지의 지시에 따라 답을 하시기 바랍니다.

18. 다음 글의 목적으로 가장 적절한 것은?

Dear Mrs. Coling,

My name is Susan Harris and I am writing on behalf of the students at Lockwood High School. Many students at the school have been working on a project about the youth unemployment problem in Lockwood. You are invited to attend a special presentation that will be held at our school auditorium on April 16th. At the presentation, students will propose a variety of ideas for developing employment opportunities for the youth within the community. As one of the famous figures in the community, we would be honored by your attendance. We look forward to seeing you there.

Sincerely,

Susan Harris

① 학생들이 준비한 발표회 참석을 부탁하려고
② 학생들을 위한 특별 강연을 해 준 것에 감사하려고
③ 청년 실업 문제의 해결 방안에 관한 강연을 의뢰하려고
④ 학생들의 발표회에 대한 재정적 지원을 요청하려고
⑤ 학생들의 프로젝트 심사 결과를 알리려고

19. 다음 글에 드러난 'I'의 심경 변화로 가장 적절한 것은?

On December 6th, I arrived at University Hospital in Cleveland at 10:00 a.m. I went through the process of admissions. I grew anxious because the time for surgery was drawing closer. I was directed to the waiting area, where I remained until my name was called. I had a few hours of waiting time. I just kept praying. At some point in my ongoing prayer process, before my name was called, in the midst of the chaos, an unbelievable peace embraced me. All my fear disappeared! An unbelievable peace overrode my emotions. My physical body relaxed in the comfort provided, and I looked forward to getting the surgery over with and working hard at recovery.

① cheerful → sad
② worried → relieved
③ angry → ashamed
④ jealous → thankful
⑤ hopeful → disappointed

20. 다음 글에서 필자가 주장하는 바로 가장 적절한 것은?

It can be tough to settle down to study when there are so many distractions. Most young people like to combine a bit of homework with quite a lot of instant messaging, chatting on the phone, updating profiles on social-networking sites, and checking emails. While it may be true that you can multi-task and can focus on all these things at once, try to be honest with yourself. It is most likely that you will be able to work best if you concentrate on your studies but allow yourself regular breaks — every 30 minutes or so — to catch up on those other pastimes.

① 공부할 때는 공부에만 집중하라.
② 평소 주변 사람들과 자주 연락하라.
③ 피로감을 느끼지 않게 충분한 휴식을 취하라.
④ 자투리 시간을 이용하여 숙제를 하라.
⑤ 학습에 유익한 취미 활동을 하라.

21. 밑줄 친 <u>information blinded</u>가 다음 글에서 의미하는 바로 가장 적절한 것은? [3점]

Technology has doubtful advantages. We must balance too much information versus using only the right information and keeping the decision-making process simple. The Internet has made so much free information available on any issue that we think we have to consider all of it in order to make a decision. So we keep searching for answers on the Internet. This makes us <u>information blinded</u>, like deer in headlights, when trying to make personal, business, or other decisions. To be successful in anything today, we have to keep in mind that in the land of the blind, a one-eyed person can accomplish the seemingly impossible. The one-eyed person understands the power of keeping any analysis simple and will be the decision maker when he uses his one eye of intuition.

* intuition: 직관

① unwilling to accept others' ideas
② unable to access free information
③ unable to make decisions due to too much information
④ indifferent to the lack of available information
⑤ willing to take risks in decision-making

22. 다음 글의 요지로 가장 적절한 것은?

Recent studies show some interesting findings about habit formation. In these studies, students who successfully acquired one positive habit reported less stress; less impulsive spending; better dietary habits; decreased caffeine consumption; fewer hours spent watching TV; and even fewer dirty dishes. Keep working on one habit long enough, and not only does it become easier, but so do other things as well. It's why those with the right habits seem to do better than others. They're doing the most important thing regularly and, as a result, everything else is easier.

① 참을성이 많을수록 성공할 가능성이 커진다.
② 한 번 들인 나쁜 습관은 쉽게 고쳐지지 않는다.
③ 나이가 들어갈수록 좋은 습관을 형성하기 힘들다.
④ 무리한 목표를 세우면 달성하지 못할 가능성이 크다.
⑤ 하나의 좋은 습관 형성은 생활 전반에 긍정적 효과가 있다.

23. 다음 글의 주제로 가장 적절한 것은?

While some sand is formed in oceans from things like shells and rocks, most sand is made up of tiny bits of rock that came all the way from the mountains! But that trip can take thousands of years. Glaciers, wind, and flowing water help move the rocky bits along, with the tiny travelers getting smaller and smaller as they go. If they're lucky, a river may give them a lift all the way to the coast. There, they can spend the rest of their years on the beach as sand.

① things to cause the travel of water
② factors to determine the size of sand
③ how most sand on the beach is formed
④ many uses of sand in various industries
⑤ why sand is disappearing from the beach

24. 다음 글의 제목으로 가장 적절한 것을 고르시오.

Studies from cities all over the world show the importance of life and activity as an urban attraction. People gather where things are happening and seek the presence of other people. Faced with the choice of walking down an empty or a lively street, most people would choose the street with life and activity. The walk will be more interesting and feel safer. Events where we can watch people perform or play music attract many people to stay and watch. Studies of benches and chairs in city space show that the seats with the best view of city life are used far more frequently than those that do not offer a view of other people.

① The City's Greatest Attraction: People
② Leave the City, Live in the Country
③ Make More Parks in the City
④ Feeling Lonely in the Crowded Streets
⑤ Ancient Cities Full of Tourist Attractions

25. 다음 도표의 내용과 일치하지 <u>않는</u> 것은?

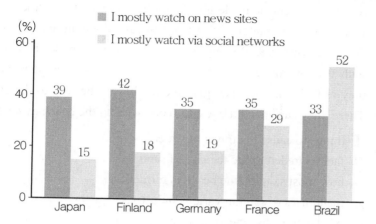

News Video Consumption: on News Sites vs. via Social Networks

The above graph shows how people in five countries consume news videos: on news sites versus via social networks. ① Consuming news videos on news sites is more popular than via social networks in four countries. ② As for people who mostly watch news videos on news sites, Finland shows the highest percentage among the five countries. ③ The percentage of people who mostly watch news videos on news sites in France is higher than that in Germany. ④ As for people who mostly watch news videos via social networks, Japan shows the lowest percentage among the five countries. ⑤ Brazil shows the highest percentage of people who mostly watch news videos via social networks among the five countries.

26. chuckwalla에 관한 다음 글의 내용과 일치하지 <u>않는</u> 것은?

　　Chuckwallas are fat lizards, usually 20-25 cm long, though they may grow up to 45 cm. They weigh about 1.5 kg when mature. Most chuckwallas are mainly brown or black. Just after the annual molt, the skin is shiny. Lines of dark brown run along the back and continue down the tail. As the males grow older, these brown lines disappear and the body color becomes lighter; the tail becomes almost white. It is not easy to distinguish between male and female chuckwallas, because young males look like females and the largest females resemble males.

* molt: 탈피

① 길이가 45cm까지 자랄 수 있다.
② 대부분 갈색이거나 검은색이다.
③ 등을 따라 꼬리까지 짙은 갈색 선들이 나 있다.
④ 수컷의 몸통 색깔은 나이가 들수록 짙어진다.
⑤ 어린 수컷의 생김새는 암컷과 비슷하다.

27. L-19 Smart Watch 사용에 관한 다음 안내문의 내용과 일치하는 것은?

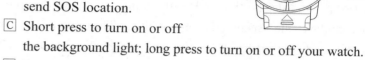

L-19 Smart Watch
User Guide

KEY FUNCTIONS

A　Short press to confirm; long press to enter the sports mode.
B　Short press to return to the 'home' menu; long press to send SOS location.
C　Short press to turn on or off the background light; long press to turn on or off your watch.
D　Press to go up. (In time, date or other settings, press the key to increase the value.)
E　Press to go down. (In time, date or other settings, press the key to decrease the value.)

CAUTION
Make sure the battery level of your watch has at least two bars, in order to avoid an upgrading error.

* confirm: 설정값을 확정하다

① A를 짧게 누르면 스포츠 모드로 들어간다.
② B를 길게 누르면 '홈' 메뉴로 돌아간다.
③ C를 길게 누르면 배경 화면의 불빛이 켜지거나 꺼진다.
④ D를 누르면 설정값이 내려간다.
⑤ 업그레이드 오류를 피하려면 배터리 잔량 표시가 최소 두 칸은 되어야 한다.

28. 2017 Happy Voice Choir Audition에 관한 다음 안내문의 내용과 일치하지 <u>않는</u> 것은?

2017 Happy Voice Choir Audition

Do you love to sing? Happy Voice, one of the most famous school clubs, is holding an audition for you. Come and join us for some very exciting performances!

- Who: Any freshman
- When: Friday, March 24, 3 p.m.
- Where: Auditorium

All applicants should sing two songs:
- 1st song: *Oh Happy Day!*
- 2nd song: You choose your own.

To enter the audition, please email us at hvaudition@qmail.com.

For more information, visit the school website.

① 학교 동아리가 개최한다.
② 신입생이면 누구나 참가할 수 있다.
③ 3월 24일에 강당에서 열린다.
④ 지원자는 자신이 선택한 두 곡을 불러야 한다.
⑤ 참가하려면 이메일을 보내야 한다.

29. 다음 글의 밑줄 친 부분 중, 어법상 틀린 것은?

Bad lighting can increase stress on your eyes, as can light that is too bright, or light that shines ① <u>directly</u> into your eyes. Fluorescent lighting can also be ② <u>tiring</u>. What you may not appreciate is that the quality of light may also be important. Most people are happiest in bright sunshine — this may cause a release of chemicals in the body ③ <u>that</u> bring a feeling of emotional well-being. Artificial light, which typically contains only a few wavelengths of light, ④ <u>do</u> not seem to have the same effect on mood that sunlight has. Try experimenting with working by a window or ⑤ <u>using</u> full spectrum bulbs in your desk lamp. You will probably find that this improves the quality of your working environment.

* fluorescent lighting: 형광등

30. 다음 글의 밑줄 친 부분 중, 문맥상 낱말의 쓰임이 적절하지 않은 것은? [3점]

Painters have in principle an infinite range of colours at their disposal, especially in modern times with the chromatic ① <u>explosion</u> of synthetic chemistry. And yet painters don't use all the colours at once, and indeed many have used a remarkably ② <u>restrictive</u> selection. Mondrian limited himself mostly to the three primaries red, yellow and blue to fill his black-ruled grids, and Kasimir Malevich worked with similar self-imposed restrictions. For Yves Klein, one colour was ③ <u>enough</u>; Franz Kline's art was typically black on white. There was nothing ④ <u>new</u> in this: the Greeks and Romans tended to use just red, yellow, black and white. Why? It's impossible to generalize, but both in antiquity and modernity it seems likely that the ⑤ <u>expanded</u> palette aided clarity and comprehensibility, and helped to focus attention on the components that mattered: shape and form.

* chromatic: 유채색의 ** grid: 격자무늬

[31~34] 다음 빈칸에 들어갈 말로 가장 적절한 것을 고르시오.

31. In small towns the same workman makes chairs and doors and tables, and often the same person builds houses. And it is, of course, impossible for a man of many trades to be skilled in all of them. In large cities, on the other hand, because many people make demands on each trade, one trade alone — very often even less than a whole trade — is enough to support a man. For instance, one man makes shoes for men, and another for women. And there are places even where one man earns a living by only stitching shoes, another by cutting them out, and another by sewing the uppers together. Such skilled workers may have used simple tools, but their _____ did result in more efficient and productive work. [3점]

* trade: 직종

① specialization ② criticism
③ competition ④ diligence
⑤ imagination

32. All mammals need to leave their parents and set up on their own at some point. But human adults generally provide a comfortable existence — enough food arrives on the table, money is given at regular intervals, the bills get paid and the electricity for the TV doesn't usually run out. If teenagers didn't build up a fairly major disrespect for and conflict with their parents or carers, they'd never want to leave. In fact, _____ is probably a necessary part of growing up. Later, when you live independently, away from them, you can start to love them again because you won't need to be fighting to get away from them. And you can come back sometimes for a home-cooked meal. [3점]

① developing financial management skills
② learning from other people's experiences
③ figuring out your strengths and interests
④ managing relationship problems with your peers
⑤ falling out of love with the adults who look after you

01회

33. What do advertising and map-making have in common? Without doubt the best answer is their shared need to communicate a limited version of the truth. An advertisement must create an image that's appealing and a map must present an image that's clear, but neither can meet its goal by _____. Ads will cover up or play down negative aspects of the company or service they advertise. In this way, they can promote a favorable comparison with similar products or differentiate a product from its competitors. Likewise, the map must remove details that would be confusing. [3점]

① reducing the amount of information
② telling or showing everything
③ listening to people's voices
④ relying on visual images only
⑤ making itself available to everyone

34. It is difficult to know how to determine whether one culture is better than another. What is the cultural rank order of rock, jazz, and classical music? When it comes to public opinion polls about whether cultural changes are for the better or the worse, looking forward would lead to one answer and looking backward would lead to a very different answer. Our children would be horrified if they were told they had to go back to the culture of their grandparents. Our parents would be horrified if they were told they had to participate in the culture of their grandchildren. Humans tend to _____. After a certain age, anxieties arise when sudden cultural changes are coming. Our culture is part of who we are and where we stand, and we don't like to think that who we are and where we stand are short-lived. [3점]

① seek cooperation between generations
② be forgetful of what they experienced
③ adjust quickly to the new environment
④ make efforts to remember what their ancestors did
⑤ like what they have grown up in and gotten used to

35. 다음 글에서 전체 흐름과 관계 <u>없는</u> 문장은?

Today car sharing movements have appeared all over the world. In many cities, car sharing has made a strong impact on how city residents travel. ① Even in strong car-ownership cultures such as North America, car sharing has gained popularity. ② In the U.S. and Canada, membership in car sharing now exceeds one in five adults in many urban areas. ③ Strong influence on traffic jams and pollution can be felt from Toronto to New York, as each shared vehicle replaces around 10 personal cars. ④ The best thing about driverless cars is that people won't need a license to operate them. ⑤ City governments with downtown areas struggling with traffic jams and lack of parking lots are driving the growing popularity of car sharing.

[36~37] 주어진 글 다음에 이어질 글의 순서로 가장 적절한 것을 고르시오.

36.

> Collaboration is the basis for most of the foundational arts and sciences.

(A) For example, his sketches of human anatomy were a collaboration with Marcantonio della Torre, an anatomist from the University of Pavia. Their collaboration is important because it marries the artist with the scientist.

(B) It is often believed that Shakespeare, like most playwrights of his period, did not always write alone, and many of his plays are considered collaborative or were rewritten after their original composition. Leonardo Da Vinci made his sketches individually, but he collaborated with other people to add the finer details.

(C) Similarly, Marie Curie's husband stopped his original research and joined Marie in hers. They went on to collaboratively discover radium, which overturned old ideas in physics and chemistry.

* anatomy: 해부학적 구조

① (A) − (C) − (B)　　② (B) − (A) − (C)
③ (B) − (C) − (A)　　④ (C) − (A) − (B)
⑤ (C) − (B) − (A)

37.

> Andrew Carnegie, the great early-twentieth-century businessman, once heard his sister complain about her two sons.

(A) Within days he received warm grateful letters from both boys, who noted at the letters' end that he had unfortunately forgotten to include the check. If the check had been enclosed, would they have responded so quickly?

(B) They were away at college and rarely responded to her letters. Carnegie told her that if he wrote them he would get an immediate response.

(C) He sent off two warm letters to the boys, and told them that he was happy to send each of them a check for a hundred dollars (a large sum in those days). Then he mailed the letters, but didn't enclose the checks.

* enclose: 동봉하다

① (A) − (C) − (B)　　② (B) − (A) − (C)
③ (B) − (C) − (A)　　④ (C) − (A) − (B)
⑤ (C) − (B) − (A)

[38 ~ 39] 글의 흐름으로 보아, 주어진 문장이 들어가기에 가장 적절한 곳을 고르시오.

38.

> When you hit puberty, however, sometimes these forever-friendships go through growing pains.

Childhood friends — friends you've known forever — are really special. (①) They know everything about you, and you've shared lots of firsts. (②) You find that you have less in common than you used to. (③) Maybe you're into rap and she's into pop, or you go to different schools and have different groups of friends. (④) Change can be scary, but remember: Friends, even best friends, don't have to be exactly alike. (⑤) Having friends with other interests keeps life interesting — just think of what you can learn from each other.

* puberty: 사춘기

39.

> However, if you tried to copy the original rather than your imaginary drawing, you might find your drawing now was a little better.

Imagine in your mind one of your favorite paintings, drawings, cartoon characters or something equally complex. (①) Now, with that picture in your mind, try to draw what your mind sees. (②) Unless you are unusually gifted, your drawing will look completely different from what you are seeing with your mind's eye. (③) Furthermore, if you copied the picture many times, you would find that each time your drawing would get a little better, a little more accurate. (④) Practice makes perfect. (⑤) This is because you are developing the skills of coordinating what your mind perceives with the movement of your body parts. [3점]

* coordinate ~ with ...: ~와 …을 조화시키다

40. 다음 글의 내용을 한 문장으로 요약하고자 한다. 빈칸 (A), (B)에 들어갈 말로 가장 적절한 것은?

> A large American hardware manufacturer was invited to introduce its products to a distributor with good reputation in Germany. Wanting to make the best possible impression, the American company sent its most promising young executive, Fred Wagner, who spoke fluent German. When Fred first met his German hosts, he shook hands firmly, greeted everyone in German, and even remembered to bow the head slightly as is the German custom. Fred, a very effective public speaker, began his presentation with a few humorous jokes to set a relaxed atmosphere. However, he felt that his presentation was not very well received by the German executives. Even though Fred thought he had done his cultural homework, he made one particular error. Fred did not win any points by telling a few jokes. It was viewed as too informal and unprofessional in a German business setting.
>
> * distributor: 배급 업체

↓

> This story shows that using ___(A)___ in a business setting can be considered ___(B)___ in Germany.

	(A)		(B)
①	humor	······	essential
②	humor	······	inappropriate
③	gestures	······	essential
④	gestures	······	inappropriate
⑤	first names	······	useful

[41~42] 다음 글을 읽고, 물음에 답하시오.

Researchers brought two groups of 11-year-old boys to a summer camp at Robbers Cave State Park in Oklahoma. The boys were strangers to one another and upon arrival at the camp, were randomly separated into two groups. The groups were kept apart for about a week. They swam, camped, and hiked. Each group chose a name for itself, and the boys printed their group's name on their caps and T-shirts. Then the two groups met. A series of athletic competitions were set up between them. Soon, each group considered the other an (a) enemy. Each group came to look down on the other. The boys started food fights and stole various items from members of the other group. Thus, under competitive conditions, the boys quickly (b) drew sharp group boundaries.

The researchers next stopped the athletic competitions and created several apparent emergencies whose solution (c) required cooperation between the two groups. One such emergency involved a leak in the pipe supplying water to the camp. The researchers assigned the boys to teams made up of members of both groups. Their job was to look into the pipe and fix the leak. After engaging in several such (d) cooperative activities, the boys started playing together without fighting. Once cooperation replaced competition and the groups (e) started to look down on each other, group boundaries melted away as quickly as they had formed.

* apparent: ~인 것으로 보이는

41. 윗글의 제목으로 가장 적절한 것은?

① How Are Athletic Competitions Helpful for Teens?
② Preparation: The Key to Preventing Emergencies
③ What Makes Group Boundaries Disappear?
④ Respect Individual Differences in Teams
⑤ Free Riders: Headaches in Teams

42. 밑줄 친 (a)~(e) 중에서 문맥상 낱말의 쓰임이 적절하지 않은 것은?

① (a)　　② (b)　　③ (c)　　④ (d)　　⑤ (e)

[43~45] 다음 글을 읽고, 물음에 답하시오.

(A)

Once in a village lived a rich man. He had many slaves and servants for work. The rich man was very unkind and cruel to them. One day one of the slaves made a mistake while cooking food. (a) He overcooked the food. When the rich man saw the food, he became angry and punished the slave. He kept the slave in a small room and locked it from outside.

(B)

After a few days the lion recovered. The slave and the lion became very close friends. A few days went by but one day the slave was caught by one of the guards of the rich man. The guard took (b) him to the rich man, who decided to punish him severely. The rich man ordered guards to put him in the lion's cage.

(C)

Somehow the slave escaped from that room and ran away. (c) He went to a forest. There he saw a lion. Instead of becoming afraid of the lion and running away, he went close to the lion. He saw the lion was injured and one of his legs was bleeding. The slave searched for herbs to cure the lion's wound and took care of the lion.

(D)

The whole village got the news about it and came to see. As soon as the slave was locked in the lion's cage, the lion came near (d) him and started licking his hand and hugged him. It was the same lion that the slave had helped in the forest. Seeing this, everyone was surprised. The rich man thought that the slave was such a great person that the lion didn't kill him. (e) He freed the slave, made him his friend and started to treat all his servants and slaves better.

43. 주어진 글 (A)에 이어질 내용을 순서에 맞게 배열한 것으로 가장 적절한 것은?

① (B) - (D) - (C)　　② (C) - (B) - (D)
③ (C) - (D) - (B)　　④ (D) - (B) - (C)
⑤ (D) - (C) - (B)

44. 밑줄 친 (a)~(e) 중에서 가리키는 대상이 나머지 넷과 다른 것은?

① (a)　　② (b)　　③ (c)　　④ (d)　　⑤ (e)

45. 윗글의 내용으로 적절하지 않은 것은?

① 부자는 노예가 요리한 음식을 보고 화가 났다.
② 노예는 부자의 경비병에게 잡혔다.
③ 노예는 사자를 보자 재빨리 달아났다.
④ 사자의 다리에서 피가 나고 있었다.
⑤ 노예는 사자 우리에 갇혔다.

* 확인 사항
◦ 답안지의 해당란에 필요한 내용을 정확히 기입(표기)했는지 확인하시오.

※ QR 코드를 스캔하시면 듣기 방송이 나옵니다. 듣기 방송을 들으며 다음 빈칸을 채우시오.
● 제한 시간 : 25분

01

다음을 듣고, 남자가 하는 말의 목적으로 가장 적절한 것을 고르시오.

M : Hello, students. This is your vice principal Mike Westwood. I have ✿ _____ _____ _____ today. As the student lockers are getting old, we've been receiving complaints from many of you. So we've decided to _____ _____ _____ over the weekend. We ask that you empty your lockers and leave them open by this Friday, March 22. Make sure to take all the items from your lockers and leave nothing behind. Any items that are not removed _____ _____ _____ _____. Thank you for your cooperation.

02

대화를 듣고, 여자의 의견으로 가장 적절한 것을 고르시오.

W : Paul, what did you do on the weekend?
M : I went to the new bookstore downtown. Have you been there?
W : Yes. They put lots of cozy chairs in the bookstore. I like that.
M : Actually, I wonder why they did that.
W : I think _____ _____ _____ _____ _____ _____.
M : Really? What if people just read books sitting on the chairs without buying them?
W : I heard that the longer people stay, _____ _____ _____ _____ _____.
M : That makes sense.
W : More chairs can ✿ _____ _____ _____ and the sales will go up.
M : You're right.

03

대화를 듣고, 두 사람의 관계를 가장 잘 나타낸 것을 고르시오.

M : Hello, Ally! Long time no see.
W : Hi, Robert. It's been a long time since I came to your store.
M : You _____ _____ _____ _____.
W : Yeah. Did I tell you that I had to prepare for an exhibition?
M : Oh, yeah. I remember. _____ _____ _____ _____?
W : It went well. It was finally over last week.

M : Good. So what kind of hat are you looking for today?
W : Actually I've changed my hair style, so I'm not sure ✿ _____ _____ _____ _____ _____.
M : Oh, you cut your hair short! Why don't you try this hat? It goes well with short hair.
W : Let me try. [Pause] I love it!
M : It looks great on you.
W : Thanks. I'll take it.

04

대화를 듣고, 그림에서 대화의 내용과 일치하지 않는 것을 고르시오.

W : Harry, have a look at this picture. It's from the flea market yesterday.
M : Wow! There's _____ _____ _____ in the air.
W : Yeah. Look at the man playing the guitar on the left. He's selling old guitars.
M : Interesting. _____ _____ _____ _____ _____ _____ Kevin. He's playing with a yoyo!
W : Right. He bought it there.
M : I see. Oh, you're ✿ _____ _____ _____ _____ _____. It's pretty.
W : Thanks. I got it there for just one dollar.
M : Great. You're eating ice cream. Did you buy it from the ice cream cart on the right?
W : Yes. It was delicious.
M : _____ _____ _____ you had a good time there.

05

대화를 듣고, 남자가 여자를 위해 할 일로 가장 적절한 것을 고르시오.

W : What are you doing, Sam?
M : ✿ _____ _____ _____ _____ _____ _____ to join the school movie club.
W : Really? I'm also interested in that club.
M : Let's join together then.
W : I'd love to, but I already belong to the science club.
M : _____ _____ _____ _____.
W : You're right. I'll have to check the movie club's meeting schedule first, though.
M : Then I'll pick up the movie club's brochure for you from the club room later.
W : That'll be great. Thanks.
M : No problem. I'll have to _____ _____ _____ _____ anyway.

06

대화를 듣고, 두 사람이 지불할 금액을 고르시오. [3점]

M : Honey, I think Paul needs new shoes.

W : You're right. His shoes are ✪ _____ _____ _____ _____ _____.

M : Let's buy a pair online. I know a good store. *[Clicking sound]* Have a look.

W : Oh, how about these shoes? They're originally $100 a pair, but they're 30% off now.

M : That's a good deal. _____ _____ _____ _____.

W : Oh, there are shoe bags, too. Why don't we buy one?

M : Okay. There are two kinds, a $10 bag and a $15 bag. Which one do you like?

W : The $10 one looks good enough.

M : Then let's take it. Is that all we need?

W : Yes. Oh, _____ _____ _____ that if you're a member of this online store, you'll get $5 off.

M : That's good. I'm a member. Let's buy them now.

W : Okay.

07

대화를 듣고, 여자가 뉴욕 여행을 취소한 이유를 고르시오.

M : Sabina, have you finished packing for your trip?

W : You mean the trip to New York?

M : Yes, you're leaving this weekend, right?

W : Oh, actually ✪ _____ _____ _____ _____.

M : Why? Do you have a new project coming up?

W : No. It's just because of my parents.

M : Is there something wrong with them?

W : Not really. I just want to spend my vacation at my parents' house.

M : Oh, right. They _____ _____ _____ _____ last year.

W : Yeah. I _____ _____ _____ _____ _____. It'll be great to stay with them.

M : Sure. They'll be happy to have you there.

08

대화를 듣고, Fun Town Amusement Park에 관해 언급되지 않은 것을 고르시오.

W : Honey, what are you looking at?

M : It's the website of the Fun Town Amusement Park. ✪ _____ _____ _____ _____ _____ there this weekend?

W : Good idea. It's located in Southern California, right?

M : Yes. _____ _____ _____ _____ _____ _____ to get there by car.

W : What time shall we leave here?

M : About 8 in the morning. The park is open from 9 a.m. to 8 p.m.

W : Okay. Are there any programs that our kids will find interesting?

M : Yeah, they offer many special programs _____ _____ _____.

W : Great. I'll go tell the kids now.

M : Go ahead. They'll be excited to hear that.

09

2019 Riverside High School Musical에 관한 다음 내용을 듣고, 일치하지 않는 것을 고르시오.

W : Hello, students. This is Janice Hawkins, your drama teacher. I'm happy to invite you and your family to the 2019 Riverside High School Musical. This year we're presenting *Shrek*, ✪ _____ _____ _____ _____ _____ _____. It's full of singing, dancing, romance and lots of fun. The auditions for the show were in December last year. The cast and crew have been rehearsing for months to _____ _____ _____. The musical will be held _____ _____ _____ _____ _____ _____ on March 15 and 16. Tickets are $8 per person. You can buy tickets in the drama club room. For more details, visit the school website. Thank you.

10

다음 표를 보면서 대화를 듣고, 남자가 구매할 토스터를 고르시오.

W : Hello. How may I help you, sir?

M : I'm looking for a toaster.

W : Okay. These five are our bestsellers. How about this one-slice toaster?

M : It's nice. But I want _____ _____ _____ _____ _____ _____ at a time.

W : Then you need to choose one ✪ _____ _____ _____ _____ _____. May I ask your price range?

M : Well, I don't want to spend more than fifty dollars.

W : You have two options left then. Which color do you like better?

M : _____ _____ _____ _____ _____.

W : Okay. Good choice.

11

대화를 듣고, 여자의 마지막 말에 대한 남자의 응답으로 가장 적절한 것을 고르시오.

W : Grandpa, is that a Spanish book you're reading?

M : Yes, I just started to learn Spanish. You know learning a foreign language is good for your brain.

W : Sounds great. Are you ✪ _____ _____ _____ _____?

12

대화를 듣고, 남자의 마지막 말에 대한 여자의 응답으로 가장 적절한 것을 고르시오.

M : Lydia, have you finished writing the history essay?

W : Yes, I have. I brought it today. How about you?

M : Me, too. ✪ _____ _____ _____ _____ _____ the essay now?

13

대화를 듣고, 남자의 마지막 말에 대한 여자의 응답으로 가장 적절한 것을 고르시오.

M : What are you reading, Lily?

W : It's a book for my English class, Dad. We have to read a book and _____ _____ _____ _____.

M : Do you like the book?

W : Well, I'm not sure. Frankly it's too difficult for me.

M : Why did you choose to read that book then?

W : _____ _____ _____ _____ _____ _____ and it looked interesting. It's very challenging, though.

M : Maybe you should try another book _____ _____ _____ _____.

W : I know what you mean, but ✪ _____ _____ _____ _____ from reading a difficult book?

M : Well, what's the use of reading it if you can't understand it?

14

대화를 듣고, 여자의 마지막 말에 대한 남자의 응답으로 가장 적절한 것을 고르시오. [3점]

M : _____ _____ _____ _____ _____, Monica?

W : Oh, I'm looking for a birthday gift for my son Willy.

M : I see. Did you find anything good?

W : Not yet. Do you have any ideas?

M : Hmm. Why don't you get him a drone?

W : A drone? I'm not sure if he'll like it.

M : Of course, he will. Boys are _____ _____ _____ these days.

W : Willy is just nine years old. Do you think he can fly a drone?

M : I guess so. There are ✪ _____ _____ _____ _____ _____ for kids.

W : Are you sure _____ _____ _____ _____ for a nine-year-old?

15

다음 상황 설명을 듣고, Lily가 John에게 할 말로 가장 적절한 것을 고르시오. [3점]

M : Lily is a freshman in high school. She is planning to run for class president this year. She really wants to _____ _____ _____. She thinks she needs a poster with a cool slogan to ✪ _____ _____ _____. But she _____ _____ _____ _____ _____ a good slogan. Lily knows her friend John is very creative and has a lot of great ideas. So she wants to ask him for help. In this situation, what would Lily most likely say to John?

16~17

다음을 듣고, 물음에 답하시오.

W : Hello, class. You must have heard of the proverb, 'Birds of a feather flock together.' We all know what this proverb means because ✪ _____ _____ _____. Like this, there are many proverbs _____ _____ _____ _____. Let's talk about them today. First one is, 'When the cat's away, the mice will play.' It is using the fun relationship between the two animals. We can easily guess the meaning of this proverb: the weaker do whatever they want when _____ _____ _____ _____ _____. The next one is, 'Don't count your chickens before they're hatched.' It's using a chicken's life cycle. From this proverb, we can learn the lesson that we should not _____ _____ _____. Now it's your turn to talk about a few proverbs like these. You may have already thought about one with dogs, like 'Every dog has its day.' Let's talk about some together.

▶ 정답 : 해설편 182쪽

18

001	on behalf of	~을 대신하여, ~을 대표하여
002	work on	~을 수행하다
003	unemployment	⑪ 실업
004	attend	⑭ 참석하다
005	hold	⑭ (행사 등을) 열다
006	auditorium	⑪ 강당
007	propose	⑭ 제안하다
008	a variety of	여러 가지의
009	opportunity	⑪ 기회
010	within	prep ~의 이내에
011	community	⑪ 주민, 지역 사회
012	figure	⑪ 인물
013	be honored	영광스럽다
014	attendance	⑪ 출석, 참석
015	look forward to	~을 기대하다, 고대하다

19

016	process	⑪ 절차
017	admission	⑪ 입원, 입장
018	anxious	ⓐ 불안해하는, 염려하는
019	surgery	⑪ 수술
020	direct	⑭ 길을 안내하다
021	remain	⑭ 계속[여전히] …이다
022	pray	⑭ 기도하다
023	ongoing	ⓐ 진행 중인
024	prayer	⑪ 기도 (내용)
025	midst	⑪ 중앙, 한가운데
026	chaos	⑪ 혼돈
027	peace	⑪ 평화
028	embrace	⑭ 감싸다, 포옹하다
029	override	⑭ (~의 위로) 퍼지다
030	comfort	⑪ 편안함
031	get ~ over with	~을 끝마치다
032	recovery	⑪ 회복
033	cheerful	ⓐ 발랄한, 쾌활한

20

034	tough	ⓐ 힘든, 어려운
035	settle down to	마음을 가라앉히고 ~하기 시작하다
036	distraction	⑪ 마음을 산만하게 하는 것, 집중력을 흩뜨리는 것
037	combine	⑭ 합치다
038	quite	ad 꽤, 상당히
039	instant	ⓐ 즉각적인, 즉시의
040	chat	⑭ 담소를 나누다, 수다를 떨다
041	multi-task	여러 가지 일을 동시에 처리하다
042	focus on	~에 주력하다, 집중하다
043	once	ad 한번에
044	honest	ⓐ 솔직한
045	concentrate on	~에 집중하다
046	allow	⑭ 허락하다
047	regular	ⓐ 규칙적인
048	break	⑪ (작업 중의) 휴식
049	catch up on	~을 처리하다, 따라잡다, 만회하다
050	pastime	⑪ 소일거리, 취미

21

051	doubtful	ⓐ 의문의 여지가 있는, 의심스러운
052	advantage	⑪ 이점, 장점

22(53)

053	balance	⑭ 균형을 이루다
054	information	⑪ 정보
055	versus	prep ~에 비해
056	decision-making	의사 결정
057	simple	ⓐ 단순한, 간소한
058	available	ⓐ 이용 가능한
059	blind	ⓐ 눈이 먼
060	deer	⑪ 사슴
061	personal	ⓐ 사적인, 개인적인
062	blind	⑪ 눈이 먼, 맹인인
063	accomplish	⑭ 달성하다, 성취하다
064	seemingly	ad 겉보기에
065	analysis	⑪ 분석
066	intuition	⑪ 직감, 직관
067	unwilling	ⓐ (~하기를) 꺼리는, 마지못해 하는
068	access	⑭ 접근하다, 이용하다
069	indifferent	ⓐ 무관심한
070	lack	⑪ 부족, 결여
071	take a risk	위험을 감수하다

22

072	recent	ⓐ 최근의
073	finding	⑪ 결과, 결론
074	habit	⑪ 버릇
075	formation	⑪ 형성
076	successfully	ad 성공적으로
077	acquire	⑭ 습득하다, 얻다
078	positive	ⓐ 긍정적인
079	report	⑭ 보고하다, 알리다
080	impulsive	ⓐ 충동적인
081	dietary	ⓐ 식사의
082	decrease	⑪ 감소, 하락
083	consumption	⑪ 소비[소모]
084	work on	~하려고 노력하다
085	regularly	ad 규칙적으로
086	as a result	결과적으로
087	else	ad 다른

23

088	sand	⑪ 모래
089	form	⑭ 형성하다, 만들다
090	shell	⑪ 조개껍데기
091	be made up of	~로 이루어지다
092	bit	⑪ (작은) 조각
093	glacier	⑪ 빙하
094	flow	⑭ 흐르다
095	rocky	ⓐ 바위로 된
096	give a lift	~을 실어다 주다, 태워주다, 들어 올리다
097	coast	⑪ 해안
098	rest	⑪ (어떤 것의) 나머지
099	factor	⑪ 요인, 인자
100	determine	⑭ 결정하다
101	various	ⓐ 여러 가지의, 다양한

24

102	activity	⑪ 활동
103	urban	ⓐ 도시의
104	attraction	⑪ 매력, 끌림, 명소
105	gather	⑭ 모이다
106	seek	⑭ 찾다, 구하다

24(107)

107	presence	⑪ 존재
108	empty	ⓐ 비어 있는, 빈
109	lively	ⓐ 활기찬
110	safer	ⓐ 안전한, 안심할 수 있는
111	perform	⑭ 공연하다, 연기하다, 수행하다
112	attract	⑭ 끌어들이다, 마음을 끌다
113	frequently	ad 자주
114	leave	⑭ 떠나다
115	crowded	ⓐ (사람들이) 붐비는
116	ancient	ⓐ 고대의

25

117	consume	⑭ 소비하다, 쓰다
118	via	prep ~을 통하여, ~을 경유하여
119	mostly	ad 주로, 대개
120	among	prep ~사이에, ~중에

26

121	lizard	⑪ 도마뱀
122	up to	~까지
123	weigh	⑭ 무게가 ~이다
124	mature	⑭ 다 자라다, 성숙한
125	mainly	ad 주로
126	annual	ⓐ 매년의, 1년의
127	molt	⑪ 탈피
128	shiny	ⓐ 빛나는, 반짝거리는
129	tail	⑪ 꼬리
130	male	⑪ 남자, 수컷
131	disappear	⑭ 사라지다
132	distinguish	⑭ 구별하다
133	female	⑪ 여성, 암컷
134	resemble	⑭ 닮다

27

135	function	⑪ 기능
136	press	⑭ 누르다
137	confirm	⑭ 확정하다
138	return	⑭ 돌아오다[가다]
139	location	⑪ 장소[곳/위치]
140	background light	배경화면 불빛
141	caution	⑪ 경고[주의](문)
142	at least	적어도[최소한]

28

143	choir	⑪ 합창단
144	freshman	⑪ 신입생
145	auditorium	⑪ 강당, 방청석, 청중석
146	applicant	⑪ 지원자
147	enter	⑭ 참가하다, 들어가다, 입장하다
148	information	⑪ 정보, 자료

29

149	lighting	⑪ 조명, 빛
150	increase	⑭ 증가하다, 인상되다
151	bright	ⓐ 밝은
152	directly	ad 곧장, 똑바로
153	fluorescent lighting	형광등
154	appreciate	⑭ 이해하다
155	release	⑪ 분비, 방출
156	chemical	⑪ 화학 물질
157	emotional	ⓐ 정서적인
158	artificial	ⓐ 인공의

29(159)

159	typically	ad 일반적으로
160	contain	⑭ …이 들어[함유되어] 있다
161	wavelength	⑪ 파장, 주파수
162	experiment	⑭ 실험하다 ⑪ 실험
163	bulb	⑪ 전구
164	probably	ad 아마
165	improve	⑭ 향상시키다, 개선하다
166	working environment	근로 환경

30

167	in principle	원칙적으로, 이론상으로
168	infinite	ⓐ 무한한
169	at one's disposal	~의 마음대로 이용할 수 있는
170	especially	ad 특히
171	modern	ⓐ 현대의, 근대의
172	explosion	⑪ 폭발적 증가, 폭발
173	synthetic	ⓐ 합성한
174	indeed	ad 사실
175	remarkably	ad 눈에 띄게, 두드러지게
176	restrictive	ⓐ 제한적인
177	primary	ⓐ 원색 ⑪ 주요한, 기본적인
178	grid	⑪ 격자무늬
179	similar	ⓐ 비슷한, 유사한
180	self-imposed	스스로 부과한, 자진해서 하는
181	restriction	⑪ 제한
182	generalize	⑭ 일반화하다
183	antiquity	⑪ 고대, 아주 오래됨
184	modernity	⑪ 현대, 현대적임
185	expand	⑭ 확장시키다
186	palette	⑪ 팔레트
187	aid	⑭ (일이 수월해지도록) 돕다
188	clarity	⑪ 명확성
189	comprehensibility	⑪ 이해 가능성
190	component	⑪ 구성 요소

31

191	workman	⑪ 일꾼, 노동자, 직공
192	often	ad 자주, 흔히, 종종
193	impossible	ⓐ 불가능한
194	trade	⑪ 직종
195	skilled	ⓐ 숙련된
196	on the other hand	반면에
197	demand	⑭ 필요로 하다, 요구되다
198	for instance	예를 들어
199	place	⑪ 경우
200	stitch	⑭ 깁다, 꿰매다, 바느질하다
201	sew	⑭ 꿰매다, 깁다
202	upper	⑪ (구두의) 윗부분
203	tool	⑪ 연장, 도구
204	result in	~로 이어지다, ~을 초래하다
205	efficient	ⓐ 효율적인
206	productive	ⓐ 생산적인
207	specialization	⑪ 특수[전문]화
208	criticism	⑪ 비판
209	diligence	⑪ 근면
210	imagination	⑪ 상상력, 상상

32

211	mammal	⑪ 포유동물
212	point	⑪ 지점

213 ☐ **generally** [ad] 대개, 보통
214 ☐ **comfortable** ⓐ 편안한
215 ☐ **existence** ⓝ 생활, 생계, 존재, 현존
216 ☐ **interval** ⓝ 간격
217 ☐ **bill** ⓝ 고지서, 청구서
218 ☐ **run out** (공급품 등이) 다 떨어지다
219 ☐ **fairly** [ad] 상당히, 꽤
220 ☐ **major** ⓐ 심각한
221 ☐ **disrespect** ⓝ 불손, 무례, 결례
222 ☐ **conflict** ⓝ 갈등, 충돌
223 ☐ **carer** ⓝ 간병인, 보호자
224 ☐ **independently** [ad] 독립하여
225 ☐ **away from** ~에서 떠나서
226 ☐ **home-cooked** 가정에서 만든
227 ☐ **financial** ⓐ 재정적인, 금전적인
228 ☐ **figure out** ~을 이해하다[알아내다]
229 ☐ **strength** ⓝ 강점, 힘
230 ☐ **manage** ⓥ 살아 나가다, 지내다
231 ☐ **relationship** ⓝ 관계
232 ☐ **peer** ⓝ 동료, 친구
233 ☐ **fall out of love with** ~와 정을 떼다

33
234 ☐ **advertising** ⓝ 광고
235 ☐ **map-making** 지도 제작, 지도 만들기
236 ☐ **have in common** (관심사나 생각을) 공통 적으로 지니다
237 ☐ **communicate** ⓥ 전달하다
238 ☐ **appealing** ⓐ 매력적인
239 ☐ **present** ⓥ 제시하다
240 ☐ **meet** ⓥ (목표나 기한 등을) 달성하다, 맞추다
241 ☐ **play down** 약화시키다, 낮추다
242 ☐ **aspect** ⓝ 측면
243 ☐ **promote** ⓥ 홍보하다, 촉진하다
244 ☐ **favorable** ⓐ 호의적인
245 ☐ **comparison** ⓝ 비교
246 ☐ **differentiate** ⓥ 차별화하다
247 ☐ **competitor** ⓝ 경쟁자, 경쟁 상대
248 ☐ **confusing** ⓐ 혼란을 주는, 혼란스러운

34
249 ☐ **determine** ⓥ 결정하다, 정하다
250 ☐ **culture** ⓝ 문화
251 ☐ **public opinion poll** 여론 조사
252 ☐ **horrified** ⓐ 겁에 질린, 무서워하는
253 ☐ **participate in** ~에 참여하다
254 ☐ **grandchildren** ⓝ 손자
255 ☐ **certain** ⓐ 특정한, 일정한
256 ☐ **anxiety** ⓝ 불안, 걱정
257 ☐ **arise** ⓥ 생기다, 발생하다
258 ☐ **short-lived** 오래 가지 못하는, 단기적인
259 ☐ **seek** ⓥ 찾다
260 ☐ **cooperation** ⓝ 협력
261 ☐ **adjust** ⓥ 적응하다
262 ☐ **ancestor** ⓝ 조상

35
263 ☐ **have an impact on** ~에 영향을 미치다
264 ☐ **resident** ⓝ 거주민, 거주자
265 ☐ **ownership** ⓝ 소유
266 ☐ **popularity** ⓝ 인기

267 ☐ **membership** ⓝ 회원 수, 회원들
268 ☐ **exceed** ⓥ 넘어서다, 능가하다
269 ☐ **traffic jam** 교통 체증
270 ☐ **vehicle** ⓝ 차량, 탈것
271 ☐ **replace** ⓥ 대체하다
272 ☐ **driverless car** 무인 자동차
273 ☐ **operate** ⓥ 조작하다, 가동하다
274 ☐ **struggle with** ~에 시달리다, ~로 고전하다

36
275 ☐ **collaboration** ⓝ 협업, 협동, 공동 작업
276 ☐ **basis** ⓝ 근거, 이유
277 ☐ **foundational** ⓐ 기초적인, 기본의
278 ☐ **sketch** ⓝ 개요
279 ☐ **anatomist** ⓝ 해부학자
280 ☐ **marry** ⓥ (서로 다른 두 가지 사상·사물을 성공적으로) 결합시키다
281 ☐ **playwright** ⓝ 극작가
282 ☐ **period** ⓝ 기간, 시기
283 ☐ **rewrite** ⓥ 개작하다, 다시 쓰다
284 ☐ **composition** ⓝ 작성, 작곡, 작품
285 ☐ **individually** [ad] 개인적으로, 따로
286 ☐ **fine** ⓐ 세밀한, 섬세한, 촘촘한
287 ☐ **join** ⓥ 합류하다
288 ☐ **overturn** ⓥ 뒤엎다, 전복시키다

37
289 ☐ **businessman** ⓝ 사업가
290 ☐ **complain** ⓥ 불평하다
291 ☐ **warm** ⓐ 따뜻한, 열띤, 다정한
292 ☐ **grateful** ⓐ 감사해하는, 고마워하는
293 ☐ **note** ⓥ 언급하다, 말하다
294 ☐ **unfortunately** [ad] 안타깝게도, 불행히도
295 ☐ **check** ⓝ 수표
296 ☐ **enclose** ⓥ 동봉하다
297 ☐ **rarely** [ad] 좀처럼 ~하지 않는
298 ☐ **immediate** ⓐ 즉각적인, 즉시의
299 ☐ **send off** 보내다, 발송하다
300 ☐ **sum** ⓝ 액수
301 ☐ **mail** ⓥ (우편물을) 부치다, 보내다

38
302 ☐ **puberty** ⓝ 사춘기
303 ☐ **go through** ~을 겪다
304 ☐ **growing pains** 성장통
305 ☐ **share** ⓥ 함께 하다, 공유하다
306 ☐ **less than** ~보다 적은
307 ☐ **scary** ⓐ 무서운, 겁나는
308 ☐ **exactly** [ad] 정확히
309 ☐ **alike** ⓐ (아주) 비슷한
310 ☐ **interest** ⓝ 관심사, 흥미
311 ☐ **learn** ⓥ 배우다, 학습하다
312 ☐ **each other** 서로

39
313 ☐ **copy** ⓥ 베끼다
314 ☐ **rather than** ~보다
315 ☐ **imaginary** ⓐ 상상의, 가상적인
316 ☐ **drawing** ⓝ (색칠을 하지 않은) 그림, 소묘, 데생
317 ☐ **cartoon characters** 만화 속 등장인물들

318 ☐ **equally** [ad] 똑같이
319 ☐ **complex** ⓐ 복잡한
320 ☐ **unless** [conj] ~하지 않는 한
321 ☐ **unusually** [ad] 특별하게
322 ☐ **gifted** ⓐ 재능 있는
323 ☐ **completely** [ad] 완전히
324 ☐ **furthermore** [ad] 게다가, 더욱이
325 ☐ **accurate** ⓐ 정확한
326 ☐ **practice** ⓝ 연습
327 ☐ **coordinating ~ with …** ~와 …을 조화 시키다
328 ☐ **movement** ⓝ 움직임
329 ☐ **perceive** ⓥ 인지하다, 인식하다

40
330 ☐ **manufacturer** ⓝ 제조 업체, 생산자
331 ☐ **invite** ⓥ 초대하다, 초청하다
332 ☐ **introduce** ⓥ 소개하다, 도입하다
333 ☐ **distributor** ⓝ 배급 업체, 배급자
334 ☐ **reputation** ⓝ 명성
335 ☐ **impression** ⓝ 인상
336 ☐ **promising** ⓐ 촉망받는, 전도 유망한
337 ☐ **executive** ⓝ 임원, 중역
338 ☐ **shake hands** 악수하다
339 ☐ **firmly** [ad] 굳게, 단단히, 단호히
340 ☐ **greet** ⓥ 인사하다, 환영하다
341 ☐ **bow** ⓥ (고개를) 숙이다
342 ☐ **slightly** [ad] 약간, 조금
343 ☐ **custom** ⓝ 관습
344 ☐ **presentation** ⓝ 발표, 프레젠테이션
345 ☐ **humorous** ⓐ 재미있는, 유머러스한
346 ☐ **joke** ⓝ 농담
347 ☐ **relaxed** ⓐ 편안한
348 ☐ **atmosphere** ⓝ 분위기
349 ☐ **particular** ⓐ 특정한
350 ☐ **informal** ⓐ 비격식적인, 허물없는
351 ☐ **essential** ⓐ 본질적인
352 ☐ **inappropriate** ⓐ 부적절한
353 ☐ **useful** ⓐ 유용한

41~42
354 ☐ **stranger** ⓝ 모르는 사람
355 ☐ **one another** 서로
356 ☐ **arrival** ⓝ 도착
357 ☐ **randomly** [ad] 무작위로
358 ☐ **separate** ⓥ 나누다, 분리하다
359 ☐ **apart** [ad] 떨어져, 따로
360 ☐ **hike** ⓥ 하이킹[도보 여행]을 가다
361 ☐ **a series of** 일련의
362 ☐ **athletic** ⓐ 운동의, 육상의
363 ☐ **look down on** ~을 얕잡아보다, 깔보다
364 ☐ **competitive** ⓐ 경쟁적인
365 ☐ **quickly** [ad] (속도를) 빨리[빠르게]
366 ☐ **sharp** ⓐ 선명한, 뚜렷한, 분명한
367 ☐ **boundary** ⓝ 경계
368 ☐ **several** ⓐ (몇)몇의
369 ☐ **apparent** ⓐ …인 것처럼 보이는[여겨지는]
370 ☐ **emergency** ⓝ 비상사태
371 ☐ **solution** ⓝ 해법, 해결
372 ☐ **leak** ⓝ (물이) 새는 곳, 구멍 ⓥ (물이나 기체가) 새다
373 ☐ **pipe** ⓝ 관[배관/파이프]

374 ☐ **assign** ⓥ 배정하다
375 ☐ **melt away** 차츰 사라지다
376 ☐ **helpful** ⓐ 도움이 되는
377 ☐ **preparation** ⓝ 준비[대비]
378 ☐ **disappear** ⓥ 사라지다
379 ☐ **headaches** ⓝ 두통[골칫]거리

43~45
380 ☐ **slave** ⓝ 노예
381 ☐ **servant** ⓝ 하인, 종
382 ☐ **unkind** ⓐ 불쾌한, 박정한
383 ☐ **cruel** ⓐ 잔인한
384 ☐ **mistake** ⓝ 실수, 잘못
385 ☐ **overcooked** ⓐ 너무 익힌[구운]
386 ☐ **punish** ⓥ 처벌하다
387 ☐ **lock** ⓥ 잠그다[잠기다]
388 ☐ **lion** ⓝ 사자
389 ☐ **recover** ⓥ 회복하다, 낫다
390 ☐ **close** ⓐ (사이가) 친한, 가까운
391 ☐ **catch** ⓥ 잡다, 붙잡다
392 ☐ **guard** ⓝ 경비 요원
393 ☐ **decided** ⓥ 결정하다
394 ☐ **severely** [ad] 엄하게, 심하게
395 ☐ **order** ⓥ 명령하다
396 ☐ **cage** ⓝ (쇠창살이나 철사로 만든 짐승의) 우리
397 ☐ **escape** ⓥ 달아나다, 탈출하다
398 ☐ **instead of** ~ 대신에
399 ☐ **run away** 도망치다, 달아나다
400 ☐ **injure** ⓥ 상처를 입히다
401 ☐ **bleed** ⓥ 피를 흘리다, 출혈하다
402 ☐ **search for** ~을 찾다
403 ☐ **herb** ⓝ 약초
404 ☐ **cure** ⓥ 치료하다
405 ☐ **wound** ⓝ 상처, 부상
406 ☐ **whole** ⓐ 전체의, 모든
407 ☐ **as soon as** ~하자마자
408 ☐ **lick** ⓥ 핥다
409 ☐ **hug** ⓥ 껴안다[포옹하다]
410 ☐ **free** ⓥ 풀어 주다 ⓐ 자유로운
411 ☐ **treat** ⓥ 대하다, 대접하다

● 채점 : 맞은 개수 _____ / 80

TEST A-B 각 단어의 뜻을 [A] 영어는 우리말로, [B] 우리말은 영어로 쓰시오.

A	English	Korean
01	on behalf of	
02	embrace	
03	catch up on	
04	indifferent	
05	finding	
06	give a lift	
07	consume	
08	mature	
09	at one's disposal	
10	generalize	
11	diligence	
12	run out	
13	interval	
14	competitor	
15	exceed	
16	note	
17	go through	
18	promising	
19	boundary	
20	bleed	

B	Korean	English
01	참석하다	
02	제안하다	
03	기도하다	
04	편안함	
05	마음을 산만하게 하는 것, 집중력을 흩뜨리는 것	
06	분석	
07	위험을 감수하다	
08	매력, 끌림, 명소	
09	사라지다	
10	이해하다	
11	눈에 띄게, 두드러지게	
12	~로 이어지다, ~를 초래하다	
13	(목표 등을) 달성하다, 맞추다	
14	조상	
15	대체하다	
16	명성	
17	(물이) 새는 곳, 새다	
18	잔인한	
19	처벌하다	
20	상처를 입히다	

▶ A-D 정답 : 해설편 182쪽

TEST C-D 각 단어의 뜻을 골라 기호를 쓰시오.

C	English			Korean
01	admission	(	)	ⓐ 습득하다, 얻다
02	seemingly	(	)	ⓑ 원색, 주요한
03	acquire	(	)	ⓒ 닮다
04	glacier	(	)	ⓓ 동료
05	urban	(	)	ⓔ 겁에 질린, 무서워하는
06	via	(	)	ⓕ 정서적인
07	resemble	(	)	ⓖ 재능 있는
08	emotional	(	)	ⓗ 빙하
09	infinite	(	)	ⓘ 배정하다
10	primary	(	)	ⓙ ~을 통하여, ~을 경유하여
11	sew	(	)	ⓚ 입원, 입장
12	peer	(	)	ⓛ 즉각적인
13	horrified	(	)	ⓜ 상상의, 가상의
14	driverless car	(	)	ⓝ 인상
15	immediate	(	)	ⓞ 회복하다
16	imaginary	(	)	ⓟ 꿰매다, 깁다
17	gifted	(	)	ⓠ 겉보기에
18	impression	(	)	ⓡ 무인 자동차
19	assign	(	)	ⓢ 무한한
20	recover	(	)	ⓣ 도시의

D	Korean			English
01	실업	(	)	ⓐ accomplish
02	절차	(	)	ⓑ regularly
03	즉각적인, 즉시의	(	)	ⓒ freshman
04	달성하다, 성취하다	(	)	ⓓ artificial
05	규칙적으로	(	)	ⓔ synthetic
06	나머지	(	)	ⓕ vehicle
07	존재	(	)	ⓖ unemployment
08	신입생	(	)	ⓗ wavelength
09	인공의	(	)	ⓘ puberty
10	합성한	(	)	ⓙ informal
11	효율적인	(	)	ⓚ process
12	포유류	(	)	ⓛ atmosphere
13	불안, 걱정	(	)	ⓜ severely
14	차량, 탈것	(	)	ⓝ mammal
15	사춘기	(	)	ⓞ efficient
16	~하지 않는 한	(	)	ⓟ instant
17	분위기	(	)	ⓠ rest
18	비격식적인, 허물없는	(	)	ⓡ anxiety
19	엄하게, 심하게	(	)	ⓢ presence
20	파장, 주파수	(	)	ⓣ unless

영어 영역

● 문항수 45개 | 배점 100점 | 제한 시간 70분
● 점수 표시가 없는 문항은 모두 2점 ● 출처 : 고1 학력평가

1번부터 17번까지는 듣고 답하는 문제입니다. 1번부터 15번까지는 한 번만 들려주고, 16번부터 17번까지는 두 번 들려줍니다. 방송을 잘 듣고 답을 하시기 바랍니다.

1. 다음을 듣고, 여자가 하는 말의 목적으로 가장 적절한 것을 고르시오.

① 개관 시간 연장을 알리려고
② 작가 초청 행사를 안내하려고
③ 사진 촬영 자제를 당부하려고
④ 미술 강좌 회원을 모집하려고
⑤ 전시 장소 변경을 공지하려고

2. 대화를 듣고, 남자의 의견으로 가장 적절한 것을 고르시오.

① 다양한 영양소의 섭취는 성장에 필수적이다.
② 식품 구매 시 영양 성분의 확인이 필요하다.
③ 새우를 섭취하는 것은 건강에 도움이 된다.
④ 체중 관리는 균형 잡힌 식단에서 비롯된다.
⑤ 음식을 조리할 때 위생 관리가 중요하다.

3. 대화를 듣고, 두 사람의 관계를 가장 잘 나타낸 것을 고르시오.

① 교사 — 학부모   ② 의사 — 환자
③ 간병인 — 보호자   ④ 상담사 — 학생
⑤ 편집장 — 신문 기자

4. 대화를 듣고, 그림에서 대화의 내용과 일치하지 않는 것을 고르시오.

5. 대화를 듣고, 남자가 여자에게 부탁한 일로 가장 적절한 것을 고르시오.

① 음식 만들기   ② 꽃 사러 가기
③ 친구 초대하기   ④ 거실 청소하기
⑤ 식료품 구입하기

6. 대화를 듣고, 남자가 지불할 금액을 고르시오.

① $15   ② $30   ③ $48   ④ $54   ⑤ $60

7. 대화를 듣고, 여자가 남자와 함께 뮤지컬을 보러 갈 수 없는 이유를 고르시오.

① 표를 구하지 못해서
② 회사에 출근해야 해서
③ 해외여행을 가기로 해서
④ 다른 친구를 만나기로 해서
⑤ 부모님과 주말을 보내야 해서

8. 대화를 듣고, Career Vision Camp에 관해 언급되지 않은 것을 고르시오.

① 참가 대상   ② 등록 비용   ③ 지원 마감일
④ 기념품   ⑤ 행사 장소

9. Book Review Contest에 관한 다음 내용을 듣고, 일치하지 않는 것을 고르시오. [3점]

① 독서의 달을 기념하는 행사이다.
② 학생들은 누구나 참여할 수 있다.
③ 지정 도서에 대한 독후감을 작성해야 한다.
④ 독후감은 이달 말까지 제출해야 한다.
⑤ 우수작 세 편은 학교 잡지에 실릴 것이다.

10. 다음 표를 보면서 대화를 듣고, 여자가 구입할 전기면도기를 고르시오.

Electric Shaver

	Model	Price	Battery Life	Waterproof	Color
①	A	$ 55	20 minutes	×	black
②	B	$ 70	40 minutes	×	white
③	C	$ 85	60 minutes	○	black
④	D	$ 90	70 minutes	○	white
⑤	E	$ 110	80 minutes	○	black

11. 대화를 듣고, 여자의 마지막 말에 대한 남자의 응답으로 가장 적절한 것을 고르시오.

① I've never been there.
② I really liked the food.
③ It sounds like a good idea.
④ I didn't eat breakfast today.
⑤ It wasn't open last weekend.

12. 대화를 듣고, 남자의 마지막 말에 대한 여자의 응답으로 가장 적절한 것을 고르시오.

① Okay. I'll take the subway then.
② No. I didn't take your umbrella.
③ Right. It was too much work.
④ Yes. It will rain tomorrow.
⑤ Sorry. I can't drive a car.

13. 대화를 듣고, 남자의 마지막 말에 대한 여자의 응답으로 가장 적절한 것을 고르시오. [3점]

Woman: _____

① I told her a scary story.
② I said goodbye to her mother.
③ I asked her to do the homework.
④ I apologized for my silly mistake.
⑤ I thanked her for helping me study.

14. 대화를 듣고, 여자의 마지막 말에 대한 남자의 응답으로 가장 적절한 것을 고르시오.

Man: _____

① You're welcome. I'm glad that you really enjoyed the gift.
② Don't worry about that. Everyone can learn from mistakes.
③ Yeah, I've sung the song. I want to sing in harmony now.
④ Okay, I'll sing for you. I hope you won't expect too much.
⑤ I don't think so. It's not easy to choose a wedding ring.

15. 다음 상황 설명을 듣고, Julie가 Eric에게 할 말로 가장 적절한 것을 고르시오. [3점]

Julie: _____

① That's great. I've always wanted to meet your parents.
② Sure, you can bring him. The more people, the better.
③ Please don't bring anything. I'll get everything ready.
④ Never mind. Let's have dinner together another time.
⑤ Thank you for the invitation. I'll be there on time.

[16 ~ 17] 다음을 듣고, 물음에 답하시오.

16. 남자가 하는 말의 주제로 가장 적절한 것은?

① foods at risk due to climate change
② reasons why sea temperatures rise
③ animals and plants in the water
④ requirements of growing crops
⑤ ways to solve global warming

17. 언급된 음식이 <u>아닌</u> 것은?

① coffee   ② avocados   ③ apples
④ strawberries   ⑤ coconuts

이제 듣기 문제가 끝났습니다. 18번부터는 문제지의 지시에 따라 답을 하시기 바랍니다.

---

18. 다음 글의 목적으로 가장 적절한 것은?

> Dear Parents,
>
> As you know, Sandy Brown, our after-school swimming coach for six years, retired from coaching last month. So, Virginia Smith, who swam for Bredard Community College and has won several awards in national competitions, has been named the school's new swimming coach. This is her first job as a coach, and she is going to start working from next week. She will teach her class in the afternoons, and continue with our summer program. By promoting the health benefits of swimming, she hopes that more students will get healthy through her instruction.
>
> Sincerely,
> Fred Wilson
> Principal, Riverband High School

① 새로운 수영 코치를 소개하려고
② 수영 강좌의 폐강을 통보하려고
③ 수영 코치의 퇴임식을 공지하려고
④ 수영부의 대회 입상을 축하하려고
⑤ 수영의 건강상 이점을 홍보하려고

19. 다음 글에 드러난 Rowe의 심경 변화로 가장 적절한 것은?

Rowe jumps for joy when he finds a cave because he loves being in places where so few have ventured. At the entrance he keeps taking photos with his cell phone to show off his new adventure later. Coming to a stop on a rock a few meters from the entrance, he sees the icy cave's glittering view. He says, "Incredibly beautiful!" stretching his hand out to touch the icy wall. Suddenly, his footing gives way and he slides down into the darkness. He looks up and sees a crack of light about 20 meters above him. 'Phone for help,' he thinks. But he realizes there's no service this far underground. He tries to move upward but he can't. He calls out, "Is anyone there?" There's no answer.

① delighted → grateful
② disappointed → ashamed
③ indifferent → regretful
④ bored → frightened
⑤ excited → desperate

20. 다음 글에서 필자가 주장하는 바로 가장 적절한 것은?

Language play is good for children's language learning and development, and therefore we should strongly encourage, and even join in their language play. However, the play must be owned by the children. If it becomes another educational tool for adults to use to produce outcomes, it loses its very essence. Children need to be able to delight in creative and immediate language play, to say silly things and make themselves laugh, and to have control over the pace, timing, direction, and flow. When children are allowed to develop their language play, a range of benefits result from it.

① 아이들이 언어 놀이를 주도하게 하라.
② 아이들의 질문에 즉각적으로 반응하라.
③ 아이들에게 다양한 언어 자극을 제공하라.
④ 대화를 통해 아이들의 공감 능력을 키워라.
⑤ 언어 놀이를 통해 자녀와의 관계를 회복하라.

영어 영역

3

21. 밑줄 친 at the "sweet spot"이 다음 글에서 의미하는 바로 가장 적절한 것은? [3점]

For almost all things in life, there can be too much of a good thing. Even the best things in life aren't so great in excess. This concept has been discussed at least as far back as Aristotle. He argued that being virtuous means finding a balance. For example, people should be brave, but if someone is too brave they become reckless. People should be trusting, but if someone is too trusting they are considered gullible. For each of these traits, it is best to avoid both deficiency and excess. The best way is to live at the "sweet spot" that maximizes well-being. Aristotle's suggestion is that virtue is the midpoint, where someone is neither too generous nor too stingy, neither too afraid nor recklessly brave.

* excess: 과잉 ** gullible: 잘 속아 넘어가는

① at the time of a biased decision
② in the area of material richness
③ away from social pressure
④ in the middle of two extremes
⑤ at the moment of instant pleasure

22. 다음 글의 요지로 가장 적절한 것은?

If you walk into a room that smells of freshly baked bread, you quickly detect the rather pleasant smell. However, stay in the room for a few minutes, and the smell will seem to disappear. In fact, the only way to reawaken it is to walk out of the room and come back in again. The exact same concept applies to many areas of our lives, including happiness. Everyone has something to be happy about. Perhaps they have a loving partner, good health, a satisfying job, a roof over their heads, or enough food to eat. As time passes, however, they get used to what they have and, just like the smell of fresh bread, these wonderful assets disappear from their consciousness. As the old proverb goes, you never miss the water till the well runs dry.

① 새로움을 추구하는 삶이 가치 있다.
② 작은 행복이 모여서 큰 행복이 된다.
③ 즐거움은 어느 정도의 고통을 수반한다.
④ 익숙함이 소중한 것의 가치를 잊게 한다.
⑤ 결과보다 과정에 집중하는 삶이 행복하다.

23. 다음 글의 주제로 가장 적절한 것은?

If you've ever seen a tree stump, you probably noticed that the top of the stump had a series of rings. These rings can tell us how old the tree is, and what the weather was like during each year of the tree's life. Because trees are sensitive to local climate conditions, such as rain and temperature, they give scientists some information about that area's local climate in the past. For example, tree rings usually grow wider in warm, wet years and are thinner in years when it is cold and dry. If the tree has experienced stressful conditions, such as a drought, the tree might hardly grow at all during that time. Very old trees in particular can offer clues about what the climate was like long before measurements were recorded.

* stump: 그루터기

① use of old trees to find direction
② traditional ways to predict weather
③ difficulty in measuring a tree's age
④ importance of protecting local trees
⑤ tree rings suggesting the past climate

24. 다음 글의 제목으로 가장 적절한 것은?

Many people suppose that to keep bees, it is necessary to have a large garden in the country; but this is a mistake. Bees will, of course, do better in the midst of fruit blossoms in May and white clovers in June than in a city where they have to fly a long distance to reach the open fields. However, bees can be kept with profit even under unfavorable circumstances. Bees do very well in the suburbs of large cities since the series of flowers in the gardens of the villas allow a constant supply of honey from early spring until autumn. Therefore, almost every person — except those who are seriously afraid of bees — can keep them profitably and enjoyably.

① The Best Season for Honey Harvest in Cities
② Myth and Truth about Where to Keep Bees
③ How Can We Overcome Fear of Bees?
④ Benefits of Bee Farming on Nature
⑤ Bee Farming: Not an Easy Job

25. 다음 도표의 내용과 일치하지 <u>않는</u> 것은?

Smartphone Average Prices

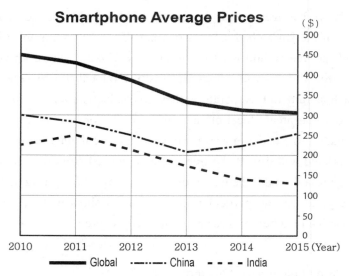

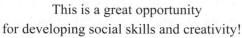

The above graph shows the smartphone average prices in China and India between 2010 and 2015, compared with the global smartphone average price during the same period. ① The global smartphone average price decreased from 2010 to 2015, but still stayed the highest among the three. ② The smartphone average price in China dropped between 2010 and 2013. ③ The smartphone average price in India reached its peak in 2011. ④ From 2013, China and India took opposite paths, with China's smartphone average price going down and India's going up. ⑤ The gap between the global smartphone average price and the smartphone average price in China was the smallest in 2015.

26. Nauru에 관한 다음 글의 내용과 일치하지 <u>않는</u> 것은?

Nauru is an island country in the southwestern Pacific Ocean. It is located about 800 miles to the northeast of the Solomon Islands; its closest neighbor is the island of Banaba, some 200 miles to the east. Nauru has no official capital, but government buildings are located in Yaren. With a population of about 10,000, Nauru is the smallest country in the South Pacific and the third smallest country by area in the world. The native people of Nauru consist of 12 tribes, as symbolized by the 12-pointed star on the Nauru flag, and are believed to be a mixture of Micronesian, Polynesian, and Melanesian. Their native language is Nauruan, but English is widely spoken as it is used for government and business purposes.

① 솔로몬 제도로부터 북동쪽에 위치해 있다.
② 공식 수도는 없으나 Yaren에 정부 건물이 있다.
③ 면적이 세계에서 세 번째로 작은 국가이다.
④ 원주민은 12개의 부족으로 구성되어 있다.
⑤ 모국어가 있어 다른 언어는 사용하지 않는다.

27. Summer Camp 2019에 관한 다음 안내문의 내용과 일치하는 것은?

Summer Camp 2019

This is a great opportunity
for developing social skills and creativity!

Period & Participation
• July 1−5 (Monday−Friday)
• 8−12 year olds (maximum 20 students per class)

Programs
• Cooking
• Outdoor Activities (hiking, rafting, and camping)

Cost
• Regular: $100 per person
• Discounted: $90 (if you register by June 15)

Notice
• The programs will run regardless of weather conditions.
• To sign up, email us at summercamp@standrews.com.

For more information, visit our website: www.standrews.com.

① 참가 연령 제한이 없다.
② 야외 프로그램은 운영되지 않는다.
③ 할인된 가격은 100달러이다.
④ 기상 조건에 관계없이 프로그램이 진행될 것이다.
⑤ 이메일을 통해 등록을 할 수 없다.

28. Family Activities at the Basque Museum에 관한 다음 안내문의 내용과 일치하지 <u>않는</u> 것은?

Family Activities at the Basque Museum

Whether you are a new or regular visitor, this is your guide to the family activities coming up at the Basque Museum.

■ **Dates & Hours**
• June 1 − 30
• Weekdays: 9:00 a.m. − 5:00 p.m.
• Weekends: 10:00 a.m. − 6:00 p.m.

■ **Activities**
• **Treasure Hunt**
 - Age 5+, lasts 30 minutes, 3 times a day
• **Making History Books**
 - For kids of all ages, weekends only

■ **Notices**
• All activities are free, donations are welcome.
• Reservations are required for all activities.
• Children must be accompanied by an adult.

① 주중과 주말 운영 시간이 다르다.
② 보물찾기 활동은 하루에 세 번 진행한다.
③ 역사 책 만들기 활동은 주중에만 운영한다.
④ 모든 활동은 예약이 필수이다.
⑤ 어린이들은 성인과 함께 와야 한다.

29. 다음 글의 밑줄 친 부분 중, 어법상 틀린 것은? [3점]

Are you honest with yourself about your strengths and weaknesses? Get to really know ① yourself and learn what your weaknesses are. Accepting your role in your problems ② mean that you understand the solution lies within you. If you have a weakness in a certain area, get educated and do ③ what you have to do to improve things for yourself. If your social image is terrible, look within yourself and take the necessary steps to improve ④ it, TODAY. You have the ability to choose how to respond to life. Decide today to end all the excuses, and stop ⑤ lying to yourself about what is going on. The beginning of growth comes when you begin to personally accept responsibility for your choices.

30. 다음 글의 밑줄 친 부분 중, 문맥상 낱말의 쓰임이 적절하지 않은 것은?

The overabundance of options in today's marketplace gives you more freedom of choice. However, there may be a price to pay in terms of happiness. According to research by psychologists David Myers and Robert Lane, all this choice often makes people ① depressed. Researchers gave some shoppers 24 choices of jams to taste and others only 6 choices. Those who had ② fewer choices were happier with the tasting. Even more surprisingly, the ones with a smaller selection purchased jam 31% of the time, while those with a wider range of choices only purchased jam 3% of the time. The ironic thing about this is that people nearly always say they want ③ more choices. Yet, the more options they have, the more ④ relieved they become. Savvy restaurant owners provide fewer choices. This allows customers to feel more relaxed, ⑤ prompting them to choose easily and leave more satisfied with their choices.

* savvy: 사리에 밝은

[31 ~ 34] 다음 빈칸에 들어갈 말로 가장 적절한 것을 고르시오.

31. Creativity is a skill we usually consider uniquely human. For all of human history, we have been the most creative beings on Earth. Birds can make their nests, ants can make their hills, but no other species on Earth comes close to the level of creativity we humans display. However, just in the last decade we have acquired the ability to do amazing things with computers, like developing robots. With the artificial intelligence boom of the 2010s, computers can now recognize faces, translate languages, take calls for you, write poems, and beat players at the world's most complicated board game, to name a few things. All of a sudden, we must face the possibility that our ability to be creative is not _____.

[3점]

① unrivaled　　② learned　　③ universal
④ ignored　　⑤ challenged

32. In 1995, a group of high school students in Miner County, South Dakota, started planning a revival. They wanted to do something that might revive their dying community. Miner County had been failing for decades. Farm and industrial jobs had slowly dried up, and nothing had replaced them. The students started investigating the situation. One finding in particular disturbed them. They discovered that half of the residents had been shopping outside the county, driving an hour to Sioux Falls to shop in larger stores. Most of the things that could improve the situation were out of the students' control. But they did uncover one thing that was very much in their control: inviting the residents to _____ . They found their first slogan: Let's keep Miner dollars in Miner County. [3점]

* resident: 주민

① work out regularly
② spend money locally
③ drive their cars safely
④ treat strangers nicely
⑤ share work equally

33. The mind is essentially a survival machine. Attack and defense against other minds, gathering, storing, and analyzing information — this is what it is good at, but it is not at all creative. All true artists create from a place of no-mind, from inner stillness. Even great scientists have reported that their creative breakthroughs came at a time of mental quietude. The surprising result of a nationwide inquiry among America's most famous mathematicians, including Einstein, to find out their working methods, was that thinking "plays only a subordinate part in the brief, decisive phase of the creative act itself." So I would say that the simple reason why the majority of scientists are *not* creative is not because they don't know how to think, but because they don't know how to _____!

* quietude: 정적 ** subordinate: 부수적인

① organize their ideas
② interact socially
③ stop thinking
④ gather information
⑤ use their imagination

34. One real concern in the marketing industry today is how to _____ in the age of the remote control and mobile devices. With the growing popularity of digital video recorders, consumers can mute, fast-forward, and skip over commercials entirely. Some advertisers are trying to adapt to these technologies, by planting hidden coupons in frames of their television commercials. Others are desperately trying to make their advertisements more interesting and entertaining to discourage viewers from skipping their ads; still others are simply giving up on television advertising altogether. Some industry experts predict that cable providers and advertisers will eventually be forced to provide incentives in order to encourage consumers to watch their messages. These incentives may come in the form of coupons, or a reduction in the cable bill for each advertisement watched. [3점]

* mute: 음소거하다

① guide people to be wise consumers
② reduce the cost of television advertising
③ keep a close eye on the quality of products
④ make it possible to deliver any goods any time
⑤ win the battle for broadcast advertising exposure

35. 다음 글에서 전체 흐름과 관계 <u>없는</u> 문장은?

Words like 'near' and 'far' can mean different things depending on where you are and what you are doing. If you were at a zoo, then you might say you are 'near' an animal if you could reach out and touch it through the bars of its cage. ① Here the word 'near' means an arm's length away. ② If you were telling someone how to get to your local shop, you might call it 'near' if it was a five-minute walk away. ③ It seems that you had better walk to the shop to improve your health. ④ Now the word 'near' means much longer than an arm's length away. ⑤ Words like 'near', 'far', 'small', 'big', 'hot', and 'cold' all mean different things to different people at different times.

[36 ~ 37] 주어진 글 다음에 이어질 글의 순서로 가장 적절한 것을 고르시오.

36.

In early 19th century London, a young man named Charles Dickens had a strong desire to be a writer. But everything seemed to be against him.

(A) Moreover, he had so little confidence in his ability to write that he mailed his writings secretly at night to editors so that nobody would laugh at him. Story after story was refused.

(B) He had never been able to attend school for more than four years. His father had been in jail because he couldn't pay his debts, and this young man often knew the pain of hunger.

(C) But one day, one editor recognized and praised him. The praise that he received from getting one story in print changed his whole life. His works have been widely read and still enjoy great popularity.

① (A) − (C) − (B)　　　　② (B) − (A) − (C)
③ (B) − (C) − (A)　　　　④ (C) − (A) − (B)
⑤ (C) − (B) − (A)

37.

The next time you're out under a clear, dark sky, look up. If you've picked a good spot for stargazing, you'll see a sky full of stars, shining and twinkling like thousands of brilliant jewels.

(A) It might be easier if you describe patterns of stars. You could say something like, "See that big triangle of bright stars there?" Or, "Do you see those five stars that look like a big letter W?"

(B) But this amazing sight of stars can also be confusing. Try and point out a single star to someone. Chances are, that person will have a hard time knowing exactly which star you're looking at.

(C) When you do that, you're doing exactly what we all do when we look at the stars. We look for patterns, not just so that we can point something out to someone else, but also because that's what we humans have always done. [3점]

① (A) − (C) − (B)　　② (B) − (A) − (C)
③ (B) − (C) − (A)　　④ (C) − (A) − (B)
⑤ (C) − (B) − (A)

[38 ~ 39] 글의 흐름으로 보아, 주어진 문장이 들어가기에 가장 적절한 곳을 고르시오.

38.

Throw away your own hesitation and forget all your concerns about whether you are musically talented or whether you can sing or play an instrument.

Music appeals powerfully to young children. (①) Watch preschoolers' faces and bodies when they hear rhythm and sound—they light up and move eagerly and enthusiastically. (②) They communicate comfortably, express themselves creatively, and let out all sorts of thoughts and emotions as they interact with music. (③) In a word, young children think music is a lot of fun, so do all you can to make the most of the situation. (④) They don't matter when you are enjoying music with your child. (⑤) Just follow his or her lead, have fun, sing songs together, listen to different kinds of music, move, dance, and enjoy.

39.

Instead of that, say to them, 'I can't deal with that now but what I can do is I can ask Brian to give you a hand and he should be able to explain them.'

Whenever you say what you can't do, say what you can do. This ends a sentence on a positive note and has a much lower tendency to cause someone to challenge it. (①) Consider this situation — a colleague comes up to you and asks you to look over some figures with them before a meeting they are having tomorrow. (②) You simply say, 'No, I can't deal with this now.' (③) This may then lead to them insisting how important your input is, increasing the pressure on you to give in. (④) Or, 'I can't deal with that now but I can find you in about half an hour when I have finished.' (⑤) Either of these types of responses are better than ending it with a negative. [3점]

40. 다음 글의 내용을 한 문장으로 요약하고자 한다. 빈칸 (A)와 (B)에 들어갈 말로 가장 적절한 것은?

According to an Australian study, a person's confidence in the kitchen is linked to the kind of food that he or she tends to enjoy eating. Compared to the average person, those who are proud of the dishes they make are more likely to enjoy eating vegetarian food and health food. Moreover, this group is more likely than the average person to enjoy eating diverse kinds of food: from salads and seafood to hamburgers and hot chips. In contrast, people who say "I would rather clean than make dishes." don't share this wide-ranging enthusiasm for food. They are less likely than the average person to enjoy different types of food. In general, they eat out less than the average person except for when it comes to eating at fast food restaurants.

↓

In general, people who are confident in ___(A)___ are more likely to enjoy ___(B)___ foods than those who are not.

	(A)		(B)
①	cooking	······	various
②	cooking	······	specific
③	tasting	······	organic
④	dieting	······	healthy
⑤	dieting	······	exotic

[41 ~ 42] 다음 글을 읽고, 물음에 답하시오.

Many advertisements cite statistical surveys. But we should be (a) underline cautious because we usually do not know how these surveys are conducted. For example, a toothpaste manufacturer once had a poster that said, "More than 80% of dentists recommend *Smiley Toothpaste*." This seems to say that most dentists (b) prefer *Smiley Toothpaste* to other brands. But it turns out that the survey questions allowed the dentists to recommend more than one brand, and in fact another competitor's brand was recommended just as often as *Smiley Toothpaste*! No wonder the UK Advertising Standards Authority ruled in 2007 that the poster was (c) misleading and it could no longer be displayed.

A similar case concerns a well-known cosmetics firm marketing a cream that is supposed to rapidly reduce wrinkles. But the only evidence provided is that "76% of 50 women agreed." But what this means is that the evidence is based on just the personal opinions from a small sample with no objective measurement of their skin's condition. Furthermore, we are not told how these women were selected. Without such information, the "evidence" provided is pretty much (d) useful. Unfortunately, such advertisements are quite typical, and as consumers we just have to use our own judgment and (e) avoid taking advertising claims too seriously.

41. 윗글의 제목으로 가장 적절한 것은?

① The Link between Advertisements and the Economy
② Are Statistical Data in Advertisements Reliable?
③ Statistics in Advertisements Are Objective!
④ The Bright Side of Public Advertisements
⑤ Quality or Price, Which Matters More?

42. 밑줄 친 (a)~(e) 중에서 문맥상 낱말의 쓰임이 적절하지 <u>않은</u> 것은?

① (a)　　② (b)　　③ (c)　　④ (d)　　⑤ (e)

[43 ~ 45] 다음 글을 읽고, 물음에 답하시오.

(A)

It was evening when I landed in Kuching, Malaysia. I felt alone and homesick. I was a 19-year-old Dubai-raised kid away from home for the first time to start my university studies in mechanical engineering. I took my luggage and headed to the airport exit. I looked around and found my driver waiting for me in front of (a) his gray van with the name of my university on it.

(B)

With a sigh of relief, I took my wallet and thanked him. I could imagine a horrible scenario if he had not returned it. The man welcomed me to Kuching and drove away. As my driver dropped me off, (b) he smiled and wished me luck with my university studies. Thanks to the kindness of these strangers, the initial doubt I had had about my decision to study away from home was replaced with hope and excitement.

(C)

This continued more aggressively and my driver started to panic. Honks and more flashes followed, so (c) he pulled the van over to the roadside. My heart was pounding as the man from the car behind approached us. As he reached my window, I lowered it and then looked down at (d) his hands to see that he was holding my wallet. I had left it in the airport and I realized he had been trying to return it to me ever since we had left the airport.

* honk: 경적 소리

(D)

As we left the airport, he began talking about the city and its people. As I loved driving very much, we moved onto talking about cars and driving in Kuching. "Never make Kuching people angry," (e) he warned. "No road rage. Very dangerous!" He then went on to list his experiences of road rage and advised me to drive very cautiously. A bit later, the car behind started to flash its lights at us.

* road rage: 도로에서 벌어지는 운전자의 난폭 행동

43. 주어진 글 (A)에 이어질 내용을 순서에 맞게 배열한 것으로 가장 적절한 것은?

① (B) − (D) − (C)　　② (C) − (B) − (D)
③ (C) − (D) − (B)　　④ (D) − (B) − (C)
⑤ (D) − (C) − (B)

44. 밑줄 친 (a)~(e) 중에서 가리키는 대상이 나머지 넷과 <u>다른</u> 것은?

① (a)　　② (b)　　③ (c)　　④ (d)　　⑤ (e)

45. 윗글의 'I'에 관한 내용으로 적절하지 <u>않은</u> 것은?

① 기계 공학을 공부하려고 집을 떠나왔다.
② 처음에는 유학 결정에 대해 의구심을 가졌다.
③ 지갑을 자동차에 두고 내렸다.
④ 운전하는 것을 매우 좋아했다.
⑤ 조심스럽게 운전하라는 충고를 들었다.

＊ 확인 사항
○ 답안지의 해당란에 필요한 내용을 정확히 기입(표기)했는지 확인하시오.

※ QR 코드를 스캔하시면 듣기 방송이 나옵니다. 듣기 방송을 들으며 다음 빈칸을 채우시오.

● 제한 시간 : 25분

01

다음을 듣고, 여자가 하는 말의 목적으로 가장 적절한 것을 고르시오.

W : Good afternoon. I'm the director of the Modern Gallery. I hope you are ✿ _____ _____ _____ of the works of Steve Kim, the world-famous photographer. Today, there will be a special event for our visitors. We invited Steve Kim to the gallery to meet his fans and _____ _____ _____ _____ _____ _____ _____. It will be a great opportunity to meet the artist in person. The event will start at three p.m. in the Design Hall and last for about an hour. If you're interested, please come to the hall and _____ _____ _____ _____ _____ _____. For more information, you can get a pamphlet at the reception desk. Thank you.

02

대화를 듣고, 남자의 의견으로 가장 적절한 것을 고르시오.

M : Brenda, my uncle bought a shrimp pizza. Help yourself.

W : Oh! But I don't like shrimp.

M : Really? Do you have _____ _____ _____ _____ ?

W : No. I've heard shrimp is a little high in cholesterol. So, I think it isn't good for our health.

M : Hmm, that's a misunderstanding about shrimp.

W : You mean eating shrimp _____ _____ _____ _____ _____ _____ ?

M : Of course. It can increase your level of good cholesterol.

W : Oh, I didn't know that.

M : Eating shrimp can give us vitamins and minerals. Plus, shrimp is low-calorie.

W : Then it might be good to ✿ _____ _____ _____ _____ _____ .

M : Sure. It would be helpful to your health.

W : I guess I didn't know much about shrimp. I'll give it a try.

03

대화를 듣고, 두 사람의 관계를 가장 잘 나타낸 것을 고르시오.

[Telephone Rings.]

W : Hello. This is Monica Jones.

M : Hello. This is John Lewis, Sally's father.

W : Hello, Mr. Lewis. Has Sally gotten any better?

M : Yes. ✿ _____ _____ _____ _____ _____ _____ _____ anymore.

W : Glad to hear that.

M : But the doctor said that Sally needs to stay home this week.

W : I see. Do you think she'll _____ _____ _____ next Monday?

M : I think so. But, Sally's worried that she won't be able to _____ _____ _____ _____ _____ .

W : Oh, please tell her not to worry about it. The newspaper editor is also taking my class, so I'll talk to him.

M : Thank you so much.

04

대화를 듣고, 그림에서 대화의 내용과 일치하지 않는 것을 고르시오.

M : Mom, this is a picture from Science Day.

W : Let me see. The woman wearing glasses must be your science teacher.

M : Yes, she is. She helped me a lot. Do you see _____ _____ _____ _____ _____ _____ ?

W : Oh, it looks fantastic! Who made it?

M : I made it myself. I received a lot of good comments about it.

W : Good job. What are the two pictures on the wall?

M : They are _____ _____ _____ _____ _____ .

W : I see. And there is a robot in front of the window.

M : Yeah, my class put all the parts of the robot together.

W : Sounds great. I can see ✿ _____ _____ _____ on the table, too.

M : My teacher showed us _____ _____ _____ _____ _____ _____ _____ , and it was very exciting.

W : You must've had a great time.

05

대화를 듣고, 남자가 여자에게 부탁한 일로 가장 적절한 것을 고르시오.

W : Dad, where are you going?

M : I'm going to the grocery store. We're having a surprise party this evening.

W : Really? Is it a special day today?

M : Yes. Mom _____ _____ _____ _____ , so we're going to celebrate.

W : Oh, good for her. I'm sure she'll love the party.

M : I hope so. I'm thinking of making steak and seafood pasta for dinner.

W : Sounds perfect. Will there be any guests?

M : Yes. I invited a couple of our friends.

W : Good. I also want to help. Shall I _____ _____ _____ for the dinner table?

M : No. I'll do that. Can you clean the living room instead?

W : Sure. I'll ✿ _____ _____ _____ _____ _____ before you come back.

M : Thanks. That's very kind of you.

Dictation 02

06

대화를 듣고, 남자가 지불할 금액을 고르시오.

W : Hello. Can I help you?

M : Yes. I want to buy a baseball bat for my son. He is 11 years old.

W : How about this baseball bat? It's the most popular. It's 30 dollars.

M : Okay. I'll take one bat. Do you also have baseball gloves?

W : Sure. How about this glove? It's _____ _____.

M : How much is it?

W : It's 15 dollars.

M : Hmm... That's reasonable. I'll buy two gloves.

W : Okay. Don't you need _____ _____ _____ _____ _____? They are light and soft.

M : I think I've got all I need. Can I use this coupon?

W : Of course. Then you can get ✪ _____ _____ _____ _____ _____.

M : Great. I'll use the coupon and pay by credit card.

07

대화를 듣고, 여자가 남자와 함께 뮤지컬을 보러 갈 수 없는 이유를 고르시오.

M : Hi, Jane. I got two free tickets for the musical *Lion King*. Can you go with me this Saturday?

W : I'd love to, but I don't think I can.

M : Do you have to work that day?

W : No, it's not about work.

M : Then, why not? I thought you were _____ _____ _____ _____.

W : Of course, I am. But my parents are coming ✪ _____ _____ _____ _____ _____ to see me.

M : Oh, that's great. When did you last see them?

W : Two years ago. So I think I need to spend this weekend with them.

M : Okay. No problem. I'll find _____ _____ _____ _____ _____ _____ then.

08

대화를 듣고, Career Vision Camp에 관해 언급되지 <u>않은</u> 것을 고르시오.

[Door knocks.]

M : Can I come in, Ms. Wilson?

W : Sure, come on in. *[Pause]* Oh, Peter. I was waiting for you to come. _____ _____ _____ _____ _____?

M : I'm still trying to find some information about my future career.

W : Good. So I'd like to recommend the Career Vision Camp to you.

M : Okay. I heard that the camp is _____ _____ _____ _____. Is that right?

W : Yes. It'll be helpful. Plus, there's ✪ _____ _____ _____.

M : Great. Hmm, can you tell me when the application deadline is?

W : It's December 14th. You should hurry since it's first come, first served.

M : I see. I will apply for the camp as soon as possible.

W : It'll be held at the Lincoln Center near school. You can get there easily.

M : Okay. Thank you.

09

Book Review Contest에 관한 다음 내용을 듣고, 일치하지 <u>않는</u> 것을 고르시오.

[3점]

W : Good morning, Central High School. This is Kathy Miller, the school librarian. ✪ _____ _____ _____ _____ _____ this year's reading month, our school is going to hold a Book Review Contest. All students are invited to participate in the contest. You can write a review on any type of book, but the review _____ _____ _____ _____ _____ _____. You can download a form from our school website. Reviews should be submitted through e-mail by the end of this month. The best three works will be selected and _____ _____ _____ _____ _____ _____. For more details, please visit the school website. Thank you.

10

다음 표를 보면서 대화를 듣고, 여자가 구입할 전기면도기를 고르시오.

M : Katie, what are you doing with your smartphone?

W : I'm searching for an electric shaver for my dad's birthday. Will you help me find a good one?

M : Sure. Let me see... *[Pause]* How about this one?

W : Well, that's too expensive. I can't spend more than $100.

M : Okay. And I think a 20-minute battery life is ✪ _____ _____ _____ _____ _____.

W : I think so, too. It _____ _____ _____.

M : You're right. Does it need to be waterproof?

W : Of course. He _____ _____ _____ _____ every morning.

M : Then we have only two options left. Which color do you think is better?

W : Dad likes black, so I'll buy the black one.

M : I think it's a nice choice.

11

대화를 듣고, 여자의 마지막 말에 대한 남자의 응답으로 가장 적절한 것을 고르시오.

W : Hey, look! There's an Italian restaurant over there.

M : It's newly opened. Last weekend I ✪ _____ _____ _____ with my friends.

W : Really? _____ _____ _____ _____ _____ _____ _____?

12

대화를 듣고, 남자의 마지막 말에 대한 여자의 응답으로 가장 적절한 것을 고르시오.

M : Honey, look out the window. It's raining a lot.

W : Yeah, I think it might be _____ _____ _____ _____ _____ _____.

M : You're right. You'd better ✪ _____ _____ _____ today.

13

대화를 듣고, 남자의 마지막 말에 대한 여자의 응답으로 가장 적절한 것을 고르시오. [3점]

W : Chris, _____ _____ _____ _____ _____ _____ yesterday.

M : Oh, really? Tell me about it.

W : After school I visited Mina's house to do homework with her. Then I came back home before dinner.

M : Well, I don't see why that's funny.

W : Hey, I'm not finished yet. While I was having dinner, I got a phone call from Mina.

M : What did she say?

W : She said _____ _____ _____ _____ _____ _____ _____!

M : Oh, what happened?

W : By mistake, I came home wearing her shoes instead of mine. Her shoes looked ✪ _____ _____ _____ _____ _____.

M : _____ _____ _____ _____ _____ _____. So, what did you say to Mina?

14

대화를 듣고, 여자의 마지막 말에 대한 남자의 응답으로 가장 적절한 것을 고르시오. [3점]

M : Hi, Emily! How are your wedding preparations going?

W : They're going well so far. I reserved a wedding hall and ordered invitation cards.

M : Good. ✪ _____ _____ _____. It's on the first Saturday of July, right?

W : Yes. Can you come?

M : Of course. Is there anything that I can help you with?

W : Actually, I _____ _____ _____ _____ _____ _____ _____. So, would you sing for me?

M : I'd love to, but I've never done anything like that before.

W : I heard you singing at the college song festival, so I know you're a good singer.

M : Thanks, but I'm afraid I may not sing well enough to do so at a wedding.

W : Oh, please! I'm sure _____ _____ _____ _____ _____. I'd look forward to it.

15

다음 상황 설명을 듣고, Julie가 Eric에게 할 말로 가장 적절한 것을 고르시오. [3점]

W : Julie's going to throw a birthday party this Friday evening. She invites her friend Eric to the party. Eric wants to ✪ _____ _____ _____, but he has a problem. His parents will go out for dinner on Friday, so his eight-year-old brother will have to stay home alone if he goes out. Eric can't _____ _____ _____, so he asks Julie if he can come to the party with his brother. Julie wants to say it's okay because she'd like to _____ _____ _____ _____ _____ _____. In this situation, what would Julie most likely say to Eric?

16~17

다음을 듣고, 물음에 답하시오.

M : Hello, everyone. Last class we learned about the dangers of climate change. Today, I'll tell you about some foods that might disappear because of ✪ _____ _____. First of all, 70 percent of the world's coffee could disappear by 2080 due to climate change. In Africa, the amount of coffee produced has dropped by more than 50 percent. Secondly, _____ _____ _____ _____ _____. It usually takes 72 gallons of water to make just one pound of avocados. Climate change in California _____ _____ _____ _____ _____ _____ _____, so the avocado plants aren't producing enough fruit. Thirdly, warmer temperatures affect apple trees, too. To grow properly, apple trees need a certain period of cold weather. Lack of cold weather time leads to lower apple production. Finally, the _____ _____ _____ _____ _____ _____ are causing a decrease in strawberry production in Florida. Specifically, hotter-than-normal weather has delayed the flowering and production of strawberries. Now, let me show you some slides about this issue.

▶ 정답 : 해설편 197쪽

18
- 001 ☐ retire from ~에서 은퇴하다
- 002 ☐ several ⓐ 여럿의
- 003 ☐ award ⓝ (부상이 딸린) 상
- 004 ☐ national ⓐ 국가의
- 005 ☐ competition ⓝ 대회, 경쟁
- 006 ☐ name ⓥ 임명하다, 지명하다, 명명하다
- 007 ☐ promote ⓥ 증진하다, 촉진하다
- 008 ☐ health ⓝ 건강, 보건, 건전
- 009 ☐ hope ⓥ ~을 희망하다, 바라다, 생각하다 ⓝ 희망
- 010 ☐ instruction ⓝ 강습, 교육, 지시, 방법
- 011 ☐ principal ⓝ 교장, 학장, 총장

19
- 012 ☐ cave ⓝ 동굴
- 013 ☐ venture ⓥ 탐험하다
- 014 ☐ entrance ⓝ (출)입구, 문
- 015 ☐ show off 뽐내다, 과시하다
- 016 ☐ adventure ⓝ 모험
- 017 ☐ glittering ⓐ 반짝이는
- 018 ☐ incredibly ⓐ (너무 좋아서) 믿을 수 없게
- 019 ☐ stretch out ~을 내밀다, 뻗다
- 020 ☐ wall ⓝ 담, 벽
- 021 ☐ suddenly ⓐ 갑자기, 급작스럽게
- 022 ☐ footing ⓝ 발을 디딤, 딛고 선 자리
- 023 ☐ give way 무너지다, 내려앉다
- 024 ☐ slide down 미끄러지다
- 025 ☐ crack ⓝ (좁은) 틈
- 026 ☐ underground ⓐ 지하에
- 027 ☐ upward ⓐ 위쪽을 향한
- 028 ☐ calls out ~를 부르대[외치다]
- 029 ☐ indifferent ⓐ 무관심한
- 030 ☐ desperate ⓐ 필사적인, 절박한, (상황이) 절망적인

20
- 031 ☐ development ⓝ 발달
- 032 ☐ strongly ⓐ 튼튼하게, 강력하게
- 033 ☐ encourage ⓥ 장려하다, 격려하다
- 034 ☐ own ⓥ 주도하다, 소유하다
- 035 ☐ educational ⓐ 교육적인
- 036 ☐ produce ⓥ 만들어 내다
- 037 ☐ outcome ⓝ 결과
- 038 ☐ essence ⓝ 본질
- 039 ☐ delight ⓥ 많은 기쁨을 주다
- 040 ☐ immediate ⓐ 즉각적인, 즉시의
- 041 ☐ laugh ⓥ 웃다
- 042 ☐ direction ⓝ 방향, 지시, 길, 목표
- 043 ☐ a range of 광범위한, 넓은
- 044 ☐ benefit ⓝ 이익, 혜택

21
- 045 ☐ excess ⓝ (어떤 정도를) 지나침
- 046 ☐ discuss ⓥ 상의[의논/논의]하다
- 047 ☐ as far back as ~만큼 오래전부터
- 048 ☐ argue ⓥ 언쟁을 하다, 주장하다
- 049 ☐ virtuous ⓐ 도덕적인, 고결한
- 050 ☐ brave ⓐ 용감한 ⓥ 용감하다
- 051 ☐ reckless ⓐ 무모한
- 052 ☐ trusting ⓐ 사람을 믿는
- 053 ☐ gullible ⓐ 잘 속아 넘어가는

054 ☐ trait ⓝ 특성
- 055 ☐ deficiency ⓝ 부족, 결핍
- 056 ☐ sweet spot 가장 좋은 점, 최고의 상황
- 057 ☐ maximize ⓥ 극대화하다
- 058 ☐ suggestion ⓝ 제안, 의견
- 059 ☐ virtue ⓝ 미덕, 덕목
- 060 ☐ midpoint ⓝ 중간, 중심점
- 061 ☐ neither A nor B A도 아니고 B도 아니다
- 062 ☐ generous ⓐ 관대한
- 063 ☐ stingy ⓐ (특히 돈에) 인색한
- 064 ☐ recklessly ⓐ 무모하게, 개의치 않고
- 065 ☐ biased ⓐ 편향된
- 066 ☐ material ⓐ 물질[물리]적인
- 067 ☐ richness ⓝ 풍요로움
- 068 ☐ pressure ⓝ 압박, 압력
- 069 ☐ extreme ⓝ 극단

22
- 070 ☐ freshly ⓐ 갓, 신선하게
- 071 ☐ bake ⓥ (음식을) 굽다
- 072 ☐ detect ⓥ 알아차리다, 감지하다
- 073 ☐ rather ⓐ 꽤, 다소
- 074 ☐ pleasant ⓐ 기분 좋은, 유쾌한
- 075 ☐ disappear ⓥ 사라지다, 없어지다
- 076 ☐ in fact 사실은
- 077 ☐ reawaken ⓥ 다시 일깨우다
- 078 ☐ exact ⓐ 정확한, 정밀한
- 079 ☐ concept ⓝ 개념
- 080 ☐ apply ⓥ 쓰다, 적용하다
- 081 ☐ perhaps ⓐ 아마, 어쩌면
- 082 ☐ satisfying ⓐ 만족감을 주는, 만족스러운
- 083 ☐ asset ⓝ 자산
- 084 ☐ consciousness ⓝ 의식
- 085 ☐ proverb ⓝ 속담
- 086 ☐ run dry (물 등이) 마르다, 말라붙다

23
- 087 ☐ stump ⓝ (나무의) 그루터기
- 088 ☐ notice ⓥ ~을 의식하다[보거나 듣고 알다]
- 089 ☐ a series of 일련의
- 090 ☐ sensitive ⓐ 민감한, 예민한
- 091 ☐ local ⓐ 지역의
- 092 ☐ climate ⓝ 기후
- 093 ☐ temperature ⓝ 온도
- 094 ☐ tree ring 나이테
- 095 ☐ stressful ⓐ 스트레스가 많은, 짜증나는
- 096 ☐ drought ⓝ 가뭄
- 097 ☐ hardly ⓐ 거의 ~할 수 없다
- 098 ☐ in particular 특히
- 099 ☐ clue ⓝ 단서, 증거
- 100 ☐ measurement ⓝ 측정, 관측
- 101 ☐ direction ⓝ 방향
- 102 ☐ traditional ⓐ 전통적인
- 103 ☐ predict ⓥ 예측하다
- 104 ☐ measure ⓥ 측정하다, 재다
- 105 ☐ protect ⓥ 보호하다, 지키다
- 106 ☐ suggest ⓥ 시사[암시]하다

24
- 107 ☐ suppose ⓥ 생각하다, 추정[추측]하다
- 108 ☐ keep ⓥ (동물을) 기르다[치다]
- 109 ☐ necessary ⓐ 필요한

110 ☐ bee ⓝ 벌
- 111 ☐ in the midst of 한창일 때, ~ 가운데
- 112 ☐ blossom ⓝ (특히 과수의) 꽃
- 113 ☐ distance ⓝ 거리
- 114 ☐ open ⓐ 탁 트인, 너른
- 115 ☐ unfavorable ⓐ 적합하지 못한, 불리한
- 116 ☐ circumstance ⓝ 환경, 상황
- 117 ☐ suburb ⓝ 교외
- 118 ☐ constant ⓐ 지속적인, 끊임없는
- 119 ☐ supply ⓝ 공급 ⓥ 공급하다
- 120 ☐ seriously ⓐ 심하게, 진지하게
- 121 ☐ afraid ⓥ 두려워하는
- 122 ☐ profitably ⓐ 이윤을 내며, 유리하게
- 123 ☐ enjoyably ⓐ 즐겁게
- 124 ☐ harvest ⓥ 수확하다
- 125 ☐ farming ⓝ 영농, 농업, 농사

25
- 126 ☐ average ⓐ 평균의
- 127 ☐ compared with ~과 비교하여
- 128 ☐ reach one's peak 정점에 달하다
- 129 ☐ opposite ⓐ 정반대의

26
- 130 ☐ close ⓐ 가까운
- 131 ☐ official ⓐ 공식적인
- 132 ☐ capital ⓝ 수도
- 133 ☐ population ⓝ 인구
- 134 ☐ consist ⓥ 되어[이루어져] 있다
- 135 ☐ tribe ⓝ 부족
- 136 ☐ symbolize ⓥ 나타내다, 상징하다
- 137 ☐ mixture ⓝ 혼합
- 138 ☐ native language 모국어
- 139 ☐ purpose ⓝ 목적

27
- 140 ☐ opportunity ⓝ 기회
- 141 ☐ develop ⓥ 발달시키다
- 142 ☐ social skill 사교 기술
- 143 ☐ creativity ⓝ 창의력
- 144 ☐ period ⓝ 기간, 시기
- 145 ☐ participation ⓝ 참가, 참여
- 146 ☐ maximum ⓐ 최대의
- 147 ☐ outdoor ⓐ 옥외[야외]의
- 148 ☐ cost ⓝ 값, 비용
- 149 ☐ regardless of ~에 관계없이
- 150 ☐ sign up 등록하다, 참가하다

28
- 151 ☐ regular ⓐ 상시의, 규칙적인
- 152 ☐ visitor ⓝ 방문객, 손님
- 153 ☐ treasure ⓝ 보물
- 154 ☐ donation ⓝ 기부(금)
- 155 ☐ reservation ⓝ 예약
- 156 ☐ accompany ⓥ ~와 동반하다

29
- 157 ☐ strength ⓝ 강점
- 158 ☐ weakness ⓝ 약점
- 159 ☐ accept ⓥ 받아들이다, 수용하다
- 160 ☐ role ⓝ 역할
- 161 ☐ certain ⓐ 특정한

110 추가...

- 162 ☐ improve ⓥ 나아지게 하다, 향상시키다
- 163 ☐ social ⓐ 사회의, 사회적인
- 164 ☐ necessary ⓐ 필요한
- 165 ☐ respond to ~에 응답하다
- 166 ☐ excuse ⓝ 변명
- 167 ☐ growth ⓝ 성장
- 168 ☐ personally ⓐ 직접, 개인적으로
- 169 ☐ responsibility ⓝ 책임

30
- 170 ☐ overabundance ⓝ 과잉, 지나치게 풍부함
- 171 ☐ in terms of ~의 관점에서
- 172 ☐ depressed ⓐ 우울한
- 173 ☐ researcher ⓝ 연구자
- 174 ☐ surprisingly ⓐ 놀랍게도
- 175 ☐ purchase ⓥ 구매하다
- 176 ☐ relieved ⓐ 안도한
- 177 ☐ savvy ⓐ 사리에 밝은
- 178 ☐ prompt ⓥ 촉진하다
- 179 ☐ satisfied ⓐ 만족한

31
- 180 ☐ creativity ⓝ 창조성, 독창성
- 181 ☐ uniquely ⓐ 고유하게
- 182 ☐ nest ⓝ 둥지
- 183 ☐ come close to ~에 근접하다
- 184 ☐ display ⓥ 드러내다, 내보이다
- 185 ☐ artificial intelligence 인공 지능
- 186 ☐ translate ⓥ 번역하다
- 187 ☐ poem ⓝ 시
- 188 ☐ complicated ⓐ 복잡한
- 189 ☐ to name a few things 몇 가지만 보더라도
- 190 ☐ face ⓥ 직면하다
- 191 ☐ unrivaled ⓐ 경쟁할 상대가 없는
- 192 ☐ universal ⓐ 일반적인, 보편적인

32
- 193 ☐ revival ⓝ 부흥, 부활, 회복
- 194 ☐ dying ⓐ 죽어가는
- 195 ☐ industrial ⓐ 산업의
- 196 ☐ dry up 줄어들다, 고갈되다, 말라붙다
- 197 ☐ replace ⓥ 대체하다
- 198 ☐ investigate ⓥ 조사하다, 수사하다
- 199 ☐ in particular 특히
- 200 ☐ disturb ⓥ (마음을) 불편하게 하다, 방해하다
- 201 ☐ out of control 통제력을 벗어난
- 202 ☐ uncover ⓥ 알아내다, 적발하다
- 203 ☐ invite ⓥ 부탁하다, 요청하다
- 204 ☐ slogan ⓝ 표어, 슬로건

33
- 205 ☐ essentially ⓐ 본질적으로
- 206 ☐ survival ⓝ 생존
- 207 ☐ machine ⓝ 기계
- 208 ☐ defense ⓝ 방어
- 209 ☐ against prep ~에 반대하여[맞서]
- 210 ☐ gather ⓥ 모으다, 수집하다
- 211 ☐ storing ⓝ 저장
- 212 ☐ analyze ⓥ 분석하다
- 213 ☐ inner ⓐ 내부[안쪽]의

214 ☐ stillness ⓝ 고요함
215 ☐ breakthrough ⓝ 돌파구
216 ☐ quietude ⓝ 정적, 고요
217 ☐ nationwide ⓐ 전국적인
218 ☐ inquiry ⓝ 조사, 연구
219 ☐ mathematician ⓝ 수학자
220 ☐ method ⓝ 방법
221 ☐ subordinate ⓐ 부수적인
222 ☐ brief ⓐ 짧은
223 ☐ decisive ⓐ 결정적인
224 ☐ phase ⓝ 단계
225 ☐ majority ⓝ 다수, 대부분
226 ☐ organize ⓥ 정리하다, 체계화하다
227 ☐ socially ⓐ 사회적으로
228 ☐ imagination ⓝ 상상력

34
229 ☐ concern ⓝ 관심사, 걱정
230 ☐ industry ⓝ 산업
231 ☐ remote ⓐ 원격의
232 ☐ device ⓝ 장치, 기구, 장비
233 ☐ popularity ⓝ 인기
234 ☐ recorder ⓝ 녹음기, 녹화기
235 ☐ consumers ⓝ 소비자
236 ☐ mute ⓥ ~의 소리를 줄이다
237 ☐ fast-forward 앞으로 빨리 감다
238 ☐ skip over ~을 건너뛰다, ~을 묵과하다
239 ☐ commercial ⓝ 광고 ⓐ 상업의
240 ☐ entirely ⓐ 아예, 전부, 전적으로
241 ☐ advertiser ⓝ 광고주
242 ☐ adapt to ~에 적응하다
243 ☐ plant ⓥ 놓다, 두다
244 ☐ desperately ⓐ 절박하게, 간절하게
245 ☐ entertaining ⓐ 재미있는, 즐거움을 주는
246 ☐ discourage ⓥ 막다[말리다]
247 ☐ give up on ~을 포기하다
248 ☐ altogether ⓐ 아예, 완전히
249 ☐ expert ⓝ 전문가
250 ☐ predict ⓥ 예측하다
251 ☐ eventually ⓐ 결국
252 ☐ be forced to ~하도록 강요 당하다
253 ☐ incentive ⓝ 장려책
254 ☐ encourage ⓥ 부추기다, 조장하다
255 ☐ in the form of ~의 형태로
256 ☐ reduction ⓝ 축소, 삭감, 절감
257 ☐ deliver ⓥ 배달하다
258 ☐ battle ⓝ 전투, 투쟁
259 ☐ broadcast ⓝ 방송
260 ☐ exposure ⓝ 노출, 폭로

35
261 ☐ depending on ~에 따라
262 ☐ reach out (잡으려고 손을) 뻗다
263 ☐ arm's length 팔을 뻗으면 닿는 (가까운) 거리
264 ☐ improve ⓥ 개선되다, 나아지다

36
265 ☐ early ⓐ 초(창)기의
266 ☐ desire ⓝ 열망, 갈망
267 ☐ confidence ⓝ 자신감, 믿음
268 ☐ mail ⓥ (우편으로) 보내다[부치다]

269 ☐ secretly ⓐ 몰래
270 ☐ refuse ⓥ 거절하다
271 ☐ attend ⓥ (…에) 다니다
272 ☐ jail ⓝ 교도소
273 ☐ debt ⓝ 빚, 부채
274 ☐ hunger ⓝ 배고픔
275 ☐ recognize ⓥ 알아보다, 인정하다
276 ☐ praise ⓥ 칭찬하다
277 ☐ whole ⓐ 전체의
278 ☐ widely ⓐ 널리

37
279 ☐ spot ⓝ 특정한 곳
280 ☐ stargazing ⓝ 별 보기
281 ☐ twinkle ⓥ 반짝거리다
282 ☐ brilliant ⓐ 눈부신, 훌륭한
283 ☐ jewel ⓝ 보석
284 ☐ describe ⓥ 묘사하다
285 ☐ triangle ⓝ 삼각형
286 ☐ amazing ⓐ 놀라운
287 ☐ sight ⓝ 보기, 봄
288 ☐ confuse ⓥ 혼란시키다, 혼란스럽게 만들다
289 ☐ point out 가리키다
290 ☐ chances are that ~할 가능성이 있다
291 ☐ exactly ⓐ 정확히

38
292 ☐ hesitation ⓝ 망설임, 주저함
293 ☐ musically ⓐ 음악적으로
294 ☐ talented ⓐ 재능이 있는
295 ☐ instrument ⓝ 기구, 악기
296 ☐ appeal to ~에 어필하다, ~에 호소하다
297 ☐ powerfully ⓐ 강력하게, 대단하게
298 ☐ preschooler ⓝ 미취학 아동
299 ☐ light up (안색이) 밝아지다
300 ☐ eagerly ⓐ 열렬히
301 ☐ enthusiastically ⓐ 열정적으로
302 ☐ communicate ⓥ 의사소통하다
303 ☐ comfortably ⓐ 편안하게
304 ☐ express ⓥ 나타내다, 표현하다
305 ☐ creatively ⓐ 창의적으로
306 ☐ emotion ⓝ 감정, 정서
307 ☐ interact with ~와 상호작용하다
308 ☐ make the most of ~을 최대한 활용하다
309 ☐ situation ⓝ 상황, 처지, 환경
310 ☐ matter ⓥ (사건, 일 등이) 중요하다

39
311 ☐ instead of ~ 대신에
312 ☐ give a hand 도와주다
313 ☐ explain ⓥ 설명하다
314 ☐ sentence ⓝ 문장
315 ☐ positive ⓐ 긍정적인
316 ☐ note ⓝ 어조
317 ☐ tendency ⓝ 성향, 경향
318 ☐ challenge ⓥ 이의를 제기하다, 도전하다
319 ☐ colleague ⓝ 동료
320 ☐ come up to ~에게 다가가다
321 ☐ figure ⓝ 수치
322 ☐ simply ⓐ 그저 (단순히)
323 ☐ insist ⓥ 주장하다, 고집하다
324 ☐ input ⓝ 참여, 투입

325 ☐ increase ⓥ 상승시키다
326 ☐ pressure ⓝ 압박, 압력
327 ☐ response ⓝ 대답, 응답
328 ☐ negative ⓐ 부정적인

40
329 ☐ according to ~에 따르면
330 ☐ confidence ⓝ 자신(감)
331 ☐ be linked to ~와 연관되다
332 ☐ compared to ~와 비교하여
333 ☐ average ⓐ 평균의, 보통의
334 ☐ vegetarian ⓐ 채식의, 채식주의의
335 ☐ diverse ⓐ 다양한
336 ☐ in contrast 그에 반해서
337 ☐ wide-ranging 광범위한
338 ☐ enthusiasm ⓝ 열정
339 ☐ in general 일반적으로
340 ☐ eat out 외식하다
341 ☐ except for ~을 제외하고
342 ☐ specific ⓐ 특정한
343 ☐ healthy ⓐ 건강한
344 ☐ exotic ⓐ 이국적인

41~42
345 ☐ advertisement ⓝ 광고
346 ☐ cite ⓥ 들다, 인용하다
347 ☐ statistical ⓐ 통계적인
348 ☐ surveys ⓝ (설문) 조사
349 ☐ cautious ⓐ 조심스러운, 신중한
350 ☐ usually ⓐ 보통, 대개
351 ☐ conduct ⓥ 수행하다, 행동을 하다
352 ☐ toothpaste ⓝ 치약
353 ☐ manufacturer ⓝ 제조 회사
354 ☐ dentist ⓝ 치과 의사
355 ☐ recommend ⓥ 추천하다
356 ☐ prefer ⓥ 선호하다
357 ☐ turn out 판명되다, 밝혀지다
358 ☐ allow ⓥ 허락[허용]하다
359 ☐ competitor ⓝ (특히 사업에서) 경쟁자
360 ☐ no wonder 당연히도, 그도 그럴 것이
361 ☐ rule ⓥ 결정하다, 판결하다
362 ☐ misleading ⓐ 오해의 소지가 있는
363 ☐ display ⓥ 진열하다, 전시하다
364 ☐ similar ⓐ 비슷한, 유사한
365 ☐ concern ⓥ ~에 관련되다
366 ☐ well-known ⓐ 유명한
367 ☐ cosmetic ⓝ 화장품
368 ☐ rapidly ⓐ 빨리, 급속히
369 ☐ reduce ⓥ 줄이다[축소하다]
370 ☐ wrinkle ⓝ 주름
371 ☐ evidence ⓝ 증거
372 ☐ provide ⓥ 제공하다, 주다
373 ☐ based on ~에 근거하여
374 ☐ personal ⓐ 개인의[개인적인]
375 ☐ objective ⓐ 객관적인
376 ☐ measurement ⓝ 측정, 측량
377 ☐ condition ⓝ 상태
378 ☐ quite ⓐ 꽤, 상당히
379 ☐ typical ⓐ 전형적인
380 ☐ judgment ⓝ 판단, 심판
381 ☐ avoid ⓥ 회피하다, 모면하다
382 ☐ claim ⓝ 주장

383 ☐ seriously ⓐ 심각하게, 진심으로
384 ☐ link ⓝ 관련(성)
385 ☐ between prep 사이[중간]에
386 ☐ economy ⓝ 경제
387 ☐ reliable ⓐ 믿을만한, 신뢰할만한

43~45
388 ☐ evening ⓝ 저녁, 밤, 야간
389 ☐ land ⓥ 도착[착륙/상륙]하다
390 ☐ homesick ⓐ 향수를 느끼는
391 ☐ university ⓝ 대학
392 ☐ mechanical engineering 기계 공학
393 ☐ luggage ⓝ 짐, 수하물
394 ☐ relief ⓝ 안도, 안도감
395 ☐ wallet ⓝ 지갑
396 ☐ horrible ⓐ 끔찍한, 무서운
397 ☐ scenario ⓝ 시나리오, 각본
398 ☐ drive away ⓥ (차를 몰고[타고]) 떠나다
399 ☐ kindness ⓝ 친절, 다정함
400 ☐ initial ⓐ 처음의, 초기의
401 ☐ excitement ⓝ 흥분, 신남
402 ☐ aggressively ⓐ 공격적으로
403 ☐ panic ⓥ 허둥대다, 겁에 질려 어쩔 줄 모르다
404 ☐ honk ⓥ (자동차의) 경적
405 ☐ pull ⓥ (차량 등을 한쪽으로) 틀다
406 ☐ van ⓝ 승합차, 밴
407 ☐ roadside ⓝ 갓길, 길가
408 ☐ pound ⓥ (심장이) 쿵쾅거리다, 방망이질 치다
409 ☐ approach ⓥ 다가가다[오다]
410 ☐ reach ⓥ …에 이르다[닿다/도달하다]
411 ☐ warn ⓥ 경고하다, 주의를 주다
412 ☐ road rage (도로에서 운전 중) 분통 터뜨리기
413 ☐ advise ⓥ 조언하다, 권고하다
414 ☐ cautiously ⓐ 조심해서, 조심스럽게

● 채점 : 맞은 개수 _____ / 80

TEST A-B 각 단어의 뜻을 [A] 영어는 우리말로, [B] 우리말은 영어로 쓰시오.

A	English	Korean
01	retire from	
02	argue	
03	run dry	
04	hardly	
05	unfavorable	
06	reach one's peak	
07	sign up	
08	relieved	
09	universal	
10	industrial	
11	organize	
12	phase	
13	refuse	
14	stargazing	
15	chances are that	
16	hesitation	
17	give a hand	
18	vegetarian	
19	rule	
20	cautiously	

B	Korean	English
01	증진하다, 촉진하다	
02	임명하다, 명명하다	
03	장려하다, 격려하다	
04	개념	
05	만족감을 주는	
06	단서	
07	거리	
08	되어(이루어져) 있다	
09	~에 관계없이	
10	~에 응답하다	
11	인공지능	
12	다수, 대부분	
13	결국	
14	개선되다, 나아지다	
15	빚, 부채	
16	혼란시키다	
17	(사건 등이) 중요하다	
18	성향, 경향	
19	판명되다, 밝혀지다	
20	향수를 느끼는	

▶ A-D 정답 : 해설편 197쪽

TEST C-D 각 단어의 뜻을 골라 기호를 쓰시오.

C	English		Korean
01	incredibly	( )	ⓐ 본질
02	essence	( )	ⓑ 편향된
03	a range of	( )	ⓒ 환경, 상황
04	reckless	( )	ⓓ 돌파구
05	biased	( )	ⓔ 광범위한, 넓은
06	temperature	( )	ⓕ 수도
07	circumstance	( )	ⓖ 눈부신, 훌륭한
08	capital	( )	ⓗ 수치
09	accompany	( )	ⓘ 믿을 수 없게
10	strength	( )	ⓙ 열망, 갈망
11	overabundance	( )	ⓚ 무모한
12	translate	( )	ⓛ ~을 건너뛰다
13	uncover	( )	ⓜ (안색이) 밝아지다
14	breakthrough	( )	ⓝ 알아내다, 적발하다
15	skip over	( )	ⓞ 과잉
16	desire	( )	ⓟ 온도
17	brilliant	( )	ⓠ 강점
18	light up	( )	ⓡ 번역하다
19	figure	( )	ⓢ 오해의 소지가 있는
20	misleading	( )	ⓣ ~와 동반하다

D	Korean		English
01	필사적인	( )	ⓐ awareness
02	가장 좋은 점, 최고의 상황	( )	ⓑ desperate
03	의식	( )	ⓒ compared with
04	가뭄	( )	ⓓ defense
05	이윤을 내며, 유리하게	( )	ⓔ recognize
06	~과 비교하여	( )	ⓕ interact with
07	모국어	( )	ⓖ prompt
08	공식적인	( )	ⓗ unrivaled
09	기부금	( )	ⓘ insist
10	촉진하다	( )	ⓙ native language
11	경쟁할 상대가 없는	( )	ⓚ profitably
12	방어	( )	ⓛ initial
13	아예, 전적으로	( )	ⓜ donation
14	알아보다, 인정하다	( )	ⓝ appeal to
15	~에 호소하다	( )	ⓞ official
16	~와 상호작용하다	( )	ⓟ colleague
17	주장하다	( )	ⓠ eat out
18	동료	( )	ⓡ sweet spot
19	외식하다	( )	ⓢ entirely
20	처음의, 초기의	( )	ⓣ drought

제 3 교시

영어 영역

03회

● 문항수 45개 | 배점 100점 | 제한 시간 70분   ● 점수 표시가 없는 문항은 모두 2점 ● 출처 : 고1 학력평가

1번부터 17번까지는 듣고 답하는 문제입니다. 1번부터 15번까지는 한 번만 들려주고, 16번부터 17번까지는 두 번 들려줍니다. 방송을 잘 듣고 답을 하시기 바랍니다.

1. 다음을 듣고, 남자가 하는 말의 목적으로 가장 적절한 것을 고르시오.

① 도서 대출 기한 변경을 안내하려고
② 도서관 조명 시설 교체를 요청하려고
③ 도서관 운영 시간 연장을 건의하려고
④ 도서관 공사로 인한 소음에 대해 사과하려고
⑤ 도서관 보수로 인한 임시 휴관을 공지하려고

2. 대화를 듣고, 여자의 의견으로 가장 적절한 것을 고르시오.

① 수면 부족은 신체 건강에 해롭다.
② 적절한 스트레스는 일의 능률을 높인다.
③ 잠자기 전 휴대폰 사용은 숙면에 방해가 된다.
④ 수면 장애 해결을 위해 원인을 파악해야 한다.
⑤ 집중력 향상을 위해 규칙적인 운동이 필요하다.

3. 대화를 듣고, 두 사람의 관계를 가장 잘 나타낸 것을 고르시오.

① 신문 기자 - 작가   ② 녹음 기사 - 성우
③ 영화감독 - 배우   ④ 매니저 - 가수
⑤ 의사 - 환자

4. 대화를 듣고, 그림에서 대화의 내용과 일치하지 않는 것을 고르시오.

5. 대화를 듣고, 남자가 할 일로 가장 적절한 것을 고르시오.

① 배낭 빌려주기   ② 항공권 예매하기
③ 은행에서 환전하기   ④ 여행 안내 책자 주문하기
⑤ 호텔 숙박비 비교 앱 알려 주기

6. 대화를 듣고, 남자가 지불할 금액을 고르시오. [3점]

① $27   ② $36   ③ $40   ④ $45   ⑤ $63

7. 대화를 듣고, 여자가 building expo에 갈 수 없는 이유를 고르시오.

① 오디션에 참가해야 해서
② 건축학 특강을 들어야 해서
③ 연극 관람을 하러 가야 해서
④ 다른 박람회에 갈 계획이어서
⑤ 집짓기 봉사 활동을 해야 해서

8. 대화를 듣고, Stress Free Program에 관해 언급되지 않은 것을 고르시오.

① 활동 종류   ② 등록 방법   ③ 운영 장소
④ 참가비   ⑤ 운영 시간

9. 2017 Student Design Competition에 관한 다음 내용을 듣고, 일치하지 않는 것을 고르시오. [3점]

① 학생의 창의력 향상을 목표로 한다.
② 참가자는 2층 건물 디자인을 제출해야 한다.
③ 전 세계 대학생이 참가할 수 있다.
④ 제출한 디자인은 네 개의 기준에 의해 평가된다.
⑤ 출품작은 10월 1일까지 제출해야 한다.

10. 다음 표를 보면서 대화를 듣고, 여자가 주문할 블루투스 키보드를 고르시오.

Bluetooth Keyboards

	Model	Price	Weight	Battery Life	Foldable
①	A	$45	160g	100 hours	×
②	B	$38	250g	82 hours	○
③	C	$30	280g	48 hours	×
④	D	$26	350g	10 hours	○
⑤	E	$15	420g	24 hours	×

11. 대화를 듣고, 여자의 마지막 말에 대한 남자의 응답으로 가장 적절한 것을 고르시오.

① Why don't you give it a try?
② I want to visit other countries, too.
③ I really liked noodle soup with pork.
④ It took one hour to get to the beach.
⑤ Can you pick me up from the airport?

12. 대화를 듣고, 남자의 마지막 말에 대한 여자의 응답으로 가장 적절한 것을 고르시오.

① All right. Either day is fine with me.
② I'm sorry. You can't choose the date.
③ Really? I didn't know about the change.
④ Thanks. I enjoyed the volunteer program.
⑤ Good. I'm looking forward to this weekend.

13. 대화를 듣고, 남자의 마지막 말에 대한 여자의 응답으로 가장 적절한 것을 고르시오. [3점]

Woman: _____

① I think I received the wrong items.
② Fortunately, my students really liked the gifts.
③ I'll check if your order can be canceled or not.
④ Your baseball club did a great job. Congratulations!
⑤ I'll upload the list to your bulletin board in an hour.

14. 대화를 듣고, 여자의 마지막 말에 대한 남자의 응답으로 가장 적절한 것을 고르시오. [3점]

Man: _____

① We can post the notice on social media.
② Let's move our instruments indoors, then.
③ I've already cancelled our outdoor concert.
④ We'd better change the location right away.
⑤ We can check the weather forecast using an app.

15. 다음 상황 설명을 듣고, Kate가 종업원에게 할 말로 가장 적절한 것을 고르시오.

Kate: _____

① Would you refill the drinks?
② I think he's still eating that.
③ Can I get the check, please?
④ Thank you for cleaning the table.
⑤ I would like to order a shrimp dish.

[16 ~ 17] 다음을 듣고, 물음에 답하시오.

16. 여자가 하는 말의 주제로 가장 적절한 것은?

① benefits of sharing things
② ways to sell used stuff online
③ steps in the recycling process
④ necessity of sharing information
⑤ problems caused by online markets

17. 언급된 물품이 <u>아닌</u> 것은?

① a dress ② toys ③ a car ④ books ⑤ a bicycle

이제 듣기 문제가 끝났습니다. 18번부터는 문제지의 지시에 따라 답을 하시기 바랍니다.

---

18. 다음 글의 목적으로 가장 적절한 것은?

To whom it may concern:

My wife and I have lived in Smalltown for more than 60 years and have enjoyed Freer Park for all that time. When we were young and didn't have the money to go anywhere else, we would walk there almost every day. Now we are seniors, and my wife must use a wheelchair for extended walks. We find that the beautiful walking paths through the park are all but impassable to her. The paths are cracked and littered with rocks and debris that make it impossible to roll her chair from place to place. We hope you will devote resources to restoring the walking paths in Freer Park for all visitors.

Sincerely,
Craig Thomas

* debris: 파편, 쓰레기

① 공원 산책로 복구를 요청하려고
② 노인 복지 서비스 개선을 건의하려고
③ 휠체어 대여 서비스에 대해 안내하려고
④ 청소년 야외 활동 시설에 대해 문의하려고
⑤ 공원 내 주차 공간 부족에 대해 항의하려고

19. 다음 글에 드러난 'I'의 심경 변화로 가장 적절한 것은?

I board the plane, take off, and climb out into the night sky. Within minutes, the plane shakes hard, and I freeze, feeling like I'm not in control of anything. The left engine starts losing power and the right engine is nearly dead now. Rain hits the windscreen and I'm getting into heavier weather. I'm having trouble keeping up the airspeed. When I reach for the microphone to call the center to declare an emergency, my shaky hand accidentally bumps the carburetor heat levers, and the left engine suddenly regains power. I push the levers to full. Both engines backfire and come to full power. Feeling that the worst is over, I find my whole body loosening up and at ease.

* carburetor heat lever: 기화기 열 레버

① ashamed → delighted   ② terrified → relieved
③ satisfied → regretful   ④ indifferent → excited
⑤ hopeful → disappointed

20. 다음 글에서 필자가 주장하는 바로 가장 적절한 것은?

It is easy to judge people based on their actions. We are often taught to put more value in actions than words, and for good reason. The actions of others often speak volumes louder than their words. However, when someone exhibits some difficult behavior, you might want to reserve judgement for later. People are not always defined by their behavior. It is common to think, "He is so bossy," or "She is so mean," after observing less-than-desirable behavior in someone. But you should never make such assumptions right away. You should give someone a second chance before you label them and shut them out forever. You may find a great co-worker or best friend in someone, so don't eliminate a person from your life based on a brief observation.

① 단시간의 관찰로 타인을 성급하게 판단하지 마라.
② 자신의 적성을 찾기 위해 다양한 경험을 쌓아라.
③ 바람직하지 않은 습관을 고치기 위해 노력하라.
④ 원만한 인간관계를 위해 칭찬을 아끼지 마라.
⑤ 말보다는 행동으로 삶의 모범을 보여라.

21.

밑줄 친 "There is no there there."가 다음 글에서 의미하는 바로 가장 적절한 것은? [3점]

I believe the second decade of this new century is already very different. There are, of course, still millions of people who equate success with money and power — who are determined to never get off that treadmill despite the cost in terms of their well-being, relationships, and happiness. There are still millions desperately looking for the next promotion, the next million-dollar payday that they believe will satisfy their longing to feel better about themselves, or silence their dissatisfaction. But both in the West and in emerging economies, there are more people every day who recognize that these are all dead ends — that they are chasing a broken dream. That we cannot find the answer in our current definition of success alone because — as Gertrude Stein once said of Oakland — "There is no there there."

① People are losing confidence in themselves.
② Without dreams, there is no chance for growth.
③ We should not live according to others' expectations.
④ It is hard to realize our potential in difficult situations.
⑤ Money and power do not necessarily lead you to success.

22.

다음 글의 요지로 가장 적절한 것은?

Study the lives of the great people who have made an impact on the world, and you will find that in virtually every case, they spent a considerable amount of time alone thinking. Every political leader who had an impact on history practiced the discipline of being alone to think and plan. Great artists spend countless hours in their studios or with their instruments not just doing, but exploring their ideas and experiences. Time alone allows people to sort through their experiences, put them into perspective, and plan for the future. I strongly encourage you to find a place to think and to discipline yourself to pause and use it because it has the potential to change your life. It can help you to figure out what's really important and what isn't.

① 예술적 감수성을 키우기 위해 다양한 활동이 필요하다.
② 공동의 문제를 해결하기 위해 협동심을 발휘해야 한다.
③ 자신의 성장을 위해 혼자 생각할 시간을 가질 필요가 있다.
④ 합리적 정책을 수립하기 위해 비판적 의견을 수용해야 한다.
⑤ 성공적인 지도자가 되기 위해 규율을 엄격하게 적용해야 한다.

23.

다음 글의 주제로 가장 적절한 것은?

Social relationships benefit from people giving each other compliments now and again because people like to be liked and like to receive compliments. In that respect, social lies such as making deceptive but flattering comments ("I like your new haircut.") may benefit mutual relations. Social lies are told for psychological reasons and serve both self-interest and the interest of others. They serve self-interest because liars may gain satisfaction when they notice that their lies please other people, or because they realize that by telling such lies they avoid an awkward situation or discussion. They serve the interest of others because hearing the truth all the time ("You look much older now than you did a few years ago.") could damage a person's confidence and self-esteem.

① ways to differentiate between truth and lies
② roles of self-esteem in building relationships
③ importance of praise in changing others' behaviors
④ balancing between self-interest and public interest
⑤ influence of social lies on interpersonal relationships

24.

다음 글의 제목으로 가장 적절한 것은?

Overprotective parents spare kids from all natural consequences. Unfortunately, their kids often lack a clear understanding of the reasons behind their parents' rules. They never learn how to bounce back from failure or how to recover from mistakes because their parents prevented them from making poor choices. Rather than learning, "I should wear a jacket because it's cold outside," a child may conclude, "I have to wear a jacket because my mom makes me." Without an opportunity to experience real-world consequences, kids don't always understand why their parents make certain rules. Natural consequences prepare children for adulthood by helping them think about the potential consequences of their choices.

① Dark Sides of the Virtual World
② Let Natural Consequences Teach Kids
③ The More Choices, the More Mistakes
④ Listen to Kids to Improve Relationships
⑤ The Benefits of Overprotective Parenting

25. 다음 도표의 내용과 일치하지 <u>않는</u> 것은?

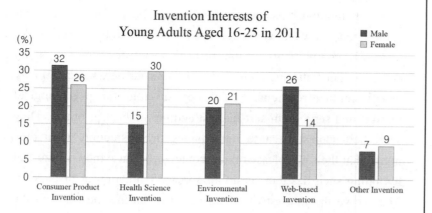

Invention Interests of
Young Adults Aged 16-25 in 2011

The graph above shows the results of a survey on invention interests in young adults aged 16 to 25 in 2011. ① Among the five invention categories, the highest percentage of male respondents showed interest in inventing consumer products. ② For health science invention, the percentage of female respondents was twice as high as that of male respondents. ③ The percentage point gap between males and females was the smallest in environmental invention. ④ For web-based invention, the percentage of female respondents was less than half that of male respondents. ⑤ In the category of other invention, the percentage of respondents from each gender group was less than 10 percent.

26. Dorothy Hodgkin에 관한 다음 글의 내용과 일치하지 <u>않는</u> 것은?

Dorothy Hodgkin was born in Cairo in 1910, where her father worked in the Egyptian Education Service. Her interest in chemistry started when she was just ten years old. In 1949, she worked on the structure of penicillin with her colleagues. Her work on vitamin B12 was published in 1954, which led to her being awarded the Nobel Prize in Chemistry in 1964. She also became the first woman to receive the Copley Medal and was a winner of the Lenin Peace Prize. Hodgkin showed great concern for social inequalities and resolving conflicts. As a result, she was president of the Pugwash Conferences from 1976 to 1988.

① 10세 때 화학에 대한 흥미가 생겼다.
② 동료와 함께 페니실린의 구조를 연구했다.
③ 1954년에 노벨 화학상을 받았다.
④ Copley 메달을 수상한 최초의 여성이다.
⑤ 사회 불평등과 갈등 해소에 큰 관심을 보였다.

27. Robotic Vacuum Cleaner 사용에 관한 다음 안내문의 내용과 일치하는 것은?

Robotic Vacuum Cleaner
- User Manual -

■ **Charging the Battery**
· It takes 90 minutes for the battery to be fully charged.
· The robotic vacuum can operate for 40 minutes when fully charged.
· While the robotic vacuum is charging, the battery indicator light blinks red.
· When fully charged, the battery indicator light turns blue.

■ **Operating the Vacuum**
· Press the power button to turn on the vacuum.
· The following cleaning modes are provided: Auto Mode, Spot Mode, and Manual Mode.
· Turning off the vacuum will reset all settings except for the current time.
· The time can be set only with the remote control.

① 배터리를 완전히 충전하는 데 40분이 소요된다.
② 완전히 충전되면 배터리 표시등이 빨간색으로 변한다.
③ 네 가지 종류의 청소 모드를 제공한다.
④ 전원을 끄면 현재 시각이 리셋된다.
⑤ 시각은 리모컨을 사용하여 설정한다.

28. Passing on My Favorites에 관한 다음 안내문의 내용과 일치하지 <u>않는</u> 것은?

Passing on My Favorites

Do you have anything you don't use anymore? Passing on My Favorites is a flea market event that takes place at our school every year.

Bring Your Goods
■ When: September 4 - 6 (12:00 - 13:00)
■ Where: the student council room
■ What: anything you don't use anymore
　　　(clothing, bags, shoes, stationery, etc.)
＊You will receive coupons according to how much you bring.

Buy What You Want
■ When: September 8 (10:00 - 12:00)
■ Where: the gymnasium
■ How: The coupons mentioned above will be your only way to purchase goods.
＊No food will be sold because it might spoil in the hot weather.

① 벼룩시장 행사이다.
② 학생회실로 물건을 가져와야 한다.
③ 물건을 사는 날은 9월 8일이다.
④ 현금을 주고 물건을 구입할 수 있다.
⑤ 음식은 판매되지 않는다.

29. 다음 글의 밑줄 친 부분 중, 어법상 틀린 것은? [3점]

In perceiving changes, we tend to regard the most recent ① ones as the most revolutionary. This is often inconsistent with the facts. Recent progress in telecommunications technologies is not more revolutionary than ② what happened in the late nineteenth century in relative terms. Moreover, in terms of the consequent economic and social changes, the Internet revolution has not been as ③ important as the washing machine and other household appliances. These things, by vastly reducing the amount of work needed for household chores, ④ allowing women to enter the labor market and virtually got rid of professions like domestic service. We should not "put the telescope backward" when we look into the past and underestimate the old and overestimate the new. This leads us ⑤ to make all sorts of wrong decisions about national economic policy, corporate policies, and our own careers.

30. 다음 글의 밑줄 친 부분 중, 문맥상 낱말의 쓰임이 적절하지 않은 것은?

Technological development often forces change, and change is uncomfortable. This is one of the main reasons why technology is often resisted and why some perceive it as a ① threat. It is important to understand our natural ② hate of being uncomfortable when we consider the impact of technology on our lives. As a matter of fact, most of us prefer the path of ③ least resistance. This tendency means that the true potential of new technologies may remain ④ unrealized because, for many, starting something new is just too much of a struggle. Even our ideas about how new technology can enhance our lives may be ⑤ encouraged by this natural desire for comfort.

[31~34] 다음 빈칸에 들어갈 말로 가장 적절한 것을 고르시오.

31. _____ provides a change to the environment for journalists. Newspaper stories, television reports, and even early online reporting (prior to communication technology such as tablets and smartphones) required one central place to which a reporter would submit his or her news story for printing, broadcast, or posting. Now, though, a reporter can shoot video, record audio, and type directly on their smartphones or tablets and post a news story instantly. Journalists do not need to report to a central location where they all contact sources, type, or edit video. A story can be instantaneously written, shot, and made available to the entire world. The news cycle, and thus the job of the journalist, never takes a break. Thus the "24-hour" news cycle that emerged from the rise of cable TV is now a thing of the past. The news "cycle" is really a constant.

① Mobility　　② Sensitivity　　③ Creativity
④ Accuracy　　⑤ Responsibility

32. It's hard enough to stick with goals you want to accomplish, but sometimes we make goals we're not even thrilled about in the first place. We set resolutions based on what we're supposed to do, or what others think we're supposed to do, rather than what really matters to us. This makes it nearly impossible to stick to the goal. For example, reading more is a good habit, but if you're only doing it because you feel like that's what you're supposed to do, not because you actually want to learn more, you're going to have a hard time reaching the goal. Instead, make goals based on _____. Now, this isn't to say you should read less. The idea is to first consider what matters to you, then figure out what you need to do to get there. [3점]

① your moral duty
② a strict deadline
③ your own values
④ parental guidance
⑤ job market trends

33. Houston Airport executives faced plenty of complaints regarding baggage claim time, so they increased the number of baggage handlers. Although it reduced the average wait time to eight minutes, complaints didn't stop. It took about a minute to get from the arrival gate to baggage claim, so the passengers spent seven more minutes waiting for their bags. The solution was to move the arrival gates away from the baggage claim so it took passengers about seven minutes to walk there. It resulted in complaints reducing to almost zero. Research shows occupied time feels shorter than unoccupied time. People usually exaggerate about the time they waited, and what they find most bothersome is time spent unoccupied. Thus, occupying the passengers' time by ＿＿＿＿＿＿＿ gave them the idea they didn't have to wait as long. [3점]

* baggage claim (area): 수하물 찾는 곳

① having them wait in line
② making them walk longer
③ producing more advertisements
④ bothering them with complaints
⑤ hiring more staff to handle bags

34. Vision is like shooting at a moving target. Plenty of things can go wrong in the future and plenty more can change in unpredictable ways. When such things happen, you should be prepared to ＿＿＿＿＿＿＿. For example, a businessman's optimistic forecast can be blown away by a cruel recession or by aggressive competition in ways he could not have foreseen. Or in another scenario, his sales can skyrocket and his numbers can get even better. In any event, he will be foolish to stick to his old vision in the face of new data. There is nothing wrong in modifying your vision or even abandoning it, as necessary. [3점]

* recession: 경기 침체

① explain your vision logically to others
② defend the wrong decisions you've made
③ build a community to share your experience
④ make your vision conform to the new reality
⑤ consult experts to predict the future economy

35. 다음 글에서 전체 흐름과 관계 없는 문장은?

Studying history can make you more knowledgeable or interesting to talk to or can lead to all sorts of brilliant vocations, explorations, and careers. ① But even more importantly, studying history helps us ask and answer humanity's Big Questions. ② If you want to know why something is happening in the present, you might ask a sociologist or an economist. ③ But if you want to know deep background, you ask historians. ④ A career as a historian is a rare job, which is probably why you have never met one. ⑤ That's because they are the people who know and understand the past and can explain its complex interrelationships with the present.

[36 ~ 37] 주어진 글 다음에 이어질 글의 순서로 가장 적절한 것을 고르시오.

36.

We always have a lot of bacteria around us, as they live almost everywhere — in air, soil, in different parts of our bodies, and even in some of the foods we eat. But do not worry!

(A) But unfortunately, a few of these wonderful creatures can sometimes make us sick. This is when we need to see a doctor, who may prescribe medicines to control the infection.

(B) Most bacteria are good for us. Some live in our digestive systems and help us digest our food, and some live in the environment and produce oxygen so that we can breathe and live on Earth.

(C) But what exactly are these medicines and how do they fight with bacteria? These medicines are called "antibiotics," which means "against the life of bacteria." Antibiotics either kill bacteria or stop them from growing.

① (A) - (C) - (B)   ② (B) - (A) - (C)
③ (B) - (C) - (A)   ④ (C) - (A) - (B)
⑤ (C) - (B) - (A)

[해설편 p.206]

37.

From a correlational observation, we conclude that one variable is related to a second variable. But neither behavior could be directly causing the other even though there is a relationship.

(A) They found the best predictor to be the number of tattoos the rider had. It would be a ridiculous error to conclude that tattoos cause motorcycle accidents or that motorcycle accidents cause tattoos.

(B) The following example will illustrate why it is difficult to make causal statements on the basis of correlational observation. The researchers at the U.S. Army conducted a study of motorcycle accidents, attempting to correlate the number of accidents with other variables such as socioeconomic level and age.

(C) Obviously, a third variable is related to both — perhaps preference for risk. A person who is willing to take risks likes to be tattooed and also takes more chances on a motorcycle.

[3점]

* variable: 변인

① (A) − (C) − (B) ② (B) − (A) − (C)
③ (B) − (C) − (A) ④ (C) − (A) − (B)
⑤ (C) − (B) − (A)

[38 ~ 39] 글의 흐름으로 보아, 주어진 문장이 들어가기에 가장 적절한 곳을 고르시오.

38.

The other main clue you might use to tell what a friend is feeling would be to look at his or her facial expression.

Have you ever thought about how you can tell what somebody else is feeling? (①) Sometimes, friends might tell you that they are feeling happy or sad but, even if they do not tell you, I am sure that you would be able to make a good guess about what kind of mood they are in. (②) You might get a clue from the tone of voice that they use. (③) For example, they may raise their voice if they are angry or talk in a shaky way if they are scared. (④) We have lots of muscles in our faces which enable us to move our face into lots of different positions. (⑤) This happens spontaneously when we feel a particular emotion.

39.

But as soon as he puts skis on his feet, it is as though he had to learn to walk all over again.

Reading is like skiing. When done well, when done by an expert, both reading and skiing are graceful, harmonious activities. When done by a beginner, both are awkward, frustrating, and slow. (①) Learning to ski is one of the most embarrassing experiences an adult can undergo. (②) After all, an adult has been walking for a long time; he knows where his feet are; he knows how to put one foot in front of the other in order to get somewhere. (③) He slips and slides, falls down, has trouble getting up, and generally looks — and feels — like a fool. (④) It is the same with reading. (⑤) Probably you have been reading for a long time, too, and starting to learn all over again would be humiliating.

40. 다음 글의 내용을 한 문장으로 요약하고자 한다. 빈칸 (A), (B)에 들어갈 말로 가장 적절한 것은? [3점]

In a study, psychologist Laurence Steinberg of Temple University and his co-author, psychologist Margo Gardner divided 306 people into three age groups: young adolescents, with a mean age of 14; older adolescents, with a mean age of 19; and adults, aged 24 and older. Subjects played a computerized driving game in which the player must avoid crashing into a wall that appears, without warning, on the roadway. Steinberg and Gardner randomly assigned some participants to play alone or with two same-age peers looking on. Older adolescents scored about 50 percent higher on an index of risky driving when their peers were in the room — and the driving of early adolescents was fully twice as reckless when other young teens were around. In contrast, adults behaved in similar ways regardless of whether they were on their own or observed by others.

* reckless: 무모한

⬇

The ___(A)___ of peers makes adolescents, but not adults, more likely to ___(B)___.

(A)	(B)
① presence	…… take risks
② presence	…… behave cautiously
③ indifference	…… perform poorly
④ absence	…… enjoy adventures
⑤ absence	…… act independently

[41 ~ 42] 다음 글을 읽고, 물음에 답하시오.

A quick look at history shows that humans have not always had the abundance of food that is enjoyed throughout most of the developed world today. In fact, there have been numerous times in history when food has been rather scarce. As a result, people used to eat more when food was available since the availability of the next meal was (a) questionable. Overeating in those times was essential to ensure survival, and humans received satisfaction from eating more than was needed for immediate purposes. On top of that, the highest pleasure was derived from eating the most calorie-dense foods, resulting in a (b) longer lasting energy reserve.

Even though there are parts of the world where, unfortunately, food is still scarce, most of the world's population today has plenty of food available to survive and thrive. However, this abundance is new, and your body has not caught up, still naturally (c) rewarding you for eating more than you need and for eating the most calorie-dense foods. These are innate habits and not simple addictions. They are self-preserving mechanisms initiated by your body, ensuring your future survival, but they are (d) irrelevant now. Therefore, it is your responsibility to communicate with your body regarding the new environment of food abundance and the need to (e) strengthen the inborn habit of overeating.

* innate: 타고난

41. 윗글의 제목으로 가장 적절한 것은?

① Which Is Better, Tasty or Healthy Food?
② Simple Steps for a More Balanced Diet
③ Overeating: It's Rooted in Our Genes
④ How Calorie-dense Foods Ruin Our Bodies
⑤ Our Eating Habits Reflect Our Personalities

42. 밑줄 친 (a) ~ (e) 중에서 문맥상 낱말의 쓰임이 적절하지 않은 것은? [3점]

① (a)　　② (b)　　③ (c)　　④ (d)　　⑤ (e)

[43 ~ 45] 다음 글을 읽고, 물음에 답하시오.

(A)

A long time ago, there was a boy. He was smart, talented, and handsome. However, he was very selfish, and his temper was so difficult that nobody wanted to be his friend. Often, (a) he got angry and said hurtful things to people around him.

(B)

The number of nails the boy drove into the fence each day gradually decreased. Eventually, the boy started to understand that holding his temper was easier than driving nails into the fence. (b) He didn't need the hammer and nails anymore when he learned to hold his temper. He went to his father and shared (c) his achievement. "Now every time you hold your temper all day long, pull out one nail."

(C)

Much time passed. At last, the boy was proud of himself as all the nails were gone. He found his father and explained this. Together, they went to the fence, and (d) he said, "You did a good job, my son, but pay attention to the holes left from the nails. The fence will never be the same. The same happens when you say hurtful things to people. Your words leave scars in their hearts like those holes in the fence."

(D)

The boy's parents were concerned about his bad temper. One day, the father had an idea. He called his son and gave (e) him a hammer and a bag of nails. The father said, "Every time you get angry, take a nail, and drive it into that old fence as hard as you can." The fence was very tough, and the hammer was heavy. Nevertheless, he was so furious that during the very first day he drove in 37 nails.

43. 주어진 글 (A)에 이어질 내용을 순서에 맞게 배열한 것으로 가장 적절한 것은?

① (B) − (D) − (C)　　　　② (C) − (B) − (D)
③ (C) − (D) − (B)　　　　④ (D) − (B) − (C)
⑤ (D) − (C) − (B)

44. 밑줄 친 (a) ~ (e) 중에서 가리키는 대상이 나머지 넷과 다른 것은?

① (a)　　② (b)　　③ (c)　　④ (d)　　⑤ (e)

45. 윗글의 내용으로 적절하지 않은 것은?

① 어느 누구도 소년과 친구가 되기를 원치 않았다.
② 소년이 하루에 박은 못의 수는 점점 늘어났다.
③ 소년은 모든 못을 제거하고 스스로를 자랑스러워했다.
④ 소년의 부모는 아들의 못된 성질을 걱정했다.
⑤ 소년은 못을 박기 시작한 첫날 37개의 못을 박았다.

* 확인 사항
◦ 답안지의 해당란에 필요한 내용을 정확히 기입(표기)했는지 확인하시오.

※ QR 코드를 스캔하시면 듣기 방송이 나옵니다. 듣기 방송을 들으며 다음 빈칸을 채우시오.   ● 제한 시간 : 25분

01

다음을 듣고, 남자가 하는 말의 목적으로 가장 적절한 것을 고르시오.

M : Attention, please. This is your vice principal, Mr. Stevens. There will be some renovations _____ _____ _____ next week. First, we will replace worn-out carpets with new ones. Meanwhile, old tables and chairs will be repaired or replaced. We will also _____ _____ _____ _____ and install LED lighting. For these reasons, the library will be closed for a week. During this period, you will not be able to check out or return books. I'm sorry ✿ _____ _____ _____ _____ _____, but I expect the renovation will make it more convenient to use. Thank you for your cooperation.

02

대화를 듣고, 여자의 의견으로 가장 적절한 것을 고르시오.

W : David, is there something wrong? You don't look well.
M : I'm just sleepy. I _____ _____ _____ _____ finishing the science project.
W : Again? Don't you know that a lack of sleep is bad for your health?
M : For my health? In what way?
W : If you don't get ✿ _____ _____ _____ _____ _____, you are more likely to have health problems like the common cold or even heart disease.
M : Really? Why's that?
W : It can _____ _____ _____ _____, so your body won't be able to fight viruses.
M : I didn't know that. I'll try to get enough sleep.

03

대화를 듣고, 두 사람의 관계를 가장 잘 나타낸 것을 고르시오.

M : Hi, Kate. How do you feel today?
W : I feel better, but I still have a sore throat. How does my voice sound?
M : It sounds fine, so don't worry about it.
W : Thanks. Did you hear about one of the audio books we recorded in this studio last year?
M : You mean "The Dreaming Tree?" I heard it was the _____ _____ _____ _____ _____ _____.
W : It was. The sound effects you added made the story feel alive.
M : Thank you. Most of all, _____ _____ _____ _____ _____ in the various roles.

W : I'm flattered. Okay, I think I'm ready now. Is this the script for the radio drama we're working on today?
M : Yes. We can begin once you ✿ _____ _____ _____ _____ _____. I'll check the microphone.
W : All right. I'll start when you give me the signal.

04

대화를 듣고, 그림에서 대화의 내용과 일치하지 않는 것을 고르시오.

M : Anna, can you check out my campaign poster?
W : Sure. I see you wrote the title "PROTECT THE POLAR BEARS!" at the top of the poster. It looks great.
M : Thanks. Do you think I should make the phrase "By switching off" bigger?
W : No, you don't have to. It should be _____ _____ _____ _____.
M : Okay. Also, I ✿ _____ _____ _____ _____ on an ice cap to make people think they should save the polar bears.
W : Good. I like the "OFF" button _____ _____ _____ _____ _____ _____. The word "OFF" on the button makes the message very clear.
M : That's the idea. One last thing — I'm worried that the round logo at the bottom isn't in the right place.
W : Don't worry. I think it's okay.

05

대화를 듣고, 남자가 할 일로 가장 적절한 것을 고르시오.

M : Hey, Lucy! Where are you going?
W : Hi, Steve. I'm _____ _____ _____ _____ _____ to exchange some money.
M : Oh, is it for your trip to Europe? You must be excited. Did you buy the big backpack you needed?
W : No, but I borrowed a nice one from my cousin. And I _____ _____ _____ _____ _____.
M : That's good. It'll be very useful. You seem to be all set for your trip.
W : Almost. I've renewed my passport and booked the flight. But I haven't decided on a hotel yet.
M : How come?
W : Because there are so many different options. It's difficult to find the right deal.
M : Why don't you ✿ _____ _____ _____ _____ the hotel prices? It'll save you time and money.
W : Mobile apps? Do you know of any good ones?
M : Yes, I know a few. I'll text you and let you know their names.
W : Thanks. I'll try them out.

06

대화를 듣고, 남자가 지불할 금액을 고르시오. [3점]

W : Hello, sir. How can I help you?

M : _____ _____ _____ _____ _____ for my mother. She enjoys having tea with her friends.

W : Okay. How about this teapot with a simple and classic design? It'll never go out of style.

M : I think she'll like it. How much is it?

W : It's $20. But if you like this design, we also have _____ _____ _____ _____ _____ _____ _____ _____. It's only $30.

M : Great! I'll take the set. Can you recommend some tea as well?

W : Sure. How about this lavender tea? It's ✪ _____ _____ _____ _____, and it's $10 a package.

M : Sounds good. I'll take two packages. Can I use this discount coupon?

W : Absolutely. You'll get a 10% discount from the total price.

M : Great. Here's my credit card.

07

대화를 듣고, 여자가 building expo에 갈 수 <u>없는</u> 이유를 고르시오.

M : The Central Park Museum will _____ _____ _____ _____ soon.

W : What's it about?

M : It's a building expo titled "New Home Builders."

W : Sounds interesting. When does it open?

M : It will start tomorrow at nine a.m. I'm going to the exhibition in the afternoon. Do you want to go with me?

W : I'm sorry, but I can't.

M : Why not? ✪ _____ _____ _____ _____, aren't you?

W : Yes, but I have to do something else.

M : What's your plan?

W : Actually, _____ _____ _____ _____ _____ tomorrow.

M : Oh, I see now. I hope you make it.

08

대화를 듣고, Stress Free Program에 관해 언급되지 <u>않은</u> 것을 고르시오.

W : Hey, Ryan, did you hear about the Stress Free Program?

M : Stress Free Program? No, what is it?

W : It's a new school program for students. You might want to join it. You look really stressed out these days.

M : Yeah, I really need to relax. _____ _____ _____ _____ _____ _____?

W : You can take part in various activities like coloring, e-sports, and board games.

M : Sounds interesting! How can I register for the program?

W : You can register ✪ _____ _____ _____ _____ _____ _____ _____.

M : Where's the program held?

W : It's held on the second floor of the Student Union building.

M : All right. Is the program available anytime?

W : No, it _____ _____ _____ _____ _____ _____ p.m. There's a schedule for each activity.

M : Okay, I'll check the schedule first.

W : Great. I hope you can refresh your mind there.

09

2017 Student Design Competition에 관한 다음 내용을 듣고, 일치하지 <u>않는</u> 것을 고르시오. [3점]

W : Do you think you're a great designer? Then join the 2017 Student Design Competition. The goal of this competition is to ✪ _____ _____ _____ by _____ _____ _____ _____ steel-framed buildings. Participants should submit the design of a two-story building. The winning design will be used for a museum. The competition is _____ _____ _____ _____ _____ _____ _____ _____. Submissions will be judged using three standards: efficiency, constructability, and creativity. The entry should be submitted to info@designcom.org by October 1st. We are looking forward to _____ _____ _____ _____ _____.

10

다음 표를 보면서 대화를 듣고, 여자가 주문할 블루투스 키보드를 고르시오.

M : Jessica, what are you doing on the computer?

W : I'm looking for a bluetooth keyboard that works with my smartphone.

M : What do you need it for?

W : I need to _____ _____ _____ _____ _____. Can you help me choose one?

M : Sure. How about this model? It looks great and is ✪ _____ _____.

W : I already have that model, but it's too heavy to carry around.

M : Then, why don't you get something that _____ _____ _____ _____ _____?

W : Yeah. That makes sense.

M : You can get this one. It also has a battery life of 100 hours.

W : It's nice, but _____ _____ _____. I want to buy that one, instead.

M : You mean this foldable keyboard?

W : Yeah, it'll take up much less space in my bag. I think I'll order it now.

11

대화를 듣고, 여자의 마지막 말에 대한 남자의 응답으로 가장 적절한 것을 고르시오.

W : How was your trip to Jeju Island?

M : It was great. The food _____ _____ _____ _____.

W : What did you ✪ _____ _____ _____ _____? I want to try it when I go there.

12

대화를 듣고, 남자의 마지막 말에 대한 여자의 응답으로 가장 적절한 것을 고르시오.

[Telephone rings.]
M : Hello. This is the Youth Volunteer Center. What can I do for you?
W : I'm supposed to join the volunteer program tomorrow, but
_____ _____ _____ _____ _____ ?
M : Sure. You can choose ✪ _____ _____ _____ _____ .

13

대화를 듣고, 남자의 마지막 말에 대한 여자의 응답으로 가장 적절한 것을 고르시오. [3점]

[Telephone rings.]
M : Hello. This is Gift Variety. How can I help you?
W : Hello. I ordered 30 water bottles on your site two days ago, but I want to put a design on them.
M : I'll check _____ _____ _____ _____ _____ . Can I have your order number?
W : AE13043.
M : One moment. [Typing sound] It looks like you can still do that.
W : Good. The bottles will be a gift ✪ _____ _____ _____ _____ _____ , so I want to _____ _____ _____ _____ _____ on the bottles.
M : I see, but it will cost you an extra 30 dollars.
W : No problem. Can I still get them before next Monday?
M : If that's the case, you'll have to _____ _____ _____ _____ _____ _____ by today.

14

대화를 듣고, 여자의 마지막 말에 대한 남자의 응답으로 가장 적절한 것을 고르시오. [3점]

W : Chris, did you hear the weather forecast?
M : No, what did it say?
W : It said there would be heavy rain and strong winds this afternoon.
M : Oh, no! Our outdoor concert is supposed to start at 4 p.m. What should we do?
W : The teacher said we have to _____ _____ _____ _____ _____ _____ to the school auditorium.
M : Okay. We still have several hours to set up the stage. But how can we inform people of the change?
W : I'll make a notice and _____ _____ _____ _____ _____ _____ at the outdoor concert hall.
M : Good. I'll go and ask the school broadcasting station to make an announcement about it.
W : Good idea. Is there any other way for us to ✪ _____ _____ _____ _____ _____ ?

15

다음 상황 설명을 듣고, Kate가 종업원에게 할 말로 가장 적절한 것을 고르시오.

M : Kate and David love a new seafood buffet restaurant in their town. One day, they ✪ _____ _____ _____ _____ , fill up their plates, and bring them to their table. Then, as David is eating his favorite shrimp dish, he decides to get something to drink. So, he leaves the table _____ _____ _____ _____ _____ . When Kate is eating alone at the table, a waiter comes and tries to take away David's almost empty plate. Kate wants to tell the waiter that David is _____ _____ _____ _____ _____ . In this situation, what would Kate most likely say to the waiter?

16~17

다음을 듣고, 물음에 답하시오.

W : Hello, everyone! Today, I want you to consider this: do you have something you're not using in your home? Then, _____ _____ _____ _____ _____ _____ ? It enables products to be recycled and reused, reducing the negative effects on the environment. For example, if you have a nice dress for a party, lend it to others who need it. Then the materials used in making a new dress can be saved. _____ _____ _____ _____ _____ . Every year, millions of toys that children no longer play with are thrown away. By sharing things with others, you can reduce waste. Also, you can benefit financially by sharing your goods. If you have books you've finished reading, register them on online sharing systems. Then, someone who wants to read your books can rent them and you can make money by sharing. Similarly, if you ✪ _____ _____ _____ , you can find some people who share theirs on bike-sharing systems and save money. Why don't you _____ _____ _____ _____ ?

▶ 정답 : 해설편 211쪽

18

001 to whom it may concern (주로 편지에서) 담당자 귀하
002 wheelchair ⓝ 휠체어
003 extended ⓐ 길어진, 장시간에 걸친
004 through prep ~을 통해
005 impassable ⓐ 지나갈 수 없는, 통행 불가한
006 cracked ⓐ 갈라진
007 littered with ~가 널린, ~로 어질러진
008 debris ⓝ 파편, 잔해
009 roll ⓥ 구르다, 굴러가다, (기계를) 돌리다
010 from place to place 이곳저곳, 이리저리
011 devote ⓥ 바치다, 헌신하다
012 resource ⓝ 자원
013 restore ⓥ 복원[복구]하다
014 path ⓝ (사람·사물이 나아가는) 길

19

015 board ⓥ 탑승하다
016 plane ⓝ 비행기
017 take off 이륙하다[날아오르다]
018 climb ⓥ 오르다, 올라가다
019 shake ⓥ 흔들리다, 흔들다
020 freeze ⓥ 얼다[얼리다]
021 in control of ~을 통제하는
022 engine ⓝ 엔진
023 nearly ad 거의
024 windscreen ⓝ 앞 유리
025 get into ~에 들어가다
026 weather ⓝ 날씨, 기상
027 keep up ~을 계속하다, 유지하다
028 airspeed ⓝ (항공기의) 대기 속도
029 reach for ~에 손을 뻗다
030 declare ⓥ 신고하다, 선언하다
031 shaky ⓐ 떨리는[휘청거리는]
032 accidentally ad 우연히
033 bump ⓥ (~에) 부딪치다
034 regain ⓥ 되찾다[회복하다]
035 worst ⓐ 가장 나쁜, 최악의
036 loosen up 긴장을 풀다
037 at ease (마음이) 편안한
038 delighted ⓐ 기뻐하는
039 regretful ⓐ 후회하는

20

040 judge ⓥ 판단하다[여기다]
041 based on ~에 근거하여
042 value ⓝ 가치
043 exhibit ⓥ 보이다, 드러내다
044 behavior ⓝ 행동
045 reserve ⓥ 유보하다
046 define ⓥ 정의하다
047 bossy ⓐ 거들먹거리는
048 mean ⓐ 심술궂은, 비열한
049 assumption ⓝ 추측, 가정, 추정
050 right away 곧바로, 즉시
051 label ⓥ (특히 부당하게) 꼬리표를 붙이다
052 shut out 차단하다
053 co-worker 동료
054 brief ⓐ 짧은, 단시간의
055 observation ⓝ 관찰, 관측

21

056 decade ⓝ 10년
057 already ad 이미, 벌써
058 equate ⓥ 동일시하다
059 determined ⓐ 단호한, 완강한
060 treadmill ⓝ (다람쥐) 쳇바퀴, 러닝머신
061 despite prep ~에도 불구하고
062 well-being 안녕, 행복
063 desperately ad 필사적으로
064 promotion ⓝ 승진, 진급
065 payday ⓝ 월급날
066 satisfy ⓥ 충족시키다[채우다]
067 silence ⓥ 침묵시키다
068 dissatisfaction ⓝ 불만
069 emerging ⓐ 신흥의, 최근 생겨난
070 recognize ⓥ 인정[인식]하다
071 dead end 막다른 길
072 chase ⓥ 좇다, 추구하다
073 definition ⓝ 의미[정의]
074 confidence ⓝ 믿음, 자신감
075 expectation ⓝ 예상, 기대
076 realize ⓥ (꿈 등을) 실현하다
077 not necessarily 꼭 ~한 것은 아니다

22

078 virtually ad 거의, 실제로
079 considerable ⓐ 상당한
080 amount ⓝ (무엇의) 양
081 political ⓐ 정치의, 정치적인
082 practice ⓥ 실천하다, 실행하다
083 discipline ⓝ 훈련 ⓥ 단련시키다
084 countless ⓐ 셀 수 없이 많은
085 instrument ⓝ 도구
086 explore ⓥ 탐구[분석]하다
087 experience ⓝ 경험
088 sort through 정리하다, 자세히 살펴보다
089 put into perspective ~을 통찰하다, 넓게 보다
090 future ⓝ 미래, 장래
091 encourage ⓥ 권장하다, 장려하다
092 pause ⓥ 잠시 멈추다
093 potential ⓝ 잠재력

23

094 benefit from ~에서 이로움을 얻다
095 compliment ⓝ 칭찬 ⓥ 칭찬하다
096 in that respect 그 점에서는
097 deceptive ⓐ 속이는
098 flattering ⓥ 비위를 맞추는
099 comment ⓝ 논평, 언급
100 mutual ⓐ 상호의
101 self-interest ⓝ 사리사욕
102 liar ⓝ 거짓말쟁이
103 satisfaction ⓝ 만족
104 avoid ⓥ 피하다
105 awkward ⓐ 어색한, 곤란한
106 discussion ⓝ 논의, 상의
107 damage ⓥ 해치다, 손상시키다
108 self-esteem 자존감
109 differentiate between A and B A와 B를 구별하다
110 role ⓝ 역할

24

111 praise ⓝ 칭찬, 찬사
112 behavior ⓝ 행동
113 balance between A and B A와 B 사이에서 균형을 잡다
114 public ⓐ 공공의
115 influence ⓝ 영향
116 interpersonal ⓐ 대인관계에 관련된

24

117 overprotective ⓐ 과잉보호하는
118 spare A from B A가 B를 겪지 못하게 막다
119 natural ⓐ 자연의
120 consequence ⓝ 결과
121 unfortunately ad 불행히도, 안타깝게도
122 lack ⓥ ~이 없다, ~을 결여하다
123 behind prep 뒤에, 배후에
124 rule ⓝ 규칙
125 bounce back 다시 회복하다
126 failure ⓝ 실패
127 recover ⓥ 회복하다
128 prevent ⓥ 막다[예방/방지하다]
129 wear ⓥ 입고 있다
130 conclude ⓥ 결론 짓다
131 opportunity ⓝ 기회
132 real-world 실제 세계의
133 certain ⓐ 특정한
134 adulthood ⓝ 성인기
135 virtual ⓐ 가상의
136 parenting ⓝ 육아

25

137 invention ⓝ 발명
138 consumer product 소비재
139 twice ad 두 배[갑절]로
140 environmental ⓐ 환경의
141 web-based 웹 기반의
142 gender ⓝ 성, 성별

26

143 born ⓥ 태어나다
144 chemistry ⓝ 화학
145 structure ⓝ 구조
146 colleague ⓝ 동료
147 publish ⓥ 발표하다, 출판하다
148 award ⓥ 상을 주다, 수여하다
149 receive ⓥ 받다
150 concern ⓝ 관심, 우려
151 inequality ⓝ 불평등
152 resolve ⓥ (문제 등을) 해결하다
153 conflict ⓝ 갈등
154 president ⓝ (기관의) 장, 회장

27

155 robotic vacuum cleaner 로봇 진공청소기
156 charging ⓝ 충전
157 fully ad 완전히, 충분히
158 operate ⓥ 작동[가동]되다
159 indicator ⓝ 표시기
160 blink ⓥ 깜박이다
161 turn ⓥ 바뀌다

28

162 except for ~을 제외하고
163 current ⓐ 현재의, 지금의
164 remote control 리모콘

28

165 flea market 벼룩시장
166 take place 열리다, 개최되다
167 student council 학생회
168 stationery ⓝ 문구류
169 according to ~에 따라
170 gymnasium ⓝ 체육관
171 mention ⓥ 언급하다, 말하다
172 purchase ⓥ 구입하다, 사다
173 spoil ⓥ 상하다

29

174 perceive ⓥ 인식하다, 이해하다
175 revolutionary ⓐ 혁신적인, 혁명적인
176 inconsistent ⓐ 일치하지 않는, 부합하지 않는
177 progress ⓝ 발전, 진보
178 relative ⓐ 상대적인
179 in terms of ~의 관점에서
180 consequent ⓐ ~의 결과로 일어나는
181 household appliance 가전제품
182 vastly ad 막대하게, 방대하게
183 virtually ad 사실상, 거의
184 get rid of ~을 없애다, 제거하다
185 underestimate ⓥ 과소평가하다
186 overestimate ⓥ 과대평가하다
187 corporate ⓐ 기업의

30

188 resist ⓥ 저항하다
189 perceive ⓥ 감지하다
190 threat ⓝ 위협
191 impact ⓝ 영향
192 as a matter of fact 사실, 실상은
193 prefer ⓥ 선호하다
194 tendency ⓝ 경향
195 unrealized ⓐ 실현되지 않은
196 struggle ⓝ 힘든 일, 투쟁
197 enhance ⓥ 향상시키다

31

198 prior to ~의 이전에
199 require ⓥ 필요로 하다
200 central ⓐ 중심적인
201 submit ⓥ 제출하다
202 directly ad 곧장
203 instantly ad 즉시
204 instantaneously ad 즉석에서
205 take a break 멈추다, 휴식을 취하다
206 emerge ⓥ 나타나다
207 rise ⓥ 성장, 상승, 증가
208 constant ⓝ 일정불변의 것

32

209 stick with ~을 고수하다
210 accomplish ⓥ 성취하다, 달성하다
211 thrilled ⓐ 아주 흥분된[신이 난]
212 resolution ⓝ 다짐, 결심

213 □ impossible ⓐ 불가능한
214 □ actually 〔ad〕 실제로
215 □ reach ⓥ ~에 이르다[닿다/도달하다]
216 □ figure out 알아내다, 이해하다
217 □ moral ⓐ 도의[도덕]적인
218 □ duty ⓝ 의무
219 □ guidance ⓝ 지도, 지침

33
220 □ executive ⓝ 임원, 중역
221 □ face ⓥ 직면하다, 맞서다
222 □ complaint ⓝ 불평[항의] (거리), 고소
223 □ regarding 〔prep〕 ~에 관하여
224 □ baggage ⓝ 수하물, 짐
225 □ claim ⓥ 얻다, 차지하다
226 □ reduce ⓥ 줄이다, 감소시키다
227 □ passenger ⓝ 승객
228 □ solution ⓝ 해결책
229 □ result in ~을 가져오다, ~을 초래하다
230 □ occupied ⓐ 차지된, 점거된
231 □ exaggerate ⓥ 과장하다
232 □ bothersome ⓐ 성가신, 귀찮은
233 □ advertisement ⓝ 광고

34
234 □ shoot at ~을 쏘아 맞히다
235 □ target ⓝ 표적[목표물]
236 □ plenty ⓝ 많음 〔ad〕 많이
237 □ wrong ⓐ 틀린, 잘못된
238 □ unpredictable ⓐ 예측할 수 없는
239 □ prepare ⓥ 준비하다[시키다]
240 □ optimistic ⓐ 낙관적인
241 □ forecast ⓝ 예측
242 □ blow ⓥ 날리다, 날려 보내다
243 □ cruel ⓐ 잔혹한, 고통스러운
244 □ recession ⓝ 경기 침체
245 □ aggressive ⓐ 공격적인
246 □ foresee ⓥ 예견하다
247 □ sale ⓝ 매출(량)
248 □ skyrocket ⓥ 급등하다
249 □ in any event 어떤 경우에도
250 □ foolish ⓐ 어리석은
251 □ stick to ~을 고수하다
252 □ in the face of ~에 직면하여
253 □ modify ⓥ 수정하다
254 □ abandon ⓥ 버리다
255 □ defend ⓥ 방어하다
256 □ conform to ~에 맞추다, 순응하다

35
257 □ knowledgeable ⓐ 유식한, 정통한
258 □ brilliant ⓐ 멋진, 훌륭한
259 □ vocation ⓝ 직업, 천직
260 □ exploration ⓝ 탐구
261 □ career ⓝ 경력, 직업
262 □ importantly 〔ad〕 중요한, 유력한
263 □ humanity ⓝ 인류
264 □ present ⓝ 현재
265 □ sociologist ⓝ 사회학자
266 □ historian ⓝ 사학자
267 □ probably 〔ad〕 아마
268 □ interrelationship ⓝ 연관성, 상호 관계

36
269 □ almost 〔ad〕 거의
270 □ soil ⓝ 토양
271 □ creature ⓝ 생명이 있는 존재, 생물
272 □ sick ⓐ 아픈, 병든
273 □ prescribe ⓥ 처방하다
274 □ medicine ⓝ 약, 약물
275 □ infection ⓝ 감염
276 □ digestive ⓐ 소화의
277 □ produce ⓥ 생산하다
278 □ breathe ⓥ 호흡하다, 숨을 쉬다
279 □ antibiotics ⓝ 항생제
280 □ either A or B A이거나 B인; A나 B 둘 중 하나

37
281 □ correlational ⓐ 상관관계의
282 □ conclude ⓥ 결론 짓다
283 □ variable ⓝ (실험에서) 변인, 변수
284 □ related to ~와 관련 있는
285 □ directly 〔ad〕 직접적으로
286 □ predictor ⓝ 예측 변수
287 □ tattoo ⓝ 문신 ⓥ 문신을 새기다
288 □ rider ⓝ (오토바이를) 타는[탄] 사람
289 □ ridiculous ⓐ 우스꽝스러운
290 □ motorcycle ⓝ 오토바이
291 □ accident ⓝ (특히 자동차) 사고[재해]
292 □ illustrate ⓥ 보여주다, 예증하다
293 □ causal ⓐ 인과관계의, 인과의
294 □ statement ⓝ 성명, 진술
295 □ conduct ⓥ (수행)하다
296 □ attempt ⓥ 시도하다
297 □ correlate ⓥ 연관시키다, 상관관계를 보여주다
298 □ socioeconomic ⓐ 사회 경제적인
299 □ obviously 〔ad〕 명백히, 분명히
300 □ preference ⓝ 선호(도), 애호
301 □ be willing to 기꺼이 ~하다

38
302 □ main ⓐ 주된, 주요한
303 □ facial expression 얼굴 표정
304 □ sometimes 〔ad〕 때때로, 가끔
305 □ make a guess 추측하다
306 □ mood ⓝ 기분
307 □ clue ⓝ 실마리, 힌트
308 □ shaky ⓐ 떨리는
309 □ muscle ⓝ 근육
310 □ position ⓝ (자리 잡고 있는) 위치
311 □ spontaneously 〔ad〕 자동적으로
312 □ particular ⓐ 특정한, 특별한

39
313 □ as soon as ~하자마자
314 □ put something on ~을 입다
315 □ ski ⓝ 스키
316 □ as though 마치 ~처럼
317 □ expert ⓝ 전문가
318 □ graceful ⓐ 우아한
319 □ harmonious ⓐ 조화로운
320 □ beginner ⓝ 초보자, 초심자
321 □ awkward ⓐ 어색한, 불편한

40
329 □ co-author 공동 저자
330 □ divide ⓥ 나누다
331 □ adolescent ⓝ 청소년
332 □ mean ⓐ 평균의
333 □ computerized ⓐ 컴퓨터화된
334 □ crash into ~에 충돌하다
335 □ appear ⓥ 나타나다, 보이기 시작하다
336 □ roadway ⓝ 도로, 차도
337 □ randomly 〔ad〕 무작위로
338 □ assign ⓥ 맡기다[배정하다/부과하다]
339 □ peer ⓝ 또래[동배]
340 □ score ⓥ 득점을 매기다[기록하다]
341 □ index ⓝ (물가·임금 등의) 지수
342 □ risky ⓐ 위험한
343 □ early ⓐ 빠른[이른]
344 □ reckless ⓐ 무모한
345 □ regardless of ~에 상관없이
346 □ observe ⓥ 관찰하다
347 □ presence ⓝ 있음, 존재(함)
348 □ cautiously 〔ad〕 조심스럽게
349 □ indifference ⓝ 무관심
350 □ perform ⓥ 행하다[수행하다/실시하다]
351 □ poorly 〔ad〕 저조하게, 형편없이
352 □ absence ⓝ 결석, 부재
353 □ independently 〔ad〕 독립적으로

41~42
354 □ abundance ⓝ 풍부함
355 □ numerous ⓐ 수많은
356 □ scarce ⓐ 부족한
357 □ availability ⓝ 이용 가능성
358 □ meal ⓝ 식사[끼니]
359 □ questionable ⓐ 확실치 않은, 의심스러운
360 □ overeating ⓝ 과식
361 □ essential ⓐ 필수적인 ⓝ 필수적인 것
362 □ ensure ⓥ 보장하다
363 □ survival ⓝ 생존
364 □ immediate ⓐ 당면한, 목전의
365 □ on top of that 설상가상으로, 더욱이
366 □ highest ⓐ 가장 높은, 최고의
367 □ pleasure ⓝ 기쁨, 즐거움
368 □ derive A from B B에서 A를 얻다
369 □ calorie-dense 칼로리가 높은
370 □ reserve ⓝ 비축(물)
371 □ even though 비록 ~일지라도
372 □ population ⓝ 인구, (모든) 주민
373 □ thrive ⓥ 번영하다
374 □ catch up ~을 따라잡다
375 □ reward ⓥ 보상[보답/사례]하다
376 □ innate ⓐ 타고난, 선천적인
377 □ addiction ⓝ 중독
378 □ self-preserving 자기 보존의
379 □ initiate ⓥ 시작하다

322 □ frustrating ⓐ 좌절감을 주는
323 □ embarrassing ⓐ 당혹스러운
324 □ undergo ⓥ 겪다
325 □ in front of ~의 앞쪽에[앞에]
326 □ slip ⓥ (어떤 위치나 손을 벗어나) 미끄러지다
327 □ slide ⓥ 미끄러지다
328 □ humiliating ⓐ 창피한, 굴욕적인

380 □ irrelevant ⓐ 부적절한, 관계없는
381 □ regarding 〔prep〕 ~에 관련하여
382 □ strengthen ⓥ 강화하다
383 □ inborn ⓐ 타고난
384 □ rooted in ~에 뿌리박힌
385 □ gene ⓝ 유전자
386 □ ruin ⓥ 망치다
387 □ reflect ⓥ 반영하다

43~45
388 □ talented ⓐ 재능 있는
389 □ selfish ⓐ 이기적인
390 □ temper ⓝ 성질, 기질
391 □ difficult ⓐ 까다로운
392 □ hurtful ⓐ 상처를 주는, 아프게 하는
393 □ around 〔prep〕 둘레에, 주위에
394 □ nail ⓝ 못
395 □ drive into (못 등을) 박다
396 □ fence ⓝ 울타리
397 □ gradually 〔ad〕 점차, 서서히
398 □ eventually 〔ad〕 결국, 종내
399 □ hammer ⓝ 망치[해머]
400 □ share ⓥ 함께 나누다
401 □ achievement ⓝ 성취
402 □ pull out (잡아) 뽑다
403 □ explain ⓥ 설명하다
404 □ pay attention to ~에 주목하다
405 □ leave ⓥ 남기다
406 □ scar ⓝ 흉터, 상처
407 □ heart ⓝ 마음[가슴]
408 □ hole ⓝ 구멍
409 □ be concerned about ~을 걱정하다
410 □ nevertheless 〔ad〕 그럼에도 불구하고
411 □ furious ⓐ 화가 난, 격분한

● 채점 : 맞은 개수 _____ / 80

TEST A-B 각 단어의 뜻을 [A] 영어는 우리말로, [B] 우리말은 영어로 쓰시오.

A	English	Korean
01	extended	
02	nearly	
03	define	
04	not necessarily	
05	flattering	
06	consequence	
07	structure	
08	spoil	
09	inconsistent	
10	resist	
11	prior to	
12	stick with	
13	occupied	
14	optimistic	
15	knowledgeable	
16	antibiotics	
17	ridiculous	
18	scarce	
19	derive A from B	
20	furious	

B	Korean	English
01	바치다, 헌신하다	
02	우연히	
03	불만	
04	잠재력	
05	상당한	
06	칭찬, 칭찬하다	
07	자존감	
08	불평등	
09	~을 없애다, 제거하다	
10	선호하다	
11	필요로 하다	
12	과장하다	
13	버리다	
14	직업, 천직	
15	처방하다	
16	인과관계의, 인과의	
17	마치 ~처럼	
18	이기적인	
19	수행하다	
20	시도하다	

▶ A-D 정답 : 해설편 211쪽

TEST C-D 각 단어의 뜻을 골라 기호를 쓰시오.

C	English			Korean
01	littered with	(	)	ⓐ 심술궂은, 비열한
02	board	(	)	ⓑ 깜빡이다
03	take place	(	)	ⓒ ~가 널린, ~로 어질러진
04	mean	(	)	ⓓ 상관관계의
05	emerging	(	)	ⓔ 탑승하다
06	deceptive	(	)	ⓕ 감염
07	conclude	(	)	ⓖ 흉터
08	blink	(	)	ⓗ 결론 짓다
09	corporate	(	)	ⓘ 속이는
10	enhance	(	)	ⓙ 신흥의, 최근 생겨난
11	resolution	(	)	ⓚ 열리다, 개최되다
12	regarding	(	)	ⓛ 기업의
13	conform to	(	)	ⓜ 예견하다
14	foresee	(	)	ⓝ 향상시키다
15	infection	(	)	ⓞ 다짐, 결심
16	correlational	(	)	ⓟ 조화로운
17	spontaneously	(	)	ⓠ 평균의
18	harmonious	(	)	ⓡ ~에 맞추다, 순응하다
19	mean	(	)	ⓢ 자동적으로
20	scar	(	)	ⓣ ~에 관하여

D	Korean			English
01	파편, 잔해	(	)	ⓐ discipline
02	(마음이) 편안한	(	)	ⓑ stationery
03	추측, 가정, 추정	(	)	ⓒ digestive
04	훈련, 단련시키다	(	)	ⓓ humiliating
05	정리하다, 자세히 살펴보다	(	)	ⓔ household appliance
06	상호의	(	)	ⓕ assumption
07	성인기	(	)	ⓖ at ease
08	발표하다, 출판하다	(	)	ⓗ adulthood
09	표시기	(	)	ⓘ submit
10	문구류	(	)	ⓙ result in
11	~의 관점에서	(	)	ⓚ sociologist
12	가전제품	(	)	ⓛ adolescent
13	제출하다	(	)	ⓜ indicator
14	알아내다, 이해하다	(	)	ⓝ skyrocket
15	~을 가져오다, ~을 초래하다	(	)	ⓞ publish
16	급등하다	(	)	ⓟ mutual
17	사회학자	(	)	ⓠ in terms of
18	소화의	(	)	ⓡ sort through
19	창피한, 굴욕의	(	)	ⓢ debris
20	청소년	(	)	ⓣ figure out

영어 영역

● 문항수 45개 | 배점 100점 | 제한 시간 70분 　　● 점수 표시가 없는 문항은 모두 2점 ● 출처 : 고1 학력평가

1번부터 17번까지는 듣고 답하는 문제입니다. 1번부터 15번까지는 한 번만 들려주고, 16번부터 17번까지는 두 번 들려줍니다. 방송을 잘 듣고 답을 하시기 바랍니다.

1. 다음을 듣고, 여자가 하는 말의 목적으로 가장 적절한 것을 고르시오.

① 강의 일정 변경을 공지하려고
② 감사 일기 쓰는 것을 권장하려고
③ 건강 관리의 중요성을 강조하려고
④ 자기소개서 작성 요령을 설명하려고
⑤ 효과적인 시간 활용법을 안내하려고

2. 대화를 듣고, 남자의 의견으로 가장 적절한 것을 고르시오.

① 운동은 자신감 향상에 도움이 된다.
② 격렬한 운동 전에 스트레칭을 해야 한다.
③ 스트레칭은 많은 면에서 건강에 유익하다.
④ 바른 자세를 유지하는 습관을 가져야 한다.
⑤ 자신에게 맞는 스트레스 해소 방법을 찾아야 한다.

3. 대화를 듣고, 두 사람의 관계를 가장 잘 나타낸 것을 고르시오.

① 안과 의사 – 환자　　　② 보건 교사 – 학생
③ 프로젝트 팀장 – 팀원　④ 컴퓨터 판매원 – 구매자
⑤ 약사 – 제약 회사 직원

4. 대화를 듣고, 그림에서 대화의 내용과 일치하지 <u>않는</u> 것을 고르시오.

5. 대화를 듣고, 남자가 여자를 위해 할 일로 가장 적절한 것을 고르시오.

① 감자 사 오기　　　② 케이크 만들기
③ 장학금 신청하기　④ 스테이크 주문하기
⑤ 식료품점 위치 검색하기

6. 대화를 듣고, 남자가 지불할 금액을 고르시오. [3점]

① $40　② $45　③ $50　④ $54　⑤ $60

7. 대화를 듣고, 여자가 거리 공연을 보러 갈 수 없는 이유를 고르시오.

① 학교 축제를 위한 부스를 만들어야 해서
② 좋아하는 밴드의 팬 사인회에 가야 해서
③ 동아리 부원들과 기타 연습을 해야 해서
④ 학급 친구들과 합창 대회 준비를 해야 해서
⑤ 과학 프로젝트를 위해 조원들을 만나야 해서

8. 대화를 듣고, Junior Badminton Competition에 관해 언급되지 <u>않은</u> 것을 고르시오.

① 대회 일시　　② 참가비　　③ 준비물
④ 우승 상품　　⑤ 신청 방법

9. Forest Concert에 관한 다음 내용을 듣고, 일치하지 <u>않는</u> 것을 고르시오.

① 10월 7일에 열린다.
② 주제는 '꿈을 찾아서'이다.
③ 무료로 입장할 수 있다.
④ 사전 예약이 필요하다.
⑤ 집에서 TV로 시청할 수 있다.

10. 다음 표를 보면서 대화를 듣고, 여자가 선택할 미술용품 세트를 고르시오.

Art Supplies Set for Children

	Model	Price	Coloring Tool	Number of Colors	Sketchbook
①	A	$12	Crayons	24	×
②	B	$16	Crayons	32	○
③	C	$17	Watercolors	28	○
④	D	$18	Markers	32	×
⑤	E	$22	Markers	36	○

11. 대화를 듣고, 여자의 마지막 말에 대한 남자의 응답으로 가장 적절한 것을 고르시오.

① You should be honest about your ideas.
② I can help to choose the right class for you.
③ I already took the career counseling program.
④ I'm thinking of making an English debate club.
⑤ You'll get all the academic advice as you need.

12. 대화를 듣고, 남자의 마지막 말에 대한 여자의 응답으로 가장 적절한 것을 고르시오.

① The building is too far from here.
② We don't need to bring umbrellas.
③ We can buy one on the first floor.
④ I don't know where your umbrella is.
⑤ You'd better check the weather forecast.

13. 대화를 듣고, 여자의 마지막 말에 대한 남자의 응답으로 가장 적절한 것을 고르시오. [3점]

Man: _____

① Come on. You'll do fine if you volunteer with a kind heart.
② Okay, will you search for volunteer opportunities for me?
③ Sure. Let's check the list of art schools you could attend.
④ Yeah, you'd better plan your trip to Africa in advance.
⑤ You're right. We should have watched that movie.

14. 대화를 듣고, 남자의 마지막 말에 대한 여자의 응답으로 가장 적절한 것을 고르시오. [3점]

Woman: _____

① Great. I should try to keep a weekly budget.
② Good luck. I hope you can find a part-time job.
③ Come on. You can coach me on my eating habits.
④ No way. You can't spend so much money shopping.
⑤ I know. I need to spend more time with my friends.

15. 다음 상황 설명을 듣고, Ted가 Linda에게 할 말로 가장 적절한 것을 고르시오.

Ted: _____

① Why don't you use a calendar app as a reminder?
② I recommend you ask your friends for some help.
③ Do you prefer a wall calendar or a desk calendar?
④ I wonder why you didn't submit your paper on time.
⑤ Could you tell me how you overcame your bad habit?

[16 ~ 17] 다음을 듣고, 물음에 답하시오.

16. 남자가 하는 말의 주제로 가장 적절한 것은?

① the best souvenirs to bring home from travel
② popular places in the world to photograph nature
③ tips on how to save money on souvenir shopping
④ the variety of cultural environments around the world
⑤ the most important travel safety rules to keep in mind

17. 언급된 지역이 <u>아닌</u> 것은?

① Beijing   ② Paris   ③ Sydney   ④ Hawaii   ⑤ Venice

┌───┐
│ 이제 듣기 문제가 끝났습니다. 18번부터는 문제지의 지 │
│ 시에 따라 답을 하시기 바랍니다.   │
└───┘

18. 다음 글의 목적으로 가장 적절한 것은?

┌───┐
│ To the Principal of Alamda High School,   │
│   │
│   On behalf of the Youth Soccer Tournament   │
│ Series, I would like to remind you of the 2019 │
│ Series next week. Surely, we understand the   │
│ importance of a player's education. Regrettably,│
│ however, the Series will result in players   │
│ missing two days of school for the competition. │
│ The games will be attended by many college   │
│ coaches scouting prospective student athletes. │
│ Therefore, the Series can be a great   │
│ opportunity for young soccer players to   │
│ demonstrate their capabilities as athletes. I   │
│ would like to request your permission for the   │
│ absence of the players from your school during │
│ this event. Thank you for your understanding.   │
│ Best regards,   │
│ Jack D'Adamo, Director of the Youth Soccer   │
│ Tournament Series   │
└───┘

① 선수들의 학력 향상 프로그램을 홍보하려고
② 대학 진학 상담의 활성화 방안을 제안하려고
③ 선수들의 훈련 장비 추가 구입을 건의하려고
④ 선수들의 대회 참가를 위한 결석 허락을 요청하려고
⑤ 대회 개최를 위한 운동장 대여 가능 여부를 문의하려고

19. 다음 글에 드러난 'I'의 심경 변화로 가장 적절한 것은?

One night, my family was having a party with a couple from another city who had two daughters. The girls were just a few years older than I, and I played lots of fun games together with them. The father of the family had an amusing, jolly, witty character, and I had a memorable night full of laughter and joy. While we laughed, joked, and had our dinner, the TV suddenly broadcast an air attack, and a screeching siren started to scream, announcing the "red" situation. We all stopped dinner, and we squeezed into the basement. The siren kept screaming and the roar of planes was heard in the sky. The terror of war was overwhelming. Shivering with fear, I murmured a panicked prayer that this desperate situation would end quickly.

① indifferent → satisfied   ② relaxed → envious
③ frustrated → relieved   ④ excited → bored
⑤ pleased → terrified

20. 다음 글에서 필자가 주장하는 바로 가장 적절한 것은?

If you were at a social gathering in a large building and you overheard someone say that "the roof is on fire," what would be your reaction? Until you knew more information, your first inclination might be toward safety and survival. But if you were to find out that this particular person was talking about a song called "The Roof Is on Fire," your feelings of threat and danger would be diminished. So once the additional facts are understood — that the person was referring to a song and not a real fire — the context is better understood and you are in a better position to judge and react. All too often people react far too quickly and emotionally over information without establishing context. It is so important for us to identify context related to information because if we fail to do so, we may judge and react too quickly.

① 갈등을 해결하려면 상대방의 감정을 파악해야 한다.
② 정보에 대해 판단하고 반응하기 전에 맥락을 확인해야 한다.
③ 위험한 상황에 처할 때일수록 타인의 의견을 경청해야 한다.
④ 많은 정보보다 정확한 정보 제공을 통해 신뢰성을 높여야 한다.
⑤ 신속한 의사결정을 위해 핵심 정보와 주변 정보를 구별해야 한다.

21. 밑줄 친 "learn and live"가 다음 글에서 의미하는 바로 가장 적절한 것은? [3점]

There is a critical factor that determines whether your choice will influence that of others: the visible consequences of the choice. Take the case of the Adélie penguins. They are often found strolling in large groups toward the edge of the water in search of food. Yet danger awaits in the icy-cold water. There is the leopard seal, for one, which likes to have penguins for a meal. What is an Adélie to do? The penguins' solution is to play the waiting game. They wait and wait and wait by the edge of the water until one of them gives up and jumps in. The moment that occurs, the rest of the penguins watch with anticipation to see what happens next. If the pioneer survives, everyone else will follow suit. If it perishes, they'll turn away. One penguin's destiny alters the fate of all the others. Their strategy, you could say, is "learn and live."

* perish: 죽다

① occupy a rival's territory for safety
② discover who the enemy is and attack first
③ share survival skills with the next generation
④ support the leader's decisions for the best results
⑤ follow another's action only when it is proven safe

22. 다음 글의 요지로 가장 적절한 것은?

Imagine that your body is a battery and the more energy this battery can store, the more energy you will be able to have within a day. Every night when you sleep, this battery is recharged with as much energy as you spent during the previous day. If you want to have a lot of energy tomorrow, you need to spend a lot of energy today. Our brain consumes only 20% of our energy, so it's a must to supplement thinking activities with walking and exercises that spend a lot of energy, so that your internal battery has more energy tomorrow. Your body stores as much energy as you need: for thinking, for moving, for doing exercises. The more active you are today, the more energy you spend today and the more energy you will have to burn tomorrow. Exercising gives you more energy and keeps you from feeling exhausted.

* supplement: 보충하다

① 많은 에너지를 얻기 위해 적극적인 신체 활동이 필요하다.
② 가벼운 산책을 통해 창의적 사고력을 증진할 수 있다.
③ 에너지의 소비와 회복의 불균형은 건강을 해친다.
④ 과도한 운동은 효율적인 두뇌 활동을 방해할 수 있다.
⑤ 원활한 에너지 충전을 위해서는 충분한 수면이 중요하다.

23. 다음 글의 주제로 가장 적절한 것은?

You can say that information sits in one brain until it is communicated to another, unchanged in the conversation. That's true of *sheer* information, like your phone number or the place you left your keys. But it's not true of knowledge. Knowledge relies on judgements, which you discover and polish in conversation with other people or with yourself. Therefore you don't learn the details of your thinking until speaking or writing it out in detail and looking back critically at the result. "Is what I just said foolish, or is what I just wrote a deep truth?" In the speaking or writing, you uncover your bad ideas, often embarrassing ones, and good ideas too, sometimes fame-making ones. Thinking requires its expression.

① critical roles of speaking or writing in refining thoughts
② persuasive ways to communicate what you think to people
③ important tips to select the right information for your writing
④ positive effects of logical thinking on reading comprehension
⑤ enormous gaps between spoken language and written language

24. 다음 글의 제목으로 가장 적절한 것은?

In a competitive environment, such as a college admissions process or a job application situation, almost everyone has strong qualifications. Almost everyone has facts in their favor. But how valuable are facts alone? Think back to the most recent lecture or presentation you attended. How many facts do you remember from it? If you're like most people, you can't recall many, if any. Chances are good, however, that you remember stories, anecdotes, and examples from the event, even if you can't think of their exact context. The average person today is flooded with facts and data, and we let most of this pass through our brains with minimal retention or reaction — unless something makes the information stand out in a meaningful way. That's where story comes in.

* retention: 기억

① Make Yourself Outstanding by Using Accurate Terms
② The Power of Story: Why We Need More Than Facts
③ What Is the Key Qualification of a Storyteller?
④ How Big Is Our Average Memory Capacity?
⑤ A Single Fact Is Worth a Whole Story

25. 다음 표의 내용과 일치하지 <u>않는</u> 것은?

Wellness Tourism Trips and Expenditures by Region in 2015 and 2017

Destination	Number of Trips (millions)		Expenditures ($ billions)	
	2015	2017	2015	2017
North America	186.5	204.1	$215.7	$241.7
Europe	249.9	291.8	$193.4	$210.8
Asia-Pacific	193.9	257.6	$111.2	$136.7
Latin America-The Caribbean	46.8	59.1	$30.4	$34.8
The Middle East-North Africa	8.5	11.0	$8.3	$10.7
Africa	5.4	6.5	$4.2	$4.8
Total	**691.0**	**830.0**	**$563.2**	**$639.4**

• Note: Figures may not sum to total due to rounding.

The table above shows the number of trips and expenditures for wellness tourism, travel for health and well-being, in 2015 and 2017. ① Both the total number of trips and the total expenditures were higher in 2017 compared to those in 2015. ② Of the six listed regions, Europe was the most visited place for wellness tourism in both 2015 and 2017, followed by Asia-Pacific. ③ In 2017, the number of trips to Latin America-The Caribbean was more than five times higher than that to The Middle East-North Africa. ④ While North America was the only region where more than 200 billion dollars was spent in 2015, it was joined by Europe in 2017. ⑤ Meanwhile, expenditures in The Middle East-North Africa and Africa were each less than 10 billion dollars in both 2015 and 2017.

26. Charles Henry Turner에 관한 다음 글의 내용과 일치하지 <u>않는</u> 것은?

Born in 1867 in Cincinnati, Ohio, Charles Henry Turner was an early pioneer in the field of insect behavior. His father owned an extensive library where Turner became fascinated with reading about the habits and behavior of insects. Proceeding with his study, Turner earned a doctorate degree in zoology, the first African American to do so. Even after receiving his degree, Turner was unable to get a teaching or research position at any major universities, possibly as a result of racism. He moved to St. Louis and taught biology at Sumner High School, focusing on research there until 1922. Turner was the first person to discover that insects are capable of learning, illustrating that insects can alter behavior based on previous experience. He died of cardiac disease in Chicago in 1923. During his 33-year career, Turner published more than 70 papers. His last scientific paper was published the year after his death.

* cardiac: 심장의

① 곤충의 습성과 행동에 관한 독서에 매료되었다.
② 아프리카계 미국인 최초로 동물학 박사 학위를 받았다.
③ Sumner 고등학교에서 생물학을 가르쳤다.
④ 곤충이 학습할 수 있다는 것을 최초로 발견했다.
⑤ 마지막 과학 논문은 사망한 해에 발표되었다.

27. Introduction to Furniture Making에 관한 다음 안내문의 내용과 일치하는 것은?

Introduction to Furniture Making

Throughout this four-week workshop, students will build a solid foundation for their new venture into woodworking.

• Age Requirement: 16 and older
• Location: Hoboken Community Center
• Dates: Dec 7 – Dec 28 (Every Saturday)
• Time: 1:00 p.m. – 5:00 p.m.
• Price: $399
• Note:
 - Previous woodworking experience is not necessary.
 - We offer full refunds if you cancel at least 10 days in advance.

With the guidance of an instructor, each student will leave with a hand-crafted side table.

For more information or to register, contact Dave Malka (davemalka@woodfurniture.org).

---

① 연령에 제한이 없다.
② 토요일에 5시간씩 진행된다.
③ 목공 경험이 없는 사람도 참여할 수 있다.
④ 적어도 일주일 전에 취소하면 전액을 환불해 준다.
⑤ 수강생들은 수작업으로 만든 의자를 가지고 가게 된다.

28. Poetry in the Park에 관한 다음 안내문의 내용과 일치하지 <u>않는</u> 것은?

Poetry in the Park
Saturday, October 13, 11:00 a.m.— 6:00 p.m.

This annual festival, now in its sixth year, is held with the support of Riverside Public Library.

◈ **Poetry Workshop**
• Meet and talk with renowned poets about their poems.
 Jane Kenny(11:30 a.m.), Michael Weil(12:30 p.m.)
• Learn how to express your feelings poetically.

◈ **Poetry Contest**
• Theme for this year's contest is "Arrivals and Departures."
• Only one poem per participant
• Due by 3:00 p.m.
• The winners will be announced at 5:00 p.m. on the day on site.

For questions about the festival,
please visit our website at www.poetryinthepark.org.

---

① 매년 개최되며 올해가 여섯 번째이다.
② 저명한 시인들과 만나 시에 대해 이야기할 수 있다.
③ 감정을 시적으로 표현하는 방법을 배울 수 있다.
④ 1인당 1편의 시만 콘테스트에 제출할 수 있다.
⑤ 행사 다음 날 오전에 콘테스트의 수상자를 발표한다.

29. 다음 글의 밑줄 친 부분 중, 어법상 **틀린** 것은? [3점]

Non-verbal communication is not a substitute for verbal communication. Rather, it should function as a supplement, ① serving to enhance the richness of the content of the message that is being passed across. Non-verbal communication can be useful in situations ② where speaking may be impossible or inappropriate. Imagine you are in an uncomfortable position while talking to an individual. Non-verbal communication will help you ③ get the message across to him or her to give you some time off the conversation to be comfortable again. Another advantage of non-verbal communication is ④ what it offers you the opportunity to express emotions and attitudes properly. Without the aid of non-verbal communication, there are several aspects of your nature and personality that will not be adequately expressed. So, again, it does not substitute verbal communication but rather ⑤ complements it.

* supplement: 보충

30. 다음 글의 밑줄 친 부분 중, 문맥상 낱말의 쓰임이 적절하지 **않은** 것은? [3점]

Random errors may be detected by ① repeating the measurements. Furthermore, by taking more and more readings, we obtain from the arithmetic mean a value which approaches more and more closely to the true value. Neither of these points is true for a systematic error. Repeated measurements with the same apparatus neither ② reveal nor do they eliminate a systematic error. For this reason systematic errors are potentially more ③ dangerous than random errors. If large random errors are present in an experiment, they will manifest themselves in a large value of the final quoted error. Thus everyone is ④ unaware of the imprecision of the result, and no harm is done — except possibly to the ego of the experimenter when no one takes notice of his or her results. However, the concealed presence of a systematic error may lead to an apparently ⑤ reliable result, given with a small estimated error, which is in fact seriously wrong.

* arithmetic mean: 산술 평균 ** apparatus: 도구

[31~34] 다음 빈칸에 들어갈 말로 가장 적절한 것을 고르시오.

31. If you follow science news, you will have noticed that _____ among animals has become a hot topic in the mass media. For example, in late 2007 the science media widely reported a study by Claudia Rutte and Michael Taborsky suggesting that rats display what they call "generalized reciprocity." They each provided help to an unfamiliar and unrelated individual, based on their own previous experience of having been helped by an unfamiliar rat. Rutte and Taborsky trained rats in a cooperative task of pulling a stick to obtain food for a partner. Rats who had been helped previously by an unknown partner were more likely to help others. Before this research was conducted, generalized reciprocity was thought to be unique to humans.

① friction ② diversity ③ hierarchy
④ cooperation ⑤ independence

32. The title of Thomas Friedman's 2005 book, *The World Is Flat*, was based on the belief that globalization would inevitably bring us closer together. It has done that, but it has also inspired us _____. When faced with perceived threats — the financial crisis, terrorism, violent conflict, refugees and immigration, the increasing gap between rich and poor — people cling more tightly to their groups. One founder of a famous social media company believed social media would unite us. In some respects it has, but it has simultaneously given voice and organizational ability to new cyber tribes, some of whom spend their time spreading blame and division across the World Wide Web. There seem now to be as many tribes, and as much conflict between them, as there have ever been. Is it possible for these tribes to coexist in a world where the concept of "us and them" remains? [3점]

① to build barriers
② to achieve equality
③ to abandon traditions
④ to value individualism
⑤ to develop technologies

33. From an economic perspective, a short-lived event can become an innovative event if it generates goods and services that can be sold to people, in particular to those from outside the locality. The remarkable growth of art exhibitions, cultural festivals and sports competitions, for example, can be analysed in this light. They are temporary activities that can attract large numbers of outsiders to a locality, bringing in new sources of income. But even here, there is a two-way interaction between the event and the context. The existence of an infrastructure, a reputation, a history of an activity for an area may have important effects on the economic success or failure of an event. In other words, events do not take place in a vacuum. They depend on an existing context which has been in the making for a long time. The short-lived event, therefore, would _____. [3점]

* infrastructure: 기반 시설

① build a new context with other short-lived events
② take place free from this spatial and temporal limit
③ be performed in relation to this long-term context
④ interact with well-known events from another locality
⑤ evolve itself from a local event to a global one in the end

34. There is a famous Spanish proverb that says, "The belly rules the mind." This is a clinically proven fact. Food is the original mind-controlling drug. Every time we eat, we bombard our brains with a feast of chemicals, triggering an explosive hormonal chain reaction that directly influences the way we think. Countless studies have shown that the positive emotional state induced by a good meal _____. It triggers an instinctive desire to repay the provider. This is why executives regularly combine business meetings with meals, why lobbyists invite politicians to attend receptions, lunches, and dinners, and why major state occasions almost always involve an impressive banquet. Churchill called this "dining diplomacy," and sociologists have confirmed that this principle is a strong motivator across all human cultures. [3점]

* banquet: 연회

① leads us to make a fair judgement
② interferes with cooperation with others
③ does harm to serious diplomatic occasions
④ plays a critical role in improving our health
⑤ enhances our receptiveness to be persuaded

35. 다음 글에서 전체 흐름과 관계 없는 문장은?

Wouldn't it be nice if you could take your customers by the hand and guide each one through your store while pointing out all the great products you would like them to consider buying? ① Most people, however, would not particularly enjoy having a stranger grab their hand and drag them through a store. ② Rather, let the store do it for you. ③ Have a central path that leads shoppers through the store and lets them look at many different departments or product areas. ④ You can use this effect of music on shopping behavior by playing it in the store. ⑤ This path leads your customers from the entrance through the store on the route you want them to take all the way to the checkout.

[36~37] 주어진 글 다음에 이어질 글의 순서로 가장 적절한 것을 고르시오.

36.

Making a small request that people will accept will naturally increase the chances of their accepting a bigger request afterwards.

(A) After this, the salesperson asks you if you are interested in buying any cruelty-free cosmetics from their store. Given the fact that most people agree to the prior request to sign the petition, they will be more likely to purchase the cosmetics.

(B) For instance, a salesperson might request you to sign a petition to prevent cruelty against animals. This is a very small request, and most people will do what the salesperson asks.

(C) They make such purchases because the salesperson takes advantage of a human tendency to be consistent in their words and actions. People want to be consistent and will keep saying yes if they have already said it once.

* petition: 청원서

① (A) – (C) – (B) ② (B) – (A) – (C)
③ (B) – (C) – (A) ④ (C) – (A) – (B)
⑤ (C) – (B) – (A)

[해설편 p.221]

37.

> Color can impact how you perceive weight. Dark colors look heavy, and bright colors look less so. Interior designers often paint darker colors below brighter colors to put the viewer at ease.

(A) In fact, black is perceived to be twice as heavy as white. Carrying the same product in a black shopping bag, versus a white one, feels heavier. So, small but expensive products like neckties and accessories are often sold in dark-colored shopping bags or cases.

(B) In contrast, shelving dark-colored products on top can create the illusion that they might fall over, which can be a source of anxiety for some shoppers. Black and white, which have a brightness of 0% and 100%, respectively, show the most dramatic difference in perceived weight.

(C) Product displays work the same way. Place bright-colored products higher and dark-colored products lower, given that they are of similar size. This will look more stable and allow customers to comfortably browse the products from top to bottom.

① (A) − (C) − (B)
② (B) − (A) − (C)
③ (B) − (C) − (A)
④ (C) − (A) − (B)
⑤ (C) − (B) − (A)

[38 ~ 39] 글의 흐름으로 보아, 주어진 문장이 들어가기에 가장 적절한 곳을 고르시오.

38.

> The stage director must gain the audience's attention and direct their eyes to a particular spot or actor.

Achieving focus in a movie is easy. Directors can simply point the camera at whatever they want the audience to look at. (①) Close-ups and slow camera shots can emphasize a killer's hand or a character's brief glance of guilt. (②) On stage, focus is much more difficult because the audience is free to look wherever they like. (③) This can be done through lighting, costumes, scenery, voice, and movements. (④) Focus can be gained by simply putting a spotlight on one actor, by having one actor in red and everyone else in gray, or by having one actor move while the others remain still. (⑤) All these techniques will quickly draw the audience's attention to the actor whom the director wants to be in focus.

39.

> However, as society becomes more diverse, the likelihood that people share assumptions and values diminishes.

The way we communicate influences our ability to build strong and healthy communities. Traditional ways of building communities have emphasized debate and argument. (①) For example, the United States has a strong tradition of using town hall meetings to deliberate important issues within communities. (②) In these settings, advocates for each side of the issue present arguments for their positions, and public issues have been discussed in such public forums. (③) Yet for debate and argument to work well, people need to come to such forums with similar assumptions and values. (④) The shared assumptions and values serve as a foundation for the discussion. (⑤) As a result, forms of communication such as argument and debate become polarized, which may drive communities apart as opposed to bringing them together.

40. 다음 글의 내용을 한 문장으로 요약하고자 한다. 빈칸 (A), (B)에 들어갈 말로 가장 적절한 것은?

> The perception of the same amount of discount on a product depends on its relation to the initial price. In one study, respondents were presented with a purchase situation. The persons put in the situation of buying a calculator that cost $15 found out from the vendor that the same product was available in a different store 20 minutes away and at a promotional price of $10. In this case, 68% of respondents decided to make their way down to the store in order to save $5. In the second condition, which involved buying a jacket for $125, the respondents were also told that the same product was available in a store 20 minutes away and cost $120 there. This time, only 29% of the persons said that they would get the cheaper jacket. In both cases, the product was $5 cheaper, but in the first case, the amount was 1/3 of the price, and in the second, it was 1/25 of the price. What differed in both of these situations was the price context of the purchase.

↓

> When the same amount of discount is given in a purchasing situation, the _____(A)_____ value of the discount affects how people _____(B)_____ its value.

	(A)	(B)		(A)	(B)
①	absolute	modify	②	absolute	express
③	identical	produce	④	relative	perceive
⑤	relative	advertise			

[41~42] 다음 글을 읽고, 물음에 답하시오.

Behavioral ecologists have observed clever copying behavior among many of our close animal relatives. One example was uncovered by behavioral ecologists studying the behavior of a small Australian animal called the quoll. Its survival was being (a) threatened by the cane toad, an invasive species introduced to Australia in the 1930s. To a quoll, these toads look as tasty as they are (b) poisonous, and the quolls who ate them suffered fatal consequences at a speedy rate. Behavioral ecologists identified a clever solution by using quolls' instincts to imitate. Scientists fed small groups of quolls toad sausages containing harmless but nausea-inducing chemicals, conditioning them to (c) avoid the toads. Groups of these 'toad-smart' quolls were then released back into the wild: they taught their own offspring what they'd learned. Other quolls copied these (d) constructive behaviors through a process of social learning. As each baby quoll learned to keep away from the hazardous toads, the chances of the survival of the whole quoll species — and not just that of each individual quoll — were (e) reduced. The quolls were saved via minimal human interference because ecologists were able to take advantage of quolls' natural imitative instincts.

*nausea: 메스꺼움

41. 윗글의 제목으로 가장 적절한 것은?

① Imitative Instinct as a Key to Survival for Animals
② Copy Quickly and Precisely to Be Productive
③ How to Stop the Spread of Invasive Species
④ The Role of Threats in Animal Cooperation
⑤ Ideal Habitats for Diverse Wildlife

42. 밑줄 친 (a)~(e) 중에서 문맥상 낱말의 쓰임이 적절하지 않은 것은? [3점]

① (a)　　② (b)　　③ (c)　　④ (d)　　⑤ (e)

[43~45] 다음 글을 읽고, 물음에 답하시오.

(A)

Rangan opened his cycle shop early in the morning. Yesterday he could not attend to business as he was laid up with high fever, but today he made it up to the shop to earn money for his family. Shouting to the tea boy in the next shop for a strong cup of tea, (a) he lined up all the bicycles to be repaired outside. He took a sip of the tea, thinking about the order in which he had to go ahead with his job.

(B)

Rangan worked hard to finish what he had to do. It was already late evening but there was no sign of the old man. Doubts filled (b) him. What if the old man does not return with the money? He regretted fixing up the old man's bicycle. Suddenly (c) he lost all hope and he could wait no longer. He locked up his shop later than usual and cursed himself for getting tricked by an old man.

(C)

At home, Rangan was confused. Washing his greasy hands, he heard a knock at his door. It was the old man and the tea boy. The old man said, "Your shop was closed when I returned. Luckily, I saw this boy in front of the shop." Handing over the money to Rangan, he continued, "Thanks for your hospitality." Rangan grinned at the kind words the old man spoke to (d) him. The fact that he had suspected the old man pained his heart.

(D)

Rangan's thoughts were disturbed by an old man walking with his bicycle towards his shop. The old man was wearing an old turban on his head. His hands and face were covered in wrinkles. In a gloomy tone, (e) he said, "Would you please replace the tire? I'll pay you this evening." Feeling sympathy for him, Rangan fixed the bicycle. He even treated the old man to a cup of tea. The old man thanked Rangan and left.

43. 주어진 글 (A)에 이어질 내용을 순서에 맞게 배열한 것으로 가장 적절한 것은?

① (B) − (D) − (C)　　② (C) − (B) − (D)
③ (C) − (D) − (B)　　④ (D) − (B) − (C)
⑤ (D) − (C) − (B)

44. 밑줄 친 (a)~(e) 중에서 가리키는 대상이 나머지 넷과 다른 것은?

① (a)　　② (b)　　③ (c)　　④ (d)　　⑤ (e)

45. 윗글에 관한 내용으로 적절하지 않은 것은?

① Rangan은 어제 열이 심해 일을 할 수 없었다.
② Rangan은 노인의 자전거를 수리한 것을 후회한 적이 있다.
③ Rangan은 그의 가게를 평소보다 늦게 닫았다.
④ 노인은 홀로 Rangan의 집을 방문했다.
⑤ 노인은 머리에 오래된 터번을 쓰고 있었다.

* 확인 사항
○ 답안지의 해당란에 필요한 내용을 정확히 기입(표기)했는지 확인하시오.

[해설편 p.224]

※ QR 코드를 스캔하시면 듣기 방송이 나옵니다. 듣기 방송을 들으며 다음 빈칸을 채우시오. ● 제한 시간 : 25분

01

다음을 듣고, 여자가 하는 말의 목적으로 가장 적절한 것을 고르시오.

W : Hello and welcome back to 'Happy Life.' I'm Christine Brown, professional life coach. When was the last time you sat down and _____ _____ _____ _____ _____ in your life? With our busy schedules, we easily _____ _____ _____ _____ _____ we already have. However, according to a recent study, people who are more grateful for what they have are more hopeful and physically healthier. So here is today's tip. _____ _____ _____. A gratitude journal is a diary in which you can express all the things you're thankful for. Just invest five to ten minutes each day in the journal. You'll feel more thankful and stay healthier.

02

대화를 듣고, 남자의 의견으로 가장 적절한 것을 고르시오.

M : Good morning, Lily!

W : Hi, Sean! Are you exercising?

M : Yeah. I'm just doing some stretching.

W : Oh, it's good for making your muscles flexible, right?

M : Not only for that. Stretching can _____ _____ _____ by making our mind and body more alert.

W : I can imagine. I think _____ _____ _____ _____ as well.

M : You're right. It also _____ _____ _____ to the muscles, so you can feel less tired.

W : I see. I _____ _____ _____ _____ _____.

M : As you see, stretching is very good for your health in many ways.

W : I think I should do some stretching right away.

M : Of course. Let's do it together.

03

대화를 듣고, 두 사람의 관계를 가장 잘 나타낸 것을 고르시오.

[Door knocks.]

W : Come on in. [Pause] Have a seat, please.

M : Thanks!

W : _____ _____ _____ _____ _____ _____, Mr. Williams?

M : My eyes are red and sore, and I can't see things clearly.

W : Okay. Let me check your eyes first. Put your chin on the machine and don't move.

M : Alright.

W : [Pause] Oh, you have dry eyes. Have you been using your computer more than usual?

M : Yes, _____ _____ _____ _____ _____ on an important project.

W : You should rest your eyes and _____ _____ _____.

M : I see. I was worried I got an eye infection.

W : No, you didn't. Just put some eyedrops in your eyes. I'll give you a prescription.

M : Okay. Do I have to come again?

W : I _____ _____ _____ _____ _____ _____ again next week. The nurse will help you make an appointment.

M : All right. Thank you.

04

대화를 듣고, 그림에서 대화의 내용과 일치하지 않는 것을 고르시오.

M : What are you looking at, honey?

W : It's the picture Sally sent to me. She recommended that _____ _____ _____ _____ _____ _____ _____ near her house.

M : Let me see it. [Pause] I like this big round table on the left. We can have some sandwiches and talk there.

W : Sounds great. Look at the elephant face at the top of the slide. It looks cute.

M : Yeah, there are also swings next to it. Our son would like this park, too.

W : He sure would. Oh, there is _____ _____ _____ _____ _____ _____ _____.

M : Wow, this park has everything a child could want.

W : It's great to find a place where parents and children can have a good time together.

M : It really is. Take a look at these flowers placed _____ _____ _____ _____ _____ _____ _____!

W : They're beautiful. How about going there this weekend?

M : Terrific! I can't wait to go there.

05

대화를 듣고, 남자가 여자를 위해 할 일로 가장 적절한 것을 고르시오.

[Cellphone rings.]

W : Benjamin, I'm sorry to call you during work, but I have great news to share.

M : No problem, mom. _____ _____ _____ _____ my office. What's up?

W : Your brother Wilson got the football scholarship! Let's _____ _____ _____ _____ _____ to celebrate.

M : Wow, wonderful. I'll buy a cake for him on my way home.

W : Good! I'll cook his favorite steak.

M : Oh, he'll love it!

W : Yeah, I hope so. But I think something is missing from the meal. How about _____ _____ _____ as a side dish?

M : Great, it goes well with steak.

W : Right, but we're out of potatoes.

M : Don't worry. I'll buy some for you. The grocery store is near the bakery. I'll be at home in an hour.

W : Thanks. _____ _____ _____. We still have some time.

06

대화를 듣고, 남자가 지불할 금액을 고르시오. [3점]

W : Welcome to Good Aroma Candle. How may I help you?
M : Hi. I'm looking for _____ _____ _____ _____ _____. They like flower scents.
W : Come over here and try this flower scent.
M : Thanks. *[Pause]* I like this rose scented candle. How much is it?
W : Large candles and medium ones are on sale now. Large ones are $20 and medium ones are $10 each.
M : Well then, I'll take two large candles.
W : If you buy any three candles, _____ _____ _____ _____ _____ _____ _____.
M : Great. Then I'll have a medium one ✪ _____ _____ _____ as well. Did you say they're $10?
W : Exactly. You're getting two large candles and one medium candle.
M : That's right. Can I also use this mobile coupon?
W : Of course, you get 10% off the total price with that.
M : Thank you. I'll pay by credit card.

07

대화를 듣고, 여자가 거리 공연을 보러 갈 수 없는 이유를 고르시오.

M : Hi, Charlotte, long time no see!
W : Hi, Andrew. Are you doing well at your new school?
M : I think _____ _____ _____. All of my new classmates are nice.
W : Good to hear that. Are you still playing the guitar? I loved your performance at the school festival last year.
M : Yeah, I joined my new school's rock band. ✪ _____ _____ _____ _____ with the other members.
W : Great! I'd like to listen to your band play.
M : Actually, our band will _____ _____ _____ _____ at Union Square. Will you come and watch?
W : Sure, I'd love to. When exactly will it be?
M : Next Saturday at 2 o'clock. Can you make it?
W : Oh, sorry but unfortunately not. I have to meet my group members next Saturday afternoon for the science project.
M : Okay. There should be another performance soon.
W : I'll try to make it then!

08

대화를 듣고, Junior Badminton Competition에 관해 언급되지 않은 것을 고르시오.

M : Kelly, did you see this Junior Badminton Competition leaflet?
W : No, not yet. Let me see. The competition is on November 21st, at 10 a.m.
M : It's after the midterm exams. Why don't we sign up for the competition as a team?
W : Sounds exciting. It would be _____ _____ _____ _____ _____.
M : Exactly. The participation fee is only $8.
W : That's reasonable. Oh, look at this. They provide lunch for free.

M : But here it says we have to ✪ _____ _____ _____ _____.
W : Then, we should bring ours. How can we apply for the competition?
M : It says we can _____ _____ _____. Let's do it together now.
W : Okay. I'm really looking forward to it.

09

Forest Concert에 관한 다음 내용을 듣고, 일치하지 않는 것을 고르시오.

W : Hello, listeners! We have some good news for music lovers. The Grand Philharmonic will hold the Forest Concert in Central Park on October 7th. The legendary Russian conductor, Alexander Ivanov, will _____ _____ _____ with the theme of 'In Search of a Dream.' This concert is a gift from the Grand Philharmonic to all music lovers so everyone can _____ _____ _____ to this 90-minute musical treat. Seats are on a ✪ _____ _____ _____ _____, so prior reservation is not required. You can also watch it live on TV at home, but seeing it live at the park could be a once in a lifetime experience.

10

다음 표를 보면서 대화를 듣고, 여자가 선택할 미술용품 세트를 고르시오.

M : Hey, Cathy! What are you looking at?
W : Hi, Steve. I was searching for _____ _____ _____ _____. I'm thinking about sending it as a Christmas gift to children in need.
M : You're so kind. Do you need help choosing one?
W : Yeah, thank you. I want it to be under $20.
M : All right. Let me see. Which type of coloring tool would be good for them?
W : Hmm... I think ✪ _____ _____ _____ _____ _____. The kids would need extra things like brushes.
M : I agree. The other tools would be better.
W : Right. How about the number of colors?
M : They'll need more than thirty colors to express what they want.
W : You're right. Then, there are two choices left.
M : Yeah. Oh, there is a model _____ _____ _____ _____.
W : Perfect! They might need it in their art classes. I'll choose that one.

11

대화를 듣고, 여자의 마지막 말에 대한 남자의 응답으로 가장 적절한 것을 고르시오.

W : Hey, James, did you choose which club you're going to join?
M : Not yet. To be honest, I'd like to _____ _____ _____ _____ _____.
W : Great idea! What ✪ _____ _____ _____ do you want to make?

12

대화를 듣고, 남자의 마지막 말에 대한 여자의 응답으로 가장 적절한 것을 고르시오.

M : Mom, look! It's raining outside. But we don't have umbrellas.

W : I think we need to buy one in this building.

M : Okay. ✪ _____ _____ _____ _____?

13

대화를 듣고, 여자의 마지막 말에 대한 남자의 응답으로 가장 적절한 것을 고르시오. [3점]

W : That was a great documentary film, wasn't it, David?

M : Yeah, I was really impressed by the Korean man, _____ _____ _____ _____ the poorest people of Africa.

W : Right, his life was so beautiful. Living one's life for others is truly meaningful.

M : I think so, too. Evelyn, would you like to volunteer with me?

W : Great! What kind of volunteer work are you thinking about?

M : Actually, I've been working at the children's hospital as a volunteer teacher.

W : Volunteer teacher?

M : Yeah, I teach children _____ _____ _____. The hospital is now looking for more teachers.

W : I'd like to, but can I be helpful?

M : Sure, your major is art, so you _____ _____ _____ _____ _____.

W : ✪ _____ _____ _____ _____ _____ _____, so I'm worried whether I can teach them well.

14

대화를 듣고, 남자의 마지막 말에 대한 여자의 응답으로 가장 적절한 것을 고르시오. [3점]

M : Bonnie, what are you doing?

W : I'm checking my bank account. I'm running out of money again.

M : Haven't you gotten paid for your part-time job yet?

W : I have, but I already spent most of the money hanging out with my friends. At the end of month, _____ _____ _____.

M : Then, how about setting a weekly budget?

W : A weekly budget? What do you mean by that?

M : I usually set a budget for each week, and don't spend more than it allows. So I've _____ _____ _____ _____ _____ on chips and soda.

W : Good for you. Can I save money if I make it a habit, too?

M : Of course, you can. If you consider your budget, you'll think twice before you spend money.

W : That makes sense. ✪ _____ _____ _____ _____ _____.

M : Now that I keep a weekly budget, I spend money only where I need it. I bet it'll work for you, too.

15

다음 상황 설명을 듣고, Ted가 Linda에게 할 말로 가장 적절한 것을 고르시오.

M : Ted and Linda are classmates. Linda has some trouble with her friends because she _____ _____ _____ _____ _____ _____. In contrast, Ted is always on time and the other classmates think he's very responsible and reliable. Today, Linda even forgets to submit an important paper. She knows what she has to do, but it's not easy for her to remember everything. _____ _____ _____, she asks Ted for some help on how she can overcome her habit of forgetting. He thinks using a ✪ _____ _____ could _____ _____ _____ _____ _____ _____.

So Ted wants to advise Linda to try using a calendar app to remind her of important things. In this situation, what would Ted most likely say to Linda?

16~17

다음을 듣고, 물음에 답하시오.

M : Welcome to 'Smart Traveler.' I'm your host, Brian Lewis. While traveling, ✪ _____ _____ _____ is one of the greatest pleasures, and many people enjoy bringing small souvenirs back home. Today I'll introduce some of the best souvenirs from around the world! First, when you travel to Beijing, jasmine tea is a great souvenir. _____ _____ _____ _____ _____ will become a wonderful reminder of all those memories there. Second, in Paris, Eiffel Tower keychains are popular. With this little metal item hanging on your keys, you can remember the special moment of being at the top of the Eiffel Tower. Third, when visiting Hawaii, bring back a Hawaiian dancing doll. It'll _____ _____ _____ _____ _____ _____, crystal clear water, and amazing beaches. Last, in Venice, you can buy a traditional Venetian mask. Hanging the mask on the wall as a decoration, you can feel the spirit of Venice at home long afterwards. I hope these tips will help you in your souvenir shopping.

▶ 정답 : 해설편 226쪽

18

001 on behalf of ~을 대표하여, 대신하여
002 remind A of B ⓥ A에게 B를 상기시키다
003 surely 〔ad〕 물론, 틀림없이
004 importance ⓝ 중요성
005 education ⓝ 교육[지도/훈련]
006 regrettably 〔ad〕 유감스럽게도
007 result in ⓥ ~을 야기하다
008 attend ⓥ 참석하다
009 scout ⓥ 스카우트[발굴]하다
010 prospective ⓐ 유망한
011 athletes ⓝ (운동)선수
012 therefore 〔ad〕 그러므로, 그러니
013 demonstrate ⓥ 보여주다, 입증하다
014 capability ⓝ 역량, 능력
015 request ⓥ 요청[신청]하다
016 permission ⓝ 허락, 허가
017 absence ⓝ 결석

19

018 amusing ⓐ 재미있는
019 jolly ⓐ 쾌활한
020 witty ⓐ 재치 있는
021 character ⓝ 성격, 기질
022 memorable ⓐ 기억할 만한
023 laughter ⓝ 웃음(소리)
024 joke ⓥ 농담하다
025 suddenly 〔ad〕 갑자기
026 broadcast ⓥ 널리 알리다, 광고하다
027 air attack 공습
028 screeching ⓐ 날카로운 소리를 내는
029 announce ⓥ 발표하다, 알리다
030 squeeze into ~로 비집고 들어가다
031 basement ⓝ (건물의) 지하층
032 roar ⓝ 굉음, 함성
033 terror ⓝ 두려움, 공포(심)
034 overwhelming ⓐ 압도적인
035 shiver ⓥ 떨다
036 fear ⓝ 공포, 두려움
037 murmur ⓥ 중얼거리다
038 panick ⓥ 겁에 질려 어쩔 줄 모르다
039 desperate ⓐ 절망적인
040 indifferent ⓐ 무관심한
041 envious ⓐ 부러워하는
042 frustrated ⓐ 좌절한
043 terrified ⓐ 공포에 질린

20

044 social gathering 사교 모임
045 overhear ⓥ 우연히 듣다, 엿듣다
046 reaction ⓝ 반응
047 inclination ⓝ ~하려는 뜻, 경향, 의향
048 toward 〔prep〕 (어떤 방향을) 향하여
049 safety ⓝ 안전(함)
050 diminish ⓥ 줄이다, 감소하다
051 additional ⓐ 추가의
052 fact ⓝ 사실
053 refer to ~을 언급하다
054 context ⓝ 맥락
055 emotionally 〔ad〕 감정적으로
056 establish ⓥ 설정하다, 확고히 하다
057 identify ⓥ 확인하다, 알아보다

21

058 critical ⓐ 중요한
059 factor ⓝ 요인, 인자
060 determine ⓥ 확정[결정]하다
061 influence ⓥ 영향을 미치다 ⓝ 영향
062 visible ⓐ 가시적인, 눈에 보이는
063 consequence ⓝ 결과
064 stroll ⓥ 다니다, 거닐다
065 edge ⓝ 끝, 가장자리
066 await ⓥ ~을 기다리다
067 leopard seal 표범 물개
068 play the waiting game ⓥ 대기 전술을 펼치다, 기회를 기다리다
069 moment ⓝ 순간
070 occur ⓥ 일어나다, 발생하다
071 anticipation ⓝ 기대
072 follow suit ⓥ 방금 남이 한 대로 따라하다
073 perish ⓥ 죽다
074 destiny ⓝ 운명
075 alter ⓥ 바꾸다
076 fate ⓝ 운명
077 strategy ⓝ 계획[전략]
078 occupy ⓥ 차지하다
079 rival ⓝ 경쟁자
080 territory ⓝ 영토
081 discover ⓥ 찾다[알아내다]
082 enemy ⓝ 장애물, 적
083 share ⓥ 공유하다
084 generation ⓝ 세대
085 decision ⓝ 결정, 판단
086 prove ⓥ 입증[증명]하다

22

087 imagine ⓥ 상상하다
088 store ⓥ 저장하다
089 be able to ~할 수 있다
090 recharge ⓥ 재충전하다
091 spend ⓥ 들이다[소비하다]
092 previous ⓐ 이전[전]의
093 consume ⓥ 소비하다, 쓰다
094 must ⓝ 필수사항
095 supplement ⓥ 보충하다
096 activity ⓝ 활동
097 exercise ⓝ 운동
098 internal ⓐ 내부의
099 exhausted ⓐ 기진맥진한, 진이 다 빠진

23

100 communicate ⓥ 전달하다
101 conversation ⓝ 대화, 회화
102 true of ~에 관해 사실인, ~에 해당되는
103 sheer ⓐ 순전한
104 rely on ⓥ ~에 의존하다
105 judgement ⓝ 판단
106 polish ⓥ 다듬다
107 detail ⓝ 세부 사항
108 critically 〔ad〕 비판적으로
109 uncover ⓥ 발견하다
110 embarrassing ⓐ 당황스러운
111 fame ⓝ 명성
112 require ⓥ 필요[요구]하다
113 expression ⓝ 표현, 표출

24

114 refine ⓥ 정제하다, 다듬다
115 persuasive ⓐ 설득력 있는
116 select ⓥ 선발[선정/선택]하다
117 effect ⓝ 영향
118 comprehension ⓝ 이해력
119 enormous ⓐ 엄청난

24

120 competitive ⓐ 경쟁의, 경쟁적인
121 admission ⓝ (승인을 받고) 입학, 가입
122 process ⓝ 과정[절차]
123 application ⓝ 지원, 신청
124 qualification ⓝ 자격, 자질
125 in one's favor ~에게 유리하게
126 recent ⓐ 최근의
127 lecture ⓝ 강의, 강연
128 presentation ⓝ 발표[설명]
129 recall ⓥ 기억하다, 회상하다
130 anecdote ⓝ 일화, 개인적인 진술
131 be flooded with ~이 넘쳐나다, 쇄도하다
132 pass through ~을 빠져나가다
133 minimal ⓐ 최소한의
134 retention ⓝ 기억(력)
135 unless 〔conj〕 ~하지 않는 한
136 stand out 두드러지다, 눈에 띄다
137 meaningful ⓐ 의미 있는, 중요한
138 outstanding ⓐ 뛰어난, 탁월한
139 accurate ⓐ 정확한
140 term ⓝ 용어, 말
141 qualification ⓝ 자격[자질/능력]
142 capacity ⓝ 용량, 수용력, 능력

25

143 wellness ⓝ 건강
144 tourism ⓝ 관광
145 expenditure ⓝ 경비, 지출
146 destination ⓝ 목적지, 도착지
147 rounding ⓝ 반올림
148 listed 표[명단]에 실린
149 meanwhile 〔ad〕 한편

26

150 early ⓐ 초(창)기의
151 pioneer ⓝ 선구자, 개척자
152 field ⓝ 분야
153 insect ⓝ 곤충
154 own ⓥ 소유하다
155 extensive ⓐ 폭넓은, 광범위한
156 fascinated with ~에 매료된, 마음을 빼앗긴
157 proceed with ~을 계속하다
158 earn ⓥ 얻다[받다]
159 doctorate ⓝ 박사 학위
160 zoology ⓝ 동물학
161 possibly 〔ad〕 아마
162 racism ⓝ 인종 차별
163 biology ⓝ 생물학
164 focus on ~에 집중[주력]하다
165 capable ⓐ ~을 할 수 있는
166 illustrate ⓥ 설명하다, 분명히 보여주다, 예증하다
167 alter ⓥ 바꾸다, 고치다

27

168 cardiac ⓐ 심장의
169 disease ⓝ 질병, 병
170 publish ⓥ 발표하다, 게재하다
171 scientific ⓐ 과학의

27

172 introduction ⓝ 도입, 입문(서)
173 furniture ⓝ 가구
174 throughout 〔prep〕 ~동안 쭉, 내내
175 solid ⓐ 탄탄한
176 foundation ⓝ 기초
177 venture ⓝ 도전, 모험
178 woodworking ⓝ 목공
179 refund ⓥ 환불하다
180 at least 적어도[최소한]
181 in advance 미리, 사전에
182 hand-crafted ⓐ 수작업의, 손으로 만든
183 register ⓥ 등록[기재]하다

28

184 poetry ⓝ 시, 시가
185 annual ⓐ 연례의
186 with the support of ~의 후원으로
187 renowned ⓐ 저명한, 유명한
188 express ⓥ 나타내다, 표현하다
189 poetically 〔ad〕 시적으로
190 arrival ⓝ 도착
191 departure ⓝ 출발
192 participant ⓝ 참가자
193 on site 현장에서

29

194 verbal ⓐ 언어[말]의
195 substitute ⓝ 대체물 ⓥ 대체하다
196 function ⓝ 기능 ⓥ 기능하다
197 serve ⓥ 제공하다, 돕다
198 enhance ⓥ 강화하다
199 richness ⓝ 풍부함
200 content ⓝ 내용
201 pass across ⓥ 전달하다
202 useful ⓐ 유용한
203 inappropriate ⓐ 부적절한
204 uncomfortable ⓐ 불편한
205 get A across to B ⓥ A를 B에게 전하다, 이해시키다
206 attitude ⓝ 태도[자세]
207 properly 〔ad〕 적절하게
208 aid ⓝ 도움
209 aspect ⓝ 측면
210 personality ⓝ 성격, 인격
211 adequately 〔ad〕 적절하게
212 complement ⓥ 보완하다

30

213 random error ⓝ 랜덤 오차(원인을 알 수 없거나 알더라도 보정할 수 없는 무작위적인 오차)
214 detect ⓥ 발견하다
215 repeat ⓥ 반복[되풀이]하다
216 measurement ⓝ 측정
217 reading ⓝ 측정값, 눈금값
218 arithmetic mean 산술 평균
219 approach ⓥ 다가가다, 접근하다

220 ☐ closely ad 철저하게, 면밀히
221 ☐ systematic error ⓝ 계통 오차(발생한 원인이 분명한 오차)
222 ☐ apparatus ⓝ 도구, 기구, 장치
223 ☐ reveal ⓥ 드러내다
224 ☐ eliminate ⓥ 제거하다
225 ☐ potentially ad 잠재적으로
226 ☐ present ⓐ 있는, 존재하는
227 ☐ manifest ⓥ (분명히) 나타내다, 드러내 보이다
228 ☐ unaware ⓐ ~을 알지 못하는
229 ☐ imprecision ⓝ 부정확성
230 ☐ harm ⓝ 해, 피해
231 ☐ conceal ⓥ 감추다, 숨기다
232 ☐ apparently ad 겉보기에
233 ☐ reliable ⓐ 신뢰할 수 있는
234 ☐ estimated ⓐ 추정된
235 ☐ seriously ad 심(각)하게

31
236 ☐ notice ⓥ 관심을 기울이다
237 ☐ topic ⓝ 화제, 주제
238 ☐ widely ad 널리
239 ☐ report ⓥ 보도하다
240 ☐ suggest ⓥ 시사[암시]하다
241 ☐ rat ⓝ 쥐
242 ☐ display ⓥ 보여주다
243 ☐ generalize ⓥ 일반화하다
244 ☐ reciprocity ⓝ 호혜성, 이익 교환
245 ☐ unfamiliar ⓐ 낯선, 익숙하지 않은
246 ☐ unrelated ⓐ 무관한, 관계없는, 친족이 아닌
247 ☐ train ⓥ 훈련시키다[훈련하다]
248 ☐ cooperative ⓐ 협동적인
249 ☐ obtain ⓥ 얻다
250 ☐ previously ad 이전에, 사전에, 미리
251 ☐ conduct ⓥ 수행하다
252 ☐ unique ⓐ 고유의, 특유의
253 ☐ friction ⓝ 마찰
254 ☐ diversity ⓝ 다양성
255 ☐ hierarchy ⓝ 계급, 계층
256 ☐ independence ⓝ 독립(성)

32
257 ☐ title ⓝ 제목, 표제
258 ☐ belief ⓝ 생각, 믿음
259 ☐ globalization ⓝ 세계화
260 ☐ inevitably ad 필연적으로, 불가피하게
261 ☐ inspire ⓥ 고무하다, 자극하다
262 ☐ face with 직면하다
263 ☐ threat ⓝ 위협
264 ☐ financial ⓐ 금융[재정]의
265 ☐ crisis ⓝ 위기
266 ☐ violent ⓐ 폭력적인
267 ☐ conflict ⓝ 분쟁, 갈등
268 ☐ refugee ⓝ 난민
269 ☐ immigration ⓝ 이주[이민]
270 ☐ gap between rich and poor ⓝ 빈부 격차
271 ☐ cling to ⓥ ~에 달라붙다
272 ☐ tightly ad 단단히
273 ☐ founder ⓝ 설립자
274 ☐ unite ⓥ 결합시키다

275 ☐ simultaneously ad 동시에
276 ☐ organizational ⓐ 조직(상)의
277 ☐ ability ⓝ 능력
278 ☐ tribe ⓝ 부족, 종족
279 ☐ spread ⓥ 퍼뜨리다
280 ☐ blame ⓝ 책임, 탓
281 ☐ division ⓝ 분열
282 ☐ coexist ⓥ 공존하다
283 ☐ concept ⓝ 개념
284 ☐ remains ⓝ 남은 것, 나머지
285 ☐ barrier ⓝ 장벽
286 ☐ achieve ⓥ 달성하다, 성취하다
287 ☐ equality ⓝ 평등
288 ☐ tradition ⓝ 전통
289 ☐ individualism ⓝ 개인주의

33
290 ☐ perspective ⓝ 관점, 시각
291 ☐ short-lived 단기의
292 ☐ innovative ⓐ 획기적인, 혁신적인
293 ☐ generate ⓥ 만들어 내다
294 ☐ goods ⓝ 상품, 제품
295 ☐ locality ⓝ (~이 존재하는) 곳
296 ☐ remarkable ⓐ 눈에 띄는, 놀라운, 주목할 만한
297 ☐ exhibition ⓝ 전시회
298 ☐ analyse ⓥ 분석하다
299 ☐ in this light 이러한 관점에서
300 ☐ temporary ⓐ 일시적인
301 ☐ attract ⓥ 끌다, 매혹시키다
302 ☐ sources ⓝ 원천, 근원
303 ☐ two-way ⓐ 쌍방의
304 ☐ interaction ⓝ 상호 작용
305 ☐ existence ⓝ 존재, 있음
306 ☐ infrastructure ⓝ 기반 시설
307 ☐ reputation ⓝ 명성
308 ☐ failure ⓝ 실패
309 ☐ vacuum ⓝ 진공, 공백
310 ☐ free from ~에서 벗어나, ~의 염려가 없는
311 ☐ spatial ⓐ 공간의, 공간적인
312 ☐ temporal ⓐ 시간의, 시간의 제약을 받는
313 ☐ in relation to ~와 관련하여
314 ☐ long-term ⓐ 장기간의
315 ☐ evolve ⓥ 발달[진전]하다

34
316 ☐ proverb ⓝ 속담
317 ☐ belly ⓝ 배
318 ☐ clinically ad 임상적으로
319 ☐ drug ⓝ 약
320 ☐ bombard A with B ⓥ A에 B를 퍼붓다
321 ☐ feast ⓝ 향연
322 ☐ trigger ⓥ 유발하다
323 ☐ explosive ⓐ 폭발적인
324 ☐ hormonal ⓐ 호르몬의
325 ☐ chain reaction 연쇄 반응
326 ☐ directly ad 곧장, 똑바로
327 ☐ countless ⓐ 무수한, 셀 수 없이 많은
328 ☐ state ⓝ 국가
329 ☐ induce ⓥ 유도하다
330 ☐ instinctive ⓐ 본능적인
331 ☐ desire ⓝ 욕구, 갈망

332 ☐ executive ⓝ 경영진
333 ☐ regularly ad 정기[규칙]적으로
334 ☐ combine ⓥ 결합하다
335 ☐ invite ⓥ 초대[초청]하다
336 ☐ politician ⓝ 정치인
337 ☐ reception ⓝ 환영회
338 ☐ major ⓐ 주요한
339 ☐ occasion ⓝ 행사[의식/축하]
340 ☐ impressive ⓐ 인상적인
341 ☐ banquet ⓝ 연회[만찬]
342 ☐ diplomacy ⓝ 외교
343 ☐ confirm ⓥ 사실임을 보여주다[확인해 주다]
344 ☐ principle ⓝ 원리
345 ☐ motivator ⓝ 동기 부여
346 ☐ fair ⓐ 공정한
347 ☐ interfere with ~을 방해하다
348 ☐ do harm to ~에 해를 끼치다
349 ☐ diplomatic ⓐ 외교의
350 ☐ enhance ⓥ 높이다, 향상시키다
351 ☐ receptiveness ⓝ 수용성, 감수성
352 ☐ persuade ⓥ 설득하다

35
353 ☐ customer ⓝ 손님, 고객
354 ☐ point out ~을 가리키다, 지적하다
355 ☐ particularly ad 특히
356 ☐ grab ⓥ 붙잡다[움켜잡다]
357 ☐ drag ⓥ 끌다
358 ☐ entrance ⓝ 입구
359 ☐ route ⓝ 길[경로/루트]
360 ☐ checkout ⓝ 계산대, 체크아웃

36
361 ☐ accept ⓥ 받아 주다[수락하다]
362 ☐ naturally ad 자연스럽게
363 ☐ afterwards ad 나중에
364 ☐ salesperson ⓝ 판매원
365 ☐ cruelty ⓝ 잔인함
366 ☐ petition ⓝ 청원서
367 ☐ purchase ⓥ 구입[구매/매입]하다
368 ☐ take advantage of ~을 이용하다
369 ☐ tendency ⓝ 경향
370 ☐ consistent ⓐ 일관적인
371 ☐ already ad 이미, 벌써

37
372 ☐ impact ⓥ 영향을 주다 ⓝ 영향
373 ☐ perceive ⓥ 인식하다, 인지하다
374 ☐ at ease 편안한, 걱정 없는
375 ☐ shelve ⓥ 선반에 얹다
376 ☐ illusion ⓝ 착각, 환상
377 ☐ anxiety ⓝ 불안, 염려, 걱정거리
378 ☐ brightness ⓝ 명도, 밝음
379 ☐ respectively ad 각각
380 ☐ dramatic ⓐ 극적인
381 ☐ stable ⓐ 안정적인
382 ☐ browse ⓥ 훑어보다, 둘러보다

38
383 ☐ emphasize ⓥ 강조하다
384 ☐ glance ⓝ 흘긋 봄
385 ☐ guilt ⓝ 죄책감

386 ☐ draw A's attention to B A의 관심을 B로 돌리다

39
387 ☐ diverse ⓐ 다양한
388 ☐ likelihood ⓝ 가능성
389 ☐ assumption ⓝ 가정, 추정
390 ☐ diminish ⓥ 줄어들다, 감소하다
391 ☐ emphasize ⓥ 강조하다
392 ☐ deliberate ⓥ 숙고하다, 신중히 생각하다
393 ☐ advocate ⓝ 옹호자
394 ☐ serve as ~의 역할을 하다, ~로 기능하다
395 ☐ polarize ⓥ 양극화를 초래하다, 양극화되다
396 ☐ drive apart ~을 멀어지게 하다, 소원하게 하다
397 ☐ as opposed to ~이 아니라, ~와는 대조적으로

40
398 ☐ perception ⓝ 인식
399 ☐ initial ⓐ 최초의
400 ☐ be presented with ⓥ ~을 제시받다
401 ☐ calculator ⓝ 계산기
402 ☐ promotional ⓐ 판촉의, 홍보의
403 ☐ differ ⓥ 다르다
404 ☐ absolute ⓐ 절대적인
405 ☐ identical ⓐ 동일한

41~42
406 ☐ ecologist ⓝ 생태학자
407 ☐ uncover ⓥ 밝히다
408 ☐ threaten ⓥ 위협하다
409 ☐ invasive ⓐ 침입의
410 ☐ introduce ⓥ 도입하다
411 ☐ fatal ⓐ 치명적인
412 ☐ consequence ⓝ 결과
413 ☐ identify ⓥ 찾아내다, 확인하다
414 ☐ instinct ⓝ 본능
415 ☐ harmless ⓐ 무해한
416 ☐ induce ⓥ 유발하다
417 ☐ offspring ⓝ 자손
418 ☐ constructive ⓐ 건설적인
419 ☐ hazardous ⓐ 위험한
420 ☐ interference ⓝ 개입, 간섭
421 ☐ take advantage of ~을 이용하다
422 ☐ precisely ad 정확히

43~45
423 ☐ attend to business 일을 보다, 사무를 보다
424 ☐ lay up ~을 드러눕게 하다, 꼼짝 못하게 하다
425 ☐ earn ⓥ (돈을) 벌다, 얻다
426 ☐ take a sip 한 모금을 홀짝 마시다
427 ☐ curse ⓥ 비난하다, 욕하다, 저주하다
428 ☐ greasy ⓐ 기름투성이의
429 ☐ hospitality ⓝ 호의, 환대
430 ☐ suspect ⓥ 의심하다
431 ☐ disturb ⓥ 방해하다
432 ☐ gloomy ⓐ 우울한, 침울한

04회

TEST A-B 각 단어의 뜻을 [A] 영어는 우리말로, [B] 우리말은 영어로 쓰시오.

A	English	Korean
01	prospective	
02	overwhelming	
03	overhear	
04	critical	
05	recharge	
06	enormous	
07	in one's favor	
08	stand out	
09	expenditure	
10	pioneer	
11	foundation	
12	aid	
13	reciprocity	
14	inevitably	
15	vacuum	
16	bombard A with B	
17	perceive	
18	diverse	
19	absolute	
20	offspring	

B	Korean	English
01	A에게 B를 상기시키다	
02	좌절한	
03	~을 언급하다	
04	영향을 미치다, 영향	
05	저장하다	
06	정제하다, 다듬다	
07	자격, 자질	
08	용량, 수용력, 능력	
09	인종 차별	
10	미리, 사전에	
11	저명한, 유명한	
12	대체물, 대체하다	
13	신뢰할 수 있는	
14	협동적인	
15	고무하다, 자극하다	
16	~에서 벗어나, ~의 염려가 없는	
17	유발하다	
18	~을 이용하다	
19	불안, 염려, 걱정거리	
20	비난하다, 욕하다, 저주하다	

▶ A-D 정답 : 해설편 226쪽

TEST C-D 각 단어의 뜻을 골라 기호를 쓰시오.

C	English		Korean
01	demonstrate	( )	ⓐ 굉음, 함성
02	roar	( )	ⓑ 건강
03	inclination	( )	ⓒ 측정값, 눈금값
04	anticipation	( )	ⓓ 연례의
05	must	( )	ⓔ 단기의
06	polish	( )	ⓕ 임상적으로
07	be flooded with	( )	ⓖ 계산대, 체크아웃
08	wellness	( )	ⓗ 강조하다
09	alter	( )	ⓘ 입증하다
10	annual	( )	ⓙ 기대
11	adequately	( )	ⓚ 개인주의
12	individualism	( )	ⓛ ~하려는 뜻, 경향, 의향
13	reading	( )	ⓜ 적절하게
14	short-lived	( )	ⓝ ~이 넘쳐나다, 쇄도하다
15	clinically	( )	ⓞ 바꾸다, 고치다
16	checkout	( )	ⓟ 다듬다
17	shelve	( )	ⓠ 줄어들다, 감소하다
18	emphasize	( )	ⓡ 환대
19	diminish	( )	ⓢ 선반에 얹다
20	hospitality	( )	ⓣ 필수사항

D	Korean		English
01	결석	( )	ⓐ anecdote
02	떨다	( )	ⓑ extensive
03	확인하다, 알아보다	( )	ⓒ shiver
04	운명	( )	ⓓ manifest
05	~에 의존하다	( )	ⓔ apparently
06	일화	( )	ⓕ fate
07	반올림	( )	ⓖ identical
08	폭넓은, 광범위한	( )	ⓗ drag
09	도전, 모험	( )	ⓘ disturb
10	참가자	( )	ⓙ rounding
11	부적절한	( )	ⓚ induce
12	(분명히) 나타내다, 드러내 보이다	( )	ⓛ glance
13	겉보기에	( )	ⓜ participant
14	공존하다	( )	ⓝ deliberate
15	유도하다	( )	ⓞ identify
16	끌다	( )	ⓟ inappropriate
17	흘끗 봄	( )	ⓠ rely on
18	숙고하다, 신중히 생각하다	( )	ⓡ venture
19	동일한	( )	ⓢ absence
20	방해하다	( )	ⓣ coexist

영어 1등급
결론은~ 빈순삽!

20일 완성
[빈칸·순서·삽입]

하루 12문제씩! 20일 완성으로 영어 영역 1등급 OK!

| 하루 20분 20일 완성 | 영어 독해 [빈칸 · 순서 · 삽입] |

기본(고1)   완성(고2)   실전(고3)

영어 1등급 핵심은 '빈순삽'
빈칸·순서·삽입 이 세 가지 유형의 문제는 수능과 내신에서도
비슷한 유형으로 출제되기 때문에
반드시 정복해야만 하는 '필수 유형' 입니다.

● 영어 독해 20일 완성 [빈칸·순서·삽입] 특징

• 기본(고1), 완성(고2), 실전(고3)
• 최근 5개년 수능기출 학력평가 [빈칸 · 순서 · 삽입] 총 240문항 수록
• 하루 12문제를 20분씩 학습하는 효율적인 20일 완성 PLAN
• 평이한 2점, 3점 문항과 [고난도 2점, 3점] 문제를 매회 체계적으로 배치
• 다양한 유형의 지문과 [고난도 문항] 문제 해결 꿀~팁 수록
• A4 사이즈로 제작해 간편한 휴대와 편리한 학습

REAL
리얼 오리지널 BOOK LIST

575만권 수능기출 베스트셀러 2006~2024

예비 [고1] 전과목
고등학교 첫 시험 & 3월 대비
- 반 배치 + 3월 [전과목]
- 3월 전국연합 [전과목]

[고1] 전과목
학력평가 & 중간·기말 대비
- 6월 학평+기말고사
- 9월 학평+기말고사
- 11월 학평+기말고사

[고1] 3개년 | 16회
3개년 전국연합 12회+실전 4회
- 국어 영역
- 영어 영역
- 수학 영역

[고1] 3개년 | 12회
3개년 전국연합 모의고사 12회
- 국어 영역
- 영어 영역

[고2] 3개년 | 16회
3개년 전국연합 12회+실전 4회
- 국어 영역
- 영어 영역
- 수학 영역

[고2] 3개년 | 12회
3개년 전국연합 모의고사 12회
- 국어 영역
- 영어 영역

[고3] 3개년
3개년 교육청+평가원 [총17회]
- 국어(공통+화작·언매)
- 영어 영역
- 수학(공통+확통·미적)

영어 독해 [빈·순·삽]
하루 20분 20일 완성 빈·순·삽
- 기본(고1)
- 완성(고2)
- 실전(고3)

[고3] 5개년
6·9·수능 평가원 기출만 15회
- 국어(공통+화작·언매)
- 영어 영역
- 수학(공통+확통·미적)

[고3] 사탐·과탐
기출 최다 문항 1000제 50회 수록
- 사회·문화
- 생활과 윤리
- 지구과학 I
- 생명과학 I

영어 독해
영어 독해 문제만 회차별 구성
- 고1 영어 독해
- 고2 영어 독해
- 고3 영어 독해

영어 듣기
영어 듣기 문제만 회차별 구성
- 고1 영어 듣기
- 고2 영어 듣기
- 고3 영어 듣기

[고1·2] 미니 모의고사
하루 20분 30일 완성 모의고사
- 고1 국어 영역
- 고1 영어 영역
- 고2 국어 영역
- 고2 영어 영역

[고3] 미니 모의고사
하루 20분 30일 완성 모의고사
- 고3 독서
- 고3 문학
- 고3 영어

▶ 문제편 뒤 표지와 본책을 펼쳐서 누르면 쉽게 분리됩니다. 문제편이 분리되는 것은 파본이 아닙니다.

We are all of us star and deserve to twinkle.

우리는 모두 별이고 반짝일 권리가 있다.

리얼 오리지널 | 전국연합 학력평가 3개년 기출 모의고사 16회 [고1 영어]

발행처 수능 모의고사 전문 출판 입시플라이   **발행일** 2024년 11월 18일   **등록번호** 제 2017-0022호
홈페이지 www.ipsifly.com   **대표전화** 02-433-9979   **구입문의** 02-433-9975   **팩스** 02-433-9905
발행인 조용규   **편집책임** 양창열 김유 이혜민 임명선 김선영   **물류관리** 김소희 이혜리   **주소** 서울특별시 중랑구 용마산로 615 정민빌딩 3층

※ 페이지가 누락되었거나 파손된 교재는 구입하신 곳에서 교환해 드립니다. ※ 발간 이후 발견되는 오류는 입시플라이 홈페이지 정오표를 통해서 알려드립니다.

리얼 오리지널

2025 학력평가 + 내신 대비

전국연합 학력평가 3개년 기출 모의고사

16회 [학력평가 기출 12회 실전 모의고사 4회]

- 2022~2024 최신 3개년 [고1] 전국연합 학력평가 12회
- 학평+내신 대비 3·6·9·11월 [고1] 실전 모의고사 4회
- 어려운 발음 훈련으로 점수를 올려주는 [딕테이션] 16회
- 매회 어휘를 복습할 수 있는 [어휘 리뷰 TEST] 16회
- 친절한 입체적 해설로 [직독직해·구문풀이·고난도 꿀팁]
- 회차별 [SPEED 정답 체크표·STUDY 플래너·정답률]
- 듣기 파일 [QR 코드] 수록 & MP3 파일 제공
- [특별 부록] 회차별 영단어

고1 영어

4회분
실전 모의고사
수록

The Real series ipsifly provide questions in previous real test and you can practice as real college scholastic ability test.

모바일로 학습하는
회차별 영단어 QR 코드 제공

• 해 설 편 •

수능 모의고사 전문 출판
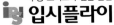 입시플라이

하루 20분
루틴으로 1등급 Fix!
30일 완성
[미니 모의고사]

하루 20분! 30일 완성으로 국어·영어 1등급 Fix!

| 하루 20분 30일 완성 | 수능기출 미니 모의고사 |

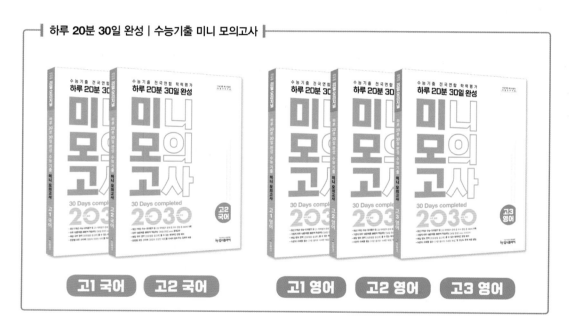

고1 국어　**고2 국어**　　**고1 영어**　**고2 영어**　**고3 영어**

가볍게 '하루 20분'
하루 12문제씩 20분을 학습하는
매일 루틴(Routine)은 수능에 대한 감을 잡아주기 때문에
꾸준한 '수능 대비'가 가능합니다.

• 수능기출 미니 모의고사 [30일 완성] 특징

- 고1 국어, 고2 국어 | 고1 영어, 고2 영어, 고3 영어
- 최근 7개년 수능기출 학력평가 문제 중 [우수 문항 선별] 후 총 360문항 수록
- 매일 정기적인 학습으로 수능의 감을 잡는 꾸준한 연습
- 하루 12문제를 20분씩 학습하는 효율적인 30일 완성 PLAN
- 과목별로 매일 전 유형을 골고루 풀어 볼 수 있는 체계적인 문항 배치
- A4 사이즈로 제작해 간편한 휴대와 편리한 학습

REAL

REAL ORIGINAL

전국연합학력평가
3개년 기출 모의고사

고1 영어 16회 | 해설편

Contents

※ 수록된 정답률은 실제와 차이가 있을 수 있습니다. 문제 난도를 파악하는데 참고용으로 활용하시기 바랍니다.

SPEED 정답 체크 전국연합학력평가 3개년 기출 모의고사 [16회] 고1·영어

01회 2024학년도 3월 전국연합학력평가
01⑤ 02② 03⑤ 04⑤ 05② 06③ 07⑤ 08④ 09④ 10③
11③ 12⑤ 13② 14① 15① 16① 17④ 18③ 19① 20②
21① 22③ 23① 24⑤ 25③ 26④ 27④ 28④ 29② 30③
31② 32③ 33③ 34⑤ 35④ 36④ 37③ 38① 39② 40①
41① 42④ 43⑤ 44④ 45②

02회 2023학년도 3월 전국연합학력평가
01⑤ 02⑤ 03③ 04⑤ 05② 06② 07① 08③ 09④ 10②
11② 12① 13③ 14① 15③ 16③ 17④ 18③ 19② 20⑤
21⑤ 22① 23① 24② 25⑤ 26⑤ 27③ 28④ 29⑤ 30④
31① 32③ 33① 34② 35④ 36④ 37② 38④ 39⑤ 40①
41② 42③ 43④ 44④ 45④

03회 2022학년도 3월 전국연합학력평가
01① 02③ 03② 04④ 05④ 06③ 07① 08④ 09⑤ 10③
11① 12⑤ 13② 14① 15① 16④ 17④ 18② 19③ 20⑤
21⑤ 22① 23④ 24② 25⑤ 26③ 27④ 28⑤ 29③ 30③
31② 32③ 33① 34① 35④ 36③ 37② 38④ 39② 40①
41⑤ 42⑤ 43③ 44④ 45⑤

04회 2024학년도 6월 전국연합학력평가
01③ 02① 03④ 04⑤ 05① 06② 07④ 08② 09⑤ 10④
11① 12③ 13⑤ 14① 15③ 16③ 17④ 18② 19② 20①
21② 22① 23⑤ 24① 25③ 26⑤ 27④ 28⑤ 29③ 30⑤
31② 32② 33⑤ 34① 35④ 36③ 37② 38③ 39④ 40④
41① 42④ 43⑤ 44② 45④

05회 2023학년도 6월 전국연합학력평가
01② 02① 03④ 04④ 05⑤ 06③ 07④ 08③ 09⑤ 10④
11① 12③ 13② 14⑤ 15⑤ 16③ 17④ 18② 19① 20⑤
21① 22③ 23② 24① 25④ 26② 27⑤ 28④ 29④ 30②
31④ 32① 33② 34③ 35④ 36② 37⑤ 38② 39⑤ 40②
41① 42③ 43④ 44② 45③

06회 2022학년도 6월 전국연합학력평가
01② 02① 03⑤ 04⑤ 05① 06③ 07① 08⑤ 09⑤ 10④
11① 12③ 13③ 14④ 15④ 16② 17③ 18② 19② 20⑤
21③ 22① 23② 24⑤ 25④ 26③ 27④ 28② 29④ 30③
31① 32③ 33③ 34② 35④ 36③ 37⑤ 38④ 39⑤ 40③
41① 42④ 43④ 44② 45④

07회 2024학년도 9월 전국연합학력평가
01③ 02③ 03⑤ 04⑤ 05② 06③ 07④ 08④ 09④ 10④
11① 12② 13① 14① 15① 16① 17③ 18⑤ 19⑤ 20②
21⑤ 22③ 23④ 24① 25④ 26② 27⑤ 28③ 29⑤ 30④
31② 32① 33① 34④ 35④ 36② 37④ 38③ 39② 40④
41③ 42④ 43④ 44③ 45②

08회 2023학년도 9월 전국연합학력평가
01⑤ 02① 03④ 04⑤ 05① 06③ 07④ 08③ 09④ 10④
11① 12④ 13① 14③ 15⑤ 16③ 17③ 18⑤ 19② 20②
21⑤ 22④ 23② 24① 25④ 26④ 27④ 28⑤ 29④ 30②
31① 32③ 33② 34① 35② 36② 37③ 38⑤ 39④ 40①
41② 42⑤ 43④ 44③ 45④

09회 2022학년도 9월 전국연합학력평가
01③ 02⑤ 03② 04④ 05④ 06③ 07② 08② 09⑤ 10③
11③ 12① 13① 14③ 15④ 16① 17④ 18⑤ 19② 20④
21③ 22① 23② 24① 25③ 26④ 27④ 28④ 29③ 30⑤
31② 32① 33④ 34① 35④ 36② 37⑤ 38④ 39⑤ 40①
41② 42④ 43④ 44③ 45③

10회 2023학년도 11월 전국연합학력평가
01② 02① 03⑤ 04④ 05① 06⑤ 07⑤ 08④ 09③ 10③
11② 12② 13④ 14③ 15⑤ 16① 17⑤ 18⑤ 19① 20④
21④ 22⑤ 23② 24⑤ 25③ 26③ 27⑤ 28⑤ 29④ 30④
31① 32② 33④ 34③ 35④ 36④ 37③ 38① 39④ 40①
41⑤ 42③ 43④ 44② 45③

11회 2022학년도 11월 전국연합학력평가
01① 02① 03② 04④ 05⑤ 06④ 07① 08③ 09④ 10②
11① 12② 13① 14① 15② 16② 17④ 18② 19② 20⑤
21① 22① 23⑤ 24④ 25④ 26④ 27⑤ 28③ 29④ 30④
31③ 32② 33④ 34④ 35④ 36③ 37⑤ 38⑤ 39③ 40④
41① 42⑤ 43④ 44③ 45④

12회 2021학년도 11월 전국연합학력평가
01② 02③ 03① 04⑤ 05② 06③ 07① 08④ 09④ 10③
11① 12① 13⑤ 14④ 15⑤ 16① 17⑤ 18⑤ 19⑤ 20③
21④ 22③ 23① 24② 25④ 26④ 27② 28④ 29④ 30⑤
31② 32① 33② 34④ 35③ 36③ 37⑤ 38④ 39⑤ 40②
41① 42④ 43① 44② 45⑤

[특별 부록] 실전 모의고사

01회 3월 학력평가 대비 실전 모의고사
01④ 02② 03⑤ 04④ 05① 06① 07③ 08④ 09③ 10④
11② 12③ 13② 14⑤ 15④ 16① 17③ 18① 19② 20①
21③ 22⑤ 23③ 24① 25③ 26④ 27⑤ 28④ 29④ 30⑤
31① 32⑤ 33② 34⑤ 35④ 36③ 37③ 38④ 39③ 40②
41③ 42④ 43② 44⑤ 45③

02회 6월 학력평가 대비 실전 모의고사
01② 02③ 03① 04⑤ 05④ 06④ 07⑤ 08④ 09③ 10③
11② 12① 13④ 14④ 15② 16① 17⑤ 18① 19⑤ 20①
21④ 22④ 23⑤ 24② 25④ 26⑤ 27④ 28③ 29② 30④
31① 32② 33③ 34⑤ 35③ 36② 37② 38④ 39④ 40①
41② 42④ 43⑤ 44④ 45③

03회 9월 학력평가 대비 실전 모의고사
01⑤ 02② 03② 04⑤ 05⑤ 06④ 07① 08④ 09④ 10②
11③ 12① 13⑤ 14① 15② 16① 17③ 18① 19② 20①
21⑤ 22③ 23⑤ 24② 25④ 26③ 27⑤ 28④ 29④ 30⑤
31① 32② 33② 34④ 35④ 36③ 37③ 38④ 39④ 40①
41③ 42⑤ 43④ 44④ 45②

04회 11월 학력평가 대비 실전 모의고사
01② 02③ 03① 04② 05① 06② 07⑤ 08④ 09④ 10②
11④ 12③ 13① 14① 15① 16① 17③ 18④ 19⑤ 20②
21⑤ 22① 23④ 24② 25⑤ 26⑤ 27③ 28⑤ 29④ 30④
31④ 32④ 33③ 34④ 35④ 36② 37⑤ 38④ 39⑤ 40④
41① 42⑤ 43④ 44④ 45④

---

01 폭우로 인한 셔틀 버스 일정 조정 안내 방송   정답률 94% | 정답 ⑤

다음을 듣고, 남자가 하는 말의 목적으로 가장 적절한 것을 고르시오.
① 학교 체육관 공사 일정을 알리려고
② 학교 수업 시간표 조정을 안내하려고
③ 학교 통학 시 대중교통 이용을 권장하려고
④ 학교 방과 후 수업 신청 방식을 설명하려고
☑ 학교 셔틀버스 운행 시간 변경을 공지하려고

M : Good afternoon, students!
좋은 오후입니다. 학생 여러분!
This is your vice principal, Jack Eliot.
저는 교감 선생님인 Jack Eliot이에요.
Due to the heavy rain last night, there's some damage on the road and the road condition is not good.
어젯밤 내린 폭우로 인해서, 도로에 손상이 있었고 도로 상태가 좋지 않습니다.
So we decided to make some rearrangements to the school shuttle bus schedule.
그래서 우리는 학교 셔틀 버스 스케줄을 조정하기로 결정했어요.
From tomorrow, keep in mind that the bus schedule will be delayed by 15 minutes.
내일부터 버스 스케줄이 15분씩 미뤄지는 것을 기억하세요.
We want to make sure all of you are safe.
여러분 모두가 안전하길 원해요.
This bus schedule change will continue for one week.
버스 스케줄 변동은 일주일 간 지속될 겁니다.
We appreciate your understanding and cooperation.
여러분의 이해와 협조에 감사드립니다.
Thank you for your attention!
집중해 주셔서 감사합니다!

Why? 왜 정답일까?

비가 많이 와 학교 셔틀 버스 스케줄이 조정되었다는(So we decided to make some rearrangements to the school shuttle bus schedule.) 내용이므로, 여자가 하는 말의 목적으로 가장 적절한 것은 ⑤ '학교 셔틀버스 운행 시간 변경을 공지하려고'이다.

- vice principal ⓝ 교감
- damage ⓝ 손상
- decide ⓥ 결정하다
- delay ⓥ 지연되다
- schedule ⓝ 일정
- appreciate ⓥ 감사하다
- cooperation ⓝ 협조
- heavy rain ⓝ 폭우
- condition ⓝ 상태
- rearrangement ⓝ 조정
- safe ⓐ 안전한
- continue ⓥ 계속되다
- understanding ⓝ 이해

---

02 전기 자전거를 탈 때 주의할 점   정답률 85% | 정답 ②

대화를 듣고, 여자의 의견으로 가장 적절한 것을 고르시오.
① 전기 자전거 이용 전에 배터리 상태를 점검하여야 한다.
☑ 전기 자전거 운행에 관한 규정이 더 엄격해야 한다.
③ 전기 자전거의 속도 규정에 대한 논의가 필요하다.
④ 전기 자전거 구입 시 가격을 고려해야 한다.
⑤ 전기 자전거 이용 시 헬멧을 착용해야 한다.

W : Brian, I heard that you are thinking of buying an electric bicycle.
Brian, 나 네가 전기 자전거 사는 것을 고려하고 있다고 들었어.
M : Yes, that's right.
응, 맞아.
W : That's good. But be careful when you ride it.
좋아. 하지만 탈 때 조심해.
M : Yeah, I know what you mean. On my way here I saw a man riding an electric bicycle without wearing a helmet.
응, 무슨 말인지 알아. 여기 오는 길에 나는 헬멧 없이 전기 자전거를 타고 있는 사람을 봤어.
W : Some riders don't even follow basic traffic rules.
어떤 사람들은 심지어 기본적인 교통 법규도 안 지키더라.
M : What do you mean by that?
그건 무슨 말이야?
W : These days many people ride electric bicycles on sidewalks.
요즘 많은 사람들이 전기 자전거를 인도에서 타.
M : Yes, it's so dangerous.
맞아, 그거 진짜 위험해.
W : Right. There should be stricter rules about riding electric bicycles.
맞아. 전기 자전거를 타는 것에 대한 더 엄격한 규칙들이 있어야 해.
M : I totally agree with you.
나 너에게 완전 동의해.

Why? 왜 정답일까?

전기 자전거를 타는 것에 대한 더 엄격한 규칙이 있어야 한다고(Right. There should be stricter rules about riding electric bicycles.) 말했기 때문에, 여자의 의견으로 가장 적절한 것은 ② '전기 자전거 운행에 관한 규정이 더 엄격해야 한다.'이다.

- electric bicycle ⓝ 전기 자전거
- ride ⓥ 탑승하다
- way ⓝ 길
- basic ⓐ 기본적인
- sidewalk ⓝ 보행로, 인도
- strict ⓐ 엄격한
- be careful 조심하다
- mean ⓥ 의미하다
- helmet ⓝ 헬멧
- traffic rule ⓝ 교통 법규
- dangerous ⓐ 위험한
- agree ⓥ 동의하다

---

03 신입생을 위한 시간관리 팁   정답률 87% | 정답 ⑤

다음을 듣고, 여자가 하는 말의 요지로 가장 적절한 것을 고르시오.
① 학업 목표를 분명히 설정하는 것이 필요하다.
② 친구와의 협력은 학교생활의 중요한 덕목이다.
③ 과제 제출 마감 기한을 확인하고 준수해야 한다.
④ 적절한 휴식은 성공적인 과업 수행의 핵심 요소이다.
☑ 할 일의 목록을 활용하는 것이 시간 관리에 유용하다.

W : Hello, this is your student counselor, Susan Smith.
안녕하세요 여러분, 저는 학생 상담사, Susan Smith입니다.
You might be worried about your new school life as a freshman.
신입생으로서 여러분의 새로운 학교 생활에 대해 걱정이 될 수도 있어요.
You have a lot of things to do in the beginning of the year.
연초에 해야할 게 아주 많아요.
Today, I'm going to give you a tip about time management.
오늘, 전 여러분에게 시간 관리에 대한 팁을 줄 거예요.
Make a to-do list! Write down the tasks you have to do on a list and check off what you finish, one by one.
할 일 목록을 만드세요! 여러분이 해야 하는 것들을 목록에 쓰고, 완료하면 하나씩 지우세요.
By doing this, you won't miss the things you need to do.
이렇게 함으로써, 여러분은 해야 할 것들을 놓치지 않을 거예요.
Using a to-do list will help you manage your time efficiently.
할 일의 목록을 사용하는 것은 여러분이 시간을 효과적으로 관리하는 것을 도울 거예요.
Good luck to you and don't forget to start today.
행운을 빌고, 오늘 시작하는 것을 잊지 마세요.

Why? 왜 정답일까?

시간 관리의 팁으로 할 일의 목록을 작성하라 하였으므로(Using a to-do list will help you manage your time efficiently.) 여자가 하는 말의 요지로 가장 적절한 것은 ⑤ '할 일의 목록을 활용하는 것이 시간 관리에 유용하다.'이다.

- counselor ⓝ 상담사
- freshman ⓝ 1학년
- tip ⓝ 도움
- to-do list ⓝ 할 일 목록
- list ⓝ 목록
- one by one 하나씩
- manage ⓥ 관리하다
- forget ⓥ 잊다
- worry ⓥ 걱정하다
- beginning ⓝ 시작
- time management ⓝ 시간 관리
- task ⓝ 과업
- finish ⓥ 끝내다
- miss ⓥ 놓치다
- efficiently ⓐⓓ 효율적으로
- start ⓥ 시작하다

---

04 영어 뉴스 동아리방 사진   정답률 90% | 정답 ⑤

대화를 듣고, 그림에서 대화의 내용과 일치하지 않는 것을 고르시오.

M : Hi, Amy. I heard that you've joined the English Newspaper Club.
안녕 Amy. 네가 영어 신문 동아리에 가입했다는 것을 들었어.
W : Yes, Tom. I went to the club room yesterday and took a picture of it. Look.
맞아 Tom. 나는 어제 동아리방에 갔다가 사진을 찍었어. 봐봐.
M : Wow, the place looks nice. 「I like the lockers on the left.」 ①의근거 일치
우와, 동아리 좋아 보인다. 왼쪽에 사물함이 마음에 드는걸.
W : Yes, they're good. 「We also have a star-shaped mirror on the wall.」 ②의근거 일치
응, 사물함 좋아. 우리는 벽에 별 모양 거울도 있어.
M : It looks cool. What's that on the bookshelf?
멋지다. 책장에는 뭐야?
W : 「Oh, that's the trophy my club won for 'Club of the Year'.」 ③의근거 일치
아, '올해의 동아리'상에서 받은 우리 동아리 상패야.
M : You must be very proud of it. 「There's also a computer on the right side of the room.」 ④의근거 일치
너 아주 자랑스럽겠다. 방 오른쪽에 컴퓨터도 있네.
W : Yeah, we use the computer when we need it.
응, 우리 필요할 때 컴퓨터 사용해.
M : Great. I can see a newspaper on the table.
좋다. 책상에 신문도 보이네.
W : 「Yes, it was published last December.」 ⑤의근거 불일치
응, 저건 지난 12월에 발행됐어.

Why? 왜 정답일까?

대화에서 책상 위 신문이 지난 12월에 발행되었다고 했으나 그림에서는 3월(March)에 발행되었기 때문에, 그림에서 대화의 내용과 일치하지 않는 것은 ⑤이다.

- join ⓥ 들어가다
- club ⓝ 동아리
- locker ⓝ 사물함
- mirror ⓝ 거울
- bookshelf ⓝ 책장
- newspaper ⓝ 신문
- picture ⓝ 사진
- star-shaped ⓐ 별 모양의
- wall ⓝ 벽
- trophy ⓝ 상패

- publish ⓥ 발행하다
- December ⓝ 12월

05 캠핑 가기 전 준비
정답률 94% | 정답 ②

대화를 듣고, 남자가 할 일로 가장 적절한 것을 고르시오.
① 따뜻한 옷 챙기기　　　　✓ 체스 세트 가져가기
③ 읽을 책 고르기　　　　④ 간편식 구매하기
⑤ 침낭 준비하기

W : Mike, I think we've got most of the camping supplies ready now.
　Mike, 내 생각에 우리 이제 캠핑 준비물 거의 다 챙긴 것 같아.
M : Yeah, the tent, sleeping bags, and cooking tools are all set.
　응, 텐트, 침낭, 그리고 조리 도구까지 모두 준비됐어.
W : Perfect. I bought some easy-to-cook meals and snacks for us.
　완벽해. 나 우리 먹을 간편식과 간식을 샀어.
M : Great. What about some warm clothes? It might get cold at night.
　좋아. 따뜻한 옷은 챙겼어? 밤에 추워질 수도 있어.
W : I've packed some warm jackets for us, too. Anything else we need to consider?
　우리를 위해서 따뜻한 잠바도 좀 챙겼어. 또 생각해야 할 게 있을까?
M : We need something fun for the camping night. I already packed some books to read.
　캠핑 밤을 위해서 우리 좀 재미있는 게 필요해. 나는 이미 읽을 책을 몇 권 챙겼어.
W : How about playing board games?
　보드 게임 하는 건 어때?
M : Nice. I have a chess set at home.
　멋져. 집에 체스 세트가 있어.
W : Cool, can you bring it?
　좋아, 그거 가져올 수 있어?
M : Of course! I'll take it with me.
　당연하지! 내가 가져갈게.

Why? 왜 정답일까?

남자가 체스 세트를 가져 간다고 했으므로(Of course! I'll take it with me.) 남자가 할 일로 가장 적절한 것은 ② '체스 세트 가져가기'이다.

- most [ad] 대부분의
- ready ⓐ 준비된
- cooking tool ⓝ 요리 도구
- snack ⓝ 간식
- cold ⓐ 추운
- warm ⓐ 따뜻한
- fun ⓐ 재미있는
- chess ⓝ 체스
- take ⓥ 가지고 가다
- camping supplies ⓝ 캠핑 용품
- sleeping bag ⓝ 침낭
- easy-to-cook meal ⓝ 간편식
- clothes ⓝ 옷
- pack ⓥ (짐을) 챙기다
- consider ⓥ 생각하다
- board game ⓝ 보드게임
- bring ⓥ 가지고 오다

06 과일 가게에서 사과와 당근 사기
정답률 87% | 정답 ③

대화를 듣고, 여자가 지불할 금액을 고르시오. [3점]
① $15　　② $20　　✓ $27　　④ $30　　⑤ $33

M : Hello, what can I help you with today?
　안녕하세요. 오늘 무엇을 도와드릴까요?
W : Hi! I want to buy some fruit and vegetables. What's fresh today?
　안녕하세요! 과일과 채소를 사고 싶어요. 오늘 신선한 것은 무엇인가요?
M : We just got some apples in.
　방금 사과가 들어왔어요.
W : How much are they?
　얼마인가요?
M : They are ten dollars for one bag.
　한 봉지에 10달러입니다.
W : Fantastic! I'll take two bags of apples.
　멋지네요! 사과 두 봉지 주세요.
M : Okay, what else do you need?
　알겠습니다. 또 무엇이 필요하신가요?
W : I'd like to buy some carrots, too.
　당근도 사고 싶어요.
M : The carrots are five dollars for one bag. How many do you need?
　당근은 한 봉지에 5달러입니다. 몇 봉지 필요하신가요?
W : I need two bags of carrots.
　당근 두 봉지 필요해요.
M : Okay, you need two bags of apples and two bags of carrots.
　알겠습니다. 사과 두 봉지와 당근 두 봉지가 필요하군요.
W : Right. And I have a coupon. I can get a discount with this, right?
　맞아요. 그리고 쿠폰이 있어요. 이걸로 할인 받을 수 있죠?
M : Yes. You can get a ten percent discount off the total price.
　네. 총 금액에 10% 할인 받으실 수 있습니다.
W : Good. Here's the coupon and my credit card.
　좋아요. 여기 쿠폰과 제 신용카드예요.

Why? 왜 정답일까?

한 봉지에 10달러인 사과를 두 봉지, 한 봉지에 5달러인 당근을 두 봉지 구매했고 총 금액에서 10% 할인 받는 쿠폰을 사용했으므로 {(10×2)+(5×2)}×9÷10＝27, 여자가 지불할 금액은 ③ '$27'이다.

- help ⓥ 도와주다
- fruit ⓝ 과일
- fresh ⓐ 신선한
- fantastic ⓐ 굉장한
- carrot ⓝ 당근
- coupon ⓝ 쿠폰
- price ⓝ 가격
- buy ⓥ 사다
- vegetable ⓝ 채소, 야채
- bag ⓝ 가방, 봉지
- some [ad] 약간의, 일부
- need ⓥ 필요하다
- discount ⓝ 할인
- credit card ⓝ 신용 카드

07 운동회 연습에 참가할 수 없는 이유
정답률 95% | 정답 ⑤

대화를 듣고, 남자가 체육 대회 연습을 할 수 없는 이유를 고르시오.

① 시험공부를 해야 해서
② 동아리 면접이 있어서
③ 축구화를 가져오지 않아서
④ 다리가 완전히 회복되지 않아서
✓ 가족 식사 모임에 참석해야 해서

W : Hey, Jake! How was your math test yesterday?
　안녕, Jake! 어제 수학 시험은 어땠어?
M : Better than I expected.
　생각보다 잘 봤어.
W : That's great. Let's go and practice for Sports Day.
　정말 다행이네. 이제 운동회 연습하러 가자.
M : I'm so sorry but I can't make it.
　미안하지만 오늘은 못 갈 것 같아.
W : Come on, Jake! Sports Day is just around the corner.
　왜 그래, Jake! 운동회가 코앞이잖아.
M : I know. That's why I brought my soccer shoes.
　알아. 그래서 축구화를 가져왔어.
W : Then, why can't you practice today? Do you have a club interview?
　그런데 왜 오늘 연습을 못 해? 동아리 면접이라도 있어?
M : No, I already had the interview last week.
　아니, 이미 지난주에 면접 봤어.
W : Then, does your leg still hurt?
　그럼 다리가 아직도 아파?
M : Not really, it's okay, now. Actually, I have to attend a family dinner gathering tonight for my mother's birthday.
　아니, 이제 괜찮아. 사실 오늘 밤에 엄마 생일이라 가족 저녁 모임에 가야 해.
W : Oh, that's important! Family always comes first. Are you available tomorrow, then?
　아, 그거 중요하지! 가족이 우선이니까. 그럼 내일은 시간 돼?
M : Sure. Let's make up for the missed practice.
　물론이지. 못한 연습을 내일 보충하자.

Why? 왜 정답일까?

대화에서 남자는 오늘 밤에 엄마 생일이라 가족 저녁 모임에 가야한다(Actually, I have to attend a family dinner gathering tonight for my mother's birthday.) 했으므로, 남자가 체육 대회 연습을 할 수 없는 이유는 ⑤ '가족 식사 모임에 참석해야 해서'이다.

- math ⓝ 수학
- yesterday ⓝ 어제
- expect ⓥ 기대하다
- already [ad] 이미
- last [ad] 지난
- hurt ⓥ 아프다
- attend ⓥ 참여하다
- important ⓐ 중요한
- tomorrow ⓝ 내일
- test ⓝ 시험
- better ⓐ 더 나은
- practice ⓝ 연습
- interview ⓝ 면접
- still [ad] 아직, 여전히
- actually [ad] 사실은
- birthday ⓝ 생일
- available ⓐ 참석 가능한
- make up 보충하다

08 과학 프로그램 참여하기
정답률 85% | 정답 ④

대화를 듣고, Science Open Lab Program에 관해 언급되지 않은 것을 고르시오.
① 지원 가능 학년　　　　② 실험 재료 구입 필요성
③ 지원서 제출 기한　　　✓ 참가 인원수
⑤ 시상 여부

W : Hey, Chris. Have you heard about the Science Open Lab Program?
　안녕, Chris. 과학 오픈 랩 프로그램에 대해 들어 봤어?
M : Yes, I heard about it. But I don't know what it is exactly.
　응, 들어 봤어. 그런데 정확히 뭔지는 잘 몰라.
W : In that program, we can design any science experiment we want.
　그 프로그램에서는 우리가 원하는 과학 실험을 설계할 수 있어.
M : That sounds pretty cool. Do you want to join the program?
　정말 멋지다. 그 프로그램에 참여할래?
W : Sure, 「it's only for freshmen like us.」 ①의 근거 일치 Let's join it together.
　물론이지, 그건 우리 같은 신입생들만을 위한 거야. 같이 참여하자.
M : Great! Do we need to buy some materials for experiments?
　좋아! 실험 재료는 우리가 사야 하나?
W : No, 「they'll prepare everything for us.」 ②의 근거 일치 We just need to send the application form online.
　아니, 그쪽에서 모든 거 준비해 줄 거야. 우리는 온라인으로 신청서만 제출하면 돼.
M : When is the deadline for applying?
　신청 마감일이 언제야?
W : 「It's tomorrow.」 ③의 근거 일치 We need to hurry.
　내일이야. 서둘러야 해.
M : Oh, I see. Is there any special prize?
　아, 그렇구나. 특별한 상이 있니?
W : Yes. 「I heard they're giving out prizes for the most creative projects.」 ⑤의 근거 일치
　응, 가장 창의적인 프로젝트에 상을 준다고 들었어.
M : Perfect! I'm so excited.
　완벽해! 정말 기대된다.

.Why? 왜 정답일까?

과학 오픈 랩 프로그램에서 언급 된 것은 지원 가능 학년, 실험 재료 구입 필요성, 지원서 제출 기한, 시상 여부이므로 언급되지 않은 것은 ④ '참가 인원수'이다.

- lab ⓝ 실험실
- exactly [ad] 정확히
- pretty [ad] 꽤
- experiment ⓝ 실험
- prepare ⓥ 준비하다
- deadline ⓝ 제출 기한
- give out 주다
- know ⓥ 알다
- design ⓥ 설계하다
- join ⓥ 참여하다
- material ⓝ 재료
- application form ⓝ 지원서
- prize ⓝ 상
- creative ⓐ 창의적인

09 어르신들 휴대폰 가르쳐드리기 봉사

정답률 91% | 정답 ④

Triwood High School Volunteer Program에 관한 다음 내용을 듣고, 일치하지 <u>않는</u> 것을 고르시오.
① 노인을 도와주는 봉사 활동이다.
② 봉사자는 대면으로 활동한다.
③ 스마트폰 사용 방법 교육을 한다.
④ 봉사자는 매주 토요일에 세 시간씩 참여한다.
⑤ 지원자는 이메일로 참가 신청서를 보내야 한다.

W : Hello, students! Are you looking for a chance to help others?
안녕하세요. 학생 여러분! 다른 사람들을 도울 기회를 찾고 계신가요?
Then, I recommend you to join Triwood High School Volunteer Program to help senior citizens.
그렇다면, Triwood 고등학교 자원봉사 프로그램에 참여하여 어르신들을 도와드리는 것을 추천합니다.
『You're supposed to help the senior citizens face-to-face.』 ①, ②의 근거 일치
여러분은 어르신들을 직접 대면하여 도와드리게 될 것입니다.
『You teach them how to use their smartphones for things such as sending text messages or taking pictures.』 ③의 근거 일치
문자 메시지를 보내거나 사진을 찍는 등 스마트폰 사용 방법을 가르쳐 드리게 됩니다.
You will also teach seniors how to use various apps.
또한 다양한 앱 사용법도 가르쳐 드릴 것입니다.
『The program will require volunteers to participate for two hours every Saturday.』
이 프로그램은 자원봉사자들이 매주 토요일에 2시간씩 참여해야 합니다. ④의 근거 불일치
『If you are interested in joining our program, please send us an application form through email.』 ⑤의 근거 일치
이 프로그램에 관심이 있으시면, 이메일로 신청서를 보내주세요.

Why? 왜 정답일까?
Triwood High School Volunteer Program의 봉사자는 매주 토요일에 두 시간씩 참여해야 하기 (The program will require volunteers to participate for two hours every Saturday.) 때문에, 일치하지 않는 것은 ④ '봉사자는 매주 토요일에 세 시간씩 참여한다.'이다.

- **look for** 찾다
- **recommend** ⓥ 추천하다
- **senior** ⓐ 노인의
- **face-to-face** 대면(으로)
- **take picture** 사진을 찍다
- **require** ⓥ 요구하다
- **be interested in** ~에 관심이 있다
- **chance** ⓝ 기회
- **volunteer** ⓝ 봉사 활동
- **citizen** ⓝ 시민
- **text message** 문자 메시지
- **various** ⓐ 다양한
- **participate** ⓥ 참여하다
- **application** ⓝ 지원

10 휴대용 선풍기 고르기

정답률 82% | 정답 ③

다음 표를 보면서 대화를 듣고, 여자가 주문할 휴대용 선풍기를 고르시오.

Portable Fan

	Model	Number of Speed Options	Color	LED Display	Price
①	A	1	blue	×	$15
②	B	3	white	○	$26
③ ✓	C	3	yellow	×	$31
④	D	4	pink	×	$37
⑤	E	5	green	○	$42

M : Sophie, what are you looking for?
Sophie, 무엇을 찾고 있어?
W : I'm trying to choose one of these portable fans as a gift for my friend Cathy.
친구 Cathy에게 줄 선물로 이 휴대용 선풍기 중 하나를 고르려고 해.
M : Oh, let me help you. How many speed options do you think she would want?
아, 내가 도와줄게. 몇 가지 속도 옵션이 있으면 좋을까?
W : 『She would like it if the fan has more than two options.』 근거1 Number of Speed Options 조건
두 가지 이상의 옵션이 있으면 좋아할 것 같아.
M : Okay, then, what color do you have in mind?
알겠어, 그럼 어떤 색깔을 생각하고 있어?
W : Cathy's old one was white. 『I want to choose a different color.』 근거2 Color 조건
Cathy의 예전 것은 흰색이었어. 이번엔 다른 색을 고르고 싶어.
M : Good idea. Do you want an LED display to show the remaining battery power?
좋은 생각이야. 남은 배터리 용량을 보여주는 LED 디스플레이가 있으면 좋겠어?
W : 『Hmm, I don't think she will need it.』 근거3 LED Display 조건
음, 그건 필요 없을 것 같아.
M : You're left with two options. Which one do you prefer?
그럼 두 가지 옵션이 남아. 어느 걸로 할래?
W : 『Well, I'll take the cheaper one.』 근거4 Price 조건
음, 더 저렴한 걸로 할게.

Why? 왜 정답일까?
속도 옵션이 2개 이상이고, 색깔은 흰색 외의 다른 색이며, LED 디스플레이가 없는 모델 중 저렴한 옵션은 C이므로 답은 ③이다.

- **portable** ⓐ 휴대용의
- **speed** ⓝ 속도
- **remain** ⓥ 남다
- **cheap** ⓐ (값이) 싼
- **fan** ⓝ 선풍기
- **option** ⓝ 선택지
- **prefer** ⓥ 선호하다

11 잃어버린 지갑 찾기

정답률 82% | 정답 ③

대화를 듣고, 남자의 마지막 말에 대한 여자의 응답으로 가장 적절한 것을 고르시오.
① I can help you find it. – 네가 지갑 찾는 걸 도와줄 수 있어.
② I already bought a new one. – 나 이미 새 거 샀어.

✓③ I had it before biology class. – 생물 시간 전에 가지고 있어.
④ You should report it to the police. – 경찰에 신고해야 해.
⑤ It was a birthday gift from my dad. – 아버지가 사주신 내 생일 선물이었어.

M : What's wrong, Jane? You look so upset.
무슨 일이야, Jane? 기분이 안 좋아 보이네.
W : I lost my purse! I have been searching for it for an hour, but I can't find it.
지갑을 잃어버렸어! 한 시간 동안 찾고 있었는데, 못 찾겠어.
M : When did you last have it?
마지막으로 지갑을 가졌던 게 언제야?
W : I had it before biology class.
생물 시간 전에 가지고 있었어.

Why? 왜 정답일까?
마지막으로 지갑을 가지고 있었던 것이 언제인지 물었으므로 시간을 나타내는 표현이 포함된 ③ 'I had it before biology class.'(나는 지갑을 생물학 시간에 가지고 있었어.)이 남자의 마지막 말에 대한 여자의 응답으로 가장 적절하다.

- **upset** ⓐ 당황한
- **search for** 찾다
- **biology** ⓝ 생물학
- **purse** ⓝ 지갑
- **last** ⓐⓓ 마지막으로

12 토요일 점심 예약하기

정답률 72% | 정답 ⑤

대화를 듣고, 여자의 마지막 말에 대한 남자의 응답으로 가장 적절한 것을 고르시오.
① Thank you. Everything looks delicious. – 고마워. 모든 게 맛있어 보인다.
② Yes. I have an appointment this Saturday. – 응. 나 이번 주 토요일에 약속 있어.
③ You're welcome. I made it with my dad's recipe. – 천만에, 아빠의 레시피로 만들었어.
④ Sounds good. What time did you make a reservation? – 좋아. 예약 몇 시로 했어?
✓⑤ That's too bad. Why don't we try another restaurant? – 그거 별로네. 다른 식당 찾아볼까?

W : Honey, what do you have in mind for lunch this Saturday?
자기야, 이번 토요일 점심은 뭐 먹을까?
M : I was thinking we should try the new Italian restaurant.
새로 생긴 이탈리아 식당에 가보면 어떨까 생각 중이었어.
W : Hmm... I heard that it's hard to make a reservation there these days.
음... 요즘 거기 예약하기 어렵다고 들었어.
M : That's too bad. Why don't we try another restaurant?
그거 별로네. 다른 식당 찾아볼까?

Why? 왜 정답일까?
토요일 점심 예약을 하던 중, 가고 싶은 식당은 예약하기가 어렵다고 들었다는 말에 대한 응답으로 'That's too bad. Why don't we try another restaurant?' (그거 별로네. 다른 식당 찾아볼까?) 가 가장 적합하므로 여자의 마지막 말에 대한 남자의 응답으로 적절한 것은 ⑤번이다.

- **reservation** ⓝ 예약
- **recipe** ⓝ 요리법
- **delicious** ⓐ 맛있는

13 오디오북 녹음하기

정답률 88% | 정답 ②

대화를 듣고, 남자의 마지막 말에 대한 여자의 응답으로 가장 적절한 것을 고르시오. [3점]
Woman:
① No problem. You can find other projects at the organization
문제 없어. 넌 기관에서 다른 프로젝트를 찾아볼 수 있어.
✓② Sure. Let's choose one from your old children's books.
당연하지. 네 옛날 어린이 책에서 하나 골라 보자.
③ Congratulations. You finally made your first audiobook.
축하해. 드디어 네 첫 오디오북을 만들었네.
④ I hope so. You're going to be a wonderful writer.
그러길 바라. 넌 훌륭한 작가가 될 거야.
⑤ Exactly. Kids grow faster than you think.
정확해. 아이들은 네가 생각하는 것보다 더 빨리 자란단다.

M : Mom! I've started to record audiobooks for kids.
엄마! 아이들을 위한 오디오북 녹음을 시작했어요.
W : That's great! How did you get involved in that?
정말 좋네! 어떻게 그 일을 시작하게 됐니?
M : My teacher told me that a local organization is looking for students to record audiobooks.
선생님이 지역 단체에서 오디오북을 녹음할 학생들을 찾고 있다고 알려 주셨어요.
W : Fantastic! Are you having fun with it?
멋지구나. 그 일 재미있니?
M : Well, actually, I'm struggling with my voice acting.
음, 사실 목소리 연기가 좀 어려워요.
W : Oh? Is that so?
오? 그래?
M : Yes, it's a bit challenging to get the right tone for kids.
네, 아이들에게 맞는 톤을 찾는 게 좀 힘들어요.
W : I'm sure you'll get better with practice soon.
연습하면 곧 나아질 거야.
M : Thanks. I'm trying my best.
고마워요. 최선을 다하고 있어요.
W : That's wonderful. Anything I can help you with?
정말 좋구나. 내가 도와줄 게 있을까?
M : Can you recommend a good book for my audiobook recording?
오디오북 녹음을 위해 좋은 책 좀 추천해 줄 수 있어요?
W : Sure. Let's choose one from your old children's books.
당연하지. 네 옛날 어린이 책에서 하나 골라 보자.

Why? 왜 정답일까?
어린이를 위한 오디오북 녹음을 위해 좋은 책을 추천해 달라 했기 때문에 ② 'Sure. Let's choose one from your old children's books.'(당연하지. 네 옛날 어린이책 중에서 한 권을 골라 보자.)가 남자의 마지막 말에 대한 여자의 응답으로 가장 적절하다.

- record ⓥ 녹음하다
- local ⓐ 지역의, 현지의
- struggle ⓥ 고군분투하다
- right ⓐ 알맞은
- practice ⓥ 연습하다
- project ⓝ 계획, 기획
- involve ⓥ 참여시키다
- organization ⓝ 단체
- challenging ⓐ 도전적인
- tone ⓝ 어조
- recommend ⓥ 추천하다

---

14 역사 프로젝트 시작하기 　　　　　정답률 85% | 정답 ①

대화를 듣고, 여자의 마지막 말에 대한 남자의 응답으로 가장 적절한 것을 고르시오.

Man:

☑ Well, let's do the presentation together. – 음, 발표는 같이하자.
② Cheer up! I know you did your best. – 힘내! 네가 최선을 다 한 걸 알아.
③ Yes, I got a good grade on science. – 응, 나 과학 성적 잘 받았어.
④ Wow! it was a really nice presentation. – 와! 진짜 좋은 발표였어.
⑤ Right. I have already finished the project. – 맞아. 나 이미 과제 끝냈어.

W : Hi, Fred. What should we do for our history project?
　안녕, Fred. 역사 프로젝트를 어떻게 할까?
M : Actually, I was thinking about it. Why don't we divide the roles for the project?
　사실, 나도 생각하고 있었어. 프로젝트 역할을 나누는 게 어떨까?
W : Okay. Good idea. We have the research part, the visual material part, and the presentation part.
　좋아. 좋은 생각이야. 연구 파트, 시각 자료 파트, 그리고 발표 파트가 있잖아.
M : Hmm, is there any part you want to take on?
　음, 너는 어떤 파트를 맡고 싶어?
W : Well, I would like to do the research. I've been collecting news articles about history.
　음, 나는 연구 파트를 맡고 싶어. 역사에 관한 기사를 모아 왔거든.
M : Excellent. You are good at gathering necessary information.
　훌륭해. 필요한 정보를 잘 모으잖아.
W : Thanks. Can you handle the visual material?
　고마워. 너는 시각 자료를 맡아줄 수 있겠니?
M : Okay. I'll take care of it. I have done it before.
　좋아. 내가 맡을게. 전에 해본 적 있어.
W : All right. Then, the only part left is the presentation.
　알았어. 그럼 발표 파트만 남았네.
M : Well, let's do the presentation together.
　음, 발표는 같이하자.

Why? 왜 정답일까?

발표 준비를 하며 역할을 분배하던 중 발표 파트만 역할을 분배하면 되므로 ① 'Well, let's do the presentation together.'(음, 발표는 같이 하자.)가 여자의 마지막 말에 대한 남자의 응답으로 가장 적절하다.

- history ⓝ 역사
- role ⓝ 역할
- visual material ⓝ 시각 자료
- take on 맡다
- article ⓝ (신문 등의) 기사
- necessary ⓐ 필요한
- handle ⓥ 다루다
- divide ⓥ 나누다
- research ⓝ 조사
- presentation ⓝ 발표
- collect ⓥ 모으다
- gather ⓥ 모으다
- information ⓝ 정보

---

15 도서관 개장 시간 질문하기 　　　　　정답률 68% | 정답 ①

다음 상황 설명을 듣고, Robert가 Michelle에게 할 말로 가장 적절한 것을 고르시오. [3점]

Robert:

☑ When can I use the library? – 도서관을 언제 이용할 수 있어?
② Where can I find the library? – 도서관 어디에 있어?
③ How can I join the reading club? – 독서 동아리에 어떻게 가입해?
④ Why do you want to go to the library? – 왜 도서관에 가고 싶어해?
⑤ What time does the lost and found open? – 분실물 보관소가 몇 시에 여니?

W : Robert and Michelle are attending their high school orientation.
　Robert와 Michelle은 고등학교 오리엔테이션에 참석하고 있습니다.
　After short greetings, the teacher begins to explain student clubs, school activities, and school facilities.
　간단한 인사 후, 선생님은 동아리, 학교 활동, 그리고 학교 시설에 대해 설명하기 시작합니다.
　Robert is focusing very carefully on the explanation.
　Robert는 설명에 매우 집중하고 있습니다.
　However, while writing down important things about the school library, Robert drops his pen.
　하지만 학교 도서관에 대한 중요한 내용을 적는 도중, Robert는 펜을 떨어뜨립니다.
　Trying to find his pen, Robert misses important information about the opening hours of the library, so now, Robert wants to ask Michelle when the library is open.
　펜을 찾으려다가, Robert는 도서관 개관 시간에 대한 중요한 정보를 놓치고, 이제 Michelle에게 도서관이 언제 여는지 물어보려 합니다.
　In this situation, what would Robert most likely say to Michelle?
　이 상황에서, Robert는 Michelle에게 뭐라고 말할 가능성이 가장 높을까요?
Robert : When can I use the library?
　도서관을 언제 이용할 수 있어?

Why? 왜 정답일까?

Robert는 도서관 개관 시간에 대한 중요한 정보를 놓치고, Michelle에게 도서관 개장 시간을 물어보고 싶기 때문에 ① 'When can I use the library?'(도서관을 언제 이용할 수 있어?)가 Michelle에게 할 말로 가장 적절하다.

- attend ⓥ 참석하다
- greetings ⓝ 인사
- facility ⓝ 시설
- library ⓝ 도서관
- orientation ⓝ 설명회
- explain ⓥ 설명하다
- explanation ⓝ 설명
- drop ⓥ 떨어뜨리다

16-17 감기에 좋은 음식들

M : Hello, listeners. Thank you for tuning in to our Happy Radio Show.
　안녕하세요, 청취자 여러분. 해피 라디오 쇼를 들어 주셔서 감사합니다.
　Are you taking good care of your health in the early spring?
　초봄에 건강 잘 챙기고 계신가요?
　「Today, I want to recommend some foods that can reduce the symptoms of a cough.」 16번의 근거
　오늘은 기침 증상을 줄이는 데 도움이 되는 몇 가지 음식을 추천 드리고자 합니다.
　Ginger is a popular home remedy for coughs.
　생강은 기침을 줄이는 인기 있는 민간 요법입니다.
　「A cup of hot ginger tea can be helpful for reducing your cough.」 17번 ①의 근거 일치
　따뜻한 생강차 한 잔이 기침 완화에 도움이 될 수 있습니다.
　Lemon is a rich source of vitamin C.
　레몬은 비타민 C가 풍부한 과일입니다.
　「Lemon tea can help you relieve your cough.」 17번 ②의 근거 일치
　레몬차는 기침 완화에 도움이 됩니다.
　「Surprisingly, pineapple is another excellent food to help relieve a cough.」 17번 ③의 근거 일치
　놀랍게도, 파인애플도 기침 완화에 탁월한 음식입니다.
　「When you are suffering from a cough, eating bananas also helps to get rid of the symptoms more easily.」 17번 ⑤의 근거 일치
　기침을 할 때 바나나를 먹으면 증상도 더 쉽게 완화하는 데 도움이 됩니다.
　These foods are rich in vitamins and they are recommended for people suffering from a cough.
　이 음식들은 비타민이 풍부하며 기침을 겪고 있는 사람들에게 추천됩니다.
　I hope you have a healthy week.
　건강한 한 주 되시길 바랍니다.

- tune in 주파수를 맞추다
- cough ⓝ 기침
- symptom ⓝ 증상
- popular ⓐ 인기 있는
- relieve ⓥ 완화하다
- get rid of 없애다
- source ⓝ 공급원
- healthy ⓐ 건강한
- recommend ⓥ 추천하다
- reduce ⓥ 줄이다
- ginger ⓝ 생강
- remedy ⓝ 치료법
- suffer ⓥ 고생하다
- rich ⓐ 풍부한
- vitamin ⓝ 비타민

---

16 주제 파악 　　　　　정답률 85% | 정답 ①

남자가 하는 말의 주제로 가장 적절한 것은?

☑ useful foods to relieve coughs – 기침 완화에 좋은 음식들
② importance of proper food recipes – 적절한 음식 레시피의 중요성
③ various causes of cough symptoms – 감기 증상의 다양한 원인들
④ traditional home remedies for fever – 미열을 위한 전통적인 가정 치료법들
⑤ connection between weather and cough – 날씨와 기침 간의 연관성

Why? 왜 정답일까?

기침에 좋은 음식에 대해 이야기하고 있으므로(Today, I want to recommend some foods that can reduce the symptoms of a cough.), 남자가 하는 말의 주제로 가장 적절한 것은 ① 'useful foods to relieve coughs'이다.

---

17 언급 유무 파악 　　　　　정답률 89% | 정답 ④

언급된 음식 재료가 아닌 것은?

① ginger – 생강　　② lemon – 레몬　　③ pineapple – 파인애플
☑ honey – 꿀　　⑤ banana – 바나나

Why? 왜 정답일까?

생강, 레몬, 파인애플, 바나나는 언급된 음식 재료이다. 따라서 언급되지 않은 것은 ④ 'honey'(꿀)이다.

---

18 특별 강연 초청 편지 　　　　　정답률 94% | 정답 ③

다음 글의 목적으로 가장 적절한 것은?

① 환경 보호의 중요성을 강조하려고
② 글쓰기에서 주의할 점을 알려 주려고
☑ 특강 강사로 작가의 방문을 요청하려고
④ 작가의 팬 사인회 일정 변경을 공지하려고
⑤ 작가가 쓴 책의 내용에 관하여 문의하려고

Dear Ms. Jane Watson,
친애하는 Jane Watson 씨,
I am John Austin, a science teacher / at Crestville High School.
저는 John Austin입니다. / Crestville 고등학교의
Recently, / I was impressed / by the latest book / you wrote about the environment.
최근에, / 저는 감명 받았습니다. / 최신 도서에 / 당신이 환경에 관해 쓴
Also, / my students read your book / and had a class discussion about it.
또한, / 저의 학생들은 당신의 책을 읽었고 / 그것에 대해 토론 수업을 하였습니다.
They are big fans of your book, / so I'd like to ask you / to visit our school / and give a special lecture.
그들은 당신의 책을 아주 좋아하고, / 그래서 저는 당신에게 요청합니다. / 우리 학교에 방문하여 / 특별 강연을 해 주시기를
We can set the date and time / to suit your schedule.
우리는 날짜와 시간을 정할 수 있습니다. / 당신의 일정에 맞춰
Having you at our school / would be a fantastic experience for the students.
당신이 우리 학교에 와주신다면 / 학생들에게 멋진 경험이 될 것 같습니다.
We would be very grateful / if you could come.
우리는 정말 감사하겠습니다. / 당신이 와 주신다면
Best regards, // John Austin
안부를 전하며, // John Austin

친애하는 Jane Watson 씨, 저는 Crestville 고등학교의 과학 교사 John Austin입니다. 최근에, 저는 환경에 관해 당신이 쓴 최신 도서에 감명받았습니다. 또한 저의 학생들은 당신의 책을 읽었고 그것에 대해 토론 수업을 하였습니다. 그들은 당신의 책을 아주 좋아하고, 그래서 저는 당신이 우리 학교에 방문하여 특별 강연을 해 주시기를 요청드리고 싶습니다. 우리는 당신의 일정에 맞춰 날짜와 시간을 정하겠습니다. 당신이 우리 학교에 와 주신다면 학생들에게 멋진 경험이 될 것 같습니다. 우리는 당신이 와 주신다면 정말 감사하겠습니다. 안부를 전하며, John Austin

Why? 왜 정답일까?

Jane Watson에게 Crestville 고등학교에 방문하여 특별 강연을 해 주기를 요청하고 있기 때문에 (I'd like to ask you to visit our school and give a special lecture.), 글의 목적으로 가장 적절한 것은 ③ '특강 강사로 작가의 방문을 요청하려고'이다.

- science ⓝ 과학
- impressed ⓐ 감명을 받은
- discussion ⓝ 토론
- suit ⓥ 맞추다
- recently ⓐ 최근에
- environment ⓝ 환경
- lecture ⓝ 강의
- grateful ⓐ 감사한

구문 풀이

3행 Recently I was impressed by the latest book (that) you wrote about the environment.
수동태 by 행위자 / 최상급, 선행사 / 목적격 관계대명사 생략

---

19 모래성 만들기의 의의
정답률 92% | 정답 ①

다음 글에 드러난 Sarah의 심경 변화로 가장 적절한 것은?

✓① sad → excited
　슬픈　신난
② envious → anxious
　부러운　불안한
③ bored → joyful
　지루한　즐거운
④ relaxed → regretful
　안정된　후회하는
⑤ nervous → surprised
　긴장한　놀란

Marilyn and her three-year-old daughter, Sarah, took a trip to the beach, / where Sarah built her first sandcastle.
Marilyn과 세 살 된 딸 Sarah는 해변으로 여행을 떠났다, / 그곳에서 Sarah는 처음으로 모래성을 쌓았다.
Moments later, / an enormous wave destroyed Sarah's castle.
잠시 후, / 거대한 파도가 Sarah의 성을 무너뜨렸다.
In response to the loss of her sandcastle, / tears streamed down Sarah's cheeks / and her heart was broken.
모래성을 잃은 것에 반응하여 / 눈물이 Sarah의 뺨을 타고 흘러내렸고, / 그녀의 마음은 무너졌다.
She ran to Marilyn, / saying she would never build a sandcastle again.
그녀는 Marilyn에게 달려갔다, / 그녀가 다시는 모래성을 쌓지 않겠다고 말하며
Marilyn said, / "Part of the joy of building a sandcastle / is that, in the end, / we give it as a gift / to the ocean."
Marilyn은 말했다, / "모래성을 쌓는 즐거움 중 일부는 / 결국에는 / 우리가 그것을 선물로 주는 것이란다. / 바다에게" 라고
Sarah loved this idea / and responded with enthusiasm / to the idea of building another castle — / this time, even closer to the water / so the ocean would get its gift sooner!
Sarah는 이 생각이 마음에 들었고 / 열정적으로 반응했다. / 다른 모래성을 만들 생각에 / 이번에는 바다와 훨씬 더 가까운 곳에서 / 바다가 그 선물을 더 빨리 받을 수 있도록

Marilyn과 세 살 된 딸 Sarah는 해변으로 여행을 떠났고, 그곳에서 Sarah는 처음으로 모래성을 쌓았다. 잠시 후, 거대한 파도가 Sarah의 성을 무너뜨렸다. 모래성을 잃은 것에 반응하여 눈물이 Sarah의 뺨을 타고 흘러내렸고, 그녀의 마음은 무너졌다. 그녀는 다시는 모래성을 쌓지 않겠다고 말하며 Marilyn에게 달려갔다. Marilyn은 "모래성을 쌓는 즐거움 중 일부는 결국에는 우리가 그것을 바다에게 선물로 주는 것이란다."라고 말했다. Sarah는 이 생각이 마음에 들었고 또 다른 모래성을 만들 생각에 이번에는 바다와 훨씬 더 가까운 곳에서 바다가 그 선물을 더 빨리 받을 수 있도록 하겠다며 열정적으로 반응했다.

Why? 왜 정답일까?

Sarah가 해변에서 처음으로 쌓은 모래성을 파도가 무너뜨리자 울었다. 그러자 Marilyn은 Sarah에게 모래성을 바다에게 선물로 준 것이라 말한다. 이에 Sarah는 Marilyn의 말에 열정적으로 반응했다. 따라서 Sarah의 심정 변화로 적절한 것은 ① 'sad(슬픈) → excited(신난)'이다.

- sandcastle ⓝ 모래성
- destroy ⓥ 부수다
- ocean ⓝ 바다
- enthusiasm ⓝ 열정
- enormous ⓐ 거대한
- stream ⓥ 흐르다
- respond ⓥ 반응하다

구문 풀이

5행 She ran to Marilyn, saying she would never build a sandcastle again.
현재분사(~하면서) / 조동사 + 동사원형 / 부정어

---

20 긍정적인 진술의 마법
정답률 73% | 정답 ②

다음 글에서 필자가 주장하는 바로 가장 적절한 것은?

① 목표한 바를 꼭 이루려면 생각을 곧바로 행동으로 옮겨라.
✓② 자신감을 얻으려면 어려움을 긍정적인 진술로 바꿔 써라.
③ 어려운 일을 해결하려면 주변 사람에게 도움을 청하라.
④ 일상에서 자신감을 향상하려면 틈틈이 마술을 배워라.
⑤ 실생활에서 마주하는 도전을 피하지 말고 견뎌 내라.

Magic is what we all wish for / to happen in our life.
마법은 우리 모두가 바라는 것이다. / 자신의 삶에 일어나기를
Do you love the movie Cinderella / like me?
여러분은 신데렐라 영화를 사랑하는가? / 나처럼
Well, / in real life, / you can also create magic.
그러면, / 실제 삶에서, / 여러분도 마법을 만들 수 있다.
Here's the trick.
여기 그 요령이 있다.

Write down / all the real-time challenges / that you face and deal with.
적어라. / 모든 실시간의 어려움을 / 여러분이 직면하고 처리하는
Just change the challenge statement / into positive statements.
어려움에 관한 진술을 바꾸기만 해라. / 긍정적인 진술로
Let me give you / an example here.
여러분에게 제시하겠다. / 예시를 여기에
If you struggle with / getting up early in the morning, / then write a positive statement / such as "I get up early in the morning / at 5:00 am every day."
만약 여러분이 어려움을 겪는다면 / 아침 일찍 일어나는 것에 / 그러면 긍정적인 진술을 작성해라. / 나는 일찍 일어난다. / 매일 아침 5시에
Once you write these statements, / get ready to witness magic and confidence.
이러한 진술을 작성하고 나면, / 마법과 자신감을 목격할 준비를 하라.
You will be surprised / that just by writing these statements, / there is a shift / in the way you think and act.
당신은 놀랄 것이다. / 단지 이러한 진술들을 작성함으로써 / 변화가 있다는 것에 / 당신이 생각하고 행동하는 방식에
Suddenly / you feel more powerful and positive.
어느 순간 / 여러분은 더 강력하고 긍정적이라고 느끼게 된다.

마법은 우리 모두 자신의 삶에서 일어나기를 바라는 바이다. 여러분도 나처럼 신데렐라 영화를 사랑하는가? 그러면, 실제 삶에서, 여러분도 마법을 만들 수 있다. 여기 그 요령이 있다. 여러분이 직면하고 처리하는 모든 실시간의 어려움을 적어라. 그 어려움에 관한 진술을 긍정적인 진술로 바꾸어라. 여기서 여러분에게 한 예시를 제시하겠다. 만약 여러분이 아침 일찍 일어나는 것에 어려움을 겪는다면, 그러면 '나는 매일 일찍 아침 5시에 일어난다.'와 같은 긍정적인 진술을 써라. 일단 여러분이 이러한 진술을 적는다면, 마법과 자신감을 목격할 준비를 하라. 여러분은 단지 이러한 진술을 적음으로써 여러분이 생각하고 행동하는 방식에 변화가 있다는 것에 놀랄 것이다. 어느 순간 여러분은 더 강력하고 긍정적이라고 느끼게 된다.

Why? 왜 정답일까?

일상생활에서 마법을 이루는 방법으로 긍정적인 진술 작성을 제시하고 있기 때문에(Just change the challenge statement into positive statements.), 필자가 주장하는 바로 가장 적절한 것은 ② '자신감을 얻으려면 어려움을 긍정적인 진술로 바꿔 써라.'이다.

- magic ⓝ 마법, 마술
- statement ⓝ 진술
- struggle ⓥ 어려움을 겪다
- confidence ⓝ 자신감
- shift ⓝ 변화
- challenge ⓝ 어려움, 도전
- positive ⓐ 긍정적인
- witness ⓥ 목격하다
- surprise ⓥ 놀라게 하다
- powerful ⓐ 강력한

구문 풀이

10행 You will be surprised that just by writing these statements, there is a shift in the way you think and act.
조동사 + 동사원형 수동태 / 종속접속사 / 관계부사 the way(= how)

---

21 Aristotle이 정의한 감각
정답률 49% | 정답 ①

밑줄 친 push animal senses into Aristotelian buckets가 다음 글에서 의미하는 바로 가장 적절한 것은? [3점]

✓① sort various animal senses into fixed categories
　동물의 감각을 고정된 체계로 분류하다
② keep a balanced view to understand real senses
　진짜 감각을 이해하기 위해서 균형잡힌 시각을 유지하다
③ doubt the traditional way of dividing all senses
　모든 감각을 나누는 전통적인 방법을 의심하다
④ ignore the lessons on senses from Aristotle
　Aristotle의 감각에 대한 지식을 무시하다
⑤ analyze more animals to find real senses
　진짜 감각을 찾기 위해서 더 많은 동물을 분석하다

Consider the seemingly simple question / "How many senses are there?"
겉으로 보기에 단순한 질문을 고려해 보아라. / '얼마나 많은 감각이 존재하는가?'
Around 2,370 years ago, / Aristotle wrote / that there are five, in both humans and animals / — sight, hearing, smell, taste, and touch.
약 2,370년 전 / Aristotle은 썼다. / 인간과 동물 둘 다에게 다섯(감각)이 있다고 / 시각, 청각, 후각, 미각, 그리고 촉각의
However, / according to the philosopher Fiona Macpherson, / there are reasons to doubt it.
그러나 / 철학자 Fiona Macpherson에 따르면, / 그것을 의심할 이유가 존재한다.
For a start, / Aristotle missed a few in humans: / the perception of your own body / which is different from touch / and the sense of balance / which has links to both touch and vision.
우선, / Aristotle은 인간에게서 몇 가지를 빠뜨렸는데, / 그것은 자신의 신체에 대한 인식과, / 촉각과는 다른 / 그리고 균형의 감각 이었다. / 촉각과 시각 모두에 관련되어 있는
Other animals have senses / that are even harder to categorize.
다른 동물들도 감각을 가지고 있다. / 범주화하기 더욱 어려운
Many vertebrates have a different sense system / for detecting odors.
많은 척추동물들은 다른 감각 체계를 가지고 있다. / 냄새를 탐지하기 위한
Some snakes can detect the body heat / of their prey.
어떤 뱀들은 체열을 감지할 수 있다. / 그들의 먹잇감의
These examples tell us / that "senses cannot be clearly divided / into a limited number of specific kinds," / Macpherson wrote in The Senses.
이러한 예시들은 우리에게 알려 준다. / '감각은 명확하게 나누어지지 않을 수 있다. / 제한된 수의 특정한 종류로' / Macpherson이 'The Senses'에서 쓰기를
Instead of trying to push animal senses into Aristotelian buckets, / we should study them / for what they are.
동물의 감각을 Aristotle의 양동이로 밀어 넣는 대신, / 우리는 그것들을 연구해야 한다. / 존재하는 그대로

'얼마나 많은 감각이 존재하는가?'라는 겉으로 보기에 단순한 질문을 고려해 봐라. 약 2,370년 전 Aristotle은 인간과 동물 둘 다에게 시각, 청각, 후각, 미각, 그리고 촉각의 다섯(감각)이 있다고 썼다. 그러나, 철학자 Fiona Macpherson에 따르면, 그것을 의심할 이유가 존재한다. 우선, Aristotle은 인간에게서 몇 가지를 빠뜨렸는데, 그것은 촉각과는 다른 여러분 자신의 신체에 대한 인식과, 촉각과 시각 모두에 관련되어 있는 균형 감각이었다. 다른 동물들은 훨씬 더 범주화하기 어려운 감각을 가지고 있다. 많은 척추동물은 냄새를 탐지하기 위한 다른 감각 체계를 가지고 있다. 어떤 뱀은 그들의 먹잇감의 체열을 감지할 수 있다. Macpherson이 'The Senses'에서 쓰기를, 이러한 사례는 우리에게 '감각은 제한된 수의 특정한 종류로 명확하

게 나누어지지 않을 수 있다.'라는 것을 알려 준다. 동물의 감각을 Aristotle의 양동이로 밀어 넣는 대신, 우리는 그것들을 존재하는 그대로 연구해야 한다.

Why? 왜 정답일까?

Aristotelian buckets가 의미하는 바는 Aristotle이 주장한 바이므로 다섯 개의 감각이 존재하는 것이다. Aristotelian bucket으로 밀어 넣는 것은 Aristotle의 주장을 받아들이는 것이므로, ① 'sort various animal senses into fixed categories'가 가장 적절하다.

- consider ⓥ 고려하다
- philosopher ⓝ 철학자
- perception ⓝ 인식
- link ⓝ 연결
- detect ⓥ 감지하다
- divide ⓥ 나누다
- bucket ⓝ 양동이
- sight ⓝ 시각
- doubt ⓥ 의심하다
- balance ⓝ 균형
- categorize ⓥ 분류하다
- prey ⓝ 먹잇감
- specific ⓐ 특정한

구문 풀이

12행 These examples tell us that "senses cannot be clearly divided into a limited number of specific kinds," Macpherson wrote in *The Senses*.
(주어 / 동사 / 간접목적어 / 직접목적어절 / ~으로 나누어지다.)

---

22 리더로써의 잠재력 정답률 80% | 정답 ③

다음 글의 요지로 가장 적절한 것은?

① 훌륭한 리더는 고귀한 목표를 위해 희생적인 삶을 산다.
② 위대한 인물은 위기의 순간에 뛰어난 결단력을 발휘한다.
✓③ 공동체를 위한 아이디어를 발전시키는 누구나 리더가 될 수 있다.
④ 다른 사람의 의견을 경청하는 자세는 목표 달성에 가장 중요하다.
⑤ 근면하고 경험이 풍부한 사람들은 경제적으로 성공할 수 있다.

When we think of leaders, / we may think of people / such as Abraham Lincoln or Martin Luther King, Jr.
우리가 리더에 대해서 생각할 때, / 우리는 사람들을 생각할지도 모른다. / Abraham Lincoln이나 Martin Luther King Jr.와 같은

If you consider / the historical importance and far-reaching influence / of these individuals, / leadership might seem like a noble and high goal.
만약 여러분이 고려한다면 / 역사적 중요성과 광범위한 영향력을 / 이러한 인물들의 / 리더십은 고귀하고 높은 목표처럼 보일지도 모른다.

But like all of us, / these people started out / as students, workers, and citizens / who possessed ideas / about how some aspect of daily life could be improved / on a larger scale.
그러나 우리 모두와 마찬가지로, / 이러한 인물들은 시작했다. / 학생, 근로자, 그리고 시민으로 / 생각을 가진 / 일상생활의 어느 측면이 어떻게 개선될 수 있는지에 대한 / 더 큰 규모로

Through diligence and experience, / they improved upon their ideas / by sharing them with others, / seeking their opinions and feedback / and constantly looking for the best way / to accomplish goals for a group.
근면함과 경험을 통해, / 그들은 생각을 발전시켰다. / 자신의 생각을 다른 사람들과 공유하고, / 그들의 의견과 반응을 구하며 / 끊임없이 가장 좋은 방법을 찾음으로써 / 집단의 목표를 성취할 수 있는

Thus we all have the potential to be leaders / at school, in our communities, and at work, / regardless of age or experience.
그러므로 우리는 모두 리더가 될 잠재력을 가지고 있다. / 학교, 공동체, 그리고 일터에서 / 나이나 경험에 관계 없이

우리가 리더에 대해 생각할 때, 우리는 Abraham Lincoln 혹은 Martin Luther King, Jr.와 같은 사람들에 대해 생각할지 모른다. 만약 여러분이 이러한 인물들의 역사적 중요성과 광범위한 영향력을 고려한다면, 리더십은 고귀하고 높은 목표처럼 보일지도 모른다. 그러나 우리 모두와 마찬가지로, 이러한 인물들은 일상생활의 어느 측면이 더 큰 규모로 어떻게 개선될 수 있는지에 대한 생각을 가졌던 학생, 근로자, 그리고 시민으로 시작했다. 근면함과 경험을 통해, 그들은 자신의 생각을 다른 사람들과 공유하고, 그들의 의견과 반응을 구하며, 끊임없이 집단의 목표를 성취할 수 있는 가장 좋은 방법을 찾음으로써 자신의 생각을 발전시켰다. 그러므로 우리는 모두, 나이나 경험에 관계없이, 학교, 공동체, 그리고 일터에서 리더가 될 수 있는 잠재력을 가지고 있다.

Why? 왜 정답일까?

우리 모두 리더가 될 잠재력을 가지고 있다고 말하기 때문에(Thus we all have the potential to be leaders at school, in our communities, and at work, regardless of age or experience.), 글의 요지로 가장 적절한 것은 ③ '공동체를 위한 아이디어를 발전시키는 누구나 리더가 될 수 있다.'이다.

- historical ⓐ 역사적인
- influence ⓝ 영향력
- possess ⓥ 가지다, 소유하다
- improve ⓥ 개선하다
- feedback ⓝ 피드백
- accomplish ⓥ 성취하다
- community ⓝ 공동체
- far-reaching ⓐ 광범위한
- noble ⓐ 고귀한
- aspect ⓝ 측면
- diligence ⓝ 근면
- constantly ⓐⓓ 끊임없이
- potential ⓝ 잠재력
- regardless of ~와 관계없이

구문 풀이

8행 Through diligence and experience, they improved upon their ideas by sharing them with others, seeking their opinions and feedback and constantly looking for the best way to accomplish goals for a group.
(접속사(~을 통해서) / 동명사구1 / 동명사구2 / 동명사구3 / to 부정사 부사적 용법(목적 달성을 위해서))

---

23 윤작의 방법과 특징 정답률 84% | 정답 ①

다음 글의 주제로 가장 적절한 것은?

✓① advantage of crop rotation in maintaining soil health
토지 건강을 유지하는 것에 있어서 윤작의 이점
② influence of purchasing organic food on farmers
농부들에게 유기농 음식을 사는 것의 영향
③ ways to choose three important crops for rich soil
비옥한 토양을 위해 세 가지 중요한 곡물을 고르는 방법

④ danger of growing diverse crops in small spaces
작은 공간에 다양한 곡물을 기르는 것의 위험성
⑤ negative impact of crop rotation on the environment
환경에 윤작의 부정적인 영향

Crop rotation is the process / in which farmers change the crops / they grow in their fields / in a special order.
윤작은 과정이다. / 농부가 작물을 바꾸는 / 그들이 자신의 밭에서 재배하는 / 특별한 순서로

For example, / if a farmer has three fields, / he or she may grow / carrots in the first field, / green beans in the second, / and tomatoes in the third.
예를 들어서, / 만약 한 농부가 세 개의 밭을 가지고 있다면, / 그들은 재배할 수 있다. / 첫 번째 밭에는 당근을, / 두 번째 밭에는 녹색 콩을, / 세 번째 밭에는 토마토를

The next year, / green beans will be in the first field, / tomatoes in the second, / and carrots will be in the third.
그 다음 해에 / 첫 번째 밭에는 녹색 콩을 재배할 것이고, / 두 번째 밭에는 토마토를 재배하며, / 세 번째 밭에는 당근을 재배할 것이다.

In year three, / the crops will rotate again.
3년 차에 / 작물은 다시 순환할 것이다.

By the fourth year, / the crops will go back / to their original order.
4년째에 이르면 / 작물은 되돌아 갈 것이다. / 원래의 순서로

Each crop enriches the soil / for the next crop.
각각의 작물은 토양을 비옥하게 한다. / 다음 작물을 위해

This type of farming is sustainable / because the soil stays healthy.
이 유형의 농업은 지속 가능하다. / 토양이 건강하게 유지되기 때문에

윤작은 농부가 자신의 밭에서 재배하는 작물을 특별한 순서로 바꾸는 과정이다. 예를 들면, 만약 한 농부가 세 개의 밭을 가지고 있다면, 그들은 첫 번째 밭에는 당근을, 두 번째 밭에는 녹색 콩을, 세 번째 밭에는 토마토를 재배할 수 있다. 그 다음 해에 첫 번째 밭에는 녹색 콩을, 두 번째 밭에는 토마토를, 세 번째 밭에는 당근을 재배할 것이다. 3년 차에 작물은 다시 순환할 것이다. 4년째에 이르면 작물은 원래의 순서로 되돌아 갈 것이다. 각각의 작물은 다음 작물을 위한 토양을 비옥하게 한다. 이 유형의 농업은 토양이 건강하게 유지되기 때문에 지속 가능하다.

Why? 왜 정답일까?

윤작의 정의, 예시에 이어 윤작을 통해 토양이 건강하게 유지된다고(This type of farming is sustainable because the soil stays healthy.) 말하기 때문에, 글의 주제로 가장 적절한 것은 ① 'advantage of crop rotation in maintaining soil health'이다.

- crop rotation ⓝ 윤작
- rotate ⓥ 순환하다
- enrich ⓥ 비옥하게 하다
- field ⓝ 밭
- original ⓐ 원래의
- soil ⓝ 토양

구문 풀이

1행 Crop rotation is the process in which farmers change the crops (that) they grow in their fields in a special order.
(관계부사(= where) / 선행사 / 목적격 관계대명사 생략)

---

24 그림의 완성을 결정하기 정답률 67% | 정답 ⑤

다음 글의 제목으로 가장 적절한 것은?

① Drawing Inspiration from Diverse Artists
다양한 예술가로부터로의 그림 영감
② Don't Spoil Your Painting by Leaving It Incomplete
덜 완성된 채로 둠으로써 당신의 그림을 망치지 마세요
③ Art Interpretation: Discover Meanings in a Painting
예술 해석: 그림에서 의미를 발견하라
④ Do Not Put Down Your Brush: The More, the Better
붓을 내려놓지 마세요: 더 많이 할수록, 더 낫습니다
✓⑤ Avoid Overwork and Find the Right Moment to Finish
과한 작업을 피하고 끝낼 적절한 순간을 찾으세요

Working around the whole painting, / rather than concentrating on one area at a time, / will mean / you can stop at any point / and the painting can be considered "finished."
전체 그림에 대해서 작업하는 것은 / 한 번에 한 영역에만 집중하기보다 / 의미할 것이다. / 여러분이 어떤 지점에서도 멈출 수 있고 / 그림이 '완성'된 것으로 간주될 수 있다는 것을

Artists often find it difficult / to know when to stop painting, / and it can be tempting / to keep on adding more to your work.
화가들은 종종 어렵다는 것을 발견한다. / 그림을 언제 멈춰야 할지 알기가 / 그리고 유혹을 느낄 수 있다. / 자신의 그림에 계속해서 더 추가하고 싶은

It is important to take a few steps back from the painting / from time to time to / assess your progress.
그림에서 몇 걸음 뒤로 물러나는 것이 중요하다. / 때때로 / 자신의 진행 상황을 평가하기 위해

Putting too much into a painting / can spoil its impact / and leave it looking overworked.
한 그림에 너무 많은 것을 넣는 것은 / 영향력을 망칠 수 있다 / 그리고 그것이 과하게 작업된 것처럼 보이게 둘 수 있다.

If you find yourself struggling / to decide whether you have finished, / take a break and come back to it later with fresh eyes.
만약 여러분이 어려움을 겪고 있음을 알게 된다면 / 여러분이 끝냈는지를 결정하는 데에 / 잠시 휴식을 취하고 나중에 새로운 눈으로 그림으로 다시 돌아와라.

Then you can decide / whether any areas of your painting would benefit / from further refinement.
그러면 여러분은 결정할 수 있다. / 자신의 그림 어느 부분이 득을 볼지를 / 더 정교하게 꾸며서

한 번에 한 영역에만 집중하기보다 전체 그림에 대해서 작업하는 것은 여러분이 어떤 지점에서도 멈출 수 있고 그림이 '완성'된 것으로 간주될 수 있다는 것을 의미할 것이다. 화가인 여러분은 종종 언제 그림을 멈춰야 할지 알기 어렵다는 것을 발견하고, 자신의 그림에 계속해서 더 추가하고 싶은 유혹을 느낄 수도 있다. 때때로 자신의 진행 상황을 평가하기 위해 그림에서 몇 걸음 뒤로 물러나는 것이 중요하다. 한 그림에 너무 많은 것을 넣으면 그것의 영향력을 망칠 수 있고 그것이 과하게 작업된 것처럼 보이게 둘 수 있다. 만약 여러분이 끝냈는지를 결정하는 데 자신이 어려움을 겪고 있음을 알게 된다면, 잠시 휴식을 취하고 나중에 새로운 눈으로 그것(그림)으로 다시 돌아와라. 그러면 여러분은 더 정교하게 꾸며서 자신의 그림 어느 부분이 득을 볼지를 결정할 수 있다.

Why? 왜 정답일까?

그림을 그리며 어떤 지점에서 멈춰야 할지 알기가 어렵기 때문에 과하게 작업하기가 쉬우므로, 잠시 휴식을 취하라며 과한 작업을 피해야 할 필요성을 강조하고 있다. 따라서 ⑤ 'Avoid Overwork and Find the Right Moment to Finish'가 제목으로 가장 적절하다.

- **concentrate** ⓥ 집중하다
- **spoil** ⓥ 망쳐 놓다
- **overwork** ⓥ 과하게 작업하다
- **assess** ⓥ 평가하다
- **impact** ⓝ 영향(력)
- **benefit** ⓥ 득을 보다

구문 풀이

5행 It is important to take a few steps back from the painting from time to time
가주어 it   진주어   때때로, 이따금, 가끔
to assess your progress.
to부정사 형용사적 용법(평가절)

---

25 2021년 기후 변화를 두려워하는 6개국 16-25세 인구의 순위   정답률 81% | 정답 ③

다음 도표의 내용과 일치하지 않는 것은?

The Extent of the Youth's Climate Fear in 2021
☑ Extremely worried ☐ Very worried

Philippines	49%	35%
Brazil	29%	38%
Portugal	30%	35%
France	18%	40%
United Kingdom	20%	29%
United States	19%	27%

(0 20 40 60 80 100)

The above graph shows the extent / to which young people aged 16 – 25 in six countries had fear / about climate change in 2021.
위의 그래프는 정도를 보여 준다. / 6개국의 16세에서 25세 사이 젊은 사람들이 두려움을 갖는 / 2021년 기후 변화에 대해

① The Philippines had the highest percentage of young people / who said they were extremely or very worried, / at 84 percent, / followed by 67 percent in Brazil.
필리핀은 젊은 사람들의 가장 높은 비율을 보여 준다. / 극도로 혹은 매우 걱정한다고 말한 / 84퍼센트로, / 67퍼센트로 브라질이 그 뒤를 잇고

② More than 60 percent of young people in Portugal said / they were extremely worried or very worried.
포르투갈은 60퍼센트 이상의 젊은 사람들이 말했다. / 극도로 혹은 매우 걱정하고 있다고

☑ In France, the percentage of young people who were extremely worried / was higher than that of young people / who were very worried.
프랑스는 극도로 걱정하는 젊은 사람들의 비율이 / 젊은 사람들의 비율보다 높았다. / 매우 걱정하는

④ In the United Kingdom, the percentage of young generation who said / that they were very worried / was 29 percent.
영국은 젊은 세대의 비율이 / 매우 걱정된다고 말하는 / 29퍼센트였다.

⑤ In the United States, the total percentage of extremely worried and very worried youth / was the smallest / among the six countries.
미국은 극도로 걱정하거나 매우 걱정하는 젊은 사람들의 총비율이 / 가장 작았다. / 6개국 중에서

위 그래프는 2021년 6개국의 16세에서 25세 사이 젊은 사람들이 기후 변화에 대해 두려움을 갖는 정도를 보여 준다. ① 필리핀은 극도로 혹은 매우 걱정한다고 말한 젊은 사람들의 비율이 84퍼센트로 가장 높았으며, 브라질이 67퍼센트로 그 뒤를 이었다. ② 포르투갈은 60퍼센트 이상의 젊은 사람들이 극도로 혹은 매우 걱정하고 있다고 말했다. ③ 프랑스는 극도로 걱정하는 젊은 사람들의 비율이 매우 걱정하는 젊은 사람들의 비율보다 높았다. ④ 영국은 매우 걱정한다고 말하는 젊은 세대의 비율이 29퍼센트였다. ⑤ 미국은 극도로 걱정하거나 매우 걱정하는 젊은 사람들의 총비율이 6개국 중에서 가장 작았다.

Why? 왜 정답일까?

프랑스는 극도로 걱정하는 젊은 사람들의 비율이 18%로 매우 걱정하는 젊은 사람들의 비율인 40%보다 낮기 때문에 도표의 내용과 일치하지 않는 것은 ③이다.

- **extent** ⓝ 정도
- **extremely** ⓐⓓ 극도로
- **climate** ⓝ 기후
- **generation** ⓝ 세대

구문 풀이

7행 In France, the percentage of young people who were extremely worried
선행사   주격관계대명사
was higher than that of young people who were very worried.
동사   비교급 지시대명사 the percentage 주격관계대명사

---

26 Jaroslav Heyrovsky의 일생   정답률 86% | 정답 ④

Jaroslav Heyrovsky에 관한 다음 글의 내용과 일치하지 않는 것은?

① 라틴어와 그리스어보다 자연 과학에 강한 흥미를 보였다.
② Czech University에서 화학, 물리학 및 수학을 공부했다.
③ 1910년부터 1914년까지 런던에서 학업을 이어 나갔다.
☑ 제1차 세계 대전이 끝난 후 군 병원에 복무했다.
⑤ 1959년에 노벨 화학상을 수상했다.

Jaroslav Heyrovsky was born in Prague / on December 20, 1890, / as the fifth child of Leopold Heyrovsky.
Jaroslav Heyrovsky는 Prague에서 태어났다. / 1890년 12월 20일에 / Leopold Heyrovsky의 다섯째 자녀로

In 1901 / Jaroslav went to a secondary school / called the Akademicke Gymnasium.
1901년에 / Jaroslav는 중등학교에 다녔다. / Akademicke Gymnasium이라는

『Rather than Latin and Greek, / he showed a strong interest in the natural sciences.』 ①의근거 일치
라틴어와 그리스어보다, / 그는 자연 과학에 강한 흥미를 보였다.

『At Czech University in Prague / he studied chemistry, physics, and mathematics.』 ②의근거 일치
Prague에 있는 Czech University에서 / 그는 화학, 물리학, 그리고 수학을 공부했다.

『From 1910 to 1914 / he continued his studies / at University College, London.』 ③의근거 일치
1910년부터 1914년까지 / 그는 그의 학업을 이어 나갔다. / London의 University College에서

『Throughout the First World War, / Jaroslav served in a military hospital.』 ④의근거 불일치

제1차 세계 대전 내내, / Jaroslav는 군 병원에 복무했다.

In 1926, / Jaroslav became the first Professor of Physical Chemistry / at Charles University in Prague.
1926년에, / Jaroslav는 최초의 물리화학 교수가 되었다. / Prague의 Charles University에서

『He won the Nobel Prize in chemistry / in 1959.』 ⑤의근거 일치
그는 노벨 화학상을 수상했다. / 1959년에

Jaroslav Heyrovsky는 1890년 12월 20일 Prague에서 Leopold Heyrovsky의 다섯째 자녀로 태어났다. 1901년 Jaroslav는 Akademicke Gymnasium이라고 불리는 중등학교에 다녔다. 그는 라틴어와 그리스어보다는 자연 과학에 강한 흥미를 보였다. Prague에 있는 Czech University에서 그는 화학, 물리학 및 수학을 공부했다. 1910년부터 1914년까지 그는 런던의 University College에서 학업을 이어 나갔다. 제1차 세계 대전 내내 Jaroslav는 군 병원에 복무했다. 1926년에 Jaroslav는 Prague에 있는 Charles University 최초의 물리화학 교수가 되었다. 그는 1959년에 노벨 화학상을 수상했다.

Why? 왜 정답일까?

'Throughout the First World War, Jaroslav served in a military hospital.'에서 Jaroslav Heyrovsky는 제1차 세계 대전 내내 군 병원에서 복무했다고 했으므로 글의 내용과 일치하지 않는 것은 ④ '제1차 세계 대전이 끝난 후 군 병원에 복무했다.'이다.

Why? 왜 오답일까?

① '~he showed a strong interest in the natural sciences.'의 내용과 일치한다.
② 'At Czech University in Prague he studied chemistry, physics, and mathematics.'의 내용과 일치한다.
③ 'From 1910 to 1914 he continued his studies at University College, London.'의 내용과 일치한다.
⑤ 'He won the Nobel Prize in chemistry in 1959.'의 내용과 일치한다.

- **secondary school** ⓝ 중등학교
- **physics** ⓝ 물리학
- **throughout** prep 내내
- **chemistry** ⓝ 화학
- **mathematics** ⓝ 수학
- **military** ⓐ 군대의

구문 풀이

1행 Jaroslav Heyrovsky was born in Prague on December 20, 1890, as the
수동태   전치사(~로써)
fifth child of Leopold Heyrovsky.

---

27 청소년을 위한 봄철 차 교실 안내문   정답률 96% | 정답 ④

Spring Tea Class for Young People에 관한 다음 안내문의 내용과 일치하지 않는 것은?

① 수강생은 전 세계 다양한 문화권의 차를 경험할 수 있다.
② 금요일 수업은 오후에 1시간 30분 동안 진행된다.
③ 수강생에게 차와 간식을 제공할 것이다.
☑ 15세 이하의 수강생은 30달러의 참가비를 내야 한다.
⑤ 음식 알레르기가 있는 수강생은 이메일을 미리 보내야 한다.

Spring Tea Class for Young People
청소년을 위한 봄철 차 교실

『Join us / for a delightful Spring Tea Class for young people, / where you'll experience the taste of tea / from various cultures around the world.』 ①의근거 일치
참여하세요. / 즐거운 봄철 차 교실에 / 여러분이 차를 맛보는 경험을 할 / 전 세계 다양한 문화권의

Class Schedule
수업 일정

『Friday, April 5 (4:30 p.m. – 6:00 p.m.)』 ②의근거 일치
4월 5일 금요일 (오후 4:30 ~ 오후 6:00)

Saturday, April 6 (9:30 a.m. – 11:00 a.m.)
4월 6일 토요일 (오전 9:30 ~ 오전 11:00)

Details
세부 내용

『We will give you tea and snacks.』 ③의근거 일치
우리는 여러분에게 차와 간식을 드리겠습니다.

We offer special tips / for hosting a tea party.
우리는 특별한 조언을 제공합니다. / 차 모임 주최를 위한

Participation Fee
참가비

『Age 13 – 15: $25 per person』 ④의근거 불일치
13 ~ 15세: 1인당 25달러

Age 16 – 18: $30 per person
16 ~ 18세: 1인당 30달러

Note
주의 사항

『If you have any food allergy, / you should email us in advance / at youth@seasonteaclass.com.』 ⑤의근거 일치
만약 여러분이 음식 알레르기가 있다면, / 저희에게 미리 이메일을 보내야 합니다. / youth@seasonteaclass.com으로

청소년을 위한 봄철 차 교실

청소년을 위한 즐거운 봄철 차 교실에 참여하세요.
그곳에서 여러분은 전 세계 다양한 문화권의 차를 맛보는 경험을 할 것입니다.

수업 일정
• 4월 5일 금요일 (오후 4:30 ~ 오후 6:00)
• 4월 6일 토요일 (오전 9:30 ~ 오전 11:00)

세부 내용
• 우리는 여러분에게 차와 간식을 드리겠습니다.
• 우리는 차 모임 주최를 위한 특별한 조언을 제공합니다.

참가비
• 13 ~ 15세: 1인당 25달러
• 16 ~ 18세: 1인당 30달러

주의 사항
만약 여러분이 음식 알레르기가 있다면 저희에게 미리 youth@seasonteaclass.com으로 이메일을 보내야 합니다.

Why? 왜 정답일까?
참가비 항목에 13 ~ 15세는 1인당 25달러의 참가비를 내야하므로 안내문의 내용과 일치하지 않는 것은 ④ '15세 이하의 수강생은 30달러의 참가비를 내야 한다.'이다.

Why? 왜 오답일까?
① '~you'll experience the taste of tea from various cultures around the world.'의 내용과 일치한다.
② 'Friday, April 5 (4:30 p.m. – 6:00 p.m.)'의 내용과 일치한다.
③ 'We will give you tea and snacks.'의 내용과 일치한다.
⑤ 'If you have any food allergy, you should email us in advance at youth@seasonteaclass.com.'의 내용과 일치한다.

- **delightful** ⓐ 즐거운
- **various** ⓐ 다양한
- **in advance** 미리
- **experience** ⓥ 경험하다
- **host** ⓥ (파티 등을) 주최하다

---

28 | 2024 의류 업사이클링 대회 안내문 | 정답률 88% | 정답 ④

Clothes Upcycling Contest 2024에 관한 다음 안내문의 내용과 일치하는 것은?
① Lakewood에 사는 사람이면 누구든지 참가할 수 있다.
② 참가자는 출품 사진을 직접 방문하여 제출해야 한다.
③ 참가자는 5월 14일까지 출품 사진을 제출할 수 있다.
☑ 우승 상품은 지역 상점에서 쓸 수 있는 기프트 카드이다.
⑤ 지역 신문을 통해 우승자를 발표한다.

Clothes Upcycling Contest 2024
2024 의류 업사이클링 대회
Are you passionate / about fashion and the environment?
여러분은 열정이 있으신가요? / 패션과 환경에 대한
Then we have a contest for you!
그렇다면 우리가 여러분을 위한 대회를 개최합니다!
Participants
참가자
「Anyone living in Lakewood, aged 11 to 18」 ①의 근거 불일치
Lakewood에 거주하는 11세에서 18세까지이면 누구나
How to participate
참여 방법
Take before and after photos / of your upcycled clothes.
전, 후 사진을 찍으세요. / 여러분의 업사이클된 옷의
「Email the photos at lovelw@lwplus.com.」 ②의 근거 불일치
사진은 lovelw@lwplus.com으로 이메일을 보내세요.
「Send in the photos from April 14 to May 12.」 ③의 근거 불일치
사진은 4월 14일부터 5월 12일까지 보내세요.
Winning Prize
우승 상품
「A $100 gift card to use at local shops」 ④의 근거 일치
지역 상점에서 쓸 수 있는 100달러 기프트 카드 한 장
「The winner will be announced on our website on May 30.」 ⑤의 근거 불일치
우승자를 우리 웹사이트에서 5월 30일에 발표할 것입니다.
For more details, visit our website www.lovelwplus.com.
더 많은 정보를 위해서는 우리 웹사이트(www.lovelwplus.com)를 방문하세요.

2024 의류 업사이클링 대회

여러분은 패션과 환경에 대한 열정이 있으신가요?
그렇다면 우리가 여러분을 위한 대회를 개최합니다!

• 참가자
– Lakewood에 거주하는 11세에서 18세까지이면 누구나

• 참여 방법
– 여러분의 업사이클된 옷의 전, 후 사진을 찍으세요.
– 사진은 lovelw@lwplus.com으로 이메일을 보내세요.
– 사진은 4월 14일부터 5월 12일까지 보내세요.

• 우승 상품
– 지역 상점에서 쓸 수 있는 100달러 기프트 카드 한 장
– 우승자를 우리 웹사이트에서 5월 30일에 발표할 것입니다.

더 많은 정보를 위해서는 우리 웹사이트(www.lovelwplus.com)를 방문하세요.

Why? 왜 정답일까?
우승 상품이 'A $100 gift card to use at local shops'라고 했으므로 내용과 일치하는 것은 ④ '우승 상품은 지역 상점에서 쓸 수 있는 기프트 카드이다.'이다.

Why? 왜 오답일까?
① 'Anyone living in Lakewood, aged 11 to 18'에서 Lakewood에 사는 11세에서 18세만 참가할 수 있다고 하였다.
② 'Email the photos at lovelw@lwplus.com.'에서 출품 사진을 이메일로 제출하라 하였다.
③ 'Send in the photos from April 14 to May 12.'에서 5월 12일까지 출품 사진을 제출할 수 있다고 하였다.
⑤ 'The winner will be announced on our website on May 30.'에서 우승자는 웹사이트에서 발표된다고 하였다.

- **upcycled** ⓐ 업사이클된
- **passionate** ⓐ 열정적인
- **contest** ⓝ 대회
- **local** ⓐ 지역의
- **environment** ⓝ 환경
- **fashion** ⓝ 패션, 의류
- **announce** ⓥ 발표하다

---

29 | 의미 있는 일의 중요성 | 정답률 68% | 정답 ②

다음 글의 밑줄 친 부분 중, 어법상 틀린 것은? [3점]

It would be hard to overstate / how important meaningful work is to human beings / — work ① that provides a sense of fulfillment and empowerment.
과장해서 말하기는 힘들 것이다. / 인간에게 의미 있는 일이 얼마나 중요한지를 / 성취감과 권한을 제공하는
Those who have found deeper meaning in their careers / find their days much more energizing and satisfying, / and ☑ count their employment as one of their greatest sources of joy and pride.
자신의 직업에서 더 깊은 의미를 찾은 사람은 / 자신의 하루하루가 훨씬 더 활기차고 만족감을 준다는 것을 발견하고, / 자신의 직업을 기쁨과 자부심의 가장 큰 원천 중 하나로 꼽는다
Sonya Lyubomirsky, professor of psychology at the University of California, / has conducted numerous workplace studies ③ showing / that when people are more fulfilled on the job, / they not only produce higher quality work and a greater output, / but also generally earn higher incomes.
University of California의 심리학 교수인 Sonya Lyubomirsky는 / 보여 주는 수많은 업무 현장 연구를 수행했다. / 사람이 직업에 더 많은 성취감을 느낄 때 / 그들은 더 질 높은 업무와 더 큰 성과를 만들어 낼 뿐만 아니라 / 일반적으로 더 높은 수입을 거둔다는 것을
Those most satisfied with their work / ④ are also much more likely to be happier with their lives overall.
자신의 일에 가장 만족하는 사람은 / 또한 전반적으로 자신의 삶에 더 행복할 가능성이 훨씬 더 크다.
For her book *Happiness at Work*, / researcher Jessica Pryce-Jones conducted a study of 3,000 workers in seventy-nine countries, / ⑤ finding that those who took greater satisfaction from their work / were 150 percent more likely to have a happier life overall.
자신의 저서 'Happiness at Work'를 위해 / 연구자 Jessica Pryce-Jones는 79개 국가의 3,000명의 근로자에 대한 연구를 수행했고, / 자신의 일로부터 더 큰 만족감을 갖는 사람이 / 전반적으로 더 행복한 삶을 살 가능성이 150퍼센트 더 크다는 것을 알아냈다.

인간에게 의미 있는 일, 즉 성취감과 권한을 제공하는 일이 얼마나 중요한지를 과장해서 말한다는 것은 어려울 것이다. 자신의 직업에서 더 깊은 의미를 찾은 사람은 자신의 하루하루가 훨씬 더 활기차고 만족감을 준다는 것을 발견하고, 자신의 직업을 기쁨과 자부심의 가장 큰 원천 중 하나로 꼽는다. University of California의 심리학 교수인 Sonya Lyubomirsky는 사람이 직업에 더 많은 성취감을 느낄 때 그들은 더 질 높은 업무와 더 큰 성과를 만들어 낼 뿐만 아니라 일반적으로 더 높은 수입을 거둔다는 것을 보여 주는 수많은 업무 현장 연구를 수행했다. 자신의 일에 가장 만족하는 사람은 또한 전반적으로 자신의 삶에 더 행복해 할 가능성이 훨씬 더 크다. 자신의 저서 'Happiness at Work'를 위해 연구자 Jessica Pryce-Jones는 79개 국가의 3,000명의 근로자에 대한 연구를 수행했고, 자신의 일로부터 더 큰 만족감을 갖는 사람이 전반적으로 더 행복한 삶을 살 가능성이 150퍼센트 더 크다는 것을 알아냈다.

Why? 왜 정답일까?
주어구가 'Those who have found deeper meaning in their careers'이기 때문에 등위접속사인 'and' 뒤에는 'find'와 동급인 동사 형태의 'count'가 와야 하기 때문에 ② 'to count'가 어법상 틀렸다.

Why? 왜 오답일까?
① 선행사로 **work**가 왔고, 뒷문장에 주어가 없으므로 주격관계대명사인 'that'이 쓰였다.
③ 앞 문장 전체를 수식하는 현재분사 형태인 'showing'이 쓰였다. "사람들이 더 직장에서 더 만족할 때 나타나는 결과"를 설명하고 있어 문법적으로 옳다.
④ 주어가 'Those most satisfied with their work'으로 복수이므로 be동사의 복수형태인 'are'이 쓰였다.
⑤ 앞의 문장 전체를 수식하는 현재분사로, 'study'의 결과를 보충 설명하며 덧붙이고 있어 문법적으로 옳다.

- **overstate** ⓥ 과장해서 말하다
- **empowerment** ⓝ 권한
- **satisfying** ⓐ 만족감을 주는
- **source** ⓝ 원천
- **numerous** ⓐ 수많은
- **workplace** ⓝ 업무 현장, 직장
- **output** ⓝ 성과
- **income** ⓝ 수입
- **fulfillment** ⓝ 성취감
- **energizing** ⓐ 활기찬
- **employment** ⓝ 직업, 고용
- **conduct** ⓥ 수행하다
- **psychology** ⓝ 심리
- **quality** ⓝ 질
- **generally** ⓐⓓ 일반적으로
- **overall** ⓐⓓ 전반적으로

구문 풀이

11행 Those (who are) most satisfied with their work are also much more likely to be happier with their lives overall.
지시대명사 → 주격관계대명사+be동사 생략 / 최상급 / 'be likely to: ~할 것 같은, ~할 확률이 높은'

★★★ 등급을 가르는 문제!
30 | 사람의 이동속도와 처리 능력 | 정답률 47% | 정답 ③

다음 글의 밑줄 친 부분 중, 문맥상 낱말의 쓰임이 적절하지 않은 것은? [3점]

The rate of speed at which one is traveling / will greatly determine the ability / to process detail in the environment.
사람이 이동하는 속도의 빠르기는 / 능력을 크게 결정할 것이다. / 환경 속 세세한 것을 처리하는
In evolutionary terms, / human senses are adapted to the ① speed / at which humans move through space / under their own power while walking.
진화적 관점에서, / 인간의 감각은 속도에 적응되어 있다. / 공간을 이동하는 / 그 자신의 힘으로 걷는
Our ability to distinguish detail in the environment is / therefore ideally ② suited to movement at speeds / of perhaps five miles per hour and under.
환경 속에서 세세한 것을 구별하는 우리의 능력은 / 그래서 속도의 이동에 이상적으로 맞추어져 있다. / 대략 시속 5마일 또는 그 속도 이하의
The fastest users of the street, motorists, / therefore have a much more limited ability / to process details along the street / — a motorist simply has ☑ less time or ability / to appreciate design details.
도로의 가장 빠른 사용자인 운전자는 / 그러므로 더 제한된 능력을 가지고 있고 / 도로를 따라 (이동하며) 세세한 것을 처리하는 / 그래서 운전자는 적은 시간이나 능력이 있다. / 디자인의 세세한 것을 감상할 수 있는
On the other hand, / pedestrian travel, being much slower, / allows for the ④ appreciation of environmental detail.

반면에, / 보행자 이동은 훨씬 더 느려서, / 환경의 세세한 것을 감상할 수 있도록 허용해 준다.

Joggers and bicyclists fall somewhere in between these polar opposites; / while they travel faster than pedestrians, / their rate of speed is ordinarily much ⑤ slower / than that of the typical motorist.
조깅하는 사람과 자전거를 타는 사람은 이러한 극과 극 사이의 어딘가에 해당한다. / 그들은 보행자보다 더 빨리 이동하지만, / 속도의 빠르기는 훨씬 더 느리다. / 보통 전형적인 운전자의 그것보다

사람이 이동하는 속도의 빠르기는 환경 속 세세한 것을 처리하는 능력을 크게 결정할 것이다. 진화론적 관점에서, 인간의 감각은 그 자신의 힘으로 걸으며 공간을 이동하는 ① 속도에 적응되어 있다. 환경 속에서 세세한 것을 구별하는 우리의 능력은 그래서 대략 시속 5마일 또는 그 속도 이하의 이동에 이상적으로 ② 맞추어져 있다. 그러므로 도로의 가장 빠른 사용자인 운전자는 도로를 따라서 (이동하며) 세세한 것을 처리하는 훨씬 더 제한된 능력을 가지고 있고, 그래서 운전자는 단지 디자인의 세세한 것을 감상할 수 있는 ④ 충분한(→ 적은) 시간이나 능력이 있다는 선지는 적절하지 않다. 반면에 보행자 이동은 훨씬 더 느려서, 환경의 세세한 것을 ④ 감상할 수 있도록 허용해 준다. 조깅하는 사람과 자전거를 타는 사람은 이러한 극과 극 사이의 어딘가에 해당한다. 그들은 보행자보다 더 빨리 이동하지만, 속도의 빠르기는 보통 전형적인 운전자의 그것보다 훨씬 ⑤ 더 느리다.

Why? 왜 정답일까?
인간의 감각은 보행 속도에 적응되어 있기 때문에, 도로의 가장 빠른 사용자인 운전자는 도로를 따라서 이동하며 세세한 것을 처리하는 능력이 비교적 제한되어 있다. 따라서 운전자는 디자인의 세세한 것을 감상할 수 있는 시간이 적기 때문에, ③ enough → less로 수정해야 한다.

- rate ⓝ 빠르기
- ability ⓝ 능력
- ideally ⓐⓓ 이상적으로
- motorist ⓝ 운전자
- appreciate ⓥ 감상하다, 제대로 인식하다
- allow for 가능하게 하다, 허락하다
- opposite ⓝ 반대의 것
- typical ⓐ 전형적인
- determine ⓥ 결정하다
- adapted ⓐ 맞추어진, 적응된
- suited ⓐ 적합한
- limited ⓐ 제한된
- polar ⓐ 극과 극의
- ordinarily ⓐⓓ 보통

구문 풀이

2행 In evolutionary terms, human senses are adapted to the speed at which
전치사 + 관계대명사
「be adapted to : ~에 적응되었다」 ~에 익숙하다
humans move through space under their own power while walking.
~하는 동안에

★★ 문제 해결 꿀~팁 ★★

▶ 많이 틀린 이유는?
글은 이동 속도에 따라 변화하는 주변 감상 능력에 대해서 이야기하고 있다. 'Our ability to distinguish detail in the environment is therefore ideally suited to movement at speeds of perhaps five miles per hour and under.'에서 이동 속도가 걷는 속도, 즉 시간 당 5 마일 이상일 때 주변 감상 능력과의 관계는 반비례함을 알 수 있다. 보행자(pedestrian), 조깅하는 사람(jogger), 자전거를 타는 사람(bicyclist), 자동차를 타는 사람(motorist) 순으로 속도가 빨라지므로 주변 감상 능력 역시 감소한다. 따라서 도로에서 이동 속도가 가장 빠른 사람으로 제시된 자동차를 타는 사람은 주변을 감상할 시간과 능력이 가장 적기 때문에, 자동차를 타는 사람이 주변을 감상할 충분한 시간과 능력이 있다는 선지는 적절하지 않다.

▶ 문제 해결 방법은?
글의 요지를 파악한 후, 요지에 어긋나는 선지를 고른다. 해당 문제의 경우 글에 제시된 다른 이동 속도를 가진 사람들을 주변 감상 능력의 정도에 따라 줄 세우면 더욱 쉽게 풀 수 있다.

---

31 기후 변화와 종의 변화   정답률 51% | 정답 ②

다음 빈칸에 들어갈 말로 가장 적절한 것을 고르시오.
① endurance – 인내
✓② movement – 이동
③ development – 발달
④ transformation – 변화
⑤ communication – 의사소통

Every species has certain climatic requirements / — what degree of heat or cold it can endure, for example.
모든 종은 특정한 기후 요건을 가지고 있다. / 예를 들자면 어느 정도의 더위나 추위를 견딜 수 있는지와 같은,
When the climate changes, / the places that satisfy those requirements change, too.
기후가 변할 때, / 그러한 요건을 충족시키는 장소도 역시 변한다.
Species are forced to follow.
종은 따르도록 강요받는다.
All creatures are capable of some degree of movement.
모든 생명체는 어느 정도의 이동이 가능하다.
Even creatures that appear immobile, / like trees and barnacles, / are capable of dispersal at some stage of their life / — as a seed, in the case of the tree, / or as a larva, in the case of the barnacle.
심지어 나무나 따개비처럼 움직이지 않는 것처럼 보이는 생명체도, / 그들 일생의 어느 단계에서 분산될 수 있다. / 나무의 경우는 씨앗으로, / 따개비의 경우는 유충으로,
A creature must get from the place it is born / — often occupied by its parent / — to a place where it can survive, grow, and reproduce.
생명체는 종종 자신이 태어난 장소로부터 / — 종종 자신의 부모에 의해 점유된 / — 생존하고 성장하며 번식할 수 있는 장소로 이동해야 한다.
From fossils, scientists know / that even creatures like trees / moved with surprising speed / during past periods of climate change.
화석으로부터, 과학자들은 / 심지어 나무와 같은 생명체도 / 기후 변화의 과거 시기 동안, / 놀라운 속도로 이동했다는 것을 알고 있다.

모든 종은, 예를 들자면 어느 정도의 더위나 추위를 견딜 수 있는지와 같은, 특정한 기후 요건을 가지고 있다. 기후가 변할 때, 그러한 요건을 충족시키는 장소도 역시 변한다. 종은 따르도록 강요받는다. 모든 생명체는 어느 정도의 이동이 가능하다. 심지어 나무나 따개비처럼 움직이지 않는 것처럼 보이는 생명체도, 나무의 경우는 씨앗으로, 따개비의 경우는 유충으로, 그들 일생의 어느 단계에서 분산될 수 있다. 생명체는 종종 자신의 부모에 의해서 점유된,

그래서 자신이 태어난 장소로부터 생존하고 성장하며 번식할 수 있는 장소로 이동해야 한다. 화석으로부터, 과학자들은 심지어 나무와 같은 생명체는 기후 변화의 과거 시기 동안 놀라운 속도로 이동했다는 것을 알고 있다.

Why? 왜 정답일까?
종이 견딜 수 있는 특정한 기후 요건이 있고, 기후가 변화하면 종이 이동해야 한다고 설명하고 있기 때문에 빈칸에 적절한 표현은 ② 'movement'이다.

- climatic ⓐ 기후의
- endure ⓥ 견디다
- force ⓥ 강요하다
- immobile ⓐ 움직이지 않는
- seed ⓝ 씨앗
- occupy ⓥ 점유하다
- reproduce ⓥ 번식하다
- requirement ⓝ 요건
- satisfy ⓥ 충족시키다
- creature ⓝ 생명체
- capable ⓐ ~할 수 있는
- larva ⓝ 유충
- survive ⓥ 생존하다

구문 풀이

2행 When the climate changes, the places that satisfy those requirements
관계부사   선행사   주격관계대명사
change, too.

★★★ 등급을 가르는 문제!

32 반대 의견의 장점   정답률 26% | 정답 ③

다음 빈칸에 들어갈 말로 가장 적절한 것을 고르시오. [3점]
① unconditional loyalty – 무조건적인 충성
② positive attitude – 긍정적인 태도
✓③ internal protest – 내부적인 저항
④ competitive atmosphere – 경쟁적인 분위기
⑤ outstanding performance – 눈에 띄는 수행

No respectable boss would say, / "I make it a point to discourage my staff from speaking up, / and I maintain a culture that prevents disagreeing viewpoints from ever getting aired."
존경할 만한 상사라면 누구라도 말하지는 않을 것이다. / '나는 반드시 내 직원이 자유롭게 의견을 내지 못하도록 하고, / 동의하지 않는 관점이 언제든 공공연히 알려지는 것을 가로막는 문화를 유지한다.'라고
If anything, / most bosses even say that they are pro-dissent.
오히려, / 대부분의 상사는 심지어 자신은 반대에 찬성한다고 말한다.
This idea can be found throughout the series of conversations / with corporate, university, and nonprofit leaders, / published weekly in the business sections of newspapers.
이러한 생각은 일련의 대담을 통해서 발견될 수 있다 / 기업, 대학, 그리고 비영리 (단체의) 리더와의 / 매주 발행되는 신문의 경제란에
In the interviews, / the featured leaders are asked about their management techniques, / and regularly claim to continually encourage internal protest from more junior staffers.
인터뷰에서, / (기사에) 다루어진 리더는 자신의 경영 기법에 대해 질문을 받고, / 내부적인 저항이 더 많은 부하 직원에게서 (나오기를) 계속해서 장려하고 있다고 어김없이 주장한다.
As Bot Pittman remarked in one of these conversations: / "I want us to listen to these dissenters / because they may intend to tell you why we can't do something, / but if you listen hard, / what they're really telling you is what you must do to get something done."
Bot Pittman은 이러한 대담 중 하나에서 말했다. / "저는 우리가 이러한 반대자에게 귀 기울이기를 원합니다. / 왜냐하면 그들은 여러분에게 우리가 무엇인가를 할 수 없는 이유를 말하려고 의도할 수 있겠지만, / 그러나 만약에 여러분이 열심히 귀 기울이면, / 그들이 정말로 여러분에게 말하고 있는 것은 어떤 일이 이루어지도록 하기 위해서 여러분이 무엇을 해야 하는가이기 때문입니다."라고

존경할 만한 상사라면 누구라도 '나는 반드시 내 직원이 자유롭게 의견을 내지 못하도록 하고, 동의하지 않는 관점이 언제든 공공연히 알려지는 것을 가로막는 문화를 유지한다.'라고 말하지는 않을 것이다. 오히려, 대부분의 상사는 심지어 자신은 반대에 찬성한다고 말한다. 이러한 생각은 매주 발행되는 신문의 경제란에 기업, 대학, 그리고 비영리 (단체의) 리더와의 일련의 대담을 통해서 발견될 수 있다. 인터뷰에서, (기사에) 다루어진 리더는 자신의 경영 기법에 대해 질문을 받고, 내부적인 저항이 더 많은 부하 직원에게서 (나오기를) 계속해서 장려하고 있다고 어김없이 주장한다. Bot Pittman은 이러한 대담 중 하나에서 "저는 우리가 이러한 반대자에게 귀 기울이기를 원합니다. 왜냐하면 그들은 여러분에게 우리가 무엇인가를 할 수 없는 이유를 말하려고 의도할 수 있겠지만, 그러나 만약에 여러분이 열심히 귀 기울이면, 그들이 정말로 여러분에게 말하고 있는 것은 어떤 일이 이루어지도록 하기 위해서 여러분이 무엇을 해야만 하는가이기 때문입니다."라고 말했다.

Why? 왜 정답일까?
대부분의 상사들이 반대자의 의견을 좋아함을 언급하고(most bosses even say that they are pro-dissent), 반대자의 의견의 중요성에 대해서 얘기하고 있기 때문에 반대 의견을 독려함이 적절하다. 따라서 ③ 'internal protest'(내부적인 저항)이 정답이다.

- respectable ⓐ 존경할 만한
- discourage ⓥ 못하게 하다
- maintain ⓥ 유지하다
- if anything 오히려
- corporate ⓐ 기업
- publish ⓥ 발행하다, 출판하다
- management ⓝ 경영
- regularly ⓐⓓ 어김없이, 규칙적으로
- remark ⓥ 말하다
- make it a point 반드시 ~하도록 하다
- speak up 자유롭게 의견을 내다
- get aired 공공연히 알려지다
- conversation ⓝ 대담, 대화
- nonprofit ⓐ 비영리적
- feature ⓥ (기사로) 다루다
- techniques ⓝ 기법
- claim ⓥ 주장하다

구문 풀이

4행 If anything, most bosses even say that they are pro-dissent.
오히려, 그러기는커녕   접속사

★★ 문제 해결 꿀~팁 ★★

▶ 많이 틀린 이유는?
글에 따르면 좋은 상사는 반대 의견에서 해결책을 찾아내기도 하기 때문에 부하 직원들이 반대 의견을 내는 것에 찬성한다. 반대 의견의 중요성에 대해 서술하고 있다. 따라서 인터뷰를 진행한 리더들에게 경영 기술을 물었을 때 꾸준히 반대 의견을 내는 것을 장려한다는 말이 자연스럽다.

33 잠 자는 동안의 지각 이탈   정답률 55% | 정답 ③

다음 빈칸에 들어갈 말로 가장 적절한 것을 고르시오. [3점]

① get recovered easily – 빠르게 회복된다
② will see much better – 더 선명하게 볼 것이다
✓③ are functionally blind – 기능적으로는 실명 상태이다
④ are completely activated – 완전히 활성화되어 있다
⑤ process visual information – 시각 정보를 처리한다

One of the most striking characteristics / of a sleeping animal or person / is that they do not respond normally to environmental stimuli.
가장 두드러진 특징 중 하나는 / 잠을 자고 있는 동물이나 사람의 / 그들이 환경의 자극에 정상적으로 반응하지 않는다는 것이다.

If you open the eyelids of a sleeping mammal / the eyes will not see normally — they are functionally blind.
만약 당신이 잠을 자고 있는 포유류의 눈꺼풀을 열면, / 그 눈은 정상적으로 볼 수 없을 것인데, / 즉 그 눈은 기능적으로는 실명 상태이다.

Some visual information apparently gets in, / but it is not normally processed / as it is shortened or weakened; / same with the other sensing systems.
어떤 시각적 정보는 명백히 눈으로 들어오지만, / 그것은 짧아지거나 약화되어서 정상적으로 처리되지 않는데, / 이는 다른 감각 체계도 마찬가지이다.

Stimuli are registered but not processed normally / and they fail to wake the individual.
자극은 등록되지만 정상적으로 처리되지 않고 / 사람을 깨우는 데 실패한다.

Perceptual disengagement probably serves the function of protecting sleep, / so some authors do not count it / as part of the definition of sleep itself.
지각 이탈은 추측하건대 수면을 보호하는 기능을 제공해서 / 어떤 저자는 그것을 여기지 않는다. / 수면 자체의 정의의 일부로

But as sleep would be impossible without it, / it seems essential to its definition.
그러나 수면은 그것 없이는 불가능하기 때문에 / 그것(지각 이탈)은 그것(수면)의 정의에 필수적인 것으로 보여진다.

Nevertheless, / many animals (including humans) use the intermediate state of drowsiness / to derive some benefits of sleep / without total perceptual disengagement.
그럼에도 불구하고, / (인간을 포함한) 많은 동물은 졸음이라는 중간 상태를 이용한다. / 수면의 일부 이득을 끌어내기 위해서 / 완전한 지각 이탈 없이

잠을 자고 있는 동물이나 사람의 가장 두드러진 특징 중 하나는 그들이 환경의 자극에 정상적으로 반응하지 않는다는 것이다. 만약 당신이 잠을 자고 있는 포유류의 눈꺼풀을 열면, 그 눈은 정상적으로 볼 수 없을 것인데, 즉 그 눈은 기능적으로는 실명 상태이다. 어떤 시각적 정보는 명백히 눈으로 들어오지만, 그것은 짧아지거나 약화되어서 정상적으로 처리되지 않는데, 이는 다른 감각 체계도 마찬가지이다. 자극은 등록되지만 정상적으로 처리되지 않고 사람을 깨우는 데 실패한다. 지각 이탈은 추측하건대 수면을 보호하는 기능을 제공해서 어떤 저자는 그것을 수면 자체의 정의의 일부로 여기지 않는다. 그러나 수면이 그것 없이는 불가능하기 때문에 그것(지각 이탈)은 그것(수면)의 정의에 필수적인 것으로 보여진다. 그럼에도 (인간을 포함한) 많은 동물은 완전한 지각 이탈 없이 수면의 일부 이득을 끌어내기 위해서 졸음이라는 중간 상태를 이용한다.

Why? 왜 정답일까?

잠을 잘 때 눈을 뜨면 시각 정보가 입력되기는 하지만 정보가 약화되거나 짧아져서 정상적으로 처리되지 않는다고 하였으므로 본래의 시기능을 하지 못하는 ③ 'are functionally blind'가 적절하다.

- striking ⓐ 두드러진
- eyelid ⓝ 눈꺼풀
- apparently ⓐⓓ 분명히
- shorten ⓥ 짧아지다
- register ⓥ 등록하다
- definition ⓝ 정의
- derive ⓥ 얻다

- characteristics ⓝ 특징
- mammal ⓝ 포유류
- process ⓥ 처리하다
- weaken ⓥ 약화되다
- function ⓝ 기능
- essential ⓐ 필수적인
- perceptual ⓐⓓ 지각의

구문 풀이

13행 Nevertheless, many animals (including humans) use the intermediate
접속사(그럼에도 불구하고)
state of drowsiness to derive some benefits of sleep without total perceptual
to부정사 부사적 용법(끌어내기 위해서)   전치사(~없이)
disengagement.

34 지식의 저주   정답률 50% | 정답 ⑤

다음 빈칸에 들어갈 말로 가장 적절한 것을 고르시오. [3점]

① focus on the new functions of digital devices
디지털 기기의 새로운 기능에 집중하기
② apply new learning theories recently released
최근에 알려진 새로운 학습 이론을 적용하기
③ develop varieties of methods to test students
학생을 시험할 방법의 다양성 개발하기
④ forget the difficulties that we have had as students
학생으로서 우리가 가졌던 어려움 잊기
✓⑤ look at the learning process through students' eyes
학생들의 눈을 통해 학습 과정을 보기

A number of research studies have shown / how experts in a field often experience difficulties / when introducing newcomers to that field.
많은 조사 연구는 보여 준다. / 한 분야의 전문가가 어떻게 어려움을 종종 겪는지를 / 그 분야로 초보자를 입문시킬 때

For example, in a genuine training situation, / Dr.Pamela Hinds found that people expert in using mobile phones / were remarkably less accurate than novice phone users / in judging how long it takes people to learn to use the phones.
예를 들어, 실제 교육 상황에서, / Pamela Hinds 박사는 휴대 전화를 사용하는 데 능숙한 사람들이 / 초보 휴대 전화 사용자보다 놀랍도록 덜 정확하다는 것을 알아냈다. / 휴대 전화 사용법을 배우는 것에 얼마나 오랜 시간이 걸리는지를 판단하는 데 있어서,

Experts can become insensitive / to how hard a task is for the beginner, / an effect referred to as the 'curse of knowledge'.
전문가는 무감각해질 수 있는데, / 한 과업이 초보자에게 얼마나 어려운지에 대해 / 이는 '지식의 저주'로 칭해지는 효과이다.

Dr.Hinds was able to show / that as people acquired the skill, / they then began to underestimate the level of difficulty of that skill.
Hinds 박사는 보여 줄 수 있었다. / 사람이 기술을 습득했을 때 / 그 이후에 그 기술의 어려움의 정도를 과소평가하기 시작했다는 것을

Her participants even underestimated / how long it had taken themselves / to acquire that skill in an earlier session.
그녀의 참가자는 심지어 과소평가했다. / 자신들이 얼마나 오래 걸렸는지를 / 이전 기간에 그 기술을 습득하는 데

Knowing that experts forget / how hard it was for them to learn, / we can understand the need to look at the learning process / through students' eyes, / rather than making assumptions / about how students 'should be' learning.
전문가가 잊어버린다는 것을 안다면, / 자신이 학습하는 것이 얼마나 어려웠는지를 / 우리는 학습 과정을 볼 필요성을 이해할 수 있을 것이다. / 학생들의 눈을 통해, / (근거 없는) 추정을 하기보다 / 학생이 어떻게 학습을 '해야 하는지'에 대한

많은 조사 연구는 한 분야의 전문가가 그 분야로 초보자를 입문시킬 때 어떻게 어려움을 종종 겪는지를 보여 주었다. 예를 들어, 실제 교육 상황에서 Pamela Hinds 박사는 휴대 전화기를 사용하는 데 능숙한 사람들이 휴대 전화기 사용법을 배우는 것에 얼마나 오랜 시간이 걸리는지를 판단하는 데 있어서, 초보 휴대 전화기 사용자보다 놀랍도록 덜 정확하다는 것을 알아냈다. 전문가는 한 과업이 초보자에게 얼마나 어려운지에 대해 무감각해질 수 있는데, 즉 '지식의 저주'로 칭해지는 효과이다. Hinds 박사는 사람이 기술을 습득했을 때 그 이후에 그 기술의 어려움의 정도를 과소평가하기 시작했다는 것을 보여 줄 수 있었다. 그녀의 참가자는 심지어 자신들이 이전 기간에 그 기술을 습득하는 데 얼마나 오래 걸렸는지를 과소평가했다. 전문가가 자신이 학습하는 것이 얼마나 어려웠는지를 잊어버린다는 것을 안다면, 우리는 학생이 어떻게 학습을 '해야 하는지'에 대한 (근거 없는) 추정을 하기보다 학생들의 눈을 통해 학습 과정을 바라봐야 할 필요성을 이해할 수 있을 것이다.

Why? 왜 정답일까?

기술을 습득한 후 기술의 어려움을 과소평가하는 '지식의 저주'에 대한 글이고, 학생의 학습 방법에 대한 근거 없는 추정이 학습하려는 기술의 어려움을 과소평가하고 있는 것일 수도 있음을 시사한다. 따라서 학생들의 입장에서 학습 과정을 바라봐야 한다는 ⑤ 'look at the learning process through students' eyes'가 적절하다.

- research ⓝ 연구
- difficulty ⓝ 어려움
- genuine ⓐ 실제
- accurate ⓐ 정확한
- insensitive ⓐ 무감각한
- underestimate ⓥ 과소평가하다
- assumption ⓝ 추정, 가정

- expert ⓝ 전문가
- newcomer ⓝ 초보
- remarkably ⓐⓓ 놀랍게
- judge ⓥ 판단하다
- acquire ⓥ 습득하다
- session ⓝ 기간, 시간

구문 풀이

11행 Her participants even underestimated how long it had taken themselves
→to부정사 부사적 용법(얻기 위해서)   비인칭 주어(시간)
to acquire that skill in an earlier session.
지시대명사   비교급

35 집단 음악 치료가 정신 건강에 미치는 긍정적 영향   정답률 70% | 정답 ④

다음 글에서 전체 흐름과 관계 없는 문장은?

A group of psychologists studied / individuals with severe mental illness / who experienced weekly group music therapy, / including singing familiar songs and composing original songs.
한 심리학자 그룹이 연구했다. / 심각한 정신 질환이 있는 사람들을 / 집단 음악 치료를 매주 경험한 / 친숙한 노래 부르기와 독창적인 작곡하기를 포함한

① The results showed / that the group music therapy / improved the quality of participants' life, / with those participating in a greater number of sessions / experiencing the greatest benefits.
그 연구 결과는 보여 주었다. / 집단 음악 치료가 / 참여자의 삶의 질을 개선하였음을 / 참여자가 치료 활동에 참여한 횟수가 많을수록 / 가장 큰 효과를 경험하며

② Focusing on singing, / another group of psychologists reviewed articles / on the efficacy of group singing / as a mental health treatment / for individuals living with a mental health condition in a community setting.
노래 부르기에 초점을 두고, / 또 다른 그룹의 심리학자는 논문을 검토했다. / 집단 가창의 효능에 대한 / 정신 건강 치료로써의 / 집단 생활의 환경에서 정신적 건강 문제를 가지고 살고 있는 개인들에게 미치는

③ The findings showed that, / when people with mental health conditions participated in a choir, / their mental health and wellbeing significantly improved.
발견된 결과는, / 정신적인 건강 문제를 가진 사람이 합창단에 참여했을 때, / 정신 건강과 행복이 상당히 개선되었음을 보여 주었다.

✓④ The negative effects of music / were greater than the psychologists expected.
음악의 부정적인 효과는 / 심리학자가 예상했던 것보다 더 컸다.

⑤ Group singing provided enjoyment, / improved emotional states, / developed a sense of belonging / and enhanced self-confidence.
집단 가창은 즐거움을 제공했고, / 감정 상태를 개선하였으며, / 소속감을 키웠고, / 자신감을 강화하였다.

한 심리학자 그룹이 친숙한 노래 부르기와 독창적인 작곡하기를 포함한 집단 음악 치료를 매주 경험한 심각한 정신 질환이 있는 사람들을 연구했다. ① 그 연구 결과는 참여자가 (치료) 활동에 참여한 횟수가 많을수록 가장 큰 효과를 경험했기에, 집단 음악 치료가 참여자의 삶의 질을 개선하였음을 보여 주었다. ② 노래 부르기에 초점을 두고, 또 다른 그룹의 심리학자는 집단생활의 환경에서 정신적인 건강 문제를 가지고 살고 있는 이들에게 미치는 집단 가창의 효능에 대한 논문을 검토했다. ③ 발견된 결과는, 정신적인 건강 문제를 가진 사람이 합창단에 참여했을 때, 정신 건강과 행복이 상당히 개선되었음을 보여주었다. ④ 음악의 부정적인 효과는 심리학자가 예상했던 것보다 더 컸다. ⑤ 집단 가창은 즐거움을 제공했고 감정 상태를 개선하였으며 소속감을 키웠고 자신감을 강화하였다.

Why? 왜 정답일까?

정신 질환 환자들에게 있어서의 집단 음악 치료의 장점에 대해서 이야기하고 있기 때문에, '음악의 부정적인 효과는 심리학자가 예상했던 것보다 더 컸다.'라는 ④ 'The negative effects of music were greater than the psychologists expected.'는 글의 전체 흐름과 관계가 없다.

- psychologist ⓝ 심리학자
- severe ⓐ 심각한

- **mental** [ad] 정신적
- **improve** ⓥ 개선하다
- **review** ⓥ 검토하다
- **finding** ⓝ 결과
- **wellbeing** ⓝ 행복
- **enhance** ⓥ 강화하다
- **compose** ⓥ 작곡하다
- **session** ⓝ 활동, 기간
- **treatment** ⓝ 치료
- **choir** ⓝ 합창단
- **significantly** [ad] 상당히

구문 풀이

14행 Group singing provided enjoyment, improved emotional states, developed
　　　　주어　　　　　동사1　　　　　　　동사2　　　　　　　동사3
a sense of belonging and enhanced self-confidence.
　　　　　　　　　　　　　　동사4

---

36 어린 아이들을 위한 스포츠의 조정　　정답률 72% | 정답 ④

주어진 글 다음에 이어질 글의 순서로 가장 적절한 것을 고르시오.

① (A) – (C) – (B)　　　　② (B) – (A) – (C)
③ (B) – (C) – (A)　　　　✔④ (C) – (A) – (B)
⑤ (C) – (B) – (A)

In many sports, / people realized the difficulties / and even impossibilities / of young children participating fully / in many adult sport environments.
많은 스포츠에서, / 사람들은 어려움과 심지어 불가능하다는 것을 깨달았다. / 어린아이들이 완전히 참여하는 것의 / 여러 성인 스포츠 환경에

(C) They found / the road to success for young children / is unlikely / if they play on adult fields, / courts or arenas / with equipment that is too large, too heavy or too fast / for them to handle / while trying to compete / in adult-style competition.
그들은 발견했다. / 어린아이들이 성공으로 가는 길이 / 있을 것 같지 않다는 것을 / 만약 그들이 성인용 운동장에서, / 코트 또는 경기장에서 / 너무 크거나, 너무 무겁고 또는 너무 빠른 장비를 가지고 / 그들이 다룰 수 없는 / 성인 스타일의 시합에서 경쟁하려고 할 때

Common sense has prevailed: / different sports have made adaptations/ for children.
상식이 널리 퍼졌다: / 여러 스포츠는 조정을 했다. / 어린아이들을 위해

(A) As examples, / baseball has T ball, / football has flag football / and junior soccer uses / a smaller and lighter ball / and (sometimes) a smaller field.
예를 들자면, / 야구에는 티볼이 있고, / 풋볼에는 플래그 풋볼이 있고 / 유소년 축구는 사용한다. / 더 작고 더 가벼운 공과 / (가끔은) 더 작은 경기장을

All have junior competitive structures / where children play for shorter time periods / and often in smaller teams.
모두 유소년 시합의 구조를 가진다. / 어린아이들이 더 짧은 시간 동안 경기하고 / 종종 더 작은 팀으로 경기하는

(B) In a similar way, / tennis has adapted the court areas, / balls and rackets / to make them more appropriate for children under 10.
비슷한 방식으로, / 테니스는 코트 면적, 공, 라켓을 조정했다. / 10세 미만의 어린아이에게 더 적합하도록 만들기 위해

The adaptations are progressive / and relate to the age of the child.
이러한 조정은 점진적이고 / 어린아이의 연령과 관련이 있다.

많은 스포츠에서 사람들은 어린아이들이 여러 성인 스포츠 환경에 완전히 참여하기란 어렵고 심지어 불가능하다는 것을 깨달았다.

(C) 어린아이들이 너무 크거나 너무 무겁고 또는 너무 빨라서 그들(어린아이들)이 다룰 수 없는 장비를 가지고 성인 스타일의 시합에서 경쟁하려고 하면서 성인용 운동장, 코트 또는 경기장에서 운동한다면 그들(어린아이들)이 성공으로 가는 길이 있을 것 같지 않다는 것을 그들은 발견했다. 이러한 공통된 견해가 널리 퍼졌기에 여러 스포츠는 어린아이들을 위한 조정을 했다.

(A) 예를 들자면, 야구에는 티볼이 있고, 풋볼에는 플래그 풋볼이 있고, 유소년 축구는 더 작고 더 가벼운 공과 (가끔은) 더 작은 경기장을 사용한다. 모두가 어린아이들이 더 짧아진 경기 시간 동안 그리고 종종 더 작은 팀으로 경기하는 유소년 시합의 구조를 가진다.

(B) 비슷한 방식으로, 테니스는 코트 면적, 공, 라켓을 10세 미만의 어린아이에게 더 적합하도록 만들기 위해 조정했다. 이러한 조정은 점진적이고 어린아이의 연령과 관련이 있다.

Why? 왜 정답일까?

어린아이들이 스포츠에 참여하는 데에 갖는 어려움을 언급하는 주어진 글 뒤로, 어린아이들이 스포츠에 참여하기가 어려운 이유를 제시하는 (C)가 연결된다. (C)의 후반부는 여러 스포츠가 어린아이들을 위한 조정을 했다고 밝히고, (A) 초반부에서 조정의 예시를 언급하기 때문에 (A)가 오는 것이 자연스럽다. (B) 역시 어린아이들을 위해 스포츠가 한 조정의 예시를 들고 있지만 비슷한 방식으로의 'In a similar way,'로 이전에 유사한 내용이 필요하다. 따라서 (A) 뒤에 (B)가 오는 것이 적절하다. 따라서 적절한 순서는 ④ (C) – (A) – (B)이다.

- **realize** ⓥ 깨닫다
- **competitive** ⓐ 경쟁적인
- **period** ⓝ 기간
- **appropriate** ⓐ 적절한
- **relate to** ~와 관련되다
- **equipment** ⓝ 장비
- **adaptation** ⓝ 조정
- **impossibility** ⓝ 불가능
- **structure** ⓝ 구조
- **racket** ⓝ 라켓
- **progressive** ⓐ 점진적인
- **arena** ⓝ 경기장
- **common sense** ⓝ (일반인들의) 공통된 견해, 상식

구문 풀이

9행 In a similar way, tennis has adapted the court areas, balls and rackets
　　　　　　　　　　　　　　　　　　　　　　현재완료
　　　　　　　　　　　　┌to부정사 부사적 용법(만들기 위해서)
to make them more appropriate for children under 10.
　　　　　　　　비교급

---

37 Inca 제국의 메시지 전달 방법　　정답률 52% | 정답 ③

주어진 글 다음에 이어질 글의 순서로 가장 적절한 것을 고르시오. [3점]

① (A) – (C) – (B)　　　　② (B) – (A) – (C)
✔③ (B) – (C) – (A)　　　　④ (C) – (A) – (B)
⑤ (C) – (B) – (A)

With no horses available, / the Inca empire excelled / at delivering messages on foot.
구할 수 있는 말이 없어서, / Inca 제국은 탁월했다. / 걸어서 메시지를 전달하는 데

(B) The messengers were stationed on the royal roads / to deliver the Inca king's orders and reports / coming from his lands.
전령들은 왕의 길에 배치되었다. / Inca 왕의 명령과 보고를 전달하기 위해 / 그의 영토에서 오는

Called Chasquis, / they lived in groups of four to six in huts, / placed from one to two miles apart along the roads.
Chasquis라고 불리는, / 그들은 네 명에서 여섯 명의 집단을 이루어 오두막에서 생활을 했다. / 길을 따라 1마일에서 2마일 간격으로 떨어져 배치된

(C) They were all young men / and especially good runners / who watched the road in both directions.
그들은 모두 젊은 남자였고, / 특히 잘 달리는 이들이었다. / 양방향으로 길을 주시하는

If they caught sight of another messenger coming, / they hurried out to meet them.
그들은 다른 전령이 오는 것을 발견하면 / 그들을 맞이하기 위해 서둘러 나갔다.

The Inca built the huts on high ground, / in sight of one another.
Inca 사람들은 오두막을 지었다. / 서로를 볼 수 있는 높은 지대에

(A) When a messenger neared the next hut, / he began to call out / and repeated the message three or four times / to the one who was running out to meet him.
전령은 다음 오두막에 다가갈 때, / 소리치기 시작했고 / 메시지를 서너 번 반복했다. / 자신을 만나러 달려 나오는 전령에게

The Inca empire could relay messages 1,000 miles (1,610 km) / in three or four days under good conditions.
Inca 제국은 1,000마일(1,610km) 정도 메시지를 이어 갈 수 있었다. / 사정이 좋으면 사나흘 만에

구할 수 있는 말이 없어서, Inca 제국은 걸어서 메시지를 전달하는 데 탁월했다.

(B) 전령들은 Inca 왕의 명령과 그의 영토에서 오는 보고를 전달하기 위해 왕의 길에 배치되었다. Chasquis라고 불리는, 그들은 네 명에서 여섯 명의 집단을 이루어 길을 따라 1마일에서 2마일 간격으로 떨어져 배치된 오두막에서 생활했다.

(C) 그들은 모두 젊은 남자였고, 양방향으로 길을 주시하는 특히 잘 달리는 이들이었다. 그들은 다른 전령이 오는 것을 발견하면 그들을 맞이하기 위해 서둘러 나갔다. Inca 사람들은 서로를 볼 수 있는 높은 지대에 오두막을 지었다.

(A) 전령은 다음 오두막에 다가갈 때, 자신을 만나러 달려 나오고 있는 전령에게 소리치기 시작했고 메시지를 서너 번 반복했다. Inca 제국은 사정이 좋으면 사나흘 만에 1,000마일(1,610km) 정도 메시지를 이어 갈 수 있었다.

Why? 왜 정답일까?

Inca 제국에서 말 없이 걸어서 메시지를 전달하는 전령과 Chasquis가 있음을 소개하는 (B)가 가장 먼저 오고, 전령과 Chasquis의 간단한 정보를 전달하는 (C)가 이어지는 것이 자연스럽다. (C)에서 다른 전령이 오는 것을 발견하면 그들을 맞이하기 위해 서둘러 나갔기 때문에, (A)의 자신을 만나러 달려 나오고 있는 전령에게 소리치기 시작했다는 내용이 이어져야 한다. 따라서 ③ (B) – (C) – (A)가 정답이다.

- **available** ⓐ 구할 수 있는
- **excel** ⓥ 빼어나다, 탁월하다
- **deliver** ⓥ 전달하다
- **repeat** ⓥ 반복하다
- **condition** ⓝ 사정, 상황
- **royal** ⓐ 왕의, 왕실의
- **apart** [ad] 떨어져
- **direction** ⓝ 방향
- **empire** ⓝ 제국
- **on foot** 걸어서, 도보로
- **near** ⓥ 다가가다
- **relay** ⓥ 이어가다
- **station** ⓥ 배치하다
- **hut** ⓝ 오두막
- **especially** [ad] 특히
- **hurry out** 서둘러 나오다

구문 풀이

3행 　　　　　　　　　　　　　　　　　　　　　　→to부정사 명사적 용법(부르기를)
When a messenger neared the next hut, he began to call out and repeated
　전치사　　　　　　　주격관계대명사　　　동사1　　　　　　　　　　동사2
the message three or four times to the one who was running out to meet him.
　　　　　　　　　　　부정대명사　　　　　　　　　　과거 진행형　　　to부정사 부사적 용법
　　　　　　　　　　　　　　　　　　　　　　　　　　　　　　　　　(만나기 위해서)

★★★ 등급을 가르는 문제!

38 잘못된 혀 지도　　정답률 47% | 정답 ①

글의 흐름으로 보아, 주어진 문장이 들어가기에 가장 적절한 곳을 고르시오.

The tongue was mapped into separate areas / where certain tastes were registered: / sweetness at the tip, / sourness on the sides, / and bitterness at the back of the mouth.
혀는 개별적인 영역으로 구획화되었다. / 특정 맛이 등록되는 / 끝에는 단맛, / 측면에는 신맛, / 그리고 입의 뒤쪽에는 쓴맛이 등록된다.

✔ Research in the 1980s and 1990s, / however, / demonstrated that the "tongue map" explanation of how we taste was, / in fact, totally wrong.
1980년대와 1990년대의 연구는 / 그러나 / 우리가 맛을 느끼는 방식에 대한 '혀 지도' 설명이 ~것을 증명했다. / 사실은 완전히 틀렸다는

② As it turns out, / the map was a misinterpretation and mistranslation / of research conducted in Germany / at the turn of the twentieth century.
밝혀진 바와 같이, 그 지도는 오해하고 오역한 것이었다. / 독일에서 수행된 연구를 / 20세기 초입에

Today, / leading taste researchers believe / that taste buds are not grouped / according to specialty.
오늘날, / 선도적인 미각 연구자는 믿는다. / 미뢰가 분류되지 않는다고 / 맛을 느끼는 특화된 분야에 따라

③ Sweetness, saltiness, bitterness, and sourness / can be tasted / everywhere in the mouth, / although they may be perceived / at a little different intensities at different sites.
단맛, 짠맛, 쓴맛 그리고 신맛은 / 느껴질 수 있다. / 입안 어디에서나 / 비록 그것들이 지각될지라도 / 여러 위치에서 조금씩 다른 강도로

④ Moreover, / the mechanism at work is not place, / but time.
게다가, / 작동중인 기제는 위치가 아니라, / 시간이다.

⑤ It's not that you taste sweetness / at the tip of your tongue, / but rather that you register that perception *first*.
여러분이 단맛을 느끼는 것이 아니라 / 여러분 혀 끝에서, / 오히려 그 지각(단맛)을 *가장 먼저* 등록하는 것이다.

혀는 특정 맛이 등록되는 개별적인 영역으로 구획되었는데, 즉, 끝에는 단맛, 측면에는 신맛, 그리고 입의 뒤쪽에는 쓴맛이 있었다. ① 그러나 1980년대와 1990년대의 연구는 우리가 맛을 느끼는 방식에 대한 '혀 지도' 설명이 사실은 완전히 틀렸다는 것을 보여 주었다. 밝혀진 바와 같이, 그 지도는 20세기 초입 독일에서 수행된 연구를 오해하고 오역한 것이었다. ② 오늘날, 선도적인 미각 연구자는 미뢰가 맛을 느끼는 특화된 분야에 따라 분류되지 않는다고 믿는다.

③ 비록 그것들이 여러 위치에서 조금씩 다른 강도로 지각될지도 모르겠지만, 단맛, 짠맛, 쓴맛 그리고 신맛은 입안 어디에서나 느낄 수 있다. ④ 게다가, 작동 중인 기제는 위치가 아니라 시간이다. ⑤ 여러분은 혀끝에서 단맛을 느낀다기보다 오히려 그 지각(단맛)을 '가장 먼저' 등록하는 것이다.

Why? 왜 정답일까?

특정 맛이 등록되는 개별적인 영역으로 구획된 혀 지도가 있음을 소개하고, 혀 지도가 잘못되었음을 시사하는 As it turns out, the map was a misinterpretation and mistranslation of research conducted in Germany at the turn of the twentieth century. (밝혀진 바와 같이, 그 지도는 20세기 초입 독일에서 수행된 연구를 오해하고 오역한 것이었다.) 문장 사이에 주어진 문장이 오는 것이 자연스럽다. 또한 'As it turns out,'(밝혀진 바와 같이)와 같은 전치사구 역시 앞뒤 문장을 적절하게 이어준다.

- demonstrate ⓥ 보여 주다
- explanation ⓝ 설명
- map ⓥ (지도에) 구획하다
- certain ⓐ 특정한
- tip ⓝ 끝
- bitterness ⓝ 쓴맛
- mistranslation ⓝ 오역
- leading ⓐ 선두적인
- specialty ⓝ 특화된 분야
- intensity ⓝ 강도
- mechanism ⓝ 기제
- tongue ⓝ 혀
- taste ⓝ 맛
- separate ⓐ 개별적인
- register ⓥ 등록하다
- sourness ⓝ 신맛
- misinterpretation ⓝ 오해
- conduct ⓥ 수행하다
- taste bud 미뢰
- perceive ⓥ 지각하다
- site ⓝ 위치

구문 풀이

14행 It's not that you taste sweetness at the tip of your tongue, but rather that you register that perception first.
(가주어 / 진주어 / 오히려 / 지시대명사)

★★ 문제 해결 꿀~팁 ★★

▶ 많이 틀린 이유는?
혀 지도에 대한 글이며, 글의 서두에서는 혀 지도에 대해 소개하고 있다. 그러나 글의 중반부부터는 서두에 제시된 혀 지도의 개념이 잘못 되었다고 이야기하고 있기 때문에 혀 지도에 대한 입장이 바뀌는 서두와 중반부 사이 ①에 주어진 문장이 오는 것이 자연스럽다.

▶ 문제 해결 방법은?
주어진 문장을 넣는 문제는 글의 흐름을 파악하는 것이 중요하다. 해당 문제에서는 'however'를 기점으로 제시되는 바가 달라진다. 주장하는 바가 달라지는 부분이나 새로운 개념이 나오는 부분을 잘 체크하여 어울리는 선지를 선택하자.

★★★ 등급을 가르는 문제! ★★★

39 동물마다 다른 치료법 적용의 필요성 | 정답률 45% | 정답 ②

글의 흐름으로 보아, 주어진 문장이 들어가기에 가장 적절한 곳을 고르시오.

No two animals are alike.
어떤 두 동물도 똑같지 않다.
① Animals from the same litter / will display some of the same features, / but will not be exactly the same as each other; / therefore, they may not respond in entirely the same way / during a healing session.
한 배에서 태어난 동물들은 / 똑같은 몇몇 특성을 보여 줄 수 있겠지만, / 서로 정확히 같지는 않을 것이다. / 그런 까닭에, 그들은 완전히 똑같은 방식으로 반응하지 않을지도 모른다. / 치료 활동 중에
✔ Environmental factors / can also determine how the animal will respond / during the treatment.
또한 환경적 요인은 / 동물이 어떻게 반응할지를 결정할 수 있다. / 치료 중에
For instance, / a cat in a rescue center / will respond very differently / than a cat within a domestic home environment.
예를 들어, / 구조 센터에 있는 고양이는 / 매우 다르게 반응할 것이다. / 가정집 환경 내에 있는 고양이와는
③ In addition, / animals that experience healing for physical illness / will react differently / than those accepting healing / for emotional confusion.
게다가, / 신체적 질병의 치료를 받는 동물들은 / 다르게 반응할 것이다. / 치료를 받는 동물과는 / 감정적 동요의
④ With this in mind, / every healing session needs to be explored differently, / and each healing treatment / should be adjusted / to suit the specific needs / of the animal.
이를 염두에 두어, / 모든 치료 활동은 다르게 탐구되어야 하고, / 각각의 치료법은 / 조정되어야 한다. / 특정한 필요에 맞도록 / 동물의
⑤ You will learn / as you go; / healing is a constant learning process.
여러분은 배우게 될 것이다. / 직접 겪으며 / 치료가 끊임없는 학습의 과정인 것을

어떤 두 동물도 똑같지 않다. ① 한 배에서 태어난 동물은 똑같은 몇몇 특성을 보여 줄 수 있겠지만, 서로 정확히 같지는 않을 것이다. 그런 까닭에, 그들은 치료 활동 중에 완전히 똑같은 방식으로 반응하지 않을지도 모른다. ② 또한 환경적 요인은 치료 중에 동물이 어떻게 반응할지를 결정할 수 있다. 예를 들어, 구조 센터에 있는 고양이는 가정집 환경 내에 있는 고양이와는 매우 다르게 반응할 것이다. ③ 게다가, 신체적 질병의 치료를 받는 동물은 감정적 동요의 치료를 받는 동물과는 다르게 반응할 것이다. ④ 이를 염두에 두어, 모든 치료 활동은 다르게 탐구되어야 하고, 각각의 치료법은 동물의 특정한 필요에 맞도록 조정되어야 한다. ⑤ 여러분은 치료가 끊임없는 학습의 과정인 것을 직접 겪으면서 배우게 될 것이다.

Why? 왜 정답일까?

환경적인 요소 또한 동물들이 치료에서 반응하는 것을 결정할 수 있다는 문장이 제시되었기 때문에, 환경적인 요소 외 동물들이 치료에서 반응하는 것을 결정하는 요소가 이전에 제시되어야 하고, 이후에는 환경적인 요소로 동물들이 다르게 반응하는 예시가 제시되어야 할 것이다. 따라서 동물들이 다르기 때문에 치료 활동 중에 동물들이 완전히 똑같이 반응하지 않을 것이라는 문장과 보호소의 고양이와 가정의 고양이가 다르게 반응할 것이라는 문장 사이인 ②에 오는 것이 자연스럽다.

- determine ⓥ 결정하다
- therefore ⓐ 그런 까닭에
- rescue ⓝ 구조하다
- illness ⓝ 질병
- display ⓥ 보이다
- session ⓝ 활동
- domestic ⓐ 가정의
- confusion ⓝ 동요, 혼란

- explore ⓥ 탐구하다
- constant ⓐ 끊임없는
- specific ⓐ 특정한, 구체적인
- process ⓝ 과정

구문 풀이

11행 With this in mind, every healing session needs to be explored differently, and each healing treatment should be adjusted to suit the specific needs of the animal.
(주어구 / 동사 / 수동태 / 조동사 + 동사원형 / to부정사 부사적 용법(알맞기 위해서))

★★ 문제 해결 꿀~팁 ★★

▶ 많이 틀린 이유는?
동물이 치료를 받을 때 다르게 반응할 수 있고, 이에 영향을 미치는 요소들을 이야기하고 있다. 주어진 문장은 환경적인 요소가 영향을 끼칠 수 있다는 문장이며, 'also'를 보았을 때 이전에 다른 요소가 언급되어야 하며 이후에는 환경적인 요소의 영향에 대해 설명해야 자연스럽다.

▶ 문제 해결 방법은?
주어진 문장을 글에 넣는 문제는 글의 흐름 파악이 최우선이다. 흐름이 바뀌는 부분과 새로운 개념이 제시되는 부분에 표시를 하여 직관적으로 파악할 수 있게 하자.

40 의식적 마음과 잠재의식적 마음의 두려움 형성 | 정답률 55% | 정답 ①

다음 글의 내용을 한 문장으로 요약하고자 한다. 빈칸 (A), (B)에 들어갈 말로 가장 적절한 것은?

	(A)		(B)
✔	emotions 감정	······	forming 형성하는
②	actions 행동	······	overcoming 극복하는
③	emotions 감정	······	overcoming 극복하는
④	actions 행동	······	avoiding 피하는
⑤	moralities 도덕	······	forming 형성하는

The mind has parts / that are known as the conscious mind / and the subconscious mind.
마음은 부분을 갖고 있다. / 의식적 마음이라고 알려진 부분과 / 잠재의식적 마음이라고
The subconscious mind / is very fast to act / and doesn't deal with emotions.
잠재의식적 마음은 / 매우 빠르게 작동하고 / 감정을 다루지 않는다.
It deals with memories / of your responses to life, your memories and recognition.
그것은 기억을 다룬다. / 여러분의 삶에 대한 반응의 기억, 기억 및 인식
However, / the conscious mind is the one / that you have more control over.
그러나, / 의식적 마음은 부분이다. / 여러분이 더 많은 통제력을 갖고 있는
You think.
여러분은 생각한다.
You can choose / whether to carry on a thought / or to add emotion to it / and this is the part of your mind / that lets you down frequently / because — fueled by emotions — you make the wrong decisions / time and time again.
여러분은 선택할 수 있다. / 생각을 계속할지를 / 또는 그 생각에 감정을 더할지를 / 그리고 이것은 마음의 부분이기도 하다. / 여러분을 빈번하게 낙담시키는 — 왜냐 — 감정에 북받쳐 — 잘못된 결정을 내리게 만들기 때문에 / 반복해서
When your judgment is clouded by emotions, / this puts in / biases and all kinds of other negativities / that hold you back.
감정에 의해 여러분의 판단력이 흐려질 때, / 이것은 자리잡게 만든다. / 편견과 그 밖의 모든 종류의 부정성을 / 여러분을 억제하는
Scared of spiders? // Scared of the dark?
거미를 무서워하는가? // 어둠을 무서워하는가?
There are reasons for all of these fears, / but they originate in the conscious mind.
이러한 두려움 전부 이유가 있지만, / 그것들은 의식적 마음에서 비롯된다.
They only become real fears / when the subconscious mind records your reactions.
그것들은 오직 실제 두려움이 된다. / 잠재의식적 마음이 여러분의 반응을 기록할 때
➡ While the controllable conscious mind / deals with thoughts and (A) emotions, / the fast-acting subconscious mind / stores your responses, / (B) forming real fears.
통제할 수 있는 의식적 마음은 / 생각과 감정을 다루지만, / 빠르게 작동하는 잠재의식적 마음이 / 여러분의 반응을 저장하고, / 이는 실제 두려움을 형성한다.

마음은 의식적 마음과 잠재의식적 마음이라고 알려진 부분을 갖고 있다. 잠재의식적 마음은 매우 빠르게 작동하며 감정을 다루지 않는다. 그것은 여러분의 삶에 대한 반응의 기억, 기억 및 인식을 다룬다. 그러나 의식적 마음은 여러분이 더 많은 통제력을 갖고 있는 부분이다. 여러분은 생각한다. 여러분은 생각을 계속할지 또는 그 생각에 감정을 더할지를 선택할 수 있다. 그리고 이것은 감정에 북받쳐 잘못된 결정을 반복해서 내리게 만들기 때문에 여러분을 빈번하게 낙담시키는 마음의 부분이기도 하다. 감정에 의해 여러분의 판단력이 흐려질 때 이것은 편견과 그 밖의 여러분을 억제하는 모든 종류의 부정성을 자리 잡게 만든다. 거미를 무서워하는가? 어둠을 무서워하는가? 이러한 두려움 전부 이유가 있지만 그것들은 의식적 마음에서 비롯된다. 그것들은 오직 잠재의식적 마음이 여러분의 반응을 기록할 때 실제 두려움이 된다.

➡ 통제할 수 있는 의식적 마음은 생각과 (A) 감정을 다루지만, 빠르게 작동하는 잠재의식적 마음이 여러분의 반응을 저장하고, 이는 실제 두려움을 (B) 형성한다.

Why? 왜 정답일까?

글에서 통제할 수 있는 의식적 마음과 통제가 어려운 잠재의식적 마음을 설명한다. 'However, the conscious mind is the one that you have more control over. ~ You can choose whether to carry on a thought or to add emotion to it ~.' 부분에서 의식적 마음이 생각과 감정을 다루는 것을 알 수 있고, 'They only become real fears when the subconscious mind records your reactions.'에서 잠재의식적 마음이 반응을 저장할 때 실제 두려움을 형성함을 알 수 있다.

- conscious ⓐ 의식적
- recognition ⓝ 인식
- judgment ⓝ 판단(력)
- bias ⓝ 편견
- originate ⓥ 비롯되다
- subconscious ⓐ 잠재의식(적)
- frequently ⓐ 자주, 빈번히
- cloud ⓥ (기억력, 판단력 등을) 흐리게 하다
- negativity ⓝ 부정성
- fear ⓝ 두려움

구문 풀이

2행 The subconscious mind is very fast to act and doesn't deal with emotions.
(동사1 / to부정사 부사적 용법(행동하기에) / 동사2)

41-42 문화마다 다른 규범

『Norms are everywhere, / defining what is "normal" / and guiding our interpretations of social life at every turn.』 41번의 근거
규범은 어디에나 존재한다. / 무엇이 '정상적'인지를 규정하고 / 모든 순간 사회적 생활에 대한 우리의 해석을 안내해 주며

As a simple example, / there is a norm in Anglo society / to say *Thank you* to strangers / who have just done something to (a) help, / such as open a door for you, / point out that you've just dropped something, / or give you directions.
간단한 예로, / 규범이 Anglo 사회에 있다. / 낯선 사람에게 '감사합니다'라고 말하는 / 도움을 줄 수 있는 무언가를 이제 막 해준 / 문을 열어 주거나, / 여러분이 물건을 방금 떨어뜨렸다는 것을 짚어 주거나, / 길을 알려 주는 것과 같이

There is no law / that forces you to say *Thank you*.
법은 없다. / 여러분이 '감사합니다'라고 말하도록 강요하는

But if people don't say *Thank you* / in these cases / it is marked.
하지만 사람들이 '감사합니다'라고 말하지 않으면 / 이런 상황에서 / 그것은 눈에 띄게 된다.

People expect / that you will say it.
사람들은 기대한다. / 여러분이 그렇게 말하기를

You become responsible.
여러분은 책임을 지게 되는 것이다.

(b) Failing to say it / will be both surprising and worthy of criticism.
그렇게 말하지 못하는 것은 / (주변을) 놀라게 하기도 하고 비판을 받을 만하다.

『Not knowing the norms of another community / is the (c) central problem of cross-cultural communication.』 41번의 근거
다른 집단의 규범을 모른다는 것은 / 문화 간 의사소통에서 중심적인 문제이다.

To continue the *Thank you* example, / even though another culture may have an expression / that appears translatable (many don't), / 『there may be (d) different norms for its usage,』 / for example, / such that you should say *Thank you* / only when the cost someone 42번의 근거
has caused is considerable.
'감사합니다'의 예를 이어 보자면, / 비록 또 다른 문화권이 표현을 가지고 있다 할지라도, / 번역할 수 있는 것처럼 보이는 (다수는 그렇지 못하지만) / 다른 규범이 있을 수 있다. / 예를 들어서, / '감사합니다'라고 말해야 한다는 것처럼 / 누군가가 초래한 대가가 상당할 때만

『In such a case / it would sound ridiculous (i.e., unexpected, surprising, and worthy of criticism) / if you were to thank someone / for something so (e) minor / as holding a door open for you.』 42번의 근거
그 같은 상황에서 / 우스꽝스럽게(즉, 예상치 못하게, 놀랍게, 비판을 받을 만하게) 들릴 수 있을 것이다. / 만약 여러분이 누군가에게 감사해한다면 / 아주 사소한 일에 대해 / 여러분을 위해 문을 잡아주는 것과 같이

규범은 무엇이 '정상적'인지를 규정하고 모든 순간 사회적 생활에 대한 우리의 해석을 안내해 주며 어디에나 존재한다. 간단한 예로, 문을 열어 주거나, 여러분이 물건을 방금 떨어뜨렸다는 것을 짚어 주거나, 길을 알려주는 것과 같이 (a) 도움을 줄 수 있는 무언가를 이제 막 해준 낯선 사람에게 '감사합니다'라고 말하는 규범이 Anglo 사회에 있다. 여러분이 '감사합니다'라고 말하도록 강요하는 법은 없다. 하지만 이런 상황에서 사람들이 '감사합니다'라고 말하지 않으면 그것은 눈에 띄게 된다. 사람들은 여러분이 그렇게 말하기를 기대한다. 여러분은 책임을 지게 되는 것이다. 그렇게 (b) 말하지 못하는 것은 (주변을) 놀랍게 하기도 하고 비판을 받을 만하다. 다른 집단의 규범을 모른다는 것은 문화 간 의사소통에서 (c) 중심적인 문제이다. '감사합니다'의 예를 이어 보자면, 비록 또 다른 문화권이 번역할 수 있는 것처럼 보이는 어떤 표현(다수는 그렇지 못하지만)을 가지고 있다 할지라도, 그것의 사용법에 대해, 예를 들어, 누군가가 초래한 대가가 상당할 때만 '감사합니다'라고 말해야 한다는 것처럼 (d) 유사한 (→ 다른) 규범이 있을 수 있다. 그 같은 상황에서 만약 여러분이 혹시라도, 여러분을 위해 문을 잡아주는 것과 같이 아주 (e) 사소한 일에 대해 누군가에게 감사해한다면, 그것은 우스꽝스럽게(즉, 예상치 못하게, 놀랍게, 비판을 받을 만하게) 들릴 수 있을 것이다.

- norm ⑪ 규범
- interpretation ⑪ 해석
- marked ⓐ 눈에 띄는
- worthy ⓐ 받을 만한
- central ⓐ 중심적인
- cost ⑪ 대가, 비용
- ridiculous ⓐ 우스꽝스러운
- minor ⓐ 사소한
- define ⓥ 규정하다
- stranger ⑪ 낯선 사람
- responsible ⓐ 책임이 있는
- criticism ⑪ 비난
- translatable ⓐ 번역할 수 있는
- considerable ⓐ 상당한
- unexpected ⓐ 예상치 못한

구문 풀이

18행 In such a case it would sound ridiculous (i.e., unexpected, surprising, and worthy of criticism) if you were to thank someone for something so minor as holding a door open for you.

---

41 제목 파악
정답률 59% | 정답 ①

윗글의 제목으로 가장 적절한 것은?

☑ Norms: For Social Life and Cultural Communication – 규범: 사회적 삶과 문화적 의사소통
② Don't Forget to Say "Thank you" at Any Time – 언제든 "고맙습니다" 말하기를 잊지마라
③ How to Be Responsible for Your Behaviors – 당신의 행동에 책임지는 방법
④ Accept Criticism Without Hurting Yourself – 상처받지 않고 비판을 받아들이기
⑤ How Did Diverse Languages Develop? – 어떻게 다양한 언어가 발달되었는가?

Why? 왜 정답일까?
문화마다 다른 규범에 대해 '감사합니다'를 예로 들어 설명하는 글이다. 사회가 구성원에게 갖는 규범적 기대(People expect that you will say it. You become responsible.)에 이어 같은 말이라도 문화마다 다른 사용 규범이 있다는 것(there may be different norms for its usage)을 언급한다. 따라서 글의 제목으로 가장 적절한 것은 ① '규범: 사회적 삶과 문화적 의사소통'이다.

★★★ 등급을 가르는 문제!

42 어휘 추론
정답률 38% | 정답 ④

밑줄 친 (a)~(e) 중에서 문맥상 낱말의 쓰임이 적절하지 않은 것은?

① (a)   ② (b)   ③ (c)   ☑ (d)   ⑤ (e)

Why? 왜 정답일까?
문화권마다 규범이 다르고, 한 문화권에서는 가벼운 일이라도 감사 인사를 해야하는 반면, 다른 문화권에서는 중대한 일에만 감사 인사를 하기도 함을 설명했다. "Thank you" 예시를 들며, 번역될 수 있는 것처럼 보이는 표현이라도 사용 규범이 다르다는 의미가 되어야 자연스러우므로, similar 대신 different를 쓰는 것이 적절하다. 따라서 낱말의 쓰임이 문맥상 적절하지 않은 것은 ④ (d)다.

★★ 문제 해결 꿀~팁 ★★

▶ 많이 틀린 이유는?
문화마다 다른 규범에 대해서 이야기하는 글이다. "감사합니다"를 예시로 전개하며 같은 말일지라도 문화마다 갖는 무게가 다르기 때문에 다르게 사용해야 함을 강조한다. 이 글에서 중요하게 이야기하는 것은 문화 간의 규범의 차이이기 때문에, similar norms는 적절하지 않다.

▶ 문제 해결 방법은?
글이 길 때에도 글의 서두와 말미에서 주제를 정확히 파악하여 주제와 어색한 문장을 찾는다. 헷갈릴 때에는 반대의 뜻으로 바꾸어서 해석해 보며 대조해 보는 것도 좋다.

43-45 드림캐처의 기원

(A)

『Long ago, / when the world was young, / an old Native American spiritual leader Odawa / had a dream on a high mountain.』 45번 ①의 근거 일치
오래전, / 세상이 생겨난지 오래지 않을 무렵, / 아메리카 원주민의 늙은 영적 지도자인 Odawa는 / 높은 산에서 꿈을 꾸었다.

In his dream, / Iktomi, the great spirit and searcher of wisdom, / appeared to (a) him in the form of a spider.
자신의 꿈속에서, / 위대한 신령이자 지혜의 구도자인 Iktomi가 / 거미의 형태로 그에게 나타났다.

Iktomi spoke to him / in a holy language.
Iktomi는 그에게 말했다. / 성스러운 언어로

(D)

『Iktomi told Odawa / about the cycles of life.』 45번 ⑤의 근거 일치
Iktomi는 Odawa에게 말했다. / 삶의 순환에 관해서

(d) He said, / "We all begin our lives as babies, / move on to childhood, / and then to adulthood.
그는 ~라고 말했다. / 우리는 모두 아기로 삶을 출발하고, / 유년기를 거쳐 / 그다음 성년기에 이르게 된다.

Finally, we come to old age, / where we must be taken care of / as babies again."
결국 우리는 노년기에 도달하고, / 거기서 우리는 보살핌을 받아야 한다." / 다시 아기처럼

Iktomi also told (e) him / that there are good and bad forces / in each stage of life.
또한 Iktomi는 그에게 말했다. / 좋고 나쁜 힘이 있다고 / 삶의 각 단계에는

"If we listen to the good forces, / they will guide us / in the right direction.
"우리가 좋은 힘에 귀를 기울이면 / 그들은 우리를 올바른 방향으로 인도할 것이다.

But if we listen to the bad forces, / they will lead us the wrong way / and may harm us," / Iktomi said.
하지만 만약 나쁜 힘에 귀를 기울이면 / 그들은 우리를 잘못된 길로 이끌고 / 우리를 해칠 수도 있다." / 라고 Iktomi는 말했다.

(C)

『When Iktomi finished speaking, / he spun a web / and gave it to Odawa』 45번 ③의 근거 일치
Iktomi가 말을 끝냈을 때, / 그는 거미집을 짜서 / Odawa에게 주었다

He said to Odawa, / "The web is a perfect circle with a hole in the center.
그가 Odawa에게 말하기를, / "그 거미집은 가운데 구멍이 뚫린 완벽한 원이다.

Use the web / to help your people reach their goals.
거미집을 사용해라. / 너의 마을 사람들이 자신들의 목표에 도달할 수 있도록

Make good use of / their ideas, dreams, and visions.
잘 활용해라. / 그들의 생각, 꿈, 비전을

If (c) you believe in the great spirit, / the web will catch your good ideas / and the bad ones / will go through the hole."
만약 네가 위대한 신령을 믿는다면, / 그 거미집이 네 좋은 생각을 붙잡아 줄 것이고 / 나쁜 생각은 / 구멍을 통해 빠져나갈 것이다."

『Right after Odawa woke up, / he went back to his village.』 45번 ④의 근거 일치
Odawa는 잠에서 깨자마자 / 자기 마을로 되돌아갔다.

(B)

Odawa shared Iktomi's lesson / with (b) his people.
Odawa는 Iktomi의 교훈을 나누었다. / 그의 마을 사람들과

『Today, many Native Americans / have dream catchers / hanging above their beds.』 45번 ②의 근거 불일치
오늘날 많은 미국 원주민은 / 드림캐처를 가지고 있다. / 그들 침대 위에 건

Dream catchers are believed / to filter out bad dreams.
드림캐처는 믿어진다. / 나쁜 꿈을 걸러 준다고

The good dreams / are captured in the web of life / and carried with the people.
좋은 꿈은 / 인생이라는 거미집에 걸리고 / 사람들과 동반하게 된다.

The bad dreams / pass through the hole in the web / and are no longer a part of their lives.
나쁜 꿈은 / 거미집의 구멍 사이로 빠져나가고 / 더 이상 그들의 삶의 한 부분이 되지 못한다.

(A)

오래전, 세상이 생겨난지 오래지 않을 무렵, 아메리카 원주민의 늙은 영적 지도자인 Odawa는 높은 산에서 꿈을 꾸었다. 자신의 꿈속에서 위대한 신령이자 지혜의 구도자인 Iktomi가 거미의 형태로 (a) 그에게 나타났다. Iktomi는 성스러운 언어로 그에게 말했다.

(D)

Iktomi는 Odawa에게 삶의 순환에 관해서 말했다. (d) 그는 "우리는 모두 아기로 삶을 출발하고, 유년기를 거쳐 그다음 성년기에 이르게 된다. 결국 우리는 노년기에 도달하고, 거기서 우리는 다시 아기처럼 보살핌을 받아야 한다."라고 말했다. 또한 Iktomi는 삶의 각 단계에는 좋고 나쁜 힘이 있다고 (e) 그에게 말했다. "우리가 좋은 힘에 귀를 기울이면 그들은 우리를 올바른 방향으로 인도할 것이다. 하지만 만약 나쁜 힘에 귀를 기울이면 그들은 우리를 잘못된 길로 이끌고 우리를 해칠 수도 있다."라고 Iktomi는 말했다.

(C)

Iktomi가 말을 끝냈을 때, 그는 거미집을 짜서 Odawa에게 주었다. 그가 Odawa에게 말하기를, "그 거미집은 가운데 구멍이 뚫린 완벽한 원이다. 너의 마을 사람들이 자신들의 목표에 도달할 수 있도록 거미집을 사용해라. 그들의 생각, 꿈, 비전을 잘 활용해라. 만약 (c) 네가 위대한 신령을 믿는다면 그 거미집이 네 좋은 생각을 붙잡아 줄 것이고 나쁜 생각은 구멍을 통해 빠져나갈 것이다." Odawa는 잠에서 깨자마자 자기 마을로 되돌아갔다.

(B)

Odawa는 Iktomi의 교훈을 (b) 그의 마을 사람들과 나누었다. 오늘날 많은 미국 원주민은 침대

위에 드림캐처를 건다. 드림캐처는 나쁜 꿈을 걸러 준다고 믿어진다. 좋은 꿈은 인생이라는 거미집에 걸리고 사람들과 동반하게 된다. 나쁜 꿈은 거미집의 구멍 사이로 빠져나가고 더 이상 그들의 삶의 한 부분이 되지 못한다.

- Native American ⓝ 미국 원주민
- holy ⓐ 성스러운
- cycle ⓝ 순환
- spiritual ⓐ 영적인
- spin ⓥ 짜다 (과거형 spun)

구문 풀이

(C) 1행 When Iktomi finished speaking, he spun a web and gave it to Odawa.
부사절의 접속사(~때) / 동명사 / 동사1 / 동사2

---

43 글의 순서 파악　　　정답률 70% | 정답 ⑤

주어진 글 (A)에 이어질 내용을 순서에 맞게 배열한 것으로 가장 적절한 것은?

① (B) – (D) – (C)
② (C) – (B) – (D)
③ (C) – (D) – (B)
④ (D) – (B) – (C)
☑ (D) – (C) – (B)

Why? 왜 정답일까?

Odawa가 꿈에서 Iktomi를 거미 형태로 만났다는 내용의 (A) 뒤로, Iktomi가 Odawa에게 삶의 순환에 대해 얘기했다는 내용의 (D), Iktomi가 Odawa에게 거미집을 주며 Odawa와 마을 사람들에게 이롭게 거미집을 사용하라고 말하는 내용의 (C), Odawa가 꿈에서 깨 마을 사람들과 거미집을 나눈 내용의 (B)가 순서대로 이어져야 자연스럽다. 따라서 글의 순서로 가장 적절한 것은 ⑤ (D) – (C) – (B)이다.

---

44 지칭 추론　　　정답률 71% | 정답 ④

밑줄 친 (a) ~ (e) 중에서 가리키는 대상이 나머지 넷과 다른 것은?

① (a)　② (b)　③ (c)　☑ (d)　⑤ (e)

Why? 왜 정답일까?

(a), (b), (c), (e)는 모두 Odawa를 가리키므로, (a) ~ (e) 중에서 가리키는 대상이 다른 하나는 ④ (d)이다.

---

45 세부 내용 파악　　　정답률 74% | 정답 ②

윗글에 관한 내용으로 적절하지 않은 것은?

① Odawa는 높은 산에서 꿈을 꾸었다.
☑ 많은 미국 원주민은 드림캐처를 현관 위에 건다.
③ Iktomi는 Odawa에게 거미집을 짜서 주었다.
④ Odawa는 잠에서 깨자마자 자신의 마을로 돌아갔다.
⑤ Iktomi는 Odawa에게 삶의 순환에 대해 알려 주었다.

Why? 왜 정답일까?

(B)의 'Today, many Native Americans have dream catchers hanging above their beds.'에서 많은 미국 원주민들은 드림캐처를 그들의 침대 위에 둔다고 하였기 때문에, 내용과 일치하지 않는 것은 ② '많은 미국 원주민은 드림캐처를 현관 위에 건다.'이다.

Why? 왜 오답일까?

① (A) 'Long ago, ~, Odawa had a dream on a high mountain'의 내용과 일치한다.
③ (C) 'When Iktomi finished speaking, he spun a web and gave it to Odawa.'의 내용과 일치한다.
④ (C) 'Right after Odawa woke up, he went back to his village'의 내용과 일치한다.
⑤ (D) 'Iktomi told Odawa about the cycles of life.'의 내용과 일치한다.

Dictation 01　　　문제편 009쪽

01 heavy rain last night / school shuttle bus schedule / continue for one week
02 buying an electric bicycle / wearing a helmet / follow basic traffic rules
03 tip about time management / a to-do list / manage your time efficiently
04 took a picture / star-shaped mirror on the wall / trophy my club won
05 camping supplies ready now / packed some warm jackets / playing board games
06 fruit and vegetables / for one bag / ten percent discount
07 practice for Sports Day / family dinner gathering tonight / make up for
08 only for freshmen / deadline for applying / most creative projects
09 Are you looking for / senior citizens face-to-face / will require volunteers
10 these portable fans / have in mind / take the cheaper one
11 look so upset / have been searching for / When did you
12 have in mind / we should try / make a reservation
13 to record audiobooks / I'm struggling with / a bit challenging
14 Why don't we divide / are good at / take care of it
15 are attending their high school / writing down important things / the opening hours
16-17 reduce the symptoms / relieve your cough / another excellent food to

어휘 Review Test 01　　　문제편 014쪽

A	B	C	D
01 맞추다	01 rescue	01 ⓔ	01 ⓙ
02 가지다, 소유하다	02 certain	02 ⓑ	02 ⓙ
03 요건	03 lecture	03 ⓖ	03 ⓓ
04 해석	04 define	04 ⓠ	04 ⓠ
05 감지하다	05 extremely	05 ⓘ	05 ⓚ
06 정의	06 structure	06 ⓓ	06 ⓔ
07 강도	07 acquire	07 ⓘ	07 ⓘ
08 열정	08 income	08 ⓙ	08 ⓘ
09 과하게 작업하다	09 station	09 ⓞ	09 ⓕ
10 초보	10 insensitive	10 ⓜ	10 ⓐ
11 견디다	11 divide	11 ⓢ	11 ⓗ
12 편견	12 assess	12 ⓚ	12 ⓡ
13 지각하다	13 prey	13 ⓛ	13 ⓟ
14 등록하다	14 norm	14 ⓕ	14 ⓝ
15 고귀한	15 arena	15 ⓟ	15 ⓒ
16 장비	16 output	16 ⓡ	16 ⓢ
17 작곡하다	17 treatment	17 ⓝ	17 ⓖ
18 군대의	18 rotate	18 ⓒ	18 ⓑ
19 자주, 빈번히	19 destroy	19 ⓗ	19 ⓞ
20 진술	20 illness	20 ⓐ	20 ⓜ

• 정답 •

01 ⑤ 02 ⑤ 03 ③ 04 ⑤ 05 ② 06 ② 07 ① 08 ③ 09 ④ 10 ②
11 ② 12 ① 13 ④ 14 ① 15 ③ 16 ③ 17 ④ 18 ③ 19 ② 20 ⑤
21 ⑤ 22 ① 23 ① 24 ② 25 ⑤ 26 ⑤ 27 ③ 28 ④ 29 ⑤ 30 ④
31 ① 32 ③ 33 ① 34 ② 35 ④ 36 ④ 37 ② 38 ④ 39 ⑤ 40 ①
41 ④ 42 ③ 43 ④ 44 ④ 45 ④

★ 표기된 문항은 [등급을 가르는 문제]에 해당하는 문항입니다.

---

01   아이스하키 리그 첫 경기 관람 독려   정답률 85% | 정답 ⑤

다음을 듣고, 남자가 하는 말의 목적으로 가장 적절한 것을 고르시오.

① 아이스하키부의 우승을 알리려고
② 아이스하키부 훈련 일정을 공지하려고
③ 아이스하키부 신임 감독을 소개하려고
④ 아이스하키부 선수 모집을 안내하려고
☑ 아이스하키부 경기의 관람을 독려하려고

M : Hello, Villeford High School students.
　안녕하세요, Villeford 고등학교 학생 여러분.
This is principal Aaron Clark.
　저는 교장인 Aaron Clark입니다.
As a big fan of the Villeford ice hockey team, I'm very excited about the upcoming National High School Ice Hockey League.
　Villeford 아이스하키 팀의 열렬한 팬으로서, 저는 다가오는 전국 고교 아이스하키 리그를 몹시 기대하고 있습니다.
As you all know, the first game will be held in the Central Rink at 6 p.m. this Saturday.
　여러분 모두가 알다시피, 첫 경기는 이번 주 토요일 저녁 6시에 Central Rink에서 열립니다.
I want as many of you as possible to come and cheer our team to victory.
　최대한 많이 와서 우리 팀의 승리를 응원해주기 바랍니다.
I've seen them put in an incredible amount of effort to win the league.
　선수들이 이번 리그를 이기려고 엄청난 노력을 기울이는 것을 보았습니다.
It will help them play better just to see you there cheering for them.
　여러분이 거기서 응원해주는 것을 선수들이 보기만 해도 경기를 더 잘하는 데 도움이 될 겁니다.
I really hope to see you at the rink. Thank you.
　여러분을 링크장에서 만날 수 있기를 진심으로 바랍니다. 고맙습니다.

Why? 왜 정답일까?

'I want as many of you as possible to come and cheer our team to victory.'에서 아이스하키 리그 경기 관람을 독려하는 담화임을 알 수 있으므로, 남자가 하는 말의 목적으로 가장 적절한 것은 ⑤ '아이스하키부 경기의 관람을 독려하려고'이다.

● principal ⓝ 교장
● put in effort 노력을 기울이다
● amount ⓝ 양
● excited ⓐ 기대하는, 신나는
● incredible ⓐ 엄청난, 믿을 수 없는

---

02   약을 새로 처방 받기를 권하기   정답률 89% | 정답 ⑤

대화를 듣고, 여자의 의견으로 가장 적절한 것을 고르시오.

① 과다한 항생제 복용을 자제해야 한다.
② 오래된 약을 함부로 폐기해서는 안 된다.
③ 약을 복용할 때는 정해진 시간을 지켜야 한다.
④ 진료 전에 자신의 증상을 정확히 확인해야 한다.
☑ 다른 사람에게 처방된 약을 복용해서는 안 된다.

W : Honey, are you okay?
　여보, 괜찮아요?
M : I'm afraid I've caught a cold. I've got a sore throat.
　나 감기에 걸린 것 같아요. 인후통이 있어요.
W : Why don't you go see a doctor?
　병원에 가는 게 어때요?
M : Well, I don't think it's necessary. I've found some medicine in the cabinet. I'll take it.
　음, 그게 필요한 것 같지는 않아요. 찬장에서 약을 좀 찾았어요. 그걸 먹겠어요.
W : You shouldn't take that medicine. That's what I got prescribed last week.
　그 약을 먹으면 안 돼요. 그거 내가 지난주에 처방받은 거예요.
M : My symptoms are similar to yours.
　내 증상도 당신 증상이랑 비슷해요.
W : Honey, you shouldn't take medicine prescribed for others.
　여보, 다른 사람한테 처방된 약을 먹으면 안 돼요.
M : It's just a cold. I'll get better if I take your medicine.
　그냥 감기인걸요. 당신 약을 먹으면 나을 거예요.
W : It could be dangerous to take someone else's prescription.
　다른 사람의 처방약을 먹는 것은 위험할 수도 있어요.
M : Okay. Then I'll go see a doctor this afternoon.
　알겠어요. 그럼 오늘 오후에 병원에 갈게요.

Why? 왜 정답일까?

'Honey, you shouldn't take medicine prescribed for others.'와 'It could be dangerous to take someone else's prescription.'에서 여자는 다른 사람에게 처방된 약을 먹어서는 안 된다는 의견을 말하고 있다. 따라서 여자의 의견으로 가장 적절한 것은 ⑤ '다른 사람에게 처방된 약을 복용해서는 안 된다.'이다.

● catch a cold 감기에 걸리다
● see a doctor 병원에 가다
● prescribe ⓥ 처방하다
● prescription ⓝ 처방(전)
● sore throat 인후통
● cabinet ⓝ 찬장, 캐비닛
● symptom ⓝ 증상

---

03   전시실 변경 알려주기   정답률 86% | 정답 ③

대화를 듣고, 두 사람의 관계를 가장 잘 나타낸 것을 고르시오.

① 관람객 – 박물관 관장
② 세입자 – 건물 관리인
☑ 화가 – 미술관 직원
④ 고객 – 전기 기사
⑤ 의뢰인 – 건축사

W : Hi, Mr. Thomson. How are your preparations going?
　안녕하세요, Thomson 씨. 준비 어떻게 돼 가세요?
M : You arrived at the right time. I have something to tell you.
　마침 잘 오셨어요. 말씀드릴 게 있어요.
W : Okay. What is it?
　네. 뭔가요?
M : Well, I'm afraid that we have to change the exhibition room for your paintings.
　음, 죄송하지만 선생님 그림을 둘 전시실을 바꿔야 할 것 같아요.
W : May I ask why?
　이유를 여쭤봐도 될까요?
M : Sure. We have some electrical problems there.
　물론이죠. 거기 전기 문제가 좀 있어서요.
W : I see. Then where are you going to exhibit my works?
　그렇군요. 그럼 제 작품을 어디에 전시하실 예정인가요?
M : Our gallery is going to exhibit your paintings in the main hall.
　우리 갤러리에서는 선생님 작품을 메인 홀에 전시할 계획이에요.
W : Okay. Can I see the hall now?
　그렇군요. 지금 홀을 봐도 될까요?
M : Sure. Come with me.
　물론이죠. 같이 가시죠.

Why? 왜 정답일까?

'~ we have to change the exhibition room for your paintings.', 'Then where are you going to exhibit my works?', 'Our gallery is going to exhibit your paintings in the main hall.'에서 여자가 화가이고, 남자가 미술관 직원임을 알 수 있다. 따라서 두 사람의 관계로 가장 적절한 것은 ③ '화가 – 미술관 직원'이다.

● preparation ⓝ 준비, 대비
● electrical ⓐ 전기의
● exhibition ⓝ 전시
● exhibit ⓥ 전시하다

---

04   벽화 봉사 사진 구경하기   정답률 88% | 정답 ⑤

대화를 듣고, 그림에서 대화의 내용과 일치하지 <u>않는</u> 것을 고르시오.

M : Hi, Grace. What are you looking at on your phone?
　안녕, Grace. 핸드폰으로 뭐 보고 있어?
W : Hi, James. It's a photo I took when I did some volunteer work. We painted pictures on a street wall.
　안녕, James. 내가 봉사활동을 좀 하면서 찍었던 사진이야. 거리 벽에다 그림을 그렸어.
M : Let me see. 『Wow, I like the whale with the flower pattern.』①의 근거 일치
　나도 좀 보자. 와, 꽃무늬가 있는 고래 그림이 마음에 들어.
W : I like it, too. 『How do you like the house under the whale?』②의 근거 일치
　나도 그게 좋아. 고래 밑에 있는 집은 어때?
M : It's beautiful. 『What are these two chairs for?』③의 근거 일치
　예쁘다. 이 의자 두 개는 왜 있는 거야?
W : You can take a picture sitting there. The painting becomes the background.
　거기 앉아서 사진을 찍을 수 있어. 그림이 배경이 되는 거지.
M : Oh, I see. 『Look at this tree! It has heart-shaped leaves.』④의 근거 일치
　오, 그렇구나. 이 나무 좀 봐! 하트 모양 잎이 있어.
W : That's right. We named it the Love Tree.
　맞아. 우리 그걸 '사랑의 나무'라고 이름 지었어.
M : 『The butterfly on the tree branch is lovely, too.』⑤의 근거 불일치
　나뭇가지 위의 나비도 귀여워.
W : I hope a lot of people enjoy the painting.
　많은 사람들이 그림을 즐겨주면 좋겠어.

Why? 왜 정답일까?

대화에서 나뭇가지 위에 나비가 있다고 하는데(The butterfly on the tree branch is lovely, too.), 그림 속 나뭇가지 위에는 새가 있다. 따라서 그림에서 대화의 내용과 일치하지 않는 것은 ⑤이다.

● volunteer work 봉사활동
● How do you like ~? ~는 어때?

---

05   록 콘서트 준비하기   정답률 91% | 정답 ②

대화를 듣고, 남자가 할 일로 가장 적절한 것을 고르시오.

① 티켓 디자인하기
☑ 포스터 게시하기
③ 블로그 개설하기
④ 밴드부원 모집하기
⑤ 콘서트 장소 대여하기

M : Hi, Stella. How are you doing these days?
　안녕, Stella. 요새 뭐 하고 있어?

W : Hi, Ryan. I've been busy helping my granddad with his concert. He made a rock band with his friends.
안녕, Ryan. 난 요새 우리 할아버지 콘서트 준비를 돕느라 바빴어. 친구분들하고 록 밴드를 만드셨거든.
M : There must be a lot of things to do.
할 게 많겠구나.
W : Yeah. I reserved a place for the concert yesterday.
응. 난 어제 콘서트 장소를 예약했어.
M : What about posters and tickets?
포스터랑 티켓은?
W : Well, I've just finished designing a poster.
음, 포스터 디자인은 방금 다 했어.
M : Then I think I can help you.
그럼 내가 널 도와줄 수 있을 거 같아.
W : Really? How?
정말? 어떻게?
M : Actually, I have a music blog. I think I can upload the poster there.
사실, 난 음악 블로그를 하고 있어. 거기다 포스터를 올려줄 수 있을 거 같아.
W : That's great!
그거 좋네!
M : Just send the poster to me, and I'll post it online.
나한테 포스터를 보내주기만 하면, 내가 온라인에 그걸 올릴게.
W : Thanks a lot.
정말 고마워.

Why? 왜 정답일까?

남자는 할아버지의 콘서트 준비를 도와 포스터를 만들었다는 여자에게 포스터를 보내주기만 하면 자신이 운영하는 음악 블로그에 게시해 주겠다고 한다(Just send the poster to me, and I'll post it online.). 따라서 남자가 할 일로 가장 적절한 것은 ② '포스터 게시하기'이다.

● be busy ~ing ~하느라 바쁘다 ● reserve ⓥ 예약하다

---

06 커피포트와 텀블러 구매하기 정답률 79% | 정답 ②

대화를 듣고, 여자가 지불할 금액을 고르시오. [3점]
① $70 ✓② $90 ③ $100 ④ $110 ⑤ $120

M : Good morning. How may I help you?
안녕하세요. 무엇을 도와드릴까요?
W : Hi. I want to buy a coffee pot.
안녕하세요. 전 커피포트를 사고 싶어요.
M : Okay. You can choose from these coffee pots.
알겠습니다. 여기 포트들 중에서 선택하시면 돼요.
W : I like this one. How much is it?
이거 마음에 드네요. 얼마가요?
M : It was originally $60, but it's now on sale for $50.
원래는 60달러인데, 지금 50달러로 세일 중이에요.
W : Okay, I'll buy it. I'd also like to buy this red tumbler.
그렇군요. 이걸 사겠어요. 그리고 이 빨간색 텀블러도 사고 싶어요.
M : Actually, it comes in two sizes. This smaller one is $20 and a bigger one is $30.
사실, 이것은 두 개 사이즈로 나옵니다. 이 작은 것은 20달러이고 더 큰 것은 30달러예요.
W : The smaller one would be easier to carry around. I'll buy two smaller ones.
작은 게 들고 다니기 더 편하겠네요. 작은 거로 두 개 사겠어요.
M : All right. Is there anything else you need?
알겠습니다. 더 필요하신 건 없으신가요?
W : No, that's all. Thank you.
이거면 돼요. 고맙습니다.
M : Okay. How would you like to pay?
알겠습니다. 어떻게 지불하시겠습니까?
W : I'll pay by credit card. Here you are.
신용 카드로 지불할게요. 여기 있습니다.

Why? 왜 정답일까?

대화에 따르면 여자는 본래 60달러이지만 현재 50달러로 세일 중인 커피포트를 하나 사고, 하나에 20달러인 작은 텀블러도 두 개 샀다. 이를 식으로 나타내면 '50+(20×2)=90'이므로, 여자가 지불할 금액은 ② '$90'이다.

● come in (사이즈나 색상이) 나오다 ● carry around 들고 다니다

---

07 면세점에서 지갑을 못 산 이유 정답률 92% | 정답 ①

대화를 듣고, 남자가 지갑을 구매하지 못한 이유를 고르시오.
✓① 해당 상품이 다 팔려서 ② 브랜드명을 잊어버려서
③ 계산대의 줄이 길어서 ④ 공항에 늦게 도착해서
⑤ 면세점이 문을 닫아서

[Cell phone rings.]
[휴대전화가 울린다.]
W : Hi, Brian.
안녕, Brian.
M : Hi, Mom. I'm in line to get on the plane.
엄마, 저 비행기 타려고 줄 서 있어요.
W : Okay. By the way, did you drop by the duty free shop in the airport?
그래. 그나저나 너 공항 면세점에는 들렀니?
M : Yes, but I couldn't buy the wallet you asked me to buy.
네, 그런데 엄마가 사달라고 부탁하신 지갑은 못 샀어요.
W : Did you forget the brand name?
브랜드 이름을 잊어버린 거야?
M : No. I remembered that. I took a memo.
아니요. 그건 기억했어요. 메모했는걸요.
W : Then did you arrive late at the airport?
그럼 공항에 늦게 도착했어?
M : No, I had enough time to shop.
아니요, 쇼핑할 시간은 충분했어요.

W : Then why couldn't you buy the wallet?
그럼 왜 지갑을 못 산 거니?
M : Actually, because they were all sold out.
사실, 그게 품절이 됐더라고요.
W : Oh, really?
오, 정말?
M : Yeah. The wallet must be very popular.
네. 그 지갑 무척 인기가 많은가봐요.
W : Okay. Thanks for checking anyway.
알겠어. 그래도 확인해줘서 고마워.

Why? 왜 정답일까?

대화에서 남자는 여자가 부탁한 지갑을 사지 못한 이유로 그것이 품절되었기 때문(Actually, because they were all sold out.)임을 언급한다. 따라서 남자가 지갑을 구매하지 못한 이유로 가장 적절한 것은 ① '해당 상품이 다 팔려서'이다.

● in line 줄을 선, 줄 서서 ● drop by ~에 들르다
● duty free shop 면세점

---

08 합창단 오디션 정답률 88% | 정답 ③

대화를 듣고, Youth Choir Audition에 관해 언급되지 않은 것을 고르시오.
① 지원 가능 연령 ② 날짜 ✓③ 심사 기준
④ 참가비 ⑤ 지원 방법

M : Lucy, look at this.
Lucy, 이것 좀 봐.
W : Wow. It's about the Youth Choir Audition.
와. Youth Choir Audition에 관한 거구나.
M : Yes. 「It's open to anyone aged 13 to 18.」 ①의 근거 일치
응. 13~18세인 누구나 참가할 수 있어.
W : I'm interested in joining the choir. 「When is it?
난 합창단에 드는 데 관심이 있어. 언제 해?」 ②의 근거 일치
M : April 2nd, from 9 a.m. to 5 p.m.
4월 2일 아침 9시부터 오후 5시까지야.
W : The place for the audition is the Youth Training Center. It's really far from here.
오디션 장소는 Youth Training Center네. 여기서 아주 멀어.
M : I think you should leave early in the morning.
너 아침 일찍 출발해야겠네.
W : That's no problem. 「Is there an entry fee?
그건 괜찮아. 참가비가 있나?」
M : No, it's free.」 ④의 근거 일치
아니, 무료래.
W : Good. I'll apply for the audition.
좋아. 난 오디션에 지원하겠어.
M : 「Then you should fill out an application form on this website.」 ⑤의 근거 일치
그럼 이 웹 사이트에서 신청서를 작성해야 해.
W : All right. Thanks.
알겠어. 고마워.

Why? 왜 정답일까?

대화에서 남자와 여자는 Youth Choir Audition의 지원 가능 연령, 날짜, 참가비, 지원 방법을 언급하므로, 언급되지 않은 것은 ③ '심사 기준'이다.

Why? 왜 오답일까?

① 'It's open to anyone aged 13 to 18.'에서 '지원 가능 연령'이 언급되었다.
② 'April 2nd, from 9 a.m. to 5 p.m.'에서 '날짜'가 언급되었다.
④ 'No, it's free.'에서 '참가비'가 언급되었다.
⑤ '~ you should fill out an application form on this website.'에서 '지원 방법'이 언급되었다.

● choir ⓝ 합창단 ● entry fee 참가비
● apply for ~에 신청하다, 지원하다 ● fill out (서류를) 작성하다

---

09 진로 관련 특별 행사 안내 정답률 90% | 정답 ④

2023 Career Week에 관한 다음 내용을 듣고, 일치하지 않는 것을 고르시오.
① 5일 동안 열릴 것이다.
② 미래 직업 탐색을 돕는 프로그램이 있을 것이다.
③ 프로그램 참가 인원에 제한이 있다.
✓④ 특별 강연이 마지막 날에 있을 것이다.
⑤ 등록은 5월 10일에 시작된다.

W : Hello, Rosehill High School students!
안녕하세요, Rosehill 고등학교 학생 여러분!
I'm your school counselor, Ms. Lee.
저는 진로 상담 교사인 Ms. Lee입니다.
I'm so happy to announce a special event, the 2023 Career Week.
특별행사인 2023 Career Week에 관해 알려드리게 되어 기쁩니다.
「It'll be held from May 22nd for five days.」 ①의 근거 일치
이것은 5월 22일부터 5일간 개최돼요.
「There will be many programs to help you explore various future jobs.」 ②의 근거 일치
여러분이 다양한 미래 직업을 탐색하도록 도와줄 많은 프로그램이 있을 겁니다.
「Please kindly note that the number of participants for each program is limited to 20.」 ③의 근거 일치
프로그램마다 참가자 수가 20명으로 제한된다는 것을 유념해 주세요.
「A special lecture on future career choices will be presented on the first day.」 ④의 근거 불일치
미래 직업 선택에 대한 특별 강연이 첫날 제공될 예정입니다.
「Registration begins on May 10th.」 ⑤의 근거 일치
등록은 5월 10일부터 시작됩니다.
For more information, please visit our school website.
더 많은 정보를 원하시면, 우리 학교 웹 사이트를 방문해주세요.
I hope you can come and enjoy the 2023 Career Week!
여러분이 2023 Career Week에 와서 즐길 수 있기를 바랍니다!

Why? 왜 정답일까?

'A special lecture on future career choices will be presented on the first day.'에서 미래 직업 선택에 관한 특강은 첫날 있을 것이라고 하므로, 내용과 일치하지 않는 것은 '④ 특별 강연이 마지막 날에 있을 것이다.'이다.

Why? 왜 오답일까?

① 'It'll be held from May 22nd for five days.'의 내용과 일치한다.
② 'There will be many programs to help you explore various future jobs.'의 내용과 일치한다.
③ 'Please kindly note that the number of participants for each program is limited to 20.'의 내용과 일치한다.
⑤ 'Registration begins on May 10th.'의 내용과 일치한다.

- announce ⓥ 안내하다
- note ⓥ 주목하다, 유념하다
- registration ⓝ 등록, 신청
- explore ⓥ 탐색하다
- be limited to ~로 제한되다

---

10 프라이팬 고르기   정답률 90% | 정답 ②

다음 표를 보면서 대화를 듣고, 여자가 구입할 프라이팬을 고르시오.

Frying Pans

	Model	Price	Size (inches)	Material	Lid
①	A	$30	8	Aluminum	○
②	B	$32	9.5	Aluminum	○
③	C	$35	10	Stainless Steel	×
④	D	$40	11	Aluminum	×
⑤	E	$70	12.5	Stainless Steel	○

M : Jessica, what are you doing?
　Jessica, 뭐 하고 있어?
W : I'm trying to buy one of these five frying pans.
　이 다섯 개 프라이팬 중 하나 사려고 해.
M : Let me see. This frying pan seems pretty expensive.
　좀 보자. 이 프라이팬은 꽤 비싸 보이는걸.
W : Yeah. 『I don't want to spend more than $50.』 근거1 Price 조건
　응. 난 50달러 넘게 쓰고 싶지는 않아.
M : Okay. 『And I think 9 to 12-inch frying pans will work for most of your cooking.』 근거2 Size 조건
　그래. 그리고 내 생각에 9인치에서 12인치 크기의 프라이팬이 대부분의 요리에 적합할 거야.
W : I think so, too. An 8-inch frying pan seems too small for me.
　나도 그렇게 생각해. 8인치는 나한테 너무 작아 보여.
M : What about the material? Stainless steel pans are good for fast cooking.
　소재는 어때? 스테인리스 팬이 빨리 요리하는 데 좋아.
W : I know, but they are heavier. 『I'll buy an alumium pan.』 근거3 Material 조건
　나도 알지만, 그건 더 무거워. 알루미늄 팬을 살 거야.
M : Then you have two options left. 『Do you need a lid?』 근거4 Lid 조건
　그럼 선택권이 두 개 남았네. 너 뚜껑 필요해?
W : 『Of course.』 A lid keeps the oil from splashing. I'll buy this one.
　물론이지. 뚜껑은 기름이 안 튀게 막아줘. 난 이걸 살래.
M : Good choice.
　좋은 선택이야.

Why? 왜 정답일까?

대화에 따르면 여자는 가격이 50달러를 넘지 않고, 크기는 9~12인치이며, 소재는 알루미늄으로 되어 있고, 뚜껑이 딸려 있는 프라이팬을 사려고 한다. 따라서 여자가 구입할 프라이팬은 ② 'B'이다.

- work for ~에 적합하다
- lid ⓝ 뚜껑
- splash ⓥ (물 등을) 튀기다, 철벅거리다
- material ⓝ 소재, 재료, 자재
- keep A from B A가 B하지 못하게 막다

---

11 단편 영화 프로젝트   정답률 85% | 정답 ②

대화를 듣고, 남자의 마지막 말에 대한 여자의 응답으로 가장 적절한 것을 고르시오.

① I don't think I can finish editing it by then. – 내가 그때까지 편집을 끝낼 수 있을 거 같지 않아.
② I learned it by myself through books. – 책 보고 독학했어.
③ This short movie is very interesting. – 이 단편영화 무척 재밌어.
④ You should make another video clip. – 넌 다른 영상을 만들어야 해.
⑤ I got an A⁺ on the team project. – 난 팀 프로젝트에서 A⁺를 받았어.

M : Have you finished your team's short-movie project?
　너네 팀 단편 영화 프로젝트 끝냈어?
W : Not yet. I'm still editing the video clip.
　아직. 난 아직 영상을 편집하고 있어.
M : Oh, you edit? How did you learn to do that?
　오, 네가 편집해? 그거 어디서 배웠어?
W : I learned it by myself through books.
　책 보고 독학했어.

Why? 왜 정답일까?

여자가 영상을 직접 편집하고 있다는 말에 남자는 어떻게 배웠는지(How did you learn to do that?) 물으며 관심을 보인다. 따라서 여자의 응답으로 가장 적절한 것은 ② '책 보고 독학했어.'이다.

- video clip (짧은) 영상
- learn by oneself 독학하다

---

12 차로 데리러 와달라고 부탁하기   정답률 83% | 정답 ①

대화를 듣고, 여자의 마지막 말에 대한 남자의 응답으로 가장 적절한 것을 고르시오.

① All right. I'll come pick you up now. – 그래. 내가 지금 태우러 가마.
② I'm sorry. The library is closed today. – 미안해. 도서관은 오늘 닫았어.

③ No problem. You can borrow my book. – 물론이지. 내 책을 빌려가도 된다.
④ Thank you so much. I'll drop you off now. – 무척 고맙구나. 지금 내가 널 내려줄게.
⑤ Right. I've changed the interior of my office. – 맞아. 내 사무실 인테리어를 바꿨어.

[Cell phone rings.]
[휴대전화가 울린다.]
W : Daddy, are you still working now?
　아빠, 아직 일하고 계세요?
M : No, Emma. I'm about to get in my car and drive home.
　아니, Emma. 지금 차에 타서 집으로 가려던 참이야.
W : Great. Can you give me a ride? I'm at the City Library near your office.
　잘됐네요. 저 좀 태워주실래요? 저 아빠 사무실 근처 시립 도서관에 있어요.
M : All right. I'll come pick you up now.
　그래. 내가 지금 태우러 가마.

Why? 왜 정답일까?

남자가 집으로 가려던 참이라고 말하자 여자는 남자 사무실 근처에 있는 시립 도서관으로 태우러 와달라고 부탁하고 있다(Can you give me a ride? I'm at the City Library near your office.). 따라서 남자의 응답으로 가장 적절한 것은 ① '그래. 내가 지금 태우러 가마.'이다.

- be about to ~할 참이다
- drop off ~을 (차에서) 내려주다
- pick up ~을 (차에) 태우다

---

13 농장에 함께 가도 될지 묻기   정답률 83% | 정답 ③

대화를 듣고, 남자의 마지막 말에 대한 여자의 응답으로 가장 적절한 것을 고르시오.
Woman: _____

① Try these tomatoes and cucumbers. – 이 토마토랑 오이 좀 먹어봐.
② I didn't know peppers are good for skin. – 난 고추가 피부에 좋은 줄 몰랐어.
③ Just wear comfortable clothes and shoes. – 그냥 편한 옷이랑 신발만 있으면 돼.
④ You can pick tomatoes when they are red. – 토마토가 빨간색이면 따도 돼.
⑤ I'll help you grow vegetables on your farm. – 너희 농장에서 채소 기르는 걸 도와줄게.

M : Claire, how's your farm doing?
　Claire, 너네 농장 어때?
W : Great! I harvested some cherry tomatoes and cucumbers last weekend. Do you want some?
　아주 좋아! 난 방울토마토랑 오이를 지난 주말에 좀 수확했어. 너 좀 줄까?
M : Of course. I'd like some very much.
　물론이지. 주면 아주 좋아.
W : Okay. I'll bring you some tomorrow.
　그래. 내가 내일 좀 가져다줄게.
M : Thanks. Are you going to the farm this weekend too?
　고마워. 너 이번 주일에도 농장 가?
W : Yes. The peppers are almost ready to be picked.
　응. 고추 딸 때가 거의 다 됐어.
M : Can I go with you? I'd like to look around your farm and help you pick the peppers.
　나도 가도 돼? 나도 너네 농장 좀 둘러보고 고추 따는 거 도와주고 싶어.
W : Sure. It would be fun to work on the farm together.
　물론이지, 같이 농장에서 일하면 재미있을 거야.
M : Sounds nice. Is there anything I need to prepare?
　근사할 거 같아. 내가 준비해야 할 게 있어?
W : Just wear comfortable clothes and shoes.
　그냥 편한 옷이랑 신발만 있으면 돼.

Why? 왜 정답일까?

여자네 농장에 따라가려는 남자가 준비물을 물으므로(Is there anything I need to prepare?), 여자의 응답으로 가장 적절한 것은 ③ '그냥 편한 옷이랑 신발만 있으면 돼.'이다.

- harvest ⓥ 수확하다
- cucumber ⓝ 오이

---

14 싸운 친구에게 직접 만나 사과하라고 권하기   정답률 89% | 정답 ①

대화를 듣고, 여자의 마지막 말에 대한 남자의 응답으로 가장 적절한 것을 고르시오. [3점]
Man: _____

① You're right. I'll meet her and apologize. – 네 말이 맞아. 걔를 만나서 사과하겠어.
② I agree with you. That's why I did it. – 네 말에 동의해. 그래서 내가 그렇게 했어.
③ Thank you. I appreciate your apology. – 고마워. 네 사과 고맙게 받을게.
④ Don't worry. I don't think it's your fault. – 걱정 마. 난 그게 네 잘못이라고 생각하지 않아.
⑤ Too bad. I hope the two of you get along. – 안됐네. 둘이 잘 지내길 바라.

W : Daniel, what's wrong?
　Daniel, 무슨 일이야?
M : Hi, Leila. I had an argument with Olivia.
　안녕, Leila. 나 Olivia랑 싸웠어.
W : Was it serious?
　진짜로 싸웠어?
M : I'm not sure, but I think I made a mistake.
　잘 모르겠어. 그런데 내가 실수를 한 것 같아.
W : So that's why you have a long face.
　그래서 네 얼굴이 우울하구나.
M : Yeah. I want to get along with her, but she's still angry at me.
　응. 난 걔랑 잘 지내고 싶은데, 걘 아직 나한테 화가 나 있어.
W : Did you say you're sorry to her?
　미안하다고 말했어?
M : Well, I texted her saying that I'm sorry.
　음, 미안하다는 문자를 보냈어.
W : I don't think it's a good idea to express your apology through a text message.
　문자 메시지로 사과를 표현하는 게 좋은 생각인 것 같지는 않아.
M : Do you think so? Now I know why I haven't received any response from her yet.
　그래? 이제 왜 내가 걔한테 아직 아무 답도 못 받았는지 알겠네.

W : I think it'd be best to go and talk to her in person.
내 생각에 걔한테 가서 직접 말해보는 게 최선일 거 같아.
M : You're right. I'll meet her and apologize.
네 말이 맞아. 걔를 만나서 사과할게.

Why? 왜 정답일까?

친구에게 문자로 사과했으나 답을 받지 못했다는 남자에게 여자는 직접 만나 사과하는 것이 가장 좋겠다고 충고하고 있다(I think it'd be best to go and talk to her in person.). 따라서 남자의 응답으로 가장 적절한 것은 ① '네 말이 맞아. 걔를 만나서 사과할게.'이다.

- **have a long face** 우울한 얼굴을 하다
- **get along with** ~와 잘 지내다
- **in person** 직접
- **apologize** ⓥ 사과하다
- **appreciate** ⓥ 감사하다

---

15 | 해돋이를 보기 위한 기상 시간 정하기 | 정답률 80% | 정답 ③

다음 상황 설명을 듣고, John이 Ted에게 할 말로 가장 적절한 것을 고르시오. [3점]

John:
① How can we find the best sunrise spot? – 최고의 해돋이 장소는 어떻게 찾지?
② Why do you go mountain climbing so often? – 넌 왜 그렇게 자주 등산을 가니?
☑ What time should we get up tomorrow morning? – 우리 내일 아침 몇 시에 일어나야 하지?
④ When should we come down from the mountain top? – 우리 산 정상에서 언제 내려가야 할까?
⑤ Where do we have to stay in the mountain at night? – 우리 밤에는 산 어디에서 있어야 할까?

M : Ted and John are college freshmen.
Ted와 John은 대학 신입생이다.
They are climbing Green Diamond Mountain together.
그들은 Green Diamond Mountain에 함께 오른다.
Now they have reached the campsite near the mountain top.
이제 그들은 산 정상 근처의 캠핑장에 이르렀다.
After climbing the mountain all day, they have a relaxing time at the campsite.
하루 종일 산을 오른 뒤, 그들은 캠핑장에서 여유로운 시간을 보내고 있다.
While drinking coffee, Ted suggests to John that they watch the sunrise at the mountain top the next morning.
커피를 마시던 중, Ted는 John에게 다음날 아침에 산 정상에서 해돋이를 보자고 제안한다.
John thinks it's a good idea.
John은 그게 좋은 생각인 것 같다.
So, now John wants to ask Ted how early they should wake up to see the sunrise.
그래서, 이제 John은 Ted에게 해돋이를 보려면 얼마나 일찍 일어나야 할지 물어보려고 한다.
In this situation, what would John most likely say to Ted?
이 상황에서, John은 Ted에게 뭐라고 말할 것인가?
John : What time should we get up tomorrow morning?
우리 내일 아침 몇 시에 일어나야 하지?

Why? 왜 정답일까?

상황에 따르면 John은 Ted의 제안에 따라 다음 날 산 정상에서 해돋이를 보려면 몇 시에 일어나야 할지 Ted에게 물어보려 한다(~ John wants to ask Ted how early they should wake up to see the sunrise.). 따라서 John이 Ted에게 할 말로 가장 적절한 것은 ③ '우리 내일 아침 몇 시에 일어나야 하지?'이다.

- **relaxing** ⓐ 여유로운, 느긋한
- **sunrise** ⓝ 일출, 해돋이

16-17 | 가족끼리 즐길 수 있는 운동

W : Good morning, everyone.
안녕하세요, 여러분.
Do you spend a lot of time with your family?
여러분은 가족과 시간을 많이 보내시나요?
One of the best ways to spend time with your family is to enjoy sports together.
가족과 시간을 보내는 최고의 방법 중 하나는 함께 운동을 즐기는 것입니다.
「Today, I will share some of the best sports that families can play together.」 16번의 근거
오늘, 저는 가족이 함께 즐길 수 있는 몇 가지 최고의 스포츠를 공유드리려고 합니다.
「The first one is badminton.」 17번 ①의 근거 일치
첫 번째로 배드민턴입니다.
The whole family can enjoy the sport with minimal equipment.
가족 모두가 최소의 장비로 스포츠를 즐길 수 있습니다.
「The second one is basketball.」 17번 ②의 근거 일치
두 번째로 농구입니다.
You can easily find a basketball court near your house.
집 근처에서 농구장을 쉽게 찾아볼 수 있죠.
「The third one is table tennis.」 17번 ③의 근거 일치
세 번째로 탁구입니다.
It can be played indoors anytime.
이것은 실내에서 언제든 할 수 있죠.
「The last one is bowling.」 17번 ⑤의 근거 일치
마지막으로 볼링입니다.
Many families have a great time playing it together.
많은 가족들은 볼링을 함께하며 멋진 시간을 보냅니다.
When you go home today, how about playing one of these sports with your family?
오늘 집에 가시면, 이 운동 중 하나를 가족과 해보시면 어떨까요?

- **whole** ⓐ 전체의
- **minimal** ⓐ 최소의
- **equipment** ⓝ 장비
- **table tennis** 탁구
- **the elderly** 연세 드신 분들, 노인들
- **useful** ⓐ 유용한
- **traditional** ⓐ 전통적인

---

16 | 주제 파악 | 정답률 96% | 정답 ③

여자가 하는 말의 주제로 가장 적절한 것은?
① indoor sports good for the elderly – 노인층에 좋은 실내 스포츠
② importance of learning rules in sports – 스포츠에서 규칙을 익히는 것의 중요성
☑ best sports for families to enjoy together – 가족이 함께 즐길 수 있는 최고의 운동

---

④ useful tips for winning a sports game – 운동 경기를 이기기 위한 유용한 조언
⑤ history of traditional family sports – 전통 가족 스포츠의 역사

Why? 왜 정답일까?

'Today, I will share some of the best sports that families can play together.'에서 여자는 가족이 함께 즐기기 좋은 운동을 몇 가지 소개하겠다고 하므로, 여자가 하는 말의 주제로 가장 적절한 것은 ③ '가족이 함께 즐길 수 있는 최고의 운동'이다.

---

17 | 언급 유무 파악 | 정답률 96% | 정답 ④

언급된 스포츠가 아닌 것은?
① badminton – 배드민턴
② basketball – 농구
③ table tennis – 탁구
☑ soccer – 축구
⑤ bowling – 볼링

Why? 왜 정답일까?

담화에서 여자는 가족끼리 즐기기 좋은 스포츠의 예시로 배드민턴, 농구, 탁구, 볼링을 언급한다. 따라서 언급되지 않은 것은 ④ '축구'이다.

Why? 왜 오답일까?

① 'The first one is badminton.'에서 '배드민턴'이 언급되었다.
② 'The second one is basketball.'에서 '농구'가 언급되었다.
③ 'The third one is table tennis.'에서 '탁구'가 언급되었다.
⑤ 'The last one is bowling.'에서 '볼링'이 언급되었다.

---

18 | 아파트 놀이터 시설 수리 요청 | 정답률 93% | 정답 ③

다음 글의 목적으로 가장 적절한 것은?
① 아파트의 첨단 보안 설비를 홍보하려고
② 아파트 놀이터의 임시 폐쇄를 공지하려고
☑ 아파트 놀이터 시설의 수리를 요청하려고
④ 아파트 놀이터 사고의 피해 보상을 촉구하려고
⑤ 아파트 공용 시설 사용 시 유의 사항을 안내하려고

To whom it may concern,
관계자분께
I am a resident of the Blue Sky Apartment.
저는 Blue Sky 아파트의 거주자입니다.
Recently I observed / that the kid zone is in need of repairs.
최근에 저는 알게 되었습니다. / 아이들을 위한 구역이 수리가 필요하다는 것을
I want you to pay attention / to the poor condition of the playground equipment in the zone.
저는 귀하께서 관심을 기울여 주시기를 바랍니다. / 그 구역 놀이터 설비의 열악한 상태에
The swings are damaged, / the paint is falling off, / and some of the bolts on the slide are missing.
그네가 손상되었고, / 페인트가 떨어져 나가고 있고, / 미끄럼틀의 볼트 몇 개가 빠져 있습니다.
The facilities have been in this terrible condition / since we moved here.
시설들은 이렇게 형편없는 상태였습니다. / 우리가 이곳으로 이사 온 이후로
They are dangerous / to the children playing there.
이것들은 위험합니다. / 거기서 노는 아이들에게
Would you please have them repaired?
이것들을 수리해 주시겠습니까?
I would appreciate your immediate attention / to solve this matter.
즉각적인 관심을 보여주시면 감사하겠습니다. / 이 문제를 해결하기 위해
Yours sincerely, / Nina Davis
Nina Davis 드림

관계자분께

저는 Blue Sky 아파트의 거주자입니다. 최근에 저는 아이들을 위한 구역이 수리가 필요하다는 것을 알게 되었습니다. 저는 귀하께서 그 구역 놀이터 설비의 열악한 상태에 관심을 기울여 주시기를 바랍니다. 그네가 손상되었고, 페인트가 떨어져 나가고 있고, 미끄럼틀의 볼트 몇 개가 빠져 있습니다. 시설들은 우리가 이곳으로 이사 온 이후로 이렇게 형편없는 상태였습니다. 이것들은 거기서 노는 아이들에게 위험합니다. 이것들을 수리해 주시겠습니까? 이 문제를 해결하기 위한 즉각적인 관심을 보여주시면 감사하겠습니다.

Nina Davis 드림

Why? 왜 정답일까?

'I want you to pay attention to the poor condition of the playground equipment in the zone.'와 'Would you please have them repaired?'에 놀이터 시설 수리를 요청하는 필자의 목적이 잘 드러나 있다. 따라서 글의 목적으로 가장 적절한 것은 ③ '아파트 놀이터 시설의 수리를 요청하려고'이다.

- **to whom it may concern** 담당자 귀하, 관계자 귀하
- **in need of** ~이 필요한
- **pay attention to** ~에 주의를 기울이다
- **equipment** ⓝ 장비
- **damaged** ⓐ 손상된
- **fall off** 벗겨지다, 떨어져 나가다
- **facility** ⓝ 시설
- **immediate** ⓐ 즉각적인

구문 풀이

6행 The facilities **have been** in this terrible condition **since** we **moved** here.
현재완료 / 접속사(~ 이후로) / 과거

---

19 | 야생에서 회색곰을 만난 필자 | 정답률 82% | 정답 ②

다음 글에 드러난 'I'의 심경 변화로 가장 적절한 것은?
① sad → angry
슬픈 화난
☑ delighted → scared
기쁜 겁에 질린

③ satisfied → jealous
만족한   질투하는
⑤ frustrated → excited
좌절한   신난
④ worried → relieved
걱정하는   안도한

On a two-week trip in the Rocky Mountains, / I saw a grizzly bear in its native habitat.
로키산맥에서 2주간의 여행 중, / 나는 자연 서식지에서 회색곰 한 마리를 보았다.
At first, / I felt joy / as I watched the bear walk across the land.
처음에 / 나는 기분이 좋았다. / 내가 그 곰이 땅을 가로질러 걸어가는 모습을 보았을 때
He stopped every once in a while / to turn his head about, / sniffing deeply.
그것은 이따금 멈춰 서서 / 고개를 돌려 / 깊게 코를 킁킁거렸다.
He was following the scent of something, / and slowly I began to realize / that this giant animal was smelling me!
그것은 무언가의 냄새를 따라가고 있었고, / 나는 서서히 깨닫기 시작했다! / 거대한 이 동물이 내 냄새를 맡고 있다는 것을
I froze.
나는 얼어붙었다.
This was no longer a wonderful experience; / it was now an issue of survival.
이것은 더는 멋진 경험이 아니었고, / 이제 그것은 생존의 문제였다.
The bear's motivation was to find meat to eat, / and I was clearly on his menu.
그 곰의 동기는 먹을 고기를 찾는 것이었고, / 나는 분명히 그의 메뉴에 올라 있었다.

로키산맥에서 2주간의 여행 중, 나는 자연 서식지에서 회색곰 한 마리를 보았다. 처음에 나는 그 곰이 땅을 가로질러 걸어가는 모습을 보았을 때 기분이 좋았다. 그것은 이따금 멈춰 서서 고개를 돌려 깊게 코를 킁킁거렸다. 그것은 무언가의 냄새를 따라가고 있었고, 나는 서서히 거대한 이 동물이 내 냄새를 맡고 있다는 것을 깨닫기 시작했다! 나는 얼어붙었다. 이것은 더는 멋진 경험이 아니었고, 이제 생존의 문제였다. 그 곰의 동기는 먹을 고기를 찾는 것이었고, 나는 분명히 그의 메뉴에 올라 있었다.

Why? 왜 정답일까?
처음에 회색곰을 발견하고 기분이 좋았던(At first, I felt joy as I watched the bear walk across the land.) 필자가 곰이 자신을 노린다는 것을 알고 겁에 질렸다(I froze.)는 내용이다. 따라서 'I'의 심경 변화로 가장 적절한 것은 ② '기쁜 → 겁에 질린'이다.

● grizzly bear (북미·러시아 일부 지역에 사는) 회색곰
● walk across ~을 횡단하다
● turn about 뒤돌아보다, 방향을 바꾸다
● scent ⓝ 냄새
● no longer 더 이상 ~않다
● jealous ⓐ 질투하는
● habitat ⓝ 서식지
● every once in a while 이따금
● sniff ⓥ 킁킁거리다
● freeze ⓥ 얼어붙다
● motivation ⓝ (행동의) 이유, 동기 (부여)
● frustrated ⓐ 좌절한

구문 풀이
3행 He stopped every once in a while to turn his head about, sniffing deeply.
목적(~하려고)   분사구문(~하면서)

---

20 신체 리듬이 정점일 때를 파악해 활용하기   정답률 81% | 정답 ⑤

다음 글에서 필자가 주장하는 바로 가장 적절한 것은?
① 부정적인 감정에 에너지를 낭비하지 말라.
② 자신의 신체 능력에 맞게 운동량을 조절하라.
③ 자기 성찰을 위한 아침 명상 시간을 확보하라.
④ 생산적인 하루를 보내려면 일을 균등하게 배분하라.
✓ 자신의 에너지가 가장 높은 시간을 파악하여 활용하라.

It is difficult for any of us / to maintain a constant level of attention / throughout our working day.
우리 중 누구라도 어렵다. / 일정한 수준의 주의 집중을 유지하기는 / 근무일 내내
We all have body rhythms / characterised by peaks and valleys of energy and alertness.
우리 모두 신체 리듬을 가지고 있다. / 에너지와 기민함의 정점과 저점을 특징으로 하는
You will achieve more, / and feel confident as a benefit, / if you schedule your most demanding tasks / at times when you are best able to cope with them.
여러분은 더 많은 것을 이루고, / 이득으로 자신감을 느낄 것이다. / 여러분이 가장 힘든 작업을 하도록 계획을 잡으면 / 가장 잘 처리할 수 있는 시간에
If you haven't thought about energy peaks before, / take a few days to observe yourself.
만약 여러분이 전에 에너지 정점에 관해 생각해 본 적이 없다면, / 며칠 자신을 관찰할 시간을 가져라.
Try to note the times / when you are at your best.
때를 알아차리도록 노력하라. / 여러분이 상태가 제일 좋은
We are all different.
우리는 모두 다르다.
For some, / the peak will come first thing in the morning, / but for others / it may take a while to warm up.
어떤 사람에게는 / 정점이 아침에 제일 먼저 오지만, / 다른 사람에게는 / 준비되는 데 얼마간의 시간이 걸릴 수도 있다.

우리 중 누구라도 근무일 내내 일정한 수준의 주의 집중을 유지하기는 어렵다. 우리 모두 에너지와 기민함의 정점과 저점을 특징으로 하는 신체 리듬을 가지고 있다. 가장 힘든 작업을 가장 잘 처리할 수 있는 시간에 하도록 계획을 잡으면, 더 많은 것을 이루고, 이득으로 자신감을 느낄 것이다. 만약 전에 에너지 정점에 관해 생각해 본 적이 없다면, 며칠 동안 자신을 관찰하라. 상태가 제일 좋을 때를 알아차리도록 노력하라. 우리는 모두 다르다. 어떤 사람에게는 정점이 아침에 제일 먼저 오지만, 다른 사람에게는 준비되는 데 얼마간의 시간이 걸릴 수도 있다.

Why? 왜 정답일까?
힘든 작업을 분배할 수 있도록 하루 중 신체 리듬이 가장 좋은 시간을 찾아보라(Try to note the times when you are at your best.)고 조언하는 글이므로, 필자의 주장으로 가장 적절한 것은 ⑤ '자신의 에너지가 가장 높은 시간을 파악하여 활용하라.'이다.

● maintain ⓥ 유지하다
● throughout prep ~ 내내
● peaks and valleys 정점과 저점, 부침, 성쇠
● achieve ⓥ 성취하다
● benefit ⓝ 이득
● cope with ~을 처리하다
● constant ⓐ 지속적인
● characterise ⓥ ~을 특징으로 하다
● alertness ⓝ 기민함
● confident ⓐ 자신감 있는
● demanding ⓐ 까다로운, 힘든
● warm up 준비가 되다, 몸을 풀다

구문 풀이
7행 Try to note the times when you are at your best.
선행사(시간) 관계부사

21 더 많은 기술을 받아들인 대가   정답률 55% | 정답 ⑤

밑줄 친 The divorce of the hands from the head가 다음 글에서 의미하는 바로 가장 적절한 것은? [3점]
① ignorance of modern technology
현대 기술에 대한 무지
② endless competition in the labor market
노동 시장에서의 끝없는 경쟁
③ not getting along well with our coworkers
동료와 잘 지내지 않는 것
④ working without any realistic goals for our career
경력을 위한 아무 현실적 목표도 없이 일하는 것
✓ our increasing use of high technology in the workplace
우리가 직장에서 고도의 기술을 점점 더 많이 사용하는 것

If we adopt technology, / we need to pay its costs.
만약 우리가 기술을 받아들이면, / 우리는 그것의 비용을 치러야 한다.
Thousands of traditional livelihoods / have been pushed aside by progress, / and the lifestyles around those jobs / removed.
수천 개의 전통적인 생계 수단이 / 발전 때문에 밀려났으며, / 그 직업과 관련된 생활 방식이 / 없어졌다.
Hundreds of millions of humans today / work at jobs they hate, / producing things they have no love for.
오늘날 수억 명의 사람들이 / 자기가 싫어하는 일자리에서 일한다 / 그들이 아무런 애정을 느끼지 못하는 것들을 생산하면서
Sometimes / these jobs cause physical pain, disability, or chronic disease.
때로로 / 이러한 일자리는 육체적 고통, 장애 또는 만성 질환을 유발한다.
Technology creates many new jobs / that are certainly dangerous.
기술은 많은 새로운 일자리를 창출한다 / 확실히 위험한
At the same time, / mass education and media train humans / to avoid low-tech physical work, / to seek jobs working in the digital world.
동시에, / 대중 교육과 대중 매체는 인간을 훈련시킨다 / 낮은 기술의 육체노동을 피하고 / 디지털 세계에서 일하는 직업을 찾도록
The divorce of the hands from the head / puts a stress on the human mind.
손이 머리로부터 단절되어 있는 것은 / 인간의 정신에 부담을 준다.
Indeed, / the sedentary nature of the best-paying jobs / is a health risk / — for body and mind.
실제로, / 가장 보수가 좋은 직업이 주로 앉아서 하는 특성을 지녔다는 것은 / 건강상 위험 요소이다. / 신체와 정신에

만약 우리가 기술을 받아들이면, 우리는 그것의 비용을 치러야 한다. 수천 개의 전통적인 생계 수단이 발전 때문에 밀려났으며, 그 직업과 관련된 생활 방식이 없어졌다. 오늘날 수억 명의 사람들이 자기가 싫어하는 일자리에서 일하면서 아무런 애정을 느끼지 못하는 것들을 생산한다. 때때로 이러한 일자리는 육체적 고통, 장애 또는 만성 질환을 유발한다. 기술은 확실히 위험한 많은 새로운 일자리를 창출한다. 동시에, 대중 교육과 대중 매체는 인간이 낮은 기술의 육체노동을 피하고 디지털 세계에서 일하는 직업을 찾도록 훈련시킨다. 손이 머리로부터 단절되어 있는 것은 인간의 정신에 부담을 준다. 실제로, 가장 보수가 좋은 직업이 주로 앉아서 하는 특성을 지녔다는 것은 신체 및 정신 건강의 위험 요소이다.

Why? 왜 정답일까?
첫 두 문장에서 우리는 더 많은 기술을 받아들이면서 더 많은 전통적 방식을 포기하게 되었다고 말한다. 특히 밑줄이 포함된 문장 앞뒤에서는 현대 인간이 육체노동을 덜 찾고 앉아서 하는 일을 찾도록(to avoid low-tech physical work, to seek jobs working in the digital world) 훈련되면서 더 많은 건강 위험에 노출되었다고 설명한다. 이러한 흐름으로 보아, 밑줄 부분은 결국 '인간이 기술을 더 많이 받아들인 대가로' 육체와 정신의 건강을 잃게 되었다는 뜻으로 볼 수 있다. 따라서 밑줄 친 부분의 의미로 가장 적절한 것은 ⑤ '우리가 직장에서 고도의 기술을 점점 더 많이 사용하는 것'이다.

● adopt ⓥ 수용하다, 받아들이다
● livelihood ⓝ 생계
● progress ⓝ 진보
● million ⓝ 100만
● have love for ~에 애정을 갖다
● disability ⓝ 장애
● certainly ad 분명히, 확실히
● seek ⓥ 찾다, 추구하다
● divorce A from B A와 B의 분리, A를 B로부터 분리시키다
● put a stress on ~에 스트레스[부담]를 주다
● nature ⓝ 본성, 특성
● ignorance ⓝ 무지
● competition ⓝ 경쟁
● get along (well) with ~와 잘 지내다
● cost ⓝ 비용 ⓥ (~의 비용을) 치르게 하다
● push aside 밀어치우다
● remove ⓥ 제거하다
● produce ⓥ 만들어내다
● physical ⓐ 신체적인
● chronic ⓐ 만성의
● mass ⓝ (일반) 대중 ⓐ 대중의, 대량의
● sedentary ⓐ 주로 앉아서 하는
● health risk 건강상 위험
● endless ⓐ 끝없는
● labor market 노동 시장
● realistic ⓐ 현실적인

구문 풀이
3행 Hundreds of millions of humans today work at jobs (that) they hate,
수식어   목적격 관계대명사
producing things [they have no love for.]
선행사

---

22 숙련된 학습자의 융통성   정답률 83% | 정답 ①

다음 글의 요지로 가장 적절한 것은?
✓ 숙련된 학습자는 상황에 맞는 학습 전략을 사용할 줄 안다.
② 선다형 시험과 논술 시험은 평가의 형태와 목적이 다르다.
③ 문화마다 특정 행사와 상황에 맞는 복장 규정이 있다.
④ 학습의 양보다는 학습의 질이 학업 성과를 좌우한다.
⑤ 학습 목표가 명확할수록 성취 수준이 높아진다.

When students are starting their college life, / they may approach every course, test, or learning task the same way, / using what we like to call "the rubber-stamp approach."
학생들이 대학 생활을 시작할 때 / 그들은 모든 과목, 시험, 또는 학습 과제를 똑같은 방식으로 접근하는지도 모른다. / 우리가 '고무도장 방식'이라고 부르고자 하는 방법을 이용하여

Think about it this way: / Would you wear a tuxedo to a baseball game? / A colorful dress to a funeral? / A bathing suit to religious services?
그것을 이렇게 생각해 보라. / 여러분은 야구 경기에 턱시도를 입고 가겠는가? / 장례식에 화려한 드레스를 입고 가겠는가? / 종교 예식에 수영복을 입고 가겠는가?
Probably not.
아마 아닐 것이다.
You know / there's appropriate dress for different occasions and settings.
여러분은 알고 있다. / 다양한 행사와 상황마다 적합한 옷이 있음을
Skillful learners know / that "putting on the same clothes" / won't work for every class.
숙련된 학습자는 알고 있다. / '같은 옷을 입는 것'이 / 모든 수업에 효과가 있지 않을 것이라는 걸
They are flexible learners.
그들은 유연한 학습자이다.
They have different strategies / and know when to use them.
그들은 다양한 전략을 갖고 있으며 / 그것을 언제 사용해야 하는지 안다.
They know / that you study for multiple-choice tests differently / than you study for essay tests.
그들은 안다. / 여러분이 선다형 시험은 다르게 학습한다는 것을 / 여러분이 논술 시험을 위해 학습하는 것과는
And they not only know what to do, / but they also know how to do it.
그리고 그들은 무엇을 해야 하는지 알고 있을 뿐만 아니라, / 그것을 어떻게 해야 하는지도 알고 있다.

대학 생활을 시작할 때 학생들은 우리가 '고무도장 방식(잘 살펴보지도 않고 무조건 승인 또는 처리하는 방식)'이라고 부르고자 하는 방법을 이용하여 모든 과목, 시험, 또는 학습 과제를 똑같은 방식으로 접근할지도 모른다. 그것을 이렇게 생각해 보라. 여러분은 야구 경기에 턱시도를 입고 가겠는가? 장례식에 화려한 드레스를 입고 가겠는가? 종교 예식에 수영복을 입고 가겠는가? 아마 아닐 것이다. 다양한 행사와 상황마다 적합한 옷이 있음을 여러분은 알고 있다. 숙련된 학습자는 '같은 옷을 입는 것'이 모든 수업에 효과가 있지 않을 것이라는 걸 알고 있다. 그들은 유연한 학습자이다. 그들은 다양한 전략을 갖고 있으며 그것을 언제 사용해야 하는지 안다. 그들은 선다형 시험은 논술 시험을 위해 학습하는 것과는 다르게 학습한다는 것을 안다. 그리고 그들은 무엇을 해야 하는지 알고 있을 뿐만 아니라, 그것을 어떻게 해야 하는지도 알고 있다.

Why? 왜 정답일까?
숙련된 학습자는 상황마다 적절한 학습 전략이 있음을 알고 이를 융통성 있게 사용한다(Skillful learners know that "putting on the same clothes" won't work for every class. They are flexible learners. They have different strategies and know when to use them.)는 내용이다. 따라서 글의 요지로 가장 적절한 것은 ① '숙련된 학습자는 상황에 맞는 학습 전략을 사용할 줄 안다.'이다.

- course ⓝ 수업, 강좌
- rubber-stamp ⓝ 고무도장, 잘 살펴보지도 않고 무조건 허가하는 사람
- colorful ⓐ 화려한, 색색의
- bathing suit 수영복
- appropriate ⓐ 적절한
- skillful ⓐ 숙련된
- strategy ⓝ 전략
- funeral ⓝ 장례식
- religious service 종교 의식
- occasion ⓝ 상황, 경우
- flexible ⓐ 융통성 있는
- multiple-choice test 객관식 시험, 선다형 시험

구문 풀이
1행 When students are starting their college life, they may approach every course, test, or learning task the same way, using what we like to call "the rubber-stamp approach."
분사구문 관계 →불완전한 문장
to call의 보어 대명사 (to call의 목적어가 없음)

★★★ 등급을 가르는 문제!
23 관광 산업이 성장한 배경 정답률 39% | 정답 ①
다음 글의 주제로 가장 적절한 것은?
☑ factors that caused tourism expansion – 관광 산업의 확장을 일으킨 요인
② discomfort at a popular tourist destination – 유명한 여행지에서의 불편
③ importance of tourism in society and economy – 사회와 경제에 관광 산업이 갖는 중요성
④ negative impacts of tourism on the environment – 관광 산업이 환경에 미치는 부정적 영향
⑤ various types of tourism and their characteristics – 다양한 유형의 관광 산업과 그 특징

As the social and economic situation of countries got better, / wage levels and working conditions improved.
국가들의 사회적 및 경제적 상황이 더 나아지면서, / 임금 수준과 근로 여건이 개선되었다.
Gradually / people were given more time off.
점차 / 사람들은 더 많은 휴가를 받게 되었다.
At the same time, / forms of transport improved / and it became faster and cheaper / to get to places.
동시에, / 운송 형태가 개선되었고 / 더 빠르고 더 저렴해졌다. / 장소를 이동하는 것이
England's industrial revolution / led to many of these changes.
영국의 산업 혁명이 / 이러한 변화 중 많은 것을 일으켰다.
Railways, / in the nineteenth century, / opened up now famous seaside resorts / such as Blackpool and Brighton.
철도는 / 19세기에, / 현재 유명한 해안가 리조트를 개업시켰다. / Blackpool과 Brighton 같은
With the railways / came many large hotels.
철도가 생기면서 / 많은 대형 호텔이 생겨났다.
In Canada, for example, / the new coast-to-coast railway system made possible / the building of such famous hotels / as Banff Springs and Chateau Lake Louise in the Rockies.
예를 들어, 캐나다에서는 / 새로운 대륙 횡단 철도 시스템이 가능하게 했다. / 그런 유명한 호텔 건설을 / 로키산맥의 Banff Springs와 Chateau Lake Louise 같은
Later, / the arrival of air transport / opened up more of the world / and led to tourism growth.
이후에 / 항공 운송의 출현은 / 세계의 더 많은 곳을 열어 주었고 / 관광 산업의 성장을 이끌었다.

국가들의 사회적 및 경제적 상황이 더 나아지면서, 임금 수준과 근로 여건이 개선되었다. 점차 사람들은 더 많은 휴가를 받게 되었다. 동시에, 운송 형태가 개선되었고 장소를 이동하는 것이 더 빠르고 더 저렴해졌다. 영국의 산업 혁명이 이러한 변화 중 많은 것을 일으켰다. 19세기에, 철도로 인해 Blackpool과 Brighton 같은 현재 유명한 해안가 리조트가 들어서게 되

었다. 철도가 생기면서 많은 대형 호텔이 생겨났다. 예를 들어, 캐나다에서는 새로운 대륙 횡단 철도 시스템이 로키산맥의 Banff Springs와 Chateau Lake Louise 같은 유명한 호텔 건설을 가능하게 했다. 이후에 항공 운송의 출현은 세계의 더 많은 곳(으로 가는 길)을 열어 주었고 관광 산업의 성장을 이끌었다.

Why? 왜 정답일까?
관광 산업의 성장(tourism growth)을 이끈 원인을 흐름에 따라 열거하는 글이다. 가장 먼저 사회경제적 상황이 개선되면서 임금 수준과 근로 조건이 개선되고, 이에 따라 여가가 늘어나고, 운송 사업이 발달하여 이동을 편하게 했다는 것이다. 따라서 글의 주제로 가장 적절한 것은 ① '관광 산업의 확장을 일으킨 요인'이다.

- wage ⓝ 임금
- improve ⓥ 향상되다
- time off 휴가
- industrial revolution 산업 혁명
- tourism ⓝ 관광(업)
- expansion ⓝ 확장
- tourist destination 관광지
- working condition 근무 조건
- gradually ⓐⓓ 차차, 점점
- transport ⓝ 운송, 이동
- lead to ~을 초래하다
- factor ⓝ 요인
- discomfort ⓝ 불편
- characteristic ⓝ 특징

구문 풀이
7행 In Canada, for example, the new coast-to-coast railway system made possible the building of such famous hotels as Banff Springs and Chateau Lake Louise in the Rockies.
동사
목적격 보어 목적어(길어서 뒤로 빠짐)

★★ 문제 해결 꿀~팁 ★★
▶ 많이 틀린 이유는?
사회경제적 변화 상황이 결국 '관광업의 성장'을 이끌었다는 결론이 글의 핵심이다. 따라서 첫 문장에 언급된 '사회와 경제'만 다소 두루뭉술하게 언급하는 ③은 답으로 부적합하다.
▶ 문제 해결 방법은?
시간 흐름에 따라 관광업의 성장을 이끈 배경 요인을 열거하는 글로, '그래서 결론이 무엇인지'를 파악하는 것이 중요하다.

24 성공적인 직업의 함정 정답률 67% | 정답 ②
다음 글의 제목으로 가장 적절한 것은?
① Don't Compete with Yourself – 자기 자신과 경쟁하지 말라
☑ A Trap of a Successful Career – 성공적인 직업의 함정
③ Create More Jobs for Young People – 젊은이들을 위해 더 많은 일자리를 창출하라
④ What Difficult Jobs Have in Common – 어려운 직업에는 어떤 공통점이 있는가
⑤ A Road Map for an Influential Employer – 영향력이 큰 고용주를 위한 지침

Success can lead you / off your intended path / and into a comfortable rut.
성공은 여러분을 이끌 수 있다. / 의도한 길에서 벗어나 / 틀에 박힌 편안한 생활로 들어가도록
If you are good at something / and are well rewarded for doing it, / you may want to keep doing it / even if you stop enjoying it.
여러분이 어떤 일을 잘하고 / 그 일을 하는 데 대한 보상을 잘 받는다면, / 여러분은 그걸 계속하고 싶을 수도 있다. / 여러분이 그것을 즐기지 않게 되더라도
The danger is / that one day you look around and realize / you're so deep in this comfortable rut / that you can no longer see the sun or breathe fresh air; / the sides of the rut have become so slippery / that it would take a superhuman effort / to climb out; / and, effectively, you're stuck.
위험한 점은 ~이다. / 어느 날 여러분이 주변을 둘러보고 깨닫게 된다는 것 / 여러분이 틀에 박힌 이 편안한 생활에 너무나 깊이 빠져 있어서 / 더는 태양을 보거나 신선한 공기를 호흡할 수 없다고 / 그 틀에 박힌 생활의 양쪽 면이 너무나 미끄럽게 되어 / 초인적인 노력이 필요할 것이라고 / 기어올라 나오려면 / 그리고 사실상 여러분이 꼼짝할 수 없다는 것을
And it's a situation / that many working people worry / they're in now.
그리고 이는 상황이다. / 많은 근로자가 걱정하는 / 현재 자신이 처해 있다고
The poor employment market / has left them feeling locked / in what may be a secure, or even well-paying — but ultimately unsatisfying — job.
열악한 고용 시장은 / 이들이 갇혀 있다고 느끼게 했다. / 안정적이거나 심지어 보수가 좋을 수도 있지만 궁극적으로는 만족스럽지 못한 일자리에

성공은 여러분이 의도한 길에서 벗어나 틀에 박힌 편안한 생활로 들어가도록 이끌 수 있다. 여러분이 어떤 일을 잘하고 그 일을 하는 데 대한 보상을 잘 받는다면, 그것을 즐기지 않게 되더라도 계속하고 싶을 수도 있다. 위험한 점은 어느 날 여러분이 주변을 둘러보고, 자신이 틀에 박힌 이 편안한 생활에 너무나 깊이 빠져 있어서 더는 태양을 보거나 신선한 공기를 호흡할 수 없으며, 그 틀에 박힌 생활의 양쪽 면이 너무나 미끄럽게 되어 기어올라 나오려면 초인적인 노력이 필요할 것이고, 사실상 자신이 꼼짝할 수 없다는 것을 깨닫게 된다는 것이다. 그리고 이는 많은 근로자가 현재 자신이 처해 있다고 걱정하는 상황이다. 열악한 고용 시장은 이들이 안정적이거나 심지어 보수가 좋을 수도 있지만 궁극적으로 만족스럽지 못한 일자리에 갇혀 있다고 느끼게 했다.

Why? 왜 정답일까?
첫 두 문장을 통해, 직업에서 성공하고 높은 보상을 누리게 된다면 그 일을 즐기지 않게 되거나 일에서의 만족을 느끼지 못하게 되더라도 그 일을 고수하게 된다(If you are good at something and are well rewarded for doing it, you may want to keep doing it even if you stop enjoying it.)는 주제를 파악할 수 있다. 따라서 글의 제목으로 가장 적절한 것은 ② '성공적인 직업의 함정'이다.

- intended ⓐ 의도된
- be rewarded for ~에 대해 보상받다
- slippery ⓐ 미끄러운
- superhuman ⓐ 초인적인
- be stuck 꼼짝 못하다
- well-paying ⓐ 보수가 좋은
- unsatisfying ⓐ 불만족스러운
- have ~ in common ~을 공통적으로 지니다
- rut ⓝ 틀에 박힌 생활
- breathe ⓥ 호흡하다
- take effort to ~하는 데 (…한) 노력이 들다
- effectively ⓐⓓ 실질적으로, 사실상
- employment ⓝ 고용
- ultimately ⓐⓓ 궁극적으로
- compete with ~와 경쟁하다
- influential ⓐ 영향력 있는

구문 풀이

8행 The poor employment market has left them feeling locked in [what may
be a secure, or even well-paying — but ultimately unsatisfying — job].
동사 ~~목적어~~ ~~목적격 보어(현재분사)~~ [ ]: in의 목적절
may be의 주격 보어

---

25 국내 출생자 수와 사망자 수의 변화 추이 정답률 74% | 정답 ⑤

다음 도표의 내용과 일치하지 <u>않는</u> 것은?

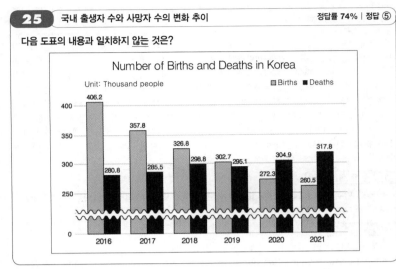

Number of Births and Deaths in Korea
Unit: Thousand people ☐ Births ■ Deaths

	2016	2017	2018	2019	2020	2021
Births	406.2	357.8	326.8	302.7	272.3	260.5
Deaths	280.8	285.5	298.8	295.1	304.9	317.8

The above graph shows the number of births and deaths in Korea / from 2016 to 2021.
위 그래프는 한국에서의 출생자 수와 사망자 수를 보여 준다. / 2016년부터 2021년까지
① The number of births / continued to decrease / throughout the whole period.
출생자 수는 / 계속 감소했다. / 전체 기간 내내
② The gap between the number of births and deaths / was the largest in 2016.
출생자 수와 사망자 수 사이의 차이는 / 2016년에 가장 컸다.
③ In 2019, / the gap between the number of births and deaths / was the smallest, / with the
number of births slightly larger than that of deaths.
2019년에는 / 출생자 수와 사망자 수 사이의 차이가 / 가장 작았는데, / 출생자 수가 사망자 수보다 약간 더 컸다.
④ The number of deaths / increased steadily during the whole period, / except the period
from 2018 to 2019.
사망자 수는 / 전체 기간 동안 꾸준히 증가했다. / 2018년과 2019년까지의 기간을 제외하고
☑ In 2021, / the number of deaths / was larger than that of births / for the first time.
2021년에는 / 사망자 수가 / 출생자 수보다 더 컸다. / 처음으로

위 그래프는 2016년부터 2021년까지 한국에서의 출생자 수와 사망자 수를 보여 준다. ① 출생자 수는 전체 기간 내내 계속 감소했다. ② 출생자 수와 사망자 수 사이의 차이는 2016년에 가장 컸다. ③ 2019년에는 출생자 수와 사망자 수 사이의 차이가 가장 작았는데, 출생자 수가 사망자 수보다 약간 더 컸다. ④ 사망자 수는 2018년과 2019년까지의 기간을 제외하고 전체 기간 동안 꾸준히 증가했다. ⑤ 2021년에는 처음으로 사망자 수가 출생자 수보다 더 컸다.

Why? 왜 정답일까?

도표에 따르면 한국의 사망자 수는 2020년에 이미 출생자 수를 추월했다. 따라서 도표와 일치하지 않는 것은 2021년에 사망자 수가 처음으로 출생자 수를 넘어섰다고 언급한 ⑤이다.

● decrease ⓥ 감소하다 ● gap between A and B A와 B 사이의 격차
● slightly ⓐⓓ 약간 ● steadily ⓐⓓ 꾸준히

구문 풀이

8행 In 2021, the number of deaths was larger than that of births for the first
time. 「비교급+than : ~보다 더 …한」 = the number

---

26 Lilian Bland의 생애 정답률 91% | 정답 ⑤

Lilian Bland에 관한 다음 글의 내용과 일치하지 <u>않는</u> 것은?
① 승마와 사냥 같은 모험적인 활동을 즐겼다.
② 스포츠와 야생 동물 사진작가로 경력을 시작했다.
③ 자신의 비행기를 설계하고 제작했다.
④ 자동차 판매원으로 일하기도 했다.
☑ 캐나다에서 생의 마지막 기간을 보냈다.

Lilian Bland was born in Kent, England in 1878.
Lilian Bland는 1878년 잉글랜드 Kent에서 태어났다.
「Unlike most other girls at the time / she wore trousers / and spent her time enjoying
adventurous activities / like horse riding and hunting.」 ①의 근거 일치
당시 대부분의 다른 여자아이와 달리 / 그녀는 바지를 입었고, / 모험적인 활동을 즐기며 시간을 보냈다. / 승마와 사냥 같은
「Lilian began her career / as a sports and wildlife photographer for British newspapers.」
Lilian은 경력을 시작했다. / 영국 신문사의 스포츠와 야생 동물 사진작가로 ②의 근거 일치
「In 1910 / she became the first woman / to design, build, and fly her own airplane.」 ③의 근거 일치
1910년에 / 그녀는 최초의 여성이 되었다. / 자신의 비행기를 설계하고 제작하고 비행한
In order to persuade her / to try a slightly safer activity, / Lilian's dad bought her a car.
그녀가 ~하도록 설득하고자 / 약간 더 안전한 활동을 하도록 / Lilian의 아버지는 그녀에게 자동차를 사주었다.
「Soon Lilian was a master driver / and ended up working as a car dealer.」 ④의 근거 일치
곧 Lilian은 뛰어난 운전자가 되었고 / 결국 자동차 판매원으로 일하게 되었다.
She never went back to flying / but lived a long and exciting life nonetheless.
그녀는 비행에 결코 다시 복귀하지 않았지만 / 그렇기는 해도 오랫동안 흥미진진한 삶을 살았다.
She married, moved to Canada, and had a kid.
그녀는 결혼하여 캐나다로 이주했고, 아이를 낳았다.
「Eventually, / she moved back to England, / and lived there for the rest of her life.」
결국 / 그녀는 잉글랜드로 돌아와 / 거기서 생의 마지막 기간을 보냈다. ⑤의 근거 불일치

Lilian Bland는 1878년 잉글랜드 Kent에서 태어났다. 당시 대부분의 다른 여자아이와 달리 그녀는 바지를 입었고, 승마와 사냥 같은 모험적인 활동을 즐기며 시간을 보냈다. Lilian은 영국 신문사의 스포츠와 야생 동물 사진작가로 경력을 시작했다. 1910년에 그녀는 자신의 비행기를 설계하고 제작하고 비행한 최초의 여성이 되었다. 그녀가 약간 더 안전한 활동을 하도록 설득하고자, Lilian의 아버지는 그녀에게 자동차를 사주었다. 곧 Lilian은 뛰어난 운전자가 되었고 결국 자동차 판매원으로 일하게 되었다. 그녀는 비행에 결코 다시 복귀하지 않았지만, 그렇기는 해도 오랫동안 흥미진진한 삶을 살았다. 그녀는 결혼하여 캐나다로 이주했고, 아이를 낳았다. 결국 그녀는 잉글랜드로 돌아와 거기서 생의 마지막 기간을 보냈다.

Why? 왜 정답일까?

'Eventually, she moved back to England, and lived there for the rest of her life.'에 따르면 Lilian Bland는 캐나다에서 살다가 잉글랜드로 돌아와 잉글랜드에서 생의 말년을 보냈다고 하므로, 내용과 일치하지 않는 것은 ⑤ '캐나다에서 생의 마지막 기간을 보냈다.'이다.

Why? 왜 오답일까?

① '~ spent her time enjoying adventurous activities like horse riding and hunting.'의 내용과 일치한다.
② 'Lilian began her career as a sports and wildlife photographer for British newspapers.'의 내용과 일치한다.
③ 'In 1910 she became the first woman to design, build, and fly her own airplane.'의 내용과 일치한다.
④ 'Soon Lilian ~ ended up working as a car dealer.'의 내용과 일치한다.

● unlike prep ~와 달리 ● adventurous ⓐ 모험적인
● wildlife ⓝ 야생 동물 ● photographer ⓝ 사진 작가
● persuade ⓥ 설득하다 ● end up ~ing 결국 ~하다
● car dealer 자동차 판매상 ● nonetheless ⓐⓓ 그럼에도 불구하고
● have a kid 자식을 낳다 ● the rest of ~의 나머지

구문 풀이

6행 In order to persuade her to try a slightly safer activity, Lilian's dad bought
her a car. 목적(~하기 위해서) 동사
간접목적어 직접목적어

---

27 잡지 기사 공모 정답률 93% | 정답 ③

Call for Articles에 관한 다음 안내문의 내용과 일치하지 <u>않는</u> 것은?
① 13세에서 18세까지의 누구나 참여할 수 있다.
② 기사는 고화질 컬러 사진을 포함해야 한다.
☑ 사진 한 장에 5센트씩 지급한다.
④ 전화번호를 원고와 함께 보내야 한다.
⑤ 원고를 이메일로 제출해야 한다.

Call for Articles
기사 모집
Do you want to get your stories published?
여러분의 이야기가 출간되기를 원하시나요?
New Dream Magazine is looking for future writers!
*New Dream Magazine*은 미래의 작가를 찾고 있습니다!
「This event is open to anyone aged 13 to 18.」 ①의 근거 일치
이 행사는 13세에서 18세까지 누구나 참여할 수 있습니다.
Articles
기사
Length of writing: 300 – 325 words
원고 길이: 300 ~ 325단어
「Articles should also include high-quality color photos.」 ②의 근거 일치
기사에는 또한 고화질 컬러 사진이 포함되어야 합니다.
Rewards
사례금
Five cents per word
단어당 5센트
「Five dollars per photo」 ③의 근거 불일치
사진당 5달러
Notes
주의 사항
「You should send us your phone number / together with your writing.」 ④의 근거 일치
여러분의 전화번호를 보내주셔야 합니다. / 원고와 함께
「Please email your writing to us / at article@ndmag.com.」 ⑤의 근거 일치
여러분의 원고를 저희에게 보내주세요. / 이메일 article@ndmag.com으로

기사 모집

여러분의 이야기가 출간되기를 원하시나요? *New Dream Magazine*은 미래의 작가를 찾고 있습니다! 이 행사는 13세에서 18세까지 누구나 참여할 수 있습니다.

기사
● 원고 길이: 300 ~ 325단어
● 기사에는 또한 고화질 컬러 사진이 포함되어야 합니다.

사례금
● 단어당 5센트
● 사진당 5달러

주의 사항
● 여러분의 전화번호를 원고와 함께 보내주셔야 합니다.
● 원고를 이메일 article@ndmag.com으로 보내주세요.

Why? 왜 정답일까?

'Five dollars per photo'에서 사진당 5달러가 지급된다고 하므로, 안내문의 내용과 일치하지 않는 것은 ③ '사진 한 장에 5센트씩 지급한다.'이다. 5센트는 단어당 정산되는 비용이다.

① 'This event is open to anyone aged 13 to 18.'의 내용과 일치한다.

② 'Articles should also include high-quality color photos.'의 내용과 일치한다.

④ 'You should send us your phone number together with your writing.'의 내용과 일치한다.

⑤ 'Please email your writing to us at article@ndmag.com.'의 내용과 일치한다.

- **publish** ⓥ 출간하다
- **high-quality** ⓐ 고품질의
- **article** ⓝ 기사

---

28 롤러스케이팅장 이용 안내 　　　　정답률 90% | 정답 ④

Greenhill Roller Skating에 관한 다음 안내문의 내용과 일치하는 것은?

① 오전 9시부터 오후 9시까지 운영한다.

② 이용료는 시간 제한 없이 1인당 8달러이다.

③ 입장하려면 예약이 필요하다.

☑④ 10세 미만 어린이는 어른과 동행해야 한다.

⑤ 추가 요금을 내면 롤러스케이트를 빌려준다.

Greenhill Roller Skating
Greenhill 롤러스케이팅

Join us for your chance / to enjoy roller skating!
기회를 함께 해요! / 롤러스케이팅을 즐길

Place: Greenhill Park, 351 Cypress Avenue
장소: Cypress Avenue 351번지 Greenhill Park

Dates: Friday, April 7 – Sunday, April 9
일자: 4월 7일 금요일 ~ 4월 9일 일요일

『Time: 9 a.m. – 6 p.m.』 ①의근거 불일치
시간: 오전 9시 ~ 오후 6시

『Fee: $8 per person for a 50-minute session』 ②의근거 불일치
요금: 50분간 1인당 8달러

Details
세부 사항

『Admission will be on a first-come, first-served basis / with no reservations.』 ③의근거 불일치
입장은 선착순입니다. / 예약 없이

『Children under the age of 10 / must be accompanied by an adult.』 ④의근거 일치
10세 미만의 어린이는 / 어른과 동행해야 합니다.

『We will lend you our roller skates for free.』 ⑤의근거 불일치
롤러스케이트는 무료로 빌려드립니다.

Contact the Community Center for more information at 013-234-6114.
더 많은 정보를 위해서 주민센터 013-234-6114로 연락하세요.

Greenhill 롤러스케이팅

롤러스케이팅을 즐길 기회를 함께 해요!

● 장소: Cypress Avenue 351번지 Greenhill Park

● 일자: 4월 7일 금요일 ~ 4월 9일 일요일

● 시간: 오전 9시 ~ 오후 6시

● 요금: 50분간 1인당 8달러

세부 사항

– 입장은 예약 없이 선착순입니다.

– 10세 미만의 어린이는 어른과 동행해야 합니다.

– 롤러스케이트는 무료로 빌려드립니다.

더 많은 정보를 위해서 주민센터 013-234-6114로 연락하세요.

Why? 왜 정답일까?

'Children under the age of 10 must be accompanied by an adult.'에서 10세 미만 어린이는 성인 동반이 필수라고 하므로, 안내문의 내용과 일치하는 것은 ④ '10세 미만 어린이는 어른과 동행해야 한다.'이다.

Why? 왜 오답일까?

① 'Time: 9 a.m. – 6 p.m.'에서 운영 시간은 오전 9시부터 오후 6시라고 하였다.

② 'Fee: $8 per person for a 50-minute session'에서 이용료 8달러에 스케이트장 이용은 50분으로 제한돼 있음을 알 수 있다.

③ 'Admission will be on a first-come, first-served basis with no reservations.'에서 입장은 예약이 필요 없이 선착순으로 이뤄진다고 하였다.

⑤ 'We will lend you our roller skates for free.'에서 롤러스케이트는 무료로 대여해준다고 하였다.

- **first-come, first-served** 선착순
- **for free** 공짜로
- **accompany** ⓥ 동반하다

---

29 동물에게 투영된 인간의 특징 　　　　정답률 62% | 정답 ⑤

다음 글의 밑줄 친 부분 중, 어법상 틀린 것은? [3점]

The most noticeable human characteristic / projected onto animals / is ① that they can talk in human language.
가장 눈에 띄는 인간의 특징은 / 동물에게 투영된 / 동물이 인간의 언어로 대화할 수 있다는 점이다.

Physically, / animal cartoon characters and toys ② made after animals / are also most often deformed / in such a way as to resemble humans.
신체적으로도, / 동물 만화 캐릭터와 장난감은 / 동물을 본떠 만든 / 또한 변형되는 경우가 아주 많다. / 인간을 닮는 그런 방식으로

This is achieved / by ③ showing them / with humanlike facial features / and deformed front legs to resemble human hands.
이것은 이뤄진다. / 그들을 보여줌으로써 / 인간과 같은 얼굴 특징을 갖고 있는 / 그리고 사람의 손을 닮게 변형된 앞다리를

In more recent animated movies / the trend has been / to show the animals in a more "natural" way.
더 최근의 만화 영화에서 / 추세는 ~였다. / 동물을 더 '자연스러운' 방식으로 묘사하는 것

However, / they still use their front legs / ④ like human hands / (for example, lions can pick up and lift small objects with one paw), / and they still talk with an appropriate facial expression.
그러나 / 이 동물들은 여전히 앞다리를 사용하고, / 사람 손처럼 / (가령 사자가 한 발로 작은 물체를 집어들 수 있는 것처럼) / 그리고 그들은 여전히 적절한 표정을 지으며 이야기한다.

A general strategy / that is used to make the animal characters more emotionally appealing, / both to children and adults, / ☑ is to give them enlarged and deformed childlike features.
일반적인 전략은 / 동물 캐릭터를 더 감정적으로 매력적이게 만들기 위해 이용하는 / 아이와 어른 모두에게 / 그것들에 확대되고 변형된 어린이 같은 특징을 부여하는 것이다.

동물에게 투영된 가장 눈에 띄는 인간의 특징은 동물이 인간의 언어로 대화할 수 있다는 점이다. 신체적으로도, 동물 만화 캐릭터와 동물을 본떠 만든 장난감은 또한 인간을 닮도록 변형되는 경우가 아주 많다. 이것은 그들이 인간과 같은 얼굴 특징과 사람의 손을 닮게 변형된 앞다리를 갖고 있는 모습을 보여줌으로써 이뤄진다. 더 최근의 만화 영화에서 추세는 동물을 더 '자연스러운' 방식으로 묘사하는 것이었다. 그러나 이 동물들은 여전히 사람 손처럼 (가령 사자가 한 발로 작은 물체를 집어들 수 있는 것처럼) 앞다리를 사용하고, 여전히 적절한 표정을 지으며 이야기한다. 동물 캐릭터를 아이와 어른 모두에게 더 감정적으로 매력적이게 만들기 위해 이용하는 일반적인 전략은 그것들에 확대되고 변형된 어린이 같은 특징을 부여하는 것이다.

Why? 왜 정답일까?

핵심 주어가 단수 명사인 **A general strategy**이므로, 동사 또한 복수형인 are 대신 단수형인 is를 쓰는 것이 적합하다. 따라서 어법상 틀린 것은 ⑤이다.

Why? 왜 오답일까?

① 주격 보어 역할의 명사절을 이끌기 위해 접속사 that을 썼다.

② animal cartoon characters and toys가 '만들어지는' 대상이므로 과거분사 made를 사용해 꾸몄다.

③ 전치사 by 뒤에 목적어로 동명사 showing을 썼다.

④ 뒤에 명사구인 human hands가 나오는 것으로 보아 전치사 like(~처럼)가 적절하게 쓰였다.

- **noticeable** ⓐ 눈에 띄는, 두드러지는
- **project onto** ~에게 투영시키다
- **deform** ⓥ 변형하다
- **resemble** ⓥ ~와 닮다
- **natural** ⓐ 자연스러운
- **emotionally** ⓐ 정서적으로
- **enlarge** ⓥ 확대하다
- **characteristic** ⓝ 특징
- **cartoon character** 만화 캐릭터
- **in such a way as to** ~한 방식으로
- **humanlike** ⓐ 인간 같은
- **paw** ⓝ (동물의) 발
- **appealing** ⓐ 매력적인
- **feature** ⓝ 특징, 이목구비

구문 풀이

2행 Physically, <u>animal cartoon characters and toys</u> <u>made after animals</u> <u>are also most often deformed</u> <u>in such a way as to resemble humans</u>.
　주어　　　　　　　　　과거분사구　　　동사구(수동태)　　　~하는 (그런) 식으로

★★★ 등급을 가르는 문제!

30 생산이 곧 수요 창출과 이득으로 이어지지 않는 시대 　　　　정답률 39% | 정답 ④

다음 글의 밑줄 친 부분 중, 문맥상 낱말의 쓰임이 적절하지 않은 것은? [3점]

The major philosophical shift in the idea of selling / came / when industrial societies became more affluent, / more competitive, / and more geographically spread out / during the 1940s and 1950s.
판매 개념에서의 주요한 철학적 변화가 / 일어났다. / 산업 사회가 더 부유해지고, / 더 경쟁적이 되고, / 지리적으로 더 확산되면서 / 1940년대와 1950년대 동안

This forced business / to develop ① closer relations with buyers and clients, / which in turn made business realize / that it was not enough / to produce a quality product at a reasonable price.
이로 인해 기업은 / ~해야 했고 / 구매자 및 고객과 더 긴밀한 관계를 발전시켜야 / 이것은 결과적으로 기업이 깨닫게 했다. / 충분하지 않다는 것을 / 합리적인 가격에 양질의 제품을 생산하는 것으로는

In fact, / it was equally ② essential / to deliver products / that customers actually wanted.
사실, / 마찬가지로 매우 중요했다. / 제품을 내놓는 것이 / 고객이 실제로 원하는

Henry Ford produced his best-selling T-model Ford / in one color only (black) / in 1908, / but in modern societies / this was no longer ③ possible.
Henry Ford는 가장 많이 팔렸던 T-모델 Ford를 생산했지만, / 한 가지 색상(검은색)으로만 / 1908년에 / 현대 사회에서는 / 이것이 더 이상 가능하지 않았다.

The modernization of society / led to a marketing revolution / that ☑ destroyed the view / that production would create its own demand.
사회의 현대화는 / 마케팅 혁명으로 이어졌다. / 견해를 파괴한 / 생산이 그 자체의 수요를 창출할 것이라는

Customers, / and the desire to ⑤ meet their diverse and often complex needs, / became the focus of business.
고객 / 그리고 이들의 다양하고 흔히 복잡한 욕구를 충족하고자 하는 욕망이 / 기업의 초점이 되었다.

산업 사회가 1940년대와 1950년대 동안 더 부유해지고, 더 경쟁적이 되고, 지리적으로 더 확산되면서 판매 개념에 주요한 철학적 변화가 일어났다. 이로 인해 기업은 구매자 및 고객과 ① 더 긴밀한 관계를 발전시켜야 했고, 이것은 결과적으로 기업이 합리적인 가격에 양질의 제품을 생산하는 것으로는 충분하지 않다는 것을 깨닫게 했다. 사실, 고객이 실제로 원하는 제품을 내놓는 것이 마찬가지로 ② 매우 중요했다. 1908년에 Henry Ford는 가장 많이 팔렸던 T-모델 Ford를 한 가지 색상(검은색)으로만 생산했지만, 현대 사회에서는 이것이 더 이상 ③ 가능하지 않았다. 사회의 현대화는 생산이 그 자체의 수요를 창출할 것이라는 견해를 ④ 강화한(→ 파괴한) 마케팅 혁명으로 이어졌다. 고객과 이들의 다양하고 흔히 복잡한 욕구를 ⑤ 충족하고자 하는 욕망이 기업의 초점이 되었다.

Why? 왜 정답일까?

현대 사회에 이르러 사람들이 전체적으로 풍족해지고 기업 간 경쟁이 치열해지면서, 합리적인 비용의 대량 생산으로 이득을 보던 시대는 지나고 고객마다의 다양한 수요에 부응할 필요성이 커졌다는 내용이다. ④가 포함된 문장 앞에서, 과거에는 Ford 처럼 한 가지 색상만으로 제품을 생산해도 괜찮았지만 현대 사회에서는 이것이 '가능하지' 않다고 한다. 이 뒤에는 생산만으로 수요가 창출되리라는 기대가 '무너졌

다'가 설명이 이어져야 적합하므로, ④의 **strengthened**를 **destroyed**로 고쳐야 한다. 따라서 문맥상 낱말의 쓰임이 적절하지 않은 것은 ④이다.

- **philosophical** ⓐ 철학적인
- **industrial** ⓐ 산업의
- **geographically** ⓐⓓ 지리적으로
- **in turn** 결과적으로
- **best-selling** ⓐ 가장 많이 팔리는, 베스트셀러인
- **revolution** ⓝ 혁명
- **complex** ⓐ 복잡한
- **shift** ⓝ 변화, 전환 ⓥ 바뀌다
- **affluent** ⓐ 부유한
- **spread** ⓥ 퍼지다
- **essential** ⓐ 매우 중요한
- **modernization** ⓝ 현대화
- **strengthen** ⓥ 강화하다

구문 풀이

3행 [This forced business to develop closer relations with buyers and clients], [ ]:선행사
which in turn made business realize that it was not enough to produce a quality
계속적 용법　사역동사　　원형부정사　가주어　　　진주어
product at a reasonable price.

★★ 문제 해결 꿀~팁 ★★

▶ 많이 틀린 이유는?
T-model Ford가 한 가지 색상으로 출시된 것이 어떤 예시인지 파악해야 한다. 색상을 한 가지로만 출시해도 차가 잘 팔렸다는 것은, 과거에는 '그저 질 좋은 제품을 합리적인 가격에 제공하는 것으로 족했다'는 의미와 같다. 하지만 지금은 상황이 달라져서, 이러한 전략이 더 이상(no longer) '가능하지' 않다는 의미로 ③은 자연스럽다.

▶ 문제 해결 방법은?
Ford 차의 예시를 일반화한 표현이 바로 'production would create its own demand'이다. 즉 '생산만으로 수요가 만들어지고 제품이 팔리는' 상황을 가리키는 것이다. 오늘날에는 이런 상황이나 견해가 '강화되는' 것이 아니라 점점 '깨지고' 있다는 것이 글의 주제이다.

---

31 비행 방향에 따른 시차 피로 차이 정답률 55% | 정답 ①

다음 빈칸에 들어갈 말로 가장 적절한 것을 고르시오.
- ✓ ① direction – 방향
- ② purpose – 목적
- ③ season – 계절
- ④ length – 길이
- ⑤ cost – 비용

People differ / in how quickly they can reset their biological clocks / to overcome jet lag, / and the speed of recovery depends on the direction of travel.
사람마다 서로 다르며, / 체내 시계를 얼마나 빨리 재설정할 수 있는지에 있어서 / 시차로 인한 피로감을 극복하기 위해서 / 그 회복 속도는 이동의 방향에 달려 있다.

Generally, / it's easier / to fly westward and lengthen your day / than it is to fly eastward and shorten it.
일반적으로, / 더 쉽다. / 서쪽으로 비행하여 여러분의 하루를 연장하는 것이 / 동쪽으로 비행하여 하루를 단축하는 것보다

This east-west difference in jet lag / is sizable enough / to have an impact on the performance of sports teams.
시차로 인한 피로감에 있어 이러한 동서의 차이는 / 충분히 크다. / 스포츠 팀의 경기력에 영향을 미칠 만큼

Studies have found / that teams flying westward perform significantly better / than teams flying eastward / in professional baseball and college football.
연구는 밝혔다. / 서쪽으로 비행하는 팀이 상당히 더 잘한다고 / 동쪽으로 비행하는 팀보다 / 프로 야구와 대학 미식 축구에서

A more recent study of more than 46,000 Major League Baseball games / found additional evidence / that eastward travel is tougher than westward travel.
46,000건 이상의 메이저 리그 야구 경기에 관한 더 최근의 연구에서는 / 추가적인 증거를 발견했다. / 동쪽으로 이동하는 것이 서쪽으로 이동하는 것보다 더 힘들다는

시차로 인한 피로감을 극복하기 위해서 체내 시계를 얼마나 빨리 재설정할 수 있는지는 사람마다 서로 다르며, 그 회복 속도는 이동의 방향에 달려 있다. 일반적으로 동쪽으로 비행하여 하루를 단축하는 것보다 서쪽으로 비행해 하루를 연장하는 것이 더 쉽다. 시차로 인한 피로감에서 이러한 동서의 차이는 스포츠 팀의 경기력에 영향을 미칠 만큼 충분히 크다. 연구에 따르면 서쪽으로 비행하는 팀이 동쪽으로 비행하는 팀보다 프로 야구와 대학 미식 축구에서 상당히 더 잘한다. 46,000건 이상의 메이저 리그 야구 경기에 관한 더 최근의 연구에서는 동쪽으로 이동하는 것이 서쪽으로 이동하는 것보다 더 힘들다는 추가적인 증거를 발견했다.

Why? 왜 정답일까?
빈칸 뒤에서 동쪽으로 이동해 하루를 줄이게 되는 경우보다 서쪽으로 이동해 하루를 연장하게 되는 경우 시차 회복이 더 쉽다고 한다(Generally, it's easier to fly westward and lengthen your day than it is to fly eastward and shorten it.). 즉, 이동의 '방향'이 중요하다는 글이므로, 빈칸에 들어갈 말로 가장 적절한 것은 ① '방향'이다.

- **biological clock** 체내 시계
- **jet lag** 시차로 인한 피로감
- **lengthen** ⓥ 연장하다
- **sizable** ⓐ 꽤 큰, 상당한
- **performance** ⓝ (선수의) 경기력, 수행, 성과
- **additional** ⓐ 추가적인
- **overcome** ⓥ 극복하다
- **depend on** ~에 좌우되다
- **shorten** ⓥ 단축하다
- **have an impact on** ~에 영향을 주다
- **significantly** ⓐⓓ 상당히, 현저히

구문 풀이

4행 This east-west difference in jet lag is **sizable enough to have an impact**
「형/부+enough+to부정사: ~할 만큼 충분히 …한」
on the performance of sports teams.

---

32 일 처리에 걸리는 시간 제대로 파악하기 정답률 54% | 정답 ③

다음 빈칸에 들어갈 말로 가장 적절한 것을 고르시오.
- ① what benefits you can get – 여러분이 어떤 이득을 얻을 수 있는지
- ② how practical your tasks are – 여러분의 과업이 얼마나 현실성 있는지
- ✓ ③ how long things are going to take – 일에 시간이 얼마나 오래 걸릴지
- ④ why failures are meaningful in life – 실패가 왜 인생에서 의미가 있는지
- ⑤ why your leisure time should come first – 왜 여러분의 여가 시간이 가장 우선이어야 하는지

If you want the confidence / that comes from achieving / what you set out to do each day, / then it's important / to understand how long things are going to take.
만약 여러분이 자신감을 원한다면 / 성취해 얻어지는 / 매일 여러분이 하고자 착수하는 일을 / 그러면 중요하다. / 일에 시간이 얼마나 오래 걸릴지 아는 것이

Over-optimism about what can be achieved / within a certain time frame / is a problem.
성취될 수 있는 것에 대한 지나친 낙관주의는 / 어떤 특정 기간 내에 / 문제다.

So work on it. // Make a practice of estimating the amount of time needed / alongside items on your 'things to do' list, / and learn by experience / when tasks take a greater or lesser time than expected.
그러므로 그것을 개선하려고 노력하라. // 필요한 시간의 양을 추산하는 것을 습관화하고, / '해야 할 일' 목록에 있는 항목과 함께, / 경험을 통해 배우라. / 언제 과제가 예상보다 더 많은 시간 또는 더 적은 시간을 필요로 하는지

Give attention / also to fitting the task to the available time.
주의를 기울이라. / 그 이용 가능한 시간에 과제를 맞추는 것에도 또한

There are some tasks / that you can only set about / if you have a significant amount of time available.
몇몇 과제가 있다. / 여러분이 비로소 시작할 수 있는 / 여러분이 이용할 시간이 상당히 많아야만

There is no point / in trying to gear up for such a task / when you only have a short period available.
무의미하다. / 그런 과제를 위해 준비하려 애쓰는 것은 / 여러분에게 이용 가능한 시간이 얼마 없을 때

So schedule the time / you need for the longer tasks / and put the short tasks into the spare moments in between.
그러므로 시간을 계획하라, / 여러분이 시간이 더 오래 걸리는 과제에 필요로 하는 / 그리고 그 사이 남는 시간에 시간이 짧게 걸리는 과제를 배치하라.

만약 매일 하고자 착수하는 일을 성취해 얻어지는 자신감을 원한다면 일에 시간이 얼마나 오래 걸릴지 아는 것이 중요하다. 어떤 특정 기간 내에 성취될 수 있는 것에 대한 지나친 낙관주의는 문제다. 그러므로 그것을 개선하려고 노력하라. '해야 할 일' 목록에 있는 항목과 함께, 필요한 시간의 양을 추산하는 것을 습관화하고, 언제 과제에 예상보다 더 많고 또 더 적은 시간이 걸리는지 경험을 통해 배우라. 그 이용 가능한 시간에 과제를 맞추는 것에도 또한 주의를 기울이라. 이용할 시간이 상당히 많아야만 시작할 수 있는 몇몇 과제가 있다. 여러분에게 이용 가능한 시간이 얼마 없을 때 그런 과제를 위해 준비하려 애쓰는 것은 무의미하다. 그러므로 시간이 더 오래 걸리는 과제에 필요한 시간을 계획하고, 그 사이 남는 시간에 시간이 짧게 걸리는 과제를 배치하라.

Why? 왜 정답일까?
과업을 끝내는 데 걸리는 시간을 정확히 추산하고 계획할 줄 알아야 한다(Make a practice of estimating the amount of time needed ~)는 내용의 글이므로, 빈칸에 들어갈 말로 가장 적절한 것은 ③ '일에 시간이 얼마나 오래 걸릴지'이다.

- **confidence** ⓝ 자신감
- **time frame** (어떤 일에 쓸 수 있는) 시간(대)
- **make a practice of** ~을 습관으로 하다
- **learn by experience** 경험을 통해 배우다
- **set about** ~을 시작하다
- **gear up** 준비를 갖추다, 대비하다
- **set out** 착수하다
- **work on** ~에 공을 들이다
- **estimate** ⓥ 추산하다
- **fit** ⓥ ~에 맞추다
- **there is no point in** ~하는 것은 의미가 없다
- **practical** ⓐ 현실성 있는, 타당한

구문 풀이

10행 There is **no point in** trying to **gear up** for such a task when you only have
「there is no point in+동명사 : ~해봐야 의미가 없다」
a short period available.

★★★ 등급을 가르는 문제!
33 진화가 거듭되어도 상황이 변하지 않는 까닭 정답률 47% | 정답 ①

다음 빈칸에 들어갈 말로 가장 적절한 것을 고르시오. [3점]
- ✓ ① just stay in place – 제자리에 머무를 뿐이다
- ② end up walking slowly – 결국 느리게 걷게 된다
- ③ never run into each other – 결코 서로 마주치지 않는다
- ④ won't be able to adapt to changes – 변화에 적응할 수 없을 것이다
- ⑤ cannot run faster than their parents – 자기 부모보다 더 빨리 달릴 수 없다

In Lewis Carroll's *Through the Looking-Glass*, / the Red Queen takes Alice / on a race through the countryside.
Lewis Carroll의 *Through the Looking-Glass*에서 / 붉은 여왕은 Alice를 데리고 간다. / 시골을 통과하는 한 경주에

They run and they run, / but then Alice discovers / that they're still under the same tree / that they started from.
그들은 달리고 또 달리는데, / 그러다 Alice는 발견한다. / 그들이 나무 아래에 여전히 있음을 / 자신들이 출발했던

The Red Queen explains to Alice: / "*here*, you see, / it takes all the running you can do, / to keep in the same place."
붉은 여왕은 Alice에게 설명한다. / "*여기서는* 네가 보다시피 / 네가 할 수 있는 모든 뜀박질을 해야 한단다. / 같은 장소에 머물러 있으려면"이라고

Biologists sometimes use this Red Queen Effect / to explain an evolutionary principle.
생물학자들은 때때로 이 '붉은 여왕 효과'를 사용한다 / 진화의 원리를 설명하기 위해.

If foxes evolve to run faster / so they can catch more rabbits, / then only the fastest rabbits will live long enough / to make a new generation of bunnies / that run even faster / — in which case, of course, / only the fastest foxes will catch enough rabbits / to thrive and pass on their genes.
만약 여우가 더 빨리 달리게 진화한다면, / 그들이 더 많은 토끼를 잡기 위해 / 그러면 가장 빠른 토끼만이 충분히 오래 살아 / 새로운 세대의 토끼를 낳을 텐데, / 훨씬 더 빨리 달리는 / 이 경우 당연히도 / 가장 빠른 여우만이 충분한 토끼를 잡을 것이다 / 번성하여 자신들의 유전자를 물려줄 만큼.

Even though they might run, / the two species just stay in place.
그들이 달린다 해도 / 그 두 종은 제자리에 머무를 뿐이다.

Lewis Carroll의 *Through the Looking-Glass*에서, 붉은 여왕은 Alice를 데리고 시골을 통과하는 한 경주에 간다. 그들은 달리고 또 달리는데, 그러다 Alice는 자신들이 출발했던 나무 아래에 여전히 있음을 발견한다. 붉은 여왕은 Alice에게 "*여기서는 보다시피 같은 장소에 머물러 있으려면 네가 할 수 있는 모든 뜀박질을 해야 한단다.*"라고 설명한다. 생물학자들은 때때로 이 '붉은 여왕 효과'를 사용해 진화의 원리를 설명한다. 만약 여우가 더 많은 토끼를 잡기 위해 더 빨리 달리게 진화한다면, 가장 빠른 토끼만이 충분히 오래 살아 훨씬 더 빨리 달리는

새로운 세대의 토끼를 낳을 텐데, 이 경우 당연히도 가장 빠른 여우만이 충분한 토끼를 잡아 번성하여 자신들의 유전자를 물려줄 것이다. 그 두 종은 달린다 해도 제자리에 머무를 뿐이다.

Why? 왜 정답일까?

원래 있던 자리를 유지하기 위해 전력 질주해야 하는(~ it takes all the running you can do, to keep in the same place.) 소설 속 상황에 빗대어 진화의 원리를 설명하는 글이다. 마지막 문장 앞에 제시된 여우와 토끼의 예시에 따르면, 여우가 토끼를 더 많이 잡기 위해 달리기가 빨라지도록 진화하면, 그 여우보다도 빠른 토끼만이 살아남아 번식하게 되므로 토끼 또한 더 빨라지도록 진화하게 된다. 이것은 다시 여우의 달리기가 더 빨라지게 하는 원인으로 작용하므로, 결과적으로 두 종의 상황은 시간이 지나도 차이가 없다. 따라서 빈칸에 들어갈 말로 가장 적절한 것은 ① '제자리에 머무를 뿐이다'이다.

- discover ⓥ 발견하다
- evolutionary ⓐ 진화적인
- generation ⓝ 세대
- pass on 물려주다
- species ⓝ (생물) 종
- adapt to ~에 적응하다
- biologist ⓝ 생물학자
- principle ⓝ 원리
- thrive ⓥ 번성하다
- gene ⓝ 유전자
- run into ~을 우연히 만나다

구문 풀이

2행 They run and they run, but then Alice discovers that they're still under
접속사
the same tree that they started from.
선행사(the same + 명) └ 목적격 관계대명사

★★ 문제 해결 꿀~팁 ★★

▶ 많이 틀린 이유는?
여우가 토끼를 더 많이 잡기 위해 더 빨리 뛰도록 진화해도, 토끼 또한 똑같이 진화하기 때문에 결국 둘 다 '제자리에 있는' 셈이라는 것이 글의 결론이다. ③은 두 동물이 '서로 절대 우연히 만나지 않는다'는 의미로, run이 있어 혼동될 수 있지만 의미상 연관이 없다.

▶ 문제 해결 방법은?
글에 인용구가 나오면 주제와 연관되는 경우가 많다. 여기서도 인용구 안의 to keep in the same place가 주제를 가리키는 핵심 표현이다.

34 머릿속 아이디어일 때 이미 완성된 미래   정답률 53% | 정답 ②

다음 빈칸에 들어갈 말로 가장 적절한 것을 고르시오. [3점]

① didn't even have the potential to accomplish – 성취할 잠재력조차 지니고 있지 않았던
✔ have mentally concluded about the future – 미래에 대해 머릿속에서 완성한
③ haven't been able to picture in our mind – (전에는) 머릿속에 그릴 수 없었던
④ considered careless and irresponsible – 조심성 없고 무책임하다고 여겼던
⑤ have observed in some professionals – 몇몇 전문가에게서 관찰해 낸

Everything in the world around us / was finished in the mind of its creator / before it was started.
우리 주변 세상의 모든 것은 / 그것을 만들어 낸 사람의 마음속에서 완성되었다 / 그것이 시작되기 전에
The houses we live in, / the cars we drive, / and our clothing / — all of these began with an idea.
우리가 사는 집, / 우리가 운전하는 자동차, / 우리 옷, / 이 모든 것이 아이디어에서 시작했다.
Each idea was then studied, refined and perfected / before the first nail was driven / or the first piece of cloth was cut.
각각의 아이디어는 그런 다음 연구되고, 다듬어지고, 완성되었다 / 첫 번째 못이 박히거나 / 첫 번째 천 조각이 재단되기에 앞서
Long before the idea was turned into a physical reality, / the mind had clearly pictured the finished product.
그 아이디어가 물리적 실체로 바뀌기 훨씬 전에 / 마음은 완제품을 분명하게 그렸다.
The human being designs his or her own future / through much the same process.
인간은 자신의 미래를 설계한다 / 거의 똑같은 과정을 통해
We begin with an idea / about how the future will be.
우리는 아이디어로 시작한다 / 미래가 어떨지에 대한
Over a period of time / we refine and perfect the vision.
일정 기간에 걸쳐서 / 우리는 그 비전을 다듬어 완성한다.
Before long, / our every thought, decision and activity / are all working in harmony / to bring into existence / what we have mentally concluded about the future.
머지않아, / 우리의 모든 생각, 결정, 활동은 / 모두 조화롭게 작용하게 된다 / 생겨나게 하려고 / 우리가 미래에 대해 머릿속에서 완성한 것을

우리 주변 세상의 모든 것은 시작되기 전에 그것을 만들어 낸 사람의 마음속에서 완성되었다. 우리가 사는 집, 우리가 운전하는 자동차, 우리 옷, 이 모든 것이 아이디어에서 시작했다. 각각의 아이디어는 그런 다음 첫 번째 못이 박히거나 첫 번째 천 조각이 재단되기에 앞서 연구되고, 다듬어지고, 완성되었다. 그 아이디어가 물리적 실체로 바뀌기 훨씬 전에 마음은 완제품을 분명하게 그렸다. 인간은 거의 똑같은 과정을 통해 자신의 미래를 설계한다. 우리는 미래가 어떨지에 대한 아이디어로 시작한다. 일정 기간에 걸쳐서 우리는 그 비전을 다듬어 완성한다. 머지않아, 우리의 모든 생각, 결정, 활동은 우리가 미래에 대해 머릿속에서 완성한 것을 생겨나게 하려고 모두 조화롭게 작용하게 된다.

Why? 왜 정답일까?

첫 문장에서 세상 모든 것은 실체가 있기 이전에 머릿속에서 이미 완성된 아이디어(finished in the mind of its creator)였다고 설명하는데, 글 중반부에서 우리 미래 역시 같은 식으로 설계된다고 말한다. 즉, 처음에 '이미 머릿속에서 만들어진' 아이디어가 다듬어지고 구현되는 과정이 똑같이 진행된다는 의미로, 빈칸에 들어갈 말로 가장 적절한 것은 ② '미래에 대해 머릿속에서 완성한'이다.

- clothing ⓝ 옷, 의복
- perfect ⓥ 완성하다, 완벽하게 하다
- turn A into B A를 B로 바꾸다
- process ⓝ 과정
- before long 머지않아
- bring into existence ~을 생겨나게 하다
- careless ⓐ 조심성 없는
- professional ⓝ 전문가 ⓐ 전문적인
- refine ⓥ 다듬다
- nail ⓝ 못
- picture ⓥ 상상하다, 그리다
- over a period of time 일정 기간에 걸쳐서
- in harmony 조화롭게
- mentally [ad] 머릿속에, 마음속으로
- irresponsible ⓐ 무책임한

구문 풀이

1행 Everything in the world around us was finished in the mind of its creator
주어(every-)   동사(단수)
before it was started.

35 서술자에 따라 다르게 이해되는 이야기   정답률 61% | 정답 ④

다음 글에서 전체 흐름과 관계 없는 문장은?

Whose story it is / affects *what* the story is.
누구의 이야기인지가 / 무슨 이야기인지에 영향을 미친다.
Change the main character, / and the focus of the story must also change.
주인공을 바꿔보라, / 그러면 이야기의 초점도 틀림없이 바뀐다.
If we look at the events through another character's eyes, / we will interpret them differently.
만약 우리가 다른 등장인물의 눈을 통해 사건을 본다면, / 우리는 그것을 다르게 해석할 것이다.
① We'll place our sympathies with someone new.
우리는 새로운 누군가에게 공감할 것이다.
② When the conflict arises / that is the heart of the story, / we will be praying for a different outcome.
갈등이 발생할 때, / 이야기의 핵심인 / 우리는 다른 결과를 간절히 바랄 것이다.
③ Consider, for example, / how the tale of Cinderella would shift / if told from the viewpoint of an evil stepsister.
예컨대, 생각해 보라 / 신데렐라 이야기가 어떻게 바뀔지 / 사악한 의붓자매의 관점에서 이야기된다면
✔ We know / Cinderella's kingdom does not exist, / but we willingly go there anyway.
우리는 알지만, / 신데렐라의 왕국이 존재하지 않는다는 것을 / 어쨌든 우리는 기꺼이 그곳에 간다.
⑤ *Gone with the Wind* is Scarlett O'Hara's story, / but what if we were shown the same events / from the viewpoint of Rhett Butler or Melanie Wilkes?
*Gone with the Wind*는 Scarlett O'Hara의 이야기이지만, / 만약 같은 사건이 우리에게 제시된다면 어떠할 것인가? / Rhett Butler나 Melanie Wilkes의 관점에서

누구의 이야기인지가 무슨 이야기인지에 영향을 미친다. 주인공을 바꾸면, 이야기의 초점도 틀림없이 바뀐다. 만약 우리가 다른 등장인물의 눈을 통해 사건을 본다면, 우리는 그것을 다르게 해석할 것이다. ① 우리는 새로운 누군가에게 공감할 것이다. ② 이야기의 핵심인 갈등이 발생할 때, 우리는 다른 결과를 간절히 바랄 것이다. ③ 예컨대, 신데렐라 이야기가 사악한 의붓자매의 관점에서 이야기된다면 어떻게 바뀔지 생각해 보라. ④ 우리는 신데렐라의 왕국이 존재하지 않는다는 것을 알지만, 어쨌든 기꺼이 그곳에 간다. ⑤ *Gone with the Wind*는 Scarlett O'Hara의 이야기이지만, 만약 같은 사건이 Rhett Butler나 Melanie Wilkes의 관점에서 우리에게 제시된다면 어떠할 것인가?

Why? 왜 정답일까?

이야기의 주인공이 누구인가에 따라 이야기 내용이 다르게 받아들여진다는 내용인데, ④는 Cinderella의 왕국에 관해서만 지엽적으로 언급하고 있다. 따라서 전체 흐름과 관계 없는 문장은 ④이다.

- affect ⓥ 영향을 미치다
- sympathy ⓝ 공감
- arise ⓥ 발생하다
- outcome ⓝ 결과
- shift ⓥ 바꾸다
- evil ⓐ 사악한 ⓝ 악
- kingdom ⓝ 왕국
- interpret ⓥ 해석하다, 이해하다
- conflict ⓝ 갈등
- pray for ~을 위해 기도하다
- tale ⓝ 이야기
- viewpoint ⓝ 관점
- stepsister ⓝ 의붓자매
- willingly [ad] 기꺼이

구문 풀이

6행 Consider, for example, [how the tale of Cinderella would shift if told from
명령문(~하라)   [ ] : 목적어   접속사 + 과거분사(~한다면)
the viewpoint of an evil stepsister].

★★★ 등급을 가르는 문제!

36 농경 생활로 인한 인간 사회의 변화   정답률 36% | 정답 ④

주어진 글 다음에 이어질 글의 순서로 가장 적절한 것을 고르시오.

① (A) − (C) − (B)
② (B) − (A) − (C)
③ (B) − (C) − (A)
✔ (C) − (A) − (B)
⑤ (C) − (B) − (A)

In the Old Stone Age, / small bands of 20 to 60 people / wandered from place to place / in search of food.
구석기 시대에는 / 20 ~ 60명의 작은 무리가 / 여기저기 돌아다녔다 / 먹을 것을 찾아
Once people began farming, / they could settle down near their farms.
일단 사람들이 농사를 짓기 시작하면서, / 그들은 자신의 농경지 근처에 정착할 수 있었다
(C) As a result, / towns and villages grew larger.
그 결과, / 도시와 마을이 더 커졌다.
Living in communities / allowed people / to organize themselves more efficiently.
공동체 생활은 / 사람들이 ~하게 했다 / 더 효율적으로 조직되게
They could divide up the work / of producing food and other things they needed.
그들은 일을 나눌 수 있었다 / 식량과 자신들에게 필요한 다른 것들을 생산하는
(A) While some workers grew crops, / others built new houses and made tools.
어떤 노동자들은 농작물을 재배하는 한편, / 다른 노동자들은 새로운 집을 짓고 도구를 만들었다.
Village dwellers also learned to work together / to do a task faster.
마을 거주자들은 또한 함께 일하는 법도 익혔다 / 일을 더 빨리 하려고
(B) For example, / toolmakers could share the work / of making stone axes and knives.
예를 들어, / 도구 제작자들은 작업을 함께 할 수 있었다 / 돌도끼와 돌칼을 만드는
By working together, / they could make more tools / in the same amount of time.
함께 일함으로 / 그들은 더 많은 도구를 만들 수 있었다. / 같은 시간 안에

구석기 시대에는 20 ~ 60명의 작은 무리가 먹을 것을 찾아 여기저기 돌아다녔다. 일단 농사를 짓기 시작하면서, 사람들은 자신의 농경지 근처에 정착할 수 있었다.

(C) 그 결과, 도시와 마을이 더 커졌다. 공동체 생활을 통해 사람들은 더 효율적으로 조직될 수 있었다. 그들은 식량과 자신들에게 필요한 다른 것들을 생산하는 일을 나눌 수 있었다.

(A) 어떤 노동자들은 농작물을 재배하는 한편, 다른 노동자들은 새로운 집을 짓고 도구를 만들었다. 마을 거주자들은 또한 일을 더 빨리 하려고 함께 일하는 법도 익혔다.

(B) 예를 들어, 도구 제작자들은 돌도끼와 돌칼을 만드는 작업을 함께 할 수 있었다. 그들은 함께 일하여 같은 시간 안에 더 많은 도구를 만들 수 있었다.

Why? 왜 정답일까?

농경이 시작되면서 사람들이 정착할 수 있었다는 내용의 주어진 글 뒤로, '그 결과' 도시와 마을이 생기고 사람들이 일을 분배할 수 있게 되었다고 설명하는 (C)가 먼저 연결된다. 이어서 (A)는 (C)에서 언급된 '분업'이 어떻게 이루어졌는지 언급하며, 사람들이 함께 일하는 법 또한 배우게 되었다고 이야기한다. (B)에서는 '함께 작업'하는 상황의 예를 제시하며 (A)를 보충 설명한다. 따라서 글의 순서로 가장 적절한 것은 ④ 'C) – (A) – (B)'이다.

- Old Stone Age 구석기 시대
- wander ⓥ 돌아다니다, 배회하다
- settle down 정착하다
- dweller ⓝ 거주자
- community ⓝ 공동체, 지역사회
- efficiently ⓐⓓ 효율적으로
- band ⓝ (소규모) 무리
- in search of ~을 찾아서
- crop ⓝ 작물
- axe ⓝ 도끼
- organize ⓥ 조직하다, 정리하다
- divide up ~을 나누다

구문 풀이

2행 Once people began farming, they could settle down near their farms.
접속사(일단 ~한다면)

★★ 문제 해결 꿀~팁 ★★

▶ 많이 틀린 이유는?

글을 자세히 읽지 않고 연결어 중심으로만 보면, (B)가 주어진 글의 예시(For example)이고 (C)가 전체 글의 결론(As a result)일 것이라고 잘못 추론할 수 있다. 하지만, 내용적 단서가 중요하다. 주어진 글은 사람들이 농경을 시작하며 정착했다는 내용인데, (B)는 갑자기 '도구 제작자'를 언급하며, 이들이 업무를 분업해 담당했다는 설명을 제시하고 있다. 서로 전혀 다른 키워드로 보아 (B)가 주어진 글에 대한 예시라고 보기 어렵기 때문에 ②를 답으로 고르는 것은 적절하지 않다.

▶ 문제 해결 방법은?

사람들이 농경지 근처에 정착하여 살게 되면서, 마을이 성장하고 분업화가 일어나(C), 누구는 농사를 짓고 누구는 도구를 만드는 한편 공동 작업도 활성화되었으며(A), 공동 작업으로 더 쉽고 빠른 작업이 가능해졌다(B)는 흐름이다.

★★★ 등급을 가르는 문제!

37 광물의 형성   정답률 42% | 정답 ②

주어진 글 다음에 이어질 글의 순서로 가장 적절한 것을 고르시오. [3점]
① (A) – (C) – (B)
✔ (B) – (A) – (C)
③ (B) – (C) – (A)
④ (B) – (A) – (B)
⑤ (C) – (B) – (A)

Natural processes form minerals in many ways.
자연 과정은 많은 방법으로 광물을 형성한다.

For example, / hot melted rock material, / called magma, / cools / when it reaches the Earth's surface, / or even if it's trapped below the surface.
예를 들어, / 뜨거운 용암 물질은 / 마그마라고 불리는 / 식는다. / 그것이 지구의 표면에 도달할 때, / 또는 그것이 심지어 표면 아래에 갇혔을 때도

As magma cools, / its atoms lose heat energy, / move closer together, / and begin to combine into compounds.
마그마가 식으면서 / 마그마의 원자는 열에너지를 잃고, / 서로 더 가까이 이동해 / 화합물로 결합하기 시작한다.

(B) During this process, / atoms of the different compounds / arrange themselves into orderly, repeating patterns.
이 과정 동안, / 서로 다른 화합물의 원자가 / 질서 있고 반복적인 패턴으로 배열된다.

The type and amount of elements / present in a magma / partly determine / which minerals will form.
원소의 종류와 양이 / 마그마에 존재하는 / 부분적으로 결정한다. / 어떤 광물이 형성될지를

(A) Also, / the size of the crystals that form / depends partly / on how rapidly the magma cools.
또한, / 형성되는 결정의 크기는 / 부분적으로는 달려 있다. / 마그마가 얼마나 빨리 식냐에

When magma cools slowly, / the crystals that form / are generally large enough / to see with the unaided eye.
마그마가 천천히 식으면, / 형성되는 결정은 / 대개 충분히 크다. / 육안으로 볼 수 있을 만큼

(C) This is because the atoms have enough time / to move together and form into larger crystals.
이것은 원자가 충분한 시간을 가지기 때문이다. / 함께 이동해 더 큰 결정을 형성할

When magma cools rapidly, / the crystals that form / will be small.
마그마가 빠르게 식으면, / 형성되는 결정은 / 작을 것이다.

In such cases, / you can't easily see individual mineral crystals.
이런 경우에는 / 여러분은 개별 광물 결정을 쉽게 볼 수 없다.

자연 과정은 많은 방법으로 광물을 형성한다. 예를 들어, 마그마라고 불리는 뜨거운 용암 물질은 지구의 표면에 도달할 때, 또는 심지어 표면 아래에 갇혔을 때도 식는다. 마그마가 식으면서 마그마의 원자는 열에너지를 잃고, 서로 더 가까이 이동해 화합물로 결합하기 시작한다.

(B) 이 과정 동안, 서로 다른 화합물의 원자가 질서 있고 반복적인 패턴으로 배열된다. 마그마에 존재하는 원소의 종류와 양이 어떤 광물이 형성될지를 부분적으로 결정한다.

(A) 또한, 형성되는 결정의 크기는 부분적으로는 마그마가 얼마나 빨리 식냐에 달려 있다. 마그마가 천천히 식으면, 형성되는 결정은 대개 육안으로 볼 수 있을 만큼 충분히 크다.

(C) 이것은 원자가 함께 이동해 더 큰 결정을 형성할 충분한 시간을 가지기 때문이다. 마그마가 빠르게 식으면, 형성되는 결정은 작을 것이다. 이런 경우에는 개별 광물 결정을 쉽게 볼 수 없다.

Why? 왜 정답일까?

마그마가 식을 때 광물이 형성될 수 있다는 내용의 주어진 글 뒤로, '이 식어가는 과정' 동안 마그마 속 원

소의 종류나 양에 따라 어떤 종류의 광물이 형성될지 결정된다고 설명하는 (B)가 먼저 연결된다. 이어서 Also로 시작하는 (A)는 추가로 마그마가 식는 속도에 따라 광물의 크기가 결정된다고 언급한다. 마지막으로 (C)는 (A) 후반부에서 언급되었듯이 마그마가 천천히 식을 때 광물의 크기가 커지는 이유에 관해 보충 설명한다. 따라서 글의 순서로 가장 적절한 것은 ② '(B) – (A) – (C)'이다.

- form ⓥ 형성하다
- melt ⓥ 녹이다, 녹다
- trap ⓥ 가두다
- combine into ~로 결합되다
- partly ⓐⓓ 부분적으로
- with the unaided eye 육안으로
- orderly ⓐⓓ 질서 있는
- in such cases 이런 경우에
- mineral ⓝ 광물
- surface ⓝ 표면
- atom ⓝ 원자
- compound ⓝ 화합물
- rapidly ⓐⓓ 빠르게
- arrange ⓥ 배열하다
- element ⓝ 원소, 구성요소

구문 풀이

6행 Also, the size of the crystals that form depends partly on how rapidly the magma cools.
「how + 형/부 + 주어 + 동사 : 얼마나 ~한지」

★★ 문제 해결 꿀~팁 ★★

▶ 많이 틀린 이유는?

(B)는 마그마가 식는 속도에 따라 그로 인해 만들어지는 결정의 종류가 달라질 수 있다는 내용으로 끝나는데, (C)를 보면 갑자기 결정의 '크기'가 커지는 이유를 언급한다. (C)에 앞서 '크기'를 처음 언급하는 단락은 Also로 시작하는 (A)이다. (A)에서 먼저 size를 언급해줘야 크기가 커지는 '이유'를 설명하는 (C)가 자연스럽게 연결된다.

▶ 문제 해결 방법은?

(A)와 (C)가 둘 다 '크기'를 언급하고 있지만, (B)에는 '크기'에 관한 언급이 없다. 따라서 Also가 있는 (A)를 먼저 연결해 '크기'에 관한 내용을 추가한다는 뜻을 밝히고, 뒤이어 (C)를 연결해야 논리적 흐름이 자연스러워진다.

38 탄수화물의 종류   정답률 57% | 정답 ④

글의 흐름으로 보아, 주어진 문장이 들어가기에 가장 적절한 곳을 고르시오.

All carbohydrates are basically sugars.
모든 탄수화물은 기본적으로 당이다.
① Complex carbohydrates are the good carbohydrates for your body.
복합 탄수화물은 몸에 좋은 탄수화물이다.
② These complex sugar compounds / are very difficult to break down / and can trap other nutrients / like vitamins and minerals / in their chains.
이러한 복당류 화합물은 / 분해하기 매우 어렵고 / 다른 영양소를 가두어 둘 수 있다. / 비타민과 미네랄 같은 / 그것의 사슬 안에
③ As they slowly break down, / the other nutrients are also released into your body, / and can provide you with fuel for a number of hours.
그것들이 천천히 분해되면서, / 다른 영양소도 여러분의 몸으로 방출되고, / 많은 시간 동안 여러분에게 연료를 공급할 수 있다.
✔ Bad carbohydrates, / on the other hand, / are simple sugars.
나쁜 탄수화물은 / 반면에 / 단당류이다.
Because their structure is not complex, / they are easy to break down / and hold few nutrients for your body / other than the sugars from which they are made.
그것의 구조는 복잡하지 않기 때문에 / 그것은 분해되기 쉬우며, / 몸을 위한 영양소를 거의 가지고 있지 않다. / 그것을 구성하는 당 말고는
⑤ Your body breaks down these carbohydrates rather quickly / and what it cannot use / is converted to fat and stored in the body.
여러분의 몸은 이러한 탄수화물을 상당히 빨리 분해하며, / 몸이 사용하지 못하는 것은 / 지방으로 바뀌어 몸에 저장된다.

모든 탄수화물은 기본적으로 당이다. ① 복합 탄수화물은 몸에 좋은 탄수화물이다. ② 이러한 복당류 화합물은 분해하기 매우 어렵고, 비타민과 미네랄 같은 다른 영양소를 그것의 사슬 안에 가두어 둘 수 있다. ③ 그것들이 천천히 분해되면서, 다른 영양소도 여러분의 몸으로 방출되고, 많은 시간 동안 여러분에게 연료를 공급할 수 있다. ④ 반면에 나쁜 탄수화물은 단당류이다. 그것의 구조는 복잡하지 않기 때문에 분해되기 쉬우며, 그것을 구성하는 당 말고는 몸을 위한 영양소를 거의 가지고 있지 않다. ⑤ 여러분의 몸은 이러한 탄수화물을 상당히 빨리 분해하며, 몸이 사용하지 못하는 것은 지방으로 바뀌어 몸에 저장된다.

Why? 왜 정답일까?

복합 탄수화물과 단당류의 차이점을 설명하는 글이다. ④ 앞의 복합당의 경우 구조가 복잡하기 때문에 분해 시간이 느리고 오랜 시간 몸에 연료를 공급한다는 내용이다. 한편 주어진 문장은 '나쁜 탄수화물'인 단당류를 언급하고, ④ 뒤에서는 이 단당류를 they로 받아 이것이 분해되기 쉽고 당 외에는 다른 영양소를 가지고 있지도 않아 몸에서 다 쓰지 못하면 지방이 되어 쌓인다는 설명을 이어 간다. 따라서 주어진 문장이 들어가기에 가장 적절한 곳은 ④이다.

- carbohydrate ⓝ 탄수화물
- break down 분해하다
- release ⓥ 방출하다
- a number of 많은
- be made from ~로 구성되다
- basically ⓐⓓ 기본적으로
- nutrient ⓝ 영양소
- provide A with B A에게 B를 공급하다
- structure ⓝ 구조
- convert ⓥ 바꾸다

구문 풀이

4행 These complex sugar compounds are very difficult to break down and can trap other nutrients like vitamins and minerals in their chains.
보어(형용사구)   부사적 용법(~하기에)

39 초기 정보와 기대의 영향   정답률 48% | 정답 ⑤

글의 흐름으로 보아, 주어진 문장이 들어가기에 가장 적절한 곳을 고르시오. [3점]

People commonly make the mistaken assumption / that because a person has one type of characteristic, / then they automatically have other characteristics / which go with it.
흔히 사람들은 잘못된 가정을 한다. / 어떤 사람이 어떤 특성 하나를 가지고 있으므로 / 그러면 그들은 자동으로 다른 특성을 지니고 있다는 / 그것과 어울리는

① In one study, / university students were given descriptions of a guest lecturer / before he spoke to the group.
한 연구에서, / 대학생들은 어떤 초청 강사에 대한 설명을 들었다. / 그가 그들 집단 앞에서 강연하기 전

② Half the students received a description / containing the word 'warm', / the other half were told / the speaker was 'cold'.
학생들 절반은 설명을 들었고, / '따뜻하다'라는 단어가 포함된 / 나머지 절반은 들었다. / 그 강사가 '차갑다'는 말을

③ The guest lecturer then led a discussion, / after which the students were asked / to give their impressions of him.
그러고 나서 그 초청 강사가 토론을 이끌었고, / 이후 학생들은 요청받았다. / 강사에 대한 인상을 말해 달라고

④ As expected, / there were large differences / between the impressions formed by the students, / depending upon their original information of the lecturer.
예상한 대로, / 큰 차이가 있었다. / 학생들에 의해 형성된 인상 간에는 / 그 강사에 대한 학생들의 최초 정보에 따라

☑ It was also found / that those students / who expected the lecturer to be warm / tended to interact with him more.
또한 밝혀졌다. / 그런 학생들이 / 그 강사가 따뜻할 거라고 기대했던 / 그와 더 많이 소통하는 경향이 있었다는 것이

This shows / that different expectations / not only affect the impressions we form / but also our behaviour and the relationship which is formed.
이것은 보여준다. / 서로 다른 기대가 / 우리가 형성하는 인상뿐만 아니라 (~에도) 영향을 미친다는 것을 / 우리의 행동 및 형성되는 관계에도

흔히 사람들은 어떤 사람이 어떤 특성 하나를 가지고 있으면 자동으로 그것과 어울리는 다른 특성을 지니고 있다는 잘못된 가정을 한다. ① 한 연구에서, 대학생들은 어떤 초청 강사가 그들 집단 앞에서 강연하기 전 그 강사에 대한 설명을 들었다. ② 학생들 절반은 '따뜻하다'라는 단어가 포함된 설명을 들었고, 나머지 절반은 그 강사가 '차갑다'는 말을 들었다. ③ 그러고 나서 그 초청 강사가 토론을 이끌었고, 이후 학생들은 강사에 대한 인상을 말해 달라고 요청받았다. ④ 예상한 대로, 학생들에 의해 형성된 인상 간에는 그 강사에 대한 학생들의 최초 정보에 따라 큰 차이가 있었다. ⑤ 또한, 그 강사가 따뜻할 거라고 기대했던 학생들은 그와 더 많이 소통하는 경향이 있었다는 것이 밝혀졌다. 이것은 서로 다른 기대가 우리가 형성하는 인상뿐만 아니라 우리의 행동 및 형성되는 관계에도 영향을 미친다는 것을 보여준다.

Why? 왜 정답일까?

대학생 집단을 대상으로 초기 정보의 영향력을 연구한 실험을 소개하는 글이다. ① 이후로 ⑤ 앞까지 대학생들 두 집단이 똑같은 강사에 관해 상반된 정보를 들었고, 이에 따라 동일한 사람에 대해 서로 다른 인상을 갖게 되었다는 실험 내용이 소개된다. 이어서 주어진 문장은 추가적인 결과(was also found)로 각 집단에 따라 강사와 소통하는 정도에도 영향이 있었다는 내용을 제시한다. 마지막으로 ⑤ 뒤에서는 서로 다른 초기 정보와 기대로 인해 강사에 대한 인상뿐 아니라 관계 맺음에도 차이가 생겼다는 최종적 결론을 제시한다. 따라서 주어진 문장이 들어가기에 가장 적절한 곳은 ⑤이다.

- **lecturer** ⓝ 강사, 강연자
- **commonly** ⓐⓓ 흔히
- **assumption** ⓝ 가정, 추정
- **description** ⓝ 설명
- **be told** ~을 듣다
- **impression** ⓝ 인상
- **original** ⓐ 최초의, 원래의
- **relationship** ⓝ 관계
- **interact with** ~와 상호작용하다
- **mistaken** ⓐ 잘못된, 틀린
- **automatically** ⓐⓓ 자동으로, 저절로
- **contain** ⓥ 포함하다, (~이) 들어 있다
- **discussion** ⓝ 토론, 논의
- **as expected** 예상된 대로
- **expectation** ⓝ 기대, 예상

---

40 사회적 증거의 위력
정답률 49% | 정답 ①

다음 글의 내용을 한 문장으로 요약하고자 한다. 빈칸 (A), (B)에 들어갈 말로 가장 적절한 것은?

	(A)	(B)		(A)	(B)
✓	numbers 숫자	uncertain 불확실한	②	numbers 숫자	unrealistic 비현실적인
③	experiences 경험	unrealistic 비현실적인	④	rules 규칙	uncertain 불확실한
⑤	rules 규칙	unpleasant 불쾌한			

To help decide what's risky and what's safe, / who's trustworthy and who's not, / we look for *social evidence*.
무엇이 위험하고 무엇이 안전한지 결정하는 것을 돕고자 / 누구를 신뢰할 수 있고 없는지를 / 우리는 *사회적 증거*를 찾는다.

From an evolutionary view, / following the group is almost always positive / for our prospects of survival.
진화의 관점에서 볼 때, / 집단을 따르는 것은 거의 항상 긍정적이다. / 우리의 생존 전망에

"If everyone's doing it, / it must be a sensible thing to do," / explains / famous psychologist and best selling writer of *Influence*, / Robert Cialdini.
"모든 사람이 그것을 하고 있다면, / 그것은 분별 있는 행동임에 틀림없다."라고 / 설명한다. / 저명한 심리학자이자 *Influence*를 쓴 베스트셀러 작가 / Robert Cialdini는

While we can frequently see this today in product reviews, / even subtler cues within the environment / can signal trustworthiness.
오늘날 우리가 상품평에서 이를 자주 볼 수 있지만, / 환경 내의 훨씬 더 미묘한 신호가 / 신뢰성을 나타낼 수 있다.

Consider this: / when you visit a local restaurant, / are they busy?
다음을 생각해보라. / 여러분이 어느 현지 음식점을 방문할 때, / 그들이 바쁜가?

Is there a line outside / or is it easy to find a seat?
밖에 줄이 있는가, / 아니면 자리를 찾기 쉬운가?

It is a hassle to wait, / but a line can be a powerful cue / that the food's tasty, / and these seats are in demand.
기다리기는 성가시지만, / 줄이라는 것은 강력한 신호일 수 있다. / 음식이 맛있다는 / 그리고 이곳의 좌석이 수요가 많다는

More often than not, / it's good / to adopt the practices of those around you.
대개는 좋다. / 주변 사람들의 행동을 따르는 것이

➡ We tend to feel safe and secure in (A) numbers / when we decide how to act, / particularly when faced with (B) uncertain conditions.
우리는 숫자에서 안전함과 안도감을 느끼는 경향이 있다. / 어떻게 행동할지 결정할 때 / 특히 불확실한 상황에 직면하고 있다면

무엇이 위험하고 무엇이 안전하며, 누구를 신뢰할 수 있고 없는지를 결정하는 것을 돕고자, 우리는 *사회적* 증거를 찾는다. 진화의 관점에서 볼 때, 집단을 따르는 것은 거의 항상 우리의 생존 전망에 긍정적이다. "모든 사람이 그것을 하고 있다면, 그것은 분별 있는 행동임에 틀림 없다."라고 저명한 심리학자이자 *Influence*를 쓴 베스트셀러 작가인 Robert Cialdini는 설명한다. 오늘날 상품평에서 이를 자주 볼 수 있지만, 환경 내의 훨씬 더 미묘한 신호가 신뢰성을 나타낼 수 있다. 다음을 생각해보라. 여러분이 어느 현지 음식점을 방문할 때, 그들(식당 사람)이 바쁜가? 밖에 줄이 있는가, 아니면 (사람이 없어서) 자리를 찾기 쉬운가? 기다리

기는 성가시지만, 줄이라는 것은 음식이 맛있고 이곳의 좌석이 수요가 많다는 강력한 신호일 수 있다. 대개는 주변 사람들의 행동을 따르는 것이 좋다.

➡ 우리는 어떻게 행동할지 결정할 때 특히 (B) 불확실한 상황에 직면해 있다면 (A) 숫자에서 안전함과 안도감을 느끼는 경향이 있다.

Why? 왜 정답일까?

불확실한 상황에서 결정을 내려야 할 때 우리는 주변 집단의 행동을 따라 안전하게 선택하려 한다(~ following the group is almost always positive for our prospects of survival. / More often than not, it's good to adopt the practices of those around you.)는 내용의 글이다. 따라서 요약문의 빈칸 (A), (B)에 들어갈 말로 가장 적절한 것은 ① '(A) numbers(숫자), (B) uncertain(불확실한)'이다.

- **risky** ⓐ 위험한
- **evidence** ⓝ 근거, 증거
- **sensible** ⓐ 분별 있는, 현명한
- **subtle** ⓐ 미묘한
- **tasty** ⓐ 맛있는
- **more often than not** 대개
- **faced with** ~와 직면한
- **unrealistic** ⓐ 비현실적인
- **unpleasant** ⓐ 불쾌한
- **trustworthy** ⓐ 신뢰할 만한
- **prospect** ⓝ 예상, 가망성
- **frequently** ⓐⓓ 자주, 빈번히
- **hassle** ⓝ 성가신 일
- **in demand** 수요가 많은
- **practice** ⓝ 관례, 실행
- **uncertain** ⓐ 불확실한
- **rule** ⓝ 규칙 ⓥ 지배하다

구문 풀이

1행 To help decide what's risky and what's safe, who's trustworthy and who's
목적(~하려면) 원형부정사   의문사절1   의문사절2
not, we look for *social evidence*.

41-42 익숙한 정보에 대한 전문가의 유리함

Chess masters shown a chess board / in the middle of a game for 5 seconds / with 20 to 30 pieces still in play / can immediately reproduce the position of the pieces from memory.
체스판을 본 체스의 달인들은 / 게임 중간에 5초 동안 / 20 ~ 30개의 말들이 아직 놓여 있는 상태로 / 그 말들의 위치를 외워서 즉시 재현할 수 있다.

Beginners, / of course, / are able to place only a few.
초보자들은 / 물론 / 겨우 몇 개만 기억해 낼 수 있다.

Now take the same pieces / and place them on the board randomly / and the (a) difference is much reduced.
이제 똑같은 말들을 가져다가 / 체스판에 무작위로 놓으라 / 그러면 그 차이는 크게 줄어든다.

「The expert's advantage is only for familiar patterns / — those previously stored in memory.」42번의 근거
전문가의 유리함은 익숙한 패턴에 대해서만 있다. / 즉 이전에 기억에 저장된 패턴

Faced with unfamiliar patterns, / even when it involves the same familiar domain, / the expert's advantage (b) disappears.
익숙하지 않은 패턴에 직면하면, / 그것이 같은 익숙한 분야와 관련 있는 경우라도 / 전문가의 유리함은 사라진다.

「The beneficial effects of familiar structure on memory / have been observed for many types of expertise, / including music.」41번의 근거
익숙한 구조가 기억에 미치는 유익한 효과는 / 여러 전문 지식 유형에서 관찰되어 왔다. / 음악을 포함해

People with musical training / can reproduce short sequences of musical notation more accurately / than those with no musical training / when notes follow (c) conventional sequences, / but the advantage is much reduced / when the notes are ordered randomly.
음악 훈련을 받은 사람 / 연속된 짧은 악보를 더 정확하게 재현할 수 있다 / 음악 훈련을 안 받은 사람보다 / 음표가 전형적인 순서를 따를 때는 / 하지만 그 유리함이 훨씬 줄어든다. / 음표가 무작위로 배열되면

Expertise also improves memory for sequences of (d) movements.
전문 지식은 또한 연속 동작에 대한 기억을 향상시킨다.

Experienced ballet dancers are able to repeat longer sequences of steps / than less experienced dancers, / and they can repeat a sequence of steps making up a routine better / than steps ordered randomly.
숙련된 발레 무용수가 더 긴 연속 스텝을 반복할 수 있다 / 경험이 적은 무용수보다 / 그리고 그들은 정해진 춤 동작을 이루는 연속 스텝을 더 잘 반복할 수 있다 / 무작위로 배열된 스텝보다

In each case, / memory range is (e) increased / by the ability to recognize familiar sequences and patterns.
각각의 경우, / 기억의 범위는 늘어난다 / 익숙한 순서와 패턴을 인식하는 능력에 의해

체스판을 게임 중간에 20 ~ 30개의 말들이 아직 놓여 있는 상태로 5초 동안 본 체스의 달인들은 그 말들의 위치를 외워서 즉시 재현할 수 있다. 물론 초보자들은 겨우 몇 개만 기억해 낼 수 있다. 이제 똑같은 말들을 가져다가 체스판에 무작위로 놓으면 그 (a) 차이는 크게 줄어든다. 전문가의 유리함은 익숙한 패턴, 즉 이전에 기억에 저장된 패턴에 대해서만 있다. 익숙하지 않은 패턴에 직면하면, 같은 익숙한 분야와 관련 있는 경우라도 전문가의 유리함은 (b) 사라진다. 익숙한 구조가 기억에 미치는 유익한 효과는 음악을 포함해 여러 전문 지식 유형에서 관찰되어 왔다. 음표가 (c) 특이한(→ 전형적인) 순서를 따를 때는 음악 훈련을 받은 사람이 음악 훈련을 안 받은 사람보다 연속된 짧은 악보를 더 정확하게 재현할 수 있지만, 음표가 무작위로 배열되면 그 유리함이 훨씬 줄어든다. 전문 지식은 또한 연속 (d) 동작에 대한 기억을 향상시킨다. 숙련된 발레 무용수가 경험이 적은 무용수보다 더 긴 연속 스텝을 반복할 수 있고, 무작위로 배열된 스텝보다 정해진 춤 동작을 이루는 연속 스텝을 더 잘 반복할 수 있다. 각각의 경우, 기억의 범위는 익숙한 순서와 패턴을 인식하는 능력에 의해 (e) 늘어난다.

- **in the middle of** ~의 한가운데에
- **reproduce** ⓥ 재현하다
- **beginner** ⓝ 초심자
- **randomly** ⓐⓓ 무작위로
- **advantage** ⓝ 유리함, 이점
- **previously** ⓐⓓ 이전에, 사전에
- **domain** ⓝ 영역, 분야
- **beneficial** ⓐ 유익한, 이로운
- **sequence** ⓝ 연속, 순서
- **accurately** ⓐⓓ 정확하게
- **experienced** ⓐ 숙련된, 경험 많은
- **guarantee** ⓥ 보장하다
- **in play** 시합 중인
- **from memory** 외워서, 기억하여
- **only a few** 몇 안 되는 (것)
- **reduce** ⓥ 줄이다, 감소시키다
- **familiar** ⓐ 익숙한, 친숙한
- **unfamiliar** ⓐ 익숙지 않은, 낯선
- **disappear** ⓥ 사라지다
- **expertise** ⓝ 전문 지식
- **musical notation** 악보
- **unusual** ⓐ 특이한
- **routine** ⓝ 습관, (정해진) 춤 동작, 루틴

구문 풀이

1행 Chess masters <u>shown</u> a chess board in the middle of a game for 5
주어 ↳과거분사 shown의 직접목적어
seconds with 20 to 30 pieces still in play <u>can immediately reproduce</u> the position
동사구
of the pieces from memory.

---

41 제목 파악 정답률 64% | 정답 ②

윗글의 제목으로 가장 적절한 것은?
① How Can We Build Good Routines? - 어떻게 하면 좋은 습관을 들일 수 있을까?
✓② Familiar Structures Help Us Remember - 익숙한 구조는 우리가 기억하는 것을 돕는다
③ Intelligence Does Not Guarantee Expertise - 지능은 전문 지식을 보장하지는 않는다
④ Does Playing Chess Improve Your Memory? - 체스를 하는 것이 기억력을 향상시킬까?
⑤ Creative Art Performance Starts from Practice - 창의적인 예술 공연은 연습에서 시작된다

Why? 왜 정답일까?
익숙한 정보가 기억력에 미치는 좋은 영향(The beneficial effects of familiar structure on memory)을 설명하는 글로, 전문가들의 경우 익숙하고 패턴화된 정보는 더 잘 기억하지만 무작위적인 정보는 전문 분야라고 하더라도 기억력 면에서 초심자와 큰 차이를 보이지 못한다는 예시를 다루고 있다. 따라서 글의 제목으로 가장 적절한 것은 ② '익숙한 구조는 우리가 기억하는 것을 돕는다'이다.

42 어휘 추론 정답률 48% | 정답 ③

밑줄 친 (a) ~ (e) 중에서 문맥상 낱말의 쓰임이 적절하지 않은 것은?
① (a) ② (b) ✓③ (c) ④ (d) ⑤ (e)

Why? 왜 정답일까?
'The expert's advantage is only for familiar patterns ~'에서 전문가의 유리함, 즉 전문가들이 자기 분야의 정보를 더 잘 기억할 수 있는 까닭은 바로 정보의 '익숙한 구조'에 있다고 한다. 이를 음악 전문가들의 사례에 적용하면, 음표에 대한 전문가들의 기억이 비전문가들을 넘어설 수 있는 경우는 음표가 '익숙한' 패턴으로 배열된 때일 것이므로, (c)에는 unusual 대신 conventional을 써야 한다. 따라서 문맥상 낱말의 쓰임이 적절하지 않은 것은 ③ '(c)'이다.

43-45 친절로 없어진 괴물

(A)
Once upon a time, / there was a king / who lived in a beautiful palace.
옛날 옛적에, / 한 왕이 있었다. / 아름다운 궁전에 사는
「While the king was away, / a monster approached the gates of the palace.」 **45번 ①의 근거 일치**
왕이 없는 동안, / 한 괴물이 궁전 문으로 접근했다.
The monster was so ugly and smelly / that the guards froze in shock.
그 괴물이 너무 추하고 냄새가 나서 / 경비병들은 충격으로 얼어붙었다.
He passed the guards / and sat on the king's throne.
괴물은 경비병들을 지나 / 왕의 왕좌에 앉았다.
The guards soon came to their senses, / went in, / and shouted at the monster, / demanding that (a) he get off the throne.
경비병들은 곧 정신을 차리고 / 안으로 들어가 / 괴물을 향해 소리치며 / 그에게 왕좌에서 내려올 것을 요구했다.

(D)
With each bad word the guards used, / the monster grew more ugly and smelly.
경비병들이 나쁜 말을 사용할 때마다, / 그 괴물은 더 추해졌고, 더 냄새가 났다.
「The guards got even angrier — / they began to brandish their swords / to scare the monster away from the palace.」 **45번 ⑤의 근거 일치**
경비병들은 한층 더 화가 났다. / 그들은 칼을 휘두르기 시작했다. / 그 괴물을 겁주어 궁전에서 쫓아내려고
But (e) he just grew bigger and bigger, / eventually taking up the whole room.
하지만 그는 그저 점점 더 커져서 / 결국 방 전체를 차지했다.
He grew more ugly and smelly than ever.
그는 그 어느 때보다 더 추해졌고, 더 냄새가 났다.

(B)
Eventually the king returned.
마침내 왕이 돌아왔다.
He was wise and kind / and saw what was happening.
그는 현명하고 친절했으며, / 무슨 일이 일어나고 있는지 알았다.
He knew what to do.
그는 어떻게 해야 할지 알고 있었다.
「He smiled and said to the monster, / "Welcome to my palace!"」 **45번 ②의 근거 일치**
그는 미소를 지으며 그 괴물에게 말했다. / "나의 궁전에 온 것을 환영하오!"라고
He asked the monster / if (b) he wanted a cup of coffee.
왕은 그 괴물에게 물었다. / 그가 커피 한 잔을 원하는지
The monster began to grow smaller / as he drank the coffee.
괴물은 더 작아지기 시작했다. / 그가 그 커피를 마시면서

(C)
The king offered (c) him some take-out pizza and fries.
왕은 그에게 약간의 테이크아웃 피자와 감자튀김을 제안했다.
The guards immediately called for pizza.
경비병들은 즉시 피자를 시켰다.
「The monster continued to get smaller / with the king's kind gestures.」 **45번 ③의 근거 일치**
그 괴물은 몸이 계속 더 작아졌다. / 왕의 친절한 행동에
(d) He then offered the monster a full body massage.
그러고 나서 그는 괴물에게 전신 마사지를 제공했다.
「As the guards helped with the relaxing massage, / the monster became tiny.」 **45번 ④의 근거 불일치**
경비병들이 편안한 마사지를 도와주자 / 그 괴물은 매우 작아졌다.
With another act of kindness to the monster, / he just disappeared.
그 괴물에게 또 한 번의 친절한 행동을 베풀자, / 그는 바로 사라졌다.

(A)
옛날 옛적에, 아름다운 궁전에 사는 한 왕이 있었다. 왕이 없는 동안, 한 괴물이 궁전 문으로

접근했다. 그 괴물이 너무 추하고 냄새가 나서 경비병들은 충격으로 얼어붙었다. 괴물은 경비병들을 지나 왕의 왕좌에 앉았다. 경비병들은 곧 정신을 차리고 안으로 들어가 괴물을 향해 소리치며 (a) 그에게 왕좌에서 내려올 것을 요구했다.

(D)
경비병들이 나쁜 말을 사용할 때마다, 그 괴물은 더 추해졌고, 더 냄새가 났다. 경비병들은 한층 더 화가 났다. 그들은 그 괴물을 겁주어 궁전에서 쫓아내려고 칼을 휘두르기 시작했다. 하지만 (e) 그는 그저 점점 더 커져서 결국 방 전체를 차지했다. 그는 그 어느 때보다 더 추해졌고, 더 냄새가 났다.

(B)
마침내 왕이 돌아왔다. 그는 현명하고 친절했으며, 무슨 일이 일어나고 있는지 알았다. 그는 어떻게 해야 할지 알고 있었다. 그는 미소를 지으며 그 괴물에게 "나의 궁전에 온 것을 환영하오!"라고 말했다. 왕은 그 괴물에게 (b) 그가 커피 한 잔을 원하는지 물었다. 괴물은 그 커피를 마시면서 더 작아지기 시작했다.

(C)
왕은 (c) 그에게 약간의 테이크아웃 피자와 감자튀김을 제안했다. 경비병들은 즉시 피자를 시켰다. 그 괴물은 왕의 친절한 행동에 몸이 계속 더 작아졌다. 그러고 나서 (d) 그는 괴물에게 전신 마사지를 제공해 주었다. 경비병들이 편안한 마사지를 도와주자 그 괴물은 매우 작아졌다. 그 괴물에게 또 한 번의 친절한 행동을 베풀자, 그는 바로 사라졌다.

- **approach** ⓥ 다가오다, 접근하다
- **ugly** ⓐ 추한
- **in shock** 충격을 받아
- **come to one's senses** 정신을 차리다
- **get off** ~을 떠나다
- **take-out** ⓐ 사서 가지고 가는
- **gesture** ⓝ 몸짓, (감정의) 표시, 표현
- **brandish** ⓥ 휘두르다
- **take up** ~을 차지하다
- **gate** ⓝ 문
- **smelly** ⓐ 냄새 나는, 악취가 나는
- **throne** ⓝ 왕좌
- **shout at** ~을 향해 소리치다
- **wise** ⓐ 현명한
- **call for** ~을 시키다, ~을 요구하다
- **tiny** ⓐ 아주 작은
- **scare away** ~을 겁주어 쫓아버리다
- **than ever** 그 어느 때보다

구문 풀이

(A) 5행 The guards soon came to their senses, went in, and shouted at the monster, demanding that he (should) get off the throne.
요구 동사   생략   동사원형
(D) 4행 But he just grew bigger and bigger, eventually taking up the whole room.
「비교급 + and + 비교급: 점점 더 ~한」   분사구문(그리고 ~하다)

43 글의 순서 파악 정답률 77% | 정답 ④

주어진 글 (A)에 이어질 내용을 순서에 맞게 배열한 것으로 가장 적절한 것은?
① (B) - (D) - (C)   ② (C) - (B) - (D)
③ (C) - (D) - (B)   ✓④ (D) - (B) - (C)
⑤ (D) - (C) - (B)

Why? 왜 정답일까?
왕이 없을 때 어느 괴물이 왕좌에 대신 앉아버렸다는 내용의 (A) 뒤에는, 경비병들이 괴물을 위협하며 쫓아내려 했으나 오히려 괴물의 몸집이 점점 커질 뿐이었다는 내용의 (D), 왕이 돌아와서는 사태를 파악하고 괴물에게 친절을 베풀기 시작했다는 내용의 (B), 왕이 음식과 마사지 등 친절한 행동을 보낼 때마다 괴물이 점점 작아져서 마침내는 없어졌다는 내용의 (C)가 차례로 연결되어야 한다. 따라서 글의 순서로 가장 적절한 것은 ④ '(D) - (B) - (C)'이다.

44 지칭 추론 정답률 75% | 정답 ④

밑줄 친 (a) ~ (e) 중에서 가리키는 대상이 나머지 넷과 <u>다른</u> 것은?
① (a) ② (b) ③ (c) ✓④ (d) ⑤ (e)

Why? 왜 정답일까?
(a), (b), (c), (e)는 the monster, (d)는 the king을 가리키므로, (a) ~ (e) 중에서 가리키는 대상이 다른 하나는 ④ '(d)'이다.

45 세부 내용 파악 정답률 83% | 정답 ④

윗글에 관한 내용으로 적절하지 않은 것은?
① 왕이 없는 동안 괴물이 궁전 문으로 접근했다.
② 왕은 미소를 지으며 괴물에게 환영한다고 말했다.
③ 왕의 친절한 행동에 괴물의 몸이 계속 더 작아졌다.
✓④ 경비병들은 괴물을 마사지해 주기를 거부했다.
⑤ 경비병들은 겁을 주어 괴물을 쫓아내려 했다.

Why? 왜 정답일까?
(C) 'As the guards helped with the relaxing massage, ~'에서 경비병들은 괴물을 마사지해주기를 거부하지 않고, 오히려 마사지를 도와줬음을 알 수 있다. 따라서 내용과 일치하지 않는 것은 ④ '경비병들은 괴물을 마사지해 주기를 거부했다.'이다.

Why? 왜 오답일까?
① (A) 'While the king was away, a monster approached the gates of the palace.'의 내용과 일치한다.
② (B) 'He smiled and said to the monster, "Welcome to my palace!"'의 내용과 일치한다.
③ (C) 'The monster continued to get smaller with the king's kind gestures.'의 내용과 일치한다.
⑤ (D) 'The guards ~ began to brandish their swords to scare the monster away from the palace.'의 내용과 일치한다.

01 come and cheer our team / an incredible amount of effort / see you at the rink

02 got a sore throat / similar to yours / shouldn't take medicine prescribed for others

03 change the exhibition room / some electrical problems / Can I see the hall

04 painted pictures on a street wall / How do you like the house / The butterfly on the tree branch

05 reserved a place / upload the poster / send the poster to me

06 buy a coffee pot / it comes in two sizes / easier to carry around

07 drop by the duty free shop / enough time to shop / all sold out

08 joining the choir / really far from here / Is there an entry fee

09 for five days / explore various future jobs / on the first day

10 work for most of your cooking / they are heavier / keeps the oil from splashing

11 editing the video clip / How did you learn to do that

12 get in my car and drive home / Can you give me a ride

13 harvested some cherry tomatoes / ready to be picked / anything I need to prepare

14 had an argument / you have a long face / talk to her in person

15 have a relaxing time / watch the sunrise / how early they should wake up

16-17 enjoy sports together / with minimal equipment / It can be played indoors anytime

어휘 Review Test 02

문제편 028쪽

A	B	C	D
01 갈등	**01** settle down	**01** ⓒ	**01** ⓗ
02 광물	**02** efficiently	**02** ⓗ	**02** ⓢ
03 탄수화물	**03** contain	**03** ⓑ	**03** ⓔ
04 토론	**04** scare away	**04** ⓜ	**04** ⓜ
05 불쾌한	**05** discover	**05** ①	**05** ⓡ
06 다가오다, 접근하다	**06** gene	**06** ⓐ	**06** ①
07 보장하다	**07** randomly	**07** ①	**07** ⓞ
08 ~을 차지하다	**08** constant	**08** ⓡ	**08** ①
09 기꺼이	**09** species	**09** ①	**09** ⓚ
10 방출하다	**10** organize	**10** ⓞ	**10** ⓑ
11 냄새	**11** jealous	**11** ⓠ	**11** ⓐ
12 좌절한	**12** motivation	**12** ⓓ	**12** ⓒ
13 자신감 있는	**13** estimate	**13** ⓚ	**13** ⓓ
14 발생하다	**14** wander	**14** ⓟ	**14** ①
15 ~로 결합되다	**15** principle	**15** ⓔ	**15** ⓖ
16 ~을 처리하다	**16** impression	**16** ①	**16** ①
17 수용하다, 받아들이다	**17** empathy	**17** ⓝ	**17** ①
18 ~에 적응하다	**18** habitat	**18** ⓢ	**18** ⓟ
19 유지하다	**19** expectation	**19** ⓥ	**19** ⓥ
20 ~을 시키다, 요구하다	**20** structure	**20** ①	**20** ⓝ

03회 | 2022학년도 3월 학력평가 [고1]

| 정답과 해설 |

· 정답 ·

01 ① 02 ③ 03 ② 04 ④ 05 ④ 06 ③ 07 ① 08 ③ 09 ⑤ 10 ③ 11 ① 12 ⑤ 13 ② 14 ② 15 ①
16 ④ 17 ④ 18 ② 19 ③ 20 ⑤ 21 ⑤ 22 ① 23 ④ 24 ② 25 ⑤ 26 ③ 27 ④ 28 ⑤ 29 ③ 30 ⑤
31 ② 32 ③ 33 ① 34 ① 35 ④ 36 ③ 37 ② 38 ④ 39 ② 40 ① 41 ⑤ 42 ③ 43 ② 44 ④ 45 ⑤

★ 표기된 문항은 [등급을 가르는 문제]에 해당하는 문항입니다.

01 농구 리그 등록 방법 변경 안내

정답률 86% | 정답 ①

다음을 듣고, 남자가 하는 말의 목적으로 가장 적절한 것을 고르시오.

☑ 농구 리그 참가 등록 방법의 변경을 알리려고
② 확정된 농구 리그 시합 일정을 발표하려고
③ 농구 리그의 심판을 추가 모집하려고
④ 농구 리그 경기 관람을 권장하려고
⑤ 농구 리그 우승 상품을 안내하려고

M : Good afternoon, everybody.
안녕하세요, 여러분.
This is Student President Sam Wilson.
저는 학생회장인 Sam Wilson입니다.
As you know, the lunch basketball league will begin soon.
여러분도 알다시피, 점심시간 농구 리그가 곧 시작됩니다.
Many students are interested in joining the league and waiting for the sign-up sheet to be handed out at the gym.
많은 학생들이 리그 참가에 관심을 보이고 있고 체육관에서 신청서가 배부되기를 기다리고 있습니다.
For easier access, we've decided to change the registration method.
보다 쉽게 접근할 수 있도록, 저희는 등록 방법을 바꾸기로 했습니다.
Instead of going to the gym to register, simply log into the school website and fill out the registration form online.
체육관에 가서 등록하는 대신, 학교 웹 사이트에 로그인해서 온라인 신청서를 작성하기만 해 주세요.
Thank you for listening and let's have a good league.
들어주셔서 감사하고, 좋은 리그 경기를 합시다.

Why? 왜 정답일까?

'For easier access, we've decided to change the registration method. Instead of going to the gym to register, simply log into the school website and fill out the registration form online.'에서 남자는 점심시간 농구 리그 참가 등록이 온라인 등록으로 바뀌었음을 공지하고 있다. 따라서 남자가 하는 말의 목적으로 가장 적절한 것은 ① '농구 리그 참가 등록 방법의 변경을 알리려고'이다.

● hand out 배부하다, 나눠주다 ● access ⓝ 접근, 이용
● registration ⓝ 등록

02 손으로 얼굴을 만지지 말라고 권하기

정답률 96% | 정답 ③

대화를 듣고, 여자의 의견으로 가장 적절한 것을 고르시오.

① 평소에 피부 상태를 잘 관찰할 필요가 있다.
② 여드름을 치료하려면 피부과 병원에 가야 한다.
☑ 얼굴을 손으로 만지는 것은 얼굴 피부에 해롭다.
④ 지성 피부를 가진 사람은 자주 세수를 해야 한다.
⑤ 손을 자주 씻는 것은 감염병 예방에 도움이 된다.

W : Daniel, what are you doing in front of the mirror?
Daniel, 거울 앞에서 뭐 하고 있어?
M : I have skin problems these days. I'm trying to pop these pimples on my face.
요새 피부에 문제가 있어. 얼굴에 난 이 여드름들을 짜려는 중이야.
W : Pimples are really annoying, but I wouldn't do that.
여드름은 정말 거슬리긴 하는데, 나라면 짜지 않겠어.
M : Why not?
왜?
W : When you pop them with your hands, you're touching your face.
네가 그걸 손으로 짜면, 얼굴을 만지게 되잖아.
M : Are you saying that I shouldn't touch my face?
내가 얼굴을 만지면 안 된다는 얘기야?
W : Exactly. You know our hands are covered with bacteria, right?
바로 그거야. 우리 손은 세균으로 뒤덮여 있는 거 알잖아, 그렇지?
M : So?
그래서?
W : You'll be spreading bacteria all over your face with your hands. It could worsen your skin problems.
넌 손으로 얼굴 전체에 세균을 퍼뜨리게 될 거야. 그건 피부 문제를 더 나빠지게 만들 수 있지.
M : Oh, I didn't know that.
오, 난 그건 몰랐어.
W : Touching your face with your hands is bad for your skin.
손으로 얼굴을 만지는 것은 피부에 해로워.
M : Okay, I got it.
그래, 알았어.

Why? 왜 정답일까?

얼굴에 난 여드름을 손으로 짜려는 남자에게 여자는 세균이 뒤덮인 손으로 얼굴을 만지는 것이 피부에 좋지 않다(Touching your face with your hands is bad for your skin.)는 것을 설명해주고 있다. 따라서 여자의 의견으로 가장 적절한 것은 ③ '얼굴을 손으로 만지는 것은 얼굴 피부에 해롭다.'이다.

● pop a pimple 여드름을 짜다 ● annoying ⓐ 거슬리는, 짜증나게 하는
● spread ⓥ 퍼뜨리다 ● worsen ⓥ 악화시키다

03 만화가와 환경 운동가의 우연한 만남
정답률 91% | 정답 ②

대화를 듣고, 두 사람의 관계를 가장 잘 나타낸 것을 고르시오.
① 방송 작가 - 연출자   ✓ 만화가 - 환경 운동가
③ 촬영 감독 - 동화 작가   ④ 토크쇼 진행자 - 기후학자
⑤ 제품 디자이너 - 영업 사원

M : Excuse me. You're Chloe Jones, aren't you?
실례합니다. Chloe Jones 씨 맞으시죠?

W : Yes, I am. Have we met before?
네, 맞아요. 전에 봬었나요?

M : No, but I'm a big fan of yours. I've watched your speeches on climate change, and they're very inspiring.
아니요, 하지만 전 당신의 열성팬이에요. 기후 변화에 대한 당신의 연설을 보았고, 그것은 매우 고무적이었어요.

W : Thank you. I'm so glad to hear that.
고맙습니다. 그 말씀을 들으니 몹시 기쁘네요.

M : And, I also think your campaign about plastic pollution has been very successful.
그리고, 플라스틱 오염에 관한 당신의 캠페인 또한 아주 성공적이었다고 생각해요.

W : As an environmental activist, that means a lot to me.
환경 운동가로서, 그것은 제게 많은 의미가 있죠.

M : May I make a suggestion? I thought it'd be nice if more children could hear your ideas.
제안을 하나 해도 될까요? 더 많은 어린이들이 당신의 생각을 접할 수 있으면 좋을 것 같아요.

W : That's what I was thinking. Do you have any good ideas?
저도 그렇게 생각했답니다. 좋은 아이디어가 있으신가요?

M : Actually, I'm a cartoonist. Perhaps I can make comic books based on your work.
사실, 전 만화가예요. 어쩌면 제가 당신의 작업물에 기반해 만화책을 만들 수 있을 거예요.

W : That is a wonderful idea. Can I contact you later to discuss it more?
멋진 생각이네요. 좀 더 논의하기 위해 나중에 연락드려도 될까요?

M : Sure. By the way, my name is Jack Perse. Here's my business card.
그럼요. 참, 제 이름은 Jack Perse입니다. 여기 제 명함이요.

Why? 왜 정답일까?

'Actually, I'm a cartoonist.'에서 남자는 만화가이고, 'As an environmental activist, that means a lot to me.'에서 여자는 환경 운동가임을 알 수 있다. 따라서 두 사람의 관계로 가장 적절한 것은 ② '만화가 - 환경 운동가'이다.

- **climate change** 기후 변화
- **pollution** ⓝ 오염, 공해
- **make a suggestion** 제안하다
- **business card** 명함
- **inspiring** ⓐ 고무하는
- **environmental activist** 환경 운동가
- **discuss** ⓥ 상의하다

04 새로 꾸민 수조 사진 구경하기
정답률 76% | 정답 ④

대화를 듣고, 그림에서 대화의 내용과 일치하지 <u>않는</u> 것을 고르시오.

W : Yesterday, I decorated my fish tank like a beach.
어제 난 내 수조를 바닷가처럼 꾸몄어.

M : I'd like to see it. Do you have a picture?
나도 보고 싶다. 사진 있어?

W : Sure. Here. [Pause] 『Do you recognize the boat in the bottom left corner?』 ①의 근거 일치
응. 여기. [잠시 멈춤] 왼쪽 아래 구석에 배 알아보겠어?

M : Yes. It's the one I gave you, isn't it?
응. 내가 너한테 준 거네, 그렇지?

W : Right. It looks good in the fish tank, doesn't it?
맞아. 수조에 넣어두니 근사하지, 그렇지?

M : It does. 『I love the beach chair in the center.』 ②의 근거 일치
그러네. 가운데 있는 해변용 의자 마음에 든다.

W : Yeah. I like it, too.
응. 나도 그게 마음에 들어.

M : 『I see a starfish next to the chair.』 ③의 근거 일치
의자 옆에 불가사리가 있네.

W : Isn't it cute? 『And do you see these two surf boards on the right side of the picture?』 ④의 근거 불일치
귀엽지 않아? 그리고 사진 오른쪽에 서핑 보드 두 개가 있는 거 보여?

M : Yeah. I like how you put both of them side by side.
응. 두 개를 나란히 배치해둔 게 좋네.

W : I thought that'd look cool.
그게 멋져 보이는 것 같더라고.

M : 『Your fish in the top left corner looks happy with its new home.』 ⑤의 근거 일치
왼쪽 위 구석에 있네 물고기도 새로운 집에 만족한 것 같네.

W : I hope so.
그러길 바라.

Why? 왜 정답일까?

대화에 따르면 사진 오른쪽에 서핑 보드가 두 개 있다(And do you see these two surf boards on the right side of the picture?)고 하는데, 그림에서는 서핑 보드가 하나 뿐이다. 따라서 그림에서 대화의 내용과 일치하지 않는 것은 ④이다.

- **fish tank** 수조
- **side by side** 나란히
- **starfish** ⓝ 불가사리

05 생일 파티 준비하기
정답률 93% | 정답 ④

대화를 듣고, 여자가 남자에게 부탁한 일로 가장 적절한 것을 고르시오.
① 장난감 사 오기   ② 풍선 달기
③ 케이크 가져오기   ✓ 탁자 옮기기
⑤ 아이들 데려오기

[Cell phone rings.]
[휴대전화가 울린다.]

M : Hello, honey. I'm on the way home. How's setting up Mike's birthday party going?
여보세요. 여보, 나 집에 가고 있어요. Mike의 생일 파티 준비는 어떻게 돼 가요?

W : Good, but I still have stuff to do. Mike and his friends will get here soon.
잘돼 가는데, 아직 할 일이 있어요. Mike와 친구들이 곧 이리로 올 거예요.

M : Should I pick up the birthday cake?
내가 생일 케이크 찾으러 갈까요?

W : No, that's okay. I already did that.
아니, 괜찮아요. 내가 이미 찾아왔어요.

M : Then, do you want me to put up the balloons around the doorway when I get there?
그럼, 내가 도착해서 현관문 주변에 풍선을 달아놓을까요?

W : I'll take care of it. Can you take the table out to the front yard?
그건 내가 할게요. 탁자를 앞마당으로 옮겨줄 수 있어요?

M : Sure. Are we having the party outside?
물론이죠. 우린 야외 파티를 하는 건가요?

W : Yes. The weather is beautiful so I made a last minute change.
네. 날씨가 좋아서 막판에 바꿨어요.

M : Great. The kids can play with water guns in the front yard.
좋아요. 아이들이 앞마당에서 물총을 갖고 놀아도 되겠네요.

W : Good idea. I'll go to the garage and grab the water guns.
좋은 생각이에요. 내가 차고에 가서 물총을 가져와야겠어요.

Why? 왜 정답일까?

아들의 생일 파티를 밖에서 하기로 마음을 바꾼 여자는 남자에게 탁자를 밖으로 옮겨달라고 하므로(Can you take the table out to the front yard?), 여자가 부탁한 일로 가장 적절한 것은 ④ '탁자 옮기기'이다.

- **put up** 달다, 올리다, 게시하다
- **grab** ⓥ 집다, 잡다
- **make a last minute change** 마지막 순간에 바꾸다

06 친환경 칫솔과 목욕용품 사기
정답률 86% | 정답 ③

대화를 듣고, 남자가 지불할 금액을 고르시오. [3점]
① $14   ② $16   ✓ $18   ④ $20   ⑤ $22

W : Welcome to Green Eco Shop. How can I help you?
Green Eco Shop에 잘 오셨습니다. 무엇을 도와드릴까요?

M : Hi, do you sell eco-friendly toothbrushes?
안녕하세요. 친환경 칫솔 파시나요?

W : Yes, we have a few types over here. Which do you like?
네, 이쪽에 몇 가지 종류가 있습니다. 어떤 것이 마음에 드세요?

M : Hmm.... How much are these?
흠... 이건 얼마인가요?

W : They're $2 each. They are made from bamboo.
하나에 2달러입니다. 대나무로 만들어졌어요.

M : All right. I'll take four of them.
좋아요. 이거 네 개 살게요.

W : Excellent choice. Anything else?
탁월한 선택입니다. 다른 거 필요하신 건요?

M : I also need bath sponges.
목욕용 스펀지도 필요해요.

W : They're right behind you. They're plastic-free and only $3 each.
바로 뒤쪽에 있어요. 플라스틱이 안 들어간 제품이고 하나에 3달러밖에 안 합니다.

M : Okay. I'll also take four of them. That'll be all.
그렇군요. 이것도 네 개 살게요. 이거면 됐어요.

W : If you have a store membership, you can get a 10% discount off the total price.
매장 회원이시면, 총 가격에서 10퍼센트 할인을 받으실 수 있어요.

M : Great. I'm a member. Here are my credit and membership cards.
좋네요. 전 회원이에요. 여기 제 신용카드랑 회원 카드요.

Why? 왜 정답일까?

대화에 따르면 남자는 하나에 2달러인 대나무 칫솔을 네 개 사고, 하나에 3달러인 목욕용 스펀지도 네 개 산 뒤, 총 가격에서 회원 할인 10퍼센트를 받았다. 이를 식으로 나타내면 '$(2 \times 4 + 3 \times 4) \times 0.9 = 18$'이므로, 남자가 지불한 총 금액은 ③ '$18'이다.

- **eco-friendly** ⓐ 친환경적인
- **plastic-free** ⓐ 플라스틱이 들어가지 않은
- **bamboo** ⓝ 대나무

07 오늘 과학 실험을 할 수 없는 이유
정답률 94% | 정답 ①

대화를 듣고, 두 사람이 오늘 실험을 할 수 <u>없는</u> 이유를 고르시오.
✓ 실험용 키트가 배달되지 않아서   ② 실험 주제를 변경해야 해서
③ 과학실을 예약하지 못해서   ④ 보고서를 작성해야 해서
⑤ 남자가 감기에 걸려서

[Cell phone rings.]
[휴대전화가 울린다.]

M : Hey, Suji. Where are you?
안녕, Suji. 어디 있어?

W : I'm in the library checking out books. I'll be heading out to the science lab for our experiment in a couple of minutes.
도서관에서 책 빌리고 있어. 몇 분만 있다가 우리 실험하는 과학실로 갈게.

M : I guess you haven't checked my message yet. We can't do the experiment today.
너 내 메시지 아직 못 확인했나 보구나. 우리 오늘 실험 못해.

W : Really? Isn't the lab available today?
진짜? 실험실 오늘 쓸 수 있는 거 아니었어?
M : Yes, it is, but I canceled our reservation.
맞는데, 내가 예약을 취소했어.
W : Why? Are you still suffering from your cold?
왜? 너 아직도 감기로 아픈 거야?
M : No, I'm fine now.
아니, 이제 괜찮아.
W : That's good. Then why aren't we doing the experiment today? We need to hand in the science report by next Monday.
다행이다. 그럼 왜 오늘 실험을 안 하는 거야? 다음 주 월요일까지 과학 보고서 내야 하잖아.
M : Unfortunately, the experiment kit hasn't been delivered yet. It'll arrive tomorrow.
안타깝게도, 실험용 키트가 아직 배달되지 않았어. 그게 내일 도착한대.
W : Oh, well. The experiment has to wait one more day, then.
오, 그렇구나. 그럼 하루 더 기다렸다가 실험해야겠네.

Why? 왜 정답일까?

대화에 따르면 남자는 실험용 키트를 아직 배송받지 못했기에 (Unfortunately, the experiment kit hasn't been delivered yet.) 예약된 실험을 취소했다고 하므로, 두 사람이 오늘 실험을 할 수 없는 이유로 가장 적절한 것은 ① '실험용 키트가 배달되지 않아서'이다.

- check out (책 등을) 대출하다
- a couple of 몇몇의, 둘의
- deliver ⓥ 배송하다
- science lab 과학실
- hand in 제출하다

---

08 프리사이클 행사
정답률 90% | 정답 ③

대화를 듣고, Stanville Free-cycle에 관해 언급되지 <u>않은</u> 것을 고르시오.
① 참가 대상
② 행사 장소
③ 주차 가능 여부 ✓
④ 행사 시작일
⑤ 금지 품목

W : Honey, did you see the poster about the Stanville Free-cycle?
여보, Stanville Free-cycle에 관한 포스터 봤어요?
M : Free-cycle? What is that?
프리사이클이요? 그게 뭐예요?
W : It's another way of recycling. You give away items you don't need and anybody can take them for free.
재활용의 또 다른 방법이에요. 필요하지 않은 물품을 버리면 누군가 그것을 공짜로 가져가는 거죠.
M : Oh, it's like one man's garbage is another man's treasure. 「Who can participate?」
오, 어떤 사람의 쓰레기가 다른 사람의 보물이라는 것 같군요. 누가 참여할 수 있나요?
W : It's open to everyone living in Stanville. 」❶의근거 일치
Stanville에 사는 누구나 참여할 수 있어요.
M : Great. 「Where is it taking place?」
좋네요. 어디서 열려요?
W : At Rose Park on Second Street. 」❷의근거 일치
Second Street에 있는 Rose Park에서요.
M : 「When does the event start?」
행사는 언제 시작해요?
W : It starts on April 12 and runs for a week. 」❹의근거 일치
4월 12일에 시작해서 일주일 동안 운영돼요.
M : Let's see what we can free-cycle, starting from the cupboard.
우리가 뭘 프리사이클할 수 있는지 찬장부터 살펴보죠.
W : Okay. 「But breakable items like glass dishes or cups won't be accepted. 」❺의근거 일치
좋아요. 하지만 유리 접시나 컵처럼 깨지기 쉬운 물품은 허용되지 않을 거예요.
M : I see. I'll keep that in mind.
알겠어요. 그 점을 기억할게요.

Why? 왜 정답일까?

대화에서 남자와 여자는 Stanville Free-cycle의 참가 대상, 행사 장소, 행사 시작일, 금지 품목에 관해 언급한다. 따라서 언급되지 않은 것은 ③ '주차 가능 여부'이다.

Why? 왜 오답일까?

① 'It's open to everyone living in Stanville.'에서 '참가 대상'이 언급된다.
② 'At Rose Park on Second Street.'에서 '행사 장소'가 언급된다.
④ 'It starts on April 12 ~'에서 '행사 시작일'이 언급된다.
⑤ 'But breakable items like glass dishes or cups won't be accepted.'에서 '금지 품목'이 언급되었다.

- give away 버리다, 거저 주다
- treasure ⓝ 보물
- for free 공짜로
- breakable ⓐ 깨지기 쉬운

---

09 음악 캠프 개최 안내
정답률 93% | 정답 ⑤

River Valley Music Camp에 관한 다음 내용을 듣고, 일치하지 <u>않는</u> 것을 고르시오.
① 4월 11일부터 5일 동안 진행된다.
② 학교 오케스트라 단원이 아니어도 참가할 수 있다.
③ 자신의 악기를 가져오거나 학교에서 빌릴 수 있다.
④ 마지막 날에 공연을 촬영한다.
⑤ 참가 인원에는 제한이 없다. ✓

M : Hello, River Valley High School students.
안녕하세요, River Valley 고등학교 학생 여러분.
This is your music teacher, Mr. Stailor.
저는 음악 교사인 Stailor 선생님입니다.
「Starting on April 11, we are going to have the River Valley Music Camp for five days. 」❶의근거 일치
4월 11일부터, River Valley Music Camp가 5일 동안 열립니다.
「You don't need to be a member of the school orchestra to join the camp. 」❷의근거 일치
캠프에 참여하기 위해 학교 오케스트라 단원일 필요는 없습니다.
「You may bring your own instrument or you can borrow one from the school. 」
자신의 악기를 가져오거나, 학교에서 하나 빌리면 됩니다. ❸의근거 일치
「On the last day of camp, we are going to film our performance and play it on screen

---

at the school summer festival. 」❹의근거 일치
캠프 마지막 날, 우리는 공연을 촬영하여 그것을 학교 여름 축제에서 스크린으로 재생할 예정입니다.
「Please keep in mind the camp is limited to 50 students. 」❺의근거 불일치
캠프 참가 인원은 50명으로 제한되어 있다는 점 유의해 주세요.
Sign-ups start this Friday, on a first-come-first-served basis.
신청은 이번 주 금요일부터 선착순으로 이루어집니다.
Come and make music together!
오셔서 함께 음악을 즐깁시다!

Why? 왜 정답일까?

'Please keep in mind the camp is limited to 50 students.'에서 참가 인원은 50명으로 제한된다고 하므로, 내용과 일치하지 않는 것은 ⑤ '참가 인원에는 제한이 없다.'이다.

Why? 왜 오답일까?

① 'Starting on April 11, we are going to have the River Valley Music Camp for five days.'의 내용과 일치한다.
② 'You don't need to be a member of the school orchestra to join the camp.'의 내용과 일치한다.
③ 'You may bring your own instrument or you can borrow one from the school.'의 내용과 일치한다.
④ 'On the last day of camp, we are going to film our performance ~'의 내용과 일치한다.

- instrument ⓝ 악기
- be limited to ~로 제한되다
- performance ⓝ 공연
- on a first-come-first-served basis 선착순으로

---

10 소형 진공청소기 구매하기
정답률 85% | 정답 ③

다음 표를 보면서 대화를 듣고, 여자가 주문할 소형 진공청소기를 고르시오.

Handheld Vacuum Cleaners

	Model	Price	Working Time	Weight	Washable Filter
①	A	$50	8 minutes	2.5 kg	✕
②	B	$80	12 minutes	2.0 kg	○
③✓	C	$100	15 minutes	1.8 kg	○
④	D	$120	20 minutes	1.8 kg	✕
⑤	E	$150	25 minutes	1.6 kg	○

W : Ben, do you have a minute?
Ben, 잠깐 시간 돼?
M : Sure. What is it?
응. 왜?
W : I'm trying to buy a handheld vacuum cleaner among these five models. Could you help me choose one?
난 소형 진공청소기를 이 다섯 개 제품 중에 사려고 해. 내가 하나 고르는 걸 도와줄래?
M : Okay. 「How much are you willing to spend?」
그래. 얼마나 쓸 생각이야?
W : No more than $130. 」근거1 Price 조건
130달러 이하로.
M : Then we can cross this one out. 「What about the working time?」
그럼 이거는 빼야겠네. 작동 시간은?
W : I think it should be longer than 10 minutes. 」근거2 Working Time 조건
10분 이상은 돼야 할 것 같아.
M : Then that narrows it down to these three.
그럼 이 세 개로 좁혀지네.
W : 「Should I go with one of the lighter ones?」
내가 좀 가벼운 것 중에 골라야 할까?
M : Yes. Lighter ones are easier to handle while cleaning. 」근거3 Weight 조건
응. 더 가벼운 게 청소할 때 들고 있기 더 편하니까.
W : All right. 「What about the filter?」
그래. 필터는 어쩌지?
M : The one with a washable filter would be a better choice. 」근거4 Washable Filter 조건
씻어 쓸 수 있는 필터가 더 좋은 선택일 거야.
W : I got it. Then I'll order this one.
알겠어. 그럼 이걸로 주문할래.

Why? 왜 정답일까?

대화에 따르면 여자는 가격이 130달러를 넘지 않으면서, 작동 시간은 10분 이상이고, 무게는 가벼운 것으로, 필터는 씻어 쓸 수 있는 청소기를 고르려고 한다. 따라서 여자가 주문할 소형 진공청소기는 ③ 'C'이다.

- handheld ⓐ 손에 들고 쓰는
- narrow down to ~로 좁히다
- cross out (선을 그어) 지우다

---

11 먼지로 눈이 아플 때 어떻게 할지 묻기
정답률 76% | 정답 ①

대화를 듣고, 남자의 마지막 말에 대한 여자의 응답으로 가장 적절한 것을 고르시오.
① Why don't you rinse your eyes with clean water? – 깨끗한 물로 눈을 좀 헹구면 어때? ✓
② Can you explain more about the air pollution? – 대기 오염에 대해 더 설명해 줄래?
③ I need to get myself a new pair of glasses. – 나는 새 안경을 하나 사야겠어.
④ I agree that fine dust is a serious problem. – 나는 미세먼지는 심각한 문제라는 데 동의해.
⑤ We should go outside and take a walk. – 우리는 밖에 좀 나가서 산책을 해야겠어.

M : My eyes are sore today.
오늘 눈이 따갑네.
W : Too bad. Maybe some dust got in your eyes.
딱해라. 아마 눈에 먼지가 좀 들어갔나봐.
M : You're probably right. What should I do?
네 말이 맞을 수도 있겠다. 어째야 하지?
W : Why don't you rinse your eyes with clean water?
깨끗한 물로 눈을 좀 헹구면 어때?

Why? 왜 정답일까?

눈에 먼지가 들어가서 따가운가보다는 여자의 말에 남자는 어떻게 해야 할지 묻고 있으므로(What should I do?), 여자의 응답으로 가장 적절한 것은 ① '깨끗한 물로 눈을 좀 헹구면 어때?'이다.

● sore ⓐ 따가운, 아픈, 화끈거리는 ● rinse ⓥ 헹구다

---

12 옆자리가 비었는지 물어보기 　정답률 77% | 정답 ⑤

대화를 듣고, 여자의 마지막 말에 대한 남자의 응답으로 가장 적절한 것을 고르시오.

① That's not fair. I booked this seat first. – 공평하지 않아요. 내가 이 자리를 먼저 예약했어요.
② Thank you. My friend will be glad to know it. – 고맙습니다. 제 친구가 알면 좋아할 거예요.
③ You're welcome. Feel free to ask me anything. – 천만에요. 어떤 것이든 편하게 물어보세요.
④ Not at all. I don't mind changing seats with you. – 아니에요. 당신과 자리를 바꿔도 괜찮아요.
✔ That's okay. I think the seat next to it is available. – 괜찮아요. 그 옆자리는 비어 있는 것 같아요.

W : Excuse me. Would you mind if I sit here?
실례합니다. 여기 좀 앉아도 될까요?
M : I'm sorry, but it's my friend's seat. He'll be back in a minute.
죄송하지만, 제 친구 자리예요. 조금 있으면 돌아올 거예요.
W : Oh, I didn't know that. Sorry for bothering you.
오, 제가 몰랐네요. 귀찮게 해 드려서 죄송해요.
M : That's okay. I think the seat next to it is available.
괜찮아요. 그 옆자리는 비어 있는 것 같아요.

Why? 왜 정답일까?

여자는 남자의 옆자리에 앉으려고 했다가 친구 자리라는 답을 듣고 귀찮게 해 미안하다며(Sorry for bothering you.) 사과하고 있다. 따라서 남자의 응답으로 가장 적절한 것은 ⑤ '괜찮아요. 그 옆자리는 비어 있는 것 같아요.'이다.

● Would you mind if~? ~해도 괜찮을까요? ● bother ⓥ 귀찮게 하다, 성가시게 하다
● feel free to 편하게 ~하다

---

13 야구 경기 함께 보기로 약속하기 　정답률 93% | 정답 ②

대화를 듣고, 남자의 마지막 말에 대한 여자의 응답으로 가장 적절한 것을 고르시오.
Woman :

① Smells good. Can I try the pizza? – 냄새 좋네. 나 피자 좀 먹어도 돼?
✔ Great. I'll bring chips and popcorn. – 좋아. 내가 과자랑 팝콘 좀 가져갈게.
③ No problem. I'll cancel the tickets. – 문제 없어. 내가 표를 취소할게.
④ Sorry. I don't like watching baseball. – 미안해. 난 야구 보는 거 안 좋아해.
⑤ Sure. Here's the hammer I borrowed. – 물론이지. 여기 내가 빌려갔던 망치야.

M : Hey, Jasmine.
안녕, Jasmine.
W : Hi, Kurt. Are you going to be at home tomorrow afternoon?
안녕, Kurt. 너 내일 오후에 집에 있을 거야?
M : Yeah, I'm going to watch the baseball game with my friends at home.
응, 내 친구들이랑 집에서 야구 경기 볼 거야.
W : Good. Can I drop by your house and give you back the hammer I borrowed?
잘됐다. 나 너네 집에 들러서 내가 빌려갔던 망치 돌려줘도 돼?
M : Sure. Come over any time. By the way, why don't you join us and watch the game?
물론이지. 아무 때나 들러. 그런데, 우리랑 함께 경기 보면 어때?
W : I'd love to. Which teams are playing?
좋지. 어느 팀이 경기해?
M : Green Thunders and Black Dragons.
Green Thunders랑 Black Dragons 경기야.
W : That'll be exciting. What time should I come?
재미있겠네. 몇 시에 갈까?
M : Come at five. We'll have pizza before the game.
5시에 와. 우린 경기 전에 피자를 먹을 거야.
W : Perfect. Do you want me to bring anything?
완벽하네. 내가 뭐 좀 가져갈까?
M : Maybe some snacks to eat while watching the game.
경기 보면서 먹을 간식이 좋을 것 같아.
W : Great. I'll bring chips and popcorn.
좋아, 내가 과자랑 팝콘 좀 가져갈게.

Why? 왜 정답일까?

남자네 집에 들러서 야구를 함께 보기로 한 여자에게 남자는 간식 거리를 좀 가져오면 좋겠다고 하므로(Maybe some snacks to eat while watching the game.), 여자의 응답으로 가장 적절한 것은 ② '좋아. 내가 과자랑 팝콘 좀 가져갈게.'이다.

● drop by ~에 들르다 ● give back ~을 돌려주다
● by the way (화제를 전환하며) 그나저나, 그런데

---

14 독서 동아리 가입 권하기 　정답률 93% | 정답 ②

대화를 듣고, 여자의 마지막 말에 대한 남자의 응답으로 가장 적절한 것을 고르시오. [3점]
Man :

① Exactly. This is a best-selling novel. – 바로 그거야. 그건 베스트셀러 소설이야.
✔ Sounds cool. I'll join a book club, too. – 괜찮을 것 같다. 나도 독서 동아리에 들래.
③ Not really. Books make good presents. – 별로 그렇지 않아. 책은 좋은 선물이 되지.
④ New year's resolutions are hard to keep. – 새해 다짐은 지키기 힘들어.
⑤ Let's buy some books for your book club. – 너희 독서 동아리를 위해 책을 좀 사자.

W : Hi, Tom.
안녕, Tom.
M : Hi, Jane. What are you reading?
안녕, Jane. 뭘 읽고 있어?

W : It's a novel by Charles Dickens. I'm going to talk about it with my book club members this weekend.
Charles Dickens의 소설이야. 이번 주말에 우리 독서 동아리 회원들하고 이 책에 대해서 이야기할 거야.
M : Oh, you're in a book club?
오, 너 독서 동아리였어?
W : Yes. I joined it a few months ago. And now I read much more than before.
응. 몇 달 전에 가입했어. 그래서 요새 전보다 훨씬 많은 책을 읽고 있어.
M : Really? Actually one of my new year's resolutions is to read more books.
진짜? 사실 내 새해 결심 중 하나가 책을 좀 더 많이 읽는 거야.
W : Then, joining a book club will surely help.
그럼 독서 동아리 드는 게 분명 도움이 될 거야.
M : Hmm.... What other benefits can I get if I join one?
흠... 내가 동아리에 들면 얻을 수 있는 이점이 또 뭐가 있지?
W : You can also share your reading experiences with others.
네 독서 경험을 다른 사람들과 공유할 수도 있어.
M : That'd be nice.
그거 괜찮겠다.
W : Yeah, it really broadens your mind. I really recommend you to join a book club.
응. 그건 정말 시각을 넓혀 줘. 난 네가 독서 동아리에 드는 걸 정말 추천해.
M : Sounds cool. I'll join a book club, too.
괜찮을 것 같다. 나도 독서 동아리에 들래.

Why? 왜 정답일까?

여자는 독서 동아리에 들었을 때의 장점을 열거하면서 남자에게 동아리에 들 것을 권하므로(I really recommend you to join a book club.), 남자의 응답으로 가장 적절한 것은 ② '괜찮을 것 같다. 나도 독서 동아리에 들래.'이다.

● resolution ⓝ 다짐, 결심 ● benefit ⓝ 이점
● broaden ⓥ 넓히다, 확장하다

---

15 안내견을 함부로 만지지 않기 　정답률 89% | 정답 ①

다음 상황 설명을 듣고, Brian이 Sally에게 할 말로 가장 적절한 것을 고르시오. [3점]
Brian :

✔ You shouldn't touch a guide dog without permission. – 안내견을 허락 없이 만져서는 안 돼.
② The dog would be happy if we give it some food. – 우리가 음식을 좀 주면 개가 좋아할 거야.
③ I'm sure it's smart enough to be a guide dog. – 분명 이 개는 안내견이 될 만큼 충분히 똑똑한가봐.
④ I suggest that you walk your dog every day. – 너희 개를 맨날 산책시키라고 제안하겠어.
⑤ I'm afraid that dogs are not allowed in here. – 유감이지만 개는 여기 들일 수 없어.

M : Brian and Sally are walking down the street together.
Brian과 Sally는 함께 거리를 걷고 있다.
A blind man and his guide dog are walking towards them.
시각 장애인과 안내견이 그들을 향해 걸어오고 있다.
Sally likes dogs very much, so she reaches out to touch the guide dog.
Sally는 개를 무척 좋아해서, 안내견을 만지려고 손을 뻗는다.
Brian doesn't think that Sally should do that.
Brian은 Sally가 그렇게 하면 안 된다고 생각한다.
The guide dog needs to concentrate on guiding the blind person.
안내견은 시각 장애인을 안내하는 데 집중해야 한다.
If someone touches the dog, the dog can lose its focus.
만일 누군가 그 개를 만지면, 개는 집중력이 흐트러질 수 있다.
So Brian wants to tell Sally not to touch the guide dog without the permission of the dog owner.
그래서 Brian은 Sally에게 개 주인의 허락 없이 안내견을 만지지 말라고 말하고 싶다.
In this situation, what would Brian most likely say to Sally?
이 상황에서, Brian은 Sally에게 뭐라고 말할 것인가?
Brian : You shouldn't touch a guide dog without permission.
안내견을 허락 없이 만져서는 안 돼.

Why? 왜 정답일까?

상황에 따르면 Brian은 안내견을 만지려는 Sally에게 주인의 허락 없이 만져서는 안 된다고 말해 주려 한다(So Brian wants to tell Sally not to touch the guide dog without the permission of the dog owner.). 따라서 Brian이 Sally에게 할 말로 가장 적절한 것은 ① '안내견을 허락 없이 만져서는 안 돼.'이다.

● reach out (손을) 뻗다 ● concentrate on ~에 집중하다
● lose one's focus 집중력을 잃다, 초점을 잃다 ● permission ⓝ 허락

16-17 관절에 무리가 되지 않는 운동 소개

W : Hello, everybody. Welcome to the health workshop.
안녕하세요, 여러분. 헬스 워크숍에 잘 오셨습니다.
I'm Alanna Reyes, the head trainer from Eastwood Fitness Center.
저는 Eastwood Fitness Center의 수석 트레이너 Alanna Reyes입니다.
As you know, joints are body parts that link bones together.
아시다피, 관절은 뼈를 함께 연결해주는 신체 부위입니다.
And doing certain physical activities puts stress on the joints.
그리고 특정한 신체 활동을 하는 것은 관절에 무리를 줍니다.
「But the good news is that people with bad joints can still do certain exercises.
하지만 좋은 소식은 관절이 안 좋은 사람들도 여전히 특정 운동을 할 수 있다는 겁니다.
They have relatively low impact on the joints.
그것들은 관절에 상대적으로 적은 충격을 줍니다.
Here are some examples.」16번의 근거
여기 몇 가지 예가 있습니다.
「The first is swimming.」17번 ①의 근거 일치
첫째는 수영입니다.
While swimming, the water supports your body weight.
수영 중에는, 물이 여러분의 체중을 받쳐줍니다.
「The second is cycling.」17번 ②의 근거 일치
두 번째는 사이클입니다.
You put almost no stress on the knee joints when you pedal smoothly.

페달을 부드럽게 밟을 때에는 무릎 관절에 거의 무리가 가지 않습니다.
「Horseback riding is another exercise that puts very little stress on your knees.」 `17번 ③의 근거` 일치
승마도 무릎에 거의 무리가 가지 않는 또 하나의 운동입니다.
「Lastly, walking is great because it's low-impact, unlike running.」 `17번 ⑤의 근거` 일치
마지막으로 걷기도 좋은데, 뛰는 것과는 달리 충격이 적기 때문입니다.
If you have bad joints, don't give up exercising.
관절이 나빠도, 운동을 포기하지 마세요.
Instead, stay active and stay healthy!
그 대신, 계속 활동하고 건강을 유지하세요!

- **joint** ⓝ 관절
- **relatively** ⓐⓓ 상대적으로, 비교적
- **smoothly** ⓐⓓ 부드럽게
- **put stress on** ~에 무리를 주다
- **impact** ⓝ 충격, 영향

---

16 주제 파악   정답률 76% | 정답 ④

여자가 하는 말의 주제로 가장 적절한 것은?

① activities that help build muscles - 근육을 키우는 데 도움이 되는 활동
② ways to control stress in daily life - 일상 스트레스를 다스리는 방법
③ types of joint problems in elderly people - 노년층에서 나타나는 관절 문제의 종류
✓ low-impact exercises for people with bad joints - 관절이 약한 사람들을 위한 충격이 적은 운동
⑤ importance of daily exercise for controlling weight - 체중 조절을 위한 매일 운동의 중요성

Why? 왜 정답일까?

'But the good news is that people with bad joints can still do certain exercises.'와 'Here are some examples.'을 통해, 여자가 관절에 무리가 되지 않는 운동을 소개하려 함을 알 수 있으므로, 여자가 하는 말의 주제로 가장 적절한 것은 ④ '관절이 약한 사람들을 위한 충격이 적은 운동'이다.

---

17 언급 유무 파악   정답률 92% | 정답 ④

언급된 운동이 아닌 것은?

① swimming - 수영
② cycling - 사이클
③ horseback riding - 승마
✓ bowling - 볼링
⑤ walking - 걷기

Why? 왜 정답일까?

담화에서 여자는 관절에 무리가 되지 않는 운동의 예로 수영, 사이클, 승마, 걷기를 언급하므로, 언급되지 않은 것은 ④ '볼링'이다.

Why? 왜 오답일까?

① 'The first is swimming.'에서 '수영'이 언급되었다.
② 'The second is cycling.'에서 '사이클'이 언급되었다.
③ 'Horseback riding is another exercise ~'에서 '승마'가 언급되었다.
⑤ 'Lastly, walking is great ~'에서 '걷기'가 언급되었다.

---

18 모금 음악회 참석 요청   정답률 87% | 정답 ②

다음 글의 목적으로 가장 적절한 것은?

① 합창 대회 결과를 공지하려고
✓ 모금 음악회 참석을 요청하려고
③ 음악회 개최 장소를 예약하려고
④ 합창곡 선정에 조언을 구하려고
⑤ 기부금 사용 내역을 보고하려고

Dear Ms. Robinson,
Robinson 씨께,
The Warblers Choir is happy to announce / that we are invited to compete in the International Young Choir Competition.
Warblers 합창단은 알려드리게 되어 기쁩니다. / 저희가 국제 청년 합창 대회에서 실력을 겨루도록 초청받은 사실을
The competition takes place in London on May 20.
대회는 5월 20일 런던에서 열립니다.
Though we wish to participate in the event, / we do not have the necessary funds to travel to London.
비록 저희는 대회에 참가하고 싶지만, / 저희에게는 런던에 가는 데 필요한 자금이 없습니다.
So we are kindly asking you to support us / by coming to our fundraising concert.
그래서 귀하께서 저희를 후원해 주시기를 정중하게 부탁드립니다. / 저희 모금 음악회에 참석하셔서
It will be held on March 26.
음악회는 3월 26일에 개최될 것입니다.
In this concert, / we shall be able to show you / how big our passion for music is.
이 음악회에서 / 저희는 귀하께 보여드릴 수 있을 것입니다. / 음악에 대한 저희의 열정이 얼마나 큰지
Thank you in advance / for your kind support and help.
미리 감사드립니다. / 귀하의 친절한 후원과 도움에 대해
Sincerely, // Arnold Reynolds
Arnold Reynolds 드림

Robinson 씨께,
저희 Warblers 합창단이 국제 청년 합창 대회에서 실력을 겨루도록 초청받은 사실을 알려드리게 되어 기쁩니다. 대회는 5월 20일 런던에서 열립니다. 비록 저희는 대회에 참가하고 싶지만, 런던에 가는 데 필요한 자금이 없습니다. 그래서 귀하께서 저희 모금 음악회에 참석하셔서 저희를 후원해 주시기를 정중하게 부탁드립니다. 음악회는 3월 26일에 개최될 것입니다. 이 음악회에서 음악에 대한 저희의 열정이 얼마나 큰지 귀하께 보여드릴 수 있을 것입니다. 귀하의 친절한 후원과 도움에 대해 미리 감사드립니다.
Arnold Reynolds 드림

Why? 왜 정답일까?

'So we are kindly asking you to support us by coming to our fundraising concert.'에서 모금 음악회에 참석하여 후원을 해주기를 바란다는 내용이 제시되므로, 글의 목적으로 가장 적절한 것은 ② '모금 음악회 참석을 요청하려고'이다.

- **compete in** ~에서 경쟁하다
- **support** ⓥ 후원하다 ⓝ 지지, 후원
- **passion** ⓝ 열정
- **take place** (행사 등이) 열리다
- **fundraising** ⓝ 모금
- **in advance** 미리

구문 풀이

8행 In this concert, we shall be able to show you how big our passion for music is.
(4형식 동사 / 간접목적어 / 직접목적어(간접의문문))

---

19 학업 최우수상을 받게 되어 기뻐하는 Zoe   정답률 80% | 정답 ③

다음 글에 드러난 Zoe의 심경 변화로 가장 적절한 것은?

① hopeful → disappointed
  기대하는 → 실망한
② guilty → confident
  죄책감을 느끼는 → 자신 있는
✓ nervous → delighted
  긴장한 → 기쁜
④ angry → calm
  화난 → 평온한
⑤ relaxed → proud
  느긋한 → 자랑스러운

The principal stepped on stage.
교장 선생님이 무대 위로 올라갔다.
"Now, I present this year's top academic award / to the student who has achieved the highest placing."
"이제, 저는 올해의 학업 최우수상을 수여합니다. / 최고 등수를 차지한 학생에게"
He smiled at the row of seats / where twelve finalists had gathered.
그는 좌석 열을 향해 미소를 지었다. / 열두 명의 최종 입상 후보자가 모여 있는
Zoe wiped a sweaty hand on her handkerchief / and glanced at the other finalists.
Zoe는 땀에 젖은 손을 손수건에 문질러 닦고는 / 나머지 다른 최종 입상 후보자들을 힐끗 보았다.
They all looked as pale and uneasy as herself.
그들은 모두 그녀만큼 창백하고 불안해 보였다.
Zoe and one of the other finalists / had won first placing in four subjects / so it came down / to how teachers ranked their hard work and confidence.
Zoe와 나머지 다른 최종 입상 후보자 중 한 명이 / 네 개 과목에서 1위를 차지했으므로, / 이제 그것은 좁혀졌다. / 그들의 노력과 자신감을 선생님들이 어떻게 평가하는가로
"The Trophy for General Excellence / is awarded to Miss Zoe Perry," / the principal declared.
"전체 최우수상을 위한 트로피는 / Zoe Perry 양에게 수여됩니다."라고 교장 선생님이 공표했다.
"Could Zoe step this way, please?"
"Zoe는 이리로 나와 주시겠습니까?"
Zoe felt as if she were in heaven.
Zoe는 마치 천국에 있는 기분이었다.
She walked into the thunder of applause with a big smile.
그녀는 활짝 웃음을 지으며 우레와 같은 박수갈채를 받으며 걸어갔다.

교장 선생님이 무대 위로 올라갔다. "이제, 최고 등수를 차지한 학생에게 올해의 학업 최우수상을 수여하겠습니다." 그는 열두 명의 최종 입상 후보자가 모여 있는 좌석 열을 향해 미소를 지었다. Zoe는 땀에 젖은 손을 손수건에 문질러 닦고는 나머지 다른 최종 입상 후보자들을 힐끗 보았다. 그들은 모두 그녀만큼 창백하고 불안해 보였다. Zoe와 나머지 다른 최종 입상 후보자 중 한 명이 네 개 과목에서 1위를 차지했으므로, 선생님들이 그들의 노력과 자신감을 어떻게 평가하는가로 좁혀졌다. "전체 최우수상 트로피는 Zoe Perry 양에게 수여됩니다."라고 교장 선생님이 공표했다. "Zoe는 이리로 나와 주시겠습니까?" Zoe는 마치 천국에 있는 기분이었다. 그녀는 활짝 웃음을 지으며 우레와 같은 박수갈채를 받으며 걸어갔다.

Why? 왜 정답일까?

학업 최우수상 수상자 발표를 앞두고 긴장했던(Zoe wiped a sweaty hand ~. ~ pale and uneasy as herself.) Zoe가 수상자로 호명된 뒤 기뻐했다(Zoe felt as if she were in heaven. She ~ with a big smile.)는 내용의 글이므로, Zoe의 심경 변화로 가장 적절한 것은 ③ '긴장한 → 기쁜'이다.

- **row** ⓝ 줄, 열
- **gather** ⓥ 모이다
- **sweaty** ⓐ 땀에 젖은
- **pale** ⓐ 창백한
- **confidence** ⓝ 자신감
- **finalist** ⓝ 최종 후보자, 결승 진출자
- **wipe** ⓥ 닦다
- **glance at** ~을 흘긋 보다
- **uneasy** ⓐ 불안한
- **applause** ⓝ 박수 갈채

구문 풀이

10행 Zoe felt as if she were in heaven.
「as if + 주어 + 과거 동사 : (실제로 ~이지 않지만) 마치 ~인 것처럼」

---

20 작은 일부터 잘 처리하기   정답률 87% | 정답 ⑤

다음 글에서 필자가 주장하는 바로 가장 적절한 것은?

① 숙면을 위해서는 침대를 깔끔하게 관리해야 한다.
② 일의 효율성을 높이려면 협동심을 발휘해야 한다.
③ 올바른 습관을 기르려면 정해진 규칙을 따라야 한다.
④ 건강을 유지하기 위해서는 기상 시간이 일정해야 한다.
✓ 큰일을 잘 이루려면 작은 일부터 제대로 수행해야 한다.

When I was in the army, / my instructors would show up in my barracks room, / and the first thing they would inspect / was our bed.
내가 군대에 있을 때, / 교관들이 나의 병영 생활관에 모습을 드러내곤 했는데, / 그들이 맨 먼저 검사하곤 했던 것은 / 우리의 침대
It was a simple task, / but every morning / we were required / to make our bed to perfection.
단순한 일이었지만, / 매일 아침 / 우리는 요구받았다. / 침대를 완벽하게 정돈하도록
It seemed a little ridiculous at the time, / but the wisdom of this simple act / has been proven to me many times over.
그 당시에는 약간 우스꽝스럽게 보였지만, / 이 단순한 행위의 지혜는 / 여러 차례 거듭하여 나에게 증명되었다.
If you make your bed every morning, / you will have accomplished the first task of the day.
그것은 여러분이 매일 아침 침대를 정돈한다면, / 여러분은 하루의 첫 번째 과업을 성취한 것이 된다.
It will give you a small sense of pride / and it will encourage you to do another task and another.

그것은 여러분에게 작은 자존감을 주고, / 그것은 또 다른 과업을 잇따라 이어가도록 용기를 줄 것이다.
By the end of the day, / that one task completed / will have turned into many tasks completed.
하루가 끝날 때쯤에는, / 완수된 그 하나의 과업이 / 여러 개의 완수된 과업으로 변해 있을 것이다.
If you can't do little things right, / you will never do the big things right.
여러분이 작은 일들을 제대로 할 수 없으면, / 여러분은 결코 큰일들을 제대로 할 수 없을 것이다.

내가 군대에 있을 때, 교관들이 나의 병영 생활관에 모습을 드러내곤 했었는데, 그들이 맨 먼저 검사하곤 했던 것은 우리의 침대였다. 단순한 일이었지만, 매일 아침 우리는 침대를 완벽하게 정돈하도록 요구받았다. 그 당시에는 약간 우스꽝스럽게 보였지만, 이 단순한 행위의 지혜는 여러 차례 거듭하여 나에게 증명되었다. 여러분이 매일 아침 침대를 정돈한다면, 여러분은 하루의 첫 번째 과업을 성취한 것이 된다. 그것은 여러분에게 작은 자존감을 주고, 또 다른 과업을 잇따라 이어가도록 용기를 줄 것이다. 하루가 끝날 때쯤에는, 완수된 그 하나의 과업이 여러 개의 완수된 과업으로 변해 있을 것이다. 작은 일들을 제대로 할 수 없으면, 여러분은 결코 큰일들을 제대로 할 수 없을 것이다.

Why? 왜 정답일까?
매일 잠자리 정돈부터 잘해야 했던 군대 시절 이야기를 토대로 작은 일부터 잘 해내야 큰일을 처리할 수 있다(If you can't do little things right, you will never do the big things right.)는 결론을 이끌어내는 글이다. 따라서 필자의 주장으로 가장 적절한 것은 ⑤ '큰일을 잘 이루려면 작은 일부터 제대로 수행해야 한다.'이다.

- inspect ⓥ 조사하다
- make the bed 잠자리를 정돈하다
- wisdom ⓝ 지혜
- turn into ~로 바뀌다
- task ⓝ 일, 과업, 과제
- ridiculous ⓐ 우스꽝스러운
- complete ⓥ 완수하다

구문 풀이
6행 If you make your bed every morning, you will have accomplished the first
접속사(조건) 동사(현재)   동사(미래완료)
task of the day.

---

21 적극적으로 구직 활동하기 정답률 58% | 정답 ⑤

밑줄 친 Leave those activities to the rest of the sheep이 다음 글에서 의미하는 바로 가장 적절한 것은? [3점]
① Try to understand other job-seekers' feelings.
 다른 구직자들의 심정을 이해하려고 노력해보라.
② Keep calm and stick to your present position.
 평정심을 유지하고 현재 입장을 지켜라.
③ Don't be scared of the job-seeking competition.
 구직 경쟁을 두려워하지 말라.
④ Send occasional emails to your future employers.
 미래 고용주들에게 가끔 이메일을 보내라.
☑⑤ Be more active to stand out from other job-seekers.
 다른 구직자들보다 두드러지기 위해 더 적극적으로 하라.

A job search is not a passive task.
구직 활동은 수동적인 일이 아니다.
When you are searching, / you are not browsing, / nor are you "just looking".
여러분이 구직 활동을 할 때, / 여러분은 이것저것 훑어보고 다니지 않으며 / '그냥 구경만 하지도 않는다.
Browsing is not an effective way / to reach a goal / you claim to want to reach.
훑어보고 다니는 것은 효과적인 방법이 아니다. / 목표에 도달할 수 있는 / 여러분이 도달하기를 원한다고 주장하는
If you are acting with purpose, / if you are serious about anything you chose to do, / then you need to be direct, / focused / and whenever possible, / clever.
만약 여러분이 목적을 가지고 행동한다면, / 만약 여러분이 하고자 선택한 어떤 것에 대해 진지하다면, / 여러분은 직접적이고, 집중해야 하며, / 가능한 모든 경우에, / 영리해야 한다.
Everyone else searching for a job / has the same goal, / competing for the same jobs.
일자리를 찾는 다른 모든 사람이 / 같은 목표를 지니고 있으며, / 같은 일자리를 얻기 위해 경쟁한다.
You must do more than the rest of the herd.
여러분은 그 무리의 나머지 사람들보다 더 많은 것을 해야 한다.
Regardless of how long it may take you / to find and get the job you want, / being proactive will logically get you results faster / than if you rely only on browsing online job boards / and emailing an occasional resume.
여러분에게 얼마나 오랜 시간이 걸리든 간에, / 원하는 직업을 찾아서 얻는 데 / 진취적인 것이 논리적으로 여러분에게 더 빨리 결과를 가져다줄 것이다. / 여러분이 온라인 취업 게시판을 검색하는 것에만 의존하는 것보다는 / 그리고 가끔 이력서를 이메일로 보내는 것
Leave those activities to the rest of the sheep.
그런 활동들은 나머지 양들이 하도록 남겨 두라.

구직 활동은 수동적인 일이 아니다. 구직 활동을 할 때, 여러분은 이것저것 훑어보고 다니지 않으며 '그냥 구경만 하지도' 않는다. 훑어보고 다니는 것은 여러분이 도달하기를 원한다고 주장하는 목표에 도달할 수 있는 효과적인 방법이 아니다. 만약 여러분이 목적을 가지고 행동한다면, 하고자 선택한 어떤 것에 대해 진지하다면, 여러분은 직접적이고, 집중해야 하며, 가능한 한 영리해야 한다. 일자리를 찾는 다른 모든 사람이 같은 목표를 지니고 있으며, 같은 일자리를 얻기 위해 경쟁한다. 여러분은 그 무리의 나머지 사람들보다 더 많은 것을 해야 한다. 원하는 직업을 찾아서 얻는 데 얼마나 오랜 시간이 걸리든 간에, 온라인 취업 게시판을 검색하고 가끔 이력서를 이메일로 보내는 것에만 의존하는 것보다는 진취적인 것이 논리적으로 여러분이 더 빨리 결과를 얻도록 해줄 것이다. 그런 활동들은 나머지 양들이 하도록 남겨 두라.

Why? 왜 정답일까?
마지막 문장 바로 앞에서 온라인 취업 게시판을 검색하고 가끔 이메일을 보내는 것보다 더 적극적인 행동을 해야 한다(being proactive will ~ get you results faster)고 언급한 뒤, 마지막 문장에서는 비교적 소극적인 행동은 남더러 하게 두라고 말하며 적극적인 행동의 필요성을 다시금 주장한다. 따라서 밑줄 친 부분의 의미로 가장 적절한 것은 ⑤ '다른 구직자들보다 두드러지기 위해 더 적극적으로 하라.'이다.

- passive ⓐ 수동적인
- herd ⓝ 무리
- proactive ⓐ 상황을 앞서서 주도하는
- occasional ⓐ 가끔씩의
- stand out from ~에서 두드러지다
- claim ⓥ 주장하다
- regardless of ~와 상관없이
- logically ⓐ 논리적으로
- resume ⓝ 이력서

구문 풀이
1행 When you are searching, you are not browsing, nor are you "just looking".
「nor + 동사 + 주어: ~도 않대(도치 구문)」

22 수면의 중요한 기능 정답률 92% | 정답 ①

다음 글의 요지로 가장 적절한 것은?
☑① 수면은 건강 유지와 최상의 기능 발휘에 도움이 된다.
② 업무량이 증가하면 필요한 수면 시간도 증가한다.
③ 균형 잡힌 식단을 유지하면 뇌 기능이 향상된다.
④ 불면증은 주위 사람들에게 부정적인 영향을 미친다.
⑤ 꿈의 내용은 깨어 있는 시간 동안의 경험을 반영한다.

Many people view sleep as merely a "down time" / when their brain shuts off and their body rests.
많은 사람이 수면을 그저 '가동되지 않는 시간'으로 본다. / 그들의 뇌는 멈추고 신체는 쉬는
In a rush to meet work, school, family, or household responsibilities, / people cut back on their sleep, / thinking it won't be a problem, / because all of these other activities seem much more important.
일, 학교, 가족, 또는 가정의 책임을 다하기 위해 서두르는 와중에, / 사람들은 수면 시간을 줄이고, / 그것이 문제가 되지 않을 것으로 생각하는데, / 왜냐하면 이러한 모든 다른 활동들이 훨씬 더 중요해 보이기 때문이다.
But research reveals / that a number of vital tasks carried out during sleep / help to maintain good health / and enable people to function at their best.
하지만 연구는 밝히고 있다. / 수면 중에 수행되는 많은 매우 중요한 과업이 / 건강을 유지하는 데 도움이 되고 / 사람들이 최상의 수준으로 기능할 수 있게 해 준다는 것을
While you sleep, / your brain is hard at work / forming the pathways / necessary for learning and creating memories and new insights.
여러분이 잠을 자는 동안, / 여러분의 뇌는 열심히 일하고 있다. / 경로를 형성하느라 / 학습하고 기억과 새로운 통찰을 만드는 데 필요한
Without enough sleep, / you can't focus and pay attention / or respond quickly.
충분한 수면이 없다면, / 여러분은 정신을 집중하고 주의를 기울이거나 / 빠르게 반응할 수 없다.
A lack of sleep may even cause mood problems.
수면 부족은 심지어 감정 문제를 일으킬 수도 있다.
In addition, / growing evidence shows / that a continuous lack of sleep / increases the risk for developing serious diseases.
게다가, / 점점 더 많은 증거가 보여 준다. / 계속된 수면 부족이 / 심각한 질병의 발생 위험을 증가시킨다는 것

많은 사람이 수면을 그저 뇌는 멈추고 신체는 쉬는 '가동되지 않는 시간'으로 본다. 일, 학교, 가족, 또는 가정의 책임을 다하기 위해 서두르는 와중에, 사람들은 수면 시간을 줄이고, 그것이 문제가 되지 않을 것으로 생각하는데, 왜냐하면 이러한 모든 다른 활동들이 훨씬 더 중요해 보이기 때문이다. 하지만 연구는 수면 중에 수행되는 매우 중요한 여러 과업이 건강을 유지하는 데 도움이 되고 사람들이 최상의 수준으로 기능할 수 있게 해 준다는 것을 밝히고 있다. 잠을 자는 동안, 여러분의 뇌는 학습하고 기억과 새로운 통찰을 만드는 데 필요한 경로를 형성하느라 열심히 일하고 있다. 충분한 수면이 없다면, 여러분은 정신을 집중하고 주의를 기울이거나 빠르게 반응할 수 없다. 수면이 부족하면 심지어 감정 (조절) 문제를 일으킬 수도 있다. 게다가, 계속된 수면 부족이 심각한 질병의 발생 위험을 증가시킨다는 것을 점점 더 많은 증거가 보여 준다.

Why? 왜 정답일까?
주제를 제시하는 'But ~ a number of vital tasks carried out during sleep help to maintain good health and enable people to function at their best.'에서 수면 중 이루어지는 많은 일이 건강 및 기능 유지에 도움이 된다고 하므로, 글의 요지로 가장 적절한 것은 ① '수면은 건강 유지와 최상의 기능 발휘에 도움이 된다.'이다.

- view A as B A를 B로 보다
- down time 정지 시간, 휴식 시간
- carry out ~을 수행하다
- develop a disease 병을 키우다
- merely ⓐ 그저, 단순히
- cut back on ~을 줄이다
- insight ⓝ 통찰력

구문 풀이
5행 But research reveals that a number of vital tasks carried out during sleep
접속사(~것)←┘ 주어(a number of + 복수 명사: 많은 ~) 과거분사구
help to maintain good health and enable people to function at their best.
동사1 목적어   동사2 목적어 목적격 보어

---

23 미래 날씨 예측에 영향을 받는 인간의 생활 정답률 63% | 정답 ④

다음 글의 주제로 가장 적절한 것은? [3점]
① new technologies dealing with climate change
 기후 변화에 대처하는 신기술
② difficulties in predicting the weather correctly
 정확한 날씨 예측의 어려움
③ weather patterns influenced by rising temperatures
 온도 상승에 영향을 받는 날씨 패턴
☑④ knowledge of the climate widely affecting our lives
 우리 삶에 광범위하게 영향을 미치는 기후에 관한 지식
⑤ traditional wisdom helping our survival in harsh climates
 혹독한 기후에서 우리의 생존을 돕는 전통적 지혜

The whole of human society / operates on knowing the future weather.
전체 인간 사회는 / 미래의 날씨를 아는 것을 기반으로 운영된다.
For example, / farmers in India know / when the monsoon rains will come next year / and so they know when to plant the crops.
예를 들어, / 인도의 농부들은 알고, / 내년에 몬순 장마가 올 시기를 / 그래서 그들은 작물을 심을 시기를 안다.
Farmers in Indonesia know / there are two monsoon rains each year, / so next year they can have two harvests.
인도네시아의 농부들은 알고, / 매년 몬순 장마가 두 번 있다는 것을 / 그래서 이듬해 그들은 수확을 두 번 할 수 있다.
This is based on their knowledge of the past, / as the monsoons have always come / at about the same time each year in living memory.
이것은 과거에 대한 그들의 지식에 기반을 두고 있는데, / 몬순은 항상 왔기 때문이다 / 살아 있는 기억 속에서 매년 거의 같은 시기에
But the need to predict goes deeper than this; / it influences every part of our lives.

[03회] 2022학년도 3월 033

그러나 예측할 필요는 이것보다 더욱더 깊어지는데 / 그것은 우리 생활의 모든 부분에 영향을 미치기 때문이다.

Our houses, roads, railways, airports, offices, and so on / are all designed for the local climate.
우리의 집, 도로, 철도, 공항, 사무실 등은 / 모두 지역의 기후에 맞추어 설계된다.

For example, / in England all the houses have central heating, / as the outside temperature is usually below 20℃, / but no air-conditioning, / as temperatures rarely go beyond 26℃, / while in Australia the opposite is true: / most houses have air-conditioning but rarely central heating.
예를 들어, / 영국에서는 모든 집은 중앙 난방을 갖추고 있지만, / 외부의 기온이 대체로 섭씨 20도 미만이기 때문에 / 냉방기는 없다. / 기온이 섭씨 26도 위로 올라가는 일은 거의 없어서 / 호주에서는 그 정반대가 사실인 반면에 / 대부분의 집은 냉방기를 갖추었지만 중앙 난방은 거의 없다.

전체 인간 사회는 미래의 날씨를 아는 것을 기반으로 운영된다. 예를 들어, 인도의 농부들은 내년에 몬순 장마가 올 시기를 알고, 그래서 그들은 작물을 심을 시기를 안다. 인도네시아의 농부들은 매년 몬순 장마가 두 번 있다는 것을 알고, 그래서 이듬해에 그들은 수확을 두 번 할 수 있다. 이것은 과거에 대한 그들의 지식에 기반을 두고 있는데, 살아 있는 기억 속에서 몬순은 매년 항상 거의 같은 시기에 왔기 때문이다. 그러나 예측할 필요는 이것보다 더욱더 깊어지는데, 그것은 우리 생활의 모든 부분에 영향을 미치기 때문이다. 우리의 집, 도로, 철도, 공항, 사무실 등은 모두 지역의 기후에 맞추어 설계된다. 예를 들어, 영국에서는 외부의 기온이 대체로 섭씨 20도 미만이기 때문에 모든 집은 중앙 난방을 갖추고 있지만, 기온이 섭씨 26도 위로 올라가는 일은 거의 없어서 냉방기는 없는 반면, 호주에서는 그 정반대가 사실이어서, 대부분의 집은 냉방기를 갖추었지만 중앙 난방은 거의 없다.

Why? 왜 정답일까?

첫 문장에서 인간 사회는 미래 날씨 예측에 기반하여 운영된다(The whole of human society operates on knowing the future weather.)는 중심 내용을 제시하는 것으로 보아, 글의 주제로 가장 적절한 것은 ④ '우리 삶에 광범위하게 영향을 미치는 기후에 관한 지식'이다.

- monsoon ⓝ (동남아 여름철의) 몬순, 우기, 장마
- harvest ⓝ 수확
- predict ⓥ 예측하다
- influence ⓥ 영향을 미치다
- harsh ⓐ 혹독한

구문 풀이

2행 For example, farmers in India know when the monsoon rains will come next year and so they know when to plant the crops.
주어1 / 동사1 / 목적어1(간접의문문)
주어2 동사2 목적어2(의문사 + to부정사)

---

24 감정을 인식하고 명명할 수 있는 능력 정답률 64% | 정답 ②

다음 글의 제목으로 가장 적절한 것은?

① True Friendship Endures Emotional Arguments – 진정한 우정은 감정적인 다툼을 견뎌낸다
✓② Detailed Labeling of Emotions Is Beneficial – 감정에 상세하게 이름을 붙이는 것은 이롭다
③ Labeling Emotions: Easier Said Than Done – 감정에 이름 붙이기: 말하기는 쉬워도 행하기는 어렵다
④ Categorize and Label Tasks for Efficiency – 효율성을 위해 작업을 분류하고 이름 붙이라
⑤ Be Brave and Communicate Your Needs – 용기를 갖고 여러분의 요구를 전달하라

Our ability to accurately recognize and label emotions / is often referred to as *emotional granularity.*
감정을 정확하게 인식하고 그것에 이름을 붙일 수 있는 우리의 능력은 / 흔히 *감정 입자도*라고 불린다.

In the words of Harvard psychologist Susan David, / "Learning to label emotions / with a more nuanced vocabulary / can be absolutely transformative."
Harvard 대학의 심리학자인 Susan David의 말에 의하면, / "이름을 붙이는 법을 배우는 것은 / 감정에 더 미묘한 차이가 있는 어휘로 / 절대적으로 변화시킬 수 있다."

David explains / that if we don't have a rich emotional vocabulary, / it is difficult / to communicate our needs / and to get the support that we need from others.
David은 설명한다. / 우리가 풍부한 감정적인 어휘를 갖고 있지 않으면, / 어렵다고 / 우리의 욕구를 전달하는 것이 / 그리고 우리가 필요로 하는 지지를 다른 사람들로부터 얻는 것이

But those / who are able to distinguish between a range of various emotions / "do much, much better / at managing the ups and downs of ordinary existence / than those who see everything in black and white."
그러나 사람들은 / 광범위한 다양한 감정을 구별할 수 있는 / "훨씬, 훨씬 더 잘한다. / 평범한 존재로 사는 중에 겪는 좋은 일들과 궂은 일들을 다스리는 것을 / 모든 것을 흑백 논리로 보는 사람들보다"

In fact, / research shows / that the process of labeling emotional experience / is related to greater emotion regulation and psychosocial well-being.
사실, / 연구 결과가 보여 준다. / 감정적인 경험에 이름을 붙이는 과정이 / 더 큰 감정 통제 및 심리 사회적인 행복과 관련되어 있다는 것을

감정을 정확하게 인식하고 그것에 이름을 붙일 수 있는 우리의 능력은 흔히 *감정 입자도*라고 불린다. Harvard 대학의 심리학자인 Susan David의 말에 의하면, "감정에 더 미묘한 차이가 있는 어휘로 이름을 붙이는 법을 배우는 것은 절대적으로 (사람을) 변화시킬 수 있다." David는 우리가 풍부한 감정적인 어휘를 갖고 있지 않으면, 우리의 욕구를 전달하고 다른 사람들로부터 우리가 필요로 하는 지지를 얻는 것이 어렵다고 설명한다. 그러나 광범위한 다양한 감정을 구별할 수 있는 사람들은 "모든 것을 흑백 논리로 보는 사람들보다 평범한 존재로 사는 중에 겪는 좋은 일들과 궂은 일들을 다스리는 일을 훨씬, 훨씬 더 잘한다." 사실, 감정적인 경험에 이름을 붙이는 과정은 더 큰 감정 통제 및 심리 사회적인 행복과 관련되어 있다는 것을 연구 결과가 보여 준다.

Why? 왜 정답일까?

마지막 문장에 따르면 감정적인 경험에 이름을 붙이는 것은 감정을 더 잘 통제하고 심리 사회적으로 더 큰 행복감을 느끼는 것과 관련되어 있다(~ the process of labeling emotional experience is related to greater emotion regulation and psychosocial well-being.)고 하므로, 글의 제목으로 가장 적절한 것은 ② '감정에 상세하게 이름을 붙이는 것은 이롭다'이다.

- accurately ⓐⓓ 정확하게
- refer to A as B A를 B라고 부르다
- absolutely ⓐⓓ 절대적으로
- transformative ⓐ 변화시키는
- communicate ⓥ 전달하다
- distinguish ⓥ 구별하다
- ups and downs 좋은 일과 궂은 일, 오르락내리락
- existence ⓝ 존재
- regulation ⓝ 통제
- psychosocial ⓐ 심리사회적인

구문 풀이

1행 Our ability to accurately recognize and label emotions is often referred to as *emotional granularity.*
주어 / 형용사적 용법 / 동사(refer to A as B의 수동태)

25 온라인 강의와 학습 자료를 이용한 영국인들의 비율 정답률 68% | 정답 ⑤

다음 도표의 내용과 일치하지 않는 것은?

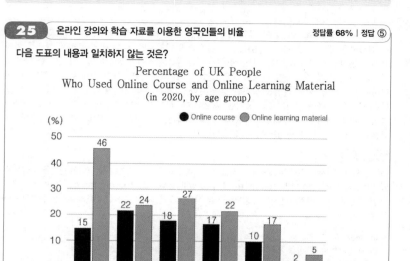

Percentage of UK People
Who Used Online Course and Online Learning Material
(in 2020, by age group)

The above graph shows the percentage of people in the UK / who used online courses and online learning materials, / by age group / in 2020.
위 도표는 영국 사람들의 비율을 보여 준다. / 온라인 강의와 온라인 학습 자료를 이용한 / 연령 집단별로 / 2020년도에

① In each age group, / the percentage of people / who used online learning materials / was higher than that of people / who used online courses.
각 연령 집단에서 / 사람들의 비율이 / 온라인 학습 자료를 이용한 / 사람들의 비율보다 더 높았다. / 온라인 강의를 이용한

② The 25 – 34 age group / had the highest percentage of people / who used online courses / in all the age groups.
25세에서 34세 연령 집단에서 / 차이는 /사람들의 비율이 / 온라인 강의를 이용한 / 모든 연령 집단 중

③ Those aged 65 and older / were the least likely to use online courses / among the six age groups.
65세 이상인 사람들이 / 온라인 강의를 이용할 가능성이 가장 낮았다. / 여섯 개의 연령 집단 가운데서

④ Among the six age groups, / the gap / between the percentage of people / who used online courses / and that of people who used online learning materials / was the greatest in the 16 – 24 age group.
여섯 개의 연령 집단 가운데서, / 차이는 / 사람들의 비율과 / 온라인 강의를 이용한 / 그리고 온라인 학습 자료를 이용한 사람들의 비율 사이의 / 16세에서 24세 연령 집단에서 가장 컸다.

✓⑤ In each of the 35 – 44, 45 – 54, and 55 – 64 age groups, / more than one in five people / used online learning materials.
35세에서 44세, 45세에서 54세, 55세에서 64세의 각 연령 집단에서 / 다섯 명 중 한 명이 넘는 비율의 사람들이 / 온라인 학습 자료를 이용했다.

위 도표는 2020년도에 온라인 강의와 온라인 학습 자료를 이용한 영국 사람들의 비율을 연령 집단별로 보여 준다. ① 각 연령 집단에서 온라인 학습 자료를 이용한 사람들의 비율이 온라인 강의를 이용한 사람들의 비율보다 더 높았다. ② 모든 연령 집단 중, 25세에서 34세 연령 집단에서 온라인 강의를 이용한 사람들의 비율이 가장 높았다. ③ 여섯 개의 연령 집단 가운데서, 65세 이상인 사람들이 온라인 강의를 이용할 가능성이 가장 낮았다. ④ 여섯 개의 연령 집단 가운데서, 온라인 강의를 이용한 사람들의 비율과 온라인 학습 자료를 이용한 사람들의 비율 차이는 16세에서 24세 연령 집단에서 가장 컸다. ⑤ 35세에서 44세, 45세에서 54세, 55세에서 64세의 각 연령 집단에서 다섯 명 중 한 명이 넘는 비율로 온라인 학습 자료를 이용했다.

Why? 왜 정답일까?

도표에 따르면 55 ~ 64세 집단에서 온라인 학습 자료를 이용한 비율은 17%로, 전체의 5분의 1에 미치지 못했다. 따라서 도표와 일치하지 않는 것은 ⑤이다.

- learning material 학습 자료
- be the least likely to ~할 가능성이 가장 낮다

26 Antonie van Leeuwenhoek의 생애 정답률 91% | 정답 ③

Antonie van Leeuwenhoek에 관한 다음 글의 내용과 일치하지 않는 것은?

① 세포 연구로 잘 알려진 과학자였다.
② 22살에 Delft로 돌아왔다.
✓③ 여러 개의 언어를 알았다.
④ 유리로 물건을 만드는 방법을 알고 있었다.
⑤ 화가를 고용하여 설명하는 것을 그리게 했다.

「Antonie van Leeuwenhoek was a scientist / well known for his cell research.」 ①의 근거 일치
Antonie van Leeuwenhoek은 과학자였다. / 세포 연구로 잘 알려진

He was born in Delft, the Netherlands, / on October 24, 1632.
그는 네덜란드 Delft에서 태어났다. / 1632년 10월 24일에

At the age of 16, / he began to learn job skills in Amsterdam.
16살에 / 그는 Amsterdam에서 직업 기술을 배우기 시작했다.

「At the age of 22, / Leeuwenhoek returned to Delft.」 ②의 근거 일치
22살에 / Leeuwenhoek은 Delft로 돌아왔다.

It wasn't easy for Leeuwenhoek to become a scientist.
Leeuwenhoek이 과학자가 되기는 쉽지 않았다.

「He knew only one language — Dutch —」 / which was quite unusual for scientists of his time. ③의 근거 불일치
그는 오직 한 가지 언어, 즉 네덜란드어만을 알고 있었는데, / 그것은 그 당시 과학자들에게는 상당히 드문 것이었다.

But his curiosity was endless, / and he worked hard.
하지만 그의 호기심은 끝이 없었고, / 그는 열심히 노력했다.

He had an important skill.
그에게는 중요한 기술이 있었다.

[문제편 p.031]

「He knew how to make things out of glass.」 ④의근거 일치
그는 유리로 물건을 만드는 법을 알고 있었다.
This skill came in handy / when he made lenses for his simple microscope.
이 기술은 도움이 되었다. / 그가 자신의 간단한 현미경에 쓰일 렌즈를 만들 때
He saw tiny veins / with blood flowing through them.
그는 미세한 혈관을 보았다. / 그 속에 피가 흐르고 있는
He also saw living bacteria in pond water.
그는 또한 연못 물 속에서 살아 있는 박테리아를 보았다.
He paid close attention to the things he saw / and wrote down his observations.
그는 자신이 본 것들에 세심한 주의를 기울였고 / 그가 관찰한 것을 기록했다.
「Since he couldn't draw well, / he hired an artist / to draw pictures of what he described.」
그가 그림을 잘 그릴 수 없었기 때문에, / 그는 화가를 고용하여 / 자신이 설명하는 것을 그림으로 그리게 했다. ⑤의근거 일치

Antonie van Leeuwenhoek은 세포 연구로 잘 알려진 과학자였다. 그는 1632년 10월 24일 네덜란드 Delft에서 태어났다. 그는 16살에 Amsterdam에서 직업 기술을 배우기 시작했다. Leeuwenhoek은 22살에 Delft로 돌아왔다. Leeuwenhoek이 과학자가 되기는 쉽지 않았다. 그는 오직 한 가지 언어, 즉 네덜란드어만을 알고 있었는데, 그것은 그 당시 과학자들에게는 상당히 드문 것이었다. 하지만 그의 호기심은 끝이 없었고, 그는 열심히 노력했다. 그에게는 중요한 기술이 있었다. 그는 유리로 물건을 만드는 법을 알고 있었다. 이 기술은 그가 자신의 간단한 현미경에 쓰일 렌즈를 만들 때 도움이 되었다. 그는 피가 흐르고 있는 미세한 혈관을 보았다. 그는 또한 연못 물속에서 살아 있는 박테리아를 보았다. 그는 자신이 본 것들에 세심한 주의를 기울였고 관찰한 것을 기록했다. 그는 그림을 잘 그릴 수 없었기 때문에, 화가를 고용하여 자신이 설명하는 것을 그림으로 그리게 했다.

Why? 왜 정답일까?

'He knew only one language — Dutch ~'에서 Antonie van Leeuwenhoek는 오직 네덜란드어만 알았다고 하므로, 내용과 일치하지 않는 것은 ③ '여러 개의 언어를 알았다.'이다.

Why? 왜 오답일까?

① 'Antonie van Leeuwenhoek was a scientist well known for his cell research.'의 내용과 일치한다.
② 'At the age of 22, Leeuwenhoek returned to Delft.'의 내용과 일치한다.
④ 'He knew how to make things out of glass.'의 내용과 일치한다.
⑤ '~ he hired an artist to draw pictures of what he described.'의 내용과 일치한다.

● curiosity ⓝ 호기심
● make A out of B B로 A를 만들다
● pond ⓝ 연못
● endless ⓐ 끝없는
● microscope ⓝ 현미경
● observation ⓝ 관찰

구문 풀이

5행 He knew only one language — Dutch — which was quite unusual for
　　　　　　　　　　　　　선행사(문장)　　　　　　계속적 용법
scientists of his time.

---

27 꽃 교실 안내　　　정답률 95% | 정답 ④

Rachel's Flower Class에 관한 다음 안내문의 내용과 일치하지 <u>않는</u> 것은?
① 플라워 박스 만들기 수업은 오후 1시에 시작된다.
② 수강료에 꽃값과 다른 재료비가 포함된다.
③ 수강생은 가위와 가방을 가져와야 한다.
✔ 수업 등록은 전화로만 할 수 있다.
⑤ 수업 당일 취소 시 환불을 받을 수 없다.

Rachel's Flower Class
Rachel의 꽃 교실
Make Your Life More Beautiful!
인생을 더 아름답게 만드세요!
Class Schedule (Every Monday to Friday)
수업 일정 (매주 월요일부터 금요일까지)

Flower Arrangement 꽃꽂이	11 a.m. – 12 p.m. 오전 11시 ~ 정오
「Flower Box Making 플라워 박스 만들기	1 p.m. – 2 p.m.」 ①의근거 일치 오후 1시 ~ 오후 2시

Price
가격
「$50 for each class (flowers and other materials included)」 ②의근거 일치
각 수업당 $50 (꽃값과 다른 재료비 포함)
「Bring your own scissors and a bag.」 ③의근거 일치
본인의 가위와 가방을 가져오세요.
Other Info.
다른 정보
「You can sign up for classes / either online or by phone.」 ④의근거 불일치
수업 등록을 할 수 있습니다. / 온라인이나 전화로
「No refund for cancellations on the day of your class」 ⑤의근거 일치
수업 당일 취소 시 환불 불가
To contact, / visit www.rfclass.com or call 03-221-2131.
연락하시려면, / www.rfclass.com을 방문하시거나 03-221-2131로 전화주세요.

Rachel의 꽃 교실
인생을 더 아름답게 만드세요!

수업 일정 (매주 월요일부터 금요일까지)

꽃꽂이	오전 11시 ~ 정오
플라워 박스 만들기	오후 1시 ~ 오후 2시

가격
• 각 수업당 $50 (꽃값과 다른 재료비 포함)

• 본인의 가위와 가방을 가져오세요.
다른 정보
• 온라인이나 전화로 수업 등록을 할 수 있습니다.
• 수업 당일 취소 시 환불 불가

연락하시려면, www.rfclass.com을 방문하시거나 03-221-2131로 전화주세요.

Why? 왜 정답일까?

'You can sign up for classes either online or by phone.'에서 수업 등록은 전화뿐 아니라 온라인으로도 가능하다고 하므로, 안내문의 내용과 일치하지 않는 것은 ④ '수업 등록은 전화로만 할 수 있다.'이다.

Why? 왜 오답일까?

① 'Flower Box Making / 01 p.m. – 02 p.m.'의 내용과 일치한다.
② '$50 for each class (flowers and other materials included)'의 내용과 일치한다.
③ 'Bring your own scissors and a bag.'의 내용과 일치한다.
⑤ 'No refund for cancellations on the day of your class'의 내용과 일치한다.

● flower arrangement 꽃꽂이
● sign up for ~에 등록하다

---

28 야간 궁궐 투어 안내　　　정답률 91% | 정답 ⑤

Nighttime Palace Tour에 관한 다음 안내문의 내용과 일치하는 것은?
① 금요일에는 하루에 두 번 투어가 운영된다.
② 8세 미만 어린이의 티켓은 5달러이다.
③ 예약은 투어 하루 전까지만 가능하다.
④ 투어 가이드의 안내 없이 궁궐을 둘러본다.
✔ 추가 비용 없이 전통 의상을 입어 볼 수 있다.

Nighttime Palace Tour
야간 궁궐 투어
Date: Friday, April 29 – Sunday, May 15
날짜: 4월 29일 금요일 ~ 5월 15일 일요일
Time
시간

Friday 금요일	7 p.m. – 8:30 p.m.」 ①의근거 불일치 오후 7시 ~ 오후 8시 30분
Saturday & Sunday 토요일과 일요일	6 p.m. – 7:30 p.m. 오후 6시 ~ 오후 7시 30분
	8 p.m. – 9:30 p.m. 오후 8시 ~ 오후 9시 30분

Tickets & Booking
티켓과 예약
$15 per person 「(free for kids under 8)」 ②의근거 불일치
1인당 15달러 (8세 미만 어린이는 무료)
「Bookings will be accepted / up to 2 hours before the tour starts.」 ③의근거 불일치
예약은 가능합니다. / 투어가 시작되기 2시간 전까지
Program Activities
프로그램 활동
「Group tour with a tour guide (1 hour)」 ④의근거 불일치
투어 가이드와 단체 투어 (1시간)
Trying traditional foods and drinks (30 minutes)
전통 음식 시식 및 음료 시음 (30분)
「You can try on traditional clothes / with no extra charge.」 ⑤의근거 일치
전통 의상을 입어 볼 수 있습니다. / 추가 비용 없이
For more information, / please visit our website, www.palacenighttour.com.
더 많은 정보를 원하시면, / 저희 웹 사이트 www.palacenighttour.com에 방문하세요.

야간 궁궐 투어

날짜: 4월 29일 금요일 ~ 5월 15일 일요일

시간

금요일	오후 7시 ~ 오후 8시 30분
토요일과 일요일	오후 6시 ~ 오후 7시 30분
	오후 8시 ~ 오후 9시 30분

티켓과 예약
• 1인당 15달러 (8세 미만 어린이는 무료)
• 예약은 투어 시작 2시간 전까지 가능합니다.

프로그램 활동
• 투어 가이드와 단체 투어 (1시간)
• 전통 음식 시식 및 음료 시음 (30분)

※ 추가 비용 없이 전통 의상을 입어 볼 수 있습니다.
※ 더 많은 정보를 원하시면, 저희 웹 사이트 www.palacenighttour.com에 방문하세요.

Why? 왜 정답일까?

'You can try on traditional clothes with no extra charge.'에서 전통 의상 착용은 추가 비용 없이도 가능하다고 하므로, 안내문의 내용과 일치하는 것은 ⑤ '추가 비용 없이 전통 의상을 입어 볼 수 있다.'이다.

Why? 왜 오답일까?

① 'Friday / 7 p.m. – 8:30 p.m.'에서 금요일 투어는 한 번만 열린다고 하였다.
② '(free for kids under 8)'에서 8세 미만 어린이는 무료 입장이라고 하였다.
③ 'Bookings will be accepted up to 2 hours before the tour starts.'에서 투어 예약은 투어 시작 2시간 전까지 가능하다고 하였다.

④ 'Group tour with a tour guide (1 hour)'에서 투어 가이드와 함께 1시간 동안 그룹 투어를 하게 된다고 하였다.

● palace ⓝ 궁전　　　　　● accept ⓥ 접수하다, 수용하다

29　비슷한 대상과 어울리기를 선호하는 경향　정답률 63% | 정답 ③

다음 글의 밑줄 친 부분 중, 어법상 틀린 것은?

We usually get along best with people / who we think are like us.
우리는 보통 사람들과 가장 잘 지낸다. / 우리가 같다고 생각하는

In fact, we seek them out.
사실, 우리는 그들을 찾아낸다.

It's why places like Little Italy, Chinatown, and Koreatown ① exist.
이 이유로 리틀 이탈리아, 차이나타운, 코리아타운과 같은 장소들이 존재한다.

But I'm not just talking about race, skin color, or religion.
하지만 나는 인종, 피부색, 또는 종교만을 말하는 것이 아니다.

I'm talking about people / who share our values / and look at the world / the same way we ② do.
나는 사람들을 말하는 것이다. / 우리의 가치관을 공유하고 / 세상을 바라보는 / 우리와 같은 방식으로

As the saying goes, / birds of a feather flock together.
속담에서처럼, / 같은 깃털을 가진 새가 함께 무리 짓는다.

This is a very common human tendency / ✔ that is rooted in how our species developed.
이것은 매우 흔한 인간의 경향이다. / 우리 종이 발전한 방식에 깊게 뿌리박혀 있는

Imagine you are walking out in a forest.
여러분이 숲에 나가 걷는다고 상상해 보라.

You would be conditioned / to avoid something unfamiliar or foreign / because there is a high likelihood / that ④ it would be interested in killing you.
여러분은 조건화되어 있을 것이다. / 친숙하지 않거나 낯선 것을 피하도록 / 가능성이 커서 / 그런 것이 여러분을 죽이는 데 관심이 있을

Similarities make us ⑤ relate better to other people / because we think / they'll understand us on a deeper level than other people.
유사점은 우리가 다른 사람들과 마음이 더 잘 통할 수 있도록 하는데, / 우리가 생각하기 때문이다. / 그들이 우리를 다른 사람들보다 더 깊이 있는 수준으로 이해할 것이라고

우리는 보통 우리와 같다고 생각하는 사람들과 가장 잘 지낸다. 사실, 우리는 그들을 찾아낸다. 이 이유로 리틀 이탈리아, 차이나타운, 코리아타운과 같은 장소들이 존재한다. 하지만 나는 인종, 피부색, 또는 종교만을 말하는 것이 아니다. 우리의 가치관을 공유하고 우리와 같은 방식으로 세상을 바라보는 사람들을 말하는 것이다. 속담에서처럼, 같은 깃털을 가진 새가 함께 무리 짓는다(유유상종이다). 이것은 우리 종이 발전한 방식에 깊게 뿌리박혀 있는 매우 흔한 인간의 경향이다. 여러분이 숲에 나가 걷는다고 상상해 보라. 친숙하지 않거나 낯선 것은 여러분을 죽이는 데 관심이 있을 가능성이 커 여러분은 그런 것을 피하도록 조건화되어 있을 것이다. 유사점(을 갖고 있는 것)은 우리가 다른 사람들과 마음이 더 잘 통할 수 있도록 하는데, 그들이 우리를 다른 사람들보다 더 깊이 있는 수준으로 이해할 것으로 생각하기 때문이다.

Why? 왜 정답일까?

관계대명사 what은 선행사를 포함하고 있는데, ③ 앞에는 선행사 a very common human tendency가 있으므로 what을 that 또는 which로 고쳐야 한다. 따라서 어법상 틀린 것은 ③이다.

Why? 왜 오답일까?

① 주어가 복수 명사인 places이므로 복수 동사 exist가 바르게 쓰였다. like Little Italy, Chinatown, and Koreatown은 주어 places를 꾸미는 전명구이다.
② 앞의 일반동사구 look at을 가리키는 대동사 do가 바르게 쓰였다.
④ something unfamiliar or foreign을 받는 단수 대명사로 it이 바르게 쓰였다.
⑤ 사역동사 make의 목적격 보어로 원형부정사 relate가 바르게 쓰였다.

● get along with ~와 잘 지내다, 어울리다
● race ⓝ 인종
● be rooted in ~에 뿌리박고 있다, ~에 원인이 있다
● relate to ~을 이해하다, ~에 공감하다
● seek out (오랫동안 공들여) 찾아다니다
● as the saying goes 속담에서 말하듯이, 옛말처럼
● condition ⓥ 조건화하다

구문 풀이

1행 We usually get along best with people [who (we think) are like us].
선행사　주격 관·대　( ): 삽입절

★★★ 등급을 가르는 문제!

30　거절에 대한 두려움 극복하기　정답률 45% | 정답 ⑤

다음 글의 밑줄 친 부분 중, 문맥상 낱말의 쓰임이 적절하지 않은 것은? [3점]

Rejection is an everyday part of our lives, / yet most people can't handle it well.
거절은 우리 삶의 일상적인 부분이지만, / 대부분의 사람은 그것을 잘 감당하지 못한다.

For many, / it's so painful / that they'd rather not ask for something at all / than ask and ① risk rejection.
많은 사람에게, / 거절이 너무 고통스러워서, / 그들은 아예 무언가를 요청하지 않으려 한다. / 요청하고 거절의 위험을 감수하기보다는

Yet, as the old saying goes, / if you don't ask, / the answer is always no.
하지만 옛말처럼, / 여러분이 요청하지 않으면 / 대답은 항상 '아니오'이다.

Avoiding rejection / ② negatively affects many aspects of your life.
거절을 피하는 것은 / 여러분의 삶의 많은 측면에 부정적으로 영향을 준다.

All of that happens / only because you're not ③ tough enough to handle it.
이 모든 것은 일어난다. / 단지 여러분이 거절을 감당할 만큼 강하지 않기 때문에

For this reason, / consider rejection therapy.
이러한 이유로 / 거절 요법을 고려해 보라.

Come up with a ④ request or an activity / that usually results in a rejection.
요청이나 활동을 생각해 내라. / 일반적으로 거절당할 만한

Working in sales is one such example.
판매 분야에서 일하는 것이 그러한 사례 중 하나이다.

Asking for discounts at the stores / will also work.
매장에서 할인을 요청하는 것은 / 또한 효과가 있을 것이다.

By deliberately getting yourself ✔ rejected / you'll grow a thicker skin / that will allow you to take on much more in life, / thus making you more successful / at dealing with unfavorable circumstances.
의도적으로 스스로를 거절당할 상황에 놓이게 함으로써 / 여러분은 더한 둔감함을 키우게 될 것이다. / 여러분이 인생에서 훨씬 더 많은 것을 떠맡을 수 있게 해주며, / 그리하여 여러분은 더 성공적이 될 것이다 / 호의적이지 않은 상황에 대처하는 것에

거절은 우리 삶의 일상적인 부분이지만, 대부분의 사람은 그것을 잘 감당하지 못한다. 많은 사람에게 거절이 너무 고통스러워서, 그들은 요청하고 거절의 ① 위험을 감수하기보다는 아예 무언가를 요청하지 않으려 한다. 하지만 옛말처럼, 요청하지 않으면 대답은 항상 '아니오'이다. 거절을 피하는 것은 여러분의 삶의 많은 측면에 ② 부정적으로 영향을 준다. 이 모든 것은 단지 여러분이 거절을 감당할 만큼 ③ 강하지 않기 때문에 일어난다. 이러한 이유로 거절 요법을 (시도하는 것을) 고려해 보라. 일반적으로 거절당할 만한 ④ 요청이나 활동을 생각해 내라. 판매 분야에서 일하는 것이 그러한 사례 중 하나이다. 매장에서 할인을 요청하는 것 또한 효과가 있을 것이다. 의도적으로 스스로를 ⑤ 환영받을(→ 거절당할) 상황에 놓이게 함으로써 여러분은 더 둔감해지고, 인생에서 훨씬 더 많은 것을 떠맡을 수 있게 되며, 그리하여 호의적이지 않은 상황에 더 성공적으로 대처할 수 있게 될 것이다.

Why? 왜 정답일까?

⑤ 앞에서 판매 분야에서 일하는 등 거절을 경험할 법한 요청이나 활동에 참여해보라고 언급하는데, 이는 거절을 부르는 상황의 예시이므로 ⑤의 welcomed는 rejected로 바뀌어야 적절하다. 따라서 문맥상 낱말의 쓰임이 적절하지 않은 것은 ⑤이다.

● rejection ⓝ 거절
● grow a thick skin 무덤덤해지다, 둔감해지다
● circumstance ⓝ 상황, 환경
● come up with ~을 생각해내다, 떠올리다
● unfavorable ⓐ 호의적이지 않은

구문 풀이

2행 For many, it's so painful that they'd rather not ask for something at all
'so ~ that …': 너무 ~해서 …하다　차라리 ~ 않다　동사원형1
than ask and risk rejection.
동사원형2

★★ 문제 해결 꿀~팁 ★★

▶ 많이 틀린 이유는?
오답 중 ③이 포함된 문장은 우리가 거절을 왜 피하려 하는지 그 이유를 설명하는 문장이다. 우리가 거절에 잘 대처할 만큼 '충분히 강하지' 않기 때문이라는 것이다. 그렇기에 훈련이 필요하다는 결론까지 자연스럽게 연결되므로, ③은 문맥상 어색하지 않다.
▶ 문제 해결 방법은?
정답인 ⑤가 포함된 문장은 예시 앞의 'Come up with a request or an activity that usually results in a rejection.'과 같은 의미이다. '일부러 거절이라는 결과를 초래할' 수 있는 상황은 '환영받는' 상황이 아니라 그야말로 '거부당하는' 상황이다.

★★★ 등급을 가르는 문제!

31　세밀한 묘사의 필요성　정답률 46% | 정답 ②

다음 빈칸에 들어갈 말로 가장 적절한 것을 고르시오.

① similarities - 유사점
✔ particulars - 세부 사항
③ fantasies - 환상
④ boredom - 지루함
⑤ wisdom - 지혜

Generalization without specific examples / that humanize writing / is boring to the listener and to the reader.
구체적인 사례가 없는 일반화는 / 글을 인간미 있게 하는 / 듣는 사람과 읽는 사람에게 지루하다.

Who wants to read platitudes all day?
누가 상투적인 말을 온종일 읽고 싶어 하겠는가?

Who wants to hear the words / great, greater, best, smartest, finest, humanitarian, on and on and on / without specific examples?
누가 듣고 싶어 하겠는가? / 위대한, 더 위대한, 최고의, 제일 똑똑한, 가장 훌륭한, 인도주의적인, 이런 말들을 계속해서 끊임없이 / 구체적인 사례가 없이

Instead of using these 'nothing words,' / leave them out completely / and just describe the particulars.
이런 '공허한 말들'을 사용하는 대신에, / 그것들을 완전히 빼고 / 세부 사항만을 서술하라.

There is nothing worse than reading a scene in a novel / in which a main character is described up front / as heroic or brave or tragic or funny, / while thereafter, the writer quickly moves on to something else.
소설 속 장면을 읽는 것보다 더 끔찍한 것은 없다. / 주인공이 대놓고 묘사되는 / 영웅적이다, 용감하다, 비극적이다, 혹은 웃긴다고 / 한편 그 후 작가가 다른 것으로 빠르게 넘어가는

That's no good, no good at all.
그건 좋지 않으며, 전혀 좋지 않다.

You have to use less one word descriptions / and more detailed, engaging descriptions / if you want to make something real.
여러분은 한 단어 묘사는 덜 사용하고 / 세밀하고 마음을 끄는 묘사를 더 많이 사용해야 한다. / 여러분이 어떤 것을 실감 나는 것으로 만들고 싶다면

글을 인간미 있게 하는 구체적인 사례가 없는 일반화는 듣는 사람에게도 읽는 사람에게도 지루하다. 누가 상투적인 말을 온종일 읽고 싶어 하겠는가? 구체적인 사례가 없이 위대한, 더 위대한, 최고의, 제일 똑똑한, 가장 훌륭한, 인도주의적인, 이런 말들을 누가 계속해서 끊임없이 듣고 싶어 하겠는가? 이런 '공허한 말들'을 사용하는 대신에, 그것들을 완전히 빼고 세부 사항만을 서술하라. 주인공을 대놓고 영웅적이다, 용감하다, 비극적이다, 혹은 웃긴다고 묘사한 후 작가가 다른 것으로 빠르게 넘어가는 소설 속 장면을 읽는 것보다 더 끔찍한 것은 없다. 그건 좋지 않으며, 전혀 좋지 않다. 어떤 것을 실감 나는 것으로 만들고 싶다면, 한 단어 짜리 묘사는 덜 사용하고, 세밀하고 마음을 끄는 묘사를 더 많이 사용해야 한다.

Why? 왜 정답일까?

마지막 문장에서 장면을 실감 나게 만들려면 세밀하고 마음을 끄는 묘사를 사용해야 한다(You have to use less one word descriptions and more detailed, engaging descriptions if you want to make something real.)고 언급하는 것으로 보아, 빈칸에 들어갈 말로 가장 적절한 것은 ② '세부 사항'이다. 이는 빈칸 앞의 specific examples을 재진술한 말이기도 하다.

● specific ⓐ 구체적인
● humanitarian ⓐ 인도주의적인
● engaging ⓐ 마음을 끄는, 몰입시키는
● humanize ⓥ 인간적으로 만들다
● leave out ~을 빼다

구문 풀이

6행 There is nothing worse than reading a scene in a novel [in which a main
「nothing + 비교급 + than ~ : ~보다 더 …한 것은 없다(최상급 의미)」   선행사   = where
character is described up front as heroic or brave or tragic or funny, while
thereafter, the writer quickly moves on to something else].

★★ 문제 해결 꿀~팁 ★★

▶ 많이 틀린 이유는?
첫 문장의 Generalization만 보고 ①을 고르면 안 된다. '특별한' 사례의 공통점을 찾아 '일반화'하라는 내용은 글 어디에도 없기 때문이다.

▶ 문제 해결 방법은?
빈칸이 주제문인 명령문에 있으므로, 마찬가지로 '~해야 한다'라는 당위의 의미를 나타내는 마지막 문장을 잘 읽어야 한다. more detailed, engaging와 같은 의미의 단어를 빈칸에 넣으면 된다.

★★★ 등급을 가르는 문제!

32 정보 공유에 있어 대면 상호작용의 중요성   정답률 49% | 정답 ③

다음 빈칸에 들어갈 말로 가장 적절한 것을 고르시오.

① natural talent – 천부적 재능
② regular practice – 규칙적인 연습
③ ✓ personal contact – 개인적인 접촉
④ complex knowledge – 복잡한 지식
⑤ powerful motivation – 강력한 동기

Face-to-face interaction / is a uniquely powerful — and sometimes the only — way / to share many kinds of knowledge, / from the simplest to the most complex.
대면 상호 작용은 / 유례 없이 강력한—때로는 유일한—방법이다. / 많은 종류의 지식을 공유하는 / 가장 간단한 것부터 가장 복잡한 것까지

It is one of the best ways / to stimulate new thinking and ideas, / too.
그것은 가장 좋은 방법의 한 가지이다. / 새로운 생각과 아이디어를 자극하는 / 또한

Most of us would have had difficulty learning / how to tie a shoelace only from pictures, / or how to do arithmetic from a book.
우리 대부분이 배웠다면 어려움을 겪었을 것이다. / 그림만으로 신발 끈 묶는 법을 / 또는 책으로부터 계산하는 방법을

Psychologist Mihàly Csikszentmihàlyi found, / while studying high achievers, / that a large number of Nobel Prize winners / were the students of previous winners: / they had access to the same literature as everyone else, / but personal contact made a crucial difference / to their creativity.
심리학자 Mihàly Csikszentmihàlyi는 발견했다. / 높은 성취도를 보이는 사람들을 연구하면서 / 다수의 노벨상 수상자가 / 이전 수상자들의 학생이라는 것을 / 그들은 다른 모든 사람들과 똑같은 문헌에 접근할 수 있었지만, / 개인적인 접촉이 결정적인 차이를 만들었다. / 이들의 창의성에

Within organisations / this makes conversation / both a crucial factor for high-level professional skills / and the most important way of sharing everyday information.
조직 내에서 / 이것은 대화를 만든다. / 고급 전문 기술을 위한 매우 중요한 요소이자 / 일상 정보를 공유하는 가장 중요한 방식으로

대면 상호 작용은 가장 간단한 것부터 가장 복잡한 것까지 많은 종류의 지식을 공유하는 유례 없이 강력한—때로는 유일한—방법이다. 그것은 새로운 생각과 아이디어를 자극하는 최고의 방법 중 하나이기도 하다. 우리 대부분이 그림으로만 신발 끈 묶는 법을 배웠거나, 책으로 셈법을 배웠다면 어려움을 겪었을 것이다. 심리학자 Mihàly Csikszentmihàlyi는 높은 성취도를 보이는 사람들을 연구하면서 다수의 노벨상 수상자가 이전 (노벨상) 수상자들의 학생이라는 것을 발견했다. 그들은 다른 모든 사람들과 똑같은 (연구) 문헌에 접근할 수 있었지만, 개인적인 접촉이 이들의 창의성에 결정적인 차이를 만들었다. 이로 인해 조직 내에서 대화는 고급 전문 기술을 위한 매우 중요한 요소이자 일상 정보를 공유하는 가장 중요한 방식이 된다.

Why? 왜 정답일까?

첫 문장과 마지막 문장에서 정보를 공유하는 가장 중요한 방법으로 대면 상호 작용(Face-to-face interaction) 또는 대화(conversation)를 언급하고 있다. 따라서 빈칸에 들어갈 말로 가장 적절한 것은 ③ '개인적인 접촉'이다.

● stimulate ⓥ 자극하다
● crucial ⓐ 아주 중요한

구문 풀이

4행 Most of us would have had difficulty learning {how to tie a shoelace} only
「have difficulty + 동명사 : ~하는 데 어려움을 겪다」
from pictures, or {how to do arithmetic} from a book.
{ } : 명사구(how + to부정사 : ~하는 방법)

★★ 문제 해결 꿀~팁 ★★

▶ 많이 틀린 이유는?
글 처음과 마지막에 many kinds of knowledge, from the simplest to the most complex 또는 high-level professional skills와 같은 표현이 등장하므로 얼핏 보면 ④가 적절해 보인다. 하지만 빈칸은 이러한 정보 공유나 전문 능력 개발에 '무엇이 영향을 미치는지' 그 요인을 밝히는 것이므로 ④를 빈칸에 넣기는 부적절하다.

▶ 문제 해결 방법은?
첫 문장의 Face-to-face interaction과 마지막 문장의 conversation이 키워드이다. 이 둘을 일반화할 수 있는 표현이 바로 '빈칸'이다.

33 영화 속 외국어 대화에 자막이 없을 때의 효과   정답률 59% | 정답 ①

다음 빈칸에 들어갈 말로 가장 적절한 것을 고르시오. [3점]

① ✓ seeing the film from her viewpoint – 그녀의 시각에서 영화를 보고 있게
② impressed by her language skills – 그녀의 언어 능력에 감명받게
③ attracted to her beautiful voice – 그녀의 아름다운 목소리에 이끌리게
④ participating in a heated debate – 열띤 토론에 참여하게
⑤ learning the language used in the film – 영화에서 사용된 언어를 배우고 있게

Most times a foreign language is spoken in film, / subtitles are used / to translate the dialogue for the viewer.
영화에서 외국어가 사용되는 대부분의 경우 / 자막이 사용된다. / 관객을 위해 대화를 통역하려

However, / there are occasions / when foreign dialogue is left unsubtitled / (and thus incomprehensible to most of the target audience).
하지만 / 경우가 있다. / 외국어 대화가 자막 없이 처리되는 / (그리하여 대부분의 주요 대상 관객이 이해하지 못하게)

This is often done / if the movie is seen / mainly from the viewpoint of a particular character / who does not speak the language.
흔히 이렇게 처리된다. / 영화가 보여지는 경우에 / 주로 특정 등장인물의 관점에서 / 그 언어를 할 줄 모르는

Such absence of subtitles / allows the audience / to feel a similar sense of incomprehension and alienation / that the character feels.
그러한 자막의 부재 / 관객이 ~하게 한다. / 비슷한 몰이해와 소외의 감정 / 그 등장인물이 느끼는

An example of this / is seen in Not Without My Daughter.
이것의 한 예는 / Not Without My Daughter에서 볼 수 있다.

The Persian language dialogue / spoken by the Iranian characters / is not subtitled / because the main character Betty Mahmoody does not speak Persian / and the audience is seeing the film from her viewpoint.
페르시아어 대화는 / 이란인 등장인물들이 하는 / 자막 없이 처리되며 / 왜냐하면 주인공 Betty Mahmoody가 페르시아어를 하지 못하기 때문에 / 관객은 그녀의 시각에서 영화를 보고 있게 된다.

영화에서 외국어가 사용되는 대부분의 경우 관객을 위해 대화를 통역하려고 자막이 사용된다. 하지만 외국어 대화가 자막 없이 (그리하여 대부분의 주요 대상 관객이 이해하지 못하게) 처리되는 경우가 있다. 영화가 그 언어를 할 줄 모르는 특정한 등장인물의 관점에서 주로 보여지는 경우에 흔히 이렇게 처리된다. 그러한 자막의 부재는 관객이 그 등장인물이 느끼는 것과 비슷한 몰이해와 소외의 감정을 느끼게 한다. 이것의 한 예를 Not Without My Daughter에서 볼 수 있다. 주인공 Betty Mahmoody가 페르시아어를 하지 못하기 때문에 이란인 등장인물들이 하는 페르시아어 대화에는 자막이 없으며, 관객은 그녀의 시각에서 영화를 보고 있게 된다.

Why? 왜 정답일까?

외국어 대화가 자막 없이 사용되는 경우는 그 언어를 할 줄 모르는 특정 등장인물의 시점에서 사건을 보게 만든다(~ if the movie is seen mainly from the viewpoint of a particular character who does not speak the language.)는 설명으로 보아, 빈칸에 들어갈 말로 가장 적절한 것은 ① '그녀의 시각에서 영화를 보고 있게'이다.

● translate ⓥ 번역하다, 통역하다
● viewpoint ⓝ 관점, 시점
● occasion ⓝ 경우, 때
● absence ⓝ 부재

구문 풀이

2행 However, there are occasions [when foreign dialogue is left unsubtitled
선행사(경우)   관계부사   5형식 수동태   보어1
(and thus incomprehensible to most of the target audience)].
보어2(형용사)   (과거분사)

★★★ 등급을 가르는 문제!

34 홈 이점이 발휘되지 못하는 경우   정답률 19% | 정답 ①

다음 빈칸에 들어갈 말로 가장 적절한 것을 고르시오. [3점]

① ✓ often welcome a road trip – 길을 떠나는 것을 흔히 반길
② avoid international matches – 국제적 경기를 피할
③ focus on increasing ticket sales – 티켓 매출을 높이는 데 집중할
④ want to have an eco-friendly stadium – 친환경적인 경기장을 갖기를 원할
⑤ try to advertise their upcoming games – 다가오는 경기를 광고하려 애쓸

One dynamic that can change dramatically in sport / is the concept of the home-field advantage, / in which perceived demands and resources seem to play a role.
스포츠에서 극적으로 바뀔 수 있는 한 가지 역학은 / 홈 이점이라는 개념으로, / 여기에는 인식된 부담과 자원이 역할을 하는 것처럼 보인다.

Under normal circumstances, / the home ground would appear / to provide greater perceived resources / (fans, home field, and so on).
일반적인 상황에서, / 홈그라운드는 보일 것이다. / 인식된 자원을 더 많이 제공하는 것처럼 / (팬, 홈 경기장 등)

However, / researchers Roy Baumeister and Andrew Steinhilber / were among the first / to point out / that these competitive factors can change; / for example, / the success percentage for home teams / in the final games of a playoff or World Series / seems to drop.
하지만, / 연구원 Roy Baumeister와 Andrew Steinhilber는 / 최초의 사람들 중 하나였다. / 지적한 / 이러한 경쟁력이 있는 요소들이 바뀔 수도 있다고 / 예를 들어, / 홈 팀들의 성공률은 / 우승 결정전이나 미국 프로 야구 선수권의 마지막 경기에서 / 떨어지는 것처럼 보인다.

Fans can become part of the perceived demands / rather than resources / under those circumstances.
팬들은 인식된 부담의 일부가 될 수 있다. / 자원보다는 / 이러한 상황에서

This change in perception can also explain / why a team that's struggling at the start of the year / will often welcome a road trip / to reduce perceived demands and pressures.
이러한 인식의 변화는 또한 설명할 수 있다. / 왜 연초에 고전하는 팀이 / 길을 떠나는 것을 흔히 반길 것인지 / 인식된 부담과 압박을 줄이기 위해

스포츠에서 극적으로 바뀔 수 있는 한 가지 역학은 홈 이점이라는 개념으로, 여기에는 인식되는 부담과 자원이 일조하는 것처럼 보인다. 일반적인 상황에서, 홈그라운드는 인식되는 자원(팬, 홈 경기장 등)을 더 많이 제공하는 것처럼 보일 것이다. 하지만, 연구원 Roy Baumeister와 Andrew Steinhilber는 이러한 경쟁력이 있는 요소들이 바뀔 수도 있다고 처음으로 지적한 사람 중 하나이다. 예를 들어, 우승 결정전이나 미국 프로 야구 선수권의 마지막 경기에서 홈 팀들의 성공률은 떨어지는 것처럼 보인다. 이러한 상황에서 팬들은 자원보다는 인식되는 부담의 일부가 될 수 있다. 이러한 인식의 변화는 왜 연초에 고전하는 팀이 인식되는 부담과 압박을 줄이기 위해 길을 떠나는 것(원정 경기를 가는 것)을 흔히 반길 것인지 또한 설명할 수 있다.

Why? 왜 정답일까?

홈그라운드의 이점은 부담에 대한 인식이나 자원에 의해 뒤집힐 수 있다(~ the concept of the home-field advantage, in which perceived demands and resources seem to play a role.)는 내용의 글이다. **for example** 뒤로 결승전 등 중요한 경기에서 팬들은 선수들에게 자원이 아닌 부담일 수 있기에 도리어 홈 팀의 성적이 부진해질 수 있다고 한다. 이를 근거로 볼 때, 마지막 문장은 부진하는 팀이 도리어 부담을 피하고자 '홈그라운드에서의 경기를 피한다'는 내용일 것이다. 따라서 빈칸에 들어갈 말로 가장 적절한 것은 ① '길을 떠나는 것을 흔히 반길'이다.

- **play a role in** ~에 역할을 하다, 일조하다
- **perception** ⓝ 인식
- **competitive** ⓐ 경쟁력 있는
- **struggle** ⓥ 고전하다, 분투하다

★★ 문제 해결 꿀~팁 ★★

▶ 많이 틀린 이유는?
home-field advantage만 보면 정답과 정반대되는 의미의 ②를 고르기 쉽다. 하지만 사실 이 글은 '홈 구장의 이점'을 긍정하는 글이 아니라 이 이점이 '없을 수도 있는' 경우에 대한 글이다.

▶ 문제 해결 방법은?
for example 뒤에서, 홈 팀의 결승전 승률이 '떨어지는' 것처럼 보인다는 예를 제시한다. 이 점이 어떤 결과를 불러올까 생각해보면, 연초에 고전 중인 팀은 오히려 '홈 팀에서 경기하기를 꺼릴' 수도 있다는 추론이 가능하다.

---

35 커피의 부정적 영향 주의하기   정답률 60% | 정답 ④

다음 글에서 전체 흐름과 관계 없는 문장은?

Who hasn't used a cup of coffee / to help themselves stay awake while studying?
커피 한 잔을 이용해 보지 않은 사람이 있을까? / 공부하는 동안 깨어 있는 것을 돕기 위해
Mild stimulants / commonly found in tea, coffee, or sodas / possibly make you more attentive / and, thus, better able to remember.
가벼운 자극제는 / 차, 커피 또는 탄산음료에서 흔히 발견되는 / 아마도 여러분을 더 주의 깊게 만들고, / 따라서 더 잘 기억할 수 있게 한다.
① However, / you should know / that stimulants are as likely / to have negative effects on memory / as they are to be beneficial.
하지만, / 여러분은 알아야 한다 / 자극제가 ~할 수도 있다는 것을 / 기억력에 부정적인 영향을 미칠 / 그것들이 이로울 수 있는 만큼
② Even if they could improve performance at some level, / the ideal doses are currently unknown.
비록 그것이 특정 수준에서 수행을 향상할 수 있다고 할지라도, / 이상적인 복용량은 현재 알려지지 않았다.
③ If you are wide awake and well-rested, / mild stimulation from caffeine can do little / to further improve your memory performance.
만약 여러분이 완전히 깨어 있고 잘 쉬었다면, / 카페인으로부터의 가벼운 자극은 거의 영향을 주지 못할 수 있다. / 여러분의 기억력을 더욱 향상하는 데
☑ In contrast, / many studies have shown / that drinking tea is healthier than drinking coffee.
반면에, / 많은 연구에서 밝혀졌다. / 커피를 마시는 것보다 차를 마시는 것이 건강에 더 좋다는 것이
⑤ Indeed, / if you have too much of a stimulant, / you will become nervous, / find it difficult to sleep, / and your memory performance will suffer.
실제로 / 만약 여러분이 자극제를 너무 많이 섭취하면, / 여러분은 신경이 과민해지고, / 잠을 자기 어려워지며, / 기억력도 저하될 것이다.

공부하는 동안 깨어 있는 것을 돕기 위해 커피 한 잔을 이용해 보지 않은 사람이 있을까? 차, 커피 또는 탄산음료에서 흔히 발견되는 가벼운 자극제는 아마도 여러분을 더 주의 깊게 만들고, 따라서 더 잘 기억할 수 있게 한다. ① 하지만, 자극제가 기억력에 이로울 수 있는 만큼 부정적인 영향을 미칠 수도 있다는 것을 알아야 한다. ② 비록 그것이 특정 수준에서 수행을 향상할 수 있다고 할지라도, (자극제의) 이상적인 복용량은 현재 알려지지 않았다. ③ 만약 여러분이 완전히 깨어 있고 잘 쉬었다면, 카페인으로부터의 가벼운 자극은 여러분의 기억력을 더욱 향상하는 데 거의 영향을 주지 못할 수 있다. ④ 반면에, 많은 연구에서 커피를 마시는 것보다 차를 마시는 것이 건강에 더 좋다는 것이 밝혀졌다. ⑤ 실제로 만약 여러분이 자극제를 너무 많이 섭취하면, 신경이 과민해지고, 잠을 자기 어려워지며, 기억력도 저하될 것이다.

Why? 왜 정답일까?

커피를 지나치게 많이 마시면 부정적 영향이 나타날 수 있다는 내용의 글인데, ④는 커피보다 차가 몸에 좋다는 무관한 설명을 제시하고 있다. 따라서 전체 흐름과 관계 없는 문장은 ④이다.

- **attentive** ⓐ 주의 깊은
- **ideal** ⓐ 이상적인
- **have an effect on** ~에 영향을 미치다
- **suffer** ⓥ 악화되다

---

36 과거 시골 건축업자들의 건축 양식   정답률 58% | 정답 ③

주어진 글 다음에 이어질 글의 순서로 가장 적절한 것을 고르시오.
① (A) - (C) - (B)   ② (B) - (A) - (C)
☑ (B) - (C) - (A)   ④ (C) - (A) - (B)
⑤ (C) - (B) - (A)

Toward the end of the 19th century, / a new architectural attitude emerged.
19세기 말이 되면서, / 새로운 건축학적 사고방식이 나타났다.
Industrial architecture, / the argument went, / was ugly and inhuman; / past styles had more to do with pretension / than what people needed in their homes.
산업 건축은 / 그 주장에 따르면, / 추하고 비인간적이었다. / 과거의 스타일은 허세와 더욱 관련이 있었다 / 사람들이 자기 집에서 필요로 했던 것보다는

(B) Instead of these approaches, / why not look at the way / ordinary country builders worked in the past?
이러한 접근 대신에, / 방식을 살펴보는 것은 어떠한가? / 평범한 시골 건축업자들이 과거에 일했던
They developed their craft skills over generations, / demonstrating mastery of both tools and materials.
그들은 세대를 거쳐 공예 기술을 발전시켰다. / 도구와 재료 둘 다에 숙달한 기술을 보이며
(C) Those materials were local, / and used with simplicity — / houses built this way / had plain wooden floors and whitewashed walls inside.
그 재료는 지역적이고, / 단순하게 사용되었는데, / 이러한 방식으로 건축된 집들은 / 실내가 평범한 나무 바닥과 회반죽을 칠한 벽으로 되어 있었다.
(A) But they supplied people's needs perfectly / and, at their best, had a beauty / that came from the craftsman's skill / and the rootedness of the house in its locality.
그러나 그것들은 사람들의 필요를 완벽하게 충족시켰고, / 가장 좋은 경우 아름다움을 갖추고 있었다. / 장인의 솜씨에서 비롯된 / 그리고 그 집이 그 지역에 뿌리내림으로써 비롯된

19세기 말이 되면서, 새로운 건축학적 사고방식이 나타났다. 그 주장에 따르면, 산업 건축은 추하고 비인간적이었다. 과거의 스타일은 사람들이 자기 집에서 필요로 했던 것보다는 허세와 더욱 관련이 있었다.

(B) 이러한 접근 대신에, 평범한 시골 건축업자들이 과거에 일했던 방식을 살펴보는 것은 어떠한가? 그들은 도구와 재료 둘 다에 숙달한 기술을 보이며, 세대를 거쳐 공예 기술을 발전시켰다.

(C) 그 재료는 지역적이었고, 단순하게 사용되었는데, 이러한 방식으로 건축된 집들은 실내가 평범한 나무 바닥과 회반죽을 칠한 벽으로 되어 있었다.

(A) 그러나 그것들은 사람들의 필요를 완벽하게 충족시켰고, 가장 좋은 경우 장인의 솜씨와 집이 그 지역에 뿌리내리며 비롯된 아름다움을 갖추고 있었다.

Why? 왜 정답일까?

산업 건축 양식을 언급하는 주어진 글 뒤로, '이 접근법' 대신 평범한 시골 건축업자들의 작업 방식을 살펴보겠다고 언급하는 (B), (B)에서 언급된 재료를 Those materials로 받으며 이것들이 단순하게 사용되었다고 설명하는 (C), '그래도' 이렇게 건축된 집들은 사람들의 필요만큼은 완벽하게 충족시켰다는 내용의 (A)가 차례로 연결된다. 따라서 글의 순서로 가장 적절한 것은 ③ '(B) - (C) - (A)'이다.

- **architectural** ⓐ 건축의
- **inhuman** ⓐ 비인간적인
- **rootedness** ⓝ 뿌리내림, 고착, 정착
- **demonstrate** ⓥ 입증하다
- **plain** ⓐ 평범한, 단순한
- **emerge** ⓥ 나타나다, 출현하다
- **craftsman** ⓝ 장인
- **locality** ⓝ (~이 존재하는) 지역, 곳
- **mastery** ⓝ 숙달한 기술

---

37 좋은 음악과 나쁜 음악   정답률 61% | 정답 ②

주어진 글 다음에 이어질 글의 순서로 가장 적절한 것을 고르시오. [3점]
① (A) - (C) - (B)   ☑ (B) - (A) - (C)
③ (B) - (C) - (A)   ④ (C) - (A) - (B)
⑤ (C) - (B) - (A)

Robert Schumann once said, / "The laws of morals are those of art."
Robert Schumann은 언젠가 말했다. / "도덕의 법칙은 예술의 법칙이다."라고
What the great man is saying here / is that there is good music and bad music.
여기서 이 위인이 말하고 있는 것은 / 좋은 음악과 나쁜 음악이 있다는 것이다.
(B) The greatest music, / even if it's tragic in nature, / takes us to a world higher than ours; / somehow the beauty uplifts us.
가장 위대한 음악은, / 심지어 그것이 사실상 비극적일지라도, / 우리의 세상보다 더 높은 세상으로 우리를 데려간다. / 어떻게든지 아름다움은 우리를 고양시킨다.
Bad music, on the other hand, degrades us.
반면에 나쁜 음악은 우리를 격하시킨다.
(A) It's the same with performances: / a bad performance isn't necessarily the result of incompetence.
연주도 마찬가지다. / 나쁜 연주가 반드시 무능의 결과는 아니다.
Some of the worst performances occur / when the performers, / no matter how accomplished, / are thinking more of themselves / than of the music they're playing.
최악의 연주 중 일부는 발생한다. / 연주자들이 ~할 때 / 아무리 숙달되었더라도 / 자기 자신을 더 생각하고 있을 / 연주하고 있는 곡보다
(C) These doubtful characters aren't really listening / to what the composer is saying / — they're just showing off, / hoping that they'll have a great 'success' with the public.
이 미덥지 못한 사람들은 정말로 듣고 있는 것이 아니다. / 작곡가가 말하는 것을 / 그들은 그저 뽐내고 있을 뿐이다. / 그들이 대중적으로 큰 '성공'을 거두기를 바라며
The performer's basic task / is to try to understand the meaning of the music, / and then to communicate it honestly to others.
연주자의 기본 임무는 / 음악의 의미를 이해하려고 노력하고서, / 그것을 다른 사람들에게 정직하게 전달하는 것이다.

Robert Schumann은 "도덕의 법칙은 예술의 법칙이다."라고 말한 적이 있다. 여기서 이 위인이 말하고 있는 것은 좋은 음악과 나쁜 음악이 있다는 것이다.

(B) 가장 위대한 음악은, 심지어 그것이 사실상 비극적일지라도, 우리의 세상보다 더 높은 세상으로 우리를 데려가며, 아름다움은 어떻게든지 우리를 고양시킨다. 반면에 나쁜 음악은 우리를 격하시킨다.

(A) 연주도 마찬가지다. 나쁜 연주가 반드시 무능의 결과는 아니다. 최악의 연주 중 일부는 연주자들이 아무리 숙달되었더라도 연주하고 있는 곡보다 자기 자신을 더 생각하고 있을 때 발생한다.

(C) 이 미덥지 못한 사람들은 작곡가가 말하는 것을 정말로 듣고 있는 것이 아니다. 그들은 대중적으로 큰 '성공'을 거두기를 바라며 그저 뽐내고 있을 뿐이다. 연주자의 기본 임무

는 음악의 의미를 이해하려고 노력하고서, 그것을 다른 사람들에게 정직하게 전달하는 것이다.

Why? 왜 정답일까?

음악에 좋은 음악과 나쁜 음악이 있음을 언급하는 주어진 글 뒤로, 두 음악의 특징을 풀어 설명하는 **(B)**, 연주에도 나쁜 연주와 좋은 연주가 있음을 덧붙이는 **(A)**, **(A)**에서 언급된 최악의 연주자를 These doubtful characters로 가리키는 **(C)**가 차례로 연결된다. 따라서 글의 순서로 가장 적절한 것은 ② '(B) – (A) – (C)'이다.

- accomplished ⓐ 숙달된, 기량이 뛰어난
- uplift ⓥ 고양시키다, 들어올리다
- doubtful ⓐ 미심쩍은
- composer ⓝ 작곡가
- show off 과시하다, 뽐내다

구문 풀이

5행 Some of the worst performances occur when the performers, no matter [주어] [동사(복수)] how accomplished (they are), are thinking more of themselves than of the music 「no matter how + 형/부 + 주어 + 동사 : 아무리 ~할지라도」 they're playing.

---

38 생물 다양성으로 인한 이득   정답률 52% | 정답 ④

글의 흐름으로 보아, 주어진 문장이 들어가기에 가장 적절한 곳을 고르시오. [3점]

When an ecosystem is biodiverse, / wildlife have more opportunities / to obtain food and shelter.
생태계에 생물 종이 다양할 때, / 야생 생물들은 더 많은 기회를 얻는다. / 먹이와 서식지를 얻을

Different species react and respond / to changes in their environment / differently.
다양한 종은 작용하고 반응한다. / 그들의 환경 변화에 / 다르게

① For example, / imagine a forest with only one type of plant in it, / which is the only source of food and habitat / for the entire forest food web.
예를 들어, / 단 한 종류의 식물만 있는 숲을 상상해 보라 / 그 식물은 유일한 먹이원이자 서식지이다. / 숲의 먹이 그물 전체에게 있어

② Now, / there is a sudden dry season / and this plant dies.
이제, / 갑작스러운 건기가 오고 / 이 식물이 죽는다.

③ Plant-eating animals / completely lose their food source and die out, / and so do the animals / that prey upon them.
초식 동물은 / 그들의 먹이원을 완전히 잃고 죽게 되고, / 동물들도 그렇게 된다, / 그들을 먹이로 삼는

✔ But, when there is biodiversity, / the effects of a sudden change / are not so dramatic.
하지만 종 다양성이 있을 때, / 갑작스러운 변화의 영향은 / 그렇게 극적이지 않다.

Different species of plants / respond to the drought differently, / and many can survive a dry season.
다양한 종의 식물들이 / 가뭄에 다르게 반응하고, / 많은 식물이 건기에 살아남을 수 있다.

⑤ Many animals have a variety of food sources / and don't just rely on one plant; / now our forest ecosystem is no longer at the death!
많은 동물은 다양한 먹이원을 가지고 있으며 / 그저 한 식물에 의존하지는 않는다. / 그래서 이제 우리의 숲 생태계는 더는 종말에 처해 있지 않다!

생태계에 생물 종이 다양할 때, 야생 생물들은 먹이와 서식지를 얻을 더 많은 기회를 얻는다. 다양한 종들은 그들의 환경 변화에 다르게 작용하고 반응한다. ① 예를 들어, 단 한 종류의 식물만 있는 숲을 상상해 보면, 그 식물은 숲의 먹이 그물 전체의 유일한 먹이원이자 서식지이다. ② 이제, 갑작스러운 건기가 오고 이 식물이 죽는다. ③ 초식 동물은 그들의 먹이원을 완전히 잃고 죽게 되고, 그들을 먹이로 삼는 동물들도 그렇게 된다. ④ 하지만 종 다양성이 있을 때, 갑작스러운 변화의 영향은 그렇게 극적이지 않다. 다양한 종의 식물들이 가뭄에 다르게 반응하고, 많은 식물이 건기에 살아남을 수 있다. ⑤ 많은 동물은 다양한 먹이원을 가지고 있으며 한 식물에만 의존하지 않기에, 이제 우리의 숲 생태계는 더는 종말에 처해 있지 않다!

Why? 왜 정답일까?

생물 다양성이 보장되면 환경 변화에 대처하기가 더 좋다는 내용의 글로, ④ 앞에서는 식물이 한 종류만 있는 숲의 예를 들어 이 경우 갑작스러운 건기라도 찾아와 식물이 죽으면 숲 전체 생태계가 망가진다는 내용을 제시한다. 한편 주어진 문장은 But으로 흐름을 반전시키며 생물 다양성이 있으면 상황이 다르다는 것을 언급한다. ④ 뒤에서는 '다양한 식물 종'을 언급하며, 이것들이 건기에 대처하는 방식이 모두 다르기에 많은 수가 살아남아 생태계가 유지될 수 있음을 설명한다. 따라서 주어진 문장이 들어가기에 가장 적절한 곳은 ④이다.

- ecosystem ⓝ 생태계
- food web 먹이 그물, 먹이 사슬 체계
- die out 멸종되다, 자취를 감추다
- prey upon ~을 잡아먹다, 괴롭히다

구문 풀이

5행 For example, imagine a forest with only one type of plant in it, which is [선행사] [계속적 용법] the only source of food and habitat for the entire forest food web.

★★★ 등급을 가르는 문제!

39 우리 생활의 다방면에 연관된 밤하늘   정답률 34% | 정답 ②

글의 흐름으로 보아, 주어진 문장이 들어가기에 가장 적절한 곳을 고르시오.

We are connected to the night sky in many ways.
우리는 많은 방식으로 밤하늘과 연결되어 있다.

① It has always inspired people / to wonder and to imagine.
그것은 항상 사람들에게 영감을 주었다. / 궁금해하고 상상하도록

✔ Since the dawn of civilization, / our ancestors created myths / and told legendary stories / about the night sky.
문명의 시작부터, / 우리 선조들은 신화를 만들었고 / 전설적 이야기를 했다. / 밤하늘에 대해

Elements of those narratives became embedded / in the social and cultural identities of many generations.
그러한 이야기들의 요소들은 깊이 새겨졌다. / 여러 세대의 사회·문화적 정체성에

③ On a practical level, / the night sky helped past generations / to keep track of time and create calendars / — essential to developing societies / as aids to farming and seasonal gathering.

[문제편 p.035]

실용적인 수준에서, / 밤하늘은 과거 세대들이 ~하도록 도왔고 / 시간을 기록하고 달력을 만들도록 / 이는 사회를 발전시키는 데 필수적이었다. / 농업과 계절에 따른 수확의 보조 도구로서

④ For many centuries, / it also provided a useful navigation tool, / vital for commerce and for exploring new worlds.
수 세기 동안, / 그것은 또한 유용한 항해 도구를 제공했다. / 무역과 새로운 세계를 탐험하는 데 필수적인

⑤ Even in modern times, / many people in remote areas of the planet / observe the night sky / for such practical purposes.
심지어 현대에도, / 지구의 외딴 지역에 있는 많은 사람이 / 밤하늘을 관찰한다. / 그러한 실용적인 목적을 위해

우리는 많은 방식으로 밤하늘과 연결되어 있다. ① 그것은 항상 사람들이 궁금해하고 상상하도록 영감을 주었다. ② 문명의 시작부터, 우리 선조들은 밤하늘에 대해 신화를 만들었고 전설적 이야기를 했다. 그러한 이야기들의 요소들은 여러 세대의 사회·문화적 정체성에 깊이 새겨졌다. ③ 실용적인 수준에서, 밤하늘은 과거 세대들이 시간을 기록하고 달력을 만들도록 도왔고 이는 농업과 계절에 따른 수확의 보조 도구로서 사회를 발전시키는 데 필수적이었다. ④ 수 세기 동안, 그것은 또한 무역과 새로운 세계를 탐험하는 데 필수적인 유용한 항해 도구를 제공하였다. ⑤ 심지어 현대에도, 지구의 외딴 지역에 있는 많은 사람이 그러한 실용적인 목적을 위해 밤하늘을 관찰한다.

Why? 왜 정답일까?

② 앞에서 인류는 밤하늘을 궁금해했다고 언급한 후, 주어진 문장은 인류가 거의 문명이 시작되던 시기부터 밤하늘에 대한 다양한 전설과 신화를 만들어냈다고 설명한다. 그리고 ② 뒤의 문장은 주어진 문장의 myths and legendary stories를 those narratives로 가리킨다. 따라서 주어진 문장이 들어가기에 가장 적절한 곳은 ②이다.

- keep track of ~을 기록하다
- gathering ⓝ 수집, 수확
- vital ⓐ 필수적인, 매우 중요한
- remote ⓐ 멀리 떨어진

구문 풀이

6행 On a practical level, the night sky helped past generations to keep track of [동사] [목적어] [목적격 보어1] time and (to) create calendars — (which are) essential to developing societies as [목적격 보어2] [선행사] [생략] aids to farming and seasonal gathering.

★★ 문제 해결 꿀~팁 ★★

▶ 많이 틀린 이유는?
③ 앞에서 밤하늘에 대한 이야기는 '사회문화적 정체성에 깊이 새겨졌다'고 하는데, ③ 뒤에서는 '실용적으로 살펴보면' 밤하늘 연구가 달력 제작 등에 영향을 미쳤다고 한다. 즉 On a practical level 앞뒤로 일반적 논의에서 더 구체적 논의로 나아가는 내용이 자연스럽게 연결된다.

▶ 문제 해결 방법은?
② 앞에서는 '이야기'로 볼 만한 내용이 없는데, ② 뒤에서는 갑자기 those narratives를 언급하므로 논리적 공백이 발생한다. 이때 주어진 문장을 보면 myths와 legendary stories가 있으므로, 이것을 ② 뒤에서 those narratives로 연결했다는 것을 알 수 있다.

---

40 경쟁자 제거에 망가니즈를 활용하는 식물   정답률 55% | 정답 ①

다음 글의 내용을 한 문장으로 요약하고자 한다. 빈칸 (A), (B)에 들어갈 말로 가장 적절한 것은?

	(A)		(B)
✔	increase 증가시키다	……	deadly 치명적인
②	increase 증가시키다	……	advantageous 이로운
③	indicate 보여주다	……	nutritious 영양가 있는
④	reduce 줄이다	……	dry 건조한
⑤	reduce 줄이다	……	warm 따뜻한

The common blackberry (*Rubus allegheniensis*) / has an amazing ability / to move manganese from one layer of soil to another / using its roots.
common blackberry(*Rubus allegheniensis*)는 / 놀라운 능력이 있다. / 토양의 망가니즈를 한 층에서 다른 층으로 옮기는 / 뿌리를 이용하여

This may seem like a funny talent / for a plant to have, / but it all becomes clear / when you realize the effect / it has on nearby plants.
이것은 기이한 재능처럼 보일 수도 있지만, / 식물이 가지기에는 / 전부 명확해진다. / 여러분이 영향을 깨닫고 나면 / 그것이 근처의 식물에 미치는

Manganese can be very harmful to plants, / especially at high concentrations.
망가니즈는 식물에 매우 해로울 수 있으며, / 특히 고농도일 때 그렇다.

Common blackberry is unaffected by damaging effects of this metal / and has evolved two different ways of using manganese to its advantage.
common blackberry는 이 금속 원소의 해로운 효과에 영향을 받지 않으며, / 망가니즈를 자신에게 유리하게 사용하는 두 가지 다른 방법을 발달시켰다.

First, / it redistributes manganese / from deeper soil layers to shallow soil layers / using its roots as a small pipe.
첫째로, / 그것은 망가니즈를 재분배한다. / 깊은 토양층으로부터 얕은 토양층으로 / 그것의 뿌리를 작은 관으로 사용하여

Second, / it absorbs manganese as it grows, / concentrating the metal in its leaves.
둘째로, / 그것은 성장하면서 망가니즈를 흡수하여 / 그 금속 원소를 잎에 농축한다.

When the leaves drop and decay, / their concentrated manganese deposits / further poison the soil around the plant.
잎이 떨어지고 부패할 때, / 그것의 농축된 망가니즈 축적물은 / 그 식물 주변의 토양을 독성 물질로 더욱 오염시킨다.

For plants / that are not immune to the toxic effects of manganese, / this is very bad news.
식물에게 / 망가니즈의 유독한 영향에 면역이 없는 / 이것은 매우 나쁜 소식이다.

Essentially, / the common blackberry eliminates competition / by poisoning its neighbors with heavy metals.
본질적으로, / common blackberry는 경쟁자를 제거한다. / 중금속으로 그것의 이웃을 중독시켜

➡ The common blackberry has an ability / to (A) increase the amount of manganese / in the surrounding upper soil, / which makes the nearby soil / quite (B) deadly for other plants.
common blackberry는 능력이 있다. / 망가니즈의 양을 증가시키는 / 주변의 위쪽 토양의 / 그것은 근처의 토양을 ~하게 만든다 / 다른 식물에게 상당히 치명적이게

common blackberry(*Rubus allegheniensis*)는 뿌리를 이용하여 토양의 한 층에서 다른 층으로 망가니즈를 옮기는 놀라운 능력이 있다. 이것은 식물이 가지기에는 기이한 재능처럼 보일 수도 있지만, 그것이 근처의 식물에 미치는 영향을 깨닫고 나면 전부 명확해진다. 망가니즈는 식물에 매우 해로울 수 있으며, 특히 고농도일 때 그렇다. common blackberry는 이 금속 원소의 해로운 효과에 영향을 받지 않으며, 망가니즈를 자신에게 유리하게 사용하는 두 가지 다른 방법을 발달시켰다. 첫째로, 그것은 뿌리를 작은 관으로 사용하여 망가니즈를 깊은 토양층으로부터 얕은 토양층으로 재분배한다. 둘째로, 그것은 성장하면서 망가니즈를 흡수하여 그 금속 원소를 잎에 농축한다. 잎이 떨어지고 부패할 때, 그것의 농축된 망가니즈 축적물은 그 식물 주변의 토양을 독성 물질로 더욱 오염시킨다. 망가니즈의 유독한 영향에 면역이 없는 식물에게 이것은 매우 나쁜 소식이다. 본질적으로, common blackberry는 중금속으로 그것의 이웃을 중독시켜 경쟁자를 제거한다.

→ common blackberry는 주변 위쪽 토양에 있는 망가니즈의 양을 (A) 증가시키는 능력이 있는데, 그것이 근처의 토양이 다른 식물에게 상당히 (B) 치명적이게 만든다.

Why? 왜 정답일까?

첫 문장과 마지막 세 문장에 따르면 common blackberry는 뿌리를 이용해 망가니즈를 끌어올리거나 이동시킬 수 있어서 주변 토양에 망가니즈가 더 많아지게 할 수 있는데, 이것은 경쟁자 제거에 도움이 된다고 한다. 따라서 요약문의 빈칸 (A), (B)에 들어갈 말로 가장 적절한 것은 ① '(A) increase(증가시키다), (B) deadly(치명적인)'이다.

- concentration ⓝ 농도, 농축
- absorb ⓥ 흡수하다
- eliminate ⓥ 제거하다
- shallow ⓐ 얕은
- be immune to ~에 면역이 있다

구문 풀이

3행 This may seem like a funny talent for a plant to have, but it all becomes
주어1　　동사1　　　　　주격 보어　　　　의미상 주어 형용사적 용법 주어2　　동사2
clear when you realize the effect [it has on nearby plants].
주격 보어2　　　　　　　　　　선행사

41-42 우리를 가로막는 이들을 이해하기

The longest journey we will make / is the eighteen inches between our head and heart.
우리가 갈 가장 긴 여정은 / 우리의 머리에서 가슴까지의 18인치이다.

「If we take this journey, / it can shorten our (a) misery in the world.」 **41번의 근거**
우리가 이 여행을 한다면, / 그것은 세상에서 우리의 비참함을 줄일 수 있다.

Impatience, judgment, frustration, and anger / reside in our heads.
조급함, 비난, 좌절, 그리고 분노가 / 우리 머릿속에 있다.

When we live in that place too long, / it makes us (b) unhappy.
우리가 그 장소에서 너무 오래 살면, / 그것은 우리를 불행하게 만든다.

But when we take the journey from our heads to our hearts, / something shifts (c) inside.
그러나 우리가 머리부터 가슴까지의 여행을 하면, / 내면에서 무엇인가 바뀐다.

What if we were able to love everything / that gets in our way?
만일 모든 것을 우리가 사랑할 수 있다면 어떻게 될까? / 우리를 가로막는

What if we tried loving the shopper / who unknowingly steps in front of us in line, / the driver who cuts us off in traffic, / the swimmer who splashes us with water during a belly dive, / or the reader who pens a bad online review of our writing?
만일 우리가 그 쇼핑객을 사랑하려고 노력한다면 어떨까? / 줄을 서 있는 우리 앞에 무심코 들어온 / 차량 흐름에서 우리 앞에 끼어든 그 운전자를, / 배 쪽으로 다이빙하면서 우리에게 물을 튄 수영하는 그 사람을, / 우리의 글에 대해 나쁜 온라인 후기를 쓴 그 독자를

「Every person who makes us miserable / is (d) like us」 **42번의 근거** — a human being, / most likely doing the best they can, / deeply loved by their parents, a child, or a friend.
우리를 비참하게 만드는 모든 사람은 / 우리와 같다. / 인간, / 아마도 분명히 최선을 다하고 있으며, / 부모, 자녀, 또는 친구로부터 깊이 사랑받는

And how many times have we unknowingly stepped / in front of someone in line?
그리고 우리는 몇 번이나 무심코 들어갔을까? / 줄을 서 있는 누군가의 앞에

Cut someone off in traffic?
차량 흐름에서 누군가에게 끼어든 적은?

Splashed someone in a pool?
수영장에서 누군가에게 물을 튄 적은?

Or made a negative statement / about something we've read?
혹은 부정적인 진술을 한 적은 몇 번이었을까? / 우리가 읽은 것에 대해

It helps to (e) remember / that a piece of us resides in every person we meet.
기억하는 것은 도움이 된다. / 우리가 만나는 모든 사람 속에 우리의 일부가 있다는 것을

우리가 갈 가장 긴 여정은 우리의 머리에서 가슴까지의 18인치이다. 우리가 이 여행을 한다면, 그것은 세상에서 우리의 (a) 비참함을 줄일 수 있다. 조급함, 비난, 좌절, 그리고 분노가 우리 머릿속에 있다. 우리가 그 장소에서 너무 오래 살면, 그것은 우리를 (b) 불행하게 만든다. 그러나 우리가 머리부터 가슴까지의 여행을 하면, (c) 내면에서 무엇인가 바뀐다. 만일 우리를 가로막는 모든 것을 우리가 사랑할 수 있다면 어떻게 될까? 만일 줄을 서 있는 우리 앞에 무심코 들어온 그 쇼핑객을, 차량 흐름에서 우리 앞에 끼어든 그 운전자를, 배 쪽으로 다이빙하면서 우리에게 물을 튄 수영하는 그 사람을, 우리의 글에 대해 나쁜 온라인 후기를 쓴 그 독자를 우리가 사랑하려고 노력한다면 어떨까? 우리를 비참하게 만드는 모든 사람은 우리와 (d) 같다. 그들은 아마도 분명히 최선을 다하고 있으며, 부모, 자녀, 또는 친구로부터 깊이 사랑받는 인간일 것이다. 그리고 우리는 몇 번이나 무심코 줄을 서 있는 누군가의 앞에 끼어 들어갔을까? 차량 흐름에서 누군가에게 끼어든 적은? 수영장에서 누군가에게 물을 튄 적은? 혹은 우리가 읽은 것에 대해 부정적인 진술을 한 적은 몇 번이었을까? 우리가 만나는 모든 사람 속에 우리의 일부가 있다는 것을 (e) 부정하는(→기억하는) 것은 도움이 된다.

- misery ⓝ 불행, 비참함
- frustration ⓝ 좌절
- cut off ~을 가로막다
- deny ⓥ 부인하다
- impatience ⓝ 조급함
- get in one's way ~을 방해하다
- splash ⓥ (물을) 튀기다, 끼얹다

구문 풀이

6행 What if we were able to love everything [that gets in our way]?
「what if + 주어 + 과거 동사 ~? : 가정법 과거(실제로 ~하지 않지만 만일 ~한다면 어떨까?)」

---

41 제목 파악   정답률 52% | 정답 ⑤

윗글의 제목으로 가장 적절한 것은?

① Why It Is So Difficult to Forgive Others – 다른 사람을 용서하기는 왜 그토록 어려울까
② Even Acts of Kindness Can Hurt Somebody – 친절한 행동조차도 누군가를 상처 입힐 수 있다
③ Time Is the Best Healer for a Broken Heart – 실연에는 시간이 가장 좋은 약이다
④ Celebrate the Happy Moments in Your Everyday Life – 매일의 일상에서 행복한 순간을 축복하라
☑ Understand Others to Save Yourself from Unhappiness – 타인을 이해하여 스스로를 불행에서 구하라

Why? 왜 정답일까?

첫 두 문장인 'The longest journey we will make is the eighteen inches between our head and heart. If we take this journey, it can shorten our misery in the world.'에서 남을 이해하는 과정을 '머리부터 가슴까지의 여행'에 빗대어, 이 여행은 우리에게 가장 멀게 느껴지지만 잘 이뤄지면 우리를 불행에서 구해줄 수 있다고 한다. 따라서 글의 제목으로 가장 적절한 것은 ⑤ '타인을 이해하여 스스로를 불행에서 구하라'이다.

42 어휘 추론   정답률 54% | 정답 ⑤

밑줄 친 (a)~(e) 중에서 문맥상 낱말의 쓰임이 적절하지 않은 것은?

① (a)　② (b)　③ (c)　④ (d)　☑ (e)

Why? 왜 정답일까?

'Every person who makes us miserable is like us ~'에서 우리를 비참하게 하는 사람들에게도 우리 자신의 모습이 있다고 설명하는 것으로 보아, 이 점을 우리가 '기억하고' 있을 때 우리 마음속의 불행이 걷어진다는 결론이 적절하다. 즉 (e)의 deny를 remember로 고쳐야 한다. 따라서 문맥상 낱말의 쓰임이 적절하지 않은 것은 ⑤ '(e)'이다.

43-45 여행자들과 수도승의 대화

(A)

One day / a young man was walking along a road on his journey / from one village to another.
어느 날 / 한 젊은이가 여행 중에 길을 따라 걷고 있었다. / 한 마을로부터 다른 마을로

「As he walked / he noticed a monk working in the fields.」 **45번 ①의 근거** 일치
그가 걸어갈 때 / 그는 들판에서 일하는 수도승을 보게 되었다.

The young man turned to the monk and said, / "Excuse me.
그 젊은이는 그 수도승을 향해 돌아보며 말했다. / "실례합니다.

Do you mind if I ask (a) you a question?"
제가 스님께 질문을 하나 드려도 되겠습니까?"라고

"Not at all," replied the monk.
"물론입니다."라고 그 수도승은 대답했다.

(C)

"I am traveling / from the village in the mountains / to the village in the valley / and I was wondering if (c) you knew what it is like in the village in the valley.
"저는 가고 있는데 / 산속의 마을로부터 / 골짜기의 마을로 / 저는 궁금합니다. / 스님께서 골짜기의 마을은 어떤지 아시는지

"Tell me," / said the monk, / "what was your experience of the village in the mountains?"
"저에게 말해 보십시오." / 수도승은 말했다. / "산속의 마을에서의 경험은 어땠습니까?"라고

"Terrible," replied the young man.
그 젊은이는 "끔찍했습니다."라고 대답했다.

"I am glad to be away from there.
"그곳을 벗어나게 되어 기쁩니다.

I found the people most unwelcoming.
저는 그곳 사람들이 정말로 불친절하다고 생각했습니다.

So tell (d) me, / what can I expect in the village in the valley?"
그러니 저에게 말씀해 주십시오. / 제가 골짜기의 마을에서 무엇을 기대할 수 있을까요?"

"I am sorry to tell you," / said the monk, / "but I think / your experience will be much the same there."
"말씀드리기에 유감이지만," / 수도승이 말했다. / "제 생각에 선생님의 경험은 그곳에서도 거의 같을 것 같다고 생각합니다."

「The young man lowered his head helplessly / and walked on.」 **45번 ④의 근거** 일치
그 젊은이는 힘없이 고개를 숙이고 / 계속 걸어갔다.

(B)

A while later / a middle-aged man journeyed down the same road / and came upon the monk.
잠시 후 / 한 중년 남자가 같은 길을 걸어와서 / 그 수도승을 만났다.

「"I am going to the village in the valley,"」 / said the man. **45번 ②의 근거** 일치
"저는 골짜기의 마을로 가고 있습니다." / 그 남자는 말했다.

「"Do you know what it is like?"」 **45번 ③의 근거** 일치
"그곳이 어떤지 아십니까?"라고

"I do," / replied the monk, / "but first tell (b) me about the village where you came from."
"알고 있습니다만." / 그 수도승은 대답했다. / "먼저 저에게 선생님께서 떠나오신 마을에 관해 말해 주십시오."라고

"I've come from the village in the mountains," / said the man.
"저는 산속의 마을로부터 왔습니다." / 그 남자는 말했다.

"It was a wonderful experience.
"그것은 멋진 경험이었습니다.

I felt / as though I was a member of the family in the village."
저는 느꼈습니다. / 마치 제가 그 마을의 가족의 일원인 것처럼"

(D)

"Why did you feel like that?" asked the monk.
그 수도승은 "왜 그렇게 느끼셨습니까?"라고 물었다.

"The elders gave me much advice, / and people were kind and generous.
"어르신들은 저에게 많은 조언을 해 주셨고 / 사람들은 친절하고 너그러웠습니다.

「I am sad to have left there.」 **45번 ⑤의 근거** 불일치
저는 그곳을 떠나서 슬픕니다.

And what is the village in the valley like?" / he asked again.
그런데 골짜기의 마을은 어떻습니까?"라고 / 그는 다시 물었다.

"(e) I think you will find it much the same," / replied the monk.
"저는 선생님은 그곳이 거의 같다고 여기실 거로 생각합니다."라고 / 수도승은 대답했다.

"I'm glad to hear that," / the middle-aged man said smiling and journeyed on.
"그 말씀을 들으니 기쁩니다." / 그 중년 남자는 미소를 지으며 말하고서 여행을 계속했다.

(A)

어느 날 한 젊은이가 한 마을로부터 다른 마을로 여행하며 길을 따라 걷고 있었다. 그는 걷다가 들판에서 일하는 한 수도승을 보게 되었다. 그 젊은이는 그 수도승을 향해 돌아보며 "실례합니다. 제가 (a) 스님께 질문을 하나 드려도 되겠습니까?"라고 말했다. "물론입니다."라고 그 수도승은 대답했다.

(C)

"저는 산속의 마을로부터 골짜기의 마을로 가고 있는데 (c) 스님께서 골짜기의 마을은 어떤지 아시는지 궁금합니다." 수도승은 "저에게 말해 보십시오. 산속의 마을에서의 경험은 어땠습니까?"라고 말했다. 그 젊은이는 "끔찍했습니다."라고 대답했다. "그곳을 벗어나게 되어 기쁩니다. 그곳 사람들이 정말로 불친절하다고 생각했습니다. 그러니 (d) 저에게 말씀해 주십시오, 제가 골짜기의 마을에서 무엇을 기대할 수 있을까요?" "말씀드리기에 유감이지만, 제 생각에 선생님의 경험은 그곳에서도 거의 같을 것 같다고 생각합니다." 수도승이 말했다. 그 젊은이는 힘없이 고개를 숙이고 계속 걸어갔다.

(B)

잠시 후 한 중년 남자가 같은 길을 걸어와서 그 수도승을 만났다. 그 남자는 "저는 골짜기의 마을로 가고 있습니다. 그곳이 어떤지 아십니까?"라고 말했다. "알고 있습니다만, 먼저 (b) 저에게 선생님께서 떠나오신 마을에 관해 말해 주십시오."라고 그 수도승은 대답했다. 그 남자는 "저는 산속의 마을로부터 왔습니다. 그것은 멋진 경험이었습니다. 저는 마치 그 마을의 가족의 일원인 것처럼 느꼈습니다."라고 말했다.

(D)

그 수도승은 "왜 그렇게 느끼셨습니까?"라고 물었다. "어르신들은 저에게 많은 조언을 해 주셨고, 사람들은 친절하고 너그러웠습니다. 그곳을 떠나서 슬픕니다. 그런데 골짜기의 마을은 어떻습니까?"라고 그는 다시 물었다. "(e) 저는 선생님은 그곳이 (산속 마을과) 거의 같다고 여기실 거로 생각합니다."라고 수도승은 대답했다. "그 말씀을 들으니 기쁩니다."라고 그 중년 남자는 미소를 지으며 말하고서 여행을 계속했다.

- **come upon** ~을 우연히 만나다
- **unwelcoming** ⓐ 불친절한, 환영하지 않는
- **generous** ⓐ 관대한
- **valley** ⓝ 골짜기
- **helplessly** 〔ad〕 힘없이, 무기력하게

구문 풀이

(B) 6행 I felt as though I was a member of the family in the village.
　　　　　접속사(마치 ~인 것처럼)

(C) 6행 I found the people most unwelcoming.
　　　　　5형식 동사　　목적어　　　목적격 보어(형용사)

(D) 2행 I am sad to have left there.
　　　　　완료부정사(am보다 과거에 일어난 일 묘사)

---

43 글의 순서 파악　　　　정답률 66% | 정답 ②

주어진 글 (A)에 이어질 내용을 순서에 맞게 배열한 것으로 가장 적절한 것은?

① (B) – (D) – (C)　　　　☑ (C) – (B) – (D)
③ (C) – (D) – (B)　　　　④ (D) – (B) – (C)
⑤ (D) – (C) – (B)

Why? 왜 정답일까?

여행 중이던 젊은이가 수도승을 만나 물어볼 것이 있다고 말했다는 (A) 뒤에는, 젊은이가 산속 마을에 대한 자신의 부정적 감상을 말하며 골짜기의 마을이 어떠한지 묻자 수도승이 산속 마을과 차이가 없을 것이라고 답했다는 내용의 (C)가 연결된다. 이어서 (B)에서는 똑같이 산속 마을에서 출발한 중년 남자가 수도승과 비슷한 대화를 나누며 산속 마을에 관해 좋은 감상을 이야기했다는 내용이 나오고, (D)에서는 수도승이 그렇다면 골짜기 마을도 좋게 느껴질 것이라 답해주었다고 한다. 따라서 글의 순서로 가장 적절한 것은 ② '(C) – (B) – (D)'이다.

---

44 지칭 추론　　　　정답률 64% | 정답 ④

밑줄 친 (a) ~ (e) 중에서 가리키는 대상이 나머지 넷과 다른 것은?

① (a)　② (b)　③ (c)　☑ (d)　⑤ (e)

Why? 왜 정답일까?

(a), (b), (c), (e)는 the monk, (d)는 the young man이므로, (a) ~ (e) 중에서 가리키는 대상이 다른 하나는 ④ '(d)'이다.

---

45 세부 내용 파악　　　　정답률 72% | 정답 ⑤

윗글에 관한 내용으로 적절하지 <u>않은</u> 것은?

① 한 수도승이 들판에서 일하고 있었다.
② 중년 남자는 골짜기에 있는 마을로 가는 중이었다.
③ 수도승은 골짜기에 있는 마을에 대해 질문받았다.
④ 수도승의 말을 듣고 젊은이는 고개를 숙였다.
☑ 중년 남자는 산속에 있는 마을을 떠나서 기쁘다고 말했다.

Why? 왜 정답일까?

(D) 'I am sad to have left there.'에 따르면 중년 남자는 산속 마을을 떠나서 슬펐다고 말했으므로, 내용과 일치하지 않는 것은 ⑤ '중년 남자는 산속에 있는 마을을 떠나서 기쁘다고 말했다.'이다.

Why? 왜 오답일까?

① (A) 'As he walked he noticed a monk working in the fields.'의 내용과 일치한다.
② (B) '"I am going to the village in the valley," said the man.'의 내용과 일치한다.
③ (B) 'Do you know what it is like?'의 내용과 일치한다.
④ (C) 'The young man lowered his head helplessly and walked on.'의 내용과 일치한다.

Dictation 03　　　　문제편 037쪽

03회

01 to be handed out / change the registration method / simply log into the school website

02 pop these pimples / shouldn't touch my face / worsen your skin problems

03 your speeches on climate change / As an environmental activist / I'm a cartoonist

04 a starfish next to the chair / how you put both of them / Your fish in the top left corner

05 put up the balloons around the doorway / take the table out / made a last minute change

06 sell eco-friendly toothbrushes / made from bamboo / need bath sponges

07 checking out books / suffering from your cold / hasn't been delivered yet / has to wait one more day

08 another man's treasure / Where is it taking place / breakable items like glass dishes or cups

09 bring your own instrument / play it on screen / limited to 50 students

10 cross this one out / easier to handle / with a washable filter

11 My eyes are sore / got in your eyes

12 Sorry for bothering you

13 drop by your house / why don't you join us / some snacks to eat

14 my new year's resolutions / share your reading experiences / it really broadens your mind

15 reaches out to touch the guide dog / lose its focus / not to touch the guide dog

16-17 link bones together / relatively low impact on the joints / put almost no stress / don't give up exercising

---

어휘 Review Test 03　　　　문제편 042쪽

A	B	C	D
01 발표하다, 알리다	01 maintain	01 ⓕ	01 ⓟ
02 책임	02 communicate	02 ⓟ	02 ⓙ
03 열정	03 regulation	03 ⓚ	03 ⓘ
04 모이다	04 flow	04 ⓡ	04 ⓗ
05 일, 과업, 과제	05 foreign	05 ⓘ	05 ⓡ
06 완수하다	06 engaging	06 ⓜ	06 ⓘ
07 진지한	07 competitive	07 ⓞ	07 ⓕ
08 통찰력	08 necessarily	08 ⓔ	08 ⓔ
09 기온	09 material	09 ⓐ	09 ⓝ
10 인식하다	10 influence	10 ⓝ	10 ⓠ
11 호기심	11 traditional	11 ⓙ	11 ⓢ
12 감당하다	12 reply	12 ⓘ	12 ⓕ
13 구체적인	13 indeed	13 ⓒ	13 ⓐ
14 이전의	14 observe	14 ⓓ	14 ⓒ
15 관점, 시점	15 civilization	15 ⓛ	15 ⓚ
16 줄이다	16 currently	16 ⓖ	16 ⓘ
17 나타나다, 출현하다	17 claim	17 ⓢ	17 ⓘ
18 생태계	18 factor	18 ⓑ	18 ⓑ
19 살아남다	19 plain	19 ⓗ	19 ⓞ
20 제거하다	20 mainly	20 ⓠ	20 ⓜ

• 정답 •

01 ③ 02 ① 03 ③ 04 ⑤ 05 ④ 06 ③ 07 ⑤ 08 ② 09 ⑤ 10 ④ 11 ① 12 ③ 13 ⑤ 14 ② 15 ③
16 ③ 17 ④ 18 ② 19 ② 20 ① 21 ② 22 ① 23 ⑤ 24 ① 25 ③ 26 ⑤ 27 ④ 28 ⑤ 29 ③ 30 ⑤
31 ② 32 ② 33 ⑤ 34 ① 35 ③ 36 ③ 37 ② 38 ③ 39 ④ 40 ① 41 ① 42 ④ 43 ⑤ 44 ② 45 ④

★ 표기된 문항은 [등급을 가르는 문제]에 해당하는 문항입니다.

---

01 스낵바 운영 안내   정답률 97% | 정답 ③

다음을 듣고, 여자가 하는 말의 목적으로 가장 적절한 것을 고르시오.
① 친환경 제품 사용을 홍보하려고
② 음식 대접에 대한 감사를 표하려고
☑ 간식이 마련되어 있음을 안내하려고
④ 휴식 시간이 변경되었음을 공지하려고
⑤ 구내식당 메뉴에 관한 의견을 구하려고

[Chime bell rings.]
[종소리가 울린다.]
W : Attention, everyone!
집중하세요, 여러분!
Our CEO, Mr. Wayne, has prepared a snack bar to celebrate our success on last month's project.
우리의 CEO인 Wayne 씨가 지난달 프로젝트 성공을 기념하기 위해 스낵바를 준비했습니다.
Please come down to the lobby and enjoy some delicious snacks.
로비로 내려와서 맛있는 간식을 즐겨주세요.
They'll be available until 4 p.m.
간식은 오후 4시까지 제공됩니다.
You'll be impressed by the amazing variety, from crispy fries and hot dogs to fresh lemonade and coffee.
바삭한 감자튀김과 핫도그에서 신선한 레모네이드와 커피까지 다양한 종류에 감탄하실 겁니다.
It'd be great if you could bring your own personal cups for the drinks.
음료를 드실 때 개인 컵을 가져오시면 좋겠습니다.
See you there.
거기서 뵙겠습니다.

Why? 왜 정답일까?

로비에 스낵바가 준비되어 있고, 내려와서 간식을 즐기라 했으므로(Please come down to the lobby and enjoy some delicious snacks.) 여자가 하는 말의 목적으로 가장 적절한 것은 ③ '간식이 마련되어 있음을 안내하려고'이다.

• prepare ⓥ 준비하다   • celebrate ⓥ 기념하다
• success ⓝ 성공   • enjoy ⓥ 즐기다
• available ⓐ 가능한   • variety ⓝ 다양성
• personal ⓐ 개인의

---

02 AI 사용 시 주의할 점   정답률 91% | 정답 ①

대화를 듣고, 남자의 의견으로 가장 적절한 것을 고르시오.
☑ 인공 지능에서 얻은 정보를 맹목적으로 믿어서는 안 된다.
② 출처를 밝히지 않고 타인의 표현을 인용해서는 안 된다.
③ 인공 지능의 도움을 통해 과제물의 질을 높일 수 있다.
④ 과제를 할 때 본인의 생각이 들어가는 것이 중요하다.
⑤ 기술의 변화에 맞추어 작업 방식을 바꿀 필요가 있다.

M : Hi, Pamela. Did you finish your history assignment?
안녕, Pamela. 역사 과제 다 했니?
W : Yes, Dad. I finished it quite easily with the help of AI.
네, 아빠. AI의 도움으로 쉽게 끝냈어요.
M : Really? Do you mean you used an artificial-intelligence website?
정말? 인공지능 웹사이트를 사용했다는 말이니?
W : Yeah. I typed in the questions and AI gave me the answers right away.
네. 질문을 입력하니 AI가 바로 답을 줬어요.
M : Well, is it a good idea to do your homework that way?
그런데 그렇게 과제를 하는 게 좋은 생각일까?
W : Why not? It saves a lot of time and gives me just the information I need.
왜요? 시간도 많이 절약되고 필요한 정보만 주잖아요.
M : I used to think so, too. But after trying it a couple of times, I found out AI sometimes uses false information as well.
나도 그렇게 생각했었지. 하지만 몇 번 사용해 보니까 AI가 가끔 잘못된 정보를 제공한다는 걸 알았어.
W : Really? I didn't know that.
정말요? 그건 몰랐어요.
M : Yeah, you shouldn't blindly trust the answers from AI.
그래. AI가 주는 답을 맹목적으로 믿으면 안 돼.
W : Okay. I'll keep that in mind next time.
알겠어요. 다음에는 명심할게요.

Why? 왜 정답일까?

과제에 AI를 사용했다는 여자에게 남자는 AI가 가끔 잘못된 정보를 제공하기도 한다(I found out AI sometimes uses false information as well.)는 것을 알려주었으므로, 남자의 의견으로 가장 적절한 것은 ① '인공 지능에서 얻은 정보를 맹목적으로 믿어서는 안 된다.'이다.

• assignment ⓝ 과제   • quite ⓐ 꽤
• easily ⓐ 쉽게   • artificial-intelligence 인공 지능
• information ⓝ 정보   • false ⓐ 틀린
• blindly ⓐ 맹목적으로

---

03 소셜 미디어에서 비교하지 말기   정답률 89% | 정답 ③

다음을 듣고, 여자가 하는 말의 요지로 가장 적절한 것을 고르시오.
① 소셜 미디어는 원만한 대인관계 유지에 도움이 된다.
② 온라인에서는 자아가 다양한 모습으로 표출될 수 있다.
☑ 소셜 미디어는 자존감에 부정적인 영향을 줄 수 있다.
④ 친밀한 관계일수록 상대의 언행에 쉽게 영향을 받는다.
⑤ 유명인 사생활 보호의 중요성은 종종 간과된다.

W : Hello, listeners. This is Kelly Watson's *Love Yourself*.
안녕하세요, 청취자 여러분. 저는 Kelly Watson의 *Love Yourself*입니다.
Have you ever thought about your social media use?
여러분은 자신의 소셜 미디어 사용에 대해 생각해 본 적이 있나요?
Social media lets you stay connected with others easily.
소셜 미디어는 다른 사람들과 쉽게 연결될 수 있게 해줍니다.
However, it can make you compare yourself with others, too.
그러나, 소셜 미디어는 여러분이 다른 사람들과 자신을 비교하게 만들 수도 있습니다.
For example, a celebrity's post about going on a luxurious trip may make you jealous.
예를 들어, 유명인이 호화로운 여행을 떠난다는 게시물이 여러분을 질투하게 만들 수 있습니다.
Continuously making such comparisons stops you from looking at yourself the way you truly are.
이런 비교를 계속하게 되면 자신을 있는 그대로 바라보지 못하게 됩니다.
You might think, "Why can't I have a better life?" and feel small about yourself.
여러분은 "왜 나는 더 나은 삶을 살 수 없을까?"라고 생각하고 자신을 작게 느낄지도 모릅니다.
As you can see, social media can have a negative effect on your self-esteem.
이처럼, 소셜 미디어는 여러분의 자존감에 부정적인 영향을 미칠 수 있습니다.
I'll be right back with some tips for healthy social media use.
잠시 후에 건강한 소셜 미디어 사용을 위한 팁을 알려드리겠습니다.

Why? 왜 정답일까?

소셜 미디어에서의 타인과 스스로를 비교하면 자존감에 부정적인 영향을 줄 수 있다(As you can see, social media can have a negative effect on your self-esteem.)고 얘기하고 있으므로, 여자가 하는 말의 요지로 가장 적절한 것은 ③ '소셜 미디어는 자존감에 부정적인 영향을 줄 수 있다'이다.

• stay ⓥ 머무르다   • celebrity ⓝ 연예인
• luxurious ⓐ 호화로운   • jealous ⓐ 질투하다
• continuously ⓐ 계속해서   • comparison ⓝ 비교
• negative ⓐ 부정적인

---

04 공원 풍경 감상하기   정답률 95% | 정답 ⑤

대화를 듣고, 그림에서 대화의 내용과 일치하지 않는 것을 고르시오.

W : Honey, I love this park!
여보, 이 공원 너무 좋아요!
M : Me, too. This park is so cool. But, oh, look! What's that in the tree?
나도요. 이 공원 너무 멋져요. 근데, 오, 저 나무에 있는 게 뭐죠?
W : 「It's just a kite stuck in the tree's branches.」 ①의 근거 일치
그냥 나무 가지에 연이 걸려 있네요.
M : I guess some kids went home without their kite.
아마도 아이들이 연을 두고 집에 갔나 봐요.
W : 「By the same tree, a woman is walking her dog. They look so lovely.」 ②의 근거 일치
같은 나무 옆에서 한 여성이 개를 산책시키고 있네요. 정말 예뻐요.
M : What about the little girl beside her?
옆에 있는 작은 소녀는요?
W : 「You mean the girl holding balloons in her hand?」 ③의 근거 일치
손에 풍선을 들고 있는 소녀요?
M : Right. She's adorable. And look there! 「Did you notice a basket full of flowers on the picnic mat?」 ④의 근거 일치
맞아요. 정말 귀엽네요. 그리고 저기 보세요! 피크닉 매트 위에 꽃이 가득 담긴 바구니 보셨나요?
W : Yes, right. It adds a touch of romance to the scene.
네, 맞아요. 그 장면에 로맨틱한 분위기를 더해 주네요.
M : I think so, too. Oh, there's a fountain. 「Next to it, a man is playing the violin.」
저도 그렇게 생각해요. 오, 저기 분수예요. 그 옆에서 한 남자가 바이올린을 연주하고 있네요. ⑤의 근거 불일치
W : The melody is beautiful. I'm glad we came here.
멜로디가 정말 아름다워요. 여기 오길 잘했어요.

Why? 왜 정답일까?

대화에서 분수 옆에서 한 남자가 바이올린을 연주하고 있다고 했지만, 그림에서는 분수 옆의 한 남자는 카메라로 사진을 찍고 있다. 따라서 그림에서 대화의 내용과 일치하지 않는 것은 ⑤이다.

• branch ⓝ 나뭇가지   • hold ⓥ 들다
• balloon ⓝ 풍선   • notice ⓥ 알아차리다
• basket ⓝ 바구니   • scene ⓝ 장면
• fountain ⓝ 분수   • glad ⓐ 기쁘다

---

05 과학 캠프   정답률 80% | 정답 ④

대화를 듣고, 남자가 할 일로 가장 적절한 것을 고르시오.

① 과학 캠프 지원하기 ② 참가 실험 결정하기
③ 체크리스트 작성하기 ✓ 실험 계획서 보여주기
⑤ 자기 소개 영상 촬영하기

M : Hey, Alice. I applied for the science camp next week. What about you?
안녕, Alice. 나는 다음 주에 과학 캠프에 지원했어. 너는 어때?

W : Me, too. But I didn't know that there were so many things to do before the camp.
나도 했어. 그런데 캠프 전에 할 일이 이렇게 많은 줄 몰랐어.

M : Right. Would you like to go over my checklist together?
맞아. 내 체크리스트를 같이 확인해 볼래?

W : Hmm, let's see. Did you upload your introduction video to the website?
음, 보자. 자기소개 영상을 웹사이트에 올렸어?

M : Yes, I tried to show my interest in science. Oh, hey, have you picked which experiment to work on?
응, 과학에 대한 나의 관심을 보여 주려고 노력했어. 그런데, 너는 어떤 실험을 할지 정했어?

W : Yes. I decided to participate in a biology experiment.
응. 나는 생물학 실험에 참여하기로 했어.

M : Me, too. Wasn't it difficult to make a plan for your experiment?
나도. 실험 계획을 세우는 게 어렵지 않았어?

W : Actually, I haven't even started yet because I've never written a plan for a biology experiment before.
사실, 아직 시작도 안 했어. 생물학 실험 계획을 세워본 적이 없거든.

M : I'll show you mine after class. Maybe you can get some ideas.
내가 수업 끝나고 내 계획을 보여 줄게. 아마 아이디어를 얻을 수 있을 거야.

W : Really? That'd be great. See you soon.
정말? 그럼 좋지. 곧 보자.

Why? 왜 정답일까?

대화에서 여자가 생물학 실험 계획을 세워본 적이 없다고 하자 남자가 수업 끝나고 자신의 계획을 보여준다고 하였으므로, 남자가 할 일로 가장 적절한 것은 ④ '실험 계획서 보여주기'이다.

● go over 검토하다   ● introduction ⓝ 소개
● interest ⓝ 관심   ● experiment ⓝ 실험
● participate ⓥ 참가하다   ● idea ⓝ 개념

06 조카를 위한 배낭 구매하기   정답률 49% | 정답 ③

대화를 듣고, 여자가 지불할 금액을 고르시오. [3점]
① $50   ② $55   ✓ $60   ④ $65   ⑤ $70

W : Hi, I'm looking for a backpack for my niece. She's going on a camping trip this summer.
안녕하세요. 제 조카를 위해 배낭을 찾고 있어요. 이번 여름에 캠핑을 갈 거예요.

M : Great. We have this blue backpack that has multiple pockets.
좋네요. 여기 여러 개의 주머니가 있는 파란색 배낭이 있습니다.

W : It looks stylish and functional. How much is it?
멋있고 기능적이네요. 가격은 얼마예요?

M : It's $50, but we have a special discount only on backpacks today. Every backpack is 10% off.
50달러인데 오늘은 배낭에만 특별 할인이 있어요. 모든 배낭이 10% 할인됩니다.

W : That's a great deal! I'll take it.
정말 좋은 거래네요! 이걸로 할게요.

M : I'm sure your niece will love it. Do you need anything else?
분명 조카분도 좋아할 거예요. 다른 건 필요하세요?

W : Yes. I like this camping hat. How much is it?
네. 이 캠핑 모자가 마음에 드네요. 얼마인가요?

M : It's $10, not on sale, though.
10달러입니다. 하지만 할인은 안 됩니다.

W : That's okay. I'll take it as well.
괜찮아요. 이것도 같이 할게요.

M : Gift wrapping for them would be a total of $5. Would you like gift wrapping?
두 개 다 포장하는데 5달러입니다. 포장 원하세요?

W : Yes, please. Here's my credit card.
네, 부탁드려요. 여기 제 신용카드예요.

Why? 왜 정답일까?

10% 할인하는 50달러 배낭과 할인하지 않는 10달러 캠핑 모자, 그리고 선물포장 5달러를 더하면 45+10+5=60이므로 여자가 지불할 금액으로 적절한 것은 ③ '$60'이다.

● look for 찾다   ● multiple ⓐ 다수의
● functional ⓐ 기능적인   ● discount ⓝ 할인
● deal ⓝ 거래   ● niece ⓝ 조카

07 동아리 축제에 갈 수 없는 이유   정답률 96% | 정답 ⑤

대화를 듣고, 남자가 마술쇼에 갈 수 없는 이유를 고르시오.
① 록 콘서트에 가야 해서
② 다른 학교 축제에 가야 해서
③ 가족 중 아픈 사람이 있어서
④ 동아리 축제를 준비해야 해서
✓ 삼촌 생일 파티에 참석해야 해서

W : Hi, Chris. How was your weekend?
안녕, Chris. 주말 어땠어?

M : Hello, Martha. I went to a rock concert and had fun. How about you?
안녕, Martha. 나는 록 콘서트에 다녀왔고 재미있었어. 너는 어땠어?

W : I've been preparing for tomorrow's club festival.
나는 내일 있을 동아리 축제를 준비하고 있었어.

M : Oh, what kind of activity are you preparing for the festival?
오, 축제를 위해 무슨 활동을 준비하고 있어?

W : Our club members are presenting a magic show. Come and watch us at 4 p.m. tomorrow if you are available.
우리 동아리 회원들이 마술 쇼를 선보일 거야. 시간 되면 내일 오후 4시에 와서 봐줘.

M : I'd love to, but I can't make it.
가고 싶지만 못 갈 것 같아.

W : Why? It'd be nice to have you there.
왜? 네가 와주면 좋을 텐데.

M : I'm sorry, but I have to attend my uncle's birthday party.
미안해. 하지만 삼촌 생일 파티에 가야 해.

W : Oh, I understand. I hope you have a wonderful time with your family.
아, 이해해. 가족과 즐거운 시간 보내길 바라.

M : Thank you, I will.
고마워, 그럴게.

Why? 왜 정답일까?

여자의 동아리 축제에 남자가 가지 못하는 이유로 삼촌 생일 파티에 가야한다고 했기 때문에(I'm sorry, but I have to attend my uncle's birthday party.), 남자가 마술쇼에 갈 수 없는 이유는 ⑤ '삼촌 생일 파티에 참석해야 해서'이다.

● weekend ⓝ 주말   ● prepare ⓥ 준비하다
● present ⓥ 보여주다   ● available ⓐ 가능한
● attend ⓥ 참석하다   ● wonderful ⓐ 놀라운

08 Victory 마라톤 정보   정답률 91% | 정답 ②

대화를 듣고, Victory Marathon에 관해 언급되지 <u>않은</u> 것을 고르시오.
① 행사 날짜   ✓ 신청 방법   ③ 출발 지점
④ 참가비   ⑤ 예상 참가 인원

W : Hey, Alex. Have you seen the announcement for the Victory Marathon?
안녕, Alex. Victory 마라톤 공지 봤어?

M : Not yet, but I'm curious about it. When's the event?
아직 못 봤어. 그런데 궁금해. 행사가 언제야?

W : 「It's on Saturday, July 13th.」 ①의근거 일치
7월 13일 토요일이야.

M : Nice. Where will the race start?
좋다. 경주는 어디서 시작해?

W : 「It will start at William Stadium.」 ③의근거 일치
William 경기장에서 시작해.

M : Oh, great. How much does it cost to participate?
오, 좋네. 참가 비용은 얼마야?

W : 「It costs $30.」 ④의근거 일치
30달러야.

M : That's reasonable. How many participants are they expecting?
적당하네. 참가자는 얼마나 예상하고 있어?

W : Last year, there were around 5,000. 「They say they expect about the same this year.」 ⑤의근거 일치
작년에는 약 5,000명이었어. 올해도 비슷할 거라고 해.

M : I didn't know that many people love marathons. I'm in!
그렇게 많은 사람들이 마라톤을 좋아하는 줄 몰랐네. 나도 참여할게!

W : Great. I look forward to running with you.
좋아. 너와 함께 달리는 게 기대돼.

Why? 왜 정답일까?

Victory Marathon에 관해 언급된 것은 행사 날짜, 출발 지점, 참가비 그리고 예상 참가 인원이므로 언급되지 않은 것은 ② '신청 방법'이다.

● announcement ⓝ 공고, 알림   ● curious ⓐ 궁금한
● cost ⓥ 비용이 들다   ● reasonable ⓐ 합리적인
● participant ⓝ 참가자   ● expect ⓥ 기대하다

09 Violet Hill 멘토링 프로그램 안내   정답률 95% | 정답 ⑤

Violet Hill Mentorship에 관한 다음 내용을 듣고, 일치하지 <u>않는</u> 것을 고르시오.
① 다음 주 금요일에 개최될 예정이다.
② 대학 생활에 관한 조언이 제공된다.
③ 신청 시 질문을 미리 제출해야 한다.
④ 신청 마감일은 다음 주 화요일이다.
✓ 전공별 참가 가능한 인원은 20명이다.

M : Good morning, students of Violet Hill High School. This is your principal speaking.
안녕하세요, Violet Hill 고등학교 학생 여러분. 교장 선생님입니다.
「I'm delighted to announce that the annual Violet Hill Mentorship will be held next Friday.」 ①의근거 일치
저는 매년 열리는 Violet Hill 멘토링 프로그램이 다음 주 금요일에 열릴 것임을 기쁘게 알립니다.
「Our school graduates who are now majoring in English literature, bioengineering, and theater and film will be giving some tips on university life.」 ②의근거 일치
현재 영문학, 생명공학, 그리고 연극 및 영화를 전공하고 있는 우리 학교 졸업생들이 대학 생활에 관한 조언을 해 줄 것입니다.
「To register for this event, visit our school website and submit two questions you would like to ask them in advance.」 ③의근거 일치
이 행사에 등록하려면, 학교 웹사이트를 방문하여 사전에 그들에게 묻고 싶은 질문 두 가지를 제출하세요.
「The deadline for registration is next Tuesday, so don't wait too long.」 ④의근거 일치
등록 마감일은 다음 주 화요일이니 너무 늦지 않게 등록하세요.
「And remember, the maximum number of participants for each major is 30 people.」 ⑤의근거 불일치
그리고 각 전공별로 최대 참가 인원은 30명입니다.
For more information, visit our school website.
자세한 사항은 학교 웹사이트를 참조하세요.

Why? 왜 정답일까?

Violet Hill Mentorship의 전공별 참가 가능한 인원은 30명이기 때문에 ⑤ '전공별 참가 가능한 인원은 20명이다.'는 일치하지 않는다.

● principal ⓝ 교장   ● delight ⓥ 기쁜
● annual ⓐ 연간의   ● graduate ⓝ 졸업생
● major ⓥ 전공하다   ● register ⓥ 신청하다
● submit ⓥ 제출하다

다음 표를 보면서 대화를 듣고, 두 사람이 구입할 무선 진공 청소기를 고르시오.

Cordless Vacuum Cleaner

	Model	Battery Life	Price	Wet Cleaning	Color
①	A	1 hour	$300	×	Red
②	B	2 hours	$330	×	White
③	C	2 hours	$370	○	Red
④✓	D	3 hours	$390	○	White
⑤	E	3 hours	$410	○	Black

M : Honey, look. This website's Summer Sale has just begun.
자기야, 봐바. 이 웹사이트에서 여름 세일이 막 시작됐어.

W : Oh, great. Why don't we buy a new cordless vacuum cleaner?
오, 좋네. 새 무선 청소기를 사는 게 어때?

M : Sure. There are five bestsellers shown here.
좋아. 여기 베스트셀러 다섯 가지가 나와 있어.

W : Let's check the battery life first.
먼저 배터리 수명을 확인해 보자.

M : 「I think it should be at least two hours so that we don't have to charge it as often.」
자주 충전하지 않게 최소 2시간은 되어야할 것 같아. **근거1** Battery Life의 조건

W : I agree. 「But let's not spend more than $400 on a vacuum cleaner.」
동의해. 하지만 청소기에 400달러 이상은 쓰지 말자. **근거2** Price의 조건

M : Fine. Oh, some of these also have a wet cleaning function.
알겠어. 오, 여기 몇몇 제품은 물청소 기능도 있네.

W : 「I'd love that. With that function, we can definitely save a lot of time.」
그거 좋겠다. 그 기능이 있으면 확실히 시간을 많이 절약할 수 있을 거야. **근거3** Wet Cleaning의 조건

M : Okay. What about the color? 「The white one looks better to me.」
좋아. 색상은 어때? 나는 흰색이 더 좋아 보이네. **근거4** Color의 조건

W : Right. It'll match the color tone of our living room.
맞아. 우리 거실 색조와도 잘 어울릴 거야.

M : Perfect. So, let's buy this one.
완벽해. 그럼 이걸로 사자.

W : Great.
좋아.

Why? 왜 정답일까?

배터리 수명은 2시간 이상이고, 가격은 400달러 이하이며 습식 청소가 가능한 모델 중 색깔은 흰색이어야 하므로 두 사람이 구입할 무선 진공청소기는 ④이다.

- cordless ⓐ 무선의
- charge ⓥ 충전하다
- definitely ⓪ⓓ 분명히
- vacuum cleaner ⓝ 진공청소기
- function ⓝ 기능
- match ⓥ 알맞다

대화를 듣고, 남자의 마지막 말에 대한 여자의 응답으로 가장 적절한 것을 고르시오.

①✓ Fine. Let's talk about it over dinner. – 그래. 저녁 먹으면서 얘기해 보자.

② Okay. Be more responsible next time. – 알았어. 다음번에는 좀 더 책임감 있는 모습을 보여주렴.

③ Great. I already ordered some pet food. – 좋아. 나 이미 사료를 주문했어.

④ Too bad. I hope your cat gets well soon. – 안 됐다. 네 고양이 낫길 바랄게.

⑤ Sorry. I can't take care of your cat tonight. – 미안해. 나 오늘밤 네 고양이 못 돌봐 줘.

M : Mom, I want to have a cat. Have you ever thought about us adopting a cat?
엄마, 저 고양이 갖고 싶어요. 고양이 입양에 대해서 생각해보신 적 있으세요?

W : Sweetie, having a pet requires a lot of responsibility.
얘야, 반려동물을 키우는 것은 많은 책임을 요구한다.

M : I'm totally ready for it. Mom, we could at least consider it.
저 완전 준비됐어요. 엄마, 그냥 생각은 해볼 수 있잖아요.

W : Fine. Let's talk about it over dinner.
그래. 저녁 먹으면서 얘기해 보자.

Why? 왜 정답일까?

고양이를 가지고 싶어 하는 남자와 반려동물을 키우는 것은 책임감이 많이 든다는 여자의 대화이다. 남자가 고양이를 정말 기르고 싶어하므로 남자의 마지막 말에 대한 여자의 응답으로 가장 적절한 것은 ① 'Fine. Let's talk about it over dinner.'이다.

- adopt ⓥ 입양하다
- responsibility ⓝ 책임감
- consider ⓥ 고려하다
- require ⓥ 필요로 하다
- totally ⓪ⓓ 완전히

대화를 듣고, 여자의 마지막 말에 대한 남자의 응답으로 가장 적한 것을 고르시오.

① I can't accept late assignments. – 늦게 제출한 과제 안 받아 줄 거야.

② You did an excellent job this time. – 이번에 아주 잘했어.

③✓ Upload your work to our school website. – 네 과제를 학교 웹사이트에 올려.

④ Try to do your homework by yourself. – 숙제를 스스로 하려고 해봐.

⑤ We can finish it before the next class. – 우리 다음 수업 전까지 끝낼 수 있어.

W : Jake, I completely forgot about the math assignment. When's the deadline?
Jake야, 나 수학 과제에 대해서 완전히 까먹고 있었어. 제출기한이 언제야?

M : You need to submit it by next Tuesday.
다음 주 화요일까지 제출하면 돼.

W : Phew, I still have some time. Where should I submit it?
휴, 아직 시간 있구나. 어디으로 제출하면 돼?

M : Upload your work to our school website.
네 과제를 학교 웹사이트에 올려.

Why? 왜 정답일까?

수학 과제 제출에 대한 대화이다. 수학 과제를 어디에 제출 하냐는 질문에 대한 답이므로 ③ 'Upload your work to our school website.'가 가장 적절한 응답이다.

- completely ⓪ⓓ 완전히
- assignment ⓝ 과제
- submit ⓥ 제출하다
- forget ⓥ 잊다
- deadline ⓝ 제출기한

대화를 듣고, 남자의 마지막 말에 대한 여자의 응답으로 가장 적절한 것을 고르시오. [3점]

Woman : _____

① Yes. I can give you the phone number of the clinic I visited.
응. 내가 갔던 병원 전화번호 너에게 줄 수 있어.

② I agree. Last evening's badminton match was awesome.
동의해. 어젯밤 배드민턴 경기는 멋졌어.

③ No problem. I'll teach you how to serve this time.
문제없어. 이번에 어떻게 서브하는지 너에게 가르쳐줄게.

④ Too bad. I hope you recover from your knee injury soon.
안 됐다. 네 무릎 부상이 빨리 낫길 바라.

⑤✓ You're right. Maybe I should start taking badminton lessons.
네가 맞아. 배드민턴 수업을 들어야할지도 몰라.

M : Hey, Cindy. Have you been playing a lot of badminton these days?
안녕, Cinday야. 요즘 배드민턴 많이 치니?

W : No, I've been experiencing some pain in my knee since a badminton match last weekend.
아니, 지난 주말 배드민턴 경기 때문에 무릎이 아파.

M : I'm sorry to hear that. Did you go see a doctor?
유감이야. 병원에 가봤어?

W : Yes, I visited a local clinic yesterday.
응, 나 어제 동네 병원에 다녀왔어.

M : I hope you feel better soon. By the way, have you ever taken a badminton lesson?
금방 낫길 바라. 그나저나, 배드민턴 수업 들어 본 적 있어?

W : No, I haven't. Why are you asking?
아니, 없어. 그건 왜 물어?

M : In my experience, that kind of injury can come from bad posture. A lesson might reduce the risk of any further injury.
내 경험상, 그런 부상은 안 좋은 자세가 원인이더라고. 수업을 들으면 더 이상의 부상의 위험을 줄여줄지도 몰라.

W : Well, I thought I didn't need those lessons.
음, 나 그런 수업은 필요 없다고 생각했어.

M : Cindy, if you want to keep playing badminton without any injuries, it's important to learn from an instructor to develop the right posture.
Cindy야, 만약 네가 더 이상 부상 없이 배드민턴을 치고 싶다면, 바른 자세를 갖기 위해 지도자에게서부터 배우는 것이 중요해.

W : You're right. Maybe I should start taking badminton lessons.
네가 맞아. 배드민턴 수업을 들어야할지도 몰라.

Why? 왜 정답일까?

배드민턴을 치다가 부상을 당한 여자에게 남자는 배드민턴의 전문가에게서 수업을 받으면 바른 자세를 가질 수 있어 부상의 위험이 줄어든다고 말하고 있다. 따라서 남자의 마지막 말에 대한 여자의 응답으로 가장 적절한 것은 ⑤ 'You're right. Maybe I should start taking badminton lessons.'이다.

- experience ⓥ 경험하다
- pain ⓝ 고통
- clinic ⓝ 병원
- match ⓝ 경기
- local ⓐ 지역의
- injury ⓝ 부상

대화를 듣고, 여자의 마지막 말에 대한 남자의 응답으로 가장 적절한 것을 고르시오. [3점]

Man : _____

① Sure. It seems like a perfect place for bears. – 그래. 곰을 위한 완벽한 장소인 것 같다.

②✓ Great. Let's think about the club name first. – 좋아. 동아리 이름부터 먼저 생각해 보자.

③ My pleasure. I can always give you a ride. – 천만에. 항상 태워줄 수 있어.

④ I agree. It's hard to give up using plastics. – 동의해. 플라스틱을 포기하는 것은 어려워.

⑤ No worries. I'll get my bike repaired. – 걱정 마. 나는 내 자전거를 고칠 거야.

W : Mike, don't you think climate change is kind of scary?
Mike야, 기후 변화가 좀 무섭게 느껴지지 않니?

M : Right. The temperature seems higher than ever.
맞아. 기온이 어느 때보다 높은 것 같아.

W : I heard it's putting a number of animals in danger these days.
요즘 그게 많은 수의 동물들을 멸종 위기로 몰아넣고 있다고 들었어.

M : Right. Maybe one day we won't be able to see polar bears anymore.
맞아. 언젠가 우리는 북극곰을 더 이상 볼 수 없을지도 몰라.

W : That's not good. What can we do?
좋지 않은걸. 우리가 무엇을 할 수 있을까?

M : Use less plastic, plant more trees. Small things matter.
플라스틱 덜 쓰기, 나무 더 심기. 작은 것들이 중요해.

W : And maybe we can ride bikes instead of always asking for rides.
그리고 항상 차 태워 달라고 하는 것 대신 자전거를 탈 수도 있겠어.

M : Yeah. Making a Tree-Planting Day at school can also be helpful.
맞아. 학교에서 나무 심는 날을 만드는 것도 도움이 될 것 같아.

W : Absolutely. Then, why don't we make our own school club to put it into action?
완전. 그럼, 우리만의 학교 동아리를 만들어서 실행해 보는 건 어때?

M : Great. Let's think about the club name first.
좋아. 동아리 이름부터 먼저 생각해 보자.

Why? 왜 정답일까?

기후 변화가 두려워 행동하자는 대화이다. 학교 동아리를 만들어 실행에 옮겨보자(Then, why don't we make our own school club to put it into action?)고 하였으므로, 여자의 마지막 말에 대한 남자의 응답으로 가장 적절한 것은 ② 'Great. Let's think about the club name first.'이다.

- climate ⓝ 기후
- temperature ⓝ 온도
- helpful ⓐ 도움이 되는
- scary ⓐ 무서운
- danger ⓝ 위험
- absolutely ⓪ⓓ 완전히

15 책상 조립 도움 청하기 정답률 78% | 정답 ③

다음 상황 설명을 듣고, Laura가 Tony에게 할 말로 가장 적절한 것을 고르시오.

Laura :
① I don't like visiting a hospital for medical checkups. – 건강 검진하러 병원에 가는 거 안 좋아해.
② I appreciate you taking me to the doctor today. – 오늘 병원에 나를 데려다 줘서 고마워.
✓③ You'd better take a break for a few days. – 너 며칠 쉬는 게 좋을 것 같아.
④ You should finish your work before the deadline. – 기한 안에 네 작업을 마쳐야 해.
⑤ I'm afraid I can't reduce your workload right now. – 네 업무량을 지금 당장 못 줄여줄 것 같아.

M : Laura and Tony are close coworkers.
Laura와 Tony는 가까운 동료이다.
Laura notices that Tony has been looking unusually tired and pale recently.
Laura는 Tony가 요즘 들어 더 피곤하고 창백해 보이는 것을 알아차렸다.
One day, she asks Tony if he's not been feeling well lately, but Tony says he's just a bit tired from work.
어느 날, 그녀는 Tony에게 요즘 몸이 안 좋은지 물어봤지만, Tony는 그저 일 때문에 조금 피곤하다고 말했다.
Laura knows that Tony sometimes works even on weekends without taking a break or getting any rest.
Laura는 Tony가 때때로 주말에도 쉬지 않고 일하는 것을 알고 있다.
However, this time, she is really worried about him and wants him to take at least a couple of days off.
그러나 이번에는 그녀가 그를 정말 걱정하고 있고, 그가 최소한 며칠은 쉬었으면 하고 있다.
In this situation, what would Laura most likely say to Tony?
이 상황에서, Laura가 Tony에게 가장 할 법한 말은 무엇일까?
Laura : You'd better take a break for a few days.
너 며칠 쉬는 게 좋을 것 같아.

Why? 왜 정답일까?
Larua는 과로하고 있는 Tony에게 며칠이라도 쉬라고 말하고 싶은 상황이므로 Laura가 Tony에게 할 말로 가장 적절한 것은 ③ 'You'd better take a break for a few days.'이다.

- coworker ⓝ 동료
- pale ⓐ 창백한
- take a break 쉬다
- appreciate ⓥ 고마워하다
- workload ⓝ 업무량, 작업량
- notice ⓥ 알아차리다
- lately ⓐ 최근에
- situation ⓝ 상황
- deadline ⓝ 기한, 마감 시간

16-17 Lincoln 고등학교의 학생 대표 선거 안내

M : Hello, Lincoln High School.
안녕하세요, Lincoln 고등학교 여러분.
This is David Newman, your current student representative, and I'm speaking to you today to let you know about the upcoming election for next year's student representative.
저는 현재 학생 대표인 David Newman이고, 오늘은 내년 학생 대표 선거에 대해 알려 드리기 위해 말씀드립니다.
『Candidates can now begin their campaigns, following these instructions.』 16번의 근거
후보자들은 이제 다음 지침에 따라 선거 운동을 시작할 수 있습니다.
『First, they can share short promotional video clips on their social media, but the video clips must not be longer than 3 minutes.』 17번 ①의 근거 일치
첫째, 후보자들은 소셜 미디어에 짧은 홍보 영상을 공유할 수 있지만, 그 영상은 3분을 넘기 않아야 합니다. 17번 ②의 근거 일치
『Second, candidates can display posters only in allowed areas, and it's important to keep the size to A3 or smaller, as larger posters will be removed without warning.』
둘째, 후보자들은 허용된 구역에만 포스터를 게시할 수 있으며, 포스터 크기는 A3 이하로 유지해야 합니다. 더 큰 포스터는 경고 없이 제거될 것입니다.
『Third, the use of pamphlets is allowed, but they must only be distributed within the school campus.』 17번 ③의 근거 일치
셋째, 팸플릿 사용은 허용되지만, 학교 캠퍼스 내에서만 배포되어야 합니다.
『Lastly, there will be an online debate broadcast on our school website among the candidates three days before the election.』 17번 ⑤의 근거 일치
마지막으로, 선거 3일 전에 후보자들 간의 온라인 토론이 학교 웹사이트에서 방송될 것입니다.
It's important to be respectful toward the other candidates during the debate.
토론 중에는 다른 후보자들을 존중하는 것이 중요합니다.
Let's make this election a success.
이번 선거를 성공적으로 치르도록 합시다.

- current ⓐ 현재의
- upcoming ⓐ 다가오는
- candidate ⓝ 후보자
- promotional ⓐ 홍보의
- warning ⓝ 경고
- representative ⓝ 대표
- election ⓝ 선거
- campaign ⓝ 캠페인
- remove ⓥ 제거하다
- distribute ⓥ 분배하다

16 주제 파악 정답률 72% | 정답 ③

남자가 하는 말의 주제로 가장 적절한 것은
① relationships between media and voters – 미디어와 유권자 간의 관계
② common ways of promoting school policy – 학교 정책을 알리는 흔한 방법
✓③ guidelines for student election campaigns – 학생 선거 캠페인에 대한 가이드라인
④ requirements for becoming a candidate – 후보자가 되기 위한 조건
⑤ useful tips for winning school debates – 학교 토론을 이기는 유용한 팁

Why? 왜 정답일까?
Lincoln 고등학교의 학생회장 선거의 주의점에 대해서 얘기하고 있으므로, 남자가 하는 말의 주제로 가장 적절한 것은 ③ 'guidelines for student election campaigns'이다.

17 언급 유무 파악 정답률 94% | 정답 ④

언급된 매체가 아닌 것은?
① social media – 소셜미디어
② poster – 포스터
③ pamphlet – 팜플렛
✓④ school newspaper – 학교 신문
⑤ school website – 학교 웹사이트

Why? 왜 정답일까?
담화에서 학생 대표 선거 홍보 매체로 social media, poster, pamphlet, school website는 모두 언급되었지만 school newspaper는 언급되지 않았기 때문에, ④ 'school newspaper'가 정답이다.

18 온라인 회원 전환 홍보 정답률 95% | 정답 ②

다음 글의 목적으로 가장 적절한 것은?
① 여행 일정 지연에 대해 사과하려고
✓② 잡지 온라인 구독을 권유하려고
③ 무료 잡지 신청을 홍보하려고
④ 여행 후기 모집을 안내하려고
⑤ 기사에 대한 독자 의견에 답변하려고

Dear Reader,
독자 여러분께,
We always appreciate / your support.
저희는 항상 감사드립니다. / 여러분의 지지에
As you know, / our service is now available / through an app.
아시다시피, / 저희의 서비스는 이제 가능합니다. / 앱을 통해서도
There has never been a better time / to switch to an online membership / of *TourTide Magazine*.
더 나은 때는 없었습니다. / 온라인 멤버십으로 바꾸기에 / *TourTide Magazine*의
At a 50% discount off your current print subscription, / you can access / a full year of online reading.
현재 여러분의 지간 구독물에서 50% 할인 된 가격으로, / 여러분은 접근할 수 있습니다. / 1년 온라인 읽기에
Get new issues and daily web pieces / at TourTide.com, / read or listen to *TourTide Magazine* / via the app, / and get our members-only newsletter.
새로운 소식과 일간 웹 이야기를 얻으세요. / TourTide.com에서 / *TourTide Magazine*에서 읽거나 들으세요. / 앱을 통해서, / 그리고 저희의 구독자 전용 뉴스레터를 얻으세요.
You'll also gain access / to our editors' selections / of the best articles.
여러분은 또한 접근 권한을 얻을 것입니다. / 저희의 편집자 선택에 / 최고 기사의
Join today!
오늘 가입하세요!
Yours,
여러분의,
TourTide Team
TourTide Team 드림

독자분께,
보내주신 성원에 항상 감사드립니다. 아시다시피, 이제앱을 통해서도 저희 서비스를 이용하실 수 있습니다. *TourTide Magazine*의 온라인 회원으로 전환하기에 이보다 더 좋은 시기는 없습니다. 당신의 현재 인쇄본 구독료에서 50% 할인된 가격으로 1년 치를 온라인으로 구독할 수 있습니다. TourTide.com에서 신간호와 일일 웹 기사를 받아보고, 앱을 통해 *TourTide Magazine*을 읽거나 청취해 보고, 회원 전용 뉴스레터도 받아보세요. 편집자들이 선정한 최고의 기사도 받아볼 수 있습니다. 오늘 가입하세요!

TourTide 팀 드림

Why? 왜 정답일까?
오프라인 서비스에서 온라인 회원으로 전환하기에 더욱 좋은 때는 없다(There has never been a better time to switch to an online membership of *TourTide Magazine*.)고 말하고 있기 때문에, 글의 목적으로 가장 적절한 것은 ② '잡지 온라인 구독을 권유하려고'이다.

- appreciate ⓥ 감사하다
- available ⓐ 가능한
- discount ⓝ 할인
- support ⓝ 지원
- switch ⓥ 전환하다
- article ⓝ 기사

구문 풀이
3행 There has never been a better time to switch to an online membership of *TourTide Magazine*.
(현재완료시제) (to부정사(형용사적 용법)) (전치사(~로))

19 대학교 합격 편지 열기 정답률 83% | 정답 ②

다음 글에 드러난 'I'의 심경 변화로 가장 적절한 것은?
① relaxed → upset
   안심한   화난
✓② anxious → delighted
   불안한   기쁜
③ guilty → confident
   죄책감이 드는 자신감 있는
④ angry → grateful
   화난   감사한
⑤ hopeful → disappointed
   희망찬   실망한

As I walked from the mailbox, / my heart was beating rapidly.
우편함에서 걸어오면서, / 내 심장은 빠르게 뛰었다.
In my hands, / I held the letter / from the university / I had applied to.
내 손에는, / 편지를 쥐었다. / 대학에서부터 온 / 내가 지원한
I thought / my grades were good enough / to cross the line / and my application letter / was well-written, / but was it enough?
난 생각했다. / 내 성적도 충분했고 / 기준을 넘기에 / 그리고 내 자기소개서도 / 잘 써졌다고 / 근데 그게 충분했나?
I hadn't slept a wink / for days.
난 한 숨도 못 잤다. / 며칠 째
As I carefully tore into the paper of the envelope, / the letter slowly emerged / with the opening phrase, / "It is our great pleasure..."
내가 조심스럽게 봉투의 종이를 뜯자, / 편지가 천천히 나타났다. / 첫줄과 함께 / "저희는 기쁘게..."라며
I shouted with joy, / "I am in!"
나는 기뻐서 소리쳤다. / "합격이다!"
As I held the letter, / I began to make a fantasy / about my college life / in a faraway city.
편지를 쥐며, / 환상을 만들기 시작했다. / 나의 대학교 생활에 대해서 / 먼 도시에서의

우체통에서 걸어올 때 내 심장은 빠르게 뛰고 있었다. 내 손에는 지원했던 대학에서 보낸 편지가 들려 있었다. 내 생각에는 합격할 만큼 성적이 좋았고 지원서도 잘 썼지만, 그것으로 충분했을까? 며칠 동안 한숨도 잘 수 없었다. 봉투의 종이를 조심스럽게 찢자 "매우 기쁘게도..."라는 첫 문구와 함께 편지가 천천히 모습을 드러냈다. 나는 기뻐서 소리 질렀다. "합격이야!" 나는 편지를 손에 쥐고 집에서 멀리 떨어진 도시에서의 대학 생활에 대해 상상하기 시작했다.

Why? 왜 정답일까?

우체통에서 편지를 꺼내어 걸어올 때 심장이 빠르게 뛰고 있었고(As I walked from the mailbox, my heart was beating rapidly.). 편지를 열어 합격임을 알고 기뻐서 소리 질렀다고 하였으니 (I shouted with joy, "I am in!") 'I'의 심경 변화로 가장 적절한 것은 ② 'anxious → delighted' 이다.

- **mailbox** ⓝ 우편함
- **rapidly** ⓐⓓ 빠르게
- **apply** ⓥ 지원하다
- **beat** ⓥ 뛰다
- **university** ⓝ 대학교
- **application** ⓝ 지원서

구문 풀이

8행 As I held the letter, I began to make a fantasy about my college life in a
~하면서　　　begin to부정사(= begin ~ing): ~하는 것을 시작하다.
faraway city.

---

20 깨끗한 방의 힘　　　정답률 95% | 정답 ①

다음 글에서 필자가 주장하는 바로 가장 적절한 것은?

☑ 자신의 공간을 정돈하여 긍정적 변화를 도모하라.
② 오랜 시간 고민하기보다는 일단 행동으로 옮겨라.
③ 무질서한 환경에서 창의적인 생각을 시도하라.
④ 장기 목표를 위해 단기 목표를 먼저 설정하라.
⑤ 반복되는 일상을 새로운 관점으로 관찰하라.

Having a messy room / can add up to / negative feelings and destructive thinking.
어지러운 방은 / 결과로 이어질 수 있다. / 부정적인 감정과 파괴적인 생각의
Psychologists say / that having a disorderly room / can indicate a disorganized mental state.
심리학자들은 말한다. / 엉망인 방은 / 정리되지 않은 정신 상태를 가리킨다고
One of the professional tidying experts says / that the moment you start cleaning your room, / you also start changing your life / and gaining new perspective.
전문 정리 전문가 중 한 명이 말한다. / 당신이 당신 방을 청소하는 순간, / 당신은 또한 당신의 삶을 바꾸기 시작한다고 / 그리고 새 관점을 갖기를
When you clean your surroundings, / positive and good atmosphere / follows.
여러분 주변을 청소할 때, / 긍정적이고 좋은 분위기가 / 따라온다.
You can do more things / efficiently and neatly.
여러분은 더 많은 것을 할 수 있다. / 효과적으로 그리고 깔끔하게
So, clean up your closets, / organize your drawers, / and arrange your things first, / then peace of mind / will follow.
그러니, 옷장을 치우고, / 서랍을 정리하고, / 물건을 먼저 배열해라. / 그러면 마음의 평화가 / 따라올 것이다.

방이 지저분한 것은 결국 부정적인 감정과 파괴적인 사고로 이어질 수 있다. 심리학자들은 방이 무질서하다는 것은 정신 상태가 혼란스럽다는 것을 나타낼 수 있다고 말한다. 정리 전문가 중 한 명이 방 청소를 시작하는 순간 당신은 인생을 변화시키고 새로운 관점을 얻기 시작한다고 말한다. 주변을 청소하면 긍정적이고 좋은 분위기가 따라온다. 당신은 더 많은 일을 효율적이고 깔끔하게 할 수 있다. 그러니 먼저 옷장을 청소하고, 서랍을 정리하고, 물건을 정돈한다면 마음의 평화가 따라올 것이다.

Why? 왜 정답일까?

깨끗하지 않은 방에서는 부정적인 감정과 파괴적인 사고가 들지만(Having a messy room can add up to negative feelings and destructive thinking.), 주변을 청소하면 긍정적이고 좋은 분위기가 따라온다(When you clean your surroundings, positive and good atmosphere follows.)고 하였으므로 글에서 필자가 주장하는 바로 가장 적절한 것은 ① '자신의 공간을 정돈하여 긍정적 변화를 도모하라.'이다.

- **messy** ⓐ 지저분한
- **feeling** ⓝ 감정
- **expert** ⓝ 전문가
- **efficiently** ⓐⓓ 효과적으로
- **negative** ⓐ 부정적인
- **destructive** ⓐ 파괴적인
- **surrounding** ⓝ 주변
- **atmosphere** ⓝ 분위기

구문 풀이

3행 One of the professional tidying experts says that the moment you
one of the 복수명사: ~들 중에 하나(단수취급)　　접속사
start cleaning your room, you also start changing your life and gaining new
start 동명사(= start to부정사): ~하는 것을 시작하다.　　동명사1　　동명사2
perspective.

---

21 작물을 위한 완벽한 토양　　　정답률 54% | 정답 ②

밑줄 친 luxury real estate가 다음 글에서 의미하는 바로 가장 적절한 것은? [3점]

① a farm where a scientist's aid is highly required – 과학자의 도움이 매우 필요한 농장
☑ a field abundant with necessities for plants – 식물에 필요한 것이 충분한 땅
③ a district accessible only for the rich – 부자들만 접근할 수 있는 구역
④ a place that is conserved for ecology – 생태계를 보존하는 장소
⑤ a region with higher economic value – 높은 경제적인 가치를 가진 지역

The soil of a farm field / is forced to be the perfect environment / for monoculture growth.
농장 땅의 흙은 / 완벽한 환경이 되도록 만들어진다. / 한 가지 작물의 성장을 위해
This is achieved / by adding nutrients to the form of fertilizer / and water by way of irrigation.
이것은 이루어진다 / 비료의 형태로 영양분을 추가하고 / 관개를 통해 물을 더함으로써
During the last fifty years, / engineers and crop scientists have helped farmers / become much more efficient / at supplying exactly the right amount of both.
지난 50년 동안, / 엔지니어들과 작물 과학자들은 농부들이 / 훨씬 더 효율적으로 되도록 도왔다 / 둘 다 정확한 양을 공급하는 데

World usage of fertilizer has tripled / since 1969, / and the global capacity for irrigation has almost doubled.
세계 비료 사용량은 세 배로 증가했다. / 1969년 이후로, / 그리고 전 세계 관개 능력은 거의 두 배로 늘었다.
We are feeding and watering our fields / more than ever, / and our crops are loving it.
우리는 우리의 농장에 비료와 물을 공급하고 있다. / 그 어느 때보다 많이, / 그리고 우리의 것것을 좋아하고 있다.
Unfortunately, / these luxurious conditions / have also excited the attention / of certain agricultural undesirables.
불행히도, / 이러한 풍족한 조건들은 / 또한 관심을 끌었다. / 특정 농업에 바람직하지 않은 것들의
Because farm fields are loaded with nutrients and water / relative to the natural land that surrounds them, / they are desired as luxury real estate / by every random weed in the area.
농장 땅은 영양분과 물이 가득 차 있기 때문에 / 그것을 둘러싼 자연 땅에 비해, / 그곳은 고급 부동산으로 여겨진다. / 주변의 모든 잡초들에 의해

농지의 토양은 단일 작물 재배를 위한 완벽한 환경이어야 한다. 이것은 비료 형태로 양분을 더하고 관개로 물을 댐으로써 이루어진다. 지난 50년 동안 기술자와 농작물 연구자들은 농부들이 양쪽 모두의 적정량을 공급하는 데 훨씬 더 효율적일 수 있도록 도움을 주었다. 전 세계 비료 사용량은 1969년 이래로 세 배가 되었고, 전체 관개 능력은 거의 두 배가 되었다. 우리는 그 어느 때보다도 들판을 기름지게 하고 물을 대고 있으며, 우리의 농작물은 이를 좋아한다. 불행히도, 이러한 호사스러운 상황은 농업에서는 달갑지 않은 것들의 관심도 끌어들였다. 농지는 주위를 둘러싼 자연 지대에 비해 영양분과 물이 풍족히 채워져 있기 때문에 그 지역의 어떤 잡초라도 원하는 고급 부동산이 된다.

Why? 왜 정답일까?

농작물 연구자들의 노력으로 작물을 위한 완벽한 토양을 만들어냈다(The soil of a farm field is forced to be the perfect environment for monoculture growth.)고 하였으므로, luxury real estate의 luxury는 물과 영양분이 충분함을 뜻하고, real estate는 땅을 뜻한다고 해석하는 것이 가장 적절하다. 따라서 답은 ② 'a field abundant with necessities for plants'이다.

- **monoculture** ⓝ 단일 작물 재배
- **efficient** ⓐ 효과적인
- **capacity** ⓝ 능력
- **achieve** ⓥ 달성하다
- **supply** ⓥ 제공하다
- **attention** ⓝ 관심

구문 풀이

4행 During the last fifty years, engineers and crop scientists have helped
~동안　　　현재완료시제
farmers become much more efficient at supplying exactly the right amount of both.
준사역동사(help) + 동사원형　　　　　동명사

---

22 사소한 관심의 영향　　　정답률 89% | 정답 ①

다음 글의 요지로 가장 적절한 것은?

☑ 사소한 관심이 타인에게 도움이 될 수 있다.
② 사람마다 행복의 기준이 제각기 다르다.
③ 선행을 통해 자신을 되돌아볼 수 있다.
④ 원만한 대인 관계는 경청에서 비롯된다.
⑤ 현재에 대한 만족이 행복의 필수조건이다.

When it comes to helping out, / you don't have to do much.
도움을 주는 일에 있어서, / 많은 것을 할 필요는 없다.
All you have to do / is come around / and show that you care.
네가 해야 할 일은 / 다가가서 / 네가 신경 쓰고 있음을 보여주는 것뿐이다.
If you notice someone who is lonely, / you could go and sit with them.
누군가가 외로워 보인다면, / 그들과 함께 가서 앉아 있을 수 있다.
If you work with someone / who eats lunch all by themselves, / and you go and sit down with them, / they will begin to be more social after a while, / and they will owe it all to you.
만약 너와 함께 일하는 사람이 있다면 / 혼자서 점심을 먹는, / 네가 가서 그들과 앉아 있으면, / 시간이 지나면 그들은 더 사교적이게 될 것이고, / 그 모든 것을 너에게 고마워할 것이다.
A person's happiness / comes from attention.
사람의 행복은 / 관심에서 온다.
There are too many people / out in the world / who feel like everyone has forgotten them or ignored them.
너무 많은 사람들이 있다. / 세상 속에 / 모두가 자신을 잊었거나 무시했다고 느끼는
Even if you say hi / to someone passing by, / they will begin to feel better about themselves, / like someone cares.
심지어 네가 인사만 해도 / 지나가는 사람에게, / 그들은 스스로에 대해 더 나은 기분을 느끼기 시작할 것이다. / 마치 누군가가 자신을 신경 쓰는 것처럼

도움을 주는 것에 관해서 당신은 많은 것을 할 필요는 없다. 그저 다가가서 관심을 갖고 있다는 것을 보여주기만 하면 된다. 외로운 사람을 발견하면 가서 함께 앉아 있으면 된다. 혼자서 점심을 먹는 사람과 함께 일한다면, 그리고 그 사람에게 다가가서 함께 앉는다면 얼마 지나지 않아 그 사람은 더 사교적으로 변하기 시작할 것이고, 이 모든 것을 당신 덕분이라고 할 것이다. 한 사람의 행복은 관심에서 비롯된다. 세상에는 모든 이가 자신을 잊었거나 무시한다고 느끼는 사람들이 너무 많다. 지나가는 사람들에게 인사만 건네도, 누군가 (그들에게) 관심을 가져주는 것처럼, 그들은 자기 자신에 대해 기분이 좋아지기 시작할 것이다.

Why? 왜 정답일까?

도움은 많은 것을 해줄 필요가 없고, 관심을 갖고 있다는 것을 보여주기만 하면 된다(When it comes to helping out, you don't have to do much.)고 말하고 있기 때문에, 글의 요지로 가장 적절한 것은 ① '사소한 관심이 타인에게 도움이 될 수 있다.'이다.

- **notice** ⓥ 알아차리다
- **social** ⓐ 사회적인
- **attention** ⓝ 관심
- **lonely** ⓐ 외로운
- **owe** ⓥ 빚지다
- **pass by** 지나가다

구문 풀이

4행 If you work with someone who eats lunch all by themselves, and you
가정법　　　　　주격관계대명사
go and sit down with them, they will begin to be more social after a while, and
동사1　동사2　　　　　　　　　　　　　　　　　곧(= soon)
they will owe it all to you.

23 고난의 교훈
정답률 77% | 정답 ⑤

다음 글의 주제로 가장 적절한 것은?

① characteristics of well-equipped athletes – 잘 정비된 운동선수의 특징
② difficulties in overcoming life's sudden challenges – 삶의 급작스런 도전을 극복하는 어려움
③ relationship between personal habit and competence – 개인적인 습관과 경쟁 사이의 관계
④ risks of enduring hardship without any preparation – 준비 없이 고난을 겪는 것의 위험
☑ importance of confronting hardship in one's life – 삶에서 고난을 마주하는 것의 중요성

We often try / to make cuts / in our challenges / and take the easy route.
우리는 종종 시도한다. / 지름길을 내려고 / 우리의 도전에서 / 그리고 쉬운 길을 선택하려고

When taking the quick exit, / we fail / to acquire the strength / to compete.
빠른 출구를 선택할 때, / 우리는 실패한다. / 힘을 얻는 데 / 경쟁할 수 있는

We often take / the easy route / to improve our skills.
우리는 종종 선택한다. / 쉬운 길을 / 우리의 기술을 향상시키기 위해

Many of us / never really work / to achieve mastery / in the key areas of life.
우리 중 많은 사람들은 / 결코 열심히 일하지 않는다. / 숙달을 이루기 위해 / 인생의 중요한 영역에서

These skills / are key tools / that can be useful / to our career, health, and prosperity.
이러한 기술은 / 중요한 도구들이다. / 유용할 수 있는 / 우리의 경력, 건강, 그리고 번영에

Highly successful athletes / don't win / because of better equipment; / they win / by facing hardship / to gain strength and skill.
매우 성공적인 운동선수들은 / 승리하지 않는다. / 더 좋은 장비 때문에; / 그들은 승리한다. / 어려움을 마주하면서 / 힘과 기술을 얻기 위해

They win / through preparation.
그들은 승리한다. / 준비를 통해

It's the mental preparation, / winning mindset, / strategy, and skill / that set them apart.
그것은 정신적 준비, / 승리하는 마음가짐, / 전략과 기술이다. / 그들을 구별하는

Strength comes / from struggle, / not from taking the path / of least resistance.
힘은 온다. / 투쟁에서, / 길을 선택하는 것에서가 아니라 / 최소한의 저항의

Hardship / is not just a lesson / for the next time / in front of us.
어려움은 / 단지 교훈이 아니다. / 다음을 위한 / 우리 앞에 있는

Hardship / will be / the greatest teacher / we will ever have / in life.
어려움은 / 될 것이다. / 가장 위대한 스승이 / 우리가 인생에 가질 / 존재 중에

우리는 종종 우리의 도전을 멈추고, 쉬운 길을 택하려고 한다. 쉬운 길을 택하면 경쟁할 수 있는 힘을 얻지 못한다. 우리는 종종 실력을 향상하기 위해 쉬운 길을 택한다. 우리 중 다수가 인생의 핵심이 되는 영역에서 숙달을 위한 노력을 하지 않는다. 이러한 기술은 경력, 건강, 번영에 도움이 될 수 있는 핵심 도구이다. 성공한 운동선수들은 더 좋은 장비 때문에 승리하는 것이 아니다. 그들은 힘과 실력을 얻기 위해 고난에 맞섬으로써 승리한다. 그들은 준비를 통해 승리한다. 그들을 돋보이게 하는 것은 바로 정신적 준비, 승리하는 마음가짐, 전략, 그리고 기술이다. 힘은 저항이 가장 적은 길을 택하는 것이 아니라 맞서 싸우는 데서 나온다. 고난은 단지 우리 앞에 놓인 다음을 위한 교훈만은 아니다. 고난은 우리 인생에서 가장 위대한 스승이 될 것이다.

Why? 왜 정답일까?

고난이 우리 인생에서 가장 위대한 스승이 될 것(Hardship will be the greatest teacher we will ever have in life.)이라 하였으므로, 글의 주제로 가장 적절한 것은 ⑤ 'importance of confronting hardship in one's life'이다.

- cut ⓝ 지름길
- route ⓝ 길
- mastery ⓝ 숙달
- hardship ⓝ 고난
- challenge ⓝ 도전
- acquire ⓥ 얻다, 획득하다
- prosperity ⓝ 번영
- preparation ⓝ 준비

구문 풀이

13행 Hardship will be the greatest teacher (which/that) we will ever have in life.
the 형용사 최상급 / 목적격 관계대명사 생략

24 행동과 정체성의 관계
정답률 68% | 정답 ①

다음 글의 제목으로 가장 적절한 것은?

☑ Action Comes from Who You Think You Are – 당신이 누구인지 생각하는 데에서 기인하는 행동
② The Best Practices for Gaining More Voters – 더 많은 유권자들을 모으는 최고의 실행
③ Stop Pursuing Undesirable Behavior Change! – 바람직하지 않은 행동 변화 추구를 그만하라!
④ What to Do When Your Exercise Bores You – 운동이 당신을 지루하게 할 때 할 것
⑤ Your Actions Speak Louder than Your Words – 말보다 행동이 우선이다

Your behaviors / are usually / a reflection / of your identity.
당신의 행동은 / 대개 / 당신의 정체성의

What you do / is an indication / of the type of person / you believe that you are — / either consciously or nonconsciously.
당신이 하는 것은 / 암시이다. / 당신이 믿는 / 사람의 유형에 대한 / 의식적으로든 무의식적으로든

Research has shown / that once a person believes in a particular aspect / of their identity, / they are more likely / to act according to that belief.
연구는 보여 주었다. / 한 사람이 특정 측면을 믿으면 / 그들의 정체성의, / 그들이 더 가능성이 높다는 것을 / 그 믿음에 따라 행동할

For example, / people who identified / as "being a voter" / were more likely / to vote / than those who simply claimed / "voting" was an action / they wanted to perform.
예를 들어, / 스스로를 규정한 사람들은 / "유권자"라고 / 더 가능성이 높았다. / 투표할 / 단순히 주장한 사람보다 / "투표"는 그들이 하고 싶었던 행동이라고

Similarly, / the person who accepts exercise / as the part of their identity / doesn't have to convince themselves / to train.
비슷하게, / 운동을 받아들이는 사람은 / 그들의 정체성의 일부로 / 스스로를 설득할 필요가 없다. / 훈련하기 위해

Doing the right thing / is easy.
올바른 일을 하는 것은 / 쉽다.

After all, / when your behavior and your identity / perfectly match, / you are no longer / pursuing behavior change.
결국, / 당신의 행동과 정체성이 / 완벽히 일치할 때, / 더 이상 / 행동 변화를 추구하지 않는다.

You are simply / acting like the type of person / you already believe yourself to be.
당신은 단순히 / 행동하고 있는 것이다. / 이미 스스로 믿고 있는 그 사람처럼

당신의 행동은 대개 당신의 정체성을 반영한다. 당신이 하는 행동은 의식적으로든 무의식적으로든 당신이 스스로를 어떤 사람이라고 믿고 있는지를 나타낸다. 연구에 따르면 자신의 정체성의 특정 측면을 믿는 사람은 그 믿음에 따라 행동할 가능성이 더 높다. 예를 들어, 자신을 "유권자"라고 느끼는 사람은 단순히 "투표"가 자신이 하고 싶은 행동이라고 주장하는 사람보다 투표할 가능성이 더 높았다. 마찬가지로, 운동을 자신의 정체성의 일부로 받아들이는 사람은 훈련하라고 스스로를 설득할 필요가 없다. 옳은 일을 하는 것은 쉽다. 결국, 자신의 행동과 정체성이 완벽하게 일치하면 더 이상 행동 변화를 추구하지 않아도 된다. 당신은 그저 당신 스스로가 그렇다고 이미 믿고 있는 유형의 사람처럼 행동하고 있을 뿐이다.

Why? 왜 정답일까?

투표를 예로 들며 생각하는 대로 행동한다(Your behaviors are usually a reflection of your identity.)는 얘기를 하고 있다. 따라서 제목으로 가장 적절한 것은 ① 'Action Comes from Who You Think You Are'이다.

- reflection ⓝ 반영
- indication ⓝ 지시
- accept ⓥ 받아들이다
- identity ⓝ 정체성
- similarly ⓐⓓ 비슷하게
- behavior ⓝ 행동

구문 풀이

6행 For example, people who identified as "being a voter" were more likely to
주격관계대명사 / be likely to : ~할 것 같다
vote than those who simply claimed "voting" was an action (which/that) they
지시대명사 주격관계대명사 / 목적격관계대명사
wanted to perform.

25 2016년과 2019년의 지역별 전자 폐기물 수거율 및 재활용률
정답률 84% | 정답 ③

다음 도표의 내용과 일치하지 않는 것은?

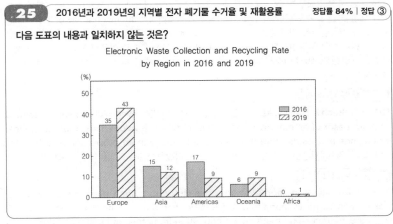

The above graph shows / the electronic waste collection and recycling rate / by region / in 2016 and 2019.
위의 표는 보여준다. / 전자 쓰레기 수거와 재활용률을 / 지역마다의 / 2016년과 2019년의

① In both years, / Europe showed / the highest electronic waste collection and recycling rates.
두 해 모두, / 유럽은 보여 주었다. / 가장 높은 전자 쓰레기 수거와 재활용률의

② The electronic waste collection and recycling rate / of Asia / in 2019 / was lower than in 2016.
전자 쓰레기 수거와 재활용률은 / 아시아의 / 2019년의 / 2019년보다 낮았다.

☑ The Americas ranked third / both in 2016 and in 2019, / with 17 percent and 9 percent / respectively.
아메리카는 3위를 차지했다. / 2016과 2019년 모두 / 17퍼센트와 9퍼센트로 / 각각

④ In both years, / the electronic waste collection and recycling rates / in Oceania / remained under 10 percent.
두 해 모두, / 전자 쓰레기 수거와 재활용률은 / 오세아니아의 / 10퍼센트 미만을 유지했다.

⑤ Africa had / the lowest electronic waste collection and recycling rates / in both 2016 and 2019, / showing the smallest gap / between 2016 and 2019.
아프리카는 가졌다. / 가장 낮은 전자 쓰레기 수거와 재활용률을 / 2016년과 2019년 모두 / 가장 작은 차이를 보여 주며 / 2016년과 2019년의

위 도표는 2016년과 2019년의 지역별 전자 폐기물 수거율 및 재활용률을 보여 준다. 두 해 모두 유럽이 가장 높은 전자 폐기물 수거율 및 재활용률을 보였다. 2019년 아시아의 전자 폐기물 수거율 및 재활용률은 2016년보다 낮았다. (남·북·중앙)아메리카는 2016년과 2019년 모두 3위를 기록했으며, 그 비율은 각각 17퍼센트와 9퍼센트였다. 오세아니아의 전자 폐기물 수거율 및 재활용률은 두 해 모두 10퍼센트 아래에 머물렀다. 아프리카는 2016년과 2019년 모두 가장 낮은 전자 폐기물 수거율 및 재활용률을 기록했으며, 두 해 사이의 비율 격차가 가장 적었다.

Why? 왜 정답일까?

아메리카는 2016년에는 2위, 2019년에는 3위를 차지하기 때문에 도표의 내용과 일치하지 않는 것은 ③이다.

- recycling ⓝ 재활용
- electronic ⓐ 전자의
- remain ⓥ 남다
- region ⓝ 지역
- respectively ⓐⓓ 각각
- collection ⓝ 수집

구문 풀이

9행 Africa had the lowest electronic waste collection and recycling rates in
최상급
both 2016 and 2019, showing the smallest gap between 2016 and 2019.
현재분사 / 최상급

26 Fritz Zwicky의 일생
정답률 81% | 정답 ⑤

Fritz Zwicky에 관한 다음 글의 내용과 일치하지 않는 것은?

① 불가리아의 Varna에서 태어났다.
② 스위스에서 수학과 물리학 교육을 받았다.
③ 미국으로 이주하여 연구를 이어갔다.

④ 우주 이해에 영향을 미친 수많은 이론을 발전시켰다.
☑ 초창기 제트 엔진을 개발한 후 교수로 임용되었다.

『Fritz Zwicky, / a memorable astrophysicist / who coined the term 'supernova', / was born in Varna, Bulgaria / to a Swiss father and a Czech mother.』 ①의근거 일치
Fritz Zwicky는 / 기억할만한 천체물리학자인 / '초신성'이라는 단어를 만든 / 불가리아의 Varna에서 태어났다. / 스위스인 아버지와 체코인 어머니에게서
At the age of six, / he was sent to his grandparents / who looked after him / for most of his childhood / in Switzerland.
6살에, / 그는 그의 조부모님께 보내졌다. / 그를 돌봐준 / 그의 유아기 대부분을 / 스위스에서
『There, / he received an advanced education / in mathematics and physics.』 ②의근거 일치
그곳에서, / 그는 고등 교육을 받았다. / 수학과 물리학의
『In 1925, / he emigrated to the United States / and continued his physics research / at California Institute of Technology (Caltech).』 ③의근거 일치
1925년에, / 그는 미국으로 이주했다. / 그리고 그의 물리학 연구를 이어나갔다. / California Institute of Technoloy(Caltech)에서
『He developed / numerous theories / that have had a profound influence / on the understanding of our universe / in the early 21st century.』 ④의근거 일치
그는 발전시켰다. / 수많은 이론들을 / 풍부한 영향을 끼친 / 우리의 우주를 이해하는 데에 / 초기 21세기에 ⑤의근거 불일치
『After being appointed / as a professor of astronomy / at Caltech in 1942, / he developed / some of the earliest jet engines / and holds more than 50 patents, / many in jet propulsion.』
임용된 후 / 천문학의 교수로써 / 1942년에 Caltech에서 / 그는 발전시켰다. / 초창기 제트 엔진을 / 그리고 50개 이상의 저작권을 가지고 있었다. / 제트 추진 분야에

'초신성'이라는 용어를 만든 유명한 천체 물리학자 Fritz Zwicky는 불가리아의 Varna에서 스위스인 아버지와 체코인 어머니 사이에서 태어났다. 여섯 살이 되던 해, 그는 스위스에서 보낸 어린 시절의 대부분 동안 그를 돌봐준 조부모에게 보내졌다. 그곳에서, 그는 수학과 물리학에 대한 고급 교육을 받았다. 1925년 미국으로 이주하여 California Institute of Technology (Caltech)에서 물리학 연구를 이어갔다. 그는 21세기 초 우주에 대한 이해에 지대한 영향을 미친 수많은 이론을 발전시켰다. 1942년 Caltech의 천문학 교수로 임용된 후 그는 초창기 제트 엔진을 개발했고, 50개 이상의 특허를 보유하고 있으며, 이 중 많은 부분이 제트 추진 분야의 특허이다.

Why? 왜 정답일까?
1942년 Caltech의 천문학 교수로 임용된 후 초창기 제트 엔진을 개발했다(After being appointed as a professor of astronomy at Caltech in 1942, he developed some of the earliest jet engines and holds more than 50 patents, many in jet propulsion.)고 했기 때문에, 글의 내용과 일치하지 않는 것은 ⑤ '초창기 제트 엔진을 개발한 후 교수로 임용되었다.'이다.

Why? 왜 오답일까?
① 'Fritz Zwicky, a memorable astrophysicist who coined the term 'supernova', was born in Varna, Bulgaria to a Swiss father and a Czech mother.'의 내용과 일치한다.
② 'There, he received an advanced education in mathematics and physics.'의 내용과 일치한다.
③ 'In 1925, he emigrated to the United States and continued his physics research at California Institute of Technology (Caltech).'의 내용과 일치한다.
④ 'He developed numerous theories that have had a profound influence on the understanding of our universe in the early 21st century.'의 내용과 일치한다.

● memorable ⓐ 기억할만한　　● astrophysicist ⓝ 천체물리학자
● coin ⓥ (단어를) 발명하다　　● develop ⓥ 발달시키다
● patent ⓝ 특허권　　● propulsion ⓝ 추진력

구문 풀이

8행　He developed numerous theories that have had a profound influence on
　　　　　　　　　　　　　　　주격관계대명사　　　현재완료시제
the understanding of our universe in the early 21st century.
　　　동명사

27　미식 베이킹 대회　　정답률 91% | 정답 ④

Gourmet Baking Competition에 관한 다음 안내문의 내용과 일치하지 않는 것은?
① 8월 3일 토요일에 개최된다.
② 온라인으로 참가 신청이 가능하다.
③ 누구나 참가할 수 있다.
☑ 참가자 한 명이 여러 부문에 참여할 수 있다.
⑤ 모든 참가자에게 기념품이 제공될 것이다.

Gourmet Baking Competition
미식가 베이킹 대회
Get out your cookbooks / and dust off / your greatest baking recipes.
당신의 요리책을 꺼내세요. / 그리고 먼지를 털어내세요. / 당신의 최고의 베이킹 레시피의
When & Where
시간 & 장소
『5 p.m. − 7 p.m. Saturday, August 3rd』 ①의근거 일치
8월 3일 토요일 오후 5시부터 7시까지
Gourmet Baking Studio
미식가 베이킹 스튜디오
Registration
등록
『Register online / at www.bakeoff.org by July 25th.』 ②의근거 일치
등록은 온라인으로 진행됩니다. / 7월 25일까지 www.bakeoff.org에서
『Anyone can participate / in the competition.』 ③의근거 일치
누구든 참여할 수 있습니다. / 대회에
Categories
분류
Pies, Cakes, and Cookies
파이, 케이크, 쿠키
『Each person can only enter / one category.』 ④의근거 불일치
한 사람은 참여할 수 있습니다. / 한 분류에만

Prizes & Gifts
상 & 선물
Prizes will be given / to the top three in each category.
상은 지급됩니다. / 각 분류의 상위 3등에게
『Souvenirs will be given / to every participant.』 ⑤의근거 일치
기념품은 주어집니다. / 모든 참가자들에게

미식 베이킹 대회

요리책을 꺼내 최고의 베이킹 레시피의 먼지를 털어내세요.

일시 및 장소
• 8월 3일 토요일 오후 5시 − 오후 7시
• Gourmet Baking Studio

참가 신청
• 7월 25일까지 www.bakeoff.org에서 온라인으로 신청하세요.
• 누구나 대회에 참가할 수 있습니다.

부문
• 파이, 케이크, 쿠키
• 참가자 한 명당 하나의 부문만 참가할 수 있습니다.

상 및 선물
• 각 부문별 최상위 3명에게는 상이 수여됩니다.
• 모든 참가자에게 기념품이 주어집니다.

Why? 왜 정답일까?
'Categories' 항목의 'Each person can only enter one category.'의 문장을 보았을 때, 참가자 한 명은 한 부문에 참여할 수 있기 때문에, 일치하지 않는 것은 ④ '참가자 한 명이 여러 부문에 참여할 수 있다.'이다.

Why? 왜 오답일까?
① 'When & Where'의 '5 p.m. − 7 p.m. Saturday, August 3rd'의 내용과 일치한다.
② 'Register online at www.bakeoff.org by July 25th.'의 내용과 일치한다.
③ 'Anyone can participate in the competition.'의 내용과 일치한다.
⑤ 'Souvenirs will be given to every participant.'의 내용과 일치한다.

● competition ⓝ 경쟁　　● cookbook ⓝ 요리책
● gourmet ⓝ 미식가　　● category ⓝ 분류
● souvenir ⓝ 기념품

28　겨울 스포츠 프로그램　　정답률 95% | 정답 ⑤

Winter Sports Program에 관한 다음 안내문의 내용과 일치하는 것은?
① 오후 2시에서 4시 사이에 실시된다.
② 네 종목의 강좌가 개설된다.
③ 참가 연령에 제한은 없다.
④ 모든 종목 강좌의 수강료는 같다.
☑ 장갑은 각자 가져와야 한다.

Winter Sports Program
겨울 스포츠 프로그램
Winter is coming! // Let's have some fun together!
겨울이 다가오고 있습니다! // 같이 즐깁시다!
Time & Location
시간 & 장소
『Every Sunday in December / from 1 p.m. to 3 p.m.』 ①의근거 불일치
12월 매주 일요일 / 오후 1시부터 3시까지
Grand Blue Ice Rink
Grand Blue 아이스 링크장에서
Lesson Details
수업 설명
『Ice Hockey, Speed Skating, and Figure Skating』 ②의근거 불일치
아이스하키, 스피드 스케이팅, 피겨 스케이팅
『Participants must be 8 years of age or older.』 ③의근거 불일치
참가자들은 8세 이상이어야 합니다.
Fee
수업료
『Ice Hockey: $200
아이스하키: 200달러
Speed Skating / Figure Skating: $150』 ④의근거 불일치
스피드 스케이팅 / 피겨 스케이팅: 150달러
Notice
알림
Skates and helmets will be provided / for free.
스케이터 헬멧은 제공될 것입니다. / 무료로
『You should bring / your own gloves.』 ⑤의근거 일치
가지고 오세요. / 여러분의 장갑을
For more information, / visit www.wintersports.com.
더 많은 정보는 / www.wintersports.com를 방문하세요.

겨울 스포츠 프로그램

겨울이 옵니다! 같이 즐겨요!

시간 및 장소
• 12월 매주 일요일 오후 1시부터 오후 3시까지
• Grand Blue Ice Rink

강좌 세부 정보
• 아이스하키, 스피드 스케이팅, 피겨 스케이팅
• 참가자는 8세 이상이어야 합니다.

수강료
- 아이스하키: $200
- 스피드 스케이팅 / 피겨 스케이팅: $150

주의 사항
- 스케이트와 헬멧은 무료로 제공됩니다.
- 장갑은 각자 가져와야 합니다.

※ 더 많은 정보를 얻고자 한다면, www.wintersports.com에 방문하세요.

Why? 왜 정답일까?

'You should bring your own gloves.'에서 얘기하듯, 장갑은 각자 가져와야하기 때문에 안내문의 내용과 일치하는 것은 ⑤이다.

Why? 왜 오답일까?

① 'Every Sunday in December from 1 p.m. to 3 p.m.'라고 하였기 때문에 오후 1시에서 3시 사이에 실시된다.
② 'Ice Hockey, Speed Skating, and Figure Skating'에서 세 종목의 강좌가 개설됨을 알 수 있다.
③ 'Participants must be 8 years of age or older.'에서 참가 연령이 8세 이상임을 알 수 있다.
④ 'Ice Hockey: $200, Speed Skating / Figure Skating: $150'에서 종목 강좌의 수강료가 다름을 알 수 있다.

- provide ⓥ 제공하다
- gloves ⓝ 장갑
- bring ⓥ 가져오다
- information ⓝ 정보

---

29 문명의 탄생 정답률 69% | 정답 ③

다음 글의 밑줄 친 부분 중, 어법상 틀린 것은? [3점]

The hunter-gatherer lifestyle, / which can ① be described as "natural" to human beings, / appears to have had much to recommend it.
수렵 채집 생활 방식은, / "인간에게 자연스러운" 것으로 묘사될 수 있는, / 추천할 만한 점이 많이 있었던 것으로 보인다.
Examination of human remains / from early hunter-gatherer societies ② has suggested / that our ancestors enjoyed abundant food, / obtainable without excessive effort, / and suffered very few diseases.
인간 유해의 연구는 시사했다. / 초기 수렵 채집 사회에서 나온 / 우리의 조상들이 풍부한 음식을 누렸다는 것, / 과도한 노력 없이 얻을 수 있었고, / 매우 적은 질병만 겪었다는 것
If this is true, / it is not clear / why so many humans settled in permanent villages / and developed agriculture, / growing crops and domesticating animals: cultivating fields / was hard work, / and it was in farming villages ✔ that epidemic diseases first took root.
만약 이것이 사실이라면, / 분명하지 않다. / 왜 그렇게 많은 사람들이 영구적인 마을에 정착했는지 / 그리고 농업을 발전시켰는지, / 작물을 재배하고 동물을 길렀는지 / 경작하는 것은 / 힘든 일이고, / 전염병이 처음으로 뿌리내린 곳은 농촌 마을이었다.
Whatever its immediate effect / on the lives of humans, / the development of settlements and agriculture / ④ undoubtedly led to a high increase in population density.
즉각적인 영향이 어떻든 간에, / 그것이 인간 삶에 미친 / 정착지와 농업의 발전은 / 틀림없이 인구 밀도의 큰 증가로 이끌었다.
This period, / known as the New Stone Age, / was a major turning point in human development, / ⑤ opening the way / to the growth of the first towns and cities, / and eventually leading to settled "civilizations."
이 시기는, / 신석기 시대로 알려진, / 인간 발전의 중요한 전환점이었다, / 길을 열며 / 첫 번째 마을과 도시의 성장을 향해, / 결국 정착된 "문명"으로 이어졌다.

수렵 채집 생활 방식은 인류에게 "자연스러운" 것으로 묘사될 수 있으며, 그것을 추천할 만한 많은 것(장점)이 있는 것으로 보인다. 초기 수렵 채집 사회의 유적 조사는 인류의 조상들이 과도한 노력 없이도 구할 수 있는 풍족한 식량을 누릴 수 있었고 질병에 걸리는 일도 거의 없었다는 것을 알려준다. 이것이 사실이라면, 왜 그렇게 많은 인류가 영구적으로 마을에 정착하여 농작물을 재배하고 동물을 기르면서 농업을 발달시켰는지 분명하지 않다. 밭을 경작하는 것은 힘든 일이고, 전염병이 처음 뿌리를 내린 곳은 농경 마을이었다. 인간의 삶에 미치는 즉각적인 영향이 무엇이든, 정착지와 농업의 발전은 의심의 여지없이 인구 밀도의 높은 증가로 이어졌다. 신석기 시대로 알려진 이 시기는 인류 발전의 중요한 전환점으로, 최초의 마을과 도시가 성장하는 길을 열었고, 결국 정착된 "문명"으로 이어졌다.

Why? 왜 정답일까?

뒷 문장이 완전하므로 관계대명사 'what' 대신 'that'이 쓰이는 것이 알맞다. 따라서 어법상 틀린 것은 ③이다.

Why? 왜 오답일까?

① 주어가 'The hunter-gather lifestyle'이기 때문에 수동태가 오는 것이 알맞다.
② 주어가 'Examination'이기 때문에 단수인 'has'가 오는 것이 알맞다.
④ 뒷문장이 불완전하고 선행사가 없으므로 선행사가 없는 관계대명사인 'what'은 적절하다.
⑤ '열면서'라는 해석이 자연스러우므로 현재분사 'opening'은 적절하다.

- describe ⓥ 묘사하다
- recommend ⓥ 추천하다
- epidemic ⓐ 전염병의
- natural ⓐ 자연적인
- remains ⓝ 유적, 유해
- permanent ⓐ 영구적인

구문 풀이

13행 This period, (which is) known as the New Stone Age, was a major turning point in human development, opening the way to the growth of the first towns and cities, and eventually leading to settled "civilizations."
(주격관계대명사+be동사 생략 / 동사 / 현재분사1 / 현재분사2)

★★★ 등급을 가르는 문제!

30 즐거움에 대한 유혹과 저축의 사용 정답률 36% | 정답 ⑤

다음 글의 밑줄 친 부분 중, 문맥상 낱말의 쓰임이 적절하지 않은 것은? [3점]

Many human and non-human animals / save commodities or money / for future consumption.
많은 인간과 비인간 동물들은 / 재화나 돈을 저축한다. / 미래 소비를 위해
This behavior / seems to reveal a preference / of a ① delayed reward / over an immediate one:
이 행동은 / 선호를 나타내는 것 같다. / 지연된 보상을 / 즉각적인 보상보다
the agent / gives up some immediate pleasure / in exchange for a future one.
행위자는 / 즉각적인 쾌락을 일부 포기한다. / 미래의 쾌락을 얻기 위해
Thus, / the discounted value / of the future reward / should be ② greater than / the un-discounted value of the present one.
따라서 / 할인된 가치가 / 미래 보상의 / 더 커야 한다. / 현재 보상의 할인되지 않은 가치보다
However / in some cases / the agent does not wait / for the envisioned occasion / but uses their savings ③ prematurely.
그러나 / 일부 경우에는 / 행위자가 기다리지 않고 / 예상된 기회를 / 저축을 미리 사용해 버린다.
For example, / early in the year / an employee might set aside money / to buy Christmas presents / but then spend it / on a summer vacation instead.
예를 들어, / 연초에 / 직원이 돈을 따로 모아둘 수 있지만 / 크리스마스 선물을 사기 위해 / 그러나 그것을 써버린다. / 대신 여름휴가에
Such cases / could be examples of ④ weakness of will.
이런 경우는 / 의지력의 약함의 예시가 될 수 있다.
That is, / the agents may judge or resolve / to spend their savings / in a certain way for the greatest benefit / but then act differently / when temptation for immediate pleasure ✔ appears.
즉, / 행위자가 판단하거나 결심할 수 있다. / 그들의 저축을 쓰기로 / 최대의 이익을 위해 특정 방식으로 / 그러나 다르게 행동한다. / 즉각적인 쾌락의 유혹이 나타날 때

많은 인간과 인간이 아닌 동물은 물건이나 돈을 미래의 소비를 위해 저축한다. 이러한 행동은 즉각적인 보상보다 ① 지연된 보상을 선호하는 것을 드러내는 듯하다. 즉, 행위자는 미래의 보상을 위해 당장의 쾌락을 포기하는 것이다. 그러므로 미래 보상의 하락된 가치는 하락되지 않은 현재의 가치보다 ② 더 커야만 한다. 그러나, 어떤 경우 자기가 계획한 일을 기다리지 않고 그들의 저축을 ③ 조기에 사용하는 경우도 있다. 예를 들어, 연초에 한 직원이 자기 돈을 크리스마스 선물을 사기 위해 모아두었지만 대신 여름휴가에 사용할 수 있다. 이러한 사례는 의지의 ④ 약함의 예시가 될 수 있다. 즉, 행위자는 그들의 저축을 가장 큰 이익을 위해 특정 방식으로 사용하기로 판단하거나 결심했으나 즉각적인 즐거움에 대한 유혹이 ⑤ 사라지면(→ 생기면) 다르게 행동할 수도 있다.

Why? 왜 정답일까?

미래의 즐거움을 위해 현재의 소비를 미루고 저축을 하지만, 즉각적인 즐거움에 대한 유혹이 생기면 소비를 한다(For example, early in the year an employee might set aside money to buy Christmas presents but then spend it on a summer vacation instead.)는 예를 들었으므로 ⑤ 'disappears'를 'appears'로 바꾸는 것이 문맥상 적절하다.

- commodity ⓝ 상품
- behavior ⓝ 행동
- preference ⓝ 선호
- envision ⓥ 계획하다
- consumption ⓝ 소비
- reveal ⓥ 드러내다
- immediate ⓐ 즉각적인
- resolve ⓥ 결심하다

구문 풀이

7행 However, in some cases the agent does not wait for the envisioned occasion but uses their savings prematurely.
(동사1 / 과거분사 / 동사2)

★★ 문제 해결 꿀~팁 ★★

▶ 많이 틀린 이유는?
글은 문제의 지문은 사람들이 미래의 소비를 위해 저축하지만, 때로는 그 돈을 너무 일찍 써버리는 상황을 설명하고 있다. 문맥은 미래의 보상과 즉각적인 보상 사이의 선택을 다루고 있다. 문맥상 유혹은 사라지는 것이 아니라 존재하는 상황에서 즉각적인 보상에 넘어가게 되는 것이므로 "disappears(사라지다)"는 부적절하다. "appears(나타나다)"가 되어야 문맥에 맞다. 따라서 ⑤가 어색하다.

▶ 문제 해결 방법은?
문맥상 단어의 의미와 논리적 흐름을 파악하면 된다. 특히, 밑줄 친 부분의 단어가 문맥과 맞지 않는지 판단할 때 문장의 앞뒤 의미와 흐름을 충분히 고려하지 않으면 실수를 할 수 있기 때문에 정확한 해설이 필수적이다.

---

31 방해의 영향 정답률 52% | 정답 ②

다음 빈칸에 들어갈 말로 가장 적절한 것을 고르시오.

① misunderstandings - 오해
✔ interruptions - 방해
③ inequalities - 불평등
④ regulations - 규칙
⑤ arguments - 주장

The costs of interruptions / are well-documented.
방해의 비용은 / 잘 기록되어 있다.
Martin Luther King Jr. / lamented them / when he described / "that lovely poem / that didn't get written / because someone knocked on the door."
Martin Luther King Jr.는 / 그것들을 한탄했다. / 그가 묘사할 때 / "아름다운 시 / 쓰이지 못한 / 누군가 문을 두드렸기 때문에"
Perhaps / the most famous literary example / happened in 1797 / when Samuel Taylor Coleridge / started writing his poem *Kubla Khan* / from a dream he had / but then was visited / by an unexpected guest.
아마도 / 가장 유명한 문학적 예시는 / 1797년에 일어났다. / 그가 그의 시 'Kubla Khan'을 쓰기 시작했을 때 / 그가 꾸었던 / 그러나 그 후 예기치 않은 손님이 찾아왔다.
For Coleridge, / by coincidence, / the untimely visitor / came at a particularly bad time.
Coleridge에게 / 우연히도 / 제때 오지 않은 손님이 / 특히 좋지 않은 시기에 왔다.
He forgot his inspiration / and left the work unfinished.
그는 영감을 잊어버리고 / 작품을 미완성으로 남겼다.
While there are many documented cases / of sudden disruptions / that have had significant consequences / for professionals in critical roles / such as doctors, nurses, control room operators, stock traders, and pilots, / they also impact most of us / in our everyday lives, / slowing down work productivity / and generally increasing stress levels.
여러 기록된 사례들이 있는 반면 / 갑작스러운 방해로 인해 / 중요한 결과를 초래한 / 예를 들어 의사, 간호사, 제어실 운영자, 주식 거래자, 그리고 조종사들 / 중요한 직업을 가진 전문가들에게 / 심각한 결과를 / 그들은 또한 우리 대부분에게 영향을 미친다. / 우리의 일상생활에서 / 업무 생산성을 저하시킴으로써 / 그리고 전반적으로 스트레스 수준을 높이며

방해로 인한 대가는 잘 기록되어 있다. Martin Luther King Jr.는 "누군가 문을 두드리는 바람에 쓰여지지 못한 사랑스러운 시"를 묘사하며 이를 슬퍼했다. 아마도 가장 유명한 문학적 사례는 1797년 Samuel Taylor Coleridge가 꿈을 꾸고 Kubla Khan이라는 시를 쓰기 시작했는데 뜻밖의 손님이 찾아왔을 때 일어났던 일일 것이다. 공교롭게도 Coleridge에게 이 불청객은 특히 좋지 않은 시기에 찾아왔다. 그는 영감을 잊고 작품을 미완성으로 남겼다. 의사, 간호사, 관제실 운영자, 주식 거래자, 조종사와 같은 중요한 역할을 담당하는 전문가들에게 심각한 결과를 초래한 갑작스러운 방해의 사례가 많이 기록되어 있지만, 갑작스러운 방해는 일상생활에서 대부분의 사람들에게도 영향을 미쳐 업무 생산성을 떨어뜨리며 일반적으로 스트레스 수준을 높인다.

Why? 왜 정답일까?

갑작스러운 방해로 영감을 잊고 작품을 완성하지 못한 예시(He forgot his inspiration and left the work unfinished.)와 같이, 집중의 흐름이 끊긴 예시를 제시한다. 따라서 빈칸에 들어갈 말로 가장 적절한 것은 ② 'interruptions'이다.

- **well-documented** 잘 기록된
- **lament** ⓥ 슬퍼하다
- **describe** ⓥ 묘사하다
- **inspiration** ⓝ 영감
- **untimely** ⓐd 때가 안 맞는
- **interruption** ⓝ 방해
- **literary** ⓐ 문학의
- **productivity** ⓝ 생산성

구문 풀이

4행 Perhaps the most famous literary example happened in 1797 when Samuel Taylor Coleridge started writing his poem Kubla Khan from a dream (which/that) he had but then was visited by an unexpected guest.

---

32 뇌를 재구조화하는 집중 　정답률 59% | 정답 ②

다음 빈칸에 들어갈 말로 가장 적절한 것을 고르시오.
① improved decision making – 향상된 의사결정
✔ the reshaping of the brain – 뇌의 재구조화
③ longterm mental tiredness – 장기적 정신 피곤
④ the development of hand skills – 손기술의 발달
⑤ increased levels of self-control – 자기통제의 향상된 정도

There's a lot of scientific evidence / demonstrating that / focused attention / leads to the reshaping of the brain.
많은 과학적 증거가 있다. / 증명하는 / 집중된 주의가 / 뇌의 재구조화로 이끎을
In animals / rewarded for noticing sound / (to hunt or to avoid being hunted for example), / we find / much larger auditory centers / in the brain.
동물들에서 / 소리를 인지한 것에 대해 보상받는 / (예를 들어 사냥을 하거나 사냥당하지 않기 위해). / 우리는 발견한다. / 훨씬 더 큰 청각 중심을 / 그들의 뇌에서
In animals / rewarded for sharp eyesight, / the visual areas are larger.
동물들에서는 / 날카로운 시력을 보상받는 / 시각 영역이 더 크다.
Brain scans of violinists / provide more evidence, / showing dramatic growth and expansion / in regions of the cortex / that represent the left hand, / which has to finger the strings precisely, / often at very high speed.
바이올리니스트의 뇌 스캔은 / 더 많은 증거를 제공한다. / 극적인 성장과 확장을 보여주며 / 대뇌 피질 영역에서 / 왼손을 담당하는 / 현을 정확하게 짚어야 하는 / 종종 매우 빠른 속도로
Other studies / have shown that the hippocampus, / which is vital for spatial memory, / is enlarged in taxi drivers.
다른 연구들은 / 해마를 보여준다. / 공간 기억에 중요한 / 택시 운전사들에게 확대되었다는 것을
The point is / that the physical architecture of the brain / changes according to / where we direct our attention / and what we practice doing.
핵심은 / 뇌의 물리적 구조가 / 변화한다는 것이다. / 우리가 어디에 주의를 기울이는지 / 그리고 우리가 무엇을 연습하는지에 따라

주의 집중이 뇌의 재구조화로 이어진다는 과학적 증거는 많이 있다. (예를 들어 사냥하거나 사냥감이 되는 것을 피하기 위해), 소리를 알아채는 것에 대한 보상을 받은 동물에서 우리는 뇌의 청각 중추가 훨씬 더 큰 것을 발견한다. 예리한 시력에 대한 보상을 받은 동물은 시각 영역이 더 크다. 바이올린 연주자의 뇌 스캔 결과는 더 많은 증거를 제공해서 종종 매우 빠른 속도로 현을 정확하게 켜야 하는 왼손을 나타내는 피질 영역의 극적인 성장과 확장을 보여준다. 다른 연구는 공간 기억에 필수적인 해마가 택시 운전사에게서 확대되는 것을 보여준다. 요점은 우리가 어디에 주의를 기울이고 무엇을 연습하느냐에 따라 뇌의 물리적 구조가 달라진다는 것이다.

Why? 왜 정답일까?

시력과 청력이 중요한 동물들과 바이올린 연주자, 택시 운전사를 예로 들며 어느 부분에 집중하느냐에 따라 뇌가 발달하는 부분이 다르다는 글이다. 따라서 집중이 뇌를 재구조한다는 ② 'the reshaping of the brain'이 빈칸에 적절하다.

- **scientific** ⓐ 과학적인
- **demonstrate** ⓥ 입증하다
- **auditory** ⓐ 청각의
- **expansion** ⓝ 확장
- **hippocampus** ⓝ 해마
- **evidence** ⓝ 증거
- **attention** ⓝ 집중
- **dramatic** ⓝ 극적인
- **cortex** ⓝ 대뇌피질
- **enlarge** ⓥ 확대되다

구문 풀이

6행 Brain scans of violinists provide more evidence, showing dramatic growth and expansion in regions of the cortex that represent the left hand, which has to finger the strings precisely, often at very high speed.

---

33 인간 생각 진화 　정답률 51% | 정답 ⑤

다음 빈칸에 들어갈 말로 가장 적절한 것을 고르시오. [3점]
① physical power to easily hunt prey – 사냥감을 쉽게 사냥하기 위한 물리적 힘
② individual responsibility in one's inner circle – 내부 원에서의 개인적 책임

---

③ instinctive tendency to avoid natural disasters – 자연 재해를 피하는 본능적인 경향
④ superiority in the number of one's descendants – 후손의 수의 우위
✔ competition and conflicts with other human tribes – 다른 인간 부족과의 경쟁과 갈등

How did the human mind evolve?
인간의 정신은 어떻게 진화했을까?
One possibility / is that competition and conflicts with other human tribes / caused our brains to evolve the way they did.
한 가지 가능성은 / 다른 인간 부족들과의 경쟁과 갈등이 / 우리의 뇌가 지금과 같은 방식으로 진화하게 만들었다는 것이다.
A human tribe / that could out-think its enemies, / even slightly, / possessed a vital advantage.
인간 부족은 / 적보다 더 생각할 수 있다면, / 조금이라도, / 중요한 이점을 가졌다.
The ability of your tribe / to imagine and predict / where and when a hostile enemy tribe might strike, / and plan accordingly, / gives your tribe a significant military advantage.
당신의 부족이 가진 능력 / 상상하고 예측하는 / 적대적인 부족이 어디에서 언제 공격할지 / 그리고 그에 맞춰 계획하는 능력이 / 당신의 부족에게 중요한 군사적 이점을 준다.
The human mind became a weapon / in the struggle for survival, / a weapon far more decisive than any before it.
인간의 정신은 무기가 되었다. / 생존을 위한 투쟁에서 / 이전의 어떤 무기보다 훨씬 더 결정적인 무기로
And this mental advantage / was applied, / over and over, / within each succeeding generation.
그리고 이 정신적 이점은 / 적용되었다. / 반복해서, / 각 후속 세대에서
The tribe that could out-think its opponents / was more likely to succeed in battle / and would then / pass on the genes / responsible for this mental advantage / to its offspring.
상대보다 더 잘 생각할 수 있는 부족은 / 전투에서 성공할 가능성이 더 높았고 / 그 후, / 유전자를 물려주었다. / 이 정신적 이점을 책임지는 / 자손에게
You and I / are the descendants of the winners.
너와 나는 / 승자의 후손이다.

인간의 생각은 어떻게 진화했을까? 한 가지 가능성은 다른 인간 부족과의 경쟁과 갈등이 우리 두뇌가 그렇게 진화하도록 했다는 것이다. 적보다 조금이라도 더 우수한 생각을 할 수 있는 인간 부족은 중요한 우위를 점했다. 적대적인 적 부족이 언제 어디서 공격할지 상상하고 예측하며 그에 따라 계획을 세울 수 있는 능력은 부족에게 상당한 군사적 우위를 가져다준다. 인간의 생각은 생존을 위한 투쟁에서 그 이전의 어떤 무기보다 훨씬 더 결정적인 무기가 되었다. 그리고 이러한 정신적 우위는 다음 세대에 걸쳐 계속해서 적용되었다. 상대보다 더 우수한 생각을 할 수 있는 부족은 전투에서 승리할 확률이 높았고, 이러한 정신적 우위를 담당하는 유전자를 자손에게 물려주었다. 당신과 나는 승자의 후손이다.

Why? 왜 정답일까?

적 부족과 경쟁을 예측하고 계획을 세울 수 있는 부족이 상당한 군사적 우위를 가졌다(The ability of your tribe to imagine and predict where and when a hostile enemy tribe might strike, and plan accordingly, gives your tribe a significant military advantage.)고 하며 조심스러운 부족이 후손을 가질 가능성이 높았다고 얘기한다. 따라서 빈칸에 들어갈 알맞은 말은 ⑤ 'competition and conflicts with other human tribes'이다.

- **evolve** ⓥ 진화하다
- **tribe** ⓝ 부족
- **apply** ⓥ 적용되다
- **weapon** ⓝ 무기
- **gene** ⓝ 유전자
- **possibility** ⓝ 가능성
- **advantage** ⓝ 장점
- **hostile** ⓐ 적대적인
- **opponent** ⓝ 상대
- **descendant** ⓝ 후손

구문 풀이

5행 The ability of your tribe to imagine and predict where and when a hostile enemy tribe might strike, and plan accordingly, gives your tribe a significant military advantage.

★★★ 등급을 가르는 문제!
34 브레인라이팅 　정답률 41% | 정답 ①

다음 빈칸에 들어갈 말로 가장 적절한 것을 고르시오. [3점]
✔ developing and assessing ideas individually – 개별적으로 아이디어를 전개하고 평가하기
② presenting and discussing ideas out loud – 아이디어를 크게 발표하고 논의하기
③ assigning different roles to each member – 각각의 구성원에게 다른 역할을 할당하기
④ coming to an agreement on these options – 선택사항에 동의하고 다르기
⑤ skipping the step of judging these options – 이 선택사항을 판단하는 단계를 건너뛰기

To find / the hidden potential in teams, / instead of brainstorming, / we're better off shifting / to a process called brainwriting.
찾기 위해서 / 팀의 숨겨진 잠재력을 / 브레인스토밍 대신 / 우리는 바꾸는 것이 낫다. / 브레인라이팅이라고 불리는 과정으로
The initial steps are solo.
첫 단계는 단독이다.
You start / by asking everyone / to generate ideas / separately.
당신은 시작한다. / 모두에게 부탁하며 / 아이디어를 만들라고 / 개별적으로
Next, / you pool them / and share them / anonymously among the group.
그다음, / 당신은 아이디어를 모은다. / 그리고 팀원들과 공유한다. / 팀에서 익명으로
To preserve independent judgment, / each member evaluates them / on their own.
독립적인 판단을 보전하기 위해서, / 각각의 팀원은 아이디어를 평가한다. / 그들 스스로
Only then / does the team come together / to select and refine / the most promising options.
그런 다음에야 / 팀은 모두 모여서 / 고르고 정제한다. / 가장 유망한 아이디어를
By developing and assessing ideas individually / before choosing and elaborating them, / teams can surface and advance possibilities / that might not get attention otherwise.
아이디어를 개별적으로 발달시키고 평가하므로써, / 아이디어를 선택하고 다듬기 전에 / 팀은 가능성을 마주하고 향상시킬 수 있다. / 그렇지 않으면 관심을 받지 못했을 아이디어의
This brainwriting process / makes sure / that all ideas are brought to the table / and all voices are brought into the conversation.
브레인라이팅 과정은 / 확실하게 만든다. / 모든 아이디어가 관심을 받고 / 모든 목소리가 대화에 참여하도록
It is especially effective in groups / that struggle to achieve / collective intelligence.
이것은 특히 팀에 효과적이다. / 달성하기 위해 고군분투하는 / 집단지성을

팀의 숨겨진 잠재력을 찾으려면 브레인스토밍 대신 브레인라이팅이라는 과정으로 전환하는

것이 좋다. 초기 단계는 혼자서 진행한다. 먼저 모든 사람에게 개별적으로 아이디어를 내도록 요청한다. 그런 다음, 아이디어를 모아 익명으로 그룹에 공유한다. 독립적인 판단을 유지하기 위해 각 구성원이 스스로 그 아이디어를 평가한다. 그러고 나서야 팀이 함께 모여 가장 유망한 옵션을 선택하고 다듬는다. 아이디어를 선택하고 구체화하기 전에 개별적으로 아이디어를 전개하고 평가함으로써 팀은 다른 방법으로는 주목받지 못했을 가능성을 드러내고 발전시킬 수 있다. 이 브레인라이팅 과정은 모든 아이디어를 테이블에 올려놓고 모든 의견을 대화에 반영할 수 있도록 한다. 특히 집단 지성을 달성하는 데 어려움을 겪는 그룹에서 효과적이다.

Why? 왜 정답일까?

기존의 'brainstorming'과는 차이가 있는 'brainwriting'의 개념을 제시하며, 'To preserve independent judgment, each member evaluates them on their own.'이라며 개인적으로 모든 의견을 고려해야함을 얘기한다. 따라서 빈칸에 들어갈 알맞은 말은 ① 'developing and assessing ideas individually'이다.

- **potential** ⓝ 가능성
- **separately** ⓐⓓ 개별적으로
- **surface** ⓥ 드러내다
- **shift** ⓥ 바꾸다
- **anonymously** ⓐⓓ 익명으로
- **struggle** ⓥ 다투다

구문 풀이

7행 Only then does the team come together to select and refine the most promising options.
도치 / 동사1 / to부정사(부사적 용법) / 동사2 / 최상급

★★ 문제 해결 꿀~팁 ★★

▶ 많이 틀린 이유는?
빈칸이 포함된 문장을 제대로 해석하지 못했거나, 앞뒤 문맥을 통해 논리적인 연결을 찾는 데 어려움을 겪었기 때문이다. 특히, 빈칸에 들어갈 적절한 표현을 찾기 위해서는 문장의 흐름과 글의 전반적인 논리를 정확하게 파악해야 하는데, 이 부분에서 실수하는 경우가 많다. 'brainstorming'과 다른 'brainwriting'의 특징을 파악하는 것이 이 문제를 풀기 위해 중요하다.

▶ 문제 해결 방법은?
빈칸 문제는 글의 흐름, 문맥 파악이 중요하다. 해당 글에서는 'brainwriting'의 절차를 설명하므로, 번호를 매기며 읽는 것이 직관적인 문제 풀이에 도움이 될 수 있다.

---

35 주인의식의 힘
정답률 53% | 정답 ③

다음 글에서 전체 흐름과 관계 없는 문장은?

Simply giving employees a sense of agency / — a feeling that they are in control, that they have genuine decision-making authority — / can radically increase how much energy and focus they bring to their jobs.
단순히 직원들에게 주도권 주는 것은 / — 그들이 통제하고 있고, 진정한 의사 결정 권한을 가지고 있다는 느낌 — / 그들이 직무에 투입하는 에너지와 집중력을 급격히 증가시킬 수 있다.

① One 2010 study / at a manufacturing plant in Ohio, / for instance, / carefully examined assembly-line workers / who were empowered / to make small decisions about their schedules and work environment.
2010년의 한 연구에서 / 오하이오의 한 제조 공장에서 / 예를 들어, / 조립 라인 노동자들을 면밀히 조사했다. / 권한을 부여받은 / 그들이 자신의 일정과 작업 환경에 대해 소규모 결정을 내릴

② They designed their own uniforms / and had authority over shifts / while all the manufacturing processes and pay scales stayed the same.
그들은 자신의 유니폼을 디자인했고 / 교대 근무에 대한 권한을 가졌으며 / 모든 제조 과정과 급여 체계는 그대로 유지되었다.

✔ It led to decreased efficiency / because their decisions / were not uniform / or focused on / meeting organizational goals.
그것은 효율성 저하로 이끌었다. / 왜냐하면 그들의 결정이 / 통일되지 않았고 / 또는 집중하지 않았기 때문이다. / 조직의 목표달성에

④ Within two months, / productivity at the plant increased by 20 percent, / with workers taking shorter breaks and making fewer mistakes.
두 달 안에, / 공장의 생산성은 20% 증가했고, / 노동자들이 더 짧은 휴식을 취하고 실수를 덜 하게 되었다.

⑤ Giving employees a sense of control / improved how much self-discipline they brought to their jobs.
직원들에게 통제감을 주는 것은 / 그들이 직무에 가져오는 자기 규율의 수준을 향상시켰다.

단순히 직원들에게 주인의식(그들이 통제하고 있다는 느낌, 진정한 의사 결정 권한이 있다는 느낌)을 주는 것만으로도 그들이 자신의 업무에 쏟는 에너지와 집중력을 급격하게 높일 수 있다. ① 예를 들어, 오하이오 주의 한 제조 공장에서 진행된 2010년의 한 연구는 그들의 일정과 작업 환경에 대한 작은 결정 권한을 부여받은 조립 라인 근로자를 주의 깊게 살펴보았다. ② 그들은 그들 자신의 유니폼을 디자인했고, 근무 교대 에 대한 권한을 가진 반면에, 모든 생산 과정과 임금 규모는 동일하게 유지되었다. ③ 결정이 합치되거나 조직의 목표 달성에 초점이 맞춰지지 않았기 때문에 그것은 효율성을 낮추는 결과를 낳았다. ④ 두 달 만에 직원들은 휴식 시간을 더 짧게 가졌고, 실수를 더 적게 하였으며, 그 공장의 생산성은 20퍼센트 증가했다. ⑤ 자신들이 통제권을 쥐고 있다는 느낌을 직원들에게 부여한 것이 그들이 업무에 끌어들이는 자기 통제력을 향상시켰다.

Why? 왜 정답일까?

직원들에게 주인의식을 주기만 함으로써 일의 효율이 높아짐을 얘기한다. 따라서 결정이 합치되거나 조직의 목표 달성에 초점이 맞춰져있지 않기 때문에 효율성을 낮춘다는 ③은 전체 흐름과 관계없다.

- **employee** ⓝ 직원
- **genuine** ⓐ 진짜의
- **examine** ⓥ 검사하다
- **agency** ⓝ 주인
- **authority** ⓝ 권한
- **decision** ⓝ 결정

구문 풀이

1행 Simply giving employees a sense of agency — a feeling that they are in
동명사 / 접속사
control, that they have genuine decision-making authority — can radically increase
접속사
how much energy and focus (which/that) they bring to their jobs.
목적격관계대명사 생략

---

36 디지털 비즈니스 활동의 환경오염
정답률 56% | 정답 ③

주어진 글 다음에 이어질 글의 순서로 가장 적절한 것을 고르시오. [3점]
① (A) – (C) – (B)
② (B) – (A) – (C)
✔ (B) – (C) – (A)
④ (C) – (A) – (B)
⑤ (C) – (B) – (A)

As businesses shift some core business activities to digital, / such as sales, marketing, or archiving, / it is assumed that the impact on the environment will be less negative.
기업들이 일부 핵심 비즈니스 활동을 디지털로 전환하면서 / 판매, 마케팅 또는 기록 보관과 같은 / 환경에 미치는 영향이 덜 부정적일 것이라고 가정된다.

(B) However, / digital business activities / can still threaten the environment. /
그러나 / 디지털 비즈니스 활동은 / 여전히 환경을 위협할 수 있다.
In some cases, / the harm of digital businesses / can be even more hazardous.
어떤 경우에는 / 디지털 비즈니스가 주는 피해가 / 훨씬 더 해로울 수 있다.
A few decades ago, / offices used to have much more paper waste / since all documents were paper based.
몇 십 년 전만 해도 / 사무실은 훨씬 더 많은 종이 폐기물을 발생시켰다. / 모든 문서가 종이 기반이었기 때문에

(C) When workplaces / shifted from paper to digital documents, invoices, and emails, / it was a promising step to save trees.
직장이 / 종이에서 디지털 문서로, 청구서와 이메일로 전환되었을 때, / 나무를 구할 수 있는 유망한 조치였다.
However, / the cost of the Internet and electricity for the environment / is neglected.
그러나 / 인터넷과 전기에 드는 환경 비용은 / 간과되고 있다.
A recent *Wired* report declared / that most data centers' energy source / is fossil fuels.
최근 *Wired* 보고서는 밝혔다. / 대부분의 데이터 센터의 에너지원이 / 화석 연료라고

(A) When we store bigger data on clouds, / increased carbon emissions / make our green clouds gray.
우리가 클라우드에 더 많은 데이터를 저장할 때, / 증가한 탄소 배출이 / 우리의 '녹색 클라우드'를 '회색 클라우드'로 만든다.
The carbon footprint of an email / is smaller than mail sent via a post office, / but still, / it causes four grams of CO_2, / and it can be as much as 50 grams if the attachment is big.
이메일의 탄소 발자국은 / 우편으로 보내는 편지보다 적지만, / 여전히 / 이로 인해 4g의 이산화탄소가 발생하고, / 첨부 파일이 크면 50g까지 될 수 있다.

기업이 영업, 마케팅, 파일 보관 등 일부 핵심 비즈니스 활동을 디지털로 전환함에 따라 환경에 미치는 영향이 덜 부정적일 것으로 예상된다.

(B) 그러나 디지털 비즈니스 활동은 여전히 환경을 위협할 수 있다. 경우에 따라서는 디지털 비즈니스가 끼치는 해악이 훨씬 더 위험할 수 있다. 수십 년 전만 해도 사무실에서는 모든 문서가 종이로 작성되었기 때문에 종이 폐기물이 훨씬 더 많았다.

(C) 직장에서 종이를 디지털 문서, (디지털) 송장, 이메일로 전환한 것은 나무를 보호할 수 있는 유망한 조치였다. 하지만 인터넷과 전기가 환경에 입히는 손실은 간과되고 있다. 최근 Wired의 보고서에 따르면 대부분의 데이터 센터의 에너지원은 화석 연료이다.

(A) 클라우드에 더 많은 데이터를 저장할수록 탄소 배출량이 증가하여 녹색 구름을 회색으로 변하게 만든다. 이메일의 탄소 발자국은 우체국을 통해 보내는 우편물보다 적지만 여전히 4g의 이산화탄소를 유발하며 첨부 파일이 크면 50g에 달할 수 있다.

Why? 왜 정답일까?

주어진 글은 비즈니스 활동을 디지털로 옮기며 환경에 미치는 영향이 부정적일 것이라고 한다. (B)에서는 디지털 비즈니스 활동이 환경에 여전히 위험할 수 있음을 언급하고, (C)는 인터넷과 전기가 환경에 입히는 손실이 간과된다며 자세히 심화 설명하고 있다. 따라서 (B)와 (A)가 이어져야 하고, 그 이후에도 가장 세부적인 예시인 클라우드를 설명하는 (C)가 마지막에 오는 순서가 알맞다. 따라서 답은 ③ '(B) – (C) – (A)'이다.

- **core** ⓐ 핵심적인, 가장 중요한
- **environment** ⓝ 환경
- **hazardous** ⓐ 위험한
- **document** ⓝ 자료
- **electricity** ⓝ 전기
- **emission** ⓝ 배출
- **carbon footprint** 탄소 발자국
- **waste** ⓝ 쓰레기
- **workplace** ⓝ 직장
- **declare** ⓥ 발표하다, 밝히다

구문 풀이

12행 A few decades ago, offices used to have much more paper waste since
a few + 가산명사 / used to 동사원형: ~하곤 했다 / 때문에
all documents were paper based.

---

37 붉은 다람쥐와 회색 다람쥐
정답률 64% | 정답 ②

주어진 글 다음에 이어질 글의 순서로 가장 적절한 것을 고르시오.
① (A) – (C) – (B)
✔ (B) – (A) – (C)
③ (B) – (C) – (A)
④ (C) – (A) – (B)
⑤ (C) – (B) – (A)

Problems often arise / if an exotic species / is suddenly introduced to an ecosystem.
문제는 종종 발생한다. / 외래종이 / 갑자기 생태계에 도입되면

(B) Britain's red and grey squirrels / provide a clear example.
영국의 붉은 다람쥐와 회색 다람쥐는 / 명확한 예를 제공한다.
When the grey arrived from America in the 1870s, / both squirrel species competed for the same food and habitat, / which put the native red squirrel populations / under pressure.
회색 다람쥐가 1870년대에 미국에서 도착했을 때, / 두 다람쥐 종은 같은 먹이와 서식지를 두고 경쟁했다. / 이는 토종 붉은 다람쥐 개체군에게 / 큰 압박을 주었다.

(A) The grey had the edge / because it can adapt its diet; / it is able, for instance, / to eat green acorns, / while the red can only digest mature acorns.
회색 다람쥐는 우위를 가졌다. / 먹이를 적응할 수 있었기 때문에 / 예를 들어, 회색 다람쥐는 / 푸른 도토리를 먹을 수 있는 반면, / 붉은 다람쥐는 성숙한 도토리만 소화할 수 있었다.
Within the same area of forest, / grey squirrels can destroy the food supply / before red squirrels even have a bite.
같은 숲 지역에서 / 회색 다람쥐는 먹이 공급을 파괴할 수 있었다. / 붉은 다람쥐가 먹이를 먹기 전에

(C) Greys can also live / more densely and in varied habitats, / so have survived more easily when woodland has been destroyed.
회색 다람쥐는 또한 살 수 있어, / 더 밀집해서 다양한 서식지에서 / 숲이 파괴되었을 때 더 쉽게 생존했다.

As a result, / the red squirrel has come close to extinction / in England.
그 결과, / 붉은 다람쥐는 멸종 위기에 처하게 되었다. / 영국에서

외래종이 갑자기 생태계에 유입되면 문제가 종종 발생한다.

(B) 영국의 붉은색 다람쥐와 회색 다람쥐가 명확한 예를 제공한다. 1870년대 미국에서 회색 다람쥐가 왔을 때, 두 다람쥐 종은 동일한 먹이와 서식지를 놓고 경쟁했고, 이것이 토종의 붉은 다람쥐 개체군을 압박했다.

(A) 회색 다람쥐는 먹이를 조절할 수 있기 때문에 우위를 점했다. 예를 들어 회색 다람쥐는 설익은 도토리를 먹을 수 있는 반면, 붉은 다람쥐는 다 익은 도토리만 소화할 수 있다. 숲의 같은 지역 내에서 회색 다람쥐는 붉은 다람쥐가 한 입 먹기도 전에 식량 공급을 파괴할 수 있다.

(C) 회색 다람쥐는 또한 더 밀집하며 다양한 서식지에서 살 수 있어서 삼림이 파괴되었을 때 더 쉽게 살아남았다. 그 결과, 붉은 다람쥐는 영국에서 거의 멸종 위기에 이르렀다.

Why? 왜 정답일까?

외래종이 생태계에 미치는 위험성에 대해 얘기하고 있다. (B)에서는 회색 다람쥐가 외래종으로 붉은색 다람쥐의 서식지에 온 것을 언급하고, (A)는 외래종인 회색 다람쥐가 왜 붉은색 다람쥐보다 우위에 있었는지 설명하고 있다. 따라서 (B)와 (A)가 이어져야 하고, 그 이후의 결과가 나오는 (C)가 마지막에 오는 순서가 알맞다. 따라서 답은 ② '(B) – (A) – (C)'이다.

- **exotic species** 외래종
- **introduce** ⓥ 소개하다
- **ecosystem** ⓝ 생태계
- **digest** ⓥ 소화하다, 소화시키다
- **bite** ⓥ 베어 물다
- **suddenly** ⓐⓓ 갑자기
- **edge** ⓝ 우위
- **acorn** ⓝ 도토리
- **destroy** ⓥ 파괴하다, 말살하다
- **survive** ⓥ 살아남다

구문 풀이

13행 Greys can also live more densely and in varied habitats, so have survived
(동사1) (수식어구1) (수식어구2) (동사2)
more easily when woodland has been destroyed.
(현재완료시제)

★★★ 등급을 가르는 문제!

38 농작물 재배와 인구 증가의 관계 　　　정답률 43% | 정답 ③

글의 흐름으로 보아, 주어진 문장이 들어가기에 가장 적절한 곳을 고르시오.

Growing crops forced people / to stay in one place.
농작물을 재배하는 것은 사람들을 / 한 곳에 머물게 했다.
Hunter-gatherers typically moved around frequently, / and they had to be able to carry / all their possessions with them / every time they moved.
수렵–채집인들은 주로 자주 이동했고, / 그들은 가지고 다닐 수 있어야 했다. / 그들의 모든 소지품을 / 그들이 이동할 때마다
① In particular, mothers / had to carry their young children.
특히 어머니들은 / 어린 자녀들을 데리고 다녀야 했다.
② As a result, hunter-gatherer mothers / could have only one baby / every four years or so, / spacing their births / so that they never had to carry more than one child at a time.
그 결과, 수렵–채집 사회의 어머니들은 / 아이를 하나만 낳을 수 있었다. / 대략 4년마다 / 출산 간격을 두어 / 한 번에 한 명 이상의 아이를 들고 다니지 않도록
☑ Farmers, on the other hand, / could live in the same place year after year / and did not have to worry about transporting young children long distances.
반면에 농부들은 / 매년 같은 장소에서 살 수 있었고 / 어린아이들을 먼 거리로 이동시키는 것에 대해 걱정할 필요가 없었다.
Societies that settled down in one place / were able to shorten their birth intervals / from four years to about two.
한 곳에 정착한 사회는 / 출산 간격을 단축할 수 있었다. / 4년에서 약 2년으로
④ This meant that each woman / could have more children / than her hunter-gatherer counterpart, / which in turn resulted in rapid population growth / among farming communities.
이는 각 여성이 / 더 많은 아이를 낳을 수 있다는 것을 의미했다. / 수렵–채집 사회의 여성들보다 / 그 결과 인구가 급격히 증가하게 되며 / 농경 사회에서
⑤ An increased population was actually an advantage / to agricultural societies, / because farming required large amounts of human labor.
증가한 인구는 실제로 장점이었다. / 농경 사회에 / 왜냐하면 농업은 많은 인간 노동을 필요로 했기 때문이다.

농작물 재배는 사람들이 한곳에 머무르게 했다. 수렵 채집인들은 일반적으로 자주 이동해야 했고, 이동할 때마다 모든 소유물을 가지고 다닐 수 있어야 했다. ① 특히, 어머니들은 어린 아이를 업고 이동해야 했다. ② 그 결과, 수렵 채집인 어머니들은 대략 4년마다 한 명의 아이만 낳을 수 있었고, 한 번에 한 명 이상의 아이를 업고 다닐 필요가 없도록 출산 간격을 두었다. ③ 반면, 농부들은 매년 같은 장소에서 살 수 있었고 어린아이를 장거리 이동시켜야 하는 걱정을 하지 않아도 되었다. 한곳에 정착하게 된 사회는 출산 간격을 4년에서 약 2년으로 단축할 수 있었다. ④ 이는 여성 한 명이 수렵 채집인인 상대보다 더 많은 아이를 낳을 수 있다는 것을 의미했고, 그 결과 그것은 농경 사회에서 급격한 인구 증가를 야기했다. ⑤ 인구 증가는 실제로 농경 사회에 유리했는데, 왜냐하면 농사는 많은 인간의 노동력을 필요로 했기 때문이다.

Why? 왜 정답일까?

글에서는 수렵 채집인들과 농작물 재배인을 비교하며 수렵 채집인들은 이동이 잦았기 때문에 아이를 많이 낳을 수 없었지만, 농작물 재배인들은 이동이 거의 없었기 때문에 아이를 많이 낳을 수 있었다는 설명을 한다. 농작물 재배인들이 아이들을 옮기지 않아도 된다는 내용은 따라서 ③에 오는 것이 가장 적절하다.

- **transport** ⓥ 이송하다
- **possession** ⓝ 소유물, 소지품
- **interval** ⓝ 간격
- **rapid** ⓐ 빠른
- **agricultural society** 농경 사회, 농업사회
- **frequently** ⓐⓓ 자주
- **settled** ⓐ 정착한
- **counterpart** ⓝ 상대
- **population** ⓝ 인구
- **labor** ⓝ 노동

구문 풀이

1행 Farmers, on the other hand, could live in the same place year after year
(동사1)
and did not have to worry about transporting young children long distances.
(동사2) (동명사)

★★ 문제 해결 꿀~팁 ★★

▶ 많이 틀린 이유는?
문단 내 문장들의 논리적 흐름을 잘못 이해했기 때문이다. 글의 전개가 사냥–채집 사회와 농경 사회의 차이점에 대한 비교로 이어진다. 수렵 채집인과 농경인의 상황을 비교하며 아이를 낳기가 불리하거나 유리하다는 결론으로 이끈다.
▶ 문제 해결 방법은?
문장 간의 인과관계와 논리적 연결을 파악해야 한다. ②번 문장은 사냥–채집 사회의 출산 간격을 설명하며, 여러 아이를 동시에 돌볼 수 없는 이유를 명시한다. ③번 문장은 농경 사회로 넘어가면서 출산 간격이 줄어든 이유를 설명한다. 이처럼 각 문장은 원인과 결과로 연결되어 있기 때문에, ②번 문장이 사냥–채집 사회의 설명을 마무리 짓고, ③번 문장에서 농경 사회로 자연스럽게 넘어가야 한다.

★★★ 등급을 가르는 문제!

39 유년기의 길이에 따른 적응의 차이 　　　정답률 35% | 정답 ④

글의 흐름으로 보아, 주어진 문장이 들어가기에 가장 적절한 곳을 고르시오. [3점]

Spending time as children allows animals / to learn about their environment.
어린 시절을 보내는 것은 동물들이 / 환경에 대해 배우게 해준다.
Without childhood, / animals must rely more fully on hardware, / and therefore be less flexible.
어린 시절이 없으면, / 동물들은 더 완전히 하드웨어에 의존해야 하고, / 따라서 덜 유연해진다.
① Among migratory bird species, / those that are born knowing how, when, and where to migrate / — those that are migrating / entirely with instructions they were born with — / sometimes have very inefficient migration routes.
철새 중에는 / 태어날 때부터 언제, 어디로, 어떻게 이동할지를 알고 태어난 종들은 / — 이주하는 종들 / 태어날 때 받은 지시만으로 — / 때때로 매우 비효율적인 이동 경로를 가진다.
② These birds, born knowing how to migrate, / don't adapt easily.
이주하는 방법을 알고 태어난 이 새들은 / 쉽게 적응하지 못한다.
③ So when lakes dry up, / forest becomes farmland, / or climate change pushes breeding grounds farther north, / those birds that are born knowing how to migrate / keep flying by the old rules and maps.
그래서 호수가 마르거나 / 숲이 농지로 바뀌거나 / 기후 변화로 인해 번식지가 더 북쪽으로 밀려나면 / 이주 방법을 알고 태어난 새들은 / 여전히 오래된 규칙과 지도를 따라 비행한다.
☑ By comparison, / birds with the longest childhoods, / and those that migrate with their parents, / tend to have the most efficient migration routes.
반면에, / 가장 긴 어린 시절을 가진 새들과 / 부모와 함께 이주하는 새들은 / 가장 효율적인 이동 경로를 가지는 경향이 있다.
Childhood facilitates / the passing on of cultural information, / and culture can evolve faster than genes.
어린 시절은 돕는다 / 문화적 정보를 전달하는 것을 / 문화는 유전자보다 더 빠르게 진화할 수 있다.
⑤ Childhood / gives flexibility / in a changing world.
어린 시절은 / 유연성을 준다 / 변화하는 세상에서

동물은 유년기를 보내면서 환경에 대해 배울 수 있다. 유년기가 없으면, 동물은 하드웨어에 더 많이 의존해야 하므로 유연성이 떨어질 수밖에 없다. ① 철새 중에서도 언제, 어디로, 어떻게 이동해야 하는지를 알고 태어나는 새들, 즉 전적으로 태어날 때부터 주어진 지침에 따라 이동하는 새들은 때때로 매우 비효율적인 이동 경로를 가지고 있다. ② 이동 방법을 알고 태어난 새들은 쉽게 적응하지 못한다. ③ 따라서 호수가 마르거나 숲이 농지로 바뀌거나 기후 변화로 번식지가 더 북쪽으로 밀려났을 때, 이동하는 방법을 알고 태어난 새들은 기존의 규칙과 지도를 따라 계속 날아간다. ④ 이에 비해 유년기가 가장 길고 부모와 함께 이동하는 새는 가장 효율적인 이동 경로를 가지고 있는 경향이 있다. 유년기는 문화적 정보의 전달을 촉진하며, 문화는 유전자보다 더 빠르게 진화할 수 있다. ⑤ 유년기는 변화하는 세상에서 유연성을 제공한다.

Why? 왜 정답일까?

유년기가 긴 동물과 유년기가 짧은 동물의 적응의 차이에 대한 글이다. 바뀐 환경에 적응하려면 유년기가 긴 것이 유리하기 때문에 유년기의 문화적 정보가 제공하는 이점의 앞부분이며 유년기가 짧은 동물들의 행동을 설명하는 문장 뒤인 ④에 주어진 문장이 오는 것이 가장 적절하다.

- **comparison** ⓝ 비교
- **migrate** ⓥ 이주하다
- **flexible** ⓐ 유연한
- **entirely** ⓐⓓ 전적으로
- **inefficient** ⓐ 비효율적인
- **dry up** (강·호수 등이) 바싹 마르다
- **facilitate** ⓥ 촉진하다
- **childhood** ⓝ 유년기
- **migration** ⓝ 이주
- **migratory bird** 철새
- **instruction** ⓝ 지시, 명령
- **adapt** ⓥ 적응하다
- **breeding ground** (야생 동물의) 번식지
- **flexibility** ⓝ 유연성

구문 풀이

5행 Without childhood, animals must rely more fully on hardware, and therefore
(~없이)　　　　　　　　　　　　　　　　　　　　　　　(동사1)
be less flexible.
(동사2)

★★ 문제 해결 꿀~팁 ★★

▶ 많이 틀린 이유는?
주어진 글은 "어린 시절이 긴 새들이 가장 효율적인 이동 경로를 가지고 있다"는 내용을 설명하고 있다. 이어지는 내용도 어린 시절을 통한 학습과 유전적 지식에만 의존하는 새들에 대한 비교를 다루고 있음을 알 수 있다. 따라서 어린 시절이 길지 않은 새들과의 비교하는 부분에 들어가야 가장 알맞다.
▶ 문제 해결 방법은?
문장 간 논리적 연결과 핵심 아이디어를 파악하는 것이 중요하다. 특히 'By comparison'과 같이 반대 의미를 담고 구를 주의해서 보자. 글을 읽으며 자신만의 기호로 글의 흐름의 변화를 표시하는 것도 도움이 된다.

40 장애를 가진 사람들의 디지털 프로젝트 　　　정답률 49% | 정답 ①

다음 글의 내용을 한 문장으로 요약하고자 한다. 빈칸 (A), (B)에 들어갈 말로 가장 적절한 것은?

(A)	(B)		(A)	(B)
✓ overlooked 간과하다	inclusive 포함하는		② accepted 받아들이다	practical 실용적인
③ considered 고려하다	inclusive 포함하는		④ accepted 받아들이다	abstract 추상적인
⑤ overlooked 간과하다	abstract 추상적인			

Over the last several decades, / scholars have developed / standards for how best to create, organize, present, and preserve digital information / for future generations.
지난 수십 년 동안, / 학자들은 개발해 왔다 / 디지털 정보를 가장 잘 창조하고, 조직하고, 제공하고, 보존하는 방법에 대한 기준들을 / 미래 세대를 위해

What has remained neglected for the most part, / however, are the needs of people with disabilities.
그러나 대체로 무시되어 온 것은 / 장애를 가진 사람들의 필요이다.

As a result, / many of the otherwise most valuable digital resources / are useless / for people who are deaf or hard of hearing, / as well as for people who are blind, have low vision, or have difficulty / distinguishing particular colors.
그 결과, / 가장 가치 있는 디지털 자원들 중 많은 것이 / 쓸모가 없다 / 귀가 들리지 않거나 난청인 사람들에게는 / 또한 시각 장애가 있거나, 저시력이거나, 어려운 사람들에게도 / 특정 색을 구별하기가

While professionals / working in educational technology and commercial web design / have made significant progress / in meeting the needs of such users, / some scholars creating digital projects / all too often fail / to take these needs into account.
전문가들이 / 교육 기술과 상업적 웹 디자인에서 일하는 / 상당한 진전을 이루었음에도, / 그러한 사용자들의 필요를 충족시키는 데 있어 / 일부 디지털 프로젝트를 만드는 학자들은 / 너무 자주 실패한다 / 이러한 필요를 고려하는 것에

This situation / would be much improved / if more projects embraced the idea / that we should always keep / the largest possible audience in mind / as we make design decisions, / ensuring that our final product / serves the needs / of those with disabilities as well as those without.
이 상황은 / 크게 개선될 것이다 / 더 많은 프로젝트가 생각을 수용한다면, / 우리가 염두에 둬야 한다는 / 가능한 가장 큰 청중을 / 우리가 디자인 결정을 내릴 때, / 최종 제품이 / 필요를 모두 충족하도록 보장하면서 / 장애를 가진 사람들과 그렇지 않은 사람들의

➡ The needs of people with disabilities / have often been (A) overlooked / in digital projects, / which could be changed / by adopting a(n) (B) inclusive design.
장애를 가진 사람들의 필요는 / 간과되어 왔다 / 디지털 프로젝트에서 / 이것은 바뀔 수 있다 / 포함적인 디자인을 받아들임으로써

지난 수십 년 동안 학자들은 미래 세대를 위해 디지털 정보를 가장 잘 만들고, 정리하고, 제시하고, 보존하는 방법에 대한 표준을 개발해 왔다. 그러나 대부분의 경우 장애가 있는 사람들의 요구는 여전히 무시되어 왔다. 그 결과, 청각 장애가 있거나 듣는 것이 힘든 사람, 시각 장애가 있거나 시력이 낮거나 특정 색상을 구분하기 어려운 사람에게는 그렇지 않은 경우라면 가장 가치 있었을 디지털 자원 중 상당수가 무용지물이 되고 있다. 교육 기술 및 상업용 웹 디자인에 종사하는 전문가들은 이러한 사용자의 요구를 충족시키는 데 상당한 진전을 이루었지만, 디지털 프로젝트를 만드는 일부 학자들은 이러한 요구를 고려하지 못하는 경우가 너무 많다. 더 많은 프로젝트에서 디자인을 결정할 때 최대한 많은 사용자를 항상 염두에 두고 최종 제품이 장애가 있는 사람들과 그렇지 않은 사람들 모두의 요구를 충족시킬 수 있도록 해야 한다는 생각을 받아들인다면 이러한 상황은 훨씬 개선될 것이다.

➡ 장애가 있는 사람들의 요구는 디지털 프로젝트에서 종종 (A) 간과되어 왔으며, 이것은 (B) 포괄(포용)적인 디자인을 채택함으로써 변화될 수 있다.

Why? 왜 정답일까?

'What has remained neglected for the most part, however, are the needs of people with disabilities.'와 'This situation would be much improved if more projects embraced the idea that we should always keep the largest possible audience in mind as we make design decisions, ensuring that our final product serves the needs of those with disabilities as well as those without.'의 문장을 보았을 때 미래 세대를 위해 만든 디지털 정보에 장애가 있는 사람들의 접근이 어려움을 언급하고 있다. 따라서 'overlooked'와 'inclusive'가 들어가는 것이 가장 알맞다.

- scholar ⓝ 학자
- organize ⓥ 정리하다
- preserve ⓥ 보존하다
- valuable ⓐ 가치가 큰, 소중한
- distinguish ⓥ 구별하다
- develop ⓥ 발전시키다
- present ⓥ 제공하다
- disability ⓝ 장애
- resource ⓝ 원천
- situation ⓝ 상황

구문 풀이

14행 This situation would be much improved if more projects embraced the idea [가정법] that we should always keep the largest possible audience in mind as we [접속사] [최상급] [~하면서] make design decisions, ensuring that our final product serves the needs of those [현재분사] [접속사] [지시대명사] with disabilities as well as those without. [마찬가지로] [지시대명사]

41-42 안전한 위협이 주는 쾌락

All humans, to an extent, seek activities / that cause a degree of pain in order to experience pleasure, / whether this is found in spicy food, strong massages, / or stepping into a too-cold or too-hot bath.
모든 인간은 어느 정도, 활동을 찾는다 / 쾌락을 경험하기 위해 어느 정도의 고통을 유발하는 / 이것이 매운 음식, 강한 마사지에서든, / 너무 차갑거나 너무 뜨거운 욕조에 들어가는 것에서든 상관없이

『The key / is that it is a 'safe threat'.』 42번의 근거
핵심은 / 이것이 '안전한 위협'이라는 것이다.

The brain perceives the stimulus to be painful / but ultimately (a) non-threatening.
뇌는 그 자극을 고통스럽게 인식하지만, / 궁극적으로는 위협적이지 않다고 여긴다.

Interestingly, / this could be similar to the way humor works: / a 'safe threat' that causes pleasure by playfully violating norms.
흥미롭게도, / 이것은 유머가 작동하는 방식과 유사할 수 있다: / 규범을 장난스럽게 위반하여 쾌락을 유발하는 '안전한 위협'

We feel uncomfortable, / but safe.
우리는 불편함을 느끼지만, / 안전함도 느낀다.

In this context, where (b) survival is clearly not in danger, / the desire for pain is actually the desire for a reward, / not suffering or punishment.
생존이 분명히 위협받지 않는 이 상황에서, / 고통에 대한 욕구는 사실 보상을 향한 욕구이다. / 고통이나 처벌을 향한 것이 아니라.

This reward-like effect / comes from the feeling / of mastery over the pain.
이 보상 같은 효과는 / 느끼는 데서 온다. / 고통에 대한 통제감을

The closer you look at your chilli-eating habit, / the more remarkable it seems.
매운 고추를 먹는 습관을 더 자세히 들여다볼수록, / 그것이 더욱 놀랍게 보인다.

When the active ingredient of chillies — capsaicin — touches the tongue, / it stimulates exactly the same receptor / that is activated when any of these tissues are burned.
고추의 활성 성분인 캡사이신이 혀에 닿으면, / 그것은 정확히 같은 수용체를 자극한다 / 우리가 조직을 데울 때 활성화되는

Knowing that our body is firing off danger signals, / but that we are actually completely safe, / (c) produces pleasure. 41번의 근거
우리의 몸이 위험 신호를 보내고 있다는 것을 알지만, / 실제로는 완전히 안전하다는 것을 알 때, / 쾌락이 생긴다.

All children start off hating chilli, / but many learn to derive pleasure from it through repeated exposure / and knowing that they will never experience any real (d) threat.
모든 아이들은 처음에 칠리를 싫어하지만, / 많은 아이들이 반복된 노출을 통해 쾌락을 얻는 법을 배운다. / 그리고 그들이 결코 진정한 해를 경험하지 않을 것임을 알면서

Interestingly, / seeking pain for the pain itself / appears to be (e) uniquely human.
흥미롭게도, / 고통 그 자체를 찾는 행위는 / 독특하게 인간만의 특징인 것 같다.

The only way / scientists have trained animals / to have a preference for chilli or to self-harm / is to have the pain / always directly associated / with a pleasurable reward.
유일한 방법은 / 동물에게 훈련시킨 / 과학자들이 고추를 선호하거나 자해하도록 / 고통이 / 직접적으로 연관되도록 하는 것이다. / 항상 쾌락적인 보상과

모든 인간은 어느 정도는 쾌락을 경험하기 위해 약간의 고통을 유발하는 활동을 추구한다. 이것이 매운 음식 또는 강한 마사지, 너무 차갑거나 뜨거운 욕조에 들어가기 중 어디에서 발견되든지 간에 말이다. 핵심은 그것이 '안전한 위험'이라는 점이다. 뇌는 자극이 고통스럽지만 궁극적으로 (a) 위협적이지 않은 것으로 인식한다. 흥미롭게도 이것은 유머가 작동하는 방식, 즉 규범을 장난스럽게 위반함으로써 쾌락을 유발하는 '안전한 위험'과 유사할 수 있다. 우리는 불편하지만 안전하다고 느낀다. (b) 생존이 위협받지 않은 이런 상황에서 고통에 대한 욕구는 실제로는 고통이나 처벌이 아닌 보상에 대한 욕구이다. 이러한 보상과 같은 효과는 고통에 대한 숙달된 느낌에서 비롯된다. 칠리를 먹는 습관을 자세히 들여다볼수록 이는 더욱 분명하게 드러난다. 칠리의 활성 성분인 캡사이신이 혀에 닿으면 피부 조직이 화상을 입었을 때 활성화되는 것과 똑같은 수용체를 자극한다. 우리 몸이 위험 신호를 보내고 있지만 실제로는 완전히 안전하다는 것을 알면 쾌감이 (c) 생긴다. 모든 아이들은 처음에는 칠리를 싫어하지만, 반복적인 노출과 실질적인 (d) 기쁨(→ 해)을 경험하지 않는다는 것을 알게 됨을 통해 그것에서 쾌락을 얻는 방법을 배우게 된다. 흥미롭게도 고통 그 자체를 위해 고통을 추구하는 것은 (e) 인간만이 할 수 있는 행동으로 보인다. 동물이 칠리를 선호하게 하거나 스스로에게 해를 가하도록 과학자들이 훈련시키는 유일한 방법은 고통을 항상 즐거운 보상과 직접적으로 연관시키는 것이다.

- seek ⓥ 찾다
- threat ⓝ 협박, 위협
- norm ⓝ 규범
- receptor ⓝ 수용체
- completely ⓐ🇩 완전히
- pleasure ⓝ 즐거움
- painful ⓐ 고통스러운, 아픈
- punishment ⓝ 처벌, 형벌
- tissue ⓝ 조직
- preference ⓝ 선호

구문 풀이

14행 When the active ingredient of chillies — capsaicin — touches the tongue, [때] it stimulates exactly the same receptor that is activated when any of these [주격관계대명사] [수동태] [때] tissues are burned.

41 제목 파악 정답률 54% | 정답 ①

윗글의 제목으로 가장 적절한 것은?

✓① The Secret Behind Painful Pleasures – 고통스러운 즐거움 뒤의 비밀
② How 'Safe Threat' Changes into Real Pain – '안전한 위험'이 진짜 고통으로 어떻게 바뀌는가
③ What Makes You Stronger, Pleasure or Pain? – 무엇이 당신을 강하게 만드는가, 즐거움인가 고통인가?
④ How Does Your Body Detect Danger Signals? – 당신의 몸이 어떻게 위험 신호를 감지하는가?
⑤ Recipes to Change Picky Children's Eating Habits – 까다로운 아이들의 식습관을 바꿀 레시피

Why? 왜 정답일까?

실질적으로 위험이 되지 않는다는 것을 알 때 보상의 원리로 고통 뒤에 쾌락이 온다고 설명하고 있다. 따라서 윗글의 제목으로 가장 적절한 것은 ① 'The Secret Behind Painful Pleasures'이다.

★★★ 등급을 가르는 문제!

42 어휘 추론 정답률 46% | 정답 ④

밑줄 친 (a) ~ (e) 중에서 문맥상 낱말의 쓰임이 적절하지 않은 것은?

① (a) ② (b) ③ (c) ✓④ (d) ⑤ (e)

Why? 왜 정답일까?

글에 따르면 많은 아이들이 칠리를 싫어하지만, 반복된 노출을 통해 이끌어진 쾌락을 배운다. 즉, 위협적이지 않은 고통인 칠리 뒤에 쾌락이 오는 것을 깨달았다고 하니 그들이 진짜 위험을 경험하지 않았다고 하는 것이 자연스럽다. 따라서 ④ (d)의 'joy'를 'threat'으로 바꾸는 것이 문맥상 자연스럽다.

★★ 문제 해결 꿀~팁 ★★

▶ 많이 틀린 이유는?
글이 길어 문맥 파악이 어려웠을 수 있다. 실질적이지 않은 위험 뒤에 보상의 원리로 쾌락이 따른다는 것이 이 글의 핵심 주제이므로, 칠리를 싫어하는 어린이들도 실질적인 위험 없이 보상의 원리로 즐거움을 경험한다는 문장이 알맞다. 진짜 위험을 겪지 않는 것이 고통 뒤의 쾌락의 핵심이기 때문이다.

▶ 문제 해결 방법은?
다른 문제와 마찬가지로 문맥 파악이 중요하다. 주제 문장을 찾아도 풀기가 어렵다면, 주제에 어울리지 않는 문장을 추린 후, 반대의 뜻을 가진 단어로 해석해보자. 반대의 뜻이 어색하지 않고 자연스러운 선택지를 고르면 된다.

(A)

An airplane flew high above / the deep blue seas / far from any land.
비행기가 위로 높이 날아가고 있었다. / 깊고 푸른 바다 / 육지에서 멀리 떨어진 곳에서

『Flying the small plane / was a student pilot / who was sitting alongside / an experienced flight instructor.』 45번 ①의 근거 일치
작은 비행기를 조종하고 있는 사람은 / 학생 조종사였고, / 그 옆에 앉아 있었다. / 경험 많은 비행 교관이

As the student looked out the window, / (a) she was filled with wonder and appreciation / for the beauty of the world.
학생이 창밖을 바라보자, / 그녀는 경이로움과 감사함으로 가득 차게 되었다. / 세상의 아름다움에 대한

Her instructor, meanwhile, / waited patiently / for the right time / to start a surprise flight emergency training exercise.
그녀의 교관은, 그동안, / 인내심 있게 기다리고 있었다. / 적절한 순간을 / 갑작스러운 비행 비상 훈련을 시작할

(D)

When the plane hit a bit of turbulence, / the instructor pushed a hidden button.
비행기가 약간의 난기류에 부딪혔을 때, / 교관이 숨겨진 버튼을 눌렀다.

『Suddenly, / all the monitors inside the plane / flashed several times / then went out completely!』 45번 ④의 근거 불일치
갑자기, / 비행기 안의 모든 모니터가 / 여러 번 깜빡이더니 / 완전히 꺼져 버렸다!

Now the student was in control of an airplane that was flying well, / but (e) she had no indication of where she was / or where she should go.
이제 학생은 잘 날고 있는 비행기를 조종하고 있었지만, / 그녀는 자신이 어디에 있는지, / 어디로 가야 할지 알 수 없었다.

『She did have a map, / but no other instruments.』 45번 ⑤의 근거 일치
그녀에게는 지도는 있었지만, / 다른 계기들은 없었다.

She was at a loss / and then the plane shook again.
그녀는 당황했고, / 비행기는 다시 흔들렸다.

(C)

When the student began to panic, / the instructor said, "Stay calm and steady. / (c) You can do it."
학생이 당황하기 시작했을 때, / 교관이 말했다. / "침착하고 안정적으로 해. / 너는 할 수 있어."

Calm as ever, / the instructor told her student, / "Difficult times always happen during flight.
언제나처럼 침착하게, / 교관은 학생에게 말했다, / "비행 중에는 언제나 어려운 순간이 찾아온다.

『The most important thing / is to focus on your flight in those situations."』 45번 ③의 근거 일치
가장 중요한 것은 / 그러한 상황에서 비행에 집중하는 거야."

Those words encouraged the student / to focus on flying the aircraft first.
그 말은 학생을 격려했고, / 학생은 먼저 비행기에 집중하게 되었다.

"Thank you, / I think (d) I can make it," / she said, / "As I've been trained, / I should search for visual markers."
"고맙습니다. / 저 해낼 수 있을 것 같아요." / 그녀는 말했다. / "제가 훈련받았던 것처럼, / 시각적 표식을 찾아봐야겠어요."

(B)

Then, the student carefully flew low enough / to see if she could find any ships / making their way across the surface of the ocean.
그 후, 학생은 조심스럽게 낮게 비행했다. / 배를 찾을 수 있는지 보기 위해 / 바다 위를 지나가고 있는

Now the instructor and the student / could see some ships.
이제 교관과 학생이 / 몇몇 배를 볼 수 있었다.

『Although the ships were far apart, / they were all sailing in a line.』 45번 ②의 근거 일치
배들이 서로 멀리 떨어져 있었지만, / 모두 한 줄로 항해하고 있었다.

With the line of ships in view, / the student could see the way / to home and safety.
배들의 줄이 보이자, / 학생은 길을 볼 수 있었다. / 집과 안전으로 가는

The student looked at (b) her in relief, / who smiled proudly back at her student.
학생은 그녀를 안도하며 바라보았고, / 교관은 자랑스러운 미소로 학생을 바라보았다.

(A)
비행기가 육지에서 멀리 떨어진 깊고 푸른 바다 위를 높이 날고 있었다. 소형 비행기를 조종하고 있는 것은 노련한 비행 교관과 나란히 앉아 있는 한 파일럿 교육생이었다. 교육생이 창문 밖을 바라볼 때, (a) 그녀는 세상의 아름다움에 대한 경이로움과 감탄으로 가득 차 있었다. 한편, 비행 교관은 비행 중 돌발 비상 상황 대처 훈련을 시작할 적절한 때를 인내심을 가지고 기다리고 있었다.

(D)
비행기가 약간의 난기류를 만났을 때, 교관은 숨겨진 버튼을 눌렀다. 갑자기, 비행기 안의 모든 모니터가 여러 번 깜빡이다가 완전히 꺼졌다! 이제 교육생은 잘 날고 있는 비행기를 조종하고 있었지만, (e) 그녀는 자신이 어디에 있는지, 어디로 가야 하는지 알 방도가 없었다. 교육생은 지도는 가지고 있었지만, 다른 도구는 가지고 있지 않았다. 그녀는 어쩔 줄 몰라 했고 그때 비행기가 다시 흔들렸다.

(C)
교육생이 당황하기 시작하자 교관은 "침착하세요. (c) 당신은 할 수 있습니다." 여느 때처럼 침착한 교관은 교육생에게 "비행 중에는 항상 어려운 상황이 발생합니다. 그러한 상황에서는 비행에 집중하는 것이 가장 중요합니다."라고 말했다. 그 말이 교육생이 먼저 비행에 집중할 수 있게끔 용기를 주었다. "감사합니다. (d) 제가 해낼 수 있을 것 같아요."라고 그녀는 말했다. "훈련받은 대로, 저는 시각 표식을 찾아야겠어요."

(B)
그런 다음 교육생은 바다 표면을 가로지르는 배가 보이는지 확인할 수 있을 정도로 충분히 낮게 조심히 비행하였다. 이제 교관과 교육생이 배 몇 척을 볼 수 있었다. 배들은 멀리 떨어져 있었지만 모두 한 줄을 이루고 항해하고 있었다. 배들이 줄을 지어있는 것이 보이자, 교육생은 안전하게 복귀하는 길을 알 수 있었다. 교육생은 안도하며 (b) 그녀를 바라봤고, 그녀도 교육생을 향해 자랑스럽게 웃어보였다.

- **instructor** ⓝ 교관
- **appreciation** ⓝ 감사
- **emergency** ⓝ 긴급 상황
- **aircraft** ⓝ 비행기
- **wonder** ⓝ 궁금증
- **patiently** [ad] 침착하게
- **relief** ⓝ 안도
- **turbulence** ⓝ 난기류

구문 풀이

[B] 1행 Then, the student carefully flew low enough to see if she could find any
　　　　　　　　　　　　　　　　　　　　to부정사(부사적 용법)◀┘　가정법
ships (that were) making their way across the surface of the ocean.
　　　　현재분사 주격관계대명사 + be동사 생략

---

43 글의 순서 파악　　　정답률 69% | 정답 ⑤

주어진 글 (A)에 이어질 내용을 순서에 맞게 배열한 것으로 가장 적절한 것은?
① (B) – (D) – (C)　　　　② (C) – (B) – (D)
③ (C) – (D) – (B)　　　　④ (D) – (B) – (C)
✓⑤ (D) – (C) – (B)

Why? 왜 정답일까?

주어진 글은 파일럿 교육생과 비행 교관이 함께 비행을 하며 시작한다. 비행기가 난기류를 만난 장면을 묘사하는 **(D)**가, 비행 교관이 격려하는 **(C)**, 마지막으로 힌트를 얻어 난기류를 잘 해결한 **(B)**의 순서가 자연스럽다. 따라서 알맞은 순서는 ⑤ **(D) – (C) – (B)**이다.

44 지칭 추론　　　정답률 65% | 정답 ②

밑줄 친 (a) ~ (e) 중에서 가리키는 대상이 나머지 넷과 다른 것은?
① (a)　　✓② (b)　　③ (c)　　④ (d)　　⑤ (e)

Why? 왜 정답일까?

(a), (c), (d), (e) 모두 비행 교육생을 가리키기 때문에, 비행 교관을 뜻하는 **(b)**는 가리키는 대상이 나머지 넷과 다르다. 따라서 답은 ② '**(b)**'이다.

45 세부 내용 파악　　　정답률 67% | 정답 ④

윗글에 관한 내용으로 적절하지 않은 것은?
① 교관과 교육생이 소형 비행기에 타고 있었다.
② 배들은 서로 떨어져 있었지만 한 줄을 이루고 있었다.
③ 교관은 어려운 상황에서는 집중이 가장 중요하다고 말했다.
✓④ 비행기 내부의 모니터가 깜박이다가 다시 정상 작동했다.
⑤ 교육생은 지도 이외의 다른 도구는 가지고 있지 않았다.

Why? 왜 정답일까?

(D)의 'Suddenly, all the monitors inside the plane flashed several times then went out completely!'에서 알 수 있듯이, 비행기의 내부 모니터는 깜박이더니 완전히 나가버렸다. 윗글에 대한 내용으로 적절하지 않은 것은 '④ 비행기 내부의 모니터가 깜박이다가 다시 정상 작동했다.'이다.

Why? 왜 오답일까?

① (A) 'Flying the small plane was a student pilot who was sitting alongside an experienced flight instructor'의 내용과 일치한다.
② (B) 'Although the ships were far apart, they were all sailing in a line.'의 내용과 일치한다.
③ (C) 'The most important thing is to focus on your flight in those situations.'의 내용과 일치한다.
⑤ (D) 'She did have a map, but no other instruments.'의 내용과 일치한다.

01 to celebrate our success / be available until / your own personal cups
02 an artificial-intelligence website / used to think so / keep that in mind
03 Social media lets you / luxurious trip may make / feel small about yourself
04 kite stuck in the / holding balloons in her / romance to the scene
05 applied for the science / go over my checklist / biology experiment before
06 looking for a backpack / special discount only on / your niece will love
07 preparing for tomorrow's club / presenting a magic show / have to attend my
08 participants are they expecting / expect about the same / look forward to
09 delighted to announce that / who are now majoring / The deadline for registration
10 new cordless vacuum cleaner / a wet cleaning function / looks better to me
11 us adopting a cat / a lot of responsibility / totally ready for it
12 about the math assignment / You need to submit / still have some time
13 Have you been playing / visited a local clinic / come from bad posture
14 climate change is kind / won't be able to / can also be helpful
15 looking unusually tired / without taking a break / really worried about him
16-17 your current student representative / following these instructions / pamphlets is allowed

어휘 Review Test 04　　문제편 056쪽

A	B	C	D
01 계획하다	01 tribe	01 ⓜ	01 ①
02 기사	02 switch	02 ①	02 ⓞ
03 지시	03 evidence	03 ⓚ	03 ⓔ
04 배출	04 relief	04 ⓓ	04 ⓗ
05 특허권	05 interval	05 ⓖ	05 ①
06 발표하다, 밝히다	06 apply	06 ⓟ	06 ⓠ
07 분위기	07 comparison	07 ①	07 ⓐ
08 뛰다	08 capacity	08 ⓔ	08 ⓢ
09 구별하다	09 migrate	09 ⓗ	09 ⓖ
10 청각의	10 struggle	10 ①	10 ⓟ
11 영감	11 rapid	11 ①	11 ⓓ
12 묘사하다	12 labor	12 ⓢ	12 ⓡ
13 드러내다	13 ecosystem	13 ⓞ	13 ⓝ
14 길	14 destructive	14 ⓒ	14 ①
15 긴급 상황	15 punishment	15 ⓑ	15 ⓚ
16 빠르게	16 document	16 ⓡ	16 ①
17 선호	17 preserve	17 ①	17 ⓑ
18 감사하다	18 souvenir	18 ⓐ	18 ⓜ
19 주변	19 supply	19 ⓠ	19 ①
20 검사하다	20 hardship	20 ⓝ	20 ⓒ

• 정답 •

01 ② 02 ① 03 ① 04 ④ 05 ⑤　06 ③ 07 ④ 08 ③ 09 ⑤ 10 ④　11 ① 12 ③ 13 ② 14 ⑤ 15 ⑤
16 ③ 17 ④ 18 ② 19 ① 20 ⑤　21 ① 22 ③ 23 ② 24 ① 25 ④　26 ② 27 ⑤ 28 ⑤ 29 ④ 30 ②
31 ④ 32 ① 33 ② 34 ③ 35 ④　36 ② 37 ⑤ 38 ② 39 ⑤ 40 ②　41 ④ 42 ③ 43 ④ 44 ② 45 ③

★ 표기된 문항은 [등급을 가르는 문제]에 해당하는 문제입니다.

01 　연례 게임 대회 자원봉사자 모집　정답률 92% | 정답 ②

다음을 듣고, 여자가 하는 말의 목적으로 가장 적절한 것을 고르시오.
① 체육대회 종목을 소개하려고
☑ 대회 자원봉사자를 모집하려고
③ 학생 회장 선거 일정을 공지하려고
④ 경기 관람 규칙 준수를 당부하려고
⑤ 학교 홈페이지 주소 변경을 안내하려고

W : Good afternoon, everybody.
　안녕하세요, 여러분.
　This is your student council president, Monica Brown.
　저는 학생회장 Monica Brown입니다.
　Our school's annual e-sports competition will be held on the last day of the semester.
　우리 학교가 매년 하는 게임 대회가 이번 학기 마지막 날에 열릴 예정입니다.
　For the competition, we need some volunteers to help set up computers.
　대회를 위해, 우리는 컴퓨터 설치를 도와줄 자원봉사자가 좀 필요합니다.
　If you're interested in helping us make the competition successful, please fill out the volunteer application form and email it to me.
　만일 여러분이 우리가 대회를 성공적으로 이끌도록 돕고 싶으시다면, 자원봉사자 신청서를 작성해서 제게 이메일로 보내주세요.
　For more information, please visit our school website.
　더 많은 정보를 보려면, 학교 웹 사이트를 방문해주세요.
　I hope many of you will join us. Thank you for listening.
　여러분들이 많이 함께해주시길 바랍니다. 들어주셔서 고맙습니다.

Why? 왜 정답일까?

게임 대회를 맞아 자원봉사자가 필요하다는(**For the competition, we need some volunteers to help set up computers.**) 내용이므로, 여자가 하는 말의 목적으로 가장 적절한 것은 ② '대회 자원봉사자를 모집하려고'이다.

● **annual** ⓐ 연마다 하는
● **competition** ⓝ 대회, 경쟁
● **application form** 신청서
● **e-sports** ⓝ 게임, e-스포츠
● **fill out** 작성하다

02 　산책으로 창의력 높이기　정답률 90% | 정답 ①

대화를 듣고, 남자의 의견으로 가장 적절한 것을 고르시오.
☑ 산책은 창의적인 생각을 할 수 있게 돕는다.
② 식사 후 과격한 운동은 소화를 방해한다.
③ 지나친 스트레스는 집중력을 감소시킨다.
④ 독서를 통해 창의력을 증진할 수 있다.
⑤ 꾸준한 운동은 기초체력을 향상시킨다.

M : Hannah, how's your design project going?
　Hannah, 네 디자인 프로젝트는 어떻게 돼 가?
W : Hey, Aiden. I'm still working on it, but I'm not making much progress.
　안녕, Aiden. 아직 작업 중인데. 그다지 진전이 안 되네.
M : Can you tell me what the problem is?
　문제가 뭔지 말해줄래?
W : Hmm... [Pause] It's hard to think of creative ideas. I feel like I'm wasting my time.
　흠… [잠시 멈춤] 창의적인 아이디어를 생각하기가 어려워. 난 시간 낭비 중인 거 같아.
M : I understand. Why don't you take a walk?
　이해해. 산책을 해보면 어때?
W : How can that help me to improve my creativity?
　그게 내 창의력을 높이는 데 어떻게 도움이 되지?
M : It will actually make your brain more active. Then you'll see things differently.
　그건 실제로 네 뇌를 더 활동적이게 만들어. 그럼 넌 사물을 다르게 볼 수 있지.
W : But I don't have time for that.
　그런데 나 그럴 시간이 없어.
M : You don't need a lot of time. Even a short walk will help you to come up with creative ideas.
　시간이 많이 필요한 게 아냐. 잠깐 산책하는 것만으로도 창의적인 생각을 하는 데 도움이 될 거야.
W : Then I'll try it. Thanks for the tip.
　그럼 시도해봐야겠어. 조언 고마워.

Why? 왜 정답일까?

창의적인 생각을 떠올리기가 어렵다는 여자에게 남자는 산책을 권하며, 짧은 산책일지라도 창의력 증진에 도움이 된다고 조언한다(**Even a short walk will help you to come up with creative ideas.**). 따라서 남자의 의견으로 가장 적절한 것은 ① '산책은 창의적인 생각을 할 수 있게 돕는다.'이다.

● **work on** ~을 작업하다
● **waste** ⓥ 낭비하다
● **have time for** ~할 시간이 있다
● **make progress** 진전되다
● **take a walk** 산책하다

03 　우체국에서 물건 부치기　정답률 88% | 정답 ①

대화를 듣고, 두 사람의 관계를 가장 잘 나타낸 것을 고르시오.

☑ 고객 – 우체국 직원　　② 투숙객 – 호텔 지배인
③ 여행객 – 여행 가이드　　④ 아파트 주민 – 경비원
⑤ 손님 – 옷가게 주인

W : Excuse me. Could you please tell me where I can put this box?
실례합니다. 제가 이 박스를 어디에 놓으면 될지 말해주실래요?
M : Right here on this counter. How can I help you today?
여기 이 카운터에 놔주세요. 오늘은 뭘 도와드릴까요?
W : I'd like to send this to Jeju Island.
이걸 제주도에 보내고 싶어요.
M : Sure. Are there any breakable items in the box?
알겠습니다. 상자 안에 깨지기 쉬운 물건이라도 들어 있나요?
W : No, there are only clothes in it.
아뇨, 옷밖에 없어요.
M : Then, there should be no problem.
그럼, 아무 문제가 없을 겁니다.
W : I see. What's the fastest way to send it?
네. 제일 빠른 배송 방법이 뭔가요?
M : You can send the package by express mail, but there's an extra charge.
급행 우편으로 보내실 수 있는데, 추가 비용이 있습니다.
W : That's okay. I want it to be delivered as soon as possible. When will it arrive in Jeju if it goes out today?
괜찮아요. 최대한 빨리 보내고 싶어요. 오늘 배송 나가면 언제 제주도에 도착할까요?
M : If you send it today, it will be there by this Friday.
오늘 보내시면 이번 주 금요일이면 도착할 겁니다.
W : Oh, Friday will be great. I'll do the express mail.
오, 금요일이면 아주 좋겠네요. 급행 우편 할게요.

Why? 왜 정답일까?

'I'd like to send this to Jeju Island.', 'Sure. Are there any breakable items in the box?', 'What's the fastest way to send it?', 'You can send the package by express mail, but there's an extra charge.', 'I'll do the express mail.'에서 여자는 물건을 부치는 고객이고, 남자는 이를 처리해주는 우체국 직원임을 알 수 있다. 따라서 두 사람의 관계로 가장 적절한 것은 ① '고객 – 우체국 직원'이다.

- breakable ⓐ 깨지기 쉬운
- express mail 급행 우편
- deliver ⓥ 배달하다
- package ⓝ 소포
- extra charge 추가 비용

---

04 버스킹 사진 구경하기　　정답률 87% | 정답 ④

대화를 듣고, 그림에서 대화의 내용과 일치하지 않는 것을 고르시오.

M : Kayla, I heard you went busking on the street last weekend.
Kayla, 나 네가 지난 주말에 거리에 버스킹하러 갔다고 들었어.
W : It was amazing! I've got a picture here. Look!
아주 멋졌어! 여기 사진이 있어. 봐봐!
M : 「Oh, you're wearing the hat I gave you.」 ①의 근거 일치
오, 너 내가 준 모자를 쓰고 있구나.
W : Yeah, I really like it.
응, 나 그거 아주 마음에 들어.
M : Looks great. 「This boy playing the guitar next to you must be your brother Kevin.」 ②의 근거 일치
잘 어울리네. 네 옆에서 기타 치는 이 남자애는 네 남동생 Kevin이겠구나.
W : You're right. He played while I sang.
맞아. 내가 노래하는 동안 걔는 연주를 했어.
M : Cool. 「Why did you leave the guitar case open?」 ③의 근거 일치
근사한걸. 기타 케이스는 왜 열어둔 거야?
W : That's for the audience. If they like our performance, they give us some money.
관객들 때문에. 우리 공연이 마음에 들면 돈을 좀 주라고.
M : 「Oh, and you set up two speakers!」 ④의 근거 불일치
오, 그리고 너네 스피커도 두 개 설치해 뒀구나!
W : I did. I recently bought them.
응. 최근에 샀어.
M : I see. 「And did you design that poster on the wall?」 ⑤의 근거 일치
그렇구나. 그리고 벽에 있는 저 포스터는 네가 디자인했어?
W : Yeah. My brother and I worked on it together.
응. 내 남동생이랑 나랑 같이 작업했어.
M : It sounds like you really had a lot of fun!
둘이 되게 재미있었겠다!

Why? 왜 정답일까?

대화에서 스피커는 두 개였다고 하는데(Oh, and you set up two speakers!), 그림 속 스피커는 하나뿐이다. 따라서 그림에서 대화의 내용과 일치하지 않는 것은 ④이다.

- busk ⓥ 버스킹하다, 거리 공연하다
- leave open 열어두다
- recently ⓐⓓ 최근에
- amazing ⓐ 멋진, 근사한
- performance ⓝ 공연, 성과

---

05 아들의 생일 파티 준비하기　　정답률 90% | 정답 ⑤

대화를 듣고, 남자가 할 일로 가장 적절한 것을 고르시오.
① 초대장 보내기　　② 피자 주문하기
③ 거실 청소하기　　④ 꽃다발 준비하기
☑ 스마트폰 사러 가기

W : Honey, are we ready for Jake's birthday party tomorrow?
여보, 우리 내일 Jake의 생일 파티 준비가 다 되었나요?
M : I sent the invitation cards last week. What about other things?
내가 지난주에 초대장을 보냈어요. 다른 건요?
W : I'm not sure. Let's check.
모르겠어요. 확인해보죠.
M : We are expecting a lot of guests. How about the dinner menu?
손님이 많이 올 거예요. 저녁 메뉴는 뭐죠?
W : I haven't decided yet.
아직 결정 못했어요.
M : We won't have much time to cook, so let's just order pizza.
우린 요리할 시간이 많지 않을 테니까, 그냥 피자를 주문하죠.
W : Okay. I'll do it tomorrow. What about the present?
알겠어요. 내가 내일 할게요. 선물은 어떻게요?
M : Oh, you mean the smartphone? I forgot to get it!
오, 스마트폰 말하는 거죠? 그걸 사는 걸 잊었네요!
W : That's alright. Can you go to the electronics store and buy it now?
괜찮아요. 지금 전자제품 가게 좀 가서 사올래요?
M : No problem. I'll do it right away.
문제 없어요. 바로 할게요.
W : Good. Then, I'll clean up the living room while you're out.
알겠어요. 그럼 당신이 외출한 동안 내가 거실을 치울게요.

Why? 왜 정답일까?

아들의 생일 선물은 스마트폰을 깜빡 잊고 못 샀다는 남자에게 여자는 지금 사 와달라고 부탁한다(Can you go to the electronics store and buy it now? / No problem. I'll do it right away.). 따라서 남자가 할 일로 가장 적절한 것은 ⑤ '스마트폰 사러 가기'이다.

- invitation card 초대장
- forget to ~해야 하는 걸 잊다
- present ⓝ 선물
- clean up 청소하다, 치우다

---

06 소파에 놓을 담요와 쿠션 구매하기　　정답률 80% | 정답 ③

대화를 듣고, 여자가 지불할 금액을 고르시오. [3점]
① $54　② $60　☑ $72　④ $76　⑤ $80

M : Good morning! How can I help you?
안녕하세요! 뭘 도와드릴까요?
W : Hi. I'm looking for a blanket and some cushions for my sofa.
안녕하세요. 전 소파에 놓을 담요랑 쿠션을 좀 찾고 있어요.
M : Okay. We've got some on sale. Would you like to have a look?
알겠습니다. 세일하는 제품이 좀 있습니다. 살펴보시겠어요?
W : Yes. How much is this green blanket?
네. 이 녹색 담요는 얼만가요?
M : That's $40.
40달러입니다.
W : Oh, I love the color green. Can you also show me some cushions that go well with this blanket?
오, 전 녹색을 좋아해요. 이 담요랑 잘 어울리는 쿠션도 좀 보여주실래요?
M : Sure! How about these?
물론이죠! 이건 어때요?
W : They look good. I need two of them. How much are they?
좋아 보이네요. 두 개 필요해요. 얼만가요?
M : The cushions are $20 each.
쿠션은 하나에 20달러입니다.
W : Okay. I'll take one green blanket and two cushions. Can I use this coupon?
알겠어요. 전 녹색 담요 하나랑 쿠션 두 개를 사겠어요. 제가 이 쿠폰을 사용해도 되나요?
M : Sure. It will give you 10% off the total.
물론이죠. 총액에서 10퍼센트 할인됩니다.
W : Thanks! Here's my credit card.
고맙습니다! 여기 제 신용 카드요.

Why? 왜 정답일까?

대화에 따르면 여자는 40달러짜리 담요 한 장과 20달러짜리 쿠션을 두 개 구입하고, 총액에서 10퍼센트를 할인받기로 했다. 이를 식으로 나타내면 '$(40 + 20 \times 2) \times 0.9 = 72$'이므로, 여자가 지불할 금액은 ③ '$72'이다.

- blanket ⓝ 담요
- have a look 살펴보다
- on sale 할인 중인
- go well with ~와 잘 어울리다

---

07 록 콘서트에 가자고 제안하기　　정답률 92% | 정답 ④

대화를 듣고, 남자가 록 콘서트에 갈 수 없는 이유를 고르시오.
① 일을 하러 가야 해서
② 피아노 연습을 해야 해서
③ 할머니를 뵈러 가야 해서
☑ 친구의 개를 돌봐야 해서
⑤ 과제를 아직 끝내지 못해서

W : Hello, Justin. What are you doing?
안녕, Justin. 뭐 하고 있어?
M : Hi, Ellie. I'm doing my project for art class.
안녕, Ellie. 나 미술 수업 프로젝트 하고 있어.
W : Can you go to a rock concert with me this Saturday? My sister gave me two tickets!
너 이번 주 토요일에 나랑 록 콘서트 갈래? 우리 언니가 표를 두 장 줬어!

M : I'd love to! *[Pause]* But I'm afraid I can't.
나도 가고 싶어! *[잠시 멈춤]* 근데 미안하지만 안 되겠어.

W : Do you have to work that day?
그날 일해야 돼?

M : No, I don't work on Saturdays.
아니, 나 토요일엔 일 안 하지.

W : Then, why not? I thought you really like rock music.
그럼 왜? 너 록 음악 되게 좋아하는 줄 알았는데.

M : Of course I do. But I have to take care of my friend's dog this Saturday.
물론 좋아하지. 근데 이번 주 토요일엔 내 친구네 개를 돌봐줘야 해.

W : Oh, really? Is your friend going somewhere?
오, 그래? 네 친구는 어디 가는 거야?

M : He's visiting his grandmother that day.
그날 자기 할머니를 뵈러 간대.

W : Okay, no problem. I'm sure I can find someone else to go with me.
알겠어, 괜찮아. 난 같이 갈 다른 사람 찾을 수 있겠지.

Why? 왜 정답일까?

남자는 토요일에 할머니를 뵈러 가는 친구네 개를 돌봐주기로 해서(But I have to take care of my friend's dog this Saturday.) 여자와 함께 콘서트에 갈 수 없다고 한다. 따라서 남자가 록 콘서트에 갈 수 없는 이유로 가장 적절한 것은 ④ '친구의 개를 돌봐야 해서'이다.

- **I'm afraid I can't.** 미안하지만 안 되겠어.
- **somewhere** ad 어딘가
- **take care of** ~을 돌보다

---

08 환경의 날 행사   정답률 93% | 정답 ③

대화를 듣고, Eco Day에 관해 언급되지 <u>않은</u> 것을 고르시오.
① 행사 시간   ② 행사 장소   ☑ 참가비
④ 준비물   ⑤ 등록 방법

W : Scott, did you see this Eco Day poster?
Scott, 너 이 Eco Day(환경의 날) 포스터 봤어?

M : No, not yet. Let me see. *[Pause]* It's an event for picking up trash while walking around a park.
아니, 아직. 나 볼래. *[잠시 멈춤]* 공원을 걸으면서 쓰레기를 줍는 행사구나.

W : Why don't we do it together? 「It's next Sunday from 10 a.m. to 5 p.m.」 ①의근거 일치
우리 이거 같이 하면 어때? 다음 주 토요일 아침 10시부터 오후 5시까지야.

M : Sounds good. I've been thinking a lot about the environment lately.
좋네. 난 최근에 환경 생각을 많이 하고 있어.

W : Me, too. 「Also, the event will be held in Eastside Park.」 You know, we often used to go there. ②의근거 일치
나도 그래. 게다가, 이 행사는 Eastside Park에서 열린대. 알다시피 우리 자주 거기 갔잖아.

M : That's great. Oh, look at this. 「We have to bring our own gloves and small bags for the trash.」 ④의근거 일치
아주 좋네. 오, 이거 봐. 우린 장갑이랑 쓰레기 담을 작은 가방을 가져와야 해.

W : No problem. I have extra. I can bring some for you as well.
문제 없어. 나 남는 거 있어. 내가 네 것도 좀 가져올 수 있어.

M : Okay, thanks. 「Do we have to sign up for the event?」
알겠어, 고마워. 우리 행사 등록해야 하나?

W : Yes. The poster says we can do it online. ⑤의근거 일치
응. 포스터에 온라인으로 하면 된다고 적혀 있어.

M : Let's do it right now. I'm looking forward to it.
지금 바로 하자. 기대된다.

Why? 왜 정답일까?

대화에서 남자와 여자는 Eco Day의 행사 시간, 행사 장소, 준비물, 등록 방법을 언급하므로, 언급되지 않은 것은 ③ '참가비'이다.

Why? 왜 오답일까?

① 'It's next Sunday from 10 a.m. to 5 p.m.'에서 '행사 시간'이 언급되었다.
② 'Also, the event will be held in Eastside Park.'에서 '행사 장소'가 언급되었다.
④ 'We have to bring our own gloves and small bags for the trash.'에서 '준비물'이 언급되었다.
⑤ 'The poster says we can do it online.'에서 '등록 방법'이 언급되었다.

- **pick up** 줍다
- **Why don't we ~?** ~하면 어때?
- **look forward to** ~을 고대하다
- **trash** n 쓰레기
- **sign up for** ~에 등록하다, 신청하다

---

09 교내 팀 댄스 대회 안내   정답률 80% | 정답 ⑤

Eastville Dance Contest에 관한 다음 내용을 듣고, 일치하지 <u>않는</u> 것을 고르시오.
① 처음으로 개최되는 경연이다.
② 모든 종류의 춤이 허용된다.
③ 춤 영상을 8월 15일까지 업로드 해야 한다.
④ 학생들은 가장 좋아하는 영상에 투표할 수 있다.
☑ 우승팀은 상으로 상품권을 받게 될 것이다.

M : Hello, Eastville High School students. This is your P.E. teacher, Mr. Wilson.
안녕하세요, Eastville 고교 학생 여러분. 체육 교사 Wilson 선생님입니다.
「I'm pleased to let you know that we're hosting the first Eastville Dance Contest.」 ①의근거 일치
여러분께 제 1회 Eastville Dance Contest가 개최된다는 것을 알리게 되어 기쁩니다.
Any Eastville students who love dancing can participate in the contest as a team.
춤추는 것을 좋아하는 모든 Eastville 학생들은 팀으로 대회에 참가할 수 있습니다.
「All kinds of dance are allowed.」 ②의근거 일치
모든 종류의 춤이 허용됩니다.
「If you'd like to participate, please upload your team's dance video to our school website by August 15th.」 ③의근거 일치
참가하고 싶다면, 8월 15일까지 여러분 팀의 댄스 영상을 우리 학교 웹 사이트에 업로드 해주세요.
「Students can vote for their favorite video from August 16th to 20th.」 ④의근거 일치
학생들은 8월 16일부터 20일까지 가장 좋아하는 영상에 투표할 수 있습니다.

05회

「The winning team will receive a trophy as a prize.」 ⑤의근거 불일치
우승팀은 상으로 트로피를 받게 됩니다.
Don't miss this great opportunity to show off your talents!
여러분의 재능을 뽐낼 이 대단한 기회를 놓치지 마세요!

Why? 왜 정답일까?

'The winning team will receive a trophy as a prize.'에서 우승팀에는 트로피가 수여된다고 하므로, 내용과 일치하지 않는 것은 ⑤ '우승팀은 상으로 상품권을 받게 될 것이다.'이다.

Why? 왜 오답일까?

① '~ we're hosting the first Eastville Dance Contest.'의 내용과 일치한다.
② 'All kinds of dance are allowed.'의 내용과 일치한다.
③ 'If you'd like to participate, please upload your team's dance video to our school website by August 15th.'의 내용과 일치한다.
④ 'Students can vote for their favorite video from August 16th to 20th.'의 내용과 일치한다.

- **pleased** a 기쁜
- **all kinds of** 모든 종류의
- **vote for** ~을 위해 투표하다
- **participate in** ~에 참가하다
- **allow** v 허용하다
- **show off** 뽐내다, 보여주다

---

10 새집에 놓을 정수기 사기   정답률 87% | 정답 ④

다음 표를 보면서 대화를 듣고, 두 사람이 구입할 정수기를 고르시오.

Water Purifiers

	Model	Price	Water Tank Capacity(liters)	Power-saving Mode	Warranty
①	A	$570	4	×	1 year
②	B	$650	5	○	1 year
③	C	$680	5	×	3 years
☑	D	$740	5	○	3 years
⑤	E	$830	6	○	3 years

M : Honey, we need a water purifier for our new house.
여보, 우리 새집에 둘 정수기가 필요해요.

W : You're right. Let's order one online.
당신 말이 옳아요. 온라인에서 하나 주문하죠.

M : Good idea. *[Clicking Sound]* Look! These are the five bestsellers.
좋은 생각이에요. *[클릭하는 소리]* 이거 봐요! 이게 베스트셀러 다섯 개예요.

W : I see. 「What's our budget?」
그렇군요. 우리 예산이 얼마죠?

M : Well, I don't want to spend more than 800 dollars. 근거1 Price 조건
음, 800달러 넘게는 쓰고 싶지 않군요.

W : 「Okay, how about the water tank capacity?」
알겠어요. 물 탱크 용량은요?

M : I think the five-liter tank would be perfect for us.」 근거2 Water Tank Capacity 조건
5리터짜리 탱크면 우리한테 딱 좋겠어요.

W : I think so, too. 「And I like the ones with a power-saving mode.」 근거3 Power-saving Mode 조건
나도 그렇게 생각해요. 그리고 난 절전 모드가 있는 게 좋아요.

M : Okay, then we can save electricity. Now, there are just two options left.
그래요, 그럼 우린 전기를 절약할 수 있겠죠. 이제, 두 가지 선택권이 남았군요.

W : 「Let's look at the warranties. The longer, the better.」 근거4 Warranty 조건
보증 기간을 보죠. 길수록 좋죠.

M : I agree. We should order this model.
동의해요. 이 제품으로 주문해야겠어요.

Why? 왜 정답일까?

대화에 따르면 남자와 여자는 금액이 800달러를 넘지 않으면서, 물 탱크 용량은 5리터이고, 절전 모드가 있으면서, 보증 기간은 더 긴 정수기를 사기로 한다. 따라서 두 사람이 구입할 정수기는 ④ 'D'이다.

- **water purifier** 정수기
- **power-saving mode** 절전 모드
- **warranty** n 보증 (기간)
- **capacity** n 용량
- **electricity** n 전기

---

11 자동차 전시회   정답률 72% | 정답 ①

대화를 듣고, 남자의 마지막 말에 대한 여자의 응답으로 가장 적절한 것을 고르시오.
☑ Great. We don't have to wait in line. - 좋아. 우린 줄 서서 기다릴 필요가 없네.
② All right. We can come back later. - 알겠어. 다음에 다시 오면 돼.
③ Good job. Let's buy the tickets. - 잘했어. 표를 사자.
④ No worries. I will stand in line. - 걱정 마. 내가 줄 서 있을게.
⑤ Too bad. I can't buy that car. - 아깝네. 난 그 차를 살 수 없어.

M : Let's get inside. I'm so excited to see this auto show.
들어가자. 난 이 자동차 전시회 보게 돼서 무척 신나.

W : Look over there. So many people are already standing in line to buy tickets.
저기 봐. 엄청 많은 사람들이 벌써 표를 사려고 줄을 서 있어.

M : Fortunately, I bought our tickets in advance.
다행히도 난 우리 표를 미리 샀어.

W : Great. We don't have to wait in line.
좋아. 우린 줄 서서 기다릴 필요가 없네.

Why? 왜 정답일까?

여자가 자동차 전시회 표를 사기 위해 늘어선 줄을 보고 하자 남자는 미리 표를 사두었다(Fortunately, I bought our tickets in advance.)고 한다. 따라서 여자의 응답으로 가장 적절한 것은 ① '좋아. 우린 줄 서서 기다릴 필요가 없네.'이다.

- **auto show** 자동차 전시회
- **in advance** 미리
- **stand in line** 줄 서서 기다리다

12 역사 시험 점수 확인 　　　　　　　　　정답률 72% | 정답 ③

대화를 듣고, 여자의 마지막 말에 대한 남자의 응답으로 가장 적절한 것을 고르시오.

① Yes. You can register online.
　응. 온라인으로 등록하면 돼.
② Sorry. I can't see you next week.
　미안. 나 다음 주에 너 못 만나.
✓③ Right. I should go to his office now.
　맞아. 지금 선생님 교무실로 가야겠어.
④ Fantastic! I'll take the test tomorrow.
　환상적이네! 내일 테스트를 치러야겠다.
⑤ Of course. I can help him if he needs my help.
　물론이지. 그분께서 도움이 필요하시면 내가 도와드릴 수 있어.

W : Hi, Chris. Did you check your grade for the history test we took last week?
　　안녕, Chris. 너 지난주 우리가 본 역사 시험 점수 확인해 봤어?
M : Yes. But I think there's something wrong with my grade.
　　응. 근데 내 성적에 뭔가 잘못된 거 같아.
W : Don't you think you should go ask Mr. Morgan about it?
　　너 Morgan 선생님께 가서 그거 여쭤봐야 한다고 생각하지 않아?
M : Right. I should go to his office now.
　　맞아. 지금 선생님 교무실로 가야겠어.

Why? 왜 정답일까?

역사 시험 점수가 잘못된 것 같다는 남자의 말에 여자는 선생님께 가서 확인해봐야 하지 않냐고(Don't you think you should go ask Mr. Morgan about it?) 말하므로, 남자의 응답으로 가장 적절한 것은 ③ '맞아. 지금 선생님 교무실로 가야겠어.'이다.

● grade ⓝ 점수
● go ask 가서 물어보다
● take a test 시험을 치다
● register ⓥ 등록하다

---

13 중고 책 안에 들어 있던 쪽지 　　　　　　　정답률 79% | 정답 ②

대화를 듣고, 여자의 마지막 말에 대한 남자의 응답으로 가장 적절한 것을 고르시오. [3점]
Man:

① I agree. You can save a lot by buying secondhand.
　같은 생각이에요. 중고를 사면 돈을 많이 아낄 수 있죠.
✓② Great idea! Our message would make others smile.
　좋은 생각이에요! 우리 메시지가 남들을 웃게 할 거예요.
③ Sorry. I forgot to write a message in the book.
　죄송해요. 전 책 안에 메시지를 써놓는다는 걸 까먹었어요.
④ Exactly. Taking notes during class is important.
　바로 그거예요. 수업 중에 필기하는 것은 중요해요.
⑤ Okay. We can arrive on time if we leave now.
　알겠어요. 우리가 지금 떠나면 제때 도착할 수 있어요.

M : Mom, did you write this note?
　　엄마, 엄마가 이 쪽지 쓰셨어요?
W : What's that?
　　그게 뭔데?
M : I found this in the book you gave me.
　　엄마가 주신 책에 이걸 찾았어요.
W : Oh, the one I bought for you at the secondhand bookstore last week?
　　오, 내가 지난 주 너한테 중고 서점에서 사다준 거 말이구나?
M : Yes. At first I thought it was a bookmark, but it wasn't. It's a note with a message!
　　네. 처음엔 책갈피인 줄 알았는데, 아니더라고요. 메시지가 적힌 쪽지였어요!
W : What does it say?
　　뭐라고 써 있는데?
M : It says, "I hope you enjoy this book."
　　'이 책을 재밌게 읽기 바랍니다.'라고 적혀 있어요.
W : How sweet! That really brings a smile to my face.
　　상냥해라! 정말 얼굴에 웃음이 지어지게 하네.
M : Yeah, mom. I love this message so much.
　　그러게요, 엄마. 전 이 메시지가 정말 마음에 들어요.
W : Well, then, why don't we leave a note if we resell this book later?
　　음, 그럼, 우리가 이 책을 나중에 다시 팔 때 쪽지를 남겨두면 어때?
M : Great idea! Our message would make others smile.
　　좋은 생각이에요! 우리 메시지가 남들을 웃게 할 거예요.

Why? 왜 정답일까?

중고 책 안에 있었던 쪽지를 읽고 기분이 좋았다는 남자의 말에 여자는 다음에 같은 책을 되팔 때 똑같이 쪽지를 써두자고(Well, then, why don't we leave a note if we resell this book later?) 제안하고 있다. 따라서 남자의 응답으로 가장 적절한 것은 ② '좋은 생각이에요! 우리 메시지가 남들을 웃게 할 거예요.'이다.

● secondhand bookstore 중고 서점
● take notes 필기하다
● resell ⓥ 되팔다

---

14 가족과 캠핑 가기 　　　　　　　　　　정답률 85% | 정답 ⑤

대화를 듣고, 남자의 마지막 말에 대한 여자의 응답으로 가장 적절한 것을 고르시오. [3점]
Woman:

① Why not? I can bring some food when we go camping.
　왜 안 되겠어? 우리 캠핑갈 때 내가 음식을 좀 가져갈 수 있어.
② I'm sorry. That fishing equipment is not for sale.
　미안해. 그 낚시 도구는 파는 게 아냐.
③ I don't think so. The price is most important.
　난 그렇게 생각 안 해. 가격이 제일 중요해.
④ Really? I'd love to meet your family.
　정말? 난 너희 가족을 만나보고 싶어.
✓⑤ No problem. You can use my equipment.
　문제 없어. 내 장비를 쓰면 돼.

M : Do you have any plans for this weekend, Sandy?
　　이번 주말 계획 있어, Sandy?
W : Hey, Evan. I'm planning to go camping with my family.
　　안녕, Evan. 가족하고 캠핑 갈 계획이야.
M : I've never gone before. Do you go camping often?
　　난 한 번도 가본 적이 없어. 넌 캠핑 자주 가?

---

15 책 대신 빌려달라고 부탁하기 　　　　　　정답률 91% | 정답 ⑤

다음 상황 설명을 듣고, Violet이 Peter에게 할 말로 가장 적절한 것을 고르시오.
Violet:

① Will you join the science club together? – 너 과학 동아리 같이 할래?
② Is it okay to use a card to pay for the drinks? – 음료 계산에 카드를 써도 될까?
③ Why don't we donate our books to the library? – 우리 책을 도서관에 기부하는 거 어때?
④ How about going to the cafeteria to have lunch? – 구내식당 가서 점심 먹는 거 어때?
✓⑤ Can you borrow the books for me with your card? – 네 카드로 나 대신 책을 빌려줄 수 있어?

W : Violet and Peter are classmates.
　　Violet과 Peter는 반 친구이다.
　　They're doing their science group assignment together.
　　그들은 과학 팀 과제를 함께 하는 중이다.
　　On Saturday morning, they meet at the public library.
　　토요일 아침, 그들은 공립 도서관에서 만난다.
　　They decide to find the books they need in different sections of the library.
　　그들은 도서관 각기 다른 구역에서 필요한 책을 찾기로 한다.
　　Violet finds two useful books and tries to check them out.
　　Violet은 유용한 책을 두 권 찾아서 대출하려고 한다.
　　Unfortunately, she suddenly realizes that she didn't bring her library card.
　　안타깝게도, 그녀는 문득 도서관 카드를 가져오지 않았음을 깨닫는다.
　　At that moment, Peter walks up to Violet.
　　그때, Peter가 Violet에게 다가온다.
　　So, Violet wants to ask Peter to check out the books for her because she knows he has his library card.
　　Peter는 도서관 카드를 갖고 있다는 것을 알기에 Violet은 그에게 자기 대신 책을 빌려달라고 부탁하려 한다.
　　In this situation, what would Violet most likely say to Peter?
　　이 상황에서, Violet은 Peter에게 뭐라고 말할 것인가?
Violet : Can you borrow the books for me with your card?
　　　　네 카드로 나 대신 책을 빌려줄 수 있어?

Why? 왜 정답일까?

상황에 따르면 Violet은 필요한 책을 찾았지만 도서관 카드가 없어 못 빌리므로, Peter에게 책을 대신 빌려달라고 부탁하려 한다(So, Violet wants to ask Peter to check out the books for her because she knows he has his library card.). 따라서 Violet이 Peter에게 할 말로 가장 적절한 것은 ⑤ '네 카드로 나 대신 책을 빌려줄 수 있어?'이다.

● group assignment 팀 과제
● section ⓝ 구역
● public ⓐ 공립의, 공공의
● check out 대출하다, 빌리다

16-17 숙면에 도움이 되는 음식

M : Hello, everyone. I'm Shawn Collins, a doctor at Collins Sleep Clinic.
　　안녕하세요, 여러분. 저는 Collins Sleep Clinic의 의사 Shawn Collins입니다.
　　Sleep is one of the most essential parts of our daily lives.
　　수면은 우리의 일상에서 가장 중요한 부분 중 하나죠.
　　「So today, I'm going to introduce the best foods for helping you sleep better.」 16번의 근거
　　그래서 오늘, 저는 여러분께 더 잘 잠드는 데 도움이 되는 최고의 음식을 소개해 드리려고 합니다.
　　「First, kiwi fruits contain a high level of hormones that help you fall asleep more quickly, sleep longer, and wake up less during the night.」 17번 ①의 근거 일치
　　첫 번째로, 키위는 더 빨리 잠들고, 더 오래 자고, 밤 시간 동안 덜 깨게 도와주는 호르몬이 많이 함유되어 있습니다.
　　「Second, milk is rich in vitamin D and it calms the mind and nerves.」 17번 ②의 근거 일치
　　둘째로, 우유는 비타민 D가 풍부하고 정신과 신경을 안정시켜 줍니다.
　　If you drink a cup of milk before you go to bed, it will definitely help you get a good night's sleep.
　　잠자리에 들기 전 우유 한 컵을 드시면, 확실히 숙면하는 데 도움이 될 것입니다.
　　「Third, nuts can help to produce the hormone that controls your internal body clock and sends signals for the body to sleep at the right time.」 17번 ③의 근거 일치
　　세 번째로, 견과류는 생체 시계를 조절하는 호르몬을 만드는 것을 도와주고, 몸이 제때 잠들도록 신호를 보냅니다.
　　「The last one is honey. Honey helps you sleep well because it reduces the hormone that keeps the brain awake!」 17번 ⑤의 근거 일치
　　마지막은 꿀입니다. 꿀은 뇌를 깨어있게 만드는 호르몬을 줄여줘서 잠을 잘 잘 수 있게 도와주죠!
　　Now, I'll show you some delicious diet plans using these foods.
　　이제, 이 음식들을 이용한 맛 좋은 식단을 알려드리겠습니다.

- essential ⓐ 필수적인
- nerve ⓝ 신경
- internal ⓐ 내부의
- disorder ⓝ 장애, 질환
- contain ⓥ 함유하다
- get a good night's sleep 숙면하다
- body clock 생체 시계

16 주제 파악 정답률 93% | 정답 ③

남자가 하는 말의 주제로 가장 적절한 것은?

① different causes of sleep disorders – 수면 장애의 다양한 원인
② various ways to keep foods fresh – 음식을 신선하게 보관하는 여러 방법
☑ foods to improve quality of sleep – 수면의 질을 높여주는 음식들
④ reasons for organic foods' popularity – 유기농 음식이 인기 있는 이유
⑤ origins of popular foods around the world – 세계의 인기 있는 음식의 기원

Why? 왜 정답일까?

잠을 더 잘 자게 해주는 음식을 소개하는 내용(So today, I'm going to introduce the best foods for helping you sleep better.)이므로, 남자가 하는 말의 주제로 가장 적절한 것은 ③ '수면의 질을 높여주는 음식들'이다.

17 언급 유무 파악 정답률 92% | 정답 ④

언급된 음식이 아닌 것은?

① kiwi fruits – 키위
② milk – 우유
③ nuts – 견과류
☑ tomatoes – 토마토
⑤ honey – 꿀

Why? 왜 정답일까?

담화에서 남자는 잠에 도움이 되는 음식으로 키위, 우유, 견과류, 꿀을 언급하므로, 언급되지 않은 것은 ④ '토마토'이다.

Why? 왜 오답일까?

① 'First, kiwi fruits contain a high level of hormones that help you fall asleep more quickly, sleep longer, and wake up less during the night.'에서 '키위'가 언급되었다.
② 'Second, milk is rich in vitamin D and it calms the mind and nerves.'에서 '우유'가 언급되었다.
③ 'Third, nuts can help to produce the hormone that controls your internal body clock and sends signals for the body to sleep at the right time.'에서 '견과류'가 언급되었다.
⑤ 'The last one is honey.'에서 '꿀'이 언급되었다.

18 여름 휴가 패키지 홍보 정답률 93% | 정답 ②

다음 글의 목적으로 가장 적절한 것은?

① 여행 일정 변경을 안내하려고
☑ 패키지 여행 상품을 홍보하려고
③ 여행 상품 불만족에 대해 사과하려고
④ 여행 만족도 조사 참여를 부탁하려고
⑤ 패키지 여행 업무 담당자를 모집하려고

ACC Travel Agency Customers:
ACC 여행사 고객님께
Have you ever wanted / to enjoy a holiday in nature?
당신은 원한 적이 있습니까? / 자연 속에서 휴가를 즐기기를
This summer is the best time / to turn your dream into reality.
이번 여름이 최고의 시간입니다. / 당신의 꿈을 현실로 바꿀
We have a perfect travel package for you.
우리에게는 당신을 위한 완벽한 패키지 여행 상품이 있습니다.
This travel package / includes special trips to Lake Madison / as well as massage and meditation to help you relax.
이 패키지 여행 상품은 / Lake Madison으로의 특별한 여행을 포함합니다. / 당신이 편히 쉴 수 있도록 돕는 마사지와 명상뿐만 아니라
Also, / we provide yoga lessons / taught by experienced instructors.
또한, / 우리는 요가 강의도 제공합니다. / 숙련된 강사에 의해 지도되는
If you book this package, / you will enjoy all this at a reasonable price.
만약 당신이 이 패키지를 예약한다면, / 당신은 이 모든 것을 합리적인 가격으로 즐길 것입니다.
We are sure / that it will be an unforgettable experience for you.
우리는 확신합니다. / 그것이 당신에게 잊지 못할 경험이 될 것이라고
If you call us, / we will be happy to give you more details.
당신이 우리에게 전화하시면, / 우리는 당신에게 더 많은 세부 사항을 기꺼이 알려드리겠습니다.

ACC 여행사 고객님께

자연 속에서 휴가를 즐기는 것을 원한 적이 있습니까? 이번 여름이 당신의 꿈을 현실로 바꿀 최고의 시간입니다. 우리에게는 당신을 위한 완벽한 패키지 여행 상품이 있습니다. 이 패키지 여행 상품은 당신이 편히 쉴 수 있도록 돕는 마사지와 명상뿐만 아니라 Lake Madison으로의 특별한 여행을 포함합니다. 또한, 우리는 숙련된 강사에 의해 지도되는 요가 강의도 제공합니다. 만약 당신이 이 패키지를 예약한다면, 당신은 이 모든 것을 합리적인 가격으로 즐길 것입니다. 우리는 그것이 당신에게 잊지 못할 경험이 될 것이라고 확신합니다. 우리에게 전화하시면, 우리는 당신에게 더 많은 세부 사항을 기꺼이 알려드리겠습니다.

Why? 왜 정답일까?

여름 휴가에 적합한 패키지 여행 상품이 있음을 홍보하는 글(We have a perfect travel package for you.)이므로, 글의 목적으로 가장 적절한 것은 ② '패키지 여행 상품을 홍보하려고'이다.

- travel agency 여행사
- experienced ⓐ 경험 많은, 숙련된
- unforgettable ⓐ 잊지 못할
- meditation ⓝ 명상
- instructor ⓝ 강사

[문제편 p.058]

구문 풀이

4행 This travel package includes special trips to Lake Madison as well as
「A+as well as+B : B뿐 아니라 A도」
massage and meditation to help you relax.
「help+목적어+원형부정사 : ~이 …하는 데 도움이 되다」

19 남편과 딸이 없어진 줄 알았다가 다시 찾는 안도한 필자 정답률 88% | 정답 ①

다음 글에 드러난 'I'의 심경 변화로 가장 적절한 것은?

☑ anxious → relieved 불안한 안도한
② delighted → unhappy 기쁜 불행한
③ indifferent → excited 무관심한 신난
④ relaxed → upset 안도한 언짢은
⑤ embarrassed → proud 당황한 자랑스러운

When I woke up in our hotel room, / it was almost midnight.
내가 호텔 방에서 깨어났을 때는 / 거의 자정이었다.
I didn't see my husband nor daughter.
남편과 딸이 보이지 않았다.
I called them, / but I heard their phones ringing in the room.
나는 그들에게 전화를 걸었지만, / 나는 그들의 전화가 방에 울리는 것을 들었다.
Feeling worried, / I went outside and walked down the street, / but they were nowhere to be found.
걱정이 되어, / 나는 밖으로 나가 거리를 걸어 내려갔지만, / 그들을 어디에서도 찾을 수 없었다.
When I decided / I should ask someone for help, / a crowd nearby caught my attention.
내가 마음 먹었을 때 / 내가 누군가에게 도움을 요청해야겠다고 / 근처에 있던 군중이 내 주의를 끌었다.
I approached, / hoping to find my husband and daughter, / and suddenly I saw two familiar faces.
나는 다가갔고, / 남편과 딸을 찾으려는 희망을 안고 / 갑자기 낯익은 두 얼굴이 보였다.
I smiled, feeling calm.
나는 안도하며 웃었다.
Just then, / my daughter saw me and called, / "Mom!"
바로 그때, / 딸이 나를 보고 외쳤다. / "엄마"라고
They were watching the magic show.
그들은 마술 쇼를 보고 있는 중이었다.
Finally, / I felt all my worries disappear.
마침내, / 나는 내 모든 걱정이 사라지는 것을 느꼈다.

내가 호텔 방에서 깨어났을 때는 거의 자정이었다. 남편과 딸이 보이지 않았다. 나는 그들에게 전화를 걸었지만, 나는 그들의 전화가 방에서 울리는 것을 들었다. 걱정이 되어, 나는 밖으로 나가 거리를 걸어 내려갔지만, 그들을 어디에서도 찾을 수 없었다. 내가 누군가에게 도움을 요청하려고 했을 때, 근처에 있던 군중이 내 주의를 끌었다. 나는 남편과 딸을 찾으려는 희망을 안고 다가갔고, 갑자기 낯익은 두 얼굴이 보였다. 나는 안도하며 웃었다. 바로 그때, 딸이 나를 보고 "엄마!"라고 외쳤다. 그들은 마술 쇼를 보고 있는 중이었다. 마침내, 나는 내 모든 걱정이 사라지는 것을 느꼈다.

Why? 왜 정답일까?

호텔 방에서 잠을 자다가 깬 필자가 남편과 딸이 없어져 걱정했다가(Feeling worried, ~) 둘이 마술 쇼를 보고 있었다는 것을 알고 안도했다(I smiled, feeling calm. / Finally, I felt all my worries disappear.)는 글이다. 따라서 'I'의 심경 변화로 가장 적절한 것은 ① '불안한 → 안도한'이다.

- worried ⓐ 걱정한
- ask for help 도움을 요청하다
- approach ⓥ 다가가다
- disappear ⓥ 사라지다
- delighted ⓐ 기쁜
- decide ⓥ 결심하다, 정하다
- catch one's attention 관심을 끌다
- familiar ⓐ 익숙한
- anxious ⓐ 불안한
- embarrassed ⓐ 당황한

구문 풀이

3행 Feeling worried, I went outside and walked down the street, but they
분사구문(~하면서)
were nowhere to be found.
수동 부정사(they 보충 설명)

20 업무와 개인 용무를 한 곳에 정리하기 정답률 78% | 정답 ⑤

다음 글에서 필자가 주장하는 바로 가장 적절한 것은?

① 결정한 것은 반드시 실행하도록 노력하라.
② 자신이 담당한 업무에 관한 전문성을 확보하라.
③ 업무 집중도를 높이기 위해 책상 위를 정돈하라.
④ 좋은 아이디어를 메모하는 습관을 길러라.
☑ 업무와 개인 용무를 한 곳에 정리하라.

Research shows / that people who work have two calendars: / one for work and one for their personal lives.
연구는 보여준다. / 일하는 사람들이 두 개의 달력을 가지고 있다는 것을 / 업무를 위한 달력 하나와 개인적인 삶을 위한 달력 하나
Although it may seem sensible, / having two separate calendars for work and personal life / can lead to distractions.
비록 이것이 현명해 보일지도 모르지만, / 업무와 개인적인 삶을 위한 두 개의 별도의 달력을 갖는 것은 / 주의를 산만하게 할 수 있다.
To check if something is missing, / you will find yourself / checking your to-do lists multiple times.
누락된 것이 있는지를 확인하고자 / 당신은 자신이 ~한다는 것을 깨닫게 될 것이다. / 당신의 할 일 목록을 여러 번 확인하고 있다는 것을
Instead, / organize all of your tasks in one place.
그렇게 하는 대신에, / 당신의 모든 일들을 한 곳에 정리하라.
It doesn't matter / if you use digital or paper media.
중요하지 않다. / 당신이 디지털 매체를 사용하든 종이 매체를 사용하든
It's okay / to keep your professional and personal tasks in one place.
괜찮다. / 당신의 업무와 개인 용무를 한 곳에 둬도
This will give you / a good idea of how time is divided between work and home.
이것은 당신에게 줄 것이다. / 일과 가정 사이에 시간이 어떻게 나뉘는지에 관한 좋은 생각을

This will allow you / to make informed decisions / about which tasks are most important.
이것은 당신이 ~하게 할 것이다. / 잘 알고 결정하게 / 어떤 일이 가장 중요한지에 대해

연구는 일하는 사람들이 두 개의 달력을 가지고 있다는 것을 보여준다. 하나는 업무를 위한 달력이고 하나는 개인적인 삶을 위한 달력이다. 비록 이것이 현명해 보일지도 모르지만, 업무와 개인적인 삶을 위한 두 개의 별도의 달력을 갖는 것은 주의를 산만하게 할 수 있다. 누락된 것이 있는지를 확인하고자 당신은 자신이 할 일 목록을 여러 번 확인하고 있다는 것을 깨닫게 될 것이다. 그렇게 하는 대신에, 당신의 모든 일들을 한 곳에 정리하라. 당신이 디지털 매체를 사용하든 종이 매체를 사용하든 중요하지 않다. 당신의 업무와 개인 용무를 한 곳에 둬도 괜찮다. 이것은 당신에게 일과 가정 사이에 시간이 어떻게 나눠지는지에 대해 잘 알게 해줄 것이다. 이것은 어떤 일이 가장 중요한지에 대해 잘 알고 결정하게 할 것이다.

Why? 왜 정답일까?

개인 용무와 일을 한 곳에 정리하라고(~ keep your professional and personal tasks in one place.) 조언하는 글이므로, 필자가 주장하는 바로 가장 적절한 것은 ⑤ '업무와 개인 용무를 한 곳에 정리하라.'이다.

- sensible ⓐ 분별 있는, 현명한
- distraction ⓝ 주의 분산, 정신을 흩뜨리는 것
- organize ⓥ 정리하다
- make an informed decision 잘 알고 결정하다
- separate ⓐ 별개의
- multiple ⓐ 여럿의, 다수의
- divide ⓥ 나누다, 분배하다

구문 풀이

4행 To check if something is missing, you will find yourself checking your
목적격(~하려면) 접속사(~인지 아닌지) 동사 목적어 목적격 보어
to-do lists multiple times.

---

21 고객의 구매 후 행동을 관찰할 필요성 정답률 56% | 정답 ①

밑줄 친 become unpaid ambassadors가 다음 글에서 의미하는 바로 가장 적절한 것은?

☑ recommend products to others for no gain – 대가 없이 다른 사람들에게 제품을 추천할
② offer manufacturers feedback on products – 제조업자들에게 제품에 대한 피드백을 제공할
③ become people who don't trust others' words – 다른 사람들의 말을 믿지 않는 사람이 될
④ get rewards for advertising products overseas – 해외에 광고를 해주고 보상을 받을
⑤ buy products without worrying about the price – 가격에 대해 걱정하지 않고 제품을 살

Why do you care / how a customer reacts to a purchase?
왜 당신은 신경 쓰는가? / 고객이 구매품에 어떻게 반응하는지
Good question.
좋은 질문이다.
By understanding post-purchase behavior, / you can understand the influence / and the likelihood of whether a buyer will repurchase the product / (and whether she will keep it or return it).
구매 후 행동을 이해함으로써, / 당신은 그 영향력을 이해할 수 있다. / 그리고 구매자가 제품을 재구매하지 하는 가능성을 / (그리고 그 사람이 제품을 계속 가질지 반품할지)
You'll also determine / whether the buyer will encourage others / to purchase the product from you.
또한 당신은 알아낼 것이다. / 구매자가 다른 사람들에게 권할지 아닐지를 / 당신으로부터 제품을 구매하도록
Satisfied customers can become unpaid ambassadors for your business, / so customer satisfaction should be on the top of your to-do list.
만족한 고객은 당신의 사업을 위한 무급 대사가 될 수 있으므로, / 고객 만족이 할 일 목록의 최상단에 있어야 한다.
People tend to believe the opinions of people they know.
사람들은 자기가 아는 사람들의 의견을 믿는 경향이 있다.
People trust friends over advertisements any day.
사람들은 언제든 광고보다 친구를 더 신뢰한다.
They know / that advertisements are paid to tell the "good side" / and that they're used / to persuade them to purchase products and services.
그들은 알고 있다. / 광고는 '좋은 면'을 말하도록 돈을 지불받고, / 그것은 이용된다는 것을 / 그들더러 제품과 서비스를 구매하게 설득하려고
By continually monitoring your customer's satisfaction after the sale, / you have the ability / to avoid negative word-of-mouth advertising.
판매 후 고객의 만족을 지속적으로 관찰하여 / 당신은 능력을 얻는다. / 부정적인 입소문 광고를 피할 수 있는

왜 당신은 고객이 구매품에 어떻게 반응하는지 신경 쓰는가? 좋은 질문이다. 구매 후 행동을 이해함으로써, 당신은 그 영향력과 구매자가 제품을 재구매할지(그리고 그 사람이 제품을 계속 가질지 반품할지) 하는 가능성을 이해할 수 있다. 또한 당신은 구매자가 다른 사람들에게 당신으로부터 제품을 구매하도록 권할지 아닐지도 알아낼 것이다. 만족한 고객은 당신의 사업을 위한 무급 대사가 될 수 있으므로, 고객 만족이 할 일 목록의 최상단에 있어야 한다. 사람들은 아는 사람들의 의견을 믿는 경향이 있다. 그들은 언제든 광고보다 친구를 더 신뢰한다. 그들은 광고는 '좋은 면'을 말하도록 돈을 지불받고, 그것은 그들더러 제품과 서비스를 구매하게 설득하려고 이용된다는 것을 알고 있다. 판매 후 고객의 만족을 지속적으로 관찰하여 당신은 부정적인 입소문 광고를 피할 수 있는 능력을 얻는다.

Why? 왜 정답일까?

구매 후 행동을 관찰하면 구매자들이 다른 사람들에게 제품을 권해줄지(~ whether the buyer will encourage others to purchase the product from you.) 알 수 있다는 내용으로 보아, 밑줄 친 부분의 의미로 가장 적절한 것은 ① '대가 없이 다른 사람들에게 제품을 추천할'이다.

- purchase ⓝ 구매 ⓥ 사다
- return ⓥ 반품하다
- unpaid ⓐ 무급의
- ambassador ⓝ (외교 시 나라를 대표하는) 대사, 사절
- advertisement ⓝ 광고
- word-of-mouth ⓐ 구전의
- likelihood ⓝ 가능성, 확률
- satisfied ⓐ 만족한
- continually ⓐ 지속적으로
- overseas ⓐ 해외에

구문 풀이

10행 They know {that advertisements are paid to tell the "good side"} and {that they're used to persuade them to purchase products and services}.
「be used to + 동사원형」: ~하기 위해 사용되다 { }: know의 목적어

---

22 컴퓨터화된 사회에서 오히려 일이 늘어난 소비자들 정답률 54% | 정답 ③

다음 글의 요지로 가장 적절한 것은?

① 컴퓨터 기반 사회에서는 여가 시간이 더 늘어난다.
② 회사 업무의 전산화는 업무 능률을 향상시킨다.
☑ 컴퓨터화된 사회에서 소비자는 더 많은 일을 하게 된다.
④ 온라인 거래가 모든 소비자들을 만족시키기에는 한계가 있다.
⑤ 산업의 발전으로 인해 기계가 인간의 일자리를 대신하고 있다.

The promise of a computerized society, / we were told, / was / that it would pass to machines all of the repetitive drudgery of work, / allowing us humans / to pursue higher purposes / and to have more leisure time.
컴퓨터화된 사회의 약속은 / 우리가 듣기로, / ~이었다. / 그것이 모든 반복적인 고된 일을 기계에 넘겨준다는 것 / 더 높은 목적을 추구하고 / 더 많은 여가 시간을 가질 수 있게
It didn't work out this way.
일은 이런 식으로 되지는 않았다.
Instead of more time, / most of us have less.
더 많은 시간 대신에, / 우리 대부분은 더 적은 시간을 가지고 있다.
Companies large and small / have off-loaded work onto the backs of consumers.
크고 작은 회사들은 / 일을 소비자들의 등에 떠넘겼다.
Things that used to be done for us, / as part of the value-added service of working with a company, / we are now expected to do ourselves.
우리를 위해 행해지던 일들을 / 회사에 맡겨 해결하던 부가가치 서비스의 일환으로, / 우리는 이제 스스로 하도록 기대받는다.
With air travel, / we're now expected / to complete our own reservations and check-in, / jobs that used to be done by airline employees or travel agents.
항공 여행의 경우, / 이제는 우리는 기대된다 / 예약과 체크인을 직접 완수하도록 / 항공사 직원이나 여행사 직원이 하던 일인
At the grocery store, / we're expected to bag our own groceries / and, in some supermarkets, / to scan our own purchases.
식료품점에서는, / 우리가 우리 자신의 식료품을 직접 봉지에 넣도록 기대받는다. / 그리고 일부 슈퍼마켓에서는 / 우리가 직접 구매한 물건을 스캔하도록

우리가 듣기로, 컴퓨터화된 사회의 약속은 그것이 모든 반복적인 고된 일을 기계에 넘겨 우리 인간들이 더 높은 목적을 추구하고 더 많은 여가 시간을 가질 수 있게 해준다는 것이었다. 일은 이런 식으로 되지는 않았다. 더 많은 시간 대신에, 우리 대부분은 더 적은 시간을 가지고 있다. 크고 작은 회사들은 일을 소비자들의 등에 떠넘겼다. 우리는 회사에 맡겨 해결하던 부가가치 서비스의 일환으로 우리를 위해 행해지던 일들을 이제 스스로 하도록 기대받는다. 항공 여행의 경우, 항공사 직원이나 여행사 직원들이 하던 일인 예약과 체크인을 이제는 우리가 직접 완수하도록 기대된다. 식료품점에서는, 우리가 우리 자신의 식료품을 직접 봉지에 넣도록, 그리고 일부 슈퍼마켓에서는 우리가 직접 구매한 물건을 스캔하도록 기대받는다.

Why? 왜 정답일까?

컴퓨터화된 사회가 도래하면 개인은 더 많은 여가 시간을 누릴 것으로 기대되었지만, 실상은 반대로 더 많은 일을 하게 되었다(Instead of more time, most of us have less. Companies large and small have off-loaded work onto the backs of consumers.)는 내용이다. 따라서 글의 요지로 가장 적절한 것은 ③ '컴퓨터화된 사회에서 소비자는 더 많은 일을 하게 된다.'이다.

- repetitive ⓐ 반복되는
- pursue ⓥ 추구하다
- as part of ~의 일환으로
- drudgery ⓝ 고된 일
- off-load ⓥ 짐을 내리다, 떠넘기다
- grocery store 슈퍼, 식료품 가게

구문 풀이

6행 Things [that used to be done for us], (as part of the value-added service
to do의 목적어   ~하곤 했다   ( ): 삽입구
of working with a company), we are now expected to do ourselves.
주어   「be expected + to부정사」: ~하도록 기대되다

---

23 자신을 평균 이상으로 보는 경향 정답률 66% | 정답 ②

다음 글의 주제로 가장 적절한 것은?

① importance of having a positive self-image as a leader
리더로서 긍정적인 자아상을 갖는 것의 중요성
☑ our common belief that we are better than average
우리가 평균보다 낫다는 일반적인 믿음
③ our tendency to think others are superior to us
남들이 우리보다 낫다고 생각하는 우리의 경향
④ reasons why we always try to be above average
우리가 늘 평균보다 나아지려고 노력하는 이유
⑤ danger of prejudice in building healthy social networks
건전한 사회적 네트워크를 구축할 때 편견의 위험성

We tend to believe / that we possess a host of socially desirable characteristics, / and that we are free of most of those / that are socially undesirable.
우리는 믿는 경향이 있다. / 우리가 사회적으로 바람직한 특성들을 많이 지니고 있고, / 우리가 특성 대부분은 지니고 있지 않다고 / 사회적으로 바람직하지 않은
For example, / a large majority of the general public thinks / that they are more intelligent, / more fair-minded, / less prejudiced, / and more skilled behind the wheel of an automobile / than the average person.
예를 들어, / 대다수의 일반 대중은 생각한다. / 자신이 더 지적이고, / 더 공정하고, / 편견을 덜 가지고, / 자동차를 운전할 때 더 능숙하다고 / 보통 사람보다
This phenomenon is so reliable and ubiquitous / that it has come to be known as the "Lake Wobegon effect," / after Garrison Keillor's fictional community / where "the women are strong, / the men are good-looking, / and all the children are above average."
이 현상은 너무 신뢰할 수 있고 어디서나 볼 수 있기 때문에 / 그것은 'Lake Wobegon effect'라고 알려지게 되었다. / Garrison Keillor의 허구적인 공동체 이름을 따서 / '여성들은 강하고, / 남성들은 잘생겼으며, / 모든 아이들은 평균 이상'인
A survey of one million high school seniors found / that 70% thought they were above average in leadership ability, / and only 2% thought they were below average.
고등학교 졸업반 학생 100만 명을 대상으로 한 설문조사는 밝혔다. / 70%는 자신이 리더십 능력에 있어 평균 이상이라고 생각했고, / 2%만이 자신이 평균 이하라고 생각했다는 것을
In terms of ability to get along with others, / all students thought they were above average, / 60% thought they were in the top 10%, / and 25% thought they were in the top 1%!
다른 사람들과 잘 지내는 능력에 있어서, / 모든 학생들은 자신이 평균 이상이라고 생각했고, / 60%는 자신이 상위 10%에 속한다고 생각했고, / 25%는 자신이 상위 1%에 속한다고 생각했다!

우리는 우리가 사회적으로 바람직한 특성들을 많이 지니고 있고, 사회적으로 바람직하지 않은 특성들 대부분은 지니고 있지 않다고 믿는 경향이 있다. 예를 들어, 대다수의 일반 대중들은 자신이 보통 사람보다 더 지적이고, 더 공정하고, 편견을 덜 가지고, 자동차를 운전할 때 더 능숙하다고 생각한다. 이 현상은 너무 신뢰할 수 있고 어디서나 볼 수 있기 때문에 '여성들은 강하고, 남성들은 잘생겼으며, 모든 아이들은 평균 이상'인 Garrison Keillor의 허구적인 공동체의 이름을 따서 'Lake Wobegon effect'라고 알려지게 되었다. 고등학교 졸업반 학생 100만 명을 대상으로 한 설문조사에서, (학생들의) 70%는 자신이 리더십 능력에 있어 평균 이상이라고 생각했고, 2%만이 자신이 평균 이하라고 생각했다는 것을 발견했다. 다른 사람들과 잘 지내는 능력에 있어서, 모든 학생들은 자신이 평균 이상이라고 생각했고, 60%는 자신이 상위 10%에 속한다고 생각했고, 25%는 자신이 상위 1%에 속한다고 생각했다!

Why? 왜 정답일까?

사람들은 스스로 바람직한 특성은 더 많이 가지고 있고, 바람직하지 않은 특성은 덜 가지고 있다고 믿는 경향이 있음(We tend to believe that we possess a host of socially desirable characteristics, and that we are free of most of those that are socially undesirable.)을 설명하는 글이다. 뒤에 이어지는 여러 예시에도 사람들이 스스로를 특정 항목에서 '평균 이상'이라고 생각한다는 내용이 주를 이룬다. 따라서 글의 주제로 가장 적절한 것은 ② '우리가 평균보다 낫다는 일반적인 믿음'이다.

- possess ⓥ 지니다, 소유하다
- desirable ⓐ 바람직한
- fair-minded ⓐ 공정한
- skilled ⓐ 능숙한
- automobile ⓝ 자동차
- reliable ⓐ 믿을 만한
- fictional ⓐ 허구의
- million ⓝ 100만
- self-image ⓝ 자아상(사람이 자기 자신에 대해 가진 이미지)
- superior to ~보다 우월한
- a host of 여러, 다수의
- characteristic ⓝ 특성
- prejudiced ⓐ 고정 관념이 있는
- behind the wheel 운전할 때, 핸들을 잡은
- phenomenon ⓝ 현상
- ubiquitous ⓐ 도처에 있는
- good-looking ⓐ 잘생긴

구문 풀이

1행 We tend to believe {that we possess a host of socially desirable characteristics}, and {that we are free of most of those that are socially undesirable}.
{ }: to believe의 목적절
대명사(= characteristics)

---

24 부유한 국가의 스트레스 요소
정답률 64% | 정답 ①

다음 글의 제목으로 가장 적절한 것은?

✔①Why Are Even Wealthy Countries Not Free from Stress?
왜 심지어 부유한 국가들도 스트레스에서 자유롭지 못한 걸까?
② In Search of the Path to Escaping the Poverty Trap
가난의 덫을 벗어나기 위한 길을 찾아서
③ Time Management: Everything You Need to Know
시간 관리: 당신이 알아야 할 모든 것
④ How Does Stress Affect Human Bodies?
스트레스는 우리 몸에 어떤 영향을 미칠까?
⑤ Sound Mind Wins the Game of Life!
건전한 정신이 인생이란 게임에서 이긴다!

Few people will be surprised / to hear that poverty tends to create stress: / a 2006 study / published in the American journal *Psychosomatic Medicine*, / for example, / noted / that a lower socioeconomic status / was associated with higher levels of stress hormones in the body.
놀랄 사람은 거의 없을 것이다. / 가난이 스트레스를 유발하는 경향이 있다는 것을 듣고 / 2006 연구는 / 미국의 저널 *Psychosomatic Medicine*에 발표된 / 예를 들어, / 언급했다. / 더 낮은 사회 경제적 지위 / 체내의 더 높은 수치의 스트레스 호르몬과 관련이 있다고

However, / richer economies have their own distinct stresses.
하지만, / 더 부유한 국가는 그들만의 독특한 스트레스를 가지고 있다.

The key issue is time pressure.
핵심 쟁점은 시간 압박이다.

A 1999 study of 31 countries / by American psychologist Robert Levine and Canadian psychologist Ara Norenzayan / found / that wealthier, more industrialized nations had a faster pace of life — which led to a higher standard of living, / but at the same time / left the population feeling a constant sense of urgency, / as well as being more prone to heart disease.
31개국을 대상으로 한 1999년 연구는 / 미국 심리학자 Robert Levine과 캐나다 심리학자 Ara Norenzayan에 의한 / 알아냈다. / 더 부유하고 더 산업화된 국가들이 더 빠른 삶의 속도를 가지고 있다는 것 / 그리고 이것이 더 높은 생활 수준으로 이어졌지만, / 동시에 / 사람들에게 지속적인 촉박함을 느끼게 했다는 것 / 심장병에 걸리기 더 쉽게 했을 뿐 아니라

In effect, / fast-paced productivity creates wealth, / but it also leads people to feel time-poor / when they lack the time / to relax and enjoy themselves.
사실, / 빠른 속도의 생산력은 부를 창출하지만, / 이는 또한 사람들이 시간이 부족하다고 느끼게 한다. / 그들이 시간이 부족할 때 / 긴장을 풀고 즐겁게 지낼

가난이 스트레스를 유발하는 경향이 있다는 것을 듣고 놀랄 사람은 거의 없을 것이다. 예를 들어, 미국의 저널 *Psychosomatic Medicine*에 발표된 2006년 연구는 더 낮은 사회 경제적 지위가 체내의 더 높은 수치의 스트레스 호르몬과 관련이 있다고 언급했다. 하지만, 더 부유한 국가는 그들 특유의 스트레스를 가지고 있다. 핵심 쟁점은 시간 압박이다. 미국 심리학자 Robert Levine과 캐나다 심리학자 Ara Norenzayan이 31개국을 대상으로 한 1999년 연구는 더 부유하고 더 산업화된 국가들이 더 빠른 삶의 속도를 가지고 있다는 것, 그리고 이것이 더 높은 생활 수준으로 이어졌지만, 동시에 사람들이 심장병에 걸리기 더 쉽게 했을 뿐 아니라 지속적인 촉박함을 느끼게 했다는 것을 알아냈다. 사실, 빠른 속도의 생산력은 부를 창출하지만, 이는 또한 사람들이 긴장을 풀고 즐겁게 지낼 시간이 없을 때 시간이 부족하다고 느끼게 한다.

Why? 왜 정답일까?

부유한 국가에 사는 사람들이 시간 압박이라는 스트레스에 시달린다(However, richer economies have their own distinct stresses. The key issue is time pressure.)는 내용이므로, 글의 제목으로 가장 적절한 것은 ① '왜 심지어 부유한 국가들도 스트레스에서 자유롭지 못한 걸까?'이다.

- poverty ⓝ 가난
- socioeconomic ⓐ 사회경제적인

- status ⓝ 지위
- psychologist ⓝ 심리학자
- industrialize ⓥ 산업화하다
- urgency ⓝ 다급함
- productivity ⓝ 생산성
- distinct ⓐ 특유의, 독특한, 뚜렷한
- wealthy ⓐ 부유한
- constant ⓐ 지속적인
- prone to ~에 걸리기 쉬운

구문 풀이

1행 Few people will be surprised to hear that poverty tends to create stress: ~
감정 형용사 원인(~해서)

---

25 지역별 산림 면적 점유율 비교
정답률 80% | 정답 ④

05회

다음 도표의 내용과 일치하지 않는 것은?

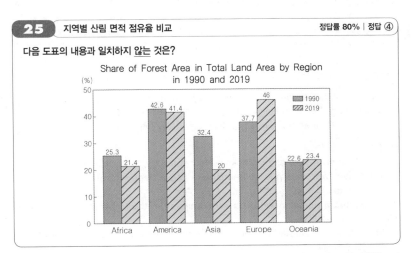

Share of Forest Area in Total Land Area by Region in 1990 and 2019

The above graph shows / the share of forest area / in total land area by region / in 1990 and 2019.
위 도표는 보여준다. / 산림 면적의 점유율을 / 지역별 총 토지 면적에서 / 1990년과 2019년의

① Africa's share of forest area in total land area / was over 20% in both 1990 and 2019.
아프리카의 전체 토지 면적에서 산림 면적의 점유율이 / 1990년과 2019년 둘 다 20%를 넘었다.

② The share of forest area in America / was 42.6% in 1990, / which was larger than that in 2019.
아메리카의 산림 면적 점유율은 / 1990년에 42.6%였고, / 이는 2019년보다 더 컸다.

③ The share of forest area in Asia / declined from 1990 to 2019 / by more than 10 percentage points.
아시아의 산림 면적 점유율은 / 1990년부터 2019년까지 감소했다. / 10퍼센트포인트 이상만큼

✔ In 2019, / the share of forest area in Europe / was the largest among the five regions, / more than three times that in Asia in the same year.
2019년 / 유럽의 산 면적 점유율은 / 다섯 개 지역 중 가장 컸고, / 같은 해 아시아의 세 배가 넘었다.

⑤ Oceania showed the smallest gap between 1990 and 2019 / in terms of the share of forest area in total land area.
오세아니아는 1990년과 2019년 사이에 가장 작은 차이를 보였다. / 총 토지 면적에서 산림 면적의 점유율에 있어

위 도표는 1990년과 2019년의 지역별 총 토지 면적에서 산림 면적의 점유율을 보여준다. ① 아프리카의 전체 토지 면적에서 산림 면적의 점유율이 1990년과 2019년 둘 다 20%를 넘었다. ② 1990년 아메리카의 산림 면적 점유율은 42.6%였고, 이는 2019년보다 더 컸다. ③ 아시아의 산림 면적 점유율은 1990년부터 2019년까지, 10퍼센트포인트 이상 감소했다. ④ 2019년 유럽의 산 면적 점유율은 다섯 개 지역 중 가장 컸고, 같은 해 아시아의 세 배가 넘었다. ⑤ 오세아니아는 1990년과 2019년 사이에 총 토지 면적에서 산림 면적의 점유율에 있어 가장 작은 차이를 보였다.

Why? 왜 정답일까?

도표에 따르면 2019년 아시아의 산림 면적 점유율은 20%인데, 유럽의 점유율은 46%이므로 두 비율은 3배 이상 차이가 나지 않는다. 따라서 도표와 일치하지 않는 것은 ④이다.

- region ⓝ 지역
- decline ⓥ 감소하다, 줄어들다

---

26 Gary Becker의 생애
정답률 86% | 정답 ③

Gary Becker에 관한 다음 글의 내용과 일치하지 않는 것은?

① New York City의 Brooklyn에서 자랐다.
② 아버지는 금융과 정치 문제에 깊은 관심이 있었다.
✔ Princeton University에서의 경제학 교육에 만족했다.
④ 1955년에 경제학 박사 학위를 취득했다.
⑤ *Business Week*에 경제학 칼럼을 기고했다.

『Gary Becker was born in Pottsville, Pennsylvania in 1930 / and grew up in Brooklyn, New York City.』 ①의 근거 일치
Gary Becker는 1930년 Pennsylvania 주 Pottsville에서 태어났고 / New York City의 Brooklyn에서 자랐다.

『His father, / who was not well educated, / had a deep interest in financial and political issues.』 ②의 근거 일치
그의 아버지는 / 교육을 제대로 받지 못했는데 / 금융과 정치 문제에 깊은 관심이 있었다.

After graduating from high school, / Becker went to Princeton University, / where he majored in economics.
고등학교를 졸업한 후, / Becker는 Princeton University로 진학했고, / 거기서 그는 경제학을 전공했다.

『He was dissatisfied / with his economic education at Princeton University / because "it didn't seem to be handling real problems."』 ③의 근거 불일치
그는 불만족했다. / Princeton University에서의 경제학 교육에 / '그것이 현실적인 문제를 다루고 있는 것처럼 보이지 않았기' 때문에

『He earned a doctor's degree in economics / from the University of Chicago / in 1955.』 ④의 근거 일치
그는 경제학 박사 학위를 취득했다. / University of Chicago에서 / 1955년에

His doctoral paper on the economics of discrimination / was mentioned by the Nobel Prize Committee / as an important contribution to economics.
차별의 경제학에 대한 그의 박사 논문은 / 노벨상 위원회에 의해 언급되었다. / 경제학에 대한 중요한 기여로

『Since 1985, / Becker had written a regular economics column in *Business Week*, / explaining economic analysis and ideas to the general public.』 ⑤의 근거 일치

1985년부터, / Becker는 *Business Week*에 경제학 칼럼을 정기적으로 기고했다. / 경제학적 분석과 아이디어를 일반 대중에게 설명하는
In 1992, / he was awarded / the Nobel Prize in economic science.
1992년에, / 그는 수상했다. / 노벨 경제학상을

Gary Becker는 1930년 Pennsylvania 주 Pottsville에서 태어났고 New York City의 Brooklyn에서 자랐다. 교육을 제대로 받지 못한 그의 아버지는 금융과 정치 문제에 깊은 관심이 있었다. 고등학교를 졸업한 후, Becker는 Princeton University로 진학했고, 거기서 그는 경제학을 전공했다. 'Princeton University에서의 경제학 교육이 현실적인 문제를 다루고 있는 것처럼 보이지 않았기' 때문에 그는 그것에 불만족했다. 그는 1955년에 University of Chicago에서 경제학 박사 학위를 취득했다. 차별의 경제학에 대한 그의 박사 논문은 노벨상 위원회에 의해 경제학에 대한 중요한 기여로 언급되었다. 1985년부터, Becker는 *Business Week*에 경제학적 분석과 아이디어를 일반 대중에게 설명하는 경제학 칼럼을 정기적으로 기고했다. 1992년에, 그는 노벨 경제학상을 수상했다.

Why? 왜 정답일까?
'He was dissatisfied with his economic education at Princeton University ~'에서 Gary Becker는 Princeton University에서의 경제학 교육에 불만족했다고 하므로, 내용과 일치하지 않는 것은 ③ 'Princeton University에서의 경제학 교육에 만족했다.'이다.

Why? 왜 오답일까?
① 'Gary Becker ~ grew up in Brooklyn, New York City.'의 내용과 일치한다.
② 'His father, who was not well educated, had a deep interest in financial and political issues.'의 내용과 일치한다.
④ 'He earned a doctor's degree in economics from the University of Chicago in 1955.'의 내용과 일치한다.
⑤ 'Since 1985, Becker had written a regular economics column in *Business Week*. ~'의 내용과 일치한다.

- financial ⓐ 재정적인
- doctoral paper 박사 논문
- mention ⓥ 언급하다
- analysis ⓝ 분석
- handle ⓥ 다루다, 대처하다
- discrimination ⓝ 차별
- contribution ⓝ 기여, 이바지
- award ⓥ 상을 주다, 수여하다

구문 풀이

13행 In 1992, he was awarded the Nobel Prize in economic science.
4형식 수동태   직접목적어

---

27 드론 레이싱 선수권 | 정답률 94% | 정답 ⑤

2023 Drone Racing Championship에 관한 다음 안내문의 내용과 일치하지 않는 것은?
① 7월 9일 일요일에 개최된다.
② 고등학생만 참가할 수 있다.
③ 자신의 드론을 가져와야 한다.
④ 상금과 메달이 우승자에게 수여될 것이다.
✓ 20명의 참가자가 기념품을 받을 것이다.

2023 Drone Racing Championship
2023 드론 레이싱 선수권
Are you the best drone racer?
여러분은 최고의 드론 레이서인가요?
Then take the opportunity / to prove you are the one!
그렇다면 기회를 잡으세요! / 여러분이 바로 그 사람이라는 것을 증명할
When & Where
일시 & 장소
「6 p.m. – 8 p.m., Sunday, July 9」 ①의 근거 일치
7월 9일 일요일 오후 6시부터 오후 8시까지
Lakeside Community Center
Lakeside 주민센터
Requirements
필수 조건
「Participants: High school students only」 ②의 근거 일치
참가자: 고등학생만
「Bring your own drone for the race.」 ③의 근거 일치
레이스를 위해 당신의 드론을 가져 오세요.
Prize
부상
「$500 and a medal will be awarded to the winner.」 ④의 근거 일치
500달러와 메달이 우승자에게 수여될 것입니다.
Note
참고 사항
「The first 10 participants will get souvenirs.」 ⑤의 근거 불일치
선착순 10명의 참가자들은 기념품을 받게 될 것입니다.
For more details, / please visit www.droneracing.com / or call 313-6745-1189.
더 많은 세부 정보를 원하시면, / www.droneracing.com을 방문하거나 / 313-6745-1189로 전화하세요.

2023 Drone Racing Championship(2023 드론 레이싱 선수권)

여러분은 최고의 드론 레이서인가요? 그렇다면 여러분이 바로 그 사람이라는 것을 증명할 기회를 잡으세요!

일시 & 장소
• 7월 9일 일요일 오후 6시부터 오후 8시까지
• Lakeside 주민센터

필수 조건
• 참가자: 고등학생만
• 레이스를 위해 당신의 드론을 가져 오세요.

부상
• 500달러와 메달이 우승자에게 수여될 것입니다.

참고 사항
• 선착순 10명의 참가자들은 기념품을 받게 될 것입니다.
더 많은 세부 정보를 원하시면, www.droneracing.com을 방문하거나 313-6745-1189로 전화하세요.

Why? 왜 정답일까?
'The first 10 participants will get souvenirs.'에서 선착순 10명의 참가자에게 기념품을 준다고 하므로, 안내문의 내용과 일치하지 않는 것은 ⑤ '20명의 참가자가 기념품을 받을 것이다.'이다.

Why? 왜 오답일까?
① '6 p.m. – 8 p.m., Sunday, July 9'의 내용과 일치한다.
② 'Participants: High school students only'의 내용과 일치한다.
③ 'Bring your own drone for the race.'의 내용과 일치한다.
④ '$500 and a medal will be awarded to the winner.'의 내용과 일치한다.

- drone ⓝ 드론, 무인 항공기
- take an opportunity 기회를 잡다
- requirement ⓝ 필수 요건
- souvenir ⓝ 기념품
- championship ⓝ 선수권
- prove ⓥ 증명하다
- bring ⓥ 가져오다, 지참하다

---

28 스쿠버 다이빙 일일 수업 광고 | 정답률 86% | 정답 ⑤

Summer Scuba Diving One–day Class에 관한 다음 안내문의 내용과 일치하는 것은?
① 오후 시간에 바다에서 다이빙 기술을 연습한다.
② 그룹 수업의 최대 정원은 4명이다.
③ 다이빙 장비를 유료로 대여할 수 있다.
④ 연령에 관계없이 참가할 수 있다.
✓ 적어도 수업 시작 5일 전까지 등록해야 한다.

Summer Scuba Diving One-day Class
여름 스쿠버 다이빙 일일 수업
Join our summer scuba diving lesson for beginners, / and become an underwater explorer!
초보자용 여름 스쿠버 다이빙 수업에 참여하여 / 수중 탐험가가 되세요!
Schedule
일정
10:00 – 12:00 Learning the basics
10시 – 12시 기초 배우기
「13:00 – 16:00 Practicing diving skills in a pool」 ①의 근거 불일치
13시 – 16시 수영장에서 다이빙 기술 연습하기
Price
가격
Private lesson: $150
개인 수업: $150
「Group lesson (up to 3 people): $100 per person」 ②의 근거 불일치
그룹 수업 (최대 3명): 1인당 $100
「Participants can rent our diving equipment for free.」 ③의 근거 불일치
참가자는 다이빙 장비를 무료로 대여할 수 있습니다.
Notice
알림
「Participants must be 10 years old or over.」 ④의 근거 불일치
참가자는 10세 이상이어야 합니다.
「Participants must register / at least 5 days before the class begins.」 ⑤의 근거 일치
참가자는 적어도 수업 시작 5일 전까지 / 등록해야 합니다. / 적어도 수업 시작 5일 전까지
For more information, / please go to www.ssdiver.com.
더 많은 정보를 원하시면, / www.ssdiver.com을 방문하세요.

Summer Scuba Diving One-day Class(여름 스쿠버 다이빙 일일 수업)

초보자용 여름 스쿠버 다이빙 수업에 참여하여 수중 탐험가가 되세요!

일정
• 10시 – 12시 기초 배우기
• 13시 – 16시 수영장에서 다이빙 기술 연습하기

가격
• 개인 수업: $150
• 그룹 수업 (최대 3명): 1인당 $100
• 참가자는 다이빙 장비를 무료로 대여할 수 있습니다.

알림
• 참가자는 10세 이상이어야 합니다.
• 참가자는 적어도 수업 시작 5일 전까지 등록해야 합니다.

더 많은 정보를 원하시면, www.ssdiver.com을 방문하세요.

Why? 왜 정답일까?
'Participants must register at least 5 days before the class begins.'에서 참가를 원하면 적어도 수업 시작 5일 전까지 등록하라고 하므로, 안내문의 내용과 일치하는 것은 ⑤ '적어도 수업 시작 5일 전까지 등록해야 한다.'이다.

Why? 왜 오답일까?
① '13:00 – 16:00 Practicing diving skills in a pool'에서 다이빙 기술을 연습하는 장소는 바다가 아니라 수영장이라고 하였다.
② 'Group lesson (up to 3 people): ~'에서 그룹 수업은 최대 3명까지라고 하였다.
③ 'Participants can rent our diving equipment for free.'에서 다이빙 장비는 무료로 대여할 수 있다고 하였다.
④ 'Participants must be 10 years old or over.'에서 참가 가능 연령은 10세 이상이라고 하였다.

- one-day class 일일 수업
- explorer ⓝ 탐험가
- private lesson 개인 레슨
- underwater ⓐ 물속의, 수중의
- basics ⓝ 기본, 필수적인 것들
- equipment ⓝ 장비

29 칭찬이 아이들의 자존감에 미치는 효과 　　정답률 55% | 정답 ④

다음 글의 밑줄 친 부분 중, 어법상 틀린 것은? [3점]

Although praise is one of the most powerful tools / available for improving young children's behavior, / it is equally powerful / for improving your child's self-esteem.
칭찬은 가장 강력한 도구 중 하나지만, / 어린 아이들의 행동을 개선하는 데 사용할 수 있는 / 그것은 똑같이 강력하다. / 아이의 자존감을 향상시키는 데에도

Preschoolers believe / what their parents tell ① them / in a very profound way.
미취학 아동은 여긴다. / 그들의 부모가 그들에게 하는 말을 / 매우 뜻 깊게

They do not yet have the cognitive sophistication / to reason ② analytically and reject false information.
그들은 인지적 정교함을 아직 가지고 있지 않다. / 분석적으로 추론하고 잘못된 정보를 거부할 수 있는

If a preschool boy consistently hears from his mother / ③ that he is smart and a good helper, / he is likely to incorporate that information into his self-image.
만약 미취학 소년이 그의 어머니로부터 계속 듣는다면, / 그가 똑똑하고 좋은 조력자라는 것을 / 그는 그 정보를 자기 자아상으로 통합시킬 가능성이 높다.

Thinking of himself as a boy / who is smart and knows how to do things / ☑ is likely to make him endure longer in problem-solving efforts / and increase his confidence in trying new and difficult tasks.
스스로를 소년으로 생각하는 것은 / 똑똑하고 일을 어떻게 하는지 아는 / 그가 문제 해결 노력에 있어 더 오래 지속하게 만들 가능성이 높다. / 그리고 새롭고 어려운 일을 시도할 때 그의 자신감을 높일

Similarly, / thinking of himself as the kind of boy / who is a good helper / will make him more likely / to volunteer ⑤ to help with tasks at home and at preschool.
마찬가지로, / 자신을 그런 부류의 소년으로 생각하는 것은 / 좋은 조력자인 / 그가 ~할 가능성이 더 커지게 할 것이다. / 집과 유치원에서 일을 자발적으로 도울

칭찬은 어린 아이들의 행동을 개선하는 데 사용할 수 있는 가장 강력한 도구 중 하나지만, 그것은 아이의 자존감을 향상시키는 데에도 똑같이 강력하다. 미취학 아동은 그들의 부모가 그들에게 하는 말을 매우 뜻 깊게 여긴다. 그들은 분석적으로 추론하고 잘못된 정보를 거부할 수 있는 인지적 정교함을 아직 가지고 있지 않다. 만약 미취학 소년이 그의 어머니로부터 그가 똑똑하고 좋은 조력자라는 것을 계속 듣는다면, 그는 그 정보를 자기 자아상으로 통합시킬 가능성이 높다. 스스로를 똑똑하고 일을 어떻게 하는지 아는 소년으로 생각하는 것은 그가 문제 해결 노력에 있어 더 오래 지속하게 하고, 새롭고 어려운 일을 시도할 때 그의 자신감을 높일 가능성이 높다. 마찬가지로, 자신을 좋은 조력자인 그런 부류의 소년으로 생각하는 것은 그가 집과 유치원에서 일을 자발적으로 도울 가능성이 더 커지게 할 것이다.

Why? 왜 정답일까?
주어인 동명사구(Thinking of himself as a boy ~) 뒤에 동사가 있어야 하므로, being을 is로 고쳐야 한다. 따라서 어법상 틀린 것은 ④이다.

Why? 왜 오답일까?
① tell의 주어는 their parents인데, 목적어는 문맥상 문장의 주어인 Preschoolers이다. 따라서 재귀대명사를 쓰지 않고, 인칭대명사 them을 썼다.
② to부정사구 to reason을 수식하는 부사 analytically이다.
③ hears의 목적절을 이끄는 접속사로 that이 알맞다. from his mother가 동사 앞으로 들어간 구조이다.
⑤ volunteer는 to부정사를 목적어로 취하므로 to help가 알맞다.

- self-esteem ⓝ 자존감
- profound ⓐ 뜻 깊은
- sophistication ⓝ 정교화(함)
- analytically ⓐⓓ 분석적으로
- incorporate A into B A를 B로 통합시키다
- preschooler ⓝ 미취학 아동
- cognitive ⓐ 인지적인
- reason ⓥ 추론하다
- consistently ⓐⓓ 지속적으로
- endure ⓥ 지속하다, 참다

구문 풀이
6행　If a preschool boy consistently hears from his mother {that he is smart and a good helper}, he is likely to incorporate that information into his self-image.
（동사 / 부사구 / [ ]: hears의 목적어）

30 광고주의 메시지 조절 　　정답률 55% | 정답 ②

다음 글의 밑줄 친 부분 중, 문맥상 낱말의 쓰임이 적절하지 않은 것은?

Advertisers often displayed considerable facility / in ① adapting their claims / to the market status of the goods they promoted.
광고주들은 상당한 능력을 자주 보여주었다. / 그들의 주장을 맞추는 데 있어 / 그들이 홍보하는 상품의 시장 지위에

Fleischmann's yeast, / for instance, / was used / as an ingredient for cooking homemade bread.
Fleischmann의 효모는 / 예를 들어, / 사용되었다. / 집에서 만든 빵을 요리하는 재료로

Yet / more and more people in the early 20th century / were buying their bread from stores or bakeries, / so consumer demand for yeast ② declined.
하지만 / 20세기 초의 점점 더 많은 사람들이 / 가게나 빵집에서 빵을 사고 있었고, / 그래서 효모에 대한 소비자 수요는 감소했다.

The producer of Fleischmann's yeast / hired the J. Walter Thompson advertising agency / to come up with a different marketing strategy / to ③ boost sales.
Fleischmann의 효모의 생산자는 / J. Walter Thompson 광고 대행사를 고용했다. / 다른 마케팅 전략을 고안하려고 / 판매를 촉진하기 위해서

No longer the "Soul of Bread," / the Thompson agency first turned yeast / into an important source of vitamins / with significant health ④ benefits.
더 이상 'Soul of Bread'를 쓰지 않고, / Thompson 광고 대행사는 먼저 효모를 바꾸었다. / 중요한 비타민 공급원으로 / 상당한 건강상의 이점이 있는

Shortly thereafter, / the advertising agency transformed yeast into a natural laxative.
그 이후 얼마 안 되어, / 광고 대행사는 효모를 천연 완하제로 바꾸었다.

⑤ Repositioning yeast / helped increase sales.
효모의 이미지 전환은 / 매출을 증가시키는 것을 도왔다.

광고주들은 그들이 홍보하는 상품의 시장 지위에 주장을 ① 맞추는 상당한 능력을 자주 보여주었다. 예를 들어, Fleischmann의 효모는 집에서 만든 빵을 요리하는 재료로 사용되었다. 하지만 20세기 초에 점점 더 많은 사람들이 가게나 빵집에서 빵을 사고 있었고, 그래서 효모에 대한 소비자 수요는 ② 증가했다(→ 감소했다). Fleischmann의 효모의 생산자는 판매를

---

③ 촉진하기 위해서 다른 마케팅 전략을 고안하려고 J. Walter Thompson 광고 대행사를 고용했다. 더 이상 "Soul of Bread"를 쓰지 않고, Thompson 광고 대행사는 먼저 효모를 상당한 건강상의 ④ 이점이 있는 중요한 비타민 공급원으로 바꾸었다. 그 이후 얼마 안 되어, 광고 대행사는 효모를 천연 완하제로 바꾸었다. 효모의 ⑤ 이미지 전환은 매출을 증가시키는 것을 도왔다.

Why? 왜 정답일까?
과거 효모는 집에서 굽는 빵의 재료로 쓰였지만, 20세기에 접어들어 사람들이 점점 가게에서 구운 빵을 사면서 효모에 대한 수요가 '떨어졌다'는 설명이 되도록 increased를 declined로 고쳐야 한다. 따라서 문맥상 낱말의 쓰임이 적절하지 않은 것은 ②이다.

- considerable ⓐ 상당한
- ingredient ⓝ 재료
- come up with 떠올리다, 고안하다
- significant ⓐ 상당한, 중요한
- laxative ⓝ 완하제(배변을 쉽게 하는 약·음식·음료)
- facility ⓝ 능력, 재능
- hire ⓥ 고용하다
- strategy ⓝ 전략
- transform ⓥ 변모시키다
- reposition ⓥ (제품의) 이미지를 바꾸다

구문 풀이
1행　Advertisers often displayed considerable facility in adapting their claims to the market status of the goods [[(that) they promoted].
（~하는 데 있어, ~할 때 / 선행사 / 생략）

★★★ 등급을 가르는 문제!

31 탁월함과 타인의 신뢰 　　정답률 50% | 정답 ④

다음 빈칸에 들어갈 말로 가장 적절한 것을 고르시오.
① Patience – 인내심
② Sacrifice – 희생
③ Honesty – 정직함
☑ Excellence – 탁월함
⑤ Creativity – 창의력

Individuals / who perform at a high level in their profession / often have instant credibility with others.
사람들은 / 자기 직업에서 높은 수준으로 수행하는 / 흔히 다른 사람들에게 즉각적인 신뢰를 얻는다.

People admire them, / they want to be like them, / and they feel connected to them.
사람들은 그들을 존경하고, / 그들처럼 되고 싶어 하고, / 그들과 연결되어 있다고 느낀다.

When they speak, / others listen — even if the area of their skill / has nothing to do with the advice they give.
그들이 말할 때, / 다른 사람들은 경청한다. / 비록 그들의 기술 분야가 / 그들이 주는 조언과 전혀 관련이 없을지라도

Think about a world-famous basketball player.
세계적으로 유명한 농구 선수에 대해 생각해 보라.

He has made more money from endorsements / than he ever did playing basketball.
그는 광고로부터 더 많은 돈을 벌었다. / 그가 농구를 하면서 그간 벌었던 것보다

Is it because of / his knowledge of the products he endorses?
그것이 ~ 때문일까? / 그가 광고하는 제품에 대한 그의 지식

No.
아니다.

It's because of / what he can do with a basketball.
그것은 ~ 때문이다. / 그가 농구로 할 수 있는 것

The same can be said of an Olympic medalist swimmer.
올림픽 메달리스트 수영 선수도 마찬가지이다.

People listen to him / because of what he can do in the pool.
사람들은 그의 말을 경청한다. / 그가 수영장에서 할 수 있는 것 때문에

And when an actor tells us / we should drive a certain car, / we don't listen / because of his expertise on engines.
그리고 어떤 배우가 우리에게 말할 때, / 우리가 특정 자동차를 운전해야 한다고 / 우리가 경청하는 것은 아니다. / 엔진에 대한 그의 전문 지식 때문에

We listen / because we admire his talent.
우리는 경청한다. / 그의 재능을 존경하기 때문에

Excellence connects.
탁월함이 연결된다.

If you possess a high level of ability in an area, / others may desire to connect with you / because of it.
만약 당신이 어떤 분야에서 높은 수준의 능력을 갖고 있다면, / 다른 사람들은 당신과 연결되기를 원할 수도 있다. / 그것 때문에

자기 직업에서 높은 수준으로 수행하는 사람들은 흔히 다른 사람들에게 즉각적인 신뢰를 얻는다. 사람들은 그들을 존경하고, 그들처럼 되고 싶어 하고, 그들과 연결되어 있다고 느낀다. 그들이 말할 때, 다른 사람들은 비록 그들의 기술 분야가 그들이 주는 조언과 전혀 관련이 없을지라도 경청한다. 세계적으로 유명한 농구 선수에 대해 생각해 보라. 그는 그가 농구를 하면서 그간 벌었던 것보다 광고로부터 더 많은 돈을 벌었다. 그것이 그가 광고하는 제품에 대한 그의 지식 때문일까? 아니다. 그것은 그가 농구로 할 수 있는 것 때문이다. 올림픽 메달리스트 수영 선수도 마찬가지이다. 사람들은 그가 수영장에서 할 수 있는 것 때문에 그의 말을 경청한다. 그리고 어떤 배우가 우리에게 특정 자동차를 운전해야 한다고 말할 때, 우리는 엔진에 대한 그의 전문 지식 때문에 경청하는 것은 아니다. 우리는 그의 재능을 존경하기 때문에 경청한다. 탁월함이 연결된다. 만약 당신이 어떤 분야에서 높은 수준의 능력을 갖고 있다면, 다른 사람들은 그것 때문에 당신과 연결되기를 원할 수도 있다.

Why? 왜 정답일까?
처음(Individuals who perform at a high level in their profession often have instant credibility with others.)과 마지막(If you possess a high level of ability in an area, others may desire to connect with you because of it.)에서 자기 분야에서 '높은 수준의 능력'을 가진 사람들은 다른 이들의 신뢰를 사기 쉽다고 언급하는 것으로 보아, 빈칸에 들어갈 말로 가장 적절한 것은 ④ '탁월함'이다.

- profession ⓝ 직업
- credibility ⓝ 신뢰
- have nothing to do with ~와 관련이 없다
- endorsement ⓝ (유명인의 텔레비전 등에서의 상품) 보증 선전
- endorse ⓥ (유명인이 광고에 나와 특정 상품을) 보증하다, 홍보하다
- medalist ⓝ 메달리스트
- patience ⓝ 인내심
- instant ⓐ 즉각적인
- admire ⓥ 존경하다
- world-famous ⓐ 세계적으로 유명한
- expertise ⓝ 전문 지식
- sacrifice ⓝ 희생

6행 He has made more money from endorsements than he ever did playing
basketball. (대동사= made money)

★★ 문제 해결 꿀~팁 ★★

▶ 많이 틀린 이유는?
빈칸 바로 앞에서 '전문 지식' 때문이 아니라 '재능' 때문에 유명인들의 말을 듣게 된다고 하는데, 이것을 ② '희생'이나 ⑤ '정직함'의 사례로 볼 수는 없다.
▶ 문제 해결 방법은?
글 처음과 마지막에 요지가 반복 제시된다. 즉 주제문인 첫 문장을 보고 빈칸을 완성하면 간단하다.

★★★ 등급을 가르는 문제!

32 도시처럼 상호작용으로 작동하는 뇌   정답률 43% | 정답 ①

다음 빈칸에 들어갈 말로 가장 적절한 것을 고르시오. [3점]
✔ operates in isolation – 독립적으로 작동하지
② suffers from rapid changes – 급속한 변화로 고생하지
③ resembles economic elements – 경제적 요소를 닮지
④ works in a systematic way – 체계적으로 작동하지
⑤ interacts with another – 서로 상호 작용하지

Think of the brain as a city.
뇌를 도시라고 생각해보라.
If you were to look out over a city / and ask "where is the economy located?" / you'd see / there's no good answer to the question.
만약 당신이 도시를 내다보며 / "경제는 어디에 위치해 있나요?"라고 묻는다면 / 당신은 알게 될 것이다. / 그 질문에 좋은 답이 없다는 것을
Instead, / the economy emerges / from the interaction of all the elements / — from the stores and the banks / to the merchants and the customers.
대신, / 경제는 나타난다. / 모든 요소의 상호 작용으로부터 / 상점과 은행에서 / 상인과 고객에 이르기까지
And so it is with the brain's operation: / it doesn't happen in one spot.
뇌의 작용도 그렇다. / 즉 그것은 한 곳에서 일어나지 않는다.
Just as in a city, / no neighborhood of the brain / operates in isolation.
도시에서처럼, / 뇌의 어떤 지역도 ~않는다. / 독립적으로 작동하지
In brains and in cities, / everything emerges / from the interaction between residents, / at all scales, / locally and distantly.
뇌와 도시 안에서, / 모든 것은 나타난다. / 거주자들 간의 상호 작용으로부터 / 모든 규모로, / 근거리든 원거리든
Just as trains bring materials and textiles into a city, / which become processed into the economy, / so the raw electrochemical signals from sensory organs / are transported along superhighways of neurons.
기차가 자재와 직물을 도시로 들여오고, / 그것이 경제 속으로 처리되는 것처럼, / 감각 기관으로부터의 가공되지 않은 전기화학적 신호는 / 뉴런의 초고속도로를 따라서 전해진다.
There / the signals undergo processing / and transformation into our conscious reality.
거기서 / 신호는 처리를 겪는다. / 그리고 우리의 의식적인 현실로의 변형을

뇌를 도시라고 생각해보라. 만약 당신이 도시를 내다보며 "경제는 어디에 위치해 있나요?"라고 묻는다면 그 질문에 좋은 답이 없다는 것을 알게 될 것이다. 대신, 경제는 상점과 은행에서 상인과 고객에 이르기까지 모든 요소의 상호 작용으로부터 나타난다. 뇌의 작용도 그렇다. 즉 그것은 한 곳에서 일어나지 않는다. 도시에서처럼, 뇌의 어떤 지역도 독립적으로 작동하지 않는다. 뇌와 도시 안에서, 모든 것은 모든 규모로, 근거리든 원거리든, 거주자들 간의 상호 작용으로부터 나타난다. 기차가 자재와 직물을 도시로 들여오고, 그것이 경제 속으로 처리되는 것처럼, 감각 기관으로부터의 가공되지 않은 전기화학적 신호는 뉴런의 초고속도로를 따라서 전해진다. 거기서 신호는 처리와 우리의 의식적인 현실로의 변형을 겪는다.

Why? 왜 정답일까?
경제가 모든 요소의 상호 작용으로 작동하는 것처럼 뇌 또한 그렇다(And so it is with the brain's operation: it doesn't happen in one spot. / ~ everything emerges from the interaction ~)는 내용이므로, 빈칸에 들어갈 말로 가장 적절한 것은 ① '독립적으로 작동하지'이다.

- think of A as B A를 B로 여기다
- element ⓝ 요소
- operation ⓝ 작동, 작용
- distantly ⓐⓓ 멀리, 원거리로
- process ⓥ 가공하다, 처리하다
- electrochemical ⓐ 전기화학의
- transport ⓥ 수송하다, 실어 나르다
- transformation ⓝ 변화, 변모
- in isolation 고립되어
- emerge ⓥ 나타나다, 생겨나다
- merchant ⓝ 상인
- locally ⓐⓓ 국지적으로
- textile ⓝ 직물
- raw ⓐ 원재료의, 날것의
- sensory organ 감각 기관
- undergo ⓥ 거치다, 겪다
- conscious ⓐ 의식적인

1행 If you were to look out over a city and ask "where is the economy
「if + 주어 + were to + 동사원형1 + ~   동사원형2 ~
located?" you'd see there's no good answer to the question.
주어 + 조동사 과거형 + 동사원형: 가정법 미래(거의 불가능한 상황에 대한 가정)

★★ 문제 해결 꿀~팁 ★★

▶ 많이 틀린 이유는?
도시가 많은 경제 주체의 상호 작용을 통해 돌아가듯이 뇌 또한 수많은 요소의 상호 작용으로 돌아간다는 내용이다. 주어가 「no + 명사」 형태이므로, 빈칸에는 주제와 반대되는 말을 넣어야 문장 전체가 주제를 나타내게 된다. 하지만 ③은 '경제 주체와 비슷하다'는 주제를 직접 제시하므로, 이를 빈칸에 넣어서 읽으면 '뇌의 그 어느 구역도 경제 주체와 비슷하지 않다'는 의미가 되어버린다. 즉 ③은 주제와 정반대의 의미를 완성한다.
▶ 문제 해결 방법은?
'뇌 = 도시'라는 비유를 확인하고, 둘의 공통점이 무엇인지 파악한 후, 선택지를 하나씩 대입하며 빈칸 문장의 의미를 주의 깊게 이해해 보자.

---

33 신체로부터 발생하는 감정   정답률 57% | 정답 ②

다음 빈칸에 들어갈 말로 가장 적절한 것을 고르시오. [3점]
① language guides our actions – 언어가 우리 행동을 이끈다
✔ emotions arise from our bodies – 감정이 우리 신체에 발생한다
③ body language hides our feelings – 신체 언어는 우리 감정을 숨긴다
④ what others say affects our mood – 다른 사람들의 말이 우리 감정에 영향을 미친다
⑤ negative emotions easily disappear – 부정적 감정은 쉽게 사라진다

Someone else's body language affects our own body, / which then creates an emotional echo / that makes us feel accordingly.
다른 사람의 신체 언어는 우리 자신의 신체에 영향을 미치며, / 그것은 그 후 감정적인 메아리를 만들어낸다. / 우리가 그에 맞춰 느끼게 하는
As Louis Armstrong sang, / "When you're smiling, / the whole world smiles with you."
Louis Armstrong이 노래했듯이, / "당신이 미소 지을 때, / 전 세계가 당신과 함께 미소 짓는다."
If copying another's smile / makes us feel happy, / the emotion of the smiler / has been transmitted via our body.
만약 다른 사람의 미소를 따라 하는 것이 / 우리를 행복하게 한다면, / 그 미소 짓는 사람의 감정은 / 우리의 신체를 통해 전달된 것이다.
Strange as it may sound, / this theory states / that emotions arise from our bodies.
이상하게 들릴지 모르지만, / 이 이론은 말한다. / 감정이 우리 신체에서 발생한다고
For example, / our mood can be improved / by simply lifting up the corners of our mouth.
예를 들어, / 우리의 기분은 좋아질 수 있다. / 단순히 입꼬리를 올리는 것으로
If people are asked / to bite down on a pencil lengthwise, / taking care not to let the pencil touch their lips / (thus forcing the mouth into a smile-like shape), / they judge cartoons funnier / than if they have been asked to frown.
만약 사람들이 요구받으면, / 연필을 긴 방향으로 꽉 물라고 / 연필이 입술에 닿지 않도록 조심하면서 / (그래서 억지로 입을 미소 짓는 것과 같은 모양이 되도록), / 그들은 만화를 더 재미있다고 판단한다. / 그들이 인상을 찌푸리라고 요구받은 경우보다
The primacy of the body / is sometimes summarized in the phrase / "I must be afraid, / because I'm running."
신체가 우선한다는 것은 / 때때로 구절로 요약된다. / "나는 분명 두려운가보다, / 왜냐하면 나는 도망치고 있기 때문이다."라는

다른 사람의 신체 언어는 우리 자신의 신체에 영향을 미치며, 그것은 그 후 우리가 그에 맞춰 (감정을) 느끼게 하는 감정적인 메아리를 만들어낸다. Louis Armstrong이 노래했듯이, "당신이 미소 지을 때, 전 세계가 당신과 함께 미소 짓는다." 만약 다른 사람의 미소를 따라 하는 것이 우리를 행복하게 한다면, 그 미소 짓는 사람의 감정은 우리의 신체를 통해 전달된 것이다. 이상하게 들릴지 모르지만, 이 이론은 감정이 우리 신체에서 발생한다고 말한다. 예를 들어, 우리의 기분은 단순히 입꼬리를 올리는 것으로 좋아질 수 있다. 만약 사람들이 연필을 긴 방향으로 꽉 물라고 요구받으면, 연필이 입술에 닿지 않도록 조심하면서 (그래서 억지로 입을 미소 짓는 것과 같은 모양이 되도록), 그들은 인상을 찌푸리라고 요구받은 경우보다 만화를 더 재미있다고 판단한다. 신체가 (감정에) 우선한다는 것은 "나는 분명 두려운가보다, 왜냐하면 나는 도망치고 있기 때문이다."라는 구절로 때때로 요약된다.

Why? 왜 정답일까?
빈칸 뒤의 실험에서 우리가 입꼬리를 올리고 있다 보면 더 기분이 좋아질 수 있다(~ our mood can be improved by simply lifting up the corners of our mouth.)고 설명하고, 이를 마지막 문장에서는 '(감정에 대한) 신체의 우선(The primacy of the body)'이라고 요약했다. 따라서 빈칸에 들어갈 말로 가장 적절한 것은 ② '감정이 우리 신체에서 발생한다'이다.

- emotional ⓐ 정서적인
- transmit ⓥ 전달하다
- theory ⓝ 이론
- lift up ~을 들어올리다
- bite down on ~을 깨물다
- frown ⓥ 얼굴을 찡그리다
- summarize ⓥ 요약하다
- hide ⓥ 숨기다
- accordingly ⓐⓓ 그에 따라
- via ⓟⓡⓔⓟ ~을 통해서
- state ⓥ 진술하다
- be asked to ~하도록 요청받다
- lengthwise ⓐⓓ 길게
- primacy ⓝ 우선함
- arise from ~에서 생겨나다

5행 Strange as it may sound, this theory states that emotions arise from our
「보어 + as + 주어 + 동사 : 비록 ~일지라도(양보 구문)」
bodies.

---

34 구매를 이끄는 희소성   정답률 59% | 정답 ③

다음 빈칸에 들어갈 말로 가장 적절한 것을 고르시오. [3점]
① Promoting products through social media
소셜 미디어를 통해 제품을 홍보하는 것
② Reducing the risk of producing poor quality items
질이 좋지 않은 제품을 생산할 위험을 낮추는 것
✔ Restricting the number of items customers can buy
고객이 구입할 수 있는 품목의 개수를 제한하는 것
④ Offering several options that customers find attractive
고객들이 매력적이라고 생각하는 몇 가지 선택 사항을 제시하는 것
⑤ Emphasizing the safety of products with research data
연구 데이터로 제품의 안전성을 강조하는 것

Restricting the number of items customers can buy / boosts sales.
고객이 구입할 수 있는 품목의 개수를 제한하는 것은 / 매출을 증가시킨다.
Brian Wansink, / Professor of Marketing at Cornell University, / investigated the effectiveness of this tactic in 1998.
Brian Wansink는 / Cornell University의 마케팅 교수인 / 1998년에 이 전략의 효과를 조사했다.
He persuaded three supermarkets in Sioux City, Iowa, / to offer Campbell's soup at a small discount: / 79 cents rather than 89 cents.
그는 Iowa 주 Sioux City에 있는 세 개의 슈퍼마켓을 설득했다. / Campbell의 수프를 약간 할인하여 제공하도록 / 즉 89센트가 아닌 79센트로
The discounted soup was sold in one of three conditions: / a control, / where there was no limit on the volume of purchases, / or two tests, / where customers were limited to either four or twelve cans.
할인된 수프는 세 가지 조건 중 하나의 조건으로 판매되었다. / 즉 하나의 통제 집단 / 구매량에 제한이 없는 / 또는 두 개의 실험 집단 / 고객이 4캔 아니면 12캔으로 제한되는
In the unlimited condition / shoppers bought 3.3 cans on average, / whereas in the scarce condition, / when there was a limit, / they bought 5.3 on average.

무제한 조건에서 / 구매자들은 평균 3.3캔을 구입했고, / 반면 희소 조건에서는 / 제한이 있던 / 그들은 평균 5.3캔을 구입했다.
This suggests / scarcity encourages sales.
이것은 보여준다. / 희소성이 판매를 장려한다는 것을
The findings are particularly strong / because the test took place / in a supermarket with genuine shoppers.
그 결과는 특히 타당하다. / 이 실험이 진행되었기 때문에 / 진짜 구매자들이 있는 슈퍼마켓에서
It didn't rely on claimed data, / nor was it held in a laboratory / where consumers might behave differently.
그것은 주장된 데이터에 의존하지 않았고, / 그것은 실험실에서 이루어진 것도 아니었다. / 소비자들이 다르게 행동할지도 모르는

고객이 구입할 수 있는 품목의 개수를 제한하는 것은 매출을 증가시킨다. Cornell University의 마케팅 교수인 Brian Wansink는 1998년에 이 전략의 효과를 조사했다. 그는 Iowa 주 Sioux City에 있는 세 개의 슈퍼마켓이 Campbell의 수프를 약간 할인하여 89센트가 아닌 79센트로 제공하도록 설득했다. 할인된 수프는 세 가지 조건 중 하나의 조건으로 판매되었다. 구매량에 제한이 없는 하나의 통제 집단, 또는 고객이 4개 아니면 12개의 캔으로 제한되는 두 개의 실험 집단이 그것이었다. 무제한 조건에서 구매자들은 평균 3.3캔을 구입했던 반면, 제한이 있던 희소 조건에서는 평균 5.3캔을 구입했다. 이것은 희소성이 판매를 장려한다는 것을 보여준다. 이 실험은 진짜 구매자들이 있는 슈퍼마켓에서 진행되었기 때문에 그 결과는 특히 타당하다. 그것은 주장된 데이터에 의존하지 않았고, 소비자들이 다르게 행동할지도 모르는 실험실에서 이루어진 것도 아니었다.

Why? 왜 정답일까?

빈칸 뒤로 소개된 연구에서, 구매 개수에 제한이 있었던 실험군이 제품을 가장 많이 구입했다고 설명하며, 희소성이 판매를 장려한다는 결론을 정리하고 있다(~ scarcity encourages sales.). 따라서 빈칸에 들어갈 말로 가장 적절한 것은 ③ '고객이 구입할 수 있는 품목의 개수를 제한하는 것'이다.

- investigate ⓥ 조사하다
- tactic ⓝ 전략
- rather than ~ 대신에
- control ⓝ 통제 집단(실험에서 처치를 가하지 않고 둔 집단)
- unlimited ⓐ 제한되지 않은, 무제한의
- genuine ⓐ 진짜의
- laboratory ⓝ 실험실
- differently ⓐ 다르게
- emphasize ⓥ 강조하다
- effectiveness ⓝ 유효성, 효과 있음
- persuade ⓥ 설득하다
- condition ⓝ 조건
- scarcity ⓝ 희소성
- rely on ~에 의존하다
- behave ⓥ 행동하다
- attractive ⓐ 매력적인

구문 풀이

13행 It didn't rely on claimed data, nor was it held in a laboratory where
부정문   「부정어 + be + 주어 + p.p. : 도치 구문(~도 없다)」
consumers might behave differently.

---

35 기술과 생산성의 관계   정답률 58% | 정답 ④

다음 글에서 전체 흐름과 관계 없는 문장은?

Although technology has the potential / to increase productivity, / it can also have a negative impact on productivity.
기술은 잠재력을 가지고 있지만, / 생산성을 높일 수 있는 / 그것은 또한 생산성에 부정적인 영향을 미칠 수 있다.
For example, / in many office environments / workers sit at desks with computers / and have access to the internet.
예를 들어, / 많은 사무실 환경에서 / 직원들은 컴퓨터가 있는 책상에 앉아 / 인터넷에 접속한다.
① They are able to check their personal e-mails / and use social media / whenever they want to.
그들은 개인 이메일을 확인하고 / 소셜 미디어를 사용할 수 있다. / 그들이 원할 때마다
② This can stop them from doing their work / and make them less productive.
이것은 그들이 일을 하는 것을 방해하고 / 생산성이 떨어지게 할 수 있다.
③ Introducing new technology / can also have a negative impact on production / when it causes a change to the production process / or requires workers to learn a new system.
새로운 기술을 도입하는 것은 / 또한 생산에 부정적인 영향을 미칠 수 있다. / 그것이 생산 공정에 변화를 야기하거나 / 직원들에게 새로운 시스템을 배우도록 요구할 때
☑ Using technology / can enable businesses / to produce more goods / and to get more out of the other factors of production.
기술을 사용하는 것은 / 기업이 ~할 수 있게 한다. / 더 많은 제품을 생산하고 / 다른 생산 요소들로부터 더 많은 것을 얻게
⑤ Learning to use new technology / can be time consuming and stressful for workers / and this can cause a decline in productivity.
새로운 기술 사용법을 배우는 것은 / 직원들에게 시간이 많이 드는 일이고 스트레스를 줄 수 있으며, / 이것은 생산성 저하를 야기할 수 있다.

기술은 생산성을 높일 수 있는 잠재력을 가지고 있지만, 또한 생산성에 부정적인 영향을 미칠 수 있다. 예를 들어, 많은 사무실 환경에서 직원들은 컴퓨터가 있는 책상에 앉아 인터넷에 접속한다. ① 그들은 원할 때마다 개인 이메일을 확인하고 소셜 미디어를 사용할 수 있다. ② 이것은 그들이 일을 하는 것을 방해하고 생산성이 떨어지게 할 수 있다. ③ 또한 새로운 기술을 도입하는 것은 생산 공정에 변화를 야기하거나 직원들에게 새로운 시스템을 배우도록 요구할 때 생산에 부정적인 영향을 미칠 수 있다. ④ 기술을 사용하는 것은 기업이 더 많은 제품을 생산하고 다른 생산 요소들로부터 더 많은 것을 얻게 할 수 있다. ⑤ 새로운 기술 사용법을 배우는 것은 직원들에게 시간이 많이 드는 일이고 스트레스를 줄 수 있으며, 이것은 생산성 저하를 야기할 수 있다.

Why? 왜 정답일까?

기술이 생산성을 떨어뜨릴 수 있다는 내용인데, ④는 기술 사용이 더 많은 제품 생산에 도움이 되고 생산 요소로부터 더 많은 것을 얻게 한다는 긍정적 내용이다. 따라서 전체 흐름과 관계 없는 문장은 ④이다.

- impact ⓝ 영향, 충격
- production ⓝ 생산, 제조
- require ⓥ 요구하다
- time-consuming ⓐ 시간이 많이 걸리는
- have access to ~에 접근하다, ~을 이용하다
- cause ⓥ 야기하다
- factor ⓝ 요인, 요소

구문 풀이

5행 This can stop them from doing their work and make them less productive.
「stop + A + from + B : A가 B하지 못하게 하다」 5형식 동사 목적어 형용사 보어

---

36 시계의 발명   정답률 78% | 정답 ②

주어진 글 다음에 이어질 글의 순서로 가장 적절한 것을 고르시오. [3점]
① (A) – (C) – (B)   ☑ (B) – (A) – (C)
③ (B) – (C) – (A)   ④ (C) – (A) – (B)
⑤ (C) – (B) – (A)

Up until about 6,000 years ago, / most people were farmers.
약 6,000년 전까지 / 대부분의 사람들은 농부였다.
Many lived in different places throughout the year, / hunting for food / or moving their livestock to areas with enough food.
많은 사람들은 일 년 내내 여러 장소에서 살았고, / 식량을 찾아다니거나 / 가축을 충분한 먹이가 있는 지역으로 옮겼다.
(B) There was no need to tell the time / because life depended on natural cycles, / such as the changing seasons or sunrise and sunset.
시간을 알 필요가 없었다. / 삶이 자연적인 주기에 달려 있었기 때문에 / 변화하는 계절이나 일출과 일몰 같은
Gradually more people started to live in larger settlements, / and some needed to tell the time.
점점 더 많은 사람들이 더 큰 정착지에서 살기 시작했고, / 어떤 사람들은 시간을 알 필요가 있었다.
(A) For example, / priests wanted to know / when to carry out religious ceremonies.
예를 들어, / 성직자들은 알고 싶었다. / 언제 종교적인 의식을 수행해야 하는지
This was when people first invented clocks / — devices that show, measure, and keep track of passing time.
이때 사람들이 처음으로 발명했다. / 시간을 보여주고, 측정하고, 흐르는 시간을 추적하는 장치인 시계를
(C) Clocks have been important ever since.
시계는 그 이후로도 중요했다.
Today, / clocks are used for important things / such as setting busy airport timetables / — if the time is incorrect, / aeroplanes might crash into each other / when taking off or landing!
오늘날, / 시계는 중요한 일에 사용된다. / 바쁜 공항 시간표를 설정하는 것과 같은 / 만약 시간이 부정확하다면, / 비행기는 서로 충돌할지도 모른다! / 이륙하거나 착륙할 때

약 6,000년 전까지 대부분의 사람들은 농부였다. 많은 사람들은 일 년 내내 여러 장소에서 살았고, 식량을 찾아다니거나 가축을 충분한 먹이가 있는 지역으로 옮겼다.

(B) 변화하는 계절이나 일출과 일몰 같은 자연적인 주기에 삶이 달려 있었기 때문에 시간을 알 필요가 없었다. 점점 더 많은 사람들이 더 큰 정착지에서 살기 시작했고, 어떤 사람들은 시간을 알 필요가 있었다.

(A) 예를 들어, 성직자들은 언제 종교적인 의식을 수행해야 하는지 알고 싶었다. 이때 사람들이 시간을 보여주고, 측정하고, 흐르는 시간을 추적하는 장치인 시계를 처음으로 발명했다.

(C) 시계는 그 이후로도 중요했다. 오늘날, 시계는 바쁜 공항 시간표를 설정하는 것과 같은 중요한 일에 사용된다. 만약 시간이 부정확하다면, 비행기는 이륙하거나 착륙할 때 서로 충돌할지도 모른다!

Why? 왜 정답일까?

사람들이 대부분 농부였던 시절을 언급하는 주어진 글 뒤로, 이때는 시계가 필요 없었다는 내용으로 시작하는 (B)가 연결된다. 한편, (B)의 후반부는 그러다 일부 사람들이 시계를 필요로 하기 시작했다는 내용이고, (A)는 그런 사람들의 예로 성직자를 언급한다. (C)는 시계가 처음 발명된 이후로 시계의 중요성이 높아졌고, 오늘날에도 시계가 중요한 역할을 담당하고 있음을 설명한다. 따라서 글의 순서로 가장 적절한 것은 ② '(B) – (A) – (C)'이다.

- hunt for ~을 사냥하다
- carry out 수행하다
- device ⓝ 장치
- keep track of ~을 추적하다, 기록하다
- gradually ⓐ 점차
- tell the time 시간을 알다
- take off 이륙하다
- livestock ⓝ 가축
- religious ⓐ 종교적인
- measure ⓥ 측정하다
- natural cycle 자연적 주기
- settlement ⓝ 정착(지)
- crash into ~에 충돌하다
- land ⓥ 착륙하다

구문 풀이

12행 Today, clocks are used for important things such as setting busy airport timetables — if the time is incorrect, aeroplanes might crash into each other when taking off or landing!
접속사를 포함한 분사구문(= when they take off or land)

---

37 생산성과 노동 분업   정답률 58% | 정답 ⑤

주어진 글 다음에 이어질 글의 순서로 가장 적절한 것을 고르시오.
① (A) – (C) – (B)   ② (B) – (A) – (C)
③ (B) – (C) – (A)   ④ (C) – (A) – (B)
☑ (C) – (B) – (A)

Managers are always looking for ways / to increase productivity, / which is the ratio of costs to output in production.
관리자들은 항상 방법을 찾고 있는데, / 생산성을 높일 수 있는 / 이것은 생산에서 비용 대비 생산량의 비율이다.
Adam Smith, / writing when the manufacturing industry was new, / described a way / that production could be made more efficient, / known as the "division of labor."
Adam Smith는 / 제조 산업이 새로 등장했을 때 저술한 / 방식을 설명했다 / 생산이 더 효율적으로 될 수 있는 / 이것은 '노동 분업'으로 알려져 있다.
(C) Making most manufactured goods / involves several different processes / using different skills.
대부분의 공산품을 만드는 것은 / 여러 가지 다른 과정을 포함한다. / 다른 기술을 사용하는
Smith's example was the manufacture of pins: / the wire is straightened, / sharpened, / a head is put on, / and then it is polished.
Smith의 예는 핀의 제조였다. / 철사가 곧게 펴지고, / 뾰족해지고, / 머리가 끼워지고, / 그러고 나서 그것은 다듬어진다.
(B) One worker could do all these tasks, / and make 20 pins in a day.
한 명의 노동자가 이 모든 작업을 할 수 있고, / 하루에 20개의 핀을 만들 수 있다.
But this work can be divided into its separate processes, / with a number of workers each performing one task.
그러나 이 일은 별개의 과정으로 분리될 수 있다. / 많은 노동자가 각각 한 가지 작업을 수행하며

(A) Because each worker specializes in one job, / he or she can work much faster / without changing from one task to another.
각 노동자는 한 가지 작업을 전문으로 하기 때문에, / 이 사람은 훨씬 더 빠르게 일할 수 있다. / 한 작업에서 다른 작업으로 옮겨가지 않으면서

Now 10 workers can produce thousands of pins in a day / — a huge increase in productivity / from the 200 / they would have produced before.
이제 10명의 노동자가 하루에 수천 개의 핀을 생산할 수 있다. / 이는 큰 증가이다 / 이는 생산성의 큰 증가이다. / 200개로부터 / 이전에 그들이 생산했던

관리자들은 항상 생산성을 높일 수 있는 방법을 찾고 있는데, / 생산성은 생산에서 비용 대비 생산량의 비율이다. 제조 산업이 새로 등장했을 때 저술한 Adam Smith는 생산이 더 효율적으로 될 수 있는 방식을 설명했고, 이것은 '노동 분업'으로 알려져 있다.

(C) 대부분의 공산품을 만드는 것은 다른 기술을 사용하는 여러 가지 다른 과정을 포함한다. Smith의 예는 핀의 제조였다. 철사를 곧게 펴고, 뾰족하게 만들고, 머리를 끼운 다음, 그것을 다듬는다.

(B) 한 명의 노동자가 이 모든 작업들을 할 수 있고, 하루에 20개의 핀을 만들 수도 있다. 그러나 이 일은 많은 노동자가 각각 한 가지 작업을 수행하며 별개의 과정으로 분리될 수 있다.

(A) 각 노동자는 한 가지 작업을 전문으로 하기 때문에, 이 사람은 한 작업에서 다른 작업으로 옮겨가지 않으면서 훨씬 더 빠르게 일할 수 있다. 이제 10명의 노동자가 하루에 수천 개의 핀을 생산할 수 있다. 이는 이전에 그들이 생산했던 200개로부터 생산성 측면에서 크게 증가한 것이다.

Why? 왜 정답일까?

'노동 분업'의 개념을 소개하는 주어진 글 뒤로, 핀 제조 과정을 예로 설명하는 (C), 이 제조 과정은 한 사람에 의해 수행될 수도 있지만, 분업으로 진행될 수도 있다고 설명하는 (B), 분업 상황의 장점을 소개하는 (A)가 차례로 이어져야 자연스럽다. 따라서 글의 순서로 가장 적절한 것은 ⑤ '(C) – (B) – (A)'이다.

- ratio ⓝ 비율
- manufacturing industry 제조업
- efficient ⓐ 효율적인
- specialize in ~에 특화되다
- involve ⓥ 포함하다, 수반하다
- sharpen ⓥ 뾰족하게 하다
- output ⓝ 산출
- describe ⓥ 설명하다
- division of labor 분업
- a number of 많은
- straighten ⓥ 곧게 펴다
- polish ⓥ 다듬다

구문 풀이

12행 But this work can be divided into its separate processes, with a number of workers each performing one task.
「with + 명사 + 분사 : ~이 …한 채로(부대상황 분사구문)」

★★★ 등급을 가르는 문제!

38 느리게라도 계속 진행되는 변화 정답률 39% | 정답 ②

글의 흐름으로 보아, 주어진 문장이 들어가기에 가장 적절한 곳을 고르시오.

Sometimes the pace of change is far slower.
때때로 변화의 속도는 훨씬 더 느리다.

① The face you saw / reflected in your mirror this morning / probably appeared no different / from the face you saw the day before — or a week or a month ago.
당신이 본 얼굴은 / 오늘 아침 거울에 비춰진 / 아마도 다르지 않게 보였을 것이다. / 당신이 그 전날에 본 얼굴과 / 또는 일주일이나 한 달 전에

✓ Yet we know / that the face that stares back at us from the glass / is not the same, / as it was 10 minutes ago.
그러나 우리는 안다. / 거울에서 우리를 마주보는 얼굴이 / 같지 않고, / 같을 수 없다는 것을 / 10분 전과

The proof is in your photo album: / Look at a photograph / taken of yourself 5 or 10 years ago / and you see clear differences / between the face in the snapshot / and the face in your mirror.
증거는 당신의 사진 앨범에 있다. / 사진을 보라 / 5년 또는 10년 전에 당신을 찍은 / 그러면 당신은 명확한 차이를 보게 될 것이다 / 스냅사진 속의 얼굴과 / 거울 속 얼굴 사이의

③ If you lived in a world without mirrors for a year / and then saw your reflection, / you might be surprised by the change.
만약 당신이 일 년간 거울이 없는 세상에 살고 / 그 이후 (거울에) 비친 당신의 모습을 본다면, / 당신은 그 변화 때문에 깜짝 놀랄지도 모른다.

④ After an interval of 10 years / without seeing yourself, / you might not at first recognize the person / peering from the mirror.
10년의 기간이 지난 후, / 스스로를 보지 않고 / 당신은 그 사람을 처음에는 알아보지 못할지도 모른다. / 거울에서 쳐다보고 있는

⑤ Even something as basic as our own face / changes from moment to moment.
심지어 우리 자신의 얼굴같이 아주 기본적인 것조차도 / 순간순간 변한다.

때때로 변화의 속도는 훨씬 더 느리다. ① 오늘 아침 당신이 거울에 비춰진 것을 본 얼굴은 아마도 당신이 그 전날 또는 일주일이나 한 달 전에 본 얼굴과 다르지 않게 보였을 것이다. ② 그러나 우리는 거울에서 우리를 마주보는 얼굴이 10분 전과 같지 않고, 같을 수 없다는 것을 안다. 증거는 당신의 사진 앨범에 있다. 5년 또는 10년 전에 찍은 당신의 사진을 보면 당신은 스냅사진 속의 얼굴과 거울 속 얼굴 사이의 명확한 차이를 보게 될 것이다. ③ 만약 당신이 일 년간 거울이 없는 세상에 살고 그 이후 (거울에) 비친 당신의 모습을 본다면, 당신은 그 변화 때문에 깜짝 놀랄지도 모른다. ④ 스스로를 보지 않고 10년의 기간이 지난 후, 당신은 거울에서 쳐다보고 있는 사람을 처음에는 알아보지 못할지도 모른다. ⑤ 심지어 우리 자신의 얼굴같이 아주 기본적인 것조차도 순간순간 변한다.

Why? 왜 정답일까?

② 앞은 오늘 아침 거울로 본 얼굴이 전날, 일주일 전, 또는 한 달 전에 본 얼굴과 다르지 않았을 것이라는 내용인데, ② 뒤는 얼굴이 명확히 '달라졌다'는 것을 알 수 있는 증거에 관한 내용이다. 즉 ② 앞뒤로 상반된 내용이 제시되어 흐름이 어색하게 끊기므로, 주어진 문장이 들어가기에 가장 적절한 곳은 ②이다.

- reflect ⓥ 반사하다
- snapshot ⓝ 스냅사진, 짧은 묘사
- surprised ⓐ 놀란
- peer ⓥ 응시하다
- clear ⓐ 명확한
- reflection ⓝ (물이나 거울에 비친) 그림자
- interval ⓝ 간격
- from moment to moment 시시각각

구문 풀이

12행 Even something as basic as our own face changes from moment to moment.
「as + 원급 + as : ~만큼 …한」

★★ 문제 해결 꿀~팁 ★★

▶ 많이 틀린 이유는?
가장 헷갈리는 ③ 앞을 보면, 우리가 5~10년 전 찍은 사진을 보면 지금 거울로 보는 얼굴과 다르다는 것을 알 수 있다는 내용이며, 주어진 문장 또한 우리 얼굴이 단 10분 사이에도 '달라진다'는 내용이다. 하지만 주어진 문장은 Yet(그럼에도 불구하고)으로 시작하므로, 이 앞에는 '다르지 않다'라는 반대되는 내용이 나와야 한다. 따라서 주어진 문장 내용과 똑같은 내용이 앞에 나오는 ③ 자리에 주어진 문장을 넣을 수는 없다.

▶ 문제 해결 방법은?
② 앞뒤로 발생하는 논리적 공백에 주목하자. ②는 거울로 보는 우리 얼굴이 '별 차이가 없어보인다'는 내용인데, ②는 사진 앨범 속 우리 얼굴이 '명확한 차이'를 보인다는 내용이다. 즉 ② 앞뒤의 의미가 '다르지 않다 ↔ 다르다'로 상반되는 상황인데, 이 경우 반드시 역접 연결어(주어진 문장의 Yet)가 있어야만 한다.

★★★ 등급을 가르는 문제!

39 나이가 들면서 호기심이 줄어드는 까닭 정답률 31% | 정답 ⑤

글의 흐름으로 보아, 주어진 문장이 들어가기에 가장 적절한 곳을 고르시오. [3점]

According to educational psychologist Susan Engel, / curiosity begins to decrease / as young as four years old.
교육 심리학자 Susan Engel에 따르면, / 호기심은 줄어들기 시작한다. / 네 살 정도라는 어린 나이에

By the time we are adults, / we have fewer questions and more default settings.
우리가 어른이 될 무렵, / 질문이 더 적어지고 기본값은 더 많아진다.

As Henry James put it, / "Disinterested curiosity is past, / the mental grooves and channels set."
Henry James가 말했듯이, / '무관심한 호기심은 없어지고, / 정신의 고랑과 경로가 자리잡는다.'

① The decline in curiosity / can be traced / in the development of the brain through childhood.
호기심의 감소는 / 원인을 찾을 수 있다. / 유년 시절 동안의 뇌의 발달에서

② Though smaller than the adult brain, / the infant brain contains millions more neural connections.
비록 성인의 뇌보다 작지만, / 유아의 뇌는 수백만 개 더 많은 신경 연결을 가지고 있다.

③ The wiring, however, is a mess; / the lines of communication between infant neurons / are far less efficient / than between those in the adult brain.
그러나 연결 상태는 엉망인데, / 유아의 뉴런 간의 전달은 / 훨씬 덜 효율적이다. / 성인 뇌 속 뉴런끼리의 전달보다

④ The baby's perception of the world / is consequently both intensely rich and wildly disordered.
세상에 대한 아기의 인식은 / 결과적으로 매우 풍부하면서도 상당히 무질서하다.

✓ As children absorb more evidence / from the world around them, / certain possibilities become much more likely and more useful / and harden into knowledge or beliefs.
아이들이 더 많은 증거를 흡수함에 따라, / 그들 주변의 세상으로부터 / 특정한 가능성들이 훨씬 더 커지게 되고 더 유용하게 되며 / 지식이나 믿음으로 굳어진다.

The neural pathways / that enable those beliefs / become faster and more automatic, / while the ones / that the child doesn't use regularly / are pruned away.
신경 경로는 / 그러한 믿음을 가능하게 하는 / 더 빠르고 자동적으로 이루어지게 되고, / 반면에 경로는 / 아이가 주기적으로 사용하지 않는 / 제거된다.

교육 심리학자 Susan Engel에 따르면, 호기심은 네 살 정도라는 어린 나이에 줄어들기 시작한다. 우리가 어른이 될 무렵, 질문은 더 적어지고 기본값은 더 많아진다. Henry James가 말했듯이, '무관심한 호기심은 없어지고, 정신의 고랑과 경로가 자리잡는다.' 호기심의 감소는 유년 시절 동안의 뇌의 발달에서 원인을 찾을 수 있다. ② 비록 성인의 뇌보다 작지만, 유아의 뇌는 수백만 개 더 많은 신경 연결을 가지고 있다. ③ 그러나 연결 상태는 엉망인데, 유아의 뉴런 간의 전달은 성인 뇌 속 뉴런끼리의 전달보다 훨씬 덜 효율적이다. ④ 결과적으로 세상에 대한 아기의 인식은 매우 풍부하면서도 상당히 무질서하다. ⑤ 아이들이 그들 주변의 세상으로부터 더 많은 증거를 흡수함에 따라, 특정한 가능성들이 훨씬 더 커지게 되고 더 유용하게 되며 지식이나 믿음으로 굳어진다. 그러한 믿음을 가능하게 하는 신경 경로는 더 빠르고 자동적으로 이루어지게 되고, 반면에 아이가 주기적으로 사용하지 않는 경로는 제거된다.

Why? 왜 정답일까?

⑤ 앞은 아기의 인식이 성인에 비해 무질서하다는 내용인데, ⑤ 뒤에서는 갑자기 '믿음'을 언급하며, 신경 경로의 자동화와 제거를 설명한다. 이때 주어진 문장을 보면, 아이들이 주변 세상에서 더 많은 근거를 얻고 더 유용한 가능성들을 취하면서 '믿음'이 굳어지기 시작한다고 한다. 이 '믿음'이 ⑤ 뒤와 연결되는 것이므로, 주어진 문장이 들어가기에 가장 적절한 곳은 ⑤이다.

- absorb ⓥ (정보를) 받아들이다
- educational ⓐ 교육의
- decrease ⓥ 감소하다
- disinterested ⓐ 무관심한
- channel ⓝ 경로
- childhood ⓝ 어린 시절
- neural ⓐ 신경의
- perception ⓝ 지각, 인식
- intensely ⓓ 대단히, 강렬하게
- pathway ⓝ 경로
- prune ⓥ 가지치기하다
- harden ⓥ 굳어지다
- curiosity ⓝ 호기심
- default setting 기본값
- groove ⓝ 고랑
- development ⓝ 발달
- infant ⓝ 유아
- mess ⓝ 엉망
- consequently ⓓ 그 결과
- disordered ⓐ 무질서한
- automatic ⓐ 자동적인

구문 풀이

1행 As children absorb more evidence from the world around them, certain possibilities become much more likely and more useful and harden into knowledge or beliefs.
접속사(~함에 따라) =children 동사1 주격 보어(비교급 형용사) 동사2

★★ 문제 해결 꿀~팁 ★★

▶ 많이 틀린 이유는?
① 뒤의 문장 이후, ②~⑤ 사이의 내용은 모두 부연 설명이다. 호기심이 감소하는 까닭은 뇌 발달에 있다는 일반적인 내용 뒤로, 아이들의 뇌가 성인의 뇌보다 작지만 연결고리가 훨씬 더 많다는 설명, 그렇지만 그 연결고리가 엉망이라는 설명, 그렇기에 아이의 세상 인식은 어른보다 풍부할지언정 무질서하다는 설명이 모두 자연스럽게 이어지고 있다. 주어진 문장은 이 모든 설명이 마무리된 후 '어쩌다' 호기심이 떨어지는 것인지 마침내 언급하는 문장이다.

▶ 문제 해결 방법은?
연결어 힌트가 없어서 난해하게 느껴질 수 있지만, 지시어 힌트를 활용하면 아주 쉽다. ⑤ 뒤에는 '그러한 믿음(those beliefs)'이라는 표현이 나오는데, 이는 앞에서 '믿음'을 언급했어야만 쓸 수 있는 표현이다. 하지만 ⑤ 앞까지는 beliefs가 전혀 등장하지 않고, 오로지 주어진 문장에만 knowledge or beliefs가 등장한다.

★★★ 등급을 가르는 문제! ★★★

40 식단의 좋고 나쁨
정답률 53% | 정답 ②

다음 글의 내용을 한 문장으로 요약하고자 한다. 빈칸 (A), (B)에 들어갈 말로 가장 적절한 것은?

(A)	(B)
① incorrect 부정확한	…… limited to ~에 한정된
✔ appropriate 적절한	…… composed of ~로 구성되는
③ wrong 틀린	…… aimed at ~을 목표로 하는
④ appropriate 적절한	…… tested on ~에 시험된
⑤ incorrect 부정확한	…… adjusted to ~에 맞춰진

Nearly eight of ten U.S. adults believe / there are "good foods" and "bad foods."
미국 성인 10명 중 거의 8명이 믿는다. / '좋은 음식'과 '나쁜 음식'이 있다고

Unless we're talking / about spoiled stew, poison mushrooms, or something similar, / however, / no foods can be labeled as either good or bad.
우리가 이야기하고 있지 않는 한, / 상한 스튜, 독버섯, 또는 이와 유사한 것에 관해 / 하지만 / 어떤 음식도 좋고 나쁨으로 분류될 수 없다.

There are, / however, / combinations of foods / that add up to a healthful or unhealthful diet.
~이 있다. / 하지만 / 음식들의 조합 / 결국 건강에 좋은 식단이나 건강에 좋지 않은 식단이 되는

Consider the case of an adult / who eats only foods thought of as "good" / — for example, / raw broccoli, apples, orange juice, boiled tofu, and carrots.
성인의 경우를 생각해보라. / '좋은' 음식이라고 생각되는 음식만 먹는 / 가령 / 생브로콜리, 사과, 오렌지 주스, 삶은 두부와 당근과 같이

Although all these foods are nutrient-dense, / they do not add up to a healthy diet / because they don't supply / a wide enough variety of the nutrients we need.
비록 이 모든 음식들이 영양이 풍부하지만, / 그것들은 결국 건강한 식단이 되지 않는다. / 그것들이 공급하진 않기에 / 우리가 필요로 하는 충분히 다양한 영양소를

Or take the case of the teenager / who occasionally eats fried chicken, / but otherwise stays away from fried foods.
또는 십 대의 경우를 예로 들어보자. / 튀긴 치킨을 가끔 먹지만, / 다른 경우에는 튀긴 음식을 멀리하는

The occasional fried chicken / isn't going to knock his or her diet off track.
가끔 먹는 튀긴 치킨은 / 이 십 대의 식단을 궤도에서 벗어나게 하지 않을 것이다.

But the person / who eats fried foods every day, / with few vegetables or fruits, / and loads up on supersized soft drinks, candy, and chips for snacks / has a bad diet.
하지만 사람은 / 매일 튀긴 음식을 먹고, / 채소나 과일을 거의 먹지 않으면서 / 간식으로 초대형 탄산음료, 사탕, 그리고 감자 칩으로 배를 가득 채우는 / 식단이 나쁜 것이다.

➡ Unlike the common belief, / defining foods as good or bad / is not (A) appropriate; / in fact, / a healthy diet is determined / largely by what the diet is (B) composed of.
일반적인 믿음과 달리, / 음식을 좋고 나쁨으로 정의하는 것은 / 적절하지 않고, / 사실 / 건강에 좋은 식단이란 결정된다. / 대체로 그 식단이 무엇으로 구성되는지에 의해

미국 성인 10명 중 거의 8명이 '좋은 음식'과 '나쁜 음식'이 있다고 믿는다. 하지만, 우리가 상한 스튜, 독버섯, 또는 이와 유사한 것에 관해 이야기하고 있지 않는 한, 어떤 음식도 좋고 나쁨으로 분류될 수 없다. 하지만, 결국 건강에 좋은 식단이나 건강에 좋지 않은 식단이 되는 음식들의 조합이 있다. 가령 생브로콜리, 사과, 오렌지 주스, 삶은 두부와 당근과 같이 '좋은' 음식이라고 생각되는 음식만 먹는 성인의 경우를 생각해보라. 비록 이 모든 음식들이 영양이 풍부하지만, 그것들은 우리가 필요로 하는 충분히 다양한 영양소를 공급하진 않기에 결국 건강한 식단이 되지 않는다. 또는 튀긴 치킨을 가끔 먹지만, 다른 경우에는 튀긴 음식을 멀리하는 십 대의 경우를 예로 들어보자. 가끔 먹는 튀긴 치킨은 이 십 대의 식단을 궤도에서 벗어나게 하지 않을 것이다. 하지만 채소나 과일을 거의 먹지 않으면서 매일 튀긴 음식을 먹고, 간식으로 초대형 탄산음료, 사탕, 그리고 감자 칩으로 배를 가득 채우는 사람은 식단이 나쁜 것이다.

➡ 일반적인 믿음과 달리, 음식을 좋고 나쁨으로 정의하는 것은 (A) 적절하지 않고, 사실 건강에 좋은 식단이란 대체로 그 식단이 무엇으로 (B) 구성되는지에 의해 결정된다.

Why? 왜 정답일까?

첫 세 문장에서 음식을 절대적으로 좋고 나쁘다고 분류할 수는 없고(~ no foods can be labeled as either good or bad.), 그 조합이 중요하다(There are, however, combinations of foods that add up to a healthful or unhealthful diet.)고 말한다. 따라서 요약문의 빈칸 (A), (B)에 들어갈 말로 가장 적절한 것은 ② '(A) appropriate(적절한), (B) composed of(~로 구성되는)'이다.

- nearly [ad] 거의
- spoiled @ 상한
- label A as B A를 B라고 분류하다
- add up to 결국 ~이 되다
- broccoli ⓝ 브로콜리
- nutrient-dense @ 영양이 풍부한
- nutrient ⓝ 영양분
- otherwise [ad] 그렇지 않으면, 다른 경우에는
- off track 제 길에서 벗어난
- composed of ~로 구성된
- unless [conj] ~하지 않는 한
- poison mushroom 독버섯
- combination ⓝ 조합
- healthful @ 건강에 좋은
- tofu ⓝ 두부
- a wide variety of 매우 다양한
- occasionally [ad] 가끔
- stay away from ~을 멀리하다
- load up on ~로 배를 가득 채우다

구문 풀이

2행 Unless we're talking about spoiled stew, poison mushrooms, or something
접속사(~하지 않는 한)
similar, however, no foods can be labeled as either good or bad.
「A+be labeled as+B : A가 B라고 분류되다」

★★ 문제 해결 꿀~팁 ★★

▶ 많이 틀린 이유는?
두 번째 문장에서 음식을 절대적으로 좋고 나쁘다고 분류할 수 없다고 언급하는 것으로 보아, 음식의 분류가 '부정확하지' 않다, 즉 '정확하다'는 의미를 완성하는 ①과 ⑤의 incorrect를 (A)에 넣기는 부적절하다.

▶ 문제 해결 방법은?
글 초반에 however가 두 번 연속해 등장하여 주제를 강조한다. Consider 이하는 이 주제에 대한 사례이므로 결론만 가볍게 확인하며 읽어도 충분하다.

41-42 농업 발전과 생활 변화

Early hunter-gatherer societies had (a) minimal structure.
초기 수렵 채집인 사회는 최소한의 구조만 가지고 있었다.

A chief or group of elders / usually led the camp or village.
추장이나 장로 그룹이 / 주로 캠프나 마을을 이끌었다.

Most of these leaders / had to hunt and gather / along with the other members / because the surpluses of food and other vital resources / were seldom (b) sufficient / to support a full-time chief or village council.
대부분의 이러한 지도자들은 / 사냥과 채집을 해야 했다. / 다른 구성원들과 함께 / 왜냐하면 식량과 기타 필수 자원의 잉여분이 / 충분한 경우가 드물었기 때문에 / 전임 추장이나 마을 의회를 지원할 만큼

『The development of agriculture changed work patterns.』 41번의 근거
농업의 발전은 작업 패턴을 변화시켰다.

Early farmers could reap 3-10 kg of grain / from each 1 kg of seed planted.
초기 농부들은 3~10kg의 곡물을 수확할 수 있었다. / 심은 씨앗 1kg마다

Part of this food/energy surplus / was returned to the community / and (c) provided support for nonfarmers / such as chieftains, village councils, men who practice medicine, priests, and warriors.
이 식량/에너지 잉여분의 일부는 / 지역 사회에 환원되었고 / 비농민에 대한 지원을 제공했다. / 족장, 마을 의회, 의술가, 사제, 전사와 같은

『In return, / the nonfarmers provided leadership and security / for the farming population, / enabling it / to continue to increase food/energy yields / and provide ever larger surpluses.』 42번의 근거
그 대가로, / 비농민들은 리더십과 안보를 제공하여, / 농업 인구에게 / 그들이 ~할 수 있게 하였다. / 식량/에너지 생산량을 지속적으로 늘리고 / 항상 더 많은 잉여를 제공할 수 있게

With improved technology and favorable conditions, / agriculture produced consistent surpluses of the basic necessities, / and population groups grew in size.
개선된 기술과 유리한 조건으로, / 농업은 기본 생필품의 지속적인 흑자를 창출했고, / 인구 집단은 규모가 커졌다.

These groups concentrated in towns and cities, / and human tasks (d) specialized further.
이러한 집단은 마을과 도시에 집중되었고, / 인간의 업무는 더욱 전문화되었다.

Specialists / such as carpenters, blacksmiths, merchants, traders, and sailors / developed their skills / and became more efficient / in their use of time and energy.
전문가들은 / 목수, 대장장이, 상인, 무역업자, 선원과 같은 / 기술을 계발하고 / 더 효율적이 되었다. / 자신의 시간과 에너지 사용 면에서

『The goods and services they provided / brought about / an (e) improved quality of life, / a higher standard of living, / and, for most societies, / increased stability.』 41번의 근거
그들이 제공한 재화와 서비스는 / 가져왔다. / 삶의 질 향상, / 생활 수준 개선, / 그리고 대부분의 사회에서, / 안정성의 향상을

초기 수렵 채집인 사회는 (a) 최소한의 구조만 가지고 있었다. 추장이나 장로 그룹이 주로 캠프나 마을을 이끌었다. 식량과 기타 필수 자원의 잉여분이 전임 추장이나 마을 의회를 지원할 만큼 (b) 충분한 경우가 드물었기 때문에 대부분의 이러한 지도자들은 다른 구성원들과 함께 사냥과 채집을 해야 했다. 농업의 발전은 작업 패턴을 변화시켰다. 초기 농부들은 심은 씨앗 1kg마다 3~10kg의 곡물을 수확할 수 있었다. 이 식량/에너지 잉여분의 일부는 지역 사회에 환원되었고 족장, 마을 의회, 의술가, 사제, 전사와 같은 비농민에 대한 지원을 (c) 제한했다(→ 제공했다). 그 대가로, 비농민들은 농업 인구에게 리더십과 안보를 제공하여, 그들이 식량/에너지 생산량을 지속적으로 늘리고 항상 더 많은 잉여를 제공할 수 있게 하였다. 개선된 기술과 유리한 조건으로, 농업은 기본 생필품의 지속적인 흑자를 창출했고, 인구 집단은 규모가 커졌다. 이러한 집단은 마을과 도시에 집중되었고, 인간의 업무는 더욱 (d) 전문화되었다. 목수, 대장장이, 상인, 무역업자, 선원과 같은 전문가들은 기술을 계발하고 자신의 시간과 에너지 사용을 더 효율적으로 하게 되었다. 그들이 제공한 재화와 서비스로 인해 삶의 질 (e) 향상, 생활 수준 개선, 그리고 대부분의 사회에서 안정성의 향상을 가져왔다.

- hunter-gatherer ⓝ 수렵 채집인
- vital @ 필수적인, 매우 중요한
- reap ⓥ (농작물을) 베어내다
- practice medicine 의사로 개업하다, 의술을 행하다
- warrior ⓝ 전사
- yield ⓝ 수확량
- concentrate ⓥ 집중되다
- blacksmith ⓝ 대장장이
- bring about ~을 야기하다, 초래하다, 가져오다
- surplus ⓝ 잉여, 흑자
- sufficient @ 충분한
- chieftain ⓝ 수령, 두목
- security ⓝ 안보
- basic necessity 기본 필수품
- carpenter ⓝ 목수
- sailor ⓝ 선원
- stability ⓝ 안정성

구문 풀이

20행 The goods and services [they provided] brought about an improved quality
주어   동사   목적어1
of life, a higher standard of living, and, for most societies, increased stability.
목적어2   목적어3

41 제목 파악
정답률 61% | 정답 ①

윗글의 제목으로 가장 적절한 것은?
✔ How Agriculture Transformed Human Society
농업은 어떻게 인간 사회를 바꿨나
② The Dark Shadow of Agriculture: Repetition
농업의 어두운 그늘: 반복

③ How Can We Share Extra Food with the Poor?
우리는 가난한 사람들과 남은 음식을 어떻게 나눌 수 있을까?
④ Why Were Early Societies Destroyed by Agriculture?
왜 초기 사회는 농업으로 파괴되었나?
⑤ The Advantages of Large Groups Over Small Groups in Farming
농업에 있어 대규모 집단이 소규모 집단보다 유리한 점

Why? 왜 정답일까?

농업 이전 사회에서는 비교적 단순했던 사회 구조가 농업 이후로 어떻게 변화했는지 설명하는 내용이다. 우선 작업의 패턴이 변하고(The development of agriculture changed work patterns.), 잉여 생산물이 늘어남에 따라 사회 규모도 바뀌면서 삶의 질도 향상되었다(~ an improved quality of life, a higher standard of living, and, for most societies, increased stability.)는 설명이 주를 이룬다. 따라서 글의 제목으로 가장 적절한 것은 ① '농업은 어떻게 인간 사회를 바꿨나'이다.

42 어휘 추론   정답률 58% | 정답 ③

밑줄 친 (a) ~ (e) 중에서 문맥상 낱말의 쓰임이 적절하지 <u>않은</u> 것은? [3점]
① (a)   ② (b)   ✓(c)   ④ (d)   ⑤ (e)

Why? 왜 정답일까?

In return 앞뒤는 농민이 비농민에게 무언가를 해준 '보답으로' 비농민 또한 농민에게 안보를 제공하여 생산에 집중하게 했다는 내용이다. 즉 (c)는 농민의 잉여 생산물이 비농민에 대한 지원을 '제공하는 데' 쓰였다는 의미일 것이므로, limited 대신 provided를 써야 자연스럽다. 따라서 문맥상 낱말의 쓰임이 적절하지 않은 것은 ③ '(c)'이다.

43-45 모르는 노인의 임종을 지킨 군인

(A)

A nurse took a tired, anxious soldier to the bedside.
한 간호사가 피곤하고 불안해하는 군인을 침대 곁으로 데려갔다.
"Jack, your son is here," / the nurse said to an old man / lying on the bed.
"Jack, 당신 아들이 왔어요."라고 / 간호사가 노인에게 말했다. / 침대에 누워있는
She had to repeat the words several times / before the old man's eyes opened.
그녀는 그 말을 여러 번 반복해야 했다. / 그 노인이 눈을 뜨기 전에
『Suffering from the severe pain / because of heart disease, he barely saw the young uniformed soldier standing next to him.』 **45번 ①의 근거** 일치
극심한 고통을 겪고 있던 / 심장병 때문에 / 그는 제복을 입은 젊은 군인을 간신히 보았다. / 자기 옆에 서 있는
(a) He reached out his hand to the soldier.
그는 손을 그 군인에게 뻗었다.

(D)

The soldier gently wrapped his fingers / around the weak hand of the old man.
그 군인은 부드럽게 자기 손가락을 감쌌다. / 노인의 병약한 손 주위로
『The nurse brought a chair / so that the soldier could sit beside the bed.』 **45번 ④의 근거** 일치
간호사는 의자를 가져왔다. / 군인이 침대 옆에 앉을 수 있도록
All through the night / the young soldier sat there, / holding the old man's hand / and offering (e) him words of support and comfort.
밤새 / 젊은 군인은 거기에 앉아, / 노인의 손을 잡고 / 그에게 지지와 위로의 말을 건넸다.
『Occasionally, / she suggested / that the soldier take a rest for a while.』
가끔, / 그녀는 제안했다. / 군인에게 잠시 쉬라고
He politely said no.』 **45번 ⑤의 근거** 일치
그는 정중하게 거절했다.

(B)

Whenever the nurse came into the room, / she heard the soldier say a few gentle words.
간호사가 병실에 들어올 때마다, / 그녀는 그 군인이 상냥한 말을 하는 것을 들었다.
The old man said nothing, / only held tightly to (b) him all through the night.
노인은 아무 말도 하지 않았다. / 밤새도록 그에게 손만 꼭 잡힌 채로
Just before dawn, / the old man died.
동트기 직전에, / 그 노인은 죽었다.
『The soldier released the old man's hand / and left the room to find the nurse.』
그 군인은 노인의 손을 놓고 / 간호사를 찾기 위해 병실을 나갔다. **45번 ②의 근거** 일치
After she was told what happened, / she went back to the room with him.
그녀가 무슨 일이 있었는지 들은 후, / 그녀는 그와 함께 병실로 돌아갔다.
The soldier hesitated for a while and asked, / "Who was this man?"
군인은 잠시 머뭇거리고는 물었다. / "그분은 누구였나요?"라고

(C)

She was surprised and asked, / "Wasn't he your father?"
그녀는 깜짝 놀라서 물었다. / "그가 당신의 아버지가 아니었나요?"
『"No, he wasn't. / I've never met him before," / the soldier replied.』 **45번 ③의 근거** 불일치
"아니요. / 저는 그분을 이전에 만난 적이 없어요."라고 / 군인이 대답했다.
She asked, / "Then why didn't you say something / when I took you to (c) him?"
그녀는 물었다. / "그러면 당신은 왜 아무 말도 하지 않았나요 / 내가 당신을 그에게 안내했을 때"
He said, / "I knew there had been a mistake, / but when I realized / that he was too sick to tell / whether or not I was his son, / I could see how much (d) he needed me. / So, I stayed."
그가 말했다. / "저는 실수가 있었다는 것을 알았지만, / 제가 알게 되었을 때, / 그분이 너무도 위독해서 구별할 수 없다는 걸 / 제가 아들인지 아닌지 / 저는 그가 얼마나 저를 필요로 하는지 알 수 있었습니다. / 그래서 저는 머물렀습니다."

(A)
한 간호사가 피곤하고 불안해하는 군인을 침대 곁으로 데려갔다. "Jack, 당신 아들이 왔어요."라고 간호사가 침대에 누워있는 노인에게 말했다. 그 노인이 눈을 뜨기 전에 그녀는 그 말을 여러 번 반복해야 했다. 심장병 때문에 극심한 고통을 겪고 있던 그는 제복을 입은 젊은 군인이 자기 옆에 선 것을 간신히 보았다. (a) 그는 손을 그 군인에게 뻗었다.

(D)
그 군인은 노인의 병약한 손을 부드럽게 감쌌다. 간호사는 군인이 침대 옆에 앉을 수 있도록 의자를 가져왔다. 밤새 젊은 군인은 거기에 앉아, 노인의 손을 잡고 (e) 그에게 지지와 위로의 말을 건넸다. 가끔, 그녀는 군인에게 잠시 쉬라고 제안했다. 그는 정중하게 거절했다.

(B)
간호사가 병실에 들어올 때마다, 그녀는 그 군인이 상냥한 말을 하는 것을 들었다. 밤새도록

(b) 그에게 손만 꼭 잡힌 채로 노인은 아무 말도 하지 않았다. 동트기 직전에, 그 노인은 죽었다. 그 군인은 노인의 손을 놓고 간호사를 찾기 위해 병실을 나갔다. 그녀가 무슨 일이 있었는지 들은 후, 그녀는 그와 함께 병실로 돌아갔다. 군인은 잠시 머뭇거리고는 "그분은 누구였나요?"라고 물었다.

(C)
그녀는 깜짝 놀라서 물었다. "그가 당신의 아버지가 아니었나요?" "아니요. 저는 그분을 이전에 만난 적이 없어요."라고 군인이 대답했다. 그녀는 물었다. "그러면 내가 당신을 (c) 그에게 안내했을 때 왜 아무 말도 하지 않았나요?" 그가 말했다. "저는 실수가 있었다는 것을 알았지만, 그분이 너무도 위독해서 제가 아들인지 아닌지 구별할 수 없다는 걸 알게 되었을 때, 저는 (d) 그가 얼마나 저를 필요로 하는지 알 수 있었습니다. 그래서 저는 머물렀습니다."

- severe ⓐ 극심한
- reach out one's hand 손을 뻗다
- hesitate ⓥ 주저하다
- barely ⓪ 간신히 ~하다, 거의 못 ~하다
- dawn ⓝ 새벽

구문 풀이

[A] 4행 Suffering from the severe pain because of heart disease, he barely saw
분사구문 / 전치사(~ 때문에) / 지각동사
the young uniformed soldier standing next to him.
목적어 / 현재분사

[D] 2행 The nurse brought a chair so that the soldier could sit beside the bed.
접속사(~하도록)

43 글의 순서 파악   정답률 77% | 정답 ④

주어진 글 (A)에 이어질 내용을 순서에 맞게 배열한 것으로 가장 적절한 것은?
① (B) - (D) - (C)   ② (C) - (B) - (D)
③ (C) - (D) - (B)   ✓(D) - (B) - (C)
⑤ (D) - (C) - (B)

Why? 왜 정답일까?

간호사가 한 군인을 임종이 임박한 노인에게 데려갔다는 내용의 (A) 뒤로, 군인이 노인 곁에 밤새 있었다는 내용의 (D), 마침내 노인이 임종한 뒤 군인이 그 노인이 누구였는지 물었다는 내용의 (B), 간호사가 놀라서 왜 노인 곁에 있었는지 묻고 군인이 답했다는 내용의 (C)가 순서대로 이어져야 자연스럽다. 따라서 글의 순서로 가장 적절한 것은 ④ '(D) - (B) - (C)'이다.

44 지칭 추론   정답률 64% | 정답 ②

밑줄 친 (a) ~ (e) 중에서 가리키는 대상이 나머지 넷과 <u>다른</u> 것은?
① (a)   ✓(b)   ③ (c)   ④ (d)   ⑤ (e)

Why? 왜 정답일까?

(a), (c), (d), (e)는 the old man, (b)는 the soldier를 가리키므로, (a) ~ (e) 중에서 가리키는 대상이 다른 하나는 ② '(b)'이다.

45 세부 내용 파악   정답률 75% | 정답 ③

윗글에 관한 내용으로 적절하지 <u>않은</u> 것은?
① 노인은 심장병으로 극심한 고통을 겪고 있었다.
② 군인은 간호사를 찾기 위해 병실을 나갔다.
✓군인은 노인과 이전에 만난 적이 있다고 말했다.
④ 간호사는 군인이 앉을 수 있도록 의자를 가져왔다.
⑤ 군인은 잠시 쉬라는 간호사의 제안을 정중히 거절하였다.

Why? 왜 정답일까?

(C) "No, he wasn't. I've never met him before."에서 군인은 노인을 만난 적이 없다고 말하므로, 내용과 일치하지 않는 것은 ③ '군인은 노인과 이전에 만난 적이 있다고 말했다.'이다.

Why? 왜 오답일까?

① (A) 'Suffering from the severe pain because of heart disease, ~'의 내용과 일치한다.
② (B) 'The soldier ~ left the room to find the nurse.'의 내용과 일치한다.
④ (D) 'The nurse brought a chair so that the soldier could sit beside the bed.'의 내용과 일치한다.
⑤ (D) 'Occasionally, she suggested that the soldier take a rest for a while. He politely said no.'의 내용과 일치한다.

Dictation 05

01 help set up computers / fill out the volunteer application form / will join us
02 not making much progress / take a walk / improve my creativity
03 any breakable items / there's an extra charge / do the express mail
04 went busking on the street / leave the guitar case open / set up two speakers
05 What about the present / go to the electronics store / clean up the living room
06 some on sale / go well with this blanket / two of them
07 go to a rock concert / take care of my friend's dog / visiting his grandmother
08 picking up trash / used to go there / I have extra
09 as a team / vote for their favorite video / show off your talents
10 a water purifier / water tank capacity / look at the warranties
11 this auto show / bought our tickets in advance
12 something wrong with my grade / you should go ask
13 at the secondhand bookstore / it was a bookmark / brings a smile
14 spending time in nature / relieve all my stress / don't have any equipment
15 science group assignment / bring her library card / check out the books for her
16-17 the most essential parts / rich in vitamin D / controls your internal body clock

어휘 Review Test 05

A	B	C	D
01 명상	01 familiar	01 ⓗ	01 ⑨
02 불안한	02 possess	02 ⓞ	02 ①
03 가능성, 확률	03 productivity	03 ①	03 ①
04 ~보다 우월한	04 experienced	04 ⓢ	04 ⓡ
05 허구의	05 unpaid	05 ⓠ	05 ⓠ
06 지위	06 decline	06 ⓝ	06 ⓚ
07 지속적으로	07 award	07 ⓚ	07 ⓐ
08 도움을 요청하다	08 hire	08 ⓓ	08 ⓑ
09 능력, 재능	09 state	09 ⓔ	09 ⓟ
10 나타나다, 생겨나다	10 emphasize	10 ①	10 ⓜ
11 응시하다	11 curiosity	11 ⓟ	11 ⓢ
12 잉여, 흑자	12 barely	12 ⓕ	12 ⓒ
13 주저하다	13 vital	13 ①	13 ⓓ
14 지속하다, 참다	14 stability	14 ⓜ	14 ⓞ
15 지역	15 contribution	15 ⓐ	15 ①
16 특유의, 독특한, 뚜렷한	16 embarrassed	16 ⓑ	16 ①
17 현상	17 considerable	17 ⓒ	17 ⓔ
18 바람직한	18 composed of	18 ⓖ	18 ①
19 추구하다	19 unless	19 ⓡ	19 ⓝ
20 주의 산만, 정신을 흩뜨리는 것	20 reflect	20 ①	20 ⓗ

06회 | 2022학년도 6월 학력평가   고1

정답

01② 02② 03⑤ 04⑤ 05① 06③ 07① 08⑤ 09⑤ 10④ 11① 12③ 13③ 14④ 15④
16② 17③ 18② 19② 20⑤ 21③ 22① 23② 24① 25⑤ 26③ 27④ 28② 29④ 30②
31① 32② 33③ 34② 35④ 36③ 37⑤ 38④ 39⑤ 40③ 41① 42④ 43④ 44② 45④

★ 표기된 문항은 [등급을 가르는 문제]에 해당하는 문항입니다.

01   건물 벽 페인트 작업 공지   정답률 97% | 정답 ②

다음을 듣고, 남자가 하는 말의 목적으로 가장 적절한 것을 고르시오.
① 사생활 보호의 중요성을 강조하려고
☑ 건물 벽 페인트 작업을 공지하려고
③ 회사 근무시간 변경을 안내하려고
④ 새로운 직원 채용을 공고하려고
⑤ 친환경 제품 출시를 홍보하려고

M : Good afternoon, this is the building manager, Richard Carson.
안녕하세요, 건물 관리인인 Richard Carson입니다.
We are planning to have the walls painted on our building next week.
다음 주에 우리 건물 벽에 페인트를 칠할 계획입니다.
The working hours will be from 9 a.m. to 6 p.m.
작업 시간은 오전 9시부터 오후 6시로 예정되어 있습니다.
Don't be surprised to see workers outside your windows.
창문 밖으로 작업자들을 보고 놀라지 마세요.
Please keep your windows closed while they are painting.
그들이 칠하는 동안, 창문을 닫고 계시기 바랍니다.
There might be some smell from the paint.
페인트 냄새가 조금 날 수도 있습니다.
But don't worry. It is totally safe and eco-friendly.
하지만 걱정 마세요. 완전히 안전하고 친환경적입니다.
Sorry for any inconvenience and thank you for your cooperation.
불편을 끼쳐 사과드리고 협조에 감사합니다.

Why? 왜 정답일까?

건물 벽 페인트 작업이 예정되어 있다(We are planning to have the walls painted on our building next week.)는 내용으로 보아, 남자가 하는 말의 목적으로 가장 적절한 것은 ② '건물 벽 페인트 작업을 공지하려고'이다.

● eco-friendly ⓐ 친환경적인   ● cooperation ⓝ 협조

02   속도 제한 준수   정답률 96% | 정답 ①

대화를 듣고, 여자의 의견으로 가장 적절한 것을 고르시오.
☑ 운전자는 제한 속도를 지켜야 한다.
② 교통경찰을 더 많이 배치해야 한다.
③ 보행자의 부주의가 교통사고를 유발한다.
④ 교통사고를 목격하면 즉시 신고해야 한다.
⑤ 대중교통을 이용하면 이동시간을 줄일 수 있다.

M : Hello, Veronica.
안녕, Veronica.
W : Hi, Jason. I heard that you are trying to get a driver's license these days. How is it going?
안녕, Jason. 나 네가 요새 운전 면허를 따려고 한다고 들었어. 어떻게 돼 가?
M : You know what? I already got it. Look!
있잖아, 이미 땄어. 이거 봐!
W : Oh, good for you! How was the driving test?
오, 잘됐다! 운전 시험은 어땠어?
M : Well, while taking the driving test, I was very nervous because some people were driving so fast.
음, 운전 시험을 보는 동안, 몇몇 사람들이 너무 빨리 달려서 난 아주 긴장했어.
W : But there are speed limit signs everywhere.
그치만 모든 곳에 속도 제한 표시가 있잖아.
M : Right, there are. But so many drivers ignore speed limits these days.
맞아, 있지. 하지만 요새 속도 제한을 무시하는 사람들이 너무 많아.
W : That's terrible. Those drivers could cause serious car accidents.
끔찍해. 그런 운전자들은 심각한 교통사고를 낼 수도 있어.
M : That's true. Driving too fast can be dangerous for everybody.
맞아. 너무 빨리 운전하는 건 모두에게 위험할 수 있어.
W : Exactly. In my opinion, all drivers should follow the speed limits.
바로 그 말이야. 내 생각에, 모든 운전자들은 속도 제한을 지켜야 해.
M : I totally agree with you.
네 말에 전적으로 동의해.

Why? 왜 정답일까?

모든 운전자들은 제한 속도를 따라야 한다(In my opinion, all drivers should follow the speed limits.)는 여자의 말로 보아, 여자의 의견으로 가장 적절한 것은 ① '운전자는 제한 속도를 지켜야 한다.'이다.

● get a driver's license 운전 면허를 따다   ● speed limit 속도 제한
● follow ⓥ 지키다, 따르다

03   숙제를 위해 책 빌리기   정답률 96% | 정답 ⑤

대화를 듣고, 두 사람의 관계를 가장 잘 나타낸 것을 고르시오.

① 작가 – 출판사 직원　　　　② 관람객 – 박물관 해설사
③ 손님 – 주방장　　　　　　④ 탑승객 – 항공 승무원
✔ 학생 – 사서

W : Excuse me. Can you help me find some books for my homework?
　실례합니다. 제가 숙제에 필요한 책을 좀 찾게 도와주실래요?
M : Sure. What is your homework about?
　물론이죠. 어떤 숙제인가요?
W : It's for my history class. The topic is the relationship between France and Germany.
　역사 수업 숙제고요. 주제는 프랑스와 독일의 관계예요.
M : What about this world history book?
　이 세계사 책은 어떠세요?
W : It looks good. Do you have any other books?
　괜찮아 보여요. 다른 책도 있나요?
M : I can also recommend this European history book.
　이 유럽사 책도 추천해 드릴게요.
W : Great. How many books can I borrow at a time?
　좋아요. 제가 한 번에 책을 몇 권 빌릴 수 있나요?
M : You can borrow up to four books for three weeks each.
　한 권당 3주 동안 네 권까지 빌릴 수 있어요.
W : Okay. I'll take these two books, then.
　알겠습니다. 그럼 이 두 권을 빌릴게요.
M : All right. [Beep sound] Don't forget to return them on time.
　알겠습니다. [삐 소리] 제때 반납하는 것 잊지 마세요.

Why? 왜 정답일까?

'Can you help me find some books for my homework?', 'You can borrow up to four books for three weeks each.' 등에서 여자는 숙제에 참고할 책을 찾는 학생이고, 남자는 도서관 사서임을 알 수 있으므로, 두 사람의 관계로 가장 적절한 것은 ⑤ '학생 – 사서'이다.

● up to ~까지
● on time 제때
● return ⓥ 반납하다

04　아이 방 구경하기　　　정답률 85% | 정답 ⑤

대화를 듣고, 그림에서 대화의 내용과 일치하지 <u>않는</u> 것을 고르시오.

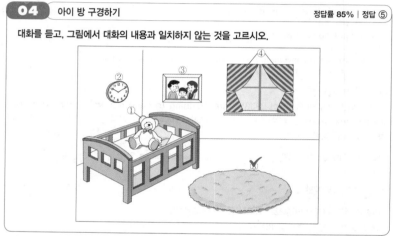

M : Honey, come to Lucy's room. Look at what I did for her.
　여보, Lucy 방에 좀 와 봐요. 내가 아이를 위해 해놓은 것 좀 봐요.
W : It looks great. 「Is that a toy bear on the bed?」①의 근거 일치
　근사해 보이네요. 침대 위에 있는 저건 곰 인형이에요?
M : Yes. That's right. She can sleep with the toy bear.
　네, 맞아요. 아이는 곰 인형과 함께 잠들 수 있어요.
W : It's cute. 「Oh, and I like the round clock on the wall.」②의 근거 일치
　귀여워요. 오, 그리고 벽에 걸린 동그란 시계가 마음에 드네요.
M : The round clock goes well with the room, doesn't it? 「How do you like the family picture next to the window?」③의 근거 일치
　동그란 시계가 방에 잘 어울리죠, 그렇죠? 창문 옆에 있는 가족사진은 어때요?
W : That's so sweet. 「I also love the striped curtains on the window.」④의 근거 일치
　정말 보기 좋아요. 창문에 걸린 줄무늬 커튼도 마음에 들어요.
M : I'm happy you like them. 「What do you think of the star-shaped rug on the floor?」
　당신이 좋아해주니 기뻐요. 바닥에 깔린 별 모양 깔개는 어때요? ⑤의 근거 불일치
W : It is lovely. Lucy will feel safe and warm on the rug.
　귀여워요. Lucy가 깔개 위에서 안전하고 따뜻한 기분을 느낄 거예요.
M : Looks like everything's prepared.
　모든 게 준비된 것 같네요.
W : Thanks, honey. You've done a great job.
　고마워요, 여보. 정말 잘했어요.

Why? 왜 정답일까?

대화에서는 바닥에 별 모양 깔개가 있다(What do you think of the star-shaped rug on the floor?)고 하는데, 그림의 깔개는 동그란 모양이다. 따라서 그림에서 대화의 내용과 일치하지 않는 것은 ⑤이다.

● toy bear 곰 인형
● go well with ~와 잘 어울리다
● What do you think of ~? ~을 어떻게 생각해요?
● round ⓐ 원형의
● How do you like ~? ~이 어때요?

05　영화 약속 전에 보고서 내기　　　정답률 95% | 정답 ①

대화를 듣고, 남자가 할 일로 가장 적절한 것을 고르시오.

✔ 보고서 제출하기　　　　② 티켓 예매하기
③ 자전거 수리하기　　　　④ 축구 연습하기
⑤ 팝콘 구입하기

W : David, did you fix your bicycle yesterday?
　David, 너 어제 네 자전거 고쳤어?

M : Yes. Luckily, I was able to fix it by myself. How was your soccer practice, Christine?
　응. 다행히도 혼자 고칠 수 있었어. 너 축구 연습은 어땠어, Christine?
W : A new coach came to our soccer club and we practiced very hard.
　우리 축구 동아리에 새로운 코치님이 와서 우린 아주 열심히 연습했어.
M : You must be so tired. Do you still want to see a movie this afternoon?
　되게 피곤하겠네. 그래도 오늘 오후에 영화 보러 가는 거 괜찮겠어?
W : Of course, I booked the tickets two weeks ago.
　물론이지, 난 표를 2주 전에 예매한걸.
M : All right. Let's get going.
　알겠어. 같이 가자.
W : Wait, did you email your science report to Mr. Smith? It's due today.
　잠깐만, 너 Smith 선생님께 이메일로 과학 보고서 냈어? 오늘이 마감이야.
M : [Pause] Oh, no! I finished it but forgot to send it. What should I do?
　[잠시 멈춤] 오, 이런! 나 그거 끝냈는데 보내는 걸 깜빡했어. 어떻게 해야 하지?
W : Why don't you send it before meeting me at the movie theater?
　나랑 영화관에서 만나기 전에 그걸 보내 놓으면 어때?
M : Good idea. I'll go home quickly and send the report, but can you buy some popcorn for me before I get there?
　좋은 생각이야. 빨리 집으로 가서 보고서 낼게. 근데 내가 도착하기 전에 네가 팝콘 좀 사 놓을 수 있어?
W : No problem. See you there.
　문제 없지, 거기서 봐.

Why? 왜 정답일까?

남자는 과학 보고서를 다 작성했지만 제출하는 것을 깜빡 잊어서, 여자를 영화관에서 만나기 전에 보고서를 메일로 제출하고 오겠다(I'll go home quickly and send the report, ~)고 하므로, 남자가 할 일로 가장 적절한 것은 ① '보고서 제출하기'이다.

● fix ⓥ 고치다
● due ⓐ 기한인, ~하기로 되어 있는

06　놀이공원 표 사기　　　정답률 85% | 정답 ③

대화를 듣고, 여자가 지불할 금액을 고르시오. [3점]

① $40　② $60　✔ $80　④ $100　⑤ $120

M : Good morning. Welcome to Happy Land.
　안녕하세요. Happy Land에 잘 오셨습니다.
W : Hello. I'd like to buy some tickets. How much are they?
　안녕하세요. 전 표를 좀 사고 싶어요. 얼마인가요?
M : $20 for the amusement park and $10 for the water park. How many tickets do you need?
　놀이공원 표는 20달러이고, 워터파크 표는 10달러입니다. 표가 몇 장 필요하신가요?
W : We're five people in total, and we only want to go to the amusement park.
　저희는 총 다섯 명이고, 놀이공원만 가고 싶어요.
M : Okay. Do you have any discount coupons?
　알겠습니다. 할인 쿠폰 가지고 계신가요?
W : I printed out a birthday coupon from your website. It's my birthday today.
　웹 사이트에서 생일 쿠폰을 출력해 왔어요. 오늘 제 생일이거든요.
M : It's your birthday? Just let me check your ID, please.
　생일이세요? 그럼 신분증만 확인할게요.
W : Here you are.
　여기 있어요.
M : Oh, happy birthday! With your birthday coupon, your ticket is free.
　오, 생일 축하드립니다! 생일 쿠폰이 있으면 본인 표는 무료예요.
W : That's great. Please give me five tickets including my ticket.
　잘됐네요. 제 거 포함해서 표 다섯 장 주세요.
M : Let me see. That'll be four people at the original price, and one person with a birthday coupon.
　확인하겠습니다. 네 분은 정가이고, 한 분은 생일 쿠폰이 있으시고요.
W : Right. Here is my credit card.
　맞아요. 여기 제 신용 카드요.

Why? 왜 정답일까?

대화에 따르면 여자는 일행 넷과 함께 놀이공원에 입장하려 하는데, 여자 본인은 생일 쿠폰이 있어 표 값을 내지 않아도 된다. 놀이공원 표는 1인당 20달러이므로, 여자가 지불할 금액은 4인 표의 정가인 ③ '$80'이다.

● amusement park 놀이공원
● original price 정가
● print out ~을 출력하다

07　음식 부스에 갈 수 없는 이유　　　정답률 97% | 정답 ①

대화를 듣고, 남자가 음식 부스에 갈 수 <u>없는</u> 이유로 가장 적절한 것을 고르시오.

✔ 밴드 오디션 연습을 해야 해서
② 보드게임 부스를 설치해야 해서
③ 영어 프로젝트를 끝내야 해서
④ 샌드위치를 준비해야 해서
⑤ 친구를 만나러 가야 해서

W : Hi, Alex. How is it going?
　안녕, Alex. 잘 지내니?
M : I'm good. Thanks. I've just finished my English project. How about you, Tracy?
　잘 지내. 고마워. 영어 프로젝트를 막 끝낸 참이야. 넌 어때, Tracy?
W : I'm a little busy preparing for my food booth.
　난 음식 부스를 준비하느라 약간 바빠.
M : A food booth? What for?
　음식 부스? 왜?
W : My school festival is next Tuesday. I'm running a food booth that day.
　우리 학교 축제가 다음 주 화요일이야. 난 그날 음식 부스를 운영해.
M : That is so cool. What is on the menu?
　근사하네. 메뉴가 뭐야?
W : We're making sandwiches. You should come.
　우린 샌드위치를 만들 거야. 너도 와.
M : I'd love to, but I can't.
　나도 가고 싶은데 그럴 수가 없어.

W : You can't? I was really looking forward to seeing you at my school.
못 온다고? 난 우리 학교에서 널 만나길 고대했는데.

M : I'm terribly sorry. I have to practice for a band audition.
진짜 미안해. 난 밴드 오디션을 위해 연습해야 해.

W : Oh, I see. Well, good luck with your audition.
오, 그렇구나. 그럼, 오디션에 행운을 빌어줄게.

M : Thank you.
고마워.

Why? 왜 정답일까?

남자는 밴드 오디션 연습 때문에(I have to practice for a band audition.) 여자가 학교 축제 때 운영하는 음식 부스에 가볼 수 없다고 하므로, 남자가 음식 부스에 갈 수 없는 이유로 가장 적절한 것은 ① '밴드 오디션 연습을 해야 해서'이다.

- be busy ~ing ~하느라 바쁘다
- look forward to ~을 고대하다
- run ⓥ 운영하다
- terribly [ad] 너무, 대단히

---

08 스페인 문화 수업　　　　정답률 97% | 정답 ⑤

대화를 듣고, Spanish culture class에 관해 언급되지 <u>않은</u> 것을 고르시오.
① 강사　　　② 활동 종류　　　③ 수업 요일
④ 준비물　　　✓ 수강료

[Telephone rings.]
[전화벨이 울린다.]

W : Hello, this is the World Culture Center. How can I help you?
안녕하세요, World Culture Center입니다. 무엇을 도와드릴까요?

M : Hi, I'm calling about a Spanish culture class for my teenage son.
안녕하세요, 전 제 십 대 아들을 위한 스페인 문화 수업 때문에 전화 드렸어요.

W : Okay. We have an interesting class for teenagers.
그러시군요. 저희는 십대 들을 위한 흥미로운 수업을 열고 있어요.

M : Great. 『Who teaches it?
좋아요. 강사가 누구인가요?

W : A Korean teacher and a native speaker teach it together.』 ①의 근거 일치
한국인 선생님 한 분과 원어민 선생님 한 분이 함께 가르쳐요.

M : 『What kind of activities are there in the class?
수업에서 어떤 활동을 하나요?

W : Students can cook traditional foods, learn new words, and try on traditional clothing.』 ②의 근거 일치
학생들은 전통 음식을 만들고, 새로운 단어를 배우고, 전통 복장도 체험해요.

M : 『On what day is the class?
수업이 무슨 요일에 있나요?

W : It's on Wednesday and Friday afternoons…』 ③의 근거 일치
수요일과 금요일 오후입니다.

M : I see. 『Is there anything my son should prepare before the class?
그렇군요. 제 아들이 수업 전에 준비해야 할 게 있나요?

W : He just needs to bring a pen and a notebook.』 The center provides all the other class materials. ④의 근거 일치
그냥 펜하고 공책만 지참하시면 돼요. 다른 수업 자료는 센터에서 다 제공합니다.

M : Perfect. Thanks for the information.
완벽해요. 정보 감사합니다.

Why? 왜 정답일까?

대화에서 남자와 여자는 Spanish culture class의 강사, 활동 종류, 수업 요일, 준비물을 언급하므로, 언급되지 않은 것은 ⑤ '수강료'이다.

Why? 왜 오답일까?

① 'A Korean teacher and a native speaker teach it together.'에서 '강사'가 언급되었다.
② 'Students can cook traditional foods, learn new words, and try on traditional clothing.'에서 '활동 종류'가 언급되었다.
③ 'It's on Wednesday and Friday afternoons.'에서 '수업 요일'이 언급되었다.
④ 'He just needs to bring a pen and a notebook.'에서 '준비물'이 언급되었다.

- native speaker 원어민
- try on ~을 입어보다
- traditional ⓐ 전통적인
- class material 수업 자료

---

09 벼룩시장 행사 안내　　　　정답률 91% | 정답 ⑤

Summer Flea Market에 관한 다음 내용을 듣고, 일치하지 <u>않는</u> 것을 고르시오. [3점]
① 일주일 동안 진행된다.
② 학교 주차장에서 열린다.
③ 장난감, 양초와 같은 물품을 살 수 있다.
④ 상태가 좋은 중고 물품을 판매할 수 있다.
✓ 첫날 방문하면 할인 쿠폰을 선물로 받는다.

W : Good afternoon, residents.
안녕하세요, 주민 여러분.

This is the head of the Pineville Community Center.
Pineville 주민센터장입니다.

『We're holding the Summer Flea Market for one week.』 ①의 근거 일치
저희는 일주일 동안 Summer Flea Market을 개최할 예정입니다.

『It'll be held in the parking lot of Pineville Middle School.』 ②의 근거 일치
이 행사는 Pineville 중학교 주차장에서 열립니다.

『You can get many different kinds of items such as toys and candles at reasonable prices.』 ③의 근거 일치
장난감과 양초 같은 아주 다양한 종류의 물건을 합리적인 가격에 구매할 수 있습니다.

『You can also sell any of your own used items if they are in good condition.』 ④의 근거 일치
또한 여러분의 중고 물품이 상태가 좋다면 어떤 것이든 팔 수 있습니다.

『On the first day, every resident visiting the market will get a shopping bag as a gift.』 ⑤의 근거 불일치
첫날에는 장을 방문하는 모든 주민에게 쇼핑백을 선물로 드립니다.

For more information, please check out the community center's website.
더 많은 정보를 얻으시려면, 주민센터 웹 사이트를 확인해 주세요.

Why? 왜 정답일까?

'On the first day, every resident visiting the market will get a shopping bag as a gift.'에서 첫날 방문하는 주민 전원에게 선물로 쇼핑백을 준다고 하므로, 내용과 일치하지 않는 것은 ⑤ '첫날 방문하면 할인 쿠폰을 선물로 받는다.'이다.

Why? 왜 오답일까?

① 'We're holding the Summer Flea Market for one week.'의 내용과 일치한다.
② 'It'll be held in the parking lot of Pineville Middle School.'의 내용과 일치한다.
③ 'You can get many different kinds of items such as toys and candles at reasonable prices.'의 내용과 일치한다.
④ 'You can also sell any of your own used items if they are in good condition.'의 내용과 일치한다.

- flea market 벼룩시장
- reasonable ⓐ 합리적인, 적당한
- parking lot 주차장
- used item 중고품

---

10 운동화 사기　　　　정답률 86% | 정답 ④

다음 표를 보면서 대화를 듣고, 여자가 구입할 운동화를 고르시오.

Sneakers

	Model	Price	Style	Waterproof	Color
①	A	$50	casual	×	black
②	B	$60	active	×	white
③	C	$65	casual	○	black
✓	D	$70	casual	○	white
⑤	E	$85	active	○	white

W : Kyle, I'm looking for some sneakers. Can you help me find some good ones?
Kyle, 나 운동화를 찾고 있는데. 좋은 거 좀 찾게 도와줄래?

M : Of course. Let me see… [Pause] Look. These are the five best-selling ones.
물론이지. 어디 보자… [잠시 멈춤] 봐바. 이게 제일 잘 나가는 제품 다섯 개네.

W : Wow, they all look so cool. It's hard to choose among them.
와, 다 근사해 보이네. 여기서 고르기 어려워.

M : 『Well, what's your budget?
음, 예산이 얼마야?

W : I don't want to spend more than 80 dollars.』 근거1 Price 조건
80달러 넘게 쓰고 싶지는 않아.

M : All right. 『Which style do you want, active or casual? 근거2 Style 조건
알겠어. 어떤 스타일이 좋아, 활동적인 거 아니면 캐주얼한 거?

W : I prefer casual ones.』 I think they match my clothes better.
캐주얼한 게 더 좋아. 그게 내 옷하고 잘 어울릴 것 같아.

M : Good. 『And I'd like to recommend waterproof shoes for rainy days.』 근거3 Waterproof 조건
그래. 그리고 난 비 오는 날을 대비해서 방수가 되는 신발을 추천하겠어.

W : Okay, I will take your advice.
그래, 네 충고를 따를게.

M : So you have two options left. 『Which color do you prefer?
그럼 선택권이 둘 남았어. 어떤 색을 선호해?

W : Most of my shoes are black, so I'll buy white ones this time.』 근거4 Color 조건
내 운동화 대부분 검은색이라, 이번에는 흰색을 사겠어.

M : You made a good choice.
잘 골랐네.

Why? 왜 정답일까?

대화에 따르면 여자는 가격이 80달러를 넘지 않고, 캐주얼한 스타일에, 방수가 되고, 색이 흰색인 운동화를 골랐으므로, 여자가 구입할 운동화는 ④ 'D'이다.

- cool ⓐ 근사한, 멋진
- waterproof ⓐ 방수의
- make a choice 선택하다, 고르다
- match ⓥ 어울리다
- take an advice 충고를 따르다

---

11 서점 행사 광고　　　　정답률 60% | 정답 ①

대화를 듣고, 여자의 마지막 말에 대한 남자의 응답으로 가장 적절한 것을 고르시오.
✓ All children's books are 20% off. - 모든 어린이 책이 20% 할인이래.
② It takes time to write a good article. - 좋은 기사를 쓰려면 시간이 걸리지.
③ I like to read action adventure books. - 난 액션 어드벤처 책을 읽는 걸 좋아해.
④ There are too many advertisements on TV. - TV에 광고가 너무 많이 나와.
⑤ The store has been closed since last month. - 그 매장은 지난 달부터 문을 닫았어.

W : Justin, what are you reading?
Justin, 뭐 읽고 있어?

M : An advertisement. There's a special event at Will's Bookstore downtown.
광고야. 시내에 있는 Will's Bookstore에서 특별 행사가 있대.

W : What kind of event is it?
무슨 행사야?

M : All children's books are 20% off.
모든 어린이 책이 20% 할인이래.

Why? 왜 정답일까?

서점 행사 광고를 읽고 있다는 남자에게 여자는 무슨 행사인지 물어보므로(What kind of event is it?), 남자의 응답으로 가장 적절한 것은 ① '모든 어린이 책이 20% 할인이래.'이다.

- advertisement ⓝ 광고
- article ⓝ 기사, 논문
- take time to ~하는 데 시간이 걸리다

---

12 걱정거리 묻기　　　　정답률 85% | 정답 ③

대화를 듣고, 남자의 마지막 말에 대한 여자의 응답으로 가장 적절한 것을 고르시오.

① You're welcome. I'm happy to help you. – 천만에. 도와주게 돼 기뻐.
② That's not true. I made it with your help. – 그건 사실이 아냐. 네 도움이 있어 내가 해낸 거지.
✔ Okay. Good food always makes me feel better. – 그래. 맛있는 음식은 언제나 날 기분 좋게 해.
④ Really? You should definitely visit the theater later. – 정말? 그 영화관 나중에 꼭 가 봐.
⑤ Never mind. You'll do better on the next presentation. – 신경 쓰지 마. 다음 번 발표는 더 잘할 거야.

M : You look so worried. What's wrong, Liz?
　　너 되게 걱정하는 것 같아 보이네. 무슨 일이야, Liz?
W : I didn't do well on my presentation yesterday.
　　난 어제 발표를 잘하지 못했어.
M : Sorry about that. To help take your mind off of it, how about having a nice meal?
　　안됐네. 생각을 떨쳐내기 위해서 맛있는 밥을 먹는 건 어때?
W : Okay. Good food always makes me feel better.
　　그래. 맛있는 음식은 언제나 날 기분 좋게 해.

Why? 왜 정답일까?

발표를 잘하지 못해서 속상하다는 여자에게 남자는 기분 전환 겸 맛있는 것을 먹어보라고 제안하므로(To help take your mind off of it, how about having a nice meal?), 여자의 응답으로 가장 적절한 것은 ③ '그래. 맛있는 음식은 언제나 날 기분 좋게 해.'이다.

● do well on ~을 잘하다　　　● take one's mind off of ~의 생각을 떨쳐내다
● definitely ad 꼭, 반드시

---

13 방학 때 들을 수업 고르기　　　정답률 85% | 정답 ③

대화를 듣고, 여자의 마지막 말에 대한 남자의 응답으로 가장 적절한 것을 고르시오.
Man: _____

① I'm excited to buy a new guitar. – 난 새 기타를 살 생각에 신나.
② Summer vacation starts on Friday. – 여름방학은 금요일부터야.
✔ You can find it on the school website. – 학교 웹 사이트에서 볼 수 있어.
④ Let's go to the school festival together. – 학교 축제 같이 가자.
⑤ You can get some rest during the vacation. – 넌 방학 동안에 좀 쉴 수 있겠네.

M : Jenny, what class do you want to take this summer vacation?
　　Jenny, 너 여름 방학 때 무슨 수업 듣고 싶어?
W : Well, [Pause] I'm thinking of the guitar class.
　　음, [잠시 멈춤] 난 기타 수업을 생각 중이야.
M : Cool! I'm interested in playing the guitar, too.
　　멋지다! 나도 기타 연주에 관심 있어.
W : Really? It would be exciting if we took the class together.
　　정말? 같이 수업 들으면 재밌겠다.
M : I know, but I am thinking of taking a math class instead. I didn't do well on the final exam.
　　그러게. 그런데 난 대신 수학 수업을 들을까 해. 기말고사를 망쳤거든.
W : Oh, there is a math class? I didn't know that.
　　오, 수학 수업이 있어? 몰랐네.
M : Yes. Mrs. Kim said she is offering a math class for first graders.
　　응. Kim 선생님이 1학년을 대상으로 수학 수업을 열 거래.
W : That might be a good chance to improve my skills, too. Where can I check the schedule for the math class?
　　내 수학 실력도 늘릴 수 있는 좋은 기회가 될지도 모르겠네. 수학 수업 시간표는 어디서 확인할 수 있어?
M : You can find it on the school website.
　　학교 웹 사이트에서 볼 수 있어.

Why? 왜 정답일까?

방학 때 수학 수업이 열린다는 남자의 말에 여자는 수학 수업 시간표를 어디서 확인하면 되는지 물어보므로(Where can I check the schedule for the math class?), 남자의 응답으로 가장 적절한 것은 ③ '학교 웹 사이트에서 볼 수 있어.'이다.

● first grader 1학년생　　　● improve ⓥ 향상시키다
● get rest 휴식을 취하다

---

14 온라인 운동 수업　　　정답률 92% | 정답 ④

대화를 듣고, 남자의 마지막 말에 대한 여자의 응답으로 가장 적절한 것을 고르시오.
Woman: _____

① I agree. There are many benefits of exercising at the gym.
　　동의해. 체육관에서 운동하면 이점이 많아.
② You're right. Not all exercise is helpful for your brain.
　　네 말이 맞아. 모든 운동이 머리에 도움이 되는 건 아냐.
③ Don't worry. It's not too difficult for me to exercise.
　　걱정 마. 내가 운동하기에 그렇게 어렵진 않아.
✔ That sounds great. Can I join the course, too?
　　그거 괜찮다. 나도 거기 합류할 수 있나?
⑤ That's too bad. I hope you get well soon.
　　안됐네. 빨리 낫길 바랄게.

M : Hi, Claire! How are you doing?
　　안녕, Claire! 어떻게 지내?
W : I'm good. You're looking great!
　　좋아. 너 멋져 보인다!
M : Thanks. I've been working out these days.
　　고마워. 난 요새 운동하고 있어.
W : I need to start working out, too. What kind of exercise do you do?
　　나도 운동 시작해야 해. 무슨 운동 하고 있어?
M : I do yoga and some stretching at home.
　　난 집에서 요가랑 스트레칭 좀 하고 있어.
W : At home? Do you exercise alone?
　　집에서? 혼자 운동하는 거야?
M : Yes and no. I exercise online with other people.
　　맞기도 하고 아니기도 해. 난 온라인에서 다른 사람들하고 운동해.
W : Exercising online with others? What do you mean by that?
　　온라인에서 다른 사람들과 운동을 한다고? 그게 무슨 말이야?

072　고1·3개년 영어 [리얼 오리지널]

M : I'm taking an online fitness course. We work out together on the Internet every evening at 7.
　　난 온라인 운동 수업을 듣고 있어. 우린 인터넷에서 매일 저녁 7시에 같이 운동해.
W : That sounds great. Can I join the course, too?
　　그거 괜찮다. 나도 거기 합류할 수 있나?

Why? 왜 정답일까?

온라인 운동 수업을 통해 집에서 다른 사람들과 함께 운동하고 있다(I'm taking an online fitness course. We work out together on the Internet every evening at 7.)는 남자의 말에 대한 여자의 응답으로 가장 적절한 것은 ④ '그거 괜찮다. 나도 거기 합류할 수 있나?'이다.

● work out 운동하다　　　● benefit ⓝ 이점, 이득
● get well (병 등이) 낫다

---

15 선거 포스터 제작 부탁하기　　　정답률 83% | 정답 ④

다음 상황 설명을 듣고, Ted가 Monica에게 할 말로 가장 적절한 것을 고르시오. [3점]
Ted: _____

① Can I draw your club members on the poster? – 내가 포스터에 너희 동아리 회원을 그려도 돼?
② Are you interested in joining my drawing club? – 너 우리 그림 동아리 드는 거 관심 있어?
③ Could you tell me how to vote in the election? – 선거 투표 방법을 알려줄 수 있니?
✔ Can you help me make posters for the election? – 내가 선거 포스터 만드는 거 도와줄래?
⑤ Would you run in the next school president election? – 너 다음 전교 회장 선거에 출마해줄래?

M : Ted is a high school student.
　　Ted는 고등학생이다.
　　He is planning to run for school president this year.
　　그는 올해 전교 회장에 입후보할 계획이다.
　　He really wants to win the election.
　　그는 정말로 선거에서 이기고 싶다.
　　He thinks using posters is an effective way to make a strong impression on his schoolmates.
　　그는 포스터를 사용하는 것이 자기 학우들에게 강한 인상을 주는 데 효과적인 방법이라고 생각한다.
　　But he is not good at drawing.
　　하지만 그는 그림을 잘 그리지 못한다.
　　His friend, Monica, is a member of a drawing club and she is good at drawing.
　　그의 친구인 Monica는 그림 동아리 회원이고 그림을 잘 그린다.
　　So, he wants to ask her to help him draw posters.
　　그래서 그는 그녀에게 포스터 그리는 것을 도와달라고 청하고 싶다.
　　In this situation, what would Ted most likely say to Monica?
　　이 상황에서, Ted는 Monica에게 뭐라고 말할 것인가?
Ted : Can you help me make posters for the election?
　　내가 선거 포스터 만드는 거 도와줄래?

Why? 왜 정답일까?

상황에 따르면 전교 회장 선거에 쓸 포스터를 만들려는 Ted는 본인이 그림을 잘 그리지 못해 친구 Monica에게 도와달라고 부탁하려 하므로(So, he wants to ask her to help him draw posters.), Ted가 Monica에게 할 말로 가장 적절한 것은 ④ '내가 선거 포스터 만드는 거 도와줄래?'이다.

● run for ~에 입후보하다　　　● school president 전교 회장
● election ⓝ 선거　　　● make an impression on ~에게 인상을 주다

16-17 건강한 아침 식사를 위한 식품 소개

W : Good morning, listeners.
　　안녕하세요, 청취자 여러분.
　　This is your host Rachel at the Morning Radio Show.
　　Morning Radio Show의 진행자 Rachel입니다.
　　What do you eat for breakfast?
　　아침으로 뭘 드셨나요?
　　「Today I will introduce a healthy breakfast food list.」 16번의 근거
　　오늘 저는 건강한 아침 식사 음식 목록을 소개하려고 합니다.
　　「Eggs are an excellent choice because they are high in protein.」 17번 ①의 근거 일치
　　달걀은 단백질 함량이 높아서 탁월한 선택입니다.
　　High-protein foods such as eggs provide energy for the brain.
　　달걀 같은 고단백 음식은 뇌에 에너지를 공급해 주죠.
　　「Cheese is another good option.」 17번 ②의 근거 일치
　　치즈도 또 다른 좋은 선택입니다.
　　It reduces hunger so it supports weight loss.
　　이것은 배고픔을 줄여서 체중 감량을 도와주죠.
　　「Yogurt is also great to eat in the morning.」 17번 ④의 근거 일치
　　요거트도 아침에 먹기 아주 좋습니다.
　　It contains probiotics that can improve digestion.
　　여기에는 소화를 증진할 수 있는 프로바이오틱스가 들어 있습니다.
　　「Eating berries such as blueberries or strawberries is another perfect way to start the morning.」 17번 ⑤의 근거 일치
　　블루베리나 딸기 같은 베리를 먹는 것도 아침을 시작하는 데 완벽한 또 한 가지 방법입니다.
　　They are lower in sugar than most other fruits, but higher in fiber.
　　이것들은 대부분의 과일보다 당이 적지만, 섬유소는 더 많습니다.
　　Add them to yogurt for a tasty breakfast.
　　이것들을 요거트에 넣어 맛있는 아침을 만들어 보세요.
　　Start every day with a healthy meal. Thank you.
　　매일을 건강한 식사로 시작하세요. 고맙습니다.

● protein ⓝ 단백질　　　● weight loss 체중 감량
● digestion ⓝ 소화　　　● fiber ⓝ 섬유소
● downside ⓝ 단점

---

16 주제 파악　　　정답률 97% | 정답 ②

여자가 하는 말의 주제로 가장 적절한 것은?

① downsides of fatty food – 지방이 많은 식품의 단점
✓ healthy foods for breakfast – 아침 식사를 위한 건강 식품
③ ways to avoid eating snacks – 간식 섭취를 피하는 방법
④ easy foods to cook in 5 minutes – 5분만에 요리하기 쉬운 음식
⑤ the importance of a balanced diet – 균형 잡힌 식사의 중요성

Why? 왜 정답일까?
'Today I will introduce a healthy breakfast food list.'에서 여자는 아침에 먹기 좋은 건강한 식품을 소개하겠다고 하므로, 여자가 하는 말의 주제로 가장 적절한 것은 ② '아침 식사를 위한 건강 식품'이다.

---

17 언급 유무 파악   정답률 94% | 정답 ③

언급된 음식이 아닌 것은?
① eggs – 달걀   ② cheese – 치즈   ✓ potatoes – 감자
④ yogurt – 요거트   ⑤ berries – 베리

Why? 왜 정답일까?
담화에서 여자는 아침에 먹기 좋은 건강식의 예로 달걀, 치즈, 요거트, 베리를 언급하므로, 언급되지 않은 것은 ③ '감자'이다.

Why? 왜 오답일까?
① 'Eggs are an excellent choice because they are high in protein.'에서 '달걀'이 언급되었다.
② 'Cheese is another good option.'에서 '치즈'가 언급되었다.
④ 'Yogurt is also great to eat in the morning.'에서 '요거트'가 언급되었다.
⑤ 'Eating berries is another perfect way to start the morning.'에서 '베리'가 언급되었다.

---

18 분실물 확인 요청   정답률 96% | 정답 ②

다음 글의 목적으로 가장 적절한 것은?
① 제품의 고장 원인을 문의하려고
✓ 분실물 발견 시 연락을 부탁하려고
③ 시설물의 철저한 관리를 당부하려고
④ 여행자 보험 가입 절차를 확인하려고
⑤ 분실물 센터 확장의 필요성을 건의하려고

Dear Boat Tour Manager,
보트투어 담당자께
On March 15, / my family was on one of your Glass Bottom Boat Tours.
3월 15일에 / 저희 가족은 귀사의 Glass Bottom Boat Tours 중 하나에 참여했습니다.
When we returned to our hotel, / I discovered that I left behind my cell phone case.
저희가 호텔에 돌아왔을 때, / 제가 휴대 전화 케이스를 놓고 왔다는 것을 발견했습니다.
The case must have fallen off my lap and onto the floor / when I took it off my phone to clean it.
제 무릎에서 케이스가 바닥으로 떨어졌던 것이 틀림없습니다. / 제가 케이스를 닦기 위해 휴대 전화에서 분리했을 때
I would like to ask you / to check if it is on your boat.
저는 당신에게 부탁드리고 싶습니다. / 그것이 보트에 있는지 확인해 주시길
Its color is black / and it has my name on the inside.
그것의 색깔은 검은색이며 / 안쪽에 제 이름이 있습니다.
If you find the case, / I would appreciate it if you would let me know.
만약 케이스가 발견된다면, / 저에게 알려주시면 감사하겠습니다.
Sincerely, // Sam Roberts
Sam Roberts 드림

보트 투어 담당자께

3월 15일에 저희 가족은 귀사의 Glass Bottom Boat Tours 중 하나에 참여했습니다. 호텔에 돌아왔을 때, 제가 휴대 전화 케이스를 놓고 왔다는 것을 발견했습니다. 케이스를 닦기 위해 휴대 전화에서 분리했을 때 케이스가 제 무릎에서 바닥으로 떨어졌던 것이 틀림없습니다. 그 것이 보트에 있는지 확인해 주시길 부탁드립니다. 그것의 색깔은 검은색이며 안쪽에 제 이름이 있습니다. 만약 케이스가 발견된다면, 저에게 알려주시면 감사하겠습니다.

Sam Roberts 드림

Why? 왜 정답일까?
보트 투어 중 잃어버린 휴대 전화 케이스가 보트에 있는지 확인해줄 것을 부탁하는(I would like to ask you to check if it is on your boat.) 글이다. 따라서 글의 목적으로 가장 적절한 것은 ② '분실물 발견 시 연락을 부탁하려고'이다.

● leave behind ~을 남겨놓고 오다   ● fall ⓥ 떨어지다
● lap ⓝ 무릎   ● appreciate ⓥ 감사하다

구문 풀이
4행 The case must have fallen off my lap and onto the floor when I took it off
「must have+과거분사 : ~했음에 틀림없다」
my phone to clean it.
부사적 용법(~하기 위해)

---

19 공원에 놀러갔다가 얼마 못 놀고 돌아가게 된 Matthew   정답률 93% | 정답 ②

다음 글에 드러난 Matthew의 심경 변화로 가장 적절한 것은?
① embarrassed → indifferent   ✓ excited → disappointed
  당황한   무관심한   신난   실망한
③ cheerful → ashamed   ④ nervous → touched
  즐거운   수치스러운   긴장한   감동한
⑤ scared → relaxed
  겁에 질린   느긋한

One Saturday morning, / Matthew's mother told Matthew / that she was going to take him to the park.
어느 토요일 아침, / Matthew의 어머니는 Matthew에게 말했다. / 자신이 그를 공원으로 데리고 가겠다고
A big smile came across his face.
그의 얼굴에 환한 미소가 드리워졌다.
As he loved to play outside, / he ate his breakfast and got dressed quickly / so they could go.
그가 밖에 나가서 노는 것을 좋아했기 때문에, / 그는 서둘러 아침을 먹고 옷을 입었다. / 그들이 나가기 위해
When they got to the park, / Matthew ran all the way over to the swing set.
그들이 공원에 도착했을 때, / Matthew는 그네를 향해 바로 뛰어갔다.
That was his favorite thing to do at the park.
그것은 그가 공원에서 가장 좋아하는 것이었다.
But the swings were all being used.
하지만 그네는 이미 모두 이용되고 있었다.
His mother explained / that he could use the slide / until a swing became available, / but it was broken.
그의 어머니는 말했지만, / 그가 미끄럼틀을 탈 수 있다고 / 그네를 이용할 수 있을 때까지 / 그것은 부서져 있었다.
Suddenly, his mother got a phone call / and she told Matthew they had to leave.
갑자기 그의 어머니가 전화를 받고 / 그녀는 Matthew에게 떠나야 한다고 말했다.
His heart sank.
그는 가슴이 내려앉았다.

어느 토요일 아침, Matthew의 어머니는 Matthew에게 공원으로 데리고 가겠다고 말했다. 그의 얼굴에 환한 미소가 드리워졌다. 그는 밖에 나가서 노는 것을 좋아했기 때문에, 나가기 위해 서둘러 아침을 먹고 옷을 입었다. 공원에 도착했을 때, Matthew는 그네를 향해 바로 뛰어갔다. 그것은 그가 공원에서 가장 좋아하는 것이었다. 하지만 그네는 이미 모두 이용되고 있었다. 그의 어머니는 그네를 이용할 수 있을 때까지 미끄럼틀을 탈 수 있다고 말했지만, 그것은 부서져 있었다. 갑자기 그의 어머니가 전화를 받고 Matthew에게 떠나야 한다고 말했다. 그는 가슴이 내려앉았다.

Why? 왜 정답일까?
아침에 어머니와 함께 공원으로 가게 되어 기뻐하던 Matthew가(A big smile came across his face.) 제대로 놀지도 못한 채 갑자기 떠나야 한다는 이야기를 듣고 실망했다는(His heart sank.) 내용의 글이다. 따라서 Matthew의 심경 변화로 가장 적절한 것은 ② '신난 → 실망한'이다.

● swing ⓝ 그네   ● slide ⓝ 미끄럼틀
● broken ⓐ 고장난, 부서진   ● sink ⓥ 가라앉다
● embarrassed ⓐ 당황한   ● touched ⓐ 감동한

구문 풀이
3행 As he loved to play outside, he ate his breakfast and got dressed quickly
접속사(이유)   동사1   동사2
so (that) they could go.
접속사(목적 : ~하도록)

---

20 회의 안건을 사전에 작성해 공유하기   정답률 88% | 정답 ⑤

다음 글에서 필자가 주장하는 바로 가장 적절한 것은?
① 회의 결과는 빠짐없이 작성해서 공개해야 한다.
② 중요한 정보는 공식 회의를 통해 전달해야 한다.
③ 생산성 향상을 위해 정기적인 평가회가 필요하다.
④ 모든 참석자의 동의를 받아서 회의를 열어야 한다.
✓ 회의에서 다룰 사항은 미리 작성해서 공유해야 한다.

Meetings encourage creative thinking / and can give you ideas / that you may never have thought of on your own.
회의는 창의적 사고를 촉진하며 / 아이디어들을 당신에게 제공할 수 있다. / 당신이 혼자서는 절대 떠올리지 못할 만한
However, on average, / meeting participants consider / about one third of meeting time / to be unproductive.
그러나, 평균적으로, / 회의 참석자들은 여긴다. / 회의 시간의 대략 3분의 1 정도를 / 비생산적이라고
But you can make your meetings / more productive and more useful / by preparing well in advance.
하지만 당신은 회의를 만들 수 있다. / 더 생산적이고 유용하게 / 사전에 잘 준비함으로써
You should create a list of items to be discussed / and share your list with other participants / before a meeting.
당신은 논의하게 될 사항들의 목록을 만들고 / 다른 회의 참석자들에게 공유해야 한다. / 회의 전에
It allows them / to know what to expect in your meeting / and prepare to participate.
그것은 참석자들이 ~하도록 만들어 준다. / 회의에서 무엇을 기대하는지를 알고 / 회의 참석을 준비할 수 있도록

회의는 창의적 사고를 촉진하며, 당신이 혼자서는 절대 떠올리지 못했을 만한 아이디어들을 당신에게 제공할 수 있다. 그러나, 평균적으로, 회의 참석자들은 회의 시간의 대략 3분의 1 정도를 비생산적으로 여긴다. 하지만 당신은 사전에 잘 준비함으로써 회의를 더 생산적이고 유용하게 만들 수 있다. 당신은 논의하게 될 사항들의 목록을 만들어 그 목록을 회의 전에 다른 회의 참석자들에게 공유해야 한다. 그것은 참석자들이 회의에서 무엇을 기대할지를 알고 회의 참석을 준비할 수 있도록 만들어 준다.

Why? 왜 정답일까?
'You should create a list of items to be discussed and share your list with other participants before a meeting.'에서 회의 전 논의 사항을 미리 작성해 공유하는 것이 좋다고 하므로, '필자가 주장하는 바로 가장 적절한 것은 ⑤ '회의에서 다룰 사항은 미리 작성해서 공유해야 한다.'이다.

● encourage ⓥ 촉진하다, 격려하다   ● on one's own 혼자서, 스스로
● on average 평균적으로   ● unproductive ⓐ 비생산적인

구문 풀이
7행 It allows them to know {what to expect in your meeting} and (to) prepare
동사 목적어 목적격 보어1   { } : 명사구(무엇을 ~할지)   목적격 보어2
to participate.

21 스트레스 관리의 원칙   정답률 80% | 정답 ③

밑줄 친 put the glass down이 다음 글에서 의미하는 바로 가장 적절한 것은? [3점]

① pour more water into the glass – 잔에 물을 더 부어야
② set a plan not to make mistakes – 실수하지 않기 위해 계획을 세워야
③ let go of the stress in your mind – 마음속에서 스트레스를 떨쳐내야
④ think about the cause of your stress – 스트레스의 원인을 생각해 보아야
⑤ learn to accept the opinions of others – 다른 사람들의 의견을 받아들이는 법을 배워야

A psychology professor raised a glass of water / while teaching stress management principles to her students, / and asked them, / "How heavy is this glass of water I'm holding?"
한 심리학 교수가 물이 든 유리잔을 들어 올리고 / 학생들에게 스트레스 관리 원칙을 가르치던 중 / 그들에게 물었다. / "제가 들고 있는 이 물 잔의 무게는 얼마나 될까요?"라고

Students shouted out various answers.
학생들은 다양한 대답을 외쳤다.

The professor replied, / "The absolute weight of this glass doesn't matter. / It depends on how long I hold it. / If I hold it for a minute, / it's quite light.
그 교수가 답했다. / "이 잔의 절대 무게는 중요하지 않습니다. / 이는 제가 이 잔을 얼마나 오래 들고 있느냐에 달려 있죠. / 만약 제가 이것을 1분 동안 들고 있다면, / 꽤 가볍죠.

But, if I hold it for a day straight, / it will cause severe pain in my arm, / forcing me to drop the glass to the floor.
하지만, 만약 제가 이것을 하루종일 들고 있다면 / 이것은 제 팔에 심각한 고통을 야기하고 / 잔을 바닥에 떨어뜨릴 것입니다.

In each case, / the weight of the glass is the same, / but the longer I hold it, / the heavier it feels to me."
각 사례에서 / 잔의 무게는 같지만, / 제가 오래 들고 있을수록 / 그것은 저에게 더 무겁게 느껴지죠."

As the class nodded their heads in agreement, / she continued, / "Your stresses in life are like this glass of water. / If you still feel the weight of yesterday's stress, / it's a strong sign / that it's time to put the glass down."
학생들은 동의하며 고개를 끄덕였고, / 교수는 이어 말했다. / "여러분이 인생에서 느끼는 스트레스들도 이 물 잔과 같습니다. / 만약 아직도 어제 받은 스트레스의 무게를 느낀다면, / 그것은 강한 신호입니다. / 잔을 내려놓아야 할 때라는"

한 심리학 교수가 학생들에게 스트레스 관리 원칙을 가르치던 중 물이 든 유리잔을 들어 올리고 "제가 들고 있는 이 물 잔의 무게는 얼마나 될까요?"라고 물었다. 학생들은 다양한 대답을 외쳤다. "이 잔의 절대 무게는 중요하지 않습니다. 이는 제가 이 잔을 얼마나 오래 들고 있느냐에 달려 있죠. 만약 제가 이것을 1분 동안 들고 있다면, 꽤 가볍죠. 하지만, 만약 제가 이것을 하루종일 들고 있다면 이것은 제 팔에 심각한 고통을 야기하고 잔을 바닥에 떨어뜨릴 수밖에 없게 할 것입니다. 각 사례에서 잔의 무게는 같지만, 제가 오래 들고 있을수록 그것은 저에게 더 무겁게 느껴지죠." 학생들은 동의하며 고개를 끄덕였고, 교수는 이어 말했다. "여러분이 인생에서 느끼는 스트레스들도 이 물 잔과 같습니다. 만약 아직도 어제 받은 스트레스의 무게를 느낀다면, 그것은 잔을 내려놓아야 할 때라는 강한 신호입니다."

Why? 왜 정답일까?

물 잔의 무게를 느낄 때 중요한 것은 잔의 절대적 무게가 아니라 얼마나 오래 들고 있는지(It depends on how long I hold it.)이며, 같은 잔이라고 할지라도 더 오래 들고 있을수록 더 무겁게 느껴진다(the longer I hold it, the heavier it feels to me.)고 한다. 이를 스트레스 상황에 적용하면, 스트레스의 무게가 더 무겁게 느껴질수록 그 스트레스를 오래 안고 있었다는 뜻이므로 '스트레스를 떨쳐내기' 위해 노력해야 한다는 것을 알 수 있다. 따라서 밑줄 친 부분이 의미하는 바로 가장 적절한 것은 ③ '마음속에서 스트레스를 떨쳐내야'이다.

- principle ⓝ 원칙, 원리
- nod ⓥ 끄덕이다
- put down ~을 내려놓다
- let go of ~을 내려놓다, 버리다, 포기하다
- severe ⓐ 심각한
- in agreement 동의하며
- pour ⓥ 쏟다, 붓다

구문 풀이

6행 But, if I hold it for a day straight, it will cause severe pain in my arm,
접속사(조건)   ↳ 동사(현재)   동사(미래)
forcing me to drop the glass to the floor.
분사구문(= and will force ~)

22 상황을 오해하게 하는 감정   정답률 82% | 정답 ①

다음 글의 요지로 가장 적절한 것은?

① 자신의 감정으로 인해 상황을 오해할 수 있다.
② 자신의 생각을 타인에게 강요해서는 안 된다.
③ 인간관계가 우리의 감정에 영향을 미친다.
④ 타인의 감정에 공감하는 자세가 필요하다.
⑤ 공동체를 위한 선택에는 보상이 따른다.

Your emotions deserve attention / and give you important pieces of information.
당신의 감정은 주목할 만하고 / 당신에게 중요한 정보를 준다.

However, / they can also sometimes be / an unreliable, inaccurate source of information.
그러나, / 감정은 또한 될 수도 있다. / 가끔 신뢰할 수 없고, 부정확한 정보의 원천이

You may feel a certain way, / but that does not mean / those feelings are reflections of the truth.
당신이 분명하게 느낄지 모르지만, / 그것은 뜻하지는 않는다. / 그러한 감정들이 사실의 반영이라는 것을

You may feel sad / and conclude that your friend is angry with you / when her behavior simply reflects / that she's having a bad day.
당신은 슬플지도 모르고 / 그녀가 당신에게 화가 났다고 결론을 내릴지도 모른다. / 단지 친구의 행동이 나타낼 때에도, / 그 친구가 안 좋은 날을 보내고 있음을

You may feel depressed / and decide that you did poorly in an interview / when you did just fine.
당신은 기분이 우울할지도 모르고 / 자신이 면접에서 못했다고 판단할지도 모른다. / 당신이 잘했을 때도

Your feelings can mislead you into thinking things / that are not supported by facts.
당신의 감정은 당신을 속여 생각하게 할 수 있다. / 사실에 의해 뒷받침되지 않는 것들을

당신의 감정은 주목할 만하고 당신에게 중요한 정보를 준다. 그러나, 감정은 또한 가끔 신뢰할 수 없고, 부정확한 정보의 원천이 될 수도 있다. 당신이 특정하게 느낄지 모르지만, 그것은 그러한 감정들이 사실의 반영이라는 뜻은 아니다. 친구의 행동이 단지 그 친구가 안 좋은 날을 보내고 있음을 나타낼 때에도, 당신이 슬프기 때문에 그녀가 당신에게 화가 났다고 결론을 내릴지도 모른다. 당신은 기분이 우울해서 면접에서 잘했을 때도 못했다고 판단할지도 모른다. 당신의 감정은 당신을 속여 사실에 의해 뒷받침되지 않는 것들을 생각하게 할 수 있다.

Why? 왜 정답일까?

'However, they can also sometimes be an unreliable, inaccurate source of information.'와 'Your feelings can mislead you into thinking things that are not supported by facts.'을 통해, 감정이 상황을 오해하게 하는 경우가 생길 수 있다는 중심 내용을 파악할 수 있으므로, 글의 요지로 가장 적절한 것은 ① '자신의 감정으로 인해 상황을 오해할 수 있다.'이다.

- deserve ⓥ ~을 받을 만하다
- inaccurate ⓐ 부정확한
- reflection ⓝ 반영
- depressed ⓐ 우울한
- support 뒷받침하다, 지지하다
- unreliable ⓐ 믿을 만하지 않은
- source of information 정보 출처
- conclude ⓥ 결론 짓다
- mislead A into B A를 속여 B하게 하다

구문 풀이

8행 Your feelings can mislead you into thinking things [that are not supported by facts].
「mislead + A + into + B : A를 잘못 인도해 B하게 하다」   선행사 주격 관·대

23 아이들이 수학적 개념을 익혀 가는 방식   정답률 78% | 정답 ②

다음 글의 주제로 가장 적절한 것은?

① difficulties of children in learning how to count – 아이들이 수를 세는 법을 배우는 데 있어 어려움
② how children build mathematical understanding – 아이들은 수학적 이해를 어떻게 쌓아나가는가
③ why fingers are used in counting objects – 수를 셀 때 왜 손가락을 쓰는가
④ importance of early childhood education – 아동 조기 교육의 중요성
⑤ advantages of singing number songs – 숫자 노래 부르기의 이점

Every day, / children explore and construct relationships among objects.
매일, / 아이들은 사물 사이의 관계를 탐구하고 구성한다.

Frequently, / these relationships focus on / how much or how many of something exists.
빈번히, / 이러한 관계는 ~에 초점을 맞춘다. / 무언가 얼마만큼 혹은 몇 개 존재하는지

Thus, / children count / — "One cookie, / two shoes, / three candles on the birthday cake, / four children in the sandbox."
따라서, / 아이들은 센다. / "쿠키 하나, / 신발 두 개, / 생일 케이크 위에 초 세 개, / 모래놀이 통에 아이 네 명."

Children compare / — "Which has more? Which has fewer? Will there be enough?"
아이들은 비교한다. / "무엇이 더 많지? 무엇이 더 적지? 충분할까?"

Children calculate / — "How many will fit? Now, I have five. I need one more."
아이들은 계산한다. / "몇 개가 알맞을까? 나는 지금 다섯 개가 있어. 하나 더 필요하네."

In all of these instances, / children are developing a notion of quantity.
이 모든 예시에서, / 아이들은 양의 개념을 발달시키는 중이다.

Children reveal and investigate mathematical concepts / through their own activities or experiences, / such as figuring out how many crackers to take at snack time / or sorting shells into piles.
아이들은 수학적 개념을 밝히고 연구한다. / 그들만의 활동이나 경험을 통해 / 간식 시간에 몇 개의 크래커를 가져갈지 알아내거나 / 조개껍질들을 더미로 분류하는 것과 같은

매일, 아이들은 사물 사이의 관계들을 탐구하고 구성한다. 빈번히, 이러한 관계들은 무언가 얼마만큼 혹은 몇 개 존재하는지에 초점을 맞춘다. 따라서, 아이들은 센다. "쿠키 하나, 신발 두 개, 생일 케이크 위에 초 세 개, 모래놀이 통에 아이 네 명." 아이들은 비교한다. "무엇이 더 많지? 무엇이 더 적지? 충분할까?" 아이들은 계산한다. "몇 개가 알맞을까? 나는 지금 다섯 개가 있어. 하나 더 필요하네." 이 모든 예시에서, 아이들은 수량의 개념을 발달시키는 중이다. 아이들은 간식 시간에 몇 개의 크래커를 가져갈지 알아내거나 조개껍질들을 더미로 분류하는 것과 같은, 그들만의 활동이나 경험을 통해 수학적 개념을 밝히고 연구한다.

Why? 왜 정답일까?

아이들은 자기만의 활동이나 경험을 통해 수학적 개념을 익혀 간다(Children reveal and investigate mathematical concepts through their own activities or experiences ~)는 것이 핵심 내용이므로, 글의 주제로 가장 적절한 것은 ② '아이들은 수학적 이해를 어떻게 쌓아나가는가'이다.

- explore ⓥ 탐구하다
- sandbox ⓝ (어린이가 안에서 노는) 모래놀이 통
- fit ⓥ 맞다, 적합하다
- notion ⓝ 개념
- investigate ⓥ 연구하다, 조사하다
- shell ⓝ (조개 등의) 껍데기
- construct ⓥ 구성하다
- calculate ⓥ 계산하다
- instance ⓝ 예시, 사례
- quantity ⓝ (측정 가능한) 양, 수량
- sort A into B A를 B로 분류하다

구문 풀이

2행 Frequently, these relationships focus on {how much or how many of something exists}. [〕 : 「how + 형/부 + 주어 + 동사 : 얼마나 ~한지」

24 알고리듬의 시대   정답률 76% | 정답 ①

다음 글의 제목으로 가장 적절한 것은?

① We Live in an Age of Algorithms – 우리는 알고리듬의 시대에 산다
② Mysteries of Ancient Civilizations – 고대 문명의 미스터리
③ Dangers of Online Banking Algorithms – 온라인 뱅킹 알고리듬의 위험성
④ How Algorithms Decrease Human Creativity – 알고리듬은 어떻게 인간의 창의력을 떨어뜨리는가
⑤ Transportation: A Driving Force of Industry – 교통: 산업 발달의 원동력

Only a generation or two ago, / mentioning the word *algorithms* / would have drawn a blank from most people.

[문제편 p.073]

한두 세대 전만 해도, / *알고리듬*이라는 단어를 언급하는 것은 / 대부분의 사람들로부터 아무 반응을 얻지 못했을 것이다.
Today, algorithms appear in every part of civilization.
오늘날, 알고리듬은 문명의 모든 부분에서 나타난다.
They are connected to everyday life.
그것들은 일상에 연결되어 있다.
They're not just in your cell phone or your laptop / but in your car, your house, your appliances, and your toys.
그것들은 당신의 휴대 전화나 노트북 속뿐 아니라 / 당신의 자동차, 집, 가전과 장난감 안에도 있다.
Your bank is a huge web of algorithms, / with humans turning the switches here and there.
당신의 은행은 알고리듬의 거대한 망이다. / 인간들이 여기저기서 스위치를 돌리고 있는
Algorithms schedule flights / and then fly the airplanes.
알고리듬은 비행 일정을 잡고 / 비행기를 운항한다.
Algorithms run factories, / trade goods, / and keep records.
알고리듬은 공장을 운영하고, / 상품을 거래하며, / 기록 문서를 보관한다.
If every algorithm suddenly stopped working, / it would be the end of the world / as we know it.
만일 모든 알고리듬이 갑자기 작동을 멈춘다면, / 이는 세상의 끝이 될 것이다. / 우리가 알고 있는

한두 세대 전만 해도, *알고리듬*이라는 단어를 언급하는 것은 대부분의 사람들로부터 아무 반응을 얻지 못했을 것이다. 오늘날, 알고리듬은 문명의 모든 부분에서 나타난다. 그것들은 일상에 연결되어 있다. 그것들은 당신의 휴대 전화나 노트북 속뿐 아니라 당신의 자동차, 집, 가전과 장난감 안에도 있다. 당신의 은행은 인간들이 여기저기서 스위치를 돌리고 있는, 알고리듬의 거대한 망이다. 알고리듬은 비행 일정을 잡고 비행기를 운항한다. 알고리듬은 공장을 운영하고, 상품을 거래하며, 기록 문서를 보관한다. 만일 모든 알고리듬이 갑자기 작동을 멈춘다면, 이는 우리가 알고 있는 세상의 끝이 될 것이다.

Why? 왜 정답일까?

오늘날 문명의 모든 영역에서 알고리듬을 찾아볼 수 있다(Today, algorithms appear in every part of civilization.)는 것이 핵심 내용이므로, 글의 제목으로 가장 적절한 것은 ① '우리는 알고리듬의 시대에 산다'이다.

- generation ⓝ 세대
- civilization ⓝ 문명
- fly an airplane 비행기를 운항하다
- draw a blank 아무 반응을 얻지 못하다
- appliance ⓝ 가전 (제품)
- trade ⓥ 거래하다, 교역하다

구문 풀이

8행 If every algorithm suddenly stopped working, it would be the end of the
「If + 주어 + 과거시제 동사 ~, 주어 + 조동사 과거형 + 동사원형 : 가정법 과거(현재 사실 반대)」
world as we know it.

---

25 미국에서 반려동물을 키우는 가정의 비율　　　정답률 88% | 정답 ⑤

다음 도표의 내용과 일치하지 않는 것은?

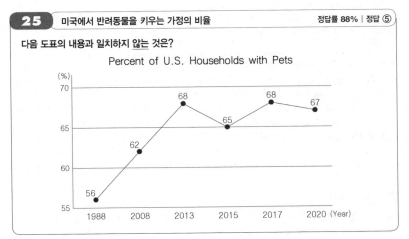

Percent of U.S. Households with Pets

The graph above shows the percent of households with pets / in the United States (U.S.) / from 1988 to 2020.
위 그래프는 반려동물을 기르는 가정의 비율을 보여준다. / 미국의 / 1988년부터 2020년까지
① In 1988, / more than half of U.S. households owned pets, / and more than 6 out of 10 U.S. households / owned pets from 2008 to 2020.
1988년에는 / 절반 이상의 미국 가정이 반려동물을 길렀고, / 10개 중 6개 이상의 미국 가정이 / 2008년에서 2020년까지 반려동물을 길렀다.
② In the period between 1988 and 2008, / pet ownership increased among U.S. households / by 6 percentage points.
1988년과 2008년 사이, / 반려동물 보유가 미국 가정들에서 증가했다. / 6퍼센트포인트만큼
③ From 2008 to 2013, / pet ownership rose an additional 6 percentage points.
2008년과 2013년 사이, / 반려동물 보유가 6퍼센트포인트가 추가적으로 올랐다.
④ The percent of U.S. households with pets in 2013 / was the same as that in 2017, / which was 68 percent.
2013년의 반려동물을 기르는 미국 가정의 비율은 / 2017년의 비율과 같고, / 68퍼센트였다.
⑤ In 2015, / the rate of U.S. households with pets / was 3 percentage points lower than in 2020.
2015년에는, / 반려동물을 기르는 미국 가정의 비율이 / 2020년보다 3퍼센트포인트 더 낮았다.

위 그래프는 1988년부터 2020년까지 반려동물을 기르는 미국 가정의 비율을 보여준다. ① 1988년에는 절반 이상의 미국 가정이 반려동물을 길렀고, 2008년에서 2020년까지 10개 중 6개 이상의 미국 가정이 반려동물을 길렀다. ② 1988년과 2008년 사이, 반려동물 보유는 미국 가정들에서 6퍼센트포인트 증가했다. ③ 2008년과 2013년 사이, 반려동물 보유는 6퍼센트포인트가 추가적으로 올랐다. ④ 2013년의 반려동물을 기르는 미국 가정의 비율은 2017년의 비율과 같고, 68퍼센트였다. ⑤ 2015년에는, 반려동물을 기르는 미국 가정의 비율이 2020년보다 3퍼센트포인트 더 낮았다.

Why? 왜 정답일까?

도표에 따르면 미국에서 반려동물을 기르는 가정의 비율은 **2015년 65%, 2020년 67%**로, 두 해 간 비율은 **2퍼센트포인트**의 격차를 보인다. 따라서 도표와 일치하지 않는 것은 ⑤이다.

- household ⓝ 가정, 가구
- rise ⓥ 오르다
- ownership ⓝ 보유, 소유

---

26 Claude Bolling의 생애　　　정답률 93% | 정답 ③

Claude Bolling에 관한 다음 글의 내용과 일치하지 않는 것은?

① 1930년에 프랑스에서 태어났다.
② 학교 친구를 통해 재즈를 소개받았다.
☑ 20대에 Best Piano Player 상을 받았다.
④ 성공적인 영화 음악 작곡가였다.
⑤ 1975년에 플루트 연주자와 협업했다.

「Pianist, composer, and big band leader, / Claude Bolling, was born on April 10, 1930, / in Cannes, France, / but spent most of his life in Paris.」 ①의 근거 일치
피아니스트, 작곡가, 그리고 빅 밴드 리더인 / Claude Bolling은 1930년 4월 10일 태어났지만, / 프랑스 칸에서 / 삶의 대부분을 파리에서 보냈다.
He began studying classical music as a youth.
그는 젊었을 때 클래식 음악을 공부하기 시작했다.
「He was introduced to the world of jazz / by a schoolmate.」 ②의 근거 일치
그는 재즈의 세계를 소개받았다. / 학교 친구를 통해
Later, / Bolling became interested in the music of Fats Waller, / one of the most excellent jazz musicians.
후에, / Bolling은 Fats Waller의 음악에 관심을 가졌다. / 최고의 재즈 음악가들 중 한 명인
「Bolling became famous as a teenager / by winning the Best Piano Player prize / at an amateur contest in France.」 ③의 근거 불일치
그는 10대 때 유명해졌다. / Best Piano Player 상을 수상하며 / 프랑스의 아마추어 대회에서
「He was also a successful film music composer, / writing the music for more than one hundred films.」 ④의 근거 일치
그는 또한 성공적인 영화 음악 작곡가였고, / 100편이 넘는 영화의 음악을 작곡했다.
「In 1975, he collaborated with flutist Rampal / and published *Suite for Flute and Jazz Piano Trio*, / which he became most well-known for.」 ⑤의 근거 일치
1975년에, 그는 플루트 연주자 Rampal과 협업했고, / *Suite for Flute and Jazz Piano Trio*를 발매했으며, / 이것으로 가장 잘 알려지게 되었다.
He died in 2020, / leaving two sons, David and Alexandre.
그는 2020년 사망했다. / 두 아들 David와 Alexandre를 남기고

피아니스트, 작곡가, 그리고 빅 밴드 리더인 Claude Bolling은 1930년 4월 10일 프랑스 칸에서 태어났지만, 삶의 대부분을 파리에서 보냈다. 그는 젊었을 때 클래식 음악을 공부하기 시작했다. 그는 학교 친구를 통해 재즈의 세계를 소개받았다. 후에 Bolling은 최고의 재즈 음악가들 중 한 명인 Fats Waller의 음악에 관심을 가졌다. 그는 10대 때 프랑스의 아마추어 대회에서 Best Piano Player 상을 수상하며 유명해졌다. 그는 또한 성공적인 영화 음악 작곡가였고, 100편이 넘는 영화의 음악을 작곡했다. 1975년에, 그는 플루트 연주자 Rampal과 협업했고, *Suite for Flute and Jazz Piano Trio*를 발매했으며, 이것으로 가장 잘 알려지게 되었다. 그는 두 아들 David와 Alexandre를 남기고 2020년 사망했다.

Why? 왜 정답일까?

'Bolling became famous as a teenager by winning the Best Piano Player prize at an amateur contest in France.'에서 Claude Bolling이 아마추어 재즈 연주자 대회에서 **Best Piano Player** 상을 받은 것은 **10대** 시절이었다고 하므로, 내용과 일치하지 않는 것은 ③ '20대에 **Best Piano Player** 상을 받았다.'이다.

Why? 왜 오답일까?

① 'Claude Bolling, was born on April 10, 1930, in Cannes, France, ~'의 내용과 일치한다.
② 'He was introduced to the world of jazz by a schoolmate.'의 내용과 일치한다.
④ 'He was also a successful film music composer, ~'의 내용과 일치한다.
⑤ 'In 1975, he collaborated with flutist Rampal ~'의 내용과 일치한다.

- composer ⓝ 작곡가
- introduce ⓥ 소개하다
- flutist ⓝ 플루티스트
- well-known for ~로 유명한
- youth ⓝ 젊은 시절, 청춘
- collaborate with ~와 협업하다
- publish ⓥ 발매하다, 출간하다

구문 풀이

1행 Pianist, composer, and big band leader, Claude Bolling, was born on
주어 동격　　　주어　　　동사1
April 10, 1930, in Cannes, France, but spent most of his life in Paris.
동사2

---

27 여름방학 태권도 프로그램　　　정답률 94% | 정답 ④

Kids Taekwondo Program에 관한 다음 안내문의 내용과 일치 하지 않는 것은?

① 8월 8일부터 3일간 운영한다.
② 5세 이상의 어린이가 참가할 수 있다.
③ 자기 방어 훈련 활동을 한다.
☑ 참가비에 간식비는 포함되지 않는다.
⑤ 물병과 수건을 가져와야 한다.

Kids Taekwondo Program
Kids Taekwondo Program(어린이 태권도 프로그램)
Enjoy our taekwondo program this summer vacation.
이번 여름방학에 태권도 프로그램을 즐기세요.
Schedule
일정
「Dates: August 8th – August 10th」 ①의 근거 일치
날짜: 8월 8일 ~ 8월 10일
Time: 9:00 a.m. – 11:00 a.m.
시간: 오전 9시 ~ 오전 11시
Participants
참가자
「Any child aged 5 and up」 ②의 근거 일치
5세 이상 어린이 누구나
Activities
활동

『Self-defense training』 ③의근거 일치
자기 방어 훈련
Team building games to develop social skills
사교성 발달을 위한 팀 빌딩 게임
Participation Fee
참가비
『$50 per child (includes snacks)』 ④의근거 불일치
1인당 $50 (간식 포함)
Notice
알림
『What to bring: water bottle, towel』 ⑤의근거 일치
가져올 것: 물병, 수건
What not to bring: chewing gum, expensive items
가져오지 말아야 할 것: 껌, 비싼 물건

Kids Taekwondo Program(어린이 태권도 프로그램)

이번 여름방학에 태권도 프로그램을 즐기세요.
□ 일정
• 날짜: 8월 8일 ~ 8월 10일
• 시간: 오전 9시 ~ 오전 11시
□ 참가자
• 5세 이상 어린이 누구나
□ 활동
• 자기 방어 훈련
• 사교성 발달을 위한 팀 빌딩 게임
□ 참가비
• 1인당 $50 (간식 포함)
□ 알림
• 가져올 것: 물병, 수건
• 가져오지 말아야 할 것: 껌, 비싼 물건

Why? 왜 정답일까?
'$50 per child (includes snacks)'에서 참가비는 50달러인데, 간식이 포함된 금액이라고 한다. 따라서 안내문의 내용과 일치하지 않는 것은 ④ '참가비에 간식비는 포함되지 않는다.'이다.

Why? 왜 오답일까?
① 'Dates: August 8th – August 10th'의 내용과 일치한다.
② 'Participants / Any child aged 5 and up'의 내용과 일치한다.
③ 'Activities / Self-defense'의 내용과 일치한다.
⑤ 'What to bring: water bottle, towel'의 내용과 일치한다.

● self-defense ⓝ 자기 방어   ● social skill 사교성
● expensive ⓐ 비싼

---

28 초콜릿 공장 투어   정답률 93% | 정답 ②

Moonlight Chocolate Factory Tour에 관한 다음 안내문의 내용과 일치하는 것은?
① 주말 오후 시간에 운영한다.
✓ 초콜릿 제조 과정을 볼 수 있다.
③ 네 가지 종류의 초콜릿을 시식할 수 있다.
④ 마스크 착용은 참여자의 선택 사항이다.
⑤ 공장 내부에서 사진 촬영이 가능하다.

Moonlight Chocolate Factory Tour
Moonlight Chocolate Factory Tour(Moonlight 초콜릿 공장 투어)
Take this special tour / and have a chance to enjoy our most popular chocolate bars.
이 특별한 투어에 참여하여 / 우리의 가장 인기 있는 초콜릿 바를 즐길 기회를 가지세요.
Operating Hours
운영 시간
『Monday – Friday, 2:00 p.m. – 5:00 p.m.』 ①의근거 불일치
월요일 ~ 금요일, 오후 2시 ~ 오후 5시
Activities
활동
『Watching our chocolate-making process』 ②의근거 일치
초콜릿 제조 과정 견학
『Tasting 3 types of chocolate (dark, milk, and mint chocolate)』 ③의근거 불일치
초콜릿 3종 (다크, 밀크 및 민트 초콜릿) 시식
Notice
알림
Ticket price: $30
티켓 가격 : $30
『Wearing a face mask is required.』 ④의근거 불일치
마스크 착용은 필수입니다.
『Taking pictures is not allowed inside the factory.』 ⑥의근거 불일치
공장 내부에서 사진 촬영은 허용되지 않습니다.

Moonlight Chocolate Factory Tour
(Moonlight 초콜릿 공장 투어)

이 특별한 투어에 참여하여 우리의 가장 인기 있는 초콜릿 바를 즐길 기회를 가지세요.
□ 운영 시간
• 월요일 ~ 금요일, 오후 2시 ~ 오후 5시
□ 활동
• 초콜릿 제조 과정 견학
• 초콜릿 3종 (다크, 밀크 및 민트 초콜릿) 시식
□ 알림

• 티켓 가격 : $30
• 마스크 착용은 필수입니다.
• 공장 내부에서 사진 촬영은 허용되지 않습니다.

Why? 왜 정답일까?
'Activities / Watching our chocolate-making'에서 초콜릿 제조 과정을 견학할 수 있다고 하므로, 안내문의 내용과 일치하는 것은 ② '초콜릿 제조 과정을 볼 수 있다.'이다.

Why? 왜 오답일까?
① 'Monday – Friday, 2:00 p.m. – 5:00 p.m.'에서 운영 시간은 평일 오후라고 하였다.
③ 'Tasting 3 types of chocolate (dark, milk, and mint chocolate)'에서 시식할 수 있는 초콜릿은 세 종류라고 하였다.
④ 'Wearing a face mask is required.'에서 마스크 착용은 필수라고 하였다.
⑤ 'Taking pictures is not allowed inside the factory.'에서 공장 내부 사진 촬영은 불가하다고 하였다.

● have a chance to ~할 기회를 갖다   ● operating hour 운영 시간

---

29 더 많은 것을 소비하게 하는 첨단 생활방식   정답률 59% | 정답 ④

다음 글의 밑줄 친 부분 중, 어법상 틀린 것은?

Despite all the high-tech devices / that seem to deny the need for paper, / paper use in the United States / ① has nearly doubled recently.
모든 첨단 기기들에도 불구하고, / 종이의 필요성을 부정하는 것처럼 보이는 / 미국에서 종이 사용은 / 최근 거의 두 배로 증가했다.
We now consume more paper than ever: / 400 million tons globally and growing.
우리는 현재 그 어느 때보다도 더 많은 종이를 소비하고 있어서, / 전 세계에서 4억 톤을 쓰고 있으며 그 양은 증가하고 있다.
Paper is not the only resource / ② that we are using more of.
자원은 종이만이 아니다. / 우리가 더 많이 사용하고 있는
Technological advances often come / with the promise of ③ using fewer materials.
기술의 발전은 흔히 온다. / 더 적은 재료의 사용 가능성과 함께
However, / the reality is / that they have historically caused more materials use, / making us ✓ dependent on more natural resources.
그러나, / 현실은 ~이다. / 그것들이 역사적으로 더 많은 재료 사용을 야기해 / 우리가 더 많은 천연자원 사용에 의존하게 한다는 것
The world now consumes far more "stuff" / than it ever has.
세계는 이제 훨씬 더 많은 '것'을 소비한다. / 그것이 어느 때 그랬던 것보다
We use twenty-seven times more industrial minerals, / such as gold, copper, and rare metals, / than we ⑤ did just over a century ago.
우리는 산업 광물을 27배 더 많이 사용한다. / 금, 구리, 희귀 금속과 같은 / 우리가 고작 1세기 이전에 그랬던 것보다
We also each individually use more resources.
우리는 또한 각자 더 많은 자원을 사용한다.
Much of that is due to our high-tech lifestyle.
그중 많은 부분은 우리의 첨단 생활방식 때문이다.

종이의 필요성을 부정하는 것처럼 보이는 모든 첨단 기기들에도 불구하고, 미국에서 종이 사용은 최근 거의 두 배로 증가했다. 우리는 현재 그 어느 때보다도 더 많은 종이를 소비하고 있어서, 전 세계에서 4억 톤을 쓰고 있으며 그 양은 증가하고 있다. 우리가 더 많이 사용하고 있는 자원은 종이만이 아니다. 기술의 발전은 흔히 더 적은 재료의 사용 가능성을 수반한다. 그러나, 현실은 그것들이 역사적으로 더 많은 재료 사용을 야기해 우리가 더 많은 천연자원에 의존하게 한다는 것이다. 세계는 이제 그 어느 때보다 훨씬 더 많은 '재료'를 소비한다. 우리는 금, 구리, 희귀 금속과 같은 산업 광물을 고작 1세기 이전보다 27배 더 많이 사용한다. 우리는 또한 각자 더 많은 자원을 사용한다. 그중 많은 부분은 우리의 첨단 생활방식 때문이다.

Why? 왜 정답일까?
make는 형용사를 목적격 보어로 취하는 5형식 동사이므로, 부사 **dependently**를 형용사 **dependent**로 고쳐 **making**의 보어 자리를 채워야 한다. 따라서 어법상 틀린 것은 ④이다.

Why? 왜 오답일까?
① 주어 **paper use**가 불가산명사이므로 단수 동사 **has**가 어법상 적절하다.
② 선행사 **the only resource** 뒤로 목적어가 없는 불완전한 절을 이끌고자 관계대명사 **that**이 알맞게 쓰였다. 참고로 선행사에 **the only**가 있으면 관계대명사 **that**이 주로 쓰인다.
③ 전치사 **of** 뒤에 목적어인 동명사 **using**이 알맞게 쓰였다.
⑤ 앞에 나온 일반동사 **use**를 대신하는데 시제가 과거이므로(**over a century ago**) 대동사 **did**가 알맞게 쓰였다.

● high-tech ⓐ 첨단 기술의   ● consume ⓥ 소비하다
● material ⓝ 물질, 자재, 재료   ● historically ⓐⓓ 역사적으로
● dependently ⓐⓓ 의존적으로, 남에게 의지하여   ● industrial ⓐ 산업의
● rare ⓐ 희귀한

구문 풀이

6행 However, the reality is {that they have historically caused more materials use, making us dependently on more natural resources}. { } : 명사절(주격 보어)
분사구문(=and they make ~)

---

30 삶을 사랑하는 법   정답률 61% | 정답 ②

다음 글의 밑줄 친 부분 중, 문맥상 낱말의 쓰임이 적절하지 않은 것은? [3점]

Do you sometimes feel like / you don't love your life?
당신은 가끔 느끼는가? / 당신이 삶을 사랑하지 않는다고
Like, deep inside, something is missing?
마치 마음 깊은 곳에서 뭔가가 빠진 것처럼?
That's because we are living someone else's life.
왜냐하면 우리가 타인의 삶을 살고 있기 때문이다.
We allow other people to ① influence our choices.
우리는 타인이 우리의 선택에 영향을 주도록 허용한다.
We are trying to meet their expectations.

우리는 그들의 기대감을 만족시키기 위해 노력하고 있다.
Social pressure is deceiving / — we are all impacted without noticing it.
사회적 압력은 현혹시킨다. / 우리 모두는 그것을 눈치채지도 못한 채 영향을 받는다.
Before we realize / we are losing ownership of our lives, / we end up ✔envying how other people live.
우리가 깨닫기 전에, / 우리의 삶에 대한 소유권을 잃었다는 것을 / 우리는 결국 다른 사람들이 어떻게 사는지를 부러워하게 된다.
Then, we can only see the greener grass / — ours is never good enough.
그러면, 우리는 더 푸른 잔디만 볼 수 있게 된다. / 우리의 삶은 만족할 만큼 충분히 좋아질 수 없다.
To regain that passion for the life you want, / you must ③ recover control of your choices.
당신이 원하는 삶에 대한 열정을 되찾기 위해서는 / 당신은 당신의 선택에 대한 통제력을 회복해야 한다.
No one but yourself / can choose how you live.
당신 자신을 제외한 그 누구도 / 당신이 어떻게 살지를 선택할 수 없다.
But, how?
하지만 어떻게 해야 할까?
The first step to getting rid of expectations / is to treat yourself ④ kindly.
기대감을 버리는 첫 단계는 / 자신을 친절하게 대하는 것이다.
You can't truly love other people / if you don't love yourself first.
당신은 다른 사람을 진정으로 사랑할 수 없다. / 당신이 자신을 먼저 사랑하지 않으면
When we accept who we are, / there's no room for other's ⑤ expectations.
우리가 우리 있는 그대로를 받아들일 때, / 타인의 기대를 위한 여지는 남지 않는다.

당신은 가끔 삶을 사랑하지 않는다고 느끼는가? 마치 마음 깊은 곳에서 뭔가가 빠진 것처럼? 왜냐하면 우리가 타인의 삶을 살고 있기 때문이다. 우리는 타인이 우리의 선택에 ① 영향을 주도록 허용한다. 우리는 그들의 기대감을 만족시키기 위해 노력하고 있다. 사회적 압력은 (우리를) 현혹시켜서, 우리 모두는 그것을 눈치채지도 못한 채 영향을 받는다. 우리의 삶에 대한 소유권을 잃어가고 있다는 것을 깨닫기도 전에, 우리는 결국 다른 사람들이 어떻게 좋아 사는지를 ② 무시하게(→ 부러워하게) 된다. 그러면, 우리는 더 푸른 잔디(타인의 삶이 더 좋아 보이는 것)만 볼 수 있게 되어, 우리의 삶은 (만족할 만큼) 충분히 좋아질 수 없다. 당신이 원하는 삶에 대한 열정을 되찾기 위해서는 당신의 선택에 대한 통제력을 ③ 회복해야 한다. 당신 자신을 제외한 그 누구도 당신이 어떻게 살지를 선택할 수 없다. 하지만 어떻게 해야 할까? 기대감을 버리는 첫 단계는 자기 자신에게 ④ 친절하게 대하는 것이다. 자신을 먼저 사랑하지 않으면 다른 사람을 진정으로 사랑할 수 없다. 우리가 우리 있는 그대로를 받아들일 때, 타인의 ⑤ 기대를 위한 여지는 남지 않는다.

Why? 왜 정답일까?
타인의 기대를 만족시키는 삶을 살아갈 때에는 삶을 사랑할 수 없기에 자신을 친절하게 대하며 삶에 대한 주도권을 회복해 나가야 한다는 내용의 글이다. 흐름상 ② 앞뒤가 타인의 삶을 살다 보면 자신의 삶에 대한 통제력을 잃었음을 알기도 전에 이미 타인의 삶을 더 좋게 보고 '부러워하게' 된다는 문맥이므로, ignoring을 envying으로 고쳐야 한다. 따라서 문맥상 낱말의 쓰임이 적절하지 않은 것은 ②이다.

● missing ⓐ 빠진, 실종된
● meet the expectation 기대를 충족하다
● impact ⓥ 영향을 미치다
● recover ⓥ 회복하다
● influence ⓥ 영향을 미치다 ⓝ 영향
● deceiving ⓐ 현혹시키는, 속이는
● ownership ⓝ 소유권
● get rid of ~을 없애다

구문 풀이
9행 No one but yourself can choose {how you live}. [ ] : 간접의문문(어떻게 ~할지)
~을 제외하고(= except)

★★★ 등급을 가르는 문제!
31 혁신 지속에 도움이 되는 가상 환경의 특징 | 정답률 49% | 정답 ①
다음 빈칸에 들어갈 말로 가장 적절한 것을 고르시오.
✔ restrictions - 제한점
② responsibilities – 책임감
③ memories - 기억
④ coincidences - 우연의 일치
⑤ traditions - 전통

One of the big questions faced this past year / was how to keep innovation rolling / when people were working entirely virtually.
작년에 직면한 가장 큰 질문 중 하나는 / 어떻게 혁신을 지속할 것인가 하는 것이었다. / 사람들이 완전히 가상 공간에서 작업할 때
But experts say / that digital work didn't have a negative effect / on innovation and creativity.
그러나 전문가들은 말한다. / 디지털 작업이 부정적인 영향을 미치지 않았다고 / 혁신과 창의성에
Working within limits / pushes us to solve problems.
한계 내에서 일하는 것 / 우리에게 문제를 해결하도록 독려한다.
Overall, / virtual meeting platforms put more constraints / on communication and collaboration / than face-to-face settings.
전반적으로, / 가상 미팅 플랫폼은 더 많은 제약들을 가한다. / 의사소통과 협업에 / 대면 설정보다
For instance, / with the press of a button, / virtual meeting hosts can control the size of breakout groups / and enforce time constraints; / only one person can speak at a time; / nonverbal signals, / particularly those below the shoulders, / are diminished; / "seating arrangements" are assigned by the platform, / not by individuals; / and visual access to others may be limited / by the size of each participant's screen.
예를 들어, / 버튼을 누르면, / 가상 회의 진행자는 소모임 그룹의 크기를 제어하고 / 시간 제한을 시행할 수 있다. / 한 번에 한 사람만이 말할 수 있다. / 비언어적 신호, / 특히 어깨 아래의 신호는 / 줄어든다. / '좌석 배치'는 플랫폼에 의해 할당된다. / 개인이 아닌 / 그리고 다른 사람에 대한 시각적 접근은 제한될 수 있다. / 각 참가자의 화면 크기에 따라
Such restrictions are likely to stretch participants / beyond their usual ways of thinking, / boosting creativity.
이러한 제한점은 참가자들을 확장시킬 가능성이 높다. / 일반적 사고방식 너머까지 / 그리고 창의력을 증진시킬

작년에 직면한 가장 큰 질문 중 하나는 사람들이 완전히 가상 공간에서 작업할 때 어떻게 혁신을 지속할 것인가 하는 것이었다. 그러나 전문가들은 디지털 작업이 혁신과 창의성에 부정적인 영향을 미치지 않았다고 말한다. 한계 내에서 일하는 것은 우리에게 문제를 해결하도록 독려한다. 전반적으로, 가상 미팅 플랫폼은 대면 환경보다 의사소통과 협업에 더 많은 제약들을 가한다. 예를 들어, 버튼을 누르면, 가상 회의 진행자는 소모임 그룹의 크기를 제어하고 시간 제한을 시행할 수 있다. 한 번에 한 사람만이 말할 수 있다. 비언어적 신호, 특히 어깨 아래의 신호는 줄어든다. '좌석 배치'는 개인이 아닌 플랫폼에 의해 할당된다. 그리고 다른 사람에 대한 시각적 접근은 각 참가자의 화면 크기에 따라 제한될 수 있다. 이러한 제한점은 참가자들을 일반적인 사고방식 너머까지 확장시켜 창의력을 증진시킬 가능성이 높다.

Why? 왜 정답일까?
'Working within limits pushes us to solve problems.'에서 한계 내에서 작업하는 것이 문제 해결을 독려한다고 언급하는 것으로 보아, 빈칸에 들어갈 말로 가장 적절한 것은 ① '제한점'이다.

● virtually ⓐⓓ (컴퓨터를 이용해) 가상으로
● have a negative effect on ~에 부정적 영향을 미치다
● constraint ⓝ 제한, 한계
● enforce ⓥ 시행하다
● seating arrangement 좌석 배치
● stretch ⓥ 늘이다, 확장하다
● breakout group (전체에서 나누어진) 소집단
● diminish ⓥ 줄이다
● assign ⓥ 배정하다, 할당하다
● coincidence ⓝ 우연의 일치, 동시 발생

구문 풀이
1행 One of the big questions faced this past year was {how to keep innovation
주어(one of the + 복수명사) 과거분사 동사(단수)
rolling when people were working entirely virtually}.
[ ] : 주격 보어(how+to부정사 : ~하는 방법)

★★ 문제 해결 꿀~팁 ★★
▶ 많이 틀린 이유는?
Working within limits가 핵심 표현으로, 제약이나 제한이 혁신과 업무 수행에 도움이 된다는 것이 이 글의 주제이다. 최다 오답인 ②의 responsibilities는 '책임, (맡은) 책무'라는 뜻이므로 글 내용과 관련이 없다.
▶ 문제 해결 방법은?
핵심어인 limits, constraints와 동의어를 찾으면 된다. 빈칸 앞에 not 등 부정어도 없어, 복잡하게 사고할 필요가 없는 비교적 단순한 빈칸 문제이다.

★★★ 등급을 가르는 문제!
32 전통적 수요 법칙의 예외인 기펜재 | 정답률 56% | 정답 ②
다음 빈칸에 들어갈 말로 가장 적절한 것을 고르시오. [3점]
① order more meat - 더 많은 고기를 주문한다
✔ consume more rice - 더 많은 쌀을 소비한다
③ try to get new jobs - 새로운 일자리를 구하려 한다
④ increase their savings - 저축액을 늘린다
⑤ start to invest overseas - 해외에 투자하기 시작한다

The law of demand is / that the demand for goods and services increases / as prices fall, / and the demand falls / as prices increase.
수요의 법칙은 ~이다. / 상품과 서비스에 대한 수요가 증가하고, / 가격이 하락할수록 / 수요가 감소하는 것 / 가격이 상승할수록
Giffen goods are special types of products / for which the traditional law of demand does not apply.
기펜재는 특별한 유형의 상품이다. / 전통적인 수요 법칙이 적용되지 않는
Instead of switching to cheaper replacements, / consumers demand more of giffen goods / when the price increases / and less of them when the price decreases.
저렴한 대체품으로 바꾸는 대신 / 소비자들은 기펜재를 더 많이 필요로 한다. / 가격이 상승할 때 / 그리고 가격이 하락할 때 덜
Taking an example, / rice in China is a giffen good / because people tend to purchase less of it / when the price falls.
예를 들어, / 중국의 쌀은 기펜재이다. / 사람들이 그것을 덜 구매하는 경향이 있기 때문에 / 가격이 하락할 때
The reason for this is, / when the price of rice falls, / people have more money / to spend on other types of products / such as meat and dairy / and, therefore, change their spending pattern.
그 이유는 ~이다. / 쌀값이 하락하면, / 사람들이 돈이 많아지고, / 다른 종류의 상품에 쓸 / 고기나 유제품 같은 / 그 결과 소비 패턴을 바꾸기 때문에
On the other hand, / as rice prices increase, / people consume more rice.
반면에, / 쌀값이 상승하면, / 사람들은 더 많은 쌀을 소비한다.

수요의 법칙은 가격이 하락할수록 상품과 서비스에 대한 수요가 증가하고, 가격이 상승할수록 수요가 감소하는 것이다. 기펜재는 전통적인 수요 법칙이 적용되지 않는 특별한 유형의 상품이다. 저렴한 대체품으로 바꾸는 대신 소비자들은 가격이 상승할 때 기펜재를 더 많이, 가격이 하락할 때 덜 필요로 한다. 예를 들어, 중국의 쌀은 가격이 하락할 때 사람들이 덜 구매하는 경향이 있기 때문에 기펜재이다. 그 이유는, 쌀값이 하락하면, 사람들이 고기나 유제품 같은 다른 종류의 상품에 쓸 돈이 많아지고, 그 결과 소비 패턴을 바꾸기 때문이다. 반면에, 쌀값이 상승하면, 사람들은 더 많은 쌀을 소비한다.

Why? 왜 정답일까?
전통적인 수요 법칙에 따르면 가격과 수요는 반비례하지만, 이 법칙의 예외에 있는 기펜재는 가격과 상승 및 하락 흐름을 같이한다(Instead of switching to cheaper replacements, consumers demand more of giffen goods when the price increases and less of them when the price decreases.)는 내용의 글이다. 중반부 이후로 중국의 쌀이 기펜재의 예시로 언급되므로, 쌀 가격이 오를 때 오히려 사람들은 '쌀을 더 산다'는 내용이 결론이어야 한다. 따라서 빈칸에 들어갈 말로 가장 적절한 것은 ② '더 많은 쌀을 소비한다'이다.

● demand ⓝ 수요 ⓥ 필요로 하다, 요구하다
● switch to ~로 바꾸다
● dairy ⓝ 유제품
● apply for ~에 적용되다
● replacement ⓝ 대체(품)
● overseas ⓐⓓ 해외에

구문 풀이
3행 *Giffen goods* are special types of products [for which the traditional law
선행사 「전치사+관계대명사」
of demand does not apply].

★★ 문제 해결 꿀~팁 ★★
▶ 많이 틀린 이유는?
기펜재의 개념을 잘 이해하고 사례에 적용해야 하는 빈칸 문제이다. 최다 오답 ④는 '저축액을 늘린다'는 의미인데, 글에서 기펜재와 저축액을 연결짓는 내용은 언급되지 않았다.

▶ 문제 해결 방법은?
글에 따르면 기펜재는 일반적 재화와 달리 가격이 오를 때 수요도 오르고, 가격이 떨어질 때 수요도 떨어지는 재화이다. 빈칸 문장에서는 '쌀 가격이 오르는' 상황을 상정하고 있으므로, '쌀에 대한 수요도 덩달아 오른다'는 결과를 예측할 수 있다.

★★★ 등급을 가르는 문제!

33 지적 능력 발달에 있어 천성보다 중요한 양육 정답률 44% | 정답 ③

다음 빈칸에 들어갈 말로 가장 적절한 것을 고르시오. [3점]

① by themselves for survival – 생존을 위해 스스로
② free from social interaction – 사회적 상호작용 없이
✓③ based on what is around you – 여러분 주변에 있는 것에 따라
④ depending on genetic superiority – 유전적 우월성에 따라
⑤ so as to keep ourselves entertained – 우리 자신을 계속 즐겁게 하기 위해

In a study at Princeton University in 1992, / research scientists looked at two different groups of mice.
1992년 프린스턴 대학의 연구에서, / 연구 과학자들은 두 개의 다른 쥐 집단을 관찰했다.
One group was made intellectually superior / by modifying the gene for the glutamate receptor.
한 집단은 지적으로 우월하게 만들어졌다. / 글루타민산염 수용체에 대한 유전자를 변형함으로써
Glutamate is a brain chemical / that is necessary in learning.
글루타민산염은 뇌 화학 물질이다. / 학습에 필수적인
The other group was genetically manipulated / to be intellectually inferior, / also done by modifying the gene for the glutamate receptor.
다른 집단도 유전적으로 조작되었다 / 지적으로 열등하도록 / 역시 글루타민산염 수용체에 대한 유전자를 변형함으로써 이루어진
The smart mice were then raised in standard cages, / while the inferior mice were raised in large cages / with toys and exercise wheels / and with lots of social interaction.
그 후 똑똑한 쥐들은 표준 우리에서 길러졌다. / 열등한 쥐들은 큰 우리에서 길러진 반면 / 장난감과 운동용 쳇바퀴가 있고 / 사회적 상호작용이 많은
At the end of the study, / although the intellectually inferior mice were genetically handicapped, / they were able to perform just as well / as their genetic superiors.
연구가 끝날 무렵, / 비록 지적 능력이 떨어지는 쥐들이 유전적으로 장애가 있었지만, / 그들은 딱 그만큼 잘 수행할 수 있었다. / 그들의 유전적인 우월군들만큼
This was a real triumph for nurture over nature.
이것은 천성에 대한 양육의 진정한 승리였다.
Genes are turned on or off / based on what is around you.
유전자는 작동하거나 멈춘다. / 여러분 주변에 있는 것에 따라

1992년 프린스턴 대학의 한 연구에서, 연구 과학자들은 두 개의 다른 쥐 집단을 관찰했다. 한 집단은 글루타민산염 수용체에 대한 유전자를 변형함으로써 지적으로 우월하게 만들어졌다. 글루타민산염은 학습에 필수적인 뇌 화학 물질이다. 다른 집단도 역시 글루타민산염 수용체에 대한 유전자를 변형함으로써, 지적으로 열등하도록 유전적으로 조작되었다. 그 후 똑똑한 쥐들은 표준 우리에서 길러진 반면 열등한 쥐들은 장난감과 운동용 쳇바퀴가 있고 사회적 상호작용이 많은 큰 우리에서 길러졌다. 연구가 끝날 무렵, 비록 지적 능력이 떨어지는 쥐들이 유전적으로 장애가 있었지만, 그들은 딱 유전적인 우월군들만큼 잘 수행할 수 있었다. 이것은 천성(선천적 성질)에 대한 양육(후천적 환경)의 진정한 승리였다. 유전자는 여러분 주변에 있는 것에 따라 작동하거나 멈춘다.

Why? 왜 정답일까?

빈칸이 있는 문장 바로 앞에서 양육, 즉 후천적 환경이 타고난 천성을 이겼다(a real triumph for nurture over nature)는 말로 연구 결과를 정리하고 있다. 따라서 빈칸에 들어갈 말로 가장 적절한 것은 '환경, 양육'과 같은 의미의 ③ '여러분 주변에 있는 것에 따라'이다.

● intellectually ⓐ 지적으로
● receptor ⓝ 수용체
● inferior ⓐ 열등한
● triumph ⓝ 승리
● free from ~ 없이, ~을 면하여
● modify ⓥ 수정하다, 바꾸다
● genetically ⓐ 유전적으로
● handicapped ⓐ 장애가 있는, 불리한 입장인
● nurture ⓝ 양육

구문 풀이

5행 The other group was genetically manipulated to be intellectually inferior,
선행사
(which was) also done by modifying the gene for the glutamate receptor.
생략(계속적 용법) 과거분사

★★ 문제 해결 꿀~팁 ★★

▶ 많이 틀린 이유는?
지적으로 우월하게(superior) 만들어진 쥐와 열등하게(inferior) 만들어진 쥐를 비교하는 실험 내용상 '유전적 우월함'을 언급하는 ④가 정답처럼 보인다. 하지만 실험의 결과를 보면, 결국 유전적으로 지능이 우월하게 만들어진 쥐와 열등하게 만들어진 쥐 사이에 차이가 없었다는 것이 핵심이다. 따라서 '유전적 우월함에 따라' 유전자가 작동하거나 작동하지 않을 수 있다는 의미를 완성하는 ④는 빈칸에 적절하지 않다.

▶ 문제 해결 방법은?
유전적으로 유도된 지능 차이보다도, 다른 어떤 요인이 쥐의 수행에 영향을 미칠 수 있었는지 살펴봐야 한다. 글 중반부를 보면, 열등한 쥐들이 자란 환경은 우월한 쥐들이 자란 환경에 비해 사회적 상호작용이 활발한 공간이었다고 한다. 나아가 빈칸 앞에는 이 실험 결과가 유전보다도 양육, 즉 후천적 환경(nurture)의 중요성을 말해준다고 한다. 따라서 빈칸에도 '환경'과 관련된 내용이 들어가야 한다.

★★★ 등급을 가르는 문제!

34 기후 변화에 대한 대처가 '현재' 이루어지지 않는 이유 정답률 45% | 정답 ②

다음 빈칸에 들어갈 말로 가장 적절한 것을 고르시오. [3점]

① it is not related to science – 그것이 과학과 관련이 없다
✓② it is far away in time and space – 그것이 시공간적으로 멀리 떨어져 있다

---

③ energy efficiency matters the most – 에너지 효율이 가장 중요하다
④ careful planning can fix the problem – 신중한 계획이 문제를 해결할 수 있다
⑤ it is too late to prevent it from happening – 그것이 일어나지 않도록 막기에는 너무 늦었다

Researchers are working on a project / that asks coastal towns / how they are preparing for rising sea levels.
연구원들은 프로젝트를 진행하고 있다. / 해안가 마을들에 묻는 / 해수면 상승에 어떻게 대비하고 있는지
Some towns have risk assessments; / some towns even have a plan.
어떤 마을들은 위험 평가를 하고 / 어떤 마을들은 심지어 계획을 가지고 있다.
But it's a rare town / that is actually carrying out a plan.
하지만 마을은 드물다. / 실제로 계획을 실행하고 있는
One reason we've failed to act on climate change / is the common belief / that it is far away in time and space.
우리가 기후 변화에 대처하는 데 실패한 한 가지 이유는 / 일반적인 믿음 때문이다. / 그것이 시공간적으로 멀리 떨어져 있다는
For decades, / climate change was a prediction about the future, / so scientists talked about it in the future tense.
수십 년 동안, / 기후 변화는 미래에 대한 예측이었기 때문에 / 과학자들은 미래 시제로 기후 변화에 대해 이야기했다.
This became a habit / — so that even today / many scientists still use the future tense, / even though we know / that a climate crisis is ongoing.
이것이 습관이 되어 / 그 결과 오늘날에도 / 많은 과학자들이 여전히 미래 시제를 사용하고 있다. / 우리가 알고 있음에도, / 기후 위기가 진행중이라는 것을
Scientists also often focus on regions / most affected by the crisis, / such as Bangladesh or the West Antarctic Ice Sheet, / which for most Americans are physically remote.
과학자들은 또한 지역에 초점을 맞추고 있으며, / 위기의 영향을 가장 많이 받는 / 방글라데시나 서남극 빙상처럼 / 그 지역은 대부분의 미국인들에게는 물리적으로 멀리 떨어져 있다.

연구원들은 해안가 마을들이 해수면 상승에 어떻게 대비하고 있는지 묻는 프로젝트를 진행하고 있다. 어떤 마을들은 위험 평가를 하고 어떤 마을들은 심지어 계획을 가지고 있다. 하지만 실제로 계획을 실행하고 있는 마을은 드물다. 우리가 기후 변화에 대처하는 데 실패한 한 가지 이유는 그것이 시공간적으로 멀리 떨어져 있다는 일반적인 믿음 때문이다. 수십 년 동안, 기후 변화는 미래에 대한 예측이었기 때문에 과학자들은 미래 시제로 기후 변화에 대해 이야기했다. 이것이 습관이 되어, 비록 우리가 기후 위기가 진행중이라는 것을 알고 있음에도, 많은 과학자들이 오늘날에도 여전히 미래 시제를 사용하고 있다. 과학자들은 또한 방글라데시나 서남극 빙상처럼 위기의 영향을 가장 많이 받는 지역에 초점을 맞추고 있으며, 그 지역은 대부분의 미국인들에게는 물리적으로 멀리 떨어져 있다.

Why? 왜 정답일까?

빈칸 뒤에 따르면, 기후 변화는 현재가 아닌 미래의 사건으로 여겨져 늘 미래 시제로 묘사되며(use the future tense), 기후 위기에 취약한 지역 또한 과학자들에게는 물리적으로 멀리 떨어진(physically remote) 곳이다. 다시 말해 기후 변화와 그로 인한 여파는 늘 '지금 여기와는 동떨어진' 사건으로 취급되고 있다는 것이 글의 핵심 내용이므로, 빈칸에 들어갈 말로 가장 적절한 것은 ② '그것이 시공간적으로 멀리 떨어져 있다'이다.

● sea level 해수면
● prediction ⓝ 예측
● crisis ⓝ 위기
● Antarctic ⓐ 남극의
● remote ⓐ 멀리 떨어진
● assessment ⓝ 평가
● tense ⓝ (문법) 시제
● ongoing ⓐ 진행 중인
● physically ⓐⓓ 물리적으로, 신체적으로

구문 풀이

4행 One reason [we've failed to act on climate change] is the common belief
주어 [ ]: 관계부사절 동사(단수) 주격 보어
{that it is far away in time and space}. [ ]: 동격절(=the common belief)

★★ 문제 해결 꿀~팁 ★★

▶ 많이 틀린 이유는?
⑤는 일반적으로 많이 언급되는 내용이지만 글에서 보면 기후 변화를 막기에 '시간적으로 너무 늦었다'는 내용은 글에 다뤄지지 않았다.

▶ 문제 해결 방법은?
빈칸이 글 중간에 있으면 주로 뒤에 답에 대한 힌트가 있다. 여기서도 빈칸 뒤를 보면, 과학자들은 기후 변화에 관해 아직도 미래 시제로 말하며, 지리적으로도 멀리 떨어진 곳을 연구하는 데 집중한다는 점을 지적하고 있다. 이는 기후 변화를 '시간·공간적으로 동떨어진' 일로 여기는 경향을 비판하는 것이다.

35 패션의 의미 정답률 66% | 정답 ④

다음 글에서 전체 흐름과 관계 없는 문장은?

According to Marguerite La Caze, / fashion contributes to our lives / and provides a medium for us / to develop and exhibit important social virtues.
Marguerite La Caze에 따르면, / 패션은 우리의 삶에 기여하고 / 우리에게 수단을 제공한다. / 중요한 사회적 가치를 개발하고 나타내는
① Fashion may be beautiful, innovative, and useful; / we can display creativity and good taste in our fashion choices.
패션은 아름다울 수 있고, 혁신적일 수 있으며, 유용할 수 있다. / 우리는 패션을 선택하는 데 있어서 창의성과 좋은 취향을 드러낼 수 있다.
② And in dressing with taste and care, / we represent / both self-respect and a concern for the pleasure of others.
그리고 취향과 관심에 따라 옷을 입을 때, / 우리는 보여준다. / 자아존중과 타인의 즐거움에 대한 관심 모두를
③ There is no doubt / that fashion can be a source of interest and pleasure / which links us to each other.
의심의 여지가 없다. / 패션은 흥미와 즐거움의 원천이 될 수 있다는 것은 / 우리와 타인을 연결해 주는
✓④ Although the fashion industry / developed first in Europe and America, / today it is an international and highly globalized industry.
비록 패션 산업은 / 유럽과 미국에서 처음 발달했지만, / 오늘날에는 국제적이고 매우 세계화된 산업이 되었다.
⑤ That is, / fashion provides a sociable aspect / along with opportunities to imagine oneself differently / — to try on different identities.
다시 말해, / 패션은 친교적인 측면을 제공한다. / 자신을 다르게 상상하는 기회와 더불어 / 즉, 다른 정체성을 시도하는

Marguerite La Caze에 따르면, 패션은 우리의 삶에 기여하고, 우리가 중요한 사회적 가치를 개발하고 나타낼 수단을 제공한다. ① 패션은 어쩌면 아름다울 수 있고, 혁신적일 수 있으며, 유용할 수 있다. 우리는 패션을 선택하는 데 있어서 창의성과 좋은 취향을 드러낼 수 있다. ② 그리고 취향과 관심에 따라 옷을 입을 때, 우리는 자아존중과 타인의 즐거움에 대한 관심 모두를 보여준다. ③ 의심의 여지없이, 패션은 우리를 서로 연결해 주는 흥미와 즐거움의 원천이 될 수 있다. ④ 패션 산업은 유럽과 미국에서 처음 발달했지만, 오늘날에는 국제적이고 매우 세계화된 산업이 되었다. ⑤ 다시 말해, 패션은 자신을 다르게 상상하는, 즉 다른 정체성을 시도하는 기회와 더불어 친교적인 측면을 제공한다.

Why? 왜 정답일까?

패션이 삶에서 갖는 의미를 설명한 글로, 개인의 삶과 타인과의 상호작용에서 어떤 의미를 갖는지가 주로 언급된다. 하지만 ④는 패션 사업의 발달에 관해 언급하며 글의 흐름에서 벗어나므로, 전체 흐름과 관계 없는 문장은 ④이다.

- **contribute to** ~에 기여하다, ~의 원인이 되다
- **medium** ⓝ 수단, 매체
- **exhibit** ⓥ 보여주다, 드러내다
- **taste** ⓝ 취향
- **represent** ⓥ 나타내다, 표현하다
- **concern** ⓝ 관심, 우려
- **link A to B** A와 B를 연결하다
- **highly** ⓐⓓ 매우
- **sociable** ⓐ 사교적인, 사람들과 어울리기 좋아하는
- **along with** ~와 더불어

구문 풀이

6행 There is no doubt {that fashion can be a source of interest and pleasure [which links us to each other]}.
부정 주어 { }: doubt의 동격절 / 선행사 / 주격 관·대

---

36 선생님에게 그림으로 감사를 표현한 Douglas   정답률 79% | 정답 ③

주어진 글 다음에 이어질 글의 순서로 가장 적절한 것을 고르시오.
① (A) – (C) – (B)
② (B) – (A) – (C)
✔ (B) – (C) – (A)
④ (C) – (A) – (B)
⑤ (C) – (B) – (A)

Mrs. Klein told her first graders / to draw a picture of something to be thankful for.
Klein 선생님은 1학년 학생들에게 말했다. / 감사히 여기는 것을 그려보라고

She thought / that most of the class would draw turkeys or Thanksgiving tables.
그녀는 생각했다. / 반 아이들 대부분이 칠면조나 추수감사절 식탁을 그릴 것으로

But Douglas drew something different.
하지만 Douglas는 색다른 것을 그렸다.

(B) Douglas was a boy / who usually spent time alone and stayed around her / while his classmates went outside together during break time.
Douglas는 소년이었다. / 보통 혼자 시간을 보내고 그녀 주변에 머무르는 / 그의 반 친구들이 쉬는 시간에 함께 밖으로 나가 있는 동안

What the boy drew was a hand.
그 소년이 그린 것은 손이었다.

But whose hand?
그런데 누구의 손일까?

His image immediately attracted the other students' interest.
그의 그림은 즉시 다른 학생들의 관심을 끌었다.

(C) So, / everyone rushed to talk / about whose hand it was.
그래서, / 모두가 앞다투어 말하려 했다. / 그것이 누구의 손인지에 관해

"It must be the hand of God / that brings us food," / said one student.
"그것은 신의 손이 틀림없어. / 우리에게 음식을 가져다주는" / 한 학생이 말했다.

"A farmer's," / said a second student, / "because they raise the turkeys."
"농부의 손이야," / 두 번째 학생이 말했다. / "왜냐하면 그들은 칠면조를 기르거든."이라고

"It looks more like a police officer's," / added another, / "they protect us."
"경찰관의 손과 더 비슷해 보여," / 또 다른 학생이 덧붙였다. / "그들은 우리를 보호해 줘."라고

(A) The class was so responsive / that Mrs. Klein had almost forgotten about Douglas.
반 아이들이 몹시 호응해서 / Klein 선생님은 Douglas에 대해 하마터면 잊어버릴 뻔했다.

After she had the others at work on another project, / she asked Douglas whose hand it was.
그녀가 나머지 아이들에게 다른 과제를 하도록 지도한 후, / 그녀는 Douglas에게 그 손이 누구 손인지 물었다.

He answered softly, / "It's yours. Thank you, Mrs. Klein."
그는 조용히 대답했다. / "선생님 손이에요. 고마워요, Klein 선생님."이라고

Klein 선생님은 1학년 학생들에게 감사히 여기는 것을 그려보라고 말했다. 그녀는 반 아이들 대부분이 칠면조나 추수감사절 식탁을 그릴 것으로 생각했다. 하지만 Douglas는 색다른 것을 그렸다.

(B) Douglas는 그의 반 친구들이 쉬는 시간에 함께 밖으로 나가 있는 동안, 보통 혼자 시간을 보내고 그녀 주변에 머무르는 소년이었다. 그 소년이 그린 것은 손이었다. 그런데 누구의 손일까? 그의 그림은 즉시 다른 학생들의 관심을 끌었다.

(C) 그래서, 모두들 그것이 누구의 손인지에 관해 앞다투어 말하려 했다. "그것은 우리에게 음식을 가져다주는 신의 손이 틀림없어."라고 한 학생이 말했다. "농부의 손이야, 왜냐하면 그들은 칠면조를 기르거든."이라고 두 번째 학생이 말했다. "경찰관의 손과 더 비슷해 보여, 그들은 우리를 보호해 줘."라고 또 다른 학생이 덧붙였다.

(A) 반 아이들의 호응에 Klein 선생님은 Douglas에 대해 하마터면 잊어버릴 뻔했다. 그녀는 나머지 아이들에게 다른 과제를 하도록 지도한 후, Douglas에게 그 손이 누구 손인지 물었다. "선생님 손이에요. 고마워요, Klein 선생님."이라고 그는 조용히 대답했다.

Why? 왜 정답일까?

고마운 것을 그려보는 시간에 Douglas가 무언가 색다른 것을 그렸다는 내용의 주어진 글 뒤에는, Douglas가 그린 것이 손이었다는 내용의 (B), 아이들이 누구의 손인지 맞춰보려 했다는 내용의 (C), 나중에 Douglas가 그것이 선생님의 손을 말했다는 내용의 (A)가 차례로 이어져야 자연스럽다. 따라서 글의 순서로 가장 적절한 것은 ③ '(B) – (C) – (A)'이다.

- **turkey** ⓝ 칠면조
- **responsive** ⓐ 즉각 반응하는, 관심을 보이는
- **immediately** ⓐⓓ 즉시
- **attract one's interest** ~의 관심을 끌다
- **raise** ⓥ 기르다, 키우다

구문 풀이

1행 Mrs. Klein told her first graders to draw a picture of something to be thankful for.
동사 / 목적어 / 목적격 보어 / 대명사(-thing) / 형용사적 용법

---

37 흡혈귀가 존재했을 수 없는 이유   정답률 62% | 정답 ⑤

주어진 글 다음에 이어질 글의 순서로 가장 적절한 것을 고르시오. [3점]
① (A) – (C) – (B)
② (B) – (A) – (C)
③ (B) – (C) – (A)
④ (C) – (A) – (B)
✔ (C) – (B) – (A)

According to legend, / once a vampire bites a person, / that person turns into a vampire / who seeks the blood of others.
전설에 따르면, / 흡혈귀가 사람을 물면 / 그 사람은 흡혈귀로 변한다. / 다른 사람의 피를 갈구하는

A researcher came up with some simple math, / which proves that these highly popular creatures can't exist.
한 연구자는 간단한 계산법을 생각해냈다. / 이 잘 알려진 존재가 실존할 수 없다는 것을 증명하는

(C) University of Central Florida physics professor / Costas Efthimiou's work breaks down the myth.
University of Central Florida의 물리학과 교수인 / Costas Efthimiou의 연구가 그 미신을 무너뜨렸다.

Suppose / that on January 1st, 1600, / the human population was just over five hundred million.
가정해 보자. / 1600년 1월 1일에 / 인구가 5억 명이 넘는다고

(B) If the first vampire came into existence / that day and bit one person a month, / there would have been two vampires by February 1st, 1600.
그날 최초의 흡혈귀가 생겨나서 / 한 달에 한 명을 물었다면, / 1600년 2월 1일까지 흡혈귀가 둘 있었을 것이다.

A month later there would have been four, / the next month eight, / then sixteen, / and so on.
한 달 뒤면 넷이 되었을 것이고 / 그다음 달은 여덟, / 그리고 열여섯 / 등등이 되었을 것이다.

(A) In just two-and-a-half years, / the original human population / would all have become vampires / with no humans left.
불과 2년 반 만에, / 원래의 인류는 / 모두 흡혈귀가 되었을 것이다. / 인간이 하나도 남지 않은 채로

But look around you.
하지만 주위를 둘러보라.

Have vampires taken over the world?
흡혈귀가 세상을 정복하였는가?

No, because there's no such thing.
아니다. 왜냐하면 흡혈귀는 존재하지 않으니까.

전설에 따르면, 흡혈귀가 사람을 물면 그 사람은 다른 사람의 피를 갈구하는 흡혈귀로 변한다. 한 연구자는 이 대단히 잘 알려진 존재가 실존할 수 없다는 것을 증명하는 간단한 계산법을 생각해냈다.

(C) University of Central Florida의 물리학과 교수 Costas Efthimiou의 연구가 그 미신을 무너뜨렸다. 1600년 1월 1일에 인구가 막 5억 명을 넘겼다고 가정해 보자.

(B) 그날 최초의 흡혈귀가 생겨나서 한 달에 한 명을 물었다면, 1600년 2월 1일까지 흡혈귀가 둘 있었을 것이다. 한 달 뒤면 넷, 그다음 달은 여덟, 그리고 열여섯 등등으로 계속 늘어났을 것이다.

(A) 불과 2년 반 만에, 원래의 인류는 모두 흡혈귀가 되어 더 이상 남아 있지 않았을 것이다. 하지만 주위를 둘러보라. 흡혈귀가 세상을 정복하였는가? 아니다. 왜냐하면 흡혈귀는 존재하지 않으니까.

Why? 왜 정답일까?

흡혈귀가 존재했음을 부정하는 계산식을 생각해낸 사람이 있다는 내용의 주어진 글 뒤에는, 먼저 1600년 1월 1일에 인구가 5억 명 넘었다고 가정해 보자며 계산식에 관해 설명하기 시작하는 (C)가 연결된다. 이어서 (B)는 (C)에서 언급한 날짜를 that day로 가리키며, 흡혈귀가 달마다 두 배씩 늘어가는 상황을 가정해 보자고 설명한다. 마지막으로 (A)는 (C) – (B)의 상황이 성립한다면 5억 명의 사람들이 불과 2년 반 만에 모두 흡혈귀로 변했을 것인데, 인류는 현재까지 지속되고 있으므로 흡혈귀가 존재했을 수 없다는 결론을 제시하고 있다. 따라서 글의 순서로 가장 적절한 것은 ⑤ '(C) – (B) – (A)'이다.

- **legend** ⓝ 전설
- **take over** ~을 지배하다, 장악하다
- **come into existence** 생기다, 나타나다
- **break down** 무너뜨리다
- **myth** ⓝ 미신, (잘못된) 통념

구문 풀이

5행 In just two-and-a-half years, the original human population would all have become vampires with no humans left.
「would have+과거분사」: ~했을 것이다(가정법 과거완료 주절) / 「with+명사+과거분사」: ~이 …된 채로

---

38 마찰력의 특징   정답률 73% | 정답 ④

글의 흐름으로 보아, 주어진 문장이 들어가기에 가장 적절한 곳을 고르시오.

Friction is a force / between two surfaces / that are sliding, or trying to slide, / across each other.
마찰력은 힘이다. / 두 표면 사이에 작용하는 / 미끄러지거나 미끄러지려고 하는 / 서로 엇갈리게

For example, / when you try to push a book along the floor, / friction makes this difficult.
예를 들어, / 당신이 바닥 위 책을 밀려고 할 때, / 마찰이 이를 어렵게 만든다.

Friction always works in the direction / opposite to the direction / in which the object is moving, or trying to move.
마찰은 항상 방향으로 작용한다. / 방향과 반대인 / 물체가 움직이거나 움직이려 하는

So, friction always slows a moving object down.
그래서 마찰은 항상 움직이는 물체를 느리게 만든다.

① The amount of friction depends on the surface materials.
마찰의 양은 표면 물질에 따라 달라진다.

② The rougher the surface is, / the more friction is produced.
표면이 거칠수록 / 더 많은 마찰력이 발생한다.

③ Friction also produces heat.
마찰은 또한 열을 발생시킨다.

✔ For example, / if you rub your hands together quickly, / they will get warmer.
예를 들어, / 만약 당신이 손을 빠르게 비비면, / 손이 더 따뜻해질 것이다.

Friction can be a useful force / because it prevents our shoes slipping on the floor / when we walk / and stops car tires skidding on the road.
마찰력은 유용한 힘으로 작용할 수 있다. / 그것이 신발이 바닥에서 미끄러지는 것을 방지하고 / 우리가 걸을 때 / 자동차 타이어가 도로에서 미끄러지는 것을 막아주어

⑤ When you walk, / friction is caused / between the tread on your shoes and the ground, / acting to grip the ground and prevent sliding.
당신이 걸을 때, / 마찰은 발생하며, / 당신의 신발 접지면과 바닥 사이에 / 땅을 붙잡아 미끄러지는 것을 방지하는 역할을 한다.

마찰력은 서로 엇갈리게 미끄러지거나 미끄러지려고 하는 두 표면 사이에 작용하는 힘이다. 예를 들어, 당신이 바닥 위 책을 밀려고 할 때, 마찰이 이를 어렵게 만든다. 마찰은 항상 물체가 움직이거나 움직이려고 하는 방향과 반대 방향으로 작용한다. 그래서 마찰은 항상 움직이는 물체를 느려지게 만든다. ① 마찰의 양은 표면 물질에 따라 달라진다. ② 표면이 거칠수록 더 많은 마찰력이 발생한다. ③ 마찰은 또한 열을 발생시킨다. ④ 예를 들어, 만약 당신이 손을 빠르게 비비면, 손이 더 따뜻해질 것이다. 마찰력은 우리가 걸을 때 신발이 바닥에서 미끄러지는 것을 방지하고 자동차 타이어가 도로에서 미끄러지는 것을 막아주므로 유용한 힘이 될 수 있다. ⑤ 걸을 때, 마찰은 당신의 신발 접지면과 바닥 사이에 발생하여 땅을 붙잡아 미끄러지는 것을 방지하는 역할을 한다.

Why? 왜 정답일까?
주어진 문장은 마찰과 열을 관련지어 설명하고 있으므로, 앞에 열에 관한 내용이 언급된 후 예시(For example)로 이어질 수 있다. 글에서 열에 관해 언급하는 문장은 ④ 앞의 문장이므로, 주어진 문장이 들어가기에 가장 적절한 곳은 ④이다.

- rub ⓥ 문지르다
- surface ⓝ 표면
- slow down ~을 느려지게 하다
- slip ⓥ (넘어지거나 넘어질 뻔하게) 미끄러지다
- friction ⓝ 마찰
- opposite ⓐ 반대의
- rough ⓐ 거친
- grip ⓥ 붙잡다

구문 풀이
9행 The rougher the surface is, the more friction is produced.
「the + 비교급 ~, the + 비교급 … : ~할수록 더 …하다」

★★★ 등급을 가르는 문제!
39 선천적 시각장애인의 세상 이해 정답률 46% | 정답 ⑤

글의 흐름으로 보아, 주어진 문장이 들어가기에 가장 적절한 곳을 고르시오.

Humans born without sight / are not able to collect visual experiences, / so they understand the world / entirely through their other senses.
선천적으로 시각장애가 있는 사람은 / 시각적 경험을 수집할 수 없어서, / 그들은 세상을 이해한다. / 전적으로 다른 감각을 통해

① As a result, / people with blindness at birth / develop an amazing ability / to understand the world / through the collection of experiences and memories / that come from these non-visual senses.
그 결과, / 선천적으로 시각장애가 있는 사람들은 / 놀라운 능력을 발달시킨다. / 세상을 이해하는 / 경험과 기억의 수집을 통해 / 이러한 비시각적 감각에서 오는

② The dreams of a person / who has been without sight since birth / can be just as vivid and imaginative / as those of someone with normal vision.
사람이 꾸는 꿈은 / 선천적으로 시각장애가 있는 / 생생하고 상상력이 풍부할 수 있다. / 정상 시력을 가진 사람의 꿈처럼

③ They are unique, however, / because their dreams are constructed / from the non-visual experiences and memories / they have collected.
그러나 그들은 특별하다. / 그들의 꿈은 구성되기 때문에 / 비시각적 경험과 기억으로부터 / 그들이 수집한

④ A person with normal vision / will dream about a familiar friend / using visual memories of shape, lighting, and colour.
정상적인 시력을 가진 사람은 / 친숙한 친구에 대해 꿈을 꿀 것이다. / 형태, 빛 그리고 색의 시각적 기억을 사용하여

✔ But, / a blind person will associate the same friend / with a unique combination of experiences / from their non-visual senses / that act to represent that friend.
하지만, / 시각장애인은 그 친구를 연상할 것이다. / 독특한 조합의 경험으로 / 비시각적 감각에서 나온 / 그 친구를 구현하는 데 작용하는

In other words, / people blind at birth / have similar overall dreaming experiences / even though they do not dream in pictures.
다시 말해, / 선천적 시각장애인들은 / 전반적으로 비슷한 꿈을 경험한다. / 그들이 시각적인 꿈을 꾸지는 않지만

선천적으로 시각장애가 있는 사람은 시각적 경험을 수집할 수 없어서, 전적으로 다른 감각을 통해 세상을 이해한다. ① 그 결과, 선천적으로 시각장애가 있는 사람들은 이러한 비시각적 감각에서 오는 경험과 기억의 수집을 통해 세상을 이해하는 놀라운 능력을 발달시킨다. ② 선천적으로 시각장애가 있는 사람이 꾸는 꿈은 정상 시력을 가진 사람의 꿈처럼 생생하고 상상력이 풍부할 수 있다. ③ 그러나 그들의 꿈은 그들이 수집한 비시각적 경험과 기억으로부터 구성되기 때문에 특별하다. ④ 정상적인 시력을 가진 사람들은 형태, 빛 그리고 색의 시각적 기억을 사용하여 친숙한 친구에 대해 꿈을 꿀 것이다. ⑤ 하지만, 시각장애인은 그 친구를 구현하는 데 작용하는 자신의 비시각적 감각에서 나온 독특한 조합의 경험으로 바로 그 친구를 연상할 것이다. 다시 말해, 선천적 시각장애인들은 시각적인 꿈을 꾸지는 않지만, 전반적으로 비슷한 꿈을 경험한다.

Why? 왜 정답일까?
선천적 시각장애인은 시각적 경험이 없지만 비시각적 경험과 기억을 통해 세상을 이해하는 특별한 방법을 구성해 나간다는 내용의 글로, ② 이후로 시각장애인이 꿈꾸는 방식을 예로 들고 있다. ⑤ 앞에서 비시각장애인은 시각적 경험을 이용해 친구에 관한 꿈을 꾼다고 언급하는데, 주어진 문장은 But으로 흐름을 뒤집으며 선천적 시각장애인은 비시각적 감각 경험을 토대로 친구를 연상한다고 설명한다. In other words로 시작하는 ⑤ 뒤의 문장은 주어진 문장의 의미를 풀어볼 때 시각장애인도 결국 꿈을 비슷하게 경험한다는 것을 알 수 있다고 결론 짓는다. 따라서 주어진 문장이 들어가기에 가장 적절한 곳은 ⑤이다.

- associate A with B A와 B를 연결 짓다, 연상하다
- combination ⓝ 조합
- vivid ⓐ 생생한
- sight ⓝ 시력
- imaginative ⓐ 상상력이 풍부한

구문 풀이
9행 The dreams of a person [who has been without sight since birth] can be
주어(복수)   주격 관·대(a person 수식)   전치사(~ 이후로)   동사
just as vivid and imaginative as those of someone with normal vision.
└→ 「as + 원급 + as : ~만큼 …한」   대명사(= the dreams)

★★ 문제 해결 꿀~팁 ★★
▶ 많이 틀린 이유는?
가장 헷갈리는 ③ 앞을 보면, 선천적 시각 장애인의 꿈도 비장애인의 꿈과 마찬가지로 생생하고 상상력이 풍부하다는 내용이다. 이어서 ③ 뒤에서는 however와 함께, '그런데' 이들의 꿈은 비시각적 경험과 기억에 바탕을 두기 때문에 '특별하다'는 내용을 추가하고 있다. 즉, ③ 앞뒤는 역접어 however를 기점으로 '우리와 다르지 않다 → 특별하다'로 자연스럽게 전환되는 흐름인 것이다.
▶ 문제 해결 방법은?
⑤ 앞에서 언급된 a familiar friend가 주어진 문장의 the same friend, that friend로 이어진다. 또한, In other words로 시작하는 ⑤ 뒤의 문장은 주어진 문장을 일반화한 내용이다.

40 권위가 있는 부모 밑에서 자란 자녀들의 학업 성취 정답률 65% | 정답 ③

다음 글의 내용을 한 문장으로 요약하고자 한다. 빈칸 (A), (B)에 들어갈 말로 가장 적절한 것은? [3점]

	(A)		(B)
①	likely 가능성이 크며	……	random 무작위적인
②	willing 자발적이며	……	minimal 최소한의
✔	willing 자발적이며	……	active 적극적인
④	hesitant 망설이며	……	unwanted 원치 않는
⑤	hesitant 망설이며	……	constant 지속적인

According to a study of Swedish adolescents, / an important factor of adolescents' academic success / is how they respond to challenges.
스웨덴 청소년들에 대한 연구에 따르면, / 청소년들의 학업 성공의 중요한 요인은 / 그들이 어려움에 반응하는 방식이다.

The study reports / that when facing difficulties, / adolescents exposed to an authoritative parenting style / are less likely to be passive, helpless, and afraid to fail.
이 연구는 보고하고 있다. / 어려움에 직면했을 때 / 권위가 있는 양육 방식에 노출된 청소년들은 / 덜 수동적이고, 덜 무기력하며, 실패를 덜 두려워한다고

Another study of nine high schools / in Wisconsin and northern California / indicates / that children of authoritative parents do well in school, / because these parents put a lot of effort / into getting involved in their children's school activities.
9개 고교에서 진행된 또 다른 연구는 / Wisconsin과 northern California의 / 밝히고 있다. / 권위가 있는 부모들의 아이들이 학습을 잘하는데, / 그 이유는 이러한 부모들이 많은 노력을 기울이기 때문이라고 / 아이들의 학교 활동에 관여하고자

That is / authoritative parents are significantly more likely / to help their children with homework, / to attend school programs, / to watch their children in sports, / and to help students select courses.
즉, / 권위가 있는 부모들은 ~할 가능성이 훨씬 더 크다. / 아이들의 숙제를 도와주고, / 학교 프로그램에 참여하며, / 스포츠에 참여하는 아이들을 지켜보고, / 아이들의 과목 선택을 도와줄

Moreover, / these parents are more aware / of what their children do and how they perform in school.
게다가, / 이러한 부모들은 더 잘 인지하고 있다. / 아이들이 학교에서 하고 있는 일과 수행하는 방식에 대해

Finally, / authoritative parents / praise academic excellence and the importance of working hard more / than other parents do.
마지막으로, / 권위가 있는 부모들은 / 학문적 탁월함과 근면함의 중요성을 더 많이 칭찬한다. / 다른 부모들에 비해

➡ The studies above show / that the children of authoritative parents / often succeed academically, / since they are more (A) willing to deal with their difficulties / and are affected by their parents' (B) active involvement.
위 연구는 보여준다. / 권위가 있는 부모의 아이들이 / 학업 성취가 좋다는 것을 / 그들이 어려움에 대처하는 데 더 자발적이며, / 그 부모들의 적극적인 관여에 영향을 받기 때문에

스웨덴 청소년들에 대한 연구에 따르면, 청소년들의 학업 성공의 중요한 요인은 그들이 어려움에 반응하는 방식이다. 이 연구는 어려움에 직면했을 때 권위가 있는 양육 방식에 노출된 청소년들은 덜 수동적이고, 덜 무기력하며, 실패를 덜 두려워한다고 보고하고 있다. Wisconsin과 northern California의 9개 고교에서 진행된 또 다른 연구는 권위가 있는 부모들의 아이들이 학습을 잘하는데, 그 이유는 이러한 부모들이 아이들의 학교 활동에 관여하고자 많은 노력을 기울이기 때문이라고 밝히고 있다. 즉, 권위가 있는 부모들은 아이들의 숙제를 도와주고, 학교 프로그램에 참여하며, 스포츠에 참여하는 아이들을 지켜보고, 아이들의 과목 선택을 도와줄 가능성이 훨씬 더 크다. 게다가, 이러한 부모들은 아이들이 학교에서 무엇을 하는지, 어떤 성과를 내는지 더 잘 인지하고 있다. 마지막으로, 권위가 있는 부모들은 다른 부모들에 비해 학문적 탁월함과 근면함의 중요성을 더 많이 칭찬한다.

➡ 위 연구는 권위가 있는 부모의 아이들이 어려움에 대처하는 데 더 (A) 자발적이며, 그 부모들의 (B) 적극적인 관여에 영향을 받기 때문에 학업 성취가 좋다는 것을 보여준다.

Why? 왜 정답일까?
두 번째 문장인 '~ when facing difficulties, adolescents exposed to an authoritative parenting style are less likely to be passive ~'에서 권위적인 양육 방식에 노출된 자녀는 어려움 앞에서 덜 수동적이라고 한다. 이어서 '~ children of authoritative parents do well in school, because these parents put a lot of effort into getting involved in their children's school activities.'에서 권위가 있는 부모는 자녀의 학습에 더 적극 관여하기 때문에, 이들 자녀의 학업 성취가 실제로 더 좋다는 연구 결과를 언급하고 있다. 따라서 요약문의 빈칸 (A), (B)에 들어갈 말로 가장 적절한 것은 ③ 'A) willing(자발적이며), (B) active(적극적인)'이다.

- adolescent ⓝ 청소년
- authoritative ⓐ 권위적인
- factor ⓝ 요인
- helpless ⓐ 무기력한

- put effort into ~에 노력을 쏟다
- significantly ad 상당히
- hesitant a 망설이는

3행 The study reports that when facing difficulties, adolescents exposed to
분사구문(~할 때) 주어 과거분사
an authoritative parenting style are less likely to be passive, helpless, and
동사구(~할 가능성이 적다) 주격 보어1 주격 보어2
afraid to fail.
주격 보어3

41-42 취침 시간과 심장 건강의 연관관계

『U.K. researchers say / a bedtime of between 10 p.m. and 11 p.m. is best.
영국 연구원들은 이야기한다. / 밤 10시와 밤 11시 사이의 취침 시간이 가장 좋다고

They say / people who go to sleep between these times / have a (a) lower risk of heart
disease.』 41번의 근거
그들은 이야기한다. / 이 시간대 사이에 잠드는 사람들이 / 더 낮은 심장 질환의 위험성을 가지고 있다고

Six years ago, / the researchers collected data / on the sleep patterns of 80,000 volunteers.
6년 전, / 그 연구원들은 데이터를 수집했다. / 8만 명의 자원자들의 수면 패턴에 관해

The volunteers had to wear a special watch for seven days / so the researchers could collect
data / on their sleeping and waking times.
그 자원자들은 7일간 특별한 시계를 착용해야 했고, / 그래서 연구원들은 데이터를 수집할 수 있었다. / 그들의 수면과 기상 시간에 대한

The scientists then monitored the health of the volunteers.
그러고 나서 연구원들은 그 자원자들의 건강을 관찰했다.

Around 3,000 volunteers later showed heart problems.
약 3천 명의 자원자들이 이후에 심장 문제를 보였다.

『They went to bed earlier or later / than the (b) ideal 10 p.m. to 11 p.m. timeframe.』
그들은 더 이르거나 더 늦게 잠자리에 들었다. / 밤 10시에서 밤 11시 사이라는 이상적인 시간대보다 42번의 근거

One of the authors of the study, Dr. David Plans, / commented on his research / and the
(c) effects of bedtimes on the health of our heart.
그 연구 저자 중 한 명인 Dr. David Plans는 / 자신의 연구에 대해 언급했다. / 그리고 취침 시간이 우리의 심장 건강에 끼치는 영향에 대해

He said / the study could not give a certain cause for their results, / but it suggests / that
early or late bedtimes may be more likely / to disrupt the body clock, / with (d) negative
consequences for cardiovascular health.
그는 이야기했다. / 그 연구가 결과에 특정한 원인을 시사하지는 못하지만, / 그것은 제시한다고 / 이르거나 늦은 취침 시간이 ~할 가능성이 더 높을 수 있다는 것을 / 체내 시계를 혼란케 할 / 심혈관 건강에 부정적인 결과와 함께

He said / that it was important for our body / to wake up to the morning light, / and that the
worst time to go to bed / was after midnight / because it may (e) reduce the likelihood of
seeing morning light / which resets the body clock.
그는 말했다. / 우리의 몸에 중요하고, / 아침 빛에 맞추어 일어나는 것이 / 잠자리에 드는 가장 나쁜 시간이 / 자정 이후인데, / 그것이 아침 빛을 볼 가능성을 낮출 수도 있기 때문이라고 / 우리의 체내 시계를 재설정하는

He added / that we risk cardiovascular disease / if our body clock is not reset properly.
그는 덧붙였다. / 우리가 심혈관 질환의 위험을 안게 된다고 / 만약 우리의 체내 시계가 적절하게 재설정되지 않으면

영국 연구원들은 밤 10시와 밤 11시 사이의 취침 시간이 가장 좋다고 이야기한다. 그들은 이 시간대 사이에 잠드는 사람들이 (a) 더 낮은 심장 질환의 위험성을 가지고 있다고 이야기한다. 6년 전, 그 연구원들은 8만 명의 자원자들의 수면 패턴에 대한 데이터를 수집할 수 있도록 7일간 특별한 시계를 착용해야 했다. 그러고 나서 연구원들은 그 자원자들의 건강을 관찰했다. 약 3천 명의 자원자들이 이후에 심장 문제를 보였다. 그들은 밤 10시에서 밤 11시 사이라는 (b) 이상적인 시간대보다 더 이르거나 더 늦게 잠자리에 들었다.

그 연구 저자 중 한 명인 Dr. David Plans는 자신의 연구와 취침 시간이 우리의 심장 건강에 끼치는 (c) 영향에 대해 언급했다. 그는 그 연구가 결과의 특정한 원인을 시사하지는 못하지만, 이르거나 늦은 취침 시간이 심혈관 건강에 (d) 긍정적인(→ 부정적인) 결과와 함께 체내 시계를 혼란케 할 가능성이 더 높을 수 있다는 것을 제시한다고 이야기했다. 그는 우리의 몸이 아침 빛에 맞추어 일어나는 것이 중요하고, 잠자리에 드는 가장 나쁜 시간이 자정 이후인데, 우리의 체내 시계를 재설정하는 아침 빛을 볼 가능성을 (e) 낮출 수도 있기 때문이라고 말했다. 그는 만약 우리의 체내 시계가 적절하게 재설정되지 않으면 우리가 심혈관 질환의 위험을 안게 된다고 덧붙였다.

- author n 저자
- consequence n 결과, 영향
- likelihood n 가능성, 공산
- sound a 좋은, 건전한
- body clock 생체 시계
- reduce v 낮추다, 줄이다
- properly ad 적절하게

15행 He said {that it was important for our body to wake up to the morning
가주어 의미상주어 진주어(주어1)
light,} and {that the worst time to go to bed was after midnight because it may
주어2 형용사적용법 동사2 접속새(이유)
reduce the likelihood of seeing morning light [which resets the body clock]}.
선행사 주격 관·대

---

41 제목 파악

정답률 67% | 정답 ①

윗글의 제목으로 가장 적절한 것은?

✓① The Best Bedtime for Your Heart – 당신의 심장을 위한 최적의 취침 시간
② Late Bedtimes Are a Matter of Age – 늦은 취침 시간은 나이 문제이다
③ For Sound Sleep: Turn Off the Light – 숙면을 위해: 불을 끄세요
④ Sleeping Patterns Reflect Personalities – 수면 패턴은 성격을 반영한다
⑤ Regular Exercise: A Miracle for Good Sleep – 규칙적인 운동: 숙면을 위한 기적

Why? 왜 정답일까?

취침 시간이 심혈관 건강에 미치는 영향에 관한 연구 내용을 들어 적절한 취침 시간의 중요성을 설명하는 글로, 첫 두 문장에 화제가 잘 제시된다(~ a bedtime of between 10 p.m. and 11 p.m. is

---

best. ~ people who go to sleep between these times have a lower risk of heart disease.)이다. 따라서 글의 제목으로 가장 적절한 것은 ① '당신의 심장을 위한 최적의 취침 시간'이다.

42 어휘 추론

정답률 68% | 정답 ④

밑줄 친 (a) ~ (e) 중에서 문맥상 낱말의 쓰임이 적절하지 않은 것은?

① (a)   ② (b)   ③ (c)   ✓④ (d)   ⑤ (e)

Why? 왜 정답일까?

연구 결과를 언급하는 첫 문단의 마지막 두 문장에 따르면, 이상적인 취침 시간보다 이르거나 늦게 잠드는 사람들은 이후 심장 문제가 생길 가능성이 높았다(Around 3,000 volunteers later showed heart problems. They went to bed earlier or later than the ideal 10 p.m. to 11 p.m. timeframe.)고 한다. 즉 이상적인 취침시간보다 빨리 자든 늦게 자든, 그로 인해 '부정적인' 영향을 입을 수 있다는 것이므로, (d)의 positive를 negative로 고쳐야 한다. 따라서 문맥상 낱말의 쓰임이 적절하지 않은 것은 ④ '(d)'이다.

43-45 한 소년의 도움으로 잃어버린 시계를 찾은 농부

(A)

Once, / a farmer lost his precious watch / while working in his barn.
어느 날, / 한 농부가 그의 귀중한 시계를 잃어버렸다. / 헛간에서 일하는 동안

It may have appeared to be an ordinary watch to others, / but 『it brought a lot of happy
childhood memories to him.』 45번 ①의 근거 일치
그것은 다른 이들에게는 평범한 시계로 보일 수도 있었지만 / 그것은 그에게 어린 시절의 많은 행복한 기억을 불러왔다.

It was one of the most important things to (a) him.
그것은 그에게 가장 중요한 것들 중 하나였다.

After searching for it for along time, / the old farmer became exhausted.
오랜 시간 동안 그것을 찾아본 뒤에 / 그 나이 든 농부는 지쳐버렸다.

(D)

However, / the tired farmer did not want to give up / on the search for his watch / and
asked a group of children playing outside to help him.
그러나, / 그 지친 농부는 포기하고 싶지 않았기에 / 자기 시계를 찾는 것을 / 밖에서 놀던 한 무리의 아이들에게 도와 달라고 요청했다.

(e) He promised an attractive reward / for the person who could find it.
그는 매력적인 보상을 약속했다. / 자기 시계를 찾는 사람에게

『After hearing about the reward, / the children hurried inside the barn / and went through
and round the entire pile of hay / looking for the watch.』 45번 ④의 근거 불일치
보상에 대해 듣고 난 뒤, / 그 아이들은 헛간 안으로 서둘러 들어갔고 / 전체 건초 더미 사이와 주변으로 걸어갔다. / 시계를 찾으러

『After a long time searching for it, / some of the children got tired and gave up.』
시계를 찾느라 오랜 시간을 보낸 후, / 아이들 중 일부는 지쳐서 포기했다. 45번 ⑤의 근거 일치

(B)

The number of children looking for the watch / slowly decreased / and only a few tired
children were left.
시계를 찾는 아이들의 숫자가 / 천천히 줄어들었고 / 지친 아이들 몇 명만이 남았다.

The farmer gave up all hope of finding it / and called off the search.
그 농부는 시계를 찾을 거라는 모든 희망을 포기하고 / 찾는 것을 멈추었다.

『Just when the farmer was closing the barn door, / a little boy came up to him / and asked
the farmer to give him another chance.』 45번 ②의 근거 일치
농부가 막 헛간 문을 닫고 있었을 때 / 한 어린 소년이 그에게 다가와서 / 자신에게 또 한 번의 기회를 달라고 요청했다.

The farmer did not want / to lose out on any chance of finding the watch / so let (b) him in
the barn.
농부는 원하지 않아서 / 시계를 찾을 어떤 가능성도 놓치는 것을 / 그를 헛간 안으로 들어오게 해주었다.

(C)

『After a little while / the boy came out with the farmer's watch in his hand.』 45번 ③의 근거 일치
잠시 후 / 그 소년이 한 손에 농부의 시계를 들고 나왔다.

(c) He was happily surprised / and asked how he had succeeded to find the watch / while
everyone else had failed.
그는 행복에 겨워 놀랐고 / 소년이 어떻게 시계를 찾는 데 성공했는지를 물었다. / 다른 모두가 실패했던 반면

He replied / "I just sat there and tried listening for the sound of the watch. / In silence, / it
was much easier / to hear it and follow the direction of the sound."
그는 답했다. / "저는 거기에 앉아서 시계의 소리를 들으려고 했어요. / 침묵 속에서, / 훨씬 쉬웠어요, / 그것을 듣고 소리의 방향을 따라가는 것이"

(d) He was delighted to get his watch back / and rewarded the little boy as promised.
그는 시계를 되찾아 기뻤고 / 그 어린 소년에게 약속했던 대로 보상해 주었다.

(A)

어느 날, 한 농부가 헛간에서 일하는 동안 그의 귀중한 시계를 잃어버렸다. 그것은 다른 이들에게는 평범한 시계로 보일 수도 있었지만 그것은 그에게 어린 시절의 많은 행복한 기억을 불러일으켰다. 그것은 (a) 그에게 가장 중요한 것들 중 하나였다. 오랜 시간 동안 그것을 찾아본 뒤에 그 나이 든 농부는 지쳐버렸다.

(D)

그러나, 그 지친 농부는 자기 시계를 찾는 것을 포기하고 싶지 않았기에 밖에서 놀던 한 무리의 아이들에게 도와 달라고 요청했다. (e) 그는 자기 시계를 찾는 사람에게 매력적인 보상을 약속했다. 보상에 대해 듣고 난 뒤, 그 아이들은 헛간 안으로 서둘러 들어갔고 시계를 찾으러 전체 건초 더미 사이와 주변을 다녔다. 시계를 찾느라 오랜 시간을 보낸 후, 아이들 중 일부는 지쳐서 포기했다.

(B)

시계를 찾는 아이들의 숫자가 천천히 줄어들었고 지친 아이들 몇 명만이 남았다. 그 농부는 시계를 찾을 거라는 모든 희망을 포기하고 찾는 것을 멈추었다. 농부가 막 헛간 문을 닫고 있었을 때 한 어린 소년이 그에게 다가와서 자신에게 또 한 번의 기회를 달라고 요청했다. 농부는 시계를 찾을 어떤 가능성도 놓치고 싶지 않아서 (b) 그를 헛간 안으로 들어오게 해주었다.

(C)

잠시 후 그 소년이 한 손에 농부의 시계를 들고 나왔다. (c) 그는 행복에 겨워 놀랐고 다른 모두가 실패했던 반면 소년이 어떻게 시계를 찾는 데 성공했는지를 물었다. 그는 "저는 거기에 앉아서 시계의 소리를 들으려고 했어요. 침묵 속에서, 그것을 듣고 소리의 방향을 따라가는

[문제편 p.078]

[06회] 2022학년도 6월 **081**

것이 훨씬 쉬웠어요."라고 답했다. (d) 그는 시계를 되찾아 기뻤고 그 어린 소년에게 약속했던 대로 보상해 주었다.

- precious ⓐ 소중한, 귀중한
- lose out on ~을 놓치다, ~에게 지다
- pile ⓝ 더미
- call off ~을 중단하다, 멈추다
- attractive ⓐ 매력적인
- hay ⓝ 건초

구문 풀이

[B] 1행 The number of children looking for the watch slowly decreased and
주어1(the number of+복수명사 : ~의 수)   현재분사   동사1

only a few tired children were left.
주어2   동사2

[C] 5행 In silence, it was much easier to hear it and follow the direction of the
가주어   비교급 강조(훨씬)   진주어
sound.

---

43 글의 순서 파악   정답률 77% | 정답 ④

주어진 글 (A)에 이어질 내용을 순서에 맞게 배열한 것으로 가장 적절한 것은?
① (B) - (D) - (C)
② (C) - (B) - (D)
③ (C) - (D) - (B)
✔ (D) - (B) - (C)
⑤ (D) - (C) - (B)

Why? 왜 정답일까?

아끼던 시계를 잃어버린 농부를 소개하는 (A) 뒤로, 농부가 아이들에게 시계 찾기를 맡겼다는 내용의 (D), 모두가 실패한 가운데 한 소년이 다시 자원했다는 내용의 (B), 소년이 시계를 찾아냈다는 내용의 (C)가 차례로 이어져야 자연스럽다. 따라서 글의 순서로 가장 적절한 것은 ④ '(D) - (B) - (C)'이다.

---

44 지칭 추론   정답률 73% | 정답 ②

밑줄 친 (a)~(e) 중에서 가리키는 대상이 나머지 넷과 다른 것은?
① (a)   ✔ (b)   ③ (c)   ④ (d)   ⑤ (e)

Why? 왜 정답일까?

(a), (c), (d), (e)는 the farmer, (b)는 a little boy이므로, (a)~(e) 중에서 가리키는 대상이 다른 하나는 ② '(b)'이다.

---

45 세부 내용 파악   정답률 76% | 정답 ④

윗글에 관한 내용으로 적절하지 않은 것은?
① 농부의 시계는 어린 시절의 행복한 기억을 불러일으켰다.
② 한 어린 소년이 농부에게 또 한 번의 기회를 달라고 요청했다.
③ 소년이 한 손에 농부의 시계를 들고 나왔다.
✔ 아이들은 시계를 찾기 위해 헛간을 뛰쳐나왔다.
⑤ 아이들 중 일부는 지쳐서 시계 찾기를 포기했다.

Why? 왜 정답일까?

(D) 'After hearing about the reward, the children hurried inside the barn ~'에서 아이들은 농부가 잃어버린 시계를 찾기 위해 헛간을 나온 것이 아니라 들어갔다고 하므로, 내용과 일치하지 않는 것은 ④ '아이들은 시계를 찾기 위해 헛간을 뛰쳐나왔다.'이다.

Why? 왜 오답일까?

① (A) '~ it brought a lot of happy childhood memories to him.'의 내용과 일치한다.
② (B) 'a little boy came up to him and asked the farmer to give him another chance.'의 내용과 일치한다.
③ (C) 'After a little while the boy came out with the farmer's watch in his hand.'의 내용과 일치한다.
⑤ (D) 'After a long time searching for it, some of the children got tired and gave up.'의 내용과 일치한다.

---

01 have the walls painted / surprised to see workers / safe and eco-friendly
02 get a driver's license / many drivers ignore speed limits / follow the speed limits
03 the relationship between France and Germany / borrow up to four books / return them on time
04 a toy bear on the bed / the round clock / How do you like / the star-shaped rug on the floor
05 email your science report / send it before meeting me / buy some popcorn
06 want to go to the amusement park / printed out a birthday coupon / your ticket is free
07 a little busy preparing / running a food booth / practice for a band audition
08 Who teaches it / try on traditional clothing / bring a pen and a notebook
09 many different kinds of items / if they are in good condition / a shopping bag as a gift
10 active or casual / recommend waterproof shoes / buy white ones
11 What kind of event is it
12 help take your mind off of it
13 interested in playing the guitar / a math class for first graders / Where can I check the schedule
14 I've been working out / yoga and some stretching / online fitness course
15 run for school president / make a strong impression / help him draw posters
16-17 introduce a healthy breakfast food list / supports weight loss / can improve digestion / higher in fiber

---

어휘 Review Test 06   문제편 084쪽

A		B		C	D
01 현혹시키는, 속이는		01 process		01 ①	01 ⓓ
02 매력적인		02 overseas		02 ⓝ	02 ①
03 원칙, 원리		03 consume		03 ①	03 ⓞ
04 자기 방어		04 participant		04 ⓐ	04 ①
05 논의하다		05 surface		05 ⓜ	05 ⓝ
06 탐구하다		06 modify		06 ⓟ	06 ⓖ
07 물리적으로, 신체적으로		07 raise		07 ⓡ	07 ⓢ
08 붙잡다		08 superior		08 ⓖ	08 ①
09 반영		09 household		09 ⓔ	09 ⓕ
10 믿을 만하지 않은		10 construct		10 ⓠ	10 ⓑ
11 우연의 일치, 동시 발생		11 recover		11 ①	11 ⓠ
12 예측		12 inaccurate		12 ⓑ	12 ⓗ
13 유전적으로		13 assessment		13 ⓢ	13 ①
14 독특한		14 sink		14 ⓓ	14 ⓚ
15 보유, 소유		15 historically		15 ⓗ	15 ⓔ
16 양, 수량		16 introduce		16 ⓚ	16 ⓐ
17 결과, 영향		17 precious		17 ①	17 ①
18 양육		18 constraint		18 ⓞ	18 ⓜ
19 감동한		19 comment		19 ⓒ	19 ⓟ
20 발매하다, 출간하다		20 concern		20 ①	20 ⓒ

・정답・

01 ③ 02 ③ 03 ⑤ 04 ④ 05 ② 06 ③ 07 ④ 08 ③ 09 ④ 10 ④ 11 ① 12 ③ 13 ① 14 ① 15 ①
16 ⑤ 17 ③ 18 ⑤ 19 ⑤ 20 ② 21 ⑤ 22 ③ 23 ④ 24 ① 25 ④ 26 ② 27 ⑤ 28 ③ 29 ⑤ 30 ④
31 ② 32 ① 33 ① 34 ④ 35 ④ 36 ② 37 ④ 38 ③ 39 ② 40 ④ 41 ③ 42 ③ 43 ⑤ 44 ③ 45 ②

★ 표기된 문항은 [등급을 가르는 문제]에 해당하는 문항입니다.

01 불꽃놀이 축제 지하철 연장 운행 | 정답률 89% | 정답 ③

다음을 듣고, 여자가 하는 말의 목적으로 가장 적절한 것을 고르시오.

① 축제 기간 연장을 요청하려고
② 신설된 지하철 노선을 홍보하려고
☑ 축제 당일의 지하철 연장 운행을 안내하려고
④ 축제 방문객에게 안전 수칙 준수를 당부하려고
⑤ 축제 기간 중 도심 교통 통제 구간을 공지하려고

W : Hello! I'm Olivia Parker from Pineview City Subway.
안녕하세요! 전 Pineview City Subway의 Olivia Parker입니다.
I have an announcement for this Saturday's fireworks festival.
이번 주 토요일의 불꽃놀이 축제에 대해 안내사항이 있습니다.
Many people are expected to visit and enjoy the festival late into the night.
많은 사람들이 밤늦게 축제를 방문하고 즐길 것이라 기대됩니다.
For smooth transportation and visitor safety, we're extending the operational hours of the subway on the day of the festival.
원활한 교통과 방문자들의 안전을 위해서, 축제 날 지하철 운행 시간을 연장하려고 합니다.
The subway will run for an extra two hours after the regular last train from the festival area stations.
축제 근처 지하철역에서 지하철이 기존보다 두 시간 더 운행합니다.
For a comfortable and safe journey from the event, we encourage you to take advantage of our extended subway services.
행사에서 편안하고 안전한 시간을 위해, 연장된 지하철 서비스를 이용하시길 권합니다.
We hope you enjoy this fantastic festival with convenience. Thank you!
환상적인 행사를 편안하게 즐기시길 바랍니다. 감사합니다!

Why? 왜 정답일까?

불꽃놀이 축제 중 혼잡을 대비하여 근처 지하철역에서 지하철 연장 운행을 한다고(The subway will run for an extra two hours after the regular last train from the festival area stations.) 하였으므로, 여자가 하는 말의 목적으로 가장 적절한 것은 ③ '축제 당일의 지하철 연장 운행을 안내하려고' 이다.

● announcement ⓝ 안내
● smooth ⓐ 원활한
● extend ⓥ 연장하다
● expect ⓥ 기대하다
● transportation ⓝ 운송수단, 교통

02 휴대폰 사용과 수면의 질의 관계 | 정답률 95% | 정답 ③

대화를 듣고, 남자의 의견으로 가장 적절한 것을 고르시오.

① 불규칙한 수면 습관은 청소년의 뇌 발달을 방해한다.
② 스마트폰의 화면 밝기를 조절하여 눈을 보호해야 한다.
☑ 취침 전 스마트폰 사용을 줄여야 수면의 질이 높아진다.
④ 집중력 향상을 위해 디지털 기기 사용을 최소화해야 한다.
⑤ 일정한 시간에 취침하는 것이 생체 리듬 유지에 도움을 준다.

M : Hi, Emma. What's up? You look tired.
안녕, Emma. 무슨 일 있어? 너 피곤해 보여.
W : Hey, David. I always feel tired. Even though I sleep many hours, I guess I don't get any good sleep.
안녕, David. 나 항상 피곤해. 심지어 내가 많이 잤을 때에도 그렇거든, 잠을 잘 못자는 것 같아.
M : That's too bad. Is there anything you do before you go to bed?
안 됐다. 자기 전에 하는 거 있어?
W : I usually read webtoons on my smartphone for a few hours.
나 몇 시간 동안 내 휴대폰으로 웹툰을 봐.
M : Ah, that's the problem. Having too much screen time right before bed is not good.
아, 그게 문제네. 잠들기 전 바로 휴대폰을 보는 것은 좋지 않아.
W : Really? But I'm so used to spending time on my phone at night!
진짜? 하지만 나는 밤에 휴대폰 보는 게 익숙한데!
M : Long exposure to the screen light can make your brain stay awake.
휴대폰 빛에 오랫동안 노출되는 것은 네 뇌를 깨어있게 할 수 있어.
W : I never knew using smartphones had a negative impact on sleep.
휴대폰 사용이 잠자는 것에 부정적인 영향을 끼치는 줄 몰랐어.
M : Reducing your smartphone use before going to bed will increase the quality of your sleep.
잠들기 전에 휴대폰 사용을 줄이는 것이 네 수면의 질을 올릴 거야.
W : Okay, I can give it a try.
응, 시도해 볼게.

Why? 왜 정답일까?

수면의 질이 낮다는 여자의 말에 남자는 잠자기 전 휴대폰을 하는 것이 수면의 질을 떨어뜨릴 수 있다고(Long exposure to the screen light can make your brain stay awake.)하고 있기 때문에, 남자의 의견으로 가장 적절한 것은 ③ '취침 전 스마트폰 사용을 줄여야 수면의 질이 높아진다.'이다.

● guess ⓥ 추측하다
● negative ⓐ 부정적인
● increase ⓥ 향상시키다
● spend ⓥ 소비하다
● impact ⓝ 영향

[문제편 p.085]

03 스트레스 관리의 팁 | 정답률 93% | 정답 ⑤

다음을 듣고, 남자가 하는 말의 요지로 가장 적절한 것을 고르시오.

① 과도한 컴퓨터 사용은 스트레스 지수를 증가시킨다.
② 컴퓨터 관련 취미 활동은 IT 활용 능력을 향상시킨다.
③ 직업을 선택할 때 자신의 흥미와 적성을 고려해야 한다.
④ 다양한 악기 연주를 배우는 것은 인생을 풍요롭게 만든다.
☑ 직업과 관련 없는 취미 활동이 스트레스 감소에 도움이 된다.

M : Hello, listeners! Welcome to your *Daily Tips*.
안녕하세요, 청취자 여러분! *Daily Tips*에 오신 것을 환영합니다.
Today, I'll tell you a helpful way to relieve your stress.
오늘, 전 여러분에게 스트레스를 풀 수 있는 유용한 방법을 알려드릴 겁니다.
Recent research shows that having hobbies completely unrelated to your job can significantly reduce stress.
최근 연구에서는 여러분의 일과 전혀 관련이 없는 취미를 가지는 것이 스트레스를 확연히 줄일 수 있다고 합니다.
For example, if you work in IT, consider exploring activities that are far from the digital field.
예를 들어서, 여러분이 IT에서 일하신다면, 디지털 분야와 동떨어진 활동을 탐험하는 것을 고려해 보세요.
Playing the guitar might be a good option rather than playing computer games.
컴퓨터 게임을 하는 것보다 기타를 연주하는 것이 좋은 선택이 되겠네요.
Let's enjoy hobbies that are different from our work!
우리의 일과 다른 취미를 즐깁시다!
That'll be the best way to get a refreshing break.
재정비하는 시간을 가질 최고의 방법이 될 것입니다.
Remember, a well-chosen hobby can be a powerful tool for stress relief.
기억하세요, 잘 고른 취미는 스트레스 해소에 강력한 도구가 됩니다.
Tune in tomorrow for more helpful daily tips!
더 많은 유용한 일상 팁들을 위해 내일도 만나요!

Why? 왜 정답일까?

스트레스 해소 방법으로 직업과 전혀 관련 없는 취미를 배우는 것이 좋다고 말하고 있기 때문에(Recent research shows that having hobbies completely unrelated to your job can significantly reduce stress.), 남자가 하는 말의 요지로 가장 적절한 것은 ⑤ '직업과 관련 없는 취미 활동이 스트레스 감소에 도움이 된다.'이다.

● significantly ⓐ 상당히
● option ⓝ 선택권
● relief ⓝ 해소
● consider ⓥ 고려하다
● hobby ⓝ 취미

04 새로운 녹음 스튜디오 | 정답률 82% | 정답 ④

대화를 듣고, 그림에서 대화의 내용과 일치하지 않는 것을 고르시오.

M : Hey, Amy. Here is the new recording studio for our band. How do you like it?
안녕, Amy. 여기가 우리 밴드의 새로운 녹음 스튜디오야. 어때?
W : 「Wow, these two speakers are impressive!」①의 근거 일치
와, 이 두 스피커 정말 인상 깊다!
M : Yes, they are. The sound quality is excellent.
응. 음질이 훌륭해.
W : 「Also, the long desk between the speakers looks great.」②의 근거 일치
또한, 스피커 사이의 긴 책상도 멋져 보여.
「③의 근거 일치」
M : Yeah. 「And on the desk, there is a microphone.」We can use it to give recording directions.
맞아. 책상 위에 마이크가 있어, 녹음 감독할 때 쓸 수 있어.
W : Nice. Oh, this chair looks comfortable. It could be helpful for long recordings.
좋다. 아, 이 의자 편안해 보인다. 오래 녹음할 때 도움이 될 것 같아.
M : Agreed. And the rug under the chair gives the room a cozy feeling, doesn't it?
동의해. 의자 밑의 러그가 방에 포근한 느낌을 주는 것 같아, 그렇지?
W : 「Yes, and I like the flower patterns on the rug.」④의 근거 불일치
응, 러그의 꽃무늬도 마음에 든다.
M : 「I like it, too. How about the poster on the wall?」⑤의 근거 일치
나도 마음에 들어. 벽의 포스터는 어때?
W : It's cool. This studio feels like where music truly comes alive!
멋지다. 이 스튜디오는 음악이 진정으로 살아나는 곳 같아!
M : I'm glad you like this place.
네가 여기를 좋아해서 기뻐.
W : Absolutely. I can't wait to start recording here.
완전 좋아. 여기서 녹음하는 거 기대된다.

Why? 왜 정답일까?

러그의 꽃무늬가 마음에 든다고(Yes, and I like the flower patterns on the rug.) 하였는데, 그림에서 러그는 격자무늬이기 때문에 대화의 내용과 일치하지 않는 것은 ④이다.

● impressive ⓐ 인상적인
● microphone ⓝ 마이크
● cozy ⓐ 포근한
● quality ⓝ 질
● record ⓥ 녹음하다
● glad ⓐ 기쁜

05 친환경 행사 참여 준비하기 | 정답률 77% | 정답 ②

대화를 듣고, 여자가 할 일로 가장 적절한 것을 고르시오.

① 선물 준비하기　　　　　　☑ 온라인 초대장 보내기
③ 음식 주문하기　　　　　　④ 초대 손님 명단 확인하기
⑤ 전시 부스 설치하기

W : Tony, I'm so excited for our Go-Green event!
　　Tony야, 나 우리의 Go-Green 행사 가는 거 신나.
M : Me too. The event is almost here. Why don't we go over our preparations together?
　　나도. 행사가 곧이야. 우리 가서 같이 준비하지 않을래?
W : Okay. I think the exhibition booths are very important for our event. How are they going?
　　그래. 전시회 부스가 우리의 행사에 아주 중요한 것 같아. 어떻게 되어 가고 있어?
M : Almost ready. I'm working on the booth setup this afternoon. What about the welcome gifts?
　　거의 준비됐어. 오늘 오후에 부스 설치 준비할게. 환영 선물은 어떻게 되어 가고 있어?
W : I've already prepared some eco-friendly bags.
　　나는 이미 친환경 가방들을 준비했어.
M : Perfect! What's next?
　　완벽해! 다음은 뭐야?
W : We need to confirm the list of guests for the ceremony.
　　우리는 행사 손님 목록을 확인해야 해.
M : I double-checked the list. But I haven't sent the online invitation cards, yet.
　　목록은 내가 두 번 확인했어. 하지만 아직 온라인 초대장을 보내지 않았어.
W : No problem. I'll deal with it right away. How about the food and drinks?
　　문제없어. 그건 내가 지금 당장 해결할게. 음식이랑 음료는 어떻게 되어 가고 있어?
M : I've scheduled food and drink services and I'll serve the guests with reusable dishes.
　　나는 음식이랑 음료 서비스를 예약했고, 손님들한테 재사용 가능한 접시에 대접할 거야.
W : Nice! I'm confident our event will be a great success.
　　멋제! 우리의 행사가 크게 성공할 거야.

Why? 왜 정답일까?

남자가 온라인 초대장을 보내지 않았다고 하자, 여자가 해결하겠다고 하였으므로(I'll deal with it right away.) 여자가 할 일로 가장 적절한 것은 ② '온라인 초대장 보내기'이다.

● preparation ⓝ 준비　　　　● exhibition ⓝ 전시회
● important ⓐ 중요한　　　　● eco-friendly ⓐ 친환경적인
● confirm ⓥ 확인하다

06 캠핑 용품 구매하기　　　　　정답률 87% | 정답 ③

대화를 듣고, 남자가 지불할 금액을 고르시오. [3점]
① $63　　② $70　　☑ $81　　④ $86　　⑤ $90

W : Welcome to the Riverside Camping store. How can I help you?
　　Riverside Camping 가게에 오신 것을 환영합니다. 어떻게 도와드릴까요?
M : I'm looking for a camping table for my family. Can you recommend one?
　　전 가족을 위한 캠핑 테이블을 찾고 있어요. 추천해 주시겠어요?
W : Sure. How about this one? It's light and easy to fold, so it's our best-selling product.
　　당연하죠. 이건 어때요? 가볍고 접기도 쉬워서 저희 가게에서 가장 잘 팔리는 상품이에요.
M : It looks good. How much is it?
　　좋아 보여요. 얼마예요?
W : It comes in two sizes. The small one is 30 dollars and the large one is 50 dollars.
　　사이즈가 두 가지 있습니다. 작은 건 30달러이고, 큰 건 50달러입니다.
M : I'll buy the large one. Are there folding chairs, too?
　　큰 거 살게요. 저건 접이식 의자인가요?
W : Yep. These folding chairs might go well with the table. They're 10 dollars each.
　　네. 이 접이식 의자들은 테이블이랑도 잘 어울려요. 각각 10달러입니다.
M : Sounds good. I'll buy four of those chairs.
　　좋네요. 의자 4개 살게요.
W : Okay. That's one large camping table and four chairs.
　　네. 큰 캠핑 테이블과 의자 4개 확인 도와드리겠습니다.
M : That's right. Can I use this discount coupon now?
　　맞아요. 이 할인 쿠폰 지금 쓸 수 있나요?
W : Of course. You can get a 10% discount on the total price.
　　당연하죠. 총 금액에서 10% 할인 받으실 수 있습니다.
M : Perfect. Here's my credit card.
　　완벽해요. 여기 제 신용 카드입니다.

Why? 왜 정답일까?

큰 테이블 50달러, 10달러 접이식 의자 4개를 사고 10% 할인 쿠폰을 사용한다고 하였으므로 {(50×1)+(10×4)}×0.9=81이라서 남자가 지불할 금액은 ③ '$81'이다.

● look for 찾다　　　　　● recommend ⓥ 추천하다
● light ⓐ 가벼운　　　　● folding chair 접이식 의자
● discount ⓝ 할인

07 암벽 등반에 갈 수 없는 이유　　　　정답률 97% | 정답 ④

대화를 듣고, 여자가 이번 주말에 등산을 갈 수 없는 이유를 고르시오.
① 아르바이트를 해야 해서
② 학교 시험공부를 해야 해서
③ 폭우로 인해 등산로가 폐쇄되어서
☑ 경연을 위한 춤 연습을 해야 해서
⑤ 주문한 등산 장비가 도착하지 않아서

W : Lately, the weather has been lovely. This is a perfect time for climbing.
　　요즘 날씨가 좋아. 등반하기 딱인 때야.
M : Indeed. Oh, would you like to go mountain climbing together?
　　진짜 그래. 아, 산 등반하러 같이 갈래?
W : Sounds awesome. I have all the climbing equipment.
　　좋아. 등반 장비를 가지고 있어.
M : Great. How about this upcoming weekend? I'll find a nice mountain for us.
　　멋져. 오는 주말은 어때? 좋은 산을 찾아볼게.

W : Hold on, this weekend? I don't think I can make it then.
　　잠깐만, 이번 주말? 나 그때는 안 될 것 같아.
M : Really? All school tests are finally done, so I thought this weekend would be good for us.
　　진짜? 학교 시험이 다 끝나서, 이번 주 주말이 괜찮을 거라 생각했어.
W : Sorry, but I have something important to do this weekend.
　　미안, 주말에 해야 할 중요한 일이 있어.
M : Do you have a part-time job?
　　너 아르바이트 해?
W : No. Actually, I need to practice dancing for the entire weekend.
　　아니. 사실, 나 주말 동안 춤 연습을 해야 해.
M : Ah, for the dance competition you mentioned before?
　　아, 전에 말했던 춤 대회 때문에?
W : Yes. Surprisingly, I made it through the first round, and it's the finals next Monday.
　　응. 놀랍게도 내가 첫 번째 라운드를 통과했지 뭐야. 그리고 다음 주 월요일이 결승전이야!
M : That's fantastic! I wish you the best of luck.
　　멋지다! 행운을 빌어.

Why? 왜 정답일까?

여자가 주말에 춤 연습을 해야 한다고 했기 때문에(No. Actually, I need to practice dancing for the entire weekend.), 여자가 이번 주말에 등산을 갈 수 없는 이유는 ④ '경연을 위한 춤 연습을 해야 해서'이다.

● lovely ⓐ 사랑스러운　　　● climb ⓥ 오르다
● equipment ⓝ 장비　　　　● part-time job 아르바이트
● competition ⓝ 경연　　　● mention ⓥ 언급하다

08 요가 프로그램 참여하기　　　　정답률 92% | 정답 ③

대화를 듣고, Lakestate Apartment Yoga Program에 관해 언급되지 않은 것을 고르시오.
① 대상 연령　　　② 운영 요일　　　☑ 모집 인원
④ 등록 방법　　　⑤ 등록 준비물

W : Grandpa, take a look at this. It's a Lakestate Apartment Yoga Program poster.
　　할아버지, 이것 좀 보세요. Lakestate 아파트의 요가 프로그램 포스터예요.
M : Wow, a new program for the residents. I've always wanted to join a yoga program.
　　와, 입주민을 위한 새로운 프로그램이구나. 난 항상 요가 프로그램에 참여해 보고 싶었어.
W : 「I know, and this one is only for those aged 60 and above.」 ①의 근거 일치
　　알아요. 그리고 이 프로그램은 60세 이상을 위한 거예요.
M : That's perfect for me. [Pause] 「Oh, it says it's held at 8 a.m. every Tuesday and Friday.」 ②의 근거 일치
　　나에게 딱 맞구나. [잠시 멈춤] 오, 매주 화요일과 금요일 아침 8시에 열리는구나.
W : It'll be a good time for you. You're an early bird.
　　할아버지께 좋은 시간인 것 같아요. 일찍 일어나시잖아요.
M : Yes, I am. How do I register?
　　그치. 어떻게 등록해?
W : 「You just need to fill out an application form at the apartment fitness center.」 ④의 근거 일치
　　아파트 피트니스 센터의 신청서만 작성하시면 돼요.
M : Okay, I think I'll go right now.
　　그래, 지금 가야겠다.
W : Good. 「But don't forget to take your ID card with you.」 ⑤의 근거 일치
　　좋아요. 신분증 꼭 챙기세요.
M : Oh, do I need that for the registration?
　　아, 등록하려면 신분증이 필요하니?
W : Yes. It says that on the poster. Would you like me to go with you?
　　네. 포스터에 쓰여 있어요. 같이 가 드릴까요?
M : That would be lovely.
　　그럼 좋지.

Why? 왜 정답일까?

Lakestate 아파트의 요가 프로그램에 대해서 언급 된 것은 대상 연령, 운영 요일, 등록 방법, 등록 준비물로, 언급되지 않은 것은 ③ '모집 인원'이다.

● join ⓥ 참가하다　　　　● register ⓥ 등록하다
● application ⓝ 신청서　　● forget ⓥ 잊다
● early bird 일찍 일어나는 새

09 글로벌 음식 마켓 안내하기　　　　정답률 95% | 정답 ④

Global Food Market에 관한 다음 내용을 듣고, 일치하지 않는 것을 고르시오.
① 학교 주차장에서 열린다.
② 이틀간 진행된다.
③ 8개 국가의 음식을 즐길 수 있다.
☑ 음식마다 가격이 다르다.
⑤ 채식주의자를 위한 메뉴가 있다.

W : Good morning! This is Allison from the student council.
　　좋은 아침입니다! 학생 위원회의 Allison입니다.
　　I'm happy to announce the Global Food Market right here at Westhill High School.
　　이곳 Westhill 고등학교에서 Global Food Market이 열림을 알리게 되어 전 기쁩니다.
　　「Get ready for a delicious journey around the world in the school parking lot.」 ①의 근거 일치
　　학교 주차장에서 전 세계의 맛 여행을 떠날 준비를 하세요.
　　「Our Global Food Market will take place for two days, on September 25th and 26th.」 ②의 근거 일치
　　Global Food Market은 9월 25일과 26일, 이틀간 진행됩니다.
　　「You can enjoy food from eight different countries, including Mexico and France.」 ③의 근거 일치
　　멕시코와 프랑스를 포함한 8개국의 음식을 즐길 수 있습니다.
　　And there's no need to worry about prices.
　　가격에 대해서 걱정할 필요도 없습니다.
　　「Every single dish is only five dollars.」 ④의 근거 불일치
　　요리 하나당 오직 5달러입니다.
　　Wait! You don't eat meat? No problem!
　　잠만요! 고기를 안 드신다고요? 문제없습니다!
　　「We also have menus for vegetarians.」 ⑤의 근거 일치 So, join us at the Global Food Market.
　　채식주의자를 위한 메뉴도 있습니다. Global Food Market에 오세요.

It's not just about food, but a celebration of culture and diversity.
음식뿐만이 아니라, 문화와 다양성의 축하이기도 합니다.
Don't miss this chance to taste the world!
세상을 맛볼 기회를 놓치지 마세요!

Why? 왜 정답일까?

Global Food Market의 모든 음식은 5달러라고 했기 때문에, 내용과 일치하지 않는 것은 ④ '음식마다 가격이 다르다.'이다.

- council ⑩ 위원회
- journey ⑪ 여행
- diversity ⑪ 다양성
- announce ⑨ 알리다
- vegetarian ⑪ 채식주의자

---

10 디지털 텀블러 고르기　　　정답률 86% | 정답 ④

다음 표를 보면서 대화를 듣고, 남자가 주문할 디지털 텀블러를 고르시오.

Digital Tumblers

	Model	Price	Size	Water Intake Display	Color
①	A	$35	350ml	×	White
②	B	$40	470ml	×	Gold
③	C	$45	470ml	○	Black
✓④	D	$55	550ml	○	White
⑤	E	$65	550ml	○	Gold

W : Honey, what are you looking at?
　자기야, 뭐 보고 있어?
M : I'm looking at digital tumblers. They show the temperature on an LED screen. Would you like to help me choose one?
　디지털 텀블러 보고 있어. LED 스크린에 온도를 보여 준대. 고르는 거 도와줄래?
W : Sure, let me see. [Pause] The price differs by model.
　그럼, 같이 보자. [잠시 멈춤] 모델마다 가격이 다르네.
M : 「Hmm, I don't want to pay more than 60 dollars.」 근거1 Price 조건
　흠, 60달러 넘게 내고 싶지는 않아.
W : That sounds reasonable. Look, there are various sizes to choose from.
　합리적이네. 봐, 다양한 사이즈를 고를 수 있어.
M : 「Less than 400ml would be too small for me.」 근거2 Size 조건
　400ml보다 작으면 나한테 부족할 거야.
W : Alright. Oh, there's a new function. Do you need the water intake display? It'll show you how much water you drink in a day.
　그래. 오, 새로운 기능이 있네. 물 섭취량 화면도 필요해? 하루에 물을 얼마나 마셨는지 보여 준대.
M : That sounds smart. 「I'd love to have it.」 Then, I have just two options left. 근거3 Water Intake Display 조건
　그거 똑똑하네. 있으면 좋겠다. 그럼, 두 가지 옵션이 남네.
W : What color do you like? You have too many black items and they're boring.
　무슨 색이 좋아? 자기 검은색이 너무 많아서 좀 지루해.
M : Okay. 「I'll go with the one that's not black.」 Then, I'll order this one. 근거4 Color 조건
　그래. 검은색 아닌 걸로 골라야겠다. 이거 주문할게.
W : Great idea!
　좋은 생각이야!

Why? 왜 정답일까?

가격은 60달러 아래이고, 크기는 400ml 이상이며 물 섭취량 화면이 있고 검은색이 아닌 것은 모델 D로, ④이다.

- look ⓥ 쳐다보다
- temperature ⑪ 온도
- function ⑪ 기능
- show 보여주다
- differ ⓥ 다르다
- option ⑪ 선택지

---

11 감기와 습도의 관계　　　정답률 58% | 정답 ①

대화를 듣고, 여자의 마지막 말에 대한 남자의 응답으로 가장 적절한 것을 고르시오.

✓① If it's too dry inside, you can easily get a cold. – 내부가 너무 건조하면, 감기에 쉽게 걸릴 수 있어.
② When you cough, you should cover your mouth. – 기침할 때, 입을 가려야해.
③ You need to wash your hands not to get a cold. – 감기에 걸리지 않으려면 손을 씻어야해.
④ It's really important to keep yourself warm. – 따뜻하게 있는 것이 중요해.
⑤ Drinking water can make your skin soft. – 물을 마시는 것은 네 피부를 부드럽게 만들 수 있어.

W : I easily catch a cold these days.
　나 요즘 감기에 쉽게 걸려.
M : That's too bad. It's a good idea to keep some moisture in your room.
　안 됐다. 방에 습도를 유지하는 것이 좋아.
W : Oh, how does that relate to a cold?
　아, 그게 감기랑 연관이 있어?
M : If it's too dry inside, you can easily get a cold.
　내부가 너무 건조하면, 감기에 쉽게 걸릴 수 있어.

Why? 왜 정답일까?

남자가 방의 습도를 유지하라고 하였고, 여자는 습도가 감기와 연관이 있냐고 물었으므로 ① 'If it's too dry inside, you can easily get a cold.'가 적절한 응답이다.

- catch a cold 감기에 걸리다
- moisture ⑪ 습도
- keep ⓥ 유지하다
- relate ⓥ 연관되다

---

12 책장 정리하기　　　정답률 72% | 정답 ②

대화를 듣고, 남자의 마지막 말에 대한 여자의 응답으로 가장 적절한 것을 고르시오.

① Awesome. The new bookshelf looks good in your room. – 멋지다. 새 책장이 네 방에 잘 어울리네.
✓② Right. Then, shall we sell them at a used bookstore? – 맞아. 그럼, 중고책 서점에 책을 팔까?
③ I see. Can you borrow them from the library? – 그렇구나. 도서관에서 빌릴 수 있어?

---

④ Okay. I'll buy you books in a good condition. – 맞아. 좋은 상태의 책을 살게.
⑤ I'm sorry. I haven't finished the book yet. – 미안해. 책을 아직 덜 읽었어.

M : Mom, the bookshelf in my room is full of books. There's no space for new ones.
　엄마, 제 방의 책장이 책으로 가득 찼어요. 새 책을 꽂을 자리가 없어요.
W : Well, how about throwing away the books you don't read anymore?
　음, 더 이상 읽지 않는 책을 버리는 건 어때?
M : But some of them are in too good condition to throw away.
　하지만 몇 권은 버리기에는 상태가 좋아요.
W : Right. Then, shall we sell them at a used bookstore?
　맞아. 그럼, 중고책 서점에 책을 팔까?

Why? 왜 정답일까?

책을 버리기에는 상태가 좋다고 하였으므로, ② 'Right. Then, shall we sell them at a used bookstore?'가 여자의 응답으로 가장 적절하다.

- bookshelf ⑪ 책장
- throw away 버리다
- space ⑪ 자리
- condition ⑪ 상태

---

13 조별활동의 역할 분배　　　정답률 55% | 정답 ①

대화를 듣고, 여자의 마지막 말에 대한 남자의 응답으로 가장 적절한 것을 고르시오. [3점]
Man :

✓① I'll clarify each group member's specific role. – 조원들 각자에게 특정한 역할을 분명히 할게요.
② I'll collect more data for our group research. – 저희 조 조사를 위해 더 많은 정보를 모을게요.
③ I should challenge myself for the competition. – 대회에 도전해야겠어요.
④ I need to change the topic of our group project. – 저희 조 프로젝트의 주제를 바꿀 필요가 있겠어요.
⑤ I'll let you know how to analyze data effectively. – 정보를 효과적으로 분석하는 방법을 알려 드릴게요.

W : Hey, Peter. How's your group project going?
　Peter야 안녕, 조별 과제 어떻게 돼 가고 있어?
M : Hello, Ms. Adams. It's my first time as a leader, so it's quite challenging.
　안녕하세요 Adams 선생님. 조장은 처음이라, 꽤 어려워요.
W : I thought your group was working well together.
　네 조는 함께 잘 작업하고 있는 줄 알았어.
M : Yes. We're all motivated and working hard, but progress is slow.
　네. 저희 모두 적극적이고 열심히 하는데, 진도가 느려요.
W : Well, what are you all working on at this moment?
　음, 지금 다들 뭐하고 있니?
M : Everyone is focusing on gathering data as much as possible.
　모두 가능한 많이 정보를 많이 모으는 데에 집중하고 있어요.
W : Hmm, did you assign individual tasks to each member?
　흠, 각자 할 일을 할당해 주었니?
M : Oh, we haven't discussed it yet. We're not exactly sure who does what.
　아, 아직 그건 얘기 안 해봤어요. 저희 아직 누가 뭘 하는지 정확하게 정하지 않았어요.
W : That's crucial. Otherwise, it can lead to overlapping tasks in a group project.
　그거 중요해. 그렇지 않으면, 조별 과제에서 작업이 겹칠 수 있어.
M : That makes sense. That's why our progress is not that fast.
　말이 되네요. 그래서 저희 진도가 빠르지 않았던 거네요.
W : Then, as the leader, what do you think you should do now?
　그럼, 조장으로서, 네가 이제 뭘 해야 할 것 같니?
M : I'll clarify each group member's specific role.
　조원들 각자에게 특정한 역할을 분명히 할게요.

Why? 왜 정답일까?

조별 과제에서 조원들에게 각자 할 일을 할당하지 않아서 진도가 느린 것 같다고 하였으므로, 여자의 마지막 말에 대한 남자의 응답으로 가장 적절한 것은 ① 'I'll clarify each group member's specific role.'이다.

- challenge ⓥ 도전하다
- moment ⑪ 순간
- assign ⓥ 할당하다
- motivate ⓥ 동기를 붙하다
- gather ⓥ 모으다
- discuss ⓥ 토의하다

---

14 체중 감량하기　　　정답률 58% | 정답 ①

대화를 듣고, 남자의 마지막 말에 대한 여자의 응답으로 가장 적절한 것을 고르시오. [3점]
Woman :

✓① Trust me. When we eat makes a big difference.
　믿어봐. 언제 먹느냐가 큰 차이를 만들어.
② Okay. I'll check my meals to get in better shape.
　그래. 살을 빼기 위해서 내 식사를 확인할게.
③ Thank you for your tip. But I don't think I can do it.
　네 팁을 알려 줘서 고마워. 근데 나는 못할 것 같아.
④ Of course. I'll make sure to follow your workout routine.
　당연하지. 네 운동 루틴을 따라할게.
⑤ Sure. That's why I didn't succeed at keeping a balanced diet.
　응. 그게 내가 균형 잡힌 식단을 유지하지 못한 이유야.

M : Hey, Emily! You're looking great these days.
　안녕 Emily! 요즘 좋아 보인다.
W : Thanks, Isaac. I've been trying hard to get in better shape.
　고마워 Isaac. 나 요즘 몸매 관리 중이야.
M : Good for you! I'm trying to get fit, too. But it's tough.
　좋네! 나도 관리하고 싶어. 근데 어렵더라고.
W : Haven't you been working out a lot lately?
　요즘 운동 하지 않아?
M : Yeah, but I don't see a big difference. What's your secret?
　응, 근데 큰 차이를 모르겠어. 네 비법이 뭐야?
W : Well, I started being careful about when I eat.
　음, 나는 언제 먹느냐를 신경 쓰기 시작했어.
M : You mean like not eating right before bed?
　자기 전에 안 먹는 것처럼 말야?
W : Kind of. I noticed I was eating a lot at night. So now I don't eat after 7 p.m.
　그런 셈이지. 내가 밤에 많이 먹더라고. 그래서 이제 저녁 7시 이후로는 안 먹어.

M : Hmm... I don't know if that's enough to get me in better shape.
흠... 내가 살 빼는 데에 그게 충분할지 모르겠어.

W : Trust me. When we eat makes a big difference.
믿어봐. 언제 먹느냐가 큰 차이를 만들어.

Why? 왜 정답일까?

저녁 7시 이후로 안 먹는다는 것이 여자의 살을 빼는 비법이었기 때문에, 이것에 의구심을 갖는 남자의 마지막 말에 대한 여자의 응답으로 가장 적절한 것은 ① 'Trust me. When we eat makes a big difference.'이다.

- tough ⓐ 어려운
- difference ⓝ 차이점
- enough ⓐ 충분한
- lately 【ad】 최근에
- careful ⓐ 신경 쓰는

---

15 책상 조립 도움 청하기　　　　　정답률 76% | 정답 ①

다음 상황 설명을 듣고, Julia가 Sophie에게 할 말로 가장 적절한 것을 고르시오.

Julia :
✓ Could you help me assemble my desk? – 내 책상 조립하는 거 도와줄 수 있어?
② Can you share where you bought your desk? – 책상 어디서 샀는지 알려 줄 수 있어?
③ How about choosing a new computer together? – 새 컴퓨터를 같이 고르는 거 어때?
④ Why don't you repair the furniture by yourself? – 스스로 가구를 수리해 보는 건 어때?
⑤ Do you have any ideas for decorating my room? – 방 꾸미기에 대한 생각이 있니?

M : Julia is a college student, living in the dormitory.
Julia는 기숙사에 사는 대학교 학생이다.
Recently, she ordered a new computer desk.
최근에, 그녀는 컴퓨터 책상을 시켰다.
Upon receiving the desk, she realized that the desk was a DIY product.
책상을 받고, 그녀는 책상이 DIY 상품인 것을 깨달았다.
It means she needs to put the pieces together to build the desk.
그녀가 책상을 조립하기 위해서 부품들을 끼워야 한다는 뜻이었다.
However, it was complicated to assemble it by herself.
하지만 그녀 혼자서 조립하는 것은 복잡했다.
Julia knows that Sophie, her best friend, is good at assembling DIY furniture and enjoys it.
Julia는 그녀의 친한 친구인 Sophie가 DIY 가구를 잘 조립하고, 즐기는 것을 알고 있다.
So, Julia wants to ask Sophie to help her with the desk.
그래서 Julia는 Sophie에게 책상 조립을 도와달라고 부탁하고 싶다.
In this situation, what would Julia most likely say to Sophie?
이 상황에서, Julia가 Sophie에게 할 말로 가장 적절한 것은 무엇인가?
Julia : Could you help me assemble my desk?
내 책상 조립하는 거 도와줄 수 있어?

Why? 왜 정답일까?

Julia는 Sophie에게 책상 조립을 도와달라고 말하고 싶기 때문에, Julia가 Sophie에게 할 말로 가장 적절한 것은 ① 'Could you help me assemble my desk?'이다.

- dormitory ⓝ 기숙사
- receive ⓥ 받다
- assemble ⓥ 조립하다
- repair ⓥ 수리하다
- order ⓥ 주문하다
- complicate ⓥ 복잡하게 만들다
- situation ⓝ 상황

16-17 천연 재료 옷 빨래하기

W : Hello, *Family-Life* subscribers!
안녕하세요, *Family-Life* 구독자 여러분!
These days, many people are looking for clothes made from natural materials for their family.
요즘, 많은 사람들이 가족들을 위해 천연 재료로 만든 옷을 찾고 있습니다.
『Today, I'd like to introduce some tips for how to properly wash natural material clothes.』 16번의 근거
오늘 전 천연 재료 옷을 제대로 빨래하는 방법을 소개할 거에요.
『First, for cotton, like 100% cotton t-shirts, you should hand-wash in cool water to avoid shrinking or wrinkling.』 17번 ①의 근거 일치
첫째로, 100% 순면 티셔츠와 같은 면일 때, 줄어듦과 주름짐을 방지하기 위해서 찬물로 손세탁해야 합니다.
『Second, silk should be washed separately and quickly to keep its shape and color.』 17번 ②의 근거 일치
둘째로, 실크는 모양과 색깔을 유지하기 위해 따로 빠르게 세탁해야 합니다.
Also, when you dry silk clothes such as blouses, avoid direct sunlight and dry them in the shade.
또한 블라우스와 같은 실크 옷을 말릴 때, 직사광선은 피하고 그늘에서 말려 주세요.
『Third, linen is a sensitive material to wash.』 17번 ④의 근거 일치
세 번째로, 린넨은 세탁하기에 섬세한 재료입니다.
For example, to wash linen jackets, use vinegar instead of fabric softener.
예를 들어, 린넨 자켓을 세탁할 때, 섬유 유연제 대신 식초를 사용하세요.
『Lastly, for wool, the best way is to wash as little as possible.』 17번 ⑤의 근거 일치
마지막으로, 울은 최대한 적게 빨래하는 것이 좋습니다.
If you have to wash wool sweaters, use special wool washing soap.
울 스웨터를 빨아야 한다면, 울 특수 세제를 사용하세요.
Apply these tips so you can keep and enjoy natural clothes for a longer time!
이 방법을 적용하면 천연 재료 옷을 더 오래 갖고 즐길 수 있어요!

- natural ⓐ 자연의
- introduce ⓥ 소개하다
- wrinkle ⓥ 주름이 지다
- avoid ⓥ 피하다
- fabric softener 섬유 유연제
- material ⓝ 소재
- shrink ⓥ 줄어들다
- separately 【ad】 개별로
- sensitive ⓐ 섬세한

---

16 주제 파악　　　　　정답률 80% | 정답 ⑤

여자가 하는 말의 주제로 가장 적절한 것은?
① material trends in the fashion industry – 패션 사업의 재료 트렌드

---

② benefits of making clothes from nature – 자연으로 옷 만드는 것의 장점
③ tips to purchase natural material clothes – 천연 재료 옷을 구매하는 팁
④ development of clothes washing methods – 옷 빨래 방법의 발달
✓ proper ways to wash natural material clothes – 천연 재료 옷을 제대로 빨래하는 방법

Why? 왜 정답일까?

천연 재료 옷의 빨래 방법을 설명하고 있기 때문에(Today, I'd like to introduce some tips for how to properly wash natural material clothes.), 여자가 하는 말의 주제로 가장 적절한 것은 ⑤ 'proper ways to wash natural material clothes'이다.

---

17 언급 유무 파악　　　　　정답률 93% | 정답 ③

언급된 소재가 아닌 것은?
① cotton – 면
② silk – 실크
✓ leather – 가죽
④ linen – 린넨
⑤ wool – 울

Why? 왜 정답일까?

cotton, silk, linen, wool은 모두 언급되었지만 leather는 언급되지 않았기 때문에, ③ 'leather'가 정답이다.

---

18 유인 매표소 재운영 요구 글　　　　　정답률 88% | 정답 ⑤

다음 글의 목적으로 가장 적절한 것은?
① 승차권 발매기 수리를 의뢰하려고
② 기차표 단체 예매 방법을 문의하려고
③ 기차 출발 시간 지연에 대해 항의하려고
④ 기차역 직원의 친절한 도움에 감사하려고
✓ 기차역 유인 매표소 재운영을 요구하려고

To whom it may concern,
관계자분께,
I am writing to express my deep concern / about the recent change made by Pittsburgh Train Station.
저는 깊은 우려를 표하고자 이 글을 씁니다. / Pittsburgh Train Station에서 최근에 이루어진 변화에 대해
The station had traditional ticket offices with staff before, / but these have been replaced with ticket vending machines.
기차역에는 예전에는 직원이 있는 전통적인 매표소가 있었으나, / 이제는 자동발권기로 대체되었습니다.
However, individuals who are unfamiliar with these machines / are now experiencing difficulty accessing the railway services.
그러나, 이 기계에 익숙하지 않은 사람들은 / 지금 철도 서비스를 이용하는 데 어려움을 겪고 있습니다.
Since these individuals heavily relied on the staff assistance to be able to travel, / they are in great need of ticket offices with staff in the station.
이들은 여행하기 위해 직원의 도움에 크게 의존해 왔기 때문에, / 역에 직원이 있는 매표소가 절실히 필요합니다.
Therefore, I am urging you to consider reopening the ticket offices.
그러므로, 저는 매표소를 다시 여는 것을 검토해 주시기를 촉구합니다.
With the staff back in their positions, / many people would regain access to the railway services.
직원이 다시 그들의 자리로 돌아오면, / 많은 사람들이 철도 서비스를 다시 이용할 수 있을 것입니다.
I look forward to your prompt attention to this matter and a positive resolution.
저는 이 문제에 대해 신속한 관심과 긍정적인 해결을 기대합니다.
Sincerely, / Sarah Roberts
진심을 담아, / 사라 로버츠

관계자분께,
저는 Pittsburgh Train Station에 의한 최근의 변경에 대해 저의 깊은 우려를 표하기 위해 글을 쓰고 있습니다. 이전에는 역에 직원이 있는 전통적인 매표소가 있었지만, 이것들은 승차권 발매기로 대체되었습니다. 그러나 이러한 기계에 익숙하지 않은 사람들은 현재 철도 서비스에 접근하는 데 어려움을 겪고 있습니다. 이 사람들은 이동할 수 있기 위해 직원의 도움에 크게 의존했기 때문에, 그들은 역 내에 직원이 있는 매표소를 매우 필요로 합니다. 그러므로 저는 당신에게 매표소 재운영을 고려할 것을 촉구합니다. 직원이 그들의 자리로 돌아오면 많은 사람이 철도 서비스에 대한 접근을 다시 얻을 것입니다. 저는 이 문제에 대한 당신의 신속한 관심과 긍정적인 해결을 기대합니다.
진심을 담아,
Sarah Roberts

Why? 왜 정답일까?

Pittsburgh Train Station에 전통적인 매표소를 키오스크가 대체하자 기계에 익숙하지 않은 사람들이 현재 철도 서비스에 접근하는 데에 어려움을 겪고 있다고 하였으므로('However, individuals who are unfamiliar with these machines are now experiencing difficulty accessing the railway services.'), 글의 목적으로 가장 적절한 것은 ⑤ '기차역 유인 매표소 재운영을 요구하려고'이다.

- express ⓥ 표현하다
- traditional ⓐ 전통의, 전통적인
- unfamiliar ⓐ 익숙하지 않은
- station ⓝ 역
- reopen ⓥ 다시 열다
- prompt ⓐ 즉각적인, 지체 없는
- concern ⓝ 걱정
- vending machine 자동판매기
- experience ⓥ 경험하다
- assistance ⓝ 도움
- regain ⓥ 되찾다, 회복하다
- resolution ⓝ 해결책

구문 풀이

8행 Since these individuals heavily relied on the staff assistance to be able to travel, they are in great need of ticket offices with staff in the station.
때문에 / 의존하다(= depend) / to부정사 부사적 용법(위해서)

---

19 Arthur 살리기　　　　　정답률 82% | 정답 ⑤

다음 글에 드러난 Jeevan의 심경 변화로 가장 적절한 것은?

① thrilled → bored
긴장한 → 지루한

② ashamed → confident
부끄러운 → 자신감 있는

③ hopeful → helpless
희망에 찬 → 어찌할 수 없는

④ surprised → indifferent
놀란 → 무관심한

✔ desperate → relieved
절망한 → 안심한

All the actors on the stage were focused on their acting.
무대에 있던 모든 배우들은 연기에 집중하고 있었다.

Then, suddenly, Arthur fell into the corner of the stage.
그러다, 갑자기 Arthur가 무대 구석으로 쓰러졌다.

Jeevan immediately approached Arthur / and found his heart wasn't beating.
Jeevan은 즉시 Arthur에게 다가갔고 / 그의 심장이 뛰지 않는 것을 발견했다.

Jeevan began CPR.
Jeevan은 심폐소생술을 시작했다.

Jeevan worked silently, / glancing sometimes at Arthur's face.
Jeevan은 침묵 속에서, / 가끔 Arthur의 얼굴을 힐끗 보았다.

He thought, / "Please, start breathing again, please."
그는 생각했다, / '제발 다시 숨 쉬어 줘, 제발.'

Arthur's eyes were closed.
Arthur의 눈은 감겨 있었다.

Moments later, / an older man in a grey suit appeared, / swiftly kneeling beside Arthur's chest.
잠시 후, / 회색 정장을 입은 나이 든 남자가 나타나서 / 빠르게 Arthur의 가슴 옆에 무릎을 꿇었다.

"I'm Walter Jacobi. I'm a doctor." / He announced with a calm voice.
"나는 Walter Jacobi다. 나는 의사야." / 그는 침착한 목소리로 말했다.

Jeevan wiped the sweat off his forehead.
Jeevan은 이마의 땀을 닦았다.

With combined efforts, / Jeevan and Dr. Jacobi successfully revived Arthur.
Jeevan과 Jacobi 박사는 힘을 합쳐 / Arthur를 성공적으로 소생시켰다.

Arthur's eyes slowly opened.
Arthur의 눈이 천천히 떠졌다.

Finally, Jeevan was able to hear Arthur's breath again, / thinking to himself, / "Thank goodness. You're back."
마침내, Jeevan은 다시 Arthur의 숨소리를 들을 수 있었고, / 속으로 생각했다, / "다행이야. 네가 돌아왔구나."

무대 위의 모든 배우가 그들의 연기에 집중하고 있었다. 그 때 갑자기 Arthur가 무대의 한쪽 구석에 쓰러졌다. Jeevan이 즉각 Arthur에게 다가갔고 그의 심장이 뛰지 않는 것을 알아차렸다. Jeevan은 CPR을 시작했다. Jeevan은 때때로 Arthur의 얼굴을 흘끗 보며 조용히 작업했다. 그는 '제발, 다시 숨쉬기를 시작해요, 제발.'이라고 생각했다. Arthur의 눈은 감겨 있었다. 잠시 뒤, 회색 정장 차림의 한 노인이 나타났고, Arthur의 가슴 옆에 재빠르게 무릎을 꿇었다. "저는 Walter Jacobi입니다. 저는 의사입니다." 그는 차분한 목소리로 전했다. Jeevan은 그의 이마에서 땀을 닦아냈다. 협력하여, Jeevan과 Dr. Jacobi는 Arthur를 성공적으로 소생시켰다. Arthur의 눈이 천천히 떠졌다. 마침내 Jeevan은 Arthur의 숨을 다시 들을 수 있었고, '다행이다. 깨어났다.'라고 자신에게 되뇌었다.

Why? 왜 정답일까?

Arthur가 쓰러졌고, Jeevan은 Arthur에게 심폐소생술을 진행하며 제발 다시 숨을 쉬라고 생각했으며(He thought, "Please, start breathing again, please."), Jeevan과 Dr. Jacobi의 노력으로 Arthur가 다시 눈을 뜨자 다시 숨을 쉬어서 너무 다행이라고 생각했기 때문에(Finally, Jeevan was able to hear Arthur's breath again, thinking to himself, "Thank goodness. You're back."), Jeevan의 심경 변화로 가장 적절한 것은 ⑤ 'desperate → relieved'이다.

- stage ⓝ 무대
- immediately [ad] 즉시
- kneel ⓥ 무릎을 꿇다
- successfully [ad] 성공적으로
- focus ⓥ 집중하다
- approach ⓥ 접근하다
- wipe ⓥ 닦다
- revive ⓥ 소생하다

구문 풀이

12행 Finally, Jeevan was able to hear Arthur's breath again, thinking to himself,
be able to ~할 수 있다 / 감각동사 / 재귀대명사(목적어)
"Thank goodness. You're back."

---

20 영재 부모의 자랑 　　정답률 75% | 정답 ②

다음 글에서 필자가 주장하는 바로 가장 적절한 것은?

① 부모는 자녀를 다른 아이와 비교하지 말아야 한다.
✔ 부모는 자녀의 영재성을 지나치게 자랑하지 말아야 한다.
③ 영재교육 프로그램에 대한 맹목적인 믿음을 삼가야 한다.
④ 과도한 영재교육보다 자녀와의 좋은 관계 유지에 힘써야 한다.
⑤ 자녀의 독립성을 기르기 위해 자기 일은 스스로 하게 해야 한다.

As the parent of a gifted child, / you need to be aware of / a certain common parent trap.
재능 있는 아이의 부모로서, / 인식해야 한다. / 흔히 빠지기 쉬운 부모의 함정에 대해

Of course you are a proud parent, / and you should be.
물론 당신은 자랑스러운 부모일 것이며, / 그래야 마땅하다.

While it is very easy / to talk nonstop about your little genius / and his or her remarkable behavior, / this can be very stressful on your child.
매우 쉬운 일이지만, / 당신의 작은 천재에 대해 끊임없이 이야기하는 것은 / 그리고 그들의 놀라운 행동에 / 이것은 아이에게 매우 스트레스를 줄 수 있다.

It is extremely important / to limit your bragging behavior / to your very close friends, or your parents.
매우 중요하다. / 당신의 자랑을 제한하는 것이 / 매우 가까운 친구들이나 부모에게만

Gifted children / feel pressured / when their parents show them off too much.
재능 있는 아이들은 / 부담을 느낀다. / 부모가 자신을 너무 과시하면

This behavior creates expectations / that they may not be able to live up to, / and also creates a false sense of self for your child.
이런 행동은 기대를 만들어낸다 / 아이가 충족할 수 없을지도 모르는 / 또한 아이에게 잘못된 자아 인식을 심어줄 수 있다.

You want your child to be who they are, / not who they seem to be as defined / by their incredible achievements.
당신은 아이가 있는 그대로의 사람이 되길 원할 것이다. / 정의된 사람이 아니라, / 그들의 놀라운 성과로

If not, / you could end up with a driven perfectionist child / or perhaps a drop-out, or worse.
그렇지 않으면, / 당신은 완벽주의에 집착하는 아이나 학교를 그만두는 아이, 혹은 더 나쁜 결과를 마주할 수 있다.

영재의 부모로서, 당신은 어떤 흔한 부모의 덫을 주의할 필요가 있다. 물론, 당신은 자랑스러워하는 부모이고, 그리고 그래야 한다. 당신의 작은 천재와 그 또는 그녀의 놀라운 행동에 대해서 쉬지 않고 말하는 것은 매우 쉬우나, 이것은 당신의 아이에게 매우 스트레스가 될 수 있다. 당신의 자랑하는 행동을 당신의 아주 가까운 친구나, 당신의 부모에게로 제한하는 것이 매우 중요하다. 영재는 그들의 부모가 지나치게 그들을 자랑할 때 부담을 느낀다. 이러한 행동은 그들이 부응할 수 없을지도 모르는 기대를 만들고, 또한 당신의 자녀에게 있어 잘못된 자의식을 만든다. 당신은 당신의 자녀가 그들의 엄청난 업적에 의해서 규정지어진 대로 보이는 누군가가 아니라 있는 그대로의 그들이기를 바란다. 그렇지 않으면, 당신은 결국 지나친 완벽주의자 아이 또는 아마도 학업 중단자이거나 그보다 더 안 좋은 것을 마주하게 될 것이다.

Why? 왜 정답일까?

영재 부모가 아이에 대한 자랑을 과도하게 하면 아이가 부담을 느껴 문제를 일으킬 수도 있다고 하였으므로(This behavior creates expectations that they may not be able to live up to, and also creates a false sense of self for your child.), 필자가 주장하는 바로 가장 적절한 것은 ② '부모는 자녀의 영재성을 지나치게 자랑하지 말아야 한다.'이다.

- gifted ⓐ 재능이 있는
- remarkable ⓐ 눈에 띄는
- brag ⓥ 자랑하다
- incredible ⓐ 놀라운
- be aware of 알고 있다
- limit ⓥ 한정하다
- expectation ⓝ 기대
- achievement ⓝ 달성

구문 풀이

10행 You want your child to be who they are, not who they seem to
주격관계대명사 / 주격관계대명사
be as defined by their incredible achievements.
수동태+행위자

---

21 자조 집단의 힘 　　정답률 74% | 정답 ⑤

밑줄 친 "hanging out with the winners"가 다음 글에서 의미하는 바로 가장 적절한 것은?

① staying with those who sacrifice themselves for others
타인을 위해 스스로를 희생한 사람들과 지내기
② learning from people who have succeeded in competition
경쟁에서 이긴 사람들로부터 배우기
③ keeping relationships with people in a higher social position
높은 사회적 지위에 있는 사람들과의 관계를 유지하기
④ spending time with those who need social skill development
사회적 기술 발달을 필요로 하는 사람들과 시간을 보내기
✔ being with positive people who have overcome negative states
부정적인 상태를 극복한 긍정적인 사람들과 함께 있기

One valuable technique / for getting out of helplessness, depression, and situations / which are predominantly being run by the thought, / "I can't," / is to choose to be with other persons / who have resolved the problem / with which we struggle.
하나의 유용한 기법은 / 무력감, 우울증, 상황에서 벗어나는 / 그리고 생각이 주로 지배하는 / "나는 할 수 없어."라는 / 사람들과 함께 있는 것을 선택하는 것이다. / 문제를 해결한 / 우리가 겪고 있는

This is one of the great powers / of self-help groups.
이것이 큰 힘 중 하나이다. / 자기계발 그룹의

When we are in a negative state, / we have given a lot of energy to negative thought forms, / and the positive thought forms are weak.
우리가 부정적인 상태에 있을 때, / 우리는 많은 에너지를 부정적인 사고 형태에 주며, / 긍정적인 사고 형태는 약해진다.

Those who are in a higher vibration / are free of the energy / from their negative thoughts / and have energized positive thought forms.
더 높은 진동 상태에 있는 사람들은 / 에너지로부터 자유롭다. / 그들의 부정적인 생각에서부터의 / 그리고 긍정적인 사고 형태에 에너지를 불어넣는다.

Merely to be in their presence / is beneficial.
그들 곁에 있는 것만으로도 / 유익하다.

In some self-help groups, / this is called "hanging out with the winners."
일부 자기계발 그룹에서는 / 이것을 "승자들과 함께 어울리기"라고 부른다.

The benefit here / is on the psychic level of consciousness, / and there is a transfer / of positive energy / and relighting of one's own latent positive thought forms.
여기서의 이점은 / 의식의 심리적 차원에서 발생하며, / 전이가 있다. / 긍정적인 에너지의 / 그리고 자신의 잠재된 긍정적 사고 형태가 다시 불붙는 것

'무력함, 우울감, 그리고 '나는 할 수 없다'는 생각에 의해 현저히 지배당하는 상황에서 벗어나기 위한 한 가지 유용한 기술은 우리가 분투하고 있는 문제를 해결해 본 타인과 함께 있기로 선택하는 것이다. 이것은 자조 집단의 큰 힘 중 하나이다. 우리가 부정적인 상태에 있을 때, 우리는 부정적인 사고 형태에 많은 에너지를 투입해 왔고 긍정적인 사고 형태는 약하다. 더 높은 진동에 있는 사람들은 그들의 부정적인 사고에서 나오는 에너지가 없고, 긍정적인 사고 형태를 활기 띠게 했다. 단지 그들이 있는 자리에 있기만 하는 것도 유익하다. 일부 자조 집단에서 이것은 '승자들과 어울리기'라고 불린다. 여기에서의 이점은 의식의 정신적 수준에 있으며, 긍정적인 에너지의 전달과 자신의 잠재적인 긍정적 사고 형태의 재점화가 있다.

Why? 왜 정답일까?

자조 집단의 장점은 겪고 있는 어려움을 극복한 누군가의 에너지를 받는 것이라 얘기하고 있으므로(The benefit here is on the psychic level of consciousness, and there is a transfer of positive energy and relighting of one's own latent positive thought forms), "hanging out with the winners"가 글에서 의미하는 바는 ⑤ 'being with positive people who have overcome negative states'이다.

- valuable ⓐ 가치있는
- predominantly [ad] 지배적인
- state ⓝ 상태
- beneficial ⓐ 혜택의
- latent ⓐ 잠재적인
- technique ⓝ 기술
- negative ⓐ 부정적인
- vibration ⓝ 진동
- consciousness ⓝ 의식

구문 풀이

7행 Those who are in a higher vibration are free of the energy from their
지시대명사 주격관계대명사 / 동사1
negative thoughts and have energized positive thought forms.
동사2

다음 글의 요지로 가장 적절한 것은?
① 과거의 경험이 현재의 감정에 영향을 미친다.
② 문명의 발달에 따라 인간의 감정은 다양화되어 왔다.
✓ 감정은 인간이 생존하도록 도와왔기 때문에 존재한다.
④ 부정적인 감정은 긍정적인 감정보다 더 오래 기억된다.
⑤ 두려움의 원인을 파악함으로써 두려움을 없앨 수 있다.

Our emotions are thought to exist / because they have contributed to / our survival as a species.
우리의 감정은 존재한다고 여겨진다. / 왜냐하면 그것들이 기여했기 때문이다. / 우리 종족의 생존에

Fear has helped us avoid dangers, / expressing anger helps us scare off threats, / and expressing positive emotions helps us bond with others.
두려움은 우리가 위험을 피하도록 도와주었고, / 분노를 표현하는 것은 위협을 몰아내는 데 도움을 주며, / 긍정적인 감정을 표현하는 것은 우리가 다른 사람들과 유대감을 형성하도록 돕는다.

From an evolutionary perspective, / an emotion is a kind of "program" that, / when triggered, directs many of our activities.
진화적인 관점에서, / 감정은 일종의 '프로그램'이다. / 그것이 촉발될 때, 우리의 많은 활동을 지시하는

For example, / fear makes us very attentive, / narrows our perceptual focus to threatening stimuli, / will cause us either to face a situation (fight) or avoid it (flight), / and may cause us to remember an experience more acutely.
예를 들어, / 두려움은 우리를 매우 주의 깊게 만들고, / 우리의 지각 초점을 위협적인 자극으로 좁히며, / 상황에 맞서거나 (싸우거나) 피하도록 하고 (달아나도록), / 더 날카롭게 경험을 기억하게 만들 수 있다.

So that we avoid the threat in the future.
그리하여 우리가 미래에 그 위협을 피할 수 있게 된다.

Regardless of the specific ways / in which they activate our systems, / the specific emotions we possess / are thought to exist / because they have helped us (as a species) survive challenges within our environment long ago.
특정 방식과 상관없이 / 그것들이 우리의 시스템을 활성화하는 / 우리가 가진 특정 감정들은 / 존재한다고 여겨진다 / 우리가 (종족으로서) 도전에 생존할 수 있도록 도왔기 때문에 / 오래 전 우리의 환경에서

If they had not helped us adapt and survive, / they would not have evolved with us.
만약 그것들이 우리가 적응하고 생존하는 것을 돕지 않았다면, / 그것들은 우리와 함께 진화하지 않았을 것이다.

우리의 감정은 그것들이 종으로서 우리의 생존에 기여해 왔기 때문에 존재한다고 여겨진다. 두려움은 우리가 위험을 피하는 데 도움을 주어 왔고, 분노를 표현하는 것은 우리가 위협을 쫓아내도록 돕고, 긍정적인 감정을 표현하는 것은 우리가 다른 사람과 유대하도록 돕는다. 진화적 관점에서, 감정은 유발될 때 (주의, 지각, 기억, 움직임, 표현 등을 포함하는) 우리의 많은 활동을 지시하는 일종의 '프로그램'이다. 예를 들어, 두려움은 우리를 매우 주의 깊게 만들고, 우리의 지각의 초점을 위협적인 자극으로 좁히고, 우리로 하여금 상황을 정면으로 대하거나 (싸우거나) 그것을 피하도록 (도피하도록) 하며, 우리로 하여금 경험을 더 강렬하게 기억하도록 (그래서 우리가 미래에 위협을 피하도록) 할 수도 있다. 그것들이 우리의 시스템을 활성화하는 구체적인 방식과는 관계없이, 우리가 소유한 특정한 감정은 그것들이 오래전에 우리의 환경 내에서 우리가 (종으로서) 힘든 상황에서 생존하도록 도움을 주어 왔기 때문에 존재한다고 여겨진다. 만약 그것들이 우리가 적응하고 생존하도록 도움을 주지 않았더라면 그것들은 우리와 함께 진화해 오지 않았을 것이다.

Why? 왜 정답일까?
감정은 인간의 생존에 이롭기 때문에 존재했다고 얘기하고 있기 때문에(**Regardless of the specific ways in which they activate our systems, the specific emotions we possess are thought to exist because they have helped us (as a species) survive challenges within our environment long ago.**), 글의 요지로 가장 적절한 것은 ③ '감정은 인간이 생존하도록 도와왔기 때문에 존재한다.'이다.

● contribute ⓥ 기여하다
● avoid ⓥ 피하다
● perspective ⓝ 관점, 시각
● fear ⓝ 공포, 두려움, 무서움
● environment ⓝ 환경
● survival ⓝ 생존
● scare off 겁을 줘 쫓아내다
● trigger ⓥ 야기하다
● perceptual @ 지각의
● evolve ⓥ 진화하다

구문 풀이

1행 Our emotions are thought to exist because they have contributed to our survival as a species.
    (수동태)   (to부정사 (명사적 용법))   (현재완료)

다음 글의 주제로 가장 적절한 것은?
① jobs replaced by AI in the labour market
노동 시장에서 AI에 의해 대체된 직업들
② ethical issues caused by using AI in the workplace
AI를 직장에서 사용하며 발생하는 도덕적 문제들
③ necessity of using AI technology for language learning
언어 학습을 위해 AI를 사용하는 것의 필요성
✓ impacts of AI on supporting workers with disadvantages
장애가 있는 노동자들을 지원하는 AI의 영향
⑤ new designs of AI technology to cure people with disabilities
장애를 가진 사람들을 치료하기 위한 AI 기술의 새로운 디자인

By improving accessibility of the workplace / for workers / that are typically at a disadvantage / in the labour market, / AI can improve / inclusiveness in the workplace.
직장에서의 접근성을 향상시킴으로써 / 노동자를 위해 / 일반적으로 노동시장에서 불리한 / AI가 향상시킬 수 있다. / 직장에서 포용성을

AI-powered assistive devices / to aid workers / with visual, speech or hearing difficulties / are becoming more widespread, / improving the access to, / and the quality of work for people with disabilities.
AI 기반의 보조적 기구는 / 노동자를 돕기 위한 / 시각, 말하기 또는 청각적 불편함이 있는 / 더 널리 퍼지고 있다. / 접근성을 높이며 / 그리고 장애가 있는 사람들의 일의 질을

For example, / speech recognition solutions for people with dysarthric voices, / or live captioning systems / for deaf and hard of hearing people / can facilitate communication with colleagues / and access to jobs where inter-personal communication is necessary.
예를 들어, / 음성 인식 솔루션이나 / 발음이 부정확한 사람들을 위한 / 실시간 자막 시스템은 / 청각 장애인들을 위한 / 동료들과의 의사소통을 돕고, / 대인관계 소통이 필요한 직업에 대한 접근을 가능하게 한다.

AI can also enhance the capabilities of low-skilled workers, / with potentially positive effects / on their wages and career prospects.
AI는 또한 저숙련 근로자의 능력을 향상시킬 수 있으며, / 이는 긍정적인 영향을 미칠 수 있다. / 그들의 임금과 경력 전망에

For example, / AI's capacity to translate written and spoken word in real-time / can improve the performance of non-native speakers in the workplace.
예를 들어, / AI의 실시간 번역 능력은 / 비원어민 근로자들의 직장 내 성과를 향상시킬 수 있다.

Moreover, recent developments in AI-powered text generators / can instantly improve the performance of lower-skilled individuals / in domains such as writing, coding or customer service.
또한, 최근 AI 기반 텍스트 생성기의 발전은 / 저숙련 근로자들의 성과를 즉시 향상시킬 수 있다. / 글쓰기, 코딩, 고객 서비스와 같은 분야에서

노동 시장에서 일반적으로 불리한 위치에 있는 노동자를 위한 일터로의 접근성을 향상시킴으로써, AI는 일터에서 포괄성을 향상시킬 수 있다. 시각, 발화 또는 청각 장애가 있는 노동자들을 돕기 위한 AI 동력의 보조 장치들이 더 널리 보급되어, 장애를 지닌 사람들의 업무 접근성과 업무의 질을 향상시키고 있다. 예를 들어, 구음 장애가 있는 사람들을 위한 발화 인식 솔루션이나 청각 장애인과 난청인을 위한 실시간 자막 시스템은 동료와의 의사소통과 대인 의사소통이 필요한 일에 대한 접근을 용이하게 할 수 있다. AI는 또한 그들의 임금과 경력 전망에 잠재적으로 긍정적인 영향과 함께 저숙련 노동자들의 능력을 향상시킬 수 있다. 예를 들어, 문자 언어와 음성 언어를 실시간으로 번역하는 AI의 능력은 일터에서 비원어민의 수행을 향상시킬 수 있다. 게다가, 최근의 AI 동력의 텍스트 생성기의 발전은 글쓰기, 코딩, 고객 서비스와 같은 영역에서 저숙련된 개인의 수행을 즉시 향상시킬 수 있다.

Why? 왜 정답일까?
AI가 노동 시장에서 미칠 수 있는 긍정적인 영향을 언급하고 있기 때문에(**By improving accessibility of the workplace for workers that are typically at a disadvantage in the labour market, AI can improve inclusiveness in the workplace.**), 글의 주제로 가장 적절한 것은 ④ 'impacts of AI on supporting workers with disadvantages'이다.

● accessibility ⓝ 접근, 접근하기 쉬움
● workplace ⓝ 직장
● device ⓝ 기기
● dysarthric @ 구음 장애의
● enhance ⓥ 향상시키다
● development ⓝ 발달
● disadvantage ⓝ 불리한 점
● assistive @ 도와주는
● aid ⓥ 돕다
● colleague ⓝ 동료
● wage ⓝ 임금
● individiaul ⓝ 개인

구문 풀이

3행 AI-powered assistive devices to aid workers with visual, speech or
                            (to부정사(부사적 용법))
hearing difficulties are becoming more widespread, improving the access to, and
                (동사)   (현재분사(향상시키며))
the quality of work for people with disabilities.

다음 글의 제목으로 가장 적절한 것은?
✓ Saving Whales Saves the Earth and Us – 고래를 살리는 것이 지구와 우리를 살린다
② What Makes Whales Go Extinct in the Ocean – 바다에서 고래를 멸종하게 하는 것
③ Why Is Overpopulation of Whales Dangerous? – 왜 과도한 개체수의 고래가 위험할까?
④ Black Money: Lies about the Whaling Industry – 검은 돈: 고래 산업에 대한 거짓말
⑤ Climate Change and Its Effect on Whale Habitats – 기후 변화와 고래 거주지에 끼치는 영향

Whales are highly efficient at carbon storage.
고래는 탄소 저장에 매우 효율적이다.

When they die, / each whale sequesters an average of 30 tons of carbon dioxide, / taking that carbon out of the atmosphere for centuries.
고래가 죽을 때, / 각각의 고래는 평균적으로 30톤의 이산화 탄소를 격리하며, / 이 탄소를 수세기 동안 대기에서 제거한다.

For comparison, / the average tree absorbs only 48 pounds of CO_2 a year.
비교하자면, / 평균적인 나무는 매년 48파운드의 CO_2만을 흡수한다.

From a climate perspective, / each whale is the marine equivalent of thousands of trees.
기후 관점에서, / 각각의 고래는 수천 그루의 나무에 해당하는 해양 생물이다.

Whales also help sequester carbon / by fertilizing the ocean as they release nutrient-rich waste, / in turn increasing phytoplankton populations, / which also sequester carbon — / leading some scientists to call them the "engineers of marine ecosystems."
고래는 또한 탄소 격리에 도움을 주는데 / 영양이 풍부한 배설물을 방출하여 바다를 비옥하게 만들고, / 그 결과 식물성 플랑크톤의 개체 수를 증가시키며, / 이는 또한 탄소를 격리한다 — / 이로 인해 일부 과학자들은 고래를 "해양 생태계의 엔지니어"라고 부른다.

In 2019, economists from the International Monetary Fund (IMF) / estimated the value of the ecosystem services provided by each whale at over $2 million USD.
2019년에, 국제통화기금(IMF)의 경제학자들은 / 각각의 고래가 제공하는 생태계 서비스의 가치를 200만 달러 이상으로 추산했다.

They called for a new global program of economic incentives / to return whale populations to preindustrial whaling levels / as one example of a "nature-based solution" to climate change.
그들은 새로운 글로벌 경제적 인센티브 프로그램을 촉구했다. / 고래 개체 수를 산업화 이전의 포경 수준으로 되돌리기 위해 / 기후 변화에 대한 "자연 기반 해결책"의 한 예로서

Calls are now being made / for a global whale restoration program, / to slow down climate change.
현재 / 글로벌 고래 복원 프로그램에 대한 요청이 이루어지고 있다. / 기후 변화를 늦추기 위해

고래는 탄소 저장에 매우 효율적이다. 그들이 죽을 때, 각각의 고래는 평균 30톤의 이산화 탄소를 격리하며, 수 세기 동안 대기로부터 그 탄소를 빼내어 둔다. 비교하자면, 평균적인 나무는 연간 48파운드의 이산화 탄소만을 흡수한다. 기후의 관점에서 각각의 고래는 수천 그루의 나무에 상응하는 바다에 사는 것이다. 고래는 또한 영양이 풍부한 배설물을 내보내면서 바다를 비옥하게 함으로써 탄소를 격리하는 데 도움을 주는데, 결과적으로 식물성 플랑크톤 개체를 증가시키고 이는 또한 탄소를 격리한다. 그리하여 몇몇 과학자들은 그들을 '해양 생태계의 기술자'라고 부르게 되었다. 2019년 국제 통화 기금(IMF)의 경제학자들은 각각의 고래에 의해서 제공되는 생태계 서비스의 가치를 미화 200만 달러가 넘게 추정했다. 그들은 기후 변화에 대한 '자연 기반 해결책'의 한 예로서 고래 개체수를 산업화 이전의 고래잡이 수준으로 되돌리기 위한 새로운 글로벌 경제적 인센티브 프로그램을 요구했다. 기후 변화를 늦추기 위해 세계적인 고래 복원 프로그램에 대한 요구가 현재 제기되고 있다.

Why? 왜 정답일까?

고래가 탄소를 저장하고, 바다를 비옥하게 하여 환경에 긍정적인 영향을 끼치며, 국제 통화 기금은 고래 개체수를 늘려야 한다고 주장하고 있기 때문에(They called for a new global program of economic incentives to return whale populations to preindustrial whaling levels as one example of a "nature-based solution" to climate change.), 제목으로 가장 적절한 것은 ① 'Saving Whales Saves the Earth and Us'이다.

- efficient ⓐ 효율적인
- atmosphere ⓝ 대기
- equivalent ⓐ 상응하는, 상당하는
- increase ⓥ 증가하다
- economist ⓝ 경제학자
- solution ⓝ 해결책
- sequester ⓥ 격리하다
- comparison ⓝ 대조
- absorb ⓥ 흡수하다
- population ⓝ 개체군, 개체 수
- estimate ⓥ 추산하다
- climate ⓝ 기후

구문 풀이

1행 When they die, each whale sequesters an average of 30 tons of carbon
~할 때   각각의 단수명사
dioxide, taking that carbon out of the atmosphere for centuries.
현재분사

---

25 2022년 국가별 1인당 이산화 탄소 배출량   정답률 79% | 정답 ④

다음 도표의 내용과 일치하지 <u>않는</u> 것은?

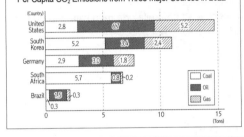

Per Capita CO₂ Emissions from Three Major Sources in 2022

The above graph shows per capita CO₂ emissions / from coal, oil, and gas by countries in 2022.
위 그래프는 각국의 1인당 CO₂ 배출량을 보여준다. / 2022년의 석탄, 석유, 가스에 의한

① The United States had the highest total per capita CO₂ emissions, / even though its emissions from coal were the second lowest among the five countries shown.
미국은 총 1인당 CO₂ 배출량이 가장 높았으나, / 석탄에 의한 배출량은 다섯 나라 중 두 번째로 낮았다.

② South Korea's total per capita CO₂ emissions were over 10 tons, / ranking it the second highest among the countries shown.
한국의 총 1인당 CO₂ 배출량은 10톤을 넘었으며, / 표시된 국가들 중 두 번째로 높았다.

③ Germany had lower CO₂ emissions per capita than South Korea / in all three major sources respectively.
독일은 세 주요 원천에서 / 각각 한국보다 1인당 CO₂ 배출량이 더 낮았다.

✔ The per capita CO₂ emissions from coal in South Africa / were over three times higher than those in Germany.
남아프리카의 석탄에 의한 1인당 CO₂ 배출량은 / 독일보다 세 배 이상 높았다.

⑤ In Brazil, oil was the largest source of CO₂ emissions per capita / among its three major sources, / just as it was in the United States and Germany.
브라질에서는 석유가 1인당 CO₂ 배출의 가장 큰 원천이었으며, / 이는 미국과 독일에서도 마찬가지였다.

위 그래프는 2022년의 국가별 석탄, 석유, 천연가스에서 나온 1인당 이산화 탄소 배출량을 보여 준다. ① 석탄에서 나온 배출량은 보여진 다섯 개의 국가 중 두 번째로 낮았음에도 불구하고, 미국은 가장 높은 1인당 이산화 탄소 총배출량을 가졌다. ② 한국의 1인당 이산화 탄소 총배출량은 10톤이 넘고, 보여진 국가 중 두 번째로 높은 순위를 차지했다. ③ 독일은 한국보다 각각의 모든 세 가지 주요 원천에서 더 낮은 1인당 이산화 탄소 배출량을 가졌다. ④ 남아프리카 공화국의 석탄으로부터의 1인당 이산화 탄소 배출량은 독일의 그것보다 세 배보다 더 높았다. ⑤ 브라질에서 석유는 브라질의 세 가지 주요한 원천 중에서 1인당 이산화 탄소 배출량의 가장 큰 원천이었고, 그것은 미국과 독일에서도 마찬가지였다.

Why? 왜 정답일까?

남아프리카 공화국의 석탄으로부터의 1인당 이산화 탄소 배출량은 5.7톤이고, 독일의 석탄으로부터의 1인당 이산화 탄소 배출량은 2.9톤이기 때문에 도표의 내용과 일치하지 않는 것은 ④이다.

- emission ⓝ 배출량
- rank ⓥ 순위에 들다
- source ⓝ 원천
- per capita 1인당
- major ⓐ 주요한

구문 풀이

2행 The United States had the highest total per capita CO₂ emissions,
최상급
even though its emissions from coal were the second lowest among the five
비록   주어
countries shown.

---

26 Émilie du Châtelet의 일생   정답률 70% | 정답 ②

Émilie du Châtelet에 관한 다음 글의 내용과 일치하지 <u>않는</u> 것은?

① 어린 시절에 수학과 과학 교육을 받았다.
✔ 불의 속성에 관한 그녀의 논문이 1737년에 출간되었다.
③ Institutions de Physique에서 공간과 시간의 개념을 설명했다.
④ 아이작 뉴턴의 Principia를 프랑스어로 번역했다.
⑤ 이룩한 업적은 당대에 인정받지 못했다.

Émilie du Châtelet, a French mathematician and physicist, / was born in Paris in 1706.

프랑스의 수학자이자 물리학자인 Émilie du Châtele는 / 1706년에 파리에서 태어났다.
「During her childhood, / with her father's support, / she was able to get mathematical and scientific education / that most women of her time did not receive.」 **①의 근거** 일치
어린 시절에, / 아버지의 지원으로 / 그녀는 수학과 과학 교육을 받을 수 있었다. / 당시 대부분의 여성들이 받지 못했던
「In 1737, / she submitted her paper on the nature of fire / to a contest sponsored by the French Academy of Sciences, / and it was published a year later.」 **②의 근거** 불일치
1737년에, / 그녀는 불의 본질에 관한 논문을 제출했다. / French Academy of Sciences가 주최한 경연에 / 그리고 그것은 1년 후에 출판되었다.
「In her book, Institutions de Physique, / Émilie du Châtelet explained the ideas of space and time / in a way that is closer to what we understand in modern relativity / than what was common during her time.」 **③의 근거** 일치
그녀의 책 Institutions de Physique에서, / Émilie du Châtelet는 공간과 시간에 대한 개념을 설명했다. / 우리가 현대의 상대성 이론에서 이해하는 방식에 더 가까운 / 그녀 시대의 일반적인 이해보다
「Her most significant achievement / was translating Isaac Newton's Principia into French / near the end of her life.」 **④의 근거** 일치
그녀의 가장 중요한 업적은 / 아이작 뉴턴의 Principia를 프랑스어로 번역한 것이다. / 그녀 생애 말년에 **⑤의 근거** 일치
「Émilie du Châtelet's work was not recognized in her time, / but she is now remembered / as a symbol of the Enlightenment and the struggle for women's participation in science.」
Émilie du Châtelet의 업적은 그녀 생애 동안 인정받지 못했지만, / 현재 그녀는 기억되고 있다. / 계몽주의와 여성의 과학 참여 투쟁의 상징으로서

프랑스 수학자이자 물리학자인 Émilie du Châtelet는 1706년에 파리에서 태어났다. 어린 시절에 아버지의 도움으로 그녀는 당대 대부분의 여성들은 받지 못했던 수학과 과학 교육을 받을 수 있었다. 1737년에 그녀는 불의 속성에 관한 논문을 French Academy of Sciences에 의해 후원되는 대회에 제출했으며, 그것은 1년 후에 출간되었다. 그녀의 책 Institutions de Physique에서 Émilie du Châtelet는 당대에 일반적이었던 것보다 현대의 상대성 이론에서 우리가 이해하는 것에 더 가까운 방식으로 공간과 시간의 개념을 설명했다. 그녀의 가장 주요한 성과는 그녀의 말년 무렵 아이작 뉴턴의 Principia를 프랑스어로 번역한 것이었다. Émilie du Châtelet의 업적은 당대에 인정받지 못했지만, 현재 그녀는 계몽주의와 여성의 과학 분야 참여를 위한 투쟁의 상징으로 기억된다.

Why? 왜 정답일까?

'In 1737, she submitted her paper on the nature of fire to a contest sponsored by the French Academy of Sciences, and it was published a year later.'에서 논문이 출간된 것은 1738년임을 알 수 있기 때문에, 글의 내용과 일치하지 않는 것은 ② '불의 속성에 관한 그녀의 논문이 1737년에 출간되었다.'이다.

Why? 왜 오답일까?

① 'During her childhood, ~ she was able to get mathematical and scientific education ~ did not receive.'의 내용과 일치한다.
③ 'In her book, Institutions de Physique, Émilie du Châtelet explained the ideas of space and time ~ during her time'의 내용과 일치한다.
④ 'Her most significant achievement was translating Isaac Newton's Principia into French near the end of her life.'의 내용과 일치한다.
⑤ 'Émilie du Châtelet's work was not recognized in her time, ~ participatio in science.'의 내용과 일치한다.

- mathematician ⓝ 수학자
- childhood ⓝ 어린 시절
- receive ⓥ 받다
- publish ⓥ 출간하다
- relativity ⓝ 상대성 이론
- enlightenment ⓝ (18세기의) 계몽주의 시대
- physicist ⓝ 물리학자
- support ⓝ 지원
- submit ⓥ 제출하다
- explain ⓥ 설명하다
- significant ⓐ 중요한, 특별한 의미가 있는

구문 풀이

7행 In her book, Institutions de Physique, Émilie du Châtelet explained the ideas of space and time in a way that is closer to what we understand in modern
주격관계대명사   관계대명사1(the thing that)
relativity than what was common during her time.
관계대명사2(the thing that)

---

27 2024 청소년 발명가 로봇 대회 안내문   정답률 90% | 정답 ⑤

2024 Young Inventors Robot Competition에 관한 다음 안내문의 내용과 일치하지 <u>않는</u> 것은?

① 세 가지 분야 중 하나에 참가할 수 있다.
② 9월 28일에 5시간 동안 열린다.
③ 고등학생이 등록할 수 있다.
④ 등록은 온라인으로만 가능하다.
✔ 수상자는 각 분야당 한 명이다.

2024 Young Inventors Robot Competition
2024년 청소년 발명가 로봇 대회
Join us for an exciting day of the Young Inventors Robot Competition!
청소년 발명가 로봇 대회의 신나는 날에 참여하세요!
Categories
분류
「Participants can compete in one of the following categories:」 **①의 근거** 일치
참가자들은 아래의 분류 중 한 개의 대회에 참여할 수 있습니다:
Robot Design
로봇 디자인
Robot Coding
로봇 코딩
Robot Remote Control
로봇 원격 조종
Date and Time
날짜와 시간
「September 28, 2024, 10 a.m. to 3 p.m.」 **②의 근거** 일치
2024년 9월 28일, 오전 10시부터 오후 3시까지

Location
장소
Computer Lab, Oakwood University
Oakwood 대학교의 컴퓨터실
Registration
등록
From August 1 to August 10, 2024
2024년 8월 1일부터 8월 10일까지
『Open to high school students』 ③의근거 일치
고등학생들 등록 가능
『Online registration only (www.younginventors.edu)』 ④의근거 일치
온라인 등록만 받습니다 (www.younginventors.edu)
Awards
상품
『In each competition category, three participants will be honored.』 ⑤의근거 불일치
각각의 분류 대회에서 세 명의 참가자들이 수상합니다.
1st place: $300
1등: 300 달러
2nd place: $200
2등: 200 달러
3rd place: $100
3등: 100달러
For more information, visit our website.
더 많은 정보는 웹사이트를 방문해주세요.

2024 Young Inventors Robot Competition

Young Inventors Robot Competition의 신나는 날에 우리와 함께하세요!

□ 분야
- 참가자들은 다음 분야 중 하나에 참가할 수 있습니다.
  • 로봇 디자인   • 로봇 코딩   • 로봇 원격 조종

□ 날짜와 시간
- 2024년 9월 28일, 오전 10시부터 오후 3시까지

□ 장소
- Oakwood University 컴퓨터실

□ 등록
- 2024년 8월 1일부터 8월 10일까지
- 고등학생이 등록 가능
- 온라인 등록만 가능 (www.younginventors.edu)

□ 시상
- 각 경쟁 분야에서 세 명의 참가자가 수상할 것입니다.
  • 1등: 300달러   • 2등: 200달러   • 3등: 100달러

※ 더 많은 정보를 원하시면, 저희 웹사이트를 방문하세요

Why? 왜 정답일까?
'Awards' 항목의 'In each competition category, three participants will be honored.'의 문장을 보았을 때, 각 분야당 수상자는 세 명이므로 안내문과 일치하지 않는 것은 ⑤ '수상자는 각 분야당 한 명이다.'이다.

Why? 왜 오답일까?
① 'Categories' 아래의 내용에서 참가자들은 주어진 세 가지 분야 중 하나에 참가할 수 있다고 제시한다.
② 'September 28, 2024, 10 a.m. to 3 p.m.'의 내용과 일치한다.
③ 'Registration'의 'Open to high school students'의 내용과 일치한다.
④ 'Online registration only'의 내용과 일치한다.

● inventor ⓝ 발명가
● category ⓝ 분류
● registration ⓝ 등록
● competition ⓝ 대회
● participant ⓝ 참여자

---

28 제8회 Saintville Art Week 스탬프 투어 안내   정답률 90% | 정답 ③

Saintville Art Week Stamp Tour에 관한 다음 안내문의 내용과 일치하는 것은?
① 참가 대상에 제한이 있다.
② 10월 둘째 주에 진행된다.
✓ Saintville Arts Center에서 스탬프 투어 지도를 받는다.
④ 적어도 다섯 곳에서 도장을 받아야 선물을 받는다.
⑤ 선물로 가방과 머그잔 중 하나를 고를 수 있다.

Saintville Art Week Stamp Tour
Saintville Art 주 스탬프 투어
The 8th annual Saintville Art Week Stamp Tour is back this year!
올해 연례 Saintville Art 주 8회 스탬프 투어가 돌아왔습니다!
『Anyone can participate in our event.』 ①의근거 불일치
누구나 행사에 참여 가능합니다.
Join us and enjoy exhibitions and new collections.
참여하시고 전시회와 새 수집품을 즐기세요.
When: 『The first week of October, 2024』 ②의근거 불일치
언제: 2024년 10월 첫째 주
Where: Saintville Arts District
어디서: Saintville Arts 구역
How:
어떻게:
Step 1. 『Take a stamp tour map from the Saintville Arts Center.』 ③의근거 일치
1단계. Saintville Arts Center에서 스탬프 투어 지도를 가져가세요.
Step 2. 『Get stamps from at least 3 out of 5 spots and receive your gift.』 ④의근거 불일치
2단계. 5 곳 중 최소 3 곳에서 스탬프를 찍고 선물을 받으세요.
『You can choose either an umbrella or a mug with printed artwork on it for your gift.』
선물로 우산 또는 예술품이 그려진 머그컵을 고를 수 있습니다. ⑤의근거 불일치

For more information, please visit our website at www.SaintvilleArtsCenter.com.
더 많은 정보는 우리의 웹사이트 www.SaintvilleArtsCenter.com.를 방문하세요.

Saintville Art Week Stamp Tour

해마다 열리는 8번째 Saintville Art Week Stamp Tour가 올해도 돌아왔습니다! 누구나 우리의 행사에 참가할 수 있습니다. 우리와 함께하여 전시와 새로운 컬렉션을 즐겨 보세요.

□ 언제: 2024년 10월 첫째 주
□ 어디서: Saintville Arts District
□ 어떻게:
  1단계: Saintville Arts Center에서 스탬프 투어 지도를 받으세요.
  2단계: 다섯 곳 중 적어도 세 곳에서 도장을 받고 선물을 받으세요.
  - 예술 작품이 인쇄된 우산이나 머그잔 중 하나를 선물로 선택할 수 있습니다.

※ 더 많은 정보를 원하시면, 저희 웹사이트 www.SaintvilleArtsCenter.com을 방문해 주세요.

Why? 왜 정답일까?
'Take a stamp tour map from the Saintville Arts Center.'에서 Saintville Arts Center에서 스탬프 투어 지도를 받는다고 안내하기 때문에 안내문의 내용과 일치하는 것은 ③이다.

Why? 왜 오답일까?
① 'Anyone can participate in our event.'라고 하였기 때문에 참가 대상에는 제한이 없다.
② 'The first week of October, 2024'에서 대회는 10월 첫째 주에 진행됨을 알 수 있다.
④ 'Get stamps from at least 3 out of 5 spots and receive your gift.'에서 선물을 받기 위해서는 세 곳에서만 도장을 받아도 된다고 알린다.
⑤ 'You can choose either an umbrella or a mug with printed artwork on it for your gift.'에서 선물로 우산과 머그잔 중 하나를 고를 수 있다고 안내한다.

● stamp ⓝ 도장
● participate ⓥ 참여하다
● join ⓥ 참여하다
● collectin ⓝ 수집품
● annual ⓐ 연간의
● event ⓝ 행사
● exhibition ⓝ 전시회

★★★ 등급을 가르는 문제!
29 터널 시야 현상   정답률 41% | 정답 ⑤

다음 글의 밑줄 친 부분 중, 어법상 틀린 것은?

From an organizational viewpoint, / one of the most fascinating examples / of how any organization may contain many different types of culture / ① is to recognize / the functional operations of different departments within the organization.
조직적 관점에서, / 가장 흥미로운 예 중 하나는 / 조직 내에 다양한 유형의 문화가 존재할 수 있다는 / 인식하는 것이다. / 조직 각 부서의 기능적 운영을

The varying departments / and divisions within an organization / will inevitably view any given situation / from their own biased and prejudiced perspective.
다양한 부서와 / 조직 내의 부문은 / 필연적으로 주어진 상황을 바라볼 것이다. / 자신들의 편향되고 선입견이 있는 시각에서

A department and its members / will acquire "tunnel vision" / which disallows them / to see things as others see ② them.
부서와 그 구성원들은 / '터널 비전'을 가지게 되어, / 못하게 될 것이다. / 다른 사람들이 보는 방식으로 상황을 보지

The very structure of organizations / can create conflict.
조직의 구조 자체가 / 갈등을 일으킬 수 있다.

The choice of ③ whether the structure / is "mechanistic" or "organic" / can have a profound influence on conflict management.
구조를 선택하는 것은 / '기계적'인지 '유기적'인지를 / 갈등 관리에 깊은 영향을 미칠 수 있다.

A mechanistic structure has / a vertical hierarchy with many rules, / many procedures, / and many levels of management ④ involved in decision making.
기계적 구조는 가지고 있다. / 의사 결정에 관여하는 많은 규칙, 절차, / 그리고 여러 관리 계층을 가진 수직적 위계 구조를

Organic structures are more horizontal in nature, / ✓ where decision making is less centralized / and spread across the plane of the organization.
유기적 구조는 더 수평적인 성격을 가지며, / 의사 결정이 덜 중앙 집중화되고 / 조직 내 여러 곳에 분산된다.

조직의 관점에서, 어떤 조직이 어떻게 많은 다른 문화 유형들을 포함할 수 있는지에 대한 가장 매력적인 예시 중 하나는 조직 내 다른 부서들의 기능적 운영을 인식하는 것이다. 조직 내 다양한 부서와 과는 필연적으로 어떤 주어진 상황이라도 그들 자신만의 편향적이고 편파적인 관점에서 볼 것이다. 한 부서와 그 구성원들은 그들을 다른 이들이 그것들을 보는 대로 볼 수 없게 하는 '터널 시야 현상'을 갖게 될 것이다. 조직의 구조 자체가 갈등을 만들어낼 수 있다. 구조가 '기계적'인지 또는 '유기적'인지의 선택은 갈등 관리에 깊은 영향을 미칠 수 있다. 기계적 구조는 많은 규칙, 많은 절차 그리고 의사결정에 포함된 많은 수준의 관리를 가진 수직적 위계를 갖는다. 유기적 구조는 본래 더 수평적이고, 여기서는 의사결정이 덜 중앙 집중화되고, 조직 전반에 걸쳐 펼쳐진다.

Why? 왜 정답일까?
뒤 문장이 완전하므로 관계대명사 'which' 대신 관계부사 'where'이 쓰이는 것이 알맞다. 따라서 어법상 틀린 것은 ⑤이다.

Why? 왜 오답일까?
① 'is'의 주어가 'one of the most fascinationg examples'이므로 단수 be 동사 'is'가 적절히 쓰였다.
② 'tunnel vision'이 그들이 타인이 그들을 보듯이 스스로를 보는 것을 방해한다고 하였기 때문에 목적어 형태인 'them'이 알맞다.
③ 'whether A or B'는 A든지 B든지라는 숙어로, 적절하다.
④ '포함한'이라고 해석되어야 자연스러우므로 과거분사 'involved'는 적절하다.

● organizational ⓐ 구조적인
● fascinate ⓥ 멋지다
● functional ⓐ 기능상의, 기능적인
● acquire ⓥ 얻다
● influence ⓝ 영향
● viewpoint ⓝ 시각
● contain ⓥ 포함되다
● biased ⓐ 편향된, 선입견이 있는
● choice ⓝ 선택
● hierarchy ⓝ 계급, 계층

구문 풀이

1행 From an organizational viewpoint, one of the most fascinating examples
(one of the 복수명사 (단수취급))
of how any organization may contain many different types of culture is to recognize
(조동사+동사원형) (동사) (to부정사(부사적 용법))
the functional operations of different departments within the organization.

★★ 문제 해결 꿀~팁 ★★

▶ 많이 틀린 이유는?
관계대명사와 관계부사의 차이와 관계대명사의 쓰임을 알아야 풀 수 있는 문제이다. 관계대명사는 뒷 문장이 불완전하며, 선행사를 필요로 한다. 해당 문장에서는 뒷 문장이 완전하기 때문에 관계대명사가 아닌 관계부사가 쓰이는 것이 적절하다.

▶ 문제 해결 방법은?
관계부사와 관계대명사의 개념을 확실히 하자. 관계부사는 뒷 문장이 완전하고, 장소, 시간, 방법 등의 정해진 단어들로 교체가 가능하다. 관계대명사는 뒷 문장이 불완전하며, 선행사를 필요로 한다. 헷갈리는 문법적 개념은 나올 때마다 정리해두자.

---

30 친환경적인 도로 만들기 · 정답률 67% | 정답 ④

다음 글의 밑줄 친 부분 중, 문맥상 낱말의 쓰임이 적절하지 않은 것은? [3점]

An excellent alternative to calming traffic / is removing it.
교통을 진정시키는 훌륭한 대안은 / 그것을 제거하는 것이다.

Some cities ① reserve / an extensive network of lanes and streets / for bikes, pedestrians, and the occasional service vehicle.
일부 도시는 예약해 둔다. / 넓은 도로와 차선을 / 자전거, 보행자, 그리고 가끔 다니는 서비스 차량을 위해 /

This motivates people to travel by bike rather than by car, / making streets safer for everyone.
이것은 사람들이 자동차 대신 자전거로 이동하게 하며, / 모두에게 더 안전한 거리를 만든다.

As bicycles become more ② popular in a city, / planners can convert more automobile lanes and entire streets / to accommodate more of them.
자전거가 도시에 점점 더 인기를 얻게 되면서, / 도시 계획자들은 더 많은 자동차 차선과 전체 도로를 전환할 수 있다. / 자전거를 수용할 수 있도록

Nevertheless, / even the most bikeable cities still ③ require motor vehicle lanes / for taxis, emergency vehicles, and delivery trucks.
그럼에도 불구하고, / 자전거 친화적인 도시들도 여전히 자동차 차선이 필요하다. / 택시, 응급 차량, 그리고 배달 트럭을 위해

Delivery vehicles are frequently a target of animus, / but they are actually an essential component to making cities greener.
배달 차량은 자주 반감의 대상이 되지만, / 사실 그것들은 도시를 더 친환경적으로 만드는 데 중요한 요소이다.

A tightly packed delivery truck / is a far more ④ efficient transporter of goods / than several hybrids carrying a few shopping bags each.
가득 실린 배달 트럭은 / 몇 개의 쇼핑 가방을 나르는 여러 대의 하이브리드 자동차보다 / 훨씬 더 효율적인 화물 운송 수단이다.

Distributing food and other goods to neighborhood vendors / ⑤ allows them to operate smaller stores close to homes / so that residents can walk, rather than drive, to get their groceries.
음식과 기타 물품을 인근 상점에 배달함으로써 / 그들이 집 근처에서 더 작은 가게를 운영할 수 있도록 허용하며, / 주민들이 장을 보기 위해 차 대신 걸을 수 있게 한다.

교통을 진정시키는 훌륭한 대안은 그것을 제거하는 것이다. 몇몇 도시는 자전거, 보행자, 그리고 수시 서비스 차량을 위한 광범위한 망의 도로와 거리를 ① 마련해 둔다. 이것은 사람들이 자동차보다 자전거로 이동을 하도록 동기를 부여하여 거리를 모두에게 더 안전하게 만든다. 자전거가 도시에서 더 ② 대중적이 되면, 계획자들은 더 많은 자동차 도로와 전체 거리를 더 많은 자전거를 수용할 수 있도록 전환할 수 있다. 그럼에도 불구하고, 가장 자전거를 타기 좋은 도시들조차도 여전히 택시, 긴급 차량, 그리고 배달 트럭을 위한 자동차 도로를 ③ 필요로 한다. 배달 차량은 자주 반감의 대상이지만, 그것들은 실제로 도시를 더 친환경적으로 만드는 필수 구성요소이다. 짐이 빽빽하게 들어찬 배달 트럭은 각각 몇 개의 쇼핑백을 실은 여러 하이브리드 차량보다 훨씬 더 ④ 비효율적인(→ 효율적인) 상품 운송 수단이다. 음식과 다른 상품을 동네 상인에게 배포하는 것은 그들이 집에 가까운 더 작은 상점을 ⑤ 운영할 수 있게 하고 그 결과 주민들은 식료품을 사기 위해 운전하기보다는 걸어갈 수 있다.

Why? 왜 정답일까?
배달 차량이 반감을 사지만 실제로는 이점이 더 많기 때문에 여러 하이브리드 차량보다 효율적인 상품 운송 수단이라고 바꾸는 것이 자연스럽다. 따라서 정답은 ④ 'inefficient'이다.

- excellent ⓐ 훌륭한
- traffic ⓝ 교통
- pedestrian ⓝ 보행자
- popular ⓐ 인기있는
- accommodate ⓥ 공간을 제공하다, 수용하다
- animus ⓝ 반감, 적대감
- component ⓝ 요소, 부품
- alternative ⓝ 대체
- remove ⓥ 제거하다
- rather ⓐd 꽤, 약간, 상당히
- convert ⓥ 바꾸다
- delivery ⓝ 배송
- essential ⓐ 극히 중요한, 가장 중요한
- tightly ⓐd 단단히, 꽉

구문 풀이

14행 Distributing food and other goods to neighborhood vendors allows them
(동명사) (neighborhood) (동사)
to operate smaller stores close to homes so that residents can walk, rather than
(to부정사(부사적 용법)) (비교급) (그래서) (동사1)
drive, to get their groceries.
(동사2) (to부정사(부사적 용법))

★★★ 등급을 가르는 문제!

31 창작의 매력 · 정답률 31% | 정답 ②

다음 빈칸에 들어갈 말로 가장 적절한 것을 고르시오.
① simple – 단순한   ✓② original – 독창적인
③ familiar – 익숙한   ④ conventional – 전통적인
⑤ understandable – 이해할 수 있는

You hear again and again / that some of the greatest composers were misunderstood / in their own day.
당신은 계속해서 듣는다. / 가장 위대한 작곡가들 중 일부가 오해받았다는 이야기를 / 그들의 시대에는

Not everyone could understand the compositions / of Beethoven, Brahms, or Stravinsky / in their day.
모두가 이해할 수 있었던 것은 아니었다. / 베토벤, 브람스, 또는 스트라빈스키의 작품을 / 그들의 시대에

The reason for this initial lack of acceptance / is unfamiliarity.
이러한 초기의 받아들임 부족의 이유는 / 익숙하지 않음이다.

The musical forms, or ideas expressed within them, / were completely new.
그 음악 형식들, 혹은 그 안에 표현된 아이디어들은 / 완전히 새로웠다.

And yet, this is exactly one of the things / that makes them so great.
그리고 이 점이 바로 / 그들을 위대하게 만드는 것들 중 하나다.

Effective composers have their own ideas.
유능한 작곡가들은 자신만의 아이디어를 가지고 있다.

Have you ever seen the classic movie *Amadeus?*
당신은 고전 영화 *Amadeus*를 본 적이 있는가?

The composer Antonio Salieri is the "host" of this movie; / he's depicted as one of the most famous non-great composers.
작곡가 Antonio Salieri는 이 영화의 "주최자"이다; / 그는 가장 유명한 비위대한 작곡가 중 한 명으로 묘사된다.

He lived at the time of Mozart / and was completely overshadowed by him.
그는 모차르트와 같은 시대에 살았으며 / 완전히 그에 의해 가려졌다.

Now, Salieri wasn't a bad composer; / in fact, he was a very good one.
Salieri는 나쁜 작곡가가 아니었다; / 사실 그는 매우 훌륭한 작곡가였다.

But he wasn't one of the world's great composers / because his work wasn't original.
그러나 그는 세계의 위대한 작곡가 중 한 명이 아니었다. / 그의 작품이 독창적이지 않았기 때문에.

What he wrote / sounded just like what everyone else was composing / at the time.
그가 쓴 음악은 / 다른 모든 사람들이 작곡하던 것과 비슷하게 들렸다. / 그 당시에

여러분은 몇몇 가장 위대한 작곡가들이 그들의 시대에 진가를 인정받지 못했다고 몇 번이고 듣는다. 그들의 시대에 베토벤, 브람스, 스트라빈스키의 곡들을 모든 사람이 이해할 수 있었던 것은 아니었다. 이러한 초기의 수용 부족의 이유는 낯섦이다. 음악적 형식, 또는 그 안에 표현된 생각은 완전히 새로운 것이었다. 그럼에도 불구하고 이것이 바로 그들을 그토록 위대하게 만드는 것들 중 하나이다. 유능한 작곡가는 그들 자신만의 생각을 갖는다. 당신은 고전 영화 *Amadeus*를 본 적이 있는가? 작곡가 Antonio Salieri가 이 영화의 '주인공'이다. 그는 가장 유명한 위대하지 않은 작곡가 중 한 명으로 묘사된다. 그는 모차르트 시대에 살았고 그에 의해 완전히 가려졌다. 인제 보니 Salieri는 형편없는 작곡가가 아니었다. 사실, 그는 매우 훌륭한 작곡가였다. 하지만 그의 작품이 독창적이지 않았기 때문에 그는 세계의 위대한 작곡가들 중 한 명은 아니었다. 그가 쓴 곡은 마치 그 당시 모든 다른 사람들이 작곡했던 것처럼 들렸다.

Why? 왜 정답일까?
'What he wrote sounded just like what everyone else was composing at the time. (그가 쓴 곡은 마치 그 당시 모든 다른 사람들이 작곡했던 것처럼 들렸다.)'를 미루어 보아 작곡의 독창성이 중요하다고 얘기하고 있으므로 ② 'original'이 빈칸에 들어갈 말로 적절하다.

- composer ⓝ 작곡가
- composition ⓝ 구성
- initial ⓐ 초기의
- acceptance ⓝ 수락
- effective ⓐ 유능한
- misunderstand ⓥ 오해하다
- reason ⓝ 이유, 까닭, 사유
- lack ⓝ 부족, 결핍
- completely ⓐd 완전히
- depict ⓥ 묘사하다

구문 풀이

1행 You hear again and again that some of the greatest composers were
(지각동사) (again and again 계속해서) (접속사) (some of the 복수명사(복수취급))
misunderstood in their own day.

★★ 문제 해결 꿀~팁 ★★

▶ 많이 틀린 이유는?
Salieri가 위대한 작곡가가 아니었던 이유가 다른 사람들의 것과 차별성이 없었기 때문이라고 설명하는 글이다. 빈칸 문장의 다음 문장인 'What he wrote sounded just like what everyone else was composing at the time.'이 가장 분명한 힌트다. 가장 많이 고른 ③ 'familiar' (익숙한)은 ② 'original' (독창적인)과 반대의 뜻으로, 'Now, Salieri wasn't a bad composer; in fact, he was a very good one.'의 문장 때문에 헷갈릴 수 있다.

▶ 문제 해결 방법은?
주어진 빈칸의 문장이 접속사 'But'으로 시작하므로 앞의 내용과 반대되어야 자연스럽다. 빈 칸 문제는 본문의 주제와 글의 흐름을 파악해야 풀 수 있는데, 주로 접속사에서 큰 힌트를 얻을 수 있다.

---

32 메시지에 매체가 끼치는 영향 · 정답률 49% | 정답 ①

다음 빈칸에 들어갈 말로 가장 적절한 것을 고르시오. [3점]

✓① see the world according to a new set of codes – 새로운 코드에 따라 세상을 바라보다.
② ignore unfamiliar messages from new media – 새로운 매체에서의 낯선 메시지를 무시하다.
③ maintain steady focus and clear understanding – 꾸준한 집중과 명료한 이해를 유지하다.
④ interpret information through a traditional lens – 전통적인 렌즈를 통해 정보를 해석하다.
⑤ enjoy various media contents with one platform – 한가지 매체에서 다양한 미디어 콘텐츠를 즐기다.

Every time a new medium comes along / — whether it's the invention of the printed book, or TV, or SNS — / and you start to use it, / it's like you are putting on a new kind of goggles, / with their own special colors and lenses.
새로운 매체가 등장할 때마다 / —그것이 인쇄된 책, TV, 또는 SNS의 발명이든 간에 / —그것을 사용하기 시작하면, / 마치 새로운 종류의 고글을 쓰는 것과 같다. / 그만의 특별한 색과 렌즈를 가진

Each set of goggles you put on / makes you see things differently.
다른 고글을 쓸 때마다 / 세상을 다르게 보게 된다.

So when you start to watch television, / before you absorb the message of any particular TV show / — whether it's *Wheel of Fortune* or *The Wire* — / you start to see the world / as being shaped like television itself.
그래서 TV를 보기 시작하면, / 특정 TV 프로그램의 메시지를 받아들이기 전에 — / 그것이 *Wheel of Fortune*이든 *The Wire* 이든 — / 세상이 보이기 시작한다. / TV 자체처럼 형성된 것처럼

That's why Marshall McLuhan said / that every time a new medium comes along / — a new way for humans to communicate — it has buried in it a message.
이것이 Marshall McLuhan이 말한 이유이다. / 새로운 매체가 등장할 때마다 / — 인간이 소통하는 새로운 방식이 — / 그 안에 메시지가 숨겨져 있다

It is gently guiding us / to see the world according to a new set of codes.
그것은 우리를 부드럽게 이끌어 / 새로운 코드 세트에 따라 세상을 보게 한다.

The way information gets to you, McLuhan argued, / is more important than the information itself.
McLuhan은 주장했다 / 정보가 전달되는 방식이 정보 자체보다 더 중요하다고

TV teaches you that the world is fast; / that it's about surfaces and appearances.
TV는 세상이 빠르다고 가르친다. / 그것은 표면과 외양에 관한 것이라고

인쇄된 책의 발명이든 텔레비전의 발명이든 SNS의 발명이든, 새로운 매체가 나타나 여러분이 그것을 쓰기 시작할 때마다 여러분은 고유의 색깔과 렌즈를 가진 새 고글을 쓰는 것과 같다. 여러분이 쓰는 각각의 고글은 세상을 다른 방식으로 바라보게 한다. 그러므로 여러분이 텔레비전을 보기 시작하면, 그것이 *Wheel of Fortune*이든 *The Wire*든, 특정 텔레비전 프로그램의 메시지를 흡수하기 이전에 이미 세상을 텔레비전 그 자체처럼 형성된 것으로 바라보게 된다. 이러한 이유로 Marshall McLuhan이 새로운 매체, 즉, 인간이 의사소통하는 새로운 방식이 나타날 때마다 그 안에 메시지가 담겨 있다고 말한 것이다. 새로운 매체는 자연스럽게 우리가 새로운 일련의 방식에 따라 세상을 바라보게 한다. McLuhan은 정보가 여러분에게 도달하는 방식이 정보 자체보다 더 중요하다고 주장했다. 텔레비전은 우리에게 세상은 빠르고, 중요한 것은 표면과 겉모습이라고 가르친다.

Why? 왜 정답일까?

인쇄된 책, 텔레비전, SNS 등의 새로운 매체가 나타날 때마다 새 고글을 쓰는 것과 같다고 하였으니 (Every time a new medium comes along — whether it's the invention of the printed book, or TV, or SNS — and you start to use it, it's like you are putting on a new kind of goggles, with their own special colors and lenses.) 매체마다 메시지가 다르게 전달된다는 것이 주제임을 알 수 있다. 따라서 빈칸에는 ① 'see the world according to a new set of codes'가 적절하다.

- medium ⓝ 매체
- invention ⓝ 발명
- absorb ⓥ 흡수하다
- particular ⓐ 특정한
- bury ⓥ 묻다
- guide ⓥ 이끌다
- appearance ⓝ 외모
- come along 따라오다
- goggle ⓝ 고글
- differently ⓐⓓ 다르게, 같지 않게
- communicate ⓥ 의사소통하다
- gently ⓐⓓ 다정하게, 부드럽게
- argue ⓥ 주장하다

구문 풀이

13행 The way information gets to you, McLuhan argued, is more important than the information itself.
관계부사 how ... 비교급 ... 재귀대명사(그 자체)

---

33 개념에 대한 집착의 위험성 정답률 47% | 정답 ①

다음 빈칸에 들어갈 말로 가장 적절한 것을 고르시오. [3점]

✓① encourage us to see things that aren't present – 존재하지 않는 것을 보도록 부추긴다.
② force scientists to simplify scientific theories – 과학적 이론을 단순화하기 위해서 과학자들을 강제한다.
③ let us think science is essential and practical – 과학이 필수적이고 실용적이라고 생각하게 만든다.
④ drive physicists to explore philosophy – 물리학자들이 철학을 탐구하게 이끈다.
⑤ lead us to ignore the unknown – 우리를 미지를 무시하도록 이끈다.

Concepts are vital to human survival, / but we must also be careful with them / because concepts open the door to essentialism.
개념은 인간의 생존에 필수적이지만, / 우리는 그것들을 주의 깊게 다뤄야 한다. / 왜냐하면 개념은 본질주의로 이어질 수 있기 때문에

They encourage us to see things that aren't present.
그것들은 우리가 존재하지 않는 것을 보도록 부추긴다.

Stuart Firestein opens his book, *Ignorance*, / with an old proverb, / "It is very difficult to find a black cat in a dark room, / especially when there is no cat."
Stuart Firestein은 그의 책 *Ignorance*을 / 오래된 속담으로 시작한다, / "어두운 방에서 검은 고양이를 찾는 것은 매우 어렵다. / 특히 고양이가 없을 때는 더더욱"

This statement / beautifully sums up / the search for essences.
이 문장은 / 아름답게 요약한다 / 본질을 찾는 과정

History has many examples of scientists / who searched fruitlessly for an essence / because they used the wrong concept to guide their hypotheses.
역사에는 많은 예가 있다. / 잘못된 개념을 사용하여 가설을 세운 결과 / 본질을 헛되이 찾은 과학자들의

Firestein gives the example of luminiferous ether, / a mysterious substance that was thought to fill the universe / so that light would have a medium to move through.
Firestein은 발광성 에테르의 예를 든다. / 우주를 채우고 있다고 여겨진 신비로운 물질을 설명하며 / 빛이 이동할 수 있는 매체로서

The ether was a black cat, / writes Firestein, / and physicists had been theorizing in a dark room, / and then experimenting in it, / looking for evidence of a cat that did not exist.
에테르는 검은 고양이였다고, / Firestein은 쓴다. / 물리학자들은 어두운 방에서 이론을 세우고 / 실험하며, / 존재하지 않는 고양이의 증거를 찾고 있었다고

개념은 인간의 생존에 필수적이지만, 개념이 본질주의로 향하는 문을 열기 때문에 우리는 또한 그것들을 주의해야 한다. 그것들은 존재하지 않는 것들을 보도록 우리를 부추긴다. Stuart Firestein은 "어두운 방에서 검은 고양이를 찾는 것은 특히 고양이가 없을 때 매우 어렵다."라는 옛 속담으로 그의 책 *Ignorance*를 시작한다. 이 말은 본질에 대한 탐구를 훌륭하게 요약한다. 역사는 가설을 이끄는 잘못된 개념을 사용했기 때문에 헛되이 본질을 탐색했던 과학자들의 많은 예를 가지고 있다. Firestein은 빛이 통과할 수 있는 매개체를 갖도록 우주를 가득 채워줄 것이라 여겨진 신비한 물질인 발광 에테르의 예를 제시한다. Firestein이 쓰기를, 에테르는 검은 고양이였고, 물리학자들은 어두운 방에서 이론을 세우고, 그러고 나서 존재하지 않았던 고양이라는 증거를 찾으며, 그 안에서 실험을 하고 있었던 것이었다.

Why? 왜 정답일까?

개념에 과도하게 집중하게 되면 본질주의로 빠질 우려가 있다며 우주를 채우고 있다는 에테르라는 성분을 예로 들며 설명한다. 어두운 방에서 검은 고양이를 찾는 비유를 하며 검은 고양이가 실제로는 존재하지

않고, 따라서 개념에 과도하게 집착하는 것은 존재하지 않는 것들을 보도록 만들기 때문에 ① 'encourage us to see things that aren't present'가 자연스럽다.

- concept ⓝ 개념
- careful ⓐ 조심스러운
- encourage ⓥ 부추기다
- fruitlessly ⓐⓓ 헛되이
- medium ⓝ 도구
- evidence ⓝ 증거
- vital ⓐ 필수적인
- essentialism ⓝ 본질주의
- statement ⓝ 표현, 진술
- luminiferous ⓐ 빛을 내는, 발광성의
- experiment ⓥ 실험하다
- exist ⓥ 존재하다

구문 풀이

12행 The ether was a black cat, writes Firestein, and physicists had been theorizing in a dark room, and then experimenting in it, looking for evidence of a cat that did not exist.
과거완료진행1 ... 과거완료진행2 ... 현재분사 ... 주격관계대명사

★★★ 등급을 가르는 문제!

34 새로운 명성의 개념 정답률 35% | 정답 ④

다음 빈칸에 들어갈 말로 가장 적절한 것을 고르시오. [3점]

① shifts to that of elite celebrity – 엘리트 유명인의 것으로 변화한다.
② disappears gradually over time – 시간이 지남에 따라 점차적으로 사라진다.
③ focuses solely on talent and class – 재능과 계층에만 집중한다.
✓④ reconstructs the meaning of fame – 명성의 의미를 재구성한다.
⑤ restricts interactions with the public – 대중과의 상호작용을 제한한다.

While social media attention is potentially an instrument / to achieve ends like elite celebrity, / some content creators desire ordinary fame / as a social end in itself.
소셜 미디어 주목은 수단이 될 수 있지만, / 엘리트 연예인과 같은 목적을 달성하는 / 일부 콘텐츠 제작자들은 평범한 명성을 원한다 / 그것 자체로서 사회적 목표로서의

Not unlike reality television stars, / social media celebrities are often criticized / for not having skills and talents / associated with traditional, elite celebrity, / such as acting or singing ability.
리얼리티 TV 스타들과 마찬가지로, / 소셜 미디어 유명인들은 종종 비판을 받는다. / 전통적인 엘리트 유명인들이 가진 / 연기나 노래와 같은 / 기술이나 재능이 없다는

This criticism highlights the fact / that digital content creators face / real barriers to crossing over / to the sphere of elite celebrity.
이 비판은 사실을 강조한다 / 디지털 콘텐츠 제작자들이 마주함은 / 실제 장벽을 넘어가는 데에 / 엘리트 유명인의 영역으로

However, the criticism also misses the point / that the phenomenon of ordinary celebrity / reconstructs the meaning of fame.
그러나, 이 비판은 또한 중요한 점을 놓치는데, / 평범한 명성의 현상이 / 명성의 의미를 재구성한다는 점이다.

The elite celebrity is symbolized by the metaphor of the star, / characterized by mystery and hierarchical distance / and associated with naturalized qualities of talent and class.
엘리트 유명인은 별의 은유로 상징되며, / 신비와 계층적 거리를 특징으로 하며 / 타고난 재능과 계급의 속성과 연결된다.

The ordinary celebrity attracts attention / through regular and frequent interactions / with other ordinary people.
평범한 유명인은 주목을 끈다. / 정기적이고 빈번한 상호작용을 통해 / 다른 일반인들과의

Achieving ordinary fame as a social media celebrity / is like doing well at a game, / because in this sphere, fame is nothing more nor less / than relatively high scores on / the metrics of subscribers, followers, Likes, or clicks built into social media applications.
소셜 미디어 유명인으로서 평범한 명성을 얻는 것은 / 게임을 잘하는 것과 같다. / 왜냐하면 이 영역에서 명성은 그 이상도 이하도 아니고 / 상대적으로 높은 점수일 뿐이다. / 소셜 미디어 애플리케이션에 내장된 구독자, 팔로워, 좋아요, 또는 클릭 수와 같은 관심의 척도에서

소셜 미디어 관심은 잠재적으로 엘리트 명성과 같은 목적을 달성하기 위한 도구인 반면, 일부 콘텐츠 제작자들은 사회적 목적 그 자체로서 평범한 명성을 원한다. 리얼리티 텔레비전 스타들과 다르지 않게, 소셜 미디어 유명인들은 연기나 가창력과 같은 전통적인 엘리트 명성과 관련된 기술과 재능을 가지고 있지 않다는 이유로 종종 비판을 받는다. 이러한 비판은 디지털 콘텐츠 제작자들이 엘리트 명성의 영역으로 넘어가는 데 있어 실질적인 장벽에 직면하고 있다는 사실을 강조한다. 그러나 이 비판은 또한 평범한 명성 현상이 명성의 의미를 재구성한다는 점을 놓친다. 엘리트 유명인은 스타라는 은유로 상징되고, 신비로움과 계층적 거리로 특징지어지며, 타고난 자질의 재능과 계층에 연관되어 있다. 평범한 유명인은 다른 평범한 사람들과의 정기적이고 빈번한 상호작용을 통해 관심을 끈다. 소셜 미디어 유명인으로서 평범한 명성을 얻는 것은 게임에서 잘하는 것과 같은데, 왜냐하면 이 영역에서 명성은 관심 척도, 즉, 소셜 미디어 애플리케이션에 내장된 구독자, 팔로워, 좋아요 또는 클릭의 측정 기준에서 상대적으로 높은 점수 그 이상도 그 이하도 아니기 때문이다.

Why? 왜 정답일까?

기존의 'elite celebrity'와 대조되는 'ordinary celebrity'의 개념을 제시하며, 'elite celebrity'는 비밀스럽고 고귀한 모습을 보이는 반면 'ordinary celebrity'는 대중과 친숙하고 소통을 잘 하는 특징을 가지고 있다고 설명한다. 따라서 'ordinary celebrity'는 명성의 의미를 재구성한다는 ④ 'reconstructs the meaning of fame'가 빈칸에 적절하다.

- celebrity ⓝ 유명인
- instrument ⓝ 도구
- content ⓝ 컨텐츠
- phenomenon ⓝ 현상
- hierarchical ⓐ 계층제의, 계층에 따른
- attention ⓝ 관심
- achieve ⓥ 달성하다
- creator ⓝ 창작자
- symbolize ⓥ 상징되다
- interaction ⓝ 상호 작용

구문 풀이

15행 Achieving ordinary fame as a social media celebrity is like doing well at a game, because in this sphere, fame is nothing more nor less than relatively high scores on attention scales, the metrics of subscribers, followers, Likes, or clicks (that are) built into social media applications.
동명사 ... 동명사 ... 그 이상도 그 이하도 아니다 ... 주격관계대명사 + be 동사 생략

35 장기기억으로 기억을 넘기기 · 정답률 75% | 정답 ④

다음 글에서 전체 흐름과 관계 없는 문장은?

Why do we have the illusion / that cramming for an exam / is the best learning strategy?
왜 우리는 착각을 할까? / 시험에 벼락치기가 / 가장 좋은 학습 방법이라는

Because we are unable to differentiate / between the various sections of our memory.
그것은 우리가 구별하지 못하기 때문이다. / 기억의 다양한 부분을

Immediately after reading our textbook or our class notes, / information is fully present in our mind.
교과서나 강의 노트를 읽고 난 직후, / 정보는 완전히 우리의 마음속에 있다.

① It sits in our conscious working memory, / in an active form.
그것은 의식적인 작업 기억에 자리 잡고 있다. / 활성화된 형태로

② We feel as if we know it, / because it is present / in our short-term storage space ... / but this short-term section has nothing to do with the long-term memory / that we will need in order to recall / the same information a few days later.
우리는 그것을 알고 있는 것처럼 느낀다. / 왜냐하면 그것이 있기 때문이다 / 우리의 단기 기억 공간에 ... / 그러나 이 단기 기억 부분은 장기 기억과는 아무런 관련이 없다. / 기억하기 위해 필요한 / 며칠 후에 같은 정보를

③ After a few seconds or minutes, / working memory already starts disappearing, / and after a few days, the effect becomes enormous: / unless you retest your knowledge, / memory vanishes.
몇 초 또는 몇 분 후에, / 작업 기억은 이미 사라지기 시작하며, / 며칠이 지나면 그 효과는 더욱 커진다: / 지식을 다시 테스트하지 않으면, / 기억은 사라진다.

☑ Focusing on exploring new topics / rather than reviewing the same material over and over again / can improve your academic performance.
같은 자료를 반복해서 복습하는 대신 / 새로운 주제를 탐구하는 데 집중하는 것이 / 학업 성과를 향상시킬 수 있다.

④ To get information into long-term memory, / it is essential to study the material, then test yourself, / rather than spend all your time studying.
정보를 장기 기억에 저장하려면, / 자료를 공부한 다음 스스로 테스트하는 것이 필수적이다. / 시간을 모두 공부에만 할애하는 대신

왜 우리는 시험을 위해 벼락 공부를 하는 것이 최고의 학습 전략이라는 착각을 하는 것일까? 우리가 우리의 기억의 다양한 구획을 구별할 수 없기 때문이다. 우리의 교과서나 수업 노트를 읽은 직후에는 정보가 우리 머릿속에 완전히 존재한다. ① 그것은 우리의 의식적인 작업 기억에 활동적인 형태로 자리한다. ② 그것은 우리의 단기 저장 공간에 존재하기 때문에 우리는 마치 우리가 그것을 알고 있는 것처럼 느끼지만, 이 단기 구획은 며칠 후 같은 정보를 기억하기 위해 우리가 필요로 할 장기 기억과는 아무런 관련이 없다. ③ 몇 초 또는 몇 분 후, 작업 기억은 이미 사라지기 시작하고, 며칠 후 그 영향은 엄청나게 되어, 여러분이 자신의 지식을 다시 테스트하지 않으면 기억은 사라진다. ④ 같은 자료를 반복해서 다시 복습하는 것보다 새로운 주제를 탐구하는 데 집중하는 것이 여러분의 학업 성취를 향상시킬 수 있다. ⑤ 정보를 장기 기억에 넣으려면, 여러분의 모든 시간을 공부하는 데에 쓰기보다는 자료를 공부하고 나서 스스로를 테스트하는 것이 필수적이다.

Why? 왜 정답일까?
단기 기억을 장기 기억으로 옮기는 방법에 대해 얘기하고 있다. 이전 지식을 다시 테스트해야 기억에 남아 있는다고 하기 때문에(After a few seconds or minutes, working memory already starts disappearing, and after a few days, the effect becomes enormous: unless you retest your knowledge, memory vanishes.) 전체 흐름과 관계 없는 문장은 ④이다.

- illusion ⓝ 환각
- strategy ⓝ 전략
- section ⓝ 부분
- information ⓝ 정보
- conscious ⓐ 의식적인
- effect ⓝ 효과
- knowledge ⓝ 정보
- cram ⓥ 벼락 공부를 하다
- differentiate ⓥ 차별화하다
- memory ⓝ 기억
- mind ⓝ 생각
- disappear ⓥ 사라지다
- enormous ⓐ 막대한, 거대한
- vanish ⓥ 사라지다

구문 풀이

13행 Focusing on exploring new topics rather than reviewing the same material
      동명사   동명사1   보다   동명사2
over and over again can improve your academic performance.
계속하여

36 관찰에 의한 모방 · 정답률 72% | 정답 ②

주어진 글 다음에 이어질 글의 순서로 가장 적절한 것을 고르시오.

① (A) - (C) - (B)　　☑ (B) - (A) - (C)
③ (B) - (C) - (A)　　④ (C) - (A) - (B)
⑤ (C) - (B) - (A)

The discovery of mirror neurons has profoundly changed / the way we think of a fundamental human capacity, / learning by observation.
거울 뉴런의 발견은 크게 바꿨다. / 우리가 인간의 근본적인 능력에 대해 생각하는 방식을 / 관찰을 통한 학습을 통해

(B) As children / we learn a lot / by observing what our parents and friends do.
어린 시절 / 우리는 많은 것을 배운다. / 부모님과 친구들이 하는 것을 관찰함으로써

Newborns, in the first week of life, / have an inborn tendency / to stick out their tongue / if their parents stick out theirs.
신생아는, 생후 첫 주에, / 타고난 경향을 가지고 있다. / 그들도 혀를 내미는 / 부모가 혀를 내밀면

Such imitation is not perfect.
그러한 모방은 완벽하지 않다.

(A) You may not see the tongue stick out each time / you stick yours out at your newborn, / but if you do it many times, / the tongue will come out more often / than if you do something different.
매번 혀를 내밀 때마다 보지 못할 수도 있다. / 신생아가 혀를 내미는 것을, / 그러나 여러 번 하면, / 혀를 더 자주 내밀게 될 것이다. / 다른 것을 해보다

Babies babble / and later start to imitate / the sounds their parents produce.
아기들은 옹알이를 하고 / 이후에는 흉내 내기 시작한다. / 부모가 내는 소리를

(C) Later still, / they play with vacuum cleaners and hammers / in imitation of their parents.
그 후에는, / 진공청소기나 망치로 놀기도 한다. / 부모를 흉내 내어

Our modern cultures, / in which we write, speak, read, build spaceships / and go to school, / can work only because we are not restricted to the behavior / we are born with or learn by trial and error.
우리 현대 문화는, / 우리가 글을 쓰고, 말하고, 읽고, 우주선을 만들고 / 학교에 다니는, / 행동에만 제한되지 않기 때문에 가능한 것이다. / 태어날 때부터 가지고 있거나 시행착오로 배우는

We can learn a lot / by simply watching others.
우리는 많은 것을 배울 수 있다. / 단순히 다른 사람들을 관찰함으로써

거울 뉴런의 발견은 관찰에 의한 학습이라는 근본적인 인간의 능력에 대해 우리가 생각하는 방식을 완전히 바꾸어 놓았다.

(B) 어린이일 때 우리는 우리의 부모와 친구들이 하는 것을 관찰하면서 많이 배운다. 갓난아기들은 생의 첫 주에 그들의 부모가 그들의 것(혀)을 내밀면 자신의 혀를 내미는 선천적인 성향을 갖고 있다. 그러한 모방은 완벽하지 않다.

(A) 당신은 당신의 갓난아기에게 당신의 것(혀)을 내밀 때마다 (아기의) 혀가 내밀어 나오는 것을 보지 못할 수도 있지만, 만약 당신이 그것을 여러 번 한다면 당신이 다른 것을 할 때보다 (아기의) 혀가 더 자주 나올 것이다. 아기들은 옹알이를 하고 이후에 그들의 부모가 내는 소리를 모방하기 시작한다.

(C) 이후에도 여전히, 그들은 부모들을 흉내 내어 진공청소기와 망치를 갖고 논다. 쓰고 말하고 읽고 우주선을 만들고 학교에 가는 우리의 현대 문화는 단지 우리가 가지고 태어나는 또는 시행착오를 통해 배우는 행동에 국한되지 않기 때문에 작동할 수 있다. 우리는 그저 다른 사람들을 관찰하는 것을 통해 많이 배울 수 있다.

Why? 왜 정답일까?
주어진 글은 거울 뉴런을 발견하며 관찰에 의한 학습이라는 생각이 바뀐다고 한다. (B)에서는 혀를 내미는 행동의 관찰에 대한 얘기를 하고 있고, (A)는 혀를 내미는 것을 너머 옹알이와 소리를 모방한다고 한다. 따라서 (B)와 (A)가 이어져야 하고, 그 이후에도 모방으로 학습한다는 (C)가 마지막에 오는 순서가 알맞다. 따라서 답은 ② '(B) - (A) - (C)'이다.

- discovery ⓝ 발견
- profoundly ⓐⓓ 풍부하게
- capacity ⓝ 능력
- babble ⓥ 옹알이하다
- imitation ⓝ 모방
- neuron ⓝ 뉴런
- fundamental ⓐ 기본적인
- observation ⓝ 관찰
- tongue ⓝ 혀

구문 풀이

4행 You may not see the tongue stick out each time you stick yours out at
            지각동사   동사원형
your newborn, but if you do it many times, the tongue will come out more often
                  가정법   조동사+동사원형
than if you do something different.

37 녹음된 목소리가 다르게 들리는 이유 · 정답률 73% | 정답 ④

주어진 글 다음에 이어질 글의 순서로 가장 적절한 것을 고르시오. [3점]

① (A) - (C) - (B)　　② (B) - (A) - (C)
③ (B) - (C) - (A)　　☑ (C) - (A) - (B)
⑤ (C) - (B) - (A)

Have you ever been surprised / to hear a recording of your own voice?
당신은 자신의 목소리가 녹음된 것을 듣고 / 놀란 적이 있는가?

You might have thought, / "Is that really what my voice sounds like?"
당신은 아마 생각했을 것이다. / "저게 정말 내 목소리야?"

(C) Maybe your accent is more pronounced in the recording / than you realized, / or your voice is higher than it seems to your own ears.
아마도 당신의 억양이 녹음에서 더 두드러지게 들릴 것이다. / 당신이 인지한 것보다. / 또는 당신의 목소리가 당신이 듣기에는 생각보다 더 높다.

This is of course quite a common experience.
이것은 물론 매우 흔한 경험이다.

The explanation is actually fairly simple.
그 설명은 사실 꽤 간단하다.

(A) There are two pathways / through which we perceive our own voice / when we speak.
두 가지 경로가 있다. / 자신의 목소리를 인지하는 / 우리가 말을 할 때

One is the route / through which we perceive most external sounds, / like waves that travel from the air through the outer, middle and inner ear.
하나는 경로인데, / 우리가 대부분의 외부 소리를 인지하는 / 공기 중의 파동이 외이, 중이, 내이를 통해 전달되는 것처럼

(B) But because our vocal cords vibrate when we speak, / there is a second internal path.
그러나 우리가 말을 할 때 성대가 진동하기 때문에, / 두 번째 내부 경로가 있다.

Vibrations are conducted through our bones / and stimulate our inner ears directly.
진동이 우리의 뼈를 통해 전달되되 / 내이를 직접 자극한다.

Lower frequencies are emphasized along this pathway.
이 경로에서는 저주파가 강조된다.

That makes your voice sound deeper and richer to yourself / than it may sound to other people.
그 때문에 당신 자신의 목소리가 더 깊고 풍부하게 들린다. / 다른 사람들이 듣는 것보다

당신은 당신의 음성 녹음을 듣고 놀랐던 적이 있는가? 당신은 '내 목소리가 정말 이렇게 들리는가?'라고 생각했을지도 모른다.

(C) 어쩌면 녹음에서는 당신이 인식한 것보다 당신의 억양이 더 강조되거나, 당신의 목소리가 당신의 귀에 들리는 것 같은 것보다 더 높다. 이것은 당연히 꽤 흔한 경험이다. 이 설명은 사실 꽤 간단하다.

(A) 우리가 말할 때 우리 자신의 목소리를 인지하는 데는 두 가지 경로가 있다. 하나는 외이, 중이, 내이를 통하는 공기로부터 이동하는 파동처럼 우리가 대부분의 외부의 소리를 인지하는 경로이다.

(B) 그러나 우리가 말할 때 우리의 성대가 진동하기 때문에 두 번째 내부의 경로가 있다. 진동은 뼈를 통해 전해지고, 우리의 내이를 직접 자극한다. 낮은 주파수는 이 경로를 따라 두드러진다. 그것은 당신의 목소리가 다른 사람에게 들릴 수 있는 것보다 당신 자신에게 더 깊고 풍부하게 들리게 한다.

Why? 왜 정답일까?

스스로의 목소리가 생각했던 것과 다르게 들리는 경험을 얘기하고 있다. 따라서 스스로의 목소리가 생각했던 것과 다르게 들리는 예시를 제시하는 (C)가 주어진 글 뒤에 오고, 이것의 이유를 설명하는 (A), 마지막으로 (A)의 구조적 설명을 자세히 하는 (B)가 오는 것이 자연스럽다. 따라서 ④ (C) – (A) – (B)가 정답이다.

- record ⓥ 녹음하다
- perceive ⓥ 인식하다
- external ⓐ 외부의
- vibrate ⓥ 진동하다
- conduct ⓥ (열·전기·소리 등을) 전도하다
- stimulate ⓥ 자극하다
- pathway ⓝ 길
- route ⓝ 경로, 길
- vocal cord ⓝ 성대
- internal ⓐ 내부의
- frequency ⓝ 주파수
- directly ⓐⓓ 직접으로

구문 풀이

> **9행** Vibrations are conducted through our bones and stimulate our inner ears directly.
> 수동태1   전치사(~을 통해서)   수동태2

---

38 상사형질과 상동형질의 차이점 정답률 57% | 정답 ③

글의 흐름으로 보아, 주어진 문장이 들어가기에 가장 적절한 곳을 고르시오.

Biologists distinguish two kinds of similarity.
생물학자는 두 가지의 유사함을 구분한다.
① "Analogous" traits / are ones that have a common function / but arose on different branches of the evolutionary tree / and are in an important sense not "the same" organ.
"유사한" 특징은 / 공통된 기능을 가지고 있는 것이다. / 하지만 다른 진화적 나무의 가지에서 나는 것이다. / 그리고 "같지 않은" 장기라는 중요한 감각이 있다.
② The wings of birds / and the wings of bees / are both used for flight and are similar in some ways / because anything used for flight / has to be built in those ways, / but they arose independently in evolution / and have nothing in common / beyond their use in flight.
새들의 날개와 / 벌들의 날개는 / 모두 비행을 위해 사용되고 어떤 방법에서는 비슷하다. / 왜냐하면 비행을 위해 사용되는 어느 것이든 / 그러한 방법으로 만들어져야 하기 때문이다. / 하지만 그들은 진화에 독립적으로 자란다. / 그리고 공통점이 없다. / 비행이라는 그들의 사용 외에는
✔ "Homologous" traits, / in contrast, / may or may not have a common function, / but they descended from a common ancestor / and hence have some common structure / that indicates their being "the same" organ.
"동종의" 특징은, / 반대로, / 공통의 기능을 가지고 있거나 가지고 있지 않을 수 있다. / 하지만 공통 조상으로부터 내려온 것이다. / 그리고 그러므로 약간의 공통 구조를 가진다. / 그들을 "같은" 장기라고 규정하는
The wing of a bat and the front leg of a horse / have very different functions, / but they are all modifications of the forelimb / of the ancestor of all mammals.
박쥐의 날개와 말의 앞다리는 / 아주 다른 기능을 가지고 있다. / 하지만 그들 모두는 앞다리의 변형이다. / 모든 포유류의 조상의
④ As a result, / they share nonfunctional traits / like the number of bones and the ways they are connected.
결과적으로, / 그들은 비기능적인 특징들을 공유한다. / 뼈의 개수 그리고 그들이 연결되어 있는 방식과 같은
⑤ To distinguish analogy from homology, / biologists usually look at the overall architecture of the organs / and focus on their most useless properties.
유사성과 동종성을 구별하기 위해서, / 생물학자들은 주로 장기의 전체적인 구조를 본다. / 그리고 그들의 가장 쓸모없는 자질에 집중한다.

생물학자들은 두 종류의 유사성을 구별한다. ① '상사' 형질은 공통된 기능을 가지는 것들이지만, 진화 계보의 다른 가지에서 생겨났고 중요한 면에서 '동일한' 기관이 아닌 형질이다. ② 새의 날개들과 벌의 날개들은 둘 다 비행에 쓰이고 비행에 쓰이는 것은 어떤 것이든 그러한 방식으로 만들어져야 하기 때문에 일부 방식에서 유사하지만, 그것들은 진화상에 별개로 생겨났고, 비행에서 그것들의 쓰임 외에는 공통점이 없다. ③ 대조적으로, '상동' 형질은 공통된 기능이 있을 수도 없을 수도 있으나 그것들은 공통의 조상으로부터 내려왔으므로 그들이 '동일한' 기관임을 보여주는 어떠한 공통된 구조를 가진다. 박쥐의 날개와 말의 앞다리는 매우 다른 기능을 가지나, 그것들은 모든 포유류의 조상의 앞다리가 모두 변형된 것들이다. ④ 그 결과, 그들은 뼈의 개수와 그것들이 연결된 방식과 같은 비기능적 형질을 공유한다. ⑤ 상사성과 상동성을 구별하기 위해, 생물학자들은 주로 그 기관의 전체적인 구성을 살펴보고 그들의 가장 쓰임이 없는 특성에 집중한다.

Why? 왜 정답일까?

상사 형질은 공통된 기능이지만 진화 계보가 다른 가지인 형질을, 상동 형질은 기능은 공통되지 않을 수 있지만 진화 계보의 가지가 같은 형질임을 설명한다. ③을 기준으로 위에는 상사 형질의 특징, 상사 형질의 특징과 다른 특징을 설명하고 있기 때문에 상동 형질에 대해 설명하는 주어진 문장이 ③에 들어가는 것이 알맞다.

- biologist ⓝ 생물학자
- analogous ⓐ 유사한
- organ ⓝ 장기
- evolution ⓝ 진화
- common ⓐ 공통의
- structure ⓝ 구조
- forelimb ⓝ (척추동물의) 앞다리
- similarity ⓝ 유사성
- arise ⓥ 생기다
- independently ⓐⓓ 독립적으로
- descend ⓥ 내려오다
- ancestor ⓝ 조상
- indicate ⓥ 가리키다
- mammals ⓝ 포유류

구문 풀이

> **1행** "Homologous" traits, in contrast, may or may not have a common
> 조동사+동사원형
> function, but they descended from a common ancestor and hence have some
> homologous traits
> common structure that indicates their being "the same" organ.
> 선행사   주격관계대명사

★★★ 등급을 가르는 문제! ★★★

39 용존 산소의 중요성 정답률 30% | 정답 ②

글의 흐름으로 보아, 주어진 문장이 들어가기에 가장 적절한 곳을 고르시오. [3점]

Seawater contains an abundance of dissolved oxygen / that all marine animals breathe to stay alive.
해수는 많은 용해된 산소를 포함한다. / 모든 해양 생물들이 살기 위해서 호흡해야하는
① It has long been established in physics / that cold water holds more dissolved oxygen / than warm water does / — this is one reason / that cold polar seas are full of life / while tropical oceans are blue, clear, and relatively poorly populated with living creatures.
물리학에서 오랫동안 정립되었다. / 차가운 물이 더 많은 용해된 산소를 포함하는 것이 / 따뜻한 물보다 / — 이것이 한 가지 이유이다. / 차가운 극지방의 바다가 생명으로 가득한 / 열대 바다는 파랗고, 맑고, 생명체가 덜 있지만
✔ Thus, as global warming raises the temperature of marine waters, / it is self-evident / that the amount of dissolved oxygen will decrease.
따라서, 지구 온난화가 해수의 온도를 올리면 / 분명하다. / 용해된 산소의 양이 감소한다는 것이
This is a worrisome / and potentially disastrous consequence / if allowed to continue to an ecosystem-threatening level.
이것은 걱정할만하다. / 그리고 파멸적인 결과를 불러올 수 있다. / 만약 생태계가 위협받는 상태까지 계속된다면
③ Now scientists have analyzed data / indicating that the amount of dissolved oxygen in the oceans / has been declining for more than a half century.
지금 과학자들은 정보를 분석했다. / 바다의 용해된 산소의 양을 가리키며 / 지난 반 세기 넘게 감소한
④ The data show that the ocean oxygen level / has been falling more rapidly than the corresponding rise in water temperature.
정보는 바다 산소 레벨을 보여준다. / 맞는 해수 온도보다 더 빠르게 떨어짐
⑤ Falling oxygen levels in water / have the potential to impact the habitat of marine organisms worldwide / and in recent years this has led to more frequent anoxic events / that killed or displaced populations / of fish, crabs, and many other organisms.
감소하는 물의 산소 레벨은 / 전세계의 해양 유기체의 거주지에 영향을 끼칠 가능성이 있다. / 그리고 최근 몇 년 간 이것은 자주 산소 결핍의 사건으로 이끌었다. / 죽거나 개체수가 도망가도록 / 물고기, 게, 그리고 많은 다른 유기체들을

해수는 모든 해양 동물이 살아있기 위해 호흡하는 다량의 용존 산소를 포함한다. ① 따뜻한 물이 보유하고 있는 것보다 차가운 물이 더 많은 용존 산소를 보유하고 있다는 사실은 물리학에서 오랫동안 확립되어 왔으며, 이는 열대 해양은 푸르고 맑고 생물이 상대적으로 적게 서식하는 반면 차가운 극지의 바다는 생명으로 가득한 하나의 이유이다. ② 따라서 지구 온난화가 해양 수온을 높임에 따라 용존 산소의 양이 감소할 것은 자명하다. 만약 생태계를 위협하는 수준까지 계속되도록 허용된다면 이는 걱정스럽고 잠재적으로 파괴적인 결과다. ③ 현재 과학자들은 해양에서 용존 산소의 양이 반세기가 넘는 기간 동안 감소해 왔다는 것을 보여 주는 데이터를 분석해 왔다. ④ 이 데이터는 해양 산소 농도가 상응하는 수온 상승보다 더 빠르게 감소해 오고 있음을 보여 준다. ⑤ 감소하는 수중 산소 농도는 세계적으로 해양 생물의 서식지에 영향을 끼칠 가능성을 갖고 있으며 최근에 이것은 물고기, 게, 그리고 많은 다른 생물의 개체군을 죽이거나 쫓아낸 더 빈번한 산소 결핍 사건을 초래해 왔다.

Why? 왜 정답일까?

해수에 용해된 산소, 즉 용존 산소가 해양 생물이 물에서 숨을 쉴 수 있게 해주어 해양 생태계에 필수적인 요소임을 말하고 있다. 용존 산소가 풍부한 극지방의 바다와 용존 산소가 부족한 열대 바다를 비교하고, 용존 산소가 생태계를 위협할 만큼 부족해지면 재앙적인 결과가 나올 것이라 얘기한다. 따라서 지구 온난화가 해수의 온도를 올리면 용존 산소가 부족해질 것이라는 주어진 문장이 ②에 오는 것이 알맞다.

- abundance ⓝ 넘칠 만큼 많음, 다량
- oxygen ⓝ 산소
- polar ⓐ 극지의
- populate ⓥ 살다, 거주하다
- temperature ⓝ 온도
- self-evident ⓐ 분명한
- potentially ⓐⓓ 잠재적으로
- consequence ⓝ 결과
- correspond ⓥ 일치하다
- dissolved ⓐ 용해된
- establish ⓥ 확립하다, 수립하다
- poorly ⓐⓓ 부족하게
- creature ⓝ 생물
- marine ⓐ 해양의
- decrease ⓥ 감소하다
- disastrous ⓐ 재앙적인
- analyze ⓥ 분석하다
- anoxic ⓐ 산소 결핍의

구문 풀이

> **1행** Thus, as global warming raises the temperature of marine waters, it is
> ~하면서
> self-evident that the amount of dissolved oxygen will decrease.
> 진주어   가주어

★★ 문제 해결 꿀~팁 ★★

▶ 많이 틀린 이유는?
글은 용존 산소의 중요성에 대해 얘기하고 있다. 'It has long been established in physics that cold water holds more dissolved oxygen than warm water does — this is one reason that cold polar seas are full of life while tropical oceans are blue, clear, and relatively poorly populated with living creatures.' → 여기서는 차가운 물이 따뜻한 물보다 더 많은 산소를 포함하고 있으며, 이것이 왜 극지방의 바다가 생명으로 가득한 반면, 열대 바다는 상대적으로 생명체가 적은지를 설명한다. 이 부분에서 주어진 문장을 넣으면 자연스럽게 이어진다. 차가운 물이 더 많은 산소를 포함한다는 사실을 바탕으로, 지구 온난화가 물의 온도를 상승시키면서 산소량을 감소시킨다는 논리가 연결된다. 따라서 ② 위치가 가장 적절하다.

▶ 문제 해결 방법은?
글의 흐름과 논리적 연관성을 파악하는 것이 우선이다. 주어진 문장은 지구 온난화로 인한 해양 온도 상승과 산소량 감소를 결과로 설명하고 있으므로, 온도와 용존 산소 간의 관계를 설명하는 ② 위치가 가장 적절하다.

40 카푸친 원숭이 실험
정답률 53% | 정답 ④

다음 글의 내용을 한 문장으로 요약하고자 한다. 빈칸 (A), (B)에 들어갈 말로 가장 적절한 것은?

	(A)		(B)
① benefit 혜택	……	protect 보호하다	
② inequality 불평등	……	share 공유하다	
③ abundance 충분함	……	yield 양보하다	
✓④ inequality 불평등	……	reject 거절하다	
⑤ benefit 혜택	……	display 보여주다	

Capuchins / — New World Monkeys that live in large social groups — / will, in captivity, trade with people all day long, / especially if food is involved.
카푸친은 / — 큰 사회적 집단으로 사는 새로운 세계의 원숭이 — / 포로로써, 사람들과 하루 종일 거래할 것이다. / 특히 음식이 걸려 있다면

I give you this rock / and you give me a treat to eat.
내가 이 돌을 너에게 주면 / 너는 나에게 먹을 간식을 준다.

If you put two monkeys in cages next to each other, / and offer them both slices of cucumber / for the rocks they already have, / they will happily eat the cucumbers.
만약 케이지에 있는 두 원숭이들을 옆에 두고, / 모두에게 오이 조각을 주면 / 그들이 이미 가지고 있는 돌과 바꿔서 / 그들은 행복하게 오이를 먹을 것이다.

If, however, you give one monkey grapes instead / — grapes being universally preferred to cucumbers — / the monkey that is still receiving cucumbers / will begin to throw them back at the experimenter.
하지만 만약 당신이 한 원숭이에게 오이 대신 포도를 준다면 / — 포도를 오이보다 전체적으로 좋아한다 — / 아직 오이를 받는 원숭이는 / 실험자에게 오이를 다시 던지기 시작할 것이다.

Even though she is still getting "paid" the same amount / for her effort of sourcing rocks, / and so her particular situation has not changed, / the comparison to another makes the situation unfair.
비록 원숭이가 여전히 같은 양으로 "보상받고 있지만" / 돌을 주는 노력으로 / 그리고 특정한 상황이 바뀌지는 않았지만, / 다른 원숭이와의 비교는 상황을 불공평하게 만든다.

Furthermore, / she is now willing to abandon all gains / — the cucumbers themselves — / to communicate her displeasure to the experimenter.
게다가, / 원숭이는 얻은 모든 것을 이제 기꺼이 버린다. / —오이를— / 실험자에게 불만을 토로하기 위해서

➡ According to the passage, / if the Capuchin monkey realizes the (A) inequality in rewards / compared to another monkey, / she will (B) reject her rewards / to express her feelings about the treatment, / despite getting exactly the same rewards as before.
글에 따르면, / 만약 카푸친 원숭이가 보상에서의 불공평함을 알아차리면 / 다른 원숭이와 비교했을 때, / 원숭이는 보상을 거절할 것이다. / 보상에 대한 감정을 표현하기 위해서 / 비록 전과 같은 보상을 받지만

대규모의 사회 집단으로 서식하는 New World Monkey인 Capuchin은 갇힌 상태에서 온종일 사람들과 거래를 할 것인데 특히 먹이가 연관된다면 그러할 것이다. '내가 너에게 이 돌을 주고 너는 나에게 먹을 간식을 준다.' 만약 당신이 두 마리의 원숭이들을 나란히 있는 우리에 넣고 그들이 이미 가지고 있는 돌의 대가로 오이 조각을 둘 모두에게 주었을 때 그들은 그 오이를 기쁘게 먹을 것이다. 하지만 만약 당신이 한 원숭이에게는 포도를 대신 준다면, 일반적으로 포도는 오이보다 더 선호되는데, 여전히 오이를 받은 원숭이는 그것들을 실험자에게 던지기 시작할 것이다. 비록 그녀가 돌을 모은 그녀의 수고에 대한 대가로 같은 양을 여전히 '받고', 그래서 그녀의 특정한 상황이 변화가 없더라도, 다른 원숭이와의 비교는 그 상황을 부당하게 만든다. 게다가, 그녀는 실험자에게 그녀의 불쾌함을 전달하기 위해 모든 얻은 것들, 즉, 오이 자체를 이제 기꺼이 포기한다.

➡ 이 글에 따르면, 만약 Capuchin 원숭이가 다른 원숭이와 비교하여 보상에서의 (A) 불평등을 알아차린다면, 그녀는 이전과 정확히 똑같은 보상을 받더라도 대우에 대한 그녀의 감정을 표현하기 위해 그녀의 보상을 (B) 거부할 것이다.

Why? 왜 정답일까?

카푸친 원숭이 실험을 설명한다. 돌을 주면 간식을 주는 거래이고, 두 원숭이가 돌을 주면 오이를 주었다. 다시 두 원숭이가 돌을 주었을 때 한 원숭이에게는 그대로 오이를 주고 한 원숭이에게는 포도를 주면 오이를 받은 원숭이가 부당하다고 느껴 오이도 먹지 않는다는 실험이었다. 따라서 보상에서의 'inequality'를 느끼면 전과 같은 보상이라도 'reject' 한다는 ④가 알맞다.

- large ⓐ 큰
- captivity ⓝ 감금, 억류, 포로
- involve ⓥ 포함하다
- cucumber ⓝ 오이
- prefer ⓥ 선호하다
- effort ⓝ 노력
- unfair ⓐ 부당한
- displeasure ⓝ 불쾌감
- social ⓐ 사회의
- trade ⓥ 거래하다
- cage ⓝ 우리
- universally ⓐⓓ 공통적으로
- experimenter ⓝ 실험자
- situation ⓝ 상황
- abandon ⓥ 버리다

구문 풀이

4행 If you put two monkeys in cages next to each other, and offer them both
가정법 / 동사1 / 동사2 two monkeys
slices of cucumber for the rocks (that/which) they already have, they will happily
목적격 관계대명사 생략 / 조동사+동사원형
eat the cucumbers.

41-42 고등 교육의 변화

Higher education has grown / from an elite to a mass system / across the world.
고등교육은 성장해왔다. / 엘리트 시스템에서 대중 시스템으로 / 전 세계적으로

In Europe and the USA, / (a) increased rates of participation / occurred in the decades / after the Second World War.
유럽과 미국에서는, / 참여율이 증가했고 / 수십 년간 일어났다. / 제2차 세계대전 이후

Between 2000 and 2014, / rates of participation in higher education / almost doubled / from 19% to 34% / across the world / among the members of the population / in the school-leaving age category / (typically 18 − 23).
2000년과 2014년 사이에, / 고등교육 참여율이 / 거의 두 배로 증가했다. / 19%에서 34%로 / 전 세계적으로 / 학교를 떠나는 연령대의 인구들 사이에서 / (보통 18세에서 23세)

The dramatic expansion of higher education / has been marked by / a wider range of institutions of higher learning / and a more diverse demographic of students.
고등교육의 극적인 확장은 / 특징지어진다. / 더 넓은 범위의 고등 교육 기관들로 / 그리고 더 다양한 학생 인구 통계로

Changes from an elite system / to a mass higher education system / are associated with / political needs / to build a (b) specialised workforce / for the economy.
엘리트 시스템에서의 변화는 / 대중 고등교육 시스템으로의 변화와 / 연관되어 있다. / 정치적 필요성과 / 경제를 위한 전문화된 노동력을 구축하기 위한

In theory, / the expansion of higher education / to develop a highly skilled workforce / should diminish / the role of examinations / in the selection and control of students, / initiating approaches to assessment / which (c) enable lifelong learning: / assessment *for* learning / and a focus on feedback for development.
이론적으로, / 고등교육의 확장은 / 고숙련 노동력을 개발하기 위해 / 줄어야 한다. / 시험의 역할을 / 학생 선발과 통제에서 / 평가 방식을 도입하면서 / 평생 학습을 촉진하는: / 학습을 *위한* 평가 / 그리고 성장을 위한 피드백에 중점을 둔

「In reality, / socio-political changes / to expand higher education / have set up / a 'field of contradictions' / for assessment in higher education.」 [41번의 근거]
현실적으로, / 사회정치적 변화가 / 고등교육을 확장하려는 / 세워 놓았다. / '모순의 장'을 / 고등교육 평가에서

「Mass higher education / requires efficient approaches to assessment, / such as examinations / and multiple-choice quizzes, with minimalist, / (d) impersonal, / or standardised feedback, / often causing students / to focus more on grades / than feedback.」 [42번의 근거]
대중 고등교육은 / 효율적 평가 방식을 요구한다. / 예를 들어 시험 / 그리고 객관식 퀴즈 같은 최소한의, / 비인격적인 / 또는 표준화된 피드백을 통해, / 종종 학생들로 하여금 / 성적에 더 집중하게 만든다. / 피드백보다

In contrast, / the relatively small numbers of students / in elite systems in the past / (e) allowed for closer relationships / between students and their teachers, / with formative feedback / shaping the minds, / academic skills, / and even the characters of students.
대조적으로, / 상대적으로 적은 수의 학생들이 / 과거의 엘리트 시스템에서 / 더 밀접한 관계를 허용했다. / 학생들과 그들의 교사들 간에 / 형성적 피드백을 통해 / 사고를 형성하고, / 학업 능력이, / 심지어 학생들의 성격까지도

고등 교육은 전 세계에 걸쳐 엘리트에서 대중 체제로 성장해 왔다. 유럽과 미국에서는 2차 세계 대전 이후 수십 년 동안 (a) 증가된 참여율이 나타났다. 2000년과 2014년 사이에 졸업 연령 범주 (대체로 18세에서 23세) 내 집단 구성원 사이에서의 고등 교육 참여율은 전 세계에 걸쳐 19%에서 34%로 거의 두 배가 되었다. 고등 교육의 극적인 확대는 더 광범위한 고등 학습 기관과 더 다양한 학생 인구 집단으로 특징지어져 왔다.
엘리트 체제에서 대중 고등 교육 체제로의 변화는 경제를 위한 (b) 전문화된 노동력을 구축하려는 정치적 필요성과 관련이 있다. 이론적으로, 고도로 숙련된 노동력을 개발하기 위한 고등 교육의 확대는 평생학습을 (c) 막는(→ 가능하게 하는) 평가로의 접근 방법, 즉, 학습을 '위한' 평가와 발달을 위한 피드백에 집중을 시작하면서, 학생의 선발과 통제에 있어 시험의 역할을 감소시킬 것이다. 실제로는 고등 교육을 확대하기 위한 사회 정치적 변화는 고등 교육에서의 평가에 있어 '모순의 장'을 조성해 왔다. 대중 고등 교육은 최소한이거나 (d) 비인격적이거나 또는 표준화된 피드백을 갖춘, 시험과 선다형 퀴즈와 같은, 평가의 효율적인 접근 방법을 필요로 하며, 이는 종종 학생이 피드백보다 성적에 더 집중하게 만든다. 대조적으로, 과거에 엘리트 체제의 상대적으로 적은 학생의 수는 형성적 피드백이 학생의 마음, 학업 기술, 그리고 심지어 학생의 성격을 형성하면서, 학생과 그들의 선생님 사이의 더 긴밀한 관계를 (e) 허용했다.

- elite ⓝ 엘리트
- increase ⓝ 증가하다
- occur ⓥ 발생하다
- population ⓝ 인구
- diverse ⓐ 다양한
- allow ⓥ 허락하다
- formative ⓐ 형태적인
- mass ⓝ 대량
- participation ⓝ 참가
- education ⓝ 교육
- category ⓝ 분류
- demographic ⓐ 인구학의
- relationship ⓝ 관계
- feedback ⓝ 평가

구문 풀이

11행 Changes from an elite system to a mass higher education system are
from A to B : A에서 B까지 / 동사
associated with political needs to build a specialised workforce for the economy.
to부정사(부사적 용법) / 과거분사

41 제목 파악
정답률 58% | 정답 ③

윗글의 제목으로 가장 적절한 것은?

① Is It Possible to Teach Without Assessment? – 평가 없이 가르치는 것이 가능한가?
② Elite vs. Public: A History of Modern Class Society – 엘리트 대 대중: 현대 계급 사회의 역사
✓③ Mass Higher Education and Its Reality in Assessment – 대중 고등 교육과 평가의 현실
④ Impacts of Mass Higher Education on Teachers' Status – 교사의 지위에 대중 고등 교육의 영향
⑤ Mass Higher Education Leads to Economic Development – 대중 고등 교육이 경제 발달로 이끈다

Why? 왜 정답일까?

고등 교육이 엘리트 집단에서 대중 체제로 이동하는 과정에서 겪는 평가의 문제에 대해 다룬 글이다. 학습을 위한 평가와 발달을 위한 피드백에 집중하며 시험의 역할이 감소하고, 이것을 '모순의 장'이라고 일컫는다. 왜냐하면 발달을 위한 피드백이 종종 학생들이 피드백보다 성적에 더 집중하게 만들기 때문이라고 설명한다. 과거 엘리트 체제의 형성적 피드백이 학생의 발달에 더 효과적이었다고 글을 마치기 때문에, 제목으로 가장 적절한 것은 ③ 'Mass Higher Education and Its Reality in Assessment'이다.

★★★ 등급을 가르는 문제!

42 어휘 추론
정답률 38% | 정답 ③

밑줄 친 (a) ~ (e) 중에서 문맥상 낱말의 쓰임이 적절하지 않은 것은? [3점]
① (a) ② (b) ✓③ (c) ④ (d) ⑤ (e)

Why? 왜 정답일까?

고등 교육이 대중을 대상으로 행해졌을 때 엘리트를 대상으로 행해졌을 때보다 평가의 측면에서 본래 목적인 학생들의 발달에 집중하지 못한다는 글이다. 따라서 'In theory, the expansion of higher education to develop a highly skilled workforce should diminish the role of examinations in the selection and control of students, initiating approaches to assessment which block lifelong learning: assessment for learning and a focus on feedback for development.'(이론적으로, 고도로 숙련된 노동력을 개발하기 위한 고등 교육의 확대는 평생학습을 막는 평가로의 접근 방법, 즉, 학습을 '위한' 평가와 발달을 위한 피드백에 집중을 시작하면서, 학생의 선발과 통제에 있어 시험의 역할을 감소시킬 것이다.)는 문장은 어색하다. 따라서 답은 ③ '(c)'이다.

▶ 많이 틀린 이유는?
고등 교육이 대중을 대상으로 행해졌을 때와 엘리트를 대상으로 행해졌을 때의 차이를 이해해야 풀 수 있다. 고숙련 노동력 개발을 위해 고등 교육이 대중화된 것이라면, 평생 학습을 지향해야 논리적이므로 'diminish'는 'enable'로 바꿔야 자연스럽다.
▶ 문제 해결 방법은?
개념이 두 개 이상 나오는 지문일 경우, 개념마다 해당되는 개념을 분리해서 이해해야한다. 자신만의 기호를 사용하여 표시하는 것도 직관적인 문제 풀이에 도움이 되니 활용해보자.

43-45 시인의 옷차림 바꾸기

(A)

Once upon a time / in the Iranian city of Shiraz, / there lived / the famous poet Sheikh Saadi.
옛날 옛적 / 이란의 시라즈라는 도시에, / 살고 있었다 / 유명한 시인 세이크 사디가
Like most other poets and philosophers, / he led / a very simple life.
다른 대부분의 시인과 철학자들처럼, / 그는 살았다 / 매우 소박한 삶을
A rich merchant of Shiraz / was preparing / for his daughter's wedding / and invited
(a) him / along with a lot of big businessmen / of the town.
시라즈의 한 부유한 상인이 / 준비하고 있었다 / 딸의 결혼식을 / 그리고 그를 초대했다 / 많은 부유한 상인들과 함께 / 그 마을의
『The poet accepted the invitation / and decided / to attend.』 45번 ①의 근거 일치
시인은 그 초대를 수락했고 / 결정했다 / 참석하기로

(D)

『On the day of the wedding, / the rich merchant, / the host of the wedding, / was receiving the guests / at the gate.』 45번 ④의 근거 일치
결혼식 날, / 그 부유한 상인이, / 결혼식의 주최자인, / 손님을 맞이하고 있었다. / 문 앞에서
『Many rich people of the town / attended the wedding.』 45번 ⑤의 근거 일치
그 마을의 많은 부유한 사람들이 / 그 결혼식에 참석했다.
They had come out / in their best clothes.
그들은 나왔다. / 최고의 옷을 입고
The poet wore simple clothes / which were neither grand / nor expensive.
시인은 간단한 옷을 입었다. / 그것은 화려하지도 / 비싸지도 않았다.
He waited / for someone to approach him / but no one gave (e) him / as much as even a second glance.
그는 기다렸다. / 누군가가 그에게 다가오기를 / 하지만 아무도 그에게 주지 않았다. / 두 번째 눈길조차도
Even the host / did not greet him / and looked away.
심지어 주최자조차도 / 그를 맞이하지 않았고 / 외면했다.

(C)

『Seeing all this, / the poet quietly left the party / and went / to a shop / where he could rent clothes.』 45번 ③의 근거 일치
이 모든 것을 보고, / 시인은 조용히 파티를 떠났고 / 가게로 갔다. / 그가 옷을 빌릴 수 있는
There he chose / a richly decorated coat, / which made him / look like a new person.
그곳에서 그는 골랐고 / 화려하게 장식된 코트를, / 그것은 그를 만들었다. / 새로운 사람처럼 보이게
With this coat, / he entered the party / and this time was welcomed / with open arms.
이 코트를 입고, / 그는 파티에 들어갔고 / 이번에는 환영받았다. / 따뜻하게
The host / embraced him / as (c) he would do / to an old friend / and complimented him / on the clothes / he was wearing.
주최자는 / 그를 포옹했다. / 그가 할 법한 것처럼 / 오랜 친구에게 / 그리고 칭찬했다 그를 / 그가 입고 있는 옷을
The poet / did not say a word / and allowed the host / to lead (d) him / to the dining room.
시인은 / 한 마디도 하지 않았고 / 주최자가 이끌도록 했다. / 그를 / 식당으로

(B)

The host personally led the poet / to his seat / and served out / chicken soup / to him.
주최자는 직접 시인을 이끌어 / 그의 자리로 / 그리고 대접했다. / 치킨 수프를 / 그에게
『After a moment, the poet suddenly dipped / the corner of his coat in the soup / as if he fed it.』 45번 ②의 근거 불일치
잠시 후, 시인은 갑자기 담갔다. / 그의 코트의 자락을 수프에 / 마치 그것을 먹이는 것처럼
All the guests / were now staring / at (b) him / in surprise.
모든 손님들이 / 이제 쳐다보고 있었다. / 그를 / 놀란 표정으로
The host said, / "Sir, what are you doing?"
주최자가 말했다. / "선생님, 무엇을 하고 계신 겁니까?"
The poet very calmly replied, / "Now that I have put on / expensive clothes, / I see / a world of difference / here.
시인은 매우 침착하게 대답했다. / "이제 내가 입었으니, / 비싼 옷을, / 나는 본다. / 여기에 엄청난 차이가 있음을
All that I can say now is that / this feast / is meant for my clothes, / not for me."
내가 이제 할 수 있는 말은 / 이 잔치는 / 내 옷을 위한 것이고, / 나를 위한 것이 아니라는 것이다."

(A)

옛날 옛적에 이란의 도시 Shiraz에 유명한 시인 Sheikh Saadi가 살았다. 대부분의 다른 시인들과 철학자들처럼 그는 매우 검소한 생활을 했다. Shiraz의 부유한 상인이 그의 딸의 결혼식을 준비하고 있었고 (a) 그를 그 마을의 많은 큰 사업가들과 함께 초대했다. 그 시인은 초대를 수락했고 참석하기로 결정했다.

(D)

결혼식 날, 결혼식의 혼주인 부유한 상인은 입구에서 손님을 맞이하고 있었다. 마을의 많은 부유한 사람들이 결혼식에 참석했다. 그들은 자신의 가장 좋은 옷차림으로 나왔다. 시인은 거창하지도 비싸지도 않은 소박한 옷을 입었다. 그는 누군가가 자신에게 다가오기를 기다렸지만 아무도 (e) 그에게 단 일 초의 눈길도 주지 않았다. 혼주조차도 그에게 인사하지 않고 눈길을 돌렸다.

(C)

이 모든 것을 보고 시인은 조용히 파티를 떠나 그가 옷을 빌릴 수 있는 가게로 갔다. 그곳에서 그는 화려하게 장식된 외투를 골랐고, 그것은 그를 새로운 사람처럼 보이게 만들었다. 이 외투를 입고, 그는 파티에 들어갔고 이번에는 두 팔 벌려 환영을 받았다. 혼주는 (c) 그가 오랜 친구에게 하듯이 그를 껴안았고, 그가 입고 있는 옷에 대해 그에게 칭찬했다. 시인은 한마디도 하지 않고 혼주가 (d) 그를 식당으로 안내하도록 허락했다.

(B)

혼주는 직접 시인을 그의 자리로 안내하고 그에게 닭고기 수프를 내주었다. 잠시 후에 시인은 마치 음식을 먹이듯 그의 외투 자락을 수프에 갑자기 담갔다. 모든 손님이 바로 (b) 그를

놀라서 바라보고 있었다. 혼주가 말했다. "선생님, 뭐 하는 겁니까?" 시인은 매우 침착하게 대답했다. "내가 비싼 옷을 입으니, 이곳에서 엄청난 차이를 봅니다. 내가 지금 할 수 있는 모든 말은 이 진수성찬이 내 옷을 위한 것이지, 나를 위한 것이 아니라는 것뿐입니다."

● famous ⓐ 유명한
● poet ⓝ 시인
● invite ⓥ 초대하다
● accept ⓥ 받아들이다
● attend ⓥ 참석하다
● philosopher ⓝ 철학가
● prepare ⓥ 준비하다
● businessmen ⓝ 사업가
● ivitation ⓝ 초대장

구문 풀이

(C) 1행 Seeing all this, the poet quietly left the party and went to a shop where
분사구문(= After he saw)   동사1   동사2   관계부사
he could rent clothes.

43 글의 순서 파악 정답률 61% | 정답 ⑤

주어진 글 (A)에 이어질 내용을 순서에 맞게 배열한 것으로 가장 적절한 것은?
① (B) - (D) - (C)
② (C) - (B) - (D)
③ (C) - (D) - (B)
④ (D) - (B) - (C)
✓ (D) - (C) - (B)

Why? 왜 정답일까?

주어진 글은 Shiraz의 부유한 상인이 결혼식을 준비하며 사업가들을 초대했다고 한다. 시인이 파티 초대를 받아들인 후 파티를 하는 결혼식 날 시작을 묘사하는 (D)가, 아무도 반겨주지 않아 시인이 파티를 떠나는 (C), 시인이 기존에 입었던 옷보다 화려한 옷을 입은 (C), 마지막으로 옷차림에 따라 대우가 달라진다는 (B)의 순서가 자연스럽다. 따라서 알맞은 순서는 ⑤ (D) - (C) - (B)이다.

44 지칭 추론 정답률 65% | 정답 ③

밑줄 친 (a) ~ (e) 중에서 가리키는 대상이 나머지 넷과 다른 것은?
① (a) ② (b) ✓ (c) ④ (d) ⑤ (e)

Why? 왜 정답일까?

(a), (b), (d), (e) 모두 시인을 가리키기 때문에, 파티 주최자를 뜻하는 (c)는 가리키는 대상이 나머지 넷과 다르다. 따라서 답은 ③ '(c)'이다.

45 세부 내용 파악 정답률 69% | 정답 ②

윗글에 관한 내용으로 적절하지 않은 것은?
① 시인은 상인의 초대를 받아들였다.
✓ 상인은 시인의 외투 자락을 수프에 담갔다.
③ 시인은 옷을 빌릴 수 있는 가게로 갔다.
④ 결혼식 날 상인은 입구에서 손님을 맞이했다.
⑤ 마을의 많은 부유한 사람들이 결혼식에 참석했다.

Why? 왜 정답일까?

(B)의 'After a moment, the poet suddenly dipped the corner of his coat in the soup as if he fed it'에서 'he'는 시인을 가리키기 때문에 시인이 외투 자락을 수프에 담근 것이므로 윗글에 대한 내용으로 적절하지 않은 것은 '② 상인은 시인의 외투 자락을 수프에 담갔다.'이다.

Why? 왜 오답일까?

① (A) 'The poet accepted the invitation and decided to attend.'의 내용과 일치한다.
③ (C) 'Seeing all this, the poet quietly left the party and went to a shop where he could rent clothes.'의 내용과 일치한다.
④ (D) 'On the day of the wedding, the rich merchant, the host of the wedding, was receiving the guests at the gate.'의 내용과 일치한다.
⑤ (D) 'Many rich people of the town attended the wedding.'의 내용과 일치한다.

01 are expected to visit / the regular last train / fantastic festival with convenience
02 before you go to bed / used to spending / will increase the quality
03 hobbies completely unrelated to / different from our work / be a powerful tool
04 sound quality is excellent / helpful for long recordings / like where music truly
05 go over our preparations / some eco-friendly bags / serve the guests
06 a camping table / our best-selling product / this discount coupon now
07 go mountain climbing / something important to do / competition you mentioned
08 program for the residents / fill out an application / take your ID card
09 happy to announce / to worry about prices / have menus for vegetarians
10 pay more than / the water intake display / go with the one
11 easily catch a cold / keep some moisture
12 no space for / throwing away the books / some of them are
13 was working well together / assign individual tasks / lead to overlapping tasks
14 working out a lot / about when I eat / enough to get me
15 living in the dormitory / complicated to assemble it / is good at assembling
16-17 from natural materials / how to properly wash / washed separately and quickly

어휘 Review Test 07

문제편 098쪽

A	B	C	D
01 표현하다	01 climate	01 ⓘ	01 ⓢ
02 걱정	02 emission	02 ⓗ	02 ⓑ
03 되찾다, 회복하다	03 major	03 ⓣ	03 ⓗ
04 접근하다	04 source	04 ⓠ	04 ⓕ
05 닦다	05 physicist	05 ⓝ	05 ⓓ
06 소생하다	06 support	06 ⓜ	06 ⓘ
07 눈에 띄는	07 submit	07 ⓚ	07 ⓜ
08 놀라운	08 inventor	08 ⓞ	08 ⓛ
09 달성	09 category	09 ⓓ	09 ⓖ
10 지배적인	10 participant	10 ⓛ	10 ⓥ
11 상태	11 annual	11 ⓐ	11 ⓟ
12 의식	12 participate	12 ⓡ	12 ⓔ
13 기여하다	13 exhibition	13 ⓒ	13 ⓕ
14 관점, 시각	14 viewpoint	14 ⓔ	14 ⓘ
15 공포, 두려움, 무서움	15 functional	15 ⓛ	15 ⓡ
16 도와주는	16 acquire	16 ⓘ	16 ⓝ
17 기기	17 alternative	17 ⓑ	17 ⓚ
18 향상시키다	18 rather	18 ⓢ	18 ⓞ
19 효율적인	19 component	19 ⓟ	19 ⓐ
20 추산하다	20 initial	20 ⓖ	20 ⓒ

08회 | 2023학년도 9월 학력평가

| 정답과 해설 |

고1

• 정답 •

01⑤ 02① 03③ 04⑤ 05① 06③ 07④ 08③ 09④ 10④ 11① 12④ 13① 14③ 15⑤
16③ 17③ 18⑤ 19② 20② 21⑤ 22④ 23② 24① 25④ 26④ 27④ 28⑤ 29④ 30②
31① 32③ 33② 34① 35② 36② 37③ 38⑤ 39⑤ 40① 41④ 42⑤ 43④ 44③ 45④

★ 표기된 문항은 [등급을 가르는 문제]에 해당하는 문항입니다.

01 록 밴드 콘서트장 변경 안내
정답률 93% | 정답 ⑤

다음을 듣고, 남자가 하는 말의 목적으로 가장 적절한 것을 고르시오.
① 강당의 천장 수리 기간을 공지하려고
② 콘서트 관람 규칙 준수를 요청하려고
③ 학교 축제에서 공연할 동아리를 모집하려고
④ 폭우에 대비한 교실 시설 관리를 당부하려고
☑ 학교 록 밴드 공연의 장소 변경을 안내하려고

M : Attention, Fargo High School students.
집중해 주세요, Fargo 고등학교 학생 여러분.
This is your music teacher, Mr. Nelson.
저는 음악 교사인 Nelson 선생님입니다.
Our school rock band was supposed to hold its concert in the auditorium today.
우리 학교 록 밴드가 오늘 강당에서 콘서트를 열 예정이었습니다.
I'm sure you've been looking forward to the concert.
분명 여러분은 이 콘서트를 기다려 왔겠죠.
Unfortunately, the rain yesterday caused a leak in the ceiling of the auditorium.
유감스럽게도, 어제 온 비로 강당 천장에 누수가 생겼습니다.
The ceiling needs to be fixed, so we decided to change the location of the concert.
천장을 수리해야 해서, 우리는 콘서트 장소를 바꾸기로 했습니다.
The rock band will now perform in the school theater.
록 밴드는 이제 학교 극장에서 공연할 계획입니다.
The time for the concert hasn't changed.
콘서트 시간은 바뀌지 않았습니다.
I hope you'll enjoy the performance.
여러분이 공연을 즐기기를 바랍니다.

Why? 왜 정답일까?

'~ we decided to change the location of the concert. The rock band will now perform in the school theater.'에서 학교 록 밴드 콘서트 공연장이 강당에서 극장으로 바뀌었다고 공지하고 있다. 따라서 남자가 하는 말의 목적으로 가장 적절한 것은 ⑤ '학교 록 밴드 공연의 장소 변경을 안내하려고'이다.

● be supposed to ~할 예정이다
● leak ⓝ 누수
● theater ⓝ 극장
● auditorium ⓝ 강당
● location ⓝ 장소, 위치

02 달리기에 적합한 신발 신기
정답률 98% | 정답 ①

대화를 듣고, 여자의 의견으로 가장 적절한 것을 고르시오.
☑ 달리기를 할 때 적합한 신발을 신어야 한다.
② 운동을 한 후에 충분한 물을 섭취해야 한다.
③ 야외 활동 전에 일기예보를 확인하는 것이 좋다.
④ 달리기 전 스트레칭은 통증과 부상을 예방해 준다.
⑤ 초보자의 경우 달리는 거리를 점진적으로 늘려야 한다.

W : Simon, are you doing anything after school?
Simon, 너 학교 끝나고 할 거 있어?
M : Nothing special. What about you?
별다른 거 없어. 넌?
W : I'm planning to go for a run in the park. It's a five-kilometer route.
난 공원에 달리기하러 가려고. 5킬로미터 코스야.
M : The weather is perfect for running. Can I go with you?
날씨가 달리기하기 제격이네. 나도 가도 돼?
W : Why not? [Pause] Wait! You're wearing slippers. Those aren't good for running.
당연하지. [잠시 멈춤] 잠깐! 너 슬리퍼를 신었잖아. 그건 달리기에 좋지 않아.
M : It's okay. I can run in slippers.
괜찮아. 슬리퍼 신고도 뛸 수 있어.
W : No way. Slippers aren't designed for running. You can get hurt if you run in them.
절대 안 돼. 슬리퍼는 달리기를 위해 만들어진 게 아냐. 그걸 신고 뛰면 넌 다칠 수도 있어.
M : You mean I need to put on running shoes?
네 말은 내가 러닝화를 신어야 한다는 거야?
W : You got it. You need to wear the right shoes for running.
바로 그거야. 넌 달리기에 적합한 신발을 신어야 해.
M : All right. I'll go home and change.
알겠어. 집에 가서 바꿔 신을게.

Why? 왜 정답일까?

'You need to wear the right shoes for running.'에서 달리기에 적합한 신발을 신으라고 말하는 것으로 보아, 여자의 의견으로 가장 적절한 것은 ① '달리기를 할 때 적합한 신발을 신어야 한다.'이다.

● go for a run 달리기하러 가다
● No way. 절대 안 돼.
● route ⓝ 길
● get hurt 다치다

03 영화 의상 디자이너 인터뷰하기
정답률 90% | 정답 ③

대화를 듣고, 두 사람의 관계를 가장 잘 나타낸 것을 고르시오.

① 관객 – 영화감독 ② 연극 배우 – 시나리오 작가
✓ 잡지 기자 – 의상 디자이너 ④ 토크쇼 진행자 – 영화 평론가
⑤ 배우 지망생 – 연기 학원 강사

M : Good morning, Ms. Clapton. It's nice to meet you.
안녕하세요, Ms. Clapton. 만나서 반가워요.
W : Nice to meet you, too. I'm a fan of your articles.
저도 만나서 반가워요. 전 당신 기사의 팬이에요.
M : You won many awards at the film festival this year. Congratulations!
당신은 올해 영화제에서 상을 많이 받았죠. 축하드려요!
W : Thank you. I was lucky to work with a great director and talented actors.
고맙습니다. 훌륭한 감독님과 재능 있는 배우들과 작업해서 운이 좋았죠.
M : The clothes and accessories in the movie are impressive. How do you start your costume designs?
영화 속 의상과 액세서리가 인상적이던데요. 의상 디자인을 어떻게 시작하시나요?
W : I read the script to fully understand the characters. Then I research the characters' backgrounds.
등장인물들을 완전히 이해하기 위해 대본을 읽어요. 그런 다음 인물들의 배경을 연구하죠.
M : That sounds like a lot of work. Which of the costumes from this film is your favorite?
일이 많으실 것 같아요. 이번 영화에서는 어떤 의상이 가장 마음에 드셨나요?
W : It's hard to pick just one because I love all of my designs.
전 제 디자인을 다 좋아해서 하나만 고르기가 어려워요.
M : I totally understand. Thank you for sharing your story with the readers of our magazine.
전적으로 이해되는 말씀이에요. 저희 잡지 독자분들께 당신의 이야기를 공유해주셔서 고맙습니다.
W : It was my pleasure.
제가 감사하죠.

Why? 왜 정답일까?

'I'm a fan of your articles.', 'How do you start your costume designs?', 'Thank you for sharing your story with the readers of our magazine.' 등을 통해, 잡지 기자인 남자가 영화 의상 디자이너인 여자를 인터뷰하는 대화임을 알 수 있다. 따라서 두 사람의 관계로 가장 적절한 것은 ③ '잡지 기자 – 의상 디자이너'이다.

● talented ⓐ 재능 있는 ● impressive ⓐ 인상적인
● costume ⓝ 의상

04 새 열람실 구경하기 정답률 83% | 정답 ⑤

대화를 듣고, 그림에서 대화의 내용과 일치하지 <u>않는</u> 것을 고르시오.

W : Come look at the new reading room in the library.
와서 도서관의 새 열람실 좀 봐봐.
M : Wow! It's much better than I thought.
왜! 내가 생각한 것보다 훨씬 근사해.
W : Same here. 「I like the rug in the center of the room.
나도 그렇게 생각해. 방 가운데 있는 러그가 마음에 들어.
M : The striped pattern of the rug makes the room feel warm.」 ①의근거 일치
러그의 줄무늬가 방이 따뜻해 보이게 해주네.
W : I agree. 「I think putting the sofa between two plants was a good idea.」 ②의근거 일치
동의해. 내 생각엔 두 화분 사이에 소파를 둔 게 좋은 아이디어인 것 같아.
M : Right. We can sit there and read for hours.
그러게. 저기 앉아서 몇 시간이고 책을 읽을 수 있겠어.
W : 「There's a round clock on the wall.」 ③의근거 일치
벽에는 둥근 시계가 있네.
M : I have the same clock at home. 「Oh, the bookshelf under the clock is full of books.」
나 집에 똑같은 시계 있어. 오, 시계 밑에 있는 책장에 책이 가득하네. ④의근거 일치
W : We can read the books at the long table.
긴 책상에 앉아서 책을 읽을 수 있겠네.
M : Yeah, it looks like a good place to read. 「The two lamps on the table will make it easy to focus.」 ⑤의근거 불일치
그러게, 독서하기 좋은 장소로 보여. 책상에 있는 전등 두 개가 집중하기 편하게 해줄 거야.
W : Good lighting is important for reading.
좋은 조명은 독서에 중요하지.
M : I can't wait to start using the reading room.
열람실을 이용하기 시작할 게 몹시 기대돼.

Why? 왜 정답일까?

대화에서는 책상에 조명이 두 개 있다(The two lamps on the table will make it easy to focus.)고 하는데, 그림 속 책상에는 조명이 하나뿐이다. 따라서 그림에서 대화의 내용과 일치하지 않는 것은 ⑤이다.

● Same here. 나도 그렇게 생각해.

05 뮤지컬 공연 준비 정답률 89% | 정답 ①

대화를 듣고, 여자가 할 일로 가장 적절한 것을 고르시오.

✓ 관객용 의자 배치하기 ② 마이크 음향 점검하기
③ 공연 포스터 붙이기 ④ 무대 조명 설치하기
⑤ 배터리 구매하기

M : Kelly, the school musical is tomorrow. Shall we go over the final checklist together?
Kelly, 학교 뮤지컬이 내일이야. 최종 체크리스트를 같이 검토할까?
W : Let's do it. What's first? [Pause] Oh, the posters. We put them up around school last week.
그렇게 하자. 뭐가 제일 먼저지? [잠시 멈춤] 아, 포스터. 우린 그걸 지난주에 학교 전체에 붙였어.
M : Right. Do we have extra batteries for the wireless microphones?
맞아. 우리 무선 마이크에 넣을 여분 배터리 있나?
W : Yeah. I bought them yesterday. We should check that the microphones work well with the sound system.
응, 내가 어제 샀어. 우린 마이크가 음향 시스템하고 같이 잘 작동하는지 확인해야 해.
M : I did that this morning. They sound terrific.
내가 오늘 아침에 했어. 소리 근사하더라.
W : How about the stage lights?
무대 조명은?
M : They work perfectly. I think everyone will love the lighting design you made.
그것도 완벽하게 작동해. 네가 한 조명 디자인을 모두가 좋아할 것 같아.
W : Really? Thanks. It looks like we've finished everything.
정말? 고마워. 우리 다 끝낸 거 같아.
M : No, wait. The chairs for the audience haven't been arranged yet.
아냐, 잠깐. 관객용 의자가 아직 배치되지 않았어.
W : You're right! I'll go take care of that now.
맞다! 내가 그거 지금 처리할게.
M : The musical is going to be fantastic.
뮤지컬은 환상적일 거야.

Why? 왜 정답일까?

남자가 관객용 의자가 아직 세팅되지 않았다고 하자(The chairs for the audience haven't been arranged yet.) 여자는 자신이 가서 처리하겠다고 한다(You're right! I'll go take care of that now.). 따라서 여자가 할 일로 가장 적절한 것은 ① '관객용 의자 배치하기'이다.

● go over 검토하다 ● put up 게시하다
● terrific ⓐ 근사한, 훌륭한

06 꽃 바구니 주문하기 정답률 79% | 정답 ③

대화를 듣고, 남자가 지불할 금액을 고르시오. [3점]
① $37 ② $45 ✓ $55 ④ $60 ⑤ $80

W : Welcome to Libby's Flowers. How can I help you?
Libby's Flowers에 잘 오셨어요. 무엇을 도와드릴까요?
M : I'd like to order a rose basket for my parents' wedding anniversary.
저희 부모님 결혼기념일을 위해 장미꽃 바구니를 주문하려고요.
W : All right. Our rose baskets come in two sizes.
알겠습니다. 저희 장미꽃 바구니는 두 가지 크기로 나와요.
M : What are the options?
어떻게 나오죠?
W : The regular size is 30 dollars, and the large size is 50 dollars.
보통 크기는 30달러이고, 큰 것은 50달러입니다.
M : Hmm.... I think the bigger one is better.
흠... 전 더 큰 게 좋을 것 같아요.
W : Good choice. So, you'll get one rose basket in the large size. By the way, we're giving a 10-percent discount on all purchases this week.
잘 고르셨네요. 그럼, 장미꽃 바구니 하나 큰 사이즈로 하시는 거고요. 그런데 이번 주 모든 구매에 대해서 10퍼센트 할인을 해 드리고 있어요.
M : Excellent! When will my order be ready?
아주 좋아요! 제 주문은 언제 다 될까요?
W : It'll be ready around 11 a.m. If you can't pick it up, we offer a delivery service. It's 10 dollars.
오전 11시 정도에 다 될 겁니다. 수령하실 수 없으면, 배달 서비스를 제공해 드려요. 10달러입니다.
M : Oh, great. I'd like it to be delivered. Here's my credit card.
오, 좋네요. 배송받고 싶어요. 여기 제 신용 카드요.

Why? 왜 정답일까?

대화에 따르면, 남자는 부모님의 결혼 기념일을 위해 50달러짜리 큰 장미꽃 바구니를 하나 주문하고 10퍼센트 할인을 적용받았으며, 추가로 10달러를 내고 배송 서비스도 이용하기로 하였다. 이를 식으로 나타내면 '50×0.9+10=55'이므로, 남자가 지불할 금액은 ③ '$55'이다.

● anniversary ⓝ 기념일 ● come in (제품이 특정 색상이나 크기로) 나오다
● delivery ⓝ 배송

07 스키 여행에 함께하지 못하는 이유 정답률 92% | 정답 ④

대화를 듣고, 여자가 스키 여행을 갈 수 없는 이유를 고르시오.
① 카페에서 일해야 해서 ② 숙소를 예약하지 못해서
③ 역사 시험 공부를 해야 해서 ✓ 수술받은 고양이를 돌봐야 해서
⑤ 캐나다에 사는 친척을 방문해야 해서

M : You seem busy this morning, Olivia.
너 오늘 아침 바빠 보이네, Olivia.
W : I am. I had to see Professor Martin about my history test.
바쁜 거 맞아. 역사 시험 관련해서 Martin 교수님을 뵈어야 했어.
M : Oh, I see. Do you remember that our club's ski trip is this weekend?
오, 그렇구나. 너 우리 동아리 스키 여행이 이번 주말인 거 기억해?
W : Yeah. I heard that a nice ski resort has been booked for the trip.
응, 여행을 위해 근사한 스키 리조트를 예약했다는 거 들었어.
M : I didn't know that. I'm so excited to go skiing at a nice resort.
그건 몰랐네. 근사한 리조트로 스키 타러 갈 생각에 몹시 신나.
W : I bet it'll be great, but I don't think I can go this time.
근사할 게 분명해. 그런데 난 이번엔 못 갈 거 같아.
M : Why? You don't work at the cafe on the weekends, do you?
왜? 너 주말에는 카페에서 일 안 하잖아, 맞지?
W : No, I don't. But I need to take care of my cat. She's recovering from surgery.
어, 안 하지. 그런데 내 고양이를 돌봐야 해. 수술 받고 회복 중이거든.

M : Isn't there anyone else who can look after your cat?
네 고양이를 돌봐줄 다른 사람은 없는 거야?

W : No one but me. My parents are visiting relatives in Canada. They won't be back for two weeks.
나밖에 없어. 우리 부모님은 캐나다 친척 집에 가셨어. 2주 동안 안 계실 거야.

M : I'm sorry that you can't join us.
네가 올 수 없다니 유감이네.

W : Me, too. Have fun this weekend.
나도 그래. 이번 주말 재미있게 보내.

여자는 수술을 받고 회복 중인 고양이를 돌봐야 해서(But I need to take care of my cat. She's recovering from surgery.) 스키 여행에 동행할 수 없다고 한다. 따라서 여자가 스키 여행을 가지 못하는 이유로 가장 적절한 것은 ④ '수술받은 고양이를 돌봐야 해서'이다.

- recover from ~에서 회복하다
- look after ~을 돌보다
- surgery ⓝ 수술
- relative ⓝ 친척

08 일상 사진 대회   정답률 88% | 정답 ③

대화를 듣고, Street Photography Contest에 관해 언급되지 않은 것을 고르시오.
① 참가 대상 ② 주제 ✓③ 심사 기준 ④ 제출 마감일 ⑤ 우승 상품

W : What are you doing, Tim?
뭐 하고 있어, Tim?

M : I'm looking at the Street Photography Contest website.
난 Street Photography Contest 웹사이트를 보고 있어.

W : I've heard about that. 『It's a contest for college students, right?』
나도 그거 들었어. 대학생을 대상으로 한 대회지, 맞지?

M : Actually, it's open to high school students, too. Why don't you try it? 『①의 근거 일치』
사실, 고등학생도 대상으로 해. 너도 참가하면 어때?

W : Really? Maybe I will. 『Does the contest have a theme?』
정말? 해볼까 봐. 대회에 주제가 있어?

M : Sure. This year's theme is Daily Life. 『②의 근거 일치』
그럼. 올해의 주제는 일상이야.

W : That sounds interesting. 『When is the deadline?』
그거 재미있겠다. 기한이 언제야?

M : You have to submit your photographs by September 15. 『④의 근거 일치』
9월 15일까지는 네 사진을 내야 해.

W : That's sooner than I expected.
예상보다 금방이네.

M : You should hurry and choose your photos. 『The winner will receive a laptop as a prize.』 『⑤의 근거 일치』
서둘러서 사진을 골라봐. 우승자는 상품으로 노트북을 받을 거야.

W : Okay! Wish me luck.
그래! 행운을 빌어줘.

남자와 여자는 Street Photography Contest의 참가 대상, 주제, 제출 마감일, 우승 상품을 언급하고 있으므로, 언급되지 않은 것은 ③ '심사 기준'이다.

① 'It's a contest for college students, right? / Actually, it's open to high school students, too.'에서 '참가 대상'이 언급되었다.
② 'This year's theme is Daily Life.'에서 '주제'가 언급되었다.
④ 'You have to submit your photographs by September 15.'에서 '제출 마감일'이 언급되었다.
⑤ 'The winner will receive a laptop as a prize.'에서 '우승 상품'이 언급되었다.

- photography ⓝ 사진
- deadline ⓝ 기한
- Wish me luck. 행운을 빌어줘.
- daily life 일상
- laptop ⓝ 노트북 컴퓨터

09 초콜릿 박물관에서 여는 특별 행사   정답률 91% | 정답 ④

Twin Stars Chocolate Day에 관한 다음 내용을 듣고, 일치하지 않는 것을 고르시오.
① 11월 12일 오후에 열린다.
② 초콜릿의 역사에 관한 강의가 진행된다.
③ 초콜릿 5개를 만든다.
✓④ 사전 등록 없이 참가할 수 있다.
⑤ 등록비에 재료비가 포함된다.

M : Hello, listeners. I'm Charlie Anderson from the Twin Stars Chocolate Museum.
안녕하세요, 청취자 여러분. 저는 Twin Stars 초콜릿 박물관에서 나온 Charlie Anderson입니다.
I'm happy to introduce the Twin Stars Chocolate Day, a special opportunity to create your own delicious chocolates.
여러분만의 맛있는 초콜릿을 만들어볼 수 있는 특별한 기회인 Twin Stars Chocolate Day를 소개해 드리게 되어 기쁩니다.
『It'll be held on November 12 from 1 p.m. to 4 p.m.』 『①의 근거 일치』
이것은 11월 12일 오후 1시부터 4시까지 열립니다.
『First, you'll listen to a lecture about the history of chocolate.』 『②의 근거 일치』
먼저 여러분은 초콜릿의 역사에 관한 강의를 들으시게 됩니다.
Then you'll have a chance to taste our most popular flavors.
그런 다음, 저희의 가장 인기 있는 맛을 시식하실 기회가 있습니다.
『At the end of the event, you'll make five chocolates yourself.』 『③의 근거 일치』
행사 끝무렵에, 여러분은 직접 5개의 초콜릿을 만드실 겁니다.
『If you want to take part in the event, you must register in advance.』 『④의 근거 불일치』
이 행사에 참여하고 싶으시다면, 사전 등록을 해주셔야 합니다.
You can sign up on our website until November 1.
11월 1일까지 저희 웹사이트에서 등록하실 수 있습니다.
『The registration fee is 20 dollars, which includes the cost of ingredients.』 『⑤의 근거 일치』
등록비는 20달러로, 여기에는 재료비가 포함됩니다.
Don't miss this sweet opportunity!
이 달콤한 기회를 놓치지 마세요!

'If you want to take part in the event, you must register in advance.'에서 참여를 희망한다면 미리 등록해달라고 하므로, 내용과 일치하지 않는 것은 ④ '사전 등록 없이 참가할 수 있다.'이다.

① 'It'll be held on November 12 from 1 p.m. to 4 p.m.'의 내용과 일치한다.
② 'First, you'll listen to a lecture about the history of chocolate.'의 내용과 일치한다.
③ 'At the end of the event, you'll make five chocolates yourself.'의 내용과 일치한다.
⑤ 'The registration fee is 20 dollars, which includes the cost of ingredients.'의 내용과 일치한다.

- delicious ⓐ 맛있는
- take part in ~에 참여하다
- ingredient ⓝ 재료
- lecture ⓝ 강의
- in advance 미리

10 실내 자전거 주문하기   정답률 89% | 정답 ④

다음 표를 보면서 대화를 듣고, 두 사람이 주문할 실내 사이클링 자전거를 고르시오.

Indoor Cycling Bikes

	Model	Price	Color	Foldable	Customer Rating
①	A	$100	White	×	★★★★
②	B	$150	Black	×	★★★
③	C	$190	Black	○	★★★★
✓④	D	$250	Black	○	★★★★★
⑤	E	$320	White	×	★★★★★

M : Honey, what are you looking at?
여보, 뭘 보고 있어요?

W : I'm looking at indoor cycling bikes. Would you like to choose one together?
실내 사이클링 자전거를 보고 있어요. 같이 하나 고를래요?

M : Sure, let me see. [Pause] The price differs by model.
그래요, 나도 볼래요. [잠시 멈춤] 가격이 제품별로 다르군요.

W : 『I don't want to pay more than 300 dollars. That's too expensive.』 『근거1 Price 조건』
난 300달러 이상 지불하고 싶지 않아요. 너무 비싸요.

M : I agree. 『Which color do you like?』
동의해요. 어느 색이 마음에 들어요?

W : I prefer a dark color because it goes well with our living room.
어두운 색이 좋아요, 우리 거실하고 잘 어울리니까요.

M : Okay. Then we shouldn't get a white one.』 『What do you think about the foldable one? 『근거2 Color 조건』 『근거3 Foldable 조건』
알겠어요. 그럼 우린 흰색을 사면 안 되겠어요. 접을 수 있는 건 어때요?

W : We definitely need that.』 It'll take up less storage space.
당연히 그게 필요해요. 보관 공간을 덜 차지할 거예요.

M : We have just two options left. Which one should we get?
선택권이 두 개 남았어요. 어느 걸 살까요? 『근거4 Customer Rating 조건』

W : 『I think we should go with the one with a higher customer rating.』 The reviews are based on actual customers' experiences.
고객 평점이 더 높은 걸 사야 할 것 같아요. 리뷰는 실제 고객 경험에 바탕을 두잖아요.

M : Sounds good. Let's order this one.
좋은 거 같아요. 이걸로 주문할게요.

대화에 따르면 두 사람은 가격이 300달러를 넘지 않으면서, 색상은 흰색이 아니고, 접을 수 있으면서, 고객 평점이 더 높은 자전거를 사려고 한다. 따라서 두 사람이 주문할 실내 사이클링 자전거는 ④ 'D'이다.

- go with ~와 어울리다
- take up 차지하다
- foldable ⓐ 접을 수 있는
- storage ⓝ 보관, 저장

11 스웨터를 어디서 샀는지 물어보기   정답률 90% | 정답 ①

대화를 듣고, 여자의 마지막 말에 대한 남자의 응답으로 가장 적절한 것을 고르시오.
✓① Sure. I'll send you a link to the website. - 물론이지. 내가 웹사이트 링크를 보내줄게.
② It would look better in a different color. - 다른 색이면 더 잘 어울릴 텐데.
③ Sorry. I forgot to bring your sweater. - 미안해. 네 스웨터 가져오는 걸 잊어버렸어.
④ You need your receipt to return it. - 그거 환불하려면 영수증이 필요해.
⑤ My brother bought it on sale, too. - 내 남동생도 세일 때 그걸 샀어.

W : Jason, is that a new sweater? It looks good on you.
Jason, 그거 새 스웨터야? 너한테 잘 어울리네.

M : Thanks. I bought it online. It was on sale.
고마워. 온라인에서 샀어. 세일하더라고.

W : I'd love to buy the same one for my brother. Can you tell me where you got it?
내 남동생한테도 똑같은 거 사주고 싶어. 어디서 샀는지 말해줄래?

M : Sure. I'll send you a link to the website.
물론이지. 내가 웹사이트 링크를 보내줄게.

여자는 남자가 입은 스웨터가 잘 어울린다면서 자신의 남동생에게도 똑같은 것을 사주고 싶으니 어디서 샀는지 말해달라고 한다(Can you tell me where you got it?). 따라서 여자의 말에 대한 남자의 응답으로 가장 적절한 것은 ① '물론이지. 내가 웹사이트 링크를 보내줄게.'이다.

- look good on ~에게 잘 어울리다
- on sale 할인 중인

12 식사 주문 확인하기   정답률 79% | 정답 ④

대화를 듣고, 남자의 마지막 말에 대한 여자의 응답으로 가장 적절한 것을 고르시오.
① Let's take the leftovers home. - 남은 걸 집에 싸 가자.
② I prefer fried chicken over pizza. - 난 피자보다 치킨이 더 좋아.

③ I don't want to go out for lunch today. - 오늘은 점심 먹으러 나가고 싶지 않아.
✓ I'll call the restaurant and check our order. - 내가 식당에 전화해서 우리 주문 확인해볼게.
⑤ The letter was delivered to the wrong address. - 편지가 잘못된 주소로 배달됐어.

M : Becky, did you order our food for dinner?
Becky, 우리 저녁 식사 주문했어?
W : Yes. I ordered pizza about an hour ago.
응. 한 시간쯤 전에 피자 시켰어.
M : An hour ago? Delivery usually takes less than 40 minutes.
한 시간 전이라고? 배달은 보통 40분도 안 걸려.
W : I'll call the restaurant and check our order.
내가 식당에 전화해서 우리 주문 확인해볼게.

Why? 왜 정답일까?

남자는 여자가 저녁 식사로 한 시간쯤 전에 피자를 주문했다는 말에 배달이 평소 40분도 안 걸린다며 의아해하고 있다(An hour ago? Delivery usually takes less than 40 minutes.) 따라서 남자의 말에 대한 여자의 응답으로 가장 적절한 것은 ④ '내가 식당에 전화해서 우리 주문 확인해볼게.'이다.

● leftover ⓝ 남은 음식 　　　● prefer A over B A를 B보다 선호하다

13　식사를 거르지 않도록 조언하기　　정답률 86% | 정답 ①

대화를 듣고, 여자의 마지막 말에 대한 남자의 응답으로 가장 적절한 것을 고르시오.

Man :
✓ You're right. I won't skip meals anymore.
네 말이 맞아. 더 이상 식사를 거르지 않을게.
② Thank you for the lunch you prepared for me.
나를 위해 준비해준 점심 식사 고마워.
③ You need to check when the cafeteria is open.
넌 언제 구내식당이 열리는지 확인해 봐야 해.
④ Trust me. I can teach you good table manners.
날 믿어. 내가 식사 예절을 알려줄게.
⑤ No problem. We'll finish the science project on time.
문제 없어. 우리 과학 프로젝트를 제때 끝낼 거야.

W : I haven't seen you in the cafeteria this week. Where have you been?
이번주에 널 구내식당에서 못 봤어. 어디 있었어?
M : I've been in the library working on my science project.
과학 프로젝트 하느라 도서관에 있었어.
W : Does that mean you've been skipping lunch?
점심밥을 거르고 있었다는 거야?
M : Yeah. This project is really important for my grade.
어, 이 프로젝트는 내 성적에 정말 중요하거든.
W : You shouldn't do that. It's not good for your health.
그렇게 하면 안 돼. 건강에 좋지 않아.
M : Don't worry. I always have a big dinner when I get home.
걱정 마. 난 항상 집에 가면 저녁을 많이 먹어.
W : That's the problem. Skipping meals makes you overeat later.
그게 문제야. 식사를 거르면 나중에 과식하게 돼.
M : I hadn't thought of that. Then what should I do?
그건 생각 못 해봤네. 그럼 나 어떻게 하지?
W : It's simple. You should eat regularly to stay healthy.
간단하지. 건강을 유지하려면 규칙적으로 먹으면 돼.
M : You're right. I won't skip meals anymore.
네 말이 맞아. 더 이상 식사를 거르지 않을게.

Why? 왜 정답일까?

남자가 식사를 거르고 과학 프로젝트를 하고 있었다는 말에 여자는 건강에 해롭다면서 식사를 규칙적으로 챙겨 먹으라고 한다(You should eat regularly to stay healthy.). 따라서 여자의 말에 대한 남자의 응답으로 가장 적절한 것은 ① '네 말이 맞아. 더 이상 식사를 거르지 않을게.'이다.

● skip ⓥ 건너뛰다　　　● overeat ⓥ 과식하다
● regularly ⓐⒹ 규칙적으로, 정기적으로

14　스페인어 공부에 관해 조언 구하기　　정답률 76% | 정답 ③

대화를 듣고, 남자의 마지막 말에 대한 여자의 응답으로 가장 적절한 것을 고르시오. [3점]

Woman :
① No. It isn't difficult for me to learn Spanish.
아니. 난 스페인어 배우는 게 어렵지 않아.
② I'm glad you finally passed the vocabulary test.
네가 단어 테스트를 마침내 통과해서 기쁘구나.
✓ Exactly. Learning a language starts with repetition.
바로 그거야. 언어를 배우는 것은 반복으로 시작돼.
④ It's very helpful to use a dictionary while writing.
글쓰기를 하는 동안 사전을 쓰는 것은 도움이 많이 돼.
⑤ You should turn in your homework by this afternoon.
오늘 오후까지 네 숙제를 제출해야 해.

M : Excuse me, Ms. Lopez. Can I ask you something?
실례합니다. Lopez 선생님. 뭐 좀 여쭤도 될까요?
W : Sure, Tony. What can I do for you?
물론이지, Tony. 뭘 도와줄까?
M : I want to do better in Spanish, but I don't know how to improve.
전 스페인어를 더 잘하고 싶은데, 어떻게 실력을 키울지 모르겠어요.
W : You seem to do well during class. Do you study when you're at home?
수업 시간에는 잘 하는 거 같은데. 집에 있을 때 공부하니?
M : I do all my homework and try to learn 20 new words every day.
숙제 다 하고 하루에 새로운 단어 20개씩 외우려고 해요.
W : That's a good start. Do you also practice saying those words repeatedly?
좋은 출발이네. 그 단어를 반복해서 말하는 연습도 하니?
M : Do I need to do that? That sounds like it'll take a lot of time.
그것도 해야 하나요? 그럼 시간이 많이 들 것 같아요.
W : It does. But since you're still a beginner, you have to put in more effort to get used to new words.
그렇긴 하지만 네가 아직 초보자니까, 새로운 단어에 익숙해지려면 노력을 더 기울여야 해.

M : I see. So are you suggesting that I practice them over and over?
알겠습니다. 그럼 선생님 말씀은 제가 단어를 반복해서 연습해야 한다는 거죠?
W : Exactly. Learning a language starts with repetition.
바로 그거야. 언어를 배우는 것은 반복으로 시작돼.

Why? 왜 정답일까?

여자는 스페인어 실력을 키우고 싶다는 남자에게 단어를 반복해서 연습하도록 조언해준다. 마지막 말에서 남자는 조언 내용을 한 번 더 확인하고 있으므로(So are you suggesting that I practice them over and over?), 남자의 말에 대한 여자의 응답으로 가장 적절한 것은 ③ '바로 그거야. 언어를 배우는 것은 반복으로 시작돼.'이다.

● repeatedly ⓐⒹ 반복적으로　　　● take time 시간이 걸리다
● put in effort 노력을 기울이다　　　● get used to ~에 익숙해지다
● turn in 제출하다

15　에너지 절약을 촉구하는 스티커 만들기　　정답률 85% | 정답 ⑤

다음 상황 설명을 듣고, Brian이 Melissa에게 할 말로 가장 적절한 것을 고르시오. [3점]

Brian :
① Let's clean the classroom after art class.
미술 시간 끝나고 교실을 치우자.
② Did you remove the stickers from the board?
네가 게시판에 있던 스티커 뗐어?
③ Please turn off the heater when you leave the room.
네가 방을 나갈 때 히터를 꺼줘.
④ When is the final date to sign up for the design class?
디자인 수업에 등록할 수 있는 마지막 날짜가 언제야?
✓ Will you design stickers that encourage energy saving?
네가 에너지 절약을 권하는 스티커를 만들어줄래?

W : Brian is a class leader.
Brian는 반장이다.
He is passionate about environmental issues and saving energy.
그는 환경 문제와 에너지 절약에 열성이다.
Recently, he's noticed that his classmates don't turn the lights off when they leave the classroom.
최근에 그는 자기 반 친구들이 교실 밖으로 나갈 때 불을 끄지 않는다는 것을 알았다.
Brian thinks this is very careless.
Brian은 이것이 매우 부주의하다고 생각한다.
He wants to make stickers that remind his classmates to save energy by turning off the lights.
그는 반 친구들에게 전등을 꺼서 에너지를 절약할 것을 상기시키는 스티커를 만들고 싶다.
He tells this idea to his classmate Melissa, and she agrees it's a good idea.
그는 이 아이디어를 반 친구인 Melissa에게 말하고, 그녀는 이것이 좋은 생각이라고 동의한다.
Brian knows Melissa is a great artist, so he wants to ask her to design stickers that encourage their classmates to save energy.
Brain은 Melissa가 미술을 매우 잘한다는 것을 알기에, 그녀에게 반 친구들더러 에너지를 아끼라고 권하는 스티커를 디자인해 달라고 부탁하고 싶다.
In this situation, what would Brian most likely say to Melissa?
이 상황에서, Brain은 Melissa에게 뭐라고 말하겠는가?
Brian : Will you design stickers that encourage energy saving?
네가 에너지 절약을 권하는 스티커를 만들어줄래?

Why? 왜 정답일까?

상황에 따르면 Brian은 미술을 잘하는 친구 Melissa에게 에너지 절약을 촉구하는 스티커를 디자인해 줄 것을 부탁하려고 한다(~ he wants to ask her to design stickers that encourage their classmates to save energy.). 따라서 Brain이 Melissa에게 할 말로 가장 적절한 것은 ⑤ '네가 에너지 절약을 권하는 스티커를 만들어줄래?'이다.

● passionate ⓐ 열성적인, 열정적인　　　● save energy 에너지를 절약하다
● careless ⓐ 부주의한

16-17　과잉 관광으로 인해 생기는 문제에 대처하기

M : Good afternoon, everyone.
안녕하세요, 여러분.
Last time, we learned that overtourism happens when there are too many visitors to a particular destination.
지난 시간에 우리는 특정 목적지에 너무 많은 관광객이 있으면 과잉 관광이 발생한다고 배웠죠.
「Today, we'll learn how cities deal with the problems caused by overtourism.」　16번의 근거
오늘 우리는 과잉 관광으로 생기는 문제를 여러 도시가 어떻게 처리하는지 배우겠습니다.
First, some cities limit the number of hotels so there are fewer places for visitors to stay.
첫째로, 어떤 도시에서는 관광객이 머물 곳이 더 적어지도록 호텔 수를 제한하고 있습니다.
「In Barcelona, building new hotels is not allowed in the city center.」　17번 ①의 근거 일치
바르셀로나에서는, 새로운 호텔을 도심에 짓는 것이 허용되지 않습니다.
Second, other cities promote areas away from popular sites.
둘째로, 다른 도시들에서는 인기 있는 장소와 멀리 떨어진 곳을 홍보합니다.
「For instance, Amsterdam encourages tourists to visit less-crowded areas.」　17번 ②의 근거 일치
예컨대, 암스테르담에서는 관광객들이 덜 혼잡한 지역을 방문하도록 권장하지요.
Third, many cities have tried to limit access.
셋째로, 많은 도시가 출입 제한을 시도했습니다.
「For example, Venice has tried to reduce tourism overall by stopping large cruise ships from docking on the island.」　17번 ④의 근거 일치
예를 들어 베니스는 큰 여객선이 섬에 정박하는 것을 막아서 전반적으로 관광을 줄이려는 시도를 해왔습니다.
「Similarly, Paris has focused on reducing tourism to certain parts of the city by having car-restricted areas.」　17번 ⑤의 근거 일치
비슷한 예로, 파리에서는 차량 제한 지역을 두어서 도시 특정 구역의 관광을 줄이는 데 집중해 왔죠.
Now, let's watch some video clips.
이제, 영상을 몇 개 보겠습니다.

● overtourism ⓝ 과잉 관광(지역 규모에 비해 관광객이 너무 많은 현상)
● promote ⓥ 홍보하다　　　● crowded ⓐ 혼잡한
● correlation ⓝ 상관 관계

16 주제 파악
정답률 80% | 정답 ③

남자가 하는 말의 주제로 가장 적절한 것은?
① advantages of renting houses in cities – 도시에서 집을 세 드는 것의 이점
② reasons tourists prefer visiting old cities – 관광객들이 오래된 도시를 방문하기를 선호하는 이유
✓③ ways cities deal with overtourism problems – 여러 도시가 과잉 관광 문제에 대처하는 방식
④ correlation between cities' sizes and overtourism – 도시 규모와 과잉 관광 간의 상관 관계
⑤ how cities face their aging transportation systems – 도시에서 노후화된 교통 체계에 직면하는 방식

Why? 왜 정답일까?
여러 도시에서 과잉 관광으로 발생하는 문제를 어떻게 처리하는지 배우겠다(Today, we'll learn how cities deal with the problems caused by overtourism.)는 내용으로 보아, 남자가 하는 말의 주제로 가장 적절한 것은 ③ '여러 도시가 과잉 관광 문제에 대처하는 방식'이다.

17 언급 유무 파악
정답률 91% | 정답 ③

언급된 도시가 아닌 것은?
① Barcelona – 바르셀로나 ② Amsterdam – 암스테르담 ✓③ London – 런던
④ Venice – 베니스 ⑤ Paris – 파리

Why? 왜 정답일까?
담화에서 남자는 과잉 관광 문제를 각 도시에서 어떻게 처리하는지 설명하기 위해 바르셀로나, 암스테르담, 베니스, 파리를 예로 들어 설명한다. 따라서 언급되지 않은 곳은 ③ '런던'이다.

Why? 왜 오답일까?
① 'In Barcelona, building new hotels is not allowed in the city center.'에서 '바르셀로나'가 언급되었다.
② 'For instance, Amsterdam encourages tourists to visit less-crowded areas.'에서 '암스테르담'이 언급되었다.
④ '~ Venice has tried to reduce tourism overall by stopping large cruise ships from docking on the island.'에서 '베니스'가 언급되었다.
⑤ '~ Paris has focused on reducing tourism to certain parts of the city by having car-restricted areas.'에서 '파리'가 언급되었다.

18 학생 인력 추천 요청
정답률 86% | 정답 ⑤

다음 글의 목적으로 가장 적절한 것은?
① 과학 박물관 내 시설 이용 제한을 안내하려고
② 화학 박람회 일정이 변경된 이유를 설명하려고
③ 중학생을 위한 화학 실험 특별 강연을 부탁하려고
④ 중학교 과학 수업용 실험 교재 집필을 의뢰하려고
✓⑤ 화학 박람회에서 실험을 도울 대학생 추천을 요청하려고

Dear Professor Sanchez,
Sanchez 교수님께
My name is Ellis Wight, / and I'm the director of the Alexandria Science Museum.
제 이름은 Ellis Wight이고 / 저는 Alexandria 과학 박물관의 관장입니다.
We are holding a Chemistry Fair / for local middle school students / on Saturday, October 28.
저희는 화학 박람회를 개최합니다. / 지역 중학교 학생을 위한 / 10월 28일 토요일에
The goal of the fair is / to encourage them to be interested in science / through guided experiments.
이 박람회의 목적은 ~입니다. / 학생들이 과학에 관한 관심을 갖도록 장려하는 것 / 안내자가 있는 실험을 통해
We are looking for college students / who can help with the experiments during the event.
저희는 대학생을 모집하고자 합니다. / 행사 기간 동안 실험을 도와줄 수 있는
I am contacting you / to ask you to recommend some students / from the chemistry department at your college / who you think are qualified for this job.
저는 당신께 연락드렸습니다. / 학생 몇 명을 추천해 달라는 요청을 드리고자 / 귀교의 화학과 소속인 / 당신이 이 일에 적합하다고 생각하는
With their help, / I'm sure / the participants will have a great experience.
그 학생들의 도움으로 / 저는 확신합니다. / 참가자들이 훌륭한 경험을 하게 될 것이라고
I look forward to hearing from you soon.
빠른 시일 내에 귀하로부터 연락 받기를 기대하겠습니다.
Sincerely, // Ellis Wight
Ellis Wight 드림

Sanchez 교수님께
제 이름은 Ellis Wight이고 Alexandria 과학 박물관의 관장입니다. 저희는 10월 28일 토요일에 지역 중학교 학생을 위한 화학 박람회를 개최합니다. 이 박람회의 목적은 안내자가 있는 실험을 통해 학생들이 과학에 관한 관심을 갖도록 장려하는 것입니다. 저희는 행사 기간 동안 실험을 도와줄 수 있는 대학생을 모집하고자 합니다. 저는 이 일에 적합하다고 생각되는 귀교의 화학과 학생 몇 명을 추천해 달라는 요청을 드리고자 연락드렸습니다. 그 학생들의 도움으로 참가자들이 훌륭한 경험을 하게 될 것이라 확신합니다. 빠른 시일 내에 귀하로부터 연락 받기를 기대하겠습니다.

Ellis Wight 드림

Why? 왜 정답일까?
박람회에서 진행할 실험을 도와줄 화학과 학생을 추천해달라는(I am contacting you to ask you to recommend some students from the chemistry department at your college who you think are qualified for this job.) 내용이므로, 글의 목적으로 가장 적절한 것은 ⑤ '화학 박람회에서 실험을 도울 대학생 추천을 요청하려고'이다.

- hold ⓥ 개최하다
- fair ⓝ 박람회
- experiment ⓝ 실험
- department ⓝ 학과, 부서
- chemistry ⓝ 화학
- local ⓐ 지역의, 지역의
- recommend ⓥ 추천하다
- qualified for ~에 적합한, 자격을 갖춘

[문제편 p.100]

구문 풀이
7행 I am contacting you to ask you to recommend some students from the
'ask + 목적어 + to부정사 : ~에 …하기를 요청하다'
chemistry department at your college [who (you think) are qualified for this job].
주격 관·대 삽입절 동사

19 암벽 등반 중 위기를 맞이한 필자 일행
정답률 69% | 정답 ②

다음 글에 나타난 'I'의 심경 변화로 가장 적절한 것은?
① joyful → bored 즐거운 지루한
✓② confident → fearful 자신 있는 겁에 질린
③ nervous → relieved 긴장한 안도한
④ regretful → pleased 후회하는 즐거운
⑤ grateful → annoyed 고마운 짜증 난

Gregg and I had been rock climbing since sunrise / and had had no problems.
Gregg와 나는 일출 이후에 암벽 등반을 하고 있었고, / 아무런 문제가 없었다.
So we took a risk.
그래서 우리는 위험을 감수했다.
"Look, the first bolt is right there. / I can definitely climb out to it. / Piece of cake," / I persuaded Gregg, / minutes before I found myself pinned.
"봐, 첫 번째 볼트가 바로 저기야. / 난 분명히 거기까지 올라갈 수 있어. / 식은 죽 먹기야."라고 / 나는 Gregg를 설득했고, / 얼마 지나지 않아 나는 내가 꼼짝 못하게 되었다는 것을 알게 되었다.
It wasn't a piece of cake.
그것은 식은 죽 먹기가 아니었다.
The rock was deceptively barren of handholds.
그 바위는 믿을 수 없게도 손으로 잡을 곳이 없었다.
I clumsily moved back and forth across the cliff face / and ended up with nowhere to go...but down.
나는 서툴게 절벽 면을 이리저리 가로질러 보았지만 / 갈 곳이 … 결국 아래쪽밖에는 없었다.
The bolt that would save my life, / if I could get to it, / was about two feet above my reach.
내 목숨을 구해줄 볼트는 / 만약 내가 거기까지 갈 수 있다면, / 내 손이 닿을 수 있는 곳에서 약 2피트 위에 있었다.
My arms trembled from exhaustion.
내 팔은 극도의 피로로 떨렸다.
I looked at Gregg.
나는 Gregg를 쳐다보았다.
My body froze with fright / from my neck down to my toes.
내 몸은 공포로 얼어붙었다. / 목에서부터 발끝까지
Our rope was tied between us.
우리 사이에 밧줄이 묶여 있었다.
If I fell, / he would fall with me.
내가 떨어지면, / 그도 나와 함께 떨어질 것이었다.

Gregg와 나는 일출 이후에 암벽 등반을 하고 있었고, 아무런 문제가 없었다. 그래서 우리는 위험을 감수했다. "봐, 첫 번째 볼트가 바로 저기야. 난 분명히 거기까지 올라갈 수 있어. 식은 죽 먹기야."라고 나는 Gregg를 설득했고, 얼마 지나지 않아 나는 내가 꼼짝 못하게 되었다는 것을 알게 되었다. 그것은 식은 죽 먹기가 아니었다. 그 바위는 믿을 수 없게도 손으로 잡을 곳이 없었다. 나는 서툴게 절벽 면을 이리저리 가로질러 보았지만 갈 곳이… 결국 아래쪽밖에는 없었다. 만약 내가 거기까지 갈 수 있다면, 내 목숨을 구해줄 볼트는 내 손이 닿을 수 있는 곳에서 약 2피트 위에 있었다. 내 팔은 극도의 피로로 떨렸다. 나는 Gregg를 쳐다보았다. 내 몸은 목에서부터 발끝까지 공포로 얼어붙었다. 우리 사이에 밧줄이 묶여 있었다. 내가 떨어지면, 그도 나와 함께 떨어질 것이었다.

Why? 왜 정답일까?
첫 번째 볼트까지 쉽게 오를 수 있다며 자신했던(I can definitely climb out to it. Piece of cake, ~) 필자가 생각과 다른 현실에 공포감에 휩싸였다는(My body froze with fright ~)는 내용이다. 따라서 'I'의 심경 변화로 가장 적절한 것은 ② '자신 있는 → 겁에 질린'이다.

- sunrise ⓝ 일출
- bolt ⓝ 볼트, 나사못
- piece of cake 식은 죽 먹기, 몹시 쉬운 일
- deceptively ⓐ 현혹될 정도로
- clumsily ⓐ 서툴게
- cliff ⓝ 절벽
- exhaustion ⓝ 피로
- fright ⓝ 공포
- fearful ⓐ 겁에 질린
- take a risk 위험을 감수하다
- definitely ⓐ 확실히, 분명히
- pinned ⓐ 고정된
- handhold ⓝ (등반 도중) 손으로 잡을 수 있는 곳
- back and forth 이리저리
- end up with 결국 ~에 처하다
- freeze ⓥ 얼어붙다
- confident ⓐ 자신 있는
- regretful ⓐ 유감스러운, 후회하는

구문 풀이
7행 The bolt [that would save my life], (if I could get to it), was about two feet
주어 주격 관·대 삽입절 동사(단수) 대략, 약
above my reach.

20 자녀에게 행동으로 모범을 보이기
정답률 93% | 정답 ②

다음 글에서 필자가 주장하는 바로 가장 적절한 것은?
① 자녀를 타인과 비교하는 말을 삼가야 한다.
✓② 자녀에게 행동으로 삶의 모범을 보여야 한다.
③ 칭찬을 통해 자녀의 바람직한 행동을 강화해야 한다.
④ 훈육을 하기 전에 자녀 스스로 생각할 시간을 주어야 한다.
⑤ 자녀가 새로운 것에 도전할 때 인내심을 가지고 지켜봐야 한다.

We are always teaching our children something / by our words and our actions.
우리는 항상 우리 자녀에게 무언가를 가르치고 있다. / 우리의 말과 행동으로
They learn from seeing.
그들은 보는 것으로부터 배운다.
They learn from hearing and from *overhearing*.
*그들은 듣거나 *우연히* 들은 것으로부터 배운다.*
Children share the values of their parents / about the most important things in life.
아이들은 부모의 가치관을 공유한다. / 인생에서 가장 중요한 것에 관한

Our priorities and principles and our examples of good behavior / can teach our children to take the high road / when other roads look tempting.
우리의 우선순위와 원칙, 그리고 훌륭한 행동에 대한 본보기는 / 우리 자녀에게 올바른 길로 가도록 가르칠 수 있다. / 다른 길이 유혹적으로 보일 때

Remember / that children do not learn the values / that make up strong character / simply by being *told* about them.
기억하라. / 아이들은 가치를 배우지 않는다는 것을 / 확고한 인격을 구성하는 / 단순히 그것에 관해 들어서

They learn / by seeing the people around them / *act* on and *uphold* those values in their daily lives.
그들은 배운다. / 주변 사람들을 보면서 / 일상생활에서 그러한 가치를 좇아 행동하고 유지하는 것을

Therefore / show your child good examples of life / by your action.
그러므로 / 여러분의 자녀에게 삶의 모범을 보이라. / 행동으로

In our daily lives, / we can show our children / that we respect others.
우리 일상생활에서, / 우리는 자녀에게 보여줄 수 있다. / 우리가 타인을 존중하는 것을

We can show them our compassion and concern / when others are suffering, / and our own self-discipline, courage and honesty / as we make difficult decisions.
우리는 그들에게 우리의 연민과 걱정을 보여줄 수 있다. / 타인이 괴로워할 때 / 그리고 우리 자신의 자제력과 용기와 정직을 / 우리가 어려운 결정을 할 때

우리는 항상 우리 자녀에게 말과 행동으로 무언가를 가르치고 있다. 그들은 보는 것으로부터 배운다. 그들은 듣거나 우연히 들은 것으로부터 배운다. 아이들은 인생에서 가장 중요한 것에 관한 부모의 가치관을 공유한다. 우리의 우선순위와 원칙, 그리고 훌륭한 행동에 대한 본보기는 우리 자녀가 다른 길이 유혹적으로 보일 때 올바른 길로 가도록 가르칠 수 있다. 아이들은 확고한 인격을 구성하는 가치를 단순히 그것에 관해 들어서 배우지 않는다는 것을 기억하라. 그들은 주변 사람들이 일상생활에서 그러한 가치를 좇아 행동하고 *유지하는* 것을 보면서 배운다. 그러므로 여러분의 자녀에게 행동으로 삶의 모범을 보이라. 우리 일상생활에서, 우리는 자녀에게 우리가 타인을 존중하는 것을 보여줄 수 있다. 우리는 타인이 괴로워할 때 우리의 연민과 걱정을, 어려운 결정을 할 때 우리 자신의 자제력과 용기와 정직을 그들에게 보여줄 수 있다.

Why? 왜 정답일까?

글 중반부에서 행동을 통해 자녀에게 삶의 본보기를 보여주라고(Therefore show your child good examples of life by your action.) 조언하는 것으로 볼 때, 필자가 주장하는 바로 가장 적절한 것은 ② '자녀에게 행동으로 삶의 모범을 보여야 한다.'이다.

- overhear ⓥ 엿듣다, 우연히 듣다
- priority ⓝ 우선순위
- take the high road 확실한 길로 가다
- make up ~을 구성하다
- uphold ⓥ 유지하다, 떠받치다
- concern ⓝ 걱정, 우려
- self-discipline ⓝ 자제
- value ⓝ 가치 ⓥ 중시하다
- principle ⓝ 원칙
- tempting ⓐ 유혹적인, 솔깃한
- act on ~에 따라 행동하다
- compassion ⓝ 연민
- suffer ⓥ 고통받다, 괴로워하다

구문 풀이

7행 Remember that children do not learn the values [that make up strong
　　　　　　접속사　　　　　　　　　　　　　선행사　　주격 관·대
character] simply by being *told* about them.
　　　　　　　　　동명사의 수동태(~되는 것)

---

21 출판을 넘어 독자에게 이해되어야 비로소 완성되는 과학 연구　　정답률 45% | 정답 ⑤

밑줄 친 fall silently in the woods가 다음 글에서 의미하는 바로 가장 적절한 것은? [3점]

① fail to include the previous study
　이전 연구를 포함하지 못한다
② end up being considered completely false
　결국 완전히 틀렸다고 간주된다
③ become useless because they are not published
　출판되지 않아서 쓸모없게 되어버린다
④ focus on communication to meet public demands
　대중의 요구를 맞추기 위해 커뮤니케이션에 집중한다
✔ are published yet readers don't understand them
　출판되지만 독자가 그것을 이해하지 못한다

Most people have no doubt heard this question: / If a tree falls in the forest / and there is no one there to hear it fall, / does it make a sound?
대부분의 사람들은 틀림없이 이 질문을 들어 봤을 것이다. / 만약 숲에서 나무가 쓰러지고 / 그것이 쓰러지는 것을 들을 사람이 거기 없다면, / 그것은 소리를 낼까?

The correct answer is no.
정답은 '아니요'이다.

Sound is more than pressure waves, / and indeed there can be no sound without a hearer.
소리는 압력파 이상이며, / 정말로 듣는 사람 없이는 소리가 있을 수 없다.

And similarly, / scientific communication is a two-way process.
마찬가지로, / 과학적 커뮤니케이션은 양방향 프로세스이다.

Just as a signal of any kind is useless / unless it is perceived, / a published scientific paper (signal) is useless / unless it is both received *and* understood / by its intended audience.
어떠한 종류의 신호든 쓸모가 없는 것처럼, / 그것이 감지되지 않으면 / 출판된 과학 논문(신호)은 쓸모가 없다. / 그것이 수신되고 *나아가* 이해되지 않으면 / 목표 독자에 의해

Thus we can restate the axiom of science as follows: / A scientific experiment is not complete / until the results have been published *and understood*.
따라서 우리는 과학의 자명한 이치를 다음과 같이 풀어 말할 수 있다. / 과학 실험은 완성된 것이 아니다. / 결과가 출판되고 *나아가 이해될* 때까지는

Publication is no more than pressure waves / unless the published paper is understood.
출판은 압력파에 지나지 않는다. / 출판된 논문이 이해되지 않으면

Too many scientific papers / fall silently in the woods.
너무 많은 과학 논문이 / 소리 없이 숲속에서 쓰러진다.

대부분의 사람들은 틀림없이 이 질문을 들어 봤을 것이다. 만약 숲에서 나무가 쓰러지고 그것이 쓰러지는 것을 들을 사람이 거기 없다면, 그것은 소리를 낼까? 정답은 '아니요'이다. 소리는 압력파 이상이며, 정말로 듣는 사람 없이는 소리가 있을 수 없다. 마찬가지로, 과학적 커뮤니케이션은 양방향 프로세스이다. 어떠한 종류의 신호든 감지되지 않으면 쓸모가 없는 것처럼, 출판된 과학 논문(신호)은 그것이 목표 독자에게 수신되고 *나아가* 이해까지 되지 않으면 쓸모가 없다. 따라서 우리는 과학의 자명한 이치를 다음과 같이 풀어 말할 수 있다. 과학 실험은 결과가 출판되고 *나아가 이해될* 때 비로소 완성된다. 출판된 논문이 이해되지 않으면 출판은 압력파에 지나지 않는다. 너무 많은 과학 논문이 소리 없이 숲속에서 쓰러진다.

Why? 왜 정답일까?

글에 따르면, 소리가 청자가 있을 때 비로소 만들어지듯이, 과학 논문 또한 출판되고 독자에게 '이해될' 때 비로소 완성된다고 한다. 밑줄 부분 또한 독자의 이해를 강조하는 비유로, 독자에게 '이해되지' 않으면 논문은 '진정한 소리'가 되어 나오지 못하고 그저 사라져버린다는 뜻이다. 따라서 밑줄 친 부분의 의미로 가장 적절한 것은 ⑤ '출판되지만 독자가 그것을 이해하지 못한다'이다.

- no doubt 분명히, 틀림없이
- pressure wave 압력파(압력 크기의 변화로 생성되는 파동)
- similarly ⓐⁿ 비슷하게, 마찬가지로
- signal ⓝ 신호 ⓥ 알리다
- publish ⓥ 출판하다, 게재하다
- intend ⓥ 목표로 하다, 의도하다
- as follows 다음과 같이
- publication ⓝ 출판, 게재
- previous ⓐ 이전의
- meet the demand 요구에 맞추다
- scientific ⓐ 과학적인
- useless ⓐ 쓸모없는
- paper ⓝ 논문, 서류
- restate ⓥ (더 분명하게) 고쳐 말하다
- complete ⓥ 완성되
- no more than 단지 ~일 뿐인
- false ⓐ 틀린

구문 풀이

8행 Thus we can restate the axiom of science as follows: A scientific experiment is not complete until the results have been published *and understood*.
「not + A + until + B : B하고 나서야 비로소 A하다」

---

22 원원을 추구하여 협상 상대와 건전한 관계를 유지하기　　정답률 83% | 정답 ④

다음 글의 요지로 가장 적절한 것은?

① 협상 상대의 단점뿐 아니라 장점을 철저히 분석해야 한다.
② 의사소통 과정에서 서로의 의도를 확인하는 것이 바람직하다.
③ 성공적인 협상을 위해 다양한 대안을 준비하는 것이 중요하다.
✔ 양측에 유리한 협상을 통해 상대와 좋은 관계를 유지해야 한다.
⑤ 원만한 인간관계를 위해 상호독립성을 인정하는 것이 필요하다.

We all negotiate every day, / whether we realise it or not.
우리 모두는 매일 협상한다. / 우리가 알든 모르든

Yet few people ever learn *how* to negotiate.
하지만 이제까지 *어떻게* 협상하는지를 배운 사람은 거의 없다.

Those who do / usually learn the traditional, win-lose negotiating style / rather than an approach / that is likely to result in a win-win agreement.
그렇게 하는 사람들은 / 대개 이기고 지는 쪽이 생기는 전통적인 협상 방식을 배운다. / 접근법보다는 / 양쪽 모두에 유리한 합의를 도출할 가능성이 있는

This old-school, adversarial approach / may be useful in a one-off negotiation / where you will probably not deal with that person again.
이런 구식의 적대적인 접근법은 / 일회성 협상에서는 유용할지도 모른다. / 아마도 여러분이 그 사람을 다시 상대하지 않을

However, / such transactions are becoming increasingly rare, / because most of us deal with the same people repeatedly / — our spouses and children, our friends and colleagues, our customers and clients.
하지만 / 이런 식의 거래는 점점 더 드물어지고 있다. / 우리 대부분은 동일한 사람들을 반복적으로 상대하기 때문에, / 배우자와 자녀, 친구와 동료, 고객과 의뢰인같이

In view of this, / it's essential / to achieve successful results for ourselves / and maintain a healthy relationship with our negotiating partners at the same time.
이러한 관점에서, / 중요하다. / 우리 자신을 위해 성공적인 결과를 얻어내는 것 / 그리고 동시에 협상 파트너들과 건전한 관계를 유지하는 것

In today's interdependent world of business partnerships and long-term relationships, / a win-win outcome is fast becoming the *only* acceptable result.
오늘날 비즈니스 파트너십과 장기적 관계의 상호 의존적인 세계에서, / 양측에 유리한 성과는 수용 가능한 유일한 결과로 빠른 속도로 자리잡고 있다.

우리 모두는 우리가 알든 모르든 매일 협상한다. 하지만 이제까지 *어떻게* 협상하는지를 배운 사람은 거의 없다. (협상 방식을) 배우는 사람들은 대개 양쪽 모두에 유리한 합의를 도출할 가능성이 있는 접근법보다는, 이기고 지는 쪽이 생기는 전통적인 협상 방식을 배운다. 이런 구식의 적대적인 접근법은 아마도 여러분이 그 사람을 다시 상대하지 않을 일회성 협상에서는 유용할지도 모른다. 하지만 우리 대부분은 배우자와 자녀, 친구와 동료, 고객과 의뢰인이 동일한 사람들을 반복적으로 상대하기 때문에, 이런 식의 거래는 점점 더 드물어지고 있다. 이러한 관점에서, 우리 자신을 위해 성공적인 결과를 얻어내는 동시에 협상 파트너들과 건전한 관계를 유지하는 것이 중요하다. 오늘날 비즈니스 파트너십과 장기적 관계의 상호 의존적인 세계에서, 양측에 유리한 성과는 수용 가능한 유일한 결과로 빠른 속도로 자리잡고 있다.

Why? 왜 정답일까?

협상 시 서로에게 모두 유리한 성과를 도출하면서 상대와 건전한 관계를 유지해야 한다(~ it's essential to achieve successful results for ourselves and maintain a healthy relationship with our negotiating partners at the same time.)고 조언하는 글이다. 따라서 글의 요지로 가장 적절한 것은 ④ '양측에 유리한 협상을 통해 상대와 좋은 관계를 유지해야 한다.'이다.

- negotiate ⓥ 협상하다
- usually ⓐⁿ 보통
- agreement ⓝ 합의, 동의
- adversarial ⓐ 적대적인
- transaction ⓝ 거래
- rare ⓐ 드문
- spouse ⓝ 배우자
- essential ⓐ 필수적인, 아주 중요한
- interdependent ⓐ 상호 의존적인
- outcome ⓝ 결과, 성과
- whether ~ or not ~이든 아니든
- traditional ⓐ 전통적인
- old-school ⓐ 구식의
- one-off ⓐ 단 한 번의
- increasingly ⓐⁿ 점점 더
- repeatedly ⓐⁿ 반복해서
- in view of ~을 고려하면
- maintain ⓥ 유지하다
- long-term ⓐ 장기의
- acceptable ⓐ 수용 가능한

구문 풀이

4행 This old-school, adversarial approach may be useful in a one-off
negotiation [where you will probably not deal with that person again].
　　　　　　　　　　선행사(상황)
　　　관계부사

23 문화적 다양성이 너무 클 때의 문제점 　　　　정답률 58% | 정답 ②

다음 글의 주제로 가장 적절한 것은?

① roles of culture in ethnic groups
　민족 집단에서 문화의 역할
✓ contrastive aspects of cultural diversity
　문화적 다양성의 대립적 양상
③ negative perspectives of national identity
　국가 정체성에 대한 부정적인 시각
④ factors of productivity differences across countries
　국가 간 생산성 차이의 요인
⑤ policies to protect minorities and prevent discrimination
　소수자를 보호하고 차별을 방지하려는 정책

The interaction of workers from different cultural backgrounds with the host population / might increase productivity / due to positive externalities like knowledge spillovers.
다른 문화적 배경을 가진 노동자들과 현지 주민의 상호 작용은 / 생산성을 증가시킬 수 있다. / 지식의 확산과 같은 긍정적인 외부 효과로 인해

This is only an advantage / up to a certain degree.
이것은 오로지 장점이다. / 어느 정도까지만

When the variety of backgrounds is too large, / fractionalization may cause excessive transaction costs for communication, / which may lower productivity.
배경의 다양성이 너무 크면, / 분열은 의사소통에 대한 과도한 거래 비용을 초래하고, / 이는 생산성을 저하시킬 수 있다.

Diversity not only impacts the labour market, / but may also affect the quality of life in a location.
다양성은 노동 시장에 영향을 줄 뿐만 아니라 / 한 지역의 삶의 질에도 영향을 미칠 수 있다.

A tolerant native population / may value a multicultural city or region / because of an increase in the range of available goods and services.
관용적인 원주민은 / 다문화 도시나 지역을 가치 있게 여길 수 있다 / 이용 가능한 재화와 용역 범위의 증가로 인해

On the other hand, / diversity could be perceived as an unattractive feature / if natives perceive it / as a distortion of what they consider to be their national identity.
반면에, / 다양성은 매력적이지 않은 특징으로 인지될 수 있다. / 원주민들이 그것을 왜곡으로 인식한다면 / 그들이 국가 정체성이라고 여기는 것에 대한

They might even discriminate against other ethnic groups / and they might fear / that social conflicts between different foreign nationalities / are imported into their own neighbourhood.
그들은 심지어 다른 민족 집단을 차별할 수도 있고, / 그들은 두려워할 수도 있다. / 다양한 외국 국적들 간의 사회적 갈등이 / 그들 인근으로 유입되는 것을

다른 문화적 배경을 가진 노동자들과 현지 주민의 상호 작용은 지식의 확산과 같은 긍정적인 외부 효과로 인해 생산성을 증가시킬 수 있다. 이것은 어느 정도까지만 장점이다. 배경의 다양성이 너무 크면, 분열은 의사소통에 대한 과도한 거래 비용을 초래하고, 이는 생산성을 저하시킬 수 있다. 다양성은 노동 시장에 영향을 줄 뿐만 아니라 한 지역의 삶의 질에도 영향을 미칠 수 있다. 관용적인 원주민은 이용 가능한 재화와 용역 범위의 증가로 인해 다문화 도시나 지역을 가치 있게 여길 수 있다. 반면에, 원주민들이 다양성을 국가 정체성이라고 여겨지는 것에 대한 왜곡으로 인식한다면 그것(다양성)은 매력적이지 않은 특징으로 인지될 수 있다. 그들은 심지어 다른 민족 집단을 차별할 수도 있고, 다양한 외국 국적들 간의 사회적 갈등이 그들 인근으로 유입되는 것을 두려워할 수도 있다.

Why? 왜 정답일까?
한 지역 사회 내에서 외지 출신 노동자들의 문화적 다양성이 일정 수준을 넘어가면 생산성 또는 삶의 질 저하나 갈등을 겪게 될 수 있다는 내용이다. 따라서 글의 주제로 가장 적절한 것은 ② '문화적 다양성의 대립적 양상'이다.

● cultural ⓐ 문화적인
● population ⓝ 인구
● externality ⓝ 외부 효과(의도하지 않았지만 부수적으로 따르는 결과)
● knowledge spillover 지식의 확산
● fractionalization ⓝ 분열
● cost ⓝ 비용, 대가
● impact ⓥ 영향을 주다, 충격을 주다
● quality of life 삶의 질
● multicultural ⓐ 다문화의
● perceive A as B A를 B로 인식하다
● identity ⓝ 정체성
● ethnic ⓐ 민족의
● import ⓥ 유입하다, 수입하다
● factor ⓝ 요인
● background ⓝ 배경
● productivity ⓝ 생산성
● variety ⓝ 다양성
● excessive ⓐ 과도한
● lower ⓥ 떨어뜨리다
● labo(u)r market 노동 시장
● tolerant ⓐ 관용적인
● on the other hand 반면에
● distortion ⓝ 왜곡
● discriminate against ~을 차별하다
● conflict ⓝ 갈등
● contrastive ⓐ 대비되는, 대립적인
● policy ⓝ 정책

구문 풀이

10행 On the other hand, diversity could be perceived as an unattractive
　　　　　　　　　　　　　　　　　　　　　　　　~로 인식되다
feature if natives perceive it as a distortion of [what they consider to be their
　　　　　　　　　　　　　　　　　　　전치사 관계대명사(~것)
national identity].

24 인간의 생활방식에 깊은 영향을 주는 건물과 개발 　　　　정답률 60% | 정답 ①

다음 글의 제목으로 가장 적절한 것은?

✓ Buildings Transform How We Live! – 건물이 우리의 삶의 방식을 바꾼다!
② Why Do We Build More Than We Need? – 우리는 왜 필요 이상으로 건물을 지을까?
③ Copying Ancient Buildings for Creativity – 창의성을 위해 고대 건물을 베끼기
④ Was Life Better in Hunter-gatherer Times? – 수렵 채집인 시대에는 삶이 더 괜찮았을까?
⑤ Innovate Your Farm with New Constructions – 새로운 건축물로 농장을 혁신하라

We think we are shaping our buildings.
우리는 우리가 건물을 형성하고 있다고 생각한다.

But really, / our buildings and development are also shaping us.
그러나 실제로 / 우리의 건물과 개발도 또한 우리를 형성하고 있다.

One of the best examples of this / is the oldest-known construction: / the ornately carved rings of standing stones at Göbekli Tepe in Turkey.
이것의 가장 좋은 예 중 하나는 / 가장 오래된 것으로 알려진 건축물인 / 튀르키예의 Göbekli Tepe에 있는, 화려하게 조각된 입석의 고리

Before these ancestors got the idea / to erect standing stones / some 12,000 years ago, / they were hunter-gatherers.
이 조상들이 아이디어를 얻기 전에, / 입석을 세우는 / 약 12,000년 전에 / 그들은 수렵 채집인이었다.

It appears / that the erection of the multiple rings of megalithic stones / took so long, / and so many successive generations, / that these innovators were forced to settle down / to complete the construction works.
~인 것으로 보인다. / 거석으로 된 여러 개의 고리를 세우는 것은 / 오랜 시간을 필요로 하고 / 그리고 많은 잇따른 세대 / 이 혁신가들은 정착해야만 했던 것으로 보인다. / 건설 작업을 완료하기 위해

In the process, / they became the first farming society on Earth.
그 과정에서, / 그들은 지구상 최초의 농업 사회가 되었다.

This is an early example of a society constructing something / that ends up radically remaking the society itself.
이것은 무언가를 건설하는 사회의 초기 예이다. / 결국 사회 자체를 근본적으로 재구성하는

Things are not so different in our own time.
우리 시대에도 상황이 그렇게 다르지 않다.

우리는 우리가 건물을 형성하고 있다고 생각한다. 그러나 실제로 우리의 건물과 개발도 또한 우리를 형성하고 있다. 이것의 가장 좋은 예 중 하나는 가장 오래된 것으로 알려진 건축물인, 튀르키예의 Göbekli Tepe에 있는 화려하게 조각된 입석의 고리이다. 이 조상들이 약 12,000년 전에 입석을 세우는 아이디어를 얻기 전에, 그들은 수렵 채집인이었다. 거석으로 된 여러 개의 고리를 세우는 데 오랜 시간이 걸리고 많은 잇따른 세대를 거쳐야 했기에, 이 혁신가들은 건설 작업을 완료하기 위해 정착해야만 했던 것으로 보인다. 그 과정에서, 그들은 지구상 최초의 농업 사회가 되었다. 이것은 결국 사회 자체를 근본적으로 재구성하는 무언가를 건설하는 사회의 초기 예이다. 우리 시대에도 상황이 그렇게 다르지 않다.

Why? 왜 정답일까?
튀르키예의 초기 인류가 입석을 건설하며 수렵 채집인에서 농경인으로 정착하게 된 예시를 들어, 건물이나 개발이 인간 (사회)를 형성한다(~ our buildings and development are also shaping us.)는 점을 설명하는 글이다. 따라서 글의 제목으로 가장 적절한 것은 ① '건물이 우리의 삶의 방식을 바꾼다!'이다.

● shape ⓥ 형성하다
● ornately ⓐⓓ 화려하게
● erect ⓥ 세우다
● multiple ⓐ 여럿의
● successive ⓐ 연속된, 잇따른
● settle down 정착하다
● transform ⓥ 바꾸다, 변모시키다
● construction ⓝ 건설, 구성
● carve ⓥ 새기다
● hunter-gatherer ⓝ 수렵 채집인
● megalithic ⓐ 거석의
● be forced to 어쩔 수 없이 ~하다
● radically ⓐⓓ 근본적으로, 급진적으로

구문 풀이

6행 It appears that the erection of the multiple rings of megalithic stones
　　　　~한 것으로 보인다
took so long, and so many successive generations, that these innovators
　　　　　　「so ~ that ... : 너무 ~해서 ...하다」
were forced to settle down to complete the construction works.
　어쩔 수 없이 ~했다

25 미국 내의 연령대별 소셜 미디어 사용자 비율 　　　　정답률 77% | 정답 ④

다음 도표의 내용과 일치하지 않는 것은?

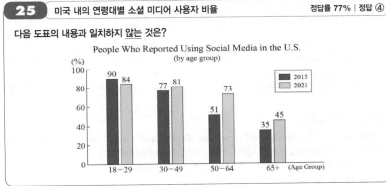

People Who Reported Using Social Media in the U.S. (by age group)

The graph above shows the percentages of people in different age groups / who reported using social media / in the United States / in 2015 and 2021.
위 그래프는 다양한 연령 집단 내 사람들의 비율을 보여 준다. / 소셜 미디어를 사용한다고 보고한 / 미국에서 / 2015년과 2021년에

① In each of the given years, / the 18-29 group had the highest percentage of people / who said they used social media.
주어진 각각의 해에, / 18~29세 집단에서 사람들의 비율이 제일 높았다. / 소셜 미디어를 사용한다고 말한

② In 2015, / the percentage of people / who reported using social media in the 30-49 group / was more than twice that in the 65 and older group.
2015년에 / 사람들의 비율은 / 소셜 미디어를 사용한다고 보고한 / 30~49세 집단에서 / 65세 이상 집단의 두 배 이상이었다.

③ The percentage of people / who said they used social media / in the 50-64 group in 2021 / was 22 percentage points higher / than that in 2015.
사람들의 비율은 / 소셜 미디어를 사용한다고 말한 / 2021년에 50~64세 집단에서 / 22퍼센트포인트 더 높았다. / 2015년의 비율보다

✓ In 2021, / except for the 65 and older group, / more than four-fifths of people in each age group / reported using social media.
2021년에 / 65세 이상 집단을 제외하고 / 각 연령 집단에서 5분의 4가 넘는 사람들이 / 소셜 미디어를 사용한다고 보고했다.

⑤ Among all the age groups, / only the 18-29 group showed a decrease / in the percentage of people / who reported using social media / from 2015 to 2021.
모든 연령 집단 중에서 / 18~29세 집단만이 감소를 보였다. / 사람들의 비율에서 / 소셜 미디어를 사용한다고 보고한 / 2015년에서 2021년까지

위 그래프는 2015년과 2021년에 미국에서 소셜 미디어를 사용한다고 보고한 다양한 연령 집단 내 사람들의 비율을 보여 준다. ① 주어진 각각의 해에, 18~29세 집단에서 소셜 미디어를 사용한다고 말한 사람들의 비율이 제일 높았다. ② 2015년에 30~49세 집단에서 소셜 미디어를 사용한다고 보고한 사람들의 비율은 65세 이상 집단의 두 배 이상이었다. ③ 2021년에 50~64세 집단에서 소셜 미디어를 사용한다고 말한 사람들의 비율은 2015년보다 22퍼센트포인트 더 높았다. ④ 2021년에 65세 이상 집단을 제외한 각 연령 집단에서 5분의 4가 넘는 사람들이 소셜 미디어를 사용한다고 보고했다. ⑤ 모든 연령 집단 중에서 18~29세 집단만이 2015년에서 2021년까지 소셜 미디어를 사용한다고 보고한 사람들의 비율에서 감소를 보였다.

도표에 따르면 2021년에 미국에서 소셜 미디어를 사용하고 있다고 보고한 50~64세 인구는 73%인데, 이는 5분의 4인 80%에 미치지 못하는 수치이다. 따라서 도표와 일치하지 않는 것은 ④이다.

- social media 소셜 미디어
- more than ~ 이상
- decrease ⓝ 감소
- given ⓐ 주어진 prep ~을 고려하면
- except for ~을 제외하고

---

26 Bill Evans의 생애 정답률 80% | 정답 ④

Bill Evans에 관한 다음 글의 내용과 일치하지 <u>않는</u> 것은?
① 6세에 피아노 수업을 받기 시작했다.
② Southeastern Louisiana 대학에서 학위를 취득했다.
③ 군 복무 이후 뉴욕에서 작곡을 공부했다.
✓ 작곡가 George Russell을 고용했다.
⑤ 1964년에 자신의 첫 번째 그래미상을 수상했다.

American jazz pianist Bill Evans / was born in New Jersey in 1929.
미국인 재즈 피아니스트 Bill Evans는 / 뉴저지에서 1929년에 태어났다.

His early training was in classical music.
그의 초기 교육은 클래식 음악이었다.

「At the age of six, / he began receiving piano lessons, / later adding flute and violin.」 ①의근거 일치
6세에 / 그는 피아노 수업을 받기 시작해서, / 나중에 플루트와 바이올린도 추가했다.

「He earned bachelor's degrees in piano and music education / from Southeastern Louisiana College / in 1950.」 ②의근거 일치
그는 피아노와 음악 교육에서 학사 학위를 취득했다. / Southeastern Louisiana 대학에서 / 1950년에

He went on to serve in the army from 1951 to 1954 / and played flute in the Fifth Army Band.
그는 1951에서 1954년까지 군 복무를 하며 / 제5군악대에서 플루트를 연주했다.

「After serving in the military, / he studied composition / at the Mannes School of Music in New York.」 ③의근거 일치
군 복무 이후 / 그는 작곡을 공부했다. / 뉴욕에 있는 Mannes School of Music에서

「Composer George Russell admired his playing / and hired Evans / to record and perform his compositions.」 ④의근거 불일치
작곡가 George Russell은 그의 연주에 감탄하여 / Evans를 고용했다. / 자신의 곡을 녹음하고 연주하게 하려고

Evans became famous for recordings / made from the late-1950s through the 1960s.
Evans는 음반으로 유명해졌다. / 1950년대 후반부터 1960년 동안 만들어진

「He won his first Grammy Award in 1964 / for his album *Conversations with Myself*.」 ⑤의근거 일치
그는 1964년에 자신의 첫 번째 그래미상을 수상했다. / 자신의 앨범 *Conversations with Myself*로

Evans' expressive piano works and his unique harmonic approach / inspired a whole generation of musicians.
Evans의 표현이 풍부한 피아노 작품과 그의 독특한 화성적 접근은 / 전 세대의 음악가들에게 영감을 주었다.

미국인 재즈 피아니스트 Bill Evans는 뉴저지에서 1929년에 태어났다. 그의 초기 교육은 클래식 음악이었다. 그는 6세에 피아노 수업을 받기 시작해서, 나중에 플루트와 바이올린도 추가했다. 그는 1950년에 Southeastern Louisiana 대학에서 피아노와 음악 교육에서 학사 학위를 취득했다. 그는 1951에서 1954년까지 군 복무를 하며 제5군악대에서 플루트를 연주했다. 군 복무 이후 그는 뉴욕에 있는 Mannes School of Music에서 작곡을 공부했다. 작곡가 George Russell은 그의 연주에 감탄하여 Evans를 고용해 자신의 곡을 녹음하고 연주하게 했다. Evans는 1950년대 후반부터 1960년대 동안 만들어진 음반으로 유명해졌다. 그는 자신의 앨범 *Conversations with Myself*로 1964년에 자신의 첫 번째 그래미상을 수상했다. Evans의 표현이 풍부한 피아노 작품과 그의 독특한 화성적 접근은 전 세대의 음악가들에게 영감을 주었다.

Why? 왜 정답일까?

'Composer George Russell admired his playing and hired Evans to record and perform his compositions.'에서 Evans는 작곡가 George Russell을 고용한 것이 아니고, 그에게 고용되어 그의 음악을 녹음하고 연주했다고 한다. 따라서 내용과 일치하지 않는 것은 ④ '작곡가 George Russell을 고용했다.'이다.

Why? 왜 오답일까?

① 'At the age of six, he began receiving piano lessons, ~'의 내용과 일치한다.
② 'He earned bachelor's degrees in piano and music education from Southeastern Louisiana College in 1950.'의 내용과 일치한다.
③ 'After serving in the military, he studied composition at the Mannes School of Music in New York.'의 내용과 일치한다.
⑤ 'He won his first Grammy Award in 1964 ~'의 내용과 일치한다.

- add ⓥ 추가하다
- bachelor's degree 학사 학위
- military ⓝ 군대 ⓐ 군사적인
- admire ⓥ 감탄하다, 존경하다
- expressive ⓐ 표현이 풍부한
- harmonic ⓐ (음악) 화성의
- earn ⓥ 얻다, 취득하다, 벌다
- serve in the army 군 복무하다
- composition ⓝ 작곡
- recording ⓝ 음반, 녹음
- unique ⓐ 독특한

구문 풀이

9행 Composer George Russell admired his playing and hired Evans to record and perform his compositions.
동사1 / 동사2 / 목적(~하기 위해)

---

27 보석 만들기 수업 정답률 95% | 정답 ④

Silversmithing Class에 관한 다음 안내문의 내용과 일치하지 <u>않는</u> 것은?
① 두 시간 동안 진행된다.
② 10월 1일부터 등록할 수 있다.
③ 등록 인원은 6명으로 제한된다.
✓ 참가 연령에 제한이 없다.
⑤ 수업 당일 취소 시 환불이 불가하다.

Silversmithing Class
Silversmithing Class(은세공 수업)

Kingston Club is offering a fine jewelry making class.
Kingston Club은 정교한 보석 만들기 수업을 제공합니다.

Don't miss this great chance / to make your own jewelry!
이런 좋은 기회를 놓치지 마세요! / 여러분만의 보석을 만들어볼

When & Where
시간 & 장소

「Saturday, October 21, 2023 (2 p.m. to 4 p.m.)」 ①의근거 일치
2023년 10월 21일 토요일(오후 2시부터 오후 4시까지)

Kingston Club studio
Kingston Club 스튜디오

Registration
등록

Available only online
온라인으로만 가능

「Dates: October 1 – 14, 2023」 ②의근거 일치
일자: 2023년 10월 1 ~ 14일

Fee: $40 (This includes all tools and materials.)
비용: 40달러(이것은 모든 도구와 재료를 포함합니다.)

「Registration is limited to 6 people.」 ③의근거 일치
등록은 6명으로 제한됩니다.

Note
유의 사항

「Participants must be at least 16 years old.」 ④의근거 불일치
참가자는 16세 이상이어야 합니다.

「No refund for cancellation on the day of the class」 ⑤의근거 일치
수업 당일 취소 시 환불 불가

Silversmithing Class(은세공 수업)

Kingston Club은 정교한 보석 만들기 수업을 제공합니다. 여러분만의 보석을 만들어볼 이런 좋은 기회를 놓치지 마세요!

시간 & 장소
- 2023년 10월 21일 토요일(오후 2시부터 오후 4시까지)
- Kingston Club 스튜디오

등록
- 온라인으로만 가능
- 일자: 2023년 10월 1 ~ 14일
- 비용: 40달러(이것은 모든 도구와 재료를 포함합니다.)
- 등록은 6명으로 제한됩니다.

유의 사항
- 참가자는 16세 이상이어야 합니다.
- 수업 당일 취소 시 환불 불가

Why? 왜 정답일까?

'Participants must be at least 16 years old.'에서 참가자는 16세 이상이어야 한다고 하므로, 안내문의 내용과 일치하지 않는 것은 ④ '참가 연령에 제한이 없다.'이다.

Why? 왜 오답일까?

① 'Saturday, October 21, 2023 (2 p.m. to 4 p.m.)'의 내용과 일치한다.
② 'Dates: October 1–14, 2023'의 내용과 일치한다.
③ 'Registration is limited to 6 people.'의 내용과 일치한다.
⑤ 'No refund for cancellation on the day of the class'의 내용과 일치한다.

- silversmith ⓝ 은세공하는 사람
- jewelry ⓝ 보석
- cancellation ⓝ 취소
- fine ⓐ 정교한, 미세한
- miss a chance 기회를 놓치다

---

28 해양 인식 관련 영상 대회 정답률 93% | 정답 ⑤

2023 Ocean Awareness Film Contest에 관한 다음 안내문의 내용과 일치하는 것은?
① 세 가지 주제 중 하나를 선택해야 한다. ② 중학생이 참가할 수 있다.
③ 영상은 10분을 넘길 수 없다. ④ 1인당 두 개까지 출품할 수 있다.
✓ 수상자는 웹사이트에 공지될 것이다.

2023 Ocean Awareness Film Contest
2023 Ocean Awareness Film Contest(2023 해양 보존 인식 영상 대회)

Join our 7th annual film contest / and show your knowledge of marine conservation.
우리 일곱 번째 연례 영상 대회에 참여해서 / 해양 보존에 관한 여러분의 지식을 보여 주세요.

Theme
주제

「Ocean Wildlife / Ocean Pollution
해양 야생 생물 / 해양 오염

(Choose one of the above.)」 ①의근거 불일치
(위에서 하나를 선택하세요.)

Guidelines
지침

「Participants: High school students」 ②의근거 불일치
참가자: 고등학생

Submission deadline: September 22, 2023
제출 기한: 2023년 9월 22일

「The video must be between 10 and 15 minutes.」 ③의근거 불일치
영상은 10분에서 15분 사이여야 합니다.

All entries must be uploaded to our website.
모든 출품작은 우리 웹사이트에 업로드되어야 합니다.

「Only one entry per person」 ④의근거 불일치
1인당 출품작 하나만 가능

Prizes
상금

1st place: $100 / 2nd place: $70 / 3rd place: $50
1등: 100달러 / 2등: 70달러 / 3등: 50달러
『(Winners will be announced on our website.)』 ᴏᴊ근거 일치
(수상자는 우리 웹사이트에 공지될 것입니다.)
For more information, / please visit www.oceanawareFC.com.
더 많은 정보를 위해 / www.oceanawareFC.com을 방문하세요.

2023 Ocean Awareness Film Contest
(2023 해양 보존 인식 영상 대회)

우리 일곱 번째 연례 영상 대회에 참여해서 해양 보존에 관한 여러분의 지식을 보여 주세요.

☐ **주제**
  – 해양 야생 생물 / 해양 오염
    (위에서 하나를 선택하세요.)

☐ **지침**
  – 참가자: 고등학생
  – 제출 기한: 2023년 9월 22일
  – 영상은 10분에서 15분 사이여야 합니다.
  – 모든 출품작은 우리 웹사이트에 업로드되어야 합니다.
  – 1인당 출품작 하나만 가능

☐ **상금**
  • 1등: 100달러 • 2등: 70달러 • 3등: 50달러
    (수상자는 우리 웹사이트에 공지될 것입니다.)

더 많은 정보를 위해 www.oceanawareFC.com을 방문하세요.

Why? 왜 정답일까?
'(Winners will be announced on our website.)'에서 수상자는 웹사이트에서 알려준다고 하므로, 안내문의 내용과 일치하는 것은 ⑤ '수상자는 웹사이트에 공지될 것이다.'이다.

Why? 왜 오답일까?
① 'Ocean Wildlife / Ocean Pollution / (Choose one of the above.)'에서 주제는 2개 중 하나를 선택하는 것이라고 하였다.
② 'Participants: High school students'에서 참가자는 고등학생으로 명시되었다.
③ 'The video must be between 10 and 15 minutes.'에서 영상 길이는 10~15분 사이면 된다고 하였다.
④ 'Only one entry per person'에서 출품은 1인당 하나의 영상만 가능하다고 하였다.

- awareness ⓝ 인식, 앎
- conservation ⓝ 보존
- pollution ⓝ 오염
- entry ⓝ 출품작, 참가, 입장
- annual ⓐ 매년의
- wildlife ⓝ 야생 생물
- submission ⓝ 제출

★★★ 등급을 가르는 문제!

29 다른 사람들의 사후 비판을 유독 많이 듣는 스포츠 업계 사람들   정답률 33% | 정답 ④

다음 글의 밑줄 친 부분 중, 어법상 틀린 것은?

There is a reason / the title "Monday Morning Quarterback" exists.
이유가 있다. / 'Monday Morning Quarterback'이라는 명칭이 존재하는
Just read the comments on social media from fans / discussing the weekend's games, / and you quickly see / how many people believe / they could play, coach, and manage sport teams more ① successfully / than those on the field.
팬들의 소셜 미디어의 댓글만 읽어보더라도 / 주말 경기에 대해 토론하는 / 그러면 여러분은 금방 알 수 있다. / 얼마나 많은 사람들이 믿는지 / 자기가 더 성공적으로 경기를 뛰고, 감독하고, 스포츠팀을 관리할 수 있다고 / 경기장에 있는 이들보다
This goes for the boardroom as well.
이것은 이사회실에서도 마찬가지이다.
Students and professionals / with years of training and specialized degrees in sport business / may also find themselves ② being given advice / on how to do their jobs / from friends, family, or even total strangers without any expertise.
학생들과 전문가들 / 스포츠 사업에서 수년간의 훈련을 받고 전문 학위를 가진 / 또한 충고를 듣고 있는 자신을 발견할지도 모른다. / 어떻게 일해야 할지에 관해 / 전문 지식이 전혀 없는 친구나 가족이나 혹은 심지어 생판 남으로부터
Executives in sport management / ③ have decades of knowledge and experience / in their respective fields.
스포츠 경영 임원들은 / 수십 년의 지식과 경험을 가지고 있다. / 각자 자기 분야에서
However, / many of them face criticism / from fans and community members / telling ✔them how to run their business.
하지만, / 그들 중 많은 사람들이 비난에 직면한다. / 팬들과 지역 사회 구성원들로부터의 / 그들에게 사업 운영 방식을 알려주는
Very few people tell / their doctor how to perform surgery / or their accountant how to prepare their taxes, / but many people provide feedback / on ⑤ how sport organizations should be managed.
알려주는 사람은 거의 없지만, / 의사에게 수술하는 방법을 알려주거나, / 회계사에게 세금을 준비하는 방법을 / 많은 이들이 피드백을 제공한다. / 스포츠 조직이 어떻게 관리되어야 하는지에 대한

'Monday Morning Quarterback(월요일 아침 쿼터백: 일이 이미 있고 난 뒤 이러쿵저러쿵하는 사람)'이라는 명칭이 존재하는 이유가 있다. 주말 경기에 대해 토론하는 팬들의 소셜 미디어의 댓글만 읽어봐도, 여러분은 얼마나 많은 사람들이 경기장에 있는 이들보다 자기가 더 성공적으로 경기를 뛰고, 감독하고, 스포츠팀을 관리할 수 있다고 믿는지 금방 알 수 있다. 이것은 이사회실에서도 마찬가지이다. 스포츠 사업에서 수년간의 훈련을 받고 전문 학위를 가진 학생들과 전문가들 또한, 전문 지식이 전혀 없는 친구나 가족이나 혹은 심지어 생판 남으로부터 어떻게 일해야 할지에 관해 충고를 듣고 있는 자신을 발견할지도 모른다. 스포츠 경영 임원진들은 각자 자기 분야에서 수십 년의 지식과 경험을 가지고 있다. 하지만, 그들 중 많은 사람들이 자신에게 사업 운영 방식을 알려주는 팬들과 지역 사회 구성원들의 비난에 직면한다. 의사에게 수술하는 방법을 알려주거나, 회계사에게 세금을 준비하는 방법을 알려주는 사람은 거의 없지만, 스포츠 조직이 어떻게 관리되어야 하는지에 대한 피드백은 많은 이들이 제공한다.

Why? 왜 정답일까?
telling의 의미상 주어가 fans and community members인데, 목적어는 many of them(=

[문제편 p.103]

---

executives)이므로, 둘은 서로 다른 대상을 지칭한다. 재귀대명사는 주어와 목적어가 일치할 때만 쓰므로, themselves 대신 them을 써야 어법상 맞다. 따라서 어법상 틀린 것은 ④이다.

Why? 왜 오답일까?
① 동사구인 could play, coach, and manage를 꾸미기 위해 부사 more successfully를 쓴 것이다.
② may also find의 목적어인 themselves가 '충고를 듣는' 입장이므로, 수동을 나타내는 『being + 과거분사』 형태를 적절하게 썼다.
③ 복수 명사 주어인 Executives에 맞춰 복수 동사 have를 쓴 것은 어법상 맞다.
⑤ 완전한 문장인 sport organizations should be managed를 이끌기 위해 의문부사 how(어떻게)를 쓴 것은 어법상 맞다.

- boardroom ⓝ 이사회실
- specialized ⓐ 전문화된
- expertise ⓝ 전문 지식
- respective ⓐ 각자의
- criticism ⓝ 비평
- accountant ⓝ 회계사
- organization ⓝ 조직, 단체
- professional ⓝ 전문가
- total stranger 생판 남
- executive ⓝ 임원, 중역
- face ⓥ 마주하다, 직면하다
- run ⓥ (가게나 사업을) 운영하다
- tax ⓝ 세금

구문 풀이

14행 Very few people [tell] their doctor [how to perform surgery] or their accountant [how to prepare their taxes], but many people provide feedback on [how sport organizations should be managed].
→4형식 동사 / ~하는 사람은 거의 없다 / 간접목적어1 / 직접목적어1 / 간접목적어2 / 직접목적어2

★★ 문제 해결 꿀~팁 ★★

▶ 많이 틀린 이유는?
themselves가 사람이므로 '충고를 주는' 주체처럼 보여서 ②를 고르기 쉽다. 하지만 문맥을 보면, 이들은 일을 어떻게 할지에 대한 충고를 남에게 '받는' 입장이 맞다.

▶ 문제 해결 방법은?
재귀대명사를 쓰려면, 행위를 나타내는 동사 또는 준동사를 기준으로 (의미상) 주어와 목적어가 같아야 한다. 여기서는 현재분사 telling을 중심으로 판단해야 하는데, 현재분사의 의미상 주어는 분사가 꾸미는 명사이고, 목적어는 분사 뒤에 나오는 명사이므로, 두 대상이 같은지 다른지 비교하면 된다.

30 새로운 환경을 상상하기 어려워하는 어린 아이들   정답률 58% | 정답 ②

다음 글의 밑줄 친 부분 중, 문맥상 낱말의 쓰임이 적절하지 <u>않은</u> 것은? [3점]

While moving is difficult for everyone, / it is particularly stressful for children.
이사는 모두에게 힘들지만, / 아이들에게 특히 스트레스가 된다.
They lose their sense of security / and may feel disoriented / when their routine is disrupted / and all that is ① familiar is taken away.
그들은 안정감을 잃고, / 혼란스러움을 느낄 수도 있다. / 그들의 일상이 무너지고 / 익숙한 모든 것이 사라질 때
Young children, ages 3-6, / are particularly affected by a move.
3세에서 6세 사이의 어린아이들은 / 이사에 특히 영향을 받는다.
Their understanding at this stage / is quite literal, / and it is ✔hard for them / to imagine beforehand a new home and their new room.
이 시기 그들의 이해력은 / 꽤 융통성이 없어서, / 그들로서는 어렵다. / 새로운 집과 자신의 새로운 방을 미리 상상하기가
Young children may have worries / such as "Will I still be me in the new place?" / and "Will my toys and bed come with us?"
어린아이들은 걱정들을 가질지도 모른다. / "내가 새로운 곳에서도 여전히 나야?"와 / "내 장난감과 침대는 우리랑 같이 가?"와 같은
It is important / to establish a balance / between validating children's past experiences / and focusing on helping them ③ adjust to the new place.
중요하다. / 균형을 잡는 것이 / 아이들의 과거 경험을 인정하는 것 / 그리고 그들이 새로운 곳에 적응하도록 돕는 데 집중하는 것 사이에
Children need to have opportunities / to share their backgrounds / in a way that ④ respects their past / as an important part of who they are.
아이들은 기회를 가져봐야 한다. / 자신의 배경을 나눌 / 자기 과거를 존중하는 방식으로 / 자신의 존재에 대한 중요한 부분으로서
This contributes to building a sense of community, / which is essential for all children, / especially those in ⑤ transition.
이것은 공동체 의식을 형성하는 데 기여하고, / 이는 모든 아이들에게 몹시 중요하다. / 특히 변화를 겪는 아이들

이사는 모두에게 힘들지만, 아이들에게 특히 스트레스가 된다. 그들은 안정감을 잃고, 그들의 일상이 무너지고 ① 익숙한 모든 것이 사라질 때 혼란스러움을 느낄 수도 있다. 3세에서 6세 사이의 어린아이들은 이사에 특히 영향을 받는다. 이 시기에 그들의 이해력은 꽤 융통성이 없어서, 그들이 새로운 집과 자신의 새로운 방을 미리 상상하기란 ② 쉽다(→ 어렵다). 어린아이들은 "내가 새로운 곳에서도 여전히 나야?"와 "내 장난감과 침대는 우리랑 같이 가?"와 같은 걱정들을 가질지도 모른다. 아이들의 과거 경험을 인정하는 것, 그리고 그들이 새로운 곳에 ③ 적응하도록 돕는 데 집중하는 것 사이에 균형을 잡는 것이 중요하다. 아이들은 자신의 존재에 대한 중요한 부분으로서 자기 과거를 ④ 존중하는 방식으로 자신의 배경을 나눌 기회를 가져봐야 한다. 이것은 공동체 의식을 형성하는 데 기여하고, 이는 모든 아이들, 특히 ⑤ 변화를 겪는 아이들에게 몹시 중요하다.

Why? 왜 정답일까?
② 뒤로 아이들은 새로운 곳에 가도 자기 존재가 그대로일지, 물건도 그대로 있을지 잘 상상하지 못한다는 예시가 나오는 것으로 보아, 아이들은 새로운 환경에 처하기 전에 미리 그 환경을 상상해보는 것을 '어려워한다'는 설명이 적합하다. 즉 easy를 hard로 바꾸어야 하므로, 문맥상 쓰임이 적절하지 않은 단어는 ②이다.

- particularly [ad] 특히
- disoriented ⓐ 혼란스러워 하는
- disrupt ⓥ 무너뜨리다, 지장을 주다, 방해하다
- take away 없애다, 빼앗다
- literal ⓐ 융통성 없는, 문자 그대로의
- establish ⓥ 설정하다, 쌓다
- validate ⓥ 인정하다, 승인하다, 입증하다
- share ⓥ 나누다, 공유하다
- transition ⓝ 변화
- security ⓝ 안정
- routine ⓝ 일상, 루틴
- familiar ⓐ 익숙한
- understanding ⓝ 이해(력)
- beforehand [ad] 미리
- balance ⓝ 균형, 균형을 맞추다
- adjust to ~에 적응하다
- contribute to ~에 기여하다, ~의 원인이 되다

14행 This contributes to building a sense of community, which is essential for
　　　　　　　　　　　　　　　　　　　　　　　선행사　　　　계속적 용법
all children, especially those in transition.
　　　　　　　　　　= children

---

31 사실보다 감정에 기반한 우리의 선택　　　　　　정답률 54% | 정답 ①

다음 빈칸에 들어갈 말로 가장 적절한 것을 고르시오.

☑ ① anxiety – 불안감　　② boredom – 지루함　　③ confidence – 자신감
④ satisfaction – 만족감　　⑤ responsibility – 책임감

Many people are terrified to fly in airplanes.
많은 사람들은 비행기를 타는 것을 두려워한다.

Often, / this fear stems from a lack of control.
종종, / 이 두려움은 통제력의 부족에서 비롯된다.

The pilot is in control, / not the passengers, / and this lack of control instills fear.
조종사는 통제를 하지만 / 승객은 그렇지 않으며, / 이러한 통제력의 부족은 두려움을 스며들게 한다.

Many potential passengers are so afraid / they choose to drive great distances / to get to a destination / instead of flying.
많은 잠재적인 승객들은 너무 두려운 나머지 / 그들은 먼 거리를 운전하는 것을 선택한다. / 목적지에 도착하기 위해 / 비행기를 타는 대신

But / their decision to drive / is based solely on emotion, / not logic.
그러나 / 운전을 하기로 한 그들의 결정은 / 오직 감정에 근거한다. / 논리가 아닌

Logic says / that statistically, / the odds of dying in a car crash / are around 1 in 5,000, / while the odds of dying in a plane crash / are closer to 1 in 11 million.
논리에 따르면, / 통계적으로 / 자동차 사고로 사망할 확률은 / 약 5,000분의 1인데 반면, / 비행기 사고로 사망할 확률은 / 1,100만분의 1에 가까운 반면

If you're going to take a risk, / especially one that could possibly involve your well-being, / wouldn't you want the odds in your favor?
만약 여러분이 위험을 감수할 것이라면, / 특히 여러분의 안녕을 혹시 포함할 수 있는 위험을 / 여러분에게 유리한 확률을 원하지 않겠는가?

However, / most people choose the option / that will cause them the least amount of anxiety.
그러나 / 사람들 대부분은 선택을 한다. / 그들에게 최소한의 불안감을 야기할

Pay attention to the thoughts / you have about taking the risk / and make sure you're basing your decision on facts, / not just feelings.
생각에 주의를 기울여보고 / 여러분이 위험을 감수하는 데 관해 하고 있는 / 여러분이 사실에 기반하여 결정을 내리고 있는지 확인하라. / 단지 감정이 아니고

많은 사람들은 비행기를 타는 것을 두려워한다. 종종, 이 두려움은 통제력의 부족에서 비롯된다. 조종사는 통제를 하지만 승객은 그렇지 않으며, 이러한 통제력의 부족은 두려움을 스며들게 한다. 많은 잠재적인 승객들은 너무 두려운 나머지 비행기를 타는 대신 먼 거리를 운전해 목적지에 도착하기를 선택한다. 그러나 운전을 하기로 한 그들의 결정은 논리가 아닌 오직 감정에 근거한다. 논리에 따르면, 통계적으로 자동차 사고로 사망할 확률은 약 5,000분의 1인 반면, 비행기 사고로 사망할 확률은 1,100만분의 1에 가깝다고 한다. 만약 여러분이 위험을 감수할 것이라면, 특히 여러분의 안녕을 혹시 포함할 수 있는 위험을 감수할 것이라면, 여러분에게 유리한 확률을 원하지 않겠는가? 그러나 사람들 대부분은 그들에게 최소한의 불안감을 야기할 선택을 한다. 여러분이 위험을 감수하는 데 관해 하고 있는 생각에 주의를 기울여보고, 단지 감정이 아니고 사실에 기반하여 결정을 내리고 있는지 확인하라.

Why? 왜 정답일까?

글에서 사람들이 비행기를 타는 대신 장거리 운전을 하기로 결심하는 것은 사실상 사고의 실질적 확률을 고려하지 않은, 감정 중심의 선택(their decision to drive is based solely on emotion)이라고 지적하고 있다. 즉, 사람들은 실제 통계적으로 교통사고 확률이 비행기 사고 확률보다 높은데도 오로지 '불안'을 피하려고 운전을 선택한다는 것이므로, 빈칸에 들어갈 말로 가장 적절한 것은 ① '불안감'이다.

- terrified ⓐ 겁에 질린
- lack ⓝ 부족, 결여
- potential ⓐ 잠재적인
- solely ⓐ 오로지
- statistically ⓐ 통계적으로
- in one's favor ~에 유리한
- well-being ⓝ 안녕, 행복
- base ⓥ ~에 근거를 두다, 기반으로 하다
- boredom ⓝ 지루함
- stem from ~에서 기원하다
- instill ⓥ 스며들게 하다, 주입하다
- destination ⓝ 목적지
- logic ⓝ 논리
- odds ⓝ 공산, 가능성
- crash ⓝ (차나 비행기의) 사고, 충돌
- make sure 반드시 ~하다
- anxiety ⓝ 불안

3행 Many potential passengers are so afraid (that) they choose to drive great
　　　　　　　　　　　　　　　　　「so ~ that : 너무 ~해서 …하다」　목적어(~것)
distances to get to a destination instead of flying.
　　　　　부사적 용법(~하기 위해)

---

32 언어적 수법으로 다른 동물과 거리를 두는 인간　　　정답률 43% | 정답 ③

다음 빈칸에 들어갈 말로 가장 적절한 것을 고르시오. [3점]

① define human instincts – 인간의 본능을 정의하는
② overestimate chimps' intelligence – 침팬지의 지능을 과대평가하는
☑ ③ distance the other animals from us – 우리와 다른 동물들 사이에 거리를 두는
④ identify animals' negative emotions – 동물의 부정적 감정을 식별하는
⑤ correct our misconceptions about nature – 자연에 대한 우리의 오해를 정정하는

The famous primatologist Frans de Waal, of Emory University, / says / humans downplay similarities / between us and other animals / as a way of maintaining our spot / at the top of our imaginary ladder.
Emory 대학의 유명한 영장류학자 Frans de Waal은 / 말한다. / 인간은 유사성을 경시한다고 / 우리와 다른 동물들 사이의 / 우리 위치를 유지할 방법으로 / 상상 속 사다리의 꼭대기에 있는

Scientists, / de Waal points out, / can be some of the worst offenders / — employing technical language / to distance the other animals from us.

과학자들은 / de Waal은 지적한다. / 최악의 죄를 범하는 자들 중 일부일 수 있다고 / 전문 언어를 사용하는 / 우리와 다른 동물들 사이에 거리를 두기 위해

They call "kissing" in chimps "mouth-to-mouth contact"; / they call "friends" between primates "favorite affiliation partners"; / they interpret evidence / showing that crows and chimps can make tools / as being somehow qualitatively different / from the kind of toolmaking said to define humanity.
그들은 침팬지의 '키스'를 '입과 입의 접촉'이라고 부르고, / 그들은 영장류 사이의 '친구'를 '좋아하는 제휴 파트너'라고 부르며, / 그들은 증거를 해석한다 / 까마귀와 침팬지가 도구를 만들 수 있다는 것을 보여주는 / 아무래도 질적으로 다르다고 / 인류를 정의한다고 하는 종류의 도구 제작과는

If an animal can beat us at a cognitive task / — like how certain bird species can remember the precise locations of thousands of seeds — / they write it off as instinct, / not intelligence.
만약 동물이 인지적인 과업에서 우리를 이길 수 있다면, / 특정 종의 새들이 수천 개의 씨앗의 정확한 위치를 기억할 수 있듯이, / 그들은 그것을 본능으로 치부한다 / 지능이 아니라

This and so many more tricks of language / are what de Waal has termed "linguistic castration."
이것과 더 많은 언어적 수법은 / de Waal이 '언어적 거세'라고 명명한 것이다.

The way we use our tongues / to disempower animals, / the way we invent words / to maintain our spot at the top.
우리의 언어를 사용하는 방식이며, / 우리가 동물로부터 힘을 빼앗기 위해 / 우리가 단어들을 만들어내는 방식이다. / 우리의 꼭대기 위치를 지키려고

Emory 대학의 유명한 영장류학자 Frans de Waal은 인간은 상상 속 사다리의 꼭대기에 있는 우리 위치를 유지할 방법으로 우리와 다른 동물들 사이의 유사성을 경시한다고 말한다. de Waal은 과학자들이 전문 언어를 사용해 우리와 다른 동물들 사이에 거리를 두는 최악의 죄를 범하는 자들 중 일부일 수 있다고 지적한다. 그들은 침팬지의 '키스'를 '입과 입의 접촉'이라고 부르고, 영장류 사이의 '친구'를 '좋아하는 제휴 파트너'라고 부르며, 그들은 까마귀와 침팬지가 도구를 만들 수 있다는 것을 보여주는 증거를 인류를 정의한다고 하는 종류의 도구 제작과는 아무래도 질적으로 다르다고 해석한다. 만약 특정 종의 새들이 수천 개의 씨앗의 정확한 위치를 기억할 수 있는 경우처럼, 동물이 인지적인 과업에서 우리를 이길 수 있다면, 그들은 그것을 지능이 아니라 본능으로 치부한다. 이것과 더 많은 언어적 수법은 de Waal이 '언어적 거세'라고 명명한 것이다. 우리가 동물로부터 힘을 빼앗기 위해 우리의 언어를 사용하는 방식이며, 우리의 꼭대기 위치를 지키려고 단어들을 만들어내는 방식이다.

Why? 왜 정답일까?

우리가 인간과 동물이 서로 다름을 강조하는(humans downplay similarities between us and other animals) 언어 사용으로 교묘하게 우월한 입지를 지키려 한다는 것을 지적하는 내용이므로, 빈칸에 들어갈 말로 가장 적절한 것은 ③ '우리와 다른 동물들 사이에 거리를 두는'이다.

- primatologist ⓝ 영장류학자
- similarity ⓝ 유사성
- imaginary ⓐ 상상의
- offender ⓝ 범죄자, 나쁜 짓을 하는 사람
- technical ⓐ 전문적인
- chimp ⓝ 침팬지
- affiliation ⓝ 제휴
- crow ⓝ 까마귀
- toolmaking ⓝ 도구 제작
- humanity ⓝ 인류
- cognitive ⓐ 인지적인
- write off as ~라고 치부하다
- intelligence ⓝ 지능
- term ⓥ (특정 용어로) 칭하다 ⓝ 용어
- overestimate ⓥ 과대평가하다
- identify ⓥ 식별하다, 알아보다, 확인하다
- downplay ⓥ 경시하다
- spot ⓝ 위치 ⓥ 파악하다
- ladder ⓝ 사다리
- employ ⓥ 이용하다, 고용하다
- language ⓝ 언어
- primate ⓝ 영장류
- interpret A as B A를 B로 해석하다
- qualitatively ⓐ 질적으로
- define ⓥ 정의하다
- beat ⓥ 이기다
- precise ⓐ 정확한
- instinct ⓝ 본능
- trick ⓝ 수법, 트릭
- disempower ⓥ ~로부터 힘을 빼앗다
- distance A from B A와 B 사이에 거리를 두다
- misconception ⓝ 오해

6행 ~ they interpret evidence (showing that crows and chimps can make tools)
　　　　　　　　　　interpret + A +
as being somehow qualitatively different from the kind of toolmaking [(that is)
as + B : A를 B로 해석하다　　　　　　　　　　　　　　　　　　　　　생략
said to define humanity].

---

33 학습자의 관심사에 맞는 읽기 자료 제공　　　정답률 56% | 정답 ②

다음 빈칸에 들어갈 말로 가장 적절한 것을 고르시오.

① examples from official textbooks – 공식 교과서에서 뽑은 예시
☑ ② relevant texts they will be interested in – 학생이 관심 있어 할 적절한 글
③ enough chances to exchange information – 정보를 교환할 충분한 기회
④ different genres for different age groups – 각 연령대마다 다른 장르
⑤ early reading experience to develop logic skills – 논리력을 키우기 위한 조기 읽기 경험

A key to engagement and achievement / is providing students with relevant texts / they will be interested in.
참여와 성취의 핵심은 / 적절한 글을 학생들에게 제공하는 것이다. / 그들이 관심 있어 할

My scholarly work and my teaching / have been deeply influenced / by the work of Rosalie Fink.
내 학문적 연구와 수업은 / 깊이 영향을 받아왔다 / Rosalie Fink의 연구에 의해

She interviewed twelve adults / who were highly successful in their work, / including a physicist, a biochemist, and a company CEO.
그녀는 열두 명의 성인들과 면담했다. / 자기 직업에서 매우 성공한 / 물리학자, 생화학자, 회사의 최고 경영자를 포함해

All of them had dyslexia / and had had significant problems with reading / throughout their school years.
그들 모두가 난독증이 있었고, / 읽기에 상당한 문제를 겪었다. / 학령기 내내

While she expected to find / that they had avoided reading / and discovered ways to bypass it or compensate with other strategies for learning, / she found the opposite.
그녀는 알게 되리라고 예상했다 / 그들이 학습할 때 읽기를 피하고, / 방법을 찾아냈다는 것을 / 그것을 우회하거나 다른 전략들로 학습을 보완할 / 하지만 그녀는 정반대를 알아냈다.

"To my surprise, / I found / that these dyslexics were enthusiastic readers... / they rarely avoided reading. / On the contrary, / they sought out books."
"놀랍게도, / 나는 알아냈다. / 난독증이 있는 이런 사람들이 열성적인 독자인 것을... / 이들이 좀처럼 읽기를 피하지 않는 것을 / 거꾸로, 그들은 책을 찾았다."

The pattern Fink discovered / was / that all of her subjects had been passionate / in some personal interest.
Fink가 발견한 패턴은 / ~이었다. / 그녀의 실험 대상자 모두가 열정적이었다는 것 / 어떤 개인적인 관심사에

The areas of interest included / religion, math, business, science, history, and biography.
관심 분야는 포함했다. / 종교, 수학, 상업, 과학, 역사 그리고 생물학을

What mattered was / that they read voraciously to find out more.
중요한 것은 ~이었다. / 그들이 더 많이 알아내기 위해 탐욕스럽게 읽었다는 것

참여와 성취의 핵심은 학생들이 관심 있어 할 적절한 글을 그들에게 제공하는 것이다. 내 학문적인 연구와 수업은 Rosalie Fink의 연구에 깊이 영향을 받았다. 그녀는 물리학자, 생화학자, 회사의 최고 경영자를 포함해 자기 직업에서 매우 성공한 열두 명의 성인들과 면담했다. 그들 모두가 난독증이 있었고, 학령기 내내 읽기에 상당한 문제를 겪었다. 그녀는 그들이 학습할 때 읽기를 피하고, 그것을 우회하거나 다른 전략들로 학습을 보완할 방법을 찾아냈다는 것을 알게 되리라고 예상했으나, 정반대를 알아냈다. "놀랍게도, 나는 난독증이 있는 이런 사람들이 열정적인 독자인 것을… 이들이 좀처럼 읽기를 피하지 않는 것을 알아냈다. 거꾸로, 그들은 책을 찾았다." Fink가 발견한 패턴은 그녀의 실험 대상자 모두가 어떤 개인적인 관심사에 열정적이었다는 것이었다. 관심 분야는 종교, 수학, 상업, 과학, 역사 그리고 생물학을 포함했다. 중요한 것은 그들이 더 많이 알아내기 위해 탐욕스럽게 읽었다는 것이었다.

Why? 왜 정답일까?

마지막 두 문장에서 어린 시절 난독증을 겪었으나 성공한 사람들을 연구한 결과, 자신이 관심을 두었던 분야에 대해 열정을 갖고 있었으며(passionate in some personal interest) 더 많은 것을 알기 위해 닥치는 대로 글을 읽었다는 것을 알아냈다고 한다. 이를 통해 결국 학생을 좋은 학습자로 만들려면 '흥미를 가질 만한 글'을 제시하라는 결론을 도출할 수 있다. 따라서 빈칸에 들어갈 말로 가장 적절한 것은 ② '학생들이 관심 있어 할 적절한 글'이다.

- engagement ⓝ 참여, 몰입
- provide A with B A에게 B를 제공하다
- biochemist ⓝ 생화학자
- significant ⓐ 상당한, 심각한
- bypass ⓥ 우회하다
- opposite ⓝ 정반대
- seek out ~을 찾아내다
- personal ⓐ 개인적인
- biography ⓝ (인물의) 전기
- official ⓐ 공식적인
- achievement ⓝ 성취
- physicist ⓝ 물리학자
- dyslexia ⓝ 난독증
- discover ⓥ 찾아내다, 발견하다
- compensate for ~을 보완하다, 보상하다
- enthusiastic ⓐ 열정적인, 열성적인
- subject ⓝ 실험 대상자
- religion ⓝ 종교
- voraciously ⓐⅾ 탐욕스럽게
- relevant ⓐ 적절한

구문 풀이

8행 While she expected to find [that they had avoided reading and
「expect + to부정사 : ~하기를 기대하다」 동사1
discovered ways to bypass it or compensate with other strategies for learning],
동사2   수식(형용사적 용법)
she found the opposite.

★★★ 등급을 가르는 문제!
34 수행으로 자기 자신의 가치를 매길 때   정답률 37% | 정답 ①

다음 빈칸에 들어갈 말로 가장 적절한 것을 고르시오. [3점]

✔ ① it is the sole determinant of one's self-worth – 그것이 자신의 가치를 결정하는 유일한 요소일
② you are distracted by others' achievements – 다른 사람의 성취에 의해 주의가 분산될
③ there is too much competition in one field – 한 분야의 경쟁이 너무 심할
④ you ignore feedback about a performance – 수행에 관한 피드백을 무시할
⑤ it is not accompanied by effort – 그것에 노력이 따르지 않을

For many people, / *ability* refers to intellectual competence, / so they want everything they do / to reflect how smart they are — / writing a brilliant legal brief, / getting the highest grade on a test, / writing elegant computer code, / saying something exceptionally wise or witty in a conversation.
많은 사람들에게 / 능력은 지적 능력을 의미하기 때문에, / 그들은 자신이 하는 모든 것이 ~하기를 원한다. / 자신이 얼마나 똑똑한지를 보여주기를 / 훌륭한 소송 의견서를 작성하는 것, / 시험에서 최고의 성적을 받는 것, / 명쾌한 컴퓨터 코드를 작성하는 것, / 대화 도중 탁월하게 현명하거나 재치 있는 말을 하는 것

You could also define ability / in terms of a particular skill or talent, / such as how well one plays the piano, / learns a language, / or serves a tennis ball.
여러분은 또한 능력을 정의할 수도 있다. / 특정한 기술이나 재능의 관점에서 / 피아노를 얼마나 잘 치는지, / 언어를 얼마나 잘 배우는지, / 테니스공을 얼마나 잘 서브하는지와 같은

Some people focus on their ability / to be attractive, entertaining, up on the latest trends, / or to have the newest gadgets.
어떤 사람들은 능력에 초점을 맞춘다. / 매력적이고, 재미있고, 최신 유행에 맞출 수 있는 / 혹은 최신 기기를 가질 수 있는

However ability may be defined, / a problem occurs / when it is the sole determinant of one's self-worth.
능력이 어떻게 정의되든지, / 문제가 발생한다. / 그것이 자신의 가치를 결정하는 유일한 요소일 때

The performance becomes the *only* measure of the person; / nothing else is taken into account.
수행이 그 사람의 유일한 척도가 되며, / 다른 것은 고려되지 않는다.

An outstanding performance means an outstanding person; / an average performance means an average person. // Period.
뛰어난 수행은 뛰어난 사람을 의미하고, / 평범한 수행은 평범한 사람을 의미한다. // 끝.

많은 사람들에게 능력은 지적 능력을 의미하기 때문에, 그들은 자신이 하는 모든 것이 자신이 얼마나 똑똑한지를 보여주기를 원한다. 예컨대, 훌륭한 소송 의견서를 작성하는 것, 시험에서 최고의 성적을 받는 것, 명쾌한 컴퓨터 코드를 작성하는 것, 대화 도중 탁월하게 현명하거나 재치 있는 말을 하는 것이다. 여러분은 또한 피아노를 얼마나 잘 치는지, 언어를 얼마나 잘 배우는지, 테니스공을 얼마나 잘 서브하는지와 같은 특정한 기술이나 재능의 관점에서 능력을 정의할 수도 있다. 어떤 사람들은 매력적이고, 재미있고, 최신 유행에 맞추거나, 최신 기기를 가질 수 있는 능력에 초점을 맞춘다. 능력이 어떻게 정의되든, 그것이 자신의 가치를 결정하는 유일한 요소일 때 문제가 발생한다. 수행이 그 사람의 유일한 척도가 되며, 다른 것은 고려되지 않는다. 뛰어난 수행은 뛰어난 사람을 의미하고, 평범한 수행은 평범한 사람을 의미한다. 끝.

Why? 왜 정답일까?

빈칸 뒤에서 수행을 자신의 가치에 대한 유일한 평가 척도로 삼는 경우(The performance becomes the *only* measure of the person; nothing else is taken into account.)의 부작용을 언급하는 것으로 보아, 빈칸에 들어갈 말로 가장 적절한 것은 ① '그것이 자신의 가치를 결정하는 유일한 요소일'이다.

- competence ⓝ 능력, 역량
- brilliant ⓐ 뛰어난
- elegant ⓐ 명쾌한, 멋들어진
- witty ⓐ 재치 있는
- serve a ball 서브를 넣다
- entertaining ⓐ 재미있는, 즐거움을 주는
- measure ⓝ 척도
- outstanding ⓐ 뛰어난
- determinant ⓝ 결정 요소
- distracted ⓐ 정신이 팔린
- reflect ⓥ 반영하다
- brief ⓝ (법률) 취지서, 의견서, 보고서
- exceptionally ⓐⅾ 탁월하게
- in terms of ~의 면에서
- attractive ⓐ 매력적인
- gadget ⓝ 장비, 기기
- take into account ~을 고려하다, 참작하다
- sole ⓐ 유일한
- self-worth ⓝ 자존감, 자부심

구문 풀이

10행 However ability may be defined, a problem occurs when it is the sole
복합관계부사(어떻게 ~하든 간에 = no matter how)
determinant of one's self-worth.

★★ 문제 해결 꿀~팁 ★★

▶ 많이 틀린 이유는?
특정 분야의 재능이나 역량을 보여주려 한다는 내용 때문에, 빈칸 뒤를 제대로 읽지 않으면 남과의 비교를 언급하는 ②나 수행에 대한 피드백을 언급하는 ④가 빈칸에 적절해 보인다. 하지만 빈칸 문제를 풀 때는 해당 지문 자체의 내용에 충실해야 한다.

▶ 문제 해결 방법은?
빈칸 뒤에서 수행이 '한 사람을 평가하는 유일한 척도(the *only* measure of the person)'가 될 때를 언급하는데, 이 표현이 거의 그대로 ①에서 재진술되었다(the sole determinant of one's self-worth).

★★★ 등급을 가르는 문제!
35 감각 신경의 작용   정답률 38% | 정답 ②

다음 글에서 전체 흐름과 관계 없는 문장은? [3점]

Sensory nerves have specialized endings in the tissues / that pick up a particular sensation.
감각 신경은 특화된 말단을 조직에 가지고 있다. / 특정 감각을 포착하는

If, for example, / you step on a sharp object such as a pin, / nerve endings in the skin / will transmit the pain sensation up your leg, / up and along the spinal cord to the brain.
만약 예를 들어, / 여러분이 핀과 같이 날카로운 물체를 밟는다면, / 피부의 신경 말단이 / 통증 감각을 여러분의 다리 위로 전달할 것이다. / 그리고 척수를 따라 위로 뇌까지

① While the pain itself is unpleasant, / it is in fact acting as a protective mechanism for the foot.
통증 자체는 불쾌하지만, / 이것은 사실 발을 보호하는 메커니즘으로 작용하고 있다.

② That is, / you get used to the pain / so the capacity with which you can avoid pain decreases.
즉, / 여러분은 그 통증에 익숙해진다 / 그래서 통증을 피할 수 있는 능력이 감소한다.

③ Within the brain, / nerves will connect to the area / that controls speech, / so that you may well shout 'ouch' / or something rather less polite.
뇌 안에서, / 신경은 부분에 연결될 것이고, / 언어를 통제하는 / 그래서 여러분은 '아야'를 외칠 것이다. / 또는 다소 덜 공손한 무언가를

④ They will also connect to motor nerves / that travel back down the spinal cord, / and to the muscles in your leg / that now contract quickly / to lift your foot away from the painful object.
그것들은 또한 운동 신경에 연결될 것이다. / 척수를 타고 다시 내려오는 / 그리고 여러분의 다리 근육에 / 이제 재빨리 수축하여 / 고통을 주는 물체로부터 발을 떼서 들어 올리게 하는

⑤ Sensory and motor nerves / control almost all functions in the body / — from the beating of the heart / to the movement of the gut, sweating and just about everything else.
감각 신경과 운동 신경은 / 신체의 거의 모든 기능을 통제한다. / 심장의 박동에서부터 / 장 운동, 발한 그 밖에 모든 것에 이르기까지

감각 신경은 특정 감각을 포착하는 특화된 말단을 조직에 가지고 있다. 예를 들어, 만약 여러분이 핀과 같이 날카로운 물체를 밟는다면, 피부의 신경 말단이 통증 감각을 여러분의 다리 위로, 그리고 척수를 따라 위로 뇌까지 전달할 것이다. ① 통증 자체는 불쾌하지만, 이것은 사실 발을 보호하는 메커니즘으로 작용하고 있다. ② 즉, 여러분은 그 통증에 익숙해져 통증을 피할 수 있는 능력이 감소한다. ③ 뇌 안에서, 신경은 언어를 통제하는 부분에 연결될 것이고, 그래서 여러분은 '아야' 또는 다소 덜 공손한 무언가를 외칠 것이다. ④ 그것들은 또한 척수를 타고 다시 내려오는 운동 신경에 연결될 것이고, 그리고 이제 재빨리 수축하여 고통을 주는 물체로부터 발을 떼서 들어 올리게 하는 여러분의 다리 근육에 연결될 것이다. ⑤ 감각 신경과 운동 신경은 심장의 박동에서부터 장 운동, 발한과 그 밖에 모든 것에 이르기까지 신체의 거의 모든 기능을 통제한다.

Why? 왜 정답일까?

통증이 위험을 피하는 보호 기제 역할을 한다는 예시를 들어 감각 신경의 작용을 설명하는 글인데, ②는 통증에 익숙해져 둔감해진다는 내용이다. 따라서 전체 흐름과 관계 없는 문장은 ②이다.

- sensory ⓐ 감각의
- tissue ⓝ (생체) 조직
- transmit ⓥ 전달하다
- unpleasant ⓐ 불쾌한
- capacity ⓝ 능력
- painful ⓐ 고통스러운
- gut ⓝ 내장, 소화관
- nerve ⓝ 신경
- sensation ⓝ 감각
- spinal cord 척수
- protective mechanism 보호 기제
- lift ⓥ 들어올리다
- motor ⓐ 운동 신경의
- sweating ⓝ 발한, 땀이 남

구문 풀이

6행 That is, you get used to the pain so the capacity [with which you can
주어1 동사1(~에 익숙해지다)   주어2 「전치사 + 목적격 관·대」
avoid pain] decreases.
동사2

36 결정의 형성 정답률 72% | 정답 ②

주어진 글 다음에 이어질 글의 순서로 가장 적절한 것을 고르시오. [3점]

① (A) − (C) − (B)
✓ (B) − (A) − (C)
③ (B) − (C) − (A)
④ (C) − (A) − (B)
⑤ (C) − (B) − (A)

Maybe you've heard this joke: / "How do you eat an elephant?"
아마 여러분은 이 농담을 들어본 적이 있을 것이다. / "코끼리를 어떻게 먹지?"

The answer is "one bite at a time."
정답은 '한 번에 한 입'이다.

(B) So, how do you "build" the Earth?
그렇다면, 여러분은 어떻게 지구를 '건설'하는가?

That's simple, too: / one atom at a time.
이것도 간단하다. / 한 번에 하나의 원자이다.

Atoms are the basic building blocks of crystals, / and since all rocks are made up of crystals, / the more you know about atoms, / the better.
원자는 결정의 기본 구성 요소이고, / 모든 암석은 결정으로 이루어져 있기 때문에, / 여러분이 원자에 대해 더 많이 알수록 / 더 좋다.

Crystals come in a variety of shapes / that scientists call *habits*.
결정은 다양한 모양으로 나온다. / 과학자들이 습성이라고 부르는

(A) Common crystal habits / include squares, triangles, and six-sided hexagons.
일반적인 결정 습성은 / 사각형, 삼각형, 육면의 육각형을 포함한다.

Usually crystals form / when liquids cool, / such as when you create ice cubes.
보통 결정이 형성된다. / 액체가 차가워질 때 / 여러분이 얼음을 만들 때와 같이

Many times, / crystals form in ways / that do not allow for perfect shapes.
많은 경우, / 결정은 방식으로 형성된다. / 완벽한 모양을 허용하지 않는

If conditions are too cold, too hot, / or there isn't enough source material, / they can form strange, twisted shapes.
조건이 너무 차갑거나, 너무 뜨겁거나, / 혹은 원천 물질이 충분하지 않으면 / 그것들은 이상하고 뒤틀린 모양을 형성할 수 있다.

(C) But when conditions are right, / we see beautiful displays.
하지만 조건이 맞을 때, / 우리는 아름다운 배열을 본다.

Usually, / this involves a slow, steady environment / where the individual atoms have plenty of time to join / and fit perfectly into what's known as the *crystal lattice*.
보통, / 이것은 느리고 안정적인 환경을 수반한다. / 개별적인 원자들이 충분한 시간을 들여 결합해서 / *결정격자*라고 알려진 것에 완벽하게 들어맞게 되는

This is the basic structure of atoms / that is seen time after time.
이것은 원자의 기본적인 구조이다. / 반복하여 보이는

아마 여러분은 이 농담을 들어본 적이 있을 것이다. "코끼리를 어떻게 먹지?" 정답은 '한 번에 한 입'이다.

(B) 그렇다면, 여러분은 어떻게 지구를 '건설'하는가? 이것도 간단하다. 한 번에 하나의 원자이다. 원자는 결정의 기본 구성 요소이고, 모든 암석은 결정으로 이루어져 있기 때문에, 여러분은 원자에 대해 더 많이 알수록 더 좋다. 결정은 과학자들이 습성이라고 부르는 다양한 모양으로 나온다.

(A) 일반적인 결정 습성은 사각형, 삼각형, 육면의 육각형을 포함한다. 보통 여러분이 얼음을 만들 때와 같이 액체가 차가워질 때 결정이 형성된다. 많은 경우, 결정은 완벽한 모양을 허용하지 않는 방식으로 형성된다. 조건이 너무 차갑거나, 너무 뜨겁거나, 혹은 원천 물질이 충분하지 않으면 이상하고 뒤틀린 모양을 형성할 수 있다.

(C) 하지만 조건이 맞을 때, 우리는 아름다운 배열을 본다. 보통, 이것은 개별적인 원자들이 충분한 시간을 들여 결합해서 *결정격자*라고 알려진 것에 완벽하게 들어맞게 되는 느리고 안정적인 환경을 수반한다. 이것은 반복하여 보이는 원자의 기본적인 구조이다.

Why? 왜 정답일까?

주어진 글에서 '코끼리를 어떻게 먹나'라는 물음에 '한 번에 한 입씩' 먹으면 된다는 농담이 있다고 하는데, (B)는 이것이 지구가 만들어진 과정에도 적용될 수 있다면서 결정의 습성을 언급한다. (A)는 이 결정의 습성을 설명하면서, 많은 경우 결정이 뒤틀린 모양으로 형성된다고 언급하는데, (C)는 But으로 흐름을 반전시키며 아름다운 배열을 지닌 결정도 만들어진다고 설명한다. 따라서 글의 순서로 가장 적절한 것은 ② '(B) − (A) − (C)'이다.

- bite ⓝ 한 입 (베어문 조각) ⓥ 베어 물다
- hexagon ⓝ 육각형
- ice cube 얼음 조각
- twisted ⓐ 뒤틀린
- be made up of ~로 구성되다
- plenty of 많은
- lattice ⓝ 격자 (모양)

- crystal ⓝ 결정
- liquid ⓝ 액체
- allow for ~을 허용하다
- atom ⓝ 원자
- steady ⓐ 안정된, 꾸준한
- fit into ~에 들어 맞다
- time after time 자주, 매번, 되풀이해서

구문 풀이

15행 Usually, this involves a slow, steady environment [where the individual atoms have plenty of time to join and fit perfectly into {what's known as the crystal lattice}].
선행사(상황) / 관계부사 / 형용사적용법 / 전치사 / 명사절

37 기타가 소리를 내는 과정 정답률 63% | 정답 ③

주어진 글 다음에 이어질 글의 순서로 가장 적절한 것을 고르시오.

① (A) − (C) − (B)
② (B) − (A) − (C)
✓ (B) − (C) − (A)
④ (C) − (A) − (B)
⑤ (C) − (B) − (A)

When you pluck a guitar string / it moves back and forth hundreds of times every second.
여러분이 기타 줄을 뜯을 때 / 그것은 매초 수백 번 이리저리 움직인다.

(B) Naturally, / this movement is so fast / that you cannot see it / — you just see the blurred outline of the moving string.
당연히, / 이 움직임은 너무 빨라서 / 여러분이 볼 수 없다. / 여러분은 그저 움직이는 줄의 흐릿한 윤곽만 본다.

Strings vibrating in this way on their own / make hardly any noise / because strings are very thin / and don't push much air about.
이렇게 스스로 진동하는 줄들은 / 거의 소리가 나지 않는데, / 이는 줄이 매우 가늘고 / 많은 공기를 밀어내지 못하기 때문이다.

(C) But if you attach a string to a big hollow box / (like a guitar body), / then the vibration is amplified / and the note is heard loud and clear.
하지만 여러분이 속이 빈 커다란 상자에 줄을 달면, / (기타 몸통 같은) / 그 진동은 증폭되어 / 그 음이 크고 선명하게 들린다.

The vibration of the string is passed on / to the wooden panels of the guitar body, / which vibrate back and forth / at the same rate as the string.
그 줄의 진동은 전달된다 / 기타 몸통의 나무판으로 / 그리고 그것은 이리저리 떨린다. / 줄과 같은 정도로

(A) The vibration of the wood / creates more powerful waves in the air pressure, / which travel away from the guitar.
그 나무의 진동은 / 공기의 압력에 더 강력한 파동을 만들어 내고 / 그것은 기타로부터 멀리 퍼진다.

When the waves reach your eardrums / they flex in and out / the same number of times a second / as the original string.
그 파동이 여러분의 고막에 도달할 때 / 그것은 굽이쳐 들어가고 나온다. / 초당 동일한 횟수로 / 원래의 줄과

여러분이 기타 줄을 뜯을 때 그것은 매초 수백 번 이리저리 움직인다.

(B) 당연히, 이 움직임은 너무 빨라서 여러분이 볼 수 없다. 여러분은 그저 움직이는 줄의 흐릿한 윤곽만 본다. 이렇게 스스로 진동하는 줄들은 거의 소리가 나지 않는데, 이는 줄이 매우 가늘어 많은 공기를 밀어내지 못하기 때문이다.

(C) 하지만 여러분이 (기타 몸통 같이) 속이 빈 커다란 상자에 줄을 달면, 그 진동은 증폭되어 그 음이 크고 선명하게 들린다. 그 줄의 진동은 기타 몸통의 나무판으로 전달되어 줄과 같은 정도로 이리저리 떨린다.

(A) 그 나무의 진동은 공기의 압력에 더 강력한 파동을 만들어 내어 기타로부터 멀리 퍼진다. 그 파동이 여러분의 고막에 도달할 때 원래의 줄과 초당 동일한 횟수로 굽이쳐 들어가고 나온다.

Why? 왜 정답일까?

기타 줄을 뜯으면 줄이 떨린다는 주어진 글에 이어, (B)는 우리가 이 움직임을 평소에는 볼 수 없으며, 혼자서 진동하는 줄은 공기를 충분히 밀어내지 못해 소리도 내지 못한다고 언급한다. (C)는 But으로 흐름을 반전시키며, 줄을 기타 몸통 같은 상자에 담아서 진동을 증폭시키는 상황을 제시하고, (A)는 이 진동이 소리로 나오게 되는 내용으로 글을 맺는다. 따라서 글의 순서로 가장 적절한 것은 ③ '(B) − (C) − (A)'이다.

- pluck ⓥ (현악기를) 뜯다
- vibration ⓝ 진동
- flex ⓥ (근육을) 수축시키다. (관절을) 구부리다
- thin ⓐ 얇은
- hollow ⓐ (속이) 빈
- panel ⓝ 판

- string ⓝ 줄, 현악기
- eardrum ⓝ 고막
- blur ⓥ 흐리게 하다
- attach A to B A를 B에 부착하다
- amplify ⓥ 증폭시키다
- rate ⓝ 속도, 비율

구문 풀이

9행 Strings (vibrating in this way on their own) make hardly any noise
주어 / 현재분사 / 동사(복수) / 거의 전혀 ~않다
because strings are very thin and don't push much air about.

★★★ 등급을 가르는 문제!
38 일과 가정의 경계 정답률 26% | 정답 ⑤

글의 흐름으로 보아, 주어진 문장이 들어가기에 가장 적절한 곳을 고르시오. [3점]

Boundaries between work and home / are blurring / as portable digital technology makes it increasingly possible / to work anywhere, anytime.
직장과 가정의 경계가 / 흐릿해지고 있다. / 휴대용 디지털 기술이 점차 가능하게 하면서, / 언제 어디서든 작업하는 것을

Individuals differ / in how they like to manage their time / to meet work and outside responsibilities.
사람들은 서로 다르다. / 자기 시간을 관리하기를 바라는 방식에 있어서 / 직장과 외부의 책임을 수행하기 위해

① Some people prefer to separate or segment roles / so that boundary crossings are minimized.
어떤 사람들은 역할을 분리하거나 분할하기를 선호한다. / 경계 교차 지점이 최소화되도록

② For example, / these people might keep separate email accounts / for work and family / and try to conduct work at the workplace / and take care of family matters / only during breaks and non-work time.
예를 들어, / 이러한 사람들은 별개의 이메일 계정을 유지하고 / 직장과 가정을 위한 / 직장에서 일하려고 하며, / 집안일을 처리하려고 할지도 모른다. / 쉴 때나 일하지 않는 시간 중에만

③ We've even noticed / more of these "segmenters" / carrying two phones / — one for work and one for personal use.
우리는 심지어 알게 되었다. / 더 많은 이러한 '분할자들'이 / 전화기 두 대를 가지고 다니고 있음을 / 하나는 업무용이고 다른 하나는 개인용인

④ Flexible schedules work well for these individuals / because they enable greater distinction / between time at work and time in other roles.
유연근무제는 이런 사람들에게 잘 작동되는데, / 이것은 더 큰 구별을 가능하게 하기 때문이다. / 직장에서의 시간과 다른 역할에서의 시간 간에

✓ Other individuals prefer / integrating work and family roles all day long.
다른 사람들은 선호한다. / 하루 종일 직장과 가정의 역할을 통합하기를

This might entail / constantly trading text messsages with children from the office, / or monitoring emails at home and on vacation, / rather than returning to work to find hundreds of messages in their inbox.
이것을 수반할 수도 있다. / 사무실에서 아이들과 문자 메시지를 계속 주고받는 것을 / 혹은 집에 있을 때나 휴가 중에 이메일을 체크하는 것을 / 직장으로 돌아가서 받은 편지함에서 수백 개의 메시지를 발견하는 대신

휴대용 디지털 기술이 언제 어디서든 작업하는 것을 점차 가능하게 하면서, 직장과 가정의 경계가 흐릿해지고 있다. 사람들은 직장과 외부의 책임을 수행하기 위해 자기 시간을 관리하기를 바라는 방식이 서로 다르다. ① 어떤 사람들은 경계 교차 지점이 최소화되도록 역할을 분리하거나 분할하기를 선호한다. ② 예를 들어, 이러한 사람들은 직장과 가정을 위한 별개의 이메일 계정을 유지하고 직장에서 일하려고 하며, 쉴 때나 일하지 않는 시간 중에만 집안일을 처리하려고 할지도 모른다. ③ 우리는 더 많은 이러한 '분할자들'이 하나는 업무용이고 다른 하나는 개인용인 전화기 두 대를 가지고 다니고 있음을 심지어 알게 되었다. ④ 유연근무제는 이런 사람들에게 잘 적용되는데, 직장에서의 시간과 다른 역할에서의 시간 간에 더 큰 구별을 가능하게 하기 때문이다. ⑤ 다른 사람들은 하루 종일 직장과 가정의 역할을 통합하기를 선호한다. 이것은 직장으로 돌아가서 받은 편지함에서 수백 개의 메시지를 발견하는 대신, 사무실에서 아이들과 문자 메시지를 계속 주고받거나, 집에 있을 때와 휴가 중에 이메일을 체크하는 것을 수반할 수도 있다.

Why? 왜 정답일까?

⑤ 앞까지 일과 가정을 '분리하는' 사람들을 언급하는데, ⑤ 뒤에는 직장에서도 가족들과 연락하고, 집에 있을 때도 업무 처리를 하는 등 둘을 '통합하는' 사람들을 언급하고 있다. 따라서 '통합자들'에 관한 화제로 처음 넘어가는 주어진 문장이 들어가기에 가장 적절한 곳은 ⑤이다.

- integrate ⓥ 통합하다
- boundary ⓝ 경계
- outside ⓐ 외부의
- segment ⓥ 분할하다, 나누다
- account ⓝ 계정
- carry ⓥ 들고 다니다
- distinction ⓝ 구별
- constantly ⓐⓓ 계속
- monitor ⓥ 확인하다, 감독하다, 점검하다
- inbox ⓝ 수신함
- all day long 하루 종일
- portable ⓐ 휴대용의
- separate ⓥ 분리하다 ⓐ 분리된, 개별의
- minimize ⓥ 최소화하다
- conduct ⓥ 수행하다
- flexible schedule 유연근무제
- entail ⓥ 수반하다
- trade ⓥ 교환하다
- on vacation 휴가 중인

구문 풀이

3행 Boundaries between work and home are blurring as portable digital
　　　접속사(~ 때문에)
technology makes it increasingly possible to work anywhere, anytime.
　　5형식 동사　가목적어　목적격 보어　진목적어

★★ 문제 해결 꿀~팁 ★★

▶ 많이 틀린 이유는?
주어진 문장이 Other로 시작하므로, 앞에 Some이 있는 ②를 고르기 쉽다. 「Some ~ Other …」의 대구가 자연스러워 보이기 때문이다. 하지만 ② 뒤의 these people이 문맥상 ② 앞의 Some people이므로, 주어진 문장을 ②에 넣어 대명사의 흐름을 끊으면 안 된다. 또한 뒤에 갑자기 '유연근무제'라는 새로운 소재가 등장하는 ④도 정답처럼 보이기 쉽지만, ④ 앞뒤가 여전히 '일과 가정을 분리하는' 사람들에 대해서 설명하고 있어서 흐름이 끊기지 않기 때문에 다른 문장이 필요하지 않다.

▶ 문제 해결 방법은?
⑤ 뒤의 'trading ~ or monitoring ~'이 주어진 문장의 'integrating ~'에 대한 예시임을 파악해야 한다.

39　보완재의 개념　　정답률 50% | 정답 ⑤

글의 흐름으로 보아, 주어진 문장이 들어가기에 가장 적절한 곳을 고르시오.

A "complementary good" is a product / that is often consumed alongside another product.
'보완재'는 제품이다. / 종종 또 다른 제품과 함께 소비되는

① For example, / popcorn is a complementary good to a movie, / while a travel pillow is a complementary good / for a long plane journey.
예를 들어, / 팝콘은 영화에 대한 보완재인 한편, / 여행 베개는 보완재이다. / 긴 비행기 여행에 대한

② When the popularity of one product increases, / the sales of its complementary good / also increase.
한 제품의 인기가 높아지면 / 그것의 보완재 판매량도 / 또한 늘어난다.

③ By producing goods / that complement other products / that are already (or about to be) popular, / you can ensure a steady stream of demand for your product.
제품을 생산해서 / 다른 제품을 보완하는 / 이미 인기가 있는 (또는 곧 있을) / 여러분은 여러분의 제품에 대한 꾸준한 수요 흐름을 보장할 수 있다.

④ Some products enjoy perfect complementary status / — they *have* to be consumed together, / such as a lamp and a lightbulb.
일부 제품들은 완벽한 보완적 상태를 누리고 있고, / 그것들은 함께 소비되어*야* 한다. / 램프와 전구와 같이

✔ However, / do not assume / that a product is perfectly complementary, / as customers may not be completely locked in to the product.
그러나 / 가정하지 말라. / 어떤 제품이 완벽하게 보완적이라고 / 고객들이 그 제품에 완전히 고정되어 있지 않을 수 있으므로

For example, / although motorists may seem required to purchase gasoline / to run their cars, / they can switch to electric cars.
예를 들어, / 비록 운전자들이 휘발유를 구매할 필요가 있는 것처럼 보이는 해도, / 차를 운전하기 위해 / 이들이 전기 자동차로 바꿀 수도 있다.

'보완재'는 종종 또 다른 제품과 함께 소비되는 제품이다. ① 예를 들어, 팝콘은 영화에 대한 보완재인 한편, 여행 베개는 긴 비행기 여행에 대한 보완재이다. ② 한 제품의 인기가 높아지면 그것의 보완재 판매량도 늘어난다. ③ 여러분은 이미 인기가 있는 (또는 곧 있을) 다른 제품을 보완하는 제품을 생산해서 여러분의 제품에 대한 꾸준한 수요 흐름을 보장할 수 있다. ④ 일부 제품들은 완벽한 보완적 상태를 누리고 있고, 그것들은 램프와 전구와 같이 함께 소비되어야 한다. ⑤ 그러나 고객들이 그 제품에 완전히 고정되어 있지 않을 수 있으므로, 어떤 제품이 완벽하게 보완적이라고 가정하지 말라. 예를 들어, 비록 운전자들이 차를 운전하기 위해 휘발유를 구매할 필요가 있는 것처럼 보이는 해도, 이들이 전기 자동차로 바꿀 수도 있다.

Why? 왜 정답일까?

보완재에 관해 설명하는 글이다. ⑤ 앞에서 일부 제품은 램프 – 전구의 예시처럼 완벽히 서로 보완 관계에 있다고 하는데, ⑤ 뒤에서는 자동차 – 기름의 예시를 들며, 운전자들이 전기 차로 넘어갈 수도 있기 때문에 둘을 완벽한 보완 관계로 볼 수 없다고 한다. 즉, ⑤ 앞뒤로 내용이 서로 반대된다. 이때 주어진 문장

은 '보완재인 두 재화가 항상 보완 관계에 있을 거라고 가정하지 말라'는 내용으로, However가 있어 흐름 전환을 적절히 유도한다. 따라서 주어진 문장이 들어가기에 가장 적절한 곳은 ⑤이다.

- assume ⓥ 가정하다
- locked in 갇힌, 고정된
- complement ⓥ 보완하다, 보충하다
- stream ⓝ 흐름
- motorist ⓝ 운전자
- switch to ~로 바꾸다
- complementary ⓐ 보완하는
- alongside prep ~와 함께
- ensure ⓥ 확실히 하다, 보장하다
- status ⓝ 지위, 입지
- gasoline ⓝ 휘발유
- electric ⓐ 전기의

구문 풀이

14행 For example, although motorists may seem required to purchase gasoline
　　　　　접속사(~에도 불구하고)　2형식 동사　주격 보어
to run their cars, they can switch to electric cars.
~하기 위해

40　규범에서 약간 벗어나는 옷차림을 좋게 보는 우리들　정답률 50% | 정답 ①

다음 글의 내용을 한 문장으로 요약하고자 한다. 빈칸 (A), (B)에 들어갈 말로 가장 적절한 것은?

	(A)		(B)	
✔①	positively 긍정적으로	······	challenges 도전할	
②	negatively 부정적으로	······	challenges 도전할	
③	indifferently 무관심하게	······	neglects 등한시할	
④	negatively 부정적으로	······	meets 일치할	
⑤	positively 긍정적으로	······	meets 일치할	

It's not news to anyone / that we judge others based on their clothes.
누구에게도 새로운 일이 아니다. / 우리가 남들을 옷으로 판단한다는 것은

In general, / studies that investigate these judgments / find / that people prefer clothing that matches expectations / — surgeons in scrubs, little boys in blue — / with one notable exception.
일반적으로, / 이러한 판단을 조사하는 연구는 / 발견한다. / 사람들이 예상에 맞는 의복을 선호한다는 것을 / 수술복을 입은 외과 의사, 파란 옷을 입은 남자아이와 같이 / (그러면서) 눈에 띄는 예외가 하나 있는

A series of studies / published in an article in June 2014 / in the *Journal of Consumer Research* / explored observers' reactions to people / who broke established norms only slightly.
일련의 연구는 / 2014년 6월 논문에 실린 / *Journal of Consumer Research*의 / 사람들에 대한 관찰자들의 반응을 탐구했다. / 확립된 규범을 아주 약간 어긴

In one scenario, / a man at a black-tie affair / was viewed as having higher status and competence / when wearing a red bow tie.
한 시나리오에서는, / 정장 차림의 행사에 있는 남자가 / 더 높은 지위와 능력을 지녔다고 여겨졌다. / 빨간 나비 넥타이를 맸을 때

The researchers also found / that valuing uniqueness / increased audience members' ratings of the status and competence of a professor / who wore red sneakers while giving a lecture.
연구자들은 또한 발견했다. / 독특함을 중시하는 것이 / 교수의 지위와 역량에 대한 청중들의 평가를 높였다는 것을 / 강의 중에 빨간 운동화를 신은

The results suggest / that people judge these slight deviations from the norm as positive / because they suggest / that the individual is powerful enough / to risk the social costs of such behaviors.
그 결과들은 시사하는데, / 사람들이 이런 식으로 규범을 약간 어긴 것을 긍정적으로 판단한다는 것을 / 왜냐하면 그것들은 암시하기 때문이다. / 그 사람이 충분히 강하다는 것을 / 그러한 행동으로 인한 사회적 비용을 감수할 만큼

➡ A series of studies show / that people view an individual (A) positively / when the individual only slightly (B) challenges the norm / for what people should wear.
일련의 연구는 나타낸다. / 사람들이 어떤 개인을 긍정적으로 본다는 것을 / 그 사람이 규범에 아주 약간 도전할 때 / 사람들이 무엇을 입을지에 대한

우리가 남들을 옷으로 판단한다는 것은 누구에게도 새로운 일이 아니다. 일반적으로, 이러한 판단을 조사하는 연구는 사람들이 수술복을 입은 외과 의사, 파란 옷을 입은 남자아이와 같이 예상에 맞는 의복이되 눈에 띄는 예외가 하나 있는 것을 선호한다는 것을 발견한다. *Journal of Consumer Research*의 2014년 6월 논문에 실린 일련의 연구는 확립된 규범을 아주 약간 어긴 사람들에 대한 관찰자들의 반응을 탐구했다. 한 시나리오에서는, 정장 차림의 행사에서 한 남자가 빨간 나비 넥타이를 맸을 때 더 높은 지위와 능력을 지녔다고 여겨졌다. 연구자들은 또한, 독특함을 중시하는 것이 강의 중에 빨간 운동화를 신은 교수의 지위와 역량에 대한 청중들의 평가를 높였다는 것을 발견했다. 그 결과들은 사람들이 이런 식으로 규범을 약간 어긴 것을 긍정적으로 판단한다는 것을 시사하는데, 왜냐하면 그것들은 그 사람이 그러한 행동으로 인한 사회적 비용을 감수할 만큼 충분히 강하다는 것을 암시하기 때문이다.

➡ 일련의 연구는 사람들이 무엇을 입을지에 대한 규범에 개인이 아주 약간 (B) 도전할 때 사람들이 그 사람을 (A) 긍정적으로 본다는 것을 나타낸다.

Why? 왜 정답일까?

의복에 대한 규범을 살짝 어기는 사람이 더 긍정적으로 여겨진다(people judge these slight deviations from the norm as positive)는 연구를 소개하는 글이다. 따라서 요약문의 빈칸 (A), (B)에 들어갈 말로 가장 적절한 것은 ① '(A) positively(긍정적으로), (B) challenges(도전할)'이다.

- in general 일반적으로
- match ⓥ 일치하다, 맞다, 부합하다
- scrubs ⓝ 수술복
- exception ⓝ 예외
- reaction ⓝ 반응
- black-tie affair 격식을 차리는 모임
- uniqueness ⓝ 독특함, 고유함
- powerful ⓐ 영향력 있는, 강력한
- challenge ⓥ 반박하다, 도전하다
- neglect ⓥ 등한시하다, 소홀히 하다
- investigate ⓥ 연구하다, 조사하다
- surgeon ⓝ 외과 의사
- notable ⓐ 눈에 띄는
- explore ⓥ 탐구하다
- established ⓐ 확립된, 정해진
- bow tie 나비 넥타이
- deviation ⓝ 일탈
- risk ⓥ 위태롭게 하다
- negatively ⓐⓓ 부정적으로

구문 풀이

10행 The researchers also found that valuing uniqueness increased audience
　　　　　　　　　　　접속사　동명사구 주어
members' ratings of the status and competence of a professor [who wore red
　　　　　　　　　　　　　　　　　주격 관·대
sneakers while giving a lecture].
분사구문(= while he or she gave ~)

『Claims / that local food production cut greenhouse gas emissions / by reducing the burning of transportation fuel / are usually not well founded.』 41번의 근거
주장들은 / 로컬푸드 생산이 온실가스 배출을 줄였다는 / 운송 연료의 연소를 줄여서 / 대개 근거가 충분하지 않다.

Transport is the source of only 11 percent of greenhouse gas emissions / within the food sector, / so reducing the distance / that food travels after it leaves the farm / is far (a) less important / than reducing wasteful energy use on the farm.
운송은 원천이다 / 온실가스 배출의 11퍼센트만을 차지하는 / 식품 부문 내에서 / 그래서 거리를 줄이는 것은 / 식품이 농장을 떠난 후 이동하는 / 훨씬 덜 중요하다. / 농장에서 낭비되는 에너지 사용을 줄이는 것보다

Food coming from a distance / can actually be better for the (b) climate, / depending on how it was grown.
먼 곳에서 오는 식품은 / 실제로 기후에 더 좋을 수 있다. / 그것이 어떻게 재배되었느냐에 따라

For example, / field-grown tomatoes / shipped from Mexico in the winter months / will have a smaller carbon footprint / than (c) local winter tomatoes / grown in a greenhouse.
예를 들어, / 밭에서 재배된 토마토는 / 겨울에 멕시코로부터 수송된 / 탄소 발자국이 더 적을 것이다. / 현지의 겨울 토마토보다 / 온실에서 재배된

In the United Kingdom, / lamb meat that travels 11,000 miles from New Zealand / generates only one-quarter the carbon emissions per pound / compared to British lamb / because farmers in the United Kingdom / raise their animals on feed / (which must be produced using fossil fuels) / rather than on clover pastureland.
영국에서는, / 뉴질랜드에서 11,000마일을 이동하는 양고기는 / 파운드당 탄소 배출량의 4분의 1만 발생시키는데, / 영국의 양고기에 비해 / 영국의 농부들은 / 사료로 자신의 동물들을 기르기 때문에 / (화석 연료를 사용하여 생산되어야 하는) / 클로버 목초지에서가 아닌

When food does travel, / what matters most is not the (d) distance traveled / but the travel mode (surface versus air), / and most of all the load size.
식품이 이동할 때, / 가장 중요한 것은 이동 거리가 아니고, / 이동 방식(지상 대 공중) / 그리고 무엇보다도 적재량의 규모이다.

Bulk loads of food can travel halfway around the world by ocean freight / with a smaller carbon footprint, per pound delivered, / than foods traveling just a short distance but in much (e) smaller loads.
대량의 적재된 식품은 해상 화물 운송으로 세계 절반을 이동할 수 있다. / 배달된 파운드당 탄소 발자국이 더 적게 / 단거리만 이동하지만 적재량이 훨씬 더 적은 식품에 비해

『For example, / 18-wheelers carry much larger loads than pickup trucks / so they can move food 100 times as far / while burning only one-third as much gas / per pound of food delivered.』 42번의 근거
예를 들어, / 18륜 대형트럭은 픽업트럭보다 훨씬 더 많은 적재량을 운반하므로, / 그것들은 100배 멀리 식품을 이동시킬 수 있다. / 3분의 1의 연료만 연소하면서 / 배달된 식품 파운드당

로컬푸드 생산이 운송 연료의 연소를 줄여서 온실가스 배출을 줄였다는 주장들은 대개 근거가 충분하지 않다. 운송은 식품 부문 내에서 온실가스 배출의 11퍼센트만을 차지하는 원천이기에, 식품이 농장을 떠난 후 이동하는 거리를 줄이는 것은 농장에서 낭비되는 에너지 사용을 줄이는 것보다 (a) 덜 중요하다. 먼 곳에서 오는 식품은 그것이 어떻게 재배되었느냐에 따라 실제로 (b) 기후에 더 좋을 수 있다. 예를 들어, 겨울에 멕시코로부터 수송된 밭에서 재배된 토마토는 온실에서 재배된 (c) 현지의 겨울 토마토보다 탄소 발자국이 더 적을 것이다. 영국에서는, 뉴질랜드에서 11,000마일을 이동하는 양고기는 영국의 양고기에 비해 파운드당 탄소 배출량의 4분의 1만 발생시키는데, 영국의 농부들은 클로버 목초지에서가 아닌 (화석 연료를 사용하여 생산되어야 하는) 사료로 자신의 동물들을 기르기 때문이다. 식품이 이동할 때, 가장 중요한 것은 이동 (d) 거리가 아니고, 이동 방식(지상 대 공중)과 무엇보다도 적재량의 규모이다. 대량의 적재된 식품은 단거리만 이동하지만 적재량이 훨씬 (e) 더 많은(→ 더 적은) 식품에 비해, 해상 화물 운송으로 배달된 파운드당 탄소 발자국을 더 적게 들여 세계 절반을 이동할 수 있다. 예를 들어, 18륜 대형트럭은 픽업트럭보다 훨씬 더 많은 적재량을 운반하므로, 배달된 식품 파운드당 3분의 1의 연료만 연소하면서 100배 멀리 식품을 이동시킬 수 있다.

- greenhouse gas 온실가스
- well founded 근거가 충분한
- wasteful ⓐ 낭비하는
- ship ⓥ 운송하다, 수송하다
- lamb ⓝ 어린 양
- raise ⓥ 기르다, 키우다
- fossil fuel 화석 연료
- travel mode 이동 수단
- load ⓝ 적재량 ⓥ (짐을) 싣다
- freight ⓝ 화물 운송
- shorten ⓥ 짧게 줄이다
- agriculture ⓝ 농업

- emission ⓝ 배출(량)
- sector ⓝ 부문
- depending on ~에 따라
- carbon footprint 탄소 발자국
- generate ⓥ 발생시키다, 생성하다
- feed ⓝ 사료, 먹이
- pastureland ⓝ 목초지
- surface ⓝ 지면
- bulk ⓝ 대량 ⓐ 대량의
- pickup truck 픽업트럭, 소형 오픈 트럭
- ruin ⓥ 파괴하다, 망치다

구문 풀이

17행 When food does travel, what matters most is not {the distance traveled}
　　　　　　　　　　　　　　　　　　　동사 강조
but {the travel mode (surface versus air), and most of all the load size}.
not + (A) +
but + (B) : A가 아니라 B인

41 제목 파악
정답률 56% | 정답 ②

윗글의 제목으로 가장 적절한 것은?
① Shorten the Route, Cut the Cost
　거리를 줄여서 비용을 줄이라
✓② Is Local Food Always Better for the Earth?
　로컬푸드가 지구에 항상 더 좋을까?
③ Why Mass Production Ruins the Environment
　왜 대량 생산이 환경을 망치나
④ New Technologies: What Matters in Agriculture
　신기술: 농업에서 중요한 것
⑤ Reduce Food Waste for a Smaller Carbon Footprint
　더 적은 탄소 발자국을 위해 음식물 쓰레기를 줄이라

Why? 왜 정답일까?

로컬푸드로 식품 수송의 거리를 줄여 탄소 발자국을 줄일 수 있다는 주장에 대한 반박으로, 거리보다는 수송 수단이나 적재량 등 다른 요소가 더 중요하다(When food does travel, what matters most is not the distance traveled but the travel mode ~ and most of all the load size.)고 주장하는 글이다. 따라서 글의 제목으로 가장 적절한 것은 ② '로컬푸드가 지구를 위해 항상 더 좋을까?'이다.

★★★ 등급을 가르는 문제! ★★★

42 어휘 추론
정답률 38% | 정답 ⑤

밑줄 친 (a) ~ (e) 중에서 문맥상 낱말의 쓰임이 적절하지 않은 것은?
① (a)　② (b)　③ (c)　④ (d)　✓⑤ (e)

Why? 왜 정답일까?

마지막 문장에서 적재량이 더 많을 때 탄소 발자국을 훨씬 줄여 이동할 수 있다(~ 18-wheelers carry much larger loads than pickup trucks so they can move food 100 times as far while burning only one-third as much gas per pound of food delivered.)는 예를 드는 것으로 보아, 적재량이 '더 적을' 때보다 많을 때가 낫다는 설명이 적합하다. 즉 (e)의 larger를 smaller로 고쳐야 하므로, 문맥상 낱말의 쓰임이 적절하지 않은 것은 ⑤ '(e)'이다.

★★ 문제 해결 꿀~팁 ★★

▶ 많이 틀린 이유는?
첫 문장의 내용을 잘 이해하지 못하면 ①이 어색해 보일 수 있다. 하지만 식품 수송 거리를 줄인다고 해서 탄소 발자국을 줄일 수 있다는 주장에 '근거가 부족하다'는 말은 결국 거리 단축이 비교적 '덜 중요하다'는 뜻이 맞다.

▶ 문제 해결 방법은?
마지막 문장의 예시는 더 가까운 거리를 가더라도 적재량이 '더 적은' 경우보다. 더 먼 거리를 가도 양이 많은 편이 더 낫다는 핵심 내용으로 귀결된다. (e)가 than 뒤에 나온다는 점에 주의해야 한다.

(A)

『Long ago, / an old man built a grand temple / at the center of his village.』 45번 ①의 근거 일치
옛날, / 한 노인이 큰 사원을 지었다. / 마을 중심부에

People traveled to worship at the temple.
사람들이 사원에서 예배를 드리기 위해 멀리서 왔다.

So the old man made arrangements for food and accommodation / inside the temple itself.
그래서 노인은 음식과 숙소를 준비했다. / 사원 안에

He needed someone / who could look after the temple, so (a) he put up a notice: / Manager needed.
그는 사람이 필요했고, / 사원을 관리할 수 있는 / 그래서 그는 공고를 붙였다. / '관리자 구함'이라는

(D)

『Seeing the notice, / many people went to the old man.』 45번 ⑤의 근거 일치
공고를 보고, / 많은 사람들이 노인을 찾아갔다.

But he returned all the applicants after interviews, / telling them, / "I need a qualified person for this work."
그러나 그는 면접 후 모든 지원자들을 돌려보냈다. / 그들에게 말하면서 / "이 일에는 자격을 갖춘 사람이 필요합니다."라고

The old man would sit on the roof of (d) his house every morning, / watching people go through the temple doors.
노인은 매일 아침 자기 집 지붕에 앉아 있곤 했다. / 사람들이 사원의 문을 통과하는 것을 지켜보며

One day, / (e) he saw a young man come to the temple.
어느 날 / 한 젊은이가 사원으로 오는 것을 보았다.

(B)

『When that young man left the temple, / the old man called him and asked, / "Will you take care of this temple?"』 45번 ②의 근거 일치
젊은이가 사원을 나설 때, / 노인이 그를 불러 질문했다. / "이 사원의 관리를 맡아 주겠소?"라고

『The young man was surprised by the offer / and replied, / "I have no experience caring for a temple. / I'm not even educated."』 45번 ③의 근거 일치
젊은이는 그 제안에 놀라서 대답했다. / "저는 사원을 관리한 경험이 없습니다. / 저는 심지어 교육도 받지 못했습니다."라고

The old man smiled and said, / "I don't want any educated man. / I want a qualified person."
노인은 웃으며 말했다. / "나는 교육을 받은 사람이 필요한 게 아니오. / 나는 자격 있는 사람을 원하오."라고

Confused, / the young man asked, / "But why do (b) you consider me a qualified person?"
혼란스러워하며, / 젊은이는 물었다. / "그런데 당신은 왜 제가 자격이 있는 사람이라고 여기시나요?"라고

(C)

『The old man replied, / "I buried a brick on the path to the temple. / I watched for many days / as people tripped over that brick. / No one thought to remove it. / But you dug up that brick."』 45번 ④의 근거 불일치
노인은 대답했다. / "나는 사원으로 통하는 길에 벽돌 한 개를 묻었소. / 나는 여러 날 동안 지켜보았소. / 사람들이 그 벽돌에 발이 걸려 넘어질 때 / 아무도 그것을 치울 생각을 하지 않았소. / 하지만 당신은 그 벽돌을 파냈소."

The young man said, / "I haven't done anything great. / It's the duty of every human being / to think about others. / (c) I only did my duty."
젊은이는 말했다. / "저는 대단한 일을 한 것이 아닙니다. / 모든 사람의 의무인 걸요. / 타인을 생각하는 것은 / 전 제 의무를 다했을 뿐입니다."라고

The old man smiled and said, / "Only people who know their duty and perform it / are qualified people."
노인은 미소를 지으며 말했다. / "자신의 의무를 알고 그 의무를 수행하는 사람만이 / 자격이 있는 사람이오."라고

(A)

옛날, 한 노인이 마을 중심부에 큰 사원을 지었다. 사람들이 사원에서 예배를 드리기 위해 멀리서 왔다. 그래서 노인은 사원 안에 음식과 숙소를 준비했다. 그는 사원을 관리할 수 있는 사람이 필요했고, 그래서 (a) 그는 '관리자 구함'이라는 공고를 붙였다.

(D)

공고를 보고, 많은 사람들이 노인을 찾아갔다. 그러나 그는 "이 일에는 자격을 갖춘 사람이 필요합니다."라고 말하며 면접 후 모든 지원자들을 돌려보냈다. 노인은 사람들이 사원의 문을 통과하는 것을 지켜보며 매일 아침 (d) 자기 집 지붕에 앉아 있곤 했다. 어느 날 (e) 그는 한 젊은이가 사원으로 오는 것을 보았다.

(B)

젊은이가 사원을 나설 때, 노인이 그를 불러 "이 사원의 관리를 맡아 주겠소?"라고 질문했다. 젊은이는 그 제안에 놀라서 "저는 사원을 관리한 경험이 없고, 심지어 교육도 받지 못했습니다."라고 대답했다. 노인은 웃으며 "나는 교육을 받은 사람이 필요한 게 아니오. 나는 자격

있는 사람을 원하오."라고 말했다. 혼란스러워하며, 젊은이는 "그런데 (b) 당신은 왜 제가 자격이 있는 사람이라고 여기시나요?"라고 물었다.

(C)

노인은 대답했다. "나는 사원으로 통하는 길에 벽돌 한 개를 묻었소. 나는 여러 날 동안 사람들이 그 벽돌에 발이 걸려 넘어지는 것을 지켜보았소. 아무도 그것을 치울 생각을 하지 않았소. 하지만 당신은 그 벽돌을 파냈소." 젊은이는 "저는 대단한 일을 한 것이 아닙니다. 타인을 생각하는 것은 모든 사람의 의무인 걸요. (c) 전 제 의무를 다했을 뿐입니다."라고 말했다. 노인은 미소를 지으며 "자신의 의무를 알고 그 의무를 수행하는 사람만이 자격이 있는 사람이오."라고 말했다.

- grand ⓐ 큰, 위대한
- worship ⓥ 예배하다
- accommodation ⓝ 숙소
- bury ⓥ 묻다
- trip over ～에 걸려 넘어지다
- duty ⓝ 의무
- temple ⓝ 사원, 절
- make arrangements for ～을 준비하다
- care for ～을 관리하다, 돌보다
- brick ⓝ 벽돌
- dig up 파내다
- applicant ⓝ 지원자

구문 풀이

(B) 6행 Confused, the young man asked, "But why do you consider me a qualified person?"
분사구문(Being 생략) / 5형식 동사 / 목적어(me a qualified) / 목적격 보어

(D) 3행 The old man would sit on the roof of his house every morning, watching people go through the temple doors.
조동사(과거 습관) / 지각동사 / 목적어(people) / 원형부정사(go)

---

43 글의 순서 파악 　　　　　　　정답률 83% | 정답 ④

주어진 글 (A)에 이어질 내용을 순서에 맞게 배열한 것으로 가장 적절한 것은?
① (B) – (D) – (C)
② (C) – (B) – (D)
③ (C) – (D) – (B)
④ (D) – (B) – (C) ✔
⑤ (D) – (C) – (B)

Why? 왜 정답일까?

한 노인이 사원을 짓고 관리자 모집에 나섰다는 (A) 뒤로, 지원자들이 몰려들었지만 노인은 계속 자격 있는 사람을 기다렸다는 (D), 어떤 젊은이가 다녀가는 것을 보고 노인이 관리자 직을 제안했다는 (B), 왜 자신을 채용하려 하는지 묻는 젊은이에게 노인이 답을 주었다는 (C)가 차례로 연결된다. 따라서 글의 순서로 가장 적절한 것은 ④ '(D) – (B) – (C)'이다.

---

44 지칭 추론 　　　　　　　정답률 84% | 정답 ③

밑줄 친 (a)～(e) 중에서 가리키는 대상이 나머지 넷과 다른 것은?
① (a)　②(b)　③(c) ✔　④(d)　⑤(e)

Why? 왜 정답일까?

(a), (b), (d), (e)는 the old man을, (c)는 the young man을 가리키므로, (a)～(e) 중에서 가리키는 대상이 다른 하나는 ③ '(c)'이다.

---

45 세부 내용 파악 　　　　　　　정답률 79% | 정답 ④

윗글에 관한 내용으로 적절하지 않은 것은?
① 노인은 마을 중심부에 사원을 지었다.
② 젊은이가 사원을 나설 때 노인이 그를 불렀다.
③ 젊은이는 노인의 제안에 놀랐다.
④ 노인은 사원으로 통하는 길에 묻혀있던 벽돌을 파냈다. ✔
⑤ 공고를 보고 많은 사람들이 노인을 찾아갔다.

Why? 왜 정답일까?

(C) "I buried a brick on the path to the temple. I watched for many days as people tripped over that brick. No one thought to remove it. But you dug up that brick."에서 노인이 자신이 묻어뒀던 벽돌을 파낸 사람이 젊은이라고 말하고 있으므로, 내용과 일치하지 않는 것은 ④ '노인은 사원으로 통하는 길에 묻혀있던 벽돌을 파냈다.'이다.

Why? 왜 오답일까?

① (A) 'Long ago, an old man built a grand temple at the center of his village.'의 내용과 일치한다.
② (B) 'When that young man left the temple, the old man called him ～'의 내용과 일치한다.
③ (B) 'The young man was surprised by the offer ～'의 내용과 일치한다.
⑤ (D) 'Seeing the notice, many people went to the old man.'의 내용과 일치한다.

Dictation 08 　　　　　　　문제편 107쪽

01 caused a leak / change the location / the school theater
02 go for a run / run in slippers / wear the right shoes
03 a fan of your articles / won many awards / your costume designs
04 the rug in the center / the bookshelf under the clock / The two lamps
05 have extra batteries / They sound terrific / go take care of that
06 a rose basket / in the large size / offer a delivery service
07 recovering from surgery / No one but me / visiting relatives in Canada
08 sooner than I expected / receive a laptop / Wish me luck
09 create your own delicious chocolates / taste our most popular flavors / the cost of ingredients
10 differs by model / less storage space / a higher customer rating
11 buy the same one / where you got it
12 about an hour ago / less than 40 minutes
13 Where have you been / have a big dinner / makes you overeat
14 learn 20 new words / practice saying those words / get used to
15 this is very careless / turning off the lights / ask her to design
16-17 the problems caused by overtourism / fewer places for visitors to stay / having car-restricted areas

어휘 Review Test 08 　　　　　　　문제편 112쪽

A	B	C	D
01 박람회	01 hold	01 ①	01 ①
02 위험을 감수하다	02 complete	02 ⓐ	02 ⓕ
03 분명히, 틀림없이	03 confident	03 ⓗ	03 ⓖ
04 지식의 확산	04 whether ~ or not	04 ⓑ	04 ⓕ
05 협상하다	05 essential	05 ⓚ	05 ⓚ
06 배우자	06 outcome	06 ⓒ	06 ⓑ
07 ~을 차별하다	07 population	07 ①	07 ⓒ
08 어쩔 수 없이 ~하다	08 construction	08 ⓓ	08 ⓠ
09 주어진, ~을 고려하면	09 conservation	09 ⓕ	09 ①
10 인식, 앎	10 destination	10 ⓔ	10 ⓓ
11 전문 지식	11 precise	11 ⓢ	11 ⓐ
12 ~에 적응하다	12 compensate for	12 ①	12 ⓙ
13 열정적인	13 competence	13 ⓡ	13 ⓟ
14 ~을 고려하다, 참작하다	14 tissue	14 ⓠ	14 ①
15 ~로 구성되다	15 vibration	15 ①	15 ⓢ
16 통합하다	16 separate	16 ⓖ	16 ⓗ
17 보완하는	17 status	17 ⓜ	17 ⓔ
18 근거가 충분한	18 ship	18 ⓞ	18 ⓝ
19 예배하다	19 duty	19 ⓝ	19 ⓜ
20 유지하다, 떠받치다	20 ensure	20 ⓟ	20 ⓞ

· 정답 ·

01 ③ 02 ⑤ 03 ② 04 ④ 05 ④ 06 ③ 07 ② 08 ② 09 ⑤ 10 ③ 11 ③ 12 ① 13 ① 14 ③ 15 ④
16 ① 17 ④ 18 ⑤ 19 ② 20 ④ 21 ③ 22 ① 23 ② 24 ① 25 ③ 26 ④ 27 ② 28 ④ 29 ③ 30 ⑤
31 ② 32 ⑤ 33 ① 34 ⑤ 35 ④ 36 ② 37 ⑤ 38 ④ 39 ⑤ 40 ① 41 ② 42 ④ 43 ④ 44 ③ 45 ③

★ 표기된 문항은 [등급을 가르는 문제]에 해당하는 문항입니다.

01　시립 도서관 독서 습관 프로그램 소개　　정답률 93% | 정답 ③

다음을 듣고, 여자가 하는 말의 목적으로 가장 적절한 것을 고르시오.

① 도서관 확장 이전을 공지하려고
② 도서관 이용 안내 영상을 소개하려고
✔ 독서 습관 형성 프로그램을 홍보하려고
④ 독해력 향상 방안에 대한 의견을 구하려고
⑤ 독서 프로그램 만족도 조사 참여를 요청하려고

W : Good evening, Vermont citizens.
　안녕하세요, Vermont 시민 여러분.
　I'm Elizabeth Bowen, the Director of the Vermont City Library.
　저는 Vermont 시립 도서관장인 Elizabeth Bowen입니다.
　I'd like to tell you about our online 15-Minute Book Reading program.
　저희 온라인 15-Minute Book Reading 프로그램에 대해 말씀드리려고 합니다.
　This program is designed to help your children form good reading habits at home.
　이 프로그램은 여러분의 아이들이 집에서 좋은 독서 습관을 형성하는 데 도움을 주기 위해 고안되었습니다.
　Every day, individual tutoring is provided for 15 minutes.
　매일 15분 간 개별 지도가 제공됩니다.
　It's completely personalized to your child's reading level!
　여러분 자녀의 읽기 수준에 완전히 맞춰서 진행됩니다!
　Don't hesitate to sign up your children for this amazing opportunity to build their reading habits!
　자녀들의 독서 습관을 길러줄 이 놀라운 기회에 주저하지 말고 등록하세요!
　For more information, please visit the Vermont City Library.
　더 많은 정보를 원하시면, Vermont 시립 도서관을 방문하세요.
　Thank you.
　감사합니다.

Why? 왜 정답일까?

'I'd like to tell you about our online 15-Minute Book Reading program.' 이후로 시립 도서관에서 계획한 독서 습관 형성 프로그램을 소개하는 내용이 이어지고 있다. 따라서 여자가 하는 말의 목적으로 가장 적절한 것은 ③ '독서 습관 형성 프로그램을 홍보하려고'이다.

● **individual tutoring** 개별 지도
● **personalize** ⓥ 개인의 필요에 맞추다, 개별화하다

02　중고품 구매 시 세부 사항을 꼼꼼히 확인하기　　정답률 93% | 정답 ⑤

대화를 듣고, 남자의 의견으로 가장 적절한 것을 고르시오.

① 중고품은 직접 만나서 거래해야 한다.
② 물품 구매 시 여러 제품을 비교해야 한다.
③ 계획적으로 예산을 세워 물품을 구매해야 한다.
④ 온라인 거래 시 개인 정보 유출에 유의해야 한다.
✔ 중고품 구매 시 세부 사항을 꼼꼼히 확인해야 한다.

M : Clara, why the long face?
　Clara, 왜 우울한 얼굴이니?
W : Aw, Dad, I bought this hair dryer, but the cool air mode doesn't work.
　어휴, 아빠, 제가 이 헤어 드라이기를 샀는데, 차가운 바람 설정이 작동하지 않아요.
M : Where did you get it?
　어디서 샀는데?
W : I bought it second-hand online.
　온라인에서 중고로요.
M : Did you check the condition before you ordered it?
　주문하기 전에 상태를 살펴본 거니?
W : I did, but I missed the seller's note that said the cool air mode doesn't work.
　네, 그런데 차가운 바람이 나오지 않는다는 판매자 공지를 놓쳤어요.
M : Oh dear. It's important to check all the details when you buy second-hand items.
　이런, 중고품을 살 때는 모든 세부 사항을 확인하는 게 중요해.
W : You're right. I was just so excited because it was much cheaper than other hair dryers.
　아빠 말씀이 맞아요. 다른 드라이기보다 훨씬 싸니까 제가 그냥 너무 들떴어요.
M : Some second-hand items are almost like new, but others are not. So, you should read every detail of the item carefully.
　어떤 중고품은 거의 새것 같지만, 다른 것들은 그렇지 않아. 그래서, 상품의 모든 세부 사항을 꼼꼼히 읽어봐야 해.
W : Thanks, Dad. I'll keep that in mind.
　고맙습니다, 아빠. 염두에 둘게요.

Why? 왜 정답일까?

'It's important to check all the details when you buy second-hand items.'와 'So, you should read every detail of the item carefully.'에서 남자는 딸인 여자에게 중고품을 살 때는 반드시 모든 세부 사항을 주의 깊게 확인하라고 조언하고 있으므로, 남자의 의견으로 가장 적절한 것은 ⑤ '중고품 구매 시 세부 사항을 꼼꼼히 확인해야 한다.'이다.

● **Why the long face?** 왜 우울한 얼굴이야?
● **second-hand** ⓐ 중고로 ⓐ 중고의

03　시력 검사 후 안경 맞추기　　정답률 94% | 정답 ②

대화를 듣고, 두 사람의 관계를 가장 잘 나타낸 것을 고르시오.

---

① 의사 – 간호사　　✔ 안경사 – 고객
③ 보건 교사 – 학부모　　④ 사진사 – 모델
⑤ 앱 개발자 – 의뢰인

M : Hello, Ms. Adams! It's been a while since you were here.
　안녕하세요, Adams 씨! 여기 오신 지 꽤 되었죠.
W : Last time I came, you told me I should get a checkup every year.
　마지막으로 왔을 때, 저한테 매년 검진을 받아야 한다고 얘기하셨죠.
M : That's right. When did you last visit us?
　맞아요. 언제 마지막으로 오셨죠?
W : I guess I came here last October.
　작년 10월에 여기 왔던 것 같아요.
M : Okay. Then, let me check your vision. Please sit here. [Pause] Hmm... your eyesight got a little worse.
　그렇군요. 그럼, 시력 검사를 해 볼게요. 여기 앉으세요. [잠시 멈춤] 흠… 시력이 약간 나빠졌군요.
W : Yeah, maybe it's because I've been working on a computer for too long.
　네, 아마 컴퓨터로 너무 오래 일해서 그런가봐요.
M : Actually, the blue light from computers and smartphones makes your eyes tired.
　사실, 컴퓨터와 스마트폰에서 나오는 블루라이트가 눈을 피로하게 만들어요.
W : Really? Is there a lens that blocks the light?
　정말요? 블루라이트를 차단해주는 렌즈가 있나요?
M : Sure. You can wear these blue light blocking lenses.
　물론입니다. 이 블루라이트 차단 렌즈를 착용하시면 돼요.
W : That sounds perfect. But I'd like to use this frame again.
　딱 좋네요. 하지만 전 이 테는 또 쓰고 싶어요.
M : No problem, you can just change the lenses. You can come pick them up in a week.
　문제 없어요. 렌즈만 바꾸시면 됩니다. 일주일 뒤에 오셔서 찾아가시면 돼요.
W : Okay, thank you so much. See you then.
　알겠습니다. 정말 고맙습니다. 그때 뵐게요.

Why? 왜 정답일까?

'Then, let me check your vision.', 'Is there a lens that blocks the light?', 'But I'd like to use this frame again.', 'No problem, you can just change the lenses.' 등에서 안경점에서 이뤄지는 대화임을 알 수 있으므로, 두 사람의 관계로 가장 적절한 것은 ② '안경사 – 고객'이다.

● **get a checkup** 검진을 받다
● **eyesight** ⓝ 시력

04　할머니할아버지 댁 사진 구경하기　　정답률 94% | 정답 ④

대화를 듣고, 그림에서 대화의 내용과 일치하지 <u>않는</u> 것을 고르시오.

W : Carl, what are you looking at?
　Carl, 뭘 보고 있어?
M : Oh, hi, Amy. Come take a look. It's a picture of my grandparents' house. I was there last weekend.
　오, 안녕, Amy. 와서 봐봐. 우리 할머니할아버지 댁 사진이야. 지난 주말에 갔었어.
W : What a beautiful house! 「There's even a pond under the tree!」 ①의 근거 일치
　아름다운 집이구나! 나무 밑에 연못도 있네!
M : Yes, my grandfather dug it himself. 「And how about that flower-patterned tablecloth?」 ②의 근거 일치
　응, 우리 할아버지가 그걸 직접 파셨어. 그리고 이 꽃무늬 식탁보는 어때?
W : I love it. It makes the table look cozy.
　마음에 들어. 식탁이 안락해 보여.
M : 「Did you see the painting of a bear on the door?」 ③의 근거 일치
　문에 있는 곰 그림 봤어?
W : Oh! Did you paint that?
　오! 네가 그린 거야?
M : Yeah, I did it when I was 8 years old.
　응, 내가 여덟 살 때 그렸어.
W : It's cute. 「And there are two windows on the roof.」 ④의 근거 불일치
　귀엽네. 그리고 지붕에 창문이 두 개 있네.
M : Right, we get a lot of sunlight through the windows.
　맞아, 창문으로 햇빛이 많이 들지.
W : I like that! 「And can you still ride the swings next to the house?」 ⑤의 근거 일치
　좋다! 집 옆에 있는 그네를 아직 탈 수 있어?
M : Of course. That's the best spot to see the sunset.
　물론이지. 노을을 보기 가장 좋은 장소야.
W : Wow, your grandparents' house looks like a nice place!
　와, 너네 할머니할아버지 댁 정말 근사한 곳처럼 보인다!

Why? 왜 정답일까?

대화에서 지붕에 창문이 두 개 나 있다고 하는데(And there are two windows on the roof.), 그림에서는 지붕에 창문이 하나뿐이다. 따라서 그림에서 대화의 내용과 일치하지 않는 것은 ④이다.

● **cozy** ⓐ 안락한
● **swing** ⓝ 그네

05　식료품 배달 확인　　정답률 76% | 정답 ④

대화를 듣고, 여자가 할 일로 가장 적절한 것을 고르시오.

① 식료품 주문하기　　② 자동차 수리 맡기기

③ 보고서 제출하기　　　　　　　✔ 고객 센터에 전화하기
⑤ 냉장고에 식료품 넣기

M : Honey, there's a box in the doorway. What is it?
여보, 현관에 상자가 하나 있네요. 뭐죠?
W : I ordered some groceries online. Would you bring it in?
온라인으로 식료품을 좀 주문했어요. 갖고 들어와 줄래요?
M : Sure. Is this for the house-warming party today?
물론이죠. 오늘 있을 집들이에 쓸 거예요?
W : Yeah. Since I had to have my car repaired, I couldn't go shopping yesterday.
네, 내가 차를 수리해야 했어서, 어제 장을 보러 못 갔거든요.
M : Sorry, I should've taken you to the market.
미안해요, 내가 당신을 시장에 데려다줬어야 하는데.
W : That's okay. You worked late to meet the deadline for your report. Would you open the box for me?
괜찮아요. 당신 보고서 마감을 맞추느라 늦게까지 일했잖아요. 상자를 열어줄래요?
M : Sure. [Pause] Oh no, some eggs are broken! Have a look.
물론이죠. [잠시 멈춤] 이런, 달걀 몇 개가 깨져 있어요! 봐봐요.
W : Ah... that's never happened before.
아… 전에는 이런 적이 없었는데.
M : Why don't we call the customer center about it?
고객 센터에 전화하는 게 어때요?
W : Okay. I'll do it right now.
알겠어요. 내가 바로 할게요.
M : While you do that, I'll put the other food in the fridge.
당신 전화하는 동안, 난 다른 식품을 냉장고에 넣어둘게요.
W : Thanks.
고마워요.

Why? 왜 정답일까?

'Why don't we call the customer center about it? / Okay. I'll do it right now.'을 통해, 깨진 달걀을 배달 받은 여자가 고객 센터에 전화하기로 했음을 알 수 있다. 따라서 여자가 할 일로 가장 적절한 것은 ④ '고객 센터에 전화하기'이다.

● house-warming party 집들이　　　● meet the deadline 마감을 맞추다

06 당근 케이크 사기　　　　　　정답률 84% | 정답 ③

대화를 듣고, 남자가 지불할 금액을 고르시오. [3점]
① $27　　② $30　　✔ $36　　④ $40　　⑤ $45

W : Hello, welcome to Kelly's Bake Shop. How can I help you?
안녕하세요, Kelly's Bake Shop에 잘 오셨습니다. 무엇을 도와드릴까요?
M : Hi, I'd like to order a carrot cake.
안녕하세요, 전 당근 케이크를 주문하려고요.
W : Okay, we have two sizes. A small one is $25 and a large one is $35. Which one would you like?
네, 두 가지 사이즈가 있어요. 작은 것은 25달러이고, 큰 것은 35달러입니다. 어느 것으로 하시겠어요?
M : Well, we're four people, so a large one would be good.
음, 우린 네 명이라서, 큰 것이 좋겠어요.
W : Great. Do you need candles?
좋습니다. 초 필요하세요?
M : No thanks, but can you write on the cake?
아뇨, 그런데 케이크에 문구를 써주실 수 있나요?
W : We can. It costs $5. What would you like the message to say?
가능합니다. 5달러입니다. 메시지를 어떻게 써드릴까요?
M : Please write "Thank You Mom" on it.
'고마워요, 엄마'라고 위에 써주세요.
W : Sure. It takes about half an hour. Is that okay?
알겠습니다. 30분 정도 걸립니다. 괜찮으세요?
M : No problem. Can I use this 10% off coupon?
괜찮아요, 이 10퍼센트 할인 쿠폰을 써도 되나요?
W : Certainly. You get 10% off the total.
물론입니다. 총 가격에서 10퍼센트를 할인받으실 거예요.
M : Thanks. Here's my credit card.
고맙습니다. 여기 제 신용 카드요.

Why? 왜 정답일까?

대화에 따르면 남자는 35달러짜리 큰 당근 케이크를 사고, 문구를 추가하는 비용으로 5달러를 추가 지불한 뒤, 총 가격에서 10퍼센트를 할인받았다. 이를 식으로 나타내면 '$(35+5) \times 0.9 = 36$'이므로, 여자가 지불할 금액은 ③ '$36'이다.

● bake shop 제과점, 빵집　　　● cost ⓥ ~의 비용이 들다

07 여자가 가방을 산 이유　　　　정답률 94% | 정답 ②

대화를 듣고, 여자가 가방을 구입한 이유를 고르시오.
① 유명 연예인들이 착용해서　　✔ 재활용 소재를 사용해서
③ 많은 친구들이 추천해서　　　④ 디자인이 독특해서
⑤ 가격이 저렴해서

M : Anna, I haven't seen you use this bag before. Did you buy a new one?
Anna, 나 네가 이 가방 쓰는 거 전에는 못 봤어. 새 거 샀어?
W : Hi, Jason. Yeah, I bought it online last week.
안녕, Jason. 응, 지난 주에 온라인에서 샀어.
M : I saw some celebrities posting about it on their social media.
연예인 몇 명이 소셜 미디어에 이것에 관해 올린 거 봤어.
W : Really? I didn't know that, but this bag seems to be popular.
정말? 난 그건 몰랐어, 그런데 이 가방이 인기가 많은 것 같네.
M : It does, but its design isn't that unique. It's too plain.
그렇더라고, 그런데 이 디자인은 그렇게 독특하진 않아. 너무 평범해.
W : Yeah, and it's a little expensive compared to other bags.
맞아, 그리고 다른 가방에 비해서 조금 비싸.

[문제편 p.113]

M : Well, then why did you buy it?
그럼 왜 산 거야?
W : I bought it because it's made from recycled materials.
이게 재활용 소재로 만들어져서 샀어.
M : Oh, you're a responsible consumer.
오, 넌 책임감 있는 소비자구나.
W : Exactly. So, I'm recommending it to all my friends.
바로 그거지. 그래서 이 가방을 친구들한테 다 추천하고 있어.
M : Good idea. I'll check the website for more information.
좋은 생각이야. 나도 웹사이트에서 더 많은 정보를 찾아봐야겠다.

Why? 왜 정답일까?

여자가 새로 산 가방은 디자인이 독특하지는 않지만 재활용 소재로 만들어졌으며(I bought it because it's made from recycled materials.), 이 점 때문에 여자도 가방을 샀다고 한다. 따라서 여자가 가방을 구입한 이유로 가장 적절한 것은 ② '재활용 소재를 사용해서'이다.

● celebrity ⓝ 유명 인사, 연예인　　　● recycled material 재활용 소재

08 스트릿 댄스 대회 알아보기　　　　정답률 94% | 정답 ②

대화를 듣고, Youth Street Dance Contest에 관해 언급되지 않은 것을 고르시오.
① 신청 마감일　　✔ 심사 기준　　③ 우승 상금액
④ 참가 부문　　　⑤ 신청 방법

W : Jimmy, what are you doing with your smartphone?
Jimmy, 너 스마트폰으로 뭐 하고 있어?
M : I'm looking at a poster about the Youth Street Dance Contest.
Youth Street Dance Contest에 관한 포스터를 보고 있어.
W : Oh, isn't it a street dance contest for high school students?
오, 그거 고등학생을 위한 스트릿 댄스 대회 아니야?
M : Yeah. Why don't you enter? I know you're good at dancing.
맞아. 너 참가해 보면 어때? 너 춤 잘 추잖아.
W : Hmm... 『when is it?』
흠… 언제야?
M : The competition is October 22nd, but the deadline for entry is September 30th.』　①의 근거 일치
대회는 10월 22일인데, 참가 신청 마감은 9월 30일이야.
W : Okay, good. I have a few months to practice.
그래, 좋네. 몇 달 연습할 수 있겠어.
M : And look! 『The winner gets $2,000!』 ③의 근거 일치
그리고 이것 봐! 우승자는 2천 달러를 받는대!
W : That's amazing! 『What types of dancing are there?』
그거 멋지네! 댄스 부문은 뭐가 있어?
M : It says participants should choose one of these three types: hip-hop, locking, and breakdancing.』 ④의 근거 일치
참가자들은 힙합, 락킹, 그리고 브레이크댄스 이렇게 세 가지 부문 중에 하나를 선택해야 한대.
W : I'm really into breakdancing lately, so I'll enter with that. 『How do I apply?』
난 최근에 브레이크댄스에 푹 빠져 있어, 그러니 그걸로 참가할래. 어떻게 신청하지?
M : You just download the application form from the website and submit it by email.』 ⑤의 근거 일치
그냥 참가 신청서를 웹사이트에서 다운받아서 이메일로 그걸 제출하면 돼.
W : Okay! It'll be a great experience for me to try out.
그래! 내가 시도해보면 대단히 좋은 경험이 될 거야.

Why? 왜 정답일까?

대화에서 남자와 여자는 Youth Street Dance Contest의 신청 마감일, 우승 상금액, 참가 부문, 신청 방법을 언급하므로, 언급되지 않은 것은 ② '심사 기준'이다.

Why? 왜 오답일까?

① '~ the deadline for entry is September 30th.'에서 '신청 마감일'이 언급되었다.
③ 'The winner gets $2,000.'에서 '우승 상금액'이 언급되었다.
④ 'It says participants should choose one of these three types: hip-hop, locking, and breakdancing.'에서 '참가 부문'이 언급되었다.
⑤ 'You just download the application form from the website and submit it by email.'에서 '신청 방법'이 언급되었다.

● street dance (다양한 대중문화 기반의) 스트릿 댄스
● application form 신청서 양식

09 플로깅 행사 안내　　　　　　정답률 64% | 정답 ⑤

Lakewoods Plogging에 관한 다음 내용을 듣고, 일치하지 않는 것을 고르시오.
① 참가자는 운동복과 운동화를 착용해야 한다.
② 쓰레기를 담을 봉투가 배부될 것이다.
③ 10월 1일 오전 7시부터 진행될 것이다.
④ 학교 웹사이트에서 신청할 수 있다.
✔ 참가자 모두 스포츠 양말을 받을 것이다.

M : Hello, Lakewoods High School students!
안녕하세요, Lakewoods 고등학교 학생 여러분!
I'm Lawrence Cho, president of the student council.
저는 학생회장인 Lawrence Cho입니다.
I'm happy to announce a special new event to reduce waste around our school: Lakewoods Plogging!
우리 학교 주변의 쓰레기를 줄일 수 있는 새로운 특별 행사를 소개하게 되어 기쁩니다. 바로 Lakewoods Plogging입니다!
Since plogging is the activity of picking up trash while running, 『all participants should wear workout clothes and sneakers.』 ①의 근거 일치
플로깅은 뛰는 도중 쓰레기를 줍는 활동이므로, 모든 참가자는 운동복과 운동화를 착용해야 합니다.
『We provide eco-friendly bags for the trash, so you don't need to bring any.』 ②의 근거 일치
우리는 쓰레기를 넣을 환경 친화적인 봉투를 제공하니, 봉투는 가져오실 필요가 없습니다.
『The event will be held on October 1st from 7 a.m. to 9 a.m.』 ③의 근거 일치
이 행사는 10월 1일 아침 7시부터 9시까지 진행됩니다.

「You can sign up for the event on the school website starting tomorrow.」 ④의근거 일치
내일부터 여러분은 학교 웹사이트에서 행사 참가 신청을 할 수 있습니다.
「The first 30 participants will get a pair of sports socks.」 ⑤의근거 불일치
최초 30명의 참가자에게는 스포츠 양말 한 켤레가 제공됩니다.
For more information, please visit our school website.
더 많은 정보를 얻으시려면, 우리 학교 웹사이트를 방문해 주세요.
Don't miss this fun opportunity!
이 재미있는 기회를 놓치지 마세요!

Why? 왜 정답일까?

'The first 30 participants will get a pair of sports socks.'에서 모든 참가자가 아닌 최초 등록 30인에게만 스포츠 양말을 제공한다고 하므로, 내용과 일치하지 않는 것은 ⑤ '참가자 모두 스포츠 양말을 받을 것이다.'이다.

Why? 왜 오답일까?

① '~ all participants should wear workout clothes and sneakers.'의 내용과 일치한다.
② 'We provide eco-friendly bags for the trash, so you don't need to bring any.'의 내용과 일치한다.
③ 'The event will be held on October 1st from 7 a.m. to 9 a.m.'의 내용과 일치한다.
④ 'You can sign up for the event on the school website starting tomorrow.'의 내용과 일치한다.

● plogging ⓝ 플로깅(조깅하며 쓰레기를 줍는 활동) ● workout ⓝ 운동

---

10 휴대용 캠핑 히터 구매하기 정답률 93% | 정답 ③

다음 표를 보면서 대화를 듣고, 두 사람이 주문할 휴대용 캠핑 히터를 고르시오.

Portable Camping Heater

	Model	Weight(kg)	Price	Energy Source	Customer Rating
①	A	4.2	$85	Oil	★★★
②	B	3.6	$90	Oil	★★★★
✔③	C	3.4	$92	Electricity	★★★★★
④	D	3.2	$95	Electricity	★★★★
⑤	E	2.8	$115	Electricity	★★★★★

M : Honey, what are you doing?
여보, 뭐 하고 있어요?
W : I'm looking at a website to order a portable heater for winter camping. Would you like to choose one together?
겨울 캠핑을 위해 휴대용 히터를 주문하려고 웹사이트를 보고 있어요. 하나 같이 골라볼래요?
M : Sure, let me see.
좋아요, 나도 보여줘요.
W : We should be able to carry it easily, so its weight is important.「I think we should get one of these under 4kg.」 근거1 Weight 조건
쉽게 들고 다닐 수 있어야 하니, 무게가 중요해요. 우리 4킬로그램 밑으로 나가는 것을 골라야겠어요.
M : Good point. Oh, this one is pretty expensive.
좋은 지적이네요. 오, 이것은 꽤 비싸네요.
W : I know.「Let's choose one of these for less than $100.」 근거2 Price 조건
그러게요. 100달러 이하인 이 제품들 중에서 하나 골라봅시다.
M : Okay.「And I think an electric heater would be good.」 What do you think? 근거3 Energy Source 조건
좋아요. 그리고 난 전기 히터가 좋을 것 같아요. 어떻게 생각해요?
W : I agree. It's safer to use.
동의해요. 사용하기 더 안전하죠.
M : Now we have these two models left.
이제 두 가지 제품이 남았어요.
W :「I'd like the one with a five-star customer rating.」 근거4 Customer Rating 조건
고객 평점이 별 5개인 것이 좋겠어요.
M : All right. Let's order this one.
그래요. 이걸로 주문합시다.

Why? 왜 정답일까?

대화에 따르면 남자와 여자는 무게가 4kg보다 적게 나가면서, 가격은 100달러를 넘지 않고, 전기로 작동하며, 고객 평점이 별 5개인 캠핑용 히터를 사려고 한다. 따라서 두 사람이 주문할 히터는 ③ 'C'이다.

● weight ⓝ 무게 ● Good point. 좋은 지적이에요.

---

11 자전거 투어 계획 정답률 66% | 정답 ③

대화를 듣고, 여자의 마지막 말에 대한 남자의 응답으로 가장 적절한 것을 고르시오.
① You can join the tour, too. – 너도 여행 같이 가도 돼.
② The bike wasn't that expensive. – 이 자전거는 그렇게 비싸지 않았어.
✔③ I haven't decided the place, yet. – 장소는 아직 안 정했어.
④ I'm going to rent a bike in the park. – 난 공원에서 자전거를 빌리려고.
⑤ Autumn is the best season for the tour. – 가을이 여행 가기 제일 좋은 계절이지.

W : Kevin, is this bike yours?
Kevin, 이 자전거 네 거야?
M : Yes, I bought it for my bike tour.
응, 나 자전거 여행 때문에 샀어.
W : Really? Where are you planning to go?
정말? 어디로 갈 계획이야?
M : I haven't decided the place, yet.
장소는 아직 안 정했어.

Why? 왜 정답일까?

자전거 여행을 가려고 자전거를 샀다는 남자에게 여자는 어디로 갈 예정인지 묻고 있으므로(Where are you planning to go?), 남자의 응답으로 가장 적절한 것은 ③ '장소는 아직 안 정했어.'이다.

● rent ⓥ 빌리다, 대여하다

---

12 치과 진료 예약하기 정답률 89% | 정답 ①

대화를 듣고, 남자의 마지막 말에 대한 여자의 응답으로 가장 적절한 것을 고르시오.
✔① Great. I'll be there at that time. – 좋네요. 그때 가겠습니다.
② Okay. I'll change my toothbrush. – 알겠습니다. 제 칫솔을 바꿀게요.
③ Too bad. I hope you get well soon. – 안됐네요. 곧 낫길 바랍니다.
④ No worries. Your painkillers work well. – 걱정 마세요. 당신의 진통제는 효과가 좋아요.
⑤ Sure. Let me know when he's available. – 알겠어요. 그가 언제 시간이 되는지 알려주세요.

[Telephone rings.]
[전화벨이 울린다.]
M : Hello, this is Ashley's Dental Clinic. How may I help you?
안녕하세요. Ashley 치과입니다. 무엇을 도와드릴까요?
W : Hello, this is Emily Gibson. Can I see the dentist today? I have a terrible toothache.
안녕하세요, 저는 Emily Gibson이라고 합니다. 오늘 진료 볼 수 있을까요? 치통이 심해요.
M : Just a second. Let me check. [Pause] He's available at 4:30 this afternoon.
조금만 기다려주세요. 확인해 보겠습니다. [잠시 멈춤] 오늘 오후 4시 30분에 진료 가능하세요.
W : Great. I'll be there at that time.
좋네요. 그때 가겠습니다.

Why? 왜 정답일까?

치통이 심해 오늘 치과 진료를 보고 싶다는 여자에게 남자는 오후 4시 반에 예약이 가능하다고 알려주므로(He's available at 4:30 this afternoon.), 여자의 응답으로 가장 적절한 것은 ① '좋네요, 그때 가겠습니다.'이다.

● dental clinic 치과 ● painkiller ⓝ 진통제

---

13 배드민턴 팀 결성하기 정답률 79% | 정답 ①

대화를 듣고, 여자의 마지막 말에 대한 남자의 응답으로 가장 적절한 것을 고르시오.
Man:
✔① Fantastic! We'll be a really good team.
환상적이다! 우리 아주 좋은 팀이 될 거야.
② Sorry. I don't understand why you like it.
미안. 난 네가 그걸 왜 좋아하는지 모르겠어.
③ Good idea! I'll find another partner for you.
좋은 생각이야! 내가 너에게 다른 파트너를 구해 줄게.
④ No problem. I can use my racket to practice.
문제 없어. 난 연습할 때 내 라켓을 쓰면 돼.
⑤ I know. Everyone loves watching sports competitions.
맞아. 모두가 스포츠 대회 보는 것을 좋아하지.

W : Hey, Justin. Do you know where those students are going?
안녕, Justin. 너 저 학생들이 어디 가는지 알아?
M : They're probably going to the gym to practice badminton.
아마 배드민턴 연습하러 체육관에 갈 거야.
W : Why are so many students practicing badminton?
왜 저렇게 많은 학생들이 배드민턴을 연습하고 있을까?
M : Haven't you heard about the School Badminton Tournament? Many of the students have already signed up for it.
너 교내 배드민턴 토너먼트 얘기 못 들었어? 벌써 많은 학생들이 신청했어.
W : Really? Why is it so popular?
정말? 그게 왜 그렇게 인기가 많은 거야?
M : The winners will get a big scholarship and there are lots of other prizes as well.
우승자는 큰 액수의 장학금을 받을 거고, 다른 부상도 많아.
W : That's nice! Why don't you sign up for it, too?
근사하네! 너도 등록하는 게 어때?
M : I'd like to, but only doubles can participate. And I haven't found a partner, yet.
해보고 싶은데, 복식으로만 참가 가능해. 그리고 난 아직 파트너를 못 찾았어.
W : Actually, I used to be a badminton player in my elementary school.
사실, 나 초등학교 때 배드민턴 선수였어.
M : Wow! I have a top expert right here! How about we partner up?
와! 바로 여기 최고의 전문가가 있었네! 우리 파트너가 되는 게 어때?
W : Sure. Not an expert, but I can try.
그래. 전문가는 아니지만, 해볼게.
M : Fantastic! We'll be a really good team.
환상적이다! 우리 아주 좋은 팀이 될 거야.

Why? 왜 정답일까?

복식 배드민턴 대회에 파트너를 구하지 못해 신청하지 못하고 있던 남자는 초등학교 때 선수였다는 여자에게 팀이 되자고 제안하고(How about we partner up?), 여자는 이에 응한다(Sure.). 따라서 남자의 응답으로 가장 적절한 것은 ① '환상적이다! 우리 아주 좋은 팀이 될 거야.'이다.

● get a scholarship 장학금을 받다 ● partner up (~와) 협력하다, 짝을 이루다

---

14 재미있는 발표를 위해 퀴즈 만들기 정답률 88% | 정답 ③

대화를 듣고, 남자의 마지막 말에 대한 여자의 응답으로 가장 적절한 것을 고르시오. [3점]
Woman:
① Nice! I'm curious about what you'll ask. – 좋았어! 네가 뭐 물어볼지 궁금하다.
② Sure. You should study hard for the quiz. – 물론이지. 넌 퀴즈 공부를 열심히 해야 해.
✔③ Okay. I'll make some questions right away. – 알겠어. 바로 질문을 만들어볼게.
④ All right. I'll see if I can add more pictures. – 그래. 사진을 더 넣을 수 있나 볼게.
⑤ Don't worry. It won't take too long to answer. – 걱정 마. 대답하는 데 너무 오래는 안 걸릴 거야.

M : Hey, Natalie. What are you doing on your computer?
안녕, Natalie. 너 컴퓨터로 뭐 해?
W : Hi, Dave. I'm working on my presentation for social studies class. It's about traditional games in Asia.
안녕, Dave. 난 사회 수업 발표를 준비하고 있어. 아시아의 전통 게임에 관한 거야.
M : Sounds interesting. Can I see it?
재미있겠다. 나 봐도 돼?

W : Sure. I'll introduce some games with these pictures.
물론이지. 난 이 사진과 함께 몇 가지 게임을 소개하려고.

M : That's a great idea, but I think you have too many words on the slides.
좋은 생각인데, 슬라이드에 글이 너무 많은 것 같아.

W : You're right. I'm worried it might be boring.
네 말이 맞아. 지루할까봐 걱정돼.

M : Then, how about shortening your explanation and using some questions? It would make your presentation more interesting.
그럼, 설명을 줄이고 질문을 몇 개 넣으면 어때? 그게 네 발표를 더 재미있게 만들어줄 거야.

W : Great idea! What do you think about True-or-False questions?
멋진 생각이야! OX 문제를 좀 넣으면 어떨 것 같아?

M : That's good. Your audience will be able to focus on your presentation while thinking about the answers.
좋네. 네 청중들이 그 답에 대해 생각해보면서 네 발표에 더 집중할 수 있을 거야.

W : But... what if they don't know the answers?
그런데… 그들이 답을 모르면 어떡하지?

M : It doesn't matter. They'll have fun just doing it.
그건 상관 없어. 그냥 하는 거로 재미있을 거야.

W : Okay. I'll make some questions right away.
알겠어. 바로 질문을 만들어볼게.

Why? 왜 정답일까?

남자의 권유에 따라 발표 슬라이드의 설명을 줄이고 퀴즈를 넣어보려는 여자가 청중들이 답을 모를까봐 걱정하자, 남자는 그저 해보는 것으로 재미있을 것이라고 말해준다(It doesn't matter. They'll have fun just doing it.). 따라서 여자의 응답으로 가장 적절한 것은 ③ '알겠어. 바로 질문을 만들어볼게.'이다.

● social studies (과목) 사회 ● curious ⓐ 궁금해하는, 호기심 많은

---

15 롤모델의 책 사인회 소식 알려주기 　정답률 72% | 정답 ④

다음 상황 설명을 듣고, Ms. Olson이 Steven에게 할 말로 가장 적절한 것을 고르시오. [3점]

Ms. Olson:
① You can come see me any time you want. – 네가 원할 때 언제든 날 만나러 와도 돼.
② I'm happy to hear that you've met the CEO. – 네가 그 CEO를 만나봤다니 기뻐.
③ Why do you want to run a gaming company? – 넌 왜 게임 회사를 운영하고 싶은 거니?
④ How about going to your role model's book-signing? – 네 롤모델의 책 사인회에 가보는 것이 어떠니?
⑤ You should buy more books written by your role model. – 넌 네 롤모델이 쓴 책을 더 사야 해.

W : Steven is a high school student and Ms. Olson is a career counselor at his school.
Steven은 고등학교 학생이고 Ms. Olson은 학교 진로 상담 교사이다.
Steven has much interest in the video game industry.
Steven은 비디오 게임 산업에 관심이 많다.
A few days ago, Ms. Olson recommended a book written by a CEO who runs a famous gaming company.
며칠 전에, Ms. Olson은 유명 게임 회사를 운영하는 CEO가 쓴 책을 한 권 추천했다.
After reading the book, Steven told her that the CEO is his role model.
그 책을 읽고 나서, Steven은 그녀에게 그 CEO가 자신의 롤모델이라고 말했다.
This morning, Ms. Olson hears the news that the CEO is going to have a book-signing at a bookstore nearby.
오늘 아침, Ms. Olson은 그 CEO가 근처 서점에서 책 사인회를 열 예정이라는 소식을 들었다.
She thinks Steven would love to meet his role model in person.
그녀는 Steven이 자신의 롤모델을 직접 만나보고 싶어할 것이라고 생각한다.
So, Ms. Olson wants to tell Steven that he should go see the CEO at the event.
그래서 Ms. Olson은 Steven에게 그 행사에 가서 CEO를 만나보라고 말해주고 싶다.
In this situation, what would Ms. Olson most likely say to Steven?
이 상황에서, Ms. Olson은 Steven에게 뭐라고 말할 것인가?
Ms. Olson : How about going to your role model's book-signing?
네 롤모델의 책 사인회에 가보는 것이 어떠니?

Why? 왜 정답일까?

상황에 따르면 Ms. Olson은 유명 게임 회사 CEO를 롤모델로 삼고 있는 Steven에게 그 CEO의 책 사인회에 가볼 것을 권하려고 한다(So, Ms. Olson wants to tell Steven that he should go see the CEO at the event.). 따라서 Ms. Olson이 Steven에게 할 말로 가장 적절한 것은 ④ '네 롤모델의 책 사인회에 가보는 것이 어떠니?'이다.

● career counselor 진로 상담사 ● book-signing ⓝ 책 사인회

16-17 악기 관리법 소개

M : Hello, students.
안녕하세요, 여러분.
Last class, we took a brief look at how to tune your musical instruments.
지난 시간에 우리는 여러분의 악기를 조율하는 방법을 잠깐 살펴봤었죠.
『Today, we're going to talk a bit about how to take care of and maintain your instruments.』 16번의 근거
오늘은 악기를 어떻게 관리하고 유지할지 조금 이야기해보겠습니다.
『First, let's take flutes.』 17번 ①의 근거 일치
먼저, 플루트를 얘기해보죠.
They may have moisture from the air blown through them, so you should clean and wipe the mouth piece before and after playing.
플루트는 그 안에 불어 넣어지는 공기로부터 습기를 먹을 수 있어서, 연주 전후에 마우스피스 부분을 청소하고 닦아줘야 합니다.
『Next are trumpets.』 17번 ②의 근거 일치
다음으로는 트럼펫입니다.
They can be taken apart, so you should air dry the parts in a cool dry place, away from direct sunlight.
이것들은 분리될 수 있어서, 여러분은 직사광선을 피해 서늘하고 건조한 곳에 각 부분을 두어 자연 건조시켜야 합니다.
『And as for pianos, they don't need everyday care, but it's essential to protect the keys by covering them with a protective pad when not in use.』 17번 ③의 근거 일치
피아노에 관해서라면, 매일 관리가 필요하진 않지만, 피아노를 치지 않을 때에는 보호 패드로 덮어두어서 건반을 보호하는 것이 필수입니다.

『The last ones are string instruments like guitars.』 17번 ⑤의 근거 일치
마지막으로는 기타 같은 현악기입니다.
Their strings need replacement.
기타 줄은 교체가 필요합니다.
When you replace the strings, it's good to do it gradually, one at a time.
줄을 교체할 때는, 한 번에 하나씩, 점차적으로 해주는 것이 좋습니다.
Proper care can lengthen the lifespan of your musical instruments.
적절한 관리는 여러분 악기의 수명을 연장시킬 수 있습니다.
I hope this lesson helps you to keep your musical instruments safe from damage.
이 강의가 여러분이 악기를 손상되지 않게 안전하게 관리하는 데 도움이 되길 바랍니다.

● tune ⓥ 조율하다 ● take apart 분리하다
● not in use 사용하지 않는

---

16 주제 파악 　정답률 85% | 정답 ①

남자가 하는 말의 주제로 가장 적절한 것은?
✓① tips for caring for musical instruments – 악기 관리에 관한 조언
② ways to choose a good musical instrument – 좋은 악기를 고르는 방법
③ effects of the weather on musical instruments – 날씨가 악기에 미치는 영향
④ benefits of learning musical instruments as a child – 어릴 때 악기를 배우는 것의 이점
⑤ difficulties of making your own musical instruments – 자신만의 악기를 만드는 것의 어려움

Why? 왜 정답일까?

'Today, we're going to talk a bit about how to take care of and maintain your instruments.'에서 남자는 악기 유지 및 관리법을 설명하겠다고 하므로, 남자가 하는 말의 주제로 가장 적절한 것은 ① '악기 관리에 관한 조언'이다.

---

17 언급 유무 파악 　정답률 96% | 정답 ④

언급된 악기가 아닌 것은?
① flutes – 플루트 ② trumpets – 트럼펫 ③ pianos – 피아노
✓④ drums – 드럼 ⑤ guitars – 기타

Why? 왜 정답일까?

담화에서 남자는 악기 손질법을 언급하기 위한 예시로 플루트, 트럼펫, 피아노, 기타를 언급하므로, 언급되지 않은 것은 ④ '드럼'이다.

Why? 왜 오답일까?

① 'First, let's take flutes.'에서 '플루트'가 언급되었다.
② 'Next are trumpets.'에서 '트럼펫'이 언급되었다.
③ 'And as for pianos, ~'에서 '피아노'가 언급되었다.
⑤ 'The last ones are string instruments like guitars.'에서 '기타'가 언급되었다.

---

18 학급 파티에 가져올 음식에 관한 유의 사항 　정답률 93% | 정답 ⑤

다음 글의 목적으로 가장 적절한 것은?
① 학급 파티 일정 변경을 공지하려고
② 학교 식당의 새로운 메뉴를 소개하려고
③ 학생의 특정 음식 알레르기 여부를 조사하려고
④ 학부모의 적극적인 학급 파티 참여를 독려하려고
✓⑤ 학급 파티에 가져올 음식에 대한 유의 사항을 안내하려고

Dear Parents/Guardians,
부모님들 / 보호자들께,
Class parties will be held / on the afternoon of Friday, December 16th, 2022.
학급 파티가 열릴 것입니다. / 2022년 12월 16일 금요일 오후에
Children may bring in / sweets, crisps, biscuits, cakes, and drinks.
아이들은 가져올 수 있습니다. / 사탕류, 포테이토 칩, 비스킷, 케이크, 그리고 음료를
We are requesting / that children do not bring in home-cooked or prepared food.
우리는 요청합니다. / 아이들이 집에서 만들거나 준비한 음식을 가져오지 않기를
All food should arrive in a sealed packet / with the ingredients clearly listed.
모든 음식은 밀봉된 꾸러미로 가져와야 합니다. / 성분이 명확하게 목록으로 작성되어
Fruit and vegetables are welcomed / if they are pre-packed in a sealed packet from the shop.
과일과 채소는 환영합니다. / 그것이 가게에서 밀봉된 꾸러미로 사전 포장된 것이라면
Please DO NOT send any food into school / containing nuts / as we have many children with severe nut allergies.
음식은 어떤 것도 학교에 보내지 '마십시오'. / 견과류가 포함된 / 심각한 견과류 알레르기가 있는 학생들이 많이 있기 때문에
Please check the ingredients of all food / your children bring / carefully.
모든 음식의 성분을 확인해 주십시오. / 아이들이 가져오는 / 주의 깊게
Thank you for your continued support and cooperation.
여러분의 지속적인 지원과 협조에 감사드립니다.
Yours sincerely, // Lisa Brown, Headteacher
교장 Lisa Brown 드림

부모님들 / 보호자들께,

학급 파티가 2022년 12월 16일 금요일 오후에 열릴 것입니다. 아이들은 사탕류, 포테이토 칩, 비스킷, 케이크, 그리고 음료를 가져올 수 있습니다. 우리는 아이들이 집에서 만들거나 준비한 음식을 가져오지 않기를 요청합니다. 모든 음식은 성분을 명확하게 목록으로 작성하여 밀봉된 꾸러미로 가져와야 합니다. 과일과 채소는 가게에서 밀봉된 꾸러미로 사전 포장된 것이라면 환영합니다. 심각한 견과류 알레르기가 있는 학생들이 많이 있기 때문에 견과류가 포함된 음식은 어떤 것도 학교에 보내지 마십시오. 아이들이 가져오는 모든 음식의 성분을 주의 깊게 확인해 주십시오. 여러분의 지속적인 지원과 협조에 감사드립니다.

교장 Lisa Brown 드림

두 번째 문장부터 학급 파티에 어떤 음식을 가져올 수 있는지 열거한 뒤, 음식의 성분을 꼭 확인해달라고 요청하고 있다(Please check the ingredients of all food ~). 따라서 글의 목적으로 가장 적절한 것은 ⑤ '학급 파티에 가져올 음식에 대한 유의 사항을 안내하려고'이다.

- **guardian** ⓝ 보호자
- **sealed** ⓐ 밀봉한
- **pre-packed** 사전 포장된
- **headteacher** ⓝ (공립학교) 교장
- **home-cooked** ⓐ 집에서 요리한
- **ingredient** ⓝ 성분, 재료
- **severe** ⓐ 심각한

구문 풀이

4행 We are requesting that children do not bring in homecooked or prepared food.
(현재진행) (접속사(~것))

---

19 뉴스 마감 전 고장 난 타자기를 고치고 안도한 필자   정답률 90% | 정답 ②

다음 글에 나타난 'I'의 심경 변화로 가장 적절한 것은?
① confident → nervous (자신 있는 / 긴장한)
✓② frustrated → relieved (절망한 / 안도한)
③ bored → amazed (지루한 / 놀란)
④ indifferent → curious (무관심한 / 호기심 많은)
⑤ excited → disappointed (신난 / 실망한)

It was two hours before the submission deadline / and I still hadn't finished my news article.
제출 마감 시간 두 시간 전이었고 / 나는 여전히 나의 뉴스 기사를 끝내지 못했다.

I sat at the desk, / but suddenly, the typewriter didn't work.
나는 책상에 앉았는데, / 갑자기 타자기가 작동하지 않았다.

No matter how hard I tapped the keys, / the levers wouldn't move to strike the paper.
내가 아무리 세게 키를 두드려도, / 레버는 종이를 두드리려 움직이지 않았다.

I started to realize / that I would not be able to finish the article on time.
나는 깨닫기 시작했다. / 내가 제시간에 그 기사를 끝낼 수 없으리라는 것을

Desperately, / I rested the typewriter on my lap / and started hitting each key / with as much force as I could manage.
필사적으로, / 나는 타자기를 내 무릎 위에 올려놓고 / 각각의 키를 누르기 시작했다. / 내가 감당할 수 있는 최대의 센 힘으로

Nothing happened.
아무 일도 일어나지 않았다.

Thinking something might have happened inside of it, / I opened the cover, / lifted up the keys, / and found the problem / — a paper clip.
타자기 내부에 무슨 일이 일어났을지도 모르겠다고 생각하면서, / 나는 그 덮개를 열고, / 키들을 들어 올리고, / 문제를 발견했다 / 종이 집게였다.

The keys had no room to move.
키들이 움직일 공간이 없었다.

After picking it out, / I pressed and pulled some parts.
그것을 집어서 꺼낸 후에, / 나는 몇 개의 부품들을 누르고 당겼다.

The keys moved smoothly again.
키들이 매끄럽게 다시 움직였다.

I breathed deeply and smiled.
나는 깊게 숨을 내쉬고 미소 지었다.

Now I knew / that I could finish my article on time.
이제는 나는 알았다. / 내가 제시간에 기사를 끝낼 수 있음을

제출 마감 시간 두 시간 전이었고 나는 여전히 나의 뉴스 기사를 끝내지 못했다. 나는 책상에 앉았는데, 갑자기 타자기가 작동하지 않았다. 내가 아무리 세게 키를 두드려도, 레버는 종이를 두드리려 움직이지 않았다. 나는 내가 제시간에 그 기사를 끝낼 수 없으리라는 것을 깨닫기 시작했다. 필사적으로, 나는 타자기를 내 무릎 위에 올려놓고 각각의 키를 최대한 센 힘으로 누르기 시작했다. 아무 일도 일어나지 않았다. 타자기 내부에 무슨 일이 일어났을지도 모르겠다고 생각하면서, 나는 그 덮개를 열고, 키들을 들어 올리고, 문제를 발견했다 — 종이 집게였다. 키들이 움직일 공간이 없었다. 그것을 집어서 꺼낸 후에, 나는 몇 개의 부품들을 누르고 당겼다. 키들이 매끄럽게 다시 움직였다. 나는 깊게 숨을 내쉬고 미소 지었다. 이제 나는 내가 제시간에 기사를 끝낼 수 있음을 알았다.

Why? 왜 정답일까?

뉴스 마감을 앞두고 타자기가 작동하지 않아 기사를 끝내지 못할까봐 절망했던(~ I would not be able to finish the article on time.) 필자가 무사히 타자기를 고치고 안도의 미소를 지었다(I breathed deeply and smiled.)는 내용의 글이다. 따라서 'I'의 심경 변화로 가장 적절한 것은 ② '절망한 → 안도한'이다.

- **strike** ⓥ 치다, 때리다, 두드리다
- **lift up** 들어올리다
- **frustrated** ⓐ 좌절한
- **desperately** ⓐ 필사적으로
- **smoothly** ⓐ 부드럽게

구문 풀이

5행 Desperately, I rested the typewriter on my lap and started hitting each
(부사(문장 수식))
key with as much force as I could manage.
「as + 원급 + as + 주어 + can[could] : ~할 수 있는 한 최대로」

---

20 글보다 많은 단어를 필요로 하는 말하기   정답률 70% | 정답 ④

다음 글에서 필자가 주장하는 바로 가장 적절한 것은?
① 연설 시 중요한 정보는 천천히 말해야 한다.
② 좋은 글을 쓰려면 간결한 문장을 사용해야 한다.
③ 말하기 전에 신중히 생각하는 습관을 길러야 한다.
✓④ 글을 쓸 때보다 말할 때 더 많은 단어를 사용해야 한다.
⑤ 청중의 이해를 돕기 위해 미리 연설문을 제공해야 한다.

Experts on writing say, / "Get rid of as many words as possible."
글쓰기 전문가들은 말한다. / '가능한 한 많은 단어를 삭제하라'고

Each word must do something important.
각 단어는 무언가 중요한 일을 해야 한다.

If it doesn't, / get rid of it.
만일 그렇지 않다면 / 그것을 삭제하라.

Well, this doesn't work for speaking.
자, 이 방법은 말하기에서는 통하지 않는다.

It takes more words / to introduce, express, and adequately elaborate an idea in speech / than it takes in writing.
더 많은 단어가 필요하다. / 말로 아이디어를 소개하고, 표현하며, 적절히 부연 설명하는 데 / 글을 쓸 때보다

Why is this so?
이것은 왜 그러한가?

While the reader can reread, / the listener cannot rehear.
독자는 글을 다시 읽을 수 있으나 / 청자는 다시 들을 수 없다.

Speakers do not come equipped with a replay button.
화자는 반복 재생 버튼을 갖추고 있지 않다.

Because listeners are easily distracted, / they will miss many pieces of what a speaker says.
청자들은 쉽게 주의력이 흐려지기 때문에 / 그들은 화자가 말하는 것 중 많은 부분을 놓칠 것이다.

If they miss the crucial sentence, / they may never catch up.
그들이 중요한 문장을 놓친다면, / 그들은 절대로 따라잡을 수 없을 것이다.

This makes it necessary / for speakers to talk *longer* about their points, / using more words on them / than would be used to express the same idea in writing.
이것은 필요가 있게 한다. / 화자들이 요점을 *더 길게* 말할 / 그것에 관해 더 많은 단어를 사용하여 / 글을 쓸 때 같은 아이디어를 표현하기 위해 사용할 것보다

글쓰기 전문가들은 '가능한 한 많은 단어를 삭제하라'고 말한다. 각 단어는 무언가 중요한 일을 해야 한다. 만일 그렇지 않다면 그것을 삭제하라. 자, 이 방법은 말하기에서는 통하지 않는다. 말을 할 때는 아이디어를 소개하고, 표현하며, 적절히 부연 설명하는 데 글을 쓸 때보다 더 많은 단어가 필요하다. 이것은 왜 그러한가? 독자는 글을 다시 읽을 수 있으나 청자는 다시 들을 수 없다. 화자는 반복 재생 버튼을 갖추고 있지 않다. 청자들은 쉽게 주의력이 흐려지기 때문에 화자가 말하는 것 중 많은 부분을 놓칠 것이다. 그들이 중요한 문장을 놓친다면, 절대로 따라잡을 수 없을 것이다. 이것은 화자들이 글을 쓸 때 같은 아이디어를 표현하기 위해 사용할 단어 수보다 더 많은 단어를 사용하여 요점을 *더 길게* 말할 필요가 있게 한다.

Why? 왜 정답일까?

'It takes more words to introduce, express, and adequately elaborate an idea in speech than it takes in writing.'에서 글보다 말에서 더 많은 단어가 필요하다고 언급하고, 그 이유를 부연 설명한 뒤 다시 논지를 반복하고 있다. 따라서 필자가 주장하는 바로 가장 적절한 것은 ④ '글을 쓸 때보다 말할 때 더 많은 단어를 사용해야 한다.'이다.

- **get rid of** ~을 제거하다
- **elaborate** ⓥ 부연 설명하다, 자세히 말하다
- **crucial** ⓐ 아주 중요한
- **adequately** ⓐ 적절하게
- **distract** ⓥ 주의를 분산시키다
- **catch up** 따라잡다

구문 풀이

8행 This makes it necessary for speakers to talk longer about their points,
(목적격 보어) (의미상 주어) (진목적어)
(가목적어)
using more words on them than would be used to express the same idea in
(분사구문) (선행사) (유사관계대명사(비교급 선행사 뒤에 불완전한 절 연결))
writing.

---

21 고객에게 아니라고 말해야 할 순간   정답률 71% | 정답 ③

밑줄 친 fire a customer가 다음 글에서 의미하는 바로 가장 적절한 것은?
① deal with a customer's emergency – 고객의 응급 상황을 해결해야
② delete a customer's purchasing record – 고객의 구매 기록을 지워야
✓③ reject a customer's unreasonable demand – 고객의 불합리한 요구를 거절해야
④ uncover the hidden intention of a customer – 고객의 숨은 의도를 밝혀야
⑤ rely on the power of an influential customer – 영향력 있는 고객의 힘에 의존해야

Is the customer *always* right?
고객은 항상 옳은가?

When customers return a broken product to a famous company, / which makes kitchen and bathroom fixtures, / the company nearly always offers a replacement / to maintain good customer relations.
한 유명한 회사에 고객들이 고장 난 제품을 반품할 때 / 주방과 욕실 설비를 만드는 / 그 회사는 거의 항상 대체품을 제공한다. / 좋은 고객 관계를 유지하기 위해

Still, / "there are times you've got to say 'no,'" / explains the warranty expert of the company, / such as when a product is undamaged or has been abused.
그럼에도, / "'안 돼요.'라고 말을 해야 할 때가 있다."고 / 그 회사의 상품 보증 전문가는 설명한다. / 상품이 멀쩡하거나 남용되었을 때와 같이

Entrepreneur Lauren Thorp, / who owns an e-commerce company, / says, / "While the customer is 'always' right, / sometimes you just have to fire a customer."
기업가 Lauren Thorp는 / 전자 상거래 회사를 소유한 / 말한다. / "고객이 '항상' 옳지만, / 때로는 고객을 해고해야만 한다."고

When Thorp has tried everything to resolve a complaint / and realizes that the customer will be dissatisfied no matter what, / she returns her attention to the rest of her customers, / who she says are "the reason for my success."
Thorp가 고객의 불만을 해결하기 위해 최선을 다했는데 / 그 고객이 어떠한 경우에도 만족하지 않을 것이란 사실을 깨달을 때, / 그녀는 나머지 다른 고객들에게로 관심을 돌리는데, / 그 고객들이 "내 성공의 이유"라고 그녀는 말한다.

고객은 항상 옳은가? 주방과 욕실 설비를 만드는 한 유명한 회사에 고객들이 고장 난 제품을 반품할 때 그 회사는 좋은 고객 관계를 유지하기 위해 거의 항상 대체품을 제공한다. 그럼에도, 그 회사의 상품 보증 전문가는 상품이 멀쩡하거나 남용되었을 때와 같이, "'안 돼요.'라고 말을 해야 할 때가 있다."고 설명한다. 전자 상거래 회사를 소유한 기업가 Lauren Thorp는 "고객이 '항상' 옳지만, 때로는 고객을 해고해야만 한다."고 말한다. Thorp가 고객의 불만을 해결하기 위해 최선을 다했는데 그 고객이 어떠한 경우에도 만족하지 않을 것이란 사실을 깨달을 때, 그녀는 나머지 다른 고객들에게로 관심을 돌리는데, 그 고객들이 "내 성공의 이유"라고 그녀는 말한다.

Why? 왜 정답일까?

고객에게 '안 된다'고 말하는 순간이 필요하다(there are times you've got to say 'no,' ~)는 내용

의 글로, 마지막 두 문장에서 불만 해결에 최선을 다했는데도 결코 만족하지 않은 고객에 대해서는 과감히 '신경을 끄고' 다른 고객들에 집중하는 사업가의 사례를 언급하고 있다. 따라서 밑줄 친 부분이 의미하는 바로 가장 적절한 것은 ③ '고객의 불합리한 요구를 거절해야'이다.

- **fixture** ⓝ 설비, 살림, 세간
- **replacement** ⓝ 대체(품)
- **undamaged** ⓐ 멀쩡한, 손상되지 않은
- **abuse** ⓥ 남용하다
- **entrepreneur** ⓝ 기업가, 사업가
- **dissatisfied** ⓐ 불만족한

구문 풀이

8행 When Thorp has tried everything to resolve a complaint and realizes that
　　　　　　　　　　　　　　　　　　　동사1　　　　　　　　　　부사절 용법(목적)　　　　동사2
the customer will be dissatisfied no matter what, she returns her attention to the
　　　　　　　　　　　　　　　　무엇을 하든 간에
rest of her customers, who (she says) are "the reason for my success."
　　　　　　　선행사　　주격 관·대　삽입절　동사

22　교실 장식이 적당할 필요성　　정답률 82% | 정답 ①

다음 글의 요지로 가장 적절한 것은?
☑ 아이들의 집중을 돕기 위해 과도한 교실 장식을 지양할 필요가 있다.
② 아이들의 인성과 인지 능력을 균형 있게 발달시키는 것이 중요하다.
③ 아이들이 직접 교실을 장식하는 것은 창의력 발달에 도움이 된다.
④ 다양한 교실 활동은 아이들의 수업 참여도를 증진시킨다.
⑤ 풍부한 시각 자료는 아이들의 학습 동기를 높인다.

A recent study from Carnegie Mellon University in Pittsburgh, / called "When Too Much of a Good Thing May Be Bad," / indicates / that classrooms with too much decoration / are a source of distraction for young children / and directly affect their cognitive performance.
피츠버그시 Carnegie Mellon University에서 이루어진 최근 연구는 / '너무 많은 좋은 것이 나쁠 수도 있을 때'라고 불리는 / 나타낸다. / 너무 많은 장식이 있는 교실은 / 어린이들의 주의 산만의 원인이고 / 그들의 인지적인 수행에 직접적으로 영향을 미친다는 것을
Being visually overstimulated, / the children have a great deal of difficulty concentrating / and end up with worse academic results.
시각적으로 지나치게 자극되었을 때, / 아이들은 집중하는 데 많이 어려워하고 / 결국 학습 결과가 더 나빠진다.
On the other hand, / if there is not much decoration on the classroom walls, / the children are less distracted, / spend more time on their activities, / and learn more.
반면에, / 교실 벽에 장식이 많지 않으면, / 아이들은 덜 산만해지고, / 수업 활동에 더 많은 시간을 사용하고, / 더 많이 배운다.
So it's our job, / in order to support their attention, / to find the right balance / between excessive decoration and the complete absence of it.
그래서 우리가 할 일이다. / 이들의 집중을 도우려면 / 적절한 균형을 찾는 것이 / 지나친 장식과 장식이 전혀 없는 것 사이의

피츠버그시 Carnegie Mellon University에서 이루어진, '너무 많은 좋은 것이 나쁠 수도 있을 때'라고 불리는 최근 한 연구에 따르면, 너무 많은 장식이 있는 교실은 어린이들의 주의 산만의 원인이고 그들의 인지적인 수행에 직접적으로 영향을 미친다. 시각적으로 지나치게 자극되었을 때, 아이들은 집중하는 데 많이 어려워하고 결국 학습 결과가 더 나빠진다. 반면에, 교실 벽에 장식이 많지 않으면, 아이들은 덜 산만해지고, 수업 활동에 더 많은 시간을 사용하고, 더 많이 배운다. 그래서 이들의 집중을 도우려면 지나친 장식과 장식이 전혀 없는 것 사이의 적절한 균형을 찾는 것이 우리가 할 일이다.

Why? 왜 정답일까?

교실 장식이 과하면 아이들의 집중력이 떨어진다는 연구 내용을 토대로, 아이들의 집중력을 높여주려면 적당한 교실 장식의 균형을 찾아야 한다(~ in order to support their attention, to find the right balance between excessive decoration and the complete absence of it.)는 결론을 이끌어내고 있다. 따라서 글의 요지로 가장 적절한 것은 ① '아이들의 집중을 돕기 위해 과도한 교실 장식을 지양할 필요가 있다.'이다.

- **decoration** ⓝ 장식
- **overstimulate** ⓥ 과도하게 자극하다
- **a great deal of** 상당한, 큰, 많은
- **end up with** 결국 ~하다
- **excessive** ⓐ 과도한
- **absence** ⓝ 부재

구문 풀이

5행 Being visually overstimulated, the children have a great deal of difficulty
　　　　분사구문　　　　　　　　　　　　　　　　　　　「have difficulty + 동명사 : ~하는 데 어려움을 겪다」
concentrating and end up with worse academic results.

23　인간 진화와 소속 욕구　　정답률 59% | 정답 ②

다음 글의 주제로 가장 적절한 것은?
① skills for the weak to survive modern life - 약자가 현대 생활에서 생존하는 기술
☑ usefulness of belonging for human evolution - 인간 진화에 있어 소속의 유용성
③ ways to avoid competition among social groups - 사회적 집단 간의 경쟁을 피하는 방법
④ roles of social relationships in children's education - 아이들의 교육에 있어 사회적 관계의 역할
⑤ differences between two major evolutionary theories - 두 가지 주요 진화론의 차이

For creatures like us, / evolution smiled upon those / with a strong need to belong.
우리와 같은 창조물에게 있어, / 진화는 이들에게 미소지어 주었다. / 강한 소속 욕구를 지닌
Survival and reproduction / are the criteria of success by natural selection, / and forming relationships with other people / can be useful for both survival and reproduction.
생존과 번식은 / 자연 선택에 의한 성공의 기준이고, / 다른 사람들과 관계를 형성하는 것은 / 생존과 번식 모두에 유용할 수 있다.
Groups can share resources, / care for sick members, / scare off predators, / fight together against enemies, / divide tasks so as to improve efficiency, / and contribute to survival in many other ways.
집단은 자원을 공유하고, / 아픈 구성원을 돌보고, / 포식자를 쫓아버리고, / 적에 맞서서 함께 싸우고, / 효율성을 향상시키기 위해 일을 나누고, / 많은 다른 방식으로 생존에 기여한다.
In particular, / if an individual and a group want the same resource, / the group will generally prevail, / so competition for resources / would especially favor a need to belong.
특히, / 한 개인과 한 집단이 같은 자원을 원하면, / 집단이 일반적으로 우세하고, / 그래서 자원에 대한 경쟁은 / 소속하려는 욕구를 특별히 좋아할 것이다.

Belongingness will likewise promote reproduction, / such as by bringing potential mates into contact with each other, / and in particular by keeping parents together / to care for their children, / who are much more likely to survive / if they have more than one caregiver.
마찬가지로 소속되어 있다는 것은 번식을 촉진시키는데, / 이를테면 잠재적인 짝을 서로 만나게 해주거나, / 특히 부모가 함께 있도록 하면서 / 자녀를 돌보기 위해, / 자녀들은 훨씬 더 생존하기 쉬울 것이다. / 한 명 이상의 돌보는 이가 있으면

우리(인간)와 같은 창조물에게 있어, 진화는 강한 소속 욕구를 가진 이들에게 미소지어 주었다. 생존과 번식은 자연 선택에 의한 성공의 기준이고, 다른 사람들과 관계를 형성하는 것은 생존과 번식 모두에 유용할 수 있다. 집단은 자원을 공유하고, 아픈 구성원을 돌보고, 포식자를 쫓아버리고, 적에 맞서서 함께 싸우고, 효율성을 향상시키기 위해 일을 나누고, 많은 다른 방식으로 생존에 기여한다. 특히, 한 개인과 한 집단이 같은 자원을 원하면, 집단이 일반적으로 우세하고, 그래서 자원에 대한 경쟁은 소속하려는 욕구를 특별히 좋아할 것이다. 마찬가지로 소속되어 있다는 것은 이를테면 잠재적인 짝을 서로 만나게 해주거나, 특히 부모가 자녀를 돌보기 위해 함께 있도록 하면서 번식을 촉진시키는데, 자녀들은 한 명 이상의 돌보는 이가 있으면 훨씬 더 생존하기 쉬울 것이다.

Why? 왜 정답일까?

첫 문장인 'For creatures like us, evolution smiled upon those with a strong need to belong.'에서 진화의 과정은 강한 소속 욕구를 지닌 이들을 선호했다는 주제를 제시한 후, 소속 욕구가 진화에 어떤 식으로 도움이 되었는지 구체적으로 부연하고 있다. 따라서 글의 주제로 가장 적절한 것은 ② '인간 진화에 있어 소속의 유용성'이다.

- **reproduction** ⓝ 번식, 재생
- **criterion** ⓝ 기준
- **natural selection** 자연 선택
- **scare off** ~을 겁주어 쫓아버리다
- **fight against** ~에 맞서 싸우다
- **prevail** ⓥ 우세하다
- **belongingness** ⓝ 소속, 귀속, 친밀감
- **caregiver** ⓝ 양육자

구문 풀이

4행 Groups can share resources, care for sick members, scare off predators,
　　　　　　　　동사1　　　　　　　동사2　　　　　　　동사3
fight together against enemies, divide tasks so as to improve efficiency, and
　　동사4　　　　　　　　　　동사5　　　　목적(~하기 위해)
contribute to survival in many other ways.
　동사6

24　용기가 불러오는 기회　　정답률 65% | 정답 ①

다음 글의 제목으로 가장 적절한 것은?
☑ More Courage Brings More Opportunities - 더 큰 용기가 더 많은 기회를 부른다
② Travel: The Best Way to Make Friends - 여행: 친구를 사귀는 가장 좋은 방법
③ How to Turn Mistakes into Success - 실수를 성공으로 바꾸는 방법
④ Satisfying Life? Share with Others - 만족스러운 삶? 남들과 나누라
⑤ Why Is Overcoming Fear So Hard? - 공포를 극복하는 것은 왜 이리 어려울까?

Many people make a mistake / of only operating along the safe zones, / and in the process / they miss the opportunity / to achieve greater things.
많은 사람들이 실수를 저지르고, / 안전 구역에서만 움직이는 / 그 과정에서 / 그들은 기회를 놓친다. / 더 위대한 일들을 달성할
They do so / because of a fear of the unknown / and a fear of treading the unknown paths of life.
그들은 그렇게 한다. / 미지의 세계에 대한 두려움 때문에 / 그리고 알려지지 않은 삶의 경로를 밟는 것에 대한 두려움
Those / that are brave enough / to take those roads less travelled / are able to get great returns / and derive major satisfaction out of their courageous moves.
사람들은 / 충분히 용감한 / 사람들이 잘 다니지 않는 길을 택할 만큼 / 엄청난 보상을 받을 수 있고 / 용감한 행동으로부터 큰 만족감을 끌어낼 수 있다.
Being overcautious will mean / that you will miss / attaining the greatest levels of your potential.
지나치게 조심하는 것은 의미할 것이다. / 여러분이 놓친다는 것을 / 잠재력의 최고 수준을 달성하는 것
You must learn to take those chances / that many people around you will not take, / because your success will flow from those bold decisions / that you will take along the way.
여러분은 기회를 택하는 법을 배워야 하는데, / 주변에 있는 많은 사람들이 선택하지 않을 / 왜냐하면 여러분의 성공은 용감한 결정으로부터 나올 것이기 때문이다. / 삶의 과정에서 여러분이 내릴

많은 사람들이 안전 구역에서만 움직이는 실수를 저지르고, 그 과정에서 더 위대한 일들을 달성할 기회를 놓친다. 그들은 미지의 세계에 대한 두려움과 알려지지 않은 삶의 경로를 밟는 것에 대한 두려움 때문에 그렇게 한다. 사람들이 잘 다니지 않는 길을 택할 만큼 충분히 용감한 사람들은 엄청난 보상을 받을 수 있고 용감한 행동으로부터 큰 만족감을 끌어낼 수 있다. 지나치게 조심하는 것은 잠재력의 최고 수준을 달성하는 것을 놓친다는 의미일 것이다. 여러분은 주변에 있는 많은 사람들이 선택하지 않을 기회를 택하는 법을 배워야 하는데, 왜냐하면 여러분의 성공은 삶의 과정에서 여러분이 내릴 용감한 결정으로부터 나올 것이기 때문이다.

Why? 왜 정답일까?

결론을 제시하는 마지막 문장에서 많은 기회와 성공은 용기에서 파생되므로 더 과감해질 필요가 있다(You must learn to take those chances that many people around you will not take, because your success will flow from those bold decisions that you will take along the way.)고 조언하므로, 글의 제목으로 가장 적절한 것은 ① '더 큰 용기가 더 많은 기회를 부른다'이다.

- **safe zone** 안전 구역
- **unknown** ⓐ 미지의, 알지 못하는
- **derive** ⓥ 끌어내다, 도출하다
- **courageous** ⓐ 용감한
- **overcautious** ⓐ 지나치게 조심하는

구문 풀이

4행 Those that are brave enough to take those roads less travelled are able
　　　　　　　　　　「형/부 + enough + to부정사 : ~할 만큼 충분히 …한」　　과거분사
to get great returns and derive major satisfaction out of their courageous moves.

[문제편 p.115]

25 대륙별 도시 인구 점유율 비교   정답률 86% | 정답 ③

다음 도표의 내용과 일치하지 <u>않는</u> 것은?

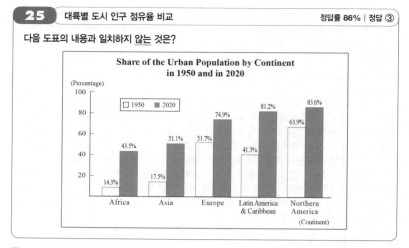

The graph above shows / the share of the urban population by continent / in 1950 and in 2020.
위 그래프는 보여준다. / 대륙별 도시 인구 점유율을 / 1950년과 2020년의

① For each continent, / the share of the urban population in 2020 / was larger than that in 1950.
각 대륙에서, / 2020년의 도시 인구 점유율이 / 1950년에 비해 더 컸다.

② From 1950 to 2020, / the share of the urban population in Africa / increased from 14.3% to 43.5%.
1950년부터 2020년까지 / 아프리카의 도시 인구 점유율은 / 14.3%에서 43.5%로 증가했다.

☑ The share of the urban population in Asia / was the second lowest in 1950 / but not in 2020.
아시아의 도시 인구 점유율은 / 1950년에는 두 번째로 낮았지만, / 2020년에는 그렇지 않았다.

④ In 1950, / the share of the urban population in Europe / was larger than that in Latin America and the Caribbean, / whereas the reverse was true in 2020.
1950년에는 / 유럽의 도시 인구 점유율이 / 라틴 아메리카 및 카리브해 지역보다 더 컸지만, / 2020년에는 그 반대가 사실이었다.

⑤ Among the five continents, / Northern America was ranked in the first position / for the share of the urban population / in both 1950 and 2020.
다섯 개 대륙 중, / 북아메리카는 1위를 차지했다. / 도시 인구 점유율에서 / 1950년과 2020년 모두

위 그래프는 1950년과 2020년의 대륙별 도시 인구 점유율을 보여준다. ① 각 대륙에서, 2020년의 도시 인구 점유율이 1950년에 비해 더 컸다. ② 1950년부터 2020년까지 아프리카의 도시 인구 점유율은 14.3%에서 43.5%로 증가했다. ③ 아시아의 도시 인구 점유율은 1950년에는 두 번째로 낮았지만, 2020년에는 그렇지 않았다. ④ 1950년에는 유럽의 도시 인구 점유율이 라틴 아메리카 및 카리브해 지역보다 더 컸지만, 2020년에는 역전이 일어났다. ⑤ 다섯 개 대륙 중, 북아메리카는 도시 인구 점유율에서 1950년과 2020년 모두 1위를 차지했다.

Why? 왜 정답일까?

도표에 따르면 2020년 아시아 대륙에서의 도시 인구 점유율은 **51.1%**로 전체에서 두 번째로 낮는데, 이는 **1950년**과 동일한 순위이다. 따라서 도표와 일치하지 않는 것은 ③이다.

- urban ⓐ 도시의
- reverse ⓝ 반대, 역전, 전환
- population ⓝ 인구(수)

구문 풀이

5행 The share of the urban population in Asia was the second lowest in 1950 but not in 2020.
「서수＋최상급: 몇 번째로 ～한」

---

26 Wilbur Smith의 생애   정답률 82% | 정답 ④

Wilbur Smith에 관한 다음 글의 내용과 일치하지 <u>않는</u> 것은?

① 역사 소설을 전문으로 하는 소설가였다.
② 아버지는 그가 글 쓰는 것을 지지하지 않았다.
③ 첫 번째 소설은 1962년까지 20번 거절당했다.
☑ 소설 *When the Lion Feeds*는 영화화되었다.
⑤ 죽기 전까지 49편의 소설을 출간했다.

「Wilbur Smith was a South African novelist / specialising in historical fiction.」 ①의근거 일치
Wilbur Smith는 남아프리카 소설가였다. / 역사 소설을 전문으로 하는

Smith wanted to become a journalist, / writing about social conditions in South Africa, / but 「his father was never supportive of his writing / and forced him to get a real job.」 ②의근거 일치
Smith는 언론인이 되고 싶었으나, / 남아프리카의 사회 환경에 관해 글을 쓰는 / 그의 아버지는 그가 글을 쓰는 것을 절대로 지지하지 않았고 / 그가 현실적인 직업을 갖도록 강요했다.

Smith studied further / and became a tax accountant, / but he finally turned back to his love of writing.
Smith는 더 공부하여 / 세금 회계사가 되었으나 / 결국에는 그가 사랑하는 글 쓰는 일로 돌아왔다.

「He wrote his first novel, *The Gods First Make Mad*, / and had received 20 rejections by 1962.」 ③의근거 일치
그는 첫 번째 소설, *The Gods First Make Mad*를 썼고 / 1962년까지 20번의 거절을 당했다.

In 1964, / Smith published another novel, *When the Lion Feeds*, / and it went on to be successful, / selling around the world.
1964년에 / Smith는 또 다른 소설, *When the Lion Feeds*를 출간했고 / 그것은 성공을 거두었다. / 전 세계에 팔리면서

「A famous actor and film producer / bought the film rights for *When the Lion Feeds*, / although no movie resulted.」 ④의근거 불일치
한 유명한 배우이자 영화 제작자가 / *When the Lion Feeds*에 대한 영화 판권을 샀다. / 비록 영화화되지는 않았지만

「By the time of his death in 2021 / he had published 49 novels, / selling more than 140 million copies worldwide.」 ⑤의근거 일치
2021년 죽기 전까지 / 그는 49편의 소설을 출간했으며 / 전 세계적으로 1억 4천만 부 이상을 판매했다.

Wilbur Smith는 역사 소설을 전문으로 하는 남아프리카 소설가였다. Smith는 남아프리카의 사회 환경에 관해 글을 쓰는 언론인이 되고 싶었으나, 그의 아버지는 그가 글을 쓰는 것을 절

대로 지지하지 않았고 그가 현실적인 직업을 갖도록 강요했다. Smith는 더 공부하여 세금 회계사가 되었으나 결국에는 그가 사랑하는 글 쓰는 일로 돌아왔다. 그는 첫 번째 소설, *The Gods First Make Mad*를 썼고 1962년까지 20번의 거절을 당했다. 1964년에 Smith는 또 다른 소설, *When the Lion Feeds*를 출간했고, 그것이 전 세계에 팔리면서 성공을 거두었다. 비록 영화화되지는 않았지만, 한 유명한 배우이자 영화 제작자가 *When the Lion Feeds*에 대한 영화 판권을 샀다. 2021년 죽기 전까지 그는 49편의 소설을 출간했으며 전 세계적으로 1억 4천만 부 이상을 판매했다.

Why? 왜 정답일까?

'A famous actor and film producer bought the film rights for *When the Lion Feeds*, although no movie resulted.'에서 소설 *When the Lion Feeds*의 영화 판권은 팔렸지만, 실제로 이것이 영화화되지는 않았다고 하므로, 내용과 일치하지 않는 것은 ④ '소설 *When the Lion Feeds*는 영화화되었다.'이다.

Why? 왜 오답일까?

① 'Wilbur Smith was a South African novelist specialising in historical fiction.'의 내용과 일치한다.
② '～ his father was never supportive of his writing ～'의 내용과 일치한다.
③ 'He wrote his first novel, *The Gods First Make Mad*, and had received 20 rejections by 1962.'의 내용과 일치한다.
⑤ 'By the time of his death in 2021 he had published 49 novels, ～'의 내용과 일치한다.

- novelist ⓝ 소설가
- fiction ⓝ 소설, 허구
- tax accountant 세무사
- rejection ⓝ 거절
- historical ⓐ 역사적인
- be supportive of ～을 지지하다
- turn back to ～로 돌아오다

구문 풀이

11행 By the time of his death in 2021 he had published 49 novels, selling more
～할 무렵   과거완료   분사구문(그리고 ～하다)
than 140 million copies worldwide.

---

27 야외 요가 수업 광고   정답률 95% | 정답 ④

2022 Springfield Park Yoga Class에 관한 다음 안내문의 내용과 일치하지 <u>않는</u> 것은?

① 온라인으로도 참여할 수 있다.
② 9월 중 토요일마다 진행된다.
③ 수업 시작 2시간 전까지 등록해야 한다.
☑ 매트가 제공된다.
⑤ 날씨가 좋지 않으면 취소될 것이다.

2022 Springfield Park Yoga Class
2022 Springfield Park Yoga Class(2022 Springfield Park 요가 수업)

The popular yoga class in Springfield Park / returns!
Springfield Park에서의 인기 있는 요가 수업이 / 돌아옵니다!

Enjoy yoga hosted on the park lawn.
공원 잔디밭에서 열리는 요가를 즐겨보세요.

「If you can't make it to the park, / join us online on our social media platforms!」 ①의근거 일치
만약 여러분이 공원에 오지 못한다면, / 저희의 소셜미디어 플랫폼에서 온라인으로 저희와 함께하세요!

When: 「Saturdays, 2 p.m. to 3 p.m., September」 ②의근거 일치
일시: 9월 매주 토요일 오후 2시부터 3시까지

Registration: / 「At least TWO hours before each class starts, / sign up here.」 ③의근거 일치
등록: / 매 수업이 시작하기 적어도 2시간 전까지, / 여기서 등록하세요.

Notes
주의 사항

For online classes: / find a quiet space with enough room / for you to stretch out.
온라인 수업: / 충분한 공간을 가진 조용한 장소를 찾으세요. / 여러분이 스트레칭을 할 만큼

For classes in the park: 「mats are not provided, / so bring your own!」 ④의근거 불일치
공원 수업: / 매트는 제공되지 않으니, / 본인 것을 가져오세요!

「The class will be canceled / if the weather is unfavorable.」 ⑤의근거 일치
수업은 취소될 것입니다. / 만약 날씨가 좋지 않으면

For more information, / click here.
더 많은 정보를 위해서는, / 여기를 클릭하세요.

2022 Springfield Park Yoga Class
(2022 Springfield Park 요가 수업)

Springfield Park에서의 인기 있는 요가 수업이 돌아옵니다! 공원 잔디밭에서 열리는 요가를 즐겨보세요. 만약 여러분이 공원에 오지 못한다면, 저희의 소셜미디어 플랫폼에서 온라인으로 저희와 함께하세요!

◈ **일시:** 9월 매주 토요일 오후 2시부터 3시까지

◈ **등록:** 매 수업이 시작하기 적어도 2시간 전까지, 여기서 등록하세요.

◈ **주의 사항**
- 온라인 수업: 여러분이 스트레칭을 할 만큼 충분한 공간을 가진 조용한 장소를 찾으세요.
- 공원 수업: 매트는 제공되지 않으니, 본인 것을 가져오세요!

※ 만약 날씨가 좋지 않으면 수업은 취소될 것입니다.

더 많은 정보를 위해서는, 여기를 클릭하세요.

Why? 왜 정답일까?

'For classes in the park: mats are not provided, so bring your own!'에서 매트는 제공되지 않아 수업을 듣는 사람이 직접 지참해야 한다고 했으므로, 안내문의 내용과 일치하지 않는 것은 ④ '매트가 제공된다.'이다.

Why? 왜 오답일까?

① '～ join us online on our social media platforms!'의 내용과 일치한다.

② 'Saturdays, 2 p.m. to 3 p.m., September'의 내용과 일치한다.
③ 'At least TWO hours before each class starts'의 내용과 일치한다.
⑤ 'The class will be canceled if the weather is unfavorable.'의 내용과 일치한다.

- **lawn** ⓝ 잔디밭
- **stretch out** 몸을 뻗고 눕다
- **make it** 참석하다, 성공하다, 해내다
- **unfavorable** ⓐ (형편이) 나쁜, 우호적이지 않은

구문 풀이

9행 ~ find a quiet space with enough room for you to stretch out.
「enough+명사+의미상 주어+to부정사: ~가 … 할 만큼 충분한 (명사)」

---

28 수질 오염 대책 아이디어 공모전
정답률 86% | 정답 ④

Kenner High School's Water Challenge에 관한 다음 안내문의 내용과 일치하는 것은?

① 제안서는 직접 방문하여 제출해야 한다.
② 9월 23일부터 제안서를 제출할 수 있다.
③ 제안서는 한 팀당 4개까지 제출할 수 있다.
④ 제공된 제안서 양식을 사용해야 한다.
⑤ 2등은 10달러의 상품권을 받는다.

Kenner High School's Water Challenge
Kenner High School's Water Challenge(Kenner 고등학교 물 챌린지)

Kenner High School's Water Challenge is a new contest / to propose measures against water pollution.
Kenner High School's 고등학교 물 챌린지는 새로운 대회입니다. / 수질 오염에 대한 대책을 제안하는

Please share your ideas / for dealing with water pollution!
여러분의 아이디어를 공유해 주세요! / 수질 오염에 대처하기 위한

Submission
제출

「How: / Submit your proposal by email / to admin@khswater.edu.」①의 근거 불일치
방법: / 여러분의 제안서를 이메일로 제출해 주세요. / admin@khswater.edu로

「When: September 5, 2022 to September 23, 2022」②의 근거 불일치
일시: 2022년 9월 5일부터 2022년 9월 23일까지

Details
세부 사항

Participants must enter in teams of four / and can only join one team.
참가자들은 반드시 4인으로 구성된 팀으로 참가해야 하며, / 오직 한 팀에만 참여할 수 있습니다.

「Submission is limited to one proposal per team.」③의 근거 불일치
한 팀당 한 개의 제안서만 제출할 수 있습니다.

「Participants must use the proposal form / provided on the website.」④의 근거 일치
참가자들은 제안서 양식을 사용해야 합니다. / 웹사이트에 제공된

Prizes
상품

1st: $50 gift certificate
1등: 50달러 상품권

「2nd: $30 gift certificate」⑤의 근거 불일치
2등: 30달러 상품권

3rd: $10 gift certificate
3등: 10달러 상품권

Please visit www.khswater.edu / to learn more about the challenge.
www.khswater.edu를 방문해 주세요. / 대회에 대해 더 알고 싶으면

Kenner High School's Water Challenge
(Kenner 고등학교 물 챌린지)

Kenner 고등학교 물 챌린지는 수질 오염에 대한 대책을 제안하는 새로운 대회입니다. 수질 오염에 대처하기 위한 여러분의 아이디어를 공유해 주세요!

제출
– **방법:** 여러분의 제안서를 이메일 admin@khswater.edu로 제출해 주세요.
– **일시:** 2022년 9월 5일부터 2022년 9월 23일까지

세부 사항
– 참가자들은 반드시 4인으로 구성된 팀으로 참가해야 하며, 오직 한 팀에만 참여할 수 있습니다.
– 한 팀당 한 개의 제안서만 제출할 수 있습니다.
– 참가자들은 웹사이트에 제공된 제안서 양식을 사용해야 합니다.

상품
– 1등: 50달러 상품권
– 2등: 30달러 상품권
– 3등: 10달러 상품권

대회에 대해 더 알고 싶으면, www.khswater.edu를 방문해 주세요.

Why? 왜 정답일까?

'Participants must use the proposal form provided on the website.'에서 제안서는 제공된 양식을 사용해 작성되어야 한다고 공지하므로, 안내문의 내용과 일치하는 것은 ④ '제공된 제안서 양식을 사용해야 한다.'이다.

Why? 왜 오답일까?

① 'Submit your proposal by email to admin@khswater.edu.'에서 제안서는 이메일로 제출하면 된다고 하였다.
② 'When: September 5, 2022 to September 23, 2022'에서 9월 23일은 제출 시작일이 아니라 마감일이라고 하였다.
③ 'Submission is limited to one proposal per team.'에서 팀별로 제안서는 하나만 제출할 수 있다고 하였다.
⑤ '2nd: $30 gift certificate'에서 2등은 30달러짜리 상품권을 받는다고 하였다.

- **measure** ⓝ 대책, 조치
- **gift certificate** 상품권
- **water pollution** 수질 오염

---

29 인간의 뇌 크기 감소
정답률 67% | 정답 ③

다음 글의 밑줄 친 부분 중, 어법상 틀린 것은? [3점]

The human brain, / it turns out, / has shrunk in mass / about 10 percent / since it ① peaked in size 15,000-30,000 years ago.
인간의 뇌는 / 밝혀졌다. / 부피가 약 10퍼센트 줄어들었다는 것이 / 그것이 15,000년에서 30,000년 전 정점에 도달한 이래

One possible reason is / that many thousands of years ago / humans lived in a world of dangerous predators / ② where they had to have their wits about them at all times / to avoid being killed.
한 가지 가능한 이유는 ~이다. / 수천 년 전에 / 인간은 위험한 포식자의 세계에서 살았다는 것 / 그들이 늘 기지를 발휘해야 했던 / 죽임을 당하는 것을 피하기 위해

Today, / we have effectively domesticated ourselves / and many of the tasks of survival / — from avoiding immediate death / to building shelters / to obtaining food — / ✓ have been outsourced to the wider society.
오늘날, / 우리는 우리 자신을 효율적으로 길들여 왔고 / 생존의 많은 과업이 / 즉각적인 죽음을 피하는 것부터 / 쉴 곳을 짓고 / 음식을 얻어 내는 일까지 / 더 넓은 사회로 위탁되어 왔다.

We are smaller than our ancestors too, / and it is a characteristic of domestic animals / ④ that they are generally smaller than their wild cousins.
우리는 우리의 조상보다 더 작기도 한데, / 가축의 특징 중 하나는 / 이들이 그들의 야생 사촌보다 일반적으로 더 작다는 것

None of this may mean we are dumber — / brain size is not necessarily an indicator of human intelligence — / but it may mean / that our brains today are wired up differently, / and perhaps more efficiently, / than ⑤ those of our ancestors.
이중 어떤 것도 우리가 더 어리석다는 뜻은 아니지만 / 뇌 크기가 반드시 인간의 지능의 지표는 아니다 / 그것은 뜻할 수도 있다. / 오늘날 우리의 뇌가 다른 식으로 장착되어 있음을 / 그리고 아마도 더 효율적으로 / 우리 조상들의 뇌보다

인간의 뇌는 15,000년에서 30,000년 전 크기가 정점에 도달한 이래 부피가 약 10퍼센트 줄어들었다는 것이 밝혀졌다. 한 가지 가능한 이유는 수천 년 전에 인간은 죽임을 당하는 것을 피하기 위해 그들이 늘 기지를 발휘해야 했던 위험한 포식자의 세계에서 살았다는 것이다. 오늘날, 우리는 우리 자신을 효율적으로 길들여 왔고 생존의 많은 과업이 — 즉각적인 죽음을 피하는 것부터 쉴 곳을 짓고 음식을 얻어 내는 일까지 — 더 넓은 사회로 위탁되어 왔다. 우리는 우리의 조상보다 더 작기도 한데, 가축이 그들의 야생 사촌보다 일반적으로 더 작다는 것은 이들의 특징 중 하나이다. 이중 어떤 것도 우리가 더 어리석다는 뜻은 아니지만 — 뇌 크기가 반드시 인간의 지능의 지표는 아니다 — 그것은 오늘날 우리의 뇌가 다른 식으로, 그리고 우리 조상보다 아마도 더 효율적으로 장착되어 있음을 뜻할 수도 있다.

Why? 왜 정답일까?

and 뒤에 새로 나온 주어가 **many of the tasks of survival**이라는 복수 명사구이므로, 단수형 **has**를 복수형 **have**로 고쳐야 한다. 따라서 어법상 틀린 것은 ③이다.

Why? 왜 오답일까?

① '주어+현재완료 동사 ~, since+주어+과거 동사 ~' 형태가 알맞게 쓰였다.
② 선행사가 바로 앞의 **predators**가 아닌 **a world**이므로, 장소의 관계부사 **where**가 알맞게 쓰였다.
④ **it**이 가주어이고, 'they are generally smaller ~'가 진주어이므로 명사절을 이끄는 접속사 **that**을 알맞게 썼다.
⑤ **than** 앞의 복수 명사 **brains**를 가리키기 위해 복수 대명사 **those**를 썼다.

- **shrink** ⓥ 줄어들다
- **have one's wits about one** ~의 기지를 발휘하다
- **domesticate** ⓥ 길들이다
- **wire** ⓥ 연결하다, 장착하다
- **mass** ⓝ 부피, 질량
- **indicator** ⓝ 지표

구문 풀이

3행 One possible reason is that many thousands of years ago humans lived in a world of dangerous predators where they had to have their wits about them at all times to avoid being killed.
장소 선행사 / 관계부사 / =predators / 수동 동명사(~되는 것)

---

30 허브의 건강상 효과
정답률 58% | 정답 ⑤

다음 글의 밑줄 친 부분 중, 문맥상 낱말의 쓰임이 적절하지 않은 것은? [3점]

It is widely believed / that certain herbs somehow magically improve the work of certain organs, / and "cure" specific diseases as a result.
널리 알려져 있다. / 어떤 허브는 왜인지는 몰라도 마법처럼 특정 장기의 기능을 향상시키고, / 그 결과 특정 질병을 '치유한다'고

Such statements are unscientific and groundless.
그러한 진술은 비과학적이고 근거가 없다.

Sometimes herbs appear to work, / since they tend to ① increase your blood circulation / in an aggressive attempt by your body / to eliminate them from your system.
때때로 허브는 효과가 있는 것처럼 보이는데, / 그것이 혈액 순환을 증가시키는 경향이 있기 때문이다. / 당신 몸이 적극 시도하는 과정에서 / 신체로부터 그것을 제거하려고

That can create a ② temporary feeling of a high, / which makes it seem / as if your health condition has improved.
이는 일시적으로 좋은 기분을 만들어 줄 수 있고, / 마치 보이게 만든다. / 당신의 건강 상태가 향상된 것처럼

Also, / herbs can have a placebo effect, / just like any other method, / thus helping you feel better.
또한 / 허브는 위약 효과를 가지고 있다 / 여느 다른 방법과 마찬가지로, / 그래서 당신이 더 나아졌다고 느끼도록 도와준다.

Whatever the case, / it is your body / that has the intelligence to ③ regain health, / and not the herbs.
어떠한 경우든, / 바로 당신의 몸이다. / 건강을 되찾게 하는 지성을 가진 것 / 허브가 아니라

How can herbs have the intelligence / needed to direct your body into getting healthier?
어떻게 허브가 지성을 가질 수 있겠는가? / 당신의 몸을 더 건강해지는 방향으로 인도하는 데 필요한

That is impossible.
그것은 불가능하다.

Try to imagine / how herbs might come into your body / and intelligently ④ fix your problems.
상상해 보라. / 어떻게 허브가 당신의 몸 안으로 들어가 / 영리하게 당신의 문제를 해결할 수 있는지

If you try to do that, / you will see how impossible it seems.
만약 당신이 그렇게 해 본다면 / 당신은 그것이 얼마나 불가능하게 보이는지를 알게 될 것이다.
Otherwise, / it would mean / that herbs are ✓more intelligent than the human body, / which is truly hard to believe.
그렇지 않다면, / 그것은 의미할 텐데, / 허브가 인간의 몸보다 더 지적이라는 것을 / 이는 정말로 믿기 어렵다.

어떤 허브는 왜인지는 몰라도 마법처럼 특정 장기의 기능을 향상시키고, 그 결과 특정한 질병을 '치유한다'고 널리 알려져 있다. 그러한 진술은 비과학적이고 근거가 없다. 때때로 허브는 효과가 있는 것처럼 보이는데, 이는 당신 몸이 신체로부터 그것을 제거하려고 적극 시도하는 과정에서 그것이 혈액 순환을 ① 증가시키는 경향이 있기 때문이다. 이는 ② 일시적으로 좋은 기분을 만들어 줄 수 있고, 마치 당신의 건강 상태가 향상된 것처럼 보이게 만든다. 또한 여느 다른 방법과 마찬가지로, 당신은 위약 효과를 가지고 있어서, 당신이 더 나아졌다고 느끼도록 도와준다. 어떠한 경우든, 건강을 ③ 되찾게 하는 지성을 가진 것은 허브가 아니라 바로 당신의 몸이다. 허브가 어떻게 당신의 몸을 더 건강해지는 방향으로 인도하는 데 필요한 지성을 가질 수 있겠는가? 그것은 불가능하다. 어떻게 허브가 당신의 몸 안으로 들어가 영리하게 당신의 문제를 ④ 해결할 수 있는지 상상해 보라. 만약 그렇게 해 본다면 당신은 그것이 얼마나 불가능하게 보이는지를 알게 될 것이다. 그렇지 않다면, 그것은 허브가 인간의 몸보다 ⑤ 덜(→더) 지적이라는 것을 의미할 텐데, 이는 정말로 믿기 어렵다.

Why? 왜 정답일까?

허브가 몸 안에서 어떻게 건강 문제를 해결해줄 수 있는지 상상해보면 얼마나 어려운지 깨닫게 될 것이라는 내용 뒤에는 허브가 인간의 몸보다 '더 똑똑하다' 생각은 믿기 어렵다는 결론이 이어져야 하므로, ⑤의 less를 more로 고쳐야 한다. 따라서 문맥상 낱말의 쓰임이 적절하지 않은 것은 ⑤이다.

- groundless ⓐ 근거가 없는
- eliminate ⓥ 제거하다, 없애다
- high ⓐ 도취감
- aggressive ⓐ 적극적인, 공격적인
- temporary ⓐ 일시적인
- whatever the case 어떤 경우이든지

구문 풀이

9행 Whatever the case, it is your body that has the intelligence to regain health, and not the herbs.
어느 경우이든 간에 "it is ~ that ··· : ···한 것은 바로 ~이다」

★★★ 등급을 가르는 문제!

31 우리의 판단력을 앗아가는 로봇   정답률 46% | 정답 ②

다음 빈칸에 들어갈 말로 가장 적절한 것을 고르시오. [3점]
① reliability – 신뢰성
✓ judgment – 판단력
③ endurance – 인내
④ sociability – 사교성
⑤ cooperation – 협력

We worry that the robots are taking our jobs, / but just as common a problem is / that the robots are taking our judgment.
우리는 로봇이 우리의 직업을 빼앗고 있다고 걱정하지만, / 그만큼 흔한 문제는 ~이다. / 로봇이 우리의 판단력을 빼앗고 있다는 것
In the large warehouses / so common behind the scenes of today's economy, / human 'pickers' hurry around / grabbing products off shelves / and moving them to where they can be packed and dispatched.
거대한 창고에서, / 오늘날의 경제 배후에 있는 아주 흔한 / 인간 '집게'는 서둘러서 / 선반에서 상품을 집어내고, / 그것들이 포장되고 발송될 수 있는 곳으로 이동시킨다.
In their ears are headpieces: / the voice of 'Jennifer', / a piece of software, / tells them where to go and what to do, / controlling the smallest details of their movements.
그들의 귀에는 헤드폰이 있는데, / 'Jennifer'의 목소리가 / 한 소프트웨어 프로그램인 / 이들에게 어디로 가고 무엇을 할지 말해준다. / 이들 움직임의 가장 작은 세부 사항들을 조종하면서
Jennifer breaks down instructions into tiny chunks, / to minimise error and maximise productivity / — for example, / rather than picking eighteen copies of a book off a shelf, / the human worker would be politely instructed to pick five.
Jennifer는 지시 사항을 아주 작은 덩어리로 쪼개는데, / 실수를 줄이고 생산성을 최대화하기 위해 / 가령 / 선반에서 책 18권을 집어내기보다는, / 인간 작업자는 5권을 집어내라고 정중하게 지시받을 것이다.
Then another five. // Then yet another five. // Then another three.
그다음 또 5권. // 그다음 또 5권. // 그다음 또 3권.
Working in such conditions / reduces people to machines / made of flesh.
그러한 조건에서 일하는 것은 / 사람을 기계로 격하시킨다. / 살로 만들어진
Rather than asking us to think or adapt, / the Jennifer unit takes over the thought process / and treats workers as an inexpensive source / of some visual processing and a pair of opposable thumbs.
우리에게 생각하거나 적응하라고 요구하기보다는, / Jennifer라는 장치는 사고 과정을 지배하고, / 작업자들을 값싼 자원으로 다룬다. / 약간의 시각적 처리 과정과 마주 볼 수 있는 엄지 한 쌍이 있는

우리는 로봇이 우리의 직업을 빼앗고 있다고 걱정하지만, 그만큼 흔한 문제는 로봇이 우리의 판단력을 빼앗고 있다는 것이다. 오늘날의 경제 배후에 있는 아주 흔한 거대한 창고에서, 인간 '집게'는 서둘러서 선반에서 상품을 집어내고, 그것들이 포장되고 발송될 수 있는 곳으로 이동시킨다. 그들의 귀에는 헤드폰이 있는데, 한 소프트웨어 프로그램인 'Jennifer'의 목소리가 이들 움직임의 가장 작은 세부 사항들을 조종하면서, 이들에게 어디로 가고 무엇을 할지 말해준다. Jennifer는 실수를 줄이고 생산성을 최대화하기 위해 지시 사항을 아주 작은 덩어리로 쪼개는데, 가령 인간 작업자는 선반에서 책 18권을 집어내기보다는, 5권을 집어내라고 정중하게 지시받을 것이다. 그다음 또 5권. 그다음 또 5권. 그다음 또 3권을 집으라는 지시를 받을 것이다. 그러한 조건에서 일하는 것은 사람을 살로 만들어진 기계로 격하시킨다. Jennifer라는 장치는 우리에게 생각하거나 적응하라고 요구하기보다는, 사고 과정을 지배하고, 작업자들을 약간의 시각적 처리 과정과 마주 볼 수 있는 엄지 한 쌍이 있는 값싼 자원으로 다룬다.

Why? 왜 정답일까?

창고 노동자들이 기계에게 아주 작은 행동까지 지시받으며 일한다(~ tells them where to go and what to do, controlling the smallest details of their movements.)는 예시를 통해, 인간이 기계로 격하되고 사고 과정을 박탈당하는 상황에 놓여 있음을 설명하는 글이다. 따라서 빈칸에 들어갈 말로 가장 적절한 것은 로봇에 지배당한 사고 과정(thought process)을 다르게 표현한 말인 ② '판단력' 이다.

- warehouse ⓝ 창고
- headpiece ⓝ 헤드폰, 머리에 쓰는 것, 지성, 판단력
- break down 쪼개다
- take over 지배하다, 장악하다
- endurance ⓝ 인내
- grab ⓥ 집어내다
- flesh ⓝ (사람, 동물의) 살
- opposable ⓐ 마주볼 수 있는

구문 풀이

12행 Working in such conditions reduces people to machines made of flesh.
동명사구 주어   동사(단수)   과거분사구

★★ 문제 해결 꿀~팁 ★★

▶ 많이 틀린 이유는?
로봇 때문에 인간의 신뢰성이나 사교성이 떨어진다는 내용은 아니므로 ①이나 ④로 답으로 적절하지 않다.

▶ 문제 해결 방법은?
예시의 결론을 정리하는 'Rather than asking us to think or adapt, the Jennifer unit takes over the thought process ~'가 핵심이다. 이 thought process와 통하는 단어를 골라야 한다.

32 자신의 발달 환경을 주도적으로 만드는 인간   정답률 53% | 정답 ⑤

다음 빈칸에 들어갈 말로 가장 적절한 것을 고르시오.
① mirrors of their generation – 자기 세대의 거울
② shields against social conflicts – 사회적 갈등을 막는 방패
③ explorers in their own career path – 자기 진로의 탐색가
④ followers of their childhood dreams – 어린 시절의 꿈을 좇는 사람
✓ manufacturers of their own development – 자신의 발달을 생산하는 사람

The prevailing view among developmental scientists / is / that people are active contributors to their own development.
발달 과학자들 사이에서 지배적인 견해는 / ~이다. / 사람들이 자신의 발달에 능동적인 기여자라는 것이다.
People are influenced by the physical and social contexts / in which they live, / but they also play a role / in influencing their development / by interacting with, and changing, those contexts.
사람들은 물리적 및 사회적 환경의 영향을 받지만, / 자신이 사는 / 그들은 또한 역할을 한다. / 그 환경들과 상호 작용하고 그것을 변화시켜 / 그 환경을 / 자신의 발달에 영향을 주는 데 있어
Even infants influence the world around them / and construct their own development / through their interactions.
심지어 유아도 자기 주변의 세상에 영향을 주고, / 자신의 발달을 구성한다. / 상호작용을 통해
Consider an infant / who smiles at each adult he sees; / he influences his world / because adults are likely to smile, / use "baby talk," / and play with him / in response.
유아를 생각해 보라. / 그가 바라보는 어른마다 미소 짓는 / 그는 자신의 세상에 영향을 준다. / 어른들은 미소 짓고, / '아기 말'을 사용하고, / 그와 함께 놀아줄 것이기 때문에 / 이에 반응하여
The infant brings adults into close contact, / making one-on-one interactions / and creating opportunities for learning.
그 유아는 어른들을 친밀한 연결로 끌어들여서, / 일대일 상호작용을 하고 / 학습의 기회를 만든다.
By engaging the world around them, / thinking, / being curious, / and interacting with people, objects, and the world around them, / individuals of all ages / are manufacturers of their own development.
주변 세상의 관심을 끌고, / 생각하고, / 호기심을 가지고, / 주변 사람, 사물, 세상과 상호작용함으로써, / 모든 연령대의 개인은 / '자신의 발달을 생산하는 사람'이다.

발달 과학자들 사이에서 지배적인 견해는 사람들이 자신의 발달에 능동적인 기여자라는 것이다. 사람들은 자신이 사는 물리적 및 사회적 환경의 영향을 받지만, 그들은 또한 그 환경들과 상호작용하고 그것을 변화시켜 자신의 발달에 영향을 주는 역할을 한다. 심지어 유아도 자기 주변의 세상에 영향을 주고, 상호작용을 통해 자신의 발달을 구성한다. 그가 바라보는 어른마다 미소 짓는 유아를 생각해 보라. 어른들은 이에 반응하여 미소 짓고, '아기 말'을 사용하고, 그와 함께 놀아줄 것이기 때문에 그는 자신의 세상에 영향을 준다. 그 유아는 어른들을 친밀한 연결로 끌어들여, 일대일 상호작용을 하고 학습의 기회를 만든다. 주변 세상의 관심을 끌고, 생각하고, 호기심을 가지고, 주변 사람, 사물, 세상과 상호작용함으로써, 모든 연령대의 개인은 '자신의 발달을 생산하는 사람'이다.

Why? 왜 정답일까?

주제문인 첫 문장에서 인간은 자신의 발달에 능동적으로 기여하는 주체(~ people are active contributors to their own development.)라고 언급하므로, 빈칸에 들어갈 말로 가장 적절한 것은 ⑤ '자신의 발달을 생산하는 사람'이다.

- prevailing ⓐ 지배적인, 만연한
- close ⓐ 친밀한
- conflict ⓝ 갈등
- developmental ⓐ 발달의
- baby talk 아기 말(말을 배우는 유아나 어린이에게 어른이 쓰는 말투)
- one-on-one ⓐ 일대일의

구문 풀이

7행 Consider an infant who smiles at each adult [he sees]; he influences his
명령문(~하라)   목적어   주격 관계대명사
world because adults are likely to smile, use "baby talk," and play with him in
~할 것이다 동사원형1   동사원형2   동사원형3
response. [ ]: 목적격 관계대명사절

33 신선함의 환경적 대가   정답률 48% | 정답 ①

다음 빈칸에 들어갈 말로 가장 적절한 것을 고르시오. [3점]
✓ have hidden environmental costs – 숨겨진 환경적인 대가를 지니고 있을
② worsen the global hunger problem – 세계 기아 문제를 악화시킬
③ bring about technological advances – 기술 진보를 가져올
④ improve nutrition and quality of food – 영양과 음식 질을 개선할
⑤ diversify the diet of a local community – 지역 사회의 식단을 다양화할

The demand for freshness / can have hidden environmental costs.
신선함에 대한 요구는 / 숨겨진 환경적인 대가를 지니고 있을 수 있다.
While freshness is now being used / as a term in food marketing / as part of a return to nature, / the demand for year-round supplies of fresh produce / such as soft fruit and exotic vegetables / has led to / the widespread use of hot houses in cold climates / and increasing reliance on total quality control / — management by temperature control, use of pesticides and computer/satellite-based logistics.
현재 신선함이 사용되고 있는 한편, / 식품 마케팅에서 하나의 용어로 / 자연으로 돌아가는 것의 일환으로 / 신선한 식품의 연중 공급에 대한 요구는 / 부드러운 과일이나 외국산 채소와 같은 / ~로 이어져 왔다. / 추운 기후에서의 광범위한 온실 사용과 / 총체적인 품질 관리에 대한 의존성의 증가로 / 즉 온도 조절에 의한 관리, 살충제 사용, 그리고 컴퓨터/위성 기반물류
The demand for freshness / has also contributed to concerns about food wastage.
신선함에 대한 요구는 / 또한 식량 낭비에 대한 우려의 원인이 되었다.
Use of 'best before', 'sell by' and 'eat by' labels / has legally allowed institutional waste.
'유통 기한', '판매 시한', '섭취 시한' 등의 라벨 사용은 / 제도적인 폐기물 생산을 법적으로 허용해 왔다.
Campaigners have exposed the scandal of over-production and waste.
운동가들은 과잉 생산이나 폐기물에 대한 추문을 폭로해 왔다.
Tristram Stuart, / one of the global band of anti-waste campaigners, / argues / that, with freshly made sandwiches, / over-ordering is standard practice across the retail sector / to avoid the appearance of empty shelf space, / leading to high volumes of waste / when supply regularly exceeds demand.
Tristram Stuart는 / 폐기물 반대 세계 연대 소속 운동가 중 한 명인 / 주장한다. / 신선하게 만들어진 샌드위치와 함께, / 초과 주문이 소매 산업 분야 전반에서 이루어지는 일반적인 행태이며, / 판매대가 비어 보이는 것을 막기 위한 / 이것은 엄청난 양의 폐기물로 이어진다고 / 공급이 정기적으로 수요를 초과하면

신선함에 대한 요구는 숨겨진 환경적인 대가를 지니고 있을 수 있다. 자연으로 돌아가는 것의 일환으로 현재 신선함이 식품 마케팅에서 하나의 용어로 사용되고 있는 한편, 부드러운 과일이나 외국산 채소와 같은 신선한 식품의 연중 공급에 대한 요구는 추운 기후에서의 광범위한 온실 사용과 총체적인 품질 관리— 온도 조절에 의한 관리, 살충제 사용, 그리고 컴퓨터/위성 기반 물류 — 에 대한 의존성의 증가로 이어져 왔다. 신선함에 대한 요구는 또한 식량 낭비에 대한 우려의 원인이 되었다. '유통 기한', '판매 시한', '섭취 시한' 등의 라벨 사용은 제도적인 폐기물 생산을 법적으로 허용해 왔다. (환경) 운동가들은 과잉 생산이나 폐기물에 대한 추문을 폭로해 왔다. 폐기물 반대 세계 연대 소속 운동가 중 한 명인 Tristram Stuart는 신선하게 만들어진 샌드위치와 함께, 판매대가 비어 보이는 것을 막기 위한 초과 주문이 소매 산업 분야 전반에서 이루어지는 일반적인 행태이며, 이것은 공급이 정기적으로 수요를 초과하면 엄청난 양의 폐기물로 이어진다고 주장한다.

Why? 왜 정답일까?
빈칸 뒤에서 '신선한' 식품 공급에 대한 요구가 커지면서 환경적 비용을 많이 야기하는 온실 또는 품질 관리 기법에 대한 의존성이 증가했으며, 폐기물 또한 더 많이 용인되는 사태가 일어났다고 한다. 따라서 빈칸에 들어갈 말로 가장 적절한 것은 ① '숨겨진 환경적인 대가를 지니고 있을'이다.

- year-round ⓐ 연중 계속되는
- reliance ⓝ 의존
- institutional ⓐ 제도적인, 기관의
- diversify ⓥ 다양화하다
- exotic ⓐ 외국의, 이국적인
- satellite ⓝ 위성
- bring about ~을 가져오다, 야기하다

구문 풀이

2행 While freshness is now being used as a term in food marketing as part of
       접속사(~인 한편)
a return to nature, the demand (for year-round supplies of fresh produce) (such
                    주어
as soft fruit and exotic vegetables) has led to the widespread use of hot houses
                                     동사(단수)
in cold climates and increasing reliance on total quality control — {management
by temperature control, use of pesticides and computer/satellite-based logistics}.
                                          { }: total quality control 보충 설명

---

34 두 가지 다른 정보를 동시에 처리할 수 없는 인간   정답률 51% | 정답 ⑤

다음 빈칸에 들어갈 말로 가장 적절한 것을 고르시오. [3점]
① decide what they should do in the moment – 그들이 그 순간 뭘 해야 하는지를 판단할
② remember a message with too many words – 너무 긴 메시지를 기억할
③ analyze which information was more accurate – 어떤 정보가 더 정확한지 분석할
④ speak their own ideas while listening to others – 다른 사람들의 말을 들으면서 자기 생각을 말할
✓ process two pieces of information at the same time – 두 개의 정보를 동시에 처리할

In the studies of Colin Cherry / at the Massachusetts Institute for Technology / back in the 1950s, / his participants listened to voices in one ear at a time / and then through both ears / in an effort to determine / whether we can listen to two people talk at the same time.
Colin Cherry의 연구에서, / 메사추세츠 공과대학 소속이었던 / 1950년대 / 참가자들은 한 번은 한쪽 귀로만 목소리를 듣고, / 그다음에는 양쪽 귀로 들었다. / 판단하기 위해 / 우리가 두 사람이 이야기하는 것을 동시에 들을 수 있는지
One ear always contained a message / that the listener had to repeat back / (called "shadowing") / while the other ear included people speaking.
한쪽 귀로는 메시지를 계속 들려주었고 / 듣는 사람이 다시 반복해야 하는 / ('새도잉'이라 불림) / 다른 한쪽 귀로는 사람들이 말하는 것을 들려주었다.
The trick was to see / if you could totally focus on the main message / and also hear someone talking in your other ear.
속임수는 알아보기 위한 것이었다. / 사람들이 주된 메시지에 완전히 집중하면서 / 다른 귀로는 다른 사람이 말하는 것 또한 들을 수 있는지를
Cleverly, / Cherry found / it was impossible / for his participants to know / whether the message in the other ear / was spoken by a man or woman, / in English or another language, / or was even comprised of real words at all!
영리하게도, / Cherry는 발견했다! / 불가능했다는 것을 / 참가자들이 알아차리는 것이 / 다른 한쪽 귀로 들리는 메시지가 / 남자가 말한 것인지 혹은 여자가 말한 것인지, / 영어인지 다른 외국어인지, / 심지어 실제 단어로 구성된 것인지조차 전혀
In other words, / people could not process two pieces of information at the same time.
다시 말해서, / 사람들은 두 개의 정보를 동시에 처리할 수 없었다.

1950년대 메사추세츠 공과대학 소속이었던 Colin Cherry의 연구에서, 우리가 두 사람이 이야기하는 것을 동시에 들을 수 있는지 판단하기 위해 참가자들은 한 번은 한쪽 귀로 목소리를 듣고, 그다음에는 양쪽 귀로 들었다. 한쪽 귀로는 듣는 사람이 다시 반복해야 하는('새도잉'이라 불림) 메시지를 계속 들려주었고 다른 한쪽 귀로는 사람들이 말하는 것을 들려주었

다. 속임수는 사람들이 주된 메시지에 완전히 집중하면서 다른 귀로는 다른 사람이 말하는 것 또한 들을 수 있는지를 알아보기 위한 것이었다. 영리하게도, Cherry는 참가자들이 다른 한쪽 귀로 들리는 메시지가 남자가 말한 것인지 혹은 여자가 말한 것인지, 영어인지 다른 외국어인지, 심지어 실제 단어로 구성된 것인지조차 전혀 알아차리지 못했다는 것을 발견했다! 다시 말해서, 사람들은 두 개의 정보를 동시에 처리할 수 없었다.

Why? 왜 정답일까?
실험 결과를 제시하는 '~ it was impossible for his participants to know whether the message in the other ear was spoken by a man or woman, in English or another language, or was even comprised of real words at all!'에서 사람들은 양쪽 귀에서 각기 다른 정보가 들어올 때 이를 동시에 처리하지 못하여, 화자가 남자였는지 여자였는지, 사용된 언어가 영어였는지 다른 언어였는지 등등을 제대로 판별하지 못했다고 한다. 따라서 빈칸에 들어갈 말로 가장 적절한 것은 ⑤ '두 개의 정보를 동시에 처리할'이다.

- at a time 한 번에
- contain ⓥ 수용하다, 담다
- shadowing ⓝ 섀도잉(남의 말을 듣는 동시에 따라서 하는 것)
- trick ⓝ 속임수, 요령
- accurate ⓐ 정확한
- in an effort to ~하기 위해서
- comprise ⓥ ~을 구성하다

구문 풀이

7행 The trick was to see if you could totally focus on the main message and
                            주격 보어(~것)   접속사(~인지 아닌지)
also hear someone talking in your other ear.
지각동사   목적어   목적격 보어

---

35 기술 진보로 가능해진 새로운 서비스 제공   정답률 49% | 정답 ④

다음 글에서 전체 흐름과 관계 없는 문장은?

The fast-paced evolution of Information and Communication Technologies (ICTs) / has radically transformed / the dynamics and business models of the tourism and hospitality industry.
정보와 의사소통 기술(ICTs)의 빠른 진화는 / 급격하게 변화시켰다. / 관광업과 서비스업의 역학과 비즈니스 모델을
① This leads to new levels/forms of competitiveness among service providers / and transforms the customer experience through new services.
이것은 서비스 제공자 간 새로운 수준/형식의 경쟁으로 이어지고, / 새로운 서비스를 통해 고객 경험을 변화시킨다.
② Creating unique experiences / and providing convenient services to customers / leads to satisfaction, and, eventually, / customer loyalty / to the service provider or brand (i.e., hotels).
독특한 경험을 만드는 것과 / 고객에게 편리한 서비스를 제공하는 것은 / 만족감을 낳고, / 종국에는 고객 충성도로 이어진다. / 서비스 제공자나 브랜드(즉, 호텔)에 대한
③ In particular, / the most recent *technological* boost / received by the tourism sector / is represented by mobile applications.
특히, / 가장 최근의 기술적 부상은 / 관광업 분야에서 받아들여진 / 모바일 애플리케이션으로 대표된다.
✓④ Increasing competitiveness among service providers / does not necessarily mean / promoting quality of customer services.
서비스 제공자 간의 경쟁을 증가시키는 것이 / 반드시 의미하지는 않는다. / 고객 서비스의 질을 증진시키는 것을
⑤ Indeed, / empowering tourists with mobile access to services / such as hotel reservations, airline ticketing, and recommendations for local attractions / generates strong interest and considerable profits.
사실, / 서비스에 대한 모바일 접근 권한을 관광객에게 주는 것은 / 호텔 예약, 항공권 발권, 그리고 지역 관광지 추천과 같은 / 강력한 흥미와 상당한 수익을 만들어 낸다.

정보와 의사소통 기술(ICTs)의 빠른 진화는 관광업과 서비스업의 역학과 비즈니스 모델을 급격하게 변화시켰다. ① 이것은 서비스 제공자 간 새로운 수준/형식의 경쟁으로 이어지고, 새로운 서비스를 통해 고객 경험을 변화시킨다. ② 독특한 경험을 만드는 것과 고객에게 편리한 서비스를 제공하는 것은 만족감을 낳고, 종국에는 서비스 제공자나 브랜드(즉, 호텔)에 대한 고객 충성도로 이어진다. ③ 특히, 관광업 분야에서 받아들여진 가장 최근의 기술적 부상은 모바일 애플리케이션으로 대표된다. ④ 서비스 제공자 간의 경쟁을 증가시키는 것이 반드시 고객 서비스의 질을 증진시키는 것을 의미하지는 않는다. ⑤ 사실, 관광객에게 호텔 예약, 항공권 발권, 그리고 지역 관광지 추천과 같은 서비스에 대한 모바일 접근 권한을 주는 것은 강력한 흥미와 상당한 수익을 만들어 낸다.

Why? 왜 정답일까?
빠른 기술적 진보로 소비자에게 새로운 경험과 서비스를 제공하는 것이 가능해졌고, 이것이 고객 만족도나 충성도, 수익 면에서 모두 좋은 결과를 이끌어낼 수 있다는 내용이다. ③과 ⑤는 특히 관광업의 모바일 애플리케이션을 예로 들고 있다. 한편 ④는 서비스 제공자 간 경쟁의 증가가 고객 서비스 질을 반드시 높이지는 않는다는 내용이어서 흐름상 무관하다. 따라서 전체 흐름과 관계 없는 문장은 ④이다.

- fast-paced ⓐ 빠른
- dynamics ⓝ 역학, 역동성
- loyalty ⓝ 충성도
- profit ⓝ 수익
- radically ⓐⓓ 급진적으로
- competitiveness ⓝ 경쟁력, 경쟁적인 것
- empower ⓥ 권한을 부여하다

구문 풀이

8행 In particular, the most recent technological boost received by the tourism
                    주어(최상급)   과거분사
sector is represented by mobile applications.
        동사(수동태)

---

36 식량 문제와 그 해결   정답률 64% | 정답 ②

주어진 글 다음에 이어질 글의 순서로 가장 적절한 것을 고르시오.
① (A) - (C) - (B)   ✓② (B) - (A) - (C)
③ (B) - (C) - (A)   ④ (C) - (A) - (B)
⑤ (C) - (B) - (A)

With nearly a billion hungry people in the world, / there is obviously no single cause.
전 세계에 거의 10억 명의 굶주리는 사람들이 있는데, / 분명 원인이 단 하나만 있는 것은 아니다.

(B) However, / far and away the biggest cause is poverty.
그렇지만, / 가장 큰 원인은 단연 빈곤이다.

Seventy-nine percent of the world's hungry / live in nations / that are net exporters of food.
세계의 굶주리는 사람들의 79퍼센트가 / 나라에 살고 있다. / 식량 순 수출국인

How can this be?
어떻게 이럴 수가 있을까?

(A) The reason people are hungry in those countries / is / that the products produced there / can be sold on the world market for more / than the local citizens can afford to pay for them.
그러한 국가에서 사람들이 굶주리는 이유는 / ~이다. / 그곳에서 생산된 산물들이 / 세계 시장에서 더 비싸게 팔릴 수 있기 때문이다. / 현지 시민들이 그것들에 지불할 수 있는 것보다

In the modern age / you do not starve because you have no food, / you starve because you have no money.
현대에는 / 여러분이 식량이 없어서 굶주리는 것이 아니라, / 여러분은 돈이 없어서 굶주리는 것이다.

(C) So the problem really is / that food is, in the grand scheme of things, too expensive / and many people are too poor to buy it.
그래서 진짜 문제는 ~이다. / 식량이 거대한 체계로 볼 때 너무 비싸고 / 많은 사람들은 너무 가난하여 그것을 구매할 수 없다는 것

The answer will be / in continuing the trend of lowering the cost of food.
해답은 있을 것이다. / 식량의 가격을 낮추는 추세를 지속하는 데

전 세계에 거의 10억 명의 굶주리는 사람들이 있는데, 분명 원인이 단 하나만 있는 것은 아니다.

(B) 그렇지만, 가장 큰 원인은 단연 빈곤이다. 세계의 굶주리는 사람들의 79퍼센트가 식량 순 수출국에 살고 있다. 어떻게 이럴 수가 있을까?

(A) 그러한 국가에서 사람들이 굶주리는 이유는 그곳에서 생산된 산물들이 현지 시민들이 그것들에 지불할 수 있는 것보다 더 비싸게 세계 시장에서 팔릴 수 있기 때문이다. 현대에는 여러분이 식량이 없어서 굶주리는 것이 아니라, 돈이 없어서 굶주리는 것이다.

(C) 그래서 진짜 문제는 거대한 체계로 볼 때 식량이 너무 비싸고 많은 사람들은 너무 가난하여 그것을 구매할 수 없다는 것이다. 해답은 식량의 가격을 낮추는 추세를 지속하는 데 있을 것이다.

Why? 왜 정답일까?

식량 문제의 원인이 다양함을 언급하는 주어진 글 뒤로, 빈곤이 가장 큰 원인임을 제시하는 (B), 빈곤한 국가의 굶주리는 사람들은 말 그대로 돈이 없어서 굶주린다는 설명을 이어 가는 (A), 해결책을 언급하며 글을 맺는 (C)가 차례로 이어져야 한다. 따라서 글의 순서로 가장 적절한 것은 ② 'B) - (A) - (C)'이다.

- billion ⑩ 10억
- afford to ~할 여유가 되다
- poverty ⑩ 가난, 빈곤
- obviously [ad] 분명히
- starve ⑰ 굶주리다

구문 풀이

3행 The reason (that) people are hungry in those countries is that the
〔주어〕〔생략〕〔동사(단수)〕〔접속사(~것)〕
products produced there can be sold on the world market for more than the local
〔조동사 수동태(조동사+be p.p.)〕
citizens can afford to pay for them.

★★★ 등급을 가르는 문제!

37 생산성이 최악인 시간에 오히려 더 발휘되는 창의성   정답률 44% | 정답 ⑤

주어진 글 다음에 이어질 글의 순서로 가장 적절한 것을 고르시오. [3점]
① (A) - (C) - (B)   ② (B) - (A) - (C)
③ (B) - (C) - (A)   ④ (C) - (A) - (B)
✓⑤ (C) - (B) - (A)

Most people have a perfect time of day / when they feel they are at their best, / whether in the morning, evening, or afternoon.
대부분의 사람들은 완벽한 시간을 갖는다. / 하루 중 그들이 최고의 상태에 있다고 느끼는 / 아침이든 저녁이든 혹은 오후든

(C) Some of us are night owls, / some early birds, / and others in between / may feel most active during the afternoon hours.
우리 중 몇몇은 저녁형 인간이고, / 몇몇은 아침형 인간이며, / 그 사이에 있는 누군가는 / 오후의 시간 동안 가장 활력을 느낄지도 모른다.

If you are able to organize your day / and divide your work, / make it a point / to deal with tasks that demand attention / at your best time of the day.
여러분이 하루를 계획할 수 있다면 / 그리고 업무를 분배할 / ~하기로 정하라. / 집중을 요구하는 과업을 처리하기로 / 하루 중 최적의 시간에

(B) However, / if the task you face demands creativity and novel ideas, / it's best to tackle it / at your "worst" time of day!
그러나, / 만약 여러분이 직면한 과업이 창의성과 새로운 아이디어를 요구한다면, / 처리하는 것이 최선이다! / 하루 중 '최악의' 시간에

So if you are an early bird, / make sure to attack your creative task in the evening, / and vice versa for night owls.
그래서 만약 여러분이 아침형 인간이라면 / 반드시 저녁에 창의적인 작업에 착수하고, / 저녁형 인간이라면 반대로 하라.

(A) When your mind and body / are less alert than at your "peak" hours, / the muse of creativity awakens / and is allowed to roam more freely.
여러분의 정신과 신체가 / '정점' 시간보다 주의력이 덜할 때, / 창의성의 영감이 깨어나 / 더 자유롭게 거니는 것이 허용된다.

In other words, / when your mental machinery is loose / rather than standing at attention, / the creativity flows.
다시 말해서, / 여러분의 정신 기제가 느슨하게 풀려있을 때 / 차렷 자세로 있을 때보다 / 창의성이 샘솟는다.

대부분의 사람들은 아침이든 저녁이든 혹은 오후든, 하루 중 그들이 최고의 상태에 있다고 느끼는 완벽한 시간을 갖는다.

(C) 우리 중 몇몇은 저녁형 인간이고, 몇몇은 아침형 인간이며, 그 사이에 있는 누군가는 오후의 시간 동안 가장 활력을 느낄지도 모른다. 여러분이 하루를 계획하고 업무를 분배할 수 있다면, 집중을 요구하는 과업을 하루 중 최적의 시간에 처리하기로 정하라.

(B) 그러나, 만약 여러분이 직면한 과업이 창의성과 새로운 아이디어를 요구한다면, 하루 중 '최악의' 시간에 처리하는 것이 최선이다! 그래서 만약 여러분이 아침형 인간이라면 반드시 저녁에 창의적인 작업에 착수하고, 저녁형 인간이라면 반대로 하라.

(A) 여러분의 정신과 신체가 '정점' 시간보다 주의력이 덜할 때, 창의성의 영감이 깨어나 더

자유롭게 거니는 것이 허용된다. 다시 말해서, 여러분의 정신 기제가 차렷 자세로 있을 때보다(힘과 긴장이 바짝 들어가 있을 때보다) 느슨하게 풀려있을 때 창의성이 샘솟는다.

Why? 왜 정답일까?

사람들에게는 자기 신체와 잘 맞는 시간이 있다고 언급하는 주어진 글 뒤로, 집중력이 필요한 과업은 최적의 시간대에 처리해야 한다는 (C), '반면에' 창의성이 필요한 과업은 최악의 시간대에 처리하는 것이 좋다는 (B), 그 이유를 보충 설명하는 (A)가 연결되어야 자연스럽다. 따라서 글의 순서로 가장 적절한 것은 ⑤ '(C) - (B) - (A)'이다.

- whether A or B A이든 B이든
- stand at attention 차렷 자세를 취하다
- tackle ⑰ 해결하다, 처리하다, 다루다
- vice versa 그 반대도 같다
- make it a point to ~하기로 정하다, 으레 ~하다
- loose ⓐ 느슨한
- novel ⓐ 새로운, 신기한
- early bird 아침형 인간
- night owl 저녁형 인간

구문 풀이

11행 Some of us are night owls, some (are) early birds, and others in between
〔주어1〕 〔주어2(여럿 중 일부)〕 〔생략(중복)〕 〔주어3(또 다른 일부)〕
may feel most active during the afternoon hours.

★★ 문제 해결 꿀~팁 ★★

▶ 많이 틀린 이유는?
(C) - (A)를 잘못 연결하기 쉽지만, (C)는 '정점' 시간에 수행할 과업(= 집중력이 필요한 일)을 언급하는 반면 (A)는 정점 시간이 '아닐' 때 수행할 과업(= 창의력이 필요한 일)을 언급한다. 즉 두 단락은 다루는 소재가 다르므로 적절한 흐름 전환의 연결어가 없으면 연결될 수 없다.
▶ 문제 해결 방법은?
하루 중 최적의 시간대가 개인마다 다르다는 주어진 글 뒤로, 누구는 아침이 좋고, 또 누구는 밤이 좋으니 각자 정점의 시간마다 집중력이 필요한 일을 처리하는 것이 좋다는 (C)가 먼저 연결된다. 즉 주어진 글과 (C)는 '일반적 내용 - 구체적 사례'의 흐름으로 자연스럽게 연결된다. 이어서 (A), (B)는 모두 (C)와는 달리 '창의력 과업을 수행하기 좋은 시간대'에 관한 내용인데, 이렇듯 흐름이나 소재가 달라질 때는 역접어가 있는 단락을 먼저 연결해야 한다. 따라서 (B) - (A)의 순서가 적합하다.

★★★ 등급을 가르는 문제!

38 사회적 활동 시간을 줄이는 텔레비전   정답률 47% | 정답 ④

글의 흐름으로 보아, 주어진 문장이 들어가기에 가장 적절한 곳을 고르시오.

Television is the number one leisure activity / in the United States and Europe, / consuming more than half of our free time.
텔레비전은 제1의 여가활동으로, / 미국과 유럽에서 / 우리의 자유 시간 중 절반 이상을 소비한다.

① We generally think of television / as a way to relax, tune out, and escape from our troubles / for a bit each day.
일반적으로 우리는 텔레비전을 취급한다. / 휴식하고, 관심을 끄고, 우리의 문제로부터 탈출하는 한 가지 방법으로서 / 매일 잠시나마

② While this is true, / there is increasing evidence / that we are more motivated / to tune in to our favorite shows and characters / when we are feeling lonely / or have a greater need for social connection.
이것이 사실이긴 하지만, / 증거가 늘어나고 있다. / 우리가 동기가 더 부여된다는 / 우리가 좋아하는 쇼들과 등장인물들을 보려는 / 우리가 외롭다고 느끼고 있거나 / 사회적 관계를 위한 더 큰 욕구를 가질 때

③ Television watching does satisfy these social needs / to some extent, / at least in the short run.
텔레비전을 보는 것이 이러한 사회적인 욕구를 정말로 만족시킨다. / 어느 정도까지는 / 적어도 단기적으로는

✓Unfortunately, / it is also likely to "crowd out" other activities / that produce more sustainable social contributions to our social well-being.
불행히도, / 그것은 또한 다른 활동들을 '몰아내기' 쉽다. / 우리의 사회적 행복에 더 지속적인 사회적 기여를 만들어 내는

The more television we watch, / the less likely we are / to volunteer our time / or to spend time with people / in our social networks.
텔레비전을 더 많이 볼수록, / 우리는 가능성이 더 적다. / 우리의 시간을 기꺼이 할애하거나 / 사람들과 함께 시간을 보낼 / 사회적 관계망 속에서

⑤ In other words, / the more time we make for *Friends*, / the less time we have for friends in real life.
다시 말해, / 우리가 *Friends*를 위해 더 많은 시간을 낼수록, / 우리는 실제 친구들을 위한 시간은 덜 갖게 된다.

텔레비전은 미국과 유럽에서 제1의 여가활동으로, 우리의 자유시간 중 절반 이상을 소비한다. ① 일반적으로 우리는 휴식하고, 관심을 끄고, 매일 잠시나마 우리의 문제로부터 탈출하는 한 가지 방법으로서 텔레비전을 취급한다. ② 이것이 사실이긴 하지만, 우리가 외롭다고 느끼고 있거나 사회적 관계를 위한 더 큰 욕구를 가질 때 우리가 좋아하는 쇼들과 등장인물들을 보려는 동기가 더 부여된다는 증거가 늘어나고 있다. ③ 적어도 단기적으로는, 텔레비전을 보는 것이 이러한 사회적인 욕구를 어느 정도까지는 정말로 만족시킨다. ④ 불행히도, 그것은 또한 우리의 사회적 행복에 더 지속적인 사회적 기여를 만들어 내는 다른 활동들을 '몰아내기' 쉽다. 텔레비전을 더 많이 볼수록, 우리는 사회적 관계망 속에서 우리의 시간을 기꺼이 할애하거나 사람들과 함께 시간을 보낼 가능성이 더 적다. ⑤ 다시 말해서, 우리가 *Friends*를 위해 더 많은 시간을 낼수록, 실제 친구들을 위한 시간은 덜 갖게 된다.

Why? 왜 정답일까?

주어진 문장에 역접어인 Unfortunately가 있으므로, 글의 흐름이 갑자기 반전되는 지점에 주어진 문장이 들어갈 것이다. ④ 앞에서 텔레비전은 어느 정도 사회적 욕구 충족에 도움이 된다고 하는데, ④ 뒤에서는 갑자기 텔레비전을 볼수록 사회적 활동 시간이 줄어든다고 한다. 즉 ④ 앞뒤로 글의 논리적 흐름이 단절되는 것으로 보아, 주어진 문장이 들어가기에 가장 적절한 곳은 ④이다.

- crowd out 몰아내다
- leisure ⑩ 여가, 레저
- tune in to ~에 채널을 맞추다
- sustainable ⓐ 지속 가능한
- tune out 주의를 돌리다, 관심을 끄다
- in the short run 단기적으로

구문 풀이

5행 We generally think of television as a way to relax, tune out, and escape
〔「think of + A + as + B : A를 B로 여기다」〕 〔형용사적 용법(a way 수식)〕
from our troubles for a bit each day.

★★★ 등급을 가르는 문제! ★★★

39 정확한 온도 측정   정답률 42% | 정답 ⑤

글의 흐름으로 보아, 주어진 문장이 들어가기에 가장 적절한 곳을 고르시오. [3점]

We often associate the concept of temperature / with how hot or cold an object feels / when we touch it.
우리는 흔히 온도 개념을 연관 짓는다. / 얼마나 뜨겁게 또는 차갑게 느껴지는지와 / 우리가 물건을 만졌을 때

In this way, / our senses provide us / with a qualitative indication of temperature.
이런 식으로, / 우리의 감각은 우리에게 제공한다. / 온도의 정성적 지표를

① Our senses, / however, / are unreliable / and often mislead us.
우리의 감각은, / 그러나, / 신뢰할 수 없으며 / 종종 우리를 잘못 인도한다.

② For example, / if you stand in bare feet / with one foot on carpet / and the other on a tile floor, / the tile feels colder than the carpet *even though both are at the same temperature.*
예를 들어, / 여러분이 맨발로 / 한쪽 발은 카펫 위에, / 다른 한쪽 발은 타일 바닥 위에 놓고 / 서 있다면, / 카펫보다 타일이 더 차갑게 느껴질 것이다. / 둘 다 같은 온도임에도 불구하고

③ The two objects feel different / because tile transfers energy by heat / at a higher rate than carpet does.
그 두 물체는 다르게 느껴진다. / 타일이 에너지를 열의 형태로 전달하기 때문에 / 카펫보다 더 높은 비율로

④ Your skin "measures" the rate of energy transfer by heat / rather than the actual temperature.
여러분의 피부는 열에너지 전도율을 '측정한다'. / 실제 온도보다는

✓ What we need / is a reliable and reproducible method / for measuring the relative hotness or coldness of objects / rather than the rate of energy transfer.
우리가 필요로 하는 것은 / 신뢰할 수 있고 재현 가능한 수단이다. / 물체의 상대적인 뜨거움과 차가움을 측정하기 위한 / 에너지 전도율보다는

Scientists have developed a variety of thermometers / for making such quantitative measurements.
과학자들은 다양한 온도계를 개발해 왔다. / 그런 정량적인 측정을 하기 위해

우리는 흔히 물건을 만졌을 때 얼마나 뜨겁게 또는 차갑게 느껴지는지를 온도 개념과 연관 짓는다. 이런 식으로, 우리의 감각은 우리에게 온도의 정성적 지표를 제공한다. ① 그러나, 우리의 감각은 신뢰할 수 없으며 종종 우리를 잘못 인도한다. ② 예를 들어, 여러분이 맨발로 한쪽 발은 카펫 위에, 다른 한쪽 발은 타일 바닥 위에 놓고 서 있다면, 둘 다 같은 온도임에도 불구하고 카펫보다 타일이 더 차갑게 느껴질 것이다. ③ 타일이 카펫보다 더 높은 비율로 에너지를 열의 형태로 전달하기 때문에 그 두 물체는 다르게 느껴진다. ④ 여러분의 피부는 실제 온도보다는 열에너지 전도율을 '측정한다'. ⑤ 우리가 필요로 하는 것은 에너지 전도율보다는 물체의 상대적인 뜨거움과 차가움을 측정하기 위한 신뢰할 수 있고 재현 가능한 수단이다. 과학자들은 그런 정량적인 측정을 하기 위해 다양한 온도계를 개발해 왔다.

Why? 왜 정답일까?

우리의 감각은 온도에 대한 정성적 지표를 제공하기는 하지만 완전히 정확한 정보를 주지는 못한다는 내용의 글로, ⑤ 앞의 문장은 이것이 피부가 실제 온도보다는 열에너지 전도율을 측정하기 때문이라고 설명한다. 한편 주어진 문장에서는 이 상황에서 우리에게 필요한 것이 상대적 온도를 신뢰도 높게 측정할 수 있는 도구라고 언급하고, ⑤ 뒤에서는 이 도구가 바로 정량적 측정이 가능한 온도계라고 밝힌다. 따라서 주어진 문장이 들어가기에 가장 적절한 곳은 ⑤이다.

- reproducible ⓐ 재현 가능한
- qualitative ⓐ 정성적인, 질적인
- bare ⓐ 맨, 벌거벗은
- energy transfer 에너지 전도
- mislead ⓥ 잘못 이끌다
- quantitative ⓐ 정량적인

구문 풀이

[10행] The two objects feel different because tile transfers energy by heat at a
　　　　　　　감각동사 ↑ 형용사 보어
higher rate than carpet does.
　　　　　　　　대동사(= transfers)

★★★ 등급을 가르는 문제! ★★★

40 기부하도록 설득하기   정답률 43% | 정답 ①

다음 글의 내용을 한 문장으로 요약하고자 한다. 빈칸 (A), (B)에 들어갈 말로 가장 적절한 것은?

	(A)	(B)
✓①	simultaneously 동시에	convinced 설득될
②	separately 따로	confused 혼란을 느낄
③	frequently 자주	annoyed 짜증을 낼
④	separately 따로	satisfied 만족할
⑤	simultaneously 동시에	offended 기분 상할

My colleagues and I ran an experiment / testing two different messages / meant to convince thousands of resistant alumni to make a donation.
내 동료들과 나는 한 연구를 진행했다. / 두 개의 다른 메시지들을 실험하는 / 저항하는 졸업생 수천 명에게 기부하도록 설득할 의도로 작성된

One message emphasized the opportunity to do good: / donating would benefit students, faculty, and staff.
하나의 메시지는 좋은 일을 할 기회를 강조했다. / '기부하는 것은 학생들, 교직원, 그리고 직원들에게 이익을 줄 것이다.'

The other emphasized the opportunity to feel good: / donors would enjoy the warm glow of giving.
다른 하나는 좋은 기분을 느끼는 기회를 강조했다. / '기부자들은 기부의 따뜻한 온기를 즐길 것이다.'

The two messages were equally effective: / in both cases, / 6.5 percent of the unwilling alumni ended up donating.
두 메시지들은 똑같이 효과적이었다. / 두 경우 모두에서, / 마음 내키지 않아했던 졸업생 6.5%가 결국에는 기부했다.

Then we combined them, / because two reasons are better than one. // Except they weren't.
그리고 나서 우리는 그것들을 결합했는데, / 두 개 이유가 한 개보다 더 낫기 때문이었다. // 안 그럴 경우를 제외한다면 말이다.

When we put the two reasons together, / the giving rate dropped below 3 percent.
우리가 두 이유를 합쳤을 때, / 기부율은 3% 아래로 떨어졌다.

Each reason alone / was more than twice as effective / as the two combined.
각각의 이유를 따로 봤을 때 / 두 배 이상 효과적이었다. / 둘을 합친 것보다

The audience was already skeptical.
청중은 이미 회의적이었다.

When we gave them different kinds of reasons to donate, / we triggered their awareness / that someone was trying to persuade them / — and they shielded themselves against it.
우리가 그들에게 기부할 다양한 이유를 주었을 때, / 우리는 그들이 인식하게 했고 / 누군가가 그들을 설득하려고 하는 중이라고 / 그리고 그들은 그것에 맞서 스스로를 보호했다.

→ In the experiment mentioned above, / when the two different reasons to donate / were given (A) simultaneously, / the audience was less likely to be (B) convinced / because they could recognize the intention / to persuade them.
위에 언급한 실험에서, / 기부할 이유 두 가지가 / (A) 동시에 주어졌을 때, / 청중은 설득될 가능성이 더 적었는데, / 그들이 의도를 인식했기 때문이었다. / 그들을 설득하려는

내 동료들과 나는 (기부에) 저항하는 졸업생 수천 명이 기부하도록 설득할 의도로 작성된 두 개의 다른 메시지들을 실험하는 한 연구를 진행했다. 하나의 메시지는 좋은 일을 할 기회를 강조했다. '기부하는 것은 학생들, 교직원, 그리고 직원들에게 이익을 줄 것이다.' 다른 하나는 좋은 기분을 느끼는 기회를 강조했다. '기부자들은 기부의 따뜻한 온기를 즐길 것이다.' 두 메시지들은 똑같이 효과적이었다. 두 경우 모두에서, 마음 내키지 않아했던 졸업생 6.5%가 결국에는 기부했다. 그리고 나서 우리는 그것들을 결합했는데, 두 개 이유가 한 개보다 더 낫기 때문이었다. 안 그럴 경우를 제외한다면 말이다. 우리가 두 이유를 합쳤을 때, 기부율은 3% 아래로 떨어졌다. 각각의 이유를 따로 봤을 때 둘을 합친 것보다 두 배 이상 효과적이었다. 청중은 이미 회의적이었다. 우리가 그들에게 기부해야 할 다양한 이유를 주었을 때, 우리는 그들이 누군가가 그들을 설득하려고 하는 중이라고 인식하게 했고 — 그리고 그들은 그것에 맞서 스스로를 보호했다.

→ 위에 언급된 실험에서, 기부할 이유 두 가지가 (A) 동시에 주어졌을 때, 청중들은 (B) 설득될 가능성이 더 적었는데, 그들을 설득하려는 의도를 인식했기 때문이었다.

Why? 왜 정답일까?

실험 결과를 제시하는 마지막 문장에서, 기부해야 할 여러 이유를 한꺼번에 주면 청중들은 이미 기부해달라고 설득하려는 화자의 의도를 알아차리기 때문에 더 방어적이 된다고 한다. 따라서 요약문의 빈칸 (A), (B)에 들어갈 말로 가장 적절한 것은 ① '(A) simultaneously(동시에), (B) convinced(설득될)'이다.

- make a donation 기부하다
- faculty ⓝ 교직원
- end up ~ing 결국 ~하다
- trigger ⓥ 유발하다
- benefit ⓥ ~에게 이득이 되다
- glow ⓝ 빛, (기쁨이나 만족감을 동반한) 감정
- put together 합치다
- simultaneously ⓐd 동시에

구문 풀이

[11행] Each reason alone was more than twice as effective as the two combined.
「배수사＋as＋원급＋as : 몇 배 더 ~한」

41-42 곤충 섭취에 대한 태도 바꾸기

In a society / that rejects the consumption of insects / there are some individuals / who overcome this rejection, / but most will continue with this attitude.
곤충 섭취를 거부하는 / 몇몇 개인들이 있지만, / 이러한 거부를 극복하는 / 대부분은 이러한 태도를 지속할 것이다.

It may be very (a) difficult / to convince an entire society / that insects are totally suitable for consumption.
매우 어려울지도 모른다. / 전체 사회를 납득시키기는 / 곤충이 섭취에 완전히 적합하다는 것을

However, / there are examples / in which this (b) reversal of attitudes about certain foods / has happened to an entire society.

Several examples in the past 120 years from European-American society / are: / considering lobster a luxury food / instead of a food for servants and prisoners; / considering sushi a safe and delicious food; / and considering pizza / not just a food for the rural poor of Sicily.
지난 120년 간 유럽–아메리카 사회로부터의 몇몇 사례는 / ~이다. / 로브스터를 고급진 음식으로 여기는 것, / 하인과 죄수용 음식 대신에 / 초밥을 안전하고 맛있는 음식으로 여기는 것, / 그리고 피자를 여기는 것이다. / 단지 시칠리아 시골의 가난한 사람들이 먹는 음식이 아니라고

In Latin American countries, / where insects are already consumed, / a portion of the population hates their consumption / and (c) associates it with poverty.
라틴 아메리카 국가들에서는 / 곤충이 이미 섭취되는 / 일부 인구는 곤충 섭취를 싫어하며, / 이를 빈곤과 연관 짓는다.

There are also examples of people / who have had the habit of consuming them / and (d) abandoned that habit due to shame, / and 『because they do not want to be categorized / as poor or uncivilized.』 42번의 근거
또한 사람들의 사례도 있다. / 그것을 섭취하는 습관이 있었으나 / 수치심 때문에 그 습관을 버린 / 그리고 분류되고 싶지 않아서 / 가난하거나 미개하다고

『According to Esther Katz, an anthropologist, / if the consumption of insects as a food luxury / is to be promoted, / there would be more chances / that some individuals who do not present this habit / overcome ideas / under which they were educated.
인류학자인 Esther Katz에 따르면, / 만약 호사스러운 음식으로써의 곤충 섭취가 / 장려된다면, / 가능성이 더 커질 것이다. / 이러한 습관을 보이지 않는 몇몇 개인들이 / 생각을 극복할 / 자신이 교육받았던

And this could also help / to (e) revalue the consumption of insects / by those people who already eat them.』 41번의 근거
그리고 이것은 또한 도움을 줄 수 있다. / 곤충 섭취를 재평가하는 데에도 / 이미 곤충을 먹고 있는 사람들에 의한

곤충 섭취를 거부하는 사회에서는 이러한 거부를 극복한 몇몇 개인들이 있지만, 대부분은 이러한 태도를 지속할 것이다. 곤충이 섭취에 완전히 적합하다는 것을 전체 사회에 납득시키기는 매우 (a) 어려울지도 모른다. 하지만, 특정 음식에 대한 이러한 태도의 (b) 역전이 전체 사회에 발생한 사례들이 있다. 지난 120년 간 유럽–아메리카 사회로부터의 몇몇 사례는 로브스터를 하인과 죄수용 음식 대신에 고급진 음식으로 여기는 것, 초밥을 안전하고 맛있는 음식으로 여기는 것, 그리고 피자를 단지 시칠리아 시골의 가난한 사람들이 먹는 음식으로 여기지 않는 것이다. 곤충이 이미 섭취되는 라틴 아메리카 국가들에서는 일부 인구는 곤충 섭취를 싫어하며, 이를 빈곤과 (c) 연관 짓는다. 또한 그것을 섭취하는 습관이 있었으나 수치심 때문에 가난하거나 미개하거나 분류되고 싶지 않아서 그 습관을 (d) 권장한(→ 버린) 사람들의 사례도 있다. 인류학자인 Esther Katz에 따르면, 만약 호사스러운 음식으로써의 곤충 섭취가 장려된다면, 이러한 습관을 보이지 않는 몇몇 개인들이 자신이 교육받았던 생각을 극복할 가능성이 더 커질 것이다. 그리고 이것은 또한 이미 곤충을 먹고 있는 사람들에 의한 곤충 섭취를 (e) 재평가하는 데에도 도움을 줄 수 있다.

- consumption ⓝ 섭취, 소비
- convince ⓥ 납득시키다, 설득하다
- prisoner ⓝ 죄수
- associate A with B A와 B를 연관 짓다
- categorize A as B A를 B라고 분류하다
- promote ⓥ 장려하다, 촉진하다, 홍보하다
- shortage ⓝ 부족
- overcome ⓥ 극복하다
- suitable for ~에 적합한
- rural ⓐ 시골의
- shame ⓝ 수치심
- anthropologist ⓝ 인류학자
- edible ⓐ 먹을 수 있는

구문 풀이

17행 According to Esther Katz, an anthropologist, if the consumption of
〔동격(= Esther Katz)〕
insects as a food luxury is to be promoted, there would be more chances [that
〔be to 용법(~하려면)〕
some individuals who do not present this habit overcome ideas under which they
were educated]. [ ] : chances 동격

41 제목 파악 　　　　　　　　　　　정답률 56% | 정답 ②

윗글의 제목으로 가장 적절한 것은?
① The More Variety on the Table, The Healthier You Become
식탁에 놓인 음식 종류가 다양할수록, 더 건강해진다
✓② Edible or Not? Change Your Perspectives on Insects
먹을 수 있는가, 없는가? 곤충에 대한 당신의 관점을 바꾸라
③ Insects: A Key to Solve the World Food Shortage
곤충: 세계 식량 부족을 해결하는 열쇠
④ Don't Let Uniqueness in Food Culture Disappear
식문화의 고유성이 사라지게 내버려두지 말라
⑤ Experiencing Various Cultures by Food
음식으로 다양한 문화 경험하기

Why? 왜 정답일까?

곤충 섭취에 대한 부정적 태도가 바뀐 사례나, 반대로 부정적 인식 때문에 곤충 섭취 습관을 포기했던 사례를 언급한 후, 이 부정적 태도를 전환할 방법을 제시하는 글이다. 따라서 글의 제목으로 가장 적절한 것은 ② '먹을 수 있는가, 없는가? 곤충에 대한 당신의 관점을 바꾸라'이다.

42 어휘 추론 　　　　　　　　　　　정답률 56% | 정답 ④

밑줄 친 (a)~(e) 중에서 문맥상 낱말의 쓰임이 적절하지 않은 것은?
① (a)　　② (b)　　③ (c)　　✓④ (d)　　⑤ (e)

Why? 왜 정답일까?

(d) 뒤의 '~ due to shame, and because they do not want to be categorized as poor or uncivilized.'는 곤충을 섭취하던 사람들이 수치감이나, 가난 또는 미개한 사람들로 분류되고 싶지 않은 마음 때문에 이 습관을 '포기했음'을 설명하는 것이므로, (d)의 encouraged를 abandoned로 고쳐야 한다. 따라서 문맥상 낱말의 쓰임이 적절하지 않은 것은 ④ '(d)'이다.

43-45 손자에게 최고의 학교를 찾아주려 한 할아버지

(A)
A boy had a place at the best school in town.
한 소년이 마을에 있는 가장 좋은 학교에 한 자리를 얻었다.

In the morning, / his granddad took him to the school.
아침에 / 그의 할아버지는 그를 학교에 데리고 갔다.

When (a) he went onto the playground with his grandson, / the children surrounded them.
그가 손자와 함께 운동장으로 들어갔을 때, / 아이들이 그들을 둘러쌌다.

"What a funny old man," / one boy smirked.
"진짜 우스꽝스러운 할아버지다."라며 / 한 소년이 히죽히죽 웃었다.

『A girl with brown hair / pointed at the pair / and jumped up and down.』 45번① 근거 일치
갈색 머리 소녀가 / 그 둘에게 손가락질하며 / 위아래로 뛰었다.

Suddenly, / the bell rang / and the children ran off to their first lesson.
갑자기 / 종이 울렸고, / 아이들이 첫 수업에 급히 뛰어갔다.

(D)
The old man took his grandson firmly by the hand, / and led him out of the school gate.
노인은 손자의 손을 꽉 잡고, / 그를 교문 밖으로 데리고 나갔다.

『"Brilliant, I don't have to go to school!" / the boy exclaimed.』 45번⑤ 근거 일치
"굉장한걸, 나 학교에 가지 않아도 되네!"라고 / 소년이 소리쳤다.

"You do, but not this one," / his granddad replied. / "I'll find you a school myself."
"가긴 가야지, 그렇지만 이 학교는 아니야."라고 / 할아버지가 대답했다. / "내가 직접 네게 학교를 찾아주마."

Granddad took his grandson back to his own house, / asked grandma to look after him, / and went off to look for a teacher (e) himself.
할아버지는 손자를 집으로 데리고 돌아가 / 할머니에게 그를 돌봐달라고 하고 나서, / 자신이 선생님을 찾아 나섰다.

Every time he spotted a school, / the old man went onto the playground, / and waited for the children to come out at break time.
그가 학교를 발견할 때마다, / 노인은 운동장으로 들어가서 / 아이들이 쉬는 시간에 나오기를 기다렸다.

(B)
In some schools / the children completely ignored the old man / and in others, / they made fun of (b) him.
몇몇 학교에서는 / 아이들이 노인을 완전히 무시했고, / 다른 학교들에서는 / 아이들이 그를 놀렸다.

When this happened, / he would turn sadly and go home.
이런 일이 일어났을 때, / 그는 슬프게 돌아서서 집으로 가곤 했다.

『Finally, / he went onto the tiny playground of a very small school, / and leant against the fence, / exhausted.』 45번② 근거 일치
마침내, / 그는 매우 작은 학교의 아주 작은 운동장으로 들어섰고, / 울타리에 기댔다. / 지쳐서

The bell rang, / and the crowd of children ran out onto the playground.
종이 울렸고, / 아이들 무리가 운동장으로 달려 나왔다.

"Sir, are you all right? / Shall I bring you a glass of water?" / a voice said.
"할아버지, 괜찮으세요? / 물 한 잔 가져다드릴까요?" / 누군가가 말했다.

"We've got a bench in the playground / — come and sit down," / another voice said.
"우리 운동장에 벤치가 있어요, / 오셔서 앉으세요." / 또 다른 누군가가 말했다.

Soon a young teacher came out onto the playground.
곧 한 젊은 선생님이 운동장으로 나왔다.

(C)
The old man greeted (c) him and said: / "Finally, I've found my grandson the best school in town."
노인은 그에게 인사하면서 이렇게 말했다. / "마침내, 제가 손자에게 마을 최고의 학교를 찾아주었네요."

"You're mistaken, sir. / Our school is not the best / — it's small and cramped."
"잘못 아신 겁니다, 어르신. / 우리 학교는 최고가 아니에요. / 작고 비좁은걸요."

『The old man didn't argue with the teacher.』 45번③ 근거 불일치
노인은 선생님과 논쟁을 벌이지 않았다.

Instead, / he made arrangements / for his grandson to join the school, / and then the old man left.
대신, / 노인은 준비해주고, / 손자가 그 학교에 다닐 수 있도록 / 그런 다음에 그 노인은 떠났다.

That evening, / the boy's mom said to (d) him: / "Dad, you can't even read." / How do you know / you've found the best teacher of all?" 45번④ 근거 일치
그날 저녁, / 소년의 어머니는 그에게 말했다. / "아버지, 글을 읽을 줄도 모르시잖아요. / 아버지는 어떻게 아세요? / 최고의 선생님을 찾았다는 것을"

"Judge a teacher by his pupils," / the old man replied.
"선생님은 그 제자를 보고 판단해야 해."라고 / 노인이 대답했다.

(A)
한 소년이 마을에 있는 가장 좋은 학교에 한 자리를 얻었다. 아침에 그의 할아버지는 그를 학교에 데리고 갔다. (a) 그가 손자와 함께 운동장으로 들어갔을 때, 아이들이 그들을 둘러쌌다. "진짜 우스꽝스러운 할아버지다."라며 한 소년이 히죽히죽 웃었다. 갈색 머리 소녀가 그 둘에게 손가락질하며 위아래로 뛰었다. 갑자기 종이 울렸고, 아이들이 첫 수업에 급히 뛰어갔다.

(D)
노인은 손자의 손을 꽉 잡고, 그를 교문 밖으로 데리고 나갔다. "굉장한걸, 나 학교에 가지 않아도 되네!"라고 소년이 소리쳤다. "가긴 가야지, 그렇지만 이 학교는 아니야."라고 할아버지가 대답했다. "내가 직접 네게 학교를 찾아주마." 할아버지는 손자를 집으로 데리고 돌아가 할머니에게 그를 돌봐달라고 하고 나서, (e) 자신이 선생님을 찾아 나섰다. 학교를 발견할 때마다, 노인은 운동장으로 들어가서 아이들이 쉬는 시간에 나오기를 기다렸다.

(B)
몇몇 학교에서는 아이들이 노인을 완전히 무시했고, 다른 학교들에서는 아이들이 (b) 그를 놀렸다. 이런 일이 일어났을 때, 그는 슬프게 돌아서서 집으로 가곤 했다. 마침내, 그는 매우 작은 한 학교의 아주 작은 운동장으로 들어섰고, 지쳐서 울타리에 기댔다. 종이 울렸고, 아이들 무리가 운동장으로 달려 나왔다. "할아버지, 괜찮으세요? 물 한 잔 가져다드릴까요?" 누군가가 말했다. "우리 운동장에 벤치가 있어요, 오셔서 앉으세요." 또 다른 누군가가 말했다. 곧 한 젊은 선생님이 운동장으로 나왔다.

(C)
노인은 (c) 그에게 인사하면서 이렇게 말했다. "마침내, 제가 손자에게 마을 최고의 학교를 찾아주었네요." "잘못 아신 겁니다, 어르신. 우리 학교는 최고가 아니에요. 작고 비좁은걸요." 노인은 선생님과 논쟁을 벌이지 않았다. 대신, 노인은 손자가 그 학교에 다닐 수 있도록 준비해주고, 그런 다음에 떠났다. 그날 저녁, 소년의 어머니는 (d) 그에게 말했다. "아버지, 글을 읽을 줄도 모르시잖아요. 최고의 선생님을 찾았다는 것을 어떻게 아세요?" "선생님은 그 제자를 보고 판단해야 해."라고 노인이 대답했다.

- grandson ⓝ 손자
- run off to ~로 뛰어가다, 달아나다
- make fun of ~을 조롱하다
- surround ⓥ 둘러싸다, 에워싸다
- ignore ⓥ 무시하다
- tiny ⓐ 아주 작은

- lean against ~에 기대다
- You are mistaken. 잘못 생각하고 계세요. 오해예요.
- make arrangements for ~을 준비하다
- firmly [ad] 단단히, 꽉
- look after ~을 돌보다
- exhausted ⓐ 지친, 소진된
- pupil ⓝ 학생, 제자
- exclaim ⓥ 소리치다, 외치다
- spot ⓥ 찾다, 발견하다

구문 풀이

(D) 2행 "Brilliant, I don't have to go to school!" the boy exclaimed. "You do, but
대동사(= go to school)
not this one," his granddad replied. "I'll find you a school myself."
대명사(= school)   강조 용법(주어 I 강조)

---

43 글의 순서 파악   정답률 69% | 정답 ④

주어진 글 (A)에 이어질 내용을 순서에 맞게 배열한 것으로 가장 적절한 것은?

① (B) – (D) – (C)
② (C) – (B) – (D)
③ (C) – (D) – (B)
④ (D) – (B) – (C) ✔
⑤ (D) – (C) – (B)

Why? 왜 정답일까?

한 할아버지가 손자를 데리고 마을 최고의 학교로 갔다가 아이들에게 놀림을 받았다는 내용의 (A) 뒤에는, 할아버지가 손자를 집에 데려다 놓고 직접 다른 학교를 찾아나섰다는 내용의 (D), 할아버지가 어느 예의 바른 아이들 무리와 선생님을 만나게 되었다는 내용의 (B), 할아버지가 학교를 결정했고, 그 결정이 어떻게 내려진 것인지 결론 짓는 내용의 (C)가 차례로 연결되어야 한다. 따라서 글의 순서로 가장 적절한 것은 ④ '(D) – (B) – (C)'이다.

---

44 지칭 추론   정답률 69% | 정답 ③

밑줄 친 (a) ~ (e) 중에서 가리키는 대상이 나머지 넷과 다른 것은?

① (a)   ② (b)   ③ (c) ✔   ④ (d)   ⑤ (e)

Why? 왜 정답일까?

(a), (b), (d), (e)는 the old man[grandad], (c)는 a young teacher를 가리키므로, (a) ~ (e) 중에서 가리키는 대상이 다른 하나는 ③ '(c)'이다.

---

45 세부 내용 파악   정답률 73% | 정답 ③

윗글에 관한 내용으로 적절하지 않은 것은?

① 갈색 머리 소녀가 노인과 소년을 향해 손가락질했다.
② 노인은 지쳐서 울타리에 기댔다.
③ 노인은 선생님과 논쟁을 벌였다. ✔
④ 노인은 글을 읽을 줄 몰랐다.
⑤ 소년은 학교에 가지 않아도 된다고 소리쳤다.

Why? 왜 정답일까?

(C) 'The old man didn't argue with the teacher.'에서 노인은 선생님과 논쟁을 벌이지 않았다고 하므로, 내용과 일치하지 않는 것은 ③ '노인은 선생님과 논쟁을 벌였다.'이다.

Why? 왜 오답일까?

① (A) 'A girl with brown hair pointed at the pair and jumped up and down.'의 내용과 일치한다.
② (B) '~ leant against the fence, exhausted.'의 내용과 일치한다.
④ (C) 'Dad, you can't even read.'의 내용과 일치한다.
⑤ (D) '"Brilliant, I don't have to go to school!" the boy exclaimed.'의 내용과 일치한다.

---

01 form good reading habits / completely personalized to / for this amazing opportunity

02 missed the seller's note / much cheaper than other hair dryers / read every detail of the item

03 get a checkup / check your vision / use this frame / pick them up in a week

04 dug it himself / ride the swings / see the sunset

05 have my car repaired / some eggs are broken / call the customer center

06 order a carrot cake / Do you need candles / write on the cake

07 some celebrities posting about it / made from recycled materials / a responsible consumer

08 deadline for entry / really into breakdancing lately / download the application form from the website

09 reduce waste around our school / picking up trash while running / wear workout clothes and sneakers

10 its weight is important / an electric heater would be good / with a five-star customer rating

11 bought it / Where are you planning to go

12 Can I see the dentist today / have a terrible toothache

13 get a big scholarship / only doubles can participate / How about we partner up

14 traditional games in Asia / shortening your explanation / have fun just doing it

15 runs a famous gaming company / have a book-signing at a bookstore nearby / meet his role model in person

16-17 maintain your instruments / can be taken apart / when not in use / lengthen the lifespan

---

어휘 Review Test 09   문제편 126쪽

A	B	C	D
01 보호자	01 dynamics	01 ⓕ	01 ⓗ
02 주의를 돌리다, 관심을 끄다	02 temporary	02 ⓖ	02 ⓜ
03 빠른	03 shortage	03 ⓚ	03 ⓚ
04 밀봉한	04 close	04 ⓑ	04 ⓛ
05 길들이다	05 smoothly	05 ⓜ	05 ⓑ
06 부연 설명하다, 자세히 말하다	06 entrepreneur	06 ⓛ	06 ⓙ
07 연결하다, 장착하다	07 spot	07 ⓝ	07 ⓢ
08 번식, 재생	08 dissatisfied	08 ⓐ	08 ⓠ
09 끌어내다, 도출하다	09 comprise	09 ⓒ	09 ⓡ
10 기준	10 endurance	10 ⓞ	10 ⓓ
11 (형편이) 나쁜, 우호적이지 않은	11 shrink	11 ⓟ	11 ⓐ
12 지표	12 unknown	12 ⓡ	12 ⓝ
13 의존	13 contain	13 ⓢ	13 ⓞ
14 굶주리다	14 ingredient	14 ⓠ	14 ⓒ
15 느슨한	15 groundless	15 ⓛ	15 ⓕ
16 제도적인, 기관의	16 surround	16 ⓗ	16 ⓟ
17 분명히	17 consumption	17 ⓔ	17 ⓣ
18 지속 가능한	18 benefit	18 ⓘ	18 ⓖ
19 유발하다	19 measure	19 ⓙ	19 ⓔ
20 먹을 수 있는	20 prevail	20 ⓓ	20 ⓘ

• 정답 •

01 ② 02 ① 03 ⑤ 04 ④ 05 ① 06 ⑤ 07 ⑤ 08 ④ 09 ③ 10 ③ 11 ① 12 ② 13 ④ 14 ③ 15 ⑤
16 ① 17 ⑤ 18 ⑤ 19 ① 20 ④ 21 ④ 22 ⑤ 23 ④ 24 ② 25 ⑤ 26 ③ 27 ⑤ 28 ⑤ 29 ④ 30 ④
31 ① 32 ② 33 ④ 34 ④ 35 ④ 36 ④ 37 ③ 38 ⑤ 39 ④ 40 ① 41 ⑤ 42 ③ 43 ④ 44 ② 45 ③

★ 표기된 문항은 [등급을 가르는 문제]에 해당하는 문항입니다.

---

01 컨벤션 센터 내 로봇 가이드 서비스 안내
정답률 95% | 정답 ②

다음을 듣고, 남자가 하는 말의 목적으로 가장 적절한 것을 고르시오.
① 로봇 프로그램 만족도 조사 참여를 독려하려고
☑ 관람객을 위한 안내 로봇 서비스를 소개하려고
③ 전시 작품 해설 서비스 중단을 안내하려고
④ 오디오 가이드 대여 장소를 공지하려고
⑤ 전시관 온라인 예약 방법을 설명하려고

[Chime bell rings.]
[차임벨이 울린다.]
M : Hello, visitors. This is Scott Wolfman from the Edison Convention Center management office.
안녕하세요, 관람객 여러분. Edison Convention Center 관리실의 Scott Wolfman입니다.
We're doing our best to make sure that visitors have a wonderful experience in our convention center.
저희는 컨벤션 센터에서 방문객들이 멋진 경험을 할 수 있도록 최선을 다하고 있습니다.
As part of our effort, our center provides a robot guide service.
우리 센터는 노력의 일환으로 로봇 가이드 서비스를 제공합니다.
The robot offers guided-tours of our exhibitions.
로봇은 우리 전시회의 가이드 투어를 제공합니다.
Foreign languages, such as Chinese and Spanish, are available.
중국어와 스페인어 같은 외국어도 가능합니다.
And if you lose your way, the robot will accompany you to where you want to go.
그리고 길을 잃으면, 로봇이 여러분이 가고 싶은 곳까지 동행할 것입니다.
So, please feel free to ask our friendly robot guide, and it'll kindly help you.
그러니 언제든지 친절한 로봇 가이드에게 문의해 주시면, 그들이 친절하게 도와드릴 것입니다.
I hope this service makes your experience even better.
저는 이 서비스가 여러분의 경험을 더 좋게 만들기를 바랍니다.
Thank you.
감사합니다.

Why? 왜 정답일까?
관람객의 더 나은 경험을 위해 로봇 가이드 서비스를 제공한다(As part of our effort, our center provides a robot guide service.)는 내용이므로, 남자가 하는 말의 목적으로 가장 적절한 것은 ② '관람객을 위한 안내 로봇 서비스를 소개하려고'이다.

● management ⓝ 관리
● effort ⓝ 노력, 분투, 수고
● offer ⓥ 제공하다
● foreign ⓐ 외국의
● accompany ⓥ 동반하다
● kindly 〈ad〉 친절하게
● experience ⓝ 경험
● provide ⓥ 제공하다
● exhibition ⓝ 전시회
● available ⓐ 이용할 수 있는
● friendly ⓐ 친절한

---

02 번역 프로그램 결과 확인하기
정답률 95% | 정답 ①

대화를 듣고, 여자의 의견으로 가장 적절한 것을 고르시오.
☑ 번역 프로그램으로 번역한 글은 검토가 필요하다.
② 읽기 학습을 통해 쓰기 능력을 향상시킬 수 있다.
③ 글을 인용할 때는 출처를 명확히 밝혀야 한다.
④ 예상 독자를 고려하여 글을 작성해야 한다.
⑤ 번역기 사용은 외국어 학습에 효과적이다.

W : Kevin, what are you doing?
Kevin, 뭐하고 있니?
M : Mom, I'm writing a letter to my sponsored child in Congo.
엄마, 저는 콩고에 있는 후원자 아이에게 편지를 쓰고 있어요.
W : That's why you're writing in French. Your French has gotten better and better.
그래서 프랑스어로 쓰고 있었구나. 너의 프랑스어가 점점 좋아졌구나.
M : Actually, I got help from a translation program.
사실, 전 번역 프로그램의 도움을 받았어요.
W : I see. [Pause] Did you check the translated text before copying it?
그렇구나. [잠시 정지] 그걸 복사하기 전에 번역된 글을 확인했니?
M : No, I didn't. Do you think I have to?
아니요. 제가 해야 된다고 생각하세요?
W : Yes. You'd better check the translation.
응. 번역을 확인하는 게 좋을 거야.
M : Well, I think the translation program does a better job than I can.
음, 번역 프로그램이 제가 하는 것 보다 더 일을 잘한다고 생각하는데요.
W : Not exactly. The translation could have meanings different from what you intended.
꼭 그렇지 않아. 번역이 네가 의도했던 것과 다른 의미를 가질 수도 있단다.
M : Hmm, you may be right. The translated text often loses the meaning of my original writing.
음, 엄마 말이 맞는 것 같아요. 번역된 글이 종종 제 원래 글의 의미를 잃어버려요.
W : See? When translating a text with a translation program, you need to check the results.
그렇지? 글이 번역 프로그램에서 번역될 때 그 결과를 확인할 필요가 있어.
M : Okay. Thanks for your advice.
알겠어요. 조언 감사해요.

Why? 왜 정답일까?
콩고에 있는 후원자 아이에게 외국어로 편지를 보내기 위해 번역 프로그램을 사용하는 아들에게 번역 결과를 검토함으로써 의도했던 의미와 일치하는지 확인해 보라고 조언한다(When translating a text with a translation program, you need to check the results.). 따라서 여자의 의견으로 가장 적절한 것은 ① '번역 프로그램으로 번역한 글은 검토가 필요하다.'이다.

● sponsored ⓐ 후원을 받는, 후원하는
● copy ⓥ 복사하다
● intended ⓐ 의도한
● original ⓐ 원래의, 진짜의
● translation ⓝ 번역
● exactly 〈ad〉 정확히
● lose ⓥ 잃다
● adice ⓝ 조언

---

03 온라인 장터의 중고 에어컨 거래
정답률 83% | 정답 ⑤

대화를 듣고, 두 사람의 관계를 가장 잘 나타낸 것을 고르시오.
① 광고 제작자 – 사진작가
② 이사업체 직원 – 의뢰인
③ 고객 – 에어컨 설치 기사
④ 트럭 운전자 – 물류 창고 직원
☑ 구매자 – 중고 물품 개인 판매자

[Cell phone rings.]
[휴대 전화가 울린다.]
M : Hello. This is Johnny. We've been messaging each other on the online marketplace.
여보세요? 전 Johnny입니다. 저희는 온라인 장터에서 서로 메시지를 보내고 있습니다.
W : Oh, hi. You have more questions about the air conditioner, right?
오, 안녕하세요. 에어컨에 대해 더 질문이 있으시다고 하셨죠?
M : Yes. Could you tell me how long you've been using it?
네. 에어컨 얼마나 오래 사용하셨어요?
W : I bought it a year ago. It works well and is like new as you can see from the photo.
1년 전에 샀어요. 작동이 잘 되고 사진에서 볼 수 있듯 새것 같아요.
M : Then why do you want to sell it?
근데 왜 파시는 건가요?
W : Because I don't need it anymore. I'm moving to a place with a built-in air conditioner.
더 이상 필요 없어서요. 에어컨이 내장되어 있는 곳으로 이사갑니다.
M : I see. I'd like to buy it, then. It's $400, correct?
그렇군요. 그럼 제가 살게요. 400달러 맞죠?
W : That's right. When can you pick it up?
네. 언제 가지러 오시나요?
M : Maybe tomorrow. I need to find a truck to load it on first.
아마도 내일이요. 먼저 그걸 실을 트럭을 찾아야 합니다.
W : Okay. Let me know when you're ready.
네. 그럼 준비되면 알려주세요.
M : Thanks. I'll call you again.
감사합니다. 다시 전화 드릴게요.

Why? 왜 정답일까?
'Then why do you want to sell it?', 'Because I don't need it anymore. I'm moving to a place with a built-in air conditioner.', 'I see. I'd like to buy it, then. It's $400, correct?' 에서 여자가 중고 에어컨을 판매하고, 남자가 이를 사려고 하는 구매자임을 알 수 있다. 따라서 두 사람의 관계로 가장 적절한 것은 ⑤ '구매자 – 중고 물품 개인 판매자'이다.

● marketplace ⓝ 장터, 시장
● built-in ⓐ 내장된
● load ⓥ 싣다
● air conditioner ⓝ 에어컨
● pick up 〜을 집다, 〜을 찾다
● on first 처음에는

---

04 학생 라운지 디자인 공모전 작품 살펴보기
정답률 91% | 정답 ④

대화를 듣고, 그림에서 대화의 내용과 일치하지 않는 것을 고르시오.

W : Hi, Benjamin. Did you finish your work for the student lounge design contest?
안녕, Benjamin. 학생 라운지 디자인 공모전 작업 끝냈어?
M : Yes. I'm confident that I'm going to win. Here's my design for it.
응. 이길 자신이 있어. 여기 내 디자인이야.
W : 「Awesome. Is that a hanging plant in front of the window?」 ①의 근거 일치
대단해. 창문 앞에는 걸어 두는 식물이야?
M : Yes. The plant will give a fresh feel to the lounge. What do you think about the banner on the wall?
응. 이 식물은 라운지에 신선한 느낌을 줄 거야. 벽에 걸린 현수막은 어때?
W : I love it. 「The slogan "TO THE WORLD" goes well with the world map.」 ②의 근거 일치
마음에 들어. '세계로'라는 슬로건이 세계지도랑 잘 어울려.
M : I hope this place helps students dream big.
난 이 공간이 학생들의 꿈을 크게 키워줬으면 좋겠어.
W : That's cool. 「And the two cushions on the sofa make the atmosphere cozier.」 ③의 근거 일치
좋다. 그리고 소파에 있는 쿠션 두 개는 분위기를 더 아늑하게 만들어.
M : You're right. 「Check out the square-shaped table as well.」 ④의 근거 불일치
맞아. 사각 테이블도 봐봐.
W : Good. It can be useful. 「Most of all, students will love the vending machine under the clock.」
좋다. 유용할 것 같아. 무엇보다도, 학생들은 시계 아래에 있는 자판기를 좋아할 것 같아. ⑤의 근거 일치
M : You bet!
틀림없어!

Why? 왜 정답일까?

대화에서 사각 테이블을 봐달라고 얘기하고 있는데(**Check out the square-shaped table as well.**), 그림 속 테이블은 원형이다. 따라서 그림에서 대화의 내용과 일치하지 않는 것은 ④이다.

- **confident** ⓐ 자신 있는
- **banner** ⓝ 현수막
- **atmosphere** ⓝ 분위기, 공기
- **square-shaped** ⓐ 사각형의
- **clock** ⓝ 시계
- **in front of** ~의 앞에
- **slogan** ⓝ 표어, 슬로건
- **cozier** ⓐ 더 아늑한
- **vending machine** 자판기

---

05 접시 비우는 날 준비하기 정답률 96% | 정답 ①

대화를 듣고, 남자가 할 일로 가장 적절한 것을 고르시오.

☑ 스티커 준비하기
② 안내문 게시하기
③ 급식 메뉴 선정하기
④ 설문 조사 실시하기
⑤ 우수 학급 시상하기

M : Ms. Kim, Empty Your Plate Day is coming. How's the preparation going?
　김 선생님, 접시 비우는 날이 다가옵니다. 준비는 어떻게 되고 있나요?
W : I've finally decided on the lunch menu for that day.
　드디어 그날 점심 메뉴를 정했습니다.
M : You did! How did you do that?
　그랬군요. 어떻게 하셨나요?
W : I did a survey of students' favorite foods.
　학생들이 좋아하는 음식에 대한 설문조사를 했습니다.
M : Good idea! Can I help you with anything?
　좋은 생각이네요! 제가 뭐 도와드릴까요?
W : Actually, Mr. Han, I'm not sure how to motivate students to participate.
　한 선생님, 사실 어떻게 학생이 참여할 수 있도록 동기를 부여해야 할지 잘 모르겠습니다.
M : How about an award for the class with the fewest leftovers?
　남은 음식이 가장 적은 반에 상을 주는 건 어때요?
W : Sounds great. But how will we find that class?
　좋네요. 그런데 그 반을 어떻게 찾죠?
M : You could give a sticker to the students who leave nothing on their plates. And then, you can find the class with the most stickers.
　접시에 아무것도 남지 않은 학생들에게 스티커를 줄 수 있습니다. 그리고 스티커가 가장 많은 반을 찾는 거죠.
W : Excellent. Could you prepare some stickers for me?
　훌륭하네요. 스티커를 준비해 주실 수 있나요?
M : Sure. I'll do that for you.
　네. 그럴게요.
W : Thanks. Then I'll put a notice on the bulletin board.
　감사합니다. 그럼 게시판에 공지를 올리겠습니다.

Why? 왜 정답일까?

음식을 가장 적게 남긴 반에 상을 주기 위해 스티커를 준비해 달라고 부탁했다(**Could you prepare some stickers for me?**). 따라서 남자가 할 일로 가장 적절한 것은 ① '스티커 준비하기'이다.

- **empty** ⓐ 빈
- **preparation** ⓝ 준비
- **survey** ⓝ 조사
- **participate** ⓝ 참여
- **fewest** ⓐ 가장 적은
- **notice** ⓝ 공지
- **plate** ⓝ 접시
- **decide** ⓥ 결심하다
- **motivate** ⓥ 동기를 부여하다
- **award** ⓝ 상
- **leftovers** ⓝ 남은 음식
- **bulletin board** 게시판

---

06 새 핸드폰의 요금제 설정하기 정답률 65% | 정답 ⑤

대화를 듣고, 남자가 매달 지불할 금액을 고르시오.
① $20　② $27　③ $30　④ $36　☑ $40

W : Welcome to Boom Telecom. How can I help you?
　Boom Telecom에 오신 걸 환영합니다. 무엇을 도와드릴까요?
M : Hi. I'm thinking of changing my internet provider. What service plans do you have?
　안녕하세요. 인터넷 업체를 바꿀까 생각 중입니다. 어떤 요금제 서비스가 있나요?
W : Okay. We have the Economic plan that's $20 per month. And the Supreme plan, which is faster, is $30 per month.
　네. Economic 플랜이 있는데 한 달에 20달러입니다. 그리고 좀 더 빠른 Supreme 플랜은 한 달에 30달러입니다.
M : I prefer the faster one.
　전 더 빠른 게 좋아요.
W : Alright. We also have an OTT service for an extra $10 per month. What do you think?
　알겠습니다. 또, 한 달에 10달러를 추가로 내시면 OTT 서비스도 제공하고 있습니다. 어떠세요?
M : Awesome. I'd like that as well.
　좋네요. 그것도 herramienta 해 주세요.
W : Excellent choice. Then you'll have the Supreme plan with the OTT service, right?
　좋은 선택입니다. 그럼 Supreme 플랜에 OTT 서비스 추가, 맞으시죠?
M : Correct. Can I get a discount?
　네. 할인 받을 수 있나요?
W : I'm afraid that the 10% discount promotion is over.
　유감스럽게도 10% 할인 프로모션이 끝났습니다.
M : That's a shame. But I'll take it anyway.
　아쉽네요. 그래도 그걸로 주세요.
W : Thank you. Please fill in this paper with your payment information.
　감사합니다. 여기 종이에 결제 정보를 기입해 주세요.
M : Okay. [Writing sound] Here you are.
　네. [적는 소리] 여기 있습니다.

Why? 왜 정답일까?

대화에 따르면 남자는 한 달에 30달러짜리 **Supreme** 플랜 요금제에 **10**달러를 추가하여 OTT 서비스도 이용하기로 했다. 할인은 없다고 했으므로, 남자가 총 지불할 금액은 ⑤ '$40'이다.

- **provider** ⓝ 제공자
- **discount** ⓝ 할인
- **that's a shame** 아쉽다
- **prefer** ⓥ 선호하다
- **I'm afraid that** ~하는 것이 유감이다
- **fill** ⓥ 채우다

---

07 여자가 좋아하는 토크쇼의 티켓 주기 정답률 96% | 정답 ⑤

대화를 듣고, 여자가 토크 쇼를 방청하러 갈 수 없는 이유를 고르시오.

① 가족 모임에 가야 해서
② 아르바이트를 해야 해서
③ 책 사인회를 준비해야 해서
④ 화학 프로젝트를 해야 해서
☑ 친구 결혼식에 참석해야 해서

[Cell phone rings.]
[휴대전화가 울린다.]
M : Hi, Isabella.
　여보세요, Isabella.
W : Hi, Lorenzo. Did you finish your part-time job?
　안녕, Lorenzo. 아르바이트 끝났어?
M : Yes. I'm on my way to a meeting for a chemistry project. What's up?
　응. 화학 프로젝트 때문에 회의에 가는 중이야. 무슨 일이야?
W : Your favorite talk show is *The Alice Mitchell Show*, right?
　네가 좋아하는 토크쇼 *The Alice Mitchell Show* 맞지?
M : Yeah, I'm a big fan of hers. I even went to her book signing event.
　응. 나 완전 그녀의 팬이야. 책 사인회에도 갔어.
W : I knew it! I got two tickets for her talk show. It's next Saturday evening.
　그럴 줄 알았어. 나 토크쇼 티켓이 두 장 있어. 다음주 토요일 저녁이야.
M : Whoa! Can you please take me with you?
　우와! 나 데려가 줄 수 있어?
W : Actually, I'm not available that day. The tickets are all yours.
　사실 내가 그날 안 될 것 같아. 티켓은 전부 네 거야.
M : Wait, why can't you go? Is it because of the family gathering you mentioned before?
　잠깐만, 왜 못 가는데? 저번에 말했던 가족 모임 때문이야?
W : No, that's in two weeks. Next Saturday I have to attend my friend's wedding.
　아니 그건 2주 후야. 다음 주 토요일에는 친구 결혼식에 참석해야 해.
M : Oh, I see. Then I'll take the tickets with pleasure. Thank you so much.
　그렇구나. 그럼 기쁘게 표를 받을게. 정말 고마워.

Why? 왜 정답일까?

여자는 친구의 결혼식에 참석해야 해서(**Next Saturday I have to attend my friend's wedding.**) 남자와 함께 토크 쇼에 갈 수 없다고 한다. 따라서 여자가 토크 쇼에 갈 수 없는 이유로 가장 적절한 것은 ⑤ '친구 결혼식에 참석해야 해서'이다.

- **part-time job** 아르바이트
- **available** ⓐ 가능한
- **mention** ⓥ 언급하다
- **pleasure** ⓝ 기쁨
- **chemistry** ⓝ 화학
- **gathering** ⓝ 모임
- **attend** ⓥ 참석하다

---

08 북극곰 수영 대회 포스터 살펴보기 정답률 93% | 정답 ④

대화를 듣고, Polar Bear Swim에 관해 언급되지 않은 것을 고르시오.

① 행사 날짜　② 제출 서류　③ 최대 참가 인원
☑ 기념품　⑤ 참가비

W : Michael, look at this poster. The Polar Bear Swim will be held soon.
　Michael, 이 포스터 봐 봐. 북극곰 수영 대회가 곧 열려.
M : I know! I've been really looking forward to it. [Pause] 「It's on December 23rd.」 ①의 근거 일치
　그러네! 정말 기대하고 있었어. [일시 장치] 12월 23일이네.
W : Yeah. We can enjoy winter sea-swimming.
　응. 겨울 바다 수영을 즐길 수 있어.
M : How nice! 「To join this event, we must hand in a medical check-up paper.」 ②의 근거 일치
　좋다! 이 행사에 참여하려면 건강검진서를 반드시 제출해야만 해.
W : I think it's a good policy for everyone's health since the water is icy cold.
　물이 얼음처럼 차갑기 때문에 모두의 건강을 위해 좋은 정책이라고 생각해.
M : I agree. 「By the way, it says that there's a limit of 100 people.」 ③의 근거 일치
　나도 그래. 그런데, 여기 100명 제한이라고 적혀 있네.
W : Oh, we must hurry. Look! Registration starts this Saturday.
　아, 서둘러야겠다. 이것 봐! 이번 주 토요일에 등록을 시작해.
M : I'll set a reminder on my phone.
　핸드폰에 알림 설정할게.
W : Great idea. 「And the entry fee is just $15.」 ⑤의 근거 일치
　좋은 생각이야. 참가비는 15 달러야.
M : Yes. And all entry fees will be donated to charity.
　응. 모든 참가비는 자선단체에 기부된다.
W : Cool. Let's have some icy fun while doing a good deed.
　좋다. 좋은 일 하면서 시원하게 놀자!

Why? 왜 정답일까?

대화에서 남자와 여자는 The Polar Bear Swim의 행사 날짜, 제출 서류, 최대 참가 인원, 참가비를 언급하므로 언급되지 않은 것은 ④ '기념품'이다.

- **looking forward to ~ing** 고대하다
- **medical check-up paper** 건강검진서
- **icy** ⓐ 얼음 같은
- **reminder** ⓝ 알림
- **donate** ⓥ 기부하다
- **hand in** 제출하다
- **policy** ⓝ 정책
- **limit** ⓝ 제한
- **entry fee** 참가비
- **deed** ⓝ 행동, 행위

---

09 1일투어 프로그램 안내 정답률 91% | 정답 ③

Walk in the Snow에 관한 다음 내용을 듣고, 일치하지 않는 것을 고르시오.

① 1일 투어 프로그램이다.
② 하이킹에 관심이 있는 누구든 참여할 수 있다.
☑ 장비를 무료로 대여할 수 있다.
④ 학생에게 등록비 할인을 해 준다.
⑤ 참여하려면 사전에 등록해야 한다.

W: Hello, listeners!
안녕하세요, 청취자 여러분!
Are you a winter person?
여러분은 겨울을 좋아하세요?
Then, Walk in the Snow might just be the adventure for you.
그렇다면, 눈 속을 걷는 것은 당신에게 모험일지 모릅니다.
「It's a one-day tour program at Great White Mountain.」 ③의 근거 일치
Great White Moutain 1일 투어 프로그램이 있습니다.
「Regardless of hiking experience, anyone who is interested in hiking can participate in the tour.」 ②의 근거 일치
하이킹 경험에 상관없이, 하이킹에 관심이 있는 사람이라면 누구나 참여할 수 있습니다.
Participants are required to bring their own snowshoes and poles.
참가자들은 스노우슈즈와 폴을 가지고 와야 합니다.
「But equipment is also available to rent for a small fee.」 ③의 근거 불일치
장비를 적은 비용으로 대여할 수 있습니다.
「The registration fee is $10, and we offer discounts to students.」 ④의 근거 일치
등록비는 10달러이며, 학생들에게는 할인이 제공됩니다.
「Don't forget that you must register in adance to participate.」 ⑤의 근거 일치
참여하기 전에는 사전에 등록해야 한다는 것을 잊지 마세요.
For more information, please visit our website, www.walkinthesnow.com.
더 많은 정보를 위해, www.walkinthesnow.com 웹사이트의 방문을 부탁드립니다.
Thank you.
감사합니다.

Why? 왜 정답일까?
'But equipment is also available to rent for a small fee.'에서 장비를 적은 돈으로 대여할 수 있다고 하므로, 내용과 일치하지 않는 것은 ③ '장비를 무료로 대여할 수 있다.'이다.

● adventure ⓝ 모험
● equipment ⓝ 장비
● regardless of ~에 상관없이
● offer ⓥ 제공하다

---

10 집에 어울리는 새 달력 사기   정답률 77% | 정답 ③

다음 표를 보면서 대화를 듣고, 두 사람이 선택할 달력을 고르시오.

Calendar

	Product	Price	Format	Recyclable Paper	Theme
①	A	$8	standing desk	×	modern art
②	B	$10	standing desk	○	classic art
③	C	$12	standing desk	○	movie
④	D	$16	wall	○	nature
⑤	E	$22	wall	×	animal

M: Honey, what are you looking at?
여보, 뭐 보고 있어?
W: It's a brochure for a new calendar. Why don't we choose one together?
새 달력을 위한 안내 책자야. 한 개 같이 고를래?
M: Great. How much do you want to spend?
좋아. 얼마를 쓸 예정이야?
W: 「I think more than $20 is not reasonable.」 근거1 Price 조건
20달러 이상은 합리적이지 않은 것 같아.
M: Agreed. How about trying a new format instead of a wall calendar? We've only used wall calendars so far.
동의해. 벽 달력 대신 새로운 형식을 시도해 보는 건 어때? 우리 지금까지 벽 달력만 썼잖아.
W: Good idea. 「Let's pick the standing desk format, then.」 근거2 Format 조건
좋은 생각이야. 탁상 달력을 고르자 그럼.
M: Okay. 「And I prefer one that's made of recyclable paper.」
좋아. 난 재활용 가능한 종이로 만든 게 좋아.
W: Me, too. 「It's more eco-friendly than those that cannot be recycled.」 근거3 Recyclable Paper 조건
나도. 이게 재활용이 불가능한 것 보다 더 친환경적이야.
M: Then, let's cross this out. Now, we have two options left. Which one do you prefer?
그럼 이건 지우자. 이제 우리에게 두 가지 옵션이 있어. 어떤 게 더 좋아?
W: 「I think the classic art theme doesn't match our interior design.」 근거4 Theme 조건
클래식 아트 테마는 우리 인테리어랑 맞지 않는 것 같아.
M: Good point. Then, let's choose this one.
좋은 지적이야. 그럼 이걸로 하자.

Why? 왜 정답일까?
대화에 따르면 남자와 여자는 금액이 20달러를 넘지 않으면서, 탁상 달력이고, 재활용이 가능한 종이로 만들어졌으면서, 클래식 아트 테마가 아닌 달력을 사기로 한다. 따라서 두 사람이 구입할 달력은 ③ 'C'이다.

● brochure ⓝ 책자
● reasonable ⓐ 합리적인
● recyclable ⓐ 재활용이 가능한
● cross out (선을 그어)지우다
● match ⓥ 잘 어울리다
● spend ⓥ 소비하다
● format ⓝ 형식
● eco-friendly ⓐ 친환경적인

★★★ 등급을 가르는 문제!
11 국회 연설 초대   정답률 48% | 정답 ①

대화를 듣고, 여자의 마지막 말에 대한 남자의 응답으로 가장 적절한 것을 고르시오.
① I covered the worrying state of marine life. - 해양 생물의 걱정에 대해 취재했어.
② I sent an article to the biology department. - 생물학부에 기사를 보냈어.
③ Whatever you did, let's not speak about it. - 무엇을 했든지, 그거에 대해서 말하지 마.
④ I spent lots of time preparing the speech. - 난 연설을 준비하는데 많은 시간을 들였어.
⑤ The article was mainly read by students. - 이 기사는 주로 학생들에게 읽혔어.

W: Congratulations, Lucas! I heard you were invited to speak at the National Assembly.
축하해, Lucas! 국회 연설에 초대되었다고 들었어.
M: Thanks. It's a real honor. I think the article I wrote in the newspaper made a strong impression.
고마워. 정말 영광이야. 내가 신문에 쓴 기사가 엄청 감명 깊었나 봐.

W: I'm so proud of you. What did you mostly write about?
자랑스럽다. 주로 뭐에 대해서 썼어?
M: I covered the worrying state of marine life.
해양 생물의 걱정에 대해 취재했어.

Why? 왜 정답일까?
여자가 주로 어떤 주제에 대해 기사를 써서 국회 연설에 초대되었는지 물었다('What did you mostly write about?'). 따라서 남자의 응답으로 가장 적절한 것은 ① '해양 생물의 걱정에 대해 취재했어.'이다.

● invite ⓥ 초대하다
● impression ⓝ 인상
● article ⓝ (신문·잡지의) 기사, 논설
● honor ⓝ 영광
● mostly ⓐⓓ 주로, 대게
● mainly ⓐⓓ 주로, 대부분

★★ 문제 해결 꿀~팁 ★★
▶ 많이 틀린 이유는?
마지막 문장에서 write라고 물었는데 답지에는 write와 관련된 동사가 없다. cover는 '취재하다, 다루다'라는 뜻을 가진 동사임으로 이 상황에서 write를 대신할 수 있음을 파악하는 것이 중요하다.
▶ 문제 해결 방법은?
마지막 문장을 잘 듣고 정확하게 무엇을 질문했는지 파악하는 것이 중요하다. 이 대화에서 남자는 what으로 시작하는 의문문에 주어가 you 동사가 write이므로 네가 무엇을 썼는지에 대해 물어보고 있다. 이에 답변에 적절하지 않은 형태인 ③번과 ⑤번은 답이 될 수 없다. ②번과 ④번은 각각 동사가 sent와 spent이므로 write에 대한 답변으로는 적절하지 않다.

12 셔틀버스 운행 안내   정답률 68% | 정답 ②

대화를 듣고, 남자의 마지막 말에 대한 여자의 응답으로 가장 적절한 것을 고르시오.
① Take care. The weather is freezing cold. - 조심해. 날씨가 너무 추워.
② Good news. Thanks for letting me know. - 좋은 소식이네. 알려 줘서 고마워.
③ Hurry up. The bus is leaving very soon. - 서둘러. 버스가 곧 떠나.
④ Seriously? I'd better try walking, then. - 진짜로? 그럼 걷는 게 더 낫겠다.
⑤ Really? I was on the shuttle bus, too. - 정말? 나도 셔틀버스에 있었어.

M: Claire, why are you sweating? It's pretty cold outside.
Claire, 왜 이렇게 땀을 흘려? 밖에 꽤 춥잖아.
W: Hey, Jamie. I ran to be in time for class. It's too far to walk from the subway station to our college, don't you think?
안녕, Jamie. 수업에 맞춰 오기 위해 뛰었어. 학교가 역에서 너무 먼 것 같아, 그렇지?
M: Yes, but the shuttle bus began running last week. You can take it instead.
응, 근데 지난주부터 셔틀 버스를 운행했어. 대신 그걸 탈 수 있어.
W: Good news. Thanks for letting me know.
좋은 소식이네. 알려 줘서 고마워.

Why? 왜 정답일까?
땀을 흘리며 지하철역에서 부터 교실까지 뛰어온 여자에게 남자가 지난주부터 셔틀버스 운행을 시작했다(Yes, but the shuttle bus began running last week.)고 말하므로, 여자의 응답으로 가장 적절한 것은 ② '좋은 소식이네. 알려 줘서 고마워.'이다.

● sweat ⓥ 땀을 흘리다
● in time 정시에
● instead ⓐⓓ 대신에
● pretty ⓐⓓ 꽤
● run ⓥ 운영하다

13 유료 어플의 무료 체험 기간 종료   정답률 83% | 정답 ④

대화를 듣고, 여자의 마지막 말에 대한 남자의 응답으로 가장 적절한 것을 고르시오. [3점]
Man: _____
① Definitely. That's why I got a refund for the app.
그래, 그게 내가 어플을 환불받은 이유야.
② Sorry. I should have repaired my tablet PC earlier.
미안해. 태블릿 PC를 더 전에 수리 받았어야 했어.
③ Exactly. Documents were filed in alphabetical order.
정확해, 서류는 알파벳순으로 정렬됐어.
④ I see. I'll give it some thought before buying this app.
알겠어. 사기 전에 생각을 좀 해 봐야겠어.
⑤ Don't worry. I still have a few more days for the free trial.
걱정하지 마. 무료 체험 기간이 며칠 더 남았어.

W: Good morning, Pablo.
좋은 아침, Pablo.
M: Hi, Eva. Look at my new tablet PC.
안녕, Eva. 내 새 태블릿 PC를 봐.
W: Wow. How do you like it?
우와. 마음에 들어?
M: It's opened a brand new world to me. But I have a small problem.
나한테 완전히 새로운 세상을 열어 줬어. 근데 약간 문제가 있어.
W: What is it? Maybe I can be of help.
원데? 내가 도울 수 있을지도 몰라.
M: This file works well on my laptop, but it won't open on my tablet.
이 파일이 노트북에서는 잘 됐는데 태블릿에서는 안 열려.
W: Did you install a file-reading app? You need one to open the file on a tablet.
파일 읽는 어플 설치했어? 태블릿에서 파일을 열기 위해서 그게 필요해.
M: I already did that a week ago.
지난주에 이미 깔았어.
W: Then, I'll check a few things. [Tapping sound] I got it. The free trial period of this app is over.
그럼 몇 개 확인해 볼게. [타자 치는 소리] 이 어플의 무료 체험 기간이 끝났어.
M: Oh, that's why it doesn't work. Do you think I should pay for this app?
아, 그래서 안 열렸던 거구나. 내가 이거 구매해야 할까?
W: Well, it depends on you. You can consider it if you need this app.
음, 너에게 달려있지. 이 어플이 필요하지 않다면 고려해봐.
M: I see. I'll give it some thought before buying this app.
알겠어. 사기 전에 생각을 좀 해 봐야겠다.

유료 어플을 구매할지 물어 보는 여자에게 남자는 어플이 필요한지 아닌지 고민해 보라고(**You can consider it if you need this app.**) 말한다. 따라서 남자의 응답으로 가장 적절한 것은 ④ '알겠어. 사기 전에 생각을 좀 해 봐야겠다.'이다.

- **brand new** 완전 새로운
- **period** ⓝ 기간
- **repair** ⓥ 수리하다
- **trial** ⓝ 체험
- **consider** ⓥ 고려하다
- **alphabetical** ⓐ 알파벳 순서의

---

14 학기 중간에 봉사활동 들어가기   정답률 88% | 정답 ③

대화를 듣고, 남자의 마지막 말에 대한 여자의 응답으로 가장 적절한 것을 고르시오. [3점]

Woman:

① Good idea. Let's learn how to read sign language.
좋은 생각이야. 수화를 읽는 법을 배우자.
② You're right. That's because I wanted to help him.
맞아. 내가 그를 돕고 싶었던 이유야.
③ Okay. Wish me luck in getting this volunteer work.
응. 이 봉사활동을 할 수 있게 행운을 빌어 줘.
④ Trust me. I bet you'll be selected as a note-taker.
날 믿어. 네가 노트테이커로 뽑는 걸 장담해.
⑤ Wonderful. Thank you for taking notes for me in class.
멋지다. 수업에서 날 위해 필기를 해 줘서 고마워.

M : Hi, Naomi. What are you up to?
안녕, Naomi. 뭐 하고 있어?
W : Hi. I'm looking for volunteer work. Didn't you say you're volunteering?
안녕. 봉사활동을 찾고 있어. 너 봉사활동 하고 있다고 하지 않았어?
M : Yes. I'm working as a note-taker.
응. 난 노트테이커로 일하고 있어.
W : You mean helping students with hearing difficulties?
그 말은 듣는 데 어려움이 있는 학생을 도와주고 있다는 거야?
M : Right. It helps deaf students understand the class better.
맞아. 청각장애인 학생들이 수업을 더 잘 이해할 수 있도록 돕는 거야.
W : Interesting. Could you tell me more?
흥미롭다. 좀 더 말해줄래?
M : I type everything during class, even jokes. The more detailed, the more understandable.
수업 중 모든 것을 타자로 쳐, 농담까지도, 더 자세할수록, 더 이해하기 쉽지.
W : It sounds like a unique and valuable experience.
독특하고 가치 있는 경험인 것 같아.
M : Yeah. Are you thinking about joining?
응. 같이할 생각 있어?
W : Absolutely. But can I join in the middle of the semester?
물론. 근데 학기 중간인데 들어갈 수 있을까?
M : It could be possible. I heard one member quit a few days ago.
가능 할거야. 한 명이 며칠 전에 그만뒀다고 들었거든.
W : Lucky me. Is the position still available?
나 운이 좋네. 그 자리 아직도 가능해?
M : Hmm, I'm not sure, but if you ask the student volunteer center, you'll get an answer immediately.
음, 잘 모르겠어. 내가 학생 봉사활동 센터에 물어보고 바로 알려 줄게.
W : Okay. Wish me luck in getting this volunteer work.
응. 이 봉사활동을 할 수 있게 행운을 빌어 줘.

봉사활동을 찾고 있는 여자에게 남자가 자기가 하고 있는 봉사활동에 참여할 것을 제안했고, 자리가 있는지 확인해 주겠다(**Hmm, I'm not sure, but if you ask the student volunteer center, you'll get an answer immediately.**)고 했다. 이에 대한 여자의 응답으로 가장 적절한 것은 ③ '응. 이 봉사활동을 할 수 있게 행운을 빌어 줘.'이다.

- **note-taker** 노트테이커(필기나 메모를 하는 사람)
- **joke** ⓝ 농담
- **valuable** ⓐ 가치 있는
- **semester** ⓝ 학기
- **position** ⓝ 자리, 위치
- **sign language** 수화
- **deaf** ⓐ 청각 장애가 있는
- **understandable** ⓐ 이해할 수 있는
- **experience** ⓝ 경험
- **quit** ⓥ 그만두다
- **immediately** ⓐd 바로, 즉시

---

15 다른 빵집에 가자고 제안하기   정답률 72% | 정답 ⑤

다음 상황 설명을 듣고, Tony가 Kate에게 할 말로 가장 적절한 것을 고르시오. [3점]

Tony:

① Why don't we post a review of this bakery? – 이 빵집에 리뷰를 남기는 게 어때?
② Let's give her the baker of the month award. – 그녀에게 이번 달의 제빵사 상을 주자
③ We'd better check if we're on the waiting list. – 대기 목록에 있는지 확인해 보는 게 좋겠어.
④ We should come later when the repairs are done. – 수리가 끝나고 다시 와야겠어.
⑤ How about finding a different bakery for the list? – 목록을 위해 다른 빵집을 찾아보는 건 어때?

M : Tony and Kate are members of the bread lovers club.
Tony와 Kate는 빵을 사랑하는 모임의 멤버입니다.
They plan to go on a bakery tour every month.
그들은 매달 빵 여행을 갈 계획이 있습니다.
To make a list of places to visit, they're sharing their ideas about must-visit bakeries.
방문할 장소 목록을 만들기 위해, 그들은 반드시 가야 할 빵집에 관한 아이디어를 공유하고 있습니다.
Kate proposes a bakery whose bread she thinks is super delicious.
Kate가 그녀가 생각하는 빵이 매우 맛있는 빵집을 제안합니다.
However, Tony finds out that the baker there quit and since then there have been lots of reviews complaining about the bread quality getting worse.
그러나, Tony는 그곳의 제빵사가 그만두었고 그 이후로 빵의 질이 나빠졌다는 것에 대해 불평하는 리뷰들이 많다는 것을 알게 됩니다.
So, he wants to suggest that they choose a better bakery for their where-to-go list.
그래서, 그는 그들의 가야 목록에 더 나은 빵집을 고르자고 제안하고자 합니다.
In this situation, what would Tony most likely say to Kate?
이 상황에서 Tony는 Kate에게 뭐라고 말할 것 같나요?
Tony : How about finding a different bakery for the list?
목록을 위해 다른 빵집을 찾아보는 건 어때?

상황에 따르면 Kate가 제안한 빵집은 제빵사가 바뀌면서 빵의 질이 바뀌었다. 이에 Tony는 다른 빵집에 가고자 제안하고자(**So, he wants to suggest that they choose a better bakery for their where-to-go list.**) 한다. 따라서 Tony가 Kate에게 할 말로 가장 적절한 것은 ⑤ '목록을 위해 다른 빵집을 찾아보는 건 어때?'이다.

- **complaining** ⓐ 불평하는
- **worse** ⓐ 더 나쁜
- **quality** ⓝ 질

16-17 개에게 안 좋은 과일

W : Hello, students. Last time, we learned why it's good for us to eat fruits and veggies.
학생 여러분, 안녕하세요. 지난 시간에는 왜 과일과 채소를 먹는 것이 좋은지에 대해 배웠습니다.
But what's good for us isn't always good for animals.
하지만 우리에게 좋은 것이 항상 동물에게 좋은 것은 아닙니다.
「Today, let's find out what fruits to avoid when feeding dogs.」 **16번의 근거**
오늘은 개에게 먹이를 줄 때 피해야 할 과일이 무엇인지 알아보겠습니다.
「First, grapes are known to be highly toxic to dogs.」 **17번 ①의 근거 일치**
먼저, 포도는 개에 독성이 매우 강한 것으로 알려져 있죠.
You should be careful because even a single grape can cause severe health damage.
포도도 한 알이라도 심각한 해를 유발할 수 있으니 조심해야 합니다.
「Now, let's take a look at cherries.」 **17번 ②의 근거 일치**
이제 체리에 대해 알아봅시다.
If a dog swallows their seeds, the dog is likely to have difficulties breathing.
만약 개가 체리의 씨앗을 삼키면, 개는 숨쉬기가 어려울 것입니다.
「Next, if your dog doesn't eat avocados, it would be for the best.」 **17번 ③의 근거 일치**
다음으로는 개가 아보카도를 먹지 않는다면 가장 좋을 것입니다.
That's because eating large amounts of avocados can make your dog sick.
아보카도를 많이 먹으면 개가 아플 수 있습니다.
「Finally, don't let your dog snack on grapefruits.」 **17번 ④의 근거 일치**
마지막으로 자몽을 간식으로 먹지 않도록 하세요.
The fruit contains so much acid that some dogs can develop stomach problems.
이 과일은 산을 많이 함유하고 있어서 몇몇 개는 위장 문제가 생길 수 있습니다.
Now, you may understand why some fruits are said to be harmful to dogs.
이제 여러분은 왜 몇몇 과일이 개에게 해롭다고 하는지 이해할 것입니다.
I hope this information will help you and your dog in living a happy life.
이 정보가 여러분과 여러분의 반려견이 행복한 삶을 사는데 도움이 되길 희망합니다.

- **veggie** ⓝ 야채
- **feed** ⓥ 먹이를 주다
- **toxic** ⓐ 독성의
- **swallow** ⓥ 삼키다
- **breathe** ⓥ 숨 쉬다
- **stomach** ⓝ 위
- **pose** ⓥ 야기하다
- **avoid** ⓥ 피하다
- **highly** ⓐd 매우
- **severe** ⓐ 심한
- **seed** ⓝ 씨앗
- **acid** ⓝ 산
- **harmful** ⓐ 해로운

---

16 주제 파악   정답률 90% | 정답 ①

여자가 하는 말의 주제로 가장 적절한 것은?

① fruits that can pose a risk to dogs' health – 과일은 개의 건강에 위험을 야기할 수 있다
② ways to help dogs develop a taste for fruits – 개가 과일에 대한 식욕을 높이는 법
③ tips for protecting garden fruits from animals – 동물로부터 정원의 과일을 지키는 방법
④ reasons fruits should be included in dogs' diets – 개의 식단에 과일이 있어야만 하는 이유
⑤ stories that use fruits and vegetables as characters – 과일과 야채를 캐릭터로 쓰는 이야기

개에게 해로운 과일을 소개하는 내용(**Today, let's find out what fruits to avoid when feeding dogs.**)이므로, 남자가 하는 말의 주제로 가장 적절한 것은 ① '과일은 개의 건강에 위험을 야기할 수 있다'이다.

---

17 언급 유무 파악   정답률 95% | 정답 ⑤

언급된 과일이 아닌 것은?

① grapes – 포도   ② cherries – 체리   ③ avocados – 아보카도
④ grapefruits – 자몽   ⑤ cranberries – 크랜베리 ✓

담화에서 여자는 개에게 위험한 과일 및 채소로 포도, 체리, 아보카도, 자몽을 언급하므로, 언급되지 않은 것은 ⑤ '크랜베리'이다.

① '**You should be careful because even a single grape can cause severe health damage.**'에서 '포도'가 언급되었다.
② '**Now, let's take a look at cherries. If a dog swallows their seeds, the dog is likely to have difficulties breathing.**'에서 '체리'가 언급되었다.
③ '**Next, if your dog doesn't eat avocados, it would be for the best.**'에서 '아보카도'가 언급되었다.
④ '**Finally, don't let your dog snack on grapefruits.**'에서 '자몽'이 언급되었다.

---

18 구직을 위해 담당자에게 보내는 편지   정답률 89% | 정답 ⑤

다음 글의 목적으로 가장 적절한 것은?

① 영업 시작일을 문의하려고
② 인터뷰 일정을 변경하려고

③ 디자인 공모전에 참가하려고
④ 제품 관련 문의에 답변하려고
✓ 의류 매장 판매직에 지원하려고

Dear Ms. MacAlpine,
친애하는 MacAlpine씨에게,
I was so excited to hear / that your brand is opening a new shop / on Bruns Street next month.
저는 듣고 매우 들떴습니다. / 당신의 브랜드가 새 매장을 연다는 것을 / 다음 달에 Bruns 거리에
I have always appreciated the way / your brand helps women to feel more stylish and confident.
저는 항상 높이 평가해 왔습니다. / 당신의 브랜드가 여성들이 더 멋지고 자신 있게 느끼도록 도와주는 방식을
I am writing in response to your ad / in the Bruns Journal.
저는 당신의 광고에 대한 응답으로 편지를 쓰고 있습니다. / Bruns Jornal에 있는
I graduated from the Meline School of Fashion / and have worked as a sales assistant / at LoganMart for the last five years.
저는 Meline 패션 학교를 졸업했습니다 / 그리고 판매 보조원으로 일해 왔습니다. / 지난 5년간 LoganMart에서
During that time, / I've developed strong customer service and sales skills, / and now I would like to apply for the sales position / in your clothing store.
그 기간 동안, / 저는 뛰어난 고객 서비스 및 판매 기술을 발달시켜 왔습니다. / 그리고 이제 판매직에 지원하고 싶습니다. / 당신의 의류 매장의
I am available for an interview / at your earliest convenience.
저는 인터뷰가 가능합니다. / 당신이 편한 가장 빠른 시간에
I look forward to hearing from you.
당신으로부터 대답을 듣게 되기를 기대합니다.
Thank you for reading my letter.
저의 편지를 읽어 주셔서 감사드립니다.
Yours sincerely, // Grace Braddock
Grace Braddock 드림

친애하는 MacAlpine씨에게,

저는 당신의 브랜드가 다음 달에 Bruns 거리에 새 매장을 연다는 것을 듣고 매우 들떴습니다. 저는 당신의 브랜드가 여성들이 더 멋지고 자신감 있게 느끼도록 도와주는 방식을 항상 높이 평가해 왔습니다. 저는 Bruns Journal에 있는 당신의 광고에 대한 응답으로 편지를 쓰고 있습니다. 저는 Meline 패션 학교를 졸업했고 지난 5년간 LoganMart에서 판매 보조원으로 일해 왔습니다. 그 기간 동안, 저는 뛰어난 고객 서비스 및 판매 기술을 발달시켜 왔고, 이제 당신의 의류 매장의 판매직에 지원하고 싶습니다. 저는 당신이 편한 가장 빠른 시간에 인터뷰가 가능합니다. 당신으로부터 대답을 듣게 되기를 기대합니다. 저의 편지를 읽어 주셔서 감사드립니다.

Grace Braddock 드림

Why? 왜 정답일까?
광고를 보고 구직을 위해 담당자에게 보내는 글(During that time, I've developed strong customer service and sales skills, and now I would like to apply for the sales position in your clothing store.)이므로, 글의 목적으로 가장 적절한 것은 ⑤ '의류 매장 판매직에 지원하려고'이다.

● confident ⓐ 자신 있는
● sales assistant 판매 보조원
● ad ⓝ 광고(advertisement)
● convenience ⓝ 편의

구문 풀이

1행 「주어 + 동사 so 형용사/부사(원인) that 주어 + 동사(결과)」
I was so excited to hear that your brand is opening a new shop on Bruns Street next month.
to 부정사 (부사적용법)

---

19 신혼여행에서 생긴 에피소드   정답률 86% | 정답 ①

다음 글에 드러난 'I'의 심경 변화로 가장 적절한 것은?

✓① excited → frustrated
  흥분한   좌절한
② pleased → jealous
  기쁜   질투난
③ nervous → confident
  긴장한   자신 있는
④ annoyed → grateful
  짜증난   감사한
⑤ relaxed → indifferent
  안도한   무관심한

I had never seen a beach / with such white sand or water / that was such a beautiful shade of blue.
나는 해변을 한 번도 본 적이 없었다. / 그렇게 하얀 모래나 물을 가진 / 그렇게 아름다운 푸른 색조의 바다를
Jane and I set up a blanket / on the sand / while looking forward to our ten days of honeymooning / on an exotic island.
Jane과 나는 담요를 깔았다. / 모래 위에 / 열흘간의 신혼여행을 기대하면서 / 이국적인 섬에서의
"Look!" / Jane waved her hand / to point at the beautiful scene / before us / — and her gold wedding ring went flying off her hand.
"저기 좀 봐!" / Jane이 그녀의 손을 흔들었다. / 아름다운 풍경을 가리키기 위해서 / 우리 앞의 / 그러자 그녀의 금으로 된 결혼반지가 날아갔다 / 그녀의 손에서 빠져
I tried to see / where it went, / but the sun hit my eyes / and I lost track of it.
나는 보기 위해 노력했다. / 그것이 날아간 곳을 / 그러나 햇빛이 눈에 들어왔다 / 그리고 나는 그것의 가던 방향을 놓쳤다.
I didn't want to lose her wedding ring, / so I started looking in the area / where I thought it had landed.
나는 그녀의 결혼 반지를 잃어버리고 싶지 않았다. / 그래서 나는 장소를 들여다보기 시작했다. / 내가 생각하기에 그것이 떨어졌
However, / the sand was so fine / and I realized / that anything heavy, like gold, / would quickly sink / and might never be found again.
하지만 / 모래가 너무 고왔다. / 그리고 나는 깨달았다. / 금처럼 무거운 것은 / 빨리 가라앉는다는 것을 / 그리고 다시는 발견되지 않을 수도 있겠다는 것을

나는 그렇게 하얀 모래나 그렇게 아름다운 푸른 색조의 바다를 가진 해변을 한 번도 본 적이 없었다. 이국적인 섬에서의 열흘간의 신혼여행을 기대하면서 Jane과 나는 모래 위에 담요를 깔았다. "저기 좀 봐!" Jane이 아름다운 풍경을 가리키기 위해서 그녀의 손을 흔들었다. 그러자 그녀의 금으로 된 결혼반지가 그녀의 손에서 빠져 날아갔다. 나는 그것이 날아간 곳을 보기 위해 노력했지만, 햇빛이 눈에 들어와 그것의 가던 방향을 놓쳤다. 나는 그녀의 결혼 반지를 잃어버리고 싶지 않아서 내가 생각하기에 그것이 떨어졌던 장소를 들여다보기 시작했다.

하지만 모래가 너무 고왔고 나는 금처럼 무거운 것은 빨리 가라앉아 다시는 발견되지 않을 수도 있겠다는 것을 깨달았다.

Why? 왜 정답일까?
신혼여행에서 아름다운 풍경을 보다 결혼반지를 잃어버리게 되었다("Look!" Jane waved her hand to point at the beautiful scene before us — and her gold wedding ring went flying off her hand.)는 글이다. 따라서 'I'의 심경 변화로 가장 적절한 것은 ① '흥분한 → 좌절한'이다.

● shade ⓝ 색조, 그늘
● exotic ⓐ 이국적인
● track ⓝ 방향, 길
● blanket ⓝ 담요
● wave ⓥ 흔들다
● sink ⓥ 가라앉다

구문 풀이

1행 I had never seen a beach with such white sand or water that was such a
      과거분사(경험)   선행사   관계대명사(주격)
beautiful shade of blue.

---

20 대학 졸업 이후 자발적 배움의 중요성   정답률 81% | 정답 ④

다음 글에서 필자가 주장하는 바로 가장 적절한 것은?

① 성공 경험을 위해 달성 가능한 목표를 수립해야 한다.
② 체계적인 경력 관리를 위해 전문가의 도움을 받아야 한다.
③ 건강을 위해 꾸준한 운동과 식습관 관리를 병행해야 한다.
✓④ 졸업 이후 성장을 위해 자발적으로 배움을 실천해야 한다.
⑤ 적성에 맞는 직업을 찾기 위해 학교 교육에 충실해야 한다.

Unfortunately, / many people don't take personal responsibility / for their own growth.
안타깝게도 / 많은 사람들이 개인적인 책임을 지지 않는다. / 그들 자신의 성장에 대해
Instead, / they simply run the race / laid out for them.
대신 / 그들은 단지 경주를 한다 / 그들에게 놓인
They do well enough in school / to keep advancing.
그들은 학교에서 제법 잘한다. / 계속 발전할 만큼
Maybe / they manage to get a good job / at a well-run company.
아마도 / 그들은 좋은 일자리를 얻는 것을 해낸다. / 잘 운영되는 회사에서
But / so many think and act / as if their learning journey ends with college.
하지만 / 아주 많은 사람들이 생각하고 행동한다. / 마치 그들의 배움의 여정이 대학으로 끝나는 것처럼
They have checked all the boxes in the life / that was laid out for them / and now lack a road map / describing the right ways / to move forward and continue to grow.
그들은 삶의 모든 사항을 체크했다. / 그들에게 놓인 / 그리고 이제는 로드맵이 없다. / 올바른 방법을 설명해 주는 / 앞으로 나아가고 계속 성장할 수 있는
In truth, / that's when the journey really begins.
사실 / 그때가 여정이 진정으로 시작되는 때이다.
When school is finished, / your growth becomes voluntary.
학교 교육이 끝나면 / 여러분의 성장은 자발적이게 된다.
Like healthy eating habits or a regular exercise program, / you need to commit to it / and devote thought, time, and energy to it.
건강한 식습관이나 규칙적인 운동 프로그램처럼 / 여러분은 그것에 전념할 필요가 있다. / 그리고 거기에 생각, 시간, 그리고 에너지를 쏟을
Otherwise, / it simply won't happen / — and your life and career are likely to stop progressing / as a result.
그렇지 않으면 / 그것은 그냥 일어나지 않을 것이다. / 그리고 여러분의 삶과 경력이 진전을 멈출 가능성이 있다. / 결과적으로

안타깝게도 많은 사람들이 그들 자신의 성장에 대해 개인적인 책임을 지지 않는다. 대신, 그들은 단지 그들에게 놓인 경주를 한다. 그들은 학교에서 계속 발전할 만큼 제법 잘한다. 아마도 그들은 잘 운영되는 회사에서 좋은 일자리를 얻는 것을 해낸다. 하지만 아주 많은 사람들이 마치 그들의 배움의 여정이 대학으로 끝나는 것처럼 생각하고 행동한다. 그들은 그들에게 놓인 삶의 모든 사항을 체크했고 이제는 앞으로 나아가고 계속 성장할 수 있는 올바른 방법을 설명해 주는 로드맵이 없다. 사실, 그때가 여정이 진정으로 시작되는 때이다. 학교 교육이 끝나면, 여러분의 성장은 자발적이게 된다. 건강한 식습관이나 규칙적인 운동 프로그램처럼 여러분은 그것에 전념하고 그것에 생각, 시간, 그리고 에너지를 쏟을 필요가 있다. 그렇지 않으면 그것은 그냥 일어나지 않을 것이고, 결과적으로 여러분의 삶과 경력이 진전을 멈출 가능성이 있다.

Why? 왜 정답일까?
대학이 끝이 아니라, 졸업 이후에도 자발적인 배움으로 계속 성장하기 위해 노력해야 한다(In truth, that's when the journey really begins. When school is finished, your growth becomes voluntary.)고 조언하는 글이므로, 필자가 주장하는 바로 가장 적절한 것은 ④ '졸업 이후 성장을 위해 자발적으로 배움을 실천해야 한다.'이다.

● unfortunately ⓐⓓ 안타깝게도
● responsibility ⓝ 책임감
● lay out 놓이다
● lack ⓥ 부족하다 ⓝ 부족
● voluntary ⓐ 자발적인
● personal ⓐ 개인적인
● growth ⓝ 성장
● manage ⓥ 관리하다
● journey ⓝ 여정, 여행
● devote ⓥ 쏟다, 몰두하다

구문 풀이

5행 But so many think and act as if their learning journey ends with college.
          주어(대명사)   동사   부사절 접속사

---

21 객관적이자 주관적으로 바라보는 색   정답률 52% | 정답 ④

밑줄 친 our brain and the universe meet가 다음 글에서 의미하는 바로 가장 적절한 것은?
[3점]

① we see things beyond the range of perception – 우리는 인식의 범위를 넘어 사물을 본다
② objects appear different by the change of light – 사물은 빛의 변화에 따라 다르게 나타난다
③ your perspectives and others' reach an agreement – 나와 타인의 관점이 합의에 도달한다
✓④ our mind and physical reality interact with each other – 정신과 물리적 현실은 서로 상호작용한다
⑤ structures of the human brain and the universe are similar – 인간 뇌의 구조와 우주는 닮았다

Many people take the commonsense view / that color is an objective property / of things, / or of the light that bounces off them.
많은 사람들이 상식적인 견해를 취한다. / 색은 객관적인 속성이다. / 사물의 / 또는 사물로부터 튕겨 나오는 빛의

They say a tree's leaves are green / because they reflect green light / — a greenness that is just as real as the leaves.
그들은 나뭇잎이 녹색이라고 말한다. / 그들이 녹색 빛을 반사하기 때문에 / 나뭇잎만큼 진짜인 녹색

Others argue / that color doesn't inhabit the physical world at all / but exists only / in the eye or mind of the viewer.
다른 사람들은 주장한다. / 색이 물리적인 세계에 전혀 존재하지 않는다고 / 보는 사람의 눈이나 정신 안에만 존재한다고

They maintain / that if a tree fell in a forest / and no one was there to see it, / its leaves would be colorless — and so would everything else.
그들은 주장한다. / 만약 나무가 숲에서 쓰러진다면 / 그리고 그것을 볼 사람이 아무도 거기에 없다면 / 그것의 잎은 색이 없을 것이다. / 그리고 다른 모든 것들도 그럴 것이라고

They say there is no such *thing* as color; / there are only the people who see it.
그들은 색 같은 '것'은 없다고 말한다 / 다시 말하면 그것을 보는 사람들만 있다고

Both positions are, in a way, correct.
두 가지 입장 모두 어떤 면에서는 옳다.

Color is objective *and* subjective / — "the place," as Paul Cézanne put it, / "where our brain and the universe meet."
색은 객관적이고 '동시에' 주관적이다. / 즉 Paul Cézanne이 말했듯이 ~이다. / '우리의 뇌와 우주가 만나는 곳'

Color is created / when light from the world is registered by the eyes / and interpreted by the brain.
색은 만들어진다. / 세상으로부터의 빛이 눈에 의해 등록될 때 / 그리고 뇌에 의해 해석될 때

많은 사람들이 색은 사물 또는 사물로부터 튕겨 나오는 빛의 객관적인 속성이라는 상식적인 견해를 취한다. 그들은 나뭇잎이 녹색 빛(정확히 나뭇잎만큼 진짜인 녹색)을 반사하기 때문에 녹색이라고 말한다. 다른 사람들은 색이 물리적인 세계에 전혀 존재하지 않고 보는 사람의 눈이나 정신 안에만 존재한다고 주장한다. 그들은 만약 나무가 숲에서 쓰러지고 그것을 볼 사람이 아무도 거기에 없다면, 그것의 잎은 색이 없을 것이고, 다른 모든 것들도 그럴 것이라고 주장한다. 그들은 색 같은 '것'은 없고 다시 말하면 그것을 보는 사람들만 있다고 말한다. 두 가지 입장 모두 어떤 면에서는 옳다. 색은 객관적이고 '동시에' 주관적이며, Paul Cézanne이 말했듯이 '우리의 뇌와 우주가 만나는 곳'이다. 색은 세상으로부터의 빛이 눈에 의해 등록되고 뇌에 의해 해석될 때 만들어진다.

Why? 왜 정답일까?

색은 사물로부터 튕겨 나오는 빛인 동시에 사람이 인식하면서 만들어진다고(Color is created when light from the world is registered by the eyes and interpreted by the brain.)고 말하는 것으로 보아, 밑줄 친 부분의 의미로 가장 적절한 것은 ④ '정신과 물리적 현실은 서로 상호작용한다'이다.

- **commonsense** ⓐ 상식적인
- **property** ⓝ 속성, 재산
- **reflect** ⓥ 반사하다
- **physical** ⓐ 물리적인
- **subjective** ⓐ 주관적인
- **perception** ⓝ 인식
- **objective** ⓐ 객관적인
- **bounce off** 반사하다
- **greenness** 녹색, 푸르름
- **position** ⓝ 입장, 위치
- **range** ⓝ 범위
- **perspective** ⓝ 관점

구문 풀이

5행 Others argue that color doesn't inhabit the physical world at all but exists only in the eye or mind of the viewer.
관계대명사(목적격) / not A but B : A가 아니라 B다

---

22 소설을 쓸 때 중요한 것 정답률 66% | 정답 ⑤

다음 글의 요지로 가장 적절한 것은?
① 작품의 완성도는 작가의 경험의 양에 비례한다.
② 작가의 상상력은 가장 훌륭한 이야기 재료이다.
③ 소설에서 사건 전개에 대한 묘사는 구체적일수록 좋다.
④ 소설을 쓸 때 독자의 관심사를 먼저 고려하는 것이 중요하다.
✔ 소설에 포함될 세부 사항은 인간의 경험을 드러내는 것이어야 한다.

When writing a novel, / research for information needs to be done.
소설을 쓸 때 / 정보를 위한 조사가 행해질 필요가 있다.

The thing is / that some kinds of fiction demand a higher level of detail: / crime fiction, for example, or scientific thrillers.
문제는 ~는 것이다. / 어떤 종류의 소설은 더 높은 수준의 세부 사항을 요구한다. / 예를 들어 범죄 소설이나 과학 스릴러와 같은

The information is never hard to find; / one website for authors even organizes trips to police stations, / so that crime writers can get it right.
정보는 찾기에 결코 어렵지 않다. / 작가들을 위한 한 웹사이트는 심지어 경찰서로의 탐방을 조직하기도 한다. / 범죄물 작가들이 정보를 제대로 얻을 수 있도록

Often, / a polite letter will earn you permission / to visit a particular location / and record all the details / that you need.
종종 / 정중한 편지는 여러분에게 허가를 얻어 줄 것이다. / 특정한 장소를 방문할 수 있는 / 그리고 모든 세부 사항을 기록할 수 있는 / 여러분이 필요한

But remember / that you will drive your readers to boredom / if you think / that you need to pack everything you discover / into your work.
하지만 기억하라. / 여러분이 독자를 지루하게 만들 것이라는 것을 / 만약 여러분이 생각할 경우 / 여러분이 발견한 모든 것을 담아야 한다고 / 여러분의 작품에

The details that matter / are those that reveal the human experience.
중요한 세부 사항은 / 인간의 경험을 드러내는 것이다.

The crucial thing is telling a story, / finding the characters, the tension, and the conflict / — not the train timetable or the building blueprint.
중요한 것은 이야기를 말하는 것이다. / 인물, 긴장, 그리고 갈등을 찾아가며 / 기차 시간표나 건물 청사진이 아니라

소설을 쓸 때 정보를 위한 조사가 행해질 필요가 있다. 문제는 예를 들어 범죄 소설이나 과학 스릴러와 같은 어떤 종류의 소설은 더 높은 수준의 세부 사항을 요구한다는 것이다. 정보는 찾기에 결코 어렵지 않다. 작가들을 위한 한 웹사이트는 범죄물 작가들이 정보를 제대로 얻을 수 있도록 심지어 경찰서로의 탐방을 조직하기도 한다. 종종 정중한 편지는 여러분에게 특정한 장소를 방문하고 필요한 모든 세부 사항을 기록할 수 있는 허가를 얻어 줄 것이다. 하지만 만약 여러분이 발견한 모든 것을 작품에 담아야 한다고 생각할 경우 여러분은 독자들을 지루하게 만들 것이라는 것을 기억하라. 중요한 세부 사항은 인간의 경험을 드러내는 것이다.

중요한 것은 기차 시간표나 건물 청사진이 아니라 인물, 긴장, 그리고 갈등을 찾아가며 이야기를 말하는 것이다.

Why? 왜 정답일까?

소설을 쓸 때 범죄 소설이나, 스릴러는 더 높은 수준의 세부 사항을 요구하는데 이때 세부 사항은 인간의 경험을 드러내야 한다(The details that matter are those that reveal the human experience.)는 내용이다. 따라서 글의 요지로 가장 적절한 것은 ⑤ '소설에 포함될 세부 사항은 인간의 경험을 드러내는 것이어야 한다.'이다.

- **demand** ⓥ 요구하다
- **author** ⓝ 작가
- **drive** ⓥ 만들다, 몰아가다
- **fiction** ⓝ 소설
- **permission** ⓝ 허락
- **boredom** ⓝ 지루함

구문 풀이

4행 The information is never hard to find; one website for authors even organizes trips to police stations, so that crime writers can get it right.
to부정사(형용사적 용법) / 접속사(~할 수 있도록)

---

23 구강 건강의 중요성 정답률 82% | 정답 ④

다음 글의 주제로 가장 적절한 것은?
① the way the immune system fights viruses
면역 체계가 바이러스와 싸우는 방법
② the effect of unhealthy eating habits on the body
건강하지 않은 식습관이 몸에 미치는 영향
③ the difficulty in raising awareness about oral health
구강 건강에 관한 인식이 증가하는 것에 대한 어려움
✔ the importance of oral health and its impact on the body
구강 건강의 중요성과 몸에 미치는 영향
⑤ the relationship between oral health and emotional well-being
구강건강과 정신적 웰빙 사이의 관계

Nearly everything has to go through your mouth / to get to the rest of you, / from food and air to bacteria and viruses.
거의 모든 것이 여러분의 구강을 거쳐야 한다. / 여러분의 나머지 부분에 도달하기 위해 / 음식과 공기에서부터 박테리아와 바이러스까지

A healthy mouth can help your body get / what it needs and prevent it from harm / — with adequate space for air to travel to your lungs, and healthy teeth and gums / that prevent harmful microorganisms from entering your bloodstream.
건강한 구강은 당신의 몸이 얻는 것을 도와줄 수 있다. / 몸이 필요한 것을 얻고, 피해로부터 몸을 지키도록 / 공기가 폐로 이동할 수 있는 적당한 공간, 그리고 건강한 치아와 잇몸으로부터 / 해로운 미생물이 혈류로 들어가는 것을 막는

From the moment you are created, / oral health affects every aspect of your life.
여러분이 생겨난 순간부터 / 구강 건강은 여러분의 삶의 모든 측면에 영향을 미친다.

What happens in the mouth / is usually just the tip of the iceberg / and a reflection / of what is happening in other parts of the body.
구강 안에서 일어나는 일은 / 대개 빙산의 일각일 뿐이다. / 그리고 반영이다. / 신체의 다른 부분에서 일어나고 있는 일의

Poor oral health can be a cause of a disease / that affects the entire body.
나쁜 구강 건강은 질병의 원인일 수 있다. / 전체 몸에 영향을 끼치는

The microorganisms in an unhealthy mouth / can enter the bloodstream / and travel anywhere in the body, / posing serious health risks.
건강하지 않은 구강 안의 미생물은 / 혈류로 들어갈 수 있다. / 그리고 신체의 어느 곳이든 이동할 수 있다. / 그 결과 심각한 건강상의 위험을 초래할 수 있다.

음식과 공기에서부터 박테리아와 바이러스까지 거의 모든 것이 여러분의 나머지 부분에 도달하기 위해 여러분의 구강을 거쳐야 한다. 건강한 구강은 공기가 폐로 이동할 수 있는 적당한 공간, 그리고 해로운 미생물이 혈류로 들어가는 것을 막는 건강한 치아와 잇몸으로부터 여러분의 몸이 필요한 것을 얻고, 피해로부터 몸을 지키도록 도와줄 수 있다. 여러분이 생겨난 순간부터 구강 건강은 여러분의 삶의 모든 측면에 영향을 미친다. 구강 안에서 일어나는 일은 대개 빙산의 일각일 뿐이며 신체의 다른 부분에서 일어나고 있는 일의 반영이다. 나쁜 구강 건강은 전체 몸에 영향을 끼치는 질병의 원인일 수 있다. 건강하지 않은 구강 안의 미생물은 혈류로 들어가고 신체의 어느 곳이든 이동하여 그 결과 심각한 건강상의 위험을 초래할 수 있다.

Why? 왜 정답일까?

건강한 구강은 몸에 필요한 것들을 전달하고 해로운 것들을 막는 역할을 한다(A healthy mouth can help your body get what it needs and prevent it from harm—with adequate space for air to travel to your lungs, and healthy teeth and gums that prevent harmful microorganisms from entering your bloodstream.)는 내용이다. 구강 건강이 나빠지면 몸에 해로운 미생물이 혈류로 들어가 위험할 수 있다는 내용이 뒤따른다. 따라서 글의 주제로 가장 적절한 것은 ④ '구강 건강의 중요성과 몸에 미치는 영향'이다.

- **prevent** ⓥ 막다
- **lung** ⓝ 폐
- **affect** ⓥ 영향을 미치다
- **iceberg** ⓝ 빙산
- **poor** ⓐ 좋지 못한
- **entire** ⓐ 전체의
- **immune system** 면역 체계
- **impact** ⓥ 영향을 주다
- **adequate** ⓐ 충분한
- **microorganism** ⓝ 미생물
- **aspect** ⓝ 측면
- **reflection** ⓝ 반영
- **disease** ⓝ 질병
- **serious** ⓐ 심각한
- **awareness** ⓝ 인식
- **emotional** ⓐ 감정적인

구문 풀이

2행 A healthy mouth can help your body get what it needs and prevent it from harm — with adequate space for air to travel to your lungs, and healthy teeth and gums that prevent harmful microorganisms from entering your bloodstream.
조동사 / 목적어 / 목적보어(동사원형) / 동사2(help와 병렬) / 선행사 / 관계대명사(주격)

---

24 신경 메커니즘에 따른 지루함 정답률 72% | 정답 ②

다음 글의 제목으로 가장 적절한 것은?
① The Brain's Brilliant Trick to Overcome Fear
두려움 극복에 대한 뇌의 뛰어난 속임수

② Boredom: Neural Mechanism for Detecting Change
지루함: 변화를 감지하는 신경 매커니즘
③ Humans' Endless Desire to Pursue Familiar Experiences
친숙한 경험을 추구하는 것에 대한 인간의 끝없는 욕망
④ The Destruction of Nature in Exchange for Human Survival
인간 생존의 대가로의 자연 파괴
⑤ How Humans Changed the Environment to Their Advantage
인간이 어떻게 환경을 자신들에게 유리하게 변화시켰는가

Kids tire of their toys, / college students get sick of cafeteria food, / and sooner or later most of us lose interest / in our favorite TV shows.
아이들은 자기들의 장난감에 지루해 한다. / 대학생들은 카페테리아 음식에 실증을 낸다. / 그리고 머지않아 우리 중 대부분은 흥미를 잃는다. / 우리가 가장 좋아하는 TV 쇼에

The bottom line is / that we humans are easily bored.
요점은 ~이다. / 우리 인간이 쉽게 지루해한다는 것

But why should this be true?
그런데 왜 이것이 사실이어야 할까?

The answer lies buried deep / in our nerve cells, / which are designed to reduce their initial excited response / to stimuli each time they occur.
답은 깊이 숨어있다. / 우리의 신경 세포 안에 / 그것에 대한 초기의 흥분된 반응을 약화하도록 설계된 / 자극이 일어날 때마다

At the same time, / these neurons enhance their responses to things that change / especially things that change quickly.
동시에 / 이 뉴런들은 변화하는 것들에 대한 반응을 강화한다. / 특히 빠르게 변화하는 것들

We probably evolved this way / because our ancestors got more survival value, / for example, / from attending to what was moving in a tree (such as a puma) / than to the tree itself.
우리는 아마도 이런 방식으로 진화했을 것이다. / 왜냐하면 우리의 조상이 더 많은 생존 가치를 얻었기 때문이다. / 예를 들어 / 나무에서 움직이는 것에 주의를 기울이는 것으로부터 (퓨마처럼) / 나무 그 자체보다

Boredom in reaction to an unchanging environment turns down / the level of neural excitation / so that new stimuli (like our ancestor's hypothetical puma threat) stand out more.
변화지 않는 환경에 대한 반응으로의 지루함은 낮춘다. / 신경 흥분의 수준을 / 그래서 새로운 자극이 더 두드러지게 한다. (우리 조상이 가정한 퓨마의 위협과 같은)

It's the neural equivalent / of turning off a front door light / to see the fireflies.
이것은 신경적 대응물이다. / 앞문의 불을 끄는 것의 / 반딧불이를 보기 위해

아이들은 자기들의 장난감에 지루해하고, 대학생들은 카페테리아 음식에 실증을 내고, 머지않아 우리 중 대부분은 우리가 가장 좋아하는 TV 쇼에 흥미를 잃는다. 요점은 우리 인간이 쉽게 지루해한다는 것이다. 그런데 왜 이것이 사실이어야 할까? 답은 자극이 일어날 때마다 그것에 대한 초기의 흥분된 반응을 약화하도록 설계된 우리의 신경 세포 안에 깊이 숨어 있다. 동시에 이 뉴런들은 변화하는 것들, 특히 빠르게 변화하는 것들에 대한 반응을 강화한다. 예를 들면 우리는 아마도 우리의 조상이 나무 그 자체보다 (퓨마처럼) 나무에서 움직이는 것에 주의를 기울이는 것으로부터 더 많은 생존 가치를 얻었기 때문에 이런 방식으로 진화했을 것이다. 변화하지 않는 환경에 대한 반응으로의 지루함은 신경 흥분의 수준을 낮춰 (우리 조상이 가정한 퓨마의 위협과 같은) 새로운 자극이 더 두드러지게 한다. 이것은 반딧불이를 보기 위해 앞문의 불을 끄는 것의 신경적 대응물이다.

Why? 왜 정답일까?

인간은 쉽게 지루함을 느끼는데, 자극이 일어날 때마다 초기의 흥분된 반응을 약화하고 빠르게 변화하는 것에 대한 반응을 강화하도록 설계되었다(The answer lies buried deep in our nerve cells, which are designed to reduce their initial excited response to stimuli each time they occur. At the same time, these neurons enhance their responses to things that change especially things that change quickly.)는 내용이므로, 글의 제목으로 가장 적절한 것은 ② '지루함: 변화를 감지하는 신경 매커니즘'이다.

- sick of ~에 실증나다
- bottom line 요점
- neuron ⓝ 뉴런(신경세포단위)
- probably ⓐⓓ 아마도
- ancestor ⓝ 조상
- stimuli ⓝ 자극(stimulus)의 복수형
- neural ⓐ 신경의
- interest ⓝ 흥미
- bury ⓥ 숨어있다
- enhance ⓥ 강화하다
- evolve ⓥ 진화하다
- excitation ⓝ 자극
- hypothetical ⓐ 가정의, 가상의
- equivalent ⓝ 대응물

구문 풀이

4행 The answer lies buried deep in our nerve cells, which are designed to
　　　　　　　　　　　　　　　　　선행사　　관계대명사(주격)
reduce their initial excited response to stimuli each time they occur.

25 청정에너지와 화석 연료에 대한 전세계 투자액 비교　　정답률 84% | 정답 ⑤

다음 도표의 내용과 일치하지 않는 것은?

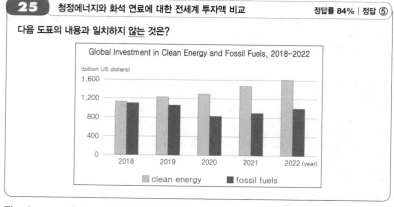

Global Investment in Clean Energy and Fossil Fuels, 2018~2022
(billion US dollars)
□ clean energy　■ fossil fuels

The above graph shows / global energy investment / in clean energy and in fossil fuels / between 2018 and 2022.
위의 그래프는 보여 준다 / 전 세계 에너지 투자액을 / 청정에너지와 화석 연료에 대한 / 2018년과 2022년 사이에

① Since 2018 / global energy investment in clean energy / continued to rise, / reaching its highest level in 2022.
2018년 이후로 / 청정에너지에 대한 전 세계 투자액은 / 계속해서 상승했다. / 그리고 2022년에 가장 높은 수준에 도달했다.

② The investment gap / between clean energy and fossil fuels in 2020 / was larger than that in 2019.
투자액 격차는 / 2020년 청정에너지와 화석 연료 사이의 / 2019년의 그것보다 컸다.

③ Investment in fossil fuels was highest in 2018 / and lowest in 2020.
화석 연료에 대한 투자액은 2018년에 가장 높았다. / 그리고 2020년에 가장 낮았다.

④ In 2021, / investment in clean energy exceeded 1,200 billion dollars, / while investment in fossil fuels did not.
2021년에는 / 청정에너지에 대한 투자액이 1조 2000억 달러를 넘었다. / 반면에 화석 연료에 대한 투자액은 그러지 않았다.

☑ In 2022, / the global investment in clean energy / was more than double / that of fossil fuels.
2022년에 / 청정에너지에 대한 전 세계 투자액이 / 두 배 이상이었다. / 화석 연료의 그것의

위의 그래프는 2018년과 2022년 사이에 청정에너지와 화석 연료에 대한 전 세계 에너지 투자액을 보여준다. ① 2018년 이후로 청정에너지에 대한 전 세계 투자액은 계속해서 상승했으며, 2022년에 가장 높은 수준에 도달했다. ② 2020년의 청정에너지와 화석 연료 사이 투자액 격차는 2019년의 그것보다 컸다. ③ 화석 연료에 대한 투자액은 2018년에 가장 높았고 2020년에 가장 낮았다. ④ 2021년에는 청정에너지에 대한 투자액이 1조 2000억 달러를 넘은 반면, 화석 연료에 대한 투자액은 그러지 않았다. ⑤ 2022년에는 청정에너지에 대한 전 세계 투자액이 화석 연료 그것의 두 배 이상이었다.

Why? 왜 정답일까?

도표에 따르면 2022년 청정에너지에 대한 전 세계 투자액은 화석 연료에 대한 투자액의 두 배 이하다. 따라서 도표와 일치하지 않는 것은 ⑤이다.

- fossil ⓝ 화석
- investment ⓝ 투자
- exceed ⓥ 초과하다
- fuel ⓝ 연료
- reach ⓥ 도달하다
- billion 10억

구문 풀이

2행 Since 2018 global energy investment in clean energy continued to rise,
reaching its highest level in 2022.
　　　　현재분사(계속적 용법)

26 Frederick Douglass의 생애　　정답률 91% | 정답 ③

Frederick Douglass에 관한 다음 글의 내용과 일치하지 않는 것은?

① Maryland에서 노예로 태어났다.
② 노예들이 탈출하는 것을 돕는 조직의 리더가 되었다.
☑ 다른 노예들로부터 읽고 쓰는 법을 배웠다.
④ 노예로서의 자신의 경험을 묘사한 자서전을 썼다.
⑤ 미국의 첫 아프리카계 미국인 부통령 후보가 되었다.

「Frederick Douglass was born into slavery / at a farm in Maryland.」 ①의 근거 일치
Frederick Douglass는 노예로 태어났다. / Maryland의 한 농장에서
His full name / at birth / was Frederick Augustus Washington Bailey.
그의 성명은 / 태어났을 때 / Frederick Augustus Washington Bailey였다.
He changed his name to Frederick Douglass / after he successfully escaped from slavery in 1838.
그는 그의 이름을 Frederick Douglass로 바꿨다. / 1838년에 노예 상태에서 성공적으로 탈출한 후
「He became a leader of the Underground Railroad / — a network of people, places, and routes / that helped enslaved people escape to the north.」 ②의 근거 일치
그는 Underground Railroad의 리더가 되었다. / 사람, 장소, 경로의 조직인 / 노예가 된 사람들을 북쪽으로 탈출하도록 돕는
He assisted other runaway slaves / until they could safely get to other areas / in the north.
그는 다른 도망친 노예들 도왔다. / 그들이 다른 지역에 안전하게 도착할 수 있을 때까지 / 북쪽에
「As a slave, / he had taught himself to read and write / and he spread / that knowledge to other slaves as well.」 ③의 근거 불일치
노예로서 / 그는 읽고 쓰는 것을 독학했다. / 그리고 그는 전파했다. / 그 지식을 다른 노예들에게도
Once free, / he became a well-known abolitionist / and strong believer in equality for all people / including Blacks, Native Americans, women, and recent immigrants.
자유로워지고 난 뒤 / 그는 유명한 노예제 폐지론자가 되었다. / 그리고 모든 사람들을 위한 평등에 대한 강한 신봉자가 되었다. / 흑인, 아메리카 원주민, 여성, 그리고 최근 이민자들을 포함한
「He wrote several autobiographies / describing his experiences as a slave.」 ④의 근거 일치
그는 몇 권의 자서전을 썼다. / 노예로서의 자신의 경험을 묘사한
「In addition to all this, / he became the first African-American candidate / for vice president of the United States.」 ⑤의 근거 일치
이 모든 것에 더하여 / 그는 첫 아프리카계 미국인 후보가 되었다. / 미국의 부통령을 위한

Frederick Douglass는 Maryland의 한 농장에서 노예로 태어났다. 태어났을 때 그의 성명은 Frederick Augustus Washington Bailey였다. 그는 1838년에 노예 상태에서 성공적으로 탈출한 후 자신의 이름을 Frederick Douglass로 바꿨다. 그는 노예가 된 사람들을 북쪽으로 탈출하도록 돕는 사람, 장소, 경로의 조직인 Underground Railroad의 리더가 되었다. 그는 다른 도망친 노예들이 북쪽의 다른 지역에 안전하게 도착할 수 있을 때까지 그들을 도왔다. 노예로서 그는 읽고 쓰는 것을 독학했고, 그 지식을 다른 노예들에게도 전파했다. 자유로워지고 난 뒤 그는 유명한 노예제 폐지론자이자 흑인, 아메리카 원주민, 여성, 그리고 최근 이민자들을 포함한 모든 사람들을 위한 평등에 대한 강한 신봉자가 되었다. 그는 노예로서의 자신의 경험을 묘사한 몇 권의 자서전을 썼다. 이 모든 것에 더하여 그는 미국의 첫 아프리카계 미국인 부통령 후보가 되었다.

Why? 왜 정답일까?

'As a slave, he had taught himself to read and write and he spread that knowledge to other slaves as well.'에서 스스로 읽고 쓰는 법을 배웠다고 하므로, 내용과 일치하지 않는 것은 ③ '다른 노예들로부터 읽고 쓰는 법을 배웠다.'이다.

Why? 왜 오답일까?

① 'Frederick Douglass was born into slavery at a farm in Maryland.'의 내용과 일치한다.
② 'He became a leader of the Underground Railroad — a network of people, places, and routes that helped enslaved people escape to the north.'의 내용과 일치한다.
④ 'He wrote several autobiographies describing his experiences as a slave.'의 내용과 일치한다.
⑤ 'In addition to all this, he became the first African-American candidate for vice president of the United States.'의 내용과 일치한다.

구문 풀이

4행 He became a leader of the Underground Railroad — a network of people, places, and routes that helped enslaved people escape to the north.
선행사 / 관계대명사(주격) / 동사 / 목적어 / 목적보어(동사원형)

---

27 게이트볼 챔피언십 정답률 89% | 정답 ⑤

2023 Australian Gateball Championships에 관한 다음 안내문의 내용과 일치하지 <u>않는</u> 것은?

① 4일 동안 진행된다.
② 복식 경기는 오전에 열린다.
③ 모든 참가자는 참가 증서를 받는다.
④ 참가비는 무료이다.
☑ 현장에서 등록하는 것이 가능하다.

2023 Australian Gateball Championships
2023 오스트레일리아 게이트볼 챔피언십
The Diamond Coast is getting set / to welcome the Australian Gateball Championships.
Diamond Coast는 준비를 하고 있다. / 오스트레일리아 게이트볼 챔피언십을 환영할
Join this great outdoor competition / and be the winner this year!
이 멋진 야외 대회에 참여하세요. / 그리고 올해 우승자가 되세요.
When & Where
언제 & 어디서
「December 19 — 22, 2023」 ①의 근거 일치
2023년 1월 19일부터 22일까지
Diamond Coast Performance Centre
Diamond Coast 공연 센터
Schedule of Matches
경기 일정
「Doubles matches (9 a.m. — 11 a.m.)」 ②의 근거 일치
복식 경기 (오전 9시부터 오전 11시까지)
Team matches (1 p.m. — 3 p.m.)
단체 경기 (오후 1시부터 오후 3시까지)
Prizes
상
「Every participant will receive a certificate for entry.」 ③의 근거 일치
모든 참가자는 참가 증서를 받을 것입니다.
Champions are awarded a medal.
우승자들은 메달을 받습니다.
Note
참고
「Participation is free.」 ④의 근거 일치
참가비는 무료입니다.
Visit www.australiangateball.com for registration.
등록을 위해 www.australiangateball.com을 방문하십시오.
「(Registration on site is not available.)」 ⑤의 근거 불일치
(현장 등록은 불가합니다.)

2023 오스트레일리아 게이트볼 챔피언십

Diamond Coast는 오스트레일리아 게이트볼 챔피언십을 환영할 준비를 하고 있습니다. 이 멋진 야외 대회에 참여해서 올해 우승자가 되세요!

언제 & 어디서
▶ 2023년 12월 19일부터 22일까지
▶ Diamond Coast 공연 센터

경기 일정
▶ 복식 경기 (오전 9시부터 오전 11시까지)
▶ 단체 경기 (오후 1시부터 오후 3시까지)

상
▶ 모든 참가자는 참가 증서를 받을 것입니다.
▶ 우승자들은 메달을 받습니다.

참고
▶ 참가비는 무료입니다.
▶ 등록을 위해 www.australiangateball.com을 방문하십시오. (현장 등록은 불가합니다.)

Why? 왜 정답일까?
'Registration on site is not available.'에서 현장 등록이 불가능하다고 하므로, 안내문의 내용과 일치하지 않는 것은 ⑤ '현장에서 등록하는 것이 가능하다'이다.

Why? 왜 오답일까?
① 'December 19 – 22, 2023'의 내용과 일치한다.
② 'Doubles matches (9 a.m. – 11 a.m.)'의 내용과 일치한다.
③ 'Every participant will receive a certificate for entry.'의 내용과 일치한다.
④ 'Participation is free.'의 내용과 일치한다.

---

28 도시 어드벤처 탐험 광고 정답률 89% | 정답 ⑤

The Amazing Urban Adventure Quest에 관한 다음 안내문의 내용과 일치하는 것은?
① 참여하는 동안 스마트폰 사용은 금지된다.

② 일 년 내내 일몰 후 참여할 수 있다.
③ 서편 코스는 나이 제한이 없다.
④ 1인당 40달러의 요금이 든다.
☑ 할인받을 수 있는 코드가 있다.

The Amazing Urban Adventure Quest
놀라운 도시 어드벤처 탐험
Explore Central Park while solving clues / and completing challenges!
단서를 해결하면서 Central Park를 탐험하세요! 그리고 도전을 완수하면서
「Guided by your smartphone, / make your way among the well-known places / in the park.」 ①의 근거 불일치
스마트폰의 안내를 받으면서 / 명소들 속 자신의 길을 만들어 보세요. / 공원의
When & How
언제 & 어떻게
「Available 365 days a year // (from sunrise to sunset)」 ②의 근거 불일치
1년 365일 이용 가능 // (일출부터 일몰까지)
Start when you want.
여러분이 원할 때 시작하세요.
Get a stamp at each checkpoint.
각 체크포인트에서 스탬프를 받으세요.
Adventure Courses
어드벤처 코스
East Side: Starts at Twilight Gardens (no age limit)
동편: Twilight Gardens에서 시작합니다. (나이 제한 없음)
「West Side: Starts at Strawberry Castle (over 15 years old)」 ③의 근거 불일치
서편: Strawberry Castle에서 시작합니다. (15세 초과)
Registration & Cost
등록 & 비용
Sign up online at www.urbanquest.com.
www.urbanquest.com에서 온라인으로 등록하세요.
「$40 for a team of 2 — 5 people」 ④의 근거 불일치
2 – 5명으로 구성된 팀 당 40달러
「Save 20% with discount code: CENTRALQUEST」 ⑤의 근거 일치
할인 코드 CENTRALQUEST로 20%를 절약하세요.

놀라운 도시 어드벤처 탐험

단서를 해결하고 도전을 완수하면서 Central Park를 탐험하세요! 스마트폰의 안내를 받으면서 공원의 명소들 속 자신의 길을 만들어 보세요.

언제 & 어떻게
• 1년 365일 이용 가능 (일출부터 일몰까지)
• 여러분이 원할 때 시작하세요.
• 각 체크포인트에서 스탬프를 받으세요.

어드벤처 코스
• 동편: Twilight Gardens에서 시작합니다. (나이 제한 없음)
• 서편: Strawberry Castle에서 시작합니다. (15세 초과)

등록 & 비용
• www.urbanquest.com에서 온라인으로 등록하세요.
• 2 – 5명으로 구성된 팀 당 40달러
• 할인 코드 CENTRALQUEST로 20%를 절약하세요.

Why? 왜 정답일까?
'Save 20% with discount code: CENTRALQUEST'에서 20% 할인 코드를 안내하고 있으므로, 안내문의 내용과 일치하는 것은 ⑤ '할인받을 수 있는 코드가 있다.'이다.

Why? 왜 오답일까?
① 'Guided by your smartphone, make your way among the well-known places in the park.'에서 스마트 폰의 안내를 받으라고 하며 이용을 권장하였다.
② 'Available 365 days a year (from sunrise to sunset)'에서 일출부터 일몰까지 참여할 수 있다고 하였다.
③ 'West Side: Starts at Strawberry Castle (over 15 years old)'에서 서편 코스는 15세 초과부터 참여 가능하다고 하였다.
④ '$40 for a team of 2 – 5 people'에서 2 – 5명의 팀 당 40달러의 요금이 든다고 하였다.

★★★ 등급을 가르는 문제!
29 뇌사 결정에 대한 엄격한 지침 정답률 47% | 정답 ④

다음 글의 밑줄 친 부분 중, 어법상 틀린 것은? [3점]

Some countries have proposed tougher guidelines / for determining brain death / when transplantation — transferring organs to others — is under consideration.
일부 국가는 더 엄격한 지침을 제안했다. / 뇌사를 결정하는 것에 대한 / 장기 이식, 즉 다른 사람에게 장기를 전달하는 것을 고려 중일 때
In several European countries, / there are legal requirements / which specify ① that a whole team of doctors must agree over the diagnosis of death / in the case of a potential donor.
몇몇 유럽 국가에는 / 법적 요건들이 있다. / 의사 팀 전체가 사망 진단에 동의해야 한다고 명시하는 / 잠재적 기증자의 경우
The reason for these strict regulations / for diagnosing brain death / in potential organ donors / ② is, / no doubt, / to ease public fears of a premature diagnosis of brain death / for the purpose of obtaining organs.
이러한 엄격한 규정들의 이유는 / 뇌사 진단에 대한 / 잠재적인 장기 기증자의 / ~것 이다. / 의심할 바 없이 / 너무 이른 뇌사 진단에 대한 대중의 두려움을 완화하기 위한 / 장기 확보를 위한
But it is questionable / whether these requirements reduce public suspicions / as much as they create ③ them.
하지만 이것은 의문이다. / 이러한 요건들이 대중의 의심을 줄여 주는지 / 그것을 만들어내는 만큼
They certainly maintain mistaken beliefs / that diagnosing brain death is an unreliable process / ☑ lacking precision.
그것들은 잘못된 믿음을 확실히 유지시킨다. / 뇌사 진단이 신뢰하기 어려운 과정이라는 / 정확성이 결여된
As a matter of consistency, / at least, / criteria for diagnosing the deaths of organ donors

should be exactly the same / as for those for ⑤ <u>whom</u> immediate burial / or cremation is intended.
일관성의 이유로 / 적어도 / 장기 기증자의 사망 진단 기준은 정확히 동일해야 한다. / 즉각적인 매장 또는 화장이 예정된 사람들에 대한 그것과

일부 국가는 장기 이식, 즉 다른 사람에게 장기를 전달하는 것을 고려 중일 때 뇌사를 결정하는 것에 대한 더 엄격한 지침을 제안했다. 몇몇 유럽 국가에는 잠재적 기증자의 경우 의사 팀 전체가 사망 진단에 동의해야 한다고 명시하는 법적 요건들이 있다. 잠재적인 장기 기증자의 뇌사 진단에 대한 이러한 엄격한 규정들의 이유는 의심할 바 없이 장기 확보를 위한 너무 이른 뇌사 진단에 대한 대중의 두려움을 완화하기 위한 것이다. 하지만 이러한 요건들이 대중의 의심을 만들어내는 만큼 그것을 줄여 주는지는 의문이다. 그것들은 뇌사 진단이 정확성이 결여되어 신뢰하기 어려운 과정이라는 잘못된 믿음을 확실히 유지시킨다. 적어도 일관성의 이유로 장기 기증자의 사망 진단 기준은 즉각적인 매장 또는 화장이 예정된 사람들에 대한 그것과 정확히 동일해야 한다.

Why? 왜 정답일까?
접속사 that 절 안에 이미 동사(is)가 있으므로, process를 수식하는 분사 형태인 lacking이 와야 한다. 따라서 어법상 틀린 것은 ④이다.

Why? 왜 오답일까?
① specify의 목적어 역할을 하는 목적격 관계대명사 that이다.
② for these ~ organ donors는 주어 the reason의 수식어구 이므로 단수 동사인 is가 오는 것이 맞다.
③ them은 suspicions의 대명사 이므로 복수형이 맞다.
⑤ those를 선행사로 하는 목적격 관계대명사 자리이므로 whom이 오는 것이 맞다.

- tough ⓐ 엄격한, 힘든
- transferring ⓝ 이동, 이송
- consideration ⓝ 고려
- diagnosis ⓝ 진단
- donor ⓝ 기증자
- regulation ⓝ 규제
- belief ⓝ 생각, 신념
- criteria ⓝ 기준
- burial ⓝ 매장
- transplantation ⓝ 이식
- organ ⓝ 장기
- specify ⓥ 구체화하다
- potential ⓐ 잠재적인
- strict ⓐ 엄격한
- premature ⓐ 정상보다 이른
- consistency ⓝ 일관성
- immediate ⓐ 즉시
- cremation ⓝ 화장

구문 풀이

9행 But it is questionable whether these requirements reduce public suspicions
부사절(~인지 아닌지)
as much as they create them.
「as much as : ~만큼」

★★ 문제 해결 꿀~팁 ★★

▶ 많이 틀린 이유는?
④번의 경우 that은 관계대명사가 아니라 동격의 that이므로 뒤에 완전한 문장이 와야 하는데 이미 is가 본동사로 쓰였으므로 동사가 두 개 올 수 없다. 따라서 lack는 process를 수식하는 현재분사 형태인 lacking으로 바꿔야한다. ⑤번은 for whom 이하의 문장이 those를 수식하고 있는 형태로, 전치사＋관계대명사 뒤에는 완벽한 문장이 와야 한다. 이 문장에는 수동태가 쓰였는데, 수동태 또한 주어 동사를 갖춘 완전한 문장임을 알아야 한다.

▶ 문제 해결 방법은?
①번은 that명사절과 what명사절을 비교하는 문제임으로 뒤에 완전한 문장인지 불완전한 문장인지 확인하여 완전한 경우 that을 고르면 된다. ②번은 단수동사 is와 복수동사 are을 비교하는 문제임으로 주어를 찾아 단수인지 복수인지 확인하면 된다. ③번은 단수 대명사 it과 복수 대명사 them을 비교하는 문제로 문장 내에서 명사를 찾아 확인하면 된다. ④번은 동격의 that 다음에 완전한 문장이 와야 하므로 문장 내에 주어와 동사가 제대로 있는지 확인하면 된다. ⑤번은 전치사＋관계대명사 뒤에 완전한 문장이 나오는지 확인해야한다.

---

30 미니멀리즘에 대한 이해 | 정답률 62% | 정답 ④

다음 글의 밑줄 친 부분 중, 문맥상 낱말의 쓰임이 적절하지 않은 것은?

The term minimalism gives a negative impression / to some people who think / that it is all about sacrificing valuable possessions.
미니멀리즘이라는 용어는 부정적인 인상을 준다. / 생각하는 일부 사람들에게 / 그것을 소중한 소유물을 희생하는 것에 관한 것으로만

This insecurity naturally stems from their ① <u>attachment</u> / to their possessions.
이러한 불안은 그들의 애착에 자연스럽게 비롯된다. / 자신의 소유물에 대한

It is difficult to distance oneself from something / that has been around for quite some time.
것으로부터 자신을 멀리 두는 것은 어렵다. / 꽤 오랫동안 곁에 있어 왔던

Being an emotional animal, / human beings give meaning to the things around them.
감정의 동물이기 때문에 / 인간은 그들의 곁에 있는 물건에 의미를 부여한다.

So, / the question arising here is that / if minimalism will ② <u>hurt</u> one's emotions, / why become a minimalist?
그래서 / 여기서 생기는 질문은 ~는 것이다. / 미니멀리즘이 사람의 감정을 상하게 한다면 / 왜 미니멀리스트가 되느냐

The answer is very simple; / the assumption of the question is fundamentally ③ <u>wrong</u>.
대답은 매우 간단하다. / 그 질문의 가정은 근본적으로 틀리다

Minimalism does not hurt emotions.
미니멀리즘은 감정을 상하게 하지 않는다.

You might feel a bit sad / while getting rid of a useless item / but sooner than later, / this feeling will be ④ <u>overcame</u> / by the joy of clarity.
여러분은 조금 슬퍼할 수도 있지만 / 쓸모없는 물건을 치우면서 / 그러나 머지않아 / 이 느낌은 명료함의 기쁨으로 극복될 것이다.

Minimalists never argue / that you should leave every convenience of the modern era.
미니멀리스트는 / 여러분이 현대의 모든 편의를 버려야 한다고 주장하지 않는다.

They are of the view / that you only need to ⑤ <u>eliminate</u> stuff / that is unused or not going to be used / in the near future.
그들은 견해를 가지고 있다. / 여러분이 물건을 없애기만 하면 된다는 / 사용되지 않거나 사용되지 않을 / 가까운 미래에

미니멀리즘이라는 용어는 그것을 소중한 소유물을 희생하는 것에 관한 것으로만 생각하는 일부 사람들에게 부정적인 인상을 준다. 이러한 불안은 자신의 소유물에 대한 ① 애착에서

자연스럽게 비롯된다. 꽤 오랫동안 곁에 있어 왔던 것으로부터 자신을 멀리 두는 것은 어렵다. 감정의 동물이기 때문에, 인간은 그들의 곁에 있는 물건에 의미를 부여한다. 그래서 여기서 생기는 질문은 미니멀리즘이 사람의 감정을 ② 상하게 한다면 왜 미니멀리스트가 되느냐는 것이다. 대답은 매우 간단하다. 그 질문의 가정은 근본적으로 ③ 틀리다. 미니멀리즘은 감정을 상하게 하지 않는다. 여러분은 쓸모없는 물건을 치우면서 조금 슬퍼할 수도 있지만 머지않아 이 느낌은 명료함의 기쁨으로 ④ 유지될(→ 극복될) 것이다. 미니멀리스트는 여러분이 현대의 모든 편의를 버려야 한다고 주장하지 않는다. 그들은 여러분이 사용되지 않거나 가까운 미래에 사용되지 않을 물건을 ⑤ 없애기만 하면 된다는 견해를 가지고 있다.

Why? 왜 정답일까?
미니멀리즘은 소요물을 전부 버리는 것이 아니라 필요 없게 되어 사용되지 않는 물건을 없애는 것이므로 버리는 순간에는 슬플 수 있지만 곧 기쁨으로 '극복될' 것이라는 설명이 알맞다. 따라서 **maintain**을 **overcame**으로 고쳐야 한다.

- term ⓝ 용어
- valuable ⓐ 가치 있는
- insecurity ⓝ 불안
- distance ⓥ 거리를 두다
- assumption ⓝ 가정
- get rid of 버리다
- maintain ⓥ 유지하다
- era ⓝ 시대
- unused ⓐ 사용되지 않는
- sacrifice ⓥ 희생하다
- possession ⓝ 소유
- stem ⓥ 비롯되다
- arise ⓥ 발생하다
- fundamentally ⓐⓓ 근본적으로
- sooner than later 머지않아
- clarity ⓝ 명료하다
- eliminate ⓥ 제거하다

구문 풀이

4행 It is difficult to distance oneself from something that has been around for quite some time.
가주어 / 진주어 / 선행사 / └→ 관계대명사(주격)

---

31 시각 체계의 특징 | 정답률 61% | 정답 ①

다음 빈칸에 들어갈 말로 가장 적절한 것을 고르시오.

✓ ① adapting itself
스스로 적응하는
② visualizing ideas
아이디어를 시각화하는
③ assessing distances
거리를 측정하는
④ functioning irregularly
불규칙적으로 기능하는
⑤ operating independently
독립적으로 작동하는

A remarkable characteristic of the visual system is / that it has the ability of adapting itself.
시각 체계의 두드러진 특징은 / 스스로 적응하는 능력이 있다는 것이다.

Psychologist George M. Stratton made this clear / in an impressive self-experiment.
심리학자 George M. Stratton은 이것을 분명히 했다. / 인상적인 자가 실험에서

Stratton wore reversing glasses for several days, / which literally turned the world upside down for him.
Stratton은 며칠 동안 반전 안경을 착용했다. / 그런데 그 안경은 말 그대로 그에게 세상을 뒤집어 놓았다.

In the beginning, / this caused him great difficulties: / just putting food in his mouth with a fork / was a challenge for him.
처음에 / 이것은 그에게 큰 어려움을 초래하였다. / 포크로 음식을 입에 넣는 것조차 / 그에게는 도전이었다.

With time, / however, / his visual system adjusted to the new stimuli from reality, / and he was able to act normally / in his environment again, / even seeing it upright / when he concentrated.
시간이 지나면서 / 그러나 / 그의 시각 체계는 현실의 새로운 자극에 적응했다. / 그리고 그는 정상적으로 행동할 수 있었다. / 다시 자신의 환경에서 / 심지어 똑바로 보면서 / 그가 집중했을 때는

As he took off his reversing glasses, / he was again confronted with problems: / he used the wrong hand / when he wanted to reach for something, / for example.
반전 안경을 벗었을 때 / 그는 다시 문제에 직면했다. / 그는 반대 손을 사용했다. / 그가 무언가를 잡기를 원할 때 / 예를 들어

Fortunately, / Stratton could reverse the perception, / and he did not have to wear reversing glasses / for the rest of his life.
다행히 / Stratton은 지각을 뒤집을 수 있었다. / 그리고 그는 반전 안경을 착용하지 않아도 되었다. / 평생

For him, / everything returned to normal after one day.
그에게 / 하루 만에 모든 것이 정상으로 돌아왔다.

시각 체계의 두드러진 특징은 스스로 적응하는 능력이 있다는 것이다. 심리학자 George M. Stratton은 인상적인 자가 실험에서 이것을 분명히 했다. Stratton은 며칠 동안 반전 안경을 착용했는데 그 안경은 말 그대로 그에게 세상을 뒤집어 놓았다. 처음에 이것은 그에게 큰 어려움을 초래하였다. 포크로 음식을 입에 넣는 것조차 그에게는 도전이었다. 그러나 시간이 지나면서 그의 시각 체계는 현실의 새로운 자극에 적응했고, 그가 집중했을 때는 심지어 똑바로 보면서, 다시 자신의 환경에서 정상적으로 행동할 수 있었다. 반전 안경을 벗었을 때 그는 다시 문제에 직면했다. 예를 들어 그가 무언가를 잡기를 원할 때 그는 반대 손을 사용했다. 다행히 Stratton은 지각을 뒤집을 수 있었고 평생 반전 안경을 착용하지 않아도 되었다. 그에게 하루 만에 모든 것이 정상으로 돌아왔다.

Why? 왜 정답일까?
처음 반전 안경을 착용했을 때 어려움을 겪었지만 시간이 지나면서 금세 적응했고(With time, however, his visual system adjusted to the new stimuli from reality, and he was able to act normally in his environment again, even seeing it upright when he concentrated.), 이후 안경을 벗었을 때도 다시 원상태에 적응했다고 얘기하고 있다. 따라서 빈칸에 들어갈 말로 가장 적절한 것은 ① '스스로 적응하는'이다.

- remarkable ⓐ 두드러진, 놀라운, 주목할 만한
- ability ⓝ 능력, 수완, 역량
- impressive ⓐ 인상적인
- literally ⓐⓓ 문자 그대로, 정말로
- adjust to ~에 적응하다
- concentrate ⓥ 집중하다
- visual ⓐ 시각의
- psychologist ⓝ 심리학자
- reverse ⓥ 뒤집다
- upside down 거꾸로, 전도되어, 뒤집혀
- upright ⓐ 똑바른
- confront ⓥ 직면하다

구문 풀이

4행 Stratton wore reversing glasses for several days, which literally turned
선행사(앞문장 전체) / 주격 관계대명사(계속적)
the world upside down for him.

32 정보의 접근여부와 지적 자신감과의 관계 　　정답률 46% | 정답 ②

다음 빈칸에 들어갈 말로 가장 적절한 것을 고르시오.

① improve their judgment skills – 그들의 판단 능력을 증가시키기
② pump up their intellectual confidence – 그들의 지적 자신감을 부풀리기
③ make them endure challenging situations – 도전 상황에서 그들을 견디도록 시키기
④ lead to a collaboration among the participants – 참가자들 사이에서 협동을 이끌어 내기
⑤ motivate them to pursue in-depth knowledge – 깊은 지식을 추구하도록 동기를 부여하기

Participants in a study were asked to answer questions / like "Why does the moon have phases?"
한 연구의 참가자들이 질문들에 답하도록 요청받았다. / '달은 왜 상을 가지고 있을까'와 같은

Half the participants were told / to search for the answers on the internet, / while the other half weren't allowed to do so.
참가자의 절반은 말을 들었다. / 인터넷에서 답을 검색하라는 / 반면 나머지 절반은 그렇게 하도록 허용되지 않았다.

Then, / in the second part of the study, / all of the participants were presented / with a new set of questions, / such as "Why does Swiss cheese have holes?"
그다음 / 연구의 두 번째 단계에서 / 모든 참가자는 제시받았다. / 일련의 새로운 질문들을 / '스위스 치즈에는 왜 구멍이 있을까'와 같은

These questions were unrelated to the ones asked / during the first part of the study, / so participants who used the internet had absolutely no advantage over those / who hadn't.
이 질문들은 질문받았던 것들과는 관련이 없었다. / 연구의 첫 번째 단계에서 / 그래서 인터넷을 사용한 참가자들은 이점이 전혀 없었다. / 그러지 않은 참가자들보다

You would think / that both sets of participants would be equally sure or unsure / about how well they could answer the new questions.
여러분은 생각할 것이다. / 두 집단의 참가자들이 동일한 정도로 확신하거나 확신하지 못할 것으로 / 그들이 새로운 질문들에 얼마나 잘 대답할 수 있을지에 대해

But / those who used the internet / in the first part of the study / rated themselves as more knowledgeable / than those who hadn't, / even about questions / they hadn't searched online for.
그러나 / 인터넷을 사용했던 참가자들은 / 연구의 첫 번째 단계에서 / 스스로 더 많이 알고 있다고 평가했다. / 그러지 않았던 참가자들보다 / 질문에 대해서조차 / 자신이 온라인에서 검색하지 않았던

The study suggests / that having access to unrelated information / was enough to pump up their intellectual confidence.
이 연구는 시사한다. / 관련 없는 정보에 접근하는 것이 ~는 것을 / 그들의 지적 자신감을 부풀리기 충분했다

한 연구의 참가자들이 '달은 왜 상을 가지고 있을까'와 같은 질문들에 답하도록 요청받았다. 참가자의 절반은 인터넷에서 답을 검색하라는 말을 들었고 나머지 절반은 그렇게 하도록 허용되지 않았다. 그다음, 연구의 두 번째 단계에서 모든 참가자는 '스위스 치즈에는 왜 구멍이 있을까'와 같은 일련의 새로운 질문들을 제시받았다. 이 질문들은 연구의 첫 번째 단계에서 질문받았던 것들과는 관련이 없어서 인터넷을 사용한 참가자들은 그러지 않은 참가자들보다 이점이 전혀 없었다. 여러분은 두 집단의 참가자들이 새로운 질문들에 얼마나 잘 대답할 수 있을지에 대해 동일한 정도로 확신하거나 확신하지 못할 것으로 생각할 것이다. 그러나 연구의 첫 번째 단계에서 인터넷을 사용했던 참가자들은 자신이 온라인에서 검색하지 않았던 질문들에 대해서조차 그러지 않았던 참가자들보다 스스로가 더 많이 알고 있다고 평가했다. 이 연구는 관련 없는 정보에 접근하는 것이 그들의 지적 자신감을 부풀리기 충분했다는 것을 시사한다.

Why? 왜 정답일까?

첫 번째 질문에서 인터넷 접근을 허용받은 사람들이 두 번째 질문에서도 스스로가 더 많이 알고 있다고 평가했다(But those who used the internet in the first part of the study rated themselves as more knowledgeable than those who hadn't, even about questions they hadn't searched online for.)는 내용이므로, 빈칸에 들어갈 말로 가장 적절한 것은 ② '그들의 지적 자신감을 부풀리기'이다.

- phase ⓝ 상
- unrelated ⓐ 관계없는
- equally ⓐⓓ 동등하게
- knowledgeable ⓐ 아는 것이 많은, 많이 아는
- intellectual ⓐ 지적의
- pursue ⓥ 추구하다
- present ⓥ 제시하다
- advantage ⓝ 이점
- rate ⓥ 평가하다
- pump up 부풀리다
- endure ⓥ 견디다
- in-depth ⓐ 깊은

구문 풀이

11행　But those who used the internet in the first part of the study rated
「those who : ~하는 사람들」　　동사
themselves as more knowledgeable than those who hadn't, even about questions they hadn't searched online for.

★★ 문제 해결 꿀~팁 ★★

▶ 많이 틀린 이유는?
지문에서 연구가 등장하면 그 연구의 결과가 글의 주제와 밀접하게 연관되어 있다. ①번, ③번, ④번은 해당 내용에서 판단 능력, 도전 상황, 협동 등이 언급되지 않았으므로 답이 될 수 없다. ⑤번 또한 참가자들이 실제로 깊은 지식을 얻도록 동기가 부여된 내용이 나오지 않았기에 답이 될 수 없다.

▶ 문제 해결 방법은?
빈칸이 포함된 문장을 먼저 정확하게 해석하는 것이 중요하다. 연구를 통해서 '정보에 접근하는 것이 ~하기에 충분했다는 것을 시사한다'는 내용을 미리 머릿속에 생각해 둔 후 다시 처음부터 읽어보며 힌트를 찾으면 된다. 먼저 연구의 결과를 파악해야하는데, 첫 번째 단계에서 인터넷을 사용한 참가자들은 후에 모르는 질문에 대해서도 알고 있다고 파악하는 경향이 많았다고 이야기하고 있다. 이는 실제로 지식을 얻은 것이 아님에도 알고 있다고 착각하는 것이므로 ⑤번은 답이 될 수 없다.

33 관점에 대한 고찰 　　정답률 61% | 정답 ④

다음 빈칸에 들어갈 말로 가장 적절한 것을 고르시오. [3점]

① using our experiences as a guide – 가이드로 우리의 경험을 이용함으로써
② breaking the framework of old ideas – 오래된 생각의 틀을 깸으로써
③ adding new information to what we know – 우리가 아는 것에 관한 새로운 정보를 추가함으로써

---

④ focusing in on particular features within it – 세상 안의 특정한 특징에 초점을 맞춤으로써
⑤ considering both bright and dark sides of it – 밝은 면과 어두운 면을 모두 고려함으로써

Anthropologist Gregory Bateson suggests / that we tend to understand the world / by focusing in on particular features within it.
인류학자 Gregory Bateson은 제안한다. / 우리가 세상을 이해하는 경향이 있다고 / 세상 안의 특정한 특징에 초점을 맞춤으로써

Take platypuses. // We might zoom in so closely to their fur / that each hair appears different.
오리너구리를 예로 들어 보자. // 우리가 그들의 털을 매우 가까이 확대하면 / 각 가닥이 다르게 보인다.

We might also zoom out / to the extent / where it appears as a single, uniform object.
우리는 또한 축소할 수도 있다. / 정도까지 / 그것이 하나의 동일한 개체로 보이는

We might take the platypus / as an individual, / or we might treat it / as part of a larger unit / such as a species or an ecosystem.
우리는 오리너구리를 취급할 수도 있다. / 개체로 / 또는 취급할 수도 있다. / 더 큰 단위의 일부로 / 종 또는 생태계와 같이

It's possible to move / between many of these perspectives, / although we may need some additional tools and skills / to zoom in on individual pieces of hair / or zoom out to entire ecosystems.
이동하는 것은 가능하다. / 이러한 많은 관점 사이에 / 비록 몇 가지 추가 도구와 기술이 필요할지도 모르지만 / 개별 머리카락을 확대하기 위해서 / 또는 전체 생태계로 축소하기 위해

Crucially, / however, / we can only take up one perspective at a time.
결정적으로 / 그러나 / 우리는 한 번에 하나의 관점만 취할 수 있다.

We can pay attention to the varied behavior of individual animals, / look at / what unites them into a single species, / or look at them as part of bigger ecological patterns.
우리는 개별 동물의 다양한 행동에 주의를 기울일 수 있다. / 그리고 살펴볼 수 있다. / 그들을 단일 종으로 합하는 것을 / 또는 더 큰 생태학적 패턴의 일부로서 그들을 살펴볼 수도 있다.

Every possible perspective / involves emphasizing certain aspects / and ignoring others.
가능한 모든 관점은 / 포함한다. / 특정 측면을 강조하는 것을 / 그리고 다른 측면을 외면하는 것을

인류학자 Gregory Bateson은 우리가 세상 안의 특정한 특징에 초점을 맞춤으로써 세상을 이해하는 경향이 있다고 제안한다. 오리너구리를 예로 들어보자. 우리가 그들의 털을 매우 가까이 확대하면 각 가닥이 다르게 보인다. 우리는 또한 그것이 하나의 동일한 개체로 보이는 정도까지 축소할 수도 있다. 우리는 오리너구리를 개체로 취급할 수도 있고 종 또는 생태계와 같이 더 큰 단위의 일부로 취급할 수도 있다. 비록 개별 머리카락을 확대하거나 전체 생태계로 축소하기 위해 몇 가지 추가 도구와 기술이 필요할지도 모르지만, 이러한 많은 관점 사이에 이동하는 것은 가능하다. 그러나 결정적으로 우리는 한 번에 하나의 관점만 취할 수 있다. 우리는 개별 동물의 다양한 행동에 주의를 기울일 수 있고, 그들을 단일 종으로 합하는 것을 살펴볼 수도 있고, 더 큰 생태학적 패턴의 일부로서 그들을 살펴볼 수도 있다. 가능한 모든 관점은 특정 측면을 강조하고 다른 측면을 외면하는 것을 포함한다.

Why? 왜 정답일까?

오리너구리를 예로 들어 사람은 관점 사이를 이동하여 이를 개체로 취급할 수도 있지만 한 번에 하나의 관점으로만 바라볼 수 있다(Crucially, however, we can only take up one perspective at a time.)는 내용이므로, 빈칸에 들어갈 말로 가장 적절한 것은 ④ '세상 안의 특정한 특징에 초점을 맞춤으로써'이다.

- anthropologist ⓝ 인류학자
- zoom out 축소하다
- ecosystem ⓝ 생태계
- take up 취하다
- unite ⓥ 합하다
- zoom in 확대하다
- object ⓝ 사물
- crucially ⓐⓓ 결정적으로
- varied ⓐ 다양한
- ecological ⓐ 생태계의

구문 풀이

4행　We might also zoom out to the extent where it appears as a single,
　　　　　　　　　　　　　　　　　　　관계부사
uniform object.

34 플라톤의 실재론 　　정답률 53% | 정답 ④

다음 빈칸에 들어갈 말로 가장 적절한 것을 고르시오. [3점]

① observable phenomena of the physical world – 물리적 세계의 관찰 가능한 현상
② our experiences shaped by external influences – 외부 영향에 의해 만들어진 경험
③ an overlapping area between emotion and reason – 감정과 이성 사이의 겹친 영역
④ an invisible but perfect world beyond our senses – 보이지 않지만 우리의 감각을 넘어선 완벽한 세계
⑤ our perception affected by stereotype or generalization – 고정관념과 일반화에 영향받은 인식

Plato's realism includes all aspects of experience / but is most easily explained / by considering the nature of mathematical and geometrical objects / such as circles.
플라톤의 실재론은 경험의 모든 측면을 포함한다. / 하지만 가장 쉽게 설명된다. / 수학적이고 기하학적인 대상의 특성을 고려함으로써 / 원과 같은

He asked the question, / what is a circle?
그는 질문을 했다. / 원이란 무엇인가?

You might indicate a particular example / carved into stone or drawn in the sand.
여러분은 특정한 예를 가리킬 수 있다. / 돌에 새겨져 있거나 모래에 그려진

However, / Plato would point out that, / if you looked closely enough, / you would see / that neither it, nor indeed any physical circle, was perfect.
그러나 / 플라톤은 지적할 것이다. / 만약 여러분이 충분히 면밀히 관찰한다면 / 여러분이 알게 될 것이다. / 그 어느 것도 진정 어떤 물리적인 원도 완벽하지 않다는 것을

They all possessed flaws, / and all were subject to change / and decayed with time.
그것들은 모두는 결함을 가지고 있다. / 그리고 모두 변화의 영향을 받는다. / 그리고 시간이 지남에 따라 쇠락한다.

So how can we talk about perfect circles / if we cannot actually see or touch them?
그렇다면 우리가 어떻게 완벽한 원에 대해 이야기할 수 있을까? / 만약 우리가 그것을 실제로 보거나 만질 수 없다면

Plato's extraordinary answer was / that the world we see is a poor reflection / of a deeper unseen reality of Forms, or universals, / where perfect cats chase perfect mice / in perfect circles around perfect rocks.
플라톤의 비범한 대답은 ~이다. / 우리가 보는 세상이 불충분한 반영물이라는 것 / '형상' 또는 '보편자'라는 더 깊은 보이지 않는 실재의 / 완벽한 고양이가 완벽한 쥐를 쫓는 / 완벽한 암석 주변에서 완벽한 원을 그리며

Plato believed / that the Forms or universals are the true reality / that exists in an invisible but perfect world beyond our senses.
플라톤은 믿었다. / '형상' 또는 '보편자'가 진정한 실재라고 / 보이지 않지만 우리의 감각을 넘어선 완벽한 세계에 존재하는

플라톤의 실재론은 경험의 모든 측면을 포함하지만, 원과 같은 수학적이고 기하학적인 대상의 특성을 고려함으로써 가장 쉽게 설명된다. 그는 '원이란 무엇인가?'라는 질문을 했다. 여러분은 돌에 새겨져 있거나 모래에 그려진 특정한 예를 가리킬 수 있다. 그러나 플라톤은 여러분이 충분히 면밀히 관찰한다면, 여러분이 그 어느 것도, 진정 어떤 물리적인 원도 완벽하지 않다는 것을 알게 될 것이라고 지적할 것이다. 그것들 모두는 결함을 가지고 있었고, 모두 변화의 영향을 받고 시간이 지남에 따라 쇠하였다. 그렇다면, 우리가 완벽한 원을 실제로 보거나 만질 수 없다면, 그것에 대해 어떻게 이야기할 수 있을까? 플라톤의 비범한 대답은 우리가 보는 세상이 완벽한 고양이가 완벽한 암석 주변에서 완벽한 원을 그리며 완벽한 쥐를 쫓는 '형상' 또는 '보편자'라는 더 깊은 보이지 않는 실재의 불충분한 반영물이라는 것이다. 플라톤은 '형상' 또는 '보편자'가 보이지 않지만 우리의 감각을 넘어선 완벽한 세계에 존재하는 진정한 실재라고 믿었다.

Why? 왜 정답일까?

플라톤은 세상이 우리가 보이지 않는 실재의 불충분한 반영물(Plato's extraordinary answer was that the world we see is a poor reflection of a deeper unseen reality of *Forms*, or *universals*, where perfect cats chase perfect mice in perfect circles around perfect rocks.)이라고 말하고 있으므로 빈칸에 들어갈 말로 가장 적절한 것은 ④ '보이지 않지만 우리의 감각을 넘어선 완벽한 세계'이다.

- nature ⓝ 특성, 본성
- indicate ⓥ 가리키다
- indeed [ad] 진정
- decay ⓥ 쇠하다, 부패하다
- form ⓝ 형상
- chase ⓥ 쫓다
- overlapping ⓐ 중복된
- generalization ⓝ 일반화
- geometrical ⓐ 기하학의
- carved ⓐ 곡선의
- possess ⓥ 소유하다
- extraordinary ⓐ 비범한
- universals ⓝ 보편자
- phenomena ⓝ 현상
- stereotype ⓝ 고정관념

구문 풀이

10행 Plato's extraordinary answer was that the world {we see} is a poor
reflection of a deeper unseen reality of *Forms*, or *universals*, where perfect cats
chase perfect mice in perfect circles around perfect rocks.

---

35 대수의 법칙 정답률 64% | 정답 ③

다음 글에서 전체 흐름과 관계 없는 문장은?

In statistics, / the law of large numbers describes / a situation where having more data is better for making predictions.
통계학에서 / 대수의 법칙은 설명한다. / 더 많은 데이터를 갖는 것이 예측하는데 더 좋은 상황을
According to it, / the more often an experiment is conducted, / the closer the average of the results can be expected / to match the true state of the world.
그것에 따르면 / 실험이 더 자주 수행될수록 / 그 결과의 평균이 예상될 수 있다. / 세상의 실제 상태에 더 맞춰지는 것으로
① For instance, / on your first encounter with the game of roulette, / you may have beginner's luck / after betting on 7.
예를 들어 / 룰렛 게임을 처음 접했을 때 / 여러분은 초보자의 운이 있을 수 있다. / 7에 베팅한 후
② But / the more often you repeat this bet, / the closer the relative frequency of wins and losses is expected to approach / the true chance of winning, / meaning that your luck will at some point fade away.
하지만 / 당신이 이 베팅을 더 자주 반복할수록 / 승패의 상대적인 빈도가 더 가까워질 것으로 예상된다. / 진짜 승률에 / 이는 당신의 운이 어느 순간 사라진다는 것을 의미한다.
☑ Each number's symbolic meanings can be interpreted / in various ways / and are promising / in situations that may change unexpectedly.
각 숫자의 상징적인 의미는 해석될 수 있다. / 다양한 방식으로 / 그리고 유망하다. / 예상치 못하게 바뀔 수 있는 상황에서
④ Similarly, / car insurers collect large amounts of data / to figure out the chances / that drivers will cause accidents, / depending on their age, region, or car brand.
마찬가지로 / 자동차 보험사는 많은 양의 데이터를 수집한다. / 확률을 파악하기 위해 / 운전자가 사고를 일으킬 / 그들의 연령, 지역 또는 자동차 브랜드에 따라
⑤ Both casinos and insurance industries / rely on the law of large numbers / to balance individual losses.
카지노와 보험 산업 모두 / 대수의 법칙에 의존한다. / 개별 손실의 균형을 맞추기 위해

통계학에서 대수의 법칙은 더 많은 데이터를 갖는 것이 예측하는데 더 좋은 상황을 설명한다. 그것에 따르면 실험이 더 자주 수행될수록 그 결과의 평균이 세상의 실제 상태에 더 맞춰지는 것으로 예상될 수 있다. ① 예를 들어 룰렛 게임을 처음 접했을 때 7에 베팅한 후 여러분은 초보자의 운이 있을 수 있다. ② 하지만 당신이 이 베팅을 더 자주 반복할수록 승패의 상대적인 빈도가 진짜 승률에 더 가까워질 것으로 예상되는데 이는 당신의 운이 어느 순간 사라진다는 것을 의미한다. ③ 각 숫자의 상징적인 의미는 다양한 방식으로 해석될 수 있으며 예상치 못하게 바뀔 수 있는 상황에서 유망하다. ④ 마찬가지로 자동차 보험사는 운전자가 그들의 연령, 지역 또는 자동차 브랜드에 따라 사고를 일으킬 확률을 파악하기 위해 많은 양의 데이터를 수집한다. ⑤ 카지노와 보험 산업 모두 개별 손실의 균형을 맞추기 위해 대수의 법칙에 의존한다.

Why? 왜 정답일까?

대수의 법칙은 데이터가 많을수록 예측에 도움이 된다는 내용인데 ③은 룰렛 게임 내 숫자의 해석에 대해 얘기하고 있다. 따라서 전체 흐름과 관계 없는 문장은 ③이다.

- statistics ⓝ 통계학
- experiment ⓝ 실험
- encounter ⓥ 접하다, 만나다
- symbolic ⓐ 상징적인
- unexpectedly [ad] 예상치 못하게
- prediction ⓝ 예측
- conduct ⓥ 수행하다
- frequency ⓝ 빈도
- promise ⓥ 유망하다
- rely on ~에 의존하다

구문 풀이

3행 According to it, the more often an experiment is conducted, the closer the average of the results can be expected to match the true state of the world.
「the 비교급 S+V ~, the 비교급 S+V ~ : ~하면 할수록 ~하다」

---

36 청소년기의 뇌 정답률 63% | 정답 ④

주어진 글 다음에 이어질 글의 순서로 가장 적절한 것을 고르시오. [3점]

① (A) − (C) − (B)　　　② (B) − (A) − (C)
③ (B) − (C) − (A)　　　☑ (C) − (A) − (B)
⑤ (C) − (B) − (A)

The adolescent brain is not fully developed / until its early twenties.
청소년기의 뇌는 완전히 발달하지 않는다. / 20대 초반까지는
This means / the way the adolescents' decision-making circuits integrate and process information / may put them at a disadvantage.
이것은 의미한다. / 청소년의 의사 결정 회로가 정보를 통합하고 처리하는 방식이 / 그들을 불리하게 만들 수 있음을
(C) One of their brain regions that matures later is the prefrontal cortex, / which is the control center, / tasked with thinking ahead and evaluating consequences.
나중에 성숙하는 뇌 영역 중 하나는 전전두엽 피질인 / 그리고 그것은 통제 센터인 / 그리고 그것은 미리 생각하고 결과를 평가하는 임무를 맡고 있다.
It is the area of the brain / responsible for preventing you / from sending off an initial angry text / and modifying it with kinder words.
그것은 뇌의 영역이다. / 당신이 막는 역할을 하는 / 초기의 화가 난 문자를 보내는 것을 / 그리고 그것을 더 친절한 단어로 수정하게 하는
(A) On the other hand, / the limbic system matures earlier, / playing a central role in processing emotional responses.
반면 / 대뇌변연계는 더 일찍 성숙한다. / 그래서 정서적 반응을 처리하는 데 중심적인 역할을 한다.
Because of its earlier development, / it is more likely to influence decision-making.
그것의 더 이른 발달로 인해 / 그것이 의사 결정에 영향을 미칠 가능성이 더 높다.
Decision-making in the adolescent brain is led / by emotional factors more than the perception of consequences.
청소년기의 뇌에서 의사 결정은 이끌어진다. / 결과의 인식보다 감정적인 요인에 의해
(B) Due to these differences, / there is an imbalance / between feeling-based decision-making / ruled by the more mature limbic system / and logical-based decision-making / by the not-yet-mature prefrontal cortex.
이러한 차이점 때문에 / 불균형이 존재한다. / 감정 기반의 의사 결정 사이에 / 더 성숙한 대뇌변연계에 의해 지배되는 / 논리 기반 의사 결정 / 아직 성숙하지 않은 전전두엽 피질에 의한
This may explain / why some teens are more likely to make bad decisions.
이것은 설명해 줄 수 있다. / 왜 일부 십 대들이 그릇된 결정을 내릴 가능성이 더 높은지를

청소년기의 뇌는 20대 초반까지는 완전히 발달하지 않는다. 이것은 청소년의 의사 결정 회로가 정보를 통합하고 처리하는 방식이 그들을 불리하게 만들 수 있음을 의미한다.
(C) 나중에 성숙하는 뇌 영역 중 하나는 통제 센터인 전전두엽 피질이며, 그것은 미리 생각하고 결과를 평가하는 임무를 맡고 있다. 그것은 당신이 초기의 화가 난 문자를 보내는 것을 막고 그것을 더 친절한 단어로 수정하게 하는 역할을 하는 뇌의 영역이다.
(A) 반면 대뇌변연계는 더 일찍 성숙하여 정서적 반응을 처리하는 데 중심적인 역할을 한다. 그것의 더 이른 발달로 인해 그것이 의사 결정에 영향을 미칠 가능성이 더 높다. 청소년기의 뇌에서 의사 결정은 결과의 인식보다 감정적인 요인에 의해 이끌어진다.
(B) 이러한 차이점 때문에 더 성숙한 대뇌변연계에 의해 지배되는 감정 기반 의사 결정과 아직 성숙하지 않은 전전두엽 피질에 의한 논리 기반 의사 결정 사이에는 불균형이 존재한다. 이것은 왜 일부 십 대들이 그릇된 결정을 내릴 가능성이 더 높은지를 설명해 줄 수 있다.

Why? 왜 정답일까?

주어진 글에서는 청소년기의 뇌는 완전히 발달하지 않는다고 이야기하고 있다. 이후 (C)에서 뇌의 영역 중 전전두엽 피질이 나중에 성숙한다고 주장을 뒷받침 하고 있으며, (A)에서는 반대로 대뇌변연계는 일찍 성숙한다고 이야기하고 있다. (B)에서 언급된 이러한 차이점은 (C)와 (A) 사이의 차이점을 언급한 것이므로 글의 순서로 가장 적절한 것은 ④ '(C) − (A) − (B)'이다.

- adolescent ⓝ 청소년
- disadvantage ⓝ 불리한 점, 약점
- limbic system 대뇌변연계
- be led by ~에 의해 이끌어지다
- imbalance ⓝ 불균형
- integrate ⓥ 통합하다
- modify ⓥ 수정하다
- mature ⓐ 성인의
- consequence ⓝ 결과
- prefrontal cortex 전전두엽 피질

구문 풀이

14행 This may explain why some teens are more likely to make bad decisions.
관계부사

---

37 딥 러닝을 기반으로 한 얼굴 인식 정답률 49% | 정답 ③

주어진 글 다음에 이어질 글의 순서로 가장 적절한 것을 고르시오.

① (A) − (C) − (B)　　　② (B) − (A) − (C)
☑ (B) − (C) − (A)　　　④ (C) − (A) − (B)
⑤ (C) − (B) − (A)

Despite the remarkable progress / in deep-learning based facial recognition approaches / in recent years, / in terms of identification performance, / they still have limitations.
눈에 띄는 발전에도 불구하고 / 딥 러닝 기반의 얼굴 인식 접근의 / 최근 몇 년 동안 / 식별 성능 측면에서 / 여전히 그것은 한계를 가지고 있다.
These limitations relate to the database / used in the learning stage.
이러한 한계는 데이터베이스와 관련이 있다. / 학습 단계에서 사용되는
(B) If the selected database does not contain enough instances, / the result may be systematically affected.
선택된 데이터베이스가 충분한 사례를 포함하지 않으면 / 그 결과가 시스템적으로 영향을 받을 수 있다.
For example, / the performance of a facial biometric system may decrease / if the person to be identified was enrolled / over 10 years ago.
예를 들어 / 안면 생체 측정 시스템의 성능이 저하될 수 있다. / 만약 식별된 사람이 등록된 경우 / 10년도 더 전에
(C) The factor to consider is / that this person may experience changes / in the texture of the face, / particularly with the appearance of wrinkles and sagging skin.
고려해야 할 요인은 ~이다. / 이 사람이 변화를 경험할 수 있다는 것 / 얼굴의 질감에서 / 특히 주름과 처진 피부가 나타나는 것을 동반한
These changes may be highlighted / by weight gain or loss.
이러한 변화는 두드러질 수 있다. / 체중 증가 또는 감소에 의해

(A) To counteract this problem, / researchers have developed models / for face aging or digital de-aging.
이 문제에 대응하기 위해 / 연구자들은 모델을 개발했다. / 얼굴 노화나 디지털 노화 완화의
It is used to compensate / for the differences in facial characteristics, / which appear over a given time period.
그것은 보완하는 데 사용된다. / 얼굴 특성의 차이를 / 주어진 기간 동안 나타나는

최근 몇 년 동안 딥 러닝 기반의 얼굴 인식 접근법의 눈에 띄는 발전에도 불구하고, 식별 성능 측면에서 여전히 그것은 한계를 가지고 있다. 이러한 한계는 학습 단계에서 사용되는 데이터베이스와 관련이 있다.

(B) 선택된 데이터베이스가 충분한 사례를 포함하지 않으면 그 결과가 시스템적으로 영향을 받을 수 있다. 예를 들어 만약 식별될 사람이 10년도 더 전에 등록된 경우 안면 생체 측정 시스템의 성능이 저하될 수 있다.

(C) 고려해야 할 요인은 이 사람이 특히 주름과 처진 피부가 나타나는 것을 동반한 얼굴의 질감에서 변화를 경험할 수 있다는 것이다. 이러한 변화는 체중 증가 또는 감소에 의해 두드러질 수 있다.

(A) 이 문제에 대응하기 위해 연구자들은 얼굴 노화나 디지털 노화 완화의 모델을 개발했다. 그것은 주어진 기간 동안 나타나는 얼굴 특성의 차이를 보완하는 데 사용된다.

Why? 왜 정답일까?
딥러닝 기반의 얼굴 인식에 한계가 있다는 주어진 글 뒤로, 데이터 베이스의 불충분한 사례를 설명하는 (B), 불충분한 사례의 원인인 성능 저하에 대해 이야기하는 (C), 그리고 대응 방법인 (A)가 차례로 이어져야 자연스럽다. 따라서 글의 순서로 가장 적절한 것은 ③ '(B) – (C) – (A)'이다.

- remarkable ⓐ 눈에 띄는
- approach ⓥ 접근하다
- identification ⓝ 인식
- biometric ⓐ 생물 측정의
- wrinkle ⓝ 주름
- counteract ⓥ 대응하다
- recognition ⓝ 식별
- in terms of ~에 관하여
- limitation ⓝ 한계
- decrease ⓥ 감소하다
- sagging ⓐ 처진
- compensate ⓥ 보완하다

구문 풀이
6행 It is used to compensate for the differences in facial characteristics,
「be used to : ~하는데 사용된다」
which appear over a given time period.
관계대명사(주격)

★★★ 등급을 가르는 문제!
38 음식 다양성의 감소 | 정답률 38% | 정답 ⑤
글의 흐름으로 보아, 주어진 문장이 들어가기에 가장 적절한 곳을 고르시오.

The decline in the diversity of our food / is an entirely human-made process.
우리 음식의 다양성의 감소는 / 전적으로 인간이 만든 과정이다.
The biggest loss of crop diversity came / in the decades / that followed the Second World War.
농작물 다양성의 가장 큰 손실은 / 수십 년 동안 / 제2차 세계 대전 이후 나타났다.
① In an attempt to save millions / from extreme hunger, / crop scientists found ways to produce grains / such as rice and wheat / on an enormous scale.
수백 만 명의 사람들을 구하고자 하는 시도에서 / 극도의 배고픔에서 / 작물 과학자들이 곡물을 생산하는 방법을 발견했다. / 쌀과 밀과 같은 / 엄청난 규모로
② And thousands of traditional varieties were replaced / by a small number of new super-productive ones.
그리고 수천 개의 전통적인 종들은 대체되었다. / 소수의 새로운 초생산적인 종들로
③ The strategy worked spectacularly well, / at least to begin with.
그 전략은 굉장히 잘 작동했다. / 적어도 처음에는
④ Because of it, / grain production tripled, / and between 1970 and 2020 / the human population more than doubled.
그것 때문에 / 곡물 생산량은 세 배가 되었다. / 그리고 1970년과 2020년 사이에 / 인구는 두 배 이상이 증가했다.
✓ Leaving the contribution of that strategy to one side, / the danger of creating more uniform crops is / that they are more at risk / when it comes to disasters.
그 전략의 기여를 차치하고 / 더 획일적인 작물을 만드는 것의 위험은 / 그것들이 더 큰 위험에 처한다는 것이다. / 재앙과 관련해
Specifically, / a global food system / that depends on just a narrow selection of plants / has a greater chance of / not being able to survive diseases, pests and climate extremes.
특히 / 세계적인 식량 시스템은 / 농작물의 좁은 선택에만 의존하는 / 더 높은 가능성을 가진다. / 질병, 해충, 및 기후 위기로부터 생존하지 못할

우리 음식의 다양성의 감소는 전적으로 인간이 만든 과정이다. 농작물 다양성의 가장 큰 손실은 제2차 세계 대전 이후 수십 년 동안 나타났다. ① 수백 만 명의 사람들을 극도의 배고픔에서 구하고자 하는 시도에서 작물 과학자들이 쌀과 밀과 같은 곡물을 엄청난 규모로 생산하는 방법을 발견했다. ② 그리고 수천 개의 전통적인 종들은 소수의 새로운 초(超)생산적인 종들로 대체되었다. ③ 그 전략은 적어도 처음에는 굉장히 잘 작동했다. ④ 그것 때문에 곡물 생산량은 세 배가 되었고 1970년과 2020년 사이에 인구는 두 배 이상 증가했다. ⑤ 그 전략의 기여를 차치하고, 더 획일적인 작물을 만드는 것의 위험은 그것들이 재앙과 관련해 더 큰 위험에 처한다는 것이다. 특히 농작물의 좁은 선택에만 의존하는 세계적인 식량 시스템은 질병, 해충 및 기후 위기로부터 생존하지 못할 더 높은 가능성을 가진다.

Why? 왜 정답일까?
⑤ 앞은 음식의 다양성이 감소한 이유는 전쟁 이후 대량 생산이 가능한 작물 위주로 농사를 지었기 때문이라고 설명하고 있으며, ⑤ 뒤에서는 좁은 선택에 의존하는 것은 생존하지 못할 가능성을 높인다고 얘기하고 있다. 주어진 문장에서는 획일적인 작물을 만드는 것에 대한 위험을 언급하고 있으므로, 주어진 문장이 들어가기에 가장 적절한 곳은 ⑤이다.

- diversity ⓝ 다양성
- attempt ⓝ 시도
- scale ⓝ 규모
- super-productive 초 생산적인
- triple ⓥ 세배가 되다
- strategy ⓝ 전략
- decade ⓐ 수십 년의
- wheat ⓝ 밀
- replace ⓥ 대체하다
- spectacularly ⓐⓓ 굉장히
- contribution ⓝ 기여
- uniform ⓝ 유니폼

[문제편 p.133]

- depend on ~에 의존하다
- pest ⓝ 해충
- disease ⓝ 질병
- extreme ⓝ 위기

구문 풀이
14행 Specifically, a global food system {that depends on just a narrow selection
주어   관계대명사(주격)   [ ]: 수식
of plants} has a greater chance of not being able to survive diseases, pests and
동사
climate extremes.

★★ 문제 해결 꿀~팁 ★★

▶ 많이 틀린 이유는?
문장을 꼼꼼하게 해석해야 한다. 주어진 글에서 전략의 기여에 대해 이야기하고 있는데 그 기여가 주어진 글 보다 먼저 나와야 하므로 ④번은 답이 될 수 없다.
▶ 문제 해결 방법은?
먼저 주어진 문장을 정확히 해석한 후, 주어진 문장에서 쓰인 대명사나 연결 접속사를 파악하여 전후 관계를 파악하면 된다. 먼저 글에서 언급된 'that strategy'와 'the danger'가 주어진 문장보다 앞에 등장해야 한다. 따라서 ①번, ②번은 답이 될 수 없다. ③번 이후에 'the strategy'가 등장하는데 전략이 잘 작동했다고 말하고 있다. 주어진 글에서 전략의 기여를 차치한다고 하였으므로 전략에 대한 기여에 대한 내용 뒤인 ⑤번에 오는 것이 맞다.

10회

39 쿠바의 야구 | 정답률 48% | 정답 ④
글의 흐름으로 보아, 주어진 문장이 들어가기에 가장 적절한 곳을 고르시오.

Between 1940 and 2000, / Cuba ruled the world baseball scene.
1940년과 2000년 사이에 / 쿠바는 세계 야구계를 지배했다.
They won 25 of the first 28 World Cups / and 3 of 5 Olympic Games.
그들은 첫 28회의 월드컵 중 25회를 이겼다. / 그리고 5회의 올림픽 게임 중 3회를 이겼다.
① The Cubans were known for wearing uniforms / covered in red from head to toe, / a strong contrast to the more conservative North American style / featuring grey or white pants.
쿠바인들은 유니폼을 입는 것으로 알려져 있다. / 머리부터 발끝까지 빨간색으로 뒤덮인 / 그런데 이것은 더 보수적인 북미 스타일과 강한 대조를 이룬다. / 회색이나 흰색 바지를 특징으로 하는
② Not only were their athletic talents superior, / the Cubans appeared even stronger from just the colour of their uniforms.
쿠바인들의 운동 재능이 뛰어났을 뿐만 아니라 / 그들은 그들의 유니폼의 색깔만으로도 훨씬 더 강하게 보였다.
③ A game would not even start / and the opposing team would already be scared.
심지어 경기가 시작하지 않았다. / 그리고 상대 팀은 이미 겁에 질리곤 했다.
✓ A few years ago, / Cuba altered that uniform style, / modernizing it and perhaps conforming to other countries' style; / interestingly, / the national team has declined / since that time.
몇 년 전 쿠바는 그 유니폼 스타일을 바꿨다. / 유니폼을 현대화하고 아마도 다른 나라의 스타일에 맞추면서 / 흥미롭게도 / 국가 대표 팀은 쇠퇴해왔다. / 그 시기부터
The country that ruled international baseball / for decades / has not been on top / since that uniform change.
국제 야구를 지배했던 그 나라는 / 수십 년 동안 / 정상에 오른 적이 없었다. / 그 유니폼 교체 이후로
⑤ Traditions are important for a team; / while a team brand or image can adjust to keep up with present times, / if it abandons or neglects its roots, / negative effects can surface.
전통은 팀에게 중요하다. / 하지만 팀 브랜드나 이미지는 현시대를 따르기 위해 조정될 수 있다 / 만약 팀이 그들의 뿌리를 버리거나 무시하면 / 부정적인 영향이 표면화될 수 있다.

1940년과 2000년 사이에 쿠바는 세계 야구계를 지배했다. 그들은 첫 28회의 월드컵 중 25회와 5회의 올림픽 게임 중 3회를 이겼다. ① 쿠바인들은 머리부터 발끝까지 빨간색으로 뒤덮인 유니폼을 입는 것으로 알려져 있었는데, 이것은 회색이나 흰색 바지를 특징으로 하는 더 보수적인 북미 스타일과 강한 대조를 이룬다. ② 쿠바인들의 운동 재능이 뛰어났을 뿐만 아니라 그들은 그들의 유니폼의 색깔만으로도 훨씬 더 강하게 보였다. ③ 심지어 경기가 시작하지 않았는데도 상대 팀은 이미 겁에 질리곤 했다. ④ 몇 년 전 쿠바는 유니폼을 현대화하고 아마도 다른 나라의 스타일에 맞추면서 그 유니폼 스타일을 바꿨다. 흥미롭게도 국가 대표 팀은 그 시기부터 쇠퇴해 왔다. 수십 년 동안 국제 야구를 지배했던 그 나라는 그 유니폼 교체 이후로 정상에 오른 적이 없었다. ⑤ 전통은 팀에게 중요하다. 팀 브랜드나 이미지는 현시대를 따르기 위해 조정될 수 있지만 만약 팀이 그들의 뿌리를 버리거나 무시하면 부정적인 영향이 표면화될 수 있다.

Why? 왜 정답일까?
④ 앞은 야구계를 지배한 쿠바의 전통적인 유니폼에 대해서 이야기하고 있는 반면 이후에는 유니폼 교체를 언급하고 있다. 주어진 글은 유니폼을 바꿨다고 이야기하고 있으므로, 주어진 문장이 들어가기에 가장 적절한 곳은 ④이다.

- be known for ~로 잘 알려진
- toe ⓝ 발끝
- conservative ⓐ 보수적인
- modernize ⓥ 현대화하다
- abandon ⓥ 버리다
- covered in ~로 뒤덮인
- contrast ⓝ 대조
- alter ⓥ 바꾸다
- decline ⓥ 쇠퇴하다
- neglect ⓥ 무시하다

구문 풀이
8행 Not only were their athletic talents superior, the Cubans appeared even
부정어   동사도치   주어
stronger from just the colour of their uniforms.

40 문화와 유전학의 관계 | 정답률 54% | 정답 ①
다음 글의 내용을 한 문장으로 요약하고자 한다. 빈칸 (A), (B)에 들어갈 말로 가장 적절한 것은? [3점]

(A)	(B)	(A)	(B)
✓ similarity 유사성	diverse 다양한	② similarity 유사성	limited 제한적인
③ difference 차이점	flexible 유연한	④ difference 차이점	complicated 복잡한
⑤ interaction 상호작용	credible 믿을 수 있는		

[10회] 2023학년도 11월 **137**

Many of the first models of cultural evolution / drew noticeable connections / between culture and genes / by using concepts from theoretical population genetics / and applying them to culture.
문화 진화의 많은 초기 모델들은 / 주목할 만한 접점을 이끌어 냈다. / 문화와 유전자 사이의 / 이론 집단 유전학의 개념을 사용함으로써 / 그리고 그것들을 문화에 적용함으로써

Cultural patterns of transmission, innovation, and selection / are conceptually likened / to genetic processes of transmission, mutation, and selection.
전파, 혁신, 선택의 문화적 방식은 / 개념적으로 유사하다. / 전달, 돌연변이, 선택의 유전적 과정과

However, / these approaches had to be modified / to account for the differences / between genetic and cultural transmission.
그러나 / 이러한 접근법은 수정되어야 했다. / 차이점을 설명하기 위해 / 유전자의 전달과 문화 전파 사이의

For example, / we do not expect / the cultural transmission to follow / the rules of genetic transmission / strictly.
예를 들어, / 우리는 예상하지 않는다. / 문화 전파가 따를 것이라고 / 유전자 전달의 규칙을 / 엄격하게

If two biological parents have different forms of a cultural trait, / their child is not necessarily equally likely to acquire / the mother's or father's form of that trait.
만약 두 명의 생물학적인 부모가 서로 다른 문화적인 특성의 형태를 가진다면 / 그들의 자녀는 반드시 동일하게 획득하지 않을 수 있다. / 엄마 혹은 아빠의 그 특성의 형태를

Further, / a child can acquire cultural traits / not only from its parents but also from nonparental adults and peers; / thus, / the frequency of a cultural trait / in the population / is relevant / beyond just the probability / that an individual's parents had that trait.
더욱이 / 아이는 문화적인 특성을 얻을 수 있다. / 부모로부터 뿐만 아니라 부모가 아닌 성인이나 또래로부터도 / 따라서 / 문화적인 특성의 빈도는 / 집단의 / 유의미하다. / 단지 확률을 넘어서 / 한 개인의 부모가 그 특성을 가졌을

➡ Early cultural evolution models used the (A) similarity / between culture and genes / but had to be revised / since cultural transmission allows for more (B) diverse factors / than genetic transmission.
초기의 문화 진화 모델들은 유사성을 사용했다. / 문화와 유전자 사이의 / 하지만 수정되어야만 했다. / 문화 전파가 더 다양한 요인을 허용하기 때문에 / 유전자의 전달보다

문화 진화의 많은 초기 모델들은 이론 집단 유전학의 개념을 사용함으로써 그리고 그것들을 문화에 적용함으로써 문화와 유전자 사이의 주목할 만한 접점을 이끌어 냈다. 전파, 혁신, 선택의 문화적 방식은 전달, 돌연변이, 선택의 유전적 과정과 개념적으로 유사하다. 그러나 이러한 접근법은 유전자의 전달과 문화 전파 사이의 차이점을 설명하기 위해 수정되어야만 했다. 예를 들어, 우리는 문화 전파가 유전자 전달의 규칙을 엄격하게 따를 것이라고 예상하지 않는다. 만약 두 명의 생물학적인 부모가 서로 다른 문화적인 특성의 형태를 가진다면, 그들의 자녀는 반드시 엄마 혹은 아빠의 그 특성의 형태를 동일하게 획득하지 않을 수 있다. 더욱이 아이는 문화적인 특성을 부모로부터 뿐만 아니라 부모가 아닌 성인이나 또래로부터도 얻을 수 있다. 따라서 집단의 문화적인 특성의 빈도는 단지 한 개인의 부모가 그 특성을 가졌을 확률을 넘어서 유의미하다.

➡ 초기의 문화 진화 모델들은 문화와 유전자 사이의 (A) 유사성을 사용했지만, 문화 전파가 유전자의 전달보다 더 (B) 다양한 요인을 허용하기 때문에 수정되어야만 했다.

Why? 왜 정답일까?

전파, 혁신, 선택의 문화적 방식은 유전학의 개념과 유사하지만(Cultural patterns of transmission, innovation, and selection are conceptually likened to genetic processes of transmission, mutation, and selection.), 차이점을 설명할 수 없기 때문에 수정되어야 했다. 문화적 방식은 유전이 아니라 성인이나 또래로부터 얻을 수 있기 때문이다.(Further, a child can acquire cultural traits not only from its parents but also from nonparental adults and peers; thus, the frequency of a cultural trait in the population is relevant beyond just the probability that an individual's parents had that trait.) 따라서 요약문의 빈칸 (A), (B)에 들어갈 말로 가장 적절한 것은 ① 'A similarity(유사성), (B) diverse(다양한)'이다.

- evolution ⓝ 진화
- concept ⓝ 개념
- genetics ⓝ 유전학
- innovation ⓝ 혁신
- mutation ⓝ 돌연변이
- trait ⓝ 특징
- peer ⓝ 동료
- revise ⓥ 수정하다
- diverse ⓐ 다양한
- difference ⓝ 차이점
- complicated ⓐ 복잡한
- credible ⓐ 믿을 수 있는
- noticeable ⓐ 주목할 만한
- theoretical ⓐ 이론적인
- transmission ⓝ 전이
- link to ~에 접근하다
- modify ⓥ 수정하다
- acquire ⓥ 얻다
- probability ⓝ 개연성
- similarity ⓝ 유사성
- limited ⓐ 제한적인
- flexible ⓐ 유연한
- interaction ⓝ 상호작용

구문 풀이

13행 Further, a child can acquire cultural traits not only from its parents but also from nonparental adults and peers; thus, the frequency of a cultural trait in the population is relevant beyond just the probability that an individual's parents had that trait.
「not only A, but also B : A뿐만 아니라 B도」

41-42 공동작용의 예시

A ball thrown into the air is acted / upon by the initial force given it, / persisting as inertia of movement / and tending to carry it / in the same straight line, / and by the constant pull of gravity downward, / as well as by the resistance of the air.
공중으로 던져진 공은 움직여진다. / 그것에 주어진 힘에 의해 / 운동의 관성으로 지속하며 / 그리고 나아가려는 경향을 보인다. / 같은 직선으로 / 그리고 아래로 지속적으로 당기는 중력에 의해서도 / 공기의 저항뿐만 아니라

It moves, / accordingly, / in a (a) curved path.
공은 움직인다. / 그에 맞춰 / 곡선의 경로로

「Now / the path does not represent / the working of any particular force; / there is simply the (b) combination / of the three elementary forces mentioned; / 「but in a real sense, / there is something in the total action / besides the isolated action of three forces, / namely, / their joint action.」 **41번의 근거**
이제 / 그 경로는 나타내지는 않는다 / 어떤 특정한 힘의 작용을 / 결합이 존재할 뿐이다. / 언급된 세 가지 기본적인 힘의 / 하지만 사실은 / 전체적인 작용에 무언가가 있다. / 세 가지 힘의 고립된 작용 외에 / 이름하여 / 그들의 공동 작용이다.

In the same way, / when two or more human individuals are together, / their mutual relationships and their arrangement into a group are things / which would not be

---

(c) uncovered / if we confined our attention to each individual separately.
같은 방식으로 / 두 명 혹은 그 이상의 인간 개인이 같이 있을 때 / 그들의 상호 관계와 그들의 집단으로의 배치는 것이다 / 드러나지 않을 / 만약 우리가 관심을 개별적으로 각각의 개인에 국한시킨다면

The significance of group behavior is greatly (d) increased / in the case of human beings / by the fact / that some of the tendencies to action of the individual / are related definitely to other persons, / and could not be aroused / except by other persons acting as stimuli.
그룹 행동의 중요성은 크게 증가된다. / 인간의 경우 / 사실로 의해 / 개인 행동의 몇몇 경향은 / 명백하게 다른 사람들과 관련이 있다는 / 그리고 유발되지 않을 수 있다는 / 자극으로 작동하는 다른 사람들은 없이는

An individual in complete (e) isolation / would not reveal / their competitive tendencies, their tendencies towards the opposite sex, their protective tendencies towards children.
완전한 고립 속의 개인은 / 드러내지 않을 것이다. / 그들의 경쟁적인 성향, 이성에 대한 그들의 성향, 아이에 대한 그들의 보호적 성향을

This shows / that the traits of human nature do not fully appear / until the individual is brought into relationships / with other individuals.
이것은 보여준다. / 인간 본성의 특성이 완전히 나타나지 않는다는 것을 / 개인이 관계에 관여될 때까지는 / 다른 개인과의

공중으로 던져진 공은 초기에 그것에 주어진 힘에 의해 움직여지는데, 운동의 관성으로 지속하며 같은 직선으로 나아가려는 경향을 보이고, 공기의 저항뿐만 아니라 아래로 지속적으로 당기는 중력에 의해서도 움직여진다. 그에 맞춰 공은 (a) 곡선의 경로로 움직인다. 이제 그 경로는 어떤 특정한 힘의 작동을 나타내지는 않는다. 언급된 세 가지 기본적인 힘의 (b) 결합이 존재할 뿐이다. 하지만 사실은 세 가지 힘의 고립된 작용 외에 전체적인 작용에 무언가가 있다. 이름하여 그들의 공동 작용이다. 같은 방식으로, 두 명 혹은 그 이상의 인간 개인이 같이 있을 때 그들의 상호 관계와 그들의 집단으로의 배치는 만약 우리가 관심을 개별적으로 각각의 개인에게 국한시킨다면 (c) 감춰지지(→ 드러나지) 않을 것이다. 개인 행동의 몇몇 경향은 명백하게 다른 사람들과 관련이 있고 자극으로 작동하는 다른 사람들 없이는 유발되지 않을 수 있다는 사실로 인해 그룹 행동의 중요성이 인간의 경우 크게 (d) 증가된다. 완전한 (e) 고립 속의 개인은 그들의 경쟁적인 성향, 이성에 대한 그들의 성향, 아이에 대한 그들의 보호적 성향을 드러내지 않을 것이다. 이것은 개인이 다른 개인과의 관계에 관여될 때까지는 인간 본성의 특성이 완전히 나타나지 않는다는 것을 보여준다.

- persist ⓥ 저항하다
- carry ⓥ 나아가다
- gravity ⓝ 중력
- resistance ⓝ 저항
- elementary ⓐ 기본의
- joint ⓐ 공동의
- arrangement ⓝ 배치
- confined ⓐ 좁은
- behavior ⓝ 행동
- tendency ⓝ 경향
- reveal ⓥ 드러내다
- opposite ⓐ 정반대의
- bring into 끌어들이다
- inertia ⓝ 관성
- constant ⓐ 끊임없는
- downward ⓐ 아래의
- combination ⓝ 결합
- isolated ⓐ 고립된
- mutual ⓐ 상호의
- conceal ⓥ 감추다
- significance ⓝ 중요성
- increase ⓥ 증가하다
- arouse ⓥ 유발하다
- competitive ⓐ 경쟁적인
- towards prep ~향하여

구문 풀이

1행 A ball thrown into the air is acted upon by the initial force given it, persisting as inertia of movement and tending to carry it in the same straight line, and by the constant pull of gravity downward, as well as by the resistance of the air.
「A as well as B : B뿐만 아니라 A도」

---

41 제목 파악   정답률 48% | 정답 ⑤

윗글의 제목으로 가장 적절한 것은?
① Common Misunderstandings in Physics – 물리학에서 흔히 볼 수 있는 오해
② Collaboration: A Key to Success in Relationships – 협력: 관계에서 성공을 위한 열쇠
③ Interpersonal Traits and Their Impact on Science – 대인 관계의 특성과 그것이 과학에 미치는 영향
④ Unbalanced Forces Causing Objects to Accelerate – 개체를 가속시키는 불균형한 힘
✓⑤ Human Traits Uncovered by Interpersonal Relationships – 대인 관계에 의해 드러난 인간의 특성

Why? 왜 정답일까?

공을 공기 중으로 던질 때 작용하는 힘 외에도 눈에 보이지 않는 힘이 있는데 바로 이들의 공동작용이다(but in a real sense, there is something in the total action besides the isolated action of three forces, namely, their joint action.). 사람의 관계에 적용했을 때를 예시로 들어 개인이 다른 개인과의 관계에 관여될 때까지는 인간 본성의 특성이 완전히 나타나지 않는다고 말하고 있으므로, 글의 제목으로 가장 적절한 것은 ⑤ '대인 관계에 의해 드러난 인간의 특성'이다.

★★★ 등급을 가르는 문제!

42 어휘 추론   정답률 42% | 정답 ③

밑줄 친 (a) ~ (e) 중에서 문맥상 낱말의 쓰임이 적절하지 않은 것은? [3점]
① (a)   ② (b)   ✓③ (c)   ④ (d)   ⑤ (e)

Why? 왜 정답일까?

'Now the path ~'에서 공이 곡선으로 움직이는 것은 어떤 특정한 힘의 작동을 나타내지 않는다고 설명하는 것으로 보아, 만약 개별에 관심을 국한시킨다면 감춰지는 것이 아니라 '드러난다'는 내용이 맞다. 따라서 concealed 대신 uncovered를 써야 자연스럽다. 낱말의 쓰임이 문맥상 적절하지 않은 것은 ③ '(c)'이다.

★★ 문제 해결 꿀~팁 ★★

▶ 많이 틀린 이유는?
공중으로 던져진 공은 초기에 주어진 힘들이 결합되어서 곡선으로 움직이게 된다고 이야기하고 있다. 이 결합된 힘은 공동 작용인데 각각의 고립된 힘과는 따로 존재한다는 것을 기억해 두어야 한다. ③번에서는 인간이 집단으로 있을 때에 대입하여 주제를 이야기하고 있는데, 집단 내에서 발생하는 공동작용을 각 개인의 고립된 힘에 집중했을 때는 드러나지 않는 것이 주제와 일치한다. ④번에서는 인간은 다른 사람들과 상호작용하여 행동이 드러나기 때문에 그룹 행동의 중요성이 증가된다는 것이 주제와 일치한다.

구문 풀이

[B] 1행 But the saint also asked if the man could do a small job for him.
부사절(~인지 아닌지)

▶ 문제 해결 방법은?
글의 큰 주제를 파악한 후에 논리적으로 주제와 일맥상통하는지 찾아보면 된다. 문장 내에서 문맥상 낱말의 쓰임이 적절한지를 파악할 때는 반의어를 염두에 두고 비교해보면 좋다.

43-45　행복에 대한 자세

(A)

There once lived a man in a village / who was not happy with his life.
옛날 어느 마을에 한 남자가 살았다. / 자신의 삶이 행복하지 않은

He was always troubled / by one problem or another.
그는 항상 어려움을 겪었다. / 하나 혹은 또 다른 문제로

One day, / a saint with his guards stopped by his village.
어느 날 / 한 성자가 그의 경호원들과 함께 그의 마을에 들렀다.

「Many people heard the news / and started going to him with their problems.」
많은 사람들이 그 소식을 들었다. / 그리고 그들의 문제를 가지고 그에게 가기 시작했다.　45번 ①의 근거 일치

The man also decided / to visit the saint.
그 남자 역시 결정했다. / 성자를 방문하기로

Even after reaching the saint's place in the morning, / (a) he didn't get the opportunity / to meet him till evening.
아침에 성자가 있는 곳에 도착하고 난 후에도 / 그는 기회를 얻지 못했다. / 저녁때까지 그를 만날

(D)

When the man got to meet the saint, / (d) he confessed / that he was very unhappy with life / because problems always surrounded him, / like workplace tension or worries about his health.
마침내 그가 성자를 만났을 때 / 그는 고백했다. / 삶이 매우 불행하다고 / 항상 문제가 자기를 둘러싸고 있어서 / 직장 내 긴장이나 건강에 대한 걱정과 같이

(e) He said, / "Please give me a solution / so that all the problems in my life will end / and I can live peacefully."
그는 말했다. / 제발 해결책을 주세요. / 나의 삶의 모든 문제가 끝나기 위해서 / 그리고 제가 평화롭게 살 수 있도록

「The saint smiled / and said / that he would answer the request the next day.」
성자는 미소지었다. / 그리고 말했다. / 그가 다음 날 그 요청에 답해주겠다고　45번 ⑤의 근거 일치

(B)

「But / the saint also asked / if the man could do a small job for him.」45번 ②의 근거 일치
그런데 / 성자는 또한 물었다. / 그 남자가 그를 위해 작은 일을 해 줄 수 있는지

「He told the man to take care of a hundred camels / in his group that night, / saying "When all hundred camels sit down, you can go to sleep."」45번 ③의 근거 불일치
그는 그 남자에게 백 마리 낙타를 돌봐 달라고 말했다. / 그날 밤에 그의 일행에 있는 / "백 마리 낙타 모두가 자리에 앉으면 당신은 자러 가도 좋습니다."라고 말하면서

The man agreed. // The next morning when the saint met that man, / (b) he asked / if the man had slept well.
그 남자는 동의했다. // 다음 날 아침에 성자가 그 남자를 만났을 때 / 그는 물어보았다. / 남자가 잠을 잘 잤는지

Tired and sad, / the man replied / that he couldn't sleep even for a moment.
피곤해 하고 슬퍼하면서 / 그 남자는 대답했다. / 한순간도 잠을 자지 못했다고

(C)

In fact, / the man tried very hard / but couldn't make all the camels sit at the same time / because every time (c) he made one camel sit, / another would stand up.
사실 / 그 남자는 열심히 노력했다. / 그러나 모든 낙타를 동시에 앉게 할 수 없었다. / 왜냐하면 그가 낙타 한 마리를 앉힐 때마다 / 다른 낙타 한 마리가 일어섰기 때문이다.

The saint told him, / "You realized that / no matter how hard you try, / you can't make all the camels sit down.
그 성자는 그에게 말했다. / 당신은 깨달았습니다. / 당신이 아무리 노력하더라도 / 당신은 모든 낙타를 앉게 할 수 없습니다.

If one problem is solved, / for some reason, / another will arise / like the camels did.
만약 한 가지 문제가 해결되면 / 어떤 이유로 / 또 다른 문제가 일어날 것입니다. / 낙타가 그런 것처럼

「So, / humans should enjoy life / despite these problems."」45번 ④의 근거 일치
그래서 / 인간은 삶을 즐겨야 합니다. / 이러한 문제에도 불구하고

(A)

옛날 어느 마을에 자신의 삶이 행복하지 않은 한 남자가 살았다. 그는 항상 하나 혹은 또 다른 문제로 어려움을 겪었다. 어느 날 한 성자가 그의 경호원들과 함께 그의 마을에 들렀다. 많은 사람들이 그 소식을 듣고 그들의 문제를 가지고 그에게 가기 시작했다. 그 남자 역시 성자를 방문하기로 결정했다. 아침에 성자가 있는 곳에 도착하고 난 후에도 (a) 그는 저녁때까지 그를 만날 기회를 얻지 못했다.

(D)

마침내 그가 성자를 만났을 때 (d) 그는 직장 내 긴장이나 건강에 대한 걱정과 같이 항상 문제가 자기를 둘러싸고 있어서 삶이 매우 불행하다고 고백했다. (e) 그는 "나의 삶의 모든 문제가 끝나고 제가 평화롭게 살 수 있도록 제발 해결책을 주세요."라고 말했다. 성자는 미소 지으면서 그가 다음 날 그 요청에 답해주겠다고 말했다.

(B)

그런데 성자는 또한 그 남자가 그를 위해 작은 일을 해 줄 수 있는지 물었다. 성자는 그 남자에게 "백 마리 낙타 모두가 자리에 앉으면 당신은 자러 가도 좋습니다."라고 말하면서 그날 밤에 그의 일행에 있는 백 마리 낙타를 돌봐 달라고 말했다. 그 남자는 동의했다. 다음 날 아침에 성자가 그 남자를 만났을 때 (b) 그는 남자가 잠을 잘 잤는지 물어보았다. 피곤해하고 슬퍼하면서 남자는 한순간도 잠을 자지 못했다고 대답했다.

(C)

사실 그 남자는 아주 열심히 노력했지만 (c) 그가 낙타 한 마리를 앉힐 때마다 다른 낙타 한 마리가 일어섰기 때문에 모든 낙타를 동시에 앉게 할 수 없었다. 그 성자는 그에게 "당신이 아무리 열심히 노력하더라도 모든 낙타를 앉게 만들 수는 없다는 것을 깨달았습니다. 만약 한 가지 문제가 해결되면 낙타가 그런 것처럼 어떤 이유로 또 다른 문제가 일어날 것입니다. 그래서 인간은 이러한 문제에도 불구하고 삶을 즐겨야 합니다."라고 말했다.

● saint ⓝ 성자　　　　　　● guard ⓝ 경호원
● stop by ~에 들르다　　　　● decide ⓥ 결심하다
● opportunity ⓝ 기회　　　　● confess ⓥ 고백하다
● surrounded ⓐ 둘러싸인　　● tension ⓝ 긴장
● take care of ~을 돌보다　　● camel ⓝ 낙타

[문제편 p.134]

43　글의 순서 파악　　　　　정답률 82% | 정답 ④

주어진 글 (A)에 이어질 내용을 순서에 맞게 배열한 것으로 가장 적절한 것은?

① (B) − (D) − (C)　　　　② (C) − (B) − (D)
③ (C) − (D) − (B)　　　　☑ (D) − (B) − (C)
⑤ (D) − (C) − (B)

Why? 왜 정답일까?

성자가 마을에 들렀다는 내용의 (A)의 뒤로, 마침내 남자가 성자를 만났다는 내용의 (D), 성자가 백마리 낙타를 돌봐달라고 요청한 내용의 (B), 아무리 노력해도 모든 낙타를 앉게 할 수 없었다는 내용의 (C)가 순서대로 이어져야 자연스럽다. 따라서 글의 순서로 가장 적절한 것은 ④ '(D) − (B) − (C)'이다.

44　지칭 추론　　　　　정답률 74% | 정답 ②

밑줄 친 (a) ~ (e) 중에서 가리키는 대상이 나머지 넷과 다른 것은?

① (a)　　☑ (b)　　③ (c)　　④ (d)　　⑤ (e)

Why? 왜 정답일까?

(a), (c), (d), (e)는 the man, (b)는 the saint를 가리키므로, (a) ~ (e) 중에서 가리키는 대상이 다른 하나는 ② '(b)'이다.

45　세부 내용 파악　　　　　정답률 67% | 정답 ③

윗글에 관한 내용으로 적절하지 않은 것은?

① 많은 사람들이 자신들의 문제를 가지고 성자에게 갔다.
② 성자는 자신을 위해 작은 일을 해 줄 수 있는지 남자에게 물었다.
☑ 성자는 남자가 낙타를 모두 재우면 잠을 자러 가도 좋다고 했다.
④ 성자는 문제가 있어도 인생을 즐겨야 한다고 말했다.
⑤ 성자는 남자의 요청에 대한 답을 다음 날 말해 주기로 했다.

Why? 왜 정답일까?

(B) 'He told the man to take care of a hundred camels in his group that night, saying "When all hundred camels sit down, you can go to sleep."'에서 낙타를 모두 앉히면 잠을 자러 가도 좋다고 했으므로, 내용과 일치하지 않는 것은 ③ '성자는 남자가 낙타를 모두 재우면 잠을 자러 가도 좋다고 했다.'이다.

Why? 왜 오답일까?

① (A) 'Many people heard the news and started going to him with their problems.'의 내용과 일치한다.
② (B) 'But the saint also asked if the man could do a small job for him.'의 내용과 일치한다.
④ (C) 'So, humans should enjoy life despite these problems.'의 내용과 일치한다.
⑤ (D) 'The saint smiled / and said / that he would answer the request the next day.'의 내용과 일치한다.

문제편 135쪽

01 The robot offers guided-tours / where you want to go / and it'll kindly help you

02 why you're writing in French / translated text before copying it / You'd better check the translation

03 how long you've been using it / can you pick it up / to load it on first

04 give a fresh feel to the lounge / the banner on the wall / make the atmosphere cozier

05 how to motivate students to participate / an award for the class / students who leave nothing on their plates

06 What service plans do you have / I prefer the faster one / Please fill in this paper

07 I'm on my way to / family gathering you mentioned before / take the tickets with pleasure

08 really looking forward to it / set a reminder on my phone / will be donated to charity

09 anyone who is interested in / are required to bring their own snowshoes and poles / you must register in advance to participate

10 instead of a wall calendar / one that's made of recyclable paper / theme doesn't match

11 you were invited to speak / I'm so proud of you

12 I ran to be in time / It's too far to walk

13 opened a brand new world to me / Did you install a file-reading app / that's why it doesn't work

14 Didn't you say you're volunteering / helps deaf students understand the class better / Is the position still available

15 plan to go on a bakery / a list of places to visit / there have been lots of reviews

16-17 we learned why it's good for us / can cause severe health damage / The fruit contains so much acid

어휘 Review Test 10

문제편 140쪽

A	B	C	D
01 자신 있는	**01** equality	**01** ⓜ	**01** ⓒ
02 편의	**02** certificate	**02** ⓟ	**02** ⓝ
03 색조, 그늘	**03** clue	**03** ⓐ	**03** ⓐ
04 흔들다	**04** diagnosis	**04** ⓕ	**04** ⓔ
05 방향, 길	**05** regulation	**05** ⓡ	**05** ⓠ
06 성장	**06** immediate	**06** ⓚ	**06** ⓖ
07 쏟다, 몰두하다	**07** specify	**07** ⓢ	**07** ⓑ
08 책임감	**08** term	**08** ⓝ	**08** ⓛ
09 상식적인	**09** possession	**09** ⓖ	**09** ⓟ
10 객관적인	**10** maintain	**10** ⓙ	**10** ⓘ
11 반사하다	**11** clarity	**11** ⓔ	**11** ⓗ
12 범위	**12** get rid of	**12** ⓘ	**12** ⓜ
13 요구하다	**13** visual	**13** ⓠ	**13** ⓙ
14 만들다, 몰아가다	**14** adjust to	**14** ⓞ	**14** ⓚ
15 막다	**15** upright	**15** ⓣ	**15** ⓞ
16 충분한	**16** reverse	**16** ⓒ	**16** ⓡ
17 인식	**17** advantage	**17** ⓛ	**17** ⓣ
18 투자, 투자액	**18** pursue	**18** ⓓ	**18** ⓓ
19 도달하다	**19** endure	**19** ⓗ	**19** ⓕ
20 초과하다	**20** unrelated	**20** ⓑ	**20** ⓢ

11회 | 2022학년도 11월 학력평가 [고1]

• 정답 •

01 ① 02 ① 03 ② 04 ④ 05 ⑤ 06 ④ 07 ① 08 ③ 09 ④ 10 ② 11 ① 12 ② 13 ③ 14 ① 15 ②
16 ② 17 ④ 18 ② 19 ② 20 ⑤ 21 ③ 22 ① 23 ⑤ 24 ④ 25 ④ 26 ③ 27 ⑤ 28 ③ 29 ④ 30 ④
31 ③ 32 ② 33 ③ 34 ③ 35 ④ 36 ③ 37 ⑤ 38 ⑤ 39 ③ 40 ② 41 ① 42 ⑤ 43 ④ 44 ③ 45 ④

★ 표기된 문항은 [등급을 가르는 문제]에 해당하는 문제입니다.

01 등산로 폐쇄 공지

정답률 87% | 정답 ①

다음을 듣고, 남자가 하는 말의 목적으로 가장 적절한 것을 고르시오.

☑ 얼음으로 덮인 일부 등산로 폐쇄를 공지하려고
② 등산객에게 야간 산행의 위험성을 경고하려고
③ 겨울 산행을 위한 안전 장비를 안내하려고
④ 긴급 제설에 필요한 작업자를 모집하려고
⑤ 일출 명소인 전망대를 소개하려고

[Chime bell rings.]
[알림벨이 울린다.]

M : Good morning. This is Ethan Cooper from the Reindeer Mountain maintenance office.
안녕하세요. Reindeer Mountain 관리 사무소의 Ethan Cooper입니다.
Last night, we had 20cm of heavy snow.
어젯밤 20센티미터의 폭설이 내렸습니다.
Most of the snow melted away with the sun out in the morning, but some of it froze in the shade.
아침에 해가 나면서 대부분의 눈이 녹았지만, 응달에 있는 일부 눈은 얼어붙었습니다.
For hikers' safety, we've closed some of the trails covered with ice.
등산객 분들의 안전을 위하여, 저희는 얼음으로 덮인 일부 등산로를 폐쇄했습니다.
At this moment, Sunrise Trail and Lakeview Trail are unavailable for hikers.
현재 Sunrise Trail과 Lakeview Trail은 등산객 분들의 이용이 불가합니다.
I'll make an announcement later when the trails are ready to be reopened.
등산로가 다시 개방될 준비가 되면 추후 안내하겠습니다.
Until then, keep in mind that Sunrise Trail and Lakeview Trail are closed.
그때까지는 Sunrise Trail과 Lakeview Trail이 폐쇄되었음을 유념해주세요.
Thank you.
감사합니다.

Why? 왜 정답일까?

'For hikers' safety, we've closed some of the trails covered with ice.'와 'Until then, keep in mind that Sunrise Trail and Lakeview Trail are closed.'에서 폭설로 인해 얼어붙은 등산로 일부가 폐쇄되었다는 내용을 알 수 있다. 따라서 남자가 하는 말의 목적으로 가장 적절한 것은 ① '얼음으로 덮인 일부 등산로 폐쇄를 공지하려고'이다.

- **melt away** 녹아버리다
- **make an announcement** 안내하다
- **unavailable** ⓐ 이용 불가한
- **keep in mind** 염두에 두다

02 조리법을 그대로 지키지는 않아도 된다고 조언하기

정답률 95% | 정답 ①

대화를 듣고, 남자의 의견으로 가장 적절한 것을 고르시오.

☑ 조리법을 있는 그대로 따를 필요는 없다.
② 요리 도구를 정기적으로 소독해야 한다.
③ 설탕 섭취는 단기 기억력을 향상시킨다.
④ 열량이 높은 음식은 건강에 좋지 않다.
⑤ 신선한 재료는 요리의 풍미를 높인다.

M : Honey, what are you doing?
여보, 뭐 하고 있어요?
W : I'm looking for the measuring spoons. Do you know where they are?
계량 스푼을 찾고 있어요. 어디 있는지 알아요?
M : They're in the first drawer. Why do you need them?
첫 번째 서랍에 있어요. 왜 그게 필요해요?
W : The recipe says four teaspoons of sugar.
조리법에 설탕을 티스푼으로 4숟갈 넣으라고 돼 있어요.
M : Dear, you don't have to follow the recipe as it is.
여보, 조리법을 있는 그대로 따를 필요는 없어요.
W : What do you mean?
무슨 말이에요?
M : A recipe is just an example. You don't need to add the same amount of ingredients as stated in the recipe.
조리법은 그냥 예시예요. 조리법에 쓰여있는 대로 재료 양을 똑같이 추가할 필요는 없어요.
W : Hmm. Right. Sometimes the food is too sweet when I cook based on the recipe instructions.
흠. 그렇군요. 가끔은 내가 조리법의 지시에 따라 요리했을 때 음식이 너무 달아요.
M : See? You don't need to stick to the recipe.
그렇죠? 조리법을 고수할 필요가 없어요.
W : Okay. I'll remember that.
알겠어요. 기억할게요.

Why? 왜 정답일까?

'Dear, you don't have to follow the recipe as it is.'와 'You don't need to stick to the recipe.'에서 남자는 조리법을 있는 그대로 따르지 않아도 된다고 여자에게 조언하고 있다. 따라서 남자의 의견으로 가장 적절한 것은 ① '조리법을 있는 그대로 따를 필요는 없다.'이다.

- **measuring spoon** 계량 스푼
- **ingredient** ⓝ 재료
- **stick to** ~을 고수하다
- **amount** ⓝ 양
- **as stated** 명시된 대로

[문제편 p.141]

03 게임 음악 제작 의뢰

정답률 92% | 정답 ②

대화를 듣고, 두 사람의 관계를 가장 잘 나타낸 것을 고르시오.
① 음악 평론가 – 방송 연출가　　② 작곡가 – 게임 제작자
③ 독자 – 웹툰 작가　　④ 삽화가 – 소설가
⑤ 영화감독 – 배우

[Door knocks.]
[문을 노크하는 소리가 난다.]

W : Can I come in?
　들어가도 될까요?

M : Yes. Oh, Ms. Smith. Did you read the email I sent?
　네. 오, Ms. Smith. 제가 보낸 이메일 읽으셨어요?

W : I did. I liked your game scenario. The characters exploring space were very mysterious. How did you create the characters?
　네. 당신의 게임 시나리오 좋았어요. 우주를 탐험하는 캐릭터들이 아주 신비로웠어요. 그 캐릭터들을 어떻게 만드신 건가요?

M : Actually, old science fiction movies inspired me to design those characters.
　사실, 오래된 공상 과학 영화들이 제가 캐릭터를 고안하는 데 영감을 줬어요.

W : Interesting. Now, could you describe the main character more specifically? It'll be helpful when I compose the theme song for the character.
　흥미롭군요. 이제, 주요 등장인물을 더 구체적으로 설명해 주실래요? 제가 인물을 위해 테마 곡을 작곡할 때 도움이 될 거예요.

M : Well, he's a thrill seeker. So, a strong, bold, and rhythmic sound would suit him.
　음, 그는 스릴을 추구하는 사람이에요. 그래서 강력하고 대담하고 리듬감 있는 소리가 그에게 어울릴 거예요.

W : Okay. Do you need anything else?
　알겠습니다. 더 필요하신 건요?

M : I also want you to make some background music.
　그리고 전 당신이 배경 음악도 좀 만들어주시면 좋겠어요.

W : Of course. When do you need them?
　물론이죠. 언제 필요하실까요?

M : By December 21st. I'd like to start putting the music into the game by then.
　12월 21일까지요. 그때쯤 음악을 게임에 넣기 시작하려고요.

W : All right. Then I'll talk to you later.
　알겠습니다. 그럼 나중에 얘기 드리죠.

Why? 왜 정답일까?

'I liked your game scenario.', 'It'll be helpful when I compose the theme song for the character.', 'I also want you to make some background music.', 'I'd like to start putting the music into the game by then.'에서 게임 제작자가 작곡가에게 게임에 들어갈 음악을 만들어 달라고 의뢰하는 상황임을 알 수 있다. 따라서 두 사람의 관계로 가장 적절한 것은 ② '작곡가 – 게임 제작자'이다.

● **explore** ⓥ 탐험하다　　● **mysterious** ⓐ 신비로운
● **compose** ⓥ 작곡하다　　● **thrill seeker** 스릴을 추구하는 사람
● **bold** ⓐ 대담한

04 방 그림 구경하기

정답률 85% | 정답 ④

대화를 듣고, 그림에서 대화의 내용과 일치하지 <u>않는</u> 것을 고르시오.

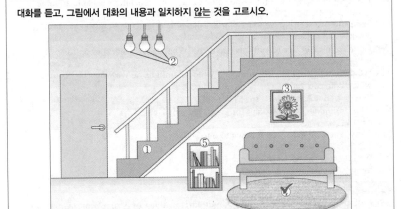

M : Hi, Chelsea. Did you finish your art assignment?
　안녕, Chelsea. 너 네 미술 숙제 끝냈어?

W : Oh, my dream room drawing? Yes. Here's the picture.
　오, 내가 꿈꾸는 방 그림 말이지? 응. 여기 그림이 있어.

M : Wow, it's so creative. 「There is a staircase next to the door.」 ①의 근거 일치
　와, 정말 창의적이야. 문 옆에 계단이 있구나.

W : Yes. I've always dreamed of a room with two floors. 「Look at the three light bulbs above the staircase.」 ②의 근거 일치
　응. 난 항상 2층짜리 방을 꿈꿨어. 계단 위의 전구 세 개를 봐.

M : They look very stylish. 「And I like the flower picture above the sofa.」 It'll bring warmth to your room. ③의 근거 일치
　정말 멋져 보이네. 그리고 난 소파 위에 있는 꽃 그림이 마음에 들어. 네 방에 온기를 더할 거야.

W : Thanks. 「Check out the square-shaped rug on the floor.」 ④의 근거 불일치
　고마워. 바닥에 있는 사각형 러그를 확인해봐.

M : It goes well with this place. 「Oh, there is a bookshelf by the sofa.」 ⑤의 근거 일치
　이곳이랑 잘 어울리네. 오, 소파 옆에 책꽂이가 있구나.

W : You're right. I want to keep my favorite books nearby.
　맞아. 난 내가 가장 좋아하는 책들을 가까이 두고 싶어.

M : That's a good idea.
　좋은 생각이야.

Why? 왜 정답일까?

대화에서 바닥에 있는 러그는 사각형이라고 하는데(Check out the square-shaped rug on the floor.), 그림 속 러그는 원형이다. 따라서 그림에서 대화의 내용과 일치하지 않는 것은 ④이다.

● **assignment** ⓝ 과제, 숙제
● **go well with** ~와 잘 어울리다
● **staircase** ⓝ 계단, 층계
● **bookshelf** ⓝ 책꽂이

05 만화가 초빙 토크쇼 준비하기

정답률 95% | 정답 ⑤

대화를 듣고, 남자가 할 일로 가장 적절한 것을 고르시오.
① 음료 구매하기　　② 연필 준비하기
③ 의자 설치하기　　④ 마이크 점검하기
⑤ 스케치북 가져오기

W : Jamie, is the cartoon artist on her way?
　Jamie, 만화가 분은 오시는 중이에요?

M : Yes. She'll arrive at our studio in an hour.
　네. 한 시간 뒤 우리 스튜디오에 도착하실 거예요.

W : Perfect. Let's check if we have everything ready for our talk show.
　완벽해요. 우리 토크쇼를 위해 모든 게 준비됐는지 확인해 보죠.

M : Okay. I set up a chair for our guest yesterday.
　그래요. 어제 제가 우리 게스트를 위해 의자를 설치했어요.

W : Great. And I bought a drink and put it on the table.
　훌륭해요. 그리고 전 음료를 사서 탁자 위에 올려뒀어요.

M : Good. Did you prepare a pencil? The artist said she'll draw caricatures of us during the live show.
　좋아요. 연필은 준비했어요? 만화가 말하길 라이브 쇼 동안에 우리의 캐리커쳐를 그려주신대요.

W : Oh, she told me that she'll bring her own pencil.
　오, 그분이 저보고 자기 연필을 가지고 올 거라고 하셨어요.

M : She did? Then we don't need it.
　그러셨어요? 그럼 그건 필요 없네요.

W : Yeah. By the way, where's the sketchbook?
　네. 그나저나 스케치북은 어디 있죠?

M : Oops. I left it in my car. I'll go get it right now.
　이런. 내 차에 놔두고 왔어요. 바로 가서 가져올게요.

W : Fine. Then I'll check the microphones.
　좋아요. 그럼 내가 마이크를 점검할게요.

M : Thanks.
　고마워요.

Why? 왜 정답일까?

게스트인 만화가가 쓸 스케치북이 어디 있느냐는 여자의 질문에(By the way, where's the sketchbook?) 남자는 깜빡하고 차에 두었다며 바로 가서 가져오겠다고 한다(I'll go get it right now.). 따라서 남자가 할 일로 가장 적절한 것은 ⑤ '스케치북 가져오기'이다.

● **cartoon artist** 만화가　　● **prepare** ⓥ 준비하다

06 치킨과 음료 주문하기

정답률 63% | 정답 ④

대화를 듣고, 여자가 지불할 금액을 고르시오. [3점]
① $17　② $22　③ $35　④ $37　⑤ $39

M : Welcome to Crispy Fried Chicken. What would you like to order?
　Crispy Fried Chicken에 잘 오셨습니다. 무엇을 주문하실 건가요?

W : What kind of chicken do you have?
　치킨 종류가 어떤 게 있죠?

M : We only have two kinds. Fried chicken is $15 and barbecue chicken is $20.
　2가지 종류밖에 없습니다. 프라이드 치킨이 15달러이고, 바비큐 치킨이 20달러입니다.

W : I'll have one fried and one barbecue chicken.
　프라이드 한 마리, 바비큐 한 마리 주세요.

M : Okay. Would you like some potato chips with your order? They're our most popular side dish.
　알겠습니다. 주문에 감자 칩도 포함하시겠어요? 그게 가장 인기 있는 사이드 메뉴입니다.

W : How much are they?
　얼마인가요?

M : One basket of potato chips is $2.
　감자칩 한 바구니에 2달러입니다.

W : Then I'll get one basket.
　그럼 한 바구니 주문할게요.

M : Will that be all?
　다 되셨을까요?

W : Yes. And can I use this coupon for a free soda?
　네. 그리고 제가 이 무료 탄산음료 쿠폰을 써도 될까요?

M : Of course. You can grab any soda from the fridge.
　물론입니다. 냉장고에서 아무 탄산음료나 가져가시면 됩니다.

W : Great. Here's my credit card.
　훌륭하군요. 여기 제 신용 카드요.

Why? 왜 정답일까?

대화에 따르면 여자는 15달러짜리 프라이드 치킨을 한 마리, 20달러짜리 바비큐 치킨을 한 마리 사고, 2달러짜리 감자 칩 바구니도 주문했다. 탄산음료는 무료 쿠폰을 이용해 추가하여 비용이 들지 않았다. 이를 식으로 나타내면 '15 + 20 + 2 = 37'이므로, 여자가 지불할 금액은 ④ '$37'이다.

● **side dish** 사이드 메뉴, 곁들이 음식
● **fridge** ⓝ 냉장고
● **grab** ⓥ 집다, 잡다

07 얼음낚시를 못 가게 되었다고 알려주기

정답률 86% | 정답 ①

대화를 듣고, 남자가 얼음낚시를 갈 수 <u>없는</u> 이유를 고르시오.
① 손목을 다쳐서　　② 병원에 입원해야 해서
③ 직장에 출근해야 해서　　④ 기상 여건이 나빠져서
⑤ 친구와 농구를 해야 해서

[Cell phone rings.]
[휴대 전화 벨이 울린다.]

W : Leo, I'm sorry I missed your call. What's up?
　Leo, 전화 못 받아서 미안해. 무슨 일이야?

M : Well, I just called to tell you that I can't go ice fishing with you this weekend.
　음, 이번 주말에 너랑 얼음낚시 못 가게 돼서 전화했어.

W : Oh, no. I heard the weather will be perfect this weekend.
오, 이런. 이번 주말에는 날씨가 완벽할 거라던데.
M : I'm sorry. I really wish I could go.
미안해. 정말 갈 수 있으면 좋겠는데.
W : Didn't you say you're off from work this weekend?
이번 주말은 일 쉰다고 하지 않았나?
M : I am. It's not because of work. Actually, I hurt my wrist.
쉬지. 일 때문이 아냐. 사실, 나 손목을 다쳤어.
W : That's terrible. Are you okay?
무척 안됐네. 괜찮은 거야?
M : Don't worry. I'll be fine.
걱정 마. 나아질 거야.
W : How did you get injured?
어쩌다 다쳤어?
M : I was playing basketball with a friend and sprained my wrist.
친구랑 농구를 하다가 손목을 삐었어.
W : Did you go to the hospital?
병원에는 가 봤어?
M : I did. The doctor told me that it'll be better in a month.
다녀왔지. 의사 선생님이 한 달 있으면 나을 거래.
W : That's good. I hope you feel better soon.
다행이다. 빨리 낫길 바라게.

Why? 왜 정답일까?

남자는 친구와 농구를 하던 중 손목을 다쳐서(Actually, I hurt my wrist.) 얼음낚시에 가지 못하게 되었다고 하므로, 남자가 얼음낚시를 갈 수 없는 이유로 가장 적절한 것은 ① '손목을 다쳐서'이다.

● hurt ⓥ 다치게 하다, 아프다   ● wrist ⓝ 손목
● sprain ⓥ 삐다

---

08 어린이 대상 도자기 수업   정답률 92% | 정답 ③

대화를 듣고, Kids' Pottery Class에 관해 언급되지 않은 것을 고르시오.
① 날짜   ② 장소   ☑수강 인원
④ 수강료   ⑤ 등록 방법

M : Honey, look at this flyer about Kids' Pottery Class.
여보, Kids' Pottery Class에 관한 이 전단지 좀 봐요.
W : Okay. Let's take a look.
알겠어요. 한번 볼게요.
M : I think our little Austin would love to make his own cereal bowl.
우리 귀여운 Austin이 자기 시리얼 그릇을 만들고 싶어할 거 같아요.
W : I think so, too. 『It says that the class is held on October 8th.』 We can take him there on that day. ①의 근거 일치
나도 그렇게 생각해요. 수업이 10월 8일날 열린다고 하네요. 그날 아이를 거기 데려가면 되겠어요.
M : Great. 『And it's held in Pottery Village. It's a 10-minute drive from our home.』
아주 좋아요. 그리고 이건 Pottery Village에서 열린대요. 우리 집에서 차로 10분 거리예요. ②의 근거 일치
W : That's so close. And check out the price. 『The class costs only $15.』 ④의 근거 일치
아주 가깝네요. 그리고 가격도 봐봐요. 수강료가 고작 15달러밖에 안 하네요.
M : That's reasonable. We should sign up. 『How can we register for the class?』
적당하네요. 등록해야겠어요. 이 수업을 어떻게 등록하죠?
W : It says you can simply scan the QR code to register online. ⑤의 근거 일치
그냥 QR코드를 스캔해서 온라인으로 등록하면 된다고 하네요.
M : Okay. Let's do it right away.
알겠어요. 당장 하죠.

Why? 왜 정답일까?

대화에서 남자와 여자는 Kids' Pottery Class의 날짜, 장소, 수강료, 등록 방법을 언급하므로, 언급되지 않은 것은 ③ '수강 인원'이다.

Why? 왜 오답일까?

① 'It says that the class is held on October 8th.'에서 '날짜'가 언급되었다.
② 'And it's held in Pottery Village.'에서 '장소'가 언급되었다.
④ 'The class costs only $15.'에서 '수강료'가 언급되었다.
⑤ 'It says you can simply scan the QR code to register online.'에서 '등록 방법'이 언급되었다.

● flyer ⓝ 전단지   ● pottery ⓝ 도자기
● sign up 등록하다

---

09 휘파람 대회 홍보   정답률 80% | 정답 ④

2022 Online Whistling Championship에 관한 다음 내용을 듣고, 일치하지 않는 것을 고르시오.
① 좋아하는 어떤 노래든 선택할 수 있다.
② 12월 4일까지 동영상을 업로드해야 한다.
③ 녹음 시 마이크의 에코 효과를 반드시 꺼야 한다.
☑운영진의 심사에 의해 수상자들이 결정될 것이다.
⑤ 결과는 웹사이트에 발표될 것이다.

W : Hello, listeners.
청취자 여러분, 안녕하세요.
The most interesting music competition is back!
가장 흥미진진한 음악 경연 대회가 다시 돌아옵니다!
You can now sign up for the 2022 Online Whistling Championship.
이제 여러분은 2022 Online Whistling Championship에 등록하실 수 있습니다.
『You can select any song that you like,』 but note that the length of your whistling video is limited to three minutes. ①의 근거 일치
좋아하는 어떤 노래를 선택하셔도 되지만, 여러분의 휘파람 영상 길이가 3분으로 제한된다는 걸 명심해 주세요.
『To enter the competition, you must upload your video on our website by December 4th.』 ②의 근거 일치
대회에 참가하시려면, 12월 4일까지 저희 웹사이트에 동영상을 업로드하셔야 합니다.

『When recording your whistling, be sure to turn off the echo effect on the microphone.』 ③의 근거 일치
휘파람을 녹음하실 때 마이크의 에코 효과를 반드시 꺼주세요.
『Winners will be decided by public online voting.』 ④의 근거 불일치
수상자는 온라인 대중 투표로 결정될 것입니다.
『The result will be announced on our website.』 ⑤의 근거 일치
결과는 저희 웹사이트에 발표될 예정입니다.
We look forward to your enthusiastic participation.
여러분의 열띤 참가를 고대합니다.

Why? 왜 정답일까?

'Winners will be decided by public online voting.'에서 수상자는 온라인 대중 투표로 결정된 다고 하므로, 내용과 일치하지 않는 것은 ④ '운영진의 심사에 의해 수상자들이 결정될 것이다.'이다.

Why? 왜 오답일까?

① 'You can select any song that you like, ~'의 내용과 일치한다.
② 'To enter the competition, you must upload your video on our website by December 4th.'의 내용과 일치한다.
③ 'When recording your whistling, be sure to turn off the echo effect on the microphone.'의 내용과 일치한다.
⑤ 'The result will be announced on our website.'의 내용과 일치한다.

● competition ⓝ 대회, 경쟁   ● whistling ⓝ 휘파람
● limited to ~로 제한되는   ● look forward to ~을 고대하다
● enthusiastic ⓐ 열띤, 열정적인

---

10 침실 커튼 고르기   정답률 62% | 정답 ②

다음 표를 보면서 대화를 듣고, 두 사람이 선택할 커튼을 고르시오.

Curtains

	Product	Price	Care Instruction	Blackout	Color
①	A	$70	machine washable	×	navy
☑②	B	$80	machine washable	○	brown
③	C	$90	dry cleaning only	○	ivory
④	D	$95	machine washable	○	gray
⑤	E	$110	dry cleaning only	×	white

M : Honey, I'm looking at a shopping site to choose curtains for our bedroom. But there are too many options to consider.
여보, 우리 침실 커튼을 고르려고 쇼핑 사이트를 보고 있어요. 그런데 고려할 선택사항이 너무 많아요.
W : Okay. Let's pick one together.
알겠어요. 같이 고르죠.
M : 『I don't think we should spend more than $100.』 근거1 Price 조건
난 우리가 100달러 이상 쓰면 안 될 것 같아요.
W : I agree. Let's drop this one. 『And some of them are machine washable at home.』
동의해요. 이건 빼죠. 그리고 일부 제품은 집에서 세탁기 세탁이 가능하군요.
M : Fantastic. We won't have to pay for dry cleaning all the time. 근거2 Care Instruction 조건
근사하네요. 매번 드라이클리닝에 돈을 쓸 필요가 없겠어요.
W : Good for us. Let's cross out this one then. 『What about a blackout option?』
우리한텐 좋죠. 그럼 이건 빼도록 하죠. 암막 옵션은요?   근거3 Blackout 조건
M : We definitely need it.』 It'll completely block sunlight, so we won't be disturbed. 『And which color do you like?』
우린 그게 꼭 필요해요. 햇빛을 완전히 차단해줄 테니, 방해를 안 받겠죠. 그리고 어떤 색깔이 마음에 들어요?
W : I don't mind any color except for gray.』 근거4 Color 조건
회색만 빼면 어느 색이든 상관 없어요.
M : Okay. Then we narrowed it down to one.
알겠어요. 그럼 하나로 좁혀지네요.
W : Well then, let's choose this one.
그럼, 이것으로 고르죠.

Why? 왜 정답일까?

대화에 따르면 남자와 여자는 가격이 100달러 미만이면서, 세탁기로 빨 수 있고, 암막 기능이 있으며, 색상 은 회색이 아닌 커튼을 사려고 한다. 따라서 두 사람이 선택할 커튼은 ② 'B'이다.

● machine washable 세탁기로 세탁할 수 있는   ● cross out 지우다, 빼다
● blackout ⓝ 빛 차단, 정전   ● disturb ⓥ 방해하다, (제자리에 있는 것을) 건드리다
● narrow down to ~로 좁히다

---

11 롤러코스터 줄 살펴보기   정답률 90% | 정답 ①

대화를 듣고, 남자의 마지막 말에 대한 여자의 응답으로 가장 적절한 것을 고르시오.
☑I've been waiting for 30 minutes. – 전 30분째 기다리고 있어요.
② I've enjoyed this ride very much. – 이번 놀이기구는 정말 재밌었어요.
③ You're standing in the correct line. – 맞는 줄에 서 계신 거예요.
④ I have enough time to wait for you. – 당신을 기다려줄 시간이 충분해요.
⑤ You may end the construction in a year. – 1년 뒤에 공사를 끝내실 거예요.

M : Excuse me. Is this really the line for the rollercoaster?
실례합니다. 이거 정말 롤러코스터 줄인가요?
W : Yes. This is the line for the ride.
네. 여기가 그 기구 줄이에요.
M : Oh, no. I can't believe it. There are so many people standing in line. How long have you been waiting here?
오, 이런. 믿을 수 없네요. 줄 서 있는 사람이 너무 많아요. 당신은 여기서 얼마나 기다리고 계신 거죠?
W : I've been waiting for 30 minutes.
전 30분째 기다리고 있어요.

Why? 왜 정답일까?

남자는 롤러코스터를 기다리는 줄이 너무 긴 것을 보고 여자에게 얼마나 기다리고 있는지(How long

have you been waiting here?) 물어보고 있다. 따라서 여자의 응답으로 가장 적절한 것은 ① '전 30분째 기다리고 있어요.'이다.

- stand in line 줄을 서다
- construction ⓝ 건설, 공사

---

12 길 잃은 아이 챙기기   정답률 83% | 정답 ②

대화를 듣고, 여자의 마지막 말에 대한 남자의 응답으로 가장 적절한 것을 고르시오.

① No way. I don't know who's lost. – 안 돼. 난 누가 길을 잃었는지 몰라.
✓ Okay. Let's see if he needs our help. – 그래. 우리 도움이 필요한지 알아보자.
③ Exactly. Just stop crying like a child. – 바로 그거야. 애처럼 우는 걸 멈춰.
④ Sure. He loves walking around the park. – 그래. 그는 공원을 걸어다니는 걸 좋아해.
⑤ Thanks. We were worried about our son. – 고마워. 우린 우리 아들을 걱정했어.

W : Chris, what are you looking at?
Chris, 뭘 보고 있어?
M : A little boy is crying and wandering around the park. He's all by himself.
어린 남자애가 울면서 공원을 돌아다니고 있어. 아이는 혼자야.
W : Oh, I see him, too. We should ask him if he's lost.
오, 나도 그 아이가 보여. 길을 잃었는지 물어봐야겠다.
M : Okay. Let's see if he needs our help.
그래. 우리 도움이 필요한지 알아보자.

Why? 왜 정답일까?

여자는 혼자 울고 있는 아이를 발견하고 길을 잃었는지 물어봐야겠다(We should ask him if he's lost.)고 하므로, 남자의 응답으로 가장 적절한 것은 ② '그래. 우리 도움이 필요한지 알아보자.'이다.

- wander ⓥ 배회하다, 돌아다니다
- all by oneself 혼자인

---

13 구직 면접에 관한 조언   정답률 89% | 정답 ③

대화를 듣고, 남자의 마지막 말에 대한 여자의 응답으로 가장 적절한 것을 고르시오. [3점]
Woman:

① Great. I believe my previous offer will benefit your company.
훌륭해. 난 네 저번 제안이 너희 회사에 이익이 될 거라고 믿어.
② I'm sorry. Your interview has been delayed to next Wednesday.
죄송합니다. 귀하의 면접은 다음 주 수요일로 밀렸어요.
✓ Good. Your effort will give a good impression on the interviewer.
좋아, 네 노력이 면접관에게 좋은 인상을 줄 거야.
④ Excellent. The second candidate's work experience caught my eye.
대단해요. 두 번째 후보의 이력이 제 눈길을 끌었네요.
⑤ No worries. You can purchase nice clothes for the upcoming party.
걱정 마. 넌 다가오는 파티를 위해 멋진 옷을 사면 돼.

M : Hi, Ava.
안녕, Ava.
W : Hi, Samuel. Are you all set for the job interview?
안녕, Samuel. 구직 면접 준비는 다 됐어?
M : I'm still working on it. I've come up with a list of questions the interviewer might ask.
아직 하고 있어. 면접관들이 물어볼 것 같은 질문 목록을 생각해봤어.
W : Good job. Preparing answers to those questions will help you for the interview.
잘했어. 그 질문들에 답을 준비하는 건 면접에 도움이 될 거야.
M : But I think I'm not ready.
하지만 준비가 안 된 것 같아.
W : Hmm. Have you thought about how you'll make a good first impression?
음. 어떻게 좋은 첫인상을 남길지 생각해 봤어?
M : Could you be more specific?
더 구체적으로 말해줄래?
W : You know a smile makes you look confident. Also, people usually dress up to give a favorable impression.
미소가 널 더 자신감 있어 보이게 해준다는 거 알지. 그리고, 사람들은 호의적인 인상을 주기 위해 보통 정장을 입어.
M : That's a good point.
그거 중요하네.
W : I believe you'll get a good interview result with a proper presentation of yourself.
난 네가 네 자신을 적절히 잘 보여주고 좋은 면접 결과를 얻을 거라고 믿어.
M : Okay. Then I'm going to practice smiling and look for my best suit.
그래. 그럼 미소 짓기를 연습하고 제일 괜찮은 정장을 찾아봐야겠다.
W : Good. Your effort will give a good impression on the interviewer.
좋아. 네 노력이 면접자에게 좋은 인상을 줄 거야.

Why? 왜 정답일까?

남자는 구직 면접에 관한 여자의 조언대로 미소와 정장을 신경쓰겠다(Then I'm going to practice smiling and look for my best suit.)고 하므로, 여자의 응답으로 가장 적절한 것은 ③ '좋아. 네 노력이 면접관에게 좋은 인상을 줄 거야.'이다.

- come up with ~을 생각하다, 떠올리다
- confident ⓐ 자신감 있는
- candidate ⓝ 후보자
- make an impression 인상을 주다
- favorable ⓐ 호의적인, 우호적인

---

14 새 신발 사기   정답률 86% | 정답 ①

대화를 듣고, 여자의 마지막 말에 대한 남자의 응답으로 가장 적절한 것을 고르시오.
Man:

✓ Please wait. I'll be back with the shoes in a minute. – 기다려주세요. 제가 금방 신발을 갖고 오겠습니다.
② Hurry up. You don't have enough time to do this. – 서둘러 주세요. 이럴 시간이 충분하지 않아요.
③ Of course. You can get a refund for these shoes. – 물론입니다. 이 신발 환불 받으실 수 있어요.
④ Don't worry. The color doesn't matter to me. – 걱정 마세요. 색상은 제게 상관없어요.
⑤ Sorry. The red ones are already sold out. – 죄송합니다. 빨간색은 이미 품절됐습니다.

W : Excuse me.
실례합니다.
M : Yes, ma'am. How can I help you?
네, 손님. 무엇을 도와드릴까요?

[문제편 p.141]

W : How much are those shoes?
이 신발은 얼마죠?
M : They're $60. But today only, we're offering a 30% discount.
60달러입니다. 하지만 오늘에 한해 저희는 30퍼센트 할인을 제공하고 있어요.
W : That's a good price. Do you have a size six?
좋은 가격이네요. 6 사이즈로 있나요?
M : Sure. Here they are. Take a seat here and try them on.
물론입니다. 여기 있습니다. 여기 앉으셔서 신어보시죠.
W : Thank you. [Pause] Well, these shoes are a little tight for me. Can I get a size six and a half?
고맙습니다. [잠시 멈춤] 음, 이 신발은 저한테 약간 끼네요. 6.5 사이즈 있을까요?
M : I'm sorry. That size in this color is sold out.
죄송합니다. 이 색상으로 이 사이즈는 품절되었어요.
W : Do you have these shoes in a different color?
이 신발 다른 색상이 있나요?
M : Let me check. [Typing sounds] We have red and green in storage.
확인해 보겠습니다. [타자 치는 소리] 빨강과 초록이 입고되어 있습니다.
W : A green pair sounds good. I want to try them on.
초록색이 괜찮을 것 같네요. 신어보고 싶어요.
M : Please wait. I'll be back with the shoes in a minute.
기다려주세요. 제가 금방 신발을 갖고 오겠습니다.

Why? 왜 정답일까?

여자는 원하던 색상의 신발이 없다는 남자의 말에 초록색으로 바꿔서 신어보겠다(A green pair sounds good. I want to try them on.)고 하므로, 남자의 응답으로 가장 적절한 것은 ① '기다려주세요. 제가 금방 신발을 갖고 오겠습니다.'이다.

- tight ⓐ 꽉 끼는
- get a refund 환불받다
- in storage 입고 중인

---

15 인터뷰 일정 재조정 요청   정답률 69% | 정답 ②

다음 상황 설명을 듣고, Amelia가 Jacob 교수에게 할 말로 가장 적절한 것을 고르시오. [3점]
Amelia:

① Could you extend the deadline for the assignment? – 과제 기한을 연장해주실 수 있을까요?
✓ Would it be possible to change our appointment? – 약속을 변경해주실 수 있을까요?
③ Why don't you join my final psychology project? – 제 심리학 기말 프로젝트에 함께하면 어떠세요?
④ Do you want to meet at the information center? – 저와 안내소에서 만나실래요?
⑤ How about visiting the doctor for a checkup? – 병원에 가서 검진 받으시면 어때요?

M : Amelia is a high school student.
Amelia는 고등학생이다.
She is working on a psychology project.
그녀는 심리학 프로젝트를 진행하고 있다.
She thinks that an interview with an expert in the field will make her project even better.
그녀는 분야 전문가와 인터뷰하는 것이 자기 프로젝트를 훨씬 더 좋게 만들어줄 것이라고 생각한다.
She emails Professor Jacob, who is a renowned psychology professor.
그녀는 유명 심리학 교수인 Jacob 교수에게 이메일을 보낸다.
Even though he's busy, she manages to set up an interview with him.
그가 비록 바쁘기는 하지만, 그녀는 어찌어찌 그와 인터뷰를 잡는다.
Unfortunately, on that morning, she eats a sandwich and feels sick.
안타깝게도, 당일 아침에 그녀는 샌드위치를 먹는 탈이 난다.
She knows this interview is important, and difficult to set up again.
그녀는 이 인터뷰가 중요한 것이고, 다시 잡기도 어렵다는 것을 안다.
But she can't go meet him because of a severe stomachache.
하지만 심한 복통 때문에 그녀는 그를 만나러 갈 수가 없다.
So she wants to ask him if he can reschedule their meeting.
그래서 그녀는 그가 미팅 일정을 바꿔줄 수 없는지 물어려고 한다.
In this situation, what would Amelia most likely say to Professor Jacob?
이 상황에서, Amelia는 Jacob 교수에게 뭐라고 말할 것인가?
Amelia : Would it be possible to change our appointment?
약속을 변경해주실 수 있을까요?

Why? 왜 정답일까?

상황에 따르면 Jacob 교수와의 인터뷰가 있는 날 아침 샌드위치를 먹고 탈이 난 Amelia는 교수에게 만남 일정을 재조정할 수 있는지 물으려 한다(So she wants to ask him if he can reschedule their meeting.). 따라서 Amelia가 Jacob 교수에게 할 말로 가장 적절한 것은 ② '약속을 변경해주실 수 있을까요?'이다.

- psychology ⓝ 심리학
- severe ⓐ 극심한
- extend ⓥ 연장하다
- renowned ⓐ 유명한
- reschedule ⓥ 일정을 바꾸다
- deadline ⓝ 마감

16-17 과거의 메시지 전달 수단

W : Good morning, students.
안녕하세요, 학생 여러분.
These days we can easily send messages to each other using phones or computers.
오늘날 우리는 핸드폰과 컴퓨터를 이용해 서로 메시지를 쉽게 보낼 수 있죠.
However, communication has not always been as simple as it is today.
하지만, 의사소통은 늘 오늘날처럼 쉬운 게 아니었습니다.
「Here are a few ways people in the past used to carry their messages.」 16번의 근거
과거 사람들이 메시지를 전달하는 데 썼던 몇 가지 방법이 있습니다.
「First, some tribes used a special drum.」 17번 ①의 근거 일치
첫째로, 어떤 부족은 특별한 북을 이용했습니다.
They were able to send warnings or important information by varying the pitch or beat.
그들은 북소리의 높이나 박자를 달리하여 경고 메시지나 중요한 정보를 보낼 수 있었습니다.
「Next, other people used smoke to send messages over long distances.」 17번 ②의 근거 일치
다음으로, 다른 사람들은 연기를 이용해 메시지를 장거리 전송했어요.
For example, our ancestors used smoke to signal attacks from enemies.

예를 들면, 우리 조상들은 적으로부터의 공격을 알리기 위해 연기를 이용했습니다.
『Third, a pigeon was a reliable means of communication.』 17번 ③의 근거 일치
셋째로, 비둘기는 믿을 만한 의사소통 수단이었죠.
It always found its way home with messages attached to its legs.
그것은 늘 다리에 메시지를 붙인 채 집으로 오는 길을 찾았습니다.
『Finally, a horse was one of the most efficient ways to communicate.』 17번 ⑤의 근거 일치
마지막으로, 말은 가장 효율적인 의사소통 수단 중 하나였어요.
The horse with a messenger on its back delivered mail more quickly than runners.
메시지 전달자를 태운 말은 뛰어오는 사람보다 더 빨리 우편을 전달했습니다.
Now you may understand the ways of sending messages back in the old days.
이제 여러분은 그 옛날 메시지를 보내던 방식을 이해할 수 있겠죠.
Then let's take a look in detail at each communication method.
그럼 각 의사소통 수단을 자세하게 살펴봅시다.

- tribe ⓝ 부족
- reliable ⓐ 믿을 만한
- deliver ⓥ 전달하다
- prehistoric ⓐ 선사시대의
- pitch ⓝ 음높이
- attached to ~에 부착된
- spread ⓥ 확산 ⓥ 퍼뜨리다

16 주제 파악   정답률 84% | 정답 ②

여자가 하는 말의 주제로 가장 적절한 것은?
① ways to stop the spread of false information – 잘못된 정보 확산을 막는 방법
☑ methods of delivering messages in the past – 과거에 메시지를 전달하던 방법
③ modes of communication in modern times – 현대의 의사소통 수단
④ types of speeches according to purposes – 목적에 따른 말하기 종류
⑤ means to survive in prehistoric times – 선사시대의 생존 수단

Why? 왜 정답일까?
'Here are a few ways people in the past used to carry their messages.'에서 여자는 과거 사람들이 어떻게 메시지를 주고받았는지 그 방법을 소개하겠다고 한다. 따라서 여자가 하는 말의 주제로 가장 적절한 것은 ② '과거에 메시지를 전달하던 방법'이다.

17 언급 유무 파악   정답률 89% | 정답 ④

언급된 수단이 아닌 것은?
① drum – 북
② smoke – 연기
③ pigeon – 비둘기
☑ flag – 깃발
⑤ horse – 말

Why? 왜 정답일까?
담화에서 여자는 과거 의사소통 수단의 예시로 북, 연기, 비둘기, 말을 언급하므로, 언급되지 않은 것은 ④ '깃발'이다.

Why? 왜 오답일까?
① 'First, some tribes used a special drum.'에서 '북'이 언급되었다.
② 'Next, other people used smoke to send messages over long distances.'에서 '연기'가 언급되었다.
③ 'Third, a pigeon was a reliable means of communication.'에서 '비둘기'가 언급되었다.
⑤ 'Finally, a horse was one of the most efficient ways to communicate.'에서 '말'이 언급되었다.

18 급여 인상 요청   정답률 79% | 정답 ②

다음 글의 목적으로 가장 적절한 것은?
① 부서 이동을 신청하려고
☑ 급여 인상을 요청하려고
③ 근무 시간 조정을 요구하려고
④ 기업 혁신 방안을 제안하려고
⑤ 신입 사원 연수에 대해 문의하려고

Dear Mr. Krull,
친애하는 Krull씨께
I have greatly enjoyed working at Trincom Enterprises / as a sales manager.
저는 Trincom Enterprises에서 일하는 것을 매우 즐겨 왔습니다. / 영업 매니저로
Since I joined in 2015, / I have been a loyal and essential member of this company, / and have developed innovative ways / to contribute to the company.
제가 2015년에 입사한 이후, / 저는 이 회사의 충성스럽고 필수적인 구성원이었고, / 혁신적인 방법들을 개발해 왔습니다. / 회사에 기여할
Moreover, in the last year alone, / I have brought in two new major clients to the company, / increasing the company's total sales by 5%.
게다가, 작년 한 해만, / 저는 두 개의 주요 고객사를 회사에 새로 유치하여, / 회사의 총매출을 5% 증가시켰습니다.
Also, / I have voluntarily trained 5 new members of staff, / totaling 35 hours.
또한, / 저는 신규 직원 5명을 자발적으로 교육해 왔고, / 그 합계가 35시간이 되었습니다.
I would therefore request your consideration / in raising my salary, / which I believe reflects my performance / as well as the industry average.
따라서 저는 고려를 요청드리며, / 제 급여를 인상하는 데 있어 / 이것이 제 성과도 반영한다고 믿습니다. / 업계 평균뿐만 아니라
I look forward to speaking with you soon.
저는 귀하와 곧 이야기하기를 기대합니다.
Kimberly Morss
Kimberly Morss 드림

친애하는 Krull씨께
저는 Trincom Enterprises에서 영업 매니저로 일하는 것을 매우 즐겨 왔습니다. 2015년에 입사한 이후, 저는 이 회사의 충성스럽고 필수적인 구성원이었고, 회사에 기여할 혁신적인 방법들을 개발해 왔습니다. 게다가, 저는 작년 한 해만 두 개의 주요 고객사를 회사에 새로 유치하여 회사의 총매출을 5% 증가시켰습니다. 또한 저는 신규 직원 5명을 자발적으로 교육해 왔고 그 합계가 35시간이 되었습니다. 따라서 저는 제 급여를 인상하는 것을 고려해 주시기

를 요청드리며, 이것이 업계 평균뿐만 아니라 제 성과도 반영한다고 믿습니다. 귀하와 곧 이야기하기를 기대합니다.

Kimberly Morss 드림

Why? 왜 정답일까?
'I would therefore request your consideration in raising my salary, ~'에서 급여 인상을 고려해달라는 요청이 나오므로, 글의 목적으로 가장 적절한 것은 ② '급여 인상을 요청하려고'이다.

- enterprise ⓝ 기업
- loyal ⓐ 충성스러운
- voluntarily ⓐⓓ 자원해서
- sales manager 영업 매니저
- essential ⓐ 핵심적인, 필수적인
- raise ⓥ 올리다, 높이다

구문 풀이
9행 I would therefore request your consideration in raising my salary, which (선행사) (주격 관·대) (I believe) reflexts my performance as well as the industry average. ( ):삽입절 (동사)

19 휴가 도중 아버지의 부상 소식을 들은 필자   정답률 83% | 정답 ②

다음 글에 드러난 'I'의 심경 변화로 가장 적절한 것은?
① nervous → confident
   긴장한   자신 있는
③ excited → indifferent
   신난   무관심한
⑤ annoyed → grateful
   짜증 난   고마워하는
☑ relaxed → worried
   여유로운   걱정하는
④ pleased → jealous
   즐거운   질투하는

On one beautiful spring day, / I was fully enjoying my day off.
어느 아름다운 봄날, / 나는 휴가를 충분히 즐기고 있었다.
I arrived at the nail salon, / and muted my cellphone / so that I would be disconnected for the hour / and feel calm and peaceful.
나는 네일 숍에 도착해서 / 내 휴대폰을 음소거했다. / 그 시간 동안 나는 단절되도록 / 그리고 차분하고 평화로운 기분을 느끼도록
I was so comfortable / while I got a manicure.
나는 아주 편안했다. / 내가 매니큐어를 받는 동안
As I left the place, / I checked my cellphone / and saw four missed calls from a strange number.
내가 그곳을 떠나면서, / 나는 나의 휴대폰을 확인했고 / 낯선 번호로 걸려 온 네 통의 부재중 전화를 봤다.
I knew immediately / that something bad was coming, / and I called back.
나는 즉시 알고 / 뭔가 나쁜 일이 생겼다는 것을 / 나는 다시 전화했다.
A young woman answered and said / that my father had fallen over a stone and was injured, / now seated on a bench.
한 젊은 여성이 전화를 받아 말했다. / 우리 아버지가 돌에 걸려 넘어져 다쳤고 / 지금 벤치에 앉아 있다고
I was really concerned / since he had just recovered from his knee surgery.
나는 정말 걱정되었다. / 아버지는 무릎 수술에서 회복한 직후라서
I rushed getting into my car / to go see him.
나는 급히 차에 올랐다. / 아버지를 보러 가기 위해

어느 아름다운 봄날, 나는 휴가를 충분히 즐기고 있었다. 나는 네일 숍에 도착해서 내 휴대폰을 음소거하고 그 시간 동안 단절되어 차분하고 평화로운 기분을 느끼고자 했다. 나는 매니큐어를 받는 동안 아주 편안했다. 그곳을 떠나면서, 나는 나의 휴대폰을 확인했고 낯선 번호에서 걸려 온 네 통의 부재중 전화를 봤다. 나는 뭔가 나쁜 일이 생겼다는 것을 즉시 알고 다시 전화했다. 한 젊은 여성이 전화를 받아 우리 아버지가 돌에 걸려 넘어져 다쳤고 지금 벤치에 앉아 있다고 말했다. 아버지는 무릎 수술에서 회복한 직후라서 나는 정말 걱정되었다. 나는 아버지를 보러 가기 위해 급히 차에 올랐다.

Why? 왜 정답일까?
네일숍에 들러 휴가를 여유롭게(feel calm and peaceful, comfortable) 즐기고 있던 필자가 아버지가 넘어져 다쳤다는 소식에 몹시 걱정했다(concerned)는 내용이다. 따라서 'I'의 심경 변화로 가장 적절한 것은 ② '여유로운 → 걱정하는'이다.

- mute ⓥ 음소거하다
- comfortable ⓐ 편안한
- fall over ~에 걸려 넘어지다
- recover from ~로부터 회복하다
- rush ⓥ 서두르다
- jealous ⓐ 질투하는
- disconnected ⓐ 단절된
- call back 전화를 회신하다
- concerned ⓐ 걱정되는
- surgery ⓝ 수술
- indifferent ⓐ 무관심한
- grateful ⓐ 고마워하는

구문 풀이
1행 I arrived at the nail salon, and muted my cellphone so that I would be (접속사 ~하기 위해) (동사1) disconnected for the hour and (would) feel calm and peaceful. (동사2)

20 상업용 블로그를 성공시킬 방법   정답률 89% | 정답 ⑤

다음 글에서 필자가 주장하는 바로 가장 적절한 것은?
① 인터넷 게시물에 대한 윤리적 기준을 세워야 한다.
② 블로그를 전문적으로 관리할 인력을 마련해야 한다.
③ 신제품 개발을 위해 상업용 블로그를 적극 활용해야 한다.
④ 상품에 대한 고객들의 반응을 정기적으로 분석할 필요가 있다.
☑ 상업용 블로그는 사람들이 흥미 있어 할 정보를 제공해야 한다.

You already have a business / and you're about to launch your blog / so that you can sell your product.
여러분은 이미 사업체를 가지고 있고 / 여러분은 블로그를 시작하려는 참이다. / 여러분의 제품을 팔 수 있도록
Unfortunately, / here is where a 'business mind' can be a bad thing.
유감스럽게도, / 이 지점에서 '비즈니스 정신'은 나쁜 것이 될 수 있다.
Most people believe / that to have a successful business blog / promoting a product, / they have to stay strictly 'on the topic.'
대부분의 사람들은 믿는다. / 성공적인 상업용 블로그를 가지기 위해서 / 제품을 홍보하는 / 엄격하게 '그 주제에' 머물러야 한다고

If all you're doing is shamelessly promoting your product, / then who is going to want to read the latest thing / you're writing about?
만일 여러분이 그저 뻔뻔스럽게 제품을 홍보하는 일만 하면, / 그렇다면 누가 최신 글을 읽고 싶어 할까? / 여러분이 쓰고 있는

Instead, / you need to give some useful or entertaining information away for free / so that people have a reason / to keep coming back.
대신에, / 여러분은 어떤 유용하거나 재미있는 정보를 무료로 줄 필요가 있다. / 사람들이 이유를 가지도록 / 계속해서 다시 방문할

Only by doing this / can you create an interested audience / that you will then be able to sell to.
이렇게 해야만 / 여러분은 관심 있는 독자를 만들 수 있다. / 여러분이 다음번에 판매할 수 있게 될

So, / the best way to be successful with a business blog / is to write about things / that your audience will be interested in.
따라서, / 상업용 블로그로 성공하기 위한 가장 좋은 방법은 / 대상들에 대해 글을 쓰는 것이다. / 여러분의 독자들이 관심을 가질 만한

여러분은 이미 사업체를 가지고 있고 여러분의 제품을 팔 수 있도록 블로그를 시작하려는 참이다. 유감스럽게도, 이 지점에서 '비즈니스 정신'은 나쁜 것이 될 수 있다. 대부분의 사람들은 제품을 홍보하는 성공적인 상업용 블로그를 가지기 위해서 엄격하게 '그 주제에' 머물러야 한다고 믿는다. 만일 여러분이 그저 뻔뻔스럽게 제품을 홍보하는 일만 하면, 그렇다면 누가 여러분이 쓰고 있는 최신 글을 읽고 싶어할까? 대신에, 사람들이 계속해서 다시 방문할 이유를 가지도록 여러분은 어떤 유용하거나 재미있는 정보를 무료로 줄 필요가 있다. 이렇게 해야만 여러분은 다음번에 판매할 수 있게 될 관심 있는 독자를 만들 수 있다. 따라서, 상업용 블로그로 성공하기 위한 가장 좋은 방법은 여러분의 독자들이 관심을 가질 만한 것들에 대해 글을 쓰는 것이다.

Why? 왜 정답일까?

'Instead, you need to give some useful or entertaining information ~.'과 'So, the best way to be successful with a business blog is to write about things that your audience will be interested in.'에서 상업용 블로그를 성공시키려면 제품이나 사업에 관한 홍보만 하지 말고 사람들이 관심을 보일 내용에 관해 글을 쓰라고 한다. 따라서 필자가 주장하는 바로 가장 적절한 것은 ⑤ '상업용 블로그는 사람들이 흥미 있어 할 정보를 제공해야 한다.'이다.

- launch ⓥ 시작하다, 출시하다
- strictly ⓐⓓ 엄격하게
- give away 공짜로 주게, 거저 주다
- audience ⓝ 청중, 독자
- promote ⓥ 홍보하다
- shamelessly ⓐⓓ 뻔뻔하게
- entertaining ⓐ 재미있는
- successful ⓐ 성공적인

구문 풀이

9행 Only by doing this can you create an interested audience that you will
부사정어(오로지 ~섬에)   조동사 주어 동사원형(도치)
then be able to sell to.

★★★ 등급을 가르는 문제! ★★★

21 노력만이 가치 있다는 믿음에 대한 반박   정답률 45% | 정답 ③

밑줄 친 challenge this sacred cow가 다음 글에서 의미하는 바로 가장 적절한 것은? [3점]

① resist the tendency to avoid any hardship
그 어떤 난관이든 피하려는 경향에 저항하다
② escape from the pressure of using formal language
공식적인 언어를 사용해야 한다는 압박에서 벗어나다
✓③ doubt the solid belief that only hard work is worthy
오로지 노력만이 가치 있다는 확고한 믿음을 의심하다
④ abandon the old notion that money always comes first
돈이 항상 먼저라는 오래된 관념을 버린다
⑤ break the superstition that holy animals bring good luck
신성한 동물은 행운을 가져다 준다는 미신을 깬다

Our language helps to reveal our deeper assumptions.
우리의 언어는 우리의 더 깊은 전제를 드러내는 것을 돕는다.

Think of these revealing phrases: / When we accomplish something important, / we say it took "blood, sweat, and tears."
이것을 잘 드러내는 다음과 같은 문구들을 생각해 보라. / 우리가 중요한 무언가를 성취할 때 / 우리는 그것이 '피, 땀, 그리고 눈물'을 필요로 했다고 말한다.

We say / important achievements are "hard-earned."
우리는 말한다. / 중요한 성과는 '힘들게 얻은' 것이라고

We recommend a "hard day's work" / when "day's work" would be enough.
우리는 '하루 동안의 고생'이라는 말을 권한다. / '하루 동안의 일이'라는 말로도 충분할 때

When we talk of "easy money," / we are implying / it was obtained through illegal or questionable means.
우리가 '쉬운 돈'이라는 말을 할 때, / 우리는 넌지시 드러낸다. / 그것이 불법적이거나 의심스러운 수단을 통해 얻어졌다는 것을

We use the phrase "That's easy for you to say" / as a criticism, / usually when we are seeking to invalidate someone's opinion.
우리는 '말은 쉽다'라는 문구를 사용한다. / 비판으로 / 우리가 보통 누군가의 의견이 틀렸음을 입증하려고 할 때

It's like we all automatically accept / that the "right" way is, inevitably, the harder one.
이는 마치 우리 모두가 저절로 받아들이는 것과 같다. / '올바른' 방법은 반드시 더 어려운 방법이라는 것을

In my experience / this is hardly ever questioned.
나의 경험상 / 여기에는 거의 한 번도 의문이 제기되지 않는다.

What would happen / if you do challenge this sacred cow?
무슨 일이 일어날까? / 만약 여러분이 정말로 이 신성한 소에 맞선다면

We don't even pause to consider / that something important and valuable / could be made easy.
우리는 잠시 멈춰 생각해 보지도 않는다. / 중요하고 가치 있는 무언가가 / 쉬워질 수 있다고

What if the biggest thing / keeping us from doing what matters / is the false assumption / that it has to take huge effort?
만약 가장 큰 것이 / 우리가 중요한 일을 하지 못하게 하는 / 잘못된 전제라면 어떨까? / 그것은 엄청난 노력이 들어가야 한다

우리의 언어는 우리의 더 깊은 전제를 드러내는 것을 돕는다. 이것을 잘 드러내는 다음과 같은 문구들을 생각해 보라. 우리는 중요한 무언가를 성취할 때 그것이 '피, 땀, 그리고 눈물'을 필요로 했다고 말한다. 우리는 중요한 성과는 '힘들게 얻은' 것이라고 말한다. 우리는 '하루 동안의 일'이라는 말로도 충분할 때 '하루 동안의 고생'이라는 말을 권한다. 우리가 '쉬운 돈'이라는 말을 할 때, 우리는 그것이 불법적이거나 의심스러운 수단을 통해 얻어졌다는 것을 넌지시 드러낸다. 우리는 보통 누군가의 의견이 틀렸음을 입증하려고 할 때, 우리는 '말은 쉽지'라는 문구를 비판으로 사용한다. 이는 마치 우리 모두가 '올바른' 방법은 반드시 더 어려운 방법이라는 것을 저절로 받아들이는 것과 같다. 나의 경험상 여기에는 거의 한 번도 의문이 제기되지 않는다. 만약 여러분이 정말로 이 신성한 소에 맞선다면 무슨 일이 일어날까? 우리는 중요하고 가치 있는 무언가가 쉬워질 수 있다고 잠시 멈춰 생각해 보지도 않는다. 만약 우리가 중요한 일을 하지 못하게 하는 가장 큰 것이 중요한 일은 엄청난 노력이 들어가야 한다는 잘못된 전제라면 어떨까?

Why? 왜 정답일까?

밑줄 친 부분 앞까지 우리는 성과가 힘들게 얻어진다는 믿음을 우리 언어를 통해 드러내는 경향이 있다는 내용이 주를 이룬다. 이어서 밑줄 친 부분은 이러한 우리의 믿음을 '신성한 소'에 비유하며, 이 믿음에 '맞선다면' 무슨 일이 생길 것인지 묻고 있다. 즉, '노력과 수고만이 가치롭다'는 믿음에 '의문을 품는다'는 것이 밑줄 친 부분의 의미이므로, 답으로 가장 적절한 것은 ③ '오로지 노력만이 가치 있다는 확고한 믿음을 의심한다'이다.

- assumption ⓝ 가정, 추정
- achievement ⓝ 성취, 성과
- imply ⓥ 암시하다
- questionable ⓐ 의심스러운
- invalidate ⓥ 틀렸음을 입증하다
- inevitably ⓐⓓ 불가피하게, 필연적으로
- sacred ⓐ 성스러운
- hardship ⓝ 고난, 난관, 어려움
- solid ⓐ 확고한
- superstition ⓝ 미신
- sweat ⓝ 땀
- hard-earned ⓐ 힘들게 얻은
- illegal ⓐ 불법적인
- criticism ⓝ 비판
- automatically ⓐⓓ 저절로
- challenge ⓥ 도전하다, 이의를 제기하다
- huge ⓐ 거대한
- formal ⓐ 공식적인
- abandon ⓥ 버리다

구문 풀이

13행 What if the biggest thing (keeping us from doing what matters) is the
~라면 어떨까?   주어   ( ): 주어 수식(현재분사구)   동사(단수)
false assumption [that it has to take huge effort]? [ ]: 동격절(= the false assumption)

★★ 문제 해결 꿀~팁 ★★

▶ 많이 틀린 이유는?
첫 문장의 주어가 '언어'이므로 얼핏 보면 언어를 언급하는 ②가 정답일 것 같지만, '공식적인 언어' 사용은 전혀 글과 관련이 없다. 이 글은 쉬운 성공을 경시하고 힘든 노력만을 가치 있게 말하는 언어 습관이 우리에게 어떤 영향을 미치는지에 관한 글이다.

▶ 문제 해결 방법은?
this sacred cow가 가리키는 것은 문맥상 'the "right" way is, inevitably, the harder one'이다. 이는 '힘든 노력만을 옳게' 여기는 사고방식인데, 밑줄 부분은 여기에 '반박을 제기한다'는 의미다.

22 두려움을 주는 뉴스의 부작용   정답률 70% | 정답 ①

다음 글의 요지로 가장 적절한 것은?

✓① 두려움을 주는 뉴스는 사람들이 문제에 덜 대처하게 할 수 있다.
② 정보를 전달하는 시기에 따라 뉴스의 영향력이 달라질 수 있다.
③ 지속적인 환경 문제 보도가 사람들의 인식 변화를 가져온다.
④ 정보 제공의 지연은 정확한 문제 인식에 방해가 될 수 있다.
⑤ 출처가 불분명한 건강 정보는 사람들에게 유익하지 않다.

The old saying is / that "knowledge is power," / but when it comes to scary, threatening news, / research suggests the exact opposite.
오래된 격언은 / '아는 것이 힘이다'이지만, / 무섭고 위험적인 뉴스에 관해서는 / 연구에서 정반대를 시사한다.

Frightening news / can actually rob people of their inner sense of control, / making them less likely / to take care of themselves and other people.
두려움을 주는 뉴스는 / 실제로 사람들로부터 내면의 통제력을 빼앗을 수 있어서, / 가능성을 더 낮아지게 한다. / 그들이 스스로와 다른 사람들을 돌볼

Public health research shows / that when the news presents health-related information / in a pessimistic way, / people are actually less likely to take steps / to protect themselves from illness / as a result.
공중 보건 연구는 보여준다. / 뉴스가 건강과 관련된 정보를 제시할 때, / 비관적인 방식으로 / 사람들이 조치를 취할 가능성이 실제로 더 낮다는 것을 / 질병으로부터 자신을 보호하기 위한 / 결과적으로

A news article / that's intended to warn people about increasing cancer rates, / for example, / can result in fewer people / choosing to get screened for the disease / because they're so terrified of what they might find.
뉴스 기사는 / 증가하는 암 발생률에 대해 사람들에게 경고하려는 / 예를 들어, / 더 적은 사람들이 하는 결과를 가져올 수 있다. / 병에 대해 검사받기로 선택하는 / 그들이 발견될지도 모르는 것을 너무 두려워하기 때문에

This is also true for issues / such as climate change.
이것은 문제에도 해당된다. / 기후 변화와 같은

When a news story is all doom and gloom, / people feel depressed and become less interested / in taking small, personal steps to fight ecological collapse.
뉴스가 온통 파멸과 암울한 상황일 때, / 사람들은 우울한 기분을 느끼고 흥미를 덜 느끼게 된다. / 생태학적 붕괴와 싸우기 위한 작고 개인적인 조치를 취하는 데

오래된 격언에 따르면 '아는 것이 힘이다'라고 하지만, 무섭고 위험적인 뉴스에 관해서는 연구에서 정반대를 시사한다. 두려움을 주는 뉴스는 실제로 사람들로부터 내면의 통제력을 빼앗을 수 있어서, 그들이 스스로와 다른 사람들을 돌볼 가능성을 더 낮아지게 한다. 공중 보건 연구는 뉴스가 건강과 관련된 정보를 비관적인 방식으로 제시할 때, 결과적으로 사람들이 질병으로부터 자신을 보호하기 위한 조치를 취할 가능성이 실제로 더 낮다는 것을 보여준다. 예를 들어, 증가하는 암 발생률에 대해 사람들에게 경고하려는 뉴스 기사는 사람들이 발견될지도 모르는 것을 너무 두려워하기 때문에 병에 대해 검사받기로 선택하는 이들이 더 적어지는 결과를 가져올 수 있다. 이것은 기후 변화와 같은 문제에도 해당된다. 뉴스가 온통 파멸과 암울한 상황일 때, 사람들은 우울한 기분을 느끼고 생태학적 붕괴와 싸우기 위한 작고 개인적인 조치를 취하는 데 흥미를 덜 느끼게 된다.

Why? 왜 정답일까?

두려움을 주는 뉴스는 사람들의 문제 대처 능력을 약화시킨다는 내용의 글로, 'Frightening news can actually rob people of their inner sense of control, making them less likely to take care of themselves and other people.'에 주제가 잘 제시된다. 따라서 글의 요지로 가장 적절한 것은 ① '두려움을 주는 뉴스는 사람들이 문제에 덜 대처하게 할 수 있다.'이다.

- **threatening** ⓐ 겁을 주는
- **public health** 공공 보건
- **take steps to** ~하기 위해 조치를 취하다
- **article** ⓝ 기사
- **screen** ⓥ (어떤 질병이 있는지) 검진하다
- **doom** ⓝ 불운, 파멸
- **collapse** ⓝ 붕괴 ⓥ 쓰러지다

- **rob A of B** A에게서 B를 빼앗다
- **pessimistic** ⓐ 염세적인, 비관적인
- **illness** ⓝ 질병
- **be intended to** ~할 의도이다
- **terrified** ⓐ 겁에 질린
- **gloom** ⓝ 우울, 어둠

구문 풀이

8행 A news article [that's intended to warn people about increasing cancer rates], for example, can result in fewer people choosing to get screened for the disease because they're so terrified of what they might find.
(주어 / 동사구 / 의미상 주어 / 명사구(in of 목적어))

---

23 해수면 상승의 결과　　정답률 70% | 정답 ⑤

다음 글의 주제로 가장 적절한 것은?

① cause of rising temperatures on the Earth
　지구의 온도가 상승하는 원인
② principles of planets maintaining their shapes
　행성들이 모양을 유지하는 원리
③ implications of melting ice on marine biodiversity
　녹는 얼음이 해양 생물 다양성에 미치는 영향
④ way to keep track of time without using any device
　어떤 장치도 쓰지 않고 시간을 아는 방법
✓⑤ impact of melting ice and rising seas on the length of a day
　녹는 얼음과 해수면 상승이 하루의 시간 길이에 미치는 영향

The most remarkable and unbelievable consequence of melting ice and rising seas / is that together they are a kind of time machine, / so real / that they are altering the duration of our day.
녹는 얼음과 상승하는 바다의 가장 놀랍고 믿을 수 없는 결과는 / 그것들이 함께 일종의 타임머신이 된다는 것인데, / 이것은 너무도 현실적이어서 / 우리 하루의 지속시간을 바꾸고 있다.
It works like this: / As the glaciers melt and the seas rise, / gravity forces more water toward the equator.
그것은 다음과 같이 작동한다. / 빙하가 녹고 바다가 높아지면서 / 중력이 적도를 향해 더 많은 물을 밀어 넣는다.
This changes the shape of the Earth ever so slightly, / making it fatter around the middle, / which in turns slows the rotation of the planet / similarly to the way / a ballet dancer slows her spin / by spreading out her arms.
이것은 지구의 모양을 아주 약간 변화시켜 / 가운데 주변으로 더 불룩해지게 만들고, / 이것은 결과적으로 행성의 회전을 늦춘다. / 방식과 유사하게 / 발레 무용수가 회전을 늦추는 / 양팔을 뻗어서
The slowdown isn't much, / just a few thousandths of a second each year, / but like the barely noticeable jump of rising seas every year, / it adds up.
이 감속이 크지는 않지만, / 매년 단지 몇천 분의 1초로 / 해마다 상승하는 바다의 거의 드러나지 않는 증가와 마찬가지로 / 그것은 쌓인다.
When dinosaurs lived on the Earth, / a day lasted only about twenty-three hours.
공룡들이 지구에 살았을 때, / 하루는 약 23시간만 지속되었다.

녹는 얼음과 상승하는 바다의 가장 놀랍고 믿을 수 없는 결과는 그것들이 함께 일종의 타임머신이 된다는 것인데, 이것은 너무도 현실적이어서 우리 하루의 지속시간을 바꾸고 있다. 그것은 다음과 같이 작동한다. 빙하가 녹고 바다가 높아지면서 중력이 적도를 향해 더 많은 물을 밀어 넣는다. 이것은 지구의 모양을 아주 약간 변화시켜 가운데 주변으로 더 불룩해지게 만들고, 이것은 결과적으로 발레 무용수가 양팔을 뻗어서 회전을 늦추는 방식과 유사하게 행성의 회전을 늦춘다. 이 감속이 매년 단지 몇천 분의 1초로 크지는 않지만, 해마다 상승하는 바다의 거의 드러나지 않는 증가와 마찬가지로 그것은 쌓인다. 공룡들이 지구에 살았을 때, 하루는 약 23시간만 지속되었다.

Why? 왜 정답일까?
지구 온난화로 인한 해수면 상승이 지구의 가운데를 더 불룩해지게 만들어 지구의 하루가 지속되는 시간을 연장할 수 있다(The most remarkable and unbelievable consequence of melting ice and rising seas ~ so real that they are altering the duration of our day.)는 내용의 글이다. 따라서 글의 주제로 가장 적절한 것은 ⑤ '녹는 얼음과 해수면 상승이 하루의 시간 길이에 미치는 영향'이다.

- **remarkable** ⓐ 현저한, 두드러지는
- **alter** ⓥ 바꾸다
- **glacier** ⓝ 빙하
- **equator** ⓝ 적도
- **rotation** ⓝ 회전
- **spread out** 벌리다, 펴지다
- **barely** [ad] 거의 ~않다, 가까스로
- **last** ⓥ 지속되다
- **implication** ⓝ 영향
- **keep track of** ~을 추적하다

- **consequence** ⓝ 결과, 영향
- **duration** ⓝ 지속 시간
- **gravity** ⓝ 중력
- **slightly** [ad] 약간
- **spin** ⓝ 회전
- **slowdown** ⓝ 둔화, 지연
- **noticeable** ⓐ 분명한, 뚜렷한
- **principle** ⓝ 원리
- **biodiversity** ⓝ 생물 다양성

구문 풀이

1행 The most remarkable and unbelievable consequence (of melting ice and rising seas) is that together they are a kind of time machine, so real that they are altering the duration of our day.
(주어(최상급) / 동사(단수) / 「so ~ that … : 너무 ~해서 …하다」)

---

24 새로운 관점에 마음 열기　　정답률 50% | 정답 ④

다음 글의 제목으로 가장 적절한 것은?

① The Value of Being Honest – 정직의 가치
② Filter Out Negative Points of View – 부정적인 관점을 걸러라
③ Keeping Your Word: A Road to Success – 약속 지키기: 성공으로 향하는 길
✓④ Being Right Can Block New Possibilities – 옳다는 것은 새로운 가능성을 차단할 수 있다
⑤ Look Back When Everyone Looks Forward – 모두가 앞을 볼 때 뒤를 봐라

Have you ever brought up an idea or suggestion to someone / and heard them immediately say / "No, that won't work."?
여러분이 누군가에게 아이디어나 제안을 내놨는데, / 그들이 즉시 말한 것을 들은 적이 있는가? / "아니, 그건 안 될 거야."라고
You may have thought, / "He/she didn't even give it a chance. / How do they know it won't work?"
여러분은 아마도 생각했을 것이다. / "그 사람은 기회조차 주지 않았는데. / 어떻게 그것이 안 될 것이라고 알지?"라고
When you are right about something, / you close off the possibility of another viewpoint or opportunity.
여러분이 어떤 일에 대해 옳다면, / 여러분은 다른 관점이나 기회의 가능성을 닫아 버린다.
Being right about something means / that "it is the way it is, period."
어떤 일에 대해 옳다는 것은 의미한다. / "그것은 원래 그런 거야, 끝."이라고 하는 것을
You may be correct.
여러분이 맞을 수도 있다.
Your particular way of seeing it / may be true with the facts.
여러분이 그것을 보는 특정한 방법이 / 사실에 부합할 수도 있다.
However, / considering the other option or the other person's point of view / can be beneficial.
하지만 / 다른 선택지나 다른 사람의 관점을 고려하는 것은 / 이로울 수 있다.
If you see their side, / you will see something new / or, at worse, learn something / about how the other person looks at life.
만약 여러분이 그들의 관점을 안다면, / 여러분은 새로운 것을 알게 되거나 / 적어도 무언가를 배울 것이다. / 다른 사람이 삶을 바라보는 방식에 대한
Why would you think / everyone sees and experiences life / the way you do?
왜 여러분은 생각하는가? / 모두가 삶을 보거나 경험할 거라고 / 여러분이 하는 방식대로
Besides how boring that would be, / it would eliminate all new opportunities, ideas, invention, and creativity.
그것이 얼마나 지루한지는 제외하고라도, / 그것은 모든 새로운 기회, 아이디어, 발명, 그리고 창의성을 없앨 것이다.

누군가에게 아이디어나 제안을 내놨는데, 그들이 즉시 "아니, 그건 안 될 거야."라고 말한 것을 들은 적이 있는가? 여러분은 아마도 "그 사람은 기회조차 주지 않았는데. 어떻게 그것이 안 될 것이라고 알지?"라고 생각했을 것이다. 여러분이 어떤 일에 대해 옳다면, 여러분은 다른 관점이나 기회의 가능성을 닫아 버린다. 어떤 일에 대해 옳다는 것은 "그것은 원래 그런 거야, 끝."이라고 하는 것을 의미한다. 여러분이 맞을 수도 있다. 여러분이 그것을 보는 특정한 방법이 사실에 부합할 수도 있다. 하지만 다른 선택지나 다른 사람의 관점을 고려하는 것은 이로울 수 있다. 만약 여러분이 그들의 관점을 안다면, 여러분은 새로운 것을 알게 되거나 적어도 다른 사람이 삶을 바라보는 방식에 대한 무언가를 배울 것이다. 왜 모두가 여러분이 하는 방식대로 삶을 보거나 경험할 거라고 생각하는가? 그것이 얼마나 지루한지를 제외하고라도, 그것은 모든 새로운 기회, 아이디어, 발명, 그리고 창의성을 없앨 것이다.

Why? 왜 정답일까?
어떤 것에 대해 옳다는 것은 새로운 가능성을 차단할 수 있다(When you are right about something, you close off the possibility of another viewpoint or opportunity.)고 지적한 뒤, 새로운 관점을 고려해보려는 태도가 필요하다고 조언하는 글이다. 따라서 글의 제목으로 가장 적절한 것은 ④ '옳다는 것은 새로운 가능성을 차단할 수 있다'이다.

- **bring up** (화제를) 꺼내다, (아이디어를) 내놓다
- **close off** 차단하다
- **period** [ad] (문장 끝에서) 끝, 이상이다, 더 말하지 마라
- **beneficial** ⓐ 이로운
- **besides** [prep] ~을 제외하더라도, ~외에도 [ad] 게다가
- **eliminate** ⓥ 제거하다
- **filter out** ~을 걸러내다, 여과하다
- **block** ⓥ 차단하다

- **suggestion** ⓝ 제안
- **viewpoint** ⓝ 관점, 견해
- **at worse** 최소한, 적어도
- **invention** ⓝ 발명
- **keep one's word** 약속을 지키다

구문 풀이

1행 Have you ever brought up an idea or suggestion to someone and heard them immediately say "No, that won't work."?
(동사1 / 목적어 / 동사2(지각동사) / 원형부정사)

---

25 고기를 덜 먹거나 먹지 않는 사람들의 이유　　정답률 74% | 정답 ④

다음 도표의 내용과 일치하지 않는 것은?

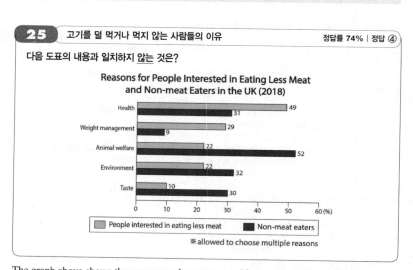

Reasons for People Interested in Eating Less Meat and Non-meat Eaters in the UK (2018)

	People interested in eating less meat	Non-meat eaters
Health	31	49
Weight management	9	29
Animal welfare	22	52
Environment	22	32
Taste	10	30

※ allowed to choose multiple reasons

The graph above shows the survey results on reasons / for people interested in eating less meat / and those eating no meat / in the UK in 2018.
위 그래프는 이유에 대한 조사 결과를 보여 준다. / 고기를 덜 먹는 것에 관심 있는 사람들과 / 고기를 먹지 않는 사람들의 / 2018년 영국에서의
① For the group of people / who are interested in eating less meat, / health is the strongest motivator / for doing so.
집단 사람들에게 / 고기를 덜 먹는 것에 관심 있는 / 가장 강력한 동기는 건강이다. / 그렇게 하려는
② For the group of non-meat eaters, / animal welfare accounts for the largest percentage among all reasons, / followed by environment, health, and taste.
고기를 먹지 않는 집단 사람들의 경우, / 모든 이유 중 동물 복지가 가장 큰 비율을 차지하고, / 환경, 건강, 그리고 맛이 그 뒤를 따른다.
③ The largest percentage point difference / between the two groups / is in animal welfare, / whereas the smallest difference is in environment.

퍼센트포인트 격차가 가장 큰 것은 / 두 집단 간 / 동물 복지에서이다. / 가장 작은 격차는 환경인 반면

☑The percentage of non-meat eaters citing taste / is four times higher / than that of people / interested in reducing their meat consumption / citing taste.
고기를 먹지 않는 사람들 중 맛을 언급한 비율은 / 4배 높다. / 사람들의 비율보다 / 고기 섭취를 줄이는 데 관심이 있는 / 맛을 언급한

⑤ Weight management ranks the lowest for people / who don't eat meat, / with less than 10 percent.
체중 관리는 사람들에게 가장 낮은 순위를 차지한다. / 고기를 먹지 않는 / 10퍼센트 미만으로

위 그래프는 고기를 덜 먹는 것에 관심 있는 사람들과 고기를 먹지 않는 사람들의 이유에 대한 2018년 영국에서의 조사 결과를 보여 준다. ① 고기를 덜 먹는 것에 관심 있는 집단 사람들에게 그렇게 하려는 가장 강력한 동기는 건강이다. ② 고기를 먹지 않는 집단 사람들의 경우, 모든 이유 중 동물 복지가 가장 큰 비율을 차지하고, 환경, 건강, 그리고 맛이 그 뒤를 따른다. ③ 두 집단 간 퍼센트포인트 격차가 가장 큰 것은 동물 복지인 반면 가장 작은 격차는 환경이다. ④ 고기를 먹지 않는 사람들 중 맛을 언급한 비율은 고기 섭취를 줄이는 데 관심이 있는 사람들 중 맛을 언급한 비율보다 4배 높다. ⑤ 체중 관리는 고기를 먹지 않는 사람들에게 10퍼센트 미만으로 가장 낮은 순위를 차지한다.

Why? 왜 정답일까?
도표에 따르면 고기를 먹지 않는 사람들 중 맛 때문이라고 언급한 사람은 30%인데, 이는 고기를 덜 먹으려는 사람들 중 맛을 이유로 언급한 비율(10%)의 3배이다. 따라서 도표와 일치하지 않는 것은 ④이다.

- survey ⓝ 설문 조사
- motivator ⓝ 동기 요인
- account for ~을 차지하다
- cite ⓥ 언급하다, 인용하다
- weight ⓝ 체중, 무게
- reason ⓝ 이유
- welfare ⓝ 복지
- followed by ~이 뒤를 잇다
- consumption ⓝ 소비

구문 풀이
9행 The percentage of non-meat eaters citing taste is four times higher than
배수사＋비교급＋than : ~보다 몇 배 더 …한
that of people (interested in reducing their meat consumption) (citing taste).
＝the percentage　　　( ) : people 수식

26 Margaret Knight의 생애　　정답률 84% | 정답 ③

Margaret Knight에 관한 다음 글의 내용과 일치하지 않는 것은?
① 기자들이 '여자 Edison'이라는 별명을 지어 주었다.
② 가족을 위해 돈을 벌려고 학교를 그만두었다.
☑직물 장비에 쓰이는 안전장치를 발명하여 많은 돈을 벌었다.
④ 밑이 평평한 종이 가방을 자르고 접고 붙이는 기계를 발명했다.
⑤ 2006년에 국립 발명가 명예의 전당에 입성했다.

「Margaret Knight was an exceptionally prolific inventor / in the late 19th century; / journalists occasionally compared her to Thomas Edison / by nicknaming her "a woman Edison."」 ①의 근거 일치
Margaret Knight는 특출나게 다작한 발명가였고, / 19세기 후반에 / 기자들은 가끔 그녀를 Thomas Edison과 비교했다. / 그녀에게 '여자 Edison'이라는 별명을 지어주며
From a young age, / she built toys for her older brothers.
어린 나이부터, / 그녀는 오빠들을 위해 장난감을 만들었다.
After her father died, / Knight's family moved to Manchester.
아버지가 돌아가신 후, / Knight의 가족은 Manchester로 이사했다.
「Knight left school in 1850, / at age 12, / to earn money for her family / at a nearby textile factory, / where she witnessed a fellow worker / injured by faulty equipment.」 ②의 근거 일치
Knight는 1850년에 학교를 그만두었는데, / 12세의 나이에 / 가족을 위해 돈을 벌기 위해 / 가까이 있는 직물 공장에서 / 그곳에서 그녀는 동료 노동자를 목격했다. / 결함이 있는 장비에 부상 당하는 것을
「That led her to create her first invention, / a safety device for textile equipment, / but she never earned money from the invention.」 ③의 근거 불일치
이로 인해 그녀는 첫 번째 발명품을 만들었지만 / 즉 직물 장비에 쓰이는 안전장치를 / 그녀는 결코 그 발명품으로 돈을 벌지 않았다.
「She also invented a machine / that cut, folded and glued flat-bottomed paper bags / and was awarded her first patent in 1871 for it.」 ④의 근거 일치
그녀는 또한 기계를 발명해 / 밑이 평평한 종이 가방을 자르고 접어 붙이는 / 1871년에 그것으로 첫 특허를 받았다.
It eliminated the need / for workers to assemble them slowly by hand.
그것은 필요가 없어지게 했다. / 작업자들이 손으로 그것들을 천천히 조립할
「Knight received 27 patents in her lifetime / and entered the National Inventors Hall of Fame in 2006.」 ⑤의 근거 일치
Knight는 일생 동안 27개의 특허를 받았고, / 2006년에 국립 발명가 명예의 전당에 입성했다.

Margaret Knight는 19세기 후반에 특출나게 다작한 발명가였고, 기자들은 가끔 '여자 Edison'이라는 별명을 지어주며 그녀를 Thomas Edison과 비교했다. 어린 나이부터, 그녀는 오빠들을 위해 장난감을 만들었다. 아버지가 돌아가신 후, Knight의 가족은 Manchester로 이사했다. Knight는 가족을 위해 가까이 있는 직물 공장에서 돈을 벌기 위해 1850년에 12세의 나이에 학교를 그만두었는데, 그곳에서 그녀는 동료 노동자가 결함이 있는 장비에 부상 당하는 것을 목격했다. 이로 인해 그녀는 첫 번째 발명품, 즉 직물 장비에 쓰이는 안전장치를 만들었지만, 그녀는 결코 그 발명품으로 돈을 벌지 않았다. 그녀는 또한 밑이 평평한 종이 가방을 자르고 접어 붙이는 기계를 발명해 1871년에 그것으로 첫 특허를 받았다. 그것은 작업자들이 손으로 그것들을 천천히 조립할 필요가 없어지게 했다. Knight는 일생 동안 27개의 특허를 받았고, 2006년에 국립 발명가 명예의 전당에 입성했다.

Why? 왜 정답일까?
'~ a safety device for textile equipment, but she never earned money from the invention.'에서 Margaret Knight는 동료가 직물 장비에 부상당하는 것을 본 후 장비에 적용할 안전장치를 만들었지만 이것으로 돈을 벌지는 않았다고 한다. 따라서 내용과 일치하지 않는 것은 ③ '직물 장비에 쓰이는 안전장치를 발명하여 많은 돈을 벌었다.'이다.

Why? 왜 오답일까?
① '~ journalists occasionally compared her to Thomas Edison by nicknaming her "a woman Edison."'의 내용과 일치한다.
② 'Knight left school in 1850, at age 12, to earn money for her family ~'의 내용과 일치한다.

④ 'She also invented a machine that cut, folded and glued flat-bottomed paper bags ~'의 내용과 일치한다.
⑤ '~ entered the National Inventors Hall of Fame in 2006.'의 내용과 일치한다.

- exceptionally ⓐⓓ 이례적으로, 특출나게
- journalist ⓝ 기자
- witness ⓥ 목격하다
- faulty ⓐ 결함이 있는
- glue ⓥ 접착하다
- assemble ⓥ 조립하다
- prolific ⓐ 다작한
- occasionally ⓐⓓ 가끔, 때때로
- fellow ⓝ 동료
- fold ⓥ 접다
- flat-bottomed ⓐ 밑이 평평한
- hall of fame 명예의 전당

구문 풀이
1행 ~ journalists occasionally compared her to Thomas Edison by nicknaming
by＋동명사 : ~함으로써
her "a woman Edison."

27 전자 폐기물 재활용 행사 공지　　정답률 88% | 정답 ⑤

E-Waste Recycling Day에 관한 다음 안내문의 내용과 일치하지 않는 것은?
① 3시간 동안 진행된다.
② Lincoln 스포츠 센터에서 열린다.
③ 전자레인지는 허용되지 않는 품목이다.
④ 기기 속 모든 개인 정보는 미리 삭제되어야 한다.
☑거주 지역에 상관없이 참가할 수 있다.

E-Waste Recycling Day
전자 폐기물 재활용의 날
E-Waste Recycling Day is an annual event in our city.
전자 폐기물 재활용의 날은 우리 시의 연례행사입니다.
Bring your used electronics / such as cell phones, tablets, and laptops / to recycle.
중고 전자 제품을 가져오세요. / 휴대폰, 태블릿, 노트북과 같이 / 재활용할
Go green!
친환경적이 되세요!
When
일시
Saturday, December 17, 2022
2022년 12월 17일 토요일
「8:00 a.m. – 11:00 a.m.」 ①의 근거 일치
오전 8시부터 오전 11시까지
Where
장소
「Lincoln Sports Center」 ②의 근거 일치
Lincoln 스포츠 센터
Notes
주의 사항
「Items NOT accepted: light bulbs, batteries, and microwaves」 ③의 근거 일치
허용되지 않는 품목들: 전구, 건전지, 전자레인지
「All personal data on the devices / must be wiped out in advance.」 ④의 근거 일치
기기 속 모든 개인 정보는 / 미리 삭제되어야 합니다.
「This event is free / but open only to local residents.」 ⑤의 근거 불일치
이 행사는 무료이나 / 지역 주민에게만 개방됩니다.
Please contact us at 986-571-0204 / for more information.
986-571-0204로 연락주세요. / 더 많은 정보를 원하시면

전자 폐기물 재활용의 날
전자 폐기물 재활용의 날은 우리 시의 연례행사입니다. 휴대폰, 태블릿, 노트북과 같이 재활용할 중고 전자 제품을 가져오세요. 친환경적이 되세요!
일시
2022년 12월 17일 토요일
오전 8시부터 오전 11시까지
장소
Lincoln 스포츠 센터
주의 사항
• 허용되지 않는 품목들: 전구, 건전지, 전자레인지
• 기기 속 모든 개인 정보는 미리 삭제되어야 합니다.
• 이 행사는 무료이나 지역 주민에게만 개방됩니다.
더 많은 정보를 원하시면 986-571-0204로 연락주세요.

Why? 왜 정답일까?
'This event is free but open only to local residents.'에서 거주민에게만 개방되는 행사라고 하므로, 안내문의 내용과 일치하지 않는 것은 ⑤ '거주 지역에 상관없이 참가할 수 있다.'이다.

Why? 왜 오답일까?
① '8:00 a.m. – 11:00 a.m.'의 내용과 일치한다.
② 'Lincoln Sports Center'의 내용과 일치한다.
③ 'Items NOT accepted: ~ microwaves'의 내용과 일치한다.
④ 'All personal data on the devices must be wiped out in advance.'의 내용과 일치한다.

- e-waste ⓝ 전자 쓰레기
- accept ⓥ 수용하다, 접수하다, 받다
- wipe out 지우다, 쓸어내다
- local resident 지역 주민
- recycling ⓝ 재활용
- microwave ⓝ 전자레인지
- in advance 미리

구문 풀이
명령문(~하라)
3행 Bring your used electronics such as cell phones, tablets, and laptops
목적어
to recycle.
형용사적 용법(목적어 수식)

Undersea Walking Activity에 관한 다음 안내문의 내용과 일치하는 것은?

① 연중무휴로 운영된다.
② 가격에 보험료는 포함되어 있지 않다.
☑ 숙련된 안전 요원이 활동 내내 동행한다.
④ 특수 수중 헬멧 착용 시 안경을 쓸 수 없다.
⑤ 현장 예약은 불가능하다.

Undersea Walking Activity
해저 걷기 활동

Enjoy a fascinating underwater walk on the ocean floor.
해저에서 매력적인 수중 걷기를 즐기세요.

Witness wonderful marine life on foot!
걸어 다니며 멋진 바다 생물을 직접 보세요!

Age Requirement
연령 요건

10 years or older
10세 이상

Operating Hours
영업시간

「from Tuesday to Sunday」①의 근거 불일치
화요일부터 일요일까지

9:00 a.m. – 4:00 p.m.
오전 9시부터 오후 4시까지

Price
가격

「$30 (insurance fee included)」②의 근거 불일치
$30 (보험료 포함)

What to Bring
준비물

swim suit and towel
수영복과 수건

Notes
주의 사항

「Experienced lifeguards accompany you / throughout the activity.」 ③의 근거 일치
숙련된 안전 요원이 여러분과 동행합니다. / 활동 내내

「With a special underwater helmet, / you can wear glasses during the activity.」 ④의 근거 불일치
특수 수중 헬멧 착용 시 / 여러분은 활동 중에 안경을 쓸 수 있습니다.

「Reservations can be made on-site or online / at www.seawalkwonder.com.」 ⑤의 근거 불일치
예약은 현장 또는 온라인으로 가능합니다. / www.seawalkwonder.com에서

해저 걷기 활동

해저에서 매력적인 수중 걷기를 즐기세요. 걸어 다니며 멋진 바다 생물을 직접 보세요!

연령 요건
10세 이상

영업시간
화요일부터 일요일까지
오전 9시부터 오후 4시까지

가격
$30 (보험료 포함)

준비물
수영복과 수건

주의 사항
• 숙련된 안전 요원이 활동 내내 여러분과 동행합니다.
• 특수 수중 헬멧 착용 시 여러분은 활동 중에 안경을 쓸 수 있습니다.
• 예약은 현장 또는 www.seawalkwonder.com에서 온라인으로 가능합니다.

Why? 왜 정답일까?

'Experienced lifeguards accompany you throughout the activity.'에서 숙련된 안전 요원이 활동 내내 동행한다고 하므로, 안내문의 내용과 일치하는 것은 ③ '숙련된 안전 요원이 활동 내내 동행한다.'이다.

Why? 왜 오답일까?

① 'from Tuesday to Sunday'에서 월요일이 휴무일임을 알 수 있다.
② '$30 (insurance fee included)'에서 입장 가격에 보험료가 포함되어 있다고 하였다.
④ 'With a special underwater helmet, you can wear glasses during the activity.'에서 특수 헬멧을 쓰면 안경 착용이 가능하다고 하였다.
⑤ 'Reservations can be made on-site ~'에서 현장 예약도 가능하다고 하였다.

• fascinating ⓐ 매혹적인
• operating hour 운영 시간
• experienced ⓐ 숙련된
• accompany ⓥ 동행하다
• on-site [ad] 현장에서 / 현장의
• ocean floor 해저
• insurance fee 보험료
• lifeguard ⓝ 안전 요원
• throughout [prep] ~ 내내

★★★ 등급을 가르는 문제!

다음 글의 밑줄 친 부분 중, 어법상 틀린 것은? [3점]

You may have seen headlines in the news / about some of the things / machines powered by artificial intelligence can do.
여러분은 헤드라인을 뉴스에서 본 적이 있을 것이다. / 몇 가지 일에 대한 / 인공 지능으로 구동되는 기계가 할 수 있는

However, / if you were to consider all the tasks / ① that AI-powered machines could actually perform, / it would be quite mind-blowing!
하지만, / 여러분이 모든 작업을 고려한다면 / AI로 구동되는 기계가 실제로 수행할 수 있는 / 꽤 놀라울 것이다!

One of the key features of artificial intelligence / ② is / that it enables machines to learn new things, / rather than requiring programming specific to new tasks.
인공 지능의 핵심 특징들 중 하나는 / ~이다. / 이것이 기계가 새로운 것을 학습할 수 있게 한다는 것 / 새로운 작업에 특화된 프로그래밍을 필요로 하기보다는

Therefore, / the core difference / between computers of the future and ③ those of the past / is / that future computers will be able to learn and self-improve.
그러므로, / 핵심 차이점은 / 미래 컴퓨터와 과거 컴퓨터 사이의 / ~이다. / 미래의 컴퓨터가 학습하고 스스로 개선할 수 있을 것이라는 점

In the near future, / smart virtual assistants will know more about you / than your closest friends and family members ☑ do.
가까운 미래에, / 스마트 가상 비서는 여러분에 관해 더 많이 알게 될 것이다. / 여러분의 가장 가까운 친구나 가족보다도

Can you imagine / how that might change our lives?
여러분은 상상할 수 있는가? / 그것이 우리의 삶을 어떻게 변화시킬지

These kinds of changes are / exactly why it is so important / ⑤ to recognize the implications / that new technologies will have for our world.
이러한 변화가 ~이다. / 아주 중요한 바로 그 이유 / 영향을 인식하는 것이 / 새로운 기술들이 우리 세계에 미칠

여러분은 인공 지능으로 구동되는 기계가 할 수 있는 몇 가지 일에 대한 헤드라인들을 뉴스에서 본 적이 있을 것이다. 하지만, AI로 구동되는 기계가 실제로 수행할 수 있는 모든 작업을 고려한다면 꽤 놀라울 것이다! 인공 지능의 핵심 특징들 중 하나는 이것에 새로운 작업에 특화된 프로그래밍이 필요하다기보다는, 이것(인공 지능)이 기계가 새로운 것을 학습할 수 있게 한다는 것이다. 그러므로, 미래 컴퓨터와 과거 컴퓨터 사이의 핵심 차이점은 미래의 컴퓨터가 학습하고 스스로 개선할 수 있을 것이라는 점이다. 가까운 미래에, 스마트 가상 비서는 여러분의 가장 가까운 친구나 가족보다도 여러분에 관해 더 많이 알게 될 것이다. 그것이 우리의 삶을 어떻게 변화시킬지 상상할 수 있는가? 이러한 변화가 바로 새로운 기술들이 우리 세계에 미칠 영향을 인식하는 것이 아주 중요한 이유이다.

Why? 왜 정답일까?

비교급 구문의 than 앞에 일반동사인 will know가 나오므로, than 뒤에 일반동사의 대동사인 do를 써야 한다. 따라서 어법상 틀린 것은 ④이다.

Why? 왜 오답일까?

① 앞에 나온 all the tasks를 꾸미면서 뒤에 목적어가 없는 문장(AI-powered machines could actually perform)을 연결하는 목적격 관계대명사 that의 쓰임이 알맞다.
② 'one of the + 복수 명사'가 주어이므로 단수동사 is는 알맞게 쓰였다.
③ 앞의 복수 명사 computers를 가리키는 복수 대명사 those가 알맞게 쓰였다.
⑤ 가주어 it에 대응되는 진주어 역할의 to부정사구 to recognize가 알맞게 쓰였다.

• artificial intelligence 인공 지능
• mind-blowing ⓐ 너무도 감동적인
• self-improve ⓥ 자가 발전하다
• assistant ⓝ 조수, 비서
• recognize ⓥ 인식하다, 깨닫다
• perform ⓥ 수행하다
• feature ⓝ 특징
• virtual ⓐ 가상의
• exactly [ad] 바로, 정확히

구문 풀이

9행 In the near future, smart virtual assistants will know more about you than your closest friends and family members do.
대동사(= know about you)

★★ 문제 해결 꿀~팁 ★★

▶ 많이 틀린 이유는?
③이 포함된 문장을 보면, 문맥상 미래의 컴퓨터와 과거의 '컴퓨터(computers)'를 비교한다는 의미를 나타내면서 컴퓨터라는 명사의 중복을 피하기 위해 those를 알맞게 썼다. 이렇듯 대명사에 밑줄이 있으면 가장 기본적으로 대명사의 수 일치를 집중적으로 살펴봐야 한다.

▶ 문제 해결 방법은?
정답인 ④ are는 대동사의 쓰임을 묻는 선택지이다. 대동사는 간단한 듯 싶어도 문맥을 전체적으로 살펴야 하기에 어렵게 나오면 한없이 어려워진다. 여기서는 비교구문의 than 앞뒤는 병렬구조를 이루므로 than 앞의 동사와 than 뒤의 동사가 서로 같은 종류여야 한다는 점에 집중하면 된다.

다음 글의 밑줄 친 부분 중, 문맥상 낱말의 쓰임이 적절하지 않은 것은? [3점]

Plant growth is controlled / by a group of hormones / called auxins / found at the tips of stems and roots of plants.
식물의 성장은 조절된다. / 호르몬 그룹에 의해 / 옥신이라고 불리는 / 식물의 줄기와 뿌리의 끝에서 발견되는

Auxins / produced at the tips of stems / tend to accumulate / on the side of the stem / that is in the shade.
옥신은 / 줄기의 끝에서 생산된 / 축적되는 경향이 있다. / 줄기 옆면에 / 그늘진 곳에 있는

Accordingly, / the auxins ① stimulate growth / on the shaded side of the plant.
따라서, / 옥신은 성장을 촉진한다. / 식물의 그늘진 면에

Therefore, / the shaded side grows faster / than the side facing the sunlight.
그러므로 / 그늘진 면은 더 빨리 자란다. / 햇빛을 마주하는 면보다

This phenomenon causes the stem / to bend and appear to be growing ② towards the light.
현상은 줄기가 ~하게 한다. / 휘어지고 빛을 향해 성장하는 것처럼 보이게

Auxins have the ③ opposite effect / on the roots of plants.
옥신은 반대 효과를 나타낸다. / 식물의 뿌리에

Auxins in the tips of roots / tend to limit growth.
뿌리 끝에 있는 옥신은 / 성장을 억제하는 경향이 있다.

If a root is horizontal in the soil, / the auxins will accumulate on the lower side / and interfere with its development.
만약 뿌리가 토양 속에서 수평이라면, / 옥신은 아래쪽에 축적되어 / 그것의 발달을 방해할 것이다.

Therefore, / the lower side of the root / will grow ☑ slower than the upper side.
그러므로 / 뿌리 아래쪽은 / 위쪽보다 더 느리게 자라게 된다.

This will, in turn, / cause the root to bend ⑤ downwards, / with the tip of the root growing in that direction.
이것은 결과적으로, / 뿌리가 아래로 휘어지게 하고, / 뿌리 끝부분은 그쪽으로 자라난다.

식물의 성장은 식물의 줄기와 뿌리의 끝에서 발견되는 옥신이라고 불리는 호르몬 그룹에 의해 조절된다. 줄기의 끝에서 생산된 옥신은 그늘진 곳에 있는 줄기 옆면에 축적되는 경향이 있다. 따라서, 옥신은 식물의 그늘진 면에서의 성장을 ① 촉진한다. 그러므로 그늘진 면은 햇빛을 마주하는 면보다 더 빨리 자란다. 이 현상은 줄기가 휘어지고 빛을 ② 향해 성장하는 것처럼 보이게 한다. 옥신은 식물의 뿌리에서는 ③ 반대 효과를 나타낸다. 뿌리 끝에 있는 옥신은 성장을 억제하는 경향이 있다. 만약 뿌리가 토양 속에서 수평이라면, 옥신은 아래쪽에 축적되어 그것의 발달을 방해할 것이다. 그러므로 뿌리 아래쪽은 위쪽보다 ④ 더 빠르게(→ 더 느리게) 자라게 된다. 이것은 결과적으로 뿌리가 ⑤ 아래로 휘어지게 하고, 뿌리 끝부분은 그쪽으로 자라난다.

Why? 왜 정답일까?

식물 생장에 있어 옥신의 작용 방식을 설명한 글이다. 줄기에 작용하는 옥신은 어두운 쪽의 성장을 자극하므로 식물은 마치 빛을 '향해' 작용하는 것처럼 보이게 되지만, 뿌리에서는 상황이 '반대'라고 한다. 즉, 뿌리 아래쪽에 축적된 옥신은 아래쪽의 성장을 오히려 '방해해서' 위쪽보다 '더 천천히' 자라게 만들 것이라는 내용을 추론할 수 있다. 따라서 문맥상 낱말의 쓰임이 적절하지 않은 것은 ④이며, **faster**를 **slower**로 바꿔야 한다.

- **tip** ⓝ 끝부분
- **accumulate** ⓥ 축적되다, 쌓이다
- **stimulate** ⓥ 자극하다, 촉진하다
- **bend** ⓥ 구부러지다
- **horizontal** ⓐ 수평적인
- **interfere with** ~을 방해하다
- **downward(s)** ⓐⓓ 아래로
- **stem** ⓝ 줄기
- **accordingly** ⓐⓓ 따라서
- **phenomenon** ⓝ 현상
- **limit** ⓥ 제한하다
- **soil** ⓝ 토양, 흙
- **in turn** 한편, 결국, 차례로

구문 풀이

12행 This will, in turn, cause the root to bend downwards, with the tip of the root growing in that direction.
「with+명사+분사 : ~이 …한 채로」

---

31 정해진 마감일이 과업 성과에 미치는 영향
정답률 56% | 정답 ③

다음 빈칸에 들어갈 말로 가장 적절한 것을 고르시오.
① offering rewards – 보상을 제공하는 것
② removing obstacles – 장애물을 제거하는 것
✓③ restricting freedom – 자유를 제한하는 것
④ increasing assignments – 과제를 늘리는 것
⑤ encouraging competition – 경쟁을 부추기는 것

To demonstrate how best to defeat the habit of delaying, / Dan Ariely, a professor of psychology and behavioral economics, / performed an experiment on students / in three of his classes at MIT.
미루는 습관을 가장 잘 무너뜨리는 방법을 설명하기 위해, / 심리학 및 행동경제학 교수인 Dan Ariely는 / 학생들을 대상으로 실험을 수행했다. / MIT에서의 수업 중 세 반에서

He assigned all classes three reports / over the course of the semester.
그는 모든 수업에 보고서 세 개를 과제로 부여했다. / 학기 과정 동안

The first class had to choose three due dates for themselves, / up to and including the last day of class.
첫 번째 수업의 학생들은 마감일 세 개를 스스로 선택해야 했다. / 종강일까지 포함해서

The second had no deadlines / — all three papers just had to be submitted / by the last day of class.
두 번째는 마감일이 없었고, / 세 개의 보고서 모두 제출되기만 하면 되었다. / 종강일까지

In his third class, / he gave students three set deadlines / over the course of the semester.
세 번째 수업에서, / 그는 학생들에게 세 개의 정해진 마감일을 주었다. / 학기 과정 동안

At the end of the semester, / he found / that students with set deadlines / received the best grades, / the students with no deadlines / had the worst, / and those who could choose their own deadlines / fell somewhere in the middle.
학기 말에, / 그는 알아냈다. / 마감일이 정해진 학생들이 / 최고의 성적을 받았으며, / 마감일이 없는 학생은 / 최하의 성적을 받았으며, / 마감일을 선택할 수 있었던 학생은 / 그 중간 어딘가의 위치에 있었다는 것을

Ariely concludes / that restricting freedom / — whether by the professor / or by students who recognize their own tendencies to delay things — / improves self-control and performance.
Ariely는 결론짓는다. / 자유를 제한하는 것은 / 교수에 의해서든 / 혹은 일을 미루는 자기 성향을 인식한 학생들에 의해서든, / 자기 통제와 성과를 향상시킨다고

미루는 습관을 가장 잘 무너뜨리는 방법을 설명하기 위해, 심리학 및 행동경제학 교수인 Dan Ariely는 MIT에서의 수업 중 세 반에서 학생들을 대상으로 실험을 수행했다. 그는 학기 과정 동안 모든 수업에 보고서 세 개를 과제로 부여했다. 첫 번째 수업의 학생들은 종강일까지 포함해서 마감일 세 개를 스스로 선택해야 했다. 두 번째는 마감일이 없었고, 세 개의 보고서 모두 종강일까지 제출되기만 하면 되었다. 세 번째 수업에서, 그는 학기 과정 동안 학생들에게 세 개의 정해진 마감일을 주었다. 학기 말에, 그는 마감일이 정해진 학생들이 최고의 성적을 받았고, 마감일이 없는 학생은 최하의 성적을 받았으며, 마감일을 선택할 수 있었던 학생들은 그 중간 어딘가의 위치에 있었다는 것을 알아냈다. Ariely가 결론짓기로, 교수에 의해서든 혹은 일을 미루는 자기 성향을 인식한 학생들에 의해서든, 자유를 제한하는 것은 자기 통제와 성과를 향상시킨다.

Why? 왜 정답일까?

연구를 소개하는 글이므로 결과 부분인 '~ he found that students with set deadlines received the best grades, ~'이 중요하다. 이 내용에 따르면, 마감일이 '정해져' 있었던 학생들이 다른 두 집단에 비해 성적이 가장 높았다고 한다. 마감을 정해둔다는 것은 결국 일정 부분 '자유를 제한한다'는 의미와 같으므로, 빈칸에 들어갈 말로 가장 적절한 것은 ③ '자유를 제한하는 것'이다.

- **demonstrate** ⓥ 입증하다
- **behavioral** ⓐ 행동의
- **for oneself** 스스로
- **set** ⓐ 정해진
- **tendency** ⓝ 경향, 성향
- **obstacle** ⓝ 장애물
- **defeat** ⓥ 무너뜨리다, 패배시키다
- **assign** ⓥ 할당하다
- **up to and including** ~까지 포함해서
- **receive** ⓥ 받다
- **self-control** ⓝ 자기 통제
- **restrict** ⓥ 제한하다

구문 풀이

12행 Ariely concludes that restricting freedom — whether by the professor or
주어(동명사)   「whether+A+or+B : A이든 B이든(부사절)」
by students who recognize their own tendencies to delay things — improves
동사(단수)
self-control and performance.

★★★ 등급을 가르는 문제!

32 혁신이 우리 삶을 바꾸는 방식
정답률 37% | 정답 ②

다음 빈칸에 들어갈 말로 가장 적절한 것을 고르시오. [3점]
① respecting the values of the old days – 과거의 가치관을 존중하는 것
✓② enabling people to work for each other – 사람들이 서로를 위해 일할 수 있게 하는 것
③ providing opportunities to think creatively – 창의적으로 사고할 기회를 주는 것
④ satisfying customers with personalized services – 개인에 맞춰진 서비스로 고객을 만족시키는 것
⑤ introducing and commercializing unusual products – 특이한 제품을 도입하고 상업화하는 것

The best way in which innovation changes our lives / is by enabling people to work for each other.
혁신이 우리의 삶을 바꾸는 최고의 방법은 / 사람들이 서로를 위해 일할 수 있게 하는 것이다.

The main theme of human history / is that we become steadily more specialized / in what we produce, / and steadily more diversified / in what we consume: / we move away / from unstable self-sufficiency / to safer mutual interdependence.
인류 역사의 주요한 주제는 / 우리가 꾸준히 더 전문화되고 / 우리가 생산하는 것에 있어 / 꾸준히 더 다양화되는 것이다. / 우리가 소비하는 것에 있어 / 즉, 우리는 옮겨간다는 것이다. / 불안정한 자급자족에서 / 더 안전한 서로 간의 상호의존으로

By concentrating on serving other people's needs / for forty hours a week / — which we call a job — / you can spend the other seventy-two hours / (not counting fifty-six hours in bed) / relying on the services / provided to you by other people.
다른 사람들의 필요를 충족시키는 것에 집중하여 / 일주일에 40시간 동안 / 즉 우리가 직업이라고 부르는 것에 / 여러분은 나머지 72시간을 보낼 수 있다. / (잠자는 56시간은 빼고) / 다른 사람들에 의지해 / 여러분에게 제공되는

Innovation has made it possible / to work for a fraction of a second / in order to be able to afford to turn on an electric lamp for an hour, / providing the quantity of light / that would have required a whole day's work / if you had to make it yourself / by collecting and refining sesame oil or lamb fat / to burn in a simple lamp, / as much of humanity did / in the not so distant past.
혁신은 가능하게 해주었는데 / 아주 짧은 시간 일하는 것을 / 전등을 한 시간 켤 수 있는 여유를 갖기 위해 / 이는 ~한 만큼의 빛을 제공해 준다. / 하루 종일의 노고가 들었을 / 여러분이 그 등을 스스로 만들어야 했다면 / 참기름이나 양의 지방을 모으고 정제해 / 그저 등 하나를 켜기 위해 / 많은 인류가 했던 것처럼 / 그리 멀지 않은 과거에

혁신이 우리의 삶을 바꾸는 최고의 방법은 사람들이 서로를 위해 일할 수 있게 하는 것이다. 인류 역사의 주요한 주제는 우리가 생산에 있어 꾸준히 더 전문화되고 소비에 있어 꾸준히 더 다양화되는 것이다. 즉, 우리는 불안정한 자급자족에서 더 안전한 서로 간의 상호의존으로 옮겨간다는 것이다. 일주일에 40시간 동안 다른 사람들의 필요를 충족시키는 것, 즉 우리가 직업이라고 부르는 것에 집중하여, 여러분은 (잠자는 56시간은 빼고) 나머지 72시간을 다른 사람들이 제공하는 서비스에 의지해 보낼 수 있다. 혁신은 아주 짧은 시간 일하고도 전등을 한 시간 켤 수 있는 여유를 갖게 해주었는데, 이는 그리 멀지 않은 과거에 많은 인류가 했던 것처럼 여러분이 그저 등 하나를 켜기 위해 참기름이나 양의 지방을 모으고 정제해 그 등을 스스로 만들어야 했다면 하루 종일의 노고가 들었을 만큼의 빛을 제공해 준다.

Why? 왜 정답일까?

생산이 꾸준히 전문화되고 소비가 꾸준히 다양해지는 과정에서 인간은 각자 맡은 일에 집중하는 동시에 타인의 서비스에도 의존해 살게 된다(By concentrating on serving other people's needs for forty hours a week ~ you can spend ~ relying on the services provided to you by other people.)고 한다. 즉 각자 세분화된 역할을 수행하는 사람들이 '서로 의존해가며' 삶이 변화되는 과정이 곧 혁신이라는 것이다. 따라서 빈칸에 들어갈 말로 가장 적절한 것은 ② '사람들이 서로를 위해 일할 수 있게 하는 것'이다.

- **innovation** ⓝ 혁신
- **specialize** ⓥ 전문화하다
- **unstable** ⓐ 불안정한
- **mutual** ⓐ 상호의
- **concentrate on** ~에 집중하다
- **serve one's needs** ~의 필요를 충족하다, ~에게 도움이 되다
- **rely on** ~에 의존하다
- **afford** ⓥ ~할 여유가 있다
- **refine** ⓥ 정제하다
- **burn up** 태우다
- **commercialize** ⓥ 상업화하다
- **steadily** ⓐⓓ 꾸준히
- **diversify** ⓥ 다양화하다
- **self-sufficiency** ⓝ 자급자족
- **interdependence** ⓝ 상호 의존성
- **a fraction of a second** 아주 짧은 시간
- **quantity** ⓝ 양
- **lamb** ⓝ (어린) 양
- **personalize** ⓥ 개인의 필요에 맞추다

구문 풀이

9행 Innovation has made it possible to work for a fraction of a second in
가목적어   진목적어
order to be able to afford to turn on an electric lamp for an hour, providing the
분사구문
quantity of light [that would have required a whole day's work if you had to make
선행사   ~했을 것이다
it yourself by collecting and refining sesame oil or lamb fat to burn in a simple
lamp, as much of humanity did in the not so distant past]. [ ] : 형용사절
대동사(=made it by themselves by collecting and refining ~)

★★ 문제 해결 꿀~팁 ★★

▶ 많이 틀린 이유는?
Innovation을 보고 creatively가 포함된 ③을 고른다거나, more specialized를 보고 personalized가 포함된 ④를 고를 수 있지만, 모두 글의 핵심 내용과 관련이 없다. 이 글의 주제는 사람들이 모든 일을 혼자 해결하던 시대에 비해 점점 각자 전문화된 일을 맡으며 각자 자기 분야가 아닌 일에 대해서는 '서로 의존할' 수밖에 없게 된다는 것이다.

▶ 문제 해결 방법은?
빈칸 뒤의 핵심어인 mutual interdependence를 재진술한 표현이 정답이다.

33 유혹을 극복하는 방법
정답률 51% | 정답 ③

다음 빈칸에 들어갈 말로 가장 적절한 것을 고르시오.

① letting go of all-or-nothing mindset - 양자택일의 사고방식을 버림
② finding reasons why you want to change - 왜 변하고 싶은지 이유를 찾음
③ locking yourself out of your temptations - 여러분 자신을 유혹으로부터 차단함 ✓
④ building a plan and tracking your progress - 계획을 세워 진행 상황을 추적함
⑤ focusing on breaking one bad habit at a time - 한 번에 하나의 나쁜 습관을 깨는 데 집중함

If you've ever made a poor choice, / you might be interested / in learning how to break that habit.
여러분이 한 번이라도 좋지 못한 선택을 한 적이 있다면, / 여러분은 관심이 있을지도 모른다. / 그런 습관을 깨는 방법을 배우는 데

One great way / to trick your brain into doing so / is to sign a "Ulysses Contract."
한 가지 좋은 방법은 / 여러분의 뇌를 속여 그렇게 하는 / 'Ulysses 계약'에 서명하는 것이다.

The name of this life tip / comes from the Greek myth about Ulysses, a captain / whose ship sailed past the island of the Sirens, / a tribe of dangerous women / who lured victims to their death with their irresistible songs.
이 인생에 대한 조언의 이름은 / Ulysses에 관한 그리스 신화에서 유래되었는데, / 그는 선장이었다. / 그의 배가 사이렌의 섬을 지나던 / 위험한 여성 부족인 / 저항할 수 없는 노래를 통해 희생자들을 죽음으로 유혹

Knowing that he would otherwise be unable to resist, / Ulysses instructed his crew / to stuff their ears with cotton / and tie him to the ship's mast / to prevent him from turning their ship towards the Sirens.
그렇게 하지 않으면 저항할 수 없다는 것을 알고, / Ulysses는 선원들에게 지시했다. / 귀를 솜으로 막고 / 자신을 배의 돛대에 묶으라고 / 그가 사이렌 쪽으로 배를 돌리지 못하게 막기 위해

It worked for him / and you can do the same thing / by locking yourself out of your temptations.
그것은 그에게 효과가 있었고, / 여러분도 똑같은 일을 할 수 있다. / 여러분 자신을 유혹으로부터 차단함으로써

For example, / if you want to stay off your cellphone / and concentrate on your work, / delete the apps that distract you / or ask a friend to change your password!
예를 들어, / 만약 여러분이 휴대폰을 멀리하고 / 일에 집중하고 싶다면, / 여러분의 주의를 산만하게 하는 앱들을 삭제하거나, / 친구에게 여러분의 비밀번호를 바꿔달라고 요청하라!

여러분이 한 번이라도 좋지 못한 선택을 한 적이 있다면, 그런 습관을 깨는 방법을 배우는 데 관심이 있을지도 모른다. 여러분의 뇌를 속여 그렇게 하는 한 가지 좋은 방법은 'Ulysses 계약'에 서명하는 것이다. 이 인생에 대한 조언의 이름은 Ulysses에 관한 그리스 신화에서 유래되었는데, 그는 저항할 수 없는 노래를 통해 희생자들을 죽음으로 유혹한 위험한 여성 부족인 사이렌의 섬을 지나던 배의 선장이었다. Ulysses는 그렇게 하지 않으면 저항할 수 없다는 것을 알고, 선원들에게 귀를 솜으로 막고 자신을 배의 돛대에 묶어 시켜 자신이 사이렌 쪽으로 배를 돌리지 못하게 했다. 그것은 그에게 효과가 있었고, 여러분은 여러분 자신을 유혹으로부터 차단함으로써 똑같은 일을 할 수 있다. 예를 들어, 만약 여러분이 휴대폰을 멀리하고 일에 집중하고 싶다면, 여러분의 주의를 산만하게 하는 앱을 지우거나, 친구에게 여러분의 비밀번호를 바꿔달라고 요청하라!

Why? 왜 정답일까?

빈칸 앞에서 신화 속 인물 Ulysses는 선원들을 시켜 자기 몸을 돛대에 묶게 해서 사이렌의 노래에 유혹되려는 자기 자신을 막았다고 한다. 빈칸에는 이러한 Ulysses의 조치를 일반화할 수 있는 표현이 필요하므로, 답으로 가장 적절한 것은 ③ '여러분 자신을 유혹으로부터 차단함'이다. 일에 집중하기 위해 일에 도움이 안 되는 앱을 지우거나 친구를 통해 비밀번호를 바꾸라는 내용 또한 '유혹에 넘어가지 않기' 위한 예시에 해당한다.

- **break a habit** 습관을 깨다
- **myth** ⓝ 신화
- **lure** ⓥ 유혹하다
- **instruct** ⓥ 지시하다, 가르치다
- **tie** ⓥ 묶다
- **distract** ⓥ 주의를 분산시키다, 산만하게 하다
- **all-or-nothing** 양자택일의, 이것 아니면 저것인
- **trick A into B** A를 속여 B하게 하다
- **sail** ⓥ 항해하다
- **irresistible** ⓐ 저항할 수 없는
- **stuff** ⓥ (속을) 채우다, 막다
- **mast** ⓝ 돛대
- **let go of** ~을 놓주다, 내려놓다
- **temptation** ⓝ 유혹

구문 풀이

3행 The name of this life tip comes from the Greek myth about Ulysses, (a captain whose ship sailed past the island of the Sirens), {a tribe of dangerous women who lured victims to their death with their irresistible songs}.
( ): Ulysses와 동격   { }: the Sirens와 동격

★★★ 등급을 가르는 문제!
34 생물의 진화 방향을 이끄는 실내 공간과 생활
정답률 46% | 정답 ③

다음 빈칸에 들어갈 말로 가장 적절한 것을 고르시오. [3점]

① produce chemicals to protect themselves
  스스로를 보호하고자 화학 물질을 만들어냄
② become extinct with the destroyed habitats
  파괴된 서식지와 함께 멸종함
③ evolve the traits they need to thrive indoors ✓
  실내에서 번성하기 위해 자신에게 필요한 특성들을 진화시킬
④ compete with outside organisms to find their prey
  먹잇감을 찾고자 야외 생물들과 경쟁함
⑤ break the boundaries between wildlife and humans
  야생 종과 인간 사이의 경계를 무너뜨릴

Our homes aren't just ecosystems, / they're unique ones, / hosting species / that are adapted to indoor environments / and pushing evolution in new directions.
우리의 집은 단순한 생태계가 아니라 / 그것은 독특한 곳이며, / 종들을 수용하고 / 실내 환경에 적응된 / 새로운 방향으로 진화를 밀어붙인다

Indoor microbes, insects, and rats / have all evolved the ability / to survive our chemical attacks, / developing resistance to antibacterials, insecticides, and poisons.
실내 미생물, 곤충, 그리고 쥐들은 / 모두 능력을 진화시켰다. / 우리의 화학적 공격에서 살아남을 수 있는 / 항균제, 살충제, 독에 대한 내성을 키우면서

German cockroaches are known / to have developed a distaste for glucose, / which is commonly used as bait in roach traps.
독일 바퀴벌레는 알려져 있는데 / 포도당에 대한 혐오감을 발달시킨 것으로 / 이것은 바퀴벌레 덫에서 미끼로 흔히 사용된다.

Some indoor insects, / which have fewer opportunities to feed / than their outdoor counterparts, / seem to have developed the ability / to survive when food is limited.
일부 실내 곤충은 / 먹이를 잡아먹을 기회가 더 적은 / 야외에 있는 상대방에 비해 / 능력을 발달시킨 것으로 보인다. / 먹이가 제한적일 때 생존할 수 있는

Dunn and other ecologists have suggested / that as the planet becomes more developed and more urban, / more species will evolve the traits / they need to thrive indoors.
Dunn과 다른 생태학자들은 말했다. / 지구가 점점 더 발전되고 도시화되면서, / 더 많은 종들이 특성들을 진화시킬 것이라고 / 실내에서 번성하기 위해 자신에게 필요한

Over a long enough time period, / indoor living could drive our evolution, too.
충분히 긴 시간에 걸쳐, / 실내 생활은 또한 우리의 진화를 이끌 수 있었다.

Perhaps my indoorsy self represents the future of humanity.
아마도 실내 생활을 좋아하는 나의 모습은 인류의 미래를 대변할 것이다.

우리의 집은 단순한 생태계가 아니라 독특한 곳이며, 실내 환경에 적응된 종들을 수용하고 새로운 방향으로 진화를 밀어붙인다. 실내 미생물, 곤충, 그리고 쥐들은 모두 항균제, 살충제, 독에 대한 내성을 키우면서 우리의 화학적 공격에서 살아남을 수 있는 능력을 진화시켰다. 독일 바퀴벌레는 바퀴벌레 덫에서 미끼로 흔히 사용되는 포도당에 대한 혐오감을 발달시킨 것으로 알려져 있다. 야외에 있는 상대방에 비해 먹이를 잡아먹을 기회가 더 적은 일부 실내 곤충은 먹이가 제한적일 때 생존할 수 있는 능력을 발달시킨 것으로 보인다. Dunn과 다른 생태학자들은 지구가 점점 더 발전되고 도시화되면서, 더 많은 종들이 실내에서 번성하기 위해 자신에게 필요한 특성들을 진화시킬 것이라고 말했다. 충분히 긴 시간에 걸쳐, 실내 생활은 또한 우리의 진화를 이끌 수 있었다. 아마도 실내 생활을 좋아하는 나의 모습은 인류의 미래를 대변할 것이다.

Why? 왜 정답일까?

첫 문장과 빈칸 뒤의 문장에서 집, 즉 실내 공간이 우리 진화를 이끌어 간다(indoor living could drive our evolution)는 주제를 반복하여 제시한다. 따라서 빈칸에 들어갈 말로 가장 적절한 것은 우리가 실내 생활에 필요한 방향으로 발전해 간다는 의미의 ③ '실내에서 번성하기 위해 자신에게 필요한 특성들을 진화시킬'이다.

- **host** ⓥ (손님을) 접대하다, 수용하다, (행사를) 주최하다
- **microbe** ⓝ 미생물
- **antibacterial** ⓐ 항균성의 ⓝ 항균제
- **cockroach** ⓝ 바퀴벌레
- **glucose** ⓝ 포도당
- **counterpart** ⓝ 상대방, 대응물
- **represent** ⓥ 표현하다, 나타내다
- **habitat** ⓝ 서식지
- **resistance** ⓝ 내성, 저항력
- **insecticide** ⓝ 살충제
- **distaste** ⓝ 혐오
- **bait** ⓝ 미끼
- **ecologist** ⓝ 생태학자
- **extinct** ⓐ 멸종한
- **prey** ⓝ 먹잇감

구문 풀이

5행 German cockroaches are known to have developed a distaste for glucose, which is commonly used as bait in roach traps.
「be known + to have p.p. : ~했다고 알려지다(완료부정사)」
선행사   계속적 용법(보충 설명)

★★ 문제 해결 꿀~팁 ★★

▶ 많이 틀린 이유는?
chemical attacks 등 지엽적 소재만 보면 ①을 답으로 고르기 쉽다. 하지만 풀이의 핵심은 생태계의 생명체들이 '어떤 방향으로' 진화하도록 유도되어 왔는지를 파악하는 데 있다.
▶ 문제 해결 방법은?
빈칸 뒤를 보면 '실내 생활이 우리 진화를 이끌 수 있었다(indoor living could drive our evolution)'는 결론이 나온다. 이 결론과 동일한 말이 빈칸에도 들어갈 것이다.

35 시 쓰기의 이점
정답률 62% | 정답 ④

다음 글에서 전체 흐름과 관계 없는 문장은?

Developing a personal engagement with poetry / brings a number of benefits to you / as an individual, / in both a personal and a professional capacity.
시와의 개인적 관계를 발전시키는 것은 / 여러분에게 많은 이점을 가져다준다. / 한 개인으로서의 / 개인적 능력과 전문적인 능력 모두에서

① Writing poetry has been shown / to have physical and mental benefits, / with expressive writing found to improve immune system and lung function, / diminish psychological distress, / and enhance relationships.
시 쓰기는 알려져 왔다. / 신체적, 정신적 이점을 지닌 것으로 / 표현적 글쓰기가 면역 체계와 폐 기능을 향상시킨다고 밝혀지면서 / 심리적 고통을 줄이고 / 그리고 관계를 증진시킨다

② Poetry has long been used / to aid different mental health needs, / develop empathy, / and reconsider our relationship with both natural and built environments.
시는 오랫동안 사용되었다. / 여러 정신 건강에 필요한 것들을 지원하고, / 공감 능력을 개발하고, / 자연 환경과 만들어진 환경 둘 다와의 관계를 재고하기 위해

③ Poetry is also / an incredibly effective way of actively targeting the cognitive development period, / improving your productivity and scientific creativity in the process.
시는 또한 / 인지 발달 시기를 적극적으로 겨냥하는 놀랍도록 효과적인 방법이며, / 그 과정에서 여러분의 생산성과 과학적 창의력을 향상시킨다.

④ Poetry is considered / to be an easy and useful means of expressing emotions, / but you fall into frustration / when you realize its complexity. ✓
시는 여겨지지만, / 감정을 표현하는 쉽고 유용한 수단이라고 / 여러분은 좌절에 빠진다. / 여러분이 그것의 복잡성을 알면

⑤ In short, / poetry has a lot to offer, / if you give it the opportunity to do so.
간단히 말해서, / 시는 많은 것을 제공할 수 있다. / 여러분이 시에게 그럴 기회를 준다면

시와의 개인적 관계를 발전시키는 것은 개인적인 능력과 전문적인 능력 모두에서 한 개인으로서의 여러분에게 많은 이점을 가져다준다. ① 표현적 글쓰기가 면역 체계와 폐 기능을 향상시키고, 심리적 고통을 줄이고, 관계를 증진시킨다고 밝혀지면서, 시 쓰기는 신체적, 정신적 이점을 지닌 것으로 알려져 왔다. ② 시는 여러 정신 건강에 필요한 것들을 지원하고, 공감 능력을 개발하고, 자연 환경과 만들어진 환경 둘 다와의 관계를 재고하기 위해 오랫동안 사용되었다. ③ 시는 또한 인지 발달 시기를 적극적으로 겨냥하는 놀랍도록 효과적인 방법이며, 그 과정에서 여러분의 생산성과 과학적 창의력을 향상시킨다. ④ 시는 감정을 표현하는 쉽고 유용한 수단으로 여겨지지만, 여러분은 그것의 복잡성을 알면 좌절에 빠진다. ⑤ 간단히 말해서, 여러분이 그럴 기회를 준다면 시는 많은 것을 제공해줄 수 있다.

시 쓰기의 이점을 두루 열거하는 글인데, ④는 시의 복잡함을 알면 우리가 좌절에 빠질 수 있다는 내용이므로 흐름상 어색하다. 따라서 전체 흐름과 관계 없는 문장은 ④이다.

- engagement ⓝ 관계, 참여
- capacity ⓝ 능력, 역량
- lung ⓝ 폐
- distress ⓝ 고통
- empathy ⓝ 공감, 감정 이입
- cognitive ⓐ 인지적인
- frustration ⓝ 좌절
- poetry ⓝ 시
- immune system 면역 체계
- diminish ⓥ 줄이다, 감소시키다
- enhance ⓥ 향상시키다
- incredibly ⓐⓓ 믿을 수 없을 정도로, 놀랍도록
- productivity ⓝ 생산성
- complexity ⓝ 복잡성

구문 풀이

1행 Developing a personal engagement with poetry brings a number of
　　　　명사구 주어　　　　　　　　　　　　　　동사(단수)
benefits to you as an individual, in both a personal and a professional capacity.
「a number of + 복수 명사: 많은 ~」

---

36 노동의 자동화로 인한 일자리 위기　　　정답률 58% | 정답 ③

주어진 글 다음에 이어질 글의 순서로 가장 적절한 것을 고르시오.

① (A) - (C) - (B)
② (B) - (A) - (C)
③ (B) - (C) - (A) ✓
④ (C) - (A) - (B)
⑤ (C) - (B) - (A)

Things are changing.
상황이 변하고 있다.

It has been reported / that 42 percent of jobs in Canada / are at risk, / and 62 percent of jobs in America / will be in danger / due to advances in automation.
보도되었다. / 캐나다의 일자리 중 42퍼센트가 / 위기에 처했으며, / 미국의 일자리 중 62퍼센트가 / 위기에 처할 것이라고 / 자동화의 발전으로 인해

(B) You might say / that the numbers seem a bit unrealistic, / but the threat is real.
여러분은 말할지 모른다 / 그 숫자들이 약간 비현실적으로 보인다고 / 하지만 그 위험은 현실이다.

One fast food franchise has a robot / that can flip a burger in ten seconds.
한 패스트푸드 체인점은 로봇을 가지고 있다. / 10초 안에 버거 하나를 뒤집을 수 있는

It is just a simple task / but the robot could replace an entire crew.
그것은 단지 단순한 일일 뿐이지만, / 그 로봇은 전체 직원을 대체할 수도 있다.

(C) Highly skilled jobs are also at risk.
고도로 숙련된 직업들 또한 위기에 처해 있다.

A supercomputer, / for instance, / can suggest available treatments / for specific illnesses / in an automated way, / drawing on the body of medical research and data on diseases.
슈퍼컴퓨터는 / 예를 들면, / 이용 가능한 치료법을 제안할 수 있다. / 특정한 질병들에 대해 / 자동화된 방식으로 / 질병에 대한 방대한 양의 의학 연구와 데이터를 이용하여

(A) However, / what's difficult to automate / is the ability / to creatively solve problems.
하지만, / 자동화하기 어려운 것은 / 능력이다 / 문제를 창의적으로 해결하는

Whereas workers in "doing" roles / can be replaced by robots, / the role of creatively solving problems / is more dependent on an irreplaceable individual.
'하는' 역할의 노동자들은 / 로봇들에 의해 대체될 수 있는 반면에, / 창의적으로 문제를 해결하는 역할은 / 대체 불가능한 개인에 더 의존한다.

상황이 변하고 있다. 캐나다의 일자리 중 42퍼센트가 위기에 처했으며, 미국의 일자리 중 62퍼센트가 자동화의 발전으로 인해 위기에 처할 것이라고 보도되었다.

(B) 여러분은 그 숫자들이 약간 비현실적으로 보인다고 말할지 모르지만, 그 위협은 현실이다. 한 패스트푸드 체인점은 10초 안에 버거 하나를 뒤집을 수 있다. 그것은 단지 단순한 일일 뿐이지만, 로봇은 전체 직원을 대체할 수도 있다.

(C) 고도로 숙련된 직업들 또한 위기에 처해 있다. 예를 들면, 슈퍼컴퓨터는 질병에 대한 방대한 양의 의학 연구와 데이터를 이용하여 특정한 질병들에 대해 이용 가능한 치료법을 자동화된 방식으로 제안할 수 있다.

(A) 하지만, 자동화하기 어려운 것은 문제를 창의적으로 해결하는 능력이다. '(기계적인 일을) 하는' 역할의 노동자들은 로봇들에 의해 대체될 수 있는 반면에, 창의적으로 문제를 해결하는 역할은 대체 불가능한 개인에 더 의존한다.

노동 시장의 상황이 변하고 있다며 경각심을 일깨우는 주어진 글 뒤로, 주어진 글에 언급된 수치들을 the numbers로 지칭한 (B)가 연결된다. (B)에서는 '이 수치들'이 비현실적인 것 같아도 사실적임을 보증 설명하는데, (C)는 여기에 이어 고도로 숙련된 직업 또한(also) 위기에 처해 있다고 설명한다. 마지막으로 상황을 반전시키는(However) (A)는 자동화하기 어려운 대상으로 인간의 창의적 문제 해결 능력을 언급한다. 따라서 글의 순서로 가장 적절한 것은 ③ '(B) - (C) - (A)'이다.

- at risk 위험에 처한
- replace ⓥ 대체하다
- unrealistic ⓐ 비현실적인
- crew ⓝ (전체) 직원, 승무원
- automation ⓝ 자동화
- irreplaceable ⓐ 대체할 수 없는
- flip ⓥ 뒤집다
- draw on ~을 이용하다

구문 풀이

1행 It has been reported [that 42 percent of jobs in Canada are at risk, and
　　　　가주어
62 percent of jobs in America will be in danger due to advances in automation].
　　　　　　　　　　　　　　　　　　　　　　　　　　[ ]: 진주어

---

37 너도밤나무의 광합성　　　정답률 52% | 정답 ⑤

주어진 글 다음에 이어질 글의 순서로 가장 적절한 것을 고르시오. [3점]

① (A) - (C) - (B)
② (B) - (A) - (C)
③ (B) - (C) - (A)
④ (C) - (A) - (B)
⑤ (C) - (B) - (A) ✓

Each beech tree grows in a particular location / and soil conditions can vary greatly / in just a few yards.
각각의 너도밤나무는 고유한 장소에서 자라고 / 토양의 조건은 크게 달라질 수 있다. / 단 몇 야드 안에서도

The soil can have a great deal of water / or almost no water.
토양은 물이 많거나 / 거의 없을 수도 있다.

It can be full of nutrients or not.
그것은 영양분이 가득할 수도 있고 아닐 수도 있다.

(C) Accordingly, / each tree grows more quickly or more slowly / and produces more or less sugar, / and thus you would expect every tree / to be photosynthesizing at a different rate.
이에 따라, / 각 나무는 더 빨리 혹은 더 느리게 자라고 / 더 많거나 더 적은 당분을 생산하는데, / 그래서 여러분은 모든 나무가 ~할 거라고 기대할 것이다. / 다른 정도로 광합성을 할 거라고

(B) However, the rate is the same.
그러나 그 정도는 동일하다.

Whether they are thick or thin, / all the trees of the same species / are using light / to produce the same amount of sugar per leaf.
그것들이 굵든 가늘든 간에, / 같은 종의 모든 나무들은 / 빛을 사용하고 있다. / 이파리당 같은 양의 당을 생산하기 위해

Some trees have plenty of sugar / and some have less, / but the trees equalize this difference between them / by transferring sugar.
어떤 나무들은 충분한 당을 지니고 / 어떤 것들은 더 적게 지니지만, / 나무들은 그들 사이의 이 차이를 균등하게 한다. / 당을 전달하여

(A) This is taking place underground through the roots.
이것은 뿌리들을 통해 지하에서 일어나고 있다.

Whoever has an abundance of sugar / hands some over; / whoever is running short / gets help.
풍부한 당을 가진 나무가 누구든 간에 / 일부를 건네주고, / 부족해지는 나무는 누구든 간에 / 도움을 받는다.

Their network acts as a system / to make sure that no trees fall too far behind.
그들의 연결망은 시스템 역할을 한다. / 그 어떤 나무도 너무 뒤처지지 않는 것을 확실히 하기 위한

각각의 너도밤나무는 고유한 장소에서 자라고 토양의 조건은 단 몇 야드 안에서도 크게 달라질 수 있다. 토양은 물이 많거나 거의 없을 수도 있다. 영양분이 가득할 수도 있고 아닐 수도 있다.

(C) 이에 따라, 각 나무는 더 빨리 혹은 더 느리게 자라고 더 많거나 더 적은 당분을 생산하는데, 그래서 여러분은 모든 나무가 다른 정도로 광합성을 할 거라고 기대할 것이다.

(B) 그러나 그 정도는 동일하다. 굵든 가늘든 간에, 같은 종의 모든 나무들은 빛을 사용하여 이파리당 같은 양의 당을 생산하고 있다. 어떤 나무들은 충분한 당을 지니고 어떤 것들은 더 적게 지니지만, 나무들은 당을 전달하여 그들 사이의 이 차이를 균등하게 한다.

(A) 이것은 뿌리들을 통해 지하에서 일어나고 있다. 풍부한 당을 가진 나무가 누구든 간에 일부를 건네주고, 부족해지는 나무는 누구든 간에 도움을 받는다. 그들의 연결망은 그 어떤 나무도 너무 뒤처지지 않는 것을 확실히 하기 위한 시스템 역할을 한다.

너도밤나무가 자라는 토양 조건이 상이할 수 있다는 내용의 주어진 글 뒤로, (C)는 그래서 (Accordingly) 광합성 정도가 나무마다 다를 것이라는 추측이 나올 수 있다고 한다. **However**로 시작하는 (B)는 사실은 그렇지 않다고 하며, 나무들끼리 서로 당을 주고받기 때문에 차이가 조절된다는 설명을 이어 간다. (A)는 이러한 '주고받음'이 뿌리를 통해 이뤄진다는 보충 설명과 함께, 나무끼리의 연결망이 각 나무에게 도움이 된다는 결론을 제시한다. 따라서 글의 순서로 가장 적절한 것은 ⑤ '(C) - (B) - (A)'이다.

- beech tree 너도밤나무
- abundance ⓝ 풍부함
- run short 부족해지다
- equalize ⓥ 동등하게 하다
- photosynthesize ⓥ 광합성하다
- a great deal of 많은
- hand over 건네주다
- fall behind 뒤처지다
- transfer ⓥ 전달하다

구문 풀이

5행 [Whoever has an abundance of sugar] hands some over; [whoever is
　　　　　　주어1　　　　　　　　　　　　　동사1(단수)　　　　　　　　주어2
running short] gets help.
　　　　　　동사2(단수)　　[ ]: 복합관계대명사절(~하는 누구든지)

★★★ 등급을 가르는 문제!

38 언어와 사고의 관계　　　정답률 42% | 정답 ⑤

글의 흐름으로 보아, 주어진 문장이 들어가기에 가장 적절한 곳을 고르시오. [3점]

Should we use language to understand mind / or mind to understand language?
우리는 사고를 이해하기 위해 언어를 사용해야 할까, / 아니면 언어를 이해하기 위해 사고를 사용해야 할까?

① Analytic philosophy historically assumes / that language is basic / and that mind would make sense / if proper use of language was appreciated.
분석 철학은 역사적으로 가정한다. / 언어가 기본이고 / 그 사고가 이치에 맞을 것이라고 / 적절한 언어 사용이 제대로 인식된다면

② Modern cognitive science, / however, / rightly judges / that language is just one aspect of mind / of great importance in human beings / but not fundamental to all kinds of thinking.
현대 인지 과학은 / 그러나 / 당연히 판단한다. / 언어가 사고의 한 측면일 뿐 / 인간에게 매우 중요한 / 하지만 모든 종류의 사고에 근본적이지 않다고

③ Countless species of animals / manage to navigate the world, / solve problems, / and learn / without using language, / through brain mechanisms / that are largely preserved in the minds of humans.
수많은 종의 동물들이 / 세계를 항해하고, / 문제를 해결하고, / 학습해낸다. / 언어를 사용하지 않고 / 두뇌의 메커니즘을 통해 / 인간의 사고 속에 대체로 보존된

④ There is no reason to assume / that language is fundamental to mental operations.
가정할 이유는 없다. / 언어가 정신 작용의 기본이라고

⑤ Nevertheless, / language is enormously important in human life / and contributes largely to our ability / to cooperate with each other / in dealing with the world. ✓
그럼에도 불구하고, / 언어는 인간의 삶에서 매우 중요하며 / 우리의 능력에 상당히 기여한다. / 서로 협력하는 / 세계를 다루는 데 있어서

Our species *homo sapiens* / has been astonishingly successful, / which depended in part on language, / first as an effective contributor / to collaborative problem solving / and much later, as collective memory / through written records.
우리 종인 호모 사피엔스는 / 놀라운 성공을 거두어 왔는데, / 이것은 언어에 부분적으로 의존했다. / 처음에는 효과적인 기여 요소로서, / 협력적인 문제 해결에 / 그리고 훨씬 나중에는 집단 기억으로서 / 글로 쓰인 기록을 통한

우리는 사고를 이해하기 위해 언어를 사용해야 할까, 아니면 언어를 이해하기 위해 사고를 사용해야 할까? ① 분석 철학은 언어가 기본이고 적절한 언어 사용이 제대로 인식된다면 그 사고가 이치에 맞을 것이라고 역사적으로 가정한다. ② 그러나 현대 인지 과학은 언어가 인간에게 매우 중요한 사고의 한 측면일 뿐 모든 종류의 사고에 근본적이지는 않다고 당연히 판단한다. ③ 수많은 종의 동물들이 인간의 사고 속에 대체로 보존된 두뇌의 메커니즘을 통해 언어를 사용하지 않고 세계를 항해하고, 문제를 해결하고, 학습해낸다. ④ 언어가 정신 작용의 기본이라고 가정할 이유는 없다. ⑤ 그럼에도 불구하고, 언어는 인간의 삶에서 매우 중요하며 세계를 다루는 데 있어서 서로 협력하는 우리의 능력에 상당히 기여한다. 우리 종족인 호모 사피엔스는 놀라운 성공을 거두어 왔는데, 이것은 처음에는 협력적인 문제 해결에 효과적인 기여 요소로서, 그리고 훨씬 나중에는 글로 쓰인 기록을 통한 집단 기억으로서의 언어에 부분적으로 의존했다.

Why? ◀ 왜 정답일까?

언어가 먼저인지 사고가 먼저인지 논하는 글로, 분석 철학과 현대 인지 과학의 시각이 대비되고 있다. ⑤ 앞까지는 주로 현대 인지 과학의 관점에서 언어가 중요하기는 해도 근본은 사고력에 있다는 내용이 제시된다. 하지만 주어진 문장은 언어가 매우 중요함을 강조하며 특히 인간의 협동 능력에 크게 기여한다는 내용으로 흐름의 반전을 이끈다. 이어서 ⑤ 뒤의 문장은 주어진 문장에서 언급한 '협력'과 관련해 언어가 중요했다는 내용을 다시금 설명한다. 따라서 주어진 문장이 들어가기에 가장 적절한 곳은 ⑤이다.

- **enormously** @ 대단히, 거대하게
- **deal with** ~을 다루다, ~에 대처하다
- **philosophy** ⓝ 철학
- **make sense** 이치에 맞다
- **fundamental** @ 근본적인
- **navigate** ⓥ 항해하다
- **contribute to** ~에 기여하다
- **analytic** @ 분석적인
- **historically** @ 역사적으로
- **appreciate** ⓥ 제대로 인식하다
- **countless** @ 무수히 많은
- **astonishingly** @ 놀랍도록

구문 풀이

13행 There is no reason to assume [that language is fundamental to mental operations]. [ ] : to assume의 목적어

★★ 문제 해결 꿀~팁 ★★

▶ 많이 틀린 이유는?
④ 앞뒤로 논리적 공백이 발생하는지 점검해 보면, 먼저 ④ 앞은 언어가 없는 동물도 세계를 항해하고 문제를 해결하는 데 문제가 없다는 내용이다. 한편 ④ 뒤는 그렇기에 언어가 정신 작용의 근간이라고 추정할 근거가 없다는 내용이다. 즉 ④ 앞을 근거로 ④ 뒤와 같은 결론을 내릴 수 있는 것이므로, ④의 위치에 논리적 공백은 발생하지 않는다.

▶ 문제 해결 방법은?
⑤ 앞은 언어가 정신 작용에 근본적이라고 추정할 필요는 없다는 내용인데, ⑤ 뒤는 호모 사피엔스의 성공에 언어가 부분적으로는 중요한 기여를 했다는 내용이다. 즉 ⑤ 앞뒤가 서로 반대되는 내용이므로, 사이에 적절한 역접어(Nevertheless)가 있어야 흐름이 자연스러워진다.

---

39 온도와 화학적 성질이 다른 물잔 섞기 정답률 48% | 정답 ③

글의 흐름으로 보아, 주어진 문장이 들어가기에 가장 적절한 곳을 고르시오.

Take two glasses of water.
물 두 잔을 가져와라.
Put a little bit of orange juice into one / and a little bit of lemon juice into the other.
하나의 잔에는 약간의 오렌지주스를 넣고, / 다른 잔에는 약간의 레몬주스를 넣어라.
① What you have / are essentially two glasses of water / but with a completely different chemical makeup.
여러분이 가지고 있는 것은 / 본질적으로 물 두 잔이다. / 완전히 다른 화학적 성질을 지닌
② If we take the glass containing orange juice / and heat it, / we will still have two different glasses of water / with different chemical makeups, / but now they will also have different temperatures.
만약 우리가 오렌지주스가 든 잔을 가져와서 / 그것을 가열한다면, / 우리는 여전히 서로 다른 물 두 잔을 가지고 있을 것이지만, / 다른 화학적 성질을 지닌 / 이제 그것들은 또한 다른 온도를 가질 것이다.
✓ If we could magically remove the glasses, / we would find / the two water bodies would not mix well.
만약 우리가 마법처럼 그 유리잔들을 없앨 수 있다면, / 우리는 알게 될 것이다. / 두 액체가 잘 섞이지 않는다는 것을
Perhaps they would mix a little / where they met; / however, / they would remain separate / because of their different chemical makeups and temperatures.
어쩌면 그것들은 조금 섞일 것이다. / 그것들이 접한 부분에서 / 하지만, / 이것은 분리된 상태로 남아 있을 것이다. / 다른 화학적 성질과 온도로 인해
④ The warmer water would float / on the surface of the cold water / because of its lighter weight.
더 따뜻한 물은 떠 있을 것이다. / 찬물의 표면에 / 그것의 무게가 더 가볍기 때문에
⑤ In the ocean we have bodies of water / that differ in temperature and salt content; / for this reason, / they do not mix.
바다에는 수역(물줄기)들이 있다. / 온도와 염분 함량이 다른 / 이러한 이유로, / 그것들은 섞이지 않는다.

물 두 잔을 가져와라. 하나의 잔에는 약간의 오렌지주스를 넣고, 다른 잔에는 약간의 레몬주스를 넣어라. ① 여러분이 가지고 있는 것은 본질적으로 물 두 잔이지만 둘은 완전히 다른 화학적 성질을 지녔다. ② 만약 우리가 오렌지주스가 든 잔을 가져와서 가열한다면, 우리는 여전히 다른 화학적 성질을 지닌 서로 다른 물 두 잔을 가지고 있을 것이지만, 이제 그것들은 또한 다른 온도를 가질 것이다. ③ 만약 우리가 마법처럼 그 유리잔들을 없앨 수 있다면, 우리는 두 액체가 잘 섞이지 않는다는 것을 알게 될 것이다. 어쩌면 그것들은 서로 접한 부분에서 조금 섞일 것이다. 하지만, 이것들은 다른 화학적 성질과 온도로 인해 분리된 상태로 남아 있을 것이다. ④ 더 따뜻한 물은 무게가 더 가볍기 때문에 찬물의 표면에 떠 있을 것이다. ⑤ 바다에는 온도와 염분이 다른 수역(물줄기)들이 있다. 이러한 이유로, 그것들은 섞이지 않는다.

Why? ◀ 왜 정답일까?

③ 앞까지는 물 두 잔에 각각 오렌지주스와 레몬주스를 섞어 성질을 달리하고, 한쪽에만 약간의 열을 더해 온도 또한 달리하는 과정을 설명한다. 여기에 이어 주어진 문장은 만일 이 상황에서 유리잔을 제거해 보면 두 액체가 서로 잘 섞이지 않는다는 사실을 알게 된다고 설명한다. ③ 뒤는 주어진 문장에 이어 두

액체가 서로 화학적 성질과 온도가 달라 섞이지 않는다고 설명한다. 따라서 주어진 문장이 들어가기에 가장 적절한 곳은 ③이다. 글은 원칙적으로 일반적 진술에서 구체적 진술로 나아가므로, ③에서 주어진 문장이 '두 액체가 안 섞인다'는 일반적 사실을 제시해야 ③ 뒤에서 '왜 안 섞이는지'에 대한 구체적 진술이 자연스럽게 이어질 수 있음을 유념해 둔다.

- **essentially** @ 본질적으로
- **separate** @ 분리된
- **content** ⓝ 함량
- **makeup** ⓝ 구성
- **float** ⓥ 뜨다

구문 풀이

1행 If we could magically remove the glasses, we would find the two water bodies would not mix well.
「if + 주어 + 과거 동사 ~」 「주어 + 조동사 과거 + 동사원형 : 가정법 과거」

---

40 성찰적 일기 쓰기의 긍정적 효과 정답률 52% | 정답 ②

다음 글의 내용을 한 문장으로 요약하고자 한다. 빈칸 (A), (B)에 들어갈 말로 가장 적절한 것은?

	(A)		(B)
①	factual 사실적인	······	rethinking 다시 생각하는 것
✓②	worthwhile 가치 있는	······	rethinking 다시 생각하는 것
③	outdated 구식인	······	generalizing 일반화하는 것
④	objective 객관적인	······	generalizing 일반화하는 것
⑤	demanding 까다로운	······	describing 기술하는 것

One of the most powerful tools / to find meaning in our lives / is reflective journaling / — thinking back on and writing about what has happened to us.
가장 강력한 도구 중 하나는 / 우리의 삶에서 의미를 찾기 위한 / 성찰적 일기 쓰기이다. / 즉 우리에게 일어난 일을 돌아보고 그것에 관해 쓰는
In the 1990s, / Stanford University researchers / asked undergraduate students on spring break / to journal about their most important personal values and their daily activities; / others were asked / to write about only the good things / that happened to them in the day.
1990년대에 / Stanford University 연구자들은 / 봄방학에 학부생들에게 요청했다. / 가장 중요한 개인적인 가치와 하루 활동에 대해 써보라고 / 다른 사람들은 요청받았다. / 좋은 일만 쓰도록 / 그날 있었던
Three weeks later, / the students who had written about their values / were happier, healthier, and more confident / about their ability to handle stress / than the ones who had only focused on the good stuff.
3주 후에, / 자신의 가치에 관해 썼던 학생들은 / 더 행복하고, 더 건강하고, 더 자신 있었다. / 스트레스에 대처할 수 있는 능력에 대해 / 좋은 것만 초점을 맞췄던 학생들보다
By reflecting on / how their daily activities supported their values, / students had gained a new perspective / on those activities and choices.
성찰하면서, / 어떻게 자신의 하루 일과가 자신의 가치관을 뒷받침하는지를 / 학생들은 새로운 관점을 얻었다. / 그 활동들과 선택들에 대해
Little stresses and hassles / were now demonstrations of their values in action.
작은 스트레스와 귀찮은 일들은 / 이제 그들의 가치가 행해지고 있음을 보여주는 것이었다.
Suddenly, / their lives were full of meaningful activities.
갑자기 / 그들의 삶은 의미 있는 활동으로 가득 찼다.
And all they had to do / was reflect and write about it / — positively reframing their experiences with their personal values.
그리고 그들이 해야 했던 일이라고는 / 그것에 대해 돌아보고 쓰는 것뿐이었다. / 그들의 경험을 개인적인 가치로 긍정적으로 재구성하면서
➡ Journaling about daily activities / based on what we believe to be (A) worthwhile / can make us feel / that our life is meaningful / by (B) rethinking our experiences in a new way.
일과에 관해 일기를 쓰는 것은 / 우리가 가치 있다고 믿는 것에 근거해 / 우리가 느끼게 만들 수 있다. / 우리 삶이 의미 있다고 / 새로운 방식으로 경험을 다시 생각하면서

우리의 삶에서 의미를 찾기 위한 가장 강력한 도구 중 하나는 성찰적 일기 쓰기, 즉 우리에게 일어난 일을 돌아보고 그것에 관해 쓰는 것이다. 1990년대에 Stanford University 연구자들은 봄방학에 학부생들에게 가장 중요한 개인적인 가치와 하루 활동에 대해 써보라고 요청했다. 다른 사람들은 그날 있었던 좋은 일만 쓰도록 요청받았다. 3주 후에, 자신의 가치에 관해 썼던 학생들은 좋은 것에만 초점을 맞췄던 학생들보다 더 행복하고, 더 건강하고, 스트레스에 대처할 수 있는 능력에 더 자신 있었다. 어떻게 자신의 하루 일과가 자신의 가치관을 뒷받침하는지를 성찰하면서, 학생들은 그 활동들과 선택들에 대해 새로운 관점을 얻었다. 작은 스트레스와 귀찮은 일들은 이제 그들의 가치가 행해지고 있음을 보여주는 것이었다. 갑자기 그들의 삶은 의미 있는 활동으로 가득 찼다. 그리고 그들이 해야 했던 일이라고는 그들의 경험을 개인적인 가치로 긍정적으로 재구성하면서 그것에 대해 돌아보고 쓰는 것뿐이었다.

➡ 우리가 (A) 가치 있다고 믿는 것에 근거해 일과에 관해 일기를 쓰는 것은 우리가 새로운 방식으로 경험을 (B) 다시 생각하면서 삶이 의미 있다고 느끼게 만들 수 있다.

Why? ◀ 왜 정답일까?

연구 결과를 정리하는 마지막 문장에서, 삶의 의미를 느끼기 위해 필요했던 일은 일과 중 있었던 경험을 가치관에 근거해 다시 생각해보고 정리하는 일뿐이었다(~ positively reframing their experiences with their personal values.)고 한다. 따라서 요약문의 빈칸 (A), (B)에 들어갈 말로 가장 적절한 것은 ② '(A) worthwhile(가치 있는), (B) rethinking(다시 생각하는 것)'이다.

- **reflective** @ 성찰적인
- **think back on** ~에 대해 되돌아보다
- **handle** ⓥ 대처하다, 다루다
- **perspective** ⓝ 관점, 시각
- **demonstration** ⓝ 입증, 시연
- **reframe** ⓥ 재구성하다
- **worthwhile** @ 가치 있는
- **demanding** @ 까다로운, 힘든
- **journaling** ⓝ 일기 쓰기
- **undergraduate** @ 학부의
- **support** ⓥ 뒷받침하다
- **hassle** ⓝ 귀찮은 일
- **in action** 활동 중인, 작용 중인
- **factual** @ 사실적인
- **outdated** @ 구식의

구문 풀이

14행 And all they had to do was reflect and write about it — positively
주어 / 동사 / 주격 보어(원형부정사)
reframing their experiences with their personal values.

Mike May lost his sight at the age of three.
Mike May는 세 살 때 시력을 잃었다.

Because he had spent the majority of his life / adapting to being blind / — and even cultivating a skiing career in this state — / his other senses compensated / by growing (a) stronger.
그는 인생 대부분을 보냈기 때문에, / 보이지 않는 데 적응하고, / 심지어 이 상태로 스키 경력을 쌓으면서 / 그의 다른 감각들은 보충되었다. / 더 강해지는 것으로

However, / when his sight was restored through a surgery in his forties, / his entire perception of reality / was (b) disrupted.
하지만 / 그의 시력이 40대에 수술로 회복되었을 때, / 현실에 대한 그의 전반적 인식은 / 지장을 받았다.

Instead of being thrilled / that he could see now, / as he'd expected, / 『his brain was so overloaded with new visual stimuli / that the world became a frightening and overwhelming place.』 42번의 근거
감격하는 대신, / 그가 이제 볼 수 있다는 데 / 그가 예상했던 것처럼, / 그의 뇌는 새로운 시각적 자극으로 과부하된 나머지 / 세상은 두렵고 압도적인 장소가 되었다.

After he'd learned to know his family / through touch and smell, / he found / that he couldn't recognize his children with his eyes, / and this left him puzzled.
그가 가족을 알아보는 것을 배운 후여서, / 만지는 것과 냄새를 통해 / 그는 알게 되었고, / 그가 자기 아이들을 눈으로는 알아볼 수 없다는 것을 / 이것은 그를 혼란스럽게 했다.

Skiing also became a lot harder / as he struggled to adapt to the visual stimulation.
스키 또한 훨씬 더 어려워졌다. / 그가 시각적인 자극에 적응하려고 힘쓰면서

This (c) confusion occurred / because his brain hadn't yet learned to see.
이 혼란은 생겼다. / 그의 뇌가 아직 보는 것을 배우지 못했기 때문에

Though we often tend to assume / our eyes function as video cameras / which relay information to our brain, / advances in neuroscientific research have proven / that this is actually not the case.
비록 우리는 흔히 가정하는 경향이 있지만, / 우리 눈이 비디오카메라 역할을 한다고 / 뇌에 정보를 전달하는 / 신경 과학 연구의 발전은 증명했다. / 이것이 실제로 그렇지 않다는 것을

『Instead, / sight is a collaborative effort / between our eyes and our brains, / and the way we process (d) visual reality / depends on the way these two communicate.』 41번의 근거
대신, / 시각은 협력적인 노력이며, / 우리의 눈과 뇌 사이의 / 우리가 시각적 현실을 처리하는 방법은 / 이 두 가지가 소통하는 방식에 달려 있다.

If communication between our eyes and our brains / is disturbed, / our perception of reality / is altered accordingly.
만약 우리의 눈과 뇌 사이의 의사소통이 / 방해된다면, / 현실에 대한 우리의 인식은 / 그에 따라 바뀐다.

And because other areas of May's brain / had adapted to process information / primarily through his other senses, / the process of learning how to see / was (e) more difficult / than he'd anticipated.
그리고 May의 뇌의 다른 부분들은 / 정보를 처리하는 것에 적응했기 때문에, / 주로 그의 다른 감각을 통해 / 보는 방법을 배우는 과정은 / 더 어려웠다. / 그가 예상했던 것보다

Mike May는 세 살 때 시력을 잃었다. 그는 보이지 않는 데 적응하고, 심지어 이 상태로 스키 경력을 쌓으면서 인생 대부분을 보냈기 때문에, 그의 다른 감각들은 (a) 더 강해지는 것으로 보충되었다. 하지만 그의 시력이 40대에 수술로 회복되었을 때, 현실에 대한 그의 전반적 인식은 (b) 지장을 받았다. 그가 예상했던 것처럼 이제 볼 수 있다는 데 감격하는 대신, 그의 뇌는 새로운 시각적 자극으로 과부하된 나머지 세상은 두렵고 압도적인 장소가 되었다. 그가 만지는 것과 냄새를 통해 가족을 알아보는 것을 배운 후여서, 그는 자기 아이들을 눈으로는 알아볼 수 없다는 것을 알게 되었고, 이것은 그를 혼란스럽게 했다. 스키 또한 그가 시각적인 자극에 적응하려고 힘쓰면서 훨씬 더 어려워졌다. 이 (c) 혼란은 그의 뇌가 아직 보는 것을 배우지 못했기 때문에 생겼다. 비록 우리는 흔히 우리 눈이 뇌에 정보를 전달하는 비디오카메라 역할을 한다고 가정하는 경향이 있지만, 신경 과학 연구의 발전은 이것이 실제로 그렇지 않다는 것을 증명했다. 대신, 시각은 우리의 눈과 뇌 사이의 협력적인 노력이며, 우리가 (d) 시각적 현실을 처리하는 방법은 이 두 가지가 소통하는 방식에 달려 있다. 만약 우리의 눈과 뇌 사이의 의사소통이 방해된다면, 현실에 대한 우리의 인식은 그에 따라 바뀐다. 그리고 May의 뇌의 다른 부분들은 주로 그의 다른 감각을 통해 정보를 처리하는 것에 적응했기 때문에, 보는 방법을 배우는 과정은 그가 예상했던 것보다 (e) 더 쉬웠다(→ 더 어려웠다).

- lose one's sight 시력을 잃다
- cultivate ⓥ 갈고 닦다, 배양하다
- restore ⓥ 회복하다, 복구하다
- overloaded ⓐ 과부하된
- overwhelming ⓐ 버거운, 압도적인
- relay ⓥ 전달하다
- anticipate ⓥ 예상하다
- ignore ⓥ 무시하다
- majority ⓝ 대다수, 대부분
- compensate ⓥ 보충하다, 보상하다
- disrupt ⓥ 지장을 주다, 방해하다
- stimulus (pl. stimuli) ⓝ 자극
- struggle to ~하느라 고생하다
- primarily ⓐⓓ 주로
- visualization ⓝ 시각화

구문 풀이

1행 Because he had spent the majority of his life adapting to being
「spend + 시간 + 동명사1 +
blind — and even cultivating a skiing career in this state — his other senses
동명사2 : ~하고 ~하면서 시간을 보내다」
compensated by growing stronger.

---

41 제목 파악   정답률 65% | 정답 ①

윗글의 제목으로 가장 적절한 것은?

✔① Eyes and Brain Working Together for Sight – 시각을 위해 함께 일하는 눈과 뇌
② Visualization: A Useful Tool for Learning – 시각화: 유용한 학습 도구
③ Collaboration Between Vision and Sound – 시각과 청각 사이의 협력
④ How to Ignore New Visual Stimuli – 새로운 시각적 자극을 어떻게 무시하는가
⑤ You See What You Believe – 여러분은 보이는 것을 믿는다

Why? 왜 정답일까?

어린 시절 시각을 잃어 다른 감각으로 사는 데 익숙해졌던 May가 시력을 회복하고서 더 어려움을 겪었던 사례를 통해, 시각적 정보 처리는 자연히 가능한 것이 아니고 눈과 뇌의 협력을 통해 가능하다는 (Instead, sight is a collaborative effort between our eyes and our brains, ~.)는 주제를 제시한 글이다. 따라서 글의 제목으로 가장 적절한 것은 ① '시각을 위해 함께 일하는 눈과 뇌'이다.

---

42 어휘 추론   정답률 55% | 정답 ⑤

밑줄 친 (a) ~ (e) 중에서 문맥상 낱말의 쓰임이 적절하지 않은 것은?

① (a)   ② (b)   ③ (c)   ④ (d)   ✔⑤ (e)

Why? 왜 정답일까?

글에 따르면 May는 시력 회복 수술 후 시각 정보로 인해 뇌가 과부하되어 일상에서 예상보다 더 큰 지장을 겪게 되었다(~ his brain was so overloaded with new visual stimuli that the world became a frightening and overwhelming place.)고 한다. 이를 근거로 볼 때, May가 '보는 법'을 익히는 것은 예상보다 더 '어려웠다'는 의미가 되도록 ⑤의 easier를 more difficult로 고쳐야 한다. 따라서 문맥상 낱말의 의미가 적절하지 않은 것은 ⑤이다.

43-45 생일 선물로 받은 곰 인형을 다시 선물한 Marie

(A)

On my daughter Marie's 8th birthday, / she received a bunch of presents / from her friends at school.
우리 딸 Marie의 8번째 생일에, / 그녀는 많은 선물을 받았다. / 학교 친구들에게

『That evening, / with her favorite present, a teddy bear, in her arms, / we went to a restaurant / to celebrate her birthday.』 45번 ①의 근거 일치
그날 저녁, / 그녀가 가장 좋아한 선물인 테디 베어를 팔에 안고 / 우리는 식당에 갔다. / 그녀의 생일을 축하하러

Our server, a friendly woman, / noticed my daughter holding the teddy bear / and said, / "My daughter loves teddy bears, too."
다정한 여성이었던 종업원은 / 우리 딸이 테디 베어를 안고 있다는 것을 알아차렸고, / 말했다. / "제 딸도 테디 베어를 좋아해요." 라고

Then, / we started chatting about (a) her family.
그러고 나서 우리는 그녀의 가족에 대해 이야기를 나누기 시작했다.

(D)

『The server mentioned during the conversation / that her daughter was in the hospital with a broken leg.』 45번 ④의 근거 불일치
대화 도중 그 종업원은 말했다. / 자신의 딸이 다리가 부러져 병원에 있다고

(e) She also said / that Marie looked about the same age as her daughter.
또한 그녀는 말했다. / Marie가 자기 딸과 거의 또래 같아 보인다고

『She was so kind and attentive all evening, / and even gave Marie cookies for free.』 45번 ⑤의 근거 일치
그녀는 저녁 내내 매우 친절하고 세심했고 / 심지어 Marie에게 쿠키를 무료로 주었다.

After we finished our meal, / we paid the bill / and began to walk to our car / when unexpectedly Marie asked me to wait / and ran back into the restaurant.
우리가 식사를 마친 후 / 우리는 값을 지불하고 / 우리 차로 걸어가기 시작했는데 / 그때 갑자기 Marie가 내게 기다려 달라고 부탁하고 / 식당으로 다시 뛰어 들어갔다.

(B)

When Marie came back out, / I asked her what she had been doing.
Marie가 돌아왔을 때 / 나는 그녀에게 뭘 하고 왔는지 물었다.

She said / that she gave her teddy bear to our server / so that she could give it to (b) her daughter.
그녀는 말했다. / 자신의 테디 베어를 종업원에게 주어 / 그녀가 자기 딸에게 그것을 갖다 줄 수 있게 했다고

『I was surprised at her sudden action / because I could see / how much she loved that bear already.』 45번 ②의 근거 일치
나는 딸의 갑작스러운 행동에 놀랐다. / 내가 알 수 있었기에 / 딸아이가 이미 그 곰인형을 얼마나 좋아하는지

(c) She must have seen the look on my face, / because she said, / "I can't imagine being stuck in a hospital bed. / I just want her to get better soon."
딸은 내 얼굴 표정을 분명히 봤을 것인데, / 왜냐하면 그녀가 말했기 때문이다. / "저는 병원 침대에 갇혀 있는 것을 상상할 수 없어요. / 그저 그 애가 빨리 나았으면 좋겠어요."라고

(C)

I felt moved by Marie's words / as we walked toward the car.
나는 그녀의 말에 감동받았다. / 우리가 차를 향해 걸어가면서

『Then, / our server ran out to our car / and thanked Marie for her generosity.』 45번 ③의 근거 일치
그때 / 우리의 종업원이 우리 차로 달려 나와 / Marie의 관대함에 고마워했다.

The server said / that (d) she had never had anyone / doing anything like that for her family before.
종업원은 말했다. / 그녀에게 한 명도 없었다고 / 전에는 자기 가족을 위해 그런 일을 해준

Later, / Marie said / it was her best birthday ever.
후에, / Marie는 말했다. / 그날이 최고의 생일이었다고

I was so proud of her empathy and warmth, / and this was an unforgettable experience for our family.
나는 그녀의 공감과 따뜻함이 너무 자랑스러웠고, / 이것은 우리 가족에게 잊을 수 없는 경험이었다.

(A)

우리 딸 Marie의 8번째 생일에, 그녀는 학교에서 친구들에게 많은 선물을 받았다. 그날 저녁, 그녀가 가장 좋아한 선물인 테디 베어를 팔에 안고 우리는 그녀의 생일을 축하하러 식당에 갔다. 다정한 여성이었던 종업원은 우리 딸이 테디 베어를 안고 있다는 것을 알아차렸고, "제 딸도 테디 베어를 좋아해요."라고 말했다. 그러고 나서 우리는 (a) 그녀의 가족에 대해 이야기를 나누기 시작했다.

(D)

대화 도중 그 종업원은 자신의 딸이 다리가 부러져 병원에 있다고 말했다. 또한 (e) 그녀는 Marie가 자기 딸과 거의 또래 같아 보인다고 말했다. 그녀는 저녁 내내 매우 친절하고 세심했고 심지어 Marie에게 쿠키를 무료로 주었다. 우리는 식사를 마친 후 값을 지불하고 차로 걸어가기 시작했는데 그때 갑자기 Marie가 내게 기다려 달라고 부탁하고 식당으로 다시 뛰어 들어갔다.

(B)

Marie가 돌아왔을 때 나는 그녀에게 뭘 하고 왔는지 물었다. 그녀는 자신의 테디 베어를 종업원에게 주어 (b) 자기 딸에게 그것을 갖다 줄 수 있게 했다고 말했다. 나는 딸아이가 이미 그 곰인형을 얼마나 좋아하는지 알 수 있었기에 딸의 갑작스러운 행동에 놀랐다. (c) 딸(Marie)은 내 얼굴 표정을 분명히 봤을 것인데, 왜냐하면 "저는 병원 침대에 갇혀 있는 것을 상상할 수 없어요. 그저 그 애가 빨리 나았으면 좋겠어요."라고 말했기 때문이다.

(C)

차를 향해 걸어가면서 나는 그녀의 말에 감동받았다. 그때 우리의 종업원이 우리 차로 달려

나와 Marie의 관대함에 고마워했다. 종업원은 전에는 (d) 그녀에게 그녀 가족을 위해 그런 일을 해준 사람이 한 명도 없었다고 했다. 후에 Marie는 그날이 최고의 생일이었다고 말했다. 나는 그녀의 공감과 따뜻함이 너무 자랑스러웠고, 이것은 우리 가족에게 잊을 수 없는 경험이었다.

- server ⓝ 종업원
- get well (병 등이) 낫다
- generosity ⓝ 관대함
- attentive ⓐ 주의 깊은, 세심한
- chat about ~에 관해 이야기하다
- moved ⓐ 감동한
- unforgettable ⓐ 잊을 수 없는

구문 풀이

(B) 5행 She must have seen the look on my face, because she said, "I can't
과거에 대한 강한 추측(~했음에 틀림없다)
imagine being stuck in a hospital bed. I just want her to get better soon."
목적어(수동 동명사)

43 글의 순서 파악   정답률 73% | 정답 ④

주어진 글 (A)에 이어질 내용을 순서에 맞게 배열한 것으로 가장 적절한 것은?
① (B) – (D) – (C)
② (C) – (B) – (D)
③ (C) – (D) – (B)
✓④ (D) – (B) – (C)
⑤ (D) – (C) – (B)

Why? 왜 정답일까?

필자가 딸인 Marie의 생일을 기념해 가족끼리 저녁 식사를 하러 갔다가 식당 종업원과 이야기를 나누었다는 내용의 (A) 뒤로, 종업원이 병원에 입원해 있는 Marie 또래의 딸에 관해 이야기했다는 내용의 (D), Marie가 그 딸을 위해 자신이 선물받은 테디 베어를 전해주었다는 내용의 (B), 필자와 종업원이 모두 감동했다는 결말의 (C)가 이어져야 자연스럽다. 따라서 글의 순서로 가장 적절한 것은 ④ '(D) – (B) – (C)'이다.

44 지칭 추론   정답률 62% | 정답 ③

밑줄 친 (a) ~ (e) 중에서 가리키는 대상이 나머지 넷과 **다른** 것은?
① (a)   ② (b)   ✓③ (c)   ④ (d)   ⑤ (e)

Why? 왜 정답일까?

(a), (b), (d), (e)는 the server, (c)는 Marie를 가리키므로, (a) ~ (e) 중에서 가리키는 대상이 다른 하나는 ③ '(c)'이다.

45 세부 내용 파악   정답률 69% | 정답 ④

윗글에 관한 내용으로 적절하지 **않은** 것은?
① Marie는 테디 베어를 팔에 안고 식당에 갔다.
② 'I'는 Marie의 갑작스러운 행동에 놀랐다.
③ 종업원은 Marie의 관대함에 고마워했다.
✓④ 종업원은 자신의 딸이 팔이 부러져서 병원에 있다고 말했다.
⑤ 종업원은 Marie에게 쿠키를 무료로 주었다.

Why? 왜 정답일까?

(D) 'The server mentioned during the conversation that her daughter was in the hospital with a broken leg.'에서 종업원의 딸은 팔이 아니라 다리가 부러져서 병원에 입원했음을 알 수 있다. 따라서 내용과 일치하지 않는 것은 ④ '종업원은 자신의 딸이 팔이 부러져서 병원에 있다고 말했다.'이다.

Why? 왜 오답일까?

① (A) 'That evening, with her favorite present, a teddy bear, in her arms, we went to a restaurant ~'의 내용과 일치한다.
② (B) 'I was surprised at her sudden action ~'의 내용과 일치한다.
③ (C) 'Then, our server ~ thanked Marie for her generosity.'의 내용과 일치한다.
⑤ (D) 'She ~ even gave Marie cookies for free.'의 내용과 일치한다.

Dictation 11
문제편 149쪽

01 melted away with the sun out / closed some of the trails / unavailable for hikers
02 follow the recipe as it is / just an example / as stated in the recipe
03 your game scenario / a thrill seeker / make some background music
04 my dream room drawing / a staircase next to the door / bring warmth to your room
05 draw caricatures of us / bring her own pencil / go get it right now
06 some potato chips / get one basket / Will that be all
07 I hurt my wrist / How did you get injured / sprained my wrist
08 make his own cereal bowl / a 10-minute drive / simply scan the QR code
09 limited to three minutes / public online voting / your enthusiastic participation
10 curtains for our bedroom / machine washable at home / completely block sunlight
11 the line for the rollercoaster / standing in line
12 all by himself / should ask him
13 Could you be more specific / usually dress up / a proper presentation of yourself
14 a little tight / in a different color / red and green in storage
15 a renowned psychology professor / eats a sandwich and feels sick / reschedule their meeting
16-17 varying the pitch or beat / over long distances / attached to its legs

어휘 Review Test 11
문제편 154쪽

A	B	C	D
01 고마워하는	01 essential	01 ⓝ	01 ⓘ
02 시작하다, 출시하다	02 recover from	02 ⓟ	02 ⓡ
03 목격하다	03 glacier	03 ⓠ	03 ⓐ
04 동행하다	04 besides	04 ⓘ	04 ⓠ
05 구부러지다	05 consumption	05 ⓑ	05 ⓘ
06 불안정한	06 afford	06 ⓚ	06 ⓓ
07 이로운	07 productivity	07 ⓜ	07 ⓔ
08 저항할 수 없는	08 capacity	08 ⓒ	08 ⓞ
09 먹잇감	09 stimulate	09 ⓔ	09 ⓑ
10 공감, 감정 이입	10 make sense	10 ⓐ	10 ⓕ
11 대체하다	11 illegal	11 ⓓ	11 ⓘ
12 ~에 기여하다	12 promote	12 ⓖ	12 ⓖ
13 성찰적인	13 jealous	13 ⓗ	13 ⓒ
14 (병 등이) 낫다	14 assemble	14 ⓘ	14 ⓚ
15 거의 ~ 않다	15 give away	15 ⓢ	15 ⓘ
16 비판	16 fascinating	16 ⓞ	16 ⓜ
17 염세적인, 비관적인	17 assign	17 ⓘ	17 ⓝ
18 미리	18 myth	18 ⓙ	18 ⓗ
19 입증하다	19 majority	19 ⓡ	19 ⓟ
20 동등하게 하다	20 habitat	20 ⓕ	20 ⓢ

• 정답 •

01 ② 02 ③ 03 ① 04 ⑤ 05 ② 06 ③ 07 ① 08 ④ 09 ④ 10 ③ 11 ① 12 ① 13 ⑤ 14 ② 15 ③
16 ④ 17 ⑤ 18 ⑤ 19 ⑤ 20 ③ 21 ④ 22 ③ 23 ① 24 ② 25 ④ 26 ④ 27 ② 28 ④ 29 ④ 30 ⑤
31 ② 32 ① 33 ② 34 ④ 35 ③ 36 ③ 37 ⑤ 38 ④ 39 ⑤ 40 ② 41 ① 42 ④ 43 ④ 44 ② 45 ⑤

★ 표기된 문항은 [등급을 가르는 문제]에 해당하는 문항입니다.

---

01 지하철 연장 운행 안내
정답률 63% | 정답 ②

다음을 듣고, 남자가 하는 말의 목적으로 가장 적절한 것을 고르시오.
① 지하철 앱 출시를 홍보하려고
☑ 지하철 연장 운행을 안내하려고
③ 지하철 운행 지연에 대해 사과하려고
④ 지하철 시설 보수 공사 일정을 공지하려고
⑤ 지하철 내 영화 촬영에 대한 양해를 구하려고

M : Hello, passengers.
안녕하세요, 승객 여러분.
I'm James Walker from the Greenville Subway System.
저는 Greenville Subway System의 James Walker입니다.
As you know, the international film festival will be held in our city next month.
아시다시피, 다음 달에 우리 시에서 국제 영화제가 열립니다.
Throughout the festival, some movies will run till late at night.
축제 기간 동안, 몇몇 영화는 밤 늦게까지 상영될 것입니다.
So, for our citizens' convenience, the Greenville City Council has decided to provide longer subway service hours during the festival.
그래서 시민 여러분의 편의를 위하여 Greenville 시의회에서는 축제 기간에 지하철 운행 시간을 연장하기로 결정했습니다.
All Greenville subway lines will run extra hours while the festival is going on.
축제가 진행되는 동안 Greenville 모든 지하철 노선이 연장 운행될 것입니다.
You can easily check the extended service schedules using the Greenville Subway App.
Greenville Subway 앱을 사용하시면 연장 운행 시간표를 쉽게 확인하실 수 있습니다.
I hope you can make the most of the festival experience with our services.
저희의 서비스로 여러분이 축제를 최대한 즐길 수 있기를 바랍니다.
Thank you.
감사합니다.

Why? 왜 정답일까?
'So, ~ the Greenville City Council has decided to provide longer subway service hours during the festival. All Greenville subway lines will run extra hours while the festival is going on.'에서 국제 영화제가 열리는 기간에 지하철이 연장 운행될 것임을 공지하고 있으므로, 남자가 하는 말의 목적으로 가장 적절한 것은 ② '지하철 연장 운행을 안내하려고'이다.

● convenience ⑪ 편의　　　　● extend ⓥ 연장하다
● make the most of ~을 최대한 활용하다

---

02 자외선 차단제를 바르도록 권하기
정답률 96% | 정답 ③

대화를 듣고, 여자의 의견으로 가장 적절한 것을 고르시오.
① 날씨가 더울수록 수분 보충이 중요하다.
② 적당한 준비 운동이 부상 위험을 줄인다.
☑ 흐린 날에도 자외선 차단제를 발라야 한다.
④ 햇빛이 강한 날에는 야외 활동을 자제해야 한다.
⑤ 화상을 입었을 때 신속하게 응급 처치를 해야 한다.

W : Good morning, Jason. It's sports day today. Do you have everything you need?
좋은 아침이야, Jason. 오늘은 운동회 날이지. 필요한 걸 다 챙겼니?
M : Yes, Mom. I put a water bottle, some snacks, and a towel in my bag. Is there anything I forgot?
네, 엄마. 전 물병이랑 간식 조금이랑 수건을 가방에 넣어뒀어요. 제가 잊은 게 있을까요?
W : What about sunblock? Did you put it on?
선크림은? 발랐니?
M : Sunblock? It's not sunny outside.
선크림이요? 밖에 햇빛이 밝지 않은 걸요.
W : Jason, you should wear sunblock even on a cloudy day.
Jason, 흐린 날에도 자외선 차단제를 발라야 해.
M : But I don't feel the sun in weather like this.
하지만 이런 날씨에는 해를 느낄 수 없잖아요.
W : Even if you don't feel the sun on your skin, the harmful light from the sun can damage your skin because the clouds don't block it.
피부로 해를 느낄 수는 없어도, 구름이 태양에서 나오는 해로운 광선을 막지 못하기 때문에 그것은 네 피부를 상하게 할 수 있어.
M : Really? You mean I can still get a sunburn even on a cloudy day?
정말요? 그럼 흐린 날에도 햇볕에 화상을 입을 수 있다는 말씀이세요?
W : Yes. That's why you shouldn't forget to wear sunblock even if it's not sunny outside.
그래. 그래서 바깥 날씨가 햇빛이 밝지 않아도 선크림을 잊지 말고 발라야 해.
M : I didn't know that. I'll put it on now.
몰랐어요. 지금 바를게요.

Why? 왜 정답일까?
'Jason, you should wear sunblock even on a cloudy day.' 이후로 여자는 아들인 남자에게 흐린 날에도 자외선 차단제를 발라야 한다고 말하며 그 이유를 설명하고 있다. 따라서 여자의 의견으로 가장 적절한 것은 ③ '흐린 날에도 자외선 차단제를 발라야 한다.'이다.

● sunblock ⑪ 자외선 차단제　　　　● harmful ⓐ 해로운
● get a sunburn 햇볕에 (심하게 타) 화상을 입다

---

03 세차 맡겼던 차 찾기
정답률 90% | 정답 ①

대화를 듣고, 두 사람의 관계를 가장 잘 나타낸 것을 고르시오.
☑ 세차장 직원 – 고객
② 청소 업체 직원 – 집주인
③ 중고차 판매원 – 구매자
④ 분실물 센터 직원 – 방문자
⑤ 액세서리 디자이너 – 의뢰인

M : Hello, Ms. Green. You came just on time.
안녕하세요, Green 씨. 시간 맞춰 오셨네요.
W : Really? I thought I was early.
정말요? 전 일찍 온 줄 알았어요.
M : No. Your car is over there. Follow me, please.
아니에요. 당신 차는 저쪽에 있어요. 저를 따라오세요.
W : Wow. All the dirt is gone. It looks like a new car.
와, 먼지가 다 없어졌네요. 새 차 같아요.
M : Yeah. But some stains were difficult to remove. It's better to have your car washed right after it gets dirty.
네. 그런데 몇몇 얼룩은 지우기 어려웠어요. 차가 더러워지면 바로 세차하시는 게 좋아요.
W : I went on a business trip for a month, so I didn't have time. I'll keep that in mind.
제가 한 달 동안 출장을 다녀와서 시간이 없었어요. 그걸 명심할게요.
M : Anyway, while cleaning the inside, we found this earring under the driver's seat.
그건 그렇고, 차 안을 치우다가 운전석 밑에서 이 귀고리를 찾았어요.
W : Really? I thought I had lost that. Thank you.
정말요? 전 잃어버린 줄 알았어요. 고맙습니다.
M : You're welcome. Would you like to pay by credit card or in cash?
천만에요. 신용카드로 결제하시겠어요, 아니면 현금으로 하시겠어요?
W : I'll pay in cash. Here you are.
현금 결제할게요. 여기요.
M : Okay. [Pause] Here is your receipt. And this is a discount coupon for our car wash center. You can use it on your next visit.
네. [잠시 멈춤] 여기 영수증이요. 그리고 이건 저희 세차장에서 쓰실 수 있는 할인 쿠폰입니다. 다음 번 방문하실 때 쓰시면 돼요.
W : That's nice. Thank you.
좋네요. 고맙습니다.

Why? 왜 정답일까?
'Your car is over there.', 'It's better to have your car washed right after it gets dirty.', 'Anyway, while cleaning the inside, we found this earring under the driver's seat.', 'And this is a discount coupon for our car wash center.' 등을 통해 남자가 세차장 직원이고, 여자가 차를 맡겼던 고객임을 알 수 있다. 따라서 두 사람의 관계로 가장 적절한 것은 ① '세차장 직원 – 고객'이다.

● stain ⑪ 얼룩　　　　● go on a business trip 출장 가다
● keep in mind 명심하다

---

04 신혼집 거실 사진 구경하기
정답률 86% | 정답 ⑤

대화를 듣고, 그림에서 대화의 내용과 일치하지 않는 것을 고르시오.

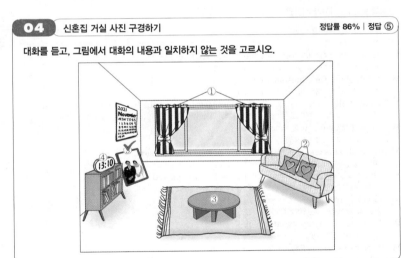

W : Hi, Harry. Congratulations on your wedding. Did you finish decorating the new house?
안녕, Harry. 결혼 축하해. 신혼집은 다 꾸몄어?
M : I just finished the living room. Look at this picture, Linda.
거실을 다 꾸민 참이야. 이 사진 봐, Linda.
W : Wow. 「I love the striped curtains on the window.」 ①의 근거 일치
와, 창문에 있는 줄무늬 커튼 마음에 들어.
M : Thanks. 「Do you see those two cushions on the sofa?」 My sister made them as wedding gifts. ②의 근거 일치
고마워. 소파에 있는 쿠션 두 개 보여? 내 여동생이 결혼 선물로 만들어줬어.
W : That's lovely. 「Oh, you put a round table on the rug.」 ③의 근거 일치
귀엽다. 오, 러그 위에 원형 탁자를 놓았네.
M : Yeah. We spend time reading books around the table. 「What do you think of the clock on the bookshelf?」 ④의 근거 일치
응. 우린 테이블 주위에서 독서하며 시간을 보내. 책장 위에 있는 시계는 어때?
W : It looks good in that room. 「By the way, is that a plant under the calendar?」 ⑤의 근거 불일치
그 방에 잘 어울리네. 그나저나, 달력 밑에 있는 건 식물이야?
M : Yes. I placed it there because the plant helps to clean the air.
응. 식물이 공기 정화에 도움이 되니까 놓아 뒀어.
W : You decorated your house really well.
넌 집을 참 잘 꾸몄구나.
M : Thanks. I'll invite you over when we have the housewarming party.
고마워. 우리가 집들이 할 때 널 초대할게.

Why? 왜 정답일까?
대화에 따르면 달력 밑에는 식물이 놓여 있다고 하는데(By the way, is that a plant under the

calendar?), 그림 속 달력 밑에는 결혼사진이 놓여 있다. 따라서 그림에서 대화의 내용과 일치하지 않는 것은 ⑤이다.

- decorate ⓥ 꾸미다, 장식하다
- spend time ~ing ~하며 시간을 보내다
- housewarming party 집들이

---

05 친환경 행사 전 마지막 점검하기 | 정답률 89% | 정답 ②

대화를 듣고, 남자가 할 일로 가장 적절한 것을 고르시오.
① 가방 준비하기　　　　　☑ 배지 가져오기
③ 스크린 점검하기　　　　④ 동영상 편집하기
⑤ 포스터 업로드하기

M : Jane, the Stop Using Plastic campaign starts tomorrow. Let's do a final check.
　Jane, Stop Using Plastic 캠페인이 내일 시작해. 마지막으로 점검하자.
W : Okay, Robin. I just finished editing a video clip about plastic waste.
　알겠어, Robin. 난 플라스틱 쓰레기에 관한 영상 편집을 막 끝냈어.
M : Then, I'm going to check the screen that we'll use for the video.
　그럼, 우리가 영상을 틀 때 쓸 스크린을 내가 확인할게.
W : No worries. I've already done it, and it works well.
　걱정 마. 내가 이미 했는데, 잘 작동하더라고.
M : That's nice. I uploaded a campaign poster on our organization's website.
　잘됐다. 난 우리 단체 웹 사이트에 캠페인 포스터를 올렸어.
W : Yeah. Some of my friends saw it and texted me they're coming.
　응. 내 친구들 중 몇몇이 그걸 보고 오겠다고 나한테 문자했어.
M : My friends, too. They showed a huge interest in the reusable bag decorating activity. The bags are ready in that box.
　내 친구들도. 그들은 재사용 가능한 가방 꾸미기 활동에 큰 관심을 보였어. 가방은 저 상자 안에 준비돼 있어.
W : Good. By the way, where are the badges you ordered for visitors?
　좋아. 그나저나, 방문객들을 위해 네가 주문했던 배지는 어디 있어?
M : Oh, I left the badges in my car. I'll bring them right away.
　오, 그 배지는 내 차에 놔 뒀어. 내가 지금 바로 가져올게.
W : Great. It seems that everything is prepared.
　좋아. 모든 게 준비된 것 같네.

Why? 왜 정답일까?

여자와 함께 행사 전 마지막 점검을 하던 남자는 방문객들을 위한 배지를 어디에 두었냐는 여자의 물음에 자신의 차에 두었다면서 바로 가져오겠다고 답한다(I'll bring them right away.). 따라서 남자가 할 일로 가장 적절한 것은 ② '배지 가져오기'이다.

- do a final check 최종 점검하다
- huge ⓐ 큰, 거대한
- reusable ⓐ 재사용 가능한

---

06 아들에게 줄 머플러와 양말 사기 | 정답률 85% | 정답 ③

대화를 듣고, 여자가 지불할 금액을 고르시오. [3점]
① $45　　② $50　　☑ $54　　④ $55　　⑤ $60

M : Welcome to Kids Clothing Club. How may I help you?
　Kids Clothing Club에 잘 오셨어요. 무엇을 도와드릴까요?
W : I'm looking for a muffler for my son. He's 5 years old.
　제 아들을 위한 머플러를 찾고 있어요. 아이는 5살이에요.
M : Okay. Follow me. [Pause] This red muffler is one of the best sellers in our shop.
　네. 따라 오시죠. [잠시 멈춤] 이 빨간 머플러가 저희 가게에서 제일 잘 나가는 상품 중 하나랍니다.
W : I love the color. How much is it?
　색이 마음에 드네요. 얼마인가요?
M : It's $50. This one is popular because of the cartoon character here.
　50달러입니다. 여기 있는 만화 캐릭터 때문에 인기가 많아요.
W : Oh, that's my son's favorite character. I'll buy one red muffler, then.
　오, 제 아들이 가장 좋아하는 캐릭터네요. 그럼 빨간 머플러 하나 살게요.
M : Great. Anything else?
　좋습니다. 더 필요한 것은 없으신가요?
W : How much are these winter socks?
　이 겨울 양말은 얼마인가요?
M : A pair of socks is $5.
　양말 한 켤레에 5달러입니다.
W : All right. I'll buy two pairs.
　좋아요. 두 켤레 사겠어요.
M : So, one red muffler and two pairs of winter socks, right?
　그럼, 빨간 머플러 하나에 겨울 양말 두 켤레 맞으시죠?
W : Yes. Can I use this discount coupon?
　네. 이 할인 쿠폰을 써도 되나요?
M : Of course. With that coupon, you can get 10% off the total price.
　물론입니다. 그 쿠폰이 있으시면 총 가격에서 10% 할인을 받으실 수 있어요.
W : Good. Here's my credit card.
　좋네요. 여기 제 신용 카드요.

Why? 왜 정답일까?

대화에 따르면 여자는 아들을 위해 50달러짜리 빨간 머플러를 하나 사고, 추가로 5달러짜리 겨울 양말을 두 켤레 구매한 뒤, 총 가격에서 10퍼센트를 할인받았다. 이를 식으로 나타내면 '50 + (5 × 2) × 0.9 = 54'이므로, 여자가 지불할 금액은 ③ '$54'이다.

- clothing ⓝ 의류
- muffler ⓝ 머플러, 목도리

---

07 런던 걷기 투어에 참여하지 못한 이유 | 정답률 88% | 정답 ①

대화를 듣고, 남자가 London Walking Tour에 참여하지 못한 이유를 고르시오.
☑ 발목에 통증이 있어서　　② 뮤지컬을 관람해야 해서
③ 투어 예약을 하지 못해서　　④ 기념품을 사러 가야 해서
⑤ 날씨로 인해 투어가 취소되어서

W : Hi, Jeremy. How was your trip to London?
　안녕, Jeremy. 런던 여행은 어땠어?
M : It was fantastic, Julia. I watched the musical you recommended.
　환상적이었어, Julia. 난 네가 추천했던 뮤지컬을 봤어.
W : Good. What about the London Walking Tour? Did you enjoy it?
　잘했어. London Walking Tour는 어땠어? 즐거웠어?
M : Unfortunately, I couldn't join the tour.
　안타깝게도, 난 투어에는 참여하지 못했어.
W : Why? Didn't you say you booked it?
　왜? 그거 예약했다고 하지 않았니?
M : Yes. I made a reservation for the tour in advance.
　응. 난 미리 투어를 예약했었지.
W : Oh, was the tour canceled because of the weather?
　오, 날씨 때문에 투어가 취소된 거야?
M : No. The weather was no problem at all.
　아니. 날씨는 전혀 문제가 아니었어.
W : Then, why couldn't you join the tour?
　그럼, 왜 투어에 참여할 수 없었던 거야?
M : Actually, I fell down the day before the tour, so I had some pain in my ankle. That's why I couldn't make it.
　사실, 난 투어 전날 넘어져서 발목이 아팠어. 그래서 갈 수가 없었어.
W : I'm sorry to hear that. Is it okay, now?
　그랬구나. 이제 괜찮아?
M : Yes. It's completely fine now. Oh, I forgot to bring the souvenir I bought for you. I'll bring it tomorrow.
　응. 지금은 완전히 멀쩡해. 오, 너한테 줄 기념품을 깜박 잊고 안 가져왔어. 내일 가져다 줄게.
W : That's so sweet. Thanks.
　상냥해라. 고마워.

Why? 왜 정답일까?

대화에 따르면 남자는 런던 걷기 투어 전날 넘어져서 발목이 아팠기에(Actually, I fell down the day before the tour, so I had some pain in my ankle.) 투어에 참가할 수 없었다. 따라서 남자가 London Walking Tour에 참여하지 못한 이유로 가장 적절한 것은 ① '발목에 통증이 있어서'이다.

- fall down 넘어지다
- ankle ⓝ 발목
- make it (시간 내에) 가다, 해내다

---

08 방학 때 가볼 겨울 축제 찾기 | 정답률 96% | 정답 ④

대화를 듣고, Winter Lake Festival에 관해 언급되지 <u>않은</u> 것을 고르시오.
① 기간　　　② 장소　　　③ 입장료
☑ 기념품　　⑤ 활동 종류

M : What are you doing, Laura?
　뭐 하고 있어, Laura?
W : Hi, Tim. I'm looking for winter festivals to visit during vacation.
　안녕, Tim. 난 방학 동안 가볼 겨울 축제를 찾아보고 있어.
M : Is there anything good?
　좋은 것 좀 있어?
W : Yes, look at this. There is a new local event called the Winter Lake Festival.
　응, 이거 봐. Winter Lake Festival이라고 불리는 새로운 지역 행사야.
M : Awesome. 『When does it start?』
　근사하네. 언제부터야?
W : December 18th and it'll be held for two weeks.』 ①의근거 일치
　12월 18일부터 2주 동안 열려.
M : Cool. 『Oh, it'll take place in Stevenson Park.』 ②의근거 일치
　멋지다. 오, Stevenson Park에서 열리네.
W : Great. It's near our school. If you don't have any plans during vacation, let's go together.
　응. 우리 학교랑 가까워. 너 방학에 계획 없으면 같이 가자.
M : Of course. 『Is there an entrance fee?』
　물론이지. 입장료가 있어?
W : Yes. Here, it says $3.』 It's not expensive. ③의근거 일치
　응. 여기 보면 3달러라고 쓰여 있어. 비싸지 않아.
M : Good. Look! 『There are so many kinds of activities to enjoy.』
　좋다. 이것 봐! 즐길 수 있는 활동이 무척 많네.
W : Yeah, there is ice skating, ice fishing, and a snowball fight.』 ⑤의근거 일치
　응. 스케이트, 얼음 낚시, 눈싸움이 있어.
M : They all sound exciting. Let's have fun there.
　다 재미있겠다. 가서 즐기자.

Why? 왜 정답일까?

대화에서 남자와 여자는 Winter Lake Festival의 기간, 장소, 입장료, 활동 종류를 언급한다. 따라서 언급되지 않은 것은 ④ '기념품'이다.

Why? 왜 오답일까?

① '~ it'll be held for two weeks.'에서 '기간'이 언급되었다.
② '~ it'll take place in Stevenson Park.'에서 '장소'가 언급되었다.
③ '~ it says $3.'에서 '입장료'가 언급되었다.
⑤ '~ there is ice skating, ice fishing, and a snowball fight.'에서 '활동 종류'가 언급되었다.

- take place (행사 등이) 열리다, 개최하다
- entrance fee 입장료

---

09 축구 팀 마스코트 디자인 경연대회 안내 | 정답률 91% | 정답 ④

Mascot Design Contest에 관한 다음 내용을 듣고, 일치하지 <u>않는</u> 것을 고르시오.
① 팀을 사랑하는 누구든 참여할 수 있다.
② 디자인은 팀 슬로건과 관련되어야 한다.
③ 수상작은 팬 투표로 선정될 것이다.
☑ 수상자는 상으로 시즌 티켓을 받게 될 것이다.
⑤ 참가 희망자는 디자인을 이메일로 보내야 한다.

W : Hello, supporters!
안녕하세요, 후원자 여러분!

I'm Christine Miller, manager of Western Football Club.
저는 Western Football Club의 매니저인 Christine Miller입니다.

This year, we're holding a Mascot Design Contest to celebrate our team's 1st championship.
올해, 저희 첫 우승을 기념하기 위해 Mascot Design Contest를 개최할 예정입니다.

「Anyone who loves our team can participate in this contest.」 ①의근거 일치
저희 팀을 사랑하는 분이라면 누구든 이 대회에 참여하실 수 있습니다.

「The mascot design should be related to our team's slogan "One team, one spirit."」 ②의근거 일치
마스코트 디자인은 저희 팀 슬로건인 '하나의 팀, 하나의 정신'과 관련되어야 합니다.

「The winning design will be chosen through a fan vote.」 ③의근거 일치
수상작은 팬 투표로 선정될 것입니다.

「And the winner will receive a team uniform as a prize.」 ④의근거 불일치
그리고 수상자는 상으로 팀 유니폼을 받게 될 것입니다.

「People who want to participate should send their design by email by December 5th.」 ⑤의근거 일치
참여하시고 싶은 분들은 12월 5일까지 이메일로 디자인을 보내주셔야 합니다.

Show your creativity and love for our team through active participation.
적극적인 참여로 여러분의 창의력과 저희 팀에 대한 사랑을 보여주세요.

For more information, please visit our website.
더 많은 정보가 필요하시면, 저희 웹 사이트를 방문해 주세요.

Thank you.
고맙습니다.

Why? 왜 정답일까?

'And the winner will receive a team uniform as a prize.'에서 수상자는 상으로 팀 유니폼을 받게 된다고 하므로, 내용과 일치하지 않는 것은 ④ '수상자는 상으로 시즌 티켓을 받게 될 것이다.'이다.

Why? 왜 오답일까?

① 'Anyone who loves our team can participate in this contest.'의 내용과 일치한다.
② 'The mascot design should be related to our team's slogan ~'의 내용과 일치한다.
③ 'The winning design will be chosen through a fan vote.'의 내용과 일치한다.
⑤ 'People who want to participate should send their design by email by December 5th.'의 내용과 일치한다.

● be related to ~와 관련되다   ● vote ⓝ 투표

---

10 캠핑장 고르기   정답률 92% | 정답 ③

다음 표를 보면서 대화를 듣고, 두 사람이 예약할 캠핑장을 고르시오.

2021 Best Campsites

	Campsite	Location	Price (per night)	Type	Kids' Playground
①	A	Seaside	$65	tent	×
②	B	Jungle Hut	$70	tent	○
③	C	Rose Valley	$85	camping car	○
④	D	Blue Forest	$90	camping car	×
⑤	E	Pine Island	$110	camping car	○

W : Honey, what are you looking at?
여보, 뭘 보고 있어요?

M : This is a list of the best campsites in 2021. How about going to one of them next month?
2021년 최고의 캠핑장 목록이에요. 다음 달에 이곳 중 한 군데에 가보면 어때요?

W : Sounds great. Let me see. [Pause] There are five different campsites.
좋아요, 나도 볼게요. [잠시 멈춤] 다섯 개 다른 캠핑장이 있네요.

M : Yeah. 「Since we went to Seaside campsite last time, let's choose among the other four.」 근거1 Location 조건
네. 지난번에 우리는 Seaside 캠핑장에 갔다 왔으니까, 다른 네 곳 중에서 고르죠.

W : Good. 「Hmm, I don't want to spend more than $100 per night.」 It's too expensive. 근거2 Price 조건
좋아요, 흠, 1박에 100달러 넘게 쓰고 싶지는 않아요. 너무 비싸요.

M : I agree with that. 「What do you think of staying in a camping car?」
동의해요. 캠핑카에서 묵는 건 어때요? 근거3 Type 조건

W : Oh, I want to try it. It'll be a special experience. 근거3 Type 조건
오, 해보고 싶어요. 특별한 경험이 될 거예요.

M : Then, we can choose between these two.
그럼, 이 두 곳 중 고르죠.

W : What about going to this campsite? 「Since this has a kids' playground, our children can have more fun.」 근거4 Kids' Playground 조건
이 캠핑장은 어때요? 아이들 놀이터가 있으니까, 우리 아이들이 더 재미있게 놀 수 있을 거예요.

M : Cool! I'll make a reservation for this campsite.
좋아요! 이 캠핑장으로 예약할게요.

Why? 왜 정답일까?

대화에 따르면 남자와 여자는 Seaside에 위치해 있지 않으면서, 가격은 1박에 100달러를 넘지 않고, 캠핑카 형태에, 아이들 놀이터를 갖추고 있는 캠핑장을 예약하기로 한다. 따라서 두 사람이 예약할 캠핑장은 ③ 'C'이다.

● campsite ⓝ 캠핑장   ● What do you think of ~? ~을 어떻게 생각해요?
● playground ⓝ 놀이터, 운동장

---

11 이사한 사무실이 어떤지 물어보기   정답률 87% | 정답 ①

대화를 듣고, 남자의 마지막 말에 대한 여자의 응답으로 가장 적절한 것을 고르시오.

✔① It takes an hour by bus. – 버스로 한 시간 걸려.
② It's bigger than your office. – 너희 사무실보다 커.
③ You should've left home earlier. – 집에서 더 일찍 나왔어야지.
④ The company moved last month. – 회사는 지난달에 이사했어.
⑤ I had a hard time getting the job. – 난 일자리를 구하느라 힘들었어.

M : Kate, I heard your company moved to a new office. How is it?
Kate, 난 너희 회사가 새 사무실로 이사했다고 들었어. 어때?

W : It's all good except one thing. It's far from my house.
하나 빼고 다 좋아. 우리 집에서 멀어.

M : Oh, really? How long does it take to get there?
아, 정말? 가는 데 얼마나 걸려?

W : It takes an hour by bus.
버스로 한 시간 걸려.

Why? 왜 정답일까?

남자는 여자가 새 사무실까지 가는 데 얼마나 걸리는지 궁금해하고 있으므로(How long does it take to get there?), 여자의 응답으로 가장 적절한 것은 ① '버스로 한 시간 걸려.'이다.

● How long does it take to ~? ~하는 데 얼마나 걸려?
● have a hard time ~ing ~하느라 힘들다

---

12 조카를 위해 피자 주문하기   정답률 95% | 정답 ①

대화를 듣고, 여자의 마지막 말에 대한 남자의 응답으로 가장 적절한 것을 고르시오.

✔① Okay. I'll order a shrimp pizza. – 알겠어요. 새우 피자를 주문할게요.
② Thanks. You're good at cooking. – 고마워요. 당신은 요리를 잘하네요.
③ No. The pizza isn't delivered yet. – 아니요. 피자 배달은 아직 안 왔어요.
④ Sure. You can come over anytime. – 물론이죠. 당신은 언제든 와도 돼요.
⑤ Yes. Skipping meals is bad for your health. – 네. 식사를 거르는 것은 건강에 나빠요.

W : Honey, you know my nephew is coming over this evening. How about ordering pizza for dinner?
여보, 당신도 알다시피 오늘 저녁에 내 조카가 와요. 저녁으로 피자를 시키는 게 어때요?

M : Sure. Which topping does he prefer, grilled beef or shrimp?
좋아요. 그는 구운 소고기랑 새우 중 어떤 토핑을 좋아하나요?

W : Oh, he doesn't like beef. He loves seafood.
오, 그는 소고기를 안 좋아해요. 해산물을 좋아해요.

M : Okay. I'll order a shrimp pizza.
알겠어요. 새우 피자를 주문할게요.

Why? 왜 정답일까?

여자가 조카를 위해 피자를 주문하자고 제안하자 남자는 조카가 어떤 토핑을 좋아하는지 묻고, 이에 여자는 조카가 해산물을 좋아한다(Oh, he doesn't like beef. He loves seafood.)고 답해준다. 따라서 남자의 응답으로 가장 적절한 것은 ① '알겠어요. 새우 피자를 주문할게요.'이다.

● come over (집에) 들르다   ● grill ⓥ (석쇠에) 굽다
● skip a meal 식사를 거르다

---

13 지역 도서관 행사에 아이 데려가기   정답률 84% | 정답 ⑤

대화를 듣고, 남자의 마지막 말에 대한 여자의 응답으로 가장 적절한 것을 고르시오.

Woman :
① Too late. The meeting is already over. – 너무 늦었어요. 미팅은 이미 끝났어요.
② Sure. There are lots of French cookbooks. – 물론이죠. 프랑스 요리책이 많아요.
③ I agree. You spend too much time reading. – 동의해요. 당신은 독서에 너무 많은 시간을 써요.
④ No. We're not allowed to eat in the library. – 아니에요. 우리 도서관에서 음식을 먹지 못하게 되어 있어요.
✔⑤ You're right. I'll change the reservation now. – 당신 말이 맞아요. 예약을 지금 바꿀게요.

M : Honey, did you read this leaflet on the table?
여보, 탁자 위에 있는 이 전단지 읽어봤어요?

W : Not yet. What's it about?
아직이요. 뭐에 관한 거예요?

M : It says the local children's library is going to hold some events to celebrate their reopening.
지역 어린이 도서관이 재개관을 기념하기 위해서 몇 가지 행사를 주최할 예정이래요.

W : Is there anything good?
좋은 게 있어요?

M : Let me see. [Pause] There will be a Meet-the-Author event. Rebecca Moore is coming.
살펴볼게요. [잠시 멈춤] 작가와의 만남 행사가 있을 거예요. Rebecca Moore가 온대요.

W : Oh, she's one of our son's favorite writers.
오, 우리 아들이 가장 좋아하는 작가 중 한 명이에요.

M : Yes. He'll be excited if he can meet her in person.
맞아요. 그 작가를 직접 만날 수 있으면 아이는 신날 거예요.

W : Let's take him to that event. When is it?
아이를 그 행사에 데려가죠. 언제예요?

M : It's next Saturday, 1 p.m.
다음 주 토요일 오후 1시예요.

W : But we have a lunch reservation at the French restaurant at that time.
하지만 그때 우리는 프렌치 식당에 점심 예약이 되어 있어요.

M : Oh, I forgot. Then how about rescheduling lunch? It's a rare chance to meet the author.
오, 내가 잊었네요. 그럼 점심 일정을 조정하는 게 어때요? 그 작가를 만나볼 드문 기회니까요.

W : You're right. I'll change the reservation now.
당신 말이 맞아요. 예약을 지금 바꿀게요.

Why? 왜 정답일까?

대화에 따르면 남자와 여자는 지역 도서관 행사에서 주최하는 작가와의 만남 행사에 아들을 데려가려 하는데, 행사 일정이 점심 예약과 겹친다. 이에 남자는 작가와의 만남은 드문 기회이니 점심 일정을 조정하자고 제안하므로(Then how about rescheduling lunch?), 여자의 응답으로 가장 적절한 것은 ⑤ '당신 말이 맞아요. 예약을 지금 바꿀게요.'이다.

● leaflet ⓝ 전단지   ● author ⓝ 작가, 저자
● in person 직접   ● rare ⓐ 드문, 희귀한

14 노트북 배터리 교체 권하기　　정답률 82% | 정답 ②

대화를 듣고, 여자의 마지막 말에 대한 남자의 응답으로 가장 적절한 것을 고르시오. [3점]

Man:

① Sorry. I forgot to bring my laptop. – 죄송해요. 제가 노트북 가져가는 걸 깜빡했어요.
✔② Then, I'd like to replace the battery. – 그럼, 배터리를 교체하고 싶어요.
③ Well, the screen still doesn't work well. – 음, 액정이 여전히 제 기능을 못하네요.
④ Good. A new repair shop opened yesterday. – 좋아요. 새 수리점이 어제 문을 열었어요.
⑤ Actually, I don't have a receipt for a refund. – 사실, 전 환불을 위한 영수증이 없어요.

[Cell phone rings.]
[휴대 전화 벨이 울린다.]

W : This is Fairview Laptop Repair. How may I help you?
　Fairview Laptop Repair입니다. 무엇을 도와드릴까요?
M : Hello, this is David Brown. I missed your call this morning.
　여보세요. 저는 David Brown입니다. 오늘 아침에 전화 주신 걸 못 받았어요.
W : Oh, Mr. Brown. You requested the screen repair yesterday, right?
　오, Brown 씨. 어제 액정 수리 요청하셨죠, 그렇죠?
M : Yes. Is there any problem?
　네. 문제가 있나요?
W : The screen is all repaired. But we found another problem with your laptop. You need to replace the battery.
　액정은 수리됐습니다. 그런데 노트북에 다른 문제가 있는 걸 발견했습니다. 배터리를 교체하셔야 해요.
M : Oh, I didn't know that. How bad is it?
　오, 그건 몰랐네요. 얼마나 심각한가요?
W : Even when the battery is fully charged, it won't last longer than an hour.
　배터리를 다 충전해도, 한 시간 이상 못 갈 거예요.
M : Really? How much does it cost to change the battery?
　정말요? 배터리를 교환하는 데 비용은 얼마나 드나요?
W : It's $70. It's on sale now.
　70달러입니다. 지금 할인 중이에요.
M : That sounds great. But, I'm worried it'll delay the laptop pick-up time, 5 p.m. today.
　괜찮네요. 그런데 그것이 노트북 수거 시간을 늦출까봐 걱정이에요. 오늘 오후 다섯 시거든요.
W : Don't worry. You can still pick it up at that time.
　걱정 마세요. 그래도 그 시간에 가져가실 수 있습니다.
M : Then, I'd like to replace the battery.
　그럼, 배터리를 교체하고 싶어요.

Why? 왜 정답일까?

대화에 따르면 여자는 액정 수리를 마친 남자의 노트북의 배터리를 함께 교체할 것을 권하는데, 남자는 만일 배터리를 교체하면 노트북 수거 일정이 늦어질까봐 고민이라고 말한다. 이에 여자는 배터리를 교체하더라도 예정된 시간에 노트북을 가져갈 수 있을 것이라고(Don't worry. You can still pick it up at that time.) 말하므로, 남자의 응답으로 가장 적절한 것은 ② '그럼, 배터리를 교체하고 싶어요.'이다.

● replace ⓥ 교체하다　　　　● last ⓥ 지속되다
● delay ⓥ 늦추다

15 포스터 글자 크기를 키워달라고 제안하기　　정답률 87% | 정답 ③

다음 상황 설명을 듣고, Amy가 Terry에게 할 말로 가장 적절한 것을 고르시오. [3점]

Amy:

① How about using a colorful font on the poster? – 포스터에 알록달록한 글자를 쓰면 어때?
② You'd better inform your friends of the concert. – 친구들에게 콘서트에 대해 알려줘야 해.
✔③ Can you make the letter size bigger on the poster? – 포스터에 있는 글자 크기를 더 키워줄 수 있어?
④ Why don't we hold a concert in the school festival? – 학교 축제에서 콘서트를 열면 어때?
⑤ You should put important information on the poster. – 포스터에는 중요한 정보를 넣어야 해.

M : Amy is the leader of a high school band and Terry is one of the band members.
　Amy는 고등학교 밴드부장이고 Terry는 부원 중 한 명이다.
　The band is going to hold a mini concert in the school festival, and Terry is in charge of making a concert poster.
　밴드에서는 학교 축제 때 미니 콘서트를 열 계획이고, Terry는 콘서트 포스터 제작 담당이다.
　When he completes the poster, he shows it to the band members.
　그가 포스터 작업을 마치고, 그는 그것을 밴드부원들에게 보여준다.
　Even though the poster has all the necessary information, it's hard to read it because the size of the letters is too small.
　포스터에 모든 정보가 다 담겨 있기는 하지만, 글자 크기가 너무 작아서 그것을 읽기 힘들다.
　Amy thinks if Terry changes the font size to a larger one, it could be easier to notice.
　Amy는 Terry가 글자 크기를 좀 더 크게 바꾼다면 눈에 띄기 쉬울 것이라 생각한다.
　So, Amy wants to suggest that Terry increase the size of the letters on the poster.
　그래서 Amy는 Terry에게 포스터에 있는 글자 크기를 키워달라고 제안하고 싶다.
　In this situation, what would Amy most likely say to Terry?
　이 상황에서, Amy는 Terry에게 뭐라고 말할 것인가?
Amy : Can you make the letter size bigger on the poster?
　포스터에 있는 글자 크기를 더 키워줄 수 있어?

Why? 왜 정답일까?

상황에 따르면 Amy는 Terry에게 포스터 글자 크기를 키워달라고 제안하고자 하므로(So, Amy wants to suggest that Terry increase the size of the letters on the poster.), Amy가 Terry에게 할 말로 가장 적절한 것은 ③ '포스터에 있는 글자 크기를 더 키워줄 수 있어?'이다.

● be in charge of ~을 담당하다　　● inform A of B A에게 B를 알리다

16-17 그늘에서도 잘 자라는 식물

W : Hello, students.
　안녕하세요, 학생 여러분.
　Previously, we discussed why gardening is a great hobby.
　지난 시간에 우리는 왜 정원 가꾸기가 훌륭한 취미인지 토의했습니다.
　But not everyone has a sunny front yard.
　하지만 모두가 볕이 잘 드는 앞마당을 갖고 있는 것은 아니죠.
　So, today we'll learn about plants that grow even in shade. 16번의 근거
　그래서 오늘은 그늘에서도 자라는 식물들에 관해 배워보겠습니다.
　First, lemon balm survives in full shade. 17번 ①의 근거 일치
　먼저, 레몬밤은 완전한 응달에서도 삽니다.
　So if your place is sunless, it's the plant you should choose.
　그래서 해가 안 드는 곳이라면, 이것이야말로 여러분이 골라야 하는 식물입니다.
　Next, ivy is the ultimate shade-loving plant. 17번 ②의 근거 일치
　다음으로, 담쟁이는 완전히 그늘을 좋아하는 식물입니다.
　Its ability to grow in shade makes it survive under trees where most plants can't.
　담쟁이가 그늘에서 자랄 수 있다는 점은 대부분의 식물이 살지 못하는 나무 아래서도 이것이 자랄 수 있게 합니다.
　Also, there's mint. 17번 ③의 근거 일치
　그리고 박하도 있죠.
　It lives well under low-light conditions, so you can grow it in a small pot indoors.
　그것은 조도가 낮은 환경에서 잘 자라서, 실내에서 작은 화분에 두고 키워도 됩니다.
　Lastly, camellia grows better in partial shade. 17번 ④의 근거 일치
　마지막으로, 동백나무는 그늘이 일부 있는 데서 더 잘 자랍니다.
　Especially when it's a young plant, it needs protection from the sun.
　특히 이것이 어린나무일 때 햇볕으로부터 보호되어야 합니다.
　Many plants like these can live even in the shade.
　이렇게 많은 식물들이 그늘에서도 살 수 있지요.
　Isn't it fascinating?
　흥미롭지 않나요?
　Now, let's watch a video clip about how to grow these plants.
　이제, 이 식물들을 어떻게 키우는지에 관한 영상을 보겠습니다.

● shade ⓝ 그늘　　　　　　● ultimate ⓐ 완전한, 궁극적인
● protection ⓝ 보호　　　　● factor ⓝ 요인

16 주제 파악　　정답률 86% | 정답 ④

여자가 하는 말의 주제로 가장 적절한 것은?

① ways to prevent plant diseases – 식물병을 예방하기 위한 방법
② factors that affect plant growth – 식물의 성장에 영향을 미치는 요인
③ benefits of growing plants at home – 집에서 식물을 키울 때의 이점
✔④ plants that can grow in shaded areas – 그늘진 곳에서도 자랄 수 있는 식물
⑤ materials that help plants grow in shade – 식물이 그늘에서 자라는 데 도움을 주는 물질

Why? 왜 정답일까?

'So, today we'll learn about plants that grow even in shade.'에서 여자는 그늘에서도 자라는 식물에 관해 배워보자고 하므로, 여자가 하는 말의 주제로 가장 적절한 것은 ④ '그늘진 곳에서도 자랄 수 있는 식물'이다.

17 언급 유무 파악　　정답률 93% | 정답 ⑤

언급된 식물이 아닌 것은?

① lemon balm – 레몬밤　　② ivy – 담쟁이　　③ mint – 박하
④ camellia – 동백나무　　✔⑤ lavender – 라벤더

Why? 왜 정답일까?

담화에서 여자는 그늘에서 자랄 수 있는 식물의 예로 레몬밤, 담쟁이, 박하, 동백나무를 언급하므로, 언급되지 않은 것은 ⑤ '라벤더'이다.

Why? 왜 오답일까?

① 'First, lemon balm survives in full shade.'에서 '레몬밤'이 언급되었다.
② 'Next, ivy is the ultimate shade-loving plant.'에서 '담쟁이'가 언급되었다.
③ 'Also, there's mint.'에서 '박하'가 언급되었다.
④ 'Lastly, camellia grows better in partial shade.'에서 '동백나무'가 언급되었다.

18 신문 이용에 관한 허락 구하기　　정답률 93% | 정답 ⑤

다음 글의 목적으로 가장 적절한 것은?

① 도서관 이용 시간 연장을 건의하려고
② 신청한 도서의 대출 가능 여부를 문의하려고
③ 도서관에 보관 중인 자료 현황을 조사하려고
④ 글쓰기 동아리 신문의 도서관 비치를 부탁하려고
✔⑤ 도서관에 있는 오래된 신문의 사용 허락을 요청하려고

To the school librarian,
학교 사서 선생님께,
I am Kyle Thomas, / the president of the school's English writing club.
저는 Kyle Thomas입니다. / 학교 영어 글쓰기 동아리 회장인
I have planned activities / that will increase the writing skills of our club members.
저는 활동들을 계획해 왔습니다. / 저희 동아리 회원들의 글쓰기 실력을 증진할
One of the aims of these activities / is / to make us aware of various types of news media / and the language used in printed newspaper articles.
이러한 활동들의 목표 중 하나는 / ~입니다. / 저희가 뉴스 미디어의 다양한 유형을 인식하게 만드는 것 / 그리고 인쇄된 신문 기사에 사용된 언어를
However, / some old newspapers are not easy to access online.
그러나 / 일부 오래된 신문은 온라인으로 접근하는 것이 쉽지 않습니다.
It is, therefore, my humble request to you / to allow us to use old newspapers / that have been stored in the school library.
그러므로 / 선생님께 드리는 저의 겸허한 요청입니다. / 저희가 오래된 신문을 사용할 수 있도록 허락해 달라는 것이 / 학교 도서관에 보관되어 온
I would really appreciate it / if you grant us permission.
정말 감사하겠습니다. / 만약 선생님께서 저희에게 허락해 주시면
Yours truly, // Kyle Thomas
Kyle Thomas 드림

학교 사서 선생님께,

저는 학교 영어 글쓰기 동아리 회장인 Kyle Thomas입니다. 저는 저희 동아리 회원들의 글쓰기 실력을 증진할 활동들을 계획해 왔습니다. 이러한 활동들의 목표 중 하나는 저희가 뉴스 미디어의 다양한 유형과 인쇄된 신문 기사에 사용된 언어를 인식하게 만드는 것입니다. 그러나 일부 오래된 신문은 온라인으로 접근하는 것이 쉽지 않습니다. 그러므로 학교 도서관에 보관되어 온 오래된 신문을 저희가 사용할 수 있도록 허락해 달라는 것이 선생님께 드리는 저의 겸허한 요청입니다. 만약 선생님께서 저희에게 허락해 주시면 정말 감사하겠습니다.

Kyle Thomas 드림

Why? 왜 정답일까?

'It is, therefore, my humble request to you to allow us to use old newspapers that have been stored in the school library.'에서 도서관에 보관된 오래된 신문을 이용할 수 있게 해 달라고 요청하므로, 글의 목적으로 가장 적절한 것은 ⑤ '도서관에 있는 오래된 신문의 사용 허락을 요청하려고'이다.

- aim ⓝ 목표, 목적
- appreciate ⓥ 감사하다
- humble ⓐ 겸손한
- grant ⓥ (공식적으로) 주다

구문 풀이

4행 주어(one of the + 복수명사: ~ 중 하나)
One of the aims of these activities is to make us aware of various types
동사(단수) 보어(~것) of의 목적어1
of news media and the language used in printed newspaper articles.
of의 목적어2 과거분사

---

19 기대했던 선물을 받지 못해 실망한 필자 | 정답률 90% | 정답 ⑤

다음 글에 드러난 "I"의 심경 변화로 가장 적절한 것은?

① worried → furious
   걱정한 → 분노한
② surprised → relieved
   놀란 → 안도한
③ ashamed → confident
   부끄러운 → 자신감에 찬
④ anticipating → satisfied
   기대하는 → 만족한
✓⑤ excited → disappointed
   신난 → 실망한

When my mom came home from the mall / with a special present for me / I was pretty sure I knew what it was.
엄마가 상점에서 집에 왔을 때 / 나를 위한 특별한 선물을 가지고 / 나는 그것이 무엇인지 안다고 꽤 확신했다.
I was absolutely thrilled / because I would soon communicate with a new cell phone!
나는 완전히 들떴는데 / 왜냐하면 내가 곧 새로운 휴대폰으로 소통할 것이기 때문이었다!
I was daydreaming about all of the cool apps and games / I was going to download.
나는 모든 멋진 앱과 게임을 상상하고 있었다. / 내가 다운로드할
But my mom smiled really big / and handed me a book.
하지만 엄마는 함박웃음을 지으며 / 나에게 책 한 권을 건네주었다.
I flipped through the pages, / figuring that maybe she had hidden my new phone inside.
나는 책장을 휙휙 넘겨보았다. / 아마도 엄마가 나의 새로운 휴대폰을 책 속에 숨겨 두었을 것이라 생각하며
But I slowly realized / that my mom had not got me a phone / and my present was just a little book, / which was so different from what I had wanted.
그러나 나는 서서히 깨달았으며, / 엄마가 나에게 휴대폰을 사 주지 않았고 / 나의 선물이 겨우 작은 책이라는 것을 / 그것은 내가 원했던 것과는 너무 달랐다.

엄마가 나를 위한 특별한 선물을 가지고 상점에서 집에 왔을 때 나는 그것이 무엇인지 안다고 꽤 확신했다. 나는 완전히 들떴는데 왜냐하면 곧 새로운 휴대폰으로 소통할 것이기 때문이었다! 나는 내가 다운로드할 모든 멋진 앱과 게임을 상상하고 있었다. 하지만 엄마는 함박웃음을 지으며 나에게 책 한 권을 건네주었다. 나는 아마도 엄마가 나의 새로운 휴대폰을 책 속에 숨겨 두었을 것이라 생각하며 책장을 휙휙 넘겨보았다. 그러나 나는 엄마가 나에게 휴대폰을 사 주지 않았고 나의 선물이 겨우 작은 책이라는 것을 서서히 깨달았으며, 그것은 내가 원했던 것과는 너무 달랐다.

Why? 왜 정답일까?

어머니에게 핸드폰을 선물로 받을 것이라 예상한 필자가 기대감에 들떠 있었다가(I was absolutely thrilled ~), 선물이 작은 책이었음을 알고 실망했다는(~ my mom had not got me a phone and my present was just a little book, which was so different from what I had wanted.) 내용의 글이다. 따라서 'I'의 심경 변화로 가장 적절한 것은 ⑤ '신난 → 실망한'이다.

- absolutely ⓐⓓ 완전히, 절대적으로
- daydream ⓥ 공상하다
- anticipate ⓥ 기대하다
- thrilled ⓐ 아주 신이 난, 황홀한
- flip through (책장을) 휙휙 넘기다, 훑어보다

구문 풀이

7행 But I slowly realized {that my mom had not got me a phone and my present was just a little book}, which was so different from what I had wanted.
선행사 [ ]: 명사절(realized의 목적어) 계속적 용법 관계대명사(~것)

---

20 교사와 학생의 관계에서 비언어적 표현의 중요성 | 정답률 87% | 정답 ③

다음 글에서 필자가 주장하는 바로 가장 적절한 것은?

① 교사는 학생 간의 상호 작용을 주의 깊게 관찰해야 한다.
② 수업 시 교사는 학생의 수준에 맞는 언어를 사용해야 한다.
✓③ 학생과의 관계에서 교사는 비언어적 표현에 유의해야 한다.
④ 학교는 학생에게 다양한 역할 경험의 기회를 제공해야 한다.
⑤ 교사는 학생 안전을 위해 교실의 물리적 환경을 개선해야 한다.

Some experts estimate / that as much as half of what we communicate / is done through the way we move our bodies.
일부 전문가들은 추정한다. / 우리가 전달하는 것의 절반 정도는 / 우리가 우리의 몸을 움직이는 방식을 통해 행해진다고
Paying attention to the nonverbal messages you send / can make a significant difference / in your relationship with students.
여러분이 보내는 비언어적인 메시지에 주의를 기울이는 것은 / 중요한 차이를 만들 수 있다. / 학생들과 여러분의 관계에

In general, / most students / are often closely tuned in to their teacher's body language.
일반적으로 / 대부분의 학생들은 / 자신의 선생님의 몸짓 언어에 종종 관심이 면밀하게 맞춰져 있다.
For example, / when your students first enter the classroom, / their initial action is to look for their teacher.
예를 들어 / 여러분의 학생들이 처음 교실에 들어갈 때 / 그들의 첫 행동은 선생님을 찾는 것이다.
Think about how encouraging and empowering it is for a student / when that teacher has a friendly greeting and a welcoming smile.
학생에게 얼마나 격려와 힘이 되는지 생각해 보자. / 그 선생님이 친근하게 인사를 하고 환영하는 미소를 지어줄 때
Smiling at students / — to let them know that you are glad to see them — / does not require a great deal of time or effort, / but it can make a significant difference in the classroom climate / right from the start of class.
학생들에게 미소 짓는 것, / 즉 그들에게 여러분이 그들을 알게 돼서 기쁘다는 것을 알려 주는 것이 / 많은 시간이나 노력을 요구하지는 않지만, / 그것은 교실 분위기에 중요한 차이를 만들 수 있다. / 수업의 바로 시작부터

일부 전문가들은 우리가 전달하는 것의 절반 정도는 우리가 몸을 움직이는 방식을 통해 행해진다고 추정한다. 여러분이 보내는 비언어적인 메시지에 주의를 기울이는 것은 학생들과 여러분의 관계에 중요한 차이를 만들 수 있다. 일반적으로 대부분의 학생들은 선생님의 몸짓 언어에 종종 관심이 면밀하게 맞춰져 있다. 예를 들어, 여러분의 학생들이 처음 교실에 들어갈 때 처음 하는 행동은 선생님을 찾는 것이다. 선생님이 친근하게 인사하고 환영하는 미소를 지어줄 때 학생에게 얼마나 격려와 힘이 되는지 생각해 보자. 학생들에게 미소 짓는 것, 즉 그들에게 여러분이 그들을 알게 돼서 기쁘다는 것을 알려 주는 것이 많은 시간이나 노력을 요구하지는 않지만, 그것은 수업의 바로 시작부터 교실 분위기를 크게 달라지게 할 수 있다.

Why? 왜 정답일까?

'Paying attention to the nonverbal messages you send can make a significant difference in your relationship with students.'에서 교사는 학생과의 관계에서 자신이 사용하는 비언어적 표현에 주의를 기울일 필요가 있음을 시사하는 것으로 보아, 필자의 주장으로 가장 적절한 것은 ③ '학생과의 관계에서 교사는 비언어적 표현에 유의해야 한다.'이다.

- estimate ⓥ 추정하다
- significant ⓐ 상당한, 유의미한
- tune in to ~에 맞추다
- empower ⓥ 권한을 주다, 힘을 주다
- nonverbal ⓐ 비언어적인
- closely ⓐⓓ 면밀하게, 밀접하게
- initial ⓐ 초기의
- a great deal of (양이) 많은

구문 풀이

1행 Some experts estimate that as much as half of what we communicate
접속사(~것) 주어(half of + 전체)
is done through the way [we move our bodies].
동사(단수) 선행사

---

21 기후 변화에 관한 우리 자신의 책임 인식하기 | 정답률 54% | 정답 ④

밑줄 친 a slap in our own face가 다음 글에서 의미하는 바로 가장 적절한 것은? [3점]

① giving the future generation room for change
   미래 세대에 변화의 여지를 주는 것
② warning ourselves about the lack of natural resources
   우리 자신에게 천연자원 부족을 경고하는 것
③ refusing to admit the benefits of fossil fuel production
   화석 연료 생산의 이점을 인정하기를 거부하는 것
✓④ failing to recognize our responsibility for climate change
   기후 변화에 대한 우리의 책임을 인식하지 못하는 것
⑤ starting to deal with environmental problems individually
   환경 문제를 따로 다루기 시작하는 것

When it comes to climate change, / many blame the fossil fuel industry for pumping greenhouse gases, / the agricultural sector for burning rainforests, / or the fashion industry for producing excessive clothes.
기후 변화에 관해 / 많은 사람들은 온실가스를 배출하는 것에 대해 화석 연료 산업을 탓한다. / 열대 우림을 태우는 것에 대해 농업 분야를, / 혹은 과다한 의복을 생산하는 것에 대해 패션 산업을
But wait, / what drives these industrial activities?
하지만 잠깐, / 무엇이 이러한 산업 활동들을 가동시키는가?
Our consumption.
우리의 소비이다.
Climate change is / a summed product of each person's behavior.
기후 변화는 / 각 개인 행위의 합쳐진 산물이다.
For example, / the fossil fuel industry / is a popular scapegoat in the climate crisis.
예를 들어 / 화석 연료 산업은 / 기후 위기에 있어서 일반적인 희생양이다.
But why do they drill and burn fossil fuels?
하지만 왜 그들은 화석 연료를 시추하고 태울까?
We provide them strong financial incentives: / some people regularly travel on airplanes and cars / that burn fossil fuels.
우리가 그들에게 강력한 금전적인 동기를 제공한다. / 어떤 사람들은 비행기와 차로 정기적으로 여행한다. / 화석 연료를 태우는
Some people waste electricity / generated by burning fuel in power plants.
어떤 사람들은 전기를 낭비한다. / 발전소에서 연료를 태워 생산된
Some people use and throw away plastic products / derived from crude oil / every day.
어떤 사람들은 플라스틱 제품을 사용하고 버린다. / 원유로부터 얻어진 / 매일
Blaming the fossil fuel industry / while engaging in these behaviors / is a slap in our own face.
화석 연료 산업을 탓하는 것은 / 이러한 행위들에 참여하면서 / 자기 얼굴 때리기이다.

기후 변화에 관해 많은 사람들은 온실가스를 배출하는 것에 대해 화석 연료 산업을, 열대 우림을 태우는 것에 대해 농업 분야를, 혹은 과다한 의복을 생산하는 것에 대해 패션 산업을 탓한다. 하지만 잠깐, 무엇이 이러한 산업 활동들을 가동시키는가? 우리의 소비이다. 기후 변화는 각 개인 행위의 합쳐진 산물이다. 예를 들어, 화석 연료 산업은 기후 위기에 있어서 일반적인 희생양이다. 하지만 왜 그들은 화석 연료를 시추하고 태울까? 우리가 그들에게 강력한 금전적인 동기를 제공한다. 예를 들어, 어떤 사람들은 화석 연료를 태우는 비행기와 차로 정기적으로 여행한다. 어떤 사람들은 발전소에서 연료를 태워 생산된 전기를 낭비한다. 어떤 사람들은 원유로부터 얻어진 플라스틱 제품을 매일 사용하고 버린다. 이러한 행위들에 참여하면서 화석 연료 산업을 탓하는 것은 자기 얼굴 때리기이다.

Why? 왜 정답일까?

For example 앞에서 기후 변화의 원인으로 지적되는 산업 활동을 촉발하는 것은 우리의 소비이고, 그러므로 기후 변화는 개인의 행위를 합친 산물로 볼 수 있다고(Our consumption. Climate change is a summed product of each person's behavior.)고 언급한다. 이어서 'But why do they drill and burn fossil fuels? We provide them strong financial incentives: ~'에서도 애초에 화석 연료를 태우는 까닭이 우리가 그럴 동기를 제공하기 때문이라는 내용을 제시한다. 이러한 흐름으로 보아, 마지막 문장은 결국 기후 변화의 원인을 화석 연료 사용에 돌리는 것이 '자기 얼굴에 침 뱉기'와 같다는 뜻이다. 따라서 밑줄 친 부분이 의미하는 바로 가장 적절한 것은 ④ '기후 변화에 대한 우리의 책임을 인식하지 못하는 것'이다.

- blame A for B B에 대해 A를 탓하다
- excessive ⓐ 과다한
- crisis ⓝ 위기
- crude oil 원유
- agricultural ⓐ 농업의
- consumption ⓝ 소비
- drill ⓥ (자원, 연료 등을) 시추하다, 구멍을 뚫다
- slap ⓝ 철썩 때리기

구문 풀이

1행 When it comes to climate change, many blame {the fossil fuel industry}
~에 관하여   「blame + (A) + for + (B) : B에 대해 A를 탓하다」
for {pumping greenhouse gases}, {the agricultural sector} for {burning rainforests}, or {the fashion industry} for {producing excessive clothes}.

---

22 고객 정보를 적절히 활용할 필요성　　　정답률 74% | 정답 ③

다음 글의 요지로 가장 적절한 것은?
① 기업 정보의 투명한 공개는 고객 만족도를 향상시킨다.
② 목표 고객층에 대한 분석은 기업의 이익 창출로 이어진다.
✓ 고객 충성도를 높이기 위해 고객 정보가 활용될 필요가 있다.
④ 일관성 있는 호텔 서비스 제공을 통해 단골 고객을 확보할 수 있다.
⑤ 사생활 침해에 대한 우려로 고객 정보를 보관하는 데 어려움이 있다.

Information is worthless / if you never actually use it.
정보는 가치가 없다. / 만약 여러분이 결코 그것을 실제로 사용하지 않는다면
Far too often, / companies collect valuable customer information / that ends up buried and never used.
너무나 자주 / 기업들은 귀중한 고객 정보를 수집한다. / 결국에는 묻히고 절대로 사용되지 않는
They must ensure / their data is accessible for use at the appropriate times.
그들은 보장해야 한다. / 그들의 정보가 적절한 때의 사용을 위해 접근 가능하도록
For a hotel, / one appropriate time for data usage / is check-in at the front desk.
호텔의 경우 / 정보 사용을 위한 하나의 적절한 때는 / 프런트데스크에서 체크인할 때이다.
I often check in at a hotel / I've visited frequently, / only for the people at the front desk to give no indication / that they recognize me as a customer.
나는 호텔에 종종 체크인하는데 / 내가 자주 방문했던 / 프런트데스크에 있는 사람들은 결국 표시를 보여 주지 않는다. / 그들이 나를 고객으로 알아차린다는
The hotel must have stored a record of my visits, / but they don't make that information / accessible to the front desk clerks.
그 호텔은 내 방문 기록을 저장하고 있음이 분명하지만 / 그들은 그 정보가 ~하도록 해 주지 않는다. / 프런트데스크 직원들에게 접근 가능하도록
They are missing a prime opportunity to utilize data / to create a better experience / focused on customer loyalty.
그들은 정보를 활용할 최적의 기회를 놓치고 있다. / 더 나은 경험을 만들 수 있도록 / 고객 충성도에 초점을 맞춘
Whether they have ten customers, ten thousand, or even ten million, / the goal is the same: / create a delightful customer experience / that encourages loyalty.
그들이 열 명, 만 명 혹은 심지어 천만 명의 고객을 보유하든 / 목표는 동일하다. / 즐거운 고객 경험을 만드는 것 / 충성도를 높이는

만약 여러분이 결코 정보를 실제로 사용하지 않는다면 그것은 가치가 없다. 너무나 자주 기업들은 결국에는 묻히고 절대로 사용되지 않는 귀중한 고객 정보를 수집한다. 그들은 그들의 정보가 적절한 때의 사용을 위해 접근 가능하도록 보장해야 한다. 호텔의 경우 정보 사용을 위한 하나의 적절한 때는 프런트데스크에서 체크인할 때이다. 나는 내가 자주 방문했던 호텔에 종종 체크인하는데, 프런트데스크에 있는 사람들은 결국 나를 고객으로 알아차린다는 표시를 보여 주지 않는다. 그 호텔은 내 방문 기록을 저장하고 있음이 분명하지만 그 정보가 프런트데스크 직원들에게 접근 가능하도록 해 주지 않는다. 그들은 고객 충성도에 초점을 맞춘 더 나은 경험을 만들 수 있도록 정보를 활용할 최적의 기회를 놓치고 있다. 그들이 열 명, 만명 혹은 심지어 천만 명의 고객을 보유하든 목표는 동일하다. 즉, 그것은 충성도를 높이는 즐거운 고객 경험을 만드는 것이다.

Why? 왜 정답일까?

첫 두 문장에서 고객 정보를 수집해 놓더라도 실제로 사용하지 않는다면 가치가 없다고 언급한 뒤, 세 번째 문장에서 고객 정보를 적절한 때 쓸 수 있도록 해 주어야 한다(They must ensure their data is accessible for use at the appropriate times.)고 주장하고 있다. 따라서 글의 요지로 가장 적절한 것은 ③ '고객 충성도를 높이기 위해 고객 정보가 활용될 필요가 있다.'이다.

- worthless ⓐ 무가치한
- ensure ⓥ 보장하다
- appropriate ⓐ 적절한
- utilize ⓥ 이용하다
- delightful ⓐ 즐거운, 기쁜
- end up 결국 ~이 되다
- accessible ⓐ 접근 가능한, 이용 가능한
- indication ⓝ 표시, 징후
- loyalty ⓝ 충성도

구문 풀이

5행 I often check in at a hotel [I've visited frequently], only for the people at
　　　　　　　　　　　선행사　　　　　　　　　　「only + 의미상 주어 +
the front desk to give no indication {that they recognize me as a customer.}
to부정사 : 결과(~가 결국 …하다)」　{ } : 동격 = indication)

---

23 행복한 뇌를 위한 습관 만들기　　　정답률 75% | 정답 ①

다음 글의 주제로 가장 적절한 것은?
✓ possibility of forming brain habits for well-being
　행복을 위한 뇌 습관을 만들어낼 수 있는 가능성
② role of brain circuits in improving body movements
　신체 움직임을 향상시키는 데 있어 뇌 회로의 역할
③ importance of practice in playing musical instruments
　악기 연주에서 연습의 중요성

④ effect of taking a break on enhancing memory capacity
　휴식이 기억력 향상에 미치는 영향
⑤ difficulty of discovering how neurons in the brain work
　뇌 속 뉴런의 작동 방식을 발견하는 것의 어려움

We used to think / that the brain never changed, / but according to the neuroscientist Richard Davidson, / we now know that this is not true / — specific brain circuits grow stronger through regular practice.
우리는 생각했었지만 / 뇌가 절대 변하지 않는다고 / 신경과학자 Richard Davidson에 따르면 / 우리는 이제 이것이 사실이 아님을 안다 / 즉 특정한 뇌 회로가 규칙적인 연습을 통해 더 강해진다는 것
He explains, / "Well-being is fundamentally no different / than learning to play the cello. / If one practices the skills of well-being, / one will get better at it."
그는 설명한다 / "행복은 기본적으로 다르지 않다. / 첼로 연주하는 것을 배우는 것과 / 만약 어떤 이가 행복의 기술을 연습한다면 / 그 사람은 그것을 더 잘하게 된다."라고
What this means is / that you can actually train your brain / to become more grateful, relaxed, or confident, / by repeating experiences / that evoke gratitude, relaxation, or confidence.
이것이 의미하는 바는 ~이다. / 여러분이 여러분의 뇌를 실제로 훈련시킬 수 있다는 것 / 더 감사하고, 편안하고 또는 자신감을 갖도록 / 경험을 반복함으로써 / 감사, 휴식 또는 자신감을 불러일으키는
Your brain is shaped by the thoughts you repeat.
여러분의 뇌는 여러분이 반복하는 생각에 의해 형성된다.
The more neurons fire / as they are activated by repeated thoughts and activities, / the faster they develop into neural pathways, / which cause lasting changes in the brain.
뉴런은 더 많이 점화할수록, / 그것이 반복된 생각과 활동에 의해 활성화되면서 / 그것은 신경 경로로 더 빠르게 발달하게 되고 / 이는 뇌에 지속적인 변화를 야기한다.
Or in the words of Donald Hebb, / "Neurons that fire together wire together."
혹은 Donald Hebb의 말을 빌리면 / "함께 점화하는 뉴런은 함께 연결된다."
This is such an encouraging premise: / bottom line / — we can intentionally create the habits / for the brain to be happier.
이는 대단히 고무적인 전제이다. / 결론은 / 즉, 우리가 습관을 의도적으로 만들 수 있다는 것 / 뇌가 더 행복해지도록

우리는 뇌가 절대 변하지 않는다고 생각했었지만, 신경과학자 Richard Davidson에 따르면 우리는 이제 이것이 사실이 아님을, 즉, 특정한 뇌 회로가 규칙적인 연습을 통해 더 강해진다는 것을 안다. 그는 "행복은 첼로 연주하는 것을 배우는 것과 기본적으로 다르지 않다. 만약 어떤 이가 행복의 기술을 연습한다면 그 사람은 그것을 더 잘하게 된다."라고 설명한다. 이것이 의미하는 바는 여러분이 감사, 휴식 또는 자신감을 불러일으키는 경험을 반복함으로써 더 감사하거나 편안하거나 자신감을 갖도록 여러분의 뇌를 실제로 훈련시킬 수 있다는 것이다. 뇌는 여러분이 반복하는 생각에 의해 형성된다. 뉴런은 반복된 생각과 활동에 의해 활성화되면서 더 많이 점화할수록 신경 경로로 더 빠르게 발달하게 되고, 이는 뇌에 지속적인 변화를 야기한다. 혹은 Donald Hebb의 말을 빌리면 "함께 점화하는 뉴런은 함께 연결된다." 이는 대단히 고무적인 전제이다. 즉, 결론은 뇌가 더 행복해지도록 우리가 습관을 의도적으로 만들 수 있다는 것이다.

Why? 왜 정답일까?

마지막 문장(~ we can intentionally create the habits for the brain to be happier.)에서 우리는 뇌를 더 행복하게 할 습관을 만들어 갈 수 있다는 결론을 제시하므로, 글의 주제로 가장 적절한 것은 ① '행복을 위한 뇌 습관을 만들어낼 수 있는 가능성'이다.

- neuroscientist ⓝ 신경과학자
- grateful ⓐ 감사하는
- bottom line 핵심, 요점, 결론
- enhance ⓥ 향상시키다
- fundamentally ⓐⓓ 기본적으로
- activate ⓥ 활성화하다
- intentionally ⓐⓓ 의도적으로

구문 풀이

9행 The more neurons fire as they are activated by repeated thoughts and
　　　　「the + 비교급 …
activities, the faster they develop into neural pathways, which cause lasting
　　　the + 비교급 … : ~할수록 더 …하다」　　　　계속적 용법(주절 보충)
changes in the brain.

---

24 현대 사회에서의 정체성　　　정답률 57% | 정답 ②

다음 글의 제목으로 가장 적절한 것은?
① What Makes Our Modern Society So Competitive?
　무엇이 우리 현대 사회를 이토록 경쟁적으로 만드는가?
✓ How Modern Society Drives Us to Discover Our Identities
　현대 사회는 어떻게 우리가 정체성을 발견하도록 부추기는가
③ Social Masks: A Means to Build Trustworthy Relationships
　사회적 가면: 믿을 만한 관계를 구축하는 수단
④ The More Social Roles We Have, the Less Choice We Have
　더 많은 사회적 역할을 가질수록, 선택권은 더 적어진다
⑤ Increasing Social Mobility Leads Us to a More Equal Society
　사회적 유동성의 증가가 더 평등한 사회로 이끈다

In modern times, / society became more dynamic.
현대에는 / 사회가 더욱 역동적이 되었다.
Social mobility increased, / and people began to exercise a higher degree of choice / regarding, for instance, their profession, their marriage, or their religion.
사회적 유동성이 증가하였고 / 사람들은 더 높은 정도의 선택권을 행사하기 시작했다. / 예를 들어 자신의 직업, 결혼 혹은 종교와 관련하여
This posed a challenge to traditional roles in society.
이것은 사회의 전통적인 역할에 이의를 제기했다.
It was less evident / that one needed to commit to the roles / one was born into / when alternatives could be realized.
덜 분명해졌다. / 개인이 역할에 전념할 필요가 있다는 것은 / 자신이 타고난 / 대안이 실현될 수 있을 때
Increasing control over one's life choices / became not only possible but desired.
자신의 삶의 선택에 대한 통제권을 늘리는 것이 / 가능해졌을 뿐만 아니라 바람직하게 되었다.
Identity then became a problem.
그러자 정체성이 문제가 되었다.
It was no longer almost ready-made at birth / but something to be discovered.
그것은 더 이상 태어날 때 대체로 주어진 것이 아닌, / 발견되어야 할 것이었다.
Traditional role identities prescribed by society / began to appear as masks imposed on people / whose real self was to be found somewhere underneath.
사회에 의해 규정된 전통적인 역할 정체성은 / 사람들에게 부여된 가면처럼 보이기 시작했다. / 그 뒤 어딘가에서 진정한 자아가 발견되어야 하는

[문제편 p.157]

현대에는 사회가 더욱 역동적이 되었다. 사회적 유동성이 증가하였고, 사람들은 가령 자신의 직업, 결혼 혹은 종교와 관련하여 더 높은 정도의 선택권을 행사하기 시작했다. 이것은 사회의 전통적인 역할에 이의를 제기했다. 대안이 실현될 수 있을 때 개인이 타고난 역할에 전념할 필요가 있다는 것은 덜 분명해졌다. 자신의 삶의 선택에 대한 통제력을 늘리는 것이 가능해졌을 뿐만 아니라 바람직하게 되었다. 그러자 정체성이 문제가 되었다. 그것은 더 이상 태어날 때 대체로 주어진 것이 아닌, 발견되어야 할 것이었다. 사회에 의해 규정된 전통적인 역할 정체성은 사람들에게 부여된 가면처럼 보이기 시작해서, 진정한 자아는 그 뒤 어딘가에서 발견되어야 하는 것처럼 여겨지기 시작했다.

Why? 왜 정답일까?

역동적인 현대 사회에서 우리의 정체성은 태어날 때 주어진 것보다는 사회적으로 발견되어야 하는 것이 되었다(Identity then became a problem. It was no longer almost ready-made at birth but something to be discovered.)는 내용의 글이다. 따라서 글의 제목으로 가장 적절한 것은 ② '현대 사회는 어떻게 우리가 정체성을 발견하도록 부추기는가'이다.

- mobility ⓝ 유동성
- pose a challenge 도전하다, 이의를 제기하다
- commit to ~에 전념하다
- prescribe ⓥ 규정하다, 처방하다
- profession ⓝ 직업
- evident ⓐ 명백한
- ready-made ⓐ 이미 주어진, 기성품의

구문 풀이

9행 Traditional role identities prescribed by society began to appear as [주어] [과거분사] [동사] [전치사(~로서)] masks imposed on people [whose real self was to be found somewhere [명사] [과거분사] [소유격 관·대] [be to 용법: ~해야 한다(의무)] underneath].

---

25 문화 활동별 참여 비율
정답률 73% | 정답 ④

다음 도표의 내용과 일치하지 않는 것은?

Percentage of U.S. Students Participating in Cultural Activities (2016)

The graph above shows / the percentage of U.S. homeschooled and public school students / participating in cultural activities in 2016.
위 도표는 보여 준다. / 미국의 홈스쿨링 학생과 공립 학교 학생의 비율을 / 2016년에 문화 활동에 참여한
① With the exception of live performances and sporting events, / the percentage of homeschooled students / participating in cultural activities / was higher than that of public school students.
라이브 공연과 스포츠 행사를 제외하고 / 홈스쿨링 학생의 비율이 / 문화 활동에 참여하는 / 공립 학교 학생의 비율에 비해 높았다.
② For each group of students, / community events accounted for the largest percentage / among all cultural activities.
각 집단의 학생에 있어 / 지역사회 행사는 가장 큰 비율을 차지했다. / 모든 문화 활동 중에서
③ The percentage point difference / between homeschooled students and their public school peers / was largest in visiting libraries.
퍼센트포인트 차이는 / 홈스쿨링 학생과 공립 학교 또래 간의 / 도서관 방문에서 가장 컸다.
✓④ The percentage of homeschooled students / visiting museums or galleries / was more than twice that of public school students.
홈스쿨링 학생의 비율은 / 박물관이나 미술관에 방문하는 / 공립 학교 학생의 비율에 비해 두 배 이상이었다.
⑤ Going to zoos or aquariums / ranked the lowest for both groups of students, / with 31 and 23 percent respectively.
동물원이나 수족관에 가는 것이 / 두 학생 집단에서 가장 낮은 순위를 차지했는데, / 각각 31퍼센트와 23퍼센트였다.

위 도표는 미국에서 2016년에 문화 활동에 참여한 홈스쿨링 학생과 공립 학교 학생의 비율을 보여 준다. ① 라이브 공연과 스포츠 행사를 제외하고 문화 활동에 참여하는 홈스쿨링 학생의 비율이 공립 학교 학생에 비해 높았다. ② 각 집단의 학생에 있어 지역사회 행사는 모든 문화 활동 중에서 가장 큰 비율을 차지했다. ③ 홈스쿨링 학생과 공립 학교 또래 간의 퍼센트포인트 차이는 도서관 방문에서 가장 컸다. ④ 박물관이나 미술관에 방문하는 홈스쿨링 학생의 비율은 공립 학교 학생에 비해 두 배 이상이었다. ⑤ 동물원이나 수족관에 가는 것이 두 학생 집단에서 가장 낮은 순위를 차지했는데, 각각 31퍼센트와 23퍼센트였다.

Why? 왜 정답일까?

도표에 따르면 홈스쿨링 학생 중 박물관이나 미술관에 가는 비율(42%)은 공립 학교 학생의 비율(25%)의 두 배에 미치지 못한다. 따라서 도표와 일치하지 않는 것은 ④이다.

- with the exception of ~을 제외하고
- respectively ⓐⓓ 각각
- account for ~을 차지하다

구문 풀이

9행 The percentage of homeschooled students visiting museums or galleries [동사(단수)] [주어] [현재분사] was more than twice that of public school students. [~ 이상인] [지시대명사(= the percentage)]

---

26 Bessie Coleman의 생애
정답률 85% | 정답 ④

Bessie Coleman에 관한 다음 글의 내용과 일치하지 않는 것은?

① 11살 때 Wright 형제의 첫 비행 소식을 들었다.
② 비행 수업을 듣기 위해 파리로 가야 했다.
③ 국제 조종사 면허를 딴 최초의 흑인 여성이 되었다.
✓④ 유럽에서 에어쇼에 첫 출현을 했다.
⑤ 다음 세대가 비행의 꿈을 추구하도록 영감을 주었다.

Bessie Coleman was born in Texas in 1892.
Bessie Coleman은 1892년에 텍사스에서 태어났다.
「When she was eleven, / she was told / that the Wright brothers had flown their first plane.」 ①의 근거 일치
그녀가 11살이었을 때 / 그녀는 들었다. / Wright 형제가 첫 비행을 했다는 것을
Since that moment, / she dreamed about the day / she would soar through the sky.
그때부터 / 그녀는 그 날을 꿈꿨다. / 자신이 하늘을 높이 날아오르는
At the age of 23, / Coleman moved to Chicago, / where she worked at a restaurant / to save money for flying lessons.
23살 때 / Coleman은 시카고로 이사했고 / 그곳에서 그녀는 식당 일을 했다. / 비행 수업을 위한 돈을 모으기 위해
「However, / she had to travel to Paris / to take flying lessons / because American flight schools at the time admitted neither women nor Black people.」 ②의 근거 일치
그러나 / 그녀는 파리로 가야 했다. / 비행 수업을 듣기 위해 / 왜냐하면 그 당시 미국 비행 학교가 여성이나 흑인의 입학을 허가하지 않았기 때문에
「In 1921, / she finally became the first Black woman / to earn an international pilot's license.」 ③의 근거 일치
1921년에 / 그녀는 마침내 최초의 흑인 여성이 되었다. / 국제 조종사 면허를 딴
「She also studied flying acrobatics in Europe / and made her first appearance / in an airshow in New York in 1922.」 ④의 근거 불일치
그녀는 또한 유럽에서 곡예 비행을 공부했고 / 첫 출현을 했다. / 1922년에 뉴욕의 에어쇼에
「As a female pioneer of flight, / she inspired the next generation / to pursue their dreams of flying.」 ⑤의 근거 일치
여성 비행 개척자로서 / 그녀는 다음 세대에게 영감을 주었다. / 비행의 꿈을 추구하도록

Bessie Coleman은 1892년에 텍사스에서 태어났다. 그녀가 11살이었을 때 그녀는 Wright 형제가 첫 비행을 했다는 것을 들었다. 그때부터 그녀는 자신이 하늘을 높이 날아오르는 그 날을 꿈꿨다. 23살 때 Coleman은 시카고로 이사했고 그곳에서 식당 일을 하여 비행 수업을 위한 돈을 모았다. 그러나 그 당시 미국 비행 학교가 여성이나 흑인의 입학을 허가하지 않았기 때문에 그녀는 비행 수업을 듣기 위해 파리로 가야 했다. 1921년에 그녀는 마침내 국제 조종사 면허를 딴 최초의 흑인 여성이 되었다. 그녀는 또한 유럽에서 곡예 비행을 공부했고 1922년에 뉴욕의 에어쇼에 첫 출현을 했다. 여성 비행 개척자로서 그녀는 다음 세대가 비행의 꿈을 추구하도록 영감을 주었다.

Why? 왜 정답일까?

'She also studied flying acrobatics in Europe and made her first appearance in an airshow in New York in 1922.'에 따르면 Coleman은 유럽에서 곡예 비행을 공부한 후 첫 에어쇼를 뉴욕에서 치렀다. 따라서 내용과 일치하지 않는 것은 ④ '유럽에서 에어쇼에 첫 출현을 했다.'이다.

Why? 왜 오답일까?

① 'When she was eleven, she was told that the Wright brothers had flown their first plane.'의 내용과 일치한다.
② 'However, she had to travel to Paris to take flying lessons ~'의 내용과 일치한다.
③ 'In 1921, she finally became the first Black woman to earn an international pilot's license.'의 내용과 일치한다.
⑤ '~ she inspired the next generation to pursue their dreams of flying.'의 내용과 일치한다.

- soar ⓥ 솟아오르다
- inspire ⓥ 영감을 주다
- pioneer ⓝ 선구자

구문 풀이

1행 When she was eleven, she was told {that the Wright brothers had flown [4형식 수동태(~을 듣다)] [과거완료] their first plane}. [ ]: 목적어

---

27 자연 사진 대회 안내
정답률 82% | 정답 ②

2021 Camptonville Nature Photo Contest에 관한 다음 안내문의 내용과 일치하지 않는 것은?

① 매년 열리는 대회이며 올해가 네 번째이다.
✓② 최대 20장의 사진을 이메일로 제출해야 한다.
③ 제출 마감 기한은 12월 1일이다.
④ 수상자는 웹 사이트에 게시될 것이다.
⑤ 모든 수상작은 시청에 전시될 것이다.

2021 Camptonville Nature Photo Contest
2021 Camptonville 자연 사진 대회
「This is the fourth year of the annual Camptonville Nature Photo Contest.」 ①의 근거 일치
올해는 매년 열리는 Camptonville 자연 사진 대회의 네 번째 해입니다.
You can show the beauty of nature in Camptonville / by sharing your most amazing photos!
여러분은 Camptonville의 자연미를 보여 줄 수 있습니다! / 자신의 가장 멋진 사진을 공유함으로써
Submission
제출
「Upload a maximum of 20 photos / onto our website www.camptonvillephotocontest.org.」 ②의 근거 불일치
최대 20장의 사진을 올리세요. / 우리 웹 사이트 www.camptonvillephotocontest.org에
「Deadline is December 1.」 ③의 근거 일치
마감 기한은 12월 1일입니다.
Prizes
상
1st Place: $500

2nd Place: $200
2위: 200달러
3rd Place: $100
3위: 100달러
(『Winners will be posted on our website on December 31.』) ④의근거 일치
(수상자는 12월 31일에 우리 웹 사이트에 게시될 것입니다.)
Details
세부 사항
『All winning photos will be exhibited at City Hall.』 ⑤의근거 일치
모든 수상작은 시청에 전시될 것입니다.
Please contact us at 122-861-3971 for further information.
더 많은 정보를 얻으시려면 122-861-3971로 연락 주세요.

2021 Camptonville 자연 사진 대회

올해는 매년 열리는 Camptonville 자연 사진 대회의 네 번째 해입니다. 여러분은 여러분이 찍은 가장 멋진 사진을 공유함으로써 Camptonville의 자연미를 보여 줄 수 있습니다!

제출
– 최대 20장의 사진을 우리 웹 사이트
  www.camptonvillephotocontest.org에 올리세요.
– 마감 기한은 12월 1일입니다.

상
• 1위: 500달러   • 2위: 200달러   • 3위: 100달러
(수상자는 12월 31일에 우리 웹 사이트에 게시될 것입니다.)

세부 사항
– 모든 수상작은 시청에 전시될 것입니다.
– 더 많은 정보를 얻으시려면 122-861-3971로 연락 주세요.

Why? 왜 정답일까?
'Upload a maximum of 20 photos onto our website ~'에서 사진은 웹 사이트에 올려 출품하라고 하므로, 따라서 안내문의 내용과 일치하지 않는 것은 ② '최대 20장의 사진을 이메일로 제출해야 한다.'이다.

Why? 왜 오답일까?
① 'This is the fourth year of the annual Camptonville Nature Photo Contest.'의 내용과 일치한다.
③ 'Deadline is December 1.'의 내용과 일치한다.
④ '(Winners will be posted on our website on December 31.)'의 내용과 일치한다.
⑤ 'All winning photos will be exhibited at City Hall.'의 내용과 일치한다.

● annual ⓐ 매년 열리는

---

28 열기구 탑승 안내   정답률 91% | 정답 ④

Willow Valley Hot Air Balloon Ride에 관한 다음 안내문의 내용과 일치하는 것은?
① 조종사를 제외하고 8인까지 탈 수 있다.
② 여름에는 오전 6시에 시작한다.
③ 요금에 보험이 포함되어 있다.
✔ ④ 예약은 온라인으로 해야 한다.
⑤ 환불은 예외 없이 불가능하다.

Willow Valley Hot Air Balloon Ride
Willow Valley 열기구 탑승
Enjoy the best views of Willow Valley from the sky / with our hot air balloon ride!
하늘에서 Willow Valley의 최고의 풍경을 즐겨보세요! / 우리의 열기구를 타고
『Capacity: up to 8 people including a pilot』 ①의근거 불일치
정원: 조종사 포함 8인까지
Time Schedule
일정표

『Spring & Summer (from April to September) 봄과 여름 (4월부터 9월까지)	②의근거 불일치 5:00 a.m. – 7:00 a.m.』 오전 5시–오전 7시
Autumn & Winter (from October to March) 가을과 겨울 (10월부터 3월까지)	6:00 a.m. – 8:00 a.m. 오전 6시–오전 8시

Duration of Flight: about 1 hour
비행 시간: 약 1시간
Fee: $150 per person / (『insurance not included』) ③의근거 불일치
요금: 인당 150달러 / (보험은 포함되지 않음)
Note
공지사항
『Reservations are required and must be made online.』 ④의근거 일치
예약은 필수이며 온라인으로 해야 합니다.
『You can get a full refund up to 24 hours in advance.』 ⑤의근거 불일치
24시간 전까지는 전액 환불을 받을 수 있습니다.
Visit www.willowvalleyballoon.com for more information.
더 많은 정보를 위해서 www.willowvalleyballoon.com을 방문해 주십시오.

Willow Valley 열기구 탑승

우리의 열기구를 타고 하늘에서 Willow Valley의 최고의 풍경을 즐겨보세요!

• 정원: 조종사 포함 8인까지

• 일정표

봄과 여름 (4월부터 9월까지)	오전 5시 – 오전 7시

가을과 겨울 (10월부터 3월까지)	오전 6시 – 오전 8시

※ 비행 시간: 약 1시간
• 요금: 인당 150달러 (보험은 포함되지 않음)
• 공지사항
– 예약은 필수이며 온라인으로 해야 합니다.
– 24시간 전까지는 전액 환불을 받을 수 있습니다.
– 더 많은 정보를 위해서 www.willowvalleyballoon.com을 방문해 주십시오.

Why? 왜 정답일까?
'Reservations are required and must be made online.'에서 예약은 필수이며 온라인으로 해야 한다고 하므로, 안내문의 내용과 일치하는 것은 ④ '예약은 온라인으로 해야 한다.'이다.

Why? 왜 오답일까?
① 'Capacity: up to 8 people including a pilot'에서 8인이라는 정원에 조종사가 포함된다고 하였다.
② 'Spring & Summer / (from April to September) / 5:00 a.m. – 7:00 a.m.'에서 봄과 여름에는 오전 5시부터 시작된다고 하였다.
③ '(insurance not included)'에서 보험은 요금에 포함되지 않는다고 하였다.
⑤ 'You can get a full refund up to 24 hours in advance.'에서 탑승 24시간 전까지는 전액 환불이 가능하다고 하였다.

● get a refund 환불을 받다   ● in advance 미리, 사전에

---

29 살충제와 비료의 사용으로 초래된 결과   정답률 45% | 정답 ④

다음 글의 밑줄 친 부분 중, 어법상 틀린 것은? [3점]

The reduction of minerals in our food / is the result of using pesticides and fertilizers / ① that kill off beneficial bacteria, earthworms, and bugs in the soil / that create many of the essential nutrients / in the first place / and prevent the uptake of nutrients into the plant.
우리의 식품 속 미네랄의 감소는 / 살충제와 비료 사용의 결과이다. / 토양에 있는 이로운 박테리아, 지렁이 그리고 벌레를 죽이고 / 많은 필수 영양소를 만들어 내는 / 우선적으로 / 식물이 영양소를 흡수하는 것을 막는
Fertilizing crops with nitrogen and potassium / ② has led to declines in magnesium, zinc, iron and iodine.
농작물에 질소와 포타슘으로 비료를 주는 것은 / 마그네슘, 아연, 철 그리고 아이오딘의 감소로 이어져 왔다.
For example, / there has been on average about a 30% decline / in the magnesium content of wheat.
예를 들어 / 평균 약 30%의 감소가 있었다. / 밀의 마그네슘 함량에서의
This is partly due to / potassium ③ being a blocker against magnesium absorption by plants.
이는 부분적으로 ~ 때문이다. / 식물이 마그네슘을 흡수하는 데 포타슘이 방해물이 되기
Lower magnesium levels in soil / also ✔ occur with acidic soils / and around 70% of the farmland on earth / is now acidic.
토양의 더 낮은 마그네슘 수치는 / 산성 토양에서도 나타나는데 / 지구상에 있는 농지의 약 70%가 / 현재 산성이다.
Thus, / the overall characteristics of soil / determine the accumulation of minerals in plants.
따라서 / 토양의 전반적인 특성은 / 식물 속 미네랄의 축적을 결정한다.
Indeed, / nowadays our soil is less healthy / and so are the plants ⑤ grown on it.
실제로 / 오늘날 우리의 토양은 덜 건강하고 / 그 위에서 길러진 식물도 그러하다.

우리의 식품 속 미네랄의 감소는 우선적으로 많은 필수 영양소를 만들어 내는 토양에 있는 이로운 박테리아, 지렁이 그리고 벌레를 죽이고 식물이 영양소를 흡수하는 것을 막는 살충제와 비료를 사용한 결과이다. 농작물에 질소와 포타슘으로 비료를 주는 것은 마그네슘, 아연, 철 그리고 아이오딘의 감소로 이어져 왔다. 예를 들어 밀의 마그네슘 함량에서 평균적으로 약 30%의 감소가 있었다. 이는 부분적으로 식물이 마그네슘을 흡수하는 데 포타슘이 방해물이 되기 때문이다. 토양의 마그네슘 수치 감소는 산성 토양에서도 나타나는데, 지구상에 있는 약 70%가 현재 산성이다. 따라서 토양의 전반적인 특성은 식물 속 미네랄의 축적을 결정한다. 실제로 오늘날 우리의 토양은 덜 건강하고 그 위에서 길러진 식물도 그러하다.

Why? 왜 정답일까?
and 앞뒤로 2개의 절이 연결되는 구조로, 첫 번째 주어인 Lower magnesium levels 뒤로 동사가 필요하기 때문에 occurring을 occur로 고쳐야 한다. 따라서 어법상 틀린 것은 ④이다.

Why? 왜 오답일까?
① pesticides and fertilizers를 꾸미는 주격 관계대명사로 that을 썼다.
② 주어가 동명사구인 'Fertilizing crops ~'이므로 단수 취급하여 has를 썼다.
③ 전치사처럼 쓰이는 'due to(~ 때문에)' 뒤로 동명사 또는 명사를 써야 하므로 being을 썼다. potassium은 being의 의미상 주어이다.
⑤ the plants가 '키워지는' 대상이므로 수동의 의미를 나타내는 과거분사 grown을 썼다.

● reduction ⓝ 감소   ● essential ⓐ 필수적인, 본질적인
● in the first place 애초에, 우선   ● uptake ⓝ 흡수, 활용
● fertilize ⓥ 비옥하게 하다, 비료를 주다   ● decline ⓝ 감소 ⓥ 감소하다
● absorption ⓝ 흡수   ● acidic ⓐ 산성의
● characteristic ⓝ 특징, 특성   ● accumulation ⓝ 축적

구문 풀이

12행 Indeed, nowadays our soil is less healthy and so are the plants grown on it.
「so + 동사 + 주어 : 동의 구문(~도 그렇다)」

★★★ 등급을 가르는 문제!
30 동물원의 포획 사육 프로그램   정답률 24% | 정답 ⑤

다음 글의 밑줄 친 부분 중, 문맥상 낱말의 쓰임이 적절하지 <u>않은</u> 것은?

For species approaching extinction, / zoos can act as a last chance for survival.
멸종에 이르고 있는 종에게 / 동물원은 생존을 위한 마지막 기회로 작용할 수 있다.
① Recovery programs are established / to coordinate the efforts of field conservationists and wildlife authorities.
회복 프로그램이 수립된다. / 현장 환경 보호 활동가와 야생 동물 당국의 노력을 통합하기 위해
As populations of those species ② diminish / it is not unusual for zoos / to start captive breeding programs.
그 종의 개체수가 감소하면서 / 동물원으로서는 드물지 않다. / 포획 사육 프로그램을 시작하는 것이
Captive breeding acts to protect against extinction.
포획 사육은 멸종을 막기 위해 작용한다.
In some cases / captive-bred individuals may be released back into the wild, / supplementing wild populations.
어떤 경우에는 / 포획 사육된 개체가 다시 야생으로 방생되어 / 야생 개체수를 보충할 수도 있다.
This is most successful in situations / where individuals are at greatest threat / during a ③ particular life stage.
이는 상황에서 가장 성공적이다. / 개체가 가장 큰 위험에 놓여 있는 / 특정한 생애 주기 동안에
For example, / turtle eggs may be removed from high-risk locations / until after they hatch.
예를 들어 / 거북이 알은 고위험 장소로부터 제거될 수도 있다. / 그들이 부화한 이후까지
This may ④ increase the number of turtles / that survive to adulthood.
이는 거북이 수를 증가시킬 수 있다. / 성체까지 생존하는
Crocodile programs have also been successful / in protecting eggs and hatchlings, / ✓ releasing hatchlings / once they are better equipped to protect themselves.
악어 프로그램 역시 성공적이었으며 / 알과 부화한 유생을 보호하는 데 있어서 / 부화한 유생을 방생한다. / 일단 그것이 스스로를 보호할 준비가 더 잘 갖추면

멸종에 이르고 있는 종에게 동물원은 생존을 위한 마지막 기회로 작용할 수 있다. 현장 환경 보호 활동가와 야생 동물 당국의 노력을 통합하기 위해 ① 회복 프로그램이 수립된다. 그 종의 개체수가 ② 감소하면서 동물원이 포획 사육 프로그램을 시작하는 것은 드물지 않다. 포획 사육은 멸종을 막기 위해 작용한다. 어떤 경우에는 포획 사육된 개체가 다시 야생으로 방생되어 야생 개체수를 보충할 수도 있다. 이는 개체가 ③ 특정한 생애 주기 동안에 가장 큰 위협에 놓여 있는 상황에서 가장 성공적이다. 예를 들어 거북이 알은 부화한 이후까지 고위험 장소로부터 제거될 수도 있다. 이는 성체까지 생존하는 거북이 수를 ④ 증가시킬 수 있다. 악어 프로그램 역시 알과 부화한 유생을 보호하는 데 있어서 성공적이었으며, 일단 그것이 스스로를 보호할 준비를 더 잘 갖추면 부화한 유생을 ⑤ 포획한다(→ 방생한다).

Why? 왜 정답일까?
멸종 위기 종의 개체수를 회복하는 데 동물원이 도움을 줄 수 있다는 내용의 글로, '~ it is not unusual for zoos to start captive breeding programs.' 뒤로 포획 사육 프로그램의 내용이 소개되고 있다. 이 포획 사육 프로그램에서는 멸종 위기 동물이나 그 알을 잡아두었다가 위험한 시기가 지나고 동물이 스스로를 보호할 준비가 되면 그 동물을 다시 야생으로 '돌려보낸다'. 이러한 흐름으로 볼 때, ⑤의 capturing을 releasing으로 고쳐야 한다. 따라서 문맥상 낱말의 쓰임이 가장 적절하지 않은 것은 ⑤이다.

- extinction ⑩ 멸종
- authority ⑩ 당국
- supplement ⑰ 보충하다
- be equipped to ~할 준비를 갖추다
- conservationist ⑩ 환경 보호 활동가
- diminish ⑰ 감소하다, 줄어들다
- hatchling ⑩ (갓 부화한) 유생

구문 풀이
7행 This is most successful in situations [where individuals are at greatest threat during a particular life stage].
선행사(추상적 공간)← 관계부사

★★ 문제 해결 꿀~팁 ★★
▶ 많이 틀린 이유는?
동물원의 포획 사육이라는 생소한 소재를 다루어 이해하기 까다로운 지문이다. 가장 헷갈리는 ④ 주변의 문맥을 살펴보면, 포획 사육이 생존에 큰 위협이 있는 시기를 지나는 동물에게 도움이 된다는 일반적인 내용 뒤로 바다거북의 사례가 언급된다. 바다거북의 알은 부화하기 전까지 고위험 지역으로부터 다른 곳으로 옮겨진다고 했다. 이는 바다거북이 무사히 부화해 성체까지 생존할 수 있도록 돕는 절차이므로, 실제로 이 조치를 통해 살아남는 바다거북의 수가 '증가'할 수 있다는 뜻의 ④ increase는 문맥상 적절하다.
▶ 문제 해결 방법은?
정답인 ⑤의 capturing은 핵심 소재인 captive (breeding programs)와 비슷한 형태의 단어이지만, 문맥적 의미는 정반대다. 포획 사육 기간에 악어가 스스로를 보호할 준비를 갖추고 나면 '계속 잡아두는' 것이 아니라 '방생해야' 야생 동물의 보호와 생존에 도움이 된다.

---

31 사전 통보로 변화에 적응할 시간을 주기 | 정답률 61% | 정답 ②

다음 빈칸에 들어갈 말로 가장 적절한 것을 고르시오.
① unite - 연합할
✓ adapt - 적응할
③ object - 반대할
④ compete - 경쟁할
⑤ recover - 회복할

We don't send telegraphs to communicate anymore, / but it's a great metaphor for giving advance notice.
우리는 소통하기 위해 더 이상 전보를 보내지 않지만 / 이것은 사전 통보를 하는 것에 대한 훌륭한 비유이다.
Sometimes, / you must inform those close to you / of upcoming change / by conveying important information well in advance.
때때로 / 여러분은 자신에게 가까운 사람들에게 알려야 한다. / 다가오는 변화를 / 중요한 정보를 미리 잘 전달함으로써
There's a huge difference / between saying, "From now on, we will do things differently," / which doesn't give people enough time / to understand and accept the change, / and saying something like, "Starting next month, we're going to approach things differently."
큰 차이가 있다. / "지금부터 우리는 일을 다르게 할 겁니다."라고 말하는 것과 / 사람들에게 충분한 시간을 주지 않는 / 그 변화를 이해하고 받아들일 / "다음 달부터 우리는 일에 다르게 접근할 겁니다." 같은 말을 하는 것 사이에
Telegraphing empowers people to adapt.
전보를 보내는 것은 사람들이 적응할 수 있도록 해 준다.
Telegraphing involves the art / of seeing an upcoming event or circumstance / and giving others enough time / to process and accept the change.
전보를 보내는 것은 기술을 포함한다. / 다가오는 사건이나 상황을 보고 / 다른 사람들에게 충분한 시간을 주는 / 그 변화를 처리하고

받아들일
Telegraph anything / that will take people out of / what is familiar and comfortable to them.
무엇이든 전보로 보내라. / 사람들을 ~에서 벗어나게 할 / 그들에게 익숙하고 편안한 것
This will allow processing time / for them to accept the circumstances / and make the most of what's happening.
이것은 처리 시간을 허락할 것이다. / 그들이 그 상황을 받아들이고 / 일어나고 있는 일을 최대한으로 활용할 수 있는

우리는 소통하기 위해 더 이상 전보를 보내지 않지만 이것은 사전 통보를 하는 것에 대한 훌륭한 비유이다. 때때로 여러분은 중요한 정보를 미리 잘 전달함으로써 다가오는 변화를 자신에게 가까운 사람들에게 알려야 한다. 사람들에게 그 변화를 이해하고 받아들일 충분한 시간을 주지 "지금부터 우리는 일을 다르게 할 겁니다."라고 말하는 것과 "다음 달부터 우리는 일에 다르게 접근할 겁니다." 같은 말을 하는 것 사이에는 큰 차이가 있다. 전보를 보내는 것은 사람들이 적응할 수 있도록 해 준다. 전보를 보내는 것은 다가오는 사건이나 상황을 보고 다른 사람들에게 그 변화를 처리하고 받아들일 충분한 시간을 주는 기술을 포함한다. 사람들을 익숙하고 편안한 것에서 벗어나게 할 무엇이든 전보로 보내라. 이것은 그들이 그 상황을 받아들이고 일어나고 있는 일을 최대한으로 활용할 수 있는 처리 시간을 허락할 것이다.

Why? 왜 정답일까?
빈칸이 포함된 문장 뒤에서 비유적 의미의 전보는 사람들이 다가오는 변화를 처리하고 받아들일 시간을 충분히 준다(Telegraphing involves the art of seeing an upcoming event or circumstance and giving others enough time to process and accept the change. / This will allow processing time for them to accept the circumstances and make the most of what's happening.)고 설명하므로, 빈칸에 들어갈 말로 가장 적절한 것은 ② '적응할'이다.

- telegraph ⑩ 전보
- convey ⑰ 전달하다
- circumstance ⑩ 상황
- metaphor ⑩ 은유
- empower ⑰ 권한을 주다
- make the most of ~을 최대한 활용하다

구문 풀이
2행 Sometimes, you must inform those close to you of upcoming change
「inform + A」 「of + B : A에게 B를 알리다」
by conveying important information well in advance.
「by + 동명사 : ~함으로써」

---

32 우리의 존재를 규정하는 기억 | 정답률 62% | 정답 ①

다음 빈칸에 들어갈 말로 가장 적절한 것을 고르시오.
✓ makes us who we are - 우리를 우리 모습으로 만들어 준다
② has to do with our body - 우리 신체와 관련이 있다
③ reflects what we expect - 우리의 예상을 반영한다
④ lets us understand others - 우리가 남을 이해하게 해준다
⑤ helps us learn from the past - 우리가 과거로부터 배우도록 도와준다

Not only does memory / underlie our ability to think at all, / it defines the content of our experiences / and how we preserve them for years to come.
기억은 ~할 뿐만 아니라 / 어쨌든 우리의 사고력의 기반이 될 / 그것은 우리의 경험의 내용을 규정한다. / 그리고 다가올 수년 간 우리가 그것을 보존하는 방식을
Memory makes us who we are.
기억은 우리를 우리 모습으로 만들어 준다.
If I were to suffer from heart failure / and depend upon an artificial heart, / I would be no less myself.
만약 내가 심부전을 앓고 / 인공 심장에 의존한다 해도 / 나는 역시 여느 때의 나일 것이다.
If I lost an arm in an accident / and had it replaced with an artificial arm, / I would still be essentially me.
만약 내가 사고로 한 팔을 잃고 / 그것을 인공 팔로 교체한다 해도 / 나는 여전히 본질적으로 나일 것이다.
As long as my mind and memories remain intact, / I will continue to be the same person, / no matter which part of my body (other than the brain) is replaced.
나의 정신과 기억이 손상되지 않은 한, / 나는 계속 같은 사람일 것이다. / (뇌를 제외하고) 내 신체의 어떤 부분이 교체될지라도
On the other hand, / when someone suffers from advanced Alzheimer's disease / and his memories fade, / people often say / that he "is not himself anymore," / or that it is as if the person "is no longer there," / though his body remains unchanged.
반면 / 누군가 후기 알츠하이머병을 앓고 / 그의 기억이 흐려진다면, / 사람들은 종종 말한다. / 그는 '더 이상 여느 때의 그가 아니다'라거나 / 마치 그 사람이 '더 이상 그곳에 없다'는 것 같다고 / 비록 그의 신체는 변하지 않은 채로 남아 있음에도 불구하고

기억은 어쨌든 우리의 사고력의 기반이 될 뿐만 아니라 우리의 경험의 내용과 다가올 수년 간 우리가 그것을 보존하는 방식을 규정한다. 기억은 우리를 우리 모습으로 만들어 준다. 만약 내가 심부전을 앓고 인공 심장에 의존한다 해도 나는 역시 여느 때의 나일 것이다. 만약 내가 사고로 한 팔을 잃고 인공 팔로 교체한다 해도 나는 여전히 본질적으로 나일 것이다. 나의 정신과 기억이 손상되지 않은 한, (뇌를 제외하고) 내 신체의 어떤 부분이 교체될지라도 나는 계속 같은 사람일 것이다. 반면 누군가 후기 알츠하이머병을 앓고 그의 기억이 흐려진다면, 비록 그의 신체는 변하지 않은 채로 남아 있음에도 불구하고 사람들은 종종 '더 이상 여느 때의 그가 아니'라거나 마치 그 사람이 '더 이상 그곳에 없'는 것 같다고 말한다.

Why? 왜 정답일까?
빈칸 뒤에서 예시를 통해 우리는 기억을 보존하는 한 같은 사람으로 여겨지지만 (As long as my mind and memories remain intact, I will continue to be the same person, ~) 기억을 잃는 경우에는 그렇지 않다는 내용을 제시하고 있다. 따라서 예시 내용을 요약하는 빈칸에 들어갈 말로 가장 적절한 것은 기억이 곧 우리 존재의 본질을 결정짓는다는 의미의 ① '우리를 우리 모습으로 만들어 준다'이다.

- underlie ⑰ (~의) 기반을 이루다
- fade ⑰ 흐려지다, (빛이) 바래다
- essentially ⑳ 본질적으로

구문 풀이
3행 If I were to suffer from heart failure and depend upon an artificial heart,
「if + 주어 + were to + 동사원형」
I would be no less myself.
주어 + 조동사 과거형 + 동사원형 : 가정법 미래(가능성이 희박한 일)

33 아기의 언어 습득에 바탕이 되는 통계 분석 능력 정답률 41% | 정답 ②

다음 빈칸에 들어갈 말로 가장 적절한 것을 고르시오. [3점]

① lack of social pressures – 사회적 압력의 부족
✓ ability to calculate statistics – 통계를 계산하는 능력
③ desire to interact with others – 타인과 상호작용하려는 욕구
④ preference for simpler sounds – 더 간단한 소리에 대한 선호
⑤ tendency to imitate caregivers – 양육자를 모방하려는 경향

Over time, / babies construct expectations / about what sounds they will hear when.
시간이 지나면서 / 아기는 기대를 형성한다. / 자신이 어떤 소리를 언제 들을지에 대한
They hold in memory the sound patterns / that occur on a regular basis.
그들은 소리 패턴을 기억한다. / 규칙적으로 발생하는
They make hypotheses / like, "If I hear *this* sound first, / it probably will be followed by *that* sound."
그들은 가설을 세운다. / '내가 이 소리를 먼저 들으면 / 그것에 아마도 저 소리가 따라올 것이다'와 같은
Scientists conclude / that much of babies' skill in learning language / is due to their ability to calculate statistics.
과학자들은 결론짓는다. / 아기의 언어 학습 능력의 상당 부분이 / 통계를 계산하는 능력 때문이라고
For babies, / this means / that they appear to pay close attention / to the patterns that repeat in language.
아기에게 있어 / 이것은 의미한다. / 그들이 세심한 주의를 기울이는 것처럼 보인다는 것을 / 언어에서 반복되는 패턴에
They remember, in a systematic way, / how often sounds occur, / in what order, / with what intervals, / and with what changes of pitch.
그들은 체계적인 방식으로 기억한다. / 소리가 얼마나 자주 발생하는지를 / 어떤 순서로, / 어떤 간격으로, / 그리고 어떤 음조의 변화로
This memory store allows them to track, / within the neural circuits of their brains, / the frequency of sound patterns / and to use this knowledge / to make predictions about the meaning in patterns of sounds.
이 기억 저장소는 그들이 추적하게 해 주고, / 자신의 뇌의 신경 회로 내에서 / 소리 패턴의 빈도를 / 이 지식을 사용하도록 해 준다. / 소리 패턴의 의미에 대한 예측을 하기 위해

시간이 지나면서 아기는 자신이 어떤 소리를 언제 들을지에 대한 기대를 형성한다. 그들은 규칙적으로 발생하는 소리 패턴을 기억한다. 그들은 '내가 이 소리를 먼저 들으면 아마도 저 소리가 따라올 것이다'와 같은 가설을 세운다. 과학자들은 아기의 언어 학습 능력의 상당 부분이 통계를 계산하는 능력 때문이라고 결론짓는다. 아기에게 있어 이것은 그들이 언어에서 반복되는 패턴에 세심한 주의를 기울이는 것처럼 보인다는 것을 의미한다. 그들은 소리가 얼마나 자주, 어떤 순서로, 어떤 간격으로, 어떤 음조의 변화로 발생하는지를 체계적인 방식으로 기억한다. 이 기억 저장소는 그들이 뇌의 신경 회로 내에서 소리 패턴의 빈도를 추적하고, 이 지식을 사용해 소리 패턴의 의미에 대해 예측하게 해준다.

Why? 왜 정답일까?

마지막 두 문장에서 아기들은 패턴이 어떻게 반복되는지에 관한 세부 사항을 기억하고, 패턴의 빈도를 추적하여 후에 의미를 예측할 때 그러한 정보를 사용한다고 설명하고 있다. 빈칸에는 이러한 일련의 인지 작용을 일반화하는 말이 필요하므로, 빈칸에 들어갈 말로 가장 적절한 것은 ② '통계를 계산하는 능력'이다.

● construct ⓥ 형성하다, 구성하다
● hypothesis ⓝ 가설
● interval ⓝ 간격
● calculate ⓥ 계산하다
● on a regular basis 규칙적으로
● systematic ⓐ 체계적인
● make a prediction 예측하다
● statistics ⓝ 통계

구문 풀이

10행 This memory store allows them to track, (within the neural circuits of
　　　　　　　　　　5형식동사　목적어　목적격 보어1
their brains), the frequency of sound patterns and to use this knowledge to make
( ): 삽입구　　　to track 목적어　　　목적격 보어2　　　부사적 용법(목적)
predictions about the meaning in patterns of sounds.

★★ 문제 해결 꿀~팁 ★★

▶ 많이 틀린 이유는?
아기들의 언어 습득에 관한 글이다. 빈칸 뒤로, 아기들이 언어에서 반복되는 소리에 주의를 기울이고, 소리의 빈도나 순서, 고저를 분석하여 언어 패턴을 익혀 나간다는 설명이 이어지고 있다. '더 간단한' 소리를 선호한다는 내용은 언급되지 않기에 ④는 답으로 적절하지 않다.

▶ 문제 해결 방법은?
아기들이 주변에서 들은 소리 데이터를 바탕으로 그 패턴을 분석하여 추후 예측에 활용한다는 설명을 '통계 자료 계산(calculate statistics)'이라는 비유적 표현으로 일반화할 수 있어야 한다.

---

34 심해 생물이 자체 발광하는 이유 정답률 55% | 정답 ④

다음 빈칸에 들어갈 말로 가장 적절한 것을 고르시오. [3점]

① send a signal for help – 도움 요청의 신호를 보내는
② threaten enemies nearby – 주위의 적을 위협하는
③ lift the veil of hidden prey – 숨어 있는 먹이의 베일을 벗기는
✓ create a cloak of invisibility – 보이지 않는 망토를 만드는
⑤ serve as a navigation system – 네비게이션 시스템의 역할을 하는

Some deep-sea organisms / are known to use bioluminescence as a lure, / to attract prey with a little glow / imitating the movements of their favorite fish, / or like fireflies, / as a sexual attractant to find mates.
일부 심해 생물은 / 가짜 미끼로 생물 발광을 활용한다고 알려져 있다. / 작은 빛으로 먹이를 유혹하기 위해 / 그들이 좋아하는 물고기의 움직임을 모방하는 / 혹은 반딧불이처럼 / 짝을 찾기 위한 성적 유인 물질로
While there are many possible evolutionary theories / for the survival value of bioluminescence, / one of the most fascinating is / to create a cloak of invisibility.
많은 가능한 진화 이론이 있지만 / 생물 발광의 생존가에 대한 / 가장 흥미로운 것 중 하나는 ~이다. / 보이지 않는 망토를 만드는 것
The color of almost all bioluminescent molecules / is blue-green, / the same color as the ocean above.
거의 모든 생물 발광 분자의 색깔은 / 청록색이다. / 바다 위층과 같은 색인

By self-glowing blue-green, / the creatures no longer cast a shadow or create a silhouette, / especially when viewed from below / against the brighter waters above.
청록색으로 자체 발광함으로써 / 생물은 더 이상 그림자를 드리우거나 실루엣을 만들어 내지 않는다. / 특히 아래에서 보여질 때 / 위쪽의 더 밝은 물을 배경으로
Rather, / by glowing themselves, / they can blend into the sparkles, reflections, and scattered blue-green glow / of sunlight or moonlight.
오히려 / 스스로 발광함으로써 / 그들은 반짝임, 반사 그리고 분산된 청록색에 섞일 수 있다. / 햇빛 혹은 달빛의
Thus, / they are most likely making their own light / not to see, but to be un-seen.
따라서 / 그들은 자신만의 빛을 분명 만들어 내고 있을 것이다. / 보기 위해서가 아니라 보이지 않기 위해서

일부 심해 생물은 그들이 좋아하는 물고기의 움직임을 모방하는 작은 빛으로 먹이를 유혹하기 위해 가짜 미끼로, 혹은 반딧불이처럼 짝을 찾기 위한 성적 유인 물질로 생물 발광을 활용한다고 알려져 있다. 생물 발광의 생존가에 대한 많은 가능한 진화 이론이 있지만, 가장 흥미로운 것 중 하나는 보이지 않는 망토를 만드는 것이다. 거의 모든 생물 발광 분자의 색깔은 바다 위층과 같은 색인 청록색이다. 청록색으로 자체 발광함으로써 생물은 특히 위쪽의 밝은 물을 배경으로 아래에서 볼 때 더 이상 그림자를 드리우거나 실루엣을 만들어 내지 않는다. 오히려 스스로 발광함으로써 그들은 햇빛 혹은 달빛의 반짝임, 반사 그리고 분산된 청록색 빛에 섞일 수 있다. 따라서 그들은 보기 위해서가 아니라 보이지 않기 위해서 분명 자신만의 빛을 만들어 내고 있을 것이다.

Why? 왜 정답일까?

마지막 두 문장에서 심해 생물들이 자체 발광하는 이유를 설명하는데, 이들은 바다 위층과 똑같은 색인 청록색으로 빛을 냄으로써 오히려 그 빛에 섞이고(~ by glowing themselves, they can blend into ~), 눈에 더 띄지 않게 될 수 있다(~ most likely making their own light not to see, but to be un-seen.)는 것이다. 따라서 빈칸에 들어갈 말로 가장 적절한 것은 '눈에 보이지 않으려' 한다는 목적을 비유적으로 설명한 ④ '보이지 않는 망토를 만드는'이다.

● attractant ⓝ 유인 물질
● cast ⓥ 드리우다, 던지다
● scatter ⓥ 흩뜨리다, 분산하다
● cloak ⓝ 망토
● fascinating ⓐ 매력적인, 흥미로운
● blend into ~에 섞이다
● threaten ⓥ 위협하다
● invisibility ⓝ 보이지 않음

구문 풀이

1행 Some deep-sea organisms are known to use bioluminescence as a lure,
　　　　　　　　　　　　　　be known + to부정사: ~한다고 알려지다
　　　　　　　　　　　　　　전치사1(~로서)
to attract prey with a little glow imitating the movements of their favorite fish, or
부사적 용법(~하기 위해)
like fireflies, as a sexual attractant to find mates.
전치사2(~로서)　　　　형용사적 용법

---

35 인간의 편향을 강화하도록 작용하는 검색 알고리즘 정답률 62% | 정답 ③

다음 글에서 전체 흐름과 관계 없는 문장은?

Internet activist Eli Pariser noticed / how online search algorithms encourage our human tendency / to grab hold of everything / that confirms the beliefs we already hold, / while quietly ignoring information / that doesn't match those beliefs.
인터넷 활동가인 Eli Pariser는 주목했다. / 온라인 검색 알고리즘이 인간의 경향을 어떻게 조장하는지에 / 모든 것을 움켜쥐고, / 우리가 이미 지닌 신념이 옳음을 확인해 주는 / 반면에 정보는 조용히 무시하는 / 그러한 신념과 맞지 않는
① We set up a so-called "filter-bubble" around ourselves, / where we are constantly exposed only to that material / that we agree with.
우리는 자신의 주변에 소위 '필터 버블'을 설치하는데 / 그곳에서 우리는 그런 자료에만 끊임없이 노출된다. / 자신이 동의하는
② We are never challenged, / never giving ourselves the opportunity / to acknowledge the existence of diversity and difference.
우리는 결코 이의를 제기 받지 않으며 / 결코 우리 자신에게 기회를 주지 않는다. / 다양성과 차이의 존재를 인정할
✓ Creating a difference that others don't have / is a way to succeed in your field, / leading to the creation of innovations.
다른 사람이 갖지 못한 차이를 만들어 내는 것이 / 자신의 분야에서 성공하는 방법이며 / 혁신의 창조를 이끈다.
④ In the best case, / we become naive and sheltered, / and in the worst, / we become radicalized with extreme views, / unable to imagine life outside our particular bubble.
최상의 경우 / 우리는 세상을 모르고 보호 받으며, / 최악의 경우 / 우리는 극단적인 시각으로 과격화되어 / 우리의 특정 버블 밖의 삶을 상상할 수 없게 된다.
⑤ The results are disastrous: / intellectual isolation and the real distortion / that comes with believing / that the little world we create for ourselves / is *the* world.
그 결과는 참담하다. / 지적 고립과 진정한 왜곡 / 믿게 되어 따라오는 / 우리가 스스로 만드는 작은 세계가 / 전 세계라고

인터넷 활동가인 Eli Pariser는 온라인 검색 알고리즘이 우리가 이미 지닌 신념이 옳음을 확인해 주는 모든 것을 움켜쥐고, 반면에 그러한 신념과 맞지 않는 정보는 조용히 무시하는 인간의 경향을 어떻게 조장하는지에 주목했다. ① 우리는 자신의 주변에 소위 '필터 버블'을 설치하는데 그곳에서 우리는 우리가 동의하는 그런 자료에만 끊임없이 노출된다. ② 우리는 결코 이의를 제기 받지 않으며 스스로에게 다양성과 차이의 존재를 인정할 기회를 주지 않는다. ③ 다른 사람이 갖지 못한 차이를 만들어 내는 것이 자신의 분야에서 성공하는 방법이며 혁신의 창조를 이끈다. ④ 최상의 경우 우리는 세상을 모르고 보호 받으며, 최악의 경우 우리는 극단적인 시각으로 과격화되어 우리의 특정 버블 밖의 삶을 상상할 수 없게 된다. ⑤ 그 결과는 참담하여, 예를 들면 지적 고립과 우리가 스스로 만드는 작은 세계가 전 세계라고 믿게 되어 따라오는 진정한 왜곡이 있다.

Why? 왜 정답일까?

첫 문장에서 온라인 검색 알고리즘은 이미 믿고 있는 신념을 확인해주는 정보를 주로 보려 하는 인간의 편향을 강화한다고 언급한다. 이어서 ①과 ②는 우리가 '필터 버블' 안에 갇혀 다양성과 차이를 인정할 기회를 갖지 못한다고 설명하고, ④와 ⑤는 그로 인한 부정적 결과를 설명한다. 하지만 ③은 다른 사람이 갖지 못한 차이를 만들어낼 때 자기 분야에서 성공할 수 있다는 내용이므로 흐름에서 벗어난다. 따라서 전체 흐름과 관계 없는 문장은 ③이다.

● grab hold of ~을 (갑자기) 움켜잡다
● filter-bubble ⓝ 필터 버블(사용자가 인터넷 알고리즘에 의해 관심 있는 정보만 접하며 왜곡된 인지 속에 갇히는 것)
● acknowledge ⓥ 인정하다
● innovation ⓝ 혁신
● isolation ⓝ 고립
● existence ⓝ 존재
● disastrous ⓐ 참담한

4행 We set up a so-called "filter-bubble" around ourselves, where we are
장소 선행사   계속적 용법
constantly exposed only to that material [that we agree with].
                                  선행사 목적격 관·대

★★★ 등급을 가르는 문제!

36 전자 상거래의 성장 · 정답률 42% | 정답 ③

주어진 글 다음에 이어질 글의 순서로 가장 적절한 것을 고르시오.
① (A) – (C) – (B)   ② (B) – (A) – (C)
✔③ (B) – (C) – (A)   ④ (C) – (A) – (B)
⑤ (C) – (B) – (A)

Roughly twenty years ago, / brick-and-mortar stores began to give way to electronic commerce.
대략 20년 전 / 오프라인 거래 상점이 전자 상거래(온라인)로 바뀌기 시작했다.
For good or bad, / the shift fundamentally changed consumers' perception of the shopping experience.
좋든 나쁘든 간에 / 그 변화는 쇼핑 경험에 대한 소비자의 인식을 근본적으로 바꾸었다.
(B) Nowhere was the shift more obvious / than with book sales, / which is how online bookstores got their start.
그 변화가 더 분명한 곳은 없었는데 / 책 판매보다 / 그렇게 해서 온라인 서점이 시작되었다.
Physical bookstores simply could not stock / as many titles as a virtual bookstore could.
물리적인 서점은 그야말로 구비할 수 없었다. / 가상 서점이 할 수 있는 만큼 많은 서적을
There is only so much space available on a shelf.
딱 책꽂이 위의 공간만큼만 이용 가능했다.
(C) In addition to greater variety, / online bookstores were also able to offer aggressive discounts / thanks to their lower operating costs.
더 많은 다양성뿐만 아니라 / 온라인 서점은 또한 대단히 적극적으로 할인을 제공할 수 있었다. / 그들의 더 낮은 운영비 덕분에
The combination of lower prices and greater selection / led to the slow, steady rise of online bookstores.
더 낮은 가격과 더 많은 선택의 결합은 / 온라인 서점의 느리지만 꾸준한 상승으로 이어졌다.
(A) Before long, / the e-commerce book market / naturally expanded to include additional categories, / like CDs and DVDs.
머지않아 / 전자 상거래 책 시장은 / 추가적인 항목을 포함하도록 자연스럽게 확장되었다. / CD와 DVD 같은
E-commerce soon snowballed / into the enormous industry it is today, / where you can buy everything / from toilet paper to cars online.
전자 상거래는 곧 눈덩이처럼 불어났고, / 오늘날의 거대 산업으로 / 여기서 여러분은 모든 것을 온라인으로 살 수 있다. / 화장실 휴지에서 자동차까지

대략 20년 전 오프라인 거래 상점이 전자 상거래(온라인)로 바뀌기 시작했다. 좋든 나쁘든 간에 그 변화는 쇼핑 경험에 대한 소비자의 인식을 근본적으로 바꾸었다.

(B) 그 변화가 책 판매보다 더 분명한 곳은 없었는데, 그렇게 해서 온라인 서점이 시작되었다. 물리적인 서점은 가상 서점이 할 수 있는 만큼 많은 서적을 그야말로 구비할 수 없었다. 딱 책꽂이 위의 공간만큼만 이용 가능했다.

(C) 더 많은 다양성뿐만 아니라 온라인 서점은 또한 더 낮은 운영비 덕분에 대단히 적극적으로 할인을 제공할 수 있었다. 더 싼 가격과 더 많은 선택의 결합은 온라인 서점의 느리지만 꾸준한 상승으로 이어졌다.

(A) 머지않아 전자 상거래 책 시장은 CD와 DVD 같은 추가적인 항목을 포함하도록 자연스럽게 확장되었다. 전자 상거래는 곧 오늘날의 거대 산업으로 눈덩이처럼 불어났고, 여기서 여러분은 화장실 휴지에서 자동차까지 모든 것을 온라인으로 살 수 있다.

Why? 왜 정답일까?
주어진 글은 약 20년 전 전자 상거래가 시작되어 쇼핑에 대한 인식을 변화시켰다는 일반적인 내용을 제시한다. 이어서 (B)는 특히 온라인 서점의 사례를 언급하며, 물리적 서점에 비해 온라인 서점이 공간적 이점을 지녔다고 설명한다. (C)는 온라인 서점이 또한 가격 우위를 지녔음을 언급하고, (A)는 온라인 서점 분야가 CD, DVD 등으로 확장되었음을 설명한다. 따라서 글의 순서로 가장 적절한 것은 ③ '(B) – (C) – (A)'이다.

● roughly [ad] 약, 대략
● fundamentally [ad] 근본적으로
● aggressive [a] 공격적인, (대단히) 적극적인
● give way to ~로 바뀌다
● enormous [a] 거대한
● operating cost 운영비

9행 Nowhere was the shift more obvious than with book sales, which is how
「장소 부사구+동사+주어: 도치 구문」   계속적 용법(선행사: 앞 문장)
online bookstores got their start.

★★ 문제 해결 꿀~팁 ★★

▶ 많이 틀린 이유는?
(B) 이후 (A)와 (C)의 순서를 잘 잡는 것이 관건이다. (B)에서 온라인 서점이 오프라인 서점보다 책을 다양하게 구비했다는 장점을 소개한 후, (A)는 온라인 서점 시장이 다른 부문으로 확장되었다는 내용을, (C)는 온라인 서점의 추가적 장점을 언급한다. 흐름상 (C)에서 온라인 서점의 장점에 관한 설명을 마무리하고, (A)에서 이 장점을 바탕으로 다른 상품 분야로의 확장이 가능했다는 결론을 내리는 것이 자연스럽다. 따라서 ② '(B) – (A) – (C)'는 답으로 부적절하다.

▶ 문제 해결 방법은?
(B)의 as many titles as a virtual bookstore가 (C)의 greater variety로 연결된다. 이어서 (C)의 결론인 the slow, steady rise of online bookstores가 (A)의 the e-commerce book market naturally expanded to include additional categories로 연결되며, 온라인 서점 사업이 책을 넘어 CD, DVD 등 다양한 부문으로 확장되었다는 최종적 결론에 이르고 있다.

★★★ 등급을 가르는 문제!

37 문학 텍스트의 이해 · 정답률 43% | 정답 ⑤

주어진 글 다음에 이어질 글의 순서로 가장 적절한 것을 고르시오. [3점]

① (A) – (C) – (B)   ② (B) – (A) – (C)
③ (B) – (C) – (A)   ④ (C) – (A) – (B)
✔⑤ (C) – (B) – (A)

Literary works, / by their nature, / suggest rather than explain; / they imply rather than state their claims boldly and directly.
문학 작품들은 / 그 본질상 / 설명하기보다는 암시하는데, / 그들은 그들의 주장을 뚜렷하고 직접적으로 진술하기보다는 함축한다.
(C) This broad generalization, / however, / does not mean / that works of literature do not include direct statements.
이 넓은 일반화는 / 그러나 / 뜻하지는 않는다. / 문학 작품들이 직접적인 진술을 포함하지 않는다는 것을
Depending on when they were written and by whom, / literary works may contain large amounts of direct telling / and lesser amounts of suggestion and implication.
그들이 언제 그리고 누구에 의해 쓰였는지에 따라 / 문학 작품들은 많은 양의 직접적 말하기를 포함할 수도 있다. / 그리고 더 적은 양의 암시와 함축을
(B) But whatever the proportion of a work's showing to telling, / there is always something for readers to interpret.
하지만 작품에서 말하기 대 보여 주기의 비율이 어떻든 간에 / 독자가 해석해야 하는 무언가가 항상 존재한다.
Thus we ask the question / "What does the text suggest?" / as a way to approach literary interpretation, / as a way to begin thinking about a text's implications.
그러므로 우리는 질문을 한다. / "그 텍스트가 무엇을 암시하는가?"라는 / 문학적 해석에 접근하는 방법이자 / 텍스트의 함축에 대해 생각하기 시작하는 방법으로
(A) What a text implies / is often of great interest to us.
텍스트가 무엇을 함축하는지는 / 종종 우리에게 매우 흥미롭다.
And / our work of figuring out a text's implications / tests our analytical powers.
그리고 / 텍스트의 함축을 알아내는 우리의 작업은 / 우리의 분석적 능력을 시험한다.
In considering what a text suggests, / we gain practice in making sense of texts.
텍스트가 무엇을 암시하는지를 고려하는 과정에서 / 우리는 텍스트를 이해하는 기량을 얻게 된다.

문학 작품들은 그 본질상 설명하기보다는 암시하는데, 그들은 주장을 뚜렷하게 직접적으로 진술하기보다는 함축한다.

(C) 그러나 이 넓은 일반화는 문학 작품들이 직접적인 진술을 포함하지 않는다는 뜻은 아니다. 그들이 언제 누구에 의해 쓰였는지에 따라, 문학 작품들은 많은 양의 직접적 말하기와 더 적은 양의 암시와 함축을 포함할 수도 있다.

(B) 하지만 작품에서 말하기 대 보여 주기의 비율이 어떻든 간에 독자가 해석해야 하는 무언가가 항상 존재한다. 그러므로 우리는 문학적 해석에 접근하는 방법이자 텍스트의 함축에 대해 생각하기 시작하는 방법으로 "그 텍스트가 무엇을 암시하는가?"라는 질문을 한다.

(A) 텍스트가 무엇을 함축하는지는 종종 우리에게 매우 흥미롭다. 그리고 텍스트의 함축을 알아내는 작업은 우리의 분석적 능력을 시험한다. 텍스트가 무엇을 암시하는지를 고려하는 과정에서 우리는 텍스트를 이해하는 기량을 얻게 된다.

Why? 왜 정답일까?
주어진 글은 문학 작품의 특징으로 함축적 진술을 언급한다. 이어서 (C)는 however로 주의를 환기하며 문학 작품 안에 직접적 진술이 전혀 없지는 않다는 점을 상기시킨다. 한편 But으로 시작하는 (B)는 직접적 진술과 함축적 진술의 비율이 어떻든 간에 문학 텍스트에는 항상 독자가 해석해야 하는 부분이 있으며, 이 때문에 우리가 '그 텍스트가 무엇을 암시하는지' 자문하게 된다고 언급한다. (A)는 (B)의 "What does the text suggest?"를 What a text implies로 바꾸어 표현하며, 텍스트가 함축하는 바를 알아내는 과정에서 우리가 텍스트를 이해하는 능력을 기르게 된다고 설명한다. 따라서 글의 순서로 가장 적절한 것은 ⑤ '(C) – (B) – (A)'이다.

● literary [a] 문학의
● boldly [ad] 뚜렷하게, 대담하게
● analytical [a] 분석적인
● generalization [n] 일반화
● nature [n] 본질, 본성
● implication [n] 함축, 암시
● interpret [v] 해석하다

3행 What a text implies is often of great interest to us.
         주어(명사절)   동사(단수)   보어(= greatly interesting)

★★ 문제 해결 꿀~팁 ★★

▶ 많이 틀린 이유는?
(B)와 (C)의 순서를 잘 파악하는 것이 관건이다. 얼핏 보면 주어진 글의 imply rather than state가 (B)의 showing과 telling으로 바로 연결되는 것 같지만, (B)의 핵심은 '독자의 해석과 이해'에 관한 것이다. 이에 반해 (C)는 주어진 글과 마찬가지로 문학적인 글의 말하기 방식에 관해서 다루고 있으므로, 화제의 흐름상 (C)가 먼저 나온 뒤 (B)로 전환되는 것이 자연스럽다.

▶ 문제 해결 방법은?
주어진 글의 'Literary works ~ imply rather than state their claims boldly and directly.'가 (C)의 This broad generalization으로 이어지고, (C)의 literary works may contain large amounts of direct telling and lesser amounts of suggestion and implication이 (B)의 the proportion of a work's showing to telling으로 연결된다. 즉 (C)까지 문학 작품 속의 말하기와 보여주기(의 비중)에 관해 설명한 뒤, (B)에서 '그 비중에 상관없이' 독자가 해석할 부분이 있다는 내용으로 넘어가는 흐름임을 파악하도록 한다.

38 보충제를 통한 영양소 섭취 · 정답률 58% | 정답 ④

글의 흐름으로 보아, 주어진 문장이 들어가기에 가장 적절한 곳을 고르시오.

According to top nutrition experts, / most nutrients are better absorbed and used by the body / when consumed from a whole food / instead of a supplement.
최고의 영양 전문가들에 의하면 / 많은 영양소가 신체에 의해 더 잘 흡수되고 사용된다. / 자연식품으로부터 섭취되었을 때 / 보충제 대신에
① However, / many people feel the need / to take pills, powders, and supplements / in an attempt to obtain nutrients / and fill the gaps in their diets.
그러나 / 많은 사람들이 필요성을 느낀다. / 알약, 분말 그리고 보충제를 섭취할 / 영양소를 얻기 위한 시도로 / 그리고 자신의 식단에 있어 부족한 부분을 채우기 위한
② We hope / these will give us more energy, / prevent us from catching a cold in the winter, / or improve our skin and hair.
우리는 바란다 / 이것들이 우리에게 더 많은 에너지를 줄 것을 / 겨울에 우리가 감기에 걸리는 것을 막아 주거나 / 또는 우리의 피부와 모발을 개선하기를

12회

우리는 바란다. / 이것들이 우리에게 더 많은 에너지를 주고, / 우리가 겨울에 감기에 걸리는 것을 막아 주거나 / 혹은 우리의 피부와 모발을 개선해 주기를

③ But in reality, / the large majority of supplements are artificial / and may not even be completely absorbed by your body.
그러나 실제로는 / 대다수의 보충제가 인위적이고 / 여러분의 신체에 의해 완전히 흡수조차 되지 않을 수도 있다.

✔Worse, / some are contaminated with other substances / and contain ingredients not listed on the label.
더 심각한 것은, / 어떤 것들은 다른 물질로 오염되어 있으며 / 라벨에 실려 있지 않은 성분을 포함한다.

For example, / a recent investigative report found heavy metals / in 40 percent of 134 brands of protein powders on the market.
예를 들어 / 최근 한 조사 보고는 중금속을 발견했다. / 시장에 있는 단백질 분말 134개 브랜드 중 40퍼센트에서

⑤ With little control and regulation, / taking supplements is a gamble and often costly.
단속과 규제가 거의 없다면 / 보충제를 섭취하는 것은 도박이며 종종 대가가 크다.

최고의 영양 전문가들에 의하면 많은 영양소가 보충제 대신에 자연식품으로부터 섭취되었을 때 신체에서 더 잘 흡수되고 사용된다. ① 그러나 많은 사람들이 영양소를 얻고 식단에 있어 부족한 부분을 채우기 위한 시도로 알약, 분말 그리고 보충제를 섭취할 필요성을 느낀다. ② 우리는 이것들이 우리에게 더 많은 에너지를 주거나, 겨울에 감기에 걸리는 것을 막아 주거나 우리의 피부와 모발을 개선해 주기를 바란다. ③ 그러나 실제로는 대다수의 보충제가 인위적이고 여러분의 신체에서 완전히 흡수조차 되지 않을 수도 있다. ④ 더 심각한 것은, 어떤 것들은 다른 물질로 오염되어 있으며 라벨에 실려 있지 않은 성분을 포함한다. 예를 들어 최근 한 조사 보고는 시장에 있는 단백질 분말 134개 브랜드 중 40퍼센트에서 중금속을 발견했다. ⑤ 단속과 규제가 거의 없다면 보충제를 섭취하는 것은 도박이며 종종 대가가 크다.

Why? 왜 정답일까?

보충제를 통해 영양소를 섭취하는 것은 생각보다 효과가 없거나 위험할 수 있다는 내용의 글이다. ④ 앞의 문장에서 대다수의 보충제가 실제로 우리 몸에서 잘 흡수되지 않는다고 설명한 후, 주어진 문장은 이것보다 더 심각한 문제(Worse)로 보충제가 다른 물질로 오염되어 있거나 라벨에 없는 성분을 포함하기도 한다고 지적한다. ④ 뒤의 문장은 주어진 문장에 대한 예시로 시중 단백질 분말 브랜드의 40%가 중금속으로 오염되어 있다는 내용을 언급한다. 따라서 주어진 문장이 들어가기에 가장 적절한 곳은 ④이다.

- **whole food** 자연식품
- **nutrition** ⓝ 영양
- **fill the gap** 부족한 부분을 채우다, 간격을 메우다
- **regulation** ⓝ 규제
- **substance** ⓝ 물질
- **absorb** ⓥ 흡수하다
- **artificial** ⓐ 인위적인

구문 풀이

7행 We hope (that) these will give us more energy, prevent us from catching a cold in the winter, or improve our skin and hair.
생략 / 동사1 / 동사2(prevent + A + from + B : A가 B하지 못하게 막다) / 동사3

★★★ 등급을 가르는 문제!

39 운동 에너지와 위치 에너지   정답률 35% | 정답 ⑤

글의 흐름으로 보아, 주어진 문장이 들어가기에 가장 적절한 곳을 고르시오. [3점]

In general, / kinetic energy is the energy associated with motion, / while potential energy represents the energy / which is "stored" in a physical system.
일반적으로, / 운동 에너지는 운동과 관련 있는 에너지이며 / 반면에 위치 에너지를 나타낸다. / 물리계에 '저장되는'

Moreover, the total energy is always conserved.
게다가 총 에너지는 항상 보존된다.

① But while the total energy remains unchanged, / the kinetic and potential parts of the total energy / can change all the time.
그러나 총 에너지가 변하지 않는 채로 있는 반면 / 총 에너지의 운동과 위치 에너지 비율은 / 항상 변할 수 있다.

② Imagine, for example, a pendulum / which swings back and forth.
예를 들어 추를 상상해 보자. / 앞뒤로 흔들리는

③ When it swings, / it sweeps out an arc / and then slows down / as it comes closer to its highest point, / where the pendulum does not move at all.
그것이 흔들릴 때 / 그것은 호 모양으로 쓸어내리듯 움직이다가 / 그리고 나서 속도가 줄어드는데, / 그것이 최고점에 가까워지면서 / 이 지점에서 추는 더 이상 움직이지 않는다.

④ So at this point, / the energy is completely given in terms of potential energy.
그래서 이 지점에서 / 에너지는 완전히 위치 에너지로 주어지게 된다.

✔But after this brief moment of rest, / the pendulum swings back again / and therefore part of the total energy is then given / in the form of kinetic energy.
하지만 이 짧은 순간의 멈춤 이후에 / 그 추는 다시 뒤로 흔들리게 되며 / 따라서 총 에너지의 일부가 그때 주어진다. / 운동 에너지의 형태로

So as the pendulum swings, / kinetic and potential energy / constantly change into each other.
그래서 그 추가 흔들리면서 / 운동과 위치 에너지는 / 끊임없이 서로 바뀐다.

일반적으로 운동 에너지는 운동과 관련 있는 에너지인 반면에, 위치 에너지는 물리계에 '저장되는' 에너지를 나타낸다. 게다가 총 에너지는 항상 보존된다. ① 그러나 총 에너지가 변하지 않는 채로 있는 반면 총 에너지의 운동과 위치 에너지 비율은 항상 변할 수 있다. ② 예를 들어 앞뒤로 흔들리는 추를 상상해 보자. ③ 그것은 흔들릴 때 호 모양으로 쓸어내리듯 움직이다가 그리고 나서 최고점에 가까워지면서 속도가 줄어드는데, 이 지점에서 추는 더 이상 움직이지 않는다. ④ 그래서 이 지점에서 에너지는 완전히 위치 에너지로 주어지게 된다. ⑤ 하지만 이 짧은 순간의 멈춤 이후에 그 추는 다시 뒤로 흔들리게 되며, 따라서 총 에너지의 일부가 그때 운동 에너지의 형태로 주어진다. 그래서 그 추가 흔들리면서 운동과 위치 에너지는 끊임없이 서로 바뀐다.

Why? 왜 정답일까?

위치 에너지와 운동 에너지는 같은 에너지 총량 안에서 계속 서로 바뀐다는 내용의 글로, ② 뒤의 문장부터 흔들리는 추를 예로 들어 이 변화를 설명하고 있다. ⑤ 앞의 두 문장에서 추의 높이가 최고점에 이르면 추는 더 이상 움직이지 않고, 모든 에너지가 위치 에너지로 바뀐다고 언급한다. 주어진 문장은 But으로 흐름을 전환하며, 이 짧은 멈춤(this brief moment of rest) 이후로 다시 추가 뒤로 흔들리면서 일부 에너지가 다시 운동 에너지로 바뀐다고 설명한다. ⑤ 뒤의 문장은 그리하여 운동 에너지와 위치 에너지는 서로 끊임없이 교환되는 관계라는 결론을 제시한다. 따라서 주어진 문장이 들어가기에 가장 적절한 곳은 ⑤이다.

- **kinetic energy** 운동 에너지
- **swing back and forth** 앞뒤로 흔들리다
- **constantly** 🄰 지속적으로, 끊임없이
- **potential energy** 위치 에너지
- **sweep out** 쓸어내리다

구문 풀이

10행 When it swings, it sweeps out an arc and then slows down as it comes
동사1 / 동사2
closer to its highest point, where the pendulum does not move at all.
선행사 / 관계부사(계속적 용법) / 접속사(~하면서, ~함에 따라)

★★ **문제 해결 꿀~팁** ★★

▶ 많이 틀린 이유는?
④ 앞의 does not move가 바로 주어진 문장의 this brief moment of rest로 연결되는 것처럼 보일 수 있지만, 사실 이 does not move는 ④ 뒤의 at this point로 연결된다. 이 '움직이지 않는' 지점에서 에너지는 모두 위치에너지로 전환되었음을 알 수 있다는 것이다.

▶ 문제 해결 방법은?
⑤ 앞뒤 문장에 모두 결론의 So가 나오므로, 이 So가 어느 내용에 이어져야 하는지에 주목하며 읽는다.

---

40 건강에 관한 과학 연구가 단순하게 소개되는 이유   정답률 48% | 정답 ②

다음 글의 내용을 한 문장으로 요약하고자 한다. 빈칸 (A), (B)에 들어갈 말로 가장 적절한 것은?

	(A)	(B)
①	satisfy 만족시키지	simple 간단한
✔②	satisfy 만족시키지	complicated 복잡한
③	ignore 무시하지	difficult 어려운
④	ignore 무시하지	simple 간단한
⑤	reject 거부하지	complicated 복잡한

There is often a lot of uncertainty / in the realm of science, / which the general public finds uncomfortable.
종종 많은 불확실성이 존재하며 / 과학의 영역에는 / 일반 대중은 그것을 불편하다고 느낀다.

They don't want "informed guesses," / they want certainties / that make their lives easier, / and science is often unequipped to meet these demands.
그들은 '정보에 근거한 추측'을 원하지 않으며 / 그들은 확실성을 원하는데, / 자신의 삶을 더 편하게 만들어 주는 / 과학은 종종 이러한 요구를 만족시키도록 갖춰져 있지 않다.

In particular, / the human body is fantastically complex, / and some scientific answers can never be provided / in black-or-white terms.
특히, / 인간의 신체는 굉장히 복잡하며 / 어떤 과학적인 답변은 절대 제공될 수 없다. / 흑백 양자택일의 말로는

All this is why / the media tends to oversimplify scientific research / when presenting it to the public.
이 모든 것은 ~한 이유이다. / 미디어는 과학적 연구를 지나치게 단순화하는 경향이 있다 / 그것을 대중에게 제시할 때

In their eyes, / they're just "giving people what they want" / as opposed to offering more accurate but complex information / that very few people will read or understand.
그들의 시각에서는 / 그들은 단지 '사람들에게 그들이 원하는 것을 제공하고' 있는 것이다. / 더 정확하지만 복잡한 정보를 제공하는 것과는 반대로 / 극소수의 사람들만이 읽거나 이해할

A perfect example of this is / how people want definitive answers / as to which foods are "good" and "bad."
이것의 완벽한 하나의 예시는 ~이다. / 사람들이 확정적인 답변을 원하는 방식 / 어떤 음식이 '좋은'지 '나쁜'지에 관해

Scientifically speaking, / there are no "good" and "bad" foods; / rather, food quality exists on a continuum, / meaning that some foods are *better* than others / when it comes to general health and well-being.
과학적으로 말하자면 / '좋고' '나쁜' 음식은 없으며, / 오히려 음식의 질은 연속체상에 존재하는데 / 이는 어떤 음식들이 다른 것들보다 더 낫다는 것을 의미한다. / 일반 건강과 웰빙 면에서

➡ With regard to general health, / science, by its nature, / does not (A) satisfy the public's demands for certainty, / which leads to the media giving less (B) complicated answers to the public.
일반 건강과 관련하여 / 과학은 본질적으로 / 확실성에 대한 대중의 요구를 만족시키지 않으며, / 이것은 미디어가 대중에게 덜 복잡한 답변을 제공하게 만든다.

과학의 영역에는 종종 많은 불확실성이 존재하며 일반 대중은 그것을 불편하다고 느낀다. 그들은 '정보에 근거한 추측'을 원하지 않으며 자신의 삶을 더 편하게 만들어 주는 확실성을 원하는데, 과학은 종종 이러한 요구를 만족시키도록 갖춰져 있지 않다. 특히 인간의 신체는 굉장히 복잡하며 어떤 과학적인 답변은 흑백 양자택일의 말로는 절대 제공될 수 없다. 이 모든 것 때문에 미디어는 과학적 연구를 대중에게 제시할 때 그것을 지나치게 단순화하는 경향이 있다. 그들의 시각에서는, 그들은 극소수의 사람들만이 읽거나 이해할 더 정확하지만 복잡한 정보를 제공하는 것과는 반대로, 단지 '사람들에게 그들이 원하는 것을 제공하고' 있는 것이다. 이것의 완벽한 하나의 예시는 어떤 음식이 '좋은'지 '나쁜'지에 관해 사람들이 확정적인 답변을 원하는 방식이다. 과학적으로 말하자면 '좋고' '나쁜' 음식은 없으며, 오히려 음식의 질은 연속체상에 존재하는데 이는 어떤 음식들이 다른 것들보다 일반 건강과 웰빙 면에서 *더 낫다*는 것을 의미한다.

➡ 일반 건강과 관련하여 과학은 본질적으로 확실성에 대한 대중의 요구를 (A) 만족시키지 않으며, 이것은 미디어가 대중에게 덜 (B) 복잡한 답변을 제공하게 만든다.

Why? 왜 정답일까?

첫 두 문장에서 대중은 과학에 확실성을 기대하지만 과학은 이러한 요구를 흔히 만족시키지 못한다(~ science is often unequipped to meet these demands.)고 언급하는데, 'All this is why the media tends to oversimplify scientific research ~'에서는 이 때문에 미디어가 연구 내용을 지나치게 단순화하여 대중이 원할 만한 답을 주려 하는 상황이 생긴다고 언급한다. 따라서 요약문의 빈칸 (A), (B)에 들어갈 말로 가장 적절한 것은 ② '(A) satisfy(만족시키지), (B) complicated (복잡한)'이다.

- **uncertainty** ⓝ 불확실성
- **informed** ⓐ 정보에 입각한
- **black-or-white** ⓐ 흑백논리의, 양자택일의
- **with regard to** ~에 관하여
- **realm** ⓝ 영역
- **fantastically** 🄰 환상적으로, 엄청나게
- **as opposed to** ~와는 반대로, ~이 아니라

구문 풀이

1행 There is often a lot of uncertainty in the realm of science, which
　　　선행사　　　　　　　　　　　계속적 용법(목적격 관·대)
the general public finds uncomfortable.
　주어　　　　　동사　　目的격 보어

41-42　단순히 유전자의 산물이 아닌 인간

Since the turn of the twentieth century / we've believed in genetic causes of diagnoses / — a theory called genetic determinism.
20세기로의 전환 이래로 / 우리는 진단의 유전적인 원인을 믿어 왔다. / 유전자 결정론이라 불리는 이론

Under this model, / our genes (and subsequent health) are determined at birth.
이 모델 하에서 / 우리의 유전자(와 차후의 건강)는 태어날 때 결정된다.

We are "destined" to inherit certain diseases / based on the misfortune of our DNA.
우리는 특정 질병을 물려받을 '운명'이다. / 자신의 DNA의 불행을 바탕으로

Genetic determinism doesn't (a) consider the role / of family backgrounds, traumas, habits, / or anything else within the environment.
유전자 결정론은 역할을 고려하지 않는다. / 가정 환경, 정신적 충격, 습관, / 또는 환경 내의 다른 어떤 것의

In this dynamic / we are not (b) active participants / in our own health and wellness.
이 역학 관계에서 / 우리는 능동적인 참여자가 아니다. / 우리 자신의 건강과 안녕에 있어

Why would we be?
우리가 왜 그러겠는가?

If something is predetermined, / it's not (c) necessary / to look at anything beyond our DNA.
만약 무언가가 미리 결정되어 있다면 / 필요하지 않다. / 우리의 DNA를 넘어서 어떤 것을 보는 것이

But the more science has learned / about the body and its interaction with the environment around it / (in its various forms, / from our nutrition to our relationships / to our racially oppressive systems), / the more (d) complex the story becomes.
하지만 과학이 더 많이 알게 될수록, / 신체와 그 주변 환경과의 상호 작용에 대해 / (다양한 형태인 / 우리의 영양에서부터 관계, / 그리고 인종적으로 억압적인 시스템에 이르기까지) / 이야기는 더욱 복잡해진다.

「We are not merely expressions of coding / but products of a remarkable variety of interactions / that are both within and outside of our control.」 42번의 근거
우리는 단지 (유전적) 코딩의 표현이 아니라 / 놀랍도록 다양한 상호 작용의 산물이다. / 우리의 통제 내부와 외부 모두에 있는

「Once we see beyond the narrative / that genetics are (e) destiny, / we can take ownership of our health.」
일단 우리가 이야기를 넘어서 보게 된다면 / 유전자가 운명이라는 / 우리는 자신의 건강에 대한 소유권을 가질 수 있다.

This allows us to see / how "choiceless" we once were / and empowers us with the ability / to create real and lasting change.」 41번의 근거
이것은 우리에게 알 수 있게 해 주며 / 자신이 한때 얼마나 '선택권이 없는' 상태였는지 / 우리에게 능력을 부여한다 / 실제적이고 지속적인 변화를 만들어 낼 수 있는

20세기로 전환된 이래로 우리는 진단의 유전적인 원인, 즉 유전자 결정론이라 불리는 이론을 믿어 왔다. 이 모델 하에서 우리의 유전자(와 차후의 건강)는 태어날 때 결정된다. 우리는 자신의 DNA의 불행을 바탕으로 특정 질병을 물려받을 '운명'이다. 유전자 결정론은 가정 환경, 정신적 충격, 습관 또는 환경 내의 다른 어떤 것의 역할을 (a) 고려하지 않는다. 이 역학 관계에서 우리는 우리 자신의 건강과 안녕에 있어 (b) 능동적인 참여자가 아니다. 우리가 왜 그러겠는가? 만약 무언가가 미리 결정되어 있다면 우리의 DNA를 넘어서 어떤 것을 보는 것이 (c) 필요하지 않다. 하지만 과학이 신체와 (우리의 영양에서부터 관계, 그리고 인종적으로 억압적인 시스템에 이르기까지 다양한 형태인) 신체 주변 환경과의 상호 작용에 대해 더 많이 알게 될수록, 이야기는 더욱 (d) 단순해진다(→ 복잡해진다). 우리는 단지 (유전적) 코딩의 표현이 아니라 우리의 통제 내부와 외부 모두에 있는 놀랍도록 다양한 상호 작용의 산물이다. 일단 우리가 유전자가 (e) 운명이라는 이야기를 넘어서 보게 된다면 우리는 자신의 건강에 대한 소유권을 가질 수 있다. 이것은 우리가 한때 얼마나 '선택권이 없는' 상태였는지 알 수 있게 해 주며 우리에게 실제적이고 지속적인 변화를 만들어 낼 수 있는 능력을 부여한다.

- **genetic** ⓐ 유전적인
- **subsequent** ⓐ 차후의, 그다음의
- **predetermined** ⓐ 미리 결정된
- **simplistic** ⓐ 단순한
- **take ownership of** ~을 갖다, 소유하다
- **diagnosis** ⓝ 진단, 진찰
- **inherit** ⓥ 물려받다
- **racially** ⓐⓓ 인종적으로
- **remarkable** ⓐ 놀랄 만한

구문 풀이

17행 This allows us to see how "choiceless" we once were and empowers us
「allow+A+to부정사: A가 ~하도록 하다」
「의문사+주어+동사: 간접의문문」
with the ability to create real and lasting change.
「empowers A with B: A가 B할 능력을 부여하다」

41　제목 파악　　　정답률 50% | 정답 ①

윗글의 제목으로 가장 적절한 것은?

✓① Health Is in Our Hands, Not Only in Our Genes
　건강은 유전자에만 있는 것이 아니라 우리 손 안에 있다
② Genetics: A Solution to Enhance Human Wellness
　유전학: 인간 건강을 증진하는 데 있어 해결책
③ How Did DNA Dominate Over Environment in Biology?
　어떻게 DNA가 생물학에서 환경을 지배했는가?
④ Never Be Confident in Your Health, but Keep Checking!
　건강을 과신하지 말고, 계속 점검하세요!
⑤ Why Scientific Innovation Affects Our Social Interactions
　왜 과학적 혁신은 사회적 상호작용에 영향을 미치는가

Why? 왜 정답일까?

마지막 세 문장에서 인간은 단순히 유전자의 산물이 아니며, 자신의 건강을 직접 통제하고 관리할 수 있는 존재임을 설명하고 있다(Once we see beyond the narrative that genetics are destiny, we can take ownership of our health). 따라서 글의 제목으로 가장 적절한 것은 ① '건강은 유전자에만 있는 것이 아니라 우리 손 안에 있다'이다.

42　어휘 추론　　　정답률 57% | 정답 ④

밑줄 친 (a) ~ (e) 중에서 문맥상 낱말의 쓰임이 적절하지 않은 것은? [3점]

① (a)　② (b)　③ (c)　✓④ (d)　⑤ (e)

Why? 왜 정답일까?

(d)가 포함된 'But the more science ~' 문장을 기점으로 글의 흐름이 반전되고 있다. 앞에서는 인간의 신체와 건강이 유전자에 의해 '운명적으로' 결정된다고 보는 유전자 결정론의 시각을 설명하는 반면, 뒤에서는 인간은 단순한 유전자의 발현이 아니라 건강을 위한 행동을 선택할 수 있는 존재라는 내용이 이어지고 있다. 이러한 흐름으로 볼 때, 유전자 외의 다른 요소를 고려하기 시작하면 건강에 대한 이해가 더 '복잡해진다'는 의미로 (d)의 simplistic을 complex로 고쳐야 한다. 따라서 문맥상 낱말의 쓰임이 적절하지 않은 것은 ④ '(d)'이다.

43-45　선물한 사람을 배려한 사려 깊은 왕자

(A)

「One day / a poor man / brought a bunch of grapes to a prince / as a gift.」 45번 ①의 근거 일치
어느 날 / 한 가난한 남자가 / 포도 한 송이를 왕자에게 가져왔다. / 선물로

He was very excited / to be able to bring a gift for (a) him / because he was too poor to afford more.
그는 매우 흥분했다. / 그를 위한 선물을 가져올 수 있어서 / 그가 너무 가난해서 그 이상의 여유가 없었기 때문에

He placed the grapes beside the prince and said, / "Oh, Prince, please accept this small gift from me."
그는 왕자의 옆에 포도를 놓고 말했다. / "오, 왕자님, 저의 이 작은 선물을 부디 받아주세요."라고

His face beamed with happiness / as he offered his small gift.
그의 얼굴은 행복으로 빛났다. / 그가 자신의 작은 선물을 바치면서

(C)

The prince thanked him politely.
왕자는 그에게 정중히 감사를 표했다.

As the man looked at him expectantly, / the prince ate one grape.
그 남자가 기대에 부풀어 그를 바라보았을 때 / 왕자는 포도 한 알을 먹었다.

Then (c) he ate another one.
그러고 나서 그는 또 다른 하나를 먹었다.

Slowly the prince finished the whole bunch of grapes by himself.
천천히 왕자는 혼자서 포도 한 송이 전부를 다 먹었다.

「He did not offer grapes to anyone near him.」 45번 ③의 근거 일치
그는 자신의 곁에 있는 어떤 이에게도 포도를 권하지 않았다.

The man who brought those grapes to (d) him / was very pleased and left.
그 포도를 그에게 가져온 남자는 / 매우 기뻐하고 떠났다.

The close friends of the prince / who were around him / were very surprised.
왕자의 가까운 친구들은 / 그의 주변에 있던 / 매우 놀랐다.

(D)

「Usually / the prince shared whatever he had with others.」 45번 ④의 근거 일치
평소에 / 왕자는 자신이 가지고 있는 어떤 것이든 다른 사람들과 나눴다.

He would offer them whatever he was given / and they would eat it together.
그는 그들에게 자신이 받은 것은 무엇이든지 권하고 / 그들은 그것을 함께 먹곤 했다.

This time was different.
이번에는 달랐다.

Without offering it to anyone, / (e) he finished the bunch of grapes by himself.
아무에게도 그것을 권하지 않고 / 그는 포도 한 송이를 혼자 다 먹었다.

One of the friends asked, / "Prince! / How come you ate all the grapes by yourself / and did not offer them to any one of us?"
그 친구들 중 한 명이 물었다. / "왕자님! / 어찌하여 혼자서 포도를 다 드시고 / 우리 중 그 누구에게도 그것을 권하지 않으셨나요?"라고

「He smiled and said / that he ate all the grapes by himself / because the grapes were too sour.」 45번 ⑤의 근거 불일치
그는 웃으며 말했다. / 그가 혼자서 모든 포도를 다 먹었다고 / 그 포도가 너무 시어서

(B)

If the prince had offered the grapes to them, / they might have made funny faces / and shown their distaste for the grapes.
만약 왕자가 그들에게 그 포도를 권했다면 / 그들은 우스꽝스러운 표정을 지으며 / 포도에 대한 불쾌감을 드러냈을 것이다.

That would have hurt the feelings of that poor man.
그것은 그 가난한 남자의 감정을 상하게 했을 것이다.

He thought to himself / that it would be better / to eat all of them cheerfully and please (b) him.
그는 혼자 생각했다. / 더 낫다고 / 모든 포도를 기분 좋게 먹고 남자를 기쁘게 하는 것이

「He did not want to hurt the feelings of that poor man.」 45번 ②의 근거 일치
그는 그 가난한 남자의 감정을 상하게 하고 싶지 않았다.

Everyone around him / was moved by his thoughtfulness.
주위의 모든 사람들은 / 그의 사려 깊음에 감동 받았다.

(A)

어느 날 한 가난한 남자가 포도 한 송이를 왕자에게 선물로 가져왔다. 그는 너무 가난해서 그 이상의 여유가 없었기 때문에 (a) 그를 위한 선물을 가져올 수 있어서 매우 흥분했다. 그는 왕자의 옆에 포도를 놓고 "오, 왕자님, 저의 이 작은 선물을 부디 받아주세요."라고 말했다. 그의 얼굴은 작은 선물을 바치면서 행복으로 빛났다.

(C)

왕자는 그에게 정중하게 감사를 표했다. 그 남자가 기대에 부풀어 그를 바라보았을 때 왕자는 포도 한 알을 먹었다. 그러고 나서 (c) 그는 또 다른 하나를 먹었다. 천천히 왕자는 혼자서 포도 한 송이 전부를 다 먹었다. 그는 자신의 곁에 있는 어떤 이에게도 포도를 권하지 않았다. 그 포도를 (d) 그에게 가져온 남자는 매우 기뻐하고 떠났다. 왕자의 주변에 있던 그의 가까운 친구들은 매우 놀랐다.

(D)

평소에 왕자는 자신이 가지고 있는 어떤 것이든 다른 사람들과 나눴다. 그는 그들에게 자신이 받은 것은 무엇이든지 권하고 그들은 그것을 함께 먹곤 했다. 이번에는 달랐다. 아무에게도 그것을 권하지 않고 (e) 그는 포도 한 송이를 혼자 다 먹었다. 그 친구들 중 한 명이 "왕자님! 어찌하여 혼자서 포도를 다 드시고 우리 중 그 누구에게도 그것을 권하지 않으셨나요?"라고 물었다. 그는 웃으며 그 포도가 너무 시어서 혼자서 모든 포도를 다 먹었다고 말했다.

(B)

만약 왕자가 그들에게 그 포도를 권했다면 그들은 우스꽝스러운 표정을 지으며 포도에 대한 불쾌감을 드러냈을 것이다. 그것은 그 가난한 남자의 감정을 상하게 했을 것이다. 그는 모든

포도를 기분 좋게 먹고 (b) 남자를 기쁘게 하는 것이 더 낫다고 속으로 생각했다. 그는 그 가난한 남자의 감정을 상하게 하고 싶지 않았다. 주위의 모든 사람들은 그의 사려 깊음에 감동받았다.

- beam with ~으로 환히 웃다
- thoughtfulness ⓝ 사려 깊음
- distaste ⓝ 불쾌감
- expectantly ⓐⓓ 기대하여

구문 풀이

[A] 2행 He was very excited to be able to bring a gift for him because he was
감정 형용사   부사적 용법(~해서)
too poor to afford more.
「too ~ to …」: 너무 ~해서 …하지 못하다」

[B] 1행 If the prince had offered the grapes to them, they might have made funny
주어 + had p.p. ~   주어 + 조동사 과거형 + have p.p. ~ : 가정법 과거완료(과거 사실의 반대)」
faces and shown their distaste for the grapes.

[D] 1행 Usually the prince shared whatever he had with others.
복합관계대명사(~하는 것은 무엇이든)

43 글의 순서 파악   정답률 73% | 정답 ③

주어진 글 (A)에 이어질 내용을 순서에 맞게 배열한 것으로 가장 적절한 것은?
① (B) – (D) – (C)   ② (C) – (B) – (D)
✓(C) – (D) – (B)   ④ (D) – (B) – (C)
⑤ (D) – (C) – (B)

Why? 왜 정답일까?

왕자가 가난한 남자로부터 포도를 선물 받았다는 내용의 (A) 뒤로, 왕자가 주변 사람에게 권하지 않고 그 포도를 다 먹었다는 내용의 (C), 평소 왕자는 가진 것은 다른 사람들과 다 나누는 성품이었기에 주변 사람들이 의아해하며 이유를 물었다는 내용의 (D), 이유를 자세히 설명하는 (B)가 차례로 이어진다. 따라서 글의 순서로 가장 적절한 것은 ③ '(C) – (D) – (B)'이다.

44 지칭 추론   정답률 71% | 정답 ②

밑줄 친 (a) ~ (e) 중에서 가리키는 대상이 나머지 넷과 다른 것은?
① (a)   ✓(b)   ③ (c)   ④ (d)   ⑤ (e)

Why? 왜 정답일까?

(a), (c), (d), (e)는 the prince, (b)는 that poor man을 가리키므로, (a) ~ (e) 중에서 가리키는 대상이 다른 하나는 ② '(b)'이다.

45 세부 내용 파악   정답률 80% | 정답 ⑤

윗글의 왕자에 관한 내용으로 적절하지 않은 것은?
① 가난한 남자에게 포도 한 송이를 선물로 받았다.
② 가난한 남자의 감정을 상하게 하고 싶지 않았다.
③ 곁에 있던 어떤 이에게도 포도를 권하지 않았다.
④ 가지고 있는 어떤 것이든 평소에 다른 사람들과 나눴다.
✓포도가 너무 시어서 혼자 다 먹지 못했다.

Why? 왜 정답일까?

(D) '~ he ate all the grapes by himself because the grapes were too sour.'에서 왕자는 가난한 남자가 가져온 포도가 너무 시어서 누구에게도 권하지 않고 혼자 다 먹었다고 하므로, 내용과 일치하지 않는 것은 ⑤ '포도가 너무 시어서 혼자 다 먹지 못했다.'이다.

Why? 왜 오답일까?

① (A) 'One day a poor man brought a bunch of grapes to a prince as a gift.'의 내용과 일치한다.
② (B) 'He did not want to hurt the feelings of that poor man.'의 내용과 일치한다.
③ (C) 'He did not offer grapes to anyone near him.'의 내용과 일치한다.
④ (D) 'Usually the prince shared whatever he had with others.'의 내용과 일치한다.

| Dictation 12 | | 문제편 163쪽 |

01 run till late at night / provide longer subway service hours / the extended service schedules
02 even on a cloudy day / the clouds don't block it / forget to wear sunblock
03 difficult to remove / found this earring / by credit card or in cash
04 the striped curtains on the window / two cushions on the sofa / clean the air
05 editing a video clip / uploaded a campaign poster / showed a huge / reusable bag decorating activity
06 because of the cartoon character / these winter socks / this discount coupon
07 couldn't join the tour / I fell down / some pain in my ankle / bring the souvenir
08 a new local event / so many kinds of activities / a snowball fight
09 related to our team's slogan / a team uniform as a prize / through active participation
10 staying in a camping car / choose between these two / a kids' playground
11 far from my house / How long does it take
12 ordering pizza for dinner / grilled beef or shrimp
13 celebrate their reopening / meet her in person / how about rescheduling lunch
14 I missed your call / replace the battery / won't last longer than an hour
15 all the necessary information / easier to notice / increase the size of the letters
16-17 survives in full shade / the ultimate shade-loving plant / in partial shade / Isn't it fascinating

---

| 어휘 Review Test 12 | | 문제편 168쪽 |

A	B	C	D
01 시추하다, 구멍을 뚫다	01 initial	01 ⓑ	01 ⓘ
02 기대하다	02 estimate	02 ⓙ	02 ⓚ
03 직업	03 circumstance	03 ⓝ	03 ⓖ
04 이미 주어진, 기성품의	04 pioneer	04 ⓠ	04 ⓜ
05 멸종	05 indication	05 ⓡ	05 ⓕ
06 공상하다	06 closely	06 ⓛ	06 ⓣ
07 거대한	07 convey	07 ⓜ	07 ⓝ
08 불확실성	08 fundamentally	08 ⓞ	08 ⓡ
09 매력적인, 흥미로운	09 innovation	09 ⓕ	09 ⓛ
10 핵심, 요점, 결론	10 enhance	10 ⓣ	10 ⓐ
11 권한을 주다	11 aggressive	11 ⓓ	11 ⓒ
12 매년 열리는	12 reduction	12 ⓐ	12 ⓠ
13 분석적인	13 inspire	13 ⓖ	13 ⓢ
14 간격	14 nature	14 ⓢ	14 ⓗ
15 접근 가능한, 이용 가능한	15 respectively	15 ⓒ	15 ⓙ
16 과다한	16 sector	16 ⓔ	16 ⓓ
17 본질적으로	17 supplement	17 ⓚ	17 ⓑ
18 규제	18 substance	18 ⓟ	18 ⓞ
19 쓸어내리다	19 remarkable	19 ⓗ	19 ⓔ
20 체계적인	20 essential	20 ⓘ	20 ⓟ

· 정답 ·

01 ④ 02 ② 03 ⑤ 04 ④ 05 ① 06 ① 07 ③ 08 ④ 09 ③ 10 ④ 11 ② 12 ③ 13 ② 14 ⑤ 15 ④
16 ① 17 ③ 18 ① 19 ② 20 ① 21 ③ 22 ⑤ 23 ④ 24 ① 25 ③ 26 ④ 27 ⑤ 28 ④ 29 ★④ 30 ⑤
31 ① 32 ⑤ 33 ★② 34 ⑤ 35 ④ 36 ② 37 ③ 38 ★⑤ 39 ④ 40 ② 41 ④ 42 ⑤ 43 ② 44 ⑤ 45 ③

★ 표기된 문항은 [등급을 가르는 문제]에 해당하는 문항입니다.

---

01 사물함 교체 안내 　　　　　　　　　　　　정답률 89% | 정답 ④

다음을 듣고, 남자가 하는 말의 목적으로 가장 적절한 것을 고르시오.

① 파손된 사물함 신고 절차를 안내하려고
② 사물함에 이름표를 부착할 것을 독려하려고
③ 사물함을 반드시 잠그고 다녀야 함을 강조하려고
✓ 사물함 교체를 위해 사물함을 비울 것을 당부하려고
⑤ 사물함 사용에 대한 학생 설문 조사 참여를 요청하려고

M : Hello, students.
안녕하세요, 학생 여러분.
This is your vice principal Mike Westwood.
저는 교감인 Mike Westwood입니다.
I have an important announcement today.
오늘 중요한 안내 사항이 있습니다.
As the student lockers are getting old, we've been receiving complaints from many of you.
학생 사물함이 노후화되어, 우리는 여러분 중 다수로부터 불만을 접수해 왔습니다.
So we've decided to replace the lockers over the weekend.
그래서 우리는 주말 동안 사물함을 교체하기로 결정했습니다.
We ask that you empty your lockers and leave them open by this Friday, March 22.
우리는 여러분이 이번 주 금요일인 3월 22일까지 사물함을 비우고 그것들을 열어두기를 요청합니다.
Make sure to take all the items from your lockers and leave nothing behind.
꼭 사물함에서 모든 물품을 챙겨가고 아무것도 남겨두지 않도록 하세요.
Any items that are not removed will be thrown away.
치우지 않은 물건들은 버려질 것입니다.
Thank you for your cooperation.
여러분의 협조에 고맙습니다.

Why? 왜 정답일까?

'So we've decided to replace the lockers over the weekend. We ask that you empty your lockers and leave them open by this Friday, March 22.'에서 주말 동안 사물함을 교체하기로 결정되었으므로 이번 금요일까지 사물함을 비우고 문을 연 채로 두기를 요청한다는 내용이 나오므로, 남자가 하는 말의 목적으로 가장 적절한 것은 ④ '사물함 교체를 위해 사물함을 비울 것을 당부하려고'이다.

● vice principal 교감
● decide ⓥ 결정하다
● leave behind ～을 두고 가다
● throw away 버리다
● complaint ⓝ 불평, 불만
● empty ⓥ 비우다
● remove ⓥ 치우다, 제거하다

---

02 서점 의자에 대한 의견 나누기 　　　　　　　정답률 92% | 정답 ②

대화를 듣고, 여자의 의견으로 가장 적절한 것을 고르시오.

① 음식물을 들고 서점에 들어가면 안 된다.
✓ 서점에 의자를 비치하면 매출에 도움이 된다.
③ 서점은 책 외에 다양한 품목을 판매해야 한다.
④ 서점은 고객들에게 추천 도서 목록을 제공해야 한다.
⑤ 온라인 서점에서 책을 구매하는 것이 더 경제적이다.

W : Paul, what did you do on the weekend?
Paul, 주말에 뭐 했어?
M : I went to the new bookstore downtown. Have you been there?
시내에 새로 생긴 서점에 갔었어. 너 거기 가봤어?
W : Yes. They put lots of cozy chairs in the bookstore. I like that.
응. 거기 안락한 의자가 많이 있던데. 마음에 들더라.
M : Actually, I wonder why they did that.
사실, 난 왜 그랬는지 궁금해.
W : I think it helps the bookstore sell more.
난 그게 서점이 장사가 더 잘되게 도와줄 거라고 생각하는데.
M : Really? What if people just read books sitting on the chairs without buying them?
정말? 만일 사람들이 책을 사지는 않고 의자에 앉아서 그냥 읽기만 하면?
W : I heard that the longer people stay, the more they're likely to buy.
내가 듣기론 사람들이 더 오래 있을수록, 살 가능성이 더 높대.
M : That makes sense.
일리가 있네.
W : More chairs can attract more customers and the sales will go up.
의자가 더 많이 있으면 더 많은 손님을 끌어모을 수 있고 매출이 올라갈 거야.
M : You're right.
네 말이 맞아.

Why? 왜 정답일까?

남자가 시내에 새로 생긴 서점에 편안한 의자가 왜 많은지 모르겠다고 말하자, 여자는 그렇게 하면 장사에 도움이 될 것(I think it helps the bookstore sell more.)이라고 말하며 그 구체적인 이유를 설명하고 있다. 따라서 여자의 의견으로 가장 적절한 것은 ② '서점에 의자를 비치하면 매출에 도움이 된다.'이다.

● bookstore ⓝ 책방, 서점
● cozy ⓐ 안락한, 편안한, 아늑한
● sell ⓥ 팔다, 팔리다
● attract ⓥ 끌어들이다, 끌어모으다
● go up (가격 등이) 오르다
● downtown ⓐⓓ 시내에
● actually ⓐⓓ 사실, 실제로
● wonder ⓥ 궁금하다
● customer ⓝ 손님, 고객

---

03 모자 가게 주인과 손님의 대화 　　　　　　　정답률 84% | 정답 ⑤

대화를 듣고, 두 사람의 관계를 가장 잘 나타낸 것을 고르시오.

① 미용사 - 고객
② 화방 점원 - 화가
③ 미술관장 - 방문객
④ 패션 디자이너 - 모델
✓ 모자 가게 주인 - 손님

M : Hello, Ally! Long time no see.
안녕하세요, Ally! 오랜만이네요.
W : Hi, Robert. It's been a long time since I came to your store.
안녕하세요, Robert. 당신의 가게에 방문한 후로 오랜 시간이 지났네요.
M : You must have been busy.
바쁘셨나봐요.
W : Yeah. Did I tell you that I had to prepare for an exhibition?
네. 제가 전시회를 준비해야 한다고 말씀 드렸었나요?
M : Oh, yeah. I remember. How did it go?
오, 네. 기억나요. 어떻게 되었나요?
W : It went well. It was finally over last week.
잘 되었어요. 그것은 지난주에 마침내 끝났어요.
M : Good. So what kind of hat are you looking for today?
좋네요. 그럼 오늘은 어떤 종류의 모자를 찾고 계신가요?
W : Actually I've changed my hair style, so I'm not sure which hat will suit me.
사실 저는 머리 스타일을 바꾸어서, 어떤 모자가 제게 어울릴지 확신이 들지 않아요.
M : Oh, you cut your hair short! Why don't you try this hat? It goes well with short hair.
오, 당신은 머리를 짧게 자르셨군요! 이 모자를 써 보시면 어때요? 그것은 짧은 머리와 잘 어울려요.
W : Let me try. [Pause] I love it!
써 볼게요. [잠시 멈춤] 마음에 들어요!
M : It looks great on you.
당신에게 근사해 보여요.
W : Thanks. I'll take it.
고맙습니다. 그걸 살게요.

Why? 왜 정답일까?

'So what kind of hat are you looking for today?', 'Why don't you try this hat?'에서 남자가 모자 가게 주인임을, 'It's been a long time since I came to your store.', 'I'm not sure which hat will suit me.', 'Let me try.'에서 여자가 손님임을 알 수 있으므로, 두 사람의 관계로 가장 적절한 것은 ⑤ '모자 가게 주인 - 손님'이다.

● long time no see. 오랜만이에요.
● suit ⓥ 어울리다(= go well with)
● prepare for ～을 준비하다
● go well with ～와 잘 어울리다

---

04 벼룩시장에서 찍은 사진에 대해 이야기하기 　　　정답률 86% | 정답 ④

대화를 듣고, 그림에서 대화의 내용과 일치하지 않는 것을 고르시오.

W : Harry, have a look at this picture. It's from the flea market yesterday.
Harry, 이 사진 좀 봐. 어제 벼룩시장에서 찍은 거야.
M : Wow! 『There's a heart-shaped balloon in the air.』 ①의근거 일치
우와! 공중에 하트 모양 풍선이 있네.
W : Yeah. 『Look at the man playing the guitar on the left.』 He's selling old guitars. ②의근거 일치
그래, 왼쪽에 기타 연주하고 있는 남자를 봐. 그는 낡은 기타를 팔고 있어.
M : Interesting. This boy must be your brother Kevin. 『He's playing with a yoyo!』 ③의근거 일치
흥미롭네. 이 남자애는 네 동생인 Kevin이구나. 요요를 갖고 놀고 있네!
W : Right. He bought it there.
맞아. 저기서 그걸 샀어.
M : I see. 『Oh, you're wearing a hat with flowers.』 It's pretty. ④의근거 불일치
그렇구나. 아, 너는 꽃이 달린 모자를 쓰고 있네. 모자 예쁘다.
W : Thanks. I got it there for just one dollar.
고마워. 저기서 단 1달러에 그걸 샀어.
M : Great. You're eating ice cream. 『Did you buy it from the ice cream cart on the right?』 ⑤의근거 일치
훌륭한데. 넌 아이스크림을 먹고 있네. 오른쪽에 있는 아이스크림 수레에서 산 거야?
W : Yes. It was delicious.
응. 맛있었어.
M : It looks like you had a good time there.
거기서 즐거운 시간을 보낸 것 같네.

Why? 왜 정답일까?

대화에서 남자는 여자가 꽃이 달린 모자를 쓰고 있다(Oh, you're wearing a hat with flowers.)고

말하는데, 그림에 따르면 여자는 리본이 달린 모자를 쓰고 있다. 따라서 그림에서 대화의 내용과 일치하지 않는 것은 ④이다.

- flea market 벼룩시장
- cart ⓝ 수레

---

05 영화 동아리 가입   정답률 55% | 정답 ①

대화를 듣고, 남자가 여자를 위해 할 일로 가장 적절한 것을 고르시오.

☑ 동아리 안내 책자 가져다주기   ② 동아리 모임 장소 예약하기
③ 동아리 방에 함께 가기   ④ 동아리 모임 일정 짜기
⑤ 동아리 가입 신청서 대신 제출하기

W : What are you doing, Sam?
Sam, 뭐 하고 있어?
M : I'm filling out an application to join the school movie club.
학교 영화 동아리에 가입하려고 신청서 작성하고 있어.
W : Really? I'm also interested in that club.
정말? 나도 그 동아리에 관심이 있어.
M : Let's join together then.
그럼 같이 가입하자.
W : I'd love to, but I already belong to the science club.
그러고 싶은데, 이미 과학 동아리에 들어갔어.
M : You can join both.
둘 다 가입할 수 있어.
W : You're right. I'll have to check the movie club's meeting schedule first, though.
네 말이 맞아. 하지만 동아리 모임 스케줄을 먼저 체크해봐야 해.
M : Then I'll pick up the movie club's brochure for you from the club room later.
그럼 나중에 내가 동아리 방에서 영화 동아리 안내 책자를 가지고 올게.
W : That'll be great. Thanks.
그러면 정말 좋겠다. 고마워.
M : No problem. I'll have to go submit this application form anyway.
고맙기는. 아무튼 난 이 신청서를 내러 가야겠어.

Why? 왜 정답일까?

여자가 영화 동아리에 관심을 보이자 남자는 함께 가입할 것을 권유하는데, 여자는 이미 영화 동아리에 들어가 있어서 모임 일정이 어떻게 되는지를 먼저 체크해야 한다고 답한다. 이에 남자는 동아리 방에서 책자를 가져다주겠다(Then I'll pick up the movie club's brochure for you from the club room later.)고 제안하므로, 남자가 여자를 위해 할 일로 가장 적절한 것은 ① '동아리 안내 책자 가져다주기'이다.

- fill out (양식 등을) 작성하다, 기입하다
- belong to ~에 속하다
- brochure ⓝ 안내 책자
- application ⓝ 신청서, 지원서
- though [ad] (문미에서) 하지만, 그래도
- submit ⓥ 제출하다

---

06 아들을 위한 새 신발 사기   정답률 76% | 정답 ①

대화를 듣고, 두 사람이 지불할 금액을 고르시오. [3점]

☑ $75   ② $80   ③ $85   ④ $105   ⑤ $110

M : Honey, I think Paul needs new shoes.
여보, 제 생각에 Paul에게 새 신발이 필요한 것 같아요.
W : You're right. His shoes are getting too tight for his feet.
당신 말이 맞아요. 그의 신발은 그의 발에 너무 끼어요.
M : Let's buy a pair online. I know a good store. [Clicking sound] Have a look.
온라인으로 한 켤레 사죠. 내가 좋은 매장을 알아요. [클릭하는 소리] 한 번 봐요.
W : Oh, how about these shoes? They're originally $100 a pair, but they're 30% off now.
오, 이 신발 어때요? 이건 원래 한 켤레에 100달러인데, 지금은 30퍼센트 세일을 하네요.
M : That's a good deal. Let's buy a pair.
괜찮은 거래네요. 한 켤레 사죠.
W : Oh, there are shoe bags, too. Why don't we buy one?
오, 신발주머니도 있네요. 하나 사는 게 어때요?
M : Okay. There are two kinds, a $10 bag and a $15 bag. Which one do you like?
그래요. 10달러짜리 주머니와 15달러짜리 주머니, 이렇게 두 종류가 있네요. 어떤 것이 좋아요?
W : The $10 one looks good enough.
10달러짜리가 충분히 좋아 보이네요.
M : Then let's take it. Is that all we need?
그럼 그것을 사죠. 이게 우리가 필요한 전부인가요?
W : Yes. Oh, here it says that if you're a member of this online store, you'll get $5 off.
네. 오, 이 온라인 매장 회원이면 5달러를 할인받는다고 여기 쓰여 있네요.
M : That's good. I'm a member. Let's buy them now.
좋네요. 난 회원이에요. 그것들을 지금 사죠.
W : Okay.
그래요.

Why? 왜 정답일까?

대화에 따르면 남자와 여자는 원래 한 켤레에 100달러인 신발을 30퍼센트 할인된 가격에 사고, 10달러짜리 신발주머니를 추가로 구매한 뒤, 전체 가격에서 5달러를 할인받았다. 이를 식으로 나타내면 '(100×0.7)+10−5=75'이므로, 두 사람이 지불할 금액은 ① '$75'이다.

- tight ⓐ 꽉 끼는
- enough [ad] 충분히
- originally [ad] 원래, 본래

---

07 Sabina가 뉴욕 여행을 취소한 이유   정답률 92% | 정답 ③

대화를 듣고, 여자가 뉴욕 여행을 취소한 이유를 고르시오.

① 부모님이 편찮으셔서
② 시골로 이사를 가게 되어서
☑ 부모님 댁에서 휴가를 보내고 싶어서
④ 새로운 프로젝트를 맡게 되어서
⑤ 휴가 기간이 짧아져서

M : Sabina, have you finished packing for your trip?
Sabina, 여행을 위해 짐은 다 쌌니?
W : You mean the trip to New York?
뉴욕 여행 말하는 거야?
M : Yes, you're leaving this weekend, right?
응. 너 이번 주말에 떠나잖아, 맞지?
W : Oh, actually I canceled the trip.
아, 사실 나 그 여행 취소했어.
M : Why? Do you have a new project coming up?
왜? 다가오는 새 프로젝트라도 있어?
W : No. It's just because of my parents.
아니, 그냥 우리 부모님 때문에.
M : Is there something wrong with them?
부모님께 무슨 문제라도 있는 거야?
W : Not really. I just want to spend my vacation at my parents' house.
그렇진 않아. 그냥 휴가를 부모님 댁에서 보내고 싶어서.
M : Oh, right. They moved to the countryside last year.
아, 맞다. 작년에 시골로 이사 가셨지.
W : Yeah. I miss them a lot. It'll be great to stay with them.
응. 무척 보고 싶어. 부모님과 함께 있으면 아주 좋을 거야.
M : Sure. They'll be happy to have you there.
물론이지. 부모님도 네가 거기 가면 행복하실 거야.

Why? 왜 정답일까?

여자가 뉴욕 여행을 취소했다는 말에 남자가 이유를 묻자 여자는 휴가를 부모님 집에서 보내고 싶기 때문(I just want to spend my vacation at my parents' house.)이라고 답한다. 따라서 답으로 적절한 것은 ③ '부모님 댁에서 휴가를 보내고 싶어서'이다.

- pack ⓥ (짐을) 싸다, 꾸리다, 챙기다
- countryside ⓝ 시골 (지역), 전원 지대
- cancel ⓥ 취소하다
- miss ⓥ 보고 싶어 하다, 그리워하다

---

08 놀이공원 특징 설명하기   정답률 93% | 정답 ④

대화를 듣고, Fun Town Amusement Park에 관해 언급되지 않은 것을 고르시오.

① 위치
② 도착 소요 시간
③ 개장 시간
☑ 입장료
⑤ 특별 프로그램

W : Honey, what are you looking at?
여보, 뭘 보고 있어요?
M : It's the website of the Fun Town Amusement Park. How about taking the kids there this weekend?
Fun Town 놀이공원 웹 사이트예요. 이번 주말에 애들을 데리고 여기 가는 건 어때요?
W : Good idea. 「It's located in Southern California, right?」 ①의 근거 일치
좋은 생각이에요. 남부 캘리포니아에 있는 것 맞죠?
M : Yes. 「It'll take about one hour to get there by car.」 ②의 근거 일치
그래요. 거기까지 차로 가려면 한 시간 정도 걸릴 거예요.
W : What time shall we leave here?
여기서 언제 출발해야 하나요?
M : About 8 in the morning. 「The park is open from 9 a.m. to 8 p.m.」 ③의 근거 일치
아침 8시 정도요. 공원은 오전 9시부터 오후 8시까지 열어요.
W : Okay. Are there any programs that our kids will find interesting?
알겠어요. 우리 애들이 재밌어 할 만한 프로그램이라도 있어요?
M : 「Yeah, they offer many special programs including animal feeding.」 ⑤의 근거 일치
있어요. 동물들 먹이 주기를 포함해서 많은 특별 프로그램을 제공해요.
W : Great. I'll go tell the kids now.
아주 좋네요. 아이들한테 지금 가서 말할게요.
M : Go ahead. They'll be excited to hear that.
그렇게 해요. 그 말을 들으면 아주 신나할 거예요.

Why? 왜 정답일까?

대화에서 남자와 여자는 Fun Town Amusement Park의 위치, 도착 소요 시간, 개장 시간, 특별 프로그램에 대해서 언급하였다. 따라서 Fun Town Amusement Park에 관해 언급되지 않은 것은 ④ '입장료'이다.

Why? 왜 오답일까?

① 'It's located in Southern California, right?'에서 '위치'가 언급되었다.
② 'It'll take about one hour to get there by car.'에서 '도착 소요 시간'이 언급되었다.
③ 'The park is open from 9 a.m. to 8 p.m.'에서 '개장 시간'이 언급되었다.
⑤ 'Yeah, they offer many special programs including animal feeding.'에서 '특별 프로그램'이 언급되었다.

- amusement park 놀이 공원
- feeding ⓝ 먹이 주기
- offer ⓥ 제공하다

---

09 교내 뮤지컬 상연 안내   정답률 87% | 정답 ③

2019 Riverside High School Musical에 관한 다음 내용을 듣고, 일치하지 않는 것을 고르시오.

① 공연작은 Shrek이다.
② 공연을 위한 오디션은 작년 12월에 있었다.
☑ 공연은 사흘간 진행된다.
④ 입장권은 1인당 8달러이다.
⑤ 입장권은 연극 동아리실에서 구입할 수 있다.

W : Hello, students.
안녕하세요, 학생 여러분.
This is Janice Hawkins, your drama teacher.
저는 여러분의 연극 선생님인 Janice Hawkins입니다.

[문제편 p.169]

I'm happy to invite you and your family to the 2019 Riverside High School Musical.
여러분과 여러분의 가족을 2019 Riverside High School Musical에 초대하게 되어 기쁩니다.
『This year we're presenting *Shrek*, based on the famous animated film.』 ①의 근거 일치
올해 저희는 유명한 만화영화에 바탕을 둔 *Shrek*을 상연합니다.
It's full of singing, dancing, romance and lots of fun.
그것은 노래와 춤, 로맨스와 많은 재미로 가득합니다.
『The auditions for the show were in December last year.』 ②의 근거 일치
공연을 위한 오디션은 작년 12월에 있었습니다.
The cast and crew have been rehearsing for months to perfect their performance.
출연진들과 제작진들이 그들의 공연을 완벽하게 만들기 위해 몇 달 간 리허설을 해 왔습니다.
『The musical will be held in the auditorium for two days on March 15 and 16.』 ③의 근거 불일치
뮤지컬은 3월 15일과 16일 이틀 동안 강당에서 열립니다.
『Tickets are $8 per person.』 ④의근거 일치
입장권은 1인당 8달러입니다.
『You can buy tickets in the drama club room.』 ⑤의 근거 일치
연극 동아리실에서 입장권을 구입할 수 있습니다.
For more details, visit the school website.
더 많은 세부사항을 위해서는, 학교 웹 사이트를 방문해주세요.
Thank you.
고맙습니다.

Why? 왜 정답일까?

'The musical will be held in the auditorium for two days on March 15 and 16.'에서 공연은 3월 15일과 16일 이틀에 걸쳐 진행된다고 하므로, 내용과 일치하지 않는 것은 ③ '공연은 사흘간 진행된다.'이다.

Why? 왜 오답일까?

① 'This year we're presenting *Shrek*, based on the famous animated film.'의 내용과 일치한다.
② 'The auditions for the show were in December last year.'의 내용과 일치한다.
④ 'Tickets are $8 per person.'의 내용과 일치한다.
⑤ 'You can buy tickets in the drama club room.'의 내용과 일치한다.

- invite ⓥ 초대하다
- based on ~에 근거하여
- animated film 만화영화
- crew ⓝ (특정한 기술을 가지고 함께 일을 하는) 팀, 반, 조
- rehearse ⓥ 예행연습을 하다
- perfect ⓥ 완벽하게 하다
- detail ⓝ 세부 사항
- present ⓥ (연극·방송 등을) 공연하다
- be full of ~로 가득 차다
- cast ⓝ 출연자들, 배역진
- hold ⓥ 개최하다
- drama club 연극 동아리

---

10 토스터 구매하기 정답률 78% | 정답 ④

다음 표를 보면서 대화를 듣고, 남자가 구매할 토스터를 고르시오.

Bestselling Toasters in K-Store

	Model	Number of Slices	Price	Color
①	A	1	$25	white
②	B	1	$30	silver
③	C	2	$40	white
✓④	D	4	$45	silver
⑤	E	4	$55	silver

W : Hello. How may I help you, sir?
안녕하세요. 어떻게 도와드릴까요, 손님?
M : I'm looking for a toaster.
토스터를 찾고 있어요.
W : Okay. These five are our bestsellers. How about this one-slice toaster?
그러시군요. 이 다섯 개가 저희 베스트셀러입니다. 이 한 조각짜리 토스터는 어떠세요?
M : It's nice. 『But I want to toast at least two slices at a time.』 근거1 Number of Slices 조건
좋은데요. 그런데 저는 한 번에 적어도 두 장을 굽고 싶어요.
W : Then you need to choose one out of these three models. May I ask your price range?
그러면 이 세 모델 중에 하나를 선택하셔야겠네요. 가격대를 여쭤봐도 될까요?
M : 『Well, I don't want to spend more than fifty dollars.』 근거2 Price 조건
음, 저는 50달러 이상을 쓰고 싶지는 않아요.
W : You have two options left then. Which color do you like better?
그러면 두 개 선택지가 남으시네요. 어떤 색을 더 좋아하세요?
M : 『I'll go with the silver one.』 근거3 Color 조건
은색으로 할게요.
W : Okay. Good choice.
알겠습니다. 잘 고르셨어요.

Why? 왜 정답일까?

대화에 따르면 남자는 한 번에 적어도 두 장 이상의 빵을 구울 수 있으면서, 가격이 50달러를 넘지 않고, 색깔은 은색인 토스터기를 선택하고자 한다. 따라서 남자가 구매할 토스터로 적절한 것은 ④ 'D'이다.

- slice ⓝ 조각
- price range 가격대
- go with ~을 고르다, ~을 받아들이다
- out of ~ 중에
- option ⓝ 선택지, 선택

---

11 스페인어 공부 정답률 78% | 정답 ②

대화를 듣고, 여자의 마지막 말에 대한 남자의 응답으로 가장 적절한 것을 고르시오.
① Sorry, but I'd rather go to Spain by myself. – 미안하지만, 난 차라리 혼자 스페인에 가겠어.
✓② No, I'm taking a class in the community center. – 아니, 나는 주민 센터에서 수업을 듣고 있어.
③ Yes, you need to eat healthy food for your brain. – 응, 넌 두뇌를 위해 건강에 좋은 음식을 먹어야 해.
④ Yeah, you don't have to worry about your brain. – 그래, 네 뇌에 대해 걱정할 필요가 없어.
⑤ Well, I'm not interested in learning Spanish. – 음, 난 스페인어를 배우는 데 관심이 없어.

W : Grandpa, is that a Spanish book you're reading?
할아버지, 읽고 계시는 게 스페인어 책인가요?
M : Yes, I just started to learn Spanish. You know learning a foreign language is good for your brain.
응, 난 막 스페인어를 배우기 시작한단다. 외국어를 배우는 게 두뇌에 좋다는 걸 너도 알지.
W : Sounds great. Are you learning it by yourself?
좋네요. 독학하시는 거예요?
M : No, I'm taking a class in the community center.
아니, 나는 주민 센터에서 수업을 듣고 있어.

Why? 왜 정답일까?

여자는 스페인어 책을 보고 있는 남자에게 혼자서 스페인어를 공부하는지 묻고 있으므로(Are you learning it by yourself?), 남자의 응답으로 가장 적절한 것은 ② '아니, 나는 주민 센터에서 수업을 듣고 있어.'이다.

- foreign language 외국어
- by oneself 혼자
- healthy ⓐ 건강에 좋은
- brain ⓝ 두뇌
- be good for ~에 좋다

---

12 역사 에세이 제출 정답률 79% | 정답 ③

대화를 듣고, 남자의 마지막 말에 대한 여자의 응답으로 가장 적절한 것을 고르시오.
① But I haven't finished writing it. – 그치만 난 그걸 다 못 썼는 걸.
② Yes, I can help you study history. – 그래, 내가 네 역사 공부를 도와줄게.
✓③ Okay, let's go to the teacher's office. – 그래, 교무실로 가자.
④ Well, take your time to write the essay. – 그럼, 천천히 에세이를 써.
⑤ Sorry, but I didn't bring my essay today. – 미안, 그런데 내가 오늘 에세이를 안 가져 왔어.

M : Lydia, have you finished writing the history essay?
Lydia, 역사 에세이 쓰는 것 다 했니?
W : Yes, I have. I brought it today. How about you?
응, 다 했어. 오늘 난 그걸 가져왔어. 너는 어때?
M : Me, too. Why don't we go submit the essay now?
나도, 우리 지금 가서 에세이를 내는 게 어때?
W : Okay, let's go to the teacher's office.
그래, 교무실로 가자.

Why? 왜 정답일까?

남자가 여자에게 역사 에세이를 다 썼는지 묻자 여자는 다 써서 에세이를 가지고 왔다며 남자의 진행 상황은 어떤지를 묻는다. 이에 남자는 자신도 마찬가지라며 가서 에세이를 내자(Why don't we go submit the essay now?)고 말하고 있으므로, 남자의 마지막 말에 대한 여자의 응답으로 가장 적절한 것은 ③ '그래, 교무실로 가자.'이다.

- bring ⓥ 가져오다, 가져가다
- why don't we ~? ~하는 게 어때?
- how about ~? ~은 어때?
- submit ⓥ 제출하다

---

13 서평 과제를 위한 책 고르기 정답률 59% | 정답 ②

대화를 듣고, 남자의 마지막 말에 대한 여자의 응답으로 가장 적절한 것을 고르시오.
Woman:
① You're right. That's why I chose this book.
아빠 말씀이 맞아요. 그것이 제가 이 책을 골랐던 이유예요.
✓② That makes sense. I'll switch to an easier book.
그 말씀이 맞네요. 더 쉬운 책으로 바꿀게요.
③ Okay. I'll choose one from the bestseller list next time.
알겠어요. 다음에는 베스트셀러 목록에서 한 권을 고를게요.
④ Don't worry. It's not too difficult for me to read.
걱정 마세요. 그것은 제가 읽기에 너무 어렵지는 않아요.
⑤ Yeah. I'll join the book club to read more books.
그래요. 책을 더 많이 읽기 위해 독서 동아리에 들 거예요.

M : What are you reading, Lily?
뭘 읽고 있니, Lily?
W : It's a book for my English class, Dad. We have to read a book and write a review.
제 영어 수업을 위한 책이에요, 아빠. 저희는 책 한 권을 읽고 서평을 써야 해요.
M : Do you like the book?
그 책이 마음에 드니?
W : Well, I'm not sure. Frankly it's too difficult for me.
음, 잘 모르겠어요. 솔직히 말하면 저한테 너무 어려워요.
M : Why did you choose to read that book then?
그럼 왜 그 책을 읽기로 결정했니?
W : It was on the bestseller list and it looked interesting. It's very challenging, though.
이게 베스트셀러 목록에 있었고 재미있어 보였거든요. 그런데 무척 어려워요.
M : Maybe you should try another book that suits your level.
아마 넌 네 수준에 맞는 다른 책을 시도해야겠구나.
W : I know what you mean, but wouldn't I learn more from reading a difficult book?
무슨 말씀이신지 알지만, 전 어려운 책을 읽어서 더 많은 걸 배우게 되지 않을까요?
M : Well, what's the use of reading it if you can't understand it?
글쎄, 네가 이해를 할 수 없다면 그것을 읽어서 무슨 소용이 있니?
W : That makes sense. I'll switch to an easier book.
그 말씀이 맞네요. 더 쉬운 책으로 바꿀게요.

Why? 왜 정답일까?

여자가 서평을 쓰기 위해 고른 책이 너무 어렵다고 말하자 남자는 수준에 맞는 책을 다시 고를 것을 권하며(Maybe you should try another book that suits your level.) 이해하지 못하는 책을 읽는 것은 소용이 없다고 이야기한다(Well, what's the use of reading it if you can't understand it?). 따라서 여자의 응답으로 가장 적절한 것은 ② '그 말씀이 맞네요. 더 쉬운 책으로 바꿀게요.'이다.

- review ⓝ 비평, 평론, 독후감
- challenging ⓐ 힘이 드는, 도전적인
- What's the use of ~? ~하는 것이 무슨 소용이니?
- frankly ⓐⓓ 솔직히, 솔직하게 말하면
- though ⓒⓞⓝⓙ 그러나
- switch ⓥ 바꾸다

14 생일 선물 고르기　　　　정답률 78% | 정답 ⑤

대화를 듣고, 여자의 마지막 말에 대한 남자의 응답으로 가장 적절한 것을 고르시오. [3점]

Man:
① Well, I'm not sure if your son likes it.
　음, 아드님이 좋아할지는 잘 모르겠어요.
② No, it's dangerous to leave kids home alone.
　아뇨, 아이들을 집에 혼자 두는 것은 위험해요.
③ Of course, they are not safe even for adults.
　물론이죠. 드론은 심지어 어른에게도 안전하지 않아요.
④ That's why it's difficult to find drones for kids.
　그게 아이들을 위한 드론을 찾는 게 어려운 이유죠.
☑ Yes, as long as you get a right drone for his age.
　그럼요. 아이 나이에 맞는 드론을 사 주기만 하면요.

M : What are you looking at, Monica?
　뭘 보고 있어요, Monica?
W : Oh, I'm looking for a birthday gift for my son Willy.
　아, 제 아들 Willy를 위한 생일선물을 찾고 있어요.
M : I see. Did you find anything good?
　그렇군요. 뭔가 좋은 걸 찾았나요?
W : Not yet. Do you have any ideas?
　아직이요. 아이디어라도 있으세요?
M : Hmm. Why don't you get him a drone?
　흠. 드론을 사주시는 건 어때요?
W : A drone? I'm not sure if he'll like it.
　드론이요? 아이가 좋아할지 모르겠네요.
M : Of course, he will. Boys are crazy about drones these days.
　당연히 좋아할 거예요. 남자애들은 요새 드론에 열광하는 걸요.
W : Willy is just nine years old. Do you think he can fly a drone?
　Willy는 아직 겨우 9살인걸요. 드론을 날릴 수 있을 거라고 생각하세요?
M : I guess so. There are quite a lot of drones for kids.
　그럴 거예요. 아이들을 위한 드론이 아주 많아요.
W : Are you sure they're safe enough for a nine-year-old?
　드론이 아홉 살짜리 아이들에게도 충분히 안전하다고 확신하나요?
M : Yes, as long as you get a right drone for his age.
　그럼요. 아이 나이에 맞는 드론을 사 주기만 하면요.

Why? 왜 정답일까?

여자가 아들의 생일 선물로 무엇을 주면 좋을지 모르겠다고 말하자 남자는 드론을 추천하는데, 여자는 아이 나이가 아홉 살로 아직 어린데 드론이 괜찮을지 모르겠다며 확실히 안전한지(Are you sure they're safe enough for a nine-year-old?)를 되묻고 있다. 이에 대한 남자의 응답으로 가장 적절한 것은 ⑤ '그럼요. 아이 나이에 맞는 드론을 사 주기만 하면요.'이다.

● drone ⓝ 드론, (지상에서 조종하는) 무인 항공기
● be crazy about ~에 열광하다, ~을 몹시 좋아하다
● quite 圓 아주, 굉장히
● as long as ~하기만 하면

15 선거 표어 만드는 데 도움 요청하기　　　정답률 74% | 정답 ④

다음 상황 설명을 듣고, Lily가 John에게 할 말로 가장 적절한 것을 고르시오. [3점]

Lily:
① Why don't you run for class president?
　너 반장 선거에 출마하는 게 어때?
② Please give me a hand putting up the poster.
　포스터 붙이는 것을 도와줘.
③ How about changing your slogan in the poster?
　네 포스터 표어를 바꾸는 게 어때?
☑ Will you help me make a slogan for the election?
　선거를 위한 표어를 만드는 것을 도와줄래?
⑤ Tell me how to keep good relationships with classmates.
　반 친구들과 어떻게 좋은 관계를 유지하는지 말해줘.

M : Lily is a freshman in high school.
　Lily는 고등학교 신입생이다.
　She is planning to run for class president this year.
　그녀는 올해 반장에 출마할 계획이다.
　She really wants to win the election.
　그녀는 선거에서 정말 이기고 싶다.
　She thinks she needs a poster with a cool slogan to impress her classmates.
　그녀는 반 친구들에게 인상을 남길 수 있는 멋진 표어가 담긴 포스터가 필요하다고 생각한다.
　But she has difficulty coming up with a good slogan.
　하지만 그녀는 좋은 표어를 생각해 내는 데 어려움이 있다.
　Lily knows her friend John is very creative and has a lot of great ideas.
　Lily는 친구인 John이 굉장히 창의적이고 좋은 아이디어가 많다는 것을 안다.
　So she wants to ask him for help.
　그래서 그녀는 그에게 도움을 구하고 싶다.
　In this situation, what would Lily most likely say to John?
　이 상황에서, Lily는 John에게 뭐라고 말할 것인가?
Lily : Will you help me make a slogan for the election?
　선거를 위한 표어를 만드는 것을 도와줄래?

Why? 왜 정답일까?

Lily는 반장 선거를 위한 포스터를 만들고 싶은데 마땅한 표어가 떠오르지 않아서(But she has difficulty coming up with a good slogan.) 반 친구들 중 창의적인 친구인 John에게 표어 고안에 대한 도움을 요청하려고 한다(So she wants to ask him for help.). 따라서 Lily가 John에게 할 말로 가장 적절한 것은 ④ '선거를 위한 표어를 만드는 것을 도와줄래?'이다.

● freshman ⓝ 신입생
● run for ~에 출마하다
● class president 반장
● election ⓝ 선거
● slogan ⓝ 표어, 슬로건
● impress ⓥ 깊은 인상을 주다
● come up with 생각해 내다, 떠올리다
● give a hand ~을 도와주다
● relationship ⓝ 관계

16-17 동물이 나오는 속담

W : Hello, class.
　안녕하세요, 여러분.

「You must have heard of the proverb, 'Birds of a feather flock together.'」
여러분은 '같은 깃털의 새들이 함께 모인다(유유상종)'이라는 속담을 분명 들어봤을 겁니다. **17번 ①의 근거** 일치
We all know what this proverb means because it's commonly used.
이것은 흔히 쓰이기 때문에 우리는 모두 이 속담이 무슨 뜻인지 알고 있습니다.
「Like this, there are many proverbs in which animals appear.」
이 속담처럼, 동물이 나오는 많은 속담들이 있습니다.
Let's talk about them today. **16번의 근거**
오늘은 그것들에 관해 이야기해 봅시다.
「First one is, 'When the cat's away, the mice will play.'」 **17번 ②의 근거** 일치
첫 번째 속담은, '고양이가 없으면 생쥐가 살맛 난다'입니다.
It is using the fun relationship between the two animals.
이것은 두 동물들의 재미있는 관계를 이용한 것입니다.
We can easily guess the meaning of this proverb: the weaker do whatever they want when the stronger are not around.
우리는 이 속담의 의미를 쉽게 추측할 수 있는데, 강자가 주변에 없으면 약자는 자기가 원하는 무엇이든 한다는 것입니다.
「The next one is, 'Don't count your chickens before they're hatched.'」 **17번 ④의 근거** 일치
다음 속담은, '병아리가 부화하기 전에 닭의 수를 헤아리지 마라(김칫국부터 마시지 마라)'입니다.
It's using a chicken's life cycle.
이것은 닭의 생애 주기를 이용하고 있습니다.
From this proverb, we can learn the lesson that we should not make hasty decisions.
이 속담으로부터, 우리는 섣부른 결정을 내려서는 안 된다는 교훈을 배울 수 있습니다.
Now it's your turn to talk about a few proverbs like these.
이제 여러분들이 이런 몇 가지 속담에 대해 이야기를 해볼 차례입니다. **17번 ⑤의 근거** 일치
「You may have already thought about one with dogs, like 'Every dog has its day.'」
여러분은 '모든 개들은 자기 날을 갖는다(쥐구멍에도 볕들 날 있다)'와 같이 개에 관한 것을 이미 하나 생각해봤을 것입니다.
Let's talk about some together.
몇 가지를 함께 이야기해 봅시다.

● proverb ⓝ 속담
● flock ⓥ 모이다, 떼 지어 가다
● appear ⓥ 나오다, 등장하다
● guess ⓥ 추측하다
● be around 존재하다
● life cycle 생애 주기
● hasty ⓐ 성급한, 서두른
● turn ⓝ 차례
● advantage ⓝ 이점
● feather ⓝ 털, 깃털
● commonly 圓 흔히, 일반적으로
● mouse ⓝ 생쥐 (pl.) mice
● hatch ⓥ 부화하다
● count ⓥ 세다
● lesson ⓝ 교훈
● decision ⓝ 결정
● Every dog has its day. 쥐구멍에도 볕 들 날이 있다.

16 주제 파악　　　정답률 79% | 정답 ①

여자가 하는 말의 주제로 가장 적절한 것은?
☑ proverbs that have animals in them – 동물이 나오는 속담
② different proverbs in various cultures – 여러 문화 속 다양한 속담
③ why proverbs are difficult to understand – 속담을 이해하기 어려운 이유
④ importance of studying animals' behavior – 동물의 행동을 연구하는 것의 중요성
⑤ advantages of teaching values through proverbs – 속담을 통해 가치관을 가르치는 것의 이점

Why? 왜 정답일까?

'Like this, there are many proverbs in which animals appear. Let's talk about them today.'에서 여자는 동물들이 나오는 속담이 많이 있다고 말하며 이에 관해 이야기해보자고 하므로, 여자가 하는 말의 주제로 가장 적절한 것은 ① '동물이 나오는 속담'이다.

17 언급 유무 파악　　　정답률 83% | 정답 ③

언급된 동물이 아닌 것은?
① birds – 새
② mice – 생쥐
☑ cows – 소
④ chickens – 닭
⑤ dogs – 개

Why? 왜 정답일까?

담화에서 여자는 속담에 등장하는 동물의 예로 새, 생쥐, 닭, 개를 언급하였다. 따라서 언급되지 않은 것은 ③ '소'이다.

Why? 왜 오답일까?

① 'Birds of a feather flock together.'에서 '새'가 언급되었다.
② 'When the cat's away, the mice will play.'에서 '생쥐'가 언급되었다.
④ 'Don't count your chickens before they're hatched.'에서 '닭'이 언급되었다.
⑤ 'Every dog has its day.'에서 '개'가 언급되었다.

18 특별 발표회 참석 부탁하기　　　정답률 79% | 정답 ①

다음 글의 목적으로 가장 적절한 것은?
☑ 학생들이 준비한 발표회 참석을 부탁하려고
② 학생들을 위한 특별 강연을 해 준 것에 감사하려고
③ 청년 실업 문제의 해결 방안에 관한 강연을 의뢰하려고
④ 학생들의 발표회에 대한 재정적 지원을 요청하려고
⑤ 학생들의 프로젝트 심사 결과를 알리려고

Dear Mrs. Coling,
Coling 선생님께,
My name is Susan Harris / and I am writing on behalf of the students / at Lockwood High School.
제 이름은 Susan Harris이고 / 학생들을 대표하여 이 글을 씁니다. / Lockwood 고교의
Many students at the school / have been working on a project / about the youth unemployment problem in Lockwood.
저희 학교의 많은 학생들은 / 프로젝트를 수행해 왔습니다. / Lockwood 지역의 청년 실업 문제에 관한
You are invited to attend a special presentation / that will be held at our school auditorium on April 16th.

[문제편 p.170]

특별 발표회에 귀하를 초대합니다. / 저희 학교 강당에서 4월 16일 열리는
At the presentation, / students will propose a variety of ideas / for developing employment opportunities / for the youth within the community.
발표회에서 / 학생들은 여러 가지 안을 제안할 것입니다. / 고용 기회를 늘리는 / 지역 사회 내 청년들을 위한
As one of the famous figures in the community, / we would be honored by your attendance.
지역 사회의 유명인사 중 한 분으로서, / 귀하가 참석하시면 영광일 것입니다.
We look forward to seeing you there.
거기서 귀하를 뵙기를 고대합니다.
Sincerely, // Susan Harris
Susan Harris 드림

Coling 선생님께,

제 이름은 Susan Harris이고 Lockwood 고교 학생들을 대표하여 이 글을 씁니다. 저희 학교의 많은 학생들은 Lockwood 지역의 청년 실업 문제를 해결하기 위한 프로젝트를 수행해 왔습니다. 저희 학교 강당에서 4월 16일 열리는 특별 발표회에 귀하를 초대합니다. 발표회에서 학생들은 지역 사회 내 청년들을 위한 고용 기회를 늘리는 여러 가지 안을 제안할 것입니다. 지역 사회의 유명인사 중 한 분으로서, 귀하가 참석하시면 영광일 것입니다. 거기서 귀하를 뵙기를 고대합니다.

Susan Harris 드림

Why? 왜 정답일까?

글 중간에서 청년 실업과 관련된 특별 발표회에 초대하겠다(You are invited to attend a special presentation that will be held at our school auditorium on April 16th.)는 뜻을 밝힌 데 이어, 마지막 두 문장에서는 참석해주면 영광일 것이고 발표회 자리에서 보게 되기를 바란다며 편지를 맺고 있으므로, 글의 목적으로 가장 적절한 것은 ① '학생들이 준비한 발표회 참석을 부탁하려고'이다.

- on behalf of ~을 대신하여, ~을 대표하여
- unemployment ⓝ 실업
- hold ⓥ (행사 등을) 열다
- propose ⓥ 제안하다
- within [prep] ~의 이내에
- work on ~을 수행하다
- attend ⓥ 참석하다
- auditorium ⓝ 강당
- opportunity ⓝ 기회
- figure ⓝ 인물

구문 풀이

5행 You are invited to attend a special presentation [that will be held at our school auditorium on April 16th].
「be invited to+동사원형: ~하도록 초청되다」 / 주격 관계대명사

---

19 수술 대기 중 경험한 안도감   정답률 86% | 정답 ②

다음 글에 드러난 'I'의 심경 변화로 가장 적절한 것은?

① cheerful → sad
  활기찬   슬픈
✓② worried → relieved
  걱정하는   안도하는
③ angry → ashamed
  화난   부끄러운
④ jealous → thankful
  질투하는   고마워하는
⑤ hopeful → disappointed
  희망찬   실망하는

On December 6th, / I arrived at University Hospital in Cleveland / at 10:00 a.m.
12월 6일 / 나는 클리블랜드에 있는 University 병원에 도착했다. / 오전 10시에
I went through the process of admissions.
나는 입원 수속을 밟았다.
I grew anxious / because the time for surgery was drawing closer.
나는 점점 불안해졌다. / 수술 시간이 다가오고 있어
I was directed to the waiting area, / where I remained until my name was called.
나는 대기실로 안내되었고 / 거기서 내 이름이 불릴 때까지 있었다.
I had a few hours of waiting time.
나는 몇 시간 동안 기다렸다.
I just kept praying.
나는 계속 기도만 했다.
At some point in my ongoing prayer process, / before my name was called, / in the midst of the chaos, / an unbelievable peace embraced me.
계속 기도하는 어느 시점에선가, / 내 이름이 불리기 전, / 혼돈 한가운데서 / 믿을 수 없는 평화가 나를 감쌌다.
All my fear disappeared!
나의 모든 두려움이 사라졌다!
An unbelievable peace overrode my emotions.
믿을 수 없는 평화가 내 감정 위로 퍼졌다.
My physical body relaxed in the comfort provided, / and I looked forward to getting the surgery over with / and working hard at recovery.
주어진 편안함 속에 몸의 긴장이 풀렸고, / 나는 수술을 끝마치기를 고대하였다. / 그리고 회복을 위해 열심히 노력하기를

12월 6일 오전 10시에 나는 클리블랜드에 있는 University 병원에 도착했다. 나는 입원 수속을 밟았다. 수술 시간이 다가오고 있어 나는 점점 불안해졌다. 나는 대기실로 안내되었고 거기서 내 이름이 불릴 때까지 있었다. 나는 몇 시간 동안 기다렸다. 나는 계속 기도만 했다. 계속 기도하는 어느 시점에선가, 내 이름이 불리기 전, 혼돈 한가운데서 믿을 수 없는 평화가 나를 감쌌다. 나의 모든 두려움이 사라졌다! 믿을 수 없는 평화가 내 감정 위로 퍼졌다. 주어진 편안함 속에 몸의 긴장이 풀렸고, 나는 수술을 끝마치고 회복을 위해 열심히 노력하기를 고대하였다.

Why? 왜 정답일까?

'I grew anxious because the time for surgery was drawing closer.'에서 수술을 기다리며 걱정하던 필자가 '~ an unbelievable peace embraced me. All my fear disappeared! An unbelievable peace overrode my emotions.' 이후로 문득 마음의 평화를 찾았음을 알 수 있으므로, 'I'의 심경 변화로 가장 적절한 것은 ② '걱정하는 → 안도하는'이다.

- process ⓝ 절차
- surgery ⓝ 수술
- pray ⓥ 기도하다
- admission ⓝ 입원, 입장
- direct ⓥ 길을 안내하다
- ongoing ⓐ 진행 중인

[문제편 p.170]

- chaos ⓝ 혼돈
- override ⓥ (~의 위로) 퍼지다
- get ~ over with ~을 끝마치다
- embrace ⓥ 감싸다, 포옹하다
- comfort ⓝ 편안함

구문 풀이

8행 My physical body relaxed in the comfort provided, / and I looked forward
  주어1   동사1(과거)   과거분사 주어2 동사2「look forward
to getting the surgery over with and working hard at recovery.
to+동명사1 +   동명사2: ~하고 …하기를 고대하다」

---

20 공부 시간과 휴식 시간을 나누기   정답률 71% | 정답 ①

다음 글에서 필자가 주장하는 바로 가장 적절한 것은?

✓① 공부할 때는 공부에만 집중하라.
② 평소 주변 사람들과 자주 연락하라.
③ 피로감을 느끼지 않게 충분한 휴식을 취하라.
④ 자투리 시간을 이용하여 숙제를 하라.
⑤ 학습에 유익한 취미 활동을 하라.

It can be tough to settle down to study / when there are so many distractions.
공부에 전념하는 것은 힘들 수 있다. / 마음을 산만하게 하는 것들이 너무 많이 있을 때
Most young people like to combine a bit of homework / with quite a lot of instant messaging, / chatting on the phone, / updating profiles on social-networking sites, / and checking emails.
많은 젊은이들이 숙제를 찔끔하는 것과 함께 하고 싶어 한다. / 즉각적으로 메시지 주고받기, / 전화로 잡담하기, / SNS에 신상 정보 업데이트하기, / 그리고 이메일 확인하기를 잔뜩 하는 것
While it may be true / that you can multi-task / and can focus on all these things at once, / try to be honest with yourself.
사실일지도 모르지만, / 여러분이 동시에 여러 가지 일을 처리할 수 있고 / 이러한 모든 일들에 집중할 수 있다는 것이 / 자신에게 솔직해지려고 노력해라.
It is most likely that you will be able to work best / if you concentrate on your studies / but allow yourself regular breaks / — every 30 minutes or so — / to catch up on those other pastimes.
여러분은 아마도 가장 잘 공부할 수 있을 것이다. / 여러분이 공부에 집중하되 / 규칙적인 휴식을 허락한다면 / 30분 정도마다 / (앞서 못했던) 그런 다른 소일거리를 하기 위해

마음을 산만하게 하는 것들이 너무 많이 있을 때, 공부에 전념하는 것은 힘들 수 있다. 많은 젊은이들이 숙제를 찔끔하는 것과 즉각적으로 메시지 주고받기, 전화로 잡담하기, SNS에 신상 정보 업데이트하기, 그리고 이메일 확인하기를 잔뜩 하는 것을 함께 하고 싶어 한다. 여러분이 동시에 여러 가지 일을 처리할 수 있고 이러한 모든 일들에 집중할 수 있다는 것이 사실일지도 모르지만, 자신에게 솔직해지려고 노력해라. 여러분이 공부에 집중하되 (공부를 하느라 못했던) 그런 다른 소일거리를 하기 위해 규칙적인 휴식을 — 30분 정도마다 — 허락한다면 여러분은 아마도 가장 잘 공부할 수 있을 것이다.

Why? 왜 정답일까?

첫 문장에서 마음을 산만하게 하는 것이 많으면 공부에 집중하기는 어렵다는 점을 언급한 뒤, 마지막 문장에서는 공부를 할 때에는 공부에 집중하되 다른 소일거리는 규칙적인 휴식시간을 두어 처리하라(It is most likely that you will be able to work best if you concentrate on your studies but allow yourself regular breaks — every 30 minutes or so — to catch up on those other pastimes.)는 결론을 내리고 있다. 따라서 필자가 주장하는 바로 가장 적절한 것은 ① '공부할 때는 공부에만 집중하라.'이다.

- tough ⓐ 힘든, 어려운
- distraction ⓝ 마음을 산만하게 하는 것, 집중력을 흩뜨리는 것
- combine ⓥ 합치다
- instant ⓐ 즉각적인, 즉시의
- once [ad] 한번에
- allow ⓥ 허락하다
- catch up on ~을 처리하다, 따라잡다, 만회하다
- settle down to 마음을 가라앉히고 ~하기 시작하다
- quite [ad] 꽤, 상당히
- multi-task 여러 가지 일을 동시에 처리하다
- concentrate on ~에 집중하다
- regular ⓐ 규칙적인
- pastime ⓝ 소일거리, 취미

구문 풀이

6행 It is most likely {that you will be able to work best / if you concentrate on
  가주어   접속사 주어 동사(~할 수 있을 것이다)   조건 접속사 동사1
your studies but allow yourself regular breaks — every 30 minutes or so — to catch
          동사2 간접목적어 직접목적어   ~하기 위해
up on those other pastimes}.
        [ ] : 진주어

---

21 정보 과잉의 역설   정답률 58% | 정답 ③

밑줄 친 information blinded가 다음 글에서 의미하는 바로 가장 적절한 것은? [3점]

① unwilling to accept others' ideas
  다른 사람들의 생각을 수용하기 꺼려하는
② unable to access free information
  무료 정보에 접근할 수 없는
✓③ unable to make decisions due to too much information
  너무나 많은 정보 때문에 의사 결정을 할 수 없는
④ indifferent to the lack of available information
  이용 가능한 정보의 부족에 무관심한
⑤ willing to take risks in decision-making
  의사 결정에서 기꺼이 위험을 무릅쓰는

Technology has doubtful advantages.
기술은 의문의 여지가 있는 이점을 지니고 있다.
We must balance too much information / versus using only the right information / and keeping the decision-making process simple.
우리는 너무 많은 정보는 조절해야 / 정확한 정보만 사용해야 / 의사 결정 과정을 간소하게 하는 것에 맞추어
The Internet has made / so much free information available / on any issue / that we think / we have to consider all of it / in order to make a decision.
인터넷은 만들어서 / 너무 많은 무료 정보를 이용 가능하게 / 어떤 문제에 대해서도 / 우리는 생각한다. / 그 모든 정보를 고려해야 한다고 / 어떤 결정을 하기 위해서

So / we keep searching for answers / on the Internet.
그래서 / 우리는 계속 답을 검색한다. / 인터넷에서

This makes us <u>information blinded</u>, / like deer in headlights, / when trying to make personal, business, or other decisions.
이것이 우리를 정보에 눈멀게 만든다. / 전조등 불빛에 노출된 사슴처럼, / 우리가 개인적, 사업적, 혹은 다른 결정을 하려고 애쓸 때

To be successful in anything today, / we have to keep in mind / that in the land of the blind, / a one-eyed person can accomplish the seemingly impossible.
오늘날 어떤 일에 있어서 성공하기 위해서는, / 우리는 명심해야 한다. / 눈먼 사람들의 세계에서는 / 한 눈으로 보는 사람이 불가능해 보이는 일을 이룰 수 있다는 것을

The one-eyed person understands / the power of keeping any analysis simple / and will be the decision maker / when he uses his one eye of intuition.
한 눈으로 보는 사람은 이해하고, / 어떤 분석이든 단순하게 하는 것의 힘을 / 의사 결정자가 될 것이다. / 직관이라는 한 눈을 사용할 때

기술은 의문의 여지가 있는 이점을 지니고 있다. 우리는 정확한 정보만 사용해서 의사 결정 과정을 간소화 하는 것에 맞추어 너무 많은 정보를 조절해야 한다. 인터넷은 어떤 문제에 대해서든 너무 많은 무료 정보를 이용 가능하게 만들어서 우리는 어떤 결정을 하기 위해서 그 모든 정보를 고려해야 한다고 생각한다. 그래서 우리는 계속 인터넷에서 답을 검색한다. 이것이 우리가 개인적, 사업적, 혹은 다른 결정을 하려고 애쓸 때, 전조등 불빛에 노출된 사슴처럼 우리를 정보에 눈멀게 만든다. 오늘날 어떤 일에 있어서 성공하기 위해서는, 우리는 눈먼 사람들의 세계에서는 한 눈으로 보는 사람이 불가능해 보이는 일을 이룰 수 있다는 것을 명심해야 한다. 한 눈으로 보는 사람은 어떤 분석이든 단순하게 하는 것의 힘을 이해하고, 직관이라는 한 눈을 사용할 때 의사 결정자가 될 것이다.

Why? 왜 정답일까?

너무 많은 정보는 의사결정에 도리어 방해가 된다는 정보의 역설을 소재로 한 글이다. 밑줄 앞의 두 문장에서 우리는 오늘날 선택의 상황과 관련된 모든 정보를 고려하려고 애쓴다는 것을 지적하고, 글의 마지막 두 문장에서는 직관을 이용하여 상황을 단순하게 바라볼 때 불가능한 일이 가능해지고 의사결정이 촉진된다는 결론을 제시한다. 따라서 정보에 눈멀게 된다는 뜻의 밑줄 친 부분은 정보의 과잉으로 인해 의사결정이 어려워지는 상황을 빗댄 표현으로 볼 수 있어, 답으로 가장 적절한 것은 ③ '너무나 많은 정보 때문에 의사 결정을 할 수 없는'이다.

- doubtful ⓐ 의문의 여지가 있는, 의심스러운
- available ⓐ 이용 가능한
- deer ⓝ 사슴
- accomplish ⓥ 달성하다, 성취하다
- analysis ⓝ 분석
- access ⓥ 접근하다, 이용하다
- lack ⓝ 부족, 결여
- versus prep ~에 비해
- blind ⓐ 눈이 먼
- personal ⓐ 사적인, 개인적인
- seemingly ⓐ 겉보기에
- unwilling ⓐ ~하기를 꺼리는, 마지못해 하는
- indifferent ⓐ 무관심한
- take a risk 위험을 감수하다

구문 풀이

[3행] The Internet has made **so** much free information available on any issue
「so + 형용사 +
that we think we have to consider all of it in order to make a decision.
that + 주어 + 동사 : 너무 ~해서 …하다」   ~하기 위해

---

22 좋은 습관 형성의 긍정적 영향   정답률 82% | 정답 ⑤

다음 글의 요지로 가장 적절한 것은?
① 참을성이 많을수록 성공할 가능성이 커진다.
② 한 번 들인 나쁜 습관은 쉽게 고쳐지지 않는다.
③ 나이가 들어갈수록 좋은 습관을 형성하기 힘들다.
④ 무리한 목표를 세우면 달성하지 못할 가능성이 크다.
✓⑤ 하나의 좋은 습관 형성은 생활 전반에 긍정적 효과가 있다.

Recent studies show some interesting findings / about habit formation.
최근의 연구에서는 몇 가지 흥미로운 결과를 보여준다. / 습관 형성에 대한

In these studies, / students who successfully acquired one positive habit / reported less stress; / less impulsive spending; / better dietary habits; / decreased caffeine consumption; / fewer hours spent watching TV; / and even fewer dirty dishes.
이런 연구들에서, / 한 가지 긍정적인 습관을 성공적으로 습득한 학생들은 / 더 적은 스트레스와 / 더 적은 충동적 소비, / 더 좋은 식습관, / 카페인 소비 감소, / TV 시청 시간 감소, / 그리고 심지어 (설거지를 안 한) 더러운 접시 수의 감소를 보고했다.

Keep working on one habit long enough, / and not only does it become easier, / but so do other things as well.
한 가지 습관에 충분히 오랜 시간을 들여 노력하라, / 그러면 그것이 쉬워질 뿐 아니라, / 다른 것들 또한 쉬워질 것이다.

It's why / those with the right habits / seem to do better than others.
이 때문에 / 올바른 습관을 가진 사람들은 / 다른 사람들보다 더 뛰어나 보이는 것이다.

They're doing the most important thing regularly / and, as a result, everything else is easier.
그들은 가장 중요한 것을 규칙적으로 하고 있다 / 그 결과로 다른 모든 것이 더 쉬워진다.

최근의 연구에서는 습관 형성에 대한 몇 가지 흥미로운 결과를 보여준다. 이런 연구들에서, 한 가지 긍정적인 습관을 성공적으로 습득한 학생들은 더 적은 스트레스와 충동적 소비, 더 좋은 식습관, 카페인 소비 감소, TV 시청 시간 감소, 그리고 심지어 (설거지를 안 한) 더러운 접시 수의 감소를 보고했다. 한 가지 습관에 충분히 오랜 시간을 들여 노력하면, 그것이 쉬워질 뿐 아니라, 다른 것들 또한 쉬워질 것이다. 이 때문에 올바른 습관을 가진 사람들은 다른 사람들보다 더 뛰어나 보이는 것이다. 그들은 가장 중요한 것을 규칙적으로 하고 있고 그 결과로 다른 모든 것이 더 쉬워진다.

Why? 왜 정답일까?

글 중간의 명령문에서 충분히 오랜 시간 노력하여 한 가지 습관을 들이면 그 습관을 행하는 것이 쉬워질 뿐 아니라 나머지 다른 것들 또한 쉽게 할 수 있을 것(Keep working on one habit long enough, and not only does it become easier, but so do other things as well.)이라 이야기하며 좋은 습관을 형성하는 것의 긍정적 영향에 대해 말하고 있으므로, 글의 요지로 가장 적절한 것은 ⑤ '하나의 좋은 습관 형성은 생활 전반에 긍정적 효과가 있다.'이다.

- finding ⓝ 결과, 결론
- formation ⓝ 형성
- acquire ⓥ 습득하다, 얻다
- work on ~하려고 노력하다
- habit ⓝ 버릇
- successfully ⓐ 성공적으로
- dietary ⓐ 식사의
- regularly ⓐ 규칙적으로

174 고1·3개년 영어 [리얼 오리지널]

구문 풀이

[5행] Keep working on one habit long enough, / and not only does it become
「keep + 동명사 : 계속해서 ~하다」   「not only + A(도치) +
easier, but so do other things as well.
but + B(긍정 동의) as well : A뿐 아니라 B도」

---

23 바닷가 모래의 형성   정답률 71% | 정답 ③

다음 글의 주제로 가장 적절한 것은?
① things to cause the travel of water – 물의 이동을 유발하는 것
② factors to determine the size of sand – 모래의 크기를 결정하는 요인
✓③ how most sand on the beach is formed – 대부분의 바닷가 모래가 형성되는 방법
④ many uses of sand in various industries – 다양한 산업에서의 모래의 많은 용도
⑤ why sand is disappearing from the beach – 해변에서 모래가 사라지고 있는 이유

While some sand is formed in oceans / from things like shells and rocks, / most sand is made up of tiny bits of rock / that came all the way from the mountains!
어떤 모래는 바다에서 만들어지기도 하지만, / 조개껍데기나 암초 같은 것들로부터 / 대부분의 모래는 암석의 작은 조각들로 이루어져 있다! / 멀리 산맥에서 온

But that trip can take thousands of years.
그런데 그 여정은 수천 년이 걸릴 수 있다.

Glaciers, wind, and flowing water / help move the rocky bits along, / with the tiny travelers getting smaller and smaller / as they go.
빙하, 바람 그리고 흐르는 물은 / 이 암석 조각들을 운반하는 데 도움이 되고, / 작은 여행자들(암석 조각들)은 점점 더 작아진다. / 이동하면서

If they're lucky, / a river may give them a lift / all the way to the coast.
만약 운이 좋다면, / 강물이 그것들을 실어다 줄지도 모른다. / 해안까지 내내

There, / they can spend the rest of their years / on the beach as sand.
거기서, / 그것들은 여생을 보낼 수 있다. / 해변에서 모래가 되어

어떤 모래는 바다에서 조개껍데기나 암초 같은 것들로부터 만들어지기도 하지만, 대부분의 모래는 저 멀리 산맥에서 온 작은 암석 조각들로 이루어져 있다! 그런데 그 여정은 수천 년이 걸릴 수 있다. 빙하, 바람 그리고 흐르는 물은 이 암석 조각들의 운반을 돕고, 작은 여행자들(암석 조각들)은 이동하면서 점점 더 작아진다. 만약 운이 좋다면, 강물이 그것들을 해안까지 내내 실어다 줄지도 모른다. 거기서, 그것들은 해변에서 모래로 여생을 보낼 수 있다.

Why? 왜 정답일까?

첫 문장에서 대부분의 바닷가 모래는 멀리 산맥에서 온 작은 암석 조각들로 이루어져 있다고 말한 뒤(~, most sand is made up of tiny bits of rock that came all the way from the mountains!), 이어지는 문장은 산맥의 모래가 바다에 이르는 여정이 수천 년에 달할 수도 있는 긴 과정임을 언급한다(But that trip can take thousands of years.). 즉 바닷가의 모래가 어떻게 바다까지 오는지를 설명하는 것이 글의 주제이므로, 답으로 가장 적절한 것은 ③ '대부분의 바닷가 모래가 형성되는 방법'이다.

- form ⓥ 형성하다, 만들다
- be made up of ~로 이루어지다
- glacier ⓝ 빙하
- rocky ⓐ 바위로 된
- coast ⓝ 해안
- shell ⓝ 조개껍데기
- bit ⓝ (작은) 조각
- flow ⓥ 흐르다
- give a lift ~을 실어다 주다, 태워주다, 들어 올리다
- rest ⓝ (어떤 것의) 나머지

구문 풀이

[4행] Glaciers, wind, and flowing water help move the rocky bits along, /
주어(복수 취급)   동사 목적어(원형부정사)
with the tiny travelers getting smaller and smaller as they go.
「with + 목적어 + 현재분사 : ~하면서」 비교급 형용사(getting의 보어) └ ~함에 따라

---

24 도시 생활의 매력   정답률 69% | 정답 ①

다음 글의 제목으로 가장 적절한 것을 고르시오.
✓① The City's Greatest Attraction: People – 도시의 가장 큰 매력: 사람들
② Leave the City, Live in the Country – 도시를 떠나 시골에서 살라
③ Make More Parks in the City – 도시에 더 많은 공원 만들기
④ Feeling Lonely in the Crowded Streets – 사람 많은 거리에서 고독함 느끼기
⑤ Ancient Cities Full of Tourist Attractions – 관광명소로 가득한 고대 도시들

Studies from cities all over the world / show the importance of life and activity / as an urban attraction.
전 세계 도시에서 이루어진 연구는 / 생활과 활동의 중요성을 보여준다. / 도시의 매력으로서

People gather where things are happening / and seek the presence of other people.
사람들은 일이 일어나고 있는 곳에 모여들고 / 타인의 존재를 찾아나선다.

Faced with the choice of walking down an empty or a lively street, / most people would choose the street with life and activity.
비어있는 거리 또는 활기찬 거리를 걷는 것에 관한 선택에 직면했을 때, / 대부분의 사람들은 활기와 활동이 있는 거리를 선택한다.

The walk will be more interesting and feel safer.
(활기찬 곳에서의) 걷기는 더 즐겁고 더 안전하게 느껴질 것이다.

Events where we can watch people perform or play music / attract many people to stay and watch.
다른 사람들이 공연하거나 음악을 연주하는 것을 볼 수 있는 행사는 / 많은 사람들을 끌어들여 자리에 머물러 보게 한다.

Studies of benches and chairs in city space / show / that the seats with the best view of city life / are used far more frequently / than those that do not offer a view of other people.
도시 공간 내 벤치나 의자에 관한 연구는 / 보여준다. / 도시 생활을 가장 잘 관망할 수 있는 자리가 / 훨씬 더 자주 이용된다는 것을 / 다른 사람의 풍경을 잘 볼 수 없는 곳보다

전 세계 도시에서 이루어진 연구는 도시의 매력으로서 생활과 활동의 중요성을 보여준다. 사람들은 일이 일어나고 있는 곳에 모여들고 타인의 존재를 찾아나선다. 비어있는 거리 또는 활기찬 거리를 걷는 것에 관한 선택에 직면했을 때, 대부분의 사람들은 활기와 활동이 있는 거리를 선택한다. (활기찬 곳에서의) 걷기는 더 즐겁고 더 안전하게 느껴질 것이다. 다른 사

[문제편 p.171]

람들이 공연하거나 음악을 연주하는 것을 볼 수 있는 행사는 많은 사람들을 끌어들여 자리에 머물러 보게 한다. 도시 공간 내 벤치나 의자에 관한 연구는 도시 생활을 가장 잘 관망할 수 있는 자리가 다른 사람의 풍경을 잘 볼 수 없는 곳보다 훨씬 더 자주 이용된다는 것을 보여준다.

Why? 왜 정답일까?

첫 문장에서 전 세계 도시에서 이루어진 연구가 도시의 매력으로서 생활과 활동이 중요하다는 것을 보여준다(Studies from cities all over the world show the importance of life and activity as an urban attraction.)고 이야기한 후 활기찬 거리, 길거리 행사, 의자나 벤치 등의 내용을 예로 제시한 글이다. 따라서 글의 제목으로 가장 적절한 것은 ① '도시의 가장 큰 매력: 사람들'이다.

- **urban** ⓐ 도시의
- **gather** ⓥ 모이다
- **presence** ⓝ 존재
- **perform** ⓥ 공연하다, 연기하다, 수행하다
- **frequently** ⓐⅾ 자주
- **attraction** ⓝ 매력, 끌림, 명소
- **seek** ⓥ 찾다, 구하다
- **lively** ⓐ 활기찬
- **attract** ⓥ 끌어들이다, 마음을 끌다

구문 풀이

6행 Events [where we can watch people perform or play music] attract many
주어 / 관계부사 / 지각 동사 / 목적어 / 목적격 보어1 / 목적격 보어2 / 동사
people to stay and watch.

---

25 5개 국가에서의 뉴스 영상 소비   정답률 81% | 정답 ③

다음 도표의 내용과 일치하지 <u>않는</u> 것은?

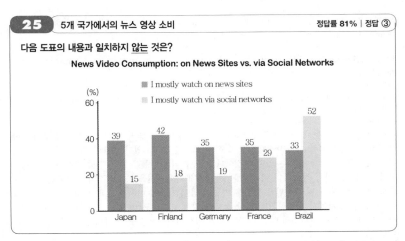

News Video Consumption: on News Sites vs. via Social Networks

The above graph shows / how people in five countries consume news videos: / on news sites versus via social networks.
위 그래프는 보여준다. / 다섯 개 국가에서 사람들이 뉴스 영상을 소비하는 방식, / 즉 뉴스 사이트에서의 뉴스 영상 소비 대 소셜 네트워크를 통한 뉴스 영상 소비를

① Consuming news videos on news sites / is more popular than via social networks / in four countries.
뉴스 영상 사이트에서의 뉴스 영상 소비는 / 소셜 네트워크를 통한 것보다 더 인기가 있다. / 네 개 국가에서

② As for people / who mostly watch news videos on news sites, / Finland shows the highest percentage / among the five countries.
사람들에 있어서는 / 주로 뉴스 사이트에서 뉴스 영상을 시청하는 / 핀란드가 가장 높은 비율을 보여 준다. / 다섯 개 국가 중에서

✓③ The percentage of people / who mostly watch news videos on news sites in France / is higher than that in Germany.
사람들의 비율은 / 프랑스에서 주로 뉴스 사이트에서 뉴스 영상을 시청하는 / 독일에서의 비율보다 더 높다.

④ As for people / who mostly watch news videos via social networks, / Japan shows the lowest percentage / among the five countries.
사람들에 있어서는 / 주로 소셜 네트워크를 통해 뉴스 영상을 시청하는 / 일본이 가장 낮은 비율을 보여 준다. / 다섯 개 국가 중에서

⑤ Brazil shows the highest percentage of people / who mostly watch news videos via social networks / among the five countries.
브라질은 사람들의 가장 높은 비율을 보여 준다. / 주로 소셜 네트워크를 통해 뉴스 영상을 시청하는 / 다섯 개 국가 중에서

위 그래프는 다섯 개 국가에서 사람들이 뉴스 영상을 소비하는 방식, 즉 뉴스 사이트에서의 뉴스 영상 소비 대 소셜 네트워크를 통한 뉴스 영상 소비를 보여준다. ① 뉴스 영상 사이트에서의 뉴스 영상 소비는 네 개 국가에서 소셜 네트워크를 통한 것보다 더 인기가 있다. ② 주로 뉴스 사이트에서 뉴스 영상을 시청하는 사람들에 있어서는 핀란드가 다섯 개 국가 중에서 가장 높은 비율을 보여 준다. ③ 프랑스에서 주로 뉴스 사이트에서 뉴스 영상을 시청하는 사람들의 비율은 독일에서의 비율보다 더 높다. ④ 주로 소셜 네트워크를 통해 뉴스 영상을 시청하는 사람들에 있어서는 다섯 개 국가 중에서 일본이 가장 낮은 비율을 보여 준다. ⑤ 브라질은 다섯 개 국가 중에서 주로 소셜 네트워크를 통해 뉴스 영상을 시청하는 사람들의 가장 높은 비율을 보여 준다.

Why? 왜 정답일까?

도표에 따르면 프랑스에서 뉴스 사이트에서 뉴스 영상을 보는 사람들의 비율은 35%인데, 독일 또한 같은 항목에서 동일한 비율을 보이므로, 도표와 일치하지 않는 것은 ③이다.

- **consume** ⓝ 소비하다, 쓰다
- **mostly** ⓐⅾ 주로, 대개
- **via** ⟮prep⟯ ~을 통하여, ~을 경유하여
- **among** ⟮prep⟯ ~사이에, ~중에

---

26 chuckwalla의 특징   정답률 90% | 정답 ④

chuckwalla에 관한 다음 글의 내용과 일치하지 <u>않는</u> 것은?

① 길이가 45cm까지 자랄 수 있다.
② 대부분 갈색이거나 검은색이다.
③ 등을 따라 꼬리까지 짙은 갈색 선들이 나 있다.
✓④ 수컷의 몸통 색깔은 나이가 들수록 짙어진다.
⑤ 어린 수컷의 생김새는 암컷과 비슷하다.

「Chuckwallas are fat lizards, usually 20-25 cm long, / though they may grow up to 45 cm.」 ①의근거 일치
Chuckwalla는 보통 20 ~ 25cm 길이의 뚱뚱한 도마뱀이다. / 비록 그들이 45cm까지 자랄 수도 있지만
They weigh about 1.5kg / when mature.
무게는 1.5kg 정도 나간다. / 다 크면

「Most chuckwallas are mainly brown or black.」 ②의근거 일치
대부분의 Chuckwalla는 주로 갈색 또는 검정색이다.
Just after the annual molt, / the skin is shiny.
매년의 탈피 직후에, / 피부는 윤이 난다.
「Lines of dark brown run along the back / and continue down the tail.」 ③의근거 일치
짙은 갈색 선들이 등을 따라 / 꼬리까지 이어져 있다.
「As the males grow older, / these brown lines disappear / and the body color becomes lighter; / the tail becomes almost white.」 ④의근거 불일치
수컷은 자라면서 / 이 갈색 선이 사라지고 몸의 색깔이 밝아진다. / 꼬리는 거의 흰색이 된다.
「It is not easy / to distinguish between male and female chuckwallas, / because young males look like females / and the largest females resemble males.」 ⑤의근거 일치
쉽지 않은데, / chuckwalla 수컷과 암컷을 구별하기는 / 어린 수컷은 암컷처럼 생겼고 / 가장 큰 암컷은 수컷을 닮기 때문에 그렇다.

Chuckwalla는 보통 20 ~ 25cm 길이의 뚱뚱한 도마뱀이지만, 45cm까지 자랄 수도 있다. 무게는 다 크면 1.5kg 정도 나간다. 대부분의 Chuckwalla는 주로 갈색 또는 검정색이다. 매년의 탈피 직후에, 피부는 윤이 난다. 짙은 갈색 선들이 등을 따라 꼬리까지 이어져 있다. 수컷은 자라면서 이 갈색 선이 사라지고 몸의 색깔이 밝아진다. 꼬리는 거의 흰색이 된다. chuckwalla 수컷과 암컷의 구별은 쉽지 않은데, 어린 수컷은 암컷처럼 생겼고 가장 큰 암컷은 수컷을 닮기 때문에 그렇다.

Why? 왜 정답일까?

'As the males grow older, these brown lines disappear and the body color becomes lighter.'에서 수컷은 자라면서 몸 색깔이 짙어지지 않고 도리어 밝아진다는 내용을 확인할 수 있다. 따라서 chuckwalla에 관한 글의 내용과 일치하지 않는 것은 ④ '수컷의 몸통 색깔은 나이가 들수록 짙어진다.'이다.

Why? 왜 오답일까?

① 'Chuckwallas are fat lizards, usually 20–25cm long, though they may grow up to 45cm.'의 내용과 일치한다.
② 'Most chuckwallas are mainly brown or black.'의 내용과 일치한다.
③ 'Lines of dark brown run along the back and continue down the tail.'의 내용과 일치한다.
⑤ '~, because young males look like females and the largest females resemble males.'의 내용과 일치한다.

- **lizard** ⓝ 도마뱀
- **weigh** 무게가 ~이다
- **annual** ⓐ 매년의, 1년의
- **distinguish** ⓥ 구별하다
- **up to** ~까지
- **mature** ⓐ 다 자란, 성숙한
- **disappear** ⓥ 사라지다
- **resemble** ⓥ 닮다

구문 풀이

7행 It is not easy to distinguish between male and female chuckwallas, /
가주어 / 진주어 / between A and B : A와 B 사이의
because young males look like females and the largest females resemble males.
~처럼 보이다 / ~을 닮다(타동사)

---

27 스마트 워치 기능 소개   정답률 75% | 정답 ⑤

L-19 Smart Watch 사용에 관한 다음 안내문의 내용과 일치하는 것은?

① A를 짧게 누르면 스포츠 모드로 들어간다.
② B를 길게 누르면 '홈' 메뉴로 돌아간다.
③ C를 길게 누르면 배경 화면의 불빛이 커지거나 꺼진다.
④ D를 누르면 설정값이 내려간다.
✓⑤ 업그레이드 오류를 피하려면 배터리 잔량 표시가 최소 두 칸은 되어야 한다.

L-19 Smart Watch
L-19 Smart Watch
User Guide
사용 설명서
KEY FUNCTIONS
주요 기능
「A Short press to confirm; / long press to enter the sports mode.」 ①의근거 불일치
설정값을 확정하려면 짧게 누르시오; / 스포츠 모드로 들어가려면 길게 누르시오.
「B Short press to return to the 'home' menu; / long press to send SOS location.」 ②의근거 불일치
'홈' 메뉴로 돌아가려면 짧게 누르시오; / 구조 요청 위치 정보를 보내려면 길게 누르시오.
「C Short press to turn on or off the background light; / long press to turn on or off your watch.」 ③의근거 불일치
배경 화면의 불빛을 켜거나 끄려면 짧게 누르시오; / 시계를 켜거나 끄려면 길게 누르시오.
「D Press to go up. / (In time, date or other settings, / press the key to increase the value.)」 ④의근거 불일치
설정값을 올리려면 누르시오. / (시간, 날짜, 혹은 다른 설정에서 / 값을 올리려면 키를 누르시오.)
「E Press to go down. / (In time, date or other settings, / press the key to decrease the value.」
설정값을 내리려면 누르시오. / (시간, 날짜, 혹은 다른 설정에서 / 값을 내리려면 키를 누르시오.)
CAUTION
주의 사항
「Make sure / the battery level of your watch / has at least two bars, / in order to avoid an upgrading error.」 ⑤의근거 일치
반드시 하십시오. / 시계의 배터리 잔량 표시가 / 최소 두 칸은 되도록 / 업그레이드 오류를 피하기 위하여

L-19 Smart Watch

사용 설명서

주요 기능
A 설정값을 확정하려면 짧게 누르시오; 스포츠 모드로 들어가려면 길게 누르시오.
B '홈' 메뉴로 돌아가려면 짧게 누르시오; 구조 요청 위치 정보를 보내려면 길게 누르시오.
C 배경 화면의 불빛을 켜거나 끄려면 짧게 누르시오; 시계를 켜거나 끄려면 길게 누르시오.
D 설정값을 올리려면 누르시오. (시간, 날짜, 혹은 다른 설정에서 값을 올리려면 키를 누르시오.)

E 설정값을 내리려면 누르시오. (시간, 날짜, 혹은 다른 설정에서 값을 내리려면 키를 누르시오.)

주의 사항

업그레이드 오류를 피하기 위하여, 반드시 시계의 배터리 잔량 표시가 최소 두 칸은 되도록 하십시오.

Why? 왜 정답일까?

'Make sure the battery level of your watch has at least two bars, in order to avoid an upgrading error.'에서 업그레이드 오류를 피하려면 시계의 배터리 잔량 표시가 반드시 최소 두 칸은 되도록 해야 한다는 내용이 나오므로, 안내문의 내용과 일치하는 것은 ⑤ '업그레이드 오류를 피하려면 배터리 잔량 표시가 최소 두 칸은 되어야 한다.'이다.

Why? 왜 오답일까?

① 'A ~ long press to enter the sports mode.'에서 스포츠 모드로 들어가려면 A를 길게 누르라고 하였다.

② 'B Short press to return to the 'home' menu; ~'에서 '홈' 메뉴로 돌아가려면 B를 짧게 누르라고 하였다.

③ 'C Short press to turn on or off the background light; ~'에서 배경화면의 불빛을 켜거나 끄려면 C를 짧게 누르라고 하였다.

④ 'D Press to go up. (In time, date or other settings, press the key to increase the value.)'에서 설정값을 올리려면 D를 누르라고 하였다.

● function ⓝ 기능　　　　● background light 배경화면 불빛

---

28 합창단 오디션 안내　　　　정답률 83% | 정답 ④

2017 Happy Voice Choir Audition에 관한 다음 안내문의 내용과 일치하지 <u>않는</u> 것은?

① 학교 동아리가 개최한다.
② 신입생이면 누구나 참가할 수 있다.
③ 3월 24일에 강당에서 열린다.
✓④ 지원자는 자신이 선택한 두 곡을 불러야 한다.
⑤ 참가하려면 이메일을 보내야 한다.

2017 Happy Voice Choir Audition
2017 Happy Voice 합창단 오디션
Do you love to sing?
노래 부르는 것을 좋아하세요?
「Happy Voice, one of the most famous school clubs, / is holding an audition for you.」
가장 인기 있는 학교 동아리 중 하나인 Happy Voice에서 / 여러분을 위한 오디션을 개최합니다. ①의 근거 일치
Come and join us for some very exciting performances!
오셔서 몇 가지 아주 즐거운 공연에 함께 하세요!
「Who: Any freshman」 ②의 근거 일치
대상: 신입생 누구나
「When: Friday, March 24, 3 p.m.」
일시: 3월 24일 금요일 오후 3시
Where: Auditorium」 ③의 근거 일치
장소: 강당
「All applicants should sing two songs:
모든 지원자 분들은 두 곡의 노래를 부르셔야 합니다.
1st song: *Oh Happy Day!*
첫 곡: *Oh Happy Day!*
2nd song: You choose your own.」 ④의 근거 불일치
두 번째 곡: 직접 선택하세요.
「To enter the audition, / please email us at hvaudition@qmail.com.」 ⑤의 근거 일치
오디션에 참가하시려면, / hvaudition@qmail.com으로 이메일을 보내주세요.
For more information, visit the school website.
더 많은 정보를 얻으시려면 학교 웹 사이트를 방문해 주세요.

2017 Happy Voice 합창단 오디션

노래 부르는 것을 좋아하세요? 가장 인기 있는 학교 동아리 중 하나인 Happy Voice에서 여러분을 위한 오디션을 개최합니다. 오셔서 몇 가지 아주 즐거운 공연에 함께 하세요!

■ 대상: 신입생 누구나
■ 일시: 3월 24일 금요일 오후 3시
■ 장소: 강당

모든 지원자 분들은 두 곡의 노래를 부르셔야 합니다.
– 첫 곡: *Oh Happy Day!*
– 두 번째 곡: 직접 선택하세요.

오디션에 참가하시려면, hvaudition@qmail.com으로 이메일을 보내주세요.

더 많은 정보를 얻으시려면 학교 웹 사이트를 방문해 주세요.

Why? 왜 정답일까?

'All applicants should sing two songs:' 문장을 통해 한 곡은 *Oh Happy Day!*라는 지정곡을, 나머지 한 곡은 본인이 선택한 곡을 부른다는 것을 알 수 있으므로, 2017 Happy Voice Choir Audition에 관한 안내문의 내용과 일치하지 않는 것은 ④ '지원자는 자신이 선택한 두 곡을 불러야 한다.'이다.

Why? 왜 오답일까?

① 'Happy Voice, one of the most famous school clubs, is holding an audition for you.'의 내용과 일치한다.
② 'Who: Any freshman'의 내용과 일치한다.
③ 'When: Friday, March 24, 3 p.m. / Where: Auditorium'의 내용과 일치한다.
⑤ 'To enter the audition, please email us at hvaudition@qmail.com.'의 내용과 일치한다.

● freshman ⓝ 신입생　　　　● auditorium ⓝ 강당, 방청석, 청중석
● applicant ⓝ 지원자　　　　● enter ⓥ 참가하다, 들어가다, 입장하다
● information ⓝ 정보, 자료

구문 풀이

1행 Happy Voice, one of the most famous school clubs, is holding an audition for you.
　　　주어　　　　동격구　　　　　동사

★★★ 등급을 가르는 문제!

29 정서에 영향을 미치는 조명　　　　정답률 49% | 정답 ④

다음 글의 밑줄 친 부분 중, 어법상 틀린 것은?

Bad lighting can increase stress on your eyes, / as can light that is too bright, / or light that shines ① directly into your eyes.
좋지 못한 조명은 여러분의 눈에 스트레스를 증가시킬 수 있다. / 너무 밝은 빛이나 / 눈에 직선으로 들어오는 빛과 마찬가지로
Fluorescent lighting can also be ② tiring.
형광등 또한 피로감을 줄 수 있다.
What you may not appreciate is / that the quality of light may also be important.
여러분이 모를 수도 있는 것은 / 빛의 질 또한 중요할 수 있다는 것이다.
Most people are happiest in bright sunshine / — this may cause a release of chemicals in the body / ③ that bring a feeling of emotional well-being.
대부분의 사람들은 밝은 햇빛 속에서 가장 행복하다 / 이것은 아마 체내 화학물질을 분비시킬지도 모른다. / 정서적인 행복감을 주는
Artificial light, / which typically contains only a few wavelengths of light, / ✓does not seem to have the same effect on mood / that sunlight has.
인공조명은 / 전형적으로 몇 개 안 되는 빛 파장만 포함하는 / 기분에 미치는 효과는 똑같지 않을 수 있다. / 햇빛이 미치는 효과와
Try experimenting / with working by a window / or ⑤ using full spectrum bulbs in your desk lamp.
실험해 보아라. / 창가에서 작업하거나 / 책상 전등에 있는 모든 파장이 있는 전구를 사용하여
You will probably find / that this improves the quality / of your working environment.
아마도 알게 될 것이다. / 이것이 질을 향상시킨다는 것을 / 여러분의 작업 환경의

너무 밝은 빛이나 눈에 직선으로 들어오는 빛과 마찬가지로 좋지 못한 조명은 여러분의 눈에 스트레스를 증가시킬 수 있다. 형광등 또한 피로감을 줄 수 있다. 여러분이 모를 수도 있는 것은 빛의 질 또한 중요할 수 있다는 것이다. 대부분의 사람들은 밝은 햇빛 속에서 가장 행복하다 — 이것은 아마 정서적인 행복감을 주는 체내 화학물질을 분비시킬지도 모른다. 전형적으로 몇 개 안 되는 빛 파장만 포함하는 인공 조명이 기분에 미치는 효과는 햇빛과 똑같지 않을 수 있다. 창가에서 작업하거나 책상 전등에 있는 모든 파장이 있는 전구를 사용하여 실험해 보아라. 이것이 여러분의 작업 환경의 질을 향상시킨다는 것을 아마도 알게 될 것이다.

Why? 왜 정답일까?

주어가 불가산명사인 Artificial light이므로 동사는 단수인 does로 쓰는 것이 적절하다. 따라서 어법상 틀린 것은 ④이다.

Why? 왜 오답일까?

① 동사 shines를 꾸미는 말로서 부사 directly의 쓰임은 어법상 맞다.
② 주어인 Fluorescent lighting이 피로감을 주는 주체이므로 능동의 현재분사 tiring의 쓰임은 어법상 맞다.
③ 선행사 chemicals를 꾸미고 뒤에 복수 동사 bring를 연결하는 말로서 주격 관계대명사 that의 쓰임은 어법상 맞다.
⑤ 등위접속사 or 앞에 동명사 experimenting이 나오므로, 이와 병렬을 이루도록 동명사인 using을 쓴 것은 어법상 맞다. 두 동명사는 명령문 동사 Try의 목적어이다.

● lighting ⓝ 조명, 빛　　　　● bright ⓐ 밝은
● directly ⓐⓓ 곧장, 똑바로　　　● appreciate ⓥ 이해하다
● release ⓝ 분비, 방출　　　　● chemical ⓝ 화학 물질
● emotional ⓐ 정서적인　　　● artificial ⓐ 인공의
● typically ⓐⓓ 일반적으로　　　● wavelength ⓝ 파장, 주파수
● experiment ⓥ 실험하다 ⓝ 실험　● improve ⓥ 향상시키다, 개선하다

구문 풀이

1행 Bad lighting can increase stress on your eyes, / as can light [that is too bright], or light [that shines directly into your eyes].
　　　　　　　　　　　　　　　　　　as+동사+주어 : ~이 …하듯이(도치 구문)

★★ 문제 해결 꿀~팁 ★★

▶ 많이 틀린 이유는?

최다 오답인 ②는 감정 유발 동사의 태를 묻고 있다. 감정 유발 동사를 분사로 바꿀 때에는 분사가 설명하는 명사에 따라 태를 결정한다. 즉 명사가 감정을 유발하는 주체라면 현재분사, 감정을 느끼게 되는 대상이라면 과거분사를 쓴다. 여기서는 분사가 주어인 '형광등'을 설명하는데 이는 피로감을 유발하는 주체로 보는 것이 타당하다. 따라서 tiring의 쓰임은 어법상 맞다.

▶ 문제 해결 방법은?

④에서 묻는 수 일치 개념은 어법 최빈출 포인트 중 하나이다. 뒤에 관계절을 수반하는 긴 주어가 나오면 관계절이 어디에서 시작되고 끝나는지, 주어의 핵심부는 무엇인지 눈여겨보고 동사의 단복수 여부를 결정하도록 한다.

---

30 화가들의 제한적인 색상 선택　　　　정답률 50% | 정답 ⑤

다음 글의 밑줄 친 부분 중, 문맥상 낱말의 쓰임이 적절하지 <u>않은</u> 것은? [3점]

Painters have in principle / an infinite range of colours at their disposal, / especially in modern times / with the chromatic ① explosion of synthetic chemistry.
이론상으로 화가들은 사용할 수 있는데, / 무한한 범위의 색을 마음대로 / 현대에 특히 그렇다. / 합성 화학을 통한 유채색의 폭발적 증가를 이룬
And yet / painters don't use all the colours at once, / and indeed many have used / a remarkably ② restrictive selection.
그러나 / 화가들이 모든 색을 동시에 사용하는 것은 아닌데, / 사실 많은 화가들은 사용해 왔다. / 눈에 띄게 제한적으로 색을 선택하여

Mondrian limited himself / mostly to the three primaries red, yellow and blue / to fill his black-ruled grids, / and Kasimir Malevich worked / with similar self-imposed restrictions.
Mondrian은 스스로를 제한했고, / 대개 빨강, 노랑, 그리고 파랑의 3원색으로 / 자신의 검정색 선이 그려진 격자무늬를 채우기 위해 / Kasimir Malevich는 작업했다. / 비슷하게 스스로 부과한 제한에 따라

For Yves Klein, one colour was ③ enough; / Franz Kline's art was typically black on white.
Yves Klein에게는 한 가지 색이면 충분했고, / Franz Klein의 예술(작품)은 보통 흰색 바탕에 검정색이었다.

There was nothing ④ new in this: / the Greeks and Romans tended to use / just red, yellow, black and white.
여기에는 새로울 것이 없었는데, / 그리스와 로마 사람들은 사용하는 경향이 있었다. / 단지 빨간색, 노란색, 검정색 그리고 흰색만을 / Why?
왜 그랬을까?

It's impossible to generalize, / but both in antiquity and modernity / it seems likely / that the ✓ limited palette aided clarity and comprehensibility, / and helped to focus attention / on the components that mattered: / shape and form.
일반화할 수는 없지만, / 고대와 현대에 모두 / ~했을 것 같다. / (범위가) 제한된 팔레트가 [색이] 명확성과 이해 가능성에 도움을 주고 / 주의를 집중할 수 있도록 도움을 주었을 / 중요한 구성소소인 / 모양과 형태에

이론상으로 화가들은 무한한 범위의 색을 마음대로 사용할 수 있는데, 합성 화학에서 유채색의 ① 폭발적 증가를 이룬 현대에 특히 그렇다. 그러나 화가들이 모든 색을 동시에 사용하는 것은 아닌데, 사실 많은 화가들은 눈에 띄게 ② 제한적으로 색을 선택하여 사용해 왔다. Mondrian은 자신의 검정색 선이 그려진 격자무늬를 채우기 위해 대개 빨강, 노랑, 그리고 파랑의 3원색으로 스스로를 제한했고, Kasimir Malevich는 비슷하게 스스로 부과한 제한에 따라 작업했다. Yves Klein에게는 한 가지 색이면 ③ 충분했고, Franz Klein의 예술(작품)은 보통 흰색 바탕 위에 검정색이었다. 여기에는 ④ 새로울 것이 없었는데, 그리스와 로마 사람들은 단지 빨간색, 노란색, 검정색 그리고 흰색만을 사용하는 경향이 있었다. 왜 그랬을까? 일반화할 수는 없지만, 고대와 현대에서 모두 (범위가) ⑤ 확대된(→ 제한된) 팔레트가[색이] 명확성과 이해 가능성에 도움을 주고 중요한 구성 요소인 모양과 형태에 주의를 집중할 수 있도록 도움을 주었던 것 같다.

Why? 왜 정답일까?

다양한 색을 이용할 수 있게 된 현대에 이르러서도 많은 화가들은 고대 시절 화가들이 그랬듯이 제한된 색을 쓰곤 하는데(And yet painters don't use all the colours at once, and indeed many have used a remarkably restrictive selection.) 이것이 모양과 형태에 보다 주의를 기울이게 도와줄 것임을 설명한 글이다. 즉 색이 '제한적으로' 선택되는 이유를 언급하는 것이 글의 핵심이므로, ⑤의 expanded를 limited로 고쳐야 한다. 따라서 낱말의 쓰임이 적절하지 않은 것은 ⑤이다.

- in principle 원칙적으로, 이론상으로
- at one's disposal ~의 마음대로 이용할 수 있는
- synthetic ⓐ 합성의
- restrictive ⓐ 제한적인
- self-imposed 스스로 부과한, 자진해서 하는
- generalize ⓥ 일반화하다
- modernity ⓝ 현대, 현대적임
- aid ⓥ (일이 수월해지도록) 돕다
- comprehensibility ⓝ 이해 가능성
- infinite ⓐ 무한한
- explosion ⓝ 폭발적 증가, 폭발
- remarkably ⓐⓓ 눈에 띄게, 두드러지게
- primary ⓝ 원색 ⓐ 주요한, 기본적인
- typically ⓐⓓ 보통, 대개, 전형적으로
- antiquity ⓝ 고대, 아주 오래됨
- expand ⓥ 확장시키다
- clarity ⓝ 명확성
- component ⓝ 구성 요소

구문 풀이

10행 It's impossible to generalize, but both in antiquity and modernity it seems
가주어   진주어   주어 동사
likely {that the limited palette aided clarity and comprehensibility, and helped to
보어   (   ) : 명사절   동사1   동사2
focus attention on the components [that mattered]: shape and form}.
                                                              = the components

---

31 대도시의 분업   정답률 48% | 정답 ①

다음 빈칸에 들어갈 말로 가장 적절한 것을 고르시오. [3점]

✓ specialization - 전문화   ② criticism - 비판
③ competition - 경쟁   ④ diligence - 근면
⑤ imagination - 상상

In small towns / the same workman makes chairs and doors and tables, / and often the same person builds houses.
작은 마을에서는 / 똑같은 일꾼이 의자와 문, 탁자를 만들고, / 바로 같은 사람이 종종 집도 짓는다.

And it is, of course, impossible / for a man of many trades / to be skilled in all of them.
그리고 물론 불가능하다. / 많은 직업을 가진 한 사람이 / 그 모든 데 능하기는

In large cities, on the other hand, / because many people make demands on each trade, / one trade alone — very often even less than a whole trade — is enough to support a man.
반면에 대도시에서는, / 많은 사람들이 각 직종을 필요로 하기에, / 한 가지 직종만으로도, / 아주 흔하게 전체 직종에 훨씬 못 미치는 / 한 사람이 먹고 사는 데 충분하다.

For instance, / one man makes shoes for men, / and another for women.
예를 들어, / 한 사람은 남자 신발을 만들고, / 다른 사람은 여자 신발을 만든다.

And there are places / even where one man earns a living / by only stitching shoes, / another by cutting them out, / and another by sewing the uppers together.
그리고 경우까지도 있다. / 어떤 사람은 생계를 꾸려가는 / 신발을 깁기만 하여 / 다른 사람은 자르기만 하고, / 또 다른 사람은 신발 위창을 꿰매기만 하여

Such skilled workers may have used simple tools, / but their specialization / did result in more efficient and productive work.
그런 숙련된 노동자들은 간단한 도구만을 썼을지도 모르지만, / 그들의 전문화는 / 정말로 더 효율적이고 생산적인 작업으로 이어졌다.

작은 마을에서는 똑같은 일꾼이 의자와 문, 탁자를 만들고, 바로 같은 사람이 종종 집도 짓는다. 그리고 물론 많은 직업을 가진 한 사람이 그 모든 데 능하기는 불가능하다. 반면에 대도시에서는, 많은 사람들이 각 직종을 필요로 하기에, 아주 흔하게 전체 직종에 훨씬 못 미치는 한 가지 직종만으로도, 한 사람이 먹고 사는 데 충분하다. 예를 들어, 한 사람은 남자 신발을 만들고, 다른 사람은 여자 신발을 만든다. 그리고 어떤 사람은 신발을 깁기만 하고, 다른 사람은 자르기만 하고, 또 다른 사람은 신발 위창을 꿰매기만 하여 생계를 꾸려가는 경우까지도 있다. 그런 숙련된 노동자들은 간단한 도구만을 썼을지도 모르지만, 그들의 전문화는 정말로 더 효율적이고 생산적인 작업으로 이어졌다.

Why? 왜 정답일까?

작은 마을과 대도시의 업무 방식을 대조한 글이다. 작은 마을에서는 한 사람이 여러 가지 일을 하게 되지만, 대도시에서는 한 사람이 한 가지 직종만 갖고서도 먹고 사는 데 충분하여 분업이 이루어진다(In large cities, ~, because many people make demands on each trade, one trade alone — very often even less than a whole trade — is enough to support a man.)고 이야기하므로, 빈칸에 들어갈 말로 적절한 것은 '분업'과 대응될 수 있는 ① '전문화'이다.

- workman ⓝ 일꾼, 노동자, 직공
- skilled ⓐ 숙련된
- stitch ⓥ 깁다, 꿰매다, 바느질하다
- result in ~로 이어지다, ~을 초래하다
- productive ⓐ 생산적인
- diligence ⓝ 근면
- impossible ⓐ 불가능한
- place ⓝ 경우
- sew ⓥ 꿰매다, 깁다
- efficient ⓐ 효율적인
- criticism ⓝ 비판

구문 풀이

7행 And there are places [even where one man earns a living by only stitching
          동사   주어   관계부사   생계를 꾸리다   「by + 동명사」: ~함으로써
shoes, another by cutting them out, and another by sewing the uppers together].
                                      (earns a living 생략)

---

32 성장 과정의 일부인 자립   정답률 45% | 정답 ⑤

다음 빈칸에 들어갈 말로 가장 적절한 것을 고르시오. [3점]

① developing financial management skills – 금전 관리 기술을 발달시키는 것
② learning from other people's experiences – 다른 사람의 경험에서 배우는 것
③ figuring out your strengths and interests – 여러분의 강점과 흥미를 알아내는 것
④ managing relationship problems with your peers – 동료와의 인간관계 문제를 관리하는 것
✓ falling out of love with the adults who look after you – 자신을 보살펴 주는 어른과 정을 떼는 것

All mammals need to leave their parents / and set up on their own / at some point.
모든 포유동물은 부모를 떠나서 / 스스로 자립해야 한다. / 어느 시점에서는

But human adults generally provide a comfortable existence / — enough food arrives on the table, / money is given at regular intervals, / the bills get paid / and the electricity for the TV doesn't usually run out.
하지만 성인 인간은 대개 안락한 생활을 제공하는데, / 충분한 음식이 식탁 위에 차려지고, / 일정한 기간마다 돈이 지급되며, / 청구서가 지불되고, / TV 전기가 대개 끊기지 않는다.

If teenagers didn't build up / a fairly major disrespect for and conflict with / their parents or carers, / they'd never want to leave.
십 대 아이가 키우지 않는다면, / 매우 심각한 불손과 갈등을 / 부모나 보호자에 대한 / 그들은 결코 떠나고 싶어 하지 않을 것이다.

In fact, / falling out of love with the adults / who look after you / is probably a necessary part of growing up.
사실, / 어른과의 정을 떼는 것은 / 보살펴 주는 / 아마도 성장의 필수적인 부분일 것이다.

Later, / when you live independently, away from them, / you can start to love them again / because you won't need to be fighting / to get away from them.
나중에, / 여러분이 그들과 떨어져서 독립적으로 생활하게 되면, / 그들을 다시 사랑하기 시작할 수 있을 것이다. / 싸울 필요가 없을 것이기 때문에 / 그들에게서 벗어나기 위해서

And you can come back sometimes / for a home-cooked meal.
그리고 여러분은 돌아올 수 있다. / 가끔 집 밥을 먹기 위해

모든 포유동물은 어느 시점에서는 부모를 떠나서 자립해야 한다. 하지만 성인 인간은 대개 안락한 생활을 제공하여, 충분한 음식이 식탁 위에 차려지고, 일정한 기간마다 돈이 지급되며, 청구서가 지불되고, TV 전기가 대개 끊기지 않는다. 십 대 아이가 부모나 보호자에 대한 매우 심각한 불손과 갈등을 키우지 않는다면, 그들은 결코 떠나고 싶어 하지 않을 것이다. 사실, 자신을 보살펴 주는 어른과 정을 떼는 것은 아마도 성장의 필수적인 부분일 것이다. 나중에, 여러분이 그들과 떨어져서 독립적으로 생활하게 되면, 그들에게서 벗어나기 위해서 싸울 필요가 없을 것이기 때문에 그들을 다시 사랑하기 시작할 수 있을 것이다. 그리고 여러분은 가끔 집 밥을 먹기 위해 돌아올 수 있다.

Why? 왜 정답일까?

첫 문장에서 모든 포유류는 어느 시점이 되면 부모를 떠나 자립해야 한다(All mammals need to leave their parents and set up on their own at some point.)는 핵심 내용이 나오므로, 강조의 연결어인 In fact 뒤의 빈칸 또한 '자립'에 관련된 내용을 언급할 것임을 유추할 수 있다. 따라서 빈칸에 들어갈 말로 가장 적절한 것은 ⑤ '자신을 보살펴 주는 어른과 정을 떼는 것'이다.

- mammal ⓝ 포유동물
- existence ⓝ 생활, 생계, 존재, 현존
- run out (공급품 등이) 다 떨어지다
- disrespect ⓝ 불손, 무례, 결례
- independently ⓐⓓ 독립하여
- financial ⓐ 재정적인, 금전적인
- manage ⓥ 살아 나가다, 지내다
- fall out of love with ~와 정을 떼다
- point ⓝ 지점
- interval ⓝ 간격
- fairly ⓐⓓ 상당히, 꽤
- conflict ⓝ 갈등, 충돌
- home-cooked 가정에서 만든
- strength ⓝ 강점, 힘
- peer ⓝ 동료, 친구

구문 풀이

2행 But human adults generally provide a comfortable existence / {— enough
                                                              (   ) : a comfortable existence의 내용 설명   주어1
food arrives on the table, money is given at regular intervals, the bills get paid
            동사1(자동사)   주어2 동사2(수동태)   주어3 동사3(수동태)
and the electricity for the TV doesn't usually run out}.
          주어4   동사4(자동사)

★★★ 등급을 가르는 문제!
33 광고와 지도 제작의 공통된 특성   정답률 39% | 정답 ②

다음 빈칸에 들어갈 말로 가장 적절한 것을 고르시오. [3점]

① reducing the amount of information – 정보의 양을 줄여서
✓ telling or showing everything – 모든 것을 말하거나 보여줌
③ listening to people's voices – 사람들의 목소리에 귀 기울여서

④ relying on visual images only – 시각 이미지에만 의존해서
⑤ making itself available to everyone – 자체로 모두가 이용 가능하게 만들어서

What do advertising and map-making have in common?
광고와 지도 제작은 무슨 공통점이 있을까?
Without doubt / the best answer is their shared need / to communicate a limited version of the truth.
의심할 여지없이 / 최고의 대답은 공통된 필요성이 있다. / 제한된 형태의 사실을 전달하는
An advertisement must create an image / that's appealing / and a map must present an image that's clear, / but neither can meet its goal / by telling or showing everything.
광고는 이미지를 만들어내야 하고 / 매력적인 / 지도는 명백한 이미지를 제시해야 하지만, / 둘 다 목표를 달성할 수는 없다. / 모든 것을 말하거나 보여줌으로써
Ads will cover up or play down / negative aspects of the company or service / they advertise.
광고는 가리거나 약화시킬 것이다. / 회사나 서비스의 부정적인 측면을 / 그들이 광고하는
In this way, / they can promote a favorable comparison with similar products / or differentiate a product from its competitors.
이런 식으로, / 그들은 유사 상품과의 유리한 비교를 홍보하거나 / 제품을 그 경쟁 제품과 차별화할 수 있다.
Likewise, the map must remove details / that would be confusing.
마찬가지로, 지도는 세부사항을 지워야 한다. / 혼란을 줄 수 있는

광고와 지도 제작은 무슨 공통점이 있을까? 의심할 여지없이 최고의 대답은 제한된 형태의 사실을 전달하는 공통된 필요성에 있다. 광고는 매력적인 이미지를 만들어내야 하고 지도는 명백한 이미지를 제시해야 하지만, 둘 다 모든 것을 말하거나 보여줌으로써 목표를 달성할 수는 없다. 광고는 그들이 광고하는 회사나 서비스의 부정적인 측면을 가리거나 약화시킬 것이다. 이런 식으로, 그들은 유사 상품과의 유리한 비교를 홍보하거나 제품을 그 경쟁 제품과 차별화할 수 있다. 마찬가지로, 지도는 혼란을 줄 수 있는 세부사항을 지워야 한다.

Why? 왜 정답일까?

광고와 지도는 서로 제한된 형태의 사실만을 전달하여 목적을 달성한다(Without doubt the best answer is their shared need to communicate a limited version of the truth.)는 내용이다. 광고가 제품의 약점을 숨기거나 축소하여 말하듯이, 지도 또한 혼란을 줄 수 있는 세부사항을 나타내지 않는다는 것을 말하고 있다. 이를 통해 오히려 '모든 것을 말하면' 광고든 지도든 목적을 달성할 수 없으리라는 내용을 유추할 수 있어, 빈칸에 들어갈 말로 가장 적절한 것은 ② '모든 것을 말하거나 보여줌'이다.

- **advertising** ⓝ 광고
- **have in common** (관심사나 생각을) 공통적으로 지니다
- **communicate** ⓥ 전달하다
- **present** ⓥ 제시하다
- **play down** 약화시키다, 낮추다
- **promote** ⓥ 홍보하다, 촉진하다
- **comparison** ⓝ 비교
- **competitor** ⓝ 경쟁자, 경쟁 상대
- **map-making** 지도 제작, 지도 만들기
- **appealing** ⓐ 매력적인
- **meet** ⓥ (목표나 기한 등을) 달성하다, 맞추다
- **aspect** ⓝ 측면
- **favorable** ⓐ 호의적인
- **differentiate** ⓥ 차별화하다
- **confusing** ⓐ 혼란을 주는, 혼란스러운

구문 풀이

2행 Without doubt / the best answer is their shared need to communicate a
의심할 여지없이   형용사적 용법
limited version of the truth.

★★ 문제 해결 꿀~팁 ★★

▶ 많이 틀린 이유는?
빈칸 문제이만큼 주제문을 찾으면 쉽게 답에 접근할 수 있으나, 빈칸 문장에 neither라는 부정어가 있으므로 주제를 거꾸로 뒤집은 내용이 답이 된다는 점에서 어려운 문제였다.
▶ 문제 해결 방법은?
글의 주제는 광고와 지도가 공통적으로 제한된 진실만을 담는다는, 즉 '다 말하지 않는' 특성이 있다는 것이다. 이를 빈칸 문장의 맥락에 맞게 뒤집어 생각하면 '다 말하면 광고나 지도가 제 기능을 못한다'는 내용을 유추할 수 있다. 최다 오답인 ⑤은 '정보 양의 제한'이라는 핵심 내용을 그대로 담고 있기에, 빈칸에 넣으면 오히려 '정보를 제한할 때 광고나 지도 제작의 목적이 달성되지 않는다'는, 주제와 정반대되는 내용을 나타내게 된다.

★★★ 등급을 가르는 문제! ★★★

34 문화적 변화에 대한 인간의 태도   정답률 36% | 정답 ⑤

다음 빈칸에 들어갈 말로 가장 적절한 것을 고르시오. [3점]
① seek cooperation between generations – 세대 간 협력을 추구하는
② be forgetful of what they experienced – 그들이 경험한 것을 잘 잊어버리는
③ adjust quickly to the new environment – 새로운 환경에 빠르게 적응하는
④ make efforts to remember what their ancestors did – 자신의 조상이 했던 것을 기억하려고 노력하는
☑ like what they have grown up in and gotten used to – 자신이 자라고 익숙해진 것을 좋아하는

It is difficult to know how to determine / whether one culture is better than another.
방법을 알기는 어렵다. / 한 문화가 다른 문화보다 더 나은지를 결정하는
What is the cultural rank order / of rock, jazz, and classical music?
문화적인 순위는 어떻게 될까? / 록, 재즈, 고전 음악의
When it comes to public opinion polls / about whether cultural changes are for the better or the worse, / looking forward would lead to one answer / and looking backward would lead to a very different answer.
여론 조사에 관한 한, / 문화적 변화가 더 나아지는 것인지 더 나빠지는 것인지에 관한 / 앞을 내다보는 것과 / 뒤돌아보는 것은 아주 다른 대답으로 이어진다.
Our children would be horrified / if they were told / they had to go back to the culture of their grandparents.
우리 아이들은 겁이 날 것이다. / 말을 들으면 / 조부모의 문화로 되돌아가야 한다는
Our parents would be horrified / if they were told / they had to participate in the culture of their grandchildren.
우리 부모님은 겁이 날 것이다. / 들으면 / 손주의 문화에 참여해야 한다고
Humans tend to like / what they have grown up in / and gotten used to.
인간은 좋아하는 경향이 있다. / 자신이 자라고 / 익숙해진 것을

After a certain age, / anxieties arise / when sudden cultural changes are coming.
특정한 나이 이후에는 / 불안감이 생긴다. / 갑작스러운 문화적 변화가 다가오고 있을 때
Our culture is part of / who we are and where we stand, / and we don't like to think / that who we are and where we stand / are short-lived.
우리 문화는 일부이고, / 우리의 정체성과 우리의 입지의 / 우리는 생각하고 싶어 하지 않는다. / 우리의 정체성과 우리의 입지가 / 오래가지 못한다고

한 문화가 다른 문화보다 더 나은지를 결정하는 방법을 알기는 어렵다. 록, 재즈, 고전 음악의 문화적인 순위는 어떻게 될까? 문화적 변화가 더 나아지는 것인지 더 나빠지는 것인지에 관한 여론 조사에 관한 한, 앞을 내다보는 것과 뒤를 돌아보는 것은 아주 다른 대답으로 이어진다. 우리 아이들은 조부모의 문화로 되돌아가야 한다는 말을 들으면 겁이 날 것이다. 우리 부모님은 손주의 문화에 참여해야 한다고 들으면 겁이 날 것이다. 인간은 자신이 자라고 익숙해진 것을 좋아하는 경향이 있다. 특정한 나이 이후에는 갑작스러운 문화적 변화가 다가오고 있을 때 불안감이 생긴다. 우리 문화는 우리의 정체성과 우리의 입지의 일부이고, 우리는 우리의 정체성과 우리의 입지가 오래가지 못한다고 생각하고 싶어 하지 않는다.

Why? 왜 정답일까?

인간은 특정한 나이가 지나면 갑작스러운 문화의 변화에 불안감을 느끼는데 이는 우리의 문화가 우리 정체성과 입지의 일부로 여겨지기 때문이라는(Our culture is part of who we are and where we stand, ~) 내용을 다룬 글이다. 우리는 우리 자신의 문화가 오래가지 못한다고 여기고 싶어 하지 않는다는 내용의 마지막 문장을 근거로 볼 때, 빈칸 앞의 두 문장에서 언급하듯이 우리가 다른 세대의 문화에 참여해야 한다고 생각하면 겁을 내는 이유는 우리가 우리 자신의 문화를 가장 편하게 여기고 좋아하기 때문임을 유추할 수 있으므로, 빈칸에 들어갈 말로 가장 적절한 것은 ⑤ '자신이 자라고 익숙해진 것을 좋아하는'이다.

- **determine** ⓥ 결정하다, 정하다
- **public opinion poll** 여론 조사
- **participate in** ~에 참여하다
- **certain** ⓐ 특정한, 일정한
- **arise** ⓥ 생기다, 발생하다
- **seek** ⓥ 찾다
- **adjust** ⓥ 적응하다
- **culture** ⓝ 문화
- **horrified** ⓐ 겁에 질린, 무서워하는
- **grandchildren** ⓝ 손자
- **anxiety** ⓝ 불안, 걱정
- **short-lived** 오래 가지 못하는, 단기적인
- **cooperation** ⓝ 협력
- **ancestor** ⓝ 조상

구문 풀이

3행 When it comes to public opinion polls about {whether cultural changes
~에 관한 한   명사구   ~인지 아닌지
are for the better or the worse}, looking forward would lead to one answer and
[ ]: 명사절(about의 목적어)   동명사구 주어1   동사1
looking backward would lead to a very different answer.
동명사구 주어2   동사2

★★ 문제 해결 꿀~팁 ★★

▶ 많이 틀린 이유는?
인간은 자신이 익숙하게 느끼는 문화를 좋아한다는 내용의 글로, 빈칸 앞의 예시와 뒤의 결론 내용을 종합하면 답을 고를 수 있다. 최다 오답인 ④는 사람들이 조상의 행동을 기억하려고 애쓴다는 뜻인데 이는 본문의 내용과 관계가 없다. 새로운 환경에 대한 적응력을 언급하는 ③은 우리가 새로운 문화에 잘 적응한다는 뜻으로 이해될 수 있으므로 주제와 상반된다.
▶ 문제 해결 방법은?
결론이 다소 추상적이므로 예시를 통해 글을 이해하면 쉽다. 아이이든 노인이든 서로 다른 세대의 문화에 참여해야 한다면 겁부터 날 것이라는 언급을 통해, 익숙한 것을 좋게 여기는 인간의 특성을 유추하도록 한다.

35 차량 공유 운동의 인기   정답률 53% | 정답 ④

다음 글에서 전체 흐름과 관계 없는 문장은?

Today car sharing movements / have appeared all over the world.
오늘날 차량 공유 운동이 / 전 세계에서 일어났다.
In many cities, / car sharing has made a strong impact / on how city residents travel.
많은 도시에서 / 차량 공유는 강한 영향을 미쳤다. / 도시 거주민의 이동 방식에
① Even in strong car-ownership cultures / such as North America, / car sharing has gained popularity.
심지어 차량 소유의 문화가 강한 지역에서도 / 북미 같은 / 차량 공유는 인기를 얻었다.
② In the U.S. and Canada, / membership in car sharing / now exceeds one in five adults in many urban areas.
미국과 캐나다에서 / 차량 공유 회원 수는 / 현재 많은 도시 지역에서 성인 5명 중 1명을 넘어섰다.
③ Strong influence on traffic jams and pollution / can be felt from Toronto to New York, / as each shared vehicle replaces around 10 personal cars.
교통 체증 및 오염에 대한 강한 영향력은 / 토론토부터 뉴욕까지 느껴질 수 있다. / 공유된 차량 한 대가 10대의 개인 차량을 대체함에 따라
☑ The best thing about driverless cars / is that people won't need a license / to operate them.
무인 자동차에 관한 가장 좋은 점은 / 사람들이 면허증을 필요로 하지 않는다는 것이다. / 차를 몰기 위해
⑤ City governments with downtown areas / struggling with traffic jams and lack of parking lots / are driving the growing popularity of car sharing.
시내 지역이 있는 시 정부에서는 / 교통 체증과 주차 공간 부족으로 시달리고 있는 / 차량 공유의 인기 증가를 부추기고 있다.

오늘날 차량 공유 운동이 전 세계에서 일어났다. 많은 도시에서 차량 공유는 도시 거주민의 이동 방식에 강한 영향을 미쳤다. ① 심지어 차량 소유의 문화가 강한 북미 같은 지역에서도 차량 공유는 인기를 얻었다. ② 미국과 캐나다에서 차량 공유 회원 수는 현재 많은 도시 지역에서 성인 5명 중 1명을 넘어섰다. ③ 공유된 차량 한 대가 10대의 개인 차량을 대체함에 따라 교통 체증 및 오염에 대한 강한 영향력을 토론토부터 뉴욕까지 느낄 수 있다. ④ 무인 자동차에 관한 가장 좋은 점은 사람들이 차를 몰기 위해 면허증을 필요로 하지 않는다는 것이다. ⑤ 시내의 교통 체증과 주차 공간 부족으로 시달리고 있는 시 정부에서는 차량 공유의 인기 증가를 부추기고 있다.

Why? 왜 정답일까?

이 글은 차량 공유 운동이 전 세계에 걸쳐, 특히 차량 소유 문화가 강한 북미 지역에서까지 인기를 누리고

있다는 내용을 설명한다. ①~③에서는 미국과 캐나다에서 차량 공유의 인기를 확인할 수 있다는 내용을, ⑤에서는 교통 체증 및 주차 공간 부족에 시달리는 시 정부들이 차량 공유를 장려하고 있다는 내용을 이야기한다. 하지만 ④는 '무인 자동차'에 관해 언급하고 있어 흐름에 맞지 않는다. 따라서 전체 흐름과 관계 없는 문장은 ④이다.

- have an impact on ~에 영향을 미치다
- ownership ⓝ 소유
- membership ⓝ 회원 수, 회원들
- traffic jam 교통 체증
- replace ⓥ 대체하다
- operate ⓥ 조작하다, 가동하다
- resident ⓝ 거주민, 거주자
- popularity ⓝ 인기
- exceed ⓥ 넘어서다, 능가하다
- vehicle ⓝ 차량, 탈것
- driverless car 무인 자동차
- struggle with ~에 시달리다, ~로 고전하다

구문 풀이

10행 City governments with downtown areas [struggling with traffic jams and
　　　　　주어　　　　　　　　　　　　　　　　　　　~로 고전하는　　명사구1
lack of parking lots] are driving the growing popularity of car sharing.
명사구2　　　　　　동사(현재진행)　　　현재분사

---

36 과학과 예술의 근간인 협업　　　　　　　정답률 58% | 정답 ②

주어진 글 다음에 이어질 글의 순서로 가장 적절한 것을 고르시오.
① (A) - (C) - (B)　　　　　　　　✔ (B) - (A) - (C)
③ (B) - (C) - (A)　　　　　　　　④ (C) - (A) - (B)
⑤ (C) - (B) - (A)

Collaboration is the basis / for most of the foundational arts and sciences.
협업은 / 대부분의 기초 예술과 과학의

(B) It is often believed / that Shakespeare, like most playwrights of his period, / did not always write alone, / and many of his plays are considered collaborative / or were rewritten after their original composition.
흔히 믿어지고, / 셰익스피어는, 당대 대부분의 극작가처럼, / 늘 혼자 작품을 썼던 것은 아니라고 / 그의 희곡 중 다수가 협업을 한 것으로 여겨지거나 / 최초의 창작 후에 개작되었다.

Leonardo Da Vinci made his sketches individually, / but he collaborated with other people / to add the finer details.
레오나르도 다빈치는 혼자서 스케치를 그렸지만, / 다른 사람들과 협업했다 / 더 세밀한 세부 묘사를 더 하기 위해

(A) For example, / his sketches of human anatomy / were a collaboration with Marcantonio della Torre, / an anatomist from the University of Pavia.
예를 들어, / 인체의 해부학적 구조를 그린 그의 스케치는 / Marcantonio della Torre와 협업한 것이었다. / Pavia 대학의 해부학자인

Their collaboration is important / because it marries the artist with the scientist.
그들의 협업은 중요하다 / 예술가와 과학자가 결합한 것이어서

(C) Similarly, / Marie Curie's husband stopped his original research / and joined Marie in hers.
마찬가지로, / Marie Curie의 남편은 원래 자신이 하던 연구를 중단하고 / Marie의 연구를 함께 했다.

They went on to collaboratively discover radium, / which overturned old ideas / in physics and chemistry.
그들은 더 나아가 협업으로 라듐을 발견했고, / 그것은 기존 개념들을 뒤집었다. / 물리학과 화학에서의

협업은 대부분의 기초 예술과 과학의 기반이다.
(B) 셰익스피어는, 당대 대부분의 극작가처럼, 늘 혼자 작품을 썼던 것은 아니라고 흔히 믿어지고, 그의 희곡 중 다수가 협업을 한 것으로 여겨지거나 최초의 창작 후에 개작되었다. 레오나르도 다빈치는 혼자서 스케치를 했지만, 더 세밀한 세부 묘사를 더하기 위해 다른 사람들과 협업했다.
(A) 예를 들어, 그의 인체 해부 구조 스케치는 Pavia 대학의 해부학자인 Marcantonio della Torre와 협업한 것이었다. 그들의 협업은 예술가와 과학자가 결합한 것이어서 중요하다.
(C) 마찬가지로, Marie Curie의 남편은 원래 자신이 하던 연구를 중단하고 Marie의 연구를 함께 했다. 그들은 더 나아가 협업으로 라듐을 발견했고, 그것은 물리학과 화학의 오래된 개념들을 뒤집었다.

Why? 왜 정답일까?

협업이 기초 예술과 과학의 기반임을 언급한 주어진 글 뒤에는, 셰익스피어와 레오나르도 다빈치의 예를 제시하는 (B), 다빈치를 단락 초반에서 his로 받아 그의 스케치 중 협동 작업의 사례를 언급하는 (A), 이어서 추가 사례를 제시하는 Similarly 뒤로 과학에서의 예로서 퀴리 부부를 언급하는 (C)가 차례로 연결되는 것이 자연스럽다. 따라서 글의 순서로 가장 적절한 것은 ② '(B) - (A) - (C)'이다.

- collaboration ⓝ 협업, 협동, 공동 작업
- foundational ⓐ 기초적인, 기본의
- anatomist ⓝ 해부학자
- marry ⓥ (서로 다른 두 가지 사상·사물을 성공적으로) 결합시키다
- playwright ⓝ 극작가
- rewrite ⓥ 개작하다, 다시 쓰다
- individually ⓐⓓ 개인적으로, 따로
- join ⓥ 합류하다
- basis ⓝ 근거, 이유
- sketch ⓝ 개요
- period ⓝ 기간, 시기
- composition ⓝ 작성, 작곡, 작품
- fine ⓐ 세밀한, 섬세한, 촘촘한
- overturn ⓥ 뒤엎다, 전복시키다

구문 풀이

7행 It is often believed {that Shakespeare, like most playwrights of his period,
　　　　　주어1(가주어) 동사1　　　　　주어 　　 ( ) : 진주어
did not always write alone}, and many of his plays are considered collaborative
　　　　→ 동사1　　　　　　　　　　　　　　주어2 　　 동사2　　　보어(형용사)
or were rewritten after their original composition.
　　　동사3

---

37 조카에게 빠른 답장을 받은 Carnegie　　　　정답률 54% | 정답 ③

주어진 글 다음에 이어질 글의 순서로 가장 적절한 것을 고르시오.
① (A) - (C) - (B)　　　　　　　② (B) - (A) - (C)
✔ (B) - (C) - (A)　　　　　　　④ (C) - (A) - (B)
⑤ (C) - (B) - (A)

[문제편 p.174]

Andrew Carnegie, the great early-twentieth-century businessman, / once heard his sister complain about her two sons.
20세기 초반의 위대한 사업가 Andrew Carnegie는 / 언젠가 누이가 자기 두 아들에 대해 불평하는 것을 들었다.

(B) They were away at college / and rarely responded to her letters.
그들은 멀리서 대학을 다니면서 / 어머니의 편지에 좀처럼 답장을 하지 않고 있었다.

Carnegie told her / that if he wrote them / he would get an immediate response.
Carnegie는 그녀에게 이야기했다. / 자신이 그들에게 편지를 쓰면 / 자신은 즉각적인 답장을 받을 것이라고

(C) He sent off two warm letters to the boys, / and told them / that he was happy / to send each of them a check for a hundred dollars / (a large sum in those days).
그는 다정한 편지 두 통을 조카들에게 보냈고, / 이야기했다. / 그가 기쁘다는 것을 / 그들 각자에게 100달러짜리 수표를 보내게 되어 / (당시 큰 액수였던)

Then he mailed the letters, / but didn't enclose the checks.
그런 다음 그는 편지를 부쳤지만, / 수표를 동봉하지는 않았다.

(A) Within days / he received warm grateful letters from both boys, / who noted at the letters' end / that he had unfortunately forgotten to include the check.
며칠 안에 / 그는 두 조카에게서 다정한 감사 편지를 받았는데, / 그들은 편지 말미에 언급했다. / 삼촌이 안타깝게도 수표를 함께 보내는 것을 잊었음을

If the check had been enclosed, / would they have responded so quickly?
만일 수표가 동봉되었더라면, / 그들이 그토록 빨리 답장을 보냈을까?

20세기 초반의 위대한 사업가 Andrew Carnegie는 언젠가 누이가 자기 두 아들에 대해 불평하는 것을 들었다.
(B) 그들은 멀리서 대학을 다니면서 어머니의 편지에 좀처럼 답장을 하지 않고 있었다. Carnegie는 자신이 그들에게 편지를 쓰면 자신은 즉각적인 답장을 받을 것이라고 이야기했다.
(C) 그는 다정한 편지 두 통을 조카들에게 보냈고, 그들 각자에게 (당시 큰 액수였던) 100달러짜리 수표를 보내게 되어 기쁘다는 것을 이야기했다. 그런 다음 그는 편지를 부쳤지만, 수표를 동봉하지는 않았다.
(A) 며칠 안에 그는 두 조카에게서 다정한 감사 편지를 받았는데, 그들은 편지 말미에 삼촌이 안타깝게도 수표를 함께 보내는 것을 잊었음을 언급했다. 만일 수표가 동봉되었더라면, 그들이 그토록 빨리 답장을 보냈을까?

Why? 왜 정답일까?

주어진 글에서는 Carnegie가 누이가 두 아들에 대해 불평하는 것을 들었다는 이야기가 나오는데 (B)에서는 이 '두 아들'을 They로 받으며 이들이 어머니의 편지에 좀처럼 답을 하지 않았다는 이야기를 이어 간다. 한편 (B)의 마지막 부분에는 Carnegie가 자신이 편지를 쓴다면 바로 답을 받을 수 있다고 말했다는 내용이 나오는데 (C)에서는 Carnegie가 조카들에게 '수표를 보내게 되어 기쁘다'라고 편지를 쓰면서 수표는 보내지 않았다는 내용을 이어서 제시한다. 마지막으로 (A)에서는 Carnegie가 며칠만에 조카들로부터 답장을 받았고 이는 수표를 동봉한다고 말했으면서 실제로 동봉하지는 않았기 때문이었다는 내용을 말한다. 따라서 주어진 글 다음에 이어질 글의 순서로 가장 적절한 것은 ③ '(B) - (C) - (A)'이다.

- businessman ⓝ 사업가
- grateful ⓐ 감사해하는, 고마워하는
- unfortunately ⓐⓓ 안타깝게도, 불행히도
- rarely ⓐⓓ 좀처럼 ~하지 않는
- send off 보내다, 발송하다
- complain ⓥ 불평하다
- note ⓥ 언급하다, 말하다
- check ⓝ 수표
- immediate ⓐ 즉각적인, 즉시의
- mail ⓥ (우편물을) 부치다, 보내다

구문 풀이

3행 Within days / he received warm grateful letters from both boys, who
　　　　　　　　　　　　　　　　　　　　　　　　　　　관계대명사(계속적 용법)
noted (at the letters' end) that he had unfortunately forgotten to include the
　동사　　　　　　　　　　　접속사　　　　　　　　　　　　　　　「forget to + 동사원형: (미래에) ~하는 것을 잊다」
check.

★★★ 등급을 가르는 문제!

38 어린 시절의 친구가 주는 이점　　　　　정답률 41% | 정답 ②

글의 흐름으로 보아, 주어진 문장이 들어가기에 가장 적절한 곳을 고르시오.

Childhood friends — friends you've known forever — / are really special.
당신이 평생 동안 알아왔던 어린 시절의 친구는 / 정말로 특별하다.

① They know everything about you, / and you've shared lots of firsts.
그들은 당신에 대해서 모든 것을 알고, / 당신은 그들과 많은 것들을 처음으로 함께 했다.

✔ When you hit puberty, however, / sometimes these forever-friendships go through growing pains.
하지만 사춘기가 되면, / 때때로 이런 영원한 우정은 성장통을 겪는다.

You find / that you have less in common than you used to.
당신은 알게 된다. / 과거보다 공유하는 것이 적다는 것을

③ Maybe you're into rap and she's into pop, / or you go to different schools / and have different groups of friends.
아마 당신은 랩을 좋아하는데 친구는 팝을 좋아한다거나, / 학교가 달라지고 / 서로 다른 친구 무리와 어울리게 될 수 있다.

④ Change can be scary, but remember:
변화는 무서울 수 있지만, 기억하라.

Friends, even best friends, / don't have to be exactly alike.
심지어 가장 친한 친구더라도 친구들이 / 완전히 똑같을 필요는 없다.

⑤ Having friends with other interests / keeps life interesting / — just think of what you can learn from each other.
다른 관심사를 가진 친구를 두는 것은 / 삶을 흥미롭게 만들 수 있다. / 그저 서로에게 무엇을 배울 수 있겠는지 생각해 보라.

당신이 평생 동안 알아왔던 어린 시절의 친구는 정말로 특별하다. ① 그들은 당신에 대해서 모든 것을 알고, 당신은 그들과 많은 것들을 처음으로 함께 했다. ② 하지만 사춘기가 되면, 때때로 이런 영원한 우정은 성장통을 겪는다. 당신은 과거보다 공유하는 것이 적다는 것을 알게 된다. ③ 아마 당신은 랩을 좋아하는데 친구는 팝을 좋아한다거나, 학교가 달라지고 서로 다른 친구 무리와 어울리게 될 수 있다. ④ 변화는 무서울 수 있지만, 기억하라. 심지어 가장 친한 친구더라도 친구들이 완전히 똑같을 필요는 없다. ⑤ 다른 관심사를 가진 친구를 두는 것은 삶을 흥미롭게 만들 수 있다. 그저 서로에게 무엇을 배울 수 있겠는지 생각해 보라.

Why? 왜 정답일까?

② 앞의 문장에서는 어린 시절의 친구가 모든 것을 서로 공유하고 많은 처음을 함께 나눈 '특별한 사이'임

을 말하는데, 주어진 문장은 이를 however로 뒤집으며 사춘기가 되면 이러한 우정에 '성장통'이 찾아온다는 내용을 제시한다. ② 뒤의 문장에서는 주어진 문장에 이어 사춘기 이후에 사람들은 어린 시절의 친구와 서로 공유하는 것이 적어지고 관심사가 달라지게 될 수 있다는 내용을 제시한다. 따라서 주어진 문장이 들어가기에 가장 적절한 곳은 ②이다.

- **puberty** ⓝ 사춘기
- **scary** ⓐ 무서운, 겁나는
- **alike** ⓐ (아주) 비슷한
- **go through** ~을 겪다
- **exactly** ⓐⓓ 정확히
- **interest** ⓝ 관심사, 흥미

구문 풀이

9행 Having friends with other interests keeps life interesting / — just think of
주어(동명사) / 동사(단수) / 목적어 / └ 목적격 보어(현재분사)
what you can learn from each other.
의문사(무엇)

★★ 문제 해결 꿀~팁 ★★

▶ 많이 틀린 이유는?
주어진 문장에 however라는 역접의 연결어가 있으므로 본문에서 앞뒤가 서로 다른 말을 하는 지점에 주어진 문장을 넣어야 한다. 최다 오답은 ④인데 ④의 앞뒤 모두 '어린 시절의 친구가 시간이 지나서 서로 안 맞게 될 수 있지만 괜찮다'는 내용으로 요약될 수 있으므로 ④를 흐름 반전의 지점으로 보기는 어렵다.

▶ 문제 해결 방법은?
주어진 문장 넣기 유형에서 주어진 문장은 보통 흐름 반전의 연결사를 포함하고 있기 마련이다. 본문을 읽을 때 각 번호 앞뒤 문장이 요약했을 때 서로 같은 말인지 다른 말인지를 계속 비교해 보면 오답을 피할 수 있다.

---

39 그림을 나아지게 할 방법   정답률 54% | 정답 ③

글의 흐름으로 보아, 주어진 문장이 들어가기에 가장 적절한 곳을 고르시오. [3점]

Imagine in your mind / one of your favorite paintings, drawings, cartoon characters / or something equally complex.
마음속으로 그려 보라. / 좋아하는 회화, 소묘, 만화의 등장인물이나 / 그 정도로 복잡한 어떤 것 중 하나를

① Now, / with that picture in your mind, / try to draw what your mind sees.
이제 / 그 그림을 염두에 두고 / 마음이 본 것을 그리려고 애써 보라.

② Unless you are unusually gifted, / your drawing will look completely different / from what you are seeing / with your mind's eye.
특별하게 재능이 있는 게 아니라면 / 여러분이 그린 그림은 완전히 다르게 보일 것이다. / 여러분이 보고 있는 것과 / 마음의 눈으로

✓ However, / if you tried to copy the original / rather than your imaginary drawing, / you might find / your drawing now was a little better.
하지만 / 원본을 베끼려고 애쓴다면 / 마음속에 존재하는 그림보다 / 알게 될 것이다. / 여러분의 그림은 이제 조금 더 나아졌다는 것을

Furthermore, / if you copied the picture many times, / you would find / that each time your drawing would get a little better, / a little more accurate.
게다가 / 그 그림을 여러 번 베낀다면 / 알게 될 것이다. / 매번 여러분의 그림이 조금 더 나아지고 / 조금 더 정확해질 거라는 것을

④ Practice makes perfect.
연습하면 완전해진다.

⑤ This is because you are developing the skills / of coordinating what your mind perceives / with the movement of your body parts.
이것은 능력이 발달되고 있기 때문이다. / 마음이 인식한 것을 조화시키는 / 신체 부위의 움직임과

좋아하는 회화, 소묘, 만화의 등장인물이나 그 정도로 복잡한 어떤 것 중 하나를 마음속으로 그려 보라. ① 이제 그 그림을 염두에 두고 마음이 보는 것을 그리려고 애써 보라. ② 특별하게 재능이 있는 게 아니라면 여러분이 그린 그림은 여러분이 마음의 눈으로 보고 있는 것과 완전히 다르게 보일 것이다. ③ 하지만 상상 속 그림보다 원본을 베끼려고 애쓴다면 여러분은 그림이 이제 조금 더 나아졌다는 것을 알게 될 것이다. 게다가 그 그림을 여러 번 베낀다면 매번 여러분의 그림이 조금 더 나아지고 조금 더 정확해질 거라는 것을 알게 될 것이다. ④ 연습하면 완전해진다. ⑤ 이것은 마음이 인식한 것을 신체 부위의 움직임과 조화시키는 능력이 발달되고 있기 때문이다.

Why? 왜 정답일까?

어떤 원본을 마음으로 상상하며 재현하려 하기보다 실제로 두고 따라 그리는 연습을 할 때 그림이 좋아질 수 있다는 내용을 다룬 글이다. ③ 앞의 문장에서 원본을 마음으로 생각하고 그리면 실제 그림은 원본과 달라진다는 내용을 말한 데 이어, However로 시작하는 주어진 문장은 실제 원본을 놓고 베끼려고 애쓴다면 그림이 나아진다는 반전된 내용을 제시한다. ③ 뒤에서는 보고 그리기를 여러 번 반복할수록 그림이 더 정확해질 것이라는 내용을 이어 간다. 따라서 주어진 문장이 들어가기에 가장 적절한 곳은 ③이다.

- **copy** ⓥ 베끼다
- **drawing** ⓝ (색칠을 하지 않은) 그림, 소묘, 데생
- **complex** ⓐ 복잡한
- **unusually** ⓐⓓ 특별하게
- **completely** ⓐⓓ 완전히
- **practice** ⓝ 연습
- **imaginary** ⓐ 상상의, 가상적인
- **equally** ⓐⓓ 똑같이
- **unless** [conj] ~하지 않는 한
- **gifted** ⓐ 재능 있는
- **accurate** ⓐ 정확한
- **perceive** ⓥ 인지하다, 인식하다

구문 풀이

→ 조건 접속사(~하지 않으면)
7행 Unless you are unusually gifted, your drawing will look completely different
현재시제 / 주어 / 미래시제 / 형용사 보어
from what you are seeing with your mind's eye.
관계대명사(~것)

---

40 문화 차이로 인해 야기된 비즈니스 실패   정답률 54% | 정답 ②

다음 글의 내용을 한 문장으로 요약하고자 한다. 빈칸 (A), (B)에 들어갈 말로 가장 적절한 것은?

	(A)		(B)
①	humor 유머	……	essential 본질적으로
✓②	humor 유머	……	inappropriate 부적절하게
③	gestures 제스처	……	essential 본질적으로
④	gestures 제스처	……	inappropriate 부적절하게
⑤	first names 이름	……	useful 유용하게

A large American hardware manufacturer / was invited to introduce its products / to a distributor with good reputation in Germany.
미국의 큰 하드웨어 제조 업체가 / 자사 제품을 소개하도록 초청받았다. / 독일에서 평판이 좋은 배급 업체에

Wanting to make the best possible impression, / the American company sent its most promising young executive, Fred Wagner, / who spoke fluent German.
최고의 인상을 심어주고 싶은 생각에, / 미국의 회사는 가장 촉망받는 젊은 임원 Fred Wagner를 보냈는데, / 그는 독일어를 유창하게 말했다.

When Fred first met his German hosts, / he shook hands firmly, / greeted everyone in German, / and even remembered to bow the head slightly / as is the German custom.
Fred가 그를 초대한 독일 쪽 사람들을 처음 만났을 때, / 그는 굳게 악수를 하고, / 독일어로 모두에게 인사를 했으며, / 고개를 살짝 숙여 인사하는 것도 잊지 않았다. / 독일의 관습대로

Fred, a very effective public speaker, / began his presentation with a few humorous jokes / to set a relaxed atmosphere.
유능한 대중 연설가인 Fred는 / 몇 가지 우스운 농담으로 발표를 시작했다. / 편안한 분위기를 조성하기 위해

However, he felt / that his presentation was not very well received / by the German executives.
하지만, 그는 느꼈다. / 발표가 아주 잘 받아들여지지 않는다고 / 독일 임원들에게

Even though Fred thought / he had done his cultural homework, / he made one particular error.
Fred는 비록 생각했지만, / 자기가 문화적인 숙제를 마쳤다고 / 그는 한 가지 특정한 실수를 저질렀다.

Fred did not win any points / by telling a few jokes.
Fred는 그 어떤 점수도 얻지 못했다. / 몇 가지 농담을 이야기하여서

It was viewed as too informal and unprofessional / in a German business setting.
이는 너무 비격식적이고 비전문적인 것으로 여겨졌다. / 독일 비즈니스 상황에서는

➡ This story shows / that using (A) humor in a business setting / can be considered (B) inappropriate / in Germany.
이 이야기는 보여준다. / 비즈니스 상황에서 유머를 쓰는 것이 / 부적절하게 여겨질 수 있다는 것을 / 독일에서

미국의 큰 하드웨어 제조 업체가 독일에서 평판이 좋은 배급 업체에 자사 제품을 소개하도록 초청받았다. 최고의 인상을 심어주고 싶은 생각에, 미국의 회사는 가장 촉망받는 젊은 임원 Fred Wagner를 보냈는데, 그는 독일어를 유창하게 말하였다. Fred가 그를 초대한 독일 쪽 사람들을 처음 만났을 때, 그는 굳게 악수를 하고, 독일어로 모두에게 인사를 했으며, 독일의 관습대로 고개를 살짝 숙여 인사하는 것도 잊지 않았다. 대중 연설을 매우 유능하게 하는 Fred는 편안한 분위기를 조성하기 위해 몇 가지 우스운 농담으로 발표를 시작했다. 하지만, 그는 발표가 독일 임원들에게 아주 잘 받아들여지지 않는다고 느꼈다. Fred는 비록 자기가 문화적인 숙제를 마쳤다고 생각했지만(독일 문화에 대한 대비를 열심히 했다고 생각했지만), 한 가지 특정한 실수를 저질렀다. Fred는 몇 가지 농담을 이야기하여서 그 어떤 점수도 얻지 못했다. 이는 독일 비즈니스 상황에서는 너무 비격식적이고 비전문적인 것으로 여겨졌다.

➡ 이 이야기는 비즈니스 상황에서 (A) 유머를 쓰는 것이 독일에서 (B) 부적절하게 여겨질 수 있다는 것을 보여준다.

Why? 왜 정답일까?

마지막 두 문장을 통해 Fred가 발표 초반에 농담을 꺼낸 것은 독일 임원들에게 도리어 비격식적이고 비전문적인 것으로 비쳐져(Fred did not win any points by telling a few jokes. It was viewed as too informal and unprofessional in a German business setting.) 비즈니스 실패로 이어지고 말았다는 것을 알 수 있으므로, 빈칸 (A)와 (B)에 들어갈 말로 적절한 것은 ② '(A) humor(유머), (B) inappropriate(부적절하게)'이다.

- **manufacturer** ⓝ 제조 업체, 생산자
- **distributor** ⓝ 배급 업체, 배급자
- **impression** ⓝ 인상
- **executive** ⓝ 임원, 중역
- **greet** ⓥ 인사하다, 환영하다
- **slightly** ⓐⓓ 약간, 조금
- **relaxed** ⓐ 편안한
- **particular** ⓐ 특정한
- **introduce** ⓥ 소개하다, 도입하다
- **reputation** ⓝ 명성
- **promising** ⓐ 촉망받는, 전도 유망한
- **firmly** ⓐⓓ 굳게, 단단히, 단호히
- **bow** ⓥ (고개를) 숙이다
- **custom** ⓝ 관습
- **atmosphere** ⓝ 분위기
- **informal** ⓐ 비격식적인, 허물없는

구문 풀이

5행 When Fred first met his German hosts, / he shook hands firmly, greeted
접속사(~할 때) / 동사1 / 동사2
everyone in German, and even remembered to bow the head slightly as is the
동사3 「remember to+동사원형: ~하는 것을 잊지 않다」 접속사(~대로)
German custom.

41-42 그룹 간의 경계심을 사라지게 하는 협동

Researchers brought two groups of 11-year-old boys to a summer camp / at Robbers Cave State Park in Oklahoma.
연구자들은 두 그룹의 11세 소년들을 주립 공원의 여름 캠프에 데려왔다. / Oklahoma에 있는 Robbers Cave

The boys were strangers to one another / and upon arrival at the camp, / were randomly separated into two groups.
그 소년들은 서로 몰랐고 / 캠프에 도착하자마자 / 무작위로 두 그룹으로 나뉘었다.

The groups were kept apart / for about a week.
그 그룹들은 서로 떨어져 있었다. / 약 1주일 동안

They swam, camped, and hiked.
그들은 수영하고, 야영하고, 하이킹을 했다.

Each group chose a name for itself, / and the boys printed their group's name / on their caps and T-shirts.
각 그룹은 자기 그룹의 이름을 지었고, / 소년들은 자신의 그룹 이름을 새겼다. / 모자와 티셔츠에

Then the two groups met.
그 후 두 그룹이 만났다.

A series of athletic competitions / were set up between them.
일련의 운동 시합이 / 그들 사이에 마련되었다.

Soon, / each group considered the other an (a) enemy.
곧, / 각 그룹은 서로를 적으로 여겼다.

Each group came to look down on the other.
각 그룹은 서로를 얕잡아 보게 되었다.

The boys started food fights / and stole various items / from members of the other group.

소년들은 먹을 것을 가지고 싸우기 시작하고 / 여러 물건을 훔쳤다. / 상대 그룹의 구성원으로부터
Thus, / under competitive conditions, / the boys quickly (b) drew sharp group boundaries.
그래서 / 경쟁적인 환경에서 / 소년들은 재빨리 뚜렷한 그룹 경계를 그었다.
The researchers / next stopped the athletic competitions / and created several apparent
emergencies / whose solution (c) required cooperation between the two groups.
연구자들은 / 그런 다음 운동 시합을 멈추고, / 몇 가지 비상사태로 보이는 상황을 만들었다. / 해결이 두 그룹 사이의 협력이 필요한
One such emergency involved a leak in the pipe / supplying water to the camp.
그러한 비상사태 중 하나는 파이프가 새는 경우를 포함한다. / 캠프에 물을 공급하는
The researchers assigned the boys to teams / made up of members of both groups.
연구자들은 소년들을 팀에 배정했다. / 두 그룹의 일원으로 구성된
Their job was / to look into the pipe / and fix the leak.
그들의 임무는 / 파이프를 조사하고 / 새는 곳을 고치는 것이었다.
After engaging in several such (d) cooperative activities, / the boys started playing together
/ without fighting.
그러한 협력적인 활동을 몇 차례 한 후에, / 소년들은 함께 놀기 시작했다. / 싸우지 않고
『Once cooperation replaced competition / and the groups (e) ceased to look down on each
other, / group boundaries melted away / as quickly as they had formed.』 41번의 근거
일단 협력이 경쟁을 대체하고 / 그룹들이 서로를 얕잡아 보기를 중단하자, / 그룹 경계가 사라져 갔다. / 형성되었던 것만큼 빠르게

연구자들은 두 그룹의 11세 소년들을 Oklahoma에 있는 Robbers Cave 주립 공원의 여름 캠프에 데려왔다. 그 소년들은 서로 몰랐고 캠프에 도착하자마자 무작위로 두 그룹으로 나뉘었다. 그 그룹들은 약 1주일 동안 서로 떨어져 있었다. 그들은 수영하고, 야영하고, 하이킹을 했다. 각 그룹은 자기 그룹의 이름을 지었고, 소년들은 자신의 그룹 이름을 모자와 티셔츠에 새겼다. 그 후 두 그룹이 만났다. 그들 사이에 일련의 운동 시합이 마련되었다. 곧, 각 그룹은 서로를 (a) 적으로 여겼다. 각 그룹은 서로를 얕잡아 보게 되었다. 소년들은 먹을 것을 가지고 싸우기 시작했고 상대 그룹 구성원의 여러 물건을 훔쳤다. 그래서 경쟁적인 환경에서 소년들은 재빨리 뚜렷한 그룹 경계를 (b) 그었다. 그런 다음, 연구자들은 운동 시합을 멈추고, 해결에 두 그룹 사이의 협력이 (c) 필요한, 몇 가지 비상사태로 보이는 상황을 만들었다. 그러한 비상사태 중 하나는 캠프에 물을 공급하는 파이프가 새는 경우를 포함한다. 연구자들은 소년들을 두 그룹 모두의 일원으로 구성된 팀에 배정했다. 그들의 임무는 파이프를 조사하고 새는 곳을 고치는 것이었다. 그러한 (d) 협력적인 활동을 몇 차례 한 후에, 소년들은 싸우지 않고 함께 놀기 시작했다. 일단 협력이 경쟁을 대체하고 그룹들이 서로를 얕잡아 보기를 (e) 시작하자(→ 중단하자), 그룹 경계가 형성되었던 것만큼 빠르게 사라져 갔다.

- **randomly** [ad] 무작위로
- **apart** [ad] 떨어져, 따로
- **look down on** ~을 얕잡아보다, 깔보다
- **boundary** [n] 경계
- **leak** [n] (물이) 새는 곳, 구멍 [v] (물이나 기체가) 새다
- **replace** [v] 대체하다
- **separate** [v] 나누다, 분리하다
- **athletic** [a] 운동의, 육상의
- **competitive** [a] 경쟁적인
- **emergency** [n] 비상사태
- **assign** [v] 배정하다
- **melt away** 차츰 사라지다

구문 풀이

14행 The researchers next stopped the athletic competitions and created
[동사1] [동사2]
several apparent emergencies [whose solution required cooperation between the
[선행사] [소유격 관계대명사]
two groups].

41 제목 파악   정답률 49% | 정답 ③

윗글의 제목으로 가장 적절한 것은?
① How Are Athletic Competitions Helpful for Teens? – 운동 시합은 어떻게 십 대에게 도움이 되는가?
② Preparation: The Key to Preventing Emergencies – 대비: 비상사태 예방의 비결
✔ ③ What Makes Group Boundaries Disappear? – 무엇이 그룹 경계를 사라지게 하는가?
④ Respect Individual Differences in Teams – 팀 내 개인차를 존중하라
⑤ Free Riders: Headaches in Teams – 무임승차자: 팀의 골칫거리

Why? 왜 정답일까?

소년들을 두 그룹으로 나누어 일련의 경쟁을 하도록 했을 때에는 그룹 간에 적개심과 경계가 형성되었지만, 그룹 간의 협력이 필요한 활동에 참여하게 하자 그 경계가 쉽게 사라졌다는(Once cooperation replaced competition ~, group boundaries melted away as quickly as they had formed.)는 내용의 실험을 소개한 글이다. 따라서 글의 제목으로 가장 적절한 것은 ③ '무엇이 그룹 경계를 사라지게 하는가?'이다.

★★★ 등급을 가르는 문제!

42 어휘 추론   정답률 35% | 정답 ⑤

밑줄 친 (a) ~ (e) 중에서 문맥상 낱말의 쓰임이 적절하지 않은 것은?
① (a)   ② (b)   ③ (c)   ④ (d)   ✔ ⑤ (e)

Why? 왜 정답일까?

마지막 문장의 and 앞에서 협력이 경쟁을 대체하였다는(cooperation replaced competition)는 내용이 언급되는 것으로 보아, and 뒤에는 그룹들이 경쟁 관계에서 벗어나 서로를 얕잡아 보기를 '그만두었다'는 내용이 이어지는 것이 적절하므로, (e)의 started는 반의어인 ceased로 고쳐야 한다. 따라서 문맥상 낱말의 쓰임이 적절하지 않은 것은 ⑤ '(e)'이다.

★★ 문제 해결 꿀~팁 ★★

▶ 많이 틀린 이유는?
문장이 어렵지는 않지만 길이로 인한 압박이 있어 전체 맥락을 파악하는 데 부담이 따르는 지문이다. 최다 오답인 ②는 앞에서 소년들이 팀 별로 경계심을 키웠음을 보여주는 사례가 나오는 것으로 볼 때 맥락상 적절하다. (b) 바로 앞의 문장을 주의 깊게 읽도록 한다.

▶ 문제 해결 방법은?
첫 단락과 두 번째 단락이 '소년들 간 반목 vs. 협동'이라는 키워드로 대조를 이루므로, 이 점에 주의하여 선택지 문장의 맥락을 파악해야 한다.

43-45 사자와의 우정으로 목숨을 건진 노예

(A)

Once in a village lived a rich man.
옛날 한 마을에 어떤 부자가 살았다.
He had many slaves and servants for work.
그는 일을 해 주는 많은 노예와 하인이 있었다.
The rich man was very unkind and cruel to them.
그 부자는 그들에게 매우 불친절하고 잔인했다.
One day one of the slaves made a mistake / while cooking food.
어느 날 노예 중 한 명이 실수를 했다. / 요리를 하다가
(a) He overcooked the food.
그는 음식을 너무 익혀버렸다.
『When the rich man saw the food, / he became angry and punished the slave.』 45번①의 근거 일치
부자가 그 음식을 보았을 때, / 그는 화가 나서 노예에게 벌을 주었다.
He kept the slave in a small room / and locked it from outside.
그는 작은 방에 노예를 가두고 / 밖에서 문을 잠가버렸다.

(C)

Somehow the slave escaped from that room / and ran away.
어찌어찌 노예는 그 방에서 탈출해서 / 도망을 쳤다.
(c) He went to a forest.
그는 숲으로 갔다.
There he saw a lion.
거기서 그는 사자 한 마리를 보았다.
『Instead of becoming afraid of the lion and running away, / he went close to the lion.』 45번③의 근거 불일치
사자를 무서워하며 도망가는 대신, / 그는 사자에게 가까이 다가섰다.
『He saw / the lion was injured / and one of his legs was bleeding.』 45번④의 근거 일치
그는 보았다. / 사자가 상처를 입은 것을 / 그리고 그의 다리 중 하나에서 피가 흐르는 것을
The slave searched for herbs / to cure the lion's wound / and took care of the lion.
그 노예는 약초를 찾아나섰고 / 사자의 상처를 치료하기 위한 / 사자를 돌봐주었다.

(B)

After a few days the lion recovered.
며칠 뒤 사자는 회복했다.
The slave and the lion became very close friends.
노예와 사자는 매우 친한 친구 사이가 되었다.
『A few days went by / but one day the slave was caught / by one of the guards of the rich
man.』 45번②의 근거 일치
며칠이 흘렀는데 / 어느 날 노예는 붙잡혔다. / 부자의 경비병 중 한 명에게
The guard took (b) him to the rich man, / who decided to punish him severely.
그 경비병은 그를 부자에게 데려갔고, / 부자는 그를 엄하게 처벌하기로 마음먹었다.
The rich man ordered guards / to put him in the lion's cage.
부자는 경비병들에게 명령했다. / 그를 사자 우리 안에 집어넣으라고

(D)

The whole village got the news about it / and came to see.
마을 전체가 이 소식을 듣고 / 보러 왔다.
『As soon as the slave was locked in the lion's cage, / the lion came near (d) him /
and started licking his hand and hugged him.』 45번⑤의 근거 일치
노예가 사자 우리에 갇히자마자, / 사자가 그에게 다가가 / 그의 손을 핥기 시작했고 그를 껴안았다.
It was the same lion / that the slave had helped in the forest.
이 사자는 바로 그 노예가 숲에서 도와주었던
Seeing this, / everyone was surprised.
이것을 보고, / 모든 사람들이 놀랐다.
The rich man thought / that the slave was such a great person / that the lion didn't kill
him.
부자는 생각했다. / 노예가 너무 대단한 사람이어서 / 사자가 그를 죽이지 않는다고
(e) He freed the slave, / made him his friend / and started to treat all his servants and slaves
better.
그는 노예를 풀어주고 / 자기 친구로 삼았으며 / 모든 하인과 노예를 더 잘 대해주기 시작했다.

(A)

옛날 한 마을에 어떤 부자가 살았다. 그는 일을 해 주는 많은 노예와 하인이 있었다. 그 부자는 그들에게 매우 불친절하고 잔인했다. 어느날 노예 중 한 명이 요리를 하다가 실수를 했다. (a) 그는 음식을 너무 익혀버렸다. 부자가 그 음식을 보았을 때, 그는 화가 나서 노예에게 벌을 주었다. 그는 작은 방에 노예를 가두고 밖에서 문을 잠가버렸다.

(C)

어찌어찌 노예는 그 방에서 탈출해서 도망을 쳤다. (c) 그는 숲으로 갔다. 거기서 그는 사자 한 마리를 보았다. 사자를 무서워하며 도망치는 대신, 그는 사자에게 가까이 다가섰다. 그는 사자가 상처를 입고 한쪽 다리에서 피를 흘리고 있는 것을 보았다. 그 노예는 사자의 상처를 치료하기 위한 약초를 찾아나섰고 사자를 돌봐주었다.

(B)

며칠 뒤 사자는 회복했다. 노예와 사자는 매우 친한 친구 사이가 되었다. 며칠이 흘렀는데 어느 날 노예는 부자의 경비병 중 한 명에게 붙잡혔다. 그 경비병은 (b) 그를 부자에게 데려갔고, 부자는 그를 엄하게 처벌하기로 마음먹었다. 부자는 경비병들에게 그를 사자 우리 안에 집어넣으라고 명령했다.

(D)

마을 전체가 이 소식을 듣고 보러 왔다. 노예가 사자 우리에 갇히자마자, 사자가 (d) 그에게 다가가 그의 손을 핥기 시작했고 그를 껴안았다. 이 사자는 노예가 숲에서 도와주었던 바로 그 사자였다. 이것을 보고, 모든 사람들이 놀랐다. 부자는 노예가 너무 대단한 사람이어서 사자가 그를 죽이지 않는다고 생각했다. (e) 그는 노예를 풀어주고 자기 친구로 삼았으며 모든 하인과 노예를 더 잘 대해주기 시작했다.

- **cruel** [a] 잔인한
- **recover** [v] 회복하다, 낫다
- **punish** [v] 처벌하다
- **order** [v] 명령하다
- **instead of** ~ 대신에
- **injure** [v] 상처를 입히다
- **search for** ~을 찾다
- **cure** [v] 치료하다
- **punish** [v] 처벌하다
- **close** [a] (사이가) 친한, 가까운
- **severely** [ad] 엄하게, 심하게
- **escape** [v] 달아나다, 탈출하다
- **run away** 도망치다, 달아나다
- **bleed** [v] 피를 흘리다, 출혈하다
- **herb** [n] 약초
- **wound** [n] 상처, 부상

- **whole** ⓐ 전체의, 모든
- **free** ⓥ 풀어 주다 ⓐ 자유로운
- **lick** ⓥ 핥다
- **treat** ⓥ 대하다, 대접하다

구문 풀이

(A) 3행 One day / one of the slaves made a mistake / while cooking food.
「one of the + 복수명사」: ~ 중 하나 ↑(he was 생략)

(B) 5행 The rich man ordered guards to put him in the lion's cage.
동사 목적어 목적격 보어(to부정사)

(D) 1행 As soon as the slave was locked in the lion's cage, / the lion came near
접속사(~하자마자) 동사1
him and started licking his hand and hugged him.
동사2 「start + 동명사: ~하기 시작하다」 동사3

---

43 글의 순서 파악　　　정답률 73% | 정답 ②

주어진 글 (A)에 이어질 내용을 순서에 맞게 배열한 것으로 가장 적절한 것은?

① (B) – (D) – (C)
② (C) – (B) – (D) ✔
③ (C) – (D) – (B)
④ (D) – (B) – (C)
⑤ (D) – (C) – (B)

Why? 왜 정답일까?

어느 날 노예가 실수로 음식을 너무 익혀버리자 주인인 부자가 그를 작은 방에 가두고 말았다는 내용을 제시한 **(A)** 뒤에는, 노예가 방에서 가까스로 탈출하여 숲으로 향했고 거기서 다친 사자를 만나 도와주게 되었다는 내용의 **(C)**가 나와야 적절하다. 이어서는 사자가 며칠 뒤 회복을 하였는데 노예는 주인인 부자에게 붙잡히게 되어 사자 우리에 집어넣어질 위기에 처했다는 내용의 **(B)**가 나와야 하고, 마지막에는 노예를 집어넣을 우리 안에 있던 사자가 사실은 노예가 며칠 전 구해준 사자였고 이 때문에 사자는 노예를 해치지 않았다는 결말을 말한 **(D)**가 나와야 자연스럽다. 따라서 **(A)**에 이어질 글의 순서로 가장 적절한 것은 ② '**(C) – (B) – (D)**'이다.

---

44 지칭 추론　　　정답률 67% | 정답 ⑤

밑줄 친 (a) ~ (e) 중에서 가리키는 대상이 나머지 넷과 다른 것은?

① (a)　② (b)　③ (c)　④ (d)　⑤ (e) ✔

Why? 왜 정답일까?

(a), (b), (c), (d)는 'the slave', (e)는 'the rich'를 나타낸다. 따라서 (a) ~ (e) 중에서 가리키는 대상이 나머지 넷과 다른 것은 ⑤ '**(e)**'이다.

---

45 세부 내용 파악　　　정답률 70% | 정답 ③

윗글의 내용으로 적절하지 <u>않은</u> 것은?

① 부자는 노예가 요리한 음식을 보고 화가 났다.
② 노예는 부자의 경비병에게 잡혔다.
③ 노예는 사자를 보자 재빨리 달아났다. ✔
④ 사자의 다리에서 피가 나고 있었다.
⑤ 노예는 사자 우리에 갇혔다.

Why? 왜 정답일까?

'Instead of becoming afraid of the lion and running away, he went close to the lion.'에서 노예는 사자를 보고 겁에 질려 도망가지 않고 사자에게 가까이 다가갔다는 내용을 확인할 수 있으므로, 윗글의 내용으로 적절하지 않은 것은 ③ '노예는 사자를 보자 재빨리 달아났다.'이다.

Why? 왜 오답일까?

① 'When the rich man saw the food, he became angry and punished the slave.'와 일치한다.
② 'A few days went by but one day the slave was caught by one of the guards of the rich man.'과 일치한다.
④ 'He saw the lion was injured and one of his legs was bleeding.'과 일치한다.
⑤ 'As soon as the slave was locked in the lion's cage, the lion came near him and started licking his hand and hugged him.'과 일치한다.

---

01 an important announcement / replace the lockers / will be thrown away

02 it helps the bookstore sell more / the more they're likely to buy / attract more customers

03 must have been busy / How did it go / which hat will suit me

04 a heart-shaped balloon / This boy must be your brother / wearing a hat with flowers / It looks like

05 I'm filling out an application / You can join both / go submit this application form

06 getting too tight for his feet / Let's buy a pair / here it says

07 I canceled the trip / moved to the countryside / miss them a lot

08 How about taking the kids / It'll take about one hour / including animal feeding

09 based on the famous animated film / perfect their performance / in the auditorium for two days

10 to toast at least two slices / out of these three models / I'll go with the silver one

11 learning it by yourself

12 Why don't we go submit

13 write a review / It was on the bestseller list / that suits your level / wouldn't I learn more

14 What are you looking at / crazy about drones / quite a lot of drones / they're safe enough

15 win the election / impress her classmates / has difficulty coming up with

16-17 it's commonly used / in which animals appear / the stronger are not around / make hasty decisions

---

어휘 Review Test 01　　　문제편 182쪽

A	B	C	D
01 ~을 대신하여, 대표하여	**01** attend	**01** ⓚ	**01** ⑨
02 감싸다, 포옹하다	**02** propose	**02** ⑨	**02** ⓚ
03 ~을 처리하다, 따라잡다, 만회하다	**03** pray	**03** ⓐ	**03** ⓟ
04 무관심한	**04** comfort	**04** ⓗ	**04** ⓐ
05 결과, 결론	**05** distraction	**05** ①	**05** ⓑ
06 ~을 실어다 주다, 태워주다	**06** analysis	**06** ①	**06** ①
07 소비하다, 쓰다	**07** take a risk	**07** ⓒ	**07** ⓢ
08 다 자란, 성숙한	**08** attraction	**08** ①	**08** ⓒ
09 ~의 마음대로 이용할 수 있는	**09** disappear	**09** ⓢ	**09** ⓓ
10 일반화하다	**10** appreciate	**10** ⓑ	**10** ⓔ
11 근면	**11** remarkably	**11** ⓟ	**11** ⓝ
12 다 떨어지다	**12** result in	**12** ⓓ	**12** ⓝ
13 간격	**13** meet	**13** ⓔ	**13** ①
14 경쟁자	**14** ancestor	**14** ①	**14** ①
15 넘어서다, 능가하다	**15** replace	**15** ①	**15** ①
16 언급하다, 말하다	**16** reputation	**16** ⓜ	**16** ①
17 ~을 겪다	**17** leak	**17** ⑨	**17** ①
18 촉망받는, 전도유망한	**18** cruel	**18** ⓗ	**18** ①
19 경계	**19** punish	**19** ①	**19** ⓜ
20 피를 흘리다	**20** injure	**20** ⓞ	**20** ⓗ

• 정답 •

01 ② 02 ③ 03 ① 04 ⑤ 05 ④ 06 ④ 07 ⑤ 08 ④ 09 ③ 10 ③ 11 ② 12 ① 13 ④ 14 ④ 15 ②
16 ① 17 ⑤ 18 ① 19 ⑤ 20 ① 21 ④ 22 ④ 23 ⑤ 24 ④ 25 ④ 26 ⑤ 27 ④ 28 ② 29 ② 30 ④
31 ① 32 ② 33 ③ 34 ④ 35 ④ 36 ② 37 ② 38 ④ 39 ④ 40 ① 41 ④ 42 ④ 43 ⑤ 44 ④ 45 ③

★ 표기된 문항은 [등급을 가르는 문제]에 해당하는 문항입니다.

01　특별 행사 안내　정답률 87% | 정답 ②

다음을 듣고, 여자가 하는 말의 목적으로 가장 적절한 것을 고르시오.
① 개관 시간 연장을 알리려고
☑ 작가 초청 행사를 안내하려고
③ 사진 촬영 자제를 당부하려고
④ 미술 강좌 회원을 모집하려고
⑤ 전시 장소 변경을 공지하려고

W : Good afternoon.
　안녕하세요.
　I'm the director of the Modern Gallery.
　Modern Gallery의 관장입니다.
　I hope you are enjoying the exhibition of the works of Steve Kim, the world-famous photographer.
　여러분께서 세계적으로 유명한 사진작가인 Steve Kim의 작품 전시회를 즐기고 계시기를 바랍니다.
　Today, there will be a special event for our visitors.
　오늘, 저희 방문객들을 위한 특별 행사가 있을 예정입니다.
　We invited Steve Kim to the gallery to meet his fans and share his ideas about photography and life.
　저희는 Steve Kim이 팬들을 만나 사진과 삶에 대한 생각을 나눌 수 있도록 그를 갤러리로 초대했습니다.
　It will be a great opportunity to meet the artist in person.
　예술가를 직접 만나는 것은 훌륭한 기회가 될 것입니다.
　The event will start at three p.m. in the Design Hall and last for about an hour.
　본 행사는 오후 3시에 Design Hall에서 시작되어 한 시간 정도 계속될 것입니다.
　If you're interested, please come to the hall and be seated before the event begins.
　관심이 있으시다면, 행사가 시작하기 전에 홀에 오셔서 착석해 주십시오.
　For more information, you can get a pamphlet at the reception desk.
　더 많은 정보를 원하신다면, 안내 데스크에서 팸플릿을 가져가시기 바랍니다.
　Thank you.
　고맙습니다.

Why? 왜 정답일까?
담화에서 여자는 특별 행사를 위해 사진작가인 **Steve Kim**을 갤러리에 초대하였다(**We invited Steve Kim to the gallery to meet his fans and share his ideas about photography and life.**)고 이야기한다. 따라서 여자가 하는 말의 목적으로 가장 적절한 것은 ② '작가 초청 행사를 안내하려고'이다.

● director ⓝ 감독, 책임자　　● world-famous 세계적으로 유명한
● opportunity ⓝ 기회　　● in person 직접, 몸소
● last ⓥ 계속되다, 지속되다　　● reception desk 안내 데스크

02　새우 섭취의 긍정적 영향　정답률 88% | 정답 ③

대화를 듣고, 남자의 의견으로 가장 적절한 것을 고르시오.
① 다양한 영양소의 섭취는 성장에 필수적이다.
② 식품 구매 시 영양 성분의 확인이 필요하다.
☑ 새우를 섭취하는 것은 건강에 도움이 된다.
④ 체중 관리는 균형 잡힌 식단에서 비롯된다.
⑤ 음식을 조리할 때 위생 관리가 중요하다.

M : Brenda, my uncle bought a shrimp pizza. Help yourself.
　Brenda, 우리 삼촌이 새우 피자를 사 오셨어. 많이 먹어.
W : Oh! But I don't like shrimp.
　오! 난 그런데 새우를 좋아하지 않아.
M : Really? Do you have an allergy to shrimp?
　그래? 너 새우 알레르기가 있니?
W : No. I've heard shrimp is a little high in cholesterol. So, I think it isn't good for our health.
　아니. 난 새우가 콜레스테롤이 조금 높다고 들었어. 그래서 나는 그게 우리 건강에 좋지 않다고 생각해.
M : Hmm, that's a misunderstanding about shrimp.
　흠, 그건 새우에 대한 오해야.
W : You mean eating shrimp has a positive effect on health?
　네 말은 새우를 먹으면 건강에 긍정적인 영향이 있다는 거야?
M : Of course. It can increase your level of good cholesterol.
　물론이지. 그것은 좋은 콜레스테롤 수치를 증가시킬 수 있어.
W : Oh, I didn't know that.
　오, 난 그건 몰랐어.
M : Eating shrimp can give us vitamins and minerals. Plus, shrimp is low-calorie.
　새우를 먹는 것은 우리에게 비타민과 무기질을 줄 수 있어. 더구나 새우는 칼로리가 낮아.
W : Then it might be good to add shrimp to my diet.
　그럼 내 식단에 새우를 첨가하는 것이 좋을지도 모르겠네.
M : Sure. It would be helpful to your health.
　물론이지. 네 건강에 도움이 될 거야.
W : I guess I didn't know much about shrimp. I'll give it a try.
　내가 새우에 대해 잘 몰랐나 봐. 시도해 볼게.

Why? 왜 정답일까?
'**You mean eating shrimp has a positive effect on health?** / **Of course.**'와 '**It would**

[문제편 p.183]

---

be helpful to your health.'에서 남자는 새우를 먹는 것이 건강에 긍정적인 영향을 준다고 생각하고 있음을 알 수 있으므로, 남자의 의견으로 가장 적절한 것은 ③ '새우를 섭취하는 것은 건강에 도움이 된다.'이다.

● misunderstanding ⓝ 오해　　● have an effect on ~에 영향을 미치다
● add A to B A를 B에 첨가하다　　● diet ⓝ 식사, 식단
● give it a try 시도하다, 한번 해 보다

03　병결 관련 통화　정답률 89% | 정답 ①

대화를 듣고, 두 사람의 관계를 가장 잘 나타낸 것을 고르시오.
☑ 교사 — 학부모
② 의사 — 환자
③ 간병인 — 보호자
④ 상담사 — 학생
⑤ 편집장 — 신문 기자

[Telephone Rings.]
[전화벨이 울린다.]
W : Hello. This is Monica Jones.
　여보세요. Monica Jones입니다.
M : Hello. This is John Lewis, Sally's father.
　여보세요. 저는 Sally의 아빠인 John Lewis입니다.
W : Hello, Mr. Lewis. Has Sally gotten any better?
　안녕하세요. Lewis 씨. Sally가 좀 나아졌나요?
M : Yes. She doesn't have a high fever anymore.
　네, 이제 고열은 없어요.
W : Glad to hear that.
　그렇다니 기쁘군요.
M : But the doctor said that Sally needs to stay home this week.
　하지만 의사 선생님이 이번 주에는 Sally가 집에 있어야 한다네요.
W : I see. Do you think she'll come to school next Monday?
　알겠습니다. 다음 주 월요일에는 Sally가 학교에 나올 수 있을까요?
M : I think so. But, Sally's worried that she won't be able to submit her school newspaper article on time.
　그럴 것 같습니다. 하지만, Sally는 학교 신문 기사를 제때 내지 못할까봐 걱정을 하고 있어요.
W : Oh, please tell her not to worry about it. The newspaper editor is also taking my class, so I'll talk to him.
　오, 걱정하지 말라고 전해주세요. 신문 편집장이 제 수업을 듣고 있으니, 제가 이야기할게요.
M : Thank you so much.
　정말 감사합니다.

Why? 왜 정답일까?
대화에서 남자는 자신이 **Sally**라는 학생의 부모임을 밝히고(**This is John Lewis, Sally's father.**), 여자는 **Sally**가 학교에 올 수 있는지를 확인하며 자신이 교사임을 드러낸다(**Do you think she'll come to school next Monday?**). 따라서 두 사람의 관계로 가장 적절한 것은 ① '교사 — 학부모'이다.

● get better (몸이) 나아지다　　● fever ⓝ 열, 열병
● submit ⓥ 제출하다　　● article ⓝ 기사
● on time 제때, 제 시간에　　● editor ⓝ 편집장, 편집자

04　과학의 날 행사 사진　정답률 86% | 정답 ⑤

대화를 듣고, 그림에서 대화의 내용과 일치하지 <u>않는</u> 것을 고르시오.

M : Mom, this is a picture from Science Day.
　엄마, 이건 과학의 날 행사 사진이에요.
W : Let me see. 『The woman wearing glasses must be your science teacher.』 ①의 근거 일치
　보자. 안경을 쓰고 있는 여자 분이 너희 과학 선생님이시겠구나.
M : Yes, she is. She helped me a lot. 『Do you see the rocket next to the flower pot?』 ②의 근거 일치
　네, 맞아요. 그녀는 저를 많이 도와주셨어요. 화분 옆에 로켓이 보이세요?
W : Oh, it looks fantastic! Who made it?
　오, 근사해 보인다! 누가 만들었니?
M : I made it myself. I received a lot of good comments about it.
　제가 직접 만들었어요. 그것에 대해 많은 호평을 받았어요.
W : Good job. 『What are the two pictures on the wall?』 ③의 근거 일치
　잘했어. 벽에 사진 두 점은 뭐니?
M : They are pictures of great scientists.
　위대한 과학자들의 사진이에요.
W : I see. 『And there is a robot in front of the window.』 ④의 근거 일치
　그렇구나. 그리고 창문 앞에 로봇이 하나 있네.
M : Yeah, my class put all the parts of the robot together.
　네, 저희 반 친구들이 그 로봇의 모든 부품을 조립했어요.
W : Sounds great. 『I can see a star-shaped clock on the table, too.』 ⑤의 근거 불일치
　멋지구나. 탁자 위에 별 모양 시계도 보여.
M : My teacher showed us how to make it with a 3D-printer, and it was very exciting.
　저희 선생님이 저희에게 3D 프린터로 그것을 어떻게 만드는지 보여주셨는데, 정말 신났어요.
W : You must've had a great time.
　분명 멋진 시간을 보냈겠구나.

Why? 왜 정답일까?

대화에서는 탁자 위에 별 모양 시계가 있다고 하는데(I can see a star-shaped clock on the table, too.), 그림에는 시계가 하트 모양이다. 따라서 그림에서 대화의 내용과 일치하지 않는 것은 ⑤이다.

- flower pot 화분
- put together ~을 조립하다
- star-shaped ⓐ 별 모양의
- comment ⓝ 의견
- part ⓝ 부품

---

05 깜짝 파티 준비   정답률 91% | 정답 ④

대화를 듣고, 남자가 여자에게 부탁한 일로 가장 적절한 것을 고르시오.
① 음식 만들기   ② 꽃 사러 가기   ③ 친구 초대하기
✔ 거실 청소하기   ⑤ 식료품 구입하기

W : Dad, where are you going?
아빠, 어디 가세요?
M : I'm going to the grocery store. We're having a surprise party this evening.
식료품 가게에 간다. 우린 오늘 저녁에 깜짝 파티를 할 거야.
W : Really? Is it a special day today?
진짜요? 오늘 특별한 날이에요?
M : Yes. Mom was promoted at work, so we're going to celebrate.
응. 네 엄마가 직장에서 승진을 해서, 축하를 할 거야.
W : Oh, good for her. I'm sure she'll love the party.
오, 잘됐네요. 엄마는 분명 파티를 좋아할 거예요.
M : I hope so. I'm thinking of making steak and seafood pasta for dinner.
그러길 바라. 저녁으로 스테이크랑 해산물 파스타를 만들까 생각 중이란다.
W : Sounds perfect. Will there be any guests?
완벽한 것 같아요. 혹시 손님도 오시나요?
M : Yes. I invited a couple of our friends.
응. 우리 친구 몇 명을 초대했어.
W : Good. I also want to help. Shall I go buy some flowers for the dinner table?
좋아요. 저도 돕고 싶어요. 저녁 식탁에 둘 꽃을 가서 좀 사올까요?
M : No. I'll do that. Can you clean the living room instead?
아냐. 내가 하마. 대신 거실을 좀 치워줄 수 있겠니?
W : Sure. I'll make it neat and tidy before you come back.
물론이죠. 아빠 오시기 전에 깔끔하고 깨끗하게 해 둘게요.
M : Thanks. That's very kind of you.
고맙다. 정말 착하구나.

Why? 왜 정답일까?

대화에서 남자는 아내의 승진을 축하하기 위해 깜짝 파티를 준비하려 한다며 딸인 여자에게 거실 청소를 부탁하고 있다(Can you clean the living room instead?). 따라서 남자가 여자에게 부탁한 일로 가장 적절한 것은 ④ '거실 청소하기'이다.

- grocery store 식료품 가게
- at work 직장에서, 일터에서
- a couple of 둘의, 몇몇의
- tidy ⓐ 깨끗한, 깔끔한
- promote ⓥ 승진하다
- celebrate ⓥ 축하하다, 기념하다
- neat ⓐ 깔끔한, 정돈된

---

06 아들을 위해 야구 용품 사기   정답률 85% | 정답 ④

대화를 듣고, 남자가 지불할 금액을 고르시오.
① $15   ② $30   ③ $48   ✔ $54   ⑤ $60

W : Hello. Can I help you?
안녕하세요. 도와드릴까요?
M : Yes. I want to buy a baseball bat for my son. He is 11 years old.
네. 전 제 아들을 위해 야구 방망이를 사고 싶어요. 그 애는 11살이에요.
W : How about this baseball bat? It's the most popular. It's 30 dollars.
이 야구 방망이는 어떠세요? 제일 인기 있는 것이에요. 30달러입니다.
M : Okay. I'll take one bat. Do you also have baseball gloves?
알겠습니다. 하나를 살게요. 야구 글러브도 있나요?
W : Sure. How about this glove? It's soft and comfortable.
물론이죠. 이 글러브는 어떠세요? 부드럽고 편합니다.
M : How much is it?
얼마죠?
W : It's 15 dollars.
15달러입니다.
M : Hmm... That's reasonable. I'll buy two gloves.
흠... 적당하네요. 글러브 두 개를 살게요.
W : Okay. Don't you need any safety balls for children? They are light and soft.
알겠어요. 아이들용 안전구가 좀 필요하지 않으신가요? 가볍고 부드러워요.
M : I think I've got all I need. Can I use this coupon?
제가 필요한 건 다 산 것 같아요. 제가 이 쿠폰을 쓸 수 있나요?
W : Of course. Then you can get 10% off the total price.
물론이죠. 그럼 총 가격에서 10퍼센트를 할인받으실 수 있어요.
M : Great. I'll use the coupon and pay by credit card.
훌륭해요. 전 이 쿠폰을 쓰고 신용 카드로 지불할게요.

Why? 왜 정답일까?

대화에 따르면 남자는 30달러짜리 야구 방망이를 한 개, 15달러짜리 야구 글러브를 두 개 산 후, 총 가격에서 10퍼센트를 할인받았다. 이를 식으로 나타내면 '(30+15×2)×0.9=54'이므로, 남자가 지불할 금액은 ④ '$54'이다.

- baseball bat 야구용 배트
- comfortable ⓐ 편한
- safety 안전(성)
- soft ⓐ 부드러운
- reasonable ⓐ (가격이) 적당한

---

07 주말 일정 이야기하기   정답률 84% | 정답 ⑤

대화를 듣고, 여자가 남자와 함께 뮤지컬을 보러 갈 수 없는 이유를 고르시오.
① 표를 구하지 못해서   ② 회사에 출근해야 해서

M : Hi, Jane. I got two free tickets for the musical *Lion King*. Can you go with me this Saturday?
안녕, Jane. 난 *Lion King* 뮤지컬 공짜 티켓을 받았어. 나랑 이번 주 토요일에 갈 수 있어?
W : I'd love to, but I don't think I can.
정말 그러고 싶은데, 못 갈 것 같아.
M : Do you have to work that day?
그날 일해야 되는 거야?
W : No, it's not about work.
아니, 일 때문은 아니야.
M : Then, why not? I thought you were a big fan of musicals.
그럼, 왜 안 돼? 난 네가 뮤지컬을 무척 좋아하는 줄 알았는데.
W : Of course, I am. But my parents are coming all the way from Canada to see me.
당연히 그렇지. 그런데 우리 부모님이 날 보러 캐나다에서 먼 길을 오실 거야.
M : Oh, that's great. When did you last see them?
오, 정말 잘됐다. 언제 마지막으로 뵀어?
W : Two years ago. So I think I need to spend this weekend with them.
2년 전에. 그래서 이번 주말에는 부모님과 있어야 할 것 같아.
M : Okay. No problem. I'll find someone else to go with me then.
알았어. 괜찮아. 그럼 같이 갈 다른 사람 찾아보지 뭐.

Why? 왜 정답일까?

대화에서 남자는 여자에게 뮤지컬을 함께 보러 가자고 제안하는데 여자는 부모님이 캐나다에서 오셔서 부모님과 함께 주말을 보내야 한다(So I think I need to spend this weekend with them.)고 이야기한다. 따라서 여자가 남자와 함께 뮤지컬을 보러 갈 수 없는 이유로 적절한 것은 ⑤ '부모님과 주말을 보내야 해서'이다.

- free ⓐ 공짜의, 무료의
- spend ⓥ (시간을) 보내다
- be a big fan of ~을 무척 좋아하다
- else ⓐ 다른

---

08 고교생 대상 진로 캠프 추천하기   정답률 80% | 정답 ④

대화를 듣고, Career Vision Camp에 관해 언급되지 않은 것을 고르시오.
① 참가 대상   ② 등록 비용   ③ 지원 마감일
✔ 기념품   ⑤ 행사 장소

[Door knocks.]
[문을 노크하는 소리가 난다.]
M : Can I come in, Ms. Wilson?
들어가도 될까요, Wilson 선생님?
W : Sure, come on in. [Pause] Oh, Peter. I was waiting for you to come. How's your career search going?
물론이지, 들어오렴. [잠시 멈춤] 오, Peter. 난 네가 오기를 기다리고 있었어. 네 진로 탐색은 어떻게 되어 가니?
M : I'm still trying to find some information about my future career.
제 미래 직업에 관한 정보를 아직 좀 찾고 있어요.
W : Good. So I'd like to recommend the Career Vision Camp to you.
좋아. 그래서 나는 네게 Career Vision Camp를 추천하려 해.
M : Okay. 「I heard that the camp is only for high school students.」 Is that right? ①의 근거 일치
그렇군요. 전 그 캠프가 고등학생만을 위한 것이라고 들었어요. 맞나요?
W : Yes. It'll be helpful. 「Plus, there's no registration fee.」 ②의 근거 일치
응. 도움이 될 거야. 게다가 등록 비용이 없어.
M : Great. 「Hmm, can you tell me when the application deadline is?」 ③의 근거 일치
훌륭하네요. 흠, 지원 마감일이 언제인지 말씀해 주실 수 있나요?
W : 「It's December 14th.」 You should hurry since it's first come, first served.
12월 14일이야. 선착순이기 때문에 서둘러야 한다.
M : I see. I will apply for the camp as soon as possible.
알겠습니다. 가급적 빨리 캠프에 지원할게요. ⑤의 근거 일치
W : 「It'll be held at the Lincoln Center near school.」 You can get there easily.
이건 학교 근처인 Lincoln Center에서 열린단다. 넌 그곳에 쉽게 갈 수 있어.
M : Okay. Thank you.
알겠습니다. 고맙습니다.

Why? 왜 정답일까?

대화에서 남자와 여자는 Career Vision Camp의 참가 대상, 등록 비용, 지원 마감일, 행사 장소를 언급하였다. 따라서 언급되지 않은 것은 ④ '기념품'이다.

Why? 왜 오답일까?

① 'I heard that the camp is only for high school students.'에서 '참가 대상'이 언급되었다.
② 'Plus, there's no registration fee.'에서 '등록 비용'이 언급되었다.
③ 'It's December 14th.'에서 '지원 마감일'이 언급되었다.
⑤ 'It'll be held at the Lincoln Center near school.'에서 '행사 장소'가 언급되었다.

- career search 진로 탐색
- application deadline 지원 마감일
- apply ⓥ 지원하다
- registration fee 등록 비용
- first come, first served 선착순

---

09 독후감 대회 개최 안내   정답률 82% | 정답 ③

Book Review Contest에 관한 다음 내용을 듣고, 일치하지 않는 것을 고르시오. [3점]
① 독서의 달을 기념하는 행사이다.
② 학생들은 누구나 참여할 수 있다.
✔ 지정 도서에 대한 독후감을 작성해야 한다.
④ 독후감은 이달 말까지 제출해야 한다.
⑤ 우수작 세 편은 학교 잡지에 실릴 것이다.

W : Good morning, Central High School.
안녕하세요, Central High School 여러분.
This is Kathy Miller, the school librarian.
학교 도서관 사서인 Kathy Miller입니다.

『In order to celebrate this year's reading month, our school is going to hold a Book Review Contest.』 [①의 근거] 일치
올해의 독서의 달을 기념하기 위해, 우리 학교는 독후감 경진대회를 개최할 예정입니다.

『All students are invited to participate in the contest.』 [②의 근거] 일치
학생 분들은 누구나 대회에 참여하실 수 있습니다.

『You can write a review on any type of book, but the review must be your own original work.』 [③의 근거] 불일치
어떤 종류의 책이든 독후감을 쓰실 수 있는데, 독후감은 본인의 독창적인 작품이어야 합니다.

You can download a form from our school website.
학교 웹 사이트를 통해 서식을 내려 받으실 수 있습니다.

『Reviews should be submitted through e-mail by the end of this month.』 [④의 근거] 일치
독후감은 이달 말까지 이메일로 제출되어야 합니다.

『The best three works will be selected and published in our school magazine.』 [⑤의 근거] 일치
우수작 세 편이 선정되어 학교 잡지에 실릴 것입니다.

For more details, please visit the school website.
더 자세한 사항을 보시려면, 학교 웹 사이트를 방문해 주세요.

Thank you.
고맙습니다.

Why? 왜 정답일까?

'You can write a review on any type of book, but the review must be your own original work.'에서 어떤 종류의 책이든 독후감을 쓸 수 있다는 말을 통해 지정 도서가 없다는 점을 유추할 수 있으므로, Book Review Contest에 관한 내용과 일치하지 않는 것은 ③ '지정 도서에 대한 독후감을 작성해야 한다.'이다.

Why? 왜 오답일까?

① 'In order to celebrate this year's reading month, our school is going to hold a Book Review Contest.'의 내용과 일치한다.
② 'All students are invited to participate in the contest.'의 내용과 일치한다.
④ 'Reviews should be submitted through e-mail by the end of this month.'의 내용과 일치한다.
⑤ 'The best three works will be selected and published in our school magazine.'의 내용과 일치한다.

- librarian ⓝ 사서
- participate in ~에 참가하다
- submit ⓥ 제출하다
- publish ⓥ (신문이나 잡지에) 싣다, 출판하다
- celebrate ⓥ 기념하다, 축하하다
- original ⓐ 독창적인
- through prep ~을 통해

---

10 전기면도기 사기 　　　　　정답률 91% | 정답 ③

다음 표를 보면서 대화를 듣고, 여자가 구입할 전기면도기를 고르시오.

Electric Shaver

	Model	Price	Battery Life	Waterproof	Color
①	A	$55	20 minutes	×	black
②	B	$70	40 minutes	×	white
✓③	C	$85	60 minutes	○	black
④	D	$90	70 minutes	○	white
⑤	E	$110	80 minutes	○	black

M : Katie, what are you doing with your smartphone?
Katie, 스마트폰으로 뭐 하고 있어?

W : I'm searching for an electric shaver for my dad's birthday. Will you help me find a good one?
난 우리 아빠 생신을 위해 전기면도기를 찾아보고 있어. 내가 좋은 걸 찾도록 도와줄래?

M : Sure. Let me see... [Pause] How about this one?
물론이지. 어디 보자... [잠시 멈춤] 이거 어때?

W : Well, that's too expensive. 『I can't spend more than $100.』 [근거1] Price 조건
음, 그건 너무 비싸. 난 100달러 이상 쓸 수 없어.

M : Okay. 『And I think a 20-minute battery life is too short to use conveniently.』 [근거2] Battery Life 조건
알겠어. 그리고 내 생각엔 20분짜리 배터리 수명은 편하게 쓰기에는 너무 짧아.

W : I think so, too. It needs frequent charging.
나도 그렇게 생각해. 그건 잦은 충전을 필요로 하지.

M : You're right. 『Does it need to be waterproof?』 [근거3] Waterproof 조건
네 말이 맞아. 그것이 방수가 되어야 할까?

W : Of course. 『He shaves in the shower every morning.』
물론이지. 아빠는 매일 샤워 중에 면도를 하셔.

M : Then we have only two options left. Which color do you think is better?
그럼 우리에겐 두 가지 선택권만 남았네. 어떤 색이 더 나은 것 같니?

W : 『Dad likes black, so I'll buy the black one.』 [근거4] Color 조건
아빠는 검은색을 좋아하시니까, 난 검은색을 사겠어.

M : I think it's a nice choice.
좋은 선택인 것 같아.

Why? 왜 정답일까?

대화에 따르면 여자는 가격이 100달러를 넘지 않으면서, 배터리 수명이 20분보다 길고, 방수 기능이 있는 검은색 전기면도기를 구입하려고 한다. 따라서 여자가 구입할 전기면도기는 ③ 'C'이다.

- search ⓥ 찾다
- battery life 배터리 수명
- charge 충전하다
- waterproof ⓐ 방수의
- electric shaver 전기면도기
- conveniently ad 편리하게
- frequent ⓐ 잦은, 빈번한

---

11 새로 연 레스토랑에 대해 이야기하기 　　정답률 82% | 정답 ②

대화를 듣고, 여자의 마지막 말에 대한 남자의 응답으로 가장 적절한 것을 고르시오.

① I've never been there. - 난 저기 가 본 적이 없어.
✓② I really liked the food. - 음식이 정말 좋았어.

---

③ It sounds like a good idea. - 좋은 생각인 것 같아.
④ I didn't eat breakfast today. - 난 오늘 아침을 안 먹었어.
⑤ It wasn't open last weekend. - 지난 주말에는 안 열렸더라.

W : Hey, look! There's an Italian restaurant over there.
저기 봐! 저기 이탈리아 레스토랑이 생겼네.

M : It's newly opened. Last weekend I had lunch there with my friends.
거긴 새로 열었어. 지난주에 친구들이랑 거기서 점심을 먹었지.

W : Really? What did you think of it?
진짜? 어땠는데?

M : I really liked the food.
음식이 정말 좋았어.

Why? 왜 정답일까?

대화에서 여자는 남자에게 새로 생긴 이탈리아 레스토랑에서 식사를 했었다는 얘기를 듣고 어떻게 생각하는지(What did you think of it?) 묻고 있으므로, 이에 대한 남자의 응답으로 가장 적절한 것은 ② '음식이 정말 좋았어.'이다.

- What do you think of ~? ~은 어떠니?

---

12 대중교통을 이용하여 출근하기 　　　　정답률 82% | 정답 ①

대화를 듣고, 남자의 마지막 말에 대한 여자의 응답으로 가장 적절한 것을 고르시오.

✓① Okay. I'll take the subway then. - 알겠어요. 그럼 난 지하철을 탈게요.
② No. I didn't take your umbrella. - 아니요. 난 당신 우산을 안 가져왔어요.
③ Right. It was too much work. - 맞아요. 그건 너무 많은 일이었어요.
④ Yes. It will rain tomorrow. - 네. 내일은 비가 올 거예요.
⑤ Sorry. I can't drive a car. - 미안해요. 난 운전을 할 수 없어요.

M : Honey, look out the window. It's raining a lot.
여보, 창밖을 봐요. 비가 많이 오고 있어요.

W : Yeah, I think it might be dangerous to drive to work.
그러게요. 내 생각엔 운전해서 출근하는 게 위험할지도 모르겠어요.

M : You're right. You'd better use public transportation today.
당신 말이 맞아요. 오늘 당신은 대중교통을 이용하는 게 좋겠어요.

W : Okay. I'll take the subway then.
알겠어요. 그럼 난 지하철을 탈게요.

Why? 왜 정답일까?

남자는 밖에 비가 많이 온다며 여자에게 대중교통을 이용해 출근할 것을 권하고 있으므로(You'd better use public transportation today.), 여자의 응답으로 가장 적절한 것은 ① '알겠어요. 그럼 난 지하철을 탈게요.'이다.

- public transportation 대중교통

---

13 친구의 신발을 바꿔 신고 온 여자 　　정답률 85% | 정답 ④

대화를 듣고, 남자의 마지막 말에 대한 여자의 응답으로 가장 적절한 것을 고르시오. [3점]
Woman : _____

① I told her a scary story. - 그 애한테 무서운 이야기를 해 주었어.
② I said goodbye to her mother. - 그 애의 어머니께 작별 인사를 했어.
③ I asked her to do the homework. - 숙제를 하라고 요청했어.
✓④ I apologized for my silly mistake. - 내 바보 같은 실수에 대해 사과했어.
⑤ I thanked her for helping me study. - 내 공부를 도와주어서 고맙다고 했어.

W : Chris, a funny thing happened to me yesterday.
Chris, 어제 나한테 웃긴 일이 있었어.

M : Oh, really? Tell me about it.
오, 정말? 얘기해 줘.

W : After school I visited Mina's house to do homework with her. Then I came back home before dinner.
학교가 끝나고 Mina네 집에 숙제를 같이 하러 갔었어. 그런 다음 저녁 먹기 전에 집으로 돌아왔거든.

M : Well, I don't see why that's funny.
음, 그게 왜 웃긴지 모르겠는데.

W : Hey, I'm not finished yet. While I was having dinner, I got a phone call from Mina.
이봐, 아직 안 끝났어. 저녁을 먹다가 나는 Mina에게 전화를 받았어.

M : What did she say?
그 애가 뭐랬는데?

W : She said my shoes were still in her house!
내 신발이 아직 자기 집에 있다는 거야!

M : Oh, what happened?
오, 무슨 일이 일어난 거야?

W : By mistake, I came home wearing her shoes instead of mine. Her shoes looked almost the same as mine.
실수로 난 내 신발 대신 그 애의 신발을 신고 온 거야. 그 애 신발이 내 것이랑 거의 똑같아 보였거든.

M : No doubt you were very embarrassed. So, what did you say to Mina?
의심할 것도 없이 굉장히 당황했겠구나. 그래서, Mina한테는 뭐라고 했어?

W : I apologized for my silly mistake.
내 바보 같은 실수에 대해 사과했지.

Why? 왜 정답일까?

대화에서 여자는 친구인 Mina의 집에 갔다가 신발을 바꾸어 신고 온 이야기(By mistake, I came home wearing her shoes instead of mine.)를 하고 있다. 이에 남자는 여자가 이러한 실수에 대해 Mina에게 뭐라고 했는지(So, what did you say to Mina?) 묻고 있으므로, 남자의 마지막 말에 대한 여자의 응답으로 가장 적절한 것은 ④ '내 바보 같은 실수에 대해 사과했지.'이다.

- visit ⓥ 가다, 방문하다, 체류하다
- instead of ~ 대신에
- by mistake 실수로
- embarrassed ⓐ 당황한, 민망한

14 결혼식 축가 부탁하기　　　　　정답률 88% | 정답 ④

대화를 듣고, 여자의 마지막 말에 대한 남자의 응답으로 가장 적절한 것을 고르시오.

Man:
① You're welcome. I'm glad that you really enjoyed the gift.
천만에. 난 네가 정말로 선물을 좋아해준 게 기뻐.
② Don't worry about that. Everyone can learn from mistakes.
그건 걱정하지 마. 모두들 실수를 통해 배울 수 있어.
③ Yeah, I've sung the song. I want to sing in harmony now.
응, 난 그 노래를 불러봤어. 이제 화음을 넣어 부르고 싶어.
✓④ Okay, I'll sing for you. I hope you won't expect too much.
알겠어, 널 위해 노래할게. 네가 너무 많이 기대하는 않길 바라.
⑤ I don't think so. It's not easy to choose a wedding ring.
난 그렇게 생각 안 해. 결혼반지를 고르는 것은 쉽지 않아.

M : Hi, Emily! How are your wedding preparations going?
안녕, Emily! 네 결혼 준비는 어떻게 되어 가?
W : They're going well so far. I reserved a wedding hall and ordered invitation cards.
지금까지는 잘되고 있어. 난 결혼식장을 예약하고 청첩장을 주문했어.
M : Good. Everything's almost settled. It's on the first Saturday of July, right?
좋네. 모든 게 거의 정해졌구나. 7월 첫 번째 토요일이지, 맞지?
W : Yes. Can you come?
응. 올 수 있니?
M : Of course. Is there anything that I can help you with?
물론이지. 뭐라도 내가 도와줄 건 없니?
W : Actually, I haven't decided who'll sing at the wedding. So, would you sing for me?
사실, 난 결혼식에서 누가 노래를 부를지 정하지 못했어. 그러니, 네가 날 위해 노래해 줄래?
M : I'd love to, but I've never done anything like that before.
그러고 싶은데, 난 그런 걸 전에 해본 적이 없어.
W : I heard you singing at the college song festival, so I know you're a good singer.
난 네가 대학 노래 축제에서 노래하는 것을 들었어서 네가 노래를 잘하는 걸 알아.
M : Thanks, but I'm afraid I may not sing well enough to do so at a wedding.
고마워, 하지만 내가 결혼식에서 노래를 할 정도로 충분히 노래를 잘하는 건 아닌 것 같아.
W : Oh, please! I'm sure it would be the best wedding gift. I'd look forward to it.
오, 제발! 분명 그건 최고의 결혼 선물이 될 거야. 기대돼.
M : Okay, I'll sing for you. I hope you won't expect too much.
알겠어, 널 위해 노래할게, 네가 너무 많이 기대하는 않길 바라.

Why? 왜 정답일까?

축가를 부탁하는 여자의 말에 남자가 망설이자 여자는 최고의 결혼 선물이 될 것이라며 남자를 거듭 설득한다(Oh, please! I'm sure it would be the best wedding gift. I'd look forward to it.). 따라서 남자의 응답으로 가장 적절한 것은 ④ '알겠어, 널 위해 노래할게. 네가 너무 많이 기대하는 않길 바라.'이다.

● preparation ⓝ 준비
● wedding hall 예식장
● settle ⓥ 해결하다
● wedding ring 결혼반지
● reserve ⓥ 예약하다
● invitation card 초대장
● sing in harmony 화음을 넣어 노래하다

---

15 동생을 생일 파티에 데리고 가도 되는지 묻기　　　정답률 70% | 정답 ②

다음 상황 설명을 듣고, Julie가 Eric에게 할 말로 가장 적절한 것을 고르시오. [3점]

Julie:
① That's great. I've always wanted to meet your parents.
그거 아주 좋다. 난 항상 너희 부모님을 뵙고 싶었어.
✓② Sure, you can bring him. The more people, the better.
물론이지, 동생을 데려와도 돼. 사람이 많을수록 더 좋아.
③ Please don't bring anything. I'll get everything ready.
부디 아무것도 가져오지 마. 모든 것을 내가 준비할게.
④ Never mind. Let's have dinner together another time.
신경 쓰지 마. 다른 때 저녁을 함께 먹자.
⑤ Thank you for the invitation. I'll be there on time.
초대해줘서 고마워. 제 시간에 갈게.

W : Julie's going to throw a birthday party this Friday evening.
Julie는 이번 주 금요일 저녁 생일 파티를 열 것이다.
She invites her friend Eric to the party.
그녀는 친구 Eric을 파티에 초대한다.
Eric wants to accept her invitation, but he has a problem.
Eric은 그녀의 초대를 받아들이고 싶은데, 문제가 있다.
His parents will go out for dinner on Friday, so his eight-year-old brother will have to stay home alone if he goes out.
그의 부모님이 금요일 저녁에 외식을 하실 것이어서, 그가 외출을 하면 8살짜리 남동생이 집에 혼자 있어야 한다.
Eric can't leave him alone, so he asks Julie if he can come to the party with his brother.
Eric은 동생을 혼자 둘 수가 없어서, Julie에게 자기 남동생을 데려가도 되는지 묻는다.
Julie wants to say it's okay because she'd like to have more guests at the party.
Julie는 파티에 손님을 더 부르고 싶기 때문에 괜찮다고 말하고 싶다.
In this situation, what would Julie most likely say to Eric?
이 상황에서, Julie는 Eric에게 뭐라고 말할 것인가?
Julie : Sure, you can bring him. The more people, the better.
물론이지, 동생을 데려와도 돼. 사람이 많을수록 더 좋아.

Why? 왜 정답일까?

Julie의 생일 파티에 초대를 받은 Eric은 자신이 외출하면 집에 홀로 남을 동생을 걱정하여 동생을 파티에 데려가고 싶어 하는데, 이에 Julie는 손님이 많을수록 더 좋다고 생각하여 괜찮다고 답하려 한다(Julie wants to say it's okay because she'd like to have more guests at the party.). 따라서 Julie가 Eric에게 할 말로 가장 적절한 것은 ② '물론이지, 동생을 데려와도 돼. 사람이 많을수록 더 좋아.'이다.

● throw a party 파티를 열다
● leave ⓥ 남겨두다
● invitation ⓝ 초대(장)

16-17 기후 변화로 인해 사라질 위험에 처한 음식

M : Hello, everyone. Last class we learned about the dangers of climate change.

186　고1·3개년 영어 [리얼 오리지널]

안녕하세요, 여러분. 지난 수업에서 우리는 기후 변화의 위험에 대해 배웠습니다.
『Today, I'll tell you about some foods that might disappear because of climate change.』 **16번의 근거**
오늘은 기후 변화로 인해 사라질지도 모르는 음식에 대해 이야기하겠습니다.
『First of all, 70 percent of the world's coffee could disappear by 2080 due to climate change.』 **17번 ①의 근거** 일치
우선 기후 변화 때문에 2080년이면 세계 커피의 70퍼센트가 사라질 수도 있습니다.
In Africa, the amount of coffee produced has dropped by more than 50 percent.
아프리카에서는 커피 생산량이 50퍼센트 이상 떨어졌습니다.
『Secondly, avocados are also in danger.』 **17번 ②의 근거** 일치
둘째로, 아보카도 또한 위험에 처해 있습니다.
It usually takes 72 gallons of water to make just one pound of avocados.
아보카도 단 1파운드를 생산하기 위해서는 보통 72갤런의 물이 필요합니다.
Climate change in California has resulted in a lack of water, so the avocado plants aren't producing enough fruit.
캘리포니아의 기후 변화는 물 부족을 초래했고, 그래서 아보카도 나무는 충분한 열매를 맺지 못하고 있습니다.
『Thirdly, warmer temperatures affect apple trees, too.』 **17번 ③의 근거** 일치
셋째로, 더 따뜻해진 기온은 사과나무에도 영향을 미칩니다.
To grow properly, apple trees need a certain period of cold weather.
사과나무는 제대로 자라기 위해서 일정 기간의 추운 날씨를 필요로 합니다.
Lack of cold weather time leads to lower apple production.
추운 날씨의 부족은 사과 생산량을 감소시킵니다.
『Finally, the unstable climatic conditions through crop season are causing a decrease in strawberry production in Florida.』 **17번 ④의 근거** 일치
마지막으로, 작물 제철 동안 불안정한 기후 조건은 플로리다의 딸기 생산량 감소를 야기하고 있습니다.
Specifically, hotter-than-normal weather has delayed the flowering and production of strawberries.
특히 보통보다 더운 날씨는 딸기의 개화와 생산을 지연시켰습니다.
Now, let me show you some slides about this issue.
이제, 이 문제에 대한 슬라이드를 좀 보여드리겠습니다.

● climate change 기후 변화
● result in ~을 낳다, 야기하다
● properly ⓐⓓ 제대로, 적절히
● production ⓝ 생산
● crop season 작물 제철
● delay ⓥ 지연시키다
● at risk 위험에 처한
● disappear ⓥ 사라지다
● affect ⓥ 영향을 미치다
● lead to ~을 야기하다
● unstable ⓐ 불안정한
● specifically ⓐⓓ 특히
● flowering ⓝ 개화

---

16 주제 파악　　　　　정답률 90% | 정답 ①

남자가 하는 말의 주제로 가장 적절한 것은?
✓① foods at risk due to climate change – 기후 변화 때문에 위험에 처한 음식들
② reasons why sea temperatures rise – 바다 수온이 상승하는 이유
③ animals and plants in the water – 물속의 동식물
④ requirements of growing crops – 작물을 키우는 데 있어 필수사항들
⑤ ways to solve global warming – 지구 온난화를 해결할 방법들

Why? 왜 정답일까?

'Today, I'll tell you about some foods that might disappear because of climate change.'에서 남자는 기후 변화로 인해 사라질지도 모르는 음식들에 관해 이야기하겠다고 하므로, 남자가 하는 말의 주제로 가장 적절한 것은 ① '기후 변화 때문에 위험에 처한 음식들'이다.

---

17 언급 유무 파악　　　　　정답률 90% | 정답 ⑤

언급된 음식이 아닌 것은?
① coffee – 커피　　② avocados – 아보카도　　③ apples – 사과
④ strawberries – 딸기　　✓⑤ coconuts – 코코넛

Why? 왜 정답일까?

담화에서 남자는 기후 변화로 인해 사라질 위험에 처한 음식의 예로서 커피, 아보카도, 사과, 딸기를 언급하였다. 따라서 언급되지 않은 음식은 ⑤ '코코넛'이다.

Why? 왜 오답일까?

① 'First of all, 70 percent of the world's coffee could disappear by 2080 due to climate change.'에서 '커피'가 언급되었다.
② 'Secondly, avocados are also in danger.'에서 '아보카도'가 언급되었다.
③ 'Thirdly, warmer temperatures affect apple trees, too.'에서 '사과'가 언급되었다.
④ 'Finally, the unstable climatic conditions through crop season are causing a decrease in strawberry production in Florida.'에서 '딸기'가 언급되었다.

---

18 새로운 수영 코치 부임 안내　　　정답률 89% | 정답 ①

다음 글의 목적으로 가장 적절한 것은?
✓① 새로운 수영 코치를 소개하려고
② 수영 강좌의 폐강을 통보하려고
③ 수영 코치의 퇴임식을 공지하려고
④ 수영부의 대회 입상을 축하하려고
⑤ 수영의 건강상 이점을 홍보하려고

Dear Parents,
학부모님께,
As you know, / Sandy Brown, our after-school swimming coach for six years, / retired from coaching last month.
아시다시피, / 6년간 저희 학교 방과 후 수영 코치였던 Sandy Brown이 / 지난달에 코치 직에서 은퇴했습니다.
So, / Virginia Smith, / who swam for Bredard Community College / and has won several awards in national competitions, / has been named the school's new swimming coach.
그래서, / Virginia Smith가 / Bredard Community 대학 수영 선수였고 / 국내 대회에서 수차례 입상한 / 학교의 새로운 코치로 임명되었습니다.

This is her first job as a coach, / and she is going to start working from next week.
그녀는 이번에 처음으로 코치가 되었으며, / 다음 주부터 근무를 시작할 예정입니다.
She will teach her class in the afternoons, / and continue with our summer program.
그녀는 오후에 수업을 할 예정이며, / 여름 프로그램을 이어서 진행할 것입니다.
By promoting the health benefits of swimming, / she hopes / that more students will get healthy through her instruction.
수영의 건강상 이득을 증진시킴으로써, / 그녀는 희망합니다. / 강습을 통해 더 많은 학생들이 건강해지기를
Sincerely, // Fred Wilson
Fred Wilson 드림
Principal, Riverband High School
Riverband 고등학교 교장

학부모님께,

아시다시피, 6년간 저희 학교 방과 후 수영 코치였던 Sandy Brown이 지난달에 코치 직에서 은퇴했습니다. 그래서, Bredard Community 대학 수영 선수였고 국내 대회에서 수차례 입상한 Virginia Smith가 학교의 새로운 코치로 임명되었습니다. 그녀는 이번에 처음으로 코치가 되었으며, 다음 주부터 근무를 시작할 예정입니다. 오후에 수업을 할 예정이며, 여름 프로그램을 이어서 진행할 것입니다. 수영의 건강상 이득을 증진시킴으로써, 그녀는 강습을 통해 더 많은 학생들이 건강해지기를 희망합니다.

Riverband 고등학교 교장
Fred Wilson 드림

Why? 왜 정답일까?
첫 두 문장에서 기존 코치의 은퇴로 인해 새 코치가 영입되었다(So, Virginia Smith, ~ has been named the school's new swimming coach.)는 내용을 안내하므로, 글의 목적으로 가장 적절한 것은 ① '새로운 수영 코치를 소개하려고'이다.

- retire from ~에서 은퇴하다
- national ⓐ 국가의
- name ⓥ 임명하다, 지명하다, 명명하다
- health ⓝ 건강, 보건, 건전
- instruction ⓝ 강습, 교육, 지시, 방법
- several ⓐ 여럿의
- competition ⓝ 대회, 경쟁
- promote ⓥ 증진하다, 촉진하다
- hope ⓥ ~을 희망하다, 바라다, 생각하다 ⓝ 희망

구문 풀이

3행 So, / Virginia Smith, [who swam for Bredard Community College and
주격 관계대명사 ↵ 동사1(과거)
has won several awards in national competitions], has been named the school's
동사2(현재완료) 「be named + 명사: ~라고 명명되다」
new swimming coach.

---

19 아무도 없는 동굴에 고립된 Rowe   정답률 87% | 정답 ⑤

다음 글에 드러난 Rowe의 심경 변화로 가장 적절한 것은?
① delighted → grateful
    기쁜   고마워하는
② disappointed → ashamed
    실망한   부끄러운
③ indifferent → regretful
    무관심한   후회하는
④ bored → frightened
    지루한   겁에 질린
✓⑤ excited → desperate
    신난   필사적인

Rowe jumps for joy / when he finds a cave / because he loves being in places / where so few have ventured.
Rowe는 기쁨에 폴짝 뛴다. / 동굴을 발견하고 / 그가 장소에 있는 것을 좋아하기 때문에 / 거의 아무도 탐험하지 않은
At the entrance / he keeps taking photos with his cell phone / to show off his new adventure later.
동굴 입구에서 / 그는 휴대폰으로 사진을 계속 찍는다. / 나중에 그의 새로운 모험을 뽐내기 위해
Coming to a stop on a rock / a few meters from the entrance, / he sees the icy cave's glittering view.
바위 위에 멈추어 서서, / 동굴 입구로부터 몇 미터 떨어진 / 그는 얼음 동굴의 빛나는 광경을 본다.
He says, "Incredibly beautiful!" / stretching his hand out to touch the icy wall.
그는 "믿을 수 없을 정도로 아름답군!"이라고 말한다. / 얼음으로 된 벽을 만지기 위해 손을 뻗으면서
Suddenly, his footing gives way / and he slides down into the darkness.
갑자기 그는 발을 헛디뎌 / 어둠 속으로 미끄러져 들어간다.
He looks up and sees a crack of light / about 20 meters above him.
그는 위를 올려다보고 틈의 빛을 본다. / 대략 20미터 위에 있는
'Phone for help,' he thinks.
'전화로 도움을 요청해야지,'라고 그는 생각한다.
But he realizes / there's no service this far underground.
하지만 그는 깨닫는다. / 이렇게 깊은 지하에서는 (통화) 서비스가 되지 않는다는 것을
He tries to move upward but he can't.
그는 위로 올라가려고 하지만 올라갈 수 없다.
He calls out, "Is anyone there?"
그는 "거기 누구 있나요?"라고 외친다.
There's no answer.
응답이 없다.

Rowe는 거의 아무도 탐험하지 않은 장소에 있는 것을 좋아하기 때문에 동굴을 발견하고 기쁨에 폴짝 뛴다. 동굴 입구에서 그는 나중에 그의 새로운 모험을 뽐내기 위해 휴대폰으로 사진을 계속 찍는다. 동굴 입구로부터 몇 미터 떨어진 바위 위에 멈추어 서서, 그는 얼음 동굴의 빛나는 광경을 본다. 그는 얼음으로 된 벽을 만지기 위해 손을 뻗으면서 "믿을 수 없을 정도로 아름답군!"이라고 말한다. 갑자기 그는 발을 헛디뎌 어둠 속으로 미끄러져 들어간다. 그는 위를 올려다보고 대략 20미터 위에 있는 틈의 빛을 본다. '전화로 도움을 요청해야지,'라고 그는 생각한다. 하지만 그는 이렇게 깊은 지하에서는 (통화) 서비스가 되지 않는다는 것을 깨닫는다. 그는 위로 올라가려고 하지만 올라갈 수 없다. 그는 "거기 누구 있나요?"라고 외친다. 응답이 없다.

Why? 왜 정답일까?
글 중간의 Suddenly를 기점으로 상황이 반전되므로, 심경 변화의 힌트를 앞뒤에서 하나씩 찾아야 한

다. 'Rowe jumps for joy when he finds a cave because he loves being in places where so few have ventured.'에서 인적이 드문 동물을 발견한 Rowe가 기뻐한다는 내용이 나온데 이어, 마지막 네 문장에서는 갑자기 발을 헛디딘 Rowe가 전화도 되지 않고 위로 올라갈 수도 없으며 도움도 구할 수 없는 어둠 속에 혼자 갇힌다는 내용이 나온다. 따라서 Rowe의 심경 변화로 가장 적절한 것은 ⑤ '신난 → 필사적인'이다.

- cave ⓝ 동굴
- glittering ⓐ 반짝이는
- stretch out ~을 내밀다, 뻗다
- give way 무너지다, 내려앉다
- desperate ⓐ 필사적인, 절박한, (상황이) 절망적인
- venture ⓥ 탐험하다
- incredibly ⓐⓓ (너무 좋아서) 믿을 수 없게
- footing ⓝ 발을 디딤, 딛고 선 자리
- slide down 미끄러지다

구문 풀이

1행 Rowe jumps for joy when he finds a cave / because he loves being in
시간 접속사   이유 접속사
places [where so few have ventured].
선행사 관계부사 주어   자동사

---

20 언어 놀이의 주도성을 아이들에게 줄 필요성   정답률 84% | 정답 ①

다음 글에서 필자가 주장하는 바로 가장 적절한 것은?
✓① 아이들이 언어 놀이를 주도하게 하라.
② 아이들의 질문에 즉각적으로 반응하라.
③ 아이들에게 다양한 언어 자극을 제공하라.
④ 대화를 통해 아이들의 공감 능력을 키워라.
⑤ 언어 놀이를 통해 자녀와의 관계를 회복하라.

Language play is good / for children's language learning and development, / and therefore we should strongly encourage, / and even join in their language play.
언어 놀이는 유익하며, / 아이들의 언어 학습과 발달에 / 그러므로 우리는 (아이들의 언어 놀이를) 강력하게 장려하고 / 나아가 그들의 놀이에 참여해야 한다.
However, the play must be owned by the children.
하지만, 그 놀이는 아이들에 의해 주도되어야 한다.
If it becomes another educational tool / for adults to use to produce outcomes, / it loses its very essence.
놀이가 또 다른 교육적 도구가 되어버린다면, / 어른들이 결과물을 내기 위해 쓰는 / 놀이는 바로 그 본질을 잃게 될 것이다.
Children need to be able to delight / in creative and immediate language play, / to say silly things and make themselves laugh, / and to have control over the pace, timing, direction, and flow.
아이들은 즐거워하고, / 창의적이고 즉각적인 언어 놀이 안에서 / 바보 같은 말을 하며 웃기도 하고, / 속도와 타이밍, 방향, 흐름을 통제할 수 있어야 한다.
When children are allowed to develop their language play, / a range of benefits result from it.
아이들이 언어 놀이를 발전시키도록 허용할 때, / 광범위한 이점이 생겨난다.

언어 놀이는 아이들의 언어 학습과 발달에 유익하며, 그러므로 우리는 아이들의 언어 놀이를 강력하게 장려하고 나아가 그들의 놀이에 참여해야 한다. 하지만, 그 놀이는 아이들에 의해 주도되어야 한다. 놀이가 어른들이 결과물을 내기 위해 쓰는 또 다른 교육적 도구가 되어버린다면, 놀이는 바로 그 본질을 잃게 될 것이다. 아이들은 창의적이고 즉각적인 언어 놀이 안에서 즐거워하고, 바보 같은 말을 하며 웃기도 하고, 속도와 타이밍, 방향, 흐름을 통제할 수 있어야 한다. 아이들이 언어 놀이를 발전시키도록 허용할 때, 광범위한 이점이 생겨난다.

Why? 왜 정답일까?
첫 두 문장에서 언어 학습 및 발달에 유익한 언어 놀이를 아이들 스스로에 의해 '주도'될 수 있도록 하라(However, the play must be owned by the children.)고 말하고, 글의 후반부에서는 이 내용을 구체적으로 풀어서 설명하고 있다. 따라서 필자가 주장하는 바로 가장 적절한 것은 ① '아이들이 언어 놀이를 주도하게 하라.'이다.

- development ⓝ 발달
- own ⓥ 주도하다, 소유하다
- outcome ⓝ 결과
- delight ⓥ 많은 기쁨을 주다
- direction ⓝ 방향, 지시, 길, 목표
- benefit ⓝ 이익, 혜택
- encourage ⓥ 장려하다, 격려하다
- educational ⓐ 교육적인
- essence ⓝ 본질
- immediate ⓐ 즉각적인, 즉시의
- a range of 광범위한, 넓은

구문 풀이

1행 Language play is good for children's language learning and development,
                          「be good for + 명사: ~에 유익하다」
/ and therefore we should strongly encourage, and even join in their language
접속부사(그러므로) 조동사   동사원형1   동사원형2
play.

---

21 아리스토텔레스가 본 미덕   정답률 62% | 정답 ④

밑줄 친 at the "sweet spot"이 다음 글에서 의미하는 바로 가장 적절한 것은? [3점]
① at the time of a biased decision - 편향된 결정의 시점에
② in the area of material richness - 물질적 풍요의 영역에
③ away from social pressure - 사회적 압력에서 벗어나서
✓④ in the middle of two extremes - 양 극단의 중간에
⑤ at the moment of instant pleasure - 즉각적인 기쁨의 순간에

For almost all things in life, / there can be too much of a good thing.
인생의 거의 모든 것에는, / 좋은 것에도 지나침이 있을 수 있다.
Even the best things in life / aren't so great in excess.
심지어 인생에서 최상의 것도 / 지나치면 그리 좋지 않다.
This concept has been discussed / at least as far back as Aristotle.
이 개념은 논의되어 왔다. / 적어도 아리스토텔레스 시대만큼 오래부터
He argued / that being virtuous means finding a balance.
그는 주장했다. / 미덕이 있다는 것은 균형을 찾는 것을 의미한다고

For example, / people should be brave, / but if someone is too brave / they become reckless.
예를 들어, / 사람들은 용감해져야 하지만, / 만약 어떤 사람이 너무 용감하다면 / 그 사람은 무모해진다.

People should be trusting, / but if someone is too trusting / they are considered gullible.
사람들은 타인을 신뢰해야 하지만, / 만약 어떤 사람이 너무 신뢰한다면 / 그들은 잘 속아 넘어가는 사람으로 여겨진다.

For each of these traits, / it is best to avoid both deficiency and excess.
이러한 각각의 특성에 있어, / 부족과 과잉 둘 다를 피하는 것이 최상이다.

The best way is / to live at the "sweet spot" / that maximizes well-being.
최상의 방법은 / '최고의 상황'에 머무르는 것이다. / 행복을 극대화하는

Aristotle's suggestion is / that virtue is the midpoint, / where someone is neither too generous nor too stingy; / neither too afraid nor recklessly brave.
아리스토텔레스의 의견은 / 미덕이란 중간 지점이라는 것이다. / 누군가 너무 관대하지도 너무 인색하지도 않고, / 너무 두려워하지도 너무 무모하게 용감하지도 않은

인생의 거의 모든 것에는, 좋은 것에도 지나침이 있을 수 있다. 심지어 인생에서 최상의 것도 지나치면 그리 좋지 않다. 이 개념은 적어도 아리스토텔레스 시대만큼 오래전부터 논의되어 왔다. 그는 미덕이 있다는 것은 균형을 찾는 것을 의미한다고 주장했다. 예를 들어, 사람들은 용감해져야 하지만, 만약 어떤 사람이 너무 용감하다면 그 사람은 무모해진다. 사람들은 타인을 신뢰해야 하지만, 만약 어떤 사람이 너무 신뢰한다면 그들은 잘 속아 넘어가는 사람으로 여겨진다. 이러한 각각의 특성에 있어, 부족과 과잉 둘 다를 피하는 것이 최상이다. 최상의 방법은 행복을 극대화하는 '최고의 상황'에 머무르는 것이다. 아리스토텔레스의 의견은, 미덕이란 누군가가 너무 관대하지도 너무 인색하지도 않고, 너무 두려워하지도 너무 무모하게 용감하지도 않은 중간 지점이라는 것이다.

Why? 왜 정답일까?

밑줄 친 부분의 앞뒤의 문장인 '~ it is best to avoid both deficiency and excess.'와 '~ virtue is the midpoint, ~'에서 부족하지도 넘치지도 않는 지점, 즉 중간 지점이 미덕임을 언급하므로, 밑줄 친 부분이 의미하는 바로 가장 적절한 것은 ④ '양 극단의 중간에'이다.

- **as far back as** ~만큼 오래전부터
- **virtuous** ⓐ 도덕적인, 고결한
- **trusting** ⓐ 사람을 믿는
- **deficiency** ⓝ 부족, 결핍
- **maximize** ⓥ 극대화하다
- **virtue** ⓝ 미덕, 덕목
- **generous** ⓐ 관대한
- **recklessly** ⓐ대 무모하게, 개의치 않고

- **argue** ⓥ 언쟁을 하다, 주장하다
- **reckless** ⓐ 무모한
- **trait** ⓝ 특성
- **sweet spot** 가장 좋은 점, 최고의 상황
- **suggestion** ⓝ 제안, 의견
- **midpoint** ⓝ 중간, 중심점
- **stingy** ⓐ (특히 돈에) 인색한
- **biased** ⓐ 편향된

구문 풀이

9행 Aristotle's suggestion is that virtue is the midpoint, / where someone is
　　　　　　　　　　　 접속사(~것)　　　　선행사　　 관계부사
neither too generous nor too stingy, neither too afraid nor recklessly brave.
「neither+A+nor+B : A도 B도 아닌」

---

22 자기가 가진 것의 가치를 잊고 사는 사람들　　정답률 74% | 정답 ④

다음 글의 요지로 가장 적절한 것은?
① 새로움을 추구하는 삶이 가치 있다.
② 작은 행복이 모여서 큰 행복이 된다.
③ 즐거움은 어느 정도의 고통을 수반한다.
④ 익숙함이 소중한 것의 가치를 잊게 한다. ✓
⑤ 결과보다 과정에 집중하는 삶이 행복하다.

If you walk into a room / that smells of freshly baked bread, / you quickly detect the rather pleasant smell.
여러분이 방에 들어가면, / 갓 구운 빵 냄새가 나는 / 여러분은 꽤 기분 좋은 그 냄새를 바로 알아차린다.

However, / stay in the room for a few minutes, / and the smell will seem to disappear.
하지만, / 몇 분 동안 그 방에 있어라, / 그러면 냄새가 사라지는 듯할 것이다.

In fact, / the only way to reawaken it / is to walk out of the room and come back in again.
사실, / 이를 다시 일깨우는 유일한 방법은 / 방을 나갔다가 다시 들어오는 것이다.

The exact same concept / applies to many areas of our lives, / including happiness.
정확히 똑같은 개념이 / 우리 삶의 많은 영역에 적용된다. / 행복을 포함해서

Everyone has something to be happy about.
모두에게는 행복을 느끼는 무언가가 있다.

Perhaps / they have a loving partner, / good health, / a satisfying job, / a roof over their heads, / or enough food to eat.
아마 / 그들에게는 사랑하는 파트너가 있을 것이다. / 건강, / 만족감을 주는 직업, / 보금자리, / 또는 먹을 충분한 양식이

As time passes, however, / they get used to what they have / and, just like the smell of fresh bread, / these wonderful assets disappear from their consciousness.
하지만 시간이 흐르면서, / 사람들은 자기가 가진 것에 익숙해지고, / 마치 갓 구운 빵 냄새와 마찬가지로, / 이 경이로운 자산들은 의식 속에서 사라지고 만다.

As the old proverb goes, / you never miss the water / till the well runs dry.
오랜 격언처럼, / 여러분은 결코 물을 그리워하지 않는다. / 우물이 마르기 전에는

갓 구운 빵 냄새가 나는 방에 들어가면, 여러분은 꽤 기분 좋은 그 냄새를 바로 알아차린다. 하지만, 몇 분 동안 그 방에 있으면, 냄새가 사라지는 듯할 것이다. 사실, 이를 다시 일깨우는 방법은 방을 나갔다가 다시 들어오는 것이다. 정확히 똑같은 개념이 행복을 포함해서 우리 삶의 많은 영역에 적용된다. 모두에게는 행복을 느끼는 무언가가 있다. 아마 사랑하는 파트너나 건강, 만족감을 주는 직업, 보금자리, 먹을 충분한 양식이 있을 것이다. 하지만 시간이 흐르면서, 사람들은 자기가 가진 것에 익숙해지고, 마치 갓 구운 빵 냄새와 마찬가지로, 이 경이로운 자산들은 의식 속에서 사라지고 만다. 오랜 격언처럼, 우물이 마르기 전에는 결코 물을 그리워하지 않는다.

Why? 왜 정답일까?

갓 구운 빵 냄새를 처음 맡으면 그 냄새를 알아차리지만 시간이 지나면 익숙해져서 더 이상 의식하지 못하는 것과 마찬가지로, 처음에는 생각하면 행복함을 느끼던 소중한 것도 시간이 지나면 의식 속에서 사라진다는 것(As time passes, however, they get used to what they have and, ~ these wonderful assets disappear from their consciousness.)이 글의 주된 내용이다. 따라서 글의 요지로 가장 적절한 것은 ④ '익숙함이 소중한 것의 가치를 잊게 한다.'이다.

- **freshly** ⓐ대 갓, 신선하게
- **rather** ⓐ대 꽤, 다소
- **disappear** ⓥ 사라지다, 없어지다
- **reawaken** ⓥ 다시 일깨우다
- **perhaps** ⓐ대 아마, 어쩌면
- **asset** ⓝ 자산
- **run dry** (물 등이) 마르다, 말라붙다

- **detect** ⓥ 알아차리다, 감지하다
- **pleasant** ⓐ 기분 좋은, 유쾌한
- **in fact** 사실은
- **concept** ⓝ 개념
- **satisfying** ⓐ 만족감을 주는, 만족스러운
- **consciousness** ⓝ 의식

구문 풀이

8행 As time passes, however, / they get used to what they have / and, (just like
　　接속사(~하면서, ~함에 따라)　접속사(하지만)　~에 익숙해지다 관계대명사(~것)　 바로 ~처럼
the smell of fresh bread), these wonderful assets disappear from their consciousness.
　　　　　　　　　　　　　　　　　　　　　자동사(사라지다)

---

23 지난 날씨에 관해 알려주는 나무의 나이테　　정답률 73% | 정답 ⑤

다음 글의 주제로 가장 적절한 것은?
① use of old trees to find direction - 방향을 찾기 위해 오래된 나무 이용하기
② traditional ways to predict weather - 날씨를 예측하는 전통적인 방법들
③ difficulty in measuring a tree's age - 나무의 나이를 측정하는 어려움
④ importance of protecting local trees - 지역 나무들을 보호하는 일의 중요성
⑤ tree rings suggesting the past climate - 과거의 기후를 알려주는 나이테 ✓

If you've ever seen a tree stump, / you probably noticed / that the top of the stump had a series of rings.
만약 여러분이 나무 그루터기를 본 적이 있다면, / 아마도 보았을 것이다. / 그루터기의 꼭대기 부분에 일련의 나이테가 있는 것을

These rings can tell us / how old the tree is, / and what the weather was like / during each year of the tree's life.
이 나이테는 우리에게 말해 줄 수 있다. / 그 나무가 몇 살인지, / 날씨가 어떠했는지를 / 그 나무가 매해 살아오는 동안

Because trees are sensitive to local climate conditions, / such as rain and temperature, / they give scientists some information / about that area's local climate in the past.
나무는 지역적 기후 조건에 민감하므로, / 비와 온도 같은 / 그것은 약간의 정보를 과학자에게 제공해 준다. / 과거의 그 지역 기후에 대한

For example, / tree rings usually grow wider in warm, wet years / and are thinner in years / when it is cold and dry.
예를 들어, / 나이테는 보통 온화하고 습한 해에는 폭이 더 넓어지고 / 해에는 더 좁아진다. / 춥고 건조한

If the tree has experienced stressful conditions, / such as a drought, / the tree might hardly grow at all / during that time.
만약 나무가 힘든 기후 조건을 경험하게 되면, / 가뭄과 같은 / 나무가 거의 성장하지 못할 수 있다. / 그러한 기간에는

Very old trees in particular / can offer clues / about what the climate was like / long before measurements were recorded.
특히 매우 나이가 많은 나무는 / 단서를 제공해 줄 수 있다. / 기후가 어떠했는지에 대한 / 관측이 기록되기 훨씬 이전에

만약 여러분이 나무 그루터기를 본 적이 있다면, 아마도 그루터기의 꼭대기 부분에 일련의 나이테가 있는 것을 보았을 것이다. 이 나이테는 그 나무가 몇 살인지, 그 나무가 매해 살아 오는 동안 날씨가 어떠했는지를 우리에게 말해 줄 수 있다. 나무는 비와 온도 같은 지역적 기후 조건에 민감하므로, 그것은 과거의 그 지역 기후에 대한 약간의 정보를 과학자에게 제공해 준다. 예를 들어, 나이테는 보통 온화하고 습한 해에는 폭이 더 넓어지고 춥고 건조한 해에는 더 좁아진다. 만약 나무가 가뭄과 같은 힘든 기후 조건을 경험하게 되면, 그러한 기간에는 나무가 거의 성장하지 못할 수 있다. 특히 매우 나이가 많은 나무는 관측이 기록되기 훨씬 이전에 기후가 어떠했는지에 대한 단서를 제공해 줄 수 있다.

Why? 왜 정답일까?

'These rings can tell us how old the tree is, and what the weather was like during each year of the tree's life.'에서 나무의 나이테는 나무의 나이뿐 아니라 나무가 살아온 동안 과거의 날씨가 어떠했는가에 대한 정보를 알려준다는 핵심 내용이 제시되므로, 글의 주제로 가장 적절한 것은 ⑤ '과거의 기후를 알려주는 나이테'이다.

- **sensitive** ⓐ 민감한, 예민한
- **climate** ⓝ 기후
- **stressful** ⓐ 스트레스가 많은, 짜증나는
- **hardly** ⓐ대 거의 ~할 수가 없다
- **clue** ⓝ 단서, 증거
- **direction** ⓝ 방향
- **predict** ⓥ 예측하다
- **protect** ⓥ 보호하다, 지키다

- **local** ⓐ 지역의
- **temperature** ⓝ 온도
- **drought** ⓝ 가뭄
- **in particular** 특히
- **measurement** ⓝ 측정, 관측
- **traditional** ⓐ 전통적인
- **measure** ⓥ 측정하다, 재다

구문 풀이

10행 Very old trees in particular can offer clues about what the climate was like
　　　　주어　　　　　　　　　　　동사　　목적어　　「what+주어+be like : ~이 어떤지」
long before measurements were recorded.
~하기 오래 전에

★★★ 등급을 가르는 문제!

24 양봉 장소에 대한 고정 관념 반박　　정답률 43% | 정답 ②

다음 글의 제목으로 가장 적절한 것은?
① The Best Season for Honey Harvest in Cities - 도시에서 꿀 수확을 하기 가장 좋은 계절
② Myth and Truth about Where to Keep Bees - 어디에서 벌을 기를 것인가에 대한 통념과 진실 ✓
③ How Can We Overcome Fear of Bees? - 벌에 대한 공포를 어떻게 극복할 수 있는가?
④ Benefits of Bee Farming on Nature - 자연에서 양봉업을 하는 것의 이점
⑤ Bee Farming: Not an Easy Job - 양봉업: 쉬운 일이 아니다

Many people suppose / that to keep bees, / it is necessary to have a large garden in the country; / but this is a mistake.
많은 사람들은 생각한다. / 벌을 키우기 위해서는 / 시골에 큰 정원을 갖고 있을 필요가 있다고 / 하지만 이는 잘못된 판단이다.

Bees will, of course, do better / in the midst of fruit blossoms in May / and white clovers in June / than in a city / where they have to fly a long distance / to reach the open fields.

물론, 벌들은 (꿀 만들기를) 더 잘한다. / 5월의 과일나무 꽃이 한창일 때 / 그리고 6월의 흰토끼풀이 / 도시에서보다 / 그들이 먼 거리를 날아가야 하는 / 탁 트인 벌판에 다다르기 위해

However, / bees can be kept with profit / even under unfavorable circumstances.
하지만, / 벌들은 이익을 낼 수 있다. / 적합하지 못한 환경에서도

Bees do very well in the suburbs of large cities / since the series of flowers in the gardens of the villas / allow a constant supply of honey / from early spring until autumn.
벌들은 대도시의 교외 지역에서도 (꿀 만들기를) 아주 잘 해내는데 / 주택 정원에 있는 일련의 꽃들이 / 지속적인 꿀 공급을 해 주기 때문이다. / 초봄부터 가을까지

Therefore, / almost every person / — except those who are seriously afraid of bees — / can keep them profitably and enjoyably.
그러므로, / 거의 모든 사람들은 / 벌을 심하게 무서워하는 사람들을 제외한 / 이윤을 내며 즐겁게 벌을 기를 수 있다.

많은 사람들은 벌을 키우기 위해서는 시골에 큰 정원을 갖고 있을 필요가 있다고 생각한다. 하지만 이는 잘못된 판단이다. 물론, 벌들은 탁 트인 벌판에 다다르기 위해 먼 거리를 날아가야 하는 도시에서보다 5월의 과일나무 꽃과 6월의 흰토끼풀이 한창일 때 (꿀 만들기를) 더 잘한다. 하지만, 벌들은 적합하지 못한 환경에서도 이익을 낼 수 있다. 벌들은 대도시의 교외 지역에서도 (꿀 만들기를) 아주 잘 해내는데 주택 정원에 있는 일련의 꽃들이 초봄부터 가을까지 지속적인 꿀 공급을 해 주기 때문이다. 그러므로, 특히 벌을 심하게 무서워하는 사람들을 제외한 거의 모든 사람들은 이윤을 내며 즐겁게 벌을 기를 수 있다.

Why? 왜 정답일까?

흔히 사람들은 양봉이 큰 정원이나 너른 벌판에서 하기 좋다고 생각하지만, 사실은 적합하지 못한 환경에서도 양봉을 충분히 잘 할 수 있다(However, bees can be kept with profit even under unfavorable circumstances.)는 내용의 글이다. 따라서 글의 제목으로 가장 적절한 것은 ② '어디에서 벌을 기를 것인가에 대한 통념과 진실'이다.

- in the midst of 한창일 때, ~ 가운데
- distance ⓝ 거리
- unfavorable 적합하지 못한, 불리한
- constant ⓐ 지속적인, 끊임없는
- seriously ⓐⓓ 심하게, 진지하게
- profitably ⓐⓓ 이윤을 내며, 유리하게
- blossom ⓝ (특히 과수의) 꽃
- open ⓐ 탁 트인, 너른
- circumstance ⓝ 환경, 상황
- supply ⓝ 공급 ⓥ 공급하다
- afraid ⓐ 두려워하는

구문 풀이

2행 Bees will, (of course), do better / in the midst of fruit blossoms in May
조동사 삽입구 동사원형 └→비교급
and white clovers in June than in a city [where they have to fly a long distance /
~보다 관계부사 완전한 문장
to reach the open fields].
부사적 용법(~하기 위해)

★★ 문제 해결 꿀~팁 ★★

▶ 많이 틀린 이유는?
but과 however 앞뒤로 통념을 반박하는 구조의 글이다. 특히 통념을 설명하는 부분의 구문이 까다로워 문장 단위의 정확한 독해가 이루어지지 않았다면 단어만 보고 ④를 고르기 쉬운 문제였다.

▶ 문제 해결 방법은?
제목 문제는 일단 본문에서 반복되는 내용을 찾고 이를 적절한 말로 압축해 나타난 선택지를 답으로 골라야 한다. but과 however 앞뒤 문장에서 각각 '사람들은 벌을 시골에서 키워야 하는 줄로 알지만, 실은 꼭 그럴 필요가 없다'는 큰 내용이 반복되는데 이를 ②에서는 '통념과 반박'이라는 말로 요약하고 있다. '통념 = 시골에서 벌을 키워야 한다고 생각하는 것, 반박 = 도시 등에서 키워도 됨'임을 파악하는 것이 풀이의 관건이다.

---

25 중국과 인도의 스마트폰 평균 가격 정답률 82% | 정답 ④

다음 도표의 내용과 일치하지 않는 것은?

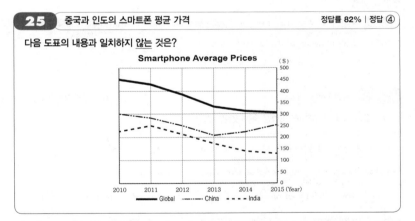

The above graph shows / the smartphone average prices in China and India / between 2010 and 2015, / compared with the global smartphone average price / during the same period.
위의 그래프는 보여준다. / 중국과 인도의 스마트폰 평균 가격 / 2010년과 2015년 사이 / 전 세계 스마트폰 평균 가격과 비교하여 / 같은 기간의

① The global smartphone average price / decreased from 2010 to 2015, / but still stayed the highest among the three.
전 세계 스마트폰 평균 가격은 / 2010년부터 2015년까지 하락했지만, / 여전히 셋 중 가장 높게 머물렀다.

② The smartphone average price in China / dropped between 2010 and 2013.
중국의 스마트폰 평균 가격은 / 2010년과 2013년 사이에는 하락했다.

③ The smartphone average price in India / reached its peak in 2011.
인도의 스마트폰 평균 가격은 / 2011년에 최고점에 도달했다.

☑ From 2013, China and India took opposite paths, / with China's smartphone average price going down / and India's going up.
2013년부터 중국과 인도는 정반대의 모습을 보여, / 중국의 스마트폰 평균 가격은 하락했고 / 인도의 스마트폰 평균 가격은 상승하였다.

⑤ The gap / between the global smartphone average price / and the smartphone average price in China / was the smallest in 2015.
차이는 / 전 세계 스마트폰 평균 가격과 / 중국의 스마트폰 평균 가격의 / 2015년에 가장 적었다.

위의 그래프는 2010년과 2015년 사이 중국과 인도의 스마트폰 평균 가격을 같은 기간의 전 세계 스마트폰 평균 가격과 비교하여 보여준다. ① 전 세계 스마트폰 평균 가격은 2010년부

터 2015년까지 하락했지만, 여전히 셋 중 가장 높게 머물렀다. ② 중국의 스마트폰 평균 가격은 2010년과 2013년 사이에는 하락했다. ③ 인도의 스마트폰 평균 가격은 2011년에 최고점에 도달했다. ④ 2013년부터 중국과 인도는 정반대의 모습을 보여, 중국의 스마트폰 평균 가격은 하락했고 인도의 스마트폰 평균 가격은 상승하였다. ⑤ 전 세계 스마트폰 평균 가격과 중국의 스마트폰 평균 가격의 차이는 2015년에 가장 적었다.

Why? 왜 정답일까?

도표에 따르면 중국과 인도의 스마트폰 가격이 2013년부터 정반대의 방향으로 변화한 것은 맞지만, 가격이 상승한 국가는 중국이며 하락한 국가는 인도이다. 따라서 도표의 내용과 일치하지 않는 것은 ④이다.

- average ⓐ 평균의
- reach one's peak 정점에 달하다
- compared with ~과 비교하여
- opposite ⓐ 정반대의

---

26 Nauru 국가 소개 정답률 85% | 정답 ⑤

Nauru에 관한 다음 글의 내용과 일치하지 않는 것은?
① 솔로몬 제도로부터 북동쪽에 위치해 있다.
② 공식 수도는 없으나 Yaren에 정부 건물이 있다.
③ 면적이 세계에서 세 번째로 작은 국가이다.
④ 원주민은 12개의 부족으로 구성되어 있다.
☑ 모국어가 있어 다른 언어는 사용하지 않는다.

Nauru is an island country / in the southwestern Pacific Ocean.
Nauru는 섬나라이다. / 남서부 태평양에 있는

『It is located about 800 miles / to the northeast of the Solomon Islands; / its closest neighbor is the island of Banaba, / some 200 miles to the east.』 ①의근거 일치
이는 800마일 정도 떨어진 곳에 위치해 있다. / 솔로몬 제도로부터 북동쪽으로 / 여기서 가장 가까운 섬은 Banaba 섬이다. / 동쪽으로 200마일 가량 떨어진

『Nauru has no official capital, / but government buildings are located in Yaren.』 ②의근거 일치
Nauru는 공식 수도가 없지만, / 정부 건물은 Yaren에 위치해 있다.

『With a population of about 10,000, / Nauru is the smallest country in the South Pacific / and the third smallest country by area in the world.』 ③의근거 일치
1만 명 정도 되는 인구가 있는 / Nauru는 남태평양에서 가장 작은 나라이고 / 면적으로는 세계에서 세 번째로 작은 나라이다.

『The native people of Nauru consist of 12 tribes, / as symbolized by the 12-pointed star on the Nauru flag, / and are believed to be a mixture / of Micronesian, Polynesian, and Melanesian.』 ④의근거 일치
Nauru의 원주민은 12개 부족으로 구성되어 있고, / 국기에 12개의 꼭짓점이 있는 별로 나타나듯이 / 혼합으로 여겨진다. / 미크로네시아인, 폴리네시아인, 말레이시아인의

『Their native language is Nauruan, / but English is widely spoken / as it is used for government and business purposes.』 ⑤의근거 불일치
이들의 모국어는 Nauru 어인데 / 영어도 널리 쓰여서 / 이것이 행정 및 사업적 목적으로 이용된다.

Nauru는 남서부 태평양에 있는 섬나라이다. 이는 솔로몬 제도로부터 북동쪽으로 800마일 정도 떨어진 곳에 위치해 있다. 여기서 가장 가까운 섬은 동쪽으로 200마일 가량 떨어진 Banaba 섬이다. Nauru는 공식 수도가 없지만, 정부 건물은 Yaren에 위치해 있다. 1만 명 정도 되는 인구가 있는 Nauru는 남태평양에서 가장 작은 나라이고 면적으로는 세계에서 세 번째로 작은 나라이다. Nauru의 원주민은 국기에 12개의 꼭짓점이 있는 별로 나타나듯이 12개 부족으로 구성되어 있고, 미크로네시아인, 폴리네시아인, 말레이시아인의 혼합으로 여겨진다. 이들의 모국어는 Nauru 어인데 영어도 널리 쓰여서 행정 및 사업적 목적으로 이용된다.

Why? 왜 정답일까?

'Their native language is Nauruan, but English is widely spoken as it is used for government and business purposes.'에서 Nauru의 모국어는 Nauru 어인데 영어 또한 행정 및 사업적 목적으로 많이 쓰인다고 이야기하므로, Nauru에 관한 글의 내용과 일치하지 않는 것은 ⑤ '모국어가 있어 다른 언어는 사용하지 않는다.'이다.

Why? 왜 오답일까?

① 'It is located about 800 miles to the northeast of the Solomon Islands; ~'의 내용과 일치한다.
② 'Nauru has no official capital, but government buildings are located in Yaren.'의 내용과 일치한다.
③ '~, Nauru is ~ the third smallest country by area in the world.'의 내용과 일치한다.
④ 'The native people of Nauru consist of 12 tribes, ~'의 내용과 일치한다.

- close ⓐ 가까운
- capital ⓝ 수도
- consist ⓥ 되어(이루어져) 있다
- symbolize ⓥ 나타나다, 상징하다
- native language 모국어
- official ⓐ 공식적인
- population ⓝ 인구
- tribe ⓝ 부족
- mixture ⓝ 혼합
- purpose ⓝ 목적

구문 풀이

7행 The native people of Nauru consist of 12 tribes, / as symbolized by the
자동사(~로 구성되다) 접속사(~대로, ~듯이) └(they are 생략)
12-pointed star on the Nauru flag, / and are believed to be a mixture of
~라고 여겨지다
Micronesian, Polynesian, and Melanesian.

---

27 여름 캠프 안내 정답률 87% | 정답 ④

Summer Camp 2019에 관한 다음 안내문의 내용과 일치하는 것은?
① 참가 연령 제한이 없다.
② 야외 프로그램은 운영되지 않는다.
③ 할인된 가격은 100달러이다.
☑ 기상 조건에 관계없이 프로그램이 진행될 것이다.
⑤ 이메일을 통해 등록을 할 수 없다.

Summer Camp 2019
Summer Camp 2019(여름캠프 2019)

This is a great opportunity / for developing social skills and creativity!
이 캠프는 훌륭한 기회입니다! / 사교 기술과 창의력을 발달시키기 위한

Period & Participation
기간 및 참가

July 1 – 5 (Monday – Friday)
7월 1일 ~ 5일(월요일 ~ 금요일)

『8 – 12 year olds (maximum 20 students per class)』 ①의근거 불일치
8세 ~ 12세(한 반당 최대 20명)

Programs
프로그램

Cooking
요리

『Outdoor Activities (hiking, rafting, and camping)』 ②의근거 불일치
야외 활동(하이킹, 래프팅, 그리고 캠핑)

Cost
비용

Regular: $100 per person
일반 가격: 1인당 100달러

『Discounted: $90 / (if you register by June 15)』 ③의근거 불일치
할인 가격: 90달러 / (6월 15일까지 등록 시)

Notice
알림

『The programs will run / regardless of weather conditions.』 ④의근거 일치
프로그램은 진행될 것입니다. / 기상 조건에 관계없이

『To sign up, / email us at summercamp@standrews.com.』 ⑤의근거 불일치
등록하시려면, / summercamp@standrews.com으로 이메일을 보내주세요.

For more information, / visit our website: www.standrews.com.
더 많은 정보가 필요하다면, / 우리 웹 사이트(www.standrews.com)를 방문해 주세요.

Summer Camp 2019

이 캠프는 사교 기술과 창의력을 발달시키기 위한 훌륭한 기회입니다!

기간 및 참가
• 7월 1일 ~ 5일(월요일 ~ 금요일)
• 8세 ~ 12세(한 반당 최대 20명)

프로그램
• 요리
• 야외 활동(하이킹, 래프팅, 그리고 캠핑)

비용
• 일반 가격: 1인당 100달러
• 할인 가격: 90달러(6월 15일까지 등록 시)

알림
• 프로그램은 기상 조건에 관계없이 진행될 것입니다.
• 등록하시려면, summercamp@standrews.com으로 이메일을 보내주세요.

더 많은 정보가 필요하다면, 우리 웹 사이트(www.standrews.com)를 방문해 주세요.

Why? 왜 정답일까?

'The programs will run regardless of weather conditions.'에서 프로그램은 기상 조건에 관계없이 진행된다고 하므로, 안내문의 내용과 일치하는 것은 ④ '기상 조건에 관계없이 프로그램이 진행될 것이다.'이다.

Why? 왜 오답일까?

① '8 – 12 year olds (maximum 20 students per class)'에서 참가 연령은 8 ~ 12세로 제한된다고 하였다.
② 'Outdoor Activities (hiking, rafting, and camping)'에서 하이킹, 래프팅, 캠핑 등의 야외 프로그램이 제공된다고 하였다.
③ 'Regular: $100 per person / Discounted: $90 (if you register by June 15)'에서 100달러가 정규 가격이며 할인가는 90달러라고 하였다.
⑤ 'To sign up, email us at summercamp@standrews.com.'에서 등록하려면 안내된 주소로 이메일을 보내달라고 하였다.

● develop ⓥ 발달시키다　　　　　● social skill 사교 기술
● maximum ⓐ 최대의　　　　　● regardless of ~에 관계없이
● sign up 등록하다, 참가하다

---

28 박물관 가족 활동 소개　　　　　정답률 82% | 정답 ③

Family Activities at the Basque Museum에 관한 다음 안내문의 내용과 일치하지 <u>않는</u> 것은?
① 주중과 주말 운영 시간이 다르다.
② 보물찾기 활동은 하루에 세 번 진행한다.
✔ 역사 책 만들기 활동은 주중에만 운영한다.
④ 모든 활동은 예약이 필수이다.
⑤ 어린이들은 성인과 함께 와야 한다.

Family Activities at the Basque Museum
Basque 박물관에서의 가족 활동

Whether you are a new or regular visitor, / this is your guide to the family activities / coming up at the Basque Museum.
귀하가 신규 관람객이든 정기 관람객이든, / 이것은 가족 활동에 대한 안내입니다. / Basque 박물관에서 있을

Dates & Hours
날짜 및 시간

June 1 – 30
6월 1 ~ 30일

『Weekdays: 9:00 a.m. – 5:00 p.m.
평일: 오전 9:00 ~ 오후 5:00

Weekends: 10:00 a.m. – 6:00 p.m.』 ①의근거 일치
주말: 오전 10:00 ~ 오후 6:00

Activities
활동

『Treasure Hunt
보물찾기

Age 5+, lasts 30 minutes, 3 times a day』 ②의근거 일치
5세 이상, 30분 소요, 하루 3번

『Making History Books
역사 책 만들기

For kids of all ages, weekends only』 ③의근거 불일치
모든 연령대 아이들, 주말만 가능

Notices
공지사항

All activities are free, / donations are welcome.
모든 활동은 무료이며 / 기부금을 환영합니다.

『Reservations are required for all activities.』 ④의근거 일치
모든 활동은 예약이 필수입니다.

『Children must be accompanied by an adult.』 ⑤의근거 일치
아이들은 성인과 함께 오셔야 합니다.

Basque 박물관에서의 가족 활동

신규 관람객 및 정기 관람객 분들께 Basque 박물관에서 있을 가족 활동에 대해 알려드립니다.

■ **날짜 및 시간**
• 6월 1 ~ 30일
• 평일: 오전 9:00 ~ 오후 5:00
• 주말: 오전 10:00 ~ 오후 6:00

■ **활동**
• 보물찾기
 – 5세 이상, 30분 소요, 하루 3번
• 역사 책 만들기
 – 모든 연령대 아이들, 주말만 가능

■ **공지사항**
• 모든 활동은 무료이며 기부금을 환영합니다.
• 모든 활동은 예약이 필수입니다.
• 아이들은 성인과 함께 오셔야 합니다.

Why? 왜 정답일까?

'• Making History Books / – For kids of all ages, weekends only'을 통해 역사 책 만들기는 주중이 아닌 주말에만 가능하다는 것을 알 수 있으므로, Family Activities at the Basque Museum에 관한 안내문의 내용과 일치하지 않는 것은 ③ '역사 책 만들기 활동은 주중에만 운영한다.'이다.

Why? 왜 오답일까?

① '• Weekdays: 9:00 a.m. – 5:00 p.m. / • Weekends: 10:00 a.m. – 6:00 p.m.'의 내용과 일치한다.
② '• Treasure Hunt / – Age 5+, lasts 30 minutes, 3 times a day'의 내용과 일치한다.
④ 'Reservations are required for all activities.'의 내용과 일치한다.
⑤ 'Children must be accompanied by an adult.'의 내용과 일치한다.

● regular ⓐ 상시의, 규칙적인　　　● donation ⓝ 기부(금)
● reservation ⓝ 예약　　　　　　● accompany ⓥ ~와 동반하다

구문 풀이

1행 Whether you are a new or regular visitor, / this is your guide to the family
접속사(~이든 아니든)　　　　　　　　　　　　　　　　~에 대한 안내
activities [coming up at the Basque Museum].
　　　　　↳ 현재분사(있을, 다가오는)

---

29 약점 파악의 중요성　　　　　정답률 59% | 정답 ②

다음 글의 밑줄 친 부분 중, 어법상 틀린 것은? [3점]

Are you honest with yourself / about your strengths and weaknesses?
당신은 스스로에게 솔직한가? / 자신의 강점과 약점에 관해

Get to really know ① yourself / and learn what your weaknesses are.
진정 자신을 알고 / 단점이 무엇인지 파악하라.

Accepting your role in your problems / ✔ means / that you understand the solution lies within you.
문제에 있어 자신의 역할을 받아들이는 것은 / 뜻한다. / 자신 안에 해결책이 있다는 것을 안다는 것

If you have a weakness in a certain area, / get educated / and do ③ what you have to do / to improve things for yourself.
특정 분야에 약점이 있다면, / 교육을 받고 / 해야 할 일을 해라. / 스스로 상황을 나아지게 하기 위해

If your social image is terrible, / look within yourself / and take the necessary steps to improve ④ it, TODAY.
만일 당신의 사회적 이미지가 심히 나쁘다면, / 자신을 들여다보고 / '당장 오늘' 그 이미지를 나아지게 하기 위해 필요한 조치를 취하라.

You have the ability / to choose how to respond to life.
당신은 능력이 있다. / 삶에 어떻게 반응할 것인지를 선택할

Decide today to end all the excuses, / and stop ⑤ lying to yourself / about what is going on.
오늘 모든 변명을 끝내기로 결심하고 / 스스로에게 거짓말하는 일을 관둬라. / 상황이 어떻게 돌아가는가에 대해

The beginning of growth comes / when you begin to personally accept responsibility for your choices.
성장의 시작은 온다. / 당신이 선택에 대한 책임을 직접 지기 시작할 때

자신의 강점 및 약점에 관해 스스로에게 솔직한가? 진정 자신을 알고 단점이 무엇인지 파악하라. 문제에 있어 자신의 역할을 받아들이는 것은 자신 안에 해결책이 있다는 것을 안다는 뜻이다. 특정 분야에 약점이 있다면, 교육을 받고 스스로 상황을 나아지게 하기 위해 해야 할 일을 해라. 만일 당신의 사회적 이미지가 심히 나쁘다면, 자신을 들여다보고 '당장 오늘' 그

이미지를 나아지게 하기 위해 필요한 조치를 취하라. 당신은 삶에 어떻게 반응할 것인지를 선택할 능력이 있다. 오늘 모든 변명을 끝내기로 결심하고 상황이 어떻게 돌아가는가에 대해 스스로에게 거짓말하는 일을 관둬라. 성장의 시작은 당신이 선택에 대한 책임을 직접 지기 시작할 때 온다.

Why? 왜 정답일까?

주어가 동명사구인 'Accepting ~'이므로 동사는 단수로 써야 하고, 이에 따라 복수동사인 mean을 means로 바꾸어야 한다. 어법상 틀린 것은 ②이다.

Why? 왜 오답일까?

① 명령문에서 동사원형 앞에 생략된 주어는 You이다. 따라서 명령문의 목적어로 you가 나오면 반드시 재귀대명사인 yourself로 쓴다.
③ 앞에 선행사가 없고 뒤에 'have to do'의 목적어가 없는 불완전한 절이 나오므로 관계대명사 what을 쓴 것은 적절하다.
④ 맥락상 대명사가 'social image'라는 단수 명사를 받으므로 it을 쓴 것은 적절하다.
⑤ 타동사 stop은 동명사 목적어와 함께 쓰일 때 '~하기를 관두다, 멈추다'라는 뜻이다. 'stop + to부정사(~하기 위해 멈추다)'와 구별해 둔다.

- strength ⓝ 강점
- accept ⓥ 받아들이다, 수용하다
- certain ⓐ 특정한
- social ⓐ 사회의, 사회적인
- respond to ~에 응답하다
- growth ⓝ 성장
- responsibility ⓝ 책임
- weakness ⓝ 약점
- role ⓝ 역할
- improve ⓥ 나아지게 하다, 향상시키다
- necessary ⓐ 필요한
- excuse ⓝ 변명
- personally [ad] 직접, 개인적으로

구문 풀이

3행 Accepting your role in your problems means that you understand the
주어(동명사) / 동사(단수) / 접속사 / (접속사 that 생략)
solution lies within you.
자동사(~에 있다)

---

30 합리적인 선택에 혼란을 주는 선택 항목 과잉   정답률 57% | 정답 ④

다음 글의 밑줄 친 부분 중, 문맥상 낱말의 쓰임이 적절하지 <u>않은</u> 것은?

The overabundance of options in today's marketplace / gives you more freedom of choice.
오늘날 시장에서 선택 항목의 과잉은 / 여러분에게 더 많은 선택의 자유를 준다.
However, / there may be a price to pay / in terms of happiness.
그러나 / 치러야 할 대가가 있을 것이다. / 행복의 관점에서
According to research / by psychologists David Myers and Robert Lane, / all this choice often makes people ① depressed.
연구에 따르면 / 심리학자 David Myers와 Robert Lane의 / 모든 이런 선택은 자주 사람들을 우울하게 만든다.
Researchers gave some shoppers 24 choices of jams to taste / and others only 6 choices.
연구자들은 일부 쇼핑객들에게는 맛볼 24개의 잼을 주었고 / 다른 사람들에게는 단 6개만 맛볼 것을 주었다.
Those who had ② fewer choices / were happier with the tasting.
더 적은 선택 항목을 가진 사람들이 / 맛볼 때 더 행복해했다.
Even more surprisingly, / the ones with a smaller selection / purchased jam 31% of the time, / while those with a wider range of choices / only purchased jam 3% of the time.
훨씬 더 놀랍게도, / 더 적은 선택 사항을 가진 사람들 중에서는 / 그 당시 31%가 잼을 구매했고, / 더 넓은 범위의 선택 사항을 가진 사람들 중 / 당시 3%만이 잼을 구매한 반면
The ironic thing about this is / that people nearly always say / they want ③ more choices.
이에 관해 아이러니한 점은 / 사람들이 거의 항상 말한다는 것이다. / 더 많은 선택 항목을 원한다고
Yet, the more options they have, / the more ✔ paralyzed they become.
그러나 더 많은 선택 항목을 가질수록 / 그들은 더 마비된다.
Savvy restaurant owners provide fewer choices.
사리에 밝은 레스토랑 사장들은 더 적은 선택 항목을 제공한다.
This allows customers to feel more relaxed, / ⑤ prompting them to choose easily / and leave more satisfied with their choices.
이는 고객들이 더 편안함을 느끼게 하고, / 그들이 쉽게 고르도록 촉진한다. / 그리고 자신의 선택에 더 만족한 상태로 남도록

오늘날 시장에서 선택 항목의 과잉은 더 많은 선택의 자유를 준다. 그러나 행복의 관점에서 치러야 할 대가가 있을 것이다. 심리학자 David Myers와 Robert Lane의 연구에 따르면 모든 이런 선택은 자주 사람들을 ① 우울하게 만든다. 연구자들은 일부 쇼핑객들에게는 24개의 잼을 맛보게 했고 다른 사람들에게는 단 6개만 맛보게 했다. ② 더 적은 선택 항목을 가진 사람들이 맛볼 때 더 행복해했다. 훨씬 더 놀랍게도, 더 넓은 범위의 선택 사항을 가진 사람들 중 오직 당시 3%만이 잼을 구매한 반면, 더 적은 선택 사항을 가진 사람들 중에서는 그 당시 31%가 잼을 구매했다. 아이러니한 점은 사람들이 거의 항상 ③ 더 많은 선택 항목을 원한다고 말한다는 것이다. 그러나 더 많은 선택 항목을 가질수록 그들은 더 ④ 안도한다(→ 마비된다). 사리에 밝은 레스토랑 사장들은 더 적은 선택 항목을 제공한다. 이는 고객들이 더 편안함을 느끼게 하고, 그들이 쉽게 고르고 선택에 더 만족하도록 ⑤ 촉진한다.

Why? 왜 정답일까?

'The overabundance of options in today's marketplace gives you more freedom of choice. However, there may be a price to pay in terms of happiness.'에서 선택 항목이 많은 것은 자유를 주는 반면 행복의 측면에서는 대가를 치르게 한다고 말하므로, ④의 경우처럼 더 많은 선택 항목을 가진 사람들은 '안도'와는 반대로 paralyzed(마비된, 불안한)한 기분을 느끼게 될 것이다. 따라서 문맥상 적절하지 않은 어휘는 ④이다.

- overabundance ⓝ 과잉, 지나치게 풍부함
- depressed ⓐ 우울한
- surprisingly [ad] 놀랍게도
- relieved ⓐ 안도한
- prompt ⓥ 촉진하다
- in terms of ~의 관점에서
- researcher ⓝ 연구자
- purchase ⓥ 구매하다
- savvy ⓐ 사리에 밝은
- satisfied ⓐ 만족한

구문 풀이

10행 The ironic thing about this is [that people nearly always say they want
주어 / 동사 / 접속사(~것) / (접속사 that 생략)
more choices].

[문제편 p.187]

★★★ 등급을 가르는 문제!

31 창의력의 위기   정답률 31% | 정답 ①

다음 빈칸에 들어갈 말로 가장 적절한 것을 고르시오. [3점]

✔ unrivaled - 경쟁할 상대가 없다   ② learned - 학습되지   ③ universal - 보편적이지
④ ignored - 무시되지   ⑤ challenged - 도전받지

Creativity is a skill / we usually consider uniquely human.
창의력은 능력이다. / 우리가 일반적으로 인간만이 고유하게 가지고 있다고 간주하는
For all of human history, / we have been the most creative beings on Earth.
인류 역사를 통틀어, / 우리는 지구상에서 가장 창의적인 존재였다.
Birds can make their nests, / ants can make their hills, / but no other species on Earth / comes close to the level of creativity / we humans display.
새는 둥지를 틀 수 있고, / 개미는 개미탑을 쌓을 수 있지만, / 지구상의 어떤 다른 종도 / 창의력 수준에 가까이 도달하지는 못한다. / 우리 인간이 보여주는
However, just in the last decade / we have acquired the ability / to do amazing things with computers, / like developing robots.
하지만, 불과 지난 10년 만에 / 우리는 능력을 습득하였다. / 컴퓨터로 놀라운 것을 할 수 있는 / 로봇 개발처럼
With the artificial intelligence boom of the 2010s, / computers can now recognize faces, / translate languages, / take calls for you, / write poems, / and beat players / at the world's most complicated board game, / to name a few things.
2010년대의 인공 지능의 급속한 발전으로 / 컴퓨터는, 이제 얼굴을 인식하고, / 언어를 번역하고, / 여러분을 대신해 전화를 받고, / 시를 쓸 수 있고 / 선수들을 이길 수 있다 / 세계에서 가장 복잡한 보드게임에서 / 몇 가지를 언급하자면
All of a sudden, / we must face the possibility / that our ability to be creative is not unrivaled.
갑작스럽게, / 우리는 가능성에 직면해야 할 것이다. / 우리의 창의력이 경쟁할 상대가 없지 않게 되는

창의력은 우리가 일반적으로 인간만이 고유하게 가지고 있다고 간주하는 능력이다. 인류 역사를 통틀어, 우리는 지구상에서 가장 창의적인 존재였다. 새는 둥지를 틀 수 있고, 개미는 개미탑을 쌓을 수 있지만, 지구상의 어떤 다른 종도 우리 인간이 보여주는 창의력 수준에 가까이 도달하지는 못한다. 하지만, 불과 지난 10년 만에 우리는 로봇 개발처럼 컴퓨터로 놀라운 것을 할 수 있는 능력을 습득하였다. 2010년대의 인공 지능의 급속한 발전으로 컴퓨터는, 몇 가지를 언급하자면, 이제 얼굴을 인식하고, 언어를 번역하고, 여러분을 대신해 전화를 받고, 시를 쓸 수 있으며 세계에서 가장 복잡한 보드게임에서 선수들을 이길 수 있다. 갑작스럽게, 우리는 우리의 창의력이 경쟁할 상대가 없지 않게 되는 가능성에 직면해야 할 것이다.

Why? 왜 정답일까?

빈칸 앞의 문장에서 컴퓨터는 얼굴 인식, 언어 번역, 전화 응대, 시 창작, 보드게임 경기 등 기존에 인간만의 영역으로 여겨졌던 다양한 활동을 할 수 있게 되었다고 언급하는 것으로 보아, 빈칸이 포함된 문장은 그간 인간만의 능력으로 간주되어 왔던 창의력도 컴퓨터의 능력에 포함될지도 모른다는 의미를 나타내야 한다. 따라서 빈칸에 들어갈 말로 가장 적절한 것은 ① '경쟁할 상대가 없지'이다.

- creativity ⓝ 창조성, 독창성
- nest ⓝ 둥지
- display ⓥ 드러내다, 내보이다
- translate ⓥ 번역하다
- complicated ⓐ 복잡한
- face ⓥ 직면하다
- universal ⓐ 일반적인, 보편적인
- uniquely [ad] 고유하게
- come close to ~에 근접하다
- artificial intelligence 인공 지능
- poem ⓝ 시
- to name a few things 몇 가지만 보더라도
- unrivaled ⓐ 경쟁할 상대가 없는

구문 풀이

3행 Birds can make their nests, ants can make their hills, but no other species
부정 주어
on Earth comes close to the level of creativity [(that) we humans display].
동사(단수) / 생략(목적격 관계대명사)
10행 All of a sudden, we must face the possibility [that our ability to be creative
타동사 / 목적어 / 동격 접속사 / 형용사적 용법
is not unrivaled].

★★ 문제 해결 꿀~팁 ★★

▶ 많이 틀린 이유는?
빈칸에 직접 대응시킬 주제문이 없고 추상적인 내용을 다루어 까다로운 지문이다. 최다 오답인 ④는 인공 지능의 발달로 인해 인간의 창의력이 '무시되지' 않을 가능성이 있다는 뜻인데, 이 글은 컴퓨터가 인간의 창의력을 따라잡을 수도 있다는 내용을 주로 다루고 있어 주제와 무관한 선택지이다. ⑤는 주제와 상충한다.

▶ 문제 해결 방법은?
글 중간에 역접의 연결어가 나오므로 전반부보다는 후반부에 무게를 실어 독해한다. 특히 빈칸이 마지막 문장에 있으므로 바로 앞의 예문을 읽고 이를 토대로 일반화된 결론을 추론해야 한다.

---

32 Minor County의 소비 지역화 운동   정답률 69% | 정답 ②

다음 빈칸에 들어갈 말로 가장 적절한 것을 고르시오. [3점]

① work out regularly - 규칙적으로 운동하도록
✔ spend money locally - 그 지역에서 돈을 쓰도록
③ drive their cars safely - 차를 안전하게 운전하도록
④ treat strangers nicely - 낯선 사람을 친절하게 대하도록
⑤ share work equally - 일을 똑같이 나누도록

In 1995, / a group of high school students in Miner County, South Dakota, / started planning a revival.
1995년, / South Dakota 주 Miner County에 사는 한 무리의 고교생들이 / 부흥을 계획하기 시작했다.
They wanted to do something / that might revive their dying community.
그들은 무언가를 하고 싶었다. / 죽어가는 자기네 지역 사회를 되살릴 수 있는
Miner County had been failing for decades.
Miner County는 몇 십 년 간 침체되고 있었다.
Farm and industrial jobs had slowly dried up, / and nothing had replaced them.
농장 및 산업 일자리가 천천히 줄어들었고 / 이를 대체하는 것은 없었다.
The students started investigating the situation.

학생들은 상황을 조사하기 시작했다.
One finding in particular disturbed them.
특히 한 가지 결과가 그들의 마음을 불편하게 했다.
They discovered / that half of the residents had been shopping outside the county, / driving an hour to Sioux Falls / to shop in larger stores.
그들은 알아냈다. / 주민의 절반이 자기들 지역 바깥에서 쇼핑을 해 오고 있었다는 것을 / Sioux Falls로 한 시간을 운전해 가서, / 더 큰 가게에서 장을 보려고
Most of the things / that could improve the situation / were out of the students' control.
대부분의 일들이 / 상황을 나아지게 할 수 있는 / 학생들의 통제력을 벗어나 있었다.
But they did uncover one thing / that was very much in their control: / inviting the residents to spend money locally.
하지만 그들은 한 가지 것을 진정 알아냈는데, / 자신들이 아주 많이 통제할 수 있는 / 주민들이 그 지역에서 돈을 쓰도록 요청하는 것이었다.
They found their first slogan: / Let's keep Miner dollars in Miner County.
그들은 첫 번째 표어를 찾았다. / Miner의 돈은 Miner County 안에 두자.

1995년, South Dakota 주 Miner County에 사는 한 무리의 고교생들이 부흥을 계획하기 시작했다. 그들은 죽어가는 자기네 지역 사회를 되살릴 수 있는 무언가를 하고 싶었다. Miner County는 몇 십 년 간 침체되고 있었다. 농장 및 산업 일자리가 천천히 줄어들었고 이를 대체하는 것은 없었다. 학생들은 상황을 조사하기 시작했다. 특히 한 가지 결과가 그들의 마음을 불편하게 했다. 그들은 주민의 절반이 더 큰 가게에서 장을 보려고 Sioux Falls로 한 시간을 운전해 가서, 자기들 지역 바깥에서 쇼핑을 해 오고 있었다는 것을 알아냈다. 상황을 나아지게 할 수 있는 대부분의 일들이 학생들의 통제력을 벗어나 있었다. 하지만 그들은 자신들이 통제할 수 있는 한 가지 것을 진정 알아냈는데, 주민들이 그 지역에서 돈을 쓰도록 요청하는 것이었다. 그들은 첫 번째 표어를 찾았다. (그것은) Miner의 돈은 Miner County 안에 두자(였다).

Why? 왜 정답일까?
글 중간에서 마을의 침체 이유를 조사한 결과 학생들은 주민들이 외부 지역에서 쇼핑을 하는 것이 문제임을 파악했다고 하는데, 이를 해결하기 위한 대책은 마지막 문장의 표어 내용대로 사람들이 지역 내부에서 돈을 쓰도록 하는 것(Let's keep Miner dollars in Miner County.)이었다. 따라서 빈칸에 들어갈 말로 가장 적절한 것은 ② '그 지역에서 돈을 쓰도록'이다.

- revival ⓝ 부흥, 부활, 회복
- industrial ⓐ 산업의
- replace ⓥ 대체하다
- in particular 특히
- out of control 통제력을 벗어난
- invite ⓥ 부탁하다, 요청하다
- dying ⓐ 죽어가는
- dry up 줄어들다, 고갈되다, 말라붙다
- investigate ⓥ 조사하다, 수사하다
- disturb ⓥ (마음을) 불편하게 하다, 방해하다
- uncover ⓥ 알아내다, 적발하다
- slogan ⓝ 표어, 슬로건

구문 풀이

6행 They discovered that half of the residents had been shopping outside the county, / driving an hour to Sioux Falls to shop in larger stores.
접속사 / 동사(과거완료 진행) / 분사구문(~하면서)

---

33 고요와 정적에서 비롯되는 창작   정답률 49% | 정답 ③

다음 빈칸에 들어갈 말로 가장 적절한 것을 고르시오.
① organize their ideas – 생각을 정리하는
② interact socially – 사회적으로 상호 작용하는
✓③ stop thinking – 생각을 멈추는
④ gather information – 정보를 모으는
⑤ use their imagination – 상상력을 활용하는

The mind is essentially a survival machine.
생각은 본질적으로 생존 기계이다.
Attack and defense against other minds, / gathering, storing, and analyzing information / — this is what it is good at, / but it is not at all creative.
다른 생각에 대해 공격하고 수비하는 것 / 정보를 수집하고 저장하고 분석하며 / 이것은 생각이 잘 하는 것이지만, / 전혀 창의적이지는 않다.
All true artists create / from a place of no-mind, / from inner stillness.
모든 진정한 예술가들은 창작을 한다. / 생각이 없는 상태, / 즉 내적인 고요함 속에서
Even great scientists have reported / that their creative breakthroughs / came at a time of mental quietude.
심지어 위대한 과학자들조차도 말했다. / 그들의 창의적인 돌파구는 / 정신적 정적의 시간에서 생겨났다고
The surprising result of a nationwide inquiry / among America's most famous mathematicians, including Einstein, / to find out their working methods, / was that thinking "plays only a subordinate part / in the brief, decisive phase of the creative act itself."
전국적인 조사의 놀라운 결과는 / 아인슈타인을 포함한 미국의 가장 유명한 수학자들을 대상으로 / 그들의 작업 방식을 알아내기 위한 / 생각이 단지 부수적인 역할만 할 뿐이다."라는 것이었다. / "창의적인 행동의 짧고 결정적인 단계에서"
So I would say / that the simple reason / why the majority of scientists are *not* creative / is not because they don't know how to think, / but because they don't know how to stop thinking!
그래서 나는 말하고 싶다. / 단순한 이유는 / 대다수의 과학자들이 창의적이지 *않은* / 그들이 생각하는 방법을 몰라서가 아니라 / 생각을 멈추는 방법을 모르기 때문이라고

생각은 본질적으로 생존 기계이다. 정보를 수집하고 저장하고 분석하며 다른 생각에 대해 공격하고 수비하는 것 — 이것은 생각이 잘 하는 것이지만, 전혀 창의적이지는 않다. 모든 진정한 예술가들은 생각이 없는 상태, 즉 내적인 고요함 속에서 창작을 한다. 심지어 위대한 과학자들조차도 그들의 창의적인 돌파구는 정신적 정적의 시간에서 생겨났다고 말했다. 아인슈타인을 포함한 미국의 가장 유명한 수학자들을 대상으로 그들의 작업 방식을 알아내기 위한 전국적인 조사의 놀라운 결과는 생각이 "창의적인 행동의 짧고 결정적인 단계에서 단지 부수적인 역할만 할 뿐이다."라는 것이었다. 그래서 나는 대다수의 과학자들이 창의적이지 않은 단순한 이유는 그들이 생각하는 방법을 몰라서가 아니라 생각을 멈추는 방법을 모르기 때문이라고 말하고 싶다.

Why? 왜 정답일까?
'All true artists create from a place of no-mind, from inner stillness. Even great scientists have reported that their creative breakthroughs came at a time of mental quietude.'에서 예술가와 과학자 모두 내적인 고요함 또는 마음의 정적 속에서 창작을 하고 창의적인 돌파구를 찾는다고 이야기하므로, 빈칸 또한 '고요, 정적'과 같은 의미를 나타내야 한다. 따라서 빈

칸에 들어갈 말로 가장 적절한 것은 ③ '생각을 멈추는'이다.

- essentially ⓐ 본질적으로
- gather ⓥ 모으다, 수집하다
- analyze ⓥ 분석하다
- breakthrough ⓝ 돌파구
- inquiry ⓝ 조사, 연구
- brief ⓐ 짧은
- phase ⓝ 단계
- organize ⓥ 정리하다, 체계화하다
- imagination ⓝ 상상력
- defense ⓝ 방어
- storing ⓝ 저장
- stillness ⓝ 고요함
- nationwide ⓐ 전국적인
- method ⓝ 방법
- decisive ⓐ 결정적인
- majority ⓝ 다수, 대부분
- socially ⓐ 사회적으로

구문 풀이

10행 So I would say that the simple reason [why the majority of scientists are *not* creative] is not because they don't know how to think, but because they don't know how to stop thinking.
접속사 / 주어 / 동사 / 'not + A + but + B : A가 아니라 B'

★★★ 등급을 가르는 문제!
34 오늘날 마케팅 산업의 과제   정답률 45% | 정답 ⑤

다음 빈칸에 들어갈 말로 가장 적절한 것을 고르시오. [3점]
① guide people to be wise consumers – 사람들이 현명한 소비자가 되도록 인도하는가
② reduce the cost of television advertising – 텔레비전 광고의 비용을 줄이는가
③ keep a close eye on the quality of products – 제품의 품질에 주의를 주시하는가
④ make it possible to deliver any goods any time – 언제든 어떤 재화를 배달하는 것을 가능하게 하는가
✓⑤ win the battle for broadcast advertising exposure – 방송 광고 노출 전쟁에서 승리하는가

One real concern in the marketing industry today is / how to win the battle for broadcast advertising exposure / in the age of the remote control and mobile devices.
오늘날 마케팅 산업에서 한 가지 실질적인 관심사는 / 어떻게 방송 광고 노출 전쟁에서 승리하는가이다. / 리모컨과 휴대 장비의 시대에
With the growing popularity of digital video recorders, / consumers can mute, / fast-forward, / and skip over commercials entirely.
디지털 영상 녹화기의 인기가 증가하면서 / 소비자들은 광고의 소리를 줄이거나, / 광고를 빨리 감거나, / 아예 건너뛰어 버릴 수 있다.
Some advertisers are trying to adapt to these technologies, / by planting hidden coupons / in frames of their television commercials.
일부 광고주들은 이러한 기술에 적응하려고 노력 중이다. / 숨겨진 쿠폰을 심어두어 / 텔레비전 광고 프레임 속에
Others are desperately trying / to make their advertisements more interesting and entertaining / to discourage viewers from skipping their ads; / still others are simply giving up on television advertising altogether.
다른 광고주들은 절박하게 노력 중이고, / 광고를 더 흥미롭고 재미있게 만들기 위해 / 시청자들이 광고를 건너뛰지 못하게 하기 위해 / 또 다른 광고주들은 완전히 텔레비전 광고를 포기해 버린다.
Some industry experts predict / that cable providers and advertisers / will eventually be forced to provide incentives / in order to encourage consumers to watch their messages.
몇몇 산업 전문가들은 예측한다. / 케이블 공급자와 광고주들이 / 결국에는 어쩔 수 없이 인센티브를 제공하게 될 것이라고 / 그들의 메시지를 소비자들이 보게 하기 위해서
These incentives may come / in the form of coupons, / or a reduction in the cable bill / for each advertisement watched.
이러한 인센티브는 나타날 것이다. / 쿠폰의 형태로 / 또는 케이블 요금의 절감 형태로 / 시청되는 매 광고마다

오늘날 마케팅 산업에서 한 가지 실질적인 관심사는 리모컨과 휴대 장비의 시대에 어떻게 방송 광고 노출 전쟁에서 승리하는가이다. 디지털 영상 녹화기의 인기가 증가하면서 소비자들은 광고의 소리를 줄이거나, 광고를 빨리 감거나, 아예 건너뛰어 버릴 수 있다. 일부 광고주들은 텔레비전 광고 프레임 속에 숨겨진 쿠폰을 심어두어 이러한 기술에 적응하려고 노력 중이다. 다른 광고주들은 시청자들이 광고를 건너뛰지 못하게 하기 위해 광고를 더 흥미롭고 재미있게 만들기 위해 절박하게 노력 중이고, 또 다른 광고주들은 완전히 텔레비전 광고를 포기해 버린다. 몇몇 산업 전문가들은 케이블 공급자와 광고주들이 결국에는 그들의 메시지를 소비자들이 보게 하기 위해서 어쩔 수 없이 인센티브를 제공하게 될 것이라 예측한다. 이러한 인센티브는 쿠폰, 또는 광고를 한 번 볼 때마다 케이블 요금을 절감해주는 형태로 나타날 것이다.

Why? 왜 정답일까?
빈칸 뒤의 문장에 따르면 오늘날 디지털 영상 녹화기의 인기가 증가하면서 사람들은 원하는 대로 광고의 소리를 줄이거나, 광고를 빨리 감거나, 아예 건너뛸 수 있게 되었는데, 이 때문에 광고주들은 쿠폰을 심어두거나 광고를 더 재미있게 만드는 등의 노력을 기울여 소비자로 하여금 광고를 보게 하려고 한다(Some advertisers are trying to adapt to these technologies, by planting hidden coupons in frames of their television commercials. Others are desperately trying to make their advertisements more interesting and entertaining to discourage viewers from skipping their ads;). 따라서 빈칸에 들어갈 말로 가장 적절한 것은 이러한 노력의 목적을 적절하게 요약한 ⑤ '방송 광고 노출 전쟁에서 승리하는가'이다.

- concern ⓝ 관심사, 걱정
- remote ⓐ 원격의
- mute ⓥ ~의 소리를 줄이다
- commercial ⓝ 광고 ⓐ 상업의
- advertiser ⓝ 광고주
- plant ⓥ 놓다, 두다
- entertaining ⓐ 재미있는, 즐거움을 주는
- altogether ⓐ 아예, 완전히
- eventually ⓐ 결국
- in the form of ~의 형태로
- industry ⓝ 산업
- popularity ⓝ 인기
- skip over ~을 건너뛰다, ~을 묵과하다
- entirely ⓐ 아예, 전부, 전적으로
- adapt to ~에 적응하다
- desperately ⓐ 절박하게, 간절하게
- give up on ~을 포기하다
- predict ⓥ 예측하다
- incentive ⓝ 장려책

구문 풀이

7행 Others are desperately trying to make their advertisements more interesting and entertaining to discourage viewers from skipping their ads; / still others are simply giving up on television advertising altogether.
'try to + 동사원형 : ~하려고 노력하다' / 목적어 / 목적격 보어 / 부사적 용법(~하기 위해) / 'discourage A from + 동명사 : A가 ~하지 못하게 하다' / ~을 포기하다

▶ 많이 틀린 이유는?

본문 중 그대로 빈칸에 대응될 말이 없고, 예시를 읽고 요약하여야 한다는 점에서 어려운 문제였다. 최다 오답인 ②는 '광고주의 비용 절감'을 언급하는데, 이는 지문 마지막 부분에서 광고주들이 소비자로 하여금 광고를 계속 보게 하기 위해서 '케이블 비용을 깎아준다'는 내용을 잘못 이해한 것이다. 이는 광고주 입장에서의 비용 절감이라기보다는 소비자 입장에서 누리는 혜택이라고 볼 수 있다.

▶ 문제 해결 방법은?

흔히 예시는 주제문을 잘 이해한 경우라면 건너뛰어도 무방할 때가 많지만 이 문제는 유일한 주제에 빈칸이 있고 나머지가 예시이기 때문에 예문들을 잘 읽어야 한다. 본격적으로 광고주에 대한 세부 내용을 말하는 'Some advisers ~. Others ~' 부분을 읽어 적절히 요약한 말을 빈칸에 넣도록 한다.

---

35 맥락에 의미가 좌우되는 단어들 　　　　　정답률 79% | 정답 ③

다음 글에서 전체 흐름과 관계 없는 문장은?

Words like 'near' and 'far' / can mean different things / depending on where you are / and what you are doing.
'near'과 'far' 같은 단어들은 / 여러 가지를 의미할 수 있다. / 여러분이 어디에 있는지와 무엇을 하고 있는지에 따라

If you were at a zoo, / then you might say you are 'near' an animal / if you could reach out / and touch it through the bars of its cage.
만약 여러분이 동물원에 있다면, / 여러분은 그 동물이 '가까이'에 있다고 말할지도 모른다. / 여러분이 손을 뻗어 / 동물 우리의 창살 사이로 동물을 만질 수 있다면

① Here the word 'near' means an arm's length away.
여기서 'near'이라는 단어는 팔 하나만큼의 길이를 의미한다.

② If you were telling someone / how to get to your local shop, / you might call it 'near' / if it was a five-minute walk away.
여러분이 누군가에게 말해주고 있는 경우 / 동네 가게에 가는 방법을 / 그것을 '가까이'라고 말할 수도 있을 것이다. / 만약 그 거리가 걸어서 5분 거리라면

☑ It seems that you had better walk to the shop / to improve your health.
당신은 그 가게로 걸어가는 것이 좋을 것 같다. / 당신의 건강을 향상시키기 위해

④ Now the word 'near' means much longer / than an arm's length away.
이제 'near'이라는 단어는 훨씬 더 긴 것을 의미한다. / 팔 하나만큼의 길이보다

⑤ Words like 'near', 'far', 'small', 'big', 'hot', and 'cold' / all mean different things / to different people at different times.
'near', 'far', 'small', 'big', 'hot', 그리고 'cold'와 같은 단어들은 / 모두 다른 것을 의미한다. / 다른 때에 다른 사람들에게

'near'과 'far' 같은 단어들은 여러분이 어디에 있는지와 무엇을 하고 있는지에 따라 여러 가지를 의미할 수 있다. 만약 여러분이 동물원에 있고, 동물 우리의 창살 사이로 손을 뻗어 동물을 만질 수 있다면 여러분은 그 동물이 '가까이'에 있다고 말할지도 모른다. ① 여기서 'near'이라는 단어는 팔 하나만큼의 길이를 의미한다. ② 여러분이 누군가에게 동네 가게에 가는 방법을 말해주고 있는 경우 만약 그 거리가 걸어서 5분 거리라면 그것을 '가까이'라고 말할 수도 있을 것이다. ③ 당신은 건강을 향상시키기 위해 그 가게로 걸어가는 것이 더 좋을 것 같다. ④ 이제 'near'이라는 단어는 팔 하나만큼의 길이보다 훨씬 더 긴 것을 의미한다. ⑤ 'near', 'far', 'small', 'big', 'hot', 그리고 'cold'와 같은 단어들은 모두 다른 때에 다른 사람들에게 다른 것을 의미한다.

Why? 왜 정답일까?

첫 문장이 주제문으로, 단어의 의미는 맥락에 따라 좌우될 수 있다는 내용을 제시하고 있다. ①, ②, ④에서 예시와 함께 부연이 이어진 뒤, ⑤는 주제와 같은 결론을 내리며 글을 맺고 있다. 반면 ③은 ②에서 언급된 shop에만 초점을 두어 근거리에 있는 가게는 건강을 위해 걸어 가야 한다는 내용을 다룬다. 따라서 전체 흐름과 관계없는 문장은 ③이다.

● depending on ~에 따라
● arm's length 팔을 뻗으면 닿는 (가까운) 거리
● reach out (잡으려고 손을) 뻗다
● improve ⓥ 개선되다, 나아지다

구문 풀이

2행 If you were at a zoo, / then you might say you are 'near' an animal if you
「if + 주어 + were ~, 주어 + 조동사 과거형 + 동사원형: 가정법 과거」
could reach out and touch it through the bars of its cage.

---

36 작가가 되고 싶었던 Charles Dickens 　　　　　정답률 65% | 정답 ②

주어진 글 다음에 이어질 글의 순서로 가장 적절한 것을 고르시오.

① (A) - (C) - (B) 　　　　☑ (B) - (A) - (C)
③ (B) - (C) - (A) 　　　　④ (C) - (A) - (B)
⑤ (C) - (B) - (A)

In early 19th century London, / a young man named Charles Dickens / had a strong desire to be a writer.
19세기 초반 런던, / Charles Dickens라는 이름의 젊은이는 / 작가가 되려는 강한 열망을 갖고 있었다.

But everything seemed to be against him.
하지만 모든 것이 그에게 불리한 것 같았다.

(B) He had never been able to attend school / for more than four years.
그는 학교에 다닌 적이 없었다. / 4년 이상

His father had been in jail / because he couldn't pay his debts, / and this young man often knew the pain of hunger.
그의 아버지는 감옥에 있었고, / 그가 자기 빚을 갚지 못했기에 / 이 젊은이는 자주 배고픔의 고통을 알았다.

(A) Moreover, / he had so little confidence / in his ability to write / that he mailed his writings secretly at night to editors / so that nobody would laugh at him.
더구나, / 그는 자신감이 너무 없어서 / 자신의 글재주에 / 그는 밤에 몰래 편집자들에게 자신의 글을 우편으로 보냈다. / 그 누구도 자신을 비웃지 못하도록

Story after story was refused.
작품들마다 거절을 당했다.

(C) But one day, / one editor recognized and praised him.
하지만 어느 날, / 한 편집장이 그를 알아보고 칭찬해 주었다.

The praise / that he received from getting one story in print / changed his whole life.
칭찬은 / 하나의 이야기를 출판하여 그가 얻은 / 그의 일생을 바꾸어 놓았다.

His works have been widely read / and still enjoy great popularity.
그의 작품들은 널리 읽히게 되었고 / 여전히 엄청난 인기를 누린다.

19세기 초반 런던, Charles Dickens라는 이름의 젊은이는 작가가 되려는 강한 열망을 갖고 있었다. 하지만 모든 것이 그에게 불리한 것 같았다.

(B) 그는 4년 이상 학교에 다닌 적이 없었다. 그의 아버지는 빚을 갚지 못해 감옥에 있었고, 이 젊은이는 자주 배고픔의 고통을 알았다.

(A) 더구나, 그는 자신의 글재주에 자신감이 너무 없어서 그 누구도 자신을 비웃지 못하도록 밤에 몰래 편집자들에게 자신의 글을 우편으로 보냈다. 작품들마다 거절을 당했다.

(C) 하지만 어느 날, 한 편집장이 그를 알아보고 칭찬해 주었다. 하나의 이야기를 출판하여 그가 얻은 칭찬은 그의 일생을 바꾸어 놓았다. 그의 작품들은 널리 읽히게 되었고 여전히 엄청난 인기를 누린다.

Why? 왜 정답일까?

Charles Dickens는 작가가 되고자 했지만 상황이 그에게 불리했다는 내용의 주어진 글 뒤에는 구체적으로 그의 불리한 조건을 묘사한, 즉 그의 교육 및 가정이 모두 불우했음을 이야기한 (B), 이어서 그가 스스로의 글재주에도 자신 없어 했다는 내용의 (A)가 차례로 나오는 것이 적절하다. '하지만' 결국 그가 작가로서 성공을 거두게 되었다는 내용의 (C)는 마지막에 나오는 것이 자연스럽다. 따라서 주어진 글 다음에 이어질 글의 순서로 가장 적절한 것은 ② '(B) - (A) - (C)'이다.

● desire ⓝ 열망, 갈망
● secretly ⓐⓓ 몰래
● jail ⓝ 교도소
● recognize ⓥ 알아보다, 인정하다
● whole ⓐ 전체의
● confidence ⓝ 자신감, 믿음
● refuse ⓥ 거절하다
● debt ⓝ 빚, 부채
● praise ⓥ 칭찬하다
● widely ⓐⓓ 널리

구문 풀이

4행 Moreover, / he had so little confidence in his ability to write that he mailed
접속부사(첨가)　　　　　　「so + 형용사 + 　　　　　that + 주어 + 동사 : 너무 ~해서 …하다」
his writings secretly at night to editors / so that nobody would laugh at him.
　　　　　　　　　　～하도록　　　　　　　　　　　～을 비웃다

---

37 패턴을 찾는 인간의 특성 　　　　　정답률 50% | 정답 ②

주어진 글 다음에 이어질 글의 순서로 가장 적절한 것을 고르시오. [3점]

① (A) - (C) - (B) 　　　　☑ (B) - (A) - (C)
③ (B) - (C) - (A) 　　　　④ (C) - (A) - (B)
⑤ (C) - (B) - (A)

The next time you're out under a clear, dark sky, / look up.
다음에 여러분이 맑고 어두운 하늘 아래에 있을 때 / 위를 올려다보아라.

If you've picked a good spot for stargazing, / you'll see a sky full of stars, / shining and twinkling / like thousands of brilliant jewels.
만약 여러분이 별을 보기에 좋은 장소를 골랐다면, / 여러분은 별로 가득한 하늘을 보게 될 것이다. / 빛나고 반짝거리는 / 수천 개의 광채가 나는 보석처럼

(B) But this amazing sight of stars / can also be confusing.
하지만 이 놀라운 별들의 광경은 / 또한 혼란스러울 수도 있다.

Try and point out a single star to someone.
어떤 사람에게 별 하나를 가리켜 보라.

Chances are, that person will have a hard time / knowing exactly which star you're looking at.
아마 그 사람은 어려울 것이다. / 여러분이 어떤 별을 보고 있는지를 정확히 알기

(A) It might be easier / if you describe patterns of stars.
그것은 더 쉬워질 수도 있다. / 만약 여러분이 별의 패턴을 묘사한다면

You could say something like, / "See that big triangle of bright stars there?"
여러분은 말을 할 수 있을 것이다. / "저기 큰 삼각형을 이루는 밝은 별들이 보이세요?"와 같은

Or, "Do you see those five stars / that look like a big letter W?"
혹은, "저 다섯 개의 별이 보이세요? / 대문자 W처럼 보이는"

(C) When you do that, / you're doing exactly what we all do / when we look at the stars.
여러분이 그렇게 하면, / 여러분은 우리 모두가 하는 것을 정확하게 하고 있는 것이다. / 우리가 별을 바라볼 때

We look for patterns, / not just so that we can point something out to someone else, / but also because that's what we humans have always done.
우리는 패턴을 찾는다. / 다른 사람에게 어떤 것을 가리켜 보여주기 위해서뿐만 아니라, / 그렇게 하는 것이 우리 인간이 항상 해왔던 것이기도 하기 때문에

다음에 여러분이 맑고 어두운 하늘 아래에 있을 때 위를 올려다보아라. 만약 여러분이 별을 보기에 좋은 장소를 골랐다면, 수천 개의 광채가 나는 보석처럼 빛나고 반짝거리는 별로 가득한 하늘을 보게 될 것이다.

(B) 하지만 이 놀라운 별들의 광경은 또한 혼란스러울 수도 있다. 어떤 사람에게 별 하나를 가리켜 보라. 아마 그 사람은 여러분이 어떤 별을 보고 있는지를 정확하게 알기 어려울 것이다.

(A) 만약 여러분이 별의 패턴을 묘사한다면 그것은 더 쉬워질 수도 있다. "저기 큰 삼각형을 이루는 밝은 별들이 보이세요?"와 같은 말을 할 수 있을 것이다. 혹은, "대문자 W처럼 보이는 저 다섯 개의 별이 보이세요?"라고 말할 수도 있을 것이다.

(C) 여러분이 그렇게 하면, 여러분은 우리가 별을 바라볼 때 우리 모두가 하는 것을 정확하게 하고 있는 것이다. 우리는 다른 사람에게 어떤 것을 가리켜 보여주기 위해서뿐만 아니라, 그렇게 하는 것이 우리 인간이 항상 해왔던 것이기도 하기 때문에 패턴을 찾는다.

Why? 왜 정답일까?

밤하늘 가득한 별을 바라보는 내용으로 시작하는 주어진 글 뒤에는, 어떤 사람에게 별 하나를 가리킨다면 정확히 어떤 별인지 파악하기 어려워할 것이라는 내용의 (B), 이때 별의 일정한 패턴을 묘사해주면 이해를 도울 수 있다는 내용의 (A), 이렇듯 패턴을 찾는 것이 인간 행동의 특징이라는 결론을 내리는 (C)가 차례로 이어지는 것이 자연스럽다. 따라서 글의 순서로 가장 적절한 것은 ② '(B) - (A) - (C)'이다.

● spot ⓝ 특정한 곳
● twinkle ⓥ 반짝거리다
● describe ⓥ 묘사하다
● stargazing ⓝ 별 보기
● brilliant ⓐ 눈부신, 훌륭한
● amazing ⓐ 놀라운

02회

- **sight** ⓝ 보기, 봄
- **point out** 가리키다
- **exactly** ⓐⓓ 정확히
- **confuse** ⓥ 혼란시키다, 혼란스럽게 만들다
- **chances are that** ~할 가능성이 있다

구문 풀이

> **9행** Chances are, that person will have a hard time knowing exactly which
> ~할 가능성이 있다   'have a hard time +동명사 : ~하는 데 어려움이 있다'
> star you're looking at.   의문형용사(어떤)

★★★ 등급을 가르는 문제!

38 어린이와 함께 음악을 즐기는 것   정답률 40% | 정답 ④

글의 흐름으로 보아, 주어진 문장이 들어가기에 가장 적절한 곳을 고르시오.

Music appeals powerfully to young children.
음악은 어린 아이들에게 강력하게 어필한다.

① Watch preschoolers' faces and bodies / when they hear rhythm and sound / — they light up and move eagerly and enthusiastically.
미취학 어린이들의 얼굴과 몸을 살펴보아라. / 그들이 리듬과 소리를 들을 때 / 그들은 밝아지고 열렬히 열정적으로 움직인다.

② They communicate comfortably, / express themselves creatively, / and let out all sorts of thoughts and emotions / as they interact with music.
그들은 편안하게 의사소통하고, / 창의적으로 자신을 표현하고, / 모든 생각과 감정을 분출해 낸다. / 그들이 음악과 상호작용하면서

③ In a word, / young children think / music is a lot of fun, / so do all you can / to make the most of the situation.
한마디로, / 어린 아이들은 생각하므로, / 음악이 아주 재미있다고 / 당신이 할 수 있는 모든 것을 하라. / 이 상황을 최대로 활용하기 위해

✔ Throw away your own hesitation / and forget all your concerns / about whether you are musically talented / or whether you can sing or play an instrument.
망설임을 버리고 / 걱정을 모두 잊어라. / 당신이 음악적으로 재능이 있는가 / 혹은 노래를 하거나 악기를 연주할 수 있는가에 대한

They don't matter / when you are enjoying music with your child.
그것들은 중요하지 않다. / 당신이 아이와 함께 음악을 즐길 때

⑤ Just follow his or her lead, / have fun, / sing songs together, / listen to different kinds of music, / move, dance, and enjoy.
그저 아이의 리드를 따라가며, / 즐기고, / 함께 노래하고, / 다양한 종류의 음악을 들으며, / 움직이고 춤추고 즐겨라.

음악은 어린 아이들에게 강력하게 어필한다. ① 미취학 어린이들이 리듬과 소리를 들을 때 그들의 얼굴과 몸을 살펴보아라. 밝아지고 열렬히 열정적으로 움직인다. ② 음악과 상호작용하면서 그들은 편안하게 의사소통하고, 창의적으로 자신을 표현하고, 모든 생각과 감정을 분출해 낸다. ③ 한마디로, 어린 아이들은 음악이 아주 재미있다고 생각하므로, 이 상황을 최대로 활용하기 위해 당신이 할 수 있는 모든 것을 하라. ④ 망설임을 버리고 당신이 음악적으로 재능이 있는가 혹은 노래를 하거나 악기를 연주할 수 있는가에 대한 걱정을 모두 잊어라. 그것들은 당신이 아이와 함께 음악을 즐길 때 중요하지 않다. ⑤ 그저 아이의 리드를 따라가며, 즐기고, 함께 노래하고, 다양한 종류의 음악을 들으며, 움직이고 춤추고 즐겨라.

Why? 왜 정답일까?

④ 앞의 문장에서 언급한 'all you can'에 대한 예시가 주어진 문장에서 제시되고 있다. 또한 ④ 뒤의 문장에서는 주어진 문장에서 예로 든 다양한 '걱정'을 They로 받으며 이것들이 아이들과 음악을 즐길 때 그다지 중요하지 않다는 점을 언급한다. 따라서 주어진 문장이 들어가기에 가장 적절한 곳은 ④이다.

- **hesitation** ⓝ 망설임, 주저함
- **appeal to** ~에 어필하다, ~에 호소하다
- **light up** (안색이) 밝아지다
- **enthusiastically** ⓐⓓ 열정적으로
- **comfortably** ⓐⓓ 편안하게
- **creatively** ⓐⓓ 창의적으로
- **make the most of** ~을 최대한 활용하다
- **talented** ⓐ 재능이 있는
- **preschooler** ⓝ 미취학 아동
- **eagerly** ⓐⓓ 열렬히
- **communicate** ⓥ 의사소통하다
- **express** ⓥ 나타내다, 표현하다
- **interact with** ~와 상호작용하다
- **matter** ⓥ (사건, 일 등이) 중요하다

구문 풀이

> **9행** In a word, / young children think music is a lot of fun, / so do all you can
> 한 마디로(요약)   (접속사 that 생략)   명령문   목적어
> to make the most of the situation.
> 부사적 용법(~하기 위해)

★★ 문제 해결 꿀~팁 ★★

▶ 많이 틀린 이유는?
대명사의 쓰임에 유의하지 않으면 자칫 오답을 고르기 쉬운 문제였다. ④에 주어진 문장을 넣지 않는다면 ④ 뒤의 They는 'young children'일 수밖에 없는데, 이렇게 되면 '어린 아이들은 당신이 아이와 함께 음악을 즐길 때 중요하지 않다'라는 의미상 모순이 생기고 만다. 문법적으로도 matter는 주로 사물 주어를 취하여 '(어떤 일이나 사안이) 중요하다'라는 뜻으로 쓰인다는 점을 기억해 둔다.

▶ 문제 해결 방법은?
주어진 문장에 역접의 연결사가 있으면 본문 중 흐름 반전의 포인트를 잡아 주어진 문장을 넣으면 되지만, 이 문제에서 본문은 하나의 논지만을 일관되게 말하고 있다. 이 경우는 대명사가 풀이에 절대적 힌트를 제공하므로, '단수 명사 – 단수 대명사, 복수 명사 – 복수 대명사'의 연결고리를 하나씩 체크하며 꼼꼼하게 독해하도록 한다.

39 할 수 없는 일에 대해 말하는 기술   정답률 50% | 정답 ④

글의 흐름으로 보아, 주어진 문장이 들어가기에 가장 적절한 곳을 고르시오. [3점]

Whenever you say what you can't do, / say what you can do.
여러분이 할 수 없는 것을 말할 때마다, / 여러분이 할 수 있는 것을 말하라.

This ends a sentence on a positive note / and has a much lower tendency / to cause someone to challenge it.
이것은 긍정적인 어조로 문장을 마무리하는 것이고 / 경향을 훨씬 더 낮추는. / 누군가의 이의 제기를 불러일으킬

① Consider this situation / — a colleague comes up to you / and asks you to look over some figures with them / before a meeting they are having tomorrow.
이 상황을 생각해 보아라. / 한 동료가 여러분에게 다가와서 / 자신들과 일부 수치를 검토해 보자고 요청하는 / 내일 회의를 하기 전에

② You simply say, / 'No, I can't deal with this now.'

여러분은 그저 말한다. / '안 돼요, 지금은 이 일을 할 수 없어요.'라고

③ This may then lead to them insisting / how important your input is, / increasing the pressure on you / to give in.
이것은 그들에게 주장하게 만들 수도 있어서, / 여러분의 참여가 얼마나 중요한지를 / 여러분에 대한 압박을 증가시킨다. / (여러분이) 양보하도록(그 요청을 들어줄 수밖에 없도록)

✔ Instead of that, say to them, / 'I can't deal with that now / but what I can do is / I can ask Brian to give you a hand / and he should be able to explain them.'
그 대신, 그들에게 말해보라. / '저는 지금 그 일을 할 수 없지만 / 제가 할 수 있는 것은 / Brian에게 당신을 도와주라고 부탁하는 것이고 / 그러면 그가 그 수치를 설명해 줄 수 있을 것 같아요.'라고

Or, 'I can't deal with that now / but I can find you in about half an hour / when I have finished.'
혹은, '저는 지금 그 일을 할 수 없지만 / 약 30분 뒤에 당신을 찾아 갈게요. / 제 일이 끝나면'

⑤ Either of these types of responses / are better than ending it with a negative.
이런 형태의 대답들 중 어느 것이라도 / 부정적인 어조로 그 상황을 끝내는 것보다 더 낫다.

여러분이 할 수 없는 것을 말할 때마다, 여러분이 할 수 있는 것을 말하라. 이것은 긍정적인 어조로 문장을 마무리하는 것이고 누군가의 이의 제기를 불러일으킬 경향을 훨씬 더 낮춘다. ① 한 동료가 여러분에게 다가와서 내일 회의를 하기 전에 일부 수치를 검토해 보자고 요청하는 상황의 대화를 생각해 보아라. ② 여러분은 그저 '안 돼요, 지금은 이 일을 할 수 없어요.'라고 말한다. ③ 이것은 그들에게 여러분의 참여가 얼마나 중요한지를 주장하게 만들 수도 있어서, 여러분이 그 요청을 들어줄 수밖에 없도록 압박을 증가시킨다. ④ 그 대신, '저는 지금 그 일을 할 수 없지만 제가 할 수 있는 것은 Brian에게 당신을 도와주라고 부탁하는 것이고 그러면 그가 그 수치를 설명해 줄 것 같아요.'라고 그들에게 말해보라. 혹은, '저는 지금 그 일을 할 수 없지만 약 30분 뒤에 제 일이 끝나면 당신을 찾아 갈게요.' ⑤ 이런 형태의 대답들 중 어느 것이라도 부정적인 어조로 그 상황을 끝내는 것보다 더 낫다.

Why? 왜 정답일까?

④ 앞의 두 문장은 동료가 어떤 일을 부탁할 때 그저 할 수 없다고만 말하면 도리어 동료로 하여금 일을 도와줄 필요성이 있음을 더 피력하게 만들어 결국에는 부탁을 들어줄 수밖에 없는 상황에 처할 수 있음을 언급하고 있다. 이에 대한 조언으로서 Instead of that으로 시작하는 주어진 문장은 무엇을 해줄 수 있는지를 언급할 것을 제안하고, ④ 뒤의 문장은 '혹은' 지금은 아니더라도 나중에 다시 찾아가겠다는 여지를 남길 것을 제안하고 있다. 따라서 주어진 문장이 들어가기에 가장 적절한 곳은 ④이다.

- **instead of** ~ 대신에
- **explain** ⓥ 설명하다
- **note** ⓝ 어조
- **challenge** ⓥ 이의를 제기하다, 도전하다
- **figure** ⓝ 수치
- **input** ⓝ 참여, 투입
- **pressure** ⓝ 압박, 압력
- **give a hand** 도와주다
- **sentence** ⓝ 문장
- **tendency** ⓝ 성향, 경향
- **colleague** ⓝ 동료
- **insist** ⓥ 주장하다, 고집하다
- **increase** ⓥ 상승시키다

구문 풀이

> **4행** This ends a sentence on a positive note and has a much lower tendency
> 동사1   동사2
> to cause someone to challenge it.
> 형용사적 용법 「cause + 목적어 + to부정사 : ~이 …하도록 야기하다」

40 요리에 대한 자신감 여부와 식습관 사이의 연관성   정답률 58% | 정답 ①

다음 글의 내용을 한 문장으로 요약하고자 한다. 빈칸 (A)와 (B)에 들어갈 말로 가장 적절한 것은?

	(A)		(B)
✔	cooking 요리	......	various 다양한
②	cooking 요리	......	specific 특정한
③	tasting 맛보기	......	organic 유기농의
④	dieting 다이어트	......	healthy 건강한
⑤	dieting 다이어트	......	exotic 이국적인

According to an Australian study, / a person's confidence in the kitchen / is linked to the kind of food / that he or she tends to enjoy eating.
호주의 한 연구에 따르면, / 한 사람이 부엌에서 보이는 자신감은 / 음식의 종류와 연관되어 있다. / 그 사람이 즐겨 먹는 경향이 있는

Compared to the average person, / those who are proud of the dishes they make / are more likely to enjoy eating vegetarian food and health food.
보통 사람들과 비교했을 때, / 자기가 만든 음식에 자부심을 갖는 사람들은 / 채식과 건강식을 더 즐겨 먹는 경향이 있었다.

Moreover, / this group is more likely than the average person / to enjoy eating diverse kinds of food: / from salads and seafood to hamburgers and hot chips.
더구나, / 이 집단은 보통 사람들에 비해 더 ~한 경향이 있었다. / 다양한 종류의 음식을 더 즐겨먹는 / 샐러드와 해산물부터 햄버거와 감자튀김에 이르기까지

In contrast, / people who say "I would rather clean than make dishes." / don't share this wide-ranging enthusiasm for food.
반대로, / "요리하느니 차라리 설거지를 할래."라고 말하는 사람들은 / 음식에 대한 이러한 광범위한 열정을 공유하지 않았다.

They are less likely than the average person / to enjoy different types of food.
그들은 보통 사람들보다 덜 ~한 경향이 있었다. / 다양한 요리를 즐기는

In general, / they eat out less than the average person / except for when it comes to eating at fast food restaurants.
일반적으로, / 그들은 보통 사람보다 외식을 덜 한다. / 패스트 푸드 점에서 먹는 경우를 제외하고는

→ In general, / people who are confident in (A) cooking / are more likely to enjoy (B) various foods / than those who are not.
일반적으로, / 요리에 자신 있는 사람들은 / 다양한 음식을 더 즐기는 경향이 있다. / 그렇지 않은 사람들보다

호주의 한 연구에 따르면, 한 사람이 부엌에서 보이는 자신감은 그 사람이 즐겨 먹는 경향이 있는 음식의 종류와 연관되어 있다. 보통 사람들과 비교했을 때, 자기가 만든 음식에 자부심을 갖는 사람들은 채식과 건강식을 더 즐겨 먹는 경향이 있었다. 더구나, 이 집단은 보통 사람들에 비해 샐러드와 해산물부터 햄버거와 감자튀김에 이르기까지 다양한 종류의 음식을 더 즐겨먹는 경향이 있었다. 반대로, "요리하느니 차라리 설거지를 할래."라고 말하는 사람들은 음식에 대한 이러한 광범위한 열정을 공유하지 않았다. 그들은 보통 사람들보다 다양한 요리를 덜 즐기는 경향이 있었다. 일반적으로, 그들은 패스트 푸드 점에서 먹는 경우를 제외하고는 보통 사람보다 외식을 덜 한다.

➡ 일반적으로, (A) 요리에 자신이 있는 사람들은 그렇지 않은 사람들보다 (B) 다양한 음식을 더 즐기는 경향이 있다.

Why? 왜 정답일까?

첫 문장에서 요리에 대한 자신감과 식습관 사이에는 연관성이 있다고 말하는데, 이어지는 두 문장에서는 그 구체적인 내용으로서 요리에 자부심을 보이는 사람들의 경우에는 채식 및 건강한 음식을 더 선호할 뿐 아니라 다양한 음식을 더욱 즐겨먹는 경향이 있음(Moreover, this group is more likely than the average person to enjoy eating diverse kinds of food ~)을 이야기한다. 따라서 빈칸 (A)와 (B)에 들어갈 말로 가장 적절한 것은 ① '(A) cooking(요리), (B) various(다양한)'이다.

- **be linked to** ~와 연관되다
- **vegetarian** ⓐ 채식의, 채식주의의
- **in contrast** 그에 반해서
- **enthusiasm** ⓝ 열정
- **except for** ~을 제외하고
- **average** ⓐ 평균의, 보통의
- **diverse** ⓐ 다양한
- **wide-ranging** 광범위한
- **eat out** 외식하다

구문 풀이

3행 Compared to the average person, / those [who are proud of the dishes
~와 비교할 때   지시대명사(~한 사람들)   ~주격 관계대명사 ~을 자랑스러워하다
they make] are more likely to enjoy eating vegetarian food and health food.
더 ~한 경향이 있다   (목적격 관계대명사 생략)

41-42 광고 속 통계 수치의 신뢰도

『Many advertisements cite statistical surveys.
많은 광고는 통계 조사를 인용한다.

But we should be (a) cautious / because we usually do not know / how these surveys are conducted.』 **41번의 근거**
하지만 우리는 신중해야 한다. / 보통 모르기 때문에 / 이러한 조사들이 어떻게 실시되는지

For example, / a toothpaste manufacturer once had a poster / that said, "More than 80% of dentists recommend *Smiley Toothpaste*."
예를 들면, / 한 치약 제조업체가 예전에 포스터를 올렸다. / "80%가 넘는 치과의사들이 Smiley Toothpaste를 추천합니다."라고 적혀있는

This seems to say / that most dentists (b) prefer *Smiley Toothpaste* to other brands.
이것은 말하는 것처럼 보인다. / 대부분의 치과의사들이 다른 브랜드보다 Smiley Toothpaste를 선호한다

But it turns out / that the survey questions allowed the dentists / to recommend more than one brand, / and in fact / another competitor's brand was recommended / just as often as *Smiley Toothpaste*!
하지만 드러난다! / 그 조사 항목이 치과의사들에게 허용했다는 것이 / 한 가지 이상의 브랜드를 추천하도록 / 그리고 실제로 / 또 다른 경쟁업체의 브랜드도 많이 추천되었다는 것이 / Smiley Toothpaste만큼

No wonder / the UK Advertising Standards Authority ruled in 2007 / that the poster was (c) misleading / and it could no longer be displayed.
당연히도 / 2007년에 영국 Advertising Standards Authority는 결정을 내렸고 / 그 포스터가 잘못된 정보를 준다고 / 그것은 더 이상 게시될 수 없었다.

A similar case concerns a well-known cosmetics firm / marketing a cream / that is supposed to rapidly reduce wrinkles.
유명 화장품 회사의 경우도 유사하다. / 크림을 판매하는 / 주름을 빠른 속도로 줄여 준다는

But the only evidence provided is / that "76% of 50 women agreed."
그러나 주어진 유일한 증거라고는 / "50명의 여성 중 76%가 동의했다."라는 것뿐이다.

『But what this means is / that the evidence is based on just the personal opinions / from a small sample / with no objective measurement of their skin's condition.
하지만 이것이 의미하는 것은 / 그 증거가 개인적 의견에만 근거한다는 것이다. / 소수의 표본에서 얻은 / 피부 상태에 대한 객관적인 측정이 없었던

Furthermore, / we are not told / how these women were selected.』 **42번의 근거**
게다가, / 우리는 알 수 없다 / 이 여성들이 어떻게 선별되었는지

Without such information, / the "evidence" provided is pretty much (d) useless.
그런 정보 없이는 / 주어진 "증거"는 아주 쓸모 없다.

Unfortunately, / 『such advertisements are quite typical, / and as consumers / we just have to use our own judgment / and (e) avoid taking advertising claims too seriously.』 **41번의 근거**
불행하게도, / 그러한 광고들은 아주 전형적이고, / 소비자로서 / 우리가 스스로 판단해야 하며 / 광고의 주장을 너무 진지하게 받아들이는 것을 피해야 한다.

많은 광고는 통계 조사를 인용한다. 하지만 우리는 보통 이러한 조사들이 어떻게 실시되는지를 모르기 때문에 (a) 신중해야 한다. 예를 들면, 한 치약 제조 업체가 예전에 "80%가 넘는 치과의사들이 Smiley Toothpaste를 추천합니다."라고 적혀 있는 포스터를 올렸다. 이것은 대부분의 치과의사들이 다른 브랜드보다 Smiley Toothpaste를 (b) 선호한다고 말하는 것처럼 보인다. 하지만 그 조사 항목이 치과의사들에게 한 가지 이상의 브랜드를 추천할 수 있게 했다는 것과, 실제로 또 다른 경쟁업체의 브랜드도 Smiley Toothpaste만큼 많이 추천되었다는 것이 드러난다! 당연히도 2007년에 영국 Advertising Standards Authority는 그 포스터가 (c) 잘못된 정보를 준다고 결정을 내렸고 그것은 더 이상 게시될 수 없었다. 주름을 빠른 속도로 줄여 준다는 크림을 판매하는 유명 화장품 회사의 경우도 유사하다. 그러나 주어진 유일한 증거라고는 "50명의 여성 중 76%가 동의했다."라는 것뿐이다. 하지만 이것이 의미하는 것은 그 증거가 피부 상태에 대한 객관적인 측정이 없었던 소수의 표본에서 얻은 개인적 의견에만 근거한다는 것이다. 게다가, 우리는 이 여성들이 어떻게 선별되었는지 알 수 없다. 그런 정보 없이는 주어진 "증거"는 아주 (d) 유용하다(→ 쓸모가 없다). 불행하게도, 그러한 광고들은 아주 전형적이고, 소비자인 우리가 스스로 판단해야 하며 광고의 주장을 너무 진지하게 받아들이는 것을 (e) 피해야 한다.

- **cite** ⓥ 들다, 인용하다
- **cautious** ⓐ 조심스러운, 신중한
- **toothpaste** ⓝ 치약
- **recommend** ⓥ 추천하다
- **turn out** 판명되다, 밝혀지다
- **misleading** ⓐ 오해의 소지가 있는
- **similar** ⓐ 비슷한, 유사한
- **rapidly** [ad] 빨리, 급속히
- **evidence** ⓝ 증거
- **quite** [ad] 꽤, 상당히
- **avoid** ⓥ 회피하다, 모면하다
- **seriously** [ad] 심각하게, 진심으로
- **statistical** ⓐ 통계적인
- **conduct** ⓥ 수행하다, 행동을 하다
- **manufacturer** ⓝ 제조 회사
- **prefer** ⓥ 선호하다
- **rule** ⓥ 결정하다, 판결하다
- **display** ⓥ 진열하다, 전시하다
- **concern** ⓥ ~에 관련되다
- **wrinkle** ⓝ 주름
- **objective** ⓐ 객관적인
- **typical** ⓐ 전형적인
- **claim** ⓝ 주장
- **reliable** ⓐ 믿을만한, 신뢰할만한

[문제편 p.190]

구문 풀이

6행 But it turns out that the survey questions allowed the dentists
~임이 판명되다 접속사   주어1   동사1
to recommend more than one brand, and in fact another competitor's brand
목적격 보어   주어2
was recommended just as often as *Smiley Toothpaste*!
동사2   원급 비교(~만큼 …한)

---

41 제목 파악   정답률 57% | 정답 ②

윗글의 제목으로 가장 적절한 것은?

① The Link between Advertisements and the Economy – 광고와 경제의 연관성
✓② Are Statistical Data in Advertisements Reliable? – 광고 속 통계 데이터가 신뢰할 만한가?
③ Statistics in Advertisements Are Objective! – 광고 속 통계 자료는 객관적이다!
④ The Bright Side of Public Advertisements – 대중 광고의 긍정적인 면
⑤ Quality or Price, Which Matters More? – 질과 가격, 무엇이 더 중요한가?

Why? 왜 정답일까?

첫 두 문장인 'Many advertisements cite statistical surveys. But we should be cautious because we usually do not know how these surveys are conducted.'에서 많은 광고가 통계 조사를 인용하지만 그 조사가 진행된 과정에 대해 소비자는 보통 잘 모르고 있기 때문에 정보의 신빙성을 판단함에 있어 주의가 필요하다는 내용을 주제로 제시하므로, 글의 제목으로 가장 적절한 것은 ② '광고 속 통계 데이터가 신뢰할 만한가?'이다.

★★★ 등급을 가르는 문제!

42 어휘 추론   정답률 43% | 정답 ④

밑줄 친 (a) ~ (e) 중에서 문맥상 낱말의 쓰임이 적절하지 않은 것은?

① (a)   ② (b)   ③ (c)   ✓④ (d)   ⑤ (e)

Why? 왜 정답일까?

'But what this means is that the evidence is based on just the personal opinions from a small sample with no objective measurement of their skin's condition. Furthermore, we are not told how these women were selected.'에서 화장품 광고에서 통계 수치를 제시할 때 보통 소비자인 우리는 표본의 객관성이나 선별 과정 등에 관해 자세히 알 수 없다는 내용이 언급되고 있다. 이에 비추어 볼 때, 이 광고에서 제시된 통계 데이터는 '믿을 만하지 않다'는 것이 예시의 결론임을 알 수 있다. 따라서 문맥상 낱말의 쓰임이 적절하지 않은 것은 ④ '(d)'이다.

★★ 문제 해결 꿀~팁 ★★

▶ 많이 틀린 이유는?
최다 오답인 (c)를 제치는 데 있어서는 '~ it could no longer be displayed.'가 가장 큰 힌트이다. 포스터가 더 이상 게시되지 못한 까닭은 포스터에 포함된 정보가 부적절했기 때문임을 유추할 수 있으므로, (c)의 misleading은 맥락상 적절하다.
▶ 문제 해결 방법은?
장문 어휘 문제에서는 밑줄 문장의 전후 맥락 파악이 가장 중요하다. (d) 또한 앞의 두 문장을 주의 깊게 읽어 맥락을 파악하면 쉽게 답임을 알 수 있다.

43-45 쿠칭에 도착한 날 있었던 일

(A)
It was evening / when I landed in Kuching, Malaysia.
저녁이었다. / 내가 말레이시아 쿠칭에 도착했을 때는

I felt alone and homesick.
나는 외로움과 향수를 느꼈다.

『I was a 19-year-old Dubai-raised kid / away from home for the first time / to start my university studies in mechanical engineering.』 **45번 ①의 근거** 일치
나는 두바이에서 자란 19살짜리 아이였다. / 처음으로 집을 멀리 떠나 온, / 기계공학을 대학에서 공부하기 위해

I took my luggage / and headed to the airport exit.
나는 내 짐을 들고 / 공항 출구로 향했다.

I looked around / and found my driver / waiting for me in front of (a) his gray van / with the name of my university on it.
나는 주위를 둘러보고 / 내 기사를 찾았다. / 그의 회색 밴 앞에서 나를 기다리는 / 내 대학교 이름이 쓰인

(D)
As we left the airport, / he began talking about the city and its people.
우리가 공항을 떠날 때 / 그는 그 도시와 그곳 사람들에 대해 이야기해 주었다.

『As I loved driving very much, / we moved onto talking about cars and driving in Kuching.』 **45번 ④의 근거** 일치
내가 운전하는 것을 아주 좋아했기에 / 우리는 차와 쿠칭에서의 운전에 대한 이야기로 넘어갔다.

"Never make Kuching people angry," (e) he warned.
"쿠칭 사람들을 화나게 하지 말아요." 그가 경고했다.

"No road rage. Very dangerous!"
"운전 중 분노는 안 돼요. 굉장히 위험해요!"

『He went on to list his experiences of road rage / and advised me to drive very cautiously.』 **45번 ⑤의 근거** 일치
그런 다음 그는 운전 중 분노에 대한 자신의 경험을 이어서 늘어놓으며 / 내게 아주 조심해서 운전하라고 당부했다.

A bit later, / the car behind started to flash its lights at us.
조금 후, / 뒤에 있던 차가 우리 쪽으로 라이트를 비추기 시작했다.

(C)
This continued more aggressively / and my driver started to panic.
이것은 점점 공격적으로 지속되었고 / 기사는 허둥대기 시작했다.

Honks and more flashes followed, / so (c) he pulled the van over to the roadside.
경적과 더 많은 불빛이 뒤따랐고, / 그는 갓길에 밴을 세웠다.

My heart was pounding / as the man from the car behind approached us.
내 심장은 쿵쾅거렸다. / 뒤차에서 내린 남자가 우리에게 다가올 때

As he reached my window, / I lowered it / and then looked down at (d) his hands / to see that he was holding my wallet.
그가 내 창문에 다가섰을 때, / 나는 창문을 내려 / 그의 손을 내려다보고는 / 그가 내 지갑을 들고 있다는 것을 알았다.
『I had left it in the airport / and I realized he had been trying to return it to me / ever since we had left the airport.』 45번 ③의근거 불일치
나는 그것을 공항에 두고 왔고, / 줄곧 그가 내게 그것을 돌려주려고 했다는 것을 깨달았다. / 우리가 공항을 떠난 이후로

(B)
With a sigh of relief, / I took my wallet and thanked him.
안도의 한숨과 함께, / 나는 지갑을 받았고 그에게 고마워했다.
I could imagine a horrible scenario / if he had not returned it.
나는 끔찍한 시나리오를 떠올릴 수 있었다. / 그가 지갑을 돌려주지 않았더라면 어땠을지
The man welcomed me to Kuching and drove away.
그는 내가 쿠칭에 온 것을 환영하고는 운전을 해서 멀어져 갔다.
As my driver dropped me off, / (b) he smiled / and wished me luck with my university studies.
내 기사는 나를 내려주면서, / 그는 미소를 짓고는 / 내게 대학 공부에 행운을 빌어 주었다.
『Thanks to the kindness of these strangers, / the initial doubt / I had had about my decision to study away from home / was replaced with hope and excitement.』 45번 ②의근거 일치
이 낯선 사람들의 친절 덕택으로, / 처음의 의구심은 / 집에서 멀리 떠나 공부를 해야겠다던 나의 결심에 대해 내가 가졌던 / 희망과 흥분으로 바뀌었다.

(A)
내가 말레이시아 쿠칭에 도착했을 때는 저녁이었다. 나는 외로움과 향수를 느꼈다. 나는 기계공학을 대학에서 공부하기 위해 처음으로 집을 멀리 떠나 온, 두바이 출신의 19살짜리였다. 나는 짐을 들고 공항 출구로 향했다. 주위를 둘러보고 나는 내 대학교 이름이 쓰인 (a) 그의 회색 밴 앞에서 나를 기다리는 기사를 찾았다.

(D)
공항을 떠나면서 그는 그 도시와 그곳 사람들에 대해 이야기해 주었다. 내가 운전하는 것을 아주 좋아했기에 우리는 차와 쿠칭에서의 운전에 대한 이야기로 넘어갔다. "쿠칭 사람들을 화나게 하지 말아요." (e) 그가 경고했다. "운전 중 분노는 안 돼요. 굉장히 위험해요!" 그런 다음 그는 운전 중 분노에 대한 자신의 경험을 이어서 늘어놓으며 내게 아주 조심해서 운전하라고 당부했다. 조금 후, 뒤에 있던 차가 우리 쪽으로 라이트를 비추기 시작했다.

(C)
이것은 점점 공격적으로 지속되었고 기사는 허둥대기 시작했다. 경적과 더 많은 불빛이 뒤따랐고, (c) 그는 갓길에 밴을 세웠다. 뒤차에서 내린 남자가 우리에게 다가올 때 내 심장은 쿵쾅거렸다. 그가 내 창문에 다가섰을 때, 나는 창문을 내려 (d) 그의 손을 내려다보고는 그가 내 지갑을 들고 있다는 것을 알았다. 나는 그것을 공항에 두고 왔고, 우리가 공항을 떠난 이후로 줄곧 그가 내게 그것을 돌려주려고 했다는 것을 깨달았다.

(B)
안도의 한숨과 함께, 나는 지갑을 받았고 그에게 고마워했다. 그가 지갑을 돌려주지 않았더라면 어땠을지 끔찍한 시나리오를 떠올릴 수 있었다. 그는 내가 쿠칭에 온 것을 환영하고는 운전을 해서 멀어져 갔다. 나를 내려주면서, (b) 기사는 미소를 짓고는 내게 대학 공부에 행운을 빌어 주었다. 이 낯선 사람들의 친절 덕택에, 집에서 멀리 떠나 공부를 해야겠던 나의 결심에 대한 처음의 의구심은 희망과 흥분으로 바뀌었다.

- homesick ⓐ 향수를 느끼는
- luggage ⓝ 짐, 수하물
- horrible ⓐ 끔찍한, 무서운
- aggressively ⓐⓓ 공격적으로
- honk ⓝ (자동차의) 경적
- cautiously ⓐⓓ 조심해서, 조심스럽게
- mechanical engineering 기계 공학
- relief ⓝ 안도, 안도감
- initial ⓐ 처음의, 초기의
- panic ⓥ 허둥대다, 겁에 질려 어쩔 줄 모르다
- pound ⓥ (심장이) 쿵쾅거리다, 방망이질 치다

구문 풀이

(A) 2행 I was a 19-year-old Dubai-raised kid away from home for the first time /
복합형용사('-'로 연결)
to start my university studies in mechanical engineering.
부사적 용법(~하기 위해)

(C) 4행 As he reached my window, / I lowered it and then looked down at his
접속사(~할 때)　동사1(과거)　동사2(과거)
hands / to see that he was holding my wallet.
~하게 되다(결과)　접속사

(D) 5행 He then went on to list his experiences of road rage / and advised me
동사1(이어서 ~하다)　동사2　목적어
to drive very cautiously.
목적격 보어(to부정사)

---

43 글의 순서 파악　　정답률 60% | 정답 ⑤

주어진 글 (A)에 이어질 내용을 순서에 맞게 배열한 것으로 가장 적절한 것은?
① (B) − (D) − (C)
② (C) − (D) − (B)
③ (C) − (D) − (B)
④ (D) − (B) − (C)
✔ (D) − (C) − (B)

Why? 왜 정답일까?

쿠칭 공항에 처음 내려 외로움을 느끼던 필자가 이동하기 위해 기사를 찾았다는 내용의 (A) 뒤에는, 기사가 쿠칭에서는 운전을 조심해야 한다고 당부했고 곧이어 뒤차로부터 라이트 세례를 받기 시작했다는 내용의 (D), 알고 보니 뒤차 사람은 내가 공항에 놓고 온 지갑을 돌려주러 쫓아온 것이었다는 내용의 (C), 기사까지 포함하여 낯선 사람들의 친절 덕택에 유학 결정에 기대감을 품게 되었다는 내용의 (B)가 차례로 이어지는 것이 적절하다. 따라서 주어진 글 (A)에 이어질 내용을 순서에 맞게 배열한 것으로 가장 적절한 것은 ⑤ '(D) − (C) − (B)'이다.

44 지칭 추론　　정답률 54% | 정답 ④

밑줄 친 (a)~(e) 중에서 가리키는 대상이 나머지 넷과 다른 것은?
① (a)　② (b)　③ (c)　✔ (d)　⑤ (e)

Why? 왜 정답일까?

(a), (b), (c), (e)는 'my driver', (d)는 'the man from the car behind'를 나타낸다. (a)~(e) 중에서 가리키는 대상이 나머지 넷과 다른 것은 ④ '(d)'이다.

45 세부 내용 파악　　정답률 57% | 정답 ③

윗글의 'I'에 관한 내용으로 적절하지 <u>않은</u> 것은?
① 기계 공학을 공부하려고 집을 떠나왔다.
② 처음에는 유학 결정에 대해 의구심을 가졌다.
✔ 지갑을 자동차에 두고 내렸다.
④ 운전하는 것을 매우 좋아했다.
⑤ 조심스럽게 운전하라는 충고를 들었다.

Why? 왜 정답일까?

'I had left it in the airport and I realized he had been trying to return it to me ever since we had left the airport.'에서 필자는 공항에 지갑을 두고 왔다는 사실을 확인할 수 있으므로, 'I'에 관한 내용으로 적절하지 않은 것은 ③ '지갑을 자동차에 두고 내렸다.'이다.

Why? 왜 오답일까?

① 'I was a 19-year-old Dubai-raised kid away from home for the first time to start my university studies in mechanical engineering.'의 내용과 일치한다.
② '~ the initial doubt I had had about my decision to study away from home ~'의 내용과 일치한다.
④ 'As I loved driving very much, ~'의 내용과 일치한다.
⑤ 'He ~ advised me to drive very cautiously.'의 내용과 일치한다.

01 enjoying the exhibition / share his ideas about photography and life / be seated before the event begins

02 an allergy to shrimp / has a positive effect on health / add shrimp to my diet

03 She doesn't have a high fever / come to school / submit her school newspaper article on time

04 the rocket next to the flower pot / pictures of great scientists / a star-shaped clock / how to make it with a 3D-printer

05 was promoted at work / go buy some flowers / make it neat and tidy

06 soft and comfortable / any safety balls for children / 10% off the total price

07 a big fan of musicals / all the way from Canada / someone else to go with me

08 How's your career search going / only for high school students / no registration fee

09 In order to celebrate / must be your own original work / published in our school magazine

10 too short to use conveniently / needs frequent charging / shaves in the shower

11 had lunch there / What did you think of it

12 dangerous to drive to work / use public transportation

13 a funny thing happened to me / my shoes were still in her house / almost the same as mine / No doubt you were very embarrassed

14 Everything's almost settled / haven't decided who'll sing at the wedding / it would be the best wedding gift

15 accept her invitation / leave him alone / have more guests at the party

16-17 climate change / avocados are also in danger / has resulted in a lack of water / unstable climatic conditions through crop season

어휘 Review Test 02

A	B	C	D
01 ~에서 은퇴하다	**01** promote	**01** ①	**01** ⓑ
02 언쟁하다, 주장하다	**02** name	**02** ⓐ	**02** ⓕ
03 (물 등이) 마르다	**03** encourage	**03** ⓔ	**03** ⓐ
04 거의 ~할 수가 없다	**04** concept	**04** ⓚ	**04** ⓣ
05 적합하지 못한, 불리한	**05** satisfying	**05** ⓑ	**05** ⓚ
06 정점에 달하다	**06** clue	**06** ⓟ	**06** ⓒ
07 등록하다	**07** distance	**07** ⓒ	**07** ⓘ
08 안도한	**08** consist	**08** ⓕ	**08** ⓞ
09 일반적인, 보편적인	**09** regardless of	**09** ①	**09** ⓜ
10 산업의	**10** respond to	**10** ⓠ	**10** ⓖ
11 정리하다, 체계화하다	**11** artificial intelligence	**11** ①	**11** ⓗ
12 단계	**12** majority	**12** ⓡ	**12** ⓓ
13 거절하다	**13** eventually	**13** ⓝ	**13** ⓢ
14 별 보기	**14** improve	**14** ⓓ	**14** ⓔ
15 ~할 가능성이 있다	**15** debt	**15** ①	**15** ⓝ
16 망설임, 주저함	**16** confuse	**16** ①	**16** ⓕ
17 도와주다	**17** matter	**17** ⓖ	**17** ①
18 채식의, 채식주의의	**18** tendency	**18** ⓜ	**18** ⓟ
19 결정하다, 판결하다	**19** turn out	**19** ⓗ	**19** ⓓ
20 조심해서, 조심스럽게	**20** homesick	**20** ⓢ	**20** ①

특별 부록 03회 | 9월 학력평가 대비 실전 모의고사 [고1]

· 정답 ·

01 ⑤	02 ①	03 ②	04 ⑤	05 ⑤	06 ④	07 ①	08 ④	09 ④	10 ②	11 ③	12 ①	13 ⑤	14 ①	15 ②
16 ①	17 ③	18 ①	19 ②	20 ①	21 ⑤	22 ③	23 ⑤	24 ②	25 ④	26 ②	27 ⑤	28 ④	29 ④	30 ⑤
31 ①	32 ③	33 ②	34 ④	35 ④	36 ②	37 ②	38 ④	39 ③	40 ①	41 ③	42 ⑤	43 ④	44 ④	45 ②

★ 표기된 문항은 [등급을 가르는 문제]에 해당하는 문항입니다.

01 | 도서관 보수로 인한 임시 휴관 안내
정답률 90% | 정답 ⑤

다음을 듣고, 남자가 하는 말의 목적으로 가장 적절한 것을 고르시오.

① 도서 대출 기한 변경을 안내하려고
② 도서관 조명 시설 교체를 요청하려고
③ 도서관 운영 시간 연장을 건의하려고
④ 도서관 공사로 인한 소음에 대해 사과하려고
✓ 도서관 보수로 인한 임시 휴관을 공지하려고

M : Attention, please.
주목해 주세요, 여러분.
This is your vice principal, Mr. Stevens.
교감인 Stevens 선생님입니다.
There will be some renovations made to our library next week.
다음 주에 우리 도서관에 약간의 보수 공사가 있을 겁니다.
First, we will replace worn-out carpets with new ones.
먼저, 닳아버린 카펫을 새것으로 교체할 것입니다.
Meanwhile, old tables and chairs will be repaired or replaced.
그 사이에 오래된 탁자와 의자를 수리하거나 교체할 것입니다.
We will also remove the old lighting and install LED lighting.
또한 낡은 조명을 없애고 LED 조명을 설치할 것입니다.
For these reasons, the library will be closed for a week.
이러한 이유로, 도서관을 일주일간 닫을 예정입니다.
During this period, you will not be able to check out or return books.
이 기간에 여러분은 도서를 대출하거나 반납할 수 없습니다.
I'm sorry for temporarily closing the library, but I expect the renovation will make it more convenient to use.
일시적으로 도서관을 닫게 되어 죄송하지만, 보수되는 사항이 (도서관) 이용을 더 편리하게 만들 것이라고 기대합니다.
Thank you for your cooperation.
협조에 감사합니다.

Why? 왜 정답일까?

담화에서 남자는 도서관에 보수가 있을 예정이라는 것(There will be some renovations made to our library next week.)과 이로 인한 휴관이 있을 것임(For these reasons, the library will be closed for a week.)을 알리므로, 남자가 하는 말의 목적으로 가장 적절한 것은 ⑤ '도서관 보수로 인한 임시 휴관을 공지하려고'이다.

- vice principal ⓝ 교감
- replace ⓥ 교체하다, 바꾸다
- repair ⓥ 수리하다, 고치다
- temporarily ⓐⓓ 일시적으로, 임시로
- cooperation ⓝ 협조, 협력
- renovation ⓝ 보수, 수리
- worn-out 닳아버린
- install ⓥ 설치하다
- convenient ⓐ 편리한

02 | 수면 부족이 건강에 미치는 악영향
정답률 93% | 정답 ①

대화를 듣고, 여자의 의견으로 가장 적절한 것을 고르시오.

✓ 수면 부족은 신체 건강에 해롭다.
② 적절한 스트레스는 일의 능률을 높인다.
③ 잠자기 전 휴대폰 사용은 숙면에 방해가 된다.
④ 수면 장애 해결을 위해 원인을 파악해야 한다.
⑤ 집중력 향상을 위해 규칙적인 운동이 필요하다.

W : David, is there something wrong? You don't look well.
David, 뭐 문제 있어? 얼굴이 안 좋네.
M : I'm just sleepy. I stayed up all night finishing the science project.
그냥 졸린 거야. 과학 프로젝트를 끝내느라 어제 밤을 꼴딱 샜거든.
W : Again? Don't you know that a lack of sleep is bad for your health?
또? 수면 부족은 건강에 나쁜 거 몰라?
M : For my health? In what way?
건강에? 어째서?
W : If you don't get a sufficient amount of sleep, you are more likely to have health problems like the common cold or even heart disease.
충분한 양의 수면을 취하지 않으면 일반 감기나 심지어 심장병 같은 건강 문제가 생기게 될 가능성이 더 높아.
M : Really? Why's that?
정말? 왜 그런 거야?
W : It can lower your body's defenses, so your body won't be able to fight viruses.
그게 네 몸의 면역력을 낮출 수 있어서, 몸이 바이러스와 싸우지 못하게 되는 거야.
M : I didn't know that. I'll try to get enough sleep.
그건 몰랐어. 잠을 충분히 자도록 노력해야겠네.

Why? 왜 정답일까?

대화에서 여자는 프로젝트를 하느라 밤을 새웠다는 남자에게 수면 부족이 건강에 문제를 일으킬 수 있는지 모르냐고 물으며(Don't you know that a lack of sleep is bad for your health?) 어떤 문제가 왜 일어나는지를 설명해 준다. 따라서 여자의 의견으로 가장 적절한 것은 ① '수면 부족은 신체 건강에 해롭다.'이다.

- sufficient ⓐ 충분한
- common cold 일반 감기
- amount ⓝ 양
- defense ⓝ 방어

03 라디오 드라마 녹음 준비 정답률 88% | 정답 ②

대화를 듣고, 두 사람의 관계를 가장 잘 나타낸 것을 고르시오.
① 신문 기자 – 작가 ☑ 녹음 기사 – 성우
③ 영화감독 – 배우 ④ 매니저 – 가수
⑤ 의사 – 환자

M : Hi, Kate. How do you feel today?
안녕하세요, Kate. 오늘 상태 어때요?
W : I feel better, but I still have a sore throat. How does my voice sound?
나아졌는데, 아직 목이 아파요. 제 목소리가 어떻게 들리나요?
M : It sounds fine, so don't worry about it.
괜찮은 것 같으니 걱정하지 말아요.
W : Thanks. Did you hear about one of the audio books we recorded in this studio last year?
고마워요. 우리가 작년에 이 스튜디오에서 녹음한 오디오북 중 한 권에 대해 이야기 들으셨나요?
M : You mean "The Dreaming Tree?" I heard it was the best-selling audio book of the year.
'The Dreaming Tree' 말하는 거예요? 그게 그 해에 가장 많이 팔린 오디오북이었다고 들었어요.
W : It was. The sound effects you added made the story feel alive.
그랬죠. 당신이 더한 음향 효과가 그 이야기를 실감 나게 만들었어요.
M : Thank you. Most of all, your voice acting was great in the various roles.
고마워요. 무엇보다도 당신의 목소리 연기가 다양한 역할에서 대단했지요.
W : I'm flattered. Okay, I think I'm ready now. Is this the script for the radio drama we're working on today?
과찬이에요. 자, 이제 준비가 된 것 같아요. 이게 우리가 오늘 작업하는 라디오 드라마 대본인가요?
M : Yes. We can begin once you step into the recording booth. I'll check the microphone.
네. 당신이 녹음실로 들어가면 우린 시작할 수 있어요. 내가 마이크를 점검할게요.
W : All right. I'll start when you give me the signal.
알겠어요. 당신이 내게 신호를 주면 시작할게요.

Why? 왜 정답일까?

'The sound effects you added made the story feel alive.'와 'I'll check the microphone.'에서 남자가 녹음 기사라는 것과, 'Most of all, your voice acting was great in the various roles.'와 'I'll start when you give me the signal.'에서 여자가 성우라는 것을 알 수 있으므로, 두 사람의 관계로 가장 적절한 것은 ② '녹음 기사 – 성우'이다.

● have a sore throat 목이 아프다
● sound effect 음향 효과
● script ⓝ 대본
● record ⓥ 녹음하다
● I'm flattered. 과찬이에요.
● recording booth 녹음실

---

04 북극곰 포스터에 대해서 이야기하기 정답률 74% | 정답 ⑤

대화를 듣고, 그림에서 대화의 내용과 일치하지 <u>않는</u> 것을 고르시오.

① PROTECT THE POLAR BEARS!
② By switching off
④ OFF
③
☑ H K High School

M : Anna, can you check out my campaign poster?
Anna, 내 캠페인 포스터 좀 확인해 줄래?
W : Sure. 「I see you wrote the title "PROTECT THE POLAR BEARS!" at the top of the poster.」 ①의 근거 일치 It looks great.
물론이지. 네가 포스터 위쪽에 "북극곰을 보호하세요!"라는 제목을 쓴 걸 봤어. 근사해 보인다.
M : Thanks. 「Do you think I should make the phrase "By switching off" bigger?」
고마워. "(전기) 스위치를 꺼서"라는 문구를 더 크게 해야 할 것 같니?
W : No, you don't have to. It should be smaller than the title.」 ②의 근거 일치
아니, 그럴 필요 없어. 그건 제목보다 작아야 해.
M : Okay. 「Also, I drew the polar bear on an ice cap to make people think they should save the polar bears.」 ③의 근거 일치
알겠어. 그리고, 난 사람들이 북극곰을 지켜야 한다고 생각하게 하려고 만년설 위에 북극곰을 그렸어.
W : Good. 「I like the "OFF" button the polar bear is pointing to. The word "OFF" on the button makes the message very clear.」 ④의 근거 일치
좋아. 북극곰이 가리키고 있는 "꺼짐" 버튼이 마음에 들어. 버튼에 있는 "꺼짐"이라는 글씨가 메시지를 무척 분명하게 만들어.
M : That's the idea. 「One last thing — I'm worried that the round logo at the bottom isn't in the right place.」 ⑤의 근거 불일치
바로 그거야. 마지막으로 난 아래쪽에 있는 둥근 로고가 적절한 위치에 있는 건지 염려가 돼.
W : Don't worry. I think it's okay.
걱정 마. 내가 생각하기엔 괜찮아.

Why? 왜 정답일까?

대화에서 포스터 하단의 로고는 둥근 로고(I'm worried that the round logo at the bottom isn't in the right place.)라고 하는데, 그림에서 로고는 사각 모양이다. 따라서 그림에서 대화의 내용과 일치하지 않는 것은 ⑤이다.

● protect ⓥ 보호하다
● switch off (전기) 스위치를 끄다
● save ⓥ 지키다, 아끼다
● phrase ⓝ 문구, 어구
● ice cap 만년설

---

05 호텔 숙박비 비교 앱 정답률 94% | 정답 ⑤

대화를 듣고, 남자가 할 일로 가장 적절한 것을 고르시오.
① 배낭 빌려주기 ② 항공권 예매하기
③ 은행에서 환전하기 ④ 여행 안내 책자 주문하기
☑ 호텔 숙박비 비교 앱 알려 주기

M : Hey, Lucy! Where are you going?
안녕, Lucy! 어디 가고 있어?
W : Hi, Steve. I'm on my way to the bank to exchange some money.
안녕, Steve. 난 은행에 돈을 좀 환전하러 가는 길이야.
M : Oh, is it for your trip to Europe? You must be excited. Did you buy the big backpack you needed?
오, 네 유럽 여행 때문에? 틀림없이 신나겠구나. 네가 필요하다던 큰 배낭은 샀어?
W : No, but I borrowed a nice one from my cousin. And I ordered the guide book you recommended.
아니, 하지만 내 사촌에게서 괜찮은 것을 빌렸어. 그리고 난 네가 추천해준 가이드북을 주문했어.
M : That's good. It'll be very useful. You seem to be all set for your trip.
잘했네. 그건 몹시 유용할거야. 넌 네 여행을 위해 준비가 다 된 것 같네.
W : Almost. I've renewed my passport and booked the flight. But I haven't decided on a hotel yet.
거의 다 됐어. 난 여권을 갱신하고 비행기를 예약했어. 하지만 아직 호텔을 정하지 못했어.
M : How come?
어째서?
W : Because there are so many different options. It's difficult to find the right deal.
왜냐면 너무 여러 다양한 선택권이 있기 때문이지. 딱 맞는 곳을 찾기가 어려워.
M : Why don't you use mobile applications to compare the hotel prices? It'll save you time and money.
호텔 가격을 비교하기 위해 모바일 앱을 이용해보는 게 어때? 그것은 네 시간과 돈을 아껴줄 거야.
W : Mobile apps? Do you know of any good ones?
모바일 앱이라고? 좀 괜찮은 것들을 알고 있어?
M : Yes, I know a few. I'll text you and let you know their names.
응, 몇 개 알아. 내가 문자로 그것들 이름을 알려줄게.
W : Thanks. I'll try them out.
고마워. 그것들을 써 볼게.

Why? 왜 정답일까?

유럽 여행 중 머물 호텔을 정하지 못했다는 여자의 말에 남자는 호텔 숙박비를 비교해 볼 수 있는 앱을 사용해 볼 것을 권하며(Why don't you use mobile applications to compare the hotel prices?) 앱의 이름을 문자로 알려주겠다(I'll text you and let you know their names.)고 한다. 따라서 남자가 할 일로 가장 적절한 것은 ⑤ '호텔 숙박비 비교 앱 알려 주기'이다.

● on one's way to ~로 가는 길에
● useful ⓐ 유용한
● renew ⓥ 갱신하다
● exchange ⓥ 환전하다
● all set 준비가 다 된
● passport ⓝ 여권

---

06 찻주전자 구매하기 정답률 70% | 정답 ④

대화를 듣고, 남자가 지불할 금액을 고르시오. [3점]
① $27 ② $36 ③ $40 ☑ $45 ⑤ $63

W : Hello, sir. How can I help you?
안녕하세요, 선생님. 무엇을 도와드릴까요?
M : I'm looking for a teapot for my mother. She enjoys having tea with her friends.
전 저의 어머니를 위한 찻주전자를 찾고 있어요. 어머니는 친구 분들하고 차 마시는 것을 좋아하세요.
W : Okay. How about this teapot with a simple and classic design? It'll never go out of style.
그러시군요. 이 심플하고 고전적인 디자인의 찻주전자는 어떠세요? 이건 절대 유행을 타지 않아요.
M : I think she'll like it. How much is it?
어머니가 좋아하실 것 같아요. 얼마죠?
W : It's $20. But if you like this design, we also have this teapot set that comes with the cups. It's only $30.
20달러입니다. 하지만 이 디자인이 마음에 드신다면, 컵이 딸려오는 이 찻주전자 세트도 있어요. 그건 30달러밖에 안 합니다.
M : Great! I'll take the set. Can you recommend some tea as well?
훌륭해요! 전 세트를 사겠어요. 차도 좀 추천해 주시겠어요?
W : Sure. How about this lavender tea? It's definitely good for relaxation, and it's $10 a package.
물론이죠. 이 라벤더 차는 어떠세요? 이건 확실히 이완에 좋고, 한 상자에 10달러입니다.
M : Sounds good. I'll take two packages. Can I use this discount coupon?
좋네요. 전 두 박스를 사겠어요. 제가 이 할인 쿠폰을 쓸 수 있나요?
W : Absolutely. You'll get a 10% discount from the total price.
물론이죠. 총 가격에서 10퍼센트를 할인받으실 거예요.
M : Great. Here's my credit card.
아주 좋아요. 여기 제 신용 카드요.

Why? 왜 정답일까?

대화에 따르면 남자는 30달러짜리 찻주전자 세트와, 상자당 10달러인 라벤더 차를 두 상자 구매하기로 하고, 총 가격에서 10퍼센트를 할인받았다. 이를 식으로 나타내면 '{30+(10×2)}×0.9=45'이므로, 남자가 지불할 금액은 ④ '$45'이다.

● teapot ⓝ 찻주전자
● recommend ⓥ 추천하다
● definitely ⓐⓓ 확실히
● package ⓝ 상자, 포장
● go out of style 유행에 뒤떨어지다
● as well 또한, 역시
● relaxation ⓝ 휴식

---

07 오디션 때문에 특별 박람회 참석을 거절하는 여자 정답률 72% | 정답 ①

대화를 듣고, 여자가 building expo에 갈 수 없는 이유를 고르시오.
☑ 오디션에 참가해야 해서
② 건축학 특강을 들어야 해서
③ 연극 관람을 하러 가야 해서

④ 다른 박람회에 갈 계획이어서
⑤ 집짓기 봉사 활동을 해야 해서

M : The Central Park Museum will have a special expo soon.
Central Park 박물관에서 곧 특별 박람회를 열 거래.
W : What's it about?
뭐에 관한 건데?
M : It's a building expo titled "New Home Builders."
"새로운 집 건축가"라는 제목의 건축 박람회야.
W : Sounds interesting. When does it open?
재미있겠는데. 언제 열리는데?
M : It will start tomorrow at nine a.m. I'm going to the exhibition in the afternoon. Do you want to go with me?
내일 아침 9시에 시작할 거야. 난 오후에 전시에 가 보려고. 나랑 같이 갈래?
W : I'm sorry, but I can't.
가고 싶은데, 그럴 수가 없어.
M : Why not? You're interested in architecture, aren't you?
왜 안 되는데? 너도 건축에 관심이 있잖아, 그렇지 않니?
W : Yes, but I have to do something else.
응, 그런데 뭔가 다른 걸 해야 해.
M : What's your plan?
계획이 뭔데?
W : Actually, I'm auditioning for the school play tomorrow.
사실, 난 내일 학교 연극 오디션이 있어.
M : Oh, I see now. I hope you make it.
오, 이제 알겠다. 잘되기를 바라.

Why? 왜 정답일까?

대화에서 남자는 여자에게 건축 박람회에 함께 가자고 제안하지만 여자는 연극 오디션이 있어(Actually, I'm auditioning for the school play tomorrow.) 갈 수 없다고 이야기한다. 따라서 여자가 building expo에 갈 수 없는 이유는 ① '오디션에 참가해야 해서'이다.

● expo ⓝ 박람회
● architecture ⓝ 건축
● actually 戌 사실은, 실은
● make it 잘되다, 성공하다
● exhibition ⓝ 전시, 전시회, 박람회
● something else 다른 것
● audition ⓝ (가수, 배우 등의) 오디션

---

08 스트레스 완화 프로그램   정답률 94% | 정답 ④

대화를 듣고, Stress Free Program에 관해 언급되지 <u>않은</u> 것을 고르시오.
① 활동 종류   ② 등록 방법   ③ 운영 장소   ✔ 참가비   ⑤ 운영 시간

W : Hey, Ryan, did you hear about the Stress Free Program?
안녕, Ryan, 너 Stress Free Program에 대해 들어 봤어?
M : Stress Free Program? No, what is it?
Stress Free Program이라고? 아니, 그게 뭔데?
W : It's a new school program for students. You might want to join it. You look really stressed out these days.
학생들을 위한 새로운 학교 프로그램이야. 넌 거기 참여해 보는 게 좋을지도 몰라. 너 요새 무척 스트레스를 많이 받는 것 같아 보여.
M : Yeah, I really need to relax. 『What do I do there?』
응, 난 정말 쉴 필요가 있어. 내가 거기서 뭘 하게 되는데?
W : 『You can take part in various activities like coloring, e-sports, and board games.』 ①의근거 일치
넌 색칠하기와 전자 스포츠와 보드 게임 같은 다양한 활동에 참여할 수 있어.
M : Sounds interesting! 『How can I register for the program?』
재미있겠다! 내가 그 프로그램에 어떻게 등록할 수 있어?
W : 『You can register in person or on the school website.』 ②의근거 일치
직접 등록하거나 학교 웹 사이트에서 할 수 있어.
M : 『Where's the program held?』
프로그램은 어디서 열리지?
W : 『It's held on the second floor of the Student Union building.』 ③의근거 일치
학생회관 2층에서 열려.
M : All right. 『Is the program available anytime?』 ⑤의근거 일치
알겠어. 프로그램은 언제든 이용할 수 있는 거야?
W : No, it runs from 3 to 7 p.m.』 There's a schedule for each activity.
아니, 그것은 3시부터 7시까지 운영돼. 각 활동마다 일정이 있어.
M : Okay, I'll check the schedule first.
그래, 난 먼저 일정을 확인하겠어.
W : Great. I hope you can refresh your mind there.
좋아. 거기서 네가 마음을 상쾌하게 하길 바라.

Why? 왜 정답일까?

대화에서 남자와 여자는 Stress Free Program의 활동 종류, 등록 방법, 운영 장소, 운영 시간을 언급하였다. 따라서 언급되지 않은 것은 ④ '참가비'이다.

Why? 왜 오답일까?

① 'You can take part in various activities like coloring, e-sports, and board games.'에서 '활동 종류'가 언급되었다.
② 'You can register in person or on the school website.'에서 '등록 방법'이 언급되었다.
③ 'It's held on the second floor of the Student Union building.'에서 '운영 장소'가 언급되었다.
⑤ 'No, it runs from 3 to 7 p.m.'에서 '운영 시간'이 언급되었다.

● You might want to ~. ~해 보는 게 좋을 거야. (완곡한 권유)
● stressed out 스트레스가 쌓인, 스트레스를 받는
● take part in ~에 참여하다
● in person 직접
● refresh 戌 새롭게 하다
● relax 戌 쉬다
● register 戌 등록하다
● available 嵒 이용 가능한

---

09 학생 건축 디자인 대회 안내   정답률 83% | 정답 ④

2017 Student Design Competition에 관한 다음 내용을 듣고, 일치하지 <u>않는</u> 것을 고르시오.
[3점]

---

① 학생의 창의력 향상을 목표로 한다.
② 참가자는 2층 건물 디자인을 제출해야 한다.
③ 전 세계 대학생이 참가할 수 있다.
✔ 제출한 디자인은 네 개의 기준에 의해 평가된다.
⑤ 출품작은 10월 1일까지 제출해야 한다.

W : Do you think you're a great designer?
당신이 훌륭한 디자이너라고 생각하세요?
Then join the 2017 Student Design Competition.
그럼 2017년 학생 디자인 대회에 참여하세요.
『The goal of this competition is to encourage students' creativity by challenging them to design steel-framed buildings.』 ①의근거 일치
이 대회의 목적은 학생들에게 철골 건물을 디자인하도록 요구함으로써 학생들의 창의력을 북돋우는 데 있습니다.
『Participants should submit the design of a two-story building.』 ②의근거 일치
참가자들은 2층 건물의 디자인을 제출해야 합니다.
The winning design will be used for a museum.
수상작 디자인은 박물관을 위해 쓰일 것입니다.
『The competition is open to college students around the world.』 ③의근거 일치
대회는 전 세계 대학생에게 열려 있습니다.
『Submissions will be judged using three standards: efficiency, constructability, and creativity.』 ④의근거 불일치
제출작들은 효율성, 시공성, 창의성이라는 세 개 기준을 이용하여 평가될 것입니다.
『The entry should be submitted to info@designcom.org by October 1st.』 ⑤의근거 일치
출품작은 10월 1일까지 info@designcom.org로 제출되어야 합니다.
We are looking forward to seeing your innovative designs.
여러분의 혁신적인 디자인을 볼 수 있기를 고대하겠습니다.

Why? 왜 정답일까?

'Submissions will be judged using three standards: efficiency, constructability, and creativity.'에서 디자인은 효율성, 시공성, 창의성이라는 세 기준에 의해 평가된다고 말하므로, 2017 Student Design Competition에 관한 내용과 일치하지 않는 것은 ④ '제출한 디자인은 네 개의 기준에 의해 평가된다.'이다.

Why? 왜 오답일까?

① 'The goal of this competition is to encourage students' creativity by challenging them to design steel-framed buildings.'와 일치한다.
② 'Participants should submit the design of a two-story building.'와 일치한다.
③ 'The competition is open to college students around the world.'와 일치한다.
⑤ 'The entry should be submitted to info@designcom.org by October 1st.'와 일치한다.

● competition ⓝ 대회, 경쟁
● creativity ⓝ 창의성
● story ⓝ (건물의) 층
● entry ⓝ 출품작
● encourage 戌 북돋우다, 장려하다
● submit 戌 제출하다
● efficiency ⓝ 효율성
● innovative 嵒 혁신적인

---

10 블루투스 키보드 고르기   정답률 89% | 정답 ②

다음 표를 보면서 대화를 듣고, 여자가 주문할 블루투스 키보드를 고르시오.

Bluetooth Keyboards

	Model	Price	Weight	Battery Life	Foldable
①	A	$45	160g	100 hours	×
✔②	B	$38	250g	82 hours	○
③	C	$30	280g	48 hours	×
④	D	$26	350g	10 hours	○
⑤	E	$15	420g	24 hours	×

M : Jessica, what are you doing on the computer?
Jessica, 컴퓨터로 뭐 하고 있어?
W : I'm looking for a bluetooth keyboard that works with my smartphone.
난 내 스마트폰하고 같이 쓸 블루투스 키보드를 찾고 있어.
M : What do you need it for?
그게 왜 필요해?
W : I need to type during meetings at work. Can you help me choose one?
회사에서 회의 중에 타자를 쳐야 하거든. 내가 하나 고르는 것을 도와줄래?
M : Sure. How about this model? 『It looks great and is the cheapest.』
물론이지. 이 모델은 어때? 이건 근사해 보이고 제일 싸.
W : I already have that model, but it's too heavy to carry around.』 근거1 Price 조건
난 이미 그 제품이 있는데, 너무 무거워서 들고 다닐 수가 없어.
M : Then, 『why don't you get something that weighs less than 300 grams?』 근거2 Weight 조건
그렇다면, 300그램보다 무게가 적게 나가는 것을 사는 게 어때?
W : Yeah. That makes sense.
응. 일리가 있어.
M : You can get this one. 『It also has a battery life of 100 hours.』 근거3 Battery Life 조건
이것을 사 봐. 이건 게다가 배터리 수명이 100시간이야.
W : It's nice,』 but it's not foldable. I want to buy that one, instead.
근사한데, 접을 수가 없네. 난 대신에 저것을 사고 싶어.
M : You mean this foldable keyboard?
이 접는 키보드 말하는 거야?   근거4 Foldable 조건
W : Yeah, it'll take up much less space in my bag.』 I think I'll order it now.
응, 그것은 내 가방 안에서 자리를 많이 차지하지 않을 거야. 난 그것을 지금 주문해야 할 것 같아.

Why? 왜 정답일까?

대화에 따르면 여자는 가격이 싼 것보다도 무게가 300g 미만으로 나가는 것, 배터리 수명이 긴 것보다도 접는 블루투스 키보드를 구매하려고 한다. 따라서 여자가 주문할 블루투스 키보드로 가장 적절한 것은 ② 'B'이다.

● carry around 가지고 다니다
● That makes sense. 일리가 있네.
● take up ~을 차지하다
● weigh 戌 무게가 ~이다
● foldable 嵒 접는

11 제주도 여행 및 음식 묻기

정답률 71% | 정답 ③

대화를 듣고, 여자의 마지막 말에 대한 남자의 응답으로 가장 적절한 것을 고르시오.

① Why don't you give it a try? – 너도 시도해 보는 게 어때?
② I want to visit other countries, too. – 나도 다른 나라들을 가 보고 싶어.
☑ I really liked noodle soup with pork. – 돼지고기를 곁들인 국수가 정말 좋았어.
④ It took one hour to get to the beach. – 해변에 가는 데 한 시간이 걸렸어.
⑤ Can you pick me up from the airport? – 공항으로 나를 데리러 나올래?

W : How was your trip to Jeju Island?
　제주도 여행 어땠어?
M : It was great. The food was especially amazing.
　아주 좋았어. 음식이 특히 근사했어.
W : What did you enjoy the most? I want to try it when I go there.
　뭐가 제일 좋았어? 나도 거기 가면 먹어 보고 싶은데.
M : I really liked noodle soup with pork.
　돼지고기를 곁들인 국수가 정말 좋았어.

Why? 왜 정답일까?

대화에서 여자는 남자에게 제주도 여행을 갔을 때 먹은 음식 중 어떤 것이 가장 좋았는지(What did you enjoy the most?) 묻고 있으므로, 남자의 응답으로 가장 적절한 것은 ③ '돼지고기를 곁들인 국수가 정말 좋았어.'이다.

● especially ad 특히
● noodle n 국수
● amazing a 근사한, 경탄할 만한

12 자원봉사 시간 변경 문의

정답률 77% | 정답 ①

대화를 듣고, 남자의 마지막 말에 대한 여자의 응답으로 가장 적절한 것을 고르시오.

☑ All right. Either day is fine with me. – 알겠습니다. 둘 중 어느 날이라도 전 좋아요.
② I'm sorry. You can't choose the date. – 죄송해요. 날짜는 고르실 수 없습니다.
③ Really? I didn't know about the change. – 정말요? 전 바뀐 것을 몰랐어요.
④ Thanks. I enjoyed the volunteer program. – 고맙습니다. 전 자원봉사 프로그램을 즐겼어요.
⑤ Good. I'm looking forward to this weekend. – 좋네요. 전 이번 주말이 기대돼요.

[Telephone rings.]
[전화벨이 울린다.]
M : Hello. This is the Youth Volunteer Center. What can I do for you?
　여보세요. Youth Volunteer Center입니다. 무엇을 도와드릴까요?
W : I'm supposed to join the volunteer program tomorrow, but can I change my volunteering schedule?
　전 내일 자원봉사 프로그램에 참여하기로 되어 있는데, 제 봉사 일정을 바꿀 수 있을까요?
M : Sure. You can choose from Thursday or Friday.
　물론입니다. 목요일이나 금요일 중에 선택하실 수 있어요.
W : All right. Either day is fine with me.
　알겠습니다. 둘 중 어느 날이라도 전 좋아요.

Why? 왜 정답일까?

다음 날 자원봉사 프로그램에 참여하기로 한 여자가 일정을 바꿀 수 없는지 문의하자, 남자는 목요일이나 금요일 중 선택할 수 있다고 한다(You can choose from Thursday or Friday.). 따라서 여자의 응답으로 가장 적절한 것은 ① '알겠습니다. 둘 중 어느 날이라도 전 좋아요.'이다.

● be supposed to ~하기로 되어 있다
● either a (둘 중) 어느 하나의
● volunteer n 자원 봉사자 v 자원 봉사하다

13 물병에 이름 새기는 것 요청하기

정답률 67% | 정답 ⑤

대화를 듣고, 남자의 마지막 말에 대한 여자의 응답으로 가장 적절한 것을 고르시오. [3점]

Woman:
① I think I received the wrong items.
　잘못된 제품을 받은 것 같아요.
② Fortunately, my students really liked the gifts.
　다행히도 제 학생들이 선물을 좋아했어요.
③ I'll check if your order can be canceled or not.
　손님 주문을 취소할 수 있는지 없는지 여부를 확인하겠습니다.
④ Your baseball club did a great job. Congratulations!
　당신의 야구 동아리는 정말 잘했어요. 축하해요!
☑ I'll upload the list to your bulletin board in an hour.
　한 시간 후에 게시판에 목록을 올릴게요.

[Telephone rings.]
[전화벨이 울린다.]
M : Hello. This is Gift Variety. How can I help you?
　여보세요. Gift Variety입니다. 무엇을 도와드릴까요?
W : Hello. I ordered 30 water bottles on your site two days ago, but I want to put a design on them.
　여보세요. 거기 사이트에서 이틀 전에 물병 30개를 주문했는데, 그 위에 디자인을 넣고 싶어서요.
M : I'll check if that's possible or not. Can I have your order number?
　가능한지 확인해 보겠습니다. 주문 번호를 말씀해 주시겠어요?
W : AE13043.
　AE13043입니다.
M : One moment. [Typing sound] It looks like you can still do that.
　잠시만요. [타자 치는 소리] 아직 그렇게 하실 수 있는 것 같네요.
W : Good. The bottles will be a gift for my students' baseball club, so I want to put our club members' names on the bottles.
　좋아요. 그 물병은 제 학생들의 야구 동아리를 위한 선물이 될 거라서, 물병에 동아리 회원 아이들의 이름을 써 주고 싶어요.
M : I see, but it will cost you an extra 30 dollars.
　그러시군요. 그런데 추가로 30달러가 듭니다.
W : No problem. Can I still get them before next Monday?
　괜찮아요. 그렇게 해도 다음 주 월요일 전에 그걸 받을 수 있나요?
M : If that's the case, you'll have to give us the list of names by today.
　그런 경우이시면, 오늘까지 이름 목록을 저희 쪽에 주셔야 합니다.

W : I'll upload the list to your bulletin board in an hour.
　한 시간 후에 게시판에 목록을 올릴게요.

Why? 왜 정답일까?

대화에서 여자는 이미 주문한 물병에 야구 동아리 학생들의 이름을 새겨서 그다음 월요일 전까지 배송을 받고 싶어 하는데, 남자는 그 경우 당일 중으로 이름 목록이 필요하다(If that's the case, you'll have to give us the list of names by today.)고 이야기한다. 따라서 이에 대한 여자의 응답으로 가장 적절한 것은 ⑤ '한 시간 후에 게시판에 목록을 올릴게요.'이다.

● order v 주문하다
● case n 경우, 사례, 사건
● still ad 아직, 여전히, 그래도
● bulletin board (전자) 게시판

14 콘서트 장소 변경

정답률 73% | 정답 ①

대화를 듣고, 여자의 마지막 말에 대한 남자의 응답으로 가장 적절한 것을 고르시오. [3점]

Man:
☑ We can post the notice on social media. – 우린 소셜 미디어에 공지를 올릴 수 있어.
② Let's move our instruments indoors, then. – 그럼 우리 악기들을 실내로 옮기자.
③ I've already cancelled our outdoor concert. – 난 이미 우리 야외 콘서트를 취소했어.
④ We'd better change the location right away. – 우린 즉시 장소를 바꾸는 게 낫겠어.
⑤ We can check the weather forecast using an app. – 우린 앱을 이용해서 일기 예보를 확인할 수 있어.

W : Chris, did you hear the weather forecast?
　Chris, 일기 예보 들었어?
M : No, what did it say?
　아니, 뭐라는데?
W : It said there would be heavy rain and strong winds this afternoon.
　오늘 오후에 폭우와 강한 바람이 있을 거랬어.
M : Oh, no! Our outdoor concert is supposed to start at 4 p.m. What should we do?
　오, 이런! 우리 야외 콘서트가 오후 4시에 시작할 예정이야. 어떻게 해야 하지?
W : The teacher said we have to change the location of the concert to the school auditorium.
　선생님께서 콘서트 장소를 학교 강당으로 바꿔야 할 것 같다고 하셨어.
M : Okay. We still have several hours to set up the stage. But how can we inform people of the change?
　알겠어. 아직 우린 몇 시간 동안 무대를 설치할 수 있어. 하지만 사람들한테 변경 사항을 어떻게 알리지?
W : I'll make a notice and put it up on the notice board at the outdoor concert hall.
　내가 공지문을 만들어서 그것을 야외 콘서트장에 있는 알림판에 붙일게.
M : Good. I'll go and ask the school broadcasting station to make an announcement about it.
　좋아. 난 방송실에 가서 그것에 관한 공지를 부탁할게.
W : Good idea. Is there any other way for us to spread the news to more people quickly?
　좋은 생각이야. 우리가 더 많은 사람들에게 빨리 뉴스를 퍼뜨릴 다른 방법이 또 있을까?
M : We can post the notice on social media.
　우린 소셜 미디어에 공지를 올릴 수 있어.

Why? 왜 정답일까?

날씨 상황이 좋지 않아 콘서트 장소를 바꾸기로 한 남자와 여자는 장소 변경에 관한 공지를 어떻게 할 것인지에 관해 논의하고 있다. 'Is there any other way for us to spread the news to more people quickly?'에서 여자는 더 많은 사람들에게 빨리 변경 소식을 알릴 방법이 더 없을지 남자에게 묻고 있으므로, 남자의 응답으로 가장 적절한 것은 ① '우린 소셜 미디어에 공지를 올릴 수 있어.'이다.

● weather forecast 일기 예보
● set up ~을 설치하다
● notice n 공고문
● instrument n 악기, 도구
● auditorium n 강당
● inform A of B A에게 B에 대해 알리다
● spread v 퍼뜨리다

15 다 먹지 않은 접시를 치우지 말아달라고 부탁하기

정답률 67% | 정답 ②

다음 상황 설명을 듣고, Kate가 종업원에게 할 말로 가장 적절한 것을 고르시오.

Kate:
① Would you refill the drinks? – 음료 리필하시겠어요?
☑ I think he's still eating that. – 그가 아직 그걸 먹고 있는 중인 것 같아요.
③ Can I get the check, please? – 계산서를 주시겠어요?
④ Thank you for cleaning the table. – 식탁을 치워주셔서 고맙습니다.
⑤ I would like to order a shrimp dish. – 새우 요리를 시키고 싶은데요.

M : Kate and David love a new seafood buffet restaurant in their town.
　Kate와 David는 시내에 있는 새로운 해산물 뷔페를 무척 좋아한다.
　One day, they go to the buffet, fill up their plates, and bring them to their table.
　어느 날 그들은 뷔페에 가서 접시를 채우고 그것을 테이블로 가져왔다.
　Then, as David is eating his favorite shrimp dish, he decides to get something to drink.
　그리고 나서, David는 자신이 가장 좋아하는 새우 요리를 먹다가 마실 것을 가져오기로 한다.
　So, he leaves the table with his shrimp dish unfinished.
　그래서 그는 새우 요리를 다 먹지 않은 채로 테이블을 떠난다.
　When Kate is eating alone at the table, a waiter comes and tries to take away David's almost empty plate.
　Kate가 혼자 테이블에서 먹고 있을 때, 종업원이 다가오더니 거의 비어 있는 David의 접시를 치우려 한다.
　Kate wants to tell the waiter that David is not done with the dish.
　Kate는 종업원에게 David가 음식을 다 먹은 게 아니라고 말해주고 싶다.
　In this situation, what would Kate most likely say to the waiter?
　이런 상황에서, Kate는 종업원에게 뭐라고 말하겠는가?
Kate : I think he's still eating that.
　그가 아직 그걸 먹고 있는 중인 것 같아요.

Why? 왜 정답일까?

상황에 따르면 Kate는 새우 요리를 다 먹지 않고 음료를 가지러 간 David를 위해 접시를 치우지 말아달라고 종업원에게 말하고 싶어 한다(Kate wants to tell the waiter that David is not done with the dish.). 따라서 Kate가 종업원에게 할 말로 가장 적절한 것은 ② '그가 아직 그걸 먹고 있는 중인 것 같아요.'이다.

- **seafood** ⓝ 해산물
- **plate** ⓝ 접시
- **take away** 치우다, 가지고 가다
- **fill up** ~을 채우다
- **unfinished** ⓐ 끝내지 않은, 마치지 않은

16-17 물건 나눔 권유

W : Hello, everyone!
안녕하세요, 여러분!
Today, I want you to consider this: do you have something you're not using in your home?
오늘 저는 여러분이 이걸 고려해보시기를 바랍니다. 집에 쓰지 않는 어떤 물건이 있으신가요?
『Then, how about sharing it with others?』 16번의 근거
그렇다면 그것을 다른 사람들과 나누는 게 어때요?
It enables products to be recycled and reused, reducing the negative effects on the environment. 17번 ①의 근거 일치
그것은 물건들이 재활용되고 재사용되는 것을 가능하게 하며, 환경에 대한 부정적 영향을 줄여줍니다.
『For example, if you have a nice dress for a party, lend it to others who need it.』
예를 들어, 만일 여러분이 멋진 파티 드레스를 갖고 있다면, 그것을 필요로 하는 다른 사람들에게 빌려주세요.
Then the materials used in making a new dress can be saved.
그러면 새로운 드레스를 만드는 데 쓰이는 재료를 아낄 수 있습니다.
『The same thing with toys.』 17번 ②의 근거 일치
장난감도 마찬가지입니다.
Every year, millions of toys that children no longer play with are thrown away.
매년, 아이들이 더 이상 갖고 놀지 않는 장난감 수백만 개가 버려집니다.
By sharing them with others, you can reduce waste.
그것을 다른 사람들과 나눔으로써, 여러분은 쓰레기를 줄일 수 있습니다.
Also, you can benefit financially by sharing your goods.
또한, 여러분의 물건을 나눔으로써 여러분은 재정적으로 이득을 볼 수 있습니다.
『If you have books you've finished reading, register them on online sharing systems.』 17번 ④의 근거 일치
만일 여러분이 다 읽은 책이 있다면, 그것들을 온라인 공유 시스템에 등록하세요.
Then, someone who wants to read your books can rent them and you can make money by sharing.
그러면, 여러분의 책을 읽고 싶어 하는 누군가가 그것을 빌려갈 수 있고 여러분은 공유를 통해 돈을 벌 수 있습니다.
『Similarly, if you need a bicycle, you can find some people who share theirs on bike-sharing systems and save money.』 17번 ⑤의 근거 일치
마찬가지로, 여러분이 자전거가 필요하면, 여러분은 자전거 공유 시스템에 자기 것을 공유하고 있는 몇몇 사람들을 찾아서 돈을 아낄 수 있습니다.
Why don't you awaken your "sleeping" goods?
여러분의 '잠자고 있는' 물건들을 깨워보시는 게 어떠세요?

- **share** ⓥ 공유하다
- **environment** ⓝ 환경
- **no longer** 더 이상 ~않다
- **benefit** ⓝ 이득 ⓥ 이득을 보다
- **awaken** ⓥ (잠에서) 깨다, 깨우다
- **negative** ⓐ 부정적인
- **material** ⓝ 재료, 물질
- **throw away** ~을 버리다
- **financially** ⓐ 재정적으로
- **necessity** ⓝ 필요성

16 주제 파악   정답률 83% | 정답 ①

여자가 하는 말의 주제로 가장 적절한 것은?
☑ ① benefits of sharing things - 물건을 공유하는 것의 이득
② ways to sell used stuff online - 중고품을 온라인으로 파는 방법들
③ steps in the recycling process - 재활용 과정의 단계
④ necessity of sharing information - 정보 공유의 필요성
⑤ problems caused by online markets - 온라인 매장이 초래하는 문제들

Why? 왜 정답일까?

'Then, how about sharing it with others?'에서 여자는 집에서 쓰지 않는 물건을 다른 사람들과 공유할 것을 권한 후 물건 공유의 여러 가지 이득을 예시와 함께 열거하고 있다. 따라서 여자가 하는 말의 주제로 가장 적절한 것은 ① '물건을 공유하는 것의 이득'이다.

17 언급 유무 파악   정답률 94% | 정답 ③

언급된 물건이 아닌 것은?
① a dress - 드레스
② toys - 장난감
☑ ③ a car - 자동차
④ books - 책
⑤ a bicycle - 자전거

Why? 왜 정답일까?

담화에서 여자는 나눌 수 있는 물건의 예시로 드레스, 장난감, 책, 자전거를 언급하였다. 따라서 언급되지 않은 것은 ③ '자동차'이다.

Why? 왜 오답일까?

① 'For example, if you have a nice dress for a party, lend it to others who need it.'에서 '드레스'가 언급되었다.
② 'The same thing with toys.'에서 '장난감'이 언급되었다.
④ 'If you have books you've finished reading, register them on online sharing systems.'에서 '책'이 언급되었다.
⑤ 'Similarly, if you need a bicycle, you can find some people who share theirs on bike-sharing systems and save money.'에서 '자전거'가 언급되었다.

18 공원 산책로 복구 요청   정답률 90% | 정답 ①

다음 글의 목적으로 가장 적절한 것은?
☑ ① 공원 산책로 복구를 요청하려고
② 노인 복지 서비스 개선을 건의하려고
③ 휠체어 대여 서비스에 대해 안내하려고
④ 청소년 야외 활동 시설에 대해 문의하려고
⑤ 공원 내 주차 공간 부족에 대해 항의하려고

To whom it may concern:
담당자 귀하.
My wife and I have lived in Smalltown / for more than 60 years / and have enjoyed Freer Park for all that time.
제 아내와 저는 Smalltown에서 살았고, / 60년 이상 / 항상 Freer Park를 즐겼습니다.
When we were young / and didn't have the money to go anywhere else, / we would walk there almost every day.
저희가 젊어서 / 다른 곳으로 갈 돈이 없었을 때, / 저희는 거의 매일 그곳을 걷곤 했습니다.
Now we are seniors, / and my wife must use a wheelchair for extended walks.
이제 저희는 노인이고, / 제 아내는 장시간 산책하려면 휠체어를 사용해야만 합니다.
We find / that the beautiful walking paths through the park / are all but impassable to her.
저희는 알게 되었습니다. / 공원 곳곳의 아름다운 산책로는 / 아내로서는 지나가기 거의 불가능하다는 것을
The paths are cracked and littered with rocks and debris / that make it impossible / to roll her chair from place to place.
산책로는 금이 가 있고 돌멩이와 파편이 널려 있어 / 불가능합니다. / 휠체어가 여기저기 다니는 것이
We hope / you will devote resources / to restoring the walking paths in Freer Park for all visitors.
우리는 희망합니다. / 귀하가 자원을 투입해 주기를 / 모든 방문객들을 위해 Freer Park에 있는 산책로를 복구하는 데
Sincerely, // Craig Thomas
Craig Thomas 드림

담당자 귀하,

제 아내와 저는 60년 이상 Smalltown에서 살았고, 항상 Freer Park를 즐겨왔습니다. 저희가 젊어서 다른 곳으로 갈 돈이 없었을 때, 거의 매일 그곳을 걷곤 했습니다. 이제 저희는 노인이고, 제 아내는 장시간 산책하려면 휠체어를 사용해야만 합니다. 저희는 아내가 공원 곳곳의 아름다운 산책로를 지나가는 것이 거의 불가능하다는 것을 알게 되었습니다. 산책로는 금이 가 있고 돌멩이와 파편이 널려 있어 휠체어가 여기저기 다니는 것이 불가능합니다. 모든 방문객들을 위해 Freer Park에 있는 산책로를 복구하는 데 자원을 투입해 주기를 희망합니다.

Craig Thomas 드림

Why? 왜 정답일까?

마지막 문장인 'We hope you will devote resources to restoring the walking paths in Freer Park for all visitors.'에서 휠체어가 다닐 수 있도록 산책로를 복구해 주기를 바란다고 이야기하므로, 글의 목적으로 가장 적절한 것은 ① '공원 산책로 복구를 요청하려고'이다.

- **to whom it may concern** (주로 편지에서) 담당자 귀하
- **extended** ⓐ 길어진, 장시간에 걸친
- **impassable** ⓐ 지나갈 수 없는, 통행 불가한
- **littered with** ~가 널린, ~로 어질러진
- **devote** ⓥ 바치다, 헌신하다
- **through** prep ~을 통해
- **cracked** ⓐ 갈라진
- **debris** ⓝ 파편, 잔해

구문 풀이

6행 We find that the beautiful walking paths through the park are all but
         접속사(~것)   주어   동사(복수)↵ 거의
impassable to her.
주격 보어

19 야간 비행 중 위기 극복   정답률 81% | 정답 ②

다음 글에 드러난 'I'의 심경 변화로 가장 적절한 것은?
① ashamed → delighted
     부끄러운   기쁜
☑ ② terrified → relieved
     겁에 질린   안도한
③ satisfied → regretful
     만족한   후회하는
④ indifferent → excited
     무관심한   신난
⑤ hopeful → disappointed
     희망에 부푼   실망한

I board the plane, / take off, / and climb out into the night sky.
나는 비행기를 타고 / 이륙해서 / 밤하늘로 올라간다.
Within minutes, / the plane shakes hard, / and I freeze, / feeling like I'm not in control of anything.
몇 분 되지 않아 / 비행기가 심하게 흔들리고 / 나는 몸이 굳는다. / 아무것도 통제할 수 없다는 것을 느끼며
The left engine starts losing power / and the right engine is nearly dead now.
왼쪽 엔진은 동력을 잃기 시작하고 / 오른쪽 엔진은 이제 거의 멈췄다.
Rain hits the windscreen / and I'm getting into heavier weather.
비가 앞 유리에 부딪히고 / 나는 더 악화되는 기상 속으로 들어간다.
I'm having trouble keeping up the airspeed.
나는 대기 속도를 유지하는 것에 어려움을 겪고 있다.
When I reach for the microphone to call the center / to declare an emergency, / my shaky hand accidentally bumps the carburetor heat levers, / and the left engine suddenly regains power.
센터에 전화하려고 마이크에 손을 뻗을 때, / 비상 상황을 신고하기 위해 / 나의 떨리는 손이 우연히 기화기 열 레버를 툭 치고, / 갑자기 왼쪽 엔진의 동력이 되살아난다.
I push the levers to full.
나는 레버를 끝까지 누른다.
Both engines backfire / and come to full power.
두 엔진이 모두 점화되어 / 최대 동력에 이르게 된다.
Feeling that the worst is over, / I find my whole body loosening up and at ease.
최악의 고비가 끝났다고 느끼며, / 나는 온몸의 긴장이 풀리고 편안해짐을 알게 된다.

나는 비행기를 타고 이륙해서 밤하늘로 올라간다. 몇 분 되지 않아 비행기가 심하게 흔들리고 나는 아무것도 통제할 수 없다는 것을 느끼며 몸이 굳는다. 왼쪽 엔진은 동력을 잃기 시작하고 오른쪽 엔진은 이제 거의 멈췄다. 비가 앞 유리에 부딪히고 나는 더 악화되는 기상 속으로 들어간다. 나는 대기 속도를 유지하는 것에 어려움을 겪고 있다. 비상 상황을 신고하기 위해 센터에 전화하려고 마이크에 손을 뻗을 때, 나의 떨리는 손이 우연히 기화기 열 레버를 툭

치고, 갑자기 왼쪽 엔진의 동력이 되살아난다. 나는 레버를 끝까지 누른다. 두 엔진이 모두 점화되어 최대 동력에 이르게 된다. 최악의 고비가 끝났다고 느끼며, 나는 온몸의 긴장이 풀리고 편안해짐을 알게 된다.

Why? 왜 정답일까?

'~ I freeze, feeling like I'm not in control of anything.'에서 이륙한지 얼마 지나지 않아 비행기가 심하게 흔들리자 필자가 두려움에 몸이 굳었다는 내용이, 'Feeling that the worst is over, I find my whole body loosening up and at ease.'에서 최악의 위기를 극복한 필자가 긴장이 풀렸다는 내용이 나온다. 따라서 'I'의 심경 변화로 가장 적절한 것은 ② '겁에 질린 → 안도한'이다.

- **board** ⓥ 탑승하다
- **nearly** [ad] 거의
- **keep up** ~을 계속하다, 유지하다
- **declare** ⓥ 신고하다, 선언하다
- **loosen up** 긴장을 풀다
- **in control of** ~을 통제하는
- **windscreen** ⓝ 앞 유리
- **reach for** ~에 손을 뻗다
- **accidentally** [ad] 우연히
- **at ease** (마음이) 편안한

구문 풀이

10행 Feeling that the worst is over, I find my whole body loosening up and
　분사구문　접속사(~것)　　5형식 동사　목적어　　목적격 보어1(분사)
at ease.
목적격 보어2(전명구)

---

20 타인에 대한 성급한 판단 경계하기　　정답률 82% | 정답 ①

다음 글에서 필자가 주장하는 바로 가장 적절한 것은?
☑ 단시간의 관찰로 타인을 성급하게 판단하지 마라.
② 자신의 적성을 찾기 위해 다양한 경험을 쌓아라.
③ 바람직하지 않은 습관을 고치기 위해 노력하라.
④ 원만한 인간관계를 위해 칭찬을 아끼지 마라.
⑤ 말보다는 행동으로 삶의 모범을 보여라.

It is easy to judge people / based on their actions.
사람들을 판단하는 것은 쉽다. / 행동에 근거하여
We are often taught / to put more value in actions than words, / and for good reason.
우리는 종종 배우는데, / 말보다 행동에 더 많은 가치를 두도록 / 그럴만한 이유가 충분하다.
The actions of others often speak volumes / louder than their words.
다른 사람의 행동은 종종 소리 크기로 말한다. / 그들의 말보다 더 큰
However, when someone exhibits some difficult behavior, / you might want to reserve judgement for later.
하지만 누군가가 난해한 행동을 보일 때, / 여러분은 판단을 나중으로 유보하고 싶을 수도 있다.
People are not always defined by their behavior.
사람들은 항상 행동으로 정의되지는 않는다.
It is common / to think, "He is so bossy," or "She is so mean," / after observing less-than-desirable behavior in someone.
흔하다. / "그는 너무 거들먹거려," 또는 "그녀는 너무 심술궂어,"라고 생각하는 것은 / 누군가에게서 별로 바람직하지 않은 행동을 관찰한 후에
But you should never make such assumptions right away.
그러나 그러한 추정을 즉시 내려서는 안 된다.
You should give someone a second chance / before you label them and shut them out forever.
여러분은 누군가에게 다시 한 번 기회를 줘야 한다. / 그들을 낙인찍고 영원히 차단해 버리기 전에
You may find a great co-worker or best friend in someone, / so don't eliminate a person from your life / based on a brief observation.
누군가가 훌륭한 동료 또는 절친한 친구라는 것을 알게 될 수도 있으니, / 어떤 사람을 삶에서 제거하지 마라. / 단시간의 관찰에 근거하여

행동에 근거하여 사람들을 판단하는 것은 쉽다. 우리는 종종 말보다 행동에 더 많은 가치를 두도록 배우는데, 그럴만한 이유가 충분하다. 다른 사람의 행동은 종종 그들이 하는 말보다 더 큰 목소리를 낸다. 하지만 누군가가 난해한 행동을 보일 때, 여러분은 판단을 나중으로 유보하고 싶을 수도 있다. 사람들은 항상 행동으로 정의되지는 않는다. 누군가에게서 별로 바람직하지 않은 행동을 관찰한 후에 "그는 너무 거들먹거려," 또는 "그녀는 너무 심술궂어,"라고 보통 생각한다. 그러나 그러한 추정을 즉시 내려서는 안 된다. 그들을 낙인찍고 영원히 차단해 버리기 전에 다시 한 번 기회를 줘야 한다. 누군가가 훌륭한 동료 또는 절친한 친구라는 것을 알게 될 수도 있으니, 단시간의 관찰로 사람을 삶에서 제거하지 마라.

Why? 왜 정답일까?

'~. so don't eliminate a person from your life based on a brief observation.'에서 한 사람의 행동에 대한 짧은 관찰에만 근거하여 그 사람을 바로 단정하지 말라고 이야기하므로, 필자가 주장하는 바로 가장 적절한 것은 ① '단시간의 관찰로 타인을 성급하게 판단하지 마라.'이다.

- **based on** ~에 근거하여
- **exhibit** ⓥ 보이다, 드러내다
- **reserve** ⓥ 유보하다
- **bossy** ⓐ 거들먹거리는
- **assumption** ⓝ 추측, 가정, 추정
- **co-worker** 동료
- **value** ⓝ 가치
- **behavior** ⓝ 행동
- **define** ⓥ 정의하다
- **mean** ⓐ 심술궂은, 비열한
- **shut out** 차단하다
- **brief** ⓐ 짧은, 단시간의

구문 풀이

1행 We are often taught to put more value in actions than words, and for
　　　　　　　　　'be taught + to부정사: ~하도록 배우다'
good reason.

---

21 성공에 대한 기존의 정의의 한계　　정답률 56% | 정답 ⑤

밑줄 친 "There is no there there."가 다음 글에서 의미하는 바로 가장 적절한 것은? [3점]
① People are losing confidence in themselves.
　사람들은 자신에 대한 믿음을 잃어가고 있다.
② Without dreams, there is no chance for growth.
　꿈이 없다면, 성장할 기회도 없다.
③ We should not live according to others' expectations.
　우리는 타인의 기대에 따라 살아서는 안 된다.

④ It is hard to realize our potential in difficult situations.
　어려운 상황에서 우리의 잠재력을 실현하는 어렵다.
☑ Money and power do not necessarily lead you to success.
　돈과 권력은 당신을 꼭 성공으로 이끄는 것은 아니다.

I believe / the second decade of this new century / is already very different.
나는 믿는다. / 이 새로운 세기의 두 번째 십 년은 / 이미 매우 다르다고
There are, of course, still millions of people / who equate success with money and power / — who are determined to never get off that treadmill / despite the cost / in terms of their well-being, relationships, and happiness.
물론 수백만의 사람들이 있다 / 여전히 돈과 권력을 성공과 동일시하는 / 쳇바퀴에서 결코 내려오려 하지 않는 / 대가를 치르고도 / 자신의 안녕, 관계, 그리고 행복의 관점에서
There are still millions / desperately looking for the next promotion, the next million-dollar payday / that they believe will satisfy their longing / to feel better about themselves, / or silence their dissatisfaction.
수백만의 사람들이 여전히 있다. / 다음번 승진과 다음번 고액 월급을 받는 날을 필사적으로 추구하는 / 바람을 충족시켜 주거나 / 자신에 대해 좋게 느끼게 하는 / 불만을 잠재워 줄 것이라고 믿는
But both in the West and in emerging economies, / there are more people every day / who recognize that these are all dead ends / — that they are chasing a broken dream.
하지만 서구와 신흥 경제 국가 모두에서 / 사람들이 매일 늘어나고 있다. / 이러한 것들은 모두 막다른 길이라는 것을 인식하는 / 즉 자신들이 부서진 꿈을 좇고 있음을
That we cannot find the answer / in our current definition of success alone / because — as Gertrude Stein once said of Oakland — / "There is no there there."
우리가 정답을 찾을 수 없다는 것을 / 성공에 대한 현재의 정의만으로는 / 언젠가 Gertrude Stein이 Oakland에 대해 말했듯이 / "그곳에는 그곳이 없기" 때문에

나는 이 새로운 세기의 두 번째 십 년은 이미 매우 다르다고 믿는다. 물론 여전히 돈과 권력을 성공과 동일시하는 수백만의 사람들, 즉 자신의 안녕, 관계, 그리고 행복의 관점에서 대가를 치르고도 쳇바퀴에서 결코 내려오려 하지 않는 사람들이 있다. 자신에 대해 더욱 좋게 느끼고자 하는 바람을 충족시켜 주거나 불만을 잠재워 줄 것이라고 믿는 다음번 승진과 다음번 고액 월급을 받는 날을 필사적으로 추구하는 수백만의 사람들이 여전히 있다. 하지만 서구와 신흥 경제 국가 모두에서 이러한 것들은 모두 막다른 길이라는 것, 즉 자신들이 부서진 꿈을 좇고 있음을 인식하는 사람들이 매일 늘어나고 있다. 언젠가 Gertrude Stein이 Oakland에 대해 말했듯이 "그곳에는 그곳이 없기" 때문에, 성공에 대한 현재의 정의만으로는 정답을 찾을 수 없다(는 것을 인식하는 사람들이 매일 늘어나고 있다).

Why? 왜 정답일까?

But 앞에서 미래의 돈과 권력을 성공과 동일시하는 수 없이 많은 사람들이 있다고 언급한 후, But 뒤에서는 그러한 것들이 모두 막다른 길과 부서진 꿈에 다를 바 없음을 지적하는 글이다. 이 내용에 비추어볼 때, '(사람들이 꿈꾸는) 그곳이 없다'는 표현은 현재 많은 사람들이 성공과 연관 지어 생각하는 돈과 권력이 실제로 성공을 가져다주지 못한다는 의미로 이해할 수 있다. 따라서 밑줄 친 부분이 의미하는 바로 가장 적절한 것은 ⑤ '돈과 권력은 당신을 꼭 성공으로 이끄는 것은 아니다.'이다.

- **treadmill** ⓝ (다람쥐) 쳇바퀴, 러닝머신
- **desperately** [ad] 필사적으로
- **dissatisfaction** ⓝ 불만
- **dead end** 막다른 길
- **confidence** ⓝ 믿음, 자신감
- **not necessarily** 꼭 ~한 것은 아니다
- **well-being** 안녕, 행복
- **payday** ⓝ 월급날
- **emerging** ⓐ 신흥의, 최근 생겨난
- **chase** ⓥ 좇다, 추구하다
- **realize** ⓥ (꿈 등을) 실현하다

구문 풀이

2행 There are, of course, still millions of people [who equate success with
　　　　　동사　　　　　　　　　　　주어(선행사)　　주격 관·대1
money and power] — [who are determined to never get off that treadmill despite
　　　　　　　　　주격 관·대2　　　　└→ ~하기로 결심하다　　　　전치사(~에도 불구하고)
the cost in terms of their well-being, relationships, and happiness].
　　└→ ~의 관점에서
'equate + A + with + B : A를 B와 동일시하다'

---

22 혼자 있는 시간의 중요성　　정답률 86% | 정답 ③

다음 글의 요지로 가장 적절한 것은?
① 예술적 감수성을 키우기 위해 다양한 활동이 필요하다.
② 공동의 문제를 해결하기 위해 협동심을 발휘해야 한다.
☑ 자신의 성장을 위해 혼자 생각할 시간을 가질 필요가 있다.
④ 합리적 정책을 수립하기 위해 비판적 의견을 수용해야 한다.
⑤ 성공적인 지도자가 되기 위해 규율을 엄격하게 적용해야 한다.

Study the lives of the great people / who have made an impact on the world, / and you will find / that in virtually every case, / they spent a considerable amount of time alone thinking.
위대한 사람들의 삶을 연구해 보라, / 세상에 영향을 끼친 / 그러면 여러분은 알게 될 것이다. / 사실상 모든 경우에, / 그들이 상당한 양의 시간을 혼자 생각하며 보냈다는 것을
Every political leader / who had an impact on history / practiced the discipline of being alone / to think and plan.
모든 정치적 지도자는 / 역사에 영향을 끼친 / 혼자 있는 훈련을 실천했다. / 생각과 계획을 하기 위해
Great artists spend countless hours / in their studios or with their instruments / not just doing, / but exploring their ideas and experiences.
위대한 예술가들은 수없이 많은 시간을 쓴다. / 자기 스튜디오에서 혹은 도구를 가지고, / 그저 무언가를 하는 것뿐 아니라 / 자신의 아이디어와 경험을 탐구하는 데에도
Time alone allows people / to sort through their experiences, / put them into perspective, / and plan for the future.
혼자 있는 시간은 사람들로 하여금 ~하게 한다. / 그들의 경험을 정리하고, / 그것들을 통찰하고, / 미래를 계획하게
I strongly encourage you / to find a place to think / and to discipline yourself / to pause and use it / because it has the potential to change your life.
나는 여러분에게 강력하게 권장한다. / 생각할 수 있는 장소를 찾아 / 스스로를 훈련시킬 것을 / 잠시 멈추고 이를 사용하도록 / 왜냐하면 그것은 여러분의 삶을 변화시킬 잠재력을 가지고 있기 때문에
It can help you to figure out / what's really important and what isn't.
이는 파악하는 데 도움을 줄 수 있다. / 무엇이 정말 중요한지와 중요하지 않은지를

세상에 영향을 끼친 위대한 사람들의 삶을 연구해 보라, 그러면 사실상 모든 경우에, 그들이 상당한 양의 시간을 혼자 생각하며 보냈다는 것을 알게 될 것이다. 역사에 영향을 끼친 모든 정치적 지도자는 생각과 계획을 하기 위해 혼자 있는 훈련을 실천했다. 위대한 예술가들은 수없이 많은 시간을 자기 스튜디오에서 혹은 도구를 가지고, 그저 무언가를 하는 것뿐 아니

라 자신의 아이디어와 경험을 탐구하는 데에도 쓴다. 혼자 있는 시간은 사람들로 하여금 그들의 경험을 정리하고, 통합하고, 미래를 계획하게 한다. 혼자 있는 시간은 여러분의 삶을 변화시킬 잠재력을 가지고 있기 때문에 나는 여러분이 생각할 수 있는 장소를 찾아 잠시 멈추고 이를 사용하도록 스스로를 훈련시킬 것을 강력하게 권장한다. 이는 무엇이 정말 중요한지와 중요하지 않은지를 파악하는 데 도움을 줄 수 있다.

Why? 왜 정답일까?

'I strongly encourage you to find a place to think and to discipline yourself to pause and use it because it has the potential to change your life.'에서 혼자 있는 시간은 삶을 변화시킬 잠재력이 있으므로 생각할 장소를 찾아 잠시 멈추고 이를 사용하도록 스스로 훈련하라고 조언하고 있다. 따라서 글의 요지로 가장 적절한 것은 ③ '자신의 성장을 위해 혼자 생각할 시간을 가질 필요가 있다.'이다.

- virtually ad 거의, 실제로
- political ⓐ 정치의, 정치적인
- discipline ⓝ 훈련 ⓥ 단련시키다
- instrument ⓝ 도구
- put into perspective ~을 통찰하다, 넓게 보다
- potential ⓝ 잠재력
- considerable ⓐ 상당한
- practice ⓥ 실천하다, 실행하다
- countless ⓐ 셀 수 없이 많은
- sort through 정리하다, 자세히 살펴보다
- encourage ⓥ 권장하다, 장려하다

구문 풀이

1행 Study the lives of the great people [who have made an impact on the
　　　　　명령문　　　　　　　　　　　　　　　주격 관계대명사
world], / and you will find [that (in virtually every case), they spent a considerable
　　　　그러면　　　　　　접속사(~것)　　　　　　　　　　　　　　　「spend +
amount of time alone thinking].
시간 + 동명사 : ~하는 데 시간을 쓰다」

---

23 사회적 거짓말이 관계에 미치는 영향　　　　정답률 75% | 정답 ⑤

다음 글의 주제로 가장 적절한 것은?

① ways to differentiate between truth and lies - 진실과 거짓말을 구별하는 방법
② roles of self-esteem in building relationships - 관계를 구축하는 데 있어 자존감의 역할
③ importance of praise in changing others' behaviors - 타인의 행동을 바꾸는 데 있어 칭찬의 중요성
④ balancing between self-interest and public interest - 사익과 공익 사이에서 균형 잡기
✓ influence of social lies on interpersonal relationships - 사회적 거짓말이 대인관계에 미치는 영향

Social relationships benefit from people / giving each other compliments now and again / because people like to be liked / and like to receive compliments.
사회적 관계는 사람들로부터 이로움을 얻는다. / 때때로 서로에게 칭찬을 해 주는 / 사람들은 사랑받기 좋아하고 / 칭찬받기 좋아하기 때문에

In that respect, / social lies such as making deceptive but flattering comments / ("I like your new haircut.") / may benefit mutual relations.
그러한 측면에서, / 속이는 말이지만 기분 좋게 만드는 말과 같은 사회적 거짓말은 / ("너 머리 자른 게 마음에 든다.") / 상호 관계에 도움이 될 수 있다.

Social lies are told for psychological reasons / and serve both self-interest and the interest of others.
사회적 거짓말은 심리적 이유로 하며 / 자신의 이익과 타인의 이익 모두에 부합한다.

They serve self-interest / because liars may gain satisfaction / when they notice that their lies please other people, / or because they realize / that by telling such lies / they avoid an awkward situation or discussion.
사회적 거짓말은 자신의 이익에 부합한다. / 거짓말을 한 사람들은 만족감을 느끼거나 / 자신의 거짓말이 다른 사람들을 즐겁게 한다는 것을 인식할 때 / 깨닫기 때문에 / 그런 거짓말을 함으로써 / 어색한 상황이나 토론을 피하는 것을

They serve the interest of others / because hearing the truth all the time / ("You look much older now / than you did a few years ago.") / could damage a person's confidence and self-esteem.
사회적 거짓말은 타인의 이익에 부합한다. / 항상 진실을 듣는 것 / ("너 지금 몇 년 전보다 훨씬 더 나이 들어 보인다. / 지금 몇 년 전보다") / 이 사람의 자신감과 자존감을 해칠 수 있기 때문에

사회적 관계는 사람들이 사랑받기 좋아하고 칭찬받기 좋아하기 때문에 때때로 서로에게 칭찬을 해 주는 것으로부터 이로움을 얻는다. 그러한 측면에서, 속이는 말이지만 기분 좋게 만드는 말과 같은 사회적 거짓말("너 머리 자른 게 마음에 든다.")은 상호 관계에 도움이 될 수 있다. 사회적 거짓말은 심리적 이유로 하며 자신의 이익과 타인의 이익 모두에 부합한다. 거짓말을 한 사람들은 자신의 거짓말이 다른 사람들을 즐겁게 한다는 것을 인식할 때 만족감을 느끼거나 그런 거짓말을 함으로써 어색한 상황이나 토론을 피한다는 것을 깨닫기 때문에 사회적 거짓말은 자신의 이익에 부합한다. 항상 진실을 듣는 것("너 지금 몇 년 전보다 훨씬 더 나이 들어 보인다.")이 사람의 자신감과 자존감을 해칠 수 있기 때문에 사회적 거짓말은 타인의 이익에 부합한다.

Why? 왜 정답일까?

거짓말이 사회적 관계에 도움이 될 수 있다는 언급 뒤로, 'Social lies are told for psychological reasons and serve both self-interest and the interest of others.'에서 사회적 거짓말은 심리적 이유 때문에 이루어지며 자신의 이익과 타인의 이익에 모두 부합한다고 설명하므로, 글의 주제로 가장 적절한 것은 ⑤ '사회적 거짓말이 대인관계에 미치는 영향'이다.

- benefit from ~에서 이로움을 얻다
- deceptive ⓐ 속이는
- mutual ⓐ 상호의
- awkward ⓐ 어색한, 곤란한
- self-esteem 자존감
- differentiate between A and B A와 B를 구별하다
- balance between A and B A와 B 사이에 균형을 잡다
- interpersonal ⓐ 대인관계에 관련된
- compliment ⓝ 칭찬 ⓥ 칭찬하다
- flattering ⓐ 비위를 맞추는
- satisfaction ⓝ 만족
- damage ⓥ 해치다, 손상시키다

구문 풀이

6행 They serve self-interest because liars may gain satisfaction (when they
　　　　　주어　　동사　　　　　　이유 접속사1
notice that their lies please other people), or because they realize {that by telling
( ) : 부사절　　　　　　　　　　　　　　이유 접속사2　　　접속사(~것) ~함으로써
such lies they avoid an awkward situation or discussion}.
　　　　　주어　　동사

---

24 아이들이 자연적 결과를 통해 배우게 하기　　　　정답률 77% | 정답 ②

다음 글의 제목으로 가장 적절한 것은?

① Dark Sides of the Virtual World - 가상 세계의 어두운 면들
✓ Let Natural Consequences Teach Kids - 자연적 결과가 아이를 가르치게 하라
③ The More Choices, the More Mistakes - 선택권이 더 많을수록 실수도 더 많다
④ Listen to Kids to Improve Relationships - 관계를 개선하기 위해 아이들의 말을 들으라
⑤ The Benefits of Overprotective Parenting - 과잉보호 육아의 이점

Overprotective parents / spare kids from all natural consequences.
과잉보호하는 부모들은 / 아이들이 모든 자연적 결과를 겪지 못하게 막는다.

Unfortunately, / their kids often lack a clear understanding / of the reasons behind their parents' rules.
불행히도, / 이들의 자녀는 종종 명확한 이해가 부족하다. / 부모가 정한 규칙 이면의 이유에 대한

They never learn / how to bounce back from failure / or how to recover from mistakes / because their parents prevented them from making poor choices.
아이들은 결코 배우지 못한다. / 실패로부터 다시 일어나거나 / 실수로부터 회복하는 법을 / 그들의 부모가 그들로 하여금 형편없는 선택을 하지 않도록 막았기 때문에

Rather than learning, / "I should wear a jacket because it's cold outside," / a child may conclude, / "I have to wear a jacket because my mom makes me."
배우는 대신, / "밖에 날씨가 춥기 때문에 외투를 입어야지,"라고 / 아이는 결론을 낼지도 모른다. / "엄마가 시키니까 외투를 입어야지,"라고

Without an opportunity to experience real-world consequences, / kids don't always understand / why their parents make certain rules.
현실이 주는 결과를 경험할 기회가 없으면, / 아이들은 항상 이해하지는 못한다. / 자기 부모가 특정한 규칙들을 왜 만드는지를

Natural consequences prepare children for adulthood / by helping them think about the potential consequences of their choices.
자연적 결과는 아이들이 성인기를 대비하게 한다. / 그들이 자신의 선택이 가져오는 잠재적인 결과에 대해 생각하게 하여

과잉보호하는 부모들은 아이들이 모든 자연적 결과를 겪지 못하게 막는다. 불행히도, 이들의 자녀는 종종 부모가 정한 규칙 이면의 이유를 명확하게 이해하지 못한다. 부모가 아이로 하여금 형편없는 선택을 하지 않도록 막았기 때문에 아이들은 결코 실패로부터 다시 일어나거나 실수로부터 회복하는 법을 배우지 못한다. 아이는 "밖에 날씨가 춥기 때문에 외투를 입어야지,"라고 배우는 대신, "엄마가 시키니까 외투를 입어야지,"라고 결론을 낼지도 모른다. 현실이 주는 결과를 경험할 기회가 없으면, 아이들은 자기 부모가 특정한 규칙들을 왜 만드는지를 항상 이해하지는 못한다. 자연적 결과는 아이들이 자신의 선택이 가져오는 잠재적인 결과에 대해 생각하게 하여 그들이 성인기를 대비하게 한다.

Why? 왜 정답일까?

'Without an opportunity to experience real-world consequences, kids don't always understand why their parents make certain rules.'에서 부모가 아이로 하여금 자연적 결과를 직접 경험하지 못하게 하면 아이는 왜 부모가 특정 규칙을 세우는지 이해하지 못하게 될 수 있다는 말을 통해, 아이에게 자연적 결과를 직접 경험시킬 필요가 있다는 내용을 간접적으로 제시하고 있다. 따라서 글의 제목으로 가장 적절한 것은 ② '자연적 결과가 아이를 가르치게 하라'이다.

- overprotective ⓐ 과잉보호하는
- consequence ⓝ 결과
- lack ⓥ ~이 없다, ~을 결여하다
- recover ⓥ 회복하다
- opportunity ⓝ 기회
- certain ⓐ 특정한
- spare A from B A가 B를 겪지 못하게 막다
- unfortunately ad 불행히도, 안타깝게도
- bounce back 다시 회복하다
- conclude ⓥ 결론 짓다
- real-world 실제 세계의
- adulthood ⓝ 성인기

구문 풀이

　　　　　　　　　　　　　　　　　목적어2 「how + to부정사 : ~하는 방법」
3행 They never learn how to bounce back from failure or how to recover from
　　　　　　동사　　목적어1
mistakes because their parents prevented them from making poor choices.
「prevent A from + 동명사 : A가 ~하지 못하게 막다」

---

25 청년들의 발명 흥미 분야　　　　정답률 78% | 정답 ④

다음 도표의 내용과 일치하지 않는 것은?

Invention Interests of Young Adults Aged 16-25 in 2011

The graph above shows the results / of a survey on invention interests / in young adults aged 16 to 25 / in 2011.
위 그래프는 결과를 보여 준다. / 발명 흥미 분야에 관한 조사 / 16세부터 25세까지의 청년들의 / 2011년

① Among the five invention categories, / the highest percentage of male respondents / showed interest in inventing consumer products.
다섯 개 발명 분야 중에서 / 가장 높은 비율의 남성 응답자가 / 소비재를 발명하는 것에 흥미를 나타냈다.

② For health science invention, / the percentage of female respondents / was twice as high as that of male respondents.
건강 과학 발명 분야에서, / 여성 응답자의 비율은 / 남성 응답자의 비율보다 2배 높았다.

③ The percentage point gap between males and females / was the smallest in environmental invention.
남성과 여성 간 퍼센트포인트의 차이가 / 환경 관련 발명 분야에서 가장 작았다.

✓ For web-based invention, / the percentage of female respondents / was less than half that of male respondents.
웹 기반 발명 분야에서, / 여성 응답자의 비율은 / 남성 응답자의 비율의 절반보다 적었다.

⑤ In the category of other invention, / the percentage of respondents from each gender group / was less than 10 percent.
기타 발명 분야의 범주에서 / 각 성별 집단의 응답자 비율은 / 10퍼센트보다 적었다.

03회

위 그래프는 16세부터 25세까지의 청년들의 발명 흥미 분야에 관한 2011년 조사의 결과를 보여 준다. ① 다섯 개 범주의 발명 분야 중에서 가장 높은 비율의 남성 응답자가 소비재를 발명하는 것에 흥미를 나타냈다. ② 건강 과학 발명 분야에서, 여성 응답자의 비율은 남성 응답자의 비율보다 2배 높았다. ③ 환경 관련 발명 분야에서 남성과 여성 간 퍼센트포인트의 차이가 가장 작았다. ④ 웹 기반 발명 분야에서, 여성 응답자의 비율은 남성 응답자의 비율의 절반보다 적었다. ⑤ 기타 발명 분야의 범주에서 각 성별 집단의 응답자 비율은 10퍼센트보다 적었다.

Why? 왜 정답일까?

도표에 따르면 웹 기반 발명 분야에서 여성 응답자의 비율은 **14%**로, 남성 응답자 비율인 **26%**의 절반보다 많다. 따라서 도표의 내용과 일치하지 않는 것은 ④이다.

- invention ⓝ 발명
- web-based 웹 기반의
- consumer product 소비재

---

26 Dorothy Hodgkin의 업적 정답률 88% | 정답 ③

Dorothy Hodgkin에 관한 다음 글의 내용과 일치하지 <u>않는</u> 것은?

① 10세 때 화학에 대한 흥미가 생겼다.
② 동료와 함께 페니실린의 구조를 연구했다.
☑ 1954년에 노벨 화학상을 받았다.
④ Copley 메달을 수상한 최초의 여성이다.
⑤ 사회 불평등과 갈등 해소에 큰 관심을 보였다.

Dorothy Hodgkin was born in Cairo in 1910, / where her father worked in the Egyptian Education Service.
Dorothy Hodgkin은 1910년에 카이로에서 태어났는데, / 그녀의 아버지는 그곳에 있는 Egyptian Education Service에서 근무했다.
『Her interest in chemistry started / when she was just ten years old.』 ①의근거 일치
화학에 대한 그녀의 흥미는 생겼다. / 그녀가 고작 10살이었을 때
『In 1949, / she worked on the structure of penicillin with her colleagues.』 ②의근거 일치
1949년에 / 그녀는 동료와 함께 페니실린의 구조를 연구했다.
『Her work on vitamin B12 / was published in 1954, / which led to her being awarded the Nobel Prize in Chemistry in 1964.』 ③의근거 불일치
비타민 B12에 관한 그녀의 연구는 / 1954년에 발표되었는데, / 이는 1964년에 그녀가 노벨 화학상을 수상하게 했다.
『She also became the first woman / to receive the Copley Medal / and was a winner of the Lenin Peace Prize.』 ④의근거 일치
그녀는 또한 최초의 여성이자 / Copley 메달을 수상한 / 레닌 평화상을 받은 사람이었다.
『Hodgkin showed great concern / for social inequalities and resolving conflicts.』 ⑤의근거 일치
Hodgkin은 큰 관심을 보였다. / 사회 불평등과 갈등 해소에
As a result, / she was president of the Pugwash Conferences / from 1976 to 1988.
그 결과 / 그녀는 Pugwash Conferences의 의장을 맡았다. / 1976년부터 1988년까지

Dorothy Hodgkin은 1910년에 카이로에서 태어났는데, 그녀의 아버지는 그곳에 있는 Egyptian Education Service에서 근무했다. 화학에 대한 그녀의 흥미는 그녀가 고작 10살이었을 때 생겼다. 1949년에 그녀는 동료와 함께 페니실린의 구조를 연구했다. 비타민 B12에 관한 연구는 1954년에 발표되었는데, 이는 1964년에 노벨 화학상을 수상하게 했다. 그녀는 또한 Copley 메달을 수상한 최초의 여성이자 레닌 평화상을 받은 사람이었다. Hodgkin은 사회 불평등과 갈등 해소에 큰 관심을 보였다. 그 결과 그녀는 1976년부터 1988년까지 Pugwash Conferences의 의장을 맡았다.

Why? 왜 정답일까?

'Her work on vitamin B12 was published in 1954, which led to her being awarded the Nobel Prize in Chemistry in 1964.'에서 Hodgkin은 B12에 대한 연구로 노벨 화학상을 수상하게 되었다고 하는데, 연구 발표는 1954년, 노벨상 수상은 1964년에 이루어졌다. 따라서 Dorothy Hodgkin에 관한 내용으로 일치하지 않는 것은 ③ '1954년에 노벨 화학상을 받았다.'이다.

Why? 왜 오답일까?

① 'Her interest in chemistry started when she was just ten years old.'와 일치한다.
② 'In 1949, she worked on the structure of penicillin with her colleagues.'와 일치한다.
④ 'She also became the first woman to receive the Copley Medal ~'와 일치한다.
⑤ 'Hodgkin showed great concern for social inequalities and resolving conflicts.'와 일치한다.

- structure ⓝ 구조
- publish ⓥ 발표하다, 출판하다
- receive ⓥ 받다
- inequality ⓝ 불평등
- president ⓝ (기관의) 장, 회장
- colleague ⓝ 동료
- award ⓥ 상을 주다, 수여하다
- concern ⓝ 관심, 우려
- conflict ⓝ 갈등

구문 풀이

4행 Her work on vitamin B12 was published in 1954, which led to her being awarded the Nobel Prize in Chemistry in 1964.
선행사 / ~로 이어지다 / 계속적 용법 / 동명사의 의미상 주어 / 동명사(being + 과거분사 : 수동)

---

27 로봇 진공청소기 정답률 72% | 정답 ⑤

Robotic Vacuum Cleaner 사용에 관한 다음 안내문의 내용과 일치하는 것은?

① 배터리를 완전히 충전하는 데 40분이 소요된다.
② 완전히 충전되면 배터리 표시등이 빨간색으로 변한다.
③ 네 가지 종류의 청소 모드를 제공한다.
④ 전원을 끄면 현재 시각이 리셋된다.
☑ 시각은 리모컨을 사용하여 설정한다.

Robotic Vacuum Cleaner
Robotic Vacuum Cleaner(로봇 진공청소기)

– User Manual –
사용자 매뉴얼
Charging the Battery
배터리 충전하기
『It takes 90 minutes / for the battery to be fully charged.』 ①의근거 불일치
90분이 소요됩니다. / 배터리를 완전히 충전하는 데
The robotic vacuum can operate for 40 minutes / when fully charged.
로봇 진공청소기는 40분간 작동할 수 있습니다. / 완전히 충전되었을 때
While the robotic vacuum is charging, / the battery indicator light blinks red.
로봇 진공청소기가 충전되는 동안 / 배터리 표시등이 빨간색으로 깜박입니다.
『When fully charged, / the battery indicator light turns blue.』 ②의근거 불일치
완전히 충전되면, / 배터리 표시등이 파란색으로 변합니다.
Operating the Vacuum
진공청소기 작동하기
Press the power button / to turn on the vacuum.
전원 버튼을 누르세요. / 진공청소기를 켜기 위해서는
『The following cleaning modes are provided: / Auto Mode, Spot Mode, and Manual Mode.』 ③의근거 불일치
다음과 같은 청소 모드가 제공됩니다: / 자동 모드, 지정 장소 모드, 수동 모드
『Turning off the vacuum will reset all settings / except for the current time.』 ④의근거 불일치
진공청소기를 끄면 모든 설정이 리셋됩니다. / 현재 시각을 제외하고
『The time can be set / only with the remote control.』 ⑤의근거 일치
시각은 설정할 수 있습니다. / 오직 리모컨만을 사용하여

Robotic Vacuum Cleaner
– 사용자 매뉴얼 –

■ 배터리 충전하기
• 배터리를 완전히 충전하는 데 90분이 소요됩니다.
• 로봇 진공청소기는 완전히 충전되었을 때 40분간 작동할 수 있습니다.
• 로봇 진공청소기가 충전되는 동안 배터리 표시등이 빨간색으로 깜박입니다.
• 완전히 충전되면, 배터리 표시등이 파란색으로 변합니다.

■ 진공청소기 작동하기
• 진공청소기를 켜기 위해서는 전원 버튼을 누르세요.
• 다음과 같은 청소 모드가 제공됩니다: 자동 모드, 지정 장소 모드, 수동 모드
• 진공청소기를 끄면 현재 시각을 제외한 모든 설정이 리셋됩니다.
• 시각은 오직 리모컨만을 사용하여 설정할 수 있습니다.

Why? 왜 정답일까?

'The time can be set only with the remote control.'에서 시각은 오로지 리모컨을 가지고 설정할 수 있다고 하므로, 안내문의 내용과 일치하는 것은 ⑤ '시각은 리모컨을 사용하여 설정한다.'이다.

Why? 왜 오답일까?

① 'It takes 90 minutes for the battery to be fully charged.'에서 배터리를 완전히 충전하기 위해서는 90분이 걸린다고 하였다.
② 'When fully charged, the battery indicator light turns blue.'에서 완전히 충전되면 배터리 표시등이 파란색으로 변한다고 하였다.
③ 'The following cleaning modes are provided: Auto Mode, Spot Mode, and Manual Mode.'에서 자동 모드, 지정 장소 모드, 수동 모드의 세 가지 청소 모드가 제공된다고 하였다.
④ 'Turning off the vacuum will reset all settings except for the current time.'에서 전원을 끄면 현재 시각을 제외한 모든 설정이 리셋된다고 하였다.

- robotic vacuum cleaner 로봇 진공청소기
- blink ⓥ 깜박이다
- indicator ⓝ 표시기
- except for ~을 제외하고

---

28 교내 연례 벼룩시장 행사 안내 정답률 91% | 정답 ④

Passing on My Favorites에 관한 다음 안내문의 내용과 일치하지 <u>않는</u> 것은?

① 벼룩시장 행사이다.
② 학생회실로 물건을 가져와야 한다.
③ 물건을 사는 날은 9월 8일이다.
☑ 현금을 주고 물건을 구입할 수 있다.
⑤ 음식은 판매되지 않는다.

Passing on My Favorites
Passing on My Favorites(내가 가장 좋아하는 것들을 넘겨주기)
Do you have anything / you don't use anymore?
물건이 있으신가요? / 여러분이 더 이상 쓰지 않는
『Passing on My Favorites is a flea market event / that takes place at our school every year.』 ①의근거 일치
Passing on My Favorites는 벼룩시장 행사입니다. / 매년 우리 학교에서 열리는
Bring Your Goods
여러분의 물건을 가져오세요
When: September 4 – 6 (12:00 – 13:00)
언제: 9월 4일 – 6일 (12시 – 13시)
『Where: the student council room』 ②의근거 일치
어디로: 학생회실
What: anything you don't use anymore / (clothing, bags, shoes, stationery, etc.)
무엇을: 여러분이 더 이상 쓰지 않는 물건 / (옷, 가방, 신발, 문구류 등)
You will receive coupons / according to how much you bring.
여러분은 쿠폰을 받게 됩니다. / 여러분이 얼마나 많이 가져오시는지에 따라
Buy What You Want
원하시는 것을 구입하세요
『When: September 8 (10:00 – 12:00)』 ③의근거 일치
언제: 9월 8일 (10시 – 12시)
Where: the gymnasium
어디로: 체육관
『How: / The coupons mentioned above / will be your only way to purchase goods.』 ④의근거 불일치
어떻게: 위에서 언급된 쿠폰이 / 물건을 구입하실 수 있는 유일한 수단이 될 것입니다. ④의근거 불일치
『No food will be sold / because it might spoil in the hot weather.』 ⑤의근거 일치
음식은 일절 판매되지 않습니다. / 그것은 더운 날씨에 상할 수 있으므로

Passing on My Favorites

더 이상 쓰지 않는 물건이 있으신가요? Passing on My Favorites는 매년 우리 학교에서 열리는 벼룩시장 행사입니다.

여러분의 물건을 가져오세요
■ 언제: 9월 4일 – 6일 (12시 – 13시)
■ 어디로: 학생회실
■ 무엇을: 더 이상 쓰지 않는 물건
　　　　　(옷, 가방, 신발, 문구류 등)
＊ 얼마나 많이 가져오시는지에 따라 쿠폰을 받게 됩니다.

원하시는 것을 구입하세요
■ 언제: 9월 8일 (10시 – 12시)
■ 어디서: 체육관
■ 어떻게: 위에서 언급된 쿠폰이 물건을 구입하실 수 있는 유일한 수단이 될 것입니다.
＊ 더운 날씨에 상할 수 있으므로 음식은 일절 판매되지 않습니다.

Why? 왜 정답일까?

'How: The coupons mentioned above will be your only way to purchase goods.'에서 쓰지 않는 물건을 내고 바꾼 쿠폰으로만 물건을 구입할 수 있다고 하였다. 따라서 Passing on My Favorites와 일치하지 않는 것은 ④ '현금을 주고 물건을 구입할 수 있다.'이다.

Why? 왜 오답일까?

① 'Passing on My Favorites is a flea market event ~'의 내용과 일치한다.
② 'Where: the student council room'의 내용과 일치한다.
③ 'When: September 8 (10:00 – 12:00)'의 내용과 일치한다.
⑤ 'No food will be sold because it might spoil in the hot weather.'의 내용과 일치한다.

- flea market 벼룩시장
- student council 학생회
- according to ~에 따라
- mention ⓥ 언급하다, 말하다
- spoil ⓥ 상하다
- take place 열리다, 개최되다
- stationery ⓝ 문구류
- gymnasium ⓝ 체육관
- purchase ⓥ 구입하다, 사다

구문 풀이

9행　You will receive coupons / according to how much you bring.
　　　　　　　　　　　　　　전치사구(~에 따라) 의문사(얼마나)

★★★ 등급을 가르는 문제!

29　변화에 대한 잘못된 인식　　정답률 49% | 정답 ④

다음 글의 밑줄 친 부분 중, 어법상 틀린 것은? [3점]

In perceiving changes, / we tend to regard the most recent ① ones / as the most revolutionary.
변화를 인식할 때 / 우리는 가장 최근의 변화를 여기는 경향이 있다. / 가장 혁신적인 것이라고

This is often inconsistent with the facts.
이는 종종 사실과 일치하지 않는다.

Recent progress in telecommunications technologies / is not more revolutionary / than ② what happened in the late nineteenth century / in relative terms.
통신기술에서의 최근의 발전은 / 더 혁명적이지는 않다. / 19세기 말에 일어났던 발전보다 / 상대적인 관점으로 볼 때

Moreover, in terms of the consequent economic and social changes, / the Internet revolution has not been as ③ important / as the washing machine and other household appliances.
게다가, 그 결과로 일어난 경제 및 사회 변화의 측면에서, / 인터넷 혁명은 중요하지는 않았다. / 세탁기 및 다른 가전제품들만큼

These things, / by vastly reducing the amount of work / needed for household chores, / ✔allow women to enter the labor market / and virtually got rid of professions like domestic service.
이런 것들은 / 일의 양을 막대하게 줄여주어서 / 가사에 필요한 / 여성들이 노동시장에 진입하도록 하였고 / 사실상 가사 서비스 같은 직업을 없애 버렸다.

We should not "put the telescope backward" / when we look into the past / and underestimate the old and overestimate the new.
우리는 "망원경을 거꾸로 놓고서" / 우리가 과거를 들여다볼 때 / 옛것을 과소평가하고 새것을 과대평가해서는 안 된다.

This leads us ⑤ to make all sorts of wrong decisions / about national economic policy, corporate policies, and our own careers.
이는 우리가 모든 종류의 잘못된 결정을 내리도록 이끈다. / 국가 경제 정책, 기업 정책 및 자기 자신의 경력에 관한

변화를 인식할 때 우리는 가장 최근의 변화를 가장 혁신적인 것으로 여기는 경향이 있다. 이는 종종 사실과 일치하지 않는다. 통신기술에서 최근의 발전은 상대적인 관점으로 볼 때 19세기 말에 일어났던 발전보다 더 혁명적이지는 않다. 게다가, 그 결과로 일어난 경제 및 사회 변화의 측면에서, 인터넷 혁명은 세탁기 및 다른 가전제품들만큼 중요하지는 않았다. 이런 것들은 가사에 필요한 일의 양을 막대하게 줄여주어서 여성들이 노동시장에 진입하도록 하였고 사실상 가사 서비스 같은 직업을 없애 버렸다. 과거를 들여다볼 때 "망원경을 거꾸로 놓고서" 옛것을 과소평가하고 새것을 과대평가해서는 안 된다. 이는 우리가 국가 경제 정책, 기업 정책 및 자기 자신의 경력에 관한 모든 종류의 잘못된 결정을 내리도록 이끈다.

Why? 왜 정답일까?

④가 있는 문장에서 주어는 These things이고 'by vastly ~ household chores'가 콤마로 삽입된 구이다. 따라서 이 문장에 동사가 없으므로 allowing을 동사 allowed로 바꾸어야 한다. 어법상 틀린 것은 ④이다.

Why? 왜 오답일까?

① 앞에 'changes'라는 복수 명사가 나왔고 이를 받는 복수대명사로서 ones가 나왔다.
② 뒤에 주어가 없는 불완전한 절이 연결되므로 관계대명사 what을 쓴 것은 적절하다.
③ 현재완료 형태로 쓰인 'has not been'의 보어 역할을 할 형용사로서 important의 쓰임은 적절하다.
⑤ 「lead + 목적어 + to부정사」는 '~가 …하도록 이끌다'라는 뜻이다. 여기서 to부정사는 lead의 목적격 보어이다.

- perceive ⓥ 인식하다, 이해하다
- inconsistent ⓐ 일치하지 않는, 부합하지 않는
- relative ⓐ 상대적인
- consequent ⓐ ~의 결과로 일어나는
- vastly [ad] 막대하게, 방대하게
- get rid of ~을 없애다, 제거하다
- overestimate ⓥ 과대평가하다
- revolutionary ⓐ 혁신적인, 혁명적인
- progress ⓝ 발전, 진보
- in terms of ~의 관점에서
- household appliance 가전제품
- virtually [ad] 사실상, 거의
- underestimate ⓥ 과소평가하다
- corporate ⓐ 기업의

구문 풀이

10행　We should not "put the telescope backward" (when we look into the past)
　　　　조동사 + not　　동사원형1　　　　　　접속사(~할 때)
/ and underestimate the old and overestimate the new.
　　동사원형2　　　　　　　　　동사원형3

★★ 문제 해결 꿀~팁 ★★

▶ 많이 틀린 이유는?
대명사 one 개념이 익숙하지 않다면 ①을 오답으로 고르기 쉬운 문제였다.
one은 앞에 나온 명사를 그대로 받지 않고 종류가 같은 것을 폭넓게 가리킬 때 쓰는 대명사이다. 이때 앞에 나온 명사가 단수라면 one, 복수라면 ones의 형태로 쓰는데 여기서는 앞에 나온 명사가 changes라는 복수 명사이므로 ones가 나왔다.

▶ 문제 해결 방법은?
정답인 ④와 같이 '준동사 vs. 동사'를 묻는 문제에서는 주변에 서술어 역할을 하는 동사가 이미 있는지, 있다면 접속사가 있는지 없는지를 따져야 한다.
만일 서술어가 있는데 접속사도 함께 있다면 뒤에 추가로 동사가 나올 수 있지만, 접속사가 없다면 준동사가 나와야 한다. 여기서는 서술어가 없으므로 접속사 유무를 따질 필요 없이 밑줄 부분을 서술어로 바꾸면 된다.

★★★ 등급을 가르는 문제!

30　과학기술이 종종 거부되는 이유　　정답률 36% | 정답 ⑤

다음 글의 밑줄 친 부분 중, 문맥상 낱말의 쓰임이 적절하지 않은 것은?

Technological development often forces change, / and change is uncomfortable.
과학기술의 발전은 흔히 변화를 강요하는데, / 변화는 불편하다.

This is one of the main reasons / why technology is often resisted / and why some perceive it as a ① threat.
이것은 주된 이유 중 하나이다. / 과학기술이 흔히 저항을 받고 / 일부 사람들이 그것을 위협으로 인식하는

It is important to understand / our natural ② hate of being uncomfortable / when we consider the impact of technology on our lives.
이해하는 것이 중요하다. / 불편함에 대한 우리의 본능적인 질색을 / 과학기술이 우리 삶에 끼치는 영향력을 고려할 때

As a matter of fact, / most of us prefer the path of ③ least resistance.
사실, / 우리 대부분은 최소한의 저항의 길을 선호한다.

This tendency means / that the true potential of new technologies / may remain ④ unrealized / because, for many, / starting something new is just too much of a struggle.
이 경향은 의미한다. / 새로운 과학기술의 진정한 잠재력이 / 실현되지 않은 채로 남아 있을 수 있다는 것을 / 많은 사람들에게 / 새로운 무엇인가를 시작하는 것이 그저 너무 힘든 일이기 때문에

Even our ideas / about how new technology can enhance our lives / may be ✔limited by this natural desire for comfort.
심지어 우리의 생각은 / 새로운 과학기술이 어떻게 우리의 삶을 향상시킬 수 있는가에 관한 / 편안함을 향한 이런 욕구에 의해 제한될 수 있다.

과학기술의 발전은 흔히 변화를 강요하는데, 변화는 불편하다. 이것은 과학기술이 흔히 저항을 받고 일부 사람들이 그것을 ① 위협으로 인식하는 주된 이유 중 하나이다. 과학기술이 우리 삶에 끼치는 영향력을 고려할 때 우리의 불편함에 대한 우리의 본능적인 ② 질색을 이해하는 것이 중요하다. 사실, 우리 대부분은 ③ 최소한의 저항의 길을 선호한다. 이 경향은 많은 사람들에게 새로운 무엇인가를 시작하는 것이 그저 너무 힘든 일이기 때문에 새로운 과학기술의 진정한 잠재력이 ④ 실현되지 않은 채로 남아 있을 수 있다는 것을 의미한다. 심지어 새로운 과학기술이 어떻게 우리의 삶을 향상시킬 수 있는가에 관한 우리의 생각은 편안함을 향한 이런 욕구에 의해 ⑤ 장려될(→ 제한될) 수 있다.

Why? 왜 정답일까?

첫 두 문장에 주제가 제시된 글로, 과학기술은 변화를 야기하여 우리에게 불편감을 주고 이로 인해 거부감을 사기도 한다는 내용을 다루고 있다. 앞에서 우리는 불편감을 본능적으로 싫어하며(our natural hate of being uncomfortable) 저항이 최소화되는 길을 선호한다(~ prefer the path of least resistance.)고 언급하는 것으로 볼 때, 과학기술이 설령 우리의 삶을 향상시킬 수 있다고 하더라도 이는 편안함을 추구하고자 하는 우리의 욕구로 인해 방해를 받을 수 있다는 내용이 이어지는 것이 적절하다. 따라서 ⑤의 encouraged를 limited로 고쳐야 한다. 문맥상 낱말의 쓰임이 적절하지 않은 것은 ⑤이다.

- resist ⓥ 저항하다
- threat ⓝ 위협
- as a matter of fact 사실, 실은
- tendency ⓝ 경향
- struggle ⓝ 힘든 일, 투쟁
- perceive ⓥ 감지하다
- impact ⓝ 영향
- prefer ⓥ 선호하다
- unrealized ⓐ 실현되지 않은
- enhance ⓥ 향상시키다

구문 풀이

9행　Even our ideas about {how new technology can enhance our lives}
　　　　　　주어　　　　전치사　　　　　　{ } : 간접의문문(about의 목적어)
may be limited by this natural desire for comfort.
조동사 수동태

★★ 문제 해결 꿀~팁 ★★

▶ 많이 틀린 이유는?
많은 수험생들이 어려워하는 과학기술을 소재로 다룬 글이다. 앞에서 우리는 저항과 불편감이 최소이기를 추구한다고 언급한 것으로 볼 때, 새로운 시작 자체를 버거워해서 새로운 기술의 잠재력 또한 종종 실현하지 못한 채로 남겨둔다는 의미의 ④는 적절하다.

▶ 문제 해결 방법은?
글에 따르면 새로운 기술의 잠재력이 충분히 실현되지 않는 까닭은 편안함을 추구하고 변화와 새로운 시작을 꺼리는 인간의 욕구 때문이다. 따라서 편안함에 대한 욕구로 인해 새로운 기술에 대한 고려가 장려된다는 ⑤의 내용은 맥락상 부적절하다.

---

31 오늘날의 뉴스 순환 · 정답률 63% · 정답 ①

다음 빈칸에 들어갈 말로 가장 적절한 것을 고르시오.

☑ Mobility - 기동성 ② Sensitivity - 민감성 ③ Creativity - 창의성
④ Accuracy - 정확성 ⑤ Responsibility - 책임감

Mobility provides a change / to the environment for journalists.
기동성은 변화를 제공한다. / 저널리스트들의 환경에 대한

Newspaper stories, television reports, and even early online reporting / (prior to communication technology / such as tablets and smartphones) / required one central place / to which a reporter would submit his or her news story / for printing, broadcast, or posting.
신문 기사, 텔레비전 보도, 그리고 심지어 초기 온라인 보도는 / (통신 기술 이전의 / 태블릿과 스마트폰과 같은) / 하나의 중심적인 장소를 필요로 했다. / 기자가 자신의 뉴스 기사를 제출할 / 인쇄, 방송, 또는 게시를 위해

Now, though, / a reporter can shoot video, / record audio, / and type directly on their smartphones or tablets / and post a news story instantly.
그러나 이제 / 기자는 비디오를 촬영하고, / 오디오를 녹음하며, / 자신의 스마트폰이나 태블릿에 직접 타이핑해서 / 즉시 뉴스 기사를 게시할 수 있다.

Journalists do not need to report to a central location / where they all contact sources, type, or edit video.
저널리스트들은 중심 장소에 보고할 필요가 없다. / 모두가 정보의 원천과 접촉하거나, 타이핑하거나, 또는 비디오를 편집하는

A story can be instantaneously written, / shot, / and made available to the entire world.
기사는 즉석에서 작성되고, / 촬영되고, / 전 세계에서 보는 것이 가능해질 수 있다.

The news cycle, and thus the job of the journalist, / never takes a break.
뉴스의 순환과 결국 저널리스트의 일은 / 결코 멈추지 않는다.

Thus the "24-hour" news cycle / that emerged from the rise of cable TV / is now a thing of the past.
그러므로 '24시간'의 뉴스 순환은 / 케이블 TV의 성장으로 나타난 / 이제 과거의 것이다.

The news "cycle" is really a constant.
뉴스 '순환'은 정말로 끊임없이 계속되는 것이다.

기동성은 저널리스트들의 환경에 대한 변화를 제공한다. 신문 기사, 텔레비전 보도, 그리고 심지어 (태블릿과 스마트폰과 같은 통신 기술 이전의) 초기 온라인 보도는 기자가 인쇄, 방송, 또는 게시를 위해 자신의 뉴스 기사를 제출할 하나의 중심적인 장소를 필요로 했다. 그러나 이제 기자는 비디오를 촬영하고, 오디오를 녹음하며, 자신의 스마트폰이나 태블릿에 직접 타이핑해서 즉시 뉴스 기사를 게시할 수 있다. 저널리스트들은 모두가 정보의 원천과 접촉하거나, 타이핑하거나, 또는 비디오를 편집하는 중심 장소에 보고할 필요가 없다. 기사는 즉석에서 작성되고, 촬영되고, 전 세계에서 보는 것이 가능해질 수 있다. 뉴스의 순환과 결국 저널리스트의 일은 결코 멈추지 않는다. 그러므로 케이블 TV의 성장으로 나타난 '24시간'의 뉴스 순환은 이제 과거의 것이다. 뉴스 '순환'은 정말로 끊임없이 계속되는 것이다.

Why? 왜 정답일까?

글 중간의 'Now, though, ~' 앞뒤로 글의 흐름이 반전되는 글이다. 예전에는 기자들이 기사를 제출할 중심적인 장소가 필요했지만 이제는 스마트폰이나 태블릿을 활용하여 언제 어디서든 기사 작성이 이루어질 수 있기 때문에 멈추지 않는 뉴스의 순환이 가능해졌다(The news cycle, and thus the job of the journalist, never takes a break.)는 내용이 언급되고 있다. 따라서 빈칸에 들어갈 말로 가장 적절한 것은 장소에 구애받지 않고 이어질 수 있는 기자 업무의 특성을 설명하기에 적합한 ① '기동성'이다.

● prior to ~의 이전에
● central ⓐ 중심적인
● directly ad 곧장
● instantaneously ad 즉석에서
● emerge ⓥ 나타나다
● constant ⓝ 일정불변의 것

● require ⓥ 필요로 하다
● submit ⓥ 제출하다
● instantly ad 즉시
● take a break 멈추다, 휴식을 취하다
● rise ⓝ 성장, 상승, 증가

구문 풀이

2행 Newspaper stories, television reports, and even early online reporting
주어(A, B, and C)
(prior to communication technology such as tablets and smartphones) required
~ 이전에   동사
one central place [to which a reporter would submit his or her news story for
목적어(선행사)   = where
printing, broadcast, or posting].

---

32 자신만의 가치 기준에 근거하여 목표를 수립할 필요성 · 정답률 71% · 정답 ③

다음 빈칸에 들어갈 말로 가장 적절한 것을 고르시오. [3점]

① your moral duty - 자신의 도덕적 의무 ② a strict deadline - 엄격한 기한
☑ your own values - 자신만의 가치 기준 ④ parental guidance - 부모의 지도
⑤ job market trends - 직업 시장의 추세

It's hard enough to stick with goals / you want to accomplish, / but sometimes we make goals / we're not even thrilled about in the first place.
목표를 고수하는 것은 매우 어렵지만, / 당신이 이루고 싶은 / 때때로 우리는 목표를 세우기도 한다. / 심지어 애초부터 우리가 감동 받지 못할

We set resolutions / based on what we're supposed to do, / or what others think we're supposed to do, / rather than what really matters to us.
우리는 다짐을 한다. / 우리가 해야만 하는 것에 기초하여 / 또는 다른 사람들이 생각하기에 우리가 해야만 하는 것 / 우리에게 진짜 중요한 것이라기보다

This makes it nearly impossible / to stick to the goal.
이는 거의 불가능하게 만든다. / 목표를 고수하는 것을

For example, reading more is a good habit, / but if you're only doing it / because you feel like / that's what you're supposed to do, / not because you actually want to learn more, /

---

you're going to have a hard time / reaching the goal.
예를 들어, 독서를 더 하는 것은 좋은 습관이지만, / 당신이 오로지 그렇게 하고 있다면, / 당신이 ~처럼 느껴서 / 그것이 당신이 해야만 하는 것처럼 / 당신이 실제로 더 배우기를 원해서가 아니라 / 당신은 어려움을 겪을 것이다. / 목표에 도달하는 데

Instead, make goals / based on your own values.
대신에, 목표를 세워라. / 자신만의 가치 기준에 기초하여

Now, this isn't to say / you should read less.
이제, 말하려는 것이 아니다. / 당신이 독서를 더 적게 해야 한다는 것

The idea is to first consider what matters to you, / then figure out what you need to do / to get there.
핵심은 우선 자신에게 무엇이 중요한지 생각하는 것이고, / 그 다음 당신이 할 필요가 있는 일을 알아내는 것이다. / 목표에 도달하기 위해

당신이 이루고 싶은 목표를 고수하는 것은 매우 어렵지만, 때때로 우리는 심지어 애초부터 우리가 감동받지 못할 목표를 세우기도 한다. 우리는 우리에게 진짜 중요한 것이라기보다 우리가 해야만 하는 것, 또는 다른 사람들이 생각하기에 우리가 해야만 하는 것에 기초하여 다짐을 한다. 이는 목표를 고수하는 것을 거의 불가능하게 만든다. 예를 들어, 독서를 더 하는 것은 좋은 습관이지만, 실제로 더 배우기를 위해서가 아니라 해야만 하는 것처럼 느껴서 그렇게 하고 있다면, 당신은 목표에 도달하는 데 어려움을 겪을 것이다. 대신에, 자신만의 가치 기준에 기초하여 목표를 세워라. 이제 독서를 더 적게 해야 한다는 것을 말하려는 것이 아니다. 핵심은 우선 자신에게 무엇이 중요한지 생각한 다음, 목표에 도달하기 위해 할 필요가 있는 일을 알아내는 것이다.

Why? 왜 정답일까?

'The idea is to first consider what matters to you, then figure out what you need to do to get there.'에서 스스로에게 뭐가 중요한지를 먼저 고민하고 목표에 도달하려면 무엇을 해야 하는지 파악하라고 이야기하는데, 여기서 핵심은 남들이 해야 한다고 말하는 것에 근거하여 결심을 하기 보다는 자기 자신에게 필요한 것을 파악하라는 데 있다. 따라서 빈칸에 들어갈 말로 가장 적절한 것은 ③ '자신만의 가치 기준'이다.

● stick with ~을 고수하다
● resolution ⓝ 다짐, 결심
● actually ad 실제로

● accomplish ⓥ 성취하다, 달성하다
● impossible ⓐ 불가능한
● figure out 알아내다, 이해하다

구문 풀이

3행 We set resolutions based on [what we're supposed to do], or [what
~에 근거하여 관계대명사(~것) ~하기로 되어 있다 관계대명사(~것)
(others think) we're supposed to do], rather than [what really matters to us].
삽입절(~가 생각하기로는)   ~라기보다는, ~ 대신에 관계대명사(~것) 자동사(~이 중요하다)

---

33 수하물 찾는 시간에 관한 불평 해결 · 정답률 59% · 정답 ②

다음 빈칸에 들어갈 말로 가장 적절한 것을 고르시오. [3점]

① having them wait in line - 그들을 줄 서서 기다리게 함
☑ making them walk longer - 탑승객들을 더 오래 걷게 함
③ producing more advertisements - 더 많은 광고를 제작함
④ bothering them with complaints - 불평으로 그들을 성가시게 한 것
⑤ hiring more staff to handle bags - 수하물을 다루는 직원 수를 늘린 것

Houston Airport executives / faced plenty of complaints / regarding baggage claim time, / so they increased the number of baggage handlers.
Houston 공항의 임원들은 / 많은 불평에 직면했고, / 수하물을 찾는 데 걸리는 시간에 관한 / 그래서 그들은 수하물 담당자들의 수를 늘렸다.

Although it reduced the average wait time to eight minutes, / complaints didn't stop.
이것이 기다리는 시간을 평균 8분으로 줄였음에도 불구하고 / 불평은 멈추지 않았다.

It took about a minute / to get from the arrival gate to baggage claim, / so the passengers spent seven more minutes / waiting for their bags.
약 1분의 시간이 걸려서 / 도착 게이트에서 수하물을 찾는 곳까지 도달하려면 / 탑승객들은 7분을 더 보냈다. / 자기 가방을 기다리며

The solution was / to move the arrival gates away from the baggage claim / so it took passengers about seven minutes / to walk there.
해결책은 / 도착 게이트를 수하물 찾는 곳으로부터 더 멀리 이동시키는 것이었고, / 그리하여 탑승객들에게 약 7분의 시간이 걸렸다. / 그곳까지 걸어가는 데

It resulted in complaints reducing to almost zero.
이는 불평이 거의 0으로 줄어드는 결과를 가져왔다.

Research shows / occupied time feels shorter than unoccupied time.
연구에서는 보여준다. / (어떤 행동으로) 소요한 시간이 빈 시간보다 더 짧게 느껴진다는 것

People usually exaggerate / about the time they waited, / and what they find most bothersome / is time spent unoccupied.
사람들은 보통 과장하며, / 그들이 기다린 시간에 대해 / 그들이 가장 성가시다고 여기는 것은 / 비어있는 시간이다.

Thus, occupying the passengers' time / by making them walk longer / gave them the idea / they didn't have to wait as long.
따라서 시간을 소요시킨 것은 / 탑승객들을 더 오래 걷게 함으로써 / 그들에게 생각을 갖게 했다. / 그들이 그렇게 오래 기다릴 필요가 없다는

Houston 공항의 임원들은 수하물을 찾는 데 걸리는 시간에 관한 많은 불평에 직면하여, 수하물 담당자들의 수를 늘렸다. 이것이 기다리는 시간을 평균 8분으로 줄였음에도 불구하고 불평은 멈추지 않았다. 도착 게이트에서 수하물을 찾는 곳까지 도달하려면 약 1분의 시간이 걸려서 탑승객들은 자기 가방을 기다리며 7분을 더 보냈다. 해결책은 도착 게이트를 수하물 찾는 곳으로부터 더 멀리 이동시키는 것이었고, 그리하여 탑승객들이 수하물을 찾는 곳까지 걷는 데 약 7분의 시간이 걸렸다. 이는 불평이 거의 0으로 줄어드는 결과를 가져왔다. 연구에서는 (어떤 행동으로) 소요한 시간이 빈 시간보다 더 짧게 느껴진다는 것을 보여준다. 사람들은 보통 기다린 시간에 대해 과장하며, 그들이 가장 성가시다고 여기는 것은 (무언가 하지 않고) 비어있는 시간이다. 따라서 탑승객들을 더 오래 걷게 함으로써 시간을 소요시킨 것은 그들로 하여금 그렇게 오래 기다릴 필요가 없다는 생각을 갖게 했다.

Why? 왜 정답일까?

'The solution was to move the arrival gates away from the baggage claim so it took passengers about seven minutes to walk there.'에서 수하물을 기다리는 시간이 너무 길다는 불평에 대처하기 위한 해결책은 탑승객들이 걷는 시간을 1분에서 7분으로 늘리는 것이었다고 이야기하므로, 빈칸에 들어갈 말로 가장 적절한 것은 ② '탑승객들을 더 오래 걷게 함'이다.

- **executive** ⓝ 임원, 중역
- **regarding** prep ~에 관하여
- **reduce** ⓥ 줄이다, 감소시키다
- **result in** ~을 가져오다, ~을 초래하다
- **exaggerate** ⓥ 과장하다
- **face** ⓥ 직면하다, 맞서다
- **baggage** ⓝ 수하물, 짐
- **solution** ⓝ 해결책
- **occupied** ⓐ 차지된, 점거된
- **bothersome** ⓐ 성가신, 귀찮은

구문 풀이

4행 It took about a minute to get from the arrival gate to baggage claim, / so
「take + 시간 + to부정사 : ~하는 데 …의 시간이 걸리다」
the passengers spent seven more minutes waiting for their bags.
「spend + 시간 + 동명사 : ~하는 데 …의 시간을 쓰다」

---

34 상황의 변화에 따라 비전을 조정할 필요성 | 정답률 61% | 정답 ④

다음 빈칸에 들어갈 말로 가장 적절한 것을 고르시오. [3점]
① explain your vision logically to others – 타인에게 당신의 비전을 논리적으로 설명할
② defend the wrong decisions you've made – 당신이 내린 잘못된 결정을 방어할
③ build a community to share your experience – 당신의 경험을 공유할 공동체를 구축할
☑ make your vision conform to the new reality – 새로운 현실에 당신의 비전을 맞출
⑤ consult experts to predict the future economy – 미래 경제를 예측하기 위해 전문가와 상담할

Vision is like shooting at a moving target.
비전은 움직이는 목표물을 쏘아 맞히는 것과 같다.
Plenty of things can go wrong in the future / and plenty more can change in unpredictable ways.
많은 것들이 미래에 잘못될 수 있고, / 더 많은 것들이 예측할 수 없는 방식들로 변할 수 있다.
When such things happen, / you should be prepared / to make your vision conform to the new reality.
그러한 일들이 일어날 때, / 당신은 준비가 되어 있어야 한다. / 새로운 현실에 당신의 비전을 맞출
For example, / a businessman's optimistic forecast / can be blown away by a cruel recession / or by aggressive competition / in ways he could not have foreseen.
예를 들어, / 한 사업가의 낙관적인 예측은 / 잔혹한 경기 침체에 의해 날아갈 수 있다 / 혹은 공격적인 경쟁에 의해 / 그가 예견할 수 없던 방식으로
Or in another scenario, / his sales can skyrocket / and his numbers can get even better.
혹은 또 다른 시나리오에서는, / 그의 매출이 급등하거나 / 그의 수익이 훨씬 더 나아질 수 있다.
In any event, / he will be foolish to stick to his old vision / in the face of new data.
어떤 상황에서든, / 그가 그의 기존의 비전을 고수하는 것은 어리석은 일이 될 것이다 / 새로운 데이터에 직면했을 때
There is nothing wrong / in modifying your vision or even abandoning it, / as necessary.
잘못된 것이 아니다. / 당신의 비전을 수정하거나 심지어 그것을 버리는 것은 / 필요에 따라

비전은 움직이는 목표물을 쏘아 맞히는 것과 같다. 많은 것들이 미래에 잘못될 수 있고, 더 많은 것들이 예측할 수 없는 방식들로 변할 수 있다. 그러한 일들이 일어날 때, 당신은 새로운 현실에 당신의 비전을 맞출 준비가 되어 있어야 한다. 예를 들어, 한 사업가의 낙관적인 예측은 그가 예견할 수 없었던 방식으로 잔혹한 경기 침체나 공격적인 경쟁에 의해 날아갈 수 있다. 혹은 또 다른 시나리오에서는 그의 매출이 급등하거나 그의 수익이 훨씬 더 나아질 수 있다. 어떤 상황에서든, 그가 새로운 데이터에 직면했을 때 그의 기존의 비전을 고수하는 것은 어리석은 일이 될 것이다. 필요에 따라 당신의 비전을 수정하거나 심지어 그것을 버리는 것은 잘못된 것이 아니다.

Why? 왜 정답일까?

마지막 문장인 'There is nothing wrong in modifying your vision or even abandoning it, as necessary.'에서 필요에 따라 비전을 수정하거나 심지어 버리는 것은 잘못된 일이 아니라고 언급하며 상황에 따라 유연하게 비전을 조정할 필요성이 있음을 시사하므로, 빈칸에 들어갈 말로 가장 적절한 것은 ④ '새로운 현실에 당신의 비전을 맞출'이다.

- **shoot at** ~을 쏘아 맞히다
- **unpredictable** ⓐ 예측할 수 없는
- **forecast** ⓝ 예측
- **aggressive** ⓐ 공격적인
- **skyrocket** ⓥ 급등하다
- **in the face of** ~에 직면하여
- **abandon** ⓥ 버리다
- **conform to** ~에 맞추다, 순응하다
- **plenty** ⓝ 많음 ad 많이
- **optimistic** ⓐ 낙관적인
- **cruel** ⓐ 잔혹한, 고통스러운
- **foresee** ⓥ 예견하다
- **stick to** ~을 고수하다
- **modify** ⓥ 수정하다
- **defend** ⓥ 방어하다

구문 풀이

4행 For example, a businessman's optimistic forecast can be blown away
조동사 수동태
by a cruel recession or by aggressive competition in ways [he could not have
전명구1   전명구2   「could not have + 과거분사 :
foreseen].   ~할 수 없었을 것이다」

---

35 역사 공부의 이점 | 정답률 66% | 정답 ④

다음 글에서 전체 흐름과 관계 없는 문장은?

Studying history / can make you more knowledgeable / or interesting to talk to / or can lead to / all sorts of brilliant vocations, explorations, and careers.
역사를 공부하는 것은 / 당신이 더 유식하게 만들어 줄 수 있거나 / 혹은 말을 걸기에 흥미롭게 / 이어질 수 있다 / 온갖 멋진 직업, 탐구 및 경력으로
① But even more importantly, / studying history helps us / ask and answer humanity's Big Questions.
하지만 훨씬 더 중요하게는, / 역사 공부는 우리에게 도움을 준다. / 인류의 중요한 질문을 묻고 답하도록
② If you want to know / why something is happening in the present, / you might ask a sociologist or an economist.
만약 당신이 알고 싶다면 / 현재 어떤 일이 왜 발생하고 있는지 / 당신은 사회학자나 경제학자에게 물어볼지도 모른다.
③ But if you want to know deep background, / you ask historians.
그러나 당신이 만약 깊은 배경지식을 알고 싶다면 / 당신은 역사가에게 질문한다.
☑ A career as a historian is a rare job, / which is probably why you have never met one.
역사가는 드문 직업이고, / 이는 아마도 당신이 역사가를 만난 적이 없는 데 대한 이유가 된다.

---

⑤ That's because they are the people / who know and understand the past / and can explain its complex interrelationships with the present.
이는 그들이 사람이기 때문이다. / 과거를 알고 이해하며 / 현재와 과거의 복잡한 연관성을 설명할 수 있는

역사 공부는 당신이 더 유식하거나 흥미롭게 말하도록 만들어 줄 수 있거나 온갖 멋진 직업, 탐구 및 경력으로 이어질 수 있다. ① 하지만 더 중요한 것은, 역사 공부는 우리가 인류의 중요한 질문을 묻고 답하는 데 도움을 준다. ② 만약 현재 어떤 일이 왜 발생하고 있는지 알고 싶다면 사회학자나 경제학자에게 물어볼지도 모른다. ③ 그러나 만약 깊은 배경지식을 알고 싶다면 역사가에게 질문한다. ④ 역사가는 드문 직업이고, 이는 아마도 당신이 역사가를 만난 적이 없는 데 대한 이유가 된다. ⑤ 이는 그들이 과거를 알고 이해하며 현재와 과거의 복잡한 연관성을 설명할 수 있는 사람이기 때문이다.

Why? 왜 정답일까?

①, ②, ③, ⑤는 역사 공부가 인류의 큰 질문을 해결하고 사건에 대한 깊은 지식과 통찰을 갖는 데 도움을 준다는 내용을 다루는데, ④는 역사가가 드문 직업임을 설명하는 내용으로 흐름에 맞지 않는다. 따라서 전체 흐름과 관계 없는 문장은 ④이다.

- **knowledgeable** ⓐ 유식한, 정통한
- **vocation** ⓝ 직업, 천직
- **present** ⓝ 현재
- **interrelationship** ⓝ 연관성, 상호 관계
- **brilliant** ⓐ 멋진, 훌륭한
- **humanity** ⓝ 인류
- **sociologist** ⓝ 사회학자

구문 풀이

7행 A career as a historian is a rare job, which is probably why you have
선행사   계속적 용법   (the reason 생략) 관계부사
never met one.

---

36 박테리아의 이로운 점과 해로운 점 | 정답률 77% | 정답 ②

주어진 글 다음에 이어질 글의 순서로 가장 적절한 것을 고르시오.
① (A) – (C) – (B)
② (B) – (A) – (C)
③ (B) – (C) – (A)
④ (C) – (A) – (B)
⑤ (C) – (B) – (A)

We always have a lot of bacteria around us, / as they live almost everywhere / — in air, soil, in different parts of our bodies, / and even in some of the foods we eat.
우리 주변에는 항상 많은 박테리아가 있는데, / 왜냐하면 그것은 거의 모든 곳에 살고 있기 때문이다. / 즉 공기, 토양, 우리 몸의 다양한 부분들, / 그리고 심지어 우리가 먹는 몇몇 음식 속에도
But do not worry!
하지만 걱정하지 마라!
(B) Most bacteria are good for us.
대부분의 박테리아는 우리에게 유익하다.
Some live in our digestive systems / and help us digest our food, / and some live in the environment / and produce oxygen / so that we can breathe and live on Earth.
어떤 것은 우리의 소화 기관에 살면서 / 우리가 음식을 소화시키는 것을 도와주고, / 어떤 것은 주변에 살면서 / 산소를 만들어낸다. / 우리가 지구에서 숨 쉬고 살 수 있도록
(A) But unfortunately, / a few of these wonderful creatures / can sometimes make us sick.
하지만 불행하게도, / 몇몇 이런 훌륭한 생명체들이 / 때로는 우리를 병들게 할 수 있다.
This is when we need to see a doctor, / who may prescribe medicines to control the infection.
이때가 우리가 의사에게 진찰을 받아야 할 때인데 / 의사는 감염을 통제할 수 있도록 약을 처방해 줄 수 있다.
(C) But what exactly are these medicines / and how do they fight with bacteria?
그런데 이런 약은 정확히 무엇이고 / 어떻게 박테리아와 싸울까?
These medicines are called "antibiotics," / which means "against the life of bacteria."
이런 약은 '항생제'라고 불리는데, / '박테리아의 생명에 대항하는 것'을 의미한다.
Antibiotics either kill bacteria / or stop them from growing.
항생제는 박테리아를 죽이거나 / 또는 그것이 증식하는 것을 막는다.

우리 주변에는 항상 많은 박테리아가 있는데, 왜냐하면 그것은 거의 모든 곳, 즉 공기, 토양, 우리 몸의 다양한 부분들, 그리고 심지어 우리가 먹는 몇몇 음식 속에도 살고 있기 때문이다. 하지만 걱정하지 마라!

(B) 대부분의 박테리아는 우리에게 유익하다. 어떤 것은 우리의 소화 기관에 살면서 우리가 음식을 소화시키는 것을 도와주고, 어떤 것은 주변에 살면서 우리가 지구에서 숨 쉬고 살 수 있도록 산소를 만들어낸다.

(A) 하지만 불행하게도, 몇몇 이런 훌륭한 생명체들이 때로는 우리를 병들게 할 수 있다. 이때가 우리가 의사에게 진찰을 받아야 할 때인데 의사는 감염을 통제할 수 있도록 약을 처방해 줄 수 있다.

(C) 그런데 이런 약은 정확히 무엇이고 어떻게 박테리아와 싸울까? 이런 약은 '항생제'라고 불리는데, '박테리아의 생명에 대항하는 것'을 의미한다. 항생제는 박테리아를 죽이거나 또는 그것이 증식하는 것을 막는다.

Why? 왜 정답일까?

박테리아는 도처에 있지만 걱정할 필요는 없다는 내용의 주어진 글 뒤에는, 박테리아가 대체로 유익하다고 설명하는 (B), 하지만 불행히도 일부는 우리에게 해를 끼치기도 한다는 내용의 (A), 박테리아 감염이 있을 때 항생제가 이용된다는 내용의 (C)가 차례로 이어지는 것이 자연스럽다. 따라서 글의 순서로 가장 적절한 것은 ② '(B) – (A) – (C)'이다.

- **soil** ⓝ 토양
- **infection** ⓝ 감염
- **produce** ⓥ 생산하다
- **either A or B** A이거나 B인, A나 B 둘 중 하나
- **prescribe** ⓥ 처방하다
- **digestive** ⓐ 소화의
- **antibiotics** ⓝ 항생제

구문 풀이

1행 We always have a lot of bacteria around us, as they live almost everywhere
이유 접속사
— in air, soil, in different parts of our bodies, and even in some of the foods [we eat].
전명구1   전명구2   전명구3

37 상관관계와 인과관계의 별개성   정답률 46% | 정답 ②

주어진 글 다음에 이어질 글의 순서로 가장 적절한 것을 고르시오. [3점]

① (A) − (C) − (B)   ✔ (B) − (A) − (C)
③ (B) − (C) − (A)   ④ (C) − (A) − (B)
⑤ (C) − (B) − (A)

From a correlational observation, / we conclude / that one variable is related to a second variable.
상관관계의 관찰로부터 / 우리는 결론을 내린다. / 하나의 변인이 제2의 변인과 연관되어 있다고

But neither behavior / could be directly causing the other / even though there is a relationship.
그러나 둘 중 어느 행동도 / 다른 행동을 직접적으로 초래하지 않을 수 있다. / 관련성이 있다 하더라도

(B) The following example will illustrate / why it is difficult to make causal statements / on the basis of correlational observation.
다음 예는 보여줄 것이다. / 인과관계의 진술을 하는 것이 왜 어려운지를 / 상관관계의 관찰에 기초하여

The researchers at the U.S. Army / conducted a study of motorcycle accidents, / attempting to correlate the number of accidents with other variables / such as socioeconomic level and age.
미 육군 연구원들은 / 오토바이 사고에 관한 연구를 수행했다. / 사고의 수를 다른 변인과 연관시키려는 시도를 하여 / 사회 경제적 수준 및 나이와 같은

(A) They found / the best predictor / to be the number of tattoos / the rider had.
그들은 발견했다. / 최상의 예측 변인이 / 문신의 수라는 것을 / 오토바이를 타는 사람이 지닌

It would be a ridiculous error / to conclude / that tattoos cause motorcycle accidents / or that motorcycle accidents cause tattoos.
우스꽝스러운 오류가 될 것이다. / 결론 내리는 것은 / 문신이 오토바이 사고를 초래한다거나 / 오토바이 사고가 문신을 초래한다고

(C) Obviously, a third variable is related to both / — perhaps preference for risk.
명백히, 제3의 변인이 둘 다와 관련이 있는데, / 아마 위험에 대한 선호일 것이다.

A person who is willing to take risks / likes to be tattooed / and also takes more chances on a motorcycle.
위험을 기꺼이 감수하려는 사람은 / 문신 새기는 것을 좋아할 것이며 / 오토바이도 탈 가능성이 더 높다.

상관관계의 관찰로부터 우리는 하나의 변인이 제2의 변인과 연관되어 있다고 결론을 내린다. 그러나 관련성이 있다 하더라도 둘 중 어느 행동도 다른 행동을 직접적으로 초래하지 않을 수 있다.

(B) 다음 예는 상관관계의 관찰에 기초하여 인과관계의 진술을 하는 것이 왜 어려운지를 보여줄 것이다. 미 육군 연구원들은 사고의 수를 사회 경제적 수준 및 나이와 같은 다른 변인과 연관시키려는 시도를 하여 오토바이 사고에 관한 연구를 수행했다.

(A) 그들은 최상의 예측 변인이 오토바이를 타는 사람이 지닌 문신의 수라는 것을 발견했다. 문신이 오토바이 사고를 초래한다거나 오토바이 사고가 문신을 초래한다고 결론 내리는 것은 우스꽝스러운 오류가 될 것이다.

(C) 명백히, 제3의 변인이 둘 다와 관련이 있는데, 아마 위험에 대한 선호일 것이다. 위험을 기꺼이 감수하려는 사람은 문신 새기는 것을 좋아할 것이며 오토바이도 탈 가능성이 더 높다.

Why? 왜 정답일까?

상관관계의 관찰에서 바로 인과관계를 추론하기는 어렵다는 내용의 주어진 글 뒤에는, 오토바이 사고 수의 예를 언급하기 시작한 (B), 연구 결과 문신 수와 사고의 수가 서로 상관관계가 있다는 점이 드러났지만 이 두 변인을 인과관계로 엮으면 우스꽝스러울 것이라는 내용의 (A), 오히려 제3의 변인이 어느 정도 관련되어 있을 것이라는 추가적인 해석을 제시하는 (C)가 차례로 이어지는 것이 자연스럽다. 따라서 주어진 글 다음에 이어질 글의 순서로 가장 적절한 것은 ② '(B) − (A) − (C)'이다.

- correlational ⓐ 상관관계의
- variable ⓝ (실험에서) 변인, 변수
- ridiculous ⓐ 우스꽝스러운
- causal ⓐ 인과관계의, 인과의
- attempt ⓥ 시도하다
- socioeconomic ⓐ 사회 경제적인
- be willing to 기꺼이 ~하다
- conclude ⓥ 결론 짓다
- directly ⓐⓓ 직접적으로
- illustrate ⓥ 보여주다, 예증하다
- conduct ⓥ (수행)하다
- correlate ⓥ 연관시키다, 상관관계를 보여주다
- obviously ⓐⓓ 명백히, 분명히

구문 풀이

6행 It would be a ridiculous error to conclude [that tattoos cause motorcycle accidents] or [that motorcycle accidents cause tattoos].
가주어 / 진주어 / 접속사(~것) / 접속사(~것)

★★ 문제 해결 꿀~팁 ★★

▶ 많이 틀린 이유는?
상관관계와 인과관계의 개념을 구별하는 까다로운 내용의 지문으로, 내용을 속속들이 파악하기보다 단서 중심으로 답을 찾는 데 주력해야 한다. 오답으로 ③이 많이 나왔는데 (A) − (C)의 순서를 정하는 것이 문제 풀이의 성패를 가르는 요인이었음을 알 수 있다.

▶ 문제 해결 방법은?
주어진 문장에서 예시로 넘어가는 (B)가 가장 먼저 나온 뒤, Researchers를 They로 받는 (A)가 일단 이어져서 '사고의 수'와 '운전자의 문신 수'가 서로 인과관계로 연결된 요인으로 보기 어렵다는 이야기가 나와야 'A third variable'을 추가하는 느낌의 (C)가 자연스럽게 이어진다. 또한 (C)의 첫 문장에 나오는 both는 (A)에서 언급한 motorcycle accidenter와 tattoo를 가리킨다. (C)부터 배치하면 (A)의 They가 '연구자'라는 단어와 한참 멀어져서 오히려 (C)에 나온 복수 명사 chances로 읽힐 수 있는데, 이 경우 맥락이 부자연스럽다.

38 다른 사람의 감정 파악하기   정답률 60% | 정답 ④

글의 흐름으로 보아, 주어진 문장이 들어가기에 가장 적절한 곳을 고르시오.

Have you ever thought / about how you can tell / what somebody else is feeling?
당신은 생각해본 적이 있는가? / 당신이 어떻게 알 수 있는지 / 다른 누군가가 어떤 기분인지를

① Sometimes, friends might tell you / that they are feeling happy or sad / but, even if they do not tell you, / I am sure that you would be able to make a good guess / about what kind of mood they are in.
때때로, 친구들이 당신에게 말할지도 모르지만, / 그들이 행복하거나 슬프다고 / 당신에게 말하지 않는다고 해도, / 나는 당신이 추측을 잘할 수 있을 것이라고 확신한다. / 그들이 어떤 기분인지에 대해

② You might get a clue / from the tone of voice that they use.
당신은 단서를 얻을지도 모른다. / 그들이 사용하는 목소리의 어조로부터

③ For example, / they may raise their voice if they are angry / or talk in a shaky way if they are scared.
예를 들어, / 그들이 화가 나 있다면 그들은 목소리를 높일 것이고, / 그들이 두려워하고 있다면 떠는 식으로 말할 것이다.

✔ The other main clue you might use / to tell what a friend is feeling / would be to look at his or her facial expression.
당신이 사용할지도 모르는 다른 주요한 단서는 / 친구가 어떤 감정인지를 알기 위해 / 그 사람의 얼굴 표정을 보는 것일 것이다.

We have lots of muscles in our faces / which enable us to move our face / into lots of different positions.
우리는 얼굴에 많은 근육들이 있는데 / 이는 우리의 얼굴을 움직일 수 있게 한다. / 많은 다른 위치로

⑤ This happens spontaneously / when we feel a particular emotion.
이것은 자동적으로 일어난다. / 우리가 특정한 감정을 느낄 때

당신은 다른 누군가가 어떤 기분인지를 당신이 어떻게 알 수 있는지 생각해본 적이 있는가? ① 때때로, 친구들이 당신에게 그들이 행복하거나 슬프다고 말할지도 모르지만, 당신에게 말하지 않는다고 해도, 나는 당신이 그들이 어떤 기분인지에 대해 추측을 잘할 수 있을 것이라고 확신한다. ② 당신은 그들이 사용하는 목소리의 어조로부터 단서를 얻을지도 모른다. ③ 예를 들어, 그들이 화가 나 있다면 그들은 목소리를 높일 것이고, 그들이 두려워하고 있다면 떠는 식으로 말할 것이다. ④ 친구가 어떤 감정인지를 알기 위해 당신이 사용할지도 모르는 다른 주요한 단서는 그 사람의 얼굴 표정을 보는 것일 것이다. 우리는 얼굴에 많은 근육들이 있는데 이는 우리의 얼굴을 많은 다른 위치로 움직일 수 있게 한다. ⑤ 이것은 우리가 특정한 감정을 느낄 때 자동적으로 일어난다.

Why? 왜 정답일까?

다른 사람의 감정을 파악하는 방법에 관해 설명한 글이다. ④ 앞의 두 문장에서 타인의 어조를 통해 그 사람의 감정에 대한 단서를 얻을 수 있다고 언급한 이후, 주어진 문장은 다른 주요한 단서(The other main clue)로서 표정을 언급한다. ④ 뒤의 두 문장은 우리 얼굴에 많은 근육이 있어 감정에 따라 다양한 위치로 움직일 수 있다는 설명을 덧붙인다. 따라서 주어진 문장이 들어가기에 가장 적절한 곳은 ④이다.

- facial expression 얼굴 표정
- clue ⓝ 실마리, 힌트
- spontaneously ⓐⓓ 자동적으로
- make a guess 추측하다
- shaky ⓐ 떨리는
- particular ⓐ 특정한, 특별한

구문 풀이

1행 The other main clue [(that) you might use / to tell what a friend is feeling] would be to look at his or her facial expression.
주어 / 목적격 관계대명사(생략) / ~하기 위해 / 동사 / 주격 보어(~것)

39 읽기와 스키 타기의 유사성   정답률 47% | 정답 ③

글의 흐름으로 보아, 주어진 문장이 들어가기에 가장 적절한 곳을 고르시오.

Reading is like skiing.
읽는 것은 스키를 타는 것과 같다.

When done well, when done by an expert, / both reading and skiing / are graceful, harmonious activities.
잘되었을 때, 즉 전문가에 의해 이뤄졌을 때 / 읽기와 스키 타기는 / 모두 우아하고 조화로운 활동이다.

When done by a beginner, / both are awkward, frustrating, and slow.
초보자가 수행하면, / 둘 다 어색하고 좌절감을 주며 느린 활동이다.

① Learning to ski / is one of the most embarrassing experiences / an adult can undergo.
스키 타기를 배우는 것은 / 가장 당혹스러운 경험들 중 하나이다. / 성인이 겪을 수 있는

② After all, an adult has been walking for a long time; / he knows where his feet are; / he knows how to put one foot in front of the other / in order to get somewhere.
어쨌든, 성인은 오랫동안 걸어 다녔고, / 자기 발이 어디 있는지 알며, / 한 발을 다른 발 앞에 어떻게 놓을지를 안다. / 어딘가로 가기 위해서

✔ But as soon as he puts skis on his feet, / it is as though he had to learn to walk all over again.
하지만 발에 스키를 신자마자, / 이는 마치 걷는 법을 처음부터 다시 배워야만 하는 것과 같다.

He slips and slides, / falls down, / has trouble getting up, / and generally looks — and feels — like a fool.
그는 발을 헛디뎌 미끄러지고, / 넘어지고, / 일어나기가 어려우며, / 대체로 바보처럼 보이고 느껴지기도 한다.

④ It is the same with reading.
읽기도 마찬가지이다.

⑤ Probably you have been reading for a long time, too, / and starting to learn all over again / would be humiliating.
아마 여러분도 역시 오랫동안 읽기를 해 왔으므로, / 처음부터 다시 배우기를 시작하는 것은 / 창피할 수 있다.

읽는 것은 스키를 타는 것과 같다. 잘되었을 때, 즉 전문가에 의해 이뤄졌을 때 읽기와 스키 타기는 모두 우아하고 조화로운 활동이다. 초보자가 수행하면, 둘 다 어색하고 좌절감을 주며 느린 활동이다. ① 스키 타기를 배우는 것은 성인이 겪을 수 있는 가장 당혹스러운 경험들 중 하나이다. ② 어쨌든, 성인은 오랫동안 걸어 다녔고, 자기 발이 어디 있는지 알며, 어딘가로 가기 위해서 한 발을 다른 발 앞에 어떻게 놓을지를 안다. ③ 하지만 발에 스키를 신자마자, 이는 마치 걷는 법을 처음부터 다시 배워야만 하는 것과 같다. 발을 헛디뎌 미끄러지고, 넘어지고, 일어나기가 어려우며, 대체로 바보처럼 보이고 느껴지기도 한다. ④ 읽기도 마찬가지이다. ⑤ 아마 여러분도 역시 오랫동안 읽기를 해 왔으므로, 처음부터 다시 배우기를 시작하는 것은 창피할 수 있다.

Why? 왜 정답일까?

③ 앞의 문장에서 성인은 어찌되었든 오랜 세월 걸어 다녀서 걸어 다니는 법을 잘 알고 있다고 말한 데 이어, 주어진 문장은 그렇다 하더라도 스키를 발에 신으면 다시 처음부터 걷는 법을 배워야 하는 것과 다름이 없다는 내용을 제시한다. ③ 뒤의 문장에서는 미끄러지고 넘어지며 '다시 걷는 법을 배우는' 이런 과

정이 매우 '바보 같고' '당혹스럽다'고 여겨질 수 있음을 지적한다. 따라서 주어진 문장이 들어가기에 가장 적절한 곳은 ③이다.

- **as soon as** ~하자마자
- **expert** ⓝ 전문가
- **harmonious** ⓐ 조화로운
- **frustrating** ⓐ 좌절감을 주는
- **undergo** ⓥ 겪다
- **humiliating** ⓐ 창피한, 굴욕적인
- **as though** 마치 ~처럼
- **graceful** ⓐ 우아한
- **awkward** ⓐ 어색한, 불편한
- **embarrassing** ⓐ 당혹스러운
- **slip** ⓥ (어떤 위치나 손을 벗어나) 미끄러지다

구문 풀이

3행 When done well, when done by an expert, both reading and skiing are
(they are 생략) (they are 생략)   동사(복수)
접속사(~할 때) 접속사(~할 때)   「both A and B : A와 B 둘 다」
graceful, harmonious activities.

★★ 문제 해결 꿀~팁 ★★

▶ 많이 틀린 이유는?
주어진 문장에 But이 있으므로 흐름 반전의 포인트를 찾아야 하는데, 최다 오답인 ④는 '스키 타기 → 독서'로 소재가 바뀌어서 얼핏 볼 때 흐름상 가장 큰 전환이 일어나는 부분이다. 이렇게 함정이 있는 문장 위치 찾기 문항은 비교적 세부적인 흐름까지 체크하며 꼼꼼히 독해해야 실수 없이 정답을 고를 수 있다.

▶ 문제 해결 방법은?
주어진 문장은 '스키 신발을 신은 직후' 상황에 대해 이야기하는데, ③ 앞의 문장은 '평소'의 상황, ③ 뒤의 문장은 '스키를 신고 걸을 때'의 상황을 말하고 있다. 따라서 '평소에는 멀쩡히 걷지만 → 스키를 신으면 처음부터 걷기를 배우는 기분이고 → 실제로 무척 넘어지며 배운다'는 흐름이 되도록 ③에 주어진 문장을 넣는 것이 가장 적절하다.

★★★ 등급을 가르는 문제! ★★★

40 또래의 존재가 청소년과 성인의 행동에 미치는 영향   정답률 41% | 정답 ①

다음 글의 내용을 한 문장으로 요약하고자 한다. 빈칸 (A), (B)에 들어갈 말로 가장 적절한 것은? [3점]

	(A)		(B)
✔①	presence 존재	·····	take risks 위험을 감수하다
②	presence 존재	·····	behave cautiously 조심스럽게 행동하다
③	indifference 무관심	·····	perform poorly 잘하지 못하다
④	absence 부재	·····	enjoy adventures 모험을 즐기다
⑤	absence 부재	·····	act independently 독립적으로 행동하다

In a study, / psychologist Laurence Steinberg of Temple University / and his co-author, psychologist Margo Gardner / divided 306 people into three age groups: / young adolescents, with a mean age of 14; / older adolescents, with a mean age of 19; / and adults, aged 24 and older.
한 연구에서, / Temple 대학교의 심리학자 Laurence Steinberg와 / 공동 저자인 심리학자 Margo Gardner는 / 306명의 사람들을 세 연령 집단으로 나누었다. / 평균 나이 14세인 어린 청소년, / 평균 나이 19세인 나이가 더 많은 청소년, / 그리고 24세 이상인 성인

Subjects played a computerized driving game / in which the player must avoid crashing into a wall / that appears, without warning, on the roadway.
피실험자들은 컴퓨터 운전 게임을 했다. / 게임 참가자가 벽에 충돌하는 것을 피해야 하는 / 도로에 경고 없이 나타나는

Steinberg and Gardner / randomly assigned some participants to play alone / or with two same-age peers looking on.
Steinberg와 Gardner는 / 무작위로 몇몇 참가자들을 혼자 게임을 하게 했다. / 혹은 두 명의 같은 나이 또래가 지켜보는 가운데

Older adolescents scored about 50 percent higher / on an index of risky driving / when their peers were in the room / — and the driving of early adolescents / was fully twice as reckless / when other young teens were around.
나이가 더 많은 청소년들은 약 50퍼센트 더 높은 점수를 기록했고, / 위험 운전 지수에서 / 그들의 또래들이 같은 방에 있을 때 / 어린 청소년들의 운전은 / 무려 두 배 더 무모했다. / 다른 어린 십대들이 주변에 있을 때

In contrast, adults behaved in similar ways / regardless of whether they were on their own / or observed by others.
대조적으로, 성인들은 유사한 방식으로 행동했다. / 그들이 혼자 있든지 상관없이 / 혹은 다른 사람이 보고 있든지

➡ The (A) presence of peers makes adolescents, / but not adults, / more likely to (B) take risks.
또래들의 존재는 청소년들을 만든다. / 성인들은 그렇지 않지만, / 더 위험을 감수하도록

한 연구에서, Temple 대학교의 심리학자 Laurence Steinberg와 공동 저자인 심리학자 Margo Gardner는 306명의 사람들을 세 연령 집단(평균 나이 14세인 어린 청소년, 평균 나이 19세인 나이가 더 많은 청소년, 그리고 24세 이상인 성인)으로 나누었다. 피실험자들은 게임 참가자가 도로에 경고 없이 나타나는 벽에 충돌하는 것을 피해야 하는 컴퓨터 운전 게임을 했다. Steinberg와 Gardner는 무작위로 몇몇 참가자들을 혼자 혹은 두 명의 같은 나이 또래들이 지켜보는 가운데 게임을 하게 했다. 나이가 더 많은 청소년들은 그들의 또래들이 같은 방에 있을 때 위험 운전 지수에서 약 50퍼센트 더 높은 점수를 기록했고, 어린 청소년들의 운전은 다른 어린 십대들이 주변에 있을 때 무려 두 배 더 무모했다. 대조적으로, 성인들은 그들이 혼자 있든지 혹은 다른 사람이 보고 있든지 상관없이 유사한 방식으로 행동했다.

➡ 성인들은 그렇지 않지만, 또래들의 (A) 존재는 청소년들이 더 (B) 위험을 감수하게 만든다.

Why? 왜 정답일까?
연구를 소개한 글이므로 결론을 제시하는 마지막 두 문장을 주의 깊게 독해하면, 청소년 집단은 또래들이 있을 때 훨씬 더 무모한 게임을 했으며, 어른들은 별 영향이 없었다는 내용이 나온다. 따라서 요약문의 빈칸 (A), (B)에 들어갈 말로 가장 적절한 것은 ① 'A presence(존재), (B) take risks(위험을 감수하다)'이다.

- **co-author** 공동 저자
- **adolescent** ⓝ 청소년
- **crash into** ~에 충돌하다
- **observe** ⓥ 관찰하다
- **divide** ⓥ 나누다
- **mean** ⓐ 평균의
- **regardless of** ~에 상관없이
- **cautiously** ⓐⓓ 조심스럽게

[문제편 p.203]

- **indifference** ⓝ 무관심
- **independently** ⓐⓓ 독립적으로
- **poorly** ⓐⓓ 저조하게, 형편없이

구문 풀이

9행 Older adolescents scored about 50 percent higher on an index of risky
주어1   동사1
driving when their peers were in the room — and the driving of early adolescents
주어2
was fully twice as reckless when other young teens were around.
동사2   「배수사 + as + 원급 + (as ~) : (~보다) … 배 더 ~한」

★★ 문제 해결 꿀~팁 ★★

▶ 많이 틀린 이유는?
크게 앞의 '연구 – 결과'의 구조를 이루는 글로, 성인과 청소년 집단을 대조하는 In contrast 앞뒤에서 어른과 달리 청소년들은 또래가 있을 때 더 무모한(reckless) 운전을 했다는 결론을 제시하고 있다. 최다 오답인 ②의 (B) 'behave cautiously'는 결론의 핵심어 reckless와 정반대의 의미를 나타내므로 답으로 적절하지 않다.

▶ 문제 해결 방법은?
두 집단을 비교하여 설명하는 글에서는 각 집단의 특성과 관련한 핵심어를 먼저 찾은 뒤 요약문 및 선택지와 맞춰보도록 한다.

41-42 음식이 부족하던 시절 인간의 자기 보호 기제로 시작된 과식

A quick look at history shows / that humans have not always had the abundance of food / that is enjoyed throughout most of the developed world today.
역사를 빠르게 살피는 것은 보여준다 / 인간은 음식의 풍부함을 항상 가졌던 것은 아니다. / 오늘날 대부분의 발전된 세상에서 누리는

In fact, there have been numerous times in history / when food has been rather scarce.
사실, 역사적으로 수많은 시기가 있었다. / 음식이 꽤 부족했던

As a result, people used to eat more / when food was available / since the availability of the next meal was (a) questionable.
그 결과, 사람들은 더 많이 먹곤 했다. / 음식이 있을 때 / 다음번 식사의 가능성이 확실치 않았기 때문에

Overeating in those times / was essential to ensure survival, / and humans received satisfaction from eating more / than was needed for immediate purposes.
그 시기의 과식은 / 생존을 보장하는 데 필수적이었고, / 인간은 더 많이 먹는 것에서 만족을 얻었다. / 당장의 목적에 필요한 것보다

On top of that, /the highest pleasure was derived / from eating the most calorie-dense foods, / resulting in a (b) longer lasting energy reserve.
더욱이, / 가장 큰 기쁨은 얻어졌고, / 가장 칼로리가 높은 음식을 먹는 것으로부터 / 이는 더 오래 지속되는 에너지 비축을 초래했다.

Even though there are parts of the world / where, unfortunately, food is still scarce, / most of the world's population today / has plenty of food available / to survive and thrive.
비록 세계의 일부 지역들이 있지만, / 불행하게도 음식이 여전히 부족한 / 오늘날 세계 인구 대부분은 / 이용 가능한 많은 음식을 가지고 있다 / 생존과 번영을 위해

『However, this abundance is new, / and your body has not caught up, / still naturally (c) rewarding you / for eating more than you need / and for eating the most calorie-dense foods.』 **41번의 근거**
그러나 이러한 풍요로움은 새로운 것이고, / 당신의 몸은 따라잡지 못하여, / 여전히 자연스럽게 보상한다. / 당신이 필요한 것보다 더 많이 먹고 / 가장 칼로리가 높은 음식을 먹는 것에 대해

These are innate habits and not simple addictions.』 **41번의 근거**
이것들은 타고난 습관이지 단순한 중독은 아니다.

『They are self-preserving mechanisms / initiated by your body, / ensuring your future survival, / but they are (d) irrelevant now.』 **42번의 근거**
그것들은 자기 보호 기제이고, / 당신의 몸에서 시작된 / 당신의 미래 생존을 보장하지만, / 그것들은 이제 부적절하다.

Therefore, it is your responsibility / to communicate with your body / regarding the new environment of food abundance / and the need to (e) change the inborn habit of overeating.
그러므로 당신의 책임이다. / 당신의 몸과 대화하는 것은 / 음식이 풍부한 새로운 환경과 / 타고난 과식 습관을 변화시킬 필요와 관련하여

역사를 빠르게 살펴보면 인간은 오늘날 대부분의 발전된 세상에서 즐기는 음식의 풍부함을 항상 누렸던 것은 아님을 알 수 있다. 사실, 역사적으로 음식이 꽤 부족했던 수많은 시기가 있었다. 그 결과, 사람들은 다음번 식사의 가능성이 (a) 확실치 않았기 때문에 음식이 있을 때 더 많이 먹곤 했다. 그 시기의 과식은 생존을 보장하는 데 필수적이었고, 인간은 당장의 목적에 필요한 것보다 더 많이 먹는 것에서 만족을 얻었다. 더욱이, 가장 큰 기쁨은 가장 칼로리가 높은 음식을 먹는 것으로부터 얻어졌고, 이는 (b) 더 오래 지속되는 에너지 비축을 초래했다.

비록 불행하게도 음식이 여전히 부족한 세계의 일부 지역들이 있지만, 오늘날 세계 인구 대부분은 생존과 번영을 위해 이용 가능한 많은 음식을 가지고 있다. 그러나 이러한 풍요로움은 새로운 것이고, 당신의 몸은 따라잡지 못하여, 당신이 필요한 것보다 더 많이 먹고 가장 칼로리가 높은 음식을 먹는 것에 대해 여전히 자연스럽게 (c) 보상한다. 이것들은 타고난 습관이지 단순한 중독은 아니다. 그것들은 당신의 몸에서 시작된 자기 보호 기제이고, 당신의 미래 생존을 보장해 주지만, 그것들은 이제 (d) 부적절하다. 그러므로 음식이 풍부한 새로운 환경과 타고난 과식 습관을 (e) 강화시킬(→ 변화시킬) 필요와 관련하여 당신의 몸과 대화하는 것은 당신의 책임이다.

- **abundance** ⓝ 풍부함
- **scarce** ⓐ 부족한
- **questionable** ⓐ 확실치 않은, 의심스러운
- **derive A from B** B에서 A를 얻다
- **reserve** ⓝ 비축(물)
- **catch up** ~을 따라잡다
- **self-preserving** 자기 보존의
- **irrelevant** ⓐ 부적절한, 관계없는
- **inborn** ⓐ 타고난
- **ruin** ⓥ 망치다
- **numerous** ⓐ 수많은
- **availability** ⓝ 이용 가능성
- **overeating** ⓝ 과식
- **calorie-dense** 칼로리가 높은
- **thrive** ⓥ 번영하다
- **addiction** ⓝ 중독
- **initiate** ⓥ 시작하다
- **regarding** prep ~에 관련하여
- **rooted in** ~에 뿌리박힌

구문 풀이

1행 A quick look at history shows that humans have not always had
주어   동사 접속사   부분부정(~해 왔던 것은 아니다)
the abundance of food [that is enjoyed throughout most of the developed world
선행사   주격 관계대명사
today].

41 제목 파악 정답률 50% | 정답 ③

윗글의 제목으로 가장 적절한 것은?

① Which Is Better, Tasty or Healthy Food? – 맛있는 음식 또는 건강한 음식, 무엇이 더 좋은가
② Simple Steps for a More Balanced Diet – 보다 균형잡힌 식단을 향한 간단한 단계들
☑ Overeating: It's Rooted in Our Genes – 과식: 그것은 우리 유전자에 뿌리박혀 있다
④ How Calorie-dense Foods Ruin Our Bodies – 칼로리가 높은 음식이 어떻게 우리 몸을 망치는가
⑤ Our Eating Habits Reflect Our Personalities – 우리의 식습관은 우리 성격을 반영한다

Why? 왜 정답일까?

'However, this abundance is new, and your body has not caught up, still naturally rewarding you for eating more than you need ~. These are innate habits and not simple addictions.'에서 음식의 풍요는 그 역사가 짧기에 우리 몸은 여전히 음식이 부족한 시대에 그랬던 것처럼 필요한 양 이상의 음식을 먹고, 이는 중독이 아니라 그저 타고난 습관의 일부라는 내용을 언급하고 있다. 따라서 글의 제목으로 가장 적절한 것은 ③ '과식: 그것은 우리 유전자에 뿌리박혀 있다'이다.

★★★ 등급을 가르는 문제!

42 어휘 추론 정답률 39% | 정답 ⑤

밑줄 친 (a) ~ (e) 중에서 문맥상 낱말의 쓰임이 적절하지 않은 것은? [3점]

① (a)   ② (b)   ③ (c)   ④ (d)   ☑ (e)

Why? 왜 정답일까?

'They are self-preserving mechanisms initiated by your body, ensuring your future survival, but they are irrelevant now.'에서 과식은 우리 몸을 보호하려는 기제에서 출발했지만 음식이 풍요로워진 현대에 이르러서는 무의미한 습관임을 설명하고 있다. 이 맥락에 비추어볼 때, 타고난 과식 습관을 '강화하기'보다는 '변화시킬' 필요가 크다는 내용이 이어져야 하므로, (e)의 strengthen을 change로 바꾸는 것이 적절하다. 따라서 문맥상 낱말의 쓰임이 적절하지 않은 것은 ⑤ '(e)'이다.

★★ 문제 해결 꿀~팁 ★★

▶ 많이 틀린 이유는?
과식 습관의 유래를 설명한 글로, 수험생들에게 다소 친숙하지 않은 내용을 다루고 있다. (c)가 포함된 문장의 '~ this abundance is new, and your body has not caught up ~'에서 현대인은 음식의 풍요를 누리고 있지만 몸이 아직 이에 맞게 발달하지 못하여 영양이 부족했던 과거와 마찬가지로 필요한 양 이상을 먹는다는 핵심 내용을 언급하고 있다. 이 문장을 근거로 할 때, 과식의 습관은 본래 미래 생존을 보장하기 위한 보호기제로 시작되었지만 현대에는 '부적절하다'는 의미를 나타내는 (d)는 맥락에 적합하다.
▶ 문제 해결 방법은?
장문 어휘 문제에서는 각 선택지가 서로 다른 선택지에 대한 근거를 제시한다. (d)가 포함된 문장에서 과식의 습관을 '부적절하다'고 언급하므로, 이에 비추어볼 때 이 습관을 '강화해야' 한다고 언급하는 (e)는 맥락상 부자연스럽다.

43-45 타인에게 상처 주는 말을 많이 하던 소년의 일화

(A)

A long time ago, there was a boy.
오래 전에, 한 소년이 있었다.
He was smart, talented, and handsome.
그는 똑똑하고 재능이 있었으며 외모가 준수했다.
However, 『he was very selfish, / and his temper was so difficult / that nobody wanted to be his friend.』 45번 ①의 근거 일치
하지만 그는 매우 이기적이고 / 그의 성질이 아주 까다로워 / 어느 누구도 그의 친구가 되기를 원하지 않았다.
Often, (a) he got angry / and said hurtful things to people around him.
종종 그는 화가 나서 / 주변 사람들에게 상처 주는 말을 했다.

(D)

『The boy's parents were concerned about his bad temper.』 45번 ④의 근거 일치
소년의 부모는 그의 못된 성질을 걱정했다.
One day, the father had an idea.
어느 날, 아버지에게 아이디어가 떠올랐다.
He called his son / and gave (e) him a hammer and a bag of nails.
그는 아들을 불러 / 그에게 망치 하나와 못이 든 가방 하나를 주었다.
The father said, / "Every time you get angry, / take a nail, and drive it into that old fence / as hard as you can."
아버지는 말했다. / "네가 화가 날 때마다, / 못을 하나 가져가 저 낡은 울타리에 박아라. / 가능한 세게"라고
The fence was very tough, / and the hammer was heavy.
그 울타리는 매우 단단했고, / 망치는 무거웠다.
『Nevertheless, / he was so furious / that during the very first day he drove in 37 nails.』 45번 ⑤의 근거 일치
그럼에도 불구하고, / 그는 너무 화가 나서 / 바로 그 첫날 동안 37개의 못을 박았다.

(B)

『The number of nails / the boy drove into the fence each day / gradually decreased.』 45번 ②의 근거 불일치
못의 수는 / 매일 소년이 울타리에 박은 / 점점 줄어들었다.
Eventually, the boy started to understand / that holding his temper was easier / than driving nails into the fence.
결국, / 소년은 이해하기 시작했다. / 화를 참는 것이 더 쉽다는 것을 / 울타리에 못을 박는 것보다
(b) He didn't need the hammer and nails anymore / when he learned to hold his temper.
그는 더 이상 망치와 못이 필요하지 않았다. / 화를 참는 법을 배웠을 때
He went to his father and shared (c) his achievement.
그는 아버지에게 가서 자신의 성취를 함께 나누었다.
"Now every time you hold your temper all day long, / pull out one nail."
"이젠 온종일 네가 화를 참을 때마다, / 못 한 개를 뽑아라."

(C)

Much time passed.
많은 시간이 흘렀다.
『At last, the boy was proud of himself / as all the nails were gone.』 45번 ③의 근거 일치
그 소년은 스스로가 자랑스러웠다. / 마침내 모든 못이 없어지자

He found his father and explained this.
그는 아버지를 찾아 이를 설명했다.
Together, they went to the fence, / and (d) he said, / "You did a good job, my son, / but pay attention to the holes / left from the nails.
그들은 함께 울타리로 갔고, / 그는 말했다. / "잘했다, 아들아, / 하지만 구멍에 주목해 보렴. / 못으로 인해 남겨진
The fence will never be the same.
울타리는 결코 전과 같지 않을 거야.
The same happens / when you say hurtful things to people.
똑같은 일이 생기지, / 네가 사람들에게 상처를 주는 말을 할 때에도
Your words leave scars in their hearts / like those holes in the fence."
네 말은 사람들의 마음에 흉터를 남긴다. / 울타리의 저 구멍처럼"

(A)
오래 전에, 한 소년이 있었다. 그는 똑똑하고 재능이 있었으며 외모가 준수했다. 하지만 그는 매우 이기적이고 성질이 아주 까다로워 어느 누구도 그의 친구가 되기를 원하지 않았다. 종종 (a) 그는 화가 나서 주변 사람들에게 상처 주는 말을 했다.

(D)
소년의 부모는 그의 못된 성질을 걱정했다. 어느 날, 아버지에게 아이디어가 떠올랐다. 그는 아들을 불러 (e) 그에게 망치 하나와 못이 든 가방 하나를 주었다. 아버지는 "네가 화가 날 때마다, 못을 하나 가져가 저 낡은 울타리에 가능한 세게 박아라."라고 말했다. 그 울타리는 매우 단단했고, 망치는 무거웠다. 그럼에도 불구하고, 그는 너무 화가 나서 바로 그 첫날 동안 37개의 못을 박았다.

(B)
매일 소년이 울타리에 박은 못의 수는 점점 줄어들었다. 결국, 소년은 울타리에 못을 박는 것보다 화를 참는 것이 더 쉽다는 것을 이해하기 시작했다. 화를 참는 법을 배웠을 때, (b) 그는 더 이상 망치와 못이 필요하지 않았다. 그는 아버지에게 가서 (c) 자신의 성취를 함께 나누었다. "이젠 온종일 네가 화를 참을 때마다, 못 한 개를 뽑아라."

(C)
많은 시간이 흘렀다. 마침내 모든 못이 없어지자 그 소년은 스스로가 자랑스러웠다. 그는 아버지를 찾았고 이를 설명했다. 그들은 함께 울타리로 갔고, (d) 그는 말했다. "잘했다, 아들아, 하지만 못으로 인해 남겨진 구멍에 주목해 보렴. 울타리는 결코 전과 같지 않을 거야. 네가 사람들에게 상처를 주는 말을 할 때에도 마찬가지야. 네 말은 울타리의 저 구멍처럼 사람들의 마음에 흉터를 남긴다."

- talented ⓐ 재능 있는
- temper ⓝ 성질, 기질
- hurtful ⓐ 상처를 주는, 아프게 하는
- drive into (못 등을) 박다
- hammer ⓝ 망치
- achievement ⓝ 성취
- pay attention to ~에 주목하다
- be concerned about ~을 걱정하다
- selfish ⓐ 이기적인
- difficult ⓐ 까다로운
- nail ⓝ 못
- gradually ⓐⓓ 점차, 서서히
- share ⓥ 함께 나누다
- pull out (잡아) 뽑다
- scar ⓝ 흉터, 상처
- furious ⓐ 화가 난, 격분한

구문 풀이

[A] 2행 However, he was very selfish, / and his temper was so difficult that nobody (접속부사(하지만)) ('so + 형용사 + that + 주어 + 동사') (너무 ~해서 …하다) wanted to be his friend.

[B] 1행 The number of nails [the boy drove into the fence each day] gradually (주어) (목적격 관계대명사 생략) decreased. (자동사(줄다, 감소하다))

[D] 3행 Every time you get angry, / take a nail, and drive it into that old fence / (~할 때마다) (명령문 동사1) (명령문 동사2) as hard as you can. (~할 수 있는 한 …하게)

43 글의 순서 파악 정답률 78% | 정답 ④

주어진 글 (A)에 이어질 내용을 순서에 맞게 배열한 것으로 가장 적절한 것은?

① (B) – (D) – (C)   ② (C) – (B) – (D)
③ (C) – (D) – (B)   ☑ (D) – (B) – (C)
⑤ (D) – (C) – (B)

Why? 왜 정답일까?

이기적이고 성질이 까다로워 종종 다른 사람들에게 상처를 주는 말을 하던 한 소년이 살았다는 내용의 (A) 뒤에는, 소년의 아버지가 그를 걱정하여 화가 날 때마다 울타리에 못을 박도록 했다는 내용의 (D), 소년이 갈수록 못을 박는 대신 화를 참는 법을 배웠다는 내용의 (C), 이어서 그 못을 모두 뽑고 난 뒤 구멍투성이가 된 울타리와 마찬가지로 소년의 말도 타인을 아프게 했을 것임을 아버지가 상기시켰다는 내용의 (C)가 차례로 이어지는 것이 자연스럽다. 따라서 주어진 글 (A)에 이어질 내용을 순서에 맞게 배열한 것으로 가장 적절한 것은 ④ '(D) – (B) – (C)'이다.

44 지칭 추론 정답률 81% | 정답 ④

밑줄 친 (a) ~ (e) 중에서 가리키는 대상이 나머지 넷과 다른 것은?

① (a)   ② (b)   ③ (c)   ☑ (d)   ⑤ (e)

Why? 왜 정답일까?

(a), (b), (c), (e)는 'the boy'를, (d)는 'his father'를 나타내므로, (a) ~ (e) 중에서 가리키는 대상이 나머지 넷과 다른 것은 ④ '(d)'이다.

45 세부 내용 파악 정답률 76% | 정답 ②

윗글의 내용으로 적절하지 않은 것은?

① 어느 누구도 소년과 친구가 되기를 원치 않았다.

☑ 소년이 하루에 박은 못의 수는 점점 늘어났다.
③ 소년은 모든 못을 제거하고 스스로를 자랑스러워했다.
④ 소년의 부모는 아들의 못된 성질을 걱정했다.
⑤ 소년은 못을 박기 시작한 첫날 37개의 못을 박았다.

Why? 왜 정답일까?

② 'The number of nails the boy drove into the fence each day gradually decreased.'에서 소년이 하루에 박은 못의 수는 점점 줄었다고 하므로, 글의 내용으로 적절하지 않은 것은 ② '소년이 하루에 박은 못의 수는 점점 늘어났다.'이다.

Why? 왜 오답일까?

① '~ his temper was so difficult that nobody wanted to be his friend.'와 일치한다.
③ 'At last, the boy was proud of himself as all the nails were gone.'과 일치한다.
④ 'The boy's parents were concerned about his bad temper.'와 일치한다.
⑤ 'Nevertheless, he was so furious that during the very first day he drove in 37 nails.'와 일치한다.

Dictation 03
문제편 205쪽

01 made to our library / remove the old lighting / for temporarily closing the library
02 stayed up all night / a sufficient amount of sleep / lower your body's defenses
03 best-selling audio book of the year / your voice acting was great / step into the recording booth
04 smaller than the title / drew the polar bear / the polar bear is pointing to
05 on my way to the bank / ordered the guide book you recommended / use mobile applications to compare
06 I'm looking for a teapot / this teapot set that comes with the cups / definitely good for relaxation
07 have a special expo / You're interested in architecture / I'm auditioning for the school play
08 What do I do there? / in person or on the school website / runs from 3 to 7
09 encourage students' creativity / challenging them to design / open to college students around the world / seeing your innovative designs
10 type during meetings at work / the cheapest / weighs less than 300 grams / it's not foldable
11 was especially amazing / enjoy the most
12 can I change my volunteering schedule / from Thursday or Friday
13 if that's possible or not / for my students' baseball club / put our club members' names / give us the list of names
14 change the location of the concert / put it up on the notice board / spread the news to more people quickly
15 go to the buffet / with his shrimp dish unfinished / not done with the dish
16-17 how about sharing it with others / The same thing with toys / need a bicycle / awaken your "sleeping" goods

어휘 Review Test 03
문제편 210쪽

A	B	C	D
01 길어진, 장시간에 걸친	01 devote	01 ⓒ	01 ⓢ
02 거의	02 accidentally	02 ⓔ	02 ⓖ
03 정의하다	03 dissatisfaction	03 ⓚ	03 ⓕ
04 꼭 ~한 것은 아니다	04 potential	04 ⓐ	04 ⓐ
05 비위를 맞추는	05 considerable	05 ⓛ	05 ⓡ
06 결과	06 compliment	06 ⓙ	06 ⓟ
07 구조	07 self-esteem	07 ⓗ	07 ⓗ
08 상하다	08 inequality	08 ⓑ	08 ⓞ
09 일치하지 않는, 부합하지 않는	09 get rid of	09 ⓘ	09 ⓜ
10 저항하다	10 prefer	10 ⓝ	10 ⓑ
11 ~이전에	11 require	11 ⓞ	11 ⓝ
12 ~을 고수하다	12 exaggerate	12 ⓕ	12 ⓔ
13 차지된, 점거된	13 abandon	13 ⓡ	13 ⓙ
14 낙관적인	14 vocation	14 ⓜ	14 ⓣ
15 유식한, 정통한	15 prescribe	15 ⓛ	15 ⓠ
16 항생제	16 causal	16 ⓓ	16 ⓝ
17 우스꽝스러운	17 as though	17 ⓢ	17 ⓚ
18 부족한	18 selfish	18 ⓟ	18 ⓒ
19 B에서 A를 얻다	19 conduct	19 ⓠ	19 ⓓ
20 화가 난, 격분한	20 attempt	20 ⓖ	20 ⓘ

03회

• 정답 •

01 ② 02 ③ 03 ① 04 ④ 05 ① 　06 ① 07 ⑤ 08 ④ 09 ④ 10 ② 　11 ④ 12 ③ 13 ① 14 ① 15 ①
16 ① 17 ④ 18 ④ 19 ⑤ 20 ② 　21 ⑤ 22 ① 23 ① 24 ② 25 ⑤ 　26 ⑤ 27 ③ 28 ⑤ 29 ④ 30 ④
31 ④ 32 ① 33 ③ 34 ⑤ 35 ④ 　36 ② 37 ⑤ 38 ③ 39★ ⑤ 40 ④ 　41 ① 42 ⑤ 43 ④ 44 ⑤ 45 ④

★ 표기된 문항은 [등급을 가르는 문제]에 해당하는 문항입니다.

---

01 감사 일기 쓰기
정답률 74% | 정답 ②

다음을 듣고, 여자가 하는 말의 목적으로 가장 적절한 것을 고르시오.

① 강의 일정 변경을 공지하려고
☑ 감사 일기 쓰는 것을 권장하려고
③ 건강 관리의 중요성을 강조하려고
④ 자기소개서 작성 요령을 설명하려고
⑤ 효과적인 시간 활용법을 안내하려고

W : Hello and welcome back to 'Happy Life.'
안녕하세요, Happy Life에 다시 오신 것을 환영해요.
I'm Christine Brown, professional life coach.
저는 전문 인생 코치인 Christine Brown입니다.
When was the last time you sat down and thought about the good things in your life?
여러분이 마지막으로 앉아서 삶의 좋은 것들을 생각해 본 게 언제였나요?
With our busy schedules, we easily forget to count the blessings we already have.
바쁜 스케줄로 인해, 우리는 우리가 이미 지난 축복들을 헤아리는 것을 쉽게 잊습니다.
However, according to a recent study, people who are more grateful for what they have are more hopeful and physically healthier.
하지만 최근의 한 연구에 따르면, 자기가 가지고 있는 것에 더 감사하는 사람들이 더 희망적이고 신체적으로 건강하다고 합니다.
So here is today's tip.
그래서 여기 오늘의 조언이 있습니다.
Write a gratitude journal.
감사 일기를 쓰세요.
A gratitude journal is a diary in which you can express all the things you're thankful for.
감사 일기는 여러분이 감사해하는 모든 것을 표현할 수 있는 일기입니다.
Just invest five to ten minutes each day in the journal.
그저 매일 5분 내지 10분을 일기에 투자하세요.
You'll feel more thankful and stay healthier.
여러분은 더 감사한 기분이 들 것이고 더 건강해질 것입니다.

Why? 왜 정답일까?

'Write a gratitude journal.'과 'Just invest five to ten minutes each day in the journal. You'll feel more thankful and stay healthier.'에서 감사한 마음과 신체 건강을 유지하기 위해 감사 일기를 쓸 것을 권한다는 내용이 나오므로, 여자가 하는 말의 목적으로 가장 적절한 것은 ② '감사 일기 쓰는 것을 권장하려고'이다.

● blessing ⓝ 축복
● invest ⓥ 투자하다, (돈이나 시간을) 들이다
● physically ⓐⓓ 신체적으로, 물리적으로

---

02 스트레칭의 이점
정답률 89% | 정답 ③

대화를 듣고, 남자의 의견으로 가장 적절한 것을 고르시오.

① 운동은 자신감 향상에 도움이 된다.
② 격렬한 운동 전에 스트레칭을 해야 한다.
☑ 스트레칭은 많은 면에서 건강에 유익하다.
④ 바른 자세를 유지하는 습관을 가져야 한다.
⑤ 자신에게 맞는 스트레스 해소 방법을 찾아야 한다.

M : Good morning, Lily!
안녕, Lily!
W : Hi, Sean! Are you exercising?
안녕, Sean! 운동하는 중이야?
M : Yeah. I'm just doing some stretching.
응, 그냥 스트레칭 좀 하고 있어.
W : Oh, it's good for making your muscles flexible, right?
오, 그건 네 근육을 유연하게 하는 데 좋지, 그렇지?
M : Not only for that. Stretching can improve energy levels by making our mind and body more alert.
그것뿐만이 아니야. 스트레칭은 우리 마음과 신체를 더 기민하게 만들어서 에너지 수준을 향상시킬 수 있어.
W : I can imagine. I think stretching can relieve stress as well.
상상이 된다. 스트레칭은 스트레스도 풀어줄 것 같아.
M : You're right. It also increases blood flow to the muscles, so you can feel less tired.
네 말이 맞아. 근육에 들어가는 혈류량도 증가시켜서, 피곤함을 덜 느낄 수 있게 돼.
W : I see. I haven't thought about that benefit.
그렇구나. 그런 이점은 생각해본 적이 없었어.
M : As you see, stretching is very good for your health in many ways.
나도 지금 바로 스트레칭을 좀 해야 할 것 같아.
W : I think I should do some stretching right away.
너도 알다시피, 스트레칭은 많은 면에서 네 건강에 아주 좋아.
M : Of course. Let's do it together.
물론이지, 같이 하자.

Why? 왜 정답일까?

'~ stretching is very good for your health in many ways.'에서 남자는 스트레칭이 여러모

로 건강에 좋다고 말하고 있으므로, 남자의 의견으로 가장 적절한 것은 ③ '스트레칭은 많은 면에서 건강에 유익하다.'이다.

● flexible ⓐ 유연한
● alert ⓐ 기민한, 초롱초롱한
● increase ⓥ 증가시키다
● improve ⓥ 향상시키다
● relieve ⓥ 완화하다, 경감하다
● benefit ⓝ 이득, 혜택

---

03 안과 진료
정답률 95% | 정답 ①

대화를 듣고, 두 사람의 관계를 가장 잘 나타낸 것을 고르시오.

☑ 안과 의사 – 환자
② 보건 교사 – 학생
③ 프로젝트 팀장 – 팀원
④ 컴퓨터 판매원 – 구매자
⑤ 약사 – 제약 회사 직원

[Door knocks.]
[문을 노크하는 소리가 난다.]
W : Come on in. [Pause] Have a seat, please.
들어오세요. [잠시 멈춤] 앉으세요.
M : Thanks!
고맙습니다!
W : What has been troubling you, Mr. Williams?
무엇 때문에 괴로우신가요, Williams 씨?
M : My eyes are red and sore, and I can't see things clearly.
눈이 빨갛고 따갑고, 사물이 분명히 보이지 않아요.
W : Okay. Let me check your eyes first. Put your chin on the machine and don't move.
알겠습니다. 눈을 먼저 확인해볼게요. 기계에 턱을 올리시고 움직이지 마세요.
M : Alright.
알겠습니다.
W : [Pause] Oh, you have dry eyes. Have you been using your computer more than usual?
[잠시 멈춤] 오, 눈이 건조하시군요. 평소보다 컴퓨터를 더 많이 쓰고 계신가요?
M : Yes, I've been working all week on an important project.
네, 전 일주일 내내 중요한 프로젝트에 공을 들이고 있어요.
W : You should rest your eyes and blink more frequently.
눈을 쉬게 하고 더 자주 깜박여 주셔야 합니다.
M : I see. I was worried I got an eye infection.
알겠습니다. 전 눈에 감염이 있나 걱정했어요.
W : No, you didn't. Just put some eyedrops in your eyes. I'll give you a prescription.
아니요, 그렇지 않았습니다. 그냥 안약을 조금 눈에 넣어주세요. 처방을 해 드릴게요.
M : Okay. Do I have to come again?
알겠습니다. 제가 다시 와야 하나요?
W : I recommend you have your eyes checked again next week. The nurse will help you make an appointment.
다음주에 다시 한 번 눈을 검사받기를 권장합니다. 간호사가 예약을 도와드릴 거예요.
M : All right. Thank you.
알겠습니다. 감사합니다.

Why? 왜 정답일까?

'Let me check your eyes first.', 'Just put some eyedrops in your eyes. I'll give you a prescription.' 등에서 여자가 안과 의사임을, 'My eyes are red and sore, and I can't see things clearly.', 'I was worried I got an eye infection.' 등에서 남자가 환자임을 알 수 있으므로, 두 사람의 관계로 가장 적절한 것은 ① '안과 의사 – 환자'이다.

● have a seat (자리에) 앉다
● chin ⓝ 턱
● frequently ⓐⓓ 자주, 빈번히
● prescription ⓝ 처방
● appointment ⓝ 예약, 약속
● sore ⓐ 따가운, 아픈
● blink ⓥ (눈을) 깜박거리다
● infection ⓝ 감염
● recommend ⓥ 권장하다, 추천하다

---

04 공원 사진 구경하기
정답률 87% | 정답 ④

대화를 듣고, 그림에서 대화의 내용과 일치하지 <u>않는</u> 것을 고르시오.

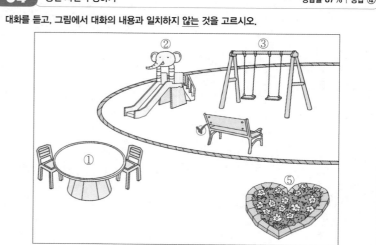

M : What are you looking at, honey?
여보, 뭘 하고 있어요?
W : It's the picture Sally sent to me. She recommended that we go to the new community park near her house.
이건 Sally가 내게 보내준 사진이에요. 그녀는 우리에게 자기 집 근처에 있는 새로운 근린 공원에 가 보라고 추천했어요.
M : Let me see it. [Pause] 「I like this big round table on the left.」 We can have some sandwiches and talk there.
나도 보여줘요. [잠시 멈춤] 왼쪽에 있는 이 커다란 원탁이 마음에 드네요. 우리 저기서 샌드위치를 먹으며 이야기할 수 있겠어요.　②의근거 일치
W : Sounds great. 「Look at the elephant face at the top of the slide.」 It looks cute.
좋을 것 같아요. 미끄럼틀 꼭대기에 있는 코끼리 얼굴 좀 봐요. 귀여워 보여요.　②의근거 일치

M : 『Yeah, there are also swings next to it.』 Our son would like this park, too. 3의근거 일치
네, 그 옆에 그네도 있어요. 우리 아들도 이 공원을 좋아하겠네요.

W : He sure would. 『Oh, there is a see-saw in front of the swings.』 4의근거 불일치
분명 그럴 거에요. 오, 그네 앞에 시소가 있어요.

M : Wow, this park has everything a child could want.
와, 이 공원에는 아이가 원할 만한 모든 것들이 있네요.

W : It's great to find a place where parents and children can have a good time together.
부모와 아이들이 함께 좋은 시간을 보낼 수 있는 장소를 찾아서요.

M : It really is. 『Take a look at these flowers placed in the shape of a heart!』 6의근거 일치
정말 그래요. 하트 모양으로 놓인 이 꽃들을 봐요.

W : They're beautiful. How about going there this weekend?
아름다워요. 이번 주말에 여기 가는 게 어때요?

M : Terrific! I can't wait to go there.
멋져요! 그곳에 갈 게 기대되네요.

Why? 왜 정답일까?

대화에서는 그네 앞에 시소가 있다(Oh, there is a see-saw in front of the swings.)고 하는데, 그림에서는 그네 앞에 벤치가 놓여 있다. 따라서 그림에서 대화의 내용과 일치하지 않는 것은 ④이다.

- recommend ⓥ 추천하다
- terrific ⓐ 아주 멋진

---

05 축하 파티 준비   정답률 92% | 정답 ①

대화를 듣고, 남자가 여자를 위해 할 일로 가장 적절한 것을 고르시오.
- ✓ 감자 사 오기
- ② 케이크 만들기
- ③ 장학금 신청하기
- ④ 스테이크 주문하기
- ⑤ 식료품점 위치 검색하기

[Cellphone rings.]
[휴대전화가 울린다.]

W : Benjamin, I'm sorry to call you during work, but I have great news to share.
Benjamin, 일하는 중에 전화해서 미안하지만, 함께 나눌 근사한 소식이 있단다.

M : No problem, mom. I'm about to leave my office. What's up?
괜찮아요, 엄마. 전 사무실을 나가려던 참이에요. 무슨 일이세요?

W : Your brother Wilson got the football scholarship! Let's throw a party tonight to celebrate.
네 동생 Wilson이 축구 장학금을 받았어! 오늘밤 축하 파티를 열자.

M : Wow, wonderful. I'll buy a cake for him on my way home.
와, 멋져요. 제가 집에 가는 길에 그를 위해 케이크를 사 갈게요.

W : Good! I'll cook his favorite steak.
좋아! 난 그 애가 가장 좋아하는 스테이크를 요리할게.

M : Oh, he'll love it!
오, 그가 좋아하겠어요!

W : Yeah, I hope so. But I think something is missing from the meal. How about adding mashed potatoes as a side dish?
응, 그러길 바라. 그런데 식사에 무언가 빠진 것 같구나. 곁들임 요리로 으깬 감자를 추가하는 건 어떠니?

M : Great, it goes well with steak.
좋아요. 스테이크랑 잘 어울려요.

W : Right, but we're out of potatoes.
맞아. 그런데 우린 감자가 다 떨어졌어.

M : Don't worry. I'll buy some for you. The grocery store is near the bakery. I'll be at home in an hour.
걱정 마세요. 제가 엄마를 위해 좀 사 갈게요. 식료품점은 빵집 근처예요. 한 시간 뒤에 집에 갈게요.

W : Thanks. No rush. We still have some time.
고마워. 서두르지 마. 우린 아직 시간이 좀 있어.

Why? 왜 정답일까?

대화에서 남자는 으깬 감자를 요리하려는데 감자가 떨어졌다(~ we're out of potatoes.)고 말하는 여자를 위해 자신이 감자를 사 가겠다(I'll buy some for you.)고 답하므로, 남자가 할 일로 가장 적절한 것은 ① '감자 사 오기'이다.

- throw a party 파티를 열다
- goes well with ~와 잘 어울리다

---

06 향초 구매하기   정답률 84% | 정답 ②

대화를 듣고, 남자가 지불할 금액을 고르시오. [3점]
① $40   ✓ $45   ③ $50   ④ $54   ⑤ $60

W : Welcome to Good Aroma Candle. How may I help you?
Good Aroma Candle에 방문하신 것을 환영합니다. 무엇을 도와드릴까요?

M : Hi. I'm looking for scented candles for my parents. They like flower scents.
안녕하세요. 전 부모님을 위한 향초를 찾고 있어요. 그분들은 꽃향기를 좋아하세요.

W : Come over here and try this flower scent.
이쪽으로 오셔서 이 꽃향기를 맡아보세요.

M : Thanks. [Pause] I like this rose scented candle. How much is it?
고맙습니다. [잠시 멈춤] 전 이 장미향 캔들이 좋아요. 얼마죠?

W : Large candles and medium ones are on sale now. Large ones are $20 and medium ones are $10 each.
큰 캔들과 중간 사이즈 캔들은 지금 세일 중입니다. 큰 것들은 20달러이고 중간 것들은 각각 10달러예요.

M : Well then, I'll take two large candles.
음, 그러면 전 큰 캔들 두 개를 사겠어요.

W : If you buy any three candles, we give you a soap for free.
어느 것이든 세 개를 사시면 저희는 비누 하나를 공짜로 드려요.

M : Great. Then I'll have a medium one with the same scent as well. Did you say they're $10?
좋아요. 그럼 전 똑같은 향이 나는 중간 크기 캔들도 하나 사겠어요. 10달러라고 하셨죠?

W : Exactly. You're getting two large candles and one medium candle.
네. 큰 캔들 두 개와 중간 것 하나요.

M : That's right. Can I also use this mobile coupon?
맞아요. 제가 이 모바일 쿠폰을 쓸 수 있나요?

W : Of course, you get 10% off the total price with that.
물론이죠. 그것으로 총 가격의 10퍼센트를 할인받게 되실 겁니다.

[문제편 p.211]

M : Thank you. I'll pay by credit card.
고맙습니다. 신용 카드로 지불할게요.

Why? 왜 정답일까?

대화에 따르면 남자는 20달러짜리 큰 장미향 캔들을 두 개와, 10달러짜리 중간 크기 캔들들을 구매하였고, 모바일 쿠폰으로 총 가격의 10퍼센트를 할인받았다. 이를 식으로 나타내면 '(20×2+10)×0.9=45'이므로, 남자가 지불할 금액은 ② '$45'이다.

---

07 거리 공연 초대   정답률 94% | 정답 ⑤

대화를 듣고, 여자가 거리 공연을 보러 갈 수 없는 이유를 고르시오.
- ① 학교 축제를 위한 부스를 만들어야 해서
- ② 좋아하는 밴드의 팬 사인회에 가야 해서
- ③ 동아리 부원들과 기타 연습을 해야 해서
- ④ 학급 친구들과 합창 대회 준비를 해야 해서
- ✓ 과학 프로젝트를 위해 조원들을 만나야 해서

M : Hi, Charlotte, long time no see!
안녕, Charlotte, 오랜만이네!

W : Hi, Andrew. Are you doing well at your new school?
안녕, Andrew. 새 학교에서 잘 지내고 있어?

M : I think I'm adjusting well. All of my new classmates are nice.
잘 적응하고 있는 것 같아. 내 반 친구들은 모두 착해.

W : Good to hear that. Are you still playing the guitar? I loved your performance at the school festival last year.
그렇다니 다행이네. 아직 기타 연주를 하고 있니? 작년에 학교 축제에서 했던 네 연주 좋았어.

M : Yeah, I joined my new school's rock band. I've been practicing hard with the other members.
응, 난 새 학교의 록밴드에 들었어. 다른 멤버들과 열심히 연습하는 중이야.

W : Great! I'd like to listen to your band play.
멋지다! 너희 밴드가 연주하는 것을 듣고 싶어.

M : Actually, our band will have a street performance at Union Square. Will you come and watch?
사실, 우리 밴드는 Union Square에서 거리 공연을 할 거야. 너 와서 볼래?

W : Sure, I'd love to. When exactly will it be?
물론이지. 그리고 싶어. 정확히 언제 해?

M : Next Saturday at 2 o'clock. Can you make it?
다음 주 토요일 오후 2시. 올 수 있니?

W : Oh, sorry but unfortunately not. I have to meet my group members next Saturday afternoon for the science project.
오, 미안하지만 안타깝게도 안 되겠어. 난 다음 주 토요일 오후에 과학 프로젝트 때문에 내 조원들을 만나야 해.

M : Okay. There should be another performance soon.
알겠어. 곧 다른 공연이 있을 거야.

W : I'll try to make it then!
그때 가보도록 노력할게!

Why? 왜 정답일까?

대화에서 여자는 거리 공연을 할 예정이라며 일정을 알려주는 남자에게 과학 프로젝트를 위한 모임이 겹쳐 못 가겠다고 말하므로(I have to meet my group members next Saturday afternoon for the science project.), 여자가 거리 공연을 보러 갈 수 없는 이유로 가장 적절한 것은 ⑤ '과학 프로젝트를 위해 조원들을 만나야 해서'이다.

- adjust ⓥ 적응하다, 조정하다
- I'd like to = I'd love to ~하고 싶다
- unfortunately ⓐⓓ 안타깝게도
- performance ⓝ 연주, 공연
- exactly ⓐⓓ 정확히

---

08 청소년 배드민턴 대회   정답률 85% | 정답 ④

대화를 듣고, Junior Badminton Competition에 관해 언급되지 않은 것을 고르시오.
- ① 대회 일시   ② 참가비   ③ 준비물   ✓ 우승 상품   ⑤ 신청 방법

M : Kelly, did you see this Junior Badminton Competition leaflet?
Kelly, 너 이 Junior Badminton Competition 전단지 봤어?

W : No, not yet. Let me see. 『The competition is on November 21st, at 10 a.m.』 1의근거 일치
아니, 아직. 좀 보자. 대회는 11월 21일 오전 10시에 열리네.

M : It's after the midterm exams. Why don't we sign up for the competition as a team?
중간고사 끝나고야. 우리 팀으로 대회에 신청하면 어때?

W : Sounds exciting. It would be an unforgettable event before graduating.
신난다. 졸업 전에 잊지 못할 일이 될 거야.

M : Exactly. 『The participation fee is only $8.』 2의근거 일치
바로 그거야. 참가비는 8달러밖에 안 돼.

W : That's reasonable. Oh, look at this. They provide lunch for free.
적당하네. 오, 이것 봐. 점심을 무료로 준대.

M : 『But here it says we have to bring our own rackets.』 3의근거 일치
하지만 여기 우리가 우리 라켓을 가져와야 한다고 쓰여 있네.

W : Then, we should bring ours. 『How can we apply for the competition?』 5의근거 일치
그럼, 우리 것을 가져가자. 우리가 대회에 어떻게 신청할 수 있지?

M : It says we can sign up online.』 Let's do it together now.
온라인으로 신청할 수 있다고 나와 있어. 지금 같이 하자.

W : Okay. I'm really looking forward to it.
알겠어. 난 정말 그게 기대돼.

Why? 왜 정답일까?

대화에서 남자와 여자는 Junior Badminton Competition의 대회 일시, 참가비, 준비물, 신청 방법을 언급하였다. 따라서 언급되지 않은 것은 ④ '우승 상품'이다.

Why? 왜 오답일까?

① 'The competition is on November 21st, at 10 a.m.'에서 '대회 일시'가 언급되었다.
② 'The participation fee is only $8.'에서 '참가비'가 언급되었다.
③ 'But here it says we have to bring our own rackets.'에서 '준비물'이 언급되었다.
⑤ 'It says we can sign up online.'에서 '신청 방법'이 언급되었다.

- competition ⑩ 대회
- reasonable ⓐ 적당한, 합리적인
- unforgettable ⓐ 잊지 못할
- art supply ⑩ 미술용품
- convenient ⓐ 편리한
- watercolor ⑩ 수채화 (물감)

---

09 무료 오케스트라 공연 안내　　　　정답률 86% | 정답 ④

Forest Concert에 관한 다음 내용을 듣고, 일치하지 않는 것을 고르시오.
① 10월 7일에 열린다.　　　　② 주제는 '꿈을 찾아서'이다.
③ 무료로 입장할 수 있다.　　④ 사전 예약이 필요하다.
⑤ 집에서 TV로 시청할 수 있다.

W : Hello, listeners!
안녕하세요, 청취자 여러분!
We have some good news for music lovers.
음악 애호가 분들께 좋은 소식이 있습니다.
「The Grand Philharmonic will hold the Forest Concert in Central Park on October 7th.」 ③의 근거 일치
Grand Philharmonic에서 10월 7일 Central Park에서 Forest Concert를 개최합니다.
「The legendary Russian conductor, Alexander Ivanov, will lead the orchestra with the theme of 'In Search of a Dream.'」 ②의 근거 일치
전설적인 러시아 지휘자인 Alexander Ivanov가 '꿈을 찾아서'라는 주제로 오케스트라를 지휘할 것입니다.
This concert is a gift from the Grand Philharmonic to all music lovers 「so everyone can enjoy free admission to this 90-minute musical treat.」 ③의 근거 일치
이 콘서트는 Grand Philharmonic에서 모든 음악 애호가들에게 드리는 선물로, 모든 분들께서는 90분간의 이 음악회에 무료로 입장할 수 있습니다.
Seats are on a first come first serve basis, 「so prior reservation is not required.」
좌석은 선착순이기 때문에 사전 예약은 필요하지 않습니다. ④의 근거 불일치
「You can also watch it live on TV at home,」 but seeing it live at the park could be a once in a lifetime experience. ⑤의 근거 일치
여러분은 집에서 TV로 그것을 생중계로 볼 수도 있지만, 공원에서 라이브로 보는 것은 일생에 한 번뿐인 경험이 될 것입니다.

Why? 왜 정답일까?

'Seats are on a first come first serve basis, so prior reservation is not required.'에서 좌석은 선착순으로 제공되기 때문에 사전 예약은 필요하지 않다고 언급하므로, 내용과 일치하지 않는 것은 ④ '사전 예약이 필요하다.'이다.

Why? 왜 오답일까?

① 'The Grand Philharmonic will hold the Forest Concert in Central Park on October 7th.'의 내용과 일치한다.
② '~ the orchestra with the theme of 'In Search of a Dream.'의 내용과 일치한다.
③ '~ so everyone can enjoy free admission to this 90-minute musical treat.'의 내용과 일치한다.
⑤ 'You can also watch it live on TV at home, ~'의 내용과 일치한다.

- first come first serve(d) 선착순의
- prior reservation 사전 예약

---

10 미술용품 세트 고르기　　　　정답률 87% | 정답 ②

다음 표를 보면서 대화를 듣고, 여자가 선택할 미술용품 세트를 고르시오.

Art Supplies Set for Children

	Model	Price	Coloring Tool	Number of Colors	Sketchbook
①	A	$12	Crayons	24	×
②	B	$16	Crayons	32	○
③	C	$17	Watercolors	28	○
④	D	$18	Markers	32	×
⑤	E	$22	Markers	36	○

M : Hey, Cathy! What are you looking at?
안녕, Cathy! 뭘 보고 있는 거야?
W : Hi, Steve. I was searching for an art supplies set. I'm thinking about sending it as a Christmas gift to children in need.
안녕, Steve. 난 미술용품 세트를 찾고 있었어. 어려운 처지의 아이들에게 그것을 크리스마스 선물로 보내려고 생각 중이야.
M : You're so kind. Do you need help choosing one?
넌 참 친절하구나. 하나 고르는 걸 도와줄까?
W : Yeah, thank you. 「I want it to be under $20.」 근거1 Price 조건
응, 고마워. 난 그게 20달러 미만이길 원해.
M : All right. Let me see. 「Which type of coloring tool would be good for them?」
알겠어. 어디 보자. 어느 색칠 도구가 아이들에게 좋을까?
W : Hmm... I think watercolors are not very convenient. The kids would need extra things like brushes.
흠... 난 수채화 물감은 그다지 편리한 것 같지 않아. 아이들한테 붓과 같은 추가 도구가 필요할 거야.
M : I agree. The other tools would be better. 근거2 Coloring Tool 조건
동의해. 다른 도구가 나을 것 같아.
W : Right. 「How about the number of colors?」
맞아. 색상 수는 어때?
M : They'll need more than thirty colors to express what they want. 근거3 Number of Colors 조건
그들이 원하는 걸 표현하려면 30가지 이상의 색깔이 필요할 거야.
W : You're right. Then, there are two choices left.
맞아. 그럼, 두 가지 선택권이 남네.
M : Yeah. 「Oh, there is a model which includes a sketchbook.」 근거4 Sketchbook 조건
응, 오. 스케치북을 포함하는 제품이 있네.
W : Perfect! They might need it in their art classes. I'll choose that one.
완벽해! 그들의 미술 수업에 그것이 필요할지도 몰라. 난 그걸 고르겠어.

Why? 왜 정답일까?

대화에 따르면 여자는 가격이 20달러 미만이면서, 수채화 물감이 아닌 다른 색칠 도구를 포함하고 있고, 색상이 30가지가 넘으면서, 스케치북이 포함된 미술용품 세트를 구매하려고 한다. 따라서 여자가 선택할 미술용품 세트는 ② 'B'이다.

---

11 동아리 만들기　　　　정답률 93% | 정답 ④

대화를 듣고, 여자의 마지막 말에 대한 남자의 응답으로 가장 적절한 것을 고르시오.
① You should be honest about your ideas. - 넌 네 생각에 솔직해야 해.
② I can help to choose the right class for you. - 난 네게 맞는 수업을 고르는 것을 도와줄 수 있어.
③ I already took the career counseling program. - 난 진로 상담 프로그램을 이미 들었어.
④ I'm thinking of making an English debate club. - 영어 토론 동아리를 만들까 생각 중이야.
⑤ You'll get all the academic advice as you need. - 넌 네가 필요한 모든 학업 조언을 얻게 될 거야.

W : Hey, James, did you choose which club you're going to join?
이봐, James, 네가 가입할 동아리 골랐니?
M : Not yet. To be honest, I'd like to create a new academic club.
아직. 솔직히 말하면, 난 새로운 학술 동아리를 만들고 싶어.
W : Great idea! What kind of club do you want to make?
좋은 생각이다! 어떤 종류의 동아리를 만들고 싶어?
M : I'm thinking of making an English debate club.
영어 토론 동아리를 만들까 생각 중이야.

Why? 왜 정답일까?

대화에서 남자가 새로운 학술 동아리를 만들고 싶다고 이야기하자, 여자는 어떤 종류의 동아리를 만들고 싶은지 묻고 있으므로(What kind of club do you want to make?), 남자의 응답으로 가장 적절한 것은 ④ '영어 토론 동아리를 만들까 생각 중이야.'이다.

---

12 우산 사기　　　　정답률 91% | 정답 ③

대화를 듣고, 남자의 마지막 말에 대한 여자의 응답으로 가장 적절한 것을 고르시오.
① The building is too far from here. - 그 빌딩은 여기서 너무 멀어.
② We don't need to bring umbrellas. - 우린 우산을 가져갈 필요가 없어.
③ We can buy one on the first floor. - 우린 1층에서 하나 살 수 있어.
④ I don't know where your umbrella is. - 난 네 우산이 어디 있는지 모르겠어.
⑤ You'd better check the weather forecast. - 넌 일기 예보를 확인해 봐야 해.

M : Mom, look! It's raining outside. But we don't have umbrellas.
엄마, 보세요! 밖에 비가 와요. 그런데 우린 우산이 없어요.
W : I think we need to buy one in this building.
내 생각엔 우린 이 건물에서 우산 하나를 사야 할 것 같아.
M : Okay. Where can we buy one?
알겠어요. 어디서 살 수 있죠?
W : We can buy one on the first floor.
우린 1층에서 하나 살 수 있어.

Why? 왜 정답일까?

밖에 비가 오고 있어 여자가 우산을 하나 건물 안에서 사야할 것 같다고 말하자 남자는 어디서 우산을 살 수 있는지 묻고 있다(Where can we buy one?). 따라서 여자의 응답으로 가장 적절한 것은 ③ '우린 1층에서 하나 살 수 있어.'이다.

- weather forecast ⑩ 일기 예보

---

13 자원봉사 권유하기　　　　정답률 86% | 정답 ①

대화를 듣고, 여자의 마지막 말에 대한 남자의 응답으로 가장 적절한 것을 고르시오. [3점]
Man : _____

① Come on. You'll do fine if you volunteer with a kind heart.
괜찮아. 친절한 마음으로 봉사한다면 잘할 거야.
② Okay, will you search for volunteer opportunities for me?
알겠어, 날 위해 자원봉사 기회를 찾아줄래?
③ Sure. Let's check the list of art schools you could attend.
물론이지, 네가 다닐 만한 미술 학교들 목록을 검토해 보자.
④ Yeah, you'd better plan your trip to Africa in advance.
응, 넌 아프리카 여행을 미리 계획해야 해.
⑤ You're right. We should have watched that movie.
네 말이 맞아. 우린 그 영화를 봤어야 했어.

W : That was a great documentary film, wasn't it, David?
그것은 훌륭한 다큐멘터리 영화였어, 그렇지 않니, David?
M : Yeah, I was really impressed by the Korean man, devoting his life to helping the poorest people of Africa.
응, 난 아프리카의 가장 가난한 사람들을 돕느라 자기 인생을 헌신한 그 한국인 남자에게 무척 감명 받았어.
W : Right, his life was so beautiful. Living one's life for others is truly meaningful.
맞아, 그의 인생은 참 아름다웠어. 다른 사람들을 위해 사는 삶은 정말 의미가 있어.
M : I think so, too. Evelyn, would you like to volunteer with me?
나도 그렇게 생각해, Evelyn. 나와 함께 자원봉사 할래?
W : Great! What kind of volunteer work are you thinking about?
멋지다! 어떤 종류의 자원봉사 활동을 생각하고 있어?
M : Actually, I've been working at the children's hospital as a volunteer teacher.
사실, 난 아동 병원에서 자원봉사 선생님으로 일하고 있어.
W : Volunteer teacher?
자원봉사 선생님이라고?
M : Yeah, I teach children how to paint. The hospital is now looking for more teachers.
응, 난 아이들에게 그림 그리는 법을 가르쳐. 병원에서 지금 선생님들을 더 찾고 있어.
W : I'd like to, but can I be helpful?
하고 싶은데, 내가 도움이 될 수 있을까?
M : Sure, your major is art, so you might be a good fit.
물론이지, 네 전공이 미술이니까 잘 맞을 거야.
W : I've never taught anyone before, so I'm worried whether I can teach them well.
난 전에 아무도 가르쳐본 적이 없어서, 내가 그 애들을 잘 가르칠 수 있을지 걱정이야.
M : Come on. You'll do fine if you volunteer with a kind heart.
괜찮아. 친절한 마음으로 봉사한다면 잘할 거야.

So Ted wants to advise Linda to try using a calendar app to remind her of important things.
그래서 Ted는 Linda에게 중요한 것들을 상기시켜 줄 달력 앱을 써보라고 조언하고 싶다.
In this situation, what would Ted most likely say to Linda?
이 상황에서, Ted는 Linda에게 뭐라고 말하겠는가?
Ted : Why don't you use a calendar app as a reminder?
(무엇을 해야 하는지) 상기시켜주는 달력 앱을 써 보는 게 어때?

Why? 왜 정답일까?

상황에 따르면 Linda는 항상 해야 할 일이나 약속을 깜박 잊는 버릇이 있어 이를 고치기 위해 Ted에게 조언을 구하고, Ted는 달력 앱을 써볼 것을 권하고 싶어 한다(So Ted wants to advise Linda to try using a calendar app to remind her of important things.). 따라서 Ted가 Linda에게 할 말로 가장 적절한 것은 ① '(무엇을 해야 하는지) 상기시켜주는 달력 앱을 써 보는 게 어때?'이다.

- **appointment** ⓝ 약속, 예약
- **submit** ⓥ 제출하다
- **overcome** ⓥ 극복하다
- **reliable** ⓐ 믿을 만한
- **disappointed** ⓐ 실망한

16-17 각 여행지에서 사 오기 좋은 기념품

M : Welcome to 'Smart Traveler.'
Smart Traveler에 오신 것을 환영합니다.
I'm your host, Brian Lewis.
저는 여러분의 진행자 Brian Lewis입니다.
While traveling, shopping for souvenirs is one of the greatest pleasures, and many people enjoy bringing small souvenirs back home.
여행을 하는 동안, 기념품을 사는 가장 큰 즐거움 중 하나이고, 많은 사람들은 작은 기념품을 가지고 집으로 돌아가기를 즐깁니다.
『Today I'll introduce some of the best souvenirs from around the world!』 **16번의 근거**
오늘 저는 세계 각지에 있는 최고의 기념품을 몇 가지 소개하려고 합니다!
『First, when you travel to Beijing, jasmine tea is a great souvenir.』 **17번 ①의 근거** 일치
먼저, 베이징으로 여행을 간다면, 자스민 차는 훌륭한 기념품입니다.
Scented tea in the morning will become a wonderful reminder of all those memories there.
아침의 향기로운 차는 그곳에서의 모든 기억을 멋지게 상기시켜주는 것이 될 것입니다.
『Second, in Paris, Eiffel Tower keychains are popular.』 **17번 ②의 근거** 일치
두 번째로, 파리에서는 에펠탑 열쇠고리가 인기 있습니다.
With this little metal item hanging on your keys, you can remember the special moment of being at the top of the Eiffel Tower.
이 작은 금속 물건을 열쇠에 달아놓으면, 여러분은 에펠탑 꼭대기에 있었던 특별한 순간을 기억할 수 있을 것입니다.
『Third, when visiting Hawaii, bring back a Hawaiian dancing doll.』 **17번 ④의 근거** 일치
세 번째로, 하와이를 방문할 때, 춤추는 하와이 인형을 가지고 돌아오세요.
It'll remind you of the intense sun, crystal clear water, and amazing beaches.
그것은 당신에게 강렬한 태양과 수정처럼 맑은 물과 놀랍도록 멋진 해변을 떠올리게 해줄 것입니다.
『Last, in Venice, you can buy a traditional Venetian mask.』 **17번 ⑤의 근거** 일치
마지막으로, 베니스에서는 전통 베네치아 가면을 살 수 있습니다.
Hanging the mask on the wall as a decoration, you can feel the spirit of Venice at home long afterwards.
벽에 장식으로 가면을 걸어두면, 여러분은 아주 오랜 뒤에도 집에서 베니스의 기운을 느낄 수 있을 것입니다.
I hope these tips will help you in your souvenir shopping.
이 조언들이 여러분의 기념품 쇼핑에 도움이 되길 바랍니다.

- **souvenir** ⓝ 기념품
- **keychain** ⓝ 열쇠고리
- **crystal clear** 수정처럼 맑은
- **keep in mind** ~을 유념하다
- **reminder** ⓝ (잊고 있던 것을) 상기시켜주는 것
- **intense** ⓐ 강렬한, 강한
- **safety rule** 안전 수칙

---

16 주제 파악 정답률 79% | 정답 ①

남자가 하는 말의 주제로 가장 적절한 것은?

☑ ① the best souvenirs to bring home from travel – 여행에서 집으로 사 오기 좋은 기념품들
② popular places in the world to photograph nature – 자연 사진을 찍기에 좋은 세계 명소들
③ tips on how to save money on souvenir shopping – 기념품 쇼핑에서 돈을 절약하는 방법에 관한 조언
④ the variety of cultural environments around the world – 세계 문화적 환경의 다양성
⑤ the most important travel safety rules to keep in mind – 유념해야 할 가장 중요한 여행 안전 수칙

Why? 왜 정답일까?

'Today I'll introduce some of the best souvenirs from around the world!'에서 남자는 여행에서 사 오기 좋은 기념품들을 몇 가지 소개하겠다고 하므로, 남자가 하는 말의 주제로 가장 적절한 것은 ① '여행에서 집으로 사 오기 가장 좋은 기념품들'이다.

---

17 언급 유무 파악 정답률 92% | 정답 ③

언급된 지역이 아닌 것은?

① Beijing – 베이징
② Paris – 파리
☑ ③ Sydney – 시드니
④ Hawaii – 하와이
⑤ Venice – 베니스

Why? 왜 정답일까?

담화에서 남자는 세계 각지의 기념품을 소개하기 위해 베이징, 파리, 하와이, 베니스를 언급하였다. 따라서 언급되지 않은 것은 ③ '시드니'이다.

Why? 왜 오답일까?

① 'First, when you travel to Beijing, jasmine tea is a great souvenir.'에서 '베이징'이 언급되었다.
② 'Second, in Paris, Eiffel Tower keychains are popular.'에서 '파리'가 언급되었다.
④ 'Third, when visiting Hawaii, bring back a Hawaiian dancing doll.'에서 '하와이'가 언급되었다.
⑤ 'Last, in Venice, you can buy a traditional Venetian mask.'에서 '베니스'가 언급되었다.

아동 병원에서 자원봉사 선생님으로 일하고 있는 남자는 병원에서 선생님을 더 모집하고 있다면서 여자에게 함께 봉사할 것을 권하는데, 여자는 이전에 다른 사람을 가르쳐본 경험이 없어 잘할 수 있을지 모르겠다(I've never taught anyone before, so I'm worried whether I can teach them well.)며 걱정하고 있다. 따라서 남자의 응답으로 가장 적절한 것은 ① '괜찮아. 친절한 마음으로 봉사한다면 잘할 거야.'이다.

- **devote A to B** A에 B를 헌신하다
- **search for** ~을 찾다, 검색하다
- **major** ⓝ (대학생의) 전공

---

14 주별 예산 설정하기 정답률 91% | 정답 ①

대화를 듣고, 남자의 마지막 말에 대한 여자의 응답으로 가장 적절한 것을 고르시오. [3점]

Woman :
☑ ① Great. I should try to keep a weekly budget.
좋아. 주별 예산 범위를 지키기 위해 노력해야겠어.
② Good luck. I hope you can find a part-time job.
행운을 빌어. 네가 아르바이트를 찾을 수 있길 바라.
③ Come on. You can coach me on my eating habits.
어서. 넌 내 식사 습관을 지도해줄 수 있어.
④ No way. You can't spend so much money shopping.
절대 안 돼. 넌 쇼핑에 그렇게 많은 돈을 쓰면 안 돼.
⑤ I know. I need to spend more time with my friends.
나도 알아. 난 내 친구들과 더 많은 시간을 보낼 필요가 있어.

M : Bonnie, what are you doing?
Bonnie, 뭐 하고 있어?
W : I'm checking my bank account. I'm running out of money again.
내 은행 계좌를 확인하고 있어. 난 또 돈이 다 떨어져 가고 있어.
M : Haven't you gotten paid for your part-time job yet?
아르바이트에서 아직 돈 안 받은 거야?
W : I have, but I already spent most of the money hanging out with my friends. At the end of month, I'll be broke.
받았는데, 친구들하고 노느라 벌써 돈을 거의 다 써 버렸어. 월말이면 난 빈털터리일 거야.
M : Then, how about setting a weekly budget?
그럼, 주별 예산을 정하는 게 어때?
W : A weekly budget? What do you mean by that?
주별 예산이라고? 그게 무슨 말이야?
M : I usually set a budget for each week, and don't spend more than it allows. So I've cut down on everyday spending on chips and soda.
난 보통 매주 예산을 정하고, 허용되는 것 이상으로 쓰지 않아. 그래서 과자와 탄산음료에 매일 쓰던 돈을 줄였어.
W : Good for you. Can I save money if I make it a habit, too?
잘됐구나. 나도 습관을 들이면 돈을 아낄 수 있을까?
M : Of course, you can. If you consider your budget, you'll think twice before you spend money.
물론이지. 네가 예산을 고려하면, 돈을 쓰기 전에 두 번 생각하게 될 거야.
W : That makes sense. Keeping a weekly budget seems advantageous.
일리가 있다. 주별 예산 안에서 쓰는 게 이로운 것 같아 보이네.
M : Now that I keep a weekly budget, I spend money only where I need it. I bet it'll work for you, too.
주별 예산 범위를 유지하니까, 난 필요한 곳에만 돈을 쓰게 돼. 너한테도 이게 효과가 있을 거라고 장담해.
W : Great. I should try to keep a weekly budget.
좋아. 주별 예산 범위를 지키기 위해 노력해야겠어.

Why? 왜 정답일까?

남자는 주별 예산을 설정하면 돈을 아낄 수 있다며 여자에게 같이 해볼 것을 권하고 있다(Now that I keep a weekly budget, I spend money only where I need it, I bet it'll work for you, too.). 따라서 여자의 응답으로 가장 적절한 것은 ① '좋아. 주별 예산 범위를 지키기 위해 노력해야겠어.'이다.

- **account** ⓝ 계좌, 계정
- **hang out with** ~와 시간을 보내다
- **cut down on** ~을 줄이다
- **advantageous** ⓐ 유리한, 유익한
- **run out of** ~을 바닥내다 [다 써버리다]
- **broke** ⓐ 빈털터리의, 무일푼의
- **keep a budget** 예산 내에서 쓰다
- **now that** ~이기 때문에

---

15 건망증 극복하기 정답률 73% | 정답 ①

다음 상황 설명을 듣고, Ted가 Linda에게 할 말로 가장 적절한 것을 고르시오.

Ted :
☑ ① Why don't you use a calendar app as a reminder?
(무엇을 해야 하는지) 상기시켜주는 달력 앱을 써 보는 게 어때?
② I recommend you ask your friends for some help.
네 친구들한테 도움을 좀 구해보기를 추천해.
③ Do you prefer a wall calendar or a desk calendar?
벽에 거는 달력이 좋니, 탁상 달력이 좋니?
④ I wonder why you didn't submit your paper on time.
난 왜 네가 보고서를 제 시간에 내지 못했는지 궁금해.
⑤ Could you tell me how you overcame your bad habit?
네 나쁜 습관을 어떻게 극복했는지 말해줄 수 있어?

M : Ted and Linda are classmates.
Ted와 Linda는 반 친구이다.
Linda has some trouble with her friends because she often forgets her appointments with them.
Linda는 친구들과 문제가 좀 있는데 종종 그들과의 약속을 잊기 때문이다.
In contrast, Ted is always on time and the other classmates think he's very responsible and reliable.
대조적으로, Ted는 항상 시간을 지키고 다른 급우들은 그가 아주 책임감 있고 믿을 만하다고 생각한다.
Today, Linda even forgets to submit an important paper.
오늘 Linda는 심지어 중요한 보고서를 제출하는 것마저 잊었다.
She knows what she has to do, but it's not easy for her to remember everything.
그녀는 무엇을 해야 하는지 알지만, 모든 것을 기억하기가 그녀로서는 쉽지 않다.
Disappointed in herself, she asks Ted for some help on how she can overcome her habit of forgetting.
스스로에게 실망한 Linda는 잊어버리는 버릇을 극복할 수 있는 방법에 관해 Ted에게 도움을 요청한다.
He thinks using a calendar app could help break her bad habit.
그는 달력 앱을 쓰는 것이 그녀가 나쁜 습관을 고치는 데 도움이 될 거라고 생각한다.

다음 글의 목적으로 가장 적절한 것은?

① 선수들의 학력 향상 프로그램을 홍보하려고
② 대학 진학 상담의 활성화 방안을 제안하려고
③ 선수들의 훈련 장비 추가 구입을 건의하려고
✓ 선수들의 대회 참가를 위한 결석 허락을 요청하려고
⑤ 대회 개최를 위한 운동장 대여 가능 여부를 문의하려고

To the Principal of Alamda High School,
Alamda 고등학교 교장 선생님께,
On behalf of the Youth Soccer Tournament Series, / I would like to remind you / of the 2019 Series next week.
청소년 축구 토너먼트 시리즈를 대표하여 / 저는 귀하에게 상기시켜 드리고 싶습니다. / 다음 주 2019 시리즈에 대해
Surely, we understand the importance of a player's education.
물론 저희는 선수 교육의 중요성을 알고 있습니다.
Regrettably, however, / the Series will result in / players missing two days of school / for the competition.
하지만, 유감스럽게도 / 시리즈는 야기할 것입니다. / 선수들이 이틀 동안 학교를 빠지는 일을 / 대회 때문에
The games will be attended / by many college coaches / scouting prospective student athletes.
이 경기들에 참석할 것입니다. / 많은 대학 코치들이 / 유망한 학생 선수들을 스카우트하는
Therefore, the Series can be a great opportunity / for young soccer players / to demonstrate their capabilities as athletes.
그러므로 이 시리즈는 엄청난 기회가 될 수 있습니다. / 어린 축구 선수들이 / 운동선수로서 자신의 역량을 보여줄 수 있는
I would like to request your permission / for the absence of the players from your school / during this event.
저는 귀하의 허락을 요청하고자 합니다. / 귀교 선수들의 학교 결석에 대한 / 이 대회 동안
Thank you for your understanding.
이해해 주셔서 감사합니다.
Best regards,
Jack D'Adamo, Director of the Youth Soccer Tournament Series
청소년 축구 토너먼트 시리즈 대표 Jack D'Adamo 드림

Alamda 고등학교 교장 선생님께,

청소년 축구 토너먼트 시리즈를 대표하여 귀하에게 다음 주 2019 시리즈에 대해 상기시켜 드리고 싶습니다. 물론 저희는 선수 교육의 중요성을 알고 있습니다. 하지만, 유감스럽게도 시리즈는 선수들이 대회 때문에 이틀 동안 학교를 빠지는 일을 야기할 것입니다. 이 경기들에 유망한 학생 선수들을 스카우트하는 많은 대학 코치들이 참석할 것입니다. 그러므로 이 시리즈는 어린 축구 선수들이 운동선수로서 자신의 역량을 보여줄 수 있는 엄청난 기회가 될 수 있습니다. 이 대회 동안 귀교 선수들의 학교 결석에 대한 귀하의 허락을 요청하고자 합니다. 이해해 주셔서 감사합니다.

청소년 축구 토너먼트 시리즈 대표 Jack D'Adamo 드림

Why? 왜 정답일까?

마지막 부분에서 대회 동안 선수들이 학교를 결석하는 것에 대한 허락을 구한다(I would like to request your permission for the absence of the players from your school during this event.)는 내용이 나오므로, 글의 목적으로 가장 적절한 것은 ④ '선수들의 대회 참가를 위한 결석 허락을 요청하려고'이다.

- on behalf of ~을 대표하여, 대신하여
- importance ⓝ 중요성
- prospective ⓐ 유망한
- capability ⓝ 역량, 능력
- remind A of B ⓥ A에게 B를 상기시키다
- result in ⓥ ~을 야기하다
- demonstrate ⓥ 보여주다, 입증하다
- absence ⓝ 결석

구문 풀이

4행 Regrettably, however, the Series will result in players missing two days of
~을 야기하다 의미상 주어 동명사
school for the competition.

다음 글에 드러난 'I'의 심경 변화로 가장 적절한 것은?

① indifferent → satisfied
　무관심한　　만족한
② relaxed → envious
　여유로운　　부러워하는
③ frustrated → relieved
　좌절한　　안도한
④ excited → bored
　신난　　지루한
✓ pleased → terrified
　유쾌한　　공포에 질린

One night, my family was having a party / with a couple from another city / who had two daughters.
어느 날 밤 우리 가족은 파티를 하고 있었다. / 다른 도시에서 온 부부와 / 두 딸이 있는
The girls were just a few years older than I, / and I played lots of fun games together with them.
그 소녀들은 나보다 단지 몇 살 많았고, / 나는 그들과 함께 많은 재미있는 게임을 했다.
The father of the family had an amusing, jolly, witty character, / and I had a memorable night / full of laughter and joy.
그 가족의 아버지는 재미있고 쾌활한 재치 있는 성격이셨고, / 나는 잊지 못할 밤을 보냈다. / 웃음과 기쁨으로 가득한
While we laughed, joked, and had our dinner, / the TV suddenly broadcast an air attack, / and a screeching siren started to scream, / announcing the "red" situation.
우리가 웃고 농담하며 저녁을 먹는 동안, / TV에서 갑자기 공습을 알렸고, / 날카로운 사이렌이 울리기 시작했다. / '긴급' 상황을 알리며
We all stopped dinner, / and we squeezed into the basement.
우리는 모두 저녁 식사를 멈추고 / 지하실로 비집고 들어갔다.
The siren kept screaming / and the roar of planes was heard in the sky.
사이렌은 계속 울렸고 / 비행기의 굉음이 하늘에서 들렸다.

The terror of war was overwhelming.
전쟁의 공포는 압도적이었다.
Shivering with fear, / I murmured a panicked prayer / that this desperate situation would end quickly.
두려움에 떨며, / 나는 겁에 질린 기도를 중얼거렸다. / 이 절망적인 상황이 빨리 끝나게 해달라는

어느 날 밤 우리 가족은 다른 도시에서 온 두 딸이 있는 부부와 파티를 하고 있었다. 그 소녀들은 나보다 단지 몇 살 많았고, 나는 그들과 함께 많은 재미있는 게임을 했다. 그 가족의 아버지는 재미있고 쾌활하며 재치 있는 성격이셨고, 나는 웃음과 기쁨으로 가득한 잊지 못할 밤을 보냈다. 우리가 웃고 농담하며 저녁을 먹는 동안, TV에서 갑자기 공습을 알렸고, 날카로운 사이렌이 '긴급' 상황을 알리며 울리기 시작했다. 우리는 모두 저녁 식사를 멈추고 지하실로 비집고 들어갔다. 사이렌은 계속 울렸고 비행기의 굉음이 하늘에서 들렸다. 전쟁의 공포는 압도적이었다. 두려움에 떨며, 나는 이 절망적인 상황이 빨리 끝나게 해달라는 겁에 질린 기도를 중얼거렸다.

Why? 왜 정답일까?

'~ the TV suddenly broadcast an air attack, ~' 앞뒤로 글의 흐름이 반전된다. 앞에서는 필자가 다른 가족과의 파티를 즐기며 웃음과 기쁨으로 가득한 밤을 보내고 있었다는(~ I had a memorable night full of laughter and joy.)는 내용이 주를 이루는 반면, 뒤에서는 사이렌이 울리고 전쟁의 공포가 상황을 압도하는 가운데 필자 일행이 두려움에 떨었다(The terror of war was overwhelming. Shivering with fear, I murmured a panicked prayer that this desperate situation would end quickly.)는 내용이 주로 묘사되고 있다. 따라서 'I'의 심경 변화로 가장 적절한 것은 ⑤ '유쾌한 → 공포에 질린'이다.

- amusing ⓐ 재미있는
- witty ⓐ 재치 있는
- squeeze into ~로 비집고 들어가다
- overwhelming ⓐ 압도적인
- murmur ⓥ 중얼거리다
- indifferent ⓐ 무관심한
- terrified ⓐ 공포에 질린
- jolly ⓐ 쾌활한
- screeching ⓐ 날카로운 소리를 내는
- roar ⓝ 굉음, 함성
- shiver ⓥ 떨다
- desperate ⓐ 절망적인
- frustrated ⓐ 좌절한

구문 풀이

10행 Shivering with fear, I murmured a panicked prayer [that this desperate
분사구문(~하면서)　　　　　　　　　　　동격 접속사(= a panicked prayer)
situation would end quickly].

다음 글에서 필자가 주장하는 바로 가장 적절한 것은?

① 갈등을 해결하려면 상대방의 감정을 파악해야 한다.
✓ 정보에 대해 판단하고 반응하기 전에 맥락을 확인해야 한다.
③ 위험한 상황에 처할 때일수록 타인의 의견을 경청해야 한다.
④ 많은 정보보다 정확한 정보 제공을 통해 신뢰성을 높여야 한다.
⑤ 신속한 의사결정을 위해 핵심 정보와 주변 정보를 구별해야 한다.

If you were at a social gathering in a large building / and you overheard someone say / that "the roof is on fire," / what would be your reaction?
당신이 큰 건물 안의 사교 모임에서 / 누군가가 말하는 것을 우연히 듣게 된다면, / '지붕이 불타고 있어'라고 / 여러분의 반응은 무엇일까?
Until you knew more information, / your first inclination might be / toward safety and survival.
더 많은 정보를 알 때까지, / 당신의 맨 처음 마음은 / 안전과 생존을 향할 것이다.
But if you were to find out / that this particular person was talking about a song / called "The Roof Is on Fire," / your feelings of threat and danger / would be diminished.
그러나 만일 당신이 알게 된다면, / 이 특정한 사람이 노래에 관해 이야기하고 있다는 것을 / '지붕이 불타고 있어'라고 불리는 / 걱정과 위험을 느끼는 마음은 / 줄어들 것이다.
So / once the additional facts are understood / — that the person was referring to a song and not a real fire — / the context is better understood / and you are in a better position / to judge and react.
그러므로 / 추가적인 사실이 일단 이해된다면 / 그 사람이 진짜 화재가 아니라 노래를 언급하고 있다는 / 맥락은 더 잘 이해되고 / 당신은 더 나은 위치에 있게 된다 / 판단하고 반응을 할
All too often / people react far too quickly and emotionally / over information / without establishing context.
너무도 자주 / 사람들은 지나치게 성급하고 감정적으로 반응한다. / 정보에 대해 / 맥락을 설정하지 않은 채
It is so important / for us to identify context / related to information / because if we fail to do so, / we may judge and react too quickly.
매우 중요한데, / 우리가 맥락을 확인하는 것이 / 정보와 관련된 / 만약 그렇게 하지 않는다면 / 우리는 너무 성급하게 판단하고 반응할 수 있기 때문이다.

당신이 큰 건물 안에서 사교 모임을 하는데 누군가가 '지붕이 불타고 있어'라고 말하는 것을 우연히 듣게 된다면, 당신의 반응은 무엇일까? 더 많은 정보를 알 때까지, 당신의 맨 처음 마음은 안전과 생존을 향할 것이다. 그러나 만일 이 특정한 사람이 '지붕이 불타고 있어'라는 노래에 관해 이야기하고 있다는 것을 알게 된다면, 당신이 걱정과 위험을 느끼는 마음은 줄어들 것이다. 그러므로 그 사람이 진짜 화재가 아니라 노래를 언급하고 있었다는 추가적인 사실이 일단 이해된다면 맥락은 더 잘 이해되고 당신은 판단하고 반응을 할 더 나은 위치에 있게 된다. 사람들은 너무도 자주 맥락을 설정하지 않은 채 지나치게 성급하고 감정적으로 정보에 반응한다. 우리가 정보와 관련된 맥락을 확인하는 것이 매우 중요한데, 만약 그렇게 하지 않는다면 우리는 너무 성급하게 판단하고 반응할 수 있기 때문이다.

Why? 왜 정답일까?

마지막 문장인 'It is so important for us to identify context related to information because if we fail to do so, we may judge and react too quickly.'에서 성급한 판단과 반응을 막을 수 있도록 먼저 맥락을 파악할 필요가 있다는 내용을 제시하므로, 필자가 주장하는 바로 가장 적절한 것은 ② '정보에 대해 판단하고 반응하기 전에 맥락을 확인해야 한다.'이다.

- social gathering 사교 모임
- inclination ⓝ ~하려는 뜻, 경향, 의향
- refer to ~을 언급하다
- establish ⓥ 설정하다, 확고히 하다
- overhear ⓥ 우연히 듣다, 엿듣다
- diminish ⓥ 줄이다, 감소하다
- emotionally ⓐⓓ 감정적으로
- identify ⓥ 확인하다, 알아보다

구문 풀이

11행 It is so important for us to identify context [related to information] /
가주어　의미상 주어　　진주어
because (if we fail to do so), we may judge and react too quickly.
이유 접속사　( ): 조건절　주어　　동사구

---

21 타인의 선택에 영향을 미치는 요인
정답률 58% | 정답 ⑤

밑줄 친 "learn and live"가 다음 글에서 의미하는 바로 가장 적절한 것은? [3점]

① occupy a rival's territory for safety
　안전을 위해 경쟁자의 영토를 차지한다
② discover who the enemy is and attack first
　누가 적인지 판단하고 먼저 공격한다
③ share survival skills with the next generation
　다음 세대와 생존 기술을 공유한다
④ support the leader's decisions for the best results
　최선의 결과를 위해 리더의 결정을 지지한다
☑ follow another's action only when it is proven safe
　다른 개체의 행동이 안전하다고 입증될 때에만 그 행동을 따른다

There is a critical factor that determines / whether your choice will influence that of others: / the visible consequences of the choice.
결정하는 중요한 한 가지 요인이 있는데, / 여러분의 선택이 다른 사람들의 선택에 영향을 미칠지를 / 바로 그 선택의 가시적 결과들이다.
Take the case of the Adélie penguins.
Adélie 펭귄들의 사례를 들어보자.
They are often found strolling in large groups / toward the edge of the water / in search of food.
그들이 큰 무리를 지어 다니는 것이 종종 발견된다. / 물가를 향해 / 먹이를 찾아
Yet danger awaits in the icy-cold water.
하지만 얼음같이 차가운 물속에 위험이 기다리고 있다.
There is the leopard seal, for one, / which likes to have penguins for a meal.
한 예로, 표범물개가 있다. / 식사로 펭귄들을 먹는 것을 좋아하는
What is an Adélie to do?
Adélie 펭귄은 무엇을 할까?
The penguins' solution / is to play the waiting game.
펭귄의 해결책은 / 대기 전술을 펼치는 것이다.
They wait and wait and wait by the edge of the water / until one of them gives up and jumps in.
그들은 물가에서 기다리고 기다리고 또 기다린다. / 자기들 중 한 마리가 포기하고 뛰어들 때까지
The moment that occurs, / the rest of the penguins watch with anticipation / to see what happens next.
그것이 일어나는 순간, / 나머지 펭귄들은 기대감을 갖고 지켜본다. / 다음에 무슨 일이 일어날지를 보기 위해
If the pioneer survives, / everyone else will follow suit.
만약 그 선두 주자가 살아남으면, / 다른 모두가 방금 그 펭귄이 한 대로 따를 것이다.
If it perishes, / they'll turn away.
만약 그 펭귄이 죽는다면, / 그들은 돌아설 것이다.
One penguin's destiny / alters the fate of all the others.
한 펭귄의 운명이 / 모든 나머지 펭귄들의 운명을 바꾼다.
Their strategy, / you could say, / is "learn and live."
그들의 전략은 / 당신은 말할 수 있을 것이다. / '배워서 사는 것이다'라고

여러분의 선택이 다른 사람들의 선택에 영향을 미칠지를 결정하는 중요한 한 가지 요인이 있는데, 바로 그 선택의 가시적 결과들이다. Adélie 펭귄들의 사례를 들어보자. 그들이 먹이를 찾아 물가를 향해 큰 무리를 지어 다니는 것이 종종 발견된다. 하지만 얼음같이 차가운 물속에 위험이 기다리고 있다. 한 예로, 식사로 펭귄들을 먹는 것을 좋아하는 표범물개가 있다. Adélie 펭귄은 무엇을 할까? 펭귄의 해결책은 대기 전술을 펼치는 것이다. 그들은 자기들 중 한 마리가 포기하고 뛰어들 때까지 물가에서 기다리고 기다리고 또 기다린다. 그것이 일어나는 순간, 나머지 펭귄들은 다음에 무슨 일이 일어날지를 보기 위해 기대감을 갖고 지켜본다. 만약 그 선두 주자가 살아남으면, 다른 모두가 방금 그 펭귄이 한 대로 따를 것이다. 만약 그 펭귄이 죽는다면, 그들은 돌아설 것이다. 한 펭귄의 운명이 모든 나머지 펭귄들의 운명을 바꾼다. 그들의 전략은 '배워서 사는 것이다'라고 할 수 있을 것이다.

Why? 왜 정답일까?

예시의 결론 부분에서 먼저 물에 뛰어든 펭귄이 살아남는지 여부에 따라 다른 펭귄들도 뛰어드는 행동을 할지 말지를 결정한다(If the pioneer survives, everyone else will follow suit. If it perishes, they'll turn away.)는 내용이 나온다. 이를 근거로 할 때, 밑줄 친 부분이 의미하는 바로 가장 적절한 것은 ⑤ '다른 개체의 행동이 안전하다고 입증될 때에만 그 행동을 따른다'이다.

● critical ⓐ 중요한
● visible ⓐ 가시적인, 눈에 보이는
● stroll ⓥ 다니다, 거닐다
● play the waiting game ⓥ 대기 전술을 펼치다, 기회를 엿보다
● anticipation ⓝ 기대
● alter ⓥ 바꾸다
● territory ⓝ 영토
● influence ⓥ 영향을 미치다 ⓝ 영향
● consequence ⓝ 결과
● await ⓥ ~을 기다리다
● follow suit ⓥ 방금 남이 한 대로 따라하다
● fate ⓝ 운명

구문 풀이

9행 The moment that occurs, the rest of the penguins watch with anticipation
~하는 순간　지시대명사　　「the rest of + 복수 명사 + 복수 동사」
to see what happens next.
~하기 위해　→ 의문사(무엇이 ~인지)

---

22 더 많은 에너지를 주는 신체 활동
정답률 86% | 정답 ①

다음 글의 요지로 가장 적절한 것은?

☑ 많은 에너지를 얻기 위해 적극적인 신체 활동이 필요하다.
② 가벼운 산책을 통해 창의적 사고력을 증진할 수 있다.
③ 에너지의 소비와 회복의 불균형은 건강을 해친다.
④ 과도한 운동은 효율적인 두뇌 활동을 방해할 수 있다.
⑤ 원활한 에너지 충전을 위해서는 충분한 수면이 중요하다.

Imagine / that your body is a battery / and the more energy this battery can store, / the more energy you will be able to have within a day.
상상해 보자. / 여러분의 몸이 배터리이고, / 이 배터리가 더 많은 에너지를 저장할수록, / 하루 안에 더 많은 에너지를 지닐 수 있다고
Every night when you sleep, / this battery is recharged / with as much energy as you spent / during the previous day.
매일 밤 여러분이 잠잘 때, / 이 배터리는 재충전된다. / 여러분이 소비했던 에너지만큼 / 그 전날
If you want to have a lot of energy tomorrow, / you need to spend a lot of energy today.
여러분이 내일 많은 에너지를 갖기를 원한다면, / 오늘 많은 에너지를 소비할 필요가 있다.
Our brain consumes only 20% of our energy, / so it's a must / to supplement thinking activities with walking and exercises / that spend a lot of energy, / so that your internal battery has more energy tomorrow.
우리의 뇌는 우리 에너지의 겨우 20퍼센트만을 소비하므로 / 반드시 필요하고, / 걷기와 운동으로 사고 활동을 보충하는 것이 / 많은 에너지를 소비하는 / 그러면 여러분의 내부 배터리는 내일 더 많은 에너지를 가지게 된다.
Your body stores / as much energy as you need: / for thinking, for moving, for doing exercises.
여러분의 몸은 저장한다. / 여러분이 필요한 만큼의 에너지를 / 사고하기 위해, 움직이기 위해, 운동하기 위해
The more active you are today, / the more energy you spend today / and the more energy you will have / to burn tomorrow.
여러분이 오늘 더 활동적일수록, / 오늘 더 많은 에너지를 소비하고 / 그러면 더 많은 에너지를 가지게 될 것이다. / 내일 소모할
Exercising gives you more energy / and keeps you from feeling exhausted.
신체 활동은 여러분에게 더 많은 에너지를 주고 / 여러분이 지치는 것을 막아 준다.

여러분의 몸이 배터리이고, 이 배터리가 더 많은 에너지를 저장할수록, 하루에 더 많은 에너지를 지닐 수 있다고 상상해 보자. 매일 밤 여러분이 잠잘 때, 이 배터리는 그 전날 여러분이 소비했던 에너지만큼 재충전된다. 여러분이 내일 많은 에너지를 갖기를 원한다면, 오늘 많은 에너지를 소비할 필요가 있다. 우리의 뇌는 우리 에너지의 겨우 20퍼센트만을 소비하므로 많은 에너지를 소비하는 걷기와 운동으로 사고 활동을 보충하는 것이 반드시 필요하고, 그러면 여러분의 내부 배터리는 내일 더 많은 에너지를 가지게 된다. 여러분의 몸은 여러분이 사고하기 위해, 움직이기 위해, 운동하기 위해 필요한 만큼의 에너지를 저장한다. 여러분이 오늘 더 활동적일수록, 여러분은 오늘 더 많은 에너지를 소비하고 내일 소모할 더 많은 에너지를 가지게 될 것이다. 신체 활동은 여러분에게 더 많은 에너지를 주고 여러분이 지친다고 느끼는 것을 막아 준다.

Why? 왜 정답일까?

'If you want to have a lot of energy tomorrow, you need to spend a lot of energy today.'에서 더 많은 에너지를 갖고 싶다면 일단 에너지를 많이 소비하라고 말한 데 이어, 'Exercising gives you more energy and keeps you from feeling exhausted.'에서는 신체 활동이 더 많은 에너지를 주고 피로해지지 않게 막아준다는 내용을 이야기한다. 따라서 글의 요지로 가장 적절한 것은 ① '많은 에너지를 얻기 위해 적극적인 신체 활동이 필요하다.'이다.

● store ⓥ 저장하다
● consume ⓥ 소비하다, 쓰다
● internal ⓐ 내부의
● recharge ⓥ 재충전하다
● must ⓝ 필수사항

구문 풀이

6행 Our brain consumes only 20% of our energy, / so it's a must to supplement
주어1　　동사1　　　　　　주어2(가주어)　동사2　진주어
thinking activities with walking and exercises [that spend a lot of energy], so that
선행사(복수)　　복수 동사　　결과(~해서 …하다)
your internal battery has more energy tomorrow.

10행 The more active you are today, / the more energy you spend today and
「the + 비교급 ~, the + 비교급 …: 더 ~할수록 …하다」
the more energy you will have to burn tomorrow.
형용사적 용법(energy 수식)

---

23 말이나 글을 통한 사고 표현의 필요성
정답률 51% | 정답 ①

다음 글의 주제로 가장 적절한 것은?

☑ critical roles of speaking or writing in refining thoughts
　사고를 정제하는 데 있어 말 또는 글의 중대한 역할
② persuasive ways to communicate what you think to people
　생각하는 바를 사람들에게 전달하는 설득력 있는 방법
③ important tips to select the right information for your writing
　글에 적절한 정보를 선별하기 위한 중요한 조언
④ positive effects of logical thinking on reading comprehension
　독해에 논리적 사고가 미치는 긍정적 영향
⑤ enormous gaps between spoken language and written language
　구어와 문어 사이의 엄청난 격차

You can say / that information sits in one brain / until it is communicated to another, / unchanged in the conversation.
여러분은 말할 수 있다. / 정보는 한 뇌에 머물러 있으며 / 그것이 다른 뇌로 전달될 때까지 / 대화 속에서 변하지 않는다고
That's true of *sheer* information, / like your phone number / or the place you left your keys.
이것은 *순전한* 정보에 대해서는 사실이다. / 여러분의 전화번호 / 혹은 여러분이 열쇠를 놓아둔 장소와 같은
But it's not true of knowledge.
하지만 이것은 지식에 대해서는 사실이 아니다.
Knowledge relies on judgements, / which you discover and polish / in conversation with other people or with yourself.
지식은 판단에 의존하는데, / 여러분은 그 판단을 발견하고 다듬는다. / 다른 사람들 혹은 자신과의 대화 속에서
Therefore you don't learn the details of your thinking / until speaking or writing it out in detail / and looking back critically at the result.
그러므로 여러분은 자신의 사고의 세부 내용을 알지 못한다. / 그것을 상세하게 이야기하거나 글로 쓰고 / 그 결과를 비판적으로 되돌아볼 때까지
"Is what I just said foolish, / or is what I just wrote a deep truth?"
"내가 방금 말한 것이 바보 같은가, / 혹은 내가 방금 쓴 것이 깊은 진실인가?"
In the speaking or writing, / you uncover your bad ideas, often embarrassing ones, / and good ideas too, / sometimes fame-making ones.
말하거나 글을 쓸 때, / 여러분은 종종 당황스러운 자신의 형편없는 생각들을 발견하게 된다. / 그리고 좋은 생각들 또한, / 때로는 유명세를 만들어주는
Thinking requires its expression.
사고는 표현이 필요하다.

여러분은 정보가 다른 뇌로 전달될 때까지 한 뇌에 머물러 있으며 대화 속에서 변하지 않는다고 말할 수 있다. 이것은 여러분의 전화번호 혹은 여러분이 열쇠를 놓아둔 장소와 같은 순전한 정보에 대해서는 사실이다. 하지만 이것은 지식에 대해서는 사실이 아니다. 지식은 판단에 의존하는데, 여러분은 다른 사람들 혹은 자신과의 대화 속에서 그 판단을 발견하고 다듬는다. 그러므로 여러분은 그것을 상세하게 이야기하거나 글로 쓰고 그 결과를 비판적으로 되돌아볼 때까지 자신의 사고의 세부 내용을 알지 못한다. "내가 방금 이야기한 것이 바보 같은가, 혹은 내가 방금 쓴 것이 깊은 진실인가?" 말하거나 글을 쓸 때 여러분은 종종 당황스러운 자신의 형편없는 생각들과, 때로는 유명세를 만들어주는 좋은 생각들을 또한 발견하게 된다. 사고는 표현이 필요하다.

Why? 왜 정답일까?

'Therefore you don't learn the details of your thinking until speaking or writing it out in detail and looking back critically at the result.'에서 사고는 상세하게 이야기되거나 글로 쓰이기 전까지는 그 세부 내용이 파악되지 않는다고 말한 데 이어, 마지막 문장에서는 사고가 그 표현을 필요로 한다(Thinking requires its expression.)는 결론을 제시하고 있다. 따라서 글의 주제로 가장 적절한 것은 ① '사고를 정제하는 데 있어 말 또는 글의 중대한 역할'이다.

- communicate ⓥ 전달하다
- sheer ⓐ 순전한
- judgement ⓝ 판단
- critically ⓪ 비판적으로
- embarrassing ⓐ 당황스러운
- refine ⓥ 정제하다, 다듬다
- true of ~에 관해 사실인, ~에 해당되는
- rely on ⓥ ~에 의존하다
- polish ⓥ 다듬다
- uncover ⓥ 발견하다
- fame ⓝ 명성
- enormous ⓐ 엄청난

구문 풀이

4행 Knowledge relies on judgements, which you discover and polish in
(선행사) (계속적 용법) (주어) (타동사구)
conversation with other people or with yourself.

---

24 이야기를 활용한 정보 전달   정답률 51% | 정답 ②

다음 글의 제목으로 가장 적절한 것은?

① Make Yourself Outstanding by Using Accurate Terms
정확한 용어를 사용함으로써 스스로를 뛰어나게 만들라
② The Power of Story: Why We Need More Than Facts
이야기의 힘: 왜 우리는 사실 그 이상을 필요로 하는가
③ What Is the Key Qualification of a Storyteller?
이야기꾼의 핵심 자질은 무엇인가?
④ How Big Is Our Average Memory Capacity?
우리의 평균 기억 용량은 얼마나 큰가?
⑤ A Single Fact Is Worth a Whole Story
하나의 사실이 전체 이야기만큼의 가치가 있다

In a competitive environment, / such as a college admissions process / or a job application situation, / almost everyone has strong qualifications.
경쟁 환경에서 / 대학 입학 과정이나 / 구직 상황과 같은 / 거의 모든 사람들은 상당한 자격 조건을 갖추고 있다.

Almost everyone has facts in their favor.
거의 모든 이들은 자기에게 유리한 사실들을 지니고 있다.

But how valuable are facts alone?
그러나 사실들만으로는 얼마나 가치가 있겠는가?

Think back to the most recent lecture or presentation / you attended.
가장 최근의 강의나 발표를 회상해 보라. / 여러분이 참석했던

How many facts do you remember from it?
여러분은 그것으로부터 얼마나 많은 사실들을 기억하는가?

If you're like most people, / you can't recall many, / if any.
만약 여러분이 대부분의 사람과 같다면, / 여러분은 많은 것을 기억해 내지 못할 것이다. / 기억한다 하더라도

Chances are good, however, / that you remember stories, anecdotes, and examples from the event, / even if you can't think of their exact context.
그러나 가능성이 높다. / 여러분은 그 행사로부터의 이야기들, 일화들, 그리고 예시들을 기억할 / 비록 여러분이 정확한 맥락을 기억하지는 못하더라도

The average person today / is flooded with facts and data, / and we let most of this pass through our brains / with minimal retention or reaction / — unless something makes the information stand out / in a meaningful way.
오늘날 보통 사람에게는 / 사실들과 데이터가 넘쳐나고, / 우리는 이것의 대부분이 우리의 뇌를 빠져나가게 둔다 / 최소한의 기억이나 반응만을 남긴 채 / 어떤 것이 그 정보를 두드러지게 하지 않는다면 / 유의미한 방식으로

That's where story comes in.
그것이 이야기가 들어서는 지점이다.

대학 입학 과정이나 구직 상황과 같은 경쟁 환경에서 거의 모든 사람들은 상당한 자격 조건을 갖추고 있다. 거의 모든 이들은 자기에게 유리한 사실들을 지니고 있다. 그러나 사실들만으로 얼마나 가치가 있겠는가? 여러분이 참석했던 가장 최근의 강의나 발표를 회상해 보라. 여러분은 그것으로부터 얼마나 많은 사실들을 기억하는가? 만약 여러분이 대부분의 사람과 같다면, 여러분은 기억한다 하더라도 많은 것을 기억해 내지 못할 것이다. 그러나 비록 여러분이 정확한 맥락을 기억하지는 못하더라도, 여러분은 그 행사에서의 이야기들, 일화들, 그리고 예시들을 기억할 가능성이 높다. 오늘날 보통 사람에게는 사실들과 데이터가 넘쳐나고, 어떤 것이 그 정보를 유의미한 방식으로 두드러지게 하지 않는다면 우리는 이것의 대부분이 최소한의 기억이나 반응만을 남긴 채 우리의 뇌를 빠져나가게 둔다. 여기에 이야기가 들어간다.

Why? 왜 정답일까?

경쟁 환경에서 남들과의 차별점을 확보하기 위해서는 이야기를 이용해야 한다는 주제를 다룬 글이다. '~ we let most of this pass through our brains with minimal retention or reaction — unless something makes the information stand out in a meaningful way. That's where story comes in.'에서 사실과 데이터의 홍수에서 어떤 정보를 유의미하게 두드러지게 하기 위해서는 이야기가 필요하다는 결론을 제시하므로, 글의 제목으로 가장 적절한 것은 ② '이야기의 힘: 왜 우리는 사실 그 이상을 필요로 하는가'이다.

- competitive ⓐ 경쟁의, 경쟁적인
- application ⓝ 지원, 신청
- in one's favor ~에게 유리하게
- anecdote ⓝ 일화, 개인적인 진술
- pass through ~을 빠져나가다
- admission ⓝ (승인을 받고) 입학, 가입
- qualification ⓝ 자격, 자질
- recall ⓥ 기억하다, 회상하다
- be flooded with ~이 넘쳐나다, 쇄도하다
- minimal ⓐ 최소한의

- stand out 두드러지다, 눈에 띄다
- accurate ⓐ 정확한
- outstanding ⓐ 뛰어난, 탁월한
- capacity ⓝ 용량, 수용력, 능력

구문 풀이

8행 The average person today is flooded with facts and data, and we let
(주어1) (동사1(~이 넘쳐나다)) (동사2(사역동사)) (주어2)
most of this pass through our brains with minimal retention or reaction / — unless
(원형부정사)   (~이 아닌 한(=if ~ not))
something makes the information stand out in a meaningful way.

---

25 지역별 건강 관광 여행 수 및 경비   정답률 75% | 정답 ⑤

다음 표의 내용과 일치하지 않는 것은?

Wellness Tourism Trips and Expenditures by Region
in 2015 and 2017

Destination	Number of Trips (millions)		Expenditures ($ billions)	
	2015	2017	2015	2017
North America	186.5	204.1	$215.7	$241.7
Europe	249.9	291.8	$193.4	$210.8
Asia-Pacific	193.9	257.6	$111.2	$136.7
Latin America-The Caribbean	46.8	59.1	$30.4	$34.8
The Middle East-North Africa	8.5	11.0	$8.3	$10.7
Africa	5.4	6.5	$4.2	$4.8
Total	**691.0**	**830.0**	**$563.2**	**$639.4**

* Note: Figures may not sum to total due to rounding.

The table above shows / the number of trips and expenditures / for wellness tourism, / travel for health and well-being, / in 2015 and 2017.
위 표는 보여 준다. / 여행 수와 경비를 / 건강 관광의 / 건강과 웰빙을 위한 여행인 / 2015년과 2017년의
① Both the total number of trips and the total expenditures / were higher in 2017 / compared to those in 2015.
① 총 여행 수와 총 경비 둘 다 / 2017년에 더 높았다. / 2015년의 그것들에 비해서
② Of the six listed regions, / Europe was the most visited place for wellness tourism / in both 2015 and 2017, / followed by Asia-Pacific.
② 목록의 여섯 개 지역 중에서, / 유럽이 건강 관광을 위해 가장 많이 방문된 장소였으며, / 2015년과 2017년 두 해 모두 / 아시아-태평양이 그 뒤를 따랐다.
③ In 2017, / the number of trips to Latin America-The Caribbean / was more than five times higher / than that to The Middle East-North Africa.
③ 2017년에 / 라틴 아메리카-카리브 해로의 여행 수가 / 5배 이상 더 많았다. / 중동-북아프리카로의 그것보다
④ While North America was the only region / where more than 200 billion dollars was spent in 2015, / it was joined by Europe in 2017.
④ 북아메리카가 유일한 지역이었던 반면 / 2015년에 2천억 달러 이상이 소비된 / 2017년에는 유럽이 합류했다.
⑤ Meanwhile, / expenditures in The Middle East-North Africa and Africa / were each less than 10 billion dollars / in both 2015 and 2017.
⑤ 한편 / 중동-북아프리카와 아프리카에서의 경비는 / 각각 100억 달러 미만이었다. / 2015년과 2017년 두 해 모두

위 표는 2015년과 2017년의 건강과 웰빙을 위한 여행인 건강 관광의 여행 수와 경비를 보여 준다. ① 총 여행 수와 총 경비 둘 다 2015년의 그것들에 비해서 2017년에 더 높았다. ② 목록의 여섯 개 지역 중에서, 유럽이 2015년과 2017년 두 해 모두 건강 관광을 위해 가장 많이 방문된 장소였으며, 아시아-태평양이 그 뒤를 따랐다. ③ 2017년에 라틴 아메리카-카리브 해로의 여행 수가 중동-북아프리카로의 그것보다 5배 이상 더 많았다. ④ 2015년에는 북아메리카가 2천억 달러 이상이 소비된 유일한 지역이었던 반면 2017년에는 유럽이 합류했다. ⑤ 한편 중동-북아프리카와 아프리카에서의 경비는 각각 2015년과 2017년 두 해 모두 100억 달러 미만이었다.

Why? 왜 정답일까?

도표에 따르면 중동-북아프리카 지역에서의 경비는 2017년에 100억 달러를 넘어 107억을 기록했다. 따라서 도표와 일치하지 않는 것은 ⑤이다.

- wellness ⓝ 건강
- rounding ⓝ 반올림
- expenditure ⓝ 경비, 지출

---

26 Charles Henry Turner의 생애   정답률 72% | 정답 ⑤

Charles Henry Turner에 관한 다음 글의 내용과 일치하지 않는 것은?

① 곤충의 습성과 행동에 관한 독서에 매료되었다.
② 아프리카계 미국인 최초로 동물학 박사 학위를 받았다.
③ Sumner 고등학교에서 생물학을 가르쳤다.
④ 곤충이 학습할 수 있다는 것을 최초로 발견했다.
⑤ 마지막 과학 논문은 사망한 해에 발표되었다.

Born in 1867 in Cincinnati, Ohio, / Charles Henry Turner was an early pioneer / in the field of insect behavior.
1867년 Ohio주의 Cincinnati에서 태어난 / Charles Henry Turner는 초기 선구자였다. / 곤충 행동 분야의
「His father owned an extensive library / where Turner became fascinated with reading / about the habits and behavior of insects.」①의 근거 일치
그의 아버지는 폭넓은 도서를 가지고 있었다. / Turner가 독서에 매료될 수 있었던 / 곤충의 습성과 행동에 관한
「Proceeding with his study, / Turner earned a doctorate degree in zoology, / the first African American to do so.」②의 근거 일치
연구를 계속하면서 / Turner는 동물학으로 박사 학위를 받았고, / 그렇게 한 최초의 아프리카계 미국인이었다.
Even after receiving his degree, / Turner was unable to get a teaching or research position / at any major universities, / possibly as a result of racism.
학위를 받은 후에도 / Turner는 교직이나 연구를 얻을 수 없었다. / 어떤 주요 대학에서도 / 아마도 인종 차별의 결과로
「He moved to St. Louis / and taught biology at Sumner High School, / focusing on research there until 1922.」③의 근거 일치

그는 St. Louis로 옮겨 / Sumner 고등학교에서 생물학을 가르쳤고 / 그곳에서 1922년까지 연구에 집중했다.

『Turner was the first person / to discover that insects are capable of learning,』 / illustrating that insects can alter behavior / based on previous experience.   ④의 근거 일치
Turner는 최초의 사람이었고, / 곤충이 학습할 수 있다는 것을 발견한 / 곤충이 행동을 바꿀 수 있다는 것을 설명했다. / 이전의 경험을 바탕으로

He died of cardiac disease / in Chicago in 1923.
그는 심장병으로 사망했다. / 1923년 Chicago에서

During his 33-year career, / Turner published more than 70 papers.
33년의 경력 동안 / Turner는 70편이 넘는 논문을 발표했다.

『His last scientific paper was published / the year after his death.』   ⑤의 근거 불일치
그의 마지막 과학 논문은 발표되었다. / 그가 사망한 해 이후에

1867년 Ohio주의 Cincinnati에서 태어난 Charles Henry Turner는 곤충 행동 분야의 초기 선구자였다. 그의 아버지는 Turner가 곤충의 습성과 행동에 관한 독서에 매료될 수 있었던 폭넓은 도서를 가지고 있었다. 연구를 계속하면서 Turner는 동물학에서 박사 학위를 받았고, 그렇게 한 최초의 아프리카계 미국인이었다. 아마도 인종 차별의 결과로, 학위를 받은 후에도 Turner는 어떤 주요 대학에서도 교직이나 연구직을 얻을 수 없었다. 그는 St. Louis로 옮겨 Sumner 고등학교에서 생물학을 가르쳤고 그곳에서 1922년까지 연구에 집중했다. Turner는 곤충이 학습할 수 있다는 것을 발견한 최초의 사람이었고, 곤충이 이전의 경험을 바탕으로 행동을 바꿀 수 있다는 것을 설명했다. 그는 1923년 Chicago에서 심장병으로 사망했다. 33년의 경력 동안 Turner는 70편이 넘는 논문을 발표했다. 그의 마지막 과학 논문은 그가 사망한 그다음 해에 발표되었다.

Why? 왜 정답일까?

'His last scientific paper was published the year after his death.'에서 Turner의 마지막 논문은 Turner가 사망하고 그다음 해에 발표되었다고 하므로, 내용과 일치하지 않는 것은 ⑤ '마지막 과학 논문은 사망한 해에 발표되었다.'이다.

Why? 왜 오답일까?

① '~ Turner became fascinated with reading about the habits and behavior of insects.'의 내용과 일치한다.
② 'Proceeding with his study, Turner earned a doctorate degree in zoology, the first African American to do so.'의 내용과 일치한다.
③ 'He moved to St. Louis and taught biology at Sumner High School, ~'의 내용과 일치한다.
④ 'Turner was the first person to discover that insects are capable of learning ~'의 내용과 일치한다.

- **pioneer** ⓝ 선구자, 개척자
- **fascinated with** ~에 매료된, 마음을 빼앗긴
- **doctorate** ⓝ 박사 학위
- **illustrate** ⓥ 설명하다, 분명히 보여주다, 예증하다
- **publish** ⓥ 발표하다, 게재하다
- **extensive** ⓐ 폭넓은, 광범위한
- **proceed with** ~을 계속하다
- **racism** ⓝ 인종 차별
- **alter** ⓥ 바꾸다, 고치다

구문 풀이

4행 Proceeding with his study, Turner earned a doctorate degree in zoology,
분사구문(~하면서)
(being) the first African American to do so.
생략(분사구문)   형용사적 용법

---

27 목공 워크숍 안내   정답률 82% | 정답 ③

Introduction to Furniture Making에 관한 다음 안내문의 내용과 일치하는 것은?
① 연령에 제한이 없다.
② 토요일에 5시간씩 진행된다.
☑ 목공 경험이 없는 사람도 참여할 수 있다.
④ 적어도 일주일 전에 취소하면 전액을 환불해 준다.
⑤ 수강생들은 수작업으로 만든 의자를 가지고 가게 된다.

Introduction to Furniture Making
가구 제작 입문

Throughout this four-week workshop, / students will build a solid foundation / for their new venture into woodworking.
이 4주간의 워크숍 동안 / 학생들은 탄탄한 기초를 세울 것입니다. / 목공을 향한 그들의 새로운 도전에

『Age Requirement: 16 and older』   ①의 근거 불일치
연령 요건: 16세 이상

Location: Hoboken Community Center
위치: Hoboken 주민 센터

『Dates: Dec 7 – Dec 28 (Every Saturday)』
날짜: 12월 7일부터 12월 28일까지(매주 토요일)

Time: 1:00 p.m. – 5:00 p.m.   ②의 근거 불일치
시간: 오후 1시부터 오후 5시까지

Price: $399
가격: 399달러

Note:
참고:

『Previous woodworking experience is not necessary.』   ③의 근거 일치
이전 목공 경험은 필요하지 않습니다.

『We offer full refunds / if you cancel at least 10 days in advance.』   ④의 근거 불일치
저희는 전액을 환불해 드립니다. / 여러분이 적어도 10일 전에 취소한다면

『With the guidance of an instructor, / each student will leave with a hand-crafted side table.』   ⑤의 근거 불일치
강사의 지도로 / 각각의 학생은 수작업으로 만든 보조 탁자를 가져가게 될 것입니다.

For more information or to register, / contact Dave Malka (davemalka@woodfurniture.org).
더 많은 정보나 등록을 위해서는 / Dave Malka(davemalka@woodfurniture.org)에게 연락하십시오.

가구 제작 입문

이 4주간의 워크숍 동안 학생들은 목공을 향한 새로운 도전에 탄탄한 기초를 세울 것입니다.

- 연령 요건: 16세 이상
- 위치: Hoboken 주민 센터
- 날짜: 12월 7일부터 12월 28일까지(매주 토요일)
- 시간: 오후 1시부터 오후 5시까지
- 가격: 399달러
- 참고:
  – 이전 목공 경험은 필요하지 않습니다.
  – 여러분이 적어도 10일 전에 취소한다면 전액을 환불해 드립니다.

강사의 지도로 각각의 학생은 수작업으로 만든 보조 탁자를 가져가게 될 것입니다.

더 많은 정보나 등록을 위해서는 Dave Malka (davemalka@woodfurniture.org)에게 연락하십시오.

Why? 왜 정답일까?

'Previous woodworking experience is not necessary.'에서 이전 목공 경험은 필요하지 않다고 하므로, 안내문의 내용과 일치하는 것은 ③ '목공 경험이 없는 사람도 참여할 수 있다.'이다.

Why? 왜 오답일까?

① 'Age Requirement: 16 and older'에서 참가자 연령은 16세 이상으로 제한된다고 하였다.
② 'Dates: Dec 7 – Dec 28 (Every Saturday) / Time: 1:00 p.m. – 5:00 p.m.'에서 4주 동안 매주 토요일에 4시간씩 진행된다고 하였다.
④ 'We offer full refunds if you cancel at least 10 days in advance.'에서 전액 환불을 받으려면 최소 10일 전에 취소해야 한다고 하였다.
⑤ 'With the guidance of an instructor, each student will leave with a hand-crafted side table.'에서 수강생들은 강사의 지도를 받아 보조 탁자를 제작하게 될 것이라고 하였다.

- **solid** ⓐ 탄탄한
- **venture** ⓝ 도전, 모험
- **in advance** 미리, 사전에
- **foundation** ⓝ 기초
- **woodworking** ⓝ 목공
- **hand-crafted** ⓐ 수작업의, 손으로 만든

---

28 시 축제 안내   정답률 92% | 정답 ⑤

Poetry in the Park에 관한 다음 안내문의 내용과 일치하지 않는 것은?
① 매년 개최되며 올해가 여섯 번째이다.
② 저명한 시인들과 만나 시에 대해 이야기할 수 있다.
③ 감정을 시적으로 표현하는 방법을 배울 수 있다.
④ 1인당 1편의 시만 콘테스트에 제출할 수 있다.
☑ 행사 다음 날 오전에 콘테스트의 수상자를 발표한다.

Poetry in the Park
Poetry in the Park(공원에서의 시)

Saturday, October 13, 11:00 a.m. – 6:00 p.m.
10월 13일 토요일 오전 11시 – 오후 6시

『This annual festival, / now in its sixth year, / is held / with the support of Riverside Public Library.』   ①의 근거 일치
이 연례 축제는 / 이제 여섯 번째 해인 / 개최됩니다. / Riverside 공립 도서관의 후원으로

Poetry Workshop
시 워크숍

『Meet and talk with renowned poets / about their poems.』   ②의 근거 일치
저명한 시인들을 만나 이야기해 보세요. / 그들의 시에 대해

Jane Kenny(11:30 a.m.), / Michael Weil(12:30 p.m.)
Jane Kenny(오전 11시 30분), / Michael Weil(오후 12시 30분)

『Learn / how to express your feelings poetically.』   ③의 근거 일치
배워 보세요. / 여러분의 감정을 시적으로 표현하는 방법을

Poetry Contest
시 콘테스트

Theme for this year's contest / is "Arrivals and Departures."
올해 콘테스트의 주제는 / '도착과 출발'입니다.

『Only one poem / per participant.』   ④의 근거 일치
1편의 시 / 참가자 1인당

Due by 3:00 p.m.
오후 3시에 마감

『The winners will be announced / at 5:00 p.m. on the day on site.』   ⑤의 근거 불일치
우승자는 발표될 것입니다. / 현장에서 당일 오후 5시에

For questions about the festival, / please visit our website at www.poetryinthepark.org.
축제에 대한 질문이 있으시면 / 저희 웹 사이트 www.poetryinthepark.org를 방문해 주십시오.

Poetry in the Park(공원에서의 시)
10월 13일 토요일 오전 11시 – 오후 6시

이제 여섯 번째 해를 맞은 이 연례 축제는 Riverside 공립 도서관의 후원으로 개최됩니다.

◈ 시 워크숍
- 저명한 시인들을 만나 그들의 시에 대해 이야기하세요.
  Jane Kenny(오전 11시 30분), Michael Weil(오후 12시 30분)
- 여러분의 감정을 시적으로 표현하는 방법을 배우세요.

◈ 시 콘테스트
- 올해 콘테스트의 주제는 "도착과 출발"입니다.
- 참가자 1인당 1편의 시
- 오후 3시에 마감
- 우승자는 현장에서 당일 오후 5시에 발표될 것입니다.

축제에 대한 질문이 있으시면 저희 웹 사이트 www.poetryinthepark.org를 방문해 주십시오.

Why? 왜 정답일까?

'The winners will be announced at 5:00 p.m. on the day on site.'에서 수상자는 행사 당일 오후 5시에 발표될 예정이라고 하므로, 안내문의 내용과 일치하지 않는 것은 ⑤ '행사 다음 날 오전에 콘테스트의 수상자를 발표한다.'이다.

Why? 왜 오답일까?

① 'This annual festival, now in its sixth year, ~'의 내용과 일치한다.
② 'Meet and talk with renowned poets about their poems.'의 내용과 일치한다.
③ 'Learn how to express your feelings poetically.'의 내용과 일치한다.
④ 'Only one poem per participant'의 내용과 일치한다.

- annual ⓐ 연례의
- renowned ⓐ 저명한, 유명한
- participant ⓝ 참가자
- with the support of ~의 후원으로
- poetically ⓐⓓ 시적으로
- on site 현장에서

---

29 비언어적 의사소통의 역할 정답률 52% | 정답 ④

다음 글의 밑줄 친 부분 중, 어법상 틀린 것은? [3점]

Non-verbal communication / is not a substitute for verbal communication.
비언어적 의사소통은 / 언어적 의사소통의 대체물이 아니다.
Rather, it should function as a supplement, / ① serving to enhance the richness of the content of the message / that is being passed across.
오히려 그것은 보충으로서 기능해야 한다. / 메시지 내용의 풍부함을 강화시키도록 도와주면서 / 전달되고 있는
Non-verbal communication / can be useful in situations / ② where speaking may be impossible or inappropriate.
비언어적 의사소통은 / 상황에서 유용할 수 있다. / 말하기가 불가능하거나 부적절할지도 모르는
Imagine you are in an uncomfortable position / while talking to an individual.
여러분이 불편한 입장에 있다고 상상해 보라. / 어떤 개인과 이야기하는 동안
Non-verbal communication will help you / ③ get the message across to him or her / to give you some time off the conversation / to be comfortable again.
비언어적 의사소통은 여러분을 도와줄 것이다. / 그 사람에게 메시지를 전하게 / 대화에서 잠깐 벗어날 시간을 달라는 / 다시 편안해지도록
Another advantage of non-verbal communication is / ✔ that it offers you the opportunity / to express emotions and attitudes properly.
비언어적 의사소통의 또 다른 장점은 / 여러분에게 기회를 제공한다는 것이다. / 감정과 태도를 적절하게 표현할
Without the aid of non-verbal communication, / there are several aspects of your nature and personality / that will not be adequately expressed.
비언어적 의사소통의 도움이 없다면 / 여러분의 본성과 성격의 여러 측면들이 있다. / 적절하게 표현되지 못할
So, again, / it does not substitute verbal communication / but rather ⑤ complements it.
따라서 다시 말하면, / 그것은 언어적 의사소통을 대체하는 것이 아니라 / 오히려 그것을 보완한다.

비언어적 의사소통은 언어적 의사소통의 대체물이 아니다. 오히려 그것은 전달되고 있는 메시지 내용의 풍부함을 강화시키도록 도와주면서 보충으로서 기능해야 한다. 비언어적 의사소통은 말하기가 불가능하거나 부적절할지도 모르는 상황에서 유용할 수 있다. 여러분이 어떤 개인과 이야기하는 동안 불편한 입장에 있다고 상상해 보라. 비언어적 의사소통은 여러분이 그 사람에게 다시 편안해지도록 대화에서 잠깐 벗어날 시간을 달라는 메시지를 전하게 도와줄 것이다. 비언어적 의사소통의 또 다른 장점은 그것이 여러분에게 감정과 태도를 적절하게 표현할 기회를 제공한다는 것이다. 비언어적 의사소통의 도움이 없다면 적절하게 표현되지 못할 여러분의 본성과 성격의 여러 측면들이 있다. 따라서 다시 말하면, 그것은 언어적 의사소통을 대체하는 것이 아니라 오히려 그것을 보완한다.

Why? 왜 정답일까?

뒤에 나오는 'it offers you the opportunity ~'가 완전한 4형식 구조임을 미루어볼 때, 뒤에 불완전한 문장을 수반하는 관계대명사 what을 쓰기에는 부적절하다. 따라서 what을 명사절 접속사인 that으로 고쳐야 한다. 어법상 틀린 것은 ④이다.

Why? 왜 오답일까?

① 완전한 주절 뒤로 '~하면서'라는 뜻의 분사구문이 적절히 연결되고 있다. 뒤에 나오는 to부정사는 serving의 목적어로, 'serve + to부정사(~하는 것을 돕다)'를 기억해 둔다.
② 앞에 추상적 공간의 선행사 situations가 나온 후 뒤에 may be가 동사인 완전한 2형식 구조가 나오는 것으로 보아 관계부사 where의 쓰임은 적절하다.
③ 준사역동사 help는 목적어와 목적격 보어가 능동 관계일 때 원형부정사 또는 to부정사를 목적격 보어로 취한다. 따라서 get의 쓰임이 적절하다.
⑤ 「not A but (rather) B(A가 아니라 B인)」 구문에서 A 자리에 주어 it에 연결되는 단수 동사 does not substitute가 나오므로, B 자리에도 단수 동사 complements가 적절하게 나왔다.

- substitute ⓝ 대체물 ⓥ 대체하다
- pass across ⓥ 전달하다
- get A across to B ⓥ A를 B에게 전하다, 이해시키다
- properly ⓐⓓ 적절하게
- adequately ⓐⓓ 적절하게
- enhance ⓥ 강화하다
- inappropriate ⓐ 부적절한
- aid ⓝ 도움
- complement ⓥ 보완하다

구문 풀이

2행 Rather, it should function as a supplement, serving to enhance the
　　　　　　　　　　　　　　　　　　　　자동사(기능하다)　　분사구문(~하면서)
richness of the content of the message [that is being passed across].
　　　　　　　　　　　　　　　　　　선행사　　　　현재진행 수동태(~되고 있다)

---

30 랜덤 오차와 계통 오차 정답률 44% | 정답 ④

다음 글의 밑줄 친 부분 중, 문맥상 낱말의 쓰임이 적절하지 않은 것은? [3점]

Random errors may be detected / by ① repeating the measurements.
랜덤 오차는 발견될 수 있다. / 측정을 반복하면
Furthermore, by taking more and more readings, / we obtain from the arithmetic mean a value / which approaches more and more closely to the true value.
더구나 더욱더 많은 측정값을 구함으로써 / 우리는 산술 평균으로부터 값을 얻는다. / 참값에 더욱더 가까이 접근하는
Neither of these points is true for a systematic error.
이 두 가지 사실 중 어떤 것도 계통 오차에는 적용되지 않는다.
Repeated measurements with the same apparatus / neither ② reveal nor do they eliminate a systematic error.
동일한 도구를 가지고 하는 반복적 측정은 / 계통 오차를 드러내지도 없애지도 않는다.

For this reason / systematic errors are potentially more ③ dangerous than random errors.
이런 이유로 / 계통 오차는 랜덤 오차보다 잠재적으로 더 위험하다.
If large random errors are present in an experiment, / they will manifest themselves in a large value of the final quoted error.
만약 어떤 실험에서 큰 랜덤 오차가 존재하면, / 그것은 최종으로 매겨진 큰 오차값으로 드러날 것이다.
Thus everyone is ✔ aware of the imprecision of the result, / and no harm is done / — except possibly to the ego of the experimenter / when no one takes notice of his or her results.
그리하여 모든 사람이 결과의 부정확성을 알게 되는데, / 어떠한 해도 가해지지 않는다. / 어쩌면 실험자의 자존심에 (가해질 수 있는 해) 말고는 / 실험자의 결과에 아무도 주목하지 않을 때에는
However, the concealed presence of a systematic error / may lead to an apparently ⑤ reliable result, / given with a small estimated error, / which is in fact seriously wrong.
그러나 계통 오차의 숨겨진 존재는, / 언뜻 신뢰할 수 있는 결과로 이어질 수 있는데, / 추정된 오차가 작다면, / 이는 사실 심각하게 잘못된 것이다.

랜덤 오차는 측정을 ① 반복하면 발견될 수 있다. 더구나 더욱더 많은 측정값을 구함으로써 우리는 산술 평균으로부터 참값에 더욱더 가까워지는 값을 얻는다. 이 두 가지 사실 중 어떤 것도 계통 오차에는 적용되지 않는다. 계통 오차는 동일한 도구를 가지고 반복적으로 측정해도 ② 드러나지도 제거되지도 않는다. 이런 이유로 계통 오차는 랜덤 오차보다 잠재적으로 더 ③ 위험하다. 만약 어떤 실험에서 큰 랜덤 오차가 존재하면, 그것은 최종적으로 매겨진 큰 오차값으로 드러날 것이다. 그리하여 모든 사람이 결과의 부정확성을 ④ 모르게(→ 알게) 되는데, 실험자의 결과에 아무도 주목하지 않을 때에는 어쩌면 실험자의 자존심에 (가해질 수 있는 해) 말고는 어떠한 해도 가해지지 않는다. 그러나 계통 오차의 숨겨진 존재는, 추정된 오차가 작다면, 언뜻 ⑤ 신뢰할 수 있는 결과로 이어질 수 있는데, 이는 사실 심각하게 잘못된 것이다.

Why? 왜 정답일까?

'If large random errors are present in an experiment, they will manifest themselves in a large value of the final quoted error.'에서 어떤 실험에 랜덤 오차가 존재하면 결국 최종적으로 큰 오차값이 매겨진다고 설명하는 것으로 보아, ④가 포함된 문장은 그 결과 사람들이 오차의 존재를 '알게' 된다는 의미를 나타내야 한다. 따라서 unaware를 반의어인 aware로 고쳐야 한다. 즉 문맥상 낱말의 쓰임이 적절하지 않은 것은 ④이다.

- random error ⓝ 랜덤 오차(원인을 알 수 없거나 알더라도 보정할 수 없는 무작위적인 오차)
- measurement ⓝ 측정
- systematic error ⓝ 계통 오차(발생한 원인이 분명한 오차)
- eliminate ⓥ 제거하다
- manifest ⓥ (분명히) 나타내다, 드러내 보이다
- apparently ⓐⓓ 겉보기에
- estimated ⓐ 추정된
- reading ⓝ 측정값, 눈금값
- potentially ⓐⓓ 잠재적으로
- imprecision ⓝ 부정확성
- reliable ⓐ 신뢰할 수 있는

구문 풀이

5행 Repeated measurements with the same apparatus neither reveal nor do they eliminate a systematic error.
「neither + A + nor + B : A도 B도 아닌」
「부정어구 + do/does/did + 주어 + 동사원형 : 도치 구문」

---

31 일반화된 호혜성에 기반한 동물의 협동 정답률 69% | 정답 ④

다음 빈칸에 들어갈 말로 가장 적절한 것을 고르시오.
① friction - 마찰
② diversity - 다양성
③ hierarchy - 계층
✔ cooperation - 협동
⑤ independence - 독립성

If you follow science news, / you will have noticed / that cooperation among animals has become a hot topic / in the mass media.
만약 여러분이 과학 뉴스에 관심을 가진다면, / 여러분은 알아차리게 될 것이다. / 동물들 사이의 협동이 뜨거운 화제가 되어 왔다는 것을 / 대중 매체에서
For example, / in late 2007 / the science media widely reported a study / by Claudia Rutte and Michael Taborsky / suggesting that rats display / what they call "generalized reciprocity."
예를 들어, / 2007년 후반에 / 과학 매체는 연구를 널리 보도했다. / Claudia Rutte와 Michael Taborsky가 / 쥐들이 보여 준다고 시사하는 / 그들에 의한 '일반화된 호혜성'이라고 부르는 것을
They each provided help / to an unfamiliar and unrelated individual, / based on their own previous experience / of having been helped by an unfamiliar rat.
그들 각각이 도움을 제공했다. / 낯설고 무관한 개체에게 / 자신의 이전 경험에 근거하여 / 낯선 쥐에 의해 도움을 받았던
Rutte and Taborsky trained rats / in a cooperative task of pulling a stick / to obtain food for a partner.
Rutte와 Taborsky는 쥐들에게 훈련시켰다. / 막대기를 잡아당기는 협동적 과업 / 파트너를 위한 음식을 얻기 위해
Rats / who had been helped previously by an unknown partner / were more likely to help others.
쥐는 / 이전에 모르는 파트너에게 도움을 받은 적이 있는 / 다른 쥐들을 돕는 경향이 더 높았다.
Before this research was conducted, / generalized reciprocity was thought / to be unique to humans.
이 연구가 수행되기 전에는, / 일반화된 호혜성은 여겨졌다. / 인간들에게 고유한 것으로

만약 여러분이 과학 뉴스에 관심을 가진다면, 여러분은 동물들 사이의 협동이 대중 매체에서 뜨거운 화제가 되어 왔다는 것을 알아차리게 될 것이다. 예를 들어, 2007년 후반에 과학 매체는 Claudia Rutte와 Michael Taborsky가 '일반화된 호혜성'이라고 부르는 것을 쥐들이 보여 준다고 시사하는, 그들에 의한 연구를 널리 보도했다. 쥐 각각이 낯선 쥐에 의해 도움을 받았던 자신의 이전 경험에 근거하여 낯설고 무관한 개체에게 도움을 제공했다. Rutte와 Taborsky는 쥐들에게 파트너를 위한 음식을 얻기 위해 막대기를 잡아당기는 협동적 과업을 훈련시켰다. 이전에 모르는 파트너에게 도움을 받은 적이 있는 쥐는 다른 쥐들을 돕는 경향이 더 컸다. 이 연구가 수행되기 전에는, 일반화된 호혜성은 인간들에게 고유한 것으로 여겨졌다.

Why? 왜 정답일까?

인간뿐 아니라 동물 또한 일반화된 호혜성(generalized reciprocity)에 근거하여 협력한다는 내용을 설명한 글로, For example 이하에서 쥐들이 낯설고 무관한 개체끼리도 서로 돕는다는 결론을 밝혀낸 실험을 소개하고 있다. 따라서 빈칸에 들어갈 말로 가장 적절한 것은 ④ '협동'이다.

[문제편 p.215]

- generalize ⓥ 일반화하다
- unfamiliar ⓐ 낯선, 익숙하지 않은
- cooperative ⓐ 협동적인
- previously [ad] 이전에, 사전에, 미리
- reciprocity ⓝ 호혜성, 이익 교환
- unrelated ⓐ 무관한, 관계없는, 친족이 아닌
- obtain ⓥ 얻다
- conduct ⓥ 수행하다

구문 풀이

5행 They each provided help to an unfamiliar and unrelated individual, based
분사구문(~에 기반을 두어)
on their own previous experience of having been helped by an unfamiliar rat.
전치사 ↵ 완료 수동 동명사 : 주절보다 먼저 일어남

★★★ 등급을 가르는 문제!

32 세계화로 강화된 집단 간 장벽   정답률 34% | 정답 ①

다음 빈칸에 들어갈 말로 가장 적절한 것을 고르시오. [3점]
- ☑ to build barriers – 장벽을 쌓도록
- ② to achieve equality – 평등을 성취하도록
- ③ to abandon traditions – 전통을 버리도록
- ④ to value individualism – 개인주의를 중시하도록
- ⑤ to develop technologies – 기술을 발전시키도록

The title of Thomas Friedman's 2005 book, *The World Is Flat*, / was based on the belief /
that globalization would inevitably bring us closer together.
Thomas Friedman의 2005년 저서의 제목인 *The World Is Flat*은 / 믿음에 근거하였다. / 세계화가 필연적으로 우리를 더 가깝게 만들 것이라는

It has done that, / but it has also inspired us to build barriers.
그것은 그렇게 해왔지만 / 또한 우리가 장벽을 쌓도록 해왔다.

When faced with perceived threats / — the financial crisis, terrorism, violent conflict,
refugees and immigration, the increasing gap between rich and poor — / people cling more
tightly to their groups.
인지된 위협들에 직면할 때, / 금융 위기, 테러 행위, 폭력적 분쟁, 난민과 이민자, 증가하는 빈부 격차 / 사람들은 자신의 집단에 더 단단히 달라붙는다.

One founder of a famous social media company / believed social media would unite us.
한 유명 소셜 미디어 회사 설립자는 / 소셜 미디어가 우리를 결합시킬 것이라고 믿었다.

In some respects it has, / but it has simultaneously given voice and organizational ability /
to new cyber tribes, / some of whom spend their time / spreading blame and division
across the World Wide Web.
어떤 면에서는 그것은 그래 왔지만 / 그것은 동시에 목소리와 조직력을 부여해 왔고, / 새로운 사이버 부족들에게 / 이들 중 일부는 그들의 시간을 보낸다. / 월드 와이드 웹(World Wide Web)에서 비난과 분열을 퍼뜨리는 데

There seem now to be as many tribes, / and as much conflict between them, / as there have
ever been.
현재 많은 부족들이 존재하는 것처럼 보인다. / 그리고 그들 사이의 많은 분쟁이 / 지금까지 존재해 온 만큼이나

Is it possible for these tribes to coexist / in a world where the concept of "us and them"
remains?
이러한 부족들이 공존하는 것이 가능할까? / '우리와 그들'이라는 개념이 남아 있는 세계에서

Thomas Friedman의 2005년 저서의 제목인 *The World Is Flat*은 세계화가 필연적으로 우리를 더 가깝게 만들 것이라는 믿음에 근거하였다. 그것(세계화)은 그렇게 해왔지만 또한 우리가 장벽을 쌓도록 해왔다. 금융 위기, 테러 행위, 폭력적 분쟁, 난민과 이민자, 증가하는 빈부 격차 같은 인지된 위협들에 직면할 때, 사람들은 자신의 집단에 더 단단히 달라붙는다. 한 유명 소셜 미디어 회사 설립자는 소셜 미디어가 우리를 결합시킬 것이라고 믿었다. 어떤 면에서는 그래 왔지만 그것은 동시에 새로운 사이버 부족들에게 목소리와 조직력을 부여해 왔고, 이들 중 일부는 월드 와이드 웹(World Wide Web)에서 비난과 분열을 퍼뜨리는 데 그들의 시간을 보낸다. 지금까지 그래 온 만큼이나 현재 많은 부족들, 그리고 그들 사이의 많은 분쟁이 존재하는 것처럼 보인다. '우리와 그들'이라는 개념이 남아 있는 세계에서 이러한 부족들이 공존하는 것이 가능할까?

Why? 왜 정답일까?

세계화로 인해 각 집단은 가까워질 것으로 기대되었지만 한편으로 서로 간 단절이 심화되었다는 점을 지적한 글이다. 특히 마지막 두 문장에서 사이버 상의 각 부족들을 별로 아직도 많은 분쟁이 존재하고 있으며 '우리'와 '그들'이라는 구별이 여전히 남아 있음(There seem now to be as many tribes, and as much conflict between them, ~.)을 언급하므로, 빈칸에 들어갈 말로 가장 적절한 것은 ① '장벽을 쌓도록'이다.

- inevitably [ad] 필연적으로, 불가피하게
- threat ⓝ 위협
- conflict ⓝ 분쟁, 갈등
- gap between rich and poor ⓝ 빈부격차
- founder ⓝ 설립자
- simultaneously [ad] 동시에
- spread ⓥ 퍼뜨리다
- equality ⓝ 평등
- inspire ⓥ 고무하다, 자극하다
- crisis ⓝ 위기
- refugee ⓝ 난민
- cling to ⓥ ~에 달라붙다
- unite ⓥ 결합시키다
- organizational ⓐ 조직(상)의
- coexist ⓥ 공존하다
- individualism ⓝ 개인주의

구문 풀이

8행 In some respects it has (united us), but it has simultaneously given voice
생략(앞 문장에 나옴)
and organizational ability to new cyber tribes, some of whom spend their time
선행사   목적격 관·대 'spend + 시간 + 동명사 :
spreading blame and division across the World Wide Web.
~하는 데 …을 들이다」

★★ 문제 해결 꿀~팁 ★★

▶ 많이 틀린 이유는?
글 중간의 'it has simultaneously given voice and organizational ability to new cyber tribes'를 긍정적으로 해석하면 세계화가 새로운 사이버 부족에게 각자의 목소리를 낼 수 있게 도왔다는 의미로 보아 ④를 답으로 고를 수 있다. 하지만 이 문장의 'some of whom ~'에서 결국 자기만의 목소리를 내기 시작한 사이버 부족들이 서로 헐뜯고 분열되어 간다는 부정적인 결과에 주목하고 있으므로, '개인주의를 중시한다'는 부분적인 진술을 빈칸에 넣는 것은 부적합하다.

▶ 문제 해결 방법은?
결론에 따르면 이 글은 세계화와 소셜 미디어 발달로 생겨난 집단 간의 '갈등(conflict)'에 주목하고 있다. 따라서 세계화가 서로간의 '장벽을 세우는 데' 일조했다는 의미의 ① 빈칸에 가장 적절하다.

33 행사와 맥락의 연관성   정답률 41% | 정답 ③

다음 빈칸에 들어갈 말로 가장 적절한 것을 고르시오. [3점]
- ① build a new context with other short-lived events
  다른 단기간 행사로 새로운 맥락을 구축할
- ② take place free from this spatial and temporal limit
  공간과 시간의 한계를 벗어나서 발생할
- ☑ be performed in relation to this long-term context
  이러한 장기간의 맥락과 관련하여 시행될
- ④ interact with well-known events from another locality
  다른 곳의 유명한 행사와 상호 작용할
- ⑤ evolve itself from a local event to a global one in the end
  결국에는 국지적 행사에서 세계적인 것으로 발전할

From an economic perspective, / a short-lived event can become an innovative event / if it
generates goods and services / that can be sold to people, / in particular to those from
outside the locality.
경제적인 관점에서 볼 때, / 단기간 행사가 혁신적인 행사가 될 수 있다. / 상품과 서비스를 만들어 낸다면 / 사람들에게 판매될 수 있는 / 특히 외부 사람들에게

The remarkable growth / of art exhibitions, cultural festivals and sports competitions, / for
example, / can be analysed in this light.
눈에 띄는 성장은 / 예술 전시회, 문화 축제 그리고 스포츠 경기의 / 예를 들어, / 이러한 관점에서 분석될 수 있다.

They are temporary activities / that can attract large numbers of outsiders to a locality, /
bringing in new sources of income.
그것들은 일시적 활동들이다. / 많은 외부인들을 그 지역으로 끌어들여 / 새로운 수입원을 가져올 수 있는

But even here, / there is a two-way interaction / between the event and the context.
그러나 심지어 여기에서도, / 쌍방향 상호 작용이 있다. / 행사와 맥락 간에

The existence / of an infrastructure, a reputation, a history of an activity / for an area / may
have important effects / on the economic success or failure of an event.
존재는 / 기반 시설, 명성, 활동의 연혁의 / 한 지역의 / 중요한 영향을 미칠 수 있다. / 행사의 경제적 성공 또는 실패에

In other words, / events do not take place in a vacuum.
다시 말해서, / 행사들은 진공 상태에서 발생하지 않는다.

They depend on an existing context / which has been in the making for a long time.
그것들은 기존의 맥락에 의존한다. / 오랜 시간 동안 만들어져 왔던

The short-lived event, / therefore, / would be performed / in relation to this long-term
context.
단기간 행사는 / 그러므로 / 시행될 것이다. / 이러한 장기간의 맥락과 관련하여

경제적인 관점에서 볼 때, 단기간 행사는 사람들, 특히 외부 사람들에게 판매될 수 있는 상품과 서비스를 만들어 낸다면 혁신적인 행사가 될 수 있다. 예를 들어, 예술 전시회, 문화 축제 그리고 스포츠 경기의 눈에 띄는 성장은 이러한 관점에서 분석될 수 있다. 그것들은 많은 외부인들을 그 지역으로 끌어들여 새로운 수입원을 가져올 수 있는 일시적 활동들이다. 그러나 심지어 여기에서도, 행사와 맥락 간에 쌍방향 상호 작용이 있다. 한 지역의 기반 시설, 명성, 활동의 연혁의 존재는 행사의 경제적 성공 또는 실패에 중요한 영향을 미칠 수 있다. 다시 말해서, 행사들은 진공 상태에서 발생하지 않는다. 그것들은 오랜 시간 동안 만들어져 왔던 기존의 맥락에 의존한다. 그러므로 단기간 행사는 이러한 장기간의 맥락과 관련하여 시행될 것이다.

Why? 왜 정답일까?

'But even here, there is a two-way interaction between the event and the context.'에서 단기 행사와 맥락 간에는 쌍방향의 상호 작용이 있다고 말한 데 이어, 'In other words, events do not take place in a vacuum. They depend on an existing context which has been in the making for a long time.'에서는 행사가 독립적으로 발생하지 않고 오랜 시간에 걸쳐 구축된 맥락에 의존하는 특성이 있음을 이야기한다. 따라서 빈칸에 들어갈 말로 가장 적절한 것은 ③ '이러한 장기간의 맥락과 관련하여 시행될'이다.

- perspective ⓝ 관점, 시각
- locality ⓝ (~이 존재하는) 곳
- in this light 이러한 관점에서
- attract ⓥ 끌다, 매혹시키다
- vacuum ⓝ 진공, 공백
- spatial ⓐ 공간의, 공간적인
- in relation to ~와 관련하여
- short-lived 단기의
- remarkable ⓐ 눈에 띄는, 놀라운, 주목할 만한
- temporary ⓐ 일시적인
- existence ⓝ 존재, 있음
- free from ~에서 벗어나, ~의 염려가 없는
- temporal ⓐ 시간의, 시간의 제약을 받는

구문 풀이

1행 From an economic perspective, a short-lived event can become an
주어   동사
innovative event / if it generates goods and services [that can be sold to people,
조건 접속사   선행사   주격 관계대명사
in particular to those from outside the locality].
~한 사람들

★★★ 등급을 가르는 문제!

34 음식이 마음에 미치는 영향   정답률 37% | 정답 ⑤

다음 빈칸에 들어갈 말로 가장 적절한 것을 고르시오. [3점]
- ① leads us to make a fair judgement – 우리가 공정한 판단을 내리게 유도한다
- ② interferes with cooperation with others – 타인과의 협력을 방해한다
- ③ does harm to serious diplomatic occasions – 심각한 외교 상황에 해를 끼친다
- ④ plays a critical role in improving our health – 우리의 건강을 증진하는 데 중요한 역할을 한다
- ☑ enhances our receptiveness to be persuaded – 설득되는 데 대한 우리의 수용성을 높인다

There is a famous Spanish proverb / that says, "The belly rules the mind."
유명한 스페인 속담이 있다. / '배가 마음을 다스린다'라고 하는

This is a clinically proven fact.
이것은 임상적으로 증명된 사실이다.

Food is the original mind-controlling drug.
음식은 원래 마음을 지배하는 약이다.

Every time we eat, / we bombard our brains with a feast of chemicals, / triggering an explosive hormonal chain reaction / that directly influences the way we think.
우리가 먹을 때마다 / 우리는 자신의 두뇌에 화학 물질의 향연을 퍼부어 / 폭발적인 호르몬 연쇄 반응을 유발한다. / 우리가 생각하는 방식에 직접적으로 영향을 미치는

Countless studies have shown / that the positive emotional state / induced by a good meal / enhances our receptiveness to be persuaded.
수많은 연구는 보여주었다 / 긍정적인 감정 상태가 / 근사한 식사로 유도된 / 설득되는 데 대한 우리의 수용성을 높인다는 것을

It triggers an instinctive desire / to repay the provider.
그것은 본능적인 욕구를 유발한다. / 그 제공자에게 보답하려는

This is why executives regularly combine business meetings with meals, / why lobbyists invite politicians / to attend receptions, lunches, and dinners, / and why major state occasions / almost always involve an impressive banquet.
이것이 경영진이 정기적으로 업무 회의와 식사를 결합하는 이유이고, / 로비스트들이 정치인들을 초대하는 이유이고, / 환영회, 점심 식사, 저녁 식사에 참석하도록 / 주요 국가 행사가 / 거의 항상 인상적인 연회를 포함하는 이유이다.

Churchill called this "dining diplomacy," / and sociologists have confirmed / that this principle is a strong motivator / across all human cultures.
Churchill은 이것을 '식사 외교'라고 불렀고, / 사회학자들은 확인해 왔다. / 이 원리가 강력한 동기 부여물이라는 것을 / 모든 인류 문화에 걸쳐

'배가 마음을 다스린다'라고 하는 유명한 스페인 속담이 있다. 이것은 임상적으로 증명된 사실이다. 음식은 원래 마음을 지배하는 약이다. 우리가 먹을 때마다 우리는 자신의 두뇌에 화학 물질의 향연을 퍼부어 우리가 생각하는 방식에 직접적으로 영향을 미치는 폭발적인 호르몬 연쇄 반응을 유발한다. 수많은 연구는 근사한 식사로 유도된 긍정적인 감정 상태가 설득되는 데 대한 우리의 수용성을 높인다는 것을 보여주었다. 그것은 그 제공자에게 보답하려는 본능적인 욕구를 유발한다. 이것이 경영진이 정기적으로 업무 회의와 식사를 결합하는 이유이고, 로비스트들이 정치인들을 환영회, 점심 식사, 저녁 식사에 참석하도록 초대하는 이유이고, 주요 국가 행사가 거의 항상 인상적인 연회를 포함하는 이유이다. Churchill은 이것을 '식사 외교'라고 불렀고, 사회학자들은 이 원리가 모든 인류 문화에 걸쳐 강력한 동기 부여물이라는 것을 확인해 왔다.

Why? 왜 정답일까?

첫 세 문장에서 스페인 속담을 예로 들며 음식이 마음을 지배한다(Food is the original mind-controlling drug.)는 것이 사실이라는 점을 언급하고, 빈칸 뒤에서는 이러한 이유로 각종 업무 상황에 연회와 식사가 포함된다고 설명한다. 따라서 빈칸에 들어갈 말로 가장 적절한 것은 근사한 식사로 긍정적인 감정 상태에 이르렀을 때의 결과를 적절히 유추한 ⑤ '설득되는 데 대한 우리의 수용성을 높인다'이다.

- **clinically** ad 임상적으로
- **feast** n 향연
- **explosive** a 폭발적인
- **instinctive** a 본능적인
- **reception** n 환영회
- **diplomacy** n 외교
- **interfere with** ~을 방해하다
- **enhance** v 높이다, 향상시키다
- **bombard A with B** v A에 B를 퍼붓다
- **trigger** v 유발하다
- **induce** v 유도하다
- **executive** n 경영진
- **impressive** a 인상적인
- **principle** n 원리
- **do harm to** ~에 해를 끼치다
- **receptiveness** n 수용성, 감수성

구문 풀이

3행 Every time we eat, we bombard our brains with a feast of chemicals,
~할 때마다 / 「bombard +A + with +B : A에 B를 퍼붓다」
triggering an explosive hormonal chain reaction [that directly influences the way
분사구문(그리고 ~하다) / 선행사 / 주격 관계대명사
we think].

★★ 문제 해결 꿀~팁 ★★

▶ 많이 틀린 이유는?
'배가 마음을 지배한다'는 말이 있듯이 사람은 특히 근사한 식사를 하면 감정과 사고과정에 영향을 받아 '설득되기 쉬운' 상태가 되고, 이 때문에 '식사 외교'라는 말이 등장할 만큼 다양한 사회적 상황에 식사가 수반된다는 내용을 다룬 글이다. ②는 근사한 식사가 도리어 '사람들 간 협력을 방해한다'는 의미를 나타내므로 주제와 상반된다.
▶ 문제 해결 방법은?
빈칸 바로 뒤의 문장에서 a good meal을 It으로 받아 근사한 식사는 식사를 제공해준 사람에게 보답하려는 본능을 일깨운다고 언급하고 있다. 이를 근거로 볼 때, 좋은 식사를 대접받으면 '(상대방의) 부탁에 설득될 가능성이 높아진다'는 내용이 빈칸에 들어가야 한다.

35 상점에 중앙 통로 두기 　　정답률 63% | 정답 ④

다음 글에서 전체 흐름과 관계 없는 문장은?

Wouldn't it be nice / if you could take your customers by the hand / and guide each one through your store / while pointing out all the great products / you would like them to consider buying?
좋지 않을까? / 만약 여러분이 고객의 손을 잡고 / 상점 안 여기저기로 고객 개개인을 안내할 수 있다면 / 모든 훌륭한 제품들을 가리키면서 / 고객에게 구매를 고려하게 하고 싶은

① Most people, / however, / would not particularly enjoy / having a stranger grab their hand / and drag them through a store.
대부분의 사람들은 / 그러나 / 특히 좋아하지 않을 것이다. / 낯선 사람이 그들의 손을 잡고 / 상점 안 여기저기로 끌고 다니도록 하는 것을

② Rather, / let the store do it for you.
차라리 / 상점이 여러분 대신 그렇게 하게 만들라.

③ Have a central path / that leads shoppers through the store / and lets them look at many different departments or product areas.
중앙 통로를 만들어라. / 고객들을 상점 안 여기저기로 이끄는 / 그래서 그 고객들이 많은 다양한 매장 또는 상품이 있는 곳을 보게 될

④ You can use this effect of music / on shopping behavior / by playing it in the store.
여러분은 음악의 이러한 효과를 사용할 수 있다. / 쇼핑 행동에 대한 / 상점에서 그것을 트는 것으로

⑤ This path leads your customers from the entrance / through the store / on the route / you want them to take / all the way to the checkout.
이 길은 입구에서부터 고객들을 이끈다. / 상점 안 여기저기를 통해 / 경로로 / 여러분이 고객들로 하여금 그리로 걷기를 바라는 / 계산대까지 내내

만약 여러분이 고객에게 구매를 고려하게 하고 싶은 모든 훌륭한 제품들을 가리키면서 고객의 손을 잡고 상점 안 여기저기로 고객 개개인을 안내할 수 있다면 좋지 않을까? ① 그러나 대부분의 사람들은 특히 낯선 사람이 그들의 손을 잡고 상점 안 여기저기로 끌고 다니도록 하는 것을 좋아하지 않을 것이다. ② 차라리 상점이 여러분 대신 그렇게 하게 만들라. ③ 고객들을 상점 안 여기저기로 이끌어 그들이 많은 다양한 매장 또는 상품이 있는 곳을 보게 해줄 중앙 통로를 만들라. ④ 여러분은 상점에서 음악을 트는 것으로 소비 행동에 대한 음악의 이러한 효과를 활용할 수 있다. ⑤ 이 길은 여러분이 고객들로 하여금 그리로 걷기를 바라는 경로로 상점 안 여기저기를 통해 입구에서부터 계산대까지 고객들을 내내 이끈다.

Why? 왜 정답일까?

①, ②, ③, ⑤는 고객들이 상점을 완전히 둘러볼 수 있도록 중앙 통로를 두라는 내용을 다루고 있는 반면, ④는 음악을 활용하라는 내용을 다루고 있다. 따라서 전체 흐름과 관계 없는 문장은 ④이다.

- **point out** ~을 가리키다, 지적하다
- **drag** v 끌다
- **checkout** n 계산대, 체크아웃
- **particularly** ad 특히
- **entrance** n 입구

구문 풀이

1행 Wouldn't it be nice if you could take your customers by the hand and
「would + 주어 + 동사원형 ~ if + 주어 + could + 동사원형」
guide each one through your store / while pointing out all the great products [you
동사원형2 : 가정법 과거 / 분사구문(~하는 동안)
would like them to consider buying]?
「would like + 목적어 + to부정사 : ~이 …하기를 원하다」

36 작은 요구를 먼저 한 후 큰 요구를 제시하는 설득의 기술 　　정답률 64% | 정답 ②

주어진 글 다음에 이어질 글의 순서로 가장 적절한 것을 고르시오.
① (A) - (C) - (B)
② (B) - (A) - (C) ✓
③ (B) - (C) - (A)
④ (C) - (A) - (B)
⑤ (C) - (B) - (A)

Making a small request / that people will accept / will naturally increase the chances / of their accepting a bigger request afterwards.
작은 요구를 하는 것은 / 사람들이 수락할 / 가능성을 자연스럽게 증가시킬 것이다. / 나중에 그들이 더 큰 요구를 수락할

(B) For instance, / a salesperson might request you to sign a petition / to prevent cruelty against animals.
예를 들어 / 한 판매원이 여러분에게 청원서에 서명하도록 요구할지도 모른다. / 동물들에 대한 잔인함을 막기 위한

This is a very small request, / and most people will do what the salesperson asks.
이것은 아주 작은 요구이고 / 대부분의 사람들은 판매원이 요구하는 바를 할 것이다.

(A) After this, the salesperson asks you / if you are interested / in buying any cruelty-free cosmetics from their store.
그 이후에 판매원은 여러분에게 물어본다. / 여러분이 관심이 있는지를 / 잔인함을 가하지 않은 어떤 화장품을 자신의 매장에서 사는 것에

Given the fact / that most people agree to the prior request / to sign the petition, / they will be more likely to purchase the cosmetics.
사실을 고려하면 / 이전 요구에 사람들이 동의한다는 / 청원서에 서명해 달라는 / 그들이 화장품을 구매할 가능성이 더 높을 것이다.

(C) They make such purchases / because the salesperson takes advantage of a human tendency / to be consistent in their words and actions.
그들은 그러한 구매를 한다. / 그 판매원이 인간의 경향을 이용하기 때문에 / 자기 말과 행동에 있어 일관되고자 하는

People want to be consistent / and will keep saying yes / if they have already said it once.
사람들은 일관되기를 원하며 / 계속 예라고 말할 것이다. / 만약 자신이 이미 한번 그렇게 말했다면

사람들이 수락할 작은 요구를 하는 것은 나중에 그들이 더 큰 요구를 수락할 가능성을 자연스럽게 증가시킬 것이다.
(B) 예를 들어 한 판매원이 여러분에게 동물들에 대한 잔인함을 막기 위한 청원서에 서명하도록 요구할지도 모른다. 이것은 아주 작은 요구이고 대부분의 사람들은 판매원이 요구하는 바를 할 것이다.
(A) 그 이후에 판매원은 여러분에게 (동물들에게) 잔인함을 가하지 않은 어떤 화장품을 자신의 매장에서 사는 것에 관심이 있는지를 물어본다. 청원서에 서명해 달라는 이전 요구에 사람들이 동의한다는 사실을 고려하면 그들이 화장품을 구매할 가능성이 더 높을 것이다.
(C) 그 판매원이 자기 말과 행동에 있어 일관되고자 하는 인간의 경향을 이용하기 때문에 그들은 그러한 구매를 한다. 사람들은 일관되기를 원하며 만약 자신이 이미 한번 그렇게 말했다면 계속 예라고 말할 것이다.

Why? 왜 정답일까?

작은 요구를 먼저 한 후 큰 요구를 제시하면 사람들이 큰 요구를 수용할 가능성이 높아질 수 있다고 언급한 주어진 글 뒤에는, 판매원이 먼저 동물 학대에 반대하는 청원서를 작성해달라고 부탁하는 예를 제시하는 (B), 이후에 판매원이 동물에게 해를 가하지 않은 화장품 구매를 권유한다는 내용의 (A), 이 경우 사람들이 화장품 구매까지 하게 될 가능성이 높아지는 이유를 설명하는 (C)가 차례로 이어지는 것이 자연스럽다. 따라서 글의 순서로 가장 적절한 것은 ② '(B) - (A) - (C)'이다.

- **cruelty** n 잔인함
- **consistent** a 일관적인
- **take advantage of** ~을 이용하다

구문 풀이

1행 Making a small request [that people will accept] will naturally increase
동명사구 주어 / 선행사 / 동사구
the chances of their accepting a bigger request afterwards.
의미상 주어 / 동명사(of의 목적어)

4행 Given the fact [that most people agree to the prior request to sign the
~을 고려할 때 / 목적어 / 동격 접속사 / ~에 동의하다
petition], they will be more likely to purchase the cosmetics.

37 색상이 무게에 대한 인식에 미치는 영향 　　정답률 42% | 정답 ⑤

주어진 글 다음에 이어질 글의 순서로 가장 적절한 것을 고르시오.
① (A) - (C) - (B)
② (B) - (A) - (C)

[문제편 p.216]

③ (B) − (C) − (A)   ④ (C) − (A) − (B)

✓⑤ (C) − (B) − (A)

Color can impact / how you perceive weight.
색상은 영향을 줄 수 있다. / 여러분이 무게를 인식하는 방식에

Dark colors look heavy, / and bright colors look less so.
어두운 색은 무거워 보이고, / 밝은 색은 덜 그렇게 보인다.

Interior designers often paint darker colors / below brighter colors / to put the viewer at ease.
실내 디자이너들은 종종 더 어두운 색을 칠한다. / 더 밝은 색 아래에 / 보는 사람을 편안하게 해 주기 위해

(C) Product displays work the same way.
상품 전시도 같은 방식으로 작동한다.

Place bright-colored products higher / and dark-colored products lower, / given that they are of similar size.
밝은 색의 상품을 더 높이 배치하라. / 어두운 색의 상품을 더 낮게 / 상품들이 비슷한 크기라면

This will look more stable / and allow customers to comfortably browse the products / from top to bottom.
이것은 더 안정적으로 보이고 / 고객이 편안하게 상품을 훑어볼 수 있도록 해 준다. / 위에서 아래로

(B) In contrast, / shelving dark-colored products on top / can create the illusion / that they might fall over, / which can be a source of anxiety for some shoppers.
반대로 / 어두운 색의 상품을 선반 맨 위에 두는 것은 / 착각을 불러일으킬 수 있으며, / 상품들이 떨어질 수 있다는 / 이것은 일부 구매자들에게 불안감의 원인이 될 수 있다.

Black and white, / which have a brightness of 0% and 100%, respectively, / show the most dramatic difference / in perceived weight.
검은색과 흰색은 / 명도가 각각 0%와 100%인 / 가장 극적인 차이를 보여준다. / 인식된 무게의

(A) In fact, / black is perceived / to be twice as heavy as white.
사실, / 검은색은 인식된다. / 흰색보다 두 배 무겁게

Carrying the same product in a black shopping bag, / versus a white one, / feels heavier.
같은 상품을 검은색 쇼핑백에 담아 드는 것이 / 흰색 쇼핑백보다 / 더 무겁게 느껴진다.

So, / small but expensive products / like neckties and accessories / are often sold / in dark-colored shopping bags or cases.
따라서 / 작지만 값비싼 상품들은 / 넥타이와 액세서리와 같이 / 대체로 판매된다. / 어두운 색의 쇼핑백 또는 케이스에 담겨

색상은 여러분이 무게를 인식하는 방식에 영향을 줄 수 있다. 어두운 색은 무거워 보이고, 밝은 색은 덜 그렇게 보인다. 실내 디자이너들은 보는 사람을 편안하게 해 주기 위해 종종 더 밝은 색 아래에 더 어두운 색을 칠한다.

(C) 상품 전시도 같은 방식으로 작용한다. 상품들이 비슷한 크기라면, 밝은 색의 상품을 더 높이, 어두운 색의 상품을 더 낮게 배치하라. 이것은 더 안정적으로 보이고 고객이 편안하게 상품들을 위에서 아래로 훑어볼 수 있도록 해 준다.

(B) 반대로 어두운 색의 상품을 선반 맨 위에 두는 것은 상품들이 떨어질 수 있다는 착각을 불러일으킬 수 있으며, 이것은 일부 구매자들에게 불안감의 원인이 될 수 있다. 명도가 각각 0%와 100%인 검은색과 흰색은 인식된 무게의 가장 극적인 차이를 보여준다.

(A) 사실, 검은색은 흰색보다 두 배 무겁게 인식된다. 같은 상품을 흰색 쇼핑백보다 검은색 쇼핑백에 담아 드는 것이 더 무겁게 느껴진다. 따라서 넥타이와 액세서리와 같이 작지만 값비싼 상품들은 대체로 어두운 색의 쇼핑백 또는 케이스에 담겨 판매된다.

Why? 왜 정답일까?

색상이 무게를 인식하는 데 영향을 미칠 수 있다고 말하며 실내 디자이너들이 이러한 사실을 활용하고 있다는 내용의 주어진 글 뒤에는, 상품 전시에서도 같은 사실을 활용하여 어두운 색의 상품을 더 낮게 배치하는 예를 언급하는 (C), 어두운 상품을 위에 두는 경우를 대조하며 선명한 검은색과 흰색이 가장 극적인 차이를 보일 수 있다는 내용을 이어서 언급하는 (B), 흑백의 무게감 대비와 관련된 사례를 드는 (A)가 차례로 연결되어야 자연스럽다. 따라서 글의 순서로 가장 적절한 것은 ⑤ '(C) − (B) − (A)'이다.

- impact ⓥ 영향을 주다 ⓝ 영향
- at ease 편안한, 걱정 없는
- illusion ⓝ 착각, 환상
- brightness ⓝ 명도, 밝음
- dramatic ⓐ 극적인
- browse ⓥ 훑어보다, 둘러보다
- perceive ⓥ 인식하다, 인지하다
- shelve ⓥ 선반에 얹다
- anxiety ⓝ 불안, 염려, 걱정거리
- respectively ⓐⓓ 각각
- stable ⓐ 안정적인

구문 풀이

9행 In contrast, / shelving dark-colored products on top can create the
            동명사구 주어   동사
illusion {that they might fall over}, which can be a source of anxiety for some
         { }: the illusion과 동격   계속적 용법(= the illusion)
shoppers.

---

38 무대에서 관객을 집중시키는 방법   정답률 58% | 정답 ③

글의 흐름으로 보아, 주어진 문장이 들어가기에 가장 적절한 곳을 고르시오.

Achieving focus in a movie is easy.
영화에서 (관객의) 집중을 얻기는 쉽다.

Directors can simply point the camera / at whatever they want the audience to look at.
감독은 단지 카메라를 향하게 하면 된다. / 자신이 관객으로 하여금 바라보기를 원하는 어떤 것에든

① Close-ups and slow camera shots / can emphasize a killer's hand / or a character's brief glance of guilt.
근접 촬영과 느린 카메라 촬영이 / 살인자의 손을 강조할 수 있다. / 또는 등장인물의 짧은 죄책감의 눈짓

② On stage, focus is much more difficult / because the audience is free to look / wherever they like.
무대 위에서는 (관객의) 집중이 훨씬 더 어려운 일이다. / 관객이 자유롭게 볼 수 있기 때문에 / 자신이 원하는 어느 곳이든

✓The stage director must gain the audience's attention / and direct their eyes to a particular spot or actor.
무대 감독은 관객의 주의를 얻고 / 그들의 시선을 특정한 장소나 배우로 향하게 해야 한다.

This can be done / through lighting, costumes, scenery, voice, and movements.
이것은 이루어질 수 있다. / 조명, 의상, 배경, 목소리, 움직임을 통해

④ Focus can be gained / by simply putting a spotlight on one actor, / by having one actor in red and everyone else in gray, / or by having one actor move / while the others remain still.
집중은 얻어질 수 있다. / 단지 한 명의 배우에게 스포트라이트를 비추거나, / 한 명의 배우는 빨간색으로 입히고 다른 모든 배우들은 회색으로 입히거나, / 한 명의 배우는 움직이게 함으로써 / 다른 배우들이 가만히 있는 동안

⑤ All these techniques / will quickly draw the audience's attention to the actor / whom the director wants to be in focus.
이러한 모든 기법들은 / 관객의 주의를 배우 쪽으로 빠르게 끌 것이다. / 감독이 (관객의) 집중 안에 들기를 원하는

영화에서 (관객의) 집중을 얻기는 쉽다. 감독은 자신이 관객으로 하여금 바라보기를 원하는 어떤 것에든 단지 카메라를 향하게 하면 된다. ① 근접 촬영과 느린 카메라 촬영이 살인자의 손이나 등장인물의 짧은 죄책감의 눈짓을 강조할 수 있다. ② 무대 위에서는 관객이 자신이 원하는 어느 곳이든 자유롭게 볼 수 있기 때문에 (관객의) 집중이 훨씬 더 어려운 일이다. ③ 무대 감독은 관객의 주의를 얻고 그들의 시선을 특정한 장소나 배우로 향하게 할 수 있다. 이것은 조명, 의상, 배경, 목소리, 움직임을 통해 이루어질 수 있다. ④ (관객의) 집중은 단지 한 명의 배우에게 스포트라이트를 비추거나, 한 명의 배우는 빨간색으로 입히고 다른 모든 배우들은 회색으로 입히거나, 다른 배우들이 가만히 있는 동안 한 명의 배우는 움직이게 함으로써 얻어질 수 있다. ⑤ 이러한 모든 기법들은 감독이 (관객의) 집중 안에 들기를 원하는 배우 쪽으로 관객의 주의를 빠르게 끌 것이다.

Why? 왜 정답일까?

③ 앞에서 무대 위에서는 관객을 집중시키기가 더 어렵다고 언급한 데 이어, 주어진 문장은 '무대 감독'이 관객의 주의를 끌어 특정한 방향으로 시선을 향하게 해야 한다고 설명한다. ③ 뒤의 문장은 주어진 문장의 내용을 This로 가리키며, 관객의 주의를 얻기 위해서는 조명, 의상, 배경, 목소리, 움직임 등이 동원될 수 있다고 한다. 따라서 주어진 문장이 들어가기에 가장 적절한 곳은 ③이다.

- emphasize ⓥ 강조하다
- guilt ⓝ 죄책감
- glance ⓝ 흘긋 봄
- draw A's attention to B A의 관심을 B로 돌리다

구문 풀이

3행 Directors can simply point the camera at whatever they want the audience
                                              복합관계대명사   「want + 목적어 + to부정사 :
to look at.   ~이 …하기를 원하다
                                              (= anything that)

12행 All these techniques will quickly draw the audience's attention to the actor
        → 목적격 관계대명사   선행사
[whom the director wants to be in focus].
    주어   동사   목적격 보어

★★★ 등급을 가르는 문제!

39 공동체 형성 방식으로서의 토론   정답률 24% | 정답 ⑤

글의 흐름으로 보아, 주어진 문장이 들어가기에 가장 적절한 곳을 고르시오.

The way we communicate / influences our ability / to build strong and healthy communities.
우리가 의사소통하는 방식은 / 우리의 능력에 영향을 미친다. / 강하고 건강한 공동체를 만드는

Traditional ways of building communities / have emphasized debate and argument.
공동체를 만드는 전통적인 방식은 / 토론과 논쟁을 강조해왔다.

① For example, / the United States has a strong tradition / of using town hall meetings / to deliberate important issues within communities.
예를 들어, / 미국은 확고한 전통을 갖고 있다. / 타운홀 미팅을 활용하는 / 공동체 내의 중요한 쟁점들을 숙고하기 위해

② In these settings, / advocates for each side of the issue / present arguments for their positions, / and public issues have been discussed / in such public forums.
이러한 환경에서 / 쟁점의 각 입장에 있는 옹호자들이 / 자신의 입장에 대한 논거를 제시하고, / 공공의 쟁점들이 논의되었다. / 그러한 공개적인 토론회에서

③ Yet for debate and argument to work well, / people need to come to such forums / with similar assumptions and values.
그러나 토론과 논쟁이 효력을 잘 발휘하기 위해서는 / 사람들이 그러한 토론회에 올 필요가 있다. / 비슷한 가정과 가치를 가지고

④ The shared assumptions and values / serve as a foundation for the discussion.
공유된 가정과 가치가 / 논의를 위한 기반의 역할을 한다.

✓However, / as society becomes more diverse, / the likelihood / that people share assumptions and values / diminishes.
하지만 / 사회가 더욱 다양해짐에 따라, / 가능성은 / 사람들이 가정과 가치를 공유할 / 줄어든다.

As a result, / forms of communication / such as argument and debate / become polarized, / which may drive communities apart / as opposed to bringing them together.
결과적으로 / 의사소통의 형태는 / 논쟁과 토론 같은 / 양극화되고, / 이것은 멀어지도록 몰아갈 수 있다. / 공동체를 결합하는 것이 아니라

우리가 의사소통하는 방식은 강하고 건강한 공동체를 만드는 우리의 능력에 영향을 미친다. 공동체를 만드는 전통적인 방식은 토론과 논쟁을 강조해왔다. ① 예를 들어, 미국은 공동체 내의 중요한 쟁점들을 숙고하기 위해 타운홀 미팅을 활용하는 확고한 전통을 갖고 있다. ② 이러한 환경에서 쟁점의 각 입장에 있는 옹호자들이 자신의 입장에 대한 논거를 제시하고, 공공의 쟁점들이 그러한 공개적인 토론회에서 논의되었다. ③ 그러나 토론과 논쟁이 효력을 잘 발휘하기 위해서는 사람들이 비슷한 가정과 가치를 가지고 그러한 토론회에 올 필요가 있다. ④ 공유된 가정과 가치가 논의를 위한 기반의 역할을 한다. ⑤ 하지만 사회가 더욱 다양해짐에 따라, 사람들이 가정과 가치를 공유할 가능성은 줄어든다. 결과적으로 논쟁과 토론 같은 의사소통의 형태는 양극화되고, 이것은 공동체를 결합하는 것이 아니라 멀어지도록 몰아갈 수 있다.

Why? 왜 정답일까?

공동체를 형성하는 방식으로서 토론과 논쟁의 역할에 대해 설명한 글로, ⑤ 앞에서는 공유된 가정과 가치가 그 기반을 이룰 때 토론이 제대로 기능할 수 있다는 점을 언급하는데 ⑤ 뒤에서는 이로 인해 의사소통이 양극화된 형태로 나타날 수 있다는 내용이 나온다. However로 시작하는 주어진 문장은 사회의 다양화로 공유된 가치나 가정을 가질 가능성이 줄어든다는 내용이므로 흐름이 반전되는 ⑤에 들어가는 것이 자연스럽다. 따라서 주어진 문장이 들어가기에 가장 적절한 곳은 ⑤이다.

- diverse ⓐ 다양한
- assumption ⓝ 가정, 추정
- emphasize ⓥ 강조하다
- advocate ⓝ 옹호자
- polarize ⓥ 양극화를 초래하다, 양극화되다
- as opposed to ~이 아니라, ~와는 대조적으로
- likelihood ⓝ 가능성
- diminish ⓥ 줄어들다, 감소하다
- deliberate ⓥ 숙고하다, 신중히 생각하다
- serve as ~의 역할을 하다, ~로 기능하다
- drive apart ~을 멀어지게 하다, 소원하게 하다

13행 As a result, forms of communication such as argument and debate
주어(복수)
become polarized, which may drive communities apart as opposed to bringing
동사 주격 보어 계속적 용법(앞의 절) ~을 멀어지게 하다 'as opposed to+동명사 : ~이 아니라,'
them together.

★★ 문제 해결 꿀~팁 ★★

▶ 많이 틀린 이유는?
토론의 공동체 형성 기능을 다룬 추상적인 지문으로, 논리적 공백에 주목하지 않으면 오답을 고르기 쉽다. 최다 오답인 ④ 앞면의 문장은 '비슷한 가정과 가치관'을 공통된 소재로 다루며, 서로 가정과 가치관이 공유되어야 이것이 건전한 토론의 기반 역할을 할 수 있다는 일관된 내용을 전개하고 있다. 즉 ④는 논리적 공백이 발생하는 지점이 아니므로 주어진 문장이 들어가기에 적절치 않다.

▶ 문제 해결 방법은?
문장 삽입 문제에서는 항상 주어진 문장을 먼저 읽고 글의 흐름을 예상하도록 한다. 주어진 문장에 However가 있으므로, 앞에는 공유된 가치나 가치관이 비교적 정립된 경우가 언급될 것이고, 뒤에는 이 정립이 잘 이루어지지 않아 공동체 의사소통이 원활하지 않다는 내용이 연결될 것이다.

---

40 동일한 할인액에 대한 인식을 좌우하는 요인 | 정답률 51% | 정답 ④

다음 글의 내용을 한 문장으로 요약하고자 한다. 빈칸 (A), (B)에 들어갈 말로 가장 적절한 것은?

	(A)		(B)		(A)		(B)
①	absolute 절대적인	·····	modify 수정하다	②	absolute 절대적인	·····	express 표현하다
③	identical 동일한	·····	produce 만들어내다	✔④	relative 상대적인	·····	perceive 인식하다
⑤	relative 상대적인	·····	advertise 광고하다				

The perception of the same amount of discount on a product / depends on its relation to the initial price.
상품의 똑같은 할인액에 대한 인식은 / 그것의 최초 가격과의 관계에 달려있다.

In one study, / respondents were presented with a purchase situation.
한 연구에서, / 응답자들은 어떤 구매 상황을 제시받았다.

The persons put in the situation of buying a calculator / that cost $15 / found out from the vendor / that the same product was available / in a different store 20 minutes away / and at a promotional price of $10.
계산기를 사는 상황에 놓인 사람들이 / 15달러 가격의 / 판매자로부터 알게 되었다. / 같은 제품이 이용 가능하다는 것을 / 20분 떨어진 다른 상점에서 / 10달러의 판촉가에

In this case, 68% of respondents / decided to make their way down to the store / in order to save $5.
이 경우 응답자의 68%가 / 그 가게까지 가기로 결심했다. / 5달러를 절약하기 위해

In the second condition, / which involved buying a jacket for $125, / the respondents were also told / that the same product was available / in a store 20 minutes away / and cost $120 there.
두 번째 상황에서, / 이는 125달러짜리 재킷을 사는 것과 관련 있었는데, / 응답자들은 또한 들었다. / 같은 제품이 이용 가능하고 / 20분 떨어진 상점에서 / 그곳에서는 120달러라고

This time, only 29% of the persons said / that they would get the cheaper jacket.
이번에는 단지 사람들의 29%만이 말했다. / 그들이 더 저렴한 재킷을 살 것이라고

In both cases, the product was $5 cheaper, / but in the first case, the amount was 1/3 of the price, / and in the second, it was 1/25 of the price.
두 경우 모두 제품은 5달러 더 저렴했으나, / 첫 번째의 경우 그 액수가 가격의 3분의 1이었고, / 두 번째의 경우 그것은 가격의 25분의 1이었다.

What differed in both of these situations / was the price context of the purchase.
이 두 상황 모두에서 달랐던 것은 / 구매의 가격 맥락이었다.

➡ When the same amount of discount is given / in a purchasing situation, / the (A) relative value of the discount / affects how people (B) perceive its value.
동일한 정도의 할인액이 주어질 때, / 구매 상황에서 / 그 할인의 상대적인 가치가 / 사람들이 그 가치를 어떻게 인식하는지에 영향을 미친다.

상품의 똑같은 할인액에 대한 인식은 그것의 최초 가격과의 관계에 달려있다. 한 연구에서, 응답자들은 어떤 구매 상황을 제시받았다. 15달러 가격의 계산기를 사는 상황에 놓인 사람들이 같은 제품을 20분 떨어진 다른 상점에서 10달러의 판촉가에 살 수 있다는 것을 판매자로부터 알게 되었다. 이 경우 응답자의 68%가 5달러를 절약하기 위해 그 가게까지 가기로 결심했다. 두 번째 상황에서, 이는 125달러짜리 재킷을 사는 것과 관련 있었는데, 응답자들은 또한 같은 제품을 20분 떨어진 상점에서 살 수 있고 그곳에서는 120달러라고 들었다. 이번에는 단지 사람들의 29%만이 더 저렴한 재킷을 살 것이라고 말했다. 두 경우 모두 제품은 5달러 더 저렴했으나, 첫 번째의 경우 그 액수가 가격의 3분의 1이었고, 두 번째의 경우 그것은 가격의 25분의 1이었다. 이 두 상황 모두에서 달랐던 것은 구매의 가격 맥락이었다.

➡ 구매 상황에서 동일한 정도의 할인액이 주어질 때, 그 할인의 (A) 상대적인 가치가 사람들이 그 가치를 어떻게 (B) 인식하는지에 영향을 미친다.

Why? 왜 정답일까?
첫 문장에서 똑같은 할인액에 대한 인식도 최초 가격에 따라 달라질 수 있다(The perception of the same amount of discount on a product depends on its relation to the initial price.)는 주제가 제시되는 것으로 보아, 요약문의 (A)와 (B)에 들어갈 말로 가장 적절한 것은 ④ '(A) relative(상대적인), (B) perceive(인식하다)'이다.

- perception ⓝ 인식
- be presented with ⓥ ~을 제시받다
- promotional ⓐ 판촉의, 홍보의
- absolute ⓐ 절대적인
- initial ⓐ 최초의
- calculator ⓝ 계산기
- differ ⓥ 다르다
- identical ⓐ 동일한

3행 The persons [put in the situation of buying a calculator {that cost $15}]
주어 과거분사 선행사 주격 관계대명사
found out from the vendor {that the same product was available in a different
동사 전명구(삽입) 접속사(~것)
store 20 minutes away and at a promotional price of $10}. { } : 목적어

41-42 주머니고양이의 모방 본능

Behavioral ecologists have observed clever copying behavior / among many of our close animal relatives.
행동 생태학자들이 영리한 모방 행동을 관찰해 왔다. / 우리와 가까운 다수의 동류 동물에게서

One example was uncovered by behavioral ecologists / studying the behavior of a small Australian animal / called the quoll.
한 예가 행동 생태학자들에 의해 발견되었다. / 작은 호주 동물의 행동을 연구하는 / 주머니고양이라고 불리는

Its survival was being (a) threatened by the cane toad, / an invasive species / introduced to Australia in the 1930s.
이들의 생존은 수수두꺼비에 의해 위협받고 있었다. / 외래종인 / 1930년대에 호주에 도입된

To a quoll, these toads look as tasty / as they are (b) poisonous, / and the quolls who ate them / suffered fatal consequences at a speedy rate.
주머니고양이에게 이 두꺼비들은 먹음직스러워 보이며 / 독성이 있는 만큼이나 / 그들을 먹은 주머니고양이는 / 빠른 속도로 치명적인 결과를 겪었다.

Behavioral ecologists identified a clever solution / by using quolls' instincts to imitate.
행동 생태학자들은 영리한 해결책을 찾아냈다. / 주머니고양이의 모방하는 본능을 이용하여

Scientists fed small groups of quolls toad sausages / containing harmless but nausea-inducing chemicals, / conditioning them to (c) avoid the toads.
과학자들은 주머니고양이 소집단에게 두꺼비 소시지를 먹여 / 무해하지만 메스꺼움을 유발하는 화학 물질을 함유한 / 그들이 두꺼비를 피하도록 조건화했다.

Groups of these 'toad-smart' quolls / were then released back into the wild: / they taught their own offspring what they'd learned.
이러한 '두꺼비에 대해 똑똑해진' 주머니고양이 집단은 / 그 후 야생으로 다시 방출되었고 / 그들은 자신이 배운 것을 자기 새끼들에게 가르쳤다.

Other quolls copied these (d) constructive behaviors / through a process of social learning.
다른 주머니고양이들은 이러한 건설적인 행동들을 모방했다. / 사회적 학습의 과정을 통해 42번의 근거

『As each baby quoll learned / to keep away from the hazardous toads,』 / the chances of the survival of the whole quoll species / — and not just that of each individual quoll — / were (e) improved.
각각의 새끼 주머니고양이가 배웠으므로, / 위험한 두꺼비를 피하는 법을 / 전체 주머니고양이 종의 생존 확률이 / 개별 주머니고양이 각각의 생존 확률 뿐만 아니라 / 높아졌다.

『The quolls were saved / via minimal human interference / because ecologists were able to take advantage of quolls' natural imitative instincts.』 41번의 근거
주머니고양이는 구해졌는데, / 최소한의 인간의 개입을 통해 / 왜냐하면 생태학자들이 주머니고양이의 타고난 모방 본능을 이용할 수 있었기 때문이다.

행동 생태학자들이 우리와 가까운 다수의 동류 동물에게서 영리한 모방 행동을 관찰해 왔다. 한 예가 주머니고양이라고 불리는 작은 호주 동물의 행동을 연구하는 행동 생태학자들에 의해 발견되었다. 이들의 생존은 1930년대에 호주에 도입된 외래종인 수수두꺼비에 의해 (a) 위협받고 있었다. 주머니고양이에게 이 두꺼비들은 (b) 독성이 있는 만큼이나 먹음직스러워 보이며 그들을 먹은 주머니고양이는 빠른 속도로 치명적인 결과를 겪었다. 행동 생태학자들은 주머니고양이의 모방하는 본능을 이용하여 영리한 해결책을 찾아냈다. 과학자들은 주머니고양이 소집단에게 무해하지만 메스꺼움을 유발하는 화학 물질을 함유한 두꺼비 소시지를 먹여 그들이 두꺼비를 (c) 피하도록 조건화했다. 이러한 '두꺼비에 대해 똑똑해진' 주머니고양이 집단은 그 후 야생으로 다시 방출되었고 자신이 배운 것을 자기 새끼들에게 가르쳤다. 다른 주머니고양이들은 사회적 학습의 과정을 통해 이러한 (d) 건설적인 행동들을 모방했다. 각각의 새끼 주머니고양이가 위험한 두꺼비를 피하는 법을 배웠으므로, 개별 주머니고양이 각각의 생존 확률뿐만 아니라 전체 주머니고양이 종의 생존 확률이 (e) 줄어들었다(→ 높아졌다). 주머니고양이는 최소한의 인간의 개입을 통해 구해졌는데, 왜냐하면 생태학자들이 주머니고양이의 타고난 모방 본능을 이용할 수 있었기 때문이었다.

- ecologist ⓝ 생태학자
- threaten ⓥ 위협하다
- introduce ⓥ 도입하다
- consequence ⓝ 결과
- instinct ⓝ 본능
- induce ⓥ 유발하다
- constructive ⓐ 건설적인
- interference ⓝ 개입, 간섭
- precisely [ad] 정확히
- uncover ⓥ 밝히다
- invasive ⓐ 침입의
- fatal ⓐ 치명적인
- identify ⓥ 찾아내다, 확인하다
- harmless ⓐ 무해한
- offspring ⓝ 자손
- hazardous ⓐ 위험한
- take advantage of ⓥ ~을 이용하다

6행 To a quoll, these toads look as tasty as they are poisonous, and the quolls
'as+원급+as : ~만큼 ~한' 주어(선행사)
[who ate them] suffered fatal consequences at a speedy rate.
=toads 타동사(~을 겪다) 목적어

---

41 제목 파악 | 정답률 56% | 정답 ①

윗글의 제목으로 가장 적절한 것은?

✔① Imitative Instinct as a Key to Survival for Animals – 동물에게 있어 생존의 열쇠인 모방 본능
② Copy Quickly and Precisely to Be Productive – 생산적이 되려면 빠르고 정확하게 복제하라
③ How to Stop the Spread of Invasive Species – 침입종의 확산을 막는 방법
④ The Role of Threats in Animal Cooperation – 동물 협력에 있어 위협의 역할
⑤ Ideal Habitats for Diverse Wildlife – 다양한 야생동물에게 이상적인 서식지

Why? 왜 정답일까?
예시의 결론을 말하는 마지막 문장에서 주머니고양이들이 인간의 최소 개입으로도 살아남을 수 있었던 까닭은 특유의 모방 본능 덕분이었다고 언급하는 것으로 볼 때, 글의 제목으로 가장 적절한 것은 ① '동물에게 있어 생존의 열쇠인 모방 본능'이다.

---

42 어휘 추론 | 정답률 46% | 정답 ⑤

밑줄 친 (a) ~ (e) 중에서 문맥상 낱말의 쓰임이 적절하지 않은 것은? [3점]
① (a) ② (b) ③ (c) ④ (d) ✔⑤ (e)

(e)가 포함된 문장의 As절에서 모방 본능을 통해 새끼 주머니고양이들이 위험한 두꺼비를 피하도록 학습했다는 내용이 나오는 것으로 보아, 각각의 주머니고양이뿐 아니라 종 전체의 생존 확률이 '올라갔다'는 결론이 뒤따라야 한다. 따라서 (e)의 reduced를 improved로 고쳐야 한다. 문맥상 낱말의 쓰임이 적절하지 않은 것은 ⑤ '(e)'이다.

43-45 노인의 자전거를 수리한 Rangan

(A)

Rangan opened his cycle shop / early in the morning.
Rangan은 자신의 자전거 가게를 열었다. / 아침 일찍

「Yesterday he could not attend to business / as he was laid up with high fever,」 but today he made it up to the shop / to earn money for his family. 45번 ①의 근거 일치
어제 그는 일을 볼 수 없었지만, / 고열로 몸져누워 있었기 때문에 / 오늘 그는 가게에 나왔다. / 자신의 가족을 위해 돈을 벌려고

Shouting to the tea boy in the next shop / for a strong cup of tea, / (a) he lined up all the bicycles to be repaired outside.
옆 가게의 차 심부름 소년을 부르며, / 진한 차 한 잔을 위해 / 그는 수리해야 할 모든 자전거를 밖에 줄 세워 놓았다.

He took a sip of the tea, / thinking about the order / in which he had to go ahead with his job.
그는 차를 한 모금 마시고, / 순서에 대해서 생각했다. / 일을 해야 할

(D)

Rangan's thoughts were disturbed by an old man / walking with his bicycle towards his shop.
Rangan의 생각은 한 노인에 의해 방해를 받았다. / 자전거를 가지고 자신의 가게를 향해 걸어오는

「The old man was wearing an old turban on his head.」 45번 ⑤의 근거 일치
그 노인은 머리에 오래된 터번을 쓰고 있었다.

His hands and face were covered in wrinkles.
그의 손과 얼굴은 주름으로 덮여 있었다.

In a gloomy tone, / (e) he said, / "Would you please replace the tire? / I'll pay you this evening."
침울한 목소리로, / 그는 말했다. / "타이어를 교체해 주시겠어요? / 제가 저녁에 돈을 지불하겠습니다."라고

Feeling sympathy for him, / Rangan fixed the bicycle.
그에게 동정심을 느껴 / Rangan은 자전거를 고쳤다.

He even treated the old man to a cup of tea.
그는 심지어 그 노인에게 차 한 잔을 대접했다.

The old man thanked Rangan / and left.
그 노인은 Rangan에게 고마워하며 / 떠났다.

(B)

Rangan worked hard / to finish what he had to do.
Rangan은 열심히 일했다. / 그가 해야 하는 것을 끝내기 위해

It was already late evening / but there was no sign of the old man.
벌써 늦은 저녁이 되었지만 / 노인이 올 기미가 없었다.

Doubts filled (b) him.
의심이 그를 가득 채웠다.

What if the old man does not return with the money?
만약에 그 노인이 돈을 가지고 돌아오지 않는다면 어쩌지?

「He regretted / fixing up the old man's bicycle.」 45번 ②의 근거 일치
그는 후회했다. / 그 노인의 자전거를 수리한 것을

Suddenly (c) he lost all hope / and he could wait no longer.
갑자기 그는 모든 희망을 잃었고 / 더 이상 기다릴 수 없었다.

「He locked up his shop later than usual, / and cursed himself / for getting tricked by an old man.」 45번 ③의 근거 일치
그는 자신의 가게를 평소보다 늦게 닫았다. / 스스로를 비난했다. / 노인에게 속았다며

(C)

At home, / Rangan was confused.
집에서 / Rangan은 심란했다.

「Washing his greasy hands, / he heard a knock at his door.」
기름투성이인 손을 씻을 때 / 그는 문을 두드리는 소리를 들었다.

It was the old man and the tea boy.」 45번 ④의 근거 불일치
그 노인과 차 심부름 소년이었다.

The old man said, / "Your shop was closed / when I returned.
그 노인이 말했다. / "당신의 가게는 닫혀 있더군요. / 제가 돌아왔을 때

Luckily, / I saw this boy in front of the shop."
다행히 / 저는 가게 앞에서 이 소년을 만났어요."

Handing over the money to Rangan, / he continued, / "Thanks for your hospitality."
Rangan에게 돈을 건네주면서 / 그는 이어 말했다. / "당신의 호의에 감사합니다."라고

Rangan grinned at the kind words / the old man spoke to (d) him.
Rangan은 그 친절한 말에 씁쓸하게 웃었다. / 노인이 그에게 건넨

The fact / that he had suspected the old man / pained his heart.
사실이 / 그 노인을 의심했다는 / 그의 마음을 아프게 했다.

(A)

Rangan은 아침 일찍 자신의 자전거 가게를 열었다. 어제 그는 고열로 몸져누워 있었기 때문에 일을 할 수 없었지만, 오늘 그는 자신의 가족을 위해 돈을 벌려고 가게에 나왔다. 진한 차 한 잔을 위해 옆 가게의 차 심부름 소년을 부르며, (a) 그는 수리해야 할 모든 자전거를 밖에 줄 세워 놓았다. 그는 차를 한 모금 마시며 일을 해야 할 순서에 대해서 생각했다.

(D)

Rangan의 생각은 자전거를 가지고 자신의 가게를 향해 걸어오는 한 노인에 의해 방해를 받았다. 그 노인은 머리에 오래된 터번을 쓰고 있었다. 그의 손과 얼굴은 주름으로 덮여 있었다. 침울한 목소리로, (e) 그는 "타이어를 교체해 주시겠어요? 제가 저녁에 돈을 지불하겠습니다."라고 말했다. 그에게 동정심을 느껴 Rangan은 자전거를 고쳤다. 그는 심지어 그 노인에게 차 한 잔을 대접했다. 그 노인은 Rangan에게 고마워하며 떠났다.

(B)

Rangan은 그가 해야 하는 것을 끝내기 위해 열심히 일했다. 벌써 늦은 저녁이 되었지만 노인이 올 기미가 없었다. 의심이 (b) 그를 가득 채웠다. 만약에 그 노인이 돈을 가지고 돌아오지 않는다면 어쩌지? 그는 그 노인의 자전거를 수리한 것을 후회했다. 갑자기 (c) 그는 모든 희망을 잃었고 더 이상 기다릴 수 없었다. 그는 자신의 가게를 평소보다 늦게 닫았고 노인에게 속았다며 스스로를 비난했다.

[문제편 p.218]

(C)

집에 온 Rangan은 심란했다. 기름투성이인 손을 씻을 때 그는 문을 두드리는 소리를 들었다. 그 노인과 차 심부름 소년이었다. 그 노인이 말했다. "제가 돌아왔을 때 당신의 가게는 닫혀 있더군요. 다행히 저는 가게 앞에서 이 소년을 만났어요." Rangan에게 돈을 건네주면서 "당신의 호의에 감사합니다."라고 그는 이어 말했다. Rangan은 노인이 (d) 그에게 건넨 그 친절한 말에 씁쓸하게 웃었다. 그 노인을 의심했다는 사실이 그의 마음을 아프게 했다.

- attend to business 일을 보다, 사무를 보다
- earn ⓥ (돈을) 벌다, 얻다
- curse ⓥ 비난하다, 욕하다, 저주하다
- hospitality ⓝ 호의, 환대
- disturb ⓥ 방해하다
- lay up ~을 드러눕게 하다, 꼼짝 못하게 하다
- take a sip 한 모금을 홀짝 마시다
- greasy ⓐ 기름투성이의
- suspect ⓥ 의심하다
- gloomy ⓐ 우울한, 침울한

구문 풀이

[A] 6행 He took a sip of the tea, / thinking about the order [in which he had to go ahead with his job].
~을 홀짝 마시다   분사구문   선행사   「전치사 + 관계대명사」

[B] 5행 He locked up his shop later than usual and cursed himself for getting tricked by an old man.
동사1   동사2 「curse + A + for + B : B에 대해 A를 비난하다」

[C] 7행 The fact {that he had suspected the old man} pained his heart.
주어   { }: 동격절   타동사(아프게 하다)

---

43 글의 순서 파악   정답률 70% | 정답 ④

주어진 글 (A)에 이어질 내용을 순서에 맞게 배열한 것으로 가장 적절한 것은?

① (B) – (D) – (C)
② (C) – (B) – (D)
③ (C) – (D) – (B)
✔ (D) – (B) – (C)
⑤ (D) – (C) – (B)

Rangan이 아침 일찍 가게를 열었다는 이야기로 시작한 (A) 뒤에는, 한 노인이 찾아와 그에게 저녁에 수리비를 줄 테니 자전거를 고쳐달라고 부탁한다는 (D), 아무리 기다려도 노인이 오지 않아 Rangan이 실망했다는 내용의 (B), 노인이 Rangan을 집으로 찾아와 돈을 지불했다는 내용의 (C)가 차례로 이어지는 것이 적절하다. 따라서 글의 순서로 가장 적절한 것은 ④ '(D) – (B) – (C)'이다.

44 지칭 추론   정답률 64% | 정답 ⑤

밑줄 친 (a)~(e) 중에서 가리키는 대상이 나머지 넷과 다른 것은?

① (a)   ② (b)   ③ (c)   ④ (d)   ✔ (e)

(a), (b), (c), (d)는 Rangan을, (e)는 The old man을 가리키므로, (a)~(e) 중에서 가리키는 대상이 나머지 넷과 다른 것은 ⑤ '(e)'이다.

45 세부 내용 파악   정답률 65% | 정답 ④

윗글에 관한 내용으로 적절하지 않은 것은?

① Rangan은 어제 열이 심해 일을 할 수 없었다.
② Rangan은 노인의 자전거를 수리한 것을 후회한 적이 있다.
③ Rangan은 그의 가게를 평소보다 늦게 닫았다.
✔ 노인은 홀로 Rangan의 집을 방문했다.
⑤ 노인은 머리에 오래된 터번을 쓰고 있었다.

(C) '~ he heard a knock at his door. It was the old man and the tea boy.'에서 Rangan은 노인과 차 심부름 소년의 방문을 받았다고 하므로, 내용과 일치하지 않는 것은 ④ '노인은 홀로 Rangan의 집을 방문했다.'이다.

① (A) 'Yesterday he could not attend to business as he was laid up with high fever, ~'의 내용과 일치한다.
② (B) 'He regretted fixing up the old man's bicycle.'의 내용과 일치한다.
③ (B) 'He locked up his shop later than usual ~'의 내용과 일치한다.
⑤ (D) 'The old man was wearing an old turban on his head.'의 내용과 일치한다.

04회

문제편 219쪽

01 thought about the good things / forget to count the blessings / Write a gratitude journal

02 improve energy levels / stretching can relieve stress / increases blood flow / haven't thought about that benefit

03 What has been troubling you / I've been working all week / blink more frequently / recommend you have your eyes checked

04 we go to the new community park / a see-saw in front of the swings / in the shape of a heart

05 I'm about to leave / throw a party tonight / adding mashed potatoes / No rush

06 scented candles for my parents / we give you a soap for free / with the same scent

07 I'm adjusting well / I've been practicing hard / have a street performance

08 an unforgettable event before graduating / bring our own rackets / sign up online

09 lead the orchestra / enjoy free admission / first come first serve basis

10 an art supplies set / watercolors are not very convenient / which includes a sketchbook

11 create a new academic club / kind of club

11 Where can we buy one

13 devoting his life to helping / how to paint / might be a good fit / I've never taught anyone before

14 I'll be broke / cut down on everyday spending / Keeping a weekly budget seems advantageous

15 often forgets her appointments with them / Disappointed in herself / calendar app / help break her bad habit

16-17 shopping for souvenirs / Scented tea in the morning / remind you of the intense sun

문제편 224쪽

A	B	C	D
01 유망한	01 remind A of B	01 ⓘ	01 ⓢ
02 압도적인	02 frustrated	02 ⓐ	02 ⓒ
03 우연히 듣다, 엿듣다	03 refer to	03 ⓛ	03 ⓞ
04 중요한	04 influence	04 ⓙ	04 ⓕ
05 재충전하다	05 store	05 ⓣ	05 ⓠ
06 엄청난	06 refine	06 ⓟ	06 ⓐ
07 ~에게 유리하게	07 qualification	07 ⓝ	07 ⓙ
08 두드러지다, 눈에 띄다	08 capacity	08 ⓑ	08 ⓑ
09 경비, 지출	09 racism	09 ⓞ	09 ⓡ
10 선구자, 개척자	10 in advance	10 ⓓ	10 ⓜ
11 기초	11 renowned	11 ⓜ	11 ⓟ
12 도움	12 substitute	12 ⓚ	12 ⓓ
13 호혜성, 이익 교환	13 reliable	13 ⓒ	13 ⓔ
14 필연적으로, 불가피하게	14 cooperative	14 ⓔ	14 ⓘ
15 진공, 공백	15 inspire	15 ⓕ	15 ⓚ
16 A에게 B를 퍼붓다	16 free from	16 ⓖ	16 ⓗ
17 인식하다, 인지하다	17 trigger	17 ⓢ	17 ⓛ
18 다양한	18 take advantage of	18 ⓗ	18 ⓝ
19 절대적인	19 anxiety	19 ⓠ	19 ⓖ
20 자손	20 curse	20 ⓡ	20 ⓘ

MEMO

MEMO